D1592980

TECHNOLOGY INNOVATION LAW AND PRACTICE CASES AND MATERIALS

LexisNexis Law School Publishing
Advisory Board

William Araiza
Professor of Law
Brooklyn Law School

Lenni B. Benson
Professor of Law & Associate Dean for Professional Development
New York Law School

Raj Bhala
Rice Distinguished Professor
University of Kansas, School of Law

Ruth Colker
Distinguished University Professor & Heck-Faust Memorial Chair in Constitutional Law
Ohio State University, Moritz College of Law

David Gamage
Assistant Professor of Law
UC Berkeley School of Law

Joan Heminway
College of Law Distinguished Professor of Law
University of Tennessee College of Law

Edward Imwinkelried
Edward L. Barrett, Jr. Professor of Law
UC Davis School of Law

David I. C. Thomson
LP Professor & Director, Lawyering Process Program
University of Denver, Sturm College of Law

Melissa Weresh
Director of Legal Writing and Professor of Law
Drake University Law School

TECHNOLOGY INNOVATION LAW AND PRACTICE

CASES AND MATERIALS

Theodore M. Hagelin
Crandall Melvin Professor of Law
Kauffman Professor of Entrepreneurship and Innovation
Director, Technology Commercialization Law Program
Director, New York State Science & Technology Law Center
Syracuse University College of Law

ISBN: 9781422486795

Library of Congress Cataloging-in-Publication Data
Hagelin, Ted.
Technology innovation law and practice : cases and materials / Ted Hagelin.
p. cm.
Includes bibliographical references and index.
ISBN 978-1-4224-8679-5
1. License agreements--United States. 2. Technological innovations--Law and legislation--United States. 3. Casebooks
I. Title.
KF3145.H34 2011
346.7304'8--dc23
2011036919

This publication is designed to provide accurate and authoritative information in regard to the subject matter covered. It is sold with the understanding that the publisher is not engaged in rendering legal, accounting, or other professional services. If legal advice or other expert assistance is required, the services of a competent professional should be sought.

LexisNexis and the Knowledge Burst logo are registered trademarks and Michie is a trademark of Reed Elsevier Properties Inc., used under license. Matthew Bender and the Matthew Bender Flame Design are registered trademarks of Matthew Bender Properties Inc.

Copyright 2011 Matthew Bender & Company, Inc., a member of the LexisNexis Group.
All Rights Reserved.

No copyright is claimed in the text of statutes, regulations, and excerpts from court opinions quoted within this work. Permission to copy material exceeding fair use, 17 U.S.C. § 107, may be licensed for a fee of 25¢ per page per copy from the Copyright Clearance Center, 222 Rosewood Drive, Danvers, Mass. 01923, telephone (978) 750-8400.

> **NOTE TO USERS**
>
> To ensure that you are using the latest materials available in this area, please be sure to periodically check the LexisNexis Law School web site for downloadable updates and supplements at www.lexisnexis.com/lawschool.

Editorial Offices
121 Chanlon Rd., New Providence, NJ 07974 (908) 464-6800
201 Mission St., San Francisco, CA 94105-1831 (415) 908-3200
www.lexisnexis.com

MATTHEW◊BENDER

DEDICATION

To my father, Theodore J. Hagelin, who gave to me the love of learning

and

To my wife, Ronile Lawrence, who gave to me the love to learn

ACKNOWLEGMENTS

This book has been a work-in-progress for many years and has benefited greatly from the countless comments, criticisms and suggestions made by generations of Syracuse University College of Law students. Although I cannot possibly thank them all individually, I am deeply grateful for their contributions. However, there are three students who I want to especially thank: Luis Ormaechea, Laura Hadley and Jared Slater, all 2009 graduates of the College of Law. The research performed by Luis, Laura and Jared was outstanding.

I also want to thank my dean, Hannah Arterian, for her generous encouragement and support throughout the writing of this book.

PREFACE

My goal in writing *Technology Innovation Law and Practice* is to bring together in a single place what I have learned over the past 25 years of studying, teaching, researching and analyzing the technology innovation process. My work has been in both classroom and clinical settings. This book is a product of both. In the classroom, I have taught nearly 150 credit hours in a course currently titled Technology Transactions. During this time, the topics which I cover have expanded from licensing law and university technology transfer to the 11 chapters included in this book. Also during this time, the reading materials have evolved from a small set of law review articles to a fully-developed set of cases and materials.

In the clinic which I have directed for over 20 years (the Technology Commercialization Research Center), we have undertaken over 100 technology commercialization research projects on behalf of start-up, early-stage, small, medium and large companies, universities, and federal laboratories. Each of these projects has included an in-depth evaluation of the technology under investigation, a comprehensive assessment of alternative market applications and market entry strategies, and a detailed analysis of the legal and regulatory obstacles to the technology's market introduction. This work has given me a keen appreciation of the crucial interrelationship between technology, business and law during the technology innovation process.

Technology Innovation Law & Practice is the result of these years of classroom and clinical teaching. The book is a comprehensive collection of cases, statutes, regulations and readings focused on the commercial development of new technologies, primarily by start-up and early-stage companies. I define the technology innovation *process* as the set of decisions and actions by which an invention is transformed from a laboratory prototype into a commercially viable product or process; and I define the technology innovation *period* as the time between the point of invention (reduction to practice) and the point of market introduction. A more informal explanation of technology innovation I sometimes give to people unfamiliar with, or only politely interested in, "innovation" is: "Technology innovation is about how to make money with an invention after it's made."

Technology innovation is a multi-trillion dollar, world-wide activity that is critical to the success of companies, industries, and regional, national and global economic growth. Nonetheless, it has thus far received scant academic attention as an independent field of study in law and engineering schools, and in many business schools. Technology innovation is most often only associated with invention. The implicit assumption is that if an invention is successful in the laboratory, the invention will be successful in the market. This assumption is flat wrong. Moving a technology from the laboratory into the market is a highly deliberative process involving multiple disciplines and multiple professionals.

Technology Innovation Law and Practice addresses the gap in academic attention paid to the field of technology innovation. The book provides students, faculty and practitioners, both in law and other disciplines, with a single source of in-depth information on the laws that affect the technology innovation process. The book is unique in its interdisciplinary focus, in its emphasis on start-up and early-stage technology companies, and in its combination of instructional and reference materials.

As noted, technology innovation is a multidisciplinary process in which science,

PREFACE

engineering, business and law must be thoroughly integrated in order to formulate successful business plans and market strategies. *Technology Innovation Law and Practice* encompasses the interdisciplinary nature of technology innovation by covering such topics as the valuation of intellectual property, market structures, financing technology development, taxation of technology creation and transfer, and business organizations and management responsibilities. As the title suggests, the book also emphasizes the *practice* of law — how law is used to achieve desired commercial outcomes. In the questions following the cases, readers are asked to consider how parties might have structured their business relationships differently to accomplish their goals more effectively. Some of the questions focus on possible changes in the parties' underlying legal relationship, while others focus on possible changes in the contract language used to implement their legal relationship.

The role of lawyers in the technology innovation process is often seen as passive. This book proposes a much more proactive role for lawyers. Unfortunately, many non-lawyers view legal services as simply transaction costs that detract from the value of technology innovation. This book seeks to train a new generation of law students who can add value to technology innovation by virtue of their understanding of the interrelated technical and business decisions that determine the course of a new technology's commercial development. The book is also intended to provide non-law students and practicing professionals a basic understanding of the law involved in the technology innovation process.

In short, *Technology Innovation Law and Practice* provides students and practicing professionals with a one-stop, multidisciplinary source of information on the laws and practices that affect the technology innovation process.

Ted Hagelin
Syracuse University College of Law
May 2011

INTRODUCTION

DEFINITIONS

The best place to begin the study of "Technology Innovation Law and Practice" is by defining the words.

Definition of "Technology Innovation"

As discussed in more detail below, the word "technology" comes from the Greek noun *technologia* which means a "systematic solution to a practical problem." The Greek definition of *technologia* fits well with the patent law definition of "reduction to practice." In patent law, "reduction to practice" is the date on which an inventor demonstrates the actual operation of an invention. "Reduction to practice" can occur in two ways; *actual* reduction to practice and *constructive* reduction to practice. "Actual" reduction to practice occurs when a physical embodiment of an invention (a prototype) is constructed that works for its intended purpose. "Constructive" reduction to practice occurs when a patent application is filed on an invention that describes the invention in sufficient detail for a person skilled in the art to practice the invention.

Under the recently enacted America Invents Act, "reduction to practice" is no longer relevant to determining patent priority. The first inventor to file a patent application will have priority when this provision of the new Act takes effect on March 16, 2013. Nonetheless, "reduction to practice" is still useful to mark the point of invention and to distinguish invention from innovation.

I will define "technology," as an invention's reduction to practice. Using the Greek definition, the point at which a technology is reduced to practice is the point at which a "systematic solution to a practical problem" has been created. This is the point at which a technology comes into existence and the "technology innovation" process begins.

Demonstrating that a technology works to accomplish its intended purpose, however, is not the same as demonstrating that a technology is commercially viable. Before a technology can be shown to be commercially viable, it must undergo a series of tests. Among these tests are alpha testing to determine whether a technology works in a limited usage setting under controlled conditions; beta testing to determine whether a technology works in normal usage and under normal operating conditions; "scale-up" testing to determine whether a technology can be produced in commercially-demanded quantities; manufacturing testing to determine whether a technology can be manufactured at a competitive cost and quality level; and customer testing to determine whether a technology can be used with minimum necessary training and experience. At the conclusion of each of these tests, the design, operation and output of a technology may be refined to maximize its competitive advantage over substitute technologies. This process of testing and refinement is an integral part of the technology innovation process.

The word "innovation" comes from the Latin word *innovationem* which is the noun form of the verb *innovare* meaning "to change." "Innovare" is a combination of the Latin words *in* (into) and *novous* (new). The contemporary definition of "innovation" is "the introduction of new things or methods." I will define "innovation" as the process by which a new technology is transformed into a commercially viable product, method or service. The "technology innovation process" is the set of technical, business and legal activities that occur between the time a new technology comes into existence and the time a new technology enters the market.

The "innovation process" can be usefully compared to the "invention process." As I have defined the term, the "innovation process" occurs between the date an invention is reduced to practice and the date an invention enters the market. The "invention process" can be defined as the date between the *conception* of an invention (in patent law, the date on which a person mentally formulates a complete and operative idea for an invention) and the time the invention is reduced to practice. The "conception" of an invention is always preceded by a period of applied research. Applied research involves the application of basic research to defined, real-world problems. Basic research generates new, fundamental knowledge of the world often in the form of discoveries of principles and theories that can explain physical phenomena, life processes or the interaction of objects and forces on atomic and cosmic scales. The culmination of applied research is the "conception" of a solution to a practical problem.

The distinction between the "invention process" and the "innovation process" is much more than a matter of semantics. The distinction is important in order to recognize the changing roles of different disciplines in the two processes. The "invention process" is largely driven by science and engineering disciplines, although input from other disciplines, for example patent law, can help to guide the "invention process" and reduce wasted time and effort. As noted above, the "innovation process" also involves science and engineering disciplines in the testing and refinement of new technologies. However, the "innovation process" also involves additional disciplines such as management, marketing, sales, finance, patent law, transactional law and business law. Factors affecting such matters as funding, manufacturing, distribution, training, support and service, as well intellectual property, licensing law, regulatory law, taxation, export controls, management responsibilities and securities law must be thoroughly researched and analyzed in order to formulate successful business plans and market strategies.

The distinction between the "invention process" and the "innovation process" is also important in order to recognize the different roles of government in funding invention and innovation. Both at the federal level and the state level, government funding is overwhelmingly directed toward research leading to invention, not innovation. The unstated assumption here is that successful laboratory research will somehow automatically be transformed into successful market innovation. This assumption is patently false. Federal and state governments will never achieve the desired economic growth from their investment in research leading to invention if they do not also invest in research leading to innovation.

A final note on "innovation." Throughout the book, I will often use the terms *innovation* and *commercialization* interchangeably. The word *commercialization* is the noun form of the verb *commercialize* which means to "offer for sale or make available as a commodity." The root word "commerce" comes from the Latin noun *commercium* which is a combination of the Latin words *com* (together) and *merx* (merchandise). The contemporary definition of "commerce" (the exchange of goods and commodities) is closely aligned with its Latin origins and encompassed within my definition of "innovation."

INTRODUCTION

Definition of "Law and Practice"

Technology innovation *law*, like other fields of law, consists of judicial and administrative cases, agency determinations and interpretations, federal and state statutes, and administrative rules and regulations. However, unlike other fields of law, technology innovation "law" is not a single, unified body of legal doctrine. Contract law, for example, consists of well-defined, interrelated core principles and rules. Technology innovation "law," on the other hand, consists of multiple fields of law that each affects the technology innovation process. The inherently *interdisciplinary* nature of the technology innovation process noted above is mirrored in the inherently *intradisciplinary* nature of technology innovation law. This book covers the main fields of law that affect the technology innovation process.

Technology innovation law *practice* focuses on the role of lawyers in participating in, and implementing, strategic decisions regarding the commercial development of new technologies. An old adage in the field of technology innovation is that the engineers tell you what is *possible*, the business people tell you what is *profitable*, and the lawyers tell you what is *permissible*. This book, however, contemplates a much more proactive role for lawyers. Unfortunately, in the eyes of many non-lawyers engaged in technology innovation, legal services are viewed as simply transaction costs at best, or as needless obstacles at worst. This book seeks to train a new generation of law students to add value to the technology innovation process through an understanding of the interrelated technical and business decisions which determine the course of a technology's commercial development.

Throughout the book, students are exposed to the practical, technical and business contexts within which disputes have arisen, and asked to consider how the parties might have structured their relationship differently to avoid the disputes, or to accomplish their objectives in more effective and efficient ways. In some cases, these practice questions may focus on changes in the parties' underlying business relationship, in others they may focus on changes in the contract language used to implement the business relationship. These practice questions may also concern overarching policies that impact the parties' business conduct. Of course, a lawyer practicing in the field of technology innovation cannot be an expert on all technical and business matters. However, the better a lawyer understands these matters, and appreciates the input of other professionals in addressing matters within their areas of expertise, the greater the value the lawyer will be able to contribute to the technology innovation process.

THE IMPORTANCE OF TECHNOLOGY INNOVATION

Commercial development of new technology is a multi-trillion dollar activity that is critical to the success of start-up, early-stage, small, medium and large companies, as well as to regional and national economies, and the global economy.

An indication of the importance of technology innovation to a company can be seen in the company's *book value* to *market capitalization value* ratio. A company's *book value* is calculated by summing the value of its tangible assets including cash, cash equivalents, marketable securities, accounts receivable, and plant, property and equipment, minus its liabilities. A company's *market capitalization value* is calculated by multiplying the number of shares of outstanding stock by the price per share of the stock. The book to market value ratio tells you the percentage of a company's value that is attributable to its

INTRODUCTION

intangible assets and intellectual property assets. The percentage of a company's value attributable to intangible and intellectual property assets is a good surrogate for the value of a company attributable to its technology innovation activities.

For leading technology companies, their book to market value ratio is striking. For example, in 2009 Google's total assets were $40,497,000 and its market capitalization value was $108,000,000,000. Google's book to market value ratio, therefore, was .037%. Less than .1% of Google's market value was attributable to its tangible assets and more than 99.9% of its market value was attributable to its intangible and intellectual property assets. Stated differently, investors in Google valued its technology innovation activities more than 2,700 times its tangible assets.

Apple's book to market value ratio is even more striking. In 2010, Apple had total tangible assets of $48,140,000 and its market capitalization value was $242,000,000,000. Apple's book to market value ratio, therefore, was .02%. Investors in Apple valued its technology innovation activities more than 5,000 times its tangible assets.

Successful technology innovation is also widely believed to be the primary engine of regional and national economic growth. The leading regions of technology-driven economic growth are generally centered around major research universities. In the U.S., Silicon Valley, Boston, Raleigh-Durham and Austin are examples of regions that have experienced dramatic economic growth due largely to the commercialization of university-generated technologies. In addition, every state has programs designed to support the creation of new companies most often through the funding of research and development, or the provision of seed-stage operating capital. The goals of these programs are to advance the economic competitiveness of the state by promoting high-value technology output, creating well-paying jobs, and attracting new firms and professional talent.

The U.S. federal government also has many programs designed to support start-up and small-business technology-based companies. Two of the most important of these federal programs are the Small Business Innovation Research (SBIR) program and the Small Business Technology Transfer (STTR) program. In 2009, these two programs awarded small business companies nearly $2 billion to pursue research of new, cutting-edge technologies. The SBIR and STTR programs are covered in detail section 11.1 of the book.

The importance of technology innovation to regional and national economic growth is reflected in global statistics. The aggregate global value of technology innovation activities is tracked by the National Science Foundation (NSF) and published annually in NSF's Science & Engineering Indicators. In the 2010 Science & Engineering Indicators, NSF reported that in 2007 knowledge-intensive and technology-intensive industries combined contributed nearly $16 trillion to the global economic output, approximately 30% of the world GDP. (Although the NSF's definitions of "knowledge-intensive" and "technology-intensive" differ somewhat from our definition of "technology innovation," these definitions are sufficiently similar to provide a fairly accurate portrait of the importance of technology innovation to the world economy.) The largest global value-added segment of these industries was commercial knowledge-intensive services which increased from $4.5 trillion in 1995 to $9.5 trillion in 2007. The United States led the world in value-added commercial knowledge-intensive services with $3.3 trillion in 2007 followed by the European Union with $2.9 trillion.

INTRODUCTION

Outside of commercial knowledge-intensive services, five high-technology industries accounted for $1.2 trillion of the value-added total in 2007; communications and semiconductors ($445 billion), pharmaceuticals ($319 billion), scientific instruments ($189 billion), aerospace ($153 billion), and computers and office machinery ($114 billion).

These NSF statistics strongly suggest that technology innovation activities are as important to the global economy and world prosperity as they are to local, regional and national economies, and their economic prosperity.

COVERAGE OF BOOK

Chapter One of the book provides a general background for the study of technology innovation law and practice. Chapter One includes an overview of intellectual property law, an introduction to basic economic concepts, a brief review of finance and accounting principles, a discussion of technology innovation business including different methods to value intellectual property, a comparison of the different perspectives of a transferor and transferee of intellectual property, a brief consideration of the advantages and disadvantages of technology transfers, a discussion of factors to be considered in formulating a technology commercialization strategy, and a brief summary of some of the more important sources of information on markets, companies and patents.

Chapter Two provides an in-depth consideration of licensing law. Licensing law governs the transfer of intellectual property. Licensing law is based on contract law which has been modified to reflect the unique features of intellectual property. Chapter Two includes a section with sample software, product and biotechnology license agreements; a section on the general rights of licensors and licensees which includes consideration of the scope of licensor rights, the relationship between patent licenses and contract law, implied licenses, licensee estoppel, co-owner licenses, license breach and breach remedies, the effect of patent invalidity on licenses, standing of licensees to sue for patent infringement, and patent misuse; a section on the basic terms included in license agreements including implied license terms, grant clauses, license warranties, most-favored licensee clauses, transfers of license agreements, post-license sale restrictions, field of use restrictions, royalties, licenses to improvements, and indemnification; and a final section that considers unilateral licenses which include box-top licenses, shrink-wrap licenses, click-wrap licenses and open source licenses.

Chapter Three covers commercialization of technologies developed by university faculty, staff and students, or through the use of university facilities or equipment. I have already noted the critical role universities play in fueling the technology commercialization process. Chapter Three includes a section on the Bayh-Dole Act, the seminal federal legislation which allows universities to elect to take title to patents resulting from federally funded research, a section on university-industry sponsored research including a discussion of the federal income tax limitations on the conduct of sponsored research, and sections on university intellectual property ownership, university patent enforcement, university-student research responsibilities and university-faculty employment contracts.

Chapter Four considers employer-employee intellectual property rights in industrial settings. Under U.S. patent law, the inventor is always the original owner of a patent. Therefore, a company must obtain patent ownership rights from an employee-inventor before the company can commercialize the invention. Chapter Four includes sections on employer shop rights, works made for hire, employer IP rights under employment contracts, state statutory restrictions on IP rights claimed by employers, hold-over agreements, non-disclosure agreements and non-competition agreements. Chapter Five considers experimental use of new technologies in three situations; experimental use as an exception to the Patent Act's public use statutory bar, experimental use as an exemption to patent infringement, and experimental use for pharmaceuticals and medical devices under the Hatch-Waxman Act infringement safe harbor.

Chapter Six considers intellectual property licenses in the case of bankruptcy. Intellectual property licenses pose special problems in bankruptcy because they are executory contracts. Congress has intervened to address some of the problems involved with intellectual property licenses in bankruptcy, but by no means all of problems. Chapter Six includes sections on licensor bankruptcy, licensee bankruptcy, perfecting security interests in copyrights, and perfecting security interests in patents. Chapter Seven covers licensing and antitrust laws. There is a fundamental tension between licensing law and antitrust law because licensing law allows a licensor to limit competition with respect to licensed technology while antitrust law seeks to increase competition in technology markets. The first section in Chapter Six considers the Sherman, Clayton and Federal Trade Commission Acts and the second section covers the Department of Justice-Federal Trade Commission antitrust guidelines for licensing intellectual property.

Chapter Eight looks at tax laws that affect technology creation and transfer. As in all areas of business activity, tax law directly affects the financial results of new technology innovation. Chapter Eight includes sections on the research and experimentation expense deduction, the research and experimentation tax credit, founders' capital contributions to new companies, issuance of stock in exchange for services, license and sale by a patent owner, and sale and exchange by a patent holder. Chapter Nine considers U.S. export controls on dual-use technologies. Dual-use technologies are technologies that are primarily used for civilian purposes, but can also be used for military purposes. Since 9/11, dual-use technologies have become an increasing concern for the Department of Commerce and U.S. technology exporters. Chapter Nine includes a section which provides an overview of the U.S. export control system, a section on "deemed" exports, and sections covering selected export controls and selected recent export violation enforcement cases.

Chapter Ten considers business organizations and management responsibilities. Lawyers who represent entrepreneurs launching start-up companies should know the alternative business forms available to entrepreneurs, and the legal, management and tax consequences associated with these alternative forms of business. Likewise, lawyers advising corporate clients on the actions of directors, officers and majority shareholders should know what fiduciary duties these individuals owe and to whom. Chapter Ten contains sections on the choice of business organization, and management responsibilities including directors', officers' and majority shareholders' fiduciary duties, shareholder direct and derivative suits, usurpation of corporate opportunities and piercing the corporate veil.

Finally, Chapter Eleven considers financing technology innovation. Lawyers representing small-business clients seeking investment capital need to have a basic understanding of government programs available to support small businesses, venture capital investment terms, private securities offerings, initial public securities offerings and the possibility of fraud claims in conjunction with private and public sales of securities. Although in many of these areas, the small-business corporate counsel may decide to retain the services of an outside securities law specialists, nonetheless a basic understanding of these areas will enable the corporate counsel to work more effectively with outside counsel and better serve as an intermediary between the corporate client and the outside counsel. Chapter Eleven is intended to provide this basic understanding, and includes sections on the Small Business Innovation Research program, the Small Business Technology Transfer program, private securities offerings, venture capital investments, initial public offerings, fraud in private and public securities offerings, and due diligence in the sale of securities. An especially useful reading in Chapter Eleven is the Glossary of Selected Private Equity Investment Terms, compiled by the Center for Private Equity and Entrepreneurship at the Tuck School of Business at Dartmouth University; reprinted with permission.

The Appendix contains practice exercises. These exercises include the valuation of an early-stage (pre-commercialization) technology, negotiating and drafting a term sheet for a venture capital investment, and negotiating and drafting a technology license agreement.

ORGANIZATION AND SELECTION OF MATERIALS

The book is intended to be used for both teaching and research purposes. Each chapter of the book begins with an overview of the topics covered in the chapter, each section of the book provides a general introduction to the law covered in the section, and each subsection of the book provides a brief review of the cases and readings contained in the subsection. At the conclusion of each case or reading, there are questions. These questions are intended to probe the readers' understanding of the case or reading and, as noted earlier, prompt critical reflection upon the practical, legal and policy implications of the case or reading. In many instances, these questions may generate opportunities for classroom and online discussions that enhance the educational value of the cases and readings.

At the end of each subsection in the book there are "Case Notes" and "Additional Information." The Case Notes consist of citations to other cases in the topic area along with parenthetical synopses of the holdings in the cases. Case Notes also include hypothetical fact questions drawn from actual cases. The Additional Information consists of treatises, texts and articles dealing with the topic subject matters. The Case Notes and Additional Information are intended to provide the reader with reference sources for further study and research.

In selecting the topics for the book, I have tried to minimize the overlap with other law school courses. My goal in preparing the book was to include in one place all of the legal topics relevant to commercial development of new technologies. Inevitably, this results in some coverage overlap between this book and other law school courses. There are two differences, however, between the topics considered in this book and the topics considered in other law school courses such as patent, bankruptcy, tax and antitrust law. First, the topics included in this book consist of a small subgroup of topics covered in other law school courses and pertain directly to technology innovation. Second, the topics included in this book are considered in a transactional context rather than a doctrinal

INTRODUCTION

context. Of course, readers who are already familiar with the material in a topic area can skip, or skim, the readings.

For the most part, the topics covered in the book are equally applicable to small and large firms. However, the focal point of the book is on small firms and the commercialization of their early-stage technologies. The chapters on Commercializing University Technologies, Business Organizations and Management Responsibilities, and Financing Technology Innovation are primarily directed to small firms. This is especially the case in the chapter on Financing Technology Innovation which includes sections on the SBIR and STTR programs, registration exemptions for private securities offerings, venture capital investments, and initial public offerings.

****

A final word. As you embark on the study of technology innovation law and practice, I hope you will find the field as interesting, as rewarding and as worthwhile as I do. I also hope you will enjoy reading this book as much as I did preparing it.

SUMMARY TABLE OF CONTENTS

Preface vii
Introduction ix

Chapter 1   TECHNOLOGY INNOVATION FUNDAMENTALS: INTELLECTUAL PROPERTY, ECONOMICS, FINANCE AND BUSINESS 1

1.1.   ETYMOLOGY OF "TECHNOLOGY TRANSFER"   1
1.2   CONTEMPORARY DEFINITIONS OF TERMS   3
1.3   NATURE OF TECHNOLOGY TRANSFER PROCESS   5
1.4   LICENSES AS PROPERTY RIGHTS   6
1.5   INTELLECTUAL PROPERTY OVERVIEW   7
1.6   BASIC ECONOMIC CONCEPTS   17
1.7   FINANCIAL AND ACCOUNTING PRINCIPLES   35
1.8   BUSINESS OF TECHNOLOGY INNOVATION   38
1.9   TECHNOLOGY TRANSFEROR/TRANSFEREE PERSPECTIVES   69
1.10   ADVANTAGES AND DISADVANTAGES OF TECHNOLOGY TRANSFERS   75
1.11   FORMULATING A TECHNOLOGY INNOVATION STRATEGY   76

Chapter 2   LICENSING LAW **91**

2.1   SAMPLE LICENSE AGREEMENTS   91
2.2   RIGHTS OF LICENSORS AND LICENSEES   124
2.3   LICENSE TERMS   252
2.4   UNILATERAL LICENSES   427

Chapter 3   COMMERCIALIZING UNIVERSITY TECHNOLOGIES **485**

3.1   THE BAYH-DOLE ACT   486
3.2   UNIVERSITY-INDUSTRY SPONSORED RESEARCH   540
3.3   UNIVERSITY INTELLECTUAL PROPERTY OWNERSHIP   576
3.4   UNIVERSITY PATENT ENFORCEMENT   635
3.5   UNIVERSITY-STUDENT RESEARCH RESPONSIBILITIES   651
3.6   UNIVERSITY-FACULTY EMPLOYMENT CONTRACTS   662

SUMMARY TABLE OF CONTENTS

Chapter 4 INDUSTRY EMPLOYER-EMPLOYEE INTELLECTUAL PROPERTY RIGHTS **693**

4.1 EMPLOYER SHOP RIGHTS 693

4.2 WORKS MADE FOR HIRE 704

4.3 EMPLOYER IP RIGHTS UNDER EMPLOYMENT CONTRACTS ... 715

4.4 STATE STATUTORY RESTRICTIONS ON EMPLOYER IP RIGHTS . 729

4.5 HOLD-OVER AGREEMENTS 743

4.6 NON-DISCLOSURE AGREEMENTS 758

4.7 NON-COMPETITION AGREEMENTS 779

Chapter 5 EXPERIMENTAL USE OF NEW TECHNOLOGY 797

5.1 EXPERIMENTAL USE EXCEPTION TO PUBLIC USE STATUTORY BAR 797

5.2 EXPERIMENTAL USE EXEMPTION TO PATENT INFRINGEMENT 807

5.3 HATCH-WAXMAN ACT INFRINGEMENT SAFE HARBOR 820

Chapter 6 BANKRUPTCY 831

6.1 LICENSOR BANKRUPTCY 832

6.2 LICENSEE BANKRUPTCY 844

6.3 PERFECTING SECURITY INTERESTS IN COPYRIGHTS 851

6.4 PERFECTING SECURITY INTERESTS IN PATENTS 861

Chapter 7 LICENSING AND ANTITRUST LAW 873

7.1 SHERMAN, CLAYTON AND FEDERAL TRADE COMMISSION ACTS 875

7.2 DOJ-FTC ANTITRUST LICENSING GUIDELINES 893

Chapter 8 TAX EFFECTS OF TECHNOLOGY CREATION AND TRANSFER 903

8.1 RESEARCH AND EXPERIMENTATION EXPENSE DEDUCTIONS . 905

8.2 RESEARCH AND EXPERIMENTATION TAX CREDITS 923

8.3 FOUNDERS' CAPITAL CONTRIBUTIONS 945

8.4 STOCK IN EXCHANGE FOR SERVICES 957

8.5 LICENSE OR SALE BY THE PATENT OWNER 985

8.6 SALE OR EXCHANGE BY THE PATENT HOLDER 1000

Chapter 9 U.S. TECHNOLOGY EXPORT CONTROLS 1027

9.1 OVERVIEW OF EXPORT CONTROL SYSTEM 1028

9.2 DEEMED EXPORTS 1063

SUMMARY TABLE OF CONTENTS

9.3   SELECTED EXPORT CONTROLS 1078

9.4   SELECTED RECENT ENFORCEMENT CASES 1096

Chapter 10   BUSINESS ORGANIZATIONS AND MANAGEMENT RESPONSIBILITIES 1107

10.1   CHOICE OF BUSINESS ORGANIZATION 1107

10.2   MANAGEMENT RESPONSIBILITIES 1116

Chapter 11   FINANCING TECHNOLOGY INNOVATION 1181

11.1   SMALL BUSINESS INNOVATION RESEARCH (SBIR) AND SMALL BUSINESS TECHNOLOGY TRANSFER (STTR) PROGRAMS 1182

11.2   PRIVATE SECURITIES OFFERINGS 1224

11.3   FRAUD IN PRIVATE SECURITIES OFFERINGS 1241

11.4   VENTURE CAPITAL INVESTMENTS 1256

11.5   OTHER FORMS OF FINANCING 1317

11.6   INITIAL PUBLIC OFFERINGS (IPOS) 1327

11.7   FRAUD IN PUBLIC SECURITIES OFFERINGS 1379

11.8   DUE DILIGENCE 1401

APPENDIX **1419**

PSA-X Valuation Exercise 1419

BioFilter Negotiation and Drafting Exercises 1422

BioFilter Venture Capital Investment Exercise 1427

BioFilter Licensing Agreement 1429

TABLE OF CASES **TC-1**

INDEX **I-1**

TABLE OF CONTENTS

Chapter 1	TECHNOLOGY INNOVATION FUNDAMENTALS: INTELLECTUAL PROPERTY, ECONOMICS, FINANCE AND BUSINESS	1

1.1.	ETYMOLOGY OF "TECHNOLOGY TRANSFER"	1
1.2	CONTEMPORARY DEFINITIONS OF TERMS	3
1.3	NATURE OF TECHNOLOGY TRANSFER PROCESS	5
1.4	LICENSES AS PROPERTY RIGHTS	6
1.5	INTELLECTUAL PROPERTY OVERVIEW	7
1.5.1	Patents	8
1.5.2	Copyrights	12
1.5.3	Trade Secrets	14
1.6	BASIC ECONOMIC CONCEPTS	17
1.6.1	Macro-Economics and Micro-Economics	18
1.6.2	Unique Economic Characteristics of Intellectual Property	26
1.6.3	Market Structures	31
1.7	FINANCIAL AND ACCOUNTING PRINCIPLES	35
1.7.1	Types of Assets	35
1.7.2	Types of Financial Reports	36
1.8	BUSINESS OF TECHNOLOGY INNOVATION	38
1.8.1	Risk and Return	39
1.8.2	Valuation of Intellectual Property	42
1.8.3	Patent Infringement Damages and Patent License Valuations	55
	Uniloc USA, Inc. v. Microsoft Corp.	56
	Questions	67
	Case Notes	67
1.9	TECHNOLOGY TRANSFEROR/TRANSFEREE PERSPECTIVES	69
1.9.1	Technology Value	69
1.9.2	Transferor Perspective	70
1.9.3	Transferee Perspective	71
1.10	ADVANTAGES AND DISADVANTAGES OF TECHNOLOGY TRANSFERS	73
1.10.1	Advantages	73
1.10.2	Disadvantages	75
1.11	FORMULATING A TECHNOLOGY INNOVATION STRATEGY	76
1.11.1	Identifying The Technology	76
1.11.2	Considering Potential Applications	77
1.11.3	The Scope of Intellectual Property Protection	78
1.11.4	Technical Advantages and Disadvantages	79
1.11.5	Defining Potential Markets	80

TABLE OF CONTENTS

1.11.6   Profiles of Firms In A Market   82

1.11.7   Terms and Conditions of a Technology Transfer   84

1.11.8   Sources of Information on Markets, Companies and Patents   88

Chapter 2   LICENSING LAW **91**

2.1   SAMPLE LICENSE AGREEMENTS   91

  2.1.1   Software License   92

              Questions   101

  2.1.2   Product License   101

              Questions   112

  2.1.3   Biotechnology License   112

              Questions   122

2.2   RIGHTS OF LICENSORS AND LICENSEES   123

  2.2.1   Scope of Licensor Rights   124

              General Talking Pictures Corporation v. Western Electric

              Company   125

              Questions   127

              Mallinckrodt v. Medipart   127

              Questions   134

              Case Notes   134

  2.2.2   Patent Licenses And Contract Law   135

              Aronson v. Quick Point Pencil Company   136

              Questions   141

              Case Notes   141

  2.2.3   Implied Licenses   142

              Suessen-Schurr v. Schubert   143

              Questions   148

              Travelers Express v. American Express Integrated Payment   148

              Questions   154

              Jacobs v. Nintendo of America, Inc.   154

              Questions   158

              Case Notes   158

  2.2.4   Licensee Estoppel   159

              Lear v. Adkins   161

              Questions   170

              Medimmune v. Genentech   170

              Questions   177

              Case Notes   177

  2.2.5   Co-Owner Licenses   180

              Ethicon v. United States Surgical Corporation   181

              Questions   188

TABLE OF CONTENTS

Case Notes 189

2.2.6   License Breach 190

Institut Pasteur v. Cambridge Biotech 190

Questions 196

Case Notes 196

2.2.7   License Breach Remedies 197

Monsanto Company v. McFarling 199

Questions 205

XCO International v. Pacific Scientific 205

Questions 209

EBay v. Mercexchange 210

Questions 213

Case Notes 214

2.2.8   Patent Invalidity 216

Tuskos Engineering v. Tuskos 217

Questions 220

Cordis v. Medtronic 220

Questions 224

Case Notes 224

2.2.9   Standing to Sue 225

Abbott Laboratories v. Diamedix Corp. 226

Questions 232

McNeilab v. Scandipharm and BASF 232

Questions 236

Case Notes 237

2.2.10   Patent Misuse 238

U.S. Philips Corporation v. Int'l Trade Comm. 240

Questions 250

Case Notes 250

2.3   LICENSE TERMS 252

2.3.1   Implied License Terms 252

Eli Lilly and Co. v. Genentech, Inc. 253

Questions 256

Hirsch-Chemie Ltd. v. Johns Hopkins University 257

Questions 265

Meijer, Inc. v. Abbott Laboratories 266

Questions 268

Case Notes 269

2.3.2   Grant Clauses 271

Apple Computer, Inc. v. Microsoft Corp. 271

Questions 276

TABLE OF CONTENTS

    Intel Corp. v. U.S. Int'l Trade Comm. 276

    Questions 280

    Case Notes 280

 2.3.3 License Warranties 282

    Chatlos Systems v. National Cash Register 283

    Questions 291

    Transport Corporation of America v. IBM 291

    Questions 297

    Meadow River v. University of Georgia 297

    Questions 302

    VRT, Inc. v. Dutton-Lainson Company 302

    Questions 305

    Case Notes 306

 2.3.4 Most-Favored Licensee Clauses 307

    Epic Systems v. Allcare Health Management 308

    Questions 313

    SGK v. Hercules, Inc. 314

    Questions 318

    Eagle Comtronics v. Pico Products 319

    Questions 320

    Wang Laboratories v. Oki Electric Industry 321

    Questions 324

    Case Notes 325

 2.3.5 License Transfers 326

    Intergraph v. Intel Corporation 328

    Questions 331

    PPG Industries, Inc. v. Guardian Industries Corp. 332

    Questions 338

    Cook Inc. v. Boston Scientific Corp. 338

    Questions 345

    Rhone-Poulenc Agro v. DeKalb Genetics 345

    Questions 350

    Case Notes 351

 2.3.6 Post-Sale Restrictions 353

    Pioneer Hi-bred Int'l v. Ottawa Plant Food 354

    Questions 360

    Adobe Systems v. Stargate Software 361

    Questions 366

    Quanta Computer, Inc. v. LG Electronics, Inc. 366

    Questions 374

    Case Notes 375

TABLE OF CONTENTS

2.3.7 Field-of-Use Restrictions 376
    Igen Int'l v. Roche Diagnostics GMBH 377
    Questions 381
    Case Notes 381
2.3.8 Best Efforts Clauses 382
    Intervisual Communications v. Volkert 383
    Questions 388
    Permanence Corporation v. Kennametal, Inc. 389
    Questions 393
    Case Notes 394
2.3.9 Royalties 395
    Scheiber v. Dolby Laboratories 397
    Questions 401
    Bayer AG v. Housey Pharmaceuticals, Inc. 401
    Questions 406
    Case Notes 407
2.3.10 Licenses to Improvements 408
    Gonser v. Leland Detroit Mfg. Co. 409
    Questions 414
    Antitrust Guidelines for the Licensing of Intellectual Property 415
    Case Notes 416
2.3.11 Indemnification 418
    RFR Industries, Inc. v. Rex-Hide Industries, Inc 419
    Questions 425
    Case Notes 425
2.4 UNILATERAL LICENSES 427
2.4.1 Box-Top Licenses 428
    Step-Saver Data Systems v. Wyse Technology 428
    Questions 436
    Case Notes 436
2.4.2 Shrink-Wrap Licenses 438
    ProCD v. Zeidenberg 438
    Questions 444
    Bowers v. Baystate Technologies 444
    Questions 450
    Case Notes 450
2.4.3 Click-Wrap Licenses 452
    Specht v. Netscape Communications Corp. 453
    Questions 460
    Case Notes 460
2.4.4 Open Source Licenses 462

TABLE OF CONTENTS

GNU General Public License, Version 2, June 1991 463

Questions 468

The SCO Group, Inc. v. Novell, Inc. 469

Questions 482

Case Notes 482

| **Chapter 3** | **COMMERCIALIZING UNIVERSITY** | |
| | **TECHNOLOGIES** . . . . | **485** |

3.1   THE BAYH-DOLE ACT 486

    3.1.1   Legislation 486

       35 U.S.C.A. §§ 200–212 486

       Questions 496

       Campbell Plastics Engineering & Mfg., Inc. v. Brownlee 496

       Questions 502

       Case Notes 503

    3.1.2   March-In Rights 504

       In The Case of Norvir® Manufactured by Abbott

       Laboratories, Inc. 505

       Questions 510

       Determination in the Case of Petition of Cellpro, Inc. 510

       Questions 516

       Case Notes 516

    3.1.3   Standing to Sue 517

       Service Engineering v. U.S.D.A. 518

       Questions 523

       Nutrition 21 v. United States 523

       Questions 529

       Case Notes 529

    3.1.4   Effect of Bayh-Dole on University-Faculty Relationship 530

       Platzer v. Sloan-Kettering Institute 530

       Questions 536

       Therien v. The Trustees of the University of Pennsylvania 536

       Questions 539

       Case Notes 540

3.2   UNIVERSITY-INDUSTRY SPONSORED RESEARCH 540

    3.2.1   University Sponsored Research Agreements 541

       Survey of Sponsored Research Contract Terms 541

    3.2.2   Income Tax Limitations on Sponsored Research 550

       Rev. Proc. 2007-47 551

       Questions 555

       Note on Public Policy Regarding Industry-Sponsored Research 556

TABLE OF CONTENTS

Questions 564

Case Notes 565

3.2.3   University-Sponsor Disputes 566

Wisconsin Alumni Research Foundation v. Xenon

Pharmaceuticals, Inc. 566

Questions 576

3.3   UNIVERSITY INTELLECTUAL PROPERTY OWNERSHIP 576

3.3.1   Sample Intellectual Property Policy 577

Syracuse University Policy on Ownership and Management of

Intellectual Property 578

Questions 580

Case Notes 581

3.3.2   University-Faculty IP Ownership Disputes 583

Fenn v. Yale University 583

Questions 595

University Patents v. Kligman 596

Questions 606

E.I. Du Pont Nemours & Co. v. Okuley 607

Questions 612

Case Notes 613

3.3.3   University-Student IP Ownership Disputes 614

University of West Virginia v. Vanvoorhies 615

Questions 624

Case Notes 624

3.3.4   University Licensing Policies 625

In the Public Interest: Nine Points to Consider in Licensing University

Technology 626

Questions 634

3.4   UNIVERSITY PATENT ENFORCEMENT 635

University of Rochester v. G.D. Searl 636

Questions 642

In re Columbia University Patent Litigation 642

Questions 650

Case Notes 650

3.5   UNIVERSITY-STUDENT RESEARCH RESPONSIBILITIES 651

Chou v. University of Chicago 651

Questions 660

Case Notes 660

3.6   UNIVERSITY-FACULTY EMPLOYMENT CONTRACTS 662

Stanford v. Roche 662

Questions 674

TABLE OF CONTENTS

Shaw v. University of California 675

Questions 682

Kucharczyk v. University of California 682

Questions 691

Case Notes (Review) 692

Chapter 4	**INDUSTRY EMPLOYER-EMPLOYEE INTELLECTUAL PROPERTY RIGHTS**	**693**

4.1   EMPLOYER SHOP RIGHTS 693

United States v. Dubilier Condenser 694

Questions 698

Schroeder v. Tracor 698

Questions 701

Case Notes 702

4.2   WORKS MADE FOR HIRE 704

MacLean Associates v. Mercer-Meidinger-Hansen 704

Questions 713

Case Notes 713

4.3   EMPLOYER IP RIGHTS UNDER EMPLOYMENT CONTRACTS ... 715

Andreaggi v. Relis 716

Questions 724

Jamesbury Corp. v. Worcester Valve Co. 725

Questions 728

Case Notes 728

4.4   STATE STATUTORY RESTRICTIONS ON EMPLOYER IP RIGHTS . 729

Minn. Stat. Ann. § 181.78 (1980) 730

Questions 730

Waterjet Tech., Inc. v. Flow Int'l Corp. 730

Questions 735

Cadence Design Sys. v. Bhandari 735

Questions 741

Case Notes 741

4.5   HOLD-OVER AGREEMENTS 743

Ingersoll-Rand Company v. Ciavatta 743

Questions 756

Case Notes 757

4.6   NON-DISCLOSURE AGREEMENTS 758

Revere Transducers, Inc. v. Deere & Comp. 759

Questions 770

Celeritas Technologies v. Rockwell International 771

Questions 776

	Case Notes	776
4.7	NON-COMPETITION AGREEMENTS	779
	Verizon Communications Inc. v. Pizzirani	780
	Questions	790
	EMSL Analytical, Inc., v. Younker	791
	Questions	794
	Case Notes	794
Chapter 5	**EXPERIMENTAL USE OF NEW TECHNOLOGY**	**797**
5.1	EXPERIMENTAL USE EXCEPTION TO PUBLIC USE STATUTORY BAR	797
	Clock Spring, L.P. v. Wrapmaster, Inc.	798
	Questions	804
	Case Notes	804
5.2	EXPERIMENTAL USE EXEMPTION TO PATENT INFRINGEMENT	807
	Madey v. Duke University	807
	Questions	817
	Case Notes	818
5.3	HATCH-WAXMAN ACT INFRINGEMENT SAFE HARBOR	820
	Merck KGaA v. Integra Lifesciences I, Ltd.	822
	Questions	828
	Case Notes	829
Chapter 6	**BANKRUPTCY**	**831**
6.1	LICENSOR BANKRUPTCY	832
	In re Cellnet Data Systems, Inc.	833
	Questions	842
	Case Notes	842
6.2	LICENSEE BANKRUPTCY	844
	In re Aerobox Composite Structures, LLC.	845
	Questions	849
	Case Notes	849
6.3	PERFECTING SECURITY INTERESTS IN COPYRIGHTS	851
	World Auxiliary Power v. Silicon Valley Bank	853
	Questions	859
	Case Notes	860
6.4	PERFECTING SECURITY INTERESTS IN PATENTS	861
	Cybernetic Services v. Matsco Financial Corporation	862
	Questions	870
	Case Notes	871

TABLE OF CONTENTS

Chapter 7	**LICENSING AND ANTITRUST LAW**	**873**

7.1	SHERMAN, CLAYTON AND FEDERAL TRADE COMMISSION ACTS	875
	Illinois Tool Works v. Independent Ink	875
	Questions	881
	Static Control Components, Inc. v. Lexmark International, Inc.	882
	Questions	891
	Case Notes	891
7.2	DOJ-FTC ANTITRUST LICENSING GUIDELINES	893
	ANTITRUST GUIDELINES FOR THE LICENSING OF INTELLECTUAL PROPERTY	893
	Questions	901

Chapter 8	**TAX EFFECTS OF TECHNOLOGY CREATION AND TRANSFER**	**903**

8.1	RESEARCH AND EXPERIMENTATION EXPENSE DEDUCTIONS .	905
	I.R.C. § 174	905
	Treas. Reg. § 1.174-1	906
	Treas. Reg. § 1.174-2	907
	Treas. Reg. § 1.174-3	910
	Treas. Reg. § 1.174-4	910
	Questions	911
	LDL Research & Development II, Ltd. v. Commissioner of Internal Revenue	912
	Questions	920
	Case Notes	921
8.2	RESEARCH AND EXPERIMENTATION TAX CREDITS	923
	I.R.C. § 41	924
	Treas. Reg. § 1.41-2	929
	Questions	931
	Eustace v. Commissioner of Internal Revenue	932
	Questions	934
	Tax and Accounting Software Corp. v. United States	935
	Questions	943
	Case Notes	944
8.3	FOUNDERS' CAPITAL CONTRIBUTIONS	945
	I.R.C. § 1001	945
	I.R.C. § 351	945
	Treas. Reg. § 1.351-1	946
	I.R.C. § 358	947
	Treas. Reg. § 1.358-1	948

TABLE OF CONTENTS

	Questions	948
	Peracchi v. Commissioner of Internal Revenue	949
	Questions	955
	Case Notes	956
8.4	STOCK IN EXCHANGE FOR SERVICES	957
	I.R.C. § 83	958
	Questions	960
	Treas. Reg. § 1.83-1	961
	Questions	964
	Treas. Reg. § 1.83-2	964
	Questions	965
	Treas. Reg. § 1.83-3	965
	Questions	971
	Treas. Reg. § 1.83-5	971
	Questions	974
	Treas. Reg. § 1.83-6	974
	Questions	975
	Treas. Reg. § 1.83-7	976
	Questions	978
	Robinson v. Commissioner of Internal Revenue	978
	Questions	981
	Pagel, Inc. v. Commissioner of Internal Revenue	981
	Questions	983
	Case Notes	983
8.5	LICENSE OR SALE BY THE PATENT OWNER	985
	I.R.C. § 61	985
	Treas. Reg. § 1.61-6	986
	Treas. Reg. § 1.61-8	987
	I.R.C. § 1221	987
	I.R.C. § 1231	988
	Questions	989
	William M. Bailey v. Commissioner of Internal Revenue	990
	Questions	994
	Gable v. Commissioner of Internal Revenue	994
	Questions	998
	Case Notes	999
8.6	SALE OR EXCHANGE BY THE PATENT HOLDER	1000
	I.R.C. § 1235	1001
	Treas. Reg. § 1.1235-1	1001
	Treas. Reg. § 1.1235-2	1003
	Questions	1006

TABLE OF CONTENTS

Busse v. United States 1006

Questions 1013

McClain v. Commissioner of Internal Revenue 1013

Questions 1019

Internal Revenue Service Technical Advice Memorandum 1020

Questions 1024

Case Notes 1024

Chapter 9   U.S. TECHNOLOGY EXPORT CONTROLS **1027**

9.1   OVERVIEW OF EXPORT CONTROL SYSTEM 1028

15 C.F.R. Part 732 1028

Questions 1037

15 C.F.R. Part 736 1037

Questions 1042

15 C.F.R. Part 738 1043

Questions 1051

15 C.F.R. Part 740 1051

Questions 1057

15 C.F.R. Part 762 1058

Case Notes 1062

9.2   DEEMED EXPORTS 1063

15 C.F.R. Part 734 1063

Questions 1065

Case Notes 1067

U.S. v. Roth 1069

Questions 1077

9.3   SELECTED EXPORT CONTROLS 1078

9.3.1   Encryption Technology 1078

15 C.F.R. Part 772 1079

Questions 1080

15 C.F.R. Part 742 1080

Questions 1082

15 C.F.R. Part 740 1083

Questions 1084

Junger v. Daley 1084

Questions 1088

9.3.2   Software Programs 1089

15 C.F.R. § 740.6 1089

Questions 1091

15 C.F.R. § 740.13 1091

Questions 1094

TABLE OF CONTENTS

Case Notes 1095

9.4   SELECTED RECENT ENFORCEMENT CASES 1096

Chapter 10   **BUSINESS ORGANIZATIONS AND MANAGEMENT RESPONSIBILITIES** **1107**

10.1   CHOICE OF BUSINESS ORGANIZATION 1107
10.1.1   Limited Partnership 1108
10.1.2   Subchapter C Corporation 1110
10.1.3   Subchapter S Corporation 1113
10.1.4   Limited Liability Company 1114
10.1.5   Comparison of Corporations and Limited Liability Companies 1115
10.2   MANAGEMENT RESPONSIBILITIES 1116
10.2.1   Directors' Fiduciary Duties 1117
        Weiss v. Swanson 1117
        Questions 1121
        Case Notes 1122
10.2.2   Officers' Fiduciary Duties 1124
        Wahlcometroflex, Inc. v. Baldwin 1125
        Questions 1128
        Case Notes 1129
10.2.3   Majority Shareholders' Fiduciary Duties 1131
        Pointer v. Castellani 1131
        Questions 1140
        Case Notes 1140
10.2.4   Shareholder Direct and Derivative Suits 1143
        Metcoff v. Lebovics 1144
        Questions 1151
        Matter of Comverse Tech., Inc. Derivative Litig. 1152
        Questions 1158
        Case Notes 1159
10.2.5   Usurpation of Corporate Opportunities 1161
        Telxon Corp. v. Meyerson 1161
        Questions 1168
        Case Notes 1168
10.2.6   Piercing The Corporate Veil 1170
        McCallum Family L.L.C. v. Winger 1170
        Questions 1178
        Case Notes 1178

TABLE OF CONTENTS

Chapter 11   **FINANCING TECHNOLOGY INNOVATION** **1181**

11.1   SMALL BUSINESS INNOVATION RESEARCH (SBIR) AND SMALL
          BUSINESS TECHNOLOGY TRANSFER (STTR) PROGRAMS 1182
  11.1.1 Overview of SBIR and STTR Programs 1182
  11.1.2 Federal Legislation 1183
          Small Business Innovation Development Act 1184
          Questions 1194
  11.1.3 SBA SBIR Policy Directive 1195
          SBIR Policy Directive 1195
          Questions 1207
  11.1.4 SBA STTR Policy Directive 1208
          STTR Policy Directive 1209
          QUESTION 1210
  11.1.5 SBIR Data Rights and Phase III Rights 1210
          Night Vision Corp. v. The United States 1210
          Questions 1223
          Case Note 1223
11.2   PRIVATE SECURITIES OFFERINGS 1224
  11.2.1 Founders, Family and Friends 1225
  11.2.2 Angel Investors 1226
          Case Notes 1226
  11.2.3 Securities Registration Exemptions 1228
          Q&A: Small Business and the SEC 1228
          Notes 1234
          Questions 1235
          Case Notes 1235
  11.2.4 Private Placement Memorandum 1237
          Case Notes 1239
11.3   FRAUD IN PRIVATE SECURITIES OFFERINGS 1241
          *Ohio Bureau of Workers' Compensation v. MDL Active Duration
          Fund, Ltd.* 1241
          Questions 1245
          H-M Wexford LLC v. Encorp, Inc. 1246
          Questions 1254
          Case Notes 1254
11.4   VENTURE CAPITAL INVESTMENTS 1256
  11.4.1 Venture Capital Industry 1257
          Size and Structure of the Venture Capital Market 1257
  11.4.2 Structuring A Venture Capital Investment 1260
          Primer on Stocks and Bonds 1260
          Key Issues in Venture Capital Investments 1261

TABLE OF CONTENTS

11.4.3	Sample Venture Capital Term Sheet		1267
11.4.4	Venture Capital Investment Disputes		1282
		Spencer Trask Software v. Rpost International	1282
		Questions	1291
		Infosage v. Mellon Ventures	1292
		Questions	1299
		Case Notes	1299
11.4.5	Glossary of Selected Private Equity Investment Terms		1302
		Private Equity Glossary	1302
11.5	OTHER FORMS OF FINANCING		1317
11.5.1	Bank Loans		1318
11.5.2	Monetization of Intellectual Property		1321
11.5.3	Securitization of Intellectual Property		1323
11.5.4	Letters of Credit		1325
11.6	INITIAL PUBLIC OFFERINGS (IPOS)		1327
11.6.1	Overview of IPO Process		1327
11.6.2	Securities Acts		1331
		Q&A: Small Business and the SEC	1331
11.6.3	Securities Registration		1338
11.7	FRAUD IN PUBLIC SECURITIES OFFERINGS		1379
11.7.1	Federal Securities Fraud		1379
		In re Stac Electronics Securities Litigation	1380
		Questions	1388
		Case Notes	1389
11.7.2	State Securities Fraud		1392
		Reardon v. Lightpath Technologies	1392
		Questions	1398
		Case Notes	1399
11.8	DUE DILIGENCE		1401
11.8.1	Due Diligence Under Federal Securities Law		1401
		Software Toolworks v. Painewebber	1402
		Questions	1409
		Case Notes	1409
11.8.2	Due Diligence Under State Securities Law		1411
		Summers v. Welltech	1411
		Questions	1416
		Case Notes	1416
APPENDIX			**1419**
PSA-X Valuation Exercise			1419
BioFilter Negotiation and Drafting Exercises			1422

TABLE OF CONTENTS

BioFilter Facts 1422
BioFilter Venture Capital Investment Exercise 1427
BioFilter License Agreement Exercise 1429

TABLE OF CASES **TC-1**

INDEX **I-1**

Chapter 1

TECHNOLOGY INNOVATION FUNDAMENTALS: INTELLECTUAL PROPERTY, ECONOMICS, FINANCE AND BUSINESS

1.1. ETYMOLOGY OF "TECHNOLOGY TRANSFER"

The subject matter of these materials is technology innovation. Technology innovation is often achieved through the transfer of the technology during the course of its commercial development. As noted in the Introduction, the word "technology" comes from the Greek noun *technologia*, which means "a systematic solution to a practical problem." The word "transfer" comes from the Latin verb *transferre*, meaning "to bear or to convey from one person or place to another." These root definitions of "technology" and "transfer" suggest the conveyance of a problem solution between people and locations. With some refinements, these ancient definitions capture the essence of contemporary technology transfer transactions.

Contemporary technologies can be thought of as systematic solutions to commercial problems. These problems arise from the need to perform certain tasks (mechanical, electrical, chemical, computational and biological) more rapidly, more accurately or more efficiently. Transferee firms seek the best problem solutions in order to provide higher-quality/lower-cost products and services to customers, and to capture market share from competitors. Transferor firms compete to provide problem solutions, to recover their research and development expenditures, and to obtain profits for reinvestment in further R&D initiatives.

Problem solutions can be provided in tangible and intangible forms. Tangible problem solutions can take the form of tools, equipment, computers, software, component parts, or fully operational (turn-key) systems. Intangible problem solutions include ideas, information and know-how that can be conveyed in the form of documents, disclosures and personal instruction. A technology transfer transaction will frequently include both tangible and intangible problem solutions, however, the proportion of each may vary widely.

In order to capture the sophistication of modern technology transfer processes, the Greek and Latin definitions require some refinement. First, the Greek definition of *technologia* implies that the problem to be solved is fully understood. Today, this is often not the case. A firm may know it has a problem because something is not working properly, but may not know the causes or nature of the problem. Until the exact causes of a problem are known, effective solutions to the problem cannot be developed. Today, a good deal of technology transfer activity is devoted to analyzing, measuring and testing a problem in order to understand which solutions are appropriate to correct it.

Second, the Greek definition suggests that solutions are developed in order to solve previously identified problems. In the modern research and development enterprise, however, solutions are often created independently of problems. A researcher, for example, might discover a new way of performing a process, or a new property of a compound, without any idea of how the discovery can be put to practical use. Under these circumstances, the discovery constitutes a solution in search of a problem to solve. These different sequential relationships between a problem and a solution have given rise to two general models of technology transfer — "market pull" and "technology push." The "market pull" model envisions an identified industry problem pulling a research solution from the laboratory. The "technology push" model envisions a known research solution pushing into an industry as a solution to an as-yet-identified problem. The development of a given technology often combines elements of both models.

Third, the Greek definition casts problem solutions in a static, final form. Today, we view technology solutions as undergoing rapid revisions and subject to continual innovation. The familiar annual versions of software programs have their counterparts in all types of technologies. In addition, any given technical solution is reached through an evolutionary process that begins with basic research and ends with a marketable product or process. A technology can be transferred at any stage of its development, and the stage at which a technology is transferred greatly influences the terms and conditions of its transfer.

Finally, the Latin definition of *transferre* envisions the physical conveyance of technology; the transportation of things and people from one place to another. Today, however, communication, rather than transportation, is the principal means for transferring technology. The shift from transportation to communication partly reflects the increasing importance of ideas and information in the technology transfer process. It also reflects the extraordinary advances in computer and communication systems within the last twenty-five years that have allowed instantaneous exchange of knowledge. The modern conception of transferring technology is better captured in another Latin word closely related to *transferre* — *translatare*, which is the root of "translate" and "translation." "Translation," in the sense of communicating and explaining complex ideas in order to transform these ideas into actions, is a more apt description of the contemporary technology transfer process.

Additional Information

1. D.P. SIMPSON, CASSELL'S LATIN & ENGLISH DICTIONARY (1987).

2. OXFORD LATIN DICTIONARY (P.G. Glare ed., Oxford University Press 1983).

3. Robert J. Moore, NTC's Dictionary of Latin and Greek Origins (1997).

4. POCKET OXFORD CLASSICAL GREEK DICTIONARY (James Morwood & John Taylor eds., Oxford University Press 2002).

1.2 CONTEMPORARY DEFINITIONS OF TERMS

For the purposes of these materials, "technology" will be defined as a proprietary problem solution; that is, a problem solution that is protected by intellectual property laws, primarily in the form of patents, copyrights or trade secrets. This definition will include technology embodied in a tangible form (e.g., a product, device or material) as well as technology embodied in an intangible form (e.g., a right to make, copy or use intellectual property). A "technology transfer" will be defined as any exchange that includes intellectual property, whether the exchange is by means of a sale or lease of goods, a contract for provision of services, or a license or assignment of intellectual property rights. "Technology innovation" will be defined as the time between a technology's reduction to practice, either by building a working prototype or filing a patent application, and its market introduction. The stages of a technology's development can be roughly divided into research, invention, reduction to practice, intellectual property protection, commercial scale-up, testing, and market entry. Technology transfer will be viewed as a means of facilitating technology innovation. Technology transfers serve to advance a technology from one development stage to the next.

Technologies are generally divided between product technologies and process technologies. Product technologies are autonomous physical units of a technical system, such as a filter or switch, or a fully assembled system, such as a drill or press. A process technology is an ordered set of steps designed to yield a particular result. Process technologies include production, testing and organization methods. Product and process technologies are often combined together in a single technology transfer agreement, and both can be provided in either a tangible or intangible form. For example, a product technology can be delivered in the form of a patented good or in the form of a right to make a patented good. Likewise, a process technology can be delivered in the form of a machine to perform a patented process or in the form of a right to utilize a patented process. There is a fundamental difference, however, between the transfer of technology in the form of a good and in the form of intellectual property rights.

Intellectual property law sharply distinguishes between goods that embody intellectual property and the intellectual property that is embodied within goods. For example, a purchaser of a patented machine acquires the right to use, repair and resell the machine; however, the purchaser of a patented machine acquires no rights to make a second machine or to authorize others to make the same machine. A licensee of the intellectual property embodied in the machine, on the other hand, might have the right to make and sell multiple machines, and might also have the right to authorize others to do the same.

Intellectual property laws specify the rights of the intellectual property owners, and it is these rights that are the subject of a technology transfer. Patent owners have the exclusive rights to make, use, sell and import a patented product or process. Copyright owners have the exclusive right to reproduce, distribute and make derivations of the copyrighted work; and trade secret owners enjoy the exclusive right to disclose and use the trade secret. Transfers of intellectual property rights are generally comprised of licenses and assignments. A technology license grants the licensee the right to do something that would be unlawful without the license. A license is similar to a lease; the technology owner retains ultimate title and control over the technology but grants limited permission to another person to use the technology in certain ways and subject to certain conditions. A technology assignment is similar to a sale; the technology owner conveys complete title and control of the technology to another party. The distinction between a license and an assignment, however, is often blurred. For example, an exclusive license may include rights more closely associated with an assignment, and an assignment may retain rights in the assignor more closely associated with a license.

An intellectual property owner may divide and condition the rights transferred in literally thousands of different ways. The ways in which a patent owner may divide and condition the rights transferred in a license include the following:

1. Scope of use

> Exclusive, limited-exclusive, non-exclusive licenses (3)

2. Right of use

> Make, use, sell, import rights (4)

3. Territory of use

> North America, Europe, Asia, worldwide regions (4)

4. Field of use

> Application #1, application #2, application #3 (3)

5. Amount of use

> Unlimited use, limited use (2)

The formula for calculating the number of unique combinations of elements is:

$$ncr = n! \div (r! \times (n - r)!),$$

where ncr = the number of unique combinations of elements,
n = the number of elements (16), and
r = the number of groups (5).

$$ncr = 16! \div (5! \times (16 - 5)!)$$
$$ncr = 16! \div (5! \times 11!)$$
$$ncr = 20,922,789,888,000 \div (120 \times 39,916,800)$$
$$ncr = 20,922,789,888,000 \div 4,790,016,000$$
$$ncr = 4,368$$

The licensor and licensee have 4,368 different ways to structure the license agreement. This should give the licensor and licensee ample opportunities to structure the license to suit their individual needs.

1.3 NATURE OF TECHNOLOGY TRANSFER PROCESS

The economic principle that underlies modern technology transfer systems is an adaptation of Adam Smith's idea of specialization of function. Smith recognized that a firm would operate more efficiently if its workers were assigned specialized tasks. Workers would gain skill and experience in performing the tasks and, as a result, produce higher-quality/quantity output per unit of time than other workers. Although Smith's idea has long been central to the organization of manufacturing and production systems, its implications for technology innovation have only recently been appreciated.

Historically, technology innovation has been pursued by individual firms through independent activities. A single firm often controlled a technology's commercial development from the earliest stages of research until the final sales to consumers; technology was rarely transferred out of, or into, the firm. Internal technology development proceeded sequentially — each development stage was completed before the next stage was begun. Today, however, the increasing complexity of technology and the pace of innovation have forced firms to pursue alternative technology innovation strategies.

Firms seek to form partnerships or collaborative networks in order to commercialize a new technology. Within these associations, each firm contributes its special competency to the development of the technology. A firm may have special competence in research, design, testing, development, manufacturing, distribution or some other task. A firm may also have special competence in marketing, management, finance, law or regulatory approvals. As with Adam Smith's workers, the specialized efforts of technology firms produce a higher-level output than can be produced by individual firms acting in isolation. In addition to aggregating the special competencies of firms, a technology transfer collaboration also serves to spread the risks inherent in technology innovation.

The passage of a technology through a series of firms in the course of commercial development is often described as a "value-added process." Each firm in the chain adds value to the technology as it incorporates its core competence (in the form of special skills, expertise or intellectual property) into the technology. Having made its contribution to the technology's commercial development, the firm then passes the technology on to another "value adder." To be an effective participant in this process, however, a "value-added reseller" firm must approach technology transfer as a two-way street. Each firm must be willing to license in technology in which it has little or no core competence and be willing to license out technology when it has exhausted its core competence.

The collaboration of firms in a technology's commercial development is mirrored in the collaboration of professionals within a firm. Technology innovation draws upon the skills and expertise of three main professional disciplines — science and engineering, business, and law. The commercial development of a technology from the moment of its invention, or reduction to practice, until its market introduction can be viewed as a series of decisions that are based upon input from multiple professional sources. These decisions regarding a technology's commercial development are highly interrelated. Technical choices greatly affect business choices, and both directly impact legal choices. For example, choices on such questions as functionality, compatibility and operating environment will greatly affect business choices on marketing strategies or strategic alliances. Similarly, these choices will affect the IP rights that arise from the technology's development as well as the means appropriate for protecting this rights. Of course, all technical and business decisions regarding a technology's development will be reflected in the terms and conditions of any technology transfer agreement.

1.4   LICENSES AS PROPERTY RIGHTS

The word "license" has two distinct meanings that are easily confused. One meaning of "license" is the contract by which parties exchange rights. The other meaning of "license" is the property right that is created by the exchange. The first meaning is analogous to a contract in a real estate transaction; the second is analogous to the title created by an exectuted deed. This section considers a license as a type of property right. A license is commonly defined as the permission to do something that would be unlawful without the license. To understand a license as a property right, it is useful to consider initially the role of private property in a market economy and the relationship between a license and other property rights.

Private property rights are the foundation of a market economy. Every society must determine who will have use of what resources and for what purposes. In a planned economy, these decisions are made by a central government authority; but in a market economy, these decisions are made by individual buyers and sellers exchanging rights to resources. A market economy steers resources to their highest valued uses by allowing buyers and sellers to negotiate freely the prices and terms of resource exchanges. In a market economy, the fundamental question of who will have use of what resources and for what purposes is answered by a series of private, voluntary transactions rather than by a single, dictated government decision; however, government nonetheless plays a critical role in a market economy.

Rights in a resource cannot be exchanged until initial entitlement to the resource is authoritatively determined. Determination of initial entitlement to a resource involves two steps. First, ownership of the resource must be established in some identified person or entity. Second, the scope of the ownership rights in the resource must be defined. If there is uncertainty either about the ownership of a resource or about the scope of ownership rights, then the value of the resource will be discounted in market exchanges to reflect this uncertainty. Government, acting through courts, administrative agencies and legislatures, plays the critical role of determining initial entitlement to resources. Government's role in determining initial entitlements is especially important and difficult in the area of intellectual property resources. In the recent past, government bodies have had to consider intellectual property in the form of computer programs, artificial intelligence, transgenic animals and human genes. Each new technical advance creates a new set of cost and benefit possibilities. Uncertainty regarding the allocation of these costs and benefits must be resolved before investment in the commercial development of a technology can begin.

Government also plays an important role in facilitating the exchange of resource rights. Government serves as the official recorder of ownership title in resources. Permanent and accurate title records are essential to efficient market exchanges of property rights whether these rights are in real property, personal property or intellectual property. Government also serves in various ways as a regulator of market transactions. Government regulation of market transactions serves many purposes, such as assuring disclosure of information about security investments, safety of consumer products, safety and efficacy of drugs, maintenance of competitive markets and orderly disposition of creditor assets. Finally, government serves as the arbiter of last resort in disputes over property rights. Disputes over rights in a resource must be finally and authoritatively settled before the resource can be traded at its true value. The resolution of disputes over property rights also serves to further define the rights and duties of parties with respect to a resource and hence to provide guidance for the arrangement of future transactions.

1.5 INTELLECTUAL PROPERTY OVERVIEW

There are three principal forms of protection for technology intellectual property — patents, copyrights and trade secrets. These three forms of protection differ in many respects. Each one covers a different subject matter; each has a different set of requirements for creation; and each affords a different scope of protection to its owner.

Intellectual property rights are intended to achieve two, often competing, objectives. First, IP rights are intended to reward the creator or inventor for the time, effort and ingenuity that it took to produce the intellectual property. Second, IP rights are intended to benefit society by advancing the progress of science and increasing the store of public knowledge. The conflict between these objectives lies in the exclusivity of control over intellectual property granted to creators and the access to intellectual property for the public.

New knowledge builds upon past knowledge. To the extent creativity is rewarded by allowing knowledge to be owned, the use of knowledge is not available to the public for further advancement of science and creation of new knowledge. These conflicting objectives have existed since the inception of intellectual property laws in the United States over two hundred years ago.

The drafters of the U.S. Constitution struggled with this conflict. Thomas Jefferson, who became the first commissioner of the U.S. Patent Office, typifies the drafters' ambivalence toward protection of intellectual property rights. England had long granted monopoly rights over the manufacture of goods to individuals and guilds. The award of these monopoly rights gave the King great control over commerce and assured fidelity to the throne. Jefferson was adamantly opposed to these royal monopolies. On the other hand, as an inventor himself, Jefferson understood the time and effort that invention required and the importance of rewarding inventors as a way to encourage new invention. In the end, Jefferson and the other drafters agreed to the language in Article 1, Section 8, Clause 8 of the Constitution. This language authorizes Congress to pass laws "To promote the progress of science and useful arts, by securing for limited times to authors and inventors the exclusive right to their respective writings and discoveries."

This language reflects the balance that the drafters attempted to strike between their abhorrence of monopolies and their recognition of the need to reward the creation of intellectual property. Congress was authorized to grant authors and inventors monopolies over their writings and discoveries, but only for limited periods of time and only to promote science and the useful arts. These monopolies could not be granted indefinitely and could not be used by the Congress to control commerce or to assure allegiance to the government. The first Patent Act, which was authored by Thomas Jefferson, was passed by Congress in 1793.

Intellectual property differs in many respects from the two other types of property with which the law deals — real property and personal property. Intellectual property cannot be defined or identified with the same precision as real and personal property. Possession of intellectual property at a given time can be shared by many persons, both lawfully and unlawfully; and intellectual property is rapidly, sometimes instantly, transportable.

On a fundamental level, however, real, personal and intellectual property laws all serve the same function in an economic system — they each determine the ownership status of property at a particular point in time and thus make possible market transfers based upon this ownership status. For an efficient exchange of ownership rights to occur, each party must be sure that the other party in fact owns the property to be transferred. Uncertainty as to ownership rights or title causes the value of property to be discounted in the market. In some cases, the cost of uncertainty may be so high that an exchange of rights cannot take place. One of the chief purposes of all property law is to minimize ownership uncertainty and thereby reduce the transaction costs associated with the exchange of rights in property.

1.5.1 Patents

[Editor's note: The America Invents Act (AIA) was signed into law on September 16th, 2011. Most of the provisions in the AIA will take effect on September 16th, 2012. The AIA includes many important changes from the current patent law. I will briefly note some of these changes in the context of the following material which was written prior to the passage of the new Patent Act.]

Patent protection is both the most difficult to obtain and the most comprehensive ownership form of intellectual property. Patent law establishes very high standards of eligibility for the grant of a patent on an invention; however, if these standards can be satisfied, the person or firm to whom the patent is issued (i.e., the patentee) obtains a true monopoly over the invention for a period of twenty years from the date the patent application is filed. No other person can make, use, sell or import the invention even if she or he developed the invention independently without access to, or knowledge of, the patented invention.

Patent Requirements

In order to obtain a patent on an invention, the patent applicant must affirmatively establish that the invention satisfies three standards — utility, novelty and non-obviousness.

Utility requires that the invention actually perform the task that it is claimed capable of performing in the patent application. Proof of an invention's utility does not require construction of a working model, although this may be necessary in some instances; however, it does require the inclusion of drawings and descriptions in the patent application that are sufficient to demonstrate the operability of the invention. In general, the utility standard requires that the patent applicant establish that the invention is capable of accomplishing an identifiable result and that this result constitutes a practical benefit in some application.

Novelty requires that the patent applicant establish that the same, or substantially identical, invention did not already exist, or was not already known to the public, prior to the date on which the applicant made his or her invention. The critical novelty date under the AIA is the date on which the patent application is filed, not the date on which the invention is made. The purpose of the novelty requirement is to ensure that the reward of patent rights is granted only to the persons who are the first and true inventors of the product or process. Events that can negate novelty, or anticipate the invention, include the prior filing or issuance of a patent, a prior printed publication, or prior public knowledge, sale or use of the invention. In order to determine whether an invention is anticipated, a search of all relevant prior art is conducted. This search covers the Patent and Trademark Office (PTO) records, scientific and technical books and journals, and inquiries of experts in the field.

Non-obviousness is by far the most difficult of the patent requirements to satisfy. The non-obviousness standard requires that an invention would not have been obvious to a reasonably skilled person having knowledge of all relevant prior art in the field. If common sense would direct a person skilled in the art to combine two known elements of prior art to solve a known problem or to provide a needed improvement, then the invention would not satisfy the non-obviousness requirement. An invention can be novel but not be non-obvious. The purpose of the non-obviousness standard is to disqualify inventions that constitute small changes in the existing field of art and which impede technology progress more than reward intellectual creativity.

Statutory Bar

Under section 102 of the current Patent Act, which will remain in effect until March 16, 2013, a patent must be filed in a timely manner or it will be subject to a statutory bar. Statutory bar is similar to novelty in terms of the events that will defeat patentability; however, there are two important differences between novelty and statutory bar. First, statutory bar is concerned with events that occur more than 12 months prior to the date a patent application is filed, whereas novelty is concerned with events that occur prior to the time an invention was conceived. Second, a statutory bar can arise from activities of either a third party or the patent claimant, whereas novelty can arise only from the activities of a third party.

The statutory bar allows a prospective patentee a 12-month grace period (beginning on the date an invention is first disclosed in a printed publication or offered for sale to customers) in which to file a patent application. Statutory bar is intended to encourage diligence on behalf of inventors in filing patent applications. It is also intended to prevent an extension of the patent monopoly period through prolonged sales of an invention followed by a patent filing. Many foreign countries, however, do not allow for a 12-month grace period and have adopted a requirement of "absolute novelty." The requirement of absolute novelty will bar the issuance of any patent if it has been disclosed or offered for sale prior to the date on which the patent application is filed. Therefore, an inventor who discloses or offers for sale patentable subject matter will have 12 months in which to file a patent application in the United States, but will be barred from gaining a patent in the many foreign countries requiring absolute novelty.

Under the AIA, with one exception, there is no longer a 12 month statutory grace period. Section 102 of the AIA states that a person shall be entitled to a patent unless "the claimed invention was patented, described in a printed publication, or in public use, or on sale, or otherwise available to the public before the effective filing date of the claimed invention." The one exception to this absolute novelty requirement under the AIA is a disclosure of the claimed invention by the inventor, joint inventor or another person who obtained the subject matter disclosed from the inventor or joint inventor. If such a disclosure is made one year or less before the effective filing date of the claimed invention it will not bar the issuance of a patent on the claimed invention. Again, section 102 of the AIA will take effect on March 16, 2013.

Patent Subject Matter

The Patent Act describes three general classes of patents — utility patents, design patents and plant patents. Utility patents are divided between product and process patents. Product patents cover the tangible embodiment of an invention in the form of a machine, manufactured article or composition of materials. Process patents cover the ordered set of steps employed to achieve a certain result.

Product and process patents involve different subject matter claims and provide the patentee with different forms of protection. A process patent does not protect the product produced by the patented process; creation of an identical product, but by a different process, will not infringe the process patent. Likewise, a product patent does not protect the process by which the product was made; the use of an identical process, but to produce a different product, will not infringe the product patent. It is possible to obtain a patent which covers both a product and process (i.e., a product-by-process patent); however, the product and process claims must each separately satisfy the utility, novelty and non-obviousness requirements. An invalid product claim cannot be saved by virtue of a process qualification, and an invalid process claim cannot be saved by virtue of a product qualification.

An interesting saga of a special type of process patent is the business method patent. For many years, the PTO and courts were unwilling to accept methods of doing business as patentable subject matter. In 1999, the Court of Appeals for the Federal Circuit (CAFC) considered the case of a patent application for a method of managing a group of mutual funds structured as a partnership. The PTO had rejected the application as un-patentable subject matter because it claimed a method of doing business. The CAFC reversed the PTO and held that methods of doing business are patentable subject matter. The CAFC found that the "the transformation of data, representing discrete dollar amounts . . . into a final share price, constitutes a practical application of a mathematical algorithm . . . because it produces a "useful, concrete and tangible result." " *See* State Street Bank &

Trust Co. v. Signature Financial Group, 149 F.3d 1368 (Fed. Cir. 1998). However, in the wake of a flood of business method patent applications, the CAFC reversed its State Street Bank decision in 2008. *See* In Re Bilski, 545 F.3d 943 (Fed. Cir. 2008). In *In Re Bilski*, the CAFC held that the sole test for patentable subject matter was whether the invention consisted of a machine or transformation of matter. The CAFC's *In Re Bilski* decision was appealed to the U.S. Supreme Court. The Supreme Court reversed the CAFC and held that the "machine-or-transformation" test is not the only test for patent subject matter and, at least, some methods of doing business are eligible for patent protection. *See* Bilski v. Kappos, 130 S. Ct. 3218 (2010). Unfortunately, the Court did not elaborate on exactly what methods of doing business would be eligible for patent protection.

Finally, two other types of patents should be briefly mentioned — improvement patents and fencing patents. An improvement patent is a patent on an improvement to an existing, or base, patent. The patentee of an improvement patent has the exclusive right to make, use, sell and import the improvement; however, the patentee of an improvement patent has no rights in the base patent unless the patentee receives a license from the patentee of the base patent. Likewise, the patentee of the base patent has no rights in the improvement patent unless the patentee receives a license from the patentee of the improvement patent.

Fencing patents are used to extend the scope of protection for a core patent. The patentees of fencing patents generally do not intend to use the patent subject matter, but do not want to allow others (usually competitors) to practice the patent subject matter. Fencing patents can be viewed as unused improvement patents. Firms would not seek to obtain fencing patents on subject matter that would not constitute a viable improvement to their core patents. It is sometimes said that fencing patents are used to make it more difficult for others to engineer around core patents. Here again, however, firms would not seek to obtain fencing patents to make it more difficult to engineer around their core patents if the engineering was not a viable alternative to their core patents.

Patent Claims

The scope of a patent is defined by the claims set forth in the patent application. The patent claims describe the boundaries of an invention in much the same way as metes and bounds measurements in a deed describe a parcel of real property. The breadth of the claims in a patent depends upon the existing state of the art in the field of invention. Broad patent claims (sometimes called "pioneer patents") are possible when the state of the art is in an early stage of development. As the state of art advances, the field becomes more crowded and claims must be narrowed in order to overcome the novelty and non-obviousness requirements. In some instances, the claims may need to be narrowed to such an extent that the value of the patent is not worth the cost of obtaining it. Generally, inventors seek to stake out broad claims in the initial patent application and the Patent Office examiners seek to narrow these claims during the course of the patent examination.

Patent Infringement

There are two types of patent infringement — literal infringement and equivalency infringement. Literal infringement is present when the alleged infringing product or process includes each and every element recited in any one of the patent's claims. Equivalency infringement, or the doctrine of equivalents, is applied when the patent claims and alleged infringing product or process perform substantially the same function, in substantially the same way, to achieve substantially the same result. Literal infringement and equivalency infringement mirror the novelty and non-obviousness requirements. A device which literally infringes a patent would also anticipate it if the device was part of the prior art when the patent was filed. Likewise, a device which infringes a patent under the doctrine of equivalents would also render the patent non-obvious if the device was part of the prior art when the patent was filed. The symmetry between novelty and literal infringement, and non-obviousness and the doctrine of equivalents, is not complete. The patent requirement of non-obviousness considers multiple prior art references to determine whether the invention would have been obvious to a person reasonably skilled in the art. The doctrine of equivalents looks only to the alleged infringing product or process to determine whether it performs substantially the same function, in substantially the same way, to achieve substantially the same result.

Non-Patentable Subject Matter

Excluded from patent protection are laws of nature, physical phenomena and naturally occurring substances. Mathematical algorithms have an interesting history under the patent laws. For many years, mathematical algorithms were not considered by the courts or the Patent Office to be eligible as patent subject matter. Courts voiced concerns over the monopolization of mathematical ideas and analogized algorithms to physical principles which were clearly excluded from patent protection. The Patent Office voiced concerns over its capacity to handle a new wave of patent applications and over the competency of patent examiners in the new field of computer science.

Today, patent law is far more receptive to protection of computer algorithms. Patents have been issued for a wide variety of algorithms from medical diagnostic programs to banking programs. However, to obtain a patent containing an algorithm, the algorithm must be integrated somehow into a physical product or process that has a tangible utility.

1.5.2   Copyrights

A copyright is much easier to obtain than a patent but affords the owner less protection. Unlike the requirements of novelty and non-obviousness that must be affirmatively established to obtain a patent, copyright only requires that the work be original and that it be fixed in some tangible medium of expression. Copyright is the principal form of intellectual property protection for literary works, artistic works and computer programs. Copyright owners have the exclusive right to reproduce the copyrighted work, prepare derivative works based upon the copyrighted work and distribute copies of the copyrighted work.

Originality and Creation

The originality requirement in copyright law does not involve any consideration of the creativity or ingenuity represented by the work. Originality is satisfied merely by showing that the work was independently created. Copyright protection is created by filing a copyright registration with the Copyright Office. (Technically, copyright protection arises at the moment of creation and fixation of a copyright work. Registration, however, is necessary to sue for copyright infringement and to obtain certain types of relief provided for in the Copyright Act.) Copyright registration is less difficult, less expensive and less time-consuming than patent prosecution. The copyright registration form consists of short, straightforward questions that the applicant can answer without the aid of an attorney. There is no search conducted of previously copyrighted works, and there are no comparisons made between existing works in a field and the work which is sought to be registered.

The lesser protection afforded the copyright holder is due to the fact that copyright protects only against the actual copying of a work. If a third party independently creates a work that is substantially similar, or even identical, to a copyrighted work, then the reproduction and sale of the third party's work will not infringe the rights of the copyright holder. This is an important difference between copyright and patent protection.

Computer Programs

The Copyright Act, unlike the Patent Act, provides specifically for the protection of computer programs. A computer program is broadly defined in the Copyright Act as "a set of statements or instructions to be used directly or indirectly in a computer in order to bring about a certain result." Less clear in the Copyright Act is the nature and extent of copyright protection which Congress intended to provide computer programs. While some of these questions have been resolved by courts, others remain very much unsettled.

Copyright protection is available for computer programs expressed in both source and object code formats. A copyright registration will protect against copying in both formats. Copyright protection is not dependent upon the medium in which the computer program is stored. Programs are copyrightable whether they are contained in disks, tapes or microprocessors. Copyright protection also does not depend upon the function that a computer program performs. Application programs, operating system programs, microcode instruction sets, user interfaces, and screen displays can all be copyrighted. The copyright owner also has the exclusive right to translate a computer program from one computer language to another and to adapt a program for use on different hardware systems.

It is possible to have patent and copyright protection in the same computer program. Patent protection covers the algorithm underlying the computer program. Copyright protection covers the code that is used to implement the program's underlying algorithm.

Ideas and Expressions

Copyright law protects only the expression of an idea, not the idea itself. The separation of ideas and expression in the context of computer programs has proven difficult. On the one hand, copyright law has sought to provide protection beyond the literal expression of the program code in order to prevent persons from avoiding copyright infringement through making minor changes. On the other hand, the extension of copyright protection beyond the literal program code immediately raises the question of where to draw the line between protectable and un-protectable aspects of the program. In general, courts have found that a program's "organization, structure and sequence" are protectable non-literal features under the copyright laws, but that functional and utilitarian aspects of a program are not protectable.

The distinction between ideas and expressions in copyright law is not black-and-white. Rather, copyright law views ideas and expressions on a continuum, extending from the most unique features of a program to the most generic. The greater the number of alternative ways in which a program can be written to perform a given function, the more unique will be the choice of individual features. Likewise, the fewer the number of alternative ways a program can perform a given function, the more generic the program features will be. Expressive features are primarily the result of the programmer's ingenuity and choice. Generic features are primarily the result of functional requirements and industry standards.

Copyright law determines the degree of copyright protection according to where a feature falls on the idea-expression continuum; more expressive features are accorded a broader scope of copyright protection, while more generic features are accorded a narrower scope of protection. A broad copyright liberally extends protection from the literal expression in a work to more generalized, but substantially similar, derivative works. A narrow copyright restricts protection to identical equivalents of the expression in a work.

Non-Copyrightable Subject Matter

The Copyright Act provides that copyright protection does not extend to any idea, procedure, process, system, method of operation, concept, principle or discovery, regardless of the form in which it is described, explained, illustrated or embodied in a work.

1.5.3 Trade Secrets

Trade secret protection of intellectual property differs in many ways from patent and copyright protection. First and foremost, trade secret protection is created by state law and enforced through state courts. Patent and copyright protection, as noted above, are created by federal law and enforced through federal courts. Trade secret protection also does not require filing of an application or registration. Instead, trade secret protection is established by the actions of the trade secret owner. Virtually any type of matter or material can be the subject of trade secret protection; ideas, discoveries, formulas, data and all types of information can be protected as trade secrets. However, third parties who have not had access to the trade secret are free to reverse engineer the trade secret. If the reverse engineering is successful, then the third party can use the trade secret without any liability to the trade secret owner.

Trade secret protection does require, however, that the subject matter be maintained as a secret and that it not be generally available to the public. Trade secret protection can be lost suddenly and forever in the event the secret becomes a matter of public knowledge. Trade secret protection also depends upon the existence of an express or implied confidential relationship between the trade secret owner and the alleged misappropriator of the trade secret.

The trade secret law of different states varies in a number of respects. In general, however, trade secret law involves three related elements — economic value, secrecy and duty of confidence.

Economic Value

To constitute a trade secret, the secret material must have some economic value. Economic value is most often established through showing that the material provides the owner with a competitive advantage in a market and that this competitive advantage would be lost in the event that other persons disclosed or used the material. Although the trade secret claimant need not attach a precise dollar value to the material, it is nonetheless helpful if the claimant can show some amount of financial investment in the material. Financial investment strengthens the reasonability of the claimant's expectation of realizing a return from the exclusive use of the material.

Secrecy

There are two questions that arise with respect to the secrecy requirement. The first is whether the material is in fact a secret within an industry. Assuming that the answer to this question is yes, the second question is whether the trade secret claimant took reasonable steps to preserve the secret status of the material.

Whether or not information is secret in an industry is obviously related to the question of economic value. If the information is generally available in an industry, it cannot provide a competitive advantage or possess economic value. However, information which is not absolutely secret, but is known to only a limited number of other persons, can still be a source of competitive advantage and have economic value. For this reason, trade secret law generally requires only a relative, rather than an absolute, standard for establishing secrecy. There is no bright dividing line between relative secrecy sufficient for a trade secret and general knowledge which will destroy a trade secret. It is clear, however, that the more persons who have access to the information, whether authorized or unauthorized, the weaker the trade secret claim becomes.

The second aspect of the secrecy requirement asks whether reasonable steps were taken to preserve the information as a secret. This involves an inquiry into the legal and practical means utilized by the claimant, internally and externally, to protect the secret information. To establish a trade secret, a claimant must show that appropriate agreements were prepared and signed and that affirmative measures were taken to enforce these agreements. Trade secret law provides that the proper focus for determining the reasonability of a claimant's efforts is the substance of the claimant's conduct, not formal documents and signatures.

In determining the reasonableness of a claimant's efforts, courts have often considered the security practices of other firms in the industry as benchmarks. These benchmarks are applied to internal and external activities. Internally, efforts to preserve trade secrets are directed toward employees, consultants, independent contractors, managers and founders. Generally, all of these persons should be required to sign nondisclosure agreements. Nondisclosure agreements protect against unauthorized disclosure or use of trade secret information. Access to trade secret information generally should be limited to those persons who have a direct need to know the information. Under some circumstances, security clearances, access codes and area restrictions may be necessary to establish reasonable effort.

Externally, efforts to preserve trade secrets are directed primarily toward customers and suppliers. Customers and suppliers who have access to any trade secret information should be required to sign nondisclosure agreements and provided only information that is strictly necessary for their purposes. Documents containing trade secret information, such as instruction manuals, maintenance materials and technical specifications, should be clearly marked as confidential and distributed on a controlled basis.

Duty of Confidence

The third requirement of a trade secret is that there exists a duty of confidence which is owed to the trade secret owner by the alleged misappropriator. A duty of confidence can be expressly created under the terms of a written agreement or it can be implied from the general nature of the parties' relationship. An implied duty of confidence is often found to exist between employees and employers and between managers and firms. In some instances, this implied duty alone may be a sufficient basis for establishing a trade secret. Implied duties, however, are always more ambiguous than express duties and should not be relied upon as substitutes for written confidentiality agreements.

In order to create an express duty, the agreement must be knowingly accepted by the party sought to be charged with the duty. Establishing acceptance is rarely a problem when the parties have personally reviewed the terms of the agreement and signed it as is the case with employees, consultants and independent contractors. Establishing acceptance is more difficult in the case of customer agreements — especially if the agreement is a standard form contract and the customer does not sign the contract. As a general rule, the closer the contact is between the trade secret owner and the alleged misappropriator, the more likely it is that a knowing acceptance will be found. Contracts resulting from personal communication between parties are generally sufficient to support acceptance of an express duty of confidence. "Shrink wrapped" contracts included with mass market products are generally insufficient.

Careful consideration should be given to the definition of a trade secret. The broader the trade secret claim, the more difficult it is to establish that the information at issue is a secret in the industry. Broad trade secret claims are also often more difficult to enforce, especially between employees and employers. Courts require that a trade secret claim not extend beyond the reasonable commercial expectations of the employer and that the claim not unnecessarily restrict former employees in obtaining future employment. The objective in defining a trade secret is to describe it as precisely as possible while not divulging key operational details of the technology.

Additional Information

1. STEPHEN ELIAS & RICHARD STIM, PATENT COPYRIGHT & TRADEMARK (6th ed. 2003).

2. SHELDON W. HALPERN, CRAIG ALLEN NARD & KENNETH L. PORT, FUNDAMENTALS OF UNITED STATES INTELLECTUAL PROPERTY LAW: COPYRIGHT, PATENT, TRADEMARK (2d ed. 2006).

3. MARY LAFRANCE, COPYRIGHT LAW IN A NUTSHELL (2008).

4. CHRISTOPHER M. ARENA, THE BUSINESS OF INTELLECTUAL Property (2008).

5. AARON SCHWABACH, INTELLECTUAL PROPERTY: A REFERENCE HANDBOOK (2007).

6. WILLIAM CORNISH & DAVID LLEWELYN, INTELLECTUAL PROPERTY: PATENTS, COPYRIGHT, TRADE MARKS AND ALLIED RIGHTS (6th ed. rev. 2007).

7. RICHARD STIM, PATENT, COPYRIGHT & TRADEMARK: AN INTELLECTUAL PROPERTY DESK REFERENCE (9th ed. rev. 2007).

8. JANICE M. MUELLER, AN INTRODUCTION TO PATENT LAW (2d ed. 2006).

9. MARSHALL LEAFFER, UNDERSTANDING COPYRIGHT LAW (4th ed. 2005).

10. ROBERT P. MERGES, INTELLECTUAL PROPERTY IN NEW TECHNOLOGICAL AGE (4th ed. 2007).

11. RICHARD W. STIM, COPYRIGHT LAW (1999).

12. WILLIAM H. H. FRANCIS & ROBERT C. COLLINS, CASES AND MATERIALS ON PATENT LAW: INCLUDING TRADE SECRETS, COPYRIGHTS, TRADEMARKS (5th ed. 2002).

13. CHERYL BESENJAK, COPYRIGHT PLAIN AND SIMPLE (2d ed. 2001).

14. ROBERT A. A. GORMAN & JANE C. GINSBURG, COPYRIGHT: CASES AND MATERIALS (6th ed. 2001).

15. MICHAEL A. EPSTEIN, EPSTEIN ON INTELLECTUAL PROPERTY (5th ed. rev. 2005).

16. HENRY H. PERRITT, TRADE SECRETS: A PRACTITIONER'S GUIDE (2d ed. 2005).

1.6 BASIC ECONOMIC CONCEPTS

A basic knowledge of economics is essential to an understanding of business. Economics is the study of how scarce resources are allocated within a society. Macroeconomics is concerned with the supply, demand and price of resources within a particular market. Microeconomics is concerned with the costs and revenues of individual firms competing to supply resources in a market. The notion of scarcity is key to economic analysis. In economics, all resources are scarce and the utilization of a given resource in one market, or by one firm, makes this resource unavailable for use in another market or by another firm — wood used in one market for pencils is not available in another market for lumber, and rubber used by one firm for erasers is unavailable to another firm for bottle stoppers. The goal of economic analysis is to predict the distribution of resources which will maximize consumer satisfaction by supplying the exact amount of products (e.g., lumber, pencils, erasers, bottle stoppers) that consumers demand.

The following section will review the core concepts of economic analysis. These concepts will be described in a simplified form, but hopefully with sufficient detail to enable the reader to appreciate their essential features and practical relevance. The next section will consider these core economic concepts in the context of intellectual property. As you will see, the economic characteristics of intellectual property are in many ways the same, and in many ways different, from those of real or personal property, which are the traditional subjects of economic analysis.

1.6.1   Macro-Economics and Micro-Economics

Efficiency

The concept of efficiency is used in many aspects of economic analysis. In its simplest form, "efficiency" can be defined as the allocation of resources according to their most highly valued uses. The ultimate goal of efficiency in a free-market economic system is to maximize consumer satisfaction by allocating resources in accordance with the consumers' willingness to pay for the resources. Consumers willing to pay more for a resource will have more of that resource available to purchase; consumers willing to pay less will have less. And no resources will be allocated to uses for which consumers are unwilling to pay. The matching of resource allocation with consumer willingness to pay, an efficient economic system, is achieved through efficiency in two other institutions — markets and firms.

An efficient market is a market in which the supply and demand for a resource are in equilibrium at a given price. If consumers are willing to pay the market price for a resource, but the resource is unavailable — or if the resource is available, but consumers are unwilling to buy the resource at the market price — then the market is operating inefficiently. The market inefficiency in the first instance will be corrected by existing firms supplying additional resources and new firms entering the market until the unmet market demand is satisfied. In the second instance, the market inefficiency will be corrected by firms decreasing the supply of the resource or exiting the market until the surplus is eliminated.

Competition between firms is critical to the operation of an efficient market. Competition forces firms in a market to provide the highest-quality goods or services possible at the lowest price possible. If the existing firms in a market provide lower quality goods or services, then firms capable of providing higher-quality goods or services at the same price will enter the market and displace the existing firms. Likewise, if existing firms in a market charge too high a price for goods or services, then firms capable of providing the same goods or services at a lower price will enter the market and displace the existing firms. Competition between firms directly benefits consumers by providing them the best possible quality-price combination at any given time.

The efficiency of a firm is the key to the firm's competitive survival in a market. A firm must always strive to minimize its cost of production and maximize the quality of its output. In order to minimize costs of production, a firm must avoid all unnecessary expenditures of money, time and effort. The firm must also have access to relatively more highly trained and dedicated employees and relatively more modern plant and equipment. Quality control is critical to a firm's competitiveness. It costs a great deal more to correct mistakes than to avoid making mistakes in the first instance. Minimizing costs at the expense of quality, therefore, is not an efficient strategy for a firm.

Supply, Demand and Price

Supply is the quantity of a good or service which suppliers are willing to provide at a given price. Supply is positively related to price — the higher the price, the greater the quantity suppliers are willing to provide; and the lower the price, the lesser the quantity suppliers are willing to provide. Demand is the quantity of a good or service which consumers are willing to buy at a given price. Demand is inversely related to price — the higher the price, the lower the quantity demanded; and the lower the price, the higher the quantity demanded. Supply and demand curves are plotted as a series of price-quantity points. The intersection of the supply and demand curves (i.e., the equilibrium point) determines the amount of a good or service which will be provided and the price which will be charged. In Figure 1 below, suppliers will provide Q number of units at P price per unit.

Figure 1: Supply and Demand Curves

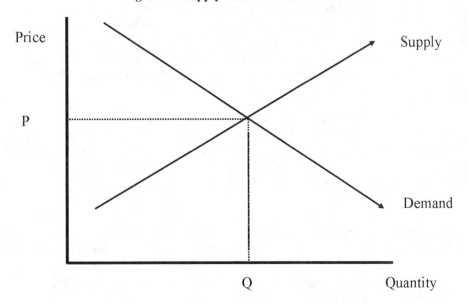

Shifts in the supply curve will affect the price and the quantity demanded. Figure 2 illustrates the effects of a shift in the supply curve. If suppliers increase the quantity of the goods or services provided (i.e., the supply curve shifts downward to S1), then the increase in supply with no change in the demand curve will result in the lower price P1 and an increase in demand to Q1. Likewise, if suppliers provide a lesser amount of goods and services (i.e., the supply curve shifts upward to S2), then the price will increase to P2 and demand will decrease to Q2.

Figure 2: Shifts in Supply Curve

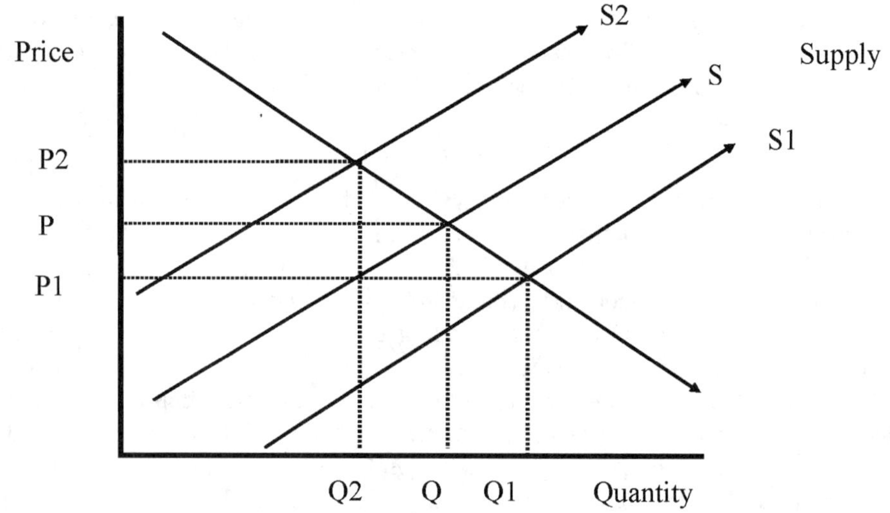

The same will occur with shifts in the demand curve. If consumers demand a lesser quantity of goods or service (i.e., the demand curve shifts downward to D1) and there is no change in the supply curve, then the price per unit will decrease to P1. If consumers demand a greater quantity of goods or services (i.e., the demand curve shifts upward to D2) and there is no change in the supply curve, then the price per unit will increase to P2. Figure 3 illustrates the effects of a shift in the demand curve.

The effect that a change in price has upon the supply or demand for a good or service is referred to as "elasticity." Elasticity measures the percentage change in the quantity of demand or supply as a function of a percentage change in price. If a one percent change in price results in a one percent change in supply or demand, the supply or demand is said to be unitary. If a one percent change in price results in less than a one percent change in supply or demand, then the supply or demand is said to be relatively inelastic. If a one percent change in price results in greater than a one percent change in supply or demand, then the supply or demand is said to be relatively elastic. In some instances, supply and demand may be completely inelastic. For example, firms may be unable to obtain the raw materials necessary to increase supply, or consumers may be unable to survive without obtaining goods or services. Figure 4 illustrates elasticity of supply and demand.

Figure 3: Shifts in Demand Curve

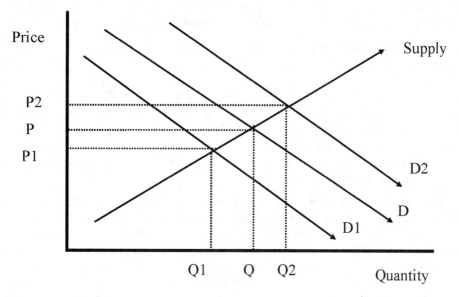

Figure 4: Elasticity of Supply and Demand

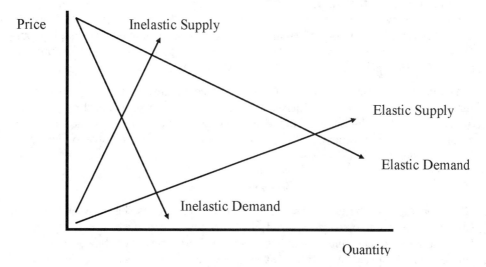

A number of factors other than the price of a given good influence the supply and demand of that good. Supply is influenced by the relative prices of other goods and the relative cost of production inputs. If other goods command a higher price and a firm can redeploy its assets to supply these other goods, the firm will shift production to the other goods. Shifting production from lower-priced to higher-priced goods is an example of what economists refer to as "opportunity costs." The investment of scarce resources in any given economic activity comes at the expense of investment in some other economic activity. Every investment has an opportunity cost associated with it — namely, the forgone opportunity to make an alternative investment. When the opportunity costs of a given investment become too high, the firm will shift its investment to reduce its opportunity costs.

The relative cost of production inputs (i.e., factors of production) such as land, labor, raw materials and equipment also affect supply. If the cost of production inputs rises and these costs cannot be passed on to consumers in the form of higher prices (i.e., demand is relatively elastic), then the firm's profit margin will decrease. As the firm's profit margin decreases, the firm will be forced to consider alternative uses of its assets which offer the potential of higher profit margins. The firm's opportunity costs are increased by a relative increase in the cost of production inputs in the same way that opportunity costs are increased by a relative increase in the price of other goods.

Demand is also affected by factors other than the price of a given good. Two of the most important factors affecting demand are the price of substitute goods and the capacity to reduce consumption through increased efficiency. There are always substitutes for a given good. The substitute good may be more or less like the original good. The more alike the substitute good is to the original good, the more the price change of one will affect the demand for the other. Even where the substitute good is quite unlike the original good, substitution will still occur if the change in price of one or the other goods is sufficiently large. For example, the substitute good may be inferior to the original good in terms of quality or functionality. Nonetheless, if the price of the original good increases sufficiently, demand may switch to the substitute good despite the inferiority of its features. This illustrates the price-performance characteristic of demand. In making purchasing decisions, consumers compare the price of a good and the performance of a good. Neither price nor performance alone determines demand.

Demand is also affected by the capacity of consumers to reduce consumption through increased efficiency. Increased efficiency may come about through elimination of waste or the introduction of new methods or processes. In either case, if consumers can obtain the same benefit or output with a reduced level of consumption, then demand will decrease.

Costs and Revenues

The relationship between costs and revenues determines the conduct of a firm. Obviously, in order to realize a profit, all firms seek to generate revenues greater than their costs. The relationship between costs and revenues, however, is more subtle than the preceding statement suggests, and economists have developed a number of ways of classifying costs and revenues in order to express this relationship. This section will first define the various types of costs and revenues and then will relate them to explain how firms determine their optimum level of output.

Fixed Cost

Fixed costs, or overhead costs, are the costs to a firm which do not vary with output. Fixed costs are the costs which must be incurred prior to producing a single unit of output. Examples of fixed costs include land, buildings and equipment.

Research and development expenditures are also a fixed cost. Fixed costs are also sometimes referred to as "sunk costs," costs that cannot be avoided before production or sales commence.

Variable Cost

Variable costs are the cost of resources which vary with the level of output. Variable costs increase or decrease as the level of output increases or decreases. Examples of variable costs include labor, raw materials and energy. Variable costs are sometimes referred to as "avoidable costs" — costs which can be avoided by altering the level of production.

Total Cost

Total costs are simply the sum of the fixed and variable costs at any given level of output.

Average Cost

Average cost is the average cost per unit produced. Average cost is determined by dividing the total cost by the number of units produced. Average cost is the sum of the average fixed cost per unit of output and the average variable cost per unit of output. Since fixed cost does not vary with output, the average fixed cost will fall as output is increased. Each additional unit produced bears a lesser percentage of the total fixed cost. Spreading fixed cost over additional units of production is referred to as "spreading the overhead." Declining average fixed cost provides existing firms in a market with a competitive price advantage over new market entrants.

Marginal Cost

Marginal cost is the change in total cost that results from a given change in output. If output increases by one unit, marginal cost tells us how much total cost will change as a result. Stated differently, marginal cost measures the rate at which total cost changes as output changes. Marginal cost is not affected by fixed cost. (Remember, fixed cost does not vary with output.) The marginal cost of an additional unit depends upon the amount and price of the variable resources required to produce that unit.

Total Revenue

Total revenue is the revenue which a firm receives from selling a given level of output at a given price. Total revenue is simply the price per unit sold multiplied by the number of units sold.

Average Revenue

Average revenue is the revenue which a firm receives per unit of output. Average revenue is computed by dividing total revenue by the number of units sold. If a firm sells its product at a uniform price, then average revenue will equal price.

Marginal Revenue

Marginal revenue is the change in total revenue which results from a given change in output. If a firm increases its output by one unit, marginal revenue tells us how much total revenue changes as a result of that one unit increase. Put differently, marginal revenue measures the rate at which total revenue changes as output changes.

We will now look at the relationship between these various types of costs and revenues. I have already noted that average fixed cost declines as the number of units produced increases because each additional unit produced bears a lesser percentage of the fixed cost. However, other cost measures (average variable cost, average cost and marginal cost) are U-shaped. That is, these costs decline initially but, at some point, begin to rise. The decline and rise of these costs reflect economies and diseconomies of scale in the production process. Economies in the production process are realized when resources are being more fully utilized. Diseconomies arise when resources are taxed beyond their capacity. The example of a single employee working on a single machine will serve to illustrate the economies and diseconomies in production. Early in the production schedule when the employee is fresh and the equipment is running well, additional units can be produced efficiently and the cost of each unit will decline. However, if production is increased beyond a certain point, the employee will become tired and less careful, the equipment will become over-used and break down, and the cost of each additional unit will begin to rise. Diseconomies reflect the simple fact that, after a certain point, it costs more and more to produce less and less.

As an aside, a dramatic example of a U shaped cost curve is health care costs in the U.S. The per capita distribution of health care costs is extremely age dependent. In the first year of life, health care costs are somewhat high, they then fall steeply during childhood, rise slowly throughout adult life and increase exponentially after age 50. Studies have shown that the oldest population group (85+) consumes three times as much health care per person as those 65-74 and twice as much as those 75-84. The macro health care cost curve is even more dramatic. It is estimated that $50 billion of annual Medicare costs are expended in the last 2 months of life and that 30% of the entire annual Medicare budget is expended in the final year of life. The inescapable fact is that ever more health care resources are required to sustain life for ever shorter periods of time.

There is a basic relationship between marginal cost, average cost and average variable cost. If marginal cost is less than the average cost or average variable cost, then the average cost and average variable cost fall as output is increased. The lower marginal cost serves to reduce the average cost and average variable cost. If marginal cost is greater than average cost or average variable cost, then average cost and average variable cost rise as output is increased. The higher marginal cost serves to increase the average cost and average variable cost.

Marginal cost is the critical determinant of a firm's output. The goal of any firm is to maximize profit. Profit is the difference between a firm's total revenue and total cost. Because a firm in a competitive market cannot affect the price it receives for its output (price is determined by the aggregate supply and demand in the market), the firm can only decide how much output to produce to maximize profit. The firm knows that increasing output will increase revenue but also increase cost. Likewise, the firm knows that reducing output will reduce cost but also reduce revenue. The optimum level of output for the firm, therefore, is the point at which the marginal revenue obtained from an additional unit of output equals the marginal cost of producing that unit. So long as marginal revenue is greater than marginal cost, the firm will continue to increase its output. Under these circumstances, each unit produced increases total revenue more than it increases total cost and the firm realizes a profit. If marginal revenue falls below marginal cost, the firm will decrease its output. Here, the cost of producing additional units is greater than the revenue which can be obtained from the additional units, and profit will be decreased. The point at which marginal revenue equals marginal cost is the firm's optimum, or equilibrium, output level and maximizes the firm's profit.

Two points should be noted regarding marginal revenue and marginal cost curves. First, the marginal revenue curve for the firm also represents the demand curve for the firm's output. Since the individual firm cannot affect market price (i.e., the output decisions of the firm will not affect aggregate supply and demand in the market), the demand curve for the firm's output is completely elastic. Viewed from the perspective of the individual firm, the firm can supply any level of output at the market-determined price.

Second, the firm's equilibrium output where marginal revenue equals marginal cost will maximize the firm's profit on additional units of output; however, maximizing profit on each additional unit of output does not guarantee the firm an economic profit. Recall that marginal cost is not affected by fixed cost. In order for the firm to earn an economic profit, the firm's total revenues must be greater than the firm's total costs, which include the firm's fixed costs. Whether the firm can earn an economic profit depends upon the relationship between the price per unit at which the firm can sell its output and the average cost of producing those units. Recall again that average cost does include fixed costs. If the price per unit is greater than the average cost of producing each unit, then total economic profit will be positive. If the price per unit is less than the average cost of producing each unit, then the total economic profit will be negative. Why would a firm continue to produce if its total economic profit is negative? Because so long as its marginal revenue on each additional unit is greater than its marginal cost, each unit produced will bring the firm closer to a point of economic profitability. Stated differently, although the firm may not be making an economic profit, each additional unit produced will decrease the firm's losses so long as marginal revenue is greater than marginal cost.

Non-Production Costs

There are two other types of costs which affect the supply and demand for goods and services, but which do not directly derive from the cost of producing the goods or services. These are transaction costs and switch-over costs. Transaction costs are the costs of implementing an exchange of resources. Transaction costs include such things as the cost of providing and obtaining information about the goods and services, and negotiating and contracting for their exchange. Transaction costs also include the cost of administering a resource exchange and monitoring against unauthorized uses of resources. Lawyers' fees, taxes, regulations, inspections and reporting requirements are common examples of transaction costs. Transaction costs act as a barrier to efficient resource exchanges. A resource exchange might be mutually beneficial to both parties and therefore serve to increase economic efficiency. However, the transaction costs associated with the exchange might be greater than the benefits that can be realized, in which case the parties will be forced to forego the exchange. Transaction costs are real costs associated with every resource exchange and can never be fully eliminated. To advance economic efficiency, however, transaction costs must be minimized.

Switch-over costs are the costs of changing over from one good or service to another, and they are particularly important in complex technical systems. Switch-over costs include such things as the loss of investment in existing goods or services, the cost of retooling production and of retraining workers, and the cost of diseconomies in the adoption of a new method or process. Switch-over costs also act as a barrier to efficient resource exchanges. For example, a new production system may be superior in every respect to an existing system, but may not be adopted because the investment in the existing system is too great or the new system requires too high a level of worker skills.

1.6.2 Unique Economic Characteristics of Intellectual Property

Modern economic theory evolved during the period of the Industrial Revolution and is based upon the supply and demand for tangible goods. Intellectual property is an intangible good. The intangible nature of intellectual property gives it a unique set of economic characteristics.

Before considering these unique economic characteristics, it is important to emphasize again the distinction between intellectual property and goods that embody intellectual property. Recall that intellectual property consists of the underlying invention, creation or idea. The intellectual property owner has the exclusive right to make, use or sell the invention (in the case of a patent); to reproduce, distribute and make derivative works (in the case of a copyright); and to disclose and use the idea (in the case of a trade secret). Ownership of intellectual property is separated from the ownership of a good which embodies the intellectual property. For example, a purchaser of a software program owns that program, including the disks, manuals, user guides, etc. and is generally free to resell that program to another person at any time. However, ownership of the software program includes no ownership rights in the underlying intellectual property. The software program owner cannot make copies of the program or authorize others to do so, nor can the software program owner distribute multiple copies of the program or make derivative works based upon the program.

The division of ownership rights in intellectual property from ownership rights in goods embodying intellectual property allows intellectual property to be exchanged independently, in a pure form, in market transactions. The transfer of pure intellectual property requires us to account for its unique economic characteristics in order to analyze the operation of intellectual property markets.

Private and Public Goods Markets

The discussion up to this point has been concerned with private goods. Private goods are goods which are supplied by private firms and generally consumed by other private firms or individuals. In a private goods market, firms and individuals unwilling to pay for the goods can be excluded from enjoyment of the goods. Firms which supply private goods, therefore, can recover the full cost of producing those goods from consumers. The availability of private goods is also inherently scarce. Two persons cannot consume the same private good at the same time; one person's consumption always comes at the expense of another person's consumption.

There is another class of goods, however, which possess none of these attributes. These goods are known as "public goods." National defense, police and fire protection are examples of public goods. A public good is a good that is indivisible among members of the community, and individuals cannot be excluded from enjoying the benefits of a public good. Public goods are also not scarce in the same way as private goods. One individual's consumption of a public good does not come at the expense of another individual's consumption. Because individuals cannot be excluded from enjoyment of public goods, a supplier of public goods cannot recover the cost of producing those goods from consumers. Public goods therefore cannot be supplied by private firms and paid for through market prices. Instead, public goods must be supplied by government and paid for through taxes.

The distinction between private and public goods, however, is not always clear. For example, highways and bridges are sometimes cited as examples of public goods. But individual users of highways and bridges can be charged a price for their use, and those unwilling to pay the price can be excluded from use. Moreover, as any traveler knows, the use of highways and bridges by some persons comes at the expense of convenient use by others. Highways and bridges can be contrasted to lighthouses. Charging for the use of the lighthouse beacon to navigate at night is far more difficult than charging for the use of a highway or bridge, and one pilot's use of the beacon in no way interferes with another pilot's use of the same beacon.

It is also important to distinguish between how public goods are paid for and who provides them. Even where taxes may be the only efficient means to pay for public goods, it does not follow that government is the most efficient means to provide these goods. Public goods might be more efficiently provided by private firms who are paid for their services under contracts with government. For example, government may contract with a private firm for the provision of garbage collection services which are paid for through taxes. And even where government may be the only entity appropriate to provide a service, such as national defense, government may rely largely upon private firms to provide the research and development and military hardware necessary for the defense mission.

Public/Private Good Nature of Intellectual Property

Intellectual property possesses characteristics of both public and private goods. The mixed character of intellectual property has stimulated much debate over the issue of according intellectual property a lesser degree of protection than is accorded real and personal property, and according government a greater involvement in intellectual property than it has with respect to real and personal property. Although some of the public good features of intellectual property do implicate a role for government, others do not. The two points most often advanced in support of classifying intellectual property as a public good are (i) consumption of intellectual property is not mutually exclusive and (ii) access to intellectual property promotes the general welfare of society. Although both arguments are valid in some respects, both contain fundamental fallacies.

It is certainly true that one person's consumption of intellectual property does not deprive another person of consuming the same intellectual property. This follows from the intangible nature of inventions, creations and ideas. Because intellectual property is intangible, one person's use of it does not exclude another person's simultaneous use, much like the lighthouse beacon. However, the economic value of intellectual property, indeed of all private property, lies in the exclusivity of its use. The owner of a trade secret is not deprived of the use of that trade secret by the unauthorized use by a competitor. However, the trade secret owner is deprived of a competitive advantage and economic value by the unauthorized use. The same is true of a copyright owner of a software program. The copyright owner is not deprived of use of the software program by another person's unauthorized use, but clearly is deprived of the income which would be paid by a lawful licensee. The essence of private property is the owner's exclusive right of enjoyment, and this is true of intellectual property as well as real and personal property.

The second argument that intellectual property promotes the general welfare of society is more complicated. It is true that all intellectual property builds upon earlier intellectual property whether it be patents, copyrights or trade secrets. It is also true that intellectual property contributes generally to the store of human knowledge and advances education and understanding throughout society. However, intellectual property laws already attempt to balance the social welfare aspects of intellectual property and private property incentives for development of intellectual property. Patent and copyright laws require public disclosure of the intellectual property as a condition to receipt of intellectual property rights. The trade-off for inventors and authors is to make their intellectual property available for others to learn from in exchange for obtaining ownership rights in the intellectual property. (Trade secrets operate differently. There is no requirement for disclosure of trade secrets; however, trade secret rights can be lost at any time in a number of ways.)

In evaluating the social welfare argument for treatment of intellectual property as a public good, it is critical to distinguish between access to intellectual property for purposes of education and development of new intellectual property and the unauthorized use of the intellectual property for its intended purpose. In the first instance, society is benefited with minimum loss of economic incentive for intellectual property owners. In the second instance, society is benefited at the direct expense of intellectual property owner's investment. One could argue that society would also benefit from the unauthorized use of real or personal property. However, this would clearly deter investment in real and personal property. The same is true for intellectual property.

Unlike true public goods, intellectual property is amenable to private market transactions. Patents, copyrights and trade secrets are exchanged all the time in negotiated private transactions. The ability of intellectual property owners to recoup the cost of their investment through fees and royalties, and to exclude the use of the intellectual property by those unwilling to pay, allows intellectual property markets to function in the same way as real and personal property markets. Although, as you will see below, the transaction costs of intellectual property exchanges may be greater than those associated with real and personal property, these transaction costs are not so high as to require government control of intellectual property markets. There is, however, one instance in which intellectual property transaction costs are so high that private markets cannot compensate for them. This is the case of basic research.

Society benefits greatly from basic research. Basic research contributes to education and understanding, and all new intellectual property derives in some way from prior basic research. However, at the time basic research is performed, it is difficult to know exactly how it will be used and who will benefit from its use. In addition, the return on investment in basic research is extremely long-term and uncertain, and much of the knowledge gained from basic research may become available to the public through scientific papers and research journals before intellectual property rights can be secured. Because the full benefits of basic research cannot be recovered in market exchanges, private firms invest very little in basic research. The problem of under-investment in basic research is dealt with through government funding of university basic research and a network of federal laboratories. Government funding of basic research attempts to make up for the shortfall in investment by private firms and to yield a level of basic research output commensurate with the social benefit of basic research.

Government funding of basic research as a public good, however, has raised important questions. In the past, a relatively small percentage of government-funded research has been utilized in commercial applications. Beginning in the early 1980s, Congress began addressing this problem through a series of special programs designed to facilitate technology transfers from universities and federal laboratories to private industry. I will discuss some of these programs in greater detail in section 3.1 of the materials. Encouraging the transfer of government-funded technology to the private sector, however, has raised a new set of questions. Government funding for basic research is, of course, ultimately paid for by taxpayers, and concerns have been raised over the transfer of taxpayer-funded technology to private industry. Some view the transfer of government-funded technologies from universities and federal laboratories as a subsidy to private firms. Others are concerned about favoritism among private firms in the selection of transferees. On the other hand, supporters of technology transfers from universities and federal laboratories point to the creation of new companies, the additional jobs and expanded tax base that these transfers stimulate, and the practice of foreign governments which provide an array of public support for their technology industries.

Regardless of whether intellectual property is classified as a public or private good, it is clear that in the future there will be ever-increasing interaction between government, universities and private industry in the development of new intellectual property in the area of basic research and early-stage technologies.

Low Marginal Costs

Many types of intellectual property goods have very low marginal costs. Computer software programs are a good example. The development of a computer program might cost millions of dollars. After these development costs have been incurred, however, the cost of producing an additional copy of the program might be only a few cents. Drugs are another example. Currently, the average cost of bringing a new drug to market is about $800 million, including research and development, testing and obtaining various regulatory approvals. Although the cost of manufacturing an additional unit of a new drug may be higher than that of a software program, this cost is only a small fraction of the fixed costs already invested in the development of the drug. The low marginal cost of many intellectual property goods has implications for pricing and for transaction costs.

Recall that in a purely competitive market, price will approximate marginal cost. The gap between price and marginal cost in many intellectual property good markets has led some to claim that these markets are non-competitive and subject to serious market failures. However, also recall that for a firm to realize an economic profit, the firm must ultimately recover its fixed costs as well as its marginal costs. The firm's marginal revenue from an additional unit of production (i.e., its sale price) must be greater than the firm's average total cost of producing the additional unit (i.e., its fixed costs plus variable costs). The pricing behavior of firms in intellectual property good markets is no different than for firms in any other market. If a software or drug company cannot recover its fixed investment in developing an intellectual property good, then the company will cease to make these investments and fewer of these intellectual property goods will be supplied in the market.

The low marginal cost of many intellectual property goods, however, does create transaction cost problems for the intellectual property owner. If a competitor misappropriates IP rights, the competitor can avoid incurring the fixed costs of development and therefore supply the intellectual property good at a price substantially lower than the intellectual property owner. The lower the marginal cost is to produce an intellectual property good, the more vigilant the intellectual property owner must be to protect the good against misappropriation. This is an acute problem for software firms, especially in foreign markets.

High Transaction Costs

There are other features of intellectual property which tend to create high transaction costs in intellectual property markets. I noted earlier the ease with which intellectual property can be transferred around the globe by means of modern telecommunication technologies. The ease of transferring intellectual property reduces, to some extent, the transaction costs of intellectual property exchanges; however, it also makes monitoring of intellectual property much more difficult and costly. A disgruntled employee or an unethical contractor can transfer a firm's intellectual property assets anywhere in the world in a second, and it might take months or years for the firm to learn of the misappropriation or to know when and where misappropriation occurred. The transaction costs of monitoring intellectual property against unauthorized use are significantly greater than the costs of monitoring real or personal property against unauthorized use.

Another source of high transaction costs in intellectual property markets is the difficulty of precisely defining intellectual property. Intellectual property consists fundamentally of ideas, and it is far more difficult to define an idea than it is to define a piece of personal property through a serial number or a parcel of real property through a metes and bounds survey in a deed. The difficulty in precisely defining intellectual property results in uncertainty in intellectual property markets and a discounting of the exchange price in light of this uncertainty. It is not uncommon for issued patents to be later found invalid because of prior art or to be held to infringe other patents. Much depends upon the interpretation of the patent claims (i.e., the definition of the intellectual property), and interpretation of language has an inherent element of ambiguity. In addition, some of the tests employed for infringement (e.g., the doctrine of equivalents in the case of patents and non-literal infringement in the case of copyrights) also inject an element of uncertainty into intellectual property titles.

Finally, unlike real and personal property, intellectual property can never be fully recovered once it has come into the possession of another. The intellectual property owner cannot strip knowledge of the intellectual property from a person who has once gained this knowledge. This is a special problem in the case of trade secrets. An owner of a trade secret who seeks to license the trade secret will have to disclose some information to a potential licensee. However, once the trade secret information has been disclosed to a potential licensee, it can never be fully recovered and the potential licensee has less incentive to pay for the trade secret. Negotiating a license for a trade secret requires a great deal of care, and this care adds substantially to the transaction costs of the exchange.

1.6.3 Market Structures

Markets can be structured in many different ways. The structure of any given market will affect the supply, demand and price in that market and, in turn, the conduct of buyers and sellers. Market structures are categorized according to their dominant features; however, no actual market fits completely within any one category, and the structure of any particular market is subject to constant change. This section will review the different types of market structures and their effect on buyers and sellers in those markets.

Perfectly Competitive Markets

The discussion of economics in the preceding section was based on the assumption of a perfectly competitive market. A perfectly competitive market is an economic model rather than a description of any actual market. This does not, however, diminish the utility of perfect competition. The model of a perfectly competitive market specifies the conditions necessary to reach perfect competition and explains how deviations from these conditions will affect market performance.

A perfectly competitive market requires that the goods or services available in the market are standardized (i.e., there exists no significant product differentiation). A perfectly competitive market also requires that there are numerous buyers and sellers who are fully informed about the conditions of the market and who are free to enter or exit the market at will. In a perfectly competitive market, no single buyer or seller can appreciably affect the demand or supply in the market. As you have seen, under conditions of perfect competition, firms can achieve optimal efficiency in resource allocation and optimal pricing of resources.

Deviations from perfect competition are referred to as "market failures." Market failures come in many forms, including barriers to market entry for potential sellers and inadequate market information for potential buyers. An important type of market failure is known as "externalities." Market externalities arise in situations where the full cost of producing a good or service is not borne by the consumers of the good or service, or the full benefit of providing a good or service is not recovered by the suppliers of the good or service. Pollution is an example of an external cost. If the production of a particular good entails pollution of the environment, and the cost of this pollution is not included in the price of the good, then consumers of the good are imposing external costs on society. Stated differently, non-consumers of the good are being forced to bear a portion of the cost of producing the good and are thereby subsidizing the price of the good to consumers. The price subsidy paid by non-consumers to consumers will result in an excess (i.e., inefficient) level of production for the good.

Education is an example of an external benefit. Society benefits in numerous ways from education. Education reduces crime, decreases welfare dependency and increases employment skills. The benefits of education, however, cannot be fully recovered through private market transactions. (The supplier of education cannot charge the police, welfare agencies and employers a price per student that fully covers the benefits each receives.) The inability of a supplier to recover the full benefit of a good or service through private market transactions will result in inefficient under-investment and under-supply of the good or service.

The solution proposed to overcome market failures is generally some form of concerted group activity, most often in the form of government intervention into the market. Pollution laws and public education, for example, have been the responses to the market failures discussed above; however, care must be taken in attempting to overcome market failures. In some instances, the cost of the remedy may be greater than the cost of the market failure and the remedy may itself create additional market inefficiencies.

Monopoly Markets

Monopoly markets are at the other extreme from purely competitive markets. In a monopoly market, a single firm provides all the goods and services in the market. True monopoly markets are characterized by extremely high fixed costs and dedicated, immovable fixed assets. The distribution (not production) of electricity is the classic example of a monopoly market. A monopoly firm can supply the total market demand at an ever-decreasing average cost. In a true monopoly market, therefore, it is inefficient to have more than one supplier. A new firm cannot enter a monopoly market because the decreasing average costs of the existing supplier will always give the existing supplier a price advantage over the new entrant.

True monopoly markets are a function of the technology employed in the market and, as the technology base changes, so does the structure of the market. During the period when long-distance telephone service was provided over land lines, telephone service was a monopoly market. However, with the advent of microwave technology for telephone transmission, it became possible for multiple firms to provide long-distance service, and the market became increasingly competitive.

The inherent efficiency of having a single supplier firm in a monopoly market comes at the expense of the market control exerted by the single firm. Since a monopoly supplier has no competition, or threat of competition, the monopoly supplier can restrict the level of output and thereby artificially increase price. There are two ways to avoid this situation — monopoly firms can be owned and operated by the government, or monopoly firms can be owned and operated privately but subject to government price regulation. Most nations of the world have opted for the first approach in dealing with monopolies. The United States has opted for the second approach. In the United States, federal and state regulatory agencies approve the prices to be charged by monopoly firms in order to assure that the price is both fair to consumers and fair to investors in the monopoly firm.

Oligopoly Markets

The word "monopoly" is often used loosely to refer to markets which are dominated by a few large sellers. Such markets are properly characterized as "oligopoly markets." In oligopoly markets, the conduct of a few large firms can directly affect market price. Oligopoly markets, however, are competitive markets. If one oligopolist firm lowers its output, another oligopolist firm will increase its output to make up the market shortfall. If one oligopolist firm increases its price and other oligopolist firms do not, consumers will buy from the lower-priced oligopolists. The oil, steel and automobile industries are examples of oligopolistic markets.

The risk of market failure in oligopoly markets comes from collusion among the oligopolist firms. If the large firms act jointly to limit output or increase price, they can directly control the market. The risk of oligopolist firms acting in concert is dealt with through the antitrust laws which prohibit price fixing and other types of joint action designed to restrain trade or to create monopolies.

Oligopolies can also exist in buyer markets. Markets which are dominated by a few large buyers are known as "monopsony markets." In a monopsonist market, the imbalance between a relatively large number of small sellers and a relatively few number of large buyers allows the monopsonist buyers to exert great pressure on sellers and to extract highly favorable supply terms. The big box retail chains are examples of monopsony buyer markets.

Vertical and Horizontal Market Structures

Markets can also be characterized according to their vertical and horizontal structures. The characterization of a market by its vertical structure looks at the successive supply stages for a good. For technical goods, these stages can generally be broken down into research and development, design and testing, manufacturing and assembling, distribution and sales, and maintenance and support. In a market that is vertically integrated, individual firms are involved in multiple stages of the supply process. A vertically integrated firm enjoys certain advantages. It has greater control over costs and quality in the supply process and can leverage its advantage in one stage of the supply process to another. Complete vertical integration, however, is very costly, and vertically integrated firms are vulnerable to more efficient competitors in any one of the supply stages. Indeed, one of the major benefits of licensing is to achieve the most efficient supply process possible by licensing out those functions in which the licensor enjoys no special competitive advantage.

Characterization of a market's horizontal structure looks at the composition of firms in a given stage of the supply process. A market that is horizontally concentrated is a market in which relatively few firms are engaged in a particular stage of the supply process. The degree of horizontal concentration may vary from one stage of the supply process to another. For example, there may be a number of firms engaged in research and development, but few firms engaged in manufacturing and distribution. A market's horizontal structure is important in licensing. It is difficult for a small firm to enter directly into a horizontally concentrated market, and licensing, therefore, is often the only alternative for a small firm.

A widely used measure of horizontal market concentration is the Herfindahl-Hirschmann Index (HHI). The HHI measures horizontal market concentration by squaring the market share of each firm in the market, summing the squares, and then dividing by 10,000. The higher the HHI, the more concentrated the market. For example, a monopoly market with only one firm in it would have a HHI of 1 while a market with 10 firms having equal market shares would have a HHI of .1.

Additional Information

1. CAMPBELL MCCONNELL, STANLEY BRUE & SEAN FLYNN, ECONOMICS (18th ed. 2008).

2. FRANK V. MASTRIANNA, BASIC ECONOMICS (14th ed. 2006).

3. THOMAS SOWELL, BASIC ECONOMICS: A COMMON SENSE GUIDE TO THE ECONOMY (3d ed. 2007).

4. N. GREGORY MANKIW, PRINCIPLES OF ECONOMICS (4th ed. 2006).

5. CAMPBELL R. MCCONNELL & STANLEY L. BRUE, MACROECONOMICS (17th ed. 2006).

6. WILLIAM J. BAUMOL & ALAN S. BLINDER, MACROECONOMICS: PRINCIPLES AND POLICY (11th ed. 2008).

7. KARL E. CASE & RAY C. FAIR, PRINCIPLES OF MACROECONOMICS (8th ed. 2006).

8. CAMPBELL R. MCCONNELL & STANLEY L. BRUE, MICROECONOMICS (17th ed. rev. 2006).

9.   ROGER A. ARNOLD, MICROECONOMICS (8th ed. 2007).

10.   N. GREGORY MANKIW, PRINCIPLES OF MICROECONOMICS (4th ed. 2006).

11.   WILLIAM M. LANDES & RICHARD A. POSNER, THE ECONOMIC STRUCTURE OF INTELLECTUAL PROPERTY LAW (2003).

12.   ECONOMICS OF INTELLECTUAL PROPERTY LAW (ECONOMIC APPROACHES TO LAW) (Robert P. Merges ed., 2008).

13.   ROBERT GUELL, ISSUES IN ECONOMICS TODAY (3d ed. 2007).

14.   ROBERTY PINDYCK & DANIEL RUBINFELD, MICROECONOMICS (7th ed. 2009).

15.   ROBERT FRANK, MICROECONOMICS AND BEHAVIOR (7th ed. 2007).

16.   FREDERIC S. MISHKIN, THE ECONOMICS OF MONEY, BANKING AND FINANCIAL MARKETS (2006).

17.   BEN BERNANKE & ROBERT H. FRANK, PRINCIPLES OF MACROECONOMICS (4th ed. 2008).

1.7   FINANCIAL AND ACCOUNTING PRINCIPLES

The value of intangible assets relative to the value of physical and financial assets has continuously increased since the early 1980s. One measure of this increase is the market-to-book (M/B) value for the S&P 500 companies. During the 1970s, the M/B ratio for the S&P 500 companies hovered around one; by 2000, the M/B ratio was over six. This means that in 2000, for every $6 of market value, less than $1 was comprised of physical and financial assets while the remaining $5 (~83.3%) was comprised of intangible assets. For many companies, the ratio of intangible assets to physical and financial assets is considerably higher. Smith and Parr, prominent experts in the field, have calculated the following percentages of intangible and intellectual property assets for the following companies: Johnson & Johnson (87.9%); Proctor & Gamble (88.5%); Merck (93.5%); Microsoft (97.8%); and Yahoo! (98.9%).

1.7.1   Types of Assets

A good starting point to consider the financial and accounting aspects of intellectual property is to define the various types of assets that comprise a firm. A firm is comprised of three basic types of assets — tangible assets, intangible assets and intellectual property assets. Tangible assets consist of physical assets (e.g., land, buildings, equipment, trucks) and financial assets (e.g., bank accounts, stocks, bonds). Intangible assets, as suggested above, consist of all other assets that are not tangible. However, there are two distinct types of intangible assets. There are some intangible assets that are not subject to property ownership rights, such as goodwill, employee training and management expertise. Because of the lack of property ownership rights, these are not truly assets, but are more accurately characterized as competitive advantages. There are other intangible assets that are subject to property ownership, such as patents, copyrights and trade secrets. In these materials, I will refer to the former type of intangible assets as "intangible assets" and the latter type of intangible assets as "intellectual property assets." Another difference between intangible assets and intellectual property assets is that intangible assets cannot be transferred separately from the firm itself, whereas intellectual property assets can be transferred separately from the firm.

Intellectual property assets can be divided into three groups — technical, operational and reputational. Technical intellectual property assets consist of utility patents, software copyrights and trade secrets. Operational intellectual property assets consist of business method patents and proprietary business processes. Reputational intellectual property assets consist of trademarks, service marks, brand names and logos. Although reputational intellectual property assets account for a significant portion of a firm's value, these materials are concerned only with technical and operational intellectual property assets — the main subjects of technology innovation.

1.7.2 Types of Financial Reports

The performance of a firm is reported in two types of accounting reports — a balance sheet and an income statement. The balance sheet is a snapshot of the firm's assets and liabilities as of the given point in time. In the left-hand column of the balance sheet, the firm reports its assets generally consisting of current assets (cash, marketable securities and accounts receivable), inventory (finished goods, work in progress and raw materials), fixed assets (plant, equipment and land) and goodwill (the value of the firm above its current assets, inventory and fixed assets). In the right-hand column of the balance sheet, the firm reports its liabilities generally consisting of current liabilities (loans due within the year), long-term liabilities (loans due beyond a year), bonds (debt owed to bond holders) and stock (shareholders' equity in the firm). Because every asset recorded is associated with a liability, the firm's total assets and total liabilities are always equal. The basic accounting equation is: Assets + Goodwill = Liabilities + Shareholder Equity.

The income statement reports the firm's operations for the past accounting year. At the top of the income statement, the firm reports its revenue — generally, the income received from the sale of goods. Next, the firm reports the "cost of goods sold" (COGS) — the raw materials, energy, labor, etc. required to produce the goods. The difference between the revenue and cost of goods sold is the firm's "gross margin." Next, the firm reports its sales, general and administrative expenses (SG&A) — this includes all of the indirect costs, such as management salaries, office overhead and advertising. Sometimes, the firm's research and development expenditures are included in SG&A; other times, research and development expenditures are reported as a separate expense item. The difference between the firm's gross margin and its sales, general and administrative expenses is the firm's "earnings before interest and taxes" (EBIT). Finally, the firm reports its interest expense and taxes. The difference between the firm's earnings before interest and taxes, and after interest and taxes is the firm's "earnings after tax" (EAT).

Although firms vary widely in their ratios between revenue and expenses, a typical set of ratios for a high-technology manufacturing company might be as follows: Cost of Goods Sold = 57% of Revenue; Sales, General and Administrative

Expenses = 25% of Revenue; Research and Development = 10% of Revenue; and Taxes = 40% of Revenue. A firm with these ratios would realize approximately $5 in profit for every $100 in revenue. Stated differently, for every $100 in revenue, the firm would have only $5 available for reinvestment in the company or distribution to shareholders.

Despite the importance of intangible and intellectual property assets, U.S. firms provide remarkably little information on these assets in their balance sheets and income statements. In balance sheets, intangible and intellectual property assets are generally lumped together under the heading of "goodwill." In income statements, as noted above, research and development expenditures may or may not be reported as separate expense items. U.S. firms have been sharply criticized for their failure to provide information on intangible and intellectual property assets. Critics claim that this lack of information leaves shareholders, market analysts and creditors in a position of having to make important decisions about a firm with minimal knowledge of its most important assets and operations.

Accounting for intangible and intellectual property assets, however, poses difficult problems. Take patents for example. How can a dollar value be assigned to a single patent that is incorporated into a product along with numerous other patents? Or, even more challenging, how can a dollar value be assigned to a recently issued patent that is not yet, and might never be, utilized by the firm? The treatment of research and development expenditures poses similar problems. Investment in research and development is expected to yield benefits well beyond the year in which the investment is made. Investments that are expected to yield benefits beyond the year in which they are made are properly treated as capital expenditures; the investment is listed as an asset on the balance sheet and amortized as an expense over the asset's useful life on the income statement. As with a patent, however, it is very difficult to assign a dollar amount to a research and development investment that might ultimately have a value far above or below the cost of the investment. For this reason, research and development expenditures are treated as expenses on the income statement. As such, they are fully written off (deducted) in the year they are made despite their potential future benefits.

A number of European firms have begun to report information on intangible and intellectual property assets. Information such as the number of patents issued to the firm in the past year, the number of patents commercialized in products, the number of research and development employees, and the amount of royalty revenue from patents has been included in reports appended to the firms' financial statements. U.S. firms, however, have been less willing to provide such information; and the gap between the financial importance of, and available information on, intangible and intellectual property assets remains wide. This has led analysts, consultants and other intellectual property professionals to develop new methods to value intellectual property assets. I will discuss intellectual property valuation methods in subsection 1.8.2 of the materials.

Additional Information

1. HERBERT B. MAYO, BASIC FINANCE: AN INTRODUCTION TO FINANCIAL INSTITUTIONS, INVESTMENTS AND MANAGEMENT (9th ed. 2006).

2. CLYDE P. STICKNEY & ROMAN L. WEIL, FINANCIAL ACCOUNTING: AN INTRODUCTION TO CONCEPTS, METHODS AND USES (12th ed. rev. 2006).

3. EUGENE F. BRIGHAM & MICHAEL C. EHRARDT, FINANCIAL MANAGEMENT: THEORY & PRACTICE (12th ed. rev. 2007).

4. STEPHEN CECCHETTI, MONEY, BANKING AND FINANCIAL MARKETS (2d ed. 2007).

1.8 BUSINESS OF TECHNOLOGY INNOVATION

As noted earlier, the transfer of technology from one organization to another is an important part of the technology innovation process. Over the last 25 years, technology transfer has become a major commercial activity. The growth of technology transfer is illustrated by the Licensing Executive Society (LES), an association of full-time professionals engaged in various types of technology transfer activities. The LES was founded in the United States in the early 1970s with about 50 members. Today, there are chapters of LES in virtually every developed country in the world, and there are over 7,000 members. The membership composition of LES is also illustrative of the nature of the technology transfer practice. Approximately one-third of the LES membership is composed of lawyers, one-third scientists and engineers and one-third business managers.

Today, every large corporation, research university and federal laboratory has a technology transfer or licensing office. There are powerful, although different, incentives for each type of organization to increase its technology transfer efforts.

For corporations, the incentive is to realize a return on their large investment in research and development, and increase profitability. Technology transfers can contribute significantly to a firm's profits. As noted above, a typical high-technology manufacturing firm's earnings after taxes (net profit) might be in the range of 5%. A firm's net profits from licensing can be far greater because the firm does incur any costs for goods sold and the licensing administration expenses are far lower than the sales, general and administrative expenses associated with the sale of goods. Even if research and development costs are charged to the license, which is problematic because research and development costs are sunk costs at the time of the license, the net profit from licensing could be nearly ten times the net profit from the sale of goods. For example, if a firm's licensing administration and research and development costs were each charged at 10% of licensing revenue, and taxes were 40% of net revenues, then the firm's net profit percentage would be 48% or $48 for every $100 of licensing revenue. Stated differently, in order to obtain the same net profit from the sale of goods as from licensing, the firm would have to increase its sales revenue 1000%.

The incentive for universities to engage in technology transfer activities is twofold. Like corporations, universities also seek to realize a return on their investments in research and development; however, unlike corporations, universities also seek to promote public welfare by making the benefits of their research available to the public within a reasonable period of time and at a reasonable cost. University technology transfer activities have been greatly encouraged by the passage of Congressional legislation. The Bayh-Dole Act, enacted in 1980 as an amendment to the Patent Act, allows universities to elect to take title to any patents resulting from federally funded research. The Bayh-Dole Act provides universities a great incentive to license patents developed with federal funding because the universities are able to retain all of the revenue received from such licenses. For most universities, federal funds constitute the large majority of their research budget. The Bayh-Dole Act, therefore, has resulted in a major expansion in university technology transfer activity and a large increase in revenue from this activity. The Bayh-Dole Act is discussed in section 3.1 of the materials.

Federal laboratories have also been encouraged to engage in technology transfer activities by Congressional legislation. The basic mission of federal laboratories is to provide research for government departments such as Defense, Energy and NASA. In an effort to stimulate economic development and make more efficient use of funds appropriated for federal laboratories, Congress passed the Stevenson-Wydler Act. The Stevenson-Wydler Act requires federal laboratories to establish offices of technology transfer in order to facilitate licenses to, and collaborative research projects with, private sector firms. Although the Stevenson-Wydler Act has not produced the same level of technology transfer activity in federal laboratories as the Bayh-Dole Act has in universities, federal laboratories are significant participants in the national technology transfer process.

As technology transfer has grown as a business, practitioners in the field have become increasingly sophisticated. Every year, numerous conferences are held and numerous articles and books are published dealing with the business of technology transfer. This section will review some of these business considerations. The first subsection will consider the fundamentals of investment risk and return. The second subsection will describe some of the methods used today to value intellectual property assets. The third subsection will discuss a recent Federal Circuit decision on the calculation of damages in patent infringement suits, and the relationship between the calculation of patent damages and the value of patent licenses.

1.8.1   Risk and Return

Risk

Risk and return are directly related. The more risk an investor assumes, the greater the return he or she will demand. The trade-off between risk and return is carefully measured and allocated in efficient capital markets, and slight changes in the magnitude of either will be rapidly reflected in the market price. Every investment has some degree of risk associated with it. U.S. Treasury bills are widely perceived to be one of the least risky investments. The rate of return on treasury bills at any given time, therefore, tends to set the benchmark against which alternative investments are measured. As the risk of realizing a return on an investment increases (e.g., from loans guaranteed by the U.S. government to loans guaranteed by a start-up company), the value of the potential return must also increase.

Risk is also related to opportunity costs. Opportunity costs are the returns foregone by not making an alternative investment. The economic cost of an investment is the sum of the actual costs of the resources expended plus the opportunity costs of alternative uses of these resources. The return offered by an investment must exceed its opportunity costs; it must offer investors a premium above alternative investments having the same risk and return characteristics. Investors value an investment only in comparison with alternative investments. The true value of an investment lies in its potential for providing lower risk or higher returns than other similar investments. The potential risk and return of comparable investments, in essence, acts to discount the value of any given investment.

Risk results from the inability to predict the future. Risk, of course, is present in all human activity — at all times and in all places. Risk can never be eliminated. Risk has two elements; an inherent probability of an event's occurrence and the amount of control which can be exercised over an event. Some risks may be subject to a relatively high level of control (avoidable risks) while others may be subject to no control at all (unavoidable risks). The capability to control a risk, however, does not assure that the risk is avoided. Individuals make mistakes. Information is misrecorded or misinterpreted, analyses are incomplete or incorrect, and errors and omissions in judgments can and do occur. Minimizing mistakes is important to a firm's welfare, however, developing a plan for mistake detection is itself an investment of resources which entails new types of risks.

Unavoidable risk ranges from such things as the sudden death of a business partner to the sudden drop in a currency's value. Unavoidable risk is beyond any direct or indirect control by a firm. There are, however, financial mechanisms by which unavoidable risk can be limited or offset. Private insurance, investments in futures markets, selling securities short or long, arbitrage transactions, and equity diversification can all be used to control levels of unavoidable risk. Again, however, these risk reduction mechanisms are themselves investments that carry with them new risks.

Patents pose a unique type of unavoidable risk — the risk that a patent might be found to be invalid or its practice found to infringe another patent. A substantial percentage of patents are found to be invalid by courts or the PTO after their issuance. If a patent is found to be invalid, the patent becomes useless because it can no longer be enforced by the patentee. The risk of patent invalidity is largely unknown to the patentee or prospective licensee. It is also not uncommon for a court to find that the practice of an issued patent infringes another patent. Again, this risk of patent infringement is largely unknown to the patentee or prospective licensee. Recently, private insurance has become available to cover the risks of patent invalidity and infringement. Although this insurance is very expensive, it does provide some risk reduction for the patentee or prospective licensee.

Return

Return on a financial investment is the value received from an investment above the value of the capital invested. A positive return is the investor's gain after full recovery of the invested capital. A negative return is the investor's loss when full recovery of the invested capital is not possible. Returns on an investment come in two forms — income and capital appreciation. Income is received over the course of the investment, and capital appreciation is received at the time the investment is sold. The total return earned from an investment is the combination of the income received during the life of the investment plus the increase in the value of the investment between its time of purchase and sale. There is generally an inverse relationship between financial returns received in the form of income and capital appreciation. The more income an investment yields, the lower its capital appreciation potential. In the case of corporate stock, this trade-off is reflected in the firm's choice to use profits either to pay dividends (income return) or to acquire new assets (capital appreciation).

Return on investment also has a time dimension; returns may be short-term or long-term, and they may be spread evenly or unevenly over the course of the investment. Short-term returns are less risky because they provide for a more prompt recovery of the invested capital. Long-term returns expose investors to greater risks and create higher opportunity costs. To realize long-term returns, investors must invest for longer time periods. This extends the duration of the risk and limits opportunities to pursue alternative investments.

Sorting out short-term and long-term returns is especially challenging in the case of investments in technology licenses. Technology licenses are generally long-term, ongoing relationships between parties. Substantial short-term returns are ordinarily not possible in a technology license, and both parties must look to profit from an investment over the entire duration of the license. Investments in technology licenses yield tangible and intangible returns. Tangible returns include such things as royalty payments, equipment purchases and access to laboratory facilities. It is relatively easy to set a dollar value on tangible returns by comparing them with the going market price of similar resources. Intangible returns include such things as know-how, intellectual property, goodwill and market recognition. Intangible returns are difficult to value in dollar terms, but must be considered in all licensing investment decisions.

Risk and return are greatly affected by the stage of a technology's development at the time of its transfer. Early-stage technology transfers involve high additional investment, high risk and delayed return for the transferees. These disadvantages are usually borne by licensees or assignees who demand in exchange a high degree of control over the technology's development and a large portion of the future gain. Later-stage technology transfers have the reverse characteristics — the technology owner, having borne the additional investment and risk, will demand to have some continuing control over the technology and to share proportionately in the profits.

Additional Information

1. Gina Colarelli O'Connor, T. Ravichandran & Daniel Robeson, *Risk Management Through Learning: Management Practices for Radical Innovation Success*, 19 J. OF HIGH TECH. MGMT. RES 70 (VOL. 1) (2008).

2. GEORGE WESTERMAN & RICHARD HUNTER, IT RISK AND RETURN: TURNING BUSINESS THREATS INTO COMPETITIVE ADVANTAGE (Harvard Business School Press) (2007).

3. RICHAR A. BREARLY, AN INTRODUCTION TO RISK AND RETURN FROM COMMON STOCKS (MIT Press) (1983).

4. Douglas G. Livingston, Yield Curve Analysis: The Fundamentals of Risk and Return (New York Institute of Finance) (1988).

5. Allan C. Reddy, A Macro Perspective on Technology Transfer (Greenwood Publishing Group) (1996).

1.8.2 Valuation of Intellectual Property

Before discussing the valuation methods, it is useful to consider briefly the meaning of "value" and the nature of valuation. Value does not equal price. Price is the dollar amount at which an asset trades in a market. Value is the worth (utility) of the asset to the buyer and seller. The distinction between value and price is the basis for asset exchanges. If the price of an asset is greater than the value of the asset to the seller and less than the value of the asset to the buyer, then the asset will be exchanged and both the buyer and seller will be better off. Price and value, however, are also integrally related. Price is an expression of the perceived value of an asset to the respective parties. Price is the concrete number at which the parties commit to an asset exchange. Value is the range of numbers which the parties use to negotiate a price.

Because value is inherently subjective and valuation methods inherently uncertain, some criticize valuation, especially intellectual property valuation, as not worth the time and money. Richard Razgaitis, a foremost authority on technology valuation, responds to this criticism by noting Aristotle's proposition "that it is a sign of an educated mind not to expect more certainty from a subject than it can possibly provide." Valuation, Razgaitis suggests, requires an intermediate perspective between certainty and ignorance, and this requires the exercise of skill, experience and judgment. Razgaitis believes that valuation tools provide very valuable guidance to intellectual property managers on a host of important questions despite their inherent uncertainty.

There are three basic valuation methods — the cost method, the market method and the income method. These methods are the core of valuation for real, personal and intellectual property.

The Cost Method

In valuing real and personal property, the cost method measures the value of an asset by the cost to replace the asset with an identical or equivalent asset. The assumption underlying the cost method of valuation is that the cost to acquire or develop a new asset is commensurate with the economic value that the asset can provide during its life. The cost method takes into account the physical depreciation and functional obsolescence of an asset in calculating the replacement cost, and is useful in determining the maximum value of an asset to a buyer. However, cost does not equal value, and the cost of an asset to the seller is irrelevant to the value of an asset to the buyer.

The cost method is no more helpful in valuing intellectual property assets. The value of an intellectual property asset is a function of the demand for the tangible products or processes which incorporate the intellectual property asset. The cost of developing an intellectual property asset (e.g., the cost of research and development), has no relationship to the market economics which determine the demand for the products or processes which embody the intellectual property asset. Empirical studies, which generally conclude that only a very few patents yield high returns while the rest are relatively worthless, confirm the disconnect between the cost of creating an intellectual property asset and its value.

The Market Method

The market method is most often associated with the appraisal of residential real estate. The market method values an asset based upon comparable transactions between unrelated parties. Four basic requirements must be met before the market method can be used to value an asset: (i) an active market must exist for the asset; (ii) there must be a sufficient number of similar asset exchanges in the recent past; (iii) price information on similar asset exchanges must be available to the public; and (iv) the exchanges must be between independent parties.

Finding comparable transactions is the key to the market valuation method. This is relatively easy in the case of residential real estate. The neighborhood, school district, square footage, number of rooms, construction quality, etc. can be used to compare past home sales and prices in order to value a prospective sale. Finding comparable transactions is more difficult in the case of intellectual property. First, there are no public trading markets for intellectual property assets. Second, the terms and conditions of intellectual property asset transactions vary widely. Third, intellectual property assets are inherently dissimilar. And finally, the details of intellectual property asset transactions are rarely made available to the public.

Despite the lack of closely comparable transactions, the market method can still serve as a useful benchmark of intellectual property value. For example, information on the range of royalty rates for a type intellectual property asset in a given market can be used to calculate an average asset value for comparison to the asset under investigation.

The Income Method

The income method values an asset based upon the net present value of the future income expected to be received over the life of the asset. The income method of valuation, often referred to as the "Discounted Cash Flow" (DCF) method, is widely used to value investments in all types of assets, including real, personal and intellectual property, businesses, stocks and bonds. Because it is so widely used, it is important to understand the basic financial concepts underlying the DCF method.

The key concepts of the DCF method all revolve around the fact that a dollar received in the future is worth less than a dollar received today. There are three basic reasons for the lesser value of a dollar received in the future. First, the inflation of prices decreases the purchasing power of money over time. For example, if prices are rising 2% per year, it would take $102 a year from now to purchase the same goods that could be purchased for $100 today; or stated differently, in terms of purchasing power, $100 today would be worth only $98 a year from now. Second, there are opportunity costs of waiting to receive a future dollar. For example, if you had $100 today to invest in a one-year U.S. Treasury Bill that paid 5% interest, you would receive $105 at the end of the year. By waiting one year to receive $100, you, therefore, lose the opportunity to earn $5. Third, there is always some risk of receiving a dollar in the future that is not present if you receive the dollar today. For example, if you hoped to receive $100 in one year, but calculated that there was a 15% chance that you would receive nothing, the value of the $100 today would be $85.

These concepts can be easily expressed mathematically. Let's begin by considering how you would calculate a return on an investment. Assume you invest $100 today in an investment that provides a 5% rate of interest. At the end of year one, you would expect your return to be $105.

$$\text{Return Yr. \#1} = \$100 + (\$100 \times .05) = \$105$$

At the end of year two, you would expect your return to be $110.25.

$$\text{Return Yr. \#2} = \$105 + (\$105 \times .05) = \$110.25$$

And at the end of year three, you would expect your return to be $115.76.

$$\text{Return Yr. \#3} = \$110.25 + (\$110.25 \times .05) = \$115.76$$

The return on an investment of any given amount, for any period of time, at any given rate of interest can be calculated by the following equation, where R is the return, I is the amount invested, r is the rate of interest and n is the investment return year.

$$R = I \times (1+r)^n$$

The equation below calculates the Return in Year #3 in the above example as follows:

$$R = \$100 \times (1+.05)^3$$
$$R = \$100 \times 1.1576$$
$$R = \$115.76$$

This same equation can be expressed differently to calculate the present value or discounted cash flow (DCF) of the return of a given amount (R), at the end of given time period (n), at discount rate (r) that reflects inflation, opportunity cost and risk.

$$DCF = R/(1+r)^n$$

You could use this equation in the above example to calculate the DCF of $115.76 received at the end of three years at a discount rate of 5%.

$$DCF = \$115.76/(1+.05)^3$$
$$DCF = \$115.76/1.1576$$
$$DCF = \$100$$

This DCF calculation is based on the receipt of a single payment. Most often, an investment will involve expenditures, and yield multiple revenues, over a period of time. Under these circumstances, the investor is interested in the net present value (NPV) of the investment over the period of the investment. The NPV of an investment is the sum of the DCFs, where each DCF is calculated as the net return (revenues minus expenses) in each year of the investment. NPV is most easily calculated using spreadsheet software such a Microsoft Excel.

The discount rate greatly affects the DCF or NPV value. Treasury Bills are considered to be the safest investment because repayment is guaranteed by the U.S. government. The yield on Treasury Bills, currently about 5%, reflects the rate of inflation in the economy. If the inflation rate is 2%, a 5% yield on Treasury Bills could be viewed as 2% for inflation and 3% for a risk-free investment return. The discount rate for an investment, therefore, must include a premium for the increased risk of the investment compared to Treasury Bills. The risk premium for an investment in bonds of a "blue chip" company (5–6%) will be far lower than the risk premium for an investment in the stock of a new public company (30–40%).

For corporations, the discount rate must not only include the risk of the investment, but also the cost of capital. Corporations are financed by stocks and bonds, and they must pay a competitive rate of return to their investors or the price of their stocks and bonds will fall in the market. For an investment to add economic value to a corporation, the return on the investment must be greater than the cost of the capital used to make the investment. A corporation's cost of capital is generally calculated as its weighted average cost of capital (WACOC). WACOC is calculated as the cost of debt (bonds) times the percentage of debt, plus the cost of equity (stock) times the percentage of equity. Assuming that a corporation is financed with 30% debt and 70% equity, and that its bonds must yield 10% and its equity must yield 18%, the corporation's WACOC would be calculated as follows.

$$WACOC = (30\% \times 10\%) + (70\% \times 18\%)$$
$$WACOC = (3\%) + (12.6\%)$$
$$WACOC = 15.6\%$$

In this example, the corporation must earn a return greater than 15.6% for the investment to add economic value to the corporation.

Again, the corporation's return must be adjusted for risk. The risk adjustment can be as low as 10% for a very low risk investment and as high as 90% for an extremely high risk investment. In calculating DCF, the discount rate is the sum of the corporation's WACOC and risk adjustment. The return on the investment at this discount rate must be greater than zero for the investment to add economic value to the corporation.

I will now discuss the valuation methods that have been developed specifically for intellectual property. These are the 25 percent rule, industry standard royalty rates, ranking methods, surrogate measures, disaggregation methods, Monte

Carlo methods, option methods and competitive advantage valuation.

The 25 Percent Rule

The 25 percent rule is a widely discussed valuation rule of thumb. Although there are many variations on the 25 percent rule, the most often given definition is that the licensor should receive 25 percent of the licensee's gross profit from the licensed technology. This statement of the 25 percent rule makes clear that its purpose is not the valuation of an intellectual property asset *per se*, but rather the apportionment of an intellectual property asset's value between the licensor and licensee. Discussions of the 25 percent rule generally provide that the percentage split between the licensor and licensee should be adjusted upwards or downwards to take into account the parties' respective investment and risk in the licensed technology.

The 25 percent rule is more easily used in the case of process technology than product technology. In the case of process technology, the 25 percent rule can be applied directly to the manufacturing cost savings attributable to the new technology. However, new product technology is generally associated with only a component portion of a product's total functionality. In this case, the 25 percent rule should be applied only to the additional profit (increased unit sales or higher unit prices) that can be attributed to the enhanced functionality. Associating sales or prices with different aspects of a product's functionality is difficult but necessary. If the 25 percent rule is applied to profits which are not attributable to the licensed technology, the licensor would receive a royalty windfall and the licensee would be deprived of a fair return on investment.

Despite difficulties in application and disagreements over its usefulness, up until recently, all commentators seemed to agree that the 25 percent rule is the simplest, most flexible and most often referenced valuation method. However, the Federal Circuit has recently held that the 25 percent rule is "fundamentally flawed" in the calculation of patent infringement damages and can no longer be introduced as evidence in infringement damages cases. *See* subsection 1.8.3 below. It remains to be seen how the Federal Circuit holding will affect the valuation of patent licenses.

Industry Standard Royalty Rates

Valuation of intellectual property by industry standard royalty rates is another widely used valuation method. The industry standards method, also referred to as the "market" or "comparable technology" method, attempts to value an intellectual property asset by reference to royalty rates in similar past transactions. Although some writers view the industry standards method as completely distinct from the 25 percent rule, in fact, they share much in common. Similar to the 25 percent rule, the industry standards method does not attempt to value an intellectual property asset *per se*, but rather it apportions the value of the intellectual property asset between the licensor and licensee. Also, similar to the 25 percent rule, the industry standards method is based on past experience. The difference between the 25 percent rule and the industry standards method is the greater degree of specificity generally associated with the industry standards method; whereas the 25 percent rule is applied across all industries and to all technologies, the industry standards method is specific to a given industry and given technology.

The industry standards method of valuation is subject to a number of limitations. Some of these limitations have to do with the comparability of transactions discussed above in connection with the market method of valuation. Intellectual property is inherently dissimilar, and intellectual property exchanges are motivated by unique strategic considerations. In addition, published royalty rates are often based on broad industry classifications and provided in terms of wide percentage ranges. There might be significant differences in royalty rates within an industry, and the wide percentage ranges might provide little guidance on an appropriate royalty rate for the intellectual property asset being valued. Finally, focusing on royalty rates in the abstract without considering a host of other factors (e.g., the presence of license fees, minimum royalties, cross-licenses; whether the licenses are exclusive or nonexclusive; the relationships between the parties and their relative bargaining power; the stage of development of the technology; changes in market demand) results in the worst of both worlds — subjective royalty rates masked by an objective methodology.

The Ranking Method

The ranking method of valuation compares the intellectual property asset to be valued to comparable intellectual property assets on a subjective or objective scale. The ranking method is often used in conjunction with the industry standards method to determine a more precise royalty rate within an industry royalty rate range. There are five components to a ranking method: (i) scoring criteria; (ii) scoring system; (iii) scoring scale; (iv) weighting factors; and (v) decision table. Scoring criteria are factors which can be used to compare intellectual property assets, such as potential market size, scope of protection and stage of development. Scoring systems are values assigned to scoring criteria, such as a 1-5 or 1-10 point system, or a high/medium/low system. Scoring scales (methods) are the means of applying the scoring system. Subjective scaling generally utilizes a panel of experts, whereas objective scaling is based on measurable past experience. Weighting factors are used to differentiate the importance of the scoring criteria. The decision table combines the scoring criteria, criteria values and criteria weights to calculate a composite score, which can then be compared to the average score for a comparable intellectual property asset.

As with the other valuation methods discussed above, selection of the comparable intellectual property asset transactions is key to using the ranking method. In addition, the ranking method requires the selection of appropriate comparative criteria and criteria weights. One of the most often-cited set of comparative criteria is the *Georgia-Pacific* criteria used to determine reasonable royalty rates for patent infringement damages. The *Georgia-Pacific* case sets forth 15 criteria (factors) to be considered in determining a reasonable royalty rate:

1. The royalties received by the patentee for the licensing of the patent in suit, proving or tending to prove an established royalty.

2. The rates paid by the licensee for the use of other patents comparable to the patent in suit.

3. The nature and scope of the license, as exclusive or non-exclusive; or as restricted or non-restricted in terms of territory or with respect to whom the manufactured product may be sold.

4. The licensor's established policy and marketing program to maintain his patent monopoly by not licensing others to use the invention or by granting licenses under special conditions designed to preserve that monopoly.

5. The commercial relationship between the licensor and licensee, such as, whether they are competitors in the same territory in the same line of business; or whether they are inventor and promoter.

6. The effect of selling the patented specialty in promoting sales of other products of the licensee; that existing value of the invention to the licensor as a generator of sales of his non-patented items; and the extent of such derivative or convoyed sales.

7. The duration of the patent and the term of the license.

8. The established profitability of the product made under the patent; its commercial success; and its current popularity.

9. The utility and advantages or the patent property over the old modes or devices, if any, that had been used for working out similar results.

10. The nature of the patented invention; the character of the commercial embodiment of it as owned and produced by the licensor; and the benefits to those who have used the invention.

11. The extent to which the infringer has made use of the invention; and any evidence probative of the value of that use.

12. The portion of the profit or of the selling price that may be customary in the particular business or in comparable businesses to allow for the use of the invention or analogous inventions.

13. The portion of the realizable profit that should be credited to the invention as distinguished from non-patented elements, the manufacturing process, business risks, or significant features or improvements added by the infringer.

14. The opinion of qualified experts.

15. The amount that a licensor (such as the patentee) and the licensee (such as the infringer) would have agreed upon (at the time the infringement began) if both had been reasonably and voluntarily trying to reach an agreement; that is, the amount which a prudent licensee — who desired, as a business proposition, to obtain a license to manufacture and sell a particular article embodying the patented invention — would have been willing to pay as a royalty and yet be able to make a reasonable profit and which amount would have been acceptable by a prudent patentee who was willing to grant a license.

Georgia-Pacific Corp. v. U.S. Plywood Corp., 318 F.Supp.1116, 1120 (S.D.N.Y. 1970).

The ranking method of valuation has many advantages. It forces the selection of criteria which affect the value of intellectual property assets as well as consideration of comparative scoring on these criteria. It provides a common basis for negotiation discussions among licensing experts while also being understandable to non-experts. Accumulated experience with the ranking method leads, over time, to more quantitative applications.

The three major disadvantages of the ranking method of valuation are the identification of comparable (benchmark) intellectual property asset transactions; the subjectivity in selection, weighting and scoring of criteria; and the translation of a decision table composite score into a royalty rate or dollar adjustment. Comparability is as much of a challenge in the ranking method as it is in the other methods, for the same reasons. Although there appears to be some agreement on the general criteria that most affect intellectual property value, selecting criteria for a specific intellectual property asset is more difficult. For example, how would one compare novel features of a new intellectual property asset to older substitute products or processes? Weighting and scoring pose similar subjectivity problems. How would one weigh the strength of intellectual property protection against the stage of technology development? How would a score be assigned to protection strength and to stage of development; and how would the two scoring systems relate to one another? Finally, regardless of how a composite score is calculated for an intellectual property asset, its translation into an adjustment to the comparable (average) royalty rate or payment is subject to further subjectivity. For example, if the composite score for the intellectual property asset being valued is 4 and a comparable average intellectual property asset has a composite score of 3, does that mean that the intellectual property asset being valued should command a 33% higher royalty rate or licensee fee?

Despite the disadvantages of the ranking method, its widespread use attests to its widely perceived usefulness.

Surrogate Measures

Surrogate measures have been developed to value patents. Surrogate measures do not value patents by reference to profits, industry standards or rankings but by reference to the patents themselves. The three most common types of surrogate measures are the number of patents issued to a company, payment of patent maintenance fees, and prior art citations. These measures have been shown to correlate, on average, with a firm's market value, suggesting that investors use these measures explicitly or implicitly in making investment decisions.

The number of patents issued to a company (i.e., patent count) is an indicator of the level of R&D expenditures and the number of product/process innovations, both of which are independently associated with market value. The payment of patent maintenance fees is an indicator of the quality of a patent portfolio — the more patents renewed, the higher the quality; the more patents lapsed, the lower the quality. There are two types of prior art citation measures — forward citations and backward citations. The forward citation measure counts the number of citations to a patent as prior art in subsequently issued patents — the greater the number of citations, the greater the importance (i.e., value) of a patent. The backward citation measure counts the number of scientific papers cited in a patent. The backward citation measure is an indicator of the level of basic science research underlying a patent. Citation-weighted patent counts have been shown to be associated with firms' market values. Citation-based measures have also been shown to be predictive of future stock returns and the market-to-book values of public companies.

Surrogate measures, especially patent-based measures, have become widely accepted valuation methods. The utility of surrogate measures, however, is limited in three respects. First, the measures themselves can be inherently misleading. For example, a patent count ignores the well-documented disparity in patent values. A portfolio with a few broad patents might be far more valuable than a portfolio with many more narrow patents. Similarly, a large number of citations to a patent might not be because the patent has current commercial value but because the patent is based on basic research which could be a long way from practical application. Second, the measures can be manipulated. Firms can inflate the value of their patent portfolios by filing more, but relatively minor, improvement patents; or by citing more, but relatively less important, scientific papers as prior art. Third, surrogate measures can only be used to value patent portfolios. Valuation of patent portfolios is very useful to investors and financial analysts. Intellectual property managers and licensing professionals, however, need to value individual, or related groups of, patents. Surrogate measures are far less useful in these valuation tasks.

Disaggregation Methods

There are two basic types of disaggregation methods — value disaggregation and income disaggregation. Value disaggregation seeks to apportion some fraction of the firm's total value to intellectual property assets, whereas income disaggregation seeks to apportion some fraction of the firm's total income to intellectual property assets.

The simplest form of value disaggregation first calculates the market value of a firm, either from the price of its outstanding common stock, in the case of a public company, or from substitute measures such as price-earnings ratios or net cash flows, in the case of a private company. The value of the firm's monetary assets (e.g., securities, working capital, receivables) and tangible assets (e.g., land, buildings, equipment) are subtracted from the market value of the firm to determine the value of the intangible assets. This form of disaggregation is useful to provide perspective on the importance of intangible assets to a firm but cannot be used to value different types of intangible assets or to value individual, or related groups of, intangible assets.

A more sophisticated value disaggregation method divides the value of a firm among its business divisions and the value of the business divisions among the products sold by the divisions. The value of a given product is then apportioned among the monetary, tangible, intangible and brand assets (e.g., trademarks, brand names) associated with the product. The monetary, tangible and intangible assets associated with the product can be based on the ratio calculated for the firm as a whole, and the value of the brand assets can be based on the difference between the value of products incorporating the brand assets and the value of generic substitute products. This method of valuation has the benefit of associating intangible assets with specific products, albeit in an undifferentiated fashion. It also has the benefit of separating out the value of brand assets from other intangible assets. This method, however, cannot value intellectual property assets (e.g., patents, copyrights, trade secrets) separately from intangible advantages (e.g., assembled work force, employee training) nor can it value individual, or related groups of, intellectual property assets.

Income disaggregation calculates the earnings of a firm or business unit and apportions a fraction of these earnings to intellectual property assets based upon various factors. One form of income disaggregation, developed for Dow Chemical Company by Arthur D. Little, is the "Tech Factor Method." The Tech Factor Method quantifies the monetary contribution of each patent as a percentage of the business's total net present revenue. The Tech Factor Method utilizes a cross-functional team of internal and/or external experts to evaluate the commercial, technical and legal aspects of a technology. Tech Factor valuation begins with a determination of the net present value of the incremental cash flow of a business unit attributable to the technology being valued. Next, a technology factor range (low, medium or high quality assessment) is assigned to the technology based on its utility and competitive advantage attributes. Finally, the net present value of the incremental cash flow is multiplied by the technology factor to calculate the value of the technology. The advantage of the Tech Factor Method is that it provides a structured, easily understood, process for valuing technology. The disadvantage of the Tech Factor Method is that it requires assembly of a large multi-functional team possessing detailed knowledge of the competitive environment, and business and marketing plans. The Tech Factor Method also does not provide a quantitative means for determining the incremental cash flow attributable to a technology or for determining the exact technology factor within a technology factor range.

Another income disaggregation method is the Knowledge Capital Scorecard developed by Professor Baruch Lev. The Knowledge Capital Scorecard first subtracts from a firm's annual normalized earnings the earnings from tangible and financial assets. The remainder of the earnings, which are generated by knowledge assets, is divided by a knowledge capital discount rate to calculate the value of knowledge assets. The advantage of the Knowledge Capital Scorecard is that it associates intangible assets with measurable earnings and calculates a realistic present value for intangible assets. The disadvantages of the Knowledge Capital Scorecard are that it cannot separate the different types of types of intangible assets and cannot value individual, or related groups of, intangible assets.

Monte Carlo Method

The Monte Carlo method of valuing intellectual property assets is primarily used as a refinement of the income method discussed earlier. Whereas the income method assigns a single value to the variables used in calculating the net present value (NPV) of an asset, the Monte Carlo method assigns a range of values to the variables. For example, two revenue variables used to determine the NPV of an intellectual property asset are the price premium and additional unit sales attributable to the asset, and two expense variables are the cost of goods sold (COGS) and sales, general and administrative expenses (SG&A) associated with the increased sales revenue. The income method would assign a single value to each of these variables; for example, the price premium might be $1000, the additional sales might be 10,000 units, the COGS might be 60% of sales revenue and SG&A might be 25% of sales revenue. The Monte Carlo method would assign a range of values to each of these variables; for example, the price premium might be between $800 and $1,200, the additional unit sales might be between 9,000 and 11,000, the COGS might be between 55% and 65%, and the SG&A might be between 15% and 35%.

In addition to assigning a range of values to each variable, the Monte Carlo method requires that a probability be assigned to the individual values within a range. The Monte Carlo method works by calculating the NPV of an intellectual property asset typically between 500 and 1000 times based upon a random selection of the probability weighted values that have been determined for each variable. Each calculation, or iteration, yields a single NPV. The multiple NPVs are then plotted by the frequency of their occurrence. This provides an indication of the most likely NPV as well as the probability of a NPV being above or below the most likely value by a given amount.

The most likely NPV calculated by the Monte Carlo method should not differ from the NPV calculated by the income method. Presumably, the single values assigned to each variable in the income method are the most probable values, so a random selection from a range of probability-weighted values would select these single values most often. The benefit of the Monte Carlo method is that it can calculate minimum and maximum NPVs and can associate intermediate NPVs with the probability of their realization. For example, the Monte Carlo method might calculate the minimum NPV to be $300K and the maximum NPV to be $600K (there is zero probability that the NPV will be below the minimum or above the maximum). Similarly, the Monte Carlo method might calculate that there is a 80% probability that the NPV will be above $400K and a 20% probability that the NPV will be above $500K. Such information is useful in licensing negotiations because it provides the parties perspective on the possible outcomes of the exchange. The Monte Carlo method is also useful to determine how different variables affect the uncertainty of the NPV calculation. For example, the Monte Carlo method can be used to determine whether the revenue or expense variables most contribute to NPV uncertainty. This information is also useful in licensing negotiations because it directs the parties' attention to monitoring and measuring the most critical variables.

The challenge in implementing the Monte Carlo method is obtaining the necessary information. The accuracy of the NPV calculations yielded by the Monte Carlo method are totally dependent on the accuracy of the value ranges and the probabilities assigned to individual values. To provide this information, extensive databases are required.

Options Method

Option methods of valuing intellectual property assets are based on a widely used method for valuing stock options, known throughout the financial industry as the Black-Scholes formula. The Black-Scholes formula values a stock option as a function of five variables: (i) the price at which the option can be exercised (the strike price); (ii) the current market price of the stock; (iii) the amount of time remaining before the option expires; (iv) the volatility of the stock price; and (v) a risk-free rate of return. Even if the strike price is higher than the current market price, the option still has value if the option period is sufficiently long and the price volatility is sufficiently great. The longer the option period and the greater the price volatility, the higher the probability that the strike price will be below the market price at some point. Under the Black-Scholes formula, the essence of a stock option's value lies in the right to wait and see what happens to a stock's price and to exercise or not exercise the option accordingly.

The adaptation of stock option valuation to intellectual property valuation is based on the same "wait and see" value. Option valuation of intellectual property views an investment in intellectual property as an option to develop the intellectual property further, or to abandon the intellectual property, depending upon future technical and market information. Option valuation is most useful for intellectual property investments which have long-term returns and high risks. The income method often undervalues these types of investments because of the compounding effect of risk over long periods of time. Option valuation compensates for this discounting effect. Option valuation recognizes that the risk of the intellectual property investment is not uniform over time but decreases as additional technical and market information is obtained, and that the owner of the intellectual property has the choice to continue to invest in the intellectual property or to abandon it at any point in time.

The advantages of option valuation are that it avoids exaggerating the risk of investing in intellectual property assets and provides an objective, repeatable means for calculating intellectual property value. The disadvantages of option valuation are its complex mathematics and its requirement of extensive information databases.

Competitive Advantage Valuation®

Competitive Advantage Valuation (CAV) is a new method to value intellectual property assets. Two patents have been issued on the CAV method: #7,188,069 — March 6, 2007 and #7,493,262 — February 17, 2009. The CAV method was developed over a number of years through a series of research projects undertaken in the Technology Commercialization Research Center at Syracuse University on behalf of a variety of client organizations. These research projects assessed the commercial potential of many different types of early-stage technologies by analyzing the science and engineering, marketing, licensing and intellectual property advantages and disadvantages associated with these technologies. When presented with the final research findings, the question most often asked by client organizations was "So, what's the invention worth"? CAV was developed to answer this question in a simple and direct way.

In comparison to other valuation methods, the CAV method combines a number of unique features. Most importantly, the CAV method is specific. It can be used to value individual intellectual property assets and to determine differences in value within a group of related intellectual property assets. The more specific a valuation method is, the more useful it is in managing intellectual property assets.

The major premise of the CAV method is that intellectual property assets have no inherent value; the value of intellectual property resides entirely in the competitive advantage which the intellectual property contributes to a product or process. The minor premise of the CAV method is that the competitive advantage contributed by an intellectual property asset can be measured, and can be used to predict the market value of the product or process incorporating the intellectual property asset. For the purpose of explanation, I will discuss the CAV method with respect to a single patent in a single pre-market product.

The CAV method is a novel combination of the income and disaggregation approaches to valuation. In its most general form, the CAV method consists of seven basic steps:

(1) Calculate the net present value of the total profits in the product's intended application market over the competitive lifetime of the product.

(2) Disaggregate the net present value of the total market profits into the portion of those profits attributable to intangible assets, reputational intellectual property assets and technical intellectual property assets. (There are three groups of intellectual property assets — technical [utility patents, functional software copyrights and technical trade secrets], reputational [trademarks, service marks and brand names] and operational [business method patents and proprietary business processes].)

(3) Define a set of price and performance parameters that determine success in the intended product application market.

(4) Calculate the competitive advantage of the product by comparing it to an average substitute product on the price and performance parameters defined above.

(5) Extrapolate from the product's competitive advantage in comparison to the average substitute product to the product's predicted market share in comparison to the average market share.

(6) Calculate the value of the patent from the net present value of the share of market profits attributable to technical intellectual property and the predicted market share of the product in its intended application market.

(7) Adjust the value of the patent for technical, market and intellectual property risks.

If the patent being valued is combined with other patents in a product, the relative competitive advantage contribution of all the patents incorporated in the product is calculated and the value of the product is apportioned among the patents in accordance with their relative competitive advantage contributions. If the patent being valued is associated with multiple products, then the patent's relative competitive advantage contribution to each product is calculated and these contributions are summed to calculate the total value of the patent. If the patent is associated with multiple parameters, then the patent's relative competitive advantage contribution for each parameter is calculated and these contributions are summed to calculate the total value of the patent.

As noted above, the CAV method is easy to use. The information required is obtainable from public domain sources and the calculations are based on simple algebra. In addition, the CAV method provides an intuitively logical association among the valuation variables. An intellectual property asset is associated with a product; the product is associated with a set of competitive advantage parameters; and the intellectual property asset is associated with one of these parameters. Finally, the CAV method provides a set of default formulas for calculating the portion of a product's net present value attributable to intellectual property assets, the weights for competition parameter groups and the weights for individual parameters within the parameter groups.

In addition to valuing intellectual property assets, the CAV method can also be used to value intellectual property licenses, alternative research and development investments, and pre-market products.

Additional Information

1. GORDON V. SMITH & RUSSELL L. PARR, INTELLECTUAL PROPERTY: VALUATION, EXPLOITATION, AND INFRINGEMENT DAMAGES (John Wiley & Sons, Inc.) (2005).

2. RICHARD RAZGAITIS, VALUATION AND PRICING OF TECHNOLOGY-BASED INTELLECTUAL PROPERTY (John Wiley & Sons, Inc.) (2003).

3. WESTON ANSON, DONNA P. SUCHY, & CHAITALI AHYA, FUNDAMENTALS OF INTELLECTUAL PROPERTY VALUATION: A PRIMER FOR IDENTIFYING AND DETERMINING VALUE (American Bar Association) (2006).

4. ROBERT F. REILLY, JR. & ROBERT SCHWEIHS, THE HANDBOOK OF BUSINESS VALUATION AND INTELLECTUAL PROPERTY ANALYSIS (McGraw Hill) (2004).

5. CHRISTOPHER M. ARENA & EDUARDO M. CARRERAS, THE BUSINESS OF INTELLECTUAL PROPERTY (Oxford University Press) (2008).

6. Ted Hagelin, *Valuation of Patent Licenses*, 12 TEX. INTELL. PROP. L. J. 423 (2004).

7. Ted Hagelin, *Competitive Advantage Valuation of Intellectual Property Assets: A New Tool for IP Managers*, 44 IDEA 79 (2003).

8. Ted Hagelin, *A New Method to Value Intellectual Property*, 30 AIPLA Q. J. 353 (2002).

9. Ted Hagelin, *Valuation of Intellectual Property Assets: An Overview*, 52 SYRACUSE L. REV. 1113 (2002).

1.8.3   Patent Infringement Damages and Patent License Valuations

The determination of damages in a patent infringement suit, and the determination of a license's value in licensing negotiations, are related calculations. Section 284 of the Patent Act provides:

　　　Upon finding for the claimant [patent owner] the court shall award the claimant damages adequate to compensate for the infringement, but in no event less than a reasonable royalty for the use made of the invention by the infringer, together with interest and costs as fixed by the court.

Courts have held that the proper determination of a reasonable royalty for purposes of calculating infringement damages is the royalty the patent owner and infringer would have agreed upon in a hypothetical, arms-length license negotiation conducted at the time the infringement began. Although parties negotiating license agreements outside of infringement suits are not bound by the courts' prescription of the proper determination of reasonable royalties for purposes of calculating infringement damages, the courts' discussions of hypothetical license negotiations, and the factors that affect the value of royalties, have clear implications for determining reasonable license values in non-litigation contexts. These implications are especially strong in cases where a patent owner and an alleged infringer are negotiating a license in order to avoid a patent infringement suit. In these cases, the value of the negotiated royalty should closely approximate the value of the reasonable royalty for purposes of calculating infringement damages because this is what the parties should expect to receive, or pay, in the event of an infringement suit.

As noted earlier, the royalty amount is a function of two variables: (1) the royalty base (the dollar amount on which royalties are calculated); and (2) the royalty rate (the percentage amount of the royalty base which is paid as royalties). In the *Unilok* case below, the Federal Circuit's most recent decision on the calculation of damages in patent infringement suits, the court directly addresses both royalty variables. The royalty rate base is addressed in the context of the "entire market value" rule which is often advanced by patent owners to establish a reasonable royalty base for a hypothetical license negotiation. The royalty rate is addressed in the context of the 25 percent rule, and other factors, including the *Georgia Pacific* factors, which are relevant to establishing a reasonable royalty rate.

UNILOC USA, INC. v. MICROSOFT CORP.
632 F.3d 1292 (Fed. Cir. 2011)

LINN, CIRCUIT JUDGE.

Uniloc USA, Inc. and Uniloc Singapore Private Limited (collectively, "Uniloc") appeal from the decision of the United States District Court for the District of Rhode Island granting Microsoft Corporation's ("Microsoft") motion for judgment as a matter of law ("JMOL") of non-infringement and no willful infringement of asserted claims of Uniloc's U.S. Patent No. 5,490,216 (" '216 patent"), and, in the alternative, granting a new trial on infringement and willfulness. Uniloc also appeals the district court's alternative grant of a new trial on damages. Microsoft cross-appeals the district court's denial of its motion for JMOL of invalidity of the '216 patent.

Because the jury's verdict on infringement was supported by substantial evidence, this court reverses the district court's grant of JMOL of non-infringement; this court also reverses the district court's alternative grant of a new trial on infringement as an abuse of discretion. Because the jury's verdict on willfulness was not supported by substantial evidence, this court affirms the district court's grant of JMOL of no willfulness; the district court's alternative grant of a new trial for willfulness is thus rendered moot. Because the jury's damages award was fundamentally tainted by the use of a legally inadequate methodology, this court affirms the grant of a new trial on damages. Finally, because the district court did not abuse its discretion in determining that the jury verdict of no invalidity of the '216 patent was supported by substantial evidence, we affirm the district court's denial of Microsoft's motion for JMOL of invalidity.

I. BACKGROUND

Commercial software manufacturers like Microsoft lose significant sales as a result of the "casual copying" of software, where users install copies of a software program on multiple computers in violation of applicable software license conditions. Uniloc's '216 patent was an early attempt to combat such software piracy. There is no dispute as to the actual functioning of Uniloc's patented invention and Microsoft's accused products. The following background information is taken from the district court's opinion.

A. The '216 Patent

Uniloc's '216 patent is directed to a software registration system to deter copying of software. The system allows the software to run without restrictions (in "use mode") only if the system determines that the software installation is legitimate. A representative embodiment functions as follows. First, a user intending to use the software in "use mode" enters certain user information when prompted, which may include a software serial number and/or name and address information. An algorithm on the user's computer (a "local licensee unique ID generating means") combines the inputted information into "a registration number unique to an intending licensee" (a "local licensee unique ID"). The user information is also sent to the vendor's system, which performs the identical algorithm (a "remote licensee unique ID generating means") to create a "remote licensee unique ID" for the user. When the application boots again, a "mode switching means" compares the local and remote licensee unique IDs. If they match, the program enters into "use mode." If they do not match, the program enters into "demo mode," wherein certain features are disabled.

****

II. DISCUSSION

****

C. New Trial on Damages

The jury here awarded Uniloc $388 million, based on the testimony of Uniloc's expert, Dr. Gemini. Dr. Gemini opined that damages should be $564,946,803. This was based on a hypothetical negotiation between Uniloc and Microsoft and the *Georgia-Pacific* factors. Gemini began with an internal pre-litigation Microsoft document that stated:

Product Keys are valuable for two major reasons. First, since Product Keys can be used to install a product and create a valid Product ID, you can associate a monetary value to them. An appraisal process found that a Product Key is worth anywhere between $10 and $10,000 depending on usage. Secondly, Product Keys contain short digital signature technology that Microsoft Research created. For these reasons, it is crucial that Product Keys are handled with maximum security.

Gemini took the lowest value, $10, and testified that this is "the isolated value of Product Activation." Gemini then applied the so-called "25 percent rule of thumb," hypothesizing that 25% of the value of the product would go to the patent owner and the other 75% would remain with Microsoft, resulting in a baseline royalty rate of $2.50 per license issued. Gemini justified the use of the rule of thumb because it has "been accepted by Courts as an appropriate methodology in determining damages, in [his] experience, in other cases." He then considered several of the *Georgia Pacific* factors, with the idea being "to adjust this 25% up or down depending on how [the *Georgia Pacific* factors] favor[ ] either party." At bottom, he concluded that the factors in favor of Uniloc and Microsoft generally balanced out and did not change the royalty rate. He then multiplied the $2.50 royalty rate by the number of new licenses to Office and Windows products, 225,978,721, to get a final reasonable royalty of $564,946,803. Gemini then "did kind of a check to determine whether that number was reasonable. It's obviously, you know, a significant amount of money. I wanted to check to make sure it was a reasonable number." The "check" was performed by "estimating the gross revenues for the accused products" by multiplying the 225,978,721 licenses by the average sales price per license of $85. The resulting gross revenue value was $19.28 billion. Gemini then calculated that his damages calculation resulted in a royalty rate over the gross revenue of Office and Windows of approximately 2.9%. Gemini presented this information in a demonstrative pie chart to accompany his testimony. In response to Uniloc's attorney's question: "And have you prepared a chart or a graph or a pie chart to show us this comparison"? Uniloc's attorney, Mr. Cronin stated, "Your honor, there's no objection," and Microsoft attorney Mr. Scherkenbach stated, "Right, there is no objection." Gemini then opined that "in my experience, and data I've seen as far as industry royalty rates for software, which are generally above-on average, above 10% or 10, 11%, I felt that this royalty was reasonable and well within that range."

Microsoft had challenged the 25% rule *in limine* and attempted to exclude Mr. Gemini's testimony. The district court noted that "the concept of a "rule of thumb" is perplexing in an area of the law where reliability and precision are deemed paramount," but rejected Microsoft's position because the rule has been widely accepted. The district court thus considered the use of the rule of thumb to be reasonable. Microsoft contested Gemini's use of the entire market value rule "check" because Product Activation was not the basis of the consumer demand for Microsoft's Office and Windows products. The district court agreed with Microsoft, and granted a new trial on damages, because the "$19 billion cat was never put back into the bag" and the jury may have "used the $19 billion figure to "check" its significant award of $388,000,000."

On appeal, the parties present the court with three damages issues: 1) the propriety of using the 25 percent rule; 2) application of the entire market value rule as a "check"; and 3) excessiveness of damages. Because this court affirms the district court's conditional grant of a new trial on damages, this court need not reach the last issue.

1. 25 Percent Rule

Section 284 of Title 35 of the United States Code provides that on finding infringement of a valid patent, damages shall "in no event [be] less than a reasonable royalty for the use made of the invention by the infringer, together with interest and costs as fixed by the court." In litigation, a reasonable royalty is often determined on the basis of a hypothetical negotiation, occurring between the parties at the time that infringement began. A reasonable royalty is the predominant measure of damages in patent infringement cases.

The 25 percent rule of thumb is a tool that has been used to approximate the reasonable royalty rate that the manufacturer of a patented product would be willing to offer to pay to the patentee during a hypothetical negotiation. Robert Goldscheider, John Jarosz and Carla Mulhern, *Use Of The 25 Per Cent Rule in Valuing IP*, 37 *les Nouvelles* 123, 123 (Dec.2002) ("*Valuing IP*"). "The Rule suggests that the licensee pay a royalty rate equivalent to 25 per cent of its expected profits for the product that incorporates the IP at issue." *Id.* As explained by its leading proponent, Robert Goldscheider, the rule takes the following form:

An estimate is made of the licensee's expected profits for the product that embodies the IP at issue. Those profits are divided by the expected net sales over that same period to arrive at a profit rate. That resulting profit rate, say 16 per cent, is then multiplied by 25 per cent to arrive at a running royalty rate. In this example, the resulting royalty rate would be 4 per cent. Going forward (or calculating backwards, in the case of litigation), the 4 per cent royalty rate is applied to net sales to arrive at royalty payments due to the IP owner.

The underlying "assumption is that the licensee should retain a majority (i.e. 75 percent) of the profits, because it has undertaken substantial development, operational and commercialization risks, contributed other technology/IP and/or brought to bear its own development, operational and commercialization contributions."

The rule was originally based on Goldscheider's observations of commercial licenses entered into by a "Swiss subsidiary of a large American company, with 18 licensees around the world, each having an exclusive territory." The rights transferred were a portfolio of patents and other intellectual property apparently related to the patented products. The term of each of these licenses was for three years, with the expectation that the licenses would be renewed. The licensees "faced strong competition," and "were either first or second in sales volume, and probably profitability, in their respective market."

According to its proponents, the veracity of the 25 percent rule has been "confirmed by a careful examination of years of licensing and profit data, across companies and industries." John C. Jarosz, Carla S. Mulhern and Michael Wagner, *The 25% Rule Lives On*, IP Law 360, Sept. 8, 2010. Goldscheider published a further empirical study in 2002, concluding that across all industries, the median royalty rate was 22.6 percent, and that the data supported the use of the 25 percent rule "as a tool of analysis." *Valuing IP*, 37 *les Nouvelles* at 132–33. Additionally, in a 1997 study of licensing organizations, 25 percent of the organizations indicated that they use the 25 percent rule as a starting point in negotiations. Stephen A. Degnan & Corwin Horton, *A Survey of Licensed Royalties*, 32 les Nouvelles 91, 95 (June 1997).

The 25 percent rule has, however, met its share of criticism that can be broadly separated into three categories. First, it fails to account for the unique relationship between the patent and the accused product. *See* Gregory K. Leonard and Lauren J. Stiroh, *Economic Approaches to Intellectual Property Policy, Litigation, and Management*, 949 PLI/Pat 425, 454–55 (Sept.–Nov. 2008) ("[The 25 percent rule] takes no account of the importance of the patent to the profits of the product sold, the potential availability of close substitutes or equally noninfringing alternatives, or any of the other idiosyncrasies of the patent at issue that would have affected a real-world negotiation."); Richard S. Toikka, *Patent Licensing Under Competitive and Non-Competitive Conditions*, 82 J. Pat. & Trademark Off. Soc'y 279, 292–93 (Apr. 2000) (arguing that it fails to "distinguish between monopoly and normal profit . . . . Thus for narrow patents, the rule may be overly generous to the patentee, and for broad patents it may be overly stingy"). Second, it fails to account for the unique relationship between the parties. *See* Ted Hagelin, *Valuation of Patent Licenses*, Tex. Intell. Prop. L.J. 423, 425–26 (Spring 2004) (noting that the rule should not be used in isolation because it fails to "account[ ] for the different levels of risk assumed by a licensor and licensee"); *Hypothetical Negotiations* at 702 ("[T]he rule is unlikely to have any basis in the accused infringer's industry, in the technology involved in either the patent or the accused product or service, or in the claimed invention's contribution to the infringing product or service."). Finally, the rule is essentially arbitrary and does not fit within the model of the hypothetical negotiation within which it is based. *See* Roy J. Epstein and Alan J. Marcus, *Economic Analysis of the Reasonable Royalty: Simplification and Extension of the Georgia-Pacific Factors*, 85 J. Pat. & Trademark Off. Soc'y 55, 574 (July 2003) ("[The 25% and the 5%] rules of thumb are best understood as special cases [ ] that may be appropriate to a given situation only by chance."); Roy J.

Epstein, *Modeling Patent Damages: Rigorous and Defensible Calculations* (2003) (paper presented at the AIPLA 2003 Annual Meeting) at 22 *available at* http://www. royepstein.com/epstein_aipla_2003_article_website.pdf (last accessed Nov. 19, 2010) (arguing that the 25% rule "shortcut" "is essentially arbitrary. Because it is based on ex post results, it does not necessarily relate to the results of a negotiation that took place prior to the infringement").

The admissibility of the bare 25 percent rule has never been squarely presented to this court. Nevertheless, this court has passively tolerated its use where its acceptability has not been the focus of the case, or where the parties disputed only the percentage to be applied (i.e. one-quarter to one-third), but agreed as to the rule's appropriateness. Lower courts have invariably admitted evidence based on the 25% rule, largely in reliance on its widespread acceptance or because its admissibility was uncontested.

****

In *Daubert* and *Kumho Tire*, the Supreme Court assigned to the district courts the responsibility of ensuring that all expert testimony must pertain to "scientific, technical, or other specialized knowledge" under Federal Rule of Evidence ("FRE") 702, which in turn required the judge to determine that the testimony was based on a firm scientific or technical grounding. "Expert testimony which does not relate to any issue in the case is not relevant and, ergo, non-helpful." *Daubert* (citing 3 Weinstein & Berger ¶ 702[02], p. 702–18).

This court now holds as a matter of Federal Circuit law that the 25 percent rule of thumb is a fundamentally flawed tool for determining a baseline royalty rate in a hypothetical negotiation. Evidence relying on the 25 percent rule of thumb is thus inadmissible under *Daubert* and the Federal Rules of Evidence, because it fails to tie a reasonable royalty base to the facts of the case at issue.

The patentee bears the burden of proving damages. *Lucent Techs., Inc. v. Gateway, Inc.* To properly carry this burden, the patentee must "sufficiently [tie the expert testimony on damages] to the facts of the case." *Daubert* ("An additional consideration under Rule 702 — and another aspect of relevancy — is whether expert testimony proffered in the case is sufficiently tied to the facts of the case that it will aid the jury in resolving a factual dispute.") If the patentee fails to tie the theory to the facts of the case, the testimony must be excluded. For example, in *General Electric Co. v. Joiner*, the Supreme Court allowed the exclusion of eight of Joiner's experts who opined that polychlorinated bi-phenyls ("PCBs") could cause cancer on the strength of several studies showing that mice receiving high doses of PCB developed cancer. The Supreme Court noted that "[t]he studies were so dissimilar to the facts presented in this litigation that it was not an abuse of discretion for the District Court to have rejected the experts' reliance on them," and affirmed the exclusion because Joiner had failed to tie the experts' opinions to the "seemingly far-removed animal studies," Likewise, in *Kumho Tire*, a products liability case arising out of a blown tire, the Supreme Court affirmed the exclusion of an expert opinion that argued that the cause of the accident at issue was a defect in the tire, based on the expert's visual and tactile inspection of the tire. The specific issue was not whether the visual and tactile inspection methodology was "reasonable[ ] *in general*," but whether "it was [reasonable to] us[e] such an approach . . . to draw a conclusion regarding *the particular matter to which the expert testimony was directly relevant*." "The relevant issue was whether the expert could reliably determine the cause of *this* tire's separation." The Court held that the expert had failed to reliably opine on this issue under *Daubert* because his general theory — "that in the absence of *at least two* of four signs of abuse . . . he concludes that a defect caused the separation," — did not take into account the facts of the particular tire at issue: that the tire "had traveled far enough so that some of the tread had been worn bald; it should have been taken out of service; it had been repaired (inadequately) for punctures; and it bore some of the very marks that the expert said indicated, not a defect, but abuse through overdeflection." In responding to the plaintiff's argument, "that a method of tire failure analysis that employs a visual/tactile inspection is a reliable method," based on "its use by other experts and to Carlson's [the expert in the case] long experience working for Michelin," the Court reaffirmed that "the question before the trial court was specific, not general. The trial court had to decide whether this particular expert had sufficient specialized knowledge to assist the jurors "in deciding the particular issues in the case." The Court held that he did not.

The bottom line of *Kumho Tire* and *Joiner* is that one major determinant of whether an expert should be excluded under *Daubert* is whether he has justified the application of a general theory to the facts of the case. Consistent with this conclusion, this court has held that "[a]ny evidence unrelated to the claimed invention does not support compensation for infringement but punishes beyond the reach of the statute."

In *ResQNet*, *Lucent Technologies* and *Wordtech Systems, Inc. v. Integrated Networks Solutions, Inc.*, this court determined that a patentee could not rely on license agreements that were "radically different from the hypothetical agreement under consideration" to determine a reasonable royalty. In *Lucent Technologies*, the patentee's expert relied in large part on "eight varied license agreements," four of which involved "PC-related patents," but either the specific subject matter of the patents was not explained to the jury or the license was "directed to a vastly different situation than the hypothetical licensing scenario of the present case," and four of which Lucent did not describe the relationship between the patented technology licensed therein and the licensee's products. This court noted that the "licenses relied on by the patentee in proving damages [must be] sufficiently comparable to the hypothetical license at issue in suit," and that the patentee's failure to do so "weighs strongly against the jury's award" relying on such non-comparable licenses. Similarly, in *ResQNet*, the patentee's expert "used licenses with no relationship to the claimed invention to drive the royalty rate up to unjustified double-digit levels," looking at licenses that did not mention the patents and had no "other discernible link to the claimed technology." This court rejected the expert's testimony, holding that the district court "must consider licenses that are commensurate with what the defendant has appropriated. If not, a prevailing plaintiff would be free to inflate the reasonable royalty analysis with conveniently selected licenses without an economic or other link to the technology in question." This court held that on remand, "the trial court should not rely on unrelated licenses to increase the reasonable royalty rate above rates more clearly linked to the economic demand for the claimed technology."

Similarly, in *Wordtech*, the patentee "introduced thirteen patent licenses that it previously granted to third parties for rights to some or all of the patents-in-suit" to argue to support the jury's damages determination. This court rejected eleven of the licenses because they were running royalty licenses (the patentee had only asked for a lump sum payment) and represented far lower rates than the jury returned. This court rejected the remaining two licenses (both for lump sum payments) because "[n]either license describe[d] how the parties calculated each lump sum, the licensees' intended products, or how many products each licensee expected to produce."

The meaning of these cases is clear: there must be a basis in fact to associate the royalty rates used in prior licenses to the particular hypothetical negotiation at issue in the case. The 25 percent rule of thumb as an abstract and largely theoretical construct fails to satisfy this fundamental requirement. The rule does not say anything about a particular hypothetical negotiation or reasonable royalty involving any particular technology, industry, or party. Relying on the 25 percent rule of thumb in a reasonable royalty calculation is far more unreliable and irrelevant than reliance on parties' unrelated licenses, which we rejected in *ResQNet* and *Lucent Technologies*. There, the prior licenses at least involved the same general industry and at least some of the same parties as the hypothetical negotiations at issue, and in *Wordtech* even involved licenses to the patents in suit entered into by the patentee-plaintiff. Lacking even these minimal connections, the 25 percent rule of thumb would predict that the same 25%/75% royalty split would begin royalty discussions between, for example, (a) TinyCo and IBM over a strong patent portfolio of twelve patents covering various aspects of a pioneering hard drive, and (b) Kodak and Fuji over a single patent to a tiny improvement in a specialty film emulsion.

It is of no moment that the 25 percent rule of thumb is offered merely as a starting point to which the *Georgia-Pacific* factors are then applied to bring the rate up or down. Beginning from a fundamentally flawed premise and adjusting it based on legitimate considerations specific to the facts of the case nevertheless results in a fundamentally flawed conclusion. This is reflected in *Lucent Technologies*, in which unrelated licenses were considered under *Georgia-Pacific* factor 1, but this court held that the entire royalty calculation was unsupported by substantial evidence.

To be admissible, expert testimony opining on a reasonable royalty rate must "carefully tie proof of damages to the claimed invention's footprint in the market place." This court has sanctioned the use of the *Georgia-Pacific* factors to frame the reasonable royalty inquiry. Those factors properly tie the reasonable royalty calculation to the facts of the hypothetical negotiation at issue. This court's rejection of the 25 percent rule of thumb is not intended to limit the application of any of the *Georgia-Pacific* factors. In particular, factors 1 and 2 — looking at royalties paid or received in licenses for the patent in suit or in comparable licenses — and factor 12 — looking at the portion of profit that may be customarily allowed in the particular business for the use of the invention or similar inventions — remain valid and important factors in the determination of a reasonable royalty rate. However, evidence purporting to apply to these, and any other factors, must be tied to the relevant facts and circumstances of the particular case at issue and the hypothetical negotiations that would have taken place in light of those facts and circumstances at the relevant time.

In this case, it is clear that Gemini's testimony was based on the use of the 25% rule of thumb as an arbitrary, general rule, unrelated to the facts of this case. When asked the basis of his opinion that the rule of thumb would apply here, Gemini testified: "[i]t's generally accepted. I've used it. I've seen others use it. It's a widely accepted rule." Upon further questioning, Dr. Gemini revealed that he had been involved in only four or five non-litigation related negotiations, and had recommended the 25% rule only once in a case involving a power tool. He did not testify that the parties here had a practice of beginning negotiations with a 25%/75% split, or that the contribution of Product Activation to Office and Word justified such a split. He did not base his 25 percent baseline on other licenses involving the patent at issue or comparable licenses. In short, Gemini's starting point of a 25 percent royalty had no relation to the facts of the case, and as such, was arbitrary, unreliable, and irrelevant. The use of such a rule fails to pass muster under *Daubert* and taints the jury's damages calculation.

This court thus holds that Microsoft is entitled to a new trial on damages.

2. Entire Market Value Rule

As discussed above, Gemini performed "a check to determine whether" his $564,946,803 royalty figure was reasonable by comparing it to his calculation of Microsoft's approximate total revenue for Office and Windows of $19.28 billion. During trial, Gemini testified that his calculated royalty accounted for only 2.9% of Microsoft's revenue, and accented his point by reference to a prepared pie chart, showing Microsoft's $19.28 billion in revenue with a 2.9% sliver representing his calculated royalty rate. He concluded that 2.9% was a reasonable royalty based on his experience that royalty rates for software are "generally above-on average, above 10% or 10, 11%."

The entire market value rule allows a patentee to assess damages based on the entire market value of the accused product only where the patented feature creates the "basis for customer demand" or "substantially create[s] the value of the component parts." This rule is derived from Supreme Court precedent requiring that "the patentee . . . must in every case give evidence tending to separate or apportion the defendant's profits and the patentee's damages between the patented feature and the unpatented features, and such evidence must be reliable and tangible, and not conjectural or speculative," or show that "the entire value of the whole machine, as a marketable article, is properly and legally attributable to the patented feature."

Microsoft argues that Uniloc employed the entire market value of Office and Windows by virtue of Gemini's pie chart, his comparison of his calculated royalty to the total revenue Microsoft earns through the accused products, and Uniloc's attorneys' belittlement of Microsoft's expert's royalty figure as representing only .0003% of total revenue. Microsoft argues that Uniloc's use of the entire market value rule was not proper because it is undisputed that Product Activation did not create the basis for customer demand or substantially create the value of the component parts. Microsoft continues that Gemini's testimony tainted the jury's damages deliberations, regardless of its categorization as a "check."

Uniloc responds that: (1) Microsoft did not object at trial and so waived any evidentiary argument to Gemini's testimony and demonstratives; (2) the entire market value of the product can be used if the royalty rate is low enough; and (3) the $19 billion figure was used only as a "check," and the jury was instructed not to base its damages determination on the entire market value, an instruction it should be presumed to have followed.

The district court agreed with Microsoft, and ordered a conditional new trial on damages. It noted that "Uniloc conceded customers do not buy Office or Windows because of [Product Activation] and said it would not base a royalty calculation on the entire market value of the products." As such, the use of the entire market value of Office and Windows in the form of the $19 billion figure was "irrelevant" and "taint[ed]" the jury's damages award. The district court also disagreed with Uniloc that Microsoft had waived its arguments to the entire market value, noting that "Microsoft objected specifically under the entire market value rule to use of a demonstrative pie chart," and that "[t]he Court preliminarily allowed it but after hearing the testimony instructed counsel to stay away from the $19 billion figure."

This court agrees with Microsoft and the district court that Uniloc's use of the $19 billion "check" was improper under the entire market value rule. First, regarding Uniloc's assertion that Microsoft has waived the issue, this court will not second-guess the district court's explicit recognition of Microsoft's objections to Gemini's testimony. FRE 103(a) notes that "Error may not be predicated upon a ruling which admits or excludes evidence unless . . . (1) Objection. — In case the ruling is one admitting evidence, a timely objection or motion to strike appears of record . . . . Once the court makes a definitive ruling on the record admitting or excluding evidence, either at or before trial, a party need not renew an objection or offer of proof to preserve a claim of error for appeal." The district court here explicitly noted that Microsoft's objection fell into the exception at the last line of FRE 103(a): "Although Microsoft did not continue to repeat an objection, it made its position on this evidence sufficiently clear to preserve the instant challenge" to Gemini's use of the entire market value rule. This is supported by Microsoft's *in limine* filings and Uniloc's response, where Uniloc explicitly said that it would not be relying on the entire market value of the accused products. This court thus agrees with the district court that Microsoft has not waived its objection.

Uniloc argues that the entire market value of the products may appropriately be admitted if the royalty rate is low enough, relying on the following statement in *Lucent Technologies:*

Simply put, the base used in a running royalty calculation can always be the value of the entire commercial embodiment, as long as the magnitude of the rate is within an acceptable range (as determined by the evidence) . . . . Microsoft surely would have little reason to complain about the supposed application of the entire market value rule had the jury applied a royalty rate of .1% (instead of 8%) to the market price of the infringing programs."

Just before this statement, however, this court held that one of the flaws in the use of the entire market value in that case was "the lack of evidence demonstrating the patented method of the Day patent as the basis — or even a substantial basis- of the consumer demand for Outlook . . . . [t]he only reasonable conclusion supported by the evidence is that the infringing use of the date-picker tool in Outlook is but a very small component of a much larger software program." Thus, in context, the passage relied on by Uniloc does not support its position. The Supreme Court and this court's precedents do not allow consideration of the entire market value of accused products for minor patent improvements simply by asserting a low enough royalty rate.

This case provides a good example of the danger of admitting consideration of the entire market value of the accused where the patented component does not create the basis for customer demand. As the district court aptly noted, "[t]he $19 billion cat was never put back into the bag even by Microsoft's cross-examination of Mr. Gemini and re-direct of Mr. Napper, and in spite of a final instruction that the jury may not award damages based on Microsoft's entire revenue from all the accused products in the case." This is unsurprising. The disclosure that a company has made $19 billion dollars in revenue from an infringing product cannot help but skew the damages horizon for the jury, regardless of the contribution of the patented component to this revenue.

****

Uniloc's final argument is that the use of the $19 billion figure was only as a check, and the jury must be presumed to have followed the jury instruction and not based its damages calculation on the entire market value rule. This argument attempts to gloss over the purpose of the check as lending legitimacy to the reasonableness of Gemini's $565 million damages calculation. Even if the jury's damages calculation was not based wholly on the entire market value check, the award was supported in part by the faulty foundation of the entire market value. Moreover, Uniloc's derision of Microsoft's damages expert by virtue of the.00003% of the entire market value that his damages calculation represented may have inappropriately contributed to the jury's rejection of his calculations. Thus, the fact that the entire market value was brought in as only a "check" is of no moment.

****

For the foregoing reasons, this court concludes that the district court did not abuse its discretion in granting a conditional new trial on damages for Uniloc's violation of the entire market value rule.

CONCLUSION

For the foregoing reasons, this court reverses the district court's grant of JMOL of non-infringement, affirms the district court's grant of JMOL of no willfulness, affirms the district court's grant of a new trial on damages, vacates the district court's grant of an alternative motion for new trial on infringement, and affirms the district court's denial of JMOL of invalidity of claim 19 of the '216. The case is remanded for proceedings consistent with this opinion.

AFFIRMED-IN-PART, REVERSED-IN-PART, VACATED-IN-PART, AND REMANDED COSTS

QUESTIONS

1. In a hypothetical negotiation with Uniloc for a license to use its Product Activation technology, what factors might Microsoft consider in determining the price, or royalty rate, that it would pay for the license?

2. Does the fact that the Product Activation technology was not a consideration in customer demand for Office and Windows products imply that the Product Activation technology was worthless to Microsoft?

3. On remand, how should the district court determine the value to Microsoft of the infringed Product Activation technology? Should the value of the Product Activation technology be determined in comparison with other features of Office and Windows? Should the value of the Product Activation technology be determined in comparison with substitute product activation technologies? Should the value of the Product Activation technology be determined by the extent to which infringement of Office and Windows products is avoided and the resulting decrease in prices enabled by the infringement avoidance?

4. If you represented Uniloc in a licensing negotiation for the Product Activation technology, how would you value the Product Activation technology?

5. Is the following formula for calculating a reasonable royalty base consistent with the *Daubert* requirements?

Reasonable Royalty Base = (Total Product Sales) × (Percentage of Sales Attributable to Technical Intellectual Property) × (Percentage of Sales Attributable to Infringing Patent)

6. Are technical, intellectual property and market risks relevant to calculating a reasonable royalty rate? Are these risks consistent with the *Daubert* requirements? Are these risks consistent with the *Georgia Pacific* factors?

CASE NOTES

1. Cornell University was the assignee of the '115 patent which claimed technology that could issue multiple, out-of-order computer processor instructions in a single computer clock cycle. The '115 patent enhanced the throughput of computer processors which perform multiple functions. In a computer server, the '115 patent performed one of the functions of the instruction reorder buffer (IRB), which is a component part of a computer processor. Computer processors are component parts of Central Processing Unit (CPU) modules. CPUs are incorporated into computer boards, which are inserted into computer servers and function as the servers' processing engines. Cornell sued Hewlett-Packard (HP) for infringement of the '115 patent in the sale of its computer servers. A jury found that the '115 patent was valid and that HP had infringed the '115. The jury awarded Cornell

$184,000,000 in infringement damages based on a royalty base of $23,000,000,000 which included HP's earnings from the sales of all of its servers incorporating the '115 patent. HP appealed the jury's damages award claiming that Cornell's damages expert had improperly applied the entire market value rule to all of HP's server sales. What result? *See* Cornell University v. Hewlett-Packard Co., 609 F.Supp.2d 279 (N.D.N.Y. 2009).

2. *See also* Lucent Technologies, Inc. v. Gateway, Inc., 580 F.3d 1301 (Fed. Cir. 2009) (Jury damage award of $357,693,056 lump-sum payment to patent owner overturned on appeal; in context of hypothetical negotiation, evidence failed to establish how often parties expected patented method to be used by consumers, how license agreements structured as running royalty agreements are probative of lump-sum payment agreements, and how license agreements involving different technologies and facts were related to the hypothetical negotiation for a license of the infringed technology; other license agreements relied on by patent owner to support damage award were radically different from the hypothetical license agreement being considered); Wordtech Sys. v. Integrated Networks Solutions, Inc., 609 F.3d 1308 (Fed. Cir. 2010) (Lump-sum license agreements relied upon by patent owner to support hypothetical license negotiation damage award provided the jury little more information than a recitation of royalty numbers; running royalty license agreements relied on by patent owner also failed to provide the jury sufficient information on which to base a hypothetical negotiation damage award); ResQNet.Com Inc. v. Lansa, Inc., 594 F.3d 860 (Fed. Cir. 2010) (Royalty rates in licenses which provided licensees finished software products and source code, as well as training, maintenance and upgrades, were not probative as to royalty rates in a straight patent license).

Additional Information

1. WESLEY KOBYLAK, 66 A.L.R. 186 (2011).

2. KATHLEEN T. PETRICH, EXPERT WITNESSES: INTELLECTUAL PROPERTY CASES § 3:32 (2008).

3. DON W. MARTENS, JOHN B. SGANGA, JR., PRE-LITIGATION PATENT ENFORCEMENT §§ 2:24–2:25, 5:29–5:31, 10:39 (2010).

4. JAY DRATLER, JR., STEPHEN M. MCJOHN, INTELLECTUAL PROPERTY LAW: COMMERCIAL CREATIVE AND INDUSTRIAL PROPERTY § 12:03 (2011).

5. TERRENCE P. ROSS, INTELLECTUAL PROPERTY LAW: DAMAGES AND REMEDIES § 3:08 (2011).

6. INTELLECTUAL PROPERTY LAW FOR BUSINESS LAWYERS § 4:25 (2010).

7. JOHN R. KENNEL ET AL., 69 C.J.S. PATENTS § 568 (2011).

8. WILLIAM O. KERR, RICHARD B. TROXEL, KERR AND TROXEL, CALCULATING IP DAMAGES §§ 5:2–5:4, 5:7–5.8, 5:16, 5:42–5:49 (2010).

9. JOHN M. SKENYON, CHRISTOPHER S. MARCHESE, JOHN LAND, PATENT DAMAGES LAW AND PRACTICE §§ 1:12–1:14, 3:32, 3:10, 3:19, 3:40–3:42 (2011).

10. Daralyn J. Durie, Mark A. Lemley, *A Structured Approach to Calculating Reasonable Royalties*, 14 Lewis & Clark L. Rev. 627 (2010).

11. Mark A. Lemley, *Distinguishing Lost Profits From Reasonable Royalties*, 51 Wm. & Mary L. Rev. 655 (2009).

12. Hal J. Singer, Kyle Smith, *What Does an Economist Have To Say About the Calculation of Reasonable Royalties*, 14 Intell. Prop. L. Bull. 7 (2009).

13. Nathan C. Love, *Nominal Reasonable Royalties for Patent Infringement*, 75 U. Chi. L. Rev. 1749 (2008).

14. Michael J. Chapman, *Using Settlement Licenses in Reasonable Royalty Determinations*, 49 IDEA 313 (2009).

15. William Choi, Roy Weinstein, *An Analytical Solution to Reasonable Royalty Calculations*, 41 IDEA 49 (2001).

1.9 TECHNOLOGY TRANSFEROR/TRANSFEREE PERSPECTIVES

Transferors and transferees of technology view the exchange from very different perspectives. As in any market transaction, both parties seek to maximize their economic gain and to realize the highest return with the lowest risk. Of course, both parties cannot simultaneously maximize their economic gain, and it is sufficient if each party believes that it will gain more from entering into the exchange than from foregoing the exchange. In negotiating a technology transfer agreement, it is important that both parties share a common understanding of how a technology is valued as well as an appreciation of each other's unique perspective.

1.9.1 Technology Value

The essence of most technology transfer agreements is an exchange of intellectual property rights. Intellectual property rights, however, do not have any inherent economic value. Rather, the value of intellectual property is derived from the value of the tangible products or processes which incorporate the intellectual property rights. Technical information alone is of little value to anyone other than research scientists, and in the case of patents and copyrights, this information is already publicly available. The commercial transferee of intellectual property rights is acquiring the right to make and utilize physical products and processes, and the transferee will value the intellectual property rights based upon the value of these products and processes.

The value which a transferee will attach to a product or process is a function of both cost and performance. It is not enough that a new product or process possesses superior performance features. The transferee is concerned with how much this superior performance will cost and how this performance/cost trade-off compares with the cost and performance of substitute products or processes. The substitute technologies might be similar to new products or processes available from other transferors, or they might be existing products or processes presently made or utilized by the transferee. Every new technology substitutes for an existing technology and can be substituted for by another new technology. The availability of substitute technologies adds another derivative function to the value of intellectual property. The value of intellectual property is derived from the value of the products or processes protected by the intellectual property, and the value of the products or processes protected by the intellectual property is derived from the value of substitute products or processes.

The cost of a new product or process is basically composed of three elements — the cost of acquiring the technology (e.g., license fees, royalties), the cost of other inputs required to utilize the technology (e.g., equipment, materials, personnel), and switch-over costs. The transferor has direct control over the transferee's cost of acquisition, but often little control over the cost of other production inputs. In instances where the cost of other inputs is high, the transferor will be forced to reduce the price of the technology to compensate for these higher costs. The transferor also has no control over the transferee's switch-over costs. If the transferee has a large investment in an existing technology, the transferor will be required to reduce the price of the new technology to compensate for the transferee's abandoned investment in the existing technology.

1.9.2   Transferor Perspective

The transferor will analyze the prospect of transferring a technology in light of the potential gain which the transferor could realize by exploiting the technology itself. An intellectual property owner always has the option of going it alone and attempting to directly enter a market. Direct market entry has the advantages of maximizing the intellectual property owner's control over the technology's development and of providing the intellectual property owner with the greatest return if the technology is successful. Direct market entry also entails the greatest risk to the intellectual property owner. In some instances, direct market entry may not be feasible or may not fit within the intellectual property owner's competitive strategy. Start-up and small firms often have no realistic opportunity to directly enter a market, especially if direct entry requires a large investment in manufacturing or marketing facilities, or if the market is dominated by large firms that already have these facilities in place. Large or established firms may also choose not to directly exploit a new technology either because the potential market is too small or because the market is outside of their core line of business. In the case of university and federal laboratory intellectual property owners, direct market entry is completely beyond their resources and expertise.

Direct market entry may also not be possible if the intellectual property consists of an improvement upon other intellectual property (a base technology). If the improvement cannot be practiced without a license to the base technology, the intellectual property owner has only two realistic choices. Either the intellectual property owner can attempt to obtain a license to the base technology and package them together for direct market entry, or the intellectual property owner can seek to license the improvement to the owner of the base technology.

If the intellectual property owner decides to transfer the technology, one of the first questions that must be addressed is the price of the transfer. Obviously, the intellectual property owner would like to recover the total investment in the intellectual property (R&D expenditures, patent prosecution costs, etc.) in the price of the transfer. The potential transferee of intellectual property, however, enjoys a substantial bargaining advantage in terms of price. The transferor's investment in the intellectual property is a sunk cost; it has already been incurred. The potential transferee's investment is an avoidable cost; it will only be incurred if the transferee consents to the transfer. The differences in the transferor's and transferee's cost calculus often mean that the transferor must settle for less than full cost recovery or spread the cost recovery over a long-term agreement.

Of course, if the transferor has already realized some return from the technology prior to the time of transfer, the need to recover investment costs in the price of the transfer is correspondingly lessened. This might occur, for example, when the technology has been utilized by the transferor for some period of time and is about to be replaced by a newer technology. Universities and federal laboratories present a special case of pre-transfer returns, and these institutions rarely seek to recover their full investment costs. In the case of universities, the intellectual property has already contributed to the education of faculty and students; and in the case of federal laboratories, the intellectual property has already served the laboratories' government missions.

The technology transferor must also consider the transaction costs and risks associated with a transfer of the technology. The transaction costs of a technology transfer will include the time and expense of identifying potential transferees and informing them about the technology, of negotiating and drafting the technology transfer agreement, of administering the technology transfer arrangement, and of policing and preventing violations of the transfer terms. The transferor will generally try to recover some of these costs through a technology transfer fee — a one-time charge to the transferee to cover the overhead costs associated with the transfer. The remainder of the costs must be covered by the royalties or other payments under the technology transfer agreement.

The risks to the transferor of a technology transfer include the potential threat to the transferor's core business, strengthening the market position of a possible competitor, and the adverse impact upon other present and future technology transfer relationships.

1.9.3 Transferee Perspective

Just as the transferor will analyze the prospect of transferring the technology as an alternative to exploiting the technology itself, the transferee will analyze the prospect of acquiring the technology as an alternative to developing the technology itself. The transferee's acquisition of technology saves the transferee the time and expense of independent development, and the magnitude of these savings is a key element in the transferee's valuation of the technology. If the potential transferee can easily "engineer around" the technology and avoid infringing the potential transferor's intellectual property rights, then the value of the technology to the transferee is significantly reduced.

The capability of the transferee to engineer around the transferor's technology depends upon the transferee's internal resources and the scope of the transferor's intellectual property rights. If the transferee has the requisite equipment, personnel and expertise and the transferor's intellectual property rights are narrowly protected, then the transferee will have an incentive to develop the technology independently. On the other hand, if the transferee lacks the requisite internal resources and the transferor's intellectual property rights are broadly protected, the transferee will have an incentive to acquire the technology from the transferor.

The transferee's ultimate goal in a technology transfer is to gain some competitive advantage in the market. This competitive advantage may come in the form of being the first firm to bring the new technology to market (market lead time), or of the capability to offer a new product with enhanced functionality, reliability or compatibility (product superiority), or of the opportunity to utilize a new process that reduces production costs or increases quality control (process superiority). Although the transferee will value all forms of competitive advantage to some extent, as a general rule, market lead time and product superiority will offer the transferee higher potential returns but with correspondingly higher risks, whereas process superiority will offer the transferee lower potential returns but a higher assurance of realizing these returns.

The transferee must also evaluate the potential risks associated with a technology transfer. If the transferee will be required to make a substantial additional investment in the technology, as will be the case with the transfer of an early-stage technology, the transferee will demand a discount in the price of the transfer to compensate for the risk of this additional investment. Likewise, if the transferee is uncertain of whether further development and design of the technology will be successful, or of whether the technology can be scaled up to commercial production levels, the transferee will seek to hedge these risks in the price of the transfer. Finally, the transferee will evaluate the risk of market acceptance of the technology. If the transferee is confident of the technology's market success, the transferee will be willing to pay a higher price for the transfer; if the transferee is doubtful of the technology's market success, the transferee will demand a lower price for the transfer or forego the transfer entirely.

There is one situation where a transferee might enter into an exchange of intellectual property rights which is not directly motivated by competitive advantage and economic gain. This is the case of an intellectual property exchange which is intended to protect the transferee from future liability for infringement. The risk of an allegation of intellectual property infringement is always present, and the cost of defending an infringement suit is great. A transferee therefore will sometimes enter into a technology transfer agreement in order to gain immunity from an infringement claim. This type of intellectual property exchange is often reciprocal with both parties granting cross-licenses to a portfolio of intellectual property rights and is frequently initiated in the context of threatened litigation by one or both parties.

Additional Information

1. F. Peter Boer, The Valuation of Technology: Business and Financial Issues in R&D (John Wiley & Sons, Inc.) (1999).

2. F. Peter Boer, Technology Valuation Solutions (John Wiley & Sons, Inc.) (2004).

3. Richard Razgaitis, Valuation and Pricing of Technology-Based Intellectual Property (John Wiley & Sons, Inc.) (2003).

4. Aswath Damodaran, The Dark Side of Valuation: Valuing Old Tech, New Tech, and New Economy Companies (Prentice Hall) (2001).

5. Christopher Gardner, The Valuation of Information Technology: A Guide for Strategy Development, Valuation, and Financial Planning (John Wiley & Sons, Inc.) (2000).

1.10   ADVANTAGES AND DISADVANTAGES OF TECHNOLOGY TRANSFERS

There are a number of important advantages which an owner of technology can realize through its transfer to a third party. The transfer of technology, however, also entails certain disadvantages. The advantages and disadvantages of technology transfer are integrally related, and the technology owner must carefully assess both before deciding upon a course of action. This section will briefly review these advantages and disadvantages as well as their potential impact upon the technology owner.

1.10.1   Advantages

The primary business advantage of transferring a technology is that the owner can leverage its resources with those of the transferee to achieve results which the owner could not achieve independently. By combining the resources of the owner with those of the transferee, a transfer of technology can provide the owner with the economic benefits of vertical integration without the costs of entering into a new vertical line of business. For example, a firm with special competence in research and development can achieve the benefits of vertical integration by transferring its technology to a firm with established manufacturing facilities for production of the technology or to a firm with established marketing and distribution channels for sales to customers. A technology transfer can also provide the owner with the benefits of horizontal market integration. For example, if a technology has potential application in more than one market and the owner has the resources to exploit the technology in only one market, then the owner might transfer the technology to a firm with an established presence in another application market.

Technology transfer also allows the owner to enter geographic markets that are beyond the owner's capability to supply. This is often the case with foreign markets and sometimes the case with domestic regional markets. Foreign markets are a very important source of potential revenue for technology firms but are also very difficult to enter directly. Obtaining local plant, equipment and personnel, and learning local customs, business practices and laws are daunting tasks for all but the largest firms. Faced with these costs and risks, many firms choose to enter foreign markets through technology transfers either in the form of licenses, joint ventures, distributorships or agency relationships. Although domestic regional markets do not pose the same challenges as foreign markets, the quickest and easiest way for a firm to expand into a new domestic market is frequently through a technology transfer to a firm that is already active in the market.

Additional benefits of technology transfer include gaining early market entry, improving cash flow, obtaining new technology and enhancing reputation and goodwill. In markets which are characterized by short product life cycles, the time required for a technology owner to prepare for direct market may result in the technology becoming obsolete before market entry can be achieved. And even if the technology does not become obsolete, it might lose its competitive edge and be surpassed by newer technology during the period of preparation for market entry. Under these circumstances, a technology transfer will allow the owner to gain rapid market entry and realize the maximum value of the technology.

A firm must maintain a solid cash flow position; at all times, the cash coming in must at least cover the cash being paid out for such things as salaries, rent, installment purchases, taxes, etc. The research expenses incurred in the development of a new technology may strain a firm's cash flow position. Although the new technology may constitute a valuable long-term asset for the firm, the firm may find it necessary to transfer the technology for a period of time in order to recover some of its research costs and improve its cash flow position. Technology transfer is the quickest way to monetize a technology (i.e., convert a technology into cash), although generally at the expense of longer-term returns.

A technology transfer can also serve as a means to obtain new technology through grantbacks and cross-licenses. Through the use of a technology, a transferee may gain a keen understanding of the technology and develop new and better ways to employ it. As a condition of the transfer, the transferor can negotiate for a grant-back license to any improvements developed by the transferee. Grant-back licenses generally take the form of nonexclusive licenses but nonetheless give the transferor the opportunity to incorporate the improvements into the base technology for purposes of further development and future transfers. In cross-licenses, the transferor and transferee exchange rights in their respective technologies. Cross-licenses generally involve the packaging of related technologies and allow the parties greater flexibility in pursuing new research and development initiatives.

Finally, technology transfer can enhance a firm's reputation and goodwill. This is especially important for start-up and small firms. The opportunity to transfer technology to a large established firm gives the small firm industry recognition and its technology industry credibility. The benefits of enhanced recognition and credibility are often so great for the small firm that they overshadow concern for financial return, at least in the short run.

1.10.2 Disadvantages

The disadvantages of technology transfer are in many respects simply the flip side of the advantages. In any technology transfer, the transferor will lose some degree of control over the technology and will become, to some extent, dependent upon the transferee. Although the transferor can attempt to minimize the loss of control through the terms of the transfer agreement, this may not be feasible because of the transferor's lesser bargaining position, or may not be wise because of the transferee's greater market expertise.

Utilizing technology transfer as a means to achieve vertical market integration clearly reduces the technology owner's incentive to enter other vertical markets directly, and this can be a source of lost opportunity for the technology owner. For example, a firm which transfers its technology to a manufacturer for production will lose the opportunity to gain knowledge of the manufacturing process, and this, in turn, will make it more difficult for the owner to perform its own manufacturing in the future. It may also deprive the owner of information necessary to refine the design of the technology in order to reduce manufacturing costs and improve production quality. The same is true for the utilization of technology transfer as a means of marketing and distributing a new technology. The technology owner will lose the opportunity to deal directly with customers and to build long-term customer relations. The loss of direct customer feedback on the technology is a particular problem for the owner. Customer feedback is the best guide to further development of the technology. Without customer feedback, the owner has no way of knowing what customers like about the technology, what they don't like, what they would like to see improved and what they don't care about.

Additional disadvantages of technology transfer include the risk of infringement, loss of a technical edge, inadequate industry recognition and dependence on other firms for revenue. We have noted earlier that the risk of infringement increases with technology transfer. The infringement may result from the transferee exceeding the scope of the transfer agreement or from a third party misappropriating the technology from the transferee. In any event, the more the technology is transferred, the more difficult it is to police and the greater the risk is that it will be infringed.

The transfer of technology may also result in the owner's loss of technical superiority. As you have seen, this can occur in the case of a transferee-user discovering improvements to the technology, in the case of a manufacturer discovering cost-saving design changes, or in the case of a distributor learning about customer preferences. In each of these instances, the technology owner can lose its technical edge because it is not actively involved in the market and is deprived of critical information.

Finally, the revenue stream that a technology owner can earn from a transfer can also be suddenly interrupted. The transferee can go into bankruptcy, breach the transfer agreement or contest the validity of the intellectual property. If any of these events occur, the technology owner is doubly disadvantaged; not only is the owner deprived of current revenue from the technology, but the owner cannot re-transfer the technology and re-establish a revenue stream until the legal uncertainty of the first transfer is resolved. To the extent that the technology owner is dependent upon this revenue to cover current expense, the owner may be forced to borrow at high interest rates, default on payments, or settle the dispute with the transferee on unfavorable terms.

Additional Information

1. PHYLLIS L. SPESER, THE ART AND SCIENCE OF TECHNOLOGY TRANSFER (John Wiley & Sons, Inc.) (2006).

2. ROGER L. GEIGER & CRESO M. SA, TAPPING THE RICHES OF SCIENCE: UNIVERSITIES AND THE PROMISE OF ECONOMIC GROWTH (Harvard University Press) (2009).

3. MOHAMMED SAAD, DEVELOPMENT THROUGH TECHNOLOGY TRANSFER: CREATING NEW CULTURAL UNDERSTANDING (Intellect Books) (2000).

1.11 FORMULATING A TECHNOLOGY INNOVATION STRATEGY

This section will attempt to synthesize the prior discussion in the context of formulating a technology innovation strategy. The first part will consider the information and analysis necessary to develop a technology innovation strategy, and the next part will look at the terms and conditions available to implement a technology innovation strategy.

1.11.1 Identifying The Technology

A technology innovation strategy should begin with a detailed knowledge of the technology to be transferred. This knowledge should include a clear definition of the technology, a review of the state of the art in the technical field, a search of related patents and copyrights, and comparisons to substitute technologies. A solid understanding of a technology is necessary before a commercial development strategy can be considered. A successful development strategy flows naturally from the special, inherent characteristics of the technology itself.

Although the relationship between the special features of a technology and a strategy for its commercial development is clear, it is surprising how often inventors fail to appreciate this connection. For example, inventors are often unclear as to exactly what they have invented, especially when the invention is incorporated into a larger system. Likewise, inventors often have difficulty specifying the design parameters of an invention. Without a clear definition of an invention and a detailed design specification, it is not possible to develop a meaningful innovation strategy. Attempting to do so is like shooting at a moving target. However, once a technology has been clearly described, its commercial possibilities can then be examined.

As you have seen, technologies can be transferred at various stages of development. In the early stages of development, technologies can be transferred in the form of research findings, data sets, or invention disclosures. In intermediate stages of development, technologies can be transferred in the form of pending or issued patents, designs and drawings, or prototype products or processes. In advanced stages of development, technologies can be transferred in the form of manufactured products or operational systems. The stage at which a technology is transferred will greatly affect the terms of the transfer.

Recall that the transfer of early-stage technologies will shift the future development risks from the transferor to the transferee. Under these circumstances, the transferee will likely demand greater control over the technology and a greater return from its investment in the technology. Early-stage transfers of technology are usually most appropriate for universities and research laboratories. Early-stage transfers allow a non-profit research entity to recoup a portion of its investment in an R&D project in order to fund future research initiatives. Early-stage transfers frequently include consultation with key research personnel and access to critical equipment and facilities.

Intermediate-stage transfers give the transferor greater bargaining leverage. At this stage, intellectual property rights have generally been secured and some of the development risks have been eliminated; however, scaling up the technology for commercial use and marketing the technology in competition with other firms still pose substantial risks for the transferee. The transferee will often seek to hedge these risks through a royalty arrangement based solely upon sales, or performance, of the technology. The transferor might seek to increase its compensation by providing services for the production and maintenance of the technology. Intermediate-stage transfers are usually most appropriate for small firms which cannot enter a market directly and larger firms which seek to leverage a core technology into new markets.

Advanced-stage transfers generally take the form of supplier agreements. Here, the transferor is usually a firm that has production capability and/or trained staff personnel, and the transferee is usually an original equipment manufacturer. The transferor supplies the transferee with component parts of a finished product or provides the transferee with system installation or support services. Parties in advanced-stage transfers tend to stand on an equal bargaining footing. The primary risk for the transferor at this stage is that the transferee will reverse engineer the component or system and terminate the contract agreement. The primary risk for the transferee is that the transferor will exploit the transferee's dependency on the components or services supplied.

1.11.2   Considering Potential Applications

A technology can have a narrow or broad range of potential applications. A technology which has been designed to solve a specific problem generally has a narrow range of potential applications; however, it should not be assumed that a technology designed to solve one problem cannot be applied to the solution of other problems as well. For example, a technology designed to solve a testing problem might also be used to solve a manufacturing problem. The key here is to focus on the similarities between the problems. Similar problems will generally be found within the same industry or technical system.

Other technologies can have a broad range of potential applications. These technologies are usually referred to as "enabling technologies." For example, a new process for making gradient index lenses might be useful in manufacturing medical instruments, research equipment, telecommunications switches and cameras. Developing technology innovation strategies for enabling technologies is highly challenging. As a general rule, enabling technologies are best introduced through high-value, high-margin products and processes. Users in these markets tend to be less price-sensitive. As market share is established in these high-end markets, the technology becomes recognized and accepted and economies of scale are realized. At this point, more price-sensitive markets, such as consumer goods, can be developed. It is very important, when transferring enabling technologies, to consider field-of-use restrictions in the transfer agreement. A transferee with great experience and competence in one market or in one application might have little value in another field.

The range of a technology's potential applications is also affected by the physical form in which the technology is embodied — hardware, software or firmware. Often, computer technologies can be developed in any one of these three forms. Generally, hardware technologies are more limited in their scope of application and more expensive to redesign for other uses. Software technologies, on the other hand, are usually much more adaptable to new applications, especially when the original software has been designed in a modular fashion. Although software technologies are generally more flexible than hardware, hardware technologies generally provide a greater degree of intellectual property protection.

1.11.3   The Scope of Intellectual Property Protection

I noted earlier that the scope of intellectual property protection is a key factor in determining the value of a technology and in developing a technology transfer strategy. Patents and copyrights do not all have the same value. A patent might be very broad and very difficult to engineer around. Broad patents tend to be issued early in the development of a technical field and are often referred to as "pioneer patents." Other patents might be quite narrow. Patents issued in a crowded technical field tend to cover small improvements over existing technologies and often can be easily circumvented. In a similar way, copyrights are often described as either deep or shallow. A deep copyright covers a substantially new way of performing a software function or of interfacing with the user. A shallow copyright constitutes a minor change from other programs or incorporates standardized methods for achieving a result.

Trade secrets are the third major means of protecting intellectual property rights in a technology. Trade secrets can also be either strong or weak. A strong trade secret is one that is extremely difficult to reverse engineer. This can be due to either the inherent nature of the technology or to the way in which the technology has been enclosed within a "black box." A weak trade secret can be easily learned by someone skilled in the field through the use of well-known reverse engineering techniques.

Obviously, the extent of intellectual property protection is very important to a potential transferee of a technology. Viewed from the standpoint of the transferee, the transfer of a technology is valuable in two respects. First, it provides the transferee savings in time and money which would otherwise be required to develop the technology independently. This is especially important to transferees in markets with very short product life cycles. Second, the technology transfer gives the transferee an advantage over its competitors in the market. This is often very important in mature markets where firms compete for customers based on offering new features or cost savings.

The value of a technology to a prospective transferee is considerably reduced when the scope of intellectual property protection is diminished. If the transferee can easily engineer around the technology and quickly develop the technology on its own, then the value of the transfer is much less. Likewise, if the transferee's competitors can do the same thing, the transferee's competitive advantage by virtue of the transfer is also reduced.

Given the importance of intellectual property protection to the commercial development of a technology, one would assume that patent, copyright and trade secret matters would be routinely considered as part of the design and development of a new technology. However, this is rarely the case. It is remarkable how often an inventor or firm will invest thousands of hours and tens of thousands of dollars in researching a technology without searching for related patents or copyrights, or without considering how best to protect the intellectual property in the technology.

1.11.4   Technical Advantages and Disadvantages

As noted earlier, in the final analysis, the value of a new technology depends upon its advantages and disadvantages with respect to existing technologies. A new technology will always serve as a substitute for an existing technology. It is critically important to compare carefully and objectively the benefits and costs of replacing an existing technology with a new technology. Such a comparison must include both technical and financial considerations. It is not sufficient to consider only the technical superiority of a new technology without also considering the costs of realizing this superiority. From the standpoint of the transferee or end user, the critical question is how much technical advantage can be gained at what cost.

Recall that one of the most important costs associated with introducing a new technology is switch-over costs. Switch-over costs include the costs of lost investment in the existing technology, installation of the new technology, the purchase of new peripheral equipment, and training of personnel on the new technology. These are very real costs to a transferee or end user and must be accounted for in any decision to adopt a new technology. Other cost concerns include compatibility, reliability, functionality and efficiency of operation.

The advantages of a new technology are best viewed from the prospective of competitors in a market. If a new technology can yield production savings in the form of time, money or fewer defective products, or can offer consumers enhanced performance benefits, these improvements can be translated quickly into competitive advantages and increased sales. In general, the more competitive a market is, the more the firms in the market will value these types of technical improvements. One should not assume, however, that the extent of the technical improvement is always related to the value of the technology. Some technologies allow users to do things that they have never done before; other technologies allow users to do things they are presently doing but in a better way. Users, however, may be wary of radical changes in a technology and may be more receptive to incremental improvements. Under these circumstances, education and information become important components of a technology transfer strategy.

The disadvantages of a new technology might come in the form of future development costs, uncertainties associated with large-scale industrial uses, problems encountered with operating a new system, or increased manufacturing costs due to beginning production schedules. Regulatory approvals and inspections may also create costs for a new technology. Regulations may be imposed on the finished products or processes, such as with drugs, chemicals and aviation systems, or they may be imposed on the production facilities, such as with health, safety and environmental requirements.

In developing a technology innovation strategy, the owner of the technology should attempt to stand in the shoes of prospective transferees and anticipate what concerns they may have. Unfortunately, the owner's zeal for its new technology often blinds the owner to the legitimate questions that transferees might raise. It is far better to anticipate these questions in advance and to have answers prepared than to have the questions raised for the first time at the negotiating table.

1.11.5   Defining Potential Markets

Once the technology has been fully described and its advantages and disadvantages identified, the next step in developing a technology innovation strategy is to analyze the various markets into which the technology can be introduced. This market analysis should include a definition of the market, its size, growth trends, entry barriers, vertical and horizontal structures, production and distribution arrangements, and product life cycles. A clear understanding of a market is essential to developing an entry strategy whether by way of a licensing agreement, a joint venture, or direct participation.

A market can be defined in terms of sellers, buyers, products and geographic areas. A good market definition will incorporate aspects of all four of these factors. Markets, however, are highly dynamic, and market definitions are never air-tight. Sellers and buyers sometimes operate in multiple markets; the same technology or product might be used in a number of different markets, and the geographic boundaries of markets often overlap.

A good starting point for defining a market is the Standard Industrial Classification (SIC) code published by the Office of Management and Budget. The SIC code classifies all industry products and processes into a two-digit primary category, a three-digit sub-category, and a four-digit product or process description. However, even with the SIC code, it is common to find that a given technology might fall within multiple categories. Trade journals and business magazines are also useful in defining markets. These publications report on recent innovations, buying trends, and production developments which are helpful in understanding how a market is evolving.

As a general rule, it is better to err on the side of defining a market too narrowly than too broadly. Although a narrow market definition might omit some sources of revenue, it will be a more precise guide to implementing a technology innovation strategy and will provide a conservative set of estimates for evaluating the worth of the venture. This is especially important for smaller firms that lack the resources to compete in broader markets. Smaller firms frequently need to carve out a niche market for themselves within a much bigger market. Establishing a niche market allows a smaller firm to conserve its resources and to focus on its core competence and competitive advantage.

The size and growth of a market obviously affect the potential revenue that can be realized from introducing a technology into the market; however, neither size nor growth can be considered in isolation. A large, growing market might already have attracted many other firms, making the entry of an additional firm very difficult. As markets mature, competition intensifies and profit margins are lowered. A new market entrant will generally incur higher costs in the short run. If profit margins in a market are already low, it will be more difficult for a new entrant to recover its higher initial costs through higher prices. Despite these problems, however, larger growing markets are preferable to smaller declining markets absent special considerations.

The Boston Consulting Group has developed a scheme that classifies markets into four categories: (i) stars, (ii) question marks, (iii) cash cows, and (iv) dogs. These categories are based upon the cash needs and the cash generation that can be expected in a market. Star markets are high-growth markets. Star markets generally require a substantial cash investment for entry. But this high cash need is offset by the prospect of generating high cash revenues through increased market share in a growing market. Question marks are markets with a high cash need but uncertain cash revenues. Question mark markets also have strong growth rates.; however, they have many competitors with relatively small market shares and low profit margins, so cash generation is more speculative. Cash cows are stable markets. For existing firms, cash-cow markets represent low cash investment and high cash revenues. Cash-cow markets, however, do not offer attractive opportunities to new entrants because these markets are not growing and because existing firms enjoy strong market positions and advantageous economies of scale in production and distribution. Finally, dogs are markets with declining growth rates and declining profits for existing firms. Obviously, these are not attractive markets for a new firm or new technology.

Recall that markets can also be categorized by their vertical and horizontal structures. "Vertical structure" refers to the organization of a market according to the different levels of market activity, such as research and development, design and production, marketing and sales, and training and support. In a market that is vertically integrated, these functions are combined in a single firm or a closely related group of firms. "Horizontal structure" refers to the organization of a market across a given level of activity. Markets in which a small number of firms dominate in a particular activity, such as manufacturing or selling, are described as "concentrated." Analyzing the vertical and horizontal structure of a market is very important to developing a successful technology transfer strategy.

Small firms are rarely able to enter directly into markets that are vertically integrated or highly concentrated. Existing firms can leverage their advantage between market activities, or can use their dominance in a given market activity, to thwart the entry of a small firm. Moreover, small firms generally have a narrow core of technology and expertise, and do not possess the resources necessary to compete with more diversified and larger firms. For these reasons, the most common strategies used by small firms to enter into vertically integrated or highly concentrated markets are technology licenses and supplier contracts.

Larger firms also have difficulty entering markets that are vertically integrated or highly concentrated. Here, the problem is not so much a lack of resources as it is undertaking a role that is beyond the firm's core competence. Larger firms, however, have a greater bargaining advantage with existing firms. A larger firm might also license its technology to an existing firm, but this license might be part of a broader relationship, such as a joint venture or strategic alliance.

1.11.6   Profiles of Firms In A Market

After a market has been defined and analyzed, the firms in that market must be researched. The Thomas Register of Manufacturers, Standard & Poors and Dunn & Bradstreet are excellent reference sources for information about firms. Knowledge of the firms in a market is important regardless of what type of entry strategy is adopted. For example, if a firm opts for direct entry, knowledge of the existing firms in the market is necessary to anticipate competitive responses. On the other hand, if a firm opts for a licensing arrangement, knowledge of existing firms is necessary to select among potential licensees.

There are many different features of a firm to consider when preparing a profile. Some of these features, and the questions they raise, are discussed below.

In preparing a profile of firms in a market, each firm should be ranked in terms of its size and market share. The larger firms and smaller firms in a market each present unique advantages and disadvantages as potential partners. The advantages of a larger firm are its greater resource base, broader market contacts, and presumably more extensive market experience. However, working with a larger firm may have a number of disadvantages — a larger firm may not be as aggressive in promoting a new technology as a smaller firm; a larger firm may have a heavy management hierarchy that causes decision-making to be slow and inflexible; and a larger firm may be prone to bully a smaller firm partner.

On the other hand, smaller firms are often perceived to be more competitive and innovative. Smaller firms are generally struggling to achieve greater market share and, as a result, are good candidates for introducing a new technology. Small firms also tend to be more flexible in their working relationships and quicker to make decisions; however, partnerships with smaller firms also pose a number of risks — a smaller firm is more vulnerable to a market challenge by its competitors and to a take-over by a third party. In either of these events, the advantages of a small firm partner might be quickly lost.

Firms tend to have special competencies. Some firms excel in research, some in manufacturing, some in marketing and sales. When considering a partnership relationship, it is important to identify the special competency of a firm. The best partnerships are between firms that have complementary competencies. For example, a firm with a strong research base might seek a partnership with a firm that has a well-established manufacturing system. Likewise, a firm with a strong manufacturing capability might seek a partnership with a firm that has a well-developed distribution system.

Firms that have a special competency in the same activity may also have an incentive to form partnership relationships. For example, two firms that are engaged in the same field of research might form a partnership to allocate their research targets and share research results, thereby saving both firms time, money and duplicative efforts. This type of relationship frequently includes a cross-licensing of patents which result from the research.

Firms may also have special competencies in management, financial and legal fields. A firm with a skillful and knowledgeable management team is always a preferable partner. Likewise, skills in raising capital and managing the finances for a joint project are extremely important. The areas of legal competency which are often important include skill in obtaining and protecting intellectual property rights, in structuring transactions, in negotiating agreements, and in achieving regulatory approval for the use of a product or process.

A technology innovation strategy will invariably create new friends and foes for the transferor and transferee firms. Markets are built upon competition between firms to supply technology. When two firms join together in a technology development project, they establish not only a new network of market friendships but also a new network of market foes. It is important to assess the benefits and risks of both.

Prospective technology transferors and transferees should both consider the organizational traits they value most in a partner. Fair dealing, trustworthiness, the ability to meet schedules, and frequent, open and accurate communication are often cited as highly desirable traits in a partner. Although these traits are difficult to define precisely, they are very important to the success of a technology development venture. The single greatest cause of failure of a technology innovation strategy is not technical or market limitations but the breakdown of interpersonal relationships and trust between the persons assigned to manage the technology innovation project. Managers should clearly communicate their own goals for a project and their performance expectations for the other partner. The more compatible persons are in terms of their management styles and perspectives, the more likely it is that they will be able to work well together and realize reciprocal success through the technology development project.

On the other side, every new friendly alliance generates a new set of competitive foes. A good technology innovation strategy should assess the potential competitors which an alliance might produce and consider how these competitors might react to the formation of the alliance. This component of a technology innovation strategy is often ignored entirely or given cursory consideration in the development of an innovation plan. As a general rule, when they do consider the reaction of competitors, technology firms tend to overestimate their own control over market outcomes and underestimate the capabilities of their competitors. This can prove to be a fatal bias.

Technology firms should generally seek to promote good relationships with competitors whenever possible. This is more a matter of practicality than of civility. Good competitor relationships are important to resolve disputes which might arise over such things as intellectual property infringement, unfair trade practices, and breaches of license agreements. Good competitor relationships are also important to preserve future options. Technology markets are highly dynamic and alliances between firms are constantly changing. Today's competitor may be tomorrow's partner.

1.11.7   Terms and Conditions of A Technology Transfer

Rights in a technology can be transferred by many means, including assignments, licenses, joint ventures, subsidiaries, distributorships and agencies. The first three forms of transfer are generally associated with exchanges of intellectual property rights, and the second three forms with the exchange of goods and services. A technology license is similar to a lease; the technology owner (the licensor) retains ultimate title and control over the technology but grants limited permission to another person (the licensee) to use the technology. A technology assignment is similar to a sale; the technology owner (the assignor) conveys complete title and control to another person (the assignee). Technology is transferred through a joint venture when the parties agree to share intellectual property rights resulting from a joint research and development project. Subsidiaries, distributorships and agencies are generally used to market goods or services. These arrangements may or may not include a transfer of the intellectual property rights embodied in the goods or services.

The various means of transferring technology are referred to collectively as technology transfer agreements.

A technology transfer agreement embodies the understanding of the parties about the subject matter of the exchange, the terms and conditions of the transfer, and the allocation of loss in the event of a failure. A threshold question in drafting a technology transfer agreement is how much detail should be included in the provisions of the agreement. One should not assume that the more detailed an agreement is the better it is. Over-concern with detail, especially in the early stages of a technology transfer relationship, can frustrate the intentions of the parties and lead to unacceptable delay in implementing a development plan. The degree of detail in a technology transfer agreement should reflect the current state of the parties' understanding of the relationship. Agreements should evolve over time and become more detailed as the parties accumulate experience in working with each other.

Regardless of detail, however, all technology transfer agreements must include certain key provisions. These provisions determine the extent of the parties' rights and duties in the technology exchange.

There are five core provisions in a technology license: (1) scope of use; (2) right of use; (3) territory of use; (4) field of use; and (5) amount of use. The scope of use in a technology license can be either (i) exclusive use, (ii) non-exclusive use, or (iii) limited exclusive use. Exclusive use gives the transferee total rights in the licensed technology within a given market and a given territory. Nonexclusive use allows the transferor to make unlimited further transfers of the technology, including transfers to a transferee's competitors. Limited exclusive use allows the transferor to transfer the technology to a specified number of transferees.

Transferees, of course, always prefer exclusive-use agreements. Exclusive-use agreements give the transferee greater potential gain from a technology and greater protection from market competitors. In the case of a new and unproven technology, an exclusive-use agreement is often the only basis on which the technology can be transferred. Nonexclusive-use agreements are most appropriate for mature technologies and large markets. If a technology becomes widely accepted by users, a single transferee might not be able to serve the full market demand. Here, multiple nonexclusive transfers increase the transferor's return without diminishing the potential return of the transferee. Nonexclusive-use agreements are also often used to transfer research tool technology. Research tool technology is technology that is used to develop end-use, commercial technology. Limited exclusive-use agreements can be used to spur competition among transferees and to reduce the risk of dependency on a single transferee.

A *right of use* restriction can be used to limit a transferee's rights to either make, use, sell, or import a technology. A *territory of use* restriction can be used to limit rights in a technology to a specified geographic location. A *field of use* restriction can be used to limit rights in a technology to a specified application. And an *amount of use* restriction can be used to limit the rights in a technology to specified number of sales, products made, instances of use or time use.

In technology transfer negotiations, exclusivity of use and restrictions on use are often bargained for together. A transferor who is pressed for an exclusive-use right will often respond by attempting to restrict the transferee's field of use and scope of use. Likewise, a transferee who is asked to accept restrictions upon the use of a technology will often respond by attempting to gain an exclusive right in the restricted domain.

The questions of exclusivity and restrictions on use call for careful analysis by both the technology transferor and transferee. From the transferor's standpoint, non-exclusivity and restricted use give the transferor greater control over the development of the technology; however, they also impose on the transferor greater administrative costs and management responsibilities. A transferor should assess its own resources and expertise and ask whether it has the capability to play an active role in a technology's development.

From the transferee's standpoint, exclusive and non-restricted use of a technology is often thought to maximize potential return. This is not always the case, however. In some market circumstances, it might be valuable to have more than one firm attempting to introduce the same technology. Multiple providers of a new technology can accelerate user knowledge and acceptance of the technology and enhance earnings for each supplier. Transferees should also be wary of overly broad market entry rights. Transferees should avoid seeking market rights in markets in which they have no prior experience. A transferee should also be careful not to over extend its resources or to undertake roles that are not part of its core competence.

The failure of the transferor or transferee to carefully assess its own capabilities, as well as those of the other party, is a major source of misunderstanding, disappointment and, too often, litigation between the parties.

The benefits of a technology innovation venture can take a number of forms and be shared by the parties in a number of ways. The benefits of technology innovation are both tangible and intangible. Tangible benefits include money payments, such as royalties and fees, and in-kind payments, such as the provision of equipment and services. Intangible benefits include technical know-how, access to research, and licenses on future intellectual property. The total package of benefits associated with a technology development project, tangible and intangible, and short-run and long-run, should be considered in reaching a final transfer agreement. Benefits are often traded and offset during the course of negotiation. Each party should consider in advance the alternative benefit packages which it is willing to accept and should prepare a negotiation plan which will lead to these outcomes.

Royalties and fees are probably the most common form of return in a technology transfer. "Royalties" refers to an ongoing stream of payments over time, and "fees" to fixed payments, usually made at the beginning of the transfer. Royalties can be structured in many ways. Minimum royalty payments can be required, and royalty percentages can be loaded toward the front end or back end of the transfer period. Royalties can also be computed using a number of different royalty bases, including gross or net sales, gross or net profits, number of sales or users, or the time during which a technology is used. Establishing a royalty computation scheme is especially difficult when the technology is a process technology or constitutes a component part of a larger technical system.

Fees are fixed payments that guarantee a return to the transferor. Minimum-level fees are often charged to recover the administrative expenses of managing a technology transfer project. Higher-level fees are charged to recover the transferor's investment in development of a technology. Royalties and fees are generally inversely related. If a transferor charges a high technology transfer fee, it should be willing to accept a lower level of royalty payments. Similarly, if a transferor sets a low fee for the transfer, it should expect to receive higher potential royalty payments.

Finally, the parties to a technology transfer agreement should allocate the risks of loss associated with the transfer. Risks come in many forms, including breach of contract, infringement of intellectual property rights, and bankruptcy. Each of these possibilities should be addressed in the technology transfer agreement.

A breach of contract may occur because of a party's failure to perform services, because of a party's violation of promises, because goods delivered failed to meet standards, or because contract milestones were not achieved on time. In a complex technology transfer arrangement, both parties sometimes fail to comply completely with the contract terms. It is important for each party to consider what types of breaches it will consider to be major and what minor.

Major breaches are the basis for an immediate termination of the agreement. Minor breaches are dealt with through discussion and adjustment of the transfer terms. Litigation over breach of contract claims should almost always be avoided. The cost of legal fees, the diversion of management time and energy, and the possibility of an adverse outcome should all be considered before a decision is made to begin a lawsuit. There are two principal ways in which the losses from a breach of contract can be lessened. The first is to use a liquidated damages clause. A liquidated damages clause sets a total dollar limit on the damages to be paid for any breach of the agreement; it reduces the cost of proving actual damages at trial and can serve as a starting point for settling damage disputes out of court.

The second way in which the costs of a breach can be lessened is through the use of an arbitration clause. An arbitration clause commits both parties to initially submit all disputes to a panel of arbitrators for resolution. The American Arbitration Association has developed rules for conducting arbitrations and can provide a list of potential arbitrators in various fields. The three major advantages of arbitration over litigation are that arbitration is less expensive, much quicker and more flexible.

Intellectual property infringement is always a risk in a technology transfer. Infringement can occur in many contexts. The transferor's title to the transferred technology might be challenged by a third party or by the transferee. A third party might infringe the intellectual property rights of the transferor or the use rights of the transferee. Finally, the transferee might exceed the scope of the rights granted in the agreement. Uncertainty over the status of intellectual property rights can seriously hinder a technology's development. Mechanisms should be established in the contract for a fair and rapid resolution of all intellectual property disputes which might arise. Litigation is even more futile in this area because courts often lack technical expertise. Parties to a technology transfer agreement should consider naming a panel of respected experts in a field who can assist in resolving intellectual property disputes should they arise.

A final, but important, source of risk in a technology transfer is the risk that one of the parties might become bankrupt. In this event, the technology's development can be seriously imperiled. In the case of bankruptcy, all of the bankrupt party's assets, including intellectual property titles and license rights, are immediately placed under the control of a trustee. The bankruptcy trustee has wide discretion in dealing with these assets in the future. The trustee has the power to sell the debtor's intellectual property and to void the debtor's technology licenses. Although bankruptcy is usually the last thing that the parties wish to address in a technology transfer agreement, this prospect cannot be ignored.

Additional Information

1.   Sten A. Thore, Technology Commercialization: Dea and Related Analytical Methods for Evaluating the Use and Implementation of Technical Innovation (Kluwer Academic Publishers) (2002).

2. Vijay K. Jolly, Commercializing New Technologies: Getting from Mind to Market (Harvard Business School Press) (1997).

1.11.8 Sources of Information on Markets, Companies and Patents

This section will briefly summarize a few major sources of information on markets, companies and patents. Most universities have subscriptions to these databases and they can be accessed by students and faculty for free.

Markets

ABI/Inform Complete: Contains indices and abstracts from leading management and business publications.

IBISWorld — Industry Market Research: Contains business reports on industry market research, company research, global industry research, and economic and demographic data.

MarketResearch.com Academic: Contains detailed market research reports prepared by leading market research firms.

Business Source Elite: Contains over 1,000 full-text business publications and economics journals, including leading management and marketing publication and the Harvard Business Review.

Lexis Nexis Academic: Contains full-text files on legal, business and industry information including newspapers, newswires and transcripts.

Companies

D&B's Million Dollar Database: Contains information on over 1,600,000 U.S. and Canadian public and private companies including SIC code, number of employees, annual sales, principal executives and biographies.

IBISWorld — Company Research: Contains industry market research, company research and global industry research.

Datamonitor 360: Contains information on companies, industries and products including business strategies, news and opinions.

ReferenceUSA: Contains detailed directory information on U.S. businesses.

Associations Unlimited: Contains information on over 400,000 U.S. national, regional, state and local nonprofit organizations in all fields including information on IRS 501(c) nonprofit organizations.

Patents

The United States Patent and Trademark Office website — http://www.uspto.gov. — is an extremely useful source of patent information. The USPTO website contains both general information about patents as well as specific information on individual patents. The general patent information includes information on patent laws and regulations, information on the requirements and processes for obtaining a patent, patent guides and manuals, and frequently-asked questions. Specific information on individual patents is obtained through a patent search. A patent search is an excellent source of competitive intelligence about competing technologies, companies' patenting strategies and important inventors in a field. Patent searches can be performed through "Quick Patent Search" or "Advanced Patent Search." The major difference between the two types of search are the number of different search fields available. In a "Quick Patent" search, the user can search using two different terms (Term 1 and Term 2) and two different fields (Field 1 and Field 2). There are over 20 different fields to choose from including Patent Abstract, Patent Number, Inventor Name, Assignee Name, Issue Date, and U.S. Patent Classification Number. The direct cite for a patent search is — http://patft.uspto.gov/netahtml/PTO/search-bool.html.

A word of caution. Performing patent searches for the purpose of obtaining competitive intelligence and performing patent searches for the purpose of determining the patentability of an invention, or infringement of a patent, are two very different things. In our research center, clients often subtly ask that we go beyond searching for competitive intelligence and provide them with an opinion on patentability or infringement. We steadfastly refuse to do this and recommend that they seek the help of a registered patent attorney.

Chapter 2

LICENSING LAW

2.1 SAMPLE LICENSE AGREEMENTS

Although as noted earlier, license agreements can take a great variety of forms, there are some standard license terms that are included in almost all license agreements. These standard terms address fundamental questions regarding the licensing relationship.

• What rights will the licensor grant to the licensee? Will the licensor obtain grant-back rights from the licensee?

• What licensor patents will be included in the license? Will the license include future patents obtained by the licensor?

• What licensee products will be covered by the license? What fields of use will be allowed under the license?

• What rights will the licensee have to sublicense or assign the license rights? What conditions will the licensor impose on the exercise of these rights?

• What will be the duration of the license? If the license is for a term of years, how will the license be renewed?

• How will the license royalties be structured? Will there be a license fee, minimum royalties, maximum royalties?

• Will the licensor be permitted to audit the records of the licensee periodically? What are the conditions of such an audit, and who will pay for it?

• How will disputes arising under the license be settled? Will the parties be required to arbitrate disputes prior to litigation?

• What warranties will the licensor give to the licensee? What warranties will the licensor disclaim?

Two excellent treatises on licensing are DAVID EPSTEIN, ECKSTROM'S LICENSING IN FOREIGN AND DOMESTIC OPERATIONS and RAYMOND T. NIMMER, JEFF DODD, MODERN LICENSING LAW. You will see these treatises cited numerous times in the materials.

Another extremely useful source of licensing material is contained in Lexis. Lexis has compiled an extensive and easily searchable database of contracts, including numerous licensing agreements. When a company registered with the Securities and Exchange Commission (SEC) enters into a "material contract" it must file the "material contract" with the SEC as part of its ongoing reporting requirements. Lexis has compiled these "material contract" filings in a database that can be searched by many different fields, including industry, Standard Industrial Classification Code (SIC), company, subject, terms and text. The Lexis database can be accessed by logging into your Lexis account and selecting the following:

> "Area of Law-By Topic > Securities > SEC Filings > Exhibit 10. Material Contracts"

All of the contracts in this section were obtained from the Lexis database.

2.1.1   Software License

U.S. ROBOTICS ACCESS CORP. — 8X8 CORP.

This Agreement is made between U.S. ROBOTICS ACCESS CORP., a Delaware corporation, with principal offices at 8100 North McCormick Boulevard, Skokie, IL 60076-2999, (herein called "USR"); and 8x8, INC., a Delaware corporation, with principal offices at 2445 Mission College Blvd., Santa Clara, CA 94027 (herein called "8x8"), effective the 5th day of May, 1997 (the "Effective Date"). The parties include any affiliate of a party; an "affiliate" is defined as the parent company of a party and any company that is controlled directly or indirectly by that party or its parent company through more than fifty percent (50%) ownership, provided such affiliate agrees to be bound by this agreement.

WHEREAS, 8x8, a developer and a supplier of videoconferencing products, intends to license certain technology to USR according to these terms and conditions; and

WHEREAS, USR, a developer and a supplier of modems, certain information access products and other products, intends to license certain technology to 8x8 according to these terms and conditions:

NOW THEREFORE, in consideration of the premises and of the mutual covenants and agreements contained hereinafter, 8x8 and USR agree as follows:

1. LICENSES.

(a) **Licensed Technology.** The license from 8x8 to USR covers:

the technology that 8x8 has relating to videoconferencing in a standalone format (i.e. in a system that is not directly connected to a personal computer), and thus includes what 8x8 calls its "videocommunicators," i.e. ViaTV, LCD Phone and variations on them (such as the Truedox design that was also displayed during 8x8's presentation on January 21, 1997), which are herein called the "VC"; VCP chip and current variations relevant to videoconferencing like LVP, which are herein called the "VCP"; any source and object code related to videoconferencing 8x8 has that will work in the VC, including H.320, H.323, H.324, and MPEG (other than on MPP or MPPex, as excluded below) and related controls of the standalone system, such as the controls from the telephone keypad, herein called the "VC Code"; any technology 8x8 has developed for direct connection to the personal computer, such as DVC6 or the Vidus CompressionCam and related technology (demonstrated to USR by Sanyo, based on its nonexclusive license of technology from 8x8's subsidiary, Vidus, Inc.) all development tools applicable to the "Licensed Technology" that 8x8 can provide to USR without violating copyright or license agreements.

All of the technology described above is herein collectively called "Licensed Technology."

Excluded from the Licensed Technology is:

the web browser technology developed by 8x8 with PlanetWeb, Inc.; the audio code 8x8 licensed from Signal Processing Associates ("SPA"); the modem technology licensed from ELSA GmbH; [though 8x8 will use its best efforts to persuade each of those parties (at the request of USR) to make available such technology to USR on the same terms and conditions as such technology is available to 8x8 (in which case thereafter USR will share enhancements to technology with 8x8 as provided below for the duration that the parties are sharing enhancements)].

Also excluded from the Licensed Technology is:

the MPP and MPPex (licensed exclusively to ESS Technology, Inc. for MPEG and CD Players), and related MPEG code and software to the extent used on MPP and MPPex; except that USR can use the MPEG on the VCP.

The Licensed Technology is as it exists on the Effective Date in written and electronic documents, including schematics, data base tapes, software, source and object code for delivery to USR, and, except for the foregoing, does not include delivery of any physical products; provided, however, future modifications and enhancements to the Licensed Technology pursuant to this Agreement shall become part of the "Licensed Technology."

(b) Grant: 8x8 will immediately deliver to USR the Licensed Technology and hereby grants to USR a nonexclusive (except as set forth in Section 4 hereof), non-assignable (except as allowed under Section 14 hereof) world-wide license to use the Licensed Technology and to make, have made, use, market and sell products containing or embodying such Licensed Technology, and enhancements as de-scribed below, including rights under any 8x8 patents or copyrights relevant thereto (including after-acquired rights). USR is free to use and market the Licensed Technology as follows:

Sell systems (what 8x8 calls its "videocommunicators," i.e., ViaTV, LCD Phone and variations on them) for itself (USR) or to Original Equipment Manufacturers under their brand names ("OEMs"), including selling systems without casing for incorporation into other manufacturers products such as television sets. Sell direct computer products (such as DVC6 and Compression Cam) for itself (USR) or to Original Equipment Manufacturers under their brand names ("OEMs"), including selling systems for incorporation into other manufacturers products. Sell "daugh-ter" cards or partial boards as subsystems for another manufacturer's video solution. USR is free to use the 8x8 H.323 stack and the H.245 and H.223 code for incorporation into its own products of all types.

(c) Consideration: In consideration therefore, USR will pay 8x8 [$X] immediately on execution of this Agreement.

(d) Royalty: On any system that USR sells that incorporates any Licensed Technology (excluding USR products in which the only use of the Licensed Technology is the incorporation of the 8x8 H.323 stack, the H.245 code or the H.223 code), USR agrees to pay 8x8 the following royalties:

CUMULATIVE NUMBER OF SYSTEMS SOLD BY USR UNDER THIS AGREEMENT AND ROYALTY PER SYSTEM OWED 8x8 ON THOSE SYSTEMS

1–20,000	[$A]
20,001–40,000	[$B]
40,001–60,000	[$C]
60,001–80,000	[$D]
80,001–100,000	[$E]
100,001–120,000	[$F]
120,001–140,000	[$G]
140,001–160,000	[$H]
160,001–180,000	[$I]
180,001–200,000	[$J]
200,001–220,000	[$K]
>220,000	[$L]

If USR elects to manufacture the VCP, then for each such chip incorporated into a system and sold (or sold on the open market as permitted herein if the option is exercised), USR agrees to pay 8x8 the following royalties:

[TABLE]

Provided, however that the chip royalty will be proportionately reduced by the die area on the chip attributable exclusively to enhancements by USR. Also, the [$X] royalty on the chip is not due on any chip purchased by USR from 8x8.

If USR uses the 8x8 H.323 stack, the H.245 code or the H.223 code on some system other than 8x8's chip USR agrees to pay 8x8 a royalty of [*] per port (or end user customer); provided further, that USR does not owe such [*] royalty if the H.323 stack, the H.245 code or the H.223 code is developed independently of 8x8's technology in good faith ("clean room" environment) and used on systems independent of 8x8's chip; and provided further, that with this exception, the VC Code may only be used on the VCP subject to royalty above.

Such royalty will be paid within 45 days of the end of each USR fiscal quarter. Royalties shall not be due, and if already paid shall be credited to USR, for systems and chips sold by USR but returned by the purchaser. 8x8 is entitled to audit the records of USR through 8x8's auditor, provided that (a) such audit shall occur no more than once per year, and (b) such auditor (i) shall be acceptable to USR and (ii) shall have executed an appropriate nondisclosure agreement. If such an audit discloses a deficiency in the royalty paid of greater than five percent (5%), then USR will pay the reasonable cost of such audit plus interest on the deficiency from the time due until paid of twelve percent (12%) simple interest per annum.

USR will give 8x8 in the report each quarter a good faith estimate of the number of systems that were for direct computer products (DVC6 or CompressionCam).

(e) Grant back from USR: USR will provide 8x8 the USR technical and other confidential and proprietary information that USR determines is necessary or useful for 8x8 to improve the modem and speakerphone functionality for the video communicator (hereinafter "USR Information") and USR hereby grants to 8x8 a paid up, royalty-free, nonexclusive, non-assignable world-wide license to use the USR Information to make, have made, use or sell products incorporating the USR Information; provided, however, (i) such products shall include 8x8's videophone technology only, and not direct computer products such as DVC6 or Compression-Cam; (ii) 8x8 shall use the USR information only for its own branded system products, and shall not sublicense or otherwise disclose the USR information to third parties for use in their products or for any other reason; and (iii) such improvements shall be included in the Licensed Technology and thereby licensed to USR for incorporation into USR's products. Notwithstanding the foregoing, in the event USR sells one or more of its products to OEMs, then 8x8 shall thereafter have the right to sell its own similar products to OEMs. Upon determining that it will sell its product(s) to OEMs, USR shall give 8x8 notice of that decision.

(f) Source Code: All source code licensed hereunder, whether from 8x8 to USR or from USR to 8x8, shall, in addition to the terms and conditions of this Agreement, be subject to the terms of the Source Code License in the form of Exhibit A attached hereto.

2. LICENSING OF ENHANCEMENTS.

Each party agrees to license to the other party any enhancements it makes to the Licensed Technology. (Such enhancements created by 8x8 shall then become Licensed Technology.) Such enhancements shall be delivered promptly upon their development, until USR discontinues the licensing of such enhancements by both parties by providing notice to 8x8 (but enhancements delivered by either party up to the date of such notice shall continue to be licensed); provided, however, that (a) 8x8 will in any event deliver the first taped out version of the VCPex, and (b) USR will in any event deliver to 8x8 the initial enhancements it makes to the VCP, VCPex, or VC relating to modem and speakerphone technology, including porting V.34 to 8x8's chip. (All such enhancements by USR are hereinafter called "USR Enhancements.") Such deliveries by 8x8 and USR, along with related development tools (to the extent delivery can be done without paying a fee to third parties or violating other agreements) will be in the same form and completeness as similar prior deliveries by 8x8 of Licensed Technology, and with engineering support as provided below. Nothing herein entitles USR to receive enhancements developed by other licensees of 8x8, and nothing herein entitles 8x8 to sublicense, distribute or otherwise disclose USR's enhancements to other licensees of 8x8; provided further that 8x8 will limit production of chips with USR Enhancements to incorporation on finished systems produced (made or have made) and sold or leased by 8x8, and in no event will 8x8 sell or otherwise make available on the open market such components in component form or on printed circuit boards for incorporation into the systems of others; and thus, the chip that 8x8 sells on the open market to its other chip customers will have deleted from it any USR Enhancements. After June 30, 2000, either party may elect to terminate sharing of enhancements developed after date of such termination.

3. ENGINEERING SUPPORT.

8x8 will provide engineering support to USR, for all Licensed Technology, including all such technology initially delivered to USR and all enhancements. Such engineering support shall be sufficient to enable USR quickly to implement the Licensed Technology and enhancements for demonstration purposes and to enable USR to achieve its objectives of volume shipments as soon as possible. USR shall provide comparable engineering support to 8x8 for the USR Enhancements. If the receiving party asks the delivering party at any time for engineers or others to travel to the receiving party's location to support the technology delivery, and the other party agrees to do so, receiving party will pay the reasonable costs associated therewith, including the traveling party's labor costs for such personnel as well as travel (coach class on the airplane), meals and lodging.

4. EXCLUSIVITY.

8x8 agrees that for a period of one year beginning on the Effective Date hereof it will not grant to any third party any licenses to use the Licensed Technology, or any portion thereof, or to make, have made, use, market or sell products with such Licensed Technology, or any portion thereof, provided 8x8 may still deliver to its customers object code with chips and reference designs for boards; 8x8 may deliver to its customers example source code needed by customers for integration of 8x8's chips into customer products, including PC driver code and microprocessor controller code for controlling VCP applications (including changing display size, logo, trademark, menu, options and features); 8x8 can honor currently outstanding licenses; and 8x8 can sell to OEMs its system level products (whether partial boards, complete boards or partial or complete systems branded as the customer desires) for resale in that form or incorporated in other systems (like TV) as the customer desires. None of the delivery of source or object code to customers shall include USR Information other than as allowed in section 1(c).

5. VCP PRICING.

8x8 agrees to sell VCP chips to USR (as enhanced with enhancements that become part of the Licensed Technology as described above) at a price [*]. USR is entitled to audit the records of 8x8 through USR's auditor, solely to verify 8x8 pricing, provided that (a) such audit shall occur no more than once per year, and (b) such auditor (i) shall be acceptable to 8x8 and (ii) shall have executed an appropriate nondisclosure agreement. If such an audit discloses a pricing discrepancy unfavorable to USR of greater than five percent (5%), then 8x8 will pay the reasonable costs of such audit plus interest on the discrepancy of twelve percent (12%) simple interest per annum.

6. WARRANTIES.

(a) 8x8 warrants that (i) all portions of the Licensed Technology owned by third party licensors of 8x8, if any, are provided to USR hereunder pursuant to appropriate authority of those third parties, and (ii) 8x8 owns all rights in and to all other portions of the Licensed Technology, free of any liens, claims, encumbrances or other restrictions that would impair USR's rights under this Agreement. The foregoing warranties exclude any warranty that the Licensed Technology does not infringe the intellectual property rights of any third party. However, 8x8 warrants that to the best of its knowledge the Licensed Technology does not infringe the intellectual property rights of any third party.

(b) 8x8 warrants that the Licensed Technology shall be free of material defects and shall function in conformance with its published documentation and other specifications customarily provided to 8x8's licensors for a period of thirty (30) days from the date of delivery of the Licensed Technology. During such thirty-day period, USR may return the Licensed Technology to 8x8 for a full refund of all moneys paid to 8x8 hereunder if USR is not satisfied with the Licensed Technology.

(c) 8x8 represents and warrants that as of the effective date of this agreement it has received no notice that the Licensed Technology infringes any patent, copyright, trade secret or other intellectual property right (collectively "Intellectual Property Rights") of any third party, though 8x8 has incorporated a patent license from DSP Group and is considering negotiating licenses of patents possibly applicable to G.723 (and USR would need to consider negotiating similar licenses for its benefit). 8x8 will immediately advise USR of any such notice received by 8x8 in the future as it applies to Licensed Technology, and whether the enhancement was done by 8x8 or USR; likewise, USR will notify 8x8 of any notice USR receives where there is a claim that applies to Licensed Technology, and whether the enhancement was done by 8x8 or USR. Each party bears the risk that some party claims or sues it with respect to alleged infringement of intellectual property rights of others; provided that the other party will cooperate in such litigation to the extent it can be helpful in defending against such claims of other third parties.

(d) EXCEPT AS SET FORTH IN SECTIONS 6(a), (b) AND (c) ABOVE, NEITHER PARTY MAKES ANY WARRANTIES, EXPRESS OR IMPLIED, AS TO THE QUALITY, PATENTS OR COPYRIGHTS OF ANYTHING DELIVERED HEREUNDER AND ENHANCEMENTS, EXCEPT AS SPECIFIED IN THIS AGREEMENT. EACH PARTY MAKES NO INDEMNITY IN THE EVENT THAT THE OTHER PARTY IS SUED FOR ANYTHING RELATED TO THE LICENSED TECHNOLOGY OR ENHANCEMENTS HEREUNDER EXCEPT AS SPECIFIED IN THIS AGREEMENT, BUT EACH PARTY WILL COOPERATE IN THE EVENT OF SUCH LITIGATION TO ASSIST THE OTHER PARTY TO DEFEND SUCH LITIGATION. THE PARTIES SPECIFICALLY DISCLAIM LIABILITY FOR CONSEQUENTIAL DAMAGES.

7. CONFIDENTIAL INFORMATION.

The parties will keep confidential any information provided to it by the other party that is proprietary to the other party and marked confidential; provided such information shall not be considered proprietary once it is in the public domain by no fault of the other party. Such confidentiality will be maintained by the other party with the same care that such party would use for its own confidential information, but in any event with reasonable care.

8. RECRUITING.

Until such time as the parties cease to share enhancements, each party agrees not to directly solicit the employment, either temporary, full time or consultancy, of any person after the effective date who was employed by the other party within one year of the date of such potential hiring.

9. COMPLETE AGREEMENT.

This is a complete agreement binding upon the parties, their heirs, successors and assigns. It may only be modified in writing signed by officers of both parties.

10. GOVERNING LAW.

This Agreement shall be governed by the laws of the State of Delaware, excluding its choice-of-law provisions.

11. PUBLIC STATEMENTS.

The parties agree immediately to publish a joint press release stating that Licensee has licensed 8x8's videoconferencing technology, and 8x8 endorses USR's "x2" and related technologies. Further, either party is free to file with the SEC any document required to be filed there on advice of counsel (redacted in a form advised by counsel). Other public statements and press releases related to this licensing agreement are subject to approval in advance by both parties; neither party shall use the name of the other party without advance approval.

12. INDEPENDENT CONTRACTORS.

The parties are independent contractors, and nothing herein shall be deemed to create any agency, joint venture or partnership relationship between them. Neither party shall have the right to bind the other to any obligation, nor have the right to incur any liability on behalf of the other.

13. FORCE MAJEURE.

Neither party shall be liable to the other for delay or failure to perform if and to the extent such delay or failure to perform is due to causes beyond the reasonable control of the party affected.

14. ASSIGNMENT.

Neither party shall assign this Agreement or its rights hereunder without the prior written consent of the other party, except to an affiliate of that party; provided, however, in the event of a change in control of one party through a merger, consolidation or other business combination or acquisition by or with a person or entity a material portion of whose business is the sale or licensing of products that are competitive with products of the other party, the other party shall have the right to terminate the licenses granted by both parties hereunder. Notwithstanding the foregoing, 8x8 agrees that USR's parent company's merger transaction with 3COM, as previously announced to the public, does not give rise to any such termination right of 8x8.

15. NON-WAIVER.

No course of dealing or failure of either party to enforce strictly any term, right, obligation or provision of this Agreement shall be construed as a waiver of such provision.

16. SEVERABILITY.

If any provision of this Agreement shall be held invalid or unenforceable, such provision shall be deemed deleted from the Agreement and replaced by a valid and enforceable provision that achieves, as much as possible, the same purpose, and the remaining provisions of the Agreement shall continue in full force and effect.

IN WITNESS WHEREOF, the parties have executed this Agreement.

U.S. ROBOTICS ACCESS CORP.   8x8, INC.
By: /s/   By: /s/

Name: _____   Name: _____

Title: _____   Title: _____

Date: _____   Date: _____

EXHIBIT A
SOURCE CODE LICENSE

This Source Code License ("License") is effective this _____ day of _____, 19_____, by and between _____ ("Licensor") and _____ ("Licensee"). This License is an addendum to the Technology License Agreement between the parties dated _____ ("Agreement"), and all Source Code licensed hereunder is subject to all terms and conditions of that Agreement as well as those terms and conditions set forth below. In the event of any conflict or inconsistency between the Agreement and this License, this License shall take precedence.

1. License Grant.

Licensor grants to Licensee, and Licensee accepts, a license to use internally and copy the Source Code described in Exhibit I attached hereto solely for the purpose of developing the products described in the Agreement.

2. Restrictions.

2.1 Licensee may make a reasonable number of copies of the Source Code solely for its own internal use under the terms of this License, provided that all legal notices set forth on the Source Code are reproduced on such copies.

2.2 Licensee shall limit access to the Source Code to those of its employees who have a need to know for the purpose of enabling Licensee to perform under this License and the Agreement. Licensee shall ensure that all of its employees given access to the Source Code shall be bound by Licensee's standard confidentiality agreement, copies of which may be requested by Licensor upon demand, and which shall contain nondisclosure and usage restrictions consistent with those set forth herein.

2.3 Except in furtherance of the license granted above, Licensee shall not (i) modify, alter or prepare derivative works based on the Source Code or (ii) engage in or cause the reverse engineering, disassembly or decompilation or similar manipulation of the Source Code. Further, Licensee acknowledges that it shall not lend, sell, assign, sublicense, lease, hypothecate, disclose, disseminate or otherwise transfer the Source Code to any third party in any media or permit any third party to use, execute, reverse engineer, disassemble, decompile or engage in any similar manipulation of the Source Code or any part thereof.

2.4 Notwithstanding the earlier termination of this License, the obligations of this section shall remain in effect until such time as the Source Code becomes publicly known, through no act or failure to act on Licensee's part.

3. Ownership of Source Code.

Source Code and all copies, in whole or in part, and all additional materials provided therewith, as described in Exhibit I, are and shall remain the property of Licensor. This Agreement grants no rights other than those set forth herein.

4. Export Control.

Both parties recognize that an export license must be obtained before the Source Code can be exported and will make all reasonable efforts to obtain such license. Licensee will not transfer any technical information that it receives from Licensor or products made using such information to any country prohibited from obtaining such data by the U.S. Department of Commerce Export Administration Regulations without first obtaining a validated export license, and Licensee will otherwise comply with all export control laws and regulations of the United States.

5. General.

This Agreement shall be governed by the laws of the State of Delaware. This License and the Agreement collectively comprise the complete and exclusive agreement between the parties relating to this subject matter and no amendments shall be effective unless in a writing signed by both parties.

LICENSOR: LICENSEE:

By:_____   By:_____

Name:_____   Name:_____

Title:_____   Title:_____

Date:_____   Date:_____

QUESTIONS

1.   The license provides that USR will not pay royalties on code developed independently of 8x8's technology in a good faith "clean room" environment. What is a "clean room" environment?

2.   The license is nonexclusive, but 8x8 agrees not to license the technology to a third party for a period of one year from the effective date of the license. What benefit does USR receive from this provision?

3.   What is a non-recruiting clause and why is it needed?

2.1.2   Product License

INTERGRAPH HARDWARE TECHNOLOGIES CO. — HEWLETT-PACKARD CO.

This Settlement Agreement, Release, and Patent Cross-License ("AGREEMENT"), effective as of January 21, 2005 (the "EFFECTIVE DATE"), is entered into by and among Hewlett-Packard Company ("HP"), a Delaware corporation, on the one hand, and Intergraph Corporation, a Delaware corporation, and Intergraph Hardware Technologies Company ("IHTC"), a Nevada corporation, on the other hand. Intergraph Corporation and IHTC shall be referred to collectively hereinafter as "INTERGRAPH." HP and INTERGRAPH may each be referred to individually as a "PARTY" and collectively as the "PARTIES."

BACKGROUND TO THIS AGREEMENT

HP and INTERGRAPH are engaged in lawsuits and actions against each other in the Eastern District of Texas, the Northern District of California, the District of Delaware and Germany, as identified more fully below;

HP and INTERGRAPH each own and/or control patents and patent applications;

HP and INTERGRAPH have agreed it would be mutually beneficial to resolve all of their litigation against each other and to grant rights to the other PARTY under certain patents and patent applications;

Now, therefore, the PARTIES agree as follows:

AGREEMENT

1. DEFINITIONS

a. "ACTIONS" means the litigation and other proceedings identified in Appendix A to this AGREEMENT.

b. "AFFILIATE" means any entity which, at any time during the term of this AGREEMENT, is the PARENT of a PARTY, a SUBSIDIARY of a PARTY, or a SUBSIDIARY of a PARENT.

c. "HP CUSTOMERS" means customers that purchased or distributed an HP PRODUCT including without limitation system integrators, distributors, retailers, resellers and end users.

d. "HP PATENTS" means all patents and patent applications anywhere in the world (a) which HP or any of its SUBSIDIARIES own and/or have the power to license, and/or which HP or any of its SUBSIDIARIES may cause to be licensed without payment of additional royalties, at any time during the term of this AGREEMENT; and (b) which claim the benefit of the filing date of a patent application filed anywhere in the world on or before January 21, 2007; and all continuation, continuation-in-part, divisional, reissue, reexamination, and counterpart patents and patent applications thereof, including without limitation all priority patents and patent applications, patents of addition and utility models.

e. "HP PRODUCT" means a product designed, made or sold by HP, its SUBSIDIARIES, or its AFFILIATES.

f. "INTERGRAPH CUSTOMERS" means customers that purchased or distributed an INTERGRAPH PRODUCT including without limitation system integrators, distributors, retailers, resellers and end users.

g. "INTERGRAPH FIELDS OF USE" means the following fields:

(i) The Mapping and Geospatial Solutions field. This field is defined by photogrammetric, mapping, and geospatial information management based solutions that have substantial value added by INTERGRAPH and which incorporate INTERGRAPH branded products.

(ii) The Process, Power and Marine field. This field is defined by information management systems that have substantial value added by INTERGRAPH and which incorporate INTERGRAPH's branded software products for the chemical, pharmaceutical, oil and gas, power generation, and shipbuilding industries. These software solutions support the project management, simulation, design, analysis, construction, material management, procurement, documentation, automation, and operation of process and power plants, offshore rigs, and ships.

(iii) The Public Safety field. This field is defined by information management systems that have substantial value added by INTERGRAPH and which incorporate INTERGRAPH's branded software products for the public safety industry. For example: video capture, enhancement and analysis systems; emergency event prediction, prevention, detection and management systems; emergency communication systems; traffic monitoring or planning systems; emergency event response planning systems; emergency resource deployment systems; event records management systems; equipment maintenance systems; mug shot systems; fingerprint systems; court management systems; prison management systems; police or fire agency management systems; emergency medical management systems; roadside assistance systems; airport, military base, campus or building security systems; fire alarms systems; utility infrastructure management systems; and workforce management systems.

(iv) The Mapping Services field. This field is defined by geospatial production services provided by INTERGRAPH that result in a hardcopy or softcopy map or chart or set of data used to create a map or chart. This production services business includes, for example: aerial data acquisition; photogrammetric and cartographic scanning; softcopy aerial triangulation; cartography; data conversion; digital nautical charts; turn-key GIS implementation; hardcopy maps; electronic charting services; full service film reprographics laboratory; digital orthographic processing; photogrammetry; image processing; and photogrammetric/GIS project management and consulting.

(v) The Personalized Solutions field. This field is defined as the integration of software, hardware, open technology, and data to produce client driven information technology solutions that have substantial value added by INTERGRAPH. These solutions include, for example: homeland security; force protection; business systems integration; integrated data environments; logistics and supply chain management; computer systems support and network support; information assurance; facility and asset management; integrated public safety/security; IT managed services; ruggedized hardware; video analysis hardware systems; multi-vendor maintenance; and financial management.

(vi) Notwithstanding anything in this AGREEMENT to the contrary, INTERGRAPH FIELDS OF USE shall not include (and no license for such products shall be granted under HP PATENTS for) ink, ink cartridges, print heads, toner cartridges or other printer consumables.

h. "INTERGRAPH PATENTS" means all patents and patent applications anywhere in the world (a) which INTERGRAPH or any of its SUBSIDIARIES own and/or have the power to license, and/or which INTERGRAPH or any of its SUBSIDIARIES may cause to be licensed without payment of additional royalties, at any time during the term of this AGREEMENT; and (b) which claim the benefit of the filing date of a patent application filed anywhere in the world on or before January 21, 2007; and all continuation, continuation-in-part, divisional, reissue, reexamination, and counterpart patents and patent applications thereof, including without limitation all priority patents and patent applications, patents of addition and utility models.

i. "INTERGRAPH PRODUCT" means a product designed, made or sold by INTERGRAPH, its SUBSIDIARIES, or its AFFILIATES.

j. "PARENT" means a corporation, company, partnership, or other entity that owns or controls more than fifty percent (50%) of the outstanding shares or securities representing the right to vote for the election of directors or other managing authority of a PARTY, but such corporation, company, partnership, or other entity shall be deemed to be a PARENT only so long as such ownership or control exists.

k. "SUBSIDIARY" means a corporation, company, partnership, or other entity in which, at any time during the term of this AGREEMENT, a PARTY (i) owns or has control over more than fifty percent (50%) of the outstanding shares or securities representing the right to vote for the election of directors or other managing authority if such entity has voting shares or other voting securities, or (ii) owns or has control over more than fifty percent (50%) of the ownership interest that represents the right to make decisions for such entity, if such entity does not have voting shares or other voting securities; provided, however, that such corporation, company, partnership, or other entity shall be deemed to be a SUBSIDIARY only so long as such ownership or control exists. Ownership of the requisite shares or ownership interest in the SUBSIDIARY may either be direct or through one or more intervening SUBSIDIARIES.

2. TERMINATION OF ALL PENDING LITIGATION AND ADMINISTRATIVE ACTIONS

Based on all of the mutual consideration exchanged under this AGREEMENT, the PARTIES agree to terminate all of the ACTIONS by dismissing with prejudice the U.S. suits and withdrawing the German administrative actions after the EFFECTIVE DATE. The PARTIES shall direct their respective counsel to cooperate in good faith to bring about this termination and/or withdrawal of all of the ACTIONS as promptly as is reasonably possible after the EFFECTIVE DATE. The PARTIES shall be responsible for payment of their own costs and fees, including attorney fees, incurred in the ACTIONS.

3. MUTUAL RELEASES

a. INTERGRAPH, on behalf of itself and its SUBSIDIARIES and AFFILIATES, hereby releases, acquits and forever discharges HP and its SUBSIDIARIES and AFFILIATES, from and against:

(i) any and all claims or liabilities asserted in the ACTIONS; and,

(ii) any and all claims or liabilities that could have been asserted in the ACTIONS; and,

(iii) any and all claims, known or unknown, that could have been asserted as of the EFFECTIVE DATE by INTERGRAPH or any of its SUBSIDIARIES and AFFILIATES against HP or any of its SUBSIDIARIES and AFFILIATES; and,

(iv) any and all claims, known or unknown, that could have been asserted as of the EFFECTIVE DATE by INTERGRAPH or any of its SUBSIDIARIES and AFFILIATES against HP CUSTOMERS based on an HP PRODUCT; and,

(v) any damages or other remedies flowing from (i)–(iv) above.

Further, INTERGRAPH, on behalf of itself and its SUBSIDIARIES and AFFILIATES, hereby releases and forever discharges HP CUSTOMERS who have acquired the right from HP to make an HP proprietary design from any and all claims for past infringement of the INTERGRAPH PATENTS based solely on the HP proprietary design licensed by HP, but only if HP owes a duty to indemnify said HP CUSTOMER against said claims.

b. HP, on behalf of itself and its SUBSIDIARIES and AFFILIATES, hereby releases, acquits and forever discharges INTERGRAPH and its SUBSIDIARIES and AFFILIATES, from and against:

(i) any and all claims or liabilities asserted in the ACTIONS; and,

(ii) any and all claims or liabilities that could have been asserted in the ACTIONS; and,

(iii) any and all claims, known or unknown, that could have been asserted as of the EFFECTIVE DATE by HP or any of its SUBSIDIARIES and AFFILIATES against INTERGRAPH and its SUBSIDIARIES and AFFILIATES; and,

(iv) any and all claims, known or unknown, that could have been asserted as of the EFFECTIVE DATE by HP or any of its SUBSIDIARIES and AFFILIATES against INTERGRAPH CUSTOMERS based on an INTERGRAPH PRODUCT; and,

(v) any damages or other remedies flowing from (i)–(iv) above.

Further, HP, on behalf of itself and its SUBSIDIARIES and AFFILIATES, hereby releases and forever discharges INTERGRAPH CUSTOMERS who have acquired the right from INTERGRAPH to make an INTERGRAPH proprietary design from any and all claims for past infringement of the HP PATENTS based solely on the INTERGRAPH proprietary design licensed by INTERGRAPH, but only if INTERGRAPH owes a duty to indemnify said INTERGRAPH CUSTOMER against said claims.

c. The PARTIES agree and acknowledge that these releases shall not extend to any obligation arising from the AGREEMENT, nor shall they release any payment obligation of a PARTY, or their respective SUBSIDIARIES and AFFILIATES, arising from the purchase of goods or services from the other PARTY, or its respective SUBSIDIARIES and AFFILIATES. The PARTIES further agree and acknowledge that HP's release is not intended to, and shall not, release any claim HP has against Intel Corporation.

d. Each PARTY, for itself, and its SUBSIDIARIES and AFFILIATES, hereby expressly waives any right that it may have under the laws or statutes of any jurisdiction which limits the extension of a general release to certain types of claims, such as California Civil Code § 1542 which provides that: "A general release does not extend to claims which the creditor does not know or suspect to exist in his favor at the time of executing the release, which if known by him must have materially affected his settlement with the debtor."

e. None of the releases in this Section 3 shall apply to claims based on events occurring after the EFFECTIVE DATE.

4. CROSS-LICENSE

a. INTERGRAPH's License to HP

(i) INTERGRAPH hereby grants to HP, and its SUBSIDIARIES and AFFILIATES, a perpetual, non-cancelable, fully paid-up, irrevocable, non-exclusive, world-wide, royalty-free license to all of the INTERGRAPH PATENTS, including, without limitation, the right for HP to make, have made, use, import, lease, offer to sell, sell or otherwise transfer products, methods, or services within the scope of the claims of the INTERGRAPH PATENTS, with no right to transfer or sublicense other than as per Section 5. The license granted by INTERGRAPH in this paragraph is not limited to any field of use.

(ii) No implied licenses are granted hereunder. Nothing contained in this AGREEMENT shall expressly or by implication or by estoppel or otherwise give HP any right to license the INTERGRAPH PATENTS to any third party except as set forth in Section 5.

b. HP's License to INTERGRAPH

(i) HP hereby grants to INTERGRAPH, and its SUBSIDIARIES and AFFILIATES, a perpetual, non-cancelable, fully paid-up, irrevocable, non-exclusive, world-wide, royalty-free license to all of the HP PATENTS, including, without limitation, the right for INTERGRAPH to make, have made, use, import, lease, offer to sell, sell or otherwise transfer products, methods, or services within the scope of the claims of the HP PATENTS, with no right to transfer or sublicense other than as per Section 5. The license granted by HP in this paragraph is limited to the INTERGRAPH FIELDS OF USE.

(ii) No implied licenses are granted hereunder. Nothing contained in this AGREEMENT shall expressly or by implication or by estoppel or otherwise give INTERGRAPH any right to license the HP PATENTS to any third party except as set forth in Section 5.

c. Anti-Foundry Provision

The rights granted under this Section 4.(a)(i) and 4.(b)(i) do not cover manufacturing activities that either PARTY, or its SUBSIDIARIES or AFFILIATES, undertakes solely as a patent foundry for a third party. This limitation applies only to the "made" and "have-made" rights of Section 4.(a)(i) and 4.(b)(i) and no others.

d. SUBSIDIARIES and AFFILIATES

Each PARTY agrees that it shall cause as of the EFFECTIVE DATE each of its SUBSIDIARIES and AFFILIATES to take all necessary action to effect the licenses granted in this Section.

5. TERM, TERMINATION AND ASSIGNABILITY

a. The term of the licenses granted in Section 4 of this AGREEMENT shall be from the EFFECTIVE DATE until the expiration of the last to expire of the INTERGRAPH PATENTS and HP PATENTS; all other rights and obligations contained in this AGREEMENT shall survive. This AGREEMENT may not be terminated, except by subsequent written agreement of the PARTIES.

b. Neither PARTY may assign its rights or obligations under this AGREEMENT, in whole or in part, outright or by way of collateral assignment, without the written consent of the other PARTY, except as follows:

(i) A PARTY can assign the licenses under this AGREEMENT to a divested or spun-off entity, as well as to an acquiring entity, as long as said licenses are limited:

(a) to those products and services manufactured and marketed by the transferred entity prior to said transfer, and any commercially reasonable improvements and extensions thereto; and,

(b) to a sales volume for said products and services that is consistent with normal business growth of the transferred entity.

(ii) Notwithstanding anything to the contrary herein, the transfer by one PARTY of any rights and obligations under this AGREEMENT as part of any internal restructuring (re-incorporation or the like) shall be permitted and shall not be considered an assignment for purposes of this AGREEMENT.

c. INTERGRAPH agrees that if it or its SUBSIDIARIES attempts to sell, assign or otherwise transfer any patent under which a license has been granted pursuant to Section 4 of this AGREEMENT, it will take all necessary and appropriate steps to ensure that such sale, assignment or transfer shall be subject to the terms and conditions of this AGREEMENT.

d. HP agrees that if it or its SUBSIDIARIES attempts to sell, assign or otherwise transfer any patent under which a license has been granted pursuant to Section 4 of this AGREEMENT, it will take all necessary and appropriate steps to ensure that such sale, assignment or transfer shall be subject to the terms and conditions of this AGREEMENT.

e. No sold, transferred, divested or spun off business to which a license has passed under Section 5(b)(i) shall be permitted to subsequently pass that license further, under Section 5(b)(i), if any part of itself is thereafter acquired, sold, transferred, divested or spun off. If under Section 5(b)(i) a PARTY assigns, sells, transfers, divests or spins off only a part of its business to which a license hereunder extends, the transferor party shall retain its original license.

6. PAYMENT BY HP

a. HP shall pay to IHTC the sum of one hundred and forty-one million, one hundred thirty-five thousand United States dollars ($141,135,000), within five (5) business days of the final execution of this AGREEMENT. The PARTIES agree that the amount of one hundred and forty-one million, one hundred thirty-five thousand dollars ($141,135,000) is a net sum to IHTC, is not refundable, and is not subject to any deductions or offsets.

b. The foregoing specified payment shall be made in United States currency by wire transfer to the escrow account of the law firm of Robins, Kaplan, Miller & Ciresi L.L.P., pursuant to a bank transfer as follows:

[Confidential information has been omitted and filed separately with the Securities and Exchange Commission]

c. The PARTIES acknowledge that the payment under this Section, the mutual releases under Section 3, and the cross-licenses made under Section 4, are not evidence of what a reasonable royalty would be as determined in a suit for infringement of any of the patents covered by this AGREEMENT because, among other reasons, the determination of a reasonable royalty in a patent infringement suit assumes that the relevant patent is valid, enforceable and infringed, while in this case, the payment under this Section as well as the mutual releases under Section 3, and the cross-licenses made under Section 4, represent a compromise settlement of disputed issues.

d. The PARTIES acknowledge that the payment hereunder is specifically based upon many considerations, including but not limited to: the issues raised by the ACTIONS, and the fact that the negotiations do not reflect what a willing licensee would pay a willing licensor in an arm's-length transaction with respect to any patent covered by this AGREEMENT.

7. CONFIDENTIALITY OF TERMS

a. Neither the PARTIES nor their AFFILIATES shall use or refer to this AGREEMENT or any of its provisions in any promotional activity, except that the PARTIES shall be allowed to issue a press release relating to this AGREEMENT. Prior to each PARTY'S press release, each PARTY will obtain the consent of the other as to the form and content of the press release, said consent not being unreasonably withheld. The PARTIES shall not make any other public statements about this AGREEMENT except as provided for in this Section.

b. Except as may be otherwise required by generally accepted accounting principles, regulatory requirements, or court order, the specific terms of this AGREEMENT shall be confidential. Notwithstanding the foregoing, the PARTIES acknowledge that HP is free to share the AGREEMENT with its suppliers on a confidential basis for purposes of seeking indemnification, and that the ACTIONS and the settlement thereof under the terms and conditions of this AGREEMENT may be material events to either or both INTERGRAPH and HP, and that each PARTY shall have the right to issue an appropriate press release and/or filing with the SEC disclosing the material provisions of this AGREEMENT. In addition, the PARTIES acknowledge and agree that the material terms of this AGREEMENT, and perhaps the AGREEMENT itself, might be subject to disclosure to the Court in the ACTIONS and agree that such disclosure shall not be considered a violation of this section.

8. CERTAIN REPRESENTATIONS, WARRANTIES AND DISCLAIMERS

a. INTERGRAPH represents and warrants to HP that it has the right to enter into this AGREEMENT, including but not limited to the grant of the rights and licenses granted herein, and including without limitation the right to license the INTERGRAPH PATENTS asserted in the ACTIONS, and that, as of the EFFECTIVE DATE, INTERGRAPH is not aware of any claims, demands or causes of action it or its SUBSIDIARIES could file or otherwise assert against HP or any of its SUBSIDIARIES or AFFILIATES other than the claims, demands, and causes of action that are released and discharged by this AGREEMENT. INTERGRAPH represents and warrants that IHTC, Intergraph GmbH, and Z/I Imaging Corporation are each a SUBSIDIARY, as that term is defined in this AGREEMENT, of Intergraph Corporation.

b. HP represents and warrants to INTERGRAPH that it has the right to enter into this AGREEMENT, including but not limited to the grant of the rights and licenses granted herein, and including without limitation the right to license the HP PATENTS asserted in the ACTIONS, and that, as of the EFFECTIVE DATE, HP is not aware of any claims, demands or causes of action it or its SUBSIDIARIES could file or otherwise assert against INTERGRAPH or any of its SUBSIDIARIES or AFFILIATES other than the claims, demands, and causes of action that are released and discharged by this AGREEMENT. HP represents and warrants that Hewlett-Packard Development Company and CPQ Holdings, Incorporated are both SUBSIDIARIES, as that term is defined in this AGREEMENT, of HP.

c. The PARTIES each warrant and represent that each has the authority to dispose of and/or grant rights with respect to the claims, suits, causes of action, rights and/or interests which are the subject matter hereto, and that such claims, suits, causes of action, rights and/or interests, in their entirety or any portion thereof, have not been assigned, transferred, sold or otherwise encumbered.

d. Nothing contained in this AGREEMENT is or shall be construed as: (i) a warranty or representation by either of the PARTIES to this AGREEMENT as to the validity, enforceability or scope of any of the INTERGRAPH PATENTS or the HP PATENTS; or (ii) a warranty or representation that any manufacture, sale, lease, use or other disposition of products will be free from infringement of any patent rights or other intellectual property rights of any third-party except with respect to the licenses granted pursuant to Section 4 of this AGREEMENT; or (iii) an obligation to furnish any technical or other information or know-how.

e. EXCEPT AS EXPRESSLY PROVIDED HEREIN, NEITHER PARTY MAKES ANY REPRESENTATIONS OR WARRANTIES, EXPRESS OR IMPLIED, REGARDING ANY MATTER, INCLUDING WITHOUT LIMITATIONS THE IMPLIED WARRANTIES OF MERCHANTABILITY, SUITABILITY, AND/OR FITNESS FOR A PARTICULAR USE OR PURPOSE.

f. LIMITATION OF LIABILITY. IN NO EVENT SHALL EITHER PARTY BE LIABLE FOR ANY SPECIAL, CONSEQUENTIAL, INDIRECT, OR INCIDENTAL DAMAGES, HOWEVER CAUSED, ON ANY THEORY OF

LIABILITY AND WHETHER OR NOT SUCH ENTITY HAS BEEN ADVISED OF THE POSSIBILITY OF SUCH DAMAGES ARISING OUT OF THIS AGREEMENT.

g. Each PARTY represents and warrants, on behalf of itself and its SUBSIDIARIES and AFFILIATES, that within the 30 days prior to the EFFECTIVE DATE neither it, nor any of its SUBSIDIARIES or AFFILIATES, have assigned patents to a third party.

9. MISCELLANEOUS PROVISIONS

a. This settlement is intended solely as a compromise of disputed claims. Neither the fact of entry into this AGREEMENT nor the terms hereof nor any acts undertaken pursuant hereto shall constitute an admission or concession of liability or of the validity of any claim or defense asserted in the ACTIONS. Neither the fact of entry into this AGREEMENT nor the terms hereof nor any acts undertaken pursuant hereto shall be offered or admitted in evidence in any legal proceeding other than to enforce rights and obligations relating to this AGREEMENT. This AGREEMENT is independent of, and shall remain unaffected by any and all rulings, findings, verdicts and/or judgments which are entered in all ACTIONS or any future actions, including, but not limited to, rulings, findings, verdicts and/or judgments, which relate to validity, enforceability and/or construction of the claims of any patents at issue in any of the ACTIONS listed in Appendix A.

b. Nothing contained in this AGREEMENT shall be construed as imposing any obligation to institute any suit or action for infringement of any patents, or to defend any suit or action brought by a third-party which challenges or concerns the validity or enforceability of any patents licensed under this AGREEMENT.

c. This AGREEMENT will not be binding until it has been signed below by all parties.

d. Nothing contained in this AGREEMENT shall be construed as an obligation to file any patent application or to secure any patent or to maintain any patent in force.

e. No express or implied waiver of any breach of any term, condition or obligation of this AGREEMENT shall be construed as a waiver of any subsequent breach of that term, condition or obligation or of any other term, condition or obligation of this AGREEMENT of the same or of a different nature.

f. Any failure to perform any obligation hereunder, except for the obligation to make payments hereunder, shall be excused to the extent such failure is caused by any controlling law, order, or regulation, or by any acts of war, acts of public enemies, fires, floods, acts of God, or any other contingency beyond the control of the PARTIES, but only so long as said law, order, regulation or contingency continues.

g. Nothing contained in this AGREEMENT shall be construed as conferring any right to use in advertising, publicity, or other promotional activities any name, trade name, trademark or other designation of either PARTY hereto and its SUBSIDIARIES (including any contraction, abbreviation or simulation of any of the foregoing).

h. This AGREEMENT shall be construed in accordance with and governed by the laws of the State of Delaware as applied to agreements entered into and fully performed therein by residents thereof, excluding conflict of laws principles thereof. However, in the event of a breach of this AGREEMENT, the exclusive venue for any and all litigation brought to enforce the AGREEMENT shall be The United States District Court, Eastern District of Texas, Marshall Division.

i. If any term, clause, or provision of this AGREEMENT shall be judged to be invalid, the validity of any other term, clause or provision shall not be affected; and such invalid term, clause or provision shall be replaced, if possible, by a valid term that reflects the intent of the PARTIES, or if such is not possible, shall be deemed deleted from this AGREEMENT.

j. This AGREEMENT is the result of negotiations between INTERGRAPH and HP, both of which have been represented by counsel during such negotiations; accordingly, this AGREEMENT shall not be construed for or against either PARTY.

k. This AGREEMENT sets forth the entire agreement and understanding as to the subject matter hereof and merges all prior discussions. Any modification to this AGREEMENT must be in writing and signed by Hewlett-Packard Company, Intergraph Corporation, and IHTC.

l. Hewlett-Packard Company, Intergraph Corporation, and IHTC shall each be responsible for the payment of its own tax liability, if any.

m. Three (3) originals of this AGREEMENT shall be fully executed.

n. This AGREEMENT and any counterpart original thereof may be executed and transmitted by facsimile or by emailed portable document format (".pdf") document. The facsimile and/or.pdf signature shall be valid and acceptable for all purposes as if it were an original. This AGREEMENT may be executed in multiple counterparts, each of which shall be deemed an original, but all of which together shall constitute one and the same instrument. In making proof of this AGREEMENT, it shall not be necessary to produce or account for more than one such counterpart.

10. NOTICES

All Notices that are required or that may be permitted to be given pursuant to the terms of this AGREEMENT shall be in writing and shall be sufficient in all respects if given in writing and delivered by courier, by facsimile, by registered mail or by certified mail, return receipt requested, as follows:

If to Intergraph Corp. or IHTC: Facsimile No.: (256) 730-2247 Intergraph Corporation Legal Department MS/HQ 034

Huntsville, AL 35894-0001 ATTN: General Counsel

With a copy to: Facsimile No.: (702) 966-4247 Intergraph Hardware Technologies Company 2215-B Renaissance Drive, Suite 14 Las Vegas, NV 89119 ATTN: Intellectual Property Manager

If to HP: Facsimile No.: (650) 857-5518

Hewlett-Packard Company 3000 Hanover Street Palo Alto, California 94304 ATTN: General Counsel

Any such Notices shall be effective upon receipt by the addressee. Changes of address for notice purposes shall be sent in accordance with the terms of this section.

IN WITNESS WHEREOF, the undersigned have caused this AGREEMENT to be executed by their duly authorized representatives.

Names and Titles

QUESTIONS

1. This is a cross-license agreement entered into in settlement of a patent infringement dispute. Do you think settlement agreement licenses are more or less likely to result in subsequent license breach claims than non-settlement agreement licenses?

2. What field of use is specifically prohibited to Intergraph? Why do you think this field of use was selected by HP for exclusion?

3. The license agreement provides that the cross-licenses are "non-cancelable" and "irrevocable." What is the difference between a license that is "non-cancelable" and one that is "irrevocable"? The license agreement also provides that the license is "fully paid-up" and "royalty free." What is the difference between a license that is "fully paid-up" and one that is "royalty free"? Is there a contract drafting lesson to be learned here?

4. What is an "Anti-Foundry" Provision"? Foundry issues involved in licenses are discussed in Section 2.3.2 — Grant Clauses.

5. Under the settlement license, HP will pay $141,135,000 to Intergraph. Does this suggest who had the superior bargaining position in the parties' respective patent infringement suits?

2.1.3 Biotechnology License

GENENTECH INC. — MEDIMMUNE INC.

This Agreement, dated as of June 4, 1997 is between Genentech, Inc., a Delaware corporation having a principal place of business at 460 Point San Bruno Blvd., South San Francisco, California 94080 (hereinafter "Genentech") and MedImmune, Inc. having a place of business at 35 West Watkins Road, Gaithersburg, Maryland 20878 (hereinafter "Licensee").

WHEREAS:

A. Genentech is the owner of certain patents and patent applications (patent rights) relating to methods and compositions in the field of immunoglobulins.

B. Genentech does not wish to have these patent rights hinder the development of immunoglobulin products and is willing to grant licenses for the development of products for public use and benefit as specified in this Agreement.

C. Licensee desires to obtain a license under the terms and conditions specified herein.

D. Genentech and Licensee believe that the subject matter of this license will be most effectively commercialized under conditions of limited exclusivity to encourage the investments required to develop and market such subject matter.

NOW, THEREFORE, the parties agree as follows:

Article I
DEFINITIONS

Unless otherwise specifically set forth herein, the following terms shall have the following meanings:

1.01. "Affiliate" of Licensee shall mean any entity that controls, is controlled by or is under common control with Licensee; and "control" for purposes of this definition shall mean the possession of the power to direct or cause the direction of the management and policies of an entity, whether through the ownership of voting stock, by contract or otherwise. In the case of a corporation, "control" shall mean the direct or indirect ownership of fifty percent (50%) or more of the outstanding voting stock together with a controlling membership on the board of directors of such corporation.

1.02. "Antigen" as used in this Agreement shall mean the respiratory syncytial virus (RSV) substance listed in Schedule A attached hereto and made a part of this Agreement. Schedule A may be amended from time to time by mutual agreement of the Parties in writing, at which time the financial terms pertaining to the newly added Antigen(s) may also be modified.

1.03. "Bulk Product" shall mean Licensed Product supplied in a form other than Finished Product which can be converted into Finished Product.

1.04. "Cost of Product" shall mean the cost of acquisition, if purchased, or the cost of manufacture, the latter being the sum of direct production costs and manufacturing overhead costs determined in accordance with generally accepted accounting principles.

1.05. "Designee" shall mean a person or entity designated by a Party to exercise the rights of and perform obligations hereunder in place of and to the exclusion of that Party in the Territory or a portion thereof.

1.06. "Effective Date" shall mean as to each Antigen, or Licensed Product based thereon, the later of the date of this Agreement or the date on which such Antigen was added to Schedule A by amendment.

1.07. "Field" shall mean the manufacture, use of sale of Licensed Product for the prevention or therapy of human diseases.

1.08. "Finished Product" shall mean any and all Licensed Products in form for use by an end user and not intended for further chemical or genetic manipulation or transformation.

1.09. "Licensed Patents" shall mean

(a) U.S. Patent No. 4,816,567 and the claims relating to chimeric antibodies found in patents or patent applications arising from divisionals, continuations or continuations-in-part of any application from which U.S. Patent No. 4,816,567 claims priority (excluding U.S.S.N. 07/205,419 and foreign counterparts thereof) as well as the foreign counterparts of the foregoing and any and all reissues, reexaminations or extensions of the foregoing ("Chimera Patents") and

(b) any patent issuing based on U.S.S.N. 07/205,419 (a continuation of the application maturing into U.S. Patent No. 4,816,567) relating to the coexpression of immunoglobulin chains in recombinant host cells, as well as the divisionals, continuations or continuations-in-part of such U.S.S.N. 07/205,419 the issued foreign counterparts of such U.S.S.N. 07/205,419 and any and all reissues, reexaminations or extensions of the foregoing ("Coexpression Patents"). Attached hereto as Schedule B is a list of patents and patent applications that Genentech in good faith believes represents Licensed Patents as of September 1, 1996. However no warranty is given as to the completeness or accuracy of Schedule B or any update thereof that might subsequently be provided to Licensee.

1.10. "Licensed Product(s)" shall mean the anti-RSV monoclonal antibody capable of binding to the Antigen listed in Schedule A hereto, the manufacture, use or sale of which substances would, if not licensed under this Agreement, infringe one or more claims of either or both of Chimera Patents or Coexpression Patents, which have neither expired nor been held invalid by a court or other body of competent jurisdiction from which no appeal has been or may be taken.

1.11. "Net Sales" shall mean the gross invoice or contract price to third party customers for Finished Products. Finished Products used or consumed by Licensee or its Affiliates or Designees as part of the delivery of services to customers shall be considered Net Sales at the gross invoice or contract price of like Finished Products which are sold to customers. If Licensed Product is sold in combination with one or more active ingredients, Net Sales shall be calculated by multiplying Net Sales of the combination product by the fraction $A/(A+B)$ where A is the sales price of the Finished Product in the combination when sold separately and B is the total sales price of all other active ingredients in the combination when sold separately. If the Finished Product and the other active ingredients are not sold separately, the percentage of the total cost of the combination product attributed to Cost of Product shall be multiplied times the sales price of the combination product to arrive at New Sales. For all Licensed Product used or consumed by others than Licensee, Licensee shall be entitled to deduct (CONFIDENTIAL TREATMENT REQUESTED) from Net Sales in lieu of all other deductions such as taxes, shipping charges, allowances and the like prior to calculating royalties due. Net Sales for Bulk Products shall be calculated by doubling the gross invoice or contract price of Bulk Products sold to non-affiliated customers. The method of calculating Net Sales of materials in form other than Finished Product or Bulk Product that can be converted into Finished Product shall be established by the parties prior to the first sale or transfer of any such material by Licensee to a non-affiliated third party.

1.12. "Party" shall mean Genentech or Licensee and when used in the plural shall mean Genentech and Licensee.

1.131 "Territory" shall mean the entire world.

Article II
GRANT

2.01. License. Subject to the fulfillment by Licensee of all the terms and conditions of this Agreement, Genentech hereby grants to Licensee and Licensee hereby accepts a co-exclusive license together with the right to sublicense its Affiliates and Designees under Licensed Patents for the term thereof to make, use and sell Licensed Products in the Field and the Territory. This grant shall be co-exclusive with Genentech, Inc., and additional licensees, if any, to be selected solely by Genentech. Genentech shall be free at its discretion to enter into agreements with such additional licensees at any time and on terms solely of its choosing. However, Genentech represents that, unless for a particular Antigen a different number of additional licenses is specified at the time such Antigen is included in Schedule A, it will not grant more than four (4) additional licenses in which both the Field and Territory are coextensive with that which is set forth herein.

2.02. Right to Appoint Designee. Licensee shall have the right to sublicense all of its rights hereunder for all or part of the Territory (including on a country-by-country basis) to a Designee of its choosing, to the exclusion of Licensee in such Territory or portion thereof, provided that Licensee agrees that it will indemnify Genentech for any failure of performance on the part of such Designee. An entity that simply acts to co-promote or to co-market Licensed Product supplied by Licensee shall not be considered a Designee and Licensee may co-promote or co-market such Licensed Product with such entity in a given country or countries, provided that (i) both Licensee and such entity obtain Licensed Products from the same manufacturing source, (ii) only one such entity shall be permitted to co-promote or co-market the same Licensed Product in a given country, and (iii) Licensee shall be responsible for the payment of royalties on Net Sales of Licensed Products by such entity and for all other acts of such entity as if such acts were those of the Licensee.

2.03. No Other License. Licensee understands and agrees that no license under any patent or application other than Licensed Patents is or shall be deemed to have been granted under this Agreement, either expressly or by implication.

2.04. Licenses Separately Available. Licensee acknowledges that separate licenses under Chimera Patents and Coexpression Patents were available from Genentech upon request prior to entering into this Agreement, but that for reasons of convenience the licenses have been combined in this Agreement. Licensee further acknowledges that it was not coerced to enter into a license under either one of Chimera or Coexpression Patents as a condition to obtaining a license under the other, and that the licenses hereunder were not offered as a mandatory package.

<h1 style="text-align:center">Article III
FEES AND ROYALTIES</h1>

3.01. License Grant Fee. Within thirty (30) days after execution of this Agreement or amendment of Schedule A to add an Antigen thereto, Licensee shall pay to Genentech a non-creditable, non-refundable license grant fee of ($X) per Antigen.

3.02. Minimum Annual Royalties. Licensee shall pay to Genentech a minimum annual royalty for each Antigen on or before January 31 of each year beginning with the third full calendar year after the Effective Date for such Antigen in accordance with the following table:

Full Calendar Year	Minimum Annual Royalty
3	($A)
4	($B)
5	($C)
6 and each subsequent year	($D)

Such payments shall be non-refundable but shall be creditable against earned royalties as provided in Section 3.05.

3.03. Earned Royalties.

(a) Licensee shall pay to Genentech a royalty of (X%) for Chimera Patents on Net Sales of Licensed Products sold by Licensee and its sublicensees.

(b) Licensee shall also pay to Genentech, if applicable, a royalty of (Y%) for Coexpression Patents on Net Sales of Licensed Products sold by Licensee.

(c) The royalties under this Article are cumulative. For example, for sales of Licensed Product falling within the scope of both Chimera Patents and Coexpression Patents in a given country, the royalty rate shall be a total of (X% + Y%).

3.04. Sales To and Between Sublicensees. No royalties shall be due upon sales of Licensed Products to and between Licensee, its Affiliates, its sublicensees, co-promoting parties or co-marketing parties as permitted under Section 2.02 for further sale; provided, however, that the royalty hereunder shall be payable upon the final sale by any of the foregoing to a non-affiliated vendee.

3.05. Credits Against Royalties.

(a) Licensee shall be entitled to reduce each earned royalty payment due under Section 3.03 for a given Antigen by up to fifty percent (50%) by applying as a one-time credit against such royalty (i) the minimum annual royalty paid for such Antigen for the calendar year for which earned royalties are then due and (ii) an amount equal to the cumulative payments previously made under Section 3.02 for the two (2) years immediately preceding the calendar year in which Licensee makes its first bona fide commercial sale in the United States, Japan or a country of the European Community of a particular Licensed Product for so long as is necessary to amortize such cumulative payments. Credits earned for one Antigen are not applicable to royalties due for other Antigens.

(b) Licensee may apply as a credit on a country-by-country basis against royalties owed to Genentech for any Licensed Product pursuant to Section 3.03(a) up to one-half of royalties actually paid during the relevant quarter to any third party for the same Licensed Product pursuant to a license agreement for the third party's patent rights covering such License Product, including royalties paid to the Medical Research Council with respect to valid and enforceable claims of United Kingdom Patent No. 2,188,638 or foreign counterparts thereof.

(c) Licensee may apply as a credit against royalties owed to Genentech for any Licensed Product pursuant to Section 3.03(b) royalties actually paid to Celltech during the relevant quarter for the same Licensed Product if a license under Celltech patents is required in order to make and sell such Licensed Product without infringing Celltech's patents.

(d) In no event shall the credits taken pursuant to subparagraphs (a), (b) and (c) of this Section 3.05 taken in the aggregate exceed fifty percent (50%) of the royalties owed to Genentech for any reporting quarter.

3.06. No Non-Monetary Consideration. Without the prior written consent of Genentech, Licensee and its Affiliates shall not solicit or accept any consideration for the sale of any Licensed Product other than as will be accurately reflected in Net Sales.

3.07. Most Favored Licensee. Should Genentech enter into a co-exclusive license with any other party after the Effective Date for the same Licensed Product and Field and any portion of the same Territory solely for monetary consideration, or monetary consideration coupled with the grant of rights as set forth in Section 2.03, and on financial terms more favorable than those set forth herein, Genentech shall notify Licensee and permit Licensee to substitute into this Agreement all of the terms of such other license that differ from those herein, including those that are less favorable.

Article IV
RECORDS, REPORTS AND PAYMENTS

4.01. Records Retention. Licensee shall keep and shall cause its sub-licensees to keep records of the sales of all Licensed Products in sufficient detail to permit Genentech to confirm the accuracy of Licensee's royalty calculations. At Genentech's request and expense, Licensee shall permit an independent certified public accountant appointed by Genentech and acceptable to Licensee to examine, upon reasonable notice and at reasonable times, such records solely to the extent necessary to verify Licensee's calculations. Such examination shall be limited to a period of time no more than three (3) years immediately preceding the request for examination. If Licensee's royalties are found to be in error such that royalties to Genetech were underpaid by more than five (5) percent then Licensee shall promptly pay any deficiency, plus interest at the prime rate, to Genentech and reimburse Genentech for its costs in examining such records.

4.02. Reports. Within sixty (60) days after the end of each calendar quarter following Licensee's or its sub-licensee's first sale of Licensed Product, Licensee shall furnish to Genentech a written report of all sales of Licensed Products subject to royalty under Section 3.03 during such calendar quarter. Such report shall include (i) the determination of Net Sales as specified in Section 1.11; (ii) detailed itemization of the credits taken pursuant to Section 3.05; and (iii) the royalty payment then due.

4.03. Payments. Concurrently with each report pursuant to Section 4.02, Licensee shall make the royalty payment then due. Payments shall be in United States dollars and, unless otherwise agreed in writing, shall be made by wire transfer to such bank as Genentech may from time to time designate in writing, without set-off and free and clear of and without any deduction or withholding for or on account of any taxes, duties, levies, imposts, fees or charges except for withholding required by tax authorities for income taxes on royalties actually payable to Genentech after application of the credits permitted by Sections 3.05. Licensee shall make any withholding payments due on behalf of Genentech and shall promptly provide Genentech with official tax receipts or other written documentation sufficient to enable Genentech to satisfy the United States tax authorities with respect to Genentech's application for a foreign tax credit for such payment.

4.04. Currency Conversion. Royalties due on Net Sales of Licensed Products made in currency other than United States dollars shall first be calculated in the foreign currency and then converted to United States dollars on the basis of the rate of exchange in effect for purchase of dollars published in the Wall Street Journal on the last business day of the period for which royalties are due.

Article V
LIABILITY

5.01. Indemnification. Licensee shall defend, indemnify and hold Genentech harmless against any and all liability, damage, loss, cost or expense resulting from any third party claim, suit or other action arising out of or based on the manufacture, use or sale of any Licensed Product by Licensee, its sub-licensees or co-promoting or co-marketing entities pursuant to Section 2.02; provided, however, that upon the filing of any such claim or suit, Genentech shall promptly notify Licensee and permit Licensee, at Licensee's cost, to handle and control such claim or suit and shall cooperate in the defense thereof.

Article VI
PATENT INFRINGEMENT

6.01. Notification of Infringement. Licensee shall notify Genentech of any infringement by third parties of any patent within Licensed Patents of which Licensee is aware and shall provide Genentech with the available evidence, if any, of such infringement.

6.02. Enforcement of Licensed Patents. Genentech shall retain the sole right, at its sole discretion and expense, to enforce Licensed Patents against third party infringers. However, if (i) a non-Affiliated third party which is not licensed under Chimera Patents or Coexpression Patents attains a market share of the greater of (a) at least (X%) of sales (in monetary volume) or (b) (Y%) in sales of a particular Licensed Product within the Field in any country, (ii) Licensee or its sub-licensee is selling the Licensed Product in such country, (iii) there is reasonable evidence that such third party is infringing either Chimera Patents or Coexpresson Patents under which Licensee is paying royalties, (iv) Licensee has paid and is not in arrears in the payment to Genentech of all royalties due under this Agreement and (v) Genentech fails to take action to abate the infringement within six (6) months after receipt of notice pursuant to Section 6.01, then Licensee shall be entitled to reduce the royalty rates to one half (½) of the rates otherwise set forth in Section 3.03 for the country in which the qualifying infringement exists. Such reduction shall continue until such time as Genentech takes action to abate the infringement or until the market share of such third party drops below (X%) of the total market or sales below (Y%) for that particular Licensed Product within the Field in the country in question. Royalties shall not be affected in countries in which such infringement is not occurring. Unlicensed infringing sales shall not affect the payment under Section 3.02 unless such sales constitute greater than (X%) of the market for such particular Licensed Product in all markets in which Licensee and its sub-licensees sell the Product, in which case the otherwise appropriate minimum shall be reduced by the percentage market share held by the unlicensed infringer. Genentech shall be entitled to recovery of all damages, costs and the like in any action brought under this Section 6.02.

6.03. No Warranty of Non-Infringement. Nothing in this Agreement shall be construed as a representation made or warranty given by Genentech that the practice by Licensee or its sub-licensees of the license granted hereunder will not infringe the patent rights of any third party.

Article VII
TERM AND TERMINATION

7.01. Term. This Agreement shall come into force as of its Effective Date and shall continue in full force and effect on a country-by-country basis unless earlier terminated as provided herein or until the expiration of the last to expire of the Licensed Patents.

7.02. Termination for Breach. Genentech shall have the right to terminate this Agreement and the licenses granted hereunder upon thirty (30) days' written notice to Licensee for Licensee's material breach of this Agreement if Licensee has failed to cure such breach within thirty (30) days of notice thereof.

7.03. Insolvency. Either Party may terminate this Agreement if, at any time, the other Party shall file in any court pursuant to any statute of any individual state or country, a petition in bankruptcy, insolvency or for reorganization or for an agreement among creditors or for the appointment of a receiver or trustee of the Party or of its assets, or if the other Party proposes a written agreement of composition or extension of its debts, or if the other Party shall be served with an involuntary petition against it filed in any insolvency proceeding, and such petition shall not be dismissed within sixty (60) days after the filing thereof, or if the other party shall propose or be a Party to any dissolution or liquidation, or if the other party shall make an assignment for the benefit of creditors.

7.04. Termination by Licensee. Licensee may terminate this Agreement in its entirety or with respect to one or more Antigens at any time upon six (6) months' written notice to Genentech.

7.05. Effect of Termination. Termination of this Agreement in whole or in part for any reason shall not relieve Licensee of its obligations to pay all fees and royalties that shall have accrued hereunder prior to the effective date of termination. Termination of this Agreement as to Licensee shall result in the termination of the licenses of Licensee and all sub-licensees of Licensee. The provisions of Sections 2.04 and 3.08 shall survive termination of the Agreement for any reason except termination for breach by Genentech.

Article VIII
MISCELLANEOUS PROVISIONS

8.01. Limitations on Assignments. Neither this Agreement nor any interests hereunder shall be assignable by either Party without the written consent of the other; provided, however, that either Party may assign this Agreement to any corporation or entity with which it may merge or consolidate, or to which it may transfer substantially all of its assets or all of its assets to which this Agreement relates without obtaining the consent of the other Party.

8.02. Jurisdiction and Choice of Laws. This Agreement shall be interpreted and construed under the laws of California, and Licensee agrees to submit to the jurisdiction of California.

8.03. Relationship of the Parties. Nothing in this Agreement is intended or shall be deemed to constitute a partnership, agency, employer-employee, or joint venture relationship between the Parties.

8.04. Further Acts and Instruments. Each Party hereto agrees to execute, acknowledge and deliver such further instruments and to do all such other acts as may be necessary or appropriate to effect the purpose and intent of this Agreement.

8.05. Entire Agreement. This Agreement constitutes and contains the entire agreement of the parties and supersedes any and all prior negotiations, correspondence, understandings and agreements between the Parties respecting the subject matter hereof. This Agreement may be amended or modified or one or more provisions thereof waived only by a written instrument signed by the Parties.

8.06. Severability. If in any jurisdiction any one or more of the provisions of this Agreement should for any reason be held by any court of authority having jurisdiction over this Agreement or any of the parties hereto to be invalid, illegal or unenforceable, such provision or provisions shall be validly reformed to as nearly approximate the intent of the Parties as possible and if unreformable, the Parties shall meet to discuss what steps should be taken to remedy the situation; in other jurisdictions, this Agreement shall not be affected.

8.07. Captions. The captions to this Agreement are for convenience only and are to be of no force or effect in construing and interpreting the provisions of this Agreement.

8.08. WARRANTIES. The Parties represent and warrant that they have the power to enter into this agreement. OTHERWISE, THE PARTIES EXPRESSLY DISCLAIM ALL WARRANTIES, EXPRESS OR IMPLIED, INCLUDING WITHOUT LIMITATION WARRANTIES OF MERCHANTABILITY, FITNESS FOR A PARTICULAR PURPOSE, OR NON-INFRINGEMENT.

8.09. Notices. Any notice, request, approval or other document required or permitted to be given under this Agreement shall be in writing and shall be deemed to have been sufficiently given when delivered in person, transmitted by telex, telecopier, telegraph or deposited in the mail, postage requested, addressed as follows:

If to Licensee, addressed to:

MedImmune, Inc.
35 West Watkins Mill Road
Gaithersburg, MD 20878
Attn.: Chief Executive Officer

If to Genentech, addressed to:

Genentech, Inc.
460 Point San Bruno Boulevard
South San Francisco, CA 94080
Attn.: Corporate Secretary

or to such other address or addresses as may be specified from time to time in a written notice.

8.10. Wire Transfer of Funds. Unless otherwise specified in writing, all payments by Licensee required hereunder shall be made by wire transfer at the direction of Genentech.

IN WITNESS WHEREOF, Genentech and Licensee have caused this Agreement to be executed by their duly authorized representatives.

Names: Titles

SCHEDULE A
Antigens

Antigens expressed by respiratory syncytial virus as described by Kenneth McIntosh and Robert M. Chanock in Virology Second Edition, pp. 1045–1067, edited by B.N. Fields, D. M. Knipe et al. Raven Press, Ltd., New York 1990 and Antigens expressed by respiratory syncytial virus as described by Peter Collins, Kenneth McIntosh and Robert M. Chanock in Virology Third Edition, pp. 1313–1351, edited by B.N. Fields, D. M. Knipe et al. Lippencott-Raven Publishers, Philadelphia 1996.

SCHEDULE B
Patents and Patent Applications

Country	Appln. Dt	Appln. No.	Patent No.	Patent Date
Australia	04/04/84	26429/84	598441	10/15/90
Austria	04/06/84	84302368.0	EPO125023	06/05/91
Belgium	04/06/84	84302368.0	EPO125023	06/05/91
Canada	04/09/84	451580	1218613	03/03/87
Denmark	04/05/84	1796/84		
European	04/06/84	84302368.0	EPO125023	06/05/91
France	04/06/84	84302368.0	EPO125023	06/05/91
Germany	04/06/84	84302368.0	P3484664.6	06/05/91
Great Britain	04/06/84	84302368.0	EPO125023	06/05/91
Ireland	04/05/84	840/84	57198	09/18/92
Israel	04/06/84	71455	71455	11/27/94
Italy	04/06/84	84302368.0	EPO125023	06/05/91
Japan	04/06/84	69874/84		
Japan	04/06/84	241576/94		
Luxembourg	04/06/84	84302368.0	EPO125023	06/05/91
Netherlands	04/06/84	84302368.0	EPO125023	06/05/91
New Zealand	04/04/84	207746	207746	10/11/91
South Africa	04/05/84	84/2583	84/2583	11/28/84
Spain	04/06/84	531372	531372	09/09/85
Sweden	04/06/84	84302368.0	EPO125023	06/15/91
Switzerland	04/06/84	84302368.0	P125023-1	06/05/91
United States	04/08/83	483457	4816567	03/28/89
United States	04/08/83	07/205419		
Australia	04/04/84	52013/90	639910	12/06/93
Denmark	04/05/84	1262/92	170895	03/04/96
Israel	04/06/84	99507	99507	07/02/95
New Zealand	04/04/84	222542	222542	08/20/91

QUESTIONS

1. Does the license agreement address the question of licensee challenges to the validity of the licensed patents? Does the license agreement address the question of the consequences of a finding that the licensed patents are invalid? These questions are considered in Section 2.2.4 — Licensee Estoppel.

Additional Information

1. ROBERT GOLDSCHEIDER, 1 ECKSTROM'S LICENSING §§ 4:28, 5:11–5:12, 5:24, 5:26, 5:29, 5:30, 5:34–5:53, 5:59–5:66, 5:68, 5:81, 7:20, 12:48–12:50, 14:23, 15:3 (2011).

2.   MORTON MOSKIN (ED.), JONATHAN E. MOSKIN, I FRED KOENIGSBERG, COMM. CONT. STRATEGIES DRAFTING & NEGOTIAION § 20:11 (2011).

3.   MICHAEL A. EPSTEIN, FRANK L. POLITANO, MICHAEL J. LENNON, DRAFTING LICENSE AGREEMENTS §§ 16.02–16.03 (2011).

4.   RICHARD RAYSMAN, PETER BROWN, COMPUTER LAW: DRAFTING AND NEGOTIATION FORMS §§ 5B.12–5B.13 (2011).

5.   RICHARD RAYSMAN ET. AL., INTELLECTUAL PROPERTY LICENSING FORMS AND ANALYSIS §§ 6.10–6.11 (2011).

6.   GARY M. LAWRENCE, CARL BARANOWSKI, REPRESENTING HIGH TECH COMPANIES § 7.16 (2011).

7.   RICHARD RAYSMAN, PETER BROWN, JEFFREY D. NEUBURGER, EMERGING TECH § 8.14 (2010).

8.   TED A. DONNER, ATTORNEY'S PRACTICE GUIDE TO NEGOTIATIONS § 41:4 (2010).

9.   CORP. COUNSEL'S GUIDE TO INTEL. PROP. § 21:3 (2010).

10. JOHN W. SCHLICHER, 1 PATENT LAW, LEGAL AND ECONOMIC PRINCIPLES § 2:51 (2d ed.) (2011).

11. JOHN W. SCHLICHER, 2 PATENT LAW, LEGAL AND ECONOMIC PRINICPLES (2d ed.) §§ 11:25, 12:10 (2011).

12. Mark S. Holmes, *Specimen Provisions From Patent License Agreements*, 979 PLI/PAT 195 (2009).

13. Peter J. Kinsella, *Hidden Risks in Patent License Agreements*, 1037 PLI/PAT 297 (2011).

14. Gerard deBlasi, *Patent & Technology Licensing: An Overview*, 879 PLI/PAT (2006).

15. Christian H. Nadan, *Software Licensing in the 21st Century: Are Software "Licenses" Really Sales and How Will the Software Industry Respond*, 858 PLI/PAT 261 (2006).

16. Darius Kharabi, *A Real Options Analysis of Pharmaceutical-Biotechnology Licensing*, 11 STAN. J.L. BUS. & FIN. 201 (2006).

2.2   RIGHTS OF LICENSORS AND LICENSEES

This section considers general principles of licensing law and how they affect the rights of licensors and licensees. Covered in this section are the scope of licensor rights, patent licenses and contract law, implied licenses, licensee estoppel, co-owner licenses, license breach and remedies, effect of patent invalidity on licenses, licensee standing to sue for infringement and license patent misuse. The following section considers the terms included in typical licenses.

2.2.1 Scope of Licensor Rights

As noted earlier, patent licensors can limit licenses in many different ways. One of the most common license limitations is on the way in which the licensed patent may be used. Subdividing patent rights into discrete fields of use and entering into separate licensing agreements in each field has many advantages. For example, if one field of use is a low-demand market (because there are many available substitute technologies) while another field of use is a high-demand market (because there are few or no available substitute technologies), then entering into separate licensing agreements in each field will allow the licensor to maximize its return on the investment in the patent by charging a lower royalty rate in the low-demand market and a higher royalty rate in the high-demand market. *See* JOHN W. SCHLICHER, PATENT LAW, LEGAL AND ECONOMIC PRINCIPLES § 11:34 (2d ed. 2008); Thomas C. Meyers, *Field of Use Restrictions as Procompetitive Elements in Patent and Know-How Licensing Agreements in the United States and European Community*, 12 NW. J. INT'L L. & BUS. 364 (1991).

Subdividing patent rights into discrete fields of use also allows the licensor to distinguish the strengths and weaknesses of different licensees. For example, a licensee who has a significant presence in one market with a high-level capability to promote and distribute the patented invention in that market might have little presence and few resources in another market. In this case, the licensor could determine which licensee is best suited to exploit the patented invention in which markets. Another situation in which a licensor might want to subdivide patent rights into discrete fields of use is when the licensor desires to retain the right to exploit the patented invention in one market but not others. It is important to note here that if the licensor grants an exclusive, unrestricted field-of-use license, any practice of the patent by the licensor will constitute a breach of the license agreement. The *General Talking Pictures* case below is an example of a licensor who desired to license its patents for one market application while reserving its right to exploit its patents in another application. The *Mallinckrodt* case that follows deals with another type of license restriction imposed by a licensor on the use of a patented product — a single-use restriction.

Restrictions imposed by a patent owner on the use of its patented product will have commercial consequences within the product market and can raise questions of anti-competitive behavior and possible violations of the antitrust laws. There is a continual tension between the rights granted to patentees under the Patent Act, the freedom of parties to negotiate private contracts, and the laws designed to promote market competition. As you read these two cases, consider how the courts have endeavored to balance these competing interests.

GENERAL TALKING PICTURES CORPORATION v.
WESTERN ELECTRIC COMPANY
304 U.S. 175 (1938)

Mr. Justice Butler delivered the opinion of the Court.

Three suits were brought by respondents against petitioner in the District Court for the Southern District of New York to restrain infringements, based on different patents for inventions in vacuum tube amplifiers which have been used in wire and radio telephony, talking motion pictures, and other fields. In all there were in suit seven patents. The cases were tried together and are treated as one. The lower courts held one of the patents invalid, and that ruling is not challenged here. They concurred in holding six of the patents valid and infringed by petitioner. This Court granted a writ of certiorari.

Under the caption "Questions Presented" the petition for writ of certiorari submits the following:

1. Can the owner of a patent, by means thereof, restrict the use made of a device manufactured under the patent, after the device has passed into the hands of a purchaser in the ordinary channels of trade, and full consideration paid therefore?

2. Can a patent owner, merely by a "license notice" attached to a device made under the patent, and sold in the ordinary channels of trade, place an enforceable restriction on the purchaser thereof as to the use to which the purchaser may put the device?

The brief supporting the petition contains specifications of error relating to decision of two other questions. One is whether, by acceptance and retention of royalties paid by the licensed manufacturer, respondents acquiesced in the infringement and are estopped from maintaining the suit. The other is whether the patents upheld are invalid because of anticipation by, or want of invention over, the prior patented art. That brief is confined to the three questions definitely stated in the petition. But petitioner's brief on the merits extends to the additional questions reflected by the specification of errors.

The respondent American Telephone & Telegraph Company owns the patents. Amplifiers having these inventions are used in different fields. One, known as the commercial field, includes talking picture equipment for theaters. Another, called the private field, embraces radio broadcast reception, radio amateur reception, and radio experimental reception. The other respondents are subsidiaries of the Telephone Company and exclusive licensees in the commercial field of recording and reproducing sound; during the time of the infringement alleged, they were engaged in making and supplying to theaters talking picture equipment including amplifiers embodying the inventions covered by the patents in suit. The petitioner also furnished to theaters talking picture equipment including amplifiers which embody the invention covered by the patents in suit. Respondents' charge is that by so doing petitioner infringes them.

The American Transformer Company was one of a number of manufacturers holding nonexclusive licenses limited to the manufacture and sale of the amplifiers for private use, as distinguished from commercial use. These licenses were granted by the Radio Corporation, acting for itself and the respondent Telephone Company, and were assented to by the latter. The Transformer Company's license was expressly confined to the right to manufacture and sell the patented amplifiers for radio amateur reception, radio experimental reception, and home broadcast reception. It had no right to sell the amplifiers for use in theaters as a part of talking picture equipment.

Nevertheless, it knowingly did sell the amplifiers in controversy to petitioner for that use. Petitioner admits that the Transformer Company knew that the amplifiers it sold to petitioner were to be used in the motion picture industry. The petitioner, when purchasing from the Transformer Company for that use, had actual knowledge that the latter had no license to make such a sale. In compliance with a requirement of the license, the Transformer Company affixed to amplifiers sold by it under the license a notice stating in substance that the apparatus was licensed only for radio amateur, experimental and broadcast reception under the patents in question. To the amplifiers sold to petitioner outside the scope of the license, it also affixed notices in the form described, but they were intended by both parties to be disregarded.

Petitioner puts its first question in affirmative form: "The owner of a patent cannot, by means of the patent, restrict the use made of a device manufactured under the patent after the device has passed into the hands of a purchaser in the ordinary channels of trade and full consideration paid therefore." But that proposition ignores controlling facts. The patent owner did not sell to petitioner the amplifiers in question or authorize the Transformer Company to sell them or any amplifiers for use in theaters or any other commercial use. The sales made by the Transformer Company to petitioner were outside the scope of its license and not under the patent. Both parties knew that fact at the time of the transactions. There is no ground for the assumption that petitioner was "a purchaser in the ordinary channels of trade."

The Transformer Company was not an assignee; it did not own the patents or any interest in them; it was a mere licensee under a nonexclusive license, amounting to no more than "a mere waiver of the right to sue." Pertinent words of the license are these: "To manufacture * * * and to sell only for radio amateur reception, radio experimental reception and radio broadcast reception. * * *" Patent owners may grant licenses extending to all uses or limited to use in a defined field. Unquestionably, the owner of a patent may grant licenses to manufacture, use, or sell upon conditions not inconsistent with the scope of the monopoly. There is here no attempt on the part of the patent owner to extend the scope of the monopoly beyond that contemplated by the patent statute. There is no warrant for treating the sales of amplifiers to petitioner as if made under the patents or the authority of their owner.

The Transformer Company could not convey to petitioner what both knew it was not authorized to sell. By knowingly making the sales to petitioner outside the scope of its license, the Transformer Company infringed the patents embodied in the amplifiers. Petitioner, having with knowledge of the facts bought at sales constituting infringement, did itself infringe the patents embodied in the amplifiers when it leased them for use as talking picture equipment in theaters. Petitioner at the time it bought the amplifiers knew that the sales constituted infringement of the patents embodied in them, petitioner's second question, as to effect of the license notice, need not be considered.

Affirmed.

Mr. Justice Roberts, Mr. Justice Cardozo, and Mr. Justice Reed took no part in the consideration or decision of this case.

Mr. Justice Black, dissenting.

QUESTIONS

1. Does the holding in *General Talking Pictures* expand the patent owner's rights (monopoly)?

2. Is the holding in *General Talking Pictures* inconsistent with ownership rights in real and personal property?

3. The American Transformer Company had a nonexclusive license to manufacture and sell amplifiers in the private use market. How did this affect the Court's analysis?

4. What difference did it make that General Talking Pictures had actual knowledge of American Talking Pictures limited nonexclusive license?

MALLINCKRODT v. MEDIPART
976 F.2d 700 (Fed. Cir. 1992)

Pauline Newman, Circuit Judge.

This action for patent infringement and inducement to infringe relates to the use of a patented medical device in violation of a "single use only" notice that accompanied the sale of the device. Mallinckrodt sold its patented device to hospitals, which after initial use of the devices sent them to Medipart for servicing that enabled the hospitals to use the device again. Mallinckrodt claimed that Medipart thus induced infringement by the hospitals and itself infringed the patent.

The district court held that violation of the "single use only" notice cannot be remedied by suit for patent infringement, and granted summary judgment of non-infringement. The district court did not decide whether the form of the "single use only" notice was legally sufficient to constitute a license or condition of sale from Mallinckrodt to the hospitals. Nor did the district court decide whether any deficiencies in the "single use only" notice were cured by Mallinckrodt's attempted subsequent notice, the release of which was enjoined by the district court on the ground that it would harm Medipart's business. Thus there was no ruling on whether, if the initial notice was legally defective as a restrictive notice, such defect was cured in the subsequent notice. The district court also specifically stated that it was not deciding whether Mallinckrodt could enforce this notice under contract law. These aspects are not presented on this appeal, and the factual premises were not explored at the summary judgment proceeding from which this appeal is taken.

Instead, the district court held that no restriction whatsoever could be imposed under the patent law, whether or not the restriction was enforceable under some other law, and whether or not this was a first sale to a purchaser with notice. This ruling is incorrect, for if Mallinckrodt's restriction was a valid condition of the sale, then in accordance with *General Talking Pictures Corp. v. Western Electric Co*, it was not excluded from enforcement under the patent law.

On review of these issues in the posture in which the case reaches us:

1. The movant Medipart did not dispute actual notice of the restriction. Thus we do not decide whether the form of the restriction met the legal requirements of notice or sufficed as a "label license," as Mallinckrodt calls it, for those questions were not presented on this motion for summary judgment.

2. Nor do we decide whether Mallinckrodt's enjoined subsequent notice cured any flaws in the first notice, for that issue was not reached by the district court.

We conclude, however, on Mallinckrodt's appeal of the grant of this injunction, that the notice was improperly enjoined.

3. We also conclude that the district court misapplied precedent in holding that there can be no restriction on use imposed as a matter of law, even on the first purchaser. The restriction here at issue does not *per se* violate the doctrine of patent misuse or the antitrust law. Use in violation of a valid restriction may be remedied under the patent law, provided that no other law prevents enforcement of the patent.

4. The district court's misapplication of precedent also led to an incorrect application of the law of repair/reconstruction, for if reuse is established to have been validly restricted, then even repair may constitute patent infringement.

BACKGROUND

The patented device is an apparatus for delivery of radioactive or therapeutic material in aerosol mist form to the lungs of a patient, for diagnosis and treatment of pulmonary disease. Radioactive material is delivered primarily for image scanning in diagnosis of lung conditions. Therapeutic agents may be administered to patients suffering various lung diseases.

The device is manufactured by Mallinckrodt, who sells it to hospitals as a unitary kit that consists of a "nebulizer" which generates a mist of the radioactive material or the prescribed drug, a "manifold" that directs the flow of oxygen or air and the active material, a filter, tubing, a mouthpiece, and a nose clip. In use, the radioactive material or drug is placed in the nebulizer, is atomized, and the patient inhales and exhales through the closed system. The device traps and retains any radioactive or other toxic material in the exhalate. The device fits into a lead-shielded container that is provided by Mallinckrodt to minimize exposure to radiation and for safe disposal after use.

The device is marked with the appropriate patent numbers, and bears the trademarks "Mallinckrodt" and "UltraVent" and the inscription "Single Use Only." The package insert provided with each unit states "For Single Patient Use Only" and instructs that the entire contaminated apparatus be disposed of in accordance with procedures for the disposal of biohazardous waste. The hospital is instructed to seal the used apparatus in the radiation-shielded container prior to proper disposal. The hospitals whose activities led to this action do not dispose of the UltraVent apparatus, or limit it to a single use.

Instead, the hospitals ship the used manifold/nebulizer assemblies to Medipart, Inc. Medipart in turn packages the assemblies and sends them to Radiation Sterilizers Inc., who exposes the packages to at least 2.5 megarads of gamma radiation, and returns them to Medipart. Medipart personnel then check each assembly for damage and leaks, and place the assembly in a plastic bag together with a new filter, tubing, mouthpiece, and nose clip. The "reconditioned" units, as Medipart calls them, are shipped back to the hospitals from whence they came. Neither Radiation Sterilizers nor Medipart tests the reconditioned units for any residual biological activity or for radioactivity. The assemblies still bear the inscription "Single Use Only" and the trademarks "Mallinckrodt" and "UltraVent."

Mallinckrodt filed suit against Medipart, asserting patent infringement and inducement to infringe. Mallinckrodt also asserted other counts including trademark infringement, unfair competition under section 43(a) of the Lanham Trademark Act, and violation of Illinois unfair competition statutes. Both parties moved for summary judgment on all counts.

The district court granted Medipart's motion on the patent infringement counts, holding that the "Single Use Only" restriction could not be enforced by suit for patent infringement. The court also held that Medipart's activities were permissible repair, not impermissible reconstruction, of the patented apparatus. The court reserved for trial Mallinckrodt's counts of trademark infringement and unfair competition, and entered final judgment on the patent aspects in accordance with Fed.R.Civ.P. 54(b).

The district court also enjoined Mallinckrodt *pendente lite* from distributing a new notice to its hospital customers. The proposed new notice emphasized the "Single Use Only" restriction and stated that the purpose of this restriction is to protect the hospital and its patients from potential adverse consequences of reconditioning, such as infectious disease transmission, material instability, and/or decreased diagnostic performance; that the UltraVent device is covered by certain patents; that the hospital is licensed under these patents to use the device only once; and that reuse of the device would be deemed infringement of the patents.

Mallinckrodt appeals the grant of summary judgment on the infringement issue, and the grant of the preliminary injunction.

I. THE RESTRICTION ON REUSE

Mallinckrodt describes the restriction on reuse as a label license for a specified field of use, wherein the field is single (*i.e.*, disposable) use. On this motion for summary judgment, there was no issue of whether this form of license gave notice of the restriction. Notice was not disputed. Nor was it disputed that sale to the hospitals was the first sale of the patented device. The issue that the district court decided on summary judgment was the enforceability of the restriction by suit for patent infringement. The court's premise was that even if the notice was sufficient to constitute a valid condition of sale, violation of that condition cannot be remedied under the patent law.

Mallinckrodt states that the restriction to single patient use is valid and enforceable under the patent law because the use is within the scope of the patent grant, and the restriction does not enlarge the patent grant. Mallinckrodt states that a license to less than all uses of a patented article is well recognized and a valid practice under patent law, and that such license does not violate the antitrust laws and is not patent misuse. Mallinckrodt also states that the restriction here imposed is reasonable because it is based on health, safety, efficacy, and liability considerations and violates no public policy. Thus Mallinckrodt argues that the restriction is valid and enforceable under the patent law. Mallinckrodt concludes that use in violation of the restriction is patent infringement, and that the district court erred in holding otherwise.

Medipart states that the restriction is unenforceable, for the reason that "the *Bauer* trilogy and *Motion Picture Patents* clearly established that *no* restriction is enforceable under patent law upon a purchaser of a sold article." (Medipart's emphasis). The district court so held. The district court also held that since the hospitals purchased the device from the patentee, not from a manufacturing licensee, no restraint on the use of the device could lawfully be imposed under the patent law.

The district court described the cases sustaining field of use and other restrictions as "in tension" with the cases prohibiting restrictions such as price-fixing and tying, and with the cases holding that the patent right is exhausted with the first sale. The court stated that policy considerations require that no conditions be imposed on patented goods after their sale and that Mallinckrodt's restriction could not "convert[ ] what was in substance a sale into a license." As we shall discuss, on the premises of this summary judgment motion the court erred in its analysis of the law, for not all restrictions on the use of patented goods are unenforceable.

The enforceability of restrictions on the use of patented goods derives from the patent grant, which is in classical terms of property: the right to exclude. 35 U.S.C. § 154. "Every patent shall contain . . . a grant . . . for the term of seventeen years . . . of the right to exclude others from making, using, or selling the invention throughout the United States . . . ."

This right to exclude may be waived in whole or in part. The conditions of such waiver are subject to patent, contract, antitrust, and any other applicable law, as well as equitable considerations such as are reflected in the law of patent misuse.

As in other areas of commerce, private parties may contract as they choose, provided that no law is violated thereby:

> [T]he rule is, with few exceptions, that any conditions which are not in their very nature illegal with regard to this kind of property, imposed by the patentee and agreed to by the licensee for the right to manufacture or use or sell the [patented] article, will be upheld by the courts.

The district court's ruling that Mallinckrodt's restriction on reuse was unenforceable was an application of the doctrine of patent misuse, although the court declined to use that designation. The concept of patent misuse arose to restrain practices that did not in themselves violate any law, but that drew anticompetitive strength from the patent right, and thus were deemed to be contrary to public policy. The policy purpose was to prevent a patentee from using the patent to obtain market benefit beyond that which inheres in the statutory patent right.

The district court's holding that Mallinckrodt's restriction to single patient use was unenforceable was, as we have remarked, based on "policy" considerations. The district court relied on a group of cases wherein resale price-fixing of patented goods was held illegal. These cases established that price-fixing and tying restrictions accompanying the sale of patented goods were *per se* illegal. These cases did not hold, and it did not follow, that all restrictions accompanying the sale of patented goods were deemed illegal. In *General Talking Pictures* the Court, discussing restrictions on use, summarized the state of the law as follows:

> That a restrictive license is legal seems clear. As was said in *United States v. General Electric Co.*, the patentee may grant a license "upon any condition the performance of which is reasonably within the reward which the patentee by the grant of the patent is entitled to secure . . . ."

The UltraVent device was manufactured by the patentee; but the sale to the hospitals was the first sale and was with notice of the restriction. Medipart offers neither law, public policy, nor logic, for the proposition that the enforceability of a restriction to a particular use is determined by whether the purchaser acquired the device from a manufacturing licensee or from a manufacturing patentee. We decline to make a distinction for which there appears to be no foundation. Indeed, Mallinckrodt has pointed out how easily such a criterion could be circumvented. That the viability of a restriction should depend on how the transaction is structured [has been] denigrated as "formalistic line drawing."

Restrictions on use are judged in terms of their relation to the patentee's right to exclude from all or part of the patent grant; and where an anticompetitive effect is asserted, the rule of reason is the basis of determining the legality of the provision. In *Windsurfing International, Inc. v. AMF, Inc.*, this court stated:

> To sustain a misuse defense involving a licensing arrangement not held to have been *per se* anticompetitive by the Supreme Court, a factual determination must reveal that the overall effect of the license tends to restrain competition unlawfully in an appropriately defined relevant market.

In support of its ruling, the district court also cited a group of cases in which the Court considered and affirmed the basic principles that unconditional sale of a patented device exhausts the patentee's right to control the purchaser's use of the device; and that the sale of patented goods, like other goods, can be conditioned. The principle of exhaustion of the patent right did not turn a conditional sale into an unconditional one.

Viewing the entire group of early cases, it appears that the Court simply applied, to a variety of factual situations, the rule of contract law that sale may be conditioned, and its kindred cases do not stand for the proposition that no restriction or condition may be placed upon the sale of a patented article. It was error for the district court to derive that proposition from the precedent. Unless the condition violates some other law or policy (in the patent field, notably the misuse or antitrust law, private parties retain the freedom to contract concerning conditions of sale. As we have discussed, the district court cited the price-fixing and tying cases as reflecting what the court deemed to be the correct policy, *viz.*, that no condition can be placed on the sale of patented goods, for any reason. However, this is not a price-fixing or tying case, and the *per se* antitrust and misuse violations found in the *Bauer* trilogy and *Motion Picture Patents* are not here present. The appropriate criterion is whether Mallinckrodt's restriction is reasonably within the patent grant, or whether the patentee has ventured beyond the patent grant and into behavior having an anticompetitive effect not justifiable under the rule of reason.

Should the restriction be found to be reasonably within the patent grant, *i.e.*, that it relates to subject matter within the scope of the patent claims, that ends the inquiry. However, should such inquiry lead to the conclusion that there are anticompetitive effects extending beyond the patentee's statutory right to exclude, these effects do not automatically impeach the restriction. Anticompetitive effects that are not *per se* violations of law are reviewed in accordance with the rule of reason. Patent owners should not be in a worse position, by virtue of the patent right to exclude, than owners of other property used in trade.

We conclude that the district court erred in holding that the restriction on reuse was, as a matter of law, unenforceable under the patent law. If the sale of the UltraVent was validly conditioned under the applicable law such as the law governing sales and licenses, and if the restriction on reuse was within the scope of the patent grant or otherwise justified, then violation of the restriction may be remedied by action for patent infringement. The grant of summary judgment is reversed, and the cause is remanded.

II. REPAIR AND RECONSTRUCTION

Even an unconditioned sale of a patented device is subject to the prohibition against "reconstruction" of the thing patented. A purchaser's right to use a patented device does not extend to reconstructing it. However, repair is permissible. Although the rule is straightforward its implementation is less so, for it is not always clear where the boundary lies: how much "repair" is fair before the device is deemed reconstructed.

Mallinckrodt charged, as an alternative ground of relief, that this prohibition was violated by Medipart's "reconditioning" of the used UltraVent devices. Medipart argued that it was merely cleaning the spent assemblies and replacing minor components. The district court found that Medipart's activities were "in the nature of repair not reconstruction. However, should Mallinckrodt's restriction on reuse be sustained on remand, then Mallinckrodt must prevail on this issue as a matter of law. If the UltraVent device is validly licensed for only a single use, any reuse is unlicensed and an infringement, and there is no need to choose between repair and reconstruction:

> The reconstruction-repair distinction is decisive, however, only when the replacement is made in a structure whose original manufacture and sale have been licensed by the patentee . . .; when the structure is unlicensed . . . the traditional rule is that even repair constitutes infringement.

This rule is dispositive if it is determined that the sale of the UltraVent device was accompanied by a valid restriction to single patient use, for "the traditional rule" is that even repair of an unlicensed device constitutes infringement. It follows that the district court's holding that the reconditioning was permissible repair is mooted, and is vacated.

III. THE INJUNCTION

The district court enjoined Mallinckrodt from issuing a new notice that stated, *inter alia*, that violation of the single patient use restriction would be deemed patent infringement.

A patentee that has a good faith belief that its patents are being infringed violates no protected right when it so notifies infringers:

> Patents would be of little value if infringers of them could not be notified of the consequences of infringement or proceeded against in the courts. Such action, considered by itself cannot be said to be illegal.

Although Medipart argues that Mallinckrodt is motivated by its commercial interest in selling new UltraVent units, and we have no doubt that all these parties' motivations are commercial, Mallinckrodt's position that infringement exists was not asserted to be in bad faith. Infringement notices have been enjoined when the patentee acted in bad faith, for example by making threats without intending to file suit, or when the patentee sent notices indiscriminately to all members of the trade, or when the patentee had no good faith belief in the validity of its patent. None of these circumstances is here asserted.

In granting the injunction, the district court found that Medipart faced irreparable harm in the loss of customers, and that Medipart had a reasonable probability of succeeding on the merits. In view of our disposition of the questions of law, *ante*, the assessment of Medipart's probability of success and the balance of harms must be adjusted accordingly. We conclude that the district court's stated grounds cannot support an injunction against giving notice to those directly involved in the asserted infringement. The court's discretionary authority does not, under these circumstances, extend to requiring the patentee to remain silent, even as it publicly litigates issues of direct concern to the objects of the intended notice.

Accordingly, the injunction is vacated.

QUESTIONS

1. What difference did it make whether Mallinckrodt could sue for patent infringement or for breach of contract for violation of the single-use restriction?

2. Where does the court draw the line between lawful and unlawful patent use restrictions?

3. What is the difference between *per se* and rule-of-reason analysis of alleged anticompetitive conduct?

4. The court acknowledges that all parties to the suit have "commercial interests." However, did Mallinckrodt have additional interests that arguably were more important than its commercial interests?

CASE NOTES

1. Chemagro, the exclusive American licensee of a patented granular insecticide, distributed the insecticide in containers with labels that prohibited the reformulation and sale of the insecticide for use by home gardeners. Chemagro contended that the specific formulation of the insecticide was highly toxic and suitable for use only by skilled commercial growers. Universal Chemical purchased and reformulated the insecticide into a presumably less toxic rose food product which it then sold in the home garden market. Universal Chemical had actual notice of the prohibition on reformulation and sale of the insecticide for use by home gardeners. Prior to the date Universal Chemical commenced sales to home gardeners, Chemagro's sales agents and employees were aware of Universal Chemical's reformulation of the insecticide, but Chemagro took no action. At a later date, however, Chemagro filed a patent infringement suit against Universal Chemical. What result? *See* Chemagro Corporation v. Universal Chemical Co., 244 F.Supp. 486 (E.D. Tex. 1965).

2. Hazeltine Research was an early pioneer in the field of radio technology. By 1948, Hazeltine had obtained over 500 patents and had about 200 patent applications pending. Hazeltine did not manufacture any radio equipment, but rather licensed its patents to a number of radio equipment manufacturers, one of whom was Automatic Radio. Hazeltine granted Automatic a nonexclusive license to use its patents to manufacture and sell radio, phonographic and other equipment, but only for use in homes, for educational purposes and for private, non-commercial use. The license agreement required Automatic to pay minimum royalties of $10,000 per year, running royalties on its gross sales of equipment regardless of whether the equipment incorporated any of the Hazeltine patents, and to mark all equipment sold incorporating Hazeltine patents with a statement that the equipment was only for use in homes, for educational purposes and for private non-commercial use. Automatic never paid the minimum royalties or the running royalties, and never marked the equipment it sold with the required statement. Hazeltine sued Automatic for the accumulated minimum royalties and an accounting for the payment of the running royalties. Automatic made two claims in defending the suit. First, Automatic claimed the license was unenforceable because the license restrictions on manufacture and sale constituted patent misuse by Hazeltine

because the license restrictions exceeded the scope of Hazeltine's patent rights. Second, Automatic claimed that because it had not marked the equipment it sold, that equipment did not constitute licensed equipment, and therefore no royalties were owed on the unmarked equipment sales. What result? *See* Automatic Radio Mfg. Co. v. Hazeltine Research, 176 F.2d 799 (1st Cir. 1949).

3. *See also* Pioneer Hi-Bred Int'l v. Ottawa Plant Food, 283 F.Supp.2d 1018 (N.D. Iowa 2003) (Conspicuously printed "label license" on bags of patented brand of seed corn provided adequate notice of the terms of the license, and clearly and unambiguously conveyed only a limited right to produce grain or forage and restricted resale of the product); (The *Pioneer Hi-Bred* case is included in Section 2.3.6 of these materials.); Jazz Photo Corp. v. Int'l Trade Com'n, 264 F.3d 1094 (Fed. Cir. 2001) (No license limitations could be implied from circumstances of sale of lens-fitted film packages; although patented cameras contained instructions and warnings printed on covers of lens-fitted film packages, statements were instructions and warnings of risk, not mutual promises or conditions placed upon sale to limit reuse of cameras); Crown Cork & Seal Co. of Baltimore City v. Brooklyn Bottle Stopper Co., 172 F.225 (E.D.N.Y. 1909) (A manufacturer of patented machines for applying a special pattern of seal or cork to bottles may lawfully sell such machines under license contracts binding purchasers to use the machines only in connection with seals or cork made by the seller, and a violation of such contract by a purchaser or by a secondhand purchaser having knowledge of such restriction will constitute an infringement of the patents).

Additional Information

1. 1 DAVID EPSTEIN, ECKSTROM'S LICENSING IN FOREIGN AND DOMESTIC OPERATIONS § 2.18 (2010).

2. 2 JOHN W. SCHLICHER, PATENT LAW, LEGAL AND ECONOMIC PRINCIPLES §§ 8:59–8:62(2d ed. 2010).

3. RAYMOND T. NIMMER, JEFF DODD, MODERN LICENSING LAW § 6:16 (2010).

4. RAYMOND T. NIMMER, 2 INFORMATION LAW § 11:7 (2010).

5. ROBERT A. MATTHEWS, 1 ANNOTATED PATENT DIGEST § 9:59 (2011).

6. Richard Stern, *Post-Sale Restrictions After Mallinckrodt — An Idea in Search of Definition*, 5 ALB. L.J. SCI. & TECH. 1 (1994).

7. Note, *Patent Use Restrictions*, 75 HARV. L. REV. 602 (1962).

2.2.2 Patent Licenses And Contract Law

Both federal and state law can regulate intellectual property. However, in the event that federal and state intellectual property laws conflict, the federal law prevails and the state law is preempted. Although there is no express preemption provision in the Patent Act, courts have implied preemption where the state law conflicts with objectives of the patent law. A series of Supreme Court decisions have generally defined the scope of federal preemption of state laws regulating intellectual property. In Sears, Roebuck & Co. v. Stiffel Co., 376 U.S. 225 (1964) and Compco Corp. v. Day-Brite Lighting, 376 U.S. 234 (1964), the Court held that state unfair competition laws that protected otherwise non-patentable mechanical and design features would conflict with the purposes of the federal Patent Act. The Court reasoned that patent law not only defines what inventions are patentable, but also what inventions are not patentable; and state law could not provide patent-like protection for un-patentable subject matter.

Similarly, in Brulotte v. Thys Co., 379 U.S. 29 (1964), the Court refused to enforce an agreement to pay royalties on a licensed patent beyond the term of the patent. Here, the Court reasoned that the enforcement of a contract to pay royalties beyond the patent term under state contract law would extend the term of the patent monopoly beyond what is permitted under the Patent Act. Thus, state contract law would conflict with the express provisions of patent law.

However, in Kewanee Oil Co. v. Bicron Corp., 416 U.S. 470 (1974), the Court held that state trade secret law was not preempted by federal patent law. The Court found that state trade secret law was consistent with federal patent law in that both encouraged innovation. The Court also found that state trade secret law did not conflict with the patent law policy of not removing works already available in the public domain because trade secrets, by definition, have never been made available in the public domain.

The following Supreme Court case deals with yet another preemption issue. Does federal patent law preempt state contract law where the contract provides for the payment of royalties, regardless of whether the licensed pending patent ever issues?

ARONSON v. QUICK POINT PENCIL COMPANY
440 U.S. 257 (1979)

Mr. Chief Justice Burger.

We granted certiorari to consider whether federal patent law pre-empts state contract law so as to preclude enforcement of a contract to pay royalties to a patent applicant, on sales of articles embodying the putative invention, for so long as the contracting party sells them, if a patent is not granted.

(1)

In October 1955 the petitioner, Mrs. Jane Aronson, filed an application, Serial No. 542677, for a patent on a new form of keyholder. Although ingenious, the design was so simple that it readily could be copied unless it was protected by patent. In June 1956, while the patent application was pending, Mrs. Aronson negotiated a contract with the respondent, Quick Point Pencil Co., for the manufacture and sale of the keyholder.

The contract was embodied in two documents. In the first, a letter from Quick Point to Mrs. Aronson, Quick Point agreed to pay Mrs. Aronson a royalty of 5% of the selling price in return for "the exclusive right to make and sell keyholders of the type shown in your application, Serial No. 542677." The letter further provided that the parties would consult one another concerning the steps to be taken "[i]n the event of any infringement."

The contract did not require Quick Point to manufacture the keyholder. Mrs. Aronson received a $750 advance on royalties and was entitled to rescind the exclusive license if Quick Point did not sell a million keyholders by the end of 1957. Quick Point retained the right to cancel the agreement whenever "the volume of sales does not meet our expectations." The duration of the agreement was not otherwise prescribed.

A contemporaneous document provided that if Mrs. Aronson's patent application was "not allowed within five (5) years, Quick Point Pencil Co. [would] pay . . . two and one half percent (2½%) of sales . . . so long as you [Quick Point] continue to sell same."

In June 1961, when Mrs. Aronson had failed to obtain a patent on the keyholder within the five years specified in the agreement, Quick Point asserted its contractual right to reduce royalty payments to 2½% of sales. In September of that year the Board of Patent Appeals issued a final rejection of the application on the ground that the keyholder was not patentable, and Mrs. Aronson did not appeal. Quick Point continued to pay reduced royalties to her for 14 years thereafter.

The market was more receptive to the keyholder's novelty and utility than the Patent Office. By September 1975 Quick Point had made sales in excess of $7 million and paid Mrs. Aronson royalties totaling $203,963.84; sales were continuing to rise. However, while Quick Point was able to pre-empt the market in the earlier years and was long the only manufacturer of the Aronson keyholder, copies began to appear in the late 1960's. Quick Point's competitors, of course, were not required to pay royalties for their use of the design. Quick Point's share of the Aronson keyholder market has declined during the past decade.

In November 1975 Quick Point commenced an action in the United States District Court for a declaratory judgment that the royalty agreement was unenforceable. Quick Point asserted that state law which might otherwise make the contract enforceable was preempted by federal patent law. This is the only issue presented to us for decision.

Both parties moved for summary judgment on affidavits, exhibits, and stipulations of fact. The District Court concluded that the "language of the agreement is plain, clear and unequivocal and has no relation as to whether or not a patent is ever granted." Accordingly, it held that the agreement was valid, and that Quick Point was obliged to pay the agreed royalties pursuant to the contract for so long as it manufactured the keyholder.

The Court of Appeals reversed, one judge dissenting. It held that since the parties contracted with reference to a pending patent application, Mrs. Aronson was estopped from denying that patent law principles governed her contract with Quick Point. Although acknowledging that this Court had never decided the precise issue, the Court of Appeals held that our prior decisions regarding patent licenses compelled the conclusion that Quick Point's contract with Mrs. Aronson became unenforceable once she failed to obtain a patent. The court held that a continuing obligation to pay royalties would be contrary to "the strong federal policy favoring the full and free use of ideas in the public domain," The court also observed that if Mrs. Aronson actually had obtained a patent, Quick Point would have escaped its royalty obligations either if the patent were held to be invalid, or upon its expiration after 17 years. Accordingly, it concluded that a licensee should be relieved of royalty obligations when the licensor's efforts to obtain a contemplated patent prove unsuccessful.

****

(3)

On this record it is clear that the parties contracted with full awareness of both the pendency of a patent application and the possibility that a patent might not issue. The clause de-escalating the royalty by half in the event no patent issued within five years makes that crystal clear. Quick Point apparently placed a significant value on exploiting the basic novelty of the device, even if no patent issued; its success demonstrates that this judgment was well founded. Assuming, *arguendo*, that the initial letter and the commitment to pay a 5% royalty was subject to federal patent law, the provision relating to the 2½% royalty was explicitly independent of federal law. The cases and principles relied on by the Court of Appeals and Quick Point do not bear on a contract that does not rely on a patent, particularly where, as here, the contracting parties agreed expressly as to alternative obligations if no patent should issue.

Commercial agreements traditionally are the domain of state law. State law is not displaced merely because the contract relates to intellectual property which may or may not be patentable; the states are free to regulate the use of such intellectual property in any manner not inconsistent with federal law. In this as in other fields, the question of whether federal law pre-empts state law "involves a consideration of whether that law "stands as an obstacle to the accomplishment and execution of the full purposes and objectives of Congress." If it does not, state law governs.

In *Kewanee Oil Co.*, we reviewed the purposes of the federal patent system. First, patent law seeks to foster and reward invention; second, it promotes disclosure of inventions, to stimulate further innovation and to permit the public to practice the invention once the patent expires; third, the stringent requirements for patent protection seek to assure that ideas in the public domain remain there for the free use of the public.

Enforcement of Quick Point's agreement with Mrs. Aronson is not inconsistent with any of these aims. Permitting inventors to make enforceable agreements licensing the use of their inventions in return for royalties provides an additional incentive to invention. Similarly, encouraging Mrs. Aronson to make arrangements for the manufacture of her keyholder furthers the federal policy of disclosure of inventions; these simple devices display the novel idea which they embody wherever they are seen. Quick Point argues that enforcement of such contracts conflicts with the federal policy against withdrawing ideas from the public domain and discourages recourse to the federal patent system by allowing states to extend "perpetual protection to articles too lacking in novelty to merit any patent at all under federal constitutional standards."

We find no merit in this contention. Enforcement of the agreement does not withdraw any idea from the public domain. The design for the keyholder was not in the public domain before Quick Point obtained its license to manufacture it. In negotiating the agreement, Mrs. Aronson disclosed the design in confidence. Had Quick Point tried to exploit the design in breach of that confidence, it would have risked legal liability. It is equally clear that the design entered the public domain as a result of the manufacture and sale of the keyholders under the contract.

Requiring Quick Point to bear the burden of royalties for the use of the design is no more inconsistent with federal patent law than any of the other costs involved in being the first to introduce a new product to the market, such as outlays for research and development, and marketing and promotional expenses. For reasons which Quick Point's experience with the Aronson keyholder demonstrate, innovative entrepreneurs have usually found such costs to be well worth paying.

Finally, enforcement of this agreement does not discourage anyone from seeking a patent. Mrs. Aronson attempted to obtain a patent for over five years. It is quite true that had she succeeded, she would have received a 5% royalty only on keyholders sold during the 17-year life of the patent. Offsetting the limited terms of royalty payments, she would have received twice as much per dollar of Quick Point's sales, and both she and Quick Point could have licensed any others who produced the same keyholder. Which course would have produced the greater yield to the contracting parties is a matter of speculation; the parties resolved the uncertainties by their bargain.

(4)

No decision of this Court relating to patents justifies relieving Quick Point of its contract obligations. We have held that a state may not forbid the copying of an idea in the public domain which does not meet the requirements for federal patent protection. Enforcement of Quick Point's agreement, however, does not prevent anyone from copying the keyholder. It merely requires Quick Point to pay the consideration which it promised in return for the use of a novel device which enabled it to pre-empt the market.

Enforcement of the royalty agreement here is also consistent with the principles treated in *Brulotte v. Thys Co.* There, we held that the obligation to pay royalties in return for the use of a patented device may not extend beyond the life of the patent. The principle underlying that holding was simply that the monopoly granted *under a patent* cannot lawfully be used to "negotiate with the leverage of that monopoly." The Court emphasized that to "use that leverage to project those royalty payments beyond the life of the patent is analogous to an effort to enlarge the monopoly of the patent." Here the reduced royalty which is challenged, far from being negotiated "with the leverage" of a patent, rested on the contingency that no patent would issue within five years.

No doubt a pending patent application gives the applicant some additional bargaining power for purposes of negotiating a royalty agreement. The pending application allows the inventor to hold out the hope of an exclusive right to exploit the idea, as well as the threat that the other party will be prevented from using the idea for 17 years. However, the amount of leverage arising from a patent application depends on how likely the parties consider it to be that a valid patent will issue. Here, where no patent ever issued, the record is entirely clear that the parties assigned a substantial likelihood to that contingency, since they specifically provided for a reduced royalty in the event no patent issued within five years.

This case does not require us to draw the line between what constitutes abuse of a pending application and what does not. It is clear that whatever role the pending application played in the negotiation of the 5% royalty, it played no part in the contract to pay the 2½% royalty indefinitely.

Our holding in *Kewanee Oil Co.* puts to rest the contention that federal law preempts and renders unenforceable the contract made by these parties. There we held that state law forbidding the misappropriation of trade secrets was not preempted by federal patent law. We observed:

> "Certainly the patent policy of encouraging invention is not disturbed by the existence of another form of incentive to invention. In this respect the two systems [patent and trade secret law] are not and never would be in conflict."

Enforcement of this royalty agreement is even less offensive to federal patent policies than state law protecting trade secrets. The most commonly accepted definition of trade secrets is restricted to confidential information which is not disclosed in the normal process of exploitation. Accordingly, the exploitation of trade secrets under state law may not satisfy the federal policy in favor of disclosure, whereas disclosure is inescapable in exploiting a device like the Aronson keyholder.

Enforcement of these contractual obligations, freely undertaken in arm's-length negotiation and with no fixed reliance on a patent or a probable patent grant, will:

> encourage invention in areas where patent law does not reach, and will prompt the independent innovator to proceed with the discovery and exploitation of his invention. Competition is fostered and the public is not deprived of the use of valuable, if not quite patentable, invention.

The device which is the subject of this contract ceased to have any secrecy as soon as it was first marketed, yet when the contract was negotiated the inventiveness and novelty were sufficiently apparent to induce an experienced novelty manufacturer to agree to pay for the opportunity to be first in the market. Federal patent law is not a barrier to such a contract.

Reversed.

MR. JUSTICE BLACKMUN, concurring in the result.

QUESTIONS

1.   If the key holder patent had issued and later been held to be invalid, would Quick Point be required to continue paying royalties?

2.   If the key holder patent had issued and later been held to be invalid, and the license provided that Quick Point would continue to pay royalties even if the patent was held to be invalid, would Quick Point be required to continue paying royalties?

CASE NOTES

1.   In 1988, Ford Motor Company contacted Ultra-Precision (founded by two former Ford industrial engineers, Herron and Beard) to help solve a problem with excessive noise in air conditioner compressors. After researching the problem for over a year, Herron and Beard believed they had found a solution and filed two patent applications in July 1989 that later issued as the '482 patent and the '647 patent. In July 1990, Herron and Beard met with a Ford employee to explain their solution and arrange for prototype testing of their invention; Ford later indicated that it was not interested in the Herron-Beard invention. Ford then formed its own team to research the problem and, in 1993, Ford incorporated a re-designed air conditioner compressor into its cars. Herron and Beard inspected the re-designed compressor and believed it incorporated elements of the solution they had developed in 1989. However, the incorporated elements had not been claimed in the '482 and '647 patents, but had been disclosed in the patent specifications. Ultra-Precision sued Ford under the Michigan unjust enrichment law which permits a plaintiff to recover the unjust benefit gained by a defendant from the use of technical information provided by the plaintiff, regardless of the plaintiff's property interest in the technical information. Ultra-Precision claimed that the proper measure of recovery for Ford's unjust enrichment was the cost savings Ford realized through the use of the Herron-Beard solution. Ford claimed that the Michigan unjust enrichment law, under the facts of this case, was preempted by federal patent law. What result? *See* Ultra-Precision Mfg., Ltd. v. Ford Motor Co., 411 F.3d 1369 (Fed. Cir. 2005).

2.   Florida enacted a statute prohibiting the use of a direct molding process to duplicate boat hulls, or the knowing sale of boat hulls duplicated by means of direct molding, regardless of whether the boat hulls were protected by federal patent laws. Bonito Boats developed a boat hull design for a fiberglass recreational boat, but never sought patent protection for the design. Thunder Craft Boats duplicated the Bonito Boats' hull design through use of a direct molding process. Bonito Boats brought suit against Thunder Craft Boats under the Florida law seeking damages and an injunction. Thunder Craft Boats defended the suit claiming the Florida law was preempted by the federal patent law. What result? *See* Bonito Boats, Inc. v. Thunder Craft Boats, Inc., 489 U.S. 141 (1989).

3.   *See also* Kiwanis Int'l. v. Ridgewood Kiwanis Club, 811 F.2d 247 (3rd Cir. 1986) (Trademark licensing agreement is contract to be interpreted and enforced

under state law).

Additional Information

1. 1 DAVID EPSTEIN, ECKSTROM'S LICENSING IN FOREIGN AND DOMESTIC OPERATIONS §§ 2:5, 2:8 (2010).

2. JANE E. LEHMAN ET. AL., 60 AM. JUR. 2D PATENTS § 1023 (2010).

3. RAYMOND T. NIMMER, 2 INFORMATION LAW § 11:50 (2010).

4. RAYMOND T. NIMMER, 10 HAWKLAND UCC SERIES UCITA § 105:2 (2010).

5. Thomas L. Lockhart; Richard McKenna, *Software License Agreements in Light of the UCC and the Convention on the International Sale of Goods*, 70 MICH. B.J. 646 (1991).

2.2.3 Implied Licenses

Although the results are the identical, analysis of implied licenses is not the same as infringement immunity based on the patent exhaustion doctrine discussed in subsection 2.3.6 of the materials. As you will see in *Quanta Computer*, the patent exhaustion doctrine focuses on the nature of the product sold and the type of sale. Implied licenses, on the other hand, focus on the conduct of the patent owner. One form of implied license is based upon *equitable estoppel.* The Supreme Court in De Forest Radio Telephone & Telegraph Co. v. United States, 273 U.S. 236 (1927) broadly described the nature of equitable estoppel giving rise to an implied license:

> No formal granting of a license is necessary in order to give [an implied license] effect. Any language used by the owner of a patent or any conduct on his part exhibited to another, from which that other may properly infer that the owner consents to his use of the patent in making or using it, or selling it, upon which the other acts, constitutes a license, and a defense to an action for a tort.

The Court of Appeals for the Federal Circuit elaborated on the doctrine of equitable estoppel in A.C. Aukerman Co. v. R.L. Chaides Construction Co., 960 F.2d 1020 (Fed. Cir. 1992). The Federal Circuit held that three underlying factual elements must be present to establish the defense of equitable estoppel. First, the patent owner must make a misleading communication to the alleged infringer, either by way of statements or conduct, indicating that the patent owner does not intend to file an infringement action against the alleged infringer. Second, the alleged infringer must undertake some action in reliance upon the patent owner's misleading communication. Third, the alleged infringer must establish that it would be materially prejudiced if the patent owner were permitted to proceed with the patent infringement suit. Unlike the related doctrine of *laches*, which is based upon the patent owner's unreasonable and inexcusable delay in filing the patent infringement suit and can bar the patent owner's claim for damages prior to the suit, *equitable estoppel* may bar all relief to the patent owner.

Another type of implied license can result from *legal estoppel.* Legal estoppel is intended to prevent a grantor of property rights from detracting from the rights granted by subsequent acts. An example of legal estoppel, sometimes referred to as "assignor estoppel," is Diamond Scientific Co. v. Ambico, *Inc.*, 848 F.2d 1220 (Fed. Cir. 1988). In *Diamond Scientific*, an employee assigned his patent rights in a vaccine to his company and then later resigned from the company to start his own company manufacturing the same vaccine. In the ensuing infringement action, the former employee claimed that the patent he had assigned was invalid and, therefore, could not be enforced. The Federal Circuit held that the former employee-assignor could not challenge the validity of the assigned patent. The court found that it was inequitable for a party to assign rights and later assert that what was assigned was worthless.

The *Suessen-Schurr* case below deals with the issue of legal estoppel in the context of a series of licenses and assignments involving an improvement patent and its corresponding base patent. The next case, *Travelers Express*, deals with the issue of equitable estoppel in the context of a poorly managed and incomplete settlement agreement. The final case, *Jacobs*, considers the question of an implied license on behalf of an express licensee's customer.

SUESSEN-SCHURR v. SCHUBERT
829 F.2d 1075 (Fed. Cir. 1987)

BALDWIN, SENIOR CIRCUIT JUDGE.

This is a consolidation of appeals from two judgments of the United States District Court for the District of South Carolina (district court) (1) declaring U.S. Patent No. 4,059,946 (the '946 patent) and U.S. Patent No. 4,175,370 (the '370 patent) valid and infringed and awarding increased damages and attorney fees based on a finding of willful infringement of the '946 patent and (2) granting a motion to enjoin subsequent infringement by a redesign of the accused device. Appeal was taken on four questions related to the district court's infringement determinations. We affirm the district court's decision with respect to each of the four questions on infringement.

Background

In 1983, the three appellees in this appeal, Hans Stahlecker, Fritz Stahlecker, and Spindelfabrik Suessen-Schurr, Stahlecker and Grill GmbH (collectively and individually "Suessen"), brought an action in the district court for infringement of two patents relating to improvements in the technology of open-end spinning devices, the '946 patent and the '370 patent. It was charged that an open-end spinning device, the Spincomat, produced and marketed by appellants, Schubert and Salzer Maschinenfabrik Aktiengesellschaft and Schubert and Salzer Machine Works, Inc. (collectively and individually "Schubert"), infringes claim 18 of the '946 patent and infringes claims 1–7, 9–13, and 17–20 of the '370 patent. The district court rejected the Schubert defenses of invalidity, unenforceability, non-infringement, and implied license, and on September 4, 1985, issued its "Order and Opinion Including Findings of Fact and Conclusions of Law" declaring the '946 and '370 patents valid and infringed. The district court awarded increased damages based on willful and deliberate infringement and attorney fees under 35 U.S.C. § 285 (1982) for infringement attributable to the '946 patent.

Six weeks later, on October 28, 1985, the district court issued an order declaring that, despite Schubert's efforts to produce a non-infringing modification, the redesigned version of the Spincomat also infringes the '946 patent.

B. The Technology

The '946 and '370 patents are directed to the automation of open-end spinning (OES), a technology whereby uniformly twisted yarn is produced from irregular strands of fiber. The findings of the district court regarding OES technology and operation of an OES device are not contested.

The '370 and '946 patents relate to a portion of the OES operation denoted as the "piecing point." As the yarn is withdrawn from the rotor, pulled by a pair of "take off" rolls and wound onto a spool, it is subject to breakage. Breakage inherently results in discontinuity in the operation, requiring reconnection and restarting of the operation. Automation of an OES device involves the implementation of a sequence of automatic steps to restart the device by cleaning out broken fiber, feeding new fiber into the rotor and reconnecting the newly spun yarn. The points of reconnection after breakage are denoted as "piecing points." Both of the patents in issue disclose improvements which avoid time lapse for reconnection and minimize non-uniformities in the yarn at the piecing points.

I. Infringement of the '946 Patent

The '946 patent, entitled "Method and Apparatus for Start Spinning a Thread on Open-End Spinning Units" issued on November 29, 1977 to Dieter Boettcher, Heinze Schulz and Fritz Stahlecker. Hans and Fritz Stahlecker were subsequently assigned the patent, and they licensed Suessen as an exclusive licensee.

The '946 patent addresses the absence in the prior art of a method and apparatus for providing precise control of fiber feed during piecing. Claim 18 recites an apparatus for performing a controlled sequence of steps for automated restart of the spinning operation, including preparation of the rotor.

The district court found that claim 18 of the '946 patent reads directly on Schubert's OES device, the Spincomat. In making this finding, the court identified an aspect of the Spincomat which corresponds to each of the elements recited in claim 18. Literal reading of the '946 patent upon Schubert's Spincomat is not contested in this appeal.

A. The Implied License Defense

Schubert argues that it has an implied license under the '946 patent. Its argument involves two agreements.

The first was a license agreement entered in 1982 between Schubert and Murata Machinery, Ltd. (Murata). That agreement, entered into before the filing of this suit in 1983, in pertinent part reads:

> Murata hereby grants to Licensee [Schubert] a non-exclusive worldwide license under the Patents to make, use and sell the patented device only as part of the open end spinning machines of the License. The License hereby granted is a limited license, and Murata reserves all rights not expressly granted.

The "Patents" were defined by the agreement as those listed in an Exhibit. They include U.S. Patent No. 4,022,011 ('011 patent) and other patents belonging to Murata in the name of Hironorai Hirai. Schubert asserts that, notwithstanding any infringement of '946, its accused infringement is merely a practicing of the '011 invention, which it is licensed to do under the 1982 agreement.

The second agreement, entered in 1984 after this lawsuit began, involved Suessen's purchase of the '011 and other Hirai patents from Murata. The agreement reads, in pertinent part:

> Suessen has been advised by Murata that a non-exclusive license of the patents and patent applications mentioned under 1. above had been granted by Murata to Messrs. Schubert & Salzer AG, Ingolstadt, F.R. Germany (hereinafter called the Licensee). Suessen hereby agrees to purchase the patents and patent applications mentioned under 1. above together with the License Agreement as of 23rd/28th July, 1982, with the said Licensee and agrees that you and your business/license concerns will maintain the licensed rights of the Licensee under the License Agreement as stipulated during the life of the patents and patent applications mentioned under 1. above.

Schubert asserts that, per the 1984 agreement, Suessen "stepped in the shoes of Murata" and by so "stepping," Suessen cannot — just as Murata cannot — sue under the '946 or any other patent for infringement based on practicing the '011 invention. To allow such a suit, Schubert argues, would unfairly take away what it paid for in 1982. Schubert labels its argument one of "legal estoppel."

The district court concluded that Schubert in 1982 could not have acquired from Murata any rights greater than those which Murata had the right to grant and that Murata had nothing more than a right to exclude others from using the Hirai patents. It then concluded, regarding the 1984 agreement:

> There is nothing whatsoever in this agreement about the '946 patent, any patent corresponding to the '946 patent, or any technology specifically covered by those patents. Nor is there any language in the agreement that can be construed as a grant by Suessen of any right to practice any particular technology which might be covered by other Suessen patent rights. All this agreement does is to convey to Suessen the entire right, title and interest in all of the Hirai patents, with the express reservation to the effect that a nonexclusive license under these Hirai patents had already been granted by Murata to [Schubert], and with the express acknowledgment by Suessen that it would continue to recognize the existence of that license under the Hirai patents. While this latter acknowledgment might seem redundant from the viewpoint of the law in this country (whereby a patent assignee under normal circumstances would be bound as a matter of

law by its assignor's prior grant to a license to a third party), it served a clear purpose under German law since, as referred to above [because] the German High Court had recently handed down a ruling, the effect of which was that an existing nonexclusive right under a German patent could be defeated by an assignment of the patent by the owner to a third party.

The net effect of the 1984 agreement, said the district court, was that Schubert is "the beneficiary of a guarantee by Suessen that the nonexclusive rights under the Hirai patents granted to [Schubert] by Murata in 1982 could not be taken away by the new patent owner, Suessen" and that the enforcement of the '946 patent against Schubert in this litigation "in no way affects that guarantee."

The district court then added:

> Beyond these two agreements, defendants offered no further evidence in support of the existence of any implied license — not even the testimony of defendants to the effect that they ever even thought they might have an implied license or that they were led to take or ever took any action upon reliance that they had rights under the '946 patents.

Discussion

The doctrines of legal estoppel and equitable estoppel have been applied by courts to imply a license. Under the facts of this case, there can be no implied license under an equitable estoppel theory. Indeed, that theory is not even argued by Schubert. Instead, Schubert asserts an implied license based on its theory of legal estoppel. Though we recognize that theory in appropriate circumstances, it does not work for Schubert here.

Legal estoppel "is merely shorthand for saying that a grantor of a property right or interest cannot derogate from the right granted by his own subsequent acts." The rationale for that is to estop the grantor from taking back that for which he received consideration. Here, however, we have a suit by a third party, Suessen, under a patent owned by Suessen. The license by the grantor, Murata, did not purport to, and indeed could not, protect Schubert from a suit by Suessen under '946. Hence, Suessen, by filing in 1983 and now maintaining its suit under '946, does not derogate from the right given by Murata in the 1982 license agreement.

Schubert nevertheless urges this three prong argument: (1) "legal estoppel" would prevent *Murata* from suing under the '946 patent if it were to acquire it; (2) Suessen "stepped into" Murata's shoes in 1984 when Suessen acquired the Hirai patents and committed to maintain Schubert's licensed rights; and hence, (3) just as Murata could not, Suessen cannot sue under the '946 patent. We reject that argument.

As a threshold matter, a patent license agreement is in essence nothing more than a promise by the licensor not to sue the licensee. Even if couched in terms of "[l]icensee is given the right to make, use, or sell X," the agreement cannot convey that absolute right because not even the patentee of X is given that right. His right is merely one to exclude others from making, using or selling X. Indeed, the patentee of X and his licensee, when making, using, or selling X, can be subject to suit under other patents. In any event, patent license agreements can be written to convey different scopes of promises not to sue, *e.g.*, a promise not to sue under a specific patent or, more broadly, a promise not to sue under any patent the licensor now has or may acquire in the future.

As stated previously, the first prong of Schubert's three part "stepping in the shoes" argument is that legal estoppel would prevent Murata from suing Schubert under the '946 patent if Murata were to acquire that patent. However, even assuming, *arguendo*, that such estoppel against Murata exists, the final two prongs of Schubert's "stepping in the shoes" argument would fail. Given the assumption of estoppel against Murata, the 1982 license agreement would necessarily be a promise by Murata not to sue under any patent, including those acquired by Murata in the future. In the 1984 agreement, Suessen incurred what Murata promised in 1982. Thus, Suessen would be committed to forebear from suit under (1) the transferred patents and (2) any of Murata's non-transferred patents (future and present). That commitment does not include a promise not to sue under Suessen's own '946 patent.

Schubert's "standing in the shoes" argument, however, would add to Suessen's commitment a promise not to sue under Suessen's separate patents that Murata never owned. On the facts of this case, we cannot interpret the 1984 agreement so broadly, at least not with respect to the '946 patent.

The district court correctly determined that there is nothing in the 1984 agreement about the '946 or other Suessen patent rights. Schubert points to no extraneous evidence tending to show any understanding on the part of either contracting party that Suessen was to forego rights under the '946 or any other patent then owned by Suessen. To the contrary, that a lawsuit under '946 was ongoing but not mentioned in the 1984 agreement indicates strongly that there was no intent by the parties to have Suessen forfeit its rights under '946. Furthermore, an implied promise by Suessen to forego its '946 suit is inconsistent not only with Suessen maintaining its lawsuit after the 1984 agreement but, also, with the course of events leading up to the 1984 contract. In sum, we agree with the district court's conclusion that the 1984 agreement did not impose on Suessen any obligation to stop its ongoing suit under the '946 patent.

Schubert argues that not implying a license in this case is unfair because Schubert paid valuable consideration for the right to practice the '011 invention but is in danger of losing that right as a result of doing no more than that for which it paid. We disagree. The right Schubert paid for in the 1982 agreement was freedom from suit by Murata, not Suessen. Indeed, when Schubert signed the 1982 agreement, it was aware of possible suit by Suessen, who had previously denied Schubert a license under the '946 patent. Moreover, Schubert has not shown us that it has lost any obligation Murata may still owe it under the 1982 license agreement, *e.g.*, not to sue under any patents Murata still has or may acquire. To rule that the Suessen acquisition of the '011 patent somehow bestows on Schubert an absolute defense to a suit already filed by Suessen under '946, would result in an unintended windfall to Schubert that makes no sense under the facts of this case.

AFFIRMED

QUESTIONS

1. If a licensor licensed an improvement patent, but not the base patent necessary to practice the improvement patent, would the licensee have an implied license to practice the base patent?

2. If a licensor licensed a base patent, but not the improvement patent necessary to practice the base patent efficiently, would the licensee have an implied license to practice the improvement patent?

3. Why did the court find that equitable estoppel did not apply under the facts of the case?

4. What is the drafting lesson here?

TRAVELERS EXPRESS v. AMERICAN EXPRESS INTEGRATED PAYMENT
80 F.Supp.2d 1033 (D. Minn. 1999)

DAVIS, DISTRICT JUDGE.

INTRODUCTION

This case has a long and tortured history. Plaintiff Travelers Express Company, Inc. ("Travelers") originally commenced this suit alleging patent infringement in 1994. The parties believed that they had reached a settlement agreement at the end of 1994, and as a result Defendants, believing a license was in place, continued on its business that used Travelers' patented technology. Ultimately, however, the parties were not able to agree on the terms of a definitive settlement, and this case is currently set for trial in January 2000. Currently before the Court are cross motions for partial summary judgment.

FACTS

Travelers is a wholly-owned subsidiary of The Dial Corp ("Dial") and the largest issuer of money orders in the United States. Defendant American Express Integrated Payment System Inc. ("IPS") is a wholly-owned subsidiary of First Data Corporation ("FDC"). FDC provides high quality, high volume information processing and related services. IPS provides payment instrument transaction processing to financial institutions and to retail customers. As part of its business, IPS markets money orders, official checks, MoneyGram® money transfer service, and other products. Defendant American Express Travel Related Services, Inc. ("TRS") is a wholly-owned subsidiary of American Express Company. IPS markets American Express® Money Orders under a Management Agreement with TRS. Under the Management Agreement, although TRS is the state-licensed issuer of the American Express® Money Orders, IPS manages the business on TRS's behalf. The Management Agreement relationship was phased out April 16, 1997.

In 1989, Travelers acquired Republic Money Orders and certain AMOD patents and patent applications Republic owned. Travelers attributed approximately $13 million of its purchase price to Republic's AMOD technology. In October 1991, Travelers sued American Express Company in this Court for infringing its AMOD patents, based on the IPS machine. In April 1993, summary judgment was granted to American Express Company based on the finding that it had not infringed the Travelers' patents. Travelers then filed this suit against IPS and TRS.

By Order of this Court, designated representatives of Travelers, IPS and TRS participated in a settlement conference on December 12–14, 1994 before Special Master Sheryl Ramstad Hvass. Apart from a short initial meeting of all participants, for two days the parties remained in separate conference rooms and communicated almost exclusively through Special Master Hvass. During the day on December 13, the parties exchanged a series of term sheets proposing terms of settlement to each other. There were no direct substantive communications between the parties except through the exchange of term sheets.

Early in the morning of December 14, 1994, at about 12:30 a.m., the parties, still in their separate rooms, each signed a largely handwritten two-page agreement entitled "Settlement Term Sheet." Each side had Special Master Hvass change the Settlement Term Sheet to correct or add terms before signing it. The Settlement Term Sheet contains thirteen paragraphs, that was meant to signify the parties' general agreement as to settlement. The Settlement Term Sheet further provided that a definitive agreement was to be signed by year end, and that the terms of settlement were subject to a definitive agreement to be drafted with the assistance of the special master.

The parties exchanged drafts of proposed "definitive agreements" the following week. The parties were unable to agree to a "definitive" agreement as provided in the Settlement Term Sheet. The Court, therefore, ordered the parties to attend another settlement conference on December 30–31, 1994, before Special Master Hvass "in order to finalize and document the terms of the settlement agreed to by the parties on December 12–14." Accordingly, on December 30 and 31, 1994, the parties again met with Special Master Hvass.

By the end of this second mediation, the parties were still not able to agree as to the specific terms of the settlement. Instead, the parties entered into an agreement that provides:

> The parties agree that they reached a Settlement Agreement as of December 14, 1994. Each party will submit its position to Judge Davis as to what the terms of the Agreement are, subject to appeal. The parties further agree that they will mutually request the Court's accelerated consideration and that there be an evidentiary hearing as to what the terms of the Agreement are.

Based upon this agreement, the parties agreed to issue the following press release on January 3, 1995:

TRAVELERS EXPRESS SIGNS PATENT AGREEMENT WITH FIRST DATA BUSINESS UNIT

MINNEAPOLIS, MN — Travelers Express Corp. Inc. (TECI) today announced that Integrated Payment Systems (IPS) has entered into a licensing agreement to employ pioneering patents owned by TECI.

The licensing agreement is part of the settlement of patent infringement litigation initiated by TECI against IPS. As part of the agreement, the parties agreed to entry of a Consent Judgment acknowledging the validity and infringement of TECI's patents.

The non-exclusive patent license will be available to IPS, First Data Corporation, and their business units and products and American Express Travel Related Services Company, Inc.

IPS will pay a substantial but undisclosed amount to use TECI patents relating to money order dispenser technology, according to the parties.

TECI is a major processor of money orders, official checks for banks, share drafts for credit unions and electronic bill payments for utility companies. Its parent company, The Dial Corp., is a $3.6 billion consumer products and services company based in Phoenix.

First Data Corporation is a leading provider of high-quality, high-volume information processing and related services to the transaction card, payment instruments, teleservices, mutual fund, healthcare, receivables and information management industries.

In January 1995, IPS tendered, and Travelers accepted, the first royalty payment in the amount of $3 million dollars as provided by the terms of the Settlement Term Sheet. Thereafter, IPS asserts it invested over $34 million in developing and deploying a new money order dispenser, made contractual commitments to provide customers with its new automated technology, and opted to convert all of its agents to its new automated technology — the result of which is to significantly increase its infringement exposure to Travelers. Further royalty payments, as called for in the Settlement Term Sheet, were made in January 1996, 1997 and 1998.

In addition to the press release issued in January 1995, Travelers made a number of public announcements with regard to the settlement of this case. For example, in an internal newsletter, Travelers announced the settlement with IPS "that recognizes the validity of our patents and brings us compensation for the use of our patents through licensing arrangements." In August 1995, Travelers issued another press release that again mentioned the settlement with IPS and that Travelers had reached a licensing agreement with IPS. In an external newsletter issued in October 1995, Travelers told its customers that it had reached a consent judgment and a licensing agreement with IPS.

Throughout the period from January 1995 through May 1998, Travelers also repeatedly asserted to this Court that Travelers had granted IPS a license, and that the parties have performed according to Travelers' views of the scope of the license.

An evidentiary hearing was held in March 1995 to determine if a settlement was in fact reached. The Court heard testimony from the principals involved in the settlement negotiations, and received other evidence to assist the Court in determining what the terms of settlement were, in the event the Court found an enforceable agreement had been entered into.

In the spring of 1997, when the March 1995 motion was still under advisement, the parties met with Magistrate Judge Boylan and were unable to resolve the disputed issues. In the spring of 1998, the parties again attended mediation sessions with a new Special Master, Roger Haydock, and again, were unable to settle their disputes. Travelers then moved the Court for a Rule 16 Conference and for an Order finding that the parties did not enter into an enforceable settlement agreement. The Defendants adamantly opposed the motion, arguing that the parties did settle and that an enforceable settlement agreement exists — the terms of which are stated in the Settlement Term Sheet.

This Court, by Order dated June 10, 1998, granted Traveler's motion on the basis that the parties clearly did not have a meeting of the minds as to the essential terms of its alleged settlement agreement. Thereafter, Traveler's filed an amended complaint, seeking to enjoin Defendants from infringing or continuing to infringe certain patents owned by Travelers, enjoining them from the continued manufacture, distribution, use or sale of devices that infringe the Traveler's patents and seeking an accounting of the profits and damages arising therefrom. In response to the amended complaint, both IPS and TRS filed amended answers, with new defenses and counterclaims that specifically address the conduct of the parties after the purported settlement agreement entered into on December 14 and December 31, 1994. Both TRS and IPS assert the affirmative defense of implied license, as well as counterclaims for breach of the settlement agreement and patent misuse. In addition, IPS has asserted counterclaims of attempted monopolization, fraud, negligent misrepresentation and the affirmative defense of equitable estoppel.

Travelers now moves the Court for summary judgment on these affirmative defenses and counterclaims. IPS also moves for summary judgment as to the affirmative defense of implied license or, in the alternative, as to the affirmative defense of equitable estoppel.

STANDARD FOR SUMMARY JUDGMENT

Summary judgment is appropriate if there is no genuine issue of material fact and the moving party is entitled to judgment as a matter of law. To determine whether genuine issues of material fact exist, the court determines materiality from the substantive law governing the claim. Disputes over facts that might affect the outcome of the lawsuit according to applicable substantive law are material. A material fact dispute is "genuine" if the evidence is sufficient to allow a reasonable jury to return a verdict for the non-moving party.

1. Implied License — IPS

Both Travelers and IPS move for summary judgment as to IPS' affirmative defense of implied license. An implied license, like an express license, is a complete defense to a claim of patent infringement.

In the area of patent law, the granting of a license "signifies a patentee's waiver of the statutory right to exclude others from making, using, or selling the patented invention." A license may be express or implied.

No formal granting of a license is necessary in order to give it effect. Any language used by the owner of the patent, or any conduct on his part exhibited to another from which that other may properly infer that the owner consents to his use of the patent in making or using it, or selling it, upon which the other acts, constitutes a license and a defense to an action for tort. An implied license may arise by acquiescence, conduct, equitable estoppel or by legal estoppel. "These labels describe not different kinds of licenses, but rather different categories of conduct which lead to the same conclusion: an implied license." Whether an implied license exists is a question of law. As the alleged infringer, IPS has the burden of establishing the existence of an implied license as an affirmative defense.

IPS asserts that it has an implied license by equitable estoppel. A license by estoppel is created if IPS can show that 1) there is infringement by IPS; 2) Travelers had knowledge of the infringement; 3) Travelers engaged in conduct that induced IPS to believe that Travelers acquiesced in the infringement; and 4) IPS relied on Travelers conduct.

There is no genuine dispute as to the first two elements. While IPS does not concede that it infringed any of Travelers' patents, Travelers believes there is infringement, and has filed suit as a result. IPS argues that the third element is met as well, based upon Travelers' numerous statements to IPS, to third parties, and to the Court, that Travelers had granted it a license, and by Travelers' acceptance of $8.7 million in royalty payments. Finally, IPS argues the fourth element is met based upon the evidence that it spent millions on automated money dispensers that utilized the allegedly infringing technology and by making future commitments to customers to provide dispensers that contain the allegedly infringing technology.

Travelers argues that the factual record does not support a finding of implied license by equitable estoppel, because IPS cannot show that it reasonably relied upon Travelers' statements or comments. It is Travelers' position that until a definitive settlement agreement was executed by the parties, any reliance by IPS to use the allegedly infringing technology was unreasonable. The Court disagrees. To establish an implied license, IPS need only show reliance. None of the authority cited by the parties requires a further showing of reasonableness. Nonetheless, the factual record supports a finding of reasonableness. For over a two and one-half year period, Travelers repeatedly asserted to the Court, the public and in internal newsletters that IPS was acting under a license. Even though the Court had not ruled on the motion to define the terms of the settlement, Travelers repeatedly conceded that IPS performed under the license consistent with Travelers' views as to its scope. Travelers was aware that IPS was utilizing its patented technology in its automated money dispenser business, and was aware that IPS had developed a new dispenser, which clearly required the expenditure of research and development costs. Yet, during the time period of January 1995 through May 1998, Travelers did not tell IPS to stop.

Travelers did benefit from this arrangement as well. Although IPS was disputing the terms of the settlement, IPS nonetheless performed according to Travelers' views during this period. Furthermore, Travelers utilized the opportunity by publicly announcing the settlement to tout the validity of its patents, and used the fact of the settlement to support its position in a separate lawsuit against Standard Register. It also received $8.7 million in royalty payments.

Travelers further asserts that given the fact that the parties could not agree as to the scope of the license, the Court will be in no better position to determine the scope of an implied license. Again, the Court does not agree. The scope of an implied license depends on the particular facts of the case. Thus, to determine the scope of the implied license, the Court must look to the course of conduct between Travelers and IPS. In a hearing before the Court in November 1997, Travelers conceded on the record that IPS conducted itself "entirely consistent" with Travelers' position on the disputed terms. IPS also concedes that the scope of the implied license must be consistent with Travelers' view of the disputed issues as of January 1995. Because both parties agree that the license was performed according to Travelers' view of the license's scope, that is the scope of the implied license.

Equity favors this result. Both parties took a risk by going forward with a licensing arrangement even though they had not hammered out its terms. By finding that IPS had an implied license, Travelers gets the benefit of the bargain it believed it reached at the end of 1994, and IPS is now protected from Travelers' reasserted claims of patent infringement.

Contrary to Travelers' assertions, the finding of an implied license does not contradict the Court's earlier decision that the parties did not enter into a settlement agreement. In March 1995, the parties asked the Court to do something it clearly had no authority to do — act as the final arbitrator and determine what the parties agreed to. By finding that an implied license exists, the Court is not making a determination as to what the parties meant when they prepared and signed the Settlement Term Sheet. Rather, the Court is simply looking to the conduct of the parties and by that conduct finding that the elements for an implied license exist.

2. Implied License — TRS

Travelers also moves for summary judgment on TRS' affirmative defense of implied license. To the extent that TRS was in business with IPS under the Management Agreement, TRS also should receive the benefit of an implied license. None of the evidence presented to the Court establishes otherwise. The Court disagrees with TRS that an implied license should extend beyond April 1997, when TRS and IPS parted ways.

Travelers asserts that in 1997, after its non-compete agreement with IPS expired, TRS approached Travelers to discuss a number of issues, including TRS' desire to re-enter the money order business. Travelers asserts that at that time, Travelers informed TRS that it was not interested in granting TRS a license. Thereafter, TRS did re-enter the money order business, utilizing technology that Travelers does not argue infringes its patents.

Although TRS disputes that it asked Travelers for a license in 1997, the facts nonetheless do not support a finding that TRS had an implied license when it re-entered the money-order business in 1998, given the fact that it does not use Travelers' patented technology.

The Court thus finds that TRS had an implied license during that period of time that it was acting under the Management Agreement with IPS. The course of conduct of the parties after the Management Agreement expired establish that no implied license exists.

QUESTIONS

1. Would the holding in the case be different if the parties had not issued a press release? If Amex had not paid, and Travelers had not accepted, royalties? If Amex had not made a significant investment in further development of the technology?

2. Who has the burden of proof as to the existence of an implied license in a patent infringement suit?

3. If you were counsel to IPS, what would you have done differently in dealing with TRS?

JACOBS v. NINTENDO OF AMERICA, INC.
370 F.3d 1097 (Fed. Cir. 2004)

BRYSON, CIRCUIT JUDGE.

Patent owner and appellant Jordan Spencer Jacobs terminated a patent infringement lawsuit against Analog Devices, Inc., by entering into a settlement and licensing agreement with Analog. Jacobs later sued appellee Nintendo of America, Inc., for infringing the same patent. As a defense, Nintendo asserted that the settlement agreement between Jacobs and Analog protected not only Analog, but also Analog's customers, including Nintendo, for making and selling devices that incorporated Analog's components. The district court agreed and entered summary judgment in Nintendo's favor. We affirm.

I

Jacobs owns U.S. Patent No. 5,059,958 ("the '958 patent"), entitled "Manually Held Tilt Sensitive Non-Joystick Control Box." The invention relates to a video game controller that the operator holds in two hands. The operator tilts the controller to achieve corresponding motion in the video game. Before suing Nintendo, Jacobs sued various hardware manufacturers, including Microsoft and Logitech, alleging that they were directly infringing the '958 patent. In the same action, Jacobs named Analog as a defendant, charging Analog with inducement and contributory infringement. Jacobs alleged that Analog provided tilt-sensitive components called accelerometers to the other defendants. Although Jacobs did not allege that Analog's accelerometers infringed the '958 patent, he alleged that the other defendants used those components in their tilt-sensitive control boxes, which allegedly infringed the '958 patent.

In July 2001, Jacobs's case against Analog was dismissed pursuant to a settlement agreement. Two provisions of the agreement are critical here:

3. License. Jacobs grants Analog an irrevocable, perpetual, fully paid up license to take any actions set forth in 35 U.S.C. § 271 which would, but for this license, constitute an infringement or violation of Jacobs' patent rights under the '958 patent. Without limiting the foregoing, the license granted hereunder includes the right to make, use, sell, import and export components, including micro-machined accelerometers, for use in tilt-sensitive control boxes.

5. Covenant-not-to-sue. Jacobs covenants not to sue Analog for any alleged infringement or violation of the '958 patent. This covenant-not-to-sue extends to any cause of action having as an element the infringement of the '958 patent by Analog or any other party, whether occurring in the past, present, or in the future.

After the settlement and dismissal of the litigation against Analog, Jacobs filed a patent infringement action against Nintendo in the United States District Court for the Middle District of Florida. The complaint charged Nintendo with infringing or inducing infringement of the '958 patent by producing the game "Kirby Tilt 'n Tumble" for its hand-held Game Boy video game systems. When the Kirby game is inserted into the system, the player can control the movement of the Kirby character in the video game by tilting the controller in the desired direction of movement.

Nintendo moved for summary judgment of non-infringement, asserting that it was entitled to practice the '958 patent by virtue of the settlement agreement between Jacobs and Analog, the supplier of the accelerometers for the Kirby game. The district court granted Nintendo's motion and entered judgment of non-infringement for Nintendo. The court held that because the settlement agreement between Jacobs and Analog permitted Analog to sell accelerometers for use in tilt-sensitive control boxes, such as the ones manufactured and sold by Nintendo, the agreement necessarily gave Nintendo an implied license to use the Analog accelerometers in its tilt-sensitive control boxes. For Jacobs to bar Analog's customer, Nintendo, from using Analog's accelerometers in the products expressly referred to in the settlement agreement, the court concluded, would undermine the provision of the agreement permitting the sale of accelerometers "for use in tilt-sensitive control boxes." The court explained that Jacobs should not be permitted to do "through the back door-by suing a customer of Analog-what he cannot do through the front door," i.e., by suing Analog.

II

The agreement between Jacobs and Analog granted Analog two important rights: (1) the right not to be sued for infringement of the '958 patent; and (2) the right to "sell . . . micro-machined accelerometers for use in tilt-sensitive control boxes." The first right (granted by paragraph 5 of the agreement) provided "peace" by assuring Analog that it would not face any further claims of infringement of the '958 patent based on any of its past or future conduct, including liability for indirect infringement, i.e., a cause of action "having as an element the infringement of the '958 patent by . . . any other party." The second right (granted by paragraph 3 of the agreement) provided "prosperity" by giving Analog a right to sell its accelerometers for a particular use.

Jacobs argues that the settlement agreement protected Analog against being sued for direct or indirect infringement, but that it did not give Nintendo a general right to use Analog's accelerometers in tilt-sensitive control boxes that infringed the '958 patent. Thus, Jacobs contends that paragraph 3 and paragraph 5 of the agreement both secured Analog against the prospect of suit for any of its conduct or any conduct by Analog's customers, but did not grant similar rights to Analog's customers. Nonetheless, Jacobs does not suggest that Nintendo obtained no rights whatsoever from the agreement between Jacobs and Analog. According to Jacobs, paragraph 3 of the agreement would give Nintendo the right to use Analog's accelerometers in infringing control boxes if it could prove that Analog's accelerometers had no non-infringing uses. In that event, according to Jacobs, the Analog-Jacobs agreement would give Nintendo an implied license to use those accelerometers without liability under the '958 patent, because otherwise the license to sell the accelerometers would be of no commercial benefit to Analog. Jacobs contends, however, that in the absence of proof that the accelerometers had no non-infringing uses, paragraph 3 provides no protection to Nintendo against an action for infringement of the '958 patent based on Nintendo's manufacture and sale of its tilt-sensitive control boxes.

In pressing its argument that Nintendo has an implied license only if it can establish that Analog's accelerometers had no non-infringing uses, Jacobs relies on this court's decision in Met-Coil Systems Corp. v. Korners Unlimited, Inc. In Met-Coil, this court held that a patent owner's sale of a machine useful only in practicing the claimed invention "plainly indicate[d] that the grant of a license [to practice the invention] should be inferred." Because there were no circumstances tending to show the contrary, this court upheld the district court's conclusion that the patent owner's customers enjoyed an implied license under the patent.

The requirement of demonstrating that there is no non-infringing use for the object in question does not apply in the context of this case. The "non-infringing use" doctrine applies when a patentee or its licensee sells an article and the question is whether the sale carries with it a license to engage in conduct that would infringe the patent owner's rights. In that setting, absent an express agreement between the parties, determining whether the sale conveys with it the implied right to use the article in an infringing manner may depend on whether there is any non-infringing use for the article. If there is no non-infringing use, it may be reasonable to infer that there has been "a relinquishment of the patent monopoly with respect to the article sold. In such a case, unless the circumstances of the sale indicate that a grant of a license should not be inferred, the patentee will be barred from asserting its patent rights against a downstream purchaser of the article.

This case is quite different. Here, there is no need to ask whether Analog was authorized to sell its accelerometers to be used in infringing devices, because the Jacobs-Analog agreement must be understood to authorize Analog to sell its accelerometers for such uses.

Jacobs's patent does not, of course, limit anyone's right to make either non-infringing devices or components for non-infringing devices. Therefore, the second sentence of paragraph 3 of the Jacobs-Analog settlement agreement, which authorizes Analog to make and sell accelerometers for use in tilt-sensitive control boxes, makes sense only if it is understood to confer on Analog the right to make and sell accelerometers for use in tilt-sensitive control boxes that would otherwise infringe Jacobs's rights under the '958 patent. For that reason, the question whether there is any non-infringing use for Analog's accelerometers is irrelevant here. The Jacobs-Analog agreement has specifically authorized the sale of those accelerometers for infringing uses. The critical question, then, is whether the clause authorizing that use protects Nintendo against suit based on the use of the accelerometers for the purposes for which Analog was authorized to sell them.

The district court held that the right given to Analog to sell its accelerometers for use in infringing tilt-sensitive control boxes would be meaningless if Jacobs could effectively prevent Analog from making any such sales by suing Analog's customers for putting the accelerometers into infringing control boxes and selling the resulting products. We agree with the district court that the clause granting Analog the right to sell its accelerometers for use in tilt-sensitive control boxes barred Jacobs from interfering with that right by prohibiting Analog's customers from using the accelerometers for that authorized purpose by making, using, and selling control boxes incorporating Analog's devices. That interpretation is in accordance with the basic contract law principle that a party may not assign a right, receive consideration for it, and then take steps that would render the right commercially worthless.

Jacobs urges us to interpret paragraph 3 of the Jacobs-Analog agreement as granting Analog only a bare license, i.e., the right not to be sued for making, using, or selling accelerometers for use in tilt-sensitive control boxes. To interpret paragraph 3 as a bare license, however, would ignore the language of the second sentence of paragraph 3 that goes beyond the creation of a license (conveying the right to make and sell accelerometers "for use in tilt-sensitive control boxes"). In addition, it would make paragraph 3 entirely redundant, because paragraph 5 already ensures Analog freedom from suit "for any alleged infringement or violation of the '958 patent." If all that Jacobs intended to do through the settlement agreement was to free Analog of its liability for infringement, paragraph 5 of the agreement (the covenant not to sue) would have been fully sufficient to serve that purpose. Paragraph 3, however, goes much further by granting Analog an affirmative right to engage in the manufacture and sale of accelerometers to be used in tilt-sensitive control boxes. That grant comes without restriction of any kind.

Jacobs seeks to explain the license granted in paragraph 3 by characterizing it as giving Analog the right to make and sell infringing control boxes on its own or, alternatively, as ensuring that Analog would be free to sell accelerometers to whomever it wanted for use in infringing control boxes, but not protecting Analog's customers from suit for making and selling those boxes. Neither explanation is plausible, however. Jacobs knew that Analog was not in the business of making game controllers, so there is no reason to believe Analog would have bargained for that right. Furthermore, as the district court noted, it is unlikely that Analog would have contracted for the right to manufacture and sell a product knowing that its customers would be unable to use the product that it sold them for the bargained-for purpose. Thus, we agree with the district court that the Jacobs-Analog settlement agreement grants to Analog's customers an implied sublicense to use Analog's accelerometers to make, use, and sell tilt-sensitive control boxes that infringe the 958 patent without interference by Jacobs. The district court therefore properly held that Jacobs was barred from suing Nintendo for infringement of the '958 patent based on Nintendo's manufacture and sale of tilt-sensitive control boxes that incorporated Analog's accelerometers.

AFFIRMED

QUESTIONS

1. In discussing the *Met-Coil Systems* case, the court said the implied license there hinged on whether or not the machine sold had any non-infringing use. How does the existence of a non-infringing use affect the determination of an implied license?

2. How does the court distinguish the facts in *Jacobs* from *Met-Coil Systems*? Why did Nintendo's implied license not require a finding of a non-infringing use for the accelerometers?

CASE NOTES

1. AMP entered into a research and development contract with the Army Signal Corps to develop and supply the Government with a device for splicing electrical wires. The contract granted the Government an irrevocable, nonexclusive, nontransferable and royalty-free license to practice the "Subject Invention." The Subject Invention was defined as any invention made during the performance of the contract. The contract specifically stated "Nothing contained in this [license] shall be deemed to grant any license under any invention other than a Subject Invention." AMP was issued patent '146 on a device for splicing electrical wires in 1955 which both parties agreed was included within the definition of Subject Invention in the contract. After conclusion of the contract, AMP discovered that any earlier issued patent (the Vinson patent) dominated its '146 patent; that is, the '146 patent could not be practiced without infringing the Vinson patent. AMP then acquired the Vinson patent. The Government ultimately contracted with another firm to supply the wire-splicing devices. AMP filed a patent infringement suit against the Government claiming the Government's purchase and use of the wire-splicing devices infringed the Vinson patent. What result? *See* AMP, Inc. v. United States, 389 F.2d 448 (Ct. Cl. 1968).

2. *See also* Zapata Industries, Inc. v. W.R. Grace & Co., 51 U.S.P.Q.2d 1619 (S.D.Fla. 1999) (An implied license can be created pursuant to several different legal theories, including acquiescence, by conduct, by equitable estoppel or by legal estoppels); Bandag Inc. v. Al Bolser's Tire Stores, Inc., 750 F.2d 903 (Fed. Cir. 1984) (Implied license of patent for cold-process tire re-treading method was not extended to defendant tire dealer by its purchase of used equipment from a former franchisee of manufacturer; the equipment had non-infringing uses, and the

possibility of infringement was simply ignored and never investigated by defendant tire dealer; equitable estoppel could not be established and thus the defendant tire dealer infringed the plaintiff manufacturer's patent; no license can be implied where equipment involved has other non-infringing uses, even if only as replacement parts); Winbond Elecs. Corp. v. ITC, 262 F.3d 1363 (Fed. Cir. 2001) (An implied license by equitable estoppel requires proof that: (1) the patentee, through statements or conduct, gave an affirmative grant of consent or permission to make, use, or sell to the alleged infringer; (2) the alleged infringer relied on that statement or conduct; and (3) the alleged infringer would be materially prejudiced if the patentee is allowed to proceed with its claim. For a finding of implied license through legal estoppel, a patentee must have licensed or assigned a right, received consideration, and then sought to derogate from the right granted); PPG Industries, Inc. v. Guardian Industries Corp., 597 F.2d 1090 (6th Cir. 1979) (A "shop right" is an implied license which accrues to an employer in cases where an employee has perfected a patentable device while working for an employer; although the employee is the owner of the patent, he is estopped from claiming infringement by the employer since the patent work has been done on the employer's time and the employer has furnished materials for experiments and financial backing to the employee). Shop rights are covered in section 4.1 of the materials.

Additional Information

1. ROBERT A. MATTHEWS JR., 2 ANNOTATED PATENT DIGEST §§ 11:47, 11:171 (2008).

2. GREGORY E. UPCHURCH, INTELLECTUAL PROPERTY LITIGATION GUIDE: PATENTS AND TRADE SECRETS § 11:9 (2008).

3. Lara J. Hodgson, *Assignor Estoppel: Fairness at What Price?*, 20 SANTA CLARA COMPUTER & HIGH TECH. L. J. 797 (2004).

4. Amber L. Hatfield, *Life After Death for Assignor Estoppel: Per Se Application to Protect Incentives to Innovate*, 68 TEX. L. REV. 251 (1989).

5. Amber Hatfield Rovner, *Practical Guide to Application of (or Defense Against) Product-Based Infringement Under the Doctrine of Patent Exhaustion and Implied License*, 12 TEX. INTELL. PROP. L.J. 227 (2004).

6. Rachel C. Clark, *Implied Licenses by Legal Estoppel*, 14 ALB. L. J. SCI. & TECH. 53 (2003).

7. Patricia Stanford, *Diamond Scientific v. Ambico: Enforcing Patent Assignor Estoppel*, 26 HOUS. L. REV. 761 (1989).

8. Michael J. Swope, *Recent Developments in Patent Law: Implied License — An Emerging Threat to Contributory Infringement Protection*, 68 TEMP. L. REV. 281 (1995).

2.2.4 Licensee Estoppel

Licensee estoppel is another field in which federal courts have held that federal law governs the relationship between parties to a patent license. Under an established common law rule, state courts have held that a buyer cannot challenge the seller's title to purchased goods as a means to repudiate the purchase agreement. The rationale for the common law rule is that if the buyer were allowed to challenge the seller's title to purchased goods, the buyer would be able to continue to possess the goods without any obligation to pay for them. State courts have extended this common law rule to patent licenses and held that a licensee could not challenge the validity of the licensed patent in a suit by the licensor for breach of the license contract. The rationale for extending the common law contract rule to patent licenses is that to hold otherwise would allow the licensee to benefit from the license agreement while at the same time claiming the agreement is invalid in order to avoid paying for that benefit. This extension of the common law rule became known as the "licensee estoppel" doctrine. As you will see in the *Lear* case below, the Supreme Court has held that the licensee estoppel doctrine, by prohibiting licensees from challenging the validity of licensed patents, stands in opposition to the important federal public interest of ensuring that all patents are valid and of having free competition in the use of ideas.

The *Lear* decision raised a number of new questions about the rights of parties to a patent contract. One question is the effect of *Lear* on assignee estoppel. The district courts that have considered this question are split, although the weight of authority appears to hold that assignee estoppel is still good law after *Lear*. *See*, STEVEN Z. SZCZEPANSKI, 1 ECKSTROM'S LICENSING IN FOR. & DOM. OPS. § 8C:7 (2008). The rationale for continuing assignee estoppel is that allowing licensees to avoid paying future royalties by challenging the validity of the licensed patent is different than allowing an assignee to avoid its contractual duty to the assignor to pay for what it has already received. *Id.* The Federal Circuit, however, has noted the anomalous position of an assignee in challenging the validity of an assigned patent; as the owner of the patent, the assignee would be in a position of simultaneously challenging and defending the validity of the patent. *Id.*

Another question raised by *Lear* is its impact on assignor estoppel. As noted earlier, in Diamond Scientific Co. v. Ambico Inc., 848 F.2d 1220 (1988), the Federal Circuit has held that an assignor is barred from challenging the validity of a patent it has assigned. The court's reasoning in *Diamond Scientific* is that the assignor has already been fully paid for the patent and, if the assignor was allowed to later challenge the validity of the patent, the assignor would be able to practice the patent and also keep the assignment payment. Other cases, however, have permitted assignors to challenge the validity of the assigned patents. *See, e.g.,* Contour Chair Lounge Co. v. True-Fit Chair, Inc., 648 F. Supp. 704 (E.D. Mo. 1986).

The question of whether the rationale of *Lear* precludes enforcement of a "no-contest" clause which prohibits the licensee from challenging the validity of the licensed patent was considered in Bendix Corp. v. Balax, Inc., 421 F.2d 809 (1970). In *Bendix*, the court held that a no-contest clause in a license agreement might constitute an illegal extension of the patent owner's rights in light of *Lear*. Given the emphasis in *Lear* on federal public policy goals, another argument against enforcing no-contest clauses in patent licenses would be that no-contest clauses are contrary to federal public policy and licensors should not be allowed to contravene federal public policy by means of contract terms.

Lear has not been extended to licenses entered into in settlement of patent infringement suits. In settlement agreements, the accused infringer is almost always required to execute a consent judgment stating that the patent in suit is valid and infringed. The consent judgment is filed with the court and precludes future challenges to the patent's validity under the doctrine of *res judicata* or collateral estoppel. *See*, 1 DAVID M. EPSTEIN, ECKSTROM'S LICENSING IN FOREIGN & DOMESTIC OPERATIONS § 8C:3 (2008).

The second case in this section, *Medimmune v. Genentech*, addresses the question of whether a licensee must breach the license agreement in order to have standing to contest the validity of the licensed patent in a declaratory judgment proceeding. *Medimmune* is generating as many questions, and stirring as much controversy, as *Lear* did nearly forty years ago.

LEAR v. ADKINS
395 U.S. 653 (1969)

MR. JUSTICE HARLAN delivered the opinion of the Court.

In January of 1952, John Adkins, an inventor and mechanical engineer, was hired by Lear, Incorporated, for the purpose of solving a vexing problem the company had encountered in its efforts to develop a gyroscope which would meet the increasingly demanding requirements of the aviation industry. The gyroscope is an essential component of the navigational system in all aircraft, enabling the pilot to learn the direction and altitude of his airplane. With the development of the faster airplanes of the 1950's, more accurate gyroscopes were needed, and the gyro industry consequently was casting about for new techniques which would satisfy this need in an economical fashion. Shortly after Adkins was hired, he developed a method of construction at the company's California facilities which improved gyroscope accuracy at a low cost. Lear almost immediately incorporated Adkins' improvements into its production process to its substantial advantage.

The question that remains unsettled in this case, after eight years of litigation in the California courts, is whether Adkins will receive compensation for Lear's use of those improvements which the inventor has subsequently patented. At every stage of this lawsuit, Lear has sought to prove that, despite the grant of a patent by the Patent Office, none of Adkins' improvements were sufficiently novel to warrant the award of a monopoly under the standards delineated in the governing federal statutes. Moreover, the company has sought to prove that Adkins obtained his patent by means of a fraud on the Patent Office. In response, the inventor has argued that since Lear had entered into a licensing agreement with Adkins, it was obliged to pay the agreed royalties regardless of the validity of the underlying patent.

The Supreme Court of California unanimously vindicated the inventor's position. While the court recognized that generally a manufacturer is free to challenge the validity of an inventor's patent, it held that "one of the oldest doctrines in the field of patent law establishes that so long as a licensee is operating under a license agreement he is estopped to deny the validity of his licensor's patent in a suit for royalties under the agreement. The theory underlying this doctrine is that a licensee should not be permitted to enjoy the benefit afforded by the agreement while simultaneously urging that the patent which forms the basis of the agreement is void."

Almost 20 years ago, in its last consideration of the doctrine, this Court also invoked an estoppel to deny a licensee the right to prove that his licensor was demanding royalties for the use of an idea which was in reality a part of the public domain. We granted certiorari in the present case to reconsider the validity of the Hazeltine rule in the light of our recent decisions emphasizing the strong federal policy favoring free competition in ideas which do not merit patent protection.

I.

At the very beginning of the parties' relationship, Lear and Adkins entered into a rudimentary one-page agreement which provided that although "(a)ll new ideas, discoveries, inventions, etc., related to * * * vertical gyros become the property of Mr. John S. Adkins," the inventor promised to grant Lear a license as to all ideas he might develop "on a mutually satisfactory royalty basis." As soon as Adkins' labors yielded tangible results, it quickly became apparent to the inventor that further steps should be taken to place his rights to his ideas on a firmer basis. On February 4, 1954, Adkins filed an application with the Patent Office in an effort to gain federal protection for his improvements. At about the same time, he entered into a lengthy period of negotiations with Lear in an effort to conclude a licensing agreement which would clearly establish the amount of royalties that would be paid.

These negotiations finally bore fruit on September 15, 1955, when the parties approved a complex 17-page contract which carefully delineated the conditions upon which Lear promised to pay royalties for Adkins' improvements. The parties agreed that if "the U.S. Patent Office refuses to issue a patent on the substantial claims" (contained in Adkins' original patent application) or if such a patent so issued is subsequently held invalid, then in any of such events Lear at its option shall have the right forthwith to terminate the specific license so affected or to terminate this entire Agreement.

As the contractual language indicates, Adkins had not obtained a final Patent Office decision as to the patentability of his invention at the time the licensing agreement was concluded. Indeed, he was not to receive a patent until January 5, 1960. This long delay has its source in the special character of Patent Office procedures. The regulations do not require the Office to make a final judgment on an invention's patentability on the basis of the inventor's original application. While it sometimes happens that a patent is granted at this early stage, it is far more common for the Office to find that although certain of the applicant's claims may be patentable, certain others have been fully anticipated by the earlier developments in the art. In such a situation, the Patent Office does not attempt to separate the wheat from the chaff on its own initiative. Instead, it rejects the application, giving the inventor the right to make an amendment which narrows his claim to cover only those aspects of the invention which are truly novel. It often happens, however, that even after an application is amended, the Patent Office finds that some of the remaining claims are unpatentable. When this occurs, the agency again issues a rejection which is subject to further amendment. And so the process of rejection and amendment continues until the Patent Office Examiner either grants a patent or concludes that none of the inventor's claims could possibly be patentable, at which time a final rejection is entered on the Office's records. Thus, when Adkins made his original application in 1954, it took the average inventor more than three years before he obtained a final administrative decision on the patentability of his ideas, with the Patent Office acting on the average application from two to four times.

The progress of Adkins' effort to obtain a patent followed the typical pattern. In his initial application, the inventor made the ambitious claim that his entire method of constructing gyroscopes was sufficiently novel to merit protection. The Patent Office, however, rejected this initial claim, as well as two subsequent amendments, which progressively narrowed the scope of the invention sought to be protected. Finally, Adkins narrowed his claim drastically to assert only that the design of the apparatus used to achieve gyroscope accuracy was novel. In response, the Office issued its 1960 patent, granting a 17-year monopoly on this more modest claim.

During the long period in which Adkins was attempting to convince the Patent Office of the novelty of his ideas, however, Lear had become convinced that Adkins would never receive a patent on his invention and that it should not continue to pay substantial royalties on ideas which had not contributed substantially to the development of the art of gyroscopy. In 1957, after Adkins' patent application had been rejected twice, Lear announced that it had searched the Patent Office's files and had found a patent which it believed had fully anticipated Adkins' discovery. As a result, the company stated that it would no longer pay royalties on the large number of gyroscopes it was producing at its plant in Grand Rapids, Michigan (the Michigan gyros). Payments were continued on the smaller number of gyros produced at the company's California plant (the California gyros) for two more years until they too were terminated on April 8, 1959.

As soon as Adkins obtained his patent in 1960, he brought this lawsuit in the California Superior Court. He argued to a jury that both the Michigan and the California gyros incorporated his patented apparatus and that Lear's failure to pay royalties on these gyros was a breach both of the 1955 contract and of Lear's quasi-contractual obligations. Although Lear sought to raise patent invalidity as a defense, the trial judge directed a verdict of $16,351.93 for Adkins on the California gyros, holding that Lear was estopped by its licensing agreement from questioning the inventor's patent. The trial judge took a different approach when it came to considering the Michigan gyros. Noting that the company claimed that it had developed its Michigan designs independently of Adkins' ideas, the court instructed the jury to award the inventor recovery only if it was satisfied that Adkins' invention was novel, within the meaning of the federal patent laws. When the jury returned a verdict for Adkins of $888,122.56 on the Michigan gyros, the trial judge granted Lear's motion for judgment notwithstanding the verdict, finding that Adkins' invention had been completely anticipated by the prior art.

Neither side was satisfied with this split decision, and both appealed to the California District Court of Appeal, which adopted a quite different approach. The court held that Lear was within its contractual rights in terminating its royalty obligations entirely in 1959, and that if Adkins desired to recover damages after that date he was "relegated to an action for infringement" in the federal courts. So far as pre-1959 royalties were concerned, the court held that the contract required the company to pay royalties on both the California and Michigan gyros regardless of the validity of the inventor's patent.

Once again both sides appealed, this time to the California Supreme Court, which took yet another approach to the problem presented. The court rejected the District Court of Appeal's conclusion that the 1955 license gave Lear the right to terminate its royalty obligations in 1959. Since the 1955 agreement was still in effect, the court concluded, relying on the language we have already quoted, that the doctrine of estoppel barred Lear from questioning the propriety of the Patent Office's grant. The court's adherence to estoppel, however, was not without qualification. After noting Lear's claim that it had developed its Michigan gyros independently, the court tested this contention by considering "whether what is being built by Lear (in Michigan) springs entirely" (emphasis supplied) from the prior art. Applying this test, it found that Lear had in fact "utilized the apparatus patented by Adkins throughout the period in question," and reinstated the jury's $888,000 verdict on this branch of the case.

II.

Since the California Supreme Court's construction of the 1955 licensing agreement is solely a matter of state law, the only issue open to us is raised by the court's reliance upon the doctrine of estoppel to bar Lear from proving that Adkins' ideas were dedicated to the common welfare by federal law. In considering the propriety of the State Court's decision, we are well aware that we are not writing upon a clean slate. The doctrine of estoppel has been considered by this Court in a line of cases reaching back into the middle of the 19th century.

B.

The estoppel rule was first stringently limited in a situation in which the patentee's equities were far more compelling than those presented in the typical licensing arrangement. Westinghouse Electric & Manufacturing Co. v. Formica Insulation Co. framed a rule to govern the recurring problem which arises when the original patent owner, after assigning his patent to another for a substantial sum, claims that the patent is worthless because it contains no new ideas. The courts of appeals had traditionally refused to permit such a defense to an infringement action on the ground that it was improper both to "sell and keep the same thing," Nevertheless, Formica imposed a limitation upon estoppel which was radically inconsistent with the premises upon which the "general rule" is based. The Court held that while an assignor may not directly attack the validity of a patent by reference to the prior state of the art, he could introduce such evidence to narrow the claims made in the patent. "The distinction may be a nice one but seems to be workable." Workable or not, the result proved to be an anomaly: if a patent had some novelty Formica permitted the old owner to defend an infringement action by showing that the invention's novel aspects did not extend to the inclusion of the old owner's products; on the other hand, if a patent had no novelty at all, the old owner could not defend successfully since he would be obliged to launch the direct attack on the patent that Formica seemed to forbid. The incongruity of this position compelled at least one court of appeals to carry the reasoning of the Formica exception to its logical conclusion. In 1940 the Seventh Circuit held that a licensee could introduce evidence of the prior art to show that the licensor's claims were not novel at all and thus successfully defend an action for royalties.

In Scott Paper Co. v. Marcalus Manufacturing Co., this Court adopted a position similar to the Seventh Circuit's, undermining the basis of patent estoppel even more than Formica had done. In Scott, the original patent owner had attempted to defend an infringement suit brought by his assignee by proving that his product was a copy of an expired patent. The Court refused to permit the assignee to invoke an estoppel, finding that the policy of the patent laws would be frustrated if a manufacturer was required to pay for the use of information which under the patent statutes, was the property of all. Chief Justice Stone, for the Court, did not go beyond the precise question presented by a manufacturer who asserted that he was simply copying an expired patent. Nevertheless it was impossible to limit the Scott doctrine to such a narrow compass. If patent policy forbids estoppel when the old owner attempts to show that he did no more than copy an expired patent, why should not the old owner also be permitted to show that the invention lacked novelty because it could be found in a technical journal or because it was obvious to one knowledgeable in the art? As Justice Frankfurter's dissent indicated there were no satisfactory answers to these questions. The Scott exception had undermined the very basis of the "general rule."

C.

At about the time Scott was decided, this Court developed yet another doctrine which was profoundly antithetic to the principles underlying estoppel. In Sola Electric Co. v. Jefferson Electric Co., the majority refused to permit a licensor to enforce the license's price-fixing provisions without permitting the licensee to contest the validity of the underlying patent. Since the price-fixing clause was per se illegal but for the existence of a valid patent, this narrow exception could be countenanced without compromising the general estoppel principle. But the Sola Court went further: it held that since the patentee had sought to enforce the price-fixing clause, the licensee could also avoid paying royalties if he could show that the patent was invalid. Five years later, the "anti-trust exception" was given an even more extensive scope in the Katzinger and MacGregor cases. Here licensors were not permitted to invoke an estoppel despite the fact that they sought only to collect their royalties. The mere existence of a price-fixing clause in the license was held to be enough to bring the validity of the patent into question. Thus in the large number of cases in which licensing agreements contained restrictions that were arguably illegal under the antitrust laws, the doctrine of estoppel was a dead letter. Justice Frankfurter, in dissent, went even further, concluding that Katzinger and MacGregor had done all but repudiate the estoppel rule: "If a doctrine that was vital law for more than ninety years will be found to have now been deprived of life, we ought at least to give it decent public burial."

D.

The lower courts, both state and federal, have also hedged the impact of estoppel by creating exceptions which have indicated a recognition of the broader policies pointing to a contrary approach. It is generally the rule that licensees may avoid further royalty payments, regardless of the provisions of their contract, once a third party proves that the patent is invalid. Some courts have gone further to hold that a licensee may notify the patent owner that he is repudiating his agreement, regardless of its terms, and may subsequently defend any action for royalties by proving patent invalidity. And even in the 19th century, state courts had held that if the licensee had not actually sold products incorporating the patent's ideas, he could challenge the validity of the patent.

III.

The uncertain status of licensee estoppel in the case law is a product of judicial efforts to accommodate the competing demands of the common law of contracts and the federal law of patents. On the one hand, the law of contracts forbids a purchaser to repudiate his promises simply because he later becomes dissatisfied with the bargain he has made. On the other hand, federal law requires, that all ideas in general circulation be dedicated to the common good unless they are protected by a valid patent. When faced with this basic conflict in policy, both this Court and courts throughout the land have naturally sought to develop an intermediate position which somehow would remain responsive to the radically different concerns of the two different worlds of contract and patent. The result has been a failure. Rather than creative compromise, there has been a chaos of conflicting case law, proceeding on inconsistent premises. Before renewing the search for an acceptable middle ground, we must reconsider on their own merits the arguments which may properly be advanced on both sides of the estoppel question.

A.

It will simplify matters greatly if we first consider the most typical situation in which patent licenses are negotiated. In contrast to the present case, most manufacturers obtain a license after a patent has issued. Since the Patent Office makes an inventor's ideas public when it issues its grant of a limited monopoly, a potential licensee has access to the inventor's ideas even if he does not enter into an agreement with the patent owner. Consequently, a manufacturer gains only two benefits if he chooses to enter a licensing agreement after the patent has issued. First, by accepting a license and paying royalties for a time, the licensee may have avoided the necessity of defending an expensive infringement action during the period when he may be least able to afford one. Second, the existence of an unchallenged patent may deter others from attempting to compete with the licensee.

Under ordinary contract principles the mere fact that some benefit is received is enough to require the enforcement of the contract, regardless of the validity of the underlying patent. Nevertheless, if one tests this result by the standard of good-faith commercial dealing, it seems far from satisfactory. For the simple contract approach entirely ignores the position of the licensor who is seeking to invoke the court's assistance on his behalf. Consider, for example, the equities of the licensor who has obtained his patent through a fraud on the Patent Office. It is difficult to perceive why good faith requires that courts should permit him to recover royalties despite his licensee's attempts to show that the patent is invalid.

Even in the more typical cases, not involving conscious wrongdoing, the licensor's equities are far from compelling. A patent, in the last analysis, simply represents a legal conclusion reached by the Patent Office. Moreover, the legal conclusion is predicated on factors as to which reasonable men can differ widely. Yet the Patent Office is often obliged to reach its decision in an ex parte proceeding, without the aid of the arguments which could be advanced by parties interested in proving patent invalidity. Consequently, it does not seem to us to be unfair to require a patentee to defend the Patent Office's judgment when his licensee places the question in issue, especially since the licensor's case is buttressed by the presumption of validity which attaches to his patent. Thus, although licensee estoppel may be consistent with the letter of contractual doctrine, we cannot say that it is compelled by the spirit of contract law, which seeks to balance the claims of promisor and promisee in accord with the requirements of good faith.

Surely the equities of the licensor do not weigh very heavily when they are balanced against the important public interest in permitting full and free competition in the use of ideas which are in reality a part of the public domain. Licensees may often be the only individuals with enough economic incentive to challenge the patentability of an inventor's discovery. If they are muzzled, the public may continually be required to pay tribute to would-be monopolists without need or justification. We think it plain that the technical requirements of contract doctrine must give way before the demands of the public interest in the typical situation involving the negotiation of a license after a patent has issued.

We are satisfied that Automatic Radio Manufacturing Co. v. Hazeltine Research, Inc., supra, itself the product of a clouded history, should no longer be regarded as sound law with respect to its "estoppel" holding, and that holding is now overruled.

B.

The case before us, however, presents a far more complicated estoppel problem than the one which arises in the most common licensing context. The problem arises out of the fact that Lear obtained its license in 1955, more than four years before Adkins received his 1960 patent. Indeed, from the very outset of the relationship, Lear obtained special access to Adkins' ideas in return for its promise to pay satisfactory compensation.

Thus, during the lengthy period in which Adkins was attempting to obtain a patent, Lear gained an important benefit not generally obtained by the typical licensee. For until a patent issues, a potential licensee may not learn his licensor's ideas simply by requesting the information from the Patent Office. During the time the inventor is seeking patent protection, the governing federal statute requires the Patent Office to hold an inventor's patent application in confidence. If a potential licensee hopes to use the ideas contained in a secret patent application, he must deal with the inventor himself, unless the inventor chooses to publicize his ideas to the world at large. By promising to pay Adkins royalties from the very outset of their relationship, Lear gained immediate access to ideas which it may well not have learned until the Patent Office published the details of Adkins' invention in 1960. At the core of this case, then, is the difficult question whether federal patent policy bars a State from enforcing a contract regulating access to an unpatented secret idea.

Adkins takes an extreme position on this question. The inventor does not merely argue that since Lear obtained privileged access to his ideas before 1960, the company should be required to pay royalties accruing before 1960 regardless of the validity of the patent which ultimately issued. He also argues that since Lear obtained special benefits before 1960, it should also pay royalties during the entire patent period (1960–1977), without regard to the validity of the Patent Office's grant. We cannot accept so broad an argument.

Adkins' position would permit inventors to negotiate all important licenses during the lengthy period while their applications were still pending at the Patent Office, thereby disabling entirely all those who have the strongest incentive to show that a patent is worthless. While the equities supporting Adkins' position are somewhat more appealing than those supporting the typical licensor, we cannot say that there is enough of a difference to justify such a substantial impairment of overriding federal policy.

Nor can we accept a second argument which may be advanced to support Adkins' claim to at least a portion of his post-patent royalties, regardless of the validity of the Patent Office grant. The terms of the 1955 agreement provide that royalties are to be paid until such time as the "patent * * * is held invalid and the fact remains that the question of patent validity has not been finally determined in this case". Thus, it may be suggested that although Lear must be allowed to raise the question of patent validity in the present lawsuit, it must also be required to comply with its contract and continue to pay royalties until its claim is finally vindicated in the courts.

The parties' contract, however, is no more controlling on this issue than is the State's doctrine of estoppel, which is also rooted in contract principles. The decisive question is whether overriding federal policies would be significantly frustrated if licensees could be required to continue to pay royalties during the time they are challenging patent validity in the courts.

It seems to us that such a requirement would be inconsistent with the aims of federal patent policy. Enforcing this contractual provision would give the licensor an additional economic incentive to devise every conceivable dilatory tactic in an effort to postpone the day of final judicial reckoning. We can perceive no reason to encourage dilatory court tactics in this way. Moreover, the cost of prosecuting slow-moving trial proceedings and defending an inevitable appeal might well deter many licensees from attempting to prove patent invalidity in the courts. The deterrent effect would be particularly severe in the many scientific fields in which invention is proceeding at a rapid rate. In these areas, a patent may well become obsolete long before its 17-year term has expired. If a licensee has reason to believe that he will replace a patented idea with a new one in the near future, he will have little incentive to initiate lengthy court proceedings, unless he is freed from liability at least from the time he refuses to pay the contractual royalties. Lastly, enforcing this contractual provision would undermine the strong federal policy favoring the full and free use of ideas in the public domain. For all these reasons, we hold that Lear must be permitted to avoid the payment of all royalties accruing after Adkins' 1960 patent issued if Lear can prove patent invalidity.

C.

Adkins' claim to contractual royalties accruing before the 1960 patent issued is, however, a much more difficult one, since it squarely raises the question whether, and to what extent, the States may protect the owners of unpatented inventions who are willing to disclose their ideas to manufacturers only upon payment of royalties. The California Supreme Court did not address itself to this issue with precision, for it believed that the venerable doctrine of estoppel provided a sufficient answer to all of Lear's claims based upon federal patent law. Thus, we do not know whether the Supreme Court would have awarded Adkins recovery even on his pre-patent royalties if it had recognized that previously established estoppel doctrine could no longer be properly invoked with regard to royalties accruing during the 17-year patent period. Our decision today will, of course, require the state courts to reconsider the theoretical basis of their decisions enforcing the contractual rights of inventors and it is impossible to predict the extent to which this reevaluation may revolutionize the law of any particular State in this regard. Consequently, we have concluded, after much consideration, that even though an important question of federal law underlies this phase of the controversy, we should not now attempt to define in even a limited way the extent, if any, to which the States may properly act to enforce the contractual rights of inventors of unpatented secret ideas. Given the difficulty and importance of this task, it should be undertaken only after the state courts have, after fully focused inquiry, determined the extent to which they will respect the contractual rights of such inventors in the future. Indeed, on remand, the California courts may well reconcile the competing demands of patent and contract law in a way which would not warrant further review in this Court.

IV.

We also find it inappropriate to pass at this time upon Lear's contention that Adkins' patent is invalid. Not only did Lear fail to raise this issue in its petition for certiorari, but the California Supreme Court has yet to pass on the question of patent validity in that clear and unequivocal manner which is so necessary for proper adjudication in this Court. As we have indicated, the California Supreme Court considered the novelty of Adkins' ideas relevant to its decision at only one stage of its extensive analysis. Since Lear claimed that it had developed its Michigan gyros completely independently of Adkins' efforts, the Supreme Court believed itself obliged to consider whether Adkins' ideas were not "entirely" anticipated by the prior art. Applying this test, the court upheld the jury's verdict of $888,000 on the Michigan gyros, finding that "Lear utilized the apparatus patented by Adkins throughout the period in question." In reaching this conclusion, however, the court did express its belief that Adkins' invention made a "significant step forward" in the art of gyroscopy.

It is far from clear that the court, in making this last statement, intended to hold that Adkins' ideas satisfied the demanding standard of invention explicated in our decision in Graham v. John Deere Co., 383 U.S. 1, 86 S.Ct. 684, 15 L.Ed.2d 545 (1966). Surely, such a holding was not required by the court's analysis, which was concerned only with the question whether Lear had benefited from Adkins' ideas in any degree. In this context, we believe that Lear must be required to address its arguments attacking the validity of the underlying patent to the California courts in the first instance.

The judgment of the Supreme Court of California is vacated and the case is remanded to that court for further proceedings not inconsistent with this opinion.

It is so ordered.

Judgment of Supreme Court of California vacated and case remanded.

QUESTIONS

1. If a licensee is obtaining a competitive advantage from the licensed patent, why would the licensee challenge the validity of the patent and put the patent into the public domain for the licensee's competitors to use?

2. Are there ways for licensors to avoid royalty litigation and thereby preempt the licensee's opportunity to challenge the validity of the licensed patent in the context of breach of license litigation?

3. Do you agree with the Court's reasoning that prohibiting licensees from challenging the validity of patent licenses stands in opposition to federal public policy? Is this claimed federal public policy enunciated in the Patent Act? Are there better alternatives to review the validity of patents?

4. Should potential licensees be required to use due diligence in researching the validity of a patent before entering into a license agreement? What if a licensor demanded a clause in the license agreement that stated that the licensee has exercised due diligence with the assistance of counsel and determined that the licensed patent is valid?

MEDIMMUNE v. GENENTECH
549 U.S. 118 (2007)

Justice Scalia.

We must decide whether Article III's limitation of federal courts' jurisdiction to "Cases" and "Controversies," reflected in the "actual controversy" requirement of the Declaratory Judgment Act, 28 U.S.C. § 2201(a), requires a patent licensee to terminate or be in breach of its license agreement before it can seek a declaratory judgment that the underlying patent is invalid, unenforceable, or not infringed.

I

Because the declaratory-judgment claims in this case were disposed of at the motion-to-dismiss stage, we take the following facts from the allegations in petitioner's amended complaint and the unopposed declarations that petitioner submitted in response to the motion to dismiss. Petitioner MedImmune, Inc., manufactures Synagis, a drug used to prevent respiratory tract disease in infants and young children. In 1997, petitioner entered into a patent license agreement with respondent Genentech, Inc. (which acted on behalf of itself as patent assignee and on behalf of the coassignee, respondent City of Hope). The license covered an existing patent relating to the production of "chimeric antibodies" and a then-pending patent application relating to "the coexpression of immunoglobulin chains in recombinant host cells." Petitioner agreed to pay royalties on sales of "Licensed Products," and respondents granted petitioner the right to make, use, and sell them. The agreement defined "Licensed Products" as a specified antibody, "the manufacture, use or sale of which would, if not licensed under th[e] Agreement, infringe one or more claims of either or both of [the covered patents,] which have neither expired nor been held invalid by a court or other body of competent jurisdiction from which no appeal has been or may be taken." The license agreement gave petitioner the right to terminate upon six months' written notice.

In December 2001, the "coexpression" application covered by the 1997 license agreement matured into the "Cabilly II" patent. Soon thereafter, respondent Genentech delivered petitioner a letter expressing its belief that Synagis was covered by the Cabilly II patent and its expectation that petitioner would pay royalties beginning March 1, 2002. Petitioner did not think royalties were owing, believing that the Cabilly II patent was invalid and unenforceable, and that its claims were in any event not infringed by Synagis. Nevertheless, petitioner considered the letter to be a clear threat to enforce the Cabilly II patent, terminate the 1997 license agreement, and sue for patent infringement if petitioner did not make royalty payments as demanded. If respondents were to prevail in a patent infringement action, petitioner could be ordered to pay treble damages and attorney's fees, and could be enjoined from selling Synagis, a product that has accounted for more than 80 percent of its revenue from sales since 1999. Unwilling to risk such serious consequences, petitioner paid the demanded royalties "under protest and with reservation of all of [its] rights." This declaratory-judgment action followed.

Petitioner sought the declaratory relief discussed in detail in Part II below. Petitioner also requested damages and an injunction with respect to other federal and state claims not relevant here. The District Court granted respondents' motion to dismiss the declaratory-judgment claims for lack of subject-matter jurisdiction, relying on the decision of the United States Court of Appeals for the Federal Circuit in *Gen-Probe Inc. v. Vysis, Inc. Gen-Probe* had held that a patent licensee in good standing cannot establish an Article III case or controversy with regard to validity, enforceability, or scope of the patent because the license agreement "obliterate[s] any reasonable apprehension" that the licensee will be sued for infringement. The Federal Circuit affirmed the District Court, also relying on *Gen-Probe*. We granted certiorari.

II

At the outset, we address a disagreement concerning the nature of the dispute at issue here-whether it involves only a freestanding claim of patent invalidity or rather a claim that, both because of patent invalidity and because of noninfringement, no royalties are owing under the license agreement. That probably makes no difference to the ultimate issue of subject-matter jurisdiction, but it is well to be clear about the nature of the case before us.

Respondents contend that petitioner "is not seeking an interpretation of its present contractual obligations." They claim this for two reasons: (1) because there is no dispute that Synagis infringes the Cabilly II patent, thereby making royalties payable; and (2) because while there is a dispute over patent validity, the contract calls for royalties on an infringing product whether or not the underlying patent is valid. The first point simply does not comport with the allegations of petitioner's amended complaint. The very first count requested a *"DECLARATORY JUDGMENT ON CONTRACTUAL RIGHTS AND OBLIGATIONS,"* and stated that petitioner "disputes its obligation to make payments under the 1997 License Agreement because [petitioner's] sale of its Synagis product does not infringe any valid claim of the [Cabilly II] Patent." These contentions were repeated throughout the complaint. And the phrase "does not infringe any *valid* claim" (emphasis added) cannot be thought to be no more than a challenge to the patent's validity, since elsewhere the amended complaint states with unmistakable clarity that "the patent is not infringed by [petitioner's] Synagis product and that [petitioner] owes no payments under license agreements with [respondents]."

As to the second point, petitioner assuredly did contend that it had no obligation under the license to pay royalties on an invalid patent. Nor is that contention frivolous. True, the license requires petitioner to pay royalties *until* a patent claim has been held invalid by a competent body, and the Cabilly II patent has not. But the license at issue in *Lear, Inc. v. Adkins* similarly provided that "royalties are to be paid until such time as the "patent is held invalid," "and we rejected the argument that a repudiating licensee must comply with its contract and pay royalties until its claim is vindicated in court. We express no opinion on whether a *nonrepudiating licensee* is similarly relieved of its contract obligation during a successful challenge to a patent's validity — that is, on the applicability of licensee estoppel under these circumstances. All we need determine is whether petitioner has alleged a contractual dispute. It has done so."

Respondents further argue that petitioner waived its contract claim by failing to argue it below. The record reveals, however, that petitioner raised the contract point before the Federal Circuit. "Here, MedImmune is seeking to define its rights and obligations under its contract with Genentech-precisely the type of action the Declaratory Judgment Act contemplates." That petitioner limited its contract argument to a few pages of its appellate brief does not suggest a waiver; it merely reflects counsel's sound assessment that the argument would be futile. The Federal Circuit's *Gen-Probe* precedent precluded jurisdiction over petitioner's contract claims, and the panel below had no authority to overrule *Gen-Probe*. Having determined that petitioner has raised and preserved a contract claim, we turn to the jurisdictional question.

III

The Declaratory Judgment Act provides that, "[i]n a case of actual controversy within its jurisdiction . . . any court of the United States . . . may declare the rights and other legal relations of any interested party seeking such declaration, whether or not further relief is or could be sought." 28 U.S.C. § 2201(a). There was a time when this Court harbored doubts about the compatibility of declaratory-judgment actions with Article III's case-or-controversy requirement. We dispelled those doubts, however, in *Nashville, C. & St. L.R. Co. v. Wallace* holding (in a case involving a declaratory judgment rendered in state court) that an appropriate action for declaratory relief *can* be a case or controversy under Article III. The federal Declaratory Judgment Act was signed into law the following year, and we upheld its constitutionality in *Aetna Life Ins. Co. v. Haworth.* Our opinion explained that the phrase "case of actual controversy" in the Act refers to the type of "Cases" and "Controversies" that are justiciable under Article III.

Aetna and the cases following it do not draw the brightest of lines between those declaratory-judgment actions that satisfy the case-or-controversy requirement and those that do not. Our decisions have required that the dispute be "definite and concrete, touching the legal relations of parties having adverse legal interests"; and that it be "real and substantial" and "admi[t] of specific relief through a decree of a conclusive character, as distinguished from an opinion advising what the law would be upon a hypothetical state of facts." In *Maryland Casualty Co. v. Pacific Coal & Oil Co.*, we summarized as follows: "Basically, the question in each case is whether the facts alleged, under all the circumstances, show that there is a substantial controversy, between parties having adverse legal interests, of sufficient immediacy and reality to warrant the issuance of a declaratory judgment."

There is no dispute that these standards would have been satisfied if petitioner had taken the final step of refusing to make royalty payments under the 1997 license agreement. Respondents claim a right to royalties under the licensing agreement. Petitioner asserts that no royalties are owing because the Cabilly II patent is invalid and not infringed; and alleges (without contradiction) a threat by respondents to enjoin sales if royalties are not forthcoming. The factual and legal dimensions of the dispute are well defined and, but for petitioner's continuing to make royalty payments, nothing about the dispute would render it unfit for judicial resolution. Assuming (without deciding) that respondents here could not claim an anticipatory breach and repudiate the license, the continuation of royalty payments makes what would otherwise be an imminent threat at least remote, if not nonexistent. As long as those payments are made, there is no risk that respondents will seek to enjoin petitioner's sales. Petitioner's own acts, in other words, eliminate the imminent threat of harm. The question before us is whether this causes the dispute no longer to be a case or controversy within the meaning of Article III.

Our analysis must begin with the recognition that, where threatened action by *government* is concerned, we do not require a plaintiff to expose himself to liability before bringing suit to challenge the basis for the threat-for example, the constitutionality of a law threatened to be enforced. The plaintiff's own action (or inaction) in failing to violate the law eliminates the imminent threat of prosecution, but nonetheless does not eliminate Article III jurisdiction. For example, in *Terrace v. Thompson*, the State threatened the plaintiff with forfeiture of his farm, fines, and penalties if he entered into a lease with an alien in violation of the State's anti-alien land law. Given this genuine threat of enforcement, we did not require, as a prerequisite to testing the validity of the law in a suit for injunction, that the plaintiff bet the farm, so to speak, by taking the violative action. Likewise, in *Steffel v. Thompson* we did not require the plaintiff to proceed to distribute handbills and risk actual prosecution before he could seek a declaratory judgment regarding the constitutionality of a state statute prohibiting such distribution. As then-Justice Rehnquist put it in his concurrence, "the declaratory judgment procedure is an alternative to pursuit of the arguably illegal activity." In each of these cases, the plaintiff had eliminated the imminent threat of harm by simply not doing what he claimed the right to do (enter into a lease, or distribute handbills at the shopping center). That did not preclude subject-matter jurisdiction because the threat-eliminating behavior was effectively coerced. The dilemma posed by that coercion — putting the challenger to the choice between abandoning his rights or risking prosecution — is "a dilemma that it was the very purpose of the Declaratory Judgment Act to ameliorate."

Supreme Court jurisprudence is more rare regarding application of the Declaratory Judgment Act to situations in which the plaintiff's self-avoidance of imminent injury is coerced by threatened enforcement action of *a private party* rather than the government. Lower federal courts, however (and state courts interpreting declaratory judgment Acts requiring "actual controversy"), have long accepted jurisdiction in such cases.

The only Supreme Court decision in point is, fortuitously, close on its facts to the case before us. *Altvater v. Freeman* held that a licensee's failure to cease its payment of royalties did not render nonjusticiable a dispute over the validity of the patent. In that litigation, several patentees had sued their licensees to enforce territorial restrictions in the license. The licensees filed a counterclaim for declaratory judgment that the underlying patents were invalid, in the meantime paying "under protest" royalties required by an injunction the patentees had obtained in an earlier case. The patentees argued that "so long as [licensees] continue to pay royalties, there is only an academic, not a real controversy, between the parties." We rejected that argument and held that the declaratory-judgment claim presented a justiciable case or controversy: "The fact that royalties were being paid did not make this a "difference or dispute of a hypothetical or abstract character." "The royalties "were being paid under protest and under the compulsion of an injunction decree," and "[u]nless the injunction decree were modified, the only other course [of action] was to defy it, and to risk not only actual but treble damages in infringement suits." We concluded that "the requirements of [a] case or controversy are met where payment of a claim is demanded as of right and where payment is made, but where the involuntary or coercive nature of the exaction preserves the right to recover the sums paid or to challenge the legality of the claim."

The Federal Circuit's *Gen-Probe* decision distinguished *Altvater* on the ground that it involved the compulsion of an injunction. But *Altvater* cannot be so readily dismissed. Never mind that the injunction had been privately obtained and was ultimately within the control of the patentees, who could permit its modification. More fundamentally, and contrary to the Federal Circuit's conclusion, *Altvater* did not say that the coercion dispositive of the case was governmental, but suggested just the opposite. The opinion acknowledged that the licensees had the option of stopping payments in defiance of the injunction, but explained that the *consequence* of doing so would be to risk "actual [and] treble damages in infringement suits" by the patentees. It significantly did not mention the threat of prosecution for contempt, or any other sort of governmental sanction. Moreover, it cited approvingly a treatise which said that an "actual or threatened serious injury to business or employment" by a private party can be as coercive as other forms of coercion supporting restitution actions at common law; and that "[t]o imperil a man's livelihood, his business enterprises, or his solvency, [was] ordinarily quite as coercive" as, for example, "detaining his property."

Jurisdiction over the present case is not contradicted by *Willing v. Chicago Auditorium Association.* There a ground lessee wanted to demolish an antiquated auditorium and replace it with a modern commercial building. The lessee believed it had the right to do this without the lessor's consent, but was unwilling to drop the wrecking ball first and test its belief later. Because there was no declaratory judgment act at the time under federal or applicable state law, the lessee filed an action to remove a "cloud" on its lease. This Court held that an Article III case or controversy had not arisen because "[n]o defendant ha[d] wronged the plaintiff or ha[d] threatened to do so." It was true that one of the colessors had disagreed with the lessee's interpretation of the lease, but that happened in an "informal, friendly, private conversation," a year before the lawsuit was filed; and the lessee never even bothered to approach the other co-lessors. The Court went on to remark that "[w]hat the plaintiff seeks is simply a declaratory judgment," and "[t]o grant that relief is beyond the power conferred upon the federal judiciary." Had *Willing* been decided after the enactment (and our upholding) of the Declaratory Judgment Act, and had the legal disagreement between the parties been as lively as this one, we are confident a different result would have obtained. The rule that a plaintiff must destroy a large building, bet the farm, or (as here) risk treble damages and the loss of 80 percent of its business, before seeking a declaration of its actively contested legal rights finds no support in Article III.

Respondents assert that the parties in effect settled this dispute when they entered into the 1997 license agreement. When a licensee enters such an agreement, they contend, it essentially purchases an insurance policy, immunizing it from suits for infringement so long as it continues to pay royalties and does not challenge the covered patents. Permitting it to challenge the validity of the patent without terminating or breaking the agreement alters the deal, allowing the licensee to continue enjoying its immunity while bringing a suit, the elimination of which was part of the patentee's *quid pro quo*. Of course even if it were valid, this argument would have no force with regard to petitioner's claim that the agreement does not call for royalties because their product does not infringe the patent. But even as to the patent invalidity claim, the point seems to us mistaken. To begin with, it is not clear where the prohibition against challenging the validity of the patents is to be found. It can hardly be implied from the mere promise to pay royalties on patents "which have neither expired nor been held invalid by a court or other body of competent jurisdiction from which no appeal has been or may be taken." Promising to pay royalties on patents that have not been held invalid does not amount to a promise *not to seek* a holding of their invalidity.

Respondents appeal to the common-law rule that a party to a contract cannot at one and the same time challenge its validity and continue to reap its benefits. *Lear*, they contend, did not suspend that rule for patent licensing agreements, since the plaintiff in that case had already repudiated the contract. Even if *Lear's* repudiation of the doctrine of licensee estoppel was so limited (a point on which, as we have said earlier, we do not opine), it is hard to see how the common-law rule has any application here. Petitioner is not repudiating or impugning the contract while continuing to reap its benefits. Rather, it is asserting that the contract, properly interpreted, does not prevent it from challenging the patents, and does not require the payment of royalties because the patents do not cover its products and are invalid. Of course even if respondents were correct that the licensing agreement or the common-law rule precludes this suit, the consequence would be that respondents win this case *on the merits-not* that the very genuine contract dispute disappears, so that Article III jurisdiction is somehow defeated. In short, Article III jurisdiction has nothing to do with this "insurance-policy" contention.

Lastly, respondents urge us to affirm the dismissal of the declaratory-judgment claims on discretionary grounds. The Declaratory Judgment Act provides that a court "*may* declare the rights and other legal relations of any interested party," 28 U.S.C. § 2201(a) (emphasis added), not that it *must* do so. This text has long been understood "to confer on federal courts unique and substantial discretion in deciding whether to declare the rights of litigants." We have found it "more consistent with the statute," however, "to vest district courts with discretion in the first instance, because facts bearing on the usefulness of the declaratory judgment remedy, and the fitness of the case for resolution, are peculiarly within their grasp." The District Court here gave no consideration to discretionary dismissal, since, despite its "serious misgivings" about the Federal Circuit's rule, it considered itself bound to dismiss by *Gen-Probe.* Discretionary dismissal was irrelevant to the Federal Circuit for the same reason. Respondents have raised the issue for the first time before this Court, exchanging competing accusations of inequitable conduct with petitioner. Under these circumstances, it would be imprudent for us to decide whether the District Court should, or must, decline to issue the requested declaratory relief. We leave the equitable, prudential, and policy arguments in favor of such a discretionary dismissal for the lower courts' consideration on remand. Similarly available for consideration on remand are any merits-based arguments for denial of declaratory relief.

****

We hold that petitioner was not required, insofar as Article III is concerned, to break or terminate its 1997 license agreement before seeking a declaratory judgment in federal court that the underlying patent is invalid, unenforceable, or not infringed. The Court of Appeals erred in affirming the dismissal of this action for lack of subject-matter jurisdiction.

The judgment of the Court of Appeals is reversed, and the cause is remanded for proceedings consistent with this opinion.

It is so ordered.

JUSTICE THOMAS, dissenting.

QUESTIONS

1. Are you persuaded that the coercive power of government to threaten criminal prosecution for violation of the law is equivalent to the coercive power of a licensor to threaten to bring a patent infringement or breach of contract suit?

2. A licensee who continues to pay royalties up until the time a patent is held to be invalid cannot recover these paid royalties after the patent is held to be invalid. Therefore, why would a licensee planning to challenge the validity of a patent not stop paying royalties prior to the litigation?

3. How might a licensor reduce the risk of a non-breaching licensee filing a declaratory judgment action?

CASE NOTES

1. SanDisk is in the flash memory storage market. STMicroelectronics (ST) decided to also enter the flash memory market. Both SanDisk and ST have patent portfolios related to flash memory storage products. In April 2004, ST sent a letter to SanDisk requesting a meeting to discuss a cross-licensing agreement. The letter listed 8 patents owned by ST that ST believed "may be of interest" to SanDisk. SanDisk responded that it would need time to review the listed patents. In July 2004, having not heard further from SanDisk, ST sent another letter to SanDisk repeating the request for a meeting to discuss a cross-licensing agreement. In August 2004, SanDisk presented ST with an analysis of three of its patents and orally offered ST a license. A licensing meeting between the parties was held at the end of August 2004. At the end of the meeting, ST gave SanDisk a packet of materials containing copies of its patents, reverse engineering reports for certain SanDisk products and diagrams showing how elements of ST's patents cover SanDisk products. ST told SanDisk that it understood the risk that the materials might allow SanDisk to file a declaratory judgment action to contest the validity of ST's patents and, therefore, ST wanted SanDisk to know that ST "has absolutely no plan whatsoever to sue SanDisk." Licensing discussions continued between ST and SanDisk through October 2004 when SanDisk filed patent infringement action against ST and sought a declaratory judgment of non-infringement and invalidity of

the ST patents. ST filed a motion to dismiss the suit claiming that there was no actual controversy between the parties at the time SanDisk filed its complaint. The district court granted ST's motion to dismiss and SanDisk appealed. What result? *See* SanDisk Corp. v. STMicroelectronics, Inc. 480 F.3d 1372 (Fed. Cir. 2007).

2. *See also* Flex-Foot, Inc. v. CRP, Inc., 238 F.3d 1362 (Fed. Cir. 2001) (Settlement agreement in which alleged infringer agreed not to challenge patent's validity in the future was not void as against public policy where settlement was voluntarily entered into during infringement litigation after parties had an opportunity to conduct discovery on validity issues); Lemelson v. Synergistics Research Corp., 669 F.Supp. 642 (S.D.N.Y. 1987) (Co-owners of patents were not precluded from challenging the validity of the patents in defense of a suit for breach of agreement to share proceeds of patents; doctrine of estoppel had to give way to federal policy of unencumbered challenges to patents believed to be invalid); Dillard Dept. Stores, Inc. v. Application Art Laboratories Co., 787 F. Supp. 49 (S.D.N.Y. 1992) (Settlement agreement by plaintiff agreeing to pay patent licensee for patent labels it affixed to its products did not estop plaintiff from challenging validity of patent; plaintiff never acknowledged validity of patent, nor had it consented to refrain from challenging the patent's validity); PPG Industries, Inc. v. Westwood Chemical, Inc., 530 F.2d 700 (6th Cir. 1976) (Patent licensing agreement, although voidable by reason of invalidity of patent, was enforceable for royalties accruing after date licensee ceased making payments, where licensee not only failed to take action to adjudicate patent invalidity but actively assisted licensor in attempting to uphold patent validity in case brought by licensor against a third party); Interconnect Planning Corp. v. Feil, 543 F.Supp. 610 (S.D.N.Y. 1982) (Rejected assignor-inventor estoppel to challenge patent validity when assignee sues assignor for infringement); Clark Equip. Co. v. Keller, 197 U.S.P.Q. 83 (D.N.D. 1976) (Rejected judicial estoppel based on party's prior validity defense of patent it now seeks to attack); Adenta GmbH v. OrthoArm, Inc. 501 F.3d 1364 (Fed. Cir. 2007) (Case or controversy existed for declaratory judgment action by licensee where licensee told assignee that it obtained legal advice that the patent was invalid and that it would not pay further royalties on sales of patented products, and assignee stated that it would "pursue its available legal remedies" if licensee breached the license agreement; licensee stopped paying royalties to assignee); Sony Electronics, Inc. v. Guardian Media Technologies, Ltd., 497 F.3d 1271 (Fed. Cir. 2007) (Patentee's continued willingness to engage in licensing negotiations with competitors did not prevent competitors from maintaining a declaratory judgment action to have patent declared invalid).

Additional Information

1. RAYMOND T. NIMMER, 2 INFORMATION LAW § 11:94 (2010).

2. JOHN G. MILLS III, ET AL., 1 PATENT LAW FUNDAMENTALS § 2:40 (2d ed. 2010).

3. DAVID M. EPSTEIN, 1 ECKSTROM'S LICENSING IN FOREIGN & DOMESTIC OPERATIONS §§ 8C:3, 8C:4, 8C:5, 8C:9 (2008).

4. RAYMOND T. NIMMER, LAW OF COMPUTER TECHNOLOGY § 7:98 (4th ed. 2008).

5.   JOHN W. SCHLICHER, 2 PATENT LAW: LEGAL AND ECONOMIC PRINCIPLES § 12:7 (2d ed. 2007).

6.   RAYMOND T. NIMMER & JEFF DODD, MODERN LICENSING LAW §§ 13:14–15 (2007).

7.   MELVIN F. JAGER, LICENSING LAW HANDBOOK § 5:14 (2008).

8.   60 AM. JUR. 2D Patents § 1055 (2008).

9.   FEDERAL PROCEDURE, LAWYERS EDITION, § 60:1226 (2008).

10.   Leslie G. Restaino, Thomas J. Dodd, *A New License to Sue? Licensees Enjoy Greater Freedom to Challenge Patents While Keeping Their Licenses Intact*, 189 N. J. L. J. 1086 (2007).

11.   Nellie A. Fisher, *The Licensee's Choice: Mechanics of Successfully Challenging a Patent Under License*, 6 TEX. INTELL. PROP. L.J. 1 (1997).

12.   George C. Best, *Licensee Estoppel Revisited: Medimmune Inc. v. Genentech, Inc.*, 25 NO. 3 INTELL. PROP. L. NEWSL. (2007).

13.   Jason Stolworthy & Ida Shum, *You Can Bet the Farm: Patent Licensees Can Now Challenge Validity Without First Breaching Their Licenses*, 50-SEP ADVOCATE IDAHO 13 (2007).

14.   Jennifer R. Saionz, *Declaratory Judgment Actions in Patent Cases: The Federal Circuit's Response to Medimmune v. Genentech*, 23 BERKELEY TECH. L.J. 161 (2008).

15.   Erik Belt & Keith Toms, *The Price of Admission: Licensee Challenges to Patents After* Medimmune v. Genentech, 51-JUN B. B.J. 10 (2007).

16.   Paul J. LaVanway, *Patent Licensing and Discretion: Reevaluating the Discretionary Prong of Declaratory Judgment Jurisdiction After Medimmune*, 92 MINN. L. REV. 1966 (2008).

17.   Stephanie Chu, *Operation Restoration: How Can Patent Holders Protect Themselves From Medimmune?*, 2007 DUKE L. & TECH. REV. 8 (2007).

18.   Elkia R. Manglona, *Reasonable Apprehension of an Infringement Suit is Not Required: Wonderful News for a Prospective Licensee*, 90 J. PAT. & TRADEMARK OFF. SOC'Y 382 (2008).

19.   Lara A. Holzman et al., *Post-Medimmune Patentees Must Act With Care: They Should Avoid Acts Giving Rise to Suits for Declaratory Judgment*, 1/21/2008 NAT'L L.J. S.3, col. 1 (2008).

20.   Ronald A. Bleeker, Michael V. O'Shaughnessy, *One Year After Medimmune — The Impact on Patent Licensing & Negotiation*, 17 FED. CIRCUIT B.J. 40 (2008).

21.   Kevin E. Noonan, *Subject Matter Jurisdiction, Declaratory Judgment Actions, and Patent Challenges by Licensees: Everything the Federal Circuit Knows is Wrong*, 19 NO. 3 INTELL. PROP. & TECH. L.J. (2007).

22.   John W. Schlicher, *Patent Licensing, What to do After Medimmune v. Genentech*, 89 J. PAT. & TRADEMARK OFF. SOC'Y 364 (2007).

2.2.5   Co-Owner Licenses

Section 116 of the Patent Act states:

> When an invention is made by two or more persons jointly, they shall apply for [a] patent jointly and each make the required oath . . . . Inventors may apply for a patent jointly even though (1) they did not physically work together or at the same time, (2) each did not make the same type or amount of contribution, or (3) each did not make a contribution to the subject matter of every claim of the patent.

> Whenever through error a person is named in an application for [a] patent as the inventor, or through error an inventor is not named in an application, and such error arose without any deceptive intention or his part, the Director may permit the application to be amended accordingly, under such terms as he prescribes. 35 U.S.C.A. § 116 (2000).

Section 262 of the Patent Act states:

> In the absence of any agreement to the contrary, each of the joint owners of a patent may make, use, offer to sell, or sell the patented invention within the United States, or import the patented invention into the United States, without the consent of and without accounting to the other owners. 35 U.S.C.A. § 262 (2000).

Courts have generally held that if a person contributes to a single claim in the patent application, that is sufficient to qualify the person as an "inventor." *See, e.g.,* Eli Lilly Co. v. Aradigm Corp., 376 F.3d 1352 (Fed. Cir. 2004).

The questions of patent inventorship and the rights of patent co-owners often arise in the context of two different types of claims by defendants in patent infringement suits. In the first type, the infringement defendant claims to have a license from one of the patent co-owners which would immunize him from infringement liability. In these cases, the court must first determine whether the co-owner licensor is an inventor of the patent and then whether the co-owner license operates to give the infringement defendant immunity from liability. In the second type, the infringement defendant claims that one of the patent co-owners has not been joined as a plaintiff. Courts have long required that all patent co-owners must join as plaintiffs in patent infringement suits. *See, e.g.,* Waterman v. Mackenzie, 138 U.S. 252 (1891). In these cases, the court need only determine whether the non-joined party is an inventor or co-owner of the patent at issue in the suit.

The *Ethicon* case below considers the questions of patent inventorship and co-ownership in the context of both types of claims by infringement defendants.

ETHICON v. UNITED STATES SURGICAL CORPORATION
135 F.3d 1456 (Fed. Cir. 1998)

RADER, CIRCUIT JUDGE.

In this patent infringement action, Dr. InBae Yoon (Yoon) and his exclusive licensee, Ethicon, Inc. (Ethicon), appeal from the judgment of the United States District Court for the District of Connecticut. In 1989, Yoon and Ethicon sued United States Surgical Corporation (U.S. Surgical) for infringement of U.S. Patent No. 4,535,773 (the '773 patent). In 1993, the parties stipulated to the intervention of Mr. Young Jae Choi (Choi) as defendant-intervenor. Choi claimed to be an omitted co-inventor of the '773 patent and to have granted U.S. Surgical a retroactive license under that patent. On U.S. Surgical's motion to correct inventorship of the '773 patent under 35 U.S.C. § 256, the district court ruled that Choi was an omitted co-inventor of two claims and subsequently granted U.S. Surgical's motion to dismiss the infringement complaint. Because the district court's determination of co-inventorship was correct, and because Choi is a joint owner of the '773 patent who has not consented to suit against U.S. Surgical, this court affirms.

I. BACKGROUND

The '773 patent relates to trocars, an essential tool for endoscopic surgery. A trocar is a surgical instrument which makes small incisions in the wall of a body cavity, often the abdomen, to admit endoscopic instruments. Trocars include a shaft within an outer sleeve. One end of the shaft has a sharp blade. At the outset of surgery, the surgeon uses the blade to puncture the wall and extend the trocar into the cavity. The surgeon then removes the shaft, leaving the hollow outer sleeve, through which the surgeon may insert tiny cameras and surgical instruments for the operation.

Conventional trocars, however, pose a risk of damage to internal organs or structures. As the trocar blade punctures the cavity wall, the sudden loss of resistance can cause the blade to lunge forward and injure an internal organ. The '773 patent claims a trocar that alleviates this danger. In one embodiment, the invention equips the trocar with a blunt, spring-loaded rod. As the trocar pierces the cavity wall, the rod automatically springs forward to precede the blade and shield against injury. A second embodiment has a retractable trocar blade that springs back into a protective sheath when it passes through the cavity wall. The patent also teaches the use of an electronic sensor in the end of the blade to signal the surgeon at the moment of puncture.

Yoon is a medical doctor and inventor of numerous patented devices for endoscopic surgery. In the late 1970s, Yoon began to conceive of a safety device to prevent accidental injury during trocar incisions. Yoon also conceived of a device to alert the surgeon when the incision was complete. In 1980, Yoon met Choi, an electronics technician, who had some college training in physics, chemistry, and electrical engineering, but no college degree. Choi had worked in the research and development of electronic devices. After Choi had demonstrated to Yoon some of the devices he had developed, Yoon asked Choi to work with him on several projects, including one for safety trocars. Choi was not paid for his work.

In 1982, after collaborating for approximately eighteen months, their relationship ended. Choi believed that Yoon found his work unsatisfactory and unlikely to produce any marketable product. For these reasons, Choi withdrew from cooperation with Yoon.

In the same year, however, Yoon filed an application for a patent disclosing various embodiments of a safety trocar. Without informing Choi, Yoon named himself as the sole inventor. In 1985, the Patent and Trademark Office issued the '773 patent to Yoon, with fifty-five claims. Yoon thereafter granted an exclusive license under this patent to Ethicon. Yoon did not inform Choi of the patent application or issuance.

In 1989, Ethicon filed suit against U.S. Surgical for infringement of claims 34 and 50 of the '773 patent. In 1992, while this suit was still pending, U.S. Surgical became aware of Choi, and contacted him regarding his involvement in Yoon's safety trocar project. When Choi confirmed his role in the safety trocar project, U.S. Surgical obtained from Choi a "retroactive license" to practice "Choi's trocar related inventions." Under the license, Choi agreed to assist U.S. Surgical in any suit regarding the '773 patent. For its part, U.S. Surgical agreed to pay Choi contingent on its ultimate ability to continue to practice and market the invention. With the license in hand, U.S. Surgical moved to correct inventorship of the '773 patent under 35 U.S.C. § 256, claiming that Choi was a co-inventor of claims 23, 33, 46, and 47. Following an extensive hearing, the district court granted U.S. Surgical's motion, finding that Choi had contributed to the subject matter of claims 33 and 47.

U.S. Surgical next moved for dismissal of the infringement suit, arguing that Choi, as a joint owner of the patent, had granted it a valid license under the patent. By its terms, the license purported to grant rights to use the patent extending retroactively back to its issuance. The district court granted U.S. Surgical's motion and dismissed the suit.

Ethicon appeals the district court's finding of co-inventorship and its dismissal of the complaint. Specifically, Ethicon contends that (1) Choi supplied insufficient corroboration for his testimony of co-invention; (2) Choi presented insufficient evidence to show co-invention of claims 33 and 47 clearly and convincingly; (3) Choi accepted illegal payment for his factual testimony which the court should therefore have excluded from the proceedings; (4) the terms of the license agreement limit it to only that part of the invention to which Choi contributed, not the entire patent; and (5) even if the agreement licenses the entire patent, it cannot release U.S. Surgical from liability for past infringement.

II. CO-INVENTORSHIP

Patent issuance creates a presumption that the named inventors are the true and only inventors. Inventorship is a question of law, which this court reviews without deference. However, this court reviews the underlying findings of fact which uphold a district court's inventorship determination for clear error.

A patented invention may be the work of two or more joint inventors. Because "[c]onception is the touchstone of inventorship," each joint inventor must generally contribute to the conception of the invention. "Conception is the "formation in the mind of the inventor, of a definite and permanent idea of the complete and operative invention, as it is hereafter to be applied in practice." " An idea is sufficiently "definite and permanent" when "only ordinary skill would be necessary to reduce the invention to practice, without extensive research or experimentation."

The conceived invention must include every feature of the subject matter claimed in the patent. Nevertheless, for the conception of a joint invention, each of the joint inventors need not "make the same type or amount of contribution" to the invention. Rather, each needs to perform only a part of the task which produces the invention. On the other hand, one does not qualify as a joint inventor by merely assisting the actual inventor after conception of the claimed invention. One who simply provides the inventor with well-known principles or explains the state of the art without ever having "a firm and definite idea" of the claimed combination as a whole does not qualify as a joint inventor. Moreover, depending on the scope of a patent's claims, one of ordinary skill in the art who simply reduced the inventor's idea to practice is not necessarily a joint inventor, even if the specification discloses that embodiment to satisfy the best mode requirement.

Furthermore, a co-inventor need not make a contribution to every claim of a patent. Thus, the critical question for joint conception is who conceived, as that term is used in the patent law, the subject matter of the claims at issue.

35 U.S.C. § 256 provides that a co-inventor omitted from an issued patent may be added to the patent by a court "before which such matter is called in question." To show co-inventorship, however, the alleged co-inventor or co-inventors must prove their contribution to the conception of the claims by clear and convincing evidence. However, "an inventor's testimony respecting the facts surrounding a claim of derivation or priority of invention cannot, standing alone, rise to the level of clear and convincing proof." Thus, an alleged co-inventor must supply evidence to corroborate his testimony. Whether the inventor's testimony has been sufficiently corroborated is evaluated under a "rule of reason" analysis. Under this analysis, "[a]n evaluation of *all* pertinent evidence must be made so that a sound determination of the credibility of the [alleged] inventor's story may be reached."

Corroborating evidence may take many forms. Often contemporaneous documents prepared by a putative inventor serve to corroborate an inventor's testimony. Circumstantial evidence about the inventive process may also corroborate. Additionally, oral testimony of someone other than the alleged inventor may corroborate.

A. Claim 33

The district court determined that Choi contributed to the conception of the subject matter of claim 33. Claim 33 (with emphasis to highlight relevant elements) reads:

> A surgical instrument for providing communication through an anatomical organ structure, comprising:

means having an abutment member and *shaft longitudinally accommo-datable within an outer sleeve*, longitudinal movement of said shaft inside said sleeve being limited by contact of said abutment member with said sleeve, said shaft having a distal end with a distal blade surface tapering into a sharp distal point, *said distal blade surface being perforated along one side by an aperture*, for puncturing an anatomical organ structure when subjected to force along the longitudinal axis of said shaft;

means having a blunt distal bearing surface, slidably extending through said aperture, for reciprocating through said aperture while said abutment member is in stationary contact with said sleeve;

means positionable between said puncturing means and said reciprocating means for biasing a distal section of said reciprocating means to protrude beyond said aperture and permitting said distal section of said reciprocating means to recede into said aperture when said bearing surface is subject to force along its axis . . .; and

means connectible to the proximal end of said puncturing means *for* responding to longitudinal movement of said reciprocating means relative to said puncturing means and *creating a sensible signal* having one state upon recision of said distal section of said reciprocating means into said aperture and another state upon protrusion of said distal section of said reciprocating means from said aperture.

To determine whether Choi made a contribution to the conception of the subject matter of claim 33, this court must determine what Choi's contribution was and then whether that contribution's role appears in the claimed invention. If Choi in fact contributed to the invention defined by claim 33, he is a joint inventor of that claim.

Figures 18 and 19 of the '773 patent illustrate an embodiment of claim 33. These figures show a trocar blade with an aperture through which a blunt rod can extend. When the trocar blade penetrates the inner wall of a cavity, a spring releases the rod, which juts out past the end of the trocar blade and prevents the blade from cutting further. The embodiment also includes a structure that gives the surgeon aural and visual signals when the blade nears penetration.

The district court found that Yoon conceived of the use of a blunt probe. However, the court found that Choi conceived of and thereby contributed two features contained in the embodiment shown in figures 18 and 19: first, Choi conceived of locating the blunt probe in the trocar shaft and allowing it to pass through an aperture in the blade surface; second, Choi conceived of the "means . . . for . . . creating a sensible signal."

If Choi did indeed conceive of "locating the blunt probe in the shaft and allowing it to pass through an aperture in the blade surface," he contributed to the subject matter of claim 33. Claim 33 requires that the "distal blade surface" be "perforated along one side by an aperture" and requires the "shaft" to be "longitudinally accommodatable within [the] outer sleeve." Properly construed, claim 33 includes the elements that Choi contributed to the invention according to the district court's findings.

In making this finding, the district court relied extensively on Choi's testimony. Choi testified that the idea of extending the blunt probe through an aperture in the trocar blade itself was his idea. To corroborate this testimony, Choi produced a series of sketches he created while working with Yoon. One sketch shows a probe inside the shaft of a trocar blade, extending through an opening in the side of the end of the blade.

To rebut Choi's showing, Yoon presented a drawing dated July 1973, which disclosed elements of claim 33. The district court determined, however, that Dr. Yoon had altered this drawing. In fact, according to the district court, it had originally depicted a device from an entirely different patent. Due to its suspicious origins, the trial court rejected it as unreliable.

The court also discounted Yoon's testimony for lack of credibility. Indeed the record supports the trial court's conclusion that Yoon altered and backdated documents to make it appear that he had independently invented trocars, shields, and electronics. Moreover, Yoon's trial testimony clashed with his earlier deposition testimony. For instance, before learning of Choi's role in the case, Yoon falsely testified at his deposition that (1) he had worked with Choi as early as 1975 and (2) the sketches at issue in this case had been drawn completely by him. However, the two did not meet until 1980, and when later questioned about authorship of the documents, Yoon replied, "If I said [that] at that time, then maybe I was confused." The district court justifiably discounted Yoon's testimony.

In sum, after full consideration of the relevant evidence, the district court determined that Choi conceived part of the invention recited in claim 33. This court detects no cause to reverse this determination.

IV. SCOPE OF THE CHOI-U.S. SURGICAL LICENSE

Questions of patent ownership are distinct from questions of inventorship. In accordance with this principle, this court has nonetheless noted that "an invention presumptively belongs to its creator."

Indeed, in the context of joint inventorship, each co-inventor presumptively owns a pro rata undivided interest in the entire patent, no matter what their respective contributions. Several provisions of the Patent Act combine to dictate this rule. 35 U.S.C. § 116, as amended in 1984 states that a joint inventor need not make a contribution "to the subject matter of every claim of the patent." In amending section 116 as to joint inventorship, Congress did not make corresponding modifications as to joint ownership. For example, section 261 continues to provide that "patents shall have the attributes of personal property." This provision suggests that property rights, including ownership, attach to patents as a whole, not individual claims. Moreover, section 262 continues to speak of "joint owners of a patent," not joint owners of a claim. Thus, a joint inventor as to even one claim enjoys a presumption of ownership in the entire patent.

This rule presents the prospect that a co-inventor of only one claim might gain entitlement to ownership of a patent with dozens of claims. As noted, the Patent Act accounts for that occurrence: "Inventors *may* apply for a patent jointly even though . . . each did not make a contribution to the subject matter of every claim." 35

U.S.C. § 116 (emphasis added). Thus, where inventors choose to cooperate in the inventive process, their joint inventions may become joint property without some express agreement to the contrary. In this case, Yoon must now effectively share with Choi ownership of all the claims, even those which he invented by himself. Thus, Choi had the power to license rights in the entire patent.

This court next examines the extent to which Choi exercised that power. This court reviews the interpretation of contractual language, including license agreements, as a question of law. State law, in this case Connecticut law, controls in matters of contract interpretation. Thus, in making its review, this court adopts the ordinary and common meaning of contract terms whenever possible.

The license which Choi granted to U.S. Surgical states:

> Choi hereby grants to U.S. Surgical an exclusive, worldwide right and license to make, have made, use, market and sell *Choi's trocar related inventions, including trocars having shields and those described and/or claimed in the '773 patent.* This license is retroactive to the date on which the '773 patent issued.

U.S. Surgical reads this language to cover all trocars "described and/or claimed in the '773 patent," encompassing the entire '773 patent and more. Ethicon reads the same language as limited to "Choi's trocar related inventions," which comprise only his contributions to claims 33 and 47 of the '773 patent.

The meaning of the phrase "including trocars . . . described and/or claimed in the '773 patent" depends on the meaning of the word "including." If construed to merely clarify the meaning of "trocar related inventions," the phrase it modifies, then "including" could limit the scope of Choi's grant. "Including," however, can also operate as a phrase of addition. Under this broader reading, the phrase "trocar related inventions" covers more than just the material specified in the "including" phrase.

If possible, this court must view a single provision of a contract in the way that gives meaning to — and provides internal harmony among — all parts of the contract. Read in context, the "including" phrase is a phrase of addition, not a limitation on the scope of "trocar related inventions." For example, the agreement states that Choi "has not . . . and shall not, grant to any other person . . . any right or license to make, use or sell any of his trocar related inventions or any device described or within the scope of *any* of the claims of the '773 patent." (emphasis added). In addition, the agreement states, "Choi hereby grants to [U.S. Surgical] the sole right to sue any infringer of the '773 patent . . . ." If the scope of the license did not encompass all of Choi's rights as a joint owner of the '773 patent, these supplementary provisions were inexplicably much too broad. Rather, in context, Choi's grant meant to license all of his rights as a joint owner under the '773 patent.

Thus, the district court's interpretation of the Choi license was correct as a matter of law.

V. RETROACTIVE LICENSURE

Finally, Ethicon argues that even if the license agreement is enforceable as to the entire patent, it should still be allowed to proceed against U.S. Surgical to recover damages for pre-license infringement. Ethicon contends that to hold otherwise would contravene the decision in *Schering Corp. v. Roussel-UCLAF SA*. This court agrees with Ethicon's challenge to the retroactive effect of Choi's license, but must affirm the dismissal of the case based on Choi's refusal to join as plaintiff in the suit.

In *Schering*, Roussel and Schering, the two co-owners of the patent in suit, entered into an agreement whereby each granted the other a unilateral right to sue third parties for infringement. Schering then sued to enjoin Zeneca, Inc. from proceeding with planned sales of an allegedly infringing product. Schering joined Roussel in the action as an involuntary plaintiff. Two weeks later, Roussel granted Zeneca a license to practice the patented invention. The district court dismissed Schering's suit. Schering appealed.

On appeal, Schering argued that because Roussel had granted Schering a unilateral right to sue, Roussel could not now grant a license to Zeneca. Schering contended that one grant was incompatible with the other. The court rejected Shering's argument, reasoning that "[t]he right to license and the unilateral right to sue are . . . not incompatible, and the granting of one does not necessarily imply the relinquishment of the other." This court acknowledged the critical distinction that a license to a third party only operates prospectively. Absent agreement to the contrary, a co-owner cannot grant a release of another co-owner's right to accrued damages. Consequently, a co-owner who has granted a unilateral right to sue to another co-owner may also license a third party. Nevertheless, by virtue of the unilateral right to sue, the second co-owner can still force the first co-owner to join an infringement action against the licensee to recover the second co-owner's accrued damages for past infringement. Thus, a prospective license is not per se incompatible with a unilateral right to sue, and, barring any other applicable contractual provision, Schering could not prevent Roussel from granting a license to Zeneca:

> [T]he grant of a license by one co-owner cannot deprive the other co-owner of the right to sue for accrued damages for past infringement. That would require a release, not a license, and the rights of a patent co-owner, absent agreement to the contrary, do not extend to granting a release that would defeat an action by other co-owners to recover damages for past infringement.

Thus, Choi's "retroactive license" to U.S. Surgical attempts to operate as the combination of a release and a prospective license. Nonetheless Choi cannot release U.S. Surgical from its liability for past accrued damages to Ethicon, only from liability to himself.

One more settled principle governs this case, however. An action for infringement must join as plaintiffs all co-owners.

Further, as a matter of substantive patent law, all co-owners must ordinarily consent to join as plaintiffs in an infringement suit. Consequently, "one co-owner has the right to impede the other co-owner's ability to sue infringers by refusing to voluntarily join in such a suit."

This rule finds support in section 262 of the Patent Act:

> In the absence of any agreement to the contrary, each of the joint owners of a patent may make, use, offer to sell, or sell the patented invention within the United States, or import the patented invention into the United States, without the consent of and without accounting to the other owners.

This freedom to exploit the patent without a duty to account to other co-owners also allows co-owners to freely license others to exploit the patent without the consent of other co-owners. Thus, the congressional policy expressed by section 262 is that patent co-owners are "at the mercy of each other."

Although in this case, the result is effectively no different than if Choi could grant a release to U.S. Surgical of any liability to Ethicon, it should be emphasized that the principle that governs this case is not incompatible with the principle enunciated in *Schering*. In *Schering*, this court noted that the granting of a unilateral right to sue is not incompatible with the right to grant a license. Similarly, this court notes that the inability to grant a release is not incompatible with the right to refuse to consent to an infringement suit. It is true that, in some circumstances, the decision of one co-owner to not join an infringement suit may have the same effect as granting a release, but this is not true in all cases. For example, when co-owners have granted each other a unilateral right to sue, each has waived his right not to join an infringement suit, and either of them can force the other to join a suit to collect accrued infringement damages.

Because Choi did not consent to an infringement suit against U.S. Surgical and indeed can no longer consent due to his grant of an exclusive license with its accompanying "right to sue," Ethicon's complaint lacks the participation of a co-owner of the patent. Accordingly, this court must order dismissal of this suit.

VI. CONCLUSION

Accordingly, the judgment of the United States District Court for the District of Connecticut is affirmed.

AFFIRMED.

QUESTIONS

1. What is the difference between allowing a patent co-owner to grant a retroactive license to an alleged patent infringer and allowing a patent co-owner to defeat an infringement action by not joining in the suit as a plaintiff?

2. How could patent co-owners prevent this type of situation from arising?

3. Is it fair that a co-owner who contributed to only one claim in a patent can negate the rights of another co-owner who contributed to the other 5 claims in the patent? What might be the rationale underlying § 116 of the Patent Act?

4. Why would a co-owner not want to join an infringement suit against an alleged infringer with whom he does not have a license agreement?

CASE NOTES

1. Schering and Roussel (an involuntary plaintiff in the suit) are co-owners of the '382 patent, a combination of drugs for the treatment of prostate cancer. Both Schering and Roussel obtained their rights by means of assignments from the two inventors of the '382 patent. In 1989, when a dispute arose regarding the validity of the Schering assignment, Schering and Roussel entered into a co-owner agreement to resolve their respective rights in the '382 patent. The co-owner agreement provided that either party shall diligently notify the other party upon discovery of any infringement, that in the event of an infringement suit both parties shall share the expenses and damages award equally, and that if one party does not wish to join in an infringement suit, that party "shall render all reasonable assistance" to the other party pursing the infringement suit. In 1994, Zeneca contacted Roussel to explore the possibility of licensing the '382 patent. At about the same time, Schering contacted Roussel seeking to obtain exclusive rights under the '382 patent. In 1995, Roussel decided to negotiate a nonexclusive license with Zeneca for the '382 patent. Schering advised Roussel by letter that it thought any Zeneca sales of drugs covered by the '382 patent would constitute infringement. Shortly after, Schering requested Roussel's assistance in an infringement suit against Zeneca. Roussel responded that it had entered into a licensing agreement with Zeneca and would not join the infringement suit. Schering then filed an infringement complaint against Zeneca. Zeneca claimed that the license from Roussel was a complete defense to the infringement action. Schering claimed the co-owner agreement barred Roussel from granting a license to the '382 patent. What result? *See* Schering Corp. v. Roussel-UCLAF SA and Zeneca Inc., 104 F.3d 341 (Fed. Cir. 1997).

2. *See also* Israel Bio-Engineering Project v. Amgen Inc., 475 F.3d 1256 (Fed. Cir. 2007) (Patent co-owner does not have standing to sue for patent infringement without voluntary joinder of other co-owner); Digeo, Inc. v. Audible, Inc., 2006 U.S. Dist. LEXIS 87266 (W.D. Wash. 2006) (Forged assignment does not convey one patent co-owner's rights to other co-owners to establish standing to sue for infringement).

Additional Information

1. RAYMOND T. NIMMER & JEFF DODD, MODERN LICENSING LAW § 6:4 (2010).

2. 69 C.J.S.PATENTS § 315 (2010).

3. 60 AM. JUR. 2D PATENTS § 9 (2010).

4. JOHN G. MILLS, ET AL., 3 PATENT LAW FUNDAMENTALS § 17:29 (2d ed., 2010).

5. ROBERT A. MATTHEWS JR., ANNOTATED PATENT DIGEST, §§ 26:123, 9:42 (2010).

6. Richard F. Cahaly, *At Each Other's Mercy: Do Courts Fairly Apply Rule 19 of the Federal Rules of Civil Procedure to Protect Patent Co-owners' Property Rights*, 35 SUFFOLK U.L. REV. 671 (2001). (Rule 19 of the Federal Rules of Civil Procedure provides for involuntary joinder of parties where

the absent party is "indispensable" to providing complete relief in the suit.)

7. Dale L. Carlson, James R. Barney, *The Division of Rights Among Joint Inventors: Public Policy Concerns After Ethicon v. U.S. Surgical*, 39 IDEA 251 (1999).

8. Howard L. Speight, *Misunderstanding of Standing is Plaintiffs' Pitfall: Co-Inventors and Licensing are Among Potential Complications in Bringing Infringement Suits*, 6/22/98 Nat'l L.J. C22 (1998).

9. Rivka Monheit, *The Importance of Correct Inventorship*, 7 J. Intell. Prop. L. 191 (1999).

2.2.6   License Breach

A patent licensee may sue the patent licensor for damages if the patent licensor breaches the license agreement. *See, e.g.*, Shaw v. E.I. DuPont De Nemours & Co., 204 A.2d 159 (Vt. 1964). One situation in which a patent licensee may sue a patent licensor is where the license grants the licensee an exclusive right within a defined territory and the licensor practices the patent in that defined territory. *See, e.g.*, N.V. Philips Gloeilampenfabrieken v. Atomic Energy Commission, 316 F.2d 401 (D.C. Cir. 1963). Likewise, if the patent license grants the licensee an unrestricted worldwide license, the practice of the patent by the licensor anywhere in the world would constitute a breach of the license agreement. As you will see in subsection 2.3.4 of these materials, patent licensors are also often sued by patent licensees for breach of a most-favored licensee clause.

The *Institut Pasteur* case below involves a claim by a cross-licensee against the cross-licensor that it was authorized to practice certain patents because the cross-licensor acquired the company that held an exclusive license to the patents.

INSTITUT PASTEUR v. CAMBRIDGE BIOTECH
186 B.R. 9 (D. Mass. 1995)

James F. Queenan, Jr., Bankruptcy Judge.

Institut Pasteur ("Pasteur") and Genetic Systems Corporation ("Genetic") bring this adversary proceeding alleging that Cambridge Biotech Corporation (the "Debtor"), a chapter 11 debtor here, is infringing three patents owned by Pasteur and licensed to Genetic. The patents cover methods for the detection of Acquired Immune Deficiency Syndrome ("AIDS"). The plaintiffs seek both injunctive and compensatory relief.

Before the court are three motions. The Debtor moves for summary judgment on all the infringement claims. Pasteur and Genetic move for summary judgment on one infringement claim. They also move to dismiss Counts I and II of the Debtor's Answer and Counterclaim. In Count I, the Debtor requests a declaratory judgment that it has an existing license from a third party encompassing two of the patents in dispute, and that this license is valid notwithstanding the exclusive license held by Genetic. In Count II, the Debtor seeks damages from Pasteur, which is a signatory to the license agreement, for breach of the license agreement.

The plaintiffs contend these counts of the Answer and Counterclaim should be dismissed for failure to join the Debtor's licensor, an indispensable party. All the motions were taken under advisement after argument. Because it was apparent a decision on them would be largely dispositive of the entire case, the trial was continued generally.

The parties have engaged in some preliminary skirmishing. Immediately after filing their complaint, the plaintiffs requested the district court to withdraw the reference of this adversary proceeding. That was denied. The Debtor sought and obtained an order from this court declaring this adversary proceeding to be a core proceeding because it is in essence a claim against the Debtor's bankruptcy estate. I have also denied the plaintiffs' request for a jury trial because of the core and equitable nature of this proceeding.

The undisputed facts shall be set forth in discussion of the relevant legal issues.

I. THE PATENTS

In 1983, scientists at Pasteur's laboratories in Paris discovered what is now known as HIV-1 (Human Immunodeficiency Virus Type 1). HIV-1 was thought to be the sole cause of AIDS, until several years later, when Pasteur's scientists discovered what is now known as HIV-2. Both HIV-1 and HIV-2 belong to a family of viruses known as retroviruses. It is likely, but not certain, that persons infected with HIV-1 or HIV-2 will acquire AIDS.

Pasteur is the owner of the following United States patents:

United States Patent 5,217,861 ("the '861 patent"), entitled "ANTIGEN OF A HUMAN RETROUIRUS [sic], NAMELY, P18 PROTEIN OF HUMAN IMMUNODEFICIENCY VIRUS (HIV), COMPOSITIONS CONTAINING THE ANTIGEN, A DIAGNOSTIC METHOD FOR DETECTING ACQUIRED IMMUNODEFICIENCY SYNDROME (AIDS) AND PRE-AIDS, AND A KIT THEREFOR," which the United States Patent and Trademark Office ("PTO") issued on June 8, 1993.

United States Patent 5,055,391 ("the '391 patent"), entitled "METHOD AND KIT OR [sic] DETECTING ANTIBODIES TO ANTIGENS OF HUMAN IMMUNODEFICIENCY VIRUS TYPE 2 (HIV-2)," which the PTO issued on October 8, 1991.

United States Patent 5,051,496 ("the '496 patent"), entitled "PEPTIDES RELATED TO HUMAN IMMUNODEFICIENCY VIRUS II (HIV-2)," which the PTO duly and legally issued on September 24, 1991.

Genetic has, through license, obtained exclusive rights in the United States under all three patents, including the right to sue for infringement. The continued validity of two of those licenses is at issue here.

II. EFFECT OF THE CLAIMS BAR DATE

The Debtor argues it should be granted summary judgment on the plaintiffs' claim for pre-petition damages because the plaintiffs have not filed proofs of claim for those damages, and the bar date of January 2, 1995 has long since passed. The plaintiffs have filed nothing designated as a proof of claim. Because the present complaint was filed on March 8, 1995, it cannot be considered a timely proof of claim.

The plaintiffs contend it was unnecessary for them to file a proof of claim because they do not possess a "claim" within the meaning of the Code. The Code defines "claim" as encompassing both the right to payment and the right to an equitable remedy for breach of performance if such breach gives rise to a right to payment. 11 U.S.C. § 101(5) (1988). The plaintiffs seek damages and an injunction. As I have previously ruled, the allegations contained in the complaint give rise to a "claim" within the meaning of the Code.

The Debtor did not list the plaintiffs on its schedules or formally give them notice of the bar date. This does not matter. On July 15, 1994, an entity now known as Pasteur Sanofi Diagnostics filed a notice of appearance. It stated it was a creditor and requested that it be served with all papers filed in the case. As a result, by notice dated November 15, 1994, the Debtor gave it due notice of the January 2, 1995 bar date. As appears in greater detail later, Pasteur Sanofi Diagnostics is the party with whom the Debtor signed a license agreement concerning two of the patents. Pasteur Sanofi Diagnostics owns all the stock of Genetic and is in turn owned by an entity in which Pasteur holds a substantial minority interest. Both plaintiffs learned of the bar date through the notice to Pasteur Sanofi Diagnostics. Indeed, it was the lawyer representing the plaintiffs in this adversary proceeding who filed the notice of appearance on behalf of Pasteur Sanofi Diagnostics. Due knowledge of an event makes any deficiency in the manner of notice irrelevant. The plaintiffs do not contend otherwise.

The plaintiffs' failure to file a claim by the bar date requires disallowance of their pre-petition claims. Prior to the Bankruptcy Reform Act of 1994, which does not govern this case, the Code contained no provision requiring proofs of claim to be filed by the bar date as a condition precedent to allowance. The Federal Rules of Bankruptcy Procedure, however, set times by which claimants must file their proofs of claim. In a chapter 11 case, the Rules require a proof of claim to be filed by the date the court sets.

Failure to file timely proofs of claim does not mean the plaintiffs have no rights against the Debtor. If they hold valid patent rights, they have infringement claims to the extent the Debtor's post-petition conduct constitutes infringement. Such conduct occurring after the petition filing date and prior to confirmation of the Debtor's plan would create an administrative expense claim entitled to first priority. Infringement conduct occurring after confirmation would create a claim that is not discharged at confirmation (confirmation discharges debts that "arose before the date of confirmation"). I now turn to the validity of the patent infringement claims.

III. THE '391 AND '496 PATENTS

The Debtor does not contest the validity of the '391 and '496 patents. Nor does the Debtor contend the HIV-2 Kits which it manufactures and sells do not encompass the subject matter of these two patents. The Debtor asserts, rather, that the patents are included within a cross-license agreement entered into on October

25, 1989 between the Debtor and an entity then named Diagnostic Pasteur ("DP"). Pasteur's signature, after the words "For approval," appears on the agreement, below the signature of DP. Harvard College also signed in a similar capacity, below the signature of the Debtor.

Through a license arrangement with Harvard, the Debtor then held the right to produce certain proteins associated with HIV-1, such as gp110/120 and p27 and other proteins related to HTLV-1 (Human T-Cell Leukemia Virus Type 1), such as gp61. Pasteur held patents and patent applications on proteins associated with HIV-1, such as gp110/120 and p27. Pasteur also held patent applications on technology associated with HIV-2 which were exclusively licensed to DP. To avoid conflict between the various claims, the parties executed the October 25, 1989 cross-license agreement, which is royalty-bearing.

Under the cross-license agreement, the Debtor and DP each licensed to the other its various patent rights. At that time, DP did not have the right to license rights under the '391 and '496 patents. It had already licensed the United States rights on these patents to the co-plaintiff here, Genetic. The cross-license agreement between the Debtor and DP contains the following provision on this subject:

> 2.2 The license granted to CBS [the Debtor] by DP under paragraph 2.1. shall be automatically extended under the Licensed Patents as defined herein and as enclosed in Exhibit C upon recovery by DP from GENETIC SYSTEMS of the right to practice DP's letter patent included in Exhibit C, which DP shall use its best efforts to recover. DP represents that it is currently discussing such recovery with GENETIC SYSTEMS and will inform CBS with the progress and results of such discussions.

The '391 and '496 patent rights are among those included in the patent applications set forth in Exhibit C of the cross-license agreement. As stated in the quoted clause, DP was then in discussion with Genetic concerning "recovery" by DP from Genetic of rights under the '391 and '496 patents. Genetic is a United States biotech research company. DP and Genetic had previously, in 1984, entered into a joint venture and formed a corporate entity known as Blood Virus Diagnostics, Inc. ("BVD"). It was pursuant to this joint venture that DP had licensed to it the '391 and '496 patent rights.

In late 1988, DP began to renegotiate its 1984 agreement with Genetic, which was then owned by Bristol-Myers, Inc. At the time of the cross-license agreement, October 25, 1989, DP and Genetic had held no discussion of a possible acquisition of Genetic by DP or by any other party. The discussions related only to restructuring the 1984 agreement so as to re-vest in DP (and hence in the Debtor) rights in the two patents then licensed to Genetic. Similarly, at the time of the October 25, 1989 cross-license agreement, there had been no discussion between DP and the Debtor concerning DP acquiring ownership of Genetic rather than these license rights.

The corporate structures involving Pasteur, DP and Genetic are complex. And the names are confusing. At the time of the cross-license agreement, Pasteur owned (and still does) a minority stock interest in DP. The majority interest in DP was and is held by Sanofi, S.A. Shortly after execution of the cross-license agreement, Sanofi learned Bristol-Myers wanted to sell Genetic. Sanofi then began discussions with

Bristol-Myers for the purchase of Genetic. These discussions culminated in an agreement under which a subsidiary of Sanofi, Elf Sanofi, Inc., acquiring all the outstanding capital stock of Genetic in April of 1990. Thereafter, the stock was transferred to Kallestad Diagnostics. The latter entity is a wholly-owned subsidiary of DP. Its name has been changed to Sanofi Diagnostics Pasteur, Inc. DP, which is now called Pasteur Sanofi Diagnostics, continues to hold all the outstanding stock of Sanofi Diagnostics (formerly Kallestad Diagnostics), which in turn continues to hold all the stock of Genetic.

In summary, DP (now Pasteur Sanofi Diagnostics) owns all the stock of a corporation which in turn owns all the stock of Genetic.

When the Debtor learned of the acquisition of Genetic, it believed DP had succeeded in performing its obligation to use "its best efforts to recover" license rights for the '391 and '496 patents. The Debtor therefore forwarded royalty checks to DP (by then called "Pasteur Sanofi Diagnostics"), which declined to retain them. DP asserted the Debtor had no license rights in the patents, and reserved all rights to proceed against the Debtor.

A. Is Pasteur an "Affiliated Company"?

The Debtor mounts several arguments. It contends, first of all, that Pasteur is jointly obligated with DP (Pasteur Sanofi Diagnostics) under the 1989 cross-license agreement because the agreement obligates not only the named parties but also a so-called "affiliated company." The agreement contains this provision concerning an affiliated company:

> 1.4 "Affiliated Company" shall mean an organization which controls or is controlled by a party or an organization which is under common control with a party hereto and/or an organization qualifying as above (control shall mean direct or indirect legal or beneficial ownership of 51% or more of the voting stock). Unless the contrary is clearly indicated by the text hereof in every instance of this Agreement it is understood that reference to a party includes Affiliated Companies of such party as well. And [sic] that such party may extend to its Affiliated Companies the benefits of this Agreement so that such party shall remain responsible with regard all obligations placed upon such party by the basis of this Agreement. For the purposes of this Agreement, the parties confirm that the companies SANOFI DIAG-NOSTICS and DIAGNOSTICS TRANSFUSION, two companies within the SANOFI Group, shall be deemed to be Affiliated Companies of DP, as long as their relationship remain unchanged.

Pasteur is not an "Affiliated Company." It neither controls, nor is it under common control with, DP (Pasteur Sanofi Diagnostics). Sanofi, S.A. controls DP but does not control Pasteur.

B. Is Pasteur guilty of "action intended [to] frustrate"?

The Debtor also points to section 8.4 of the 1989 cross-license agreement, which reads as follows:

Institut Pasteur and the President and Fellows of Harvard College, by executing this Agreement, each hereby signifies its assent to the terms hereof and agrees to take no action intended frustrate [sic] the operation of this Agreement.

Pasteur has taken no action "intended [to] frustrate" operation of the agreement. Sanofi, S.A., which is not an affiliate of Pasteur, purchased Genetic and placed its ownership in the hands of a subsidiary of DP (Pasteur Sanofi Diagnostics). Pasteur owns only a minority interest in DP.

C. Has there been "recovery" by DP of the patent rights?

The Debtor's principal argument is that DP's ownership of a corporation whose wholly-owned subsidiary owns all the stock of Genetic constitutes "recovery" by DP of Genetic's '391 and '496 patent license rights within the meaning of the cross-license agreement, so that those rights are now "automatically" licensed to the Debtor pursuant to the terms of the agreement.

I conclude the agreement is not subject to this interpretation. There is a significant difference between ownership of patent license rights and ownership of a corporation whose wholly-owned subsidiary holds those rights. Acquisition of ownership of Genetic, furthermore, was not within the contemplation of the parties at the time they signed the cross-license agreement. The discussions then going on between Genetic and DP concerned only acquisition of license rights. It was not until Genetic went on the block for sale a few months later that a possible purchase of its capital stock came to the fore. And then it was Sanofi, S.A. rather than DP that made the purchase.

D. Application of the Equitable Maxim-Equity Treats as Done That Which in Good Conscience Should be Done

The Debtor's plight is nevertheless disturbing. DP (now Pasteur Sanofi Diagnostics) obligated itself to use its "best efforts" to acquire these patent rights. It now owns all the stock of the parent of a corporation which holds the rights. Yet it has not sought to own the rights themselves. Pasteur, DP's minority stockholder, refuses in this court to do anything about the situation and insists upon the real but technical distinction between ownership of stock and ownership of patent rights. This is presumably with the consent of Sanofi, S.A., DP's majority stockholder.

It is inequitable for DP not to be treated as owning the rights. There is an old maxim in equity. Equity treats as done that which in good conscience should be done.

Independent Wireless Telegraph was also a patent infringement case. An exclusive licensee had brought suit in its name, not the name of the patent owner. Because the suit was a general equity action, it did not fall within the scope of a statute permitting a licensee to sue in its own right. The licensee was unable to join the patent owner because the latter was outside the trial court's jurisdiction. The patent owner declined to authorize suit in its name, even though it was obligated to do so. The Supreme Court approved the licensee's use of the patent owner's name as co-plaintiff, resting its decision on the maxim that equity regards as done that which should be done.

Bankruptcy courts are essentially courts of equity, governed by equitable principles. They have used their equitable powers to resolve a wide variety of issues before them. These powers "have been invoked to the end that fraud will not prevail, that substance will not give way to form, that technical considerations will not prevent substantial justice from being done."

Treating these patent rights to be outside the Debtor's license would be inequitable. It is obviously a simple matter for DP (Pasteur Sanofi Diagnostics) to obtain the rights through its wholly-owned subsidiary which in turn owns Genetic. Yet it has failed to do so, clearly breaching its best efforts obligation. That DP should perhaps pay consideration for the transfer is immaterial. Its "best efforts" obligation under the cross-license agreement obviously assumes consideration may have to be paid to Genetic, which was not then a controlled entity.

QUESTIONS

1. Why would Pasteur and Genetic bring an infringement action against a company in bankruptcy?

2. Could Cambridge Biotech have argued that Diagnostic Pasteur's failure to use its best efforts to obtain Genetic's patent rights voided Cambridge Biotech's grant of its patent rights in the cross-license agreement?

3. If you were counsel to CBS, how would you have structured the relationship with DP differently to strengthen CBS' claim to the '391 and '496 patents? If the cross-license agreement had provided that that DP "hereby assigns all right, title and interest in the '391 and '496 patents that it presently owns, or that it may own in the future," would this have strengthened CBS' claim to the disputed patents? *See* Stanford v. Roche, 583 F.3d 832 (Fed. Cir. 2009) discussed in section 3.6 of the materials.

CASE NOTES

1. Robert Dray, Sr. (Dray) was issued three patents on an "internal piston valve," which regulates the flow of molten plastic in an injection-molding process. In 1991, in order to commercialize the internal piston valve, Dray, his son Bobby Dray and Brian Ricci jointly formed U.S. Valves. Dray granted U.S. Valves an exclusive right to manufacture, use, sell, advertise and distribute the internal piston valve, and U.S. Valves agreed to pay Dray a royalty of 20% on the net sales of the internal piston valve. In January 1994, Bobby Dray asked his father to reduce the royalty rate to 15% on sales to a prospective new customer — Van Dorn. Dray agreed to this request, but it was never memorialized in writing. In October 1994, a number of disagreements arose between the Drays and Ricci, and Ricci purchased the Drays' stock in U.S. Valves. By the end of 1994, both Drays were completely dissociated from U.S. Valves. In August 1995, Dray began selling internal piston valves. In October 1995, Dray asked U.S. Valves to provide him information to verify the accuracy of the royalty payments under the license. After reviewing the informa-

tion, Dray informed U.S. Valves that he believed it had underpaid royalties, partly because it had paid a royalty of 15% on all sales to Van Dorn, not just on the initial sale, which was all Dray claimed he agreed to. U.S. Valves sued Dray for breach of the license agreement. Dray claimed U.S. Valves breached the license agreement by underpaying royalties, and sought an accounting of, and damages for, unpaid royalties. What result? *See* U.S. Valves. Inc. v. Dray, 212 F.3d 1368 (Fed. Cir. 2000).

2. *See also* Corebrace LLC v. Star Seismic LLC, 566 F.3d 1069 (Fed. Cir. 2009) (Nonexclusive license to "make, use and sell" licensed products was not breached where licensee used third party to manufacture licensed products for its own use; licensor could not terminate license agreement and sue for breach of license agreement on same day where license provided that it can be terminated only after written notice of the breach and thirty-day opportunity to cure breach); Allan Block Corp. v. County Materials Corp., 512 F.3d 912 (7th Cir. 2008) (License provision that provided license could be terminated upon 120 days written notice or upon declaration of default and 10 day opportunity to cure was a condition precedent to terminating license, not to suing for breach of license; licensor who terminated license agreement pursuant to notice provision, therefore, could sue for breach of the license agreement without giving the licensee an opportunity to cure; post-termination covenants not to compete in license agreement were not subject to license's provision requiring non-defaulting party to give notice and opportunity to cure default); Duval Wiedmann, LLC v. Inforocket.Com, Inc., 620 F.3d 496 (5th Cir. 2010) (Notice of license termination sent to licensor's trustee in bankruptcy during course of bankruptcy proceeding was effective to terminate license); Nano-Proprietary, Inc. v. Canon, Inc., 537 F.3d 394 (5th Cir. 2008) (License agreement that granted licensee an "irrevocable, fully paid-up and perpetual license" upon payment to the licensor of $5,555,555.55 could not be terminated by licensor even for licensee's material breach of license provision stating the licensee did not have the right to sublicense).

Additional Information

1. John R. Kennel Et al., 69 C.J.S. Patents §§ 386–389, 391–392 (2011).

2. Barry Kramer, Allen D. Brufsky, 2 Patent Law Practice Forms §§ 77:24, 77:41 (2011).

3. Robert A. Matthews, Jr., 5 Annotated Patent Digest § 36:14 (2011).

4. James A. Patrick, *Jurisdiction Cases Involving Breach of a Patent License,* 45 S.C. L. Rev. 187 (1993).

5. Philip B.C. Jones, *Violation of a Patent License Restriction: Breach of Contract or Patent Infringement,* 33 IDEA 225 (1993).

2.2.7 License Breach Remedies

The two main remedies for breach of license agreements are damages and injunctions. The breach of a license agreement can be both a breach of contract (an action brought in state court) and a patent infringement (an action brought in federal court). When the breach of a license agreement is brought as a breach of contract action, damages are calculated under state contract law, which generally provides that the non-breaching party can recover the profits it lost as a result of breach. A breach of license is generally brought as a breach of contract action when the damages have been incurred within the scope of the license. For example, a breach of license for underpayment of royalties or unauthorized assignment would be brought as a breach of contract action.

When the breach of license is brought as a patent infringement action, damages are calculated under the Patent Act. A breach of license is generally brought as an infringement action when the damages have been incurred outside the scope of the license. For example, breach of license for uses outside the licensed field of use or after license termination would be brought as patent infringement actions.

Section 284 of the Patent Act provides:

Damages

Upon finding for the claimant the court shall award the claimant damages adequate to compensate for the infringement, but in no event less than a reasonable royalty rate for the use made of the invention by the infringer . . .

Courts have interpreted Section 284 as providing for two types of damage calculations — lost profits and reasonable royalties. Lost profits are the profits that the patentee lost because of the presence of the infringing product in the market. Calculation of lost profits under the Patent Act is similar to calculation of lost profits under state contract law. The four factors which determine lost profits are: (i) the demand for the patented product, (ii) the absence of acceptable non-infringing substitute products, (iii) the manufacturing and marketing capability of the patentee, and (iv) the profit margin.

When a patentee cannot prove the four factors necessary for calculation of lost profits, the patentee is entitled to the recovery of reasonable royalties. Reasonable royalties have been defined as the amount that a willing licensee would pay to a willing licensor in a hypothetical negotiation. Georgia-Pacific Corp. v. U.S. Plywood Corp., 318 F. Supp. 1116 (S.D.N.Y. 1970) set forth the definitive list of fifteen factors to be considered in determining a reasonable royalty. Among the most important of these factors are royalties received by the patentee from other licenses of the patented product, royalties paid by the licensee for comparable patented products, the established profitability of the patented product, the advantages of the patented product over other products and the opinion testimony of qualified experts. *See also* Uniloc USA, Inc. v. Microsoft, 632 F.3d 1292 (Fed. Cir. 2011) discussed in subsection 1.8.3.

Proof of damages in either a breach of contract suit or a patent infringement suit is often difficult, costly and uncertain. One way in which the parties can minimize the problems associated with the proof of damages is to agree to a specific damage amount in the event of breach before the license agreement is executed. However, *ex ante* agreements on damages, commonly called *liquidated damages*, are scrutinized by courts in a way that other contract clauses are not. If a court finds that a liquidated damages clause is a penalty rather than a reasonable prediction of future damages, the court can invalidate the liquidate damages clause.

The second main remedy for license breach is an injunction which prohibits a defendant from continuing to engage in the breaching or infringing conduct. Injunctions can be obtained under state contract law or under the Patent Act. Section 283 of the Patent Act provides:

Injunction

The several courts having jurisdiction of cases under this title may grant injunctions in accordance with the principles of equity to prevent the violation of any right secured by the patent, on such terms as the court deems reasonable.

Although the distinction between an action at law and an action at equity is a historical remnant of English common law, courts nonetheless continue to require plaintiffs to satisfy a four-factor test before granting an injunction. The plaintiff must show (i) that it has suffered irreparable harm, (ii) that the remedy at law (damages) is inadequate, (iii) that the balance of hardships as between the plaintiff and defendant resulting from the injunction favors the plaintiff, and (iv) that the public interest would not be disserved by an injunction.

Historically, courts have issued permanent injunctions in patent infringement suits almost automatically once the court has found that the patent is valid and that the patent has been infringed. In issuing permanent injunctions, courts have reasoned that the patentees' most fundamental right is the right to *exclude* others from making, using, offering for sale, selling and importing the invention and that this right is only meaningful if backed by an injunction. 35 U.S.C. 271. As you will see below, this long-standing tradition of granting permanent injunctions has been abruptly ended by the Supreme Court.

In the first case of this subsection, Monsanto sued McFarling for breach of contract and patent infringement. The court calculated reasonable royalty damages under the Patent Act. The following case, *XCO*, deals with the question of liquidated damages and when liquidated damages should be invalidated as a penalty. The final case in this section, *eBay*, is the Supreme Court's recent pronouncement on how and when a permanent injunction should be granted in patent infringement cases.

MONSANTO COMPANY v. McFARLING
488 F.3d 973 (Fed. Cir. 2007)

BRYSON, CIRCUIT JUDGE.

I

This is the third time this case has been before us. In the first appeal, we affirmed the district court's entry of a preliminary injunction in favor of the plaintiff, Monsanto Company, and against the defendant, Homan McFarling. *Monsanto Co. v. McFarling*, 302 F.3d 1291 (Fed. Cir. 2002) (*McFarling I*). In the second appeal, we upheld the district court's rulings holding Mr. McFarling liable for breach of contract and rejecting Mr. McFarling's counterclaims and affirmative defenses. We reversed the judgment in that case, however, holding that the liquidated damages provision in the parties' contract was an unenforceable penalty, and we remanded for a determination of Monsanto's actual damages. *Monsanto Co. v. McFarling*, 363 F.3d 1336 (Fed. Cir. 2004) (*McFarling II*). After a damages trial, the district court entered an award of damages for patent infringement, rejected Mr. McFarling's arguments for vacating the judgment of liability, and refused Monsanto's request to modify the permanent injunction. We affirm on both Mr. McFarling's appeal and Monsanto's cross-appeal.

Monsanto developed a system for weed control that employs genetically modified crops that resist glyphosphate herbicide. Upon planting such crops, farmers can spray glyphosphate herbicide over their fields to kill weeds while sparing the resistant crops, a technique that allows for much more efficient weed control than is possible with unmodified plants. Monsanto sells the glyphosphate herbicide under the trade name Roundup and sells seeds of the genetically modified crops, in this case soybeans, under the trade name Roundup Ready.

Two patents of importance here protect aspects of Monsanto's Roundup Ready technology. First, Monsanto's U.S. Patent No. 5,633,435 ("the '435 patent") claims a plant cell containing a DNA molecule that encodes a genetically modified enzyme. That enzyme allows plants to survive exposure to glyphosphate herbicide. Second, Monsanto's U.S. Patent No. 5,352,605 ("the '605 patent") claims a plant cell containing a genetic promoter sequence that facilitates a plant's production of the modified enzyme. Although the '605 patent does not explicitly claim a seed containing a specific genetic sequence, as does the '435 patent, the parties do not dispute that Roundup Ready soybeans contain the plant cells and the promoter sequences claimed in the '605 patent.

Monsanto distributed the patented seeds by authorizing various companies to produce the seeds and sell them to farmers. Monsanto required those seed companies to obtain a signed "Technology Agreement" from purchasers. The Technology Agreement licensed the '435 and '605 patents to farmers on several conditions and required that farmers promise not to violate those conditions. Of relevance here, farmers promised not to replant seeds that were produced from the purchased seeds or to supply those seeds to others for replanting. Those promises ensure that a farmer who uses Roundup Ready seeds buys the seeds that he plants each year.

The purchasers also paid a fee to Monsanto for the license. For the time periods relevant here, Monsanto charged a license fee of $6.50 per 50-pound bag of Roundup Ready soybean seed. Mr. McFarling also would have had to pay a seed company between $19 and $22 for each bag of the seed that he purchased.

In 1998, Mr. McFarling purchased Roundup Ready soybean seeds from a seed company. He signed the Technology Agreement for that year and paid the required fees. In violation of the license agreement, however, he saved seeds from his 1998 soybean crop and planted those seeds in 1999. He did the same thing the next year, saving soybeans from his 1999 crop and planting them in 2000. The saved seeds contained the patented genetic traits, but Mr. McFarling did not pay the license fee for the 1999 or 2000 growing seasons.

Upon learning of Mr. McFarling's conduct, Monsanto sued him in the United

States District Court for the Eastern District of Missouri, asserting that he had breached the Technology Agreement and infringed the '435 and '605 patents. The district court granted Monsanto's motion for a preliminary injunction prohibiting Mr. McFarling from continuing to plant saved Roundup Ready soybeans, and we affirmed that decision on appeal.

Monsanto then moved in the district court for summary judgment on some but not all of the pending claims-namely, the breach of contract claim, the claim of infringement of the '605 patent, and all of Mr. McFarling's counterclaims. Monsanto did not move for summary judgment on its '435 patent claim. In response, Mr. McFarling raised various defenses, including patent misuse and preemption by the Plant Variety Protection Act. The district court rejected those defenses and granted Monsanto's motion in full except as it concerned damages for breach of contract and infringement of the '605 patent. With liability resolved, the parties stipulated to the amount of liquidated damages under the license agreement, and the district court entered judgment on Monsanto's breach of contract claim and on Mr. McFarling's counterclaims. The court then entered an order under Federal Rule of Civil Procedure 54(b) allowing an immediate appeal on the decided claims.

On appeal, we affirmed the dismissal of Mr. McFarling's antitrust counterclaim and the rejection of his defenses of patent misuse and preemption by the Plant Variety Protection Act. However, we vacated the liquidated damages award as an unenforceable penalty and remanded for further proceedings.

After our decision in the second appeal, Monsanto withdrew all of its claims other than the '605 patent claim, on which it had already secured a liability ruling; it then proceeded to try the issue of damages to a jury on that claim alone. During the trial on damages, Mr. McFarling moved for judgment as a matter of law based on his patent misuse defense, contending that the patent misuse defense was given new life by Monsanto's withdrawal of one of its two claims for patent infringement. The district court denied that motion.

During the damages trial, Mr. McFarling also moved for a directed verdict that an established royalty for his infringing conduct limited the size of a damages award. The district court denied the motion and submitted the issue of damages to the jury.

The jury returned a damages verdict of $40 per bag of saved seed, well in excess of the $6.50 per bag for which Mr. McFarling had argued, but substantially less than the $80.65 per bag (for 1999) and $73.20 per bag (for 2000) urged by Monsanto based on the analysis of its expert. Mr. McFarling again moved to limit the damages award to what he contended was Monsanto's $6.50 per bag established royalty for use of its patented technology. The district court denied the motion, adopted the jury's verdict, and awarded Monsanto approximately $375,000 in damages. The district court also permanently enjoined Mr. McFarling from future unauthorized use of the patented technology.

****

III

Mr. McFarling next challenges the amount of the damages award. He contends that it grossly exceeds the amount that is justified, which should be limited to the "established royalty" for Roundup Ready seeds, i.e., the "Technology Fee" of $6.50 per bag that Monsanto charged licensees who purchased Roundup Ready seeds under its Technology Agreement.

A.

By statute, damages for patent infringement are to be "adequate to compensate for the infringement, but in no event less than a reasonable royalty for the use made of the invention by the infringer, together with interest and costs as fixed by the court." 35 U.S.C. § 284. After our remand in *McFarling II*, Monsanto elected to pursue the reasonable royalty measure of its damages. In response, Mr. McFarling argued that there is an established royalty of $6.50 per bag that should apply to his infringing conduct, and he asked the court to limit the amount of the reasonable royalty to that amount. The district court found "some legitimacy" in that argument but ultimately denied the motion and submitted the damages issue to the jury.

An established royalty is usually the best measure of a "reasonable" royalty for a given use of an invention because it removes the need to guess at the terms to which parties would hypothetically agree. When the patentee has consistently licensed others to engage in conduct comparable to the defendant's at a uniform royalty, that royalty is taken as established and indicates the terms upon which the patentee would have licensed the defendant's use of the invention.

Monsanto has consistently licensed farmers to use its Roundup Ready technology pursuant to the terms of a standard license agreement. For the relevant years, Monsanto agreed to let soybean farmers use the patented traits in planting and growing soybean crops and to let them sell the harvested seeds as a commodity. In exchange, farmers agreed to pay Monsanto a Technology Fee and to refrain from planting Roundup Ready seed saved from a previous season's crop and from selling Roundup Ready seed from their crop to others for planting. Those promises ensured that the farmers had to purchase the Roundup Ready seed they planted in a given year from an authorized distributor. The distributor seed companies, some of which were owned by Monsanto and some of which were independent, also charged a fee for each bag of Roundup Ready soybeans they sold.

Mr. McFarling's infringing conduct consisted of planting patent-protected seeds in 1999 and 2000 without purchasing them from a seed company licensed or owned by Monsanto. Because Mr. McFarling neither paid Monsanto the Technology Fee nor purchased the Roundup Ready seed from an authorized distributor, the value to Monsanto of both performances provides one measure of the "reasonable royalty for the use made of the invention by the infringer." 35 U.S.C. § 284. The parties agree that the amount of the Technology Fee was $6.50 per 50-pound bag of

Roundup Ready soybean seed for the pertinent years, 1999 and 2000. Because that fee does not take into account the added obligation imposed on all authorized licensees under the Technology Agreement — to purchase seed from an authorized seed store — the trial court was correct to refuse to treat the $6.50 Technology Fee as the established royalty for a license comparable to the infringing conduct.

Monsanto in effect decided that under its standard licensing program it would extract $6.50 in direct payment and would also extract an undertaking to buy seed from a seed company, which imposed an additional cost of $19 to $22 per bag on the farmers. The fact that Monsanto elected to allocate its licensing fees by obtaining a direct payment of $6.50 and ensuring a payment to the seed companies of another $19 to $22 does not mean that the royalty for its standard license was only $6.50. It means that, for a variety of economic reasons, Monsanto decided to split the royalty up into two parts and to direct part of the royalty to the third-party seed companies, which promoted and distributed Monsanto's products. The out-of-pocket cost that the farmers paid for the right to use Monsanto's technology was thus $25.50 to $28.50. In effect, the amount of that cost that can be characterized as a pure royalty payment was $25.50 to $28.50 minus the modest cost of cleaning and bagging the seeds and other transaction costs.

Picking $6.50 as the upper limit for the reasonable royalty would create a windfall for infringers like McFarling. Such infringers would have a huge advantage over other farmers who took the standard Monsanto license and were required to comply with the provisions of the license, including the purchase-of-seed and non-replanting provisions. The evidence at trial showed that Monsanto would not agree to an unconditional license in exchange for a payment of $6.50, and the explanation-that Monsanto would lose all the benefits it gets from having the cooperation of seed companies in promoting Monsanto's product and controlling its distribution-is a reasonable commercial strategy.

By insisting that the established royalty is $6.50 per bag, Mr. McFarling does not acknowledge the significance of the requirement that licensees not only pay the $6.50, but also purchase the genetically modified seeds from a seed company rather than replanting saved seed. He does not argue, even in the alternative, that the court should have limited the reasonable royalty to the total amount paid by licensed farmers for patent-protected seeds. In any event, for the reasons given below it would be improper to hold that Monsanto's reasonable royalty damages are limited to $25.50 to $28.50 per bag, the total amount charged for the seeds and the Technology Fee.

Monsanto's evidence at trial showed that the requirement that farmers purchase their seed each year instead of saving seed from the previous year had particular benefits to Monsanto above and beyond the monetary payments represented by the Technology Fee and the seed prices charged by the seed companies. Monsanto's experts testified that the no-saving-seed requirement (1) decreased the risk of underreporting and the consequent reputation harm to Monsanto with farmers, (2) ensured Monsanto's knowledge of the quality of seed planted each year, and (3) provided a bargaining chip for signing up new seed companies. It is difficult to assign a dollar value to those benefits, but the benefits nonetheless justify the jury's finding that a reasonable royalty for a license to engage in conduct like Mr. McFarling's would exceed the amount of the payments made by farmers who participated in the licensing program.

In determining the amount of a reasonable royalty, it was proper for the jury to consider not only the benefits of the licensing program to Monsanto, but also the benefits that Monsanto's technology conferred on farmers such as Mr. McFarling. Monsanto's expert testified at length regarding the valuation of Monsanto's damages. He began by estimating the value conferred on a farmer such as Mr. McFarling by the use of the Roundup Ready product. Because using conventional soybeans was the most logical alternative to either licensing or infringing, that value provided a reasonable basis for estimating the advantages conferred by the use of the patented technology.

The expert testified that the use of Roundup Ready seeds increased the yield of soybeans in an amount valued at $14 to $25 per acre as compared to conventional seeds. In addition, the expert testified that the use of Roundup Ready seeds reduced the costs of weed control in an amount valued at $26 to $36 per acre as compared to conventional seeds; he based that estimate on three studies that showed cost savings for the Roundup Ready system ranging from a low of $17 to a high of $36. Even using the lowest dollar amount disclosed in any of the studies as the minimum amount for savings on weed control ($17), and even disregarding the expert's testimony about other possible savings associated with the use of the Roundup Ready system, those two items alone result in an estimated savings of $31 to $61 per acre as compared to conventional seeds. Given that one 50-pound bag of seed is sufficient to plant about an acre of farmland, the savings of $31 to $61 per acre was equivalent to a savings of $31 to $61 per bag of seed. Based on those advantages alone, it was reasonable for the jury to suppose that, in a hypothetical negotiation, a purchaser would pay a royalty of $40 per bag for the Roundup Ready seed. The jury's verdict was therefore justified even without considering some of the other more sharply controverted aspects of the expert's valuation opinion, such as his use of a multiplier to account for the risks to Monsanto from infringement by farmers.

In reviewing damages awards in patent cases, we give broad deference to the conclusions reached by the finder of fact. As we explained recently in another "saved seed" case, a jury's damages award "must be upheld unless the amount is grossly excessive or monstrous, clearly not supported by the evidence or based only on speculation or guesswork." In this case, we hold that the jury's verdict was supported by evidence and was not grossly excessive, particularly in light of the evidence of the savings Mr. McFarling achieved by his infringement, the benefits to Monsanto from requiring farmers to adhere to the terms of its standard licensing agreement, and the benefits conferred by the patented technology over the use of conventional seeds.

IV

The district court enjoined Mr. McFarling from infringing the '605 patent by planting any seed harvested from a crop of Roundup Ready soybeans, "except that Mr. McFarling may plant Roundup Ready soybeans acquired from any lawful dealer, but to do so McFarling must sign any applicable technology agreement required by Monsanto." Monsanto objects to that clause in the court's decree because Monsanto understands the clause as requiring it to issue a standard license to Mr. McFarling if he agrees to comply with the license terms.

We do not understand the injunction to compel Monsanto to license its technology to Mr. McFarling if it chooses not to. Rather, the injunction simply reflects that if Monsanto enters a binding technology agreement with Mr. McFarling through a dealer, then Monsanto will have licensed Mr. McFarling to engage in conduct that would otherwise infringe the '605 patent; the injunction will not prohibit that licensed conduct.

Monsanto's real concern may be that, in light of the complexity and scale of its distribution and licensing system, it may enter into a binding license with Mr. McFarling even if it does not wish to do so. Thus, Monsanto requests that we direct the district court to enjoin Mr. McFarling from obtaining Roundup Ready soybean seed absent "express authorization from Monsanto."

We decline that invitation. The district court acted well within its discretion in not enjoining conduct that would not infringe Monsanto's patent. It is up to Monsanto, not the district court, to ensure that Monsanto's representatives do not enter into a binding contract with Mr. McFarling absent "express authorization from Monsanto" or whatever other licensing standard Monsanto wishes to adopt. We therefore reject Monsanto's challenge to the district court's injunction.

Each party shall bear its own costs for this appeal and cross-appeal.

AFFIRMED.

QUESTIONS

1.   Monsanto is a multibillion dollar company, and McFarling is a small farmer. Nonetheless, the jury found damages that were clearly on the high side of a reasonable royalty rate. Why do you think the jury favored Monsanto in its damage award?

2.   Why was the fee per bag paid to Monsanto plus the amount per bag paid to the distributors not sufficient for the reasonable royalty?

3.   What factors do you think are most important in determining a reasonable royalty rate?

XCO INTERNATIONAL v. PACIFIC SCIENTIFIC
369 F.3d 998 (7th Cir. 2004)

POSNER, CIRCUIT JUDGE.

The appeal in this diversity breach of contract suit governed mainly by Illinois law presents issues involving the enforceability of a liquidated damages clause (found by the district judge to be a penalty), contract interpretation, patent law, and sanctions for making frivolous claims.

The plaintiff, XCO, owned U.S. and foreign (mainly European) patents on heat-sensitive cables. In 1991 it assigned the patents to the defendant, PacSci, which wanted to use them in making products for fire control and related uses. PacSci agreed to pay XCO $725,000 down, plus $100,000 or 5 percent of PacSci's sales of products utilizing the patented technology — whichever amount was greater — annually from 1995 through 2000; after that it would pay 5 percent of annual sales until the patents expired. As part of the deal, PacSci licensed the patents that it had just bought back to XCO for use in making heat-sensitive cables for lining refractory process vessels (used for processing petroleum products), which was the core of XCO's business, its principal market being in Europe. As the consideration for this license XCO agreed to pay PacSci $100,000 plus royalties on sales of the cables for the licensed use. The parties further agreed that PacSci would be "responsible for all expenses of any kind relating to" the patent rights that it was buying, including the fees charged by European patent authorities to maintain patents in effect. The U.S. Patent and Trademark Office charges patent-maintenance fees for U.S. patents, but payment of those fees is not in issue.

The agreement was to continue until the last of the patents expired in 2003. Beginning in 1993, however, just two years after the agreement had been signed, PacSci stopped paying maintenance fees on those patents that it wasn't using. It took the position that notwithstanding the "responsibility" clause of the contract, it could pick and choose which patents to keep alive. As a result, by 1998 a number of the patents had lapsed. XCO declared a breach that year and terminated the contract, as it was entitled to do (without liability) if in fact PacSci had committed a breach. A provision in a section of the contract captioned "Breach and Liquidated Damages" states that in the event of such a termination all money owed XCO by PacSci, "including such amounts which constitute overdue, delinquent or otherwise unpaid amounts . . . plus one hundred thousand dollars ($100,000) per year from and including the year of such termination to and including the year of the last to expire of the patent rights, shall then constitute liquidated damages under this Agreement." Another provision, also in the "Breach and Liquidated Damages" section, states that if XCO breaks the contract, PacSci will have no further obligations except to pay XCO any amounts that came due before the breach; in other words, from the date of a breach by XCO forward, PacSci would have a royalty-free license. So damages were specified for a breach by either party.

Because XCO terminated the contract in 1998 and the last patent expired in 2003, and because the $100,000 in liquidated damages was due in both the year in which the contract was terminated and the year in which the last patent expired, as well as in all the intermediate years, the clause, if valid, entitles XCO to $600,000 in damages. The district judge held that it is a penalty clause, hence invalid. He ruled so on summary judgment, while rejecting PacSci's interpretation of the "responsibility" clause. He found, in other words, that PacSci had broken the contract; but since XCO did not attempt to prove its actual damages, instead seeking only liquidated damages, XCO got no relief for the breach.

XCO's appeal challenges the district judge's denial of its motion for sanctions as well as his refusal to enforce the liquidated damages clause. In defending the latter ruling PacSci not only embraces the judge's penalty-clause determination but also argues that letting the patents lapse was not a breach of contract after all.

When damages for breach of contract would be difficult for a court to determine after the breach occurs, it makes sense for the parties to specify in the contract itself what the damages for a breach shall be; this reduces uncertainty and litigation costs and economizes on judicial resources as well. Indeed, even if damages wouldn't be difficult to determine after the fact, it is hard to see why the parties shouldn't be allowed to substitute their own ex ante determination for the ex post determination of a court. Damages would be just another contract provision that parties would be permitted to negotiate under the general rubric of freedom of contract. One could even think of a liquidated damages clause as a partial settlement, as in cases in which damages are stipulated and trial confined to liability issues. And of course settlements are favored.

Yet it is a rule of the common law of contracts, in Illinois as elsewhere, that unless the parties' ex ante estimate of damages is reasonable, their liquidated damages provision is unenforceable, as constituting a penalty intended to "force" performance. The reason for the rule is mysterious; it is one of the abiding mysteries of the common law. At least in a case such as this, where both parties are substantial commercial enterprises (ironically, it is the larger firm, PacSci, that is crying "penalty clause"), and where damages are liquidated for breach by either party, making an inference of fraud or duress implausible, it is difficult to see why the law should take an interest in whether the estimate of harm underlying the liquidation of damages is reasonable. Courts don't review the other provisions of contracts for reasonableness; why this one?

It is true that if there is a very stiff penalty for breach, parties will be discouraged from committing "efficient" breaches, that is, breaches that confer a greater benefit on the contract breaker than on the victim of the breach, in which event breach plus compensation for the victim produces a net gain with no losers and should be encouraged. (This is a reason why injunctions are not routinely granted in contract cases — why, in other words, the party who breaks his contract is usually allowed to walk away from it, provided only that he compensates the other party for the cost of the breach to that party.) But against this consideration must be set the worthwhile effect of a penalty as a signal that the party subject to it is likely to perform his contract promise. This makes him a more attractive contract partner, since if he doesn't perform he will be punished severely. His willingness to assume that risk signals his confidence that he will be able to perform and thus avoid the penalty. It makes him a credible person to do business with, and thus promotes commerce.

Granted, the case for a contractual specification of damages is stronger the more difficult it is to estimate damages and so the greater the expense to the parties and the judiciary, and hence to society, of determining the plaintiff's damages by the clumsy and costly methods of litigation. That presumably is why the enforceability of liquidated damages clauses depends on the difficulty of estimating, when the contract is signed, what the damages will be if the contract is broken. Yet in such cases the plaintiff will often be able to obtain injunctive relief instead of damages, on the ground that his damages remedy is inadequate, that being the standard criterion for injunctive relief; and an injunction often has a punitive effect because the cost to the defendant of complying with it will often exceed the harm to the plaintiff from the enjoined conduct. The fact that injunctions are sometimes granted in contract cases shows, therefore, that "punishment" is not wholly alien to contractual remedies. At a minimum one might suppose penalty clauses tolerable to the extent that the penalty portion approximated the costs in attorneys' fees and other expenses of proving damages for breach of contract.

The rule against penalty clauses, though it lingers, has come to seem rather an anachronism, especially in cases in which commercial enterprises are on both sides of the contract. As we noted "it is easy to assign non-exploitive reasons for contractual penalties and hard to give convincing reasons why in the absence of fraud or unconscionability consenting adults that are, moreover, substantial organizations rather than mere consumers should be prohibited from agreeing to such provisions." The rule hangs on, but is chastened by an emerging presumption against interpreting liquidated damages clauses as penalty clauses.

Whatever the strength and contours of the rule in Illinois today, PacSci is wholly in error in arguing that a liquidated damages clause is invalid unless it recites, or extrinsic evidence shows, that the parties determined that, yes, it really would be difficult to determine damages for breach after the breach occurred. No case in Illinois or anywhere else so holds or implies, and the rejection of the argument is implicit in the numerous cases that hold such clauses valid which do not contain such recitals, even when there is no extrinsic evidence to fill the gap. PacSci has tried to reverse the burden of proof, which, as in the case of other affirmative defenses, rests on the party resisting enforcement of a liquidated damages clause to show that the agreed-upon damages are clearly disproportionate to a reasonable estimate of the actual damages likely to be caused by a breach.

The burden of proving the invalidity of the liquidated damages clause in the contract with XCO thus remained on PacSci and it is apparent from the nature of the breach of contract — failing to pay patent-maintenance fees, as a predictable result of which the patents lapsed — that PacSci failed to carry it. And breach it was; PacSci's argument that because it was made "responsible" for the fees it could decide not to pay them-an interpretation that deprives the "responsibility" clause of all force, as well as wreaking semantic havoc ("responsibility" signifies duty, not right) — does not merit discussion.

The premature lapse of XCO's European patents exposed XCO to competition that the patents, had they remained valid, might well have prevented-or might not have. That would be a costly and uncertain issue for a court to resolve. About all the court could say would be that given the scale of XCO's operations, $100,000 a year from the breach to the termination of the last patent was not an outlandish estimate of the damages that XCO might sustain as a result of PacSci's allowing the patents to lapse. This case thus illustrates how a liquidated damages clause can spare the parties and the court the anxiety and expense of protracted and uncertain remedy proceedings.

The element common to most liquidated damages clauses that get struck down as penalty clauses is that they specify the same damages regardless of the severity of the breach. One can see the problem: if a contract provides that breaches of different gravity shall be sanctioned with equal severity, it is highly likely that the sanction specified for the mildest breach is a penalty (that, or the sanctions for all the other possible breaches must be inadequate). That would have been the case here if instead of fixing the damages at $100,000 per year, the damages clause had recited for example that in the event of breach PacSci must pay XCO $500,000, period. Then if PacSci failed to pay only the maintenance fee due six months before the last patent expired, it would owe the same damages that it would owe had it never paid any of the maintenance fees and as a result all of XCO's patents had lapsed within a year after the contract was signed. That isn't how the clause works. Instead, by proportioning damages to the remaining life of the patents, it sanctions PacSci more heavily the longer the life that remained to them when PacSci allowed them to lapse.

Yet the proportionality of the damages specification highlights by way of contrast the only halfway decent argument that PacSci has against the validity of the liquidated damages clause. This is that the clause fails to differentiate between different *kinds* of breach, some more serious than others, as distinct from different degrees of seriousness within a given kind. Suppose the breach had taken the form of PacSci's failing not to keep the patents in force but to make a royalty payment of $1,000 when it was due. The liquidated damages clause read literally would require PacSci not only to pay the $1,000 but to pay $100,000 on top of it for each year from the breach to the expiration of the last patent. That would be pretty outlandish- depending on the date of breach it could cost PacSci more than $1 million though it had harmed XCO to the tune of $1,000 at most — but it is an argument not for invalidating the clause but for interpreting it reasonably. It is apparent from the reference in the clause to the date of expiration of the last patent that the $100,000 a year damages provision is intended only for the case in which a breach by PacSci endangers the patents. It is not intended for other breaches, such as failure to pay agreed-upon amounts.

Even if the clause were read literally, and as a result would be deemed a penalty if invoked in a case in which the breach consisted merely of a failure to pay royalties or other amounts due under the contract to XCO, the proper judicial remedy would be to reform the clause to limit it to those breaches, such as the one that occurred in this case, for which it constituted a reasonable specification of damages. There would be no reason to invalidate the clause in its entirety.

We conclude that XCO is entitled to its liquidated damages but not to sanctions and that the rejection of PacSci's counterclaim must stand. The judgment is affirmed in part and reversed in part and the case is remanded to the district court for the entry of a new judgment consistent with this opinion.

QUESTIONS

1.   Could liquidated damages be established for each individual potential breach of contract?

2.   Could liquidated damages be established for major and minor breaches of contract? Would this satisfy the concern over imposing the same damages regard- less of the severity of the breach?

3.   Could parties recite that the liquidated damages amount represents their best effort determination of damages *ex ante*?

4.   Would a reciprocal liquidated damages clause be less likely to be struck down as a penalty?

EBAY v. MERCEXCHANGE
547 U.S. 388 (2006)

JUSTICE THOMAS.

Ordinarily, a federal court considering whether to award permanent injunctive relief to a prevailing plaintiff applies the four-factor test historically employed by courts of equity. Petitioners eBay Inc. and Half.com, Inc., argue that this traditional test applies to disputes arising under the Patent Act. We agree and, accordingly, vacate the judgment of the Court of Appeals.

I

Petitioner eBay operates a popular Internet Web site that allows private sellers to list goods they wish to sell, either through an auction or at a fixed price. Petitioner Half.com, now a wholly owned subsidiary of eBay, operates a similar Web site. Respondent MercExchange, L.L.C., holds a number of patents, including a business method patent for an electronic market designed to facilitate the sale of goods between private individuals by establishing a central authority to promote trust among participants. MercExchange sought to license its patent to eBay and Half.com, as it had previously done with other companies, but the parties failed to reach an agreement. MercExchange subsequently filed a patent infringement suit against eBay and Half.com in the United States District Court for the Eastern District of Virginia. A jury found that MercExchange's patent was valid, that eBay and Half.com had infringed that patent, and that an award of damages was appropriate.

Following the jury verdict, the District Court denied MercExchange's motion for permanent injunctive relief. The Court of Appeals for the Federal Circuit reversed, applying its "general rule that courts will issue permanent injunctions against patent infringement absent exceptional circumstances." We granted certiorari to determine the appropriateness of this general rule.

II

According to well-established principles of equity, a plaintiff seeking a permanent injunction must satisfy a four-factor test before a court may grant such relief. A plaintiff must demonstrate: (1) that it has suffered an irreparable injury; (2) that remedies available at law, such as monetary damages, are inadequate to compensate for that injury; (3) that, considering the balance of hardships between the plaintiff and defendant, a remedy in equity is warranted; and (4) that the public interest would not be disserved by a permanent injunction. The decision to grant or deny permanent injunctive relief is an act of equitable discretion by the district court, reviewable on appeal for abuse of discretion.

These familiar principles apply with equal force to disputes arising under the

Patent Act. As this Court has long recognized, "a major departure from the long tradition of equity practice should not be lightly implied." Nothing in the Patent Act indicates that Congress intended such a departure. To the contrary, the Patent Act expressly provides that injunctions "may" issue "in accordance with the principles of equity." 35 U.S.C. § 283.

To be sure, the Patent Act also declares that "patents shall have the attributes of personal property," § 261, including "the right to exclude others from making, using, offering for sale, or selling the invention," § 154(a)(1). According to the Court of Appeals, this statutory right to exclude alone justifies its general rule in favor of permanent injunctive relief. But the creation of a right is distinct from the provision of remedies for violations of that right. Indeed, the Patent Act itself indicates that patents shall have the attributes of personal property "[s]ubject to the provisions of this title," 35 U.S.C. § 261, including, presumably, the provision that injunctive relief "may" issue only "in accordance with the principles of equity," § 283.

This approach is consistent with our treatment of injunctions under the Copyright Act. Like a patent owner, a copyright holder possesses "the right to exclude others from using his property." Like the Patent Act, the Copyright Act provides that courts "may" grant injunctive relief "on such terms as it may deem reasonable to prevent or restrain infringement of a copyright." 17 U.S.C. § 502(a). And as in our decision today, this Court has consistently rejected invitations to replace traditional equitable considerations with a rule that an injunction automatically follows a determination that a copyright has been infringed.

Neither the District Court nor the Court of Appeals below fairly applied these traditional equitable principles in deciding respondent's motion for a permanent injunction. Although the District Court recited the traditional four-factor test; it appeared to adopt certain expansive principles suggesting that injunctive relief could not issue in a broad swath of cases. Most notably, it concluded that a "plaintiff's willingness to license its patents" and "its lack of commercial activity in practicing the patents" would be sufficient to establish that the patent holder would not suffer irreparable harm if an injunction did not issue. But traditional equitable principles do not permit such broad classifications. For example, some patent holders, such as university researchers or self-made inventors, might reasonably prefer to license their patents, rather than undertake efforts to secure the financing necessary to bring their works to market themselves. Such patent holders may be able to satisfy the traditional four-factor test, and we see no basis for categorically denying them the opportunity to do so. To the extent that the District Court adopted such a categorical rule, then, its analysis cannot be squared with the principles of equity adopted by Congress. The court's categorical rule is also in tension with *Continental Paper Bag Co. v. Eastern Paper Bag Co.*, which rejected the contention that a court of equity has no jurisdiction to grant injunctive relief to a patent holder who has unreasonably declined to use the patent.

In reversing the District Court, the Court of Appeals departed in the opposite direction from the four-factor test. The court articulated a "general rule," unique to patent disputes, "that a permanent injunction will issue once infringement and validity have been adjudged." The court further indicated that injunctions should be denied only in the "unusual" case, under "exceptional circumstances" and " "in rare instances . . . to protect the public interest." " Just as the District Court erred in its categorical denial of injunctive relief, the Court of Appeals erred in its categorical grant of such relief.

Because we conclude that neither court below correctly applied the traditional four-factor framework that governs the award of injunctive relief, we vacate the judgment of the Court of Appeals, so that the District Court may apply that framework in the first instance. In doing so, we take no position on whether permanent injunctive relief should or should not issue in this particular case, or indeed in any number of other disputes arising under the Patent Act. We hold only that the decision whether to grant or deny injunctive relief rests within the equitable discretion of the district courts, and that such discretion must be exercised consistent with traditional principles of equity, in patent disputes no less than in other cases governed by such standards.

Accordingly, we vacate the judgment of the Court of Appeals, and remand for further proceedings consistent with this opinion.

It is so ordered.

CHIEF JUSTICE ROBERTS, with whom JUSTICE SCALIA and JUSTICE GINSBURG join, concurring.

I agree with the Court's holding that "the decision whether to grant or deny injunctive relief rests within the equitable discretion of the district courts, and that such discretion must be exercised consistent with traditional principles of equity, in patent disputes no less than in other cases governed by such standards," *ante*, at 1841, and I join the opinion of the Court. That opinion rightly rests on the proposition that "a major departure from the long tradition of equity practice should not be lightly implied."

From at least the early 19th century, courts have granted injunctive relief upon a finding of infringement in the vast majority of patent cases. This "long tradition of equity practice" is not surprising, given the difficulty of protecting a right to *exclude* through monetary remedies that allow an infringer to *use* an invention against the patentee's wishes-a difficulty that often implicates the first two factors of the traditional four-factor test. This historical practice, as the Court holds, does not *entitle* a patentee to a permanent injunction or justify a *general rule* that such injunctions should issue. The Federal Circuit itself so recognized in *Roche Products, Inc. v. Bolar Pharmaceutical Co.* At the same time, there is a difference between exercising equitable discretion pursuant to the established four-factor test and writing on an entirely clean slate. "Discretion is not whim, and limiting discretion according to legal standards helps promote the basic principle of justice that like cases should be decided alike."

JUSTICE KENNEDY, with whom JUSTICE STEVENS, JUSTICE SOUTER, and JUSTICE BREYER join, concurring.

The Court is correct, in my view, to hold that courts should apply the well-established, four-factor test-without resort to categorical rules-in deciding whether to grant injunctive relief in patent cases. THE CHIEF JUSTICE is also correct that history may be instructive in applying this test. The traditional practice of issuing injunctions against patent infringers, however, does not seem to rest on "the difficulty of protecting a right to *exclude* through monetary remedies that allow an infringer to *use* an invention against the patentee's wishes." Both the terms of the Patent Act and the traditional view of injunctive relief accept that the existence of a right to exclude does not dictate the remedy for a violation of that right. To the extent earlier cases establish a pattern of granting an injunction against patent infringers almost as a matter of course, this pattern simply illustrates the result of the four-factor test in the contexts then prevalent. The lesson of the historical practice, therefore, is most helpful and instructive when the circumstances of a case bear substantial parallels to litigation the courts have confronted before.

In cases now arising trial courts should bear in mind that in many instances the nature of the patent being enforced and the economic function of the patent holder present considerations quite unlike earlier cases. An industry has developed in which firms use patents not as a basis for producing and selling goods but, instead, primarily for obtaining licensing fees. For these firms, an injunction, and the potentially serious sanctions arising from its violation, can be employed as a bargaining tool to charge exorbitant fees to companies that seek to buy licenses to practice the patent. When the patented invention is but a small component of the product the companies seek to produce and the threat of an injunction is employed simply for undue leverage in negotiations, legal damages may well be sufficient to compensate for the infringement and an injunction may not serve the public interest. In addition injunctive relief may have different consequences for the burgeoning number of patents over business methods, which were not of much economic and legal significance in earlier times. The potential vagueness and suspect validity of some of these patents may affect the calculus under the four-factor test.

The equitable discretion over injunctions, granted by the Patent Act, is well suited to allow courts to adapt to the rapid technological and legal developments in the patent system. For these reasons it should be recognized that district courts must determine whether past practice fits the circumstances of the cases before them. With these observations, I join the opinion of the Court.

QUESTIONS

1. Would any of the following provisions aid a licensor in an infringement suit?

"Licensee acknowledges damages to licensor are insufficient."

"Licensee acknowledges licensor is engaged in an active R&D program to further develop technology."

"In the event of breach, licensee will pay X times greater royalty payments to licensor."

"If licensee continues to use patent after finding of infringement and validity, damages paid to licensor shall be trebled."

2.   If an infringer refuses a license and continues to infringe after a court finding of infringement and validity, what is the licensor's remedy?

3.   Do you think *eBay* favors large or small firm patentees?

4.   The Court in *eBay* was concerned with the problem of "patent trolls" and their ability to extract excessive settlement payments from infringers by virtue of the threat of a permanent injunction, even when the alleged infringing patent constitutes a minor part of a much larger system; but could not courts award proportional damages to patentees according to the competitive advantage which the alleged infringing patent contributes to the larger system? Could courts fashion a proportional permanent injunction according to the alleged infringing patent's competitive advantage contribution? Possibly enjoining sales above a certain level?

CASE NOTES

1.   Gjerlov sued Schuyler in the early 1990s for infringement of its '396 patent covering a psyllium-based calf oral rehydrant. The '396 patent claimed a rehydrant formulation containing electrolytes and glucose in an amount equal to, or less than, 49.99% by weight. The case was settled in October 1993 by an agreement between the parties. The agreement provided that "Nothing hereunder shall prohibit Schuyler from manufacturing and selling a product containing electrolytes, glucose and psyllium so long as the amount of electrolytes and glucose is greater or equal to 69.5% by weight and the amount of pysllium is equal to or less than 28.5% by weight." In October 1994, Gjerlov determined that Schuyler was selling a product that contained 57.99% electrolytes and glucose by weight, below the minimum amount stipulated in the agreement. Gjerlov then filed a second action against Schuyler to enforce the agreement. The district court held that Schuyler had breached the settlement agreement and calculated reasonable royalty damages under § 284 of the Patent Act. In addition, the district court found that Schuyler had willfully infringed the '396 patent and awarded Gjerlov attorney fees under § 285 of the Patent Act. On appeal, Schuyler argued that the district court should have calculated damages based on Iowa contract law and not the Patent Act. What result? *See* Gjerlov v. Schuyler Laboratories, Inc., 131 F.3d 1016 (Fed. Cir. 1997).

2.   In an earlier *Monsanto v. McFarling* case, Monsanto sought to enforce a liquidated damages clause in the Technology Agreement which provided that in the event of a breach, the licensee would pay Monsanto 120 times the license fee. The district court found that the liquidated damages clause was valid and enforceable, and entered judgment for $780,000 in damages. On appeal, McFarling claimed the 120-times license fee multiplier constituted a penalty that was unenforceable under Missouri contract law. Missouri contract law provides that "For a damage clause to be valid as fixing liquidated damages: (1) the amount fixed as damages must be a reasonable forecast for the harm caused by the breach; and (2) the harm must be of a kind difficult to accurately estimate." In support of the 120-times multiplier,

Monsanto argued that soybeans can self-replicate at an exponential rate. According to Monsanto, one bag of soybean seed can yield 36 bags of soybean seed to save for the following season; and if a farmer planted 36 bags of soybean seed in year two, that would yield 1,296 bags of soybean seed to plant in year three, which would then yield 46,656 bags of soybean seed to plant in year four. What result? *See* Monsanto Co. v. McFarling, 363 F.3d 1336 (Fed. Cir. 2004).

3.　*See also* Universal Gym Equipment v. ERWA Exercise Equipment Ltd., 827 F.2d 1542 (Fed. Cir. 1987) (Patent law does not preclude application of state law to validate and award damages for licensee's breach of contract when licensee agreed not to manufacture products which included unpatented features and designs of licensor's product after termination of the license agreement); Nano-Proprietary, Inc. v. Canon, Inc., 537 F.3d 394 (5th Cir. 2008) (District court damages instructions to jury in suit for patent licensee's alleged breach of license agreement by sublicensing patented technology to corporation that was not a subsidiary did not warrant remand where patent holder failed to prove its damages with reasonable certainty).

4.　In the post-*eBay* cases, courts have generally found that the crucial factor in determining whether to issue a permanent injunction is whether the patentee is actively practicing the patent. In Z4 Technologies, Inc. v. Microsoft Corp., 434 F.Supp. 2d (E.D. Texas 2006), the court found that Microsoft infringed Z4's patented software technology but refused to grant a permanent injunction because Z4 was not actively practicing the patent and, therefore, failed to show it would suffer irreparable harm by continuing infringement by Microsoft. The court also found that monetary damages for future infringement was an adequate remedy at law, that the harm to Microsoft outweighed the hardships to Z4, and that the public interest would be negatively affected by a permanent injunction. However, in Commonwealth Sci. & Indus. Research Organisation v. Buffalo Tech. Inc., 492 F. Supp. 2d 600 (E.D. Texas 2007), the court found that the patentee was entitled to a permanent injunction where the patentee was not selling the patented devices, but was actively engaged in research and development of the patented devices and relied upon licensing income to support its research and development program.

Additional Information

1.　ROBERT A. MATTHEWS, JR.,4 ANNOTATED PATENT DIGEST § 30:74 (2010).

2.　ROBERT A. MATTHEWS, JR., 5 ANNOTATED PATENT DIGEST § 32:167 (2010).

3.　GREGORY E. UPCHURCH, 2 IP LITIGATION GUIDE: PATENTS AND TRADES SECRETS §§ 20:2, 20:6 (2010).

4.　JOHN M. SKENYON ET AL., PATENT DAMAGES LAW AND PRACTICE § 3:10 (2008).

5.　WESLEY KOBYLAK, AMERICAN LAW REPORTS, 66 A.L.R. FED. 186.

6.　RAYMOND T. NIMMER, JEFF DODD, MODERN LICENSING LAW § 11:58 (2010).

7.　25 C.J.S. DAMAGES § 262 (2008).

8.　60 AM. JUR. 2D PATENTS § 943 (2010).

9.　ROBERT A. MATTHEWS, JR. ANNOTATED PATENT DIGEST § 32:159 (2010).

10. GREGORY E. UPCHURCH, 2 IP LITIGATION GUIDE: PATENTS AND TRADE SECRETS § 20:2 (2010).

11. MELVIN F. JAGER, LICENSING LAW HANDBOOK § 1:27 (2010).

12. JOHN G. MILLS III, ET AL, 4 PATENT LAW FUNDAMENTALS §§ 20:57, 20:65 (2010).

13. John F. Sweeney, *Types of Injunctions*, PAT. LITIG § 10:1.1. (2010).

14. Benjamin Petersen, *Injunctive Relief in the Post-EBAY World*, 23 BERKELEY TECH. L.J. 193 (2008).

15. Jeremy Mulder, *The Aftermath of EBAY: Predicting When District Courts Will Grant Permanent Injunctions in Patent Cases*, 22 BERKELEY TECH. L.J. 67 (2007).

16. Howard Susser & Jerry Cohen, *Supreme Court Ends Special Treatment for Patent Injunctions*, 50-Dec. B. B.J. 9, (2006).

17. Yixin H. Tang, *The Future of Patent Enforcement After EBay v. Mercexchange*, 20 HARV. J.L. & TECH. 235, (2006).

18. Andrew Beckerman-Rodau, *The Aftermath of EBay v. Mercexchange, 126 S. Ct. 1837 (2006): A Review of Subsequent Judicial Decisions*, 89 J. PAT. & TRADEMARK OFF. SOC'Y 631 (2007).

19. Stephen L. Poe, Teressa L. Conover, *The Use and Legality of Technology-Based Remedies by Vendors in Software Contracts*, 56 ALB. L. REV. 609 (1993).

20. Christopher S. Marchese, *Patent Infringement and Future Lost Profits Damages*, 26 ARIZ. ST. L.J. 747, (1994).

2.2.8 Patent Invalidity

Courts have universally held that a final judicial declaration that a licensed patent is invalid terminates the license agreement and relieves the licensee from any further obligation to pay royalties. *See, e.g.*, Studiengesellschaft Kohle, M.B.H. v. Shell Oil Co., 112 F.3d 1561 (Fed. Cir. 1997). Courts have also universally held that licensees cannot recover royalty payments made prior to a patent validity challenge unless the licensor has committed fraud. *See, e.g.*, Troxel Mfg. Co. v. Schwinn Bicycle Co., 465 F.2d 1253 (6th Cir. 1972).

Courts have considered two types of licensor fraud that would render the license void *ab initio*, thereby allowing the licensee to recover royalty payments already made. The first type of licensor fraud that would allow a licensee to recover royalty payments is fraud committed on the Patent and Trademark Office. If the licensee can show that the licensor obtained the patent by means of fraudulent conduct during the prosecution of the patent, the licensee can recover royalty payments previously made. *See, e.g.*, Nashua Corp. v. RCA Corp., 431 F.2d 220 (1st Cir. 1970). The second type of licensor fraud that would allow the licensee to recover royalty payments is fraud committed on the licensee. If the licensee can show that the licensor fraudulently induced the licensee into entering the license agreement, the licensee can recover royalty payments previously made. *See, e.g.*, Transitron

Electronic Co. v. Hughes Aircraft Co., 649 F.2d 871 (1st Cir. 1981). However, courts have rarely found the necessary licensor fraud to allow recovery of royalties paid finding either insufficient allegations of fraud or insufficient evidence of fraud. *See*, 86 A.L.R. FED. 455, (1988).

A related question is whether the licensee can be required to pay royalties until such time as there is a final declaration of patent invalidity. You will recall that in *Lear* the Supreme Court held that a licensee could not be required to pay royalties until a final declaration of patent invalidity, even if the patent license had a provision to this effect, because this would allow licensors to engage in dilatory tactics to lengthen the litigation. However, the licensee must take some affirmative step to suspend its obligation to pay royalties under the license agreement. One such affirmative step is the filing of a declaratory judgment action to have the licensed patent declared invalid. Cases have generally held that the licensee's obligation to pay royalties is suspended upon the licensee filing an action challenging the validity of the patent, but that the licensor can recover unpaid royalties prior to this point in time. *See, e.g.*, American Sterilizer Co. v. Sybron Corp., 614 F.2d 890 (3rd Cir. 1980).

The second affirmative step that a licensee can take to suspend its obligation to pay royalties is to cease paying royalties and give notice to the licensor that it believes the licensed patent is invalid, and that it intends to challenge the validity of the patent either in a declaratory judgment action or as a counterclaim to a breach of contract or infringement suit by the licensor. The licensor, however, is entitled to recover unpaid royalties that accrued prior to the date of the licensee notice. *See, e.g.*, Rite-Nail Packaging Corp. v. Berryfast, Inc., 706 F.2d 933 (9th Cir. 1983).

The first case in this section, *Tuskos Engineering*, considers the licensee's right to recover paid royalties under a claim that the licensor committed fraud on the Patent Office. The second case in this section, *Cordis*, considers whether a licensee has the right to deposit royalty payments in escrow and to obtain a preliminary injunction enjoining the licensor from terminating the license agreement.

TUSKOS ENGINEERING v. TUSKOS
676 S.W. 2d 794 (Ky. Ct. App. 1984)

PAXTON, JUDGE.

Tuskos Engineering Corporation appeals from a judgment of the Jefferson Circuit Court requiring it to pay Michael E. Tuskos the sum of $7,380.00 and dismissing its counterclaim.

Appellee, Michael E. Tuskos, is an individual listed as inventor and owner of patents on the following devices: Lectro-Tabler, patent no. 3,439,438; Ultra-Pleater, patent no. 3,696,515; and Mark-N-Trim, patent no. 3,738,007. Appellant, Tuskos Engineering Corporation, was originally organized by Michael E. Tuskos and his wife, Irma, who were the sole stockholders until July, 1972, when they sold 25% of their stock to Wade Morgan.

On October 7, 1972, Michael entered into a license agreement with Tuskos

Engineering while he was a stockholder and president and chairman of its board of directors. Pursuant to the terms of the license agreement, Michael represented that he was the owner of a certain patent and certain patent applications pertaining to a Lectro-Tabler machine, and a Ultra-Pleater machine and that he had the right to grant certain licenses in respect to the machines. Although the Mark-N-Trim device was not mentioned in the agreement, it has been considered as an integral part of the suit, apparently because it is merely an addition to the Lectro Tabler. Tuskos was granted the right to make, use, and sell the machines throughout the United States, territories and possessions in Canada and in consideration of which the corporation agreed to pay royalties to Michael at the rate of 10% of the selling price of each machine sold. Michael was given the option to terminate the agreement upon certain conditions and Tuskos was given the absolute right to terminate the agreement at the end of any calendar year by simply giving written notice to Michael on or before September 20th of such calendar year.

Michael filed his complaint against Tuskos on July 12, 1976, alleging that Tuskos had breached the licensing agreement and should be required to make an accounting as to royalty payments due and owing him pursuant to terms of the agreement. Tuskos admitted execution of the license agreement but denied its validity on account of the "failure of consideration because of the invalidity of each of said patents." Tuskos then counterclaimed alleging that Michael had obtained the patents by fraud and demanded that the patents be declared invalid and that it be granted judgment for all payments made to Michael pursuant to terms of the agreement and that it also be awarded punitive damages. Prior to stopping payments, Tuskos had paid $31,556.29 to Michael.

The case was referred to a commissioner who, after hearing proof, entered detailed and comprehensive findings to the effect that Michael's patents were invalid because of misleading statements made to the patent office by Michael, but that Michael was not guilty of intentional fraud. The commissioner recommended that Michael retain royalties received, but that he not recover any additional royalties from Tuskos. He further recommended that Tuskos take nothing on its counterclaim against Michael.

The trial court accepted the recommendations of the commissioner, except it was of the opinion that it was unnecessary to make a determination on the validity of the patents. Consequently, the trial court refused to invalidate the patents but held that Michael was entitled to royalties due him up to the time of the termination of the agreement, in the sum of $7,380.00.

Tuskos argues that the trial court erred in:

1. Failing to find the existence of clear and convincing evidence that Michael, prior to and on October 7, 1972, the date of the license agreement made between Michael and Tuskos Engineering, knew and fraudulently concealed the fact that the three alleged inventions, the subject matter of the license agreement, had been in public use or on sale, either by himself or by others, or had been published or used by others prior to Michael's alleged invention thereof and but for the fraudulent concealment of these facts from the patent office, the patents would not have issued and the license agreement could not have been made, or but for the intentional concealment of said facts from the directors of said corporation the

license agreement would not have been made.

2. Failing to find a fiduciary duty on Michael, as chief executive officer and a director of Tuskos Engineering, to disclose to Tuskos Engineering at the combined stockholders and directors meeting, held on October 7, 1972, and at the time of execution of the license agreement on October 7, 1972, facts solely within his knowledge, relative to public use, offers for sale or sales, either by himself or others of the alleged inventions contained in said applications prior to Michael's alleged invention thereof and but for Michael's intentional concealment of said facts from Tuskos Engineering and but for Michael's breach of said fiduciary duty in concealing facts from said Tuskos Engineering, the license agreement would never have been executed.

The trial commissioner found that Michael neither intentionally deceived nor concealed transactions from Tuskos Engineering. We find from reviewing the record that the evidence is conflicting on both issues. We cannot, therefore, say that the findings of the commissioner are clearly erroneous. The commissioner concluded that the patents were invalid; that Tuskos Engineering could not recover royalties paid Michael; and that Michael could not recover royalties claimed due after Tuskos Engineering stopped payments. The trial court accepted the commissioner's report except that it was of the opinion that Michael was entitled to $7,380.00 in royalties earned after Tuskos Engineering stopped payments and that it was unnecessary to consider whether the patents were valid.

We are not required to consider Michael's entitlement to the $7,380.00 in royalties alleged to have accrued during the interim when Tuskos Engineering stopped payments and its termination of the agreement because Tuskos did not raise the issue in its brief. Nevertheless, because Michael does not have a brief, we will consider the issue on its merits and sustain the commissioner's determination. The patents are invalid because of erroneous statements made by Michael in securing them. The license agreement is also invalid, but not void *ab initio*, because Michael is not guilty of intentional fraud. Michael is therefore entitled to retain the royalties paid him by Tuskos Engineering, but he is not entitled to any royalties alleged due and owing after Tuskos stopped making payments to him. As stated in *Troxel Manufacturing Co. v. Schwinn Bicycle Co.*:

> The public interest is protected adequately . . . without imposing on the patent holder the obligation to refund royalties paid under the license of a patent procured and asserted in good faith. A licensee may at any time cease royalty payments, secure in the knowledge that the invalidity of a patent may be urged when the licensor sues for the unpaid royalties.

The judgment of the Jefferson Circuit Court is reversed and this case remanded with directions for the trial court to enter a judgment dismissing Michael's complaint; declaring the three patents and the license agreement void; and assessing costs.

All concur.

QUESTIONS

1. Given the *Lear* decision's favorable treatment of licensees, what policy reasons might justify denying licensees the right to recover royalties when they have successfully challenged the validity of the patent?

2. Could a licensee ever be bound by a clause in the license agreement requiring it to continue to pay royalties until a final determination of patent validity?

3. If a third party challenged the validity of the patent rather than the licensee, would the licensee be obligated to pay royalties until a final validity determination were made?

CORDIS v. MEDTRONIC
780 F.2d 991 (Fed. Cir. 1985)

BISSELL, CIRCUIT JUDGE.

This appeal is from the Order of the District Court for the Southern District of Florida granting the motion for relief *pendente lite* of Cordis Corporation (Cordis):

(a) permitting Cordis to deposit into an escrow account all future royalty payments due Medtronic, Inc. (Medtronic) pursuant to the license agreement between the parties; and

(b) enjoining Medtronic from terminating the license agreement because of Cordis' failure to make royalty payments pursuant to the agreement.

This in effect protects Cordis from patent infringement or breach of contract counterclaims.

The issuance of the Order by the district court is vacated. The motion for relief *pendente lite* is remanded for further consideration not inconsistent with this opinion.

I

Cordis filed suit against Medtronic seeking a declaratory judgment that the two licensed Medtronic patents, U.S. Patent Nos. 3,902,501 ('501) and 3,939,843 ('843), are invalid (Count I of the Complaint) and that the license agreement between Cordis and Medtronic "is void in its inception" (Count II of the Complaint). Contemporaneous with filing of the declaratory judgment action, Cordis moved for an order to establish a court escrow account into which the royalty payments due Medtronic, *pendente lite*, would be deposited. Additionally, Cordis sought a preliminary injunction to enjoin Medtronic from terminating the license agreement during the pendency of the patent invalidity suit.

The district court, relying on *Precision Shooting Equipment Co. v. Allen* granted the motion and permitted Cordis to deposit any royalty payments due Medtronic *pendente lite* into an interest bearing escrow account, with all funds accumulated in the escrow account to be paid to the prevailing party. The district court enjoined Medtronic from terminating the license agreement during the pendency of the action.

Consequently, the issue on appeal to this court is whether the district court properly granted the preliminary injunction and Cordis' motion for establishment of the escrow account.

****

III

The Supreme Court, in *Lear, Inc. v. Adkins* held that a licensee to a patent license agreement is not estopped from contesting the validity of the patent subject to the agreement. *Lear* further held that licensees cannot be required to continue to pay royalties during the time they are challenging patent validity in the courts. In *C.R. Bard, Inc. v. Schwartz* this court held that a patent licensee may seek a federal declaratory judgment to declare a patent, subject to a license, invalid without prior termination of the license.

It is well settled that the purpose of an interlocutory injunction is to preserve the status quo and to protect the respective rights of the parties pending a determination on the merits. The status of these parties before the district court is that of a patentee-licensor of two patents, each presumptively valid pursuant to 35 U.S.C. § 282, and that of a licensee of those patents.

This court exercises a very narrow scope of review over the district court's grant of injunctive relief. The district court's determination can be overturned only upon a showing that it abused its discretion, committed an error of law, or seriously misjudged the evidence.

In determining whether to grant or deny the requested injunction, a court must exercise sound discretion and examine the appropriate factors in granting the motion. The factors to be considered in granting a preliminary injunction in the Federal Circuit are the same as those of the Eleventh Circuit. The district court must examine and balance the parties' asserted rights, the acts sought to be enjoined, the likelihood that the movant will prevail on the merits, the irreparable nature of the harm if the injunction is not granted, and whether the public interest is better served by issuing rather than denying the injunction.

We find that several errors of law and a misjudgment of evidence occurred when the district court considered the preliminary injunction factors. Initially, the district court erred in ruling that the *Lear* decision is implicit authority for permitting a licensee to deposit royalties due *pendente lite* into an escrow account pending a determination on the merits. A second error of law appears in the district court's reading that the Sixth Circuit *Troxel (I)* opinion is authority for the proposition that a licensee may never recoup royalties. Finally, it was a misjudgment of evidence to use evidence of patent invalidity to establish the movant's likelihood of success on the claim that the license "is void in its inception."

Turning to the error committed in reading the *Lear* opinion, we find no authority in *Lear* for establishing an escrow account for royalties due *pendente lite* or preliminarily enjoining a licensor from cancelling the license agreement and, thus, from counterclaiming for patent infringement when this material breach of the license occurs.

Cordis argued and the district court agreed that the Supreme Court decision in *Lear* encouraging vigorous and prompt litigation of invalid patents supports the entry of the requested interlocutory relief. In *Lear*, the Court examined the interests of the licensor, the licensee, and the general public in light of the federal patent policy encouraging prompt adjudication of patent validity, stating:

> Surely the equities of the licensor do not weigh very heavily when they are balanced against the important public interest in permitting full and free competition in the use of ideas which are in reality a part of the public domain. Licensees may often be the only individuals with enough economic incentive to challenge the patentability of an inventor's discovery. If they are muzzled, the public may continually be required to pay tribute to would-be monopolists without need or justification. We think it plain that the technical requirements of contract doctrine must give way before the demands of the public interest in the typical situation involving the negotiation of a license after a patent has issued.

This public policy statement *does* permit a licensee to cease payments due under a contract while challenging the validity of a patent. It *does not* permit the licensees to avoid facing the consequences that such an action would bring. The holding of *Lear* only prevents the affirmative enforcement by the licensor of the royalty payment provisions of the license agreement while the patent's validity is being challenged by the licensee.

We believe that the reasoning succinctly stated by the Second Circuit in *Warner-Jenkinson Co. v. Allied Chemical Corp*, and followed by the Eighth Circuit in *Nebraska Engineering Corp. v. Shivvers*, is in keeping with the holding of and policy statements in *Lear*:

> We believe that if the plaintiffs wish to continue to invoke the protections of their licensing agreements, they should be required to continue paying their royalties to the defendant. Ultimately, all royalties paid after the filing of the complaint *may* have to be returned to the plaintiffs . . . . At present, plaintiffs already have the option of withholding royalties and thereby breaching the licensing agreement; of course, they would then run the risk of an injunction if they should lose on the merits. It would not be fair for the plaintiffs to be allowed simultaneously to reap all the benefits of the licensing agreement and to deprive the licensor of all his royalties. Patents are presumed to be valid, 35 U.S.C. § 282; until invalidity is proven, the patentee should ordinarily be permitted to enjoy the fruits of his invention. The principal effect of an escrow arrangement would be to put undeserved pressure on the defendant.

In addition to the misapplication of *Lear* in evaluating the rights and obligations of the parties and the interest of the public, the district court made errors of law in determining whether irreparable harm would occur to the licensee if the preliminary injunction was not granted.

To support its request for injunctive relief, Cordis argued that absent such relief it would experience irreparable harm in one of the following four ways: (1) being exposed to a potential patent infringement suit, (2) risking forfeiture of royalties paid while litigating the validity of the patents, (3) foregoing contesting the validity of the patents, or (4) terminating any manufacture, use or sale of the tined leads covered by the '501 and '843 patents.

Cordis argued to the district court that any one of these alternatives, when balanced against the harm suffered by Medtronic in receiving delayed royalty payments, tips the scales of equity in favor of permitting royalties due *pendente lite* to be deposited into an interest bearing escrow account.

With regard to Cordis' first, third, and fourth assertions of irreparable harm, for the reasons stated above, *Lear* provides no reprieve. Moreover, Cordis made no showing that Medtronic is financially irresponsible or might be judgment-proof at the end of the litigation. "Only a viable threat of serious harm which cannot be undone authorizes exercise of a court's equitable power to enjoin before the merits are fully determined. A preliminary injunction will not issue simply to prevent a mere possibility of injury, even where prospective injury is great."

With regard to Cordis' second assertion of irreparable harm, the district court's reliance on *Troxel (I)* is misplaced. Neither the *Troxel (I)* nor *Troxel (II)* decisions by the Sixth Circuit prohibit the licensee from recouping royalties paid *pendente lite* once the patent subject to the license agreement is proved invalid. The *Troxel* decisions only prohibit the licensee from recovering and retaining royalties paid or due prior to the adjudication of invalidity when the challenge to the patent was made by a third party. Since the district court improperly evaluated the rights of the parties and the interest of the general public under *Lear*, we need not address the risk of forfeiture question any further than the district court's application of *Troxel (I)*. Nor do we decide which party is entitled to royalties paid or accrued *pendente lite.*

Finally, the district court erred in evaluating the likelihood of success factor. To show likelihood of success on the merits, Cordis offered only the affidavit of an engineer employed by Medtronic's competitor, Pacesetter, which set forth that Pacesetter publicly disclosed and/or developed certain devices covered by claims of the patents in suit prior to Medtronic's alleged date of invention. The district court's error occurred in using evidence of patent invalidity to establish the movant's likelihood of success on the claim that the license "is void in its inception" (Count II). The affidavit by an employee of Medtronic's competitor setting forth facts is arguably sufficient to prove that the patents in suit are invalid under the provisions of 35 U.S.C. § 102(a) and (b). However, this affidavit alone is insufficient to support the movant's likelihood of success on the second count of the complaint, that is, that the license agreement "is void in its inception." Patents are issued by the government after examination and evaluation of the patent application by the United States Patent and Trademark Office and are presumed valid once issued. 28 U.S.C. § 282. As observed by the Sixth Circuit, "Congress has not seen fit to create an implied warranty of validity in license agreements." "Absent fraud or misconduct, a patentee should not be held responsible for the issuance of an invalid patent."

Consequently, because the analysis underlying the district court's order is erroneous, the order is vacated and the motion remanded for further consideration not inconsistent with this opinion.

VACATED AND REMANDED.

QUESTIONS

1. How might the Federal Circuit decision in *Cordis* be affected by the Supreme Court decision in *MedImmune*?

2. If the licensee does not have to breach the license agreement before seeking a declaratory judgment of patent invalidity, how is the licensor harmed by the licensee's deposit of royalty payments in escrow pending a final determination of validity? Is there any benefit to the licensor from allowing the licensee to deposit royalty payments in escrow rather than stopping royalty payments and terminating the license agreement?

3. If a licensee cannot recover royalty payments made prior to a final judicial determination of patent invalidity, why would a licensee continue to make payments during the pending litigation as is allowed under *Medimmune*?

CASE NOTES

1. Allied owns patents for the chemical composition and production of a red food color known as Red. No. 40. Another red food color, Red No. 2, was the dominant red color additive in the food industry until the FDA announced the imminent delisting of Red No. 2 for public health reasons. Because Red No. 40 was the only practicable alternative to Red No. 2, Warner-Jenkinson, a food processor, sought a manufacturing license from Allied which Allied refused. Warner Jenkinson nonetheless proceeded to manufacture Red No. 40, and Allied filed a patent infringement suit. The parties entered into a settlement agreement whereby the court issued a "Stipulation and Order" which dismissed Warner-Jenkinson's patent invalidity claim without prejudice and Allied's infringement claim without prejudice. The parties also agreed to a "Settlement Agreement" under which Warner-Jenkinson would pay Allied $200,000 for a release from liability for past infringement and a royalty of 17.5% on net sales of food products containing Red No. 40. The Settlement Agreement was also made non-terminable for a period of two years. When the FDA finally delisted Red No. 2, Red No. 40 became the only alternative red food coloring, and Warner-Jenkinson asked Allied to lower its royalty rate. Allied refused. Warner-Jenkinson then filed another suit to have Allied's patent declared invalid. Allied claimed the suit was barred by the settlement agreement. Warner-Jenkinson claimed the Settlement Agreement did not bar the suit because its patent invalidity claim was dismissed without prejudice and the agreement contained no express prohibition on licensee suits during some future period. Warner-Jenkinson also claimed that the non-termination provision of the Settlement Agreement for two years was analogous to liquidated damages and did not bar a suit to have the patent declared invalid. What result? *See* Warner-Jenkinson Co. v. Allied Chemical Corp., 567 F.2d 184 (2nd Cir. 1977).

2. *See also* Transitron Electronic Co. v. Hughes Aircraft Co., 649 F.2d 871 (1st Cir. 1981) (Evidence supported district court's finding that patentee had not committed knowing and willful fraud in obtaining patent and implied finding that patentee had not committed fraud on licensee in connection with the licensing transaction); Precision Shooting Equipment, Inc. v. Holless W. Allen, Inc., 492 F.Supp. 79 (D.C. Ill. 1980) (If licensee's suit challenging the validity of a patent is successful, licensee can recover all royalties accruing or paid to the patentee after the legal challenge is filed, but cannot recover royalties accruing or paid prior to the legal challenge); Atlas Chemical Industries, Inc. v. Moraine Products, 509 F.2d 1 (6th Cir. 1974) (Licensee was entitled to return of royalties which were deposited in escrow pending outcome of litigation).

Additional Information

1. TERESIA B. JOVANOVIC, RIGHT OF LICENSOR TO RECEIVE AND RETAIN ROYALTIES ON PATENT FOR PERIOD PRIOR TO JUDICIAL DECLARATION OF PATENT'S INVALIDITY, 86 A.L.R. FED. 455 (1988).

2. 60 AM. JUR. 2D PATENTS, §§ 976, 1055–1056 (2010).

3. 69 C.J.S. PATENTS, §§ 376, 384 (2010).

4. RAYMOND T. NIMMER, JEFF DODD, MODERN LICENSING LAW § 8:13 (2010).

5. MARGARET M. LEE, 82 N.Y. JUR. 2D §§ 16–18 (2010).

6. Nellie A. Fisher, *The Licensee's Choice: Mechanics of Successfully Challenging a Patent Under License*, 6 TEX. INTELL. PROP. L.J. 1, (1997).

2.2.9 Standing to Sue

Section 281 of the Patent Act states: "A patentee shall have remedy by civil action for infringement of the patent;" and section 100(d) of the Patent Act states: "The word patentee includes not only the patentee to whom the patent was issued but also the successors in title to the patentee." The question of who has standing to sue for patent infringement hinges on the definition of who is a "successor in title to the patentee."

Courts have held that nonexclusive patent licensees only have immunity from suit by the licensor, and do not have an interest in the licensed patent sufficient to qualify as successor "patentees" giving them standing to sue for infringement. *See, e.g.*, Western Elec. Co. v. Pacent Reproducer Corp., 42 F. 2d. 116 (2nd Cir. 1930). On the other hand, courts have held that assignees who have acquired all substantial rights in the patent are successor "patentees" and can sue for infringement in their own names without joinder of the assignor. *See*, Pope Mfg. Co. v. Gormully & Jeffery Mfg. Co., 144 U.S. 248 (1892).

Exclusive licenses lie between nonexclusive licenses and assignments. In Waterman v. Mackenzie, 138 U.S. 252 (1891), the Supreme Court set forth the situations under which an exclusive licensee has standing to sue for infringement of the licensed patent. According to the Court, three types of exclusive licenses are tantamount to assignments:

The patentee or his assigns may, by instrument in writing, assign, grant, and convey, either (1) the whole patent, comprising the exclusive right to make, use, and vend the invention throughout the United States; or (2) an undivided part or share of that exclusive right; or (3) the exclusive right under the patent within and throughout a specified portion of the United States . . . . A transfer of either of these three kinds of interests is an assignment, properly speaking, and vests in the assignee a title in so much of the patent itself, with a right to sue infringers. In the second case, jointly with the assignor. In the first and third cases, in the name of the assignee alone. Any assignment or transfer, short of one of these, is a mere license, giving the licensee no title in the patent, and no right to sue at law in his own name for an infringement.

Although the Court did not discuss the duration of these three types of exclusive licenses, presumably they were for the remaining term of the patent. An exclusive license for a term of years would not constitute a transfer of substantially all rights in the patent since the licensor would retain the exclusive rights in the patent at the termination of the license term.

The cases in this section, *Abbott Laboratories* and *McNeil Lab*, consider what constitutes retention of substantial rights by the patentee requiring that the patentee be joined as a plaintiff in the infringement suit.

ABBOTT LABORATORIES v. DIAMEDIX CORP.
47 F.3d 1128 (Fed. Cir. 1995)

BRYSON, CIRCUIT JUDGE.

Diamedix Corporation appeals from an order denying its motion to intervene in a patent infringement action. The action was brought by Abbott Laboratories, which held a license from Diamedix, against a third party, Ortho Diagnostic Systems, Inc. We conclude that the district court should have permitted Diamedix to join the lawsuit as a party-plaintiff. The order of the district court denying the motion to intervene is therefore reversed.

I

United States Patents Nos. 4,474,878 (the '878 patent) and 4,642,285 (the '285 patent) were issued in 1984 and 1987, respectively, and assigned to appellant Diamedix Corporation. The two patents relate to immunoassay systems used to test blood for the presence of the hepatitis virus.

Prior to 1988, Diamedix granted eight non-exclusive licenses under the '878 and '285 patents. In August 1988, following a dispute with appellee Abbott Laboratories over alleged infringement of the patents, Diamedix entered into a "license agreement" with Abbott. In exchange for annual royalty payments, Abbott received a worldwide license to make, use, and sell products incorporating the inventions claimed in the patents. The license was exclusive to Abbott and its affiliates, but was subject to the rights previously granted to Diamedix's other licensees. In addition, the agreement reserved to Diamedix the right to make and use products that exploited the patents, as well as the right to sell such products to Diamedix's previous licensees, to Abbott's sub-licensees, to end users, and to certain other parties to fulfill Diamedix's existing contractual obligations. The agreement was to remain in effect for the life of the patents unless Abbott decided to terminate it earlier. The agreement was not assignable by either party without the consent of the other.

In addition to those general terms, the agreement contained a clause addressing the rights of the parties in suits against third parties for infringement of the patent rights. That clause provided as follows:

> If any patent included in PATENT RIGHTS is infringed, Abbott shall have the right, but not the obligation, to bring suit to suppress such infringement against any unlicensed third party. However, if such infringement continues and DIAMEDIX requests ABBOTT in writing to bring such suit, and ABBOTT declines to bring such suit against such infringer within six (6) months of such request, DIAMEDIX shall have the right to bring such suit. The party who brings suit shall control the prosecution and any settlements thereof provided, however, Abbott shall not prejudice or impair the PATENT RIGHTS in connection with such prosecution or settlements and shall not enter into any settlement which would result in DIAMEDIX receiving less than one percent (1%) of the net sales of the third party's infringing products. The other party shall be entitled to be represented therein by counsel of its own selection at its own expense.

In January 1994, Abbott filed an action in the United States District Court for the Northern District of Illinois charging appellee Ortho Diagnostic Systems, Inc., with infringing the '878 and '285 patents. Ortho denied the allegations of infringement, asserted as an affirmative defense that the patents are invalid, and claimed that Abbott is barred from seeking relief because of its delay in bringing suit.

Because Abbott did not join Diamedix as a party to the lawsuit, Diamedix promptly filed a motion to intervene and a complaint as plaintiff-intervenor alleging that Ortho had infringed its rights under the two patents. In its motion, Diamedix argued that it was entitled to intervene under Fed.R.Civ.P. 24(a)(2) based on its rights as legal owner of the patents. In the alternative, Diamedix moved to be permitted to intervene under Fed.R.Civ.P. 24(b). Diamedix also suggested that as the holder of legal title to the patents, it might be required to participate in order to give the district court jurisdiction over the suit. Ortho supported Diamedix's motion to intervene, on the ground that Diamedix retained a significant interest in the patents-in-suit under its agreement with Abbott and might be an indispensable party under Fed.R.Civ.P. 19(b).

The district court denied Diamedix's motion to intervene, based on its conclusion that Diamedix's interests in the lawsuit were adequately represented by Abbott. The court explained that Diamedix and Abbott share the common goals of enforcing the patent rights against Ortho and maximizing the recovery of monetary damages. Diamedix argued that Abbott has an incentive not to defend the validity of the patents with great vigor, since a decision invalidating the patents would free Abbott from its royalty obligations. Diamedix pointed out that shortly after entering into the licensing agreement, Abbott had requested reexamination of the '878 and '285 patents by the Patent and Trademark Office (PTO), urging that all of the claims of those patents were unpatentable in light of prior art. The district court dismissed Diamedix's contention, however, noting that under the agreement with Diamedix, Abbott had the obligation not to "prejudice or impair the patent rights," and that there was no reason to believe that Abbott would fail to honor its obligation in the action against Ortho. In addition, the court concluded that as a practical matter Diamedix's intervention "would be nothing more than a paper entry into the clerk's docket," because Abbott had the right under the licensing agreement to control the prosecution of any infringement action that it initiated.

Diamedix took an immediate appeal from the order denying its motion to intervene. This court stayed the action in the district court pending the resolution of the appeal.

II

The parties to this appeal have focused principally on whether intervention should have been granted under Fed.R.Civ.P. 24 and, in particular, whether the district court properly denied intervention on the ground that Abbott adequately represents Diamedix's interests in the infringement action. We believe, however, that this case can best be resolved by addressing a related but logically antecedent question: whether a licensee such as Abbott has the statutory right to bring an action for infringement without joining the patent owner, Diamedix. Because we conclude that Abbott may pursue its infringement action against Ortho only if Diamedix is permitted to join that action, we hold that the district court should have ordered Diamedix to be joined as a party.

A

The Patent Act of 1952 provides that a civil action for infringement may be brought by "a patentee." 35 U.S.C. § 281. The statute defines "patentee" to include the party to whom the patent was issued and the successors in title to the patent, 35 U.S.C. § 100(d), and has been interpreted to require that a suit for infringement ordinarily be brought by a party holding legal title to the patent. Parties not holding title to the patent have been accorded the right to sue (or "standing") in certain circumstances, but only upon joining or attempting to join the patent owners.

In *Waterman v. Mackenzie* the Supreme Court addressed the question of the right to sue for infringement under a predecessor patent statute. The Court stated that an assignment by the patent owner of the whole of the patent right, or of an undivided part of the right, or of all rights in a specified geographical region, gives an assignee the right to bring an action for infringement in his own name. Any less complete transfer of rights, the Court explained, is a license rather than an assignment. If the patent owner grants only a license, the title remains in the owner of the patent; and suit must be brought in his name, and never in the name of the licensee alone, unless that is necessary to prevent an absolute failure of justice, as where the patentee is the infringer, and cannot sue himself. Any rights of the licensee must be enforced through or in the name of the owner of the patent, and perhaps, if necessary to protect the rights of all parties, joining the licensee with him as a plaintiff.

Thirty-five years later, in *Independent Wireless Tel. Co. v. Radio Corp. of Am.* the Supreme Court applied the teaching of *Waterman* in a case in which an exclusive licensee sought to enforce the patent rights against an alleged infringer. The Court rejected the argument that the licensee could sue for infringement without joining the patent owner. "The presence of the owner of the patent as a party is indispensable not only to give jurisdiction under the patent laws," the Court held, "but also, in most cases, to enable the alleged infringer to respond in one action to all claims of infringement for his act, and thus either to defeat all claims in the one action, or by satisfying one adverse decree to bar all subsequent actions."

The Court recognized an exception to that rule for cases in which the owner of a patent refuses or is unable to be joined as a co-plaintiff with the exclusive licensee in an infringement action. In such a case, the Court held, "the licensee may make [the patent owner] a party defendant by process and he will be lined up by the court in the party character which he should assume." A patentee, the Court explained, "holds the title to the patent in trust for [the exclusive] licensee, to the extent that he must allow the use of his name as plaintiff in any action brought at the instance of the licensee in law or in equity to obtain damages for the injury to his exclusive right by an infringer or to enjoin infringement of it." The Court emphasized, however, that before the exclusive licensee can sue in the patent owner's name, the patent owner must be given an opportunity to join the infringement action.

Based on the analysis in *Waterman* and *Independent Wireless Tel. Co.*, this court has recognized the following principles: The right to sue for infringement is ordinarily an incident of legal title to the patent. A licensee may obtain sufficient rights in the patent to be entitled to seek relief from infringement, but to do so, it ordinarily must join the patent owner. And a bare licensee, who has no right to exclude others from making, using, or selling the licensed products, has no legally recognized interest that entitles it to bring or join an infringement action.

Abbott does not take issue with these principles. Rather, it argues that Diamedix is not required to be joined in this action because the agreement between Abbott and Diamedix transferred all substantial rights under the patents to Abbott. We disagree. Although the agreement effected a broad conveyance of rights to Abbott, Diamedix retained substantial interests under the '878 and '285 patents, and Abbott therefore does not have an independent right to sue for infringement as a "patentee" under the patent statute.

Diamedix retained the right to make and use, for its own benefit, products embodying the inventions claimed in the patents, as well as the right to sell such products to end users, to parties with whom Diamedix had pre-existing contracts, and to pre-existing licensees. Abbott's exclusive license was also made subject to prior licenses granted by Diamedix. Moreover, although Abbott was given the right of first refusal in suing alleged infringers, the agreement provides that if Diamedix asks Abbott to bring suit against an alleged infringer and Abbott declines to do so, Diamedix has the right to prosecute its own infringement action; thus, although Abbott has the option to initiate suit for infringement, it does not enjoy the right to indulge infringements, which normally accompanies a complete conveyance of the right to sue. In addition, even if Abbott exercises its option to sue for infringement, it is obligated under the agreement not to "prejudice or impair the patent rights in connection with such prosecution or settlement." Finally, the parties appear to have contemplated that Diamedix could participate in a suit brought by Abbott, because the agreement provides that Diamedix is "entitled to be represented therein by counsel of its own selection at its own expense."

In light of the various rights that Diamedix retains under the agreement, Abbott must be considered a licensee, not an assignee. Under *Waterman* and its successors, Abbott therefore may not sue on its own for infringement.

In arguing to the contrary, Abbott relies principally on this court's decision in *Vaupel Textilmaschinen KG v. Meccanica Euro Italia.* In that case, the court found that the patent grantee, Marowsky, did not have to be joined as a party to the infringement suit brought by Vaupel. The court reached that conclusion, however, only after finding that Marowsky had transferred all substantial rights under the patent to Vaupel.

The only rights retained by Marowsky with respect to the domestic patent were a veto right on sublicensing by Vaupel, a reversionary right in the patent in the event of bankruptcy or termination of production by Vaupel, and a right to receive infringement damages. The sublicensing veto constituted only a minor derogation of the patent rights, the court held, and the right to receive infringement damages was merely a form of deferred compensation under the agreement. As to Marowsky's reversionary right, the court noted that *Waterman* had made clear that a transfer does not lose its character as an assignment simply because it is liable to be defeated by nonperformance of a condition subsequent.

The *Vaupel* court emphasized that Marowsky had granted Vaupel not only an exclusive license to make, use, and sell the licensed products, but also the exclusive right to sue for infringement of the patent rights. The court found that the transfer of the exclusive right to sue was "particularly dispositive" of the question whether Vaupel was authorized to bring suit without joining Marowsky.

In this case, Diamedix has retained a significantly greater interest in the patents than Marowsky retained in *Vaupel.* Unlike in *Vaupel*, Diamedix retained a limited right to make, use, and sell products embodying the patented inventions, a right to bring suit on the patents if Abbott declined to do so, and the right to prevent Abbott from assigning its rights under the license to any party other than a successor in business.

Those retained rights are the sort that are commonly held sufficient to make a patent owner who grants an exclusive license a necessary party to an infringement action brought by the licensee. We therefore conclude that Abbott does not have a sufficient interest in the '878 and '285 patents to sue, on its own, as the "patentee" entitled by 35 U.S.C. § 271 to judicial relief from infringement.

B

While Diamedix's joinder is required as a matter of statutory standing, it is consistent with the policies underlying Fed.R.Civ.P. 19, the federal joinder rule.

Rule 19(a) provides that a person who can be joined as a party should be joined if (1) the person's absence would make it impossible to grant complete relief to the parties, or (2) the person claims an interest in the subject matter of the action and is so situated that the disposition of the action in his absence could impede his ability to protect that interest or leave any of the parties subject to a substantial risk of incurring multiple or inconsistent obligations.

Diamedix retains interests in the patents, and the disposition of Abbott's suit against Ortho could either prejudice Diamedix's interests or expose Ortho to the risk of multiple litigation or obligations, depending in part on whether Diamedix would be held to be in privity with Abbott and thus bound by any judgment against Abbott. Moreover, Abbott may labor under some disadvantages, not applicable to Diamedix, that would make its defense of the patents more difficult. For example, Diamedix may not be chargeable either with Abbott's delay in bringing suit, which Ortho has pleaded as a defense, or with the statements of Abbott's agent in urging the invalidity of the '878 and '285 patents before the PTO, which might compromise Abbott's defense of the patents in this lawsuit. The purpose of Rule 19 — to avoid multiple suits or incomplete relief arising from the same subject matter — is thus served by joinder, which permits Diamedix's dispute with Ortho to be adjudicated along with Abbott's.

That is not to say that if a patentee in Diamedix's position declines to participate, the action cannot go forward. A patentee that does not voluntarily join an action prosecuted by its exclusive licensee can be joined as a defendant or, in a proper case, made an involuntary plaintiff if it is not subject to service of process. For purposes of this case, however, we need only decide that when a patent owner retains a substantial proprietary interest in the patent and wishes to participate in an infringement action, the court must allow it to do so.

III

Although we conclude that Diamedix is entitled to participate in this case as a party, the nature of its participation is another matter. The agreement between Abbott and Diamedix provides that "[t]he party who brings suit shall control the prosecution." As Abbott points out, it negotiated and paid for that right of control under the licensing agreement. At oral argument of this case, however, Diamedix's counsel made clear that Diamedix envisions participating actively in the lawsuit and does not regard the "control" clause of the agreement as imposing a significant restraint on its participation.

We refrain from commenting on the extent to which the "control" clause will give Abbott the right to control Diamedix's conduct as a party in the case. The task of refereeing disputes over the breadth of the "control" clause will necessarily fall to the district court as part of the court's responsibility to govern the pretrial and trial proceedings in cases over which it presides. Regardless of the role Diamedix is ultimately permitted to play in light of the "control" clause, however, we are persuaded that it should have been allowed to join the case as a party.

The order of the district court denying Diamedix's motion to intervene is reversed, and the case is remanded to the district court for further proceedings in accordance with this opinion.

REVERSED AND REMANDED.

QUESTIONS

1. Why would Abbott oppose the joinder of Diamedix in the infringement action?

2. Why would Diamedix seek to be joined in the infringement action if Abbott would have control over the litigation and any settlement agreement?

McNEILAB v. SCANDIPHARM and BASF
1996 U.S. App. LEXIS 19073 (Fed. Cir. 1996)

NEWMAN, CIRCUIT JUDGE.

The principal issues of law are (1) the standing of exclusive licensee McNeilab, Inc. (herein McNeilab or McNeil) to bring this suit against Scandipharm, Inc. for patent infringement, and (2) whether the patentee, BASF Aktiengesellschaft, is a necessary party. On motion of BASF the district court had dismissed Scandipharm's third party complaint against BASF. The court then dismissed McNeilab's infringement suit against Scandipharm for absence of BASF as a necessary party. McNeilab appeals the judgment that it lacks standing without joinder of BASF. We conclude that BASF is not a necessary party to this suit, and that McNeilab has standing to sue and recover damages for infringement. The district court's decision is *affirmed in part, reversed in part*, and *remanded*.

McNEILAB'S STANDING TO SUE

It is necessary to distinguish between a licensee's standing to sue, and the requirement that the patentee be party to the suit along with the licensee. Although the considerations are related, they are not identical.

A licensee that has an insufficient property interest in the patented subject matter has no standing to bring suit for infringement, whether or not the patentee is joined in the suit. Thus a licensee that has only the non-exclusive right to practice a patented invention is deemed not to have a judicially enforceable interest against an infringer, but is viewed as possessing only an immunity from exclusion by the patent owner. A simple non-exclusive license does not encompass the legal right to exclude others, and the non-exclusive licensee does not have the right to prevent infringement of the patent by others.

In contrast, grant by the patentee of the exclusive license to make, use, and sell an invention is deemed to be the grant to the licensee of all substantial rights in the patent, including the right to exclude all others. The licensee occupies the patentee's entire property interest, with the right to protect and preserve that interest and to remedy violations thereof. Although title to the patent remains in the patentee, the patentee is not a necessary party to suit brought by the exclusive licensee, when the patentee has retained no substantial rights in the licensed subject matter. Such licensee can sue infringers in its own name and without joinder of the patentee.

Between the extremes of the fully exclusive and the bare non-exclusive license there is a continuum of practical commercial arrangements. Depending on the alignment of rights and obligations, a licensee that has a sufficiently substantial interest in the patent to be entitled to damages for infringement may nonetheless be required to join the patentee in an infringement suit, in order to protect the defendant against multiple suits for the same infraction. The retention by the patentee of an interest sufficient to support an independent action for damages is the basis of the requirement that the patentee be joined in the suit.

The Federal Rules of Civil Procedure authorize joinder of a necessary party, either voluntarily or involuntarily, as the circumstances may warrant. This procedure has long been available. Although subject to interpretation at the margins, precedent generally supports the right of the exclusive licensee to sue for infringement without joining the patentee as a party when the license transfers all substantial patent rights, leaving no patent rights with the patentee; but when the patentee has retained any substantial right under the patent, the patentee must be a party to the suit and may be involuntarily joined.

Scandipharm argues that the exclusive license to McNeil did not impart standing to sue without joinder of BASF because (1) McNeil was not licensed for all of the products within the scope of the two BASF patents, (2) BASF retained certain security interests, (3) there was a restriction against assignment of the license, and (4) BASF may have retained the right to sue infringers. We review these points *seriatim*.

1. The Licensed Product

The licensed product is a cylindrical microtablet containing a specific pancreatic enzyme, described and claimed in BASF's United States Patents No. 4,797,287 and No. 4,828,843. Claim 1 of the '287 patent is as follows:

> 1. A cylindrical pharmaceutical microtablet consisting essentially of pancreatin, said microtablet having a convex upper face and convex lower face, wherein the cylinder diameter and the height independently of one another are each from 1.0 to 2.5 mm, the ratio from the said diameter to the said height being from 1:0.5 to 1:1.5, and the radius of curvature r of the convex upper and lower faces of the cylindrical microtablet is from 0.6 to 1.5 times the diameter of the cylinder.

BASF, through its subsidiary Knoll AG (KAG), granted McNeilab and its McNeil Pharmaceutical Division the exclusive patent and know-how license to make, use, and sell the product. At the time the agreement was entered into, the license grant was as follows:

> KAG hereby grants to McNeil a right and license to use the Know-How relating to the Product and the Patent Rights to make, use and sell the Product within the Territory. Such right and license shall be exclusive.

Scandipharm argued that because the patents include formulations or dimensions other than the precise "Product" that is made and sold by McNeil, the license is not an exclusive license and does not impart standing to sue without joinder of BASF. The district court agreed.

McNeil states that BASF retained no right to make, use, or sell the product that is exclusively licensed by the agreement, and that there is no other substantial patent right. McNeil states that since BASF retained no substantial patent right, McNeil's property interest as exclusive licensee is in substance that of an assignee. On the facts of this case McNeil's standing was not diminished because the exclusive license, at the time of its grant, defined the licensed subject matter as the product of commercial interest.

2. BASF's Retained Interests

The agreement provides that either BASF or McNeil can terminate the license in the event of default and certain other events. As summarized by the district court:

> Either party may terminate the agreement on ninety days' written notice of default by the other party if there is failure to cure the default within the ninety day period. Either party may terminate the Agreement immediately if the Agreement becomes void or unenforceable as a result of governmental action, if unreasonable burdens or excessive liabilities are imposed on a party with respect to its performance, or if the other party is insolvent, bankrupt, or liquidated. KAG may terminate the Agreement if McNeil Pharmaceutical Division becomes unaffiliated with Johnson & Johnson.

The right of the patentee to terminate the license in the event of the licensee's failure of performance does not negate the substantiality of the exclusive transfer of all rights to make, use, and sell the licensed product. Recovery of the patent right, should the arrangement fail through no fault of the patentee, is a common security provision when payment depends on the licensee's future performance. Such provision for contingencies that may defeat the entire arrangement does not change the fundamental nature of the agreement. Reasonable provision for unintended possibilities or force majeure does not defeat the substantiality of the transfer of the exclusive right to make, use, and sell the patented subject matter.

3. The Restriction on Alienation

The agreement required that McNeilab obtain the consent of the patentee to any assignment of the license other than to an affiliated company. The district court held that this contractual restraint on assignability "substantially impaired McNeilab's claim that it is an assignee."

When payment depends on the licensee's commercial performance in the future, the grant of the exclusive right to make, use, and sell the licensed subject matter is not significantly diminished by reasonable conditions to assure that the license remains with the chosen licensee.

The restriction on alienation did not restrain McNeilab's full exercise of the exclusive license to make, use, and sell the patented subject matter. This was not a retention by BASF of a substantial right under the patent, but a safeguard of the bargained-for consideration, which was based on the licensee's performance. Thus this contract term did not of itself defeat McNeilab's standing to sue, and its right to do so without joining the patentee.

4. The Right to Sue Infringers

The license agreement states that the patentee is not obligated to sue infringers, in the following provision:

> 6.10 *Negation of Warranties.* Nothing in this Agreement shall be construed as:
>
> (a) a warranty [that the licensed product] is or will be free of infringement of patents of third parties; or
>
> (b) an obligation to bring or prosecute actions or suits against third parties for infringement. However, should KAG choose not to enforce any of the rights licensed to McNeil hereunder within a reasonable amount of time after learning of such infringement, McNeil shall be permitted to bring or prosecute such actions or suits in its own right and with the right to retain all awards recovered thereby.

The district court described clause 6.10(b) as a "significant retention of rights by KAG," stating that "the right to sue therefore rests with KAG, not McNeil." The district court concluded that despite the clause's permission to McNeil to sue in its own right, McNeil did not have standing to sue without KAG's presence as a party.

We read this clause to different effect. Clause 6.10 is a "negation," not a grant or retention of a right. Clause 6.10(b) states that KAG is not obligated to sue infringers: the parties stated their contractual intent to negate any such obligation, thus resolving any potential future question on this point, as is the role of well-drafted agreements. Thus McNeil cannot, by this contract, require BASF (KAG) to bring or prosecute this infringement action. Nor can BASF bar McNeil's enforcement of the patents against infringers; indeed, it states that McNeil need not share any proceeds with the patentee, again resolving possible uncertainty in this fuzzy area of law. Clause 6.10(b) does not place on BASF the obligation to sue infringers; it negates such obligation.

Clause 6.10(b) does not change McNeil's exclusive license to make, use, and sell the licensed product. This contractual "negation" of any obligation upon BASF to sue infringers is not the retention by BASF of a substantial right in the licensed patents.

5. The Totality of These Provisions

Scandipharm argues that even if any one of these provisions is not viewed as the retention of a substantial patent right, taken together they weigh as substantial. Viewing the totality of the challenged provisions, we conclude that they do not defeat the completeness of the transfer. BASF can neither practice the licensed invention nor authorize anyone else to do so. BASF's right to terminate in the event of default or nonperformance, the restriction on alienation, and BASF's negation of any obligation to enforce the patent against infringers, do not affect the exclusivity of McNeil's license; they are merely safeguards against conditions subsequent.

Thus the courts have viewed the licensee with the exclusive right to make, use, and sell the patented subject matter as legally equivalent to the assignee for the purpose of determining standing to sue for infringement. The courts have recognized that there is no substantive difference between the property interests of the exclusive licensee and the assignee of the patent, and thus have sometimes used the terms interchangeably, subordinating the purity of the distinction to the reality of the legal rights. We agree that there is no substantive difference between the property interests of an assignee and of an exclusive licensee who has been granted all substantial patent rights including the right to exclude the patentee. Although it would be more accurate to preserve the distinction whereby the term "assignment" is reserved for transfers that include nominal title, we agree with precedent that when the transfer includes all substantial patent rights including the right to exclude the transferor, there is no significant difference between the rights transferred by assignment and those transferred by exclusive license.

On the facts of this case and in accordance with precedent, we conclude that McNeil has standing to sue in its own name and without joinder of BASF.

*****

SUMMARY

The dismissal of McNeilab's suit against Scandipharm is reversed. The dismissal of the third party complaint is affirmed. The case is remanded for further proceedings.

QUESTIONS

1. If a patentee grants an exclusive license to make and use a patented product, but not the right to sell and import, for the remaining term of the patent, could the licensee bring suit against an alleged infringer who was making and selling the patented product without joining the patentee?

2. If a patentee grants an exclusive license to make, use, sell and import a patented product for the remaining term of the patent, but limited to a specific territory, could the licensee bring suit against an alleged infringer in the licensed territory without joining the patentee?

3. If a patentee assigns a 50% interest in a patent to a corporation founded by the patentee, could the corporation bring suit against an alleged infringer without joining the patentee?

4. If a patentee grants an exclusive license to make, use, sell and import a patented product for a term of years, and the agreement also provides that the licensee may sue for infringement without joining the patentee, can the licensee bring suit against an alleged infringer without joining the patentee?

CASE NOTES

1. In 1985, Ortho entered into a product license agreement with Amgen for the rights to manufacture and sell EPO, a synthetic hormone that stimulates production of red blood cells that was claimed in the '008 patent. The product license agreement stated that Amgen grants Ortho an exclusive license to make, use and sell the Licensed Products, in the Licensed Territory for the Licensed Field. The agreement defined the Licensed Products as EPO, the Licensed Territory as the United States, and the Licensed Field as all indications for human use except dialysis and diagnostics. The product license agreement also stated that Ortho's exclusive license was subject to Amgen's right to make, use and sell EPO in the United States. Finally, the product license agreement contained a third-party infringement clause that granted Amgen the right to sue alone and Ortho the right to sue if Amgen failed to sue. In October 1987, Amgen filed a patent infringement action against Genetics and Chugai. Ortho sought to intervene in this suit based on its rights under the product license agreement. Amgen objected to Ortho's intervention in the suit, claiming that Ortho had neither the right nor the need to intervene. The court agreed with Amgen and denied Ortho's motion to intervene finding that Ortho's interests were adequately protected by Amgen. Ortho then filed a separate infringement suit against Genetics and Amgen in the same court. Ortho claimed it had standing under the product license agreement to file an infringement action as a co-plaintiff. Genetics and Amgen filed motions to dismiss Ortho's suit based on Ortho's lack of standing. What result? *See* Ortho Pharmaceutical Corp. v. Genetics Institute, Inc., 52 F.3d 1026 (Fed. Cir. 1995).

2. *See also* Arcade Inc. v. Minnesota Min. and Mfg. Co. 43 U.S.P.Q.2d 1511 (E.D.Tenn. 1997) (Patentee is not an indispensable party to an infringement suit brought by an exclusive licensee, and therefore need not be joined pursuant to Fed.R.Civ.P. 19(a), when the license agreement provides the patentee with a limited right to sue for infringement in situations where the licensee declines to do so, but does not obligate the patentee to sue for infringement or to join as a party to an infringement suit brought by the licensee); Mentor H/S, Inc. v. Medical Device Alliance, Inc., 240 F.3d 1016 (Fed. Cir. 2001) (Agreement between patentee and exclusive licensee did not transfer all substantial rights in patent giving the exclusive licensee the right to sue for infringement in its own name where patentee could supervise and control exclusive licensee's product development, was obligated to pay maintenance fees for the patent, and had the first obligation to sue for infringement); Prima Tek II, L.L.C. v. A-Roo Co., 222 F.3d 1372 (Fed. Cir. 2000) (To determine whether a license agreement has conveyed all substantial rights in a patent, the court must ascertain the intention of the parties and examine the substance of what was granted and what was retained by the grantor); Textile Productions, Inc. v. Mead Corp., 134 F.3d 1481 (Fed.Cir. 1998) (Plaintiff who had assigned its rights to defendant co-inventor was not an exclusive licensee under the patent and therefore lacked standing to bring an infringement action); Sicom Systems, Ltd. v. Agilent Technologies, Inc., 427 F.3d 971 (Fed. Cir. 2005) (Licensee who has the exclusive right to sue for commercial infringement does not signify that licensee has the exclusive right to sue for all infringement, especially where licensor has specifically retained the right to sue for non-commercial infringement); Great Lakes Intellectual Prop. v. Sakar Int'l, Inc., 516 F. Supp. 2d 880 (W.D.Mich. 2007)

(Exclusive licensee within a limited field of use did not have all substantial rights in the patent where licensor reserved the right to practice the patent in other, larger fields of use, the right to sublicense others within the retained field of use, and the exclusive license was expressly subject to preexisting licenses in favor of prior licensees); InternetAd Systems, L.L.C. v. Opodo Ltd., 481 F.Supp.2d 596 (N.D.Tex. 2007) (Licensor's retention of the right to approve licensee's choice of counsel in the event of an infringement suit, the right to share in proceeds, and the right to be informed regarding the infringement litigation were not significant enough to destroy the grant of all substantial rights to the licensee.; Mission I-Tech Hockey, Ltd. v. Oakley, Inc., 394 F.Supp.2d 1270 (S.D.Cal. 2005) (Exclusive patent licensee did not have all substantial rights in patent where licensee lacked the right to sublicense and patentee had the obligation to enforce patent infringement against third parties, the right to approve licensee's advertisements and the right to obtain equivalent foreign patents).

Additional Information

1. CHARLES A. WRIGHT ET AL., 6A FED. PRAC. & PROC. CIV. § 1547 (3d ed.) (2010).

2. 60 AM. JUR. 2D PATENTS § 861 (2010).

3. RAYMOND T. NIMMER & JEFF C. DODD, MODERN LICENSING LAW, §§ 5:30, 5:32 (2010).

4. 1 ROBERT A. MATTHEWS, JR., ANNOTATED PATENT DIGEST, §§ 9:27, 9:64–65 (2010).

5. Steven Walker, *Challenging a Plaintiff's Right to Sue for Patent Infringement: The Affirmative Defense of Standing*, 20 No. 6 INTELL. PROP. & TECH. L. J. 17 (2008).

6. Roger D. Blair, *The Elusive Logic of Standing Doctrine in Intellectual Property Law*, 74 TUL. L. REV. 1323 (2000).

7. William F. Lee et al., *When an Exclusive License is Not an Exclusive License: The Standing of "Exclusive" Patent Licensees to Sue After Ortho Pharmaceutical v. Genetics Institute, Inc.*, 7 FED. CIRCUIT B.J. 1,(1997).

2.2.10 Patent Misuse

The patent misuse doctrine was created by courts to prevent patent owners from extending their patent rights beyond the rights granted under the Patent Act. Although akin to antitrust law, patent misuse and antitrust law are distinct in two respects: patent misuse is rooted entirely in judicial decisions, while antitrust law is rooted primarily in federal statutes; and patent misuse focuses solely on the conduct of the patent owner, while antitrust law focuses on the anticompetitive impact of the patent owner's conduct. The seminal patent misuse case is *Morton Salt Co. v. G.S. Suppiger Co.*, 314 U.S. 488 (1942). In *Morton Salt*, the patent owner conditioned licenses of patented salt dispenser machines on the purchase of unpatented salt tablets. The Supreme Court held that conditioning the license of a patented product on the purchase of an unpatented product unlawfully extended the patent owner's rights and, therefore, constituted patent misuse. The Court found that patent misuse rendered the patent unenforceable; and that's patent misuse was an affirmative defense to a claim of patent infringement, even though the alleged infringer in *Morton Salt* was not itself subject to the patent misuse.

Since the *Morton Salt* decision, the courts and the Congress have sparred over the patent misuse doctrine with the courts generally seeking to enforce patent misuse separately from the antitrust laws and the Congress generally seeking to align patent misuse with the antitrust laws. Currently, Section 271(d) of the Patent Act provides:

> No patent owner otherwise entitled to relief for infringement or contributory infringement of a patent shall be denied relief or deemed guilty of misuse or illegal extension of the patent right by reason of his having done one or more of the following: (1) derived revenue from acts which if performed by another without his consent would constitute contributory infringement of the patent; (2) licensed or authorized another to perform acts which if performed without his consent would constitute contributory infringement of the patent; (3) sought to enforce his patent rights against infringement or contributory infringement; (4) refused to license or use any rights to the patent; or (5) conditioned the license of any rights to the patent or the sale of the patented product on the acquisition of a license to rights in another patent or purchase of a separate product unless, in view of the circumstances, the patent owner has market power in the relevant market for the patent or patented product on which the license or sale is conditioned. 35 U.S.C. § 271(d).

Section 271(d) is closely linked to Section 271(c) — contributory infringement. Section 271(c) provides:

> Whoever offers to sell or sells within the United States or imports into the United States a component of a patented machine, manufacture, combination or composition, or a material or apparatus for use in practicing a patented process, constituting a material part of the invention, knowing the same to be especially made or especially adapted for use in an infringement of such patent, and not a staple article or commodity of commerce suitable for substantial noninfringing use, shall be liable a contributory infringer.

Under sections 271(d)(3) and 271(c) a patent owner has the right to condition the sale or license of a patented product on the purchase of a nonpatented product that is especially adapted for use with the patented product (a "nonstaple" product). The patent owner can sue for contributory infringement to enforce this right, whether or not the patent owner has market power in the patented product market. On the other hand, under section 271(d)(5) if a patent owner conditions the sale or license of a patented product on the purchase of a nonpatented product that is a "staple" product having substantial noninfringing use, the patent owner will not be denied relief for infringement unless the patent owner is proven to have market power in the patented product market.

The question of patent misuse continues to arise in a variety of contexts including attempts to collect royalties after the expiration of the patent term and attempts to collect royalties on the sales of products that have been invented using a patented licensed research tool (reach through royalties). The *Philips* case below considers the question of patent misuse in the context of a license for a package (pool) of patents.

We will consider antitrust laws in more detail in Chapter 7 — Licensing and Antitrust Laws.

U.S. PHILIPS CORPORATION v. I.T.C
424 F.3d 1179 (Fed. Cir. 2005)

BRYSON, CIRCUIT JUDGE.

U.S. Philips Corporation appeals from a final order of the United States International Trade Commission, in which the Commission held six of Philips's patents for the manufacture of compact discs to be unenforceable because of patent misuse. The Commission ruled that Philips had employed an impermissible tying arrangement because it required prospective licensees to license packages of patents rather than allowing them to choose which individual patents they wished to license and making the licensing fee correspond to the particular patents designated by the licensees. We reverse and remand.

I

Philips owns patents to technology for manufacturing recordable compact discs ("CD-Rs") and rewritable compact discs ("CD-RWs") in accordance with the technical standards set forth in a publication called the Recordable CD Standard (the "Orange Book"), jointly authored by Philips and Sony Corporation. Since the 1990s, Philips has been licensing those patents through package licenses. Philips specified that the same royalty was due for each disc manufactured by the licensee using patents included in the package, regardless of how many of the patents were used. Potential licensees who sought to license patents to the technology for manufacturing CD-Rs or CD-RWs were not allowed to license those patents individually and were not offered a lower royalty rate for licenses to fewer than all the patents in a package.

Initially, Philips offered four different pools of patents for licensing: (1) a joint CD-R patent pool that included patents owned by Philips and two other companies (Sony and Taiyo Yuden); (2) a joint CD-RW patent pool that included patents owned by Philips and two other companies (Sony and Ricoh); (3) a CD-R patent pool that included only patents owned by Philips; and (4) a CD-RW patent pool that included only patents owned by Philips. After 2001, Philips offered additional package options by grouping its patents into two categories, which Philips denominated "essential" and "nonessential" for producing compact discs compliant with the technical standards set forth in the Orange Book.

In the late 1990s, Philips entered into package licensing agreements with Princo Corporation and Princo America Corporation (collectively, "Princo"); GigaStorage Corporation Taiwan and GigaStorage Corporation USA (collectively, "GigaStorage"); and Linberg Enterprise Inc. ("Linberg"). Soon after entering into the agreements, however, Princo, GigaStorage, and Linberg stopped paying the licensing fees. Philips filed a complaint with the International Trade Commission that Princo, GigaStorage, and Linberg, among others, were violating section 337(a)(1)(B) of the Tariff Act of 1930, 19 U.S.C. § 1337(a)(1)(B), by importing into the United States certain CD-Rs and CD-RWs that infringed six of Philips's patents.

The Commission instituted an investigation and identified 19 respondents, including GigaStorage and Linberg. Additional respondents, including Princo, were added through intervention. In the course of the proceedings before an administrative law judge, the respondents raised patent misuse as an affirmative defense, alleging that Philips had improperly forced them, as a condition of licensing patents that were necessary to manufacture CD-Rs or CD-RWs, to take licenses to other patents that were not necessary to manufacture those products. In particular, the respondents argued that a number of the patents that Philips had included in the category of "essential" patents were actually not essential for manufacturing compact discs compliant with the Orange Book standards, because there were commercially viable alternative methods of manufacturing CD-Rs and CD-RWs that did not require the use of the technology covered by those patents.

The administrative law judge ruled that the intervenors had infringed various claims of the six asserted Philips patents. The administrative law judge further ruled, however, that all six of the asserted patents were unenforceable by reason of patent misuse. Among the grounds invoked by the administrative law judge for finding patent misuse was his conclusion that the package licensing arrangements constituted tying arrangements that were illegal under analogous antitrust law principles and thus rendered the subject patents unenforceable.

Philips petitioned the Commission for review of the administrative law judge's decision. In an order that addressed only the findings concerning patent misuse, the Commission affirmed the administrative law judge's ruling that Philips's package licensing practice "constitutes patent misuse per se as a tying arrangement between (1) licenses to patents that are essential to manufacture CD-Rs or CD-RWs according to Orange Book standards and (2) licenses to other patents that are not essential to that activity." The Commission found that the Farla, Iwasaki, Yamamoto, and Lokhoff patents were not essential to manufacturing CD-Rs or CD-RWs. Specifically, the Commission found that the Farla and Lokhoff patents were nonessential with respect to the Philips-only CD-RW and CD-R licenses, and that the Farla, Iwasaki, Yamamoto, and Lokhoff patents were nonessential with respect to the joint CD-RW license. The Commission concluded that the four nonessential patents were impermissibly tied to patents that were essential to manufacturing CD-Rs and CD-RWs, because "none of the so-called essential patents could be licensed individually for the manufacture of CD-RWs and CD-Rs apart from the package" that Philips denominated as "essential." The Commission also found, based on the administrative law judge's findings and analysis, that the joint license for CD-R and CD-RW technology unlawfully tied patents for CD-Rs and CD-RWs in accordance with the Orange Book standards to patents that were not essential to manufacture such discs.

The Commission explained why it concluded that each of the four patents was nonessential. According to the Commission, the Farla and Iwasaki patents were not essential because there was an economically viable alternative method of writing information to discs that did not require the producer to practice those patents; the Yamamoto patent was not essential because there was a potential alternative method of creating master discs that did not require the producer to practice that patent; and the Lokhoff patent was not essential because there were alternative possible methods of accomplishing copy protection that did not require the producer to practice that patent. Based on those findings, the Commission concluded that the four "nonessential" patents constituted separate products from the patents that were essential to the manufacture of the subject discs.

The Commission ruled that Philips's patent package licensing arrangement constituted per se patent misuse because Philips did not give prospective licensees the option of licensing individual patents (presumably for a lower fee) rather than licensing one or more of the patent packages as a whole. The Commission took no position on the administrative law judge's ruling that patent pooling arrangements between Philips and its co-licensors constituted patent misuse per se based on the theories of price fixing and price discrimination, and it took no position on the administrative law judge's conclusion that the royalty structure of the patent pools was an unreasonable restraint of trade.

As an alternative ground, the Commission concluded that even if Philips's patent package licensing practice was not per se patent misuse, it constituted patent misuse under the rule of reason. Adopting the administrative law judge's findings, the Commission ruled that the anticompetitive effects of including nonessential patents in the packages of so-called essential patents outweighed the pro-competitive effects of that practice. In particular, the Commission held that including such nonessential patents in the licensing packages could foreclose alternative technologies and injure competitors seeking to license such alternative technologies to parties who needed to obtain licenses to Philips's "essential" patents. The Commission took no position with respect to the portion of the administrative law judge's rule of reason analysis in which the administrative law judge concluded that the royalty rate structure of the patent pooling arrangements constituted an unreasonable restraint on competition.

Philips took this appeal from the Commission's order.

II

Patent misuse is an equitable defense to patent infringement. It "arose to restrain practices that did not in themselves violate any law, but that drew anticompetitive strength from the patent right, and thus were deemed to be contrary to public policy." The purpose of the patent misuse defense "was to prevent a patentee from using the patent to obtain market benefit beyond that which inheres in the statutory patent right." As the Supreme Court has explained, the doctrine of patent misuse bars a patentee from using the "patent's leverage" to "extend the monopoly of his patent to derive a benefit not attributable to the use of the patent's teachings," such as requiring a licensee to pay a royalty on products that do not use the teaching of the patent. The "key inquiry is whether, by imposing conditions that derive their force from the patent, the patentee has impermissibly broadened the scope of the patent grant with anticompetitive effect."

This court summarized the principles of patent misuse as applied to "tying" arrangements in *Virginia Panel Corp. v. MAC Panel Co.* The court there explained that because of the importance of anticompetitive effects in shaping the defense of patent misuse, the analysis of tying arrangements in the context of patent misuse is closely related to the analysis of tying arrangements in antitrust law. The court further explained that, depending on the circumstances, tying arrangements can be viewed as per se patent misuse or can be analyzed under the rule of reason. The court noted that certain specific practices have been identified as constituting per se patent misuse, "including so-called "tying" arrangements in which a patentee conditions a license under the patent on the purchase of a separable, staple good, and arrangements in which a patentee effectively extends the term of its patent by requiring post-expiration royalties." If the particular licensing arrangement in question is not one of those specific practices that has been held to constitute per se misuse, it will be analyzed under the rule of reason. We have held that under the rule of reason, a practice is impermissible only if its effect is to restrain competition in a relevant market.

The Supreme Court's decisions analyzing tying arrangements under antitrust law principles are to the same effect. The Court has made clear that tying arrangements are deemed to be per se unlawful only if they constitute a "naked restrain[t] of trade with no purpose except stifling of competition" and "always or almost always tend to restrict competition and decrease output" in some substantial portion of a market. The Supreme Court has applied the per se rule only when "experience with a particular kind of restraint enables the Court to predict with confidence that the rule of reason will condemn it."

While the doctrine of patent misuse closely tracks antitrust law principles in many respects, Congress has declared certain practices not to be patent misuse even though those practices might otherwise be subject to scrutiny under antitrust law principles. In 35 U.S.C. § 271(d), Congress designated several specific practices as not constituting patent misuse. The designated practices include "condition[ing] the license of any rights to the patent or the sale of the patented product on the acquisition of a license to rights in another patent or purchase of a separate product," unless, in view of the circumstances, the patent owner "has market power for the patent or patented product on which the license or sale is conditioned." Because the statute is phrased in the negative, it does not require that patent misuse be found in the case of all such conditional licenses in which the patent owner has market power; instead, the statute simply excludes such conditional licenses in which the patent owner lacks market power from the category of arrangements that may be found to constitute patent misuse.

Although section 271(d)(5) does not define the scope of the defense of patent misuse, but merely provides a safe harbor against the charge of patent misuse for certain kinds of conduct by patentees, the statute makes clear that the defense of patent misuse differs from traditional antitrust law principles in an important respect, as applied to tying arrangements involving patent rights. In the case of an antitrust claim based on a tying arrangement involving patent rights, this court has held that ownership of a patent on the tying good is presumed to give the patentee monopoly power. Section 271(d)(5) makes clear, however, that such a presumption does not apply in the case of patent misuse. To establish the defense of patent misuse, the accused infringer must show that the patentee has power in the market for the tying product.

Philips argues briefly that it lacks market power and that it is thus shielded from liability by section 271(d)(5). Based on detailed analysis by the administrative law judge, however, the Commission found that Philips has market power in the relevant market and that section 271(d)(5) is therefore inapplicable to this case. We sustain that ruling.

Apart from its specific challenge to the Commission's ruling on the market power issue, Philips launches a more broad-based attack on the Commission's conclusion that Philips's patent licensing policies constitute per se patent misuse. In so doing, Philips makes essentially two arguments: first, that the Commission was wrong as a legal matter in ruling that the package licensing arrangements at issue in this case are among those few practices that the courts have identified as so clearly anticompetitive as to warrant being condemned as per se illegal; and second, that the Commission erred as a factual matter in concluding that Philips's package licensing arrangements reflect the use of market power in one market to foreclose competition in a separate market. We address the two arguments separately.

A

In its brief, the Commission argues that it is "hornbook law" that mandatory package licensing has been held to be patent misuse. While that broad characterization can be found in some treatises, Philips invites us to consider whether that broad proposition is sound. Upon consideration, we conclude that the proposition as applied to the circumstances of this case is not supported by precedent or reason.

In its opinion, the Commission acknowledged that the *Virginia Panel* case and many other patent tying cases "involve a tying patent and a tied *product*, rather than a tying patent and a tied *patent*" (emphasis in original). The Commission nonetheless concluded that "finding patent misuse based on a tying arrangement between patents in a mandatory package license is a reasonable application of Supreme Court precedent." In so ruling, the Commission relied primarily on two Supreme Court cases: *United States v. Paramount Pictures, Inc.* and United States v. Loew's, Inc. Those cases condemned the practice of "block-booking" movies to theaters (in the *Paramount* case) and to television stations (in the *Loew's* case) as antitrust violations.

Block-booking is the practice in which a distributor licenses one feature or group of features to exhibitors on the condition that the exhibitors agree to license another (presumably inferior) feature or group of features released by the distributor during a given period. In *Paramount* and *Loew's*, the Court held that block-booking, as practiced in those cases, was per se illegal. The Commission reasoned that the practice of block-booking that was the focus of the Court's condemnation in *Paramount* and *Loew's* is similar to the package licensing agreements at issue in this case and that under the analysis employed in *Paramount* and *Loew's*, Philips's package licensing agreements must be condemned as per se patent misuse.

We do not agree with the Commission that the decisions in *Paramount* and *Loew's* govern this case. In *Paramount*, the district court held that the defendant movie distributor had engaged in unlawful conduct because it offered to permit exhibitors to show the films they wished to license only if they agreed to license and exhibit other films that they were not interested in licensing. The Supreme Court affirmed that ruling. The Court held that block-booking was illegal because it "prevents competitors from bidding for single features on their individual merits," and because it "adds to the monopoly of a single copyrighted picture that of another copyrighted picture which must be taken and exhibited in order to secure the first." The result, the Court explained, "is to add to the monopoly of the copyright in violation of the principle of the patent cases involving tying clauses."

Because the block-booking arrangement at issue in *Paramount* required the licensee to exhibit all of the films in the group for which a license was taken, the *Paramount* block-booking was more akin to a tying arrangement in which a patent license is tied to the purchase of a separate product, rather than to an arrangement in which a patent license is tied to another patent license. Indeed, all of the patent tying cases to which the Supreme Court referred in *Paramount* involved tying arrangements in which, as the Court described them, "the owner of a patent [conditioned] its use on the purchase or use of patented or unpatented materials." Because the arrangement in the *Paramount* case was equivalent in substance to a patent-to-product tying arrangement, *Paramount* does not stand for the proposition that a pure patent-to-patent tying arrangement, such as Philips's package licensing agreement, is per se unlawful.

Philips gives its licensees the option of using any of the patents in the package, at the licensee's option. Philips charges a uniform licensing fee to manufacture discs covered by its patented technology, regardless of which, or how many, of the patents in the package the licensee chooses to use in its manufacturing process. In particular, Philips's package licenses do not require that licensees actually use the technology covered by any of the patents that the Commission characterized as nonessential. In that respect, Philips's licensing agreements are different from the agreements at issue in *Paramount*, which imposed an obligation on the purchasers of package licenses to exhibit films they did not wish to license. That obligation not only extended the exclusive right in one product to products in which the distributor did not have exclusive rights, but it also precluded exhibitors, as a practical matter, from exhibiting other films that they may have preferred over the tied films they were required to exhibit. Because Philips's package licensing agreements do not compel the licensees to use any particular technology covered by any of the licensed patents, the *Paramount* case is not a sound basis from which to conclude that the package licensing arrangements at issue in this case constitute patent misuse per se.

In the *Loew's* case, the district court determined that the licensee television stations were required to pay fees not only for the feature films they wanted, but also for additional, inferior films. As in *Paramount*, the fact that the package arrangement required the television stations to purchase exhibition rights for the package at a price that was greater than the price attributable to the desired films made the tying arrangement very much like a tying arrangement involving products. Thus, the Supreme Court explained that a "substantial portion of the licensing fees represented the cost of the inferior films which the stations were required to accept." Following the approach employed in *Paramount*, the Supreme Court applied the principles of cases involving tying arrangements between patents and unpatented products and concluded that the tying arrangements in the case before it had all the anticompetitive features of the block-booking arrangements in *Paramount* and no redeeming pro-competitive features.

In this case, unlike in *Loew's*, there is no evidence that a portion of the royalty was attributable to the patents that the Commission characterized as nonessential. While the administrative law judge found that GigaStorage "inquired into obtaining a license to less than all of the patents on Philips's patent list," the administrative law judge noted that GigaStorage did so because it "hoped that by eliminating some patents the royalty rate would be lower." There is no evidence that GigaStorage had any basis for its expectation that a smaller patent package might result in a lower royalty rate. In fact, the administrative law judge found that Philips had responded to that overture from GigaStorage by explaining that "the royalty is the same regardless of the number of patents used." Moreover, the administrative law judge found that the royalty rate for licensing Philips's patents "remains the same regardless of which option(s) in the agreement one selects," and that the royalty rate "does not increase or decrease if more or fewer patents are used." Thus, it is clear that the royalty charged by Philips was not increased because of the inclusion of the Farla, Iwasaki, Yamamoto, and Lokhoff patents. There is therefore no basis for conjecture that a hypothetical licensing fee would have been lower if Philips had offered to license the patents on an individual basis or in smaller packages.

Aside from *Paramount* and *Loew's*, the Commission relies on cases involving tying arrangements in which the patent owner conditions the availability of a patent license on the patentee's agreement to purchase a staple item of commerce from the patentee. Those cases, however, are readily distinguishable because of the fundamental difference between an obligation to purchase a product and the extension of a nonexclusive license to practice a patent.

A nonexclusive patent license is simply a promise not to sue for infringement. The conveyance of such a license does not obligate the licensee to do anything; it simply provides the licensee with a guarantee that it will not be sued for engaging in conduct that would infringe the patent in question.

In the case of patent-to-product tying, the patent owner uses the market power conferred by the patent to compel customers to purchase a product in a separate market that the customer might otherwise purchase from a competitor. The patent owner is thus able to use the market power conferred by the patent to foreclose competition in the market for the product.

By contrast, a package licensing agreement that includes both essential and nonessential patents does not impose any requirement on the licensee. It does not bar the licensee from using any alternative technology that may be offered by a competitor of the licensor. Nor does it foreclose the competitor from licensing his alternative technology; it merely puts the competitor in the same position he would be in if he were competing with unpatented technology.

A package license is in effect a promise by the patentee not to sue his customer for infringing any patents on whatever technology the customer employs in making commercial use of the licensed patent. That surrender of rights might mean that the customer will choose not to license the alternative technology offered by the patentee's competition, but it does not compel the customer to use the patentee's technology. The package license is thus not anticompetitive in the way that a compelled purchase of a tied product would be.

Contrary to the Commission's characterization, the intervenors were not "forced" to "take" anything from Philips that they did not want, nor were they restricted from obtaining licenses from other sources to produce the relevant technology. Philips simply provided that for a fixed licensing fee, it would not sue any licensee for engaging in any conduct covered by the entire group of patents in the package. By analogy, if Philips had decided to surrender its "nonessential" patents or had simply announced that it did not intend to enforce them, there would have been no way for the manufacturers to decline or reject Philips's decision. Yet the economic effect of the package licensing arrangement for Philips's patents is not fundamentally different from the effect that such decisions would have had on third parties seeking to compete with the technology covered by those "nonessential" patents. Thus, we conclude that the Commission erred when it characterized the package license agreements as a way of forcing the intervenors to license technology that they did not want in order to obtain patent rights that they did.

Aside from the absence of evidence that the package licensing arrangements in this case had the effect of impermissibly broadening the scope of the "essential" patents with anticompetitive effect, Philips argues that the Commission failed to acknowledge the unique pro-competitive benefits associated with package licensing. Philips points to the federal government's guidelines for licensing intellectual property, which recognize that patent packages "may provide pro-competitive benefits by integrating complementary technologies, reducing transaction costs, clearing blocking positions, and avoiding costly infringement litigation. By promoting the dissemination of technology, cross-licensing and pooling arrangements are often pro-competitive."

Philips introduced evidence that package licensing reduces transaction costs by eliminating the need for multiple contracts and reducing licensors' administrative and monitoring costs. Package licensing can also obviate any potential patent disputes between a licensor and a licensee and thus reduce the likelihood that a licensee will find itself involved in costly litigation over unlicensed patents with potentially adverse consequences for both parties, such as a finding that the licensee infringed the unlicensed patents or that the unlicensed patents were invalid. Thus, package licensing provides the parties a way of ensuring that a single licensing fee will cover all the patents needed to practice a particular technology and protecting against the unpleasant surprise for a licensee who learns, after making a substantial investment, that he needed a license to more patents than he originally obtained. Finally, grouping licenses in a package allows the parties to price the package based on their estimate of what it is worth to practice a particular technology, which is typically much easier to calculate than determining the marginal benefit provided by a license to each individual patent. In short, package licensing has the pro-competitive effect of reducing the degree of uncertainty associated with investment decisions.

In light of the efficiencies of package patent licensing and the important differences between product-to-patent tying arrangements and arrangements involving group licensing of patents, we reject the Commission's conclusion that Philips's conduct shows a "lack of any redeeming virtue" and should be "conclusively presumed to be unreasonable and therefore illegal without elaborate inquiry as to the precise harm they have caused or the business excuse for their use. We therefore hold that the analysis that led the Commission to apply the rule of per se illegality to Philips's package licensing agreements was legally flawed."

III

In the alternative, the Commission held that Philips's package licensing agreements constituted patent misuse under the rule of reason. The Commission's analysis under the rule of reason largely tracked the analysis that led it to conclude that the package licensing agreements constituted per se patent misuse.

As in the case of its ruling on per se patent misuse, the fulcrum of the Commission's conclusion that Philips was guilty of patent misuse under the rule of reason was its conclusion that the package licenses at issue in this case had "the anticompetitive effect of foreclosing competition in the alternative technology that competes with the technology covered by a nonessential patent that was included as a so-called "essential" patent." On that issue, the Commission adopted the administrative law judge's analysis and conclusions with respect to the Farla, Iwasaki, Yamamoto, and Lokhoff patents, but it took no position with respect to other patents that the administrative law judge found to be nonessential.

Under the rule of reason, the finder of fact must determine if the practice at issue is "reasonably within the patent grant, i.e., that it relates to subject matter within the scope of the patent claims." If the practice does not "broaden the scope of the patent, either in terms of covered subject matter or temporally," then the patentee is not chargeable with patent misuse. More specifically, "the finder of fact must decide whether the questioned practice imposes an unreasonable restraint on competition, taking into account a variety of factors, including specific information about the relevant business, its condition before and after the restraint was imposed, and the restraint's history, nature and effect."

The Commission's rule of reason analysis is flawed for two reasons. Most importantly, its conclusion was largely predicated on the anticompetitive effect on competitors offering alternatives to the four so-called nonessential patents in the Philips patent packages. Yet, as we have already held, the evidence did not show that including those patents in the patent packages had a negative effect on commercially available technology. The Commission assumed that there was a foreclosure of competition because compact disc manufacturers would be induced to accept licenses to the technology covered by the Farla and Iwasaki patents and therefore would be unwilling to consider alternatives. As noted, however, there was no evidence before the Commission that any manufacturer had actually refused to consider alternatives to the technology covered by those patents or for that matter that any commercially viable alternative actually existed.

In addition, as in its per se analysis, the Commission did not acknowledge the problems with licensing patents individually, such as the transaction costs associated with making individual patent-by-patent royalty determinations and monitoring possible infringement of patents that particular licensees chose not to license. The Commission also did not address the problem, noted above, that changes in the technology for manufacturing compact discs could render some patents that were indisputably essential at the time of licensing arguably nonessential at some later point in the life of the license. To hold that a licensing agreement that satisfied the rule of reason when executed became unreasonable at some later point because of technological development would introduce substantial uncertainty into the market and displace settled commercial arrangements in favor of uncertainty that could only be resolved through expensive litigation.

Finally, the Commission failed to consider the efficiencies that package licensing may produce because of the innovative character of the technology at hand. Given that the technology surrounding the Orange Book standard was still evolving, there were many uncertainties regarding what patents might be needed to produce the compact discs. As noted, package license agreements in which the royalty was based on the number of units produced, not the number of patents used to produce them, can resolve in advance all potential patent disputes between the licensor and the licensee, whereas licensing patent rights on a patent-by-patent basis can result in continuing disputes over whether the licensee's technology infringes certain ancillary patents owned by the licensor that are not part of the group elected by the licensee.

We therefore conclude that the line of analysis that the Commission employed in reaching its conclusion that Philips's package licensing agreements are more anticompetitive than pro-competitive, and thus are unlawful under the rule of reason, was predicated on legal errors and on factual findings that were not supported by substantial evidence. For these reasons, we cannot uphold the Commission's decision that Philips's patents are unenforceable because of patent misuse under the rule of reason.

Because the Commission did not address all of the issues presented by the administrative law judge's decision under both the per se and rule of reason analysis, further proceedings before the Commission may be necessary with respect to whether Philips's patents are enforceable and, if so, whether Philips is entitled to any relief from the Commission. Accordingly, we reverse the Commission's ruling on patent misuse for the reasons stated, and we remand this case to the Commission for further proceedings consistent with this opinion.

REVERSED AND REMANDED.

QUESTIONS

1.   How is the license of a patent that is tied to the license or sale of a product different from the license of a patent that is tied to the license of other patents?

2.   Would Philips have been better advised to put all of its patents into a single patent pool rather than grouping them as essential and non-essential?

3.   The court finds that it was erroneous for the Commission to assume that the royalty price charged by Philips would be lower if the non-essential patents were not included under the license. What would the price of the non-essential patents have to be in order for their exclusion not to have reduced the royalty price charged by Philips? Would a licensee having paid this price for the non-essential patents have any incentive to license substitute patents?

4.   In performing its rule-of-reason analysis, the court sought to balance the pro-competitive and anticompetitive effects of PhilIPS' licensing arrangement. What did the court list as the pro-competitive effects? What did the court list as the anticompetitive effects?

CASE NOTES

1.   Windsurfing International (WSI) owned a patent on a sailboard ('167 patent). WSI filed a patent infringement action against AMF based on the '167 patent and AMF then sought a declaratory judgment that the '167 patent was invalid for obviousness, unenforceable because of patent misuse and not infringed. AMF's claim of patent misuse was based on a provision in WSI's licenses that required licensees to acknowledge that the trademarks "WINDSURFER," "WINDSURF-ING" AND "WIND SURF" were valid registered trademarks owned by WSI and prohibited licensees from using these trademarks in any way. AMF claimed that these trademarks had become common descriptive names. The district court found that these trademarks were generic and that the provision enforcing these trademarks in the WSI license agreements inhibited competition beyond the scope of the patent. WSI appealed the district court decision arguing these were lawfully registered trademarks that it was free to enforce in its license agreements. What result? *See* Windsurfing Int'l Inc. v. AMF Inc., 782 F.2d 995 (Fed. Cir. 1986).

2.   *See also* Princo Corp. v. I.T.C., 616 F.3d 1318 (Fed. Cir. 2010) (Patent misuse is intended to prevent patentees from using patents to obtain market benefits beyond those granted in statutory patent rights; the key inquiry in patent misuse is whether the patentee has broadened the physical or temporal scope of the patent grant resulting in anticompetitive effects; ordinary license conditions, such as field of use limitations, are generally upheld, but price-fixing conditions and tying restraints may render the patent unenforceable); Cordance Corp. v. Amazon.Com, Inc., 727 F.Supp.2d 310 (D. Del. 2010) (Patent misuse is an affirmative defense to infringement; to establish patent misuse an alleged infringer must show that the patentee impermissibly broadened the physical or temporal scope of the patent with anticompetitive results; post-expiration royalty obligations do not dictate that a court find patent misuse *per se* or hold a patent unenforceable in its entirety); Lucent Technologies, Inc. v. Microsoft Corp., 544 F.Supp.2d 1080 (S.D. Calif. 2008)

(In determining patent misuse, courts must apply the "rule of reason" and ask whether the questioned practice imposes an unreasonable restraint on competition, taking into account multiple factors including market conditions before and after the restraint was imposed, and the restraints history, nature and effect).

Additional Information

1. RAYMOND T. NIMMER & JEFF C. DODD, MODERN LICENSING LAW §§ 13:30–31 (2009).

2. 1 WILLIAM C. HOLMES, INTELLECTUAL PROPERTY AND ANTITRUST LAW § 1:7 (2009).

3. 10A FLETCHER CYC. CORP. § 5027.10 (2009).

4. Arthur M. Peslak, *Drafting License Agreements to Avoid Patent Misuse and Antitrust Problems*, 161-JUN N.J. LAW 36 (1994).

5. MICHAEL A. EPSTEIN & FRANK L. POLITANO, DRAFTING LICENSE AGREEMENTS § 4.02 (4th ed. 2009).

6. 37 AM. JUR. *Proof of Facts* 3d 315 (2009).

7. Patricia A. Martone, Richard M. Feustel, *The Patent Misuse Defense — Does It Still Have Vitality*, 832 PLI/PAT 145 (2005).

8. Joe Potenza et al., *Patent Misuse — The Critical Balance, A Patent Lawyer's View*, 15 FED. CIRCUIT B.J. 69 (2005).

9. David W. Van Etten, *Everyone in the Patent Pool: U.S. Philips Corp. v. International Trade Commission*, 22 BERKELEY TECH. L.J. 241 (2007).

10. Somnath Bhattacharyya, *U.S. Philips Corp. v. International Trade Commission: Seeking a Better Tie between Antitrust Law and Package Licensing*, 40 COLUM. J.L. & SOC. PROBS. 267 (2007).

11. Daniel P. Homiller, *Patent Misuse in Patent Pool Licensing: From National Harrow to "The Nine No-Nos" to Not Likely*, 2006 DUKE L. & TECH. REV. 7 (2006).

12. Thomas F. Cotter, *Misuse*, 44 HOUS. L. REV. 901 (2007).

13. David McGowan, *What Tool Works Tells Us About Tailoring Patent Misuse Remedies*, 102 NW. U. L. REV. 421 (2008).

14. Philip B.C. Jones, *When the Reach Through Exceeds the Grasp: Court Rulings on a COX-2 Inhibitor Patent Lead Others to Consider Alternatives for Protecting Early-Stage Technology*, July 2004 MODERN DRUG DISCOVERY, 21–22, available at http://pubs.acs.org/subscribe/archive/mdd/v07/i07/pdf/704business2.pdf.

2.3 LICENSE TERMS

This section considers selected terms in license agreements. Included in this section are implied license terms, license grant clauses, license warranties, most-favored licensee clauses, license transfer restrictions, license post-sale restrictions, field-of-use restrictions, best efforts clauses, license royalties, licenses to improvements and indemnification clauses.

2.3.1 Implied License Terms

With one notable exception (i.e., the implied covenant of good faith and fair dealing), courts are generally loath to find implied contract terms or covenants. However, where the implication of a contract term is clearly necessary to effectuate the intentions of the parties in entering into the contract, and is consistent with language used in the contract and the external facts surrounding the contract, courts have been willing to imply contract terms. One author has cited five factors that must be considered before a term can be implied in a contract: (1) the term must be reasonable and equitable; (2) the term must be necessary to give business efficacy to the contract; (3) the term must be so obvious that "it goes without saying"; (4) the term must be capable of clear expression; and (5) the term must not contradict any express term in the contract. *See*, Sarah Hambury, *Implied License Terms in a Software License*, 6 CYBERSPACE LAWYER 29 (2006).

Courts will not imply a contract term merely because it seems reasonable, or because the contract is overly advantageous to one party, or because the implication of the contract term would be consistent with some real or supposed public policy. *See*, PAUL M. CULTOFF ET AL., 17A CORPUS JURIS SECUNDUM, § 346 (2008).

Courts are generally more willing to imply covenants of good faith and fair dealing in contracts. Indeed, as you will see, in New York and some other states, a covenant of good faith and fair dealing is implied in the performance of every contract; however, even here, a covenant of good faith and fair dealing cannot be implied if doing so would effectively nullify other express terms in the contract.

The three cases in this section deal with implied license terms in a variety of factual contexts. The first case, *Eli Lilly*, addresses the question of whether a use limitation in a patent license implies a negative covenant not to practice the patent for any other uses. The second case, *Hirsch*, involves a sponsored research agreement at a university. The issue raised in *Hirsch* is whether the sponsored research agreement and the parties' subsequent actions created an implied license. The final case, *Meijer*, involves a claim by a pharmaceutical company licensee that the licensor breached an implied covenant of good faith and fair dealing when it raised the wholesale price of the licensed drug by 400%.

ELI LILLY AND CO. v. GENENTECH, INC.
17 U.S.P.Q.2d 1531 (S.D. Ind. 1990)

DILLIN, J.

This cause is before the Court on the motions of Genentech, Inc. for partial summary judgment and Rule 11 sanctions, and the motion of Eli Lilly and Company for disqualification of Genentech's counsel. For the following reasons, these motions are denied.

Background

On August 25, 1978, Plaintiff Genentech, Inc. (Genentech), a California corporation, and Defendant Eli Lilly and Company (Lilly), an Indiana corporation, entered into a contract regarding the synthetic production of human insulin (the Insulin Agreement). The contract stated that Genentech had demonstrated an ability "to genetically engineer microorganisms capable of producing human polypeptide hormones and has acquired related patent rights." The contract further stated that Lilly had experience in the production of human insulin from animal pancreas glands. The contract provides that its terms shall be governed by California law. Dr. Walter E. Buting, then a Lilly patent lawyer, negotiated the Insulin Agreement on behalf of Lilly.

In essence, the Insulin Agreement gave Lilly access to Genentech biological material which Lilly in turn was to use in developing and marketing synthetically produced human insulin. Lilly agreed to pay Genentech a royalty fee in exchange. Under Article VI of the agreement, Genentech granted to Lilly an exclusive license to use its biological material "for the limited purpose of manufacturing, selling and using Recombinant Insulin without regard to Genentech Patent Rights. . ." In its complaint, Genentech claims, *inter alia*, that Lilly's research and production exceeded the scope of this limited patent license. Specifically, Genentech contends that Lilly used the biological material referred to in the agreement to develop a human growth hormone (hGH) product in order to compete with Genentech's hGH product. Genentech asserts that such production beyond the scope of the license is a breach of the parties' contract.

Lilly and Genentech are also embroiled in a related patent infringement suit. In the Patent Action, Lilly seeks a declaratory judgment that several Genentech patents for the synthetic expression and purification of hGH are invalid and not infringed by Lilly's hGH process. The Genentech expression patents were prosecuted before the Patent and Trademark Office in part by Dr. Walter E. Buting.

Dr. Buting, who served as a Lilly patent lawyer from 1965 through 1984, accepted a position as Chief Patent Counsel of Genentech on February 24, 1984. While realizing that "potential conflicts" of interest were inevitable in his new employment, the only constraint Lilly placed on Buting's future employment was that he carefully examine "where he got what and of the line between Lilly trade secrets and other confidential information . . . ."

After Buting joined Genentech, Lilly officials were aware that he was engaged in activity substantially similar to his former duties at Lilly which was potentially adverse to Lilly. In fact, Lilly contacted Buting directly as Genentech's legal representative on at least two occasions regarding such activity. Lilly contacted Buting in 1985 to resolve questions of interpretation under the 1978 Insulin Agreement. In 1986, Lilly officials again contacted Buting to inform him that Lilly had moved to revoke Genentech rDNA patents in the United Kingdom (U.K.) which are parallel to the patents-in-suit herein. In his affidavit, Buting states that he told Lilly's counsel that he assumed Lilly would have no objection to his participation in the U.K. revocation proceedings. Lilly does not dispute Buting's recollection, but claims that it only agreed that Buting could play a "peripheral" role in the U.K. proceedings.

Lilly now asserts that Buting breached duties that he owed to it under the rules of professional responsibility through his legal work for Genentech. As a result, Lilly argues that Buting, Genentech's in-house legal counsel and outside litigation counsel must be disqualified from representing Genentech in the co-pending cases. Genentech has responded by claiming that Lilly breached Rule 11, F.R.Civ.P. by filing its disqualification motion.

Discussion

I. Motion for Partial Summary Judgment:

The motion for partial summary judgment is focused on Genentech's contention that Lilly used Genentech materials to develop products other than insulin. Genentech argues that this alleged practice by Lilly breaches the following section of the license agreement:

Article VI

GRANT OF RIGHTS TO LILLY

6.01 Use of Recombinant Microorganisms and Know-how Free of Genentech Patent Rights. Subject to the payments of royalty as provided in Article VIII and the fulfillment of the other terms and conditions of this Agreement, Genentech hereby grants to Lilly the exclusive, irrevocable world-wide right with the right to grant sublicenses, to use all Genentech Recombinant Microorganisms for the limited purpose of manufacturing, selling and using Recombinant Insulin without regard to Genentech Patent Rights, and in connection only with such production, sale and use, to use all technical information and know-how supplied by Genentech hereunder. Rights granted hereunder shall include the right to practice under any applicable Genentech Patent Right.

The license agreement also included an integration clause which stated that the written contract "constitutes the entire Agreement between the Parties . . . supersedes all previous Agreements, whether written or oral," and can be modified only "in [a] writing . . . signed by the Party against whom such modification or waiver is sought."

Genentech seeks judgment as a matter of law that § 6.01 of the Insulin Agreement includes a covenant by Lilly not to use Genentech Recombinant Microorganisms (G.R.M.s) for non-insulin purposes. In short, Genentech's motion for summary judgment must be denied because such a negative covenant cannot be implied as a matter of law.

The United States Supreme Court approved the use of limited patent licenses in 1938, recognizing them as essentially a waiver of the patentee's right to sue. In *Talking Pictures*, the defendant-licensee was given the right to "manufacture . . . and to sell [amplifiers] only for radio amateur reception and radio broadcast reception." The Court observed that the patent license at issue "amount[ed] to no more than a mere waiver of the right to sue." Thus, the Court reasoned that "[b]y knowingly making sales . . . outside the scope of the license, the transformer company infringed the patents embodied in the amplifiers."

Subsequent caselaw has followed *Talking Pictures* by interpreting limited licenses as waivers of the right to sue so that violation of the license restriction gives rise to a patent infringement suit. These subsequent cases have also reasoned that violation of the license restriction does not give rise to an action for breach of contract.

In *Lanova Corporation v. Atlas Imperial Diesel*, the license granted to Atlas the right "to manufacture engines . . . embodying the inventions of its patents, said license being limited to stationary, marine, industrial and automotive engines" having a limited piston displacement. Atlas allegedly used the patented technology to manufacture engines which were larger than the license specified. Following the reasoning of *Talking Pictures* that a limited license is a mere waiver of a patent infringement suit, the court reasoned that the license did not prohibit Atlas from manufacturing larger engines:

> [T]he only thing which the defendant has given up by signing the license is its promise to pay royalties for the use of the patents in making engines within the license limits. The contract itself does not *restrain* it from doing anything which it could not have done otherwise; in effect, the license merely binds the defendant to pay for a limited use without fear of being sued for infringement.

The court stated that Atlas' use of patented technology to produce larger engines:

> is not barred by the license itself; the contract merely does not give that right. If the defendant should use the patents over and above the limitation, the plaintiff would have no remedy under the contract but could sue for infringement.

In *B&J Manufacturing Co. v. Hennessy Industries, Inc.*, then District Judge Flaum further developed rules to apply when a licensee has allegedly produced goods beyond the scope of the limited patent license. Judge Flaum followed the rule set down in *Lanova* and *Florida Canada Corp.* that a negative covenant could not be implied as a matter of law in the following excerpt, which is closely analogous to the case at hand:

[T]he purpose of the [license] agreement is to grant Hennessy the limited use of plaintiff's patents in return for the payment of royalties. As long as defendant has paid the royalties the plaintiff is receiving the benefits of his bargain. Moreover, it is not as if the plaintiff will lose any rights by the court's failure to imply such a negative covenant since B & J can, as it has, sue for patent infringement on those items manufactured outside the license grant. Therefore, this court agrees with the position enunciated in *Florida Canada Corp. v. Union Carbide & Carbon Co.*, that no such negative covenant should be implied as a matter of law, especially in the face of an express integration clause.

Judge Flaum also noted that a very high standard of proof must be met before a negative covenant could be implied under the facts of *B&J Manufacturing Co*:

As a general rule, covenants may only be implied into an integrated agreement "when the implied term is not inconsistent with some express term of the contract and where there arises from the language of the contract itself, and the circumstances under which it was entered into, an inference that it is absolutely necessary to introduce the term to effectuate the intention of the parties."

The court concluded that a negative covenant could not be implied under the facts in *B & J Manufacturing Co.* because the evidence showed that the subject of manufacturing items beyond the scope of the license was never considered by the parties. Rather, the evidence indicated that the intent of the parties in drafting the license was "to delineate what Hennessy could do under the agreement and not what Hennessy was prohibited from doing."

Based on the above cited law, the Court cannot imply a covenant by Lilly not to produce non-insulin products into its Insulin Agreement with Genentech as a matter of law. Unlike *B&J Manufacturing Co.*, however, disputed issues of fact remain regarding whether implying a covenant by Lilly prohibiting its non-insulin use of G.R.M.s into the Insulin Agreement is "absolutely necessary" to effectuate the intent of the parties. In *B&J Manufacturing Co.*, the evidence on summary judgment showed that the intent of the parties in drafting the licensing agreement was "to delineate what Hennessy could do under the agreement and not what Hennessy was prohibited from doing." In this case, the parties have presented conflicting affidavits regarding their intent in drafting § 6.01 of the agreement. It is also clear that discovery regarding the negotiation of the Insulin Agreement is far from complete.

For the above stated reasons, the Court cannot imply a negative covenant into the integrated Insulin Agreement as a matter of law. The Court is similarly unable to grant summary judgment because the facts regarding the parties' intent in drafting § 6.01 are in dispute and not yet fully developed. Thus, Genentech's motion for partial summary judgment is denied.

QUESTIONS

1. Why can't a negative covenant be implied as a matter of law?

2. What difference does it make whether the suit is for breach of contract or for infringement of the patent?

3. How would you draft a license to sue for breach of contract in the event the licensee uses the licensed technology beyond the use expressly granted in the license?

HIRSCH-CHEMIE LTD. v. JOHNS HOPKINS UNIVERSITY
36 U.S.P.Q.2d 1395 (4th Cir. 1995)

PHILLIPS, S.J.

In this diversity case, Hirsch-Chemie Limited and its subsidiaries, Hirsch-Scionics Limited and Hirsch Cinemedic Corporation, (collectively, "Hirsch") appeal from orders granting summary judgment in favor of The Johns Hopkins University ("Johns Hopkins") on Hirsch's two breach of contract claims and on one of Johns Hopkins's two counterclaims, and granting prejudgment interest to Johns Hopkins on its second counterclaim after a bench trial. With one modification respecting the rate of prejudgment interest to be recovered on the second counterclaim, we affirm.

I

Hirsch-Chemie Limited and its subsidiaries are all Virginia corporations engaged in biotechnology-related businesses. Johns Hopkins is a major research university in the state of Maryland. In 1983, Hirsch and Johns Hopkins entered into two contracts. Under the first, the Joint Development Agreement ("J.D.A."), Hirsch provided Johns Hopkins with approximately one million dollars in cash and equipment to further certain cancer research. In return for its investment, Hirsch obtained a "first option to acquire a worldwide royalty-bearing license . . . to make, have made, use and sell" products and inventions developed through the research. By its terms, the J.D.A. was to expire three years from its effective date (July 27, 1983) "unless sooner terminated or extended by mutual consent" or unless a license was granted, in which case the J.D.A. would continue in effect for the duration of the license. Any license granted was to be in effect for at least eleven years. The J.D.A. could also be terminated by either party for a material breach of its terms by the other.

Johns Hopkins developed a product from the research and, in conformity with its contract obligations, notified Hirsch by letter dated October 30, 1985. Hirsch responded by letter dated November 22, 1985, that it wished to exercise its option and enter a licensing agreement. The parties dispute whether a license was ever created. On January 14, 1987, approximately three years and five months after the effective date of the J.D.A. (five months after the natural expiration date of the J.D.A.), Johns Hopkins notified Hirsch that it believed Hirsch had breached the J.D.A. by failing to submit production and sales goals necessary for the granting of a license agreement for that product. On April 16, 1987, after giving Hirsch time to cure its default, Johns Hopkins purported to terminate the J.D.A. and subsequently entered non-exclusive license agreements with at least three other licensees.

The second agreement between the parties, the License Agreement ("L.A."), gave Hirsch the exclusive right to develop and market products based upon a certain invention that Johns Hopkins had patented. Within thirty days of the effective date of the L.A. (August 18, 1983), Johns Hopkins was to turn over to Hirsch "all technical information and know-how" related to the invention that it had in its possession, "including prototypes." In return, Hirsch was to advance to Johns Hopkins approximately thirty thousand dollars. Hirsch also obligated itself to pay royalties to Johns Hopkins upon commercial sales of any products that it developed from the information given to it by Johns Hopkins and subsequently licensed and marketed. If no commercial sales took place within three years of the effective date of the L.A., Hirsch agreed to pay minimum annual royalties from the end of the third year. Each royalty payment was due within thirty days after the end of the royalty year.

Hirsch never licensed any products based on the invention or made any commercial sales covered by the L.A. On September 18, 1986, the first minimum royalty payment of fifteen thousand dollars became due; Hirsch made the payment on June 24, 1987. On September 18, 1987, the second royalty payment of thirty thousand dollars became due, but Hirsch never paid it. On November 4, 1987, Johns Hopkins terminated the L.A. on the ground that Hirsch had failed to make the required royalty payment after giving Hirsch notice and time to cure its default pursuant as required by the J.D.A.

On April 12, 1990, Hirsch sued Johns Hopkins for breach of contract based on the allegedly wrongful termination of the two agreements. Johns Hopkins filed two counterclaims against Hirsch, one for the second royalty payment due under the L.A. and one for breach of contract based on failure to pay maintenance costs of certain items of loaned equipment pursuant to an oral agreement between the parties.

Johns Hopkins moved for summary judgment on Hirsch's claims. The district court granted Johns Hopkins's motion, holding that Johns Hopkins was justified in terminating both contracts. As to the J.D.A., it held that summary judgment in favor of Johns Hopkins was appropriate because "Johns Hopkins terminated the J.D.A. according to its terms" and therefore had not breached the contract. It held that "the three year natural life of the [J.D.A.] had passed" and that, even if the parties had mutually agreed to extend the J.D.A. (which it doubted), Hirsch had breached the J.D.A. by failing to provide an essential term of the license, the "production and sales goals" for the marketing of the invention, and thus Johns Hopkins had properly terminated the J.D.A. for Hirsch's breach.

The district court also held that Johns Hopkins terminated the L.A. according to its terms. It explained that it was Hirsch's responsibility to obtain any necessary government approval for sales, that Hirsch neither sought nor obtained government approval nor made any sales, that Hirsch owed but failed to pay the second minimum royalty payment, and that Johns Hopkins was therefore justified in terminating the agreement due to Hirsch's breach. The district court rejected Hirsch's argument that it was excused from its obligation to seek government approval because Johns Hopkins did not provide it with a prototype of the invention. The district court concluded that Johns Hopkins had not breached the L.A. while Hirsch had, and that, as a matter of law, Johns Hopkins was therefore justified in terminating the L.A.

Johns Hopkins then moved for partial summary judgment on its counterclaim for the unpaid royalty installment and Hirsch moved for partial summary judgment on the counterclaim for maintenance costs. The district court granted Johns Hopkins's motion, awarding it $30,000, but denied Hirsch's motion on the ground that there were genuine issues of material fact regarding the alleged oral agreement for Hirsch to maintain the equipment. After a bench trial on the counterclaim for maintenance costs, a magistrate judge entered judgment in favor of Johns Hopkins, awarding it $16,704 plus prejudgment interest.

Hirsch now appeals from the summary judgments in Johns Hopkins's favor and from the magistrate judge's award of prejudgment interest on the maintenance costs counterclaim.

III

Hirsch argues first that its claim regarding Johns Hopkins's breach of the J.D.A. should not have been disposed of by summary judgment because genuine issues existed as to at least three material facts, namely: (1) whether and when a license was created; (2) whether and how long the parties extended the J.D.A.; and (3) whether Hirsch failed to use "best efforts" to market the allegedly licensed product. We disagree and therefore affirm the district court's grant of summary judgment.

Maryland contract law governs the construction of the J.D.A. Under Maryland law, as generally, where the language of a contract "is clear and unambiguous, the construction of the contract is a matter of law for the court and it must be presumed that the parties meant what they expressed." Moreover, "[t]he written language embodying the terms of an agreement will govern the rights and liabilities of the parties, irrespective of the intent of the parties at the time they entered into the contract."

The terms governing the duration of the J.D.A. are clear and unambiguous. The J.D.A. was to expire on July 26, 1986, so long as it was not extended by one of several means. It could have been extended by mutual consent of the parties. If a license were created, the J.D.A. would have been extended for the duration of the license. In addition, once Johns Hopkins developed a product that could be licensed, Hirsch had 180 days to exercise its option to obtain an exclusive license; if Johns Hopkins notified Hirsch that it had developed a product within 180 days of the expiration of the J.D.A., the J.D.A. would have been extended as necessary to allow Hirsch its allotted 180 days to exercise its option to obtain a license, the creation of which would have itself extended the J.D.A. even longer.

None of these eventualities occurred, and the J.D.A. consequently expired on July 26, 1986, three years after its execution. Johns Hopkins notified Hirsch Chemie that it had developed a product for which it had the option to obtain an exclusive license on October 30, 1985, more than 180 days before the natural expiration date of the J.D.A., July 26, 1986. Therefore, the 180-day option period did not extend the J.D.A.

Neither was the J.D.A. extended by the creation of a license. Hirsch argues that the J.D.A. itself created a license or, in the alternative, that a license was created by an exchange of letters between agents of the two parties. We disagree. The J.D.A. did not contain all the essential terms of a license, but instead contemplated the creation of future licenses. Paragraph 8.4 states that the J.D.A. "shall not be construed to grant any license from . . . Johns Hopkins to Hirsch except as expressly provided herein." Paragraph 4.2 expressly provides that Johns Hopkins grants Hirsch an option to acquire licenses as opposed to actually granting a license itself. Other paragraphs refer to licenses to be granted in the future and terms to be specified later. We therefore conclude that, by its unambiguous terms, the J.D.A. did not convey a license to Hirsch, but merely granted it the first right to negotiate for an exclusive license on all products developed by Johns Hopkins during certain research.

The parties did negotiate and attempt to create a license agreement but were unsuccessful in that endeavor. An agent of Johns Hopkins wrote to Hirsch on October 30, 1985, notifying Hirsch that it had developed a product for licensing and that, if Hirsch wished to exercise its option to acquire a license, it should respond in writing and then Johns Hopkins would draft a proposed license agreement. Hirsch agents responded twice, once by letter dated November 22, 1985, and once by letter dated February 25, 1986, stating that Hirsch did indeed desire to exercise its option. These letters referred to the draft license agreement, noting that its consummation would be "subject to approval by all parties involved." An agent of Johns Hopkins wrote another letter on September 5, 1986, in which it assigned a license number to the item in question and discussed the matter of Hirsch's paying the costs of patenting the invention. Hirsch argues that the initial exchange of letters constitutes a binding offer and acceptance of a license. Hirsch also contends that the September letter, and Hirsch's subsequent payment of the patenting costs, is proof that a license existed, noting specifically that Hirsch was obliged to pay patent costs only for licensed products according to J.D.A. Hirsch contends that the written license agreement anticipated by the parties would only have memorialized their already-existent contract and would have been a mere formality.

We disagree with these contentions. The parties were simply in the process of negotiating the terms of a license agreement. They clearly anticipated consummating the license only after the material terms, as formulated in a draft written license agreement, were agreed upon. No such agreement ever materialized, apparently due largely to the inability of the parties to agree upon one material term of the license, production and sales goals for marketing the invention. The September 5, 1986, letter itself noted that the same term was still unsettled, leaving the license agreement incomplete; this statement negates any inference to be drawn from that letter that the granting of a license number and payment of patent fees were anything more than good faith gestures along the way to the ultimate agreement. Apparently, the parties never finalized a written license agreement despite repeated requests by Johns Hopkins for Hirsch to provide production and sales goals for approval and despite Hirsch's implicit acknowledgment that producing proposed goals was its responsibility by asking for more time to produce them.

The controlling principle of contract formation here is that expressed in the Restatement (Second) of Contracts Section 27 (1979):

> Manifestations of assent that are in themselves sufficient to conclude a contract will not be prevented from so operating by the fact that the parties also manifest an intention to prepare and adopt a written memorial thereof; *but the circumstances may show that the agreements are preliminary negotiations.*

The undisputed circumstances here establish as a matter of law that the parties were merely engaging in preliminary negotiations and meant to form a binding license agreement only with the execution of a written license agreement. We therefore conclude that the parties never extended the J.D.A. by creating a license.

Finally, the J.D.A. was not extended by the mutual consent of the parties to or beyond April 16, 1987, the date upon which Johns Hopkins purported to terminate the J.D.A., and therefore its three year term expired on July 26, 1986. The J.D.A. never was extended in writing, as is required by J.D.A. Para. 8.10, which states that "no modification or amendment to this Agreement shall be effective unless agreed to in writing, executed by both parties." The record indicates that there may have been an oral agreement to extend the J.D.A., but only for one month, at Hirsch's request, for the limited purpose of allowing Hirsch more time to develop a production and sales plan. This one-month extension also expired without finalization of a license agreement.

Hirsch argues that the behavior of the parties implies that they mutually agreed to an extension of the J.D.A., noting that Johns Hopkins did not try to terminate the J.D.A. on July 26, 1986, that the parties continued to negotiate towards a license agreement for several months after the natural expiration date of the J.D.A., and that Johns Hopkins eventually wrote two letters in which it purported to terminate the J.D.A. on April 16, 1987, implying that it believed the J.D.A. was still in force at that time. We disagree that such an inference properly could be drawn from the parties' behavior.

At most, such activity may be evidence of a subsequent oral agreement with the same terms as the original agreement. The controlling principle here is that expressed, for example, in 17A C.J.S. *Contracts* Section 449, at 561 (1963): "the fact that the parties by their acts and declarations indicate an intention to treat a written contract as continuing after the time prescribed in it for its termination will not have the effect of continuing such contract, although it may show a subsequent oral agreement on the same terms." Hirsch did not argue or offer proof that the parties made a subsequent express oral agreement on the same terms as the J.D.A. Therefore, because the unambiguous terms of the J.D.A. mandate that it expired on July 26, 1986, or August 26, 1986, at the latest, without any provision for its automatic extension, any activity by the parties indicating that they believed the J.D.A. to continue in effect after that time was ineffective to extend the J.D.A.

Moreover, even if the parties had somehow extended the J.D.A. by implicit mutual consent, the claim was properly dismissed via summary judgment. Paragraph 6.1 provides that Hirsch "will devote its best efforts to establishing and expanding a market for the various [licensed] products manufactured pursuant hereto." Hirsch argues that the "best efforts" requirement applies only to actual marketing efforts and not to the requirement in paragraph 6.3 that it "specify production and sales goals." In addition, it contends that it did make significant efforts to market the invention and that there is a genuine issue as to whether those efforts met the best efforts requirement. However, Hirsch could not very well establish and expand a market for Johns Hopkins's invention without setting production and sales goals, gaining Johns Hopkins's approval of those goals, and obtaining a license to make and sell the products. Having failed to take those steps, it therefore failed to use its best efforts to market the invention and Johns Hopkins would have been justified in terminating the J.D.A. for cause had it not already expired. See J.D.A. Para. 6.3 ("[F]uture license agreements for licensed products will specify production and sales goals to be mutually agreed upon and . . . failure of Hirsch and its licensees to meet these goals could result in termination of the license or conversion to nonexclusive."); Para. 6.5 ("Either party may terminate this Agreement if the other party shall breach any material provision of this Agreement and such breach shall continue un-remedied for a period of ninety (90) days after written notice of such breach is sent to the breaching party.").

In sum, we hold that there is no genuine issue of material fact warranting a trial regarding Hirsch's claim that Johns Hopkins breached the J.D.A. The J.D.A. expired on July 26, 1986, or on August 26, 1986, at the latest, and Johns Hopkins could not therefore have breached it at a later date. Additionally, even if the J.D.A. was extended by implicit mutual consent, Johns Hopkins was justified in terminating it for cause on grounds of Hirsch's material breach and did so according to its terms by giving Hirsch the required notice and opportunity to cure its default.

IV

We likewise conclude that the district court properly granted summary judgment dismissing Hirsch's claim that Johns Hopkins breached the L.A. and granting Johns Hopkins's motion for summary judgment on its counterclaim for royalties due under the L.A. Hirsch argues that genuine issues existed as to several material facts, including (1) when royalties became due, if ever; (2) whose responsibility it was to obtain government approval of products to be sold; and (3) whether Hirsch's failure to obtain government approval was excused by Johns Hopkins's failure to develop its invention to the point of commercial marketability or by Johns Hopkins's failure to give Hirsch a prototype of its invention. We disagree, and therefore affirm the district court's grants of summary judgment of both the claim and the counterclaim.

Maryland contract law also governs the construction of the L.A. The L.A. provided that, if no commercial sales of the invention occurred within the first three years after the effective date of the L.A., minimum royalty payments would become due beginning at the end of the third year. Delay of payment would only be excused if the first sale was postponed "by reason of a delay in receiving the required governmental approval for such sale." If Hirsch failed to pay the minimum royalties when due, Johns Hopkins had the option of terminating the contract. Hirsch contends that, because no government approval was ever obtained, no royalty payment was ever due, and that, because no royalty was due, Johns Hopkins breached the L.A. by purporting to terminate it without justification. Hirsch also maintains that it was not responsible for seeking and obtaining government approval and, in the alternative, was prevented from obtaining government approval by Johns Hopkins's failure to provide a prototype of the invention and a commercially marketable product that could be approved, or that there is at least a genuine issue as to these facts.

We disagree. First, we agree with the district court that under the L.A.'s provisions, Hirsch was responsible, as a matter of law, for obtaining government approval. Although the L.A. does not explicitly state this, the contract as a whole plainly so contemplates. In the agreement's preamble, Hirsch declares that it "wishes to obtain rights to the above-noted invention, and technical information and know how in support of its development and sales efforts in this area." Paragraph 2.1 then provides that Hirsch receives "the rights to make, have made, use, have used, sell, and have sold the Licensed Products" developed from Johns Hopkins's invention. These provisions and others clarify that Hirsch is responsible for developing, making, marketing and selling licensed products based upon the invention. Included in these obligations would naturally fall the obligation to seek necessary government approval for any sale of any product developed by Hirsch. Hirsch never proffered any evidence to contradict the plain implication of these provisions save for an affidavit of one of its officers stating that Hirsch subjectively believed the responsibility to be Johns Hopkins's. That of course could not suffice to put the intended meaning of this matter in issue.

Neither did Hirsch sufficiently counter Johns Hopkins's plain showing that the custom in the industry is for the licensee, not the licensor, to obtain government approval for sales. Relying on the rule that "a usage, to be admissible, must be proved to be known to the parties, and to be so general and well established that knowledge and adoption of it may be presumed," Hirsch proffered that it had no actual knowledge, but "knowledge of a trade usage will be imputed to persons in the same trade." And, where a usage exists in reference to a particular trade or business, the contracts of parties engaged in that business "must be presumed to be cognizant of the usage," unless it is expressly excluded. Here, it is indisputable on the summary judgment record that Hirsch is a biotechnology company, engaged in the business of marketing medical technology, contracting for a license to market an invention under the L.A., and attempting to contract for a license to market a product under the J.D.A. There is no suggestion that the parties expressly excluded this trade usage from implicit inclusion in the L.A. Construing the instrument as a whole and in light of this trade usage, we therefore conclude that there is no genuine issue of material fact on this point and that as a matter of law Hirsch, as licensee under the L.A., bore the responsibility for obtaining government approval for any products it developed from Johns Hopkins's invention.

Second, we agree with the district court that Hirsch was not prevented from obtaining government approval by Johns Hopkins's failure to provide a prototype of its invention. Paragraph 4.3 of the L.A. provides:

4.3 Within thirty (30) days after execution of this Agreement, [Johns Hopkins] shall furnish to [Hirsch] . . . all technical information and know-how, *including prototypes*, which it has *in its possession* and which relate to the [invention].

The district court held that Johns Hopkins had complied with this paragraph by turning over any information in its possession. It also held that Johns Hopkins did not have to turn over a prototype because it had none in its possession except a very primitive device unusable to Hirsch and because paragraph 4.3 did not require it to create one. We agree. Johns Hopkins offered proof that (1) the only existing prototype was primitive and unusable to Hirsch; (2) it could only be operated in a hospital with the special power lines and x-ray shields available there, so Hirsch always brought interested buyers to the hospital for demonstrations; (3) the invention's inventor was the only person able to operate the primitive prototype; (4) an agent of Hirsch admitted that no prototype existed at the time the L.A. was signed; and (5) an agent of Hirsch admitted in a 1987 meeting that the inventor had done everything and delivered everything requested by Hirsch. Hirsch never offered evidence to contradict Johns Hopkins's offered proof. We therefore conclude that Hirsch has failed to make a showing sufficient to raise a genuine issue as to whether Johns Hopkins was obliged to supply a prototype of its invention and whether Hirsch can be excused from seeking government approval by any failure to do so.

Third, Hirsch was not prevented from obtaining government approval by Johns Hopkins's failure to provide a commercially marketable product. Hirsch did not bargain for a commercially marketable product. In the preamble to the L.A., Johns Hopkins merely warranted that it was "the owner of an invention relating to on-line treatment monitoring for radiation teletherapy" and made no representations regarding its stage of development. All Hirsch contracted for under the clear terms of the contract was a license for the invention as it existed as of August 1983; no provision of the L.A. required Johns Hopkins to improve or further develop the invention. Moreover, several provisions state that Hirsch itself would develop the invention into marketable products. Hirsch proffered some evidence of its subjective expectation that Johns Hopkins's invention would be commercially marketable without further development by Hirsch, but it is irrelevant.

Because the terms of the L.A. clearly did not require Johns Hopkins to provide a commercially marketable invention, no genuine issue exists as to whether Hirsch is excused from its obligation to obtain government approval by the non-marketability of Johns Hopkins's invention.

Finally, there is no genuine issue regarding when, if ever, the royalties became due. Hirsch argues that, because government approval was not, and could not be, obtained, no royalties ever became due. However, because Hirsch never sought or obtained government approval, there was no delay in receiving government approval that could operate to delay the due date of the first royalty payment under paragraph 3.3. There is therefore no doubt that the first royalty payment of $15,000 became due on September 18, 1986, and the second royalty payment of $30,000 became due on September 18, 1987. Hirsch paid the first, albeit late, but did not pay the second.

Johns Hopkins's right to terminate the contract for nonpayment of royalties is governed by L.A. Paragraphs 5.3 and 5.4. These paragraphs provide:

> 5.3 Upon breach or default of any of the terms and conditions of this Agreement, the defaulting party shall be given notice of such default in writing and a period of thirty (30) days after receipt of such notice to correct the breach or default.

> 5.4 In the event that the minimum annual royalties required under Section 3.2 hereinabove are not paid, [Johns Hopkins] may, at its option, terminate this Agreement or convert the exclusive license granted under Section 2.1 hereinabove to a non-exclusive license.

Because Hirsch withheld the second royalty payment without justification, Johns Hopkins properly terminated the L.A. Because Johns Hopkins gave Hirsch the required 30 days notice and otherwise complied with the requirements of the L.A., it did not breach the L.A. In contrast, Hirsch did breach the L.A. by withholding the second royalty payment.

We therefore affirm the district court's grant of summary judgment in favor of Johns Hopkins both on Hirsch's breach of contract claim and Johns Hopkins's counterclaim for the unpaid royalty.

QUESTIONS

1. Hirsch paid Johns Hopkins $1 million in cash and equipment to conduct cancer research under the Joint Development Agreement? Do you think Hirsch was entitled to more deferential treatment by Johns Hopkins?

2. Hopkins and Hirsch exchanged letters on the License Agreement. Hopkins assigned a number to the License Agreement and Hirsch paid the patent fees. Why were these actions not sufficient to constitute an implied license?

3. How could Hirsch have submitted production and sales goals for marketing the product developed under the J.D.A. when the product was still in the laboratory stages of research?

4. The court held that Hirsch breached the License Agreement by failing to pay royalties on the invention and failing to obtain government approval of the invention. Johns Hopkins, on the other hand, offered proof that the invention only existed in a primitive, prototype form and that it could only be operated in a hospital with special power lines and x-ray shields. On what basis were royalties owed to Johns Hopkins? Could Hirsch have obtained government approval of the invention without the active cooperation of Johns Hopkins?

5. If you were counsel to Hirsch, how would you have structured the Joint Development Agreement and License Agreement?

MEIJER, INC. v. ABBOTT LABORATORIES
544 F.Supp.2d 995 (N.D. Cal. 2008)

CLAUDIA WILKEN, DISTRICT JUDGE.

Defendant Abbott Labs moves to dismiss the complaint in each of these related actions, arguing that Plaintiffs' claims for monopolization and attempted monopolization of the market for boosted protease inhibitors are foreclosed by the recent Ninth Circuit case, *Cascade Health Solutions v. PeaceHealth*, 515 F.3d 883 (9th Cir.2008). Abbott moves separately to dismiss GlaxoSmithKline's (GSK) claims in the *SmithKline Beecham* case for breach of the implied covenant of good faith and fair dealing, violation of the North Carolina Unfair Trade Practices Act and violation of the North Carolina Prohibition Against Monopolization. Finally, Abbott moves to transfer the *SmithKline Beecham* case to Illinois. Plaintiffs oppose each of these motions. The matters were heard on March 6, 2008. Having considered oral argument and all of the papers submitted by the parties, the Court denies Abbott's motions.

BACKGROUND

Protease inhibitors (PIs) are considered the most potent class of drugs to combat the HIV virus. In 1996, Abbott introduced Norvir as a stand-alone PI with a daily recommended dose of 1,200 milligrams (twelve 100-mg capsules a day), priced at approximately eighteen dollars per day. Norvir is the brand name for a patented compound called ritonavir.

After Norvir's release, it was discovered that, when used in small quantities with another PI, Norvir would "boost" the antiviral properties of that PI. Not only did a small dose of Norvir — about 100 to 400 milligrams per day — make other PIs more effective and decrease the side effects associated with high doses, but it also slowed the rate at which HIV developed resistance to the effects of those PIs. The use of Norvir as a "booster" has enabled HIV patients to live longer. But the use of Norvir as a booster, and not a stand-alone PI, has also meant that the average daily price of Norvir has plummeted since Norvir was first introduced, because patients need a much smaller daily dose of Norvir when it is used as a booster compared to when it is used as a stand-alone PI. By 2003, the average price for a daily dose of Norvir was $1.71.

In 2000, Abbott introduced Kaletra, a single pill containing the PI lopinavir as well as ritonavir, which is used to boost the effects of lopinavir. Although effective and widely used, Kaletra causes some patients to experience significant side effects.

In 2003, two new PIs, Bristol-Myers Squibb's Reyataz and GSK's Lexiva, were about to be introduced to the market. Studies showed that, when boosted with Norvir, the new PIs were as effective as Kaletra, and were more convenient. In July, 2003, Reyataz was successfully introduced to the market. As a result, Kaletra's market share fell more than Abbott had anticipated. The average daily dose of Norvir also fell. Before Reyataz's release, the most common boosting dose of Norvir ranged from 200 milligrams to 400 milligrams a day. Clinical trials, however, showed that a Norvir dose of only 100 milligrams a day effectively boosted Reyataz.

On December 3, 2003, Abbott raised the wholesale price of Norvir by 400 percent while keeping the price of Kaletra constant. Abbott contends that it did this so that the price of Norvir would be more in line with the drug's enormous clinical value. Plaintiffs contend that the Norvir price increase was an illegal attempt to achieve an anti-competitive purpose in the "boosted market," which Plaintiffs define as the market for those PIs, such as Reyataz, Lexiva and Kaletra, that are prescribed for use with Norvir as a booster. Plaintiffs sued for, among other things, monopolization and attempted monopolization in violation of the Sherman Act, 15 U.S.C. § 2.

LEGAL STANDARD

I. Motion to Dismiss

A complaint must contain a "short and plain statement of the claim showing that the pleader is entitled to relief." Fed.R.Civ.P. 8(a). On a motion under Rule 12(b)(6) for failure to state a claim, dismissal is appropriate only when the complaint does not give the defendant fair notice of a legally cognizable claim and the grounds on which it rests. In considering whether the complaint is sufficient to state a claim, the court will take all material allegations as true and construe them in the light most favorable to the plaintiff.

DISCUSSION

****

B. State Law Claims

1. Breach of the Implied Covenant of Good Faith and Fair Dealing

GSK asserts a claim for breach of the implied covenant of good faith and fair dealing under New York law, which applies pursuant to the choice-of-law provision in the license agreement. In connection with this claim, GSK asserts that it was deprived of the benefit of the license agreement's bargain when Abbott raised the price of Norvir. GSK maintains that, when it agreed to pay substantial royalties for the right to market its PIs for use in conjunction with Norvir, it had a "reasonable expectation that Norvir would continue to be commercially available for use as a PI boosting agent and that future increases in the price of Norvir would be consistent with past increases." When Abbott raised the price of Norvir, GSK claims it acted in bad faith by intentionally "thwart[ing] GSK's ability to benefit from [its] contracted rights."

Under New York law, "[i]mplicit in all contracts is a covenant of good faith and fair dealing in the course of contract performance." Abbott has cited lower court cases from New York holding that a claim for breach of the implied covenant of good faith and fair dealing cannot take the place of a substantively nonviable breach of contract claim, and that a claim for the breach of the implied covenant of good faith and fair dealing may not be asserted independently of a breach of contract claim when it is based on the same facts. Neither of these is the situation here.

In addition, the New York Court of Appeals has held that a breach of the implied covenant of good faith and fair dealing can itself serve as the basis for a breach of contract claim. In *511 West 232nd Owners Corp. v. Jennifer Realty Co.*, the court permitted the plaintiffs to proceed on a breach of contract claim based on their allegation that the offering plan for the conversion of an apartment building into a cooperative included an implied promise by the sponsor to sell all unsold units within a reasonable time. Such a promise was not explicitly contained in the contract. The court held that, "[w]hile the duties of good faith and fair dealing do not imply obligations inconsistent with other terms of the contractual relationship," they do require that "neither party shall do anything which will have the effect of destroying or injuring the right of the other party to receive the fruits of the contract." Accordingly, a party may pursue a breach of contract claim for violation of "any promises which a reasonable person in the position of the promisee would be justified in understanding were included."

Here, GSK's second cause of action is entitled, "Breach of Covenant of Good Faith and Fair Dealing," not breach of contract. To the extent Abbott argues that this claim should be dismissed because it must be stated as a breach of contract claim, its argument fails. "The form of the complaint and the label attached by the pleader are not controlling, and it is enough that the pleader state the facts making out a cause of action." GSK alleges that Abbott undertook an implied obligation to continue to make Norvir commercially available and to keep future increases in the price of Norvir in line with past increases. Whether Abbott in fact undertook such an obligation is an issue of fact that is not appropriately determined on a motion to dismiss. Because such an implied obligation would not necessarily be inconsistent with the express terms of the license agreement, the Court finds that GSK has sufficiently plead a claim for breach of an implied term of the license agreement.

CONCLUSION

For the foregoing reasons, Abbott's motions to dismiss are DENIED. Abbott's motion to transfer the *SmithKline Beecham* case is also DENIED.

IT IS SO ORDERED.

QUESTIONS

1.   What was the contractual relationship between GSK and Abbott? How did GSK claim it was harmed by the wholesale price increase for Norvir?

2.   Prior to the discovery of Norvir's antiviral boosting properties, the price of Norvir was about $18.00/day. After the discovery of Norvir's antiviral boosting

properties, the price of Norvir fell to about $1.71/day. Assuming the wholesale price of Norvir was 75% of the retail price, the wholesale price at this time would have been approximately $1.28/day. Abbott increased the wholesale price of Norvir by 400% which would be about $6.40/day. Do you think this price increase is unreasonable given the initial price of Norvir and its powerful antiviral boosting properties?

3. The court finds that, under New York law, a breach of the implied covenant of good faith and fair dealing is itself a breach of contract. What difference would it make if the plaintiff were required to establish the breach of an express contract term in order to establish a breach of the implied covenant of good faith and fair dealing?

CASE NOTES

1. Lilly entered into a research collaboration and licensing agreement with Emisphere for development and use of Emisphere's "carrier compounds," which could potentially be used for oral administration of therapeutic proteins. Currently, therapeutic proteins, such as insulin, can only be administered through injections. The research collaboration and license focused on the oral administration of a parathyroid hormone (PTH) which regulates bone metabolism and can be used to treat osteoporosis. Under the terms of the license, Emisphere granted Lilly an exclusive license to use all of its technology for the "Field," which was defined as oral delivery of PTH. The license agreement stated that "Lilly shall not have any rights to use Emisphere Technology or Emisphere Program Technology other than insofar as they relate directly to the Field and are expressly granted herein." Unbeknownst to Emisphere, Lilly later initiated a secret research project using Emisphere's technology to develop a carrier compound for oral delivery of a glucagon-like peptide (GLP) used to treat diabetes and obesity. Lilly filed an international patent application for the GLP carrier compound and, after the application was published, Emisphere notified Lilly that it believed Lilly had breached the license agreement by using Emisphere's technology outside the licensed Field. Lilly claimed that the license restriction merely precluded implied license rights beyond those expressly stated, that Lilly was free to use Emisphere's technology in any way not expressly prohibited by the license, and that Emisphere's sole legal remedy was to sue for patent infringement. What result? *See* Eli Lilly and Company v. Emisphere Technologies, Inc., 408 F.Supp.2d 668 (S.D.Ind. 2006).

2. *See also* Shaw v. E.I. DuPont De Nemours & Co., 226 A.2d 903 (Vt. 1967) (Patent holder granted a license to manufacture, use and sell filaments with a maximum cross-sectional dimension; licensee manufactured and sold filaments with a larger cross-sectional dimension than allowed in the license; court held that patent holder was not limited to a federal lawsuit for infringement but could also assert a claim for breach of contract in state court; reaching the opposite conclusion from *Genentech*, the court found that there was an implied covenant not to exceed the scope of the license); Frederick B. Stevens, Inc. v. Steel & Tubes, 114 F.2d 815 (6th Cir. 1940) (Where owner of a patent grants a licensee the right to use a patented machine, the grant carries with it, by necessary implication, a license under any other patent of the licensor which would be infringed by operation under the grant);

Vacuum Concrete Corp. of America v. American Mach. & Foundry Co., 321 F.Supp. 771 (S.D.N.Y. 1972) (Where exclusive license agreement provided that licensor could manufacture and sell up to $300,000 worth of licensed product annually within licensed territory, that licensee was required to pay minimum royalties of $25,000 annually, and that licensor could terminate license if annual royalty payments did not amount to $100,000 at the end of four years, court could not imply a covenant on part of licensee to exercise alleged standard of diligence in exploiting the licensed device); Havel v. Kelsey-Hayes Co., 83 A.D.2d 380 (N.Y. App. Div. 1981) (Where exclusive license agreement for use and dissemination of a patented process provided that licensor would receive 25% of all lump sum payments and 40% of all royalties paid to licensee by sub-licensees, that licensee would pay minimum royalties of $20,000 per year, but that licensor's sole remedy for failure to receive minimum royalties was to terminate license, court could imply promise by licensee to exercise reasonable diligence to exploit the patented process; where the essence of the contract is the grant of a license under which the fate of the subject matter is placed exclusively with the licensee for the purposes of exploitation and profit, implicit in such an agreement is the licensee's obligation to exploit the license); Western Geophysical Co. of America, Inc. v. Bolt Associates, Inc., 584 F.2d 1164 (2d Cir. 1978) (Where exclusive license required licensee to use its best efforts to promote worldwide licensing and use of patented device, but did not mandate that licensee sublicense patented device, licensee's attempts to improve patented device before use and sublicense satisfied best efforts requirement); Beraha v. Baxter Health Care Corp., 956 F.2d 1436 (7th Cir. 1992) (Even if letter formed part of the exclusive patent license agreement, statement of licensee in the letter that it would "do [its] very best to make this project a success" was too vague to be enforceable as a best efforts clause under Illinois law); Mechanical Ice Tray Corp. v. General Motors Corp., 144 F.2d 720 (2d Cir. 1944) (Where consideration for a grant of property lies wholly in payments based upon earnings of property transferred, a covenant to exploit transferred property in good faith to make it produce income will ordinarily be implied).

Additional Information

1. Lawrence J. Eckstrom, 1 Eckstrom's Licensing in Foreign and Domestic Operations §§ 2:13, 3:42 (2010).

2. John G. Mills Et al., 3 Patent Law Fundamentals § 19:7 (2010).

3. 69 C.J.S. Patents § 355 (2010).

4. Raymond T. Nimmer, Jeff Dodd, Modern Licensing Law § 9:48 (2010).

5. Corporate Counsel Guide to Licensing § 13:8 (2010).

6. Modern Patent Law Precedent B210 (8th ed. 2007).

7. Kenneth A. Adams, *Understanding "Best Efforts" and its Variants (including drafting recommendations)*, 50 No. 4 Prac. Law 11 (2004).

8. J. C. Bruno, *"Best Efforts" Defined*, 71 Mich. B.J. 74 (1992).

9. Philip B.C. Jones, *Violation of a Patent License Restriction: Breach of Contract or Patent Infringement?*, 33 IDEA 225 (1993).

2.3.2   Grant Clauses

The grant clause in a license agreement defines the intellectual property being licensed and how the licensed intellectual property may be used. In the case of patent licenses, the definition of the intellectual property being licensed is most often described in terms of issued or pending patent application numbers (e.g., U.S. Patent No. 7,188,069). However, patent licenses can also describe the licensed intellectual property in terms of a specific technology product or process (e.g., Ritonavir and the process for making it). In the case of copyright licenses, the definition of the intellectual property being licensed is most often described by the name of a computer program (e.g., Multilink Advanced Operating System). However, copyright licenses can also be described in terms of a registered copyright number (e.g., TXu001597925).

The grant clause also must define how the licensed intellectual property may be used. In the case of patents, the patent owner has the exclusive right to make, use, sell and import the patent subject matter. The grant clause must provide which of these exclusive rights is being conveyed in the license agreement. In the case of copyrights, the copyright owner has the exclusive right to reproduce, prepare derivative works, distribute and display the copyrighted work. Again, the grant clause must provide which of these exclusive rights is being conveyed in the license agreement.

The first case in this section, *Apple v. Microsoft*, deals with an ambiguous description of a licensed audio-visual copyright. Does the license cover individual visual displays in a graphical user interface (GUI) or does the license cover only the specific GUI itself? The second case, *Intel v. U.S. Int'l Trade Comm.*, deals with an ambiguous description of the licensed rights. Does the license allow the licensee to make the licensed products (serve as a foundry) for third-party firms or is the licensee only permitted to make the licensed products for its own use and sale? As you read the cases, consider how you would have drafted the licenses to avoid these ambiguities.

APPLE COMPUTER, INC. v. MICROSOFT CORP.
35 F.3d 1435 (9th Cir. 1994)

RYMER, CIRCUIT JUDGE.

Lisa and Macintosh are Apple computers. Each has a graphical user interface ("GUI") which Apple Computer, Inc. registered for copyright as an audiovisual work. Both GUIs were developed as a user-friendly way for ordinary mortals to communicate with the Apple computer; the Lisa Desktop and the Macintosh Finder are based on a desktop metaphor with windows, icons and pull-down menus which can be manipulated on the screen with a hand-held device called a mouse. When Microsoft Corporation released Windows 1.0, having a similar GUI, Apple complained. As a result, the two agreed to a license giving Microsoft the right to use and sublicense derivative works generated by Windows 1.0 in present and future products. Microsoft released Windows 2.03 and later, Windows 3.0; its licensee, Hewlett-Packard Company (HP), introduced NewWave 1.0 and later,

NewWave 3.0, which run in conjunction with Windows to make IBM-compatible computers easier to use. Apple believed that these versions exceed the license, make Windows more "Mac-like," and infringe its copyright. This action followed.

In a series of published rulings, the district court construed the agreement to license visual displays in the Windows 1.0 interface, not the interface itself; determined that all visual displays in Windows 2.03 and 3.0 were in Windows 1.0 except for the use of overlapping windows and some changes in the appearance and manipulation of icons; dissected the Macintosh, Windows and NewWave interfaces based on a list of similarities submitted by Apple to decide which are protectable; and applied the limiting doctrines of originality, functionality, standardization, *scenes a faire* and merger to find no copying of protectable elements in Windows 2.03 or 3.0, and to limit the scope of copyright protection to a handful of individual elements in NewWave. The court then held that those elements in NewWave would be compared with their equivalent Apple elements for substantial similarity, and that the NewWave and Windows 2.03 and 3.0 works as a whole would be compared with Apple's works for virtual identity. When Apple declined to oppose motions for summary judgment of noninfringement for lack of virtual identity, however, judgments in favor of Microsoft and HP were entered.

Apple asks us to reverse because of two fundamental errors in the district court's reasoning. First, Apple argues that the court should not have allowed the license for Windows 1.0 to serve as a partial defense. Second, Apple contends that the court went astray by dissecting Apple's works so as to eliminate unprotectable and licensed elements from comparison with Windows 2.03, 3.0 and NewWave as a whole, incorrectly leading it to adopt a standard of virtual identity instead of substantial similarity. We disagree.

The district court's approach was on target. In so holding, we readily acknowledge how much more complex and difficult its task was than ours. The district court had to grapple with graphical user interfaces in the first instance — and for the first time, with a claim of copying a computer program's artistic look as an audiovisual work instead of program codes registered as a literary work. In this case there is also the unusual, added complexity of a license that arguably covers some or most of the allegedly infringing works. The district court therefore had to cut new paths as it went along; we have the luxury of looking at the case at the end of the trip. From this vantage point, it is clear that treatment of Apple's GUIs, whose visual displays are licensed to a great degree and which are a tool for the user to access various functions of a computer in an aesthetically and ergonomically pleasing way, follows naturally from a long line of copyright decisions which recognizes that works cannot be substantially similar where analytic dissection demonstrates that similarities in expression are either authorized, or arise from the use of common ideas or their logical extensions.

We therefore hold:

(1) Because there was an agreement by which Apple licensed the right to make certain derivative works, the district court properly started with the license to determine what Microsoft was permitted to copy. Infringement cannot be founded on a licensed similarity. We read Microsoft's license as the district court did, to cover visual displays — not the Windows 1.0 interface itself. That being so, the

court correctly decided first to identify which visual displays in Windows 2.03, 3.0 and NewWave are licensed and which are not.

(2) The district court then properly proceeded to distinguish ideas from expression, and to "dissect" unlicensed elements in order to determine whether the remaining similarities lack originality, flow naturally from basic ideas, or are one of the few ways in which a particular idea can be expressed given the constraints of the computer environment. Dissection is not inappropriate even though GUIs are thought of as the "look and feel" of a computer, because copyright protection extends only to protectable elements of expression.

(3) Having found that the similarities in Windows 2.03 and 3.0 consist only of unprotectable or licensed elements, and that the similarities between protectable elements in Apple's works and NewWave are de minimis, the district court did not err by concluding that, to the extent there is creative expression left in how the works are put together, as a whole they can receive only limited protection. When the range of protectable and unauthorized expression is narrow, the appropriate standard for illicit copying is virtual identity. For these reasons, the GUIs in Windows 2.03, 3.0 and NewWave cannot be compared for substantial similarity with the Macintosh interface as a whole. Instead, as the district court held, the works must be compared for virtual identity.

Apple also challenges dismissal of the Macintosh Finder as a work in suit. Although we agree that the Finder, which is registered as a derivative work of the Lisa Desktop, should not have been dismissed as a work in suit because the underlying copyright on the Lisa has not expired, Apple's non-opposition to judgment as to the Lisa applies to the Finder as well. The Macintosh Finder is not incrementally different from the Lisa Desktop in any respect material to Apple's claims of infringement. There is accordingly no basis in the record for reversal on account of the erroneous dismissal of the Finder.

****

I

Analysis of Apple's infringement claims must start with an agreement signed in 1985 by Apple and Microsoft, which resolved a dispute about visual displays generated by Microsoft software products. The 1985 Agreement licensed the right to use the visual displays generated by Apple's Lisa and Macintosh graphic user interface programs which appeared as derivative works in Windows 1.0. As a result, to the extent that later versions of Windows and NewWave use the visual displays in Windows 1.0 (which came from Apple), that use is authorized.

Apple's appeal turns on whether the Agreement, properly construed, gives Microsoft the right to transfer individual elements or design features used in Windows 1.0. Apple particularly objects to any interpretation that would permit later Windows products to look more like the Macintosh than Windows 1.0 looked.

The plain language of the Agreement disposes of Apple's argument. It licenses Microsoft to use "these derivative works." "These derivative works" can only refer to Microsoft's acknowledgment that the "visual displays" generated by Windows 1.0 "are derivative works of the visual displays generated by Apple's Lisa and Macintosh graphic user interface programs." As the district court explained:

> Had it been the parties' intent to limit the license to the Windows 1.0 interface, they would have known how to say so. Instead, the "derivative works" covered by the license are identified as the "visual displays" in the Windows 1.0 interface, not the interface itself. And there is nothing in the 1985 Agreement that indicates that it was intended as a product license restricting Microsoft and its licensees to the use of the Windows 1.0 interface as a whole.

Apple contends that the term "visual displays" is ambiguous and can reasonably be construed (against Microsoft, as drafter) to distinguish audiovisual copyrights protecting visual works from literary copyrights protecting programs, and to cover use of so much of Apple's visual copyrights as were used in Windows 1.0 but no more. This argument fails because Apple tried to limit Microsoft's license to Windows 1.0 as a whole — but did not succeed. Apple's first draft included language providing that "at no time shall this grant extend to any appearance, look, feel, visual feature or operation other than that incorporated in Microsoft Windows." Microsoft, however, rejected this limitation. Thus, the parties had already staked out their positions by the time Microsoft produced the final draft. Accordingly, there is no basis for construing the Agreement to grant the narrow license Apple bargained for but gave up.

Apple relies on statements by various Microsoft employees in support of its ambiguity argument. These are unavailing because the Agreement has an integration clause which precludes contradicting its terms by collateral understandings. In any event, testimony by the two employees who opined that the phrase "visual displays" is ambiguous lacks force because both are engineers who took no part in negotiating the 1985 Agreement. Likewise, an internal Microsoft memorandum by Bill Gates, which states that Microsoft must "be careful not to take additional things from apple screens when we make enhancements — everything we do today is fine," raises no triable issue as it is consistent with Gates's understanding that the license was for individual displays, not the interface as a whole, and with testimony by Apple's chief negotiator that Apple's license from Microsoft gave Apple the right to incorporate into the Macintosh interface any "new visual feature" developed by Microsoft for Windows.

Apple's further contention that the district court's interpretation of the Agreement must be wrong because it would be unreasonable to suppose that Apple knowingly gave away its most valuable technological asset ignores the fact that Apple itself received valuable consideration under the license together with Microsoft's promises to delay release of an IBM-compatible version of Excel and to release an improved version of Microsoft Word for the Macintosh. Under these circumstances, the district court properly concluded that the Agreement is not reasonably susceptible to Apple's interpretation.

II

Apple also appeals denial of its own motion for partial summary judgment that the works, viewed overall as they are viewed by users, are unlicensed derivative works substantially similar to Apple's works. Our resolution of its argument for reversal of judgments in favor of Microsoft and HP essentially disposes of this issue.

Apple raises one additional point, however, which we address here because Apple treats it as connected to its motion. The argument is that even if the 1985 Agreement does confer a partial license to use visual displays, Microsoft and HP exceeded its scope and therefore infringed Apple's copyrights. The cases on which Apple relies, however, merely establish that the breach of a prohibition in the license agreement can lead to a finding of infringement. Where, as here, the accused works include both licensed and unlicensed features, infringement will depend on whether the unlicensed features are entitled to protection. Finally, contrary to Apple's suggestion, by concluding that the 1985 Agreement provides a partial defense, the district court did not preclude Apple from prevailing on its infringement claims; the court merely required Apple to prove that Microsoft and HP copied unlicensed, *protected* expression. We see no error in the court's ruling.

III

Apple makes a number of related arguments challenging the district court's copyright analysis. It contends that the district court deprived its works of meaningful protection by dissecting them into individual elements and viewing each element in isolation. Because the Macintosh GUI is a dynamic audiovisual work, Apple argues that the "total concept and feel" of its works — that is, the selection and arrangement of related images and their animation — must be compared with that of the Windows and NewWave GUIs for substantial similarity. Apple further asserts that in this case, the court had no occasion to dissect its works into discrete elements because Microsoft and HP virtually mimicked the composition, organization, arrangement and dynamics of the Macintosh interface, as shown by striking similarities in the animation of overlapping windows and the design, layout and animation of icons. Apple also argues that even if dissection were appropriate, the district court should not have eliminated from jury consideration those elements that are either licensed or unprotected by copyright. Though stated somewhat differently, all of these contentions boil down to the same thing: Apple wants an *overall comparison* of its works to the accused works for *substantial similarity* rather than virtual identity.

The fact that Apple *licensed* the right to copy almost all of its visual displays fundamentally affects the outcome of its infringement claims. Authorized copying accounts for more than 90% of the allegedly infringing features in Windows 2.03 and 3.0, and two-thirds of the features in NewWave. More than that, the 1985 Agreement and negotiations leading up to Microsoft's license left Apple no right to complain that selection and arrangement of *licensed* elements make the interface as a whole look more "Mac-like" than Windows 1.0.

Thus, we do not start at ground zero in resolving Apple's claims of infringement. Rather, considering the license and the limited number of ways that the basic ideas of the Apple GUI can be expressed differently, we conclude that only "thin" protection, against virtually identical copying, is appropriate. Apple's appeal, which depends on comparing its interface as a whole for substantial similarity, must therefore fail.

****

AFFIRMED IN PART; REVERSED AND REMANDED IN PART.

QUESTIONS

1. What is the difference between a registered copyright for computer code as a "literary" work and a registered copyright for a GUI as a "audiovisual" work? Is there a difference in the scope of copyright protection? Is there a difference in the proof of copyright infringement?

2. What is the difference between visual displays contained in a GUI and the GUI interface itself? How did this difference affect the court's analysis?

3. What is the difference between "ideas" and "expression" in a copyrighted work? What is the difference between the tests for infringement of "ideas" and "expressions"?

4. Why did the court reject Apple's claim that the term "visual displays" is ambiguous?

5. Would Microsoft's promise to delay the release of an IBM-compatible version of Excel as part of the license agreement raise any antitrust concerns?

INTEL CORP. v. U.S. INT'L TRADE COMM.
946 F.2d 821 (Fed. Cir. 1991)

ARCHER, CIRCUIT JUDGE.

Intel Corporation (Intel), Atmel Corporation (Atmel), and General Instrument Corporation and Microchip Technology Incorporated (collectively GI/M) have each filed an appeal from certain aspects of the Opinion (Decision) and Order, issued March 16, 1989, by the United States International Trade Commission (Commission), in *Certain Erasable Programmable Read Only Memories, Components Thereof, Products Containing Such Memories, And Processes For Making Such Memories*, 12 ITRD 1088 (1989). The Order prohibited Atmel and GI/M (and other parties in that proceeding) from importing into the United States certain Erasable Programmable Read-Only Memories (hereinafter EPROMs) found to infringe one or more of Intel's United States patents. We affirm-in-part, reverse-in-part, and vacate-in-part.

I

An investigation was begun by the Commission in September 1987, under section 337 of the Tariff Act of 1930, codified as amended at 19 U.S.C. § 1337 (1988), in response to a complaint filed by Intel alleging unfair acts and unfair methods of competition in the importation and sale of certain EPROMs by seven respondents, including Atmel and GI/M. *See* 19 U.S.C. § 1337(a)(1) (1988).

In the complaint, Intel alleged that the respondents violated section 337 by importing EPROMs which infringed six Intel U.S. product patents and two Intel U.S. process patents (one of which was withdrawn from consideration). Section 337 permits the Commission to exclude from the United States any goods that violate the provisions of that section. 19 U.S.C. § 1337(e)(1). The Commission may also order any party violating section 337 "to cease and desist from engaging in the unfair methods or acts involved." 19 U.S.C. § 1337(f)(1).

The respondents challenged the validity and enforceability of the asserted patents, as well as Intel's allegations of infringement. The investigation was assigned to an administrative law judge (ALJ) who produced a 350-page initial determination (ID) detailing the facts and resolving the numerous issues presented by the parties. On review of the ID, the Commission affirmed many of the ALJ's determinations, ordered review of certain portions of the ID, and requested written submissions on those and other issues. In another prodigious effort, the Commission made 143 pages of additional findings and conclusions.

****

On the basis of its Decision, the Commission entered a limited exclusion order preventing the importation of, *inter alia*, the EPROMs manufactured abroad by or for Atmel (64K, 256K, 51 Series, and 1024K), and GI/M (256K and 51 Series). In addition, the Commission ordered Atmel and GI/M to cease and desist from "importing, selling for importation, assembling, testing, performing manufacturing steps with respect to, using, marketing, distributing, offering for sale, or selling" EPROMs which were determined to be infringing.

The issues before us on appeal and cross-appeal include: (1) Atmel's claim that its EPROMs are non-infringing because they are manufactured by Sanyo Electric Co., Ltd. and Tokyo Sanyo Electric Co., Ltd. (collectively Sanyo) under a broad cross-licensing agreement between Sanyo and Intel; (2) Atmel's claim that the '084 patent is invalid; (3) Atmel's and GI/M's challenge to the Commission's finding that their "old" 51 Series EPROM's infringe the '084 patent; (4) Atmel's and GI/M's claim that Intel's '050 patent is invalid and not infringed; (5) GI/M's challenge to the validity of claim 2 of the '394 patent; (6) Intel's argument that GI/M cannot challenge the '394 patent's validity because of the doctrine of assignor estoppel; and (7) Atmel's and GI/M's claim that their EPROMs do not infringe claim 2 of the '394 patent.

II

A. Atmel argues that its EPROMs did not infringe any of the Intel patents because the EPROMs were made by Sanyo under Sanyo's cross-licensing agreement with Intel (the Intel/Sanyo agreement). The agreement grants Sanyo the right to make, use and sell "any Sanyo . . . products" under Intel's patents. Intel contends that Sanyo is not licensed to manufacture another corporation's goods, *i.e.*, under industry terminology Sanyo may not act as a "foundry." Because Intel licensed only *Sanyo* products, Intel argues that the cross-license did not authorize Sanyo to manufacture Atmel-designed EPROMs for Atmel, for that would be the manufacture of "Atmel" products rather than "Sanyo" products. The ALJ framed the license defense issue as "whether Sanyo was licensed by Intel to make an Atmel EPROM, using Atmel's design, putting Atmel's name and product designation on the EPROM, and selling the EPROM to Atmel for resale as an Atmel product."

If the Intel/Sanyo agreement permits Sanyo to act as a foundry for another company for products covered by the Intel patents, the purchaser of those licensed products from Sanyo would be free to use and/or resell the products. Such further use and sale is beyond the reach of the patent statutes.

Section 14.5 of the Intel/Sanyo agreement states that "[t]his Agreement shall be governed by and subject to and construed according to the laws of the State of California." Under California law, the interpretation of a contract is a question of law, to the extent that it is based on the language of the agreement. When interpreting a contract, we must, where possible, give meaning and purpose to every term used in the contract. In resolving what the parties meant by limiting the license only to Sanyo products, we try to ascertain and give effect to the intent of the parties at the time the contract was signed.

In determining that the Intel/Sanyo agreement did not cover foundry rights, the ALJ reasoned:

> It is reasonable to assume that the parties meant to exclude parts that one party made as foundry for another company, using the other company's design, parts intended to be sold as the other company's parts under the other company's name, and not just used as Sanyo components in a larger product made by another company.

The interpretation of the licensing agreement as proposed by Atmel would mean that any company that was unable to obtain a license from Intel but still wanted to make its own parts practicing Intel patents could employ Sanyo as a foundry and circumvent Intel's patents. *Without something to explain why the parties would have intended such a result, the agreement will not be given this strained construction.*

By not reviewing the ALJ's decision on this issue, the Commission adopted that decision.

While there is no indication in the agreement as to what the parties meant by the "Sanyo" limitation, the use of that language in paragraph 3.5 clearly evinces that the parties intended to restrict the grant in some manner.

Atmel argues that the "Sanyo" limitation in paragraph 3.5 was only intended to prevent the transfer of "have made" rights to Sanyo, *i.e.*, to prevent Sanyo from hiring another company to manufacture licensed products for Sanyo. Atmel urges that its interpretation of paragraph 3.5 is supported by a letter containing a summary of the amendments prepared by a member of Intel's negotiating team in connection with a later extension of the Intel/Sanyo agreement. This letter describes the amended agreement as being unchanged insofar as it is a "[g]eneral patent cross license without "have made" rights." In this connection, Atmel contends that paragraph 3.8 cannot be read as excluding "have made" rights. Further, it argues that if any portion of the contract excludes "have made" rights, as suggested in the letter, it must be the "Sanyo" limitation in paragraph 3.5. Finally, because the letter expressly states that the agreement excludes "have made" rights and fails to say that foundry rights are similarly excluded, Atmel draws the conclusion that Intel believed its license to Sanyo included foundry rights.

Although the ALJ did not specifically mention the letter, she did fully consider and reject Atmel's arguments regarding the source of the "have made" exclusion. In referring to paragraph 3.8, the ALJ said that neither party intended to rely upon any implied license from Intel to Sanyo and that this provision "prevent[s] any implication of "have made" rights under the license." Noting that there was no evidence indicating that Intel knew Sanyo might act as a foundry for other unlicensed companies, that Sanyo's license in paragraph 3.5 was world-wide and royalty-free, and that Intel would not receive any further consideration no matter how many companies went to Sanyo for parts that infringed Intel patents, the ALJ posed the hypothetical question: Could Intel have intended that any company in the world could get Sanyo to make its parts without having to get its own license from Intel on Intel's patents? The ALJ's answer was that, in the absence of evidence of any such intent on the part of the parties to the contract, this construction of the license agreement would not be adopted. The ALJ concluded:

> The language at issue in the license agreement lends itself to another meaning that is more plausible: that both parties intended that Sanyo and Intel would have the right to make, use and sell their own parts without the constraints imposed by the patent rights of the other party.

> It seems unlikely that the word "Sanyo" was used here to prevent Sanyo from having parts that use Intel patents made for Sanyo by others. The license already prevents the implication of "have made" rights. The use of the word "Sanyo" to impose a restriction against "have made" rights would have been ambiguous and not the customary way to express this restriction.

We agree that Atmel has not established its license defense to infringement, and that the ALJ's reasoning is persuasive. Moreover, the ALJ's interpretation is consistent with other provisions of the agreement.

The language of paragraph 3.5 grants Sanyo a world-wide, royalty-free license to practice "Intel Patents." The agreement defines the term "Intel Patents" broadly, covering "any and all" patents that Intel "owns or controls," including those of its subsidiaries. The only limitations in paragraph 3.5 are that Sanyo (1) may not sublicense, except to subsidiaries, and (2) may only make, use and sell "Sanyo . . . products." Atmel's argument is that the "Sanyo" limitation precludes *only* "have made" rights, and Sanyo otherwise has an unlimited, royalty-free right to practice all Intel patents. Put another way, *anything* manufactured by Sanyo that utilizes *any* Intel patent is subject to the royalty-free license of paragraph 3.5.

Atmel's interpretation, however, tends to create an internal inconsistency in the agreement. Paragraphs 4.3 and 4.4 of the agreement require that Sanyo pay royalties to Intel on the sales of specific Intel chips made by Sanyo and on derivative products based on those chips, whether developed jointly or by Sanyo. Interpreting paragraph 3.5 as broadly as Atmel desires would encompass these chips and derivative products as royalty-free. For consistency of the agreement as a whole, the words "Sanyo . . . products" as used in paragraph 3.5 are properly construed to cover only Sanyo designed and manufactured products and to exclude parts designed by others.

Such a consistent reading precludes the royalty-free, foundry manufacture by Sanyo of an "Atmel EPROM, using Atmel's design, putting Atmel's name and product designation on the EPROM, and selling the EPROM to Atmel for resale as an Atmel product." Atmel had the burden of proving its defense to infringement, and we are convinced that the Commission properly determined that Atmel failed to do so.

****

AFFIRMED-IN-PART, REVERSED-IN-PART, AND VACATED-IN-PART.

QUESTIONS

1. What are "have made" rights in a license agreement? Why would Intel seek to exclude "have made" rights for Sanyo in the cross-license agreement?

2. How did Atmel interpret the exclusion of "have made" rights in the Intel-Sanyo cross license agreement? On what basis did the court reject Atmel's interpretation of the "have made" rights exclusion?

3. If Sanyo had manufactured EPROMs incorporating Intel patents and sold these EPROMs to Atmel to combine with Atmel-designed EPROMs, would this have violated the Intel-Sanyo cross-license?

4. If Atmel and Sanyo worked jointly to develop an EPROM based partly on Intel patents and partly on Atmel designs, and Sanyo manufactured the jointly developed EPROM and sold it to Atmel which, in turn, sold the EPROM under its own brand name, would this have violated the Intel-Sanyo cross license?

5. How would you have drafted the Intel-Sanyo cross license to eliminate any ambiguity regarding Sanyo's right to manufacture EPROMs incorporating Intel patents for another company?

CASE NOTES

1. Cyrix designs and sells microprocessors, but does not have facilities to manufacture the microprocessors it designs. Cyrix contracts with other companies (foundries) to manufacture the microprocessors it designs. The foundries then sell the microprocessors to Cyrix which, in turn, sells the microprocessors to OEMs under its own brand name. Because some of Cyrix's microprocessor designs may contain features patented by Intel, Cyrix only contracts with foundries that have a license to Intel patents. IBM was one of the foundries that manufactured

Cyrix-designed microprocessors. The IBM-Intel license agreement provides that IBM is granted "a world-wide, royalty-free, nonexclusive license [to] Intel licensed patents . . . to make, use, lease, sell and otherwise transfer IBM Licensed Products and to practice any method or process involved in the manufacture or use thereof." IBM Licensed Products are defined in the license agreement as "IHS (information handling system) Products, IHS Complexes, IHS Programs, Supplies and any combination of any, some or all of the forgoing . . ." An IHS Product is defined as "any instrumentality . . . designed for incorporation in an Information Handling System" and an IHS Program is defined as "a plurality of instructions capable of being executed by an IHS Product or Complex." In a declaratory judgment action filed by Cyrix against Intel, Cyrix argued that the IBM-Intel agreement did not prohibit IBM from acting as a foundry in supplying microprocessors to Cyrix. Intel argued that IBM Licensed Products included only products designed by IBM and that the term "IBM Products" should be construed as a "Sanyo limitation." What result? *See* Cyrix Corp. v. Intel Corp., 77 F.3d 1381 (Fed. Cir. 1996).

2. Genencor and Novo Nordisk entered into a licensing agreement as part of a settlement of patent infringement suit. Under the Agreement, Novo Nordisk granted Genencor a license to develop two Licensed Products using Novo Nordisk's protease patents. With respect to the first Licensed Product, called the Paragraph 2.2(a) product, Novo Nordisk granted Genencor a license to use five of its published patents. With respect to the second Licensed Product, called the Paragraph 2.2(b) product, Novo Nordisk granted Genencor a license to use the same five published patents and, in addition, five of its unpublished patents. The representations and warranties clause provided that the list of five unpublished patents were the only patents that needed to disclosed in order to develop the 2.2(b) product. A month after the Agreement had been executed, Novo Nordisk informed Genencor that a sixth unpublished patent had been inadvertently omitted from the list of the five unpublished patents. Novo Nordisk proposed that the Agreement be amended and that the sixth unpublished patent be added to the list of the five unpublished patents that could be used to develop the 2.2(b) product. Genencor refused and proposed that the sixth unpublished patent be treated as a published patent under the Agreement which would allow Genencor to use the sixth unpublished patent to develop both the 2.2(a) product and the 2.2(b) product. Genencor argued that Novo Nordisk should be estopped from asserting infringement of the sixth unpublished patent by its use to develop both of the Licensed products. What result? *See* Genencor Int'l., Inc. v. Novo Nordisk, 766 A.2d 8 (Del. 2000).

3. *See also* Intel Corp. v. VIA Techs., Inc., 174 F. Supp. 2d 1038 (N.D. Cal. 2001) (Reciprocal, royalty-free patent license to technology to increase the volume and speed of communications between computer components covered all features described in the Accelerated Graphics Port (AGP) Interface Specifications, not just baseline features; doctrine of *contra preferentem* which construes ambiguous contract language against the drafter precluded interpretation of license agreement to exclude optional features of AGP Specification); Intel Corp. v. ULSI Sys. Technology, 995 F.2d 1566 (Fed. Cir. 1993) (Foundry agreement for manufacture of math coprocessors by licensee of math coprocessor patents was not a *de facto* sublicense prohibited by the license agreement because the licensee did not grant the alleged infringer the right to make, use or sell patented chips except those

lawfully manufactured and sold by the licensee); Unidisco, Inc. v. Schattner, 824 F.2d 965 (Fed. Cir. 1987) (Sale of patented sterilization compound by licensee to distributor did not constitute an unauthorized sublicense rendering the distributor's resales as infringing); E.I. du Pont de Nemours and Comp., Inc. v. Shell Oil Comp., 498 A.2d 1108 (Del. 1985) (Arrangement under which Carbide would manufacture a chemical compound for Shell under the "have made" provision in Shell's nonexclusive license from DuPont, and Shell would then immediately sell the compound back to Carbide under a separate purchase and sale agreement, constituted a sublicense which is impliedly prohibited in nonexclusive licenses, unless express permission to sublicense is granted to the nonexclusive licensee).

Additional Information

1. CORP. COUNS. GD.TO LICENSING § 1:2 (2010).

2. 3 TRANSNATIONAL JT. VENTURES §§ 52:61, 52:62 (2010).

3. KEVIN L. RUSSELL, 1 FEDERAL CIRCUIT PATENT CASE DIGESTS § 3:70 (1996).

3. Leonard T. Nuara, *The Importance of the Scope of the License Grant Clause for Internet Website Development Agreements*, 520 PLI/PAT 539 (1998).

4. Rodger R. Cole, *Substantial Similarity in the Ninth Circuit: A "Virtually Identical" "Look and Feel"? Apple Computer, Inc. v. Microsoft, 35 F.3d 1435 (9th Cir. 1994)*, 11 SANTA CLARA COMPUTER & HIGH TECH. L.J. 417 (1995).

5. Joseph Myers, *Apple v. Microsoft: Virtual Identity in the GUI Wars*, 1 RICH. J.L. & TECH. 5 (1995).

2.3.3 License Warranties

A warranty is an assertion of fact generally made by a transferor to a transferee. In the context of a sale of goods, covered under Article 2 of the Uniform Commercial Code (UCC), the law of warranties is highly developed. The UCC defines two types of warranties — express warranties (UCC § 2-313) and implied warranties (UCC § 2-314 and § 2-315). Almost any statement of fact about the goods being sold can be found to be an express warranty and therefore an essential part of the contract consideration. The seller does not have to use any special words to create an express warranty, such as *warrant* or *guarantee*, and once an express warranty has been given, it cannot be disclaimed by other language in the contract. The question that most often arises with respect to express warranties is whether the language used is a statement of fact or an expression of opinion (i.e., puffing).

The UCC establishes a number of implied warranties, including a warranty that the goods shall be merchantable, a warranty that the goods are fit for a particular purpose and a warranty that the seller has full title to the goods. The *implied warranty of merchantability*, which applies only to sellers who are merchants in the goods, is a warranty that the goods would be generally acceptable in the market under the contract description. The *implied warranty of fitness for a particular purpose*, which arises if the seller knows that the buyer is relying on the seller's judgment, is a warranty that the goods are suitable for the purpose for which the buyer is purchasing the goods. The *implied warranty of title* is a warranty that the seller has full title to the goods being sold and the authority to sell the goods.

The UCC provides that implied warranties can be disclaimed in a contract if the language of the disclaimer is clear and apparent to the buyer (UCC § 2-316). The UCC also allows a seller to disclaim consequential (indirect) damages that result from a breach of the contract (UCC § 2-719(3)) so long as the disclaimer is not unconscionable (UCC § 2-302) and does not leave the buyer without any effective remedy for the breach.

The law of warranties is less well developed in the context of transfers of intellectual property. There are two general types of intellectual property transfers. The first is the transfer of intellectual property rights in the context of the sale or lease of a physical product or method. An example of this type of intellectual property transfer is the sale or lease of computer hardware with accompanying software. Courts have held that the sale or lease of a computer system with accompanying software is a "sale of goods" under Article 2 of the UCC. Likewise, courts have held that the sale or license of a pre-packaged software program is a "sale of goods." However, the provision of software programming services, or the development of customized software programs, have been held to be a provision of services not covered in Article 2 of the UCC.

The second type of intellectual property transfer is the transfer of intellectual property rights alone without any physical product or method embodying the intellectual property rights. One of the most common forms of this type of intellectual property transfer is a patent license. Courts have found that the transfer of intellectual property rights alone is governed by contract common law, not the UCC.

The first two cases in this section, *Chatlos Systems* and *Transport Corporation of America* deal with warranty issues in the context of the sale or lease of a computer system. The second two cases, *Meadow River* and *VRT, Inc.*, deal with warranty issues in the context of patent licenses.

CHATLOS SYSTEMS v. NATIONAL CASH REGISTER
479 F.Supp. 738 (D. N.J. 1979)

WHIPPLE, SENIOR DISTRICT JUDGE.

This case was tried before the Court sitting without a jury during May and June of 1979. The action arises out of the sale, through a leasing arrangement, of computer hardware and software. The plaintiff alleges breach of contract, breach of express and implied warranties, fraudulent misrepresentation, and seeks compensatory and punitive damages. The parties have submitted extensive trial memoranda and proposed findings and conclusions. After careful consideration of all testimony, exhibits admitted into evidence, oral argument, and trial memoranda, the Court hereby adopts the following findings of fact and conclusions of fact pursuant to Fed.R.Civ.Pro. 52.

The plaintiff, Chatlos Systems, Inc. (hereinafter CSI) is a New Jersey corporation engaged in the design and manufacture of cable pressurization equipment for the telecommunications industry. Edward Chatlos is the president of CSI. The defendant, NCR Corporation (hereinafter NCR) previously known as National Cash Register Corporation, is a Maryland corporation having its principal place of business in Dayton, Ohio. NCR designs, manufactures and sells computer systems, programming and services.

The action was originally filed in the New Jersey Superior Court. It was removed on motion of the defendant citing diversity of citizenship and an amount in controversy exceeding $10,000.00.

In the spring of 1974 the plaintiff became interested in purchasing a computer system in order to modernize the control of data which had become increasingly difficult since the incorporation of CSI in 1967. Mr. Chatlos made inquiries of several computer companies and was visited by Sam Long, a NCR salesman. After discussions wherein NCR was apprised of CSI's detailed business history and operations, Mr. Long recommended that CSI acquire a computer known as the NCR 399 Magnetic Ledger Card System (330 MAG).

It was represented that the 399 MAG would provide six functions for CSI through the use of computer programs. The six functions were Accounts Receivable, Payroll, Order Entry, Inventory Deletion, State Income Tax, and Cash Receipts.

On July 11, 1974 Mr. Chatlos in his capacity as chief executive of CSI signed a System Services Agreement for the sale of a 399 MAG. Shortly thereafter he had discussions with a representative of Burroughs Corporation, a major competitor of NCR. In these discussions Mr. Chatlos learned of a more advanced method of storing data than magnetic ledger cards which was known as a disc system. When he brought this information to the attention of Mr. Long, he was told that NCR also sold a disc system which could be utilized with the basic 399 unit. The computer was called the 399/656 Disc System.

It was represented by NCR that the 399/656 Disc would perform the same functions as the 399 MAG. It was further represented that the more advanced system was a good investment for CSI's present and future needs, that it would solve inventory problems, would result in direct savings of labor costs, would be programmed by capable NCR personnel, and would be "up and running" within six months.

In reliance upon these representations CSI entered into the transaction. On July 24, 1974 CSI entered into a System Services Agreement with NCR as part of the transaction. CSI paid $5,621.22 under this agreement. Because both NCR and an independent leasing company disapproved CSI's credit, on February 4, 1975 CSI entered into a leasing arrangement with the Midlantic National Bank whereby CSI agreed to pay $70,162.09 in sixty-six equal payments. This is a common practice in the trade; the computer company sells the system to a bank who in turn leases it to the "purchaser."

On December 11, 1974 the computer hardware was delivered to CSI. At this point Mr. Chatlos, on behalf of CSI, understood that it would take slightly longer, that is three months from the date of delivery, to have the system "up and running." Based upon the representations of NCR, CSI expected the machine to be fully operational by March 1975.

After the hardware was delivered, Frank Hicks, an experienced NCR programmer began learning the CSI payroll program. Though experienced in the 399 unit, Mr. Hicks had not attended the Disc school. He arrived at CSI in January 1975 and attempted to program and install the 399/656 Disc until February 1976. The payroll program became operational in March 1975, yet the State Income Tax programs were not successfully installed until September 1, 1976.

After programming the payroll function Mr. Hicks attempted to install the inventory deletion and order entry programs which involved the use of a procedure known as multiple records per sector. Placing multiple records in a sector means that several pieces of data or information are stored in one sector or section of the disc. Mr. Hicks had problems with the process in that he could not delete one piece of information within the same sector. CSI's business involves the assembly of technical equipment using many component parts. If the information contained in a sector was the existence of several specific parts in inventory, when one part was deleted (because it had been used in the assembly of equipment), the existence of the other parts was also deleted. Thus the functions of inventory deletion and order entry were inoperative.

On January 1, 1976 Richard Moody, Branch Service Manager of NCR's Newark District Office became responsible for the CSI installation. In February 1976 Mr. Moody assigned Pasquale Turi and Edward Tuosto to replace Mr. Hicks at the CSI site. Assurances were given to CSI that the computer would soon be demonstrated. On March 9 and 10, 1976 several NCR system analysts attempted to demonstrate the order entry and accounts receivable functions. This demonstration revealed significant problems with both functions.

On June 7, 1976 CSI asked that the lease be cancelled and the computer removed. NCR asked for additional time to make the 399/656 Disc fully operational and CSI agreed.

In July and August 1976 several meetings took place between NCR and CSI. Two other NCR analysts, Doug Russo and Bob Zebroski began another attempt to program the computer. On August 31, 1976 CSI experienced problems with the payroll function, the only job the computer had been performing. On that same day Mr. Tuosto installed the State Income Tax programs and on September 1, 1976 the problems with it were corrected.

On September 2, 1976 Mr. Moody arrived at CSI and announced that he was ready to install the order entry program. CSI refused. On September 3, 1976 Mr. Chatlos sent a letter to NCR describing the events of that summer and asked to cancel the lease and have the computer removed from the CSI premises. NCR refused stating that it had no ownership rights in the 399/656 Disc because it had been paid by the Midlantic Bank in August 1975.

Though Mr. Hicks worked on the programming problems for over one year, and other NCR personnel attempted to correct them, the 399/656 Disc only performed the payroll function and never performed the other four functions. Moreover, Mr.

Chatlos and the other personnel of CSI gave full cooperation to NCR up until September 2, 1976.

This transaction was for the "sale of goods" notwithstanding the incidental service aspects and the lease arrangement; therefore Article 2 of the Uniform Commercial Code, as adopted by the State of New Jersey, is the applicable law. Because of this application and the following conclusions it is unnecessary to consider the common law breach of contract claim.

WARRANTY

Under N.J.S.A. 12A:2-313(1)(a) and (b) express warranties are created by a seller as follows:

(a) Any affirmation of fact or promise made by the seller to the buyer which relates to the goods and becomes part of the basis of the bargain creates an express warranty that the goods shall conform to the affirmation or promise.

(b) Any description of the goods which is made part of the basis of the bargain creates an express warranty that the goods shall conform to the description.

Express written warranties were made by NCR in the Equipment Order and Sales Contract where it specifically stated that NCR warranted the described equipment for "12 months after delivery against defects in material, workmanship and operational failure from ordinary use." Furthermore the July 24, 1976 System Services Agreement specifically states, "NCR warrants that the services will be performed in a skillful and workmanlike manner." Though for services, this was part and parcel of the entire transaction for a sale of goods.

Together with the written warranties, Mr. Long, the NCR salesman, made verbal warranties as outlined in the facts. All of these warranties were memorialized in the Purchase Order prepared by the Midlantic National Bank where it is written at paragraph 6:

Since the above goods (the 399/656 Disc) are purchased by us expressly for the use of the lessee, (CSI) you (NCR) further warrant that the goods are in good working order, fit for the use for which the Lessee intends them, fulfill all representations made by you to Lessee, . . .

Since the written and verbal representations were obviously a basis of the bargain, it is clear that NCR created express warranties.

Under N.J.S.A. 12A:2-315 an implied warranty of fitness for a particular purpose is created:

Where a seller at the time of contracting has reason to know of any particular purpose for which the goods are required and has reason to know that the buyer is relying on the seller's skill or judgment to select or furnish suitable goods, there is . . . an implied warranty that the goods shall be fit for such purpose.

NCR states in their trial brief that language in the Equipment Order and Sales Contract and the Systems Services Agreement effectively disclaimed all implied warranties. This argument merits little discussion because in the pre-trial order, by stipulation, NCR agreed they had represented the 399/656 Disc would perform the six functions and that NCR would provide the requisite know-how necessary to put the system into operation. While those stipulations all but admit express warranties, NCR also agreed it had expertise in the computer field and that it recommended the 399/656 Disc for the plaintiff's "express purpose." Furthermore, NCR was well aware that CSI was relying upon NCR's skill and judgment. Nothing was presented at trial to contradict the conclusion that under N.J.S.A. 12A:2-315 there was an implied warranty of fitness for the particular purposes of CSI.

Moreover, CSI having met their burden of proof and based upon the facts outlined, it is clear that NCR breached both express warranties and the implied warranty of fitness. It is unnecessary to outline each breach because the statutory remedies provided in N.J.S.A. 12A:2-714 become applicable after any breach of warranty is established.

REMEDY FOR BREACH OF WARRANTY

Having concluded that NCR breached express and implied warranties, plaintiff is entitled to the remedies as provided in the Uniform Commercial Code as follows:

(2) The measure of damages for breach of warranty is the difference . . . between the value of the goods accepted and the value they would have had if they had been as warranted, unless special circumstances show proximate damages of a different amount.

(3) In a proper case incidental and consequential damages under the next section (2-715) may also be recovered.

The Court does not lightly view the admonition of N.J.S.A. 12A:1-106(1) which states that:

(t)he remedies provided by this Act shall be liberally administered to the end that the aggrieved party may be put in as good a position as if the other party had fully performed but neither consequential or special nor penal damages may be had except as specifically provided in this Act or by other rule of law.

A two-step process is necessary in order to fully consider the initial question of damages herein. The first inquiry must be to determine the value of the goods if they had been as warranted. This is not the "market value" since that term is conspicuously absent from s 2-714(2). The appropriate starting place is the $70,162.09 the plaintiff indebted itself to pay the bank for the computer system. It includes the amount the defendant received, the sales tax, together with the interest charges under the lease arrangement. The $5,621.22 paid by the plaintiff for the service contract is added because it was an inseparable element of the entire transaction. The Court finds the total value of the computer system if it had been as warranted to be $75,783.31.

The value of what was accepted must be deducted from the $75,783.31. Plaintiff's expert testified that the value of the hardware presently located at CSI is between $5,000.00 and $7,000.00. Taking the average, the Court finds the present value to be $6,000.00. An additional element must be calculated; the value of the payroll function which plaintiff admits was used from March 1975 until October 1976. Since neither plaintiff nor defendant presented any evidence of this value, the Court will assign a value as follows. The payroll function was one of the six that were promised, therefore, it is reasonable to recognize this benefit as one-sixth of the value if as warranted, or one-sixth of $75,783.31. This equals $12,630.55. The sum of the two adjustments is $18,630.55. When this figure is deducted from $75,783.31 the $57,152.58 result is the amount to which plaintiff is entitled as the direct measure of damages for breach of warranty, before discussion of incidental and/or consequential damages.

NCR maintains that an effective limitation on recovery of consequential damages appears in the System Services Agreement. The written warranties previously discussed conclude that "NCR's obligation is limited to correcting any error in any program as appears within 60 days after such has been furnished." Later language in the System Services Agreement states, "in no event shall NCR be liable for special or consequential damages from any cause whatsoever." These phrases clearly attempt to limit the purchaser's remedy to having any error corrected within sixty days after the appropriate programs are furnished. Since four of the six functions were never furnished, the attempted limitation falls squarely within N.J.S.A. 12A:2-719(2) which provides that:

> Where circumstances cause an exclusive or limited remedy to fail of its essential purpose, remedy may be had as provided in this Act.

Uniform Commercial Code Comment 1 following N.J.S.A. 12A:2-719 states:

> (I)t is of the very essence of a sales contract that at least minimum adequate remedies be available. If the parties intend to conclude a contract for sale within this Article they must accept the legal consequences that there must be at least a fair quantum of remedy for breach of the obligations or duties outlined in the contract. Thus any clause purporting to modify or limit the remedial provisions of this Article in an unconscionable manner is subject to deletion and in that event the remedies made available by this Article are applicable as if the stricken clause had never existed. Similarly, Under subsection (2), where an apparently fair and reasonable clause because of circumstances fails in its purpose or operates to deprive either party of the substantial value of the bargain, it must give way to the general remedy provision in this Article.

This reasoning has been adopted by several courts. In Beal v. General Motors, a motion to strike allegations of consequential damages was denied, despite an apparently valid exclusive remedy clause. There the district court noted that:

> (t)he purpose of an exclusive remedy of replacement or repair of defective parts, whose presence constitute a breach of an express warranty, is to give the seller an opportunity to make the goods conforming while limiting the risks to which he is subject by excluding direct and consequential damages that might otherwise arise. From the point of view of the buyer The

> purpose of the exclusive remedy is to give him goods that conform to the contract within a reasonable time after a defective part is discovered. When the warrantor fails to correct the defect as promised within a reasonable time he is liable for a breach of that warranty . . . . The limited, exclusive remedy fails of its purpose and is thus avoided under s 2-719(2), whenever the warrantor fails to correct the defect within a reasonable period.

Because NCR never furnished four of the six promised functions, their attempted limitation of remedy failed of its essential purpose. CSI was thereby deprived of the substantial value of its bargain. For these reasons NCR is liable for consequential and incidental damages as provided for in N.J.S.A. 12A:2-714(3) and defined in N.J.S.A. 12A:2-715.

Though not arising out of the contract, a major limitation does exist on plaintiff's claim for consequential damages. When CSI refused to accept Mr. Moody's offer of September 2, 1976, CSI's claim for consequential damages terminated. Initially CSI asked that the computer system be removed by letter of June 7, 1976. When NCR asked for additional time to make all functions operable, CSI granted them more time. Here CSI was acting in a commercially reasonable manner. During the summer of 1976 NCR was making a renewed effort. New people had been brought in. CSI's own memo of events shows that by September 1, 1976 the State Income Tax program was installed and operational. When Mr. Moody offered to continue the installation CSI should have accepted.

N.J.S.A. 12A:2-715(2)(a) limits the recovery of consequential damages to situations where they "could not reasonably be prevented by cover or Otherwise." CSI was not in a position to "cover" by spending large sums of money for a replacement computer system. Until September 2, 1976 they were relying upon NCR to supply it. However, they could have prevented many of their consequential damages "otherwise," that is by continuing their cooperation. In Fablok Mills Inc. v. Cocker Machine & Foundry Corp. it was stated that:

> In certain situations continued use of (the) goods by the buyer may be the most appropriate means of achieving mitigation, i. e., where the buyer is unable to purchase a suitable substitute for the goods.

This was precisely the situation CSI faced. Because they could not reasonably be expected to replace the system in September of 1976, they should have continued their cooperation by accepting the installation of the other programs.

A time limitation on damages was imposed in Clements Auto Company v. Service Bureau Corp. Clements involved a similar factual situation where the district court concluded that fraudulent misrepresentations were made and awarded substantial damages. On appeal the United States Court of Appeals for the Eighth Circuit limited the damages awarded to the time period in which the plaintiff was justified in relying upon the misrepresentations. That is not the situation at bar, however, Clements has been relied upon by CSI in support of their various damage claims, while CSI has ignored the time limitation. Clements demonstrates that commercially reasonable standards can create a limited time period during which the damages are recoverable. For purposes of this case, all recoverable elements of consequential and incidental damages will be determined from March 1975 (when the system was promised) until September 1976 (when CSI ceased their cooperation), a total of eighteen months when NCR was liable for breach of warranties.

Incidental and consequential damages are defined as follows:

(1) Incidental damages resulting from the seller's breach include expenses reasonably incurred in inspection, receipt, transportation and Care and custody of goods rightfully rejected, any commercially reasonable charges, expenses or commissions in connection with effecting cover and Any other reasonable expense incident to the delay or other breach.

(2) Consequential damages resulting from the seller's breach include:

(a) Any loss resulting from general or particular requirements and needs of which the seller at the time of contracting had reason to know.

The plaintiff has offered exhibits and testimony to substantiate their claim for these damages. The first loss to be considered is what plaintiff calls increased labor cost for accounting, inventory, sales, and executive salaries. These costs largely occurred after September 1976 and are disallowed with an important exception. Having found NCR expressly warranted that CSI would save labor costs by implementation of the 399/656 Disc, and that warranty having been breached, it is necessary to compensate plaintiff for the consequential costs.

It was estimated that by implementation of the NCR computer system, CSI would save the cost of two employees whose services would no longer have been needed. NCR knew this was a major reason CSI entered the transaction. The United States Supreme Court has determined that:

Damages are not rendered uncertain because they cannot be calculated with absolute exactness. It is sufficient if a reasonable basis of computation is afforded, although the result be only approximate.

From the proofs it appears the cost for each employee of this type was $15,000 annually. Therefore plaintiff is entitled to the cost (for eighteen months) for each of the employees receiving $15,000 per year, a total of $45,000.

Plaintiff also seeks damages for executive salaries for the time devoted to working with NCR. These are reasonable with the exception of the time spent by Mr. Chatlos. As Chief Executive Officer he assumed the risk of all corporate problems and is not entitled to reimbursement of compensation by NCR. The expenses for the Plant Operations Manager (12% Of salary for twenty-six weeks or $2620.00) and the Chief Bookkeeper (30% Of salary for the eighteen month period or $5,107.20) are reasonable. Plaintiff is therefore awarded $7,727.20.

Plaintiff also seeks losses in profits for excesses and deficiencies in inventory. These were a consequence of the failure of the inventory deletion and order entry functions to operate. This was another major reason CSI entered into the transaction. Plaintiff presented evidence and testimony to show lost profits because of excess inventory in 1975 totaling $5,080.95. Similarly for 1976 CSI showed a deficiency in inventory causing a profit loss of $3,325.24. When adjusted to include only the eighteen-month period these figures are reduced to $4,234.13 for 1975 and

$2,216.83 for 1976, a total of $6,450.96. CSI paid $1,750.00 for a manual inventory system which could not perform the functions as well as a computer system. Plaintiff is entitled to the $1,750.00 in addition to $6,450.96 for profit losses.

CSI will receive the cost of various supplies purchased in an attempt to make the computer function. Evidence disclosed this amount to be $1,433.00. Moreover, plaintiff is entitled to the cost of the space occupied by the machine. Testimony revealed a formula for the annual rental; the cost per square foot multiplied by the measured size of the computer. After adjusting the figure to include only the eighteen months, plaintiff is entitled to $1,197.00.

Plaintiff's requests for the value of the space occupied by Mr. Hicks, cost of the power line, and for maintenance of the area where the computer was kept, are denied. Mr. Hicks was trying to make it operate, the power line was needed for the payroll function to be performed, and maintenance would have been done whether the machine worked or not.

QUESTIONS

1. What could NCR have done to avoid the risk of incidental and consequential damages?

2. On what basis did the court determine that the transaction was a "sale of goods"?

3. Do you agree that computer programs are incidental to the computer hardware?

4. If statements are made during contract negotiations regarding future or contingent events and those statements turn out to be false, could this be considered misrepresentation?

TRANSPORT CORPORATION OF AMERICA v. IBM
30 F.3d 953 (8th Cir. 1994)

McMILLIAN, CIRCUIT JUDGE.

Transport Corporation of America, Inc. (TCA), appeals from a final order entered in the District Court for the District of Minnesota granting summary judgment in favor of International Business Machines Corp. (IBM) and Innovative Computing Corp. (ICC). For reversal TCA argues that the district court erred in holding that (1) the economic loss doctrine bars its tort claims, (2) IBM's disclaimer of implied warranties is effective against TCA as a sub-purchaser, (3) IBM's limited remedy of repair and replace did not fail of its essential purpose, (4) ICC effectively disclaimed liability for consequential damages, and (5) the limited remedy provisions by IBM and ICC are not unconscionable. For the reasons discussed below, we affirm the judgment of the district court.

I. BACKGROUND

TCA is a Minnesota corporation that operates a national trucking business, with its principal place of business in Minnesota. IBM is a Delaware corporation that manufactures and sells computers, with its principal place of business in New York. ICC is an Oklahoma corporation that produces software and resells IBM computers, with its principal place of business in Oklahoma.

In 1989 TCA decided to update its computer system, which is used to process incoming orders, issue dispatching assignments and store all distribution records. The information entered into the computer system is stored onto a backup system at 2:00 a.m. every day. TCA entered into an agreement to purchase an IBM computer system from ICC for $541,313.38. TCA subsequently executed a lease agreement which assigned to IBM Credit Corporation its right to purchase the IBM equipment from ICC, but TCA retained possession and use of the computer system. The computer system was installed at TCA's offices in Minneapolis on December 29, 1989.

On December 19, 1990, almost a year later, the computer system went down and one of the disk drives revealed an error code. TCA properly contacted IBM, and IBM dispatched a service person. Although TCA requested a replacement disk drive, the error code indicated that the service procedure was not to replace any components but to analyze the disk drive. TCA had restarted the computer system and did not want to shut it down for the IBM service procedure. IBM informed TCA that replacement was not necessary under the limited warranty of repair or replace, and agreed to return on December 22, 1990, to analyze the disk drive. On December 21, 1990, the same disk drive completely failed, resulting in the computer system being inoperable until December 22, 1990.

TCA alleges that the cumulative down-time for the computer system as a result of the disk drive failure was 33.91 hours. This includes the time to replace the disk drive, reload the electronic backup data and manually reenter data which had been entered between 2:00 a.m. and the time the system failed. TCA alleges that it incurred a business interruption loss in the amount of $473,079.46 ($468,514.46 for loss of income; $4,565.00 for loss of data and replacement media).

TCA originally brought this action against IBM and ICC in Minnesota state court, based on the failure of the disk drive purchased through IBM and ICC, alleging strict liability, negligence, breach of implied warranty, and breach of express warranty. IBM removed the action to the United States District Court for the District of Minnesota on diversity of citizenship grounds. IBM and ICC then moved for summary judgment on all counts. The district court granted the motions in favor of IBM and ICC on all counts. The district court applied Minnesota law and held that the economic loss doctrine barred TCA's tort claims, the terms of IBM's remarketer agreement with ICC "passed through" to TCA, IBM effectively disclaimed implied warranties, the remedy of repair or replace in IBM's express warranty did not fail of its essential purpose, and ICC's disclaimer of liability for consequential damages was not unconscionable. This appeal followed.

II. DISCUSSION

A. Economic Loss Doctrine

TCA argues that, under Minnesota law, tort claims are not barred by the economic loss doctrine if two conditions are met: there is damage to other property and the parties are not "merchants in goods of the kind." Because TCA is not a merchant in computer systems and the loss of data due to the failed disk drive constitutes damage to other property, TCA argues that the district court erred in holding claims for negligence and strict liability are barred. IBM argues that TCA did not suffer damage to other property because the data on the disk drive was integrated into the computer system. IBM also argues that the risk of failure of the disk drive (and the risk of loss of data due to failure of the disk drive) was reasonably contemplated by TCA. Thus, IBM argues that the Uniform Commercial Code (U.C.C.) as adopted in Minnesota controls the remedy in a transaction between sophisticated commercial parties.

The economic loss doctrine in Minnesota bars recovery under the tort theories of negligence or strict liability for economic losses that arise out of commercial transactions, except those involving personal injury or damage to other property. There are two issues in applying this doctrine to TCA's claim: whether the damages arose out of a commercial transaction and whether the damages claimed fall under the "damage to other property" exception.

In interpreting *Superwood*, the Minnesota Supreme Court has held that the U.C.C. controls exclusively with respect to remedies for property damage in a commercial transaction. In *Hapka*, the plaintiff and the defendant were both commercial farmers who grew seed potatoes. When contaminated seed potatoes sold by the defendant to the plaintiff infected other seed potatoes owned by the plaintiff, the plaintiff brought an action asserting negligence and strict liability. In applying *Superwood* to bar the tort action for economic loss based on damage to other property caused by the defective product, the Minnesota Supreme Court emphasized that the U.C.C. is intended to displace tort liability, and that tort exceptions for economic losses are applicable to consumer transactions only.

TCA argues that because it does not buy and sell computer systems, the purchase was not between "merchants in goods of the kind" and therefore not a commercial transaction within the meaning of *Hapka*. TCA further argues that the loss of data on the disk drive constitutes damage to property other than the computer system, and that under *Den-Tal-Ez* the tort remedies of negligence and strict liability are therefore available.

In *Den-Tal-Ez*, a motorized dental chair caught fire and allegedly caused substantial building damage. The plaintiff brought suit both in tort and for breach of warranties against the chair manufacturer for damage to other property (that is, damage to property other than the allegedly defective dental chair). The court stated:

> [w]hen there is a claim by a buyer for damage to the defective product itself (and this includes consequential damages), the U.C.C. remedy is exclusive and tort will not lie . . . . A sub-purchaser is also limited to the U.C.C.

remedy. In this situation . . . the product lacks its bargained-for value and fails to meet the buyer's or sub-buyer's performance expectations. This is exactly the kind of loss that the Code and its warranty protections are designed to cover. This economic loss includes the consequential damages for repair and loss of profits resulting from inability to use the defective product during the period of its replacement or repair.

As the district court correctly noted, this pronouncement from *Den-Tal-Ez* applies directly to the instant case.

TCA is not a dealer in computers and thus not a merchant in goods of the kind. Therefore, the transaction between TCA and IBM and ICC was not a commercial transaction for purposes of the economic loss doctrine. However, we hold that the economic loss doctrine does apply here because TCA did not experience damage to other property within the meaning of the doctrine. Under Minnesota law, "where a defect in a component part damaged the product into which that component was incorporated, economic losses to the product as a whole were not losses to "other property." "

In *Minneapolis Society of Fine Arts*, a claim was made that defective bricks damaged the building into which they had been incorporated. In discussing the economic loss caused by the allegedly defective bricks, the court stated that "[t]o hold that buildings constitute "other property" would effectively overrule *Superwood* as to every seller of basic building materials . . . because the "other property" exception would always apply. The U.C.C. provisions as applicable to component suppliers would be totally emasculated." Thus, damage to other components integrated into a single unit are not considered damage to other property for purposes of the economic loss doctrine.

Here, the electronic data stored on the disk drive was integrated into the computer system. If the disk drive had started a fire that caused damage to property outside of the computer system, then the exception to the economic loss doctrine as applied in *Den-Tal-Ez* would be applicable.

Furthermore, TCA was aware of the risk of computer system failure and possible loss of data. In applying *Superwood*, the Court of Appeals of Minnesota held that "tort claims [are] allowed only in limited situations where the nature of the defect or damage is other than that which could ordinarily be contemplated by the parties to a commercial transaction." The fact that TCA backed up the disk drive at 2:00 a.m. every day objectively demonstrates that TCA realized the risk of its failure.

TCA argues that *Superwood* and *Holstad* were expressly overruled by the Minnesota Supreme Court in *Hapka*, and that under *Den-Tal-Ez* tort claims are never barred in commercial transactions so long as the parties are not "merchants in goods of the kind." We disagree. *Hapka* overruled *Superwood* and its progeny only to the extent that they are contrary to the U.C.C.'s exclusive damages in commercial transactions involving property damage only. Minnesota courts have consistently held that the U.C.C. should apply to commercial transactions where the product merely failed to live up to expectations and the damage did not result from a hazardous condition. Because failure of the disk drive was contemplated by the parties and the damage was limited in scope to the computer system (into which the disk drive and its data were integrated), TCA must look exclusively to the U.C.C. for its remedy.

B. IBM's Disclaimer of Implied Warranties

TCA next argues that because it was not a party to the negotiations between ICC and IBM, it is not bound by the terms of the remarketer agreement, including IBM's disclaimer of implied warranties. TCA also argues that any disclaimers of implied warranties by IBM are not binding because they were not delivered at the time of the sale. IBM argues that the remarketer agreement between IBM and ICC included a valid disclaimer of implied warranties, and the U.C.C. as enacted in Minnesota operates to extend the disclaimer as a matter of law to TCA as the ultimate purchaser or end user.

The U.C.C. as adopted in Minnesota has a privity provision that operates to extend all warranties, express or implied, to third parties who may reasonably be expected to use the warranted goods. The seller can disclaim implied warranties. Disclaimers of implied warranties are extended to third party purchasers by operation of § 336.2-318.

The remarketer agreement between IBM and ICC included a disclaimer of "ALL OTHER WARRANTIES, EXPRESS OR IMPLIED, INCLUDING, BUT NOT LIMITED TO, THE IMPLIED WARRANTIES OF MERCHANTABILITY AND FITNESS FOR A PARTICULAR PURPOSE." As the district court correctly noted, this language complies with the requirements of Minn.Stat.Ann. § 336.2-316(2) (that is, it was in writing, conspicuous and mentioned merchantability) and thus effectively disclaimed all implied warranties.

Even assuming that TCA did not receive a copy of the warranty disclaimer, TCA's claim of breach of implied warranties by IBM fails as a matter of law. *Noel Transfer* is distinguishable from the present case because it did not involve a third party transaction. Thus, operation of Minn.Stat.Ann. §§ 336.2-316,.2-318 extends IBM's disclaimer of implied warranties to TCA as a matter of law.

C. IBM's Limited Remedy of Repair or Replace

TCA next argues that the district court erred in holding that IBM and ICC effectively limited the remedy to repair or replace. TCA argues IBM's limited warranty of repair or replace failed of its essential purpose because there was a latent defect and the remedy provided for in the warranty was not provided.

Under Minnesota law, "[a]n exclusive remedy fails of its essential purpose if circumstances arise to deprive the limiting clause of its meaning or one party of the substantial value of its bargain." A repair or replace clause does not fail of its essential purpose so long as repairs are made each time a defect arises.

It is undisputed that IBM repaired the disk drive after it failed. TCA argues that latency of the defect in and of itself mandates that the limited remedy of repair or replace fails of its essential purpose. TCA cites no cases that hold that a remedy of repair failed of its essential purpose when, after a single failure, the system was fully repaired within one day, and so the rule from *Durfee* controls and the remedy is adequate.

TCA further claims that IBM's failure to replace the defective disk drive before the malfunction occurred caused the remedy to fail of its essential purpose. The computer system was fully operational between the time the computer system first revealed an error code for the disk drive and the time the disk drive failed. The drive failure occurred two days after the error code was revealed and one day before IBM was scheduled to perform diagnostic service. When the disk failed, IBM provided warranty service on the disk drive and repaired it. Given these undisputed facts, IBM's remedy of repair or replace did not, as a matter of law, fail of its essential purpose.

D. ICC's Disclaimer of Consequential Damages Liability

TCA next argues that ICC's disclaimer for consequential damages fails of its essential purpose. A seller may limit or exclude consequential damages unless the limitation is unconscionable. The U.C.C. encourages negotiated agreements in commercial transactions, including warranties and limitations. "It is at the time of contract formation that experienced parties define the product, identify the risks, and negotiate a price of the goods that reflects the relative benefits and risks to each." An exclusion of consequential damages set forth in advance in a commercial agreement between experienced business parties represents a bargained-for allocation of risk that is conscionable as a matter of law.

In the agreement between ICC and TCA, TCA expressly agreed to an ICC disclaimer that stated in part "IN NO EVENT SHALL ICC BE LIABLE FOR ANY INDIRECT, SPECIAL OR CONSEQUENTIAL DAMAGES SUCH AS LOSSES OF ANTICIPATED PROFIT OR OTHER ECONOMIC LOSS IN CONNECTION WITH . . . THIS AGREEMENT."

We agree with the district court that the disclaimer of consequential damages was not unconscionable and that the damages claimed by TCA, for business interruption losses and replacement media, were consequential damages. Furthermore, TCA and ICC were sophisticated business entities of relatively equal bargaining power. ICC's disclaimer was not unconscionable and TCA is therefore precluded from recovering consequential damages.

III. CONCLUSION

In sum, TCA's procurement of an IBM computer system through ICC, for purposes of conducting its business, was a transaction between sophisticated parties. Potential failure of the disk drive was contemplated by the parties, and any property damage was to property integrated into the computer system. The economic loss doctrine therefore bars TCA's tort claims and limits TCA's remedies to those provided by the U.C.C. as enacted by Minnesota. IBM properly disclaimed implied warranties in its remarketer agreement with ICC, and this disclaimer passed through to TCA as a matter of law, limiting TCA's remedy to the warranty provision of repair or replace, which did not fail of its essential purpose. Finally,

ICC properly disclaimed consequential damages in the agreement between ICC and TCA.

Accordingly, the judgment of the district court is affirmed.

QUESTIONS

1. What is the purpose of the "economic loss" doctrine?

2. What other property did TCA claim was damaged as a result of the disk drive failure?

3. Is the data stored on a disk drive a defective component of the computer system?

4. Is electronic data stored on a disk drive integrated into the computer system?

5. What would be the result if the lost data resulted in federal income tax liability? Civil? Criminal?

6. What are the differences between contract law and tort law?

7. Can a seller limit or exclude consequential damages and provide only a remedy of repair or replace?

MEADOW RIVER v. UNIVERSITY OF GEORGIA
233 Ga. App. 169 (Ga. App. 1998)

BEASLEY, JUDGE.

Meadow River Lumber Company and Curlpak, Inc. (appellants) are licensee and sub-licensee respectively to certain exclusive rights to two patents owned by University of Georgia Research Foundation related to an apparatus and method for making curled wood flakes which are used in the potpourri industry. After learning of alleged use of the device more than one year prior to the Foundation's application for the patents, appellants brought suit alleging the Foundation breached the patent licensing agreement, committed fraud in the inducement, and is liable to indemnify appellants against claims of other sub-licensees who relied on the validity of the patent. The Foundation filed a motion to dismiss under OCGA § 9-11-12(b)(6) which was converted into a motion for summary judgment under OCGA § 9-11-56 and granted on all counts.

A party is entitled to summary judgment "if the pleadings, depositions, answers to interrogatories, and admissions on file, together with the affidavits, if any, show that there is no genuine issue as to any material fact and that the moving party is entitled to a judgment as a matter of law." The evidence is construed most strongly against the movant.

In appellants' favor is evidence that on May 26, 1992, the Foundation licensed to Meadow River the exclusive right to make, use, and sell "wood curls" produced on the patented machine in the United States. An amendment gave Meadow River a worldwide exclusive license to make, have made, use and lease the patented equipment. As authorized by the agreement, Meadow River sub-licensed the rights to Curlpak and two others. Curlpak further sub-licensed its rights.

On March 21, 1995, Meadow River became aware of facts upon which it bases a claim that the patents were never valid in that allegedly they had been exploited commercially more than one year in advance of the patent application. Since that time, Meadow River has demanded that the Foundation take steps to stop any infringing use of the patents. On August 8, 1996, Meadow River and Curlpak filed this suit. Meadow River has not made any royalty payments since February 1994, and the Foundation counterclaimed alleging breach of contract for this and other reasons.

Certain background matters set this case in context.

(a) State court jurisdiction involving patents.

Federal district courts have original jurisdiction of "any civil action arising under any Act of Congress relating to patents," but that jurisdiction is narrowly defined to include only "those cases in which a well-pleaded complaint establishes either that federal patent law creates the cause of action or that the plaintiff's right to relief necessarily depends on resolution of a substantial question of federal patent law, in that patent law is a necessary element of one of the well-pleaded claims." The test requires that patent law be essential to each of several alternative theories of recovery under at least one claim for federal jurisdiction to exist. Where no federal jurisdiction exists, state courts may address questions of patent validity.

The United States District Court for the Middle District of Georgia already determined that it did not have jurisdiction over Meadow River's claims. It held that though the claims "may relate to patents," they are state law claims and belong in state court. Meadow River did not appeal this decision.

(b) Application of Georgia law.

Patents are based exclusively on federal law, and state courts are advised to look to the decisions of the Circuit Court for the Federal Circuit for guidance on questions involving patent law. But patent licenses are not governed by the patent act. Accordingly, the construction of patent license agreements is solely a matter of state law.

Under Georgia law, two actions are available to one who was fraudulently induced by misrepresentations into entering a contract: affirm the contract and sue for breach or seek to rescind and sue in tort for fraud and deceit. Appellants assert both claims. Although appellants' brief is written as if Meadow River and Curlpak stood on equal footing, Meadow River is the only party in a direct contractual relationship with the Foundation. Curlpak, a sub-licensee of Meadow River, has no standing to bring any of these claims.

1. In Count 1 of its complaint, Meadow River alleges the Foundation breached the licensing agreement by failure of consideration because "the patents that are

the subject matter of the . . . agreement and the sole consideration provided by the Foundation were improperly issued, and are unenforceable and of no value whatsoever." This contention is based on the contention that the product was in public use or on sale more than one year prior to the date of the application for the patents, which, if it had been disclosed to the Patent Office, would have been fatal to a patent application under federal law, and that therefore the patents are invalid. For the purpose of this appeal we accept as true that the evidence presents a question of fact as to whether prior use or sale of the device should have prevented acceptance of the patent application by the Patent Office under 35 USC § 102(b) or otherwise rendered the patent invalid.

But Meadow River did not bargain for a warranty of patent validity. "A mere license is not deemed to constitute any interest in the patent. A license is but a promise by one having an interest in a patent to forbear from suing one who would commit what would be, but for the license, an infringement of that interest." As stated by the Supreme Court, "a manufacturer gains only two benefits if he chooses to enter a licensing agreement . . . . First, . . . the licensee may have avoided the necessity of defending an expensive infringement action during the period when he may be least able to afford one. Second, the existence of an unchallenged patent may deter others from attempting to compete with the licensee."

In accord with the definition of a patent license, Meadow River's license agreement makes no representations about the validity of the patents. On appeal, appellants now admit that they "did not bargain for patents warranted to be valid, instead, they bargained for patents that were not known by [the Foundation] to be invalid." Because validity of the patent is not part of the consideration, there is no claim for failure of consideration as a matter of law.

Further, any claim of breach of warranty regarding the validity of the patent or the nature of the rights obtained is precluded by the terms of the license agreement. As noted by the trial court, the license expressly disclaims any representations or warranties associated with the patents. The license states "[THE FOUNDATION] MAKES NO REPRESENTATION OR WARRANTY OF ANY KIND WITH RESPECT TO THE LICENSED PATENTS OR LICENSED TECHNOLOGY AND EXPRESSLY DISCLAIMS ANY WARRANTIES OF MERCHANTABILITY OR FITNESS FOR A PARTICULAR PURPOSE AND ANY OTHER IMPLIED WARRANTIES WITH RESPECT TO THE CAPABILITIES, SAFETY, UTILITY, OR COMMERCIAL APPLICATION OF LICENSED PATENTS OR LICENSED TECHNOLOGY." The license agreement also contains a clause which states that the agreement "constitutes the entire agreement between [the Foundation] and LICENSEE with respect to the subject matter hereof and shall not be modified, amended or terminated except as herein provided or except by another agreement in writing executed by the parties hereto."

Meadow River urges that the second clause is not a "merger clause." A merger clause typically includes a provision which merges into the agreement any prior representations between the parties. But Meadow River does not complain about alleged prior representations or understandings. The provisions quoted above bar all aspects of Meadow River's breach of contract claim. Where "the allegedly defrauded party elected to affirm the contract, that party is bound by the contract's terms and is subject to any defenses which may be based on the contract."

Meadow River argues its claim survives application of the disclaimer and entire agreement clause. It quotes *SCM Corp. v. Thermo Structural Products*: "Even though a party electing to affirm a contract is ordinarily bound by a merger clause contained therein, a merger clause is without application where the fraud allegedly perpetrated concerned intrinsic defects in the article forming the subject matter of the contract and was such as to prevent the defrauded party from exercising its own judgment."

As stated in the quotation, this rule applies only where there is an intrinsic defect and the seller has prevented the purchaser from exercising his own judgment. That has not happened here. There is no intrinsic defect in what Meadow River received. The nature of a patent and a patent license simply does not include a warranty of validity of the patent.

Meadow River argues in support of its breach of contract claim that although the Foundation did not make any warranty of validity, it licensed patents which it knew to be invalid.

This theory addresses the concept of passive concealment similar to that used in connection with the purchase and sale of real estate. In real estate transactions, there is an exception to the general rule of caveat emptor which "places upon the seller a duty to disclose in situations where he or she has special knowledge not apparent to the buyer and is aware that the buyer is acting under a misapprehension as to facts which would be important to the buyer and would probably affect its decision" if such action constitutes fraud.

Passive concealment does not apply to a breach of contract action but rather to one for fraud. Meadow River's fraud claim is addressed in Division 2. Even if the theory had been urged in connection with the charge of fraud, the result would be the same.

We see no grounds for extending this exception to the general rule of caveat emptor to patent license agreements. The *Wilhite*-applied exception is limited "to controversies between residential homeowners and residential builder/sellers" and "is concerned with concealed defects that purchasers in the exercise of due diligence could not detect. "It is only when the defects in the property are of a nature that the buyer could not discover them through the exercise of due diligence that any burden is placed on the seller to disclose the seriousness of the problems of which he is aware, provided the seller knows that the buyer is acting under a misapprehension as to the facts which would be important to the buyer in making his decision." "

No evidence shows that, through the exercise of due diligence, Meadow River could not have discovered all the information about the early possible commercial exploitation of the device that it alleges supports its cause of action.

The court properly granted summary judgment as to Meadow River's claim for damages and as to Curlpak.

2. Count 2 of Meadow River's complaint is a claim in tort for fraud. "One who seeks rescission of a contract for fraud must restore or offer to restore the consideration received thereunder, as a condition precedent to bringing the action; however, restoration by the purchaser is not an absolute rule, and does not require that the defrauding party be placed in exact status quo, but only that he be placed substantially in his original position and that the party rescinding derives no unconscionable advantage from the rescission. One seeking to rescind a contract for fraud must restore or tender back the benefits received under the contract, or show a sufficient reason for not doing so; he need not tender back what he is entitled to keep, and need not offer to restore where the defrauding party has made restoration impossible, or when to do so would be unreasonable. The defrauded party must act promptly."

The Foundation asserts that Meadow River has not rescinded the license agreement because it never offered or tendered to the Foundation the benefits it received under the contract, i.e., the licensed technology and the right to use it, and therefore is not entitled to sue in tort for fraudulent inducement. Meadow River did not request rescission in its complaint, nor did it allege rescission was impossible. "Critical to rescission is the tender of benefits, the prompt restoration or offer to restore whatever the complaining party received by virtue of the contract."

Meadow River concedes it failed to tender or offer to tender the benefits it received but instead argues it was excused in that (1) "[s]ince the patents are of no value, to return what was obtained under the License Agreement is unnecessary," and (2) rescission is not possible because appellants have sub-licensed the patents. Meadow River's arguments are inconsistent, unsubstantiated and without merit. The license agreement gives Meadow River an unrestricted right to terminate the agreement at any time. Although Meadow River has sub-licensed the patent rights to Curlpak and others, it provides no evidence that these sub-licenses restrict its right to terminate the license with the Foundation. Its mere assertion is an insufficient response to the motion for summary judgment.

Further, the sub-licenses, including Curlpak's, contain a provision permitting Meadow River to freely assign the agreement without the consent of the sub-licensee. Appellants have not explained why they could not assign the sub-licenses back to the Foundation. Their argument that the sub-licenses prohibit rescission belies their contention that the patents are without value. If the patents have no value, then what have appellants sub-licensed? *Crews v. Cisco Bros.* is distinguishable because Meadow River does not contend and has not shown it is unconditionally obligated to the sub-licensees.

In fact, rather than rescinding, Meadow River has affirmed the license. After March 21, 1995, the day Meadow River admits it knew the facts upon which the allegations of fraudulent inducement are based, it began demanding that the Foundation "immediately end the infringement of the patents," and it continued to sub-license the patent technology. "Where a party who is entitled to rescind a contract on ground of fraud or false representations, and who has full knowledge of the material circumstances of the case, freely and advisedly does anything which amounts to a recognition of the transaction, or acts in a manner inconsistent with a repudiation of the contract, such conduct amounts to acquiescence, and, though originally impeachable, the contract becomes unimpeachable in equity. If a party to a contract seeks to avoid it on the ground of fraud or mistake, he must, upon discovery of the facts, at once announce his purpose and adhere to it. Otherwise he cannot avoid or rescind such contract."

Summary judgment on appellants' claim in tort for fraudulent inducement was properly granted.

Judgment affirmed.

QUESTIONS

1. If Meadow River had proven that the University of Georgia technology transfer office knew about the public use and sale of the wood curls machine more than 12 months prior to the date the patent application was filed, and failed to disclose this fact to Meadow River at the time the license agreement was executed, would the warranty disclaimer clause in the license agreement have shielded the University of Georgia from liability for breach of contract?

2. Why did the court not extend the real estate passive concealment doctrine to a breach of contract action? Is concealment of facts regarding a patent's background easier to detect than concealment of facts regarding the condition of a house?

3. Why did the court find that Meadow River's fraud claim failed?

4. What could Meadow River have done prior to the case to avoid the court's holding?

5. What could Meadow River do after the decision to mitigate the court's holding?

VRT, INC. v. DUTTON-LAINSON COMPANY
530 N.W.2d 619 (Neb. 1995)

CAPORALE, JUSTICE.

The plaintiff-appellee seller, VRT, Inc., formerly known as Sanitas, Inc., sought a judgment declaring its right to past and future royalties under a provision within a purchase and sale contract. VRT alleged that the defendant-appellant buyer, Dutton-Lainson Company, breached its contract with VRT by failing to pay VRT royalties contemplated under the royalty provision. The district court ruled that Dutton-Lainson was obligated to pay both past-due and future royalties as provided in the contract. Dutton-Lainson thereupon appealed to the Nebraska Court of Appeals, asserting, in summary, that the district court erred in finding that VRT had substantially performed its obligation under the contract. Under our authority to regulate the caseloads of the appellate courts, we, on our motion, ordered the matter removed to this court. For the reasons hereinafter set forth, we now reverse the judgment of the district court and remand the cause for dismissal.

Sanitas was formed to manufacture, market, and distribute James

Vanderheiden's invention, which improved devices used in hospitals and nursing homes to lift and move patients, hereinafter referred to as the patient care equipment.

After retaining an attorney to file a patent application on the patient care equipment, Sanitas sought out a manufacturer. Having been told by Sanitas that a patent application on the patient care equipment had been filed and having been assured by its own patent attorney that there was good reason to expect that a patent would issue, Dutton-Lainson and Sanitas executed a contract whereunder Sanitas sold and Dutton-Lainson purchased those Sanitas assets which related to the patient care equipment. Section 1 of the contract, entitled *"Purchased Assets,"* provides that in addition to certain inventory, tooling, jigs, fixturing devices, and equipment, Sanitas shall sell and assign and Dutton-Lainson shall purchase and acquire the following assets:

> All current patents, patent applications, inventions, blueprints, drawings, plans, specifications, procedures and confidential information related to the production and marketing of Sanitas' Patient Care Equipment and any such items acquired, applied for or produced by Sanitas during the five-year period following the date of this Agreement; all vendor and sales information related to the marketing of the Sanitas Patient Care Equipment including customer lists and other marketing information; and the name "Sanitas, Inc." and any other related or similar trade names used in the production or marketing of the Patient Care Equipment.

Section 2 of the contract is labeled *"Payment"* and provides in relevant part:

> The purchase price of the assets described above shall be an amount equal to five percent (5%) of the annual billed and collected sales of the Patient Care Equipment products produced by Dutton-Lainson from the plans and inventions acquired from Sanitas. Such amount shall be payable for the 10-year period following the close of this purchase and sale or, if longer, the period of any patent or patents issued upon the Patient Care Equipment; provided, however, that Dutton-Lainson shall not be required to make any payments for any period after the ten-year period described above, if (1) Dutton-Lainson reasonably determines that the value of the patent claims or the likelihood of success in an infringement action does not justify the cost of litigating the validity of the patent or of seeking to enjoin infringement; (2) Dutton-Lainson ceases to use the invention disclosed by the patent claims; or (3) Dutton-Lainson receives an opinion from qualified patent counsel that the patent claims are invalid and thereafter institutes no action to enforce them. Dutton-Lainson's billed and collected sales shall be determined for each quarter of the year and payment shall be made to Sanitas within thirty (30) days following the close of each quarter of the year.

The contract further requires Sanitas to deliver to Dutton-Lainson at the closing "[s]pecific assignments to the assets described . . . above as shall be reasonably required by Dutton-Lainson."

At the closing, Sanitas delivered to Dutton-Lainson a document labeled "BILL

OF SALE AND ASSIGNMENT," assigning to Dutton-Lainson all of its "current inventions, blueprints, drawings, plans, specifications, procedures and confidential information; all vendor and sales information including customer lists and other marketing information; and the name Sanitas, Inc. and any other related or similar trade name relating to the production and marketing of Sanitas, Inc.'s Patient Care Equipment." Sanitas also delivered documents purporting to assign to Dutton-Lainson the patent application and Sanitas' interest in the invention disclosed therein. Sanitas thereafter changed its name to VRT, Inc. Although the contract refers to patents and applications for patents, there was but one application and it referred to the patent being sought. There was no other patent. Dutton-Lainson produced the patient care equipment and sold it with some modifications to the invention; part of the invention was not being used at all because the design was unstable.

It turns out that Sanitas' attorney had not filed the patent application when he represented that he had and did not file it until after the parties executed the contract. It was stipulated that because of the late filing, a patent could not issue. As a result, VRT filed an action for professional negligence against its attorney, claiming that the attorney had been negligent in failing to file the patent application, in concealing his failure, and in providing false information. VRT further claimed that as a result of those actions, it was forced to incur substantial legal fees to enforce the royalty contract against Dutton-Lainson and sought recovery from its attorney for the loss of royalties beyond the 10th year. In addition, VRT claimed its future royalty payments would be reduced because Dutton-Lainson would not have the exclusive right to manufacture and market the patient care equipment. VRT and its attorney ultimately settled the action.

To successfully bring an action on a contract, a plaintiff must first establish that the plaintiff substantially performed the plaintiff's obligations under the contract. To establish substantial performance under a contract, any deviations from the contract must be relatively minor and unimportant. If there is substantial performance, a contract action may be maintained but without prejudice to any showing of damage on the part of the defendant for failure to receive full and complete performance.

Substantial performance is shown when the following circumstances are established by the evidence: (1) The party made an honest endeavor in good faith to perform its part of the contract, (2) the results of the endeavor are beneficial to the other party, and (3) such benefits are retained by the other party. If any one of the circumstances is not established, the performance is not substantial and the party has no right to recover. Substantial performance is a relative term and whether it exists is a question to be determined in each case with reference to the existing facts and circumstances.

The relationship between attorney and client is one of agency. Therefore, the general agency rules of law apply to the relation of attorney-client.

Consequently, the omissions and commissions of an attorney are to be regarded as the acts of the client whom the attorney represents, and the attorney's neglect is equivalent to the neglect of the client. Moreover, a principal holding out an agent as having authority to represent the principal and thereby asserting or impliedly admitting that the agent is worthy of trust and confidence is bound by all the agent's acts within the apparent scope of the employment. Hence, the principal may be held responsible for the fraudulent acts of the agent. Indeed, we have written: " "Where one of two innocent persons must suffer through the misfeasance of the agent of one, that one must suffer who has placed the agent in a position to perpetrate the fraud complained of." "

Accordingly, the client is bound by the acts, omissions, neglect, and fraud of the client's attorney when such is within the attorney's scope of express, implied, apparent, or ostensible authority. The misrepresentation of VRT's attorney is therefore imputable to VRT.

The contract reveals that the very essence of the transaction was to enable Dutton-Lainson to manufacture, market, and distribute the improvements which were the subject of the patent application. While Dutton-Lainson took the risk that, for reasons beyond the control of the parties, a patent might not issue, Dutton-Lainson did not bargain for the certainty that a patent would not issue because, contrary to the representation made to it, no application had been filed.

Thus, VRT's failure to deliver and assign a filed application was not a relatively minor and unimportant deviation from VRT's obligation. As a consequence, VRT's misrepresentation with regard to the application means there was no honest endeavor in good faith on its part to perform its part of the contract. It therefore necessarily follows that there was no substantial performance on its part and that it is precluded from maintaining this action against Dutton-Lainson.

As revealed in the first paragraph hereof, the judgment of the district court is reversed and the cause remanded for dismissal.

REVERSED AND REMANDED.

QUESTIONS

1. From Dutton-Lainson's standpoint, what difference does it make if Dutton-Lainson pays royalties on a patent application that never issues, on an invalid patent, or on a patent application that is never filed?

2. If Dutton-Lainson sold the patient care equipment based on VRT's blue-prints, drawings, plans, trade secrets, marketing information, customer lists, etc., should Dutton-Lainson be required to pay royalties for the use of these other VRT assets?

3. When a licensor licenses a pending patent application and the licensee pays royalties until the patent application is finally denied, can the licensee recover the royalties paid? Is the licensee still bound by the license agreement and required to continue paying royalties after the patent application is finally denied?

CASE NOTES

1.   Applied Digital Data Systems (ADDS), a manufacturer of computer terminals (CRTs), contracted with Consolidated Data Terminals (CDT) for the distribution of ADDS's CRTs in California. ADDS later introduced a new line of CRTs (Regent 100s), which, in written specifications and promotional literature, ADDS claimed would operate at the speed of 19,200 baud. In fact, the Regent 100 terminals did not operate properly at any speed above 4,800 baud, and occasionally did not operate properly at speeds above 1,200 baud. After CDT received a stream of complaints from its customers regarding the Regent 100 terminals, CDT brought suit against ADDS claiming breach of express warranty and seeking direct and consequential damages. ADDS contended that the warranty disclaimer clause included in the sales contracts with CDT for every Regent 100 terminal negated any other ADDS statement contained in the written specifications and promotional literature. The warranty clause in the sales contracts stated that ADDS's sole obligation was to repair any defective terminals and that "ADDS makes no other warranty, express or implied." The sales contracts also stated that CDT's remedies were limited to repair of defective equipment and that recovery of consequential damages were excluded. What result? *See* Consolidated Data Terminals v. Applied Digital Data Systems, Inc., 708 F.2d 385 (9th Cir. 1983).

2.   *See also* Triple Point Tech., Inc. v. D.N.L. Risk Mgmt., Inc. 41 U.C.C. Rep. Serv. 2d (CBC) 421 (D.N.J. 2000) (Where contract provided for purchase of intellectual property and also payment of royalties, the purchase payments received for the intellectual property provide some return to the seller/licensor and protect the seller/licensor against the possibility that the purchaser/licensee will not diligently exploit the intellectual property assets; when purchasers bargain for consideration apart from scheduled royalty payments, courts will not imply a best efforts obligation); CBS Inc. v. Ziff-Davis Pub. Co., 553 N.E.2d 997 (N.Y. 1990) (Once express warranty is shown to have been relied on as part of the contract, the right to be indemnified in damages for its breach does not depend on proof that buyer thereafter believed that assurances of fact made in warranty would be fulfilled; right to indemnification depends only on establishing that the warranty was breached); S.M. Wilson & Co. v. Smith Int'l., Inc., 587 F.2d 1363 (9th Cir. 1978) (Where contract limited seller's liability to replacing or repairing, free of charge, any defective parts of the machine that the seller manufactured, and disclaimed seller's liability for consequential damages, seller's good faith but futile efforts to repair machine does not mean that the disclaimer of consequential damages should be eliminated; whether a consequential damages disclaimer survives failure of the limited repair remedy to serve its essential purpose depends on the facts of each case); Barazzotto v. Intelligent Systems, Inc., 532 N.E.2d 148 (Ohio Ct. App. 1987) (Disclaimer of warranties appearing on software package constituted a disclaimer by manufacturer, and not by resellers, and thus resellers were liable to buyer for breach of implied warranty of fitness for a particular purpose); Bunge Corp. v. Northern Trust Co., 623 N.E.2d 785 (Ill. App. Ct. 1993) (Warranty in stock purchase agreement providing that "The Corporation owns, is permitted to use, or licensed under all formulae, secret processes, know-how, patents, patent applications, trademarks, trade names and copyrights, if any, used by it in its present business" was a non-infringement warranty, and was breached by issuer's representation that

it had a license to use particular patent); Prudential Ins. Co. of America v. Premit Group, Inc., 270 A.D.2d 115 (N.Y. App. Div. 2000) (Federal court judgment determining that two additional individuals had contributed to the invention of patented system, and were therefore co-owners of the patent that had been licensed, established incurable material breach of patent license agreement's warranty of sole ownership of the patent, and supported release of licensee from any obligation to make further royalty payments); Solomon v. 21st Century Envelope Co., Inc., 1991 U.S. Dist. LEXIS 3511 (E.D. N.Y. 1991) (Plaintiff, patentee warranted that it owned all proprietary rights to two-way envelopes. Claim of breach of warranty as an affirmative defense because other similar patents existed was without merit).

Additional Information

1. Raymond T. Nimmer, *Performance Warranties in Licensing*, SB29 ALI-ABA 315 (1996).

2. RAYMOND T. NIMMER, LAW OF COMPUTER TECHNOLOGY §§ 6:61, 7:162 (4th ed. 2010).

3. LARRY LAWRENCE, 4A ANDERSON U.C.C. § 2-714:7 (2008).

4. ALOIS V. GROSS, 37 A.L.R.4TH 110 (2010).

5. Eric M. Reifschneider; Barbara A. Walkowski, *Warranties, Indemnification, and Limitation of Liability Provisions in Software License Agreements*, 1410 PLI/CORP 1059 (2004).

2.3.4 Most-Favored Licensee Clauses

A most-favored licensee (MFL) clause is intended to protect a nonexclusive or limited-exclusive licensee from the disadvantage the licensee might suffer in the event that the licensor grants a subsequent license on more favorable terms. In some cases, the subsequent license might be granted to a competitor of the first licensee, thus giving the subsequent licensee a substantial competitive advantage over the first licensee. Generally, an MFL clause provides that the licensor will not grant a license to a subsequent licensee at a more favorable royalty rate than the royalty rate set in the current license. MFL clauses also generally require the licensor to give notice to the current licensee of any subsequent licenses, provide the current licensee with the full text of the subsequent license, and grant the current licensee the option to substitute the royalty rate in the subsequent license for the royalty rate in the current license.

Although MFL clauses initially appear to be a straightforward means to apportion the licensing risk between licensors and licensees, in practice they have been fraught with problems. These problems include interpreting the term "more favorable royalty rate" when the subsequent license provides for a lump-sum payment, or the subsequent license arises out of a litigation settlement that includes past damages as well as future royalties. MFL clauses are also complicated where there are different royalty rates coupled with different use restrictions or different licensing relationships. For a good discussion of these problems *See*, 2 Information Law § 11:104, Chapter 11 — Licensing Information Assets; Part F — Royalty Issues, Raymond T. Nimmer (2008).

The first case in this section, *Epic Systems*, deals with the interpretation of an MFL clause in the context of a lump-sum payment in settlement of a patent infringement suit. The second case, *SGK*, involves the application of an MFL clause to a subsequent license granted over twenty-five years after the MFL clause license. The third case, *Eagle Comtronics*, decided in the New York Supreme Court Appellate Division Fourth Department, considers whether the subsequent revision of a license agreement entered into prior to the MFL clause license agreement constitutes a subsequent license. The final case, *Wang Laboratories*, considers whether a damage recovery in settlement of an infringement suit constitutes a royalty payment under an MFL clause.

EPIC SYSTEMS v. ALLCARE HEALTH MANAGEMENT
2002 U.S. Dist. LEXIS 17110 (N.D. Tex. 2002)

McBryde, District J.

Came on for consideration the cross-motions of plaintiff, Epic Systems Corporation, and defendant, Allcare Health Management System, Inc., for summary judgment. The court, having considered the motions, the responses, the replies, the record, the summary judgment evidence, and applicable authorities, finds that plaintiff's motion should be granted in part, as set forth herein, and that defendant's motion should be denied.

I.

Plaintiff's Claims

On February 21, 2002, plaintiff filed its original complaint in this action. Plaintiff alleges:

> On or about August 6, 1999, plaintiff and defendant entered into a license agreement pursuant to which plaintiff pays annual royalties and additional royalties to defendant for a nonexclusive, nontransferable, limited license under U.S. Patent No. 5,301,105 (the "patent"). The license agreement contains a "most favored nations" provision pursuant to which plaintiff may substitute the financial terms of any license that defendant grants to any third parties in the same field of use as plaintiff if those terms are more favorable than the financial terms in the license agreement between plaintiff and defendant. Defendant has entered into other license agreements with third parties in the same field of use as plaintiff that contain financial terms that are more favorable to those third-party licensees than are the terms between plaintiff and defendant. Plaintiff has requested, but defendant has refused to provide, information regarding all licenses defendant has entered into with third parties in the same field of use as plaintiff. Defendant did provide information that the financial terms in a

license granted to MedicaLogic are more favorable than those granted to plaintiff. On October 30, 2001, plaintiff exercised its right to substitute the financial terms in the license agreement with the financial terms provided by defendant to MedicaLogic, but defendant has refused to honor the exercise of plaintiff's rights.

Plaintiff seeks a declaratory judgment that (1) it has the right to substitute more beneficial financial terms in any of the licenses defendant has entered into with third parties in the same field of use, and (2) all amounts it has paid to defendant under the license agreement to date be applied against any amounts that would be due if more favorable financial terms were substituted. Plaintiff also asserts a claim for breach of contract arising out of defendant's failure to comply with the terms of the license agreement, and seeks to recover its costs and attorney's fees.

II.

Grounds of the Motions

Plaintiff seeks judgment that its interpretation of the "most favored nations" provision is the correct one. Specifically, plaintiff says that it is entitled to substitute a paid-up license for its running royalty payments. And, it says that it is entitled to an offset on its lump-sum payment for fees previously paid to defendant. Plaintiff additionally urges that it is entitled to judgment on its breach of contract claim, and corresponding request for attorney's fees.

Defendant, on the other hand, urges that plaintiff is not entitled to substitute the terms of any of the allegedly more favorable license agreements to which it refers, because the "most favored nations" provision limits substitution to similar running royalties. Moreover, an exception to the "most favored nations" provision applies to prevent the substitution of terms. And, defendant urges that it did not breach the contract and that, in any event, plaintiff would not be entitled to an offset for amounts already paid pursuant to the license agreement.

****

IV.

Undisputed Evidence

The following is an overview of evidence pertinent to the motions for summary judgment that is undisputed in the summary judgment record:

The license agreement provides, in pertinent part:

7. Entire Agreement

This Agreement (including any rider, exhibits and schedules which are attached hereto and made a part hereof by this reference), constitutes the entire understanding between the parties with respect to the subject matter hereof and supersedes any and all prior and contemporaneous promises, agreements and understandings between them, whether written or oral. There are no terms, obligations, covenants, representations, statements or conditions other than those contained herein. No agreements altering or supplementing the terms hereof may be made except by means of a written document signed by the duly authorized representatives of the parties.

Further,

1. Most-Favored Nations

a. If after the Effective Date, Licensor shall enter into a License Agreement with any third party in the same Field of Use as Licensee ("Third Party License" and "Third Party Licensee," respectively) on financial terms that are more favorable to such Third Party Licensee than the financial terms set forth in this Agreement, Licensee shall be entitled to substitute the financial terms of such Third Party License for the counterpart or equivalent terms herein, provided that this License Agreement has been in effect continuously since the Effective Date and provided further that all such financial terms in such Third Party License are more favorable to the Third Party Licensee than the counterpart or equivalent terms in the License Agreement are to Licensee hereunder. If less than all financial terms in such Third Party License are more favorable, Licensee shall be entitled to substitute the more favorable terms for the counterpart or equivalent terms in this Agreement, if Licensee also substitutes those terms which are not more favorable. The foregoing terms notwithstanding, this provision shall not apply with respect to any Third Party License: (i) to a U.S. government agency or health care program such as HCFA, DOD, VA or Medicare, or (ii) which relates to, in whole or in part, the sale or provision of equipment, goods or services to, for, or by any such agency or program.

b. For purposes of [the preceding paragraph], the "financial terms" shall be construed to mean the following paragraphs of the Agreement: Paragraphs A-3.3, A-3.6 of Exhibit A of the Agreement, and Paragraphs R-1.1, R-1.2, R-3.6 of this Rider.

Paragraph A-3.3 is titled "Annual Royalty Payments" and includes the formula pursuant to which annual royalties are determined. Paragraph A-3.6 is titled "Royalty for Licensee's Customers" and contains the formula for determining the royalty to be paid on behalf of plaintiff's customers. Paragraph R-1.1 and R-1.2 also concern annual royalty payments, specifically, a cap for the initial and subsequent extended terms and the maximum and minimum annual royalties to be paid. Paragraph R-3.6 is titled "Royalty for Licensee's Customers" and reduces the royalty rate provided in Paragraph A-3.6 to two percent.

Plaintiff was one of the first healthcare software providers to enter into a license agreement with defendant. In June 1999, defendant filed suit against twelve companies, alleging infringement of the patent. MedicaLogic, Inc., was one of the defendants in that action. Plaintiff was not sued, because it was negotiating with defendant for a license. Its license agreement became effective August 6, 1999, and included the "most favored nations" provision so that plaintiff could take advantage of any more favorable terms subsequently granted to another licensee in plaintiff's field of use.

In mid-December 1999, a consultant for both plaintiff and defendant informed plaintiff that defendant had entered into a settlement agreement with MedicaLogic, granting MedicaLogic and its customers a nonexclusive paid-up license for $350,000.00. MedicaLogic was a competitor of plaintiff's and was in the same "field of use." Plaintiff demanded that defendant disclose the terms of the MedicaLogic license in order to verify that it included more favorable financial terms than those provided to plaintiff. Defendant refused to provide the information. By letter dated October 30, 2001, plaintiff stated that it was exercising its right under the "most favored nations" clause to substitute the financial terms of the MedicaLogic license for the terms of its own agreement. Plaintiff enclosed a check in the amount of $145,920.00, the difference between the $350,000.00 paid by MedicaLogic for a paid-up license and the sums previously paid by plaintiff to defendant as royalty fees prior to that date. Defendant refused to honor the demand and returned the check to plaintiff.

In 2000, plaintiff filed another lawsuit alleging infringement of the patent by other companies. The defendants in the second lawsuit included Argus Health Systems, Inc., ("Argus"), Consultec, L.L.C., ("Consultec") and Oacis Healthcare Systems, Inc., ("Oacis"). Oacis, Consultec, and Argus are in the same "field of use" as plaintiff and paid defendant lump sums for paid-up licenses for themselves and their customers. Information provided by defendant after this action was filed shows that it entered into such a license agreement with Oacis for $175,000.00, effective April 21, 2000; with Argus for $225,000.00 effective March 7, 2001; and, with Consultec for $325,000.00 effective February 9, 2001; and, the information confirmed such a license with MedicaLogic for $350,000.00 effective December 14, 1999.

To date, plaintiff has paid defendant $538,295.88 in royalties, plus another $197,406.14 to an escrow account pending resolution of this action.

V.

Law Applied to the Facts

The parties seem to be in agreement that Texas substantive law governs in this diversity action. They agree on the basic rules governing interpretation of contracts, including the license agreement: Under Texas law, courts must enforce unambiguous agreements as written. The court determines the parties' intent from the four corners of the written contract. The court may construe the contract in light of the surrounding circumstances in which the contract was executed. Words are to be given their plain grammatical meaning unless it definitely appears that the intent of the parties would thereby be defeated. The court will attempt to harmonize and give effect to all provisions so that none are rendered meaningless. The mere fact that the parties disagree as to the meaning of the contract or urge different interpretations does not mean that the contract is ambiguous. For ambiguity to exist, the interpretation urged by each party must be reasonable.

Applying the foregoing rules of construction, the court concludes that the license agreement is not ambiguous. The interpretation urged by plaintiff is the only reasonable interpretation, because defendant's interpretation would render the "most favored nations" clause meaningless.

The license agreement entitles plaintiff "to substitute the financial terms of such Third Party License for the counterpart or equivalent terms herein." Counterpart terms would be the same terms, i.e., "running royalties." Equivalent terms would encompass lump-sum or paid-up royalties. As other courts interpreting "most favored nations" clauses have held, there is no distinction between one who makes an up-front, lump-sum payment and one who makes continuing royalty payments. The purpose of a "most favored nations" clause is to guarantee that no other licensee will be given the opportunity to use the patent at a more favorable rate. The purpose would be defeated if the contract were limited as defendant urges. Had the parties intended to exclude lump-sum payments from the comparison, they could have done so. The court does not read the definition of "financial terms" to limit the application of the "most favored nations" provision. Rather, the definition merely identifies the financial provisions of the license agreement that would be affected by a substitution of terms. This is consistent with the language of the "most favored nations" provision allowing substitution of terms even if less than all the terms are more favorable, as long as the less favorable terms are also substituted. For example, a similarly situated licensee might have an agreement pursuant to which royalty payments might be more favorable and the royalty for customers less favorable, but substitution would be allowed as long as all terms were substituted.

In a further attempt to avoid liability, defendant argues that the "most favored nations" provision does not apply to any of the third-party licenses to which plaintiff refers because each of them "relates to, in whole or in part, the sale or provision of equipment, goods or services to, for or by [a U.S. government agency or program]." In support of this contention, defendant relies upon hearsay and speculation. In any event, to allow defendant to go searching for any relationship whatever between a licensee and a government agency or program to call into effect the exception to application of the "most favored nations" provision would vitiate the purpose of the provision. In other words, the exception would be allowed to swallow the rule. The more reasonable interpretation of the exception is that it should apply where defendant has granted some sort of discount to a licensee because of the fact that that entity is or provides equipment, goods or services to, a governmental agency or healthcare program. Certainly, defendant would know whether such a concession had been made and would not be urging a need for "third party discovery on the issue." Thus, the court is not persuaded that there is evidence that the exception applies.

As for plaintiff's second cause of action, there is really no dispute that if the contract is interpreted as plaintiff urges, defendant breached the contract by failing to timely provide necessary information so that plaintiff could determine whether more favorable financial terms had been granted to other licensees. Although the license agreement does not specifically provide that defendant must notify plaintiff upon entering into a license agreement with a third party upon more favorable financial terms, such an obligation is implicit. Otherwise, if defendant could hide such information, the "most favored nations" provision would be rendered nugatory.

Moreover, defendant breached the contract by failing to allow plaintiff to exercise its rights under the "most favored nations" provision to substitute more favorable financial terms. That any of the lump sums paid by other licensees may have included payment of past damages for infringement does not support defendant's position. That would simply mean that third-party licenses were granted on even more favorable terms. In other words, it would be to plaintiff's benefit to argue that the licenses were worth less than the amounts paid in settlement, but plaintiff is willing to accept that the entire amount paid by each of the third-party licensees was for the license for such third-party licensee and its customers.

Finally, plaintiff seeks a credit for the royalties it has already paid under the license agreement. Defendant argues that there is no entitlement to an offset, since plaintiff has never tendered the full lump-sum amount paid by any other licensee. The license agreement, however, does not provide a mechanism for the substitution of terms.

The court has concluded that defendant is entitled to an offset, but not as large as it contends. The summary judgment record reflects that, although plaintiff gave notice in January of 2000 that it believed MedicaLogic had been granted more favorable license terms and that it was entitled to substitute those terms, it was not until October 30, 2001, that plaintiff gave formal notice that it was exercising its rights under the "most favored nations" provision to substitute the financial terms in the agreement with MedicaLogic for those in the agreement between plaintiff and defendant. Accordingly, that date should be the one used to determine the amount due. The court agrees with the holdings of cases cited by the parties that a licensee is not entitled to credit for royalty payments made prior to the making of an election.

Thus, plaintiff is entitled to a paid-up license effective October 30, 2001, in exchange for the same lump sum as paid by MedicaLogic, less the total of royalties defendant paid after October 30, 2001. Also, plaintiff is entitled to recover from defendant any excess over $350,000 it paid as royalties after October 30, 2001.

Plaintiff is also entitled to recover damages on its breach of contract claim. The court is satisfied that the damages should be the license fees paid between the date defendant refused to provide plaintiff with the terms of the license agreement made with MedicaLogic so that plaintiff could elect to substitute the more favorable financial terms and the date when plaintiff made known its election to substitute terms. The summary judgment evidence establishes that the date of demand for information was January 4, 2000.

Pursuant to TEX. CIV. PRAC. & REM. CODE ANN. § 38.001, plaintiff is entitled to recover its reasonable attorney's fees.

QUESTIONS

1. Do you agree that running royalties and up-front, lump-sum payments are equivalent?

2. The court implied an obligation on the part of the licensor to notify the licensee of any further licenses. Why?

3. Are there any differences between licenses that are entered into in settlement of patent infringement suits and other licenses?

4. If you were counsel to Alcare, how could you have avoided the result in this case?

SGK v. HERCULES, INC.
105 F.3d 629 (Fed. Cir. 1997)

MAYER, CIRCUIT JUDGE.

In 1986, Studiengesellschaft Kohle m.b.H. (SGK) sued Hercules, Inc.; Himont U.S.A., Inc.; and Himont, Inc. (collectively "Hercules") for patent infringement. Hercules counterclaimed, alleging that SGK had breached the most favored licensee provision of their license agreement by failing to offer Hercules a license with the same terms it offered other licensees. But for the breach, Hercules argued, it would have been licensed under the patents at issue during the period in question, thereby insulating it from infringement. The district court agreed and entered judgment for Hercules. Because SGK has not established that the court made any clearly erroneous findings of fact or error of law, we affirm. We remand for the court to determine whether SGK is entitled to interest on its license fee.

Background

SGK is the licensing arm of the Max-Planck Institute for Coal Research in Germany and the successor-in-interest to Professor Karl Ziegler, the Institute's former head, who died in 1973. For simplicity, we refer to both Professor Ziegler and SGK as SGK. Hercules manufactured and sold plastics from the 1950s through 1983, when it sold its polypropylene business to Himont U.S.A., Inc.

In the early 1950s, SGK invented a catalyst that could be used to make plastics, such as polyethylene and polypropylene. In 1954, SGK and Hercules entered a "polyolefin contract" (the "1954 contract") granting Hercules a nonexclusive license under SGK's "Patent Applications and Patents Issued Thereon." Although the United States had not issued SGK any patents at that time, the contract contemplated that Hercules would be licensed under any SGK patent issued in the future in the plastics field. The contract included a most favored licensee provision, set forth in pertinent part:

> If a license shall hereafter be granted by [SGK] to any other licensee in the United States or Canada to practice the Process or to use and sell the products of the Process under [SGK's] inventions, Patent Applications or Patents or any of them, then [SGK] shall notify Hercules promptly of the terms of such other license and if so requested by Hercules, shall make available to Hercules a copy of such other license and Hercules shall be entitled, upon demand if made three (3) months after receiving the aforementioned notice, to the benefit of any lower royalty rate or rates for its operations hereunder in the country or countries (U.S. and Canada) in which such rates are effective, as of and after the date such more favorable

rate or rates became effective under such other license but only for so long as and to the same extent and subject to the same conditions that such . . . lower royalty rate or rates shall be available to such other licensee; provided, however, that Hercules shall not be entitled to such more favorable rate or rates without accepting any less favorable terms that may have accompanied such more favorable rate or rates.

The contract also contained a termination clause, which granted SGK the right to terminate the agreement and the licenses upon sixty days written notice if Hercules failed to make royalty payments when due. However, Hercules had the right to cure its default by paying SGK "all sums then due under [the] Agreement," in which case the licenses would remain in full force and effect. The contract would be construed under Delaware law.

The parties amended the contract in 1962 and 1964, revising, *inter alia*, the royalty rates Hercules was to pay SGK. Both amendments contained savings provisions, stating that the 1954 contract remained effective except to the extent modified by those two amendments. SGK does not allege that these amendments modified the most favored licensee provision.

In 1972, the parties again amended the 1954 contract by granting Hercules "a fully paid-up" license through December 3, 1980, the date the '115 patent expired, under SGK's "U.S. Patent rights with respect to polypropylene . . . up to a limit of six hundred million pounds (600,000,000) per year sales." For sales exceeding that amount, Hercules was obligated to pay SGK royalties of one percent of its "Net Sales Price." As to SGK's patents expiring after December 3, 1980, Hercules possessed the right, upon request, to obtain "a license on terms no worse than the most favored other paying licensee of [SGK]." SGK concedes that this provision granted Hercules the "right to the most favored paying licensee's terms regardless of whether those terms had been granted before or after 1972." The amendment also provided that the terms and conditions of the 1954 contract remained in full force and effect except as modified by, or inconsistent with, this amendment. SGK concedes that "the notice provision, indeed the whole [most-favored licensee] clause, "survived the 1972 Agreement." "

On November 14, 1978, SGK was issued U.S. Patent No. 4,125,698 ('698 patent) for the "Polymerization of Ethylenically Unsaturated Hydrocarbons." The parties agree that under the 1972 amendment Hercules was licensed under the '698 patent, without any additional payment, through December 3, 1980. It is also undisputed that this patent is covered by the 1954 agreement, as amended.

In March 1979, SGK sent Hercules a letter terminating the 1954 contract and the licenses granted under it "for failure to account and make royalty payments" when due. In accordance with the agreement, the letter stated that the termination would become effective in sixty days unless the "breach" had been corrected and the payments made. Hercules paid SGK $339,032 within the sixty-day period, which SGK accepted. Although SGK possessed the right to question any royalty statement made by Hercules, and to have a certified public accountant audit Hercules' books to verify or determine royalties paid or payable, it did not do so.

On May 1, 1980, more than seven months before the expiration of Hercules' "paid-up" license, SGK granted Amoco Chemicals Corporation (Amoco) a nonexclusive "paid-up" license to make, use, and sell products covered by SGK's polypropylene patents in the United States. In exchange, Amoco paid SGK $1.2 million. SGK does not dispute that the '698 patent is covered by this license or that it failed to apprise Hercules of the license at the time it was granted. Hercules first learned of Amoco's license in 1987, after SGK commenced this action. It demanded an equivalent license retroactive to December 3, 1980. SGK refused, contending that (1) Amoco was not a "paying licensee," as contemplated by the 1972 amendment; (2) Hercules' request was too late; and (3) Amoco's license was granted as part of a settlement agreement.

Prior to that time, in 1983, SGK saw a publication of industry-wide production figures, suggesting that Hercules had produced 890 million pounds of polypropylene in 1980. It asked Hercules why it had not made any royalty payment for the amount exceeding the 600 million pound royalty-free limit. Hercules claimed that while it had used or sold 747 million pounds of polypropylene, less than 600 million pounds met the definition of polypropylene requiring royalty payment. SGK argued that the excess use or sales required the payment of royalties under either the original 1954 contract or the 1972 amendment. Hercules responded that it believed it had fulfilled all of its royalty obligations.

On December 3, 1986, SGK filed suit in the United States District Court for the District of Delaware, charging Hercules with infringement of the '698 patent. Hercules counterclaimed, alleging that the 1954 license, as amended, required SGK to notify it of the Amoco agreement in 1980, the terms of which it was entitled to obtain via the most favored licensee provision of the 1954 contract, as amended. Hercules argued that it would have exercised its right to obtain a license on Amoco's terms had SGK not breached that provision. It claimed, therefore, that it was entitled to such license, retroactive to December 3, 1980, upon paying SGK $1.2 million. The court agreed and entered judgment for Hercules. This appeal followed.

Discussion

SGK first argues that the court erred in holding that it was contractually required to give Hercules notice of the terms of the Amoco license. Under Delaware law, we must "give effect to the intent of the parties as evidenced by the terms of the contract." We look first to the plain language. In May 1980, SGK granted Amoco a "paid-up" license to make, use, or sell products covered by the '698 patent in exchange for $1.2 million. At that time, Hercules was also licensed under the '698 patent, but only until December 3, 1980, approximately fifteen years prior to its scheduled expiration. The most favored licensee provision of the 1954 contract, which SGK agrees survived the agreement's three subsequent amendments, provides that if SGK grants any other license in the United States or Canada to practice the process or to use or sell products under SGK's patents, including the '698 patent, then SGK "shall notify Hercules promptly of the terms of such other license."

SGK concedes that the notice provision was effective but argues that it was only obligated to provide Hercules with notice of any license with terms more favorable than Hercules' license. In 1972, Hercules obtained a "paid-up" license under SGK's patents through December 3, 1980. In 1978, the '698 patent issued. Hercules was licensed under that patent, without additional cost, by virtue of the 1972 license. Because Hercules obtained a "free" license under the '698 patent for the first 600 million pounds, no terms could be more favorable, according to SGK. So, it had no duty to apprise Hercules of the Amoco license.

SGK's interpretation does violence to the plain language of the 1954 contract. The notice clause did not condition SGK's obligation to inform Hercules of other licenses on whether such licenses were more favorable. It required SGK to notify Hercules promptly of the terms of a license granted "to any other licensee." Under SGK's construction, the power to determine whether another license was more favorable resided not with Hercules, but with SGK. That simply was not what the agreement provided. It is true that the 1954 contract granted Hercules the right, upon demand, to the benefit of any "more favorable rate or rates." However, that clause signified nothing more than the commercial reality that Hercules would opt only for a license whose terms it thought were more favorable than its own. It did not divest Hercules of the right to decide which terms were more favorable. Indeed, such a decision will not always be apparent when one considers the myriad combinations of royalty payments, lump-sum payments, and technology transfers a license can effect. Consequently, the court was correct that SGK's failure to provide notice constituted a breach of the license agreement.

SGK next says that it had no obligation to grant Hercules a license with terms equivalent to those in the Amoco license because Amoco was not a "paying licensee" within the meaning of the 1972 amendment. Again, we turn to the plain language of the license and interpret it anew. The 1972 amendment provided that for any of SGK's patents expiring after December 3, 1980, including the '698 patent, SGK would "grant Hercules, upon request, a license on terms no worse than the most favored other paying licensee of [SGK]." SGK contends that Amoco was not a "paying licensee" because it made just one lump-sum payment and no royalty payments; only licensees that make ongoing royalty payments are "paying licensee[s]."

In construing the term "paying licensee," we must give the words their ordinary meaning unless a contrary intent appears. The ordinary meaning of the term "paying licensee" is one who gives money for a license. SGK has not established that the parties intended that the term should mean something else. We see no distinction between one who makes an up-front, lump-sum payment and one who makes continuing royalty payments. Indeed, such a distinction would be doubly doubtful because a "paid-up" license presumably includes potential future royalty payments discounted to their net present value.

SGK also argues that the $1.2 million payment was in settlement of litigation; Amoco was not intended to be a "paying licensee." But the court found that Amoco paid SGK $1.2 million for a paid-up license for unlimited production under, *inter alia*, the '698 patent. SGK has not shown how this finding is clearly erroneous: Amoco was a "paying licensee."

Even were we to accept SGK's interpretation as reasonable, however, the provision would be ambiguous because Hercules' construction is also reasonable. Under such circumstances, and in the absence of any extrinsic evidence clearly establishing the parties' intent, we construe the term "paying licensee" against the drafter of the language — SGK — under the doctrine of *contra proferentem.* ("It is a well-accepted principle that ambiguities in a contract should be construed against the drafter."). So, Hercules' interpretation would still prevail.

According to SGK, even if Hercules is entitled to terms equivalent to those in the Amoco license, it exercised its option too late to be effective. This argument fails because the only requirement in the 1954 contract or its amendments that limits the time in which Hercules must request a license is that it be within three months of receiving the required notice. Because SGK failed to notify Hercules of the Amoco license, that time limitation never began. The court found that Hercules first became aware of the Amoco license in 1987 through discovery in this case. Hercules demanded an equivalent license on or about March 16, 1987, so even if constructive notice could trigger the three-month limitation, Hercules met it.

SGK also contends that the court erred in concluding that Hercules was entitled to a license retroactive to December 3, 1980. It argues that for six years Hercules intentionally manufactured products covered by the '698 patent, which it thought was invalid, without a license. Only after this court ruled that the patent had not been proven invalid did Hercules become interested in obtaining a license. It requested a license retroactive to the date its allegedly infringing activities began, thereby insulating itself from any infringement claim. SGK argues that "nothing in Hercules' option provides for such a right."

To be sure, neither we nor the parties can know with certainty whether Hercules would have exercised its right to a license on Amoco's terms in 1980, had it received the required notice. To that extent the prospect of absolving six years of alleged infringement via a retroactive license is troubling. But the uncertainty was caused by SGK's breach, the consequences of which it must bear. The 1954 contract expressly and unambiguously provides Hercules with the right to obtain the terms of another license "effective, as of and after the date such more favorable rate or rates became effective under such other license." The agreement must stand as written. Hercules is entitled to the terms of the Amoco license effective May 1980, when the Amoco license became effective.

Finally, the parties disagree on whether Hercules must pay interest on the $1.2 million license fee. Because the court has not addressed this issue, we remand.

Conclusion

Accordingly, the judgment of the United States District Court for the District of Delaware is affirmed, and the case is remanded.

AFFIRMED AND REMANDED.

QUESTIONS

1. What is the doctrine of *contra proferentem?* What effect did this doctrine have on the court's decision?

2.   The SGK-Hercules contract provided that Hercules must request the substitution of a more favorable license within three months. Why did the court excuse Hercules from this requirement?

3.   On what basis did the court find that Amoco was a "paying licensee"?

4.   If SGK had notified Hercules of the Amoco license, and Hercules had elected to accept the terms of the Amoco license, what license rights would Hercules have as a result of its 1972 license and the 1980 Amoco license terms?

EAGLE COMTRONICS v. PICO PRODUCTS
705 N.Y.S.2d 758 (N.Y. App. Div. 2000)

PIGOTT, JR., P.J. PINE, WISNER AND HURLBUTT, JJ.

This dispute arises out of a June 1988 patent license agreement entered into between plaintiff, Eagle Comtronics, Inc. (Eagle), as licensee, and defendant, Pico Products, Inc. (Pico), as licensor. On a prior appeal, we granted that part of Pico's motion seeking dismissal of the causes of action for unjust enrichment and unfair competition leaving only the causes of action for breach of contract and fraud. Pico appeals from an order granting Eagle's motion seeking partial summary judgment on the issue of liability and seeking dismissal of the affirmative defenses and counterclaims and denying Pico's cross motion seeking summary judgment dismissing the complaint. In granting Eagle's motion, Supreme Court determined that Eagle "is entitled to a paid-up license on the same terms as those obtained by [Arcom] in the [r]evised [l]icense [a]greement signed on behalf of Pico and Arcom on October 11, 1988," and ordered an inquest on damages.

We agree with Pico that the court erred in granting Eagle's motion and denying Pico's cross motion. Pico contends that the June 1988 Pico-Eagle agreement provided that Eagle was entitled to amend the agreement to include more favorable terms subsequently granted only to a licensee who was not then holding a written license. Pico contends in the fourth affirmative defense that the "most favored" provision of the Pico-Eagle agreement was not triggered because Arcom held a written license before the Pico-Eagle agreement was made. Eagle counters, however, that the Pico-Arcom agreement of 1984 was terminated automatically by article 10 of that agreement and that the 1988 revised Pico-Arcom agreement triggered the "most favored" provision of the Pico-Eagle agreement.

Under the terms of the Pico-Eagle agreement, if Arcom was "a company presently holding a written license from" Pico in June 1988, then Pico had no obligation to offer Eagle the same favorable terms "subsequently extend[ed]" to Arcom when Pico and Arcom revised their license agreement in October 1988. There is no merit to Eagle's contention that, when Arcom ceased paying royalties in 1987, the 1984 Pico-Arcom license arrangement was terminated, automatically and without any action or choice on Pico's part. Read as a whole, paragraph 10 of the 1984 Pico-Arcom agreement, particularly its explicit references to the "Licensor's right to terminate this Agreement" and to the "exercise of Licensor's right to terminate this Agreement," gave Pico the right, but not the obligation, to terminate the license upon Arcom's default in paying royalties. Nothing in the 1984 contract prevented Pico from accepting deficient performance by Arcom, from waiving any provision made for Pico's benefit, or from electing to continue the agreement in force despite Arcom's breach. "If a performance differing from that required by the contract is approved or accepted, such action may constitute a waiver of performance in accordance with the contract."

Pico's submissions on the motion and cross motion establish that the Pico-Arcom license arrangement was not terminated by Pico. Principals of Arcom and Pico aver as much, without contradiction in the record. The continuation of the 1984 agreement is likewise demonstrated by the actions of Pico and Arcom in adhering to most of its provisions and in expressly revising it. That revision did not, by itself, trigger the "most favored terms" provision of the Pico-Eagle agreement. On the contrary, the June 1988 Pico-Eagle agreement explicitly provided that such a revision in favor of a present licensee, such as Arcom, would not inure to Eagle's benefit. Eagle thus failed to demonstrate its entitlement to judgment as a matter of law on the issue of Pico's liability for breach of contract. In contrast, Pico sustained its burden on the cross motion by demonstrating that it was not obligated to offer to Eagle the same favorable terms granted to Arcom, and Eagle failed to raise a triable issue of fact.

Our analysis of the fraud cause of action is similar. The alleged misrepresentations were Pico's assertions that the revised Arcom agreement did not include a royalty cap and did not confer a paid-up license upon Arcom. In order to prevail on the fraud cause of action, Eagle had to establish that the alleged misrepresentations or omissions were material and that Eagle actually and justifiably relied on them to its detriment. Because Eagle had no contractual right to enjoy its license on the same favorable terms granted to Arcom, Eagle has failed to meet its burden in seeking summary judgment to establish the essential elements of materiality and detrimental reliance. Eagle is therefore not entitled to partial summary judgment on the fraud cause of action. Pico, on the other hand, has established its entitlement to summary judgment under the fourth affirmative defense dismissing the fraud cause of action.

In view of our determination, we need not address the propriety of the court's granting that part of Eagle's motion seeking dismissal of the remaining affirmative defenses. However, because there is no merit to Eagle's interpretation of the contract, there is no basis for the court's granting that part of Eagle's motion seeking dismissal of the counterclaims. Those counterclaims must be reinstated.

Order unanimously reversed on the law with costs, motion denied in part, fourth affirmative defense and counterclaims reinstated, cross motion granted and complaint dismissed.

QUESTIONS

1.   What is the purpose of a "most favored terms" license provision?

2.   Assuming Eagle and Arcom are competitors, does it make any difference to Eagle that Arcom was granted more favorable terms by the revision of an existing license rather than by the grant of a new license?

3. If you were counsel to Eagle, how would you have drafted the Pico-Eagle agreement to avoid the result in this case?

WANG LABORATORIES v. OKI ELECTRIC INDUSTRY
15 F.Supp.2d 166 (D. MASS. 1998)

LINDSAY, DISTRICT JUDGE.

The plaintiff, Wang Laboratories ("Wang"), seeks summary judgment on its claim of entitlement to royalties from the defendant, Oki Electric Industry Company ("Oki"), pursuant to a licensing agreement granting Oki permission to use two Wang patents for computer memory modules. Oki contends that it does not owe royalties to Wang because: (1) Wang's patents are invalid and (2) Wang's patents do not cover Oki's modules. Oki also seeks partial summary judgment in its favor on grounds that the licensing agreement between Wang and Oki is unenforceable due to a breach of the agreement by Wang. On November 16, 1995, the court bifurcated Oki's claims, holding in abeyance Oki's claim that the patents are invalid pending a determination of whether Oki's modules are covered by the Wang patents. By separate order dated September 6, 1996, the court referred the case to a special master, Alan Kirkpatrick. The special master conducted a non-jury evidentiary proceeding on December 10–12, 1996, and issued a report on May 14, 1997.

The special master carefully analyzed the issues the parties raised in the motions referred to him. The court agrees with a number of the special master's findings, but reaches different conclusions with respect to others. The areas of agreement and disagreement are set forth below, in response to the parties' objections to the special master's report.

Facts

On April 7, 1987, Wang (through James Clayton, a Wang employee) obtained United States patent # 4,656,605 (the " '605 patent") for a "single in-line memory module" or "SIMM." On February 23, 1988, Wang obtained Patent # 4,727,513 (the " '513 patent") on a continuation of the '605 application.

In its first application for what ultimately was issued as the '605 patent, Wang described a module to hold computer memory chips. Wang initially sought to cover several types of memory module with its patent application, but the patent and trademark examiner rejected Wang's first effort as overbroad. A second version met the same fate. On its third and successful attempt, Wang restricted its application to cover just memory modules holding chips in a single row (i.e., the "Leaded Classic" and, arguably, a version without leads called the "Leadless Classic"). As so written, the patent and its continuation excluded two other types of modules, the "3-Pack" and the "Lateral." Each of the excluded types houses more than a single row of chips.

Having foregone its claims to multiple-row module coverage, Wang could not later assert that the '605 and '513 patents covered this type of module. That is because the doctrine of "prosecution history estoppel" precludes a patentee from regaining, through litigation, coverage of subject matter relinquished during prosecution of the patent application.

Nevertheless, Wang brought suit in the United States District Court for the Eastern District of Virginia against Toshiba Corporation, alleging infringement of the '605 and '513 patents by both single and multiple-row module types. Wang also initiated an infringement action against Oki and others with the International Trade Commission ("ITC"), based on sales of single row, 3-Pack, and Lateral modules. Oki and Wang settled the ITC dispute by agreeing to a non-exclusive licensing agreement on March 25, 1992. The instant action arises from that licensing agreement.

The terms of the licensing agreement included the following: in addition to a single $850,000 payment to Wang, Oki covenanted to pay running royalties (i.e., royalties triggered by actual sales as they occurred) to Wang on sales of any modules subject to "one or more valid and unexpired claims" of the '605 and '513 patents. Even though Oki had raised a prosecution history estoppel defense in the ITC action as to multiple-row modules, Oki nevertheless consented in the licensing agreement to pay royalties on sales of both single and multiple-row modules occurring after January 1, 1992.

On May 10, 1993, on appeal from a ruling of the district court in the litigation between Toshiba and Wang, the Court of Appeals for the Federal Circuit held that Wang had relinquished coverage of multiple-row module types, including the 3-Pack and Lateral, during the prosecution of the '605 and '513 patents. Realizing that the Federal Circuit's Toshiba decision was likely to bind Wang in its dealings with Oki, Wang informed Oki that it no longer owed royalties on sales of 3-Pack and Lateral modules after the date of the Federal Circuit decision.

Oki continued to pay royalties on both single row modules with leads ("Leaded" modules) and on single row modules without leads ("Leadless modules") marketed up to September 30, 1992. However, Oki announced in a letter to Wang dated May 27, 1993, that it would no longer pay royalties on Leadless modules marketed on or after October 1, 1992. Oki stated that it had "reconsidered" the scope of the Wang patents and believed that the Oki Leadless modules were not covered under its licensing agreement with Wang.

"Most Favored Licensee" Claim

In addition to the primary issue of patent coverage, Oki raises a threshold challenge to its contract with Wang. Oki claims that Wang violated a "most favored licensee" ("MFL") provision in the Wang-Oki licensing agreement pursuant to which Oki agreed to pay royalties based on its use of the '605 and '513 patents. The "most favored licensee" provision required Wang to notify and to grant equally beneficial terms to Oki should Wang provide another licensee with more favorable running royalty rates or a more favorable running royalty base (i.e., one calculated on the basis of fewer patents).

In support of its claim Oki asserts that, on June 21, 1993, Wang entered into a more favorable license agreement with Hyundai involving the '605 and '513 patents (the "June 21 agreement"). Pursuant to that agreement, Hyundai's royalties were based on sales of single-row modules only, with Wang reserving the right to collect royalties on multiple-row modules should the Toshiba decision be reversed. The June 21 agreement therefore provided Hyundai with a more favorable royalty base than the one to which Oki originally had agreed.

Wang contends that the June 21 agreement did not disadvantage Oki, because Wang had relieved Oki of the obligation to pay royalties on 3-Pack and Lateral modules as of May 10, 1993. The June 21 agreement, however, contained language to the effect that it ran retroactively from January 1, 1993 forward to December 31, 1994. Due to this allegedly retroactive time frame, Wang's agreements with Hyundai and Oki overlapped (on paper, if not in fact) for slightly over five months before their royalty bases were made equal.

The June 21 agreement required Hyundai to make a lump sum payment of $750,000 to Wang, which payment the parties termed a "pre-paid running royalty" — that is, an arrangement in which money is paid up front and then drawn against as royalties accrue (as opposed to a periodic accounting and payment). Despite this contract terminology, common sense dictates that this sum could only have been "pre-paid" for events after June 21, 1993. Prepayments could not be made for uses of the patents before the June 21 agreement was concluded. Therefore, some portion of the lump sum was intended to compensate Wang for past uses of its patent.

The MFL dispute turns on how one characterizes that portion of the lump sum intended to cover past events. The special master viewed the June 21 agreement as retroactively affording Hyundai royalty terms more favorable than those Oki enjoyed. Consequently, the special master deemed Wang's claims against Oki unenforceable due to Wang's breach of the MFL clause. Upon de novo consideration, however, the court determines that the relevant precedents and the language of the contract give rise to the conclusion that the portion of the lump sum payment relating to the period before June 21, 1993 represented a settlement for past infringement, rather than retroactive royalties. Therefore, the court disagrees with the special master's conclusion as to this issue and concludes that Wang did not violate Oki's MFL provision by dint of its contract with Oki.

Monies received as a settlement for past tortious use of patents are not the equivalent of royalties. Since a settlement is not a royalty, imposing a penalty for past tortious uses that is more favorable than the royalty rate does not violate an MFL clause.

Nearly all the relevant court decisions addressing this question are summarized in Studiengesellschaft Kohle m.b.H. v. Novamont Corp. In that case, the Court of Appeals for the Second Circuit considered whether a settlement for past infringement that breaks down to a lower rate than the rate at which royalties are paid violates an MFL clause. The Second Circuit acknowledged that truly parallel treatment of licensees and past infringers might require "that the licensor must insist upon an exaction from the later licensee for past infringement which is equivalent to the royalty terms governing the [MFL] during the same period, or must make a refund . . . ." However, the Studiengesellschaft court concluded:

"MFL clauses do not seem to have been drawn so as to compel that degree of equivalency . . . ."

Courts confronting this issue have been motivated in part by a desire to encourage settlements for patent infringement. Indeed, enabling patent owners to negotiate settlements independent of the MFL rate fosters resolution of patent infringement disputes without recourse to the courts. Moreover, this policy safeguards the interests of MFLs. A non-exclusive license — like the one involved in the instant case and the relevant precedents — confers no standing on a licensee to protect the patent against other infringers. Each non-exclusive licensee therefore must rely on the patent holder to prevent competition, with no legal redress if the patent holder chooses not to act. Forcing a patent owner to resolve license infringements only at the risk of forfeiting a portion of the royalties paid by an MFL could actually create a disincentive to protect the MFL patent interest, giving rise to a situation in which infringers would compete unchecked against MFLs.

In addition, there is authority to the effect that the concepts of both royalty and license are necessarily prospective, rendering a "retroactive royalty agreement" a legal nullity. The courts that have dealt with this issue have concluded that a license is a prospective grant of permission to use the patents.

Finally, the language of the June 21 agreement supports the conclusion that the pre-June 21, 1993 portion of the lump-sum payment was intended to settle Wang's claims for past infringement. Section 4 of the June 21 agreement, titled "Release," states that, effective upon payment of the lump sum, Wang "irrevocably releases Licensee . . . from any and all claims of past infringement." Section 5.2, describing the lump sum, states that Hyundai shall pay the $750,000 to Wang "as consideration for the release granted to Licensee herein."

For the reasons stated above then, the court disagrees with the findings of the special master and finds that the portion of Hyundai's lump sum payment to Wang attributable to the period before June 21, 1993 represented a settlement for past infringement, rather than royalties calculated at a rate more favorable than that which Oki enjoyed. As such, the lump sum payment did not violate Wang's contract with Oki, and Wang is entitled to seek royalties from Oki pursuant to that contract.

So Ordered.

QUESTIONS

1. What is the difference between a lump-sum payment for a retroactive license and running royalties going forward, and a lump-sum payment for past infringement and running royalties going forward?

2. What is the court's concern about requiring equivalency between the settlement amount in an infringement suit and the royalties paid under a license with a MFL provision?

CASE NOTES

1.   Beginning in 2000, Rambus filed patent infringement suits against Samsung and a number of Samsung's competitors in the semiconductor memory industry, including Hynix, Micron and Infineon. Rambus claimed that any semiconductor manufacturer who chose to litigate would be forced to pay higher royalties than those who chose to license. Samsung chose to license and signed a license agreement with Rambus that included a MFL provision. In Rambus's suit against Infineon, the district court ruled on remand that Rambus had spoiled evidence and that it would dismiss Rambus's infringement claim. Before the district court could issue its findings of fact and conclusions of law, Rambus and Infineon entered into a settlement agreement which required Infineon to pay a quarterly lump-sum payment of $5,800,000 in exchange for a license to all of Rambus's existing patents. After Rambus's settlement with Infineon, Rambus sought to terminate the Samsung license, but Samsung continued to practice the licensed patents. When Rambus finally sued Samsung, Samsung asserted a number of counter claims, including that Rambus had breached the MFL provision in the license agreement by failing to notify Samsung of Infineon's lower royalty payments and failing to negotiate a new license agreement in good faith. Rambus claimed that the phrase "royalty rate" in the MFL provision covered only a running royalty rate on net sales, and did not cover a quarterly lump-sum payment divorced from the amount of sales. Samsung claimed that the phrase "royalty rate" could encompass both a percentage of net sales and also a dollar amount per periods of time. What result? *See* Rambus Inc. v. Samsung Electronics Co., 2008 U.S. Dist. LEXIS 63027 (N.D.Cal. 2008).

2.   *See also* Qualcomm Inc. v. Texas Instruments Inc., 875 A.2d 626 (Del. 2005) (Suit by Texas Instruments (TI) against Qualcomm for breach of Most Favored Nation provision in cross-license agreement because Qualcomm granted more favorable pass-through royalties to purchasers of its own integrated circuits than to purchasers of integrated circuits from TI did not violate another cross-license provision that provided TI may not sue Qualcomm over pass-through rights agreements between Qualcomm and third parties in existence at time cross-license was executed); CBS, Inc. v. American Society of Composers, Authors and Publishers, 714 N.Y.S.2d 44 (N.Y. App. Div. 2000) (Most Favored Nation clause in CBS-ASCAP license agreement, which provided that ASCAP would not provide a competitor of CBS a more favorable license, was not breached by NBC-ASCAP license that allowed NBC to make payments at a later point in time, albeit in a higher gross amount; the plain language of the MFN clause indicated that it encompassed absolute money value and was not intended to encompass the time value of money); Core Laboratories, Inc. v. Hayward-Wolff Research Corp., 136 A.2d 553 (Del. 1957) (Patent owner's agreement not to sue infringer during period that validity of patents was being determined did not constitute a royalty-free license that would violate a Most Favored Licensee clause in an earlier license entered into by patent owner).

Additional Information

1.   Robert Goldscheider, Eckstrom's Licensing Forms: Model Clauses Clause 15-1[a] — 15-1[q] (2011).

2. JOHN G. MILLS III ET AL., 3 PATENT LAW FUNDAMENTALS § 19:21 (2d ed. 2010).

3. RAYMOND T. NIMMER, LAW OF COMPUTER TECHNOLOGY § 7:108 (4th ed. 2010).

4. 2 KURTIS A. KEMPER, COMPUTER AND INFORMATION LAW DIGEST § 7:11 (2d ed. 2010).

5. RAYMOND T. NIMMER, MODERN LICENSING LAW §§ 7:13, 7:22 (2010).

6. MELVIN F. JAGER, LICENSING LAW HANDBOOK § 10:14 (2010-2011 ed.).

7. JAY DRATLER, JR., LICENSING INTELL. PROP. § 9.05 (2011).

8. MARK S. HOLMES, LICENSING: STRATEGY, NEGOTIATION & FORMS § 15:14 (2010).

9. Stirling Adams, *Negotiating a Commercial "Most Favored Nation" Clause*, 1 INT'L L. & MGMT. REV. 79 (2005).

10. Joseph Kattan, Scott A. Stemple, *Antitrust Enforcement and Most Favored Nation Clauses*, 10 SUM ANTITRUST 20 (1996).

11. Anthony Dennis, *Most Favored Nations Contract Clauses Under the Antitrust Laws*, 20 U. DAYTON L. REV. 821 (1995).

2.3.5 License Transfers

Issues involving the transfer of rights under a patent license arise in two general contexts. The first context is when the initial transferee of the patent license seeks to transfer rights under the patent license to a third party. Within this context, there are four variations:

(1) an initial *non-exclusive* licensee seeks to transfer the license rights by way of an *assignment*;

(2) an initial *non-exclusive* licensee seeks to transfer the license rights by way of a *sublicense*;

(3) an initial *exclusive* licensee seeks to transfer the license rights by way of an *assignment*; and

(4) an initial *exclusive* licensee seeks to transfer the license rights by way of a *sublicense.*

The second context involving the transfer of rights under a patent license arises when the initial transferee of the patent license is either merged with, or acquired by, another company. Here, the issues generally revolve around the structure of the merger or acquisition and the effect of a license prohibition against assignment and sublicensing patent rights on the merger or acquisition.

Courts have held that the transfer of patent licenses is governed by federal law. Under federal law, a non-exclusive patent license cannot be assigned without the consent of the licensor because federal law provides that a non-exclusive license does not convey any rights to the licensee, but only immunity from an infringement suit by the licensor. *See*, JOHN R. KENNEL ET AL. 69 C.J.S. PATENTS § 351 (2008). The same result would follow in the event a nonexclusive licensee sought to sublicense the patent rights without the consent of the licensor. Again, because the nonexclusive licensee has not received any rights under the license, the nonexclusive licensee would not have any rights that could be sublicensed to a third party.

The federal law with respect to the transfer of patent rights by an exclusive licensee is less clear. Under federal law, an exclusive patent license does give the licensee specific rights in the patent and, therefore, arguably these rights can be transferred, at least in some ways, without the consent of the licensor. *See* RAYMOND T. NIMMER, LICENSING OF INTELLECTUAL PROPERTY AND OTHER INFORMATION ASSETS (2d ed.), 260 (2004). The cases which have considered this question have generally found that an exclusive licensee has the right to sublicense the patent rights unless the right to sublicense is expressly denied in the license. *See* Moraine Products v. ICI America, Inc., 538 F.2d 134 (7th Cir. 1976). However, an exclusive licensee's assignment of its patent rights is void, or voidable at the option of the licensor, unless assignment is expressly permitted in the license. *See*, 69 C.J.S. PATENTS, § 351 (2008).

The patent licensor is generally allowed to assign its interest in the patent license, unless expressly prohibited from doing so in the license, even where the patent licensor has agreed to indemnify the licensee.

In the case of a valid sublicense or assignment of the rights under a patent license, the sublicensee or assignee acquires these rights subject to the same terms and conditions contained in the initial patent license. In addition, after a valid sublicense or assignment, the initial patent licensee continues to be liable to the licensor unless the licensor consents to a novation of the license relieving the initial licensee from further obligations under the license. Similarly, in the event of a valid assignment by the licensor of its rights under the patent license, the assignee assumes all the rights and obligations of the licensor under the license. Likewise, in the case of a transfer of patent license rights by means of a merger or acquisition, the successor to the initial licensor or licensee would assume all the rights and obligations of the initial licensor or licensee.

The Patent Act requires that the assignment of "applications for patent, patents, or any interest therein" must be in writing. 35 U.S.C. § 261. There is no writing requirement for patent licenses. The Patent Act also provides:

> An assignment, grant or conveyance shall be void as against any subsequent purchaser or mortgagee for valuable consideration, without notice, unless it is recorded in the Patent and Trademark Office within three months from its date or prior to the date of such subsequent purchase or mortgage.

Failure to record a patent assignment will not invalidate the assignment, but it does render the assignment vulnerable to a subsequent assignment. There is no recording provision in the Patent Act for patent licenses.

The first case in this section, *Intergraph*, considers the rights of a patent licensee under a cross-license agreement where the patent licensor acquires another firm owning patents. The second case, *PPG Industries*, considers the effect of a merger between the licensee and another firm on the licensed patent rights where the license is silent with respect to mergers and acquisitions. The third case, *Cook*, considers whether a prohibition on assignment and sublicensing can be circumvented by means of a purchase-sale contract with another party. The issue in the final case, *Rhone-Poulenc*, is whether a sublicensee can raise the UCC defense of a *bona fide* purchaser for value when the initial licensee has been found guilty of fraud and the initial license has been rescinded.

INTERGRAPH v. INTEL CORPORATION
241 F.3d 1353 (Fed. Cir. 2001)

PAULINE NEWMAN, CIRCUIT JUDGE.

Intergraph Corporation appeals the decision of the United States District Court for the Northern District of Alabama, granting summary judgment that Intel Corporation is licensed to practice the inventions of Intergraph's United States Patents Nos. 4,860,192, 4,884,197, 4,933,835, and 5,091,846 (together "the Clipper patents"), and dismissing Intergraph's claims for patent infringement. We conclude that Intel is not licensed under these patents.

BACKGROUND

The Clipper patents relate to certain microprocessor technology developed by the Advanced Processor Division of Fairchild Semiconductor Corporation. Intergraph, a manufacturer of computer graphics workstations, used the Clipper technology in its workstations. In 1987, when Intergraph learned that Fairchild was to be sold by its parent company to National Semiconductor Company, Intergraph arranged to purchase the Advanced Processor Division from Fairchild, including the Clipper technology and pending patent applications. Intergraph, National Semiconductor, and Fairchild entered into a Purchase Agreement dated September 30, 1987, referring to National's forthcoming purchase of Fairchild and providing that National will, at the closing, "cause Fairchild to sell, assign, transfer, convey and deliver to Intergraph" all of the assets of the Advanced Processor Division. The agreement defines Fairchild as "Seller" of these assets, and sets forth the documents to be delivered to Intergraph at the closing, including assignment of the Clipper applications.

At the closing on October 8, 1987 these transactions were all carried out. National acquired Fairchild, which became a subsidiary of National; and the Advanced Processor Division was conveyed to Intergraph, including assignment of the Clipper patent applications from Fairchild to Intergraph. Since the Fairchild officers had resigned earlier in the day, the patent assignment documents were executed on behalf of Fairchild by Lawrence Ludgus, who was designated by National to act as attorney-in-fact for Fairchild. The question is whether, in the course of these proceedings, the Clipper patent applications and the patents granted to Intergraph thereon became included in the existing cross-license agreement between National Semiconductor and Intel. The district court so held.

The issue may be resolved upon review of the various contracts: the cross-license agreement between National and Intel, and the documents showing the intent as well as the implementation among Fairchild, Intergraph, and National.

The cross-license agreement between National Semiconductor and Intel, entered in 1976 and in effect at the time of these events, provides that National grants to Intel non-exclusive, non-transferrable, royalty-free, world-wide licenses under NATIONAL PATENTS and NATIONAL PATENT APPLICATIONS to make, to have made, to use, to sell (either directly or indirectly), to lease and to otherwise dispose of LICENSED PRODUCTS.

It is not disputed that the general subject matter of the Clipper patent applications is within the technological scope of "Licensed Products" as defined in the cross-license agreement. That agreement includes the following definitions:

> "NATIONAL PATENTS" means all classes or types of patents . . . in respect of which, as of the EFFECTIVE DATE, or thereafter during the term of this Agreement, NATIONAL owns or controls, or under which and to the extent to which and subject to the conditions under which NATIONAL may have, as of the EFFECTIVE DATE, or may thereafter during the term of this Agreement acquire, the right to grant licenses of the scope granted herein without the payment of royalties or other consideration to third persons, . . .

> "NATIONAL PATENT APPLICATIONS" means any applications . . . which, when issued, will become NATIONAL PATENTS.

The district court held that the Clipper patent applications were "National Patent Applications" because "National Semiconductor Corporation did, in fact, acquire "control" of the subject patents within the meaning of the cross-licensing agreement between itself and Intel Corporation dated June 1, 1976, and that Intel was then and is now licensed to use such patents as set out in the cross-licensing agreement."

Challenging the correctness of this ruling, Intergraph presents three principal arguments: first, that the Clipper patent applications were not within the license agreement's definition of "National Patent Applications" because they would not, when issued, become "National Patents"; second, that the events of the closing did not give National "ownership or control" of the patents that later issued on the Clipper patent applications; and third, that in all events no license was available to Intel because the agreement requires consent by any subsidiary before its patents are included in the cross-license. Thus Intergraph argues that no license to Intel vested during the procedures of the closing.

DISCUSSION

The cross-license agreement between National and Intel defines "National Patent Applications" as any applications "which, when issued, will become National Patents." "National Patents" are defined as all patents that "during the term of this Agreement, NATIONAL owns or controls . . . ." Since the Clipper patent applications were assigned by Fairchild directly to Intergraph, they could not issue as patents owned or controlled by National. The plain reading of the license definition of "National Patent Applications" is patent applications that *will* become "National Patents." The term "ownership or control" in the Intel cross-license agreement applies not to "National Patent Applications" but to "National Patents." The license agreement requires that the patent application, when issued, will become a patent that National owns or controls. As this provision was not met, and was plainly not intended to be met, the Clipper patent applications did not meet the definition of "National Patent Applications," even fleetingly on the day of the closing.

National was obligated to assure that the Advanced Processor Division, including the Clipper patent applications, were transferred from Fairchild to Intergraph "concurrently with or immediately following the acquisition of Fairchild." This obligation, and its performance, did not convert these patent applications into "National Patent Applications" with the right to encumber the later-issued Clipper patents with a third party royalty-free license. At the closing the paperwork for National's acquisition of Fairchild was completed first, followed by completion of the paperwork for Intergraph's acquisition of the Advanced Processor Division. Intel states that this placed the Clipper patent applications within the ownership or control of National for an hour or two. Intel also argues that National was a "party" to the sale by Fairchild to Intergraph, based on National's agreement "to cause Fairchild" to perform this transfer at the closing.

The transfers of Fairchild to National and of the Advanced Processor Division to Intergraph were conducted in sequence on the same day. The order of proceedings did not vest National with the right to encumber any property that it momentarily possessed until the next document was signed. Intel's citation of cases whereby the sole shareholder of a corporation may dispose of corporate property does not establish that National had the right, for an hour or two, to encumber the Advanced Processor Division and its patent property in a way that would contravene the terms of the sale to Intergraph. In the assignment by Fairchild to Intergraph there is transferred "the full and exclusive right, title and interest to the Clipper patent applications," without hint that unknown persons might acquire a free license from National during the hour of closing. Intel's contrary interpretation of these documents is too strained to be supported.

No contract or other document, and no other evidence, supports the interpretation that Fairchild, Intergraph, and National intended that the Advanced Processor Division and its patent applications could be encumbered by National before the transfer to Intergraph was completed. The Purchase Agreement, dated a week before the closing, provides that National will cause Fairchild to sell the Advanced Processor Division assets directly to Intergraph, free and clear of all encumbrances not assumed by Intergraph:

> Such sale, conveyance, transfer and delivery of the [Advanced Processor Division] assets defined above shall be free and clear of all debts, liabilities, obligations, title defects, liens and encumbrances, except for those expressly assumed by Intergraph.

This transaction was required to occur "concurrently with or immediately following the acquisition of Fairchild by National." Intergraph did not "expressly assume" that National's cross-licensees would be granted free licenses to the Clipper patent applications and ensuing patents based on the sequential mechanics of the closing. The district court erred in construing these events as giving National "ownership or control" of the patents that issued some years later to Intergraph.

In further support of its position that Intel did not acquire a license to the Clipper patents, Intergraph points out that Fairchild became a subsidiary of National, and that the National-Intel cross-license agreement provides that the patents and applications of the parties' subsidiaries are not included in the cross-license agreement unless the subsidiary expressly agrees to include them in exchange for a license to the Intel patents:

> § 2. INTEL agrees that NATIONAL shall have the right to extend the licenses granted pursuant to section 1 hereof only to those of its SUBSID-IARIES which will agree to include their patents, utility models, and design patents and applications therefor covering LICENSED PROD-UCTS in NATIONAL PATENTS and NATIONAL PATENT APPLICA-TIONS.

It is undisputed that Fairchild did not agree to include the Clipper patent applications in the cross-license agreement. Indeed Fairchild, when it became National's subsidiary, could not agree to include the Clipper patent applications in the cross-license agreement, for Fairchild had sold these applications to Intergraph exclusively and free of encumbrances.

Intel proposes an alternative reading of this contract provision, and argues that it does not exclude all patents owned by National's subsidiaries unless they elect to join the cross-license agreement, but instead provides a means whereby a subsidiary whose patents are not controlled by National may choose to enjoy the benefits of a cross-license with Intel. We discern no support for Intel's theory that this clause means that a subsidiary's patents are necessarily licensed to Intel without the subsidiary's consent, or is intended to apply only to those subsidiaries over which Intel lacks control. The cross-license agreement defines "subsidiary" as an entity at least fifty percent of whose stock is owned or controlled by a party to the agreement. Since such a subsidiary is by this definition within National's "control," yet this clause requires the subsidiary's agreement to the cross-license, there is no merit to Intel's position that the Fairchild subsidiary's patents became licensed to Intel even if the subsidiary did not agree.

CONCLUSION

The district court erred in ruling that Intel is licensed under the Clipper patents. That ruling is reversed. The case is remanded for appropriate further proceedings.

REVERSED AND REMANDED.

QUESTIONS

1. Why did the court find that Fairchild's Clipper patent applications were not included within the National-Intel cross-license agreement?

2. Why did the court find that Fairchild's Clipper patent applications did not come under the ownership or control of National upon National's acquisition of Fairchild?

3. Which firm ultimately received the payment for the patents?

4. If you were counsel to Fairchild, how would you have structured the transaction to avoid Intel's license claim?

PPG INDUSTRIES, INC. v. GUARDIAN INDUSTRIES CORP.
597 F.2d 1090 (6th Cir. 1979)

LIVELY, CIRCUIT JUDGE.

The question in this case is whether the surviving or resultant corporation in a statutory merger acquires patent license rights of the constituent corporations. The plaintiff, PPG Industries, Inc. (PPG), appeals from a judgment of the district court dismissing its patent infringement action on the ground that the defendant, Guardian Industries, Corp. (Guardian), as licensee of the patents in suit, was not an infringer. Guardian cross-appeals from a holding by the district court that its alternate defense based on an equipment license agreement was ineffective.

I

Prior to 1964 both PPG and Permaglass, Inc., were engaged in fabrication of glass products which required that sheets of glass be shaped for particular uses. Independently of each other the two fabricators developed similar processes which involved "floating glass on a bed of gas, while it was being heated and bent." This process is known in the industry as "gas hearth technology" and "air float technology"; the two terms are interchangeable. After a period of negotiations PPG and Permaglass entered into an agreement on January 1, 1964 whereby each granted rights to the other under "gas hearth system" patents already issued and in the process of prosecution. The purpose of the agreement was set forth in the preamble as follows:

> WHEREAS, PPG is desirous of acquiring from PERMAGLASS a worldwide exclusive license with right to sublicense others under PERMAGLASS Technical Data and PERMAGLASS Patent Rights, subject only to reservation by PERMAGLASS of non-exclusive rights thereunder; and

> WHEREAS, PERMAGLASS is desirous of obtaining a nonexclusive license to use Gas Hearth Systems under PPG Patent Rights, excepting in the Dominion of Canada.

This purpose was accomplished in the two sections of the agreement quoted below:

SECTION 3. GRANT FROM PERMAGLASS TO PPG

3.1 Subject to the reservation set forth in Subsection 3.3 below, PERMAGLASS hereby grants to PPG an exclusive license, with right of sublicense, to use PERMAGLASS Technical Data in Gas Hearth Systems throughout the United States of America, its territories and possessions, and all countries of the world foreign thereto.

3.2 Subject to the reservation set forth in Subsection 3.3 below, PERMA-GLASS hereby grants to PPG an unlimited exclusive license, with right of sublicense, under PERMAGLASS Patent Rights.

3.3 The licenses granted to PPG under Subsections 3.1 and 3.2 above shall be subject to the reservation of a non-exclusive, non-transferable, royalty-free, world-wide right and license for the benefit and use of PERMA-GLASS.

SECTION 4. GRANT FROM PPG TO PERMAGLASS

4.1 PPG hereby grants to PERMAGLASS a non-exclusive, non-transferable, royalty-free right and license to heat, bend, thermally temper and/or anneal glass using Gas Hearth Systems under PPG Patent Rights, excepting in the Dominion of Canada, and to use or sell glass articles produced thereby, but no license, express or implied, is hereby granted to PERMAGLASS under any claim of any PPG patent expressly covering any coating method, coating composition, or coated article.

Assignability of the agreement and of the license granted to Permaglass and termination of the license granted to Permaglass were covered in the following language:

SECTION 9. ASSIGNABILITY

9.1 This Agreement shall be assignable by PPG to any successor of the entire flat glass business of PPG but shall otherwise be non-assignable except with the consent of PERMAGLASS first obtained in writing.

9.2 This Agreement and the license granted by PPG to PERMAGLASS hereunder shall be personal to PERMAGLASS and non-assignable except with the consent of PPG first obtained in writing.

SECTION 11. TERMINATION

11.2 In the event that a majority of the voting stock of PERMAGLASS shall at any time become owned or controlled directly or indirectly by a manufacturer of automobiles or a manufacturer or fabricator of glass other than the present owners, the license granted to PERMAGLASS under Subsection 4.1 shall terminate forthwith.

Eleven patents are involved in this suit. Nine of them originated with Permaglass and were licensed to PPG as exclusive licensee under Section 3.2, Supra, subject to the non-exclusive, non-transferable reservation to Permaglass set forth in Section 3.3. Two of the patents originated with PPG. Section 4.1 granted a non-exclusive, non-transferable license to Permaglass with respect to the two PPG patents. In Section 9.1 and 9.2 assignability was treated somewhat differently as between the parties, and the Section 11.2 provisions with regard to termination apply only to the license granted to Permaglass.

As of December 1969 Permaglass was merged into Guardian pursuant to applicable statutes of Ohio and Delaware. Guardian was engaged primarily in the business of fabricating and distributing windshields for automobiles and trucks. It had decided to construct a facility to manufacture raw glass and the capacity of that facility would be greater than its own requirements. Permaglass had no glass manufacturing capability and it was contemplated that its operations would utilize a large part of the excess output of the proposed Guardian facility.

The "Agreement of Merger" between Permaglass and Guardian did not refer specifically to the 1964 agreement between PPG and Permaglass. However, among Permaglass' representations in the agreement was the following:

> (g) Permaglass is the owner, assignee or licensee of such patents, trademarks, trade names and copyrights as are listed and described in Exhibit "C" attached hereto. None of such patents, trademarks, trade names or copyrights is in litigation and Permaglass has not received any notice of conflict with the asserted rights of third parties relative to the use thereof.

Listed on Exhibit "C" to the merger agreement are the nine patents originally developed by Permaglass and licensed to PPG under the 1964 agreement which are involved in this infringement action.

Shortly after the merger was consummated PPG filed the present action, claiming infringement by Guardian in the use of apparatus and processes described and claimed in eleven patents which were identified by number and origin. The eleven patents were covered by the terms of the 1964 agreement. PPG asserted that it became the exclusive licensee of the nine patents which originated with Permaglass under the 1964 agreement and that the rights reserved by Permaglass were personal to it and non-transferable and non-assignable. PPG also claimed that Guardian had no rights with respect to the two patents which had originated with PPG because the license under these patents was personal to Permaglass and non-transferable and non-assignable except with the permission of PPG. In addition it claimed that the license with respect to these two patents had terminated under the provisions of Section 11.2, Supra, by reason of the merger.

One of the defenses pled by Guardian in its answer was that it was a licensee of the patents in suit. It described the merger with Permaglass and claimed it "had succeeded to all rights, powers, ownerships, etc., of Permaglass, and as Permaglass' successor, defendant is legally entitled to operate in place of Permaglass under the January 1, 1964 agreement between Permaglass and plaintiff, free of any claim of infringement of the patents . . . ."

After holding an evidentiary hearing the district court concluded that the parties to the 1964 agreement did not intend that the rights reserved by Permaglass in its nine patents or the rights assigned to Permaglass in the two PPG patents would not pass to a successor corporation by way of merger. The court held that there had been no assignment or transfer of the rights by Permaglass, but rather that Guardian acquired these rights by operation of law under the merger statutes of Ohio and Delaware. The provisions of the 1964 agreement making the license rights of Permaglass non-assignable and non-transferable were held not to apply because of the "continuity of interest inherent in a statutory merger that distinguishes it from the ordinary assignment or transfer case."

With respect to the termination provision in Section 11.2 of the 1964 agreement, the district court again relied on "the nature of a statutory merger in contrast to an outright sale or acquisition of stock" in holding that a majority of the voting stock of Permaglass did not become owned or controlled by Guardian.

II

Questions with respect to the assignability of a patent license are controlled by federal law. It has long been held by federal courts that agreements granting patent licenses are personal and not assignable unless expressly made so. This has been the rule at least since 1852 when the Supreme Court decided *Troy Iron & Nail v. Corning.* The district court recognized this rule in the present case, but concluded that where patent licenses are claimed to pass by operation of law to the resultant or surviving corporation in a statutory merger there has been no assignment or transfer.

There appear to be no reported cases where the precise issue in this case has been decided. At least two treatises contain the statement that rights under a patent license owned by a constituent corporation pass to the consolidated corporation in the case of a consolidation, W. Fletcher, Cyclopedia of the Law of Corporations s 7089 (revised ed. 1973); and to the new or resultant corporation in the case of a merger, A. Deller, Walker on Patents s 409 (2d ed. 1965). However, the cases cited in support of these statements by the commentators do not actually provide such support because their facts take them outside the general rule of non-assignability. Both texts rely on the decision in Hartford-Empire Co. v. Demuth Glass Works, Inc. The agreement involved in that case specified that the patent license was assignable and its assignability was not an issue. Clearly the statement in the Hartford-Empire opinion that the merger conveyed to the new corporation the patent licenses owned by the old corporation results from the fact that the licenses in question were expressly made assignable, not from any general principle that such licenses pass to the resultant corporation where there is a merger. It is also noteworthy that the surviving corporation following the merger in Hartford-Empire was the original licensee, whereas in the present case the original licensee was merged into Guardian, which was the survivor.

****

Guardian relies on two classes of cases where rights of a constituent corporation have been held to pass by merger to the resultant corporation even though such rights are not otherwise assignable or transferable. It points out that the courts have consistently held that "shop rights" do pass in a statutory merger. A shop right is an implied license which accrues to an employer in cases where an employee has perfected a patentable device while working for the employer. Though the employee is the owner of the patent he is estopped from claiming infringement by the employer. This estoppel arises from the fact that the patent work has been done on the employer's time and that the employer has furnished materials for the experiments and financial backing to the employee.

The rule that prevents an employee-inventor from claiming infringement against a successor to the entire business and good will of his employer is but one feature of the broad doctrine of estoppel which underlies the shop right cases. No element of estoppel exists in the present case. The license rights of Permaglass did not arise by implication. They were bargained for at arm's length and the agreement which defines the rights of the parties provides that Permaglass received non-transferable, non-assignable personal licenses. We do not believe that the express prohibition against assignment and transfer in a written instrument may be held ineffective by analogy to a rule based on estoppel in situations where there is no written contract and the rights of the parties have arisen by implication because of their past relationship.

The other group of cases which the district court and Guardian found to be analogous hold that the resultant corporation in a merger succeeds to the rights of the constituent corporations under real estate leases. The most obvious difficulty in drawing an analogy between the lease cases and those concerning patent licenses is that a lease is an interest in real property. As such, it is subject to the deep-rooted policy against restraints on alienation. Applying this policy, courts have construed provisions against assignability in leases strictly and have concluded that they do not prevent the passage of interests by operation of law. There is no similar policy which is offended by the decision of a patent owner to make a license under his patent personal to the licensee, and non-assignable and non-transferable. In fact the law treats a license as if it contained these restrictions in the absence of express provisions to the contrary.

We conclude that the district court misconceived the intent of the parties to the 1964 agreement. We believe the district court put the burden on the wrong party in stating:

> Because the parties failed to provide that Permaglass' rights under the 1964 license agreement would not pass to the corporation surviving a merger, the Court finds that Guardian succeeded to Permaglass' license.

The agreement provides with respect to the license which Permaglass granted to PPG that Permaglass reserved "a non-exclusive, non-transferable, royalty-free, world-wide right and license for the benefit and use of Permaglass." (emphasis added). Similarly, with respect to its own two patents, PPG granted to Permaglass "a non-exclusive, non-transferable, royalty-free right and license . . . ." Further, the agreement provides that both it and the license granted to Permaglass "shall be personal to PERMAGLASS and non-assignable except with the consent of PPG first obtained in writing."

The quoted language from Sections 3, 4 and 9 of the 1964 agreement evinces an intent that only Permaglass was to enjoy the privileges of licensee. If the parties had intended an exception in the event of a merger, it would have been a simple matter to have so provided in the agreement. Guardian contends such an exception is not necessary since it is universally recognized that patent licenses pass from a licensee to the resultant corporation in case of a merger. This does not appear to be the case. In Packard Instrument Co. v. ANS, Inc., a license agreement provided that rights thereunder could not be transferred or assigned "except . . . . (b) if the entire ownership and business of ANS is transferred by sale, merger, or consolidation, . . ." Similarly, the agreement construed in Freeman v. Seiberling Rubber Co. provided that the license was not assignable except with the entire business and good will of the licensee. We conclude that if the parties had intended an exception in case of a merger to the provisions against assignment and transfer they would have included it in the agreement. It should be noted also that the district court in Packard, *supra*, held that an assignment had taken place when the licensee was merged into another corporation.

The district court also held that the patent licenses in the present case were not transferred because they passed by operation of law from Permaglass to Guardian. This conclusion is based on the theory of continuity which underlies a true merger. However, the theory of continuity relates to the fact that there is no dissolution of the constituent corporations and, even though they cease to exist, their essential corporate attributes are vested by operation of law in the surviving or resultant corporation. It does not mean that there is no transfer of particular assets from a constituent corporation to the surviving or resultant one.

The Ohio merger statute provides that following a merger all property of a constituent corporation shall be "deemed to be transferred to and vested in the surviving or new corporation without further act or deed, ..." This indicates that the transfer is by operation of law, not that there is no transfer of assets in a merger situation. The Delaware statute, which was also involved in the Permaglass-Guardian merger, provides that the property of the constituent corporations "shall be vested in the corporation surviving or resulting from such merger or consolidation, ..." The Third Circuit has construed the "shall be vested" language of the Delaware statute as follows:

> In short, the underlying property of the constituent corporations is transferred to the resultant corporation upon the carrying out of the consolidation or merger . . . .

In his opinion in Koppers, Judge Biggs disposed of arguments very similar to those of Guardian in the present case, based on the theory of continuity. Terming such arguments "metaphysical" he found them completely at odds with the language of the Delaware statute. Finally, on this point, the parties themselves provided in the merger agreement that all property of Permaglass "shall be deemed transferred to and shall vest in Guardian without further act or deed . . . ." A transfer is no less a transfer because it takes place by operation of law rather than by a particular act of the parties. The merger was effected by the parties and the transfer was a result of their act of merging.

Thus, Sections 3, 4 and 9 of the 1964 agreement between PPG and Permaglass show an intent that the licenses held by Permaglass in the eleven patents in suit not be transferable. While this conclusion disposes of the license defense as to all eleven patents, it should be noted that Guardian's claim to licenses under the two patents which originated with PPG is also defeated by Section 11.2 of the 1964 agreement. This section addresses a different concern from that addressed in Sections 3, 4 and 9. The restrictions on transferability and assignability in those sections prevent the patent licenses from becoming the property of third parties. The termination clause, however, provides that Permaglass' license with respect to the two PPG patents will terminate if the ownership of a majority of the voting stock of Permaglass passes from the 1964 stockholders to designated classes of persons, even though the licenses themselves might never have changed hands.

Apparently PPG was willing for Permaglass to continue as licensee under the nine patents even though ownership of its stock might change. These patents originated with Permaglass and so long as Permaglass continued to use the licenses for its own benefit a mere change in ownership of Permaglass stock would not nullify the licenses. Only a transfer or assignment would cause a termination. However, the agreement provides for termination with respect to the two original PPG patents in the event of an indirect takeover of Permaglass by a change in the ownership of a majority of its stock. The fact that PPG sought and obtained a stricter provision with respect to the two patents which it originally owned in no way indicates an intention to permit transfer of licenses under the other nine in case of a merger. None of the eleven licenses was transferable; but two of them, those involving PPG's own development in the field of gas hearth technology, were not to continue even for the benefit of the licensee if it came under the control of a manufacturer of automobiles or a competitor of PPG in the glass industry "other than the present owners" of Permaglass. A consistency among the provisions of the agreement is discernible when the different origins of the various patents are considered.

****

The judgment of the district court is reversed on appeal and affirmed on cross-appeal, and the cause is remanded for further proceedings. Costs are taxed to Guardian.

QUESTIONS

1. How could the merger have been structured in a way to avoid any transfer of Permaglass' license rights?

2. Would the decision have been the same if Permaglass had been the surviving corporation?

3. Why did Permaglass reserve a "non-exclusive, non-transferable" right to use its patents?

4. Do you agree with the district court's or the appellate court's reasoning in the case?

5. What is the takeaway message regarding assignability clauses and mergers?

COOK INC. v. BOSTON SCIENTIFIC CORP.
333 F.3d 737 (7th Cir. 2003)

POSNER, CIRCUIT JUDGE.

The plaintiff brought suit seeking a declaration that it had not violated a contract to which it and the defendant, along with a third firm, are parties. Jurisdiction is based on diversity of citizenship, and the governing substantive law is that of the state of Washington, though no peculiarities of Washington law have been drawn to our attention. The defendant counterclaimed, charging that the plaintiff had indeed broken the contract. On cross-motions for summary judgment, the district court ruled for the defendant and entered a permanent injunction against the plaintiff, precipitating this appeal.

The contract involves a medical device known as a stent. The narrowing of an artery, as by atherosclerosis, is called "stenosis" and one way of treating it is by balloon angioplasty, a procedure in which a small balloon is inserted into the affected artery to press against the artery wall restoring it to its normal dimensions. The stent is a metal tube that encloses the balloon and remains in the artery after the procedure. Yet sometimes despite the stent the stenosis reappears — this is called "restenosis" — and there is medical opinion that the likelihood of this happening can be reduced by coating the stent with a suitable drug. One candidate to be such a drug is paclitaxel, which gained fame as an anticancer drug under the trade name Taxol. The patent rights for use of paclitaxel on stents are held by a Canadian company called Angiotech Pharmaceuticals. Angiotech does not manufacture either stents or drugs, and so it decided to license the use of paclitaxel for coating stents. It granted "co-exclusive" licenses to Cook Incorporated and Boston Scientific Corporation (BSC), firms involved in the development of drug-coated stents for preventing restenosis. Each license grants the licensee "worldwide right[s] and license to use, manufacture, have manufactured, distribute and sell, and to grant sublicenses to its Affiliates to use, manufacture, have manufactured, distribute and sell [paclitaxel] . . . solely for use in [stents]." The licenses are exclusive in the sense that Angiotech promises not to license the use of paclitaxel for coating stents to any other firm, but co-exclusive in the sense that each licensee has the same rights. Critically, the licenses forbid the licensee to assign his license, or to grant a sublicense to anyone except an affiliate, unless all parties to the two licenses, which is to say Angiotech, BSC, and Cook, agree. We'll call this provision the "anti-assignment" clause, although it covers sublicenses as well. Why the distinction between assignment to an affiliate, which is forbidden, and sublicensing an affiliate, which is permitted, is unclear, since, while an assignment and a sublicense are not identical, a sublicense can be drafted in such a way as to have the same effect.

The two licenses were granted in a single contract, so that both the licensees and Angiotech are contractually bound to one another. The contract provides for the arbitration of disputes arising under it, but the parties have waived that provision. Angiotech is not a party to this suit; it may be indifferent to the outcome or reluctant to take sides in a dispute between its most important partners in the development of restenosis-resisting stents.

Why *co-exclusive* licenses? No evidence has been presented or arguments made concerning the reason for the co-exclusive feature. The lawyers either have not bothered to inquire or have not bothered to inform us or the district judge concerning the commercial setting of such a contract. They seem insensitive to the importance to the sound interpretation of contracts of understanding the business purpose served by a contract's provisions, and to the limitations of generalist judges' knowledge of the customs and practices of specific industries. We are left to speculate, having found no secondary literature on co-exclusive licenses either.

A patentee's choice between granting exclusive and nonexclusive licenses is similar to a seller's choice between granting exclusive and nonexclusive rights to his dealers. The dealer who is granted an exclusive right will have an enhanced incentive to devote his sales efforts to the seller's product. Dealers who do not receive exclusive rights will have enhanced incentives to minimize their margins by competing among themselves, thus maximizing the price that the seller can charge. Consumers' demand is a function of the dealer's as well as the original seller's profit margin. For both margins are components of the retail price, and so the lower the dealer's margin is, the lower that price will be, the more therefore will be sold, and so the greater will be the original seller's total profits.

Thus a patentee can ordinarily be expected either to grant nonexclusive licenses in order to exploit the effect of competition in minimizing the licensees' margins or to grant an exclusive license in order to encourage the licensee to invest in the further development of the licensed process or product by protecting the licensee from the competition of other licensees, which might prevent the licensee from recouping his investment. There are other considerations bearing on the choice between exclusive and nonexclusive licensing as well, but we needn't get into them.

The second goal that we have mentioned, that of encouraging investment by the licensee, is the relevant one in this case. Angiotech does not manufacture or coat stents itself. It depends on its licensees to develop the product (that is, the coated stents) and obtain the Food and Drug Administration's approval so that the product can be marketed. If, therefore, Cook or BSC were essentially interchangeable, or one were clearly a superior developer to the other, we would expect Angiotech to grant an exclusive license to one of them. Probably the reason it did not is that the two firms use different coating methods, requiring each to obtain separate approval from the FDA before being permitted to market a drug-coated stent in the United States. When the contract was made, and indeed to this day, neither Cook nor BSC had yet obtained FDA approval. Their products are *still* being tested for safety and efficacy. Angiotech would not have wanted to risk betting on the wrong horse — granting BSC an exclusive license, for example, when Cook's stent might turn out to be the only drug-coated stent that the FDA would approve, or might be approved earlier than BSC's product, or might prove to be the superior product.

At the same time — and here we approach the crux of the appeal — Cook and BSC might be reluctant to accept nonexclusive licenses. To obtain FDA approval for a new drug or medical device (a paclitaxel-coated stent is what the FDA calls a "combination product" and is assigned to the division of FDA that handles devices) requires a substantial investment, which the manufacturer of the device might have difficulty recouping if it faced competition from another licensee. With Angiotech reluctant to grant an exclusive license and Cook and BSC reluctant to settle for nonexclusive licenses, coexclusive licenses were a natural compromise.

The compromise might be undone by assignment or sublicensing. Suppose Cook fell behind BSC in the race to develop an approved and marketable paclitaxel-coated stent and tried to recover the lead by assigning its license to a firm with greater resources or other advantages that would enable it to overtake BSC. The effect would be to confront the latter with more competition than it had reckoned on when it took out its license from Angiotech. Hence the bar on assignment without the permission of the other licensee (plus Angiotech, though that is not a factor here). Although competition is generally a good thing, there is no argument that Angiotech would have violated antitrust law or been guilty of patent misuse had it granted an exclusive, non-assignable license. And so we cannot see how Angiotech's action in granting two licenses and forbidding the licensees to increase the number of competitors by means of assignment or sublicensing could raise an antitrust or patent-misuse issue. Notice that the licenses do not forbid the acquisition of the licensee by another firm — to which as an affiliate the licensee could grant a sublicense without obtaining the permission of the other parties to the contract with Angiotech — that might be a more formidable competitor of the other licensee.

Angiotech granted the co-exclusive licenses in 1997. Four years later Cook made a contract (actually five simultaneous contracts, but that is a detail of no legal significance) with Advanced Cardiovascular Systems, Inc. (ACS), a manufacturer of medical devices and a subsidiary of Guidant Corporation. Under the contract, Cook is to purchase stents from ACS, coat them with paclitaxel, and sell the coated stents back to ACS for resale to hospitals and other purchasers of medical devices. The price received by Cook for the stents that it sells to ACS is to be one-third of the resale price charged by ACS. Before reselling the stents to hospitals or other users of stents, ACS is to mount them on a catheter (which it manufactures) for inserting the balloon and stent into the artery. So what it is selling is really a stent system rather than merely a stent. The stent system is called "ACHIEVE," an ACS brand, though Cook's name will also appear on the package. The contract requires ACS to obtain the regulatory rulings necessary to enable ACHIEVE stent systems actually to be sold, such as approval by the FDA.

BSC argues and the district judge found that the transaction between Cook and ACS is a de facto assignment and so violates the contract because BSC did not consent. (ACS like Angiotech is not a party to the suit — which is a surprise, as one might have expected BSC to join ACS as a counterdefendant on the theory that ACS committed the tort of interference with BSC's contract with Angiotech and Cook.) Cook argues that since the finding was made in a summary judgment proceeding rather than after a trial, we should review it de novo, that is, without according any deference to the district judge's ruling. This is a strange argument. A judge makes findings in a trial or other evidentiary hearing; a grant of summary judgment is a determination that there are no triable issues. So one would expect Cook to be asking not for de novo review of the district judge's findings, but for a trial. One possibility is that Cook thinks (incorrectly, as we'll see) that the question whether the de facto assignment violated the contract is a pure question of law. Another is that Cook consented to have the district judge decide the question of contractual violation on the basis of the pleadings, the briefs, and the limited discovery that had been conducted before the motion for summary judgment was made. Both inferences are supported by Cook's opposition to BSC's completing discovery.

When litigants waive trial, and ask the judge to decide the case as if the record compiled in the pretrial proceedings were a trial record, appellate review is as of findings made after a trial, not as of a grant of summary judgment. "[S]ometimes both parties move for summary judgment because they do not want to bear the expense of trial but instead want the trial judge to treat the record of the summary judgment proceeding as if it were the trial record. In effect the judge is asked to decide the case as if there had been a bench trial in which the evidence was the depositions and other materials gathered in pretrial discovery." It is true that the mere fact that cross-motions for summary judgment are filed, as was done in this case, does not operate as a waiver of the right to a trial. But though there was no explicit waiver, it is reasonably clear that Cook didn't want a trial (more precisely, it either wanted a trial limited to the summary judgment record or thought the issue of contractual violation could be resolved without a factual record) and so waived its right to a (fuller) trial. In its opening brief on appeal, Cook belatedly requested a trial if summary judgment in its favor was rejected. BSC replied that the demand comes too late — and Cook apparently agrees, for its reply brief is silent on the point: a second waiver.

The interpretation of a written contract, when no extrinsic evidence (evidence other than the contract itself) is presented, is treated as an issue of law, and thus is decided by the appellate court de novo, that is, without giving the trial judge's interpretation any special weight. But the rule is otherwise when as in this case the resolution of the interpretive issue requires a comparison of written documents and thus an inference from multiple pieces of evidence, a traditional task of a finder of fact, rather than requiring merely "gazing" at a single document. No matter. The district judge's ruling was not erroneous at all, and so the precise standard of review is unimportant.

Had the contract between Cook and ACS provided that Cook would license to ACS the use of paclitaxel in the ACHIEVE stent system, this would have been an assignment or sublicense in violation of the anti-assignment clause; and as that part of the contract was intended, in part anyway, to protect BSC, BSC has a right to enforce it. This conclusion would be unaffected if besides licensing the use of paclitaxel to coat ACS's ACHIEVE stents, Cook had agreed to do the coating itself (as it did agree in its "sale" contracts with ACS). Cook would still be licensing the distribution and sale of paclitaxel in stents to ACS, a firm with which Cook is not affiliated.

This means that Cook's defense to BSC's charge of breach of contract hinges on the fact that Cook is to sell the coated stents to ACS rather than assigning its patent license to ACS. Cook describes the "sale" as the exercise of the right granted to it by Angiotech to distribute and sell Angiotech's patented product. But the sale of ACS's stents back to ACS has no commercial purpose or substance; it is merely a device for defeating the anti-assignment clause. Suppose a Mr. Guidant asks a Mr. Cook to paint his house. And Cook says, fine, but let's do it this way: you sell me your house, I'll paint it (supplying both the paint and the labor to apply the paint to the house), and then I'll sell the house, painted, back to you. That would make no commercial sense, and so one would delve for an improper motive. Confronted at argument by the house painting hypothetical, Cook's lawyer was unable to distinguish it from this case.

It is obvious what is going on. Cook wanted to improve its competitive posture vis-à-vis BSC by obtaining the resources of a firm that had a better stent than Cook itself. It could have done so without breaking its contract, by affiliating with ACS; affiliation, as by the sale of Cook to Guidant (a transaction actually contemplated at one point, as we'll see), would have allowed Cook to grant a sublicense to ACS. This would not have been an evasion of the three-cornered contract, because the sublicensing of an affiliate is authorized by the licenses. It might appear to be a case of taking advantage of a loophole, but maybe not; it is more costly to merge with another firm than to execute an assignment or the series of five contracts that in substance were an assignment. We know it's more costly because after the district court enjoined the assignment, Cook entered into merger discussions with Guidant, which failed; had they succeeded, the cost to Guidant would have been in the neighborhood of $3 billion.

But while a merger plus an assignment or a sublicense differs in substantial and not merely formal respects from an assignment, the five contracts between Cook and ACS, realistically treated as one, differ from an assignment only in formal, in the sense of economically empty, respects. Not that sale-and-leaseback arrangements, which the Cook-ACS transaction superficially resembles, are characteristically devoid of economic substance, though they can be, since a common purpose is to give the buyer-lessor tax benefits. But emphasis falls on "superficially." Cook didn't buy stents from ACS and then lease them back; it bought them from ACS and then resold them to ACS, the only purpose of the transaction being to transfer Cook's patent rights to ACS in circumvention of the anti-assignment clause.

A further issue discussed in the briefs is whether Cook also violated the clause in the contract that makes it responsible for obtaining the necessary regulatory approvals for the sale of a paclitaxel-coated stent. BSC argues that Cook shifted that responsibility to ACS, and Cook replies that it retained ultimate responsibility and anyway that Angiotech hardly cares whether Cook or ACS takes the laboring oar in obtaining the necessary approvals. Cook is probably right; but the debate is beside the point. The significance of the provision in the contract between Cook and ACS that assigns to ACS the task of obtaining regulatory approvals is merely as further evidence that the contract actually assigned the sale of paclitaxel to ACS, because ACS did everything except the coating to bring the paclitaxel to market.

So Cook broke its contract with BSC and the next question is the propriety of the relief granted by the district court. As BSC points out, it would be very difficult for a court to estimate the damages that it has incurred as a result of Cook's breach. The reason is that neither party has yet obtained the FDA's approval to sell its product. The de facto assignment to ACS undoubtedly gave Cook a leg up, but to translate this insight into a dollar amount of lost expected profits to BSC is impossible. No one knows whether or when, as a consequence of the assignment, Cook will obtain FDA approval or how well its product will succeed in the market. No one knows whether or when BSC will obtain approval of its paclitaxel-coated stent and how successful that product will be in the market. There is injury to BSC in a probabilistic sense — enough injury to establish standing and entitle it to relief of some sort — but whether the injury will prove to be $1 or $100 million is unknown and unknowable.

When a breach of contract is proved but damages cannot be estimated with reasonable certainty, the plaintiff is entitled to an injunction. But the injunction the district court issued goes too far. It not only forbids Cook to perform its contract with ACS or otherwise to violate its contract with Angiotech and BSC; it also provides that "no information, data or technology generated or gathered in connection with the ACS deal shall be used for any commercial purpose, *including the purpose of obtaining regulatory approval to sell paclitaxel-coated stents in the United States or elsewhere.*" The passage that we have italicized violates the principle that in determining the appropriate scope of an injunction the judge must give due weight to the injunction's possible effect on innocent third parties. In this case they are the sufferers from atherosclerosis who might benefit from a device that prevents restenosis. Those effects must be balanced against the harm to BSC from narrowing the injunction by lancing the italicized phrase — but as it happens that harm is zero in a legal sense of "harm," which differs from harm in the lay sense. The difference is brought out in the legal slogan *damnum absque injuria*, i.e., harm without a legally cognizable injury.

What would harm BSC in a legal sense would be the competitive impact on it of having to compete with the Cook-assisted ACHIEVE stent system; it would not be the regulatory approval of that sale if the injunction against sale remained in place so that Cook could not use the approval to enable ACS to sell ACHIEVE in competition with BSC. When pressed at argument BSC's lawyer named only one harm to BSC from the grant of such approval itself — and that a shocker: that the FDA might discover in the course of considering Cook's application (prosecuted on its behalf by ACS) for approval that paclitaxel-coated stents are harmful or ineffective, and that the discovery would hurt BSC, whose own product is also paclitaxel-coated. Indeed it would — and should. We shall therefore modify the district court's injunction by striking the italicized phrase.

Should Cook obtain the FDA's approval before BSC does, it will, as we have been at pains to emphasize, still be enjoined from selling its product though authorized by the FDA to do so. But at that point we imagine that the parties will be able to negotiate the dissolution of the injunction on terms that compensate BSC for having been beaten to the punch. Of course, this suggests that Cook will derive a commercial advantage from being able to continue seeking the FDA's approval to sell a product that Cook is enjoined from selling. But that advantage, which will in any event be shared with BSC in the terms of settlement, seems slight in relation to the social costs of delaying the process of FDA approval. Indeed, should the negotiations we envisage (on the assumption that Cook obtains the FDA's approval before BSC does) fail, the district court might well decide to modify the injunction so that people suffering from atherosclerosis can obtain the benefit of Angiotech's technology at the earliest possible opportunity. While Cook errs in suggesting that 35 U.S.C. § 271(e)(1), which broadens the experimental-use defense to patent infringement as explained in *SmithKline Beecham Corp. v. Apotex Corp.* is a defense to a breach of contract suit (the provision is expressly limited to patent infringement suits), the section does reflect a policy of allowing the use of patented technology to obtain regulatory approval of non-infringing technologies. There is no suggestion that in using paclitaxel to obtain FDA approval Cook would be infringing Angiotech's patent. And so the policy that we have just mentioned is something the district court could and should consider if it is ever asked to modify the injunction to enable paclitaxel to be made available to the public.

One loose end remains to be tied up. In the course of the limited discovery that took place before the district court granted summary judgment in favor of BSC, Cook inadvertently turned over to BSC documents that were privileged. The judge held that the disclosure waived privilege, but he did not consider the documents in making his decision, and BSC has since returned them to Cook. Cook argues that the judge erred, but acknowledges that the argument is moot unless we reverse the finding of liability and remand for proceedings in which the documents might unless privileged be used by BSC as evidence against Cook. The documents relate to liability rather than to relief and so their admissibility is indeed a moot point.

The judgment, as modified to narrow the injunction, is affirmed.

QUESTIONS

1. In what way was the Cook-ASC purchase-sale agreement a *de facto* assignment?

2. The court says that Cook could have avoided the anti-assignment clause by affiliating with ACS through a merger or acquisition. Would this be any less harmful to BSC? Why might Cook not want to affiliate with ACS through a merger or acquisition?

3. The court says that the Cook-ACS contract has no economic substance. Are there circumstances under which such a contract may have economic substance?

4. One of the factors considered in granting an injunction is whether the injunction may harm the public in some way. Is there a potential public harm in this case?

RHONE-POULENC AGRO v. DeKALB GENETICS
284 F.3d 1323 (Fed. Cir. 2002)

DYK, CIRCUIT JUDGE.

Rhône-Poulenc Agro, S.A. ("RPA") appeals from the decision of the United States District Court for the Middle District of North Carolina granting summary judgment of non-infringement on the ground that Monsanto Co. ("Monsanto") has a valid license to U.S. Patent No. 5,510,471, reissued on December 14, 1999 as RE 36,449 ("the '471 patent"). The issue here is whether a sub-licensee (Monsanto) that acquired the sublicense from a licensee (DeKalb Genetics Corp. ("DeKalb")), that acquired the original license by fraud, may retain the sublicense by establishing that the sub-licensee was a bona fide purchaser for value. On November 19, 2001, this court affirmed the district court's grant of summary judgment in favor of Monsanto Company ("Monsanto") on the basis of this court's earlier panel decision in *Heidelberg Harris, Inc. v. Loebach.*

RPA filed a combined petition for rehearing or rehearing *en banc* which the court *en banc* granted today. As a result of the *en banc* order, we are no longer bound by this court's earlier decision in *Heidelberg Harris*. We hold that the bona fide purchaser defense is governed by federal law and is not available to non-exclusive licensees in the circumstances of this case. Accordingly, we vacate the decision of the district court and remand for further proceedings consistent with this opinion.

BACKGROUND

Briefly the facts are these. From 1991 through 1994, RPA and DeKalb collaborated on the development of biotechnology related to specific genetic materials. During this time, a scientist at RPA, Dr. DeRose, developed an optimized transit peptide ("OTP") with a particular maize gene, which proved useful in growing herbicide resistant corn plants. The OTP is covered by the claims of the '471 patent and is the subject of RPA's patent infringement claim against Monsanto.

In 1994, RPA, DeKalb, and non-party Calgene, Inc. ("Calgene") entered into an agreement (the "1994 Agreement") that provided:

> RPA and CALGENE hereby grant to DEKALB the world-wide, paid-up right to use the RPA/CALGENE Technology and RPA/CALGENE Genetic Material in the field of use of corn. DEKALB shall have the right to grant sublicenses to the aforementioned right to use without further payment being made to RPA or CALGENE.

The RPA/CALGENE Technology and RPA/CALGENE Genetic Material included the invention claimed in the '471 patent. In 1996, DeKalb sublicensed its rights to the RPA/Calgene Technology and Genetic Material to Monsanto. At the same time Monsanto granted to DeKalb licenses to use certain intellectual property related to genetically-engineered corn. Monsanto also acquired a forty percent equity interest in DeKalb, and ten percent of DeKalb Class A (voting) stock.

On October 30, 1997, RPA filed suit against DeKalb and Monsanto, seeking, *inter alia*, to rescind the 1994 Agreement on the ground that DeKalb had procured the license (the "right to use") by fraud. RPA also alleged that DeKalb and Monsanto were infringing the '471 patent and had misappropriated RPA's trade secrets. Monsanto defended, *inter alia*, on the ground that it had a valid license to practice the invention of the patent and use the trade secrets, based on the rights owned under the 1994 Agreement that were transferred by DeKalb to Monsanto in 1996. At trial, a jury found, *inter alia*, that DeKalb had fraudulently induced RPA to enter into the 1994 Agreement. The district court ordered rescission of the 1994 Agreement. Nonetheless, Monsanto moved the district court for summary judgment that it had a valid license to the '471 patent and the right to use RPA's trade secrets because under the 1996 Agreement Monsanto was a bona fide purchaser for value of the sublicense to the patent and the trade secrets. The district court orally granted this motion and dismissed the infringement and misappropriation claims against Monsanto. RPA moved for reconsideration of the district court's dismissal, but the district court, relying on *Heidelberg Harris*. reaffirmed its grant of summary judgment in its February 8, 2000, opinion.

The district court found that, as a sublicensee of the '471 patent and the trade secrets, Monsanto was "entitled to be considered a bona fide purchaser, because it paid value for the right to use the technology without knowledge of any wrongdoing by DeKalb." Because "Monsanto [was] a bona fide purchaser of the . . . technology, [it] therefore [could not] be liable as a patent infringer or a trade secret misappropriater." The district court explicitly did not reach the issues of whether Monsanto's bona fide purchaser defense would apply to any future licenses of RPA's technology or whether, in light of the 1994 RPA-DeKalb-Monsanto Agreement granting DeKalb the right to sublicense, the bona fide purchaser defense would benefit sub-licensees of Monsanto.

RPA filed this timely appeal, which concerns only the validity of Monsanto's license to practice the '471 patent. On this appeal, RPA does not challenge the district court's dismissal of RPA's claim for trade secret misappropriation.

DISCUSSION

I

We have jurisdiction over this appeal pursuant to 28 U.S.C. § 1295(a)(1). Summary judgment is appropriate when "there is no genuine issue as to any material fact and . . . the moving party is entitled to a judgment as a matter of law." We review a district court's grant of a motion for summary judgment without deference.

II

In *Rhône-Poulenc I*, we affirmed the judgment of the district court, rescinding the 1994 licensing agreement based on a jury verdict finding that DeKalb acquired its patent license by fraud. RPA asserts that it necessarily follows that the Monsanto sublicense to the '471 patent is void, and that Monsanto can be sued for patent infringement. We agree, since the court *en banc* has held that we are not bound by the decision in *Heidelberg Harris*.

III

Under some circumstances the bona fide purchaser defense in patent cases is governed by a federal statute, 35 U.S.C. § 261. The statute provides that "[a]n assignment, grant or conveyance shall be void as against any subsequent purchaser or mortgagee for a valuable consideration, without notice, unless it is recorded in the Patent and Trademark Office within three months from its date or prior to the date of such subsequent purchase or mortgage." 35 U.S.C. § 261.

But this case does not involve a situation covered by § 261. That statute is by its terms limited to situations in which the patent owner makes inconsistent assignments, grants, or conveyances to two entities, and the question is whether the later assignee should prevail. Section 261 provides that a later bona fide purchaser for value without notice (a later assignee) prevails if the earlier assignment was not timely recorded in the patent office. This case, however, involves a different situation — the circumstance in which the interest in the patent held by the grantor is voidable and the question is whether a grantee may retain its interest even if the grantor's interest is voided. Section 261 does not directly govern the resolution of this question.

Since section 261 does not apply directly, we must turn to other provisions of the Patent Act. Section 271 of the Act provides: "whoever without authority makes, uses, offers to sell, or sells any patented invention . . . infringes the patent." 35 U.S.C. § 271(a). We are charged with the task of determining the meaning of the term "without authority." Under this provision, as under other provisions of the Patent Act, the courts have developed a federal rule, where appropriate, and have deferred to state law, where that is appropriate. This issue of whether to apply state or federal law has particular importance in this case because North Carolina state law, the law of the forum state, does not recognize a bona fide purchaser defense unless there has been a title transfer.

In general, the Supreme Court and this court have turned to state law to determine whether there is contractual "authority" to practice the invention of a patent. Thus, the interpretation of contracts for rights under patents is generally governed by state law. Just as the interpretation of patent license contracts is generally governed by state law, so too the consequences of fraud in the negotiation of such contracts is a matter generally governed by state law, as we have recognized in our companion case, *Rhône-Poulenc I.* It may be argued that the impact of fraud upon the validity of a license as against a bona purchaser defense should also be governed by state law. However, we confront here a unique situation in which a federal patent statute explicitly governs the bona fide purchaser rule in some situations but not in all situations. It would be anomalous for federal law to govern that defense in part and for state law to govern in part. There is quite plainly a need for a uniform body of federal law on the bona fide purchaser defense.

On the related question of the transferability of patent licenses, many courts have concluded that federal law must be applied. In so holding, courts generally have acknowledged the need for a uniform national rule that patent licenses are personal and non-transferable in the absence of an agreement authorizing assignment, contrary to the state common law rule that contractual rights are assignable unless forbidden by an agreement.

So too we have held that the question of whether an invention is the subject of a commercial offer for sale more than one year before a patent is filed is a question of federal rather than state law. We noted that that rule was necessary to avoid the possibility of a patent's being valid in one state and invalid in another state.

In short, because of the importance of having a uniform national rule, we hold that the bona fide purchaser defense to patent infringement is a matter of federal law. Because such a federal rule implicates an issue of patent law, the law of this circuit governs the rule. Of course, the creation of a federal rule concerning the bona fide purchaser defense is informed by the various state common law bona fide purchaser rules as they are generally understood.

IV

Congress has specifically provided that patents are to be treated as personal property. 35 U.S.C. § 261. At common law, a bona fide purchaser (also known as a "good faith buyer") who acquired title to personal property was entitled to retain the property against the real owner who had lost title to the property, for example, by fraud. Generally, a bona fide purchaser is one who purchases legal title to property in good faith for valuable consideration, without notice of any other claim of interest in the property. The bona fide purchaser rule exists to protect innocent purchasers of property from competing equitable interests in the property because "[s]trong as a plaintiff's equity may be, it can in no case be stronger than that of a purchaser, who has put himself in peril by purchasing a title, and paying a valuable consideration, without notice of any defect in it, or adverse claim to it . . . ."

At common law, however, it was quite clear that one who did not acquire title to the property could not assert the protection of the bona fide purchaser rule. Many courts have held that a party to an executory contract to purchase title, the owner of a lease, or a purchaser from a vendor who did not have title cannot benefit from the bona fide purchaser rule.

It is clear under the law of North Carolina (the state in which RPA filed suit) that "[i]n the absence of an estoppel, one is not entitled to protection as a bona fide purchaser unless he holds the legal title to the property in dispute."

Monsanto urges that the cases requiring that one obtain title to benefit from the bona fide purchaser defense are "antiquated," and the Uniform Commercial Code's ("U.C.C.") modern approach has rejected the requirement of title. In fact, the title rule is recognized in modern property law, and has been confirmed by the U.C.C., Articles 2 and 2B. Under U.C.C. Article 2-403, even "[a] person with voidable title has power to transfer a good title to a good faith purchaser for value." Article 2B of the U.C.C. was recently adopted as the Uniform Computer Information Transactions Act ("UCITA"), U.C.I.T.A. and is relevant to the application of the bona fide purchaser rule to intellectual property. To be sure, the scope of UCITA is limited to "computer information transactions," UCITA § 103(a), and therefore is not applicable to all patent licensing cases. Nevertheless, UCITA (pertaining to the licensing of intangible property) provides guidance on the U.C.C.'s view of the common law.

Official comment 3 to UCITA § 506(b) makes clear that the drafters of the U.C.C. concluded that at common law the bona fide purchaser rule does not apply to the licensing of intellectual property:

> Subsection (b) provides that as a general rule, a licensee's transferee acquires only those contractual or other rights that the licensee was authorized to transfer. *There is no principle of bona fide purchaser of a mere contract right.*
>
> Similarly, *neither copyright nor patent recognize concepts of protecting a buyer in the ordinary course (or other good faith purchaser)* by giving that person greater rights than were authorized to be transferred even if the transfer includes delivery of a copy associated with the contract. Transfers that exceed or are otherwise unlicensed by a patent or copyright owner

create no rights of use in the transferee. Indeed, such transfers may in themselves be an infringing act.

Monsanto has been unable to cite a single common law case in which the bona fide purchaser rule was applied to the holder of a mere contract right, such as a license.

V

Even if the general common law extended the protection of the bona fide purchaser rule to holders of non-exclusive licenses, it would not be appropriate for us to extend such protection to non-exclusive licenses as a matter of federal common law. Section 261 of title 35 reflects a determination by Congress that only those who have obtained an "assignment, grant or conveyance" may benefit from the protection of the statute. This provision thus reflects a congressional judgment that the protections of the bona fide purchaser rule extend only to those who have received an "assignment, grant or conveyance." Under such circumstances, the Supreme Court has made clear that we must consider the purposes of federal statutes in framing a rule of federal common law, even if the statutes are not directly applicable. We have specifically held that non-exclusive licensees are not "assignees" under the statute.

Although our precedent has recognized that in some circumstances an exclusive patent license may be tantamount to an assignment of title to the patent, this is so only when "the licensee holds "all substantial rights" under the patent." Here the license is non-exclusive, and there is no contention that the license agreement transferred "all substantial rights." Thus, an assignment did not occur, and in the absence of an "assignment, grant or conveyance," Congress contemplated that there would be no bona fide purchaser defense.

CONCLUSION

In sum, the bona fide purchaser defense does not apply to non-exclusive licensees. We accordingly vacate the decision of the district court and remand for further proceedings consistent with this opinion.

QUESTIONS

1. Would the federal *bona fide* purchaser defense be available to an exclusive licensee for the term of the patent? Would it be available to an assignee of the patent?

2. When a *bona fide* purchaser defense is accepted, what happens to the original license? What is the license status of the *bona fide* purchaser?

3. The *bona fide* purchaser rule is intended to promote economic activity by protecting purchasers who have entered into a transaction in good faith. Will this decision tend to impede the exchange of future licenses and diminish market activity in patent rights?

4. As counsel to a firm desiring *bona fide* purchaser protection, could you

provide this protection through contract language?

CASE NOTES

1. In early 1987, Altera and Monolithic Memories, Inc. (MMI) settled a patent dispute by entering into a cross-license agreement. The cross-license agreement provided that neither party shall assign or transfer the license rights without written consent of the other party. However, the cross-license agreement also provided that the license rights "shall be extendible" to any corporation succeeding to the entire business of one of the parties, and that the successor corporation shall agree in writing to be bound by the cross-license agreement. Later in 1987, Advanced Micro Devices (AMD) acquired MMI and promptly wrote to Altera informing Altera of the acquisition and agreeing to be bound by the terms of the cross-license agreement. In 1995, AMD sued Altera for infringement of patents which had not been acquired by AMD through its acquisition of MMI. Altera claimed it had a license to practice the AMD patents based on the Altera-MMI cross-license and AMD's agreement to be bound by the terms of the cross-license. Altera based its claim on the language in the cross-license that provided that the license rights "shall be extendible" to a successor corporation of either party. Under Altera's interpretation of this language, AMD was required to license to Altera any AMD patents in field because these patent were "extendible" from the cross-license. The district court found that the "shall be extendible" language was sufficiently ambiguous to admit parole evidence and, based upon the parol evidence, a jury found that AMD, upon agreeing to become bound by the Altera-MMI Agreement, became obligated to license to Altera its own patents in the field of the Altera-MMI agreement. AMD appealed the district court decision arguing that the "shall be extendible" language in the Altera-MMI Agreement should be found as a matter of law to be unambiguous, and therefore the district court should not have admitted parole evidence and should not have submitted the question to the jury. What result? *See* Advanced Micro Devices, Inc. v. Altera Corp., 217 F.3d 849 (Fed. Cir. 1999).

2. In November 2001, Benetton entered into a settlement agreement with K-2 to settle two lawsuits among them relating to patents for in-line skates. One lawsuit involved an infringement action brought by K-2 against Benetton for infringement of Meibock patents; the second lawsuit involved an infringement action brought by Benetton against K-2 for infringement of the Olson, Spaulding, Doop patent. As part of the settlement agreement, K-2 covenanted not to sue Benetton, or any related party, for infringement of any patents at issue in the suit and, in return, Benetton covenanted not to sue K-2, or any related party, for infringement of the patent held by Benetton. In January 2002, V-Formation filed a suit against K-2 alleging infringement of patents owned by V-Formation. In the settlement agreement reached in this lawsuit, K-2 agreed to assign to V-Formation "the entire right, title and interest in the Meibock patents, including the right to sue for past infringement." V-Formation then immediately filed an infringement action against Benetton claiming infringement of the Meibock patents. Benetton claimed it could not be liable for infringement of the Meibock patents because of the covenant not sue it was granted in the K-2 — Benetton settlement agreement. V-Formation claimed that the K-2 — Benetton settlement agreement could not insulate Benetton

from infringement liability because that settlement agreement had not been recorded pursuant to 35 U.S.C. § 261 prior to the date of the K-2 — V-Formation settlement agreement, and V-Formation had no knowledge of the K-2 — Benetton settlement agreement. 35 U.S.C. § 261 provides: "An assignment, grant, or conveyance [of a patent interest] shall be void as against any subsequent purchaser or mortgagee for a valuable consideration, without notice, unless it is recorded in the Patent and Trademark Office within three months from its date or prior to the date of such subsequent purchase or mortgage." What result? *See* V-Formation, Inc. v. Benetton Group SPA, 2006 U.S. Dist. LEXIS 13352 (D. Colo. 2006).

3. *See also* Cincom Systems Inc. v. Novelis Corp., 2007 U.S. Dist. LEXIS 2721 (S.D. Ohio 2007) (Federal law that a patent license is non-assignable unless expressly made so, and that a merger results in a transfer of a patent license when the original licensee does not survive the merger, is unaffected by the fact that the merger is between two subsidiaries of a parent corporation); Yeda Research and Development Co., Ltd. v. ImClone, 2005 U.S. Dist. LEXIS 26689 (S.D.N.Y. 2005) (Doctrine of *bona fide* purchaser inapplicable to patent license from named inventors when unnamed alleged inventors challenge patent validity based on inventorship); Heidelberg Harris Inc., v. Loebach, 145 F.3d 1454 (Fed. Cir. 1998) (Purported patent licensee was a *bona fide* purchaser of license because licensee had no notice of inventor claims of rights in the patent at time of license and paid consideration for license, even though license term would not commence until seven years after the date of the license); Intel Corp. v. ULSI Sys. Technology, 995 F.2d 1566 (Fed. Cir. 1993) (A licensed seller of a patented product need not own intellectual property rights in the product in order for there to be a sale that places the patented product beyond the reach of the patent); TXO Production Co. v. M.D. Mark, Inc., 999 S.W.2d 137 (Tex. App. 1999) (Merger of subsidiary into parent company did not constitute disclosure of trade secrets to a third party prohibited by the confidentiality provision of subsidiary's contract with trade secret owner).

Additional Information

1. HOWARD C. ANWALT, IP STRATEGY: COMPLETE INTELLECTUAL PROPERTY PLANNING §§ 2:4–2:47 (2010).

2. ROBERT A. MATTHEWS, JR., 5 ANNOTATED PATENT DIGEST §§ 35:1–35:4 (2010).

3. JOHN G. MILLS III, ET AL., PATENT LAW FUNDAMENTALS, §§ 19:1, 19:19, 19:37 (2d ed. 2010).

4. 69 C.J.S. PATENTS § 351 (2008).

5. 60 AM. JUR. 2D PATENTS § 1059 (2008).

6. DEBORAH H. HARRIS, 49 A.L.R. FED. 890 (2010).

7. GREGORY E. UPCHURCH, INTELL. PROP. LIT. GUIDE § 14:39 (2008).

8. Sung Yang, *Considerations for the Patent Holder: The Transfer of Patent Licenses in the Context of a Merger*, 42 IDEA 515 (2002).

9. Kevin T. Duncan, Thomas J. Scott, Jr., *"Intel" Case Illustrates the Perils of Cross-Licenses: Patent Holders Should Clearly Define Scope of Patent,*

Extent of License, 10/22/01 Nat'l L.J. C16, (2001).

10.   Elaine D. Ziff, *The Effect of Corporate Acquisitions on the Target Companies License Rights*, 57 Bus. Law. 767, (2002).

11.   Steven E. Ballew, *The Assignment of Rights, Franchises, and Obligations of the Disappearing Corporation in a Merger*, 38 Bus. Law 45, (1982).

12.   Peter Macaulay, *The Effect of Mergers on Anti-Assignment Provisions in Contracts: A Case Note on TXO Production Co. v. M.D. Mark*, 53 Baylor L. Rev. 489, (2001).

13.   Jessica L. Braeger, *Anti-Assignment Clauses, Mergers, and the Myth about Federal Preemption of Application of State Contract Law to Patent License Agreements*, 50 Drake L. Rev. 639, (2002).

14.   Kevin L. Russell, *Rhone-Poulenc Agro, S.A. v. DeKalb Genetics Corp.*, 4 Patdigest § 18:58, (2008).

15.   Alice Haemmerli, *Why Doctrine Matters: Patent and Copyright Licensing and the Meaning of Ownership in Federal Context*, 30 Colum. J.L. & Arts 1, (2006).

2.3.6   Post-Sale Restrictions

Post-sale restrictions on the downstream use or transfer of patented products have spawned a long and complex body of case law. Post-sale restrictions have generally been analyzed under the so-called "patent exhaustion doctrine." The patent exhaustion doctrine was first applied by the Supreme Court nearly 140 years ago in *Adams v. Burke*, 84 U.S. 453 (1873). In *Adams*, the patentee of coffin lids authorized a licensee to make, use and sell the patented coffin lids only within a ten-mile radius of Boston. A customer of the licensee purchased the patented coffin lids within a ten-mile radius of Boston, but then resold the coffin lids outside of the ten-mile radius. The patentee sued the customer for patent infringement. The Supreme Court held that once a patented product has been lawfully sold, the patentee's rights are exhausted and the patentee cannot impose restrictions on a purchaser from an authorized licensee.

The Supreme Court continued its development of the patent exhaustion doctrine nearly 70 years later in *U.S. v. Univis Lens Co.*, 316 U.S. 241 (1942). *Univis* involved a complex set of arrangements between the patentee of eyeglass lenses, a licensed manufacturer of glass blanks that partly practiced the patent and eyeglass retailers who ground the blanks into finished lenses. The object of these arrangements was to control the retail price of the patented eyeglasses lenses. In analyzing these arrangements under the patent exhaustion doctrine, the Supreme Court held that:

> The first vending of any article manufactured under a patent puts the article beyond the reach of the monopoly which that patent confers. Whether the licensee sells the patented article in its completed form or sells it before completion for the purpose of enabling the buyer to finish and sell it, he has equally parted with the article, and made it the vehicle for

transferring to the buyer ownership of the invention with respect to the article.

The application of the patent exhaustion doctrine in the Federal Circuit has, however, often been confusing and inconsistent. In *Mallinckrodt, Inc. v. Medipart, Inc.*, 976 F.2d 700 (Fed. Cir. 1992), the Federal Circuit held that a "single use only" notice on a patented medical device constituted a conditional sale and the patent exhaustion doctrine only applied to unconditional sales. However, in *Kendall Co. v. Progressive Medical Technology, Inc.*, 85 F.3d 1570 (Fed. Cir. 1996), the Federal Circuit reached a different conclusion on facts similar to *Mallincktodt*. *Kendall* involved the sale of a medical device marked with a notice "single patient use only, do not reuse." Here, the Federal Circuit held that when the patentee sold medical devices, it granted customers an implied license to use the devices for their useful life and this includes an implied right to repair and reuse the medical devices. The repair and reuse of the medical devices, therefore, did not infringe the patentee's rights.

As the *Kendall* case makes clear, the patent exhaustion doctrine is closely associated with implied licenses. *See*, § 2.2.3 of the materials. The association with implied licenses, as well as the close connection with laws dealing with anticompetitive practices, further complicates the patent exhaustion case law.

The three cases in this section consider the doctrine of patent exhaustion in three very different contexts. The first case, *Pioneer Hi-Bred*, considers the patent exhaustion doctrine in the context of the sale of seed corn subject to restrictions on resale. The second case, *Adobe*, considers the patent exhaustion doctrine in the context of the sale of software subject to resale only restrictions to students and educators. The final case, *Quanta Computer*, is the Supreme Court's most recent decision on the patent exhaustion doctrine. *Quanta Computer* deals with the sale of licensed microprocessors subject to a restriction on combining the microprocessors with parts from only one manufacturer.

As you read these cases, consider how the results are affected by whether the transaction is structured as a sale or a license, or as a conditional or unconditional transfer of rights.

PIONEER HI-BRED INT'L v. OTTAWA PLANT FOOD
283 F.Supp.2d 1018 (N.D. Iowa 2003)

BENNETT, CHIEF JUDGE.

This action, which involves a claim of alleged infringement of patents for hybrid and inbred seed corn by an unlicensed reseller, comes before the court pursuant to the parties' cross-motions for summary judgment or partial summary judgment. Also before the court is the defendant's motion to strike certain paragraphs of an affidavit offered by the plaintiff as part of the summary judgment record. The court heard oral arguments on the motions on September 18, 2003. The motions are now fully submitted and some expedition in the disposition of the motions is required, as this matter is set for trial to begin on November 3, 2003.

I. INTRODUCTION

A. Procedural Background

Plaintiff Pioneer Hi-Bred International, Inc., commenced this patent infringement action on February 20, 1998, against eight defendants not including the present defendant, Ottawa Plant Food, Inc., alleging that each of the defendants, none of whom were authorized Pioneer Sales Representatives, had illegally sold or offered for sale Pioneer® brand seed corn. Ottawa was added as a defendant when Pioneer filed an Amended Complaint on September 11, 1998, apparently after Pioneer learned, through discovery, that Ottawa had acquired Pioneer® brand seed corn from one of the original defendants, Farm Advantage, Inc. The claims against all other defendants have since been settled, so that this litigation is continuing only between Pioneer and Ottawa. Pioneer's specific claim against Ottawa, pursuant to 35 U.S.C. § 271, is that Ottawa is not an authorized Pioneer Sales Representative, but that it has nevertheless, for some time past, and still is, infringing one or more of numerous patents-in-suit for Pioneer® brand hybrid and inbred seed corn by making, using, selling, or offering for sale Pioneer® brand seed corn, and will continue to do so unless enjoined by the court. Pioneer seeks injunctive relief, an accounting for damages, including damages for willful infringement, and assessments for interest and costs. Ottawa answered the Amended Complaint on November 3, 1998 (docket no. 104), denying Pioneer's claim and asserting affirmative defenses of patent exhaustion, laches, waiver, and estoppel.

B. Factual Background

Whether or not a party is entitled to summary judgment ordinarily turns on whether or not there are genuine issues of material fact for trial. Nevertheless, the court will not attempt here a comprehensive review of the undisputed and disputed facts in the record. Rather, the court will present here only sufficient factual background to put in context the parties' arguments for and against the motions for summary judgment on Pioneer's patent infringement claim. More attention will be given to specific factual disputes, where necessary, in the court's legal analysis, below.

Plaintiff Pioneer, an Iowa corporation with its principal place of business in Des Moines, Iowa, is the world's largest producer of seed corn. Pioneer has developed and sells a wide range of hybrid and inbred seed corn varieties subject to one or more of the numerous patents-in-suit. Pioneer sells its seed through a "dual" distribution system, using licensed sales representatives — who never take title to the seed, and are licensed to sell it only to actual end users, *i.e.*, farmers, who plant the seed — and licensed dealers — who do take title to the seed, and are licensed to resell it only to other authorized dealers or end users. Defendant Ottawa, an Illinois corporation with its principal place of business in Ottawa, Illinois, is a seller and wholesaler of agricultural products, including seed corn. However, Ottawa is not now, and has never been, a licensed dealer or sales representative for Pioneer.

The parties agree that, from 1992 until 1998, Ottawa purchased and resold a number of bags of different varieties of Pioneer® brand seed corn. Pioneer alleges that, during the time period in question, Ottawa sold 4,061 bags of Pioneer® brand seed corn for a total of $315,110. The parties agree that Ottawa bought Pioneer® brand seed corn from several different Pioneer Sales Representatives and licensed dealers and that Ottawa only bought Pioneer® brand seed corn in its original packaging, as sold by Pioneer. Ottawa never altered the Pioneer seed bags or their contents, removed any bag tags, or repackaged the seed. Rather, Ottawa resold the seed to farmers and other dealers, including some Pioneer dealers or representatives who were having trouble obtaining a supply of certain Pioneer® brand seed corn varieties. What the parties dispute is whether or not Ottawa's "resale" of Pioneer® brand seed corn infringed Pioneer's patent rights in that seed corn.

Pioneer contends that, from at least 1986 onward, all of its seed corn was sold subject to a "limited label license," which appeared on each bag and/or bag tag of Pioneer® brand seed corn. That "limited label license" prohibited any purchaser from using the seed corn for any purpose other than production of forage or grain for feeding or processing. Thus, Pioneer contends that no purchaser was licensed to resell the seed corn unless granted a separate license to do so by Pioneer. The parties agree that, before or during the period of Ottawa's alleged wrongdoing, Pioneer had turned down Ottawa's request for a license to resell Pioneer® brand seed corn as a dealer or sales representative.

Although Pioneer admits that the language on the bag labels and bag tags changed somewhat over time, it contends that the essence of the limited license granted to buyers did not. Somewhat more specifically, Pioneer contends that, beginning in sales year 1986 and continuing through sales year 1995, the language on the label on the seed bags read, in pertinent part, as follows:

THE FOLLOWING PROVISIONS ARE PART OF THE TERMS OF SALE OF THIS PRODUCT

One or more of the parental lines used in producing this hybrid are the exclusive property of Pioneer Hi-Bred International, Inc. Buyer intends to purchase and seller intends to sell only hybrid seed. *Buyer agrees that purchase of this bag of seed does not give any rights to use any such parental line seed* which may be found herein, or any plant, pollen or seed produced from such parental line seed, for breeding, research or seed production purposes or *for any purpose other than production of forage or grain for feeding or processing.*

* * * * * *

By acceptance of the seed or other products the Buyer acknowledges that the foregoing terms are conditions of the sale and constitute the entire agreement between the parties regarding warranty or other liabilities and the remedy therefore.

Ottawa contends that the "limited label licenses" used before the 1999 sales season restricted the "use" of the products, but did not restrict the "resale" of the products, which is a legal question, which will be addressed below. As to factual contentions, however, Ottawa also contends that Pioneer has failed to produce any evidence of what "limited label license" or bag tag appeared on any Pioneer® brand seed corn sold by Ottawa. Ottawa asserts that no such language appeared on some of the bag tags that it has retained. Ottawa also contends that, even if the "limited label license" language appeared on bags of Pioneer® brand seed corn that Ottawa acquired and resold, Ottawa's employees did not read and had no reason to read the labels, beyond verification of the type, size, and maturity of the seed. The parties do agree that Ottawa does not produce grain or forage, but instead resold all of the Pioneer® brand seed corn that it acquired, either to other dealers or to corn producers.

In May 1994, Pioneer sent Ottawa a letter notifying Ottawa that it had come to Pioneer's attention that Ottawa was reselling Pioneer® brand seed corn; asserting that Ottawa could only have obtained that seed corn from Pioneer Sales Representatives; advising Ottawa that sales of Pioneer® brand seed corn by Pioneer's Sales Representatives to anyone other than farmers were prohibited by the Sales Representatives' contracts; and advising Ottawa that Ottawa's purchase of seed corn from Pioneer Sales Representatives might have caused the Sales Representatives to breach their contracts with Pioneer, opening Ottawa up to liability for tortious interference with the contractual relations between Pioneer and its Sales Representatives. Pioneer contends that this letter placed Ottawa on notice that its acquisition and resale of Pioneer® brand seed corn was in derogation of Pioneer's patent rights. Ottawa contends that this letter provided no such notice, but instead appeared to be a complaint about the conduct of Pioneer's own sales force. Upon receiving the May 1994 letter, however, Ottawa contends that it contacted the Federal Trade Commission and the Illinois Attorney General's Office, and was advised by both bodies that Ottawa was not violating any laws by reselling Pioneer seed. However, Ottawa did not receive a written opinion from either body on the matter. Ottawa contends that it received no notice that Pioneer was asserting "patent infringement" until this lawsuit was filed against it, at which time Ottawa ceased acquiring or reselling Pioneer® brand seed corn. However, Pioneer points to testimony of Ottawa's former controller, Lester Borden, to the effect that Ottawa's managers and sales representatives simply did not care whether or not Pioneer objected to Ottawa's acquisition or resale of Pioneer® brand seed corn.

****

IV. LEGAL ANALYSIS OF SUMMARY JUDGMENT MOTIONS

A. Issues Presented

Ottawa's motion for summary judgment involves seven issues pertaining to liability and damages, while Pioneer's motion for partial summary judgment is essentially the "mirror image" of Ottawa's as to the first three issues. The cross-motions, therefore, present the following issues: (1) whether Ottawa's purchase and resale of Pioneer® brand seed corn is immunized from liability for patent infringement under the "first sale" or "patent exhaustion" doctrine; (2) whether Ottawa had notice of and was bound by Pioneer's restrictions in its "limited label license"; (3) whether Pioneer's "limited label license" restrictions are enforceable or are instead unenforceable as against public policy owing to their anticompetitive effect or unenforceable under applicable contract principles; (4) whether Pioneer has any evidence of notice to Ottawa of the patents-in-suit and alleged infringement supporting Pioneer's claim for compensatory damages under 35 U.S.C. § 287; (5) whether Pioneer has any evidence that any of the seed tags or seed bags purchased and resold by Ottawa contained any language prohibiting resale supporting Pioneer's claim for damages under 35 U.S.C. § 284; (6) whether Pioneer has already recovered its full profits in connection with the first sale of any seed, so that it is not entitled to any compensatory damages; and (7) whether Pioneer has any evidence supporting its claim for increased damages based on "willful" infringement. Issues (1) through (3) — the issues on which there are cross-motions for summary judgment — thus go to "liability," while issues (4) through (7) — which are the subject only of Ottawa's motion for summary judgment — go to "damages" or the prerequisites for any damages. The court will consider these issues in turn, subdividing its discussion into "liability" issues, on which, coincidentally, there are cross-motions for summary judgment, and "damages" issues, which are raised only in Ottawa's motion for summary judgment.

B. Liability Issues

1. "First sale" or "patent exhaustion"

In its motion for summary judgment, Ottawa contends, first, that Pioneer's patent infringement claims are barred by the "first sale" or "patent exhaustion" doctrine. However, in its motion for summary judgment, Pioneer contends that it, not Ottawa, is entitled to summary judgment on Ottawa's "patent exhaustion" defense.

a. Arguments of the parties

In its own motion for summary judgment, Ottawa argues that, while the patent laws grant a patent holder the exclusive right to make, use, and sell a patented invention, once the patentee sells the patented item, he effectively surrenders or "exhausts" this monopoly and forfeits the ability to control use of the invention by the buyer. In this case, Ottawa contends that Pioneer's patent rights were "exhausted" by a "first sale" when Pioneer or a Pioneer dealer first sold the seed corn that Ottawa bought. Ottawa contends, further, that it is presumed that, in pricing for the "first sale," Pioneer was fully compensated for the value of its invention and can no longer assert any control over the patented product or obtain any "damages" for its resale. More importantly, Ottawa argues that the "first sale" immunizes Ottawa's subsequent resale from any claim of patent infringement.

In response to Ottawa's motion for summary judgment and in support of its own motion for summary judgment on Ottawa's "patent exhaustion" defense, Pioneer contends that Ottawa cannot establish the prerequisite for application of the "first sale" or "patent exhaustion" rule, which is an *unconditional* sale of the patented product. Here, Pioneer contends that any prior sale of the seed corn at issue before

Ottawa's resale was specifically conditioned by the terms of the "limited label license," which grants only a right to use the seed corn to produce grain or forage. Pioneer also contends that distribution of Pioneer® brand seed corn to Pioneer authorized Sales Representatives or dealers does not constitute an unconditional "first sale." Rather, Pioneer argues that such sales were conditioned by the terms of the representatives' or dealers' limited licenses to resell the patented products, which prohibited sales representatives from selling to individuals or groups for resale, and permitted dealers to resell only to other licensed dealers or persons who would use the seed to produce grain or forage. Pioneer argues, further, that any price it received for transfers of the seed corn prior to the resale by Ottawa reflected only the value of the limited license to use the seed corn to produce grain or forage, not the full value of the patented invention or the retained patent rights. Pioneer points out that Ottawa admits that it was never granted a license to resell Pioneer® brand seed corn, so that Ottawa never acquired that "stick" from Pioneer's "bundle" of patent rights.

In its reply in further support of its own motion for summary judgment, Ottawa contends that Pioneer's "limited label license" simply does not restrict or prohibit Ottawa's right to "resell" Pioneer® brand seed corn. Ottawa argues that the "limited label license" restricts only certain "uses," but is silent as to "resale," so that the "first sale" exhausted any patent rights with regard to "resale." Ottawa did not, however, directly address that part of Pioneer's motion for partial summary judgment seeking summary judgment on Ottawa's "patent exhaustion" defense in its resistance to Pioneer's motion for partial summary judgment.

b. Applicable law

As the Federal Circuit Court of Appeals recently reiterated, "when a patented product has been sold the purchaser acquires "the right to use and sell it, and . . . the authorized sale of an article which is capable of use only in practicing the patent is a relinquishment of the patent monopoly with respect to the article sold." " It is not *any* sale that invokes this "first sale" or "patent exhaustion" rule, however. Rather, the *unrestricted* sale of a patented article, by or with the authority of the patentee, "exhausts" the patentee's right to control further sale and use of that article by enforcing the patent under which it was first sold. In *United States v. Masonite Corp.*, the Court explained that *exhaustion of the patent right depends on "whether or not there has been such a disposition of the article that it may fairly be said that the patentee has received his reward for the use of the article."*

In *Mallinckrodt, Inc. v. Medipart, Inc.*, the Federal Circuit Court of Appeals noted that the Supreme Court had "considered and affirmed the basic principles that *unconditional* sale of a patented device exhausts the patentee's right to control the purchaser's use of the device," but that "the sale of patented goods, like other goods, can be conditioned." Furthermore, the court explained that "[t]he principle of exhaustion of the patent right d[oes] not turn a conditional sale into an unconditional one."

c. Analysis

The court concludes that it is Pioneer, not Ottawa, that is entitled to summary judgment on Ottawa's "patent exhaustion" defense. Ottawa has failed to generate a genuine issue of material fact that the sale of Pioneer® brand seed corn was *not always* conditional, so that, in the face of undisputed evidence that the sales *were* conditional, the "patent exhaustion" defense is simply inapplicable as a matter of law. Treating the winning party on this issue as the movant and the losing party as the party charged with adequately resisting the motion, the court finds that Pioneer has met its initial burden by pointing to evidence that, from 1986 on, its bag label restricted the uses for which the seed corn was sold to production of grain or forage. Even giving Ottawa the benefit of all reasonable inferences, Ottawa's attempts to generate a genuine issue of material fact on its "patent exhaustion" defense are unavailing.

Ottawa attempts to generate a genuine issue of material fact by asserting that certain bag tags from bags it resold did not include any restrictions on use of the seed corn. However, the bag tags to which Ottawa points are dated 1992 and 1993, which means that they antedate the sales season in which Pioneer represents that it first included the restrictions *on the bag tags*, which was 1996. Ottawa has pointed to nothing suggesting that the *bag labels* did not always carry restrictions on use. Ottawa also points to evidence that the purchase orders and invoices for the Pioneer® brand seed corn that it bought from Pioneer Sales Representatives or dealers did not contain any limitations on the sale of the seed corn, but the bag labels and bag tags on the seed corn itself expressly stated that the terms thereon are terms and conditions of the sale. Although Ottawa argues that it is Pioneer's burden to show that the sale was conditional, the burdens at summary judgment require Ottawa to point to evidence that it bought bags of seed with no limitations, and Ottawa has not done so, nor has Ottawa denied that the bags it sold carried the label license. Because "[t]he principle of exhaustion of the patent right did not turn a conditional sale into an unconditional one," there was no unconditional sale in this case upon which "patent exhaustion" could be founded.

Finally, the court is unpersuaded by Ottawa's arguments, in its reply in further support of its own motion for summary judgment, that Pioneer's "limited label license" simply does not restrict or prohibit Ottawa's right to "resell" Pioneer® brand seed corn, even if it restricts other "uses." While this argument is relevant to the nature of the conditions on the first sale of the patented seed corn by Pioneer — a matter that the court must address below — it is not responsive to the pertinent issue at this point in the analysis, which is whether or not there ever was an *unconditional* sale of the seed corn.

Therefore, unless the court determines that the conditions Pioneer placed on its initial sale of the seed corn are unenforceable, Ottawa's "patent exhaustion" defense must fail as a matter of law, because there was no "first" *unconditional* sale.

QUESTIONS

1. When is the sale of a patented product conditional? When is the sale of a patented product unconditional?

2. As counsel to a company desiring to impose post-sale restrictions on the sale of a patented product, how would you draft the sales agreement?

3. Why might Pioneer have pursued a dual distribution system rather than selling directly to farmers?

4. Why might Pioneer have not received full compensation for the sales of seed corn to licensed sales representatives?

ADOBE SYSTEMS v. STARGATE SOFTWARE
216 F. Supp.2d 1051 (N.D. Cal. 2002)

WARE, DISTRICT JUDGE.

I. INTRODUCTION

Plaintiff, Adobe Systems Inc., ("Adobe") filed this action against Defendant, Stargate Systems Inc., ("Stargate") for copyright infringement of Adobe's educational software. Presently before the Court are the Parties' Cross-Motions for Summary Judgment. Based upon all papers filed to date and oral argument of counsel at the hearing, Stargate's Motion for Summary Judgment is DENIED and Adobe's Motion for Summary Judgment is GRANTED.

II. BACKGROUND

Adobe is one of the leading software development and publishing companies in the United States. Some of its copyrighted software products include Adobe Illustrator, Adobe Pagemaker, and Adobe Acrobat. Adobe contends that it distributes its software products under license to a network of distributors and original equipment manufacturers. These distributors sign license agreements that permit them to engage in limited re-distribution to entities or individuals authorized by Adobe. Adobe claims all Adobe software products are subject to a shrink-wrap End User License Agreement ("EULA") that prohibits copying or commercial re-distribution.

Adobe also makes "Educational" versions of its software packages available for license to students and educators at a discount. Adobe Educational distributors are licensed to transfer Educational software only to resellers who have signed Off or On Campus Educational Reseller Agreements ("OCRA") with Adobe. In turn, the OCRA requires that re-distribution of Educational software be limited to students and educators. Adobe claims that the Educational versions are prominently marked "Education Version — Academic ID Required" and include the legend, "Notice to users: Use of the enclosed software is subject to the license agreement contained in the package."

Stargate is a discount software distributor wholly owned by Leonid Kelman. Neither Stargate nor Mr. Kelman are authorized distributors of Adobe products. In 1995, Mr. Kelman co-founded a software distribution company called Action Software with Alexander Belfer. Together they incorporated Stargate Software

Inc. In 1997, Stargate began acquiring software from two businesses, Dallas Computer and D.C. Micro, with the majority of the software being Adobe Educational software. Adobe contends that Stargate's suppliers acquired Adobe Educational software from Adobe Educational distributor Douglas Stewart Co. pursuant to valid OCRAs. However, Stargate alleges that all of the Adobe software products that Stargate sold were purchased through either D.C. Micro, Inc. or Dallas Computers, Inc.

Between March 1998 and April 1999, Stargate, purchased between 1795–2189 packages of "Educational" software produced by Adobe. Stargate distributed this Educational software at below-market prices to retail customers and unauthorized resellers through magazine advertisements, trade shows, action websites and its website "www.stargatesoftware.com." Adobe learned of this practice, made a trap purchase of the Educational software in April 1999, and filed suit in this Court against Stargate and Mr. Kelman soon thereafter.

Adobe alleges that Stargate infringed Adobe's copyrights by obtaining and selling Educational versions of Adobe software without Adobe's authorization. Stargate contends that it was the rightful owner of the Adobe software products and therefore did not infringe Adobe's copyright by reselling those products, pursuant to the "first sale" doctrine, codified at 17 U.S.C. § 109. Presently before the Court are the Parties' Cross-Motions for Summary Judgment.

****

IV. DISCUSSION

A. Copyright Infringement Claim

Section 106 of the Copyright Act (the "Act") outlines the exclusive rights enjoyed by owners of a copyright including the exclusive right "to distribute copies or phonorecords of the copyrighted work to the public by sale or other transfer of ownership, or by rental, lease, or lending." 17 U.S.C. § 106(3). Under this provision, the copyright owner would have the "right to control the first public distribution of an authorized copy or phonorecord of his work, whether by sale, gift, loan, or some rental or lease arrangement." 17 U.S.C. § 106(3). Section 109(a) of the Act, makes clear that "the copyright owner's rights under § 106(3) cease with respect to a particular copy or phonorecord once he has parted with *ownership* of it." 17 U.S.C. § 109(a) (emphasis added). Also pursuant to § 109(a), "the *owner* of a particular copy or phonorecord lawfully made under this title, or any person authorized by such owner, is entitled without the authority of the copyright owner, to sell or otherwise dispose of the possession of that copy or phonorecord." 17 U.S.C. § 109(a) (emphasis added). One significant effect of § 109(a) is to limit the exclusive right to distribute copies to their first voluntary disposition, and thus negate copyright owner control over further or "downstream" transfer to a third party. Thus, under the first sale doctrine, "a sale of a lawfully made copy terminates a copyright holder's authority to interfere with subsequent sales or distribution of that particular copy." "[T]he copyright owner is entitled to realize no more and no less than full value of each copy or phonorecord upon its disposition."

A. Sale or License

The issue before the Court is whether Adobe, through its OCRA and EULA, transferred *ownership* of each particular copy of its software to its distributors D.C. Micro and Dallas Computers. Having transferred such ownership would bar Adobe from claiming copyright infringement by Stargate under the first sale doctrine. An issuance via license, however, would not. Rather, the establishment of a license by Adobe would protect Adobe under the first sale doctrine.

Implacably, Stargate concedes that Adobe retains title to the objective coded software of the intellectual property contained on the CD-ROM. Nevertheless, Stargate claims, however, that whenever there is a sale, Adobe has parted with title to that particular copy of its copyrighted intellectual property, thereby divesting itself of the exclusive right to vend that particular copy. In essence, Stargate contends that each time Adobe is paid by a distributor or reseller for a package of software, it has "received its rewards" for that package and has parted with title to that particular copy. Stargate argues that after examining the "economic realities" of the initial transaction between Adobe and its distributors, Adobe's distribution of its educational software constitutes a sale, rather than a license of each particular copy.

Stargate further alleges that nowhere in either the OCRA or in the EULA, does Adobe purport in any manner to retain title to that particular copy of its software, that is, the package including a CD-ROM on which the program is stored, and any manuals or other materials included within it. Therefore, Stargate argues that further transfers of that package do not infringe Adobe's copyright.

Adobe contends, on the other hand, that "a common method of distribution for software products is through licensing agreements, which permit the copyright holder to place restrictions upon the distribution of its products." Adobe alleges that Mr. Kelman, Stargate's sole owner, was aware that Adobe's software is distributed pursuant to licensing agreements. Specifically, Kelman testified that, "I've seen that there was a licensing agreement (in the software box)." Furthermore it was Adobe's intent to license the software rather than to make an outright sale. According to Adobe, "Adobe does not sell its software. Instead, Adobe distributes its software products under license to a network of distributors . . ."

Adobe also argues that under the Act, the first sale doctrine does not turn on whether the copyright owner "received its reward" for a particular piece of software, but whether the software has been *sold.* In this case, Adobe has elected to distribute its products via license rather than sale. Adobe alleges that their OCRA and EULA are clearly licenses. According to Adobe, multiple restrictions on title are placed on each distributor through the express terms of its OCRA. Additionally, Adobe asserts that it was their intention to affect a license agreement, through their OCRAs, rather than a sale.

1. The term "Software"

In this case, it is important to draw a distinction between the objective code "software" and the medium and packaging through which it is sold on the market. Section 202 of the Act recognizes a distinction between tangible property rights in copies of the work and intangible property rights in the creation itself. "Ownership of a copyright, or of any of the exclusive rights under a copyright, is distinct from ownership of any material object in which the work is embodied." 17 U.S.C. § 202. In this case, both Parties are in agreement that Adobe is the rightful owner of the intangible portion of the software, i.e. the intellectual property.

The dispute arises, however, as to who is the rightful owner of the package, or physical manifestation of this intellectual property. The CD-ROM itself is worth not much more than a nominal amount, and it is the code that justifies the purchase price of the product. That being the case, the economic reality of this transaction is that a consumer is ultimately paying for the software contained on the CD-ROM, rather than the CD-ROM itself. Despite this fact, this case is still based on the *ownership* of each particular copy of software distributed by Adobe. The determination of ownership in turn is based primarily on an examination of the OCRA, the agreement between Adobe and its distributors.

2. The OCRA

The Court looks to the language, content, and intent of the OCRA, in determining whether its terms affect a sale or license of the software. In the OCRA, Adobe contends that "Adobe is the owner and developer of Adobe Educational Software Products." According to the OCRA, "Educational Software Products," consist of "the respective software program in object code ("Software"), supporting documentation ("Documentation"), and all other related material, if any, supplied to Reseller in a commercial package." Adobe characterizes each transaction it concluded throughout the entire stream of commerce relevant to this action as a license. Accordingly, Adobe argues that it retains ownership of its software, the accompanying documentation, and all other related materials pursuant to the OCRA.

a. Terminology

In *One Stop Micro, supra*, Adobe filed suit against One Stop, a software distributor for copyright infringement, claiming that One Stop was illegally distributing copies of its software intended for educational end users to the general public. The OCRA and EULA in *One Stop* are substantially similar to the agreements relevant to this case. In *One Stop*, the Court found in favor of Adobe and held that (1) the agreement under which the software was distributed was a licensing agreement; and, (2) the license agreement applied to the distributor, even though it was not a signatory of the OCRA.

Stargate argues, however, that the language of Adobe's OCRA is evidence of a sale rather than a license. For example, in ¶ 11(c)(iv)(A), the OCRA reads, "Reseller shall submit to Adobe within (10) ten days after the effective date of termination a summary of the number of the respective Educational Software

Products *owned by Reseller* as of the effective date of termination." Also in the same paragraph is a sentence that provides, "Adobe may, at its option *repurchase* any or all of such Educational Software Products from Reseller upon written notice of its intention to do so. The question arises therefore, as to whether this language creates a sale, or a license of the product." The Court in *One Stop* concluded that "The OCRA contains additional language indicating that it only confers a license."

Similarly, the Court in this case also concludes that the language in Adobe's OCRA is evidence of a license, rather than a sale. Although the OCRA contains language such as "repurchase" and "owned," additional language indicates that the OCRA only confers a license. For instance, Paragraph 9 of the OCRA is titled, "*Ownership* of Proprietary Rights and Nondisclosure" (Referring to Adobe). Under that same paragraph, the OCRA furthers states, "Reseller acknowledges that the structure and organization of the *Software is proprietary to Adobe* and that *Adobe retains exclusive ownership of the Software* and Trademarks." The OCRA further states, "Reseller . . . to *protect Adobe's proprietary rights* in the Educational Software Products. Except as provided herein, *reseller is not granted any rights* to patents, copyrights, trade secrets, trade names, trademarks (whether registered or unregistered), or any other rights, franchises, or licenses with respect to the Software or Educational Software Products." As explained by the Court in *One Stop*, "evidence of trade usage demonstrates that it is commonplace for sales terminology to be used in connection with software licensing agreements." This Court concurs.

b. Content

In light of the fact that the OCRA in this case is substantially similar to the OCRA in *One Stop*, this Court agrees that the OCRA in the present case contains numerous restrictions on title that are imposed on the reseller, limiting the reseller's ability to re-distribute Adobe software, and thereby conferring a license between Adobe and the reseller. It is clear to the Court that the terms of the OCRA substantially and undeniably interfere with a reseller's ability to distribute and/or convey title to the products in question. 17 U.S.C. § 106.

This Court notes that software is unique from other forms of copyrighted information. Technology and software, in particular, has radically transformed the way information is created and exchanged. Software fundamentally differs from more traditional forms of medium, such as print or phonographic materials, in that software can be both, more readily and easily copied on a mass scale in an extraordinarily short amount of time and relatively inexpensively. One of the primary advantages of software, its ability to record, concentrate and convey information with unprecedented ease and speed, makes it extraordinarily vulnerable to illegal copying and piracy. This Court finds that it is important to acknowledge these special characteristics of the software industry and provide enhanced copyright protection for its inventors and developers.

Lastly, as a matter of general principle, this Court finds that no colorable reason exists in this case as to why Adobe and its distributors should be barred from characterizing the transaction that has been forged between them as a license. In light of the restrictions on title that have been incorporated into the OCRA, as well as the parties' free and willing consent to enter into and execute its terms, the Parties should be free to negotiate and/or set a price for the product being exchanged, as well as set the terms by which the product is exchanged. Fundamental to any free society is the liberty of its members to formulate contracts in accordance with the terms that they agree and consent to mutually execute. "The right to contract freely with the expectation that the contract shall endure according to its terms is as fundamental to the society as the right to write and to speak without restraint." While exceptions are made in the case of unfair or exploitive contracts, or where an inequitable end results as a result of the agreement, commercial parties are generally free to contract as they desire.

The Court, therefore, concludes that based on the clear and unambiguous language of the relevant contracts, coupled with the multiple restrictions on title placed on the reseller in the above agreements, the transaction should be characterized as a license, rather than a sale.

V. CONCLUSION

For all of the aforementioned reasons, Defendant, Stargate's Motion for Summary Judgment is DENIED and Plaintiff, Adobe's Motion for Summary Judgment is GRANTED.

QUESTIONS

1. Could Adobe license CD ROMs and specify the schools to which distributors can resell?

2. Section 117 of the Copyright Act allows "owners" of a copy of a software program to make archival copies of the program and to modify the program to run with different computer hardware configurations. Can Microsoft "license" CD ROMs and prohibit what the Copyright Act allows?

3. If you were counsel to Adobe, how would you revise the Off or On Campus Educational Reseller Agreements in light of *Adobe v. Stargate*?

4. If you were counsel to Adobe, how would you draft a license provision to clearly distinguish between the license of the software program and the license of the CD ROM on which the software program is recorded?

QUANTA COMPUTER, INC. v. LG ELECTRONICS, INC.
553 U.S. 617 (2008)

JUSTICE THOMAS

For over 150 years this Court has applied the doctrine of patent exhaustion to limit the patent rights that survive the initial authorized sale of a patented item. In this case, we decide whether patent exhaustion applies to the sale of components of a patented system that must be combined with additional components in order to practice the patented methods. The Court of Appeals for the Federal Circuit held that the doctrine does not apply to method patents at all and, in the alternative, that it does not apply here because the sales were not authorized by the license agreement. We disagree on both scores. Because the exhaustion doctrine applies to method patents, and because the license authorizes the sale of components that substantially embody the patents in suit, the sale exhausted the patents.

I

Respondent LG Electronics, Inc. (LGE), purchased a portfolio of computer technology patents in 1999, including the three patents at issue here: U.S. Patent Nos. 4,939,641 ('641); 5,379,379 ('379); and 5,077,733 ('733) (collectively LGE Patents). The main functions of a computer system are carried out on a microprocessor, or central processing unit, which interprets program instructions, processes data, and controls other devices in the system. A set of wires, or bus, connects the microprocessor to a chipset, which transfers data between the microprocessor and other devices, including the keyboard, mouse, monitor, hard drive, memory, and disk drives.

The data processed by the computer are stored principally in random access memory, also called main memory. Frequently accessed data are generally stored in cache memory, which permits faster access than main memory and is often located on the microprocessor itself. When copies of data are stored in both the cache and main memory, problems may arise when one copy is changed but the other still contains the original "stale" version of the data. The '641 patent addresses this problem. It discloses a system for ensuring that the most current data are retrieved from main memory by monitoring data requests and updating main memory from the cache when stale data are requested.

The '379 patent relates to the coordination of requests to read from, and write to, main memory. Processing these requests in chronological order can slow down a system because read requests are faster to execute than write requests. Processing all read requests first ensures speedy access, but may result in the retrieval of outdated data if a read request for a certain piece of data is processed before an outstanding write request for the same data. The '379 patent discloses an efficient method of organizing read and write requests while maintaining accuracy by allowing the computer to execute only read requests until it needs data for which there is an outstanding write request. Upon receiving such a read request, the computer executes pending write requests first and only then returns to the read requests so that the most up-to-date data are retrieved.

The '733 patent addresses the problem of managing the data traffic on a bus connecting two computer components, so that no one device monopolizes the bus. It allows multiple devices to share the bus, giving heavy users greater access. This patent describes methods that establish a rotating priority system under which each device alternately has priority access to the bus for a preset number of cycles and heavier users can maintain priority for more cycles without "hogging" the device indefinitely.

LGE licensed a patent portfolio, including the LGE Patents, to Intel Corporation (Intel). The cross-licensing agreement (License Agreement) permits Intel to manufacture and sell microprocessors and chipsets that use the LGE

Patents (the Intel Products). The License Agreement authorizes Intel to " " make, use, sell (directly or indirectly), offer to sell, import or otherwise dispose of" " its own products practicing the LGE Patents. Notwithstanding this broad language, the License Agreement contains some limitations. Relevant here, it stipulates that no license " " is granted by either party hereto . . . to any third party for the combination by a third party of Licensed Products of either party with items, components, or the like acquired . . . from sources other than a party hereto, or for the use, import, offer for sale or sale of such combination." "

The License Agreement purports not to alter the usual rules of patent exhaustion, however, providing that, " "[n]ot withstanding anything to the contrary contained in this Agreement, the parties agree that nothing herein shall in any way limit or alter the effect of patent exhaustion that would otherwise apply when a party hereto sells any of its Licensed Products." "

In a separate agreement (Master Agreement), Intel agreed to give written notice to its own customers informing them that, while it had obtained a broad license " "ensur[ing] that any Intel product that you purchase is licensed by LGE and thus does not infringe any patent held by LGE," " the license " "does not extend, expressly or by implication, to any product that you make by combining an Intel product with any non-Intel product." " The Master Agreement also provides that " a breach of this Agreement shall have no effect on and shall not be grounds for termination of the Patent License." "

Petitioners, including Quanta Computer (collectively Quanta), are a group of computer manufacturers. Quanta purchased microprocessors and chipsets from Intel and received the notice required by the Master Agreement. Nonetheless, Quanta manufactured computers using Intel parts in combination with non-Intel memory and buses in ways that practice the LGE Patents. Quanta does not modify the Intel components and follows Intel's specifications to incorporate the parts into its own systems.

LGE filed a complaint against Quanta, asserting that the combination of the Intel Products with non-Intel memory and buses infringed the LGE Patents. The District Court granted summary judgment to Quanta, holding that, for purposes of the patent exhaustion doctrine, the license LGE granted to Intel resulted in forfeiture of any potential infringement actions against legitimate purchasers of the Intel Products. The court found that, although the Intel Products do not fully practice any of the patents at issue, they have no reasonable non-infringing use and therefore their authorized sale exhausted patent rights in the completed computers. In a subsequent order limiting its summary judgment ruling, the court held that patent exhaustion applies only to apparatus or composition-of-matter claims that describe a physical object, and does not apply to process, or method, claims that describe operations to make or use a product. Because each of the LGE Patents includes method claims, exhaustion did not apply.

The Court of Appeals for the Federal Circuit affirmed in part and reversed in part. It agreed that the doctrine of patent exhaustion does not apply to method claims. In the alternative, it concluded that exhaustion did not apply because LGE did not license Intel to sell the Intel Products to Quanta for use in combination with non-Intel products.

We granted certiorari.

II

The longstanding doctrine of patent exhaustion provides that the initial authorized sale of a patented item terminates all patent rights to that item. This Court first applied the doctrine in 19th-century cases addressing patent extensions on the Woodworth planning machine. Purchasers of licenses to sell and use the machine for the duration of the original patent term sought to continue using the licenses through the extended term. The Court held that the extension of the patent term did not affect the rights already secured by purchasers who bought the item for use "in the ordinary pursuits of life "[W]hen the machine passes to the hands of the purchaser, it is no longer within the limits of the monopoly" "; Bloomer v. Millinger, 17 L.Ed. 581, 1 Wall. 340, 351 (1864). In Adams v. Burke, 21 L.Ed. 700, 17 Wall. 453 (1873), the Court affirmed the dismissal of a patent holder's suit alleging that a licensee had violated post-sale restrictions on where patented coffin-lids could be used. "[W]here a person ha[s] purchased a patented machine of the patentee or his assignee," the Court held, "this purchase carrie[s] with it the right to the use of that machine so long as it [is] capable of use."

This Court most recently discussed patent exhaustion in Univis, 316 U.S. 241, 62 S.Ct. 1088, 86 L.Ed. 1408, on which the District Court relied. Univis Lens Company, the holder of patents on eyeglass lenses, licensed a purchaser to manufacture lens blanks by fusing together different lens segments to create bi- and tri-focal lenses and to sell them to other Univis licensees at agreed-upon rates. Wholesalers were licensed to grind the blanks into the patented finished lenses, which they would then sell to Univis-licensed prescription retailers for resale at a fixed rate. Finishing retailers, after grinding the blanks into patented lenses, would sell the finished lenses to consumers at the same fixed rate. The United States sued Univis under the Sherman Act, 15 U.S.C. §§ 1,3,15, alleging unlawful restraints on trade. Univis asserted its patent monopoly rights as a defense to the antitrust suit. The Court granted certiorari to determine whether Univis' patent monopoly survived the sale of the lens blanks by the licensed manufacturer and therefore shielded Univis' pricing scheme from the Sherman Act.

The Court assumed that the Univis patents containing claims for finished lenses were practiced in part by the wholesalers and finishing retailers who ground the blanks into lenses, and held that the sale of the lens blanks exhausted the patents on the finished lenses. The Court explained that the lens blanks "embodi[ed] essential features of the patented device and [were] without utility until . . . ground and polished as the finished lens of the patent." The Court noted that:

> "where one has sold an uncompleted article which, because it embodies essential features of his patented invention, is within the protection of his patent, and has destined the article to be finished by the purchaser in conformity to the patent, he has sold his invention so far as it is or may be embodied in that particular article."

In sum, the Court concluded that the traditional bar on patent restrictions following the sale of an item applies when the item sufficiently embodies the patent

— even if it does not completely practice the patent — such that its only and intended use is to be finished under the terms of the patent.

With this history of the patent exhaustion doctrine in mind, we turn to the parties' arguments.

III

A

LGE argues that the exhaustion doctrine is inapplicable here because it does not apply to method claims, which are contained in each of the LGE Patents. LGE reasons that, because method patents are linked not to a tangible article but to a process, they can never be exhausted through a sale. Rather, practicing the patent-which occurs upon each use of an article embodying a method patent is permissible only to the extent rights are transferred in an assignment contract. Quanta, in turn, argues that there is no reason to preclude exhaustion of method claims, and points out that both this Court and the Federal Circuit have applied exhaustion to method claims. It argues that any other rule would allow patent holders to avoid exhaustion entirely by inserting method claims in their patent specifications.

Quanta has the better of this argument. Nothing in this Court's approach to patent exhaustion supports LGE's argument that method patents cannot be exhausted. It is true that a patented method may not be sold in the same way as an article or device, but methods nonetheless may be "embodied" in a product, the sale of which exhausts patent rights. Our precedents do not differentiate transactions involving embodiments of patented methods or processes from those involving patented apparatuses or materials. To the contrary, this Court has repeatedly held that method patents were exhausted by the sale of an item that embodied the method.

Eliminating exhaustion for method patents would seriously undermine the exhaustion doctrine. Patentees seeking to avoid patent exhaustion could simply draft their patent claims to describe a method rather than an apparatus. Apparatus and method claims "may approach each other so nearly that it will be difficult to distinguish the process from the function of the apparatus." By characterizing their claims as method instead of apparatus claims, or including a method claim for the machine's patented method of performing its task, a patent drafter could shield practically any patented item from exhaustion.

This case illustrates the danger of allowing such an end-run around exhaustion. On LGE's theory, although Intel is authorized to sell a completed computer system that practices the LGE Patents, any downstream purchasers of the system could nonetheless be liable for patent infringement. Such a result would violate the longstanding principle that, when a patented item is "once lawfully made and sold, there is no restriction on [its] use to be implied for the benefit of the patentee." We therefore reject LGE's argument that method claims, as a category, are never exhaustible.

B

We next consider the extent to which a product must embody a patent in order to trigger exhaustion. Quanta argues that, although sales of an incomplete article do not necessarily exhaust the patent in that article, the sale of the microprocessors and chipsets exhausted LGE's patents in the same way the sale of the lens blanks exhausted the patents in Univis. Just as the lens blanks in Univis did not fully practice the patents at issue because they had not been ground into finished lenses, Quanta observes, the Intel Products cannot practice the LGE Patents-or indeed, function at all-until they are combined with memory and buses in a computer system. If, as in Univis, patent rights are exhausted by the sale of the incomplete item, then LGE has no post-sale right to require that the patents be practiced using only Intel parts. Quanta also argues that exhaustion doctrine will be a dead letter unless it is triggered by the sale of components that essentially, even if not completely, embody an invention. Otherwise, patent holders could authorize the sale of computers that are complete with the exception of one minor step-say, inserting the microprocessor into a socket-and extend their rights through each downstream purchaser all the way to the end user.

LGE, for its part, argues that Univis is inapplicable here for three reasons. First, it maintains that Univis should be limited to products that contain all the physical aspects needed to practice the patent. On that theory, the Intel Products cannot embody the patents because additional physical components are required before the patents can be practiced. Second, LGE asserts that in Univis there was no "patentable distinction" between the lens blanks and the patented finished lenses since they were both subject to the same patent. In contrast, it describes the Intel Products as "independent and distinct products" from the systems using the LGE Patents and subject to "independent patents." Finally, LGE argues that Univis does not apply because the Intel Products are analogous to individual elements of a combination patent, and allowing sale of those components to exhaust the patent would impermissibly "ascrib[e] to one element of the patented combination the status of the patented invention in itself."

We agree with Quanta that Univis governs this case. As the Court there explained, exhaustion was triggered by the sale of the lens blanks because their only reasonable and intended use was to practice the patent and because they "embodie[d] essential features of [the] patented invention." Each of those attributes is shared by the microprocessors and chipsets Intel sold to Quanta under the License Agreement.

First, Univis held that "the authorized sale of an article which is capable of use only in practicing the patent is a relinquishment of the patent monopoly with respect to the article sold." The lens blanks in Univis met this standard because they were "without utility until [they were] ground and polished as the finished lens of the patent." Accordingly, "the only object of the sale [was] to enable the [finishing retailer] to grind and polish it for use as a lens by the prospective wearer." Here, LGE has suggested no reasonable use for the Intel Products other than incorporating them into computer systems that practice the LGE Patents. Nor can we can discern one: A microprocessor or chipset cannot function until it is connected to buses and memory. And here, as in Univis, the only apparent object of Intel's sales to Quanta was to permit Quanta to incorporate the Intel Products into computers that would practice the patents.

Second, the lens blanks in Univis "embodie[d] essential features of [the] patented invention." The essential, or inventive, feature of the Univis lens patents was the fusing together of different lens segments to create bi- and tri-focal lenses. The finishing process performed by the finishing and prescription retailers after the fusing was not unique. As the United States explained:

> "The finishing licensees finish Univis lens blanks in precisely the same manner as they finish all other bifocal lens blanks. Indeed, appellees have never contended that their licensing system is supported by patents covering methods or processes relating to the finishing of lens blanks. Consequently, it appears that appellees perform all of the operations which contribute any claimed element of novelty to Univis lenses."

Like the Univis lens blanks, the Intel Products constitute a material part of the patented invention and all but completely practice the patent. Here, as in Univis, the incomplete article substantially embodies the patent because the only step necessary to practice the patent is the application of common processes or the addition of standard parts. Everything inventive about each patent is embodied in the Intel Products. They control access to main and cache memory, practicing the '641 and '379 patents by checking cache memory against main memory and comparing read and write requests. They also control priority of bus access by various other computer components under the '733 patent. Naturally, the Intel Products cannot carry out these functions unless they are attached to memory and buses, but those additions are standard components in the system, providing the material that enables the microprocessors and chipsets to function. The Intel Products were specifically designed to function only when memory or buses are attached; Quanta was not required to make any creative or inventive decision when it added those parts. Indeed, Quanta had no alternative but to follow Intel's specifications in incorporating the Intel Products into its computers because it did not know their internal structure, which Intel guards as a trade secret. Intel all but practiced the patent itself by designing its products to practice the patents, lacking only the addition of standard parts.

We are unpersuaded by LGE's attempts to distinguish Univis. First, there is no reason to distinguish the two cases on the ground that the articles in Univis required the removal of material to practice the patent while the Intel Products require the addition of components to practice the patent. LGE characterizes the lens blanks and lenses as sharing a "basic nature" by virtue of their physical similarity, while the Intel Products embody only some of the "patentably distinct elements and steps" involved in the LGE Patents. But we think that the nature of the final step, rather than whether it consists of adding or deleting material, is the relevant characteristic. In each case, the final step to practice the patent is common and non-inventive: grinding a lens to the customer's prescription, or connecting a microprocessor or chipset to buses or memory. The Intel Products embody the essential features of the LGE Patents because they carry out all the inventive processes when combined, according to their design, with standard components.

With regard to LGE's argument that exhaustion does not apply across patents, we agree on the general principle: The sale of a device that practices patent A does not, by virtue of practicing patent A, exhaust patent B. But if the device practices patent A while substantially embodying patent B, its relationship to patent A does not prevent exhaustion of patent B. For example, if the Univis lens blanks had been composed of shatter-resistant glass under patent A, the blanks would nonetheless have substantially embodied, and therefore exhausted, patent B for the finished lenses. This case is no different. While each Intel microprocessor and chipset practices thousands of individual patents, including some LGE patents not at issue in this case, the exhaustion analysis is not altered by the fact that more than one patent is practiced by the same product. The relevant consideration is whether the Intel Products that partially practice a patent-by, for example, embodying its essential features-exhaust that patent.

C

Having concluded that the Intel Products embodied the patents, we next consider whether their sale to Quanta exhausted LGE's patent rights. Exhaustion is triggered only by a sale authorized by the patent holder.

LGE argues that there was no authorized sale here because the License Agreement does not permit Intel to sell its products for use in combination with non-Intel products to practice the LGE Patents. It cites General Talking Pictures Corp. v. Western Elec. Co., 304 U.S. 175, 58 S.Ct. 849, 82 L.Ed. 1273 (1938), and General Talking Pictures Corp. v. Western Elec. Co., 305 U.S. 124, 59 S.Ct. 116, 83 L.Ed. 81 (1938), in which the manufacturer sold patented amplifiers for commercial use, thereby breaching a license that limited the buyer to selling the amplifiers for private and home use. The Court held that exhaustion did not apply because the manufacturer had no authority to sell the amplifiers for commercial use, and the manufacturer "could not convey to petitioner what both knew it was not authorized to sell." LGE argues that the same principle applies here: Intel could not convey to Quanta what both knew it was not authorized to sell, i.e., the right to practice the patents with non-Intel parts.

LGE overlooks important aspects of the structure of the Intel-LGE transaction. Nothing in the License Agreement restricts Intel's right to sell its microprocessors and chipsets to purchasers who intend to combine them with non-Intel parts. It broadly permits Intel to " "make, use, [or] sell" " products free of LGE's patent claims. To be sure, LGE did require Intel to give notice to its customers, including Quanta, that LGE had not licensed those customers to practice its patents. But neither party contends that Intel breached the agreement in that respect. In any event, the provision requiring notice to Quanta appeared only in the Master Agreement, and LGE does not suggest that a breach of that agreement would constitute a breach of the License Agreement. Hence, Intel's authority to sell its products embodying the LGE Patents was not conditioned on the notice or on Quanta's decision to abide by LGE's directions in that notice.

LGE points out that the License Agreement specifically disclaimed any license to third parties to practice the patents by combining licensed products with other components. But the question whether third parties received implied licenses is irrelevant because Quanta asserts its right to practice the patents based not on implied license but on exhaustion. And exhaustion turns only on Intel's own license to sell products practicing the LGE Patents.

Alternatively, LGE invokes the principle that patent exhaustion does not apply to post-sale restrictions on "making" an article. But this is simply a rephrasing of its argument that combining the Intel Products with other components adds more than standard finishing to complete a patented article. As explained above, making a product that substantially embodies a patent is, for exhaustion purposes, no different from making the patented article itself. In other words, no further "making" results from the addition of standard parts-here, the buses and memory-to a product that already substantially embodies the patent.

The License Agreement authorized Intel to sell products that practiced the LGE Patents. No conditions limited Intel's authority to sell products substantially embodying the patents. Because Intel was authorized to sell its products to Quanta, the doctrine of patent exhaustion prevents LGE from further asserting its patent rights with respect to the patents substantially embodied by those products.

IV

The authorized sale of an article that substantially embodies a patent exhausts the patent holder's rights and prevents the patent holder from invoking patent law to control post-sale use of the article. Here, LGE licensed Intel to practice any of its patents and to sell products practicing those patents. Intel's microprocessors and chipsets substantially embodied the LGE Patents because they had no reasonable non-infringing use and included all the inventive aspects of the patented methods. Nothing in the License Agreement limited Intel's ability to sell its products practicing the LGE Patents. Intel's authorized sale to Quanta thus took its products outside the scope of the patent monopoly, and as a result, LGE can no longer assert its patent rights against Quanta. Accordingly, the judgment of the Court of Appeals is reversed.

It is so ordered.

QUESTIONS

1. Why did the Court find that the patent exhaustion doctrine applied to method patents as well as product patents?

2. To what extent is the result in *Quanta* attributable to the ambiguity of the language used in the License Agreement and Master Agreement? According to the Court, the License Agreement did not restrict Intel's right to sell its microprocessors and chipsets to purchasers who intended to combine them with non-Intel parts. LGE did require Intel to give notice to its customers that LGE had not licensed them to practice its patents in combination with non-Intel parts. However, the Court found that this notice provision appeared only in the Master Agreement and that LGE did not contend that a breach of the Master Agreement would constitute a breach of the License Agreement. The Court concluded, therefore, that Intel's authority to sell its products embodying the LGE Patents was not conditioned on

the notice provided or on Quanta's decision to abide by LGE's directions in that notice.

3. If you were counsel to LGE, how would you structure the license agreement to be more in line with *General Talking Pictures* and, therefore, less likely to run afoul of the patent exhaustion doctrine?

CASE NOTES

1. Lexmark manufactures printers and patented toner cartridges for its printers. Lexmark sells the patented toner cartridges to distributors who, in turn, sell the toner cartridges to end-users. On the carton of each toner cartridge is a statement that "[o]pening this package or using the patented cartridge inside confirms your acceptance of the following license agreement." The essential terms of the license agreement, also printed on each toner cartridge carton, provide that "This patented Return Program cartridge is sold at a special [discount] price subject to a restriction that it may be used only once. Following this initial use, you agree to return the empty cartridge only to Lexmark for remanufacturing and recycling." SCC collects used toner cartridges and supplies them to remanufacturers who repair them, refill the toner and resell the cartridges to end-user consumers. SCC also sells the remanufacturers parts and supplies for remanufacturing the used toner cartridges. Lexmark sued SCC for contributory infringement of its toner cartridge patents. SCC defended the infringement suit claiming that Lexmark's sale of the toner cartridges to distributors exhausted Lexmark's patent rights, that the license terms printed on the toner cartridge cartons were not valid contracts because the parties never had a meeting of the minds on the terms of the contract, and that, even if the license terms were enforceable against the distributors to whom Lexmark sold, they were not enforceable against the end-users. What result? *See* Static Control Components, Inc. v. Lexmark Int'l, Inc., 487 F. Supp. 2d 830 (E.D. Ky. 2007).

2. *See also* Monsanto Co. v. Scruggs, 459 F.3d 1328 (Fed. Cir. 2006) (Doctrine of patent exhaustion is inapplicable when the use of seeds by seed growers was conditioned on obtaining a license from the patentee and new seeds grown from the original seeds have never been sold); Vernor v. Autodesk, Inc., 555 F.Supp.2d 1164 (W.D.Wash. 2008) (Copyright owner's transfer of rights in software program were sufficiently substantial to constitute a "sale" rather than a "license" for the purposes of the Copyright Act's first sale doctrine).

Additional Information

1. Melvin F. Jager, Licensing Law Handbook, § 1:23 (1. ed. 2010-2011).

2. Raymond T. Nimmer, Law of Computer Technology § 2:43 (2010).

3. 1 John W. Schlicher, Patent Law, Legal and Economic Principles §§ 1:69,1:71 (2d ed. 2010).

4. 2 John W. Schlicher, Patent Law, Legal and Economic Principles §§ 8:13, 8:15 (2d ed. 2010).

5. Raymond T. Nimmer & Jeff Dodd, Modern Licensing Law § 10:29 (2010).

6. John Carlin, Christopher Loh, *Patent Exhaustion Revitalized? Supreme Court's "Quanta" Ruling Continues Recent Trend of Narrowing Rights of Patentees*, 8/18/2008 NAT'L L.J. S1, col. 2 (2008).

7. Lawrence T. Kass, *Patent Exhaustion, Litigation, Licensing After "Quanta"*, Outside Counsel, N.Y.L.J., col. 4 (2008).

8. William P. Skladony, *Commentary on Select Patent Exhaustion Principles in Light of the LG Electronics Cases*, 47 IDEA 235 (2007).

9. Peter Carstensen, *Post-Sale Restraints Via Patent Licensing: A "Seedcentric" Perspective*, 16 FORDHAM INTELL. PROP. MEDIA & ENT. L.J. 1053 (2006).

10. Amber H. Rovner, *Practical Guide to Application of (or Defense Against) Product-Based Infringement Immunities Under the Doctrines of Patent Exhaustion and Implied Licenses*, 12 TEX. INTELL. PROP. L.J. 227 (2004).

11. John W. Osborne, *A Coherent View of Patent Exhaustion: A Standard Based on Patentable Distinctiveness*, 20 SANTA CLARA COMPUTER & HIGH TECH. L.J. 643 (2004).

12. Christian H. Nadan, *Software Licensing in the 21st Century: Are Software "Licenses" Really Sales, and How Will the Software Industry Respond?*, 32 AIPLA Q.J. 555 (2004).

2.3.7 Field-of-Use Restrictions

Field-of-use restrictions are closely related to post-sale restrictions and patent exhaustion considered in the previous section. Conceptually, however, it is possible to distinguish field-of-use restrictions from post-sale restrictions and patent exhaustion. Field-of-use retractions most often limit the licensee to practicing the patent in a specified application market, such as human medicine or veterinary medicine. Post-sale restrictions and patent exhaustion, on the other hand, involve attempts by the seller/licensor to dictate how the transferred technology may be used downstream, often in ways that will increase the seller's/licensor's financial return on the patented technology.

Despite the conceptual differences between field-of-use restrictions, post-sale restrictions and patent exhaustion, field-of-use restrictions nonetheless raise similar concerns about potential anticompetitive effects. Field-of-use restrictions are generally perceived to be commercially reasonable and pro-competitive, and, therefore, are most often reviewed under the more lenient rule-of-reason standard. The Antitrust Licensing Guidelines promulgated by the Justice Department Antitrust Division and the Federal Trade Commission expressly adopt the rule-of-reason analysis for field-of-use restrictions unless they involve attempts to fix prices, divide markets or customers, or limit production output or the introduction of new, competing technologies. (The Antitrust Licensing Guidelines are covered in Section 7.2 of the materials.)

Field-of-use restrictions allow the patent owner to maximize its return on the licensed technology in two ways. First, the patent owner can engage in price differentiation and set the license price in different application markets according to the demand for the technology in those application markets: where the demand for the technology is high, the license price will be the high; where the demand for the technology is the low, the license price will be low. Second, the patent owner can maximize its return on the licensed technology by selecting the licensee(s) in each application market that has the greatest experience, capability and resources to exploit the licensed technology in the application market. If a licensee operates outside of the specified field of use, the licensor has causes of action for breach of the license agreement and infringement of the licensed patent.

Field-of-use restrictions also provide benefits to patent licensees. Different application markets often require different technical expertise, different plant and equipment, different personnel, different marketing skills, and different organizational structures. A licensee with great competence in one application market may have very little competence in another application market. Field-of-use restrictions, therefore, allow licensees to enter into licenses that are tailored to their unique competency. Licensees, who enter into licenses only in application markets where they have special competency, are also less likely to confront challenges later on that they have not exercised their best efforts to exploit the licensed technology when, in fact, the licensees' failure is due to a lack of competency, not a lack of effort. (Best efforts clauses are considered in the next subsection of the materials.) For a good discussion of field-of-use restraints *See* JAY DRATLER, JR., LICENSING INTELLECTUAL PROPERTY, Chapter 7. Common Restrictive Practices in Licensing: An International Overview, § 7.04 Field-of-Use Restrictions.

The *IGEN* case below involves the enforcement of a field-of-use restriction where the licensor granted the licensee the right to exploit the technology for assays performed by hospitals, blood banks and clinical laboratories, but reserved to itself the rights to all other application markets, in particular the patient point-of-care diagnostic market.

IGEN INT'L v. ROCHE DIAGNOSTICS GmbH
203 F.3d 821 (4th Cir. 1999)

Before WILKINSON, CHIEF JUDGE, and WILKINS and MICHAEL, CIRCUIT JUDGES.

PER CURIAM.

Roche Diagnostics GmbH (Roche) appeals an order of the district court granting a preliminary injunction to IGEN International, Inc. (IGEN) in IGEN's suit alleging that Roche was violating a licensing agreement. Roche also appeals the denial of its motion to alter or amend the injunction. Finding no error, we affirm.

I.

IGEN is a biotechnology firm that is incorporated in Delaware with its principal place of business in Gaithersburg, Maryland. IGEN develops and markets technologies for use in medical diagnosis, including a diagnostic process based on electrochemiluminescence ("ECL"). In 1992, IGEN entered into a licensing agreement regarding the ECL technology with Roche. Pursuant to the agreement, Roche was to develop, manufacture, and market applications of the ECL ("instruments") and the tests and supplies used with the instruments. The agreement limited Roche to marketing its instruments within a "field" defined in the agreement. The agreement defined the field as:

> the use of any Instrument to perform Assays, solely for use in hospitals (except where the performance of the Assay takes place at the side of the patient), blood banks and clinical reference laboratories. "Field" does not include, among other things, use of any Instrument or Assay in the presence or the proximity of the patient, e.g., for home, patient bedside, ambulance or physician office uses.

The agreement also contained a provision explicitly reserving rights in all non-field applications of the ECL technology to IGEN:

> [Roche] agrees and acknowledges that IGEN retains for itself and its licensees the rights to any and all fields of use other than the Field and to any and all instruments other than those falling within the definition of Instruments herein, including, without limitation, the exclusive right to develop . . . and sell or license an instrument for use in intensive care, emergency room, and other hospital patient bedside settings where the assay is performed at the patient's side, as well as home and physician office applications.

Pursuant to the agreement, Roche developed and, in 1996, began marketing two instruments using the ECL technology, the Elecsys 1010 and the Elecsys 2010. Each instrument weighs between 150 and 250 pounds and is intended for use in a laboratory, rather than at the side of the patient. Roche has marketed both instruments to non-hospital laboratories, including laboratories located within the office of a physician or group of physicians.

Since 1992, IGEN has been attempting to develop an instrument based on the ECL technology for application in the point-of-care diagnostic market. IGEN envisions a miniaturized instrument employing the ECL technology (an "ECLM") that can be used at the side of a patient and that will provide accurate results within 15 minutes, allowing physicians to make immediate decisions about patient care. Although IGEN thus far has been unsuccessful in developing such an instrument, it has been attempting to engage a corporate partner to invest in the development of the ECLM.

In the summer or fall of 1997, a Roche representative visited the office of Dr. Daniel Cohen, a shareholder of IGEN, for the purpose of selling Dr. Cohen and his partner an Elecsys instrument for use in their in-office laboratory. In October, Dr. Cohen mentioned the potential sale to IGEN's chief financial officer, who asked Dr. Cohen to learn more about Roche's sales of the Elecsys to other doctors' offices. In March 1998, Dr. Cohen sent IGEN a letter summarizing his findings that five practices had purchased an Elecsys instrument for use in their in-office laboratories.

Shortly thereafter, IGEN moved in the district court for a preliminary injunction preventing Roche from making further sales of Elecsys instruments to physicians' offices for use in in-house laboratories. IGEN asserted that Roche was marketing the Elecsys instruments to physicians' offices in violation of the licensing agreement and that Roche's marketing activities were deterring potential partners from investing in IGEN's attempts to develop the ECLM. After nearly three months of discovery, Roche filed an opposition to the motion for preliminary injunction claiming, *inter alia*, that injunctive relief was improper because IGEN had failed to comply with dispute resolution procedures outlined in the licensing agreement.

The district court granted the preliminary injunction after considering evidence obtained during discovery and hearing arguments from the parties. First, the court rejected Roche's argument that IGEN should be required to pursue contractual dispute resolution procedures, reasoning that Roche waived the argument by failing to raise it before discovery was conducted. With respect to IGEN's request for preliminary injunctive relief, the court concluded that IGEN had demonstrated that the denial of a preliminary injunction would cause it irreparable harm in that IGEN was losing a potential market for the ECLM and was having difficulty attracting corporate partners to invest in the ECLM technology. The court further found that Roche faced only a loss of sales during the course of the litigation. Based on these determinations, the court ruled that the balance of hardships favored IGEN. The court also concluded that IGEN had shown a substantial likelihood of success on the merits, reasoning that the plain language of the agreement indicated that the field in which Roche could market its instruments did not include any physician's office, irrespective of whether the instrument would be used in an in-office laboratory or at a patient's side.

The district court directed the parties to negotiate the specific terms of the injunction, which they did over the course of the next several months. IGEN and Roche were unable to agree to all of the details of the injunction and accordingly submitted proposals to the district court, which then drafted an order. As relevant to this appeal, the injunction prohibits Roche from marketing Elecsys instruments and "any products and accessories that can be used only with the Elecsys system" to "physicians' offices or physicians' office laboratories." The injunction defines "physicians' office laboratories" as:

(a) laboratories that are located within the office suites of physicians' practices and

(b) laboratories that are located outside of physicians' offices but that are operated by or under the control of one or more treating physicians.

This definition of physicians' office laboratories expressly includes all laboratories that are operated by or under the control of physicians with practices of all types and sizes, including large group practices and conglomerations of such group practices, no matter where located. This definition excludes physician-controlled or operated laboratories that have no relationship with and are not operated as part of the practice or practices of the controlling or operating physicians. That is, physician ownership or operation in and of itself does not define a "physicians' office laboratory"; rather, to be considered a physicians' office laboratory (1) the owning, operating, or controlling physicians must send a significant portion of their patient samples to that laboratory or (2) the laboratory must conduct a significant portion of its overall testing on samples from patients of the owning, operating, or controlling physicians.

Shortly thereafter, Roche moved to alter or amend the judgment, arguing that the definition of "physicians' office laboratories" did not account for the manner in which diagnostic laboratories are operated in Germany, and thus might preclude Roche from marketing its product to those laboratories even though they were clinical reference laboratories as contemplated in the licensing agreement. The district court denied the motion to alter or amend.

II.

When ruling on a request for a preliminary injunction, a district court must consider four factors. Those factors are:

(1) the likelihood of irreparable harm to the plaintiff if the preliminary injunction is denied,

(2) the likelihood of harm to the defendant if the requested relief is granted,

(3) the likelihood that the plaintiff will succeed on the merits, and

(4) the public interest.

After deciding whether the plaintiff will suffer irreparable harm if an injunction is denied and determining the nature of the harm, if any, that defendant will suffer if the injunction is granted, the district court must balance these hardships against one another. The result of this balancing determines the degree to which the plaintiff must establish a likelihood of success on the merits. If the balance of harms "tips decidedly in favor of the plaintiff," it is only necessary for the plaintiff to "raise[ ] questions going to the merits so serious, substantial, difficult and doubtful, as to make them fair ground for litigation and thus for more deliberate investigation." If, however, the balance of harms is in equipoise or does not favor the plaintiff, the plaintiff must make a correspondingly higher showing of the likelihood of success. We review a decision of the district court granting or denying preliminary injunctive relief for abuse of discretion, and we review underlying factual findings for clear error. We review the grant or denial of a motion to alter or amend for abuse of discretion.

Having reviewed the record and the parties' briefs, and having had the benefit of oral argument, we conclude that the district court correctly decided the issues before it. Accordingly, we affirm.

AFFIRMED.

QUESTIONS

1.   Would the result change if Roche sold to clinical laboratories and the clinical laboratories then sold to physicians for in-house use?

2.   Would the result change if IGEN licensed another firm for patient point-of-care applications, rather than reserving these applications for itself?

3. Does it matter that IGEN had not been able to develop a patient-point-of-care ECLM in seven years?

4. If you were counsel to IGEN, what courses of action might you suggest other than suing Roche?

CASE NOTES

1. Dr. Ziegler, who was, at the time, the Director of the Max Planck Institute, invented a new process for the production of aluminum trialklys (ATAs), a catalytic agent and chemical reactant used in the manufacture of many products, including biodegradable household detergents and synthetic rubber for tires. Dr. Ziegler's invention, for which he was awarded the Nobel Prize in Chemistry, allowed the production of ATAs at 5% of what it cost to produce ATAs using the prior art. Dr. Ziegler was issued a number of U.S. patents on his process for production of ATAs. However, since ATAs were well known at the time of Dr. Ziegler's invention, he did not receive any patents on the ATAs themselves. Dr. Ziegler entered into a non-exclusive license agreement with Hercules under which Hercules was granted the right to manufacture ATAs using the Ziegler process for use in Hercules' own, internal manufacturing operations. Hercules was also granted an exclusive license to sell ATAs it manufactured using the Ziegler process in the United States. Dr. Ziegler granted other non-exclusive licenses in the United States to manufacture ATAs using his patented process, but these licensees were only permitted to use the ATAs for internal purposes. The United States filed an antitrust suit against Dr. Ziegler and Hercules claiming the license agreement constituted an attempt to monopolize the ATAs market in violation of § 2 of the Sherman Act. Dr. Ziegler and Hercules claimed that they were immune from suit under the antitrust laws because the Ziegler ATAs manufacturing process was patented and they were operating within the scope of their patent rights. The district court held that the patent laws did not protect the Ziegler-Hercules licensing arrangement because a restriction on sales of the unpatented ATAs by the non-exclusive process licensees exceeded the scope of the process patent. Dr. Ziegler and Hercules appealed the district court's decision. What result? *See* U.S. v. Studiengesell Schaft Kohle, 670 F.2d 1122 (D.C. Cir. 1981).

2. *See also* SuperGuide Corp. v. DirectTV Enterprises, Inc., 141 F.Supp.2d 616 (W.D. N.C. 2001) (Lawyer for plaintiff-licensor in action claiming defendant-licensee had exceeded its licensed field of use, which lawyer had formerly represented defendant-licensee in multiple infringement suits, would be disqualified from representing plaintiff-licensor in instant suit); Int'l Gamco, Inc. v. Multimedia Games, Inc., 504 F.3d 1273 (Fed. Cir. 2007) (Exclusive field-of-use license, unlike exclusive territorial license, does not grant the licensee substantially all rights in the patent so that exclusive field-of-use licensee can bring an infringement action in its own name without joining the patentee; there is a risk of multiple suits in the case an exclusive field-of-use licensee which is not present in the case of an exclusive territorial licensee).

Additional Information

1. JOHN W. SCHLICHER, 2 PATENT LAW, LEGAL AND ECONOMIC PRINCIPLES §§ 11:34, 11:39 (2d ed. 2010).

2. ROBERT A. MATTHEWS, JR., 5 ANNOTATED PATENT DIGEST § 35:45 (2010).

3. ROBERT A. MATTHEWS, JR., 1 ANNOTATED PATENT DIGEST § 9:60 (2010).

4. MODERN PATENT LAW PRECEDENT, F510 (8th ed. 2010).

5. ROBERT GOLDSCHEIDER, 2 ECKSTROM'S LICENSING IN FOREIGN AND DOMESTIC OPERATIONS: THE FORMS AND SUBSTANCE OF LICENSING §§ 5:16, 5:39 (2010).

6. JEFFREY L. KESSLER & SPENCER W. WALLER, INTERNATIONAL TRADE AND U.S. ANTITRUST LAW § 10:8 (2d ed. 2010).

7. MELVIN F. JAGER, 2 TRADE SECRETS LAW § 11:8 (2010).

8. MELVIN F. JAGER, LICENSING LAW HANDBOOK § 5:8 (2010-2011 Edition).

9. RAYMOND T. NIMMER, JEFF DODD, MODERN LICENSING LAW §§ 6:15, 14:37 (2010).

10. JOHN G. MILLS ET AL., 3 PATENT LAW FUNDAMENTALS § 19:10 (2d ed. 2010).

11. WILLIAM C. HOLMES, 2 INTELLECTUAL PROPERTY AND ANTITRUST LAW § 36:4 (2008).

12. Penelope A. Preovolos, *Licensing Pitfalls: Territorial, Field of Use and Customer Restrictions, Resale Price Maintenance, Output Restrictions, Royalty Provisions and Grantbacks*, 708 PLI/PAT 671 (2002).

13. Mark R. Paterson, *Contractual Expansion of the Scope of Patent Infringement Through Field-of-Use Licensing*, 49 WM. & MARY L. REV. 157 (2007).

14. Thomas C. Meyers, *Field-of-Use Restrictions as Procompetitive Elements in Patent and Know-How Licensing Agreements*, 12 NW. J. INT'L L. & BUS. 364 (1991).

2.3.8 Best Efforts Clauses

Best efforts clauses in license agreements can be either express or implied. In the case of *express* best efforts clauses, in the absence of license provisions defining what constitutes best efforts or specifying the specific acts that must be performed by the licensee, courts are left with the challenge of determining what constitutes best efforts within the context of the commercial relationship between the licensor and licensee. Generally, in determining what constitutes best efforts, courts seek to balance the interests of the licensor and licensee. The interests of the licensor are weighted more heavily in cases where the licensor is highly dependent on the licensee to realize any return on the licensee. This would be the case, for example, where the licensor has granted the licensee an unrestricted exclusive license solely in return for running royalties on sales made by the licensee. On the other hand, if the licensor has received a large up-front license fee or a large pre-paid royalty payment, the interests of the licensor would be weighted less heavily.

In terms of the licensee, the licensee's interests are weighted more heavily where the best efforts actions demanded of the licensee could result in the licensee suffering a competitive disadvantage or sacrificing business opportunities. This would be the case, for example, where the licensor is demanding that the licensee invest in development or marketing efforts which have no reasonable likelihood of earning profits for the licensee. In cases such as these, courts respect the licensee's reasonable business decisions in terms of supply, demand and competition within a market. However, even if a court finds that a licensee is not required to exercise its best efforts, the licensee is nonetheless still required to operate fairly and in good faith with the licensor.

Courts have *implied* best efforts clauses, sometimes called "due diligence" or "reasonable efforts" clauses, where equity, commercial fairness and the reasonable expectations of the licensor and licensee indicate that the parties would have agreed to a best efforts clause had they considered it at the time of the license. Courts never imply a best efforts clause in the case of non-exclusive licenses because the licensors can always grant additional licenses if they are dissatisfied with the efforts of the current licensees. Whether or not courts imply a best efforts clause in the case of exclusive licenses depends upon a host of factors. As with the courts' determination of the meaning of an express best efforts clause, the more thoroughly dependent the licensor is on the licensee's conduct in order to realize a return on the licensed patents, the more likely courts will be to imply a best efforts clause. In addition to the factors discussed above, such as large up-front license fees and large prepaid royalties that mitigate against an implied best efforts clause, courts have to also consider the licensor's reserved right to practice the licensed patents, the licensor's right to terminate the license agreement at will or on very short notice, and other factors diminishing the licensor's dependence on the licensee in deciding whether to imply a best efforts clause.

The *Intervisual* and *Permanence* cases below illustrate how courts proceed in their analysis of whether or not to imply a best effort clause in an exclusive license agreement.

INTERVISUAL COMMUNICATIONS v. VOLKERT
975 F.Supp. 1092 (N.D. Ill. 1997)

KEYS, UNITED STATES MAGISTRATE JUDGE.

This matter is before the Court on Plaintiff's Complaint, seeking declaratory judgment, injunctive relief, and damages for interference with prospective economic advantage and for lost profits. Additionally, Defendants have counterclaimed for declaratory judgment, injunctive relief, and damages based on patent infringement as well as Plaintiff's alleged failure to use its "best efforts" to market Defendants' goods. For the following reasons, the Court enters declaratory judgment in favor of Plaintiff and against Defendants. Accordingly, the Court awards $567,667 to Plaintiff for damages. Plaintiff's claims for interference with prospective economic advantage and injunctive relief fail, as do Defendants' counterclaims.

FINDINGS OF FACT

Plaintiff, Intervisual Communications, Inc., ("Intervisual"), is a Delaware corporation with its principal place of business in California. Intervisual markets interactive advertising devices, such as hand-assembled and machine-made "pop-ups" and talking advertisements to marketing firms. Intervisual contracts with third parties to manufacture its advertising devices. Intervisual, under a succession of names, has operated in the hand-assembled pop-up market since 1962.

Defendant John Volkert is an Illinois resident. Mr. Volkert is the president of One-Up, Inc., ("One-Up"), a separately-named defendant. One-Up is a corporation with its principal place of business in Illinois. Mr. Volkert is an inventor and a salesman, with many years of experience designing and manufacturing machine-made pop-ups. He began working for F.N. Volkert and Company, his family's bookbinding business, in 1958. Starting out as a factory worker, Mr. Volkert rose through the ranks and eventually became president of the company. In 1982, Mr. Volkert began working for Papermasters, Inc., and One-Up, developing and licensing patents relating to creative advertising concepts. Mr. Volkert, through One-Up, currently owns as many as fifteen patents involving pop-up products and methods for making pop-ups.

Intervisual and Mr. Volkert first developed a business relationship in 1987, when Messrs. Volkert and Richwine met and talked about merging Intervisual and One-Up. However, according to Mr. Richwine, Mr. Volkert was "having some other legal problems" at that time, so talk of merging their companies "went away." Merger discussion resumed in 1990, and, even though Mr. Volkert was still involved in litigation, Intervisual and Mr. Volkert entered into an exclusive license agreement on October 21, 1991.

This exclusive license agreement, which was amended on January 24, 1992, and renegotiated on January 20, 1993, is the focus of the dispute between Intervisual and Mr. Volkert. The essence of the 1991 agreement was that Mr. Volkert granted Intervisual the exclusive right to use and market his patents, in exchange for annual royalties on the sale of any products using one of his patents. Additionally, Mr. Volkert agreed to provide his expertise to help design and manufacture pop-ups, assist in training Intervisual's sales force, develop new concepts utilizing pop-ups, attend trade shows with Intervisual, and participate in sales presentations with Intervisual.

Specifically, the contract required Mr. Volkert to devote at least 1,380 hours per year to providing consulting services to Intervisual to support the exclusive license agreement. In exchange, Intervisual would pay Mr. Volkert a nonrefundable sum of $50,000 upon signing the agreement. Twenty-five thousand dollars of this $50,000 advance was to be paid directly to Mr. Volkert, and $25,000 was to be escrowed to pay for Mr. Volkert's legal costs relating to pending litigation. In addition, Intervisual agreed to pay Mr. Volkert a $100,000 advance against future royalty payments and an annual license fee of $5,000 for the duration of the agreement. Intervisual also agreed to pay Mr. Volkert annual royalties in the amount of 7% for the first $3,000,000 of annual revenue for patented pop-ups, and 5% for all such revenues thereafter. After the fifth anniversary of the agreement, the annual royalty rate dropped to 5% on all patented pop-up revenue.

The exclusive license agreement provided for termination, by either party, under a variety of circumstances. Mr. Volkert could terminate the agreement, upon 30-days' notice, if Intervisual did not meet a minimum level of annual sales of patented pop-ups for two consecutive years. Intervisual had the right to terminate the agreement, upon giving Mr. Volkert twelve months' notice, after the tenth anniversary of the effective date of the agreement. Both parties could rightfully terminate the agreement "on thirty (30) days prior written notice if the other party is in breach of this Agreement," provided that the breaching party failed to cure "to the nonbreaching party's reasonable satisfaction during such thirty (30) day period." Otherwise, the agreement would last until the expiration of the last patent involved in the agreement.

After signing the 1991 agreement with Mr. Volkert, Intervisual was "excited" by the prospect of marketing in-line pop-ups, and planned to "aggressively sell them." Intervisual moved its office from Chicago to Northbrook, where Mr. Volkert was headquartered, in an effort to give its sales staff an opportunity to learn about machine-made pop-ups from Mr. Volkert. Not long after signing the agreement, however, the relationship between Mr. Volkert and Intervisual began to deteriorate. Mr. Volkert was displeased that Intervisual was "selling other products instead of just in-line pop-ups."

As a result, Messrs. Richwine and Volkert negotiated, and signed, an amendment to the 1991 agreement on January 24, 1992. That amendment waived the previous requirement that Mr. Volkert completely resolve the pending litigation with Penick and Webcraft before Intervisual would exercise its option to add the two patents at issue to the exclusive license agreement. Pursuant to the renegotiated agreement, Intervisual exercised its option to incorporate the two patents into its agreement with Mr. Volkert, and paid a $50,000 advance to Mr. Volkert immediately.

Despite over $2,000,000 in sales of his patented pop-ups in 1992, Mr. Volkert continued to be "unhappy with Intervisual." According to Mr. Richwine, Mr. Volkert complained that Intervisual should be "putting all of [its] efforts . . . on selling in-line pop-ups." Eventually, Mr. Volkert's dissatisfaction grew to such an extent that he forced Intervisual to leave his office space in Northbrook. Again, as a result of Mr. Volkert's displeasure, Messrs. Volkert and Richwine negotiated another amended agreement on January 20, 1993.

The 1993 agreement reduced the number of hours per year that Mr. Volkert was expected to devote to consulting services from 1,380 to 920. The $100,000 and $50,000 advances against future royalties paid by Intervisual to Mr. Volkert pursuant to the 1991 and 1992 agreements, respectively, were deemed "non-refundable." As a result, Mr. Volkert did not have to count those amounts against sales. According to Mr. Richwine, "it was basically giving him another $150,000."

Mr. Volkert's royalty schedule was altered such that Intervisual was required to pay him royalties at a rate of 6% on the first $1,000,000 in annual patented pop-up revenue, and 5% for all patented pop-up sales thereafter. A provision was added to pay Mr. Volkert a royalty if non-pop-up pieces were sold that he had a role in developing. Another provision was added allowing Mr. Volkert to terminate the agreement if Intervisual did not pay him a minimum royalty of $110,000 per year.

Relations between Mr. Volkert and Intervisual remained strained, despite having amended the exclusive license agreement twice. On February 29, 1996, Mr. Volkert delivered a letter to Mr. Richwine, serving notice that he found Intervisual to be in breach of the exclusive license agreement. Mr. Volkert alleged, in his letter and subsequent pleadings, that Intervisual had breached the agreement by failing to use its "best efforts" to sell machine-made pop-ups, failing to pay royalties on a monthly basis, failing to provide access to verify invoice amounts, failing to subcontract with him on certain retail sales, failing to mark patented pieces, failing to pay royalties on particular jobs, failing to use him in sales presentations, and failing to deal in good faith where it maintained a minimum purchase contract for hand-made pop-ups with Carvajal, a manufacturer in Mexico.

On March 25, 1996, Intervisual's Director of Finance, Bruce Shiney, sent a letter to Mr. Volkert, addressing each of the breaches alleged in the February 29, 1996, letter. On April 2, 1996, Mr. Volkert replied with a letter to Mr. Richwine, officially terminating the exclusive license agreement. Mr. Volkert insisted that the breaches he had alleged were not cured to his reasonable satisfaction, as was required by the exclusive license agreement.

On September 24, 1996, Mr. Volkert, operating under the assumption that the agreement with Intervisual had been officially terminated, negotiated a non-exclusive license agreement between One-Up and The Lehigh Press, Inc., Cadillac Commercial Products Division ("Lehigh Press"). One-Up granted Lehigh Press a non-exclusive license to many of the same patents included in Mr. Volkert's agreement with Intervisual. In exchange, Lehigh Press agreed to pay Mr. Volkert royalties of $45,000. This amount was an advance against future royalties, expected to be earned by Mr. Volkert at a rate of 15% for the first $4 million in annual sales of patented pieces, and 10% for all such sales thereafter.

As a result of Mr. Volkert's attempted termination of the exclusive license agreement, Intervisual was quite reluctant to sell patented pop-ups. According to Mr. Richwine, Intervisual was leery of selling patented pop-ups because its "customers could get into a patent infringement lawsuit, because John Volkert owns the patents." As a result, Intervisual sold no patented pop-ups from April 1, 1996, through May 28, 1997. Even so, Intervisual attempted to uphold its end of the exclusive license agreement by placing Mr. Volkert's minimum annual royalty payment of $110,000 for 1996 "in escrow."

Intervisual brought this action for a declaratory judgment that it did not breach its exclusive license agreement with Mr. Volkert, and that the agreement, therefore, remains in full force and effect. Further, Intervisual maintains that Mr. Volkert has tortiously interfered with its prospective economic advantage, and seeks damages for lost sales, as well as an injunction to prevent future interference. Mr. Volkert counterclaims for a declaratory judgment that Intervisual has breached the exclusive license agreement and that his termination of the agreement was rightful. Mr. Volkert also counterclaims for lost royalties and for an injunction against Intervisual's further use of his patents. Both parties plead for any additional relief the Court may deem fair and just.

ANALYSIS

A. Legal Standard for Breach of Contract

For Intervisual to succeed in this declaratory judgment action, it must prove that it has not breached the exclusive license agreement with Mr. Volkert, and that, therefore, Mr. Volkert's allegations of breach of contract are without merit. For Mr. Volkert to prove a prima facie breach of contract claim, he would have to show that: 1) a valid contract with definite and certain terms exists between him and Intervisual; 2) he has performed his obligations under the contract; 3) Intervisual has failed to perform its contractual duties; and 4) he has suffered damages as a result of Intervisual's breach.

The first element of a breach of contract claim, the existence of a valid contract, is not in dispute here. Both parties agree, at the very least, that the exclusive license agreement was in force and effect from October 21, 1991, through February 29, 1996. Hence, Intervisual cannot disprove Mr. Volkert's allegation of breach of contract by claiming that a valid contract did not exist.

The second element of a breach of contract claim, the requirement that Mr. Volkert perform his obligations under the contract, is very much in dispute. Intervisual maintains that Mr. Volkert has improperly terminated the exclusive license agreement. In so doing, Intervisual implicitly argues that Mr. Volkert cannot satisfy this second element of a breach of contract action and that, therefore, Mr. Volkert's breach of contract claim must fail. However, proof that Mr. Volkert has improperly terminated the exclusive license agreement and, therefore, has not performed his obligations under the contract, is dependent on the third element of a breach of contract — whether Intervisual has breached the exclusive license agreement.

Hence, the success or failure of Intervisual's plea for declaratory judgment turns on the third element of the breach of contract formula. To satisfy the third element necessary to maintain a breach of contract action, Mr. Volkert must show that Intervisual has failed to perform its contractual duties. Thus, if Intervisual can prove that it has not breached its contractual duties, Mr. Volkert's allegations of breach of contract must fail, and Intervisual will be granted declaratory judgment.

To prove that it has performed its contractual duties, Intervisual must repudiate the breaches alleged by Mr. Volkert in his termination letter of February 29, 1996, according to Illinois' standard for determining a contractual "breach." It is well-settled that only a material breach will justify the non-breaching party's failure to perform its contractual duties. A minor, non-material breach will not preclude specific performance. The *Arrow Master* court considered a breach to be "material" when "the matter, in respect to which the failure of performance occurs, is of such a nature and of such importance that the contract would not have been made without it." With these standards in mind, the Court next examines each of the breaches alleged by Mr. Volkert in his termination letter of February 29, 1996.

B. Intervisual's Alleged Contractual Breaches

1. Failure to Use "Best Efforts" to Market Patented Pop-Ups

Mr. Volkert argues that Intervisual failed to use its "best efforts" to market his patented pop-ups, even though there is no express term in the exclusive license agreement requiring Intervisual to use its "best efforts" to market Mr. Volkert's pop-ups. By failing to use its "best efforts," Mr. Volkert argues, Intervisual has breached the exclusive license agreement. However, a party is not required to use its "best efforts" where an explicit "best efforts" term is absent from the contract, and consideration, in the form of substantial advance royalties, already exists to satisfy the mutuality requirement of the otherwise valid contract.

In *Beraha*, a case relied upon by both parties, the plaintiff/licensor of a patent for a biopsy needle, urged the court to find an implied "best efforts" clause in its license agreement with the defendant/licensee. The *Beraha* court, however, declined to find such an implied "best efforts" clause because the licensor was receiving substantial advance royalties. Such advance royalties provided a sufficient incentive for the licensee to aggressively market the licensed patent. The advance royalties also provided the licensor a degree of security, in the event that the patent proved to be unmarketable.

Beraha is instructive in the instant case. Here, Mr. Volkert argues that Intervisual failed to use its best efforts, and in so doing, breached the exclusive license agreement. However, the exclusive license agreement does not include an express "best efforts" clause. Following the rationale of Beraha, because Mr. Volkert negotiated for substantial advance royalties, and failed to include an express "best efforts" provision, a "best efforts" provision cannot be implied. Accordingly, Mr. Volkert's first alleged breach of the exclusive license contract, that Intervisual failed to use its "best efforts" to market patented pop-ups, is rejected.

QUESTIONS

1. If the Intervisual license had included a "best efforts" clause, could Volkert have claimed breach of the "best efforts" clause?

2. If the Intervisual license had only provided for the payment of minimum royalties in the amount of $110,000 per year, would this have been sufficient to negate the implication of a best efforts clause?

3. How can parties to a license make a "best efforts" clause less ambiguous?

4. Can a "best efforts" clause ever be implied in a nonexclusive license? Can a best efforts clause ever be included in a nonexclusive license?

5. If you were counsel to Intervisual, how could you draft the Intervisual-Volkert agreement to limit Volkert's opportunity to enter into agreements with Intervisual's competitors such as Lehigh Press?

PERMANENCE CORPORATION v. KENNAMETAL, INC.
908 F.2d 98 (6th Cir. 1990)

Contie, Senior Circuit Judge.

Plaintiff-appellant, Permanence Corp., appeals the district court's grant of summary judgment to defendant-appellee, Kennametal, Inc., holding that defendant did not have an implied best efforts obligation in the contract between Permanence and Kennametal. For the following reasons, we affirm.

I.

Permanence is a closely-held Michigan corporation, which was formed by its president and majority shareholder Charles S. Baum in 1969 for the purpose of developing and exploiting certain processes developed by Baum. In the 1970s Permanence conducted research and manufactured products in the tungsten carbide field. On May 24, 1977, Permanence obtained U.S. Patent No. 4,024,902 (hereinafter "Patent '902") for a process to form an alloy by incorporating tungsten carbide into a steel matrix. The patent was entitled "metal sintered tungsten carbide composites and method of forming the same."

On December 8, 1977, plaintiff executed a non-exclusive license agreement for the use of Patent '902 to Masco Corp., a Detroit corporation. The agreement included a plan of reorganization and plan of merger between Masco and Permanence, an employment agreement concerning Baum, and an agreement not to compete concerning Baum. The agreement also contained a clause providing for its termination. The patented process was not developed by Masco and Masco chose to terminate the agreement pursuant to the contract clause, but retained its non-exclusive license to use Patent '902.

On September 19, 1979, Permanence sued Masco, claiming that Masco failed to fulfill an implied obligation to use best efforts to exploit the patent. The Michigan trial court found that Masco had no implied obligation to use best efforts as the contract for the non-exclusive right to use the patent was adequately supported by consideration in the form of the employment contract given by Masco to Mr. Baum. The Michigan Court of Appeals affirmed.

On February 8, 1979, Permanence executed a written agreement with defendant Kennametal, a publicly traded corporation specializing in the manufacture of tools, tooling systems, and supplies for the metal working industry. Kennametal's principal office is in Latrobe, Pennsylvania.

In the contract between the parties, Permanence granted Kennametal the non-exclusive right to the licensed patents (existing Patent '902 and patents that would issue from applications owned by Permanence) for a period of 24 months subject to the non-exclusive license previously granted to Masco Corp. for Patent '902. For the non-exclusive license, Kennametal agreed to pay Permanence a consideration of a $150,000 fee and a royalty rate of 2 3/4 % on the net sales price of products made by Kennametal using processes that fell under valid claims of the licensed patents. Advance royalties of $100,000 were to be paid upon the signing of the agreement for the non-exclusive license.

The agreement also provided that Kennametal would have the option to obtain the exclusive license to the patents, subject to the non-exclusive license previously granted to Masco, exercisable within 24 months from the date of the agreement. If after 24 months, the option was not exercised, Kennametal agreed to pay a royalty rate of 3½% except on products sold by Kennametal in direct competition with products manufactured under Masco's non-exclusive license. The royalty rate for competing products was 2%.

Kennametal agreed to pay Permanence a second $150,000 fee and a second $100,000 in advance royalties upon the exercise of the option for an exclusive license. Under the exclusive agreement, the royalty rate was 3½% with the exception of a 2% rate on products sold in direct competition with Masco products manufactured under its non-exclusive license.

On February 8, 1979, the parties signed the agreement and a $150,000 up-front fee and an advance payment of royalties in the amount of $100,000 was paid to Permanence for the non-exclusive right to the patents. On February 5, 1981, Kennametal exercised its option and paid an additional $250,000 for the grant of the exclusive agency — $150,000 for the exercise of the option and a second $100,000 in advance royalties.

Seven years later on April 18, 1988, Permanence filed a one-count complaint alleging that Kennametal had breached the contract by not fulfilling an obligation to use best efforts to exploit the patents. As there was no express "best efforts" provision in the contract, plaintiff argued that the grant of an exclusive agency imposes on the licensee (Kennametal) an implied duty to use best efforts to exploit. On February 1, 1989, Kennametal moved for summary judgment, arguing that it had spent $500,000 for the use of the patented technology of Permanence and that a best efforts obligation had specifically been negotiated out of the agreement.

On May 18, 1989, the district court granted defendant's motion for summary judgment, holding that no obligation on defendant's part to use its best efforts to exploit the patents could be implied in the parties' contract. Plaintiff timely filed this appeal.

II.

The sole issue before this court on appeal is whether the district court erred in its order granting summary judgment that as a matter of law an implied best efforts obligation did not arise in the contract between the parties. When an appeals court reviews the grant of summary judgment below, the district court's legal conclusions are reviewed de novo. Federal district courts sitting in diversity cases must apply the law of the appropriate state as declared by the legislature or highest court of the state. In the present case the contract at issue states that the agreement is to be interpreted under the law of Pennsylvania and the parties are therefore agreed that Pennsylvania law applies.

Plaintiff's legal theory that the court will imply a duty on the part of an exclusive licensee to use "best efforts" to bring profits and revenues into existence finds its ultimate support in the landmark opinion of Judge Cardozo, *Wood v. Lucy, Lady Duff-Gordon.* There, the defendant, a fashion designer, gave the plaintiff the exclusive privilege of marketing defendant's designs. The court implied an obligation to exploit the design, although there was not an express obligation to do so in the contract, because defendant's sole revenue from the grant of the exclusive agency was to be derived from plaintiff's sale of clothes designed by defendant, and defendant was thus at plaintiff's mercy. In subsequent cases, an obligation to employ best efforts has generally been implied in contracts in which the only consideration for a grant of property lies in payment of royalties.

In *Maxwell v. Schaefer,* the Pennsylvania Supreme Court stated that since plaintiff's profits for granting the exclusive contract depended entirely on the volume of sales defendant was able to create for the product, "it may fairly be inferred that all parties to the agreement fully intended and expected [defendant] to devote reasonable effort to the promotion of [the product]." Thus, under Pennsylvania law an obligation to use "best efforts" will be implied in a contract granting an exclusive agency if the plaintiff depends for its consideration solely upon sales of the licensed product.

In cases such as *Wood* and *Maxwell,* courts have found it necessary to imply a covenant to employ best efforts as a matter of law because otherwise the contract at issue would lack mutuality of obligation and be inequitable. It would be inherently "unfair to place the productiveness of the licensed property solely within the control of the licensee, thereby putting the licensor at his mercy, without imposing [a reciprocal] obligation upon the licensee."

The issue before this court is thus whether an implied covenant to use best efforts is necessary to establish mutuality of obligation in the present case. The existence of a best efforts obligation should not be lightly inferred since "such an obligation subjects the licensee to significant litigation exposure and deprives him of the fundamental power of determining for himself the reasonableness of his marketing efforts." Where it is unnecessary to imply such an obligation in order to give effect to the terms of the contract, the obligation will not be implied.

In making the determination of whether a covenant to use best efforts should be implied as a matter of law, this court must focus its attention on the terms of the written contract between the parties, and the circumstances surrounding the making of the agreement.

Plaintiff argues that in order to give effect to the meaning of the contract a best efforts obligation must be implied because the contract provides for royalties to be paid to Permanence by Kennametal on products produced by the processes of the licensed patents to which Kennametal had exclusive rights. Plaintiff argues that the district court erred in determining that Permanence had received sufficient consideration, $500,000, in exchange for its rights to the patents, because $250,000 of the money paid by Kennametal was for the grant of the non-exclusive license. Plaintiff contends that in spite of the additional $150,000 paid for the exercise of the option to obtain exclusive rights to the patents and the second payment of $100,000 in advance royalties, a best efforts obligation must be implied because the contract contemplates the payment of royalties and royalties under an exclusive agency will be generated only if defendant is under a duty to exploit the patented processes. Plaintiff contends that because of the grant of an exclusive, rather than non-exclusive, right to the patented processes, plaintiff bargained for and received an increase in the rate of royalty from 2¾% to 3½%.

First, plaintiff's argument that it received an increase in royalty rate as consideration for the grant of the exclusive, as opposed to non-exclusive, license is negated by the terms of the contract. Paragraph 5.2 of the contract stated that if the option was not exercised within 24 months and Kennametal chose instead to continue the non-exclusive license, the royalty rate would increase from 2¾% to 3½%. This rate — 3½% — was the same rate which was negotiated as the royalty rate to be paid under the exclusive license. Thus, contrary to plaintiff's assertions, no increase in the rate of royalty was granted for the right to use the patents exclusively after 24 months. This fact bolsters defendant's argument that the consideration given for the exclusive, as opposed to the non-exclusive, right to the patented processes was the $150,000 fee paid up front for the exercise of the option and the additional $100,000 paid in advance royalties under the exclusive license.

Plaintiff concedes that there was no best efforts obligation to exploit the non-exclusive license initially granted to Kennametal for a $150,000 fee and $100,000 in advance royalties. Yet royalties (2¾%) were also to be paid on products manufactured under the non-exclusive license. Moreover, the royalty rate for both the exclusive license and the non-exclusive license after 24 months was contingent on whether the products manufactured by Kennametal under the patents were ones which directly competed with products sold by Masco that had been produced under the non-exclusive license previously granted to it. The fact that the relationship with Masco subsequently proved to be unproductive and did not generate royalties for Permanence does not justify imposing an implied covenant to exploit on Kennametal.

The key provisions of the contract between Permanence and Kennametal which militate against implying a covenant to use best efforts are Kennametal's obligation to pay $150,000 in order to exercise the option for the exclusive license and the $100,000 in additional advance royalties paid under the exclusive license. Courts have held that by imposing a substantial minimum or advance royalty payment, the licensor, in lieu of obtaining an express agreement to use best efforts, has protected himself against the possibility that the licensee will do nothing. Rather than leaving the licensor at the mercy of the licensee, the demand for a substantial up-front or advance royalty payment creates an incentive for the licensee to exploit the invention or patent. In the present case, Permanence received a substantial total advance payment of $250,000 for its right to the exclusive license and, unlike the licensor in the majority of cases where a duty to exploit has been implied, did not depend for its consideration solely on Kennametal's sale of products developed under the patents.

Although the advance royalty clause and up-front payment alone might not preclude the finding of an implied obligation to exploit, these provisions of the contract must be considered with the other express provisions already discussed. Moreover, the contract contained a merger or integration clause. By emphasizing that the formal contract, which contained no express agreement by Kennametal to "exploit" the patents, constituted the entire agreement between the parties, this clause further negates the implication that a duty to use best efforts was assumed.

In most of the cases on which plaintiff relies, including the seminal *Wood v. Lucy, Lady Duff-Gordon*, no advance payments were made and the licensor had to rely entirely on the good faith of the licensee in order to receive any consideration in return for the grant of the exclusive agency. These cases are therefore distinguishable from the present case in which Permanence received a total of $250,000 for Kennametal's exclusive use of its patents, subject to Masco's non-exclusive use of Patent 902.

Plaintiff relies on two cases, *Perma Research and Dev. v. Singer Co.* and *Dwight & Lloyd Sintering Co. v. American Ore Reclamation Co.*, in which the courts implied a covenant to employ best efforts despite the payment of other consideration for the grant of the exclusive agency. We believe that these cases have misapplied the doctrine first articulated in *Wood v. Lucy, Lady Duff-Gordon* where it was necessary to imply "best efforts" in order to provide mutuality of obligation to save the agreement. In *Wood*, the court stated:

> [Defendant's] *sole* compensation for the grant of an exclusive agency is to be one-half of all the profits resulting from the plaintiff's efforts. *Unless he gave his efforts, she could never get anything.* Without an implied promise, the transaction cannot have such business "efficacy, as both parties must have intended that at all events it should have."

It is not necessary for a court to interject a covenant to employ best efforts, a doctrine developed in the context of lack of mutuality of obligation, into every contract in which there is a grant of an exclusive agency. Especially, as is true in the present case, when an inventor grants a license to patented technology, the application of which is unknown, a commitment on the part of the licensee to devote best efforts to the development of the technology is a substantial commitment which should not be automatically inferred.

In the present case, we do not believe that Kennametal impliedly promised to perfect an incompletely developed technology, which is what plaintiff, in effect, asserts. The total payment of $250,000 for the exclusive license to the patents provided sufficient incentive and demonstration of good faith that Kennametal would attempt to commercialize and market the Permanence process. This is not a case where the licensor (Permanence) depended for its sole compensation for the licensed patents upon royalties generated by the exclusive agency granted to Kennametal. The implication of a best efforts obligation is therefore not necessary to establish mutuality of obligation. Moreover, we find that if Permanence wished to bind Kennametal to a best efforts commitment in the circumstances of the present case, it was incumbent upon Permanence to spell out this obligation in the formal written agreement. For these reasons, the decision of the district court is affirmed.

QUESTIONS

1. Would Permanence have prevailed if the license had included a "best efforts" clause to complete the technical development?

2.   How large must an upfront payment be in order to negate an implied "best efforts" clause?

3.   When is a licensor solely dependent upon a licensee to receive consideration under the license?

4.   If you were counsel to Permanence, how could you draft a license clause that required Kennametal's best efforts to complete technical development, despite the payment of large advanced royalties and option fees?

CASE NOTES

1.   Beraha, a physician specializing in urology, designed a new biopsy needle for prostate biopsies. While Beraha's patent application for the new biopsy needle was pending, Beraha entered into license negotiations with Baxter who currently marketed another prostate biopsy needle. After considerable negotiation, Beraha and Baxter entered into a license agreement under which Beraha would receive $50,000 in advance royalties, and royalties in the amount of 3.5% of sales for the life of the patent if the patent issued, and for four years if the patent did not issue. Although there was some discussion at the final negotiation session regarding Baxter's plans to develop the biopsy needle, the license agreement did not contain a best efforts clause. When Beraha received the final license agreement to sign, he initially refused to sign the agreement because it contained no best efforts clause. Beraha telephoned his contacts at Baxter to receive some assurance from Baxter regarding the effort it would exert to develop the biopsy needle. Behara received no representation from Baxter regarding a specific level of effort, but was told that Baxter would provide him a letter when he visited Baxter's research facilities. Based on this telephone conversation, Beraha signed the license agreement. When Beraha visited Baxter's research facility, he received a hand-delivered letter which read: "Although we work in an environment that is always subject to changing conditions, you can be assured that our present intent is to do our best to make this project a success, not only for obvious business reasons but also because such a new product could be a step forward in prostate biopsies." Included with the letter was a $50,000 check for the advance royalties. After four years, Baxter had still not developed and marketed the Behara biopsy needle. Behara filed suit against Baxter claiming that the letter he received constituted an express best effort clause, or, in the alternative, the court should imply a best efforts clause. Behara also claimed that Baxter had breached the implied covenant of good faith and fair dealing. The district court granted Baxter's motion for summary judgment on Behara's claims for breach of an implied best efforts clause and breach of an implied covenant of good faith and fair dealing. However, the district court held that the letter Beraha received from Baxter presented a disputed factual issue as to whether the license contained an express best effort clause. Beraha appealed the district court's decision. What result? *See* Beraha v. Baxter Health Care Corp., 956 F.2d 1436 (7th Cir. 1992).

2.   *See also* William Hodges & Co., Inc. v. Sterwood Corp., 348 F.Supp. 383 (E.D.N.Y. 1972) (An implied best efforts obligation is not binding on an exclusive licensee if it prevents the licensee from competing in the market with some reasonable chance of success); TDS Healthcare Systems Corp. v. Humana Hosp.

Illinois, Inc., 880 F. Supp. 1572 (N.D. Ga. 1995) (Best efforts obligation to protect the confidentiality of information relating to hospital software was breached where the party subject to the best efforts obligation released the confidential information intentionally); G. Golden Associates of Oceanside, Inc. v. Arnold Foods Co., Inc., 870 F. Supp. 472 (E.D.N.Y. 1994) (New York law implies a best efforts obligation on behalf of an exclusive licensee when it is essential as a matter of equity to give meaning and effect to the license agreement as a whole); First Union Nat. Bank v. Steele Software Sys. Corp., 154 Md. App. 97 (Md. Ct. Spec. App. 2003) (Party subject to a best efforts clause is not required to relinquish all self interest); Kardios Systems Corp. v. Perkin-Elmer Corp., 645 F. Supp. 506 (D.Md. 1986) (Best efforts clause will not be implied when it was contained in the first draft of the license agreement but not in the final draft).

Additional Information

1. RAYMOND T. NIMMER, 2 INFORMATION LAW § 11:76 (2010).

2. MODERN PATENT LAW PRECEDENT B210 (8th ed. 2010).

3. MELVIN F. JAGER, LICENSING LAW HANDBOOK (2010-2011 Edition) § 10:8 (2010).

4. RAYMOND T. NIMMER & JEFF DODD, MODERN LICENSING LAW §§ 5:27, 9:45–48 (2010).

5. RAYMOND T. NIMMER, LAW OF COMPUTER TECHNOLOGY § 7:74 (2010).

6. DAVID M. EPSTEIN, 1 ECKSTROM'S LICENSING LAW IN FOREIGN AND DOMESTIC OPERATIONS §§ 2:28, 3:34 (2010).

7. MARK S. HOLMES, *BEST EFFORTS*, PAT. LICENSING STRATEGY, NEGOTIATIONS & FORMS § 1:3.2 (2009).

8. 69 C.J.S. PATENTS, § 355 (2008).

9. Zachary Miller, *Best Efforts? Differing Judicial Interpretations of a Familiar Term*, 48 ARIZ. L. REV. 615 (2006).

10. Rob Park, *Putting the "Best" in Best Efforts*, 73 U. CHI. L. REV. 505 (2006).

11. E. Allan Farnsworth, *On Trying to Keep One's Promises: The Duty of Best Efforts in Contract Law*, 46 U. PITT. L. REV. 1 (1984).

12. J. C. Bruno, *"Best Efforts" Defined*, 71 MICH. B.J. 74 (1992).

13. Victor P. Goldberg, *Desperately Seeking Consideration: The Unfortunate Impact of U.C.C. Section 2-306 on Contract Interpretation*, 68 OHIO ST. L.J. 103 (2007).

2.3.9   Royalties

There are two components to the determination of royalties: the royalty rate and the royalty base.

The royalty rate is always expressed as a percentage and there is no legal limit on how high this percentage can be. There are, however, market limits. The higher the royalty rate demanded by a licensor, the more likely the licensee will consider alternative licenses for near-substitute technologies. Likewise, the higher the royalty rate demanded by a licensor, the more likely the licensee will be at a competitive disadvantage in its market. Royalties paid to the licensor must be covered by the licensee's sales revenue. In addition, the licensee's sales revenue must provide a competitive rate of return to the licensee for its investment and risk. If a royalty rate is set too high, the licensee faces a draconian choice — either raise the price of its product sufficiently to cover the high royalty rate and lose sales to lower-priced products, or offer its products at a competitive market price and absorb the high royalty rate through a lower profit margin. Neither of these situations benefits the licensor either. In the first instance, the higher-priced products will result in lower sales revenue and lower royalty payments to the licensor. In the second instance, the licensee's lower rate of return will threaten the viability of the licensee's financial condition and, in turn, the viability of the licensor's license agreement.

Unlike the choice of a royalty rate, the choice of a royalty base raises a number of legal issues, all involving consideration of potential anticompetitive effects resulting from the licensing arrangement. The royalty base is most often comprised of product net sales, although product net quantity sold (units, pounds, etc.) is also sometimes used. There are five general royalty base situations that raise anticompetition questions.

The first is when the royalty base consists of sales that occur after the expiration of the licensed patent. Here, the concern is that royalties charged on sales after the patent expires operate to extend the patent term beyond what is allowed under the Patent Act.

The second is when the royalty base consists of related products that do not include any of the licensed patents. The concern here is that the patent monopoly has been extended to extract royalties on products not covered by the patent.

The third is when the royalty base consists of products that embody the licensed patents and also non-licensed patents. The concern here is the balance between the anticompetitive effects of charging royalties on total product sales and the difficulties of apportioning the contribution of the licensed patents to total product sales.

The fourth is when the royalty base consists of a pool of patents, some of which the licensee might want and some of which the licensee might not want. The concern here is with requiring the licensee to license patents that the licensee does not want (tied patents) as a condition of obtaining a license to patents that the licensee does want (tying patents).

The fifth is when the royalty base consists of end-products discovered or produced using a licensed patented research tool. Here, the concern is with leveraging the patented research tool to collect royalties on end-products not covered by the licensed patents.

The first case below, *Scheiber*, involves the payment of royalties after the expiration of the patent term. Although Judge Posner questions the economic rationale underlying the prohibition on payment of post-term royalties, he nonetheless feels compelled to follow the Supreme Court precedent on this issue. The second case, *Bayer AG*, involves the payment of royalties on drug compounds discovered or produced using a licensed patented research tool. The issue in *Bayer AG* is whether royalties collected on drug compounds after the expiration of the patent on the research tool used to discover or produce the drug compounds constitute post-term royalties.

SCHEIBER v. DOLBY LABORATORIES
293 F.3d 1014 (7th Cir. 2002)

Posner, Circuit Judge.

The plaintiff in a suit to enforce a patent licensing agreement appeals to us from the grant of summary judgment to the defendants, Dolby for short. Scheiber, the plaintiff, a musician turned inventor who held U.S. and Canadian patents on the audio system known as "surround sound," sued Dolby in 1983 for infringement of his patents. The parties settled the suit by agreeing that Scheiber would license his patents to Dolby in exchange for royalties. The last U.S. patent covered by the agreement was scheduled to expire in May 1993, while the last Canadian patent was not scheduled to expire until September 1995. During the settlement negotiations Dolby suggested to Scheiber that in exchange for a lower royalty rate the license agreement provide that royalties on all the patents would continue until the Canadian patent expired, including, therefore, patents that had already expired. That way Dolby could, it hoped, pass on the entire royalty expense to its sub-licensees without their balking at the rate. Scheiber acceded to the suggestion and the agreement was drafted accordingly, but Dolby later refused to pay royalties on any patent after it expired, precipitating this suit. Federal jurisdiction over the suit is based on diversity of citizenship, because a suit to enforce a patent licensing agreement does not arise under federal patent law. The presence of a federal defense (here, patent misuse) is irrelevant to jurisdiction.

Dolby argues that the duty to pay royalties on any patent covered by the agreement expired by the terms of the agreement itself as soon as the patent expired, because the royalties were to be based on Dolby's sales of equipment within the scope of the patents and once a patent expires, Dolby argues, there is no equipment within its scope. The argument would make meaningless the provision that Dolby itself proposed for continuing the payment of royalties until the last patent expired. Anyway the reference to equipment within the scope of the patent was clearly meant to *identify* the equipment on which royalties would be based (Dolby makes equipment that does not utilize Scheiber's patents as well as equipment that does) rather than to limit the duration of the obligation to pay royalties.

Dolby's principal argument is that the Supreme Court held in a decision that has never been overruled that a patent owner may not enforce a contract for the payment of patent royalties beyond the expiration date of the patent. The decision was *Brulotte v. Thys Co.*, 379 U.S. 29 (1964), dutifully followed by lower courts, including our own. *Brulotte* involved an agreement licensing patents that expired at different dates, just like this case; the two cases are indistinguishable. The decision has, it is true, been severely, and as it seems to us, with all due respect, justly, criticized, beginning with Justice Harlan's dissent and continuing with our opinion in *USM Corp. v. SPS Technologies, Inc.* The Supreme Court's majority opinion reasoned that by extracting a promise to continue paying royalties after expiration of the patent, the patentee extends the patent beyond the term fixed in the patent statute and therefore in violation of the law. That is not true. After the patent expires, anyone can make the patented process or product without being guilty of patent infringement. The patent can no longer be used to exclude anybody from such production. Expiration thus accomplishes what it is supposed to accomplish. For a licensee in accordance with a provision in the license agreement to go on paying royalties after the patent expires does not extend the duration of the patent either technically or practically, because, as this case demonstrates, if the licensee agrees to continue paying royalties after the patent expires the royalty rate will be lower. The duration of the patent fixes the limit of the patentee's power to extract royalties; it is a detail whether he extracts them at a higher rate over a shorter period of time or a lower rate over a longer period of time.

This insight is not original with us. "The Brulotte rule incorrectly assumes that a patent license has significance after the patent terminates. When the patent term ends, the exclusive right to make, use or sell the licensed invention also ends. Because the invention is available to the world, the license in fact ceases to have value. Presumably, licensees know this when they enter into a licensing agreement. If the licensing agreement calls for royalty payments beyond the patent term, the parties base those payments on the licensees' assessment of the value of the license during the patent period. These payments, therefore, do not represent an extension in time of the patent monopoly. Courts do not remove the obligation of the consignee to pay because payment after receipt is an extension of market power — it is simply a division of the payment-for-delivery transaction. Royalties beyond the patent term are no different. If royalties are calculated on post-patent term sales, the calculation is simply a risk-shifting credit arrangement between patentee and licensee. The arrangement can be no more than that, because the patentee at that time has nothing else to sell."

These criticisms might be wide of the mark if *Brulotte* had been based on a interpretation of the patent clause of the Constitution, or of the patent statute or any other statute; but it seems rather to have been a free-floating product of a misplaced fear of monopoly ("a patentee's use of a royalty agreement that projects beyond the expiration date of the patent is unlawful *per se*. If that device were available to patentees, the free market visualized for the post-expiration period would be subject to monopoly influences that have no proper place there," that was not even tied to one of the antitrust statutes. The doctrinal basis of the decision was the doctrine of patent misuse, of which more later.

A patent confers a monopoly, and the longer the term of the patent the greater the monopoly. The limitation of the term of a patent, besides being commanded by the Constitution and necessary to avoid impossible tracing problems (imagine if some caveman had gotten a perpetual patent on the wheel), serves to limit the monopoly power conferred on the patentee. But as we have pointed out, charging royalties beyond the term of the patent does not lengthen the patentee's monopoly; it merely alters the timing of royalty payments. This would be obvious if the license agreement between Scheiber and Dolby had become effective a month before the last patent expired. The parties could have agreed that Dolby would pay royalties for the next 100 years, but obviously the royalty rate would be minuscule because of the imminence of the patent's expiration.

However, we have no authority to overrule a Supreme Court decision no matter how dubious its reasoning strikes us, or even how out of touch with the Supreme Court's current thinking the decision seems.

Now it is true that in *Aronson v. Quick Point Pencil Co.*, a case decided some years after *Brulotte*, the Supreme Court upheld an agreement superficially similar to the one invalidated in *Brulotte* and at issue in the present case: a patent applicant granted a license for the invention it hoped to patent to a firm that agreed, if a patent were not granted, to pay the inventor-applicant royalties for as long as the firm sold products embodying the invention. The Court was careful to distinguish *Brulotte*, and not a single Justice suggested that any cloud had been cast over the earlier decision. Since no patent was granted, the doctrine of patent misuse could not be brought into play, and there was no other federal ground for invalidating the license. The Court emphasized that *Brulotte* had been based on the "leverage" that the patent had granted the patentee to extract royalties beyond the date of expiration and that leverage was of course missing in *Aronson*.

If *Aronson* and *Brulotte* were inconsistent with each other and the Court had not reaffirmed *Brulotte* in *Aronson*, then we would have to follow *Aronson*, the later opinion, since to follow *Brulotte* in those circumstances would be to overrule *Aronson*. But the reaffirmation of *Brulotte* in *Aronson* tells us that the Court did not deem the cases inconsistent, and so, whether we agree or not, we have no warrant for declaring *Brulotte* overruled.

Scheiber has another ground for disregarding *Brulotte* that deserves consideration (again a ground supported by a lone district court decision but one that misreads *Brulotte* as having been held to be inapplicable to package-licensing agreements that contain expired patents unless the licensees were coerced into making the agreements). The ground is that Dolby comes into court with "unclean hands" that should not be allowed to touch and stain the Supreme Court's decision. Scheiber points out that it was Dolby that asked him to stretch out the royalties until the last patent expired and that now seeks to get out of the obligation it not only accepted but volunteered to shoulder.

The doctrine of "unclean hands" — colorfully named, equitable in origin, and reflecting, in its name at least, the moralistic background of equity in the decrees of the clerics who filled the office of lord chancellor of England during the middle ages — nowadays just means that equitable relief will be refused if it would give the plaintiff a wrongful gain. "Today, "unclean hands" really just means that in equity as in law the plaintiff's fault, like the defendant's, is relevant to the question of what if any remedy the plaintiff is entitled to. An obviously sensible application of this principle is to withhold an equitable remedy that would encourage or reward (and thereby encourage) illegal activity. In what may have been the earliest application of the principle of unclean hands, a highwayman was refused an accounting against his partner in crime (and later hanged, to boot, along with the partner)." That is an apt description of the relief (in effect a partial rescission of the license agreement, and so equitable in character sought by Dolby. But unfortunately for Scheiber it is an apt description of almost any case in which a party to a contract seeks relief on the basis that the contract is illegal. Dolby is in effect a private attorney general, charged by *Brulotte* with preventing Scheiber from seeking to "extend" his patent and being rewarded for this service to the law by getting out of a freely negotiated royalty obligation.

The obvious problem is that Dolby is not seeking equitable relief; it just doesn't want to pay what it owes Scheiber under their licensing agreement on the ground that the agreement, or at least so much of it as creates the duty to pay that Dolby is flouting, is unlawful and therefore unenforceable. That is how the Court put it in *Brulotte.* The effect is the same as rescission but that is true in any case where the payee in a contract is allowed to refuse payment because the contract is unenforceable. In contrast, the remedy sought in the highwayman's case, an accounting, is an equitable remedy. But as if this weren't complicated enough, patent misuse — the doctrine applied in *Brulotte* and invoked here by Dolby — is an equitable defense, and unclean hands can be asserted in opposition to an equitable defense as well as being assertible as a defense to a claim for equitable relief. The "theory" that makes this possible is that before the joinder of law and equity, an equitable defense to a legal claim had to be asserted in a separate proceeding in equity, in which the plaintiff in the law case would be the defendant and so could plead the defense of unclean hands against the law defendant-equity plaintiff.

We needn't get deeper into this thicket of archaic distinctions, since it is apparent that to apply the doctrine of unclean hands in a case such as the present one would fatally undermine the policy of refusing enforcement to contracts for the payment of patent royalties after expiration of the patent. It would be (given the antimonopoly basis of *Brulotte*) inconsistent with the Supreme Court's rejection of the defense of *in pari delicto* ("equally at fault") in antitrust cases since the effect of that rejection is to give a party to a contract that violates the antitrust laws a defense to a suit to enforce the contract even if he entered into the contract with full knowledge. We even said in *General Leaseways, Inc. v. National Truck Leasing Ass'n.* in words that might have been uttered with the present case in mind, that "ever since the Supreme Court, in *Perma Life*, rejected the defense of *in pari delicto* in antitrust cases, it has been clear that whenever some maxim of equity (such as that to get equitable relief you must have "clean hands") collides with the objectives of the antitrust laws, the equity maxim must give way." Later the Supreme Court equated "unclean hands" to *in pari delicto.*

What is true is that a contract that is voided on grounds of illegality — Dolby's defense to Scheiber's suit for the agreed-upon royalties — is ordinarily treated as rescinded, meaning that the parties are to be put back, so far as possible, in the positions they would have occupied had the contract never been made in the first place. For example, even if a contract is unenforceable because it violates the statute of frauds, the performing party can still claim the value of his performance, net of any payment received before the contract was rescinded, on a theory of *quantum meruit*, a type of restitution. *Cox* and *Amdahl* involved contracts that were illegal, and not just unenforceable (there is nothing remotely "wrongful" about failing to memorialize in writing a contract that is enforceable only if so memorialized), yet *quantum meruit* would still have been available had the voiding party been unduly enriched by being able to walk away from the contract. But Scheiber is not arguing that if indeed the contract is unenforceable, as we believe it is, he is entitled to some form of restitution of the benefits received by Dolby under it as a result of Dolby's being allowed to use Scheiber's patents without paying the full price that they had agreed upon. Scheiber would be entitled to such relief only if the amount of royalties that Dolby did pay was less than the fair market value of Dolby's use of the patents, which of course it may not have been. In any event he makes no claim of *quantum meruit*.

Dolby was indeed entitled to summary judgment.

QUESTIONS

1. If the royalties had not been associated with specific patents but with products embodying any unexpired patents, would this have changed the result in the case?

2. If the license agreement had also included know-how, and the royalty payments were specified to be for the combination of the licensed patents and know-how, would this have changed the result in the case?

3. Are you persuaded that applying the equitable doctrine of unclean hands under the facts of this case would undermine the Supreme Court's holding in *Brulotte*?

4. Are you persuaded by the court's distinction between *Aronson* and *Brulotte*? Could the court have followed *Aronson* rather than *Brulotte* in its holding?

5. If you were counsel to Scheiber, how could you have structured the license agreement to avoid the problem of post-patent term royalties?

BAYER AG v. HOUSEY PHARMACEUTICALS, INC.
228 F. Supp.2d 467 (D. Del. 2002)

SUE L. ROBINSON, CHIEF JUDGE.

I. INTRODUCTION

Plaintiffs Bayer AG and Bayer Corporation filed this action on March 6, 2001 seeking a declaratory judgment that four patents assigned to defendant Housey Pharmaceuticals, Inc. are invalid, unenforceable and not infringed. Defendant has filed a counterclaim of infringement. The court has jurisdiction over this action pursuant to 28 U.S.C. §§ 1331,1338(a) and 2201(a). Currently before the court are plaintiffs' motion for summary judgment of unenforceability of the patents in suit on grounds of misuse and defendant's motion for summary judgment on plaintiffs' affirmative defense of patent misuse. For the following reasons, the court shall deny plaintiffs' motion and grant defendant's motion.

II. BACKGROUND

The ICT (Housey) patents, each entitled, "Method of Screening for Protein Inhibitors and Activators," generally relate to research methods used by pharmaceutical companies for discovering drugs. The patented methods enable companies to screen substances for active compounds that indicate a potential for development as pharmaceuticals. This court's October 17, 2001 order found that the defendant's patents cover only research methods, not manufacturing methods. Thus, the patent claims at issue do not cover end products, but rather the identification and generation of data used to develop new pharmaceuticals.

Defendant has licensed the ICT patents to over 30 companies. Among the licensees are SCIOS, Inc. ("SCIOS"), Eli Lilly and Company ("Eli Lilly"), and Takeda Chemical Industries, Ltd. ("Takeda"). Defendant also sent several letters to plaintiffs attempting to negotiate a license.

Defendant has agreed to, and proposed, two different types of licensing arrangements with licensees and potential licensees. One type is a running royalty license that requires the licensee to pay a royalty for sales of pharmaceutical products discovered using the subject invention. This is the type of license accepted by SCIOS and Eli Lilly. The second type is a lump sum payment license that requires the licensee to pay a lump sum royalty based upon the licensee's research and development budget. This is the type of license accepted by Takeda. Both types of licenses were offered to plaintiffs.

****

IV. DISCUSSION

Patent misuse is an equitable defense to a charge of patent infringement. The basic allegation is that the patentee has "extend[ed] the economic benefit beyond the scope of the patent grant." Patent misuse "requires that the alleged infringer show that the patentee has impermissibly broadened the physical or temporal scope of the patent grant with anticompetitive effect."

Plaintiffs assert defendant has committed the following acts of patent misuse: (1) extracting and attempting to extract royalties on products and activities that are not covered by the claims of any of the patents in suit; (2) imposing a requirement of royalty payments beyond the term of the patent; and (3) attempting to muzzle licensees. Defendant denies each of these allegations and asserts that, regardless of whether the above acts were committed, patent misuse requires an anti-competitive effect that is lacking in this case. The court will discuss each of plaintiffs' allegations in turn.

A. Extracting and Attempting to Extract Royalties on Products and Activities
That Are Not Covered by the Claims of Any of the Patents in Suit

1. License Agreements and Proposals Based on Products and Activities not
Covered by the Patents

Citing both the existing licensing agreements and the licensing proposals,
plaintiffs argue that defendant has insisted upon licenses that impose royalties on
products and activities not covered by the patents. According to plaintiffs, this
constitutes patent misuse. Defendant asserts that it has not conditioned the grant
of a license on the inclusion of unpatented products and activities and, thus, cannot
have committed patent misuse. Defendant further argues that license agreements
based on products and activities not covered by the patent are not patent misuse if
the license agreements are for the convenience of the parties.

Plaintiffs rely on *Zenith Radio Corp. v. Hazeltine Research, Inc.* for their
contention that defendant's licensing activities constitute patent misuse. In *Zenith
Radio*, the Supreme Court held "that conditioning the grant of a patent license
upon payment of royalties on products which do not use the teaching of the patent
does amount to patent misuse." The Court, however, limited the holding to
particularly egregious circumstances. In refusing to reverse the district court's
injunction, the Court stated:

> The trial court's injunction does not purport to prevent the parties from
> serving their mutual convenience by basing royalties on the sale of all
> radios and television sets, irrespective of the use of [the patentee's]
> inventions. The injunction reaches only situations where the patentee
> directly or indirectly "conditions" his license upon the payment of royalties
> on unpatented products-that is, where the patentee refuses to license on
> any other basis and leaves the licensee with the choice between a license so
> providing and no license at all.

The key consideration of whether the patentee "conditions" a license upon the
payment of royalties on unpatented products and activities is "the voluntariness of
the licensee's agreement to the royalty provisions." If the license agreement is for
the convenience of the parties in measuring the value of the license, then the
agreement cannot constitute patent misuse.

Plaintiffs have provided no evidence that defendant has impermissibly "conditioned" its licenses upon royalty provisions covering unpatented products and
activities. Plaintiffs have only established that licensees, including themselves, have
objected to the terms proposed by defendant. Specifically, after receiving the initial
offer from defendant, plaintiffs determined that the patents were invalid and the
proposed licensing terms were improper. Defendant continued to make numerous
offers to plaintiffs over the next several years. Plaintiffs make much of the fact that
the license terms and proposals were drafted by defendant. However, plaintiffs
provide no evidence of ever offering other terms they felt were equally convenient
and more appropriate. In *Zenith Radio*, relied on by plaintiffs, the Supreme Court
stated that "misuse inheres in a patentee's insistence on a percentage-of-sales
royalty . . . and his *rejections* of licensee proposals to pay for actual [use]." In the

case at bar, plaintiffs provided no evidence of proposing a licensing arrangement to pay for actual use. Rather, they blame defendant for not doing so.

Moreover, and contrary to plaintiffs' assertions, defendant has provided evidence that existing license agreements were not "conditioned" on a license with royalty provisions covering unpatented products and activities. The license with SCIOS specifically states that the licensee "selected the royalty payment option . . . as the most appropriate and convenient approach to determine the value of the Licensed Patent Rights." In addition, defendant's deposition testimony and correspondence to plaintiffs indicate a willingness to consider other licensing terms.

The court finds that defendant has not impermissibly conditioned a license upon royalty provisions covering unpatented products and activities. Thus, on this point, plaintiffs' motion for summary judgment is denied and defendant's motion for summary judgment is granted.

B. Imposing a Requirement of Royalty Payments Beyond the Term of the Patent

The license agreement with SCIOS Inc. ("SCIOS") contains the following section regarding royalty payments:

> In the case of an End Product that is not a Licensed Product and is not covered per se or for a given purpose by any patents obtained by LICENSEE, the obligation to pay royalties shall end ten (10) years after the last to expire of the patents in the Licensed Patent Rights having a claim or claims for a Licensed Method utilized in discovering, creating, identifying, characterizing, isolating, developing, manufacturing, evaluating or establishing the pharmacological properties or condition of use of the End Product (or a component thereof) for the given purpose.

Plaintiffs assert that this royalty clause in the SCIOS license requires the payment of royalties after the expiration of the patent. Relying on the Supreme Court's holding in *Brulotte v. Thys Co.*, plaintiffs argue this constitutes patent misuse *per se*.

Plaintiffs also argue that other licenses, such as the license with Eli Lilly, require post-expiration royalties. Although the language of these agreements regarding the reporting requirements is somewhat ambiguous, the agreement clearly states: "The term of this Agreement shall extend from the above effective date until expiration of the last to expire of Licensed Patent Rights." Thus, the agreement does not extend beyond the term of the patent.

Defendant asserts that the license provision is not patent misuse *per se* for two reasons. First, the license provision only imposes royalties for use of the subject invention during the life of the patent. The royalties paid after the expiration of the patent, on pharmaceuticals sold after the expiration of the patent, are actually royalties for use of the invention during the research phase of the pharmaceutical — the research phase that occurred prior to the expiration of the patent. Second, defendant argues, the license provision is not patent misuse unless defendant actually attempts to collect post-expiration royalties. The mere presence of a clause permitting collection of post-expiration royalties is not patent misuse.

In *Brulotte*, the Supreme Court held that patent misuse occurs when a licensing agreement "allows royalties to be collected which *accrued* after the last of the patents . . . [has] expired." In the case at bar, the royalties to be paid after the expiration of the patent are for the use of the subject invention prior to the expiration of the patent. Royalties are collected based on later pharmaceutical sales, but the royalties are being *accrued* as the invention is practiced during the research phase. Collecting royalties after the expiration of the patent has expired is not *per se* patent misuse as plaintiffs assert. Indeed, the Supreme Court has recognized that a patentee may collect royalties post-expiration without violating *Brulotte*. The Court acknowledged "that the patentee could lawfully charge a royalty for practicing a patented invention prior to its expiration date and that *the payment of this royalty could be postponed beyond that time*[.]" The problem arises when "the post-expiration royalties were not for prior use but for current use, and were nothing less than an effort by the patentee to extend the term of his monopoly beyond that granted by law." Thus, the SCIOS license does not violate *Brulotte* and defendant has not committed patent misuse.

The court finds that plaintiffs have not proven patent misuse on the issue of imposing royalties beyond the term of the patent. Thus, on this point, plaintiffs' motion for summary judgment is denied and defendant's motion for summary judgment is granted.

C. Attempting to Muzzle Licensees

Plaintiffs allege defendant has attempted to muzzle licensees in violation of *Lear, Inc. v. Adkins*. Defendant argues that the license provision does not violate *Lear* because the licensing agreement specifically acknowledges that the licensee can contest validity or enforceability at any time. In addition, defendant argues that even if the provision is unenforceable under *Lear*, the mere presence of the provision does not constitute patent misuse.

In *Lear*, the Supreme Court held that a licensee is not estopped from challenging the validity of a patent. Thus, contract provisions attempting to preclude licensees from challenging the validity of a patent were rendered unenforceable. The Court further held that a licensee could not be required to make royalty payments while challenging validity.

Defendant's license with SCIOS includes the following provision:

> ICT acknowledges the LICENSEE is not estopped from contesting the validity or enforceability of the Licensed Patent Rights. However, LICENSEE acknowledges that such an attack on validity or enforceability of the Licensed Patent Rights is inconsistent with the purposes of this License Agreement. Accordingly, LICENSEE hereby agrees that if it decides to assert its right to contest the Licensed Patent Rights, in whole or in part, that ICT shall have the right, at ICT's option, to terminate this License Agreement by giving written notice thereof to LICENSEE. Further, unless terminated by ICT, LICENSEE agrees to make all payments due under this License Agreement notwithstanding any chal-

lenge, by LICENSEE or others (if any) to the Licensed Patent Rights, so long as the applicable patent(s) or patent application(s) remain in effect.

Essentially, section 7.3 reserves to defendant: (1) the right to terminate the license if a challenge to validity is made or (2) the right to require SCIOS to continue making royalty payments during a pending validity challenge.

The portion of section 7.3 giving defendant the right to require the licensee to continue making royalty payments if the licensee chooses to challenge validity is unenforceable under *Lear*.

The inclusion of a provision in a license agreement that is unenforceable under *Lear*, however, does not constitute patent misuse.

Plaintiffs have not provided the court with any authority to the contrary. Thus, the court finds that while section 7.3 of the SCIOS license may very well be unenforceable under *Lear*, the inclusion of the provision does not constitute patent misuse. Accordingly, on this point, plaintiffs' motion for summary judgment is denied and defendant's motion for summary judgment is granted.

V. CONCLUSION

For the reasons stated, the court shall deny plaintiffs' motion for summary judgment of unenforceability of the patents in suit on grounds of misuse and grant defendant's motion for summary judgment on plaintiff's affirmative defense of patent misuse. An appropriate order shall issue.

QUESTIONS

1. *Bayer AG* deals with a patented research tool. A "research tool" is defined as a technology that is used to discover or produce an end-product, but that is not itself included in the end product. Patentees of research tools often license their research tools in exchange for "reach-through royalties" — royalties on the sales of the end-products discovered or produced using the research tool. Assuming there were alternative methods of screening for protein inhibitors and activators available in the market, how would ICT prove that its patented method was the one used in the discovery or production of a particular drug compound? If ITC had attempted to claim royalties on all licensee end-product sales, regardless of whether its patented research tool had been used, could this create patent misuse problems?

2. Are there other ways in which a research tool patentee can structure licensing arrangements?

3. What are the pros and cons of licensing research tools on a non-exclusive, limited exclusive or exclusive basis?

4. The *Bayer AG* court finds that the royalties on the end-product sales accrued at the time ICT's patented tool was used, although the royalties were not paid until the end-product sales were made, possibly after the expiration of the patented method. How exactly can royalties on sales accrue prior to the time the sales occur?

5.   How could you measure the value of a license for a research tool in order to establish a running royalty rate on products developed using the research tool?

CASE NOTES

1.   Tinnell invented a liquid solution to treat lesions caused by the herpes virus. After applying for a patent on his invention, he acquired a defunct corporation, Zila, for marketing and selling the product, Zilactin. In September 1980, Tinnell entered into an agreement with Zila under which Tinnell assigned all of his rights to Zilactin, the pending patent application, and any improvement patents, in exchange for stock in Zila and a five percent royalty on Zila's gross sales of Zilactin. Tinnell's initial patent issued in 1981 and an improvement patent issued in 1992. Sales of Zilactin were very successful and, by 2000, Zila owed Tinnell nearly half a million dollars in annual royalties on sales of over $8 million. In 2000, Zila's patent counsel advised the company to terminate royalty payments to Tinnell because, under the holding in the *Brulotte*, Tinnell's right to royalties expired in 1998 upon the termination of Tinnell's 1981 patent. Zila stopped paying royalties to Tinnell on sales of Zilactin and filed suit seeking a declaratory judgment that Tinnell's right to royalties under the 1980 agreement ceased in 1998 upon the termination of Tinnell's patent. Zila also sought reimbursement for the royalties paid to Tinnell for the two years after the 1981 patent expired. Tinnell counterclaimed for a declaratory judgment that his right to royalties did not terminate with the expiration of the 1981 patent. Tinnell also filed counterclaims for breach of contract and fraud. The district court granted Zila's motion for summary judgment on its declaratory judgment claim that it did not owe royalties to Tinnell after the termination of the 1981 patent. Tinnell appealed. What result? *See* Zila, Inc. v. Tinnell, 502 F.3d 1014 (9th Cir. 2007).

2.   *See also* The Adm'r of the Tulane University Educational Fund v. Debio Holding, S.A., 177 F.Supp. 2d 545 (E.D. LA 2001) (License agreement calling for royalty payments beyond expiration of patent term was *per se* unlawful warranting grant of summary judgment to defendant on this claim; but question of fact existed as to whether a subsequent letter agreement was a separate agreement or part of the initial agreement warranting denial of summary judgment to defendant on this claim); Meehan v. PPG Industries, Inc., 802 F.2d 881 (7th Cir. 1986) (Rule that license agreements extending royalty payments beyond life of patent are unlawful applies to license agreements entered into prior to filing the patent application); American Securit Co. v. Shatterproof Glass Corp., 268 F.2d 769 (3rd Cir. 1959) (Patent license for multiple patents providing for royalty payments to continue until the last patent expired constitutes patent misuse because it requires payment of royalties on patents already expired); Compton v. Metal Products Inc., 453 F.2d 38 (4th Cir. 1971) (License granted for multiple patents that provided for royalties to continue until last of the patents expired was not patent misuse where royalty rates tied to specific patents and royalty rates changed as patents expired); Rocform Corp. v. Acitelli-Standard Concrete Wall, Inc., 367 F.2d 678 (6th Cir. 1966) (License agreement for multiple patents expiring at different times was invalid where it did not provide for a reduction of license fees after the expiration of the first package of patents which was key to practice of patented process); Beckman Instruments, Inc. v. Technical Dev. Corp., 433 F.2d 55 (7th Cir. 1970) (License agreement that required payment of royalties beyond expiration of some, but not all, of the licensed

patents did not constitute patent misuse and was valid); Va. Panel Corp. v. MAC Panel Co., 133 F.3d 860 (Fed. Cir. 1997) (Patent misuse is an affirmative defense to accusation of patent infringement, successful assertion of which requires that the alleged infringer show that the patentee has impermissibly broadened the physical or temporal scope of the grant with anticompetitive consequences; the courts have identified certain specific practices as constituting *per se* patent misuse, including tying arrangements in which a patentee conditions a license under the patent on the purchase of a separable, staple good, and arrangements in which a patentee effectively extends the term of its patent by requiring post-term royalties).

Additional Information

1. John W. Schlicher, 2 Patent Law Legal and Economic Principles §§ 11:24, 11:26–28, 13:22 (2d ed. 2010).

2. Robert A. Matthews Jr., 4 Annotated Patent Digest §§ 28:29–30 (2010).

3. David M. Epstein, 2 Eckstrom's Licensing in Foreign and Domestic Operations §§ 8E:15–18 (2010).

4. J. C. Vance, 3 A.L.R.3D 770 (2010).

5. 60 Am. Jur. 2d Patents § 140 (2010).

6. Spencer W. Waller, *Antitrust and American Business Abroad Today*, 44 DePaul L. Rev. 1251 (1995).

7. Richard Li-dar Wang, *Biomedical Upstream Patenting and Scientific Research: The Case for Compulsory Licenses Bearing Reach-Through Royalties*, 10 Yale J.L. & Tech. 251 (2007-2008).

8. Kimberlee A. Stafford, *Reach-Through Royalties in Biomedical Research Tool Patent Licensing: Implications of NIH Guidelines on Small Biotechnology Firms*, 9 Lewis & Clark L. Rev. 699 (2005).

9. Steven J. Hultquist, *Reach-Through Royalties: The Scope of Research Tool Patents*, 86 J. Pat. & Trademark Off. Soc'y 285, (2004).

10. Michael Koenig, *Patent Royalties Extending Beyond Expiration: An Illogical Ban From Brulotte to Scheiber*, 2003 Duke L. & Tech. Rev. 5, (2003).

11. Michael J. Stimson, *Damages for Infringement of Research Tool Patents: The Reasonableness of Reach Through Royalties*, 2003 Stan. Tech. L. Rev. 3, (2003).

2.3.10   Licenses to Improvements

Disputes over licenses to improvements can arise in two contexts. The first, and most common, is where the licensor claims rights to improvements made to the licensed technology by the licensee under a "grant-back provision" in the license agreement. The second is where the licensee claims rights to improvements to the licensed technology made by the licensor under a "grant-forward provision" in the license agreement.

In both of these situations, the claimed improvement can fall into three general fact classes. In the *first* fact class are improvements defined in terms of the claims in the licensed patent. Here, the courts use the claims of the licensed patent to determine whether an improvement is covered by the license. If the improvement cannot be practiced without infringing the licensed patent, the improvement will very likely be covered under the grant-back or grant-forward provision in the license. In the *second* fact class are improvements that consist of a competing, independent invention that can be practiced without infringing the licensed patent. Here, the courts balance the equities between the parties to decide whether the improvement is covered by the license. In the case of a grant-back provision, the balance is between the unfairness to the licensor of allowing the licensee to practice an improvement without payment of any additional royalties, and the unfairness to the licensee of denying the licensee the opportunity to earn a return on its investment in improving the licensed technology. In the case of a grant-forward provision, the balance is between the unfairness to the licensee of allowing the licensor to own an improvement to the technology which renders the initially licensed technology less valuable, and the unfairness to the licensor of allowing the licensee to claim any future licensor inventions related to the licensed technology. In the *third* fact class of improvements are all future inventions no matter whether they are related to the claims in the licensed patent or compete with the licensed technology. *See*, Hal Milton, *"Improvements" in Patent Licenses: Presumptions and Clauses Derived From Case Law*, 34 AIPLA Q.J. 333 (2006).

The *Gosner* case below involves a competing, independent improvement made by the licensee which was claimed by the licensor under a grant-back clause in the license agreement.

Grant-back and grant-forward provisions can be structured either as exclusive, limited-exclusive, or non-exclusive licenses. In the case of a grant-back provision, a limited-exclusive or non-exclusive license would allow the licensee to exploit the improvement through other persons than the licensor. In the case of a grant-forward provision, a limited-exclusive or non-exclusive license would allow the licensor to exploit the improvement through other persons than the licensee.

Grant-back provisions can also raise antitrust issues. The U.S. Department of Justice and the Federal Trade Commission considered the antitrust issues involved in grant-back provisions in ANTITRUST GUIDELINES IN LICENSING INTELLECTUAL PROPERTY (1995). The relevant portions of these GUIDELINES are presented below. The full text of the ANTITRUST GUIDELINES is presented in section 7.2 of the materials.

GONSER v. LELAND DETROIT MFG. CO.
291 N.W. 631 (Mich. 1940)

Suit by John C. Gonser against the Leland Detroit Manufacturing Company for specific performance of a contract to assign improvements and modifications of a patent to plaintiff. From a decree granting specific performance, the defendant appeals.

Decree set aside and case remanded for an accounting and adjudication of other rights plaintiff might establish under contract relating to the invention.

BUTZEL, JUSTICE.

Plaintiff invented a "Meat Tenderizer and Cutter" and was granted patent No. 2,025,505 on December 24, 1935. The invention differed in some limited but important details from the devices known in the prior art. Defendant is a manufacturer of automotive parts and other specialties. Plaintiff and defendant entered into a contract whereby defendant agreed to manufacture and sell the machine invented by plaintiff, and to make a proper accounting and pay the agreed royalties. It was provided that the rights of the parties should terminate in 30 days after notice to that effect. Such notice had been given. The clause occasioning the present litigation provides:

> "It is mutually agreed that should second party make any improvements or modifications of said invention, that said first party shall have the right to the use thereof during the life of this contract, and that should said first party, at any time, hereafter, make any improvements or modifications of said invention, that such improvements and modifications shall become the property of the said second party and first party does hereby assign and transfer to second party all such modifications and improvements, and said first party shall manufacture all tenderizers in accordance with such specifications and designs as shall be approved by second party."

Plaintiff contends that defendant has made an improvement or modification of the invention which in equity belongs to him; defendant contends that its new device is entirely different from the patented features of plaintiff's machine, that its new tenderizer is based on different principles or the prior art which is now public domain. Defendant also refers us to unexpired patents belonging to third parties. We are reviewing the decree of the trial court granting specific performance of the contract.

To laymen, the device would immediately suggest a narrow old-fashioned wash wringer with rolls about six inches long placed far enough apart to permit a piece of meat to be run between them. The steel rolls resemble large, symmetrical ears of corn with rows of kernels of uniform size, in the middle of which are inserted small projecting steel knives that are perpendicular to the roller shaft. The kernels or teeth are arranged in the same plane with those of the opposing roll and mesh when the rolls are turned, each kernel or tooth projecting into the interdental space on the opposite roll. The entire mechanism is enclosed in a steel box, for which no claim is made here. The box has a wide slot opening at the top through which a piece of meat may be inserted. The meat is tenderized at it passes between the rolls by the cutting action of the knives and the crushing process of the teeth.

We think the main claim of novelty in plaintiff's patent is described in the first claim:

> "In a meat tenderizer, a supporting casing, a shaft supported rotatively therein, pairs of crushing gears carried by the shaft, cutter members arranged between the gears of each pair of gears, spacers arranged between the said pairs of gears to space the pairs apart, a stationary shaft having oppositely threaded ends, bearings for said threaded ends, the said bearings being provided with springs arranged to act against the interior of

the casing whereby said bearings are normally pressed away from said revoluble shaft, the said bearings and the casing having engaging inclined portions whereby when said stationary shaft is turned said bearings move the stationary shaft parallel with respect to said revoluble shaft, and a revoluble mandrel on said stationary shaft, the said mandrel being provided with pairs of crushing gears with interposed cutter members and spacers, and the said cutter members carried by either shaft being constructed and arranged to extend between the pairs of gears on the other shaft and to the said spacers."

It appears that defendant was not successful in selling this device, it having sold only 550 or 600 up to the time it received notice of the termination of the contract. The failure is ascribed to the breaking off of the small knives, of which there were over 350 on the two rolls. Frequently the broken steel would get into the meat, and defendant claims it was threatened with suits for personal injuries by persons who claimed to have been injured by eating processed steak in which bits of the knife blades were embedded. Defendant further claims that it was constantly called upon to replace the broken knives, and many customers complained that the device was difficult to clean and maintain in a sanitary condition.

After plaintiff had given notice of termination of the contract, but before the expiration of the thirty-day period, defendant was manufacturing and preparing to market a new machine, on which it has applied for letters patent. The new machine is housed in the same box, but the rolls do not have any cutter knives or blades. It does not have gears which crush the meat. The rolls have a series of star-shaped discs which have concave edged teeth, as distinguished from the convex teeth of plaintiff's machine. Each disc of the two rolls is not arranged in the same plane with the corresponding disc of the opposite roll so as to mesh, as they do in plaintiff's machine, but each meets its correspondent side-by-side in the plane adjacent; a tooth on one roll projects beside the interdental space of the opposite roll, so that there is a scissor-like action on the meat instead of a crushing and cutting operation.

It is contended by defendant that its new tenderizer had been made after the contract had been terminated and that, therefore, the contract gave plaintiff no rights therein. The trial court found that "this improvement was contemplated and largely developed before the termination of the contract." This finding is amply supported by the evidence, and we are not inclined to disturb it.

The main question concerns the construction to be given the contractual expression "improvements or modifications of said invention." Did the contract grant to plaintiff every device that defendant might conceive in the art in general, or is this language to be given a more limited scope? Defendant claims that its new machine is for the most part copied from the prior art, with possibly some new feature on which it is seeking letters patent, and that the contract does not deprive it of the right which it would otherwise have with the rest of the world to partake of the public domain; plaintiff contends, as the trial court found, that "defendant undertook to develop a market for a rather special device, and had built up somewhat of a trade through the use of the Gonser patent, and the fruits of such business development was contemplated by the parties to be a valuable right which Gonser had a right to reserve and which the defendant agreed to regard as his own property." We think this conclusion is erroneous. The tenderizing of meat by rollers was not a new art. There were other devices on the market. There was no agreement by defendant not to go into the same line of business before the termination of the contract or not to use old processes open to the public or new ones constituting new inventions; it agreed to regard as plaintiff's property only improvements "of said invention." The trial court's holdings are not in accord with the language of the contract and the decided cases interpreting similar contracts.

American Cone & Wafer Co. v. Consolidated Wafer Co. was a bill for specific performance of a contract to assign a patent "together with all rights and privileges thereunder, as well as all improvements that may be made thereto or thereunder." Judge Learned Hand wrote: "We think it clear that the purpose of the language used was not to subject every future cone baker which Groset might devise to the assignment; the improvements covered by the phrase were those to that machine, not to the art in general. Every more efficient machine would be an improvement "upon" it, in common speech, but not "to" it." We attach significance to the word "thereto," and we should attach an added significance as well to "thereunder," if we could find any meaning for it. As it is, it seems to us rather a bit of scrivener's verbiage. It is, of course, true that any improved cone baker might supersede that purchased by the plaintiff's predecessors, and would therefore defeat the grant. Perhaps it would have been legal to bind Groset to assign any future machine against such a possibility; we need not pass upon that question. All we say is that, if the purpose is so broad, the language must not be so vague. Groset was free to make a new cone baker, which might successfully compete with the plaintiff, so long as it was not an improvement "to" the disclosure of his first patent.

Other decisions are clear in holding that such an assignment includes only improvements to the machine secured by the patent assigned. Examples of language assigning all similar machines developed in the art as well as improvements on the original patented machine are found in New Haven Sand Blast Co. v. Dreisbach, Birkery Mfg. Co. v. Jones and Registering Co. v. Sampson. There is broad language in an early decision of the United States Supreme Court, Littlefield v. Perry which might seem to justify plaintiff's contention: "It is clear, also, that the idea which Littlefield had in mind, and which he was endeavoring by his devices to make practically useful, was greater economy in the use of the inflammable gases of coal to produce combustion. It is not important in this suit that the patent, which had been then obtained, was not in fact suited for that purpose. It is sufficient that it was intended to be so. The subsequent devices, better adapted to the end to be accomplished, may therefore properly be regarded as improvements upon the original invention. They produce a stove doing the same thing which the first was intended to do, but doing it better. This is the proper office of an improvement."

However, it is quite clear from the rest of the opinion that the court was discussing an improvement on a particular machine. It was further said that: "Without considering whether the invention upon which the patent of 1854 issued was not, in fact, the same to all intents and purposes as that of 1852, it is sufficient for the purposes of this case that it was an improvement upon it, or perhaps more properly, that invention perfected. An assignment of an imperfect invention, with all improvements upon it that the inventor may make, is equivalent in equity to an assignment of the perfected results."

We hold, then, that the trial court was in error in construing the contract before us now as contemplating any machine that defendant might produce which would compete with the very limited market built through the use of the Gonser patent. The terms of the contract do not preclude defendant from entering the somewhat competitive field of manufacture of meat tenderizing machines, nor do we think the contract bars defendant from making use of methods in the public domain of the prior art, or gives plaintiff the right to a new invention which is different from and in no way infringes on the old invention. We do not say here that we approve or disapprove of a contract that is so worded as to express plaintiff's construction; we only hold that the language before us now is not so comprehensive.

Our next task is to determine whether defendant's machine is merely an improvement over plaintiff's invention, or more closely resembles devices covered by other patents. The problem is one of identity: we must determine whether the identity of plaintiff's patent continues or is lost in defendant's machine. Although many of the elements must be identical because of the nature of the art, at some point the departures may take the later device beyond the scope and identity of the original invention. We examine the devices and compare their respective purpose and function, but no yardstick rule or formula can be laid down for any decision-we can only state in a given case that in our judgment the kinship between the devices either persists or is lost.

We are met at the threshold of our investigation by the charge in plaintiff's bill that "the machine now being manufactured and sold by defendant is different from plaintiff's machine in mechanical construction and in results obtained." Although we would be warranted in construing the statement against the pleader, we nevertheless base our decision on examination of the machines and the law. We turn to the patent claims to determine "where the progress claimed by the patent begins and where it ends." The state of the prior art must be examined in construing any claim to determine what progress has been made. Plaintiff's patent is not a primary patent of an original invention, but is merely an improvement on a known machine, and as a secondary patent it is given a narrower construction than would be given a primary patent.

We are told that to determine the prior state of the art, we are not to examine inventions for breaking the stems and leaves of tobacco, for cocoanut graters, or for cutting and splitting corn, because they are not in an analogous art and were never designed or actually used for the purpose of tenderizing meat. Our search is not so limited. We think the correct rule has been stated by Circuit Judge Sanborn in Mallon v. William C. Gregg & Co.: "It is only when the new use is so recondite and remote from that to which the old device has been applied, or for which it was conceived, that its application to the new use would not occur to the mind of the ordinary mechanic, skilled in the art, seeking to devise means to perform the desired function, with the old machine or combination present before him, that its conception rises to the dignity of invention. "If the new use be so nearly analogous to the former one that the applicability of the device to its new use would occur to a person of ordinary mechanical skill, it is only a case of double use; but if the relations between them be remote, and especially if the use of the old device produce a new result, it may, at least, involve an exercise of the inventive faculty [citations omitted]." " We think the slight adjustment of the rollers required to adapt these disintegrating machines to the partial disintegration process for tenderizing steak would occur to the mind of the ordinary mechanic of skill in the art.

We think the important claim of novelty in plaintiff's patent is in the "pairs of crushing gears with interposed cutter members and spacers, and the said cutter members carried by either shaft being constructed and arranged to extend between the pairs of gears on the other shaft and to the said spacers." This element is absent in the second device, and for this reason, we think defendant's construction follows more closely the prior art. Certain unexpired patents of machines for tenderizing or slitting meat have been brought to our attention, but further discussion would serve no useful purpose. The scheme of parallel rollers with sets of gears in each that interfit with the teeth of the opposite roller in the same plane or in adjacent planes is a common one. Defendant was at liberty to avail itself of the idea so long as the novelty of plaintiff's patent does not appear in the result, and in doing so defendant was not acting beyond the orbit of its contractual engagement.

Because of the view we take, we need not consider the propriety of the part of the decree denying defendant's petition to reopen the case.

A decree in conformance with this opinion may be entered setting aside the decree of the lower court and remanding the case solely for an accounting and adjudication of other rights plaintiff may establish under the original contract as far as it relates to plaintiff's invention, but not to the machine now being manufactured by defendant. Costs to defendant.

QUESTIONS

1. Do you agree with the court's definition of "improvement" and "new invention"?

2. Does the analysis of licenses to improvements differ where the licensor claims *exclusive* rights to improvements made by the licensee? Where the licensor claims exclusive rights to any competing technology developed by the licensee? *See* ANTITRUST GUIDELINES FOR THE LICENSING OF INTELLECTUAL PROPERTY in Section 7.2.

3. In the first instance, the inventor of an improvement to a patent owns the rights to the improvement, but cannot practice the improvement without a license from the owner of the base patent. In analyzing licenses to improvements, is it useful to ask whether the licensee's practice of the improvement would infringe the base patent absent the license agreement?

4. As noted above, disputes also arise over the licensee's rights to improvements to the licensed patent made by the licensor. Does this situation involve the same definitional questions? What is an "improvement" to the licensed patent and what is a "distinct" new invention?

5. A licensor could refuse to license improvements to the licensed patent. However, if the licensor licensed improvements to a base patent but not the base patent itself, could the licensee claim an implied license to the base patent? This situation often arises in university research when a company funds follow-on research on a pre-existing patent. Inventions resulting from the follow-on research

are referred to as "foreground intellectual property" and the pre-existing patents are referred to as "background intellectual property." Could a university grant a corporate sponsor rights in the foreground intellectual property but not the background intellectual property necessary to practice the invention?

6.   If you were counsel to a licensor, how could you draft an improvement clause in a license agreement to lessen uncertainty as to what is and what is not an "improvement." How would you do the same if you were counsel to a licensee?

ANTITRUST GUIDELINES FOR THE LICENSING OF INTELLECTUAL PROPERTY
1995 WL 1146232 (D.O.J.)
Issued By The U.S. Department Of Justice And The Federal Trade Commission

5.6 Grantbacks

A grantback is an arrangement under which a licensee agrees to extend to the licensor of intellectual property the right to use the licensee's improvements to the licensed technology. Grantbacks can have pro-competitive effects, especially if they are nonexclusive. Such arrangements provide a means for the licensee and the licensor to share risks and reward the licensor for making possible further innovation based on or informed by the licensed technology, and both promote innovation in the first place and promote the subsequent licensing of the results of the innovation. Grantbacks may adversely affect competition, however, if they substantially reduce the licensee's incentives to engage in research and development and thereby limit rivalry in innovation markets.

A non-exclusive grantback allows the licensee to practice its technology and license it to others. Such a grantback provision may be necessary to ensure that the licensor is not prevented from effectively competing because it is denied access to improvements developed with the aid of its own technology. Compared with an exclusive grantback, a non-exclusive grantback, which leaves the licensee free to license improvements technology to others, is less likely to have anticompetitive effects.

The Agencies will evaluate a grantback provision under the rule of reason, considering its likely effects in light of the overall structure of the licensing arrangement and conditions in the relevant markets. An important factor in the Agencies' analysis of a grantback will be whether the licensor has market power in a relevant technology or innovation market. If the Agencies determine that a particular grantback provision is likely to reduce significantly licensees' incentives to invest in improving the licensed technology, the Agencies will consider the extent to which the grantback provision has offsetting pro-competitive effects, such as (1) promoting dissemination of licensees' improvements to the licensed technology, (2) increasing the licensors' incentives to disseminate the licensed technology, or (3) otherwise increasing competition and output in a relevant technology or innovation market. In addition, the Agencies will consider the extent to which grantback provisions in the relevant markets generally increase licensors' incentives to innovate in the first place.

CASE NOTES

1. Deering Milliken granted a license to Leesona which allowed Lessona to manufacture and sell to Deering Miliken's use licensees apparatus designed by Deering Miliken for use in the manufacture of an elasticized nylon yarn called Agilon. The license agreement contained a grantback clause which provided that "Any improvements made on the apparatus or process which is the subject matter of this agreement [by Leesona] shall become the property of [Deering Miliken]." The subject matter of the agreement was defined as "certain inventions and technical information relating to elasticized yarn and the apparatus and processes employed in the manufacture of such yarn, which process and apparatus comprise passing yarn under predetermined tension about a sharp edge and equipment therefore . . ." Agilon was a crimped yarn that had the appearance of a natural fiber. The Deering Milliken method for manufacturing Agilon was a two-step process. First, smooth nylon yarn was drawn over a sharp-edged, angled knife blade at a critical temperature and tension to crimp the yarn. Second, the crimped yarn was then permanently crimped by finishing the knitted fabric in hot water at specific temperatures. Leesona developed a process which permanently crimped yarn by applying heat to the crimped yarn after it was drawn over the knife blade and before it was knitted into a fabric. The Deering Miliken method produced yarn that had high stretch characteristics, desirable for products such as hosiery, and the Leesona method produced products with high bulk characteristics, desirable for products such as sweaters. Deering Miliken claimed ownership of the Leesona process as an improvement to its licensed apparatus and process. What result? *See* Deering Milliken Research Corp. v. Leesona Corp., 315 F.2d 475 (2nd Cir. 1963).

2. *See also* United States Valves, Inc. v. Dray, 212 F.3d 1368 (Fed. Cir. 2000) (Licensor continued to sell valves in competition with licensee claiming the "sliding ring" valves it was selling were not covered by the license agreement; the license agreement granted the licensee the right to "[a]ll future improvements, modifications or enhancements of the Licensed Product made by the Licensor;" appeals court remanded to district court to determine whether the sliding ring valve was an improvement covered by the license agreement); New Britain Machine Co. v. W. Lloyd Yeo, 358 F.2d 397 (6th Cir. 1966) (Provisions in contract are not sufficiently clear and unambiguous to cover all future inventions that might be made by the licensor pertaining to "non-indexing, non-continuous boring machines;"); R.B. Jenkins & Co. v. Southern Suction and Equipment Co., 298 F.Supp. 1368 (W.D.N.C. 1969) (License agreement provided that any improvements relating to licensed subject matter made by licensee during the term of the license would become the property of the licensor; the interdependence between the licensed subject matter and the improvement to an improvement made by the licensor was sufficient to become the property of the licensor; but licensee was entitled to continue using improvement without paying royalties after termination of licensing agreement); De Long Corp. v. Lucas, 176 F. Supp. 104 (S.D.N.Y. 1959) ("It is well settled that an agreement to assign a patent and improvements thereon covers only the improvements existing at the time the agreement was entered into unless the language

specifically refers to future improvements; the law does not look favorably upon covenants which place "a mortgage on a man's brain, to bind all future products" ").

3. For cases dealing with grantback clauses and antitrust law, *see* Transparent-Wrap Machine Corp. v. Stokes & Smith Co., 329 U.S. 637 (1947) (Inclusion in the license of a condition requiring the licensee to assign improvement patents is not *per se* illegal and unenforceable); Hull v. Brunswick Corp., 704 F.2d 1195 (10th Cir. 1983) (Trial court properly rejected claim that grantback clause was *per se* illegal and considered how the provision was employed by Brunswick and Hull under the rule of reason standard); Santa Fe-Pomeroy, Inc. v. P & Z Co., 569 F.2d 1084 (9th Cir. 1978) (Grantback clause which was limited in duration and allowed bidders to use alternative methods did not constitute patent misuse or a violation of antitrust laws).

Additional Information

1. 69 C.J.S PATENTS § 335 (2008).

2. ROBERT GOLDSCHEIDER, ECKSTROMS LICENSING FORMS: MODEL CLAUSES CLAUSES 12-8, 14-2[c] (2011).

3. ROBERT GOLDSCHEIDER, 1 LICENSING AND THE ART OF TECHNOLOGY MANAGEMENT § 6:10 (2010).

4. LISA M. BROWNLEE, IP DUE DILIGENCE IN CORP. TRANSACTIONS § 5:79 (2010).

5. RICHARD RAYSMAN ET AL, INTELLECTUAL PROPERTY LICENSING: FORMS AND ANALYSIS § 13.03 (2010).

6. DAVID M. EPSTEIN, ECKSTROM'S LICENSING IN FOREIGN AND DOMESTIC OPERATIONS §§ 8E:28, 3:36 (2010).

7. RAYMOND T. NIMMER, JEFF DODD, MODERN LICENSING LAW § 14:31 (2009).

8. CORP. COUNSEL'S ANTITRUST DESKBOOK § 14:21 (2009).

9. WILLIAM C. HOLMES, INTELLECTUAL PROPERTY AND ANTITRUST LAW § 23:2 (2010).

10. Kenneth J. Dow, Traci D. Quigley, *Improvements for Handling Improvement Clauses in IP Licenses: An Analytical Framework*, 20 SANTA CLARA COMPUTER & HIGH TECH. L.J. 577 (2004).

11. Timothy J. Engling, *Improvements in Patent Licensing*, 78 J. PAT. & TRADEMARK OFF. SOC'Y 739 (1996).

12. Robert T. Canavan, *Unsolved Mysteries of Section 365(n) — When a Bankrupt Technology Licensor Rejects an Agreement Granting Rights to Future Improvements*, 21 SETON HALL L. REV 800 (1991).

13. Gerald Sobel, *The Antitrust Interface with Patents and Innovations: Acquisition of Patents, Improvement Patents and Grant-Backs, Non-Use, Fraud on the Patent Office, Development of New Products and Joint Research*, 53 ANTITRUST L.J. 681 (1985).

2.3.11 Indemnification

In an indemnification agreement, the indemnitor agrees to indemnify the indemnitee for damages suffered by the indemnitee as a result of the indemnitor's product or conduct. One of the most common examples of an indemnification agreement is when a seller of goods agrees to indemnify a buyer for damages in the event the buyer's use or resale of the goods is found to infringe a third party's intellectual property rights. However, indemnification agreements are used in a wide variety of other contexts to allocate risk between contracting parties, including joint ventures where the parties may be licensed to use one another's intellectual property and university technology transfers where licensor universities seek to limit any damages they may incur as a result of the licensee's use or sale of the licensed intellectual property.

Indemnification agreements can be tailored to cover different types of damages (compensatory damages or consequential damages), the amount of damages (maximum damages limit or liquidated damages) and the sources of damages (attorney's fees or litigation costs). Indemnification agreements generally require the indemnitee to provide the indemnitor prompt notice of an infringement claim and to assist the indemnitor in resolving the infringement claim. The indemnitor usually reserves the right to control the resolution of an infringement claim whether by settlement or litigation. If the indemnitee provides notice of an infringement claim to the indemnitor, and the indemnitor fails to take action to defend the infringement claim, the indemnitor will be bound by any reasonable settlement of the infringement claim to which the indemnitee agrees. On the other hand, if the indemnitee fails to provide notice of an infringement claim as required in the indemnification agreement and the indemnitee then proceeds to settle the infringement claim without notice to the indemnitor, the indemnitor may be relieved of liability under the indemnification agreement.

The great majority of indemnification agreements are based on express contract terms. Express indemnification agreements allow the contracting parties to carefully allocate future risks among themselves. However, in some cases, indemnification agreements can be implied or imposed by courts. U.C.C. § 2-312(3) creates implied warranties by sellers who regularly deal in goods, and buyers who furnish specifications for the production of goods, that the goods are noninfringing. U.C.C § 2-312(3) provides:

> Unless otherwise agreed a seller who is a merchant regularly dealing in goods of the kind warrants that the goods shall be delivered free of the rightful claim of any third person by way of infringement or the like but a buyer who furnishes specifications to the seller must hold the seller harmless against any such claim which arises out of compliance with the specifications.

Although U.C.C. § 2-312(3) can be disclaimed or modified by parties to contracts for sales of goods, if the parties do not do so, the implied warranty of noninfringement will give rise to an implied indemnification agreement.

Courts have also imposed implied indemnification agreements through the exercise of equity powers in cases dealing with principal-agent relationships, torts and personal injuries, fraud and misrepresentation, strict liability, and contribution among joint tortfeasors.

Courts have struck down express indemnification agreements when they have found the agreements to be unconscionable, contrary to public policy, punitive liquidated damages, and meaningless in providing a remedy.

The *RFR* case below involves a convoluted set of facts surrounding two indemnification agreements. RFR agreed to indemnify Century for any claim made against Century as a result of any claim made by RFR against any Century supplier. Rex-Hide was a Century supplier which Century agreed to indemnify in the event that Rex-Hide was sued for infringement for supplying Century. RFR sued Rex-Hide for infringement, Rex-Hide then sued Century under its indemnification agreement with Century, and Century then sued RFR under its indemnification agreement with RFR. What result?

RFR INDUSTRIES, INC. v. REX-HIDE INDUSTRIES, INC
2007 U.S. App. LEXIS 7015 (Fed. Cir. 2007)

PROST, CIRCUIT JUDGE.

RFR Industries, Inc. ("RFR") appeals from a final judgment of the United States District Court for the Northern District of Texas. RFR appeals the district court's determination that RFR cannot recover damages for patent infringement from Defendant/Third Party Plaintiff Rex-Hide Industries, Inc. ("Rex-Hide"). RFR also appeals the district court's grants of attorney fees to Rex-Hide and Third Party Defendant Century Steps, Inc. ("Century"). Finally, RFR appeals the district court's entry of a permanent injunction prohibiting RFR from pursuing certain claims against Century in arbitration and ordering RFR to file all future related actions in the Northern District of Texas in Judge Kinkeade's court. We affirm-in-part, reverse-in-part, vacate-in-part, and remand for further proceedings consistent with this opinion.

BACKGROUND

RFR is the assignee of two patents relating to an embedded railway track system, U.S. Patent No. 5,577,662 (" '662 patent") and U.S. Patent No. 5,535,947 (" '947 patent"). The '662 patent is directed to a railway system that utilizes a rubber product referred to by the parties as "flangeway filler," and the '947 patent is directed to a method of installing the flangeway filler.

In 1998, RFR sued Century for patent infringement, alleging that Century's sale of flangeway filler infringed the '662 and '947 patents. In 2000, RFR and Century entered into a written agreement to settle their dispute ("the 2000 settlement agreement"). The 2000 settlement agreement contained a number of provisions relevant to this appeal. First, Century agreed not to make, use, sell, offer to sell, or import flangeway filler that infringed the '662 or '947 patents, and Century consented to the entry of a permanent injunction prohibiting it from doing any of these activities. Second, Century agreed to pay a sum of money to RFR.

Third, Century agreed to purchase a specified amount of flangeway filler from RFR, and the 2000 settlement agreement provided Century with an express license under the '662 and '947 patents to use, sell, and offer to sell any flangeway filler it had purchased from RFR.

Fourth, the 2000 settlement agreement provided that RFR was releasing Century from RFR's patent infringement claims in the underlying lawsuit. The agreement provided, however, that notwithstanding RFR's release of Century, "nothing in this Agreement shall be construed as a release by RFR of Rex-Hide . . . or any other extruder that manufactured for Century [Flangeway] Filler ("Century Extruders") . . . ." RFR further agreed "to indemnify and hold harmless Century . . . from any claim made against Century . . . by any Century Extruder as a result of any RFR claim against any Century Extruder." Finally, in a section of the 2000 settlement agreement entitled "FUTURE DISPUTE RESOLUTION," RFR and Century agreed to submit to binding arbitration all claims arising out of the 2000 settlement agreement except for "motions for contempt for alleged violation of the permanent injunction or . . . complaints for patent infringement," which were to be filed in federal district court.

On March 29, 2004, RFR filed this action against Rex-Hide, a custom rubber extruder who had been Century's main supplier of the allegedly infringing flangeway filler. The complaint alleged that Rex-Hide's manufacture and sale of flangeway filler to Century constituted induced and contributory infringement of the '662 and '947 patents. Rex-Hide then filed a third-party complaint against Century, alleging that Century was required to indemnify it against RFR's infringement claims. Century, in turn, filed a cross-claim against RFR, alleging that the 2000 settlement agreement required RFR to indemnify it. Finally, RFR filed a counterclaim against Century, seeking a declaration that the 2000 settlement agreement did not require RFR to indemnify Century against Rex-Hide's claim.

On January 13, 2005, the district court granted partial summary judgment to Century, holding that the 2000 settlement agreement required RFR to indemnify Century against Rex-Hide's claim. On August 11, 2005, after a bench trial, the court determined that Century was required to indemnify Rex-Hide against RFR's claims pursuant to (1) the flangeway filler sales contract between Rex-Hide and Century and (2) the Texas Business & Commerce Code. The court also held that RFR's duty to indemnify Century and Century's duty to indemnify Rex-Hide "creates a circular indemnity that extinguishes RFR's patent-infringement claims against Rex-Hide."

In addition, the district court considered Century's and Rex-Hide's applications for attorney fees and expenses. In its Summary Judgment Order, the court held that RFR's duty to indemnify Century included paying any attorney fees and expenses incurred by Century while defending against Rex-Hide's claim. In its Circular Indemnity Order, the court held that Century's duty to indemnify Rex-Hide included paying any attorney fees and expenses incurred by Rex-Hide while defending against RFR's claim. In addition, the court held that RFR's duty to indemnify Century required RFR to pay Century for Rex-Hide's recovery from Century of Rex-Hide's attorney fees and expenses. Finally, in yet another order, the court determined that Rex-Hide was entitled to $222,860.21 in attorney fees and expenses and Century was entitled to $79,679.24 in attorney fees and expenses.

While all of this was going on in the district court, the parties were involved in a number of collateral disputes. When RFR first refused to indemnify Century in this action, Century withheld the remaining payments it owed RFR under the 2000 settlement agreement. Century also refused to pay RFR for some flangeway filler it had ordered from RFR pursuant to the 2000 settlement agreement. RFR responded to Century's nonpayment in three ways. First, RFR filed an arbitration demand seeking both payment of the owed settlement amounts and payment for the flangeway filler Century had ordered from RFR. Second, in October 2004 RFR filed a new patent infringement suit against Century, alleging that Century's nonpayment for and subsequent resale of the flangeway filler constituted infringement of the '662 and '947 patents. Third, RFR filed a petition to show cause in the 1998 lawsuit, alleging that Century's nonpayment for and subsequent resale of the flangeway filler it had ordered from RFR violated the permanent injunction entered in that case.

All of the collateral disputes led the district court to take action in this case. On August 11, 2005, the district court entered a preliminary injunction prohibiting RFR from pursuing its arbitration claims and ordering RFR "to file any and all future actions relating to the RFR patents, or the RFR-Century Settlement Agreement in the Northern District of Texas in Judge Kinkeade's Court." The court later made the injunction permanent. Finally, on June 27, 2006, while RFR's appeal to this court was pending, the district court on its own initiative issued a memorandum opinion clarifying the scope of the permanent injunction and requesting leave of this court to make the clarification.

DISCUSSION

RFR makes, essentially, four arguments on appeal. First, RFR argues that the district court's determination that RFR could not recover patent infringement damages from Rex-Hide was erroneous because Century was not required to indemnify Rex-Hide against RFR's infringement claims. Second, RFR argues that the district court's determination that RFR could not recover damages from Rex-Hide was erroneous because RFR was not required to indemnify Century against Rex-Hide's claim. Third, RFR argues that the district court erred by awarding attorney fees and expenses to Century and Rex-Hide. Finally, RFR argues that the district court improperly entered a permanent injunction prohibiting RFR from pursuing its arbitration claims and ordering RFR to file any future related claims in the Northern District of Texas in Judge Kinkeade's court.

A

RFR first takes issue with the district court's determination that Century was required to indemnify Rex-Hide. On August 11, 2005, after a bench trial, the court determined that Century was required to indemnify Rex-Hide against RFR's infringement claims under both (1) the Rex-Hide/Century flangeway filler sales contract and (2) the Texas Business & Commerce Code.

Specifically, the district court found that Century provided Rex-Hide with specifications for the flangeway filler. Rex-Hide, in turn, gave Century a price quotation form, which stated the terms under which Rex-Hide would manufacture the flangeway filler for Century. This form contained the following indemnification provision:

> In the event any of the parts produced under this contract infringe or are claimed to infringe any patent, copyright, or trademark, you agree to indemnify and save us harmless from any and all damages, losses or expenses, direct or indirect, to which we may be subjected on that account including but not limited to losses resulting from judgments, attorneys' fees or settlements with or without your consent.

After receiving Rex-Hide's quotation form, Century sent Rex-Hide a purchase order for the flangeway filler, which was accepted by Rex-Hide. The district court found that Century's purchase order did not contradict the terms of Rex-Hide's quotation form and that the indemnification provision on Rex-Hide's quotation form became part of the contract between Rex-Hide and Century. The court also determined that the indemnification provision required Century to indemnify Rex-Hide against RFR's patent infringement claims.

RFR argues that the district court erred in two respects. First, RFR argues that the indemnification provision was not part of the contract between Rex-Hide and Century. Specifically, RFR contends that the quotation form was not an offer that could be accepted by Century because the quotation form reserved the final right of acceptance to Rex-Hide. But even if the quotation form was not an offer, RFR has not provided this court with any basis to assign error to the district court's determination that the terms on the quotation form became part of the contract. Accordingly, we reject RFR's first argument.

Second, RFR argues that even if the indemnification provision became part of the contract, Rex-Hide is only entitled to indemnification if the parts Rex-Hide produced directly infringed the patents, but not if Rex-Hide is found to be liable for contributory or induced infringement. RFR points out that the indemnification provision only requires Century to indemnify Rex-Hide "[i]n the event any of the parts produced under th[e] contract infringe or are claimed to infringe any patent." RFR argues that Rex-Hide is not entitled to indemnification under this provision because RFR does not claim that the parts Rex-Hide produced directly infringed RFR's patents.

We agree with the district court, however, and reject RFR's second argument. Parts don't infringe a patent by themselves; it is Rex-Hide's making and selling the parts that can give rise to a claim of infringement. Accordingly, the provision is best read to protect Rex-Hide from a claim of infringement arising from its making and selling the flangeway filler. RFR has not provided us with a persuasive basis to reverse the district court's determination that the provision encompasses claims of indirect infringement. Therefore, we affirm the district court's determination that Century was required to indemnify Rex-Hide under the terms of the flangeway filler sales contract.

B

RFR next takes issue with the district court's determination that the 2000 settlement agreement required RFR to indemnify Century. The 2000 settlement agreement provided that RFR would "indemnify and hold harmless Century . . . from any claim made against Century . . . by any Century Extruder as a result of any RFR claim against any Century Extruder." The agreement specifically identified Rex-Hide as a "Century Extruder." The district court held that the 2000 settlement agreement was unambiguous and that it required RFR to indemnify Century against Rex-Hide's claim.

On appeal, RFR argues that this provision should not be given effect because it conflicts with another provision of the 2000 settlement agreement, which states that "nothing in this Agreement shall be construed as a release by RFR of Rex-Hide . . . ." We agree with the district court, however, and reject RFR's argument. It is apparent from the 2000 settlement agreement that the parties anticipated that RFR might sue Rex-Hide, who might, in turn, sue Century. And the agreement explicitly protects Century in such a situation. It is only in combination with Century's duty to indemnify Rex-Hide that RFR is precluded from recovering damages from Rex-Hide. This is not a "release" of Rex-Hide; for instance, had RFR chosen to do so, RFR could have pursued injunctive relief against Rex-Hide.

C

Next, RFR assigns error to the district court's grants of attorney fees and expenses to Century and Rex-Hide. RFR first argues that neither Century nor Rex-Hide is entitled to any attorney fees and expenses. We reject RFR's argument because RFR has not provided this court with a persuasive basis to reverse the district court's determination that, under Texas law, the indemnity provision in the 2000 settlement agreement entitled Century to recover attorney fees and expenses for defending against Rex-Hide's claim. Nor has RFR provided this court with a persuasive basis to reverse the district court's determination that the indemnity provision in the Rex-Hide/Century sales contract entitled Rex-Hide to recover attorney fees or expenses for defending against RFR's claims.

In the alternative, RFR argues that under Texas law Rex-Hide and Century may not recover fees and expenses incurred in the process of establishing their respective rights to indemnification. Accordingly, RFR argues that the district court improperly allowed Rex-Hide and Century to recover attorney fees and expenses insofar as those fees and expenses were incurred while establishing their rights to indemnification. On appeal, Rex-Hide and Century do not take issue with RFR's interpretation of the law. Nevertheless, Rex-Hide and Century assert two bases for affirming the district court's grants of attorney fees and expenses.

First, Rex-Hide and Century argue that they should be able to recover attorney fees and expenses for establishing their rights to indemnification because establishing their rights to indemnification essentially eliminated their liabilities as effectively as if Rex-Hide had obtained a judgment of non-infringement or invalidity. Were we to accept this argument, however, it would mean that a party could always recover attorney fees and expenses for establishing its right to indemnification. And Rex-Hide and Century do not dispute RFR's assertion that a party may not recover fees and expenses for establishing the party's right to indemnification. We therefore reject this argument.

During oral argument, Rex-Hide suggested a second basis for affirming the district court's grants of attorney fees and expenses. Specifically, Rex-Hide contended that the district court reduced Rex-Hide's and Century's awards to take into account the fees and expenses Rex-Hide and Century incurred while establishing their rights to indemnification. We cannot affirm the awards on this basis. It is true that the district court made a downward adjustment of 30% of Rex-Hide's and Century's requested amounts; however, the district court did not state that it was reducing Rex-Hide's or Century's award because some of the fees were incurred while establishing the right to indemnification. Instead, the district court cited "the time and amount involved, the nature of the case, fee awards in similar cases and that the case only required a one day bench trial." Thus, it appears that the district court improperly allowed Rex-Hide and Century to recover fees for establishing their respective rights to indemnification. Consequently, we vacate the district court's Attorney Fees Order and remand to the district court.

On remand, the district court should determine the portion of Rex-Hide's requested fees and expenses incurred while establishing Rex-Hide's right to indemnification from Century and adjust Rex-Hide's award accordingly. Similarly, the district court should determine the portion of Century's requested fees and expenses incurred while establishing Century's right to indemnification under the 2000 settlement agreement and adjust Century's award accordingly.

D

Next, RFR appeals the district court's entry of a permanent injunction. The permanent injunction, as elucidated by the district court in its Clarification Opinion, prohibits RFR from pursuing its arbitration claims and directs RFR to bring all future actions against Century or Rex-Hide related to the '662 and '947 patents in the Northern District of Texas in Judge Kinkeade's court.

We deal first with the portion of the injunction prohibiting RFR from pursuing its arbitration claims. The district court held that RFR had substantially invoked the judicial machinery, and thus had waived arbitration for its claim for payment of the settlement amounts owed by Century and its claim for payment for the flangeway filler Century had ordered from RFR. RFR argues that it should be allowed to submit those claims to arbitration because it has not invoked the judicial machinery with respect to those claims. In response, Century argues that RFR waived its right to arbitration because some of the issues raised by RFR's claims overlap with some of the issues resolved by the district court, for example, whether RFR had a duty under the 2000 settlement agreement to indemnify Century.

We do not conclude that RFR's actions in this case constituted a waiver of arbitration with respect to its two claims arising under the 2000 settlement agreement: its claim for payment of the settlement amounts owed by Century, and its claim for payment for the flangeway filler Century had ordered from RFR. RFR has not attempted to litigate these specific claims that it now seeks to arbitrate and, therefore, arbitration may be available for these claims.

Because RFR may seek arbitration on its claims arising under the 2000 settlement agreement, we also reverse the portion of district court's injunction directing RFR to file all future related actions in the Northern District of Texas in Judge Kinkeade's court. While this court understands and appreciates the district court's desire to prevent duplicative litigation, we anticipate that any court or arbitrator confronted with these parties and issues in the future will enter such orders as necessary to prevent unnecessary costs, delays, and inconsistent judgments.

CONCLUSION

We affirm the district court's determination that RFR cannot recover damages for patent infringement from Rex-Hide. We vacate the grants of attorney fees and remand for the district court to recalculate the amounts of the awards. We reverse the permanent injunction.

QUESTIONS

1. RFR's agreement to indemnify Century for any costs Century incurred through its indemnification agreement with a Century extruder, naming Rex-Hide as one of Century's extruders, and providing that RFR's release of Century from infringement liability did not extend to a release of Rex-Hide, would suggest that RFR contemplated suing Rex-Hide for infringement at the time of the RFR-Century agreement knowing that RFR would have to indemnify Century for Century's indemnification of Rex-Hide due to the infringement action. What were RFR's attorneys thinking?

2. What is the rationale for disallowing attorneys' fees and expenses incurred while establishing the right to indemnification?

3. If you were counsel to RFR, how could you draft the indemnification clause in the RFR-Century agreement to avoid indemnification in the event RFR successfully sued Rex-Hide?

CASE NOTES

1. Olan Mills operates more than 1,000 portrait studios throughout the United States. Linn Photo sells photographic equipment and supplies, and also reproduces photographs. Olan Mills discovered that Linn Photo was reproducing copyrighted photographs owned by Olan Mills and requested Linn Photo to cease this activity. Olan Mills took photographs of its employees and registered copyrights on the photographs with the U.S. Copyright Office. The photographs were also clearly marked with a copyright notice. Olan Mills then hired a private investigator to investigate Linn Photo's alleged infringing activity. The private investigator took four of the copyrighted photographs to Linn Photo and requested that they be reproduced. Linn Photo refused to reproduce the photographs unless the investigator signed a "Permission to Copy Agreement" which provided:

This is to state that I am the owner of this photograph and have not given anyone else permission to copy this photograph. I am submitting it to Linn Photo Company for a copy at my request. This copy is for my personal use, and I agree to hold harmless, Linn Photo Company or any of its agents, from any liability arising from the copying of this photograph.

Olan Mills sued Linn Photo in federal district court for copyright infringement. The district court granted summary judgment to Linn Photo on the ground that the private investigator was an agent of Olan Mills and that the "Permission to Copy Agreement" was binding on Olan Mills. The district court also awarded attorney's fees to Linn Photo based on the "hold harmless" language in the "Permission to Copy Agreement." Olan Mills appealed the district court's decision. What result? *See* Olan Mills, Inc. v. Linn Photo Co., 23 F.3d 1345 (8th Cir. 1994).

2. *See also* Mass Engineered Design, Inc. v. Ergotron, Inc. 633 F. Supp. 2d 361 (E.D. Tex. 2008) (Under California law, it is well settled that an indemnitee is not required to give notice of a claim to the indemnitor unless expressly required to do so in the indemnification agreement); Williams v. White Mountain Constr. Co., 749 P.2d 423 (Colo. 1988) (Indemnification provisions are scrutinized more closely than other contract provisions, and ambiguities in indemnification agreements will be resolved against the party seeking indemnity); Levin v. Septodont Inc., 2002 U.S. App. LEXIS 7359 (4th Cir. 2002) (Indemnification agreements generally contemplate reimbursement when the indemnitee is required to pay damages on a third-party claim but not reimbursement of attorney's fees in suits between contracting parties); Jordache Enterprise, Inc. v. Global Union Bank, 688 F. Supp. 939 (S.D.N.Y. 1988) (Liquidated damages clause in indemnification agreement was punitive and not enforceable); Nippon Elec. Glass Co., Ltd. v. Sheldon, 489 F. Supp. 119 (S.D.N.Y. 1980) (Infringement claim need not be made directly to declaratory judgment plaintiff, but may be made to its customers or the industry at large); Carter-Wallace, Inc. v. Tambrands, Inc. 295 A.D.2d 176 (N.Y. Sup. Ct. 2002) (Indemnification agreement excludes infringement caused by changes in design after delivery); Metabolite Labs., Inc. v. Lab. Corp. of Am. Holdings, 370 F.3d 1354 (Fed. Cir. 2004) (Specific exclusion of listed patent in an indemnification agreement should put defendant on notice to investigated listed patent).

Additional Information

1. ROBERT GOLDSCHEIDER, ECKSTROMS LICENSING FORMS: MODEL CLAUSES CLAUSE 13-3[g], 13-1[g][i], 13-1[k], 13-1[l], 13-3[e], 13-3[g], 35-13 (2011).

2. RAYMOND T. NIMMER & JEFF DODD, MODERN LICENSING LAW §§ 8:46–8:47, 8:50 (2009).

3. MICHAEL A. EPSTEIN, ET. AL., DRAFTING LICENSE AGREEMENTS §§ 2.02–2.04, Appendix 2-A (2010).

4. ROBERT A. MATTHEW, JR., 2 ANNOTATED PATENT DIGEST § 11:225 (2010).

5. DONALD S. CHISUM, CHISUM ON PATENTS § 17.04 (2000).

6. L. J. KUTTEN, 2 COMPUTER Software §§ 9:34–9:35 (2010).

7.   KATHERYN A. ANDRESEN, 1 LAW AND BUSINESS OF COMPUTER SOFTWARE (2d ed.) § 15:46 (2010).

8.   DAVID M. KLEIN, IP IN MERGERS & ACQUISITIONS § 6:27 (2010).

9.   CORP COUNS GD TO DOMESTIC JT VENTURES § 16:26 (2010).

10. Brian Naylor, *Selected Intellectual Property License Clauses: Indemnification and Audit Provisions*, 722 PLI/PAT 837 (2002).

11. Mark S. Holmes, *Patent Licensing: Indemnification*, Chapter 8, 960 PLI/PAT 343 (2009).

12. Ray J. Artiano & James F. Holtz, *California Contractual Indemnity*, 16 PAC. L. J. 768 (1984-1985).

2.4   UNILATERAL LICENSES

This section deals with license agreements which are formed without negotiation between the licensor and licensee. In unilateral licenses, the license agreement is formed as a result of some action taken by the licensee. In the case of "box-top" licenses, the license agreement is formed when the licensee opens the box containing the licensed technology, generally computer hardware or software. In the case of "shrink-wrap" licenses, the license agreement is formed when the licensee opens the package containing the licensed CD ROM software. (Courts and authors sometimes use the terms "box-top licenses" and "shrink-wrap licenses" interchangeably.) In the case of "click-wrap" licenses, the license agreement is formed when the licensee clicks an "I accept" button prior to accessing licensed software for either download or online use. And in the case of "open source" licenses, the license agreement is formed when the licensee uses software subject to an open source license.

Contracts which are formed without negotiation between the parties have generally been disfavored in common law and under the Uniform Commercial Code. In common law, standard form contracts that were presented to a buyer on a take-it-or-leave-it basis could be found to be "contracts of adhesion" which courts could refuse to enforce. Contracts of adhesion are most often formed between sellers, who have superior bargaining power, and buyers, who have little or no bargaining power. The rationale for not enforcing contracts of adhesion is that the disparity of bargaining power between the seller and buyer is such that the buyer could not meaningfully assent to the contract.

Under the Uniform Commercial Code, courts can find contracts, or contract clauses, to be "unconscionable" and refuse to enforce the entire contract, or refuse to enforce the unconscionable contract clauses and enforce the remainder of the contract. *See* UCC § 2-302. A contract can be found unconscionable either because of its oppressive terms or the way in which it was formed.

As you will see in the cases in this section, the historical disfavor for non-negotiated contracts has given way to the imperatives of modern commerce.

2.4.1   Box-Top Licenses

As the *Step-Saver* case below illustrates, box-top licenses often raise questions regarding which contract prevails when there are two contracts with different terms or conditions. This situation, commonly referred to as the "battle of the forms" is addressed in UCC § 2-207 which provides:

(1) A definite and seasonable expression of acceptance or a written confirmation which is sent within a reasonable time operates as an acceptance even though it states terms additional to or different from those offered or agreed upon, unless acceptance is expressly made conditional on assent to the additional or different terms.

(2) The additional terms are to be construed as proposals for additions to the contract. Between merchants such terms become part of the contract unless:

(a) the offer expressly limits acceptance to the terms of the offer;

(b) they materially alter it; or

(c) notification of objection to them has already been given or is given within a reasonable time after notice of them is received.

(3) Conduct by both parties which recognizes the existence of a contract is sufficient to establish a contract for sale although the writings of the parties do not otherwise establish a contract. In such case the terms of the particular contract consist of those terms on which the writings of the parties agree, together with any supplementary terms incorporated under any other provisions of this Act.

Issues involving UCC § 2-207 most often arise in transactions initiated by telephone, fax or online orders followed by written confirmations. The *Step-Saver* case involves the following communications between the parties: (i) Step-Saver placed a telephone order with a software vendor; (ii) the software vendor shipped the software to Step-Saver; (iii) Step-Saver mailed a written purchase order to the software vendor detailing the software, the price, and the shipping and payment terms; (iv) the software vendor included a written invoice with the software containing the same terms as the Step-Saver purchase order. None of these communications included a disclaimer of implied warranties under the Uniform Commercial Code. However, the box in which the software was shipped did have a disclaimer of implied warranties printed on the outside of the box.

STEP-SAVER DATA SYSTEMS v. WYSE TECHNOLOGY
939 F.2d 91 (3rd Cir. 1991)

Wisdom, Circuit Judge:

The "Limited Use License Agreement" printed on a package containing a copy of a computer program raises the central issue in this appeal. The trial judge held that the terms of the Limited Use License Agreement governed the purchase of the package, and, therefore, granted the software producer, The Software Link,

Inc. ("TSL"), a directed verdict on claims of breach of warranty brought by a disgruntled purchaser, Step-Saver Data Systems, Inc. We disagree with the district court's determination of the legal effect of the license, and reverse and remand the warranty claims for further consideration.

I. FACTUAL AND PROCEDURAL BACKGROUND

The growth in the variety of computer hardware and software has created a strong market for these products. It has also created a difficult choice for consumers, as they must somehow decide which of the many available products will best suit their needs. To assist consumers in this decision process, some companies will evaluate the needs of particular groups of potential computer users, compare those needs with the available technology, and develop a package of hardware and software to satisfy those needs. Beginning in 1981, Step-Saver performed this function as a value added retailer for International Business Machine (IBM) products. It would combine hardware and software to satisfy the word processing, data management, and communications needs for offices of physicians and lawyers. It originally marketed single computer systems, based primarily on the IBM personal computer.

As a result of advances in micro-computer technology, Step-Saver developed and marketed a multi-user system. With a multi-user system, only one computer is required. Terminals are attached, by cable, to the main computer. From these terminals, a user can access the programs available on the main computer.

After evaluating the available technology, Step-Saver selected a program by TSL, entitled Multilink Advanced, as the operating system for the multi-user system. Step-Saver selected WY-60 terminals manufactured by Wyse, and used an IBM AT as the main computer. For applications software, Step-Saver included in the package several off-the-shelf programs, designed to run under Microsoft's Disk Operating System ("MS-DOS"), as well as several programs written by Step-Saver. Step-Saver began marketing the system in November of 1986, and sold one hundred forty-two systems mostly to law and medical offices before terminating sales of the system in March of 1987. Almost immediately upon installation of the system, Step-Saver began to receive complaints from some of its customers.

Step-Saver, in addition to conducting its own investigation of the problems, referred these complaints to Wyse and TSL, and requested technical assistance in resolving the problems. After several preliminary attempts to address the problems, the three companies were unable to reach a satisfactory solution, and disputes developed among the three concerning responsibility for the problems. As a result, the problems were never solved. At least twelve of Step-Saver's customers filed suit against Step-Saver because of the problems with the multi-user system.

Once it became apparent that the three companies would not be able to resolve their dispute amicably, Step-Saver filed suit for declaratory judgment, seeking indemnity from either Wyse or TSL, or both, for any costs incurred by Step-Saver in defending and resolving the customers' law suits. The district court dismissed this complaint, finding that the issue was not ripe for judicial resolution. We affirmed the dismissal on appeal. Step-Saver then filed a second complaint alleging breach of warranties by both TSL and Wyse and intentional misrepresentations by TSL. The district court's actions during the resolution of this second complaint provide the foundation for this appeal.

On the first day of trial, the district court specifically agreed with the basic contention of TSL that the form language printed on each package containing the Multilink Advanced program ("the box-top license") was the complete and exclusive agreement between Step-Saver and TSL under § 2-202 of the Uniform Commercial Code (UCC). Based on § 2-316 of the UCC, the district court held that the box-top license disclaimed all express and implied warranties otherwise made by TSL. The court therefore granted TSL's motion in limine to exclude all evidence of the earlier oral and written express warranties allegedly made by TSL. After Step-Saver presented its case, the district court granted a directed verdict in favor of TSL on the intentional misrepresentation claim, holding the evidence insufficient as a matter of law to establish two of the five elements of a prima facie case: (1) fraudulent intent on the part of TSL in making the representations; and (2) reasonable reliance by Step-Saver. The trial judge requested briefing on several issues related to Step-Saver's remaining express warranty claim against TSL. While TSL and Step-Saver prepared briefs on these issues, the trial court permitted Wyse to proceed with its defense. On the third day of Wyse's defense, the trial judge, after considering the additional briefing by Step-Saver and TSL, directed a verdict in favor of TSL on Step-Saver's remaining warranty claims, and dismissed TSL from the case.

Step-Saver appeals on four points. (1) Step-Saver and TSL did not intend the box-top license to be a complete and final expression of the terms of their agreement. (2) There was sufficient evidence to support each element of Step-Saver's contention that TSL was guilty of intentional misrepresentation. (3) There was sufficient evidence to submit Step-Saver's implied warranty of merchantability claim against Wyse to the jury. (4) The trial court abused its discretion by excluding from the evidence a letter addressed to Step-Saver from Wyse, and by refusing to permit Step-Saver to introduce rebuttal testimony on the ordinary uses of the WY-60 terminal.

II. THE EFFECT OF THE BOX-TOP LICENSE

The relationship between Step-Saver and TSL began in the fall of 1984 when Step-Saver asked TSL for information on an early version of the Multilink program. TSL provided Step-Saver with a copy of the early program, known simply as Multilink, without charge to permit Step-Saver to test the program to see what it could accomplish. Step-Saver performed some tests with the early program, but did not market a system based on it.

In the summer of 1985, Step-Saver noticed some advertisements in Byte magazine for a more powerful version of the Multilink program, known as Multilink Advanced. Step-Saver requested information from TSL concerning this new version of the program, and allegedly was assured by sales representatives that the new version was compatible with ninety percent of the programs available "off-the-shelf" for computers using MS-DOS. The sales representatives allegedly made a number of additional specific representations of fact concerning the capabilities of the Multilink Advanced program.

Based on these representations, Step-Saver obtained several copies of the Multilink Advanced program in the spring of 1986, and conducted tests with the program. After these tests, Step-Saver decided to market a multi-user system which used the Multilink Advanced program. From August of 1986 through March of 1987, Step-Saver purchased and resold 142 copies of the Multilink Advanced program. Step-Saver would typically purchase copies of the program in the following manner. First, Step-Saver would telephone TSL and place an order. (Step-Saver would typically order twenty copies of the program at a time.) TSL would accept the order and promise, while on the telephone, to ship the goods promptly. After the telephone order, Step-Saver would send a purchase order, detailing the items to be purchased, their price, and shipping and payment terms. TSL would ship the order promptly, along with an invoice. The invoice would contain terms essentially identical with those on Step-Saver's purchase order: price, quantity, and shipping and payment terms. No reference was made during the telephone calls, or on either the purchase orders or the invoices with regard to a disclaimer of any warranties.

Printed on the package of each copy of the program, however, would be a copy of the box-top license. The box-top license contains five terms relevant to this action:

(1) The box-top license provides that the customer has not purchased the software itself, but has merely obtained a personal, non-transferable license to use the program.

(2) The box-top license, in detail and at some length, disclaims all express and implied warranties except for a warranty that the disks contained in the box are free from defects.

(3) The box-top license provides that the sole remedy available to a purchaser of the program is to return a defective disk for replacement; the license excludes any liability for damages, direct or consequential, caused by the use of the program.

(4) The box-top license contains an integration clause, which provides that the box-top license is the final and complete expression of the terms of the parties' agreement.

(5) The box-top license states: "Opening this package indicates your acceptance of these terms and conditions. If you do not agree with them, you should promptly return the package unopened to the person from whom you purchased it within fifteen days from date of purchase and your money will be refunded to you by that person."

The district court, without much discussion, held, as a matter of law, that the box-top license was the final and complete expression of the terms of the parties' agreement. Because the district court decided the questions of contract formation and interpretation as issues of law, we review the district court's resolution of these questions *de novo*.

Step-Saver contends that the contract for each copy of the program was formed when TSL agreed, on the telephone, to ship the copy at the agreed price. The box-top license, argues Step-Saver, was a material alteration to the parties' contract which did not become a part of the contract under UCC § 2-207. Alternatively, Step-Saver argues that the undisputed evidence establishes that the parties did not intend the box-top license as a final and complete expression of the terms of their agreement, and, therefore, the parol evidence rule of UCC § 2-202 would not apply.

TSL argues that the contract between TSL and Step-Saver did not come into existence until Step-Saver received the program, saw the terms of the license, and opened the program packaging. TSL contends that too many material terms were omitted from the telephone discussion for that discussion to establish a contract for the software. Second, TSL contends that its acceptance of Step-Saver's telephone offer was conditioned on Step-Saver's acceptance of the terms of the box-top license. Therefore, TSL argues, it did not accept Step-Saver's telephone offer, but made a counteroffer represented by the terms of the box-top license, which was accepted when Step-Saver opened each package. Third, TSL argues that, however the contract was formed, Step-Saver was aware of the warranty disclaimer, and that Step-Saver, by continuing to order and accept the product with knowledge of the disclaimer, assented to the disclaimer.

In analyzing these competing arguments, we first consider whether the license should be treated as an integrated writing under UCC § 2-202, as a proposed modification under UCC § 2-209, or as a written confirmation under UCC § 2-207. Finding that UCC § 2-207 best governs our resolution of the effect of the box-top license, we then consider whether, under UCC § 2-207, the terms of the box-top license were incorporated into the parties' agreement.

A. Does UCC § 2-207 Govern the Analysis?

As a basic principle, we agree with Step-Saver that UCC § 2-207 governs our analysis. We see no need to parse the parties' various actions to decide exactly when the parties formed a contract. TSL has shipped the product, and Step-Saver has accepted and paid for each copy of the program. The parties' performance demonstrates the existence of a contract. The dispute is, therefore, not over the existence of a contract, but the nature of its terms. When the parties' conduct establishes a contract, but the parties have failed to adopt expressly a particular writing as the terms of their agreement, and the writings exchanged by the parties do not agree, UCC § 2-207 determines the terms of the contract.

As stated by the official comment to § 2-207:

1. This section is intended to deal with two typical situations. The one is the written confirmation, where an agreement has been reached either orally or by informal correspondence between the parties and is followed by one or more of the parties sending formal memoranda embodying the terms so far as agreed upon and adding terms not discussed . . . .

2. Under this Article a proposed deal which in commercial understanding has in fact been closed is recognized as a contract. Therefore, any additional matter contained in the confirmation or in the acceptance falls within subsection (2) and must be regarded as a proposal for an added term unless

the acceptance is made conditional on the acceptance of the additional or different terms.

Although UCC § 2-202 permits the parties to reduce an oral agreement to writing, and UCC § 2-209 permits the parties to modify an existing contract without additional consideration, a writing will be a final expression of, or a binding modification to, an earlier agreement only if the parties so intend. It is undisputed that Step-Saver never expressly agreed to the terms of the box-top license, either as a final expression of, or a modification to, the parties' agreement. In fact, Barry Greebel, the President of Step-Saver, testified without dispute that he objected to the terms of the box-top license as applied to Step-Saver. In the absence of evidence demonstrating an express intent to adopt a writing as a final expression of, or a modification to, an earlier agreement, we find UCC § 2-207 to provide the appropriate legal rules for determining whether such an intent can be inferred from continuing with the contract after receiving a writing containing additional or different terms.

B. Application of § 2-207

TSL advances several reasons why the terms of the box-top license should be incorporated into the parties' agreement under a § 2-207 analysis. First, TSL argues that the parties' contract was not formed until Step-Saver received the package, saw the terms of the box-top license, and opened the package, thereby consenting to the terms of the license. TSL argues that a contract defined without reference to the specific terms provided by the box-top license would necessarily fail for indefiniteness. Second, TSL argues that the box-top license was a conditional acceptance and counter-offer under § 2-207(1). Third, TSL argues that Step-Saver, by continuing to order and use the product with notice of the terms of the box-top license, consented to the terms of the box-top license.

1. Was the contract sufficiently definite?

TSL argues that the parties intended to license the copies of the program, and that several critical terms could only be determined by referring to the box-top license. Pressing the point, TSL argues that it is impossible to tell, without referring to the box-top license, whether the parties intended a sale of a copy of the program or a license to use a copy. TSL cites *Bethlehem Steel Corp. v. Litton Industries* in support of its position that any contract defined without reference to the terms of the box-top license would fail for indefiniteness.

From the evidence, it appears that the following terms, at the least, were discussed and agreed to, apart from the box-top license: (1) the specific goods involved; (2) the quantity; and (3) the price. TSL argues that the following terms were only defined in the box-top license: (1) the nature of the transaction, sale or license; and (2) the warranties, if any, available. TSL argues that these two terms are essential to creating a sufficiently definite contract. We disagree.

Section 2-204(3) of the UCC provides:

Even though one or more terms are left open a contract for sale does not fail for indefiniteness if the parties have intended to make a contract and there is a reasonably certain basis for giving an appropriate remedy.

Unlike the terms omitted by the parties in *Bethlehem Steel Corp.*, the two terms cited by TSL are not "gaping holes in a multi-million dollar contract that no one but the parties themselves could fill." First, the rights of the respective parties under the federal copyright law if the transaction is characterized as a sale of a copy of the program are nearly identical to the parties' respective rights under the terms of the box-top license. Second, the UCC provides for express and implied warranties if the seller fails to disclaim expressly those warranties. Thus, even though warranties are an important term left blank by the parties, the default rules of the UCC fill in that blank.

We hold that contract was sufficiently definite without the terms provided by the box-top license.

3. Did the parties' course of dealing establish that the parties had excluded any express or implied warranties associated with the software program?

TSL argues that because Step-Saver placed its orders for copies of the Multilink Advanced program with notice of the terms of the box-top license, Step-Saver is bound by the terms of the box-top license. Essentially, TSL is arguing that, even if the terms of the box-top license would not become part of the contract if the case involved only a single transaction, the repeated expression of those terms by TSL eventually incorporates them within the contract.

Ordinarily, a "course of dealing" or "course of performance" analysis focuses on the actions of the parties with respect to a particular issue. If, for example, a supplier of asphaltic paving material on two occasions gives a paving contractor price protection, a jury may infer that the parties have incorporated such a term in their agreement by their course of performance. Because this is the parties' first serious dispute, the parties have not previously taken any action with respect to the matters addressed by the warranty disclaimer and limitation of liability terms of the box-top license. Nevertheless, TSL seeks to extend the course of dealing analysis to this case where the only action has been the repeated sending of a particular form by TSL. While one court has concluded that terms repeated in a number of written confirmations eventually become part of the contract even though neither party ever takes any action with respect to the issue addressed by those terms, most courts have rejected such reasoning.

For two reasons, we hold that the repeated sending of a writing which contains certain standard terms, without any action with respect to the issues addressed by those terms, cannot constitute a course of dealing which would incorporate a term of the writing otherwise excluded under § 2-207. First, the repeated exchange of forms by the parties only tells Step-Saver that TSL *desires* certain terms. Given TSL's failure to obtain Step-Saver's express assent to these terms before it will ship the program, Step-Saver can reasonably believe that, while TSL desires certain terms, it has agreed to do business on other terms — those terms expressly agreed upon by the parties. Thus, even though Step-Saver would not be surprised to learn that TSL desires the terms of the box-top license, Step-Saver might well be surprised to learn that the terms of the box-top license have been incorporated into the parties' agreement.

Second, the seller in these multiple transaction cases will typically have the opportunity to negotiate the precise terms of the parties' agreement, as TSL sought to do in this case. The seller's unwillingness or inability to obtain a negotiated agreement reflecting its terms strongly suggests that, while the seller would like a court to incorporate its terms if a dispute were to arise, those terms are not a part of the parties' commercial bargain. For these reasons, we are not convinced that TSL's unilateral act of repeatedly sending copies of the box-top license with its product can establish a course of dealing between TSL and Step-Saver that resulted in the adoption of the terms of the box-top license.

4. Public policy concerns.

TSL has raised a number of public policy arguments focusing on the effect on the software industry of an adverse holding concerning the enforceability of the box-top license. We are not persuaded that requiring software companies to stand behind representations concerning their products will inevitably destroy the software industry. We emphasize, however, that we are following the well-established distinction between conspicuous disclaimers made available before the contract is formed and disclaimers made available only after the contract is formed. When a disclaimer is not expressed until after the contract is formed, UCC § 2-207 governs the interpretation of the contract, and, between merchants, such disclaimers, to the extent they materially alter the parties' agreement, are not incorporated into the parties' agreement.

If TSL wants relief for its business operations from this well-established rule, their arguments are better addressed to a legislature than a court. Indeed, we note that at least two states have enacted statutes that modify the applicable contract rules in this area, but both Georgia and Pennsylvania have retained the contract rules provided by the UCC.

C. The Terms of the Contract

Under section 2-207, an additional term detailed in the box-top license will not be incorporated into the parties' contract if the term's addition to the contract would materially alter the parties' agreement. Step-Saver alleges that several representations made by TSL constitute express warranties, and that valid implied warranties were also a part of the parties' agreement. Because the district court considered the box-top license to exclude all of these warranties, the district court did not consider whether other factors may act to exclude these warranties. The existence and nature of the warranties is primarily a factual question that we leave for the district court, but assuming that these warranties were included within the parties' original agreement, we must conclude that adding the disclaimer of warranty and limitation of remedies provisions from the box-top license would, as a matter of law, substantially alter the distribution of risk between Step-Saver and TSL. Therefore, under UCC § 2-207(2)(b), the disclaimer of warranty and limitation of remedies terms of the box-top license did not become a part of the parties' agreement.

****

VI.

We will reverse the holding of the district court that the parties intended to adopt the box-top license as the complete and final expression of the terms of their agreement. We will remand for further consideration of Step-Saver's express and implied warranty claims against TSL. Finding a sufficient basis for the other decisions of the district court, we will affirm in all other respects.

QUESTIONS

1. If you were counsel to TSL, how would you ensure that the warranty disclaimers were included in the contract?

2. Should the party urging a warranty disclaimer carry the burden of proof to establish that the disclaimer is included in the contract?

3. The court distinguishes between "conspicuous disclaimers made available" before the contract is formed and "disclaimers made available" after the contract is formed. Which of these types of disclaimers may be held invalid under UCC § 2-207?

4. Could a state legislature modify its UCC contract law so that box-top license provisions are incorporated into all contracts? If you were counsel to the legislative committee charged with drafting the new box-top license contract law, and asked by the committee to draft a memorandum on the pros and cons of such a new law, what points would you emphasize?

CASE NOTES

1. Hill placed an order for a computer with Gateway by telephone specifying the type of computer and providing his credit card number. Inside the box in which Gateway shipped the computer was a list of printed terms which provided that they would govern the transaction unless the customer returned the computer within 30 days. One of the printed terms provided that any dispute arising between the customer and Gateway must be resolved by arbitration. Hill did not return the computer within 30 days, but later complained that the computer and its components were defective. Hill filed suit in U.S. district court arguing that the product defects were such that Gateway was a racketeer under the RICO act and subject to treble damages to Hill and a class of all other customers. At trial, Hill conceded that he noticed the statement of terms contained in the shipping box, but said he did not read it carefully enough to see the arbitration clause. Gateway requested the court to enforce the arbitration clause and the court refused holding that "[t]he present record is insufficient to support a finding of a valid arbitration agreement between the parties or that the plaintiffs were given adequate notice of the arbitration

clause." Gateway appealed the district court decision. What result? *See* Hill v. Gateway 2000, Inc., 105 F.3d 1147 (7th Cir. 1997).

2. *See also* M.A. Mortenson Company, Inc. v. Timberline Software Corp., 970 P.2d 803 (Wash. Ct. App. 1999) (Installation and use of software manifested buyer's assent to license terms included with the software, including an accept-or-return provision that limited the remedies available to the buyer, unless the limitation of remedies is found to be illegal or unconscionable); Arizona Retail Systems, Inc. v. Software Link, Inc., 831 F. Supp. 759 (D. Ariz. 1993) (If parties enter into an agreement before buyer opened software package containing a limited-use license, limited-use license would constitute proposed modification of original agreement requiring buyer's express assent to become part of original agreement); Wachter Management Company v. Dexter & Chaney, Inc., 144 P.3d 747 (Kan. 2006) (Contract was formed when buyer accepted vendor's offer to sell software by signing written proposal prepared by vendor; licensing agreement printed on software package containing terms not included in the original contract are considered request to amend original contract requiring buyer's express assent); Klocek v. Gateway, Inc., 104 F. Supp. 2d 1332 (D. Kan. 2000) (Seventh Circuit cases holding that licenses included in computer shipping box are binding on buyers concluded without support that UCC § 2-207 did not apply because there was only one written agreement; but nothing in the language of § 2-207 requires a second written agreement for its application).

Additional Information

1. 2 RAYMOND T. NIMMER, INFORMATION LAW §§ 11:144, 11:147 (2008).

2. RAYMOND T. NIMMER, LAW OF COMPUTER TECHNOLOGY §§ 7:126, 7:128 (2010).

3. RICHARD GILLMAN, MICHAEL R. COHEN, WEST'S LEGAL FORMS, SPECIALIZED FORMS (4th ed.), 27-A, § 10:35 (2008).

4. MITCHELL WALDMAN, NTS AM. JUR. 2D COMPUTERS AND THE INTERNET § 16 (2010).

5. 2 RICHARD A. LORD, WILLISTON ON CONTRACTS § 6:17 (4th ed. 2010).

6. 3 DAVID M. EPSTEIN ET AL, ECKSTROM'S LICENSING IN FOR. & DOM. OPPS. § 12:75 (2008).

7. KEVIN W. GRIERSON, 106 A.L.R.5th 309 (2003).

8. Batya Goodman, *Honey, I Shrink-Wrapped the Consumer: The Shrink-Wrap Agreement as an Adhesion Contract*, 21 CARDOZO L. REV. 319 (1999).

9. Jane M. Rolling, *The UCC Under Wraps: Exposing the Need for More Notice to Consumers of Computer Software with Shrink Wrapped Licenses*, 104 COM. L.J. 197 (1999).

10. Richard Raysman & Peter Brown, *Shrink Wrap License Agreements*, N.Y.L.J., Apr. 9, 1996, at col. 1.

11. Peter Brown, *Clickwrap Licenses*, 533 PLI/PAT 209 (1998).

12. D.C. Toedt III, *Shrinkwrap License Enforceability Issues*, 453 PLI/PAT 613 (1996).

13. Steven J. Davidson, Michael J. Wurzer, *Shrink-Wrap Licenses: The Continuing Controversy*, 453 PLI/PAT 673 (1996).

14. David A. Einhorn, *Shrink-Wrap Licenses: The Debate Continues*, 38 IDEA 383 (1998).

15. Thomas Finkelstein, Douglas C. Wyatt, *Shrinkwrap Licenses: Consequences of Breaking the Seal*, 71 ST. JOHN'S L. REV. 839 (1997).

16. Kristin J. Hazelwood, *Let the Buyer Beware: The Seventh Circuit's Approach to Accept-or-Return Offers*, 55 WASH. & LEE L. REV. 1287 (1998).

17. David A. Einhorn, *Box-Top Licenses and the Battle-Of-The-Forms*, 5 SOFTWARE L.J. 401 (1992).

2.4.2 Shrink-Wrap Licenses

In addition to questions of enforceability of box-top and shrink-wrap licenses under state contract laws, these licenses can also raise issues of preemption under the Copyright Act when the terms in a license govern activities that are covered within the provisions of the Copyright Act. Section 301(a) of the Copyright Act provides "[a]ll legal or equitable rights that are equivalent to any of the exclusive rights within the general scope of copyright . . . are governed exclusively by this title." The *ProCD* case considers the issue of Copyright Act preemption in the case of a shrink-wrap license that restricted the use of the software to consumer use only. The following case, *Bowers*, considers the issue of Copyright Act preemption in the case of a shrink-wrap license that prohibited reverse engineering of the licensed software.

PROCD v. ZEIDENBERG
86 F.3d 1447 (7th Cir. 1996)

EASTERBROOK, CIRCUIT JUDGE.

Must buyers of computer software obey the terms of shrinkwrap licenses? The district court held not, for two reasons: first, they are not contracts because the licenses are inside the box rather than printed on the outside; second, federal law forbids enforcement even if the licenses are contracts. The parties and numerous amici curiae have briefed many other issues, but these are the only two that matter — and we disagree with the district judge's conclusion on each. Shrinkwrap licenses are enforceable unless their terms are objectionable on grounds applicable to contracts in general (for example, if they violate a rule of positive law, or if they are unconscionable). Because no one argues that the terms of the license at issue here are troublesome, we remand with instructions to enter judgment for the plaintiff.

I

ProCD, the plaintiff, has compiled information from more than 3,000 telephone directories into a computer database. We may assume that this database cannot be copyrighted, although it is more complex, contains more information (nine-digit zip codes and census industrial codes), is organized differently, and therefore is more original than the single alphabetical directory at issue in *Feist Publications, Inc. v. Rural Telephone Service Co.* ProCD sells a version of the database, called SelectPhone (trademark), on CD-ROM discs. (CD-ROM means "compact disc — read only memory." The "shrinkwrap license" gets its name from the fact that retail software packages are covered in plastic or cellophane "shrinkwrap," and some vendors, though not ProCD, have written licenses that become effective as soon as the customer tears the wrapping from the package. Vendors prefer "end user license," but we use the more common term.) A proprietary method of compressing the data serves as effective encryption too. Customers decrypt and use the data with the aid of an application program that ProCD has written. This program, which is copyrighted, searches the database in response to users' criteria (such as "find all people named Tatum in Tennessee, plus all firms with "Door Systems" in the corporate name"). The resulting lists (or, as ProCD prefers, "listings") can be read and manipulated by other software, such as word processing programs.

The database in SelectPhone (trademark) cost more than $10 million to compile and is expensive to keep current. It is much more valuable to some users than to others. The combination of names, addresses, and SIC codes enables manufacturers to compile lists of potential customers. Manufacturers and retailers pay high prices to specialized information intermediaries for such mailing lists; ProCD offers a potentially cheaper alternative. People with nothing to sell could use the database as a substitute for calling long distance information, or as a way to look up old friends who have moved to unknown towns, or just as an electronic substitute for the local phone book. ProCD decided to engage in price discrimination, selling its database to the general public for personal use at a low price (approximately $150 for the set of five discs) while selling information to the trade for a higher price. It has adopted some intermediate strategies too: access to the SelectPhone (trademark) database is available via the America Online service for the price America Online charges to its clients (approximately $3 per hour), but this service has been tailored to be useful only to the general public.

To make price discrimination work, however, the seller must be able to control arbitrage. An air carrier sells tickets for less to vacationers than to business travelers, using advance purchase and Saturday-night-stay requirements to distinguish the categories. A producer of movies segments the market by time, releasing first to theaters, then to pay-per-view services, next to the videotape and laserdisc market, and finally to cable and commercial TV. Vendors of computer software have a harder task. Anyone can walk into a retail store and buy a box. Customers do not wear tags saying "commercial user" or "consumer user." Anyway, even a commercial-user-detector at the door would not work, because a consumer could buy the software and resell to a commercial user. That arbitrage would break down the price discrimination and drive up the minimum price at which ProCD would sell to anyone.

Instead of tinkering with the product and letting users sort themselves — for example, furnishing current data at a high price that would be attractive only to commercial customers, and two-year-old data at a low price — ProCD turned to the institution of contract. Every box containing its consumer product declares that the software comes with restrictions stated in an enclosed license. This license, which is encoded on the CD-ROM disks as well as printed in the manual, and which appears on a user's screen every time the software runs, limits use of the application program and listings to non-commercial purposes.

Matthew Zeidenberg bought a consumer package of SelectPhone (trademark) in 1994 from a retail outlet in Madison, Wisconsin, but decided to ignore the license. He formed Silken Mountain Web Services, Inc., to resell the information in the SelectPhone (trademark) database. The corporation makes the database available on the Internet to anyone willing to pay its price — which, needless to say, is less than ProCD charges its commercial customers. Zeidenberg has purchased two additional SelectPhone (trademark) packages, each with an updated version of the database, and made the latest information available over the World Wide Web, for a price, through his corporation. ProCD filed this suit seeking an injunction against further dissemination that exceeds the rights specified in the licenses (identical in each of the three packages Zeidenberg purchased). The district court held the licenses ineffectual because their terms do not appear on the outside of the packages. The court added that the second and third licenses stand no different from the first, even though they are identical, because they *might* have been different, and a purchaser does not agree to — and cannot be bound by — terms that were secret at the time of purchase.

II

Following the district court, we treat the licenses as ordinary contracts accompanying the sale of products, and therefore as governed by the common law of contracts and the Uniform Commercial Code. Whether there are legal differences between "contracts" and "licenses" (which may matter under the copyright doctrine of first sale) is a subject for another day. Zeidenberg does not argue that Silken Mountain Web Services is free of any restrictions that apply to Zeidenberg himself, because any effort to treat the two parties as distinct would put Silken Mountain behind the eight ball on ProCD's argument that copying the application program onto its hard disk violates the copyright laws. Zeidenberg does argue, and the district court held, that placing the package of software on the shelf is an "offer," which the customer "accepts" by paying the asking price and leaving the store with the goods. In Wisconsin, as elsewhere, a contract includes only the terms on which the parties have agreed. One cannot agree to hidden terms, the judge concluded. So far, so good — but one of the terms to which Zeidenberg agreed by purchasing the software is that the transaction was subject to a license. Zeidenberg's position therefore must be that the printed terms on the outside of a box are the parties' contract — except for printed terms that refer to or incorporate other terms. But why would Wisconsin fetter the parties' choice in this way? Vendors can put the entire terms of a contract on the outside of a box only by using microscopic type, removing other information that buyers might find more useful (such as what the software does, and on which computers it works), or both.

The "Read Me" file included with most software, describing system requirements and potential incompatibilities, may be equivalent to ten pages of type; warranties and license restrictions take still more space. Notice on the outside, terms on the inside, and a right to return the software for a refund if the terms are unacceptable (a right that the license expressly extends), may be a means of doing business valuable to buyers and sellers alike. Doubtless a state could forbid the use of standard contracts in the software business, but we do not think that Wisconsin has done so.

[In] . . . the software industry . . . only a minority of sales take place over the counter, where there are boxes to peruse. A customer may place an order by phone in response to a line item in a catalog or a review in a magazine. Much software is ordered over the Internet by purchasers who have never seen a box. Increasingly software arrives by wire. There is no box; there is only a stream of electrons, a collection of information that includes data, an application program, instructions, many limitations ("MegaPixel 3.14159 cannot be used with BytePusher 2.718"), and the terms of sale. The user purchases a serial number, which activates the software's features. On Zeidenberg's arguments, these unboxed sales are unfettered by terms — so the seller has made a broad warranty and must pay consequential damages for any shortfalls in performance, two "promises" that if taken seriously would drive prices through the ceiling or return transactions to the horse-and-buggy age.

According to the district court, the UCC does not countenance the sequence of money now, terms later. One of the court's reasons — that by proposing as part of the draft Article 2B a new UCC § 2-2203 that would explicitly validate standard-form user licenses, the American Law Institute and the National Conference of Commissioners on Uniform Laws have conceded the invalidity of shrinkwrap licenses under current law — depends on a faulty inference. To propose a change in a law's *text* is not necessarily to propose a change in the law's *effect*. New words may be designed to fortify the current rule with a more precise text that curtails uncertainty. To judge by the flux of law review articles discussing shrinkwrap licenses, uncertainty is much in need of reduction — although businesses seem to feel less uncertainty than do scholars, for only three cases (other than ours) touch on the subject, and none directly addresses it. See *Step-Saver Data Systems, Inc. v. Wyse Technology*, *Vault Corp. v. Quaid Software Ltd.*, *Arizona Retail Systems, Inc. v. Software Link, Inc.* As their titles suggest, these are not consumer transactions. Step-Saver is a battle-of-the-forms case, in which the parties exchange incompatible forms and a court must decide which prevails. Our case has only one form; UCC § 2-207 is irrelevant. *Vault* holds that Louisiana's special shrinkwrap-license statute is preempted by federal law, a question to which we return. And *Arizona Retail Systems* did not reach the question, because the court found that the buyer knew the terms of the license before purchasing the software.

What then does the current version of the UCC have to say? We think that the place to start is § 2-204(1): "A contract for sale of goods may be made in any manner sufficient to show agreement, including conduct by both parties which recognizes the existence of such a contract." A vendor, as master of the offer, may invite acceptance by conduct, and may propose limitations on the kind of conduct that constitutes acceptance. A buyer may accept by performing the acts the vendor proposes to treat as acceptance. And that is what happened. ProCD proposed a contract that a buyer would accept by *using* the software after having an opportunity to read the license at leisure. This Zeidenberg did. He had no choice, because the software splashed the license on the screen and would not let him proceed without indicating acceptance. So although the district judge was right to say that a contract can be, and often is, formed simply by paying the price and walking out of the store, the UCC permits contracts to be formed in other ways. ProCD proposed such a different way, and without protest Zeidenberg agreed. Ours is not a case in which a consumer opens a package to find an insert saying "you owe us an extra $10,000" and the seller files suit to collect. Any buyer finding such a demand can prevent formation of the contract by returning the package, as can any consumer who concludes that the terms of the license make the software worth less than the purchase price. Nothing in the UCC requires a seller to maximize the buyer's net gains.

Section 2-606, which defines "acceptance of goods," reinforces this understanding. A buyer accepts goods under § 2-606(1)(b) when, after an opportunity to inspect, he fails to make an effective rejection under § 2-602(1). ProCD extended an opportunity to reject if a buyer should find the license terms unsatisfactory; Zeidenberg inspected the package, tried out the software, learned of the license, and did not reject the goods. We refer to § 2-606 only to show that the opportunity to return goods can be important; acceptance of an offer differs from acceptance of goods after delivery, but the UCC consistently permits the parties to structure their relations so that the buyer has a chance to make a final decision after a detailed review.

Some portions of the UCC impose additional requirements on the way parties agree on terms. A disclaimer of the implied warranty of merchantability must be "conspicuous." UCC § 2-316(2), incorporating UCC § 1-201(10). Promises to make firm offers, or to negate oral modifications, must be "separately signed." UCC §§ 2-205, 2-209(2). These special provisos reinforce the impression that, so far as the UCC is concerned, other terms may be as inconspicuous as the forum-selection clause on the back of the cruise ship ticket in *Carnival Lines*. Zeidenberg has not located any Wisconsin case — for that matter, any case in any state — holding that under the UCC the ordinary terms found in shrinkwrap licenses require any special prominence, or otherwise are to be undercut rather than enforced. In the end, the terms of the license are conceptually identical to the contents of the package. Just as no court would dream of saying that SelectPhone (trademark) must contain 3,100 phone books rather than 3,000, or must have data no more than 30 days old, or must sell for $100 rather than $150 — although any of these changes would be welcomed by the customer, if all other things were held constant — so, we believe, Wisconsin would not let the buyer pick and choose among terms. Terms of use are no less a part of "the product" than are the size of the database and the speed with which the software compiles listings. Competition among vendors, not judicial revision of a package's contents, is how consumers are protected in a market economy. ProCD has rivals, which may elect to compete by offering superior software, monthly updates, improved terms of use, lower price, or a better compromise among these elements. As we stressed above, adjusting terms in buyers' favor might help Matthew Zeidenberg today (he already has the software) but would lead to a response, such as a higher price, that might make consumers as a whole worse off.

III

The district court held that, even if Wisconsin treats shrinkwrap licenses as contracts, § 301(a) of the Copyright Act, 17 U.S.C. § 301(a), prevents their enforcement. The relevant part of § 301(a) preempts any "legal or equitable rights [under state law] that are equivalent to any of the exclusive rights within the general scope of copyright as specified by section 106 in works of authorship that are fixed in a tangible medium of expression and come within the subject matter of copyright as specified by sections 102 and 103." ProCD's software and data are "fixed in a tangible medium of expression," and the district judge held that they are "within the subject matter of copyright." The latter conclusion is plainly right for the copyrighted application program, and the judge thought that the data likewise are "within the subject matter of copyright" even if, after Feist, they are not sufficiently original to be copyrighted. One function of § 301(a) is to prevent states from giving special protection to works of authorship that Congress has decided should be in the public domain, which it can accomplish only if "subject matter of copyright" includes all works of a *type* covered by sections 102 and 103, even if federal law does not afford protection to them.

But are rights created by contract "equivalent to any of the exclusive rights within the general scope of copyright"? Three courts of appeals have answered "no." The district court disagreed with these decisions, but we think them sound. Rights "equivalent to any of the exclusive rights within the general scope of copyright" are rights established *by law* — rights that restrict the options of persons who are strangers to the author. Copyright law forbids duplication, public performance, and so on, unless the person wishing to copy or perform the work gets permission; silence means a ban on copying. A copyright is a right against the world. Contracts, by contrast, generally affect only their parties; strangers may do as they please, so contracts do not create "exclusive rights." Someone who found a copy of SelectPhone (trademark) on the street would not be affected by the shrinkwrap license — though the federal copyright laws of their own force would limit the finder's ability to copy or transmit the application program.

Although Congress possesses power to preempt even the enforcement of contracts about intellectual property — or railroads — courts usually read preemption clauses to leave private contracts unaffected. *American Airlines, Inc. v. Wolens* provides a nice illustration. A federal statute preempts any state "law, rule, regulation, standard, or other provision . . . relating to rates, routes, or services of any air carrier." Does such a law preempt the law of contracts — so that, for example, an air carrier need not honor a quoted price (or a contract to reduce the price by the value of frequent flyer miles)? The Court allowed that it is possible to read the statute that broadly but thought such an interpretation would make little sense. Terms and conditions offered by contract reflect private ordering, essential to the efficient functioning of markets. Although some principles that carry the name of contract law are designed to defeat rather than implement consensual transactions, the rules that respect private choice are not preempted by a clause such as § 1305(a)(1). Section 301(a) plays a role similar to § 1301(a)(1): it prevents states from substituting their own regulatory systems for those of the national government. Just as § 301(a) does not itself interfere with private transactions in intellectual property, so it does not prevent states from respecting those transactions. Like the Supreme Court in *Wolens*, we think it prudent to refrain from adopting a rule that anything with the label "contract" is necessarily outside the preemption clause: the variations and possibilities are too numerous to foresee. *National Car Rental* likewise recognizes the possibility that some applications of the law of contract could interfere with the attainment of national objectives and therefore come within the domain of § 301(a). But general enforcement of shrinkwrap licenses of the kind before us does not create such interference.

REVERSED AND REMANDED.

QUESTIONS

1. Are there examples of other consumer products with contract terms that are contained in the box and can only be read after the box is opened?

2. Would a license that is fully set forth and visible in a shrink-wrapped CD ROM be enforceable under *ProCD*?

3. Is return and refund a sufficient remedy if a purchaser refuses to agree to license terms?

4. Why were the terms of the shrink-wrap license not preempted by the Copyright Act?

5. The court mentions that whether there are legal differences between contracts and licenses may make a difference under the copyright doctrine of "first sale." Why is this so?

6. If you were counsel to a company that is distributing software by means of a shrink-wrapped CD ROM and asked for your advice on a procedure for such distribution, what would you advise the company?

BOWERS v. BAYSTATE TECHNOLOGIES
320 F.3d 1317 (Fed. Cir. 2003)

RADER, CIRCUIT JUDGE.

Following trial in the United States District Court for the District of Massachusetts, the jury returned a verdict for Harold L. Bowers on his patent infringement, copyright infringement, and breach of contract claims, while rejecting Baystate Technologies, Inc.'s claim for patent invalidity. The jury awarded Mr. Bowers separate damages on each of his claims. The district court, however, omitted the copyright damages as duplicative of the contract damages. Because substantial evidence supports the jury's verdict that Baystate breached the contract, this court affirms that verdict. This court holds also that the district court did not abuse its discretion in modifying the damages award. Nevertheless, because no reasonable jury could find that Baystate infringes claim 1 as properly construed, this court reverses the patent infringement verdict.

I.

Harold L. Bowers (Bowers) created a template to improve computer aided design (CAD) software, such as the CADKEY tool of Cadkey, Inc. Mr. Bowers filed a patent application for his template on February 27, 1989. On June 12, 1990, United States Patent No. 4,933,514 ('514 patent) issued from that application.

Generally, a CAD software program has many commands that the software presents to the user in nested menus many layers deep. The layering often makes it difficult for a user to find quickly a desired command. To address this problem, the claimed template works with a CAD system as illustrated in Fig. 1 of the '514 patent. In that figure, the '514 patent template lies on top of the digitizing tablet of a CAD computer. The user selects data from the template with a pointing device. The template places the many CAD commands in a claimed visual and logical order.

Since the early 1980s, CAD programs have assisted engineers to draft and design on a computer screen. George W. Ford, III, a development engineer and supervisor of quality control at Heinemann Electric, envisioned a way to improve Mr. Bowers' template and CAD software. Specifically, Mr. Ford designed Geodraft, a DOS-based add-on program to operate with CAD. Geodraft allows an engineer to insert technical tolerances for features of the computer-generated design. These tolerances comply with the geometric dimensioning and tolerancing (GD & T) requirements in ANSI Y14.5M, a standard promulgated by the American National Standards Institute (ANSI). Geodraft works in conjunction with the CAD system to ensure that the design complies with ANSI Y14.5M — a task previously error-prone due to the standard's complexity. Geodraft automatically includes symbols specifying the correct GD & T parameters. Mr. Ford obtained a registered copyright, TX 2-939-672, covering Geodraft.

In 1989, Mr. Ford offered Mr. Bowers an exclusive license to his Geodraft software. Mr. Bowers accepted that offer and bundled Geodraft and Cadjet together as the Designer's Toolkit. Mr. Bowers sold the Designer's Toolkit with a shrink-wrap license that, *inter alia*, prohibited any reverse engineering.

In 1989, Baystate also developed and marketed other tools for CADKEY. One of those tools, Draft-Pak version 1 and 2, featured a template and GD & T software. In 1988 and 1989, Mr. Bowers offered to establish a formal relationship with Baystate, including bundling his template with Draft-Pak. Baystate rejected that offer, however, telling Mr. Bowers that it believed it had "the in-house capability to develop the type of products you have proposed."

In 1990, Mr. Bowers released Designer's Toolkit. By January 1991, Baystate had obtained copies of that product. Three months later, Baystate introduced the substantially revised Draft-Pak version 3, incorporating many of the features of Designer's Toolkit. Although Draft-Pak version 3 operated in the DOS environment, Baystate later upgraded it to operate with Microsoft Windows®.

Baystate's introduction of Draft-Pak version 3 induced intense price competition between Mr. Bowers and Baystate. To gain market share over Baystate, Mr. Bowers negotiated with Cadkey, Inc., to provide the Designer's Toolkit free with CADKEY. Mr. Bowers planned to recoup his profits by selling software upgrades to the users that he hoped to lure to his products. Following pressure from Baystate, however, Cadkey, Inc., repudiated its distribution agreement with Mr. Bowers. Eventually, Baystate purchased Cadkey, Inc., and eliminated Mr. Bowers from the CADKEY network — effectively preventing him from developing and marketing the Designer's Toolkit for that program.

On May 16, 1991, Baystate sued Mr. Bowers for declaratory judgment that 1) Baystate's products do not infringe the '514 patent, 2) the '514 patent is invalid, and 3) the '514 patent is unenforceable. Mr. Bowers filed counterclaims for copyright infringement, patent infringement, and breach of contract.

Following trial, the jury found for Mr. Bowers and awarded $1,948,869 for copyright infringement, $3,831,025 for breach of contract, and $232,977 for patent infringement. The district court, however, set aside the copyright damages as duplicative of the contract damages and entered judgment for $5,270,142 (including pre-judgment interest). Baystate filed timely motions for judgment as a matter of law (JMOL), or for a new trial, on all of Mr. Bowers' claims. Baystate appeals the district court's denial of its motions for JMOL or a new trial, while Mr. Bowers appeals the district court's denial of copyright damages. This court has jurisdiction under 28 U.S.C. § 1295(a)(1) (2000).

II.

A.

Baystate contends that the Copyright Act preempts the prohibition of reverse engineering embodied in Mr. Bowers' shrink-wrap license agreements. Swayed by this argument, the district court considered Mr. Bowers' contract and copyright claims coextensive. The district court instructed the jury that "reverse engineering violates the license agreement only if Baystate's product that resulted from reverse engineering infringes Bowers' copyright because it copies protectable expression." Mr. Bowers lodged a timely objection to this instruction. This court holds that, under First Circuit law, the Copyright Act does not preempt or narrow the scope of Mr. Bowers' contract claim.

Courts respect freedom of contract and do not lightly set aside freely-entered agreements. Nevertheless, at times, federal regulation may preempt private contract. The Copyright Act provides that "all legal or equitable rights that are equivalent to any of the exclusive rights within the general scope of copyright . . . are governed exclusively by this title." 17 U.S.C. § 301(a) (2000). The First Circuit does not interpret this language to require preemption as long as "a state cause of action requires an extra element, beyond mere copying, preparation of derivative works, performance, distribution or display." Nevertheless, "[n]ot every "extra element" of a state law claim will establish a qualitative variance between the rights protected by federal copyright law and those protected by state law."

In *Data General*, Data General alleged that Grumman misappropriated its trade secret software. Grumman obtained that software from Data General's customers and former employees who were bound by confidentiality agreements to refrain from disclosing the software. In defense, Grumman argued that the Copyright Act preempted Data General's trade secret claim. The First Circuit held that the Copyright Act did not preempt the state law trade secret claim. Beyond mere copying, that state law claim required proof of a trade secret and breach of a duty of confidentiality. These additional elements of proof, according to the First Circuit, made the trade secret claim qualitatively different from a copyright claim. In contrast, the First Circuit noted that claims might be preempted whose extra elements are illusory, being "mere label[s] attached to the same odious business conduct." For example, the First Circuit observed that "a state law misappropriation claim will not escape preemption . . . simply because a plaintiff must prove that copying was not only unauthorized but also commercially immoral."

The First Circuit has not addressed expressly whether the Copyright Act preempts a state law contract claim that restrains copying. This court perceives, however, that *Data General's* rationale would lead to a judgment that the Copyright Act does not preempt the state contract action in this case. Indeed, most courts to examine this issue have found that the Copyright Act does not preempt contractual constraints on copyrighted articles.

In *ProCD*, for example, the court found that the mutual assent and consideration required by a contract claim render that claim qualitatively different from copyright infringement. Consistent with *Data General's* reliance on a contract element, the court in *ProCD* reasoned: "A copyright is a right against the world. Contracts, by contrast, generally affect only their parties; strangers may do as they please, so contracts do not create "exclusive rights." Indeed, the Supreme Court recently noted "[i]t goes without saying that a contract cannot bind a nonparty." This court believes that the First Circuit would follow the reasoning of *ProCD* and the majority of other courts to consider this issue. This court, therefore, holds that the Copyright Act does not preempt Mr. Bowers' contract claims.

In making this determination, this court has left untouched the conclusions reached in *Atari Games v. Nintendo* regarding reverse engineering as a statutory fair use exception to copyright infringement. In *Atari*, this court stated that, with respect to 17 U.S.C. § 107 (fair use section of the Copyright Act), "[t]he legislative history of section 107 suggests that courts should adapt the fair use exception to accommodate new technological innovations." This court noted "[a] prohibition on all copying whatsoever would stifle the free flow of ideas without serving any legitimate interest of the copyright holder." Therefore, this court held "reverse engineering object code to discern the un-protectable ideas in a computer program is a fair use." Application of the First Circuit's view distinguishing a state law contract claim having additional elements of proof from a copyright claim does not alter the findings of *Atari*. Likewise, this claim distinction does not conflict with the expressly defined circumstances in which reverse engineering is not copyright infringement under 17 U.S.C. § 1201(f) (section of the Digital Millennium Copyright Act) and 17 U.S.C. § 906 (section directed to mask works).

Moreover, while the Fifth Circuit has held a state law prohibiting all copying of a computer program is preempted by the federal Copyright Act, *Vault Corp. v. Quaid Software, Ltd.*, no evidence suggests the First Circuit would extend this concept to include private contractual agreements supported by mutual assent and consideration. The First Circuit recognizes contractual waiver of affirmative defenses and statutory rights. Thus, case law indicates the First Circuit would find that private parties are free to contractually forego the limited ability to reverse engineer a software product under the exemptions of the Copyright Act. Of course, a party bound by such a contract may elect to efficiently breach the agreement in order to ascertain ideas in a computer program unprotected by copyright law. Under such circumstances, the breaching party must weigh the benefits of breach against the arguably de minimus damages arising from merely discerning non-protected code.

This court now considers the scope of Mr. Bowers' contract protection. Without objection to the choice of law, the district court applied Massachusetts contract law. Accordingly, contract terms receive "the sense and meaning of the words which the parties have used; and if clear and free from ambiguity the words are to be taken and understood in their natural, usual and ordinary sense."

In this case, the contract unambiguously prohibits "reverse engineering." That term means ordinarily "to study or analyze (a device, as a microchip for computers) in order to learn details of design, construction, and operation, perhaps to produce a copy or an improved version." Thus, the contract in this case broadly prohibits any "reverse engineering" of the subject matter covered by the shrink-wrap agreement.

The record amply supports the jury's finding of a breach of that agreement. As discussed above, the district court erred in instructing the jury that copyright law limited the scope of Mr. Bowers' contract protection. Notwithstanding that error, this court may affirm the jury's breach of contract verdict if substantial record evidence would permit a reasonable jury to find in favor of Mr. Bowers based on a correct understanding of the law. The shrink-wrap agreements in this case are far broader than the protection afforded by copyright law. Even setting aside copyright violations, the record supports a finding of breach of the agreement between the parties. In view of the breadth of Mr. Bowers' contracts, this court perceives that substantial evidence supports the jury's breach of contract verdict relating to both the DOS and Windows versions of Draft-Pak.

The record indicates, for example, that Baystate scheduled two weeks in Draft-Pak's development schedule to analyze the Designer's Toolkit. Indeed, Robert Bean, Baystate's president and CEO, testified that Baystate generally analyzed competitor's products to duplicate their functionality.

The record also contains evidence of extensive and unusual similarities between Geodraft and the accused Draft-Pak — further evidence of reverse engineering. James Spencer, head of mechanical engineering and integration at the Space and Naval Warfare Systems Center, testified that he examined the relevant software programs to determine "the overall structure of the operating program" such as "how the operating programs actually executed the task of walking a user through creating a [GD&T] symbol." Mr. Spencer concluded: "In the process of taking the

[ANSI Y14.5M] standard and breaking it down into its component parts to actually create a step-by-step process for a user using the software, both Geodraft and Draft-Pak [for DOS] use almost the identical process of breaking down that task into its individual pieces, and it's organized essentially identically." This evidence supports the jury's verdict of a contract breach based on reverse engineering.

Mr. Ford also testified that he had compared Geodraft and Draft-Pak. When asked to describe the Draft-Pak interface, Mr. Ford responded: "It looked like I was looking at my own program [i.e., Geodraft]." Both Mr. Spencer and Mr. Ford explained in detail similarities between Geodraft and the accused Draft-Pak. Those similarities included the interrelationships between program screens, the manner in which parameter selection causes program branching, and the manner in which the GD&T symbols are drawn.

Both witnesses also testified that those similarities extended beyond structure and design to include many idiosyncratic design choices and inadvertent design flaws. For example, both Geodraft and Draft-Pak offer "straightness tolerance" menu choices of "flat" and "cylindric," unusual in view of the use by ANSI Y14.5M of the terms "linear" and "circular," respectively. As another example, neither program requires the user to provide "angularity tolerance" secondary datum to create a feature control frame — a technical oversight that causes creation of an incomplete symbol. In sum, Mr. Spencer testified: "Based on my summary analysis of how the programs function, their errors from the standard and their similar nomenclatures reflecting nonstandard items, I would say that the Draft-Pak [for DOS] is a derivative copy of a Geodraft product."

Mr. Ford and others also demonstrated to the jury the operation of Geodraft and both the DOS and Windows versions of the accused Draft-Pak. Those software demonstrations undoubtedly conveyed information to the jury that the paper record on appeal cannot easily replicate. This court, therefore, is especially reluctant to substitute its judgment for that of the jury on the sufficiency and interpretation of that evidence. In any event, the record fully supports the jury's verdict that Baystate breached its contract with Mr. Bowers.

Baystate does not contest the contract damages amount on appeal. Thus, this court sustains the district court's award of contract damages. Mr. Bowers, however, argues that the district court abused its discretion by dropping copyright damages from the combined damage award. To the contrary, this court perceives no abuse of discretion.

The shrink-wrap license agreement prohibited, *inter alia*, all reverse engineering of Mr. Bowers' software, protection encompassing but more extensive than copyright protection, which prohibits only certain copying. Mr. Bowers' copyright and contract claims both rest on Baystate's copying of Mr. Bowers' software. Following the district court's instructions, the jury considered and awarded damages on each separately. This was entirely appropriate. The law is clear that the jury may award separate damages for each claim, "leaving it to the judge to make appropriate adjustments to avoid double recovery." In this case, the breach of contract damages arose from the same copying and included the same lost sales that form the basis for the copyright damages. The district court, therefore, did not abuse its discretion by omitting from the final damage award the duplicative copyright damages. Because this court affirms the district court's omission of the copyright damages, this court need not reach the merits of Mr. Bowers' copyright infringement claim.

QUESTIONS

1. Are you persuaded by the court's distinction between the instant case and *Atari* and *Vault*?

2. Will a licensor's breach of contract claim always be duplicative of an intellectual property infringement claim?

3. What was the "extra element" in Bowers' state law claim that distinguished the claim from a claim of unauthorized copying of software under the Copyright Act?

4. Is there a way in which a software programmer can reduce the burden of proving copyright infringement?

CASE NOTES

1. Meridian is a software company that provides software (Prolog Manager) for the management of large construction projects. Hardin is a construction company which, for many years, purchased licenses to use various versions of Prolog Manager. When a customer submits an order, Meridian sends the customer a standard form box containing a CD with the Prolog Manager software. The box also contains Meridian's End User License Agreement (EULA) which imposes restrictions relating to the use of Prolog Manager. Customers are given the right to return the software if they do not agree to the terms of the EULA. In 2000, Hardin began discussions with Computer Methods to use a new project management software program. Hardin wanted the new project management software to have the same functionality as Prolog Manager, so it requested one of its employees to prepare drafts of desired software specifications to be included in the Hardin-Computer Methods contract. Hardin's chief information officer sent these specifications to Computer Methods as email attachments. Meridian claimed that the email attachments contained over thirty pages of detailed descriptions copied from the Prolog Manager help files. Meridian filed suit against Hardin claiming breach of contract and copyright infringement. Hardin claimed that the EULA was unenforceable under California contract law because Hardin paid for the software prior to receiving it, and that the EULA was unconscionable because Hardin did not see the EULA before purchasing the software and opening the package. Hardin also claimed that Meridian's breach of contract action was preempted by the Copyright Act. What result? *See* Meridian Project Systems, Inc. v. Hardin Construction Company, LLC, 426 F. Supp. 2d 1101 (E.D. Cal. 2006).

2. *See also* Salco Distribs. LLC v. Icode, Inc., 2006 U.S. Dist. LEXIS 9483 (M.D. Fla. 2006) (Purchase order which stated that "This document is bound by and subject to the conditions of the Software End User License and Service Agreements" incorporated the terms of the Software End User License and Service Agreements, including choice of law provision, even though End User License and

Service Agreements were not provided to the purchaser until the software CD was received); Davidson & Associates v. Jung, 422 F.3d 630 (8th Cir. 2005) (Private parties are free to forego the ability to reverse engineer software, to waive the right to assert a fair use defense and to restrict the right to engage in other acts that are permitted by copyright law); Madison River Management Company v. Business Management Software Corporation, 351 F. Supp. 2d 436 (M.D.N.C. 2005) (Breach of contract claim preempted by Copyright Act where there is no extra element in the breach of contract claim that makes it "qualitatively different" from a copyright infringement claim); Vault Corporation v. Quaid Software Limited, 847 F. 2d 255 (5th Cir. 1988) (Louisiana License Act which permits software producer to prohibit copying, modifying or adapting software in any way for any purpose conflicts with the rights of computer program owners under Section 117 of the Copyright Act and is, therefore, preempted by federal law and unenforceable); SAS Institute, Inc. v. S & H Computer Systems, Inc., 605 F. Supp. 816 (M.D. Tenn. 1985) (Licensee's use of copyrighted statistical analysis software on an unauthorized computer, making many copies of the software for unauthorized purposes, and continued use of software after lawful termination of the license agreement constituted copyright infringement).

Additional Information

1. RAYMOND T. NIMMER, LAW OF COMPUTER TECHNOLOGY § 1:118 (2010).

2. RAYMOND T. NIMMER & JEFF DODD, MODERN LICENSING LAW §§ 9:31, 13:2, 17:22 (2010).

3. MELVIN F. JAGER, LICENSING LAW HANDBOOK § 9:1 (2010).

4. 2 MELVIN F. JAGER, TRADE SECRETS LAW § 15:11 (2010).

5. BRUCE P. KELLER, JEFFREY P. CUNARD, COPYRIGHT LAW § 2:13 (2009).

6. Lateef Mtima, *Protecting and Licensing Software: Copyright and Common Law Contract Considerations*, SM049 ALI-ABA 81 (2006).

7. Kathleen K. Olson, *Preserving the Copyright Balance: Statutory and Constitutional Preemption of Contract-Based Claims*, 11 COMM. L. & POL'Y 83 (2006).

8. David N. Pruitt, *Beyond Fair Use: The Right to Contract Around Copyright Protection of Reverse Engineering in the Software Industry*, 6 CHI.-KENT J. INTELL. PROP. 66 (2006).

9. David R. Rice, *Copyright and Contract: Preemption After Bowers v. Baystate*, 9 ROGER WILLIAMS U. L. REV. 595 (2004).

10. Jeffrey A. Andrews, *Reversing Copyright Misuse: Enforcing Contractual Prohibitions on Software Reverse Engineering*, 41 HOUS. L. REV. 975 (2004).

11. Deanna L. Kwong, *The Copyright-Contract Intersection: Softman Products v. Adobe Systems, Inc. & Bowers v. Baystate Technologies, Inc.*, 18 BERKELEY TECH. L. J. 349 (2003).

12. Nathan Smith, *The Shrinkwrap SNAFU: Untangling the "Extra Element" in Breach of Contract Claims Based on Shrinkwrap Licenses*, 2003 BYU L. Rev. 1373 (2003).

13. Maureen A. O'Rourke, *Copyright Preemption After the ProCD Case: A Market-Based Approach*, 12 Berkeley Tech. L.J. 53 (1997).

14. David A. Einhorn, *Shrink-Wrap Licenses: The Debate Continues*, 38 IDEA 383 (1998).

15. D.C. Toedt, *Shrink-Wrap Enforceability Issues*, 453 PLI/Pat 613 (1996).

2.4.3 Click-Wrap Licenses

Unlike box-top licenses and shrink-wrap licenses, which involve a manual, physical act in the formation of the contract, click-wrap licenses are formed electronically, most often during the installation of software from either a CD ROM or an Internet website. Click-wrap licenses can increase the efficiency of software transactions for both the software publisher and software consumer. For publishers, click-wrap licenses allow for low-cost widespread distribution and sale of software; and for consumers, click-wrap licenses allow for convenient and immediate access to software — all without the need of extraneous communications between the parties. However, the efficiency of click-wrap licenses often comes at the expense of the parties' full understanding of license provisions, such as forum selection, choice of law, agreements to arbitrate, terms of use and service, and limitations of liability and damages.

Courts have considered the enforceability of click-wrap licenses in many different contexts. The issues raised in these cases generally revolve around the application of the traditional contract concepts of *notice* and *assent* to the world of electronic commerce. In order to be bound by a contract, a party must have notice of the contract. In the case of click-wrap licenses, is notice that some contract exists, provided either expressly or impliedly, sufficient to satisfy the contract requirement of notice? Or must the notice be of the actual terms in the contract? Likewise, in order to be bound by a contact, a party must assent to the contract. In the case of click-wrap licenses, is the download or installation of software sufficient to satisfy the contract requirement of assent, assuming express or implied knowledge that some contract exists? Or must assent be evidenced by clicking an "I agree" button?

The *Specht* case below, decided by now Justice Sotomayor, deals with the relatively unusual case of a publisher providing free software. As you read the case, consider how the fact that the software was offered for free affected Justice Sotomayor's analysis of the notice and assent requirements.

SPECHT v. NETSCAPE COMMUNICATIONS CORP.
306 F.3d 17 (2nd Cir. 2002)

SOTOMAYOR, CIRCUIT JUDGE.

This is an appeal from a judgment of the Southern District of New York denying a motion by defendants-appellants Netscape Communications Corporation and its corporate parent, America Online, Inc. (collectively, "defendants" or "Netscape"), to compel arbitration and to stay court proceedings. In order to resolve the central question of arbitrability presented here, we must address issues of contract formation in cyberspace. Principally, we are asked to determine whether plaintiffs-appellees ("plaintiffs"), by acting upon defendants' invitation to download free software made available on defendants' webpage, agreed to be bound by the software's license terms (which included the arbitration clause at issue), even though plaintiffs could not have learned of the existence of those terms unless, prior to executing the download, they had scrolled down the webpage to a screen located below the download button. We agree with the district court that a reasonably prudent Internet user in circumstances such as these would not have known or learned of the existence of the license terms before responding to defendants' invitation to download the free software, and that defendants therefore did not provide reasonable notice of the license terms. In consequence, plaintiffs' bare act of downloading the software did not unambiguously manifest assent to the arbitration provision contained in the license terms.

We also agree with the district court that plaintiffs' claims relating to the software at issue — a "plug-in" program entitled SmartDownload ("SmartDownload" or "the plug-in program"), offered by Netscape to enhance the functioning of the separate browser program called Netscape Communicator ("Communicator" or "the browser program") — are not subject to an arbitration agreement contained in the license terms governing the use of Communicator. Finally, we conclude that the district court properly rejected defendants' argument that plaintiff website owner Christopher Specht, though not a party to any Netscape license agreement, is nevertheless required to arbitrate his claims concerning SmartDownload because he allegedly benefited directly under SmartDownload's license agreement. Defendants' theory that Specht benefited whenever visitors employing SmartDownload downloaded certain files made available on his website is simply too tenuous and speculative to justify application of the legal doctrine that requires a nonparty to an arbitration agreement to arbitrate if he or she has received a direct benefit under a contract containing the arbitration agreement.

We therefore affirm the district court's denial of defendants' motion to compel arbitration and to stay court proceedings.

BACKGROUND

I. Facts

In three related putative class actions, plaintiffs alleged that, unknown to them, their use of SmartDownload transmitted to defendants private information about plaintiffs' downloading of files from the Internet, thereby effecting an electronic surveillance of their online activities in violation of two federal statutes, the Electronic Communications Privacy Act, 18 U.S.C. §§ 2510 *et seq.*, and the Computer Fraud and Abuse Act, 18 U.S.C. § 1030.

Specifically, plaintiffs alleged that when they first used Netscape's Communicator — a software program that permits Internet browsing — the program created and stored on each of their computer hard drives a small text file known as a "cookie" that functioned "as a kind of electronic identification tag for future communications" between their computers and Netscape. Plaintiffs further alleged that when they installed SmartDownload — a separate software "plug-in" that served to enhance Communicator's browsing capabilities — SmartDownload created and stored on their computer hard drives another string of characters, known as a "Key," which similarly functioned as an identification tag in future communications with Netscape. According to the complaints in this case, each time a computer user employed Communicator to download a file from the Internet, SmartDownload "assume[d] from Communicator the task of downloading" the file and transmitted to Netscape the address of the file being downloaded together with the cookie created by Communicator and the Key created by SmartDownload. These processes, plaintiffs claim, constituted unlawful "eavesdropping" on users of Netscape's software products as well as on Internet websites from which users employing SmartDownload downloaded files.

In the time period relevant to this litigation, Netscape offered on its website various software programs, including Communicator and SmartDownload, which visitors to the site were invited to obtain free of charge. It is undisputed that five of the six named plaintiffs — Michael Fagan, John Gibson, Mark Gruber, Sean Kelly, and Sherry Weindorf — downloaded Communicator from the Netscape website. These plaintiffs acknowledge that when they proceeded to initiate installation of Communicator, they were automatically shown a scrollable text of that program's license agreement and were not permitted to complete the installation until they had clicked on a "Yes" button to indicate that they accepted all the license terms. If a user attempted to install Communicator without clicking "Yes," the installation would be aborted. All five named user plaintiffs expressly agreed to Communicator's license terms by clicking "Yes." The Communicator license agreement that these plaintiffs saw made no mention of SmartDownload or other plug-in programs, and stated that "[t]hese terms apply to Netscape Communicator and Netscape Navigator" and that "all disputes relating to this Agreement (excepting any dispute relating to intellectual property rights)" are subject to "binding arbitration in Santa Clara County, California."

Although Communicator could be obtained independently of SmartDownload, all the named user plaintiffs, except Fagan, downloaded and installed Communicator in connection with downloading SmartDownload. Each of these plaintiffs allegedly arrived at a Netscape webpage captioned "SmartDownload Communicator" that urged them to "Download With Confidence Using SmartDownload!" At or near the bottom of the screen facing plaintiffs was the prompt "Start Download" and a tinted button labeled "Download." By clicking on the button, plaintiffs initiated the download of SmartDownload. Once that process was complete, SmartDownload, as its first plug-in task, permitted plaintiffs to proceed with downloading and installing Communicator, an operation that was accompanied by the clickwrap display of Communicator's license terms described above.

The signal difference between downloading Communicator and downloading SmartDownload was that no clickwrap presentation accompanied the latter operation. Instead, once plaintiffs Gibson, Gruber, Kelly, and Weindorf had clicked on the "Download" button located at or near the bottom of their screen, and the downloading of SmartDownload was complete, these plaintiffs encountered no further information about the plug-in program or the existence of license terms governing its use. The sole reference to SmartDownload's license terms on the "SmartDownload Communicator" webpage was located in text that would have become visible to plaintiffs only if they had scrolled down to the next screen.

Had plaintiffs scrolled down instead of acting on defendants' invitation to click on the "Download" button, they would have encountered the following invitation: "Please review and agree to the terms of the *Netscape SmartDownload software license agreement* before downloading and using the software." Plaintiffs Gibson, Gruber, Kelly, and Weindorf averred in their affidavits that they never saw this reference to the SmartDownload license agreement when they clicked on the "Download" button. They also testified during depositions that they saw no reference to license terms when they clicked to download SmartDownload, although under questioning by defendants' counsel, some plaintiffs added that they could not "remember" or be "sure" whether the screen shots of the SmartDownload page attached to their affidavits reflected precisely what they had seen on their computer screens when they downloaded SmartDownload.

In sum, plaintiffs Gibson, Gruber, Kelly, and Weindorf allege that the process of obtaining SmartDownload contrasted sharply with that of obtaining Communicator. Having selected SmartDownload, they were required neither to express unambiguous assent to that program's license agreement nor even to view the license terms or become aware of their existence before proceeding with the invited download of the free plug-in program. Moreover, once these plaintiffs had initiated the download, the existence of SmartDownload's license terms was not mentioned while the software was running or at any later point in plaintiffs' experience of the product.

Even for a user who, unlike plaintiffs, did happen to scroll down past the download button, SmartDownload's license terms would not have been immediately displayed in the manner of Communicator's clickwrapped terms. Instead, if such a user had seen the notice of SmartDownload's terms and then clicked on the underlined invitation to review and agree to the terms, a hypertext link would have taken the user to a separate webpage entitled "License & Support Agreements." The first paragraph on this page read, in pertinent part:

The use of each Netscape software product is governed by a license agreement. You must read and agree to the license agreement terms BEFORE acquiring a product. Please click on the appropriate link below to review the current license agreement for the product of interest to you before acquisition. For products available for download, you must read and agree to the license agreement terms BEFORE you install the software. If you do not agree to the license terms, do not download, install or use the software.

Below this paragraph appeared a list of license agreements, the first of which was "*License Agreement for Netscape Navigator and Netscape Communicator Product Family* (Netscape Navigator, Netscape Communicator and Netscape SmartDownload)." If the user clicked on that link, he or she would be taken to yet another webpage that contained the full text of a license agreement that was identical in every respect to the Communicator license agreement except that it stated that its "terms apply to Netscape Communicator, Netscape Navigator, and Netscape SmartDownload." The license agreement granted the user a nonexclusive license to use and reproduce the software, subject to certain terms:

> BY CLICKING THE ACCEPTANCE BUTTON OR INSTALLING OR USING NETSCAPE COMMUNICATOR, NETSCAPE NAVIGATOR, OR NETSCAPE SMARTDOWNLOAD SOFTWARE (THE "PRODUCT"), THE INDIVIDUAL OR ENTITY LICENSING THE PRODUCT ("LICENSEE") IS CONSENTING TO BE BOUND BY AND IS BECOMING A PARTY TO THIS AGREEMENT. IF LICENSEE DOES NOT AGREE TO ALL OF THE TERMS OF THIS AGREE-MENT, THE BUTTON INDICATING NON-ACCEPTANCE MUST BE SELECTED, AND LICENSEE MUST NOT INSTALL OR USE THE SOFTWARE.

Among the license terms was a provision requiring virtually all disputes relating to the agreement to be submitted to arbitration:

> Unless otherwise agreed in writing, all disputes relating to this Agreement (excepting any dispute relating to intellectual property rights) shall be subject to final and binding arbitration in Santa Clara County, California, under the auspices of JAMS/EndDispute, with the losing party paying all costs of arbitration.

Unlike the four named user plaintiffs who downloaded SmartDownload from the Netscape website, the fifth named plaintiff, Michael Fagan, claims to have downloaded the plug-in program from a "shareware" website operated by ZDNet, an entity unrelated to Netscape. Shareware sites are websites, maintained by companies or individuals, that contain libraries of free, publicly available software. The pages that a user would have seen while downloading SmartDownload from ZDNet differed from those that he or she would have encountered while download-ing SmartDownload from the Netscape website. Notably, instead of any kind of notice of the SmartDownload license agreement, the ZDNet pages offered only a hypertext link to "more information" about SmartDownload, which, if clicked on, took the user to a Netscape webpage that, in turn, contained a link to the license agreement. Thus, a visitor to the ZDNet website could have obtained SmartDownload, as Fagan avers he did, without ever seeing a reference to that program's license terms, even if he or she had scrolled through all of ZDNet's webpages.

The sixth named plaintiff, Christopher Specht, never obtained or used Smart-Download, but instead operated a website from which visitors could download certain electronic files that permitted them to create an account with an internet service provider called WhyWeb. Specht alleges that every time a user who had previously installed SmartDownload visited his website and downloaded WhyWeb-related files, defendants intercepted this information. Defendants allege that Specht would receive a representative's commission from WhyWeb every time a user who obtained a WhyWeb file from his website subsequently subscribed to the WhyWeb service. Thus, argue defendants, because the "Netscape license agreement . . . conferred on each user the right to download and use both Communicator and SmartDownload software," Specht received a benefit under that license agreement in that SmartDownload "assisted in obtaining the WhyWeb file and increased the likelihood of success in the download process." This benefit, defendants claim, was direct enough to require Specht to arbitrate his claims pursuant to Netscape's license terms. Specht, however, maintains that he never received any commissions based on the WhyWeb files available on his website.

DISCUSSION

****

III

Whether the User Plaintiffs Had Reasonable Notice of and Manifested Assent to the SmartDownload License Agreement

Whether governed by the common law or by Article 2 of the Uniform Commercial Code ("UCC"), a transaction, in order to be a contract, requires a manifestation of agreement between the parties. Mutual manifestation of assent, whether by written or spoken word or by conduct, is the touchstone of contract. Although an onlooker observing the disputed transactions in this case would have seen each of the user plaintiffs click on the SmartDownload "Download" button, a consumer's clicking on a download button does not communicate assent to contractual terms if the offer did not make clear to the consumer that clicking on the download button would signify assent to those terms. California's common law is clear that "an offeree, regardless of apparent manifestation of his consent, is not bound by inconspicuous contractual provisions of which he is unaware, contained in a document whose contractual nature is not obvious."

Arbitration agreements are no exception to the requirement of manifestation of assent. "This principle of knowing consent applies with particular force to provisions for arbitration." Clarity and conspicuousness of arbitration terms are important in securing informed assent. "If a party wishes to bind in writing another to an agreement to arbitrate future disputes, such purpose should be accomplished in a way that each party to the arrangement will fully and clearly comprehend that the agreement to arbitrate exists and binds the parties thereto." Thus, California contract law measures assent by an objective standard that takes into account both what the offeree said, wrote, or did and the transactional context in which the offeree verbalized or acted.

A. The Reasonably Prudent Offeree of Downloadable Software

Defendants argue that plaintiffs must be held to a standard of reasonable prudence and that, because notice of the existence of SmartDownload license terms was on the next scrollable screen, plaintiffs were on "inquiry notice" of those terms. We disagree with the proposition that a reasonably prudent offeree in plaintiffs' position would necessarily have known or learned of the existence of the Smart-Download license agreement prior to acting, so that plaintiffs may be held to have assented to that agreement with constructive notice of its terms. It is true that "[a] party cannot avoid the terms of a contract on the ground that he or she failed to read it before signing." But courts are quick to add: "An exception to this general rule exists when the writing does not appear to be a contract and the terms are not called to the attention of the recipient. In such a case, no contract is formed with respect to the undisclosed term."

Most of the cases cited by defendants in support of their inquiry-notice argument are drawn from the world of paper contracting . . . . [R]eceipt of a physical document containing contract terms or notice thereof is frequently deemed, in the world of paper transactions, a sufficient circumstance to place the offeree on inquiry notice of those terms. "Every person who has actual notice of circumstances sufficient to put a prudent man upon inquiry as to a particular fact, has constructive notice of the fact itself in all cases in which, by prosecuting such inquiry, he might have learned such fact." These principles apply equally to the emergent world of online product delivery, pop-up screens, hyperlinked pages, clickwrap licensing, scrollable documents, and urgent admonitions to "Download Now!." What plaintiffs saw when they were being invited by defendants to download this fast, free plug-in called SmartDownload was a screen containing praise for the product and, at the very bottom of the screen, a "Download" button. Defendants argue that under the principles set forth in the cases cited above, a "fair and prudent person using ordinary care" would have been on inquiry notice of SmartDownload's license terms.

We are not persuaded that a reasonably prudent offeree in these circumstances would have known of the existence of license terms. Plaintiffs were responding to an offer that did not carry an immediately visible notice of the existence of license terms or require unambiguous manifestation of assent to those terms. Thus, plaintiffs' "apparent manifestation of . . . consent" was to terms "contained in a document whose contractual nature [was] not obvious." Moreover, the fact that, given the position of the scroll bar on their computer screens, plaintiffs may have been aware that an unexplored portion of the Netscape webpage remained below the download button does not mean that they reasonably should have concluded that this portion contained a notice of license terms. In their deposition testimony, plaintiffs variously stated that they used the scroll bar "[o]nly if there is something that I feel I need to see that is on — that is off the page," or that the elevated position of the scroll bar suggested the presence of "mere[ ] formalities, standard lower banner links" or "that the page is bigger than what I can see." Plaintiffs testified, and defendants did not refute, that plaintiffs were in fact unaware that defendants intended to attach license terms to the use of SmartDownload.

We conclude that in circumstances such as these, where consumers are urged to download free software at the immediate click of a button, a reference to the existence of license terms on a submerged screen is not sufficient to place consumers on inquiry or constructive notice of those terms. The SmartDownload webpage screen was "printed in such a manner that it tended to conceal the fact that it was an express acceptance of [Netscape's] rules and regulations." Internet users may have, as defendants put it, "as much time as they need[ ]" to scroll through multiple screens on a webpage, but there is no reason to assume that viewers will scroll down to subsequent screens simply because screens are there. When products are "free" and users are invited to download them in the absence of reasonably conspicuous notice that they are about to bind themselves to contract terms, the transactional circumstances cannot be fully analogized to those in the paper world of arm's-length bargaining.

B. Shrinkwrap Licensing and Related Practices

Defendants cite certain well-known cases involving shrinkwrap licensing and related commercial practices in support of their contention that plaintiffs became bound by the SmartDownload license terms by virtue of inquiry notice. For example, in *Hill v. Gateway 2000, Inc.* the Seventh Circuit held that where a purchaser had ordered a computer over the telephone, received the order in a shipped box containing the computer along with printed contract terms, and did not return the computer within the thirty days required by the terms, the purchaser was bound by the contract. In *ProCD, Inc. v. Zeidenberg*, the same court held that where an individual purchased software in a box containing license terms which were displayed on the computer screen every time the user executed the software program, the user had sufficient opportunity to review the terms and to return the software, and so was contractually bound after retaining the product.

These cases do not help defendants. To the extent that they hold that the purchaser of a computer or tangible software is contractually bound after failing to object to printed license terms provided with the product, *Hill* and *Brower* do not differ markedly from the cases involving traditional paper contracting discussed in the previous section. Insofar as the purchaser in *ProCD* was confronted with conspicuous, mandatory license terms every time he ran the software on his computer, that case actually undermines defendants' contention that downloading in the absence of conspicuous terms is an act that binds plaintiffs to those terms. In *Mortenson*, the full text of license terms was printed on each sealed diskette envelope inside the software box, printed again on the inside cover of the user manual, and notice of the terms appeared on the computer screen every time the purchaser executed the program. In sum, the foregoing cases are clearly distinguishable from the facts of the present action.

After reviewing the California common law and other relevant legal authority, we conclude that under the circumstances here, plaintiffs' downloading of SmartDownload did not constitute acceptance of defendants' license terms. Reasonably

conspicuous notice of the existence of contract terms and unambiguous manifestation of assent to those terms by consumers are essential if electronic bargaining is
to have integrity and credibility. We hold that a reasonably prudent offeree in
plaintiffs' position would not have known or learned, prior to acting on the invitation
to download, of the reference to SmartDownload's license terms hidden below the
"Download" button on the next screen. We affirm the district court's conclusion that
the user plaintiffs, including Fagan, are not bound by the arbitration clause
contained in those terms.

CONCLUSION

For the foregoing reasons, we affirm the district court's denial of defendants'
motion to compel arbitration and to stay court proceedings.

QUESTIONS

1.   How can you most securely bind a user who is downloading software from
either a webpage or CD ROM to a license agreement?

2.   If a CD ROM has a license agreement that appears when the CD ROM is
initially run which requires the user to click an "I agree" button before proceeding
to open the software program, must this license and "I agree" button appear every
time the software is opened? What if users could open the software without clicking
the "I agree" button? What if multiple users were using the same computer
terminal and could open the software without seeing the initial license?

3.   This case began in 2000, relatively early in the Internet Age. Today, should
an average Internet user be held to a higher standard of inquiry notice that all
software downloads are accompanied by a license agreement? Does the fact that the
software in *Specht* was provided for free have any bearing on the standard of
inquiry notice?

CASE NOTES

1.   Adobe sold its software package "Adobe Collections" (Collections) to distributors, who then resold the software package to distributors in the secondary
market, who then resold the software package to consumers. SoftMan is a software
distributor who distributes software programs, including Collections, through its
website. Collections contains an End User License Agreement (EULA) which
prohibits users from unbundling the software and selling individual software
programs included in the Collections package. The EULA is recorded on the CD
ROM containing the Collections software package and users are required to agree
to the terms of the EULA by clicking an "I agree" button prior to installing the
software. SoftMan admitted to unbundling the Collections package and selling
individual pieces of the software. Adobe sued SoftMan for copyright infringement
arguing that SoftMan's unbundling and sale of the Collections package violated the
terms of the EULA. SoftMan argued that it was not bound by the terms of the
EULA because the EULA was not provided in print with the Collections software

disk. What result? *See* Softman Products Co. v. Adobe Systems Inc., 171 F.Supp.2d 1075 (C.D. Cal. 2001).

2. iLan provides companies services to manage their computer networks. NextPoint sells software that monitors computer network traffic. In 1998, iLan and NextPoint entered into a detailed Value Added Reseller Agreement (VAR) under which iLan agreed to resell NextPoint's software to iLan's customers. In 1999, iLan purchased the unlimited right to use NextPoint's software, including perpetual upgrades and support, for $85,253. The NextPoint software contained a click-wrap license which limited NextPoint's liability to refund of the purchase price. iLan clicked "I agree" each time it installed NextPoint's software on a customer's network. The VAR agreement contained nearly identical terms as those contained in the click-wrap license. However, the purchase order that iLan sent to NextPoint contained no limitations of liability. iLan and NextPoint disagreed over the terms of their relationship and iLan filed a complaint alleging breach of contract. iLan sought specific performance of NextPoint's perpetual upgrade and support of its network monitoring software. NextPoint claimed that specific performance was not allowed under the click-wrap license agreement. iLan claimed that the terms of the click-wrap license were additional to the terms of its purchase order which could only be effective if iLan explicitly accepted the terms of the click-wrap license. What result? *See* I.Lan Sys. v. NetScout Serv. Level Corp., 183 F. Supp. 2d 328 (D. Mass. 2002).

3. *See also* Feldman v. Google, Inc., 513 F.Supp.2d 229 (E.D. Pa. 2007) (On-line AdWords agreement was a valid express contract which provided reasonable notice and mutual assent); Forest v. Verizon Communications, Inc., 805 A.2d 1007 (D.C. Cir. 2002) (Click-wrap agreement provided adequate notice where users had to click "Agree" and a warning was included at the top of the agreement in capital letters to read the agreement carefully, even though the agreement was thirteen pages long with only a small portion of the agreement visible at a time and the choice of forum clause was located in the final section of the agreement); Pollstar v. Gigmania Ltd., 170 F.Supp.2d 974 (E.D. Cal. 2000) (Reasonable notice of terms in click-wrap license was not provided when a hyperlink to the terms appeared in small gray print on a gray background); Compuserve Inc. v. Patterson, 89 F.3d 1257 (6th Cir. 1996) (Typing the word "agree" at several points in the click-wrap license manifested assent to be bound by the terms of the license); Hotmail Corp. v. Van$ Money Pie, Inc., 1998 U.S. Dist. LEXIS 10729 (N.D. Cal. 1998) (Click-wrap service agreement that prohibited sending spam, pornographic or obscene material enforceable where users registered on-line to use email services); Caspi v. The Microsoft Network, LLC., 732 A.2d 528 (N.J. Super. Ct. App. Div. 1999) (A "click" is a binding acceptance so long as the user had sufficient opportunity to review the contract); Register.com, Inc. v. Verio, Inc., 356 F.3d 393 (2nd Cir. 2004) (Requirement of unambiguous assent not necessary where user was a repeat visitor to website and received license information every time it performed a search).

Additional Information

1. 2 Raymond T. Nimmer, Information Law § 12:32 (2010).

2. Howard O. Hunter, Modern Law of Contracts § 4:32 (2010).

3. Nathan J. Davis, *Presumed Assent: The Judicial Acceptance of Clickwrap*, 22 BERKELEY TECH. L.J. 577 (2007).

4. Juliet M. Moringiello, *Signals, Assent and Internet Contracting*, 57 RUT-GERS L. REV. 1307 (2005).

5. Stephen J. Davidson, et al., *Open, Click, Download, Send . . . What Have You Agreed To? The Possibilities Seem Endless*, 2003 WL 22002079 (Georgetown CLE) (2003).

6. Jennifer Femminella, *Online Terms and Conditions Agreements: Bound by the Web*, 17 ST. JOHN'S J. LEGAL COMMENT. 87 (2003).

7. Lothar Determan, Saralyn M. Ang-Olson, *Comment on Specht v. Netscape*, 796 PLI/PAT 543 (2004).

8. James C. Hoye, Note, *Click — Do We Have A Deal?*, 6 SUFFOLK J. TRIAL & APP. ADVOC. 163 (2001).

9. Francis M. Buono, Jonathan A. Friedman, *Maximizing the Enforceability of Click Wrap Agreements*, 4 J. TECH. L. & POL'Y 3 (1999).

10. Zachary M. Harrison, *Just Click Here: Article 2B's Failure to Guarantee Adequate Manifestation of Assent in Click-Wrap Contracts*, 8 FORDHAM INTELL. PROP. MEDIA & ENT. L.J. 907 (1998).

2.4.4 Open Source Licenses

An open source license is another form of unilateral license. When a user downloads a software program subject to an open source license, the user is presumed to assent to the terms of the open source license. An open source license is granted without fees or royalties; however, an open source license does not place the software program in the public domain where it can be used without restrictions on future modification and distribution. An open source license is a true license, the breach of which can be remedied through money damages and injunctions. There are many different types of open source licenses, including the Berkeley Software Distribution license (BSD), the MIT license, the Apache 2.0 license, the Mozilla 1.1 license and the Free Software Foundation's (FSF) GNU General Public License Version 2 (GPLv2).

However, all open source licenses must comply with ten principles promulgated by the Open Source Initiative (OSI) to be an "OSI Certified" open source license. These ten principles are: (1) free distribution of the software; (2) availability of the source code; (3) permission to make derivative works; (4) maintenance of the integrity of the author's source code; (5) non-discrimination against users and groups; (6) non-discrimination against fields of use; (7) distribution of the original license with any copy or modification of the software; (8) no restriction of the software to a particular product; (9) no restrictions on other software that is distributed with the licensed software; and (10) no limitation on how the software is accessed or distributed.

There are two general theories underlying open source licenses. The first, exemplified in the FSF GPLv2 license, emphasizes political goals of "freedom" and "free speech." The second, exemplified in the BSD license, emphasizes utilitarian goals of speed, efficiency and quality in software development through collaborative efforts of multiple persons. In line with the disparate theories underlying open source licenses, the GPLv2 license and the BSD license take very different approaches to the commercialization of software developed under their respective licenses. Section 2(b) of the GPLv2 license states: "You must cause any work that you distribute or publish, that in whole or in part contains or is derived from the Program or any part thereof, to be licensed as a whole at no charge to all third parties under the terms of this License." Open source software that can only be re-licensed at no charge pursuant to the terms of the original open source license has come to be known as a "copyleft" license. The BSD license, on the other hand, imposes no restraints on the subsequent commercial distribution of the licensed software in a modified or derivative form.

Companies are increasingly integrating open source software with their own proprietary software. In part, these companies are motivated by a desire to be independent of Microsoft's dominance in the operating system and application program software markets. In part, these companies are motivated by the desire to avoid the cost of "reinventing the wheel" when open source software is readily available. Licensing open source software also allows companies to focus their software development efforts on areas in which they have unique core competencies. However, integrating open source software with proprietary software can create significant risks for customers and users of the integrated software. Open source licenses usually disclaim all warranties, limit liability and provide for no indemnification. Customers of integrated open source software, therefore, may be sued for copyright or patent infringement without any recourse against the vendor. Users of integrated open source software may also be sued for copyright or patent infringement and required to pay damages or enjoined from further use of the software.

There is also a risk that the open source software itself may infringe third-party copyrights. IBM, HP, Intel, Fujitsu, Red Hat, Novell, Sun Microsystems, General Motors and other major firms have invested billions of dollars in developing Linux, an open source operating system, as an alternative to Microsoft's server and PC proprietary operating systems. The case in this section, *SCO Group v. Novell*, is the latest development in a long-running copyright infringement challenge to the Linux operating system.

GNU GENERAL PUBLIC LICENSE, VERSION 2, JUNE 1991
Copyright (C) 1989, 1991 Free Software Foundation, Inc.

Everyone is permitted to copy and distribute verbatim copies of this license document, but changing it is not allowed.

Preamble

The licenses for most software are designed to take away your freedom to share and change it. By contrast, the GNU General Public License is intended to guarantee your freedom to share and change free software — to make sure the software is free for all its users. This General Public License applies to most of the Free Software Foundation's software and to any other program whose authors commit to using it. (Some other Free Software Foundation software is covered by the GNU Lesser General Public License instead.) You can apply it to your programs, too.

When we speak of free software, we are referring to freedom, not price. Our General Public Licenses are designed to make sure that you have the freedom to distribute copies of free software (and charge for this service if you wish), that you receive source code or can get it if you want it, that you can change the software or use pieces of it in new free programs; and that you know you can do these things.

To protect your rights, we need to make restrictions that forbid anyone to deny you these rights or to ask you to surrender the rights. These restrictions translate to certain responsibilities for you if you distribute copies of the software, or if you modify it.

For example, if you distribute copies of such a program, whether gratis or for a fee, you must give the recipients all the rights that you have. You must make sure that they, too, receive or can get the source code. And you must show them these terms so they know their rights.

We protect your rights with two steps: (1) copyright the software, and (2) offer you this license which gives you legal permission to copy, distribute and/or modify the software.

Also, for each author's protection and ours, we want to make certain that everyone understands that there is no warranty for this free software. If the software is modified by someone else and passed on, we want its recipients to know that what they have is not the original, so that any problems introduced by others will not reflect on the original authors' reputations.

Finally, any free program is threatened constantly by software patents. We wish to avoid the danger that redistributors of a free program will individually obtain patent licenses, in effect making the program proprietary. To prevent this, we have made it clear that any patent must be licensed for everyone's free use or not licensed at all.

The precise terms and conditions for copying, distribution and modification follow.

GNU GENERAL PUBLIC LICENSE TERMS AND CONDITIONS FOR COPYING, DISTRIBUTION AND MODIFICATION

0. This License applies to any program or other work which contains a notice placed by the copyright holder saying it may be distributed under the terms of this General Public License. The "Program," below, refers to any such program or work, and a "work based on the Program" means either the Program or any derivative work under copyright law: that is to say, a work containing the Program or a portion of it, either verbatim or with modifications and/or translated into another language. (Hereinafter, translation is included without limitation in the term "modification.") Each licensee is addressed as "you."

Activities other than copying, distribution and modification are not covered by this License; they are outside its scope. The act of running the Program is not restricted, and the output from the Program is covered only if its contents constitute a work based on the Program (independent of having been made by running the Program). Whether that is true depends on what the Program does.

1. You may copy and distribute verbatim copies of the Program's source code as you receive it, in any medium, provided that you conspicuously and appropriately publish on each copy an appropriate copyright notice and disclaimer of warranty; keep intact all the notices that refer to this License and to the absence of any warranty; and give any other recipients of the Program a copy of this License along with the Program.

You may charge a fee for the physical act of transferring a copy, and you may at your option offer warranty protection in exchange for a fee.

2. You may modify your copy or copies of the Program or any portion of it, thus forming a work based on the Program, and copy and distribute such modifications or work under the terms of Section 1 above, provided that you also meet all of these conditions:

a) You must cause the modified files to carry prominent notices stating that you changed the files and the date of any change.

b) You must cause any work that you distribute or publish, that in whole or in part contains or is derived from the Program or any part thereof, to be licensed as a whole at no charge to all third parties under the terms of this License.

c) If the modified program normally reads commands interactively when run, you must cause it, when started running for such interactive use in the most ordinary way, to print or display an announcement including an appropriate copyright notice and a notice that there is no warranty (or else, saying that you provide a warranty) and that users may redistribute the program under these conditions, and telling the user how to view a copy of this License. (Exception: if the Program itself is interactive but does not normally print such an announcement, your work based on the Program is not required to print an announcement.)

These requirements apply to the modified work as a whole. If identifiable sections of that work are not derived from the Program, and can be reasonably considered independent and separate works in themselves, then this License, and its terms, do not apply to those sections when you distribute them as separate works. But when you distribute the same sections as part of a whole which is a work based on the Program, the distribution of the whole must be on the terms of this License, whose permissions for other licensees extend to the entire whole, and thus to each and every part regardless of who wrote it.

Thus, it is not the intent of this section to claim rights or contest your rights to work written entirely by you; rather, the intent is to exercise the right to control the distribution of derivative or collective works based on the Program.

In addition, mere aggregation of another work not based on the Program with the Program (or with a work based on the Program) on a volume of a storage or distribution medium does not bring the other work under the scope of this License.

3. You may copy and distribute the Program (or a work based on it, under Section 2) in object code or executable form under the terms of Sections 1 and 2 above provided that you also do one of the following:

a) Accompany it with the complete corresponding machine-readable source code, which must be distributed under the terms of Sections 1 and 2 above on a medium customarily used for software interchange; or,

b) Accompany it with a written offer, valid for at least three years, to give any third party, for a charge no more than your cost of physically performing source distribution, a complete machine-readable copy of the corresponding source code, to be distributed under the terms of Sections 1 and 2 above on a medium customarily used for software interchange; or,

c) Accompany it with the information you received as to the offer to distribute corresponding source code. (This alternative is allowed only for noncommercial distribution and only if you received the program in object code or executable form with such an offer, in accord with Subsection b above.)

The source code for a work means the preferred form of the work for making modifications to it. For an executable work, complete source code means all the source code for all modules it contains, plus any associated interface definition files, plus the scripts used to control compilation and installation of the executable. However, as a special exception, the source code distributed need not include anything that is normally distributed (in either source or binary form) with the major components (compiler, kernel, and so on) of the operating system on which the executable runs, unless that component itself accompanies the executable.

If distribution of executable or object code is made by offering access to copy from a designated place, then offering equivalent access to copy the source code from the same place counts as distribution of the source code, even though third parties are not compelled to copy the source along with the object code.

4. You may not copy, modify, sublicense, or distribute the Program except as expressly provided under this License. Any attempt otherwise to copy, modify, sublicense or distribute the Program is void, and will automatically terminate your rights under this License. However, parties who have received copies, or rights, from you under this License will not have their licenses terminated so long as such parties remain in full compliance.

5. You are not required to accept this License, since you have not signed it. However, nothing else grants you permission to modify or distribute the Program or its derivative works. These actions are prohibited by law if you do not accept this License. Therefore, by modifying or distributing the Program (or any work based on the Program), you indicate your acceptance of this License to do so, and all its terms and conditions for copying, distributing or modifying the Program or works based on it.

6. Each time you redistribute the Program (or any work based on the Program), the recipient automatically receives a license from the original licensor to copy, distribute or modify the Program subject to these terms and conditions. You may

not impose any further restrictions on the recipients' exercise of the rights granted herein. You are not responsible for enforcing compliance by third parties to this License.

7. If, as a consequence of a court judgment or allegation of patent infringement or for any other reason (not limited to patent issues), conditions are imposed on you (whether by court order, agreement or otherwise) that contradict the conditions of this License, they do not excuse you from the conditions of this License. If you cannot distribute so as to satisfy simultaneously your obligations under this License and any other pertinent obligations, then as a consequence you may not distribute the Program at all. For example, if a patent license would not permit royalty-free redistribution of the Program by all those who receive copies directly or indirectly through you, then the only way you could satisfy both it and this License would be to refrain entirely from distribution of the Program.

If any portion of this section is held invalid or unenforceable under any particular circumstance, the balance of the section is intended to apply and the section as a whole is intended to apply in other circumstances.

It is not the purpose of this section to induce you to infringe any patents or other property right claims or to contest validity of any such claims; this section has the sole purpose of protecting the integrity of the free software distribution system, which is implemented by public license practices. Many people have made generous contributions to the wide range of software distributed through that system in reliance on consistent application of that system; it is up to the author/donor to decide if he or she is willing to distribute software through any other system and a licensee cannot impose that choice.

This section is intended to make thoroughly clear what is believed to be a consequence of the rest of this License.

8. If the distribution and/or use of the Program is restricted in certain countries either by patents or by copyrighted interfaces, the original copyright holder who places the Program under this License may add an explicit geographical distribution limitation excluding those countries, so that distribution is permitted only in or among countries not thus excluded. In such case, this License incorporates the limitation as if written in the body of this License.

9. The Free Software Foundation may publish revised and/or new versions of the General Public License from time to time. Such new versions will be similar in spirit to the present version, but may differ in detail to address new problems or concerns.

Each version is given a distinguishing version number. If the Program specifies a version number of this License which applies to it and "any later version," you have the option of following the terms and conditions either of that version or of any later version published by the Free Software Foundation. If the Program does not specify a version number of this License, you may choose any version ever published by the Free Software Foundation.

10. If you wish to incorporate parts of the Program into other free programs whose distribution conditions are different, write to the author to ask for

permission. For software which is copyrighted by the Free Software Foundation, write to the Free Software Foundation; we sometimes make exceptions for this. Our decision will be guided by the two goals of preserving the free status of all derivatives of our free software and of promoting the sharing and reuse of software generally.

NO WARRANTY

11. BECAUSE THE PROGRAM IS LICENSED FREE OF CHARGE, THERE IS NO WARRANTY FOR THE PROGRAM, TO THE EXTENT PERMITTED BY APPLICABLE LAW. EXCEPT WHEN OTHERWISE STATED IN WRITING THE COPYRIGHT HOLDERS AND/OR OTHER PARTIES PROVIDE THE PROGRAM "AS IS" WITHOUT WARRANTY OF ANY KIND, EITHER EXPRESSED OR IMPLIED, INCLUDING, BUT NOT LIMITED TO, THE IMPLIED WARRANTIES OF MERCHANTABILITY AND FITNESS FOR A PARTICULAR PURPOSE. THE ENTIRE RISK AS TO THE QUALITY AND PERFORMANCE OF THE PROGRAM IS WITH YOU. SHOULD THE PROGRAM PROVE DEFECTIVE, YOU ASSUME THE COST OF ALL NECESSARY SERVICING, REPAIR OR CORRECTION.

12. IN NO EVENT UNLESS REQUIRED BY APPLICABLE LAW OR AGREED TO IN WRITING WILL ANY COPYRIGHT HOLDER, OR ANY OTHER PARTY WHO MAY MODIFY AND/OR REDISTRIBUTE THE PROGRAM AS PERMITTED ABOVE, BE LIABLE TO YOU FOR DAMAGES, INCLUDING ANY GENERAL, SPECIAL, INCIDENTAL OR CONSEQUENTIAL DAMAGES ARISING OUT OF THE USE OR INABILITY TO USE THE PROGRAM (INCLUDING BUT NOT LIMITED TO LOSS OF DATA OR DATA BEING RENDERED INACCURATE OR LOSSES SUSTAINED BY YOU OR THIRD PARTIES OR A FAILURE OF THE PROGRAM TO OPERATE WITH ANY OTHER PROGRAMS), EVEN IF SUCH HOLDER OR OTHER PARTY HAS BEEN ADVISED OF THE POSSIBILITY OF SUCH DAMAGES.

QUESTIONS

1. The GPLv2 license provides that modified and derivative works must be distributed for free, but that independent works or the aggregation of another work with the open source software are not subject to distribution restrictions. Which of these scenarios would fall under the modified or derivative work category, and which under the independent or aggregation work category?

- The open source software and the proprietary software are distributed together on a CD ROM, but do not interact;

- The open source software is an operating system, and the proprietary software is an application program that runs on top of the operating system through standard interfaces;

- The open source software is a library or subroutine, kept in a separate directory, but is called by the proprietary program at runtime (dynamic linking);

- The open source software is a library or subroutine, kept in a separate directory, but is compiled with the proprietary program prior to runtime, and the resulting object code contains both the open source and proprietary software (static linking);

- The open source software is an operating system, and the proprietary software is an application that directly accesses the kernel of the operating system;

- The open source and proprietary software have been combined by a software engineer to form a single computer program.

These scenarios are discussed in Alan Stern, *Open Source Licensing*, 915 PLI/Pat 187 (2007).

2. If a licensee combines multiple open source software programs and combines them into a new, single software program by means of proprietary interfaces, can the licensee file a copyright on the new software program? Can the licensee distribute the new software program for a fee? Would it matter whether the open source license was the GPLv2 license or the BSD license?

The SCO GROUP, INC. v. NOVELL, INC.
578 F.3d 1201 (10th Cir. 2009)

[Editor's Case Note: As you will see in the case below, SCO claims to own copyrights in the Unix and UnixWare operating system source code allegedly acquired from Novell. SCO also claims that the Unix and UnixWare source code is incorporated in the open source Linux operating system used by many major companies throughout the U.S. and abroad. In pursuit of its copyright claim, SCO initiated a litigation strategy targeted initially at IBM, the most prominent user and booster of Linux. In 2007, the U.S. District for the District of Utah found that SCO did not own the copyrights in the Unix and UnixWare source code because these copyrights had never been transferred by Novell. Following its defeat in district court, SCO was forced to file for bankruptcy. However, a private equity firm came to SCO's rescue with a $100M investment conditioned on SCO aggressively continuing to pursue its copyright claims against IBM. The Court of Appeals decision, issued on September 24, 2009, gives new life to SCO's litigation against IBM — and new hope to the investors in the litigation.]

McConnell, Circuit Judge

This case primarily involves a dispute between SCO and Novell regarding the scope of intellectual property in certain UNIX and UnixWare technology and other rights retained by Novell following the sale of part of its UNIX business to Santa Cruz, a predecessor corporate entity to SCO, in the mid-1990s. Following competing motions for summary judgment, the district court issued a detailed opinion granting summary judgment to Novell on many of the key issues. We affirm the judgment of the district court in part, reverse in part, and remand for trial on the remaining issues.

I. Background

We begin by laying out some of the basic facts underlying Novell's transfer of certain UNIX-related assets to Santa Cruz, as well as the background to the instant litigation. Other facts will be discussed as the issues require.

A. The UNIX Business and the Sale to Santa Cruz

UNIX is a computer operating system originally developed in the late 1960s at AT & T. By the 1980s, AT & T had developed UNIX System V ("SVRX"); it built a substantial business by licensing UNIX source code to a number of major computer manufacturers, including IBM, Sun, and Hewlett-Packard. These manufacturers, in turn, would use the SVRX source code to develop their own individualized UNIX-derived "flavors" for use on their computer systems. Licensees could modify the source code and create derivative products mostly for internal use, but agreed to keep the UNIX source code confidential.

In 1993, Novell paid over $300 million to purchase UNIX System Laboratories, the AT & T spin-off that owned the UNIX copyrights and licenses. Only two years later, however, Novell decided to sell its UNIX business. Although Novell may have initially intended "to sell the complete UNIX business," both parties agree that Santa Cruz was either unwilling or unable to commit sufficient financial resources to purchase the entire UNIX business outright. The deal was therefore structured so that Novell would retain a 95% interest in SVRX license royalties, which had totaled $50 million in 1995.

The transfer of Unix-related rights occurred pursuant to three documents: an asset purchase agreement ("APA") executed on September 19, 1995; "Amendment No. 1" signed by the parties at the actual closing on December 6, 1995; and "Amendment No. 2" on October 16, 1996. The APA provided that:

> "Buyer will purchase and acquire from Seller on the Closing Date . . . all of Seller's right, title, and interest in and to the assets and properties of Seller relating to the Business (collectively the "Assets") identified on Schedule 1.1(a). Notwithstanding the foregoing, the Assets to be so purchased shall not include those assets (the "Excluded Assets") set forth on Schedule 1.1(b)."

Schedule 1.1(a) included within the list of "Assets" transferred, "[a]ll rights and ownership of UNIX and UnixWare." Section V of the Asset Schedule, entitled "Intellectual property" provided that Santa Cruz would obtain "[t]rademarks UNIX and UnixWare as and to the extent held by Seller" but did not explicitly mention copyrights. In contrast, Schedule 1.1(b), the list of assets excluded from the deal, did expressly speak to copyrights. Section V — "Intellectual Property" — explained that "*All copyrights* and trademarks, except for the trademarks UNIX and UnixWare," as well as "[a]ll [p]atents," were excluded from the deal. (emphasis added).

Less than a year after the deal closed, the parties agreed to Amendment No. 2, which amended the APA's treatment of copyrights. Amendment No. 2 provided that:

> With respect to Schedule 1.1(b) of the Agreement, titled "Excluded Assets," Section V, Subsection A shall be revised to read:

> All copyrights and trademarks, except for the copyrights and trademarks owned by Novell as of the date of the Agreement required for SCO to exercise its rights with respect to the acquisition of UNIX and UnixWare technologies. However, in no event shall Novell be liable to SCO for any claim brought by any third party pertaining to said copyrights and trademarks.

The APA separately purported to give Novell certain residual control over "SVRX Licenses." Section 4.16(b) of the agreement provided that:

> Buyer shall not, and shall not have the authority to, amend, modify or waive any right under or assign any SVRX License without the prior written consent of Seller. In addition, at Seller's sole discretion and direction, Buyer shall amend, supplement, modify or waive any rights under, or shall assign any rights to, any SVRX License to the extent so directed in any manner or respect by Seller.

The parties differ markedly in their characterization of the rights transferred to Santa Cruz and the value of the deal. According to SCO, Santa Cruz purchased the bulk of the business, including the core UNIX copyrights, for $250 million, but Novell retained a 95% interest in royalties as a "financing device." According to Novell, SCO's $250 million figure improperly inflates the value of the deal, by accounting not only for the value of assets actually transferred by SCO to Novell, but including the share of the SVRX royalty stream *retained* by Novell. Novell calculates that it received only about $50 million in stock, as well as a promised share of the "UnixWare" revenue stream exceeding certain targets. Novell contends that it retained ownership of the UNIX copyrights, extending only an implied license to Santa Cruz to use the copyrights, for instance, to develop and distribute an improved version of Novell's "UnixWare" product.

In support of its understanding of the transaction, SCO relies heavily on extrinsic evidence of the parties' intent at the time of the APA-including testimony from *Novell's* leadership at the time-suggesting that the parties' intent was to transfer the copyrights. For instance, Robert Frankenberg, then President and CEO of Novell, testified that it was his "initial intent," his "intent at the time when the APA was signed," and his "intent when that transaction closed" that "Novell would transfer the copyrights to UNIX and UnixWare technology to Santa Cruz" and that "that intent never changed." Similarly, Ed Chatlos, a Senior Director for UNIX Strategic Partnerships and Business Development within Novell's Strategic Relations and Mergers and Acquisitions organization, submitted an affidavit affirming SCO's version of the facts:

> In or about June 1995, I became the lead negotiator for Novell in the negotiations with SCO and headed the day-to-day responsibility for the potential deal . . . . During these negotiations, I met regularly with SCO representatives . . . . Early in our discussions, it became apparent that

SCO could not pay the full purchase price as contemplated by Novell. To bridge the price gap, it was ultimately agreed that Novell would retain certain binary royalty payments under UNIX licenses. It was my understanding and intent, on behalf of Novell-that the complete UNIX business would be transferred to SCO.

Novell, in contrast, defends its interpretation of the transaction largely by pointing to the language of the contract itself, and by arguing that the witnesses put forward by SCO to offer extrinsic evidence of the parties' intent lacked any familiarity with the actual drafting of the APA's language or Amendment No. 2. At oral argument, Novell suggested that whatever the intent of the business negotiators involved in the deal, it was superseded by the work of those lawyers who ultimately negotiated the language of the contract that governs the transaction.

B. Proceedings Below

In May 2001, Santa Cruz sold its UNIX business to Caldera, the immediate predecessor to SCO. Santa Cruz purported to transfer its interest in the UNIX and UnixWare copyrights to Caldera/SCO. In 2002 and 2003, tensions increased between Novell and SCO. SCO asserted that users of Linux, an alternative to UNIX, might be infringing on SCO's UNIX-related intellectual property rights. It purported to offer Linux users the opportunity to purchase an intellectual property license in order to continue using Linux without infringing any of SCO's copyrights. In March 2003, SCO brought contract and copyright claims against IBM on the basis of SCO's alleged intellectual property rights in UNIX. Novell then directed SCO "to waive any purported right SCO may claim to terminate [certain of] IBM's SVRX Licenses," on the basis of its aforementioned waiver rights, set out in Section 4.16 of the APA. After SCO refused, Novell ultimately claimed publicly that it-rather than SCO-maintained ownership over the UNIX copyrights.

SCO filed a slander of title action against Novell. Novell asserted counterclaims for slander of title, breach of contract, and unjust enrichment. Both parties then proceeded to amend their pleadings to add additional claims and counterclaims. After the parties filed dueling motions for summary judgment, the United States District Court for the District of Utah issued a detailed memorandum decision and order on August 10, 2007.

The district court first concluded that Novell is the owner of the UNIX and UnixWare copyrights. It reviewed the APA and Amendment No. 2 separately and sequentially. The court found that the plain language of the APA indicated that the UNIX copyrights were not transferred to Santa Cruz. The court also determined that Amendment No. 2 did not transfer ownership of the copyrights. It reasoned that "[u]nlike the APA, Amendment No. 2 was not accompanied by a separate "Bill of Sale" transferring any assets." In addition, it found persuasive that Amendment No. 2 amended only the list of excluded assets from the transaction (Schedule 1.1(b)), but did not alter the language of the list of included assets (Schedule 1.1(a)). Finally, the court determined that Amendment No. 2 did not sufficiently identify which copyrights were to change hands, and therefore failed to satisfy the requirements necessary to transfer ownership of a copyright under Section 204(a) of the Copyright Act.

Having found that SCO's assertions of copyright ownership were false, the court granted summary judgment to Novell on SCO's claims alleging slander of title and seeking specific performance of Novell's alleged duty to transfer ownership of the UNIX and UnixWare copyrights to SCO. The court also rejected SCO's claims against Novell for unfair competition under Utah common law or statutory law, or for breach of the implied covenant of good faith under California law.

On appeal, SCO challenges various aspects of the decision below. It argues that the district court erred by concluding, *as a matter of law*, that (1) Santa Cruz did not obtain the UNIX and UnixWare copyrights from Novell, but instead acquired only an implied license; (2) SCO was not now entitled to specific performance-the transfer of any copyrights not transferred by the APA; (3) Novell has the right under the APA to force SCO to waive legal claims against IBM for its alleged breach of software and sublicensing agreements; (4) Novell did not have to comply with the implied covenant of good faith and fair dealing in exercising any waiver rights; (5) Novell retained an interest in royalties from SCO's 2003 agreement with Sun Microsystems and other post-APA contracts related to SVRX technology. We address each argument in turn.

II. The Ownership of UNIX and UnixWare Copyrights

SCO argues that the district court erred by interpreting the APA and Amendment No. 2 as separate and independent. It further contends that the text of the APA and Amendment No. 2 is at least ambiguous concerning whether the parties intended to transfer ownership of the copyrights, making it appropriate to consider extrinsic evidence. SCO asserts that a thorough review of extrinsic evidence makes summary judgment inappropriate on whether the copyrights were transferred by the transaction. Finally, SCO argues that the language in the APA and Amendment No. 2 was sufficient to meet the requirements to transfer ownership of a copyright under the Section 204(a) of the Copyright Act.

Novell, in contrast, argues that we ought to consider the APA and Amendment No. 2 separately. It asserts that the plain language of the APA itself unambiguously did not transfer copyright ownership, making consideration of parol evidence inappropriate. As for Amendment No. 2, Novell contends that no admissible extrinsic evidence shows that it was intended to transfer copyright ownership. Additionally, Novell claims that "SCO presented no evidence that copyright ownership was *required* to exercise its APA rights." Because Amendment No. 2 revised the excluded assets schedule so as to allow only for transfer of those "copyrights . . . owned by Novell as of the date of the Agreement required for SCO to exercise its rights with respect to the acquisition of UNIX and UnixWare technologies," Novell argues that SCO has failed to demonstrate that any copyrights were transferred. Finally, Novell argues that any purported transfer of copyrights did not meet the requirements for transfer of ownership under the Copyright Act.

We will proceed in three steps, asking first, whether the APA and Amendment No. 2 should be considered separately or together; second, whether the APA and Amendment No. 2 satisfy any requirements imposed by the Copyright Act in order to effect a transfer of copyright ownership; and third, whether the district court erred by concluding, as a matter of law, that the transaction's language and any admissible extrinsic evidence could not support the conclusion that Novell and Santa Cruz intended the copyrights to transfer.

A. Should We Consider APA and Amendment No. 2 Separately or Together?

The parties initially contest whether Amendment No. 2 should be read separately from the APA or together with it, as a successive writing elucidating the parties' intent in the original document. As we explain below, our disposition on this point is important primarily because it operates to fix the scope of extrinsic evidence admissible to clarify the contract.

California law "generally prohibits the introduction of any extrinsic evidence to vary or contradict the terms of an integrated written instrument." California's parol evidence rule provides that "[t]erms set forth in a writing intended by the parties as a final expression of their agreement . . . may not be contradicted by evidence of any prior agreement or of a contemporaneous oral agreement." Such a writing "may not be contradicted by even the most persuasive evidence of collateral agreements. Such evidence is legally irrelevant." The rule "is based upon the premise that the written instrument *is* the agreement of the parties."

On the other hand, "[e]ven if a contract appears unambiguous on its face, California law permits the use of extrinsic evidence to expose "a latent ambiguity . . ." which reveals more than one possible meaning to which the *language* of the contract is yet reasonably susceptible." The test of admissibility of extrinsic evidence to explain the meaning of a written instrument is not whether it appears to the court to be plain and unambiguous on its face, but whether "the offered evidence is relevant to prove a meaning to which the language of the instrument is reasonably susceptible." Thus, California law does not permit the use of extrinsic evidence to establish an ambiguity in the parties' intent independent from the terms of the contract; instead, it can only be used to expose or resolve a latent ambiguity in the language of the agreement itself.

If we were to interpret the contract based initially only on the APA itself-without regard to Amendment No. 2-we agree that its language unambiguously excludes the transfer of copyrights. Although SCO argues that the asset schedule approves of the transfer of "[a]ll rights and ownership of UNIX and UnixWare" to SCO, this ignores that the APA explicitly provides that "Notwithstanding [those assets listed on the Asset Schedule], the Assets to be so purchased shall not include those assets (the "Excluded Assets") set forth on Schedule 1.1(b)." Schedule 1.1(b), in turn, explains straightforwardly that "all copyrights" were excluded from the transaction. None of SCO's extrinsic evidence explains how the actual *language* of the APA is "reasonably susceptible" to its interpretation of the transaction — namely, that all relevant copyrights were transferred (or in other words, the exact opposite of what the APA's language suggests). Novell argues, therefore, that we ought not consider any of SCO's extrinsic evidence bearing on the development of the APA itself, and limit any inquiry beyond the text of the agreement to the course of the parties' negotiations over Amendment No. 2.

But if we understand Amendment No. 2 to clarify the parties' original intent as to the transfer of copyrights, SCO's extrinsic evidence concerning the business negotiations may be relevant to resolving ambiguity concerning the content of that original intent. Indeed, SCO argues that Amendment No. 2 was designed to bring the language of the transaction in line with the parties' original intent to transfer the copyrights. Of course, Novell disputes this characterization of Amendment No. 2. But unlike the language of the APA itself, the contractual language of Amendment No. 2 concerning the transfer of copyrights is ambiguous. Amendment No. 2 revises the excluded asset schedule to limit those copyrights excluded from the transaction to "[a]ll copyrights and trademarks, *except for the copyrights* and trademarks owned by Novell as of the date of the Agreement *required for SCO to exercise its rights with respect to the acquisition of UNIX and Unix Ware technologies.*" Because what copyrights are "required" for SCO to exercise its rights under the agreement is not clear on its face, California law allows courts to consider extrinsic evidence to resolve the ambiguity. Thus, to the extent that it is proper for us to read Amendment No. 2 as clarifying the APA, SCO's extrinsic evidence of the business negotiators' intent concerning the transaction ought to be admissible.

Having closely considered the parties' arguments, as well as the district court's reasoning, we find that Amendment No. 2 must be considered together with the APA as a unified document. Under California law, "[s]everal contracts relating to the same matters, between the same parties, and made as parts of substantially one transaction, are to be taken together." Even if we considered the language of the APA and Amendment No. 2 to be mutually antagonistic, California law still dictates that we construe them together, following Amendment No. 2 wherever its language contradicts the APA. Where "two contracts are made at different times, [but where] the later is not intended to entirely supersede the first, but only modif[y] it in certain particulars [,][t]he two are to be construed as parts of one contract, the later superseding the earlier one wherever it is inconsistent therewith."

In so doing, we note that SCO paid no additional consideration for Novell's agreement to Amendment No. 2. That makes sense if Amendment No. 2 was a clarification of the agreement, to bring the language of the APA into line with the parties' intent. If Amendment No. 2 were a change in the agreement (and a commercially significant one, at that), it is hard to see why Novell would have agreed to it without compensation.

Therefore, we construe the contract and Amendment No. 2 together for the purpose of assessing any ambiguities in the contract. This means that extrinsic evidence regarding the parties' intent is relevant to our interpretation of the combined instrument.

B. Does the Amended APA Satisfy the Requirements of the Copyright Act?

We next consider whether the amended APA constituted a writing sufficient to transfer copyrights under federal law. Under the Copyright Act, "[a] transfer of copyright ownership, other than by operation of law, is not valid unless an instrument of conveyance, or a note or memorandum of the transfer, is in writing and signed by the owner of the rights conveyed or such owner's duly authorized agent." Section 204 is intended "to protect copyright holders from persons mistakenly or fraudulently claiming oral licenses [or transfers]." As a result, Section 204 "enhances predictability and certainty of ownership — "Congress's paramount goal" when it revised the [Copyright] Act in 1976." Novell argues that the Copyright Act imposes not only the requirement that a copyright transfer be in writing, but also that it state with sufficient clarity the copyrights to be transferred. Novell contends that Amendment No. 2 fails this test because its language is ambiguous. Since it is not clearly apparent which copyrights are "required for Novell to exercise its rights with respect to the acquisition of UNIX and UnixWare technologies," Novell asserts that Amendment No. 2 was not a valid "instrument of conveyance."

As an initial matter, we note that the language of 17 U.S.C. § 204(a) does not readily lend itself to the construction Novell seeks to give it. Section 204(a), by its terms, imposes only the requirement that a copyright transfer be in writing and signed by the parties from whom the copyright is transferred; it does not on its face impose any heightened burden of clarity or particularity. Likewise, Novell points to nothing in the legislative history of Section 204 which suggests that Congress envisioned it to invalidate copyright transfer agreements carrying material language subject to multiple reasonable interpretations. Nonetheless, some courts have understood Section 204(a) to impose requirements similar to that necessary to satisfy the statute of frauds. They have found that a writing is insufficient to transfer copyrights unless (1) it reasonably identifies the subject matter of the agreement, (2) is sufficient to indicate that the parties have come to an agreement, and (3) states with reasonable certainty the essential terms of the agreement.

Novell argues that Section 204's writing requirement would disserve the goals of "predictability and certainty of copyright ownership" if parties could fulfill it without making clear what copyrights they intend to transfer. But it is hardly clear that imposing strict requirements of clarity in order to effect a copyright transfer will always aid "predictability and certainty of copyright ownership." "[A]mbiguities in copyright grants are anything but rare in the jurisprudence." 3 Melville B. Nimmer and David Nimmer, Nimmer on Copyright § 10.08 (2009). "The written memorialization of [an] agreement [transferring copyrights] inevitably fails to mandate only one pellucid interpretation." If every copyright transaction were vulnerable to challenge whenever a party is able to point out some ambiguity within the governing agreement, parties might be forced to engage in costly, protracted litigation to determine whether the transfer is valid, putting into doubt the proper holder of the copyright.

In the absence of any support from the language or legislative history, we are unwilling to read into Section 204 such an onerous restraint on the alienability of copyrights. As the Second Circuit has commented, "[t]he need for interpretation of a contract does not necessarily mean that there is a bona fide issue as to whether the contract is a writing for purposes of section 204(a). In most cases, there will be no doubt that the contract is a section 204(a) writing, and the only substantial issue will be contract interpretation." In copyright as elsewhere, "[t]he making of a contract depends not on the agreement of two minds in one intention, but on the agreement of two sets of external signs-not on the parties having meant the same thing but on their having said the same thing." Nimmer on Copyright, § 10.08. Where ambiguity persists in the language of a parties' shared agreement concerning a copyright transfer, the transfer is not invalidated; instead, we look to parol evidence to construe the terms of the agreement.

We think that Section 204's writing requirement is best understood as a means of ensuring that parties intend to transfer copyrights themselves, as opposed to other categories of rights. But when it is clear that the parties contemplated that copyrights transfer, we do not think that a linguistic ambiguity concerning which particular copyrights transferred creates an insuperable barrier invalidating the transaction. Thus, the majority of cases that Novell draws our attention to, in which alleged copyright transfers are found not to satisfy Section 204, involve transactions where it is not clear whether the parties intended that copyrights would transfer at all — not disputes over which specific copyrights were within the scope of an intended transfer.

Notwithstanding the above, the district court found Amendment No. 2 insufficient to convey Novell's copyrights under Section 204 for several additional reasons. It first determined that Amendment No. 2 "[did] not include any provision that purports to transfer ownership of copyrights," because it did not profess to "amend Schedule 1.1(a)," the Asset Schedule, and because "[u]nlike the APA, Amendment No. 2 was not accompanied by a separate "Bill of Sale" transferring any assets." We are not persuaded that either prevents our recognition of a copyright transfer.

Although Amendment No. 2 did not purport to amend Schedule 1.1(a), this does not mean that the balance of assets transferred to Santa Cruz remained unchanged. The transaction was structured such that Santa Cruz would acquire "all of Seller's right, title and interest in and to the assets . . . identified on Schedule 1.1(a)," but that "the Assets to be so purchased not include those assets (the "Excluded Assets") set forth on Schedule 1.1(b)." Schedule 1.1(a), in turn, provided that Santa Cruz would receive "*[a]ll rights and ownership* of UNIX and UnixWare . . . including all source code," a broad set of assets limited only by Schedule 1.1(b). As a result, any change to the set of Excluded Assets in Schedule 1.1(b) necessarily implicated those copyrights actually transferred under Schedule 1.1(a).

Of course, it is not always the case that the absence of certain or all copyrights from an "excluded asset" schedule will suffice to indicate the inclusion of copyrights in the transaction. But a written asset transfer agreement may satisfy Section 204(a) even when it "does not mention the word "copyright" " itself. And when a party acquires "[a]ll rights and ownership" in a set of items, as was the case here, courts have generally found such language sufficient to satisfy Section 204(a) in the absence of language excepting copyrights or other special circumstances. Of course, under the language of the original agreement, copyrights were expressly excluded from the assets transferred. But here, where a written agreement to the contract excised certain copyrights from that exclusion, we think the Copyright Act's writing requirement is satisfied.

We also do not see why the absence of a Bill of Sale is fatal to an alleged transfer under the Copyright Act. Section 204 makes clear that the writing requirement can be satisfied not only by "an instrument of conveyance" but also by "a note or memorandum of the transfer." Amendment No. 2 was a writing signed by both parties evincing a clear intent to revise or clarify the formal schedule of copyrights transferred by Novell to Santa Cruz. The Copyright Act did not require more. For similar reasons, we reject the significance that the district court attributed to the fact that Amendment No. 2 revised the APA "[a]s of the 16th day of October, 1996" as opposed to the date of the Bill of Sale. The Copyright Act does not require its writing requirement be fulfilled concurrently with the production of a Bill of Sale.

We therefore conclude that the APA, as revised by Amendment No. 2, satisfied the Copyright Act's writing requirement.

C. Is Summary Judgment Appropriate on the Ownership of the Copyrights?

We come finally to the question of whether the district court was correct to enter summary judgment on the issue of whether Novell or SCO owns the UNIX and UnixWare copyrights under the APA as revised by Amendment No. 2. In contract actions, the interpretation of a written agreement is a question of fact. When a contract is ambiguous, and parties present conflicting evidence regarding their intent at the time of the agreement, a genuine issue of material fact exists which cannot be determined summarily by the court. Of course, the party opposing summary judgment "must do more than simply show that there is some metaphysical doubt as to the material facts." But so long as sufficient evidence could lead a rational trier of fact to resolve the dispute in favor of either party, granting either party's dueling motions for summary judgment would be inappropriate.

This case, involving a complicated, multi-million dollar business transaction involving ambiguous language about which the parties offer dramatically different explanations, is particularly ill-suited to summary judgment. We recognize that Novell has powerful arguments to support its version of the transaction, and that, as the district court suggested, there may be reasons to discount the credibility, relevance, or persuasiveness of the extrinsic evidence that SCO presents. Moreover, we appreciate the difficulties that follow when the resolution of ambiguous language in a ten-year-old contract is left to trial. At trial in a case like this, the intention of the parties often "must be divined from self-serving testimony offered by partisan witnesses whose recollection is hazy from passage of time and colored by their conflicting interests." Even though the parties may have shared a common understanding of a transaction at the time of the deal, now that "circumstances have changed and new financial incentives have arisen, one side may wish it had a different agreement." Nevertheless, when conflicting evidence is presented such that the ambiguities in a contract could legitimately be resolved in favor of either party, it is for the ultimate finder of fact — not the court on summary judgment — to interpret the contract. As we now explain, Novell's arguments do not convince us that the admissible evidence concerning the ambiguous contract language concerning contract ownership is so one-sided as to warrant summary judgment.

Novell contends that SCO has failed to establish a disputed issue of material fact as to copyright ownership for several reasons. It first claims that SCO has failed to present any evidence to support that the APA, as revised by Amendment No. 2, clarified the agreement to indicate that SCO received ownership of some or all UNIX and UnixWare copyrights as a result of the transaction. In the alternative, it argues that SCO has failed to present any evidence to suggest that ownership of UNIX and UnixWare copyrights was "required" for Santa Cruz to exercise its rights under the APA.

In support of its initial argument, Novell argues that it has introduced undisputed evidence that (1) Santa Cruz admitted that the initial APA excluded copyrights from the asset sale and that (2) Novell expressly rejected Santa Cruz's proposal to use Amendment No. 2 to transfer copyrights to Santa Cruz. As to the first point, Santa Cruz's admission that the initial APA excluded copyrights is not inconsistent with SCO's position that this exclusion was a mistake and failed to reflect the parties' intent. Novell itself admits that the negotiations that led to the language of Amendment No. 2 concerning copyrights began when Santa Cruz's attorney contacted Novell, informing them that "the Original APA explicitly excluded copyrights to UNIX and UnixWare as assets being sold by Novell to Santa Cruz and that it shouldn't have."

As to the second point, Novell directs us to various pieces of evidence supporting its claim that Amendment No. 2 was not intended to affirm that ownership of copyrights had transferred to Santa Cruz, but only "to affirm that Santa Cruz had a license under the Original APA to use Novell's UNIX and UnixWare copyrighted works in its business." Novell primarily relies on evidence of the negotiations over Amendment No. 2. Santa Cruz initially proposed a draft of Amendment No. 2 that would have revised the Intellectual Property section of the Excluded Assets Schedule to read:

> All copyrights and trademarks, except for the copyrights and trademarks owned by Novell as of the date of this Amendment No. 2, which pertain to the UNIX and UnixWare technologies and which SCO has acquired hereunder. However, in no event shall Novell be liable to SCO for any claim brought by any third party pertaining to said copyrights and trademarks.

Novell rejected this language, and the final language of Amendment No. 2 instead reformed the Excluded Assets Schedule to read:

> All copyrights and trademarks, except for the copyrights owned by Novell as of the date of the Agreement required for SCO to exercise its rights with respect to the acquisition of UNIX and UnixWare technologies. However, in no event shall Novell be liable to SCO for any claim brought by any third party pertaining to said copyrights and trademarks.

The revised language contains two relevant changes. Instead of excepting from the Excluded Assets Schedule "the copyrights . . . which *pertain* to UNIX and UnixWare technologies" the final language refers to "the copyrights . . . *required* for SCO to exercise its rights with respect to the acquisition of UNIX and UnixWare technologies." In addition, instead of referring to "the copyrights . . . owned by Novell as of the date of this Amendment No. 2 . . . and which SCO has acquired hereunder," the final language refers to "the copyrights . . . owned by Novell as of the date of the Agreement."

Novell contends that because it did not accept Santa Cruz's initial proposal, there is no basis for construing Amendment No. 2 as SCO would-an affirmation of the transfer of all UNIX and UnixWare copyrights. It insists that the language reflects its explanation of Amendment No. 2 as a mere affirmation of Santa Cruz's implied license to use the copyrights. SCO, in contrast, claims that the final language of Amendment No. 2 only represented "a different way" of saying what its initial draft proposed-a clarification that the parties had intended for ownership of the UNIX copyrights to transfer.

As an initial matter, we are skeptical of Novell's interpretation of the Amendment. Whatever the Amendment means, it refers to the ownership of copyrights, not to licenses. A rational trier of fact could surely find that Amendment No. 2 clarified the APA so as to indicate that at least some copyrights transferred to SCO. It is true that the final language of Amendment No. 2, by referring to "required copyrights" rather than "copyrights that pertain to" UNIX, is narrower than that initially proposed by Santa Cruz. But is it plausible to think that Santa Cruz would have found the final language equally sufficient for its purposes, given its insistence that all the UNIX copyrights *were* required for it to exercise its rights under the deal. Alternatively, the final language of Amendment No. 2 may have represented a compromise whereby Novell agreed to confirm that Santa Cruz obtained ownership only of those copyrights "necessary" for Santa Cruz to run its business.

Our conclusion that a rational trier of fact could find that Amendment No. 2 clarified the APA to affirm that the parties intended to transfer certain UNIX and UnixWare copyrights to Novell is bolstered by SCO's extrinsic evidence of the transaction. SCO presents testimony from a variety of witnesses involved in the business negotiations on both sides of the deal, which generally supports its version of the transaction. It is true, as Novell points out, that many of these witnesses were involved in the business negotiations, as opposed to the actual drafting of the contract. But because we cannot exclude the possibility that Amendment No. 2 was designed to restore the language of the transaction to the parties' actual intent during the business negotiations over the deal, such testimony is not irrelevant. Moreover, SCO's extrinsic evidence extends not only to the business negotiations preceding the contract, but also to the parties' understanding of the contractual language itself. For instance, Novell points out that the Board resolution approving the transaction on its side of the deal stated that "Novell will retain all of its patents, copyrights and trademarks." But SCO notes that Mr. Frankenberg, then Novell's CEO, testified that he understood the Board resolution's reference to Novell's retention of copyrights to refer to Netware copyrights, as opposed to the core UNIX intellectual property.

Finally, SCO presents evidence of the parties' course of performance following the transaction. Under California law, "course of performance" evidence may be used to interpret an ambiguous contractual provision. SCO points to a variety of steps taken by the parties following the signing of the APA and Amendment No. 2 that it claims supports its interpretation of the contract. These include Novell's modification of copyright notices on certain UnixWare source code, certain statements related to the transfer of intellectual property within transition documents following the deal, and the publication of a press release in 1995 stating that "SCO will acquire Novell's UnixWare business and UNIX intellectual property." Of course, such documents are not dispositive of the companies' intent at the time of the transaction. But they illustrate the difficulties with granting summary judgment here.

Novell finally argues that SCO has failed to show what UNIX copyrights are "required" for Santa Cruz to exercise its rights under the APA. The parties each argue for plausible, but diametrically opposed, interpretations of the word "required." SCO argues that the bulk of the UNIX and UnixWare copyrights are "required" in order for it to exercise its rights. For instance, the APA transferred to Santa Cruz "all of [Novell's] claims arising after the Closing Date against any parties relating to any right, property or asset included in the Business." SCO argues that it could not defend any of its intellectual property against software piracy or other business harm without ownership of the copyrights. Indeed, a key reason why this litigation is so important to SCO is that it has claimed that other companies, including IBM, are infringing on the proprietary technology that it supposedly received through its transaction with Novell.

Novell, in contrast, asserts that the class of "required" copyrights constitutes a null set. The district court agreed, noting amongst other things that "Santa Cruz had been able to pursue its UNIX business from December 6, 1995 until October 16, 1996 [the date of Amendment No. 2] without any problems due to its [alleged] lack of ownership of the copyrights." But the fact that SCO did not need to assert ownership of the UNIX copyrights publicly following the closing of the transaction does not indicate that the UNIX copyrights are unnecessary to SCO's full exercise of its rights under the agreement. Indeed, it would seem that neither party asserted public ownership of the copyrights until the events leading to the instant litigation, almost a decade after the closing of the transaction.

We need not determine at the summary judgment stage which copyrights were "required." If the evidence presented on a dispositive issue is subject to conflicting, reasonable interpretations, summary judgment is improper. Although the district court found that "there is . . . significant evidence that Santa Cruz did not "require" the UNIX and UnixWare copyrights," we think SCO has presented sufficient evidence to create a triable fact as to whether at least some UNIX copyrights were required for it to exercise its rights under the agreement. Although the district court acknowledged that "SCO has submitted testimony from witnesses stating generally that the copyrights were necessary to running a software business," it found that "none of those witnesses give specific examples of how a lack of copyright ownership impeded Santa Cruz's ability to exercise its rights under the APA." But the documents detailing the actions of the transition team at least create ambiguity over whether the transfer of copyrights was required to support SCO's rights under the APA. And we think it a commonsense proposition that intellectual property at least *may* be required to protect the underlying assets in SCO software business should, for instance, a UNIX licensee have attempted to resell technology licensed from SCO.

Because we conclude summary judgment is inappropriate on the question of which party owns the UNIX and UnixWare copyrights, we must likewise reverse the district court's determination that "Novell is entitled to summary judgment [on SCO's claim] seeking an order directing Novell to specifically perform its alleged obligations under the APA by executing all documents needed to transfer ownership of the UNIX and UnixWare copyrights to SCO." We take no position on which party ultimately owns the UNIX copyrights or which copyrights were "required" for Santa Cruz to exercise its rights under the agreement. Such matters are for the finder of fact on remand.

****

QUESTIONS

1. The court found that the Asset Purchase Agreement was unambiguous and, therefore, SCO could not submit extrinsic evidence as to the meaning of the Asset Purchase Agreement. However, the court also found that Amendment 2 was ambiguous and, therefore, SCO could submit extrinsic evidence as to the meaning of Amendment 2. Did the extrinsic evidence SCO sought to submit pertain to the Asset Purchase Agreement or Amendment 2?

2. The court found that Amendment 2 satisfied the Copyright Act § 204 writing requirement despite its ambiguity. In explaining its finding, the court quoted from Nimmer quoting from a case: "[t]he making of a contract depends not on the agreement of two minds in one intention, but on the agreement of two sets of external signs — not on the parties having meant the same thing but on their having said the same thing." What does this mean? How does it bear on the satisfaction of the Copyright Act § 204 writing requirement?

3. Why might Novell want to thwart SCO's suit against IBM rather than joining in the suit based upon its purported ownership of the copyrights in the Unix and UnixWare source code?

4. The SCO litigation has been going on for five years. If you were advising SCO on the heels of its latest victory, would you advise them to go full speed ahead in litigation against IBM and other Linux users, or would you advise them to pursue a settlement and licensing strategy?

CASE NOTES

1. Jacobsen manages an open source software group called Java Model Railroad Interface (JMRI). JMRI created a computer program that allows model railroad hobbyists to use their computers to program chips that can control model trains (the DecoderPro program). The DecoderPro files are available for download from an open source website called SourceForge. The downloadable files contain copyright notices and refer the user to a "Copying" file which sets forth the terms of the open source license. These terms include requirements that users who modify and distribute the DecoderPro files include the JMRI copyright notice and make reference to the original source files available at the SourceForge website. Katzer admittedly downloaded and distributed the DecoderPro files without including the copyright notice and without identification of the original source files from the SourceForge website. Jacobsen sued Katzer for copyright infringement and moved for a preliminary injunction. The district court held that Katzer's violation of the open source license terms constituted a breach of license "covenants" which could support an action for breach of contract, but did not constitute a copyright infringement which could support a motion for a preliminary injunction. The district court reasoned that an open source license was an "intentionally broad" nonexclusive license which was unlimited in the scope of use. Jacobsen appealed the district court's holding arguing that the open source license terms were "conditions" of the

license and that violation of license conditions constituted copyright infringement. What result? *See* Jacobsen v. Katzer, 535 F.3d 1373 (Fed. Cir. 2008).

2. *See also* Red Hat, Inc. v. SCO Group, Inc., 2004 U.S. Dist. LEXIS 7077 (D. Del. 2004) (SCO's public statements regarding its intention to sue Linux users like IBM and Red Hat created a reasonable apprehension of an infringement suit sufficient to give Red Hat standing to file a declaratory judgment action); The SCO Group v. IBM, 2005 U.S. Dist. LEXIS 4493 (C.D. Utah) (Denying IBM's motion for partial summary judgment on SCO's breach of contract claims and copyright infringement claims); Planetary Motion, Inc. v. Techsplosion, Inc., 261 F.3d 1188 (11th Cir. 2001) (Software distributed under a GPL license is not placed in the public domain); Wallace v. IBM, 467 F.3d 1104 (7th Cir. 2006) (GPL licensees are not antitrust conspirators and the GPL license does not violate price fixing prohibition of the antitrust laws).

Additional Information

1. CORP COUNS GD TO SOFTWARE TRANS §§ 13:3–13:7, 13:9, 14:2, 20:3–20:7, 20:9 (2010).

2. L. J. KUTTEN, 2 COMPUTER SOFTWARE §§ 9:78, 9:82–9:84 ((2010).

3. RAYMOND T. NIMMER, LAW OF COMPUTER TECHNOLOGY § 11:10 (2010).

4. LISA M. BROWNLEE, IP DUE DILIGENCE IN CORP. TRANSACTIONS § 8:75.1 (2010).

5. STEVEN Z. SZCZEPANSKI, DAVID M. EPSTEIN, 3 ECKSTROM'S LICENSING IN FOR. & DOM. OPS. § 12:30.75 (2010).

6. IAN C. BALLON, 1 E-COMMERCE AND INTERNET LAW 18.03[7] (2011).

7. ALAN S. GUTTERMAN, 1 CORP COUNS GD TO TECH MGMT & TRANS § 24:84.10 (2010).

8. Ibrahim Haddad, *Free and Open Software Compliance: The Basics You Must Know*, 1036 PLI/PAT 17 (2011).

9. Karen F. Copenhaver, *Compliance with Open Source Software Licenses*, 1035 PLI/PAT 773 (2011).

10. Carolyn Blankenship, Elana Bertram, *Open Source Software and Patent Protection*, 1029 PLI/PAT 347 (2010).

11. Katherine A. Franco, *Protecting Free and Open Source Software: Solutions in the Digital Millenium Copyright Act*, 12 COLUM. SCI. & TECH. L. REV. 160 (2011).

12. Alan Stern, *Open Source Licensing*, 915 PLI/PAT 187 (2007).

13. Ronald J. Mann, *Commercializing Open Source Software: Do Property Rights Still Matter?*, 20 HARV. J.L. & TECH. 1 (2006).

14. John C. Yates, Paul H. Arne, *Open Source Software Licenses: Perspectives of the End User and the Software Developer*, 823 PLI/PAT 97 (2005).

15.   Lori E. Lesser, *A Hard Look at the Tough Issues in Open Source Licenses,* 846 PLI/Pat 7 (2005).

16.   David McGowen, *Legal Implications of Open Source Software,* 2001 U. Ill. L. Rev. 241 (2001).

Chapter 3

COMMERCIALIZING UNIVERSITY TECHNOLOGIES

The commercial development of university-based technologies has become very important to the U.S. economy, to research universities and to faculty inventors. A recent report estimates that over the period from 1996 to 2007, university-licensed technologies contributed at least $47 billion, and as much as $187 billion, to the U.S. GDP. The same report estimates that university-licensed technologies have created more than 279,000 jobs during the same time period. *See* The Economic Impact of Licensed Commercialized Inventions Originating in University Research, 1996-2007, Biotechnology Industry Organization (2009), available at http://www.bio.org/techtransfer/BIO_final_report_9_3_09_rev.2pdf.

The commercial development of university technologies has also become a major source of local and regional economic development. In its FY 2007 annual survey, the Association of University Technology Managers (AUTM) identified 686 new products that were marketed, 555 new companies that were created and 5,109 new licenses that were granted. The AUTM survey also estimated that since 1980, more than 6,270 new companies have been established to develop and market academic R&D.

However, these impressive statistics on the success of university technology commercialization obscure fundamental asymmetries among and within universities. More than ninety percent of technology licensing revenue is earned by less than ten percent of universities. The majority of start-up companies are launched in only a handful of universities. And in the most successful universities, whether measured by licensing revenue or start-up companies, the success is attributable to a small fraction of the universities' patent portfolio.

This chapter will consider the commercialization of university technologies from a number of different perspectives. The first section will look at the Bayh-Dole Act, which many researchers believe is largely responsible for the growing economic importance of university technology innovation. This section will consider the Bayh-Dole legislation and legislative history, standing to sue under the Bayh-Dole Act, faculty rights to royalties arising under the Bayh-Dole Act and "march-in" rights (i.e., the right of the federal government to reclaim title to inventions made with federal funding). The second section will look at university/industry sponsored research including sponsored research policies and practices, tax issues affecting sponsored research and university-sponsored IP disputes.

The third section will cover university intellectual property ownership, including intellectual property policies, university-faculty and university-student IP ownership disputes, and university licensing policies. The fourth section will cover university patent enforcement, the fifth section will cover university research responsibilities to students, and the sixth section will cover university-faculty employment contracts, including the recent Supreme Court decision in *Stanford v. Roche*.

3.1 THE BAYH-DOLE ACT

The Bayh-Dole Act, passed in 1980, was intended to promote U.S. competitiveness and technological innovation by making the fruits of federally funded research available to the private sector for commercial development. Prior to 1980, patents resulting from federally funded research at U.S. universities were owned by the U.S. government and managed by the federal funding agency. It was estimated that only 5% of government-owned patents were ever licensed to the private sector. There were many barriers to licensing government-owned patents, including the length of negotiations with agency bureaucracies, the availability of only non-exclusive licenses and the myriad agency policies regarding licensing; the House Report accompanying the Bayh-Dole Act noted that the 26 federal funding agencies each had its own unique licensing policy.

The Bayh-Dole Act was designed to replace this ineffective and fragmented system with a single, uniform national policy centered on allowing universities to elect to take title to patents resulting from federally funded research. The rationale underlying the Bayh-Dole Act was that, by allowing universities to elect to take title to patents resulting from federally funded research, universities would have a direct incentive to license these patents to the private sector for royalty income.

The Bayh-Dole Act also covers domestic and foreign protection of federally owned inventions, promulgation of regulations governing licensing of federally owned inventions and licensing of federally owned inventions.

3.1.1 Legislation

35 U.S.C.A. §§ 200–212

§ 200.   Policy and objective

It is the policy and objective of the Congress to use the patent system to promote the utilization of inventions arising from federally supported research or development; to encourage maximum participation of small business firms in federally supported research and development efforts; to promote collaboration between commercial concerns and nonprofit organizations, including universities; to ensure that inventions made by nonprofit organizations and small business firms are used in a manner to promote free competition and enterprise without unduly encumbering future research and discovery; to promote the commercialization and public availability of inventions made in the United States by United States industry and labor; to ensure that the Government obtains sufficient rights in federally supported inventions to meet the needs of the Government and protect the public against nonuse or unreasonable use of inventions; and to minimize the costs of administering policies in this area.

§ 201.   Definitions

As used in this chapter —

(a) The term "Federal agency" means any executive agency as defined in section 105 of title 5, and the military departments as defined by section 102 of title 5.

(b) The term "funding agreement" means any contract, grant, or cooperative agreement entered into between any Federal agency, other than the Tennessee Valley Authority, and any contractor for the performance of experimental, developmental, or research work funded in whole or in part by the Federal Government. Such term includes any assignment, substitution of parties, or subcontract of any type entered into for the performance of experimental, developmental, or research work under a funding agreement as herein defined.

(c) The term "contractor" means any person, small business firm, or nonprofit organization that is a party to a funding agreement.

(d) The term "invention" means any invention or discovery which is or may be patentable or otherwise protectable under this title or any novel variety of plant which is or may be protectable under the Plant Variety Protection Act (7 U.S.C. 2321 et seq.).

(e) The term "subject invention" means any invention of the contractor conceived or first actually reduced to practice in the performance of work under a funding agreement: *Provided*, That in the case of a variety of plant, the date of determination (as defined in section 41(d) of the Plant Variety Protection Act (7 U.S.C. 2401(d))) must also occur during the period of contract performance.

(f) The term "practical application" means to manufacture in the case of a composition or product, to practice in the case of a process or method, or to operate in the case of a machine or system; and, in each case, under such conditions as to establish that the invention is being utilized and that its benefits are to the extent permitted by law or Government regulations available to the public on reasonable terms.

(g) The term "made" when used in relation to any invention means the conception or first actual reduction to practice of such invention.

(h) The term "small business firm" means a small business concern as defined at section 2 of Public Law 85-536 (15 U.S.C. 632) and implementing regulations of the Administrator of the Small Business Administration.

(i) The term "nonprofit organization" means universities and other institutions of higher education or an organization of the type described in section 501(c)(3) of the Internal Revenue Code of 1986 (26 U.S.C. 501(c)) and exempt from taxation under section 501(a) of the Internal Revenue Code (26 U.S.C. 501(a)) or any nonprofit scientific or educational organization qualified under a State nonprofit organization statute.

§ 202.   Disposition of rights

(a) Each nonprofit organization or small business firm may, within a reasonable time after disclosure as required by paragraph (c)(1) of this section, elect to retain title to any subject invention: *Provided, however,* That a funding agreement may provide otherwise (i) when the contractor is not located in the United States or does not have a place of business located in the United States or is subject to the control of a foreign government, (ii) in exceptional circumstances when it is determined by the agency that restriction or elimination of the right to retain title to any subject invention will better promote the policy and objectives of this chapter (iii) when it is determined by a Government authority which is authorized by statute or Executive order to conduct foreign intelligence or counter-intelligence activities that the restriction or elimination of the right to retain title to any subject invention is necessary to protect the security of such activities or, (iv) when the funding agreement includes the operation of a Government-owned, contractor-operated facility of the Department of Energy primarily dedicated to that Department's naval nuclear propulsion or weapons related programs and all funding agreement limitations under this subparagraph on the contractor's right to elect title to a subject invention are limited to inventions occurring under the above two programs of the Department of Energy. The rights of the nonprofit organization or small business firm shall be subject to the provisions of paragraph (c) of this section and the other provisions of this chapter.

(b) (1) The rights of the Government under subsection (a) shall not be exercised by a Federal agency unless it first determines that at least one of the conditions identified in clauses (i) through (iv) of subsection (a) exists. Except in the case of subsection (a)(iii), the agency shall file with the Secretary of Commerce, within thirty days after the award of the applicable funding agreement, a copy of such determination. In the case of a determination under subsection (a)(ii), the statement shall include an analysis justifying the determination. In the case of determinations applicable to funding agreements with small business firms, copies shall also be sent to the Chief Counsel for Advocacy of the Small Business Administration. If the Secretary of Commerce believes that any individual determination or pattern of determinations is contrary to the policies and objectives of this chapter or otherwise not in conformance with this chapter, the Secretary shall so advise the head of the agency concerned and the Administrator of the Office of Federal Procurement Policy, and recommend corrective actions.

(2) Whenever the Administrator of the Office of Federal Procurement Policy has determined that one or more Federal agencies are utilizing the authority of clause (i) or (ii) of subsection (a) of this section in a manner that is contrary to the policies and objectives of this chapter, the Administrator is authorized to issue regulations describing classes of situations in which agencies may not exercise the authorities of those clauses.

(3) At least once every 5 years, the Comptroller General shall transmit a report to the Committees on the Judiciary of the Senate and House of Representatives on the manner in which this chapter is being implemented by

the agencies and on such other aspects of Government patent policies and practices with respect to federally funded inventions as the Comptroller General believes appropriate.

(4) If the contractor believes that a determination is contrary to the policies and objectives of this chapter or constitutes an abuse of discretion by the agency, the determination shall be subject to the section 203(b).

(c) Each funding agreement with a small business firm or nonprofit organization shall contain appropriate provisions to effectuate the following:

(1) That the contractor disclose each subject invention to the Federal agency within a reasonable time after it becomes known to contractor personnel responsible for the administration of patent matters, and that the Federal Government may receive title to any subject invention not disclosed to it within such time.

(2) That the contractor make a written election within two years after disclosure to the Federal agency (or such additional time as may be approved by the Federal agency) whether the contractor will retain title to a subject invention: *Provided*, That in any case where publication, on sale, or public use, has initiated the one year statutory period in which valid patent protection can still be obtained in the United States, the period for election may be shortened by the Federal agency to a date that is not more than sixty days prior to the end of the statutory period: *And provided further*, That the Federal Government may receive title to any subject invention in which the contractor does not elect to retain rights or fails to elect rights within such times.

(3) That a contractor electing rights in a subject invention agrees to file a patent application prior to any statutory bar date that may occur under this title due to publication, on sale, or public use, and shall thereafter file corresponding patent applications in other countries in which it wishes to retain title within reasonable times, and that the Federal Government may receive title to any subject inventions in the United States or other countries in which the contractor has not filed patent applications on the subject invention within such times.

(4) With respect to any invention in which the contractor elects rights, the Federal agency shall have a nonexclusive, nontransferable, irrevocable, paid-up license to practice or have practiced for or on behalf of the United States any subject invention throughout the world: *Provided*, That the funding agreement may provide for such additional rights, including the right to assign or have assigned foreign patent rights in the subject invention, as are determined by the agency as necessary for meeting the obligations of the United States under any treaty, international agreement, arrangement of cooperation, memorandum of understanding, or similar arrangement, including military agreement relating to weapons development and production.

(5) The right of the Federal agency to require periodic reporting on the utilization or efforts at obtaining utilization that are being made by the contractor or his licensees or assignees: *Provided*, That any such information as well as any information on utilization or efforts at obtaining utilization

obtained as part of a proceeding under section 203 of this chapter shall be treated by the Federal agency as commercial and financial information obtained from a person and privileged and confidential and not subject to disclosure under section 552 of title 5.

(6) An obligation on the part of the contractor, in the event a United States patent application is filed by or on its behalf or by any assignee of the contractor, to include within the specification of such application and any patent issuing thereon, a statement specifying that the invention was made with Government support and that the Government has certain rights in the invention.

(7) In the case of a nonprofit organization, (A) a prohibition upon the assignment of rights to a subject invention in the United States without the approval of the Federal agency, except where such assignment is made to an organization which has as one of its primary functions the management of inventions (provided that such assignee shall be subject to the same provisions as the contractor); (B) a requirement that the contractor share royalties with the inventor; (C) except with respect to a funding agreement for the operation of a Government-owned-contractor-operated facility, a requirement that the balance of any royalties or income earned by the contractor with respect to subject inventions, after payment of expenses (including payments to inventors) incidental to the administration of subject inventions, be utilized for the support of scientific research or education; (D) a requirement that, except where it proves infeasible after a reasonable inquiry, in the licensing of subject inventions shall be given to small business firms; and (E) with respect to a funding agreement for the operation of a Government-owned-contractor-operated facility, requirements (i) that after payment of patenting costs, licensing costs, payments to inventors, and other expenses incidental to the administration of subject inventions, 100 percent of the balance of any royalties or income earned and retained by the contractor during any fiscal year up to an amount equal to 5 percent of the annual budget of the facility, shall be used by the contractor for scientific research, development, and education consistent with the research and development mission and objectives of the facility, including activities that increase the licensing potential of other inventions of the facility; provided that if said balance exceeds 5 percent of the annual budget of the facility, that 75 percent of such excess shall be paid to the Treasury of the United States and the remaining 25 percent shall be used for the same purposes as described above in this clause (D); and (ii) that, to the extent it provides the most effective technology transfer, the licensing of subject inventions shall be administered by contractor employees on location at the facility.

(8) The requirements of sections 203 and 204 of this chapter.

(d) If a contractor does not elect to retain title to a subject invention in cases subject to this section, the Federal agency may consider and after consultation with the contractor grant requests for retention of rights by the inventor subject to the provisions of this Act and regulations promulgated hereunder.

(e) In any case when a Federal employee is a co-inventor of any invention made with a nonprofit organization, a small business firm, or a non-Federal inventor, the Federal agency employing such co-inventor may, for the purpose of consolidating rights in the invention and if it finds that it would expedite the development of the invention —

(1) license or assign whatever rights it may acquire in the subject invention to the nonprofit organization, small business firm, or non-Federal inventor in accordance with the provisions of this chapter; or

(2) acquire any rights in the subject invention from the nonprofit organization, small business firm, or non-Federal inventor, but only to the extent the party from whom the rights are acquired voluntarily enters into the transaction and no other transaction under this chapter is conditioned on such acquisition.

(f) (1) No funding agreement with a small business firm or nonprofit organization shall contain a provision allowing a Federal agency to require the licensing to third parties of inventions owned by the contractor that are not subject inventions unless such provision has been approved by the head of the agency and a written justification has been signed by the head of the agency. Any such provision shall clearly state whether the licensing may be required in connection with the practice of a subject invention, a specifically identified work object, or both. The head of the agency may not delegate the authority to approve provisions or sign justifications required by this paragraph.

(2) A Federal agency shall not require the licensing of third parties under any such provision unless the head of the agency determines that the use of the invention by others is necessary for the practice of a subject invention or for the use of a work object of the funding agreement and that such action is necessary to achieve the practical application of the subject invention or work object. Any such determination shall be on the record after an opportunity for an agency hearing. Any action commenced for judicial review of such determination shall be brought within sixty days after notification of such determination.

§ 203.   March-in rights

(a) With respect to any subject invention in which a small business firm or nonprofit organization has acquired title under this chapter, the Federal agency under whose funding agreement the subject invention was made shall have the right, in accordance with such procedures as are provided in regulations promulgated hereunder to require the contractor, an assignee or exclusive licensee of a subject invention to grant a nonexclusive, partially exclusive, or exclusive license in any field of use to a responsible applicant or applicants, upon terms that are reasonable under the circumstances, and if the contractor, assignee, or exclusive licensee refuses such request, to grant such a license itself, if the Federal agency determines that such —

(1) action is necessary because the contractor or assignee has not taken, or is not expected to take within a reasonable time, effective steps to achieve practical application of the subject invention in such field of use;

(2) action is necessary to alleviate health or safety needs which are not reasonably satisfied by the contractor, assignee, or their licensees;

(3) action is necessary to meet requirements for public use specified by Federal regulations and such requirements are not reasonably satisfied by the contractor, assignee, or licensees; or

(4) action is necessary because the agreement required by section 204 has not been obtained or waived or because a licensee of the exclusive right to use or sell any subject invention in the United States is in breach of its agreement obtained pursuant to section 204.

(b) A determination pursuant to this section or section 202(b)(4) shall not be subject to the Contract Disputes Act (41 U.S.C. § 601 et seq.). An administrative appeals procedure shall be established by regulations promulgated in accordance with section 206. Additionally, any contractor, inventor, assignee, or exclusive licensee adversely affected by a determination under this section may, at any time within sixty days after the determination is issued, file a petition in the United States Court of Federal Claims, which shall have jurisdiction to determine the appeal on the record and to affirm, reverse, remand or modify, as appropriate, the determination of the Federal agency. In cases described in paragraphs (1) and (3) of subsection (a), the agency's determination shall be held in abeyance pending the exhaustion of appeals or petitions filed under the preceding sentence.

§ 204. Preference for United States industry

Notwithstanding any other provision of this chapter, no small business firm or nonprofit organization which receives title to any subject invention and no assignee of any such small business firm or nonprofit organization shall grant to any person the exclusive right to use or sell any subject invention in the United States unless such person agrees that any products embodying the subject invention or produced through the use of the subject invention will be manufactured substantially in the United States. However, in individual cases, the requirement for such an agreement may be waived by the Federal agency under whose funding agreement the invention was made upon a showing by the small business firm, nonprofit organization, or assignee that reasonable but unsuccessful efforts have been made to grant licenses on similar terms to potential licensees that would be likely to manufacture substantially in the United States or that under the circumstances domestic manufacture is not commercially feasible.

§ 205. Confidentiality

Federal agencies are authorized to withhold from disclosure to the public information disclosing any invention in which the Federal Government owns or may own a right, title, or interest (including a nonexclusive license) for a reasonable time in order for a patent application to be filed. Furthermore, Federal agencies shall not be required to release copies of any document which is part of an application for patent filed with the United States Patent and Trademark Office or with any foreign patent office.

§ 206. Uniform clauses and regulations

The Secretary of Commerce may issue regulations which may be made applicable to Federal agencies implementing the provisions of sections 202 through 204 of this chapter and shall establish standard funding agreement provisions required under this chapter. The regulations and the standard funding agreement shall be subject to public comment before their issuance.

§ 207. Domestic and foreign protection of federally owned inventions

(a) Each Federal agency is authorized to —

(1) apply for, obtain, and maintain patents or other forms of protection in the United States and in foreign countries on inventions in which the Federal Government owns a right, title, or interest;

(2) grant nonexclusive, exclusive, or partially exclusive licenses under federally owned inventions, royalty-free or for royalties or other consideration, and on such terms and conditions, including the grant to the licensee of the right of enforcement pursuant to the provisions of chapter 29 of this title as determined appropriate in the public interest;

(3) undertake all other suitable and necessary steps to protect and administer rights to federally owned inventions on behalf of the Federal Government either directly or through contract, including acquiring rights for and administering royalties to the Federal Government in any invention, but only to the extent the party from whom the rights are acquired voluntarily enters into the transaction, to facilitate the licensing of a federally owned invention; and

(4) transfer custody and administration, in whole or in part, to another Federal agency, of the right, title, or interest in any federally owned invention.

(b) For the purpose of assuring the effective management of Government-owned inventions, the Secretary of Commerce is authorized to —

(1) assist Federal agency efforts to promote the licensing and utilization of Government-owned inventions;

(2) assist Federal agencies in seeking protection and maintaining inventions in foreign countries, including the payment of fees and costs connected therewith; and

(3) consult with and advise Federal agencies as to areas of science and technology research and development with potential for commercial utilization.

§ 208. Regulations governing Federal licensing

The Secretary of Commerce is authorized to promulgate regulations specifying the terms and conditions upon which any federally owned invention, other than inventions owned by the Tennessee Valley Authority, may be licensed on a nonexclusive, partially exclusive, or exclusive basis.

§ 209. Licensing federally owned inventions

(a) Authority. — A Federal agency may grant an exclusive or partially exclusive license on a federally owned invention under section 207(a)(2) only if —

(1) Granting the license is a reasonable and necessary incentive to —

(A) call forth the investment capital and expenditures needed to bring the invention to practical application; or

(B) otherwise promote the invention's utilization by the public;

(2) the Federal agency finds that the public will be served by the granting of the license, as indicated by the applicant's intentions, plans, and ability to bring the invention to practical application or otherwise promote the invention's utilization by the public, and that the proposed scope of exclusivity is not greater than reasonably necessary to provide the incentive for bringing the invention to practical application, as proposed by the applicant, or otherwise to promote the invention's utilization by the public;

(3) the applicant makes a commitment to achieve practical application of the invention within a reasonable time, which time may be extended by the agency upon the applicant's request and the applicant's demonstration that the refusal of such extension would be unreasonable;

(4) granting the license will not tend to substantially lessen competition or create or maintain a violation of the Federal antitrust laws; and

(5) in the case of an invention covered by a foreign patent application or patent, the interests of the Federal Government or United States industry in foreign commerce will be enhanced.

(b) Manufacture in United States. — A Federal agency shall normally grant a license under section 207(a)(2) to use or sell any federally owned invention in the United States only to a licensee who agrees that any products embodying the invention or produced through the use of the invention will be manufactured substantially in the United States.

(c) Small business. — First preference for the granting of any exclusive or partially exclusive licenses under section 207(a)(2) shall be given to small business firms having equal or greater likelihood as other applicants to bring the invention to practical application within a reasonable time.

(d) Terms and conditions. — Any licenses granted under section 207(a)(2) shall contain such terms and conditions as the granting agency considers appropriate, and shall include provisions —

(1) retaining a non-transferrable, irrevocable, paid-up license for any Federal agency to practice the invention or have the invention practiced throughout the world by or on behalf of the Government of the United States;

(2) requiring periodic reporting on utilization of the invention, and utilization efforts, by the licensee, but only to the extent necessary to enable the Federal agency to determine whether the terms of the license are being complied with, except that any such report shall be treated by the Federal agency as

commercial and financial information obtained from a person and privileged and confidential and not subject to disclosure under section 552 of title 5; and

(3) Empowering the Federal agency to terminate the license in whole or in part if the agency determines that —

(A) the licensee is not executing its commitment to achieve practical application of the invention, including commitments contained in any plan submitted in support of its request for a license, and the licensee cannot otherwise demonstrate to the satisfaction of the Federal agency that it has taken, or can be expected to take within a reasonable time, effective steps to achieve practical application of the invention;

(B) the licensee is in breach of an agreement described in subsection (b);

(C) termination is necessary to meet requirements for public use specified by Federal regulations issued after the date of the license, and such requirements are not reasonably satisfied by the licensee; or

(D) the licensee has been found by a court of competent jurisdiction to have violated the Federal antitrust laws in connection with its performance under the license agreement.

(e) Public notice. — No exclusive or partially exclusive license may be granted under section 207(a)(2) unless public notice of the intention to grant an exclusive or partially exclusive license on a federally owned invention has been provided in an appropriate manner at least 15 days before the license is granted, and the Federal agency has considered all comments received before the end of the comment period in response to that public notice. This subsection shall not apply to the licensing of inventions made under a cooperative research and development agreement entered into under section 12 of the Stevenson-Wydler Technology Innovation Act of 1980 (15 U.S.C. 3710a).

(f) Plan. — No Federal agency shall grant any license under a patent or patent application on a federally owned invention unless the person requesting the license has supplied the agency with a plan for development or marketing of the invention, except that any such plan shall be treated by the Federal agency as commercial and financial information obtained from a person and privileged and confidential and not subject to disclosure under section 552 of title 5.

****

§ 211. Relationship to antitrust laws

Nothing in this chapter shall be deemed to convey to any person immunity from civil or criminal liability, or to create any defenses to actions, under any antitrust law.

§ 212. Disposition of rights in educational awards

No scholarship, fellowship, training grant, or other funding agreement made by a Federal agency primarily to an awardee for educational purposes will contain any provision giving the Federal agency any rights to inventions made by the awardee.

QUESTIONS

1.   Who has the benefit of the federal non-exclusive, non-transferable, royalty-free license?

2.   Does Bayh-Dole require universities to monitor licensees?

3.   Can universities assign patents obtained with federal research funding?

4.   Must universities grant licenses to small businesses?

5.   Can the inventor ever take title to an invention?

6.   Can a federal agency require a university to license patents not obtained with federal research funding?

7.   What are "march in" rights?

8.   What factors can trigger the exercise of "march in" rights?

9.   Must a federally funded invention be manufactured in the United States?

10.   Can a federal agency obtain a patent on an invention made by a federal employee?

11.   How do you manage a research project that is partially funded with federal, industry and university funds?

12.   Should Bayh-Dole-type legislation be enacted by states?

CAMPBELL PLASTICS ENGINEERING & MFG., INC. v. BROWNLEE
389 F.3d 1243 (Fed. Cir. 2004)

CLEVENGER, CIRCUIT JUDGE.

Campbell Plastics Engineering & Mfg., Inc. ("Campbell Plastics") appeals the decision by the Armed Services Board of Contract Appeals ("ASBCA" or "Board") upholding an Administrative Contracting Officer's ("ACO's") demand for title to an invention developed pursuant to a contract between Campbell Plastics and the U.S. Army Chemical Research, Development and Engineering Center ("Army" or "government"). Because we conclude that Campbell Plastics failed to comply with the invention disclosure provisions of the contract, we affirm.

I

On September 25, 1992, Campbell Plastics (named Venture Plastics, Inc., at the time) entered into a cost-plus-fixed-fee contract with the Army to develop certain components of an aircrew protective mask, as part of a program for small disadvantaged business concerns pursuant to section 8(a) of the Small Business Act.

Section I of the contract incorporates numerous clauses from the Federal Acquisition Regulations ("FARs"), including a "Patent Rights-Retention by the

Contractor" clause that requires a contractor to disclose any subject invention developed pursuant to a government contract and sets forth certain substantive requirements for doing so. The clause further provides that the government may obtain title if the contractor fails to disclose the invention within two months from the date upon which the inventor discloses it in writing to contractor personnel responsible for patent matters. Section I also incorporates from 48 C.F.R. § 252.227-7039 (1991) ("FAR 252.227-7039") a "Patents-Reporting of Subject Inventions" clause which requires the contractor to disclose subject inventions in interim reports furnished every twelve months and final reports furnished within three months after completion of the contracted work. Subsection H.11 of the contract, titled "Patent Rights Reports," requires the contractor to submit all "interim and final invention reports required by patent clause in Section I" on a "DD Form 882, Report of Inventions and Subcontracts."

On October 11, 1992, Mr. Richard Campbell, President of Campbell Plastics, submitted to the Army a DD Form 882 wherein he expressly stated "no inventions." At a post-award conference on November 17, an Army representative told Mr. Campbell that a DD form 882 was due at least once every twelve months from the date upon which the contract was awarded. Shortly thereafter, on December 14, Mr. Campbell faxed several handwritten drawings to Mr. Jeff Hofmann, an ACO Representative. One of the drawings identified a location for a "sonic weld or snap fit." Mr. Campbell's submission was the first in a series of progress reports and drawings submitted during Campbell Plastics's work under the contract that referenced sonic welding to varying degrees.

On December 19, 1992, Mr. Campbell faxed a handwritten letter to Mr. Hofmann seeking to "reopen the question of the sonic welding." The letter included an explanation of the advantages of sonic welding and the assembly concept. On January 20, 1993, Mr. Campbell provided Mr. Hofmann with two protective masks that had sonic-welded side ports. In a January 27 monthly progress report, Campbell Plastics noted, "We are also testing Sonic Welding the Kapton Film in a housing. This also has to be tested for leakage and tension." On February 11, Mr. Campbell faxed Mr. Hofmann a drawing of a side port having a sonic weld. In a monthly progress report submitted on March 2, Campbell Plastics identified the task of "[t]esting of Sonic Welding the Kapton film in a housing," and reported that sonic welding "looks viable." Campbell Plastics further reported that a "prototype mold is currently being fabricated to prove out the feasibility of sonic welding the Kapton Film and maintaining tension."

On March 19, 1993, Mr. Campbell faxed Mr. Hofmann a sketch of the side port voicemitter and the following note: "I am having this sketched up and a simple mold made to test Sonic Weld/Kapton Concept." On March 22 and 24, Mr. Campbell faxed various diagrams of the lens retaining system and the front voicemitter housing and speaking unit, and indicated that certain joints were to be sonic welded. In monthly progress reports dated April 29 and June 30, Campbell Plastics reported on its testing of the use of sonic welding. On July 8, Mr. Campbell faxed drawings of the lens retaining system to Mr. Hoffman and stated specifically that the assembly was sonic welded. On July 21 and August 5, Mr. Campbell submitted cost estimates and noted in each that the concept of sonic welding was "nearly complete."

On October 6, 1993, Mr. Joseph J. Stehlik, ACO, wrote to Mr. Campbell to remind him that an Interim Report of Inventions and Subcontracts, preferably on a DD Form 882, must be delivered at least every twelve months from the date of the contract, listing the subject inventions during the period and also certifying that the required procedures for identifying and disclosing subject inventions have been disclosed. In the letter, Mr. Stehlik requested that Campbell Plastics submit an interim report within ten days. On October 18, Mr. Campbell submitted a DD Form 882 but did not disclose an invention.

In a monthly progress report dated June 6, 1994, Campbell Plastics stated, "Eyelens Retaining System, Branson satisfied with Sonic Weld Concept-best under design restrictions." On September 15, Mr. Campbell submitted a DD Form 882 that again indicated that no invention had been developed under the contract. Campbell Plastics did not submit another DD Form 882 for the remainder of the contract period, and it received no further request from the Army to do so. In monthly progress reports dated October 7 and November 8, Campbell Plastics reported continued work on the sonic welding process.

On February 7 and November 24, 1995, Mr. Campbell faxed Mr. Hofmann drawings that identified changes in the dimensions of the eyelens retaining system to facilitate sonic welding.

In June 1997, the Army published a report titled, "Design of the XM45 Chemical-Biological, Aircrew, Protective Mask." The report disclosed research conducted by the Army from October 1991 through July 1995, and referenced sonic welded components in the mask.

In August 1997, Campbell Plastics contacted an attorney who soon after drafted a patent application for a "Sonic Welded Gas Mask and Process." Campbell Plastics filed the application on October 9, 1997. The U.S. Patent and Trademark Office ("USPTO") made the application available to the Army for the limited purpose of making a secrecy determination pursuant to 35 U.S.C. § 181 (1994). Pursuant to the USPTO's request, the Army reviewed Campbell Plastics's application by January 30, 1998.

The patent application issued on April 20, 1999, as U.S. Patent No. 5,895,537 ("the '537 patent"). The '537 patent expressly reserved for the government a paid-up license and "the right in limited circumstances to require the patent owner to license others on reasonable terms as provided for by the terms of Contract No. DAAA15-92-C-0082 awarded by The Army." On April 28, Campbell Plastics notified the Army in writing of the '537 patent.

After an exchange of letters between the parties regarding the Army's claim to joint ownership of the subject invention, including one in which the Army admitted that it had, by June 1997, a report drafted by government employees that provided an enabling disclosure of the invention, the ACO ultimately concluded that Campbell Plastics forfeited title to the patent by failing to comply with FAR 52.227-11.

On March 14, 2001, Campbell Plastics appealed the ACO's decision. Both parties filed cross-motions for summary judgment. Though Campbell Plastics conceded in its motion that its disclosure was not in the form of a DD Form 882 as was required by the contract, Campbell Plastics argued that it disclosed all technical aspects of the invention to the Army and that the Army admittedly had an enabling disclosure of the subject invention by June 1997. Campbell Plastics furthermore argued that forfeiture is not favored by law, especially where the government suffered no genuine harm. In short, Campbell Plastics framed its failure to comply with the contract as one in form only, which should not result in the forfeiture of title to the subject invention.

In denying the appeal, the Board ruled that Campbell Plastics failed to satisfy its contractual obligation to inform the Army that it considered sonic welding to be an invention. The Board further ruled that any information the Army gleaned from its review of the patent application for secrecy determination purposes and its own June 1997 report was not provided by Campbell Plastics, and that forfeiture was appropriate under the circumstances. Finally, the Board recognized that FAR 52.227-11(d), which specifies when the government "may" obtain title to a subject invention, vests the Army with some discretion in determining whether to take title. The Board found, however, that the Army had not abused its discretion. Campbell Plastics now appeals the Board's decision. We have jurisdiction pursuant to 28 U.S.C. § 1295(a)(10) (2000).

II

The Contract Disputes Act ("CDA"), 41 U.S.C. § 609(b) (2000), governs this court's review of Board decisions. While the CDA provides for nondeferential review of the Board's legal conclusions, it specifies that the Board's factual findings shall be final and conclusive unless they are "fraudulent, or arbitrary, or capricious, or so grossly erroneous as to necessarily imply bad faith, or if such decision is not supported by substantial evidence." *Id.*

III

Because we have never before defined a contractor's obligation to disclose a "subject invention" under FAR 52.227-11, this case presents a matter of first impression for this court.

In 1980, Congress passed the Bayh-Dole Act, 35 U.S.C. §§ 200–212, the statutory scheme from which FAR 52.227-11 arises. With few exceptions, the Act allows nonprofit organizations and small business firms to elect to retain title to any invention by the contractor developed pursuant to a government contract. For purposes of the Act, Congress has termed these inventions "subject inventions." *See* 35 U.S.C. § 201(d)–(e) (1988) (defining an "invention" to mean "any invention or discovery that is or may be patentable," and "subject invention" to mean "any invention of the contractor conceived or first actually reduced to practice in the performance of work under a funding agreement").

Congress required that each government contract entered into pursuant to the Act shall contain provisions that require the contractor to "disclose each subject invention to the Federal agency within a reasonable time after it becomes known to contractor personnel responsible for the administration of patent matters, and that the Federal Government may receive title to any subject invention not disclosed to it within such time." 35 U.S.C. § 202(c)(1) (1988). The reasons for this are clear. Though the Act provides nonprofit organizations and small business firms the right to elect title to a subject invention, it also vests in the government the right to a paid-up license to practice the invention when the contractor elects to retain title, *id.* § 202(c)(4), and the right to receive title to the invention in the United States or any other country in which the contractor has not filed a patent application on the invention prior to any pertinent statutory bar date, *id.* § 202(c)(3). The disclosure provisions of section 202(c)(1) thus provide the government adequate means with which to protect these rights.

Subsection 1.53 of Campbell Plastics's contract incorporated the clause "Patent Rights-Retention by the Contractor" of FAR 52.227-11, which obligates the contractor to disclose "subject inventions" to the government and sets forth both substantive and formal requirements for the disclosure. The clause states in relevant part:

> (c) Invention disclosure, election of title, and filing of patent application by contractor.
>
> (1) The Contractor will disclose each subject invention to the Federal agency within 2 months after the inventor discloses it in writing to Contractor personnel responsible for patent matters. The disclosure to the agency shall be in the form of a written report and shall identify the contract under which the invention was made and the inventor(s). It shall be sufficiently complete in technical detail to convey a clear understanding to the extent known at the time of the disclosure, of the nature, purpose, operation, and the physical, chemical, biological or electrical characteristics of the invention . . . .
>
> (d) Conditions when the government may obtain title. The Contractor will convey to the Federal agency, upon written request, title to any subject invention-
>
> (1) If the Contractor fails to disclose or elect title to the subject invention within the times specified in paragraph (c) of this clause . . . .

FAR 52.227-11.

Subsection H.11 of Campbell Plastics's contract, titled "Patent Rights Reports," requires the contractor to submit all interim and final invention reports "required by patent clause in Section I" on a DD Form 882, "Report of Inventions and Subcontracts," and Campbell Plastics does not dispute that the DD Form 882 is the contractual means for disclosing subject inventions pursuant to FAR 52.227-11(c)(1). In addition to the disclosure requirements of FAR 52.227-11(c)(1), the form also requires a contractor to report the title of the invention, whether it elects to file a patent application in either the United States or a foreign country, and any foreign country so elected.

The language of the Patent Rights Reports clause and the incorporated FARs is clear and unambiguous. It affords the government the opportunity to take title to any invention by the contractor that is or may be patentable and was conceived or first actually reduced to practice in the performance of work under the contract if the contractor fails to disclose on a DD Form 882 the technical aspects of the invention, the inventor and the contract under which the invention was developed, within two months of disclosing the invention to contractor personnel responsible for patent matters.

This plain-meaning interpretation of the contract is buttressed by the policy considerations behind the Bayh-Dole Act. While Congress clearly intended "to promote the commercialization and public availability of inventions made in the United States by United States industry and labor," and "to encourage maximum participation of small business firms in federally supported research and development efforts," 35 U.S.C. § 200 (2000), it also provided the government with certain aforementioned rights to the inventions and sought to ensure the safeguard of those rights by requiring government contractors to disclose subject inventions. *See* 35 U.S.C. § 202 (stating that each contract shall ensure that "the contractor disclose each subject invention to the Federal agency within a reasonable time after it becomes known to contractor personnel responsible for the administration of patent matters, and that the Federal Government may receive title to any subject invention not disclosed to it within such time"); *id.* § 200 (listing the protection of the government's rights in federally supported inventions as a policy objective). A single, written report containing the information required by FAR 52.227-11(c)(1) effectively provides such a safeguard.

Neither party disputes that Campbell Plastics first disclosed the method for fabricating a sonic welded gas mask to its patent counsel in August 1997, or that the method was indeed a "subject invention." At a minimum, then, the contract required Campbell Plastics to disclose on a DD Form 882 by October 1997, the technical aspects of its method for fabricating a sonic welded gas mask, the inventor and the contract under which the invention was developed. Campbell Plastics admittedly did not do so, and instead indicated "no invention" and "none" on DD Form 882s that it did submit.

Campbell Plastics contends, however, that it continually disclosed all features of the invention throughout the contractual period. While it is at least debatable whether the various progress reports and drawings Campbell Plastics submitted to the Army together convey a clear understanding of the nature, purpose and operation of the invention as well as the invention's physical, chemical, biological or electrical characteristics, we think the contract requirement of a single, easily identified form on which to disclose inventions is sound and needs to be strictly enforced. If we were to find Campbell Plastics's style of disclosure sufficient, methods of disclosure could vary widely from case to case. The government never would be sure of which piece of paper, or which oral statement, might be part of an overall invention disclosure. But we do not so find. The contract instead demands a single form for disclosure, which enables the contracting officials to direct the inventive aspects of the contract performance to the correct personnel in the agency for a determination of whether the government has an interest in the disclosed invention, and for the government to determine how best to protect its interest. Sound policy is promoted by the rule of strict compliance with the method of disclosure demanded by the contract.

Because Campbell Plastics's piecemeal submissions do not adequately disclose the subject invention under the parties' contract, the government may take title to the invention pursuant to FAR 52.227-11(d). The arguments Campbell Plastics advances in an attempt to avoid application of that subsection are unavailing. Campbell Plastics argues that the subsection refers only to the timing of the disclosure, and not to the substance of the disclosure itself. Under Campbell Plastics's interpretation, however, it could disclose anything under the sun in any form whatsoever and still avoid forfeiture, so long as it does so within two months of disclosing the subject invention to its personnel responsible for patent matters.

Campbell Plastics also argues that the government's possession of an enabling disclosure of the subject invention by June 1997, and its review of the patent application for secrecy determination purposes, satisfied Campbell Plastics's obligations under the contract. But whatever information the government had regarding the invention, it did not get it from Campbell Plastics in the form of a proper invention disclosure.

Finally, Campbell Plastics makes much of the fact that "forfeiture" is disfavored at common law. The language of the contract is very clear, as is the statutory authority behind FAR 52.227-11, which allows the government to take title to any invention not properly disclosed. The Board was correct in holding that Campbell Plastics afforded the government the opportunity to take title to its patent because Campbell Plastics failed to disclose the invention in the manner specified in the contract. Campbell Plastics cannot use the proposition that forfeiture is a disfavored remedy as an absolute shield to thwart the government's right to enforce the terms of the contract Campbell Plastics willingly signed.

****

AFFIRMED

QUESTIONS

1. Are you persuaded by the court's reasoning that a "single, easily identified" form on which to disclose inventions is sound and needs to be strictly enforced"?

2. Do you think the court's holding is consistent with the goals of the Bayh-Dole Act?

3. What are the prospects for commercial development of the "sonic weld" technology after the *Campbell Plastics* decision? Is this something the court should have considered?

4. What interests of the government are served by allowing government agencies to take title to inventions that are not properly disclosed?

5. If you were counsel to Campell Plastics in this litigation, what additional arguments would you have made to support Campbell Plastics' position?

CASE NOTES

1.   Hillis was a graduate student at MIT working on projects partially funded by the federal Advanced Research Projects Agency (ARPA). During the course of his work, Hillis invented what he called a "connection machine" for massively parallel processors. MIT disclosed Hillis' invention to the Navy but said that because of budgetary constraints and limited commercial potential, MIT would not elect to apply for a patent. MIT waived its rights in the invention to allow Hillis to file a patent application in his own name. The waiver agreement stated that Hillis' patent application should recite that "the government has rights in this invention pursuant to a contract with the Advanced Research Projects Agency." The waiver agreement also stated that "any licenses issued to commercial concerns under the invention should acknowledge the government's royalty-free license to the invention." Hillis proceeded to file a patent application in his own name which resulted in the issuance of the '773 patent. However, the '773 patent did not include the language regarding the government's retained rights. Hillis also did not file forms with the Navy that were necessary for the Navy to release its rights in the patent. After the '773 patent issued, Hillis assigned his rights in the patent to Thinking Machines Corporation (TM). TM later sued IBM for infringement of the '773 patent. IBM partly defended the infringement action by claiming that Hillis never had title to the '773 patent because he had failed to include the required language in his patent application and never perfected his title with the Navy. What result? *See* TM Patents v. International Business Machines Corporation, 121 F.Supp.2d 349 (S.D.N.Y. 2000).

Additional Information

1.   Jeanne D. Wertz, Corporate Counsel's Guide to Licensing § 22:2 (2010).

2.   John G. Mills, Et al., Patent Law Fundamentals §§ 18:6–18:12 (2d) (2011).

3.   Wendy H. Schacht, Cong. Research Serv., RL 32076, The Bayh-Dole Act: Selected Issues in Patent Policy and the Commercialization of Technology (2008).

4.   Irwin Aisenberg, Modern Patent Law Precedents B120, B130 (8th ed. (2011).

5.   Robert Goldscheider, 3 Eckstrom's Licensing — Forms § 12:2 (2011).

6.   Stephen Z. Szczwpanski, David M. Epstein, 3 Eckstrom's Licensing in For. & Dom. Ops. §§ 14:9, 14:11 (2010).

7.   Jeanne D. Wertz, Corp Couns Gd to Licensing § 22:2 (2010).

8.   Alan S. Gutterman, 1 Corp Couns Gd to Tech Mgmt & Trans §§ 15:8–15:9 (2010).

9.   James D. Clements, *Improving Bayh-Dole: A Case for Inventor Ownership of Federally Sponsored Research Patents*, 49 IDEA 469 (2009).

10.   Dov Greenbaum, *Academia to Industry Technology Transfer: An Alternative to the Bayh-Dole System for Both Developed and Developing Nations*, 19 Fordham Intell. Prop. Media & Ent. L.J. 311 (2009).

11. David A. Kanarfogel, *Rectify the Missing Costs of University Patent Practices: Addressing Bayh-Dole Criticisms Through Faculty Involvement*, 27 CARDOZA ARTS & ENT. L.J. 533 (2009).

12. Michael S. Mireless, *Adoption of the Bayh-Dole Act in Developed Countries: Added Pressure for a Broad Research Exemption in the United States*, 59 ME. L. REV. 259 (2007).

13. Chester G. Moore, *Killing the Bayh-Dole Act's Golden Goose*, 8 TUL. J. TECH. & INTELL. PROP. 151 (2006).

14. April L. Butler, *Stealing Thunder From Government Contractors: Thwarting the Intent of the Bayh-Dole Act in Campbell Plastics v. Brownlee*, 31 U. DAYTON L. REV. 477 (2006).

15. Gary Pulsinelli, *Share and Share Alike: Increasing Access to Government-Funded Inventions Under the Bayh-Dole Act*, 7 MINN. J. L. SCI. & TECH. 393 (2006).

16. Sara Boettiger, Alan B. Bennet, *Bayh-Dole: if we knew then what we know now*, 24 Nature Biotechnology 320 (2006), *available at* http://www.nature.com/nbt/journal/v24/n3/full/nbt0306-320.html.

17. John H. Raubitschek, *Responsibilities Under the Bayh-Dole Act*, 87 J. PAT. & TRADEMARK OFF. SOC'Y 311 (2005).

18. David C. Mowery, Colloquium on Entrepreneurship Education and Technology Transfer, *The Bayh-Dole Act and High-Technology Entrepreneurship in U.S. Universities: Chicken, Egg or Something Else?*, *available at* http://entrepreneurship.eller.arizona.edu/docs/conferences/2005/colloquium/D_Mowery.pdf.

19. Thomas J. Siepmann, *The Global Exportation of the U.S. Bayh-Dole Act*, 30 U. DAYTON L. REV. 209 (2004).

20. Mark L. Gordon, *University Controlled or Owned Technology: The State of Commercialization and Recommendations*, 30 J. C. & U. L. 641 (2004).

21. Scott D. Locke, *Patent Litigation Over Federally Funded Inventions and the Consequences of Failing to Comply with Bayh-Dole*, 8 VA. J. L. & TECH. 3 (2003).

22. Rebecca S. Eisenberg, *Public Research and Private Development: Patents and Technology Transfer in Government Sponsored Research*, 82 VA. L. REV. 1663 (1996).

3.1.2 March-In Rights

Section 203 of the Bayh-Dole Act provides:

(a)With respect to any subject invention in which a small business firm or nonprofit organization has acquired title under this chapter, the Federal agency under whose funding agreement the subject invention was made shall have the right, in accordance with such procedures as are provided in regulations promulgated hereunder to require the contractor, an assignee or exclusive licensee of a subject invention to grant a nonexclusive, partially exclusive, or exclusive license in any field of use to a responsible applicant or applicants, upon terms that are reasonable under the circumstances, and if the contractor, assignee, or exclusive licensee refuses such request, to grant such a license itself, if the Federal agency determines that such —

(1) action is necessary because the contractor or assignee has not taken, or is not expected to take within a reasonable time, effective steps to achieve practical application of the subject invention in such field of use;

(2) action is necessary to alleviate health or safety needs which are not reasonably satisfied by the contractor, assignee, or their licensees;

(3) action is necessary to meet requirements for public use specified by Federal regulations and such requirements are not reasonably satisfied by the contractor, assignee, or licensees; or

(4) action is necessary because the agreement required by section 204 has not been obtained or waived or because a licensee of the exclusive right to use or sell any subject invention in the United States is in breach of its agreement obtained pursuant to section 204.

The National Institutes of Health has considered whether to exercise march-in rights under § 203(a)(1) (insufficient steps to achieve practical application of the subject invention) and § 203(a)(2) (actions necessary to alleviate unmet health of safety needs). In the *Norvir* case, NIH sought to balance alleged drug overpricing and the need for investment stability in order to bring new drugs to market. In the *CellPro* case, NIH sought to balance patient access to new medical technology and market competition under the patent laws.

IN THE CASE OF NORVIR® MANUFACTURED BY ABBOTT LABORATORIES, INC.
NATIONAL INSTITUTES OF HEALTH, OFFICE OF THE DIRECTOR (2004)

Introduction

The NIH received letters from members of Congress and the public requesting that the Government exercise its march-in rights under the Bayh Dole Act (Act), 35 U.S.C. §§ 200–212, in connection with one or more patents owned by Abbott Laboratories, Inc. (Abbott). The letters expressed concern over the price of Norvir®, which is covered by the patents and marketed by Abbott for the treatment of patients with HIV/AIDS.

The march-in provision of the Act, 35 U.S.C. § 203, implemented by 37 C.F.R. § 401.6, authorizes the Government, in certain specified circumstances, to require the funding recipient or its exclusive licensee to license a Federally-funded invention to a responsible applicant or applicants on reasonable terms, or to grant such a license itself.

After careful analysis of the Bayh-Dole Act and considering all the facts in this case as well as comments received, the National Institutes of Health (NIH) has determined that it will not initiate a march-in proceeding as it does not believe that such a proceeding is warranted based on the available information and the statutory and regulatory framework.

Background on the Invention

From 1988 through 1993, ritonavir was developed at Abbott Laboratories partly through the use of Federal funds and falls within the claims of a number of patents owned by Abbott. In 1996, ritonavir (sold under the tradename "Norvir®") was approved by the FDA for marketing.

Other U.S. and foreign patents may exist which cover certain aspects of the marketed compound including specific formulations or delivery techniques, and may not be subject inventions within the meaning of the term as defined in 35 U.S.C. § 201(e). These inventions would not be subject to the Government's march-in authority.

Statutory and Regulatory Background

The stated policy and objective of the Bayh-Dole Act is:

> to use the patent system to promote the utilization of inventions arising from federally supported research or development; to encourage maximum participation of small business firms in federally supported research and development efforts; to promote collaboration between commercial concerns and nonprofit organizations, including universities; to ensure that inventions made by nonprofit organizations and small business firms are used in a manner to promote free competition and enterprise without unduly encumbering future research and discovery; to promote the commercialization and public availability of inventions made in the United States by United States industry and labor; to ensure that the Government obtains sufficient rights in federally supported inventions to meet the needs of the Government and protect the public against nonuse or unreasonable use of inventions; and to minimize the costs of administering policies in this area. Act at § 200.

Toward this goal, the Act addresses not only rules governing the licensing of Government-owned inventions, but also addresses the rights of Federal contractors to elect title to inventions made with Federal funding.

In giving contractors the right to elect title to inventions made with Federal funding, the Act also includes various safeguards on the public investment in the research. For example, the Federal agency retains a nonexclusive, nontransferable, irrevocable, paid-up license to practice or have practiced for or on behalf of the United States any subject invention throughout the world. See 35 U.S.C. § 202(c)(4). In addition, the Act includes march-in rights which provide a Federal agency with the authority, in certain very limited and specified circumstances, to make sure that a federally funded invention is made available to the public. The march-in provisions are set out in Section 203(a), which states that:

With respect to any subject invention in which a small business firm or nonprofit organization has acquired title under this chapter, the Federal agency under whose funding agreement the subject invention was made shall have the right, in accordance with such procedures as are provided in regulations promulgated hereunder to require the contractor, an assignee or exclusive licensee of a subject invention to grant a nonexclusive, partially exclusive, or exclusive license in any field of use to a responsible applicant or applicants, upon terms that are reasonable under the circumstances, and if the contractor, assignee, or exclusive licensee refuses such request, to grant such a license itself, if the Federal agency determines that such

(1) action is necessary because the contractor or assignee has not taken, or is not expected to take within a reasonable time, effective steps to achieve practical application of the subject invention in such field of use;

(2) action is necessary to alleviate health or safety needs which are not reasonably satisfied by the contractor, assignee, or their licensees;

(3) action is necessary to meet requirements for public use specified by Federal regulations and such requirements are not reasonably satisfied by the contractor, assignee, or licensees; or

(4) action is necessary because the agreement required by section 204 has not been obtained or waived or because a licensee of the exclusive right to use or sell any subject invention in the United States is in breach of its agreement obtained pursuant to section 204.

The Department of Commerce regulations implementing the Act and specifying the procedures that govern the exercise of march in proceedings are set forth at 37 C.F.R. § 401.6. The regulations provide that whenever an agency receives information that it believes might warrant the exercise of march-in rights, it may initiate a march-in proceeding after notification of the contractor and a request to the contractor for informal written or oral comments.

Public Comments

The NIH held a public meeting on May 25, 2004 at which comments were presented by advocates for and against the use of the Government's march-in authority in connection with Norvir®. The speakers presented differing perspectives regarding the interpretation and intention of the march-in provisions, the reasons for the increase in the price of ritonavir, and the anti-competitive effect of that price increase.

The NIH also has received written comments from a variety of groups and individuals representing universities, the AIDS community, pharmaceutical interests, drafters of the Bayh-Dole Act, and other interested parties. These comments along with those submitted at the public meeting are available on the NIH Office of Technology Transfer website at http://www.ott.nih.gov/policy/meeting/mav25.htm.

The NIH is aware that members of Congress and the public have asked the Federal Trade Commission (FTC) to investigate the potential anti-competitive effects of the increase in the price of Norvir®. The NIH agrees that the FTC is the appropriate agency to address this issue. After carefully considering all the information provided and otherwise made available, the NIH does not believe the initiation of a march-in proceeding is warranted.

Discussion

The NIH is the steward of medical and behavioral research for the nation. Its mission is science in pursuit of fundamental knowledge about the nature and behavior of living systems and the application of that knowledge to extend healthy life and reduce the burdens of illness and disability. Each year, a wealth of scientific discoveries emanates from the NIH intramural laboratories and from extramural activities under grants and contracts. Bringing these discoveries from "the bench to the bedside" requires drug and product development, scale-up, clinical testing, and finally marketing and distribution. Success in accomplishing this colossal task and fulfilling our primary mission of improving public health requires the participation of industry partners.

The NIH supports fundamental research that may lead to the development of pharmaceutical products. Occasionally, the NIH funds a technology that ultimately is incorporated into a commercial product or process for making a commercial product. It is important to the NIH that pharmaceutical companies commercialize new health care products and processes incorporating NIH-funded technology thereby making the technology available to the public. A central purpose of the Bayh-Dole Act involves the development and commercialization of such products out of federally-funded research.

Section 203(a) of the Act provides in part that march-in rights may be exercised by the funding Federal agency based on any of four conditions: (1) when "practical application" of the subject invention has not been achieved or is not expected to be achieved in a reasonable time, (2) when the action is necessary to alleviate health or safety needs, (3) when action is necessary to meet requirements for public use specified by Federal regulation that the contractor has failed to meet or (4) when the U.S. industry preference of Section 204 of the Act has not been met. The third and fourth conditions are not relevant to this discussion.

Practical Application of the Subject Inventions

A composition or product, such as Norvir®, that has achieved practical application is defined in Section 201(f) to mean that it is manufactured "under such conditions as to establish that the invention is being utilized and that its benefits are to the extent permitted by law or Government regulations available to the public on reasonable terms." In 1997, the NIH reviewed a march-in request from CellPro, Inc. that asserted Baxter Healthcare Corporation (Baxter) had failed to take effective steps to achieve practical application of the subject inventions. NIH determined that Baxter "met the statutory and regulatory standard for practical application" as evidenced by its "manufacture, practice, and operation" of the invention and the invention's "availability to and use by the public . . . ." Accordingly, the NIH determined not to initiate march-in proceedings.

Similarly, the record in this instance demonstrates that Abbott has met the standard for achieving practical application of the applicable patents by its manufacture, practice, and operation of ritonavir and the drug's availability and use by the public.

Ritonavir has been on the market and available to patients with HIV/ADDS since 1996, when it was introduced and sold under the tradename Norvir® as both a standalone protease inhibitor and a booster to increase the effectiveness of protease inhibitors marketed by other companies. Thus, the invention has reached practical application because it is being utilized and has been made widely available for use by patients with HIV/AIDS for at least eight years.

Health or Safety Needs

Norvir® has been approved by the Food and Drug Administration as safe and effective and is being widely prescribed by physicians for its approved indications. No evidence has been presented that march-in could alleviate any health or safety needs that are not reasonably satisfied by Abbott. Rather, the argument advanced is that the product should be available at a lower price, which is addressed below. Thus, the NIH concludes that Abbott has met the statutory and regulatory standard for health or safety needs.

Drug Pricing

Finally, the issue of the cost or pricing of drugs that include inventive technologies made using Federal funds is one which has attracted the attention of Congress in several contexts that are much broader than the one at hand. In addition, because the market dynamics for all products developed pursuant to licensing rights under the Bayh-Dole Act could be altered if prices on such products were directed in any way by NIH, the NIH agrees with the public testimony that suggested that the extraordinary remedy of march-in is not an appropriate means of controlling prices. The issue of drug pricing has global implications and, thus, is appropriately left for Congress to address legislatively.

Conclusion

Norvir® has been available for use by patients with HIV/AIDS since 1996 and is being actively marketed by Abbott and prescribed by physicians primarily as a booster drug. Accordingly, this drug has reached practical application and met health or safety needs as required by the Bayh-Dole Act. The NIH believes that the issue of drug pricing is one that would be more appropriately addressed by Congress, as it considers these matters in a larger context. The NIH also maintains that the FTC is the appropriate agency to address the question of whether Abbott has engaged in anti-competitive behavior. The NIH is cognizant of the care with which Congress crafted the march-in language and understands that it has the responsibility to exercise its march-in authority deliberately and with great care. As such, the NIH has determined that it does not have information that leads it to believe that the exercise of march-in rights might be warranted in this case.

Elias A. Zerhouni, M.D., Director, NIH

QUESTIONS

1.   The facts underlying the NIH *Norvir* case are set forth in *Meijer, Inc. v. Abbott Laboratories* discussed in subsection 2.3.1 of the materials. Do you think Abbott's price increase for Norvir constituted an attempt to monopolize the protease inhibitor market?

2.   Why did NIH refuse to consider pricing as a factor in the availability of drugs to alleviate public health and safety needs?

3.   Section 203(a) of the Bayh-Dole Act provides that the agency which funded the research can require the contractor to "grant a nonexclusive, partially exclusive, or exclusive license in any field of use to a responsible applicant or applicants, upon terms that are reasonable under the circumstances . . ." Did NIH consider these options in the *Norvir* case? How could these options have affected the pricing of Norvir?

4.   If you were counsel to a group that wanted NIH to exercise march-in rights with respect to Norvir, what additional arguments would you make to support the exercise of march-in rights?

DETERMINATION IN THE CASE OF PETITION OF CELLPRO, INC.,
NATIONAL INSTITUTES OF HEALTH, OFFICE OF THE DIRECTOR (1997)

The National Institutes of Health (NIH) has determined that the initiation of march-in procedures, as requested under the petition outlined below, is not warranted at this time. NIH retains jurisdiction over the instant proceedings until such time as a comparable alternative product becomes available for sale in the United States.

The CellPro Petition

On March 3, 1997, CellPro, Incorporated (CellPro) filed a petition with the Secretary of Health and Human Services (Secretary) requesting that the Government exercise march-in rights under the Bayh Dole Act (Act), 35 U.S.C. §§ 202–212, in connection with certain patents owned by The Johns Hopkins University (Hopkins) and licensed first to Becton-Dickinson and then to Baxter Healthcare Corporation (Baxter). As discussed in greater detail below, the march-in provision of the Act authorizes the Government, in certain circumstances, to require the contractor (or grantee) or its exclusive licensee to license a Federally-funded invention to a responsible applicant on reasonable terms, or to grant such a license itself. CellPro asserts that such action is necessary to alleviate health or safety needs that have arisen because the United States District Court for the District of Delaware (Court) has found the stem cell separation device developed by CellPro, the Ceprate SC, to infringe two of the patents in question and has enjoined its sale. Alternatively, CellPro asserts that march-in is warranted because Hopkins and Baxter have failed to take reasonable steps to commercialize the technology. At the present time, CellPro is the only company that has an FDA-approved device commercially available.

The Department of Commerce regulations implementing the Act are set forth at 37 CFR § 401.6. According to § 401.6(b):

> [w]henever an agency receives information that it believes might warrant the exercise of march-in rights, before initiating any march-in proceedings, it shall notify the contractor in writing of the information and request informal written or oral comments from the contractor, as well as information relevant to the matter.

The regulations provide that "the agency shall, within 60 days after it receives the comment, either initiate the procedures below or notify the contractor, in writing, that it will not pursue march-in rights on the basis of the available information." Pursuant to § 401.6, the NIH, which has the delegated authority to make the march-in determination in this case, notified Hopkins of the petition and requested comment. Hopkins made its initial response on May 7, but in the interim, CellPro had made an additional submission to which Hopkins sought to respond. In sum, CellPro made supplemental filings on April 24, May 8, May 28 and July 2. After its initial response on May 7, Hopkins made supplemental filings on May 19, June 2 and July 2. Because the parties continued to make submissions and insist on the right to comment on the submissions of the other party, the NIH informed the parties that the 60 days set forth in the regulations for a determination by the agency would be calculated from June 2nd, but agreed to review and consider any submissions made by the parties through July 2. The administrative record in this matter consists of the submissions of the parties, letters from universities, corporations, members of Congress, and other members of the public on this issue, as well as other pertinent materials obtained by the NIH.

****

Jurisdiction

In its submissions, Hopkins suggested that NIH did not have jurisdiction in this matter. CellPro disagreed. It is our conclusion that NIH has jurisdiction to determine whether to exercise march-in with respect to the patents in question. The patents which were found by the Court to be valid and infringed are U.S. Patent Nos. 4,714,680 ('680 patent) and 4,965,204 ('204 patent). Documentation submitted by Hopkins clearly establishes that the inventions claimed in these patents were funded by the NIH. For instance, with regard to the '680 patent, Hopkins submitted to the NIH a letter dated October 4, 1984, notifying the NIH that Hopkins had elected title to the invention. In addition, Hopkins provided annual utilization reports filed during the 1980's and early 1990's, and a license from Hopkins to the U.S. Government, which expressly acknowledges that "the invention was made in the course of research supported by the DHHS." Since the inventions were funded by the NIH, as acknowledged by Hopkins well before the patent dispute with CellPro arose, there is a clear presumption of jurisdiction by the NIH, and Hopkins has not submitted sufficient evidence to rebut that presumption.

Decision

The NIH has evaluated the administrative record with regard to two prongs of the statutory criteria, 35 U.S.C. § 203(1)(a) and (b). The NIH has examined whether, (1) Baxter has failed to take, or is not expected to take within a reasonable time, effective steps to achieve practical application of the subject inventions; and, (2) there exists a health or safety need which is not reasonably satisfied by Hopkins or Baxter. Based on these criteria and the available information, march-in is not warranted at this time.

Practical Application of the Subject Inventions

Practical application is defined under 37 C.F.R. § 404.3(d) as "to manufacture in the case of a composition or product, to practice in the case of a process or method, or to operate in the case of a machine or system; and, in each case, under such conditions as to establish that the invention is being utilized and that its benefits are to the extent permitted by law or Government regulations available to the public on reasonable terms." The administrative record demonstrates that Hopkins and Baxter have clearly met this standard.

This technology was originally developed in the laboratory of Dr. Curt Civin at Hopkins and first published in 1984. Hopkins filed for patent protection and was awarded four patents, the first of which issued in 1987. The technology was first exclusively licensed to Becton-Dickinson & Co. (BD). BD began marketing the first anti-CD34 antibody in 1985 and has sold anti-CD34 antibodies worldwide ever since. Since BD was only interested in the diagnostic applications, the company exclusively sublicensed therapeutic rights to Baxter. Baxter began development of a therapeutic system and sublicensed rights to Applied Immune Sciences (now part of RPR Gencell) and Systemix (now part of Novartis). Baxter also held licensing discussions with CellPro, but no license agreement was signed.

By late 1991, Baxter had developed a prototype stem cell selection device. In 1992, Dr. Civin began clinical trials with the device, and Baxter started its own clinical trials in 1993. In January 1995, Baxter's Isolex 300 System received regulatory approval in Europe (CE Mark of Conformity for Medical Devices). In the United States, Baxter's systems have been installed in numerous transplant centers over the past three years; the Baxter device has been used in clinical trials to process peripheral blood and bone marrow for hematopoietic reconstitution in patients. On February 24, 1997, Baxter filed for Pre-market Approval (PMA) of its Isolex 300SA System. In addition to effectively licensing and developing the technology, Hopkins, BD and Baxter have aggressively defended the patents in court. In 1994, the three parties joined in a suit against CellPro for infringement of the Civin patents.

Accordingly, NIH concludes that Hopkins and Baxter have taken effective steps to achieve practical application, as demonstrated by Hopkins' licensing, Baxter's manufacture, practice, and operation of the Isolex 300, and the device's availability to and use by the public to the extent permitted at this time under applicable law (i.e., foreign sales as well as widespread clinical research use in the U.S.). With regard to FDA approval and commercial sale of the Baxter Isolex 300 in the United

States, the administrative record indicates that Baxter is vigorously pursuing an active application. Based on these facts, we conclude that Hopkins and Baxter have met the statutory and regulatory standard for practical application.

Health or Safety Needs

The question of whether the CellPro Ceprate SC fulfills health or safety needs not reasonably satisfied by the Baxter Isolex 300 has been the central inquiry and priority of the NIH in evaluating CellPro's petition for march-in. In this regard, we note the considerable debate among scientists and clinicians as to whether immunoselection of stem cells with selection devices prior to transplantation provides a clinically significant benefit to patients over standard hematopoietic transplantation techniques. The clinical benefit upon which the CellPro Ceprate SC device was approved by FDA consisted of a reduction of infusional toxicity associated with the administration of bone marrow prepared with standard techniques. To date, neither party has presented to the Biological Response Modifiers Advisory Committee any studies documenting that cell separation devices improve stem cell engraftment, disease-free survival, or overall survival. Thus, it is premature for either Baxter or CellPro to claim patient benefits (other than a decrease in infusional toxicities) from stem cell isolation and purification, T-cell, lymphocyte, and tumor cell purging, or other claimed uses.

It is equally premature, and inappropriate, for NIH to substitute its judgment for that of clinicians and patients seeking to avail themselves of an FDA-approved medical device. The FDA has determined that the Ceprate SC is safe and effective for selecting stem cells from autologous bone marrow for hematopoietic reconstitution. Thus, to the extent that the Ceprate SC is the only device that is available for sale in the United States for this purpose, it fulfills a health need for those who wish to use it, until such time as a comparable alternative product becomes available for sale.

As explained more fully below, the administrative record demonstrates that Hopkins and Baxter have taken appropriate steps to reasonably satisfy this need. First, they have refrained from enforcing patent rights to the full extent of the law in order to allow the continuing sale of the Ceprate SC until the Baxter product is approved for sale by the FDA. Second, they have pledged to ensure that the Baxter product is as widely available as possible through clinical trials, and to ensure patient access to the fullest extent possible.

(1) Continuing Sale of CellPro Device

In deference to the health need fulfilled by the CellPro device in the absence of an FDA-approved alternative, Hopkins and Baxter have refrained from enforcing their patent rights to the full extent of the law. Specifically, they modified a proposed order of injunction filed for consideration in the patent litigation in Federal District Court. The Order issued by the Court on July 24, 1997 states, in pertinent part:

> CellPro may continue to make, have made, use and sell SC Systems and disposable products (including the 12.8 antibody) for use with SC Systems,

within the United States, until such time as an alternative stem cell concentration device, manufactured under a license under the '204 and '680 patents, is approved for therapeutic use in the United States by the United States Food and Drug Administration . . . and for a period of three months thereafter.

CellPro argues vigorously, however, in documents filed prior to the entry of the Court's Order, that the terms of the proposed order, most specifically the requirement of payments to Baxter for sales of CellPro product, would force CellPro out of business and result in the loss of availability of the CellPro device.

First, we rely on the Court's finding that it is unlikely that the terms of the Order will result in the loss of availability of the CellPro product. This issue was specifically before the Court, supported by an exhaustive factual record resulting from years of litigation. Although NIH is determining whether to open a fact-finding proceeding, as opposed to conducting one, we also found no convincing evidence that CellPro will be unable to supply patients with its product under the terms of the Court Order. The terms of the Order may be unpalatable to CellPro, but CellPro need only operate under those constraints pending a decision on its appeal of the Court's adverse verdict on infringement. The Court specifically found that CellPro "possesses adequate cash reserves to allow it to continue operations during the pendency of its appeal," and determined that it would most likely be in CellPro's interest to continue operations pending the outcome of the appeal. Moreover, the Court has retained jurisdiction and invited the parties to apply to the Court for modification of the terms of the injunction, specifically, the payment of incremental profits to Baxter, if the amount determined by the Court "either provides inadequate relief or works an injustice inconsistent with equitable principles."

Second, the loss of availability of the CellPro product is relevant to the "health need" criteria only during the period prior to FDA approval and availability for sale of a comparable alternative product. In petitioning NIH to open a separate proceeding on this matter, CellPro argues that its continuing viability and success, even beyond FDA approval of a comparable alternative, should be a matter of concern to the NIH because CellPro has developed and is marketing an important health care product. Invoking our prior caveat as to the investigational nature of these devices, we concur that, as a general matter, NIH supports the development and success of the biotechnology industry. It is indeed very important to the NIH that biotechnology and pharmaceutical companies thrive and compete in order to bring new health care products to the public. Developing and commercializing such products out of federally-funded research is the foundation and essence of the Bayh-Dole Act.

We are wary, however, of forced attempts to influence the marketplace for the benefit of a single company, particularly when such actions may have far-reaching repercussions on many companies' and investors' future willingness to invest in federally funded medical technologies. The patent system, with its resultant predictability for investment and commercial development, is the means chosen by Congress for ensuring the development and dissemination of new and useful technologies. It has proven to be an effective means for the development of health care technologies. In exercising its authorities under the Bayh-Dole Act, NIH is mindful of the broader public health implications of a march-in proceeding, including the potential loss of new health care products yet to be developed from federally funded research.

On balance, we believe it is inappropriate for the NIH to intercede in this matter to ensure CellPro's commercial future. Viability and success in the private sector is appropriately governed by the marketplace, and significantly influenced by management practices and decisions. CellPro had the opportunity to license the invention from Baxter but decided against doing so, and instead risked patent infringement litigation. It would be inappropriate for the NIH, a public health agency, to exercise its authorities under the Bayh-Dole Act to procure for CellPro more favorable commercial terms than it can otherwise obtain from the Court or from the patent owners. CellPro's commercial viability is best left to CellPro's management and the marketplace.

Reasonable Steps to Ensure Widespread Availability of Baxter's Product

Hopkins and Baxter have also pledged to reasonably satisfy any health need created by the loss of the CellPro product in the unlikely event that patient access to this technology is restricted before a comparable alternative product is approved by the FDA and becomes available for sale.

In several of its submissions to NIH, and in a letter from Baxter CEO Vernon Loucks to Secretary Donna Shalala, Baxter committed to ensuring there would be no gap in patient access to stem cell separation technology. Baxter committed to installing its device free of charge at any site from which CellPro might withdraw, and to provide that site with the same level of support on the same terms as CellPro. Baxter also committed to obtaining all clinical and regulatory approvals necessary to place the Isolex system into operation as soon as possible.

CellPro asserted that Baxter is unable to fulfill this pledge; however, neither party submitted evidence sufficient for a definitive determination, and it would be premature for the NIH to act based on Baxter's failure to accomplish what events have not yet required it to do. In any event, we believe the likelihood of Baxter having to substitute devices in order to ensure patient access is remote, as discussed above. Nevertheless, pending FDA approval and availability for sale of a comparable alternative product, NIH will continue to monitor the situation and will retain jurisdiction to initiate march-in without the filing of a new request, in the event that health needs are not being reasonably satisfied.

Conclusion

The NIH has determined not to initiate proceedings to pursue march-in rights on the basis of the available information. NIH has examined the criteria of 35 U.S.C. § 203(1)(a) and (b) and found that march-in is not warranted under either criteria. Specifically, the NIH has determined that Hopkins and Baxter have taken, or are expected to take within a reasonable time, effective steps to achieve practical application of the applicable patents, as demonstrated by Hopkins' licensing activities and Baxter's manufacture, practice, and operation of the Isolex 300, as well as the pending applications for FDA approval. NIH also finds that the available information fails to demonstrate an unmet health need that is not reasonably satisfied by Hopkins and Baxter.

The NIH will continue to monitor issues related to patient access to the CellPro or Baxter devices during the period prior to FDA approval and availability for sale of a comparable alternative device.

Harold Varmus, M.D., Director, NIH

QUESTIONS

1. CellPro clearly had a commercial interest in asking NIH to exercise march-in rights. Should CellPro's commercial interest matter in determining whether march-in rights should be exercised in order to alleviate public health and safety needs?

2. The NIH decision discusses the district court order allowing CellPro to continue to sell the SC Systems until such time as an alternative stem cell concentration device is approved for therapeutic use by the FDA. What relevance did the district court order have to the question of exercising march-in rights to alleviate public health and safety needs? If the district court order had totally enjoined CellPro from selling the SC Systems, do you think the NIH result would have been different?

3. Why did NIH believe it was inappropriate to intercede to ensure CellPro's commercial viability? How would CellPro's bankruptcy have affected public health and safety?

4. NIH cites 37 C.F.R. § 404.3(d), which defines practical application as "to manufacture in the case of a composition or product, to practice in the case of a process or method, or to operate in the case of a machine or system; and, in each case, under such conditions as to establish that the invention is being utilized and that its benefits are to the extent permitted by law or Government regulations *available to the public on reasonable terms.*" [Emphasis added]. Does pricing affect the availability of a drug to the public on reasonable terms? Did NIH discuss this question in the *Norvir* decision?

5. If you were counsel to CellPro, what additional arguments would you have made to NIH in support of march-in rights?

CASE NOTES

1. Pfizer owns patents on Xalatan, a drug used to treat glaucoma. Xalatan was developed at Columbia University under NIH-funded grants in the 1970s and early 1980s. In 2002, the FDA approved Xalatan as a first-line treatment for glaucoma. Pfizer sold Xalatan at a higher price in the United States than in Canada and Europe. Letters to NIH urged it to exercise march-in rights in order to alleviate public health needs by having Xalatan's price in the United States the same as its price in other countries. What result? *See* In the Case of Xalatan Manufactured by Pfizer, Inc., National Institutes of Health, Office of the Director (2004).

Additional Information

1. IRWIN AISENBERG, MODERN PATENT LAW PRECEDENT M250.500 (8th ed. 2009).

2. MARK S. HOLMES, PATENT LICENSING: STRATEGY, NEGOTIATIONS & FORMS § 2:6 (2010).

3. 26 FEDERAL PROCEDURE, LAWYERS EDITION § 60:853 (2010).

4. U.S. GOV'T ACCOUNTABILITY OFFICE, GAO-09-742, FEDERAL RESEARCH: INFORMATION ON THE GOVERNMENT'S RIGHT TO ASSERT OWNERSHIP CONTROL OVER FEDERALLY FUNDED INVENTIONS (July 2009).

5. John H. Raubitschek, Norman J. Latker, *Reasonable Pricing — A New Twist for March-In Rights Under the Bayh-Dole Act*, 22 SANTA CLARA COMPUTER & HIGH TECH. L.J. 149 (2005).

6. David Halperin, *The Bayh-Dole Act and March-In Rights*, NATIONAL INSTITUTE OF HEALTH OFFICE OF TECHNOLOGY TRANSFER (May 2001), *available at* http://ott.od.nih.gov/policy/meeting/David-Halperin-Attorney-Counselor.pdf.

7. Peter Mikhail, *Hopkins v. CellPro: An Illustration That Patenting and Exclusive Licensing of Fundamental Science Is Not Always in the Public Interest*, 13 HARV. J.L. & TECH. 375 (2000).

8. Tamsen Valoir, *Government Funded Inventions: The Bayh-Dole Act and the Hopkins v. CellPro March-In Controversy*, 8 TEX. INTELL. PROP. L.J. 211 (2000).

9. Mary Eberle, Comment, *March-In Rights Under the Bayh-Dole Act: Public Access to Federally Funded Research*, 3 MARQ. INTELL. PROP. L. REV. 155 (1999).

10. Kevin W. McCabe, *Implications of the CellPro Determination on Inventions Made with Federal Assistance: Will the Government Ever Exercise Its March-In Right?*, 27 PUB. CONT. L.J. 645 (1998).

3.1.3 Standing to Sue

We saw in subsection 2.2.9 of the materials that, in the context of private party litigation, only an exclusive licensee holding substantially all of the rights under a patent has standing to sue for infringement without the joinder of the licensor-patent owner. Standing to sue under the Bayh-Dole Act raises different considerations because it involves federal legislation and the federal government. Standing issues under the Bayh-Dole Act arise in two contexts. The first is when a private party attempts to assert a claim based upon the Bayh-Dole Act. Here, the question of standing depends upon whether the Bayh-Dole Act created a cause of action on behalf of private parties. The *Service Engineering* case addresses this question. The second context in which standing issues arise under the Bayh-Dole Act is when a licensee of a US-owned patent attempts to sue a third party infringer without joining the United States as a co-plaintiff. The *Nutrition 21* case addresses this question.

SERVICE ENGINEERING v. U.S.D.A.
1999 U.S. Dist. LEXIS 21952 (1999)

Opinion Memorandum

Now pending before the court are the parties' cross-motions for summary judgment. In this lawsuit, Service Engineering Corporation and Edward G. Bounds, Jr., (collectively "Plaintiffs") sue the United States Department of Agriculture ("USDA" or "the agency") for granting an exclusive license in U.S. Patent No. 4,458,630 ("the '630 patent" or "the patent") to Embrex, Inc., in June 1986 and for extending the term of the license in April 1994. Plaintiffs contend that in taking these actions, the USDA or its predecessors in interest violated the procedural and substantive provisions of the Bayh-Dole Act of 1980, codified at 35 U.S.C. §§ 200–212. Plaintiffs further contend that the agency wrongly relied upon the Embrex license in denying Plaintiffs' application for a non-exclusive license in the patent in January 1997. In opposition, the USDA asserts alternatively that (1) Plaintiffs lack standing to pursue these claims, (2) Plaintiffs are estopped from challenging the Embrex license, (3) the decision to license the '630 patent is committed to the USDA's discretion as a matter of law, and (4) the agency fully complied with all statutory and regulatory requirements in licensing the '630 patent to Embrex. Because the court agrees that Plaintiffs lack standing to challenge the USDA's actions in this matter, the agency's motion for summary judgment will be granted.

Background

In July 1984, the United States Department of Agriculture was issued U.S. Patent No. 4,458,630 for an improved method of vaccinating poultry and other avian species against disease through embryonal inoculation. In March 1985, the USDA transferred custody of the patent for licensing purposes to the National Technical Information Service ("NTIS"), a division of the United States Department of Commerce. In accordance with 37 C.F.R. § 404.7(a)(1), availability of the patent for commercial licensing was announced in the Federal Register on September 11, 1984.

In early 1985, Merieux Laboratories, Inc., ("Merieux") a French-owned company with offices in Athens, Georgia, applied for an exclusive license to utilize the patented technology. USDA officials initially viewed Merieux's application favorably, and on May 22, 1985, notice of intent to grant Merieux an exclusive license was published in the Federal Register, as required by 35 U.S.C. § 209(c)(1). The notice fully complied with agency regulations by identifying the prospective license ("exclusive"), the subject invention ("U.S. Patent 4,458,630"), and the prospective licensee ("Merieux").

During the prescribed comment period, two companies, Embrex, Inc., and Salsbury Laboratories, submitted their own applications for licenses in the patent. Like Merieux, Embrex sought an exclusive license, while Salsbury Laboratories sought a non-exclusive license. Neither Mr. Bounds nor Service Engineering Corporation ("Service") (which was not then in existence) filed an application for a license in the '630 patent or opposed the applications filed by the other companies.

After reviewing the three applications, NTIS decided to award an exclusive license in the '630 patent to Embrex. Specifically, Embrex was granted a 10 1/2-year exclusive license in the patent, running from June 15, 1986, to December 31, 1996, followed by a non-exclusive license for the remainder of the patent term. No notice of NTIS's intent to grant Embrex (instead of Merieux) an exclusive license was ever published in the Federal Register, however, in apparent violation of both statutory and regulatory requirements. Plaintiffs now claim that the Embrex license should be declared null and void ab initio as a result of NTIS's alleged failure to publish the proper notice.

In December 1991, various provisions of the licensing agreement between NTIS and Embrex for the '630 patent were revised, but the term of exclusivity remained unchanged. Plaintiffs do not challenge any of these revisions. Sometime thereafter, responsibility for administering the patent was returned to the USDA. In April 1994, the licensing agreement was revised a second time. This time, the period of exclusivity was extended to cover the entire patent term. As a result, instead of possessing an exclusive license that expired in December 1996, followed by a non-exclusive license that ran through the end of the remaining patent period, Embrex now possessed a single exclusive license for the entire patent term.

The parties dispute how this change should be characterized. The USDA argues that this change represented a mere "modification" or "amendment" to Embrex's exclusive license previously awarded. Plaintiffs argue that this change constituted "a new, exclusive license from January 1, 1997 through the expiration of the term of the '630 patent." In any event, the parties are in agreement that no notice was ever published of the USDA's intent to grant Embrex this additional period of exclusivity. Plaintiffs contend that this lack of notice renders the 1994 revisions null and void. Plaintiffs also contend that the 1994 revisions were adopted without the statutorily required findings.

In 1995, Embrex brought suit in the United States District Court for the Eastern District of North Carolina against Plaintiffs and others for infringement of the '630 patent. This suit was dismissed without prejudice on November 10, 1995, pursuant to a settlement agreement between Embrex and Plaintiffs. The settlement agreement provided that "Embrex is the exclusive licensee of the United States of America under U.S. Patent No. 4,458,630" and required Plaintiffs to refrain from "practicing the method of any claim of the '630 patent" "for so long as the '630 patent has not been held invalid or unenforceable by a court of competent jurisdiction from which no appeal can be taken." In 1996, Embrex returned to district court seeking monetary and injunctive relief for Plaintiffs' alleged breach of the settlement agreement and infringement of the '630 patent. This action ultimately resulted in a jury verdict in Embrex's favor.

On December 30, 1996, one day before the original term of exclusivity would have expired, Plaintiffs applied to the USDA for a non-exclusive license in the '630 patent. The agency rejected Plaintiff's application on January 9, 1997, explaining that the patent "is not available for licensing because it is exclusively licensed to Embrex, Inc." Plaintiffs appealed the negative decision to the Secretary of Agriculture in accordance with agency procedures. In March 1997, the agency denied Plaintiffs' appeal. Plaintiffs filed the present lawsuit on March 21, 1997. They now seek a ruling from this court declaring Embrex's original exclusive license in the '630 patent as well as the 1994 extension of the exclusivity period illegal and invalid and ordering the USDA to reconsider Plaintiffs' application for a non-exclusive license in the patent. For the reasons that follow, the court will decline to award the relief Plaintiffs seek.

Analysis

The USDA moves for summary judgment as to all of Plaintiffs' claims on the grounds, inter alia, that Plaintiffs lack standing to challenge the agency's actions in awarding an exclusive license in the '630 patent to Embrex in 1986 and in extending the license's exclusivity period in 1994. Specifically, the agency contends that Plaintiffs have demonstrated no actual injury resulting from the agency's actions in this matter and that Plaintiffs' asserted interests do not fall within the zone of interests protected by the Bayh-Dole Act.

In opposition, Plaintiffs claim that they have suffered three distinct injuries directly caused by the challenged agency actions: First, Plaintiffs claim that they have suffered a "competitive" injury due to their inability to compete effectively with Embrex which, Plaintiffs allege, "has and is continuing to use its unlawfully obtained position to interfere with Service's development efforts in order to exclude Service from both the U.S. and international markets." Plaintiffs offer no evidence in support of this claim of economic harm. Second, Plaintiffs claim that they have been injured as a result of twice being sued by Embrex for patent infringement. And third, Plaintiffs claim that they were injured when the USDA rejected their application for a non-exclusive license in the patent. Finally, Plaintiffs argue that their interests fall within the zone of interests protected by the Bayh-Dole Act which, they contend, is intended to protect economic competitors "from undue concentration and other anticompetitive effects of government licensing policies."

Article III of the United States Constitution limits the "judicial power" of the federal courts to the resolution of "cases" and "controversies." One of the requirements of a "case" or "controversy" is that the plaintiff have "standing" to challenge the action sought to be adjudicated in the lawsuit. The law of standing comprises both constitutional requirements and prudential considerations.

The irreducible constitutional minimum of standing requires: (1) that the plaintiff personally has suffered actual or threatened injury that is concrete and particularized, not conjectural or hypothetical; (2) that the injury fairly can be traced to the challenged action; and (3) that the injury is likely to be redressed by a favorable decision from the court. "An asserted right to have the Government act in accordance with law is not sufficient, standing alone, to confer jurisdiction on a federal court."

In addition to the constitutional requirements for standing, where a plaintiff challenges agency action pursuant to the Administrative Procedure Act, 5 U.S.C. § 702 (providing that "[a] person suffering legal wrong because of agency action, or adversely affected or aggrieved by agency action within the meaning of a relevant statute, is entitled to judicial review thereof"), the interests sought to be protected by the plaintiff must " "arguably [fall] within the zone of interests to be protected or regulated by the statute . . . in question." " Here, the statute in question is the Bayh-Dole Act of 1980, codified at 35 U.S.C. §§ 200–212. Thus, in order to have standing to pursue their claims in this case, Plaintiffs must demonstrate that they have suffered an actual injury arguably within the zone of interests protected by the Bayh-Dole Act that is fairly traceable to the challenged agency actions and that is redressable by a favorable decision of this court.

In their motion for summary judgment, Plaintiffs contend, first, that the exclusive license for the '630 patent issued to Embrex in 1986 was granted in violation of the Bayh-Dole Act's mandatory notice and comment provision and its implementing regulations. 35 U.S.C. § 209(c)(1) (providing that "each Federal agency may grant exclusive or partially exclusive licenses in any invention covered by a federally owned domestic patent or patent application only if, after public notice and opportunity for filing written objections" certain determinations are made). Plaintiffs argue that the May 1985 notice of the agency's initial intent to grant an exclusive license to Merieux did not satisfy these requirements with respect to the exclusive license ultimately awarded to Embrex. The USDA disagrees. The only court that has addressed this issue assumed without discussion that where a new licensee is substituted for the originally proposed licensee, separate notice identifying the new licensee is required. This court declines to reach the merits of Plaintiffs' claim, however, because it finds that Plaintiffs lack standing to challenge NTIS's 1986 decision to grant an exclusive license in the '630 patent to Embrex.

First, to meet the requirements of the prudential standing doctrine, Plaintiffs must show that their " "interests affected by the agency action" are "among" those that Congress arguably sought to protect." The Bayh-Dole Act authorizes agencies of the federal government to "grant nonexclusive, exclusive, or partially exclusive licenses under federally owned patent applications, patents, or other forms of protection . . . as determined appropriate in the public interest." 35 U.S.C. § 207(a)(2). Congress's primary "policy and objective" in adopting the Act was "to promote the utilization of inventions arising from federally supported research and development." Congress also was concerned that the federal government "obtain[] sufficient rights in federally supported inventions to meet the needs of the Government and protect the public against nonuse or unreasonable use of inventions." In keeping with these purposes, before a federal agency may grant an exclusive or partially exclusive license in a federally-owned patent, the agency must determine that granting such a license is reasonably necessary "to bring the invention to practical application or otherwise promote the invention's utilization by the public." Furthermore, the terms of any licensing agreement must provide for "the protection of the interests of the Federal Government and the public."

In light of this statutory language, the court agrees with the USDA that the goal of the Bayh-Dole Act is to "secure the public good of commercial exploitation of patents on inventions which result from government-funded research." The court does not agree with Plaintiffs' position that the Act was intended to protect individuals, including corporations, from the "anticompetitive effects of government licensing policies." Indeed, the Act clearly anticipates, even encourages, such "anticompetitive effects" since it permits the exclusive licensing of patented government inventions. While it is true that Congress directed federal agencies not to grant exclusive or partially exclusive licenses where doing so would be "inconsistent with the antitrust laws," 35 U.S.C. § 209(c)(2), nothing in the Act indicates that Congress intended to protect the specific economic interests of parties in competition with government licensees.

Furthermore, Plaintiffs offer no persuasive evidence that the notice and comment provision, in particular, was intended to promote the interests of such competitors. Rather, the court finds that by including the notice and comment provision in the statute, Congress intended to benefit the general public by improving an agency's ability to decide whether granting an exclusive or partially exclusive license will "bring the invention to practical application or otherwise promote the invention's utilization by the public." See 35 U.S.C. § 209(c)(1)(A)–(D). Consequently, the court concludes that Plaintiffs lack prudential standing to challenge the 1986 grant of an exclusive license in the '630 patent to Embrex because Plaintiffs' interests fall outside the zone of interests protected by the Bayh-Dole Act.

In support of their standing argument, Plaintiffs cite Head Start Family Educ. Program, Inc. v. Cooperative Educ. Serv. Agency, which they suggest is "strikingly similar" to the case at bar. On the contrary, the facts and law of Head Start are quite different. In Head Start, the Administration for Children and Families ("ACF"), the division of the United States Department of Health and Human Services ("HHS") responsible for managing the Head Start program, terminated its contract with the then-designated Head Start grantee serving a seven county region of the state of Wisconsin. Thereafter, ACF solicited applications for a permanent replacement grantee for the region. Both the plaintiff and the defendant in Head Start submitted applications for the contract, as did the original grantee. After the original grantee was eliminated from consideration, the defendant's application was chosen over the plaintiff's, although the plaintiff's application had received a slightly higher score from an independent review panel.

The plaintiff subsequently filed suit in federal district court, contending that it should have been awarded the Head Start contract "because it was the only eligible applicant under the Head Start Act and HHS regulations." After the district court granted summary judgment in favor of the defendant, the plaintiff appealed. Although the Seventh Circuit affirmed the district court's judgment, it rejected the defendant's argument that the plaintiff lacked standing to challenge the award. Citing a "disappointed bidder" case from the D.C. Circuit, the court held without further explanation that the plaintiff's claim "clearly satisfies the requirements of Article III and is also sufficient to confer standing under section 702 of the APA."

It is well-established in the Fourth Circuit that parties whose applications for government contracts are improperly rejected may have standing to pursue their claims in federal court. As in Head Start and other "disappointed bidder" cases, the plaintiffs in each of these Fourth Circuit cases submitted bids for government contracts in response to the agencies' requests for proposals. Having done so, the plaintiffs were entitled to have their bids treated fairly. This "right to reasonable treatment of their bids," which derived from the "combination" of the federal procurement statute and the review provisions of the APA, provided the basis for the plaintiffs' standing to challenge the agencies' allegedly unlawful denials of their applications.

In this case, however, Plaintiffs cannot qualify as disappointed bidders for the 1986 license in the '630 patent. Although notice of the patent's availability was published in September 1984 and notice of NTIS's intent to grant an exclusive license to Merieux was published in May 1985, neither Mr. Bounds nor Service (which was not then in existence) submitted an application for the license or otherwise indicated any interest in obtaining rights to the patent. Thus, Plaintiffs' position is not at all like the positions of the plaintiffs in Head Start and the three Fourth Circuit cases. Without some clearer indication in the statute, therefore, this court simply cannot find that the Bayh-Dole Act was intended by Congress to protect the interests of parties who voluntarily fail to participate in an agency's patent licensing process — much less, parties not even then in existence — so as to confer standing on such parties to challenge an agency's licensing decision more than a decade after the final decision was made.

QUESTIONS

1.   The court finds that by including the public notice and comment provision in the statute, "Congress intended to benefit the general public by improving an agency's ability to decide whether granting an exclusive or partially exclusive license will "bring the invention to practical application or otherwise promote the invention's utilization by the public." " If the USDA did not publish public notice of its intent to extend the Embrex license for the full patent term, how could the USDA have information from the public that the extension would "promote the invention's utilization by the public"?

2.   Is it relevant that Service Engineering was not in existence at the time of the original license?

3.   Why might a court be hesitant to provide private standing under the Bayh-Dole Act?

4.   If you were counsel to Service Engineering in this case, what additional arguments would you have made?

NUTRITION 21 v. UNITED STATES
930 F.2d 862 (Fed. Cir. 1991)

RICH, CIRCUIT JUDGE.

This interlocutory appeal comes to us under 28 U.S.C. § 1292(b), the United States District Court for the Western District of Washington, Dimmick, J., having certified to this court the existence of a potentially controlling question of law as to which there is substantial ground for difference of opinion, the answer to which may advance the ultimate determination of this ongoing patent infringement litigation. The certified question is whether Nutrition 21, an "exclusive" licensee under the patent in suit, title to which is in the United States (U.S.), may, under the circumstances of this case, maintain a patent infringement action without the U.S.

as a party, when the U.S. has authorized Nutrition 21 to sue for patent infringement in its own name and on its own behalf. We have jurisdiction under 28 U.S.C. §§ 1292(c)(1), 1295(a)(1), and 1338(a). We answer the certified question affirmatively.

BACKGROUND

A. Procedural History

The lawsuit underlying this appeal is for infringement of U.S. Patent No. 4,315,927 ('927 patent), titled "Dietary Supplementation with Essential Metal Picolinates," owned by the U.S. as represented by the Secretary of Agriculture. The Department of Commerce is responsible for administration of the '927 patent. Plaintiff Nutrition 21, a California limited partnership and a licensee of the '927 patent, alleges that Thorne Research, Inc. (Thorne), a Washington corporation, and Albert F. Czap (Czap) infringe the '927 patent by their sales of chromium picolinate.

Having previously notified the U.S. of possible infringement by Thorne, Nutrition 21 invited the U.S. to join its planned infringement suit in December, 1989. When the U.S. refused, Nutrition 21 filed suit against Thorne in January, 1990, naming the U.S. as a party defendant pursuant to Fed.R.Civ.P. 19(a).

The U.S. then moved to be dismissed from the case, taking the position that the suit could be maintained by Nutrition 21 without the need for the U.S. as a party. The U.S. based its argument on (1) the enforcement rights granted to Nutrition 21 by the U.S. under the license agreement, and (2) the authorization provided to federal agencies under 35 U.S.C. § 207(a)(2) to grant patent enforcement rights to licensees. Section 207(a)(2) was enacted as part of "An Act to Amend the Patent and Trademark Laws," Pub.L. No. 96-517, 94 Stat. 3015 (1980) (§ 6(a) of which is codified at 35 U.S.C. §§ 200-11). We discuss both the terms of the license agreement and 35 U.S.C. § 207(a)(2) in greater detail below.

Opposing the U.S. motion to be dismissed, Nutrition 21 moved for realignment of the U.S. as an involuntary plaintiff, again pursuant to Fed.R.Civ.P. 19(a). Nutrition 21 acknowledged that it would not otherwise object to proceeding without the U.S., but feared that if it did so it might be caught in a "Catch-22" situation, i.e., wherein after the district court had dismissed the U.S. as an unnecessary party, and a judgment had been rendered, this court might on appeal dismiss Nutrition 21's infringement action for want of an indispensable party under Fed.R.Civ.P. 19(b).

After oral argument, the district court issued an order denying the U.S. motion to be dismissed as a party and realigning the U.S. as an involuntary plaintiff. The court stated, first, that the U.S. "owns the patent in question here" and, second, that the owner of a patent is a necessary party to a suit by an exclusive licensee for patent infringement, relying on *Independent Wireless Telegraph Co. v. Radio Corp. of America*. Therefore, the court found, the U.S. has "in effect consented to its necessary joinder in this action."

The district court also considered whether it was proper to force joinder of the U.S. in light of 28 U.S.C. § 516, which reserves to the Attorney General the conduct of litigation to which the U.S. is a party. The Attorney General's authority is not at issue here, the court concluded, because 35 U.S.C. § 207(a)(2) operates as an exception to 28 U.S.C. § 516.

Accordingly, the district court realigned the U.S. as an involuntary plaintiff. In addition, the court *sua sponte* certified its order for immediate appeal pursuant to 28 U.S.C. § 1292(b).

By order dated May 24, 1990, this court granted the U.S. permission to appeal from the district court's order. Thorne submitted a memorandum in support of the U.S. position, which we refused to consider in the absence of a petition for permission to appeal. However, our order recognized that Thorne would presumably be arguing in companion appeal No. 90-1283 that if the U.S. were not made an involuntary plaintiff, the suit should be dismissed. Accordingly, we will in this appeal address Thorne's position as stated in its Reply Brief filed in companion appeal No. 90-1283.

Happily, at oral argument before this court both Nutrition 21 and the U.S. adopted the position that the U.S. is not a necessary party to this action, and that Nutrition 21 can bring the action without the presence of the U.S. Thorne, however, maintains that the underlying lawsuit cannot go forward without participation by the U.S. Thorne's interest in stopping the suit is self-evident.

B. Nutrition 21's Rights Under the License Agreement

Answering the legal issues raised by the foregoing facts requires an understanding of the license agreement between Nutrition 21 and the U.S. Paragraph 2.1 of the agreement grants Nutrition 21 an *exclusive* license, under the Licensed Patent, to make, have made, use and sell Licensed Products which do not contain zinc picolinate as their sole metal picolinate complex. (Emphasis added).

The chromium picolinate complexes allegedly sold by Thorne come within the purview of paragraph 2.1. Paragraph 2.2 grants Nutrition 21 a *nonexclusive* license under the Licensed Patent to make, have made, use and sell Licensed Products which contain zinc picolinate as their sole metal picolinate complex..(Emphasis added).

The license agreement provides for a reservation by the U.S. of an irrevocable, nonexclusive, nontransferable, royalty-free license for the practice of all inventions encompassed within the Licensed Patent . . . .

Of great importance here, paragraph 7.2 of the license contains the following enforcement provision (emphases ours):

> During the exclusive term of this Agreement, *as provided under Paragraph 2.1 above*, LICENSEE is *empowered* pursuant to the provisions of Chapter 29 of Title 35, United States Code or other statutes
>
> (a) to bring suit in its own name, at its own expense, and on its own behalf for infringement of presumably valid claims in a Licensed Patent;

(b) in any such suit, to enjoin infringement and to collect *for its use*, damages, profits, and awards of whatever nature recoverable for such infringement; and

(c) to settle any claim or suit for infringement of the Licensed Patent.

provided, however, that NTIS and appropriate U.S. Government authorities shall have a continuing right to intervene in such suit.

DISCUSSION

We proceed to answer the certified question in the context of the narrow fact situation presented. That is, we consider whether a combination of (1) the authority granted to federal agencies by 35 U.S.C. § 207 and (2) the rights granted under the particular license agreement involved here justify the maintenance of the underlying infringement suit without the presence of the U.S., holder of the legal title to the patent and licensor.

I.

Section 207 of Title 35, titled "Domestic and Foreign Protection of Federally Owned Inventions," states in pertinent part:

(a) Each Federal agency is authorized to-

(2) grant nonexclusive, exclusive, or partially exclusive licenses under federally owned patent applications, patents, or other forms of protection obtained, royalty-free or for royalties or other consideration, and on such terms and conditions, *including the grant to the licensee of the right of enforcement pursuant to the provisions of chapter 29 of this title as determined appropriate in the public interest;*

(3) undertake all other suitable and necessary steps to protect and administer rights to federally owned inventions on behalf of the Federal Government either directly or through contract. (Emphases added).

Section 207(a)(2) is somewhat ambiguous in that the phrase "right of enforcement" is undefined; the statute does not expressly address whether "right of enforcement" encompasses a right of the licensee to maintain an infringement suit *without* the federal agency licensor as a co-party. Such a definition would admittedly be contrary to the import of *Independent Wireless*, relied upon by the district court to keep the U.S. in this lawsuit. That case held that "both the owner and the exclusive licensee are generally necessary parties in the [patent infringement] action in equity." However, *Independent Wireless* did not involve a government-owned patent, and the relevant law has been changed by Congress.

Where, as here, the words of a statute are not expressly defined, and do not fairly admit of a plain, non-ambiguous meaning, resort to the legislative history for clarification is justified. In this case, however, the legislative history is of little help. The wording of 35 U.S.C. § 207(a)(2) was derived from a portion of S. 414, "The University And Small Business Patent Procedures Act" introduced by Senator Bayh in February of 1979 [hereinafter S. 414]. That portion of S. 414, namely a proposed § 208 to be added to Title 35, was inserted by amendment into the House bill (H.R. 6933) which subsequently became Pub.L. No. 96-517. The applicable legislative history states:

> Section 208 authorizes agencies to apply for patents, to grant nonexclusive, partially exclusive, or exclusive licenses, to undertake other suitable and necessary steps to protect and administer rights to federally owned inventions, *including the right to contract with private parties for the management of Government-owned inventions;* and to transfer control of inventions to other Federal agencies.

Like the wording of 35 U.S.C. § 207(a)(2) itself, this legislative history contains no express indication of legislative intent to allow "private party" licensees to bring suit without joining the United States or its agency which owns the patent as a co-party. The applicable regulations are no more enlightening. But, one must ask, how can a private party "manage" a government-owned invention without freedom to conduct enforcement litigation?

II.

Turning to the public policy concerns underlying passage of the legislation that included 35 U.S.C. § 207(a)(2), we conclude that they support maintenance of this infringement suit without the U.S. as a party. Congress passed Pub.L. No. 96-517 in response to, inter alia, growing concerns regarding the effective private sector commercialization of inventions resulting from government-financed research. Section 6(a) of Pub.L. No. 96-517 amended Title 35 of the United States Code to add Chapter 38, titled "Patent Rights in Inventions Made With Federal Assistance." Section 200 of Title 35 states the policy and objective of Chapter 38:

> It is the policy and objective of the Congress to use the patent system to promote the utilization of inventions arising from federally supported research or development; to encourage maximum participation of small business firms in federally supported research and development efforts; to promote collaboration between commercial concerns and nonprofit organizations, including universities; to ensure that inventions made by nonprofit organizations and small business firms are used in a manner to promote free competition and enterprise; to promote the commercialization and public availability of inventions made in the United States by United States industry and labor; to ensure that the Government obtains sufficient rights in federally supported inventions to meet the needs of the Government and protect the public against nonuse or unreasonable use of inventions; and to minimize the costs of administering policies in this area.

We believe that these objectives, particularly the last one of cost minimization — presumably to the taxpayers — would be undermined if the U.S. as patent owner were required to make its limited litigation resources available any time one of its licensees sought to sue for patent infringement. The vigorous efforts of the Department of Justice *not to be involved* in this case are eloquent evidence to that effect.

III.

Considerable weight should be accorded to an agency's construction of a statutory scheme it is entrusted to administer. This is particularly true when the statute is silent or ambiguous on a specific issue, as here.

Pursuant to 35 U.S.C. § 208, the Secretary of Commerce is authorized to "promulgate regulations specifying the terms and conditions upon which any federally owned invention . . . may be licensed . . . ." Moreover, the Secretary is authorized to "assist Federal agency efforts to promote the licensing and utilization of Government-owned inventions . . . ." 35 U.S.C. § 207(b)(1). As noted above, the Commerce Department is responsible for the administration of the patent in suit. Given these facts, we defer to the Commerce Department's interpretation of its authority under 35 U.S.C. § 207(a)(2), as expressed in its license agreement with Nutrition 21. In other words, we view the Commerce Department's empowerment of Nutrition 21, pursuant to the plain terms of paragraph 7.2 of the license agreement (quoted supra), to maintain this infringement action without the participation of the U.S. as a reasonable interpretation of the authority granted to federal agencies under 35 U.S.C. § 207(a)(2).

IV.

Thorne argues that the U.S. must be considered an indispensable party under Fed.R.Civ.P. 19(b) because of the potential for prejudice to Thorne if the U.S. is not bound by the outcome of this lawsuit, either by *res judicata* or collateral estoppel. However, the question of what preclusive effect the outcome of this lawsuit may have upon the U.S. after its dismissal as a party thereto is not properly before us at this time.

We have considered the additional issues raised by the parties, but need not reach them in light of our interpretation of 35 U.S.C. § 207(a)(2) that suit may be brought by a licensee without the United States as a party. Making Fed.R.Civ.P. 19 a limitation of this statute would effectively negate the statute's purpose.

CONCLUSION

In sum, we hold that pursuant to 35 U.S.C. § 207(a)(2) and the patent license and enforcement agreement involved here, Nutrition 21 can maintain this action against Thorne without the U.S. as a party. We reverse the district court's March 14, 1990 order insofar as it held that the U.S. is a necessary party to this action and realigned the U.S. as an involuntary plaintiff, and direct the court to grant the U.S. motion for an order dismissing the U.S. as a party. The case is remanded for further proceedings consistent herewith.

REVERSED and REMANDED.

QUESTIONS

1. In the license agreement, the United States retained a continuing right to intervene in an infringement suit and also an irrevocable, nonexclusive, nontransferable, royalty-free license to practice the licensed patent. If these rights were retained by a private patent owner, would an exclusive licensee have standing to sue for infringement without joining the private patent owner as a co-plaintiff?

2. How is a private party patent owner different from the U.S. patent owner?

3. What was the U.S. interest in arguing against its required joinder in a patent infringement suit?

4. The court finds that allowing an exclusive licensee standing without joinder of the United States furthers the objectives of the Bayh-Dole Act. One of these objectives, arguably the most important, is to facilitate commercialization of federally owned patents. How does an exclusive licensee's sole standing facilitate commercialization of federally owned patents? If it does, why would this relationship between standing and commercialization not also hold when the patent owner is a private party?

5. If you were counsel to Thorne, how could you assure that the decision in Nutrition 21's suit for infringement against Thorne would preclude any subsequent suit by the U.S. for the same acts of infringement?

CASE NOTES

1. Dr. Buckberg invented a chemical solution used during heart surgery to nourish heart tissue in the absence of normal blood supply. Dr. Buckberg was employed by the University of California (UC) at the time, and the invention was made under a grant awarded by the National Institutes of Health (NIH). During patent prosecution, Dr. Buckberg designated UC has his assignee. In February 1987, UC communicated to NIH its intent to abandon its interest in the pending patent application. One month later, Dr. Buckberg wrote to NIH to request that NIH waive its patent rights so he could pursue the patent application in his personal capacity. NIH granted the waiver on the condition that Dr. Buckberg grant the United States a nonexclusive, irrevocable, royalty-free license to use the invention for government purposes. Dr. Buckberg admitted that he never executed the requested license to the United States. The patent on the invention ('515 patent) issued in January 1991. In June 1991, UC assigned its interest in the '515 patent to Dr. Buckberg who immediately granted an exclusive license to the patent to CAPS. CAPS filed an infringement action against ACS in August 2000 alleging infringement of the '515 patent. ACS argued that CAPS lacked standing to bring the infringement action because Dr. Buckberg failed to execute the required license to the United States and, therefore, neither CAPS nor Dr. Buckberg have rights in the '515 patent. What result? *See* Central Admixture Pharmacy Services, Inc. v. Advanced Cardiac Solutions, 482 F.3d 1347 (Fed. Cir. 2007).

2. *See also* Gen-Probe v. Center for Neurologic Study, 853 F. Supp. 1215 (S.D. Cal. 1993) (Private corporation does not have standing under 35 U.S.C. § 202 to sue an inventor employed by the corporation for refusing to assign patent rights

resulting from federally funded research; corporate employee is not bound by the corporate-government agreement because he is employed a corporation that receives federal research funds); Ciba-Geigy Corp. v. Alza Corp., 804 F. Supp. 614 (D.N.J. 1992) (Manufacturer licensed by the University of California to manufacture nicotine patch had standing to file an infringement action against alleged infringers without joining the University of California); Southern Research Institute v. Griffin Corp., 938 F.2d 1249 (11th Cir. 1991) (Research institute which had actual notice of National Technical Information Service's (NTIS) intent to grant an exclusive license to a corporation is required to exhaust available administrative remedies to challenge the license even though NTIS failed to publish notice with respect to the license as required by regulations).

Additional Information

1. MARTIN H. REDISH, MOORE'S FEDERAL PRACTICE — CIVIL § 101.62 (2008).

2. ROBERT A. MATTHEWS, JR., ANNOTATED PATENT DIGEST § 9:71 (2009).

3. Russell E. Levine, et. al., *Who Has Standing to Sue Third-Party Patent Infringers and the Factors Affecting Standing that Every Technology Manager Should Know*, XIX JOURNAL OF THE ASSOCIATION OF UNIV. TECH. MANAGERS 1 (2007).

4. Peter R. Afrasiabi, *Private Enforcement of Government Patents Under the Bayh-Dole Act: Standing*, THE FEDERAL LAWYER, Jul. 2007.

5. Tamsen Valoir, *The Government Purse Has Strings Attached*, INTELLECTUAL PROPERTY TODAY 32, Dec. 2006.

6. G. Kenneth Smith, *Faculty and Graduate Student Generated Inventions: Is University Ownership a Legal Certainty?*, 1 VA. J. L. & TECH. 4 (1997).

3.1.4   Effect of Bayh-Dole on University-Faculty Relationship

Section 202(c)(7)(B) of the Bayh-Dole Act requires a nonprofit organization that elects to take title to an invention made with federal funding assistance to "share royalties with the inventor." The *Platzer* case considers whether this royalty-sharing requirement implies a certain royalty percentage. The following case, *Therien*, considers the extent to which the Bayh-Dole Act alters the common law contractual relationship between universities and faculty members with respect to inventions made with federal funding assistance.

PLATZER v. SLOAN-KETTERING INSTITUTE
787 F.Supp. 360 (S.D.N.Y. 1992)

MARTIN, DISTRICT JUDGE:

Doctors Erich Platzer, Karl Welte and Roland Mertelsmann commenced this action to recover a share of the royalties stemming from a discovery they made while in the employment of Sloan-Kettering Institute for Cancer Research ("Sloan-Kettering"). Sloan-Kettering now moves to dismiss the complaint pursuant to

Fed.R.Civ.P. 12(b)(1) and 12(b)(6). For the reasons contained herein, the motion to dismiss is granted in its entirety.

FACTUAL BACKGROUND

Sloan-Kettering is a not-for-profit corporation engaged in scientific research largely funded by the federal government.

The three plaintiffs are former employees of Sloan Kettering. While employed by Sloan Kettering, the plaintiffs were part of a team of five research physicians responsible for conducting research in the area of colony stimulating factors. This research resulted in a discovery: the purification of granulocyte colony stimulating factor ("G-CSF"), a natural substance which stimulates the production of white blood cells. White blood cells are vital to the body's immune system, and are often destroyed during the course of chemotherapy, resulting in life-threatening infections. By bolstering the body's production of white blood cells, G-CSF enables cancer patients to tolerate higher dosages of chemotherapeutic drugs. It may also play a role in the treatment of AIDS.

It is not disputed that Sloan-Kettering owns the rights to all discoveries and inventions made by Sloan-Kettering employees. This assignment of rights to Sloan-Kettering is both required under federal law and under Sloan-Kettering's own "Policy on Inventions, Patents, and Technology Transfer" (the "Patent Policy").

What is disputed is whether and to what extent Sloan-Kettering is required to share royalties with the Plaintiffs.

Two agreements are relevant here. Under Sloan-Kettering's Patent Policy, Sloan-Kettering is obligated to share royalties with inventors of *patented* discoveries on a sliding scale basis. The Patent Policy expressly disclaims any obligation to share royalties with employees where the Patent office has denied a patent application. However, the Patent Policy does allow for discretionary awards to inventors of unpatented inventions.

Annual Gross Proceeds	Inventor(s) Share %
$0–$50,000	25%
$50,000–$150,000	15%
$150,000–$300,000	10%
Over $300,000	5%

The second relevant agreement is the funding agreement entered into between Sloan-Kettering and the federal government. This Institutional Patent Agreement Governing Grants and Awards between Sloan-Kettering and the Department of Health, Education, and Welfare (the "IPA") applies to inventions arising out of government-funded research which are or may be patentable. The IPA as originally drafted allowed for the sharing of royalties with inventors up to a maximum of 15% of gross royalties. However, the terms of the IPA were modified by the 1980 Bayh-Dole Act. The Bayh-Dole Act grants non-profit organizations exclusive title to inventions developed through federal funding, and allows them to freely license such inventions for profit so long as such profit is used to fund additional scientific research. The statute at issue provides in relevant part:

> Each funding agreement with a . . . nonprofit organization shall contain appropriate provisions to effectuate the following:
>
> (b) a requirement that the contractor share royalties with the inventor.
>
> 35 U.S.C. § 202(c)(7)(B).

Even though its patent application for G-CSF was denied, Sloan-Kettering exercised its discretion to share the royalties from the discovery with the team of researchers responsible for the discovery. In accordance with the sliding scale of payments called for under the Patent Policy, Sloan-Kettering distributed a 5% share of the gross royalties to the five scientists on the granucolyte team. Accordingly, each plaintiff received $505,490. Sloan-Kettering also notified the researchers that they would receive additional payments, based on the same formula, from any future royalties from domestic and foreign sales.

The plaintiffs allege that Sloan-Kettering's obligation to share royalties with inventors is non-discretionary by virtue of 35 U.S.C. § 202(c)(7)(B). Furthermore, they argue that even though § 202(c)(7)(B) does not designate any particular percentage or royalties which an institution is required to pay to inventors, the legislative history makes it clear that Congress intended the share to be reasonable and greater than 15%.

The Complaint sets forth five causes of action, the first three of which are based on the statute.

(i) Plaintiffs assert an implied private right of action under the Statute, alleging that Sloan-Kettering has breached its statutorily imposed obligation to share royalties equally or equitably with inventors.

(ii) Plaintiffs claim that they are entitled to a larger share on the ground that they are third-party beneficiaries of the IPA which, by operation of law, contains the mandated clause to share royalties with inventors.

(iii) Plaintiffs claim that they are entitled to a larger share on the ground that the Statute created an implicit term of their employment agreement.

(iv) and (v) Plaintiffs assert two state law claims, one under a contract theory and the other under an unjust enrichment theory.

Sloan-Kettering moves to dismiss the first three claims on the ground that the Court lacks subject matter jurisdiction over the claims in that they do not "arise under" the laws of the United States as required by 28 U.S.C. §§ 1331 and 1338(a). Additionally, Sloan-Kettering seeks dismissal of these claims on the ground that they do not state a cause of action in that no private right of action exists under 35 U.S.C. § 202(c)(7)(B). Once these claims are dismissed, Sloan-Kettering argues that the Court should decline to exercise its supplemental jurisdiction over the state law claims, or in the alternative should dismiss these claims for also failing to state a claim for which relief can be granted.

DISCUSSION

The First Cause of Action

For their first cause of action, Plaintiffs assert an implied private right of action under § 202(c)(7)(B), alleging that Sloan-Kettering breached its obligation to share royalties equitably with the inventors.

Sloan-Kettering seeks a dismissal of the first cause of action on the ground that this Court lacks subject matter jurisdiction and, in the alternative, on the ground that the first cause of action fails to state a claim for which relief may be granted.

Sloan-Kettering first argues that no private cause of action exists under § 202(c)(7)(B) and therefore the Court lacks subject matter jurisdiction and may not entertain the suit. This argument is clearly without merit. It is well settled that where a claim asserts an implied right of action under a statute, federal courts have the requisite federal jurisdiction to determine whether such a federal remedy exists.

Because the first claim is premised on the assertion that an implied private right of action exists under § 202(c)(7)(B), this claim arises under the laws of the United States and subject matter jurisdiction exists.

This conclusion, however, does not dispose of the issue. Rather, the private cause of action claim should nevertheless be dismissed pursuant to F.R.C.P. 12(b)(6) if the Court determines that the claim does not state a cause of action for which relief may be granted. Thus, if Congress did not intend for a private cause of action to exist under the statute, the claim will be dismissed.

In ascertaining whether a private cause of action exists under a federal statute, courts are to consider four factors: (1) whether plaintiff is part of the class for whose especial benefit the statute was passed; (2) whether the legislative history indicates a Congressional intent to confer a private right of action; (3) whether a federal cause of action would further the underlying purpose of the legislative scheme; and (4) whether the plaintiff's cause of action is a subject traditionally relegated to state law.

The first factor to be considered is whether the plaintiff is a member of the class for whose "especial" benefit the statute was enacted. A review of the legislative history does not suggest that the Bayh-Dole Act was enacted for the benefit of research scientists. The Bayh-Dole Act was intended "to promote the utilization and commercialization of inventions made with Government support, to encourage the participation of smaller firms in the Government research and development process, and to promote increased cooperation and collaboration between the nonprofit and commercial sectors." To such end, the intended beneficiaries of the Bayh-Dole Act are the institutions themselves and the government.

Similarly, the legislative history does not indicate an intent to create a private right of action. Indeed, the legislative history is completely silent with regard to a private cause of action. As such, it is safe to assume that Congress did not intend for a private right of action to exist. This conclusion is supported by the fact that elsewhere in the patent statutes, Congress did explicitly grant private causes of action. *See, e.g.*, 35 U.S.C. § 281 (1988) (a "patentee shall have remedy by civil action for infringement of his patent"); 35 U.S.C. §§ 141–145 (1988) (applicant whose patent is rejected by the Patent Office on appeal may pursue his claim in the federal courts). The fact that elsewhere in the patent statutes private rights were expressly provided indicates that "when Congress wished to provide a private damage remedy, it knew how to do so and did so expressly." Likewise, that such a right was not created under § 202(c)(7)(B) suggests that no right was intended.

Nor would implication of such a right further the purpose of the statute. The Bayh-Dole Act was enacted to foster commercial development of government funded research. As such, the statute requires that royalties be funneled back into scientific research. A private right of action allowing an inventor to demand 50% of the royalties, as is the case here, would clearly frustrate this purpose rather than further it.

In light of the foregoing, the Court concludes that no private cause of action exists under § 202(c)(7)(B) of the Bayh-Dole Act. Accordingly, the first cause of action asserting an implied right must be dismissed for failing to state a claim for which relief can be granted.

The Second and Third Causes of Action

The Plaintiff's second and third claims are brought under third-party beneficiary and breach of contract theories. Both claims require interpretation of § 202(c)(7)(B). As with the first cause of action, Sloan-Kettering argues that dismissal is warranted because the Court lacks subject matter jurisdiction and because the cause of action fails to state a claim for which relief may be granted. These arguments will be considered in turn.

As the Defendant reads *Merrell Dow*, the absence of a private right of action for an underlying federal statute where a state-law claim is asserted is dispositive. Sloan-Kettering argues that once the court has concluded that no private cause of action exists for the underlying federal violation, the court may not hear the claim unless independent jurisdictional grounds exist.

Once again, Sloan-Kettering reads *Merrell Dow* too broadly. Specifically, Sloan-Kettering attempts to extend the holding of *Merrell Dow*, which involved a state law claim in which the alleged federal violation was peripheral, to cases where the alleged violation is essential to the existence of the state-law claim.

Thus, even where no private right of action exists for the underlying federal issue, if the nature of the federal issue is sufficiently substantial, subject matter jurisdiction may still exist.

Here, the federal issues in the Plaintiffs' second and third claims are sufficiently substantial to confer "arising under" jurisdiction. Indeed, the federal issue is essential to Plaintiffs' breach of contract and third-party beneficiary claims. As such, a substantial federal issue exists and subject matter jurisdiction is proper.

Sloan-Kettering next argues that dismissal of the second and third causes of action is warranted on the ground that these causes of action fail to state a claim for which relief can be granted.

In determining whether Plaintiffs have stated a claim upon which relief may be granted, the Court must first turn to the language of the statute. The language of § 202(c)(7)(B) is clear:

> Each funding agreement with a . . . non-profit organization shall contain appropriate provisions to effectuate the following . . . (7)(B) a requirement that the contractor share royalties with the inventor. 35 U.S.C. § 202(c)(7)(B).

The Plaintiffs' second and third claims are premised on the argument that § 202(c)(7)(B) contains an implicit requirement that institutions share a specific percentage of their royalties with inventors and scientists. However, nothing in the language suggests that the share should be a specified ratio. Nor does the definition of "share" suggest that a particular ratio was intended. In common usage, the unmodified verb "share" simply means "to have a share; take part." New Webster's Dictionary of the English Language 2087 (3rd ed. 1981). Black's Law Dictionary (5th ed. 1979) specifically contrasts the unmodified word "share," which it defines as "[t]o partake; enjoy with others, have a portion of," with the term "share and share alike," which is defined as referring to "equal shares or proportions." In short, the plain language of the statute does not yield the interpretation that the Plaintiffs ask us to make, that a particular ratio of sharing was intended.

Nor does the legislative history suggest a ratio for sharing. Congress enacted the Bayh-Dole Act "to promote the utilization and commercialization of inventions made with government support." To further this aim, the Bayh-Dole Act provides that non-profit institutions receiving government funding must reinvest royalties from research into additional research. 35 U.S.C. § 202(c)(7)(C). Clearly Congress' concern was with the reinvesting of funds to further research, not with furthering the private interests of individual inventors. The provision that non-profit institutions share royalties was included merely to ensure that inventors were provided with an adequate incentive to engage in scientific research. Furthermore, that any sharing ratio should be left to the supply and demand of the market is suggested by Congress' refusal to determine a particular share: "It is not intended that Federal agencies establish sharing ratios."

The regulations established by the executive agency charged with administering § 202 support the conclusion that no particular share or minimum share was intended by Congress. Specifically, the agency has expressly declined to establish any "minimum sharing formula" on the ground that to do so would be "inconsistent with the legislative intent as manifest on p. 33 of the Senate Report 96-480." The agency has noted that "[t]he intent is that non-profit organizations share . . . in accordance with their usual policies."

In sum, a review of the language of the statute, its legislative history, and subsequent agency regulations fails to suggest that Congress intended that institutions follow a federally imposed sharing ratio or minimum share. As plaintiff's second and third claims are premised on such a minimum share, the Court must conclude that these actions fail to state a claim for which relief can be granted. Accordingly, the second and third claims are dismissed.

The State-Law Claims

With the federal claims dismissed, the only remaining claims are state law claims under contract and unjust enrichment theories. In accordance with 28 U.S.C. § 1367(c)(3), the Court declines to exercise its supplemental jurisdiction over plaintiff's remaining claims.

Accordingly, the complaint is dismissed in its entirety.

SO ORDERED

QUESTIONS

1.   Why did the court find that a private cause of action on behalf of inventors would not further the purposes of the Bayh-Dole Act?

2.   The court found "The provision that non-profit institutions share royalties was included merely to ensure that inventors were provided with an adequate incentive to engage in scientific research." Doesn't an adequate incentive require an adequate share of royalties? Is there a minimum royalty-sharing percentage that would clearly be inadequate to incentivize scientific research? 2%? 1%? .01?

3.   What practical problems would courts confront if they held that inventors had an implied private cause of action to recover royalties from non-profit organizations?

4.   As between *Service Engineering* and *Platzer*, which of the two decisions do you think is most compelling? Why?

5.   If you were counsel to Platzer, what additional arguments would you have made to the court?

THERIEN v. THE TRUSTEES OF THE UNIVERSITY OF PENNSYLVANIA
2006 U.S. Dist. LEXIS 746 (E.D. Pa. 2006)

SCHILLER, J.

Plaintiff, Dr. Michael J. Therien, brings this action against the Trustees of the University of Pennsylvania ("Penn"), alleging breach of contract, breach of fiduciary duty, negligent misrepresentation and negligence. These claims were originally brought in the Philadelphia County Court of Common Pleas in September 2004. Penn filed a notice of removal on October 12, 2004, asserting federal subject matter jurisdiction because the resolution of Therien's claims requires interpretation of the Bayh-Dole Act, a federal statute. Presently before the Court is Plaintiff's motion raising lack of subject matter jurisdiction. The Court concludes that it lacks subject matter jurisdiction over this action and, accordingly, remands this case to state court.

I. BACKGROUND

Therien, a tenured chemistry professor, has worked at Penn since 1990. He, like Defendant, is a citizen of Pennsylvania. As a requirement of his employment and of Penn's patent policy, Therien signed a Participation Agreement in which he agreed to assign to Penn his rights in any future inventions he developed while working there. Several patents have been issued to Penn based on technology developed by Therien.

In September 2004, Therien brought suit against Penn in the Philadelphia County Court of Common Pleas asserting state law claims of breach of contract, breach of fiduciary duty, negligent misrepresentation and negligence. Therien averred that Penn failed to satisfy its obligations to him under: (1) its patent policy; (2) its conflict of interest policy; (3) its internal grievance procedure; and (4) his employment contract. Therien also alleged that Penn failed to commercialize properly the technology that he developed and assigned to Penn. Therien claimed to have "suffered harm in the form of lost income, equity and other revenues and benefits, and injury to his reputation." The Complaint raises no federal claims, nor does it invoke any federal standards.

On October 12, 2004, Penn filed a notice of removal with this Court and asserted that the Court has original jurisdiction because the action arises under the federal patent laws. Penn claimed that "[w]ithout expressly stating so, this Complaint claims a breach of the obligations of the Bayh-Dole Act which provides the statutory basis for technology transfer practices and obligations with respect to inventions discovered with federal funding." Penn argued the Bayh-Dole Act provides the parameters relevant to Penn's commercialization of technology based on Therien's inventions. Likewise, in its Answer, Penn asserted the defense that the federal patent laws and the Bayh-Dole Act barred the action, and Penn noted the Bayh-Dole Act does not give rise to a private cause of action.

Since removal, Plaintiff has twice amended his Complaint, with the second amended complaint adding a claim for nominal damages and expanding his request for relief to include rescission. Discovery has ended, and the Court currently has before it Defendant's motion for summary judgment.

II. STANDARD OF REVIEW

Federal courts are courts of limited jurisdiction. Federal district courts have original jurisdiction over civil actions arising under federal law and original and exclusive jurisdiction over civil actions arising under the federal patent laws.

"The presence or absence of federal-question jurisdiction is governed by the well-pleaded complaint rule, which provides that federal jurisdiction exists only when a federal question is presented on the face of the plaintiff's properly pleaded complaint." When state law creates the cause of action, a case may arise under federal law only if the well-pleaded complaint demonstrates that the right to relief "necessarily depends on resolution of a substantial question of federal law."

The defendant bears the burden of showing federal jurisdiction exists. A court should resolve any doubts about the propriety of removal in favor of remand. Lack of subject matter jurisdiction can be raised by a party at any time during the civil action.

III. DISCUSSION

The Complaint contains four counts, none of which arise under federal law: (1) breach of contract; (2) breach of fiduciary duty; (3) negligent misrepresentation; and (4) negligence. Therien alleges Penn has failed in its duty to commercialize technology he has developed, including technology that has resulted in patents issued to Penn. That allegation, however, does not create a case arising under the patent laws; any discussion of patent law is tangential to Therien's state law claims. Therien neither asserts a claim of patent infringement nor questions Penn's existing patents or its ability to patent technology he has assigned. Rather, Therien challenges Penn's handling of the business follow-up on these patented technologies. The contracts that Therien alleges have been breached include his employment contract as well as various Penn policies, including its patent policy. The Complaint does not demonstrate a right to relief that depends on resolution of a substantial question of federal law.

In its Answer, Penn raises the Bayh-Dole Act and federal patent laws as affirmative defenses. Specifically, Penn asserts that the Bayh-Dole Act establishes that Penn has no duties to Therien as an inventor and an assignor of his invention rights. Penn claims it "has sole discretion to control the steps taken to achieve practical application of the invention, subject only to the "march-in" rights of the federal funding agency." It is well-settled that a case may not be removed to federal court based on federal issues raised by the defendant.

Furthermore, the Bayh-Dole Act may not impose any duties on Penn to commercialize an inventor's technology, but Penn fails to acknowledge that it could incur such obligations independent of Bayh-Dole, as the Act does not determine the relationship between universities and their faculty members. Rather, the Bayh-Dole Act regulates the relationship between government agencies and institutions that receive federal funding. The Bayh-Dole Act does not define the relationship between inventors and these institutions beyond specific situations such as royalty sharing or when an institution elects not to retain title to an invention. Penn claims that "Therien's demands for relief seek to alter the relationship between the federal funding agency, the university, and the faculty inventor, and require the resolution of substantial questions under Bayh-Dole." The Court disagrees and concludes that this action amounts to a contract dispute wholly-governed by state law. Neither the Bayh-Dole Act or the federal patent laws have any bearing on the resolution of this dispute.

In arguing that federal question jurisdiction exists, Penn emphasizes that Therien amended his Complaint to expand his request for relief to include rescission, a remedy which he later acquiesced would take place in accordance with any relevant requirements of the Bayh-Dole Act. Rescission is not a claim for relief or a cause of action, but rather it is an equitable remedy within a court's discretion. Rescission will not be applied when the facts indicate that a return to the status quo ante is not feasible. Here, the contracts at issue have been in place since Therien's initial employment at Penn and his receipt of tenure. Additionally,

Therien's request for rescission does not demonstrate a right to relief that "necessarily depends on resolution of a substantial question of federal law." Although complete rescission of Therien's contracts with Penn would necessarily involve the existing patents, it does not follow that the Complaint raises a substantial question of federal law. Thus, the request for rescission does not confer federal jurisdiction over this action.

Penn's reliance on *Platzer v. Sloan-Kettering Institute for Cancer Research* is misplaced. The *Platzer* complaint, unlike the Complaint in this action, contained three claims that were based explicitly on the Bayh-Dole Act's provisions for royalty sharing. Specifically, the *Platzer* plaintiffs alleged in their breach of contract claim that they were "entitled to a larger share [of royalties] on the ground that the [the Bayh-Dole Act] created an implicit term of their employment agreement." Therien's claims do not similarly invoke federal law or rely on its interpretation. The *Platzer* court concluded that two of the claims required interpretation of the Bayh-Dole Act and thus established "arising under" jurisdiction. Having found jurisdiction, the court ultimately dismissed these claims, which were based on misinterpretation of the Bayh-Dole Act, for failure to state a claim on which relief could be granted.

Penn argues that Therien's claims are preempted by the Bayh-Dole Act. Preemption exists under the following circumstances: (1) when state and federal law directly conflict so that compliance with both is not possible; or (2) when state law directly interferes with Congressional goals in the context of a specific case. Penn suggests preemption exists because the "damages that [Therien] claims to arise from these common law claims, stand as an obstacle to the purpose of Bayh-Dole, which is to promote "the utilization of inventions arising from federally supported research" and the "commercialization of and public availability of inventions made in the United States by United States industry and labor." " Penn does not support this preemption argument with case law, and it does not address the contention that Therien's claims further the goals of Bayh-Dole. The Court concludes the Bayh-Dole Act does not preempt Therien's state law claims.

****

The Court concludes that Penn has failed to meet its burden of showing that federal subject matter jurisdiction exists. Therefore, remand is required.

IV. CONCLUSION

For the reasons set forth above, Plaintiff's motion raising lack of subject matter jurisdiction is granted.

QUESTIONS

1. The court found that "the Bayh-Dole Act may not impose any duties on Penn to commercialize an inventor's technology." Is this correct? *See* 35 U.S.C. § 203(a)(1).

2. If a state court were to grant Therien's demands for relief, would this have

no effect upon the relationship between Penn and a federal funding agency?

3. How does the court distinguish the existence of federal subject matter jurisdiction in *Platzer* and the lack of federal subject matter jurisdiction in *Therien*?

4. If you were counsel to Penn, what additional arguments would you have made to the court?

CASE NOTES

1. Fenn was a faculty member at Yale who invented a new chemical mass spectometor for which he was issued patent '538. After a series of unpleasant exchanges between Fenn and Yale, Fenn sued Yale for conversion, theft, tortious interference with business relations and violations of the Connecticut Unfair Trade Practices Act. Yale asserted counterclaims against Fenn for breach of contract, breach of fiduciary duty, fraud, negligent misrepresentation, conversion, theft and unjust enrichment. After a bench trial, the court concluded that Fenn failed to prove his claims against Yale and that Yale prevailed on its breach of contract, breach of fiduciary duty and fraud claims. Post-trial, Fenn moved to dismiss Yale's counter-claims on the basis of lack of subject matter jurisdiction. Fenn argued that Yale's counterclaims required the court to make a determination regarding ownership rights of the '538 patent, that such a judicial determination is prohibited by the Bayh-Dole Act and that the Bayh-Dole Act preempted Yale's counterclaims. What result? *See* Fenn v. Yale University, 393 F.Supp.2d 133 (D. Conn. 2004).

Additional Information

1. ALAN S. GUTTERMAN, CORPORATE COUNSEL'S GUIDE TO TECHNOLOGY MANAGEMENT & TRANSACTIONS § 15:12 (2009).

2. Shashwat Purohit, EXPERT VIEWS: Prof. Karen Hersey on "Royalty Sharing: A Matter of Law or a Matter of Policy," THE INT'L TECHNOLOGY TRANSFER INSTITUTE AT PIERCE LAW, Mar. 3, 2009.

3. Michael S. Mireles, *The Bayh-Dole Act and Incentives for the Commercialization of Government-Funded Inventions in Developing Countries*, 76 UMKC L. REV. 525 (2007).

4. Peter J. Harrington, *Faculty Conflicts of Interest in an Age of Academic Entrepreneurialism: An Analysis of the Problem, the Law and Selected University Policies*, 27 J.C. & U.L. 775 (2001).

3.2 UNIVERSITY-INDUSTRY SPONSORED RESEARCH

Industry-sponsored research is important to universities both as a source research funding and as a source of information regarding the current needs and interests of industry. However, the partnership between universities and industry has a troubled past. There are many reasons for these troubles, including different cultures, different goals and different time perspectives. But regardless of the reasons, the results have become increasingly disturbing. Industry investment in research at U.S. universities has been, at best, tepid in recent years. In terms of total dollar investment, industry-sponsored research at U.S. universities declined between 2001-2004 and only increased slightly between 2005-2006. In terms of the percentage of university research supported by industry, industry-sponsored research peaked in 1999 at 7% of total U.S. university research expenditures, but has been flat at 5% since 2003. Most concerning is the increasing inclination of U.S. companies to invest in research at foreign universities, especially India and China.

The challenge of industry-sponsored research at U.S. universities has been greatly exacerbated by a narrow, but very significant, ruling by the Internal Revenue Service regarding the conduct of industry-sponsored research using university facilities developed with tax-exempt bonds. As you will see, U.S. industry believes these tax rules are unwarranted and unfair.

This section first considers selected terms in university sponsored research contracts, then delves into the intricacies of federal tax law and policy regarding sponsored research and finally considers a complex university-sponsor licensing and intellectual property dispute.

3.2.1   University Sponsored Research Agreements

SURVEY OF SPONSORED RESEARCH CONTRACT TERMS

> [Editor's Note: The material in this subsection is excerpted from a report prepared by the New York State Science & Technology Law Center at Syracuse University College of Law for the New York State Foundation for Science, Technology and Innovation (NYSTAR).]

This section summarizes university approaches to sponsored research contract issues. Each issue is examined for significant trends, highlights and outlying approaches that ultimately bear on efficient and equitable contract negotiation. Attention is given to distinctions in how each issue is addressed as these may either resolve or create contracting tension. Furthermore, the presentation and phrasing of a term governing an issue may affect a sponsor's perception and willingness to accept that term.

Equipment Ownership

An equipment ownership clause is typically included in university-sponsored research agreements in order to specify rights of ownership for equipment used or built during the proposed project. All the universities reviewed include an equipment ownership clause that provides title to any equipment purchased or built during the performance of research under a sponsored research agreement that will vest in the university. Most of the agreements employ similar language to express the manner in which the university will claim ownership of the equipment used for the project. In general, equipment ownership provisions emphasize that universities will have title to:

(1) Equipment purchased for the research project;

(2) Equipment used in performing the research; and

(3) Equipment built with funds provided for the project.

Additionally, several universities adopt distinct equipment ownership provisions. Georgia Tech, for example, provides that it may return equipment purchased by a sponsor upon request.

Contract Termination

A contract termination clause is typically included in university-sponsored research agreements in order to specify rights of termination for each party for the duration of the proposed project.

The sampled university sponsored research agreements generally treat contract termination in a similar way, stipulating that either the university or sponsor has the right to terminate the contract contingent upon giving the other party advance written notice. The agreements specify a number of days necessary to constitute advance written notice, generally either thirty or sixty days. Most universities require sponsors to reimburse the university for all expenses incurred up to the date of termination and all non-cancelable costs after the date of termination when the sponsor terminates the agreement.

Universities frequently stipulate that if a sponsor breaches a term or condition in the agreement, the sponsor will have a specified number of days to cure the breach. If the breach is not cured within the specified number of days, the university may terminate the agreement. In the case of an incurable breach, the non-breaching party is often given the right to terminate immediately. Several universities also provided for the right to terminate the agreement in situations involving the occurrence of circumstances beyond their control.

While none of the universities examined employ language that is clearly unique from the others in dealing with contract termination, certain universities employ clauses that provide greater depth on the issue, thereby helping to specify when termination may or may not occur. For example, Columbia requires automatic termination of the agreement if either party becomes bankrupt or insolvent. Columbia also allows termination of the agreement if the principal investigator becomes unavailable to oversee the project. Cornell, in its termination clause as well as in a distinct provision limiting liability, states that its liability will never be greater than the cost of the project. Georgia Tech allows termination if continuing under the agreement threatens its tax-exempt status. RPI indicates that in addition to being reimbursed for non-cancelable commitments prior to termination, it will also be reimbursed for all time and expenses. RIT specifies that any costs and commitments incurred in excess of funds provided shall be invoiced to the sponsor and payable within thirty days. Stanford includes language regarding student involvement in the project by requiring that, when a student is supported under the agreement, a sponsor will remain responsible for the full cost of the student support through the end of the academic quarter in which the agreement is terminated. Finally, in cases where a sponsor defaults on its obligations under the sponsored research agreement, SUNY [State University of New York] claims the right to either suspend the contract until an acceptable remedy is established, or to terminate the agreement upon written notification.

Confidentiality

Provisions that address confidential information are very important components of university-sponsored research agreements. Unauthorized disclosures of confidential information to a third party may not only compromise the position of the original disclosing party, usually the corporate sponsor, by revealing important business information, such as market strategy and new technical initiatives, but may also adversely affect the person responsible for the unauthorized disclosure by placing that person in breach of the agreement and potentially subjecting the person to costly litigation. For these reasons, sponsored research agreements always contain provisions that address confidential information, or provide for a separate confidentiality agreement with the sponsor. Confidentiality agreements typically address written disclosures, oral disclosures, parties covered by the agreements, and conditions imposed upon the sponsor.

Most universities do not expressly identify what should be considered confidential for purposes of the agreement. The universities that do expressly identify what should be considered confidential typically list terms such as any information, know-how, technical data, materials, or reports obtained or developed in association with the project. However, Lehigh provides that the principal investigator is responsible for identifying which materials will be considered confidential for purposes of the agreement. In addition, roughly half of the universities examined require that confidential information be clearly marked as confidential in order to be considered confidential. Berkeley even goes so far as to require the sponsor to provide advance written notice prior to delivery of any confidential information. Most of the universities do not expressly address the treatment of oral disclosures in terms of confidential information. The few universities that address oral disclosures of confidential information, such as Georgia Tech, typically require that such disclosures be reduced to writing within thirty days and marked as confidential in order to be considered confidential.

The majority of universities specifically set forth exceptions to what will be considered confidential. These universities set forth all or a combination of the following exceptions as information that will not be treated as confidential:

(1) Information in the public domain;

(2) Information lawfully possessed by the other party prior to the disclosure;

(3) Information lawfully received from a third party not under a confidentiality obligation;

(4) Information required to be disclosed by law; and

(5) Information independently developed by the other party prior to the disclosure.

In terms of identifying the individuals bound by confidentiality agreements, the universities are nearly evenly divided as to whether or not they identify the individuals bound. Universities that specify the bound individuals typically use broad language capable of including many individuals. These universities commonly draft confidentiality agreements to include all sponsor and university employees, or all individuals associated with the project which, in several instances, specifically includes graduate students. However, among the universities that specify individuals who are bound by the confidentiality agreement, Yale and Caltech are unique. Yale provides that the principal investigator and his or her assistants will enter into a separate confidentiality agreement with a sponsor, while Caltech states that a sponsor may only request that the principal investigator enter into a confidentiality agreement with the sponsor.

With respect to maintaining confidential information, most of the universities set forth a combination of protective measures governing a sponsor's treatment of confidential information received from the university. Nearly half of the universities expressly provide a standard of care required for the protection of confidential information. Such a standard of care typically requires reasonable efforts similar to those used to protect a party's own information, or security measures commonly practiced within the industry. As an additional protective measure, RIT [Rochester Institute of Technology] requires that the recipient of confidential information shall return materials upon the discloser's request at the conclusion of the agreement, while all the other universities have no such provision.

As another form of protection, several of the universities set forth a time period, usually two to three years, in which the receiving party must continue to treat information as confidential, either beginning from the date of the disclosure of such information or the termination of the agreement. However, with respect to keeping information confidential, MIT is unique as the only university that states a sponsor shall be relieved of its duty of confidentiality only when such information enters the public domain through no fault of the sponsor.

Ownership of Discoveries

Every sponsored research agreement contains language that addresses the ownership of discoveries made in connection with the research project. However, ownership of sponsored research discoveries might be subject to federal laws. The Bayh-Dole Act provides that universities may choose to retain ownership of any inventions developed under federally funded research programs. Also, IRS Revenue Procedure 97-14 provides that a university must license intellectual property developed under a sponsored research agreement for a fair market value, if the university facilities used for the sponsored research have been developed with tax-exempt bonds. The Bayh-Dole Act and IRS Revenue Procedure 97-14 will be discussed later.

The following discussion addresses the ownership of discoveries not governed by these federal laws. The chart below illustrates the general treatment of discovery ownership under different conditions. While most situations provide for relatively clear ownership rights, under some sponsored research agreements, situations may exist that are not covered, resulting in uncertainty in ownership rights.

	University Inventor	Sponsor Inventor	Joint Inventors
University Facilities	University Ownership	Uncertain Situation	Joint Ownership

	University Inventor	Sponsor Inventor	Joint Inventors
Sponsor Facilities	Uncertain Situation	Sponsor Owns	Joint Ownership

All universities assert ownership of discoveries produced by university employees using university facilities either through the use of express language in the sponsored research contract or through broad assertions of ownership over all discoveries made by university employees, often without mention of the facilities used. Also, more than half of the universities specifically provide that discoveries produced solely by sponsor employees with sponsor facilities will be owned by the sponsor.

The majority of universities provide that discoveries made jointly will be owned jointly by the sponsor and the university, without any reference to the facilities used. However, a minority of universities imply university ownership of discoveries made using university facilities, and a few university-sponsored research agreements do not contain sufficient language to make a determination regarding this issue. SUNY has the most unique approach to ownership: SUNY bases ownership of discoveries on ownership of the facilities used to make the discoveries. The SUNY-sponsored research agreement provides the sponsor with ownership of discoveries made jointly while using sponsor facilities and provides the university with ownership of discoveries made jointly while using university facilities.

None of the universities surveyed specifically address the situation of discoveries made solely by the sponsor inventors using university facilities. Even universities that indirectly address this situation through broad contract language are divided; several of the universities appear to allow sponsor ownership as a result of sole sponsor invention using university facilities; several of the universities appear to claim university ownership of discoveries made using university facilities through broad contractual assertions of ownership. The SUNY-sponsored research agreement would appear to provide for university ownership of sole sponsor discoveries made using university facilities. The remaining universities, with the exception of Caltech and Yale, do not provide sufficient language in their agreements to make an implied determination regarding this issue. Caltech and Yale are unique in this situation because they provide that ownership of discoveries made by sponsor inventors using university facilities will be owned jointly by the sponsor and the university. When discoveries are made by a university employee using sponsor facilities, it appears that Caltech and Yale claim ownership through broad contract language providing for university ownership of discoveries made during the project, as well as language basing ownership on inventorship. However, SUNY would provide for sponsor ownership based on the use of sponsor facilities; Caltech and Yale do not appear to provide for joint ownership as they do in situations where a sponsor employee uses university facilities.

The majority of universities do not expressly provide that the sponsor may request the university to file a patent on a discovery made during the project. Yet, of the universities that do provide language allowing the sponsor to request the filing of a patent, nearly all require that the sponsor is responsible for the costs associated with such filing. The most unique policy regarding this issue is practiced by Case Western, which provides that expenses for joint discoveries are shared jointly by sponsor and university.

Less than half of the universities provide language addressing situations where a sponsor elects not to file a patent application for a discovery made. The universities that address this issue generally state that, in such a case, the university may pursue the patent at its own expense with the right to license to another party, and the sponsor has no further rights to the patent. Typically, if a sponsor later wishes to license the patent the sponsor must reimburse the university for expenses incurred by filing the patent. Yale is unique in this regard because it explicitly requires a sponsor to pay patent costs while the university retains ownership rights, even after the university disclaims interest in patent protection.

Warranties & Limitation of Liability

Limiting university tort liability and disclaiming contract warranties for the performance and results of research under the sponsored research agreement are critical protective measures for universities. With the exception of the Berkeley, Cornell, SUNY, and Texas, all of the sampled sponsored research agreements employ a contractual provision addressing warranties. In all but two of those agreements, standard and highly consistent language broadly disclaims all warranties for any matter and then states specific disclaimers. Specific disclaimers tend to focus on either the character of the research results or the further use of the results. MIT and Syracuse do not broadly disclaim warranties but do indicate that no warranties are made as to the accuracy, success, or condition of the research results. Ten other universities also disclaim warranties for the success, condition, or accuracy of the research results. Nine universities expressly disclaim warranties for the fitness of the results for a particular purpose and merchantability. Four universities disclaim warranties for exclusivity or originality of the research results. Two universities disclaim warranties for the patent validity of the research results and potential patent protection. Drexel is the only university that expressly disclaims warranties for the completion of the research, though this could be inferred from other universities' disclaimers of warranties for success, condition and accuracy of research results. Five universities expressly disclaim warranties for ownership of research results. Six universities broadly disclaim warranties for the use of the research results for any purpose whatsoever. Of these, four universities also expressly disclaim warranties that the research results will not infringe upon existing intellectual property rights. Lehigh and MIT do not expressly disclaim warranties for the use of research results, but do expressly disclaim warranties for non-infringement of intellectual property rights. Stanford is unique because it employs a preamble to the warranty clause which states that all rights granted under the agreement are "as is and with all faults." The Stanford warranty provision concludes by requiring the sponsor to acknowledge that the research is a scientific undertaking and Stanford will not guarantee the research outcome under the agreement.

Eight universities expressly disclaim liability for claims, demands, costs, or judgments arising out of a sponsor's or a third party's use of research results produced under the agreement. Of these, only Georgia Tech states that even if liability is found, the money damages cannot exceed the amount paid to Georgia Tech under the research agreement during the immediately preceding twelve months. While all other agreements are silent as to sponsor liability, the Case Western agreement states that neither party shall be liable to the other for indirect, special, or consequential damages. Cornell is unique in expressly stating that it shall not assume any liability resulting from sponsor's negligence. RPI is silent on liability resulting from the use of research results, but unlike any other university, RPI expressly disclaims liability for any "work or research performed."

Publication

Each of the nineteen surveyed universities asserts the right to publish information pertaining to, and resulting from, a sponsored research agreement. All but SUNY allow the sponsor a limited period of time to review a proposed manuscript for confidential information or sensitive intellectual property disclosures before submission for publication or publication itself. Ten universities allow a sponsor to review the proposed manuscript for thirty days prior to submission for publication. Two universities allow a sponsor to review the proposed publication sixty days prior to submission for publication. Cornell and Lehigh allow a sponsor to review the proposed manuscript for thirty days immediately prior to the proposed publication date. Columbia, Drexel and Harvard each provide a sponsor an opportunity of unspecified duration to review the proposed manuscript prior to submission. If confidential information or a sensitive intellectual property disclosure is found within the proposed manuscript, three universities allow for an additional delay of thirty days for appropriate protective measures to be taken in accordance with the contract provisions governing confidentiality and ownership of discoveries, five allow an additional sixty days, three allow an additional ninety days, and one simply indicates that additional delay is negotiable. Five universities do not allow for a delay during which a sponsor may protect confidential information or sensitive intellectual property disclosures. Uniquely, RIT does not allow for additional delay if the publication is a student thesis. Texas states that despite sponsor review, it maintains the ultimate authority to determine what is to be published. Yale is unique in stating that no sponsor response within the thirty-day review period constitutes a *de facto* sponsor agreement that no revisions or delays in publication are necessary. Harvard is unique in stating that the right to publish encompasses both printed publication and other forms of public disclosure. In its publication provision, Stanford explicitly requires a sponsor to provide all reasonable cooperation in meeting Stanford's basic research objectives of generating new knowledge and the expeditious public dissemination thereof.

Indemnification

An indemnification clause is typically included in sponsored research agreements to indemnify the university or the sponsor, or both, against damages resulting from any use of research and technology developed under the agreement. Most universities include an indemnification clause that generally states that a sponsor shall defend, indemnify, and hold harmless the university and its trustees, officers, employees and agents against all liability and damage, that may be incurred by or imposed upon the university in connection with any claim, suit, demand, loss, cost, damage, liability, expense, action or judgment arising out of the sponsored research agreement.

Among the agreements reviewed, a few used clauses that were notably different. For example, Harvard includes a clause that it must promptly notify a sponsor of any claim, and it must cooperate with the sponsor in the defense of any claim. The sponsor in turn agrees to consult with Harvard regarding the defense of any claim and to submit any proposed settlement to Harvard in advance of its approval.

RIT includes a clause that limits its maximum liability to the amount paid by the sponsor for the research under the agreement. Stanford has a clause in its agreement that stipulates if a sponsor provides any materials, equipment, or other property to Stanford in connection with the research program, an indemnification clause for such property is incorporated into the agreement.

Licensing Provisions

Actual licenses to technology resulting from a sponsored research project are not included in the sponsored research agreement. Most of the sponsored research agreements do, however, include a general clause providing for future licensing possibilities.

Licensing provisions vary greatly among the universities surveyed. Although there is general consensus on the substance of these provisions, the language of the provisions varies widely. Licensing provisions are subject to IRS Rev. Proc. 97-14 if the research is performed in facilities developed with the use of tax exempt bonds. Under IRS Rev. Proc. 97-14, [Editor's note: IRS Rev. Proc. 97-14 has been superseded by IRS Rev. Proc. 2007-47 which is discussed in the following section.], a university and sponsor cannot enter into an exclusive license agreement at the time the sponsored research agreement is signed. As a result, universities often allow industry sponsors only the opportunity to negotiate a future license for discoveries arising from the sponsored research project. One university explicitly makes the right to negotiate a future license contingent upon the sponsor reimbursing the university for patent prosecution costs.

Most universities offer the sponsor a time-limited, first right to negotiate an exclusive or non-exclusive, royalty-bearing license, or an option to license any patentable invention or discovery conceived and first reduced to practice during the performance of the sponsored research project. Other universities simply provide an option to negotiate a license for a specified period of time. Harvard promises not to offer a license to sponsored research discoveries to any party other than the sponsor for a specified period of time.

All universities reserve the right to use research discoveries for internal educational and research purposes. Drexel reserves an exclusive license to use research discoveries for education and research and, in addition, requires that it shall be free to license other nonprofit organizations to use research discoveries.

Several universities grant a sponsor, at the time the sponsored research agreement is signed, a non-exclusive, royalty-free and non-transferable license to use research discoveries for internal purposes. These licenses are sometimes restricted to non-commercial research purposes. Caltech includes a clause that the non-exclusive license will not include the right to sublicense and is not transferable, except in the event of a transfer or sale of all or substantially all of a sponsor's assets to a third party. Yale grants a sponsor a free license to copy any materials for its internal purposes and a royalty-bearing license to distribute such materials to third parties on reasonable terms and conditions.

SUNY states that no license or other rights in university inventions are given to, or received by a sponsor, except as specifically provided for in the sponsored research agreement, and Berkeley states that the sponsored research agreement is not deemed to grant a license to any patents, patent applications or other proprietary interests with respect to any invention, discovery or improvement made by either the university or the sponsor.

Several universities allow a sponsor a set period of time, starting from the date of the invention disclosure, during which the sponsor may negotiate a license agreement. Berkeley allows sponsors a right to negotiate a license or an option to license for a thirty-day period. Caltech allows a sponsor six months after receiving written notice of a disclosure to negotiate a license or option agreement. If a sponsor elects to exercise its negotiations rights within the prescribed time period, the university and the sponsor agree to pursue the negotiation of license terms in good faith. Case provides a sponsor ninety days to request a non-exclusive license and 270 days to request an exclusive license. If a sponsor does not respond or declines a license, Case may then license the technology with no further obligation to the sponsor. Lehigh also provides that if a sponsor fails to pay for intellectual property expenses, then Lehigh may license the intellectual property without further obligation to the sponsor.

The calculation of the cost of a license depends on factors such as the scope of the license, the technological field, the maturity of the technology, cash flow constraints, and market competition and stability. It is extremely difficult to predict the cost of a license at the time the sponsored research agreement is signed. However, some universities do provide for a royalty rate range in the sponsored research agreement. For example, Columbia, provides that royalty rates will typically range from 1%-10%, while Michigan Tech provides that royalty rates will typically range from 5%-6%. Cornell and Drexel also require a licensee to pay minimum royalties to maintain exclusivity. As noted earlier, many universities require a licensee to reimburse the university for expenses related to the prosecution of the patent application in addition to paying royalties.

Additional Information

1. STEVEN Z. SZCZEPANSKI & DAVID EPSTEIN, ECKSTROM'S LICENSING IN FOREIGN & DOMESTIC OPS. § 11:4 (2010).

2. Robert E. Bienstock, Theresa J. Colecchia, *The Fundamentals of Sponsored Research in the University Setting*, UNIV. OF PITT. OFFICE OF GENERAL

COUNSEL, June 21, 2008, *available at* http://www.ogc.pitt.edu/publications/FundamentalsJune_2008.pdf.

3. Howard L. Dorfman, Linda P. Reig, *Avoiding Legal and Ethical Pitfalls of Industry-Sponsored Research: The Co-Existence of Research, Scholarship, and Marketing in the Pharmaceutical Industry*, 59 FOOD & DRUG L.J. 595 (2004).

4. James J. Casey, Jr., Essay, *Developing Harmonious University-Industry Partnerships*, 30 U. DAYTON L. REV. 245 (2004).

5. James Stuart, Comment, *The Academic-Industrial Complex: A Warning to Universities*, 75 U. COLO. L. REV. 1011 (2004).

6. Joshua A. Newberg, Richard L. Dunn, *Keeping Secrets in the Campus Lab: Law, Values and Rules of Engagement for Industry-University R&D Partnerships*, 39 AM. BUS. L.J. 187 (2002).

7. *Developing Sponsored Research Agreements: Considerations for Recipients of NIH Research Grants and Contracts*, 59 FED. REG. 55673, Nov. 8, 1994.

8. *Working Together, Creating Knowledge: The University-Industry Research Collaboration Initiative*, BUSINESS-HIGHER EDUCATION FORUM, available at http://www.acenet.edu/bookstore/pdf/working-together.pdf.

9. Arthur L. Sherwood, et al., *Partnering for Knowledge: A Learning Framework for Univeristy-Industry Collaboration* (2004), *available at* http://www.midwestacademy.org/Proceedings/2004/papers/Sherwood.doc.

10. Sample Sponsored Research Agreement (Harvard) available at http://able.harvard.edu/forms/osr_ISRA.pdf.

11. Sample Sponsored Research Agreement (University of California, Berkeley) available at http://ipira.berkeley.edu/docs/sratemplate-2007.doc.

12. See Sample Sponsored Research Agreement (MIT), *available at* http://www.iphandbook.org/handbook/resources/Agreements/links/3-4%20Sponsored%20Research%20Contract%20MIT.rtf.

13. *See* Sample Sponsored Research Agreement (Cornell), *available at* http://www.osp.cornell.edu/Policies/Std_Agmt_Rev_Aug2009.pdf.

13. Sample Sponsored Research Agreement (Michigan State University) available at http://www.iphandbook.org/handbook/resources/Agreements/links/3-4%20Sponsored%20Research%20Agreement%20Michigan.rft.

14. *See* Compilation of University Intellectual Property Policies, *available at* http://opened.creativecommons.org/UCOP.

3.2.2   Income Tax Limitations on Sponsored Research

As the above discussion notes, there are a number of contentious issues that divide universities and industry with respect to sponsored research. However, of all these contentious issues, Revenue Procedure (Rev. Proc.) 2007-47 is probably the most divisive. Rev. Proc. 2007-47 sets forth the conditions under which industry-sponsored research can be conducted in facilities built with tax-exempt bonds. The great majority of public, as well as many private, universities' research facilities are built with tax-exempt bonds. The benefit of using tax-exempt bonds to construct university research facilities is that money can be borrowed at a lower interest rate because the bond holders do not have to pay income tax on the interest paid on the bonds.

As you will see below, the conditions imposed by Rev. Proc. 2007-47 are highly restrictive and, from industry's perspective, very unfair. Many industry representatives believe Rev. Proc. 2007-47 positively discourages industry-sponsored research in the United States and promotes industry-sponsored research at foreign universities, especially in China and India. The first reading in this subsection sets forth the provisions of Rev. Proc. 2007-47 and the second reading compares the Rev. Proc. 2007-47 to the related income tax rules on the treatment of sponsored research payments to universities as unrelated business income.

REV. PROC. 2007-47
2007 IRB LEXIS 570 (2007)

This procedure sets forth conditions under which a research agreement does not result in private business use under section 141(b) of the Code. Rev. Proc. 97-14 modified and superseded.

SECTION 1. PURPOSE

The purpose of this revenue procedure is to set forth conditions under which a research agreement does not result in private business use under § 141(b) of the Internal Revenue Code of 1986 (the Code). This revenue procedure also addresses whether a research agreement causes the modified private business use test in § 145(a)(2)(B) of the Code to be met for qualified 501(c)(3) bonds. This revenue procedure modifies and supersedes Rev. Proc. 97-14, 1997-1 C.B. 634.

SECTION 2. BACKGROUND

.01 Private Business Use.

(1) Under § 103(a) of the Code, gross income does not include interest on any State or local bond. Under § 103(b)(1), however, § 103(a) does not apply to a private activity bond, unless it is a qualified bond under § 141(e). Section 141(a)(1) defines "private activity bond" as any bond issued as part of an issue that meets both the private business use and the private security or payment tests. Under § 141(b)(1), an issue generally meets the private business use test if more than 10 percent of the proceeds of the issue are to be used for any private business use. Under § 141(b)(6)(A), private business use means direct or indirect use in a trade or business carried on by any person other than a governmental unit. Section 150(a)(2) provides that the term "governmental unit" does not include the United

States or any agency or instrumentality thereof. Section 145(a) also applies the private business use test of § 141(b)(1) to qualified 501(c)(3) bonds, with certain modifications.

(2) Section 1.141-3(b)(1) of the Income Tax Regulations provides that both actual and beneficial use by a nongovernmental person may be treated as private business use. In most cases, the private business use test is met only if a nongovernmental person has special legal entitlements to use the financed property under an arrangement with the issuer. In general, a nongovernmental person is treated as a private business user of proceeds and financed property as a result of ownership; actual or beneficial use of property pursuant to a lease, or a management or incentive payment contract; or certain other arrangements such as a take or pay or other out-put-type contract.

(3) Section 1.141-3(b)(6)(i) provides generally that an agreement by a nongovernmental person to sponsor research performed by a governmental person may result in private business use of the property used for the research, based on all the facts and circumstances.

(4) Section 1.141-3(b)(6)(ii) provides generally that a research agreement with respect to financed property results in private business use of that property if the sponsor is treated as the lessee or owner of financed property for Federal income tax purposes.

(5) Section 1.141-1(b) provides that the term "governmental person" means a State or local governmental unit as defined in § 1.103-1 or any instrumentality thereof. Section 1.141-1(b) further provides that governmental person does not include the United States or any agency or instrumentality thereof. Section 1.141-1(b) further provides that "nongovernmental person" means a person other than a governmental person.

(6) Section 1.145-2 provides that §§ 1.141-0 through 1.141-15 apply to qualified 501(c)(3) bonds under § 145(a) of the Code with certain modifications and exceptions.

(7) Section 1.145-2(b)(1) provides that, in applying §§ 1.141-0 through 1.141-15 to § 145(a) of the Code, references to governmental persons include § 501(c)(3) organizations with respect to their activities that do not constitute unrelated trades or businesses under § 513(a).

.02 Federal Government rights under the Bayh-Dole Act.

(1) The Patent and Trademark Law Amendments Act of 1980, as amended, 35 U.S.C. § 200 *et seq.* (2006) (the "Bayh-Dole Act"), generally applies to any contract, grant, or cooperative agreement with any Federal agency for the performance of research funded by the Federal Government.

(2) The policies and objectives of the Bayh-Dole Act include promoting the utilization of inventions arising from federally supported research and development programs, encouraging maximum participation of small business firms in federally supported research and development efforts, promoting collaboration between commercial concerns and nonprofit organizations, ensuring that inventions made

by nonprofit organizations and small business firms are used in a manner to promote free competition and enterprise, and promoting the commercialization and public availability of inventions made in the United States by United States industry and labor.

(3) Under the Bayh-Dole Act, the Federal Government and sponsoring Federal agencies receive certain rights to inventions that result from federally funded research activities performed by non-sponsoring parties pursuant to contracts, grants, or cooperative research agreements with the sponsoring Federal agencies. The rights granted to the Federal Government and its agencies under the Bayh-Dole Act generally include, among others, nonexclusive, nontransferable, irrevocable, paid-up licenses to use the products of federally sponsored research and certain so-called "march-in rights" over licensing under limited circumstances. Here, the term "march-in rights" refers to certain rights granted to the sponsoring Federal agencies under the Bayh-Dole Act, 35 U.S.C. § 203 (2006), to take certain actions, including granting licenses to third parties to ensure public benefits from the dissemination and use of the results of federally sponsored research in circumstances in which the original contractor or assignee has not taken, or is not expected to take within a reasonable time, effective steps to achieve practical application of the product of that research. The general purpose of these rights is to ensure the expenditure of Federal research funds in accordance with the policies and objectives of the Bayh-Dole Act.

SECTION 3. DEFINITIONS

.01 Basic research, for purposes of § 141 of the Code, means any original investigation for the advancement of scientific knowledge not having a specific commercial objective. For example, product testing supporting the trade or business of a specific nongovernmental person is not treated as basic research.

.02 Qualified user means any State or local governmental unit as defined in § 1.103-1 or any instrumentality thereof. The term also includes a § 501(c)(3) organization if the financed property is not used in an unrelated trade or business under § 513(a) of the Code. The term does not include the United States or any agency or instrumentality thereof.

.03 Sponsor means any person, other than a qualified user, that supports or sponsors research under a contract.

SECTION 4. CHANGES

This revenue procedure modifies and supersedes Rev. Proc. 97-14 by making changes that are described generally as follows:

.01 Section 6.03 of this revenue procedure modifies the operating guidelines on cooperative research agreements to include agreements regarding industry or federally sponsored research with either a single sponsor or multiple sponsors.

.02 Section 6.04 of this revenue procedure provides special rules for applying the revised operating guidelines under section 6.03 of this revenue procedure to federally sponsored research. These special rules provide that the rights of the

Federal Government and its agencies mandated by the Bayh-Dole Act will not cause research agreements to fail to meet the requirements of section 6.03, upon satisfaction of the requirements of section 6.04 of this revenue procedure. Thus, under the stated conditions, such rights themselves will not result in private business use by the Federal Government or its agencies of property used in research performed under research agreements. These special rules do not address the use by third parties that actually receive more than non-exclusive, royalty-free licenses as the result of the exercise by a sponsoring Federal agency of its rights under the Bayh-Dole Act, such as its march-in rights.

SECTION 5. SCOPE

This revenue procedure applies when, under a research agreement, a sponsor uses property financed with proceeds of an issue of State or local bonds subject to § 141 or § 145(a)(2)(B) of the Code.

SECTION 6. OPERATING GUIDELINES FOR RESEARCH AGREEMENTS

.01 *In general*. If a research agreement is described in either section 6.02 or 6.03 of this revenue procedure, the research agreement itself does not result in private business use. In applying the operating guidelines under section 6.03 of this revenue procedure to federally sponsored research, the special rules under section 6.04 of this revenue procedure (regarding the effect of the rights of the Federal Government and its agencies under the Bayh-Dole Act) apply.

.02 *Corporate-sponsored research*. A research agreement relating to property used for basic research supported or sponsored by a sponsor is described in this section 6.02 if any license or other use of resulting technology by the sponsor is permitted only on the same terms as the recipient would permit that use by any unrelated, non-sponsoring party (that is, the sponsor must pay a competitive price for its use), and the price paid for that use must be determined at the time the license or other resulting technology is available for use. Although the recipient need not permit persons other than the sponsor to use any license or other resulting technology, the price paid by the sponsor must be no less than the price that would be paid by any non-sponsoring party for those same rights.

.03 *Industry or federally-sponsored research agreements*. A research agreement relating to property used pursuant to an industry or federally-sponsored research arrangement is described in this section 6.03 if the following requirements are met, taking into account the special rules set forth in section 6.04 of this revenue procedure in the case of federally sponsored research —

(1) A single sponsor agrees, or multiple sponsors agree, to fund governmentally performed basic research;

(2) The qualified user determines the research to be performed and the manner in which it is to be performed (for example, selection of the personnel to perform the research);

(3) Title to any patent or other product incidentally resulting from the basic

research lies exclusively with the qualified user; and

(4) The sponsor or sponsors are entitled to no more than a nonexclusive, royalty-free license to use the product of any of that research.

.04 ***Federal Government rights under the Bayh-Dole Act.*** In applying the operating guidelines on industry and federally-sponsored research agreements under section 6.03 of this revenue procedure to federally sponsored research, the rights of the Federal Government and its agencies mandated by the Bayh-Dole Act will not cause a research agreement to fail to meet the requirements of section 6.03, provided that the requirements of sections 6.03(2), and (3) are met, and the license granted to any party other than the qualified user to use the product of the research is no more than a nonexclusive, royalty-free license. Thus, to illustrate, the existence of march-in rights or other special rights of the Federal Government or the sponsoring Federal agency mandated by the Bayh-Dole Act will not cause a research agreement to fail to meet the requirements of section 6.03 of this revenue procedure, provided that the qualified user determines the subject and manner of the research in accordance with section 6.03(2), the qualified user retains exclusive title to any patent or other product of the research in accordance with section 6.03(3), and the nature of any license granted to the Federal Government or the sponsoring Federal agency (or to any third party nongovernmental person) to use the product of the research is no more than a nonexclusive, royalty-free license.

SECTION 7. EFFECT ON OTHER DOCUMENTS

Rev. Proc. 97-14 is modified and superseded.

SECTION 8. EFFECTIVE DATE

This revenue procedure is effective for any research agreement entered into, materially modified, or extended on or after June 26, 2007. In addition, an issuer may apply this revenue procedure to any research agreement entered into prior to June 26, 2007.

QUESTIONS

1. Section 6.02 of Rev. Proc. 2007-47 requires that any license of technology resulting from sponsored research conducted in tax-exempt bond facilities must be available to the sponsor and non-sponsors on the same terms. Does this require sponsors to subsidize the research of non-sponsors? What is the rationale for requiring licenses to sponsors and non-sponsors on the same terms?

2. Section 6.02 of Rev. Proc. 2007-47 states that the sponsor must pay a competitive price for the use of technology resulting from the sponsored research and that the price paid for that use must be determined at the time the resulting technology is available for use. Does this preclude negotiation of license fees and royalty rates at the time the sponsored research agreement is executed? What if a university has standard license fees and established royalty rate ranges for different types of technology? Would the grant to a sponsor of a non-exclusive, non-transferable, royalty-free license to use resulting technology for internal

research and development purposes be allowed under § 6.02?

3.   Finally, Section 6.02 of Rev. Proc. 2007-47 states: "Although the recipient [university] need not permit persons other than the sponsor to use any license or other resulting technology, the price paid by the sponsor must be no less than the price that would be paid by any non-sponsoring party for those same rights." Could a university grant a sponsor the exclusive right to *negotiate* a license to resulting technology at the time the sponsored research agreement is executed? If a university refuses to grant a license to non-sponsors, how could it establish that the price paid by the sponsor is the same price that would have been paid by a non-sponsor?

NOTE ON PUBLIC POLICY REGARDING INDUSTRY-SPONSORED RESEARCH

Introduction

There is broad consensus among universities and industry that industry-sponsored research is critical for the progress of science, the education of future generations of scientists and engineers, and the advancement of the health, safety, and economic prosperity of U.S. citizens. However, there is disagreement on the appropriate public policy to guide industry-sponsored research in the United States. One area of disagreement is over a technical, but very important, question: should U.S. universities be allowed to grant corporate research sponsors rights in the resulting intellectual property at the time the sponsored research agreement is signed, if the research is to be conducted in facilities built with tax-exempt bonds?

This note discusses two different interpretations of the "public interest" regarding industry-sponsored research set forth in U.S. tax law and some of the arguments for and against adopting one or the other of these interpretations.

The Disparate Definitions of "Public Interest" Under Revenue Procedure 2007-47 and Revenue Ruling 76-296

Under the generally accepted interpretation of Rev. Proc. 2007-47, a university cannot grant a corporate research sponsor any rights in the resulting intellectual property at the time the sponsored research agreement is signed if the research is conducted in facilities built with tax-exempt bonds. Revenue Procedure 2007-47 states that corporate-sponsored research will not be considered a "private business use" of tax-exempt bond facilities provided that:

> Any license or other use of resulting technology by the sponsor is permitted only on the same terms as the [university] would permit that use by any unrelated, non-sponsoring party (that is, the sponsor must pay a competitive price for its use), and the price paid for that use must be determined at the time the license or other resulting technology is available for use.[1]

---

[1] Rev. Proc. 2007-47, § 6.02. A research agreement that is considered a "private business use" of

Rev. Proc. 2007-47 was preceded by Rev. Proc. 97-14, which contained the same limitation on licensing intellectual property to corporate sponsors at the commencement of a sponsored research project. Support for Rev. Proc. 97-14 was based on the legislative history of the 1986 Tax Act.[2] The House Ways and Means Committee Report on the 1986 Tax Act stated that "no nongovernmental participant in [a] cooperative research arrangement is entitled to preferential use of any product of the research (including any patent)."[3]

Similarly, the Senate Finance Committee Report on the 1986 Tax Act stated that:

> The use of [tax-exempt] bond-financed property by a university to perform . . . research supported or sponsored by . . . other persons pursuant to a cooperative research arrangement is not to be treated as trade or business use by such person . . . provided that any agreed use of any resulting technology by the non-university sponsoring person is permitted only on the same terms by which the university permits such use by any other non-sponsoring unrelated party.[4]

Finally, the Conference Report on the 1986 Tax Act stated that the use of university tax-exempt bond facilities by corporate sponsors would not be treated as a private business use if "the amount charged [to] participating businesses for the use of patents or other resulting technology [is] determined at the time the patent or technology is available for use."[5]

Although Rev. Proc. 97-14 is consistent with the legislative history of the 1986 Tax Act, there is another branch of tax law that sets forth a very different "public interest" test for corporate-sponsored research at universities. This branch of tax law deals with the question of when corporate-sponsored research might constitute the conduct of unrelated trade or business by universities giving rise to taxation of unrelated trade or business income to universities.

The IRS addressed this question in Rev. Rul. 76-296, which provides that "scientific research will be considered as directed toward benefiting the public, and, therefore, regarded as carried on in the public interest if it is carried on for the purpose of obtaining scientific information, which is published in a treatise, thesis, trade publication, or in any other form that is available to the interested public."[6] Rev. Rul. 76-296 goes on to state that the relevant Income Tax Regulations "explicitly provide that [scientific] research will be regarded as carried on in the public interest even though such research is performed pursuant to a contract or agreement under which the sponsor or sponsors of the research have the right to

---

tax-exempt bond facilities could result in the loss of the tax exemption for the bond income. Rev. Proc. 2007-47, § 1.

[2] P.L. 99-514 (1986).

[3] H.R. Rep. No. 99-426, 524 (1986).

[4] S. Rep. No. 99-313, 842 (1986).

[5] H.R. Conf. Rep. No. 99-841, II-685-II-689 (1986).

[6] Income Tax Regulations, § 1.501(c)(3)-1(d)(5)(iii). The "public interest" test referred to in Rev. Rul. 76-296 is the obverse of the "private business use" test referenced in Rev. Proc. 2007-47.

obtain ownership or control of any patents, copyrights, processes, or formulae resulting from such research."[7]

There are two possible ways to reconcile the very different "public interest" tests set forth in Rev. Proc. 2007-47 and Rev. Rul. 76-296. One way is to assume that Rev. Rul. 76-296 was repealed, or rendered invalid, by the passage of the 1986 Tax Act and the IRS's subsequent promulgation of Rev. Proc. 97-14. However, a Congressional committee report and an internal IRS continuing education paper clearly indicate that Rev. Rul. 76-296 is still valid law.

The Congressional committee report was prepared for the Senate Committee on Finance by the Staff of the Joint Committee on Taxation on December 4, 2006.[8] The report noted that an "issue may arise whether commercially sponsored scientific research is carried on in the public interest . . . where the commercial sponsor has a right to ownership or control of the intellectual property resulting from the research." The report cited Rev. Rul. 76-296 as the controlling authority on this question. The report made no mention of Rev. Proc. 97-14.

The internal IRS continuing education paper, published 1999, focused on intellectual property in tax-exempt organizations.[9] In discussing the meaning of the phrase "in the public interest" as used in Income Tax Regulations § 1.501(c)(3)–1(d)(5), the paper stated: "Rev. Rul. 76-206 is the controlling authority on this subject. The revenue ruling deals with the publication requirement as well as the question of the commercial sponsor's right to exploit the results of research findings. It was published to provide a clear example of how problems involving commercially sponsored scientific research projects should be treated."

The other way to reconcile the different "private business use" tests set forth in Rev. Proc. 2007-47 and Rev. Rul. 76-296 is to limit each test to its specific factual context. Rev. Proc. 2007-47 is concerned with the use of tax-exempt bond facilities by corporate sponsors, and Rev. Rul. 76-296 is concerned with unrelated trade or business income received by 501(c)(3) tax-exempt organizations. However, the distinction between the factual contexts of Rev. Proc. 2007-47 and Rev. Rul. 76-296 is quite narrow. And the question remains: why are corporate sponsor rights in resulting intellectual property consistent with the public interest when the research is conducted in privately financed facilities and inconsistent with the public interest when the same research is conducted in tax-exempt bond financed facilities?

An initial response to this question might be that allowing corporate sponsors to own intellectual property resulting from research conducted in tax-exempt bond facilities constitutes a federal subsidy of the sponsored research. The reasoning here would be that the tax-exempt bonds allow research facilities to be built at a lower cost and corporate sponsors are the beneficiaries of these lower costs when they are allowed to take title to intellectual property created in tax-exempt bond facilities. However, this line of reasoning ignores the very large, and explicit, federal

---

[7] Income Tax Regulations, § 1.501(c)(3)-1(d)(5)(iii).

[8] Present Law and Background Relating to Tax Exemptions and Incentives for Higher Education, prepared by the Staff of the Joint Committee on Taxation (December 4, 2006).

[9] R. Darling and M. Friedlander, Intellectual Property, 1999 EO CPE Text < http://www.irs.treas.gov/pub/irs-tege/eotopic99.pdf>.

research subsidies provided through the Bayh-Dole Act and the Small Business Innovation Research (SBIR) Program (discussed in Chapter 11 of the materials).

As you have seen, the express purpose of the Bayh-Dole Act in allowing universities to take title to patents resulting from federally-funded research is to make these patents available to industry for commercial development. Likewise, the SBIR Program mandates that federal agencies set aside a percentage of their research budgets to award contracts to small business concerns which, under the terms of the SBIR Program, are permitted to retain title to any patents resulting from the federal agencies' research grants. Whatever the federal research subsidies provided by allowing corporate sponsors to own patents resulting from research conducted in tax-exempt bond facilities, these subsidies are a small fraction of the research subsidies provided through the Bayh-Dole Act and SBIR Program.

Arguments *For* Adopting the Definition of "Public Interest" in Rev. Proc. 2007-47

1. Rev. Proc. 2007-47 is not a barrier to university-industry-sponsored research collaboration.

Whether Rev. Proc. 2007-47 is a barrier to university-industry sponsored research collaboration depends on institutional perspective. Although some university representatives believe Rev. Proc. 2007-47 is not a barrier to sponsored research collaboration, the great majority of industry representatives believe it is a significant barrier to sponsored research collaboration. However, both university and industry representatives agree that Rev. Proc. 2007-47 is not the only barrier to sponsored research collaboration and that other problems, such as prolonged negotiations on license terms and disagreements over the value of intellectual property rights, as well as matters outside intellectual property area, such as indemnification, liability and publication, also impede sponsored research collaboration.

2. Rev. Proc. 2007-47 protects the academic integrity of university research.

Whether Rev. Proc. 2007-47 is necessary to protect the academic integrity of university research is not clear. First, if a university believes that the academic integrity of its research requires it to refuse to grant intellectual property rights to corporate sponsors at the commencement of sponsored research projects, the university is free to incorporate this principle into its intellectual property policy statement. Second, if the academic integrity of university research depends on universities performing only basic research, as opposed to job-shop, commercial research, this concern is dealt with by the requirement set forth in Rev. Rul. 76-296 that provides only "scientific research" will be considered to be in the "public interest."

3. Rev. Proc. 2007-47 protects universities from inappropriate corporate influence.

Whether Rev. Proc. 2007-47 is necessary to protect universities from inappropriate corporate influence also depends on institutional perspective. While some universities may believe that corporations exert undue influence over their research, other universities actively seek corporate involvement in their research enterprise to assure the relevancy of, and financial support for, their research efforts. It should also be noted that some industry representatives believe the reverse is true; that is, universities exert undue control in licensing intellectual property to corporations, especially intellectual property created with federal (taxpayer) funding.

4. Rev. Proc. 2007-47 recognizes that it is not possible to value intellectual property rights prior to the time the intellectual property is created.

With respect to the relationship between Rev. Proc. 2007-47 and the valuation of licensed intellectual property, it is true that Rev. Proc. 2007-47 requires that intellectual property resulting from a sponsored research project must be licensed at a "competitive price." However, a "competitive price" need not be stated as a fixed dollar amount, but rather can be stated as a specific royalty rate, or a range of royalty rates. Universities typically have standard royalty rates for different types of intellectual property, so a standard royalty rate can be stipulated at the commencement of a sponsored research project. A stipulated standard royalty rate would presumptively be a "competitive price" because it would be the royalty rate charged to any non-sponsor licensee.

5. Rev. Proc. 2007-47 rightly allows universities to obtain higher royalties when the resulting intellectual property has higher value.

Whether universities should obtain higher royalty rates when the resulting intellectual property has higher value is problematic from an industry perspective. Scientific research is inherently a high-risk enterprise and nobody can know at the outset of a research project whether it will be successful. From the industry perspective, the corporate sponsor assumes the research risk by funding the project. If the research project is not successful, the corporate sponsor bears the loss of the research investment. On the other hand, if the research project is successful, the corporate sponsor expects to receive the benefit of the research — without paying a premium because the research project was successful. To do otherwise would impose all of the downside risk on the corporate sponsor and give all of the upside gain to the university.

6. Rev. Proc. 2007-47 allows universities to grant corporate sponsors options to negotiate future licenses to resulting intellectual property.

Rev. Proc. 2007-47 does allow universities to grant corporate sponsors options to negotiate future licenses to resulting intellectual property. However, an option to negotiate a license is *not* a license. The grant of an option to negotiate a license does not provide the corporate sponsor with any intellectual property rights in the resulting patents or technologies. This is troublesome to many corporate sponsors, especially in light of the language in Rev. Proc. 2007-47 that provides that any license of resulting technology to the sponsor must also be available to non-sponsors on the same terms and conditions. In addition, some universities are not willing to grant sponsors options to negotiate future licenses. These universities are only willing to grant sponsors an agreement to grant an option at some future date.

Again, this is troublesome to many corporate sponsors.

7. Rev. Proc. 2007-47 allows universities to grant corporate sponsors licenses without price terms.

Whether universities can grant corporate sponsors licenses without price terms is not clear. However, assuming Rev. Proc. 2007-47 does allow this type of license, it is of little benefit to corporate sponsors. A license without a price term is, in essence, no more than an option to negotiate a license. And, as a small point of law, contracts without price terms are rarely enforced by courts because they do not manifest the parties' agreement to the most fundamental terms of the contract.

8. Rev. Proc. 2007-47 allows universities to grant corporate sponsors "private business use" of tax-exempt bond facilities up to either 5% or 10% of the amount of the bond proceeds.

It is true that Rev. Proc. 2007-47 allows "private business use" of tax-exempt bond facilities by corporate sponsors up to 5% of the bond proceeds for public universities and up to 10% of the bond proceeds for private universities.[10] This allowed private business use could include granting corporate sponsors rights in the resulting intellectual property at the commencement of the research project. There are problems, however, with this allowed "private business use" from both industry and university perspectives. From the industry perspective, the allowed "private business use," and hence the opportunity to obtain rights in the resulting intellectual property at the commencement of the research project, is very limited. From the university perspective, calculating the amount of "private business use," and attributing various fixed and variable costs to "private business use," is a very difficult and risky accounting task. For this reason, many universities are unwilling to utilize the "private business use" allowance under Rev. Proc. 2007-47.

Arguments *Against* Adopting the Definition of "Public Interest" in Rev. Proc. 2007-47

1. Rev. Proc. 2007-47 retards U.S. domestic economic development and threatens U.S. international competitiveness.

Whether Rev. Proc. 2007-47 retards U.S. domestic economic development and threatens U.S. international competitiveness is a complex question of causation and measurement. Clearly, many factors other than Rev. Proc. 2007-47 affect U.S. economic development and competitiveness; and, to the extent Rev. Proc. 2007-47 does affect U.S. economic development and competitiveness, the magnitude of this effect is difficult to measure. However, the relationship between university research and regional economic development in the United States has been clearly established; so much so that many other countries are adopting the U.S. model. Although the negative impact of Rev. Proc. 2007-47 on sponsored research and economic development in the United States may not be easy to measure, nobody, certainly in industry, would suggest that Rev. Proc. 2007-47 promotes sponsored research and

---

[10] IRC § 141(b).

economic development. The question then becomes why risk negatively impacting sponsored research and economic development, even if we do not know the precise magnitude of the negative effect?

2. Rev. Proc. 2007-47 is driving U.S. industry to increasingly invest in research at foreign universities.

Whether Rev. Proc. 2007-47 is driving U.S. industry to invest in research at foreign universities is also a complex question. Other factors, such as performing research in areas close to overseas manufacturing facilities and markets, and the growing parity in science and engineering education in a number of other countries, may drive research investment to foreign universities far more than Rev. Proc. 2007-47. However, the question here is the same as above. If the goal is to maximize U.S. industry investment in research at U.S. universities and Rev. Proc. 2007-47 poses even a small obstacle to this goal, why take this risk?

3. Rev. Proc. 2007-47 is inconsistent with the Bayh-Dole Act.

Whether Rev. Proc. 2007-47 is inconsistent with the Bayh-Dole Act depends upon how one interprets the goal of the Bayh-Dole Act. If one interprets the goal of the Bayh-Dole Act as benefiting universities by providing them title to intellectual property resulting from federally-funded research, then there is no conflict with Rev. Proc. 2007-47. Under this interpretation, universities are the primary beneficiaries of the Bayh-Dole Act and their beneficiary status is not affected by Rev. Proc. 2007-47. In fact, it may be argued Rev. Proc. 2007-47 benefits universities by strengthening their bargaining position in negotiations with corporate sponsors after an invention has been made. On the other hand, if one interprets the goal of the Bayh-Dole Act as benefiting the public by making federally-funded inventions available to the public through commercialization by private industry, then there is a conflict with Rev. Proc. 2007-47.[11] Under this interpretation, university intellectual property ownership is a means to an end, not an end in itself; that is, university intellectual property ownership is intended to facilitate the transfer of federally-funded inventions to private industry so that the inventions can be commercialized for the benefit of the public. The preamble statement of policy objective in the Bayh-Dole Act makes clear that the latter interpretation is correct; the Act was intended "to promote the commercialization and public availability of inventions made [with federal funding]," not to benefit universities.[12]

---

[11] A specific example of the conflict between Rev. Proc. 2007-47 and the public benefit interpretation of the Bayh-Dole Act occurs when a federally-funded invention requires follow-on research to be commercialized, which is very often the case. If potential corporate sponsors of the follow-on research are unsure of the rights they will receive in the intellectual property resulting from the follow-on research, they may refuse to sponsor the follow-on research, in which case the public will never receive the benefit of the federally-funded invention.

[12] 35 U.S.C.A. § 200.

4. Rev. Proc. 2007-47 is in conflict with the Small Business Technology Transfer Program ("STTR").

There is a direct conflict between Rev. Proc. 2007-47 and the Small Business Technology Transfer (STTR) Program Policy Directive. (The STTR Program is discussed in Chapter 11.) Under the STTR Program Policy Directive, a small business corporation sponsoring a research project at a university must negotiate a written agreement with the university to obtain the intellectual property rights necessary to conduct follow-on research *before receiving an STTR award.*[13] Since an STTR award precedes the commencement of the sponsored research project, the written agreement with the university on intellectual property rights would also have to precede the commencement of the sponsored research project. This is precisely prohibited by Rev. Proc. 2007-47.

5. Rev. Proc. 2007-47 can operate to force corporate research sponsors to subsidize their competitors' research.

The argument that Rev. Proc. 2007-47 can cause corporate sponsors to subsidize their competitors' research is a technical argument, but nonetheless troublesome to industry. As noted above, Rev. Proc. 2007-47 requires that any license to resulting intellectual property granted to a corporate sponsor must be available on non-sponsors on the same terms and conditions. Although Rev. Proc. 2007-47 also provides that universities need not grant licenses to non-sponsors, the possibility that a non-sponsor could obtain a license on the same terms and conditions as the sponsor is a concern to industry because the non-sponsors interested in the license could well be a competitor of the sponsor. If this occurred, the sponsor would end up funding research for the benefit of a competitor.

6. Rev. Proc. 2007-47 denies sponsors and universities the flexibility to negotiate agreements at the commencement of research projects that advance the unique needs and interests of universities and sponsors.

Not only does Rev. Proc. 2007-47 deny universities and sponsors the *flexibility* to negotiate license terms prior to the commencement of a research project according to their unique needs and interests, in practice Rev. Proc. 2007-47 denies the parties the opportunity to negotiate *any* meaningful license terms prior to commencement of a research project. This deprives universities and sponsors of the opportunity to experiment with new and creative collaborative research arrangements to benefit students, faculty, universities, and corporate sponsors.

7. Rev. Proc. 2007-47 limits the educational benefits and career opportunities that industry-sponsored research can provide students.

Industry-sponsored research projects provide important educational benefits to students. To the extent Rev. Proc. 2007-47 deters corporations from sponsoring research projects, these educational benefits are lost. Likewise, industry-sponsored research provides students with career opportunities with corporate sponsors.

---

[13] STTR Policy Directive, 70 Fed. Reg. 74,935 (2005).

These career opportunities are also lost when corporations are deterred from sponsoring research projects.

8. Rev. Proc. 2007-47 makes it very difficult for corporate sponsors to budget the cost of developing new technologies at the outset of a research project.

Rev. Proc. 2007-47 does make it very difficult for corporate sponsors to budget the cost of developing new technologies at the outset of a research project. If price terms cannot be negotiated at the time a sponsored research agreement is signed, the cost to the sponsor of the resulting patents and technology cannot be factored into the business case for going forward with the sponsored research project. In many instances, this cost uncertainty may be enough to cause the corporate sponsor to refrain from the research investment.

9. Rev. Proc. 2007-47 is anticompetitive in that it does not allow universities to independently negotiate the terms and conditions of sponsored research agreements.

Rev. Proc. 2007-47 is anticompetitive in the sense that it does not allow universities to compete for sponsored research funds by offering more attractive license terms, in addition to state-of-the-art facilities and expert researchers. As nonprofit organizations, universities are not subject to the same stringent competition laws as private entities. However, it is generally assumed that competition promotes the public good in the nonprofit sector as well as in the for-profit sector. In the case of sponsored research, changes in Rev. Proc. 2007-47 would allow more universities to better compete for sponsored research funding, and would allow more corporate sponsors to better compare the combination of research facilities, research faculty, and license terms.

Conclusion

A decline in industry-sponsored research at U.S. universities poses significant risks to universities, industry and the U.S. economy. Universities risk losing access to access to crucial funding for future research, access to cutting-edge industrial problems, and access to unique educational opportunities for students and faculty. Industry risks losing access to the latest scientific and technical knowledge, access to highly skilled and specialized scientists and engineers, access to state-of-the-art equipment and facilities, and access to highly trained pools of potential new employees. The U.S. economy risks losing opportunities for growth, opportunities for the creation of new jobs, opportunities to improve the balance of trade, and opportunities to gain new competitive advantages in global markets. The stakes are high in formulating a public policy that will advance the interests of industry and universities in collaborative research projects in the future.

QUESTIONS

1.   Which definition of the "public interest" do you think is most appropriate to foster academic research, industry innovation and U.S. competitiveness?

2. Are there additional factors you think should be taken into account in determining the definition of "public interest" as it applies to industry sponsored research at U.S. universities? What are these additional factors?

3. Why might some universities oppose adoption of the "public interest" definition contained in Rev. Rul. 2007-47? Why might some universities favor adoption of the "public interest" definition contained in Rev. Rul. 2007-47?

4. What are the political obstacles to changing the definition of the "public interest" regarding industry sponsored research conducted in tax-exempt bond facilities?

CASE NOTES

1. *See* Midwest Research Inst. v. United States, 554 F. Supp. 1379 (W.D. Mo. 1983) (Income earned by nonprofit scientific research institute was not subject to taxation as unrelated business income because private sponsor research performed by institute was done for purpose of encouraging industry within a particular geographic area); IIT Research Institute v. United States, 9 Cl. Ct. 13 (Cl. Ct. 1985) (Research projects could properly be deemed "scientific research" because virtually all projects consisted of work that could only be performed by qualified engineers and scientists with expertise in particular technical field; research directed toward solving particular industrial problem does not necessarily indicate that the research is nonscientific).

Additional Information

1. FEDERAL TAX COORDINATOR, SECOND EDITION P J-3107.1, P J-3107.3-P J-3107.4 (2009).

2. SHARON STANTON WHITE, PRIVATE ACTIVITY BOND TESTS § 3:28; § 3:31 (2010).

3. *Modified Rules Apply to Tax-Exempt Bonds Involving Certain Corporate Research*, FEDERAL TAX WEEKLY ALERT, June 28, 2007, at Art. 16.

4. Michael A. Lehmann, Yoo-Kyeong Kwon, *UBIT and Privately Funded Scientific Research*, 21 TAX'N OF EXEMPTS 34 (July/Aug. 2009).

5. Frederic L. Ballard, *Tax-Exempt Bonds and Sponsored Research*, 36 J. HEALTH L. 43 (2003).

6. Peter D. Blumberg, *From "Publish or Perish" to "Profit or Perish": Revenues from University Technology Transfer and the 501(c)(3) Tax Exemption*, 145 U. PA. L. REV. 89 (1996).

7. Suzanne R. McDowell, *Exploitation of Intellectual Property*, INTELLECTUAL PROPERTY & TECHNOLOGY MAGAZINE, 28 June 2004.

8. Robert E. Bienstock, Theresa J. Colecchia, *The Fundamentals of Sponsored Research in the University Setting*, UNIV. OF PITT. OFFICE OF GENERAL COUNSEL, June 21, 2008, *available at* http://www.ogc.pitt.edu/publications/FundamentalsJune_2008.pdf.

9. John M. Bello, *Economics 101: A Study of the Tax-Exempt Status of Colleges and Universities*, 34 SUFFOLK U. L. REV. 615 (2001).

3.2.3 University-Sponsor Disputes

The Wisconsin Alumni Research Foundation (WARF) was established in 1925 to manage inventions resulting from research performed at the University of Wisconsin-Madison. One of the earliest and most successful inventions licensed by WARF was the discovery that exposing certain foods to ultraviolet light enriched their vitamin D content. This discovery eventually led to the elimination of rickets. Since its founding, WARF has generated over $1 billion in licensing revenues to support research at the University Wisconsin. WARF currently licenses over 100 inventions a year.

The case below involves three research contracts, an option to license, an exclusive license, a faculty invention disclosure and assignment, a faculty consulting contract, and a jointly owned patent. At issue are the rights to an assay and set of compounds targeted at an enzyme that can lower cholesterol.

WISCONSIN ALUMNI RESEARCH FOUNDATION v. XENON PHARMACEUTICALS, INC.
591 F.3d 876 (7th Cir. 2010)

SYKES, CIRCUIT JUDGE.

This case arises out of a complex set of contractual relationships between the Wisconsin Alumni Research Foundation, the patent-management entity for the University of Wisconsin; certain research scientists at the University; and Xenon Pharmaceuticals, a Canadian drug company. The Foundation and Xenon jointly own the patent rights to an enzyme that can lower cholesterol levels in the human body. The enzyme's cholesterol-reducing benefits were discovered and confirmed by scientists at the University whose research was sponsored in part by Xenon. In 2001, pursuant to an option agreement between the Foundation and Xenon, the Foundation gave Xenon an exclusive license to commercialize this discovery and market any resulting products in exchange for a share of the profits.

The Foundation brought this suit against Xenon alleging violations of its contract rights and seeking damages and declaratory relief. First, the Foundation alleged that Xenon sublicensed its interest in the patented enzyme to a third party but refused to pay the Foundation a percentage of the sublicense fees as required under the 2001 license agreement. Second, the Foundation alleged that Xenon wrongly asserted ownership over a set of therapeutic compounds developed from the jointly patented enzyme; the Foundation claimed that it owned rights to these compounds pursuant to its network of written agreements with Xenon and the University researcher who confirmed the therapeutic benefits of the compounds. Xenon counterclaimed against the Foundation, and on cross-motions for summary judgment, the district court ruled in the Foundation's favor on the breach-of-contract claim and in Xenon's favor on the dispute over ownership of the compounds. A jury awarded $1 million in damages for the breach of contract; the

Foundation accepted $300,000 after Xenon successfully moved for remittitur. Both parties appealed.

We affirm in part and reverse in part and remand for entry of judgment consistent with this opinion. The district court properly granted summary judgment for the Foundation on the breach-of-contract claim. Xenon breached its license agreement with the Foundation by granting a sublicense in the jointly patented enzyme to a third party without paying the Foundation its share of the sublicense fees. A subsidiary issue is whether Xenon's breach triggered the Foundation's right to terminate the agreement. We conclude that the district court should not have voided the Foundation's attempt to do so; the Foundation was entitled to and properly terminated the agreement. We also conclude the district court erroneously entered judgment for Xenon on the issue of the Foundation's claim to an ownership interest in the compounds. Under the web of contracts at issue here, the Foundation was entitled to a declaration of its ownership interest in the compounds.

I. Background

Researchers at the University of Wisconsin became interested in an enzyme called Stearoyl CoA Desaturase ("SCD") because of its potential to help treat diabetes, obesity, and other diseases by lowering cholesterol. In 1999 the researchers discovered that suppressing SCD levels in the human body lowered cholesterol levels. Pursuant to University policy, the researchers disclosed their research results to the Foundation and in January 2000 signed a Memorandum Agreement assigning all their rights in the discovery to the Foundation. The next month, the Foundation filed a provisional patent application for the discovery.

Meanwhile, Xenon, a Canadian pharmaceutical company that was collaborating with the University on research into a separate enzyme, learned of the University's discoveries and expressed interest in jointly pursuing SCD research. The University and Xenon entered into a series of research agreements (referred to as Research Agreements 1, 2, and 3) in which Xenon agreed to jointly sponsor various SCD research projects with the University. Each research agreement identified the scope of the research, the principal researcher, the expected cost, and the period of performance. These agreements also referred to a separate Sponsor Option Agreement between the Foundation and Xenon that governed ownership of any discoveries arising from the joint research program. The Sponsor Option Agreement cross-referenced the contracts between the Foundation and the individual University researchers requiring the researchers to assign to the Foundation any property rights in the discoveries emanating from the research and gave Xenon an exclusive option to license any resulting technology. Attached to the Sponsor Option Agreement were the individual contracts between the Foundation and the University researchers.

At the same time that Xenon signed its first research agreement with the University, Xenon also entered into a series of short-term consulting agreements with individual researchers at the University who worked on SCD projects. In exchange for consulting fees, these scientists undertook specific research projects for Xenon and agreed to assign any discoveries arising from these consulting projects to Xenon.

In February 2001 Xenon and the Foundation filed a joint patent application deriving from the provisional patent application the Foundation had filed in 2000. The application covered, among other things, the SCD enzyme itself and a method (called an assay) of using the enzyme to identify compounds that lower SCD levels. A patent issued for the assay, but the patent application covering the remaining claims is still pending. Also in February 2001, Xenon exercised its option under the Sponsor Option Agreement to an exclusive license for any discoveries arising from the Xenon-sponsored SCD research at the University. As a result Xenon and the Foundation entered into an Exclusive License Agreement giving Xenon an exclusive right to make, use, and sell patented products under the joint patent application within the field of human healthcare. In exchange for these exclusive rights, Xenon agreed to pay the Foundation a percentage of any product sales, royalties, or sublicense fees it received.

After receiving the exclusive license, Xenon worked with Discovery Partners, Inc., to help identify compounds that inhibit the SCD enzyme. Using the jointly patented assay, Discovery Partners screened thousands of compounds and identified a set of 20 (referred to as the PPA compounds) with the potential to suppress SCD levels. Xenon shipped the PPA compounds to Mark Gray-Keller, a University researcher with whom it had a consulting agreement, for confirmatory testing. Gray-Keller successfully confirmed the inhibitory potential of the PPA compounds and thereafter assigned any interest he had in the compounds to Xenon. In 2002 Xenon filed a patent application covering the PPA compounds.

The Foundation objected, claiming that it had an ownership interest in the PPA compounds under the various interlocking agreements among the parties. More specifically, the Foundation noted that Gray-Keller had assigned all his rights in SCD discoveries and any improvements to the Foundation in his 2000 Memorandum Agreement. The Foundation also noted that the Sponsor Option Agreement between it and Xenon specifically acknowledged that Gray-Keller was required to assign his interest in any inventions arising from the jointly sponsored research to the Foundation. Alternatively, the Foundation claimed it had title to the compounds under the Bayh-Dole Act, 35 U.S.C. §§ 200 *et seq.*, because federal funds had been used in the research and development of the compounds.

Relations between Xenon and the Foundation continued to deteriorate in 2004 when Xenon signed a license agreement with Novartis Pharma AG ("Novartis"), a Swiss corporation. This agreement gave Novartis a license to the technology covered by the joint patent application and purported to transfer ownership of the PPA compounds. After learning of this agreement (via a press release), the Foundation demanded a percentage of the sublicense fees from Xenon under the terms of the Exclusive License Agreement. Xenon refused, claiming it had the right to license its undivided interest in the joint patent application without being subject to the terms of its license agreement with the Foundation.

The Foundation then brought this suit claiming that Xenon violated the terms of the Exclusive License Agreement and owed the Foundation a percentage of the sublicense fees it received from Novartis. The Foundation also claimed that it, not

Xenon, owned Gray-Keller's interest in the PPA compounds. The Foundation sought damages and declaratory judgment. Xenon responded with counterclaims against the Foundation. The district court, on cross-motions for summary judgment, entered a series of rulings on all issues except damages. The judge held that Xenon breached the Exclusive License Agreement by granting a sublicense to Novartis without notifying the Foundation or conforming the sublicense to the terms set out in the license agreement. The judge also held that Xenon owed royalties or sublicense fees to the Foundation under the terms of the license agreement. The judge further held that in light of Xenon's breach, the Foundation had a right to terminate the license agreement.

The court also ruled in Xenon's favor on several issues. First, the judge dismissed as moot the Foundation's claim that Xenon breached its duty of good faith by failing to abide by the terms of the license agreement. Second, the judge held that the Foundation had not given Xenon proper notice or an opportunity to cure before invoking its right to terminate the license agreement. Third, the court denied the Foundation's claims to quiet title in the PPA compounds, for conversion of those same compounds, and for a declaratory judgment that Gray-Keller's purported assignment of his rights in the compounds to Xenon was void. The court held that the Foundation could not claim title to the compounds under either the Memorandum Agreement with Gray-Keller, the Sponsor Option Agreement with Xenon, or the Bayh-Dole Act. Later, the court vacated its ruling regarding the Foundation's right to terminate the license agreement; the judge agreed with Xenon that the Foundation had not properly developed this argument in its opening summary-judgment brief.

The case proceeded to a jury trial on the question of damages for Xenon's failure to pay royalties or sublicense fees. The jury awarded $1 million, but on Xenon's motion for remittitur the court reduced the award to $300,000, which the Foundation accepted. The parties cross-appealed from the judgment, challenging various of the district court's rulings on summary judgment; Xenon also challenges the sufficiency of the evidence on damages.

II. Discussion

****

A. Exclusive License Agreement

1. Xenon's Transfer of Rights to Novartis

We begin by addressing Xenon's contention that it did not violate the terms of the Exclusive License Agreement when it licensed its interest in the joint patent application to Novartis without paying the Foundation its share of the licensing fee. As a threshold matter, Xenon argues that this dispute is resolved by federal patent law, not by contract law. The district court did not address the question whether Xenon retained a federal statutory right to freely license its interest without regard to the Foundation's contract rights. The court resolved the parties' disputes based solely on the terms of their various contracts, holding that Xenon effectively executed a sublicense with Novartis and that this transaction fell within the provision of the Exclusive License Agreement governing sublicenses. Xenon contends that federal law — specifically, 35 U.S.C. § 262 — gives it the right to freely license its undivided one-half interest in the joint patent application without accounting to the Foundation under the terms of the Exclusive License Agreement. We disagree.

Federal law provides that joint patent owners, like the Foundation and Xenon, have control over the entire property, and each co-owner may freely use the patented technology without regard to the other. See 35 U.S.C. § 262. We have previously observed that under this principle of patent law, "each co-owner is "at the mercy" of the other in that the right of each to license independently "may, for all practical purposes, destroy the monopoly and so amount to an appropriation of the whole value of the patent." " This statutory rule is subject to an important exception, however: Joint patent owners may vary their rights by contract. The statute provides that "*[i]n the absence of any agreement to the contrary*, each of the joint owners of a patent may make, use, offer to sell, or sell the patented invention . . . without the consent of and without accounting to the other owners." 35 U.S.C. § 262 (emphasis added). The statutory default rule therefore controls *unless* there is an agreement to the contrary.

Here, the Foundation and Xenon modified the statutory default rule by contract; the Exclusive License Agreement plainly qualifies as "an agreement to the contrary" for purposes of § 262. That agreement provides: "[The Foundation] hereby grants to Xenon an exclusive license, limited to the [field of human healthcare,] . . . under the Licensed Patents to make, use and sell Products." In exchange Xenon agreed to pay the Foundation a percentage of any payments, royalties, or sublicense fees it received by commercializing the technology itself or sublicensing the technology to a third party to commercialize. Under the terms of the agreement, sublicenses are expressly permitted — *provided* Xenon pays the Foundation the specified percentage of any royalties or sublicense fees — but *assignments* are prohibited without the Foundation's prior written consent.

Xenon argues that nothing in the Exclusive License Agreement explicitly revokes its statutory right to license its interest freely. True, but the agreement's provision requiring that Xenon pay the Foundation a share of the fees derived from any sublicense plainly undermines Xenon's claim that it retained an unfettered right under § 262 to transfer its interest in the technology to third parties. So does the agreement's provision prohibiting assignment of the license without the Foundation's consent. The bargained-for exchange between the parties provided that the Foundation would forego its right to separately license the patent in exchange for receiving a share of the profits from Xenon's commercialization of the technology — either directly or via a sublicense to a third party. Xenon received a significant benefit from the agreement — the exclusive right to exploit the technology protected by the joint patent application. Xenon cannot avoid paying royalties or sublicense fees to the Foundation simply by labeling the Novartis transaction a "license" rather than a "sublicense."

Accordingly, the terms of the Exclusive Licensing Agreement, not 35 U.S.C.

§ 262, govern the parties' rights and responsibilities here. Under that agreement Xenon held an exclusive license to develop the SCD discovery for commercial purposes and a corresponding obligation to share proceeds with the Foundation. The agreement gives Xenon three options: (1) commercialize the technology directly and pay royalties to the Foundation; (2) sublicense the technology to a third party and pay a percentage of the sublicense fees to the Foundation; or (3) assign its exclusive licensing rights to a third party with the prior consent of the Foundation.

Xenon suggests in the alternative that it never actually gave Novartis a license to the Foundation's interest in the jointly patented technology. The district court properly rejected this argument. The Xenon-Novartis agreement provides that Xenon grants to Novartis an exclusive license to all Xenon technology in the field of human and animal healthcare. Xenon technology includes "Xenon's interest in all Patent Rights in the Field, as specifically described in Schedule B," and Schedule B prominently lists the joint patent application owned by Xenon and the Foundation — first out of four listed patents. Xenon argues unpersuasively that the phrase "patent rights" does not include rights it obtained through the Exclusive License Agreement. In the warranty clause of the Xenon-Novartis agreement, Xenon represents that "it is the owner *or licensee* of all rights, title and interest in and to the Xenon Patent Rights." (Emphasis added.) Accordingly, Xenon granted Novartis any interest it held in the joint patent application by specifically including it in Schedule B. Put another way, Xenon effectively sublicensed its exclusive license rights in the jointly patented technology. The district court correctly concluded that the Xenon-Novartis agreement is subject to the terms of the Exclusive License Agreement governing sublicenses.

2. Sublicense Fees

After concluding that Xenon granted Novartis a sublicense in the jointly patented technology, the district court held that Xenon violated the terms of the Exclusive License Agreement by failing to pay the Foundation a share of the sublicense fees. Xenon argues that it is not obligated to make payments to the Foundation until products are actually brought to market and sold as a result of the sublicense. Because no products have yet been sold, Xenon claims it does not owe the Foundation anything. Again, we disagree. The Exclusive License Agreement requires Xenon to pay the Foundation license fees, milestones, and royalty payments as soon as they are received.

Section 4 of the Exclusive License Agreement, titled "Consideration," lays out the payment details and schedule. Subsection (B)(i) of that section states: "For all Products *sold directly by Xenon*, Xenon shall pay to [the Foundation] . . . a royalty calculated as a percentage of the Selling Price of Products . . . ." (Emphasis added.) It goes on to specify that royalties are earned on either the date the product is actually sold, the date an invoice is sent, or the date the product is transferred to a third party for promotional reasons-whichever comes first. The next subsection — the provision most relevant to this dispute-states:

> For all Products sold by Xenon sublicensees, Xenon shall pay to [the Foundation] a percentage of any license fees, milestones, and royalty

payments received by Xenon as consideration for the sublicense granted to such sublicensees under Section 2B. The percentage shall remain fixed at a rate of ten percent (10%) for years one (1) and two (2) of this Agreement and seven and one-half percent (7.5%) thereafter until this Agreement is terminated.

Because both subsections begin with the phrase "[f]or all Products *sold*" (emphasis added), Xenon argues that it does not owe the Foundation any payments for the Novartis sublicense until products are actually brought to market and sold.

We agree with the district court that Section 4, read as a whole, requires payment of the Foundation's share of the sublicense fee independent of any actual sales of products. The apparent point of the prefatory phrase "[f]or all Products sold" in each of the two subsections governing payment is to distinguish between payments required when Xenon commercialized the technology itself and payments required when Xenon issued a sublicense to a third party to do so. In the former circumstance, the payment due the Foundation is a royalty based on products sold; in the latter circumstance, the payment due the Foundation is a specified percentage of the sublicense fee Xenon receives, plus "milestones" and royalties. Because the Novartis transaction falls under the second subsection, payment is due on receipt of a sublicense fee, not on the occurrence of product sales.

This reading of the payment provision is the most plausible for several reasons. Although both subsections use the same introductory phrase, the first subsection also says that payment is due upon actual product sale while the second subsection — governing sublicenses — does not include similar language. Instead, the second subsection states that Xenon owes the Foundation a percentage of any license fees and "milestones," in addition to royalty payments, stemming from any sublicense. As the district court noted, sublicense fees and milestone payments are not contingent upon a sale; they are paid immediately or on an ongoing basis by a licensee or sublicensee in exchange for the right to make sales of products developed in the future. Finally, the parties agree that it generally takes about 15 years to bring a drug product to market. Yet the Exclusive License Agreement specifies that Xenon must pay the Foundation 10% of any license fees, milestones, and royalty payments received during the first two years of the agreement and 7.5% thereafter. This provision would make little sense if no payment was required on a sublicense until a product was brought to market. Accordingly, the district court properly concluded that Xenon breached the Exclusive Licensing Agreement by failing to pay the Foundation its share of the fee from the Novartis transaction.

****

4. The Foundation's Right to Terminate the Exclusive License Agreement

In addition to damages, the Foundation also asked for a declaration that it had a right to terminate the Exclusive License Agreement based on Xenon's breach. The district court granted summary judgment for the Foundation on this claim, and on May 17, 2006, the Foundation sent Xenon a letter terminating the Exclusive License Agreement. Xenon responded with two motions, one for reconsideration of the district court's decision and the other for a stay of execution of the judgment pending disposition of Xenon's motion for reconsideration. The district court granted Xenon's motion to stay enforcement of the judgment, holding that the Foundation's purported termination of the Exclusive License Agreement was void because the Foundation had not given Xenon notice and 90 days to cure its breach, as the agreement required. The court further held that once the Foundation filed this lawsuit, its right to terminate the license agreement depended on a finding of breach by the court. The judge concluded as follows: "[A]ny attempted termination of the agreement that has already occurred is suspended until the court has ruled on the post-trial motions and plaintiff may not take renewed action to terminate the agreement until that time." A month later, the district court granted Xenon's motion for reconsideration, agreeing that the Foundation had not properly moved for summary judgment on this claim. However, the judge also said that if the Foundation wanted to terminate the Exclusive License Agreement, it could now do so — because Xenon had been found in breach — but that the Foundation was first required under the terms of the agreement to give Xenon notice and 90 days to cure.

On appeal the Foundation challenges the district court's conclusion that its right to terminate the agreement did not arise until the court found Xenon in breach of the agreement. The Foundation maintains that its right to terminate was triggered by Xenon's breach and was not contingent upon the court's *finding* of breach. The Foundation also argues that it properly terminated the agreement. We agree on both counts.

Section 7 of the Exclusive License Agreement governs the Foundation's right to terminate:

> If Xenon at any time defaults in the timely payment of any monies due . . . or commits any breach of any other covenant herein contained, and Xenon fails to remedy any such breach or default within ninety (90) days after written notice thereof by [the Foundation,] . . . [the Foundation] may, at its option, terminate this Agreement by giving notice of termination to Xenon.

In March 2005 the Foundation sent Xenon written notice that it considered the Xenon-Novartis transaction to be a sublicense of the joint patent application and that Xenon owed the Foundation sublicense fees. The relevant portion of the letter states:

> Our analysis has led us to conclude that the Novartis agreement is, in fact, a sub-license of rights granted by [the Foundation] to Xenon and we also require that Xenon remit . . . payment of any amounts owed to [the Foundation] under the Agreement. In the event that Xenon contends that no amounts are owed to [the Foundation] or that the Novartis agreement is not a sublicense as contemplated by the Agreement, Xenon must immediately provide . . . a detailed written explanation as to why such amounts are not owed or why the Novartis agreement is not a sublicense
> . . . .

This letter plainly gave Xenon notice that the Foundation considered it to be in breach of its payment obligations under the Exclusive License Agreement. Notably, Xenon does not disagree. Instead, Xenon argues that the Foundation did not provide 90 days to cure the breach because the Foundation filed suit a month after sending Xenon this letter. The March 2005 notice, Xenon says, was therefore ineffective under the termination provision of the Exclusive License Agreement.

We disagree. A contractual obligation to provide notice and an opportunity to cure a default prior to terminating a contract does not necessarily affect the aggrieved party's right to sue for breach. Here, nothing in the Exclusive License Agreement prevented the Foundation from suing for breach within the 90-day cure period, nor was the Foundation's right to terminate somehow suspended by the filing of this lawsuit. Having filed the suit, the Foundation's right to terminate did not become contingent upon the court finding Xenon in breach. A contracting party's right to terminate arises under the terms of the contract and need not await a formal declaration of the contracting parties' rights.

****

Accordingly, the district court erroneously concluded that the Foundation's right to terminate the agreement was contingent upon the court's finding that Xenon had breached the Exclusive License Agreement. The Foundation was entitled to terminate the agreement based on Xenon's breach, and it properly did so under the agreement's termination provision. The Foundation's March 2005 letter was sufficient to give notice to Xenon that the Foundation considered it in breach. More than 90 days elapsed between the time of this notice and the Foundation's letter — on May 17, 2006 — terminating the license agreement. Nothing more was required.

B. PPA Compounds

We move now to the second set of issues on appeal concerning the ownership rights to the PPA compounds. The Foundation brought several claims pertaining to its interests in the PPA compounds: It sued for a declaratory judgment that Gray-Keller's assignment to Xenon of his interest in the compounds was void; it sought to quiet title in the PPA compounds; and it sued for conversion of its property rights. The parties filed cross-motions for summary judgment on each of these claims, and the district court entered judgment for Xenon on all three claims. On appeal the Foundation reasserts its entitlement to an ownership interest in the PPA compounds.

A brief recap of the relevant facts is in order: Xenon, with the help of Discovery Partners, used the jointly patented assay to screen thousands of compounds for therapeutic potential. Xenon and Discovery Partners identified a set of 20 "PPA compounds" with the potential to lower SCD levels in the human body, and Xenon sent these compounds to Gray-Keller for confirmatory screening. Gray-Keller confirmed the cholesterol-inhibiting potential of the PPA compounds and in July 2003 [and] purported to assign his rights to Xenon pursuant to the terms of his consulting agreement.

The Foundation contends that the interlocking network of contracts among the parties gives it ownership of Gray-Keller's interest in the PPA compounds, and therefore Gray-Keller's assignment is void. We agree. Under the Sponsor Option Agreement, all University researchers working on the Xenon-funded research program agreed to assign to the Foundation their rights to any inventions that they "conceived of or reduced to practice . . . whether solely or jointly with others." Each University researcher, including Gray-Keller, signed an individual Memorandum Agreement to that effect, and copies were attached to and incorporated as part of the Sponsor Option Agreement. The scope of the joint research program was defined by three separate research agreements-Research Agreements 1, 2, and 3.

The Foundation maintains that Gray-Keller's work on the PPA compounds fell within the scope of Research Agreement 2, and therefore Gray-Keller was required to assign his interest in the compounds to the Foundation. Research Agreement 2 generally covers research to identify compounds that will influence SCD levels in the human body for therapeutic effect on cholesterol levels. While the scientific language and acronyms keep the contract from being readily understandable to a layperson, the scope of the research program is clear enough. First, Exhibit A to Research Agreement 2 is titled "Stearoyl CoA Desaturase (SCD) as a Target for Elevation of HDL." It states that its overall goal is to "evaluate SCD as a target for the development of drugs that would increase the levels of HDL in plasma and decrease triglycerides (which should have a therapeutic impact on cardiovascular disease)." It then lists a handful of more specific goals, such as to "[s]creen and rank order substrates/inhibitors of SCD1 activity for impact on SCD1 transcription in vitro" and to "[e]valuate lead substrates/inhibitors from in vitro screen for their effect on SCD1 transcription, SCD1 enzyme activity and HDL metabolism in vivo."

Gray-Keller's work identifying and confirming the therapeutic potential of the PPA compounds derived from the SCD enzyme was expressly contemplated by Research Agreement 2, which broadly covered research "to validate SCD as a target for screening novel compounds that may elevate HDL levels in vivo." Gray-Keller performed his research on this project at the University using University resources and was required under his Memorandum Agreement to assign his interest in any discoveries to the Foundation. The fact that his work was conducted partly under Xenon's sponsorship and at its behest is not dispositive. Under the Sponsor Option Agreement and each of the individual agreements attached to it, the Foundation was entitled to ownership of any discoveries "conceived of or reduced to practice" by the researchers under the joint research program; Xenon was entitled to an exclusive license to commercialize the discoveries. Accordingly, the district court erred in granting summary judgment to Xenon on the claims pertaining to the Foundation's ownership interest in the PPA compounds. Under the Sponsor Option Agreement, the Memorandum Agreement, and Research Agreement 2, the Foundation was entitled to a declaration of its ownership interest in the PPA compounds.

III. Conclusion

For the foregoing reasons, we AFFIRM the judgment for the Foundation on its claim that Xenon breached the Exclusive License Agreement, as well as the district court's order entering judgment on the remittitur in the amount of $300,000. We REVERSE the district court's reconsideration order regarding the Foundation's right to terminate the Exclusive License Agreement; under the terms of the agreement's termination provision, the Foundation was entitled to and properly terminated the agreement. Finally, we REVERSE the judgment in favor of Xenon on the Foundation's claims to quiet title and for declaratory judgment that Gray-Keller's purported assignment of his interest in the PPA compounds to Xenon is void. On these claims, we REMAND with instructions to enter judgment in favor of the Foundation.

QUESTIONS

1.   Did the Foundation own the patent that issued for the assay? If not, why was the Foundation entitled to sublicense fees on Xenon-Novartis sublicense?

2.   Why did the court find that the Xenon-Novartis sublicense was not governed by section 262 of the Patent Act that provides for the rights of joint patent owners?

3.   Gray-Keller confirmed the inhibitory potential of the 20 PPA compounds identified by Discovery Partners. What interest did Gray-Keller obtain in the PPA compounds by virtue of his confirmatory testing? What interest did the Foundation have in the PPA compounds by virtue of Gray-Keller's Memorandum Agreement with the Foundation? The Foundation argued that it owned Gray-Keller's interest in the PPA compounds by virtue of the "interlocking network of contracts among the parties." How exactly did the court find that this "interlocking network of contracts" operated to place title to the PPA compounds in the Foundation?

4.   Did any of the contracts between the Foundation and Xenon specify the ownership rights in compounds identified using the patented SCD assay? Should they have? Would a provision for "reach-through" royalties on compounds identified using the SCD assay have been appropriate here?

5.   If you were counsel to WARF, could you have simplified the parties' relationships?

6.   It appears that WARF handles the technology transfer functions for the University and the University handles the sponsored research functions. Other universities have combined offices for sponsored research and technology transfer. What are the pros and cons of separate and combined offices for sponsored research and technology transfer?

3.3   UNIVERSITY INTELLECTUAL PROPERTY
OWNERSHIP

Conflicts between universities and faculty over IP rights are increasing. Two factors are primarily responsible for this increase. The first is the growing importance of patent licensing revenue to university finances. University licensing activity is often described as a "home run" game; only a very small number of licenses yield significant revenue. However, if a university hits a home run with a license, the additional revenue can have a major impact on the university's financial condition, and help offset losses in the university's endowment revenue and cuts in state funding. The second reason for the increase in university-faculty intellectual property conflicts is the growing awareness of faculty regarding the value of the intellectual property they create. Faculty members are aware of colleagues who become wealthy through inventions they have made whether by licensing the inventions to industry or by forming start-up companies to commercialize the inventions.

The current poster case of university-faculty intellectual property disputes involves Dr. Renee Kaswan and the University of Georgia. Dr. Kaswan invented Restasis, an extremely profitable drug for the treatment of dry eyes, while employed at the University of Georgia (UG). Dr. Kaswan assigned the Restasis invention to UG as required by the UG intellectual property policy. UG then licensed the invention to Alergan. At the time of the license, the parties estimated that Restasis would have sales of approximately $400M/year from 2008-2014 or total sales of around $2.4B. The royalty rate in the UG-Alergan license is not publicly available, but a 5% royalty rate is common for a very profitable drug such as Restasis. A 5% royalty rate would have provided UG approximately $120M over the period 2008-2014. Assuming UG shares 30% of royalty revenue with inventors, a common royalty sharing percentage, Dr. Kaswan would have received around $36M.

Unfortunately for Dr. Kaswan, the State of Georgia imposed major budget cuts on UG, and UG was forced to consider ways to cover the budget shortfall. UG decided that one way to cover the budget shortfall was to monetize the Alergan royalty revenue by converting future royalty payments into a single, current, lump-sum payment. In negotiations with Alergan, which were kept secret from Dr. Kaswan, UG accepted a $30M lump-sum payment for the future royalty revenue. If UG shared 30% of this payment with Dr. Kaswan, she would receive $9M–$27M less than her share of the royalty revenue would have been.

Dr. Kaswan was unsuccessful in challenging the UG-Alergan agreement in court and vented her frustration by starting a website for other faculty who feel unfairly treated by their universities. The website, IPAdvocate.org, has become popular with faculty inventors and unpopular with university technology transfer offices. *See* www.IPAdvocate.org.

This section considers different aspects of university intellectual property ownership. The first subsection looks at university intellectual property policies in general, the second subsection looks at university-faculty intellectual property disputes, and the third subsection looks at university-student intellectual property disputes. The final subsection looks at recommended university licensing policies.

3.3.1   Sample Intellectual Property Policy

[Editor's note: The choice of Syracuse University's Intellectual Property Policy as a sample policy was based solely on my familiarity with the content. It is not intended to suggest in any way that Syracuse University's Intellectual Property Policy is better than other universities' intellectual property policies. Some other universities' intellectual property policies are listed under "Additional Information" at the end of this subsection.]

SYRACUSE UNIVERSITY POLICY ON OWNERSHIP AND MANAGEMENT OF INTELLECTUAL PROPERTY
Copyright, Syracuse University

Syracuse University is dedicated to teaching, research, and the dissemination of knowledge. When these activities have been supported by the University and have resulted in the creation of properties that have economic interest and value, Syracuse University shall have title to, or have a fair and equitable income interest proportional to the University's investment in, those properties that will reflect the legitimate interest of University investment as well as the traditions of academic freedom and pursuit.

Members of the University: For the purpose of this policy, member(s) of the University are defined as faculty, staff, students, or any person performing research or engaging in work or study utilizing University resources or facilities, whether or not they are compensated for their services.

Technology: For the purposes of this policy, technology shall mean inventions, discoveries, creations, technical innovations, information in various forms, including computer software, and tangible research property created in the course of research. Tangible research property includes, but is not limited to, notes, sketches, drawings, results of research or experiments, computer code or records, or any embodiment of the technology into any form. For purposes of this policy, technology does not include any copyright publication.

Title and Interest in Copyright Publications: Title to any copyright publication shall belong to the member who has created the copyright publication, except in the case when it has been created under a sponsored program where there are ownership restrictions or in the case the copyright publication was created as part of a member's explicit work assignment. Copyright publication includes, without limitation, written and artistic materials (such as articles, books, compilations, and visual and performing art works), whether or not protected by copyright. Under this policy copyright publication does not include software.

Generally Available Resource(s) and University Allocated Resources(s): For the purposes of this policy, generally available resource(s) shall mean office space, library, and traditional desktop computers. In addition, the University will construe salary paid from regularly budgeted department accounts as generally available resource(s). In those cases where salary was paid to accomplish or produce certain tasks or materials that were part of the member's work assignment with the University or a part of a sponsored program, that salary shall be considered a University allocated resource(s). Other University allocated resource(s) shall mean all University resources and facilities that have not been defined as generally available resource(s).

Technology Resulting from Research Supported with Externally Sponsored or University Allocated Resources: Title to technology resulting from research, work, or study which was supported by externally sponsored or University allocated resources will belong to Syracuse University. Any revenue received by the University as a result of the license or transfer of such technology will be distributed to those who created the technology in accordance with the paragraph,

Distribution of Revenue (below). The University may transfer its interest in the technology to a member, a member's corporation, or an organization with which a member has significant financial ties. In this situation a license agreement will be negotiated between that member or organization and the University.

Technology Resulting from Research Supported with Generally Available University Resources: Title to technology except technology identified in the previous paragraph, resulting from research, work, or study solely supported with generally available resources, will belong to the member; and the University will have an equitable interest in the net revenue (as defined in the paragraph, Distribution of Revenue, below) realized from the income, sale, or transfer of the technology. When the technology identified under this paragraph is transferred or licensed by a member to a third party or is retained by the member for his/her economic development, a royalty agreement will be negotiated between Syracuse University and the member. The royalty and license agreement will reflect the University's investment in the technology.

Committee on Intellectual Property: The Vice President for Research shall appoint a Committee on Intellectual Property. The committee shall include faculty from diverse academic units of the University and shall include at least one academic professional staff member and at least one student. A normal term for service will be three years with membership renewable for one term. The Senior Vice President for Business and Finance and the Vice President for Research will serve on the committee as ex officio members. A senior member of the faculty shall serve as chair of the committee. The committee shall advise the Vice President for Research on the interpretation, administration, and implementation of this policy. Any appeals of the decisions of the Vice President for Research shall be directed to the Chancellor.

Distribution of Revenue from Technology: Net revenue (defined as gross revenues less the costs and expenses incurred and related to the securing of legal protection, marketing, licensing, and other expenses associated with the technology) received by the University from the transfer, sale, or licensing of technology, shall be distributed as follows:

Fifteen percent of net revenues will be retained by the University in support of its costs in managing its intellectual property program.

The remaining net revenues (distributable net revenues) shall be distributed 50 percent to the inventor(s) or creators(s) and 50 percent to the University in accordance with the University's schedule for calculating and dispersing distributable net revenues.

The University's share of distributable net revenues will be used for the support of the department(s) or unit(s) of the inventor(s) or creator(s), development of new intellectual property, or to support the general research and scholarly goals of the University.

Modification of the standard distribution of distributable net revenue may be made in consideration of extenuating circumstances, including but not limited to proportion or royalties retained personally by inventor(s) or creator(s), extent of investment by all parties, and the additional support needed for further development of the technology.

Any modification of the standard distribution of royalties will be made by the Vice President for Research and Computing in consultation with the Committee on Intellectual Property.

Management of University Technology: The Office of Sponsored Programs (OSP) has the primary responsibility within Syracuse University for managing and administering matters involving technology developed at Syracuse. OSP will consult with members regarding the best means for development and transfer of the technology created by members. It may be necessary, in accordance with the terms of this policy, that any assignments, licenses, transfers, applications, registrations, or any other documents that are necessary to evidence the University's ownership in technology be executed by members. [Note: the Office of Technology Transfer and Industrial Relations now manages technology developed at Syracuse University.]

Disclosure: Under some United States and foreign laws, public disclosure, use, or sale of technology prior to obtaining statutory protection may prejudice, or destroy, the availability of obtaining certain legal protection. In order to protect the University's, member's, or any licensee's rights in technology, no contractual or other legally enforceable agreement for the sale, transfer, or use of University-owned technology may be made except by the University in accordance with this policy. It is also essential to consult with OSP prior to making any technology publicly known or available.

Limited License in All Technology Created by Members: Notwithstanding any other provision of this policy, Syracuse University shall have a royalty-free, nonexclusive, and nontransferable license to use for noncommercial purposes for teaching, training, and research with the University, all technology created by its members.

Good Faith: The fair and effective implementation of this policy requires good faith cooperation, collegiality and candor on behalf of Syracuse University and all of its members. For its part, the University will seek to advise affected members promptly and fully on all matters regarding technology. Members, in turn, will communicate promptly and fully with OSP whenever their research involves technology covered by the policy.

Amendment: This policy may be amended from time to time pursuant to the University's policies and procedures in effect for amending documents setting forth University policy.

QUESTIONS

1. If a Ph.D. student invented a patentable technology while working on a federally funded research project, who would own the technology? If a Ph.D. student invented a patentable technology while working on an industry-sponsored research project, who would own the technology? If a Ph.D. student invented a patentable technology while working on a research project in a Syracuse lab as part

of her Ph.D. required course work, who would own the technology?

2.   If a professor in the finance department developed a patentable financial management business method using her office computer during work hours, who would own the business method patent?

3.   What does the Syracuse Intellectual Property Policy say about equity investments by the University in spin-out companies?

4.   Do you see any problems with a university licensing an invention to a company owned by a faculty-inventor? What complications might arise if the company used students to perform research for the company's benefit?

CASE NOTES

1.   Greenberg was employed as a research assistant in the Pathology Department of Albert Einstein College of Medicine (AECOM) from 1987-1991. Greenberg's research focused on Alzheimer's disease and in 1988 she discovered an antibody (PHF-1) that could detect particular genetic markers associated with Alzheimer's disease and a cell line that could be used to produce PHF-1. When Greenberg left AECOM she took samples of PHF-1 and the cell line to her new position to continue her research. This was allowed under AECOM's intellectual property policy which allowed continued academic research by former employees. AECOM's intellectual property policy also permitted persons to obtain biological materials for academic research under a material transfer agreement. In 1994, AECOM learned that Greenberg was distributing PHF-1 and the cell line to various entities, including commercial entities. When AECOM confronted Greenberg about these activities, Greenberg claimed she was the owner of PHF-1 and had the right to distribute it for both academic and commercial purposes without permission of AECOM. AECOM then filed suit seeking a ruling that it was the owner of PHF-1 and a permanent injunction against Greenberg's further dissemination of PHF-1 and the cell line. Greenberg counterclaimed claiming tortious interference with business relationships. What result? *See* Yeshiva University v. Greenberg, 681 N.Y.S.2d 71 (N.Y. App. Div. 1998).

2.   *See also* Rutgers Council of AAUP Chapters v. Rutgers University, 381 N.J.Super. 63 (N.J Super. Ct. App. Div. 2005) (Decision by Public Employment Relations Commission that proposed amendment to state university's patent policy regarding university's ownership of laboratory notebooks pertaining to research was subject to mandatory negotiations with association of professors was arbitrary, capricious and unreasonable; decision was based on speculative contention by association that university's assertion of ownership of notebooks and materials would impede ability of its members to publish results of their research); Pittsburg State University v. Kansas Board of Regents, 122 P.3d 336 (Kan. 2005) (Federal patent law did not preclude state university and public employee organization from entering into a memorandum of agreement under the Public Employer-Employee Relations Act regarding the subject of patent ownership between the university and faculty members; Patent Act specifically provided that parties could assign patent ownership rights).

Additional Information

1. Naoko Ohashi, *The University Inventor's Obligation to Assign: A Review of U.S. Caselaw on the Enforceability of University Patent Policies*, 18 INDUS. & HIGHER EDUC. 235 (2004).

2. B. Jean Weidemier, *Ownership of University Inventions: Practical Considerations*, INTELLECTUAL PROPERTY MANAGEMENT IN HEALTH AND AGRICULTURAL INNOVATION: A HANDBOOK OF BEST PRACTICES, *available at* http://www.iphandbook.org/handbook/chPDFs/ch05/ipHandbook-Ch%2005%2004%20Weidemier%20Ownership%20of%20Inventions.pdf.

3. Stanley P. Kowalski, *Making the Most of Intellectual Property: Developing an Institutional IP Policy*, INTELLECTUAL PROPERTY MANAGEMENT IN HEALTH AND AGRICULTURAL INNOVATION: A HANDBOOK OF BEST PRACTICES, *available at* http://www.iphandbook.org/handbook/chPDFs/ch05/ipHandbook-Ch%2005%2003%20Kowalski%20Institutional%20IP%20Policy.pdf.

4. Carmenelisa Perez-Kudzma, *Fiduciary Duties in Academia: An Uphill Battle*, 48 IDEA 491 (2008).

5. James O. Castagnera, et. al., *Protecting Intellectual Capital in the New Century: Are Universities Prepared?*, 2002 DUKE L. & TECH. REV. 10 (2002).

5. G. Kenneth Smith, *Faculty and Graduate Student Generated Inventions: Is University Ownership a Legal Certainty?*, 1 VA. J.L. & TECH. 4 (1997).

6. J.H. Reichman, *Overlapping Proprietary Rights in University-Generated Research Products: The Case of Computer Programs*, 17 COLUM.-vLA J.L. & ARTS 51 (1993).

7. Molly O'Donovan Dix, Thomas R. Culver, *Establishing and Restructuring IP Management Processes: Issues and Models*, 44 IDEA 543 (2004).

8. Kevin LaRoche, Christine Collard, Jacqueline Chernys, *Appropriating Innovation: The Enforceability of University Intellectual Property Policies*, 20 INTELL. PROP. J. 135 (2007).

9. Sandip H. Patel, *Graduate Students' Ownership and Attribution Rights in Intellectual Property*, 71 IND. L.J. 481 1996).

10. Sunil R. Kulkarni, *All Professors Create Equally: Why Faculty Should Have Complete Control Over the Intellectual Property Rights in Their Creations*, 47 HASTINGS L.J. 221 (1995).

11. K.J. Nordheden & M.H. Hoeflich, *Undergraduate Research & Intellectual Property Rights*, 6 KAN. J.L. & PUB. POL'Y 34 (1997).

12. Harvard University Office of Technology Development, *Statement of Policy in Regard to Intellectual Property Policy*, *available at* http://www.techtransfer.harvard.edu/resources/policies/IP/

13. Case Western Reserve University, *Intellectual Property Policy*, *available at* http://ora.ra.case.edu/techtransfer/forms/IntellectualPropertyPolicy.pdf.

14. Massachusetts Institute of Technology, *Guide to the Ownership, Distribution and Commercial Development of M.I.T. Technology*, http://web.mit.edu/tlo/www/downloads/pdf/guide.pdf.

15. Cornell University, *Inventions and Related Property Rights*, Policy 1.5, http://www.dfa.cornell.edu/dfa/cms/treasurer/policyoffice/policies/volumes/academic/upload/vol1_5.pdf

16. University of Pennsylvania, Patent and Tangible Research Property Policies and Procedures of the University of Pennsylvania, http://www.upenn.edu/research/RevisedPatentPolicy5-19-10.pdf

17. University of California, *University of California Patent Policy*, http://www.ucop.edu/ott/genresources/policy_pdf/patentpolicy08.pdf.

3.3.2 University-Faculty IP Ownership Disputes

Dr. Renee Kaswan and the University of Georgia were noted above as the current poster case of a university-faculty IP dispute in which the university, arguably, mistreated a faculty member. The *Fenn* case below has come to be seen as a poster case of a university-faculty IP dispute in which the faculty member mistreated the university, so much so that the court found Dr. Fenn committed fraud. The following case, *Kligman*, involves a more typical university-faculty IP dispute in which reasonable people can reasonably disagree on questions of contract interpretation, the place of invention and intellectual property ownership. The third case in this subsection, *DuPont*, introduces a third-party, corporate sponsor into a university-faculty intellectual property dispute. The *DuPont* case presents a very interesting set of facts that complicate both the jurisdictional and substantive analyses. As you read the *DuPont* case, pay careful attention to how the court distinguishes between federal patent law jurisdiction and state contract law jurisdiction as they apply to federal appellate court review.

FENN v. YALE UNIVERSITY
283 F.SUPP.2D 615 (D. Conn. 2003)

DRONEY, DISTRICT JUDGE.

The plaintiff, John B. Fenn, brought this action against the defendant, Yale University, alleging conversion, theft, tortious interference with business relationship, and violations of the Connecticut Unfair Trade Practices Act ("CUTPA"), Conn. Gen.Stat. § 42-110a, *et seq.*, regarding an invention and patent for that invention, which issued to him as United States Patent No. 5,130,538 (" '538 patent") on July 14, 1992. Yale has asserted counterclaims against Fenn, seeking an accounting and assignment of the '538 patent, as well as damages for breach of contract and fiduciary duty, fraud, negligent misrepresentation, conversion, theft, unjust enrichment, and CUTPA violations.

The following are the findings of fact and conclusions of law determined by the Court following the bench trial:

I. Findings of Fact

A. Introduction

John B. Fenn ("Dr. Fenn") is a leading scientific expert in the field of mass spectrometry, which determines the masses of atoms and molecules. Mass spectrometry has important uses in the development of medicines and the mapping of genes. In 1967, Dr. Fenn joined the faculty of Yale University ("Yale") as a tenured full professor. In 1987, as required by Yale's then-mandatory retirement policy, Dr. Fenn retired from his position as a full professor, but continued his work at Yale for another seven years as a "Professor Emeritus" and "Senior Research Scientist." In 1994, Dr. Fenn left Yale and became a research professor at Virginia Commonwealth University.

Dr. Fenn recently won the Nobel Prize for Chemistry for the mass spectrometry invention which is the subject of the instant action.

This case concerns a dispute between Yale and Dr. Fenn over an invention in the field of mass spectrometry which he developed while at Yale. In the following findings of fact, the Court will first address the various Yale policies that concern the inventions of its faculty members such as Dr. Fenn, then the particular policy that applied to him for this invention, then the particular invention here.

B. Yale's Patent Policy

From before Dr. Fenn joined its faculty, Yale's administrative policies have provided that patentable inventions resulting from a faculty member's research conducted at Yale belong to Yale and not the faculty member unless Yale expressly releases its interest in such inventions. These policies have also provided, though, that licensing royalties resulting from such inventions would be shared by Yale and the faculty member/inventor. After Dr. Fenn came to Yale in 1967, Yale made changes to its patent policy in 1975, 1984, 1988, and 1989, but these changes dealt primarily with the division of net licensing royalties between Yale and the inventor. The policy that inventions belong to Yale and not the inventor remained unchanged throughout Dr. Fenn's employment at Yale.

In 1967, when Dr. Fenn began his employment at Yale, the Faculty Handbook, dated July 1, 1966, contained provisions about Yale's patent policy with regard to inventions by its faculty members (the "1966 policy"). Pursuant to that policy, a faculty member was required to report to the university any invention resulting from "research conducted under University auspices or with the use of facilities under its control" and Yale owned the invention. The patent policy further stated that Yale did not typically keep title to patents resulting from those inventions; Yale arranged with the "Research Corporation" to carry out the patenting and commercializing of the inventions and to retain title to the subject patents. The policy also indicated that an inventor's share of any net royalty income from such inventions was "usually" 15%. The policy further stated that the University could abandon its interest in an invention and that in such circumstances, "the inventor is free to handle or dispose of his invention as he wishes." Dr. Fenn does not dispute that this patent policy applied to him.

On July 1, 1970, Yale prepared and distributed an updated Faculty Handbook with a section setting forth a patent policy identical to the 1966 policy. Subsequently, Dr. Fenn wrote a letter to Yale's Provost expressing his opinion that the inventor's share of royalty income provided by that patent policy was inadequate.

In 1974, the Yale Provost appointed a committee of faculty and administrators, including Dr. Fenn, to review the patent policy. The committee's work resulted in the 1975 patent policy, which increased the faculty member/inventor's share of net licensing royalties from 15% to 50%. The policy reiterated that all discoveries and inventions which result from "teaching, research, and other intellectual activity performed under University auspices" must be reported to Yale and provided that:

> [t]he [Yale] Treasurer shall refer inventions to Research Corporation or make other arrangements for evaluation of them in accordance with this policy . . . . In addition, the inventor may propose, even though the invention is one in the patenting or licensing of which the University wishes to participate, that the patenting of the invention or the licensing of the patent shall be arranged by the inventor at the inventor's expense, and if his proposal is accepted by the University, he shall proceed in accordance with an agreement to be made between the inventor and the University providing for such patenting or licensing by the inventor. Finally, if the University decides that although patenting or licensing of an invention is not contrary to University policy or the University does not wish to participate in the patenting or licensing, the University shall release to the inventor the University's interest in the invention, and the inventor shall be free to dispose of the invention as he wishes.

The 1975 patent policy also provided that it was "subject to revocation or amendment by the [Yale] corporation at any time." Dr. Fenn concedes that he was contractually bound by this 1975 patent policy.

In the early 1980s, a committee headed by Yale Professor Clement L. Markert ("the Markert Committee") was convened and charged with the task of reviewing the 1975 patent policy, faculty research sponsored by private entities, and commercial activities of faculty members. The Committee also recognized a need to re-examine the patent policy in light of the Bayh-Dole Act's changes in federal law and a shift in responsibilities from the Research Corporation to the Yale Office of Cooperative Research. Dr. Fenn served on the Markert Committee.

The Markert Committee produced a "Report of the Committee on Cooperative Research, Patents, and Licensing" ("the Markert Report"), setting forth specific recommendations, including changes to Yale's 1975 patent policy. The report's recommendations were embodied in a revised draft of the Faculty Handbook and a revised draft patent policy. Among other things, the Markert Report recommended reducing the share of licensing royalties for faculty members set forth in its 1975 patent policy. In particular, the Markert Report provided that inventors should receive 30% of net royalty income up to $200,000 and 20% of net royalty income in excess of $200,000.

Professor Markert presented Yale's then-president, A. Bartlett Giamatti ("President Giamatti"), with a draft of the Markert Report by letter dated November 18, 1983. In that letter, Professor Markert indicated that the report "represents a consensus of diverse views held by members of the committee." In a reply letter dated November 28, 1983, President Giamatti thanked Professor Markert for the Committee's work and informed him that the Markert Report would be circulated to the faculty for their comments. President Giamatti wrote that "[a]s I receive comments, I will share them with you and the members of the committee. Sometime early in the next semester, having taken into account the advice of the faculty, I will take, with the Provost, the report to the [Yale] Corporation. My intention is to ask the Corporation to approve as university policy those relevant portions of the report." Subsequently, President Giamatti circulated the Markert Committee Report to faculty and research scientists. Dr. Fenn received a copy of the Markert Report.

On February 29, 1984, Dr. Fenn wrote to President Giamatti concerning the Committee's Report. Dr. Fenn wrote: "In the covering letter that accompanied the draft copy of the Report of the Committee on Cooperative Research, Patents and Licensing (CCRPL), Chairman Markert indicated that the views set forth comprised a consensus of the committee membership. Lest you harbor the illusion that this consensus was unanimous I write to record one member's dissent with respect to some of those views." Dr. Fenn's letter set forth his objections to the Markert Report, particularly taking exception to the Committee's recommendation to reduce the inventor's share of royalty income through licensing.

On March 10, 1984, the Yale Corporation "[v]oted, to accept in principle "the Report of the Committee on Cooperative Research, Patent, and Licenses [the Markert Report]." " On March 23, 1984, President Giamatti responded to Dr. Fenn's February 29, 1984 letter in which he had objected to the Markert Report. In his letter, President Giamatti specifically told Dr. Fenn that "[t]he final draft has been approved by the Corporation in principle. The Report was modified in a few places, specifically with regard to copyright issues, in response to faculty comment." The draft patent policy dated March 6, 1984 became Yale's patent policy on March 10, 1984 through the approval of the Markert Report. As mentioned, that policy provided inventors with 30% of net royalty income achieved through licensing up to $200,000 and 20% of net royalty income in excess of $200,000. The policy also required that inventions be "reported promptly" to Yale and that Yale may release its interest to the inventor should it decide it does not wish and has no legal obligation to participate in the patenting or licensing of the invention. The 1984 policy, like the 1975 patent policy, specifically provided that it was "subject to revocation or amendment by the [Yale] corporation at any time."

In 1986, Yale prepared a revised edition of its Faculty Handbook which contained a section titled "Policy on Patents, Copyrights, and Licensing." The section indicated that a "full statement of the University policies on patent, copyrights, and licensing is available from the Office of the Provost, the Office of Cooperative Research, or the Office of Grant and Contract Administration." The section indicated that licensing royalties would be divided "in accord with the University patent policy," and reiterated that the patent policy required faculty to disclose "[a]ny potentially patentable invention or any potentially licensable computer program" to the Committee on Cooperative Research, Patent, and Licenses through the Office of the Director of Cooperative Research.

In June 1988, the Yale Corporation adopted a patent policy developed by the Committee on Cooperative Research, Patent, and Licenses and published the text of that policy in the October 10–17, 1988 Yale Weekly Bulletin and Calendar. The policy, consistent with the prior policies, stated that "all inventions . . . shall be reported promptly in writing to the provost through the director of the Office of Cooperative Research" and that "[i]f the University decides that it does not wish and has no legal obligation to participate in the patenting or licensing of an invention, the University may release to the inventor the University's interest in the invention, and the inventor shall then be free to dispose of the invention as he or she wishes." The 1988 policy continued the royalty sharing provisions set forth by the 1984 policy, providing 30% of net royalty income up to $200,000 to the inventor and 20% of net royalty income in excess of $200,000 to the inventor. The policy provided that it was effective as to "all inventions/discoveries made on or after June, 1988." It also provided that it was "subject to revocation or amendment by the [Yale] Corporation."

In October 1989, Yale published another patent policy which it indicated applied retroactively to "all inventions/discoveries made on or after June 1988." Like the policy set forth in the October 1988 bulletin, this policy stated that "all inventions . . . shall be reported promptly in writing to the Provost through the Director of the Office of Cooperative Research" and that "[i]f the University decides that it does not wish and has no legal obligation to participate in the patenting or licensing of an invention, the University may release to the inventor the University's interest in the invention, and the inventor shall then be free to dispose of the invention as he or she wishes." The 1989 policy changed the royalty sharing as follows: for the first $100,000, 50% to the inventor; for amounts between $100,000 and $200,000, 40% to the inventor; and for amounts exceeding $200,000, 30% to the inventor. Like all the policies since 1975, it provided that it was "subject to revocation or amendment by the [Yale] Corporation."

C. The Invention and Licensing of the '538 Patent

Prior to June 1988, Dr. Fenn, together with Matthias Mann and Chin-Kai Meng, Yale graduate students working with Dr. Fenn at Yale, invented a method for determining the molecular weight of particles through the use of multiply charged ions, which relates to the field of mass spectrometry. The research that led to that invention was conducted under Yale's auspices, on the Yale campus, and was funded by grants from the National Institutes of Health ("NIH") awarded to Yale.

Dr. Fenn first publicly disclosed this invention in San Francisco at the Annual Conference of the American Society for Mass Spectrometry ("ASMS") in June 1988. The paper he presented to the ASMS met the ASMS's novelty requirements because it demonstrated for the first time that the electrospray ionization process could produce ions from large molecules.

Fenn and others recognized the importance of the invention in medical diagnosis and treatment at the 1988 conference because it solved a "longstanding scientific problem" and was believed to "revolutionize the way that one could analyze peptides and proteins." Dr. Mann, Dr. Fenn's co-inventor, believed in 1988 that the invention was "revolutionary" and a "scientific breakthrough."

Dr. Fenn did not disclose the invention to Yale's Office of Cooperative Research ("OCR") in 1988. It was not until April 6, 1989 that Dr. Fenn submitted a completed invention disclosure form to the OCR regarding the invention. However, at least by the end of 1988, Dr. Fenn knew of the great importance of the invention and its commercial value. In his invention disclosure-which only generally and briefly summarized the invention — Dr. Fenn indicated that any patent application would have to be filed by June 1, 1989 — within one year of the patent's public disclosure at the San Francisco conference. He also noted that co-inventor Mann would be out of the country until May 15, 1989.

After the Yale OCR received Dr. Fenn's invention disclosure, Dr. Robert Bickerton ("Dr. Bickerton"), the head of the OCR, telephoned Dr. Fenn to find out more about the invention. Dr. Bickerton specifically inquired as to the potential commercial value of the invention. Dr. Fenn stated to Dr. Bickerton that he did not believe the invention had the potential for much commercial value because any patent issued on it would be a "use" patent as opposed to an "apparatus" patent and, as such, it would difficult to protect against its infringement. Dr. Fenn did not disclose that Pfizer Corporation, colleagues at the Yale Medical School and others had previously expressed a strong interest in the commercial viability of the invention. Dr. Fenn also did not disclose his own view, and the view of others, that the invention was in fact "revolutionary" or "important" and that it would likely have substantial commercial value.

Dr. Bickerton asked Dr. Fenn if Analytica of Branford, Inc. ("Analytica"), a company founded in 1987 to pursue electrospray technology by Dr. Fenn and Craig Whitehouse, one of Dr. Fenn's former graduate students, would be willing to pay for a patent application in return for Yale's commitment to license the invention to Analytica. As mentioned, Analytica was founded for the purpose of exploiting Dr. Fenn's two previous mass spectrometry inventions, which were owned by Yale, and Dr. Fenn was a 49% shareholder of Analytica. Though Dr. Fenn had already discussed the '538 invention with Mr. Whitehouse, also a 49% shareholder-owner of Analytica, he stated to Dr. Bickerton that he did not know if Analytica would be interested. Contrary to Dr. Fenn's representation to Dr. Bickerton, Dr. Fenn knew that Analytica was very much interested in the invention and its potential for commercial success.

On May 5, 1989, Dr. Bickerton called Dr. Fenn to discuss the invention again. When Dr. Bickerton noted that any patent application would have to be filed within a month, Dr. Fenn replied that he would be "up to his ears" preparing for several upcoming scientific conferences and that, beginning on May 20, 1989, he would be absent from the Yale campus for several weeks in Miami and Europe attending those conferences. Dr. Fenn stated that he was not scheduled to return from Europe until the end of June 1989, after the statutory deadline for filing a patent application had passed. Dr. Fenn did not tell Dr. Bickerton that co-inventor Meng was on the Yale campus during that same period of time and would be available to assist Yale with a patent application.

Dr. Fenn knew at that time that it would be difficult for Yale to prepare a patent application without his assistance in the limited time remaining. He also understood that he would have to assist Yale in preparing a patent application because information far beyond the inventors' disclosure document he gave the OCR would be needed for a proper patent application.

Yale did not file a patent application before the statutory deadline of June 1, 1989. In making this decision, Yale relied on Dr. Fenn's representations about the importance of the invention. Recognizing that Dr. Fenn was an expert in the technology, Yale accepted Dr. Fenn's statement that the invention and any resulting patent would have little commercial value. Dr. Fenn's representation that the invention was of limited value was very significant to the OCR staff and signaled that it should not expend its resources on a patent application.

In his own name and without Yale's knowledge, however, Dr. Fenn filed a patent application for the invention on May 19, 1989, which was financed by Analytica. In an October 19, 1989 letter to Provost Turner regarding the invention, Dr. Fenn continued to conceal from Yale that he had filed the patent application. Dr. Fenn testified that he did so in order to "let[ ] the scheme play out so the incompetence of [the OCR] would emerge." Dr. Fenn stated at trial:

> I ha[d] made a number of complaints to Yale, the fact that I thought that [OCR] was incompetent. And here was a case which I had filed a patent application, it had nothing further, and I thought we'll let it go because if it culminates in a patent this will be first rate evidence that I've been trying to convince Yale of for a long time that these guys over there weren't doing their job . . . And I knew that if I, from Bickerton's previous behavior, confirmed by subsequent behavior, that if I had told him that I had filed a patent application at that time he would have immediately said, well, that belongs to Yale. And there would have been a confrontation. And if no patent issued, the confrontation would have been pointless but, moreover, if the patent didn't issue, then he'd be off the hook in a sense because he could say, well, I knew it wasn't going to result in a patent. So I was essentially making my case.

Dr. Fenn stated that he "was trying to show up how [the OCR] handled its business which in my view was incompetent."

Also in the fall of 1989, Dr. Henry Lowendorf of the Yale OCR, not knowing of Dr. Fenn's pending patent application, wrote to the NIH that "Yale is reporting an invention which was disclosed to NIH on 17 May 1989 to be unpatentable . . . The invention is not patentable because enabling information on this invention was published in an abstract, enclosed, at a conference in June of 1988 and Yale did not file a patent application between the time the invention was disclosed to this Office, 6 April 1989, and the one year anniversary of disclosure." Dr. Fenn received a copy of Dr. Lowendorf's letter to NIH. Dr. Fenn knew that this letter was untrue, but he did nothing to correct Dr. Lowendorf's unintentional misrepresentation to the NIH that no patent application had been filed.

Without telling Yale, Dr. Fenn licensed the invention to Analytica on July 31, 1991. On July 14, 1992, United States Patent No. 5,130,538 ("the '538 patent") issued to Dr. Fenn for the "Method of Producing Multiply Charged Ions and for

Determining Molecular Weights of Molecules By Use of the Multiply Charged Ions of Molecules." Dr. Fenn also failed to let Yale known of the issuance of the patent.

Yale first learned about the '538 patent when Aldo Test, an attorney for the Finnigan Corporation, wrote to Dr. Bickerton on January 20, 1993 inquiring about the possibility of licensing the '538 patent. Mr. Test explained in his letter that he had tracked the patent to Yale through its NIH grant number. Mr. Test also indicated that the patent had issued to Dr. Fenn, that Analytica claimed control over the licensing of the patent through its assignment from Dr. Fenn, and that Analytica had refused to sub-license the invention to Finnigan. Dr. Fenn received a copy of Mr. Test's letter.

Upon receiving Mr. Test's letter, Dr. Bickerton spoke with Dr. Fenn and forwarded to him a form asking him to assign the patent to Yale pursuant to the patent policy. The form was attached to a letter dated March 2, 1993, in which Dr. Bickerton wrote:

> As we discussed last month, the University recently became aware that you had filed a patent application, and obtained one or more patents, on an invention disclosed by you to my office in 1989. The invention was made by you and your students in the course of research at Yale funded by NIH . . . We have looked into the matter and concluded that Yale's patent policy requires that the invention and the patents be assigned to the University. Enclosed is a standard assignment agreement for your signature.

Yale's Committee on Cooperative Research, Patents and Licensing had determined that Yale was the rightful owner of the invention and '553 patent, and that Dr. Fenn should assign the patent to Yale. Dr. Fenn, nevertheless, refused to assign the patent to Yale.

Concerned with its ability to pursue infringers of the '538 patent because of the question whether its assignment from Dr. Fenn was valid, Analytica then asked Dr. Fenn to also assign the patent to Yale so that Yale could then license the patent to Analytica. Although Dr. Fenn "thought Analytica had a legitimate concern," he refused to assign the patent to Yale. Analytica then asked Yale for a license to any rights Yale possessed. In a meeting with Dr. Bickerton, Mr. Whitehouse "emphasized the critical nature of the invention to his company and indicated that it was imperative that they have a license." In September 1993, Yale entered into a licensing agreement with Analytica granting Analytica a "worldwide exclusive license in and to any and all interest Yale has or may have in the licensed patents [i.e. '538 patent]."

Since January 30, 1997, Analytica has been paying into escrow amounts calculated pursuant to the royalty provisions of the Fenn-Analytica agreement to which Dr. Fenn would otherwise be entitled. Before Analytica began to deposit the royalties into the escrow accounts, it had paid out $302,435.16 in royalties to Dr. Fenn and his designees in accordance with the Fenn-Analytica license agreement. At the time of trial, the escrowed amounts through the third quarter of 2000 totaled $2,108,820.90. Analytica has been depositing in escrow only amounts calculated pursuant to the terms of the Fenn-Analytica agreement and has not also deposited additional amounts calculated pursuant to the Yale-Analytica agreement. Amounts calculated pursuant to the Yale-Analytica agreement total $1,717,975.92 of the $2,108,820.90 in escrow through the third quarter of 2000. Beginning in the first quarter of 1995, Analytica ceased making royalty payments to Yale. Up until that time, Analytica had paid Yale $43,011.30 pursuant to the Yale-Analytica license agreement. At the time of trial, the earned, but unpaid, royalties due Yale under the Yale-Analytica license amounted to $1,760,987.22.

II. Conclusions of Law

Dr. Fenn's complaint raises claims of conversion, theft, tortious interference with business relationship, and violations of the Connecticut Unfair Trade Practices Act ("CUTPA"), Conn. Gen.Stat. § 42-110a, *et seq.* Yale's counterclaims seek an accounting and assignment of the '538 patent, as well as damages for breach of contract and fiduciary duty, fraud, negligent misrepresentation, conversion, theft, and unjust enrichment. Dr. Fenn has asserted special defenses to Yale's counterclaims, including waiver, abandonment and release, estoppel, unclean hands, negligence, and statutes of limitations bars. As the Court generally finds for Yale on all these issues, it will address Yale's counterclaims first.

A. Yale's Counterclaims

1. Breach of Contract

a. Dr. Fenn Was Bound by Yale's Patent Policy

University patent policies such as Yale's have long been recognized as a valid and enforceable part of the contract of employment. This Court has held that "employment agreements [pursuant to which an employee agrees to assign to her employer inventions she developed during the course of employment] are valid and enforceable and [ ] do not violate public policy."

In *Chou v. University of Chicago*, the United States Court of Appeals for the Federal Circuit held that a research assistant was obligated to assign her inventions to the university, based on the university's patent policies. The court noted that "[a]lthough it is true that Chou never signed a contract with the University specifically obligating her to assign her inventions to the University, she accepted her academic appointment subject to the administrative policies of the University." Those administrative policies, the court noted, included the university's patent policies, which were set forth in the faculty handbook and included the obligation to assign inventions to the university. The court also noted that the research assistant had previously assigned other inventions to the university without disputing her obligation to do so.

Here, Dr. Fenn, like Chou, was bound by Yale's administrative policies, including its patent policy. Indeed, as noted above, Dr. Fenn concedes that he was contractually bound by the 1975 patent policy. Dr. Fenn argues, however, that he did not assent to any subsequent patent policies, and thus, that he was not contractually bound by them. He cites *Torosyan v. Boehringer Ingelheim Pharmaceuticals, Inc.*

as support for his argument. In *Torosyan*, the plaintiff, a chemist, was encouraged by the defendant corporation to move from California to Connecticut to work for it. The plaintiff was orally promised "long term" employment and given an employee handbook that limited the defendant's right to discharge employees, i.e., provided for discharge only "for cause." After the plaintiff was hired and moved to Connecticut, the defendant amended its employee manual to delete the limiting "for cause" language in the employee handbook section dealing with the defendant's right to discharge employees. Thereafter, the plaintiff was fired and the defendant claimed it was not bound by the for cause provision of the earlier employment manual. Affirming the trial court's finding for the plaintiff on its breach of contract claim, the Connecticut Supreme Court held that when an employer issues an employment manual after the employee starts work that substantially interferes with the employee's legitimate expectations about the terms of employment, the employee's continued work after notice of those terms is not conclusive evidence of the employee's consent to those terms.

The instant circumstances differ from those in *Torosyan*. As noted above, Dr. Fenn concedes that he was bound by and consented to Yale's 1975 patent policy. Unlike the employee handbook in *Torosyan*, Yale's 1975 patent policy explicitly provided that Yale could revoke or amend that policy at any time. Yale did amend its patent policy in 1984, 1988, and 1989, each time reserving its right to further amend the policy. Thus, unlike in *Torosyan*, Dr. Fenn has not shown that Yale's amended patent policies in 1984, 1988, and 1989 "substantially interfered" with his legitimate expectations about the terms of employment. Rather, he assented that Yale could amend those policies. Additionally, there was no evidence that he limited his assent to certain provisions of the 1975 patent policy or expressed his refusal to assent to its right to amend provision. Moreover, his continuation of work and compliance with the patent policy for two prior inventions are evidence that he agreed to the changes. Accordingly, the Court does not accept Dr. Fenn's position that only the 1975 patent policy applied to him, but rather, finds that it and the subsequent patent policies applied.

b. The 1989 Patent Policy Applies to the Invention Here

The Court also concludes that Yale's 1989 patent policy applied to the '538 invention. The patent policy published in the October 9–16, 1989 Yale Weekly Bulletin and Calendar, became Yale's official patent policy for "all inventions/ discoveries made on or after June 1988." Although Dr. Fenn argues that the '538 invention in fact was "discovered" prior to June 1988 (the effective date of the 1989 policy), the meaning of "inventions/discoveries made on or after June 1988" in the 1989 patent policy is not clear from the face of the policy. A court may admit extrinsic evidence to interpret ambiguous language of a contract. Accordingly, the Court employs extrinsic evidence to determine the meaning of the language "inventions/discoveries made on or after June 1988" contained in the 1989 patent policy. Dr. Lowendorf of the Yale OCR testified that Yale considers the date that the faculty member/inventor discloses the invention to Yale to be the date the invention is "discovered" for purposes of determining which patent policy applies because the patent policy requires that all inventions be promptly reported to the OCR. Yale's position on this issue is likely informed by the principle of patent law that the date by which a patent application must be filed is one year from the *public disclosure* of that invention, rather than the discovery date. Accordingly, the Court interprets the language "inventions/discoveries made on or after June 1988" to mean inventions or discoveries *disclosed to Yale on or after June 1988.*

Here, the '538 invention was disclosed to Yale in April 1989. Accordingly, the "invention/discovery" date under the policy is April 1989, and the 1989 patent policy applies. As noted above, although there was a 1988 patent policy, effective June 1, 1988, continuing the 80-20 division of licensing royalties of the 1984 policy, the 1989 policy changed that division to 70-30 and was made retroactive to June 1, 1988, thereby superseding the 1988 policy and its 80-20 division. Accordingly, the 1989 patent policy and its licensing royalty provisions apply as follows: for the first $100,000, 50% to the inventor; for amounts between $100,000 and $200,000, 40% to the inventor; and for amounts exceeding $200,000, 30% to the inventor.

c. Dr. Fenn Breached Yale's 1989 Patent Policy

The 1989 patent policy requires that "all inventions . . . shall be reported promptly in writing to the Provost through the Director of the Office of Cooperative Research" and that "[i]f the University decides that it does not wish and has no legal obligation to participate in the patenting or licensing of an invention, the University may release to the inventor the University's interest in the invention, and the inventor shall then be free to dispose of the invention as he or she wishes."

As to Yale's counterclaim of breach of contract, the Court concludes that Dr. Fenn violated the 1989 patent policy and committed a material breach of that policy when:

(i) he failed to "promptly" disclose the '538 invention to Yale and, rather, waited nearly a year after the '538 invention's public disclosure and approximately two months prior to the statutory deadline for filing a patent application before notifying Yale that he had discovered the invention;

(ii) he misrepresented the importance and commercial viability of the invention;

(iii) he actively discouraged Yale from preparing and filing a patent application by the statutory deadline while at the same time he was secretly preparing a patent application in his own name;

(iv) he filed a patent application in his own name without notifying Yale and the NIH;

(v) he licensed the '538 invention to Analytica without notifying Yale and the NIH;

(vi) he did not share the resulting licensing income with Yale; and

(vii) he refused to assign the '538 patent to Yale when Yale discovered what he had done and repeatedly asked that he do so.

Accordingly, Yale prevails on its breach of contract claim.

3. Fraud

The Court concludes that the evidence at trial was sufficient to establish that Dr. Fenn engaged in fraudulent misrepresentation and fraudulent nondisclosure. "The essential elements of an action in common law fraud . . . are that: (1) a false representation was made as a statement of fact; (2) it was untrue and known to be untrue by the party making it; (3) it was made to induce the other party to act upon it; and (4) the other party did so act upon that false representation to his injury."

First, the Court does not credit Dr. Fenn's testimony that he accurately represented to Yale his then belief in the limited commercial viability of the patent because of its nature as a "use patent." It was certainly clear to him by April 1989 that the invention was an important one, likely to be patented, and would likely be of significant commercial value. Yet he failed to be straightforward with Yale about that. In addition, Dr. Fenn misrepresented to Yale Analytica's interest in the invention when Dr. Bickerton inquired about that topic. Though Dr. Fenn had already discussed the '538 invention with Mr. Whitehouse, a 49% shareholder-owner of Analytica, he stated to Dr. Bickerton that he did not know if Analytica would be interested. Contrary to Dr. Fenn's representation to Dr. Bickerton, Dr. Fenn knew that Analytica was very much interested in the invention and in fact was funding the secret patent application.

Additionally, as found above, Dr. Fenn had a contractual duty to promptly disclose the '538 invention to Yale and fiduciary duties to keep Yale adequately informed about patentable inventions. Also, as found above, he breached those duties in failing to promptly disclose the invention or provide adequate and accurate information about the invention or its value and actively discouraging Yale from preparing and filing a patent application by the statutory deadline while he was preparing a patent application in his own name. Dr. Fenn also failed to disclose to Yale his view, and the view of others, that the invention was "revolutionary" or "important." He also filed the patent application in his own name without notifying Yale and licensed the '538 invention to Analytica without notifying Yale. Dr. Fenn acted purposefully and although he maintains it was only to show the "incompetence" of the Yale OCR office, his conduct was also motivated by his personal financial interests.

The Court finds that Dr. Fenn made these misrepresentations and omissions in order to induce Yale not to file a patent application and that Yale relied on Dr. Fenn's actions and information to its detriment in failing to pursue a patent or otherwise follow up with Dr. Fenn on the invention. Dr. Fenn knew that his representations and omissions did not accurately represent the facts concerning the invention and its commercial value. Accordingly, those misrepresentations and omissions constitute fraudulent misrepresentation and fraudulent nondisclosure, and Yale succeeds on its fraud claim.

III. Conclusion

Dr. Fenn's contributions to the science of mass spectrometry, including the invention that led to the '538 patent, are significant and beneficial to many. As evidenced by his receipt of the 2002 Nobel Prize for Chemistry, the invention that led to the '538 patent is one of far-reaching import and magnitude. Indeed, the Nobel Foundation stated that the invention has "revolutionised the development of new pharmaceuticals" and that "[p]romising applications are also being reported in other areas, for example foodstuff control and early diagnosis of breast cancer and prostate cancer."

However, Dr. Fenn failed to promptly disclose the '538 invention to Yale, misrepresented its importance and commercial viability, and actively discouraged Yale from preparing and filing a patent application by the statutory deadline. At the same time, Dr. Fenn secretly prepared a patent application in his own name and licensed the '538 invention to Analytica without notifying Yale and the NIH. Those actions not only violated Dr. Fenn's obligations to Yale, but also violated Connecticut state law. Moreover, his actions were intentional and without justification.

Accordingly, the Court finds for the defendant and counter-plaintiff, Yale University, as indicated above. However, in order to fashion a judgment consistent with this memorandum of decision, the Court directs the parties to file supplemental papers.

Specifically, the Court hereby orders the parties to file proposed findings of fact with factual support and proposed orders concerning the relief requested by Yale. The parties shall address: (1) Yale's request for an accounting/assignment of the patent; (2) the amount of damages under the 1989 patent policy and how they should be awarded; and (3) whether punitive damages should be awarded and their amount, including proof as to reasonable attorney's fees. Those proposed findings and orders are due within thirty days of the date of this order. Both parties are also ordered to file memoranda regarding Yale's theft and conversion claims within thirty days.

QUESTIONS

1.   The 1975 Yale Patent Policy provided that it could be revoked or amended at any time. If a university patent policy can be revoked or amended at any time by the university, what rights, if any, does a faculty member have under the patent policy? Would a faculty member's rights under a university patent policy be different if the patent policy were included by reference in the faculty member's employment contract with the university?

2.   Which of Dr. Fenn's actions did the court find constituted fraud? His failure to promptly disclose his invention? His misrepresentation of the commercial importance of the invention? Filing a patent application in his own name? Licensing the patent without notifying Yale? His refusal to assign the patent to Yale? All of the above?

3.   Dr. Fenn's defense was that he "was trying to show how incompetent the Yale OCR office was." Do you think Dr. Fenn may be a better scientist than a lawyer?

UNIVERSITY PATENTS v. KLIGMAN
762 F.Supp. 1212 (E.D. Pa. 1991)

WALDMAN, DISTRICT JUDGE.

Plaintiffs, The Trustees of the University of Pennsylvania (the University) and University Patents, Inc. (UPI), commenced this action to recover royalties allegedly owed to them by defendants for a preparation for photoaged skin invented by Dr. Kligman and marketed under license by Johnson & Johnson (J & J), and to seek a declaration of ownership in the patent rights to this product.

Presently before the court is defendants' Motion for Summary Judgment premised on the absence of any demonstrated enforceable rights of plaintiffs in Dr. Kligman's discovery. The parties have engaged in considerable discovery and have filed voluminous briefs. Oral argument was held on March 27, 1991.

****

III. FACTS

The pertinent facts from the uncontroverted evidence and the balance of the record viewed in a light most favorable to plaintiffs are as follow.

On August 11, 1965, the then President of the University of Pennsylvania, Gaylord P. Harnell, appointed a Patent Policy Committee to meet and make recommendations to the Trustees of the University. The committee consisted of five faculty members, one administrator and University counsel. The committee drafted a policy which was approved by the trustees in January 1966.

Under the policy, all inventions and discoveries resulting from work carried out on University time or at University expense were to be the property of the University. Specifically, the policy provides:

> The Trustees have declared it to be the policy of the University of Pennsylvania that any invention or discovery which may result from work carried out on University time or at University expense by special grants or otherwise is the property of the University. Patents on such inventions or discoveries may be applied for in any country by the University in which case the inventor shall assign his interest in the patent application to the University. The University will exercise its ownership of such patent, with or without profit, with due regard for the public interest as well as the interests of all persons concerned. Procedures for implementation of this policy shall be developed and promulgated by the President of the University.

This basic policy has remained unchanged since 1966. The procedures for implementing the policy, however, have been revised on several occasions.

As revised in 1973, the procedures make it clear that the policy was to apply to "all members of the staff of the University whether fully or partially affiliated." One of the primary features of the implementing procedures is the disclosure requirement which provides: "If a staff member believes he has made an invention or discovery that may be patentable he shall discuss the matter with the Director of Research Administration. The latter will recommend to the Vice Provost for Graduate Studies and Research whether or not the University shall file a patent application."

If after such disclosure the University decides to apply for a patent, two alternatives are to be considered. The University may arrange for a non-profit patent management organization ("PMO") to exploit the patent through the granting of licenses to commercial firms. If it appears more advantageous, the University may make such arrangements directly with a commercial firm. Finally, if the University decides that it is not interested in assuming the costs of the patent application, the inventor may apply in his own name and at his own expense. Under such circumstances the inventor shall grant to the University a royalty-free, irrevocable, non-exclusive license to make or use the invention for its own purposes.

Plaintiffs contend that the policy was first published and mailed to faculty members on February 25, 1966. The policy was *summarized* in the 1969 Faculty and Administration Handbook. The policy was set forth in the 1977 Research Investigators' Handbook which was distributed to faculty members through the University's internal mail system. The policy as well as new implementing procedures were disseminated in a revised Research Investigators' Handbook in 1983.

The University also had a Conflict of Interest Policy. Defendants contend that the policy was not enacted, or at least not disseminated, until 1983 when the revised Research Investigators' Handbook was released. Plaintiffs contend that the policy existed prior to that time but under a different name. It appears that, at least as of 1973, the Patent Policy Implementing Procedures contained a section captioned "Outside Consulting or Employment Agreements." This section directs the faculty member to advise the Dean or Director of any potential conflict between the member's obligation under the University's Patent Policy and any obligation assumed in connection with outside employment. On or about March 8, 1983, the University issued a "Conflict of Interest Policy" for faculty members which restated relevant existing policy and further required its faculty members to disclose to the University, in advance, any research in their respective fields in which they wish to engage for any private enterprise and first to offer such opportunities to the University.

Dr. Kligman is an Emeritus Professor of Dermatology at the University of Pennsylvania and has been affiliated with the University since 1948. Most of Dr. Kligman's scientific research has been funded through consulting agreements with various drug and cosmetic companies, and performed at private research facilities, principally Ivy Laboratories and the Simon Greenberg Foundation. Dr. Kligman established Ivy Laboratories in the 1950's and the Greenberg Foundation in March 1960. Neither have any affiliation with the University.

In the 1960's, while treating inmates at the Holmsburg Prison, Dr. Kligman discovered that Vitamin A Acid was an effective treatment for acne. In an effort to commercialize the invention, Dr. Kligman consulted J & J and later disclosed his discovery to the University.

Dr. Kligman presented his invention to J & J on or about August 3, 1967. Mr. Warner was a patent attorney for Johnson & Johnson from 1957 until February 1, 1976. Mr. Warner states that he discussed the University's Patent Policy with Dr. Kligman and stated that in his mind there was a question as to whether the Policy applied to this invention. Mr. Warner stated that Dr. Kligman maintained that the University had no claim to the invention because the bulk of the work was done on his own time and expense at Holmsburg Prison but that he intended to donate the royalties to the University because he was expected and wanted to help fund the Dermatology Department. Finally, Dr. Kligman agreed to notify the University and resolve any problems.

On August 24, 1967, Dr. Kligman wrote to Encel H. Dodge, who was then the Director of the Office of Project Research and Grants of the University. In the letter, Dr. Kligman states that he wished to bring to the University's attention his development of a new topical preparation for the treatment of acne. Dr. Kligman also stated that the innovation is "probably not patentable since the active ingredient is a Vitamin A derivative." He further stated that the formulation was developed on his own time with personal funds. Dr. Kligman stated that he was negotiating about potential royalties with J & J, and that he had proposed a 3% royalty to be paid to the University for exclusive use by the Dermatology Department. On September 11, 1967, Mr. Dodge responded stating that, in his opinion, University policy did not prohibit such a royalty arrangement. Mr. Dodge also referenced Dr. Kligman's statements that the invention was probably not patentable and was developed entirely on his own time using his own funds.

Mr. Warner then drafted a three-way agreement which makes clear that Dr. Kligman was the sole owner of the acne invention and that the "University has relinquished its rights, if any, to J & J in the "Kligman Acne Treatment." " A patent ultimately issued for the acne invention on April 24, 1973. This patent was assigned to J & J which conducted voluminous tests and thereafter secured FDA approval. The drug was introduced into the market under the name Retin-A and proved to be an enormous success. J & J has profited and the University has received millions of dollars in royalties.

Mr. Warner drafted three subsequent agreements in accordance with his understanding that the University had acknowledged that Dr. Kligman could freely license inventions made on his own time and with his own funds. The University was not made a party to these agreements which included an agreement regarding a Vitamin-A Acid/Steroid combination drug and consulting agreements entered into in 1970 and 1972.

During the 1970's and early 1980's, Dr. Kligman invented a second method of using Vitamin A Acid to retard the effects of aging of the skin. This discovery was an outgrowth of his work with Vitamin A Acid for the treatment of acne. During the 1970's, he used Vitamin A Acid to treat acne among residents of the Riverview Home for the Aged. Dr. Kligman states that this work was conducted as part of his work at Ivy Laboratories. The plaintiffs allege that Dr. Kligman discovered and reduced to practice these inventions using University funds, facilities, hospital patients and staff.

In 1971, Dr. Kligman wrote to J & J regarding the new observations and in early

1974 he sent them a manuscript outlining his findings. At this time, J & J filed an Investigational New Drug Application with the FDA and thereafter filed a Clinical Trial Protocol outlining the studies that would be run. Dr. Kligman's wife, Dr. Lorraine Kligman, who is also a member of the University's Department of Dermatology, was involved in the studies.

On June 15, 1978, J & J agreed to sponsor Dr. Lorraine Kligman's studies of the affect of Vitamin A Acid on rhino mice exposed to ultraviolet radiation. The grant from J & J was paid to the Simon Greenberg Foundation. J & J sponsored other research in this project at Ivy Laboratories and the Simon Greenberg Foundation, including grants in 1980 and 1982.

On August 28, 1981, Dr. Kligman filed a patent application for the photoaging preparation in his own name. Plaintiffs allege that this was in violation of the Patent Policy. Regarding the University, Dr. Kligman states:

> "Although I had developed the photoaging invention on my own time and at my own expense, the application did not hide my affiliation with the University or the fact that University facilities were involved in a portion of the work. Thus, the application specifically stated that I was a member of the University's Dermatology Department. It also disclosed the existence of the animal studies conducted at the University (the ones conducted by my wife Lorraine Kligman pursuant to a Johnson & Johnson grant) as well as a clinical study conducted at the University's Aging Skin Clinic."

At this time, news of the invention was carried in the popular press and was the subject of numerous magazine articles. Dr. Kligman began to discuss the discovery at various scientific lectures and conferences around the world. Anthony Merritt, the University's Director of Research Administration, was aware of this publicity. He believed, however, that the product in question was merely a new adaption of the old preparation and therefore was covered by the 1967 agreement.

On July 18, 1984, with the patent application still pending, Dr. Kligman signed a licensing agreement with J & J. The new agreement declared that Dr. Kligman was the sole owner and was free to license the invention. The agreement gave J & J the exclusive right to make, use and sell the invention and had a favorable royalty rate for Dr. Kligman, which was on a sliding scale of 5%, 3% and 1% of U.S. sales. Again, like all of the agreements which came after the first Retin-A agreement, the University was not made a party to the agreement.

Patent No. 4,603,146 issued in July 1986 for the photoaging discovery. Because Dr. Kligman filed the patent himself, his attorney claimed that small entity status entitled him to reduced filing fees. The patent application had been denied several times when, in May 1984, Dr. Kligman retained the services of another patent attorney, Mr. Schwarze. Because the licensing agreement was not yet signed, Mr. Schwarze prepared another small entity status application. Once the licensing agreement was signed, the small entity status had to be changed. Dr. Kligman waited until September 1986 to do this, and in January 1987, the Patent Office granted the change.

In June 1978, the University entered into an agreement with UPI which was amended and re-executed in August 1983 and again in September 1987. Under these agreements, UPI was required to provide certain licensing services for the University in exchange for a percentage of royalties to which the University became entitled because of rights it might acquire under its Patent Policy. UPI states that during the course of its relationship with the University it received over 322 disclosures from various University faculty members.

Plaintiffs allege that in April 1988, UPI for the first time became aware of the new invention and thereafter notified the University of its existence. Plaintiffs allege that they spent a year trying to get Dr. Kligman to provide evidence that he discovered the invention independently of the University, but that he failed to produce any such evidence. Thereafter, UPI filed its action in this court.

IV. ANALYSIS AND DISCUSSION

Defendants contend that the University can show no contractual obligation upon Dr. Kligman by which he was required to assign his rights in the photoaging invention to the University. Defendants contend that employment policies and handbooks generally are not binding under Pennsylvania law, that the Patent Policy in question is not binding, and that even if it is, it is not applicable in the context of the present dispute. Plaintiffs argue that the patent policy was binding and obligated Dr. Kligman to assign his patentable rights to the University.

Although "ownership" and "inventorship" are not identical for patent law purposes, they are related. Inventorship provides the starting point for determining ownership of patent rights. The true and original inventor must be named in the application for a patent and, absent some effective transfer or obligation to assign the patent rights, the original inventor owns the right to obtain the patent. Patents have the attributes of personal property and both patents and applications for patents are assignable. 35 U.S.C. § 261.

Since a patent is a creature of federal statutory law, it may be transferred only in the manner provided by such law. An assignment of a patent must be in writing. 35 U.S.C. § 261. The writing must show a clear and unmistakable intent to transfer ownership, and must be executed by the patentee or by the patentee's assigns or legal representatives.

An agreement to assign a patent or an interest therein is an executory contract which may be valid and enforceable. An equitable assignee may sue in law for damages or in equity for specific performance. Since contracts to assign patent rights do not have a statutory basis, but rather have a basis in common law or in equity, they need not be in writing and they may be implied as well as express. "Implied contracts may arise from the circumstances surrounding a case, such as employment or confidential relationship."

The present case arises in the context of an employment relationship. As the Pennsylvania Superior Court stated "[t]he major body of law on an employer's and employee's respective rights in the inventive or creative work of the employee evolved in the nineteenth and early twentieth centuries during our nation's industrial revolution" and the "basic" rules are fairly well-settled.

The general rule is that an individual owns the patent rights in the subject matter of which he is an inventor even though he conceived of the subject matter or reduced it to practice during the course of employment. The "mere existence of an employer-employee relationship does not of itself entitle the employer to an assignment of any inventions which the employee devises during the employment." This is true even where the employee uses the time and facilities of the employer. Even where "one is employed . . . to work in a particular line in which he is an expert, there is no inference that inventions which he makes while working belong to the employer."

To this general rule there are two exceptions and one limitation. First, an employer owns an employee's inventions if the employee is a party to a contract to that effect. Second, where an employee is hired to invent something or solve a particular problem, the property of the inventions of the employee related thereto belongs to the employer.

Where an employee uses the time or facilities of his employer, the employer may have a non-exclusive and non-transferrable royalty-free license (that is, a "shop right") to use the employee's patented invention.

These basic principles were discussed by the Supreme Court in 1933 and have remained substantially unchanged:

> One employed to make an invention, who succeeds, during his term of service, in accomplishing that task, is bound to assign to his employer any patent obtained. The reason is that he has only produced that which he was employed to invent. His invention is the precise subject of the contract of employment. A term of the agreement necessarily is that what he is paid to produce belongs to his paymaster. On the other hand, if the employment be general, albeit it covers a field of labor and effort in the performance of which the employee conceived the invention for which he obtained a patent, the contract is not so broadly construed as to require an assignment of the patent . . . .

Recognition of the nature of the act of invention also defines the limits of the so-called shop right, which, shortly stated, is that, where a servant, during his hours of employment, working with his master's materials and appliances, conceives and perfects an invention for which he obtains a patent, he must accord his master a nonexclusive right to practice the invention. This is an application of equitable principles. Since the servant uses his master's time, facilities, and materials to attain a concrete result, the latter is in equity entitled to use that which embodies his own property and to duplicate it as often as he may find occasion to employ similar appliances in his business. But the employer in such a case has no equity to demand a conveyance of the invention, which is the original conception of the employee alone, in which the employer had no part.

The courts of Pennsylvania will enforce express contracts to transfer patent rights which are clear and unambiguous. In this case, there clearly is no express written contract to assign. The University's 1977 Research Investigators' Handbook included a standard "Patent Agreement" form and there was a "policy" that "all personnel who may be involved in research must execute a Patent Agreement." Dr.

Kligman, however, never executed such an agreement and it appears that he was not even requested to do so.

Rather, plaintiffs base their contract claim on implied contract and unilateral contract theories, relying on the University's Handbook and policies and the parties' course of dealing.

In the context of patent rights, the courts have been hesitant to "imply" contracts to assign. This reluctance is based on the "nature of invention" — it being the product of original thought:

> The reluctance of courts to imply or infer an agreement by the employee to assign his patent is due to a recognition of the peculiar nature of the act of invention, which consists neither in finding out the laws of nature, nor in fruitful research as to the operation of natural laws, but in discovering how those laws may be utilized or applied for some beneficial purpose, by a process, a device, or a machine. It is the result of an inventive act, the birth of an idea and its reduction to practice; the product of original thought; a concept demonstrated to be true by practical application or embodiment in tangible form.

The law regarding implied contracts to assign patent rights in the employer-employee context has developed primarily in two areas: (1) where the employee is hired for some particular reason, see *Standard Parts, supra,* and (2) where the employee holds a position of trust as to the employer.

Plaintiffs here rely primarily on the University's Patent Policy and the handbook in which it was articulated to establish an implied contract to assign. Defendants cite a number of cases in which courts applying Pennsylvania law have declined to enforce employer handbooks and policies "against the employer," and urge the court to "rule as a matter of law that employer policies and handbooks cannot constitute implied contracts as against employees." The question of whether an employee manual can create an employment contract or can change the terms of employment has not been definitively answered in Pennsylvania. Most of the cases in the area involve discharged at-will employees who are claiming the existence of an employment contract.

The court must apply traditional patent assignment principles with the more recent and controversial employee handbook concepts. The employee handbook in question clearly was not communicated as a definite offer of employment. The 1977 Research Investigators' Handbook is a fairly detailed 110-page document describing the various policies and procedures involved in research at the University, including the Patent Policy. The first statement in the Handbook itself suggests that it is a "guide" rather than an enforceable legal document.

In addition to a discussion of the Patent Policy and procedures, the Handbook contains a patent agreement form to be signed by personnel involved in research. The Handbook states: "It is the policy of the University that all personnel who may be involved in research must execute a Patent Agreement at the time of employment." Research Investigators' Handbook at 82. The Patent Agreement provides in pertinent part:

UNIVERSITY OF PENNSYLVANIA PATENT AGREEMENT

IN CONSIDERATION of information and facilities for research made available to me by The Trustees of the University of Pennsylvania under a grant or contract with the Government of the United States, University sponsorship, or other sponsors, I hereby agree:

1. That I will promptly communicate to the Director, Officer or Research Administration, full information as to each invention, discovery and improvement conceived or first actually reduced to practice by me during my work under such grant, contract, or sponsorship.

2. That I will, if and when requested, either before or after leaving the employment of the University of Pennsylvania, execute all papers necessary to file application for patents on any such invention, discovery, or improvement, in any country, and will assign such application, invention, discovery, or improvement covered thereby, and the patents that may be issued thereon as directed in accordance with the established patent policy of the University of Pennsylvania and sponsors of research projects on which I may work.

The Handbook contained a second agreement form, captioned "Patent Agreement For U.S. Public Health Service Research And Training Grants," which was to be executed by "[a]ll persons who perform any part of the work under a grant or award from the Department of Health, Education, and Welfare."

Plaintiffs suggest that both forms were only required when the research was funded by the government. Mr. Merritt acknowledged that even the first form "was used primarily where people had federal funding." These agreement forms were left out of the 1983 Handbook because as Mr. Merritt states: "Federal laws changed. There was a uniform government patent policy implemented, Public Law 96517; and it was felt under the new law that these kinds of sign-offs weren't required for Federal grants."

It is not clear whether the University ever enforced compliance with the policy that all personnel who may be involved in research execute a Patent Agreement, but it is clear that it never did so with any vigor. At Mr. Merritt's deposition he was asked whether he had any knowledge "as to whether anyone, other than people who had government grants, were asked to sign the document or documents that's contained on page 83"? He responded that he had "no such knowledge." There is no evidence that Dr. Kligman ever signed a Patent Agreement. Indeed, there is no evidence that he was ever asked to do so.

In addition to these forms, the University had an Invention Disclosure Form which it used after a faculty member had reported an invention to the research office. The invention disclosure form requires such relevant information as the title of the invention, the name of the inventor, the names of any sponsors, and certain key dates. The Instructions for Completing the form made the import of the document clear: "The Invention Disclosure Form is a legal document and requires a reasonable degree of care in its completion. There are parts of it which may be of extreme importance to the patentability of your invention and to the protection of rights under any patent which might issue related to your invention." The faculty member is required to sign a statement which provides in pertinent part:

> To the best of my (our) knowledge, the information set forth above and in the attachments is true, correct and complete. I (we) understand that this information may be relied upon during the preparation, filing and prosecution of a patent application relating to the invention disclosed herein, and that the accuracy of this information may be important to the validity of any patent which may result from such application. I (we) understand that I (we) have a duty to disclose all information which is material to the examination of any application filed on the invention, and I (we) will, from time to time, update and correct this information during the pendency of this application. I (we) acknowledge that the invention was made pursuant to the University Patent Policy and agree to assign all right, title and interest in the invention to the University pursuant to the terms of the Patent Policy.

As a general rule, the University did not require the completion of Disclosure Forms at any time prior to actual disclosure. In the case of Dr. Kligman even this was not done. The University never requested that Dr. Kligman sign a patent agreement or disclosure form with regard to the acne or photoaging inventions.

In 1967, even after Dr. Kligman wrote to the Director of the Office of Project Research disclosing the acne invention, he was not required to sign a disclosure form. In the letter, Dr. Kligman had stated that the invention was probably not patentable and was developed on his own time. The University's Patent Policy, however, did not strictly turn on "patentability." The agreement which was ultimately executed by J & J, the University and Dr. Kligman clearly evidences the possibility that a patent would emerge.

The language of the Patent Agreement and Disclosure forms make clear that they were intended to be enforceable contracts. It cannot be said, however, that any reasonable person receiving the handbook, without more, would have understood himself to be bound by the terms of a form agreement he never executed.

Plaintiffs also cite Dr. Kligman's first letter to Mr. Dodge and his responses to deposition questions as evidence of his intention to be bound by the policy. Dr. Kligman testified that before Mr. Warner read the patent policy to him, he had no knowledge that this document existed. He testified that he sought a clarification of his position from Mr. Dodge who responded that the University had no rights in the initial discovery since it was not made on University time or at its expense. He understood the policy not to apply to him because his modus operandi was to obtain independent funding and to conduct research at private facilities, principally at Ivy.

A fair reading of Kligman's letter to Dodge of August 24, 1967 suggests that Dr. Kligman decided gratuitously to assign any royalties to the University. Since he states in the letter that he developed the anti-acne preparation "on my own time using personal funds" at a non-University facility, it is not reasonable to infer that Dr. Kligman proposed an assignment pursuant to the Patent Policy.

Dr. Kligman, however, also testified that he would be bound by the Patent Policy if he "came up with some patentable invention which arose out of work done on University time or using University resources" had he been "fully affiliated." Based at least in part on Mr. Dodge's response of September 11, 1967 to Dr. Kligman's letter, he contends that he reasonably believed he was exempt from the Patent Policy as a non-fully affiliated employee. No reasonable person reading that letter could conclude that Dodge was advising Kligman that he was exempt from the Policy. Dodge specifically referenced Dr. Kligman's assurance that no University time or resources were expended on the discovery. Further, the Patent Policy makes clear on its face that it applies "to all members of the staff of the University whether fully or partially affiliated."

Even if there may have been an offer and acceptance, however, it is not clear that there was any consideration. *See Harsco Corp. v. Zlotnick*, (agreement to employ defendant for reasonable period of time provided adequate consideration for express agreement to assign patent rights).

In *Harsco*, as in most of the other handbook cases, a handbook provision was used in an attempt to recast the terms of an at-will employment arrangement. In such circumstances, the retention of the employee for a term and his continued performance of services may constitute adequate consideration. Here, although the parties cannot agree on Dr. Kligman's exact status, it is clear that he was and is a tenured professor and thus not subject to the at-will rule. When a college grants a professor tenure, it is giving away its right to terminate the professor at will. Thus, the respective patent rights of the parties regarding Dr. Kligman's discoveries during his affiliation with the University must be analyzed in the context of a tenured employment relationship.

The unilateral conferral of a benefit on a tenured employee is not enforceable without additional consideration. It logically would appear therefrom that the unilateral imposition of a new obligation on such an employee would not be enforceable without such consideration. Even courts which have taken a liberal view of the applicability of handbook provisions have held that a handbook issued after the existence of an express or implied contract of employment is not binding in the absence of additional consideration.

Plaintiffs contend that by allowing Dr. Kligman to use the University's facilities and staff, the University provided consideration for his adherence to the Patent Policy. They particularly refer to his utilization of Dr. Lavker's time and a study he conducted of 200 University hospital patients. Pennsylvania courts define consideration as:

> "a benefit to the party promising or a loss or detriment to the party to whom the promise is made [citations omitted] as long as the promisee in return for the promise does anything legal which he is not bound to do or refrains from doing anything which he has a right to do, whether there is any actual loss or detriment to him or actual benefit to the promisor or not."

There is no evidence of record to show that unqualified access to the University's staff and facilities was available to Dr. Kligman as a condition of his employment with the University as a tenured professor. Indeed, the record contains virtually no explanation of the meaning of Dr. Kligman's employment designation or evidence of the terms and conditions of his employment.

Whether a contract was formed generally is a question of fact to be resolved by a jury. Like most jury questions, however, it can be answered by the court when the meaning is so clear that a jury's verdict to the contrary would be set aside.

"The question of interpretation of language and conduct — the question of what is the meaning that should be given by a court to the words of a contract, is a question of fact, not a question of law.

We must bear in mind, however that this question of fact is like other questions of fact in this: it may be a question that should be answered by the judge rather than by the jury.

[If] the evidence is so clear no reasonable man would determine the issue before the court in any way but one, the court will itself determine the issue."

This is a close case, particularly in view of the manner in which the University conveyed its Patent Policy and its lax enforcement thereof. On the current record, however, the court cannot conclude that no jury reasonably could find that an implied contract to assign the patent in question was formed between Dr. Kligman and the University. There is evidence, however scant, from which one could find that Dr. Kligman was aware of the Patent Policy since August 1967 and manifested an intent to be bound by it. By emphasizing that the initial discovery was on his own time and at his own expense in his letter to Mr. Dodge, Dr. Kligman may have led the University reasonably to conclude that he recognized the applicability of the Policy to any discovery achieved with the use of University resources. There is evidence that such resources were used with regard to the photoaging discovery and no evidence to refute the University's position that the placement of these resources at Dr. Kligman's disposal constituted consideration.

Accordingly, defendants' motion for summary judgment premised on the absence of a binding agreement as a matter of law will be denied at this time.

QUESTIONS

1. The court held that because Dr. Kligman was a tenured professor, he could not be bound by Penn's unilateral change in its patent policy. Why?

2. Dr. Kligman informed Penn of his invention and the license to J&J, and offered to share the license royalties with Penn. How do these actions compare with Dr. Fenn's actions?

3. The court found that there was no patent assignment, no clear evidence that Penn ever enforced compliance with its patent policy, no evidence that Dr. Kligman signed the patent agreement and no evidence that Dr. Kligman had unqualified access to Penn's facilities. Nonetheless, the court still found that this was a "close case" and denied Dr. Kligman's motion for summary judgment. Why?

E.I. DU PONT NEMOURS & CO. v. OKULEY
344 F.3D 578 (6th Cir. 2003)

BOGGS, CIRCUIT JUDGE.

The defendant, Dr. John Joseph Okuley, appeals the summary judgment for the plaintiff, E.I. Du Pont de Nemours and Company ("DuPont"), in a dispute involving both contract and patent elements. Okuley helped discover FAD2, one of the genes encoding the Fatty Acid Desaturase enzyme, while an employee of Washington State University ("WSU"), which had a research collaboration agreement ("RCA") with DuPont that assigned to DuPont rights to intellectual property discovered in the course of the collaboration. When Okuley ceased cooperating with the processing of DuPont's application for a patent on FAD2, DuPont filed suit in the United States District Court for the Southern District of Ohio for a declaratory judgment that it owned FAD2 and for specific enforcement of Okuley's agreement to cooperate with DuPont. Okuley counterclaimed for a declaratory judgment that he was the inventor of FAD2 and to rescind his personal assignment of patent rights to DuPont. The district court granted summary judgment to DuPont on all issues. After initially appealing the district court's decision to this court, Okuley moved to transfer the appeal to the Court of Appeals for the Federal Circuit. We take appellate jurisdiction of this matter and affirm the judgment of the district court.

I

In 1991, Okuley, a Ph.D. in molecular biology, began work at WSU on a project on plant fat metabolism, with the aim of isolating and patenting genes that could increase the ratio between beneficial fatty acids and harmful saturated fats. Under the WSU Faculty Manual ("Faculty Manual"), employees assigned to WSU any intellectual property arising out of their employment, and WSU and DuPont were operating under the RCA regarding the assignment of the intellectual property arising out of this project. In August 1992, while still employed at WSU, but while working at a borrowed laboratory at Ohio State University ("OSU"), Okuley successfully identified the FAD2 gene and immediately informed both his supervisor at WSU and DuPont of his discovery. On November 17, DuPont initiated the patent process on FAD2. After some initial disagreement about the inventorship of FAD2, the issue was resolved in May 1993 by DuPont agreeing that inventorship was shared between Okuley and another WSU scientist and Okuley agreeing to assign to DuPont his "entire right, title and interest" in FAD2 and obligating himself to "execute all applications, papers or instruments necessary or required" for DuPont to obtain the patent. In December 1994, relations under this agreement between DuPont and Okuley broke down over Okuley's refusal to sign any more of the papers necessary for the patent application, unless he received "a reasonable royalty for the use of this invention." DuPont thereafter filed a petition with the Patent and Trademark Office ("PTO") to process the FAD2 patent application without Okuley's consent. At the time briefs in this case were filed, both the petition and the application were still pending, but on April 16, 2002, the PTO issued the patent litigated here.

On November 3, 1997, DuPont filed a three-count complaint against Okuley in the United States District Court for the Southern District of Ohio. Subject matter jurisdiction was based on diversity, DuPont being a Delaware corporation, with its principal place of business in Delaware, and Okuley a citizen of Ohio, and the matter in controversy meeting the jurisdictional amount. The first count sought a declaratory judgment that DuPont had exclusive ownership of the FAD2 gene, at least *vis-a-vis* Okuley. The second count sought specific enforcement of Okuley's contractual duties to continue executing documents necessary for DuPont to pursue the FAD2 patent. The third count sought the same relief on the basis of Okuley's common law duties. Okuley counterclaimed, seeking rescission of his personal assignment of FAD2 to DuPont and a judicial declaration that Okuley was the sole owner and inventor of FAD2. On November 1, 2000, after extensive discovery, the parties filed cross-motions for summary judgment on all counts. The district court granted summary judgment to DuPont on all issues. It concluded that it had no jurisdiction to entertain Okuley's claim to inventorship, that DuPont owned the rights to FAD2 under its agreement with WSU, that Okuley was bound by the Faculty Manual to assign all interests in FAD2 to DuPont; and that Okuley's personal, written assignment to DuPont was valid, enforceable, and not subject to rescission. Okuley timely appealed the district court's judgment to this court. After filing his proof brief in this court, Okuley moved to transfer the appeal to the Court of Appeals for the Federal Circuit, on the basis that it had exclusive appellate jurisdiction in this case.

II

We first turn to the issue of proper appellate jurisdiction. This court has jurisdiction over almost all appeals from final decisions of district courts within its geographical boundaries. 28 U.S.C. § 1294. However, the Court of Appeals for the Federal Circuit has exclusive jurisdiction over appeals from final decisions of a district court, if the jurisdiction of that court was based, in whole or in part, on 28 U.S.C. § 1338(a), subject to certain exceptions not applicable here. 28 U.S.C. § 1295. District court jurisdiction under § 1338(a) extends "only to those cases in which a well-pleaded complaint establishes either that federal patent law creates the cause of action or that the plaintiff's right to relief necessarily depends on resolution of a substantial question of federal patent law, in that patent law is a necessary element of one of the well-pleaded claims." The seemingly amorphous "substantial question of federal patent law" component of the test merely makes clear that a plaintiff cannot avoid federal patent jurisdiction by leaving out an element necessary to the success of his claim, any more than a plaintiff can create federal jurisdiction by including extraneous references to federal law. Moreover, it is important to note that only inventorship, the "question of who actually invented the subject matter claimed in a patent," is a question of federal patent law. "Ownership, however, is a question of who owns legal title to the subject matter claimed in a patent, patents having the attributes of personal property" and is not a question of federal patent law.

These principles are illustrated by *Rustevader Corp. v. Cowatch*. In that case, Rustevader sued its former employee, Cowatch, and Cowatch's father in state court. The defendants had jointly taken out a patent and Rustevader demanded assignment of the patent under a breach of employment contract theory. The defendants removed to federal court on the basis of federal patent jurisdiction and Rustevader asked for remand on the basis that there was no federal jurisdiction. The court reasoned that if the suit had been filed exclusively against the former employee, the court could have ordered an assignment to the employer on the basis of contract, regardless of whether the son was the inventor, and a resolution of the inventorship issue would not have been necessary. However, the plaintiff also made a claim against the father, who was not in contractual privity with the plaintiff. If the father was in fact, as the patent application claimed, an inventor of the disputed patent, Rustevader had no right to the assignment of his interest. If the son was the sole inventor and the contract assigned his rights to Rustevader, Rustevader had a right to the assignment of both father's and son's interest. Therefore, Rustevader's claim against the father required a resolution of the question of inventorship and unintentionally invoked federal patent jurisdiction.

This court has appellate jurisdiction if, and only if, DuPont's well-pleaded complaint [does not] necessarily require[s] resolution of the question of inventorship. The only claim in DuPont's complaint relevant to this question is the request for a declaratory judgment that DuPont had "sole title to [the FAD2] intellectual property." At first blush, to determine the validity of such a broad claim would appear to require resolution of the inventorship question, but a focus on the issues facing the court leads to the opposite conclusion. First, the district court only had the power to adjudicate the relative rights of the parties. Even if a hypothetical third party X had been the true inventor of the FAD2 gene, no judgment could have affected X's rights, as the district court never took personal jurisdiction over X. Therefore, the court needed concern itself only with the relative rights of DuPont and Okuley, regardless of the language of the complaint. The broad language of the complaint was extraneous to the resolution of the matter between the parties to the case. DuPont could not create federal patent jurisdiction by making the unnecessarily broad claim. Okuley cannot now use the overbreadth of DuPont's complaint to claim federal patent jurisdiction.

Second, as between Okuley and DuPont, the district court could have resolved the relative interests in FAD2 on several theories. For example, it could have determined that one of DuPont's other researchers was the sole inventor of FAD2 and that Okuley therefore had no right to the intellectual property. That would have required answering the inventorship question. Alternatively, the district court could have reasoned, as in fact it ultimately did, that if Okuley was the inventor of FAD2, he contractually assigned all his interests to DuPont. That would not have required answering the inventorship question. If there are several alternative theories on which a claim may succeed, patent law jurisdiction is only invoked when *all* alternative theories necessarily state a complaint under the patent law. As DuPont's assignment theory sounded in contract, not patent law, DuPont's claim to the sole ownership of the gene did not invoke patent law jurisdiction. Therefore, appellate jurisdiction lies with this court.

A separate jurisdictional issue arises with respect to Okuley's counter-claim of sole inventorship, which the district court had dismissed for lack of jurisdiction. In the proceedings below, Okuley had argued that the district court had been granted jurisdiction in two sections of the patent code.

Whenever through error a person is *named in an application for patent* as the inventor, or through error an inventor is not named in an application, and such error arose without any deceptive intention on his part, the Director *may* permit the application to be amended accordingly, under such terms as he prescribes. 35 U.S.C. § 116 (emphases added).

Whenever through error a person is named in *an issued patent* as the inventor, or through error an inventor is not named in *an issued patent* and such error arose without any deceptive intention on his part, the Director may, on application of all the parties and assignees, with proof of the facts and such other requirements as may be imposed, issue a certificate correcting such error . . . . *The court* before which such matter is called in question may order correction of the patent on notice and hearing of all parties concerned and the Director *shall* issue a certificate accordingly. 35 U.S.C. § 256 (emphases added).

We affirm the holding of the district court on the basis of the language of § 116 and § 256 and their notable differences. At the time of the trial and the briefs, no patent had yet been issued. Therefore, only § 116 applied. Section 116 does not mention courts, but rather gives discretion to the Director of the PTO to permit amendments to patent applications and to do so under such terms as the Director deems proper. Section 256, by contrast, explicitly mentions the courts and the authority of the courts to compel action by the Director. Comparing these two sections, it is clear that Congress intended to draw a distinction between patent applications and issued patents. While the patent is still in the process of gestation, it is solely within the authority of the Director. As soon as the patent actually comes into existence, the federal courts are empowered to correct any error that the Director may have committed. Such a scheme avoids premature litigation and litigation that could become futile if the Director declined to grant a patent or voluntarily acceded to the claims of the would-be inventor prior to issue. We conclude, therefore, that the district court lacked jurisdiction to review the inventorship of an unissued patent.

After the briefs in this case were filed, the PTO issued a patent naming Okuley, among others, as inventor. While this may have created § 256 jurisdiction to review Okuley's inventorship claim, in reviewing the district court's judgment we consider the facts as faced by that court, without prejudice to a § 256 claim should Okuley choose to file such an action. In this appeal, Okuley has dropped any argument that § 256 was applicable and merely made a perfunctory statement that § 116 vests jurisdiction in the courts implicitly because "inventorship is a question of law." However, federal courts have not been granted jurisdiction to settle all questions of law.

III

Having disposed of the somewhat thorny issues of federal patent jurisdiction, we now turn to the substance of the claims adjudicated by the district court and appealed here. These are questions of property and contract law and, as explained above, do not arise under federal law, patent law or otherwise. The district court's jurisdiction was based on the diversity of the parties. When sitting in diversity, a federal court applies the substantive law of the state. Hence, our source of law with respect to the contracts WSU entered with Okuley and DuPont in Washington is Washington law. With respect to the assignment executed in Ohio and the interpretation of Ohio statutes, the source is Ohio law.

The judgment appealed was a grant of summary judgment, so we apply the well-known summary judgment standard.

****

DuPont's claim of ownership to FAD2 rests on the basis of two contracts: the Faculty Manual and the RCA. According to the Faculty Manual, WSU holds "ownership in patents and other non-patentable intellectual products . . . developed by its employees as a result of their employment." The parties do not dispute that this manual was a legally binding part of Okuley's employment contract with WSU. Under the RCA between DuPont and WSU, WSU's interest in FAD2 was transferred to DuPont. In combination, these two contracts serve to transfer FAD2 from Okuley to WSU and from WSU to DuPont. Therefore DuPont owns FAD2. Against this conclusion, Okuley raises a series of objections.

Okuley's first and most novel objection is based on the fact that he discovered FAD2 while working under a WSU employment contract, but in an OSU laboratory and using OSU equipment. Under Ohio statutory law, "[a]ll rights to and interests in discoveries, inventions, or patents which result from research or investigation conducted in any . . . facility of any state college or university, . . . shall be the sole property of that college or university" Ohio Rev. Code § 3345.14(B). Therefore *ab initio* the ownership of FAD2 vested in OSU, not Okuley. Nevertheless, the Ohio statute did not abrogate Okuley's contract with WSU. Hence Okuley was also under an obligation to transfer FAD2 to WSU — an obligation he could not satisfy as at that time he did not own FAD2. Had matters rested in this posture, interesting, but quite different, litigation could have ensued involving WSU and OSU and including questions of the statute's constitutionality under the Takings Clause.

However, matters did not rest there. In 1993, at Okuley's insistence, OSU — as apparently is its practice — explicitly waived its rights to FAD2. If OSU's waiver was effective, releasing any statutory rights that it enjoyed, the site of the research and the statute ceased to have any effect on this case. However, even if, as Okuley argues, the mandatory language of the statute prevents OSU from waiving its interest in FAD2, the outcome is no different because the "waiver" also contained an assignment to Okuley of FAD2, an action undisputedly within OSU's power. This assignment enabled Okuley to fulfill his pre-existing contractual obligation to transfer FAD2 to WSU. Okuley argues that the assignment transferred FAD2 to him free and clear of any obligation. But even setting aside the question of whether OSU had the authority to void a contract to which it was not a party and executed in another state, the language of the assignment is unambiguous. The assignment clearly states that it was "subject to any rights of [WSU] or its research sponsor [DuPont]." Therefore Okuley's obligation to give FAD2 to WSU remained unaltered by the Ohio statute and the OSU waiver/assignment.

Next, Okuley claims that if FAD2 became property of WSU under the Faculty

Manual, WSU failed to follow the manual's procedures and thus forfeited it back to him. The Faculty Manual states that if WSU's "Intellectual Property Committee fails to notify the employee in writing of determination of ownership within fifty days of full disclosure, . . . the University's rights in the patentable property shall automatically become the property of the employee." It is a disputed question of fact whether Okuley made full disclosure to WSU, triggering the clause in the Faculty Manual. But even if the clause was triggered, it will not avail Okuley for several reasons. First, the Faculty Manual explicitly exempts property developed under an agreement with an outside sponsor from its return clause. Second, the clause only vests WSU's rights back with the employee. However, under the collaboration agreement with DuPont, WSU did not have any rights in the property and only DuPont did. Therefore, WSU had nothing to return to DuPont.

Okuley also contends that the patent for FAD2 was based on additional "transformation work" that he performed after the end of the agreement between WSU and DuPont and that DuPont incorporated in later versions of its patent application. However, this transformation work was merely used to confirm the identity and use of FAD2 covered under the original patent application. As such it was, as the district court found, a simple extension of the original patent application and hence falls under the Faculty Manual's language regarding "intellectual products . . . developed by its employees as a result of their employment" and was assigned to WSU.

Okuley's final argument is based upon a reinterpretation of the RCA, to which he was not a party and with which all parties to the contract disagree. Under the RCA, almost all intellectual property rights arising from the research belongs to DuPont. However, under a clause of the RCA, if DuPont failed to isolate a gene resulting from the research within nine months of the identification, and WSU succeeded where DuPont had failed, the gene would belong to WSU and DuPont would merely receive a license. Using strained definitions of the conditions that start the nine-month period, Okuley argues that it had expired before he even began his research. According to DuPont and WSU, Okuley's discovery of FAD2 started the period and DuPont was able to isolate the gene almost immediately thereafter. Even if Okuley had standing to challenge the interpretation of a contract to which the parties agreed, and his interpretation were correct, which seems highly unlikely, the effect would be merely to vest the property in WSU, not Okuley. For Okuley to obtain the patent, the court would also have to agree with the above argument regarding the reversion of the patent to Okuley by inaction of WSU. As we do not, this issue is moot.

IV

For the foregoing reasons, the judgment of the district court is AFFIRMED.

QUESTIONS

1. The court states that the WSU-DuPont research collaboration agreement "assigned" to DuPont the rights in intellectual property discovered during the course of the research collaboration. WSU is a public university and presumably all

of its facilities are constructed with tax-exempt bonds. Why would the WSU-DuPont research collaboration agreement not violate Rev. Proc. 2007-47's predecessor provision, Rev. Proc. 1997-14?

2. Why wasn't Okuley's counter-claim of sole inventorship sufficient to invoke federal patent law jurisdiction?

3. What is the difference between OSU waiving its state-granted rights and assigning its state-granted rights? How did this difference affect the outcome of the case?

4. The court dismissed Okuley's claim that the patent filed included "transformation work" he performed after the WSU-DuPont agreement terminated. According to the court, the transformation work "was a simple extension of the original patent application." Is this finding an interpretation of the patent claims or an interpretation of the WSU faculty manual? What difference would this make?

5. If you were counsel to DuPont during these transactions, what would you have done differently?

CASE NOTES

1. *See* University of Pittsburgh v. Townsend, 542 F.3d 513 (6th Cir. 2008) (University's tort and contract causes of action accrued when it should have learned that faculty member intended to assign his interest in the PET/CT scanner to a third party; doctrines of fraudulent concealment and continuing breach did not toll statutes of limitations; university ownership claims barred by the statutes of limitations); Regents of the University of New Mexico v. Knight, 321 F.3d 1111 (Fed. Cir. 2003) (Inventors were bound by patent policy and no genuine issue of material fact that inventors violated their contractual obligation to assign patents to the university; however, university waived its Eleventh Amendment immunity by filing suit for declaration of patent ownership and inventors' counterclaims for money damages, therefore, are not barred); Sanders v. Mount Sinai School of Medicine, 418 F. Supp. 2d 339 (S.D.N.Y. 2005) (Expert report of outside counsel was admissible in action brought by physicians against medical school because report described patent claims and identified elements of patent claims lost as a result of prior judgment of PTO); Speck v. North Carolina Dairy Foundation, 311 N.C. 679 (N.C. 1984) (University owed no fiduciary duty to faculty member to pay royalties on invention of secret process to prepare milk; secret process was not patentable and university royalty-sharing agreement applied only to royalties from patents; university intellectual property policy was silent on sharing royalties from trademarks and trade secrets; it is unthinkable that a valuable invention to combat disease developed at a public university, with public funds, by public employees could be monopolized for private gain).

Additional Information

1. KATHLEEN L. DAERR-BANNON, 20 CAUSES OF ACTION 2D 269 (2009).

2. L.J. KUTTEN, COMPUTER SOFTWARE PROTECTION-LIABILITY-LAW-FORMS § 6:28 (2010).

3.   JOHN GLADSTONE MILLS III, ET. AL., PATENT LAW FUNDAMENTALS § 17:27 (2010).

4.   ROBERT GOLDSCHEIDER, ECKSTROM'S LICENSING — Forms § 12:32 (2011).

5.   Practicing Law Institute, *University Technology Transfers: Recent Developments and Licensing Issues*, 899 PLI/PAT 848 (Jan. 2007).

6.   Sean B. Seymore, *My Patent, Your Patent, or Our Patent? Inventorship Disputes within Academic Research Groups*, 16 ALB. L.J. SCI. & TECH. 125 (2006).

7.   G. Kenneth Smith, *Faculty and Graduate Student Generated Inventions: Is University Ownership a Legal Certainty?*, 1 VA. L.J. & TECH. 4 (1997).

8.   Pat K. Chew, *Faculty-Generated Inventions: Who Owns the Golden Egg?*, 1992 WIS. L. REV. 259 (1992).

9.   Christopher G. Browning, Jr., *The Souring of Sweet Acidophilus Milk: Speck v. North Carolina Dairy Foundation and the Rights of University Faculty to Their Inventive Ideas*, 63 N.C. L. REV. 1248 (1985).

3.3.3 University-Student IP Ownership Disputes

In some situations, a university may claim ownership of an invention made by a student. One such situation is when a student invention is made during the course of a federally funded research project. Under the Bayh-Dole Act, discussed earlier, the university is entitled to elect to take title to inventions made with federal funding whether the inventions are made by faculty or students. Another such situation is when a student invention is made during the course of a corporate-sponsored research project. University intellectual property policies, as well as university-sponsored research agreements, invariably claim university title to any inventions made by faculty, students or staff during the course of a sponsored research project. Two other situations in which a university may claim title to student inventions are when a student is employed by the university to perform research (e.g., as a laboratory assistant to faculty researcher) and when the university provides a student special research facilities and equipment (e.g., dedicating a laboratory to a student's research project). Although a university's claim to ownership of student inventions can be based upon the Bayh-Dole Act, intellectual property policies or sponsored research agreements, the best practice for a university intending to claim title to a student invention is to have the student sign an invention assignment agreement prior to commencement of the research.

One situation in which universities rarely claim title to student inventions is when the invention is made during the course of a student's required course work in pursuit of an academic degree.

The *VanVoorhies* case below involves a claim of university ownership of an invention made by a Ph.D. student who was employed by the university as a research assistant. As you will see, the court was not sympathetic to Vanvoorheis' multiple state law counterclaims he asserted while representing himself *pro se.*

UNIVERSITY OF WEST VIRGINIA v. VANVOORHIES
278 F.3D 1288 (Fed. Cir. 2002)

LOURIE, CIRCUIT JUDGE.

Kurt L. VanVoorhies appeals from the decision of the United States District Court for the Northern District of West Virginia granting the University of West Virginia Board of Trustees' ("WVU's") motion for summary judgment that VanVoorhies breached his duty to assign U.S. Patent Applications 08/486,340 and 08/514,609 to WVU. He also appeals from the court's grant of WVU's motions for summary judgment on his claims based on fraud, breach of fiduciary duty, breach of contract, and invalid assignment, as well as its grant of WVU's motions to dismiss his quasi-contract claims and his claims under the Racketeer Influenced and Corrupt Organizations Act, 18 U.S.C. § 1962 (2000) ("RICO"). In addition, VanVoorhies appeals from the court's denial of his motions to disqualify WVU's counsel, compel discovery, and vacate the stay of a consolidated case. Because we decide that the district court did not err in concluding that VanVoorhies was obligated to assign his inventions to WVU, and we are not persuaded that it erred in any of its other challenged decisions, we affirm.

BACKGROUND

Dr. VanVoorhies was a Senior Design Engineer for General Motors Corporation before he enrolled in graduate school at WVU in 1990 to pursue a Ph.D. in engineering. He went to WVU specifically to work with one particular professor, Dr. James E. Smith, after which Smith and VanVoorhies investigated antennae for wireless power transmission. VanVoorhies' laboratory notebook indicates that he completed an invention for a contrawound toroidal helical antenna ("the first invention") by June 3, 1991.

In November 1991, VanVoorhies submitted an invention disclosure form to WVU describing that invention and listing Smith as a co-inventor. Smith later testified that he had discussed WVU's patent policy with him prior to submitting that invention disclosure, in June 1991. The WVU policy applies to "University personnel," who are defined as "all full-time and part-time members of the faculty and staff, and all other employees of the University including graduate and undergraduate students and fellows of the University." Under the policy, "[t]he University owns worldwide right, title and interest in any invention made at least in part by University personnel, or with substantial use of University resources, and unless otherwise agreed, this Policy applies to any invention conceived or first reduced to practice under terms of contracts, grants or other agreements." The policy also states that "[t]he inventor shall cooperate fully with the University in all respects; to the evaluation of an invention, the preparation of the filing and prosecution of an application and the transfer of rights in the same as well as the maintenance and protection of any resultant patents." The policy compensates inventors with thirty percent of the net royalty income received after subtracting expenses incurred from the procuring and licensing of the patent rights.

In November 1992, VanVoorhies and Smith as co-inventors executed a patent application directed to the first invention. On February 5, 1993, they assigned all rights to that first invention, embodied in U.S. Patent Application 07/992,970, to WVU. The '970 application subsequently issued as U.S. Patent 5,442,369 on August 15, 1995. The written assignment ("'970 assignment") extended as well to all continuation-in-part ("CIP") applications relating to the invention, as follows:

> [T]he undersigned does (do) hereby sell, assign, transfer and set over unto said assignee, its successors and assigns, the entire right, title and interest in and to said invention or inventions, as described in the aforesaid application, in any form or embodiment thereof, and in and to the aforesaid application; . . . also the entire right, title and interest in and to any and all patents or reissues or extensions thereof to be obtained in this or any foreign country upon said invention or inventions and any divisional, continuation, *continuation-in-part* or substitute applications which may be filed upon said invention or inventions in this or any foreign country; and the undersigned hereby authorize(s) and request(s) the issuing authority to issue any and all patents on said application or applications to said assignee or its successors and assigns.

On December 29, 1993, VanVoorhies completed his dissertation and received his doctoral degree from WVU. VanVoorhies asserts that he then invented a half-wave bifilar contrawound toroidal helical antenna ("the second invention") during the short interval between receiving his Ph.D. and beginning his work as a Post Graduate Research Assistant Professor at WVU on February 1, 1994. In a letter dated October 6, 1994, VanVoorhies, who became a registered patent agent that same month, suggested that WVU file a CIP of the '970 application directed to the second invention. VanVoorhies later forwarded a preliminary invention disclosure to WVU's patent counsel on January 9, 1995, urging WVU to obtain patent protection on the invention.

However, when WVU sent VanVoorhies a patent application with a declaration and corresponding assignment, VanVoorhies did not respond. WVU nonetheless filed what became U.S. Patent Application 08/486,340 as a CIP of the '970 application on June 7, 1995, listing VanVoorhies as the sole inventor. The application was filed under 37 C.F.R. § 1.47(b), which permits a party with a sufficient interest in an invention to file a patent application when an inventor refuses to execute the application. The United States Patent and Trademark Office ("PTO") subsequently accepted the '340 application after evaluating WVU's entitlement to ownership of the application under the '970 assignment covering CIPs. *Id.* The '340 application issued as U.S. Patent 6,028,558 on February 22, 2000. A continuation of that application issued as U.S. Patent 6,204,821 on March 20, 2001.

On August 14, 1995, VanVoorhies filed U.S. Patent Application No. 08/514,609, also directed to the second invention, listing himself as the sole inventor. The '609 application, unlike the '340 application, was not designated as a CIP of the original '970 application. He assigned all interest in that application to VorteKx, P.C., of which he is the president and majority shareholder. The '609 application issued as U.S. Patent 5,734,353 on March 31, 1998. U.S. Patent 5,952,978 also issued from a continuation of the '609 application on September 14, 1999.

In June 1992, before the '970 application was filed, Smith incorporated Integral

Concepts, Inc. ("ICI"), a consulting business wholly owned by Smith. Smith's company obtained an exclusive license to the first invention from the licensing division of WVU, West Virginia University Research Corporation ("WVURC"), on April 12, 1994.

WVU sued VanVoorhies on August 14, 1997, alleging that VanVoorhies breached his duty to assign the second invention to WVU. VanVoorhies filed extensive counterclaims and a third-party complaint against WVURC, Smith and ICI. He also moved to disqualify WVU's counsel, the law firm of Eckert Seamans Cherin & Mellott ("Eckert"), asserting that Eckert had represented VanVoorhies in connection with the prosecution of the '970 application. The district court denied that motion, determining that "[n]one of the usual indicia of an attorney-client relationship are present in this case."

VanVoorhies further alleged claims for breach of fiduciary duty, breach of contract, and fraud, and sought a declaration of invalidity of the '970 assignment. The district court granted Smith, ICI, and WVURC's motions for summary judgment on each of those claims. The court granted WVU's motions for summary judgment on those claims with one exception: it denied summary judgment to WVU as to any contract breaches that might be developed by later discovery in the case. The court determined that VanVoorhies' contract claims based on WVU's patent policy were only relevant with respect to WVU, the party with whom VanVoorhies had actually contracted. As for the breach of fiduciary duty claims, the court rejected VanVoorhies' theory that Smith owed VanVoorhies a fiduciary duty by virtue of their professor-student relationship. The court concluded that VanVoorhies' fraud claims were barred by a two-year statute of limitations, and in any event would have found them insufficient on the merits. It also applied the doctrine of assignor estoppel and held for WVU on VanVoorhies' claim that the '970 assignment should be declared invalid.

The court also granted WVU's motions for summary judgment that VanVoorhies breached his duty to assign the '340 and '609 applications to WVU, concluding without discussion that the '340 application was a CIP of the '970 application and was therefore subject to the '970 assignment. Similarly, the court determined that VanVoorhies was obligated to assign the '609 application because it included the technology underlying the '340 application.

DISCUSSION

On appeal, VanVoorhies raises a whole array of issues. He first argues that the court erred in granting WVU's motion for summary judgment that he breached his duty to assign the '340 and '609 applications to WVU. Specifically, he argues that the '340 application was not properly designated as a CIP of the '970 application because it is directed to an independent and distinct invention, and that it is therefore not subject to the CIP provision of the '970 assignment. He further asserts that the '609 application is not subject to assignment to WVU under the patent policy because he conceived that invention and reduced it to practice while he was not associated with WVU.

VanVoorhies also asserts that the court erred in granting WVU summary judgment on his claims for fraud, breach of fiduciary duty, and breach of contract, as well as his claim that the '970 assignment should be declared invalid. Similarly, he argues that the court erred in dismissing his implied contract and RICO claims. Finally, apparently proceeding on the unsound assumption that the more issues raised, the better the chance for success, he argues that the court abused its discretion in denying his motions to disqualify WVU's counsel for dual representation, compel discovery, and vacate the stay of the consolidated *Vortekx* case.

WVU and the third-party defendants, WVURC, Smith, and ICI, respond that the court properly considered the '340 application to be a CIP of the '970 application and therefore subject to the '970 assignment. They also assert that the '609 application, which is directed to the same subject matter as the '340 application, is subject to assignment to WVU under WVU's patent policy. They further argue that: (1) the court did not err in granting summary judgment on his fraud claims because they are barred under the statute of limitations; (2) VanVoorhies has not shown that the professor-student relationship between Smith and VanVoorhies gave rise to a fiduciary duty on Smith's part; (3) VanVoorhies has not shown any facts to support his breach of contract claim; and (4) assignor estoppel precludes his claim that the '970 assignment is invalid. They also argue that the court properly dismissed his RICO and implied contract claims, and that it did not abuse its discretion in its decisions regarding disqualification of counsel, discovery, and the stay of the *Vortekx* case.

A. Assignment

We first address the question whether VanVoorhies was obligated to assign the '340 application to WVU under the '970 assignment. While questions of contract law are matters of state law, the issue here depends on the fact question as to whether the '340 application was a CIP of the '970 application. That is a question of patent law, which we interpret according to federal law.

The parties do not dispute that there are differences between the first and second inventions. Whereas the first invention of the '970 application is directed to toroidal antennas in which the helical winding is divided into an even number of circumferential segments and wound around two distinct and separate conductors, the second invention of the '340 application has a single conductor with a different arrangement of elements. Those differences, however, do not establish that the application on the second invention is not properly designated as a CIP of the first invention and thus not subject to the '970 assignment of CIPs.

A continuation-in-part application is just what its name implies. It partly continues subject matter disclosed in a prior application, but it adds new subject matter not disclosed in the prior application. Thus, some subject matter of a CIP application is necessarily different from the original subject matter. The '340 application falls within the MPEP's guidelines for CIPs because it repeats some of the subject matter of the '970 application and adds the use of a single semiconductor and a different arrangement of the elements. The '340 application also has a common inventor with the '970 application, VanVoorhies, it was filed during the pendency of that application, and it contains a specific reference to the earlier filed application. Moreover, the PTO accepted the '340 application for filing without the signature of the inventor under 37 C.F.R. § 1.47(b) after reviewing WVU's submissions asserting its ownership interest based on the '970 assignment covering CIPs. Finally, and compellingly, VanVoorhies himself, a patent agent with knowledge of patent law, suggested to WVU that the second invention be designated as a CIP, and his contrary argument now on appeal is not credible. Whether the '340 application is entitled to the priority date of the '970 application for common subject matter, which is the principal reason why one designates an application as a CIP, is a separate question which is not before us. The '340 application did, however, constitute a CIP. We therefore conclude that the district court did not err in determining that the '340 application was properly designated as a CIP of the '970 application. Because the '970 assignment expressly required VanVoorhies to assign all CIPs of the '970 application to WVU, we affirm the court's conclusion that VanVoorhies was required to assign the '340 CIP application to WVU, and that he breached his duty by refusing to do so.

We next address the question whether VanVoorhies was obligated to assign to WVU the '609 application, which was not designated as a CIP. The district court determined that he was obligated to make that assignment because the technology underlying the '609 application was the same as that in the '340 CIP application, which he had a duty to assign under the '970 agreement. Although the parties now agree that the '609 and '340 applications are directed to the same subject matter, we do not read the '970 assignment of "continuation-in-part" applications as necessarily requiring assignment of an application that embodies the same subject matter as a CIP but is not itself designated as a CIP. We will evaluate whether VanVoorhies was obligated to assign the '609 application on a different basis, *viz.*, WVU's patent policy.

VanVoorhies asserts that he was not obligated to assign the '609 application to WVU under its patent policy because the policy was merely an option for him to elect or reject, and moreover that he was not given a copy of the patent policy and was not informed that it applied to him "until before 1994." He also argues that the policy did not apply to him because he invented the subject matter of the '609 application during the short period of time between December 19, 1993, and February 1, 1994, when VanVoorhies was not directly affiliated with WVU as a student or professor.

WVU responds that VanVoorhies admitted that he executed the '970 assignment "with the understanding that in exchange he would enjoy the benefits of the West Virginia University Patent Policy pertaining to this specific invention." WVU also identifies several admissions by VanVoorhies showing that the second invention was invented while VanVoorhies was "University personnel" and thus subject to the patent policy.

We agree with WVU that VanVoorhies was indeed obligated to assign the '609 application under WVU's patent policy. That policy broadly applies to all "University personnel," which includes "all full-time and part-time members of the faculty and staff, and all other employees of the University including graduate and undergraduate students and fellows of the University." Under the policy, WVU owns all inventions that are made by University personnel or made with substantial use of University resources. The policy states nothing about WVU's ownership interest being subject to the election of University personnel. Thus, any inventions made by VanVoorhies pursuant to his graduate studies rightfully belong to WVU.

Moreover, VanVoorhies' claim that he was ignorant of the policy's application to him until 1994 is not supported by the evidence of record. Smith testified that he discussed the policy with VanVoorhies in June of 1991. VanVoorhies admitted that he assigned the '970 application to WVU under the policy, and he also assigned an unrelated patent, U.S. Patent 5,361,737, to WVU without objection.

The evidence is also clearly contrary to VanVoorhies' assertion that he was not affiliated with WVU and thus not subject to its patent policy when he conceived his second invention. VanVoorhies presents only a few unwitnessed, unbound log book pages from January of 1994 to support that claim. WVU has identified much more reliable evidence, including statements made by VanVoorhies himself under oath, showing that he conceived the invention while he was still a graduate student. For example, in a declaration in support of a motion early in this litigation, VanVoorhies stated that he "conceived the invention which is the subject of my U.S. Patent Application 08/514,609, during my individual research on my Federally copyrighted dissertation thesis in order to get my degree. Between August 1993 and January 1994, I reduced my conception, a Single Conductor Bifilar Contrawound Toroidal Helical Antenna, to practice." In addition, VanVoorhies declared in a protest to the PTO concerning the '340 application that "[a]t the time I conceived the instant invention, I was a non-teaching student." As VanVoorhies now concedes that the '340 and '609 applications were directed to the same subject matter, that statement is a further admission that his conception of the invention of the '609 application occurred while he was still affiliated with WVU as "University personnel." While we must view the evidence favorably to VanVoorhies, we conclude that the self-serving, uncorroborated log book entries do not create a genuine issue of material fact to preclude summary judgment in light of the overwhelming evidence and admissions that the invention was conceived while he was a student at the University. We therefore affirm the district court's grant of summary judgment that VanVoorhies breached his obligation to assign the '340 and '609 applications to WVU, and we affirm its order requiring him to execute an assignment of those applications and the issued patents based thereon.

B. Fraud

VanVoorhies asserts fraud in the following alleged scenario: Smith told VanVoorhies that he would be able to influence licensing decisions, VanVoorhies relied on those statements when he executed the '970 assignment, but Smith and WVU in fact secretly intended that WVU would license the invention to ICI. VanVoorhies also asserts that the court erred in finding that the fraud claims were untimely.

WVU argues that the court properly granted summary judgment on the merits because VanVoorhies did not present any evidence that he was promised that he could influence licensing decisions, and that the written assignment of his rights contradicts that assertion. WVU also argues that the fraud claims were barred under the applicable two-year statute of limitations.

We agree with WVU that the district court did not err in its determination that

VanVoorhies' fraud claims fail on the merits as a matter of law. Under West Virginia law, a claim for fraud may be established by proof that the defendant made a fraudulent statement, that it was material and false, and that the plaintiff justifiably relied on it and was thereby damaged. VanVoorhies has presented no evidence that the allegedly inducing statements were ever made, and indeed such evidence would contradict the written assignment of his entire rights in the invention and the patent policy that broadly gives discretion to WVU in licensing decisions. VanVoorhies had no right to influence licensing decisions regarding the applications he was obligated to assign to WVU. Because no reasonable fact-finder could decide for VanVoorhies on his fraud claim on the merits, we affirm the district court's grant of WVU's motion for summary judgment.

C. Fiduciary Duty

VanVoorhies argues that Smith and VanVoorhies had a relationship of trust concerning their inventions, and that Smith breached that trust by inducing VanVoorhies to list Smith as a co-inventor of the '970 application so that Smith could share in the revenues. He argues that WVU breached its fiduciary duty to him as his employer by misappropriating his invention rights. Smith responds that there is no fiduciary relationship between a professor and a student. WVU responds that the relationship between WVU and VanVoorhies concerning patent rights is fully set forth in the patent policy and the '970 assignment, and that nothing in those agreements indicates that WVU owed VanVoorhies any fiduciary duty.

We recently addressed a similar claim regarding the existence of a fiduciary duty between a professor and a student in *Chou*, 254 F.3d 1347, 59 USPQ2d 1257. In that case, Chou, a graduate student, alleged that her mentor-professor specifically told her that he would take care to properly protect her research and inventions, that she trusted him to do so, and that he breached the resulting fiduciary trust relationship by misappropriating her inventions for himself without her knowledge. The district court dismissed her allegations for failing to state a claim. We reversed. Assuming the truth of her allegations, as we were obligated to at that stage of the proceedings, we determined that Chou had adequately pleaded the existence of special circumstances of trust between herself and her professor under Illinois law, as well as a breach of that trust by her professor. We also held that she had stated a claim against the University for breach of fiduciary duty under the theory of *respondeat superior*.

In this case, the district court granted WVU, WVURC, ICI, and Smith's motions for summary judgment on VanVoorhies' breach of fiduciary duty claims because VanVoorhies had not cited any authority that a fiduciary duty existed between Smith and VanVoorhies. Although we concluded in *Chou* that Chou had sufficiently stated a claim for purposes of Illinois fiduciary duty law, we conclude in this case, which is at a further stage in the litigation, that VanVoorhies has not shown a genuine issue of material fact to support his fiduciary duty claim under West Virginia law.

A fiduciary duty arises when a person assumes a duty to act for another's benefit, while subordinating his or her own personal interest to that other person. Even if, viewing the evidence favorably to VanVoorhies, we were to conclude that such a relationship of trust existed between VanVoorhies and Smith — a determination that we do not make — VanVoorhies did not present any evidence that Smith breached that trust by inducing VanVoorhies to list Smith as a co-inventor of the first invention. VanVoorhies was at all times aware of the patenting and inventorship decisions being made regarding the first invention, and he participated in and acceded in those decisions by jointly signing the '970 application and assignment with Smith, whom he knew would be entitled to a share of the proceeds under the patent policy. We therefore conclude that his breach of fiduciary claim against Smith was properly resolved by summary judgment, because VanVoorhies has not introduced sufficient evidence to establish an essential element of his claim, *viz.*, a breach of the purported fiduciary duty, on which he would bear the burden of proof at trial.

Similarly, his fiduciary duty claim against WVU must fail. WVU cannot be liable under the theory of *respondeat superior* if the claims against Smith are insufficient as a matter of law, and we agree with WVU that the relationship between WVU and VanVoorhies as set forth in the assignment and patent policy does not establish any fiduciary duty on WVU's part. We therefore affirm the court's grant of summary judgment on VanVoorhies' breach of fiduciary duty claims.

E. Invalidity of Assignment

VanVoorhies argues that if he prevails on his fraud and breach of contract claims, the '970 assignment should be declared invalid. He also argues that WVU and Smith's inequitable conduct in the PTO provide an independent basis for declaring that assignment invalid. WVU responds that the district court properly granted summary judgment on this issue because assignor estoppel bars VanVoorhies' challenge to the assignment's validity.

WVU misconstrues the doctrine of assignor estoppel, which is an equitable doctrine designed to prevent the injustice that would be suffered by an assignee if an assignor who assigned a patent later devalues it by raising defenses of patent invalidity. While the doctrine precludes challenges to the validity of a patent itself, it does not preclude challenges to the validity of a contract assigning the patent. Estopping an assignor from challenging the patent it has assigned is based on the evident unfairness of one receiving compensation for the transfer of an asset and then asserting that the asset has no value. There is no corresponding unfairness in a challenge to the validity of a contract. VanVoorhies in fact does not repudiate the value of what he assigned to WVU and thereby violate fair-dealing principles. On the contrary, he asserts that the patents are indeed valuable and that WVU has forfeited any rights to them because of false statements that WVU and Smith allegedly made to the PTO.

Although we agree with VanVoorhies that assignor estoppel does not preclude a challenge to the validity of the assignment, we conclude that VanVoorhies has failed to present a plausible legal basis for such a challenge. VanVoorhies principally asserts that "he may avoid the assignment, or be excused from performing thereunder" if he prevails on his fraud and breach of contract claims. He has not so prevailed. Furthermore, to the extent that inequitable conduct in the PTO were proved, it would only preclude enforcement of the patent, but would not affect WVU's right to the patent as against VanVoorhies. Moreover, because a determination of inequitable conduct would result in the patent being unenforceable, that result is inconsistent with VanVoorhies' claim that he is entitled to ownership of an enforceable patent. We therefore affirm the court's grant of summary judgment in favor of WVU on VanVoorhies' claim that the assignment should be declared invalid.

H. Disqualification of Counsel

VanVoorhies argues that the court abused its discretion in dismissing his motion to disqualify WVU's counsel, Arnold Silverman and the Eckert firm, because of their alleged representation of VanVoorhies in prosecuting the '970 application in his name. He asserts that he made confidential disclosures to Silverman for the purpose of obtaining legal advice in prosecuting the '970 patent application, and that Silverman and the Eckert firm should therefore be prohibited from representing WVU in substantially the same matter.

WVU responds that the mere act of prosecuting a patent application in the name of the inventor, as required under 35 U.S.C. § 111, does not establish an attorney-client relationship. WVU also argues that VanVoorhies' disclosures were made pursuant to his obligations under the '970 assignment, and that VanVoorhies did not seek legal advice in his communications.

We agree with WVU that the court did not abuse its discretion in dismissing VanVoorhies' motion to disqualify WVU's counsel. VanVoorhies was required under the '970 assignment to provide technical information and execute necessary documents for prosecution of the patent application. The Eckert firm was thus representing WVU when it dealt with VanVoorhies. It prosecuted the application in his (and Smith's) name, as required by law. That act did not give rise to an attorney-client relationship between WVU's counsel and VanVoorhies and thus require disqualification when WVU and VanVoorhies became adverse parties. The attorney-client privilege does not attach absent an attorney-client relationship, which VanVoorhies has not demonstrated. Finally, we note that VanVoorhies' own statements to an attorney at Eckert belie his arguments concerning the existence of an attorney-client relationship: "I realize that I am not your client, and that it is not your duty to look out for my rights." We therefore conclude that the district court did not abuse its discretion in dismissing VanVoorhies' disqualification motion.

CONCLUSION

Because VanVoorhies breached his duty to assign the '340 and '609 applications to WVU, we affirm the district court's grant of summary judgment and its final order directing VanVoorhies to fulfill his various obligations, including assignment of those applications and the patents based thereon. We also affirm the court's grant of summary judgment on VanVoorhies' claims of fraud, breach of fiduciary duty, breach of contract, and invalid assignment, as well as its grant of WVU's motions to dismiss the quasi-contract and RICO claims. We therefore

AFFIRM.

QUESTIONS

1.   VanVoorhies received his Ph.D. on 12/29/1993 and began teaching at WVU as a post-graduate research assistant professor on 2/1/1994. VanVoorhies claims to have reduced his second invention to practice between the time he received his Ph.D. and the time he started work as an assistant professor. Why did the court reject VanVoorhies' claimed date of invention?

2.   What difference did it make whether the '340 patent application was a continuation-in-part of the '970 patent application? What difference did it make whether the '609 patent application filed by VanVoorhies himself as the sole inventor was directed toward the same invention as the '340 patent application?

3.   If the '340 patent application was a continuation-in-part of the '970 patent application and the '609 patent application was directed toward the same invention as the '340 patent application, why did WVU believe it was necessary to demand assignment of the '609 patent application?

4.   How was WVU able to file the '340 patent application without an assignment from VanVoorhies as a co-inventor?

5.   VanVoorhies' claims against WVU included fraud, breach of fiduciary duty, breach of contract, invalidity of assignment and RICO claims. What do you make of Judge Lourie's statement that VanVoorhies "apparently proceeding on the unsound assumption that the more issues raised, the better the chance for success, . . . argues that the court abused its discretion in denying his motions to disqualify WVU's counsel for dual representation, compel discovery, and vacate the stay of the consolidated *Vortekx* case"?

6.   universities' claim of ownership of student intellectual property is very different, at least in one respect, from universities' claim of ownership of faculty intellectual property; in the case of students, the students are very often paying the university tuition; in the case of faculty, the university is almost always paying the faculty salary. Can you list the various circumstances under which students at a university might create intellectual property? Under which of these circumstances do you think the student-created intellectual property should be owned by the universities and under which of these circumstances do you think the student-created intellectual property should be owned by the students?

CASE NOTES

1.   Petr Taborsky was employed as an undergraduate research assistant at the University of South Florida (USF). USF entered into a sponsored research agreement with Progress Waters Technologies (PWT) to provide research in the area of municipal wastewater management and treatment. Taborsky was assigned to work on the PWT research project and signed a confidentiality agreement with PWT under which he agreed not to use information resulting from the research without PWT's consent and to return all documents relating to the research project to PWT at the end of the research project. The research project focused on the use of clinoptilolite, a clay-like substance akin to kitty litter, as a filter in sewage treatment plants. The initial research failed to yield any useful results. Taborsky,

however, working on his own and claiming to have worked nights and slept on the laboratory floor, discovered that heating clinoptilolite to 850° F increased its ability to absorb the kind of contaminants found in waste water.

Following a Christmas vacation break, Taborsky left USF and never returned. He took with him lab notebooks containing information regarding the research project and his discovery. When Taborsky refused to return the lab notebooks and provide information on his discovery, USF filed criminal charges against him, and he was convicted of one count of second-degree grand theft and one count of theft of trade secrets. Taborsky was sentenced to one year of house arrest, fifteen years probation and 500 hours of community service. As a condition of his probation, Taborsky was prohibited from using the stolen research for any purpose.

While on probation, Taborsky applied for and was issued a patent that related to the research done at USF. Florida moved to revoke his probation, and he was sentenced to three-and-one-half years incarceration and fifteen years probation. USF then filed a civil action against Taborsky seeking to enjoin him from using the clinoptilolite research. USF claimed that Taborsky's criminal conviction collaterally estopped him from contesting the civil injunction suit. The court upheld USF's claim. *See* Board of Regents of the State of Florida v. Taborsky, 648 So.2d 748 (1994). For more background on the Taborsky saga, *See*, Ron Grossman, *Patently Unfair: Researcher Scoops World with Discovery, Ends up on Chain Gang*, CHI. TRIB., Mar. 21, 1997, at 1.

Additional Information

1. K. J. Nordheden & M. H. Hoeflich, *Undergraduate Research & Intellectual Property Rights*, 6 KAN. J.L. & PUB. POL'Y 34 (1997).

2. Sean B. Seymore, *My Patent, Your Patent, or Our Patent? Inventorship Disputes within Academic Research Groups*, 16 ALB. L.J. SCI. & TECH. 125 (2005-2006).

3. Sandip H. Patel, *Graduate Students' Ownership and Attribution Rights in Intellectual Property*, 71 IND. L.J. 481 (1996).

3.3.4   University Licensing Policies

University licensing policies are the subject of considerable controversy today. Universities, individually and through AUTM, claim that university licensing policies contribute to a "better world" while at the same time providing universities with critical revenue to support future research and education. Others, including the Kauffman Foundation and a recent New York State Task Force on Industry-Higher Education Partnerships, take a different view of university licensing policies.

In the January-February 2010 issue of the Harvard Business Review, two Kauffman Foundation researchers, Lesa Mitchell and Robert Litan, claim that university technology transfer policies are an obstacle to innovation and economic growth in the United States. According to Mitchell and Litan, university technology transfer offices, formed in the wake of the Bayh-Dole Act, have become monopolies causing vital discoveries to languish in university labs and slowing the diffusion of new technologies into society.

In a similar vein, the Task Force on Diversifying the New York State Economy through Industry-Higher Education Partnerships found that New York university technology transfer policies have sought to maximize licensing revenue at the expense of collaborating with businesses to promote economic development and the creation of new jobs. The Task Force also found that New York Universities have fallen short of their potential to support the launch of new companies.

Despite the disagreement over the effectiveness of university technology transfer policies, all parties recognize that university research is central to scientific advancement and economic growth in our society. The white paper below, endorsed by some of the leading research universities in the country, purports to set forth a list of university licensing best practices. The universities that have endorsed the white paper include California Institute of Technology; Cornell University; Harvard University; Massachusetts Institute of Technology; Stanford University; University of California; University of Illinois, Chicago; University of Illinois, Urbana-Champaign; University of Washington; Wisconsin Alumni Research Foundation; Yale University; and Association of American Medical Colleges (AAMC).

IN THE PUBLIC INTEREST: NINE POINTS TO CONSIDER IN LICENSING UNIVERSITY TECHNOLOGY

Licensing approaches, even for comparable technologies, can vary considerably from case to case and from institution to institution based on circumstances particular to each specific invention, business opportunity, licensee and university. In spite of this uniqueness, universities share certain core values that can and should be maintained to the fullest extent possible in all technology transfer agreements.

In the summer of 2006, Stanford University's then Dean of Research Arthur Bienenstock convened a small meeting of research officers, licensing directors and a representative from the Association of American Medical Colleges to brainstorm about important societal, policy, legislative and other issues in university technology transfer. Representatives of the participating institutions have tried to capture in this document certain shared perspectives that emerged from that meeting. Recognizing that each license is subject to unique influences that render "cookie-cutter" solutions insufficient, it is our aim in releasing this paper to encourage our colleagues in the academic technology transfer profession to analyze each licensing opportunity individually in a manner that reflects the business needs and values of their institution, but at the same time, to the extent appropriate, also to bear in mind the concepts articulated herein when crafting agreements with industry. We recognize that many of these points are already being practiced. In the end, we hope to foster thoughtful approaches and encourage creative solutions to complex problems that may arise when universities license technologies in the public interest and for society's benefit.

Point 1

Universities should reserve the right to practice licensed inventions and to allow other non-profit and governmental organizations to do so.

In the spirit of preserving the ability of all universities to perform research, ensuring that researchers are able to publish the results of their research in dissertations and peer-reviewed journals and that other scholars are able to verify published results without concern for patents, universities should consider reserving rights in all fields of use, even if the invention is licensed exclusively to a commercial entity, for themselves and other non-profit and governmental organizations:

(1) to practice inventions and to use associated information and data for research and educational purposes, including research sponsored by commercial entities; and

(2) to transfer tangible research materials (e.g., biological materials and chemical compounds) and intangible materials (e.g., computer software, databases and know-how) to others in the non-profit and governmental sectors.

Point 2

Exclusive licenses should be structured in a manner that encourages technology development and use.

When significant investment of time and resources in a technology are needed in order to achieve its broad implementation, an exclusive license often is necessary and appropriate. However, it is important that technology transfer offices be aware of the potential impact that the exclusive license might have on further research, unanticipated uses, future commercialization efforts and markets. Universities need to be mindful of the impact of granting overly broad exclusive rights and should strive to grant just those rights necessary to encourage development of the technology.

Special consideration should be given to the impact of an exclusive license on uses of a technology that may not be appreciated at the time of initial licensing. A license grant that encompasses all fields of use for the life of the licensed patent(s) may have negative consequences if the subject technology is found to have unanticipated utility. This possibility is particularly troublesome if the licensee is not able or willing to develop the technology in fields outside of its core business. Universities are encouraged to use approaches that balance a licensee's legitimate commercial needs against the university's goal (based on its educational and charitable mission and the public interest) of ensuring broad practical application of the fruits of its research programs.

In situations where an exclusive license is warranted, it is important that licensees commit to diligently develop the technology to protect against a licensee that is unable or unwilling to move an innovation forward. In long-term exclusive licenses, diligent development should be well-defined and regularly monitored during the exclusive term of the agreement and should promote the development and broad dissemination of the licensed technology. Ideally, objective, time-limited performance milestones are set, with termination or non-exclusivity (subject to limited, but reasonable, cure provisions) as the penalty for breach of the diligence obligation.

Another means of ensuring diligent development, often used in conjunction with milestones, is to require exclusive licensees to grant sublicenses to third parties to address unmet market or public health needs ("mandatory sublicensing") and/or to diligently commercialize new applications of the licensed rights. Such a requirement could also be implemented through a reserved right of the licensor to grant direct licenses within the scope of the exclusive grant to third parties based on unmet need. In such situations, it is important to ensure that the parties have a common understanding of what constitutes a new application or unmet need for the purpose of implementing such a provision.

Absent the need for a significant investment — such as to optimize a technology for wide use — broad, non-exclusive licensing of tools such as genomic and proteomic inventions can help maximize the benefits derived from those technologies, in part by removing obstacles to further innovation. Unlike most research tools or manufacturing methods, diagnostic tests often must go through the regulatory approval process, and so may warrant exclusive licensing when the costs of test development, approval or diffusion require substantial investment of capital.

Nevertheless, licensing of diagnostic tests based on broadly applicable genomics or proteomics methods should strive to preserve sufficient flexibility to permit testing for multiple indications (i.e., not an exclusive licensee's single disease of interest) perhaps through multiple field-restricted or nonexclusive licenses. Exclusive licensing of a single gene for a diagnostic may be counterproductive in a multi-gene pathology where only a panel of genes can yield an adequate diagnosis, unless the licensee has access to the other genes of the panel. Such licenses can also be limited in other ways. For example, a university might license a genomics method exclusively for a company to optimize and sell licensed products for diagnostic use. The drafting of the exclusive grant could make it clear that the license is exclusive for the sale, but not use, of such products; in doing so, the university ensures that it is free to license non-exclusively to others the right (or may simply not assert its rights) to use the patented technology, which they may do either using products purchased from the exclusive licensee or those that they make in-house for their own use.

In general, when no alternative testing strategy is available for a given indication, consideration should be given to means of ensuring reasonable access for patients and shielding individual healthcare providers from the risk of suit for patent infringement. As with any medical technology, licenses should not hinder clinical research, professional education and training, use by public health authorities, independent validation of test results or quality verification and/or control.

Point 3

Strive to minimize the licensing of "future improvements."

Although licensees often seek guaranteed access to future improvements on licensed inventions, the obligation of such future inventions may effectively enslave a faculty member's research program to the company, thereby exerting a chilling effect on their ability to receive corporate and other research funding and to engage in productive collaborations with scientists employed by companies other than the licensee — perhaps even to collaborate with other academic scientists. In particular, if such future rights reach to inventions made elsewhere in the university, researchers who did not benefit from the licensing of the original invention may have their opportunities restricted as well, and may be disadvantaged economically relative to the original inventors if the licensing office has pre-committed their inventions to a licensee.

For these reasons, exclusive licensees should not automatically receive rights to "improvement" or "follow-on" inventions. Instead, as a matter of course, licensed rights should be limited to existing patent applications and patents, and only to those claims in any continuing patent applications that are (i) fully supported by information in an identified, existing patent application or patent and (ii) entitled to the priority date of that application or patent.

In the rare case where a licensee is granted rights to improvement patents, it is critical to limit the scope of the grant so that it does not impact uninvolved researchers and does not extend indefinitely into the future. It is important to further restrict the grant of improvements to inventions that are owned and controlled by the licensor institution — i.e., (i) not made by the inventor at another institution, should they move on or (ii) co-owned with, or controlled by, another party. One refinement to this strategy would be to limit the license to inventions that are dominated by the original licensed patents, as these could not be meaningfully licensed to a third party, at least within the first licensee's exclusive field. As was discussed earlier, appropriate field restrictions enable the licensing not only of the background technology, but also of improvements, to third parties for use outside the initial licensee's core business. In all cases, a license to improvements should be subject to appropriate diligent development requirements.

It should be recognized, however, that not all "improvements" have commercial potential (for example, they may not confer sufficient additional benefit over the existing technology to merit the expense of the development of new or modified products), in which case a licensee might not wish to develop them. In general, it may be best simply not to patent such improvements.

Point 4

Universities should anticipate and help to manage technology transfer related conflicts of interest.

Technology transfer offices should be particularly conscious and sensitive about their roles in the identification, review and management of conflicts of interest, both at the investigator and institutional levels. Licensing to a start-up founded by faculty, student or other university inventors raises the potential for conflicts of interest; these conflicts should be properly reviewed and managed by academic and administrative officers and committees outside of the technology transfer office. A technology licensing professional ideally works in an open and collegial manner with those directly responsible for oversight of conflicts of interest so as to ensure that potential conflicts arising from licensing arrangements are reviewed and managed in a way that reflects well on their university and its community. Ideally, the university has an administrative channel and reporting point whereby potential conflicts can be non-punitively reported and discussed, and through which consistent decisions are made in a timely manner.

Point 5

Ensure broad access to research tools.

Consistent with the NIH Guidelines on Research Tools, principles set forth by various charitable foundations that sponsor academic research programs and by the mission of the typical university to advance scientific research, universities are expected to make research tools as broadly available as possible. Such an approach is in keeping with the policies of numerous peer-reviewed scientific journals, on which the scientific enterprise depends as much as it does on the receipt of funding: in order to publish research results, scientists must agree to make unique resources (e.g., novel antibodies, cell lines, animal models, chemical compounds) available to others for verification of their published data and conclusions.

Through a blend of field-exclusive and non-exclusive licenses, research tools may be licensed appropriately, depending on the resources needed to develop each particular invention, the licensee's needs and the public good. As suggested with respect to genomics and proteomics method patents in Point 2 above, a university might license a research reagent, kit or device exclusively to a company to optimize and sell licensed products and services for research, diagnostic or other end uses. The drafting of such an exclusive grant should make clear that the license is exclusive for the sale, but not use, of such products and services; in doing so, the university ensures that it is free to license non-exclusively to others the right to use the patented technology, which they may do either using products purchased from the exclusive licensee or those that they make in-house for their own use.

Point 6

Enforcement action should be carefully considered.

In considering enforcement of their intellectual property, it is important that universities be mindful of their primary mission to use patents to promote technology development for the benefit of society. All efforts should be made to reach a resolution that benefits both sides and promotes the continuing expansion and adoption of new technologies. Litigation is seldom the preferred option for resolving disputes.

However, after serious consideration, if a university still decides to initiate an infringement lawsuit, it should be with a clear, mission-oriented rationale for doing so-one that can be clearly articulated both to its internal constituencies and to the public. Ideally, the university's decision to litigate is based on factors that closely track the reasons for which universities obtain and license patents in the first place, as set out elsewhere in this paper. Examples might include:

(1) Contractual or ethical obligation to protect the rights of existing licensees to enjoy the benefits conferred by their licenses; and

(2) Blatant disregard on the part of the infringer for the university's legitimate rights in availing itself of patent protection, as evidenced by refusal on the part of the infringer to negotiate with or otherwise entertain a reasonable offer of license terms.

Under all circumstances, it reflects poorly on universities to be involved in "nuisance suits." Exclusive licensees should be encouraged to approach patent enforcement in a manner that is consistent with the philosophy described in this Point 6.

Point 7

Be mindful of export regulations.

University technology transfer offices should have a heightened sensitivity about export laws and regulations and how these bodies of law could affect university licensing practices. Licensing "proprietary information" or "confidential information" can affect the "fundamental research exclusion" (enunciated by the various export regulations) enjoyed by most university research, so the use of appropriate language is particularly important. Diligence in ensuring that technology license transactions comply with federal export control laws helps to safeguard the continued ability of technology transfer offices to serve the public interest.

Point 8

Be mindful of the implications of working with patent aggregators.

As is true of patents generally, the majority of university-owned patents are unlicensed. With increasing frequency, university technology transfer offices are approached by parties who wish to acquire rights in such "overstock" in order to commercialize it through further licenses. These patent aggregators typically work under one of two models: the "added value" model and the so-called "patent troll" model.

Under the added value model, the primary licensee assembles a portfolio of patents related to a particular technology. In doing so, they are able to offer secondary licensees a complete package that affords them freedom to operate under patents perhaps obtained from multiple sources. As universities do not normally have the resources to identify and in-license relevant patents of importance, they cannot offer others all of the rights that may control practice (and, consequently, commercialization) of university inventions. By consolidating rights in patents that cover foundational technologies and later improvements, patent aggregators serve an important translational function in the successful development of new technologies and so exert a positive force toward commercialization. For example, aggregation of patents by venture capital groups regularly results in the establishment of corporate entities that focus on the development of new technologies, including those that arise from university research programs. To ensure that the potential benefits of patent aggregation actually are realized, however, license agreements, both primary and secondary, should contain terms (for example, time-limited diligence requirements) that are consistent with the university's overarching goal of delivering useful products to the public.

In contrast to patent aggregators who add value through technology-appropriate bundling of intellectual property rights, there are also aggregators (the "patent trolls") who acquire rights that cut broadly across one or more technological fields with no real intention of commercializing the technologies. In the extreme case, this kind of aggregator approaches companies with a large bundle of patent rights with the expectation that they license the entire package on the theory that any company that operates in the relevant field(s) must be infringing at least one of the hundreds, or even thousands, of included patents. Daunted by the prospect of committing the human and financial resources needed to perform due diligence sufficient to establish their freedom to operate under each of the bundled patents, many companies in this situation will conclude that they must pay for a license that they may not need. Unlike the original patent owner, who has created the technology and so is reasonably entitled to some economic benefit in recognition for its innovative contribution, the commercial licensee who advances the technology prior to sublicensing, or the added value aggregator who helps overcome legal barriers to product development, the kind of aggregator described in this paragraph typically extracts payments in the absence of any enhancement to the licensed technology. Without delving more deeply into the very real issues of patent misuse and bad-faith dealing by such aggregators, suffice it to say that universities would better serve the public interest by ensuring appropriate use of their technology by requiring their licensees to operate under a business model that encourages commercialization and does not rely primarily on threats of infringement litigation to generate revenue.

A somewhat related issue is that of technology "flipping," wherein a non-aggregator licensee of a university patent engages in sublicensing without having first advanced the technology, thereby increasing product development costs, potentially jeopardizing eventual product release and availability. This problem can be addressed most effectively by building positive incentives into the license agreement for the licensee to advance the licensed technology itself — e.g., design instrumentation, perform hit-to-lead optimization, file an IND. Such an incentive might be to decrease the percentage of sublicense revenues due to the university as the licensee meets specific milestones.

Point 9

Consider including provisions that address unmet needs, such as those of neglected patient populations or geographic areas, giving particular attention to improved therapeutics, diagnostics and agricultural technologies for the developing world.

Universities have a social compact with society. As educational and research institutions, it is our responsibility to generate and transmit knowledge, both to our students and the wider society. We have a specific and central role in helping to advance knowledge in many fields and to manage the deployment of resulting innovations for the public benefit. In no field is the importance of doing so clearer than it is in medicine.

Around the world millions of people are suffering and dying from preventable or curable diseases. The failure to prevent or treat disease has many causes. We have a responsibility to try to alleviate it, including finding a way to share the fruits of what we learn globally, at sustainable and affordable prices, for the benefit of the world's poor. There is an increased awareness that responsible licensing includes consideration of the needs of people in developing countries and members of other underserved populations.

The details involved in any agreement provisions attempting to address this issue are complex and will require expert planning and careful negotiation. The application will vary in different contexts. The principle, however, is simple. Universities should strive to construct licensing arrangements in ways that ensure that these underprivileged populations have low- or no-cost access to adequate quantities of these medical innovations.

We recognize that licensing initiatives cannot solve the problem by themselves. Licensing techniques alone, without significant added funding, can, at most, enhance access to medicines for which there is demand in wealthier countries. Diseases that afflict only the global poor have long suffered from lack of investment in research and development: the prospects of profit do not exist to draw commercial development, and public funding for diseases suffered by those who live far away from nations that can afford it is difficult to obtain and sustain. Through thoughtful management and licensing of intellectual property, however, drugs, therapies, and agricultural technologies developed at universities can at least help to alleviate suffering from disease or hunger in historically marginalized population groups.

Summary

As often is the case, guidance as to implementation of practices that will advance the mission of university technology transfer lags behind our collective awareness of both the needs that exist and our obligations to foster an environment in which they can effectively be met. While we may generally agree on the commonality of the above challenges, a multiplicity of approaches are possible to address the dual goals of nurturing future research and using the innovations of university research to provide the broadest possible benefit to the public. The participating universities put forth these considerations in an aspirational sense and we encourage all of our colleagues to stretch the boundaries of conventional technology transfer practice and share with the greater technology transfer community the insights that they gain in doing so.

[Examples of these nine point are provided in an Appendix which has been omitted.]

QUESTIONS

1. Which of the nine points do you think industry would find the most objectionable? Why?

2. Does the Bayh-Dole Act require that university licensees actively pursue the development and use of licensed, federally funded, technology?

3. What is the concern with licensing "future improvements" to a licensed technology? How does the fact that "future improvements" are included in a continuation-in-part patent application, or that they include some of the claims of the initially licensed patent, bear on this concern?

4. What is the purpose of granting an exclusive license to sell a research tool, but not the exclusive right to use the research tool?

5. What is the concern with licensing patent aggregators who do not add value to the licensed technology? What is the concern with licensees "flipping" the licensed technology?

Additional Information

1. University of Texas, License Review and License Checklist, available at http://www.utsystem.edu/ogc/intellectualproperty/lcreview.htm.

2. Cornell University, Sample License Agreement, available at http://www.cctec.cornell.edu/forms/p/Invention%20License%20Web%20200 80116.pdf.

3. University of Iowa, Sample License Agreement, available at http://research.uiowa.edu/uirf/pages/universal/forms-and-sample-agreements.html.

4. University of California, Irvine, Summary Terms for a Technology Licensing Agreement, available at http://www.ota.uci.edu/forms/Tech_license.pdf.

5. Harvard University, Policy Statement Regarding Application of Harvard University's Conflict of Interest Policies to the Granting of Licenses, available at http://www.techtransfer.harvard.edu/resources/policies/conflict/

6. Donna Bobrowicz, *A Checklist for Negotiating License Agreements*, in INTELLECTUAL PROPERTY HANDBOOK, ch. 11.11, *available at* http://www.iphandbook.org/handbook/chPDFs/ch11/ipHandbook-Ch%2011%2011%20Bobrowicz%20Licensing%20Check-list.pdf

7. BethLynn Maxwell, et. al., *Overview of Licensing Technology From Universities*, 762 PLI/PAT 507 (2003).

8. Sergio Garcia, et. al., *University Licensing: An Introduction to Licensing Technology From Universities*, 11 No. 1 CYBERSPACE LAW. 6 (2006).

9. Behfar Bastani, et. al., *Technology Transfer in Nanotechnology: Licensing Intellectual Property From Universities to Industry*, 1 NANOTECHNOLOGY L. & BUS. 166 (2004).

10. Louis Berneman & Kathleen Denis, *University Licensing Trends and Intellectual Capital*, 718 PLI/PAT 551 (2002).

11. Mary M. Styer, Jack Kerrigan, Andy Lustig, *A Guide through the Labyrinth: Evaluating and Negotiating a University Technology Transfer Deal*, 11 B.U. J. SCI. & TECH. L. 221 (2005).

12. 3 STEVEN Z. SZCZEPANSKI & DAVID EPSTEIN, ECKSTROM'S LICENSING IN FOR. & DOM. OPS. § 11:30; § 11:30.50 (2010).

3.4   UNIVERSITY PATENT ENFORCEMENT

Point 6 in the "Nine Points to Consider" white paper above deals with patent infringement actions brought by universities. It states:

> In considering enforcement of their intellectual property, it is important that universities be mindful of their primary mission to use patents to promote technology development for the benefit of society. All efforts should be made to reach a resolution that benefits both sides and promotes the continuing expansion and adoption of new technologies. Litigation is seldom the preferred option for resolving disputes.

> However, after serious consideration, if a university still decides to initiate an infringement lawsuit, it should be with a clear, mission-oriented rationale for doing so-one that can be clearly articulated both to its internal constituencies and to the public. Ideally, the university's decision to litigate is based on factors that closely track the reasons for which universities

obtain and license patents in the first place, as set out elsewhere in this paper. Examples might include:

• Contractual or ethical obligation to protect the rights of existing licensees to enjoy the benefits conferred by their licenses; and

• Blatant disregard on the part of the infringer for the university's legitimate rights in availing itself of patent protection, as evidenced by refusal on the part of the infringer to negotiate with or otherwise entertain a reasonable offer of license terms.

Under all circumstances, it reflects poorly on universities to be involved in "nuisance suits." Exclusive licensees should be encouraged to approach patent enforcement in a manner that is consistent with the philosophy described in this Point 6.

As you read the *University of Rochester* and *Columbia* cases below, consider whether these patent infringement suits would meet the guidelines set forth in Point 6.

UNIVERSITY OF ROCHESTER v. G.D. SEARL
358 F.3D 916 (Fed. Cir. 2004)

LOURIE, CIRCUIT JUDGE.

The University of Rochester ("Rochester") appeals from the decision of the United States District Court for the Western District of New York granting summary judgment that United States Patent 6,048,850 is invalid. Because we conclude that the court did not err in holding the '850 patent invalid for failing to comply with the written description requirement, and in granting summary judgment on that ground, we affirm.

BACKGROUND

Traditional non-steroidal anti-inflammatory drugs ("NSAIDs") such as aspirin, ibuprofen, ketoprofen, and naproxen are believed to function by inhibiting the activity of enzymes called cyclooxygenases. Cyclooxygenases catalyze the production of a molecule called prostaglandin H2, which is a precursor for other prostaglandins that perform various functions in the human body.

In the early 1990s, scientists discovered the existence and separate functions of two distinct cyclooxygenases, referred to as "COX-1" and "COX-2." COX-1 is expressed (*i.e.*, produced biologically) in the gastrointestinal tract, where it is involved in the production of prostaglandins that serve a beneficial role by, for example, providing protection for the stomach lining. COX-2 is expressed in response to inflammatory stimuli, and is thought to be responsible for the inflammation associated with diseases such as arthritis. It is now known that the traditional NSAIDs inhibit both COX-1 and COX-2, and as a result they not only reduce inflammation, but also can cause undesirable side effects such as stomach upset, irritation, ulcers, and bleeding.

After the separate functions of COX-1 and COX-2 were discovered, it was hypothesized that it would be possible to reduce inflammation without gastrointestinal side effects if a method could be found for selectively inhibiting the activity of COX-2 (*i.e.*, inhibiting the activity of COX-2 without inhibiting COX-1 activity). To that end, Rochester scientists developed a screening assay for use in determining whether a particular drug displayed such selectivity, and filed a U.S. patent application directed to their developments in 1992. After filing a series of continuation, continuation-in-part, and divisional applications derived from that 1992 application, the scientists eventually received United States Patent 5,837,479 in 1998, covering methods "for identifying a compound that inhibits prostaglandin synthesis catalyzed by mammalian prostaglandin H synthase-2 (PGHS-2)."

From a division of the application that led to the '479 patent, the scientists also obtained, on April 11, 2000, the '850 patent. The '850 patent contains three independent claims and five dependent claims. The three independent claims read as follows:

1. A method for selectively inhibiting PGHS-2 activity in a human host, comprising administering a non-steroidal compound that selectively inhibits activity of the PGHS-2 gene product to a human host in need of such treatment.

5. A method for selectively inhibiting PGHS-2 activity in a human host, comprising administering a non-steroidal compound that selectively inhibits activity of the PGHS-2 gene product in a human host in need of such treatment, wherein the activity of the non-steroidal compound does not result in significant toxic side effects in the human host.

6. A method for selectively inhibiting PGHS-2 activity in a human host, comprising administering a non-steroidal compound that selectively inhibits activity of the PGHS 2 gene product in a human host in need of such treatment, wherein the ability of the non-steroidal compound to selectively inhibit the activity of the PGHS-2 gene product is determined by:

a) contacting a genetically engineered cell that expresses human PGHS-2, and not human PGHS-1, with the compound for 30 minutes, and exposing the cell to a pre-determined-amount of arachidonic acid;

b) contacting a genetically engineered cell that expresses human PGHS-1, and not human PGHS-2, with the compound for 30 minutes, and exposing the cell to a pre-determined amount of arachidonic acid;

c) measuring the conversion of arachidonic acid to its prostaglandin metabolite; and

d) comparing the amount of the converted arachidonic acid converted by each cell exposed to the compound to the amount of the arachidonic acid converted by control cells that were not exposed to the compound, so that the compounds that inhibit PGHS-2 and not PGHS-1 activity are identified.

Thus, all eight claims are directed to methods "for selectively inhibiting PGHS-2 activity in a human host" by "administering a non-steroidal compound that selectively inhibits activity of the PGHS-2 gene product to [or in] a human host in need of such treatment."

On the day the '850 patent issued, Rochester sued G.D. Searle & Co., Inc., Monsanto Co., Pharmacia Corp., and Pfizer Inc. (collectively, "Pfizer"), alleging that Pfizer's sale of its COX-2 inhibitors Celebrex® and Bextra® for treatment of inflammation infringed the '850 patent, and seeking injunctive and monetary relief. In May 2002, Pfizer moved for summary judgment of invalidity of the '850 patent for failure to comply with the written description and enablement requirements of 35 U.S.C. § 112. Rochester opposed the motion and filed a cross-motion for summary judgment with respect to the written description issue.

In evaluating the parties' motions, the district court found that, although all of the claims require the use of a "non-steroidal compound that selectively inhibits activity of the PGHS-2 gene," the '850 patent neither discloses any such compound nor provides any suggestion as to how such a compound could be made or otherwise obtained other than by trial-and-error research. Indeed, the court found no evidence in the '850 patent that the inventors themselves knew of any such compound at the time their patent application was filed. Accordingly, the court concluded that the patent's claims are invalid for lack of written description.

The district court also found that practice of the claimed methods would require "a person of ordinary skill in the art . . . to engage in undue experimentation, with no assurance of success," and on that basis concluded that the claims are also invalid for lack of enablement. The court considered, but rejected as conclusory, Rochester's experts' opinions that one of skill in the art would have known to start with existing NSAIDs and would have used routine methods to make structural changes to lead compounds to optimize them, citing a general failure to point to any language in the patent supporting those opinions.

Finding no genuine issue of material fact concerning either written description or enablement, the district court accordingly granted Pfizer's motions for summary judgment of invalidity of the '850 patent for failure to meet the written description and enablement requirements, denied Rochester's cross-motion, and dismissed the complaint.

Rochester now appeals. We have jurisdiction pursuant to 28 U.S.C. § 1295(a)(1).

DISCUSSION

Rochester asserts three grounds of error on appeal. First, it argues that the district court erred by granting Pfizer's motion for summary judgment of invalidity for lack of written description. Second, it argues that the court erred by granting Pfizer's motion for summary judgment of invalidity for lack of enablement. Third, Rochester contends that the court erred by denying its cross-motion for summary judgment with regard to written description. Pfizer refutes each of those asserted grounds of error.

Summary judgment is appropriate when there are no genuine issues of material fact and the moving party is entitled to judgment as a matter of law. We review a district court's grant of summary judgment *de novo*, reapplying the summary judgment standard. In contrast, "when a district court *denies* summary judgment, we review that decision with considerable deference to the court," and "will not disturb the trial court's denial . . . unless we find that the court has indeed abused its discretion in so denying." Additionally, "[w]hen evaluating a motion for summary judgment, the court views the record evidence through the prism of the evidentiary standard of proof that would pertain at a trial on the merits." In that process, we draw all justifiable inferences in the nonmovant's favor.

An issued patent enjoys a presumption of validity, 35 U.S.C. § 282, that can be overcome only through clear and convincing evidence. Accordingly, a party "seeking to invalidate a patent at summary judgment must submit such clear and convincing evidence of invalidity."

In its first argument, Rochester asserts that the district court effectively — but erroneously — held that a patent claiming a method of obtaining a biological effect in a human by administering a compound cannot, as a matter of law, satisfy the written description requirement without disclosing the identity of any such compound. Indeed, Rochester contends that "no written description requirement exists independent of enablement." In any event, Rochester argues that its patent met the requirements of § 112 and is not invalid.

Pfizer responds to Rochester's argument by pointing out that we have "interpreted § 112 as requiring a "written description" of an invention separate from enablement," and that "the many prior precedential decisions" contrary to Rochester's position "cannot be overruled except by an *en banc* decision." Pfizer also cites *Vas-Cath Inc. v. Mahurkar* in which we explained that "[t]he purpose of the written description requirement is broader than to merely explain how to "make and use" [the invention]," and *Reiffin v. Microsoft Corp.* in which we stated that the purpose of the written description requirement is to "ensure that the scope of the right to exclude, as set forth in the claims, does not overreach the scope of the inventor's contribution to the field of art as described in the patent specification." Pfizer asserts that a patent fails to satisfy the written description requirement if it claims a method of achieving a biological effect, but discloses no compounds that can accomplish that result. It maintains that the district court correctly invalidated Rochester's '850 patent.

We agree with Pfizer that our precedent recognizes a written description requirement and that the '850 patent does not satisfy that requirement. As in any case involving statutory interpretation, we begin with the language of the statute itself. Section 112 provides, in relevant part, that:

> The specification shall contain a written description of the invention, and of the manner and process of making and using it, in such full, clear, concise, and exact terms as to enable any person skilled in the art to which it pertains, or with which it is most nearly connected, to make and use the same, and shall set forth the best mode contemplated by the inventor of carrying out his invention.

Three separate requirements are contained in that provision: (1) "[t]he specification shall contain a written description of the invention"; (2) "[t]he specification shall contain a written description . . . of the manner and process of making and using it [*i.e.*, the invention] in such full, clear, concise, and exact terms as to enable any person skilled in the art to which it pertains, or with which it is most nearly connected, to make and use the same"; and (3) "[t]he specification . . . shall set forth the best mode contemplated by the inventor of carrying out his invention."

In common parlance, as well as in our and our predecessor court's case law, those three requirements are referred to as the "written description requirement," the "enablement requirement," and the "best mode requirement," respectively. The United States Supreme Court also recently acknowledged written description as a statutory requirement distinct not only from the best mode requirement, but also from enablement. In addition, the patent application must *describe, enable, and set forth the best mode* of carrying out the invention. These latter requirements must be satisfied before issuance of the patent, for exclusive patent rights are given in exchange for disclosing the invention to the public.

Although there is often significant overlap between the three requirements, they are nonetheless independent of each other. Thus, an invention may be described without an enabling disclosure of how to make and use it. A description of a chemical compound without a description of how to make and use it, unless within the skill of one of ordinary skill in the art, is an example. Moreover, an invention may be enabled even though it has not been described. Such can occur when enablement of a closely related invention A that is both described and enabled would similarly enable an invention B *if* B were described. A specification can likewise describe an invention without enabling the practice of the full breadth of its claims. Finally, still further disclosure might be necessary to satisfy the best mode requirement if otherwise only an inferior mode would be disclosed.

The "written description" requirement serves a teaching function, as a *"quid pro quo"* in which the public is given "meaningful disclosure in exchange for being excluded from practicing the invention for a limited period of time." Rochester argues, however, that this teaching, or "public notice," function, although "virtually unchanged since the 1793 Patent Act," in fact "became redundant with the advent of claims in 1870." We disagree. Statutory language does not become redundant unless repealed by Congress, in which case it no longer exists.

We agree with Pfizer that the '850 patent is deficient in failing to adequately describe the claimed invention. First, although compliance with the written description requirement is a question of fact, Rochester's argument that a patent may not be held invalid on its face is contrary to our case law.

Second, it is undisputed that the '850 patent does not disclose any compounds that can be used in its claimed methods. The claimed methods thus cannot be practiced based on the patent's specification, even considering the knowledge of one skilled in the art. No compounds that will perform the claimed method are disclosed, nor has any evidence been shown that such a compound was known. The '850 patent does contain substantial description of the cyclooxygenases, including the nucleotide sequences of coding and promoter regions of the genes that encode human COX-1 and COX-2 and a comparison of those sequences. The patent also describes in detail how to make cells that express either COX-1 or COX-2, but not both, as well as "assays for screening compounds, including peptides, polynucleotides, and small organic molecules to identify those that inhibit the expression or activity of the PGHS-2 gene product; and methods of treating diseases characterized by aberrant PGHS-2 activity using such compounds," Such assay methods are in fact claimed in the '479 patent, *i.e.*, Rochester's *other* patent based on the same disclosure. The '850 patent specification also describes what can be done with any compounds that may potentially be identified through those assays, including formulation into pharmaceuticals, routes of administration, estimation of effective dosage, and suitable dosage forms. As pointed out by the district court, however, the '850 patent does not disclose just *"which* "peptides, polynucleotides, and small organic molecules" have the desired characteristic of selectively inhibiting PGHS-2." Without such disclosure, the claimed methods cannot be said to have been described. As we held in *Lilly*, "[a]n adequate written description of a DNA . . . "requires a precise definition, such as by structure, formula, chemical name, or physical properties," not a mere wish or plan for obtaining the claimed chemical invention." For reasons stated above, that requirement applies just as well to non-DNA (or — RNA) chemical inventions.

Rochester argues that "[t]he appealed decision vitiates universities' ability to bring pioneering innovations to the public," and that:

> Congress has determined that licensing of academia's inventions to industry is the best way to bring groundbreaking inventions to the public. *See* 35 U.S.C. § 200. By vesting in universities the patent rights to their federally funded research, the Bayh-Dole Act of 1980 encouraged "private industry to utilize government funded inventions through the commitment of the risk capital necessary to develop such inventions to the point of commercial application."

Further, *amici* the University of California and the University of Texas assert that "[t]his Court's decision will have a significant impact on the continuing viability of technology transfer programs at universities and on the equitable allocation of intellectual property rights between universities and the private sector."

That argument is unsound. The Bayh-Dole Act was intended to enable universities to profit from their federally-funded research. It was not intended to relax the statutory requirements for patentability. As pointed out by *amicus* Eli Lilly, "no connection exists between the Bayh-Dole Act and the legal standards that courts employ to assess patentability. Furthermore, none of the eight policy objectives of the Bayh-Dole Act encourages or condones less stringent application of the patent laws to universities than to other entities."

In sum, because the '850 patent does not provide any guidance that would steer the skilled practitioner toward compounds that can be used to carry out the claimed methods — an essential element of every claim of that patent — and has not provided evidence that any such compounds were otherwise within the knowledge of a person of ordinary skill in the art at the relevant time, Rochester has failed to raise any question of material fact whether the named inventors disclosed the claimed invention. Accordingly, we affirm the district court's grant of Pfizer's motion for summary judgment.

QUESTIONS

1. Could UR have sued for infringement of the assay patent?

2. How could UR have made a case for infringement of the assay patent?

3. Why do you think UR did not sue for infringement of the assay patent?

4. What was the basis for UR's argument that the teaching requirement of the written description was made redundant by the "advent of claims"?

5. What is the rationale underlying the teaching and disclosure requirements that caused UR problems in this case?

6. Isn't it contradictory to state that a patent is presumed to be valid but then use that very same patent to prove its invalidity?

7. The court states: "The Bayh-Dole Act was intended to enable universities to profit from their federally-funded research." Is there any support for this statement in the Bayh-Dole Act?

IN RE COLUMBIA UNIVERSITY PATENT LITIGATION
343 F.Supp.2d 35 (D. Mass. 2004)

WOLF, DISTRICT JUDGE.

I. SUMMARY

The Trustees of the Columbia University in the City of New York ("Columbia") have moved to dismiss the declaratory judgment claims in these multidistrict litigation cases. Columbia alleges that its covenant not to sue the plaintiff drug companies on the claims of Patent No. 6,455,275 (the " '275 patent") as they now read extinguishes the constitutionally required actual cases or controversies between the parties with regard to plaintiffs' requests for declaratory judgment. Plaintiffs oppose this motion.

For the reasons set forth in this Memorandum, however, Columbia's contention is correct. The covenant not to sue means that none of the plaintiffs now has the legally required reasonable apprehension that it will face an infringement suit if the court does not declare the '275 patent invalid and/or unenforceable. Moreover, the court has some discretion as to whether to exercise its jurisdiction even where an actual case or controversy exists. In the circumstances of these cases, even if contrary to the court's conclusion subject matter jurisdiction now exists, it would be most appropriate to dismiss the requests for declaratory judgment rather than devote a substantial amount of scarce judicial resources to rendering an essentially advisory opinion on hypothetical facts concerning contingencies that are not likely to occur.

Therefore, plaintiffs' requests for judgment will be dismissed. In addition, the parties are being ordered to: confer; identify for the court the remaining issues in this multidistrict litigation; inform the court whether they request an opportunity to attempt to settle the remaining issues; and, if not, propose a schedule for their judicial resolution.

II. FACTS

The plaintiffs are drug companies which have licensed from Columbia all patents deriving from an application that Columbia filed in 1980 (the "Axel Patents"). Plaintiffs believed that the last of the licensed Axel Patents that they were practicing expired in 2000 and that their duties to pay royalties to Columbia ended in 2002. However, plaintiffs were informed by Columbia that a new patent deriving from the 1980 application, the '275 patent, had been issued on September 24, 2002. Columbia asserted that plaintiffs were, therefore, obligated to pay royalties for another seventeen years.

Plaintiffs contend that the '275 patent is invalid pursuant to the doctrine of non-statutory double patenting and for other reasons. They also assert that, if valid, the '275 patent is unenforceable because of prosecution laches. Therefore, plaintiffs ceased paying royalties to Columbia under their respective licensing agreements.

In 2003, various plaintiffs filed suits against Columbia, in various United States District Courts, seeking declaratory judgments that the '275 patent is both invalid and unenforceable. Some of the plaintiffs also seek other relief, but the requests for declaratory judgment are the heart of each of the actions.

In 2004, Columbia notified each plaintiff that it was terminating its license as a result of its refusal to pay royalties on the '275 patent. Two of the plaintiffs, Biogen Idec MA and Genzyme, filed a motion to preliminarily enjoin the termination of their licenses.

On April 8, 2004, the Judicial Panel on Multidistrict Litigation transferred all of the cases relating to the '275 patent to this court for coordinated or consolidated pretrial proceedings.

After a hearing on June 22, 2004, this court denied Biogen Idec MA and Genzyme's motion for preliminary injunction. In reaching that decision, the court found that the plaintiffs had made a strong showing that they were likely to prevail in proving that the '275 patent is invalid under the doctrine of non-statutory double patenting and, if valid, is unenforceable because of the equitable doctrine of prosecution laches. The request for a preliminary injunction was denied, however, because Biogen Idec MA and Genzyme had failed to make the required showing that they would be irreparably harmed if Columbia was not enjoined from terminating their licenses.

The fundamental facts concerning these cases as of August 13, 2004 are described in detail in the decision denying the motion for preliminary injunction and will not be fully reiterated here. They are, in essence, as follows.

The Axel patents involve the use of recombinant DNA technology and a process called "co-transformation" to produce proteins in "host" cells which do not normally produce those proteins. These proteins are used to make drugs that are important to human health. For example, Biogen Idec MA uses the technology it has licensed from Columbia to produce AVONEX (Interferon beta-la), the world's leading treatment for relapsing forms of multiple sclerosis. AVONEX and the drugs manufactured by the other plaintiffs pursuant to their licenses with Columbia generate substantial revenues for the drug companies and substantial royalties for Columbia.

The three issued Axel patents, including the '275, each derive from application No. 06/124,513 (the "'513 application"), which was filed in 1980. Since 1980, Columbia has filed, and in some cases abandoned, a series of divisional and continuation applications. Most significantly, for the purpose of these cases:

> On June 7, 1995, Columbia filed two more continuation applications, Nos. 08/484,136 (the "'136 application") and 08/477,159 (the "'159 application"). The June 7, 1995 filing date for the '136 and '159 applications is very significant. On December 8, 1994, Public Law No. 103-465, the Uruguay Round Agreements Act, was enacted. Among other things, this legislation provided that all patents that issue based on applications filed on or after June 8, 1995 — 6 months after the Act was signed into law — would expire twenty years from the date the application was filed. The old rule was that patents expired seventeen years from the date of issuance. In order to grandfather in pending applications, the new law provided that all patents that issue based on applications filed before June 8, 1995 will last until either twenty years from the date the application was filed or seventeen years from the date the patent issues, whichever is later.

> The '159 application is still pending, now more than nine years after being filed. However, by virtue of the application being filed on June 7, 1995, if the '159 application results in a patent (a "'159 patent"), it will be effective for seventeen years. If the '159 application had been filed a day later, a '159 patent would either not now issue or would immediately be deemed expired because the twenty-year period after the 1980 filing of the original application from which it derives ended in 2000.

The '136 application ultimately matured into the '275 patent involved in this litigation. It was issued on September 24, 2000. Had the '136 application been filed one day later, the '275 patent too either would not have issued or would have been immediately deemed expired on February 25, 2000 because its application date relates back to its great-great-great-great-great-great-grandparent application, the 1980 '513 application. However, since the '136 application was, by one day, eligible for the seventeen years from issuance term, it will not expire until September 24, 2019 — seventeen years after the date on which it was issued.

In connection with their request for preliminary injunction, the plaintiffs presented the declaration of Harvey F. Lodish on the issue of non-statutory double patenting. Dr. Lodish is a professor at the Massachusetts Institute of Technology, and the lead author of an important, relevant textbook, *Molecular Cell Biology*. Dr. Lodish explained in detail "why the three independent claims of the '275 patent that he analyze[d] "are not patentably distinct over claims of the [earlier] '017 patent and are all invalid for obviousness type double patenting." " Based on his undisputed and compelling analysis, the court found that plaintiffs were likely to prevail in proving that the '275 patent is invalid.

In addition, the court found that:

> In the instant case, the '275 patent was issued twenty-two years after the application from which it derives was filed. There were several delays in the prosecution of the application. Columbia has provided no evidence, or even argument, to explain why it took twenty-two years to obtain the '275 patent or to justify the delays in that process. The timing of its issuance strongly suggests that Columbia deliberately delayed obtaining a patent that it always intended to secure in order to make it effective just as the other Axel patents expired and thus increase its commercial value by maximizing the period in which the public would have to pay Columbia royalties for the use of the Axel patents.

Accordingly, plaintiffs have made a strong showing that they are likely to prevail on the claim that, if valid, the '275 patent is unenforceable because of prosecution laches.

As indicated earlier, however, because the moving plaintiffs failed to make the required showing of an imminent threat of irreparable harm, their motion for a preliminary injunction was denied.

Also after a hearing on June 22, 2004, the court, on August 16, 2004, denied Columbia's motion for a stay of the multidistrict litigation pending the conclusion of Patent and Trademark Office (the "PTO") reexamination and reissuance proceedings concerning the '275 patent. In doing so, the court stated, in part, that:

> A stay would significantly harm the plaintiffs. While any stay is in effect, the drug companies' potential damages will mount. The uncertainty over whether they owe Columbia royalties on their products might create difficulties in pricing those products. It may also cause the drug companies to delay introduction of new products or needlessly invest money in efforts to design around an invalid patent. Such efforts are likely to be extremely costly in a highly regulated industry such as the one in which the drug companies compete because changes in their product designs or manufacturing processes may require regulatory approval.

Eliminating this uncertainty is the very reason that the plaintiffs brought these declaratory judgment actions. It is also the reason that Congress and the President created a declaratory judgment remedy.

A stay would also have the effect, if not the purpose, of causing delay in a case which involves, in part, the assertion that the '275 patent is unenforceable under the doctrine of prosecution laches because of the twenty-two year delay in prosecution that has already taken place. Now, over twenty-four years after he first filed the '513 application, John P. White, on behalf of Columbia, is telling the PTO that the patent should be re-issued because the issued claims are not broad enough. If the claims of the '275 patent are invalid as issued, the broader claims may be invalid as well. In denying the motion of Biogen and Genzyme to preliminarily enjoin termination of their license agreements, this court found that they have shown that they are likely to prevail in proving that if the '275 patent is valid, it is unenforceable because of prosecution laches. This finding militates against granting the complete stay of this case that Columbia seeks.

While the request for a complete stay was denied, the court substantially stayed what promised to be a prolonged period of wide-ranging discovery in order to focus on an issue that it perceived had the potential to resolve this multidistrict litigation efficiently. More specifically: [A]t the June 22, 2004 hearing the court identified the contention that the '275 patent is invalid under the doctrine of non-statutory double patenting as one that should be able to be quickly developed and decided in 2004, either on a motion for summary judgment or at a trial to be conducted in December 2004. Therefore, the court established a schedule for the resolution of the non-statutory double patenting issue in 2004, and otherwise substantially stayed the remainder of this case to permit the parties to focus on that issue, which may, as a practical matter, end these cases.

On September 1, 2004, Columbia filed a covenant not to sue plaintiffs for infringement of the '275 patent as it now reads for any products made, used, or sold on or before September 1, 2004. Columbia then filed a motion to dismiss all of plaintiffs' declaratory judgment claims, asserting that no actual cases or controversies any longer existed and, therefore, the court lacked subject matter jurisdiction concerning them. Columbia subsequently informed Biogen Idec MA, Genzyme, Abbott and Johnson & Johnson that their licenses were still in effect because their failures to pay royalties on the '275 patent was not a breach of their licensing agreements.

Plaintiffs opposed the motions to dismiss. Their oppositions relied primarily on the fact that Columbia's covenant not to sue covered only activities occurring before September 1, 2004. Several plaintiffs provided affidavits stating that they were engaged in research activity that potentially infringed the '275 patent and that they had taken concrete steps towards additional potentially infringing activity after September 1, 2004. Specifically, the plaintiffs stated that their ongoing research programs involved the co-transformation of Chinese Hamster Ovary cells, an activity that could potentially infringe the '275 patent. As such activity was occurring after September 1, 2004, and was not covered by Columbia's covenant, plaintiffs argued that they were still at risk of being sued for infringement.

At the October 6, 2004 hearing on the motion to dismiss, Columbia enlarged the scope of its covenant not to sue on the '275 patent. As memorialized in the Amended and Restated Covenant filed on October 12, 2004, Columbia has now agreed: 1) not to assert any claim against plaintiffs under the '275 patent as it currently reads and 2) not to assert the '275 patent as it currently reads against any plaintiff as a basis to recover royalties under such plaintiff's license agreement with Columbia. The current covenant covers "any and all methods, processes, and products made, used, offered for sale, sold, or imported by any plaintiff at any time[.]" In addition, it "covers all claims in the '275 patent as they currently read, and any claim in any reissued or reexamined version of the '275 patent that is the same as, or substantially identical to, any claim of the '275 patent as it currently reads."

Therefore, under the covenant not to sue, plaintiffs now have no potential liability for their current activities under the '275 patent or any other existing or potential Axel patent. Nor will they have any prospective liability under any reissued or reexamined '275 patent for any claim now in the '275 patent or any substantially identical claim.

The current covenant does not, however, cover any claim in any reissued or reexamined '275 patent that is not the same as, or substantially identical to, any claim of the '275 patent as it now reads. The current covenant also does not cover any claims that may issue from the '159 application, even if such claims are the same as, or substantially identical to, claims in the '275 patent as it now reads. Finally, the covenant does not cover "affiliates" of plaintiffs that are not parties to these cases.

However, as discussed more fully below, it is unlikely that a '159 patent will issue with claims that are now in the '275 patent or substantially similar claims. The PTO has issued a final rejection of the proposed '159 patent due to obvious-type double patenting and recently reaffirmed that rejection. In any event, plaintiffs are not now incurring any potential liability to Columbia, and Columbia is not explicitly or implicitly threatening to sue any of them as a result of their current activities.

III. ANALYSIS

A. The Applicable Standards

The Declaratory Judgment Act, 28 U.S.C. § 2201, provides in pertinent part that:

In a case of actual controversy within its jurisdiction . . . any court of the United States, upon the filing of an appropriate pleading, *may* declare the rights and other legal relations of any interested party seeking such declaration, whether or not further relief is or could be sought (emphasis added).

This means that a declaratory judgment may be issued only if there is a live case or controversy, as required by Article III of the Constitution, at the time a court decides the case. Moreover, "[s]imply because there is an actual controversy between the parties does not mean that the district court is required to exercise that jurisdiction." Rather, even where an actual case or controversy exists, the court must make " "a reasoned judgment whether the investment of time and resources will be worthwhile." "

In the context of patents, the Declaratory Judgment Act recognizes the potential for abuse if patentees explicitly or implicitly threaten litigation without bringing suit in order to obtain a settlement or other commercial advantage from competitors faced with the " "*in terrorem* choice between the incurrence of a growing potential liability for patent infringement and abandonment of their enterprises." "

The purpose of the Act is to enable a person who is reasonably at legal risk because of an unresolved dispute, to obtain judicial resolution of that dispute without having to await the commencement of legal action by the other side. It accommodates the practical situation wherein the interests of one side to the dispute may be served by delay in taking legal action. However, the controversy must be actual, not hypothetical or of uncertain prospective occurrence. The requirement of actual controversy encompasses concepts such as ripeness, standing, and the prohibition against advisory judicial rulings.

"In promulgating the Declaratory Judgment Act, Congress intended to prevent avoidable damages from being incurred by a person uncertain of his rights and threatened with damage by delayed adjudication." Therefore, in a patent case a plaintiff seeking a declaratory judgment generally must prove two essential elements to establish that an actual case or controversy exists. There must be both (1) an explicit threat or other action by the patentee, which creates a *reasonable* apprehension on the part of the declaratory plaintiff that it will face an infringement suit and (2) *present* activity which could constitute infringement or concrete steps taken with the intent to conduct such activity.

In this multidistrict litigation, each of the plaintiff drug companies is using a process to produce drugs which could constitute infringement of the '275 patent if it is valid and enforceable. Therefore, the second prong of the test is satisfied.

However, Columbia's covenant not to sue any plaintiff on any "claims in the '275 patent as they currently read, and any claim in any reissued or reexamined patent that is the same as, or substantially identical to any claim of the '275 patent as it currently reads" means that plaintiffs do not now have the required reasonable apprehension that they will face an infringement suit and possibly be required to pay damages for any of their current activities. The plaintiffs are not now "reasonably at legal risk because of an unresolved dispute."

This conclusion is not qualified by the fact that it is conceivable, although not likely, that claims now in the '275 patent could be included if a '159 patent is ever issued because the application for it is based on the specification that is in the '275 patent. Nor is the conclusion that these actions no longer present actual cases or controversies altered because plaintiffs allege not only that the '275 patent and the potential '159 patent are or would be invalid, but also that they are or would be unenforceable because of prosecution laches. Moreover, even if actual cases or controversies were now deemed to exist, the court would exercise its discretion to dismiss the requests for declaratory judgment.

The reasons for these conclusions are as follows. "Although the requirement that the declaratory plaintiff be under a reasonable apprehension of suit does not require that the patentee be known to be poised on the courthouse steps," defendant's actions must create an objectively reasonable apprehension of litigation on the part of a declaratory judgment plaintiff.

Covenants not to sue made after the commencement of a declaratory judgment action may eliminate a plaintiff's reasonable apprehension of infringement litigation and, therefore, the required actual case or controversy.

Columbia's current covenant similarly estopps it from ever suing plaintiffs on the claims of the '275 patent as it now reads, even if they are reissued. If the '275 patent is reissued with new or amended claims, they will be "enforceable only from the date of reissue and . . . [t]he specific things made before the date of the reissue, which infringe the new reissue claims, are absolutely free of the reissued patent and may be used or sold after the date of reissue without regard to the patent."

Therefore, plaintiffs' present rights are clear, and there is no risk that they will be required to pay Columbia damages for their current activities or products even if the '275 patent is reissued with new or amended claims. Accordingly, the reasons for the Declaratory Judgment Act no longer pertain to this case. More significantly, no actual cases or controversies any longer exist.

Plaintiffs make three other arguments in their effort to persuade the court that actual cases or controversies exist. Each is without merit.

Some of the plaintiffs contend that an actual case or controversy exists because Columbia's covenant not to sue does not cover the independent legal entities they call "affiliates." Columbia has not, however, implicitly or explicitly threatened to sue those entities. More significantly, the "affiliates" are not parties to these cases.

Plaintiffs also contend that their demands for attorneys fees pursuant to 35 U.S.C. § 285 create actual cases and controversies. Section 285 provides that "[t]he court in exceptional cases may award reasonable attorneys fees to the prevailing party." In interpreting the term "prevailing party" in another statute providing for fee-shifting, the Supreme Court has held that:

> A defendant's voluntary change in conduct, although perhaps accomplishing what the plaintiff sought to achieve by the lawsuit, lacks the necessary judicial *imprimatur* on the change. Our precedents thus counsel against holding that the term "prevailing party" authorizes an award of attorney's fees *without* a corresponding alteration in the legal relationship of the parties.

While Columbia's covenant not to sue is a form of voluntary conduct that accomplishes the major part of what the plaintiffs sought to achieve in these lawsuits, they have received no relief from the court on the merits of their claims. They are, therefore, not prevailing parties for the purposes of § 285. Thus, their claims for attorneys fees do not create actual cases or controversies.

Finally, at the October 6, 2004 hearing Biogen Idec MA and Genzyme briefly argued that actual cases and controversies are created by their obligation to pay an annual $30,000 fee to Columbia to maintain their reinstated licenses. Biogen Idec MA and Genzyme neither practice nor intend to practice the sole issued Axel patent other than the '275 patent, U.S. Patent No. 5,149,636. They are unlikely to resume paying the annual license fee in view of their manifest intent to challenge the validity and enforceability of any '159 patent that may issue, and Columbia's duty to license to them any '159 patent at a reasonable rate if they lose that challenge. If Biogen Idec MA and Genzyme pay the annual license fee, any possible case or controversy may be extinguished. Moreover, their counsel has stated that, "we wouldn't be here [in litigation] today if we were fighting over the $30,000."

Thus, plaintiffs evidently do not intend to pay the license fee in any event and would not litigate whether they have a duty to do so if it were the sole issue in dispute. Therefore, the question of the annual license fee does not create actual cases or controversies because the need for judicial attention is not real and immediate. If it did, the court would exercise its discretion to dismiss the requests for declaratory judgment concerning the license fee because at this point the investment of judicial time and resources necessary to decide them would not be worthwhile.

QUESTIONS

1. What was Columbia seeking to accomplish in filing a covenant not to sue on the '275 patent?

2. If the court had held Columbia's '275 patent valid and the plaintiff licensees refused to pay the license fees, would Columbia have succeeded in obtaining a permanent injunction?

3. Would *In Re Columbia Patent Litigation* be decided in the same way after *MedImmune*?

4. Was Columbia's exclusion of the plaintiffs' affiliates from the covenant not to sue an implicit threat of an infringement suit?

5. How would, or should, the post-grant opposition opportunities enacted in the America Invents Act affect these types of declaratory judgment cases?

6. What message do you think the *Rochester* and *Columbia* cases send to industry?

7. Are there goals universities should pursue in licensing their technologies other than licensing revenues? What are some of these other goals and how might their accomplishment be measured?

7. If you were counsel to the University of Rochester or Columbia University, how would you have advised them to proceed in these cases?

CASE NOTES

1. *See* Cornell Univ. v. Hewlett-Packard Co., 654 F.Supp.2d 119 (N.D.N.Y. 2009) (Cornell filed action against Hewlett-Packard alleging infringement of patent on technology for issuing multiple and out-of-order computer processing instructions in a single machine clock cycle; jury rendered verdict for Cornell; Hewlett-Packard moved for judgment as a matter of law that patent was invalid and not infringed, or in the alternative, for a new trial on validity and infringement; court denied motion; *see* discussion of damages in the Cornell case in subsection 1.8.3 case notes); Eolas Techs. Inc. v. Microsoft Corp., 399 F.3d 1325 (Fed. Cir. 2005) (Eolas, exclusive licensee of University of California's patent for internet browsing software, sued Microsoft for infringement; district court rejected Microsoft's inequitable conduct and invalidity defenses; court of appeals held that alleged prior art was not abandoned, and that a fact issue existed as to whether patent was invalid in light of prior art, and whether software code, sent abroad by Microsoft on master disks for copying on to hard drives by foreign computer producers, was a "component" of infringing products within the meaning of statute proscribing foreign assembly of patented product); Iowa State Univ. Research Found., Inc. v. Wiley Organics, Inc., 125 Fed. Appx. 291 (Fed. Cir. 2005) (Patent co-owners, Iowa State University and Vanderbilt University, and patent exclusive licensee, Metabolic Technologies, sued chemical manufacturer alleging contributory infringement and inducement of infringement; district court granted judgment as a matter of law that patent was not infringed; patent co-owners and exclusive licensee appealed; court of appeals held district court's construction of patent claims was erroneous and factual issues

on infringement remain); Cook Biotech Inc. v. Acell, Inc., 460 F.3d 1365 (Fed. Cir. 2006) (Cook and Purdue Research Foundation brought action for infringement of patents for tissue composition used as scaffold for tissue reconstruction; district court ruled that patent was infringed; court of Appeals held district court erred in its claim construction and that Acell's product did not literally infringe patent and patent was not infringed under doctrine of equivalents).

Additional Information

1. Rakesh H. Mehta, *University of Rochester Corp. v. G.D. Searle & Co., Inc.: How to Lose Millions in Patent Royalties*, 29 DEL. J. CORP. L. 2004).

2. N. Scott Pierce, *University of Rochester v. G.D. Searle & Co.: Writing on the Wall*, 4 J. MARSHALL REV. INTELL. PROP. L. 4006 (2005).

3. Recent Development, *Columbia Co-Transformation, Commercialization & Controversy: The Axel Patent Litigation*, 17 HARV. J.L. & TECH. 583 (2004).

4. Robert A. Bohrer, *Between a Rock and a Hard Place: University Research after Merck and Madey and the University of Rochester*, 24 BIOTECHNOLOGY L. REP. 713 (2005).

3.5   UNIVERSITY-STUDENT RESEARCH RESPONSIBILITIES

University ownership of student-created intellectual property does not relieve universities of other duties to students based on express and implied contracts, and fiduciary relationships. The *Chou* case below illustrates a particularly egregious instance of faculty disregard for students' academic welfare. The *Chou* case also has important implications for universities' liability arising from faculty misconduct and the need for universities' oversight of faculty-student research.

CHOU v. UNIVERSITY OF CHICAGO
254 F.3D 1347 (Fed. Cir. 2001)

LOURIE, CIRCUIT JUDGE.

Joany Chou appeals from the decision of the United States District Court for the Northern District of Illinois granting Bernard Roizman and Aviron Company's motions to dismiss her claims for correction of inventorship, declaratory judgment of inventorship, fraud, breach of fiduciary duty, unjust enrichment, breach of express contract, and breach of implied contract. Chou also seeks reinstatement of those same claims against the University of Chicago ("University"). Because the district court erred in its determination that Chou did not have standing to sue for correction of inventorship under 35 U.S.C. § 256, we reverse its judgment as to that claim. We also reverse the court's dismissal of most of her state law claims against Roizman and direct the court to reinstate certain of her state law claims against the University. However, we affirm that court's dismissal of her breach of express contract claim against Roizman and of all her remaining claims against Aviron. We also affirm the court's grant of Roizman's motion to strike her allegations of academic theft and fraud. Finally, we reject Chou's attempt to have her case reassigned to another district court judge. We therefore affirm-in-part, reverse-in-part, and remand.

BACKGROUND

Dr. Chou was a graduate student and subsequently a post-doctoral research assistant for Dr. Roizman at the University of Chicago's Department of Molecular Genetics and Cell Biology from 1983 to 1996. Roizman is named as the sole inventor on U.S. Patent 5,328,688 and a co-inventor on U.S. Patents 5,795,713 and 5,922,328, all of which relate to herpes simplex virus and its use in an avirulent vaccine. Roizman is also listed as an inventor on three foreign applications: WO 9204050 (based on the subject matter of the '688 patent), WO 9833933 (based on the subject matter of the '713 patent), and PCT/US96/14292 (based on the subject matter of the '328 patent) (collectively, "the foreign applications"). The inventorship of those patents and applications is disputed.

Under University policy, inventors receive 25% of the gross royalties and up-front payments from licensing of the patents, as well as 25% of the stock of new companies that are based on their inventions. Chou allegedly told Roizman in February of 1991 that her discoveries should be patented, and he allegedly disagreed. At that time, however, Roizman had already filed the '688 patent application, which was allegedly directed to the same disputed invention, and had named himself as the sole inventor of that subject matter. During prosecution of that application, the United States Patent and Trademark Office ("PTO") cited two joint Chou-Roizman publications as prior art. In response, Roizman submitted a declaration stating that those publications were not available as prior art because he was the sole inventor of the work described therein and that she merely worked under his direction and supervision.

On July 14, 1992, Roizman assigned the '688 patent application to Institut Merieux, a French company that had supported the research. Just before that assignment, however, on July 1, 1992, it appears that Aviron had received an exclusive license to the herpes simplex virus technology from ARCH Development Corporation, a wholly owned affiliate of the University established to license and commercialize the University's technology and intellectual property. Institut Merieux later assigned the patent application to ARCH, which in turn licensed Aviron. Aviron also obtained rights to the '713 and '328 patents and the foreign applications by license and assignment from ARCH. ARCH and Roizman each own Aviron stock and have received licensing revenue from NeuroVir, the sublicensee of Aviron's rights.

Later, in 1993, Roizman and Chou signed an agreement to share royalties from "the pending patent application to exploit the properties of the herpes simplex virus 34.5 gene." At the time the agreement was signed, Chou and Roizman were named inventors on a patent application relating to the subject matter of that agreement, which is not in dispute in this appeal. The '688 patent application was also pending when that agreement was signed, although Chou was not then aware of its existence. In 1996, Roizman asked Chou to resign, failing which he told her that he would fire her, allegedly because she would be in a stronger position to contest his inventorship if she were still conducting research at the University.

In 1999, Chou sued Roizman, the University/ARCH, and Aviron (collectively, "the defendants") for correction of inventorship under 35 U.S.C. § 256, seeking to be named as the sole inventor on the '688 patent, or, in the alternative, as a co-inventor along with Roizman. She additionally sought to be listed as a co-inventor on the '713 and '328 patents. Chou also sued for a declaratory judgment that she was an inventor on the U.S. patents and their corresponding foreign applications. In addition, Chou asserted claims of fraudulent concealment, breach of fiduciary duty, unjust enrichment, breach of express and implied contract, and academic theft and fraud.

The district court determined that Chou lacked standing to seek correction of inventorship under § 256 because she could claim no ownership of the patents, having surrendered all her rights to the University under an employment agreement. The court also dismissed her claim for a declaratory judgment of inventorship, finding that she had no reasonable grounds to believe that Roizman intended to file suit to settle the inventorship question.

The district court also dismissed under Fed.R.Civ.P. 12(b)(6) all of her state law claims except her count for conversion. It determined that Roizman had no duty as Chou's advisor and department chairman to inform Chou of the status of the patent applications, and that his opinion that some of Chou's work should not be patented, although perhaps an affirmative misrepresentation, was not fraudulent. The district court dismissed her unjust enrichment claim based on Roizman's alleged arrangement of the assignment of the '688 patent application to ARCH and then to Aviron, finding instead that Roizman assigned the application to Institut Merieux, which exercised its own "free will" to assign it to ARCH, which then licensed it to Aviron. The district court also dismissed her claim for breach of an express contract, finding that the contract signed by Chou and Roizman to split royalties related to a different patent application on which both were listed as inventors and was therefore not relevant to the dispute. The court similarly dismissed her claim for breach of an implied contract because Chou did not allege that Roizman and Chou had established a practice of sharing royalties for all joint inventions. The court also granted Roizman's motion to strike Chou's allegations of academic theft and fraud under Fed.R.Civ.P. 12(f).

The court dismissed all claims against Aviron because Chou did not allege that Roizman's actions came within the scope of his authority as Aviron's agent, and because "so much of what Dr. Roizman did was done before there was an Aviron that Aviron authorized none of it; it simply benefited from the acts after it was brought into existence." The court dismissed all her counts against Roizman except the conversion count. Chou then voluntarily dismissed the conversion count and stipulated to the dismissal with prejudice of all counts of her complaint against the University/ARCH to obtain a final, appealable judgment because she agreed that the reasoning of the district court's order applied with equal force to the University/ARCH.

DISCUSSION

On appeal, Chou presents three reasons why the district court erred in its conclusion that she did not have standing to bring an action under § 256 to correct inventorship: (1) she did not assign her interest in her inventions to the University; (2) she would be entitled to receive 25% of the gross royalties and up-front payments from licensing, as well as 25% of the stock of new companies based on the invention, if she were a named inventor; or (3) she has standing solely by virtue of being a true inventor under our decision in *University of Colorado Foundation v. American Cyanamid Co.* Chou also argues that the court erred in dismissing her declaratory judgment claim because she had a reasonable apprehension that the defendants would file a § 256 action to seek reassurance of their position that Chou was correctly excluded as an inventor from the patents.

With respect to her state law claims, Chou contends that the district court erred in dismissing her claim for fraudulent concealment because such a claim lies for fraudulent non-disclosure of a patent application under *University of Colorado.* She also contends that she adequately pleaded a claim for breach of fiduciary duty, which she argues is construed broadly under Illinois law. She further asserts that the court erred in dismissing her unjust enrichment claim because it did not consider her allegation that Roizman arranged the assignment of the application for the '688 patent from ARCH to Aviron even before he assigned it to Institut Merieux. She also argues that her breach of contract claim should not have been dismissed because she and Roizman expressly agreed to split any royalties resulting from the patents. Alternatively, she argues that she adequately stated a claim for breach of an implied contract because she pleaded that she and Roizman established a course of dealing to share royalties, and that Roizman unjustly retained the benefits of sole inventorship to her detriment. Finally, Chou argues that the court erred in striking her allegations of academic theft and fraud and requests that we remand the case to the Executive Committee of the United States District Court for the Northern District of Illinois for reassignment to a different judge.

The defendants respond that Chou lacks standing to sue for correction of inventorship under § 256 because she was obligated to assign her inventions to the University by virtue of accepting employment under the University's administrative policies. The University/ARCH also argues that it is not properly included as a defendant in her § 256 action because Chou stipulated that the district court's reasoning applied to the University/ARCH to the same extent that it applied to Roizman, and that Chou has no standing to sue Roizman under § 256 because she has no ownership interest in the patents at issue. The defendants also contend that Chou lacks standing to sue for a declaratory judgment because she had no reasonable ground to believe that the defendants would file suit to correct inventorship under § 256.

With regard to Chou's state law claims, the defendants argue that the fraud count was properly dismissed because Roizman owed her no duty to disclose information about the filing of the patent applications, and that her breach of fiduciary duty claim is similarly deficient because the University does not impose a fiduciary duty upon its professors to disclose to their research assistants the filing of patent applications. The defendants also contend that Chou has no unjust enrichment claim because she assigned her rights to the University and has suffered no financial detriment as a result of Roizman's alleged actions. The defendants further argue that the district court did not err in dismissing her breach of contract claim because the agreement Chou relies upon for this claim refers only to an unrelated patent application upon which both Chou and Roizman were listed as joint inventors, and that her implied contract claim fails because Chou did not allege a course of dealing with Roizman to share royalties from all of the patent applications. Finally, the defendants assert that the court did not abuse its discretion in striking Chou's allegations of academic theft and fraud, and that the case should not be remanded to a different judge because Chou has not shown the threshold of bias or partiality in the trial judge that warrants such a reassignment.

A. Standing to Sue for Correction of Inventorship under 35 U.S.C. § 256

As a preliminary matter, we agree with the defendants that Chou was obligated to assign her inventions to the University. Although it is true that Chou never signed a contract with the University specifically obligating her to assign her inventions to the University, she accepted her academic appointment subject to the administrative policies of the University. We are not persuaded by Chou's argument that the University's administrative policies do not include its patent statutes. The Faculty Handbook refers to the patent statutes as patent policies within a section entitled "Academic Policies." The University's Patent Statute section 20 provides as follows:

> Every patentable invention or discovery that results from research or other activities carried out at the University, or with the aid of its facilities or funds administered by it, shall be the property of the University, and shall be assigned, as determined by the University, to the University, to an organization sponsoring the activities, or to an outside organization deemed capable of administering patents.

It is true that the Faculty Handbook contains the following statement: "The contents of this handbook do not create a contract or agreement between an individual and the University." That statement, however, must be read in light of the statement immediately following it: "The basic terms and conditions of the employment agreement are set out in the letter of appointment received from the Provost's Office." Chou's letter of appointment stated that the appointment was subject to "the administrative policies of the University," which include the obligation to assign inventions to the University. Illinois law, which governs our determination of Chou's assignment obligations, thus obligated Chou to assign her inventions to the University even though she never specifically agreed to do so. Chou accepted her appointment, thereby assuming the obligations set out in the University's policies. Moreover, she did not dispute her obligation when she assigned to the University other inventions for which she was a recognized inventor. We therefore conclude that if Chou is indeed an inventor of the contested subject matter, she would be obligated to assign those inventions to the University.

That conclusion, however, does not defeat Chou's standing to sue for correction of inventorship under § 256. Section 256 of title 35 provides a cause of action for judicial correction of inventorship:

> The error of omitting inventors or naming persons who are not inventors shall not invalidate the patent in which such error occurred if it can be corrected as provided in this section. The court before which such matter is called in question may order correction of the patent *on notice and hearing of all parties concerned* and the Director shall issue a certificate accordingly.

The district court is indeed a court before which the matter was called into question, and notice and an opportunity for a hearing were provided. Chou, as a party "concerned," is clearly within the purview of the statute, but she must meet constitutional standing requirements in order to invoke it. That is, she must show that she has suffered an injury-in-fact, that the injury is traceable to the conduct complained of, and that the injury is redressable by a favorable decision.

The district court determined that Chou did not have standing to sue for correction of inventorship on the basis of "[t]he principle that one who claims no ownership of the patent has no standing to seek relief under § 256." The question whether a putative inventor who is obligated to assign her invention to another is entitled to sue for correction of inventorship under § 256 action is one of first impression for this court, notwithstanding the parties' arguments to the contrary. Chou argues that *University of Colorado* holds that a true inventor has the right to bring a § 256 action even absent an ownership interest. Although that case involved a § 256 action, we did not decide whether alleged inventors had an independent right to bring suit even though they had assigned their interest to the University.

We conclude that an expectation of ownership of a patent is not a prerequisite for a putative inventor to possess standing to sue to correct inventorship under § 256. The statute imposes no requirement of potential ownership in the patent on those seeking to invoke it. We have previously interpreted § 256 broadly as a "savings provision" to prevent patent rights from being extinguished simply because the inventors are not correctly listed. The same considerations apply here. Chou should have the right to assert her interest, both for her own benefit and in the public interest of assuring correct inventorship designations on patents. The interest of both inventors and the public are thus served by a broad interpretation of the statute.

Chou argues that a reputational interest alone is enough to satisfy the requirements of Article III standing. That assertion is not implausible. After all, being considered an inventor of important subject matter is a mark of success in one's field, comparable to being an author of an important scientific paper. Pecuniary consequences may well flow from being designated as an inventor. However, we need not decide that issue because Chou has alleged a concrete financial interest in the patent, albeit an interest less than ownership. Chou claims that the University is obligated to provide "[f]aculty, student and staff inventors . . . 25% of the gross royalties and up-front payments from licensing activities." She also claims the right to receive rights to 25% of the stock of new companies based on their inventions. If Chou has indeed been deprived of an interest in proceeds from licensing the invention and in stock ownership by the conduct that she alleges, then she will have suffered an injury-in-fact, *i.e.*, the loss of those benefits. That loss would be directly traceable to Roizman's alleged conduct in naming himself as the sole inventor of discoveries that she at least partly made, and it would be redressable by an order from the district court to the Director of the PTO to issue a certificate naming Chou as an inventor, which would entitle her under the University's policy to a share of the licensing proceeds and stock already received by Roizman. We therefore determine that Chou is entitled to sue for correction of inventorship under § 256.

We next address the question of which defendants Chou may sue under § 256. The validity of a patent requires that the inventors be correctly named. It follows that parties with an economic stake in a patent's validity are entitled to be heard on inventorship issues once a putative inventor has sued to correct inventorship. Moreover, we have cited with approval authority in which such parties have been subject to § 256 actions, even over their objection. We therefore conclude that parties with an economic stake in a patent's validity may be subject to a § 256 suit.

Each of the defendants in this case has an economic stake in the validity of the patents involved and hence in the correct inventorship designations on the patents. The University/ARCH owns the '688 and '713 patents and derives royalty income therefrom. Aviron owns the '328 patent and possesses exclusive licenses under the '688 and '713 patents; it derives royalties from its sublicense of those patents to NeuroVir. Roizman similarly receives a portion of the royalty income and stock benefits from those patents based on the University's policy to reward inventors. All of those benefits would be jeopardized by a determination that the patents are invalid for improper inventorship. Roizman's share of the profits would also be affected by joinder of Chou. Thus, each of the defendants has an economic stake in a correct inventorship designation on the patents at issue and each may properly be named as a defendant in this § 256 action.

Accordingly, we reverse the district court's conclusion that Chou has no standing to sue Roizman under 35 U.S.C. § 256, and instruct that court to reinstate her § 256 claim against the University and ARCH, and, if necessary, allow Chou leave to amend her § 256 claim to add Aviron as a defendant. The district court will determine whether Chou should be named as the sole inventor or a co-inventor on the '688 patent or a co-inventor on the '713 and '328 patents.

C. State Law Claims

1. Fraudulent Concealment

We agree with Chou that the district court erred in dismissing her complaint for failure to state a claim for fraudulent concealment of the '688 patent application. Fed.R.Civ.P. 9(b) requires that facts supporting a claim of fraud be pleaded with particularity. In Illinois, a plaintiff must allege that a defendant concealed a material fact when he was under a duty to disclose that fact to the plaintiff. The duty to disclose a material fact may arise if the plaintiff and defendant are in a fiduciary or confidential relationship, or if the plaintiff places trust and confidence in the defendant, thereby placing the defendant in a position of influence and superiority over the plaintiff. That position of superiority may arise out of friendship, agency, or experience.

Chou alleged that Roizman had a responsibility under University policies and by virtue of their advisor-advisee relationship to not misappropriate her inventions. Chou has also alleged that Roizman specifically told her that he would take care to properly protect her research, inventions and co-inventions. The University's patent policy requires the University to endeavor to "provide a return to the inventor or creator." Similarly, under the policy, "[t]he inventor or creator and his or her Dean or other administrative head shall be consulted and kept informed of the [patenting] arrangements." The University's patent policy also requires that the disposition of patent rights be consistent with the requirements of law and professional ethics. As a member of the University's faculty, Roizman had a duty to abide by those policies, and Chou alleged that she trusted that he would do so. Thus, we conclude that Chou alleged with particularity that Roizman had a duty to disclose material facts relating to the patenting of her discoveries.

With respect to his failure to disclose such facts, Chou alleged that she told Roizman in February 1991 that her discoveries should be patented, and that he disagreed with her but did not tell her that he had already filed an application on those discoveries. Thus, Chou alleges all of the elements of a claim of fraudulent concealment by Roizman, *viz.*, that Roizman concealed the material fact of a patent application of which she may have been a true inventor when he was under a duty to disclose that fact because he held a position of superiority with respect to her and was obligated by University patent policies to give her proper inventorship credit.

In *University of Colorado*, we stated that a claim for fraudulent nondisclosure turned on the status of the unnamed inventors as true inventors. Chou's claim for fraudulent concealment similarly depends on her status as a true inventor of the patents, a determination we have decided that the district court has jurisdiction to make. We therefore conclude that the district court erred in dismissing Chou's claim against Roizman for fraudulent concealment.

Chou has also alleged that Roizman is an agent of the University/ARCH and Aviron, and that those entities are liable for his fraudulent nondisclosure under agency principles. We agree that Chou has adequately stated a claim that the University is liable under the doctrine of respondeat superior for Roizman's alleged concealment of his misappropriation of Chou's inventions. In Illinois, employers may be liable for the actions of their employees if they are within the scope of employment, *i.e.*, if those actions are the kind the employee was hired to perform, the actions occur substantially within the authorized time and space limits, and they are actuated, at least in part, by a purpose to serve the master. While university faculty are not agents of the university with respect to the selection and conduct of their research projects, they may well be agents with respect to implementing policies of the university, including ownership of inventions and compensation therefor. The University's Faculty Handbook recognizes such an agency with respect to its patent policies, stating that "[t]he University, acting directly or through its designee, shall endeavor to license or assign such products in such a manner as to assure the greatest benefits to the University and the public, and provide a return to the inventor or creator." Roizman allegedly named himself as the sole inventor of Chou's discoveries and applied for a patent on those discoveries under the auspices of his authority as a department chairman of the University to recommend and direct patent prosecution on inventions made in his research lab. We therefore conclude that Chou has adequately stated a claim for fraudulent nondisclosure by the University/ARCH under principles of respondeat superior.

2. Breach of Fiduciary Duty

We also agree with Chou that the district court erred in dismissing her claim against Roizman for breach of fiduciary duty. A fiduciary duty in Illinois may arise in one of two ways. A fiduciary relationship automatically arises from particular relationships, such as attorney-client and principal-agent, as a matter of law. A fiduciary relationship may also arise from the special circumstances of the parties' relationship, such as when one party justifiably places trust in another so that the latter gains superiority and influence over the former. The relevant factors in determining whether the latter fiduciary relationship exists include the disparity in age, education, and business experience between the parties, and the extent to which the "servient" party entrusted the handling of its affairs to the "dominant" party and placed its trust and confidence in that party. The existence of a fiduciary relationship prohibits the dominant party with the duty from seeking or obtaining any selfish benefit for himself at the expense of the servient party while the fiduciary duty exists.

Chou alleged that Roizman held a position of superiority over her as her department chairman, and that he had specifically represented to her that he would protect and give her proper credit for her research and inventions. Given the disparity of their experience and roles, and Roizman's responsibility to make patenting decisions regarding Chou's inventions, Chou has adequately pleaded the existence of circumstances that place on Roizman a fiduciary duty with respect to her inventions. Furthermore, Chou pleaded that Roizman breached that duty by naming himself as an inventor of her discoveries. Resolving all inferences in favor of Chou, as we must at this stage of the proceedings, we conclude that she has sufficiently stated a claim of breach of fiduciary duty and that the district court erred in dismissing that claim.

We also agree with Chou that she has stated a claim against the University for breach of fiduciary duty under the theory of respondeat superior for the same reasons as for her fraudulent concealment claim.

CONCLUSION

Because the district court erred in holding that Chou did not have standing to sue for correction of inventorship under § 256, we reverse and remand for adjudication of that claim against all of the defendants. We also reverse the court's determination that Chou failed to state claims for fraudulent concealment, breach of fiduciary duty, unjust enrichment, and breach of implied contract against Roizman, and we direct the court to reinstate Chou's claims for fraudulent concealment, breach of fiduciary duty, and breach of an express contract against the University/ARCH. We affirm, however, its decision dismissing all other claims against Aviron, and its decision to strike Chou's allegations of academic theft and fraud pursuant to Fed.R.Civ.P. 12(f). We do not address the court's dismissal of her declaratory judgment claim for correction of inventorship because that issue is moot. Finally, we decline to remand the case to the Executive Committee for reassignment to a different judge. Accordingly, we

AFFIRM-IN-PART, REVERSE-IN-PART, and REMAND.

QUESTIONS

1.   What would a student research assistant have to show in order to establish standing for a correction of inventorship claim under 35 U.S.C. § 256?

2.   The court found that Chou had assigned her interest in the patents at issue. What interest did the court find that Chou had in these patents sufficient to provide her standing to correct inventorship under 35 U.S.C. § 256?

3.   On what basis did the court find that Roizman owed Chou a fiduciary duty?

4.   Could the University of Chicago have adopted any administrative policies to prevent breach of fiduciary duty claims against the University based on *respondeat superior*?

5.   If you were counsel to a major research university after the *Chou* case and asked to draft a memo outlining the main points faculty should keep in mind when supervising student research, what would these points be?

CASE NOTES

1.   Johnson was a graduate student in a doctoral program at Yale University in the School of Forestry and Environmental Studies. Skelly was a faculty member on his doctoral advisory committee, and Schmitz was the co-chair of the committee. During the course of his research, Johnson developed a novel idea for his dissertation based on the Trophic-Dynamic Theory of Redundancy (the Theory). Johnson recorded notes about his Theory in a private journal, which he later found other students had read and discussed with Schmitz. Johnson expressed concern to the other committee co-chair, Vogt, that Schmitz might misappropriate his theory. Vogt assured him that would not happen. Over the course of the next year while Johnson was continuing to pursue his research, Schmitz began steering his research along the same lines. During his oral defense of his doctoral dissertation, Johnson's Theory was aggressively criticized by Schmitz and Skelly. Johnson was told that his "thinking was flawed" and that his ideas were "ridiculous and unoriginal." However, following the oral defense, Schmitz and Skelly jointly published an article on Johnson's Theory without any attribution to Johnson. Johnson then complained again to Vogt, who assured him she would stop Schmitz from further appropriation of his Theory. When Vogt failed to do so, Johnson submitted a formal letter to the Director of Doctoral Studies complaining of academic fraud. Johnson never received a response to his letter, but shortly thereafter, Yale stopped paying his monthly salary supplement and providing his funding support. Johnson then wrote to the Dean of Yale School of Forestry and Environmental Studies, again complaining of

academic fraud. An inquiry committee was formed which, five months later, informed Johnson it had not found any reasonable grounds for his allegations of academic fraud. Finally, Johnson appealed to the Yale Provost, who declined to re-evaluate his claim. Johnson then filed suit against Yale claiming breach of express and implied contracts to safeguard students from academic misconduct and to investigate charges of academic misconduct. Johnson also claimed that Yale breached its fiduciary duty to him, was negligent in enforcing its rules and guidelines, and defamed his Theory. What result? *See* Johnson v. Schmitz, et. al., 119 F.Supp. 2d 90 (D. Conn. 2000).

2.   *See also* Cencor, Inc. v. Tolman, 868 P.2d 396 (Colo. 1994) (Students alleging school breached contractual obligation to provide educational services which students had paid stated a breach of contract claim); Gupta v. New Britain General Hospital, 239 Conn. 574 (Conn. 1996) (General allegation that educational program was inadequate was insufficient to state a cause of action for breach of residency agreement; judiciary is ill equipped to undertake review of adequacy of educational program); Doe v. Yale Univ., 252 Conn. 641 (Conn. 2000) (Action alleging that hospital's failure to adequately supervise and instruct student causing her to become exposed to HIV virus was not a breach of contract claim; action was a negligence action which court would review).

Additional Information

1.   Melissa Astala, *Wronged by a Professor: Breach of Fiduciary Duty as a Remedy in Intellectual Property Infringement Cases*, 3 Hous. Bus. & Tax L. J. 31 (2003).

2.   Kyle Grimshaw, *A Victory for the Student Researcher: Chou v. University of Chicago*, 2001 Duke L. & Tech. Rev. 35 (2001).

3.   Daniel P. Valentine, *Chou v. University of Chicago: Assigned Patent Rights — Gone But Not Forgotten*, 42 Jurimetrics J. 493 (2002).

4.   Carmen J. McCutcheon, *Fairplay or Greed: Mandating University Responsibility Toward Student Inventors*, 2003 Duke L. & Tech. Rev. 26 (2003).

5.   Brett G. Scharffs, John W. Welch, *An Analytical Framework for Understanding and Evaluating the Fiduciary Duties of Educators*, 2005 B.Y.U. Educ. & L.J. 159 (2005).

6.   Carmenelisa Perez-Kudzma, *Fiduciary Duties in Academia: An Uphill Battle*, 48 Idea 491 (2008).

7.   Kent Weeks, Rich Haglund, *Fiduciary Duties of College and University Faculty and Administrators*, 29 J.C. & U.L. 153 (2002).

8.   Terry Wright, *Graduate Student Patent Rights: Lesson Learned from University of West Virginia v. VanVoorhies*, available at http://brandlaw.org/2010/01/graduate-students-patent-rights/.

3.6   UNIVERSITY-FACULTY EMPLOYMENT CONTRACTS

University-faculty employment contracts govern many aspects of the parties' relationship, including intellectual property ownership, royalty sharing and control over licensing decisions. In many ways, university-faculty employment contracts are very similar to private sector employer-employee contracts. In both, the employer invariably claims ownership to any intellectual property created by the employee, complete discretion as to sharing profits from the intellectual property with the employee-creator, and final authority as to the ultimate disposition of employee-created intellectual property. One significant difference between faculty and private sector employees, however, is that faculty who are awarded tenure have a guaranteed job for life, whereas private sector employees are often subject to dismissal at the will of the employer. Some have suggested that the more favorable terms of faculty employment should entitle universities to more favorable terms in faculty employment contracts. However, as discussed earlier, faculty are increasingly resistant to such claims.

The cases in this section consider different aspects of the university-faculty employment relationship. In the *Stanford* case, the Supreme Court addresses the question of original patent ownership in the context of federally funded research governed by the Bayh-Dole Act? In this landmark case, the issue before the Court is whether the Bayh-Dole Act grants original patent ownership to the university or to the faculty inventor. The *Shaw* case addresses the question of whether a university can unilaterally change its patent policy and its royalty sharing agreement with a faculty inventor. The final case, *Kucharczyk*, considers a faculty member's right to royalty payments when the university decides to monetize the royalty payments in exchange for a single, lump-sum payment.

The decisions in each of these cases are heavily dependent upon the language used in the university-faculty employment contracts. As you read the cases, consider what language you would have used to lessen the risk of litigation.

STANFORD v. ROCHE
131 S. Ct. 2188 (2011)

Chief Justice Roberts

Since 1790, the patent law has operated on the premise that rights in an invention belong to the inventor. The question here is whether the University and Small Business Patent Procedures Act of 1980 — commonly referred to as the Bayh-Dole Act — displaces that norm and automatically vests title to federally funded inventions in federal contractors. We hold that it does not.

I

A

In 1985, a small California research company called Cetus began to develop methods for quantifying blood-borne levels of human immunodeficiency virus

(HIV), the virus that causes AIDS. A Nobel Prize winning technique developed at Cetus — polymerase chain reaction, or PCR — was an integral part of these efforts. PCR allows billions of copies of DNA sequences to be made from a small initial blood sample.

In 1988, Cetus began to collaborate with scientists at Stanford University's Department of Infectious Diseases to test the efficacy of new AIDS drugs. Dr. Mark Holodniy joined Stanford as a research fellow in the department around that time. When he did so, he signed a Copyright and Patent Agreement (CPA) stating that he "agree[d] to assign" to Stanford his "right, title and interest in" inventions resulting from his employment at the University.

At Stanford Holodniy undertook to develop an improved method for quantifying HIV levels in patient blood samples, using PCR. Because Holodniy was largely unfamiliar with PCR, his supervisor arranged for him to conduct research at Cetus. As a condition of gaining access to Cetus, Holodniy signed a Visitor's Confidentiality Agreement (VCA). That agreement stated that Holodniy "will assign and do[es] hereby assign" to Cetus his "right, title and interest in each of the ideas, inventions and improvements" made "as a consequence of [his] access" to Cetus.

For the next nine months, Holodniy conducted research at Cetus. Working with Cetus employees, Holodniy devised a PCR-based procedure for calculating the amount of HIV in a patient's blood. That technique allowed doctors to determine whether a patient was benefiting from HIV therapy.

Holodniy then returned to Stanford where he and other University employees tested the HIV measurement technique. Over the next few years, Stanford obtained written assignments of rights from the Stanford employees involved in refinement of the technique, including Holodniy, and filed several patent applications related to the procedure. Stanford secured three patents to the HIV measurement process.

In 1991, Roche Molecular Systems, a company that specializes in diagnostic blood screening, acquired Cetus's PCR-related assets, including all rights Cetus had obtained through agreements like the VCA signed by Holodniy. After conducting clinical trials on the HIV quantification method developed at Cetus, Roche commercialized the procedure. Today, Roche's HIV test "kits are used in hospitals and AIDS clinics worldwide."

B

In 1980, Congress passed the Bayh-Dole Act to "promote the utilization of inventions arising from federally supported research," "promote collaboration between commercial concerns and nonprofit organizations," and "ensure that the Government obtains sufficient rights in federally supported inventions." 35 U.S.C. § 200. To achieve these aims, the Act allocates rights in federally funded "subject invention[s]" between the Federal Government and federal contractors ("any person, small business firm, or nonprofit organization that is a party to a funding agreement"). §§ 201(e), (c), 202(a). The Act defines "subject invention" as "any invention of the contractor conceived or first actually reduced to practice in the performance of work under a funding agreement." § 201(e).

The Bayh-Dole Act provides that contractors may "elect to retain title to any subject invention." § 202(a). To be able to retain title, a contractor must fulfill a number of obligations imposed by the statute. The contractor must "disclose each subject invention to the [relevant] Federal agency within a reasonable time"; it must "make a written election within two years after disclosure" stating that the contractor opts to retain title to the invention; and the contractor must "file a patent application prior to any statutory bar date." §§ 202(c)(1)–(3). The "Federal Government may receive title" to a subject invention if a contractor fails to comply with any of these obligations.

The Government has several rights in federally funded subject inventions under the Bayh-Dole Act. The agency that granted the federal funds receives from the contractor "a nonexclusive, nontransferrable, irrevocable, paid-up license to practice . . . [the] subject invention." § 202(c)(4). The agency also possesses "[m]arch-in rights," which permit the agency to grant a license to a responsible third party under certain circumstances, such as when the contractor fails to take "effective steps to achieve practical application" of the invention. § 203. The Act further provides that when the contractor does not elect to retain title to a subject invention, the Government "may consider and after consultation with the contractor grant requests for retention of rights by the inventor." § 202(d).

Some of Stanford's research related to the HIV measurement technique was funded by the National Institutes of Health (NIH), thereby subjecting the invention to the Bayh-Dole Act. Accordingly, Stanford disclosed the invention, conferred on the Government a nonexclusive, nontransferable, paid-up license to use the patented procedure, and formally notified NIH that it elected to retain title to the invention.

C

In 2005, the Board of Trustees of Stanford University filed suit against Roche Molecular Systems, Inc., Roche Diagnostics Corporation, and Roche Diagnostics Operations, Inc. (collectively Roche), contending that Roche's HIV test kits infringed Stanford's patents. As relevant here, Roche responded by asserting that it was a co-owner of the HIV quantification procedure, based on Holodniy's assignment of his rights in the Visitor's Confidentiality Agreement. As a result, Roche argued, Stanford lacked standing to sue it for patent infringement. Stanford claimed that Holodniy had no rights to assign because the University's HIV research was federally funded, giving the school superior rights in the invention under the Bayh-Dole Act.

The District Court held that the "VCA effectively assigned any rights that Holodniy had in the patented invention to Cetus," and thus to Roche. But because of the operation of the Bayh-Dole Act, "Holodniy had no interest to assign." The court concluded that the Bayh-Dole Act "provides that the individual inventor may obtain title" to a federally funded invention "only after the government and the contracting party have declined to do so."

The Court of Appeals for the Federal Circuit disagreed. First, the court concluded that Holodniy's initial agreement with Stanford in the Copyright and Patent Agreement constituted a mere promise to assign rights in the future, unlike Holodniy's agreement with Cetus in the Visitor's Confidentiality Agreement, which itself assigned Holodniy's rights in the invention to Cetus. Therefore, as a matter of contract law, Cetus obtained Holodniy's rights in the HIV quantification technique through the VCA. Next, the court explained that the Bayh-Dole Act "does not automatically void ab initio the inventors' rights in government-funded inventions" and that the "statutory scheme did not automatically void the patent rights that Cetus received from Holodniy." The court held that "Roche possesse[d] an ownership interest in the patents-in-suit" that was not extinguished by the Bayh-Dole Act, "depriv[ing] Stanford of standing." The Court of Appeals then remanded the case with instructions to dismiss Stanford's infringement claim.

We granted certiorari. 562 U.S. ___ (2010).

II

A

Congress has the authority "[t]o promote the Progress of Science and useful Arts, by securing . . . to Authors and Inventors the exclusive Right to their respective Writings and Discoveries." U.S. Const. Art. I, § 8, cl. 8. The first Congress put that power to use by enacting the Patent Act of 1790. That Act provided "[t]hat upon the petition of any person or persons . . . setting forth, that he, she, or they, hath or have invented or discovered" an invention, a patent could be granted to "such petitioner or petitioners" or "their heirs, administrators or assigns." Act of Apr. 10, 1790, § 1, 1 Stat. 109-110. Under that law, the first patent was granted in 1790 to Samuel Hopkins, who had devised an improved method for making potash, America's first industrial chemical. U.S. Patent No. 1 (issued July 31, 1790).

Although much in intellectual property law has changed in the 220 years since the first Patent Act, the basic idea that inventors have the right to patent their inventions has not. Under the law in its current form, "[w]hoever invents or discovers any new and useful process, machine, manufacture, or composition of matter . . . may obtain a patent therefor." 35 U.S.C. § 101. The inventor must attest that "he believes himself to be the original and first inventor of the [invention] for which he solicits a patent." § 115. In most cases, a patent may be issued only to an applying inventor, or — because an inventor's interest in his invention is "assignable in law by an instrument in writing" — an inventor's assignee. §§ 151, 152, 261.

Our precedents confirm the general rule that rights in an invention belong to the inventor. See, *e.g.*, *Gayler v. Wilder*, 10 How. 477, 493 (1851) ("the discoverer of a new and useful improvement is vested by law with an inchoate right to its exclusive use, which he may perfect and make absolute by proceeding in the manner which the law requires"); *Solomons v. United States*, 137 U.S. 342, 346 (1890) ("whatever invention [an inventor] may thus conceive and perfect is his individual property"); *United States v. Dubilier Condenser Corp.*, 289 U.S. 178, 188, (1933) (an inventor owns "the product of [his] original thought"). The treatises are to the same effect. See, *e.g.*, 8 Chisum on Patents § 22.01, p. 22-2 (2011) ("The presumptive owner of the property right in a patentable invention is the single human inventor").

It is equally well established that an inventor can assign his rights in an invention to a third party. See *Dubilier Condenser Corp., supra*, at 187 ("A patent is property and title to it can pass only by assignment"); 8 Chisum on Patents, *supra*, § 22.01, at 22-2 ("The inventor . . . [may] transfer ownership interests by written assignment to anyone"). Thus, although others may acquire an interest in an invention, any such interest — as a general rule — must trace back to the inventor.

In accordance with these principles, we have recognized that unless there is an agreement to the contrary, an employer does not have rights in an invention "which is the original conception of the employee alone." *Dubilier Condenser Corp.*, 289 U.S., at 189. Such an invention "remains the property of him who conceived it." In most circumstances, an inventor must expressly grant his rights in an invention to his employer if the employer is to obtain those rights. See *id.*, at 187 ("The respective rights and obligations of employer and employee, touching an invention conceived by the latter, spring from the contract of employment").

B

Stanford and the United States as *amicus curiae* contend that the Bayh-Dole Act reorders the normal priority of rights in an invention when the invention is conceived or first reduced to practice with the support of federal funds. In their view, the Act moves inventors from the front of the line to the back by vesting title to federally funded inventions in the inventor's employer — the federal contractor.

Congress has in the past divested inventors of their rights in inventions by providing unambiguously that inventions created pursuant to specified federal contracts become the property of the United States. For example, with respect to certain contracts dealing with nuclear material and atomic energy, Congress provided that title to such inventions "shall be vested in, and be the property of, the [Atomic Energy] Commission." 42 U.S.C. § 2182. Congress has also enacted laws requiring that title to certain inventions made pursuant to contracts with the National Aeronautics and Space Administration "shall be the exclusive property of the United States," 51 U.S.C. § 20135(b)(1), and that title to certain inventions under contracts with the Department of Energy "shall vest in the United States." 42 U.S.C. § 5908.

Such language is notably absent from the Bayh-Dole Act. Nowhere in the Act is title expressly vested in contractors or anyone else; nowhere in the Act are inventors expressly deprived of their interest in federally funded inventions. Instead, the Act provides that contractors may "elect to retain title to any subject invention." 35 U.S.C. § 202(a). A "subject invention" is defined as "any invention of the contractor conceived or first actually reduced to practice in the performance of work under a funding agreement." § 201(e).

Stanford asserts that the phrase "invention of the contractor" in this provision "is naturally read to include all inventions made by the contractor's employees with the aid of federal funding." That reading assumes that Congress subtly set aside two centuries of patent law in a statutory definition. It also renders the phrase "of the contractor" superfluous. If the phrase "of the contractor" were deleted from the definition of "subject invention," the definition would cover "any invention . . . conceived or first actually reduced to practice in the performance of work under a funding agreement." Reading "of the contractor" to mean "all inventions made by the contractor's employees with the aid of federal funding," as Stanford would, adds nothing that is not already in the definition, since the definition already covers inventions made under the funding agreement. That is contrary to our general "reluctan[ce] to treat statutory terms as surplusage."

Construing the phrase to refer instead to a particular category of inventions conceived or reduced to practice under a funding agreement — inventions "of the contractor," that is, those owned by or belonging to the contractor — makes the phrase meaningful in the statutory definition. And "invention owned by the contractor" or "invention belonging to the contractor" are natural readings of the phrase "invention of the contractor." As we have explained, "[t]he use of the word "of" denotes ownership."

That reading follows from a common definition of the word "of." See Webster's Third New International Dictionary 1565 (2002) ("of" can be "used as a function word indicating a possessive relationship"); New Oxford American Dictionary 1180 (2d ed.2005) (defining "of" as "indicating an association between two entities, typically one of belonging"); Webster's New Twentieth Century Dictionary 1241 (2d ed.1979) (defining "of" as "belonging to").

Stanford's reading of the phrase "invention of the contractor" to mean "all inventions made by the contractor's employees" is plausible enough in the abstract; it is often the case that whatever an employee produces in the course of his employment belongs to his employer. No one would claim that an autoworker who builds a car while working in a factory owns that car. But, as noted, patent law has always been different: We have rejected the idea that mere employment is sufficient to vest title to an employee's invention in the employer. Against this background, a contractor's invention — an "invention of the contractor" — does not automatically include inventions made by the contractor's employees.

The Bayh-Dole Act's provision stating that contractors may "elect to *retain* title" confirms that the Act does not *vest* title. 35 U.S.C. § 202(a) (emphasis added). Stanford reaches the opposite conclusion, but only because it reads "retain" to mean "acquire" and "receive." That is certainly not the common meaning of "retain." "[R]etain" means "to hold or continue to hold in possession or use." You cannot retain something unless you already have it. The Bayh-Dole Act does not confer title to federally funded inventions on contractors or authorize contractors to unilaterally take title to those inventions; it simply assures contractors that they may keep title to whatever it is they already have. Such a provision makes sense in a statute specifying the respective rights and responsibilities of federal contractors and the Government.

The Bayh-Dole Act states that it "take[s] precedence over any other Act which would require a disposition of rights in subject inventions . . . that is inconsistent with" the Act. 35 U.S.C. § 210(a). The United States as *amicus curiae* argues that this provision operates to displace the basic principle, codified in the Patent Act, that an inventor owns the rights to his invention. But because the Bayh-Dole Act, including § 210(a), applies only to "subject inventions" — "inventions of the contractor" — it does not displace an inventor's antecedent title to his invention. Only when an invention belongs to the contractor does the Bayh-Dole Act come into play. The Act's disposition of rights — like much of the rest of the Bayh-Dole Act — serves to clarify the order of priority of rights between the Federal Government and a federal contractor in a federally funded invention that already belongs to the contractor. Nothing more.

The isolated provisions of the Bayh-Dole Act dealing with inventors' rights in subject inventions are consistent with our construction of the Act. Under the Act, a federal agency may "grant requests for retention of rights by the inventor . . . [i]f a contractor does not elect to retain title to a subject invention." § 202(d). If an employee inventor never had title to his invention because title vested in the contractor by operation of law — as Stanford submits — it would be odd to allow the Government to grant "requests for retention of rights by the inventor." By using the word "retention," § 202(d) assumes that the inventor had rights in the subject invention at some point, undermining the notion that the Act automatically vests title to federally funded inventions in federal contractors.

The limited scope of the Act's procedural protections also bolsters our conclusion. The Bayh-Dole Act expressly confers on contractors the right to challenge a Government-imposed impediment to retaining title to a subject invention. § 202(b)(4). As Roche correctly notes, however, "the Act contains not a single procedural protection for third parties that have neither sought nor received federal funds," such as cooperating private research institutions. Nor does the Bayh-Dole Act allow inventors employed by federal contractors to contest their employer's claim to a subject invention. The Act, for example, does not expressly permit an interested third party or an inventor to challenge a claim that a particular invention was supported by federal funding. In a world in which there is frequent collaboration between private entities, inventors, and federal contractors, that absence would be deeply troubling. But the lack of procedures protecting inventor and third-party rights makes perfect sense if the Act applies only when a federal contractor has already acquired title to an inventor's interest. In that case, there is no need to protect inventor or third-party rights, because the only rights at issue are those of the contractor and the Government.

The Bayh-Dole Act applies to subject inventions "conceived *or* first actually reduced to practice in the performance of work" "funded in whole *or in part* by the Federal Government." 35 U.S.C. §§ 201(e), 201(b) (emphasis added). Under Stanford's construction of the Act, title to one of its employee's inventions could vest in the University even if the invention was conceived before the inventor became a University employee, so long as the invention's reduction to practice was supported by federal funding. What is more, Stanford's reading suggests that the school would obtain title to one of its employee's inventions even if only one dollar of federal funding was applied toward the invention's conception or reduction to practice.

It would be noteworthy enough for Congress to supplant one of the fundamental precepts of patent law and deprive inventors of rights in their own inventions. To do so under such unusual terms would be truly surprising. We are confident that if Congress had intended such a sea change in intellectual property rights it would have said so clearly — not obliquely through an ambiguous definition of "subject invention" and an idiosyncratic use of the word "retain."

Though unnecessary to our conclusion, it is worth noting that our construction of the Bayh-Dole Act is reflected in the common practice among parties operating under the Act. Contractors generally institute policies to obtain assignments from their employees. Agencies that grant funds to federal contractors typically expect those contractors to obtain assignments. So it is with NIH, the agency that granted the federal funds at issue in this case. In guidance documents made available to contractors, NIH has made clear that "[b]y law, an inventor has initial ownership of an invention" and that contractors should therefore "have in place employee agreements requiring an inventor to "assign" or give ownership of an invention to the organization upon acceptance of Federal funds. Such guidance would be unnecessary if Stanford's reading of the statute were correct.

Stanford contends that reading the Bayh-Dole Act as not vesting title to federally funded inventions in federal contractors "fundamentally undermin[es]" the Act's framework and severely threatens its continued "successful application." We do not agree. As just noted, universities typically enter into agreements with their employees requiring the assignment to the university of rights in inventions. With an effective assignment, those inventions — if federally funded — become "subject inventions" under the Act, and the statute as a practical matter works pretty much the way Stanford says it should. The only significant difference is that it does so without violence to the basic principle of patent law that inventors own their inventions.

The judgment of the Court of Appeals for the Federal Circuit is affirmed.

****

JUSTICE BREYER, with whom JUSTICE GINSBURG joins, dissenting.

The question presented in this case is:

> Whether a federal contractor university's statutory right under the Bayh-Dole Act, 35 U.S.C. §§ 200–212, in inventions arising from federally funded research can be terminated unilaterally by an individual inventor through a separate agreement purporting to assign the inventor's rights to a third party.

In my view, the answer to this question is likely no. But because that answer turns on matters that have not been fully briefed (and are not resolved by the opinion of the Court), I would return this case to the Federal Circuit for further argument.

I

The Bayh-Dole Act creates a three-tier system for patent rights ownership applicable to federally funded research conducted by nonprofit organizations, such as universities, and small businesses. It sets forth conditions that mean (1) the funded firm; (2) failing that, the United States Government; and (3) failing that, the employee who made the invention, will likely obtain (or retain) any resulting patent rights (normally in that just-listed order). 35 U.S.C. §§ 202–203. The statute applies to "subject invention[s]" defined as "any *invention of the contractor* conceived or first actually reduced to practice in the performance of work under a funding agreement." § 201(e) (emphasis added). Since the "contractor" (*e.g.*, a university or small business) is unlikely to "conceiv[e]" of an idea or "reduc[e]" it "to practice" *other than* through its employees, the term "invention of the contractor" must refer to the work and ideas of those employees. We all agree that the term covers those employee inventions that the employee properly assigns to the contractor, *i.e.*, his or her employer. But does the term "subject invention" also include inventions that the employee fails to assign properly?

II

Congress enacted this statute against a background norm that often, but not always, denies individual inventors patent rights growing out of research for which the public has already paid. This legal norm reflects the fact that patents themselves have both benefits and costs. Patents, for example, help to elicit useful inventions and research and to assure public disclosure of technological advances. But patents sometimes mean unnecessarily high prices or restricted dissemination; and they sometimes discourage further innovation and competition by requiring costly searches for earlier, related patents or by tying up ideas, which, were they free, would more effectively spur research and development.

Thus, Thomas Jefferson wrote of "the difficulty of drawing a line between the things which are worth to the public the embarrassment of an exclusive patent, and those which are not." And James Madison favored the patent monopoly because it amounted to "compensation for" a community "benefit."

The importance of assuring this community "benefit" is reflected in legal rules that may deny or limit the award of patent rights where the public has already paid to produce an invention, lest the public bear the potential costs of patent protection where there is no offsetting need for such protection to elicit that invention. Why should the public have to pay twice for the same invention?

Legal rules of this kind include an Executive Order that ordinarily gives to the Government "the entire right, title and interest" to inventions made by Government employees who "conduct or perform research, development work, or both." They also include statutes, which, in specific research areas, give the Government title to inventions made pursuant to Government contracts.

These legal rules provide the basic background against which Congress passed the Bayh-Dole Act. And the Act's provisions reflect a related effort to assure that rights to inventions arising out of research for which the public has paid are distributed and used in ways that further specific important public interests. I agree with the majority that the Act does not simply take the individual inventors' rights and grant them to the Government. Rather, it assumes that the federal funds' recipient, say a university or small business, will possess those rights. The Act leaves those rights in the hands of that recipient, not because it seeks to make the public pay twice for the same invention, but for a special public policy reason. In doing so, it seeks to encourage those institutions *to commercialize* inventions that otherwise might not realize their potentially beneficial public use. 35 U.S.C. § 200. The Act helps assure that commercialization (while "promot[ing] free competition" and "protect[ing] the public,") by imposing a set of conditions upon the federal funds recipient, by providing that sometimes the Government will take direct control of the patent rights, and by adding that on occasion the Government will permit the individual inventor to retain those rights. §§ 202–203.

Given this basic statutory objective, I cannot so easily accept the majority's conclusion — that the individual inventor can lawfully assign an invention (produced by public funds) to a third party, thereby taking that invention out from under the Bayh-Dole Act's restrictions, conditions, and allocation rules. That conclusion, in my view, is inconsistent with the Act's basic purposes. It may significantly undercut the Act's ability to achieve its objectives. It allows individual inventors, for whose invention the public has paid, to avoid the Act's corresponding restrictions and conditions. And it makes the commercialization and marketing of such an invention more difficult: A potential purchaser of rights from the contractor, say a university, will not know if the university itself possesses the patent right in question or whether, as here, the individual, inadvertently or deliberately, has previously assigned the title to a third party.

Moreover, I do not agree that the language to which the majority points — the words "invention of the contractor" and "retain" — requires its result. As the majority concedes, Stanford's alternative reading of the phrase " "invention of the contractor" " is "plausible enough in the abstract." Nor do I agree that the Act's lack of an explicit provision for "an interested third party" to claim that an invention was not the result of federal funding "bolsters" the majority's interpretation. In any event, universities and businesses have worked out ways to protect the various participants to research.

Ultimately, the majority rejects Stanford's reading (and the Government's reading) of the Act because it believes that it is inconsistent with certain background norms of patent law, norms that ordinarily provide an individual inventor with full patent rights. But in my view, the competing norms governing rights in inventions for which the public has already paid, along with the Bayh-Dole Act's objectives, suggest a different result.

III

There are two different legal routes to what I consider an interpretation more consistent with the statute's objectives. First, we could set aside the Federal Circuit's interpretation of the licensing agreements and its related licensing doctrine. That doctrine governs interpretation of licensing agreements made *before* an invention is conceived or reduced to practice. Here, there are two such agreements. In the earlier agreement — that between Dr. Holodniy and Stanford

University — Dr. Holodniy said, "I *agree to assign* . . . to Stanford . . . that right, title and interest in and to . . . such inventions as required by Contracts and Grants." In the later agreement — that between Dr. Holodniy and the private research firm Cetus — Dr. Holodniy said, "I will assign and *do hereby assign* to Cetus, my right, title, and interest in" here relevant "ideas" and "inventions."

The Federal Circuit held that the earlier Stanford agreement's use of the words "agree to assign," when compared with the later Cetus agreement's use of the words "do hereby assign," made all the difference. It concluded that, once the invention came into existence, the latter words meant that the Cetus agreement trumped the earlier, Stanford agreement. That, in the Circuit's view, is because the latter words operated upon the invention automatically, while the former did not. Quoting its 1991 opinion in *FilmTec Corp. v. Allied-Signal, Inc.*, 939 F.2d 1568, 1572, the Circuit declared that " "[o]nce the invention is made and [the] application for [a] patent is filed, . . . legal title to the rights accruing thereunder would be in the assignee [*i.e.*, Cetus] . . ., and the assignor-inventor would have nothing remaining to assign." "

Given what seem only slight linguistic differences in the contractual language, this reasoning seems to make too much of too little. Dr. Holodniy executed his agreement with Stanford in 1988. At that time, patent law appears to have long specified that a present assignment of future inventions (as in both contracts here) conveyed equitable, but not legal, title. See, *e.g.*, G. Curtis, A Treatise on the Law of Patents for Useful Inventions § 170, p. 155 (3d ed. 1867) ("A contract to convey a future invention . . . cannot alone authorize a patent to be taken by the party in whose favor such a contract was intended to operate"); Comment, Contract Rights as Commercial Security: Present and Future Intangibles, 67 Yale L.J. 847, 854, n. 27 (1958) ("The rule generally applicable grants equitable enforcement to an assignment of an expectancy but demands a further act, either reduction to possession or further assignment of the right when it comes into existence").

Under this rule, both the initial Stanford and later Cetus agreements would have given rise only to equitable interests in Dr. Holodniy's invention. And as between these two claims in equity, the facts that Stanford's contract came first and that Stanford subsequently obtained a post-invention assignment as well should have meant that Stanford, not Cetus, would receive the rights its contract conveyed.

In 1991, however, the Federal Circuit, in *FilmTec*, adopted the new rule quoted above — a rule that distinguishes between these equitable claims and, in effect, says that Cetus must win. The Federal Circuit provided no explanation for what seems a significant change in the law. Nor did it give any explanation for that change in its opinion in this case. The Federal Circuit's *FilmTec* rule undercuts the objectives of the Bayh-Dole Act. While the cognoscenti may be able to meet the *FilmTec* rule in future contracts simply by copying the precise words blessed by the Federal Circuit, the rule nonetheless remains a technical drafting trap for the unwary. It is unclear to me why, where the Bayh-Dole Act is at issue, we should prefer the Federal Circuit's *FilmTec* rule to the rule, of apparently much longer vintage, that would treat both agreements in this case as creating merely equitable rights.

At the same time, the Federal Circuit's reasoning brings about an interpretation contrary to the intention of the parties to the earlier, Stanford, contract. See App. to Pet. for Cert. 120a (provision in Stanford contract promising that Dr. Holodniy "will not enter into any agreement creating copyright or patent obligations in conflict with this agreement"). And it runs counter to what may well have been the drafters' reasonable expectations of how courts would interpret the relevant language.

Second, we could interpret the Bayh-Dole Act as ordinarily assuming, and thereby ordinarily requiring, an assignment of patent rights by the federally funded employee to the federally funded employer. I concede that this interpretation would treat federally funded employees of contractors (subject to the Act) differently than the law ordinarily treats private sector employees. The Court long ago described the latter, private sector principles. In *United States v. Dubilier Condenser Corp.*, 289 U.S. 178 (1933), the Court explained that a "patent is property, and title to it can pass only by assignment." It then described two categories of private sector employee-to-employer assignments as follows: First, a person who is

> employed to make an invention, who succeeds, during his term of service, in accomplishing that task, is bound to assign to his employer any patent obtained.

But, second,

> if the employment be general, albeit it cover a field of labor and effort in the performance of which the employee conceived the invention for which he obtained a patent, the contract is not so broadly construed as to require an assignment of the patent.

The Court added that, because of "the peculiar nature of the act of invention," courts are "reluctan[t] . . . to imply or infer an agreement by the employee to assign his patent." And it applied these same principles governing assignment to inventions made by employees of the United States.

Subsequently, however, the President promulgated Executive Order 10096. Courts have since found that this Executive Order, not *Dubilier*, governs Federal Government employee-to-employer patent right assignments. The Bayh-Dole Act seeks objectives roughly analogous to the objectives of the Executive Order. At least one agency has promulgated regulations that require Bayh-Dole contractors to insist upon similar assignments. See NIH Policies, Procedures, and Forms, A "20-20" View of Invention Reporting to the National Institutes of Health (Sept. 22, 1995) (requiring a Government contractor, such as Stanford University, to "have in place employee agreements requiring an inventor to "assign" or give ownership of an invention to the organization upon acceptance of Federal funds," as the Bayh-Dole Act "require[s]"). And an *amicus* brief, filed by major associations of universities, scientists, medical researchers, and others, argues that we should interpret the rules governing assignments of the employees at issue here (and consequently the Act's reference to "inventions of the contractor") in a similar way.

The District Court in this case adopted roughly this approach. 487 F.Supp.2d 1099, 1118 (N.D.Cal.2007) ("[A]lthough title still vests in the named inventor, the inventor remains under a legal obligation to assign his interest either to the government or the nonprofit contractor unless the inventor acts within the statutory framework to retain title"). And since a university often enters into a grant agreement with the Government for a researcher's benefit and at his request, implying such a presumption in favor of compliance with the grant agreement, and thus with the Bayh-Dole Act, would ordinarily be equitable.

IV

As I have suggested, these views are tentative. That is because the parties have not fully argued these matters, though one *amicus* brief raises the license interpretation question, and at least one other can be read as supporting something like the equitable presumption I have described. While I do not understand the majority to have foreclosed a similarly situated party from raising these matters in a future case, I believe them relevant to our efforts to answer the question presented here. Consequently, I would vacate the judgment of the Federal Circuit and remand this case to provide the parties with an opportunity to argue these, or related, matters more fully.

Because the Court decides otherwise, with respect, I dissent.

QUESTIONS

1. The Court finds that the phrase "invention of the contractor" does not mean inventions made by the contractor's employees, but inventions that are owned by, or belong to, the contractor. If the inventor is always the original owner of the invention, how could Stanford obtain ownership of Holodniy's invention? How did the court find that Cetus obtained ownership of Holodniy's invention?

2. How does the Court reason that the Bayh-Dole Act's provision stating that contractors may "elect to *retain* title" to federally funded inventions confirms its interpretation of the Act?

3. How does the Court reason that the Bayh-Doles Act's provision stating that a federal agency may "grant requests for retention of rights by the inventor" confirms its interpretation of the Act?

4. The Court states: "With an effective assignment, those inventions — if federally funded — become "subject inventions" under the Act, and the statute as a practical matter works pretty much the way Stanford says it should." What constitutes "an effective assignment"?

5. Could either Stanford or Cetus have filed their contracts with Holodniy with the PTO as patent assignments under section 261 of the Patent Act? Why or why not?

6. How did the Federal Circuit reason that Holodniy's assignment to Cetus placed legal title in Cetus once the invention was made or the patent application was filed?

7. Can a present assignment of a future invention convey legal title to the assignee? What does the assignee of a present assignment of a future invention obtain?

8. Section 261 of the Patent Act provides: "Applications for patents, patents, or any interest therein, shall be assignable by an instrument in writing." Section 261

also provides: "An assignment, grant or conveyance [of a patent] shall be void as against any subsequent purchaser . . . . for valuable consideration, without notice, unless it is recorded in the Patent and Trademark Office within three months from its date or prior to the date of such subsequent purchase or mortgage." Do you think section 261 encompasses the Copyright and Patent Agreement Holodniy signed with Stanford or the Visitor Confidentiality Agreement Holodniy signed with Cetus?

9.   Is it possible that both the majority and minority opinions in *Stanford* can be correct?

10.   If you were counsel to a major research university after *Stanford*, what contract terms and practices would you recommend for assuring university ownership of faculty inventions?

SHAW v. UNIVERSITY OF CALIFORNIA
58 Cal. App. 4th 44 (Cal. Ct. App. 1997)

SCOTLAND, J.

This case involves a dispute over a policy of the Regents of the University of California (the University) which provides that, as a condition of employment by the University, an employee must assign to the University any of the employee's inventions and patents conceived in the course of employment; as consideration for the assignment, the employee will get a percentage of those net royalties and fees received by the University for a patented invention.

When Associate Professor Douglas V. Shaw was hired by the University to teach and do research, the patent policy specified that employees would get 50 percent of the net royalties and fees received from their inventions. The University later revised the policy to reduce this percentage. When the University announced it would pay Shaw the reduced percentage for his patented inventions conceived after the policy change, Shaw brought this action, seeking a declaration that he is entitled to 50 percent of the net royalties and fees.

The University appeals from the judgment entered in Shaw's favor following an order granting summary judgment on his complaint for declaratory relief. According to the University, the patent policy in effect at the time Shaw was hired was not part of the patent agreement signed by Shaw as a condition of his employment; rather, it is a personnel policy that the University may modify unilaterally at any time.

We shall affirm the judgment. As we shall explain, the patent agreement between Shaw and the University is a contract which incorporates the terms of the patent policy in effect at the time Shaw was hired. Although the University is entitled to revise its patent policy, it cannot do so with respect to Shaw because of its written agreement with him, specifying that he would receive 50 percent of the net royalties and fees from his inventions patented by the University.

Facts and Procedural Background

Shaw was hired in 1986 to teach and do research in the department of pomology at the University of California, Davis. Pomology is the science of the cultivation of fruits. In recent years, Shaw has concentrated his research on the genetics of strawberries.

At the time he became a member of the University faculty, Shaw was asked to sign a single-page, two-sided University form document entitled "State Oath of Allegiance and Patent Agreement." The document contains (1) a half-page "State Oath of Allegiance," (2) a half-page "Patent Agreement," and (3) the "University Policy Regarding Patents" (the Patent Policy).

The Patent Policy begins on one side of the document and continues onto the next side. It states that the University, "in administering intellectual property rights for public benefit, desire[s] to encourage and assist members of the faculties, employees, and others associated with the University in the use of the patent system with respect to their discoveries and inventions in a manner that is equitable to all parties involved."

The Patent Policy provides that "[a]n agreement to assign inventions and patents to the [University] . . . shall be mandatory for all employees, for persons not employed by the University but who use University research facilities and for those who receive grant or contract funds through the University." It also provides that exceptions to this assignment requirement may be authorized when "the mission of the University is better served" thereby.

As to those who have agreed to assign their inventions to the University, the Patent Policy states that "[t]he [University] agree[s], for and in consideration of said assignment of patent rights, to pay annually to the named inventor(s), the inventor(s)' heirs, successors, or assigns 50 percent of the net royalties and fees received by [the University]."

The patent agreement obligates the signatory to inform the University promptly of "every possibly patentable device, process, plant or product, hereinafter referred to as "invention," "which the signatory may conceive in the course of University employment. Should the University deem the invention patentable, the signatory promises thereafter "to assign to University all rights, title and interest" in the invention.

Directly under the title of the patent agreement appear the words: "Please read the Patent Policy on reverse side and above." The first paragraphs of the patent agreement state: "This agreement is made by me with The Regents of the University of California, a corporation, hereinafter called "University," in part consideration of my employment, and of wages and/or salary to be paid to me during any period of my employment, by University, and/or my utilization of University research facilities . . . . By execution of this agreement, I understand I am not waiving any rights to a percentage of royalty payments received by University, as set forth in University Policy Regarding Patents, hereinafter called "Policy." "

Shaw signed the patent agreement on February 25, 1986.

At or near the time he assumed his position at the University, Shaw also received a pamphlet from the University entitled "Patent Practices at the University of California." It summarizes the Patent Policy and states that, in exchange for their agreement to assign patents to the University, employees shall receive 50 percent of net royalties and fees received by the University for their inventions.

The Revised Patent Policy and Shaw's Inventions

In 1989, the University announced its intention to revise the Patent Policy to reduce the percentage of royalties it would pay to inventors.

In written memoranda to the University, Shaw objected to the application of a revised Patent Policy to individuals who, like him, had signed the patent agreement under the then existing Patent Policy.

In April 1990, the University officially revised its Patent Policy to reduce an inventor's share of net royalties and fees from a flat rate of 50 percent to a sliding scale in which the inventor would receive 50 percent of the first $100,000, 35 percent of the next $400,000, and 20 percent of any additional net royalties and fees. The University's president announced that the creation of this sliding scale "responds to internal criticisms of the present system and to concerns that — particularly in a public institution — the goal of such a policy should be to provide support and incentives for further productive research rather than the highest earnings for individual inventors." In the University's view, its 1990 Patent Policy increases the percentage of royalties that can be used to fund additional research and "is much more in line with what most of the other universities in the states do."

In December 1992, Shaw (as co-inventor with two other University professors) disclosed to the University his invention of six new strawberry cultivars. The University informed Shaw that these inventions "will be governed by the UC Patent Policy at the time of the disclosure," i.e., by the 1990 Patent Policy which calculates an inventor's share of net royalties on declining sliding scale.

Shaw objected and argued the University should instead "meet its obligation under the Patent Agreement that [Shaw] signed" to pay inventors 50 percent of the net royalties. The University declined, asserting that the Patent Policy is not a contract but merely a "personnel policy grounded in the employment relationship" and the University "may prospectively change its personnel policies unilaterally," provided it gives advance notice to employees of its intent to do so.

The University directed Shaw to execute an assignment of his interest in the patents of the six strawberry cultivars. The assignment provided that net royalties for the new plants would be divided in accordance with the "benefits stipulated for the inventor in the "University of California Patent Policy" revised effective April 16, 1990, which document is made by reference a part hereof and in fulfillment of the Assignor's Patent Agreement with the University of California . . . ." When Shaw refused to sign the assignment, the University agreed to modify its terms to provide that consideration for the assignment includes a share of net royalties in accordance with "the applicable University of California Patent Policy," so as to preserve the parties' respective positions on what policy should apply.

The Lawsuit

Shaw then brought this action, seeking a declaration that, (1) in consideration for his execution of the patent agreement, the University agreed to distribute to him 50 percent of the net royalties and fees accruing from any invention he might conceive, and (2) the University may not unilaterally modify the terms of the patent agreement without Shaw's written consent.

Shaw moved for summary judgment on the grounds that (1) absent the patent agreement, the University has no right or interest in any of Shaw's inventions; (2) in the text of the patent agreement, Shaw expressly reserves his rights to "a percentage of royalty payments received by University, as set forth in the University Policy Regarding Patents"; (3) the University may not unilaterally modify the patent agreement's terms without his consent; and (4) Shaw continues to own those patent rights which he did not waive, i.e., 50 percent of the net royalties and fees with respect to any invention.

In opposition to Shaw's motion, the University did not challenge Shaw's statement of undisputed facts; it opted instead to supplement the record with further undisputed facts of its own. The University also argued in pertinent part that (1) because Shaw's employment is governed by statute, not contract, he can maintain no contract action against the University; (2) the "Patent Policy" in effect at the time Shaw signed the patent agreement is not a contract and thus may be changed unilaterally by the University, so long as Shaw received notice of the new policy and a reasonable time within which to decide whether to continue under the new policy or to seek different employment; (3) the patent agreement operates as a complete transfer of Shaw's rights in all as-yet-uninvented plants or processes to the University; and (4) the University has done nothing to modify the patent agreement.

The trial court granted Shaw's motion for summary judgment and issued a statement of decision. The court found that Shaw had presented a prima facie case establishing that the patent agreement constitutes an enforceable contract with the University; that the patent agreement must be interpreted in accordance with the Patent Policy set forth on the same document; and that the University's 1990 modification of the Patent Policy cannot effectively modify the parties' patent agreement, in light of Shaw's objection. Accordingly, the court held, the patent agreement must be construed to require the University to pay Shaw 50 percent of the net royalties and fees received by the University for all inventions disclosed by Shaw.

The trial court entered judgment in favor of Shaw, and this appeal ensued.

Discussion

I

The University begins its argument on appeal by advancing a theory that it admits was not raised before the trial court. Characterizing Shaw's complaint as "a challenge to the administrative decisions of a state agency in establishing its policies," the University claims the trial court erred in applying "a straightforward contract analysis" rather than the standard of review for a mandamus action, i.e., that the University's decision to revise its Patent Policy must be upheld so long as it is not arbitrary, capricious, or entirely lacking in evidentiary support.

To support this argument, the University relies principally on the decision in *Bunnett v. Regents of University of California* which was issued after the entry of judgment in this case.

Generally, a party may not raise a new contention on appeal. An exception exists, however, in cases where a new point of law is decided after the trial or where the new theory "presents a question of law to be applied to undisputed facts in the record." Application of this rule is discretionary with the reviewing court.

We shall consider, but reject, the University's claim of error. While it is true the University's administrative decisions regarding its faculty are properly reviewed by writ of mandate, Shaw does not challenge an administrative decision of the University. He seeks an interpretation of his existing written contract with the University.

As a general proposition, mandamus is not an appropriate remedy for enforcing a contractual obligation against a public entity. Thus, the trial court correctly applied contract principles in resolving the parties' dispute over the patent agreement.

II

A motion for summary judgment "shall be granted if all the papers submitted show that there is no triable issue as to any material fact and that the moving party is entitled to judgment as a matter of law."

The University does not contend that there are material issues of triable fact. Rather, the parties' chief disagreement concerns the legal effect of the patent agreement. This poses a legal question which we consider de novo on appeal.

We first consider whether Shaw has demonstrated that he is entitled to a declaration on summary judgment that the patent agreement is an enforceable agreement which entitles him to 50 percent of the net royalties and fees from his strawberry cultivars.

An action for declaratory relief is appropriate to determine the legal rights and duties of the parties to a written contract. Where, as here, the only cause of action is one for declaratory relief, a motion for summary judgment likewise is appropriate.

The written patent agreement, signed by Shaw, contains all the essential elements of a contract: "(1) parties capable of contracting; (2) their consent; (3) a lawful object; and (4) a sufficient cause or consideration." The University's statement of undisputed facts raises no issue of material fact as to whether the patent agreement is a valid agreement.

To resolve the parties' dispute concerning the meaning and effect of the patent agreement, we resort to the traditional rules governing interpretation of contracts, which "teach us that the overriding goal of interpretation is to give effect to the parties' mutual intentions as of the time of contracting . . . . Where contract language is clear and explicit and does not lead to absurd results, we ascertain intent from the written terms and go no further."

By its terms, the patent agreement embodies Shaw's promises to disclose any inventions he may create in the future so that the University may "examine[] . . . and determine rights and equities therein in accordance with the Policy" and, if the University "desires . . . to seek patent protection thereon," to assign his interest in the invention to the University.

The clear language of the patent agreement does not, as the University argues, effect a contemporaneous and "complete transfer of plaintiff's rights to the University." Accordingly, the University's reliance upon cases in which the parties' agreement so provides is misplaced.

We turn now to the critical issue: Does the patent agreement entitle Shaw to 50 percent of the net royalties of any invention that he may create and thereafter assign to the University?

It is undisputed that the text of the patent agreement itself contains no provision identifying what percentage, if any, of net royalties shall be paid to an employee who creates a patentable invention in the course of University employment. It also is undisputed that the Patent Policy, which is printed on the same document as the patent agreement signed by Shaw, contains an agreement by the University to pay 50 percent of the net royalties to an inventor who has assigned an invention to the University.

Shaw contends that the patent agreement incorporates the Patent Policy and its 50 percent royalty provision. We agree.

"A contract may validly include the provisions of a document not physically a part of the basic contract . . . . It is, of course, the law that the parties may incorporate by reference into their contract the terms of some other document. But each case must turn on its facts. For the terms of another document to be incorporated into the document executed by the parties the reference must be clear and unequivocal, the reference must be called to the attention of the other party and he must consent thereto, and the terms of the incorporated document must be known or easily available to the contracting parties."

The contract need not recite that it "incorporates" another document, so long as it "guide[s] the reader to the incorporated document."

Our review of the patent agreement persuades us that, when Shaw signed the agreement, the parties intended it to incorporate the Patent Policy. The patent agreement (1) directs Shaw to "Please read the Patent Policy on reverse side and above," and (2) states that, in signing the patent agreement, Shaw is "not waiving any rights to a percentage of royalty payments received by University, *as set forth in University Policy Regarding Patents*[.]" (Italics added.)

Not only is reference to the Patent Policy " "clear and unequivocal," " and its terms " "easily available to the contracting parties," " the language we have italicized above expressly defines the "percentage of royalty payments received by

[the] University" that Shaw may expect to receive on his invention as that which is "set forth in" the Patent Policy, i.e., 50 percent of net royalties and fees.

We are unconvinced by the University's assertion that it "did not intend to incorporate the Patent Policy as part of the Patent Agreement." Although the intent of the parties determines the meaning of the contract, the relevant intent is "objective" — that is, the objective intent as evidenced by the words of the instrument, not a party's subjective intent. Nothing in the patent agreement hints at what the University now claims was its long-held desire that the Patent Policy's inventor royalty provision not be incorporated into the patent agreement. The true intent of a contracting party is irrelevant if it remains unexpressed.

In the trial court, the University argued that it is not bound by the terms of the pre-1990 Patent Policy because that document is not a contract. Documents which are not contracts may be incorporated into a contract, however.

We find no merit in the University's suggestion that, as a public employee who is employed pursuant to statute, not contract, Shaw has no vested contractual right in his terms of employment, such terms being subject to change by the University.

In each of the two cases upon which the University relied for this proposition, the public employee bringing a contract action had no written contract with his public employer.

When a public employer chooses instead to enter into a written contract with its employee (assuming the contract is not contrary to public policy), it cannot later deny the employee the means to enforce that agreement.

We also reject the University's argument that the Patent Policy is a mere personnel policy which it may modify unilaterally. Although the University is entitled to revise its Patent Policy, it cannot do so with respect to Shaw because of its written agreement with him. The University prepared, and Shaw signed, a patent agreement whose references to the Patent Policy are so direct as to indicate the parties' intent to incorporate the policy's then existing terms into the patent agreement, including the University's promise to pay Shaw 50 percent of the net royalties of any patentable invention. Whether, absent the incorporation, the Patent Policy would constitute a mere statement of personnel policy is immaterial. Having made the Patent Policy a part of its written agreement with Shaw, the University may not unilaterally revise it as to him.

In sum, we conclude that the patent agreement signed by Shaw incorporates the Patent Policy, and the University may not refuse to allocate the 50 percent net royalty payments attributable to Shaw's inventions in accordance with the terms of the document.

Disposition

The judgment is affirmed. The University shall pay Shaw's costs on appeal.

QUESTIONS

1.   What is the difference between *Shaw* and the prior cases which hold that universities can modify patent policies and that these modifications are binding on previously hired employees?

2.   How can universities ensure that employees are subject to changes in patent policies?

3.   University intellectual property ownership disputes most often involve language in an intellectual property policy statement or a faculty/staff handbook. Would it be better to have university members sign bilateral contracts with universities? What members? All faculty, staff and students at the time of hiring or enrollment? All faculty, staff and students working on a federally funded, or sponsor-funded, research project prior to commencement of the research? All faculty, staff and students who file invention disclosures with the university at the time the university decides to pursue intellectual property protection?

KUCHARCZYK v. UNIVERSITY OF CALIFORNIA
946 F. SUPP. 1419 (N.D. Cal. 1996)

LYNCH, DISTRICT JUDGE.

I. INTRODUCTION

Plaintiffs, both scientists who formerly worked for the University of California San Francisco ("UCSF"), are suing the Regents of the University of California ("the University"), Nycomed Salutar ("Salutar" or "Nycomed"), and Nycomed Imaging AS ("NIAS"), Salutar's parent company, alleging a number of theories in ten causes of action. Salutar has counterclaimed against plaintiffs and cross-claimed against the University.

This suit arises out of plaintiffs' invention of a process in the magnetic resonance imaging ("MRI") field and the University's subsequent licensing of that invention. The invention was eventually patented as U.S. Patent No. 5,190,744 ("'744 Patent"), entitled "Methods for Detecting Blood Perfusion Variations by Magnetic Resonance Imaging." The invention was a method of using DyDTPA-BMA, a chemical compound. Salutar owns the patent in DyDTPA-BMA. Dr. Scott Rocklage, a Salutar employee, was named on the '744 patent as a co-inventor, thereby giving Salutar an undivided right in the patent.

Plaintiffs assigned their rights in the invention to the University pursuant to a Patent Agreement they entered into upon their employment by the University. The Patent Agreement required plaintiffs to assign all inventions to the University and in turn obligated the University to pay them 50% of all royalties collected. Upon being assigned the invention, the University entered into an exclusive License Agreement with Salutar. Salutar agreed to pay the University a total of $25,000, half of which was paid to plaintiffs.

In essence, plaintiffs allege that they were the sole inventors of the process, that it was worth significantly more than $25,000, and that plaintiffs were entitled to greater rewards for their invention. Plaintiffs have alleged ten causes of action. First, plaintiffs allege that their civil rights, including their property rights, were impaired in violation of 42 U.S.C. § 1983. Second, plaintiffs seek a declaration that they were sole inventors of the invention claimed by the '744 patent. Next, they allege that when the University entered into an exclusive licensing agreement with Salutar and accepted a lump-sum payment of only $25,000, the University breached its contract with plaintiffs which required it to secure a royalty-bearing, non-exclusive license. In their third cause of action, they seek rescission of the Assignment Agreements on the grounds that there was a "fundamental lack of actual, mutual agreement." Alternately, in their fourth cause of action, they seek monetary damages for the University's breach of contract. In their fifth cause of action, plaintiffs allege a conspiracy to induce the breach of contract and seek punitive damages. In their sixth cause of action, they claim that the University's breach of its contracts was tortious and fraudulent and in breach of the implied covenant of good faith and fair dealing. The seventh cause of action claims fraud and deceit in connection with their employment contracts and Assignment Agreements. Eighthly, plaintiffs claim negligent misrepresentation. In their ninth cause of action, plaintiffs allege that they were fraudulently induced to enter into employment agreements, Assignment Agreements, and other unspecified contracts with the University. Finally, in their tenth cause of action, plaintiffs allege that defendants Salutar and NIAS have tortiously interfered with their contracts with the University.

Plaintiffs and the University have filed cross-motions for summary judgment; plaintiffs seek summary adjudication of their breach of contract claim, and the University seeks summary judgment on all of plaintiffs' causes of action except the claim seeking a declaratory judgment removing Scott Rocklage as the inventor of the '744 patent. The Court has requested and received supplemental briefing, and the matter has been extensively briefed and argued.

For the reasons set forth below, the Court will deny plaintiffs' motion for summary judgment and grant the University's motion. However, the Court will certify this case for interlocutory review.

II. FACTS

Plaintiff Moseley was hired by the University in 1982 as an Associate Professor of Radiology at UCSF. Upon being hired, Moseley executed a form Patent Agreement that required him to assign all rights in any invention developed during his employment to the University. Plaintiff Kucharczyk joined the UCSF faculty in 1988 and was a tenured member of the UCSF Department of Radiology. Prior to his employment, Kucharczyk also signed a form Patent Agreement in which he agreed to assign all invention rights to the University.

The '744 Patent grew out of plaintiffs' work at the UCSF Department of Radiology in the late 1980s. Plaintiffs' research was initially funded by Syntex to assess therapeutic drugs used for stroke treatment. However, Syntex ended its funding, and Salutar began funding plaintiffs' research. Plaintiffs claim that on February 13, 1989, they conceived of the use of DyDTPA-BMA, a chemical compound invented by Salutar, as a contrasting agent useful in detecting strokes via MRI. On February 23, 1990, plaintiffs faxed a disclosure form to the University's Patent Office discussing the invention and identifying the funding source or sponsor for the project as "Salutar, Inc." On March 9, 1990, Salutar and the University filed a patent application for the process. That application named as inventors Rocklage and both plaintiffs. In April of 1990, the University and Salutar submitted a grant application to California Department of Commerce for a CompTech grant under which Salutar sought to contribute $150,000 toward the research, and Salutar and the University asked the state to match that amount with a $150,000 grant. The University and Salutar executed an agreement entitled Memo of Understanding Under California Competitive Technology Program Grant Application (the "Research Funding Agreement"). The Research Funding Agreement designated Kucharczyk as the Principal Investigator for the University and Moseley as co-investigator. Kucharczyk signed the Research Funding Agreement. In 1990, CompTech provided $150,000 in research funds to UCSF.

Plaintiffs assigned their rights in the invention to the University in the Assignment Agreement they signed in early 1990. Rocklage assigned his rights to Salutar, which in turn assigned its rights to the University on May 7, 1990. On June 13, 1990, Salutar and the University entered into their exclusive License Agreement ("License Agreement"). In accordance with the License, Salutar paid the University $12,500 upon executing the license and paid an additional $12,500 when the patent issued in March of 1993. The University paid plaintiffs 50% of each of those payments.

****

IV. CONTRACTS

At issue in this case are several contracts: (1) the Patent Agreement between each of the plaintiffs and the University; (2) the Assignment Agreement between the plaintiffs and the University; (3) the CompTech Research Funding Agreement between the University and Salutar; and (4) the Licensing Agreement between the University and Salutar. Plaintiffs contend that the University was obligated by contract to obtain a reasonable running royalty upon licensing their invention. The Court's first task in this case is thus an analysis of the nature and content of the various contracts at issue here to determine whether they contain such an obligation as well as an analysis of the requirements of the Patent Policy, which plaintiffs argue obligates the University to obtain a reasonable royalty.

The Court first discusses the Patent Agreement and the Assignment Agreement. Though neither expressly requires the University to obtain a royalty, both of these documents refer to the University's Patent Policy. Plaintiffs contend that the Patent Policy applies to them as a matter of contract because it is incorporated by reference into the Patent and Assignment Agreements. They also contend that the Patent Policy requires a mandatory royalty. The Court agrees that the Patent Policy applies here, but for the reasons set forth in detail below, the Court finds that the Policy does not contain such an obligation. The Court also finds that neither the Research Funding Agreement nor the License Agreement contains a contract term requiring the University to obtain a royalty on the plaintiffs' invention.

A. Patent Agreement

Upon joining the University faculty, each plaintiff executed a form Patent Agreement with the University requiring them to assign to the University all rights in any invention developed in the course of their employment. Plaintiff Moseley signed a 1980 version of the Patent Agreement on October 21, 1982. Plaintiff Kucharczyk signed a 1985 version Patent Agreement on December 30, 1987. The Patent Agreements are very similar, and the parties agree that the 1985 version of the Patent Agreement is applicable here. For that reason, only the 1985 version will be described here.

B. Assignment Agreement

The Assignment Agreement too makes reference to the Patent Policy. Following their invention, Kucharczyk and Moseley entered into an Assignment Agreement with the University whereby plaintiffs assigned all their rights in their process to the University. The Assignment Agreement recited that the assignment was made:

> in consideration of One Dollar ($1.00) and in consideration of the benefits stipulated in the "University of California Policy Regarding Patents," as revised and effective as of November 18, 1985, which document is made by reference part hereof, and in fulfillment of my Patent Agreement with the University of California.

The assignment Agreement itself does not contain any term requiring the University to obtain a royalty on an invention.

C. Patent Policy

1. Contract Term

The Court now turns to a discussion of the Patent Policy, which plaintiffs argue applies to them and requires the University to obtain a royalty on their invention. The Patent Policy itself is not an agreement between the parties. Instead, as a policy of the University, it has the force and effect of statute. However, plaintiffs contend that the Patent Agreement and the Assignment Agreement incorporate by reference the Patent Policy and that the Patent Policy thereby became a term of these agreements.

"For the terms of another document to be incorporated into the document executed by the parties the reference must be clear and unequivocal, the reference must be called to the attention of the other party and he must consent thereto, and the terms of the incorporated document must be known or easily available to the contracting parties." While the Patent Agreement does not expressly state that it is incorporating the Patent Policy by reference, it clearly and unequivocally refers to it, stating that execution of the agreement does not waive the signer's "rights to a percentage of royalty payments received by University, as set forth in University Patent Policy, hereinafter called "Policy" "and making several other references to the Policy. The reference is called to the attention of both parties. Finally, the Patent Policy is easily available to the contracting parties given that it is printed on the reverse side of the Patent Agreement. The Court finds that the Patent Policy is thus incorporated by reference into the Patent Agreement. The Patent Policy is likewise expressly incorporated by reference in the Assignment Agreement, which states that the assignment is made "in consideration of the benefits stipulated in the "University of California Policy Regarding Patents," as revised and effective as of November 18, 1985, which document is made by reference part hereof." The Patent Policy thus is both an official policy of the University, with the force and effect of statute and a contract term.

Having concluded that the Patent Policy was incorporated by reference into both the Patent Agreement and the Assignment Agreement, the Court now turns to an analysis of the Patent Policy, a subject of no small dispute. In brief, plaintiffs contend that the Patent Policy contains a requirement that all licenses bear reasonable royalties; the University contends that it does not. Both parties point to different documents in support of their positions. For the reasons set forth below, the Court finds that the Patent Policy does not require all licenses to be royalty-bearing.

2. Patent Policy Statement

The University contends that the Patent Policy consists solely of the Patent Policy Statement, i.e., the words reproduced on the 1985 Patent Agreement in the section titled: "University of California Patent Policy." The Patent Policy Statement consists of three parts: (I) Preamble, (II) Statement of Policy, and (III) Patent Responsibilities and Administration. The Preamble states the purpose of the Patent Policy:

> It is the intent of the President of the University of California, in administering intellectual property rights for the public benefit, to encourage and assist members of the faculty, staff, and others associated with the University in the use of the patent system in a manner that is equitable to all parties involved.

The Preamble further states that the Patent Policy was adopted:

> To encourage the practical application of University research for the broad public benefit, to appraise and determine relative rights and equities of all parties concerned, to facilitate patent applications, licensing, equitable distribution of royalties, *if any*, to assist in obtaining funds for research, to provide for the use of invention-related income for the further support of research and education, and to provide a uniform procedure in patent matters when the University has a right or equity . . .

Sections A and B of the Statement of Policy provide that employees must promptly disclose and assign all inventions to the University. In Section C, the University "agrees, for and in consideration of said assignment of patent rights, to pay annually to the named inventor(s) . . . 50% of the net royalties and fees received by the University." The Patent Responsibilities and Administration portion of the Patent Policy Statement delegates duties to various the University personnel.

The Patent Policy Statement does not require the University to obtain a royalty on any invention, though it does impose on the University the obligation to share any royalty it does obtain with the inventor. The University thus argues that it has no duty, contractual or otherwise, to obtain a royalty on plaintiffs' invention. Plaintiffs contend that the Patent Policy Statement is not the complete Patent Policy, and that the complete Patent Policy does impose a royalty requirement on the University.

3. Exhibit 21

In support of their argument that the Patent Policy is not limited to the Patent Statement, plaintiffs rely on Exhibit 21 of the Sponsored Programs Office ("SPO") Handbook. Exhibit 21 is the subject of vigorous dispute, and so is described in some detail. Exhibit 21 in the SPO Handbook is 12 typeset pages long, and each page bears the heading "Exhibit 21 — Patent Policy." The exhibit consists of a number of documents. The first page is a memo dated September 1, 1987 from the University Provost for Research to various administrators at the University which discusses the University Patent Agreement. The memo states that "guidelines pertaining to the University of California Patent Agreement are set forth in the attachment." The next three pages consist of "Guidelines Concerning the Patent Agreement." These Guidelines are likewise dated September 1987. The next page is labeled Appendix B, and is a form Exemption to Signing Patent Agreement. The sixth page is a memo from the Vice Chancellor of Research to a number of University administrators. The memo refers to "the attached University of California Patent Policy, dated November 18, 1985" and indicates that "there are no substantive changes in the new patent policy statement." The following four pages consist of the Patent Policy Statement. The first of the four pages is labeled "University of California Patent Policy" and is dated November 18, 1985. Following those four pages is a document labeled "Attachment, November 18, 1985" and titled "University of California Patent Policy: Administrative Statements Concerning University Patent Matters." That document is a one-page list of various statements which "are to be considered in effect until such time as each is specifically rescinded or superseded." The last page of Exhibit 21, which is the source of a great deal of dispute in this case, is a document titled: "University of California Summary of Sponsor Patent Rights Applicable to Funding Agreements with Industrial (For Profit) Sponsors of Research" ("Summary"). The bottom of the Summary bears the date March 1984. Plaintiffs contend that the Patent Policy consists of the final six pages of Exhibit 21, and that the obligations they seek to enforce are contained in the Summary.

4. Summary

The Summary contains the language that plaintiffs contend impose a contractual duty to obtain royalties. The Summary, whose purpose is to provide "guidance on University of California patent rights policies to its potential industrial Sponsors of research," states that licenses to industry sponsors will:

a) be royalty-bearing, rates negotiable and based on general industry practices for the type of invention involved;

*****

c) normally require a license issue fee and appropriate minimum annual royalties.

Plaintiffs contend that the Summary is a part of the Patent Policy and has therefore been incorporated by reference into the Patent and Assignment Agreements, making the requirement of a royalty a term of their contracts with the University. They further argue that the University breached this term by entering into a Licensing Agreement with Salutar whereby Salutar was obligated to make only two lump-sum payments but was not required to pay a running royalty. The University argues that the Summary is not part of the Patent Policy, but is instead merely a summary of the "Guidelines For Patent Clauses In Agreements With For-Profit Sponsors" which is in turn contained in the University Contract and Grant Manual. The University contends that the Summary is not a part of any contract between it and the plaintiffs, and that it is therefore not liable for any failure to comply with its terms. The question of whether the Summary is part of the Patent Policy is thus crucial to the determination of this case.

a. Legal Standard

The Court finds that the evidence offered by plaintiff tends to prove a meaning of which the contract is not reasonably susceptible. An examination of the face of the Summary shows that it is not part of the Patent Policy. First, the title of the document shows that it is the summary of sponsor patent rights, not part of the Patent Policy. In addition, it states that "[t]his summary provides guidance on the University of California patent rights policies *to its potential industrial Sponsors of research.*" (Emphasis added.) Thus, the language of the Summary states that it is aimed at "potential industrial Sponsors," not employees. Moreover, unlike any other version of the Patent Policy Statement, the document provides an address and telephone number that the sponsors may use to contact the Patent, Trademark and Copyright Office. The face of the document thus indicates that it is not part of the Patent Policy.

In addition, the whole of Exhibit 21 does not support a finding that it is the Patent Policy. First, the SPO Handbook expressly states at page iv that it "is not intended to replace existing policies and procedures, but to point out those policies which may be applicable and those procedures which may need to be satisfied." Second, Exhibit 21 contains documents which are clearly not part of the Patent Policy, but are instead explanatory material, including the introductory memo, the Guidelines Concerning the Patent Agreement, a copy of an exemption form, and a memo from the Vice-Chancellor-Research regarding revisions to the Patent Policy. Plaintiffs do not contend that the entirety of Exhibit 21 constitutes the Patent Policy, but argue that it consists of the final six pages, which include the Patent Policy Statement, the administrative statements attachment, and the Summary. Plaintiff Kucharczyk contends that when he asked for the Patent Policy, he was sent these six pages, but does not otherwise explain why only the second half of Exhibit 21 should constitute the Patent Policy.

Thirdly, the December 6, 1985 letter from the Vice Chancellor of Research, which immediately precedes the Patent Policy Statement in Exhibit 21, suggests that the Summary is not part of the Patent Policy. That letter states that the Patent Policy dated November 18, 1995, supersedes the April 1, 1980 University Patent Policy, and indicates that the Patent Policy is attached. The letter further states that "[t]here are no substantive changes in the new policy statement." The Summary, which would constitute a substantive change from the 1980 Patent Policy if it were part of the Patent Policy, is dated March 1984. This indicates that the Summary is not a part of the Patent Policy.

Finally, not only do several sections of the Guidelines suggest that the Patent Policy Statement is the entirety of the Patent Policy and that the Summary is a summary of a separate guideline, but also several attachments to the Guidelines suggest that the summary is not part of the Patent Policy. For instance, Section 11-220 of the Guidelines states:

> In November, 1985, the President issued the University of California Patent Policy, pursuant to his authority under Standing Order 100.4(gg). The policy includes: Section I, Preamble, an outline of the principles upon which the policy is based; Section II, Statement of Policy, which sets forth the requirement that employees and certain others agree to assign inventions and patents to the University or other parties as appropriate, to promptly report and fully disclose potentially patentable inventions, and sets forth royalty-sharing provisions with the inventor and use of royalty income; and Section III, Patent Responsibilities and Administration, detailing responsibilities of the Intellectual Property Advisory Council charged by the Senior Vice President — Academic Affairs, and the assignment of responsibility for implementation of the policy to the Senior Vice President — Administration.

This precisely describes the Patent Policy Statement, and does not make any reference to the Summary. It therefore strongly suggests that the Patent Policy Statement is the Patent Policy. On the other hand, Section 11-341 of the Guidelines is titled *Summary of Sponsor Patent Rights Applicable to Funding Agreements With Industrial (For Profit) Sponsors of Research.* Like the Summary attached to Exhibit 21, it includes the categories established for commercial sponsors and contains the conditions that licenses be royalty-bearing. It also refers to 11-999 "for a full-text copy suitable for hand-out of the Summary of Sponsor Patent Rights Applicable to Funding Agreements With Industrial (For Profit) Sponsors of Research." This suggests that the Summary is distinct from the Patent Policy.

Section 11-999 lists a number of University References. A Patent Heading lists several documents, including:

— University of California Patent Policy

— Patent Agreement

— Summary of Sponsor Patent Rights Applicable to Funding Agreements with

---

Industrial (For Sponsors of Research)

— Standing Order 100.4(gg) Duties of the President

— *Business and Finance Bulletin*, University of California Patent Program

— *Staff Personnel Manual*, Appendix B, University Patent Agreement.

The documents which follow include (among other documents not relevant here) the three-part Patent Policy Statement; the Patent Agreement, which also includes the three-part Patent Policy Statement on its reverse; and the Summary. The Summary is separated from the Patent Policy Statement by the Patent Agreement. Both the language and the format of the Guidelines and its attachments thus demonstrate that the Patent Policy does not include the Summary.

Finally, the Summary does not help explain the Patent Policy, which states that its predominate purpose is to disseminate inventions to the public and further scholarly research. The purpose of the Summary, on the other hand, is to provide "guidance on University of California patent rights policies to its potential industrial Sponsors of research." The Summary does not, as plaintiffs argue, assist in interpreting the Patent Policy. Plaintiffs argue that the royalty requirement in the Summary must be used to interpret the Patent Policy in order to avoid destroying consideration flowing to the faculty inventors. However, the Patent Agreement itself recites the inventor's consideration: "my employment, and . . . wages and/or salary to be paid to me during any period of employment, by University, and/or my utilization of University research facilities and/or my receipt of gift, grant or contract research funds through the University." The Court finds that the contract does not provide for additional consideration in the form of a royalty.

" "If the evidence offered would not persuade a reasonable man that the instrument meant anything other than the ordinary meaning of its words, it is useless." " Here, the Court finds that a reasonable person viewing the Summary would not conclude that it was part of the Patent Policy. Because the evidence proffered by plaintiffs does not show that the Patent and Assignment Agreements are reasonably susceptible to the conclusion that the Summary is part of the Patent Policy. That evidence is therefore not admissible. The Patent and Assignment Agreements do not contain the Summary among their terms.

The Court finds that the Patent Policy Statement constitutes the entirety of the University Patent Policy. The Patent Policy does not include the Summary, upon which plaintiffs rely for the royalty requirement they seek to enforce. The Court holds that because the Patent Policy does not include the Summary or the royalty requirement imposed by the Summary, and because the Patent Policy explicitly limits its distribution to "royalties, if any," and because neither the Patent Agreement nor the Assignment Agreement explicitly require royalties by their terms, neither the Patent Agreement nor the Assignment Agreement requires the University to obtain a royalty on plaintiffs' invented process. However, the Court next turns to whether any other agreement between the parties makes binding either the Summary or a royalty requirement.

****

X. CONCLUSION

For the foregoing reasons and for good cause shown, the Court HEREBY ORDERS as follows:

1. Plaintiffs' motion for summary judgment is DENIED.

2. The University's motion for summary judgment is GRANTED to the extent set forth above and as follows:

a. Summary judgment is GRANTED in favor of the University on plaintiffs' Third Claim seeking rescission of their contracts with the University;

b. Summary judgment is GRANTED in favor of the University on plaintiffs' Fourth Claim seeking damages for breach of contract to the extent set forth above;

c. Summary judgment is GRANTED in favor of the University on plaintiffs' Fifth Claim for conspiracy to induce breach of contract;

d. Summary judgment is GRANTED in favor of the University on plaintiffs' Sixth Claim for tortious breach of contract;

e. Summary judgment is GRANTED in favor of the University on plaintiffs' Seventh Claim for fraud and deceit;

f. Summary judgment is GRANTED in favor of the University on plaintiffs' Eighth Claim for negligent misrepresentation; and

g. Summary judgment is GRANTED in favor of the University on plaintiffs' Ninth Claim for fraud in the inducement.

QUESTIONS

1. Do Kucharczk and UC have the same interests?

2. Why would UC not license a patent for the highest amount it could obtain?

3. Why are there so many agreements and documents in place here? Would it be simpler to have a single writing contain the entire agreement?

4. Would it be beneficial to grant faculty inventors the right to review a license prior to its execution?

5. Would it be beneficial to grant faculty inventors the right to approve or disapprove of a license?

6. Would it be beneficial to grant faculty inventors the right to select someone other than the university as the agent to negotiate a license, assuming the university still received the royalty revenue?

7. Why do faculty researchers agree to assign their inventions to universities that give them no control over licensing their inventions?

CASE NOTES (REVIEW)

1. E.I. Du Pont de Nemours & Co. v. Okuley, 344 F.3d 578 (6th Cir. 2003) (Washington State University's (WSU's) ownership of researcher's patentable invention, pursuant to terms of faculty manual, was not affected by fact that researcher discovered invention while employed by WSU but working in Ohio State University (OSU) laboratory; despite existence of Ohio statute giving OSU ownership of inventions resulting from research conducted there, OSU had assigned its interest to researcher, subject to rights of WSU); Chou v. University of Chicago, 254 F.3d 1347 (Fed. Cir. 2001) (Research assistant was obligated to assign her inventions to the university, although she never signed a contract with the university specifically obligating her to do so and although the faculty handbook stated its contents did not create a contract, where she accepted her academic appointment subject to the administrative policies of the university, which included the obligation to assign inventions to the university); Fenn v. Yale University, 283 F. Supp. 2d. 615 (D. Conn. 2003) (Faculty member who developed invention was bound by university's patent policy requiring assignment to university of inventions developed there, even after policy to which he expressly consented was amended, absent showing that amendment substantially interfered with his legitimate expectations about terms of employment or that he limited his assent to policy or refused to assent to university's right to amend policy, particularly where he continued working for the university and complied with policy for two prior inventions; university patent policies such as Yale's have long been recognized as a valid and enforceable part of the contract of employment).

Additional Information

1. Donna R. Euben, *The Faculty Handbook as a Contract: Is It Enforceable?*, ACADEME, Sept./Oct. 1998, *available at* http://findarticles.com/p/articles/mi_qa3860/is_199809/ai_n8809813/.

2. American Association of University Professors, *Faculty Handbooks as Enforceable Contracts, A State Guide*, (2009) (a comprehensive review of relevant cases in all fifty states) *available at* http://www.aaup.org/NR/rdonlyres/3F5000A9-F47D-4326-BD09-33DDD3DBC8C1/0/FacultyHandbooksasEnforceableContractssmall.pdf.

3. American Association of University Professors, *Sample Intellectual Property Policy & Contract Language*, *available at* http://www.aaup.org/AAUP/issues/DE/sampleIP.htm.

4. University of Rochester, *University of Rochester Intellectual Property Agreement*, *available at* http://www.urmc.rochester.edu/technology-transfer/inventors/ip-policies.cfm.

5. University of Florida, *Intellectual Property Policy*, (includes sample IP Agreement) *available at* http://www.research.ufl.edu/otl/pdf/ipp.pdf.

Chapter 4

INDUSTRY EMPLOYER-EMPLOYEE INTELLECTUAL PROPERTY RIGHTS

This chapter considers employer-employee intellectual property rights in industry. Although, as noted above, industry employer-employee intellectual property rights are similar in many respects to university-faculty intellectual property rights, there are some important differences, including employer shop rights, works made for hire, state statutory limitations on employer intellectual property rights, holdover agreements, non-disclosure agreements and non-competition agreements. Each of these areas involves a unique body of case law, or statutory law, that will be reviewed in this chapter.

4.1 EMPLOYER SHOP RIGHTS

An employer shop right is the right of an employer to use an invention made by an employee when the invention was made during normal working hours, or with the use of the employer's tools or equipment. There are two general rationales given for the existence of shop rights. The first is based on the concept of an implied license. Here, the idea is that an employer has a reasonable expectation of permission to use an employee's invention if the invention has been made during the course of employment. The second rationale is based on the concept of estoppel. Here, the idea is that an employee who has consented or acquiesced to the employer's use of his or her invention for some period of time should be estopped from refusing that use at a later time. Under both the implied license and estoppel rationales, a valid shop right is a complete defense to an infringement suit brought by an employee against an employer.

An employer's shop right is limited to the *use* of an employee's invention and cannot be transferred except in the case of a merger or acquisition. The employee is free to license or assign the patent to other parties, including competitors of the employer.

The *Dubilier* case is the seminal case in the development of the shop right doctrine. The following case, *Schroeder*, is the Federal Circuit's most recent explication of shop rights.

UNITED STATES v. DUBILIER CONDENSER
289 U.S. 178 (1933)

MR. JUSTICE ROBERTS.

Three suits were brought in the District Court for Delaware against the respondent as exclusive licensee under three separate patents issued to Francis W. Dunmore and Percival D. Lowell. The bills recite that the inventions were made while the patentees were employed in the radio laboratories of the Bureau of Standards, and are therefore, in equity, the property of the United States. The prayers are for a declaration that the respondent is a trustee for the government, and, as such, required to assign to the United States all its right, title, and interest in the patents, for an accounting of all moneys received as licensee, and for general relief. The District Court consolidated the cases for trial, and after a hearing dismissed the bills. The Court of Appeals for the Third Circuit affirmed the decree.

The courts below concurred in findings which are not challenged and, in summary, are:

The Bureau of Standards is a subdivision of the Department of Commerce. Its functions consist in the custody of standards; the comparison of standards used in scientific investigations, engineering, manufacturing, commerce, and educational institutions with those adopted or recognized by the government; the construction of standards, their multiples or subdivisions; the testing and calibration of standard measuring apparatus; the solution of problems which arise in connection with standards; and the physical properties of materials. In 1915 the Bureau was also charged by Congress with the duty of investigation and standardization of methods and instruments employed in radio communication, for which special appropriations were made. In recent years it has been engaged in research and testing work of various kinds for the benefit of private industries, other departments of the government, and the general public.

The Bureau is composed of divisions, each charged with a specified field of activity, one of which is the electrical division. These are further subdivided into sections. One section of the electrical division is the radio section. In 1921 and 1922 the employees in the laboratory of this section numbered approximately twenty men doing technical work and some draftsmen and mechanics. The twenty were engaged in testing radio apparatus and methods and in radio research work. They were subdivided into ten groups, each group having a chief. The work of each group was defined in outlines by the chief or alternate chief of the section.

Dunmore and Lowell were employed in the radio section and engaged in research and testing in the laboratory. In the outlines of laboratory work the subject of "airplane radio" was assigned to the group of which Dunmore was chief and Lowell a member. The subject of "radio receiving sets" was assigned to a group of which J. L. Preston was chief, but to which neither Lowell nor Dunmore belonged.

In May, 1921, the Air Corps of the Army and the Bureau of Standards entered into an arrangement whereby the latter undertook the prosecution of forty-four research projects for the benefit of the Air Corps. To pay the cost of such work, the Corps transferred and allocated to the Bureau the sum of $267,500. Projects Nos. 37 to 42, inclusive, relating to the use of radio in connection with aircraft, were assigned to the radio section and $25,000 was allocated to pay the cost of the work. Project No. 38 was styled "visual indicator for radio signals," and suggested the construction of a modification of what was known as an "Eckhart recorder." Project No. 42 was styled "airship bomb control and marine torpedo control." Both were problems of design merely.

In the summer of 1921 Dunmore, as chief of the group to which "airplane radio" problems had been assigned, without further instructions from his superiors, picked out for himself one of these navy problems, that of operating a relay for remote control of bombs on airships and torpedoes in the sea, "as one of particular interest and having perhaps a rather easy solution, and worked on it." In September he solved it.

In the midst of aircraft investigations and numerous routine problems of the section, Dunmore was wrestling in his own mind, impelled thereto solely by his own scientific curiosity, with the subject of substituting house-lighting alternating current for direct battery current in radio apparatus. He obtained a relay for operating a telegraph instrument which was in no way related to the remote control relay devised for aircraft use. The conception of the application of alternating current concerned particularly broadcast reception. This idea was conceived by Dunmore August 3, 1921, and he reduced the invention to practice December 16, 1921. Early in 1922 he advised his superior of his invention and spent additional time in perfecting the details. February 27, 1922, he filed an application for a patent.

In the fall of 1921 both Dunmore and Lowell were considering the problem of applying alternating current to broadcast receiving sets. This project was not involved in or suggested by the problems with which the radio section was then dealing and was not assigned by any superior as a task to be solved by either of these employees. It was independent of their work and voluntarily assumed.

While performing their regular tasks they experimented at the laboratory in devising apparatus for operating a radio receiving set by alternating current with the hum incident thereto eliminated. The invention was completed on December 10, 1921. Before its completion no instructions were received from and no conversations relative to the invention were held by these employees with the head of the radio section, or with any superior.

They also conceived the idea of energizing a dynamic type of loud speaker from an alternating current house-lighting circuit and reduced the invention to practice on January 25, 1922. March 21, 1922, they filed an application for a "power amplifier." The conception embodied in this patent was devised by the patentees without suggestion, instruction, or assignment from any superior.

Dunmore and Lowell were permitted by their chief, after the discoveries had been brought to his attention, to pursue their work in the laboratory and to perfect the devices embodying their inventions. No one advised them prior to the filing of applications for patents that they would be expected to assign the patents to the

United States or to grant the government exclusive rights thereunder.

The respondent concedes that the United States may practice the inventions without payment of royalty, but asserts that all others are excluded, during the life of the patents, from using them without the respondent's consent. The petitioner insists that the circumstances require a declaration either that the government has sole and exclusive property in the inventions or that they have been dedicated to the public so that anyone may use them.

A patent is property, and title to it can pass only by assignment. If not yet issued, an agreement to assign when issued, if valid as a contract, will be specifically enforced. The respective rights and obligations of employer and employee, touching an invention conceived by the latter, spring from the contract of employment.

One employed to make an invention, who succeeds, during his term of service, in accomplishing that task, is bound to assign to his employer any patent obtained. The reason is that he has only produced that which he was employed to invent. His invention is the precise subject of the contract of employment. A term of the agreement necessarily is that what he is paid to produce belongs to his paymaster. On the other hand, if the employment be general, albeit it covers a field of labor and effort in the performance of which the employee conceived the invention for which he obtained a patent, the contract is not so broadly construed as to require an assignment of the patent. Hapgood v. Hewitt; Dalzell v. Dueber Watch Case Mfg. Co. In the latter case it was said:

> "But a manufacturing corporation which has employed a skilled workman, for a stated compensation, to take charge of its works, and to devote his time and services to devising and making improvements in articles there manufactured, is not entitled to a conveyance of patents obtained for inventions made by him while so employed, in the absence of express agreement to that effect."

The reluctance of courts to imply or infer an agreement by the employee to assign his patent is due to a recognition of the peculiar nature of the act of invention, which consists neither in finding out the laws of nature, nor in fruitful research as to the operation of natural laws, but in discovering how those laws may be utilized or applied for some beneficial purpose, by a process, a device, or a machine. It is the result of an inventive act, the birth of an idea and its reduction to practice; the product of original thought; a concept demonstrated to be true by practical application or embodiment in tangible form.

Though the mental concept is embodied or realized in a mechanism or a physical or chemical aggregate, the embodiment is not the invention and is not the subject of a patent. This distinction between the idea and its application in practice is the basis of the rule that employment merely to design or to construct or to devise methods of manufacture is not the same as employment to invent. Recognition of the nature of the act of invention also defines the limits of the so-called shop right, which, shortly stated, is that, where a servant, during his hours of employment, working with his master's materials and appliances, conceives and perfects an invention for which he obtains a patent, he must accord his master a nonexclusive right to practice the invention. This is an application of equitable principles. Since the servant uses his master's time, facilities, and materials to attain a concrete result, the latter is in equity entitled to use that which embodies his own property and to duplicate it as often as he may find occasion to employ similar appliances in his business. But the employer in such a case has no equity to demand a conveyance of the invention, which is the original conception of the employee alone, in which the employer had no part. This remains the property of him who conceived it, together with the right conferred by the patent, to exclude all others than the employer from the accruing benefits. These principles are settled as respects private employment.

Second. Does the character of the service call for different rules as to the relative rights of the United States and its employees?

The title of a patentee is subject to no superior right of the government. The grant of letters patent is not, as in England, a matter of grace or favor, so that conditions may be annexed at the pleasure of the executive. To the laws passed by the Congress, and to them alone, may we look for guidance as to the extent and the limitations of the respective rights of the inventor and the public. And this court has held that the Constitution evinces no public policy which requires the holder of a patent to cede the use or benefit of the invention to the United States, even though the discovery concerns matters which can properly be used only by the government; as, for example, munitions of war.

No servant of the United States has by statute been disqualified from applying for and receiving a patent for his invention, save officers and employees of the Patent Office during the period for which they hold their appointments. This being so, this court has applied the rules enforced as between private employers and their servants to the relation between the government and its officers and employees.

The distinction between an employment to make an invention and a general employment in the course of which the servant conceives an invention has been recognized by the executive department of the government. A lieutenant in the Navy patented an anchor while he was on duty in the Bureau of Equipment and Recruiting, which was charged with the duty of furnishing anchors for the Navy; he was not while attached to the Bureau specially employed to make experiments with a view to suggesting improvements to anchors or assigned the duty of making or improving. The Attorney General advised that, as the invention did not relate to a matter as to which the lieutenant was specially directed to experiment with a view to suggesting improvements, he was entitled to compensation from the government for the use of his invention in addition to his salary or pay as a navy officer.

A similar ruling was made with respect to an ensign who obtained a patent for improvements in "B.L.R. ordnance" and who offered to sell the improvements, or the right to use them, to the government. It was held that the Navy might properly make a contract with him to this end.

The United States is entitled, in the same way and to the same extent as a private employer, to shop rights, that is, the free and nonexclusive use of a patent which results from efforts of its employee in his working hours and with material belonging to the government.

The statutes, decisions, and administrative practice negate the existence of a duty binding one in the service of the government different from the obligation of one in private employment.

The government's position in reality is, and must be, that a public policy, to be declared by a court, forbids one employed by the United States, for scientific research, to obtain a patent for what he invents, though neither the Constitution nor any statute so declares.

Where shall the courts set the limits of the doctrine? For, confessedly, it must be limited. The field of research is as broad as that of science itself. If the petitioner is entitled to a cancellation of the patents in this case, would it be so entitled, if the employees had done their work at home, in their own time and with their own appliances and materials? What is to be said of an invention evolved as the result of the solution of a problem in a realm apart from that to which the employee is assigned by his official superiors? We have seen that the Bureau has numerous divisions. It is entirely possible that an employee in one division may make an invention falling within the work of some other division. Indeed this case presents that exact situation, for the inventions in question had to do with radio reception, a matter assigned to a group of which Dunmore and Lowell were not members. Did the mere fact of their employment by the Bureau require these employees to cede to the public every device they might conceive?

The decrees are affirmed.

QUESTIONS

1. In the absence of a written patent assignment agreement at the time of employment, on what basis does an employer have a right to an invention made by an employee who was hired to make such an invention? How does an employer's right in this instance differ from an employer's shop right?

2. What does the court mean when it says the "distinction between the idea and its application in practice is the basis of the rule that employment merely to design or to construct or to devise methods of manufacture is not the same as employment to invent"?

3. The court notes that, in a prior case, the Attorney General had advised that a Navy lieutenant on duty charged with furnishing anchors for the Navy was not specially employed to make experiments and, therefore, he was entitled to compensation from the government for the use of his invention of an improved anchor. Did the United States have a shop right in this case?

SCHROEDER v. TRACOR
1999 U.S. App. LEXIS 30386 (Fed. Cir. 1999)

CLEVENGER, CIRCUIT JUDGE.

Dr. Klaus G. Schroeder (Schroeder) appeals from the grant of summary judgment in favor of Tracor, Inc. (Tracor) and AEL Industries, Inc. (AEL) on the grounds that AEL enjoyed a shop right in Schroeder's patented inventions. We *affirm* the district court's ruling.

I

Schroeder is the owner of U.S. Patent Nos. 4,750,000 (the '000 patent) and 4,958,167 (the '167 patent), directed to "ultra-broadband impedance matched electronically small self-complementary pair antennas." Schroeder asserts that these patents were infringed by AEL in its production of the "Piranha II" jam-on-the-move mobile electronic countermeasure system and the "TACJAM-A" mobile communication countermeasure system. Tracor and AEL do not deny that these systems incorporate designs protected under the '000 and '167 patents; however, they claim a shop right in these designs based on Schroeder's employment relationship with AEL.

Schroeder was employed by AEL between 1983 and 1988 in AEL's Antenna Division, located in Lansdale, Pennsylvania. AEL was acquired by Tracor in 1996. On May 2, 1983, Schroeder signed an employment agreement with AEL in which he agreed to "assign, transfer and set over . . . all my right, title and interest in and to any and all Inventions and Improvements." The Inventions and Improvements clause covered all inventions conceived by Schroeder, whether or not in the scope of his employment with AEL, except those inventions specifically identified and exempted by the agreement. Schroeder represented in the agreement that, prior to employment with AEL, he had conceived "10 non-patented inventions to be supplied later." Subsequently, he submitted a memorandum briefly describing nine "pre-employment proprietary techniques," including complementary pair antennas for low-profile, wide-band applications.

During the course of his employment, Schroeder offered his complementary pair antenna design to AEL as an improvement to its Piranha countermeasures product line. The parties dispute whether Schroeder demanded royalties at that time.

Schroeder applied for the '000 and '167 patents on September 16, 1987, and June 7, 1988, respectively, while employed by AEL. The '000 patent issued on June 7, 1988, while Schroeder was still employed by AEL. The '167 patent issued on September 18, 1990, after his termination. Schroeder did not inform AEL that he had applied for any patents on his complementary pair antenna design until after the '000 patent issued in 1988. Upon learning that Schroeder had independently filed two patent applications in violation of his employment agreement, AEL discharged Schroeder in September 1988.

Schroeder filed suit against Tracor and AEL in January 1997, alleging infringement of the '000 and '167 patents. AEL and Tracor moved for summary judgment based on the existence of a shop right. The district court found that Schroeder failed to raise a genuine issue of material fact sufficient to rebut AEL's shop right defense and, therefore, granted the motion for summary judgment. Schroeder appeals that decision. AEL and Tracor move for sanctions under Fed. R.App. P. 38. We have jurisdiction over this appeal pursuant to 28 U.S.C. § 1295(a)(1) (1994).

II

The "shop right" rule is an equitable doctrine controlled by state law. We follow California's choice of law rules in this case. Because Schroeder's employment with AEL took place in Pennsylvania and was governed by a Pennsylvania contract, we follow Pennsylvania law on the issue of shop rights.

The Pennsylvania courts, and the federal courts sitting in Pennsylvania, have long applied the Supreme Court's rules on employers' and employees' rights to inventions. Thus, we may follow *United States v. Dublier Condenser Corp.* and its progeny, in deciding this case. We may also apply our own case law on shop rights, to the extent that it interprets the Supreme Court's guidance on the issue.

In *McElmurry v. Arkansas Power & Light Co.*, we stated that "the proper methodology for determining whether an employer has acquired a shop right in a patented invention is to look to the totality of the circumstances [to] determine whether the facts of a particular case demand, under principles of equity and fairness, a finding that a shop right exists." *McElmurry* did not endorse any particular theory of shop rights, but called for a "factually driven analysis" to ensure that "the principles of equity and fairness underlying the shop rights rule are considered."

Among the factors considered relevant in *McElmurry* was that the inventor consented to his employer's use of the invention. Thus, an employer may establish a shop right defense based solely on equitable estoppel, provided that the facts of the case warrant recognition of the defense under the "principles of equity and fairness" explained in *McElmurry*. We hold that AEL has properly established such a defense. The only question that remains is whether Schroeder has come forth with sufficient facts to support a finding that AEL is not entitled to a shop right defense as a matter of law. We hold that Schroeder has failed to do so.

We agree with the district court that Schroeder has offered no admissible evidence to show that he did not consent to his employer's use of his invention. Although Schroeder asserts that he repeatedly demanded royalties from AEL for the use of his complementary pair antenna design, this assertion directly conflicts with statements he made in his Opposition to AEL's Motion to Dismiss. In the Opposition, Schroeder indicated that, as of April 1985, he specifically *avoided* demanding royalties from AEL for fear that he might be fired. Indeed, when Schroeder finally did reveal to AEL that he owned a patent on the complementary pair antenna design and expected royalties therefor, he was immediately terminated for breach of contract.

Based on the record before us, including statements made by Schroeder himself, it is clear that Schroeder allowed AEL to use his invention for several years without objecting or demanding royalties. Only in 1988, shortly after the '000 patent issued, did Schroeder demand royalties from AEL for the first time. For these reasons, we hold that AEL is entitled to a shop right defense covering the use of Schroeder's complementary pair antenna designs and that such use does not constitute infringement of the '000 and '167 patents.

On appeal, Schroeder does not dispute that Tracor is entitled to the benefit of AEL's shop right defense. However, in order to avoid any ambiguity as to the effect of our decision on Tracor's rights, we will briefly discuss the issue here. We note that in the proceedings below there was a dispute as to the nature of the corporate relationship between AEL and Tracor. However, for the purpose of this case, it does not matter whether Tracor and AEL have merged, as Schroeder suggested below, or whether they exist separately as parent and subsidiary. In either situation, AEL's enjoyment of a shop right (*i.e.*, the *noninfringing* use of a patented invention) cannot make Tracor liable for patent infringement. If the companies are separate, then Tracor, as the parent corporation, cannot be held liable where AEL, itself, has not committed any acts of infringement. If Tracor and AEL have merged, then Tracor, as successor in interest to AEL's entire business, is entitled to assert AEL's shop right defense.

On June 2, 1999, AEL and Tracor moved for sanctions under Fed. R.App. P. 38 on the basis that Schroeder's appeal is frivolous. Schroeder opposed the motion for sanctions. In an order dated June 29, 1999, this court deferred the motion for consideration by the merits panel. The motion is hereby denied.

CONCLUSION

Because Schroeder has failed to establish a genuine issue of material fact in challenging AEL's shop right defense, we must affirm the district court's decision granting summary judgment of non-infringement as a matter of law.

QUESTIONS

1. The court notes that Schroeder submitted a memorandum describing pre-employment inventions he had made, including complementary pair antennas, the technology at issue in the case. If this technology was specifically exempted from Schroeder's employment agreement, on what basis did AEL acquire a shop right in the technology?

2. If Schroeder had repeatedly demanded royalties from AEL for use of his complimentary pair antenna in the equipment AEL sold, how would this have affected AEL's shop right claim?

3. Why did the court find that the question of whether Schroeder had demanded royalties was not a sufficient question of fact to overcome AEL's motion for summary judgment?

4. The court held that AEL's shop right allowed AEL to include Schroeder's invention in two of the products it sold. How would AEL's shop right claim be affected if AEL contracted with a third party to manufacture these products rather than manufacturing these products on its own? What practical difference would it make to Schroeder if the products were manufactured by a third party rather than by AEL?

5. Could Schroeder have licensed his patents to a competitor of AEL? Why may Schroeder not have been able to do this?

6. If you were counsel to Schroeder in this case, what additional arguments would you have made in support of Schroeder's claim of ownership of his

complementary pair antenna?

CASE NOTES

1. David Magid (David) was the father of Eugene Magid (Eugene) and Robert Magid (Robert) was Eugene's younger brother. The Magid family was involved in the textile business. Hartford Textile purchased raw textile materials from mills and forwarded these raw materials to Wellington Print for processing which included printing, embossing and laminating the textiles. Wellington then sent the processed textiles back to Hartford which promoted and marketed the finished goods. David was the majority shareholder of both Hartford and Wellington. Eugene served as president of Wellington from 1955-1961. During this same period, Robert served as president of Hartford. On March 15, 1961, David sold all of his shares in Wellington and Hartford to Robert which gave Robert control of both companies. Also on March 15, 1961, a bank informed Eugene that he was no longer the president of Wellington. While Eugene was employed at Wellington, he did not report to anyone; he determined his own work hours and responsibilities which mostly included signing checks, executing purchase orders and settling labor disputes. In 1962, Eugene began experimenting with techniques for superimposing patterns on particular materials and laminating these materials. Eugene used Wellington's equipment and personnel to conduct his experiments, but only during the late shifts at the Wellington plant when production lines were slow. Although David expressed irritation at Eugene's "playing around with the machines instead of doing the work he was supposed to perform," Eugene's new materials became very popular and sold well. Wellington's patent attorney advised Eugene that three of his new products were patentable and Eugene applied for patents on these products. In March 1964, Eugene asked for a commission on the sales of the products he had invented. Robert refused to give Eugene a commission on the sale of these products and instead demanded that Eugene assign the patent applications to Wellington. Eugene refused and Robert then presented Eugene with an employment contract that required him to assign all patent applications he filed to Wellington. Eugene appealed to his father, David, who told him to sign the contracts or he would be fired. Eugene continued to refuse and on July 31, 1964 he was discharged. Wellington filed an action for a permanent injunction against Eugene's enforcement of his patents and for a declaratory judgment order stating that Wellington was the owner of Eugene's inventions. What result? *See* Wellington Print Works, Inc. v. Magid, 242 F.Supp. 614 (E.D. Pa. 1965).

2. *See also* McElmurry v. Arkansas Power & Light Co., 995 F.2d 1576 (Fed. Cir. 1993) (Employer's contract with a third party to install employee's invention in which employer claimed a shop right did not exceed scope of shop right); Francklyn v. Guilford Packing Co., 695 F.2d 1158 (9th Cir. 1983) (Patentee's employer acquired a shop right to patentee's clam harvester broad enough to cover the manufacture and use of a second, modified clam harvester because patentee tested and perfected the modified clam harvester during his work hours, the early work on the modification took place at employer's factory with employer's tools, employer agreed to underwrite all expenses incurred by patentee in his modification of the harvester, and patentee induced employer to manufacture and use a copy of his invention; however, a third party who manufactured and sold the modified harvester

to the employer-shop right holder and then leased the device back from the employer-shop right holder infringed the employee's invention and must pay royalties); California E. Labs., Inc. v. Gould, 896 F.2d 400 (9th Cir. 1990) (Shop right which employer possessed in patented process or invention developed by employee during hours of employment passed to corporation that purchased employer's business notwithstanding the corporation did not continue all facets of employer's business but distributed employer's assets to its various existing subsidiaries; any fraud in connection with patent application did not serve to invalidate employer's pre-existing shop right in patented process or invention); Wommack v. Durham Pecan Co., Inc., 715 F.2d 962 (5th Cir. 1983) (Employer's assistance in reducing to practice an idea is not necessary to obtain shop right in the invention, rather an employee may reduce his invention to practice on his own time before showing the invention to this employer and nevertheless subsequent employer-employee cooperation on invention may be sufficient to confer shop right upon employer; principal consideration in shop right determination is not employer's assistance, but employee's consent to use his invention).

Additional Information

1. 2 Gregory E. Upchurch, Ip Litigation Guide: Patents and Trade Secrets § 14:40 (2010).

2. Irwin Aisenberg, Modern Patent Law Precedent § 820 (8th ed. 2010).

3. 3 John Gladstone Mills Iii, Et. al., Patent Law Fundamentals § 17:22 (2010).

4. Paul C. Van Slyke, Mark M. Friedman, *Employer's Rights to Inventions and Patents of Its Officers, Directors and Employees*, 18 Aipla Q.J. 127 (1990).

5. Marc A. Lieberstein, *Employers Beware: Will You Own Your Employee's Inventions?*, 1 Hastings Bus. L.J. 183 (2005).

6. Robert P. Merges, *The Law and Economics of Employee Inventions*, 13 Harv. J.L. & Tech. 1 (1999).

7. Paul M. Rivard, *Protection of Business Investments in Human Capital: Shop Right and Related Doctrines*, 79 J. Pat. & Trademark Off. Soc'y 753 (1997).

8. Sarah Osborn, *I Quit and I Am Taking My Patents With Me: Who Owns the Patent Rights to Inventions Made in the Course of Employment*, 53-May Fed. Law 12 (2006).

9. C. T. Drechsler, 61 A.L.R.2d 356 (2010).

10. Julie Halloway, *Employees' Inventions: Who Owns What Rights?*, Intell. Prop. Strategist, Apr. 2008 (Newsletter), Vol. 14, No. 7, at 3, *available at* http://www.wsgr.com/PDFSearch/holloway0408.pdf.

4.2 WORKS MADE FOR HIRE

The work-made-for-hire doctrine is unique to copyright law. There is no work-made-for-hire doctrine in patent law. In patent law, the inventor is always the original owner of the patent, and title to the patent can only be transferred to an employer by means of a written assignment. However, in copyright law, if a work is found to be a work made for hire, the employer is deemed to be the original author of the work, and no written assignment is necessary to convey title to the work to the employer.

The counterpart to the work made for hire doctrine in copyright law is the hired-to-invent doctrine in patent law. An employer who hires an employee to invent specific items owns the patents on those items, albeit through a required written assignment to perfect patent ownership.

The work-made-for-hire doctrine in copyright law differs from the shop right doctrine in patent law. As you saw above, the shop right doctrine gives the employer a non-exclusive, non-transferrable right to use the patented invention. The work-made-for-hire doctrine, on the other hand, gives the employer complete ownership of the copyrighted work.

The *MacLean* case below considers the work-made-for-hire doctrine in the context of a complex working relationship between a computer programmer, and a benefits and compensation consulting firm.

MacLEAN ASSOCIATES v. MERCER-MEIDINGER-HANSEN
952 F.2d 769 (3rd Cir. 1991)

HUTCHINSON, CIRCUIT JUDGE.

I.

Barry MacLean (Mr. MacLean) appeals a ruling of the United States District Court for the Eastern District of Pennsylvania granting appellee, Wm. M. Mercer-Meidinger-Hansen, Inc.'s (Mercer's), motion for a directed verdict on Mr. MacLean's copyright claims against Mercer. Mr. MacLean is a former employee of Mercer, an employee benefit and compensation consulting firm. In addition to consulting, Mercer provides computer software for job evaluation to businesses. Mr. MacLean left Mercer to form a competing consulting firm, MacLean Associates, Inc. (MacLean Associates). Mr. MacLean asserts that he had a valid, enforceable copyright as creator of the Job Evaluation and Management System (JEMSystem) which Mercer infringed by incorporating it into software for a competing system, known as CompMaster, that Mercer devised.

For the reasons hereinafter set forth, we will vacate the judgment in favor of Mercer on Mr. MacLean's claim that Mercer's incorporation of the JEMSystem software into CompMaster infringed a copyright in JEMSystem belonging to Mr. MacLean as JEMsystem's creator and remand the case to the district court for further proceedings consistent with this opinion.

II.

On December 1, 1989, MacLean Associates filed a declaratory judgment action in the United States District Court for the Eastern District of Pennsylvania. It filed the action after notification from Mercer of its contention that MacLean Associates was infringing Mercer's copyright in CompMaster. MacLean Associates sought a judgment against Mercer declaring that MacLean Associates' computer software known as CARS written in the Clipper programming language (Clipper CARS) did not infringe Mercer's registered copyrights in CompMaster and that MacLean Associates did not compete unfairly with Mercer by misappropriating its trade secrets. Mercer filed an answer on January 4, 1990 and counterclaimed against MacLean Associates. Mercer then joined Mr. MacLean and Greg Darnley (Darnley), a former employee of Mercer hired by MacLean Associates, and filed third-party complaints against them.

MacLean Associates and Mr. MacLean filed an amended complaint and counterclaim on September 17, 1990. The amended complaint sought a judgment against Mercer declaring that neither MacLean Associates, Mr. MacLean nor Darnley had infringed Mercer's copyright or engaged in unfair competition. Mr. MacLean asserted two counterclaims against Mercer in his individual capacity. The first claim alleged that Mercer infringed his copyright in a computer spreadsheet program called JEMSystem by incorporating JEMSystem into a system called JES and later into CompMaster. The second claim alleged that Mercer falsely described its CompMaster program by failing to credit Mr. MacLean as an author of a portion of it in violation of section 43(a) of the Lanham Act.

All these competing claims eventually came to trial before a jury. After Mr. MacLean and MacLean Associates rested their case-in-chief, the district court directed a verdict against Mr. MacLean on his claims for infringement of his copyright in JEMSystem and false designation of origin. It held that Mercer was the owner and author of all copyrights in JEMSystem. Specifically, the district court ruled that Mr. MacLean was an employee of Mercer at the time he created JEMSystem and thus Mercer was the owner of all copyrights in JEMSystem because it was a work made for hire. Alternately, the district court ruled that Mr. MacLean gave Mercer an implied license in the JEMSystem program. As a third alternate ground for granting Mercer's motion for a directed verdict, the court held that Mr. MacLean furnished JEMSystem to Mercer when he had full knowledge that Mercer would copy and exploit it and that thus his JEMSystem claims against Mercer were barred under the doctrine of laches.

The rest of the case then proceeded before the jury. At the close of its evidence, Mercer voluntarily dismissed all of its claims against Mr. MacLean and Darnley. Mercer's claims against MacLean Associates for copyright infringement and misappropriation of trade secrets in connection with MacLean Associates' Clipper CARS software were submitted to the jury on special interrogatories. The jury found that MacLean Associates infringed Mercer's copyright in CompMaster and misappropriated Mercer trade secrets. The jury awarded Mercer an aggregate amount of $1,958,021.00 in compensatory and punitive damages.

In a judgment and injunction order dated January 9, 1991, the district court entered judgment on the verdict against MacLean Associates and enjoined it from continued infringement of Mercer's rights in CompMaster or continued unfair competition with it. Mr. MacLean and MacLean Associates moved for judgment notwithstanding the verdict, or alternately, a new trial. Additionally, MacLean Associates moved for a stay of proceedings to enforce the judgment pursuant to Federal Rule of Civil Procedure 62(b). The district court denied both of these motions in an order entered January 18, 1991. On February 15, 1991, Mr. MacLean, on his own behalf, filed a notice of appeal from the district court's order of January 18, 1991. Mr. MacLean then filed a second notice of appeal on February 19, 1991 from the district court's judgment and injunction order. Both appeals were timely.

III.

Mr. MacLean began work at Mercer in 1980. Mr. MacLean became a highly paid, high level employee of the company with the title of "principal." As a principal, he received stock as partial compensation and participated in a special compensation program. Among Mr. MacLean's responsibilities at Mercer were the creation and execution of marketing plans in the field of compensation consulting. The New York Stock Exchange (NYSE) was one of Mercer's clients for whom Mr. MacLean was responsible. In 1984 and 1985, Mr. MacLean directed a study for the NYSE in which he sought to design a job evaluation system and administrative procedures to accompany the system. A preliminary report of the study was delivered to the NYSE on September 19, 1985.

On September 30, 1985, MacLean left the formal employ of Mercer to open his own employment consulting business in New Hope, Pennsylvania under the name "MacLean Associates, Inc." Following his formal exit from Mercer, Mr. MacLean continued to provide services to the NYSE. Mr. MacLean did not inform the NYSE that he was no longer employed with Mercer. Instead, Mr. MacLean continued to administer the NYSE project on Mercer's behalf precisely as before, but now as a paid consultant. Mr. MacLean did not seek to take the NYSE account to his newly formed company since the NYSE was already under contract with Mercer and he did not think the NYSE would choose to do business directly with his new company.

While working as a paid consultant for Mercer on its job with the NYSE, Mr. MacLean's responsibilities remained the same as they were before he left Mercer. From October 1985 to June 1986, Mercer authorized Mr. MacLean to communicate with the NYSE on Mercer stationery as a Mercer principal. Mr. MacLean billed Mercer for his services and Mercer paid these bills without any specific reimbursement from the NYSE. The evidence introduced at trial also showed that Mr. MacLean had authority after he left the formal employ of Mercer to bind Mercer in its contractual relationship with the NYSE. For example, in November of 1985 Mr. MacLean absolved the NYSE of a $90,000.00 debt the NYSE owed to Mercer on the software project.

Central to the dispute in this case is the development, by both Mercer and Mr. MacLean, of computer software used to evaluate job performance. Beginning sometime in January 1986, Mr. MacLean authored a computer spreadsheet program called JEMSystem. It is a job evaluation and administration program that uses a scored questionnaire methodology. The JEMSystem software allows a business to compare different jobs in their organization, value them and determine compensation for them on its own personal computers without using a consultant. The program was written for the NYSE using the computer language Lotus 1-2-3. Mr. MacLean says that although Mercer employees provided computer-related support during this time, he designed and developed the JEMSystem software on his own using his equipment in New Hope. Mr. MacLean delivered the JEMSystem program to the NYSE on March 13, 1986. He used Mercer stationery and referred to the program as the one "we've written to administer JEMS[ystem]."

Mr. MacLean knew as early as August of 1985 that Mercer was considering the development of a personal computer-based job evaluation system. At two times during 1986, Mr. MacLean supplied disks of the JEMSystem software to Mercer employees Darnley and Linda Ison to combine the NYSE databases and export the data out of Mercer's mainframe into the JEMSystem software. He did not place any restrictions on the use of the disks or advise Mercer that he believed he had rights in the JEMSystem software at that time. Darnley testified that, at the direction of his superiors, he copied features of JEMSystem into a Mercer system in the process of development called Job Evaluation System (JES) and later incorporated JEMSystem into Mercer's CompMaster program.

By 1987, Mr. MacLean knew Mercer was marketing JES. Mercer says that one of MacLean Associates' employees had a copy of Mercer's JES program that was allegedly similar to MacLean's JEMSystem software as early as January of 1987, and so Mr. MacLean had the ability to determine then that he had a claim against Mercer for infringement. In June 1989, a client provided MacLean Associates with disks to audit and update the client's job evaluation system. The disks the client provided were CompMaster software. Mr. MacLean did not give Mercer notice that he intended to sue it for copyright infringement until July of 1990. On July 27, 1990, the United States Copyright Office issued Mr. MacLean a copyright registration certificate for JEMSystem. The district court, nevertheless, held that Mercer, and not Mr. MacLean, was the owner and author of JEMSystem.

After developing JEMSystem for the NYSE using the Lotus language, Mr. MacLean hired a programmer to write JEMSystem in a language called Clarion. The result was Clarion CARS, a larger, more sophisticated system which incorporated JEMSystem. Mercer's job evaluation program CompMaster used a computer language called Clipper. When Mr. MacLean left Mercer, he began to solicit other Mercer employees to join his new company. Among the Mercer employees he solicited was Darnley, a key employee in the development of CompMaster at Mercer. Darnley left Mercer in May of 1988 to join MacLean Associates. He took with him the CompMaster source code and instruction manual. Once Darnley joined MacLean Associates, MacLean Associates stopped working on the Clarion CARS program and began work with the Clipper language. MacLean Associates eventually produced a program called Clipper CARS which incorporated JEMSystem. Clipper CARS contains some program lines identical to those in CompMaster. Based on these facts, the jury returned its verdict in Mercer's favor on Mercer's claims that MacLean Associates had infringed its copyright and misappropriated its trade secrets by copying CompMaster into Clipper CARS.

****

V.

The district court gave several alternate justifications for its grant of a directed verdict in favor of Mercer on the issue of whether Mr. MacLean had a valid, enforceable copyright in the JEMSystem software. First, the district court held that Mr. MacLean created JEMSystem as a work for hire on Mercer's behalf. Under the work made for hire doctrine, a copyright belongs to the party who employs the work's creator while it is being created. Second, the district court held that the relationship between Mr. MacLean and Mercer created an implied license in Mercer to use the software. Last, the district court held that Mr. MacLean's claim for copyright infringement against Mercer was barred under the doctrine of laches since he failed to assert any right he might have in the JEMSystem software in a timely fashion. Each of these alternate bases for the district court's ruling is considered below. Mr. MacLean says none of the bases the district court gave for its verdict against him can survive appellate scrutiny, and accordingly, he asks us to remand for a new trial on his claims against Mercer or to direct a verdict in his favor on these claims.

A.

We consider first the argument that Mr. MacLean created JEMSystem as a work for hire. If so, the copyright belongs to Mercer, the party that hired Mr. MacLean, the creator of the work. The work made for hire doctrine is codified at 17 U.S.C.A. § 201(b). That statute states:

> Works Made for Hire. — In the case of a work made for hire, the employer or other person for whom the work was prepared is considered the author for purposes of this title, and, unless the parties have expressly agreed otherwise in a written instrument signed by them, owns all of the rights comprised in the copyright.

The statutory definition of a work made for hire is found at 17 U.S.C.A. § 101. That section provides:

> A "work made for hire" is —
>
> (1) a work prepared by an employee within the scope of his or her employment; or
>
> (2) a work specially ordered or commissioned for use as a contribution to a collective work, as part of a motion picture or other audiovisual work, as a translation, as a supplementary work, as a compilation, as an instructional text, as a test, as answer material for a test, or as an atlas, if the parties expressly agree in a written instrument signed by them that the work shall be considered a work made for hire . . . .

We must therefore consider whether Mr. MacLean was a Mercer employee within the meaning of 17 U.S.C.A. § 101(1) when he wrote the JEMSystem software. In *Community for Creative Non-Violence v. Reid*, the Supreme Court examined the work made for hire doctrine and set out a test for determining when a person is acting as an employee within the meaning of 17 U.S.C.A. § 101(1). There, the Community for Creative Non-Violence (CCNV) contacted Reid, a sculptor, and asked him to produce a sculpture displaying two adult figures and an infant as contemporary homeless people huddled around a steam grate in Washington, D.C. Reid orally agreed to produce the sculpture. During the time the sculpture was being created, Reid gave sketches of it to the CCNV and received assistance from various CCNV members.

Following completion of the sculpture, Reid delivered it to the CCNV for installation at a site where it was to be displayed for one month. After its month-long exhibition, the CCNV returned the sculpture to Reid for minor repairs. While the sculpture was back in Reid's possession, CCNV announced plans to take the sculpture on an ambitious tour of several cities to raise money for the homeless. Reid objected, claiming that the sculpture was not strong enough to survive the trip. Nevertheless, CCNV stuck to its plans and refused to have the sculpture bronzed or duplicated. Shortly thereafter, CCNV asked Reid to return the sculpture and he refused. Reid instead applied for a copyright upon the sculpture and announced his own plans to take the sculpture on a less ambitious tour. CCNV then filed a competing certificate of copyright registration. CCNV also filed suit seeking return of the sculpture and a determination of copyright ownership.

The district court held that the sculpture belonged to CCNV because Reid was an employee of CCNV within the meaning of 17 U.S.C.A. § 101(1) when he produced the sculpture, and thus the sculpture was a work made for hire. The United States Court of Appeals for the District of Columbia Circuit reversed, holding that the sculpture was not a work made for hire. The Supreme Court granted *certiorari* and affirmed the Court of Appeals' judgment.

Here, as in *Reid*, the dispositive inquiry is whether JEMSystem was a work prepared by an employee within the scope of his employment under 17 U.S.C.A. § 101(1). In *Reid*, the Supreme Court held that the statutory terms "employee" and "scope of employment" as found in 17 U.S.C.A. § 101(1) should "be understood in light of the general common law of agency." Thus, a key inquiry is whether the producer of a work is an employee or an independent contractor. The Supreme Court wrote that central to resolution of this inquiry is "the hiring party's right to control the manner and means by which the product is accomplished." The Supreme Court set forth a number of factors pertinent to whether the creator of a work is an employee:

> the skill required; the source of the instrumentalities and tools; the location of the work; the duration of the relationship between the parties; whether the hiring party has the right to assign additional projects to the hired party; the extent of the hired party's discretion over when and how long to work; the method of payment; the hired party's role in hiring and paying assistants; whether the work is part of the regular business of the hiring

party; whether the hiring party is in business; the provision of employee benefits; and the tax treatment of the hired party.

In *Reid*, the Supreme Court explained the application of these factors in light of that case's particular circumstances:

> Examining the circumstances of this case in light of these factors, we agree with the Court of Appeals that Reid was not an employee of CCNV but an independent contractor. True, CCNV members directed enough of Reid's work to ensure that he produced a sculpture that met their specifications. But the extent of control the hiring party exercises over the details of the product is not dispositive. Indeed, all the other circumstances weigh heavily against finding an employment relationship. Reid is a sculptor, a skilled occupation. Reid supplied his own tools. He worked in his own studio in Baltimore, making daily supervision of his activities from Washington practicably impossible. Reid was retained for less than two months, a relatively short time. During and after this time, CCNV had no right to assign additional projects to Reid. Apart from the deadline for completing the sculpture, Reid had absolute freedom to decide when and how long to work. CCNV paid Reid $15,000, a sum dependent on "completion of a specific job, a method by which independent contractors are often compensated." Reid had total discretion in hiring and paying assistants. "Creating sculptures was hardly "regular business" for CCNV." Indeed, CCNV is not a business at all. Finally, CCNV did not pay payroll or social security taxes, provide any employee benefits, or contribute to unemployment insurance or workers' compensation funds.

For these reasons, the Supreme Court affirmed the Court of Appeals' holding that Reid was an independent contractor. As a result, it also affirmed the Court of Appeals' holding that CCNV was not the sole author of the sculpture.

Mercer presents two arguments for upholding the district court's ruling that Mr. MacLean wrote the JEMSystem software in his capacity as a Mercer employee. It argues that an actual and apparent master-servant relationship existed between Mr. MacLean and Mercer.

We believe that consideration of the nine factors the Supreme Court listed in *Reid* could bring a rational jury to conclude that Mr. MacLean was not an actual servant of Mercer when JEMSystem was created. Mr. MacLean says he wrote the JEMSystem software after he left Mercer and continued in a consulting relationship with it on the NYSE project. His task of writing sophisticated computer software required skill and creativity. Mr. MacLean worked with his own software on his own computer at his own facility to complete Mercer's obligation under its contract with NYSE. Although Mr. MacLean was a principal of Mercer for almost five years, the duration of his relationship as a consultant for Mercer on the NYSE project was fairly short. Mercer did not have the right to assign additional projects to Mr. MacLean. Mr. MacLean had absolute discretion over when and how long to work. Mercer paid Mr. MacLean for the delivery of his services as a consultant, instead of paying him a regular periodic salary. It is obvious that Mercer's regular business is compensation consulting. It was not a part of Mercer's regular business at the relevant time to provide software for its clients' use on personal computers;

instead, prior to Mr. MacLean's creation of the JEMSystem software, Mercer took raw data its clients provided and produced for its clients computerized reports that evaluated and synthesized the data. Mercer did not pay any payroll or social security taxes on behalf of Mr. MacLean after he ceased to be one of Mercer's principals, nor did it thereafter provide him with workers' compensation coverage or contribute to unemployment insurance or workers' compensation funds. It is not known how Mercer treated its payments to Mr. MacLean for its own corporate tax purposes.

Nor does the district court's determination that Mr. MacLean was an apparent agent of Mercer at the time he wrote JEMSystem survive scrutiny. There is no doubt that Mr. MacLean, with Mercer's permission, held himself out to the NYSE as a Mercer employee even after he left the company. Under the Supreme Court's decision in *Reid* and the language of the Copyright Act, however, the central focus of the work for hire doctrine is upon the relationship between the person performing the work and the person paying him to perform the work. Here, Mr. MacLean performed the work, and Mercer paid him to perform the work. The fact that the NYSE thought that Mr. MacLean was an employee of Mercer at the relevant time is of no moment. Mercer, the party who seeks to invoke the work for hire doctrine, was aware of the true nature of its relationship with Mr. MacLean at all times. Mercer is not a third party who was fooled in any way by Mr. MacLean's representations to the NYSE.

In short, even though Mr. MacLean may have been Mercer's apparent agent at the time he developed the JEMSystem software, apparent agency is not dispositive of the question of whether Mr. MacLean was an employee of Mercer or an independent contractor. Restatement (Second) of Agency § 2(3) (1958) states:

> An independent contractor is a person who contracts with another to do something for him but who is not controlled by the other nor subject to the other's right to control with respect to his physical conduct in the performance of the undertaking. He may or may not be an agent.

To the extent that the district court focused upon the fact that Mr. MacLean appeared to be a Mercer employee in his dealings with the NYSE, its decision granting Mercer a directed verdict cannot stand. In this case, the focus should have been solely upon the nature of the relationship between Mr. MacLean and Mercer. Accordingly, the district court erred in holding that Mr. MacLean wrote his software as a work made for hire on behalf of Mercer based upon the NYSE's belief that Mr. MacLean was employed by Mercer. Both Mercer and Mr. MacLean knew the status of their relationship; any apparent employment relationship perceived by third parties is immaterial.

A consideration of the nine factors that the Supreme Court in *Reid* held control the application of the work for hire doctrine points clearly to the conclusion that a rational jury could have found Mr. MacLean was not an actual employee of Mercer at the time he wrote JEMSystem, but an independent contractor. Thus, unless one of the district court's alternate holdings survives, the district court's grant of a directed verdict against Mr. MacLean cannot stand. Therefore, we turn to the district court's two alternate holdings in support of its grant of a directed verdict in favor of Mercer.

B.

The second basis for the district court's grant of a directed verdict in favor of Mercer was its holding that Mr. MacLean gave Mercer an implied license in the JEMSystem software. The district court held Mercer had an exclusive implied license in the software. Mercer, in its brief, admits that it cannot have an exclusive implied license; however, it asks us to uphold the district court's grant of a directed verdict on the basis that Mr. MacLean gave it a nonexclusive implied license.

Under the Copyright Act, the owner of a copyright has the exclusive right to copy, distribute or display his work. The owner of a copyright can transfer ownership of the copyright by selling it or by exclusively licensing it. Exclusive licenses must, however, be in writing. Here, the parties agree that Mr. MacLean never gave Mercer any writing that could have transferred ownership of JEMSystem from Mr. MacLean to Mercer through exclusive license.

While 17 U.S.C.A. § 204 provides that all transfers of copyright ownership, including transfers by exclusive license, must be in writing, a nonexclusive license is expressly removed from the scope of section 204 because a nonexclusive license does not amount to a "transfer" of ownership. The leading treatise on copyright law, 3 M. Nimmer & D. Nimmer, *Nimmer on Copyright* § 10.03[A], at 10–37 (1991), states that "[a] nonexclusive license may be granted orally, or may even be implied from conduct." In *Effects Assocs.*, the court wrote that a nonexclusive license may arise by implication where the creator of a work at a defendant's request "hand[s] it over, intending that defendant copy and distribute it." The fact that Mr. MacLean delivered a copy of his software to two Mercer employees "does not of itself convey any rights in the copyrighted work embodied in the object." Delivery of a copy of the creation "is one factor that may be relied upon in determining that an implied license has been granted." Since a nonexclusive license does not transfer ownership of the copyright from the licensor to the licensee, the licensor can still bring suit for copyright infringement if the licensee's use goes beyond the scope of the nonexclusive license.

In holding that Mercer had an implied license to use the JEMSystem program, the district court relied on the fact that "Mr. MacLean put in writing to Mercer that you, Mercer, have developed out of the relationship with the [NYSE] a computer software that I've developed . . . ." Counsel for Mr. MacLean appears to have agreed with the district court that Mercer had an implied license to use JEMSystem in connection with the NYSE project. He stated: "[Mercer] paid the amount of money for that software and for that project, which was an ongoing project for a number of years. They're entitled to keep going on that thing. There's no doubt about it. Copyright[, however,] relates to whether or not the ownership can be transferred to other jobs and projects." The undisputed facts indicate that Mercer had a nonexclusive implied license to use JEMSystem in furtherance of its business relationship with its client, the NYSE.

If Mercer is correct that the district court meant to hold that Mr. MacLean gave Mercer a nonexclusive license in the software, we could uphold the district court's grant of a directed verdict in Mercer's favor only if the record shows that no rational jury could find Mercer exploited the JEMSystem software beyond the scope of any nonexclusive license Mr. MacLean had given it. Any nonexclusive implied license that Mr. MacLean gave Mercer in JEMSystem was, however, limited. Both Mr. MacLean and Mercer knew that Mr. MacLean was developing JEMSystem solely for the NYSE account. Never did Mr. MacLean give Mercer any indication that Mercer could exploit JEMSystem to the extent that it allegedly did by copying parts of it wholesale into computer programs it would later market generally as a business consultant in competition with Mr. MacLean's own consulting firm. The record does not anywhere indicate that Mr. MacLean gave Mercer the type of broad, nonexclusive license that Mercer would have needed to protect, against Mr. MacLean's copyright infringement claims, its act of incorporating JEMSystem into its CompMaster program. Accordingly, we also hold that the district court's directed verdict for Mercer and against Mr. MacLean on his claim of copyright infringement cannot be sustained on a theory of implied license.

QUESTIONS

1. In *Reid*, was there a difference between ownership of the copyright in the sculpture and ownership of the physical sculpture itself? Who owned the physical sculpture?

2. Of the factors listed by the Supreme Court in *Reid*, which do you think are the most unambiguous indicators of independent contractor status?

3. MacLean continued to hold himself out as an employee of Mercer in his ongoing work with the NYSE after he ceased formal employment. Why was this fact insufficient to establish MacLean's status as an employee of Mercer?

4. Can an independent contractor also be an agent of the party retaining the independent contractor?

5. Why could Mercer not have an exclusive implied license?

6. The court found that it was an undisputed fact that Mercer had a nonexclusive implied license to use the JEMSystem in furtherance of its business relationship with NYSE. Why? Is the nonexclusive implied license to use the JEMSystem for work with the NYSE different from ownership of a physical copy of the JEMSystem?

7. If Mercer had a nonexclusive implied license, on what basis did the court find that Mercer may have infringed McLean's copyright?

8. If you were counsel to a company about to hire an independent contractor and your client company wanted to own the copyright in the commissioned work, how would you advise them to do that?

CASE NOTES

1. Aymes is a computer programmer, and Island Recreational (Island) is in the business of supplying swimming pools. Island hired Aymes to develop a computer program to maintain records of cash receipts, physical inventory, sales figures, purchase orders, merchandise transfers and price changes. Aymes did most of his programming at the Island office, where he used Island's computer hardware.

Aymes worked semi-regular hours and was sometimes paid by the hour and sometimes paid through bill invoices. Aymes never received any health or other insurance benefits from Island; and Island never paid payroll taxes and never withheld federal and state taxes on the money Island paid to Aymes. Aymes resigned from Island when Island unilaterally cut his hours, which Aymes believed to be a breach of his oral contract with Island. At the time of Aymes' resignation, Island owed him $14,560 in back wages. Aymes also requested payment for the multi-site use of the computer program he had developed. Island insisted that Aymes sign a release of his rights in the software program as a condition of receiving payment of back wages. Aymes refused and was not paid. Aymes then registered a copyright in the computer program and filed a copyright infringement action against Island. What result? *See* Aymes v. Bonelli, 980 F.2d 857 (2nd Cir. 1992).

2. *See also* Schiller & Schmidt, Inc. v. Nordisco Corp., 969 F.2d 410 (7th Cir. 1192) (Photographs taken for use in office supply catalogues were not works for hire where written statement indicating that office supply company owned copyrights in the photographs was not signed by photographer before photographs were taken); Carter v. Helmsley-Spear, Inc., 71 F.3d 77 (2nd Cir. 1995) (Sculpture installed in lobby of commercial building was a work made for hire and thus not protected from modification or destruction under the Visual Artists Rights Act; although artists had significant control over work and work required great skill in execution, management company had the right to, and in fact did, assign other duties to artists; employee benefits and tax treatment of artists indicated employee status; and artists were provided with many supplies used in creating the sculpture); Warren v. Fox Family Worldwide, Inc., 328 F.3d 1136 (9th Cir. 2003) (Musical composition creator sued broadcasting corporation and network for claimed infringement of copyrights in compositions created for television series; agreements between creator and corporation conclusively showed that the musical compositions were works made for hire and creator was thus not the legal owner of the copyrights in the musical compositions; assignment of royalties did not create a beneficial interest in the copyright in a work for hire; creator could not regain legal title to copyrights even if corporation breached agreements).

Additional Information

1. 2 STEVEN C. ALBERTY & GARTH E. JANKE, ADVISING SMALL BUSINESSES § 33:22 (2010).

2. 1 JOHN W. HAZARD, JR., COPYRIGHT LAW IN BUSINESS AND PRACTICE § 4:15 (2010).

3. CORPORATE COUNSEL'S GUIDE TO INTELLECTUAL PROPERTY §§ 8:8, 9:8 (2010).

4. SCOTT K. ZESCH, 132 A.L.R FED. 301 (2010).

5. Gregory K. Laughlin, *Who Owns the Copyright to Faculty-Created Web Sites?: The Work-For-Hire Doctrine's Applicability to Internet Resources Created for Distance Learning and Traditional Classroom Courses*, 41 B.C. L. REV. 549 (2000).

6.   Jennifer S. Lubinski, *The Work For Hire Doctrine Under Community for Creative Non-Violence v. Reid: An Artist's Fair Weather Friend*, 46 Cath. U. L. Rev. 119 (1996).

7.   Sue G. Mota, *Work for Hire Revisited: Aymes v. Bonelli*, 12 Computer/L.J. 17 (1993).

8.   Alan Hyde, Christopher W. Hager, *Promoting the Copyright Act's Creator-Favoring Presumption: "Works Made for Hire" Under Aymes v. Bonelli & Avtec Systems, Inc. v. Peiffer*, 71 Denv. U. L. Rev. 693 (1994).

9.   Corey L. Wishner, *Whose Work Is It Anyway?: Revisiting Community for Creative Non-Violence v. Reid in Defining the Employer-Employee Relationship Under the "Work Made for Hire" Doctrine*, 12 Hofstra Lab. L.J. 393 (1995).

10. Scott J. Burnham, *The Intricacies of Copyright Law and Contract Law: Finding the Terms of an Implied Nonexclusive License in a Failed Work for Hire Agreement*, 46 J. Copyright Soc'y U.S.A. 333 (1999).

11. Catherine L. Fisk, *Authors at Work: The Origins of the Work for Hire Doctrine*, 15 Yale J.L. & Human 1 (2003).

12. Carolyn M. Salzmann, *You Commissioned It, You Bought It, But Do You Own It?: The Work for Hire: Why Is Something So Simple, So Complicated?*, 31 U. Tol. L. Rev. 497 (2000).

13. James B. Wadley, JoLynn M. Brown, *Working Between the Lines of Reid: Teachers, Copyrights, Work-For-Hire and a New Washburn University Policy*, 38 Washburn. L.J. 385 (1999).

14. Rinaldo Del Gallo, *Who Owns the Web Site?: The Ultimate Question When a Hiring Party Has a Falling-Out With the Web Site Designer*, 16 J. Marshall J. Computer & Info. L. 857 (1998).

15. Brock Shinen, *Effective Use of Work Made for Hire Agreements*, 46-May Orange County Law. 14 (2004).

4.3   EMPLOYER IP RIGHTS UNDER EMPLOYMENT CONTRACTS

As you saw in *Dubilier*, courts are unwilling to find employer ownership of employee inventions based merely upon the employer-employee relationship, even where the employee is hired to perform research. For this reason, companies invariably require employees to execute an assignment of rights agreement for inventions made during the course of employment. Sometimes, the assignment is limited to inventions within the scope of the employer's current, or prospective, business; sometimes, the assignment is limited to inventions made during normal working hours or with the use of employer facilities; and sometimes, the assignment is unlimited, covering inventions of any type, made at any time, with or without use of employer facilities.

Employees confronted with enforcement of invention assignments have challenged their validity on all of the traditional contract bases, including fraud, duress, unconscionability and failure of consideration. In the great majority of cases, these challenges have been rejected by courts, possibly because the employees making these challenges are often highly educated research scientists and engineers.

One aspect of employee invention assignments that courts have struggled with is what constitutes an "invention;" or, stated differently, what employee activities are necessary to make an invention, and has the employee performed these activities? Determining the existence of an invention is both a question of legal definition and a question of fact. The two cases below grapple with both questions.

ANDREAGGI v. RELIS
171 N.J. Super. 203 (NJ Super. Ct. Ch. Div. 1979)

DWYER, J. S. C.

Plaintiffs commenced this action to compel defendant Matthew J. Relis to assign his interests in certain patents. Relis asserts, among a myriad of defenses, that as a coinventor he has rights in alleged further developments reflected in the patent application and patents which were made solely by plaintiffs after Relis and plaintiffs were discharged by a common employer and plaintiffs acquired the employer's rights to the inventions. Since the alleged further developments were made after termination of employment and solely by plaintiffs, Relis alleges that he is under no duty to assign his interests in those alleged further developments because he has those rights individually and common employer never had any rights in them. Neither counsel nor the court has found any decision on the question. Plaintiffs deny that they made any further developments after the assignment and the sale of the equipment embodying the inventions to plaintiffs by Curtiss-Wright, the common employer; hence they assert that they have a right obtained from Curtiss-Wright to have Relis assign his interests in the patents which have issued.

While all three were employed by Curtiss-Wright the company undertook to develop a device that would simultaneously generate a document that could be read by the human eye and a machine. The initial focus was to develop a way-bill that could accompany goods in transit. The personnel handling the goods could read the document. For control and accounting purposes, a machine could read the document electronically and generate additional copies.

The concept to accomplish this result was to utilize a typewriter which was linked to an encoding device. The stock for the document was to be paper which had a magnetic backing. The operator would type the document on the front. Simultaneously the keys of the typewriter would trigger the encoding device that would record the same information on the magnetic field on the reverse side, as well as a code of instructions to the machine that was to read the document. The recording device was a head containing windings of wire which generated an electric field. To correct for errors, provision was made to erase the bits encoded on the magnetic coating without destroying or distorting the other bits so encoded, and inserting new bits when the new typed character was inserted to replace the erased visible typed character. The machine or device embodying the concept was constructed at Curtiss-Wright. For reasons hereinafter discussed, Curtiss-Wright terminated the project and transferred its rights to Joseph Andreaggi. In return for monies advanced by Robert J. Graf, Andreaggi assigned part of his rights to Graf.

Andreaggi, Graf and Relis signed application Serial No. 250,872 for letters patent for a visual and magnetic recording system in April 1972 as coinventors. It was filed on May 15, 1972 with the United States Patent and Trademark Office. At the time that plaintiffs requested Relis to sign the application their attorney also advised Relis that they would subsequently request an assignment of his interests in the patent. During 1973 certain amendments were made to the application and four divisional patents were issued on December 28, 1973. On July 9, 1974 Patent No. 3,823,405 issued on the basic application.

During 1973 and up to July 9, 1974, plaintiffs and their attorney requested Relis to assign his rights to plaintiffs.

On May 23, 1975 plaintiffs' attorney tendered a written assignment of Relis' rights in the patent to Relis for signature. This has not been executed.

The court notes that similar problems exist with the divisional patents. The court concludes that resolution of the questions concerning the basic patent will govern the issues on the other patents.

In this action plaintiffs, in addition to seeking an order compelling Relis to assign his rights, seek money damages sustained by his refusal to cooperate in connection with certain foreign patents, and money damages suffered because of his persistent refusal to assign the rights under the patents involved in this litigation with the consequence of substantial cost of this litigation and inability to market or sell licenses under the patent. Plaintiffs further seek to restrain Relis from disclosing the nonpublic portions of the contents of the invention disclosures obtained by plaintiffs from Curtiss-Wright. They base their action on the rights acquired from Curtiss-Wright and protection of their proprietary rights in such material.

In addition to the defense based upon the alleged further developments, Relis asserts that he is under no duty to convey any rights because: (i) he was not employed to invent, (ii) Curtiss-Wright fired him before it asked him for an assignment and (iii) Curtiss-Wright could not assign any rights under a contract for personal services. He also asserts that the action is barred by the statute of limitations and by laches.

The court will consider the following matters in the order stated.

1. What was the relationship between Relis and Curtiss-Wright?

2. What had been accomplished on the project at Curtiss-Wright?

3. What was the effect of the contract of employment, Relis' separate assignments to Curtiss-Wright and Curtiss-Wright's assignment to plaintiffs?

4. What duties, if any, did Relis owe to plaintiffs and Curtiss-Wright thereafter?

5. Is the action barred by limitations or laches?

6. Relief.

The court will set forth its findings of facts under the separate headings rather than state them separately.

1.

Relis has a B.S. degree in electrical engineering from C.C.N.Y. and a M.S. degree in electrical communications from M.I.T. He worked at the U.S. Navy's Naval Ordinance Laboratory and at another major electronics corporation as an assistant development engineer. At the suggestion of a friend, he applied to Curtiss-Wright to be hired as the assistant manager of the Digital Computer Department.

He testified that he read and understood D-2, Agreement For Services, before he signed it on December 15, 1958. On January 21, 1959 he signed another copy of the form of agreement for the purpose of adding additional patents which he had obtained prior to starting work at Curtiss-Wright. He claimed a total of seven prior patents on these two forms.

He stated that his duties as assistant manager were to perform assignments given him by the manager of the department, supervise engineers, investigate problem areas and suggest solutions, and do design work where additional work was needed.

On December 16, 1959 he was promoted to Manager, Digital Computer Department.

D-2 is a standard form of agreement. At the top of the form appears the following:

CURTISS-WRIGHT CORPORATION ELECTRONICS DIVISION
AGREEMENT FOR SERVICES

IN CONSIDERATION of my employment by the CURTISS-WRIGHT CORPORATION, ELECTRONICS DIVISION (hereinafter termed the "Corporation"), upon the terms and conditions of this agreement, I, Matthew Relis of Bayside, N.Y. agree with the Corporation as follows:

2. Without charge, to communicate promptly to the Corporation and, upon request, to assign to it all of my right, title and interest in and to any and all inventions which I may make, or with respect to which I may be a joint inventor, while in the employ of the Corporation, which relate to or are useful or may be useful in connection with business of the character carried on or contemplated by Curtiss-Wright Corporation, its subsidiaries or affiliates and all my right, title and interest in and to any and all domestic and foreign applications for patents covering said inventions, any and all patents granted for said inventions and any and all reissues and extensions of the said patents; and to do any and all acts and to execute and deliver such instruments as may be deemed by the Corporation necessary or

proper to vest all of my right, title and interest in and to said inventions, applications and patents in the Corporation and to effect the obtaining of said patents, reissues and/or extensions thereof. All necessary and proper expenses in connection with the foregoing shall be borne by the Corporation.

3. (e) I will regard and preserve as confidential all information pertaining to the Corporation's business that may be obtained by me from specifications, drawings, blueprints, reproductions and other source of any sort as a result of such employment and I will not without written authority from the Corporation so to do, disclose to others during my employment or thereafter, such or any other confidential information obtained by me while in the employ of the Corporation.

In 1961, as a result of discussions with Pennsylvania Railroad personnel, Curtiss-Wright undertook development work to see if it could devise a system to simultaneously generate a document that could be read by the human eye and by a machine and that would be sturdy enough to be handled by railroad personnel. Relis, Graf and Andreaggi were assigned to the project. It was called Magdop. Financing for the project was terminated in September 1963, but work continued until 1964 because of the enthusiasm of the three for the project.

The 16 invention disclosures filed with the Patent Department at Curtiss-Wright show that Relis participated actively in the inventive process. He explained his personal possession of the original of certain of the invention disclosures, without permission, on the grounds that he had a right to know what he had invented. He also retained certain engineering notebooks with notes concerning the work on Magdop, without authority. An attorney from Curtiss-Wright identified the documents at trial as having been corporate property which should have been delivered to plaintiffs.

The evidence establishes that all three were full-time employees. Curtiss-Wright spent over $200,000 on the project under budget controls. From the testimony of the witnesses the court finds that more was spent because the parties picked up tools and parts from other departments which had little use for them or which other departments wanted to be helpful to the project. These donations were the property of Curtiss-Wright.

The evidence does not establish that during the period that Magdop was pursued Relis ever worked on the project, its ideas, or the equipment embodying the ideas, except as a full-time employee of Curtiss-Wright.

The court finds that Relis was not hired to be the superintendent of the works, as the court found on the disputed record before it in Connelly Mfg. Co., but was hired to do some administrative work and to help out in the inventive process. The court does not find Relis credible that he did not do inventive work or was not expected to do it. It is inconsistent with the memoranda and invention disclosures which he wrote in many cases and signed either individually or with one or both of the plaintiffs. It is also inconsistent with his taking original copies of some of the invention disclosures so that he would know what he invented. If he believed that he had no duty to turn over inventions made at Curtiss-Wright, why did he file invention disclosures for four years on the Magdop project instead of taking all of them home?

As stated in International Pulverizing Corp., by Judge Jayne:

Where a person expressly or impliedly contracts to devote his mental faculties and exercise his inventive ability for the benefit of his employer, the inventions conceived by him in the course of his employment and as a consequence of its pursuit belong in equity to the employer.

Counsel for Relis urges that the agreement was never effective because no person signed it on behalf of Curtiss-Wright. The form contains no provision for such a signature. Curtiss-Wright is identified in the form. It employed Relis for seven years. The court finds that Curtiss-Wright accepted and performed under the contract. Relis has not argued that the statute of frauds requires a signature. In Marcalus Mfg. Co. and International Pulverizing Corp., the courts granted injunctive relief compelling assignments of patents under oral contracts; hence, if Relis was hired under an oral contract, the court could grant relief.

Relis urges that the terms must be construed against plaintiffs because their assignor drew the form of agreement and because it is one of adhesion. He argues that certain phrases, "upon request" and "while in the employ" in paragraph 2, supra, must be read to mean that any request for assignment had to come while he was in the employ of Curtiss-Wright.

The construction of the terms of a written instrument which are not in dispute is a question of law. There is no dispute as to the terms. The court concludes that the term "while in the employ of the Corporation" defines the inventions which are intended to be conveyed and does not limit the time period in which an assignment must be requested or forever lost.

Victor D. Behn, who has been a corporate patent attorney for Curtiss-Wright for 15 years and a patent attorney since 1942, testified that normally at the time a patent application is filed an assignment of the patent rights is also filed. The face of the application will then show the name of the assignee.

He further testified that it is not unusual not to file an assignment of a patent until the patent is issued, in an attempt to conceal the interest of a corporate employer in an invention from its competitors.

He also testified that there is no procedure to check all invention disclosures and obtain an assignment of an employee's interest in them before he or she is terminated. He has requested assignment of patent rights after employees have left the employer's employment.

The court concludes that a construction of the contract language that the employer had to request an assignment of a co-inventor's right to patents before the employee left its employ would be impractical. A review of the cases as well as the testimony in this case show that there is mobility between employers by those working on inventions. On the facts in this case, which include other litigation between Andreaggi and Curtiss-Wright and the work of the patent attorneys to perfect the patent application, six years elapsed between the assignment from Curtiss-Wright and the filing of the application. In other situations other employees might have to do further work before the concept was sufficiently developed that a patent application could be filed. The court concludes that the request under paragraph 2 did not have to be made during the period of employment.

The court finds that the work on the Magdop was related to the business of Curtiss-Wright or contemplated by it. The project on Magdop was to develop a new product to be sold by Curtiss-Wright or a subsidiary. The court concludes that such work is the ordinary work of a business engaged in research and development for new products and is covered by paragraph 2.

Finally, Relis urges that the words "any and all inventions which I may make . . . while in the employ of the Corporation" have to be interpreted to mean that the invention has to be complete, perfected and reduced to practice in the form of a working model before he is under a duty to make any assignment.

No useful purpose will be served by citing all the cases and statutory provisions of the patent law relied upon by counsel for defendant in support of this argument. Many of these deal with different problems pertaining to priority.

The purpose of this contract was to settle a problem between an employer and an employee and not to settle claims of priority between inventors.

In United States v. Dubilier Condenser Corp., the Supreme Court, in delimiting the shop right rule and an employee's right to patents made while working for another, described the act of invention as follows:

> The reluctance of courts to imply or infer an agreement by the employee to assign his patent is due to a recognition of the peculiar nature of the act of invention, which consists neither in finding out the laws of nature, nor in fruitful research as to the operation of natural laws, but in discovering how those laws may be utilized or applied for some beneficial purpose, by a process, a device or a machine. It is the result of an inventive act, the birth of an idea and its reduction to practice; the product of original thought; a concept demonstrated to be true by practical application or embodiment in tangible form.

Though the mental concept is embodied or realized in a mechanism or a physical or chemical aggregate, the embodiment is not the invention and is not the subject of a patent. The distinction between the idea and its application in practice is the basis of the rule that employment merely to design or to construct or to devise methods of manufacture is not the same as employment to invent. Recognition of the nature of the act of invention also defines the limits of the so-called shop right, which shortly stated, is that, where a servant, during his hours of employment, working with his master's materials and appliances, conceives and perfects an invention for which he obtains a patent, he must accord his master a non exclusive right to practice the invention. This is an application of equitable principles. Since the servant uses his master's time, facilities, and materials to attain a concrete result, the latter is in equity entitled to use that which embodies his own property and to duplicate it as often as he may find occasion to employ similar appliances in his business. But the employer in such a case has no equity to demand a conveyance of the invention, which is the original conception of the employee alone, in which the employer had no part. This remains the property of him who conceived it, together with the right conferred by the patent, to exclude all others than the employer from the accruing benefits.

Based on the foregoing cases, this court concludes that where an inventor or inventors have conceived the basic ideas, have drawn the schematics for the electrical circuitry, have assembled the hardware to do the work, and have documented the means of executing the idea, there is invention even under the Massachusetts doctrine quoted above. The court concludes that the model does not have to be built to the point of a salable product to the end user without further work, as Relis contends. Such a standard is even more stringent than the patent laws.

In terms of the contract with Curtiss-Wright, the relevant words are, "any and all inventions which I may make, or with respect to which I may be a joint inventor, while in the employ of the Corporation . . ." As explained hereafter, a co-inventor necessarily implies that the work of at least one other was necessary to complete the work. Hence the court concludes that this contract, unlike the one in Jamesbury, had to embrace rights less than ones which were fully patentable by themselves.

The court concludes that Relis was employed under a contract which provided that he would perform original and inventive development work as well as administrative functions, that he would assign all his right, title and interest in any inventions which he made either as an inventor or co-inventor, while in the employ of Curtiss-Wright, and that he was to honor any request to assign his rights to patents as either inventor or co-inventor while employed or thereafter.

2.

The court concludes that the inventions were made at Curtiss-Wright.

3.

In December 1963 Curtiss-Wright terminated Andreaggi's employment as part of a general cutback of its operations due to financial conditions. Andreaggi made an oral offer to purchase the equipment and rights in the Magdop project and stated that a responsible official of Curtiss-Wright accepted it. These events occurred in the early part of 1964.

Relis was out of the United States at the time. When he returned, he attempted to persuade Curtiss-Wright not to sell. He attempted to have Curtiss-Wright sell the package to him. It declined to do so because he was an employee.

On May 19, 1964, Relis executed an assignment which contained in relevant part:

> [I assign] to Curtiss-Wright, a Delaware corporation, its successors and assigns, all my interest of whatever kind in and to each of and all the following Invention Disclosures bearing the Disclosure number and title indicated: and I covenant and agree that I will, without expense to me, communicate to said Corporation, its successors and assigns and its or their representatives, any facts known to me respecting the above identified Invention Disclosures and testify in any legal proceedings, sign all lawful

papers, execute all patent application papers relating thereto, make all rightful oaths and cooperate with said Corporation, its successors, assigns, and representatives, to obtain and enforce proper patent protection for the inventions of said Disclosures in all countries.

Curtiss-Wright terminated Relis' employment for financial reasons in 1965. On March 7, 1966 Relis executed a similar assignment with a similar covenant covering Invention Disclosures 1652, 1656 and 1657. These related to Magdop.

Relis specifically assigned his rights in the 16 Invention Disclosures listed above.

In the middle of 1964 Andreaggi commenced suit against Curtiss-Wright for breach of contract. While Andreaggi was pursuing his appeal from an adverse judgment below, the matter was settled between Andreaggi and Curtiss-Wright by Andreaggi paying a sum of money.

On February 23, 1966 Andreaggi and Curtiss-Wright entered into a settlement agreement. Curtiss-Wright agreed to sell the equipment identified in paragraph 1(a) and in paragraph 1(b)

. . . . to Andreaggi and Andreaggi agrees to purchase from Curtiss-Wright all of Curtiss-Wright's right, title and interest in and to inventions made by Curtiss-Wright's employees, during their employment with Curtiss-Wright, relating to Curtiss-Wright's magnetic document processing (MAGDOP) device, which said inventions are listed in Schedule A attached hereto and made a part hereof, and in and to any and all patent applications and patents which may be based on said inventions, as fully and completely as might have been held by Curtiss-Wright, had this sale not been made:

> In furtherance of this sale of its right, title and interest in and to said inventions, Curtiss-Wright will deliver to Andreaggi on the closing date hereof all of its files, records and papers relating to each of said inventions. Curtiss-Wright makes no representation that it has accurate knowledge as to which of its employees made any of said inventions and this sale is made subject to the understanding that: . . .

> (2) Curtiss-Wright has no obligation to obtain or assist Andreaggi in obtaining the execution of any papers by its employees or former employees deemed by Andreaggi to be necessary or desirable for the filing of patent applications on said inventions, but Curtiss-Wright agrees that it will execute such papers prepared by Andreaggi for execution by Curtiss-Wright and which appear reasonably necessary to effectuate this sale of said inventions.

Three days after Relis executed the supplemental assignment of Invention Disclosures to Curtiss-Wright, dated March 7, 1966, Curtiss-Wright executed an assignment of all the Invention Disclosures for Magdop, dated March 10, 1966, and a bill of sale for the equipment.

The court finds that as of March 10, 1966 Curtiss-Wright had not only the agreement of Relis set forth in its employment agreement but his undertakings in the Relis assignments. The latter expressly stated that Relis would cooperate with the successors and assigns of Curtiss-Wright.

Relis urges that his assignments to Curtiss-Wright are not as broad as the assignment from Curtiss-Wright to Andreaggi in that he did not assign his rights to "inventions" in the Invention Disclosures but only to the Invention Disclosures; hence the omission of the word "inventions" means he preserved his right to them.

Relis simply overlooks his covenant that he will testify in any legal proceedings about any facts contained in the Invention Disclosures, sign patent applications and cooperate in getting "proper patent protection for the inventions of said Disclosures in all countries." All provisions of a document must be read, and should be harmonized where possible, in interpreting a document. There is no purpose to the covenant unless the assignor intended to convey his rights in the inventions, for they alone can be the subject of a patent. The court concludes that Relis did assign his rights to the inventions.

This court concludes that for the reasons heretofore set forth, following the assignment by Curtiss-Wright plaintiffs owned all the rights Andreaggi, Graf, Relis and Curtiss-Wright had as inventors, co-inventors and owners of proprietary information in the Invention Disclosures.

Plaintiffs are entitled to costs.

QUESTIONS

1.   Andreaggi acquired rights in the Magdop equipment through a settlement agreement with Curtiss-Wright entered into on February 23, 1966. The settlement agreement also purported to convey all of Curtis-Wrights' "right, title and interest in and to inventions made by Curtiss-Wrights' employees, during their employment with Curtiss-Wright." Andreaggi's employment at Curtiss-Wright was terminated in 1963, and Relis' employment at Curtiss-Wright was terminated in 1965. In 1972, Andreaggi, Graf and Relis filed a patent application on the Magdop device as co-inventors. What inventions had been made by Curtiss-Wrights' employees at the time of the settlement agreement which could be conveyed to Andreaggi?

2.   Relis executed an assignment of invention disclosures for Magdop in 1966 after his employment at Curtiss-Wright had terminated. Is the assignment of an invention disclosure the same thing as an assignment of a patent application? If Relis did not want to share the Magdop invention with Andreaggi, why did he assign his rights in the technology to Curtiss-Wright after his employment had terminated?

3.   The court concludes that a working model does not have to be built to constitute an invention, and that such a requirement is even more stringent than the patent laws. Do you agree with the court? What constitutes invention under patent law?

4.   If you were counsel to Curtis-Wright, how would you define "invention" for purposes the assignment clause in the employment contract?

JAMESBURY CORP. v. WORCESTER VALVE CO.
443 F.2d 205 (1st Cir. 1971)

COFFIN, CIRCUIT JUDGE.

This diversity action in contract concerns the ownership of patent No. 2,945,666 (patent '666), which was developed by Howard G. Freeman, president of The Jamesbury Corporation. Jamesbury, the appellee, initially brought suit for infringement of the '666 patent against Worcester Valve Company, Inc. E. W. Bliss Company, the appellant, intervened in that suit, claiming ownership of the '666 patent. At trial below Worcester Valve did not participate; the sole issue was that of ownership of the patent rights.

In 1940, Freeman went to work as an inventor for Rockwood Sprinkler Company, then an independent concern which has since been acquired by Bliss. Among other products, Rockwood manufactured ball valves. Rockwood's ball valves utilized only a single seal or seat, could control the flow of fluid in only one direction, and tended to leak. Rockwood's customers occasionally requested a so-called double-seal ball valve, but Rockwood never developed one during Freeman's employment. In his employment contract with Rockwood, Freeman agreed "without further consideration to give to Rockwood the full benefit and enjoyment of any and all inventions or improvements which he may make while in the employ of Rockwood relating to methods, apparatus, chemical substances, or methods of producing which are being used, manufactured or developed by Rockwood, or the use, manufacture and development of which was at the time of said invention or inventions in contemplation by Rockwood, and all inventions which are made or worked out on the time and at the expense of Rockwood * * *. Said Freeman further agrees that he will without additional consideration disclose promptly to Rockwood all of the above-described inventions or improvements which he may make while in the employ of Rockwood.

****

The major question is whether Freeman's admitted close-to-the-line actions about to be described, breached this undertaking under the applicable law. Freeman had risen to become Rockwood's director of research, and had developed nineteen patents for Rockwood. By the fall of 1953 he had the confidence that he could develop a double-seal ball valve and profitably market it through a company of his own. He proceeded to read up on techniques applicable to a double-seal ball valve. Through a friend he sought out investors, and set the date of February 2, 1954 as that to which checks should be post-dated. He arranged his timely extrication from Rockwood by demanding a large salary increase on January 13, 1954, predictably not expeditiously granted, and resigned as of January 25. The organization meeting of his new corporation, Jamesbury, was held on January 29.

Up to this point nothing apparently had been put on paper. Not until February 1 or 2 had Freeman begun to make drawings or sketches of the '666 patent concepts. Although Freeman has argued that his ideas were not even partly conceived until he left Rockwood, the district court found that before leaving

Rockwood's employment he had "virtually" but not "completely" conceived the invention — that he "had gotten to the point where no more than a few additional days or perhaps few hours of thinking was required for him to put his ideas on paper in a form substantially the same as his later patent application."

In mid-February, Freeman began testing his invention. In April, he encountered a mechanical difficulty in implementing his idea and he was assisted by Oscar R. Vaudreuil, who ran a machine shop. When the invention was finally perfected, a patent application naming Freeman and Vaudreuil as co-inventors was filed. The district court concluded that Vaudreuil was a spurious joint inventor whose name was added to the application to shield Jamesbury, to which the patent was assigned, from a claim that Freeman had made the invention while still at Rockwood. On appeal, Jamesbury strenuously argued that this finding was erroneous. The finding is clearly dictum and not binding in other litigation. There is, however, evidence to support it, and we cannot say it is clearly erroneous.

Patent '666 was finally issued in 1960. In 1966, Bliss came across testimony given by Freeman in December 1965 and January 1966 in which he claimed to have first conceived of the idea for his invention in the first week of February 1954 and to have begun his drawings on February 1 or 2. These statements caused Bliss to believe that Freeman had actually invented the ball valve while he was still with Rockwood. Under the 1940 employment contract, the '666 patent would then have been Rockwood's, and now Bliss' property. Bliss promptly raised this claim as an intervenor in the Jamesbury-Worcester Valve suit.

Freeman's Employment Contract

The central issue in this case is the interpretation of the word "invention" as it is used in the 1940 employment contract between Freeman and Rockwood. Bliss claims an undisclosed idea is an invention; Jamesbury claims an idea must be written down or otherwise converted into tangible form before it becomes an invention. The district court sided with Jamesbury and concluded that the definition of "invention" is "well settled and specific." In support of this proposition, the court relied on cases which defined "invention." It is this contract interpretation which Bliss appeals.

In interpreting contracts, "there is in fact no "one correct" meaning of an expression; and the party choosing the expression may have no clear and conscious meaning of his own." If there is a plain, ordinary, and proper meaning of a term, that is evidence of how the parties intended to use that term. Similarly, trade or business usage is also relevant. The district court concluded that "invention" did have a definite meaning in patent law. Since patent concepts are used in conjunction with the word "invention" in the employment contract, we find the patent definition to have much weight.

There is, in Massachusetts case law, a definition of "invention" which coincides with the usage of the word in patent law. We cannot distinguish the relevant facts of Lamson v. Martin from this case. Lamson also concerned an invention, made by the key man in a corporation, who was claiming a later date for his invention than that claimed by the other party. The issue was whether an invention had been made by the defendant before or after the company for which he worked, and to whom he had assigned his inventions, had sold its rights to all inventions to the plaintiff. The trial court found that the defendant had conceived of the idea before the sale but had not made a model or drawing until after the sale. It also found that a mechanic would have been competent to convert the pre-sale idea into practice. The Massachusetts Supreme Judicial Court held that an idea did not become an invention until it was put into practice or embodied in some tangible form. Its theory was that before an idea became a workable reality, "there often lie severe and long-continued labor and repeated failures, and that success is not always achieved by the one who first strikes out the idea."

There are other cases which define "invention" similarly. Bliss tries to distinguish these cases as priority cases: cases in which each of two individuals claims to have been first in making an invention. If a non-disclosed idea could constitute an invention, courts would have to read minds to determine priority. Therefore, courts will not consider an idea to be an "invention" until it is made tangible. This does not mean, Bliss says, that a non-disclosed idea cannot be an "invention"; it is merely an arbitrary definition created because of difficult problems of proof.

Those same problems of proof which Bliss claims militate in favor of a requirement of tangible evidence of an invention are also present in this case. Here, one party is attempting to prove that an invention was actually made at a point in time prior to its being reduced to drawings. Moreover, the rationale put forth by the Massachusetts court in Lamson v. Martin is not one of evidentiary convenience; it is an acknowledgement that an "invention" is generally thought to be more than a thought in the inventor's head. Finally, Lamson and United States v. Dubilier Condenser Corp. were not priority disputes between two would-be patent-holders; they were both cases in which the patent-holder attempted to prove he made the invention at a point in time later than that at which another party, asserting rights to the patent, claimed the invention was made. In sum, it would seem that the Massachusetts cases and the patent law cases hold that an idea becomes an "invention" only when it is reduced to some tangible form. No such "invention" existed when Freeman left Rockwood's employ.

Our interpretation is that Freeman had not made an invention, within the meaning of the employment contract when he left Rockwood, because he had not put any of his ideas down in any tangible form. The district court found that Freeman deliberately refrained from making any drawings in order to circumvent the contract requirements. Bliss argues that it would be sound policy to frustrate the success of such bad faith. Perhaps so, but the contract could easily have provided that Rockwood was entitled to any inventions patented by Freeman and relating to Rockwood's business, within a specified number of years after termination of employment. To rule as Bliss would have us rule would require the court to attempt to read inventors' minds in order to determine when the essential idea behind an invention was conceived. Such an interpretation is perhaps facially appealing in close cases such as Lamson, where there was some evidence that the critical ideas were conceived before the termination of the contract period, or the instant case, where reduction of ideas to paper followed quickly. But such an approach would also, in cases where ideas were not reduced to practice for many years, involve the courts in something close to retrospective telepathy. It would also require us to circumvent established doctrines of contract interpretation. We are not prepared to face any of those consequences.

Affirmed.

QUESTIONS

1.   How does the definition of "invention" in *Jamesbury* compare to the definition of "invention" in *Andreaggi*? Which of the two definitions do you think is clearer? Which of the two definitions do you think is fairer? Where do you think the line between judicial economy and equity should be drawn?

2.   How can a company protect itself against unscrupulous employees who claim to have made inventions after their employment has terminated?

3.   Freeman was the director of research at Rockwood. Would his position as a senior company officer impose obligations on him beyond those contained in his employment contract?

CASE NOTES

1.   Kennedy served as president, treasurer and chairman of the board of New Products. Kennedy was also the patentee on two patents related to roof and floor construction of grain bins. New Products sold these roofs and floors for grain bins under Kennedy's direction. Well after New Products' sales began, Kennedy gave New Products a license to the roof patent but never gave New Products a license to the floor patent. New Products filed for Chapter 11 bankruptcy and Specialized Products purchased New Products' assets in the bankruptcy liquidation for $1,250,000. Earlier in the day, before the trustee in bankruptcy and Specialized Products agreed to the sale of New Products' assets, Kennedy attempted to terminate the roof license by serving notice upon the trustee in bankruptcy. Later, Kennedy assigned his title to the roof and floor patents to his attorney under a trust established for the avowed purpose of funding a patent infringement action against Specialized Products. In the infringement suit, Kennedy claimed the roof and floor patents were not included in the assets sold in the bankruptcy liquidation, and Specialized Products claimed it owned equitable title to both patents. What result? *See* Kennedy v. Wright, 676 F. Supp. 888 (C.D. Ill. 1988), judgment aff'd 867 F.2d 616 (Fed. Cir. 1989).

2.   *See also* Brown v. Alcatel USA, Inc., 2004 Tex. App. LEXIS 5687 (Tex. App. 2004) (Perpetual injunction prohibiting former employee of telecommunications company from further developing or marketing a method for converting low-level computer code into high-level code to anyone other than his former employer was proper, given trial court's determination that former employer was entitled to full legal right to this method pursuant to the terms of an enforceable employment agreement); Harsco Corp. v. Zlotnicki, 779 F.2d 906 (3rd Cir. 1985) (Provisions in employment agreement whereby employee assigned to employer patent rights to inventions he conceived during and within scope of his employment was not invalid as entered into under duress merely because employer threatened to fire employee

if he did not sign; that general financial pressure of marketplace did not constitute duress, and, in any event, employee had opportunity to consult his attorney before signing agreement); DDB Techs., L.L.C. v. MLB Advanced Media, L.P., 517 F.3d 1284 (Fed. Cir. 2008) (Language in employment agreement stating employee "agrees to and does hereby grant and assign" all rights in future inventions falling within the scope of the agreement with employer, was not merely an agreement to assign, but an express assignment of rights in future inventions, meaning any assignment of a patent under the agreement would have occurred automatically).

Additional Information

1. JOHN G. MILLS, ET AL., PATENT LAW BASICS § 12:12 (2009).

2. 6 RICHARD A. LORD, WILLISTON ON CONTRACTS § 13:17 (4th ed. 2010).

3. 3 ROBERT B. HUGHES, LEGAL COMPLIANCE CHECKUPS § 26:25 (2009).

4. 2 L. J. KUTTEN, COMPUTER SOFTWARE § 6:28 (2010).

5. EDWARD L. RAYMOND, JR., 66 A.L.R.4th 1135 (1988).

6. KATHLEEN L. DAERR-BANNON, 20 CAUSES OF ACTION 2d 269 (2009).

7. MARY B. MORRIS, 27 AM. JUR. 2D EMPLOYMENT RELATIONSHIP § 186 (2010).

8. Steven Cherensky, *A Penny for Their Thoughts: Employee-Inventors, Preinvention Assignment Agreements, Property and Personhood*, 81 CAL. L. REV. 597 (1993).

9. Catherine L. Fisk, *Removing the "Fuel of Interest" From the "Fire of Genius": Law and the Employee Inventor, 1830–1930*, 65 U. CHI. L. REV. 1127 (1998).

10. Jack Lynch, *Employee Invention Agreements, Noncompetition Clauses, and the Inevitable Disclosure Doctrine*, 23 No. 4 INTELL. PROP. L. NEWSL. 39 (2005).

11. William P. Hovell, *Patent Ownership: An Employer's Rights To His Employee's Invention*, 58 NOTRE DAME L. REV. 863 (1983).

4.4   STATE STATUTORY RESTRICTIONS ON EMPLOYER IP RIGHTS

A number of states have sought to protect employees against overly broad assignments of inventions to employers through legislation. The Minnesota statute below is typical of such legislation. The following cases, *Waterjet* and *Cadence*, involve judicial interpretations of statutes intended to protect employees against overly broad assignments. In *Waterjet*, the issue is whether the employer had given the employee adequate notice of the invention assignment as required in the Washington state statute. In *Cadence*, the issue is whether the invention was sufficiently related to the employer's business or research interests to be included within the scope of the California state statute.

MINN. STAT. ANN. § 181.78 (1980)

Subdivision 1. Inventions not related to employment. Any provision in an employment agreement which provides that an employee shall assign or offer to assign any of the employee's rights in an invention to the employer shall not apply to an invention for which no equipment, supplies, facility or trade secret information of the employer was used and which was developed entirely on the employee's own time, and (1) which does not relate (a) directly to the business of the employer or (b) to the employer's actual or demonstrably anticipated research or development, or (2) which does not result from any work performed by the employee for the employer. Any provision which purports to apply to such an invention is to that extent against the public policy of this state and is to that extent void and unenforceable.

Subd. 2. Effect of subdivision 1. No employer shall require a provision made void and unenforceable by subdivision 1 as a condition of employment or continuing employment.

Subd. 3. Notice to employee. If an employment agreement entered into after August 1, 1977 contains a provision requiring the employee to assign or offer to assign any of the employee's rights in any invention to an employer, the employer must also, at the time the agreement is made, provide a written notification to the employee that the agreement does not apply to an invention for which no equipment, supplies, facility or trade secret information of the employer was used and which was developed entirely on the employee's own time, and (1) which does not relate (a) directly to the business of the employer or (b) to the employer's actual or demonstrably anticipated research or development, or (2) which does not result from any work performed by the employee for the employer

QUESTIONS

1. As you saw earlier, an employer's common law rights to an employee's invention include shop rights, in the case of an invention made using employer facilities, and implied invention assignment, in the case of an invention made by an employee who was hired specifically to make such an invention. The employer has no common law rights to an invention made by an employee who was hired to engage in general research activities. Does the Minnesota statute constrain employer rights in employee inventions to a greater extent than the common law?

WATERJET TECH., INC. v. FLOW INT'L CORP.
996 P.2d 598 (Wash. 2000)

JOHNSON, J.

In the following certified questions the United States District Court, Western District of Washington, asks us to discern whether an agreement (the Craigen Agreement) requiring employee Steven Craigen to assign patents to employer Waterjet Technology, Inc. (Waterjet) is enforceable in whole or in part under RCW 49.44.140 or, alternatively, under Washington common law:

1. Did the Craigen Agreement provide adequate notice to Craigen under RCW 49.44.140(3)?

2. If not, may Waterjet enforce the portion of the Craigen Agreement that is consistent with the requirements of RCW 49.44.140(1)?

3. If not, may Waterjet enforce an implied agreement that Craigen assign the patent in-suit to Waterjet, or did RCW 49.44.140 preempt an employer's common law rights to inventions invented by employees who were hired or directed by the employer to invent them?

We hold under the facts of this case the Craigen Agreement did provide adequate notice under RCW 49.44.140(3) and even were notice insufficient, the remedy would be limited to excision of the portions of the agreement inconsistent with RCW 49.44.140(1). In light of these determinations, we do not reach the third question.

In reaching our conclusions, we rely on the facts provided by the federal district court, which constitute the entirety of the record. RCW 2.60.010(4).

FACTS

Waterjet, plaintiff in this action, is a Washington corporation engaged in research and development of high pressure and abrasive waterjet cutting, drilling, and milling technology. Waterjet was formerly known as Flow Industries, Inc. In 1974, Flow International Corporation (Flow International), a defendant in this action, was formed as a subsidiary of Waterjet. In 1983, Flow International "spun off" from Waterjet, although the two companies continued to work together until 1995.

Waterjet owns, by assignment, an extensive portfolio of United States patents in its area of research and development. Waterjet has always required its employees to assign their patents to Waterjet. These patents are the result of research and development performed by Waterjet's employees at Waterjet's behest and using Waterjet's resources and facilities. For each of these patents, Waterjet pays the fees for prosecution of the patent application and the fees charged by the United States Patent and Trademark Office.

In 1983, Waterjet hired Steven Craigen as a senior laboratory technician; Waterjet later promoted Craigen to the position of associate engineer. At the date of his hire, Craigen signed an employment agreement. Paragraph three of the Craigen Agreement stated:

> 3. I will disclose promptly to [Waterjet] in writing all ideas, inventions and discoveries conceived or developed in whole or in part, during the term of my employment with [Waterjet], related to any of [Waterjet's] business whether or not conceived or developed during working hours or on the property of [Waterjet]. Such ideas, inventions and discoveries shall be the property of [Waterjet] and it shall have the right to any patents which may be issued with respect to the same. I will also, and hereby do, assign to [Waterjet] and/or its nominees all my right, title and interest in such ideas, inventions and discoveries and all rights, title and interest in any patent

applications or patents that may be issued based thereon. I agree to sign applications for patents, assignments, and other papers, and do such things as [Waterjet] may require for establishing and protecting its ownership and to effectuate the foregoing, either during my employment or thereafter.

Craigen is the named inventor on several patents. He has assigned at least three of these patents to Waterjet. In 1992, Craigen and other Waterjet employees submitted an invention disclosure form to Waterjet describing a method and apparatus for milling using high pressure waterjet-containing abrasives (1992 Invention). This invention was created by Waterjet employees, including Craigen, during Craigen's tenure of employment at Waterjet. Waterjet employees conducted the research and development for the 1992 Invention at Waterjet's direction. The 1992 Invention was subsidized by Waterjet directly and funded from Waterjet's government and commercial contracts.

The 1992 Invention became the subject of United States Patent 5,704,824 (Patent 824), prosecuted and paid for by Waterjet and issued on January 6, 1998. Of the eight members of the team that developed the invention, seven assigned their rights in Patent 824 to Waterjet; Craigen, the remaining member of the team, did not. In 1997, Craigen accepted a position with Flow International, Waterjet's former subsidiary.

In 1998, Waterjet filed an action in the United States District Court, Western District of Washington, alleging infringement by Flow International of Patent 824. The complaint also sought to compel assignment of Craigen's rights to Patent 824. In 1999, Craigen initiated an action in King County Superior Court to determine his obligation, if any, to assign his rights in Patent 824 to Waterjet. Pursuant to RCW 2.60.020, the federal district court then certified to this court the three questions listed above.

ANALYSIS

I. Did the Craigen Agreement provide adequate notice to Craigen under RCW 49.44.140(3)?

Agreements governing assignment of patents by employees to employers are governed by statute in Washington. RCW 49.44.140. The statute provides as follows:

(1) A provision in an employment agreement which provides that an employee shall assign or offer to assign any of the employee's rights in an invention to the employer does not apply to an invention for which no equipment, supplies, facilities, or trade secret information of the employer was used and which was developed entirely on the employee's own time, unless (a) the invention relates (i) directly to the business of the employer, or (ii) to the employer's actual or demonstrably anticipated research or development, or (b) the invention results from any work performed by the employee for the employer. Any provision which purports to apply to such an invention is to that extent against the public policy of this state and is to that extent void and unenforceable.

(2) An employer shall not require a provision made void and unenforceable by subsection (1) of this section as a condition of employment or continuing employment.

(3) If an employment agreement entered into after September 1, 1979, contains a provision requiring the employee to assign any of the employee's rights in any invention to the employer, the employer must also, at the time the agreement is made, provide a written notification to the employee that the agreement does not apply to an invention for which no equipment, supplies, facility, or trade secret information of the employer was used and which was developed entirely on the employee's own time, unless (a) the invention relates (i) directly to the business of the employer, or (ii) to the employer's actual or demonstrably anticipated research or development, or (b) the invention results from any work preformed [sic] by the employee for the employer.

RCW 49.44.140.

Only one reported decision in Washington interprets RCW 49.44.140(3), the notice provision of the statute. *See Machen, Inc. v. Aircraft Design, Inc.* There, Machen, Inc., a developer and manufacturer of airplane parts, hired Darwin Conrad as a salesman and, later, as a research and development coordinator. Conrad signed a written confidentiality and ownership of invention agreement. The agreement purported to apply to "all ideas, inventions, and other developments or improvements conceived by Employee, alone or with others, during the term of his or her employment, whether or not during working hours, that are within the scope of [employer's] business operations or that relate to any of [employer's] work or projects . . . ."

Eventually Machen, Inc. and its corporate successor sued Conrad for breach of the agreement. Among his defenses, Conrad alleged the agreement failed to provide adequate notice of his statutory rights under RCW 49.44.140(3). The trial court invalidated the contract for lack of consideration, but the Court of Appeals disagreed with this conclusion. Nevertheless, with no analysis of what constituted "written notification" under the statute, the Court of Appeals accepted Conrad's claim that the notice provisions of RCW 49.44.140(3) were not satisfied and held the entire contract unenforceable as a matter of law.

Defendants argue that due to the similarity between the Craigen Agreement and the *Machen, Inc.* agreement, the Craigen Agreement does not satisfy RCW 49.44.140(3). Defendants also suggest the Craigen Agreement is deficient because notice was not provided in a separate statement. Plaintiff counters that the Craigen Agreement provided adequate notice on its face and to the extent *Machen, Inc.* would have us hold otherwise, it should be overruled. Based on the nature of the Craigen Agreement, we agree with the plaintiff.

Initially, there is no reason why notice may not be provided in the employment agreement itself. All the statute requires is the employer "provide a written notification . . . ." RCW 49.44.140(3). *Machen, Inc.* does not address this issue, although nothing in the opinion states notice must be contained in a separate document. Commentators examining this and similar statutes in other states have assumed notice will be provided in the agreement itself. There is no prohibition against placing the required notice in the employment agreement.

Furthermore, the purpose of the notice provision of RCW 49.44.140 is to prevent overreaching by employers. Defendants fail to establish why the Craigen Agreement, under the facts of this case, did not fully satisfy this policy with regard to Patent 824. Nor does *Machen, Inc.*, upon which defendants heavily rely, answer this question. To the extent *Machen, Inc.* suggests an agreement may not, on its face, satisfy RCW 49.44.140(3), it is overruled.

RCW 49.44.140 expressly allows for assignment of patents related "directly to the business of the employer" or "to the employer's actual or demonstrably anticipated research or development," even if such inventions are developed on the employee's own time or without the employer's resources. RCW 49.44.140(1)(a)(i)–(ii). RCW 49.44.140(3) calls for notice that patents *outside* this scope are not assignable. But this is not such a patent. Here defendants concede Patent 824 is directly related to the business of Waterjet. With regard to Patent 824, Craigen received all the notice to which he was entitled.

We, therefore, hold that given the language of the Craigen Agreement and the fact Patent 824 "relate[d] directly to the business of the employer," RCW 49.44.140(3) required nothing further under the facts of this case. We answer the first certified question in the affirmative.

II. If the Craigen Agreement did not provide adequate notice, could Waterjet enforce the portion of the agreement consistent with the requirements of RCW 49.44.140(1)?

Even if our answer to the first certified question were otherwise, plaintiff contends the proper remedy for inadequate notice under RCW 49.44.140(3) is to sever the portions of the agreement that violate RCW 49.44.140(1). To support this argument, plaintiff notes that employment agreements exceeding the bounds of the statute are "*to that extent* against the public policy of this state and is *to that extent* void and unenforceable." RCW 49.44.140(1)(b) (emphasis added). Defendant asserts that under *Machen, Inc.* an agreement lacking the required statutory notice is void in its entirety. Once again, plaintiff has the superior argument.

The Legislature has set forth a remedy for employees subjected to an overreaching patent assignment agreement: invalidation of the offending sections. RCW 49.44.140(1). We interpret statutes "so as to give effect to the legislative intent as determined *within the context of the entire statute.*" *Machen, Inc.* provided no reason why an entire employment agreement should be invalidated especially when, as here, the agreement may contain numerous terms unrelated to patent assignments. Its holding is unpersuasive and contrary to the legislative purpose behind the statute.

We hold in cases where notice is inadequate under RCW 49.44.140(3), the remedy should be derived from RCW 49.44.140(1). Overreaching portions of the agreement should be stricken as against public policy. As established above, neither the Craigen Agreement nor its application to Patent 824 runs afoul of RCW 49.44.140(1). Therefore, even were notice inadequate here, the Craigen Agreement could still be enforced as to Patent 824. We answer the second certified question in the affirmative. Given our answers to questions one and two, we decline to reach the third certified question.

CONCLUSION

RCW 49.44.140(3) is not a vehicle for a facial challenge to an otherwise valid employment agreement; its purpose is to prevent enforcement of overbroad agreements that violate public policy. That public policy is expressly set forth in RCW 49.44.140(1). The Craigen Agreement in this case required assignment of a patent that all parties have agreed is directly related to the business of Waterjet. To invalidate this agreement based on other speculative scenarios would itself be against public policy as established by the Legislature. As *Machen, Inc.* conflicts with this opinion, its analysis of RCW 49.44.140 is overruled. We answer "yes" to certified questions one and two, and decline to reach question three.

QUESTIONS

1.   The Washington State statute provides that if an employment agreement "contains a provision requiring the employee to assign any of the employee's rights in any invention to the employer, the employer must also, at the time the agreement is made, provide a written notification to the employee that the agreement does not apply to an invention" exempted under the statute. How do you interpret the language "the employer must also, at the time the agreement is made, provide a written notification to the employee . . ."? How does the court interpret this language?

2.   What relevance did the fact that the '824 patent related directly to the business of the employer have to the question of adequate notice?

3.   The court declined to answer the question of whether, if there was inadequate notice, Waterjet could still enforce the patent assignment as an implied agreement under the common law right to own inventions made by employees who were hired or directed to invent specific items. Do you think this common law right was preempted by the statute?

CADENCE DESIGN SYS. v. BHANDARI
2007 U.S. Dist. LEXIS 83078 (N.D. Cal. 2007)

MARILYN HALL PATEL, DISTRICT JUDGE.

Plaintiffs Cadence Design Energy Laboratory Company, Inc., Magma Design Automation, Inc., Altera Corp., and Mentor Graphics Corp. brought this action against defendants Narpat Bhandari ("Bhandari") and Vanguard Systems, Inc. ("Vanguard"). Now before the court is plaintiffs' motion for summary judgment that LSI Logic, Inc. ("LSI"), who is not a party to this case, is the owner of U.S. Patent Number 5,663,900 (the " '900 patent"), and that defendants' counterclaims for infringement must be dismissed for lack of standing. Having considered the parties' arguments and submissions, and for the reasons set forth below, the court enters the following memorandum and order.

BACKGROUND

In the early 1990s, LSI was primarily engaged in the design, development, manufacture and marketing of application-specific integrated circuits ("ASICs"). ASICs are customized integrated circuits designed to meet the particular requirements of individual customers in the semiconductor industry. To create integrated circuits, semiconductor companies like LSI use sophisticated electronic design automation ("EDA") tools. EDA refers to computer-aided techniques for designing, simulating, emulating and manufacturing integrated circuits. Typically, customers brought LSI a set of requirements and specifications that an ASIC needed to satisfy. LSI then created a software model of an ASIC design meeting the customer requirements, and used EDA tools to simulate that model to check that the design operated correctly. After successfully simulating the ASIC design, LSI often emulated the design as well. Through emulation, LSI would verify that an ASIC operated in its intended environment.

Concomitant with ASIC production, LSI also invested in the research and development of its own proprietary EDA tools. EDA tools were integral to improving the quality and cost-effectiveness of LSI's ASIC products, allowing LSI to simulate and test ASICs without having to first fabricate a physical prototype. In its corporate disclosures and 10K for the period ending January 2, 1994, LSI disclosed that it "ha[d] developed and offers to its customers its proprietary design tools [that] . . . improve the circuit designer's productivity." LSI obtained patent protection for its proprietary EDA tools, including patents relating to simulation and emulation tools. LSI licensed its proprietary design tools to its customers. LSI's founder confirmed the role of EDA tools in LSI's business, stating that LSI has always been "an EDA company," and not merely an ASIC company, because EDA tools and technology facilitated LSI's competitiveness in ASIC production.

Daniel Watkins ("Watkins") is not a party to this suit, but was a business partner and co-inventor of defendant Bhandari. Watkins was an employee of LSI from1985 through 2003. As a condition of his employment with LSI, Watkins signed an Employee Invention and Confidential Information Agreement (the "Invention Agreement"). Section 3 of the Invention Agreement assigned and transferred to LSI any inventions Watkins made or conceived, while he was employed by LSI, using company resources or which related in any manner to the "actual or demonstratively anticipated business, work, or research and development of the Company or its subsidiaries." Section 10 of the Invention Agreement provided that the Agreement could not be modified except by a written, signed document.

From July 1992 through July 1995, Watkins worked exclusively in LSI's Mega-Functions and Cores group division. Watkins' work in that division related to designing and developing digital logic for ASICs. His specific duties included function development, function library management, core development, core library management and customer support. In performing these duties, Watkins used EDA tools. For instance, Watkins used LSI's proprietary test patterns and simulation models to verify that the integrated circuit designs operated correctly prior to fabricating the integrated circuits. Watkins later developed a concept for an ASIC emulator which he believed would "accelerate LSI's product development." The patent claiming this concept issued as U.S. Patent Number 4,901,259 (the " '259 patent"). It discloses an EDA tool for "the "real-time" simulation of application specific integrated circuits (ASICs) in the actual digital computer system in which they will be incorporated." Watkins is also named as inventor on U.S. Patent Number 5,220,512 (the " '512 patent") entitled "System for Simultaneous Interactive Presentation of Electronic Circuit Diagrams and Simulation Data." In addition to the '259 and '512 patents, both of which relate to EDA tools and both of which were assigned to LSI under the Invention Agreement, Watkins is a named inventor on over sixty additional patents and published patent applications assigned to LSI.

In 1993, a group including Watkins and defendant Bhandari founded Valona Systems, Inc. ("Valona") to develop and market EDA technology. During this period Watkins maintained his employment with LSI. Using his LSI email account, Watkins sent Bhandari at least one email pertaining to Valona's proposed business plan and a proposed EDA verification tool. Vasona hired the law firm of Fenwick and West LLP to prosecute a patent application for a proposed EDA system that as conceived, could be used to simulate a variety of different integrated circuits, including the ASICs developed by LSI. The Fenwick and West attorney responsible for prosecuting the patent advised Bhandari that under Watkins' Invention Agreement, LSI could claim ownership of the invention. While at LSI during working hours, Watkins used LSI's fax machines at least twice to send the law firm notes related to the patent application. On September 10, 1993 Bhandari and Watkins filed a patent application for their proposed EDA system. The resulting '900 patent issued on September 2, 1997. The '900 patent was entitled "electronic emulation and simulation system" and named Bhandari and Watkins as co-inventors and Vasona as assignee. As part of its 1994 business plan, Vasona named LSI as a target customer.

In May 1998 Watkins sent a letter disclosing the '900 patent to LSI for the first time. In this letter Watkins requested that LSI confirm that it did not have an ownership interest in the '900 patent. After an internal investigation of the matter, LSI rejected Watkins' request and informed him of its belief that the '900 patent was covered by the Invention Agreement. Subsequently, on August 4, 1998 Watkins sent another letter to LSI offering LSI a nonexclusive license of the '900 patent and proffering a proposed royalty-free license agreement. This offer was then rejected in an August 25, 1998 memorandum in which LSI opined that it owned an undivided one-half interest in the '900 patent under the Invention Agreement. Then, on September 21, 1998 Watkins and Bhandari sent LSI another letter proposing a joint ownership agreement and stating that LSI's Human Resources manager had advised Watkins that his outside consultation work relating to the development of software verification tools would not pose a conflict with his duties. LSI again rebuffed Watkins' and Bhandari's efforts in a September 21, 1998 memorandum reiterating its belief that LSI had an ownership interest in the '900 patent.

Subsequently, LSI changed the primary correspondence address in the Patent and Trademark Office ("PTO") file for the '900 patent from Vasona to LSI without first seeking or obtaining Vasona's, Watkins' or Bhandari's consent or permission.

Vasona paid development costs for the invention embodied in the '900 patent and absorbed all expenses related to the prosecution of the '900 patent. LSI did not reimburse Vasona for the these costs and expenses. Thereafter, LSI continued to correspond with the PTO and paid all required maintenance fees for the '900 patent. LSI also changed the power of attorney from Vasona to LSI without first seeking consent.

Having never sold any products or made any revenue, Vasona disbanded. Bhandari then started a new company, Vanguard, and signed a document assigning the '900 patent from Vasona to Vanguard. Bhandari is the sole owner of Vanguard. On November 11, 2006 Bhandari filed a patent infringement suit in the Eastern District of Texas against plaintiffs and other companies. The court dismissed the complaint on the grounds that Bhandari had assigned his interest to Vanguard and thus did not have standing to bring suit for infringement of the '900 patent.

Plaintiffs filed this action for declaratory judgment on February 8, 2007. On March 1, 2007 plaintiffs licensed the '900 patent from LSI. Under the license agreements, LSI released each plaintiff from any and all claims of past infringement and granted them non-exclusive licenses to practice the invention covered by the '900 patent. Plaintiffs now move for summary judgment on LSI's ownership of the '900 patent and the corresponding dismissal of defendants' counterclaims for infringement based on lack of standing.

****

DISCUSSION

The issue before the court is whether, under the Invention Agreement signed by Watkins, the '900 patent was assigned to LSI, making LSI the legitimate owner of the patent. Section 3 of the Invention Agreement states:

> I [Watkins] hereby assign and transfer to the Company [LSI] my entire right, title, and interest in and to all inventions (as used in this Agreement, "inventions" shall include ideas, improvements, designs and discoveries), whether or not patentable and whether or not reduced to practice, made or conceived by me (whether made solely by me or jointly with others) during the period of my employment with the Company which are [1] made with the Company's equipment, supplies, facilities, trade secrets, or time, *or* [2] which relate in any manner to the actual or demonstratively anticipated business, work, or research and development of the Company or its subsidiaries, *or* [3] which results from or is suggested by any task assigned to me or any work performed by me for or on behalf of the Company or its subsidiaries. This Agreement does not require assignment of an invention which is the subject of Section 2870 of the California Labor Code (hereinafter "Section 2870").

The court will address several threshold issues before turning to the parties' main dispute regarding whether the '900 patent "relates to" LSI's business. First, the agreement is an enforceable contract under California law. Both Watkins and LSI assented to its terms and Watkins received valid consideration in the form of compensation from LSI. Second, defendants argue that the agreement was modified by a later oral agreement in which LSI's human resources manager, Jon Gibson, represented to Watkins that his work with Bhandari and Vasona would not conflict with the Invention Agreement. This oral modification, if it occurred at all, however, is ineffective to change the terms of the Invention Agreement because the Agreement specifically prohibited modifications not in writing and signed by both Watkins and LSI. Third, the Invention Agreement assigns to LSI any invention conceived by Watkins, regardless of whether it was conceived solely by Watkins or in collaboration with others. That Watkins worked with Bhandari, rather than alone, is therefore immaterial. Fourth, the '900 patent is assigned to LSI if Watkins was employed at LSI when it was conceived or made. This is undisputed. Watkins was employed continuously with LSI from 1985 through 2003; the '900 patent was not only conceived but was also filed and prosecuted in 1993; and the patent was ultimately issued in 1997. Finally, assignment to LSI was automatic upon filing of the patent listing Watkins as a co-inventor. Other than execution of the Invention Agreement, no further action was necessary for the assignment to be effective. *ViChip Corp. v. Lee*, (agreement that provided that the employee "assigns" rather than "agrees to assign" automatically transfers the patent without further affirmative steps by the employer).

The court now turns to the main issue regarding the scope of the subject matter assigned to LSI under the Invention Agreement. California Labor Code section 2870 places limitations on the types of inventions that an employee can be required to assign to an employer. If the invention falls within the protection of section 2870, an agreement purporting to assign the invention is unenforceable. Lab.Code § 2870(b) ("To the extent a provision in an employment agreement purports to require an employee to assign an invention otherwise excluded from being required to be assigned under subdivision (a), the provision is against the public policy of this state and is unenforceable"). The Invention Agreement is drafted as a mirror image of California Labor Code section 2870. The language of the Agreement closely tracks the language of section 2870, and the Agreement expressly references the statute. The scope of the Invention Agreement is therefore coextensive with the scope of section 2870 — the Agreement assigns to LSI all inventions that section 2870 does not specifically prohibit. Section 2870 contemplates three independent scenarios in which an assignment is valid and enforceable, and the Invention Agreement tracks these three scenarios. The "related to" prong assigns to LSI all inventions that "relate in any manner to the actual or demonstrably anticipated business, work, or research and development of [LSI] or its subsidiaries." Under section 2870(a)(1), this type of assignment agreement is specifically exempted and is therefore enforceable. The question for the court, then, is whether the '900 patent is "related to" LSI's business or actual or anticipated research or development. The employee bears the burden to show that his invention comes within Labor Code section 2870. Lab.Code § 2872.

Courts interpreting employee assignment agreements in the context of section 2870 have construed the "related to" phrase broadly. *Cubic Corp v. Marty*. In *Cubic*, the employee signed an invention agreement which assigned all inventions "coming within the scope Company's business or related to Company's products or to any research, design experimental or production work carried on by Company." The employee invented an electronic warfare simulator, which the employer did not yet have in its product line. The warfare simulator was a stand-alone product which did not necessarily have to be used in conjunction with the employer's pilot training programs. The court held that the employee's invention was related to the employer's business and its assignment was enforceable in light of section 2870. The court found that the employee presented his invention to the employer as "something to enhance" the employer's existing product line; that he designed the warfare simulator to function with the employer's pilot training program; and that the patent application stated the "preferred embodiment" of the invention was the employer's pilot training program. The employee himself recognized that his invention was related to his employer's business.

As in *Cubic*, the '900 patent in this case is related to LSI's business. In the early 1990's, when the '900 patent was conceived, LSI's primary business was the design, development, manufacture and marketing of ASICs. EDA tools were integral to LSI's business because they improved the quality and cost-effectiveness of their ASIC products. For example, the EDA tools allowed LSI to simulate, test and verify the integrated circuit designs prior to their physical manufacture. Because of their importance, LSI invested in the research and development of its own proprietary EDA tools. Beginning in 1990, LSI began obtaining patent protection for its proprietary EDA tools and LSI profited from licensing these tools to its customers. These facts are supported by a 1994 SEC filing stating that LSI "ha[d] developed and offers to its customers its proprietary software design tools . . . [that] improve the circuit designer's productivity."

Watkins himself used EDA tools at LSI and was named an inventor on patents which were assigned to LSI under the Invention Agreement (patent 4,901,259 issued in 1990 and patent 5,220,512 issued in 1993). The '259 patent was for "the "real-time" simulation of application specific integrated circuits (ASICs)," and the '512 patent was entitled "System for Simultaneous Interactive Presentation of Electronic Circuit Diagrams and Simulation Data." It is undisputed that these two patents, developed in 1990 and 1993, were related to EDA tools.

In addition, like the employee in *Cubic*, there is evidence indicating that Watkins and Bhandari themselves recognized that the '900 patent was related to LSI's business. The '900 patent application states that EDA tools are "used to define and verify prototype systems, such as various application specific integrated circuits (ASICs)." Prior to the filing of the patent application, an attorney from the law firm of Fenwick and West LLP advised Bhandari that LSI could claim ownership of the invention under Watkins' Invention Agreement. Despite the risks, Bhandari chose to proceed with the patent application. After the application was filed, Watkins and Bhandari formed a business plan for Vasona in 1994, naming LSI as a target customer for their proposed EDA system.

It is undisputed that the '900 patent relates to EDA tools. It is also undisputed that LSI's business relied on EDA tools to manufacture ASICs, and that the design and development of EDA tools was part of LSI's business. Based on all of the evidence in the record, the court concludes that there is no genuine issue of material fact as to whether the '900 patent was related to LSI's business at the time the patent was conceived. Accordingly, defendants have no ownership interest in the

'900 patent and their counterclaims must be dismissed for lack of standing.

****

CONCLUSION

The court GRANTS plaintiff's motion for summary judgment and DISMISSES each of defendants' counterclaims.

QUESTIONS

1. Did LSI obtain Bhandari's co-ownership of the '900 patent? If not, why did Bhandari not have standing to sue for infringement of the '900 patent?

2. The court found that the assignment to LSI was automatic upon filing the patent listing Watkins as a co-inventor. According to the court, "Other than execution of the Invention Agreement, no further action was necessary for the assignment to be effective." If LSI wanted to register this assignment with the PTO under § 261, how would it do so?

3. The Fenwick and West attorney responsible for prosecuting the patent advised Bhandari that LSI could not claim ownership of the invention under Watkins' Invention Agreement? Is a skilled patent attorney necessarily an expert on interpretation of employment contracts? Do you see any potential conflict between the attorney's role in prosecuting the patent application and the attorney's role in providing advice on the interpretation of the Invention [Assignment] Agreement?

CASE NOTES

1. Burgess entered into a Consulting Agreement with VEC. VEC was in the business of manufacturing composite materials used in the manufacture of products such as boats, cars and bathtubs. The Consulting Agreement provided that VEC shall be the exclusive owner of all Confidential Information and Inventions created by the consultant (Contractor) during the period of the consulting agreement. Inventions were defined in the Consulting Agreement as:

> . . . . all ideas, formulas, designs, composition of matter, concepts, methods, techniques, machines, improvements, and discoveries (whether patentable or not) . . . . including, but not limited to those (1) relating to the existing or reasonably foreseeable business interests of the Company or (2) which relate to or which result from Work performed by the Contractor for the Company or (3) for which equipment, supplies, facilities or Confidential Information of the Company are used, or (4) which are developed on the Company's time.

After Burgess completed his consulting work at VEC, he filed a patent application on a certain type of composite molding process called Rapid Adjustable Molds (RAM) technology. VEC believed Burgess had developed the RAM technology while he was consulting for VEC. VEC also believed Burgress had transferred rights in the RAM technology to Acrylon Composites, a competitor of VEC, and that Acrylon was using the RAM technology to solicit business from major corporations that VEC was also soliciting. VEC filed suit to enjoin Acrylon and Burgess from engaging in any further use, marketing, promotion or sale of RAM technology and to require Acrylon and Burgess assign all right, title and interest in the RAM technology to VEC. In defense of the suit, Acrylon and Burgess claimed the Consulting Agreement violated Minnesota Statute § 181.78 that restricted the scope of employer claims to employee inventions, and required employers to provide notice of these restrictions at the time the employment agreement is entered into. VEC asserted that the Minnesota Statute did not apply to consultants and independent contractors, and that the statute was only intended to protect employees because of their vulnerability to broad assignment clauses when seeking employment. What result? *See* VEC Technology, L.L.C. v. Acrylon Plastics, Inc., 2004 U.S. Dist. LEXIS 23161 (D. Minn. 2004).

2. *See also* Motorola, Inc. v. Lemko Corp., 2010 U.S. Dist. LEXIS 121572 (N.D. Ill. 2010) (Former employees' claim that employment agreement did not comply with Illinois Employee Patent Act rejected on summary judgment review; employer sufficiently alleged that inventions at issue relate to its business which, if proven at trial, would be sufficient to come within two provisions of the Act upon which former employees rely); St. Clair Intellectual Property Consultants, Inc. v. Matsushita Electronic Industrial Co., Ltd., 2009 U.S. Dist. LEXIS 66359 (D. Del. 2009) (Magistrate finding that no ambiguity existed in Employment agreement, and that distinction between "inventions" under paragraphs 5 and 6 of employment agreements and "inventions" under paragraphs 3 and 4 as examples of what constitutes "Proprietary Information" is reasonable; magistrate's interpretation gives effect to all provisions of the Employment Agreement and avoids conflict with Section 2870 of the California Labor Code).

Additional Information

1. 2 L. J. Cutten, Computer Software § 6:29 (2010).

2. Raymond T. Nimmer, Law of Computer Technology § 4:9 (2010).

3. 1 Steven Z. Szczepanski & David M. Epstein, Eckstrom's Licensing in For. & Dom. Ops. § 8A:53 (2009).

4. Evelyn D. Pisegna-Cook, *Ownership Rights of Employee Inventions: The Role of Preinvention Assignment Agreements and State Statutes*, 2 U. Balt. Intell. Prop. L.J. 163 (1994).

5. Mary LaFrance, *Nevada's Employee Inventions Statute: Novel, Nonobvious and Patently Wrong*, 3 Nev. L.J. 88 (2002).

6. Henrik D. Parker, Note, *Reform for Rights of Employed Inventors*, 57 S. Cal. L. Rev. 603 (1984).

7. Ronald B. Coolley, *Recent Changes in Employee Ownership Law; Employers May Not Own Their Inventions and Confidential Information*, 41 Bus. Law. 57 (1985).

8.   Perkins Coie, *Invention Assignment Agreements in Washington*, 7 No. 8 Wash. Emp. L. Letter 1 (2000).

9.   Del. Code Ann. Tit. 19 § 805 (1985).

10.   765 Ill. Comp. Stat. Ann. 1060/2 (West 1993).

11.   Kan. Stat. Ann. § 44-130 (1986).

12.   Nev. Rev. Stat. Ann. § 600.500 (West 2009).

13.   Utah Code Ann. §§ 34-39-1 to -3 (West 1994).

14.   N.C. Gen. Stat. Ann. § 66-57.1 to 57-2 (West 1981).

4.5   HOLD-OVER AGREEMENTS

You saw in the *Jamesbury* case the difficulty employers have in establishing that an invention was made during the term of employment rather than after employment was terminated. A relatively easy way for employers to avoid this difficulty is to provide in the employment agreement that the employee will assign to the employer certain inventions made within a certain period of time following termination of employment. This type of provision is called a "hold-over" clause or "trailer" clause. Hold-over clauses, however, create new difficulties. If the hold-over clause is too broad in terms of inventions or period of time covered, an employee's opportunity to gain future employment may be seriously impaired. On the other hand, if the hold-over clause is too narrow in terms of inventions or period of time covered, the employer's opportunity to protect its investment in research and development may be seriously impaired. Courts have struggled to balance these competing interests using various tests. The *Ingersoll-Rand* case below provides a detailed discussion of these competing interests and balancing tests in the context of a major technology company and entrepreneurial engineer.

INGERSOLL-RAND COMPANY v. CIAVATTA
110 N.J. 609 (N.J. 1988)

Garibaldi, J.

The issue in this appeal is the enforceability of an employee invention "holdover" agreement. Specifically, the issue presented is whether a "holdover" clause requiring an employee to assign a post-termination invention that does not involve an employer's trade secret or proprietary information is enforceable. The products relevant to this dispute are a new type of friction stabilizer, which defendant invented and patented, and a split-set friction stabilizer, manufactured and distributed by plaintiff. Both devices are used in the mining industry to prevent the fall of rock from the roof and walls of underground mines. The Appellate Division reversed the Chancery Division's ruling in favor of plaintiff. We affirm.

I

Plaintiff Ingersoll-Rand Company is a New Jersey corporation with its corporate headquarters in Woodcliff Lakes, New Jersey. Plaintiff Ingersoll-Rand Research, Inc. is a wholly-owned subsidiary of Ingersoll-Rand and is located in Princeton, New Jersey. For purposes of this opinion, we refer to plaintiffs collectively as Ingersoll-Rand.

Ingersoll-Rand is engaged in the research, development, manufacture, and sale of products for use in various heavy industries. It does business through more than thirty divisions, which are organized into eleven business groups that cover a broad range of technology, including air compressors, construction equipment, mining machinery, oil field products, and tools. Ingersoll-Rand's sales exceed $2 billion and the company dedicates approximately 3.5% to 4.0% of its revenues, or $70–80 million, to research and development.

Historically, one of the dangers of underground mining is the potential collapse of a mine's rock roof. Several methods and devices have been employed to stabilize the strata of rock layers in the roof of a mine. In 1973, Dr. James Scott, a Professor of Mining Engineering at the University of Missouri, conceived of the friction stabilizer roof support system and communicated with Ingersoll-Rand regarding the development of this concept. Ingersoll-Rand, working with Dr. Scott, expended substantial sums on the research and development of the product. On December 2, 1975, the United States Patent Office issued the first patent for Dr. Scott's friction stabilizer. Dr. Scott subsequently assigned the patent to Ingersoll-Rand. In February 1977 Ingersoll-Rand began marketing its stabilizer under an agreement with Dr. Scott.

The Ingersoll-Rand split-set friction stabilizer consists of a tubular metal element that is larger in diameter than a pre-drilled hole formed in the roof of a mine. The stabilizer is forcibly inserted in the hole. As the stabilizer is forced into the pre-drilled hole, it undergoes radical deformation, causing the tube to react outwardly against the surface defining the hole. This force provides a frictional grip along the length of the tube, which stabilizes the rock strata of the roof. An example of a simple friction stabilizer would be a nail driven into a piece of wood. Ingersoll-Rand's friction stabilizer represented a breakthrough in mine roof support equipment.

The development of Ingersoll-Rand's roof stabilizer was well documented in the industry. Ingersoll-Rand, beginning in the mid-1970s, extensively marketed and promoted the product through advertisements, pamphlets, and technical articles. These publications thoroughly detailed the stabilizer's configuration, composition, method of operation, test results, performance capabilities, and sales information. The technology employed to manufacture the device is over fifty years old.

The split set stabilizer has been a very successful product for Ingersoll-Rand. It represented over half of all stabilizer units sold in the United States for metal and non-metal mines, with over one million units sold in 1984. Ingersoll-Rand controls over ninety percent of the sub-market for friction stabilizers. Ingersoll-Rand has never reduced the price of the split set below list in response to competition; and prior to 1983, when the defendant's company, Safeguard Energy Products, Inc., entered the market, only one other competitor was in the submarket: Atlas Copco Corporation. The design of Atlas Copco's friction stabilizer is identical to a configuration of the Ingersoll-Rand stabilizer sketched by Dr. Walter McGahan of Ingersoll-Rand Research on December 10, 1978. Friction stabilizers, however, do compete with other methods of roof stabilization.

Defendant, Armand Ciavatta, is a 57-year-old engineer. He was graduated from the Rhode Island School of Design in 1953 with a Bachelor of Science degree in machine design. Subsequently, he took classes in mining, tunneling, and heavy construction engineering as well as graduate business classes. Since 1950, Ciavatta has held a number of technical engineering positions involving a variety of engineering principles, including: working for a division of General Signal Corporation on instrumentation used in weight and volume measurement; conducting quality control tests for instrumentation used in the first commercial nuclear reactor; as chief project engineer for the Revere Corporation of America where he worked with transducers and other force-measuring devices; and as Vice President of Engineering and Quality Control for Iona Corporation, where he was responsible for engineering development and testing of the company's line of kitchen and consumer appliances. He was also self-employed for a period of six years when he provided engineering consulting services in a variety of areas, including manufacturing, valve engineering, tooling, public opinion testing, and market research. While employed by Revere Corporation, Mr. Ciavatta invented and obtained a patent for a force transducer using strain gauges. Although he had no agreement with his employer, he nevertheless assigned this patent to Revere.

Ciavatta joined the Millers Falls Division of Ingersoll-Rand as Director of Engineering and Quality Control in 1972. From 1972 to 1974, Ciavatta was responsible for quality control and materials management in the production of hand and electric tools. In the fall of 1974, the company terminated his employment in the Millers Falls Division, at which time he became Program Manager with Ingersoll-Rand Research, Inc. As a condition of his employment with Ingersoll-Rand Research, he executed an "Agreement Relating to Proprietary Matter" (Proprietary Agreement) in which he agreed, in pertinent part:

> 1. To assign and I hereby do assign, to the COMPANY, its successors and assigns, my entire right, title and interest in and to all inventions, copyrights and/or designs I have made or may hereafter make, conceive, develop or perfect, either solely or jointly with others either

> (a) during the period of such employment, if such inventions, copyrights and/or designs are related, directly or indirectly, to the business of, or to the research or development work of the COMPANY or its affiliates, or

> (b) with the use of the time, materials or facilities of the COMPANY or any of its affiliates, or

> (c) within one year after termination of such employment if conceived as a result of and is attributable to work done during such employment and relates to a method, substance, machine, article of manufacture or improvements therein within the scope of the business of the COMPANY or any of its affiliates.

Additionally, in Paragraph 4 of the Agreement, Ciavatta agreed:

> 4. Not to divulge, either during my employment or thereafter to any person, agency, firm or corporation, any secret, confidential or other proprietary information of the COMPANY or any of its affiliates which I may obtain through my employment without first obtaining written permission from the COMPANY.

Ciavatta signed this Agreement on October 1, 1974, and at that time he had read and understood its terms.

While employed by Ingersoll-Rand Research as a Program Manager from October 1974 through March 1978, Ciavatta worked on a variety of development projects, other than those relevant to this litigation, including a tunneling device and the development of coal haulage machinery. As a result of his participation in these development projects, Ciavatta became interested in underground mining and read extensively the industry literature on the subject. From 1974 to 1978, Ciavatta never was formally involved in or assigned to research or development relevant to the friction stabilizer. Nevertheless, Dr. McGahan, the Director of Research, encouraged the research staff to be creative, to discuss ideas for projects or potential projects beyond those to which they had been assigned. These ideas were to be submitted on disclosure forms. Through 1975, Ciavatta submitted thirteen patent disclosures to his employer for mining technology and instrumentation. Five of the thirteen proposals were for devices to support or stabilize roofs of underground mines. Four of the five invention disclosures were not friction stabilizers, but one was an improvement to Ingersoll-Rand's split-set. Ciavatta's work during this period was his first exposure to mining support equipment. Ingersoll-Rand chose not to pursue any of his concepts. Thereafter, defendant claims, he lost his motivation to invent and did not originate any additional concepts while employed by Ingersoll-Rand.

In March 1978, the company transferred Ciavatta to the Split Set Division of Ingersoll-Rand Equipment Corp. While there, he served as Manufacturing Manager and Quality Control Manager. Ingersoll-Rand does not fabricate the stabilizer in any of its plants. Rather, it contracts with two vendors who manufacture the Split Set roof stabilizers, which Ingersoll-Rand then sells to the mining industry. As manager of manufacturing, it was Ciavatta's position to administer the manufacturing program. His responsibilities in that post included supervising the manufacture, production, quality control, and distribution of Ingersoll-Rand's Split Set roof stabilizers. During this period, the company did not employ Ciavatta to design, invent, or modify the basic configuration of its Split Set roof stabilizer, and in fact he did not do so. Ciavatta did, however, have access to Ingersoll-Rand's manufacturing drawings, materials, and specifications. Ingersoll-Rand considers all of that information confidential, although the information had been published in industry trade publications. At the Ingersoll-Rand Research Center the company maintains a security system in order to ensure the confidentiality of its information. Drawings are stamped proprietary, visitors are escorted while in the Ingersoll-Rand Research Center, vendors must sign proprietary information agreements, and all employees must enter into a Proprietary Master Agreement similar to that at issue in this case.

In the spring of 1979, as a result of certain quality control problems, Ciavatta stopped certain shipments of the stabilizer and recommended that the vendors modify their production process. Ciavatta's superior countermanded this directive and directed the vendors to make their scheduled shipments. Subsequently, in June of that year, Ingersoll-Rand terminated Ciavatta's employment. Ciavatta claims that the company did not offer any explanation for his termination; the company claims it terminated his employment because of unsatisfactory performance and his poor relations with fellow employees.

After his termination, Ciavatta circulated more than one hundred resumes seeking employment with other engineering firms. From February to July 1980, he briefly obtained employment as general manager of a bankrupt company located in Michigan.

Ciavatta asserts, and the trial court found, that he first conceived of the invention in dispute in the summer of 1979 while unemployed and off the Ingersoll-Rand payroll. Apparently, he was installing a light fixture in his home when he first conceived of his invention, an elliptical metal tube designed to stabilize the roofs of mines. While searching for employment following his discharge from Ingersoll-Rand, Ciavatta intermittently worked on his design. He completed his first sketch of the stabilizing device on August 25, 1979, approximately two months after Ingersoll-Rand fired him. Ciavatta's stabilizer differs from Ingersoll-Rand's in two respects: its tubular portion is closed rather than split, and the tube is elliptical in shape.

As he continued to develop the stabilizing device, Ciavatta consulted a patent attorney to determine his rights with regard to the device. At his attorney's request, Ciavatta obtained a copy of the Ingersoll-Rand employee Proprietary Agreement he had signed when beginning his employment with Ingersoll-Rand Research. He did not inform Ingersoll-Rand of his activities with respect to his roof support system. By letter dated October 24, 1979, his attorney advised Ciavatta that "this invention is yours and Ingersoll has no enforceable claim thereto."

After his brief employment with the bankrupt company in Michigan, Ciavatta returned to his work on the stabilizing device and began refining the system in a more systematic manner. Although still looking for employment, he "started to go through significantly more calculations," and obtained sample tubing to run experimental tests. In March 1980, nine months after his termination, Ciavatta filed for a United States patent on the device and was awarded U.S. Patent No. 4,316677 in February 1982. Subsequently, in March 1982, Ciavatta received a second patent, U.S. Patent No. 4322183, which involved an improvement to the roof stabilizer protected by Ciavatta's first patent.

In July 1980, Ciavatta prepared a business plan and solicited venture capital from a number of firms, including Kerr McGee Co. and United Nuclear Corp. These financing efforts failed, however, and Ciavatta used his life savings and borrowed over $125,000 from his brother and a bank to take his invention to the marketplace. Ciavatta exhibited his now-patented invention at a trade show in October 1982, and sales of his product then began. He made his first sale in January 1983. Sales for 1983 totaled approximately $30,000. By the time that the trial of this case commenced in June 1985 his total sales approximated $270,000. Ciavatta's stabilizer sells for approximately 15% less than Ingersoll-Rand's stabilizer. The trial court observed "[t]he market place has begun to accept defendant's product and his device appears to be a competitive threat to plaintiff's device."

The parties disagree on when Ingersoll-Rand learned of Ciavatta's invention. The company acknowledges that it had learned of the model for his invention by December 1981 or early 1982. In July 1982, Ciavatta received a letter from Ingersoll-Rand's patent counsel requesting that he assign his patent to the company. Ciavatta communicated to Ingersoll-Rand that his lawyer had advised him that he was not obligated to assign his patent to his former employer. Simultaneously, Ingersoll-Rand employees prepared several internal memoranda analyzing the feasibility of Ciavatta's product and its potential competitive impact. Ingersoll-Rand, now aware of the challenge posed by Ciavatta's invention, began to consider competitive responses to the introduction of the invention in the market.

In September 1983, after Ciavatta had sold his product to several Ingersoll-Rand customers, the company decided to lower the price of its split set stabilizer and to commence this lawsuit.

Ingersoll-Rand initiated suit against Ciavatta on April 17, 1984, alleging that the defendant had violated the employment agreement by failing to assign the invention and related patents that he conceived after leaving Ingersoll-Rand. Specifically, Ingersoll-Rand sought assignment of the patent for Ciavatta's friction stabilizer and an accounting for profits. Ciavatta denied that he had violated the agreement or that he was obligated to make the assignment. He also asserted a number of affirmative defenses including unenforceability of the agreement, estoppel, laches, and unclean hands. The trial court rejected these claims.

The issue of Ciavatta's liability for breach of contract was tried without a jury. Ingersoll-Rand attempted to prove that Ciavatta had stolen his invention and that he had relied on Ingersoll-Rand's trade secrets or other confidential information in conceiving his product. Ciavatta argued that the "holdover" clause is unenforceable in the absence of a finding that the invention was based on the employer's trade secrets or other confidential information, relying on our decisions concerning the enforceability of an employee's covenant not to compete.

The trial court made detailed factual findings establishing that Ciavatta did not pirate any trade secrets or confidential information in conceiving his invention. Indeed, the trial court found that Ingersoll-Rand's split set technology "does not involve trade secrets or other confidential information since the specifications, methods of manufacture and operating principles relating to the device are available to the public or are easily discoverable." Ingersoll-Rand's "manufacturing process has been in existence for over 50 years. Anyone can buy plaintiff's product, observe it, measure it and analyze its steel content. In short, there does not appear to be anything secret about it or the principles it utilizes."

Nevertheless, the trial court enforced the agreement, concluding that the *Solari/Whitmyer* reasonableness test was inapplicable to holdover agreements. Instead, the court articulated a general reasonableness test and determined that the balance tilted in favor of Ingersoll-Rand because Ciavatta's "knowledge of the underground mining industry was based entirely on his employment experience with Ingersoll-Rand," and he had been "enriched" by the company's non-confidential ideas and by his access to Ingersoll-Rand's "information, experience, expertise and ideas and the creative interaction gleamed from his employment with the company." The court also determined that Ciavatta's engineering experience was so diverse that "assignment of this specific invention did not unreasonably preclude realistic employment opportunities in other fields." On March 20, 1986, the trial court entered judgment on its decision and certified it as a final judgment, although the issue of damages and defendant's counterclaim remain to be resolved. The trial court stayed its judgment pending completion of the appellate process. Defendant Ciavatta filed a timely Notice of Appeal on May 2, 1986.

The Appellate Division accepted the trial court's factual determination but reversed the judgment, reasoning that the principles enunciated in the *Solari/Whitmyer* decisions should apply. Applying the *Solari/Whitmyer* reasonableness test, the Appellate Division concluded that Ingersoll-Rand's legitimate interests were protected since none of the company's trade secrets or other confidential information was used by Ciavatta in devising his invention, that enforcement of the agreement would "impose upon the employee a prohibition effective for one-year over an unlimited geographical area, from working on mine supports for any company in the mining industry," and result in a "lessen[ing] [of] competition and keep [ing] potentially competitive products from the market."

Accordingly, the Appellate Division reversed the trial court's judgment and remanded the case to the Chancery Division for the dismissal of the company's complaint and for trial of the defendant's counterclaim. We granted Ingersoll-Rand's petition for certification,

II

Paragraph 1(c) of Ciavatta's Proprietary Agreement with Ingersoll-Rand comprises a one-year so-called "holdover" agreement under which the employee promises to assign his or her "entire right, title and interest" in any invention he or she creates during a one-year period following termination of employment if that invention is "conceived as a result of and is attributable to work done during such employment." The central question presented in this case is the enforceability of that covenant.

The common law regards an invention as the property of the inventor who conceived, developed, and perfected it. The Supreme Judicial Court of Massachusetts accurately summarized the common-law position in *National Development Co. v. Gray*:

> One by merely entering an employment requiring the performance of services of a non-inventive nature does not lose his rights to any inventions that he may make during the employment . . . and this is true even if the patent is for an improvement upon a device or process used by the employer or is of such great practical value as to supersede the devices or processes with which the employee became familiar during his employment . . . . The law looks upon an invention as the property of the one who conceived, developed and perfected it, and establishes, protects and en-

forces the inventor's rights in his invention unless he has contracted away those rights.

Thus, employment alone does not require an inventor to assign a patent to his employer. Absent a specific agreement, an employed inventor's rights and duties with respect to an invention or concept arise from the inventor's employment status when he actually designed the invention.

Generally, where an employer hires an employee to design a specific invention or solve a specific problem, the employee has a duty to assign the resulting patent. Where the employee is not hired specifically to design or invent, but nevertheless conceives of a device during working hours with the use of the employer's materials and equipment, the employer is granted an irrevocable but non-exclusive right to use the invention under the "shop right rule." A shop right is an employer's royalty or fee, a non-exclusive and non-transferable license to use an employee's patented invention.

Since the common-law doctrines are vague and ambiguous in defining the rights of employers and employees in employees' inventions, most employers use written contracts to allocate invention rights. Such contracts requiring an employee to assign to the employer inventions designed or conceived during the period of employment are valid.

The contractual allocation of invention rights between employers and employees is especially critical given the fact that 80% to 90% of all inventions in the United States are made by employed inventors. The United States is not alone in this regard. In West Germany, 60% to 75% of all inventions come from employed inventors; in France the figure is 70% to 75%. In both countries, 90% of all *useful* inventions are made by employees.

Most large, technologically advanced companies today require their employees by contract to assign their patents to their employers. Courts, however, will not enforce invention assignment contracts that unreasonably obligate an employee in each and every instance to transfer the ownership of the employee's invention to the employer. Additionally, several states have recently adopted legislation that delimits employer-employee invention assignment agreements. Those statutes restrict the instances in which employers may compel the assignment of employee inventions. See *Minn.Stat.Ann.* § 181.78 (1980); *N.C.Gen.Stat.* § 66-57.1 to 57-2 (1981); *Wash.Rev.Code Ann.* § 49.44.140 (1987); *Cal.Lab.Code* § 2870 (West 1987). All of these statutes provide that any employee invention assignment agreement that purports to give employers greater rights than they have under the statute is against public policy and, consequently, unenforceable.

In the instant case, the contract involves the assignment of future or post-employment inventions. Contractual provisions requiring assignment of post-employment inventions are commonly referred to as "trailer" or "holdover" clauses. The public policy issues involved in the enforceability of these holdover clauses reflect the dichotomy of our views on the rights of an inventor and rights of an employer. Our society has long recognized the intensely personal nature of an invention and the importance of providing stimulation and encouragement to inventors. Some commentators believe that the existing patent system does not present sufficient motivation to an employee-inventor. These commentators allege that the United States is in danger of losing its position as technology leader of the world. They cite for support that America is experiencing a declining patent balance and is less patent-productive than many foreign countries. More and more United States patents are not issued to United States citizens and companies but to foreigners. Interestingly, Japan, which began tying employed inventors' compensation to the market value of the invention in 1959, has witnessed a dramatic increase in the number of inventions generated by employed inventors.

To encourage an inventor's creativity, courts have held that on terminating his employment, an inventor has the right to use the general skills and knowledge gained through the prior employment. Moreover, an employee may compete with his former employer on termination. Nonetheless, it is acknowledged that the inventive process is increasingly being supported and subsidized by corporations and governments. It is becoming a more collective research process, the collective product of corporate and government research laboratories instead of the identifiable work of one or two individuals. Employers, therefore, have the right to protect their trade secrets, confidential information, and customer relations. Thus, employees and employers both have significant interests warranting judicial attention.

In view of the competing interests involved in holdover agreements, courts have not held them void *per se*. Rather, the courts apply a test of reasonableness. ("As a broad proposition, contracts that are unreasonable are unenforceable; that is, if the restraints imposed are unlimited as to time, space or subject matter."). Moreover, courts strictly construe contractual provisions that require assignment of post-employment inventions; they must be fair, reasonable, and just. Generally, a clause is unreasonable if it: (1) extends beyond any apparent protection that the employer reasonably requires; (2) prevents the inventor from seeking other employment; or (3) adversely impacts on the public.

New Jersey courts previously have not specifically addressed the enforceability of a "holdover" clause. We have, however, addressed the enforceability of analogous employee non-competition contracts. We find that our determination of the enforceability of those post-contracts is applicable to our determination in this case of the enforceability of "holdover" clauses.

In *Solari* and *Whitmyer*, we articulated a three-part test to determine the validity of a non-competition covenant in an employment contract. Under those cases, a court will find a non-competition covenant reasonable if it "simply protects the legitimate interests of the employer, imposes no undue hardship on the employee and is not injurious to the public." *Solari* and *Whitmyer* both recognize as legitimate the employer's interest in protecting trade secrets, confidential information, and customer relations.

Courts in other jurisdictions that have considered specifically the question of the enforceability of holdover agreements generally apply a "reasonableness" test consistent with our *Solari/Whitmyer* test. The Court of Appeals for the Sixth Circuit, in *New Britain Machine Co. v. Yeo*, reiterated the rule for interpreting a contract requiring the assignment of future patents and future improvements:

"It is well settled that an agreement to assign a patent and improvements thereon covers only improvements existing at the time the agreement was entered into unless the language specifically refers to future improvements. The law does not look favorably upon covenants which place "a mortgage on a man's brain, to bind all its future products."

*****

[T]o effect an assignment of future improvements to a patent which the inventor may thereafter produce "the language of the contract must be very plain and evidence unmistakably that such an agreement was in the mind of the inventor." "

Regarding the validity of the contractual provision requiring the employee to disclose and assign all ideas and improvements for five years following termination of employment, the court articulated a three-part test consistent with the principles or our decisions in *Solari* and *Whitmyer*:

1) Is the restraint reasonable in the sense that it is no greater than necessary to protect the employer in some legitimate interest?

2) Is the restraint reasonable in the sense that it is not unduly harsh and oppressive on the employee?

3) Is the restraint reasonable in the sense that it is not injurious to the public?

After balancing these criteria, the court held that the five-year restraint was void as against public policy. The court relied on the fact that the employee had originally been hired from a competitor and that his experience had been limited to one field of engineering design only, thus limiting any future employment opportunities.

Regardless of the results reached in the individual cases, all courts recognize the competing interests at stake. That is, the question of the enforceability of holdover covenants clearly presents the interest of the employee in enjoying the benefits of his or her own creation, on the one hand, and the interest of the employer in protecting confidential information, trade secrets, and, more generally, its time and expenditures in training and imparting skills and knowledge to its paid work force, on the other. Moreover, courts recognize that the public has an enormously strong interest in both fostering ingenuity and innovation of the inventor and maintaining adequate protection and incentives to corporations to undertake long-range and extremely costly research and development programs.

****

IV

The cases thus support the enforceability of holdover agreements if they are reasonable. In assessing the reasonableness of holdover agreements, this Court will follow the *Solari/Whitmyer* test of reasonableness. By applying the reasonableness test, the judicial analysis of holdover agreements will parallel the judicial analysis of contracts requiring an employee to assign to the employer inventions made or conceived of by an employee *during* his or her employment. We have held such contracts to be enforceable when reasonable. Likewise, we will enforce holdover agreements to the same extent that we will enforce similar post-employment restrictive agreements, giving employers "that limited measure of relief within the terms of the noncompetitive agreement which would be reasonably necessary to protect his "legitimate interests," would cause "no undue hardship" on the employee, and would "not impair the public interest." "

The first two parts of the *Solari/Whitmyer* test focus on the protection of the legitimate interests of the employer and the extent of the hardship on the employee. Plainly, the court must balance these competing interests. In cases where the employer's interests are strong, such as cases involving trade secrets or confidential information, a court will enforce a restrictive agreement. Conversely, in cases where the employer's interests do not rise to the level of a proprietary interest deserving of judicial protection, a court will conclude that a restrictive agreement merely stifles competition and therefore is unenforceable. Courts also recognize that knowledge, skill, expertise, and information acquired by an employee during his employment become part of the employee's person. "They belong to him as an individual for the transaction of any business in which he may engage, just the same as any part of the skill, knowledge and information received by him before entering the employment." An employee can use those skills in any business or profession he may choose, including a competitive business with his former employer. Courts will not enforce a restrictive agreement merely to aid the employer in extinguishing competition, albeit competition from a former employee. Ultimately, the consuming public would suffer from judicial nurturing of such naked restraints on competition.

At the same time, we recognize that employers have a right to protect their trade secrets and other confidential information. Initially, of course, employers can rely on the patent laws and their common law derivatives as a foundation for protecting their patented goods and trade secrets. Beyond such protections, employers may protect themselves contractually from the misappropriation of other company information by former employees. Through contract, an employer may protect its legitimate interest in preventing employees from using the thoughts and ideas generated by the employee and fellow workers while being paid by and using the resources of the employer to invent a product that directly competes with the employer's product.

Most courts have limited the legitimate protectable interests of an employer "to trade secrets and other proprietary information . . . and customer relations." The rationale offered for such a limitation is the broad definition of trade secret and other confidential information. There is no exact definition of a trade secret. Generally, cases rely on the broad definition of trade secret found in the *Restatement of Torts* § 757 comment b (1939):

> b. Definition of trade secret. A trade secret may consist of any formula, pattern, device or compilation of information which is used in one's business, and which gives him an opportunity to obtain an advantage over competitors who do not know or use it. It may be a formula for a chemical compound, a process of manufacturing, treating or preserving materials, a pattern for a machine or other device, or a list of customers.

The Restatement also lists six factors to determine whether a given idea or information is a trade secret: (1) the extent to which the information is known outside of the business; (2) the extent to which it is known by employees and others involved in the business; (3) the extent of measures taken by the owner to guard the secrecy of the information; (4) the value of the information to the business and to its competitors; (5) the amount of effort or money expended in developing the information; and (6) the ease or difficulty with which the information could be properly acquired or duplicated by others. In sum, a trade secret need not be novel, inventive, or patentable, and may be a device that is clearly anticipated in the prior art or one that is merely a mechanical improvement that a good mechanic can make. However, it may not be part of the general knowledge or information of an industry or a matter of public knowledge.

Ciavatta urges that holdover agreements also should be enforced only when the former employee has used the trade secrets or confidential information of the employer in developing his post-termination invention. Since it is undisputed that he did not do so in inventing his stabilizer, he argues, paragraph 1(c), the holdover clause, should not be enforced against him.

Ingersoll-Rand, however, argues that it is inequitable to limit an employer's "protectable interest" solely to trade secrets and other confidential information. Today, large corporations maintain at great expense modern research and development programs that involve synergistic processes. Such "think tanks" require the free and open exchange of new ideas among the members of a research staff using the employer's body of accumulated information and experiences. This creative process receives its impetus and inspiration from the assimilation of an employer's advanced knowledge and a spontaneous interaction among colleagues, co-employees, and superiors. Ingersoll-Rand argues that it maintains this creative atmosphere in its research and development effort at great expense and that it should be allowed to protect itself against a former employee who invents a unique, competing concept attributable to such brainstorming. Ingersoll-Rand contends that such creative brainstorming enriched Ciavatta and led to his invention and therefore that paragraph 1(c) of the proprietary agreement should be enforced.

We agree with Ingersoll-Rand that the protection afforded by holdover agreements such as the one executed by the parties in this lawsuit may under certain circumstances exceed the limitation of trade secrets and confidential information. We recognize that employers may have legitimate interests in protecting information that is not a trade secret or proprietary information, but highly specialized, current information not generally known in the industry, created and stimulated by the research environment furnished by the employer, to which the employee has been "exposed" and "enriched" solely due to his employment. We do not attempt to define the exact parameters of that protectable interest.

We expect courts to construe narrowly this interest, which will be deemed part of the "reasonableness" equation. The line between such information, trade secrets, and the general skills and knowledge of a highly sophisticated employee will be very difficult to draw, and the employer will have the burden to do so. Nevertheless, we do not hesitate to recognize what appears to us a business reality that modern day employers are in need of some protection against the use or disclosure of valuable information regarding the employer's business, which information is passed on to certain employees confidentially by virtue of the positions those employees hold in the employer's enterprise.

In sum, we conclude that holdover agreements are enforceable when reasonable, and that in determining if the post-termination restriction is reasonable, we will apply the three-prong test of *Solari/Whitmyer*. Thus, resolution of each case will depend on its own facts and circumstances. Courts must not go too far in construing holdover agreements to insulate employers from competition from former employees. That courts should not be overly zealous in protecting employers should not, however, dissuade a court from analyzing the reasonableness of a holdover covenant or from enforcing it where it is reasonable. Thus, here, we must balance the interests of Ingersoll-Rand and Ciavatta on the basis of the facts to determine whether the enforcement of the holdover agreement in this instance would be reasonable.

****

VI

We conclude that on the facts of this case, Ingersoll-Rand is not entitled to an assignment of the patent on Ciavatta's friction stabilizer. We find that Ingersoll-Rand has not substantiated that Ciavatta invented his friction stabilizer in violation of his contractual obligation under the holdover clause. Ingersoll-Rand has not established that Ciavatta "conceived" of his invention as a result of his employment at Ingersoll-Rand. The facts convince us that the holdover clause does not apply here however liberally we are willing to construe the protection afforded employers by such clauses. Furthermore, we also find that enforcement of the holdover agreement in this case would be unreasonable even if the contract by its terms applied to Ciavatta's invention.

The record shows that Armand Ciavatta was not hired to invent or to work on design improvements or other variations of the split set friction stabilizer. He was not directed by his employer into its research and development department, and even though Ciavatta himself submitted numerous product ideas to Ingersoll-Rand, the company never developed any of those ideas. Indeed, Ciavatta testified that as a result of plaintiffs' rejection of his submitted ideas, he was discouraged from creating or using his ingenuity to develop new ideas or suggest adaptations to existing Ingersoll-Rand products. Ingersoll-Rand did not assign Ciavatta to a "think tank" division in which he would likely have encountered on a daily basis the ideas of fellow Ingersoll-Rand personnel regarding how the split set stabilizer could be improved or how a more desirable alternative stabilizer might be designed.

More importantly, the information needed to invent the split set stabilizer is not that unique type of information that we would deem protectable even under our expanded definition of a protectable interest. All of the specifications and capabilities of the Ingersoll-Rand split set stabilizer were widely publicized throughout industry and trade publications.

These facts lead us to believe that the factors of the *Solari/Whitmyer* balancing test weigh heavily in favor of defendant, even assuming that paragraph 1(c) applies. Although we specifically hold today that reasonable holdover agreements may be enforceable, we decline to enforce the agreement between Ingersoll-Rand and Ciavatta because, as it relates to the patented invention in dispute, the restriction is unreasonable under *Solari/Whitmyer*. We recognize that employers may have a protectable interest in certain proprietary information that former employees may use to invent competing products. We also recognize that the range of the employer's proprietary information that may be protected by contract may narrowly exceed the specific types of information covered by the law of trade secrets and confidential information. Here, however, when we apply the reasonableness test of *Solari/Whitmyer*, we conclude that enforcement of the holdover agreement would work an undue hardship on defendant. Thus, we conclude that the restraint in this specific case is unreasonable and hence unenforceable.

Accordingly, we affirm the judgment of the Appellate Division.

QUESTIONS

1.   The hold-over clause at issue in *Ingersoll-Rand* covered any invention that was "conceived as a result of and is [sic] attributable to work done during such employment." Ciavatta submitted an employee invention disclosure on an improvement to Ingersoll-Rand's split-set friction stabilizer and worked for a period of time as the manufacturing manager for the fabrication the split-set friction stabilizer. Do you think this work enabled Ciavatta to conceive of his invention? Do you think Ciavatta's invention was attributable to this work? Or do you think this work was part of Ciavatta's acquisition of general knowledge and experience which he can take with him after employment?

2.   The court holds that under certain circumstances a hold-over agreement can protect more than just trade secrets and confidential information. As an example, the court cites "highly specialized, current information not generally known in the industry." Could such information qualify as a trade secret under the Restatement of Torts definition?

3.   The court sets forth a three-part test to determine the reasonableness of hold-over agreements: 1) Is the restraint reasonable in that it is no greater than necessary to protect some legitimate interest of the employer? 2) Is the restraint reasonable in that it is not unduly harsh and oppressive on the employee? And 3) Is the restraint reasonable in that it is not injurious to the public? Isn't competition from a former employee always a legitimate interest of an employer? Isn't requiring a former employee to assign patent rights to a former employer always harsh and oppressive on the employee? Isn't the public always injured (economically disadvantaged) when competition between a former employee and former employer is stifled?

4.   The *Solari/Whitmyer* test was developed in the context of a non-competition agreement. Are the interests at stake in the enforcement of a non-competition agreement the same as the interests at stake in the enforcement of a hold-over agreement?

5. Would a reasonableness test for hold-over agreements that protected only employer trade secrets and confidential information provide more predictable results than the *Solari/Whitmyer* test as applied by the court in *Ingersoll-Rand*?

CASE NOTES

1. Applied Materials is a California-based semi-conductor manufacturing company with roughly 15,000 employees. AMEC is a joint-venture start-up company headquartered in Shanghai, China. AMEC hired a number of employees who previously worked for Applied Materials. All Applied Materials' employees signed an assignment clause which stated:

> In case any invention is described in a patent application or is disclosed to third parties by me within one (1) year after terminating my employment with Applied, it is to be presumed that the invention was conceived or made during the period of my employment for Applied, and the invention will be assigned to Applied as provided by this Agreement, provided it relates to my work with Applied or any of its subsidiaries.

Applied Materials brought suit against AMEC to enforce the assignment clause with respect to several of its former employees who had gone to work for AMEC. Applied Materials alleged that several inventions were disclosed to AMEC by its former employees within one year of their termination of employment, and that, pursuant to the assignment clause, these inventions presumptively belong to, and should be assigned to, Applied Materials. AMEC filed a counterclaim seeking a declaratory judgment that the assignment clauses were unenforceable because they required former employees to assign inventions even if the inventions were the result of the independent research, development and investment of the former employee personally, or his or her new employer. Applied Materials responded that the assignment clauses merely created a presumption of conception during employment which could be rebutted by former employees. What result? *See* Applied Materials, Inc. v. Advanced Micro-Fabrication Equip. (Shanghai) Co., 630 F. Supp. 2d 1084 (N.D. Cal. 2009).

2. *See also* Armorlite Lens Co. v. Campbell, 340 F. Supp. 273 (S.D. Cal. 1972) (An agreement which requires a former employee to turn over to his former employer all new ideas and concepts concerning the field of work or the products of the employer which occur to the former employee within one year after the termination of his employment is unnecessarily broad; to require a former employee, who has developed a new idea or concept following the termination of his employment, and which is not based upon the employer's trade secrets or confidential information, to turn over the fruits of his labors to his former employer constitutes an unreasonable restraint of trade); General Signal Corp. v. Primary Flow Signal, Inc., 1987 U.S. Dist. LEXIS 6929 (D.R.I. 1987) (It is difficult to believe that after a long and distinguished career with plaintiff, Mr. Halmi in his musing five days after the trailer clause expired, for the first time, came up with the idea for the invention; the court finds that the concept of the invention must have existed in Mr. Halmi's mind before his employment with plaintiff ended); Dorr-Oliver, Inc. v. United States, 432 F.2d 447 (Ct. Cl. 1970) (Where inventor had not worked on cargo trailers in former employment and was not shown to have had knowledge of former

employer's activities relating to cargo trailers, cargo trailers were not included as part of "subject matter" which inventor agreed to assign back to former employer within one year after termination of his employment; accordingly, former employer was not "owner" of patent on cargo trailer conceived and reduced to practice upon subsequent employment under statute conferring on owner rights to sue for government's unlicensed use of invention).

Additional Information

1. 2 L. J. KUTTEN, COMPUTER SOFTWARE § 6:38 (2010).

2. IRWIN AISENBER, MODERN PATENT LAW PRECEDENT H 180 (8th ed. 2010).

3. 15-80 CORBIN ON CONTRACTS § 80.19 (2010).

4. MARY B. MORRIS, 27 AM. JUR. 2D § 187 (2nd ed. 2010).

5. GLENDA K. HARNAD, ET. AL., 30 C.J.S. § 148 (2010).

6. Catherine L. Fisk, *The Story of Ingersoll-Rand v. Ciavatta: Employee Inventors in Corporate Research and Development — Reconciling Innovation with Entrepreneurship* (2006) Duke Law School Faculty Scholarship Series, Paper 48, available at http://lsr.nellco.org/duke fs/48.

7. Marc B. Hershovitz, *Unhitching the Trailer Clause: The Rights of Inventive Employees and Their Employers*, 3 J. INTELL. PROP. L. 187 (1995).

8. Patents: *"Holdover Agreement" on Assignment of Post-Employment Patent is Invalid*, 36 BNA PATENT, TRADEMARK & COPYRIGHT J. 424, Issue No. 894 (1988).

9. Peter Caldwell, *Employment Agreements for the Inventing Worker: A Proposal for Reforming Trailer Clause Enforceability Guidelines*, 13 J. INTELL. PROP. L. 279 (2006).

4.6 NON-DISCLOSURE AGREEMENTS

Non-disclosure agreements, or NDAs, are used in many different contexts including employment hiring, product sales, intellectual property licensing, venture investing, and mergers and acquisitions. In any situation where one party (the disclosor) intends to disclose proprietary information to another party (the disclosee), an NDA protects against further disclosure and use of the proprietary information to the detriment of the disclosing party. An NDA can also cover implicit disclosures as where employees learn of employer proprietary information in the ordinary course of their work.

Although trade secrets can be protected against misappropriation absent an NDA, executing an NDA puts all parties on notice that the disclosed information constitutes a trade secret and that violation of the NDA will result in breach of contract liability. NDAs can also be used to protect confidential information that may not qualify as a trade secret. Examples of such confidential information are know-how, show-how, financial data, marketing strategies and testing results.

Two issues which often arise with respect to NDAs are the scope of the NDA (what information is covered by the NDA) and whether the information claimed under the NDA is in the public domain. Information in the public domain is always excluded from NDAs. The *Revere* case deals with the first question, and the *Celeritas* case deals with the second question.

REVERE TRANSDUCERS, INC. v. DEERE & COMP.
595 N.W.2d 751 (IOWA 1999)

McGIVERIN, CHIEF JUSTICE.

Several questions are presented in this appeal and cross appeal concerning plaintiff Revere Transducers, Inc.'s action against defendant Deere & Company for tortious interference with contractual relations, misappropriation of trade secrets and civil conspiracy. The basis of Revere's claims is that Deere allegedly induced two former Revere employees, Greg Eckart and Francis Delfino, to violate an employment agreement with Revere, start a company, and develop and manufacture a draft sensor device to sell to Deere, which would replace a similar device that Revere was manufacturing and selling to Deere.

A jury returned verdicts in favor of Revere on its claims for tortious interference with contractual relations and civil conspiracy and in favor of Deere concerning Revere's claim for misappropriation of trade secrets.

On Deere's appeal and Revere's cross appeal, we affirm in part, reverse in part and remand.

I. Background facts and proceedings.

A. Establishment of relationship between Revere and Deere.

Plaintiff, Revere Transducers, Inc., is a Delaware corporation with its principal place of business in California, and operates a facility in Connecticut. Revere is engaged in the manufacture, marketing and sale of devices called resistive strain gauge force transducers. A force transducer is a device which measures force. A strain gauge is an electrical conductor which measures strain and is a component part of a force transducer.

Defendant Deere & Company is a Delaware corporation with its principal place of business in Illinois. Deere is engaged in the manufacture of tractors and has a facility in Waterloo, Iowa.

In the mid-1980s Deere became interested in locating a company to develop and manufacture a draft sensor device which, when installed on its tractors, would regulate the depth of an attached plow in the ground and monitor the forces on the plow as the tractor was plowing.

In 1986, Deere contacted a number of different manufacturers of strain gauge sensing devices, including plaintiff Revere. Revere and Deere discussed the possibility of using a "Gozinta." A Gozinta is a strain gauge force sensor device developed and manufactured by Revere under the registered trademark "Gozinta."

The Gozinta is a metal capsule or cylinder-shaped device, approximately two inches long. One end of the Gozinta has a ridged or "knurled" surface, similar to the edge of a coin. The Gozinta is pressed into a hole in a member or metal strap and the knurled surface accomplishes an interference fit between the Gozinta and the receiving member. In oversimplified terms, the Gozinta measures the strain produced in the member in which it is inserted.

Inside the metal capsule is a disc with four evenly spaced holes which channel the stress toward four strain gauges mounted on the disc. The holes have a minimum diameter of one-eighth of an inch. Wire pins extend through the holes to the strain gauges and connect the strain gauges to an electric circuit board, or amplifier. The wire pins transfer the strain gauge signal or changes in resistance back through the printed circuit board or amplifier. The signal would eventually be transmitted to the tractor's computer. By drilling a hole in a hitch that attaches a plow to a tractor, and placing a Gozinta in the hole, the force on the plow can be calculated.

The concept of using Revere's Gozinta as a draft sensor in a Deere product was unique. Deere had experience using strain gauges in testing application, but had never used strain gauges in a product.

To formalize their business relationship, Revere and Deere signed an agreement entitled "Non-Disclosure Agreement for Proprietary Information" in June 1986 to protect the proprietary information of the parties.

The initial plan was that Revere would manufacture the Gozinta at its plant in Connecticut. The Gozinta would then be inserted into a Deere designed strap made of forged steel. The Deere metal strap was to be manufactured by a third party. The decision was later made that Revere would be responsible for assembling the completed device, that is, inserting the Gozinta into Deere's metal strap.

Deere was to provide the funding for the unique tooling which would be necessary for the manufacture, assembling and testing of the Gozinta. Deere agreed to purchase a fixed total quantity of Gozintas from Revere, pursuant to a blanket purchase order. The purchase order included language stating that Deere, at its discretion, could terminate the purchase order with 120 days notice. The parties estimated that production quantities of the Gozinta would increase from 5000 in 1989 to 30,000 in 1991. The original price of the Gozinta to Deere was estimated at $129.50 per part but later increased to $138.22.

Revere and Deere worked jointly on the project, and development of the Gozinta draft sensor device consumed the efforts of Deere and Revere over a three to four-year period. Each party had a team of engineers working on the project.

Francis Delfino, a manufacturing engineer, was a member of the Revere team. Delfino was responsible for designing the processes and equipment to manufacture the Gozinta and played an important role in its development. Delfino was hired by Revere on September 15, 1986.

Greg Eckart was another member of the Revere team. Eckart was not an engineer but was a product manager and was the primary contact between Revere and Deere for the Gozinta/Deere project. Eckart was hired by Revere on August 26, 1986.

At the time they were hired, Delfino and Eckart signed agreements whereby they agreed to disclose any inventions or discoveries they made during their employment to Revere and also agreed not to disclose any such inventions or discoveries to others without Revere's consent. The agreement further stated that Delfino and Eckart agreed not to disclose any inventions or discoveries relating to Revere's methods, processes, or apparatus or production of goods or materials for a period of one year following termination from Revere's employment. Delfino and Eckart also agreed to assignment of their rights to Revere in any invention or discovery made by them during their employment by Revere and agreed not to disclose to others at any time during their employment any confidential information, knowledge or data belonging to Revere without first obtaining Revere's written consent. Delfino and Eckart were not bound by any other employment agreement or noncompete agreement and thus were considered at-will employees.

B. Production problems arose.

According to Revere, Deere was late in supplying the funding for the tooling which prevented Revere from proceeding with development of the Gozinta. The strap forging company chosen by Deere also was late in providing the forged steel straps to Revere. Due to these delays, Revere was forced to begin actual production of the Gozinta without an opportunity to perform preproduction testing or a pilot run.

Revere began actual production of the Gozinta in December 1988. Production was not immediately successful. Problems developed in that the Gozinta produced an excessive output signal and produced an unpredictable output of the sensor when no load was applied. Initial yields during the first few months of production were in the 17–20% range. (Yield is defined as the percentage of parts produced that passed post-production tests and were actually shipped to Deere.) Because of the low yields, Deere was forced to ship tractors to customers with a temporary part that would have to be replaced later.

Both Deere and Revere worked to solve the problems encountered in manufacturing the Gozinta. After testing and analysis, it was determined that problems with the product were related to the physical dimensions of the Deere metal strap. Deere, however, believed that some of the problems were due to the poor quality of the knurls on the Gozinta that Revere was receiving from its vendor. Deere later learned that Revere had changed suppliers for the knurl, but had not informed Deere.

While Revere and Deere were working to solve the problems associated with the Gozinta/Deere project, Revere was experiencing significant downsizing in its personnel following its purchase in 1988 by Dobson-Park, an English corporation. Several Revere employees who worked on the Gozinta/Deere project either left or were laid off.

Eckart and Delfino were concerned about their positions at Revere. Eckart was informed by his supervisor that Revere's Connecticut plant would be closed in July 1989 and that he should start looking for another job. Delfino was initially assured by his supervisor that his job was secure and that he had nothing to worry about. That particular supervisor was laid off two weeks later. In early 1989, Delfino and Eckart told David Ramsey of Deere that they were scheduled to be let go from Revere.

C. Deere's search for another sensor supplier.

Although yields of the Gozinta had improved to 95% in the summer of 1989, the Revere Gozinta never completely met Deere's engineering qualification tests. Deere was also concerned about whether Revere would be a long-term viable supplier. Based on these concerns, in addition to the turnover in Revere personnel, Deere, unknown to Revere, started looking for an alternative part for the Gozinta.

To address some of the problems associated with the project, Deere and Revere held a meeting in Waterloo in February 1989. Eckart was not present at the meeting. During the meeting, Ramsey, a Deere engineer, suggested that perhaps the sensor could be welded rather than pressed into place. According to Deere employees, John Elengo, Revere's vice president of engineering, said that he did not think that welding the device would work because it would put too much stress on the sensor and cause it to fail.

In early 1989, Eckart, Revere's product manager for the Gozinta project, was having frequent conversations with Carl Kunath concerning product shipments of the Gozinta and problems associated with it. Kunath was employed by Deere as a buyer/purchasing agent of electronic and mechanical parts for Deere tractors and was Deere's primary contact with Revere on the Gozinta project. During a conversation in early March 1989, the subject of personnel changes at Revere came up. At some point during the conversation, Eckart told Kunath that he intended to leave Revere and develop a consulting engineering business and that he had ideas for installing Gozintas into new products, some of which may be applicable to Deere. Kunath testified he told Eckart that, if he had any ideas, to send Deere a proposal. Kunath testified that he did not invite or solicit Eckart to submit a proposal, but that Eckart mentioned he had an idea and wanted to know if Deere was interested. Kunath told Eckart that he would have to submit the proposal to Deere's engineering department because he was not in the position to receive proposals on engineering ideas or concepts.

After this conversation, Eckart approached Delfino, a lead Revere manufacturing engineer working on the Gozinta/Deere project, and inquired if he would be interested in developing a new draft sensor for Deere that would be welded, rather than pressed, into a hole. Delfino and Eckart agreed to meet one day after work to discuss their ideas. Delfino and Eckart eventually met with a lawyer at Delfino's suggestion. The record contains a letter from an attorney dated March 10, 1989, addressed to Delfino and Eckart regarding their potential liability concerning the manufacture of a welded-in disc sensor. The letter stated that if Delfino and Eckart decided to develop the welded-in sensor, it was extremely important for them not to take any documents, models, or engineering drawings from Revere. The letter also indicated that Delfino and Eckart's contractual obligation regarding disclosure of inventions and discoveries presented the most risk and that the possibility of liability hinged on the definition of inventions and discoveries, but that what Delfino and Eckart were considering was not an invention or discovery in the narrower sense.

Sometime thereafter, but before March 12, Delfino and Eckart formed a company called D E Sensor Manufacturing, Inc.

On March 12, 1989, Delfino and Eckart, through their company D E Sensor, wrote to Kunath at Deere. The letter contains a quotation of estimated cost for "the development and manufacturing of a functional equivalent to sensor assembly part number RE30962 rev H," a replacement part for the Gozinta. The letter also discusses payment schedules for development of the sensor. Attached to the letter were a number of drawings for a new strap assembly and draft sensor components.

Sometime thereafter, Delfino, Eckart and Kunath of Deere met in a hotel in Connecticut to discuss D E's proposal for a welded-in sensor. Neither Delfino nor Eckart informed Revere of the meeting.

On April 11, 1989, Kunath of Deere wrote to Eckart confirming its intention to provide a purchase order in the amount of $172,900 for design and development work by D E of a welded-in sensor, known as a "weldzinta," to replace the Gozinta.

On April 19, Delfino notified Revere that he was terminating his employment effective May 5. On April 26, Eckart notified Revere that he was terminating his employment effective April 28.

Subsequently, in July 1990, Kunath wrote to Revere stating that Deere was canceling its contract for purchasing Gozintas. The letter also stated that "we [Deere] have developed a new product that replaces RE30962 [the Gozinta]," that will begin production at Deere's facility on October 29, 1990.

D. The Connecticut and present litigation.

Revere eventually discovered that Delfino and Eckart were making a sensor similar to the Gozinta and sued Delfino and Eckart in federal district court in Connecticut in December 1992 for patent and trademark infringement and breach of contract. A noncompete injunction was entered against D E on February 4, 1993.

Revere later filed a petition in the present action against defendant Deere in Iowa district court on August 24, 1993, seeking damages for tortious interference with contractual relations, misappropriation of trade secrets, and civil conspiracy.

On November 30, 1993, Revere dismissed its claims against Delfino and Eckart in the Connecticut federal court action pursuant to a settlement agreement. In return for settlement of all pending disputes against them, and subject to any rights which Revere might have against Deere, Delfino and Eckart executed a promissory note in the amount of $60,000 in favor of Revere. Upon consent of the parties, the district court entered a permanent injunction which permanently enjoined Delfino and Eckart, acting through D E, from manufacturing certain types of sensors.

Revere's claims against Deere in the present action were tried to a jury. The jury returned verdicts on January 14, 1997 for compensatory damages in plaintiff Revere's favor concerning the tortious interference with a contract and the civil conspiracy claims, and awarded $350,000 and $200,000 in damages on those respective claims. The jury found in defendant Deere's favor regarding Revere's claim for misappropriation of trade secrets. The jury also awarded Revere punitive damages in the amount of $450,000, but also found that Deere's acts were not directed against Revere.

Judgment was promptly entered on the verdicts.

The district court later overruled Deere's motions for judgment notwithstanding the verdict and for new trial and Revere's motion for a new trial.

Deere appealed and Revere cross appealed concerning the verdicts and rulings that were adverse to them.

Other facts will be stated as we discuss the assignments of error raised by the parties.

II. Enforceability of employment agreement.

We first address Deere's contention that the district court erred in overruling Deere's motion for judgment notwithstanding the verdict concerning Deere's position that Revere's employment agreements with Delfino and Eckart were not enforceable and thus cannot be the basis for Revere's claim for tortious interference with a contract.

****

A. Language of the agreement.

At the time they were hired by Revere, Eckart and Delfino each signed an agreement concerning disclosure of confidential information and inventions and/or discoveries and assignment of such inventions and/or discoveries, hereinafter referred to as the Revere agreement or agreement. The Revere agreement included the following provisions:

> (1) *During the period of my employment* I will disclose promptly and in writing to the head of the department or the division in which I am employed, or to such other person as the Company may designate, *all inventions or discoveries which I may make, whether alone or with others, and whether during normal business hours or otherwise, and I will not disclose such inventions or discoveries to others, except as required by my employer, without prior written consent of the Company.*

> (2) *For a period of one year following the termination of my employment* for any reason, I will not disclose as hereinbefore provided, all inventions and discoveries made by me which relate to: (1) methods, processes, or apparatus concerned with the production of any character of goods or materials used or sold by the Company, or (2) in respect to any character of goods or materials sold or used by the Company.

(3) I hereby assign all of my right, title, and interest in and to such inventions and discoveries to the Company, and agree that I will, when requested at any time during my employment or thereafter execute specific assignments of any such inventions or discoveries to the Company or its nominee . . . .

(5) I acknowledge that *technical information other than that generally published and available to the public* and other confidential information regarding the Company's business of which I may obtain knowledge in the course of and by virtue of my employment by the Company constitute valuable and confidential assets of the Company's business and that unauthorized disclosure thereof would be detrimental to the Company. I therefore agree that I *will not disclose to others at any time during my employment or thereafter any confidential information, knowledge or data* belonging to the Company, without first obtaining the Company's written consent thereto, except as such disclosure may be required by my service to the Company or by law. (Emphasis added.)

On appeal, Deere contends that the Revere agreement is not enforceable because the language is overly broad and so open-ended as to include inventions and discoveries that are totally unrelated to Revere's business or its employees. Deere thus argues that because the Revere agreement is unenforceable, it cannot be the basis for a claim for tortious interference with a contract.

Before examining whether the Revere agreement is enforceable, we deem it helpful to clarify the applicable standards concerning the enforceability of employment agreements containing nondisclosure-confidentiality or assignment provisions.

We point out that the Revere agreement only addresses Delfino and Eckart's duties concerning disclosure or nondisclosure of confidential information and inventions and/or discoveries, and assignment of rights thereto, made by them during their employment with Revere; the agreement does not contain any noncompete provisions.

B. Applicable law.

At this point in the analysis, we are only concerned with whether the terms of Revere's agreement with Delfino and Eckart are reasonable. This inquiry is different from whether Delfino and Eckart breached the agreement, which will be discussed later.

We have apparently never addressed the enforceability of an employment agreement containing a nondisclosure-confidentiality provision. We have, however, established certain rules concerning how to determine the enforceability of a noncompete agreement. We believe that the rules concerning the enforceability of noncompete agreements, as restrictive covenants, may be helpful concerning the enforceability of Revere's agreement with Delfino and Eckart and we therefore briefly review those rules.

We have established the following three-pronged test to be applied in determining whether an employment contract containing a restrictive covenant is enforceable:

(1) Is the restriction reasonably necessary for the protection of the employer's business; (2) is it unreasonably restrictive of the employee's rights; and (3) is it prejudicial to the public interest?

Factors we consider in determining the enforceability of a noncompete agreement include the employee's close proximity to customers, the nature of the business, accessibility to information peculiar to the employer's business, and the nature of the occupation which is restrained.

Nondisclosure-confidentiality agreements enjoy more favorable treatment in the law than do noncompete agreements. This is because noncompete agreements are viewed as restraints of trade which limit an employee's freedom of movement among employment opportunities, while nondisclosure agreements seek to restrict disclosure of information, not employment opportunities. The distinction is based on the idea that "[o]nce a secret is disclosed, knowledge of the information cannot normally be confined to a particular area." Thus, imposition of geographic or durational limitations "would defeat the entire purpose of restricting disclosure," since confidentiality knows no temporal or geographical boundaries. Thus, nondisclosure agreements lacking in geographic or time limitations have been held to be enforceable.

Some states, however, either because of statutory law or public policy, require some form of geographic or time limitations in order for a nondisclosure agreement to be enforceable. Additionally, some states consider nondisclosure-confidentiality agreements to be a restraint of trade and such agreements are therefore regulated by state statutes governing contracts in restraint of trade.

Employment agreements requiring an employee to assign to the employer rights to inventions designed or conceived during the period of employment have been upheld. We have said that

In the absence of special agreement to the contrary, an invention and a patent secured for it belong to the inventor, even though the invention was made during the period of his employment, and the invention relates to the matter in which the inventor was employed.

C. Application of law to facts.

Upon consideration of the principles discussed above, we conclude that the following test should be applied in determining whether a nondisclosure-confidential or invention assignment agreement is enforceable:

(1) Is the restriction prohibiting disclosure reasonably necessary for the protection of the employer's business;

(2) is the restriction unreasonably restrictive of the employee's rights; and

(3) is the restriction prejudicial to the public interest?

This test is obviously the same as that used to determine the enforceability of a noncompete agreement. We further conclude, however, that the absence of restrictions concerning time or geographic location do not render a nondisclosure-confidentiality agreement presumptively unenforceable. This is because the inquiry whether the nondisclosure agreement unreasonably restricts the employee's rights would address the breadth of the restrictions regarding disclosure. Having articulated the proper standard, our next task is to apply it.

The Revere agreement imposed basically three types of restrictions on Delfino and Eckart concerning disclosure of Revere proprietary information. First, the agreement required Delfino and Eckart to disclose to Revere any inventions and/or discoveries made by them during the course of their employment and also required them to assign their rights to any such inventions or discoveries to Revere. Second, the agreement precluded Delfino and Eckart from disclosing inventions and/or discoveries related to "methods, processes or apparatus concerned with the production of any character of goods or materials used or sold by the Company." Third, the agreement precluded Delfino and Eckart from disclosing "any confidential information, knowledge or data belonging to the Company."

Upon our review, we conclude that the restrictions in the agreement concerning disclosure of, and assignment of rights to, inventions and/or discoveries and confidential information, knowledge or data are reasonably necessary to protect Revere's business interests. We believe an employer has the right to preclude its employees from disclosing such information. The language in paragraph five of the agreement regarding "technical information other than that generally published and available to the public" contemplates that an employee is only precluded from disclosing information that would not generally be known by the public. We thus conclude that the restrictions concerning disclosure are sufficiently narrow in scope such that they do not interfere with Delfino and Eckart's ability to use skills and general knowledge they acquired through employment with Revere in future employment. We further conclude that the invention assignment provision is reasonable and enforceable. Nor do we find any evidence in the record showing that enforcement of the restrictions is prejudicial to the public interest. The question of what information would constitute an invention or discovery or may be classified as confidential information, knowledge or data is more related to the inquiry regarding whether Delfino and Eckart breached the agreement and will be discussed later.

We thus conclude that Revere's agreement with Delfino and Eckart concerning disclosure of Revere's business information and assignment of inventions and discoveries is enforceable. The district court therefore properly overruled Deere's motion for judgment notwithstanding the verdict concerning this issue.

****

3. Evidence regarding breach.

In order to find in favor of Revere concerning its claim of tortious interference with business relations, the jury had to find that Delfino and Eckart violated their agreement with Revere concerning disclosure of Revere's proprietary information and assignment of rights to inventions.

Deere argued to the jury that the March 12 proposal did not contain confidential information or trade secrets belonging to Revere, but rather that the drawings were in fact based on prior art of a welded-in sensor. Deere also presented evidence that drawings of the Gozinta that Revere submitted to Deere did not contain proprietary stamps, which were required if the information was to be considered confidential between the parties. Deere thus contends that Revere cannot argue that information Delfino, and Eckart disclosed in the March 12 proposal was confidential when in fact Revere disclosed essentially the same information to Deere.

Upon our review, we conclude that substantial evidence supports the jury's verdict that Delfino and Eckart breached their agreement with Revere either based on the conclusion that they made a discovery or invention which they failed to disclose or assign to Revere, or wrongfully disclosed confidential information, knowledge or data.

First, the agreement required Delfino and Eckart to disclose or assign any inventions and/or discoveries to Revere made during the course of their employment and likewise precluded them from disclosing confidential information, knowledge or data belonging to Revere. Trade secrets would clearly fall within the definition of confidential information. Revere thus did not have to prove that the confidential information disclosed amounted to a *trade secret*, but rather only had to convince the jury that information depicted in the March 12 proposal amounted to a discovery or invention or that the proposal contained confidential information, knowledge or data belonging to Revere. This fact is consistent with the jury's finding that Deere tortiously interfered with Revere's agreement with Delfino and Eckart, but did not misappropriate Revere's trade secrets.

Second, Revere presented evidence from which the jury could conclude that Delfino and Eckart's March 12 proposal to Deere contained confidential information, knowledge or data, belonging to Revere that was not generally published or made available to the public, including to Deere. By comparing the drawings depicted in D E's March 12 proposal to Deere with Revere's original drawings of the Gozinta, Elengo of Revere testified that in his opinion the diameter of the holes depicted in the March 12 proposal were identical to those depicted in the drawings of Revere's Gozinta. Elengo also testified that the diameter of holes depicted in a document entitled Draft Sensor Development Program, D E Sensor Manufacturing, were Revere trade secrets, that this information was not publicly available and that this information was not disclosed in the Gozinta patent. Additionally, Elengo testified that Delfino and Eckart had access to Revere's drawings of the Gozinta during the course of their employment with Revere and further testified that the device described in the March 12 proposal could not have been designed in four or five days without using Revere's trade secrets.

A proprietary stamp appears on Revere's drawings of the Gozinta stating, "[t]his drawing contains proprietary information which shall not be reproduced or transferred to other drawings or disclosed to others or used for manufacturing or any other purpose without written permission of Revere Corporation of America." Delfino and Eckart were thus put on notice that Revere considered any information that appeared in the Gozinta drawings to be confidential. Delfino and Eckart likewise affixed a proprietary stamp with language similar to Revere's stamp on the drawings they submitted with the March 12 proposal, which the jury could find incorporated Revere confidential proprietary information.

Deere presented evidence through its witness, Walt Jacobson, the inventor of the Gozinta, that size and placement of the strain gauges, and all the other features of the product are allegedly common knowledge. Jacobson also testified that what he invented, or the strong part of the invention, was the knurl feature of the device. Deere also presented evidence that the idea of welding a sensor had been the subject of prior patents.

Despite this testimony, and even if true, the jury could still conclude that the Gozinta drawings as a whole, on which D E's March 12 proposal was based, represented the substantial time and money expended by Revere in how it thought the sensor should be designed and manufactured. It was this specific information that Delfino and Eckart acquired by virtue of their employment with Revere and it was this information which they were precluded from disclosing under their agreement to the detriment of Revere.

Additionally, we find no merit in Deere's contentions that the device D E actually sold to Deere was different from that outlined in the original proposal. The critical facts are that Delfino and Eckart, while still employed by Revere, began working on a device, prepared drawings and designs that incorporated Revere's confidential information, and disclosed this information to a third party. From this evidence the jury could reasonably find that D E's March 12 proposal for a sensor was substantially similar to Revere's Gozinta or at least used Revere's designs of the Gozinta as a starting point for D E's sensor. At the very least, the jury could find that Delfino and Eckart used the technology Revere had developed with respect to the Gozinta, including the problems associated with the knurl strap interface, to develop a welded-in sensor to Revere's detriment. In effect, Delfino and Eckart took Revere's proprietary information concerning what would not work and used it as a basis to develop a device that would directly compete with Revere.

We also reject Deere's contention that the terms of Revere's agreement with Deere concerning what those parties defined as proprietary information, and how that information was disclosed, somehow dictates what information is considered to be confidential under Revere's agreement with Delfino and Eckart. Each agreement establishes its own restrictions and responsibilities upon the parties governed thereunder and the terms of one are not applicable to the other.

The record also shows that Delfino and Eckart consulted with a patent attorney concerning whether the welded-in disc sensor was a patentable device and that the attorney opined that the device was patentable. We believe that the jury could conclude from this and other evidence presented that Delfino and Eckart's work on developing the replacement for the Gozinta, following their employment with Revere, amounted to an invention or discovery which Delfino and Eckart were required to disclose to Revere and which they wrongfully disclosed to Deere.

Upon our review of the record, we conclude that the jury's finding that Delfino and Eckart breached their agreement with Revere is supported by substantial evidence.

AFFIRMED IN PART, REVERSED IN PART, AND REMANDED.

QUESTIONS

1. Eckart and Delfino were about to be terminated by Revere when they approached Deere with the idea for the Weldzinta as a replacement for the Gonzita. The court didn't consider this fact in discussing the rights of Eckart and Delfino *vis-a-vis* Revere. Why not?

2. The nondisclosure agreement covered technical information learned at Revere that was not published. Would such technical information necessarily constitute trade secrets? Must technical information be published in order to be generally known by the public? How would Eckart's and Delfino's acknowledgement that the technical information constituted valuable and confidential assets of Revere affect the trade secret status of the information?

3. The court states that nondisclosure-confidentiality agreements enjoy more favorable treatment than noncompete agreements because they do not restrict an employee's freedom of movement among employment opportunities. The nondisclosure-confidentiality agreement at issue contained no geographic or time limitations. Could Eckert or Delfino ever obtain future employment in their technical field of expertise anywhere in the world without disclosing or using information learned at Revere? Might this be the reason why some states require geographical or durational limitations for nondisclosure agreements to be enforceable?

4. Deere argued that the drawings Eckert and Delfino presented on March 12 were based on prior art and, therefore, could not constitute confidential information belonging to Revere. The court's response to this argument was that the drawings did not have to amount to trade secrets in order to be covered by the nondisclosure-confidentiality agreement and that it would be sufficient if the drawings amounted to a discovery or invention, or contained confidential information belonging to Revere. If the information contained in the drawings was, in fact, based on prior art, could the drawings constitute a discovery or invention, or confidential information belonging to Revere? Along the same lines, if the information was based on prior art, would this information be necessary to protect Revere's business interests?

5. Non-disclosure agreements very often exclude information that is already in the possession of the party to whom the disclosure is made (disclosee). These exclusion clauses create an opportunity for an unethical disclosee to claim that it already possessed the disclosed information at the time of disclosure when, in fact, the disclosee "recreated" the disclosed information sometime after the disclosure. If you were counsel to a company about to disclose confidential information to another company, how would you protect your client against a claim made by the disclosee company, well after the date of disclosure, that it already possessed the disclosed information at the time of disclosure?

CELERITAS TECHNOLOGIES v. ROCKWELL INTERNATIONAL
150 F.3d 1354 (Fed. Cir. 1998)

LOURIE, CIRCUIT JUDGE.

Rockwell International Corporation appeals from the decision of the United States District Court for the Central District of California denying Rockwell's motions for judgment as a matter of law and for a new trial following a jury verdict that Rockwell willfully infringed Celeritas Technologies, Ltd.'s patent, misappropriated its trade secrets, and breached a non-disclosure agreement relating to the protected subject matter. Because substantial evidence supports the jury's verdict on the contract claim, we affirm the court's ruling with regard to both liability and damages on that claim. Because the claims of the patent have been shown to be anticipated as a matter of law, we reverse the denial of Rockwell's motion for JMOL regarding patent validity and direct entry of judgment for Rockwell on the patent claim.

Celeritas cross-appeals from the judgment, arguing that the district court should have added exemplary damages for misappropriation to the contract damages award. Because the district court did not err in determining that a stipulation precluded a recovery on more than one claim, we affirm the entry of judgment solely on the contract claim.

BACKGROUND

On July 28, 1993, Michael Dolan filed a patent application for an apparatus for increasing the rate of data transmission over analog cellular telephone networks. The resulting patent, U.S. Patent 5,386,590, assigned to Celeritas, issued on January 31, 1995 with two claims. As described in the patent, a conventional analog cellular communications system suffers from noise that the listener hears as a high frequency hiss. Analog cellular networks combat this noise by boosting the high frequency components of the transmitted signal (typically a speaker's voice) and then decreasing these components at the receiving end. From the listener's perspective, this pre-emphasis at the transmit end and de-emphasis at the receiving end has minimal effect on the sound of a speaker's voice. The de-emphasis on the receiving end, however, reduces the high frequency hiss and therefore increases the fidelity of the cellular communications channel.

A limiter circuit then "clips" the top of signals having high amplitudes so that the transmitted signal stays within an established range. The combined effect of the pre-emphasis and limiter circuits is substantially imperceptible in voice communication; however, it significantly impairs the transmission of data across the network.

The claimed invention overcomes the problem of distortion induced by the pre-emphasis and limiter circuits found in conventional analog cellular communications systems. The patent claims an apparatus that counteracts the adverse effects of the pre-emphasis and limiter circuits by de-emphasizing the data signal before presenting it to the cellular network. Claim 2, which is representative, reads as follows:

> An apparatus for increasing the data output rate from a transmit modem in a duplex analog radio communication system having a single-carrier data signal, comprising:
>
> a radio transmitter which receives said single-carrier data signal, said radio transmitter including a pre-emphasizer that increases the amplitudes of components of said single-carrier data signal in the range of 1,000 Hz to 3,000 Hz, said radio transmitter further including a limiter that limits the amplitudes of said single-carrier data signal;
>
> a transmit modem which provides said single-carrier data signal as an input signal to said radio transmitter, said transmit modem encoding digital data onto said input signal as a plurality of modulation signal components, said transmit modem *including a spectral shaper* which selectively reduces amplitudes of said modulation signal components at higher frequencies to cause said input signal from said modem to said radio transmitter to have lower amplitudes at higher frequencies than at lower frequencies to reduce the effect of said limiter on said input signal.

The spectral shaper recited in the claim performs the de-emphasis function.

In September 1993, Dolan and other officials of Celeritas met with representatives from Rockwell to demonstrate their proprietary de-emphasis technology. Rockwell is the leading manufacturer of modem "chip sets" which contain the core functions of commercial modems, including the modulation function where de-emphasis is performed. The parties entered into a non-disclosure agreement (NDA), which covered the subject matter of the meeting and provided in pertinent part that Rockwell "shall not disclose or use any Proprietary Information (or any derivative thereof) except for the purpose of evaluating the prospective business arrangements between Celeritas and Rockwell."

The agreement provided that proprietary information "shall not include information which . . . was in the public domain on the date hereof or comes into the public domain other than through the fault or negligence of [Rockwell]." Furthermore, the agreement contained the following paragraph:

> *Injunctive Relief.* Celeritas and Rockwell acknowledge that the extent of damages in the event of the breach of any provision of this Agreement would be difficult or impossible to ascertain, and that there will be available no adequate remedy at law in the event of any such breach. Each party therefore agrees that in the event it breaches any provision of this Agreement, the other party will be entitled to injunctive or other equitable relief, in addition to any other relief to which it may be entitled. The parties hereby waive any requirement for the posting of a bond or other security in connection with the granting of injunctive relief.

In March 1994, AT&T Paradyne began to sell a modem that incorporated de-emphasis technology. In that same month, Rockwell informed Celeritas that it would not license the use of Celeritas's proprietary technology, and concurrently began a development project to incorporate de-emphasis technology into its modem chip sets. Significantly, Rockwell did not independently develop its own de-emphasis technology, but instead assigned the same engineers who had learned of Celeritas's technology under the NDA to work on the de-emphasis development project. In January 1995, Rockwell began shipping its first prototype chip sets that contained de-emphasis technology. By the time of trial in 1997, Rockwell's sales were surpassing its projections.

On September 22, 1995, Celeritas sued Rockwell, alleging breach of contract, misappropriation of trade secrets, and patent infringement. In order to simplify the trial and avoid a duplicative recovery, Celeritas stipulated that it would accept the highest award under the three independent theories. The jury returned a verdict for Celeritas on each of the three theories, awarding Celeritas $57,658,000 each on the patent infringement and breach of contract claims, and $26,850,000 each in compensatory and exemplary damages on the trade secret misappropriation claim. The contract and patent infringement damages were based on a hypothetical lump-sum paid-up license for the use of the proprietary technology in Rockwell's products. The misappropriation damages were based on a finding that Celeritas's proprietary technology gave Rockwell a twenty-one month "head start" in its product development. After Rockwell moved for JMOL on liability and for a new trial on damages, the court concluded that the patent infringement award errone-ously included a royalty on post-judgment sales; the parties then agreed to a remittitur that reduced the award to $17,484,160, which was doubled to $34,968,320 in light of a finding of willful infringement. That award reflected multiplying a royalty rate by Rockwell's own 1994 projections of estimated sales through the last day of trial.

The court then entered judgment awarding Celeritas $57,658,000 for breach of contract, $85,820.05 in costs, and $900,000 in attorney fees under 35 U.S.C. § 285 (1994) (court may award prevailing party attorney fees in an exceptional patent case). The court denied Rockwell's remaining motions. Rockwell now appeals and Celeritas cross-appeals to this court. We have jurisdiction under 28 U.S.C. § 1295(a)(1) (1994).

DISCUSSION

On appeal from a judgment denying a motion for JMOL, we reapply the standards used by the district court in ruling on the motion. Following a jury trial, an appellant "must show that the jury's findings, presumed or express, are not supported by substantial evidence or, if they were, that the legal conclusion(s) implied from the jury's verdict cannot in law be supported by those findings."

A. Breach of the NDA

Rockwell first argues that the district court erred by denying its motion for JMOL on the breach of contract claim. Citing the prior art submitted to the United States Patent and Trademark Office (PTO) by Celeritas, Rockwell argues that the evidence at trial clearly demonstrates that the de-emphasis technology disclosed to Rockwell was already in the public domain. Even if the technology were proprietary at the time of disclosure, Rockwell argues, the technology had entered the public domain before Rockwell used it, concededly no later than March 1994. Specifically, Rockwell asserts that AT&T Paradyne had already placed the technology in the public domain through the sale of a modem incorporating de-emphasis technology ("the modem"). Rockwell asserts that the technology was "readily ascertainable" because any competent engineer could have reverse engineered the modem. Rockwell further argues that any confidentiality obligation under the NDA regarding de-emphasis technology was extinguished once the '590 patent issued in January 1995.

Celeritas responds that substantial evidence supports the jury's verdict that Rockwell used its proprietary information. Celeritas argues that in order for a trade secret to enter the public domain in California, it must actually have been ascertained by proper means, and not merely have been ascertainable. Celeritas maintains that, in any event, the only evidence at trial supports the jury's implicit finding that the information was not readily ascertainable from inspection of the modem. Celeritas also argues that the issuance of its patent in 1995 is immaterial because Rockwell had already breached the agreement by using its proprietary information in 1994.

We agree with Celeritas that substantial evidence supports the jury's conclusion that Rockwell breached the NDA. The jury implicitly found that the information given to Rockwell by Celeritas was proprietary. Unrebutted testimony established that Celeritas disclosed to Rockwell implementation details and techniques that went beyond the information disclosed in the patent. Thus, even if every detail disclosed in the patent were in the prior art, a fact never alleged by Rockwell, that fact would not undermine the jury's conclusion that Celeritas revealed proprietary information to Rockwell which it then used in developing its modem chip sets. Accordingly, Rockwell's reliance on the prosecution history of the '590 patent and the prior art submitted to the PTO is misplaced.

The jury also implicitly found that the technology had not been placed in the public domain by the sale of the modem. California law appears somewhat unsettled regarding whether a trade secret enters the public domain when it is "readily ascertainable" or whether it must also be "actually ascertained" by the public. Because the judgment is supportable under either standard, we need not attempt to resolve this issue of state law. Suffice it to say that substantial evidence supports a finding that the technology implementing the de-emphasis function in the modem was not "readily ascertainable." In fact, Dolan's testimony, the only evidence cited by Rockwell, belies its contentions. In the very passage cited by Rockwell, Dolan stated that (1) a spectrum analyzer would be needed to discover the de-emphasis technology, (2) most engineers that he talked to did not have spectrum analyzers, and (3) only if an engineer had a spectrum analyzer and knew what to look for could the engineer discover that the modem had de-emphasis technology. His express caveat that the use of de-emphasis could have been discovered if it was being affirmatively pursued is not an admission that the technology would be "readily ascertainable." Because substantial evidence supports the conclusion that the information disclosed to Rockwell had not entered the public domain before its unauthorized use by Rockwell, the court did not err in denying Rockwell's motion for JMOL regarding its breach of the NDA.

C. Patent Validity

The district court awarded Celeritas attorney fees under 35 U.S.C. § 285 as the prevailing party in an exceptional patent case. Rockwell argues that the infringement verdict, which is the basis for the award, cannot stand and that the district court erred by not granting its motion for JMOL on the issue of patent invalidity. Rockwell asserts that the claims of the patent are invalid as anticipated by either of two references.

One prior art reference cited by Rockwell was an article published in 1991 by the Telebit Corporation entitled, "The Static Characteristics of Analog Cellular Radio Channels and Their Effects Upon Data Transmission." Rockwell argues that the Telebit article discloses each limitation of the '590 patent claims. Celeritas responds that Rockwell has a heavy burden in sustaining that position because the Telebit article was disclosed to the PTO during prosecution of the '590 patent and the patent obviously was granted despite the existence of that reference. Celeritas further argues that substantial evidence supports the jury's implicit finding that the Telebit article fails to disclose a single carrier modem that incorporates de-emphasis (*i.e.*, the "spectral shaper" of claim 2 of the patent).

In the PTO and to the jury, Celeritas emphasized that the article taught away from the claimed invention, teaching the solution of amplitude reduction, and expressly stating that de-emphasis would not work well in a single-carrier system.

We agree with Rockwell that no reasonable jury could have determined that the Telebit article did not anticipate the claims of the patent. It is well settled that a claim is anticipated if each and every limitation is found either expressly or inherently in a single prior art reference. A reference is no less anticipatory if, after disclosing the invention, the reference then disparages it. Thus, the question whether a reference "teaches away" from the invention is inapplicable to an anticipation analysis.

As a factual matter, the Telebit article itself and the testimony offered at trial conclusively demonstrate that the article discloses the use of a single-carrier data signal, not only multi-carrier signals. As Celeritas's own witnesses testified, the Telebit article describes a test signal that sends twenty-one tones to simulate a modulated signal. The article states that the test signal, composed of twenty-one tones, has "a probability distribution of magnitude that closely matches that of a V.29 modem." Dolan, the inventor of the '590 patent, testified that the V.29 signal is a single-carrier data signal. Thus, contrary to Dolan's statement to the PTO that the Telebit article only discloses the use of a "large number of simultaneous carriers," the article actually does disclose a simulated single-carrier data signal.

Because it is beyond dispute that the Telebit article discloses each of the claimed limitations, the claims are anticipated and hence invalid. Accordingly, the district court erred by not granting Rockwell's motion for JMOL that the patent is invalid.

D. Misappropriation of Trade Secrets

Because we affirm the determination of liability under the contract claim, we also need not consider Rockwell's arguments regarding the jury's verdict for misappropriation of trade secrets. This portion of the verdict was not incorporated into the district court's judgment because Celeritas stipulated that it would accept the liability theory with the highest damage award. However, we need to consider the issue of Celeritas's cross-appeal.

CONCLUSION

The jury's verdict awarding Celeritas damages for breach of contract was supported by substantial evidence and the theory under which damages were awarded was not legally unsound. Thus, the district court did not err in denying Rockwell's motion for JMOL on liability and for a new trial on damages. Pursuant to Celeritas's stipulation, the district court properly awarded Celeritas damages only on its breach of contract claim. The district court erred, however, by not granting a JMOL that the claims of the '590 patent are anticipated by the Telebit article. The patent is invalid. Accordingly, the district court's award of attorney fees under 35 U.S.C. § 285 is reversed.

QUESTIONS

1. The court finds that the Telebit article published in 1991 disclosed each of the claim limitations in Celeritas' '590 patent on its de-emphasis technology. Celeritas first disclosed its de-emphasis technology to Rockwell in September 1993. Why did the Telebit article not put the de-emphasis technology in the public domain prior to Celeritas' disclosure to Rockwell?

2. Why did AT&T's sale of a modem that incorporated the de-emphasis technology in March 1994 not put the de-emphasis technology in the public domain? If the court had found that AT&T's sale of a modem incorporating the de-emphasis technology had put the de-emphasis technology in the public domain, how would this have affected the calculation of damages for breach of the non-disclosure agreement?

3. What is the difference between "readily ascertainable" and "actually ascertained" in determining whether a technology has entered the public domain? Which test did the court use to determine whether the de-emphasis technology had entered the public domain? Why did the court find that the de-emphasis technology had not entered the public domain under the test it used?

4. Which test does the Restatement of Torts trade secret definition adopt?

CASE NOTES

1. In early 1995, PKM's CEO, Peter Clancy, conceived of an idea for a new beverage label manufacturing and marketing process he called "Magic Windows." Magic Windows used a scrambled message on the inside of a beverage container label that could be decoded and read after the beverage container was emptied through the use of a color filter printed on a label on the opposite side of the container, directly across from the coded message. In November 1995, Clancy met with representatives of Coca-Cola to demonstrate Magic Windows. Clancy orally

informed Coca-Cola that the information regarding Magic Windows was confidential and Coca-Cola agreed to treat the information as confidential. Clancy also informed Coca-Cola that he was pursuing global patent protection for Magic Windows and would grant Coca-Cola an exclusive right to the patents. After continued discussions, in February 1996, the parties executed a written mutual Non-Disclosure Agreement in which both parties agreed not to disclose information exchanged during their discussions with third parties. Under the terms of the Non-Disclosure Agreement, confidential information did not include information that:

(i)   at the time of disclosure is available to the public;

(ii)   after disclosure, becomes available to the public by publication or otherwise;

(iii)   is in Coca-Cola's or its subsidiaries possession at the time of disclosure;

(iv)   is rightfully received from a third party; or

(v)   Coca-Cola can establish was subsequently developed by Coca-Cola or its subsidiaries independently of any disclosure [by PKM].

After additional months of discussion, in July 1996, Coca-Cola drafted a Development and License Agreement under which Coca-Cola would pay PKM a $1 million license fee and a per label royalty in exchange for an exclusive license to the Magic Windows patent. At the same time that Coca-Cola sent the proposed license agreement to PKM, it also undertook a patent search to determine if PKM could obtain a patent and be able to grant Coca-Cola exclusive patent rights. In the course of the patent search, Coca-Cola discovered a patent application published in May 1993 that it believed was prior art which anticipated PKM's Magic Windows patent application. Coca-Cola also concluded that the published patent application put PKM's Magic Windows concept in the public domain. Coca-Cola sent a copy of the published application to Clancy in October 1996 and informed Clancy in writing in November 1996 that Coca-Cola would not pursue an exclusive license with PKM and was terminating all negotiations with PKM.

In November 1995, Coca-Cola met with another company, BrightHouse, to discuss whether Magic Windows would work. BrightHouse believed it would and produced a graphic illustration and a bottle mock-up to demonstrate the concept. In September 1996, Coca-Cola met with ITW, an Argentinean company that produced labels for Coca-Cola's products in Argentina. Coca-Cola described the general idea of Magic Windows to ITW and asked whether ITW was capable of producing such labels. ITW said it could easily do so and in approximately three weeks ITW completed a bottle labeling process that produced labels substantially similar to Magic Windows. Coca-Cola then proceeded to use the ITW labels in an Argentinean marketing campaign.

When PKM learned of the Argentina marketing campaign, PKM filed a complaint against Coca-Cola alleging that Coca-Cola had misappropriated PKM's Magic Windows trade secrets, and breached the Non-Disclosure Agreement, when it disclosed information to ITW. Coca-Cola claimed that the information revealed by PKM regarding Magic Windows was not a trade secret and that it had not disclosed any PKM information to ITW or any other third party. What result? *See* Penalty Kick Management, Ltd. v. Coca Cola Co., 318 F.3d 1284 (11th Cir. 2003).

2. *See also* Kara Technology, Inc. v Stamps.Com, Inc., 582 F.3d 1341 (Fed. Cir. 2009) (Summary judgment not appropriate in patent owner's suit against competitor alleging breach of parties' non-disclosure agreement because genuine issues of material fact existed as to whether competitor misused confidential information of patent owner); Zahodnick v. International Business Machines Corp., 135 F.3d 911 (4th Cir. 1997) (Where former employee had agreed not to disclose confidential information and to return all employer property when employment was terminated, employer was entitled to an injunction prohibiting former employee from disclosing employer's confidential information, and requiring former employee to return all of employer's materials); IDX Sys. Corp. v. Epic Sys. Corp., 285 F.3d 581 (7th Cir. 2002) (Under Wisconsin law, confidentiality agreement between business management software provider and customer was not invalid because of its lack of time and place restrictions, or the fact that it was not restricted to trade secrets); Vermont Microsystems Inc. v. Autodesk Inc., 88 F.3d 142 (2nd Cir. 1996) (Computer software firm took reasonable steps to guard its trade secrets, as required to enforce its rights under invention and nondisclosure agreement it entered into with programmer who went to work for competitor; firm had employees sign nondisclosure agreements, management periodically issued reminders about the need to keep developments confidential, and when firm provided proprietary information to outsiders, appropriate confidentiality assurances were sought and obtained; and firm also maintained secure workplace); Modern Controls, Inc. v. Andreadakis, 578 F.2d 1264 (8th Cir. 1978) (In suit where corporate employer sought preliminary and permanent injunctive relief for the breach of an employee confidentiality agreement executed by a former employee, district court erred in denying former employer motion for a preliminary injunction where facts created likelihood that former employer would succeed on the merits and that former employer would suffer irreparable harm if former employee were permitted to continue working for a competitor).

Additional Information

1. ALLAN J. STERNSTEIN, ET. AL., CORPORATE COMPLIANCE SERIES: DESIGNING AN EFFECTIVE INTELLECTUAL PROPERTY COMPLIANCE PROGRAM § 3:5 (2009).

2. 3 TERRANCE F. MACLAREN, TRADE SECRETS THROUGHOUT THE WORLD § 38:42; § 38:49 (2009).

3. DONALD J. ASPELUND & STEPHEN L. LUNDWALL, EMPLOYEE NONCOMPETITION LAW § 3:12 (2009).

4. GARY M. LAWRENCE & CARL BARANOWSKI, REPRESENTING HIGH TECH COMPANIES § 3:03 (2010).

5. John Zaccaria, *Practice Tips in Negotiating Nondisclosure Agreements*, 33 WESTCHESTER B.J. 44 (2006).

6. Bob Feldman, *The Scope and Scrutiny of NDAS*, 24 No. 4 ACC DOCKET 20 (Apr. 2006).

7.   Eileen Barish, Brent Caslin, *Before Signing Your Next Nondisclosure Agreement, Count to 10*, 24 No. 1 ACC DOCKET 25 (Jan. 2006).

8.   James C. Bruno, David C. Hissong, *Enforcement of Non-Disclosure Agreements, Does MCLA 445.1901 and Related Case Law Apply in Other States?*, 81-JAN MICH. B.J. 58 (Jan. 2002).

9.   Jodi L. Short, *Killing the Messenger: The Use of Nondisclosure Agreements to Silence Whistleblowers*, 60 U. PITT. L. REV. 1207 (1999).

10.   Mark J. Chasteen, *In Search of a Smoking Gun: Tortious Interference with Nondisclosure Agreements as an Obstacle to Newsgathering*, 50 FED. COMM. L.J. 483 (1998).

11.   Robert B. Fitzpatrick, *Sample Non-Disclosure and Non-Compete Agreements*, SR010 ALI-ABA (2009).

12.   Trevor S. Norwitz, Erica M. Klien, *Blackberry Case Sends Long-Distance Message: Use Restrictions in NDAS Can Limit a Bidder's Freedom to Roam*, 13 No. 4 M & A LAW. 7 (2009).

13.   Rosanna Satttler, Joseph W. Corrigan, *Non-Competition, Non-Solicitation and Non-Disclosure Agreements, Varying Jurisdictional Approaches to the Law of Restrictive Covenants*, LAW JOURNAL NEWSLETTERS — EMPLOYMENT LAW STRATEGIST, Nov. 2007, Vol 15, No. 7, available at http://www.pbl.com/resources.php?ArticleID=35.

14.   Thomas C. Klien, *Non-Disclosure Agreements in Venture Capital Transactions*, ENCYCLOPEDIA OF PRIVATE EQUITY AND VENTURE CAPITAL, § 5.4.1 (2003).

15.   Eric Goldman, *Do Internet Companies Overuse Nondisclosure Agreements?*, 3 No. 9 E-COMMERCE L. REP. 10 (July 2001), *available at* http://www.ericgoldman.org/Articles/overusedndaarticle.htm. (ALM Properties, Inc., Law Journal Press 2005) (1999).

16.   Elizabeth A. Rowe, *When Trade Secrets Become Shackles: Fairness and the Inevitable Disclosure Doctrine*, 7 TUL. J. TECH. & INTELL. PROP. 167 (2005).

4.7   NON-COMPETITION AGREEMENTS

As you saw in the *Revere* case, noncompetition agreements are more strictly reviewed because of their direct impact upon the promisor's future employment opportunities. As you also saw in the *Revere* case, the tests for enforceability of noncompetition agreements and nondisclosure agreements are similar. The restrictive covenants must not be broader than is necessary to protect the former employer's legitimate business interests, must not impose an unreasonable burden upon the former employee, and must not harm the public interest. The tests for enforceability of noncompetition agreements and nondisclosure agreements, however, do differ with regard to geographic and time limitations. A noncompetition agreement must be reasonable in terms of its geographic territory and time duration as measured by the former employer's business needs. The determination of the former employer's business needs, and the threat posed to these needs by the former employee's new employment, are the subjects of numerous noncompetition cases. The *Verizon* and *EMSL* cases below address these issues in different contexts. In the *Verizon* case, the former employee is seeking to work for a competitor of the former employer. In the *EMSL* case, the former employee is seeking to work for a customer of the former employer.

VERIZON COMMUNICATIONS INC. v. PIZZIRANI
462 F. Supp.2d 648 (E.D. Pa. 2006)

Katz, Senior District Judge.

Plaintiffs Verizon Communications, Inc. and Verizon Services, Inc. (together "Verizon") seek enforcement of a twelve month non-competition restrictive covenant against their former employee, Defendant Christopher Pizzirani. On October 16, Defendant resigned from his position as Verizon's Vice President-Product Line Management for Broadband to accept a position with Comcast Cable Communications, Inc. ("Comcast"). In response, Verizon filed the instant Motion for Preliminary Injunction. For the reasons stated below, the court grants Plaintiffs' Motion.

I. FINDINGS OF FACT

A. Competition Between Verizon and Comcast

As a preliminary matter, the court notes that Verizon and Comcast are two of the nation's leading communication companies. Both Comcast and Verizon offer telephone service, internet access, cable television, and wireless communication. In addition to offering similar services, there is significant overlap in their service areas. Verizon's customers are primarily concentrated in New England, the Mid-Atlantic region, Florida, Texas, and California, and Comcast's customers are concentrated in New England, the Mid-Atlantic region, the Upper Midwest, Florida and California. Thus, Comcast and Verizon are direct competitors, and each other's most significant competitors in this region.

B. Defendant's Employment History With Verizon

Defendant Christopher Pizzirani began his employment with Verizon in 1990. During his sixteen years of employment, Defendant advanced steadily through the ranks to become one of Verizon's most senior executives. In 2003, Defendant was promoted to Executive Director-Broadband Solutions at Verizon. In this position, he had nationwide responsibility for Verizon's broadband products for residential and business customers. Among his other duties, Defendant was responsible for developing the business case for Verizon's new broadband products, recommending market strategies, pricing new and existing broadband products, developing customer premises equipment (such as modems) for Verizon's broadband services, negotiating prices with Verizon's equipment vendors, and distributing broadband equipment to Verizon's customers. He was also the executive responsible for the pricing and deployment strategy for Verizon's new fiber-optic FiOS broadband service, and overseeing the design and marketing of the Verizon One device, a device which combines telephone, modem, and wireless router functions.

Notably, both Comcast and Verizon are developing new broadband offerings and both seek to be "first to market" with these offerings. Verizon is in the process of deploying a fiber optic network, "FiOS," which supports broadband services, including internet access and cable television. Verizon considers FiOS crucial to its future success. Because FiOS is not yet fully deployed, and its deployment expands the areas of competition between Verizon and Comcast, Verizon's deployment plans are highly sensitive information.

On February 26, 2006, Verizon promoted Defendant to the position of Vice President-Product Line Management for Broadband. In that position, Defendant was among Verizon's most senior executives; his responsibilities and compensation put him in the top 0.2 percent of the company's workforce. At the time of Defendant's resignation from Verizon, he was receiving compensation and benefits worth approximately $597,000 per year.

C. Verizon's Non-Competition and Confidentiality Agreements

In 2003, Defendant became eligible to participate in Verizon's Long Term Incentive Program. Through this program, he was entitled to receive both Restricted Stock Units (RSUs) and Performance Stock Units (PSUs). RSUs and PSUs are units of deferred compensation that an employee may redeem after a vesting period.

In 2005, Verizon revised its Award Agreements to include a non-competition restrictive covenant. The non-competition covenant stated that for a period of twelve months after the termination of his employment, an employee may not "work for, own, manage, operate, control or participate in the ownership, management, operation, or control of, or provide consulting or advisory services to, any person, partnership, firm, corporation, institution or other entity engaged in Competitive Activities, or any company or person affiliated with such person or entity engaged in Competitive Activities."

"Competitive Activities" are defined as "business activities relating to products or services of the same type as the products or services (1) which are sold (or, pursuant to an existing business plan, will be sold) to paying customers of the Company or any Related Company, and (2) for which you have responsibility to plan, develop, manage, market, oversee or perform, or had any such responsibility within your most recent 24 months of employment with the Company or any Related Company."

The agreement further limits the definition of "Competitive Activities" to those activities carried out on behalf of products that were marketed in geographic areas that overlapped with those in which Verizon offered products and services. The Award Agreements also include a non-disclosure agreement; however, there is no dispute about the enforceability of that provision.

In 2005 and 2006, the restrictive covenants were attached as Exhibit A to Verizon's Long Term Incentive Award Agreements. Under the terms of the Award Agreements, in order to receive the benefits, a plan participant had to agree to abide by the relevant restrictive covenants.

In early March of both 2005 and 2006, Defendant received emails from Human Resources advising in bolded language:

> As you access your award online, it is important that you read and understand the terms and conditions of your Award Agreements. When accepting your award on-line, you acknowledge that you have read both the award agreements and Plan document, including the terms conditions regarding vesting, *restrictive covenants* and the provisions concerning award payouts.

Using his computer, on March 17, 2005, Defendant clicked on the "I ACKNOWL-EDGE" button at the bottom of this email, thus acknowledging that he understood that in accepting the award, he would become bound by the Award Agreements and its restrictive covenants. In 2006, Defendant did not click the "I ACKNOWLEDGE" button, prompting the Human Resources department to contact him regarding his failure to so. In response, Defendant drafted and sent an e-mail to John Arnold of Verizon's Human Resources stating, "John I will read and agree to the terms and conditions of the award agreement and Plan documents."

After certifying that he understood the importance of reading the Award Agreements, Defendant was able to access the Award Agreement online. Using an online electronic review and acceptance process Defendant expressly accepted these covenants on multiple occasions. Specifically, on March 24, 2005, Defendant accepted RSU and PSU awards in separate Agreements and confirmed that he had read the associated covenants and agreed to them. On March 30, 2006, Defendant accepted RSU and PSU awards in separate Agreements and confirmed that he had read the associated covenants and agreed to them. Finally, on April 28, 2006, Defendant accepted RSU and PSU awards in separate Agreements and confirmed that he had read the associated covenants and agreed to them.

Despite confirming on numerous occasions that he had read and understood the Award Agreements, Defendant asserts that he did not read the contracts prior to electronically signing them. In fact, he contends that he was completely unaware of the existence of the restrictive covenants until October 2006.

D. Defendant Seeks and Obtains Employment with Comcast

In April 2005, Defendant learned that Verizon intended to move its headquarters from Conshohoken, Pennsylvania to Basking Ridge, New Jersey and relocate executives from across the country to that location in April 2006. Defendant considered relocating his family to Basking Ridge, but decided against it for financial and family reasons, even though his decision not to relocate left him with a daily four hour commute (two hours in each direction) from his home.

In late November or December of 2005, Marci Dwyer an independent executive recruiter, contacted Defendant and informed him that Comcast was searching for a vice president in customer service. Defendant decided to pursue this opportunity, despite his lack of experience in this area. In December 2005, Defendant participated in two rounds of interviews for the position, including an interview with Mitch Bowling, Senior Vice President and General Manager for Comcast Online. Although he was not offered the position, Defendant did impress Comcast.

In approximately May 2006, Mr. Bowling decided to hire an executive to assist him with the day-to-day management of Comcast's high speed data services. Remembering Defendant from his earlier interviews, Mr. Bowling sought to interview Defendant for this position. Ms. Dwyer again contacted Defendant to inform him that Comcast had another position in which he might be interested. Defendant informed Ms. Dwyer he would only be interested if his compensation would be comparable to his compensation at Verizon.

In mid-July, Ms. Dwyer arranged a meeting between Defendant and Mr. Bowling. Comcast then decided to make an offer of employment to Defendant at a higher rate of compensation than normally offered for such a position, including a signing bonus of $150,000 to compensate Defendant for his unvested RSUs and PSUs. On August 17, 2006, Defendant received Comcast's offer to serve as "VP, Product Management-High Speed Data." Defendant accepted this offer of employment on August 22, 2006. Before Defendant resigned from Verizon, though, Ms. Dwyer asked Defendant whether he was positive he did not have a non-compete agreement. Ms. Dwyer had asked Defendant on numerous occasions prior to this occasion whether he had a non-compete agreement, and on each occasion he had told her did not.

This time, however, Defendant contacted Verizon's Human Resources Department to determine whether he had agreed to a non-competition covenant. In response to his inquiry, Human Resources sent him a sample Award Agreement from Verizon Wireless that did contain a non-competition agreement. Defendant then looked online to determine whether there was a similar document related to his Award Agreements. Defendant discovered that the Award Agreements that he signed for 2005 and 2006 did have non-competition covenants. As soon as he became aware that he had signed a non-competition agreement, he forwarded a copy of the Award Agreements to Ms. Dwyer, Mike Pascale, Comcast's Vice President of Human Resources, and Katherine Malgieri, a member of Mr. Pascale's staff.

Ms. Dwyer advised Defendant that Comcast's attorneys were reviewing the situation. While awaiting guidance from Comcast about his non-competition covenants and the effect they would have on his offer of employment, Defendant continued unabated in his position continuing to learn and develop Verizon's confidential and proprietary business information.

In response to the non-competition agreement, Comcast decided to modify its offer to Defendant. On October 5, 2006, Comcast offered Defendant a position as a Vice President in an executive training program, which it created specifically for Defendant, rather than in the broadband division of Comcast. The offer letter specified that Mr. Bowling would supervise Defendant in this training program. Defendant proposed line edits to the October 5 letter to confirm the calculation of his bonus. On October 13, 2006, Comcast sent a new offer letter that addressed Defendant's concerns regarding his bonus. The new letter provided that Mr.

Bowling would act not only as Defendant's supervisor but also as his "mentor" in the program and his "point of contact" for an "independent research project." On October 15, 2006, Defendant accepted this offer with Comcast, and the following day informed Verizon of his decision. Upon hearing Defendant's decision, Verizon asked Defendant to leave the building immediately.

On Tuesday, October 17, Verizon filed its Complaint in this case and Motion for a Temporary Restraining, Order, Expedited Discovery and Preliminary Injunction to enforce Defendant's non-competition agreement. The parties were able to reach a temporary agreement delaying Defendant's start date and prohibiting any communication with Verizon. Now before the court is Plaintiff's Motion for a Preliminary Injunction.

II. DISCUSSION

Defendant raises four primary challenges to Plaintiff's preliminary injunction. First, Defendant argues that the court should invalidate the non-competition covenants, because Verizon misrepresented the essential terms of the Award Agreement. Second, Defendant asserts that even if the Award Agreements are valid, the Agreements give an employee the power to revoke his acceptance at any time. Third, Defendant contends that Verizon cannot demonstrate irreparable harm. Finally, Defendant maintains that Verizon cannot demonstrate a likelihood of success on the merits because the scope of the non-competition agreement is unreasonable. For the reasons stated below the court disagrees and will grant Plaintiff's Motion for Preliminary Injunction.

Threshold Determinations

1. Choice of Law

As a preliminary matter, the court finds that New York law governs interpretation and enforcement of the Award Agreements. The Award Agreements state: "The validity, construction, interpretation and effect of the Agreement shall be governed by and construed in accordance with the laws of the State of New York, without giving effect to the conflicts of Laws provisions thereof." Pennsylvania courts give effect to choice of law provisions when the state selected enjoys a substantial relationship to the parties or the transaction and the application of the law is not contrary to the public policy of another state with a stronger interest in the transaction. In this case, New York enjoys a substantial connection to the parties as Verizon's headquarters is in New York and the company does business in that state. Additionally, neither side has alleged that the application of New York law would be contrary to the public policy of another state with stronger ties.

2. Misrepresentation

Defendant does not contest that he executed the Award Agreements via electronic signature. Defendant contends, though, that he did not read the Agreements before signing them, because Verizon misrepresented the essential terms of the Award Agreements. The Court, however, will not invalidate the non-competition covenant on these grounds.

"In New York, the case law provides that parties are bound "by the contracts they sign whether or not the party has read the contract so long as there is no fraud, duress or some other wrongful act of the other party." "

Defendant argues that the court, nevertheless, should invalidate the Award Agreements because there was fraud in the execution of the agreement. Specifically, Defendant argues that Verizon misrepresented the nature of agreement by failing to provide him with notice that it had revised the Award Agreements to include a non-competition clause to Award Agreements and by omitting any description of the non-competition agreement from summaries of the Award Agreements.

"Fraud in the execution occurs where there is a "misrepresentation as to the character or essential terms of a proposed contract," and a party signs without knowing or having a reasonable opportunity to know of its character or essential terms."

In this case, Defendant had a reasonable opportunity to know the character and essential terms of the Award Agreements. First, Verizon encouraged Defendant to read the agreement. For each Award Agreement, Verizon sent Defendant an email message warning him that, through his acceptance, he would certify that he had read and agreed to be bound by the award agreement and its *restrictive covenants*. Also, in order have the ability to execute the agreement on his computer, Verizon required the Defendant to click on a box on the computer screen to affirm that he had read and understood the document-which he did in each case.

Furthermore, Defendant was not under any time pressure to review and sign the document, giving him more than a month to read and electronically sign the agreement. Although Defendant complains that he was only able to view the agreement in a small box on the computer screen, the evidence presented at the hearing shows that he had the ability to print the document, save the document to his hard drive or to expand the default size of document viewing screen. The court further notes that Defendant is a sophisticated businessman, who admitted that in the course of his job at Verizon had read, and even marked for revision, numerous vendor contracts. Defendant also had a personal motivation to read the Award Agreements as they were worth hundreds of thousands of dollars to him.

Moreover, the Court finds that given the efforts Verizon took to make sure their employees understood the importance of reading the contract, there is little evidence to suggest Verizon intended to misrepresent the terms of the Award Agreements. In fact the only party that made direct misrepresentations was Defendant, who certified on numerous occasions to Verizon that he had read and understood the Award Agreements. Thus, the court will not invalidate the non-competition covenants on these grounds.

3. Revocation

Defendant further argues that even if a valid contract were formed, the Award Agreements give him the unilateral power to revoke his acceptance of the

Agreement at any time for any reason. Specifically, Paragraph 3 of the Award Agreements states that "[i]f the Participant does not properly accept (or revokes acceptance of) this Agreement the Participant shall not be entitled to [stock units] regardless of the extent to which the vesting requirements in paragraph 5 ("Vesting") are satisfied." There is no further explanation of the employee's ability to revoke acceptance.

The exact meaning of this language is somewhat ambiguous. The language does not explicitly give the plan participant the ability to revoke, but rather provides a contingency for what would happen if he did. Verizon contends that paragraph 3 was designed to give employees the limited right to revoke acceptance of the Award Agreements before the employees' deadline to accept the Award Agreements expires. In contrast, Defendant argues that this language gives the employee the unilateral and unfettered right to withdraw from the Award Agreements, including the restrictive covenants, at any time, even after the vesting requirements of the plan had been satisfied. Defendant's explanation of the clause is problematic. A unilateral, unfettered right of withdrawal renders a contract illusory.

"Courts will not adopt an interpretation of a contract that would render the benefit bestowed by the contract illusory." Therefore, the court will not adopt Defendant's interpretation of this alleged revocation provision.

The court, however, need not decide the exact meaning of paragraph 3. Paragraph 26(f) of the Award Agreements provide that the covenants "shall continue to apply after *any* expiration, termination, or Cancellation of [the] Agreement." (emphasis added). Through this clear language, the parties unambiguously expressed their intent to have the covenants remain binding even if the underlying agreements were no longer in effect. Thus, even if Defendant could unilaterally terminate the agreements by revoking acceptance as he contends, he would still have to abide by the terms of the restrictive covenants.

B. Preliminary Injunction

Having found that Defendant has executed a valid non-competition agreement which he does not have the ability to revoke, the court now considers whether to grant Plaintiff's Motion for a Preliminary Injunction.

To succeed on a motion for a preliminary injunction the movant must clearly establish: (a) irreparable harm and (b) either (1) likelihood of success on the merits or (2) sufficiently serious questions going to the merits to make them a fair ground for litigation and a balance of hardships tipping decidedly toward the party requesting the preliminary relief.

1. Irreparable Harm

"To establish irreparable harm, the movant must demonstrate an injury that is neither remote nor speculative, but actual and imminent and that cannot be remedied by an award of monetary damages."

It is well established that irreparable harm is presumed where a trade secret has been misappropriated. Even where there is no evidence that a trade secret has been disclosed, Plaintiff may demonstrate irreparable harm by establishing that trade secrets will be inevitably disclosed.

Here, Plaintiff has demonstrated irreparable harm as Defendant has information entitled to trade secret protection and Defendant intends to work for a direct competitor. First, Plaintiff has demonstrated Defendant is knowledgeable about highly confidential information that has trade secret protection. "A trade secret may consist of any formula, pattern, device or compilation of information which is used in one's business, and which gives [the owner] the opportunity to obtain an advantage over competitors who do not know or use it." In determining whether information is a trade secret, the most important consideration is whether that information was kept secret.

In this case, Verizon has established that Defendant's has knowledge of, and in fact designed, particularized marketing plans pertaining to Verizon's Broadband services. Defendant has inside information about Verizon's network deployment plans, financial information regarding Verizon's services, including costs and revenues all of which are entitled to trade secret protection. At the hearing Verizon entered into evidence several reports by Defendant regarding marketing strategies that he marked as confidential information. Comcast would be able to gain an unfair competitive advantage by obtaining Verizon's confidential business plans, including cost and pricing information, network capabilities and network deployment strategies.

Moreover, Comcast and Verizon are direct competitors both in terms of the services they offer and the geographic areas they serve. To the extent Defendant has any involvement in the broadband area at Comcast, he would inevitably disclose Verizon's trade secrets.

The court finds Comcast's attempt to circumvent the non-competition covenant by assigning Defendant to an ad hoc executive training program will not sufficiently insulate him from areas in which he might disclose trade secrets, in which he was initially offered employment. In particular, under the terms of the October 13, 2006 letter offering employment, Defendant will report directly to Mr. Bowling, who has primary responsibility for broadband services at Comcast. As Defendant's mentor, Mr. Bowling will meet regularly with Defendant and will supervise Defendant's participation in an independent research project. It would strain credulity beyond the breaking point to conclude that in his extensive contact with Mr. Bowling, Mr. Bowling's responsibilities for broadband will not come into discussion, and that Defendant will not consciously or unconsciously share or draw on insights gained from his work as a senior executive at Verizon.

The court is given additional pause by the fact that Defendant has already violated a confidentiality provision in the Award Agreement and the non-disclosure restrictive covenant. Specifically, Defendant admits that he forwarded a copy of the Award Agreement to Ms. Dwyer and employees of Comcast. This action was in direct contravention of the terms of paragraph 22 of the Award Agreements, which explicitly states that "except to the extent otherwise required by law, Participant shall not disclose, in whole or in part, any of the terms of this Agreement." Thus, the Defendant admittedly has violated a confidentiality provision contained in the Award Agreement.

Furthermore, in describing his duties in the resume that he provided to Comcast, Defendant specified the percentage by which he improved employee productivity and the budget for customer premise equipment which he managed. At the hearing, Defendant admitted that the data he supplied in regard to his duties at Verizon are not available to the public.

Moreover, at the hearing, Defendant admitted that after accepting the final offer of employment from Comcast he transferred files, including confidential and proprietary work documents, from his Verizon computer to his personal computer at home. He contends that he immediately erased the work documents once he transferred them to his personal computer, and that he only copied the "work files" folder to his home computer, because the "work files" folder was contained in his larger "My Documents" folder which contained music, photographs and other personal files. The Court finds this explanation problematic, as it would not have been difficult for Defendant to remove any folders which contained confidential work information from his My Documents folder prior to copying it. The revelation that Defendant copied work files onto his home computer after accepting employment with Comcast is made more disturbing by the fact that Defendant's witness statement which he adopted under oath at the hearing asserts that he had "not *copied*, printed or electronically, maintained any Verizon documents or information relating to [his] work at Verizon." Defendant has given the court reason to question his credibility in regards to his claim that he would fastidiously guard Verizon's trade secrets if worked at Comcast.

The court also notes that the Award Agreements expressly provide that "[i]rreparable damage to the Company shall result in the event that the Covenants . . . are not specifically enforced and that monetary damages will not adequately protect the Company from a breach of these Covenants." Under New York law, such a provision can "be viewed as an admission . . . that plaintiff will suffer irreparable harm were [the former employee] to breach the contract's non-compete provision."

2. Likelihood of Success on the Merits

New York law subjects non-competition covenants to "an overriding limitation of reasonableness." "A restraint is reasonable only if it: (1) is *no greater* than is required for the protection of the *legitimate interest* of the employer, (2) does not impose undue hardship on the employee, and (3) is not injurious to the public."

a. No Greater than Is Required for the Protection of a Legitimate Interest of the Employer

The non-competition is reasonable in duration, geographic scope, and is necessary to prevent the disclosure of Verizon's trade secrets. The one year duration of Verizon's non-competition covenant is reasonable. The durational reasonableness of a non-compete agreement is judged by the length of time for which the employer's confidential business information will be competitively valuable. In this case, Verizon has put forth sufficient evidence to establish that the proprietary and competitively sensitive information that Defendant obtained, considered, and developed at Verizon is likely to remain competitively valuable to Verizon and its competitors for more than a year. Additionally, on his resume, Defendant highlighted the fact that he was responsible for developing Verizon's five-year strategic plan and led a team "in outlining the long term strategic vision for the [broadband] product line." The resume also notes that Defendant's responsibilities at Verizon included preparing five-year revenue forecasts for the key areas of Verizon's business. The types of information known to and developed by Defendant concerning Verizon's broadband business will remain competitively significant through the expiration of Defendant's non-competition covenant in October 2007. Thus, the one year duration is reasonable.

The geographic scope of the covenant is reasonable as well. The non-competition covenant is tailored to prevent Defendant from working only for companies that engage in competitive activities in those areas where Verizon has a business presence. Given that Defendant had company-wide responsibility for Verizon's broadband products, the non-competition covenant's geographic scope is not unreasonable.

Even if a non-competition covenant is unreasonable in time and geographic scope, enforcement will be granted (1) to the extent necessary to prevent an employee's solicitation or disclosure of trade secrets, (2) to the extent necessary to prevent an employee's release of confidential information regarding the employer's customers, or (3) in those cases where the employee's services to employer are deemed special or unique.

Here, as applied to the facts of this case, the restriction is reasonable and necessary to prevent the disclosure of Verizon's trade secrets. As discussed earlier, the court finds that Defendant will not be able to participate in the training program mentored by Mr. Bowling, the Senior Vice President and General Manager for Comcast Online, without disclosing trade secrets. Thus, under the facts of this case, the non-competition covenant is reasonable.

b. Hardship on the Employee

The non-competition covenant will not impose an undue hardship on Defendant. At age 39, Defendant is already a highly compensated employee, whose compensation package his last year at Verizon would have totaled approximately $597,000 had he stayed. He has a bachelor's degree in Commerce and Engineering from Drexel University and an M.B.A. from Villanova. In fact, Defendant has acknowledged both in the award agreements and during his deposition in this case that he possesses broad-based, marketable skills so that enforcement of the non-competition covenant will not prevent him from earning a livelihood. Although, he may not be able to receive the same level of compensation at another job, that hardship is insufficient. Additionally the court notes that Plaintiff's evidence established that non-competition covenants are common for this industry in this area. As such the court concludes that Defendant's absence from this industry for the term of the non-competition covenant will not significantly impair his ability to earn a livelihood in the future.

c. Not Injurious to the Public

The non-competition covenant in this case is not injurious to the public. At the hearing Verizon presented unrebutted expert testimony that non-competition covenants such as the one in this case serve an important public-policy function by encouraging employers to make significant investments in training key employees and permitting employers to share confidential information with employees, which encourages the free exchange of ideas among top personnel. Additionally, any trade secrets disclosed by Defendant could lead to lessened competition in the broadband market. As Defendant presented little evidence to the contrary, the court holds this restrictive covenant is not injurious to the public. Having found irreparable harm and a likelihood of success on the merits, the court holds that the covenant is enforceable and therefore prevents Defendant from accepting employment with Comcast.

In the alternative, for the reasons stated above, the court holds that there are sufficiently serious questions going to the merits to make them a fair ground for litigation and a balance of hardships tipping decidedly toward the party requesting the preliminary relief.

An appropriate Order follows.

ORDER

AND NOW, this 7th day of November, 2006, upon consideration of the Proposed Findings of Fact and Conclusions of Law filed by the parties in this action and the argument and additional evidence presented at this court's hearing of November 6, 2006 on Plaintiff's Motion for Preliminary Injunction, it is hereby Ordered as follows:

1. Defendant Christopher G. Pizzirani shall not commence employment at or perform any work or services for, of for the benefit of, Comcast Corporation or any of its related companies ("Comcast") at anytime before October 17, 2007; and

2. Defendant shall not disclose to or discuss with Comcast, or use for the benefit of Comcast, any information learned by him during the course of his employment with Verizon or any of its related companies.

3. This injunction shall issue upon Plaintiffs' posting a bond in the amount of $5000.

QUESTIONS

1.   Do you think the Verizon non-competition agreement was reasonable in terms of the scope of activities covered? In terms of the geographic territory covered? In terms of the period of time covered?

2.   Do you think Comcast's second offer of employment, which provided that Pizzirani would engage in an independent research project under the direct supervision of Comcast's Senior Vice President and General Manager for Comcast Online, helped or hurt Verizon's case? Who do you think drafted the terms of the

second offer of employment?

3. What was the basis for the court's finding that Verizon would suffer irreparable harm if it was not granted a temporary injunction barring Pizzirani from working for Comcast?

4. An issue that often arises in litigation over noncompetition agreements is whether the court can strike unreasonable provisions and enforce reasonable provisions. How does the court in *Verizon* answer this question?

5. On what basis did the court find that enforcement of the noncompetition agreement would not impose an undue hardship on Pizzirani?

6. If you were counsel to Comcast, what steps would you suggest regarding Pizzirani's hiring?

EMSL ANALYTICAL, INC., v. YOUNKER
154 S.W.3d 693 (Tex. App. 2004)

ADELE HEDGES, CHIEF JUSTICE.

EMSL Analytical, Inc. appeals from the denial of its application for temporary injunction in its lawsuit against Diane Younker. EMSL alleges that Younker, its former employee, violated a covenant not to compete and a nondisclosure agreement when she went to work for one of its customers. Because EMSL failed to show that it would probably suffer imminent and irreparable injury in the absence of a temporary injunction, we affirm.

Background

EMSL provides environmental testing services to its customers. Younker went to work for EMSL in 2002 as a Microbiology Laboratory Manager. Prior to starting employment, EMSL required Younker to sign a covenant not to compete and nondisclosure agreement. The operative paragraph of this document reads as follows:

> The Company promises to provide Employee with some Confidential Information and/or Trade Secrets of the Company. Employee agrees not to disclose, or aid and abet the disclosure to any person of Confidential Information or Trade Secrets of the Company. To enforce Employee's promise not to disclose such Confidential Information or Trade Secrets, Employee agrees that during Employee's employment with the company and for a period of twelve (12) months after termination of Employee's employment, no matter how occasioned (or for a period of twelve (12) months after the entry of a final judgment of injunction in the event the Company seeks injunctive enforcement of this covenant), Employee will not, either for Employee's own purposes or as an employee of or for the benefit of any other entity or person, directly or indirectly:

a) Engage or have any interest in any activity, venture or environmental laboratory involving asbestos analysis, lead analysis and environmental microbiology within the states of Texas and Louisiana;

b) Work for any customer of the Company within the states of Texas and Louisiana . . . .

EMSL claims that Younker was subsequently given access to three types of confidential information: (1) a customer information database, (2) a laboratory quality assurance manual, and (3) a laboratory standard operating procedures manual.

In 2003, EMSL undertook a microbiology testing project for Lockheed Martin Space Operations. The project involved the testing of equipment to be used on the International Space Station. Younker supervised the project and reported the results to Lockheed. EMSL billed Lockheed $14,750 for the project. In 2004, Younker resigned from EMSL and began working for Lockheed at the Johnson Space Center. Her uncontroverted testimony was that she has not disclosed EMSL's confidential information to Lockheed or anyone else. She further stated that her job responsibilities were completely different at the two companies: at EMSL, she provided analytical services on samples, and at Lockheed, she provides scientific support to engineers relating to both microbiological and non-microbiological equipment. She stated that Lockheed does not have its own microbiological laboratory and that, although a separate department of NASA does and she has been there to collect data from the laboratory, she has never given NASA any advice regarding its laboratory.

EMSL sued Younker, alleging breach of contract, breach of fiduciary duty, and misappropriation of trade secrets, and requesting a temporary restraining order and temporary and permanent injunctions. The trial court initially granted a TRO but, after an evidentiary hearing, subsequently denied the application for a temporary injunction. This interlocutory appeal is from the denial of the temporary injunction. In a single issue, EMSL contends that the trial court abused its discretion in denying the temporary injunction.

Standard of Review

EMSL initially questions whether the requirements for a temporary injunction involving a covenant not to compete are governed by traditional common law rules of equity or by the Covenants Not to Compete Act. We agree with the First and Ninth Courts of Appeals, in holding that the Act does not preempt the common law relating to *temporary* injunctions. As explained in detail in *Cardinal Health*, the clear language of the Act expresses an intention to govern only final remedies. By its very nature, a temporary injunction is not a final remedy. Accordingly, we look to the common law rules governing temporary injunctions in determining whether the court below properly denied the application.

The purpose of a temporary injunction is to preserve the status quo of the litigation's subject matter pending a trial on the merits. To obtain a temporary injunction, the applicant must plead and prove: (1) a cause of action against the defendant, (2) a probable right to the relief sought, and (3) a probable, imminent, and irreparable injury in the interim. The decision to grant or deny a temporary injunction rests within the trial court's sound discretion. A reviewing court should not reverse an order on a temporary injunction unless the trial court's action was so arbitrary that it exceeded the bounds of reasonable discretion. When a consideration of the evidence is required, we view it in the light most favorable to the trial court's order, indulging every reasonable inference in its favor. When, as here, the trial court does not make findings of fact or conclusions of law, we must uphold the court's order on any legal theory supported by the record.

Analysis

We focus our attention on the third required element: that the applicant prove a probable, imminent, and irreparable injury in the interim. EMSL appears to identify two possible reasons for needing a temporary injunction: (1) to prevent the possible release of their confidential information and (2) to preserve the possibility that Lockheed might need EMSL's services in the future.

We begin by noting that this is not the typical covenant not to compete case where a former employer goes to work for a competitor and tries to take customers away. While there was evidence that Younker was violating the noncompete clause by working for a former customer of EMSL's, the agreement itself states that the sole purpose of the noncompete clause was to enforce the nondisclosure clause. However, there was no evidence offered to show that Younker was currently violating the nondisclosure clause or that there was any likelihood that she would in the future.

Jason Dobranic, EMSL's regional manager, testified that he had no knowledge of Younker disclosing any confidential information or of whether she worked in a microbiology lab for Lockheed. He further admitted that he had no knowledge of what Lockheed might ask Younker to do, but that there was a "potential" that Lockheed could ask her to do things that would involve EMSL's confidential information. He said that he was "concerned" that EMSL could suffer irreparable harm if Younker was not prevented from working for Lockheed during the pendency of the lawsuit, and he could "envision" a situation in which Younker might confer some of EMSL's confidential information to a laboratory at NASA. He also stated that EMSL's project for Lockheed was a one-time assignment but that there was a "potential" for future special projects.

Younker testified that she did not take any confidential information with her when she left EMSL and that she has not disclosed EMSL's confidential information to Lockheed, NASA, or anyone else. She further stated that her job responsibilities were different at the two companies and that she does not work in a microbiology lab for Lockheed. It was undisputed that Lockheed is not a competitor of EMSL.

Based on the evidence presented, EMSL established a theoretical possibility that Younker could take Lockheed away as a customer by doing in-house for them what they had on one occasion paid EMSL to do. However, there is no evidence showing that she is doing such work for Lockheed or has, will, or ever would do such work for Lockheed. EMSL also established a theoretical possibility that Younker could divulge EMSL's confidential information to Lockheed or some other entity, but again, there is no evidence that she has done this or likely will do this. Indeed, Younker's uncontroverted testimony refuted both of EMSL's theoretical reasons for needing a temporary injunction. Further, the evidence supports the conclusion that her job responsibilities at Lockheed would not require her to use EMSL's confidential information. At most, the testimony of EMSL's regional manager established only a fear of possible injury, and that contingency is not sufficient to support issuance of a temporary injunction.

Viewing the evidence in the light most favorable to the trial court's order, we hold that EMSL has failed to establish that it faced "probable, imminent, and irreparable injury" in the absence of a temporary injunction. Consequently, the trial court did not abuse its discretion in denying the application for temporary injunction. EMSL's sole issue is overruled.

The trial court's judgment is affirmed.

QUESTIONS

1. Do you think the customer information database or the laboratory quality assurance manual or the laboratory standard operating procedures manual would constitute confidential information known to EMSL, but to no one else? What do you think EMSL's primary concern was with Younker going to work for Lockheed?

2. Is it credible to assert that EMSL's laboratory quality assurance manual or laboratory standard operating procedures manual would provide valuable information to NASA?

3. What would EMSL have to show regarding Lockheed's business and Younker's employment role in order to establish a threat to EMSL's legitimate business interests?

CASE NOTES

1. Dowling was employed by Weed Eater as vice president of manufacturing. His responsibilities included the design and organization of the assemble line for production of string line trimmers. As a high-level corporate officer, Dowling was included in all company meetings and had access to all company trade secrets including product plans, market strategies, and sales, price and performance goals. All employees of Weed Eater were required to sign non-disclosure agreements and Weed Eater maintained a strict security system. In addition, all vice presidents of Weed Eater were required to sign non-competition agreements. Dowling's non-competition agreement provided that for one year following his termination of employment with Weed Eater he would not enter "the employ of any other . . . . person, firm, corporation or other entity engaged in activities relating to lawn and garden care." The non-competition agreement provided that it would only be applicable to areas in which Weed Eater conducted manufacturing, sales or business activities. Dowling signed the non-competition agreement in March 1977 and resigned from Weed Eater in October 1977. Immediately after his resignation, Dowling went to work for Hawaiian Motor Company (Hawaiian) as director of

manufacturing. While Dowling was employed by Weed Eater, Hawaiian was purchasing string line trimmer heads from Weed Eater to incorporate into its line of trimmer products. As director of manufacturing at Hawaiian, Dowling was responsible for control of the assembly line to manufacture string line trimmer heads. Weed Eater brought suit against Dowling claiming breach of the non-disclosure agreement and breach of the non-competition agreement. The trial court found that Dowling had breached the non-disclosure agreement and issued a temporary injunction against Dowling barring him from disclosing any confidential or trade secret information to third parties. However, the trial court did not enjoin Dowling from continuing in the employment of Hawaiian. Weed Eater appealed the trial court's decision. What result? *See* Weed Eater, Inc. v. Dowling, 562 S.W.2d 898 (Tex. App. 1978).

2. *See also* Advanced Bionics Corp. v. Medtronic, Inc., 59 P.3d 231 (Cal. 2002) (California's policy interest in protecting employees from non-competition agreements was an insufficient basis to overcome comity principle under which one state's laws may operate in another state; in the exercise of judicial restraint, California court, in which former employee and employee's new employer challenged non-competition clause in employee's employment contract with former Minnesota employer, could not issue temporary restraining order that restrained Minnesota employer from taking action in breach of contract suit Minnesota employer filed in Minnesota court); Continental Group, Inc. v. Kinsley, 422 F. Supp. 838 (D. Conn. 1976) (Whether protectable information is characterized as confidential or as a trade secret has no legal significance; considerations applicable to trade secrets are also applicable to confidential information); Sensabaugh v. Farmers Ins. Exchange, 420 F. Supp. 2d 980 (E.D. Ark. 2006) (Noncompetition covenant may be enforceable if the employer made trade secrets or confidential business information available to employee, and if employee used this information to gain unfair advantage over employer); Eaton Corp. v. Appliance Valves Corp., 526 F. Supp. 1172 (N.D. Ind. 1981) (Information is not trade secret unless employer can show that information could not have been learned by anyone skilled in the industry); Static Control Components, Inc. v. Darkprint Imaging, Inc., 135 F. Supp. 2d 722 (M.D. N.C. 2001) (Noncompete and nondisclosure provisions may be considered and enforced separately under the same or distinct provisions of employment contract).

Additional Information

1. ALAN S. GUTTERMAN, BUISNESS COUNSELOR'S LAW AND COMPLIANCE PRACTICE MANUAL §§ 13:5–13:15, 13:30 (2010).

2. 3 HR POLICIES AND PRACTICES § 256:16 (2011).

3. RAYMOND T. NIMMER, 1 INFORMATION LAW §§ 5:62–5:66 (2010).

4. 2 CALLMANN ON UNFAIR COMP., TR. & MONO § 16:13 (4th Ed. 2011).

5. CORP COUNS GD TO EMP CONTRACTS §§ 3:45–3:51 (2010).

6. RICHARD E. KAYE, 36 CAUSES OF ACTION 2D 103 (2010).

7. DONALD J. ASPELUND & STEPHEN L. LUNDWALL, EMPLOYEE NONCOMPETITION LAW § 3:2 (2009).

8.   Ferdinand S. Tinio, 61 A.L.R.3d 397 (1975).

9.   Alexis Costello, *Fourth District's "Lack of Interest" Makes Non-Competition Agreements Easier to Enforce*, 22 DCBA Brief 38 (2010).

10. Patrick M. Kinnally, *Litigating Noncompetition Agreements: The Employee's Perspective*, 95 Ill. B.J. 250 (2007).

11. Timothy P. Glynn, *Interjurisdictional Competition in Enforcing Noncompetition Agreements: Regulatory Risk Management and the Race to the Bottom*, 65 Wash. & Lee L. Rev. 1381 (2008).

12. Charles T. Graves, *Do Strict Trade Secret and Noncompetition Law Obstruct Innovation?*, 1 Entrepreneurial Bus. L.J. 323 (2007).

13. T. Leigh Anenson, The Role of Equity in Employment Noncompetition Cases, 42 Am. Bus. L.J. 1 (2005).

14. William L. Schaller, *Jumping Ship: Legal Issues Relating to Employee Mobility in High Technology Industries*, 17 Lab. Law. 25 (2001).

15. Andrew J. Gallo, *A Uniform Rule for Enforcement of Non-Competition Contracts Considered in Relation to "Termination Cases"*, 1 U. Pa. J. Lab. & Emp. L. 719 (1998).

16. Tracy L. Staidl, *The Enforceability of Noncompetition Agreements When Employment Is At Will: Reformulating the Analysis*, 2 Employee Rts. & Emp. Pol'y J. 95 (1998).

17. Jordan Leigman, Richard Nathan, *The Enforceability of Post-Employment Noncompetition Agreements Formed After At-Will Employment Has Commenced: The "Afterthought" Agreement*, 60 S. Cal. L. Rev. 1465 (1987).

Chapter 5

EXPERIMENTAL USE OF NEW TECHNOLOGY

Experimentation is a crucial activity during the course of a technology's commercial development. However, under the current Patent Act and the America Invents Act, experimentation can have important legal consequences in three particular situations, some negative and some positive. First, under the current Patent Act, experimentation more than one year prior to filing a patent application can result in a statutory bar to the patent's issuance. (Under the America Invents Act, experimentation at any time prior to filing of the patent application can result in a bar to the patent's issuance.) Second, experimentation using patented technology can result in patent infringement under both patent acts. Third, experimentation using patented drugs and medical devices can be exempted from patent infringement under both patent acts. The sections below consider these three situations.

5.1 EXPERIMENTAL USE EXCEPTION TO PUBLIC USE STATUTORY BAR

Section 102(b) of the current Patent Act states . . .

A person shall be entitled to a patent unless —

(b) the invention was . . . in public use or on sale in this country, more than one year prior to the date of the application for patent in the United States . . . (Again, the America Invents Act provides that a public use any time prior to filing the patent application will bar the issuance of the patent.)

In many instances, experimentation with a new technology must be conducted in public, arguably resulting in a "public use" of the technology. In 1878, the Supreme Court recognized the dilemma § 102(b) posed for inventors who must publicly experiment with an invention in order to perfect it. In *City of Elizabeth v. American Nicholson Paving Co.*, 97 U.S. 126 (1878), the Court held that an experimental use of an invention would not be regarded as a "public use" within § 102(b) even though the experiment was conducted in public. *City of Elizabeth* involved a new method of paving streets using wooden blocks laid in a checker-board pattern. The inventor, Nicholson, tested the new paving method on a heavily traveled carriage road in Boston for six years before filing his patent application. The Court found that testing the durability of the new paving method over an extended period of time was necessary to perfect the invention and that this testing could not be conducted anywhere other than on a public road.

Over the last 130 years, courts have greatly refined the experimental use exemption to public use in a wide variety of contexts. The *Clock Spring* case below deals with the repair of gas pipelines and considers whether the public use at issue was an experimentation or a demonstration.

CLOCK SPRING, L.P. v. WRAPMASTER, INC.
560 F.3d 1317 (Fed. Cir. 2009)

DYK, CIRCUIT JUDGE.

Clock Spring, L.P. ("Clock Spring") brought suit alleging that Wrapmaster, Inc. ("Wrapmaster") infringed the claims of U.S. Patent No. 5,632,307 (" '307 Patent") and violated section 43(a) of the Lanham Act, 15 U.S.C. § 1125(a)(1)(A). The '307 Patent claims methods for repairing damaged high-pressure gas pipes. On summary judgment the United States District Court for the Southern District of Texas held that the claims of the '307 Patent were invalid due to obviousness and that the Lanham Act claim was without merit. We affirm the summary judgment of invalidity because we conclude that the claims of the '307 Patent are invalid as a matter of law, due to prior public use. We do not reach the issue of invalidity due to obviousness. Additionally, we affirm the district court's summary judgment determination that the false advertising claim is without merit.

BACKGROUND

Both Clock Spring and Wrapmaster are high-pressure gas pipeline repair companies. Clock Spring is the exclusive licensee of the '307 Patent. The '307 Patent has five independent claims and thirty-eight dependent claims. All are method claims. Claim 1 of the '307 Patent reads as follows:

> A method for repairing a pipe adapted to carry an internal load directed radially outward therefrom, *said pipe having a defective region* defined by at least one cavity extending from an outer surface of said pipe toward the center of said pipe but not extending completely through the wall of said pipe, said method comprising the steps of:
>
> providing a filler material *having a workable uncured state* and a rigid cured state,
>
> filling said cavity to at least said outer surface of said pipe with said filler material in said workable state,
>
> providing at least one band having a plurality of elastic convolutions of high tensile strength material,
>
> *while said filler material is in said workable state*, wrapping said plurality of convolutions of said high tensile strength material about said pipe to form a coil overlying stud filler material[,]
>
> tightening said coil about said pipe so that said filler material completely fills that portion of said cavity underlying said coil[,] securing at least one of said convolutions to an adjacent one of said convolutions, and

permitting said filler material to cure to said rigid state, whereby a load carried by said pipe is transferred substantially instantaneously from said pipe to said coil.

The parties appeared to agree, or at least not contest, that the main distinctive feature over the prior art is wrapping the pipe while the filler is in an uncured state so as to ensure smooth and continuous contact between the wrap and the pipe. The other independent claims (claims 38, 39, 42, and 43) also require wrapping in an uncured state, but address different types of defects and repair methods. The various dependent claims add further limitations for the properties of the materials used in the individual steps of the method (e.g., requiring that the filler's "rigid cured state has a compressive strength of at least about 9,000 psi").

In 2005 Clock Spring filed an infringement suit against Wrapmaster alleging infringement of all the claims of the '307 Patent. It also filed a separate Lanham Act suit alleging that Wrapmaster "used in commerce a false and misleading description of fact, and false and misleading representation of fact, which in commercial advertising or promotion, misrepresents the nature, characteristics and qualities of [Clock Spring's] goods, services, and commercial activities." The two suits were consolidated.

After discovery, Wrapmaster filed a summary judgment motion of invalidity of all the claims of the '307 Patent and a separate summary judgment motion on the Lanham Act claim. Somewhat surprisingly, neither motion was supported by expert affidavits. We treat the two motions separately.

The invalidity summary judgment motion argued that the claims were invalid due to a prior public use under 35 U.S.C. § 102(b) in October 1989, in Cuero, Texas, more than one year before the patent application was filed in 1992. The motion was supported by a 1994 Gas Research Institute ("GRI") report (hereinafter "1994 GRI report") regarding the demonstration made by named inventor Norman C. Fawley ("Fawley"). GRI, since renamed the Gas Technology Institute, is a non-profit research and development organization which was entitled to receive royalty payments from Clock Spring on the '307 Patent. The motion also urged that the claims were invalid on grounds of obviousness based on a number of prior art patents.

Clock Spring opposed the motion. Clock Spring did not dispute that the 1989 demonstration was public, or that it involved the limitations of the patent with one exception. Clock Spring apparently urged that the 1989 demonstration had not involved the application of the wrap with an uncured filler, and that the use had been experimental. Clock Spring also urged that the patent claims were not obvious.

The district court referred the motion to a magistrate judge for recommendations. The magistrate judge recommended that the district court grant summary judgment of invalidity with respect to the claims of the '307 Patent.

The magistrate judge first addressed Wrapmaster's contention that the '307 Patent is invalid due to prior public use. The magistrate judge concluded that the 1994 GRI report proved that there was no genuine issue of material fact regarding whether the filler compound was uncured when the wrap was applied to the pipe. The magistrate judge also rejected Clock Spring's argument that the use was experimental. Based on this, the magistrate judge recommended finding that the 1989 demonstration triggered the public use bar under 35 U.S.C. § 102(b).

On review in the district court Clock Spring objected to the magistrate judge's recommendations, now arguing that three limitations of the claims were not present in the 1989 demonstration — the uncured state limitation, the requirement that the pipe have a "cavity," and the requirement that the "filler" be applied to the "cavity." The "defective region" with a "cavity" is described in the specification as "pits," "crevices," "gouging," and "denting." The district court did not address whether the 1989 demonstration included all claim limitations. In support of its argument on experimental use to the district court, Clock Spring submitted new evidence including additional GRI reports (some of which mentioned the 1989 demonstration) and a 28-page report by NCF Industries, Inc. ("NCF report") concerning the 1989 demonstration. Though characterizing the late submission of these documents as "clearly improper," the district court considered them and concluded that Clock Spring had "raise[d] a fact question about whether the 1989 installation was experimental," relying on the NCF report, a 1993 GRI report, and a 1998 GRI report. The district court did not explain why these reports raised a genuine issue of material fact. The district court thus rejected the magistrate's recommendation concerning the public use bar. However, the district judge agreed with the magistrate judge as to obviousness and granted summary judgment of invalidity due to obviousness.

I. DISCUSSION

Although the district court granted summary judgment of invalidity on obviousness, Wrapmaster contends that the invalidity decision can be sustained on the separate ground of prior public use. Relying on the 1994 GRI report and the NCF report, Wrapmaster contends that the 1989 demonstration was a public use of the method of claim 1 because the method was demonstrated to the public almost three years before the priority date of the '307 Patent application, September 9, 1992 (application 942,731). We agree.

We may affirm a grant of summary judgment on a ground supported in the record but not adopted by the district court if we conclude that "there [wa]s no genuine issue as to any material fact and . . . the movant [wa]s entitled to a judgment as a matter of law."

Under 35 U.S.C. § 102:

> A person shall be entitled to a patent unless . . . (b) the invention was patented or described in a printed publication in this or a foreign country or in public use or on sale in this country, more than one year prior to the date of the application for patent in the United States.

For a challenger to prove a patent claim invalid under § 102(b), the record must show by clear and convincing evidence that the claimed invention was in public use before the patent's critical date. The critical date is "one year prior to the date of the application for patent in the United States," here September 9, 1991. "[A] public use includes any public use of the claimed invention by a person other than the inventor who is under no limitation, restriction or obligation of secrecy to the inventor." In order for a use to be public within the meaning of § 102(b), there must be a public use with all of the claim limitations.

There is no dispute that the 1989 demonstration was public. In fact, representatives of several other domestic gas transmission companies were present at the demonstration, and there was no suggestion that they were under an obligation of confidentiality. This demonstration was accessible to the public. ("An invention is in public use if it is shown to or used by an individual other than the inventor under no limitation, restriction, or obligation of confidentiality.").

There is also no dispute that all the limitations of claim 1 were involved in the demonstration save for three. Clock Spring contends that three of the claim limitations of claim 1 were not met, namely, the requirements (1) that a corroded pipe "defined by at least one cavity extending from an outer surface of said pipe toward the center of said pipe" be involved; (2) that "filler material" be used to fill the "cavity"; and (3) that the pipe be wrapped while the filler material is in an "uncured state." We are skeptical whether the first two issues were preserved since they were not raised before the magistrate judge. Even if they were preserved, Clock Spring's argument is without merit.

The 1994 GRI report and the NCF report both described the demonstration. The NCF report states that "[t]he purpose of this demonstration . . . [was] to closely document the *entire process* of bell-hole repair and rehabilitation on a working pipeline." Even though the NCF report stated that "[n]o serious pitting was in evidence," the captions of the report's photographs numbered 8, 9, 10, 16 and 17 describe "[p]inhole areas of corrosion" which appear to be cavities within the meaning of the claim. Although the report does not specifically state that the filler was used to fill the pinholes, applying filler to cavities would have been obvious, particularly in light of the express statement in the NCF report that the filler compound was intended to be "used to fill in pitted areas of pipe corrosion," and the fact that the whole purpose of the experiment was to demonstrate a method of "spot repair" of pipelines. We have held that the public use bar applies to obvious variants of the demonstrated public use.

The 1989 demonstration also involved uncured filler. The patent applicant's January 17, 1995 Information Disclosure Statement to the PTO described the 1989 demonstration. Recounting the final three installations of the 1989 demonstration, it stated that "[e]mployees of Texas Eastern then installed the CLOCK SPRING bands around the pipeline before the filler material had cured to a rigid state." The 1994 GRI report also described the installation process as involving installation while the filler was in an uncured state, stating that this approach has been "adopted as standard installation practice in this program," and then describing the 1989 demonstration as a "field installation" of that process. Moreover, the detailed description of the 1989 demonstration in the NCF report proves that uncured filler was used. During the demonstration, three of the crews prepared the pipe using "splash zone compound" and adhesive. Based on the ambient temperature range during the demonstration, the splash zone compound had a minimum cure time of one hour. Within three minutes after the crew began to apply the filler compound, the adhesive was applied, and the clock spring was wrapped around the pipe. As the magistrate judge concluded, the short elapsed time demonstrates that the filler was uncured. There is no evidence that the filler was not uncured. There is no genuine issue of material fact as to whether the alleged missing elements of claim 1 of the '307 Patent were part of the 1989 demonstration.

In the alternative, Clock Spring claims that the 1989 demonstration was an experimental use and not a prior public use.

The experimental use exception is not a doctrine separate or apart from the public use bar. Rather, something that would otherwise be a public use may not be invalidating if it qualifies as an experimental use. In *Allen Engineering Corp. v. Bartell Industries, Inc.*, we catalogued a set of factors that in previous cases had been found instructive, and in some cases dispositive, for determining commercial versus experimental uses. These factors include:

> (1) the necessity for public testing, (2) the amount of control over the experiment retained by the inventor, (3) the nature of the invention, (4) the length of the test period, (5) whether payment was made, (6) whether there was a secrecy obligation, (7) whether records of the experiment were kept, (8) who conducted the experiment, (9) the degree of commercial exploitation during testing, (10) whether the invention reasonably requires evaluation under actual conditions of use, (11) whether testing was systematically performed, (12) whether the inventor continually monitored the invention during testing, and (13) the nature of contacts made with potential customers.

Though a prior commercial sale and not a prior public use was at issue in *Allen Engineering*, the factors explicated are equally relevant to an analysis of experimental use.

We have said that lack of control over the invention during the alleged experiment, while not always dispositive, may be so. *Atlanta Attachment Co. v. Leggett & Platt, Inc.* In that case, we held that a public use had occurred, finding "dispositive" the fact that the patentee "did not have control over the alleged testing," which was performed by its customer. Clock Spring argues that Fawley, a named inventor, exercised tight control over the demonstration, as shown through the detailed reports made of the demonstration. But, the detailed reports do not provide evidence that Fawley controlled the demonstration. An independent observer "analyzed and recorded" the 1989 demonstration. Three of the eleven Clock Spring installations were done by the pipeline's personnel. None of these individuals was under Fawley's control or surveillance. We need not, however, rely on lack of control as establishing public use because we conclude that the use cannot qualify as experimental for other reasons.

A use may be experimental only if it is designed to (1) test claimed features of the invention or (2) to determine whether an invention will work for its intended purpose-itself a requirement of patentability. In other words, an invention may not be ready for patenting if claimed features or overall workability are being tested. But, there is no experimental use unless claimed features or overall workability are being tested for purposes of the filing of a patent application. Indeed, the experimental use negation of the § 102(b) bar only exists to allow an inventor to perfect his discovery through testing without losing his right to obtain a patent for his invention.

Clock Spring does not urge that refining the claim limitations was the subject of the 1989 demonstration. Rather, Clock Spring argues that the demonstration was experimental because the 1989 demonstration was designed to determine durability of the method, i.e., its suitability for the intended purpose. The reports make no such explicit statement. The NCF report states that "[t]he purpose of this demonstration . . . was to demonstrate to Panhandle Eastern attendants and guests the steps of application and the ability of minimally-trained crews to make Clock Spring installations." The 1994 GRI report states that "[t]his demonstration was designed to familiarize pipeline personnel with the Clock Spring technology, and to begin training of maintenance personnel in the use of the coil pass installation *method*." The demonstration was similarly described to the United States Patent and Trademark Office ("PTO") during prosecution, where the applicant stated that the purpose of the demonstration was to seek "input from people in the industry on the performance of the bands and the practicality of their installation techniques."

To be sure, the 1994 GRI report can be read as suggesting that the 1989 demonstration was for durability testing because it states that "recovery and analysis of installed composite after several years of exposure in pipeline settings was the only means of verifying the long-term performance of [the clock spring's] composites in moist soils." Clock Spring's problem, however, is that no report in the record states, or in any way suggests, that the 1989 demonstration was designed to test durability for the purposes of the patent application to the PTO. In fact, the reports make clear that the durability testing was for "acceptance by regulators and the pipeline industry," and that the 1989 installation was not dug up and examined until almost a year after the 1992 patent application. Thus, even if durability were being tested, it was not for purposes of the patent application, and cannot bring the experimental use exception into play. By filing the 1992 application, the inventors represented that the invention was then ready for patenting, and studies done thereafter cannot justify an earlier delay in filing the application under the rubric of experimental use.

Finally, Clock Spring asserts that because the Department of Transportation did not grant any installation waivers until 1993, the 1989 demonstration must have been experimental. This terse argument is unsupported by any citation to law. That the inventors were not legally allowed to perform the method on a pipeline in commercial operation, does not mean that a public use did not occur. The former fact has absolutely nothing to do with the latter question.

In summary, during the 1989 demonstration, all elements of the repair method in claim 1 of the '307 Patent were performed. There was no evidence that the overall suitability of the '307 Patent's method nor any of the claim elements was being tested as would be required for experimental use. Accordingly, claim 1 of the '307 Patent is invalid due to prior public use.

Clock Spring has not contended that the remaining independent claims of the '307 Patent (claims 38, 39, 42, and 43) could be valid if claim 1 was invalid, under § 102(b). However, Clock Spring does argue that the dependent claims are not invalid and should have each been addressed separately. This is the first time that Clock Spring has made this argument. Wrapmaster had filed a motion for summary judgment, contending that all of the claims of the '307 Patent are invalid due to prior public use. In its opposition to Wrapmaster's motion for summary judgment, Clock Spring did not assert that the dependent claims needed to be separately addressed but, instead, essentially conceded that if claim 1 was invalid the other claims were also invalid. Clock Spring did not even address the dependent claims to the district court on review of the magistrate judge's recommendation. Clock Spring has waived its current argument that the invalidity of each of the dependent claims needs to be addressed separately.

In light of our finding of invalidity due to prior public use, we do not reach the obviousness question.

QUESTIONS

1. If all the people who observed the 1989 demonstration signed confidentiality agreements, would this have negated the public use of the invention? Is there a limit to how many confidentiality agreements can be signed and still meaningfully protect confidentiality? Twenty agreements? Two hundred agreements? One thousand agreements?

2. The court found that the public use must include all of the claim limitations contained in the patent, but that there was some question as to whether three of Clock Spring's claim limitations were included in the public use. How did the court overcome this question sufficiently to warrant a summary judgment?

3. How different is *Clock Spring* from *City of Elizabeth*? Could the method for repairing gas pipelines be tested in any way other than through a public use? Could the durability of the repair method be tested in any way other than through a public use?

4. If a client asked you to draft a memo on the best practices for assuring compliance with the experimental use exception to the public use statutory bar, what practical steps would you recommend?

CASE NOTES

1. Atlanta manufactures commercial sewing machines. Sealy manufactures mattresses. Sealy asked Atlanta to design a sewing machine that could automatically attach gussets to the panels of pillow-top mattresses. Sealy and Atlanta agreed to keep the development confidential, and Atlanta agreed to sell only to Sealy if the development was successful. Atlanta developed a total of four prototype machines for Sealy to test. The first two prototype machines were delivered to Sealy in April 1999 and January 2000 along with an invoice for the prototypes and a quotation for sales of subsequent machines. After testing, Sealy found these two prototype machines unsatisfactory and returned them to Atlanta with verbal suggestions for necessary improvements. Sealy did not pay the prototype invoice. For the third prototype, Atlanta again sent Sealy an invoice for the prototype and a quotation for sales of additional machines. This occurred on February 5, 2001. However, Atlanta

did not deliver the third prototype to Sealy for testing. Instead, Sealy representatives inspected the machine at Atlanta's facilities on February 7, 2001. Sealy paid the invoice for the third prototype machine. Atlanta did not make any profit on the prototype invoices. The final prototype was substantially similar to the third prototype. Atlanta delivered the final prototype machine to Sealy on April 10, 2001. Sealy experimented with the final prototype until June 2001 and made improvements to the prototype based on its experimentation. Ultimately, Sealy decided not to purchase the machines from Atlanta. Atlanta filed a patent application which covered the features of the final prototype on August 15, 2002, claiming a priority filing date of March 5, 2002. After the patent issued, Atlanta sued Leggett, a third party, for infringement. Leggett defended the infringement suit arguing that the patent was invalid because Atlanta had offered the prototypes for sale more than one year prior to the critical date of March 15, 2001. Atlanta claimed that the prototypes were not offered for sale, but provided to Sealy only for the purpose of testing and experimentation. What result? *See* Atlanta Attachment Co. v. Leggett & Platt Inc., 516 F.3d 1361 (Fed. Cir. 2008).

   2. *See also* Eli Lilly & Co. v. Zenith Goldline Pharms., Inc., 471 F.3d 1369 (Fed. Cir. 2006) (Several factors establish the experimental character of a use, including the length of the test period, the existence of a confidentiality agreement, maintaining records of the testing, monitoring and control of the test results and length of the test period in relation to tests of similar inventions); Sparton Corp. v. U.S., 57 Fed.Cl. 455 (Fed. Cl. 2003) (Sonobuoy deployment system reduced to practice before the critical date precluded application of experimental use exception to public use bar; experimental use exception not applicable when sea tests were conducted for the benefit of the Navy and there was no secrecy agreement between contractor and Navy); Netscape Communs. Corp. v. Konrad, 295 F.3d 1315 (Fed. Cir. 2002) (Inventor failed to maintain control of invention when he turned prototype database system on and allowed people to use it, but did not monitor the use or impose confidentiality agreement; employees' obligation of confidentiality to Department of Energy did not extend to inventor); Kolmes v. World Fibers Corp., 107 F.3d 1534 (Fed. Cir. 1997) (Distribution of cut-resistant gloves in environment in which gloves would be used to ensure invention would work for its intended purpose, where there was no commercialization and records documented experiments, fell within the experimental use exception to public use bar); Lough v. Brunswick Corp., 86 F.3d 1113 (Fed. Cir. 1996) (Alleged experiments with seal assembly for boat sterns were not experimental for purposes of public use bar when inventor installed first prototype in his own boat and later provided prototypes to friends and acquaintances without receiving comments on operation of prototypes, without supervision over prototypes during alleged testing and without keeping records of alleged testing); Baxter International Inc. v. Cobe Laboratories Inc., 88 F.3d 1054 (Fed. Cir. 1996) (Use of centrifuge by researcher unassociated with inventor was not experimental exception to public use bar where researcher's experiments were intended to customize centrifuge to work for his particular purposes and not to determine if centrifuge would work as recited in patent claims); Allied Colloids Inc. v. American Cyanamid Co., 64 F.3d 1570 (Fed. Cir. 1995) (Experimentation with patentee's sewage treatment method at city's sewage treatment plant could be found to be exception to public use bar where tests performed by patentee not city employees, patentee received no payment for tests

and patentee kept detailed records of tests; patent attorney's reference to testing as "commercial sampling" was not dispositive because virtually every contact between an inventor and potential customer has a commercial purpose); Sinskey v. Pharmacia Ophthalmics Inc., 982 F.2d 494 (Fed. Cir. 1992) (Implantations and sales of intraocular lens were not for purposes of experiment where patentee's subjective experimental intent was developed more than a decade after use and sales at issue and objective contemporaneous evidence, including fees, documents and medical records did not suggest use and sales were experimental).

Additional Information

1. 2 GREGORY E. UPCHURCH, IP LITIGATION GUIDE: PATENTS & TRADE SECRETS §§ 14:45, 15:16, 17:128; Appendix 15-2 (2009).

2. 3 ROBERT A. MATTHEWS, JR., ANNOTATED PATENT DIGEST §§ 17:154–17:156, 17:158, 17:162, 17:165, 17:177–17:178 (2009).

3. 3 STEVEN Z. SZCZDPANSKI & DAVID M. EPSTEIN, ECKSTROM'S LICENSING IN FOREIGN & DOMESTIC OPPS. § 11:17 (2009).

4. 2 JOHN GLADSTONE MILLS III ET AL., PATENT LAW FUNDAMENTALS § 10:10 (2d ed. 2009).

5. RAYMOND T. NIMMER, LAW OF COMPUTER TECHNOLOGY § 2:30 (2009).

6. 1 JOHN W. SCHLICHER, PATENT LAW, LEGAL AND ECONOMIC PRINCIPLES §§ 1:29, 1:65, 6:7, 6:24; (2d ed. 2008).

7. LAWRENCE M. SUNG & JEFF E. SCHWARTZ, PATENT LAW HANDBOOK § 3:9 (2008).

8. William J. Fisher, *Public Demonstration of Method Without Testing Claim Elements or Evaluating Overall Suitability of the Method is Not Experimental Use*, 21 No. 7 INTELL. PROP. & TECH. L.J. 17, (2009).

9. Andrew S. Baluch, *Relating the Two Experimental Uses in Patent Law: Inventor's Negation and Infringer's Defense*, 87 B.U. L. REV. 213 (2007).

10. Shashank Upadhye, *To Use or Not to Use: Reforming Patent Infringement, the Public Use Bar, and the Experimental Use Doctrine as Applied to Clinical Testing of Pharmaceuticals and Medical Device Inventions*, 4 MINN. INTELL. PROP. REV. 1 (2002).

11. Chad P. Webster, *In the Wake of Lough v. Brunswick Corp.: Who Decides Experimental Purpose in 35 U.S.C. § 102(B) Public Use Cases*, 73 WASH. L. REV. 1201 (1998).

12. William C. Rooklidge, Stephen C. Jensen, *Common Sense, Simplicity and Experimental Use Negation of the Public Use and On Sale Bars to Patentability*, 29 J. MARSHALL L. REV. 1 (1995).

5.2   EXPERIMENTAL USE EXEMPTION TO PATENT INFRINGEMENT

A number of countries have enacted a statutory experimental use exemption to patent infringement, including the United Kingdom, Japan, Germany and China. An experimental use exemption to patent infringement has also been included in a number of international agreements. The scope of these experimental use exemptions varies. The narrower experimental use exemptions permit use of patented subject matter for the purposes of determining whether a patented invention is feasible, useful or technically operable. The broader experimental use exemptions permit use of patented subject matter for the purposes of evaluating patent specifications, improving upon the patented invention or developing a new patentable invention. The broader experimental use exemptions include commercially motivated experimental uses of patented subject matter.

The United States has never enacted an experimental use exemption to patent infringement in its patent acts. The experimental use exemption in U.S. patent law has been developed through case law. Justice Story's 1813 opinion in the case of *Whittemore v. Cutter*, 29 F. Cas. 1120 (C.C.D. Mass. 1813) is widely acknowledged as the seminal statement of the experimental use exemption to patent infringement. In *Whittmore*, Justice Story stated that "it could never have been the intention of the legislature to punish a man, who constructed such a [patented] machine merely for philosophical experiments, or for the purpose of ascertaining the sufficiency of the machine to produce its described effects." In 1813, "philosophical" referred to the field of "natural philosophy" or what we call today "science." Justice Story's definition of the experimental use exemption, therefore, covered two distinct uses of patented subject matter: an exemption for the use of patented subject matter in order to perform scientific experiments and an exemption for the use of patented subject matter to test its claimed utility.

Over the nearly two centuries since Justice Story's statement of the experimental use exemption, the cases considering the scope of the common law experimental use exemption have gone from a generally broad definition of the exemption to the narrowest possible definition of the exemption set forth in *Madey v. Duke University*. As you read the *Madey* case below, consider how the result may have been different if a common law experimental use exemption existed which permitted use of patented subject matter for scientific experiments and testing its claimed utility.

MADEY v. DUKE UNIVERSITY
307 F.3d 1351 (Fed. Cir. 2002)

GAJARSA, CIRCUIT JUDGE.

Dr. John M.J. Madey ("Madey") appeals from a judgment of the United States District Court for the Middle District of North Carolina. Madey sued Duke University ("Duke"), bringing claims of patent infringement and various other federal and state law claims. Pursuant to a motion filed by Duke under Federal Rule of Civil Procedure ("FRCP") 12(b)(1), the district court dismissed-in-part certain patent infringement claims and dismissed certain other claims. After discovery, the district court granted summary judgment in favor of Duke on the remaining claims. For a first set of alleged infringing acts, it held that the experimental use defense applied to Duke's use of Madey's patented laser technology. For a second set of alleged infringing acts, it held that Duke was not the infringing party because a third-party owned and controlled the allegedly infringing laser equipment. The district court erred in its partial dismissal, erred in applying the experimental use defense, but, for the second set of alleged infringing acts, correctly determined that Duke did not infringe because it did not own or control the equipment. Accordingly, we reverse-in-part, affirm-in-part, and remand.

I. BACKGROUND

In the mid-1980s Madey was a tenured research professor at Stanford University. At Stanford, he had an innovative laser research program, which was highly regarded in the scientific community. An opportunity arose for Madey to consider leaving Stanford and take a tenured position at Duke. Duke recruited Madey, and in 1988 he left Stanford for a position in Duke's physics department. In 1989 Madey moved his free electron laser ("FEL") research lab from Stanford to Duke. The FEL lab contained substantial equipment, requiring Duke to build an addition to its physics building to house the lab. In addition, during his time at Stanford, Madey had obtained sole ownership of two patents practiced by some of the equipment in the FEL lab.

At Duke, Madey served for almost a decade as director of the FEL lab. During that time the lab continued to achieve success in both research funding and scientific breakthroughs. However, a dispute arose between Madey and Duke. Duke contends that, despite his scientific prowess, Madey ineffectively managed the lab. Madey contends that Duke sought to use the lab's equipment for research areas outside the allocated scope of certain government funding, and that when he objected, Duke sought to remove him as lab director. Duke eventually did remove Madey as director of the lab in 1997. The removal is not at issue in this appeal, however, it is the genesis of this unique patent infringement case. As a result of the removal, Madey resigned from Duke in 1998. Duke, however, continued to operate some of the equipment in the lab. Madey then sued Duke for patent infringement of his two patents, and brought a variety of other claims.

A. The Patents and Infringing Equipment

One of Madey's patents, U.S. Patent No. 4,641,103 ("the '103 patent"), covers a "Microwave Electron Gun" used in connection with free electron lasers. The other patent, U.S. Patent No. 5,130,994 ("the '994 patent"), is titled "Free-Electron Laser Oscillator For Simultaneous Narrow Spectral Resolution And Fast Time Resolution Spectroscopy." The details of these two patents are not material to the issues on appeal. Their use in the lab, however, as embodied in certain equipment, is central to this appeal.

The equipment at the Duke FEL lab that practices the subject matter disclosed and claimed in the patents is set forth in the list below, which first lists the equipment and then the patent(s) it embodies.

• An infrared FEL called the "Mark III FEL," embodying the '994 patent and the '103 patent (by incorporating the microwave electron gun in the infrared FEL).

• A "Storage Ring FEL," embodying the same patents as the Mark III FEL because it incorporates a Mark III FEL.

• A "Microwave Gun Test Stand," embodying the '103 patent (by incorporating the microwave electron gun).

The three alleged infringing devices are the Mark III FEL, the Storage Ring FEL, and the Microwave Gun Test Stand. Although it is not clear from the record, perhaps because Duke defended by asserting experimental use and government license defenses, Duke seems to concede that the alleged infringing devices and methods read on the claims of the patents. Although the three devices were housed in Duke's physics facilities, the Microwave Gun Test Stand was not Duke's asset, but rather belonged to North Carolina Central University ("NCCU").

B. Duke's Relationship with NCCU

Madey and Duke built the Microwave Gun Test Stand as a subcontractor to NCCU after the government awarded NCCU a contract to study microwave guns (the "AFOSR Contract"). Professor Jones of NCCU was the principal investigator under this government project. The Microwave Gun Test Stand was built and housed in the Duke FEL lab. The AFOSR Contract listed the Microwave Gun Test Stand as NCCU's asset.

C. The District Court's Dismissal Opinion

Duke moved to dismiss the infringement claims under the '103 patent under both FRCP 12(b)(1) for lack of subject matter jurisdiction, and under FRCP 12(b)(6) for failure to state a claim upon which relief can be granted. The district court granted the first motion in part, but denied the second motion. Madey alleges on appeal that the district court erred in its FRCP 12(b)(1) partial dismissal.

Motion to Dismiss under FRCP 12(b)(1)

The district court reasoned that Duke's alleged unauthorized use of the '103 patent fell into two categories: (i) use in furtherance of an Office of Naval Research ("ONR") grant; and (ii) use that exceeds the authorized scope of the ONR grant. The district court determined that if all the unauthorized use fell in the first category, jurisdiction would lie in the Court of Federal Claims. On the other hand, if all of the unauthorized use fell in the second category, jurisdiction would lie in federal district court. In all probability, however, the use spanned both categories.

To make the determination as to whether dismissal under FRCP 12(b)(1) was proper, the district court relied on 28 U.S.C. § 1498(a), set forth below.

(a) Whenever an invention described in and covered by a patent of the United States is *used or manufactured by or for the United States* without license of the owner thereof or lawful right to use or manufacture the same, the owner's remedy shall be by action against the United States in the United States Court of Federal Claims for the recovery of his reasonable and entire compensation for such use and manufacture.

For the purposes of this section, the use or manufacture of an invention described in and covered by a patent of the United States by a contractor, a subcontractor, or any person, firm, or corporation *for the Government and with the authorization or consent of the Government*, shall be construed as use or manufacture for the United States.

The district court reasoned that under § 1498(a) Madey must sue in the Court of Federal Claims for any use in furtherance of the ONR grant. This reasoning assumes that the ONR grant provides the "authorization or consent" of the government to be sued, and designates Duke's use as "by or for" the United States. The district court did not, however, discuss or analyze the particular statements or aspects of the ONR grant that provided the government's authorization or consent to be sued. Nor did the court discuss or characterize Duke's use or manufacture as "by or for the United States."

The district court acknowledged that the use at issue was potentially mixed between the two categories, within the scope of the ONR grant, and without. The district court applied Fourth Circuit law, under which the burden of proving subject matter jurisdiction is with the plaintiff. Thus, even at the pleading stage, according to the district court, the nonmoving party must set forth evidence of specific "jurisdictional" facts to show that a genuine issue of material fact exists; the moving party prevails only if the material jurisdictional facts are not in dispute.

The district court rejected Duke's contention that even if only some use is for the government, the claim should be dismissed. The court noted that the extent of Duke's "use of the '103 patent for private purposes is unclear." The court acknowledged that discovery would be necessary to determine the nature and extent of Duke's private use. However, for Duke's use of the patents "under the authority of the government research grant," the district court dismissed Madey's claim without prejudice.

D. The District Court's Summary Judgment Opinion

Among Duke's motions for summary judgment, two are relevant on appeal, entitled by the district court as: (i) the "Patent Motion;" and (ii) the "Test Stand Gun Motion."

The Patent Motion and the Experimental Use Defense

The district court acknowledged a common law "exception" for patent infringement liability for uses that, in the district court's words, are "solely for research, academic or experimental purposes." The district court recognized the debate over the scope of the experimental use defense, but cited this court's opinion in *Embrex, Inc. v. Service* to hold that the defense was viable for experimental, non-profit purposes.

After having recognized the experimental use defense, the district court then fashioned the defense for application to Madey in the passage set forth below.

Given this standard [for experimental use], for [Madey] to overcome his burden of establishing actionable infringement in this case, he must establish that [Duke] has not used the equipment at issue "solely for an experimental or other non-profit purpose." More specifically, [Madey] must sufficiently establish that [Duke's] use of the patent had "definite, cognizable, and not insubstantial commercial purposes."

On appeal, Madey attacks this passage as improperly shifting the burden to the plaintiff to allege and prove that the defendant's use was not experimental.

Before the district court, Madey argued that Duke's research in its FEL lab was commercial in character and intent. Madey relied on *Pitcairn v. United States* where the government used patented rotor structures and control systems for a helicopter to test the "lifting ability" and other attributes of the patented technology. The *Pitcairn* court held that the helicopters were not built solely for experimental purposes because they were also built to benefit the government in its legitimate business. Based on language in Duke's patent policy, Madey argues that Duke is in the business of "obtaining grants and developing possible commercial applications for the fruits of its "academic research." "

The district court rejected Madey's argument, relying on another statement in the preamble of the Duke patent policy which stated that Duke was "dedicated to teaching, research, and the expansion of knowledge . . . [and] does not undertake research or development work principally for the purpose of developing patents and commercial applications." The district court reasoned that these statements from the patent policy refute any contention that Duke is "in the business" of developing technology for commercial applications. According to the district court, Madey's "evidence" was mere speculation, and thus Madey did not meet his burden of proof to create a genuine issue of material fact. The court went on to state that "[w]ithout more concrete evidence to rebut [Duke's] stated purpose with respect to its research in the FEL lab, Plaintiff has failed to meet its burden of establishing patent infringement by a preponderance of the evidence."

Finally, under its discussion of the Patent Motion, the district court reasoned that Duke's argument that "essentially all" uses of the patents were covered by a license to the government was moot given the experimental use holding. Despite its mootness determination, the district court went on to partially analyze the government license issue as set forth in the passage below.

In a footnote, the district court cites to a section from the Bayh-Dole Act to support its reasoning that the government has a license to have patents practiced on its behalf when the government contributed to the funding of such patents. The relevant section is set forth below.

(c) Each funding agreement with a small business firm or nonprofit organization shall contain appropriate provisions to effectuate the following:

(4) With respect to any invention in which the contractor elects rights, the Federal agency shall have a nonexclusive, nontransferable, irrevocable,

paid-up license to practice or have practiced for or on behalf of the United States any subject invention throughout the world. 35 U.S.C. § 202(c)(4) (2000).

The district court stated that the "funding agreements for the inventions created under the '994 and '103 patents expressly provide that the Government retained rights in those inventions." Thus, the district court reasoned, in light of the Bayh-Dole Act, Duke's use of the patents that has been authorized by the government does not constitute patent infringement. Finally, the district court noted that:

> [a]lthough the parties have presented conflicting evidence as to the extent to which the patented devices have been used for a purpose consented to by the Government, because [Madey] has failed to create a genuine issue of material fact as to whether [Duke] has commercially benefited or intends to do so with respect to the patents at issue, the uses that have been made to date with respect to both patents are, at this point, exempt from infringement liability.

The Court does note, however, as it did previously when ruling upon [Duke's] Motion to Dismiss, that all uses that have been made of the patented devices that are covered by such a license are not subject to infringement liability.

The Test Stand Gun Motion

Under the Test Stand Gun Motion, Duke argued that any use of the patented equipment before June 1997 is not infringement because Madey consented to the manufacture and use of the Microwave Gun Test Stand by Duke and NCCU before this date. The district court agreed, concluding that there was no infringement before such date because Madey approved of such use via his direct involvement. Madey does not appeal this issue.

After June 1997, however, Duke's defense is that no one affiliated with Duke used the Microwave Gun Test Stand. Duke relied on attestations by Dr. Jones, the NCCU professor who was the principal investigator for the AFOSR contract. The district court determined that Dr. Jones was not an agent of Duke. It also determined that Dr. Jones controlled physical access to the Microwave Gun Test Stand because he had the key switch to operate the device. The district court held any contrary assertions by Madey to be "bald allegations and mere speculation."

Given Dr. Jones' attestation that he was unaware of any Duke faculty members or employees using the Microwave Gun Test Stand after June 1997, the district court determined that there was no genuine issue of material fact and awarded summary judgment of no infringement to Duke on this issue.

II. DISCUSSION

B. The District Court's Dismissal Opinion

On appeal, Madey argues that the district court improperly applied 28 U.S.C § 1498(a) by failing to make sufficient supporting determinations. As a result, according to Madey, partial dismissal of the '103 patent infringement claim for Duke's use under the ONR grant was improper. Specifically, Madey argues that the court did not find that Duke's use was "by or for the United States," and that the use was with the "authorization or consent" of the United States. Madey makes the distinction that a research grant is different from a contract to acquire property or services for the government. Duke, on the other hand, attacks Madey's distinction as meaningless, arguing that either a grant or a contract can meet the prerequisites of § 1498(a).

Based on the district court's findings, we agree with Madey that the district court erred in granting the partial dismissal. Madey, however, also asserts that a research grant can never meet the requirements of § 1498(a). We disagree with this proposition.

The district court did not clearly identify, discuss or analyze the particular statements or aspects of the ONR grant that may have provided the government's authorization or consent to be sued. The court seems to have assumed that a research grant by a federal agency to a university for financial support of scientific research proposed by the university constitutes activity "for the United States" and provides authorization or consent by the United States for patent infringement liability for any patents used in the course of the research. In addition, the court did not discuss or characterize Duke's use or manufacture of the '103 patent embodiments as "by or for the United States."

In general, there are two important features of § 1498(a). It relieves a third party from patent infringement liability, and it acts as a waiver of sovereign immunity and consent to liability by the United States. As a result, one possible consequence of dismissal based on this defense is a suit against the government in the Court of Federal Claims. In the sphere of this sovereign immunity influence on the defense, the teachings of *Crater* and *Manville* illustrate two errors by the district court in dismissing the claims for Duke's use of the '103 patent under the ONR grant.

First, the district court relied on the doctrine of jurisdictional facts when, as between private parties, § 1498(a) is not jurisdictional. The district court applied the Fourth Circuit's general jurisdictional facts doctrine. This is error because Federal Circuit law provides the applicable interpretation of § 1498(a). Section 1498(a) applies exclusively to patent law, meaning that Federal Circuit law applies. One might counter-argue that § 1498(a) is procedural. However, to the extent that § 1498(a) is procedural, it is unique to patent law, which also indicates that Federal Circuit law applies. Federal Circuit law, under *Crater* and *Manville*, teaches that § 1498(a) is an affirmative defense and is not jurisdictional. Because § 1498(a) is not jurisdictional, the jurisdictional facts doctrine does not apply. Therefore, the basis for the district court's partial dismissal was improper.

Second, by failing to explain or demonstrate precisely how the ONR grant authorizes the government's consent to suit or authorizes Duke to use or manufacture the patented articles for the government, the district court has provided no findings or analysis upon which we can base our review of the issue appealed from the court's *Dismissal Opinion*. Although a research grant may not meet the requirements of § 1498(a), from the limited record presented by the parties, it cannot be determined whether the ONR grant may authorize the necessary predicates for § 1498(a). However, even if Duke ultimately prevails on its assertion of § 1498(a) as an affirmative defense for its use of the '103 patent under the ONR grant, that does not mean that the district court's dismissal of the claim was without error. The ultimate factual and liability determinations are issues for the district court to determine initially on remand because in addition to evaluating the ONR grant and making the requisite findings, as it noted in its *Dismissal Opinion*, it has not yet determined which uses fall within the scope of the ONR grant and which uses are outside that scope. This determination, as well, seems necessary to support the dismissal in-part.

C. The District Court's Application of Experimental Use

On appeal, Madey asserts three primary errors related to experimental use. First, Madey claims that the district court improperly shifted the burden to Madey to prove that Duke's use was not experimental. Second, Madey argues that the district court applied an overly broad version of the very narrow experimental use defense inconsistent with our precedent. Third, Madey attacks the supporting evidence relied on by the district court as overly general and not indicative of the specific propositions and findings required by the experimental use defense, and further argues that there is no support in the record before us to allow any court to apply the very narrow experimental use defense to Duke's ongoing FEL lab operation. We substantially agree with Madey on all three points. In addition, Madey makes a threshold argument concerning the continued existence of the experimental use doctrine in any form, which we turn to first. Our precedent, to which we are bound, continues to recognize the judicially created experimental use defense, however, in a very limited form.

The Experimental Use Defense

Citing the concurring opinion in *Embrex*, Madey contends that the Supreme Court's opinion in *Warner-Jenkinson Co. v. Hilton Davis Chem. Co.*, eliminates the experimental use defense. The Supreme Court held in *Warner-Jenkinson* that intent plays no role in the application of the doctrine of equivalents. Madey implicitly argues that the experimental use defense necessarily incorporates an intent inquiry, and thus is inconsistent with *Warner-Jenkinson*. Like the majority in *Embrex*, we do not view such an inconsistency as inescapable, and conclude the experimental use defense persists albeit in the very narrow form articulated by this court in *Embrex*, and in *Roche*.

The District Court Improperly Shifted the Burden to Madey

The district court held that in order for Madey to overcome his burden to establish actionable infringement, he must establish that Duke did not use the patent-covered free electron laser equipment solely for experimental or other non-profit purposes. Madey argues that this improperly shifts the burden to the patentee and conflates the experimental use defense with the initial infringement inquiry.

We agree with Madey that the district court improperly shifted the burden to him. The district court folded the experimental use defense into the baseline assessment as to whether Duke infringed the patents. Duke characterizes the district court's holding as expressing the following sequence: first, the court recognized that Madey carried his burden of proof on infringement; second, the court held that Duke carried its burden of proof on the experimental use defense; and third, the court held that Madey was unable to marshal sufficient evidence to rebut Duke's shifting of the burden. We disagree with Duke's reading of the district court's opinion. The district court explicitly contradicts Duke's argument by stating that Madey failed to "meet its burden to establish patent infringement by a preponderance of the evidence." This statement is an assessment of whether Madey supported his initial infringement claim. It is not an assessment of which party carried or shifted the burden of evidence related to the experimental use defense. Thus, the district court did not conclude that Madey failed to rebut Duke's assertion of the experimental use defense. Instead, it erroneously required Madey to show as a part of his initial claim that Duke's use was not experimental. The defense, if available at all, must be established by Duke.

The District Court's Overly Broad Conception of Experimental Use

Madey argues, and we agree, that the district court had an overly broad conception of the very narrow and strictly limited experimental use defense. The district court stated that the experimental use defense inoculated uses that "were solely for research, academic, or experimental purposes," and that the defense covered use that "is made for experimental, non-profit purposes only." Both formulations are too broad and stand in sharp contrast to our admonitions in *Embrex* and *Roche* that the experimental use defense is very narrow and strictly limited. In *Embrex*, we followed the teachings of *Roche* and *Pitcairn* to hold that the defense was very narrow and limited to actions performed "for amusement, to satisfy idle curiosity, or for strictly philosophical inquiry." Further, use does not qualify for the experimental use defense when it is undertaken in the "guise of scientific inquiry" but has "definite, cognizable, and not insubstantial commercial purposes." The concurring opinion in *Embrex* expresses a similar view: use is disqualified from the defense if it has the "slightest commercial implication." Moreover, use in keeping with the legitimate business of the alleged infringer does not qualify for the experimental use defense.

Our precedent clearly does not immunize use that is in any way commercial in nature. Similarly, our precedent does not immunize any conduct that is in keeping with the alleged infringer's legitimate business, regardless of commercial implications. For example, major research universities, such as Duke, often sanction and fund research projects with arguably no commercial application whatsoever.

However, these projects unmistakably further the institution's legitimate business objectives, including educating and enlightening students and faculty participating in these projects. These projects also serve, for example, to increase the status of the institution and lure lucrative research grants, students and faculty.

In short, regardless of whether a particular institution or entity is engaged in an endeavor for commercial gain, so long as the act is in furtherance of the alleged infringer's legitimate business and is not solely for amusement, to satisfy idle curiosity, or for strictly philosophical inquiry, the act does not qualify for the very narrow and strictly limited experimental use defense. Moreover, the profit or non-profit status of the user is not determinative.

In the present case, the district court attached too great a weight to the non-profit, educational status of Duke, effectively suppressing the fact that Duke's acts appear to be in accordance with any reasonable interpretation of Duke's legitimate business objectives. On remand, the district court will have to significantly narrow and limit its conception of the experimental use defense. The correct focus should not be on the non-profit status of Duke but on the legitimate business Duke is involved in and whether or not the use was solely for amusement, to satisfy idle curiosity, or for strictly philosophical inquiry.

D. The District Court's Analysis of the Test Stand Gun Motion

In contrast to our conclusion that the district court erred in its dismissal-in-part of the alleged '103 patent infringement and its application of the experimental use defense, we find no error in the court's summary judgment conclusion that there is no genuine issue of material fact concerning Duke's non-use of the NCCU Microwave Gun Test Stand during the relevant time period.

Specifically, the district court found that NCCU, through the subcontractor agreement it had with Duke, owned the Microwave Gun Test Stand, and that Dr. Jones of NCCU controlled the gun with a key switch. Even though the gun was located on Duke's premises, Dr. Jones stated that no Duke faculty member or employee had used the gun during the relevant time period. This evidence of ownership, control, and no known Duke use, is sufficient to shift the summary judgment burden to Madey, who, in the district court's words, offers in response only bare allegations and speculation. Most of the response is testimony by Madey himself.

Madey contends that Duke and Dr. Jones have tacitly admitted to disputed questions of fact concerning whether Duke had any control or benefit over the Microwave Gun Test Stand. In addition, Madey contends that joint publications by Dr. Jones and Duke faculty, as well as research interests held by Duke faculty in areas potentially implicated by the Microwave Gun Test Stand, demonstrate disputed material facts about Duke's benefit and influence over the gun. Like the district court, we do not find that the record supports Madey's contentions, nor do we concur in the inferences in which Madey would have us draw.

In addition, we note that the record does not indicate that Madey plead any vicarious liability claims, such as alleging that Duke induced NCCU's infringement, or contributory infringement claims. To the extent that this was a strategic decision or tactical choice on Madey's part, he should not be allowed to overcome this choice now by acceptance of allegations and speculation as genuine issues of material fact.

E. Additional Matters

Finally, we note two additional matters in response to the parties' arguments before us and for the district court's attention on remand.

Duke's Assertion of a Government License Defense

Before this court, Duke argued vehemently that even if we did not agree with the district court's application of the experimental use defense that we could affirm the district court's judgment on alternate grounds: that the government had a license to have the patents at issue practiced on its behalf. We disagree with Duke's assertion because it overstates the information contained in the record on appeal. The only concrete evidence Duke cites is the statements on each of the patents noting that the government has rights in the patents. This, however, is insufficient because these short notations on the patents do not define the scope of the government's rights. None of the controlling contracts that would define the scope of such rights are provided in the record nor discussed by Duke in its arguments.

In addition, Duke discusses at length the Bayh-Dole Act, urging that this provides a basis to conclude that the scope of the rights granted to the government encompass Duke's use. Madey, however, notes that the provisions cited by Duke were enacted into law after Madey's two patents issued. Thus, some other provision may have generated the "government rights" notation on the two patents. In sum, this discussion serves to illustrate that the government license issue needs further development before the district court if it is to ultimately provide Duke the defense it seeks.

III. CONCLUSION

The district court erred in its application of the common law experimental use defense, and, consequently, incorrectly found that there was no genuine issue of material fact upon which Madey could prevail. In addition, the court's dismissal-in-part of Duke's use of the '103 patent embodiments under the government ONR grant was in error. Due to these errors, further proceedings are necessary. This includes the opportunity for the district court to reevaluate the issues we remand in light of this opinion, for the parties to litigate Duke's asserted government license defense, and for the court to potentially consider the state law claims in accordance with the case's progression. Accordingly, we affirm-in-part and reverse-in-part the district court's decision and remand for additional proceedings consistent with this opinion.

QUESTIONS

1. What is the impact of *Madey* on scientific research?

2. What is the impact of *Madey* on market competition?

3.   Would owners of patents on "research tools" receive compensation for their use if they could be used for "experimental purposes" without permission?

4.   Does *Madey* reach the right result for the wrong reasons?

5.   If you were counsel to a Congressional committee considering an experimental use exemption to patent infringement in a new patent reform bill, how would you draft the language for such an experimental use exemption?

CASE NOTES

1.   Applera is the exclusive licensee of the polymerase chain reaction (PCR) process covered by patents owned by Hoffman-La Roche. The PCR process is used to amplify DNA samples for various kinds of analyses. Applera sells preprogrammed thermal cyclers to perform the PCR process. Applera has a patent on the algorithm used in the program to control the temperature and time shifts necessary to perform the PCR process with an Applera thermal cycler. MJ Research also sells preprogrammed thermal cyclers that can be used to perform the PCR process. Applera sued MJ Research for direct infringement of its patented algorithm in the program used to control MJ Research's thermal cycler, and for inducing infringement of Applera's licensed PCR process by purchasers of MJ Research's thermal cyclers. MJ Research defended the infringement inducement charge, in part, by pointing to an article it distributed to customers which provided instructions on how to perform the PCR process *in situ*. In the article, MJ Research stated:

> [T]here is a common understanding that federal courts have historically interpreted patent & antitrust law to provide a "research exemption" to U.S. patents for research that has no commercial content. Should a reader wish to use the process described for a remunerative or commercial application, we strongly urge that proper patent licenses be obtained.

Applera claimed the article misinformed customers and encouraged infringement, thereby warranting enhanced damages for infringement inducement. What result? *See* Applera Corp. v. MJ Research Inc., 372 F.Supp.2d 233 (D. Conn. 2005).

Additional Information

1.   2 JOHN W. SCHLICHER, PATENT LAW, LEGAL AND ECONOMIC PRINCIPLES § 8:9 (2d ed. 2008).

2.   4 R. CARL MOY, MOY'S WALKER ON PATENTS §§ 14:75–14:80 (4th ed. 2008).

3.   Ted Hagelin, *The Experimental Use Exemption to Patent Infringement: Information on Ice, Competition on Hold*, 58 FLA. L. REV. 483 (2006).

4.   Norman Siebrasse, Keith Culver, *The Experimental Use Defense to Patent Infringement: A Comparative Assessment*, 56 U. TORONTO L.J. 333 (2006).

5.   Robert A. Migliorini, *The Narrowed Experimental Use Exception to Patent Infringement and Its Application to Patented Computer Software*, 88 J. PAT. & TRADEMARK OFF. SOC'Y 523 (2006).

6. Elizabeth A. Rowe, *The Experimental Use Exception to Patent Infringement: Do Universities Deserve Special Treatment?*, 57 HASTINGS L.J. 921 (2006).

7. Nicholas M. Zovko, *Nanotechnology and the Experimental Use Defense to Patent Infringement*, 37 MCGEORGE L. REV. 129 (2006).

8. Janice M. Mueller, *The Evanescent Experimental Use Exemption From United States Patent Infringement Liability: Implications for University and Nonprofit Research and Development*, 56 BAYLOR L. REV. 917 (2004).

9. Katherine J. Strandberg, *What Does the Public Get? Experimental Use and the Patent Bargain*, 2004 WIS. L. REV. 81 (2004).

10. Rochelle Dreyfuss, *Protecting the Public Domain of Science: Has the Time for an Experimental Use Defense Arrived?*, 46 ARIZ. L. REV. 457 (2004).

11. Melanie K. Kitzan Haindfield, *Is the Experimental Use Exemption to Patent Infringement Still Needed?*, 3 J. MARSHALL REV. INTELL. PROP. L. 103 (2003).

12. Janice M. Mueller, *No "Dilettante Affair": Rethinking the Experimental Use Exception to Patent Infringement for Biomedical Research Tools*, 76 WASH. L. REV. 1 (2001).

13. Michelle Walters, *De Minimis Use and Experimental Use Exceptions to Patent Infringement: A Comment on the Embrex Concurrence*, 29 AIPLA Q.J. 509 (2001).

14. Maureen A. O'Rourke, *Toward a Doctrine of Fair Use in Patent Law*, 100 COLUM. L. REV. 1177 (2000).

15. Eyal H. Barash, *Experimental Uses, Patents, and Scientific Progress*, 91 Nw. U. L. REV. 667 (1997).

16. David L. Parker, *Patent Infringement Exemptions for Life Science Research*, 16 HOUS. J. INT'L L. 615 (1994).

17. Jordan P. Karp, *Experimental Use as Patent Infringement: The Impropriety of a Broad Exception*, 100 YALE L.J. 2169 (1991).

18. Lauren C. Bruzzone, *The Research Exemption: A Proposal*, 21 AIPLA Q.J. 52 (1993).

19. Rebecca S. Eisenberg, *Patents and the Progress of Science: Exclusive Rights and Experimental Use*, 56 U. CHI. L. REV. 1017 (1989).

20. Richard E. Bee, *Experimental Use as an Act of Patent Infringement*, 39 J. PAT. & TRADEMARK OFF. SOC'Y 357 (1957).

21. Jeffrey R. Armstrong, *Bayh-Dole Under Siege: The Challenge to Federal Patent Policy as a Result of Madey v. Duke University*, 30 J.C. & U.L. 619 (2004).

5.3 HATCH-WAXMAN ACT INFRINGEMENT SAFE HARBOR

The complexity of health care reform is mirrored in Congress' attempt to handicap the prescription drug market. The pharmaceutical industry is composed of two types of firms — brand-name, or innovator, firms that invest heavily in research and development and introduce new drugs into the market; and generic, or follow-on, firms that manufacture copies of drugs already in the market. Both types of firms serve important social and economic goals. The safety and efficacy of all drugs, both brand-name and generic, must be reviewed and approved by the Food and Drug Administration (FDA) before they can be sold to the public. In the case of brand-name drugs, this is done by submitting a new drug application (NDA) to the FDA requesting approval to market the new drug upon satisfactory completion of clinical testing.

The development of a new drug is a lengthy process often taking 12 years or more. Some portion of this time is spent on in-house screening of chemical compounds, performing *in vitro* laboratory experiments and conducting animal test studies. However, the majority of development time is spent in clinical testing on human subjects to determine the safety, efficacy, dosage levels and adverse side effects of the new drug. Only upon satisfactory completion of these clinical tests will the FDA approve the new drug for sale to the public. However, the patent term continues to run during the FDA approval process.

In *Roach Products Inc. v. Bolar Pharmaceuticals Co.*, 733 F.2d 858 (C.A.F.C. 1984), the Court of Appeals for the Federal Circuit held that the testing of a patented brand-name drug to obtain information necessary for FDA approval of a generic version of the patented brand-name drug constituted an infringement of the brand-name patent owner's rights. Prohibiting a generic company from beginning the FDA approval process until the patent on the brand-name drug has expired is tantamount to extending the term of the brand-name drug patent. From the perspective of the brand-name drug patent owner, however, this *de facto* extension of the patent term serves to offset the time lost due to the FDA approval process.

Congress passed the Hatch-Waxman Act in 1984, which contained a series of amendments to the Patent Act and the Food, Drug and Cosmetic Act, in response to the *Bolar* decision. The stated objective of the Hatch-Waxman Act was to spur competition between brand-name and generic drug companies while also encouraging innovation by brand-name companies. The dilemma the Hatch-Waxman Act sought to solve was how to make current prescription drugs more affordable without reducing the supply of new prescription drugs in the future; or stated differently, how to limit the prices brand-name companies could charge for prescription drugs without limiting the profits available to brand-name companies to invest in the research and development of new prescription drugs.

The Hatch-Waxman Act attempted to solve this dilemma by giving new rights to both generic and brand-name manufacturers. The generic manufacturers were allowed to use brand-name patented drugs in order to obtain FDA approval for generic copies of the brand-name patented drugs. The generic manufacturers were also allowed to use the results of a brand-name drug's clinical trials to establish the safety and efficacy of a generic drug. Finally, generic manufacturers were given an incentive to challenge the patents on brand-name drugs. The first generic manufacturer that successfully challenged a brand-name drug patent by establishing that the patent was either invalid or that the generic drug did not infringe the brand-name patent was given a 180-day market exclusivity. No further generic drugs could be approved by the FDA until the first generic drug manufacturer's 180-day market exclusivity had expired.

The Hatch-Waxman Act gave brand-name manufacturers two new rights. First, brand-name manufacturers were granted an extension of their patent terms to compensate for the time lost during FDA review. However, this extension could not exceed 5 years, regardless of the length of time of the FDA review. Second, brand-name manufacturers were granted an automatic 30-month stay of FDA approval of a generic drug upon filing a patent infringement suit against a generic drug manufacturer.

The Hatch-Waxman Act allowed generic manufactures to submit a new type of drug approval application to the FDA called an "Abbreviated New Drug Application" or ANDA. In the ANDA, the generic manufacturer was required to establish that the generic drug was the bioequivalent of the previously approved brand-name drug and had the same active ingredient, method of use, dosage, strength, and labeling. Once a generic drug is shown to be the bioequivalent of a previously approved brand-name drug, the generic manufacturer is allowed to rely on the FDA's prior findings of safety and efficacy regarding the brand-name drug for approval of the generic drug. The generic manufacturer is also required to certify in the ANDA, in one of four ways, that marketing of the generic drug would not infringe patent rights in the previously approved brand-name drug.

The generic manufacturer must certify in the ANDA either that: (i) no patents have been listed for the brand-name drug; or (ii) the listed brand-name patents have expired; or (iii) FDA approval of the generic drug is not requested until expiration of the listed brand-name patents; or (iv) the listed brand-name patents are invalid or not infringed by the generic drug. When a generic manufacturer makes the last type of certification, the generic manufacturer must notify the brand-name patent owner stating the reasons why it believes the patents are invalid or not infringed. Upon receipt of the notification, the brand-name patent owner has 45 days to file an infringement suit against the generic drug manufacturer. If the infringement suit is filed within the time allowed, the brand-name patent owner is granted an automatic 30-month stay of FDA approval of the generic drug.

Under the 30-month stay, the FDA is prohibited from approving the ANDA until the expiration of the stay unless the patent at issue expires, or the court rules in favor of the generic manufacturer, at an earlier point in time. In the event the 30-month stay expires before the termination of the infringement suit, the generic manufacturer is given a 180-day period of market exclusivity beginning on the date of commercial sales. In the event of a favorable court decision, the 180-period of exclusivity begins on the date of the decision. A generic manufacturer receives no market exclusivity after a patent expires and must wait until the brand-name patent expires to enter the market if the court rules in favor of the brand-name company.

Finally, the Hatch-Waxman Act created an entirely new act of patent infringement. Recall the Act provided that use of a brand-name patented drug for purposes of obtaining FDA approval of a generic drug did not constitute patent infringement. So, on what basis could the brand-name manufacturer sue the generic manufacturer for infringement and trigger the 30-month stay? The Hatch-Waxman Act provided that it is an act of infringement to submit an ANDA to the FDA for a generic drug claimed in an existing brand-name patent. The generic manufacturer was free to use the brand-name patented drug and its clinical trials to obtain FDA approval, but it committed an act of patent infringement when it submitted this information in an ANDA. This bizarre new type of infringement is the basis for the infringement suit by the brand-name company against the generic manufacturer. The remedies for this new form of infringement include injunctive relief and money damages. However, money damages can only be awarded if there has been commercial manufacture, use or sale of the infringing generic drug product. In essence, the brand-name and generic companies both get a pass on the rules of ordinary patent litigation. The brand-name company can get an automatic 30-month stay without the need to establish the facts required for a preliminary injunction, and the generic manufacturer can get a determination of invalidity and/or non-infringement without the risk of monetary damages.

Since 1984, brand-name companies and generic companies have attempted to exploit ambiguities in the Hatch-Waxman Act and FDA rules to gain competitive advantage. These attempts have spawned numerous lawsuits, which often resolved some issues only to raise new issues. One issue of great concern to both brand-name companies and generic companies is the scope of the Hatch-Waxman infringement exemption. Section 271(e)(1) of the Patent Act states:

> "It shall not be an act of infringement to . . . use . . . a patented invention . . . solely for uses reasonably related to the development and submission of information under the Federal law which regulates the manufacture, use or sale of drugs . . ."

The *Merck* case below considers the question of whether the use of a patented invention in research which is not submitted to the FDA falls within the Hatch-Waxman safe harbor.

MERCK KGAA v. INTEGRA LIFESCIENCES I, LTD.
545 U.S. 193 (2005)

JUSTICE SCALIA.

This case presents the question whether uses of patented inventions in preclinical research, the results of which are not ultimately included in a submission to the Food and Drug Administration (FDA), are exempted from infringement by 35 U.S.C. § 271(e)(1).

I

It is generally an act of patent infringement to "mak[e], us[e], offe[r] to sell, or sel[l] any patented invention . . . during the term of the patent therefor." § 271(a). In 1984, Congress enacted an exemption to this general rule which provides:

> "It shall not be an act of infringement to make, use, offer to sell, or sell within the United States or import into the United States a patented invention (other than a new animal drug or veterinary biological product (as those terms are used in the Federal Food, Drug, and Cosmetic Act and the Act of March 4, 1913) . . .) solely for uses reasonably related to the development and submission of information under a Federal law which regulates the manufacture, use, or sale of drugs . . . ."

The Federal Food, Drug, and Cosmetic Act (FDCA), is "a Federal law which regulates the manufacture, use, or sale of drugs." Under the FDCA, a drugmaker must submit research data to the FDA at two general stages of new-drug development. First, a drugmaker must gain authorization to conduct clinical trials (tests on humans) by submitting an investigational new drug application (IND). The IND must describe "preclinical tests (including tests on animals) of [the] drug adequate to justify the proposed clinical testing." Second, to obtain authorization to market a new drug, a drugmaker must submit a new drug application (NDA), containing "full reports of investigations which have been made to show whether or not [the] drug is safe for use and whether [the] drug is effective in use." Pursuant to FDA regulations, the NDA must include all clinical studies, as well as preclinical studies related to a drug's efficacy, toxicity, and pharmacological properties.

II

A

Respondents, Integra Lifesciences I, Ltd., and the Burnham Institute, own five patents related to the tripeptide sequence Arg-Gly-Asp, known in single-letter notation as the "RGD peptide." The RGD peptide promotes cell adhesion by attaching to $\alpha_V \beta_3$ integrins, receptors commonly located on the outer surface of certain endothelial cells.

Beginning in 1988, petitioner Merck KGaA provided funding for angiogenesis research conducted by Dr. David Cheresh at the Scripps Research Institute (Scripps). Angiogenesis is the process by which new blood vessels sprout from existing vessels; it plays a critical role in many diseases, including solid tumor cancers, diabetic retinopathy, and rheumatoid arthritis. In the course of his research, Dr. Cheresh discovered that it was possible to inhibit angiogenesis by blocking the $\alpha_v \beta_3$ integrins on proliferating endothelial cells. In 1994, Dr. Cheresh succeeded in reversing tumor growth in chicken embryos, first using a monoclonal antibody (LM609) he developed himself and later using a cyclic RGD peptide (EMD 66203) provided by petitioner. Dr. Cheresh's discoveries were announced in leading medical journals and received attention in the general media.

With petitioner's agreement to fund research at Scripps due to expire in July

1995, Dr. Cheresh submitted a detailed proposal for expanded collaboration between Scripps and petitioner on February 1, 1995. The proposal set forth a 3-year timetable in which to develop "integrin antagonists as angiogenesis inhibitors," beginning with *in vitro* and *in vivo* testing of RGD peptides at Scripps in year one and culminating with the submission of an IND to the FDA in year three. Petitioner agreed to the material terms of the proposal on February 20, 1995 and on April 13, 1995, pledged $6 million over three years to fund research at Scripps. Petitioner's April 13 letter specified that Scripps would be responsible for testing RGD peptides produced by petitioner as potential drug candidates but that, once a primary candidate for clinical testing was in "the pipeline," petitioner would perform the toxicology tests necessary for FDA approval to proceed to clinical trials. Scripps and petitioner concluded an agreement of continued collaboration in September 1995.

Pursuant to the agreement, Dr. Cheresh directed *in vitro* and *in vivo* experiments on RGD peptides provided by petitioner from 1995 to 1998. These experiments focused on EMD 66203 and two closely related derivatives, EMD 85189 and EMD 121974, and were designed to evaluate the suitability of each of the peptides as potential drug candidates. Accordingly, the tests measured the efficacy, specificity, and toxicity of the particular peptides as angiogenesis inhibitors, and evaluated their mechanism of action and pharmacokinetics in animals. Based on the test results, Scripps decided in 1997 that EMD 121974 was the most promising candidate for testing in humans. Over the same period, Scripps performed similar tests on LM609, a monoclonal antibody developed by Dr. Cheresh. Scripps also conducted more basic research on organic mimetics designed to block <<alpha>>V<<beta>>3 integrins in a manner similar to the RGD peptides; it appears that Scripps used the RGD peptides in these tests as "positive controls" against which to measure the efficacy of the mimetics.

In November 1996, petitioner initiated a formal project to guide one of its RGD peptides through the regulatory approval process in the United States and Europe. Petitioner originally directed its efforts at EMD 85189, but switched focus in April 1997 to EMD 121974. Petitioner subsequently discussed EMD 121974 with officials at the FDA. In October 1998, petitioner shared its research on RGD peptides with the National Cancer Institute (NCI), which agreed to sponsor clinical trials. Although the fact was excluded from evidence at trial, the lower court's opinion reflects that NCI filed an IND for EMD 121974 in 1998.

B

On July 18, 1996, respondents filed a patent-infringement suit against petitioner, Scripps, and Dr. Cheresh in the District Court for the Southern District of California. Respondents' complaint alleged that petitioner willfully infringed and induced others to infringe respondents' patents by supplying the RGD peptide to Scripps, and that Dr. Cheresh and Scripps infringed the same patents by using the RGD peptide in experiments related to angiogenesis. Respondents sought damages from petitioner and a declaratory judgment against Dr. Cheresh and Scripps. Petitioner answered that its actions involving the RGD peptides did not infringe respondents' patents, and that in any event they were protected by the common-law research exemption and 35 U.S.C. § 271(e)(1).

At the conclusion of trial, the District Court held that, with one exception, petitioner's pre-1995 actions related to the RGD peptides were protected by the common-law research exemption, but that a question of fact remained as to whether petitioner's use of the RGD peptides after 1995 fell within the § 271(e)(1) safe harbor. With the consent of the parties, the District Court gave the following instruction regarding the § 271(e)(1) exemption:

> "To prevail on this defense, [petitioner] must prove by a preponderance of the evidence that it would be objectively reasonable for a party in [petitioner's] and Scripps' situation to believe that there was a decent prospect that the accused activities would contribute, relatively directly, to the generation of the kinds of information that are likely to be relevant in the processes by which the FDA would decide whether to approve the product in question.

> "Each of the accused activities must be evaluated separately to determine whether the exemption applies.

> "[Petitioner] does not need to show that the information gathered from a particular activity was actually submitted to the FDA."

The jury found that petitioner, Dr. Cheresh, and Scripps infringed respondents' patents and that petitioner had failed to show that its activities were protected by § 271(e)(1). It awarded damages of $15 million.

In response to post-trial motions, the District Court dismissed respondents' suit against Dr. Cheresh and Scripps, but affirmed the jury's damages award as supported by substantial evidence and denied petitioner's motion for judgment as a matter of law. With respect to the last, the District Court explained that the evidence was sufficient to show that "any connection between the infringing Scripps experiments and FDA review was insufficiently direct to qualify for the [§ 271(e)(1) exemption]."

A divided panel of the Court of Appeals for the Federal Circuit affirmed in part and reversed in part. The panel majority affirmed the denial of judgment as a matter of law to petitioner, on the ground that § 271(e)(1)'s safe harbor did not apply because "the Scripps work sponsored by [petitioner] was not clinical testing to supply information to the FDA, but only general biomedical research to identify new pharmaceutical compounds." It reversed the District Court's refusal to modify the damages award and remanded for further proceedings. Judge Newman dissented on both points. The panel unanimously affirmed the District Court's ruling that respondents' patents covered the cyclic RGD peptides developed by petitioner. We granted certiorari to review the Court of Appeals' construction of § 271(e)(1).

III

As described earlier, 35 U.S.C. § 271(e)(1) provides that "[i]t shall not be an act of infringement to . . . use . . . or import into the United States a patented invention . . . solely for uses reasonably related to the development and submission of information under a Federal law which regulates the . . . use . . . of drugs." Though the contours of this provision are not exact in every respect, the statutory text makes clear that it provides a wide berth for the use of patented drugs in activities related to the federal regulatory process.

As an initial matter, we think it apparent from the statutory text that § 271(e)(1)'s exemption from infringement extends to all uses of patented inventions that are reasonably related to the development and submission of *any* information under the FDCA. This necessarily includes preclinical studies of patented compounds that are appropriate for submission to the FDA in the regulatory process. There is simply no room in the statute for excluding certain information from the exemption on the basis of the phase of research in which it is developed or the particular submission in which it could be included.

Respondents concede the breadth of § 271(e)(1) in this regard, but argue that the only preclinical data of interest to the FDA is that which pertains to the safety of the drug in humans. In respondents' view, preclinical studies related to a drug's efficacy, mechanism of action, pharmacokinetics, and pharmacology are not reasonably included in an IND or an NDA, and are therefore outside the scope of the exemption. We do not understand the FDA's interest in information gathered in preclinical studies to be so constrained. To be sure, its regulations provide that the agency's "primary objectives in reviewing an IND are . . . to assure the safety and rights of subjects," but it does not follow that the FDA is not interested in reviewing information related to other characteristics of a drug. To the contrary, the FDA requires that applicants include in an IND summaries of the pharmacological, toxicological, pharmacokinetic, and biological qualities of the drug in animals. See § 312.23(a)(5); U.S. Dept. of Health and Human Services, Guidance for Industry, Good Clinical Practice: Consolidated Guidance 45 (Apr. 1996) ("The results of all relevant nonclinical pharmacology, toxicology, pharmacokinetic, and investigational product metabolism studies should be provided in summary form. This summary should address the methodology used, the results, and a discussion of the relevance of the findings to the investigated therapeutic and the possible unfavorable and unintended effects in humans"). The primary (and, in some cases, only) way in which a drugmaker may obtain such information is through preclinical *in vitro* and *in vivo* studies.

Moreover, the FDA does not evaluate the safety of proposed clinical experiments in a vacuum; rather, as the statute and regulations reflect, it asks whether the proposed clinical trial poses an "unreasonable risk." This assessment involves a comparison of the risks and the benefits associated with the proposed clinical trials. As the Government's brief, filed on behalf of the FDA, explains, the "FDA might allow clinical testing of a drug that posed significant safety concerns if the drug had a sufficiently positive potential to address a serious disease, although the agency would not accept similar risks for a drug that was less likely to succeed or that would treat a less serious medical condition." Accordingly, the FDA directs that an IND must provide sufficient information for the investigator to "make his/her own unbiased risk-benefit assessment of the appropriateness of the proposed trial." Such information necessarily includes preclinical studies of a drug's efficacy in achieving particular results.

Respondents contend that, even accepting that the FDA is interested in preclinical research concerning drug characteristics other than safety, the experiments in question here are necessarily disqualified because they were not conducted in conformity with the FDA's good laboratory practices regulations. This argument fails for at least two reasons. First, the FDA's requirement that preclinical studies be conducted under "good laboratory practices" applies only to experiments on drugs "to determine their safety." The good laboratory practice regulations do not apply to preclinical studies of a drug's efficacy, mechanism of action, pharmacology, or pharmacokinetics. Second, FDA regulations do not provide that even safety-related experiments not conducted in compliance with good laboratory practices regulations are not suitable for submission in an IND. Rather, such studies must include "a brief statement of the reason for the noncompliance."

The Court of Appeals' conclusion that § 271(e)(1) did not protect petitioner's provision of the patented RGD peptides for research at Scripps appeared to rest on two somewhat related propositions. First, the court credited the fact that the "Scripps-Merck experiments did not supply information for submission to the [FDA], but instead identified the best drug candidate to subject to future clinical testing under the FDA processes." The court explained:

> "The FDA has no interest in the hunt for drugs that may or may not later undergo clinical testing for FDA approval. For instance, the FDA does not require information about drugs other than the compound featured in an [IND] application. Thus, the Scripps work sponsored by [petitioner] was not "solely for uses reasonably related" to clinical testing for FDA."

Second, the court concluded that the exemption "does not globally embrace all experimental activity that at some point, however attenuated, may lead to an FDA approval process."

We do not quibble with the latter statement. Basic scientific research on a particular compound, performed without the intent to develop a particular drug or a reasonable belief that the compound will cause the sort of physiological effect the researcher intends to induce, is surely not "reasonably related to the development and submission of information" to the FDA. It does not follow from this, however, that § 271(e)(1)'s exemption from infringement categorically excludes either (1) experimentation on drugs that are not ultimately the subject of an FDA submission or (2) use of patented compounds in experiments that are not ultimately submitted to the FDA. Under certain conditions, we think the exemption is sufficiently broad to protect the use of patented compounds in both situations.

As to the first proposition, it disregards the reality that, even at late stages in the development of a new drug, scientific testing is a process of trial and error. In the vast majority of cases, neither the drugmaker nor its scientists have any way of knowing whether an initially promising candidate will prove successful over a battery of experiments. That is the reason they conduct the experiments. Thus, to construe § 271(e)(1), as the Court of Appeals did, not to protect research conducted on patented compounds for which an IND is not ultimately filed is effectively to limit assurance of exemption to the activities necessary to seek approval of a generic drug: One can know at the outset that a particular compound will be the subject of an eventual application to the FDA only if the active ingredient in the drug being tested is identical to that in a drug that has already been approved.

The statutory text does not require such a result. Congress did not limit § 271(e)(1)'s safe harbor to the development of information for inclusion in a submission to the FDA; nor did it create an exemption applicable only to the research relevant to filing an ANDA for approval of a generic drug. Rather, it exempted from infringement *all* uses of patented compounds "reasonably related" to the process of developing information for submission under *any* federal law regulating the manufacture, use, or distribution of drugs. We decline to read the "reasonable relation" requirement so narrowly as to render § 271(e)(1)'s stated protection of activities leading to FDA approval for all drugs illusory. Properly construed, § 271(e)(1) leaves adequate space for experimentation and failure on the road to regulatory approval: At least where a drugmaker has a reasonable basis for believing that a patented compound may work, through a particular biological process, to produce a particular physiological effect, and uses the compound in research that, if successful, would be appropriate to include in a submission to the FDA, that use is "reasonably related" to the "development and submission of information under . . . Federal law."

For similar reasons, the use of a patented compound in experiments that are not themselves included in a "submission of information" to the FDA does not, standing alone, render the use infringing. The relationship of the use of a patented compound in a particular experiment to the "development and submission of information" to the FDA does not become more attenuated (or less reasonable) simply because the data from that experiment are left out of the submission that is ultimately passed along to the FDA. Moreover, many of the uncertainties that exist with respect to the selection of a specific drug exist as well with respect to the decision of what research to include in an IND or NDA. As a District Court has observed, "[I]t will not always be clear to parties setting out to seek FDA approval for their new product exactly which kinds of information, and in what quantities, it will take to win that agency's approval." This is especially true at the preclinical stage of drug approval. FDA regulations provide only that "[t]he amount of information on a particular drug that must be submitted in an IND . . . depends upon such factors as the novelty of the drug, the extent to which it has been studied previously, the known or suspected risks, and the developmental phase of the drug." We thus agree with the Government that the use of patented compounds in preclinical studies is protected under § 271(e)(1) as long as there is a reasonable basis for believing that the experiments will produce "the types of information that are relevant to an IND or NDA."

****

QUESTIONS

1. The Court noted that "the District Court held that, with one exception, petitioner's pre-1995 actions related to the RGD peptide were protected by the common-law research exemption . . ." These pre-1995 activities included discovering that it was possible to inhibit angiogenesis by blocking certain integrins and

reversing tumor growth in chicken embryos. Do you think these activities would fall within the common law experimental use exemption as defined in *Madey*?

2.   How is the IND related to the NDA? Why does the Court find that the information contained in the IND is sufficient to satisfy the requirements of § 271(e)(1)?

3.   How does the Court distinguish "clinical testing to supply information to the FDA" from "general biomedical research to identify new pharmaceutical compounds"?

4.   In some cases, research with patented technology could be directed toward two possible purposes; a drug for treatment of a disease which would require FDA approval and an assay for use in laboratory research that would not require FDA approval. If you were counsel to a biotechnology company engaged in this type of dual-purpose research, how would you advise the company to proceed?

CASE NOTES

1.   Genentech and Insmed are biotechnology companies competing to develop a drug to treat children who suffer from Severe Primary Insulin-Like Growth Factor Deficiency (Severe Primary IGFD). Genentech was issued three patents related to the treatment of Severe Primary IGFD, but had not yet developed a drug based on these patents. Insmed did develop a drug called IPLEX to treat Severe Primary IGFD. Genentech claimed Insmed infringed its patents by using compounds claimed in the patents in the course of researching IPLEX. Insmed responded by claiming its research activities related to IPLEX were protected by the § 271(e)(1) safe-harbor. Genentech countered claiming that Insmed's infringing experiments were for commercial purposes and research for commercial purposes is not exempted by § 271(e)(1). What result? *See* Genentech, Inc. v. Insmed, Inc., 436 F.Supp.2d 1080 (N.D. Cal. 2006).

2.   *See also* Eli Lilly & Co. v. Medtronic, Inc., 496 U.S. 661 (The scope of the § 271(e)(1) safe-harbor extends to medical devices as well as drugs); Proveris Scientific Corp. v. Innovasystems, Inc., 536 F.3d 1256 (Fed. Cir. 2008) (Section 271(e)(1) does not cover a device used for characterizing aerosol sprays which FDA uses in approving inhaler-based drug delivery devices, but which has not itself been the subject of FDA approval); Classen Immunotherapies, Inc. v. Biogen IDEC, 381 F.Supp.2d 452 (D. Md. 2005) (Use of patented process in examining risks associated with various vaccination schedules was reasonably related to the development and submission of information required under the FDCA); Classen Immunotherapies, Inc. v. King Pharmaceuticals, Inc., 466 F.Supp.2d 621 (D. Md. 2006) (Use of a patented process in the study of a drug's bioavailability problem when the study results were submitted to the FDA is protected under § 271(e)(1)); Bristol-Meyers Squibb Co. v. Rhone-Poulenc Rorer, Inc., 2001 U.S. Dist. LEXIS 19361 (S.D.N.Y. 2001) (The scope of § 271(e)(1) extends to patented intermediary products used to produce products subject to FDA approval, but not themselves subject to FDA approval; patented products used to develop information for submission to the FDA are exempted by the § 271(e)(1) safe harbor, including patented research tools).

Additional Information

1. STEVEN Z. SZCZEPANSKI, DAVID M. EPSTEIN, 3 ECKSTROM'S LICENSING IN FOR. & DOM. OPS. §§ 13:24–13:26, 13:26.50–13:26.90 (2010).

2. R. CARL MOY, 4 MOY'S WALKER ON PATENTS §§ 14:68–14:74 (4th ed. 2010).

3. SHASHANK UPADHYE, GENERIC PHARMACEUTICAL PATENT AND FDA LAW § 9:3 (2011).

4. RONALD B. HILDRETH, PATENT LAW: A PRACTITIONER'S GUIDE, § 13:6 (2009).

5. ANN K. WOOSTER, 180 A.L.R. FED. 487 (2002).

6. Daniel Wobbekind, *Intergra Lifesciences I, Ltd. v. Merck KGAA: Re-Examining The Broad Scope Of The § 271(e)(1) Safe Harbor*, 23 BERKELEY TECH. L.J. 107 (2008).

7. Michael Sertic, *Muddying the Waters: How the Supreme Court's Decision in Merck v. Integra Fails to Resolve Problems of Judicial Interpretation of 35 U.S.C § 271(e)(1), The "Safe Habor" Provision of the Hatch-Waxman Act*, 17 HEALTH MATRIX 377 (2007).

8. Jonathan A. Hareid, *Testing Drugs and Testing Limits: Merck KGAA v. Integra Lifesciences 1, Ltd. and the Scope of the Hatch-Waxman Safe Harbor Provision*, 7 MINN. J.L. SCI. & TECH. 713 (2006).

9. Jonathan McPherson, *The Impact of the Hatch-Waxman Act's Safe Harbor Provision on Biomedical Research Tools After Merck KGAA v. Integra Lifesciences I, Ltd.*, 10 MICH. ST. U. J. MED. & L. 369 (2006).

10. Wolrad Prinz zu Waldeck und Pyrmont, *Research Tool Patents After Interga v. Merck — Have They Reached A Safe Harbor?*, 14 MICH. TELECOMM. & TECH. L. REV. 367 (2008).

11. Paul T. Nyffeler, *The Safe Harbor of 35 U.S.C. § 271(e)(1): The End of Enforceable Biotechnology Patents In Drug Discovery?*, 41 U. RICH. L. REV. 1025 (2007).

12. Rebecca Lynn, *Merck KGAA V. Integra Lifesciences I, LTD: Judicial Expansion Of § 271(e)(1) Signals A Need For A Broad Statutory Experimental Use Exemption In Patent Law*, 21 BERKELEY TECH. L.J. 79 (2006).

13. Marlan D. Walker, *The Patent Research Tool Problem After Merck V. Integra*, 14 TEX. INTELL. PROP. L.J. 1 (2005).

14. Elizabeth S. Weiswasser, Scott B. Danzis, *The Hatch-Waxman Act: History, Structure and Legacy*, 71 ANTITRUST L.J. 585 (2003).

15. Michael R. Mischnick, *Evaluating the Integraty of Biotechnology Research Tools: Merck v. Integra and the Scope of 35 U.S.C. Section 217(e)(1)*, 91 MINN. L. REV. 484 (2006).

16. Yi-Chen Su, Albert Wai-Kit Chan, *Too Costly to Defend: Who Is Benefited From the U.S. Supreme Court's Recent Holdings Concerning Biotechnology Patent Disputes*, 18 ALB. L.J. SCI. & TECH. 53 (2008).

Chapter 6

BANKRUPTCY

The word "bankrupt" comes from the sixteenth-century Italian phrase "banca rotta" which meant "to break the bench of a merchant." The word "bankruptcy" comes from seventeenth-century English and refers to the custom of creditors breaking the display counters of failing merchants. Whenever rumors swirled in London's Covent Garden that a merchant may be unable to pay his debts, creditors would siege the merchant's stall to recover any remaining goods to satisfy their loans. This first-come, first-served bankruptcy siege, not surprisingly, often resulted in fights among creditors and debtors. Modern bankruptcy laws were enacted to provide for a more orderly disposition of a debtor's assets when a debtor could no longer pay his creditors.

In the United States, the overwhelming majority of bankruptcy proceedings are Chapter 11 proceedings, which are commenced voluntarily by a debtor filing a petition of bankruptcy with the bankruptcy court. The ultimate goal of a Chapter 11 bankruptcy proceeding is to reorganize the business and restructure the debt so that the business may once again become commercially viable. Filing a petition of bankruptcy has two immediate effects. First, all of the debtor's assets are immediately placed in a bankruptcy estate under the control of the bankruptcy court. Second, there is an immediate automatic stay against creditors taking any actions to collect money from the debtor or to levy on the debtor assets. After the automatic stay, all actions affecting the debtor or the debtor's assets must be approved by the bankruptcy court. The day-to-day management of the bankruptcy estate is in the hands of the bankruptcy trustee. In a Chapter 11 bankruptcy, the debtor acts as the bankruptcy trustee and is often referred to as the "debtor in possession" or simply "debtor." All of the management decisions made by the debtor, however, must be approved by the bankruptcy court before they can be implemented.

Section 365 of the Bankruptcy Code permits the debtor, subject to the bankruptcy court's approval, to reject, assume, or assume and assign executory contracts. The most common definition of an executory contract, called the "Countryman definition" after the famed Harvard Law School professor Vern Countryman, provides that a contract is executory if the "obligations of both the bankrupt and the other party to the contract are so unperformed that the failure of either to complete performance would constitute a material breach excusing the performance of the other." Examples of material, continuing obligations are paying royalties, defending infringement actions and providing notice to the other party. If the debtor rejects an executory contract, the debtor is no longer bound by the contract; however, the rejection is deemed to be a breach of the contract which gives the non-debtor a pre-petition claim for damages. The pre-petition breach of contract damages claim is treated as an unsecured claim and included with the general creditors' claims. The practical result is that the non-breaching party will often receive pennies on the dollar for its damages claim.

If the debtor assumes an executory contract, the contract is, in essence, recreated and the debtor and non-debtor continue to perform under the contract exactly as they would absent the bankruptcy. However, in order to assume a contract, the debtor must first cure any outstanding defaults under the contract and provide adequate assurance of future performance to the non-debtor. Upon assumption of the contract, the contract obligations become the obligations of the bankruptcy estate. Breach of contract by the debtor after assumption gives rise to a post-petition damages claim, which is treated as a first-priority administrative claim and generally paid at 100 cents on the dollar.

In order to assume and assign an executory contract, the debtor must provide the non-debtor adequate assurance that the assignee can perform under the contract. Adequate assurance is loosely defined as more probable than not that the assignee will perform. Unless the license allows assignment, nonexclusive licenses cannot be assigned because nonexclusive licenses are considered to be personal rights of the licensee and not property rights. Generally, the same is true for exclusive licenses. Unless the license allows assignment, exclusive licenses cannot be assigned without the licensor's consent.

With respect to patent licenses, bankruptcy gives rise to different concerns on the part of the patent licensee and patent licensor. The patent licensee's primary concern in the case of licensor bankruptcy is with the licensee's ability to continue to use the patented technology in the event the licensor debtor rejects the license. The patent licensor's primary concern in the case of licensee bankruptcy is with the licensor's continued control over the licensed technology. As long as the licensee retains any rights under the license, the license becomes part of the bankruptcy estate and could be sold to a third party, including a competitor of the licensor.

The cases in this chapter deal with the issues of licensor and licensee bankruptcy, and the related issues of perfecting security interests in copyrights and patents in order to obtain senior creditor status. A senior creditor receives repayment of its claims before repayment of junior, unsecured creditor claims.

6.1 LICENSOR BANKRUPTCY

In *Lubrizol Enterprises v. Richmond Metal Finishers*, 756 F.2d 1043 (4th Cir. 1985), the court held that under § 365(g) of the Bankruptcy Code, a licensee's only remedy in the case of rejection of the license by a debtor licensor is money damages. The court explained that upon rejection of a license, a licensee's rights under the license were completely terminated and the licensee could not sue for specific performance, even if specific performance would ordinarily be available for breach of this type of contract. The *Lubrizol* decision sent shockwaves through industries that rely on technology licensing. Under the *Lubrizol* holding, licensees were totally at the mercy of debtor licensors. Debtor licensors could reject the license and then relicense the technology to another party, including a competitor of the original licensee, or the debtor licensors could relicense the technology to the original licensee on terms far more favorable to the debtor licensor.

Congress responded to the *Lubrizol* decision by enacting § 365(n) of the Bankruptcy Code. In general, Section 365(n) provides that, in the event that a trustee (debtor) rejects a patent license, the licensee can elect either to treat the rejection as a breach and seek damages, or to retain its rights under the license as they existed immediately prior to the rejection. A licensee who elected to retain its rights under the license would have to abide by all of the terms and conditions of the license, including payment of royalties. However, a licensee was not entitled to specific performance against the debtor licensor to enforce licensor contractual duties, such as provision of services or use of improvements to the licensed technology.

The *CellNet* case below deals with an issue of first impression under § 365(n). Can the ownership of royalties under a patent license be separated from the ownership of the patents that are the subject of the license?

IN RE CELLNET DATA SYSTEMS, INC.
327 F.3d 242 (3rd Cir. 2003)

NYGAARD, CIRCUIT JUDGE.

This appeal presents us with an issue of first impression involving elections under 11 U.S.C. § 365(n). CellNet Data Systems, Inc. sold its intellectual property to Schlumberger Resource Management Services, Inc., which specifically excluded the assets and liabilities of certain licensing agreements under the terms of the sale. After CellNet rejected those licensing agreements under 11 U.S.C. § 365(a) of the bankruptcy code, the licensee exercised its rights under § 365(n) to continue to use the intellectual property, subject to the royalty payments due under the original license. Both CellNet, as party to the contract, and Schlumberger, as holder of the intellectual property, claim the right to receive the royalty payments. The District Court determined that Schlumberger had expressly severed the royalties from the intellectual property by the terms of the purchase agreement and that the royalties remained in CellNet's estate. Although CellNet then rejected the license, the licensee, by operation of § 365(n), elected to enforce the license and thus the District Court concluded that the royalties due under the revived contract belonged to CellNet. We will affirm.

II. Background

The essential facts are not in dispute, rather how those facts operate is at issue. In 1997, CellNet, a developer of a wireless data network for meter reading, now in bankruptcy, entered into a joint venture with Bechtel Enterprises, Inc., forming a company called BCN Data Systems LLC. As part of the joint venture, CellNet entered into several licensing agreements with BCN, that provided BCN with an exclusive license to use CellNet's intellectual property outside the United States. In return, CellNet received a royalty payment equal to three percent of BCN's gross revenues. The License Agreements also contained a covenant that CellNet would provide technological support to BCN during the lifetime of the Agreements.

Three years later, with CellNet on the verge of bankruptcy, Appellant, Schlumberger, proposed the sale of CellNet's assets. Schlumberger and CellNet entered into a Proposal Letter under which Schlumberger would purchase "all or substantially all of the assets and business operations of [CellNet] and its subsidiaries." The January 31, 2000 Proposal Letter also provided that Schlumberger "would acquire all assets of [CellNet] free and clear of all liens other than certain liens to be agreed (the "Assets"), other than the Excluded Assets (as defined below), used in, held for use in, or related to the business and operations of [CellNet]." Thus, the proposal contemplated that certain assets of CellNet would not be subject to the ultimate purchase agreement. However, the term "Excluded Assets" was left open for future agreement by the parties.

CellNet filed for bankruptcy on February 4, 2000. On March 1, 2000, Schlumberger and CellNet entered into an Asset Purchase Agreement that mirrored the intent of the Proposal Letter, in that Schlumberger would purchase all of CellNet's assets, subject only to certain excluded assets. This time, however, the agreement included language that explained:

> At any time prior to March 25, 2000, [Schlumberger] shall be entitled unilaterally to amend this Agreement, including without limitation Schedules 1.01(a)(i) (Stock Acquired), 1.01(b) (Excluded Contracts) and 1.01(e) (Excluded Assets) attached hereto, solely for the purpose of excluding any or all of the stock, assets, liabilities and agreements of [CellNet] pertaining to [CellNet's] joint venture with Bechtel Enterprises, Inc., or its affiliates, (collectively, the "BCN Assets and Liabilities") from the stock, assets, liabilities and agreements being acquired or assumed by [Schlumberger] hereunder.

Thus, the Purchase Agreement provided that Schlumberger would purchase all of CellNet's intellectual property, etc., but would be able to specifically exclude all stocks, assets, liabilities, and agreements pertaining to CellNet's venture with BCN. Pursuant to a letter by counsel on March 24, 2000, Schlumberger elected to exercise its right to exclude the BCN assets and liabilities. The letter went on to specifically designate the License Agreements between CellNet and BCN as assets and liabilities excluded from the purchase under the heading "Excluded Contracts."

Despite excluding the License Agreements, Schlumberger asserted a right to the royalties under the Agreements prior to the approval of the Asset Purchase Agreement by the bankruptcy court. This was based on the belief that CellNet would have to reject the Agreements under § 365(a) as executory contracts that it could not fulfill and that Schlumberger would then be entitled to the royalties as owner of the underlying intellectual property. CellNet believed otherwise, but in an effort to complete the sale of its assets, agreed to reject the License Agreements and preserve the right of the parties to contest ownership of the royalties. The parties memorialized the decision to reject the License Agreements under § 365(a) in an additional section of the Asset Purchase Agreement. The new section read:

> [Schlumberger] has elected not to assume the License and Consulting Services Agreement between [CellNet] and BCN Data Systems, L.L.C. ("BCN"), dated January 1, 1997, the [OCDB License Agreement] between [CellNet] and BCN dated January 1, 1997 . . . (collectively, the "BCN

License Agreements"). [CellNet] shall obtain an order from the Bankruptcy Court pursuant to Section 365(a) of the Bankruptcy Code rejecting the BCN License Agreements. The parties hereto acknowledge that if BCN elects to retain its rights under the BCN License Agreements in accordance with Section 365(n)(1)(B) of the Bankruptcy Code, then the rights and obligations of the parties with respect to the License Agreements, including without limitation any royalty rights thereunder, are disputed by the parties. Each party reserves all rights under this Agreement with respect to the BCN License Agreements, and neither this Amendment nor any action taken in connection herewith, including the filing of any modified Sale Order, shall be deemed to be a waiver or admission of any matter related to the dispute between [CellNet] and [Schlumberger] regarding the BCN License Agreements.

Under this agreement, CellNet agreed to reject the License Agreements pursuant to § 365(a), but both parties acknowledged that a dispute over royalties would remain if BCN elected to retain its rights under § 365(n). On May 4, 2001, the Bankruptcy Court approved the Asset Purchase Agreement with both the addition, as well as additional language that further expressed that the sale did not alter the rights of CellNet, Schlumberger, or BCN regarding the License Agreements and the royalties due thereunder.

Following approval of the sale, CellNet moved to reject the License Agreements under § 365(a). Section 365(a) provides that "the trustee, subject to the court's approval, may assume or reject any executory contract or unexpired lease of the debtor." CellNet was permitted to act as the trustee because it was a debtor-in-possession pursuant to 11 U.S.C. § 1107(a). The Bankruptcy Court approved the motion and CellNet informed BCN of its election. BCN, in turn, chose to retain its rights under § 365(n). Section 365(n) provides that "[i]f a trustee rejects an executory contract under which the debtor is a licensor of a right to intellectual property, the licensee under such contract may elect" to either terminate the contract or retain certain rights under the license. Specifically, the licensee may elect:

> to retain its rights (including a right to enforce any exclusivity provision of such contract, but excluding any other right under applicable non-bankruptcy law to specific performance of such contract) under such contract and under any agreement supplementary to such contract, to such intellectual property . . . as such rights existed immediately before the case commenced . . . .

11 U.S.C. § 365(n)(1)(B).

If a licensee elects to retain its rights, section 365(n)(2)(B) of the Code requires it to "make all royalty payments due under such contract for the duration of such contract . . . ." By its election, and operation of § 365(n), BCN was permitted to continue to use the intellectual property originally licensed from CellNet, but was required to pay the royalties due under that license.

Rather than remain in a joint venture, CellNet and Bechtel agreed that Bechtel would acquire all of the assets and liabilities of BCN and make one lump sum payment to CellNet that would encompass the future royalty payments due under the License Agreements. The Bankruptcy Court approved the sale to Bechtel, and the negotiated amount of $2,250,000 for the future royalties was placed in escrow pending resolution of who was entitled to the royalties.

Both the Bankruptcy Court and the District Court found that CellNet was entitled to the royalties. In its opinion, the District Court addressed the same arguments now raised before us. Schlumberger argued that the Asset Purchase Agreement and its later rejection of the License Agreement did not operate to separate the right to the royalties from the underlying ownership of the intellectual property. Alternatively, Schlumberger asked the District Court to look past the original exclusion and find that because it owns the intellectual property and CellNet subsequently rejected the license under § 365(a), it has superior rights to the royalties.

In affirming the decision of the Bankruptcy Court in favor of CellNet, the District Court thoroughly analyzed the Asset Purchase Agreement and subsequent exclusion of License Agreements. After finding that the Purchase Agreement was not ambiguous, the District Court looked at the "express reservation" requirement necessary for the separation of royalties from intellectual property and decided that the Purchase Agreement could only be interpreted to separate the royalties due under the license from the intellectual property. The District Court also addressed Schlumberger's contention that it had superior rights under § 365 because it owned the intellectual property and CellNet had rejected the license pursuant to § 365(a). The District Court agreed with CellNet that the election of BCN pursuant to § 365(n) renewed certain obligations related to the license. The District Court found that under the License Agreements, the royalty payments were due to CellNet and that because Schlumberger had excluded those License Agreements from its purchase, CellNet "remains entitled to receive the BCN royalties pursuant to statutory authority even if it rejected the License Agreements and is not technically a party to them."

III. Discussion

A. The Effects of the Asset Purchase Agreement:

Schlumberger's first argument is that the Purchase Agreement and letter of March 2000 did not operate to sever the royalties from ownership of the intellectual property. Both the Bankruptcy Court and District Court disagreed and found that Schlumberger had separated ownership from its rights by the plain language of the Purchase Agreement and March Letter Amendment. These findings are clearly correct.

On appeal, Schlumberger points to two cases from the bankruptcy court that would require an express reservation to separate the components. In *Chemical Foundation, Inc. v. E.I. du Pont De Nemours & Co.* the court discussed the effects of assigning a patent on the right to receive royalties for that patent:

> Yet, as an assignment of a patent, without more, does not transfer to the
> assignee the right to recover damages or profits for prior infringements,

although royalties to accrue and damages and profits for future infringe-ments are incident to and accompany the patent unless separated by express reservation, and as a patentee may after assigning the patents sue and recover for past infringements, it would seem obvious that an assignor of a patent would have like rights with respect to royalties accrued at the time of the assignment. But the right to recover accrued royalties or damages and profits for past infringements may likewise be assigned.

Chemical espouses the proposition that royalties were inherent in ownership of a patent and flowed accordingly, although they could be divorced by an express reservation. This idea was expanded in *Crom v. Cement Gun Co.* where the court discussed the ownership of a patent. After quoting much of the above language in *Chemical*, the court found that:

> Where an assignment conveys all the assignor's right, title and interest, if the right to receive royalties is to be severed from the beneficial ownership of the patent and remain in the assignor, *there must be an express reservation or some agreement to that effect.* I do not think that the mere retention of the "license" is sufficient to make the severance, particularly where, as in the present case, it is merely for the purpose of protecting a supposed but nonexistent shop right and is in contravention of the understanding of the parties.

Unlike the cases Schlumberger cites, the unambiguous Purchase Agreement and March Letter Amendment present here did expressly sever the royalties. This conclusion has support in a straightforward reading of the documents. The Purchase Agreement permitted Schlumberger "unilaterally to amend this Agree-ment . . . solely for the purpose of excluding any or all of the stock, assets, liabilities and agreements of [CellNet] pertaining to [CellNet's] joint venture with Bechtel Enterprises, Inc." Beyond this language, the Purchase Agreement also explained that "[n]otwithstanding anything herein to the contrary, the Purchaser shall not purchase or acquire, and shall have no rights or liabilities with respect to, any Excluded Asset." The Purchase Agreement further defined "Excluded Assets" to include "all rights of the Sellers under any Excluded Asset" and "all proceeds from any Excluded Asset."

These sections must be read in concert with the March 24, 2000 Letter, which sought to specify those items excluded from the Purchase Agreement. In that letter, Schlumberger "elect[ed] to amend the Asset Purchase Agreement to exclude the BCN Assets and Liabilities from the stock, assets, liabilities and agreements of the Sellers being acquired or assumed under the Asset Purchase Agreement." The letter went on to specifically enumerate the various License Agreements between CellNet and BCN as excluded assets. Thus, Schlumberger expressly sought to exclude all rights and liabilities under the License Agreements, including its rights to all proceeds under those Agreements.

Schlumberger now attempts to argue that the Purchase Agreement and March Letter (both of which it drafted) are ambiguous and that extrinsic evidence is necessary to decide whether the Purchase Agreement contemplated severance of the royalties. This argument is unpersuasive. As the District Court correctly noted:

The Asset Purchase Agreement and March 24 letter contain no ambiguities and, by those documents, Schlumberger excluded the License Agreements from the assets it was acquiring. While Schlumberger has argued that, under this pattern of events, it is entitled to receive the royalties from BCN, either as a matter of contract law or under the Bankruptcy Code, both parties agree the Asset Purchase Agreement and March 24 letter accurately represent the parties' intentions. Thus, it is only the legal effect of the transaction that Schlumberger challenges.

Under New York law, "ambiguity does not exist "simply because the parties urge different interpretations." " When Schlumberger elected to exclude "all the proceeds from [the BCN License Agreements]" it expressly excluded the royalties from these agreements from the intellectual property it was purchasing. The effect of this exclusion is that the License Agreements remain in CellNet's estate.

Schlumberger also finds fault with the District Court's holding that "[b]ecause the right to royalties arises only from the License Agreements, Schlumberger's exclusion of those agreements (and the royalties they set forth) was unambiguous and effective." Instead, Schlumberger argues that the right to the royalties derives from ownership of the intellectual property and not from the License Agreements. As a general proposition, Schlumberger is correct that it is the intellectual property that creates the right to royalties — as an owner may parcel out its "bundle of rights." However, this argument does not alter our analysis under these factual circumstances. At the time the License Agreements were created, CellNet owned the intellectual property and thus could license the right of exclusivity outside the United States to BCN in exchange for royalties. This separation of rights from the "bundle" was memorialized in the License Agreements. When Schlumberger purchased the intellectual property owned by CellNet, the license already existed and, pursuant to § 365(n), would likely continue to exist. Based on Schlumberger's acceptance that they would be purchasing CellNet's intellectual property subject to BCN's rights, and that BCN's rights existed solely from the excluded licenses, what Schlumberger bought was less than the full "bundle of rights" associated with ownership.

Thus, the initial right to royalties arose from the ownership of the intellectual property, but after Schlumberger elected to exclude the License Agreements, it severed those rights from the bundle it was purchasing. Once the royalties were divorced from the intellectual property, the only authority for their existence was the License Agreement. Because Schlumberger had excluded the Agreements, CellNet remained a party to those Agreements and would be entitled to the royalties thereunder.

Finding that CellNet would be otherwise rightfully entitled to the royalties once Schlumberger separated the royalties from the intellectual property that it purchased, we now turn to the question of how CellNet's rejection of the License Agreements under 11 U.S.C. § 365(a) and BCN's subsequent revival under § 365(n) affects the rights of the parties.

B. After the 11 U.S.C. § 365(n) Election, Who is Entitled to the Royalties?

Under the Bankruptcy Code, a trustee may elect to reject or assume its obligations under an executory contract. This election is an all-or-nothing proposition — either the whole contract is assumed or the entire contract is rejected. 11 U.S.C. § 365(a). Pursuant to its Purchase Agreement with Schlumberger, CellNet, as trustee, rejected the License Agreements under 365(a). Normally in bankruptcy, this would end the obligations between the contracting parties and relegate the non-breaching party to an unsecured creditor. *See In Re Trans World Airlines* ("If the lease is rejected, a creditor's claim for the stream of future rental payments due under the now-rejected lease is denied post-petition administrative status and is treated as an unsecured pre-petition claim"). Congress, however, altered this system by passing an amendment that added § 365(n). Section 365(n) only applies to intellectual property and grants the licensee of intellectual property certain rights not enjoyed by other contracting parties. Specifically, if a trustee rejects an executory contract under § 365(a), the licensee of intellectual property may elect either:

> (A) to treat such contract as terminated by such rejection if such rejection by the trustee amounts to such a breach as would entitle the licensee to treat such contract as terminated by virtue of its own terms, applicable non-bankruptcy law, or an agreement made by the licensee with another entity; or

> (B) to retain its rights (including a right to enforce any exclusivity provision of such contract, but excluding any other right under applicable non-bankruptcy law to specific performance of such contract) under such contract and under any agreement supplementary to such contract, to such intellectual property (including any embodiment of such intellectual property to the extent protected by applicable non-bankruptcy law), as such rights existed immediately before the case commenced, for — (i) the duration of such contract; and (ii) any period for which such contract may be extended by the licensee as of right under applicable non-bankruptcy law.

11 U.S.C. § 365(n)(1)(A)–(B).

Looking to the facts before us, Schlumberger excluded the License Agreements from its purchase, and then CellNet rejected the Agreements under § 365(a). In turn, BCN elected to retain its rights and was thus obligated to "make all royalty payments due under such contract for the duration of such contract." 11 U.S.C. § 365(n)(2)(B). Schlumberger argues that because CellNet rejected the contract, it has not assumed the benefits of the contract and thus has no rights under the contract. Schlumberger then posits that because it owns the underlying intellectual property, it has superior rights to the royalties-despite not purchasing the License Agreements. We disagree.

The District Court found that CellNet was entitled to the royalties because "§ 365(n) of the Bankruptcy Code renews certain obligations related to the license." Despite Schlumberger's argument that because "§ 365(n)(2) does not designate that the payment of royalties must be made to any particular party," it should be entitled to the royalties, the District Court focused instead on the language stating that the "licensee shall make all royalty payments due under such contract." The District Court concluded "that Congress intended the language "due under the contract" to provide both the quantity of the royalty payments and the designation of the party intended to receive those payments, whether the debtor or its contractual assignee." Because Schlumberger excluded the contract from its purchase, "CellNet remains entitled to receive the BCN royalties pursuant to statutory authority even if it rejected the License Agreements and is not technically a party to them." The District Court concluded that "royalty payments made pursuant to § 365(n)(2)(B) of the Bankruptcy Code are the property of the licensor, even though the licensor may have transferred its intellectual property assets during the bankruptcy."

Schlumberger makes essentially three arguments related to the effects of § 365(n). First, Schlumberger claims that CellNet has no rights because it rejected the contract under § 365(a). To support this conclusion, Schlumberger cites our opinion in *In Re Bildisco* where we held that "as a matter of law, a debtor-in-possession is "[a] new entity . . . created with its own rights and duties, subject to the supervision of the bankruptcy court." " Schlumberger claims that this demonstrates that the License Agreements were not part of the estate because they were never assumed by CellNet as debtor-in-possession. Schlumberger is incorrect. In *NLRB v. Bildisco* the Supreme Court affirmed our previously cited opinion. The Court, however, stated that:

> Obviously if the [debtor-in-possession] were a wholly "new entity," it would be unnecessary for the Bankruptcy Code to allow it to reject executory contracts, since it would not be bound by such contracts in the first place. For our purposes, it is sensible to view the debtor-in-possession as the same "entity" which existed before the filing of the bankruptcy petition, but empowered by virtue of the Bankruptcy Code to deal with its contracts and property in a manner it could not have done absent the bankruptcy filing.

This implies that the License Agreements were property of the bankruptcy estate after Schlumberger excluded them and before CellNet rejected them. Schlumberger contends that the act of rejection serves to remove the contract from the bankruptcy estate and points to *In Re Access Beyond Technologies, Inc.* for the proposition that "[a]n executory contract does not become an asset of the estate until it is assumed pursuant to § 365(a) of the Code." That case however, is factually distinguishable from ours. In *Access*, the debtor attempted to assign its rights under a patent cross-license agreement. The debtor characterized the transaction as a sale under 11 U.S.C. § 363, but the court held that the debtor must first assume the agreement in order to transfer it. The court noted that otherwise, "[i]f the debtor does not assume an executory contract, it is deemed rejected. Thus, if a debtor does not assume an executory contract before he sells it . . ., the buyer may be purchasing an illusion: the executory contract will disappear on conclusion of the bankruptcy case." *Access* did not deal with our situation, which involves an executory contract *after* an election by a licensee under § 365(n). We need not specify the exact status of the contract. For our purposes it is suffice to say that after a licensee has resorted to § 365(n), the *rights* of the contract as they existed pre-petition and pre-rejection are in force.

The plain language of § 365(n)(2)(B) indicates that the renewed royalties are directly linked to the rejected contract, not the intellectual property. The section specifically provides that the "licensee shall make all royalty payments due *under such contract* for the duration *of such contract*." Thus, the contract is the primary mechanism for determining where the royalties flow. Although Schlumberger is correct that § 365(n)(2)(B) does not specify that the royalties must be paid to the trustee, the immediately preceding section says that "trustee shall allow the licensee to exercise such rights," and the next section deals with the rights of the licensee against the trustee. The several sections of § 365(n)(2) make sense only in contemplation of an ongoing relationship between the licensee and the licensor/trustee.

Schlumberger next argues that the legislative history of § 365(n) favors awarding it the royalties. It notes that the legislative history of § 365(n) explains that the subsection parallels § 365(h), which deals with real estate and allows a similar retention of rights by holders of real estate leases. With this link in place, Schlumberger analogizes that its position in this case would be the equivalent of where a purchaser bought a shopping center, but did not assume the lease of an occupying tenant. Under § 365(h), the tenant could choose to remain in possession and pay rent, but the rent would belong to the new owner. According to Schlumberger, the position taken by CellNet and the District Court would alter the above situation and provide that the tenant could still remain in possession, but would pay rent to the former owner of the shopping center.

Although this analogy is powerful, and the logic deceptively simple, Schlumberger's reasoning is specious because it rests on a flawed comparison of the parties. Although both sections of the Bankruptcy Code discuss their respective elections as being limited by non-bankruptcy law, the concept of tenants remaining in possession when a new landlord gains control is fraught with state law property principles not applicable in the intellectual property context. We find that there is no relationship between Schlumberger and the License Agreements — which it specifically did not purchase — that can be equated with the relationship of possessory control by a new landlord over a tenant remaining in possession.

Schlumberger's final argument is that the long-standing principle that the benefits of a contract should accompany the burden dictates that they should retain the royalties. Its argument, however, is trumped by the facts. It is true that the burden of the License Agreements falls on Schlumberger, who cannot use the intellectual property outside the United States and that the benefit to that burden is the royalty payments. However, state law allows the severance of the benefit from the burden and Schlumberger has done just that by excluding the License Agreement from its purchase and not contracting with CellNet for the royalties.

IV. Conclusion

We will affirm the decision of the District Court. Schlumberger expressly excluded the License Agreement from its purchase of CellNet's intellectual property and thus severed the benefit of royalties from the associated burdens. Although CellNet rejected the License Agreements pursuant to 11 U.S.C. § 365(a), certain rights were renewed under the License Agreements by operation of BCN's

§ 365(n) election. If Schlumberger had wanted the royalties, they only needed to purchase the License Agreements or contract with CellNet for the royalties as part of the Purchase Agreement. As they did neither, they are not entitled to the royalties from the BCN License Agreements.

QUESTIONS

1. Why do you think Schlumberger wanted to exclude all stocks, assets, liabilities and agreements pertaining to CellNet's venture with BCN from the Asset Purchase Agreement?

2. Schlumberger argued that even if the Asset Purchase Agreement did separate the patent licenses from the patents themselves, CellNet's rejection of the license agreements under § 365(a) terminated CellNet's right to receive royalties and, thereafter, the royalties should be paid to Schlumberger as owner of the patents. How did the court respond to this argument?

3. Is there any difference between CellNet assuming the licenses and CellNet rejecting the licenses followed by BCN's election to retain its rights under the licenses?

4. Is the debtor in possession a "new entity"? What difference would this make in the case of CellNet?

5. How do the rights of a licensee differ between the debtor licensor's assumption of the license and the debtor licensor's rejection of the license followed by the licensee's election to retain its rights pursuant to § 365(n)(1)(B)?

6. Section 365(n) applies only to executory contracts involving intellectual property. In § 101(56) of the Bankruptcy Code, Congress lists the types of intellectual property included under § 365(n) as trade secrets, inventions, processes, designs, or plants protected under title 35, patent applications, plant varieties, works of authorship protected under title 17, and mask works protected under Chapter 11 of Title 17. What important type of intellectual property is not included in this list? What problems could its omission create?

7. If you were counsel to Schlumberger, could you draft a contract provision that clearly gave Schlumberger ownership of the licenses, but also clearly immunized Schlumberger from any liability to BCN?

CASE NOTES

1. Matusa is the franchisor debtor in a Chapter 11 bankruptcy proceeding. INC. is the franchisee. The franchise agreement gives INC. the exclusive right to make rum using a secret formula, to distribute the rum and to use the trademarked name for the rum. The secret formula for making the rum was developed in 1872 in Cuba by the common ancestors of Matusa and the INC. owners. For over 100 years, the two different branches of the family worked together harmoniously in the rum-making business. In 1981, however, a bitter family feud erupted and the parties ceased to deal with one another as business partners or as family members. In 1982, Matusa claimed that INC. had breached the franchise agreement and threatened to

terminate the franchise agreement if INC. did not cure the breach within 30 days. INC. denied it had breached the franchise agreement, and Matusa brought suit in federal district court to terminate the agreement. After the district court rejected Matusa's breach claim, Matusa appealed to the Eleventh Circuit Court of Appeals, which also rejected Matusa's breach claim. Matusa then filed a Chapter 11 bankruptcy petition and sought to reject the franchise agreement as an executory contract. In Metusa's motion to the bankruptcy court to allow the rejection of the franchise agreement, Metusa argued that § 365(n) did not apply to the facts of the case because trademarks were not included as "intellectual property" in § 101(56). INC. argued in response that the secret formula for making rum was a trade secret, which is included as intellectual property in § 101(56); that Matusa had not been actively engaged in distillation, distribution or sale of rum products since 1981; that Matusa had no employees, no machinery, no equipment, no production facilities, no warehouses, no tangible assets and no inventory with which to conduct the franchise business should the rejection be allowed; that allowing Matusa's rejection of the franchise agreement would totally destroy INC.'s currently very profitable business; and that Matusa had no business plan for conducting the business in the event that the court allowed the franchise agreement to be rejected. What result? *See* In re Ron Matusalem, 158 B.R. 514 (Bankr. S.D.Fla 1993) for the witty and erudite answer.

2. *See also* In re Prize Frize, Inc., 32 F.3d 426 (9th Cir. 1994) (Regardless of the language used in the license agreement, all money to be paid by licensee under the agreement were "royalties" for purposes of the Bankruptcy Code provision authorizing licensees of debtor intellectual property to elect to retain its rights to the intellectual property for the duration of the contract following rejection by the debtor by making royalty payments due under the contract; whether payments were labeled "licensing fees" or "royalties," they must be paid by the licensee who elects to keep its license after the licensor's bankruptcy); In re Storm Tech., Inc., 260 B.R. 152 (Bankr. N.D. Cal. 2001) (Company that sold and assigned patents in scanner technology to a Chapter 7 debtor prepetition, pursuant to an agreement whereby upon default on debtor's payment obligation company would have a license in patents, could not assert a license in patents because company's rights under the agreement were frozen when debtor filed its bankruptcy petition; the debtor's default did not occur prepetition, but occurred postpetition when the debtor filed its petition in bankruptcy); Szombathy v. Controlled Shredders, Inc., No. 97 C 481, 1997 U.S. Dist. LEXIS 5168 (N.D. Ill. 1997) (When a licensee elects to retain its rights under § 365(n) after rejection of the license by the trustee, the licensee is entitled to continue to use the underlying intellectual property, but only in the state that it existed on the day of the bankruptcy filing; licensee is not entitled to any modifications or improvements which came into existence postpetition); In re Petur U.S.A. Instrument Co., Inc., 35 B.R. 561 (Bankr. W.D. Wash. 1983) (Bankruptcy court will not authorize debtor's rejection of an executory contract where granting the motion would result in destruction of the business of the nondebtor party and damages sustained by the nondebtor party would be grossly disproportionate to any benefit derived by general creditors); FutureSource LLC v. Reuters, Ltd., 312 F.3d 281 (7th Cir. 2002) (Bankruptcy court's sale order, which stated that a news service that purchased the assets of a debtor took such assets free and clear of all "liens, claims, interests and encumbrances," extinguished all "interests" in the

assets acquired by the news service, including competitor's interest or license in the intellectual property acquired by the news service).

Additional Information

1. 5 ROBERT A. MATTHEWS, JR., ANNOTATED PATENT DIGEST § 35:48 (2009).

2. BANKRUPTCY LAW MANUAL § 8:51 (5th ed. 2010).

3. NICK J. VIZY, CORPORATE COUNSEL'S GUIDE TO LICENSING § 24:8 (2010).

4. RAYMOND T. NIMMER & JEFF DODD, MODERN LICENSING LAW §§ 15:27–15:30 (2009).

5. MARK S. HOLMES, PATENT LICENSING: STRATEGY, NEGOTIATIONS AND FORMS § 3:5.7 (2008).

6. Stuart M. Riback, *Intellectual Property Licenses: The Impact of Bankruptcy*, 950 PATENTS, COPYRIGHTS, TRADEMARKS, AND LITERARY PROPERTY COURSE HANDBOOK SERIES 647 (2008).

7. Anthony Giaccio, *The Effect of Bankruptcy on the Licensing of Intellectual Property Rights*, 2 ALB. L.J. SCI. & TECH. 93 (1992).

8. Imran A. Khaliq, *The Effect of Bankruptcy on Intellectual Property License Agreements*, 8 INTELL. PROP. L. BULLETIN 12 (2003).

9. Rudolph J. Di Massa, Matthew E. Hoffman, *Assumption and Assignment of IP License Agreements in Bankruptcy: Circuit Split Continues*, 27 AM. BANKR. INST. J. 20 (Mar. 2008).

10. Karen Turner, Craig S. Blumsack, *The Licensing of Intellectual Property in Bankruptcy*, 24 AM. BANKR. INST. J. 22 (Oct. 2005).

11. Aleta A. Mills, *The Impact of Bankruptcy on Patent and Copyright Licenses*, 17 BANKR. DEV. J. 575 (2001).

6.2 LICENSEE BANKRUPTCY

Section 365(c)(1) of the Bankruptcy Code provides that the trustee may not assume or assign any executory contract if applicable nonbankruptcy law excuses the nondebtor party to the contract from accepting performance from, or rendering performance to, any entity other than the debtor. In the case of intellectual property, the applicable nonbankruptcy law is federal common law, which generally restricts the licensees' ability to transfer or assign their intellectual property rights, under both nonexclusive and exclusive licenses, without the consent of the licensor. As you will see, there is a split of authority among the federal circuits on the interpretation of § 365(c)(1). The Third, Fourth, Ninth and Eleventh Circuit Courts of Appeals have adopted what is called the "hypothetical test." Under the "hypothetical test," if the debtor licensee cannot assign the license agreement, the debtor licensee also cannot assume the license agreement. It doesn't matter whether the debtor licensee has any intent to assign the license agreement; if the debtor licensee could not hypothetically assign the license agreement, then the debtor licensee cannot assume the license agreement.

The First, Fifth, Eighth and Tenth Circuits have adopted what is called the "actual test." Under the "actual test," the court considers the issue of debtor licensee assumption on a case-by-case basis and asks whether the debtor licensee has an actual intent to assign the license. If the debtor licensee has no actual intent to assign the license, then the debtor licensee can assume the license. If the debtor licensee has an actual intent to assign the license, then the debtor licensee cannot assume the license.

In re Aerobox Composite Structures considers the relative merits of the "hypothetical" and "actual" tests, and the interpretations of § 365(c)(1) which support each test.

IN RE AEROBOX COMPOSITE STRUCTURES, LLC
373 B.R. 135 (Bkrtcy. D. N.M. 2007)

MARK B. McFEELEY, BANKRUPTCY JUDGE.

THIS MATTER is before the Court on the Motion to Compel Rejection of Patent and Technology License and/or for Relief from the Automatic Stay to Exercise Applicable Nonbankruptcy Rights ("Motion") filed by Tubus Bauer GmbH ("Tubus Bauer"), by and through its attorneys of record, Sherin and Lodgen LLP (Thomas H. Curran and Matthew L. Mitchell). The Motion requests the Court to compel the Debtor to reject the pre-petition Patent and Technology License Agreement ("License Agreement") between Tubus Bauer and Aerospace Composite Structures LLC, and/or to lift the automatic stay to permit Tubus Bauer to cancel the License Agreement. The Unsecured Creditor's Committee (the "UCC"), Aerobox Composite Structures, LLC, formerly known as Aerospace Composite Structures LLC ("Aerobox" or the "Debtor"), and Posterus Corporation, the Debtor's post-petition financier, oppose the Motion. The Court held a final hearing on the Motion on July 20, 2007 and took the matter under advisement. At issue is whether 11 U.S.C. § 365(c)(1) precludes a debtor-in-possession from assuming an executory contract, regardless of whether the debtor-in-possession has, in fact, sought to assume the contract, or intends to assign the contract to another entity. After consideration of the relevant code sections and the applicable case law, the Court finds that 11 U.S.C. § 365(c)(1) does not prohibit a debtor-in-possession from assuming an executory contract. Accordingly, the Motion will be denied.

FACTS

Aerobox filed a voluntary petition under Chapter 11 of the Bankruptcy Code on January 23, 2007. Pre-petition, Aerobox and Tubus Bauer entered into the License Agreement pursuant to which Tubus Bauer granted Aerobox an exclusive license within North America to use certain patent rights and confidential information for the "in house" manufacture and use of Tubus Polypropelene honeycomb, and a non-exclusive license in North America for the use of certain patent rights and confidential information to manufacture Tubus Polypropelene honeycomb for resale as value added thermoplastic sandwich panels.

The term of the License Agreement is for a period of 15 years, beginning January 10, 2004, with automatic renewal for an indefinite term, unless either party terminates the License Agreement with three months notice. The License Agreement provides for assignment only after prior written approval by Tubus Bauer, but provides further that Tubus Bauer will not unreasonably withhold its approval. All monetary consideration due Tubus Bauer for the use of the license and patent rights under the License Agreement has been paid in full. As of the date of the final hearing on the Motion, Tubus Bauer's representative, Rainer Duchene, testified that he is not aware of any failures of the Debtor to comply with any of the terms of the License Agreement.

The License Agreement contains an *ipso facto* clause that provides for termination of the License Agreement if Aerobox "becomes insolvent or is adjudged bankrupt, liquidates its business, makes an assignment for the benefit of creditors or a receiver or trustee is appointed to administer or conduct all or a substantial party of [Aerobox's] business or property." To date, Debtor has not sought to assume or assign the License Agreement as part of its reorganization efforts under Chapter 11.

POSITIONS OF THE PARTIES

Tubus Bauer asserts that the License Agreement is an executory contract that cannot be assumed or assigned under 11 U.S.C. § 365(c)(1), such that the Debtor must either be compelled to reject it, or the automatic stay must be lifted since the Debtor is precluded as a matter of law by operation of 11 U.S.C. § 365(c)(1) from assumption or assignment of the License Agreement. Tubus Bauer relies primarily on *In re Catapult Entertainment, Inc.* which held that the plain language of 11 U.S.C. § 365(c)(1) compels application of a "hypothetical test" to determine whether an executory contract can be assumed or assigned. Under the "hypothetical test," if applicable nonbankruptcy law precludes assignment of an executory contract to a third party, a debtor may not assume or assign the contract notwithstanding that the debtor may have no intention whatsoever of assigning the contract at issue to a third party.

The UCC acknowledges that several courts have applied the "hypothetical test" to 11 U.S.C. § 365(c)(1), but urges the Court to apply the "actual test" articulated by the First Circuit in *Institut Pasteur v. Cambridge Biotech Corp.* or the test adopted and employed by the court in *In re Footstar, Inc.* (the "Footstar Test"). Under the "actual test" the court must make a case-by-case inquiry to determine "whether the nondebtor party . . . *actually* was being "forced to accept performance under its executory contract from someone other than the debtor party with whom it originally contracted." "

The Debtor and the UCC also question whether the License Agreement is an executory contract, and contend further that Tubus Bauer's absolute refusal to consent to the Debtor's assumption or assignment of the License Agreement is contrary to the terms of the License Agreement which provide that Tubus Bauer will not unreasonably withhold consent to assignment.

DISCUSSION

As a preliminary matter the Court must determine whether the License Agreement is an executory contract, since, if it is not an executory contract, 11 U.S.C. § 365, which restricts assumption and assignment of executory contracts and unexpired leases, does not come into play. The Bankruptcy Code does not define "executory contract." Generally, a contract is executory for purposes of § 365(a) when each party to the contract has ongoing duties and obligations such that the contract remains materially unperformed on both sides. While the Court recognizes that the monetary consideration required under the License Agreement has been paid in full, the Court finds that the License Agreement is executory due to the continuing material duties and obligations of both parties to the License Agreement, including Aerobox's duty not to sell the thermoplastic core separately and to maintain confidentiality and Tubus Bauer's duty to defend the patent against validity challenges of third parties.

Pursuant to 11 U.S.C. § 365, a trustee, or a debtor-in-possession imbued with the rights and powers of a trustee, may assume or reject any executory contract or unexpired lease. 11 U.S.C. § 365(a). This power to assume or reject is not absolute, however, and is limited by subsection (c), which provides, in relevant part:

> The trustee may not assume or assign any executory contract or unexpired lease of the debtor, whether or not such contract or lease prohibits or restricts assignment of rights or delegation of duties, if-
>
> (1)(A) applicable law excuses a party, other than the debtor, to such contract or lease from accepting performance from or rendering performance to an entity other than the debtor or the debtor in possession, whether or not such contract or lease prohibits or restricts assignment of rights or delegation of duties; and
>
> (1)(B) such party does not consent to such assumption or assignment[.]

11 U.S.C. § 365(c)(1).

As noted above, there is a split in authority regarding the construction and application of 11 U.S.C. § 365(c)(1). A majority of the circuit courts construing 11 U.S.C. § 365(c)(1) have adhered to the "hypothetical test" espoused by *Catapult*. In *Catapult*, the Ninth Circuit examined the language of 11 U.S.C. § 365(c)(1), which "by its terms bars a debtor in possession from *assuming* an executory contract without the nondebtor's consent where applicable law precludes *assignment* of the contract to a third party." To read the statute otherwise and allow a debtor in possession to assume any executory contract as long as no assignment was contemplated improperly rewrites the statute to prohibit "assumption *and* assignment, rather than assumption *or* assignment." The Ninth Circuit thus held that "where applicable nonbankruptcy law makes an executory contract nonassignable because the identity of the nondebtor party is material, a debtor in possession may not assume the contract absent consent of the nondebtor party."

Using the "hypothetical test" the Court must determine whether applicable nonbankruptcy law excuses the non-debtor party from accepting performance from or rendering performance to a hypothetical third party. Because the License

Agreement involves use of a patent, "applicable law" means federal patent law. Federal patent law generally prohibits assignment of both exclusive and non-exclusive license agreements absent consent of the licensor. Tubus Bauer does not consent to the assignment of the License Agreement. Therefore, using the "hypothetical test," Tubus Bauer asserts that 365(c)(1) prohibits the Debtor from assuming or assigning the License Agreement, regardless of whether the Debtor has, in fact, attempted to assume it, and regardless of whether the Debtor has, in fact, attempted to assign it to a third party. This Court disagrees, and finds that § 365(c)(1) does not compel application of the "hypothetical test" when determining whether a debtor-in-possession is barred from assuming an executory contract.

As discussed by the court in *Cambridge Biotech*, the debtor-in-possession is not materially distinct from the pre-bankruptcy entity that is a party to the executory contract. Therefore, because the limitation contained in § 365(c)(1) is aimed at protecting non-debtor parties to personal services contracts from being forced to accept service from or render service to an entity other than the entity with whom it originally contracted, it is appropriate to determine whether the nondebtor party is *actually* being forced to accept performance under its executory contract from an entity other than the debtor.

Similarly, the bankruptcy court in *Footstar* reasons that it makes perfect sense for the statute, which uses the term, "trustee," to prohibit the trustee from assuming or assigning a contract, because the trustee *is* an "entity other than the debtor in possession" but it makes no sense to read "trustee" to mean "debtor in possession." Doing so would render the provision a virtual oxymoron, since mere assumption [by the debtor in possession] (without assignment) would *not* compel the counterparty to accept performance from or render it to "an entity other than" the debtor. This Court agrees.

Thus, where the debtor-in-possession seeks to assume, or, as is the situation in the instant case, where the debtor-in-possession has neither sought to assume nor reject the executory contract but simply continues to operate post-petition under its terms, 11 U.S.C. § 365(c)(1) does not prohibit assumption of the contract by the debtor-in-possession and cannot operate to allow the non-debtor party to the executory contract to compel the Debtor to reject the contract. In reaching this conclusion, the Court finds that the "actual test" articulated in *Cambridge Biotech*, and the reasoning of the court in *Footstar*, is the better approach to § 365(c)(1) when determining whether a debtor-in-possession is precluded from assuming an executory contract.

The UCC also argues that because the License Agreement contemplates assignment, and requires Tubus Bauer not to unreasonably withhold its consent, Tubus Bauer's categorical refusal to consent cannot be considered reasonable. The UCC, therefore, contends that the Motion should be denied because it constitutes a unilateral attempt by Tubus Bauer to alter the bargained-for terms of the License Agreement. The Court agrees that the License Agreement does not prohibit assignment, and that by requiring Tubus Bauer not to unreasonably withhold its consent to assignment, the assignment term of the License Agreement is less restrictive than the general federal common law prohibition against assignment of patents absent consent of the licensor. But because the Court concludes as a matter of law that 11 U.S.C. § 365(c)(1) cannot prevent a debtor-in-possession from assuming a pre-petition executory contract, the Court need not determine whether the assignment provision in the License Agreement constitutes "preconsent" by Tubus Bauer which would render 11 U.S.C. § 365(c)(1) inapplicable. And because Tubus Bauer asserts no grounds for relief from the automatic stay other than its argument that § 365(c)(1) bars assumption of the License Agreement as a matter of law, relief from the automatic stay is not warranted.

Based on the foregoing, the Motion is DENIED.

QUESTIONS

1.   What is the difference between a "bankruptcy trustee" and a "bankruptcy debtor in possession"? Is there any the difference between a bankruptcy trustee assuming an executory contract for the benefit of the debtor and the debtor assuming an executory contract directly? Who ultimately will perform under the executory contract?

2.   The court notes that federal patent law generally prohibits the assignment of both exclusive and nonexclusive licenses without the consent of the licensor. Are the reasons for the prohibition of assignment the same in the case of an exclusive license and an nonexclusive license? What rights does a licensee have under a nonexclusive license?

3.   What is an *ipso facto* clause? Are *ipso facto* clauses enforceable post petition?

4.   Aerobox had not yet sought to assume or assign the license agreement but did want to continue to exercise its rights under the license agreement. What is the difference between a debtor in possession assuming a license agreement and continuing to exercise its rights under the license agreement without assumption of the license agreement?

5.   Under the "actual test," can a debtor licensee assume a nonexclusive license? Can a debtor licensee assume a nonexclusive license under the "hypothetical test"?

6.   What are the policy arguments underlying the "actual test" and the "hypothetical test"? Which arguments to do find most compelling?

CASE NOTES

1.   CBC manufactures and sells retroviral diagnostic tests for detecting HIV. Pasteur owns a number of patents on procedures for diagnosing HIV. In October 1989, CBC and Pasteur entered into a cross-license agreement under which CBC acquired the right to incorporate Pasteur's HIV diagnostic procedures in any kits sold within a defined geographic territory. The cross-license agreement broadly prohibited the licensees from assigning or sublicensing the patent rights. CBC filed a Chapter 11 petition in July 1994. CBC's reorganization plan proposed that CBC assume Pasteur's cross-licenses, continue to operate its retroviral diagnostic testing business as a debtor in possession, and sell all of its stock to a subsidiary of bioMerieux, a large French biotechnology company which was a direct competitor of Pasteur in the international biotechnology market. Pasteur objected to the plan,

arguing that CBC cannot assume the licenses because the licenses prohibited assignment. Pasteur also argued that the proposed sale of CBC's stock to bioMerieux was a *de facto* assignment of the cross-licenses to a third party in contravention of the federal common law which presumed patent licenses to be nonassignable, unless expressly permitted in the license agreement, and that the *de facto* assignment was in contravention of the express prohibition of assignment in the cross-license agreement. CBC argued that the Fifth Circuit had adopted the "actual test," therefore, a prohibition on assignment did not preclude assumption, and that the sale of its stock to the subsidiary of bioMerieux was not an assignment because CBC would still be acting as the licensee just as it had prepetition. What result? *See* Institut Pasteur v. Cambridge Biotech Corp., 104 F.3d 489 (1st Cir. 1997). The bankruptcy court decision in this case is considered in § 2.2.6 of these materials.

2. *See also* Matter of Biopolymers, Inc., 136 B.R. 28 (Bankr. D. Conn. 1992) (Agreement which granted debtor exclusive license to use patented technology and to grant sublicenses to third parties, subject to approval of licensor, was an executory contract which had to be rejected or assumed within 60 days after entry of order for relief; licensor's obligation to forbear from granting licenses to others and not to unreasonably withhold permission for sublicensing sufficed to make the license agreement executory); In re Sunterra Corp., 361 F.3d 257 (4th Cir. 2004) (Disjunctive word "or" as used in the Bankruptcy Code provision prohibiting trustee from assuming *or* assigning any of debtor's executory contracts, if applicable nonbankruptcy law would excuse the other party to the contract from accepting performance from entity other than debtor or debtor in possession, had to be interpreted literally so as to prevent Chapter 11 debtor in possession from assuming licensing agreement for copyrighted computer software, because copyright law would excuse the other party to the contract from accepting performance from any hypothetical third party, although debtor did not intend to assign contract to any third party); Jones v. Greene (In re Nu-Corp Int'l Techs., Inc.), 362 B.R. 308 (Bankr. N.D. Miss. 2007) (Neither Chapter 11 debtor nor trustee could promptly cure debtor's default under license agreement granting debtor nonexclusive right to use patented technology for fuel oil recovery system by paying licensor $495,000 license fee; therefore, agreement was deemed to be rejected, and debtor, its officers, directors and shareholders had to return any materials, information and documents relating to patent and technology, and debtor was precluded from using patented technology in the future); In re Ehrenfried Technologies, Inc., No 97-24963, 1998 Bankr. LEXIS 804 (Bankr. E.D. Va. 1998) (At the debtor's confirmation hearing, creditor company raised three financial objections to the reorganization plan; the court found that, keeping in mind that the debtor's projections of future ability to cure existing default were mere guesses, there still might be a reasonable financial future for the debtor that would allow it to cure creditor company's licensing fee arrearages in permissible period of time; the court thus ordered that the reorganization plan treatment of the creditor company debt be accordingly modified); In re CFLC, Inc., 89 F.3d 673 (9th Cir. 1996) (Federal law, which makes a nonexclusive patent license personal and nonassignable absent consent of licensor, excused licensor from accepting performance from, or rendering it to, anyone other than Chapter 11 debtor-licensee; therefore, patent license was not assumable and assignable in bankruptcy).

Additional Information

1. 5 ROBERT A. MATTHEWS, JR., ANNOTATED PATENT DIGEST § 35:49 (2009).

2. RAYMOND T. NIMMER, JEFF DODD, MODERN LICENSING LAW § 15:31 (2009).

3. WARREN E. AGIN, 9 J. BANKR. L. & PRAC. 591 (2000).

4. Dan Schechter, *Licensee May Continue to Use Intellectual Property License Following Bankruptcy Filing Because Debtor-in-Possession Is the Same Entity as Prepetition Licensee. (In re Aerobox Composite Structures, LLC (Bankr. D. N.M.)*, 2007 COM. FIN. NEWSL. 64 (2007).

5. David R. Kuney, *Restructuring Dilemmas for the High Technology Licensee: Will "Plain Meaning" Bring Order to the Chaotic Bankruptcy Law for Assumption and Assignment of Technology Licenses?*, 44 GONZ. L. REV. 123 (2008).

6. Neal Batson, John P. Fry, *Nonexclusive Patent Licenses: Not Assignable — 9th Circuit Decision Precluded Debtor in Possession from Assuming Rights, Sans Consent*, Vol. 23, No. 8, NAT'L L.J., Oct. 16, 2000, at C22 (col. 2).

7. Stewart A. Kagan, Matthew P. Herenstein, *A Licensee-Debtor May Sell Patent-Based Stock — First Circuit Allows a Debtor to Effect a Transfer of Its Licenses Through the Sale of Its Shares*, Vol. 19, No. 42, NAT'L L.J., Jun. 16, 1997 at C15 (col. 1).

8. Neil S. Hirshman, et. al., *Is Silence Really Golden? Assumption and Assignment of Intellectual Property Licenses in Bankruptcy*, 3 HASTINGS BUS. L.J. 197 (2007).

9. Maureen McQuaid, Craig M. Rankin, *What Happens to a License for Intellectual Property When One Party to the Agreement Files for Bankruptcy? The Answer Depends on the Court Involved*, Vol. 18, No. 34, NAT'L L.J., Apr. 22, 1996 at B5 (col. 1).

10. David R. Kuney, *Intellectual Property Law in Bankruptcy Court: The Search for a More Coherent Standard in Dealing with a Debtor's Right to Assume and Assign Technology Licenses*, 9 AM. BANKR. INST. L. REV. 593 (2001).

11. Kenneth N. Klee; David A. Fidler, *Recent Developments Concerning Intellectual Property and Bankruptcy*, SJ082 ALI-ABA 201 (2004).

12. Marcelo Halpern, *Bankruptcy Issues in Intellectual Property Licensing*, 879 PLI/PAT 575 (2006).

6.3   PERFECTING SECURITY INTERESTS IN COPYRIGHTS

A creditor who perfects a security interest in personal property becomes a secured creditor. Secured creditors have priority over unsecured creditors in bankruptcy proceedings in the payment of creditor claims. Prior to *In re Peregrine* discussed below, there were two possible ways in which security interests in copyrights could be perfected; under a state's Uniform Commercial Code (UCC) and under the Copyright Act. Article 9 of the UCC governs the creation, perfection, priority and enforcement of security interests in personal property and fixtures. UCC § 9-109 provides that personal property includes general intangibles and UCC § 9-106 defines general intangibles. Although UCC § 9-106 does not identify intellectual property as a general intangible, the Official Comment to UCC § 9-106 does specifically state that "copyrights, trademarks and patents" are included in the definition of general intangibles. In order to perfect a security interest in a general intangible under Article 9, the creditor must file a UCC-1 financing statement with the Secretary of State of the debtor's place of business.

Section 205 of the Copyright Act provides that "Any transfer of copyright ownership or other document pertaining to a copyright may be recorded in the Copyright Office . . ." Section 101 defines a "transfer of copyright ownership" as an "assignment, mortgage, exclusive license, or any other conveyance, alienation or hypothecation of a copyright . . ." Section 205(c) provides that the recordation of a document in the Copyright Office gives constructive notice to all other persons of the transfer of copyright ownership; and § 205(d) provides that, as between two conflicting transfers, the one executed first prevails if it is recorded within one month after its execution, otherwise the later transfer prevails if it is recorded first and taken in good faith for valuable consideration.

In *In re Peregine*, a creditor bank filed a UCC-1 financing statement covering the debtor's film library with the California, Colorado and Utah secretaries of state. After filing a Chapter 11 bankruptcy petition, the debtor challenged the bank's security interest arguing that it was unperfected because it was not filed with the Copyright Office. After extensive discussion of the Copyright Act and UCC Article 9, the court held that the comprehensive scope of the Copyright Act's recording provisions indicated that Congress intended to preempt state methods of perfecting security interests in copyrights. *In re Peregrene* was decided in 1990 and has been uniformly adopted by all the federal circuit bankruptcy courts. Therefore, today, the only method by which a creditor can perfect a security interest in a *registered* copyright is by filing the security interest with the Copyright Office.

Under Section 102 of the Copyright Act, copyright protection exists at the time "original works of authorship [are] fixed in any tangible medium of expression . . ." Section 408 of the Copyright Act provides that a copyright owner *may* register the copyright claim in the Copyright Office by depositing a copy of the copyright material together with a copyright application form and fee. Section 408 also expressly states that registration is not a condition of copyright protection. The *World Auxiliary Power* case below considers the perfection of security interests in *unregistered* copyrights. Should security interests in unregistered copyrights be perfected under § 205 of the Copyright Act or under Article 9 of the UCC?

WORLD AUXILIARY POWER v. SILICON VALLEY BANK
303 F.3d 1120 (9th Cir. 2002)

KLEINFELD, CIRCUIT JUDGE:

In this case we decide whether federal or state law governs priority of security interests in unregistered copyrights.

FACTS

Basically, this is a bankruptcy contest over unregistered copyrights between a bank that got a security interest in the copyrights from the owners and perfected it under state law, and a company that bought the copyrights from the bankruptcy trustees after the copyright owners went bankrupt. These simple facts are all that matters to the outcome of this case, although the details are complex.

Three affiliated California corporations — World Auxiliary Power, World Aerotechnology, and Air Refrigeration Systems — designed and sold products for modifying airplanes. The FAA must approve modifications of civilian aircraft by issuing "Supplemental Type Certificates." The three companies owned copyrights in the drawings, technical manuals, blue-prints, and computer software used to make the modifications. Some of these copyrighted materials were attached to the Supplemental Type Certificates. The companies did not register their copyrights with the United States Copyright Office.

The companies got financing from Silicon Valley Bank, one of the appellees in this case. Two of the companies borrowed the money directly, the third guaranteed the loan. The security agreement, as is common, granted the bank a security interest in a broad array of presently owned and after-acquired collateral. The security agreement covered "all goods and equipment now owned or hereafter acquired," as well as inventory, contract rights, general intangibles, blueprints, drawings, computer programs, accounts receivable, patents, cash, bank deposits, and pretty much anything else the debtor owned or might be "hereafter acquired." The security agreement and financing statement also covered "[a]ll copyright rights, copyright applications, copyright registrations, and like protections in each work of authorship and derivative work thereof, whether published or unpublished, now owned or hereafter acquired."

The bank perfected its security interest in the collateral, including the copyrights, pursuant to California's version of Article 9 of the Uniform Commercial Code, by filing UCC-1 financing statements with the California Secretary of State. The bank also took possession of the Supplemental Type Certificates and the attached copyrighted materials. But the copyrights still weren't registered with the United States Copyright Office, and the bank did not record any document showing the transfer of a security interest with the Copyright Office.

Subsequently, the three debtor companies filed simultaneous but separate bankruptcy proceedings. Their copyrights were among their major assets. Aerocon Engineering, one of their creditors (and the appellant in this case), wanted the copyrights. Aerocon was working on a venture with another company, Advanced

Aerospace, and its President, Michael Gilsen, and an officer and director, Merritt Widen (all appellees in this case), to engineer and sell aircraft modifications using the debtors' designs. Their prospective venture faced a problem: Silicon Valley Bank claimed a security interest in the copyrights. To solve this problem, Aerocon worked out a deal with Gilsen, Widen, and a company named Erose Capital (not a party in this case) to buy the debtors' assets, including their copyrights, from the bankruptcy trustees along with the trustees' right to sue to avoid Silicon Valley Bank's security interest. Once Aerocon owned the copyrights, it planned to exercise the trustees' power to avoid Silicon Valley Bank's security interest so that the venture would own the copyrights free and clear.

The transaction to purchase the copyrights and the trustees' avoidance action worked as follows. First, Aerocon paid the bankruptcy trustees $90,000, $30,000 for each of the three bankruptcy estates. Then, the trustees, with the bankruptcy court's approval, sold the estates' assets and avoidance action to Erose Capital, Gilsen, and Widen. Gilsen and Widen then sold their two-thirds interest to their company, Advanced Aerospace.

After this transaction was completed, for reasons not relevant to this appeal, Aerocon's planned joint venture with Advanced Aerospace and Gilsen and Widen fell through. In the aftermath, Erose Capital sold its one-third interest to Aerocon and Advanced Aerospace sold its two-thirds interest to Airweld. These transactions meant that Aerocon and Airweld owned the debtors' copyrights and the trustees' avoidance action as tenants in common.

Meanwhile, Silicon Valley Bank won relief from the bankruptcy court's automatic stay and, based on its security interest, foreclosed on the copyrights. Then the bank sold the copyrights to Advanced Aerospace (Gilsen's and Widen's company) which then sold the copyrights to Airweld. Had Aerocon's joint venture with Gilsen and Widen gone through, buying off the trustees' and the bank's interests in the copyrights would have been a sensible, if expensive, way to ensure that the venture owned the copyrights free and clear. But, of course, the venture did not go through, and Gilsen and Widen's affiliations had changed. Thus Gilsen and Widen's purchase from the bank and sale to Airweld meant that Aerocon, which had paid $90,000 for the copyrights and had owned them as a tenant in common with Airweld, now had a claim adverse to Airweld's, which purportedly owned the copyrights in fee simple.

Aerocon brought an adversary proceeding in each of the three bankruptcy proceedings against Silicon Valley Bank, Advanced Aerospace, Gilsen, Widen, and Airweld. (These adversary proceedings were later consolidated.) Aerocon sued to avoid Silicon Valley Bank's security interest and to recover the copyrights or their value from subsequent transferees Advanced Aerospace, Gilsen, Widen, and Airweld. The bankruptcy court granted the subsequent transferees' motion to dismiss Aerocon's claims against them as time-barred. The bankruptcy court then granted summary judgment to Silicon Valley Bank on all of Aerocon's claims on the ground that the bank had perfected its security interest in the copyrights under California's version of Article 9 of the Uniform Commercial Code. Aerocon appealed to the Ninth Circuit Bankruptcy Appellate Panel. Silicon Valley Bank objected, and the appeal was transferred to the district court, which affirmed the bankruptcy court. Aerocon appeals from the district court's order.

ANALYSIS

Copyright and bankruptcy law set the context for this litigation, but the legal issue is priority of security interests. The bankruptcy trustees sold Aerocon their power to avoid any security interest "that is voidable by a creditor that extends credit to the debtor at the time of the commencement of the case, and that obtains, at such time and with respect to such credit, a judicial lien . . . ." Under this "strong-arm" provision, Aerocon has the status of an "ideal creditor" who perfected his lien at the last possible moment before the bankruptcy commenced, and if this hypothetical creditor would take priority over Silicon Valley Bank's lien, then Aerocon may avoid the bank's security interest.

Whether Aerocon's hypothetical lien creditor would take priority turns on whether federal or state law governs the perfection of security interests in unregistered copyrights. The bank did everything necessary to perfect its security interest under state law, so if state law governs, the bank has priority and wins. The bank did nothing, however, to perfect its interest under federal law, so if federal law governs, Aerocon's hypothetical lien creditor arguably has priority, although the parties dispute whether Aerocon might face additional legal hurdles.

We are assisted in deciding this case by two opinions, neither of which controls, but both of which are thoughtful and scholarly. The first is the bankruptcy court's published opinion in this case, *Aerocon Engineering Inc. v. Silicon Valley Bank (In re World Auxiliary Power Co.)*, which we affirm largely for the reasons the bankruptcy judge gave. The second is a published district court opinion, *National Peregrine, Inc. v. Capitol Federal Savings & Loan Association (In re Peregrine Entertainment, Ltd.)*, the holdings of which we adopt but, like the bankruptcy court, distinguish and limit.

Our analysis begins with the Copyright Act of 1976. Under the Act, "copyright protection subsists . . . in original works of authorship fixed in any tangible medium of expression." While an owner must register his copyright as a condition of seeking certain infringement remedies, registration is permissive, not mandatory, and is not a condition for copyright protection. Likewise, the Copyright Act's provision for recording "transfers of copyright ownership" (the Act's term that includes security interests) is permissive, not mandatory: "Any transfer of copyright ownership or other document pertaining to copyright may be recorded in the Copyright Office . . . ." The Copyright Act's use of the word "mortgage" as one definition of a "transfer" is properly read to include security interests under Article 9 of the Uniform Commercial Code.

Under the Copyright Act,

> [a]s between two conflicting transfers, the one executed first prevails if it is recorded, in the manner required to give constructive notice . . . within one month after its execution . . . or at any time before recordation . . . of the later transfer. Otherwise the later transfer prevails if recorded first in such manner, and if taken in good faith, for valuable consideration . . . and without notice of the earlier transfer.

The phrase "constructive notice" refers to another subsection providing that recording gives constructive notice but only if —

(1) the document, or material attached to it, specifically identifies the work to which it pertains so that, after the document is indexed by the Register of Copyrights, it would be revealed by a reasonable search under the title or registration number of the work; and

(2) registration has been made for the work.

A copyrighted work only gets a "title or registration number" that would be revealed by a search if it's registered. Since an unregistered work doesn't have a title or registration number that would be "revealed by a reasonable search," recording a security interest in an unregistered copyright in the Copyright Office wouldn't give "constructive notice" under the Copyright Act, and, because it wouldn't, it couldn't preserve a creditor's priority. There just isn't any way for a secured creditor to preserve a priority in an unregistered copyright by recording anything in the Copyright Office. And the secured party can't get around this problem by registering the copyright, because the secured party isn't the owner of the copyright, and the Copyright Act states that only "the owner of copyright . . . may obtain registration of the copyright claim . . . ."

Aerocon argues that the Copyright Act's recordation and priority scheme exclusively controls perfection and priority of security interests in copyrights. First, Aerocon argues that state law, here the California U.C.C., by its own terms "steps back" and defers to the federal scheme. Second, whether or not the U.C.C. steps back, Aerocon argues that Congress has preempted the U.C.C. as it applies to copyrights. We address each argument in turn.

A. U.C.C. Step Back Provisions

Article 9 of the Uniform Commercial Code, as adopted in California, provides that unperfected creditors are subordinate to perfected, and as between perfected security interests, the first perfected interest prevails. The bank perfected first under state law by filing a financing statement with the California Secretary of State on existing and after-acquired copyrights. The U.C.C. treats copyrights as "general intangibles." Security interests in general intangibles are properly perfected under the U.C.C. by state filings such as the one made by the bank in this case.

To avoid conflict with the federal law, the U.C.C. has two "step-back provisions," by which state law steps back and out of the way of conflicting federal law. The first, more general "step-back" provision says that Article 9 "does not apply . . . [t]o a security interest subject to any statute of the United States to the extent that such statute governs the rights of parties to and third parties affected by transactions in particular types of property . . . ." As applied to copyrights, the relevant U.C.C. Official Comment makes it clear that this step-back clause does not exclude all security interests in copyrights from U.C.C. coverage, just those for which the federal Copyright Act "governs the rights" of relevant parties:

Although the Federal Copyright Act contains provisions permitting the mortgage of a copyright and for the recording of an assignment of a copyright such a statute would not seem to contain sufficient provisions regulating the rights of the parties and third parties to exclude security interests in copyrights from the provisions of this Article.

The second step-back provision speaks directly to perfection of security interests. It exempts from U.C.C. filing requirements security interests in property "subject to . . . [a] statute . . . of the United States which provides for a national . . . registration . . . or which specifies a place of filing different from that specified in this division for filing of the security interest." Compliance with such a statute "is equivalent to the filing of a financing statement . . . and a security interest in property subject to the statute . . . can be perfected only by compliance therewith . . . ."

Under the U.C.C.'s two step-back provisions, there can be no question that, when a copyright has been registered, a security interest can be perfected only by recording the transfer in the Copyright Office. As the district court held in *Peregrine*, the Copyright Act satisfies the broad U.C.C. step-back provision by creating a priority scheme that "governs the rights of parties to and third parties affected by transactions" in registered copyrights and satisfies the narrow step-back provision by creating a single "national registration" for security interests in registered copyrights. Thus, under these step-back provisions, if a borrower's collateral is a registered copyright, the secured party cannot perfect by filing a financing statement under the U.C.C. in the appropriate state office, or alternatively by recording a transfer in the Copyright Office. For registered copyrights, the only proper place to file is the Copyright Office. We adopt *Peregrine's* holding to this effect.

However, the question posed by this case is whether the U.C.C. steps back as to unregistered copyrights. We, like the bankruptcy court in this case, conclude that it does not. As we've explained, there's no way for a secured creditor to perfect a security interest in unregistered copyrights by recording in the Copyright Office. The U.C.C.'s broader step-back provision says that the U.C.C. doesn't apply to a security interest "to the extent" that a federal statute governs the rights of the parties. The U.C.C. doesn't defer to the Copyright Act under this broad step-back provision because the Copyright Act doesn't provide for the rights of secured parties to unregistered copyrights; it only covers the rights of secured parties in *registered* copyrights. The U.C.C.'s narrow step-back provision says the U.C.C. doesn't apply if a federal statute "provides for a national . . . registration . . . or which specifies a place of filing different from that specified in this division for filing of the security interest." The U.C.C. doesn't defer to the Copyright Act under this narrow step-back provision because the Copyright Act doesn't provide a "national registration": unregistered copyrights don't have to be registered, and because unregistered copyrights don't have a registered name and number, under the Copyright Act there isn't any place to file anything regarding unregistered copyrights that makes any legal difference. So, as a matter of state law, the U.C.C. doesn't step back in deference to federal law, but governs perfection and priority of security interests in unregistered copyrights itself.

B. Federal Preemption

It wouldn't matter that state law doesn't step back, however, if Congress chose to knock state law out of the way by preemption. Federal law preempts state law under three circumstances. The first is "express preemption," where Congress explicitly preempts state law. The second is "field preemption," where Congress implicitly preempts state law by "occupy[ing] the entire field, leaving no room for the operation of state law." The third is "conflict preemption," where we infer preemption because "compliance with both state and federal law would be impossible, or state law stands as an obstacle to the accomplishment and execution of the full purposes and objectives of Congress." We presume that federal law does not preempt "state law in areas traditionally regulated by the States."

Aerocon argues, relying on *Peregrine*, that Congress intended to occupy the field of security interests in copyrights. Aerocon also argues that the U.C.C. actually conflicts with the Copyright Act's text and purpose.

Although *Peregrine* did not specify whether the copyrights at issue were registered, it is probably safe to assume that they were, and that the *Peregrine* court did not have a case involving unregistered copyrights, because the collateral at issue was a movie library that got licensed out to exhibitors and, in the ordinary course, copyrights in such films would be registered. Also, as the bankruptcy judge in the case at bar pointed out, *Peregrine*'s "analysis only works if the copyright was registered." The district court in *Peregrine* held that Congress had preempted state law because of "the comprehensive scope of the Copyright Act's recording provisions." As applied to registered copyrights, the Act's recording scheme is comprehensive; it doesn't exclude any registered copyright from its coverage. But as applied to unregistered copyrights, the Act doesn't have comprehensive recording provisions. Likewise, *Peregrine* notes that "[t]o the extent there are competing recordation schemes, this lessens the utility of each." This holds true for registered copyrights. But there aren't two competing filing systems for unregistered copyrights. The Copyright Act doesn't create one. Only the U.C.C. creates a filing system applicable to unregistered copyrights. *Peregrine* reasoned that creditors could get conflicting results under the U.C.C. and the Copyright Act, because each provides a different priority scheme. That's true only for registered copyrights. The Copyright Act wouldn't provide a conflicting answer as to unregistered copyrights because it wouldn't provide any answer at all. *Peregrine*'s holding applies to registered copyrights, and we adopt it, but as the bankruptcy court reasoned in the case at bar, it does not apply to unregistered copyrights.

We accordingly reject two other lower court opinions, *Zenith Productions, Ltd. v. AEG Acquisition Corp. (In re AEG Acquisition Corp.)* and *In re Avalon Software Inc.*, that extended *Peregrine*'s holding to unregistered copyrights. No circuit court has come to that erroneous conclusion. In both cases, the courts held that security interests in unregistered copyrights may not be perfected under the U.C.C.; perfection could be obtained only by registering the copyrights and recording the security interest with the Copyright Office. We reject these opinions because they miss the point made by the bankruptcy judge in this case, and discussed above, that *Peregrine*'s analysis doesn't work if it's applied to security interests in unregistered copyrights. Moreover, such extensions of *Peregrine* to unregistered copyrights would make registration of copyright a necessary prerequisite of perfecting a security interest in a copyright. The implication of requiring registration as a condition of perfection is that Congress intended to make unregistered copyrights practically useless as collateral, an inference the text and purpose of the Copyright Act do not warrant.

Though Congress must have contemplated that most copyrights would be unregistered, it only provided for protection of security interests in registered copyrights. There is no reason to infer from Congress's silence as to unregistered copyrights an intent to make such copyrights useless as collateral by preempting state law but not providing any federal priority scheme for unregistered copyrights. That would amount to a presumption in favor of federal preemption, but we are required to presume just the opposite. The only reasonable inference to draw is that Congress chose not to create a federal scheme for security interests in unregistered copyrights, but left the matter to States, which have traditionally governed security interests.

For similar reasons, we reject Aerocon's argument that congressional intent to preempt can be inferred from conflict between the Copyright Act and the U.C.C. There is no conflict between the statutory provisions: the Copyright Act doesn't speak to security interests in unregistered copyrights, the U.C.C. does.

Nor does the application of state law frustrate the objectives of federal copyright law. The basic objective of federal copyright law is to "promote the Progress of Science and useful Arts" by "establishing a marketable right to the use of one's expression" and supplying "the economic incentive to create and disseminate ideas." Aerocon argues that allowing perfection under state law would frustrate this objective by injecting uncertainty in secured transactions involving copyrights. Aerocon conjures up the image of a double-crossing debtor who, having gotten financing based on unregistered copyrights, registers them, thus triggering federal law, and gets financing from a second creditor, who then records its interest with the Copyright Office and takes priority. We decline to prevent this fraud by drawing the unreasonable inference that Congress intended to render copyrights useless as collateral unless registered.

Prudent creditors will always demand that debtors disclose any copyright registrations and perfect under federal law and will protect themselves against subsequent creditors gaining priority by means of covenants and policing mechanisms. The several *amici* banks and banking association in this case argue that most lenders would lend against unregistered copyrights subject to the remote risk of being "primed" by subsequent creditors; but no lender would lend against unregistered copyrights if they couldn't perfect their security interest. As we read the law, unregistered copyrights have value as collateral, discounted by the remote potential for priming. As Aerocon reads the law, they would have no value at all.

QUESTIONS

1. The court states that "While an owner must register his copyright as a condition of seeking certain infringement remedies, registration is permissive, not mandatory, and is not a condition for copyright protection." What copyright

protection exists if the copyright owner cannot sue for infringement? What kind of property right does a person have if the person cannot protect the property right through legal action?

2.   On what basis did the court find that recording a security interest in an unregistered copyright would not give constructive notice to other persons?

3.   What is the first step-back provision of UCC Article 9? Why does the court find that the first step-back provision does not apply? What is the second step-back provision in UCC Article 9? Why does the court find that the second step-back provision does not apply?

4.   The court notes that federal law preempts state law in three situations: express preemption, field preemption and conflict preemption. Why does the court find that none of these situations exist in the context of unregistered copyrights?

5.   Why would unregistered copyrights have value under the court's interpretation of the law and no value under Aerocon's interpretation of the law?

6.   If a creditor perfects a security interest in unregistered copyrights under state law and then obtains title to these copyrights in a bankruptcy proceeding, what should the creditor do immediately?

CASE NOTES

1.   Songwriters assign their copyrights in musical compositions to Broadcast Music, Inc. (BMI). BMI then licenses the public performance of the musical compositions and pays the royalties from the licenses to the songwriters. Miller is a songwriter who assigned his copyrights to BMI and received royalty payments from BMI derived from his licensed musical compositions. In order to satisfy debts Miller owed to Staenberg and Hirsch, in 1989, Miller executed an irrevocable assignment to them of all future royalties and directed BMI to pay Staenberg and Hirsch directly. Staenberg and Hirsch never recorded the royalty assignment with the Copyright Office. Subsequently, the Internal Revenue Service assessed tax deficiencies against Miller for 1992, 1993 and 1994 and recorded notices of these tax liens against his royalty income. The IRS also served BMI with notices of the levy. BMI then filed an interpleader action to resolve the conflicting claims to Miller's royalty income. Citing *In re Peregrine*, the IRS argued that the assignment of royalties to Staenberg and Hirsch was a "transfer of copyright ownership" which could only be perfected by recording the assignment with the Copyright Office. Since Staenberg and Hirsch had failed to record the assignment with the Copyright Office, the IRS claimed it was an unperfected security interest that was subordinate to the government's tax lien. Staenberg and Hirsch argued that Miller had already assigned his copyright ownership to BMI, that at best Miller held only beneficial ownership of his copyrights, and that the assignment of the right to receive future royalties was distinct from an assignment of ownership rights in the copyrights. What result? *See* Broadcast Music, Inc. v. Hirsch, 104 F.3d 1163 (9th Cir. 1997).

2.   *See also* In re AEG Acquisition Corp., 127 B.R. 34 (Bankr. C.D. Cal. 1991) (Creditor's security interest in films is perfected under Copyright Act and not under Uniform Commercial Code; creditor's filing under Uniform Commercial Code was

meaningless in perfecting its security interest in films; filing a copyright security interest in the Copyright Office is the only means of perfecting copyright security interest provided that the underlying copyright has been recorded in the Copyright Office); In re AEG Acquisition Corp., 161 B.R. 50 (BAP 9th Cir. 1993) (Perfection of a security interest in a motion picture, as in any copyright, requires two steps: the film must be registered with the Copyright Office, and the security interest must be recorded in the Copyright Office).

Additional Information

1.   CORPORATE COUNSEL'S GUIDE TO INTELLECTUAL PROPERTY: PATENTS, COPYRIGHTS, TRADEMARKS, & TRADE SECRETS § 14:3 (2009).

2.   1 SECURITY INTERESTS IN PERSONAL PROPERTY § 16:11 (2009).

3.   THOMAS M. WARD, INTELLECTUAL PROPERTY IN COMMERCE § 2:79 (2009).

4.   1 ALEXANDER LINDEY AND MICHAEL LANDAU, LINDEY ON ENTERTAINMENT, PUBLISHING & THE ARTS § 1:22 (3d ed. 2009).

5.   RAYMOND T. NIMMER, JEFF DODD, MODERN LICENSING LAW § 16:21; § 16:22 (2009).

6.   Alicia Griffin Mills, *Perfecting Security Interests in IP: Avoiding the Traps*, 125 BANKING L.J. 746 (2008).

7.   R. Scott Griffin, *A Malpractice Suit Waiting to Happen: The Conflict Between Perfecting Security Interests in Patents and Copyrights (A Note on Peregrine, Cybernetic, and Their Progeny)*, 20 GA. ST. U. L. REV. 765 (2004).

8.   Ariel Glasner, *Making Something Out of "Nothing" The Trend Towards Securitizing Intellectual Property Assets and the Legal Obstacles Remain*, 3 J. LEGAL TECH. RISK MGMT. 27 (2008).

9.   Stacey G. Jernigan, et. al., *The Perfection of Liens in Unregistered Copyrights: Aerocon and Beyond*, 28 OKLA. CITY U. L. REV. 645 (2003).

10. Thomas M. Ward, *Intellectual Property Collateral Perfection and Proceeds in Bankruptcy*, ALI-ABA COURSE OF STUDY, COMMERCIAL BANKING LAW (2009).

11. Xuan-Thao Nguyen, *Intellectual Property and Security Interests*, SM088 ALI-ABA 417 (2007).

12. Evan H. Krinick; Celeste M. Butera, *Lenders Must Take Care When Perfecting a Lien on a Borrower's Patents and Copyrights*, 117 BANKING L.J. 49 (2000).

6.4   PERFECTING SECURITY INTERESTS IN PATENTS

As noted above, the Official Comment to UCC § 9-106 specifically states that patents are included in the definition of "general intangibles." Therefore, security interests in patents can be perfected by recording a UCC-1 financing statement with the secretary of state of the debtor's place of business. Section 261 of the Patent Act provides that "Applications for patent, patents, or any interest therein, shall be assignable in law by an instrument in writing." Section 261 also provides that "An assignment, grant or conveyance shall be void as against any subsequent purchaser or mortgagee for valuable consideration, without notice, unless it is recorded in the Patent and Trademark Office within three months from its date or prior to the date of such subsequent purchase or mortgage." As with copyrights, the question then becomes whether a security interest in a patent can only be perfected by recording the security interest in the Patent and Trademark Office. The *Cybernetics Services* case below answers this question with a resounding "no."

CYBERNETIC SERVICES v. MATSCO FINANCIAL CORPORATION
252 F.3d 1039 (9th Cir. 2001)

Graber, Circuit Judge:

As is often true in the field of intellectual property, we must apply an antiquated statute in a modern context. The question that we decide today is whether 35 U.S.C. § 261 of the Patent Act, or Article 9 of the Uniform Commercial Code (UCC), as adopted in California, requires the holder of a security interest in a patent to record that interest with the federal Patent and Trademark Office (PTO) in order to perfect the interest as against a subsequent lien creditor. We answer "no"; neither the Patent Act nor Article 9 so requires. We therefore affirm the decision of the Bankruptcy Appellate Panel (BAP).

FACTUAL AND PROCEDURAL BACKGROUND

The parties stipulated to the relevant facts: Matsco, Inc., and Matsco Financial Corporation (Petitioners) have a security interest in a patent developed by Cybernetic Services, Inc. (Debtor). The patent is for a data recorder that is designed to capture data from a video signal regardless of the horizontal line in which the data is located. Petitioners' security interest in the patent was "properly prepared, executed by the Debtor and timely filed with the Secretary of State of the State of California," in accordance with the California Commercial Code. Petitioners did not record their interest with the PTO.

After Petitioners had recorded their security interest with the State of California, certain creditors filed an involuntary Chapter 7 petition against Debtor, and an order of relief was granted. The primary asset of Debtor's estate is the patent. Petitioners then filed a motion for relief from the automatic stay so that they could foreclose on their interest in the patent. The bankruptcy Trustee opposed the motion, arguing that Petitioners had failed to perfect their interest because they did not record it with the PTO.

The bankruptcy court ruled that Petitioners had properly perfected their security interest in the patent by following the provisions of Article 9. Furthermore, the court reasoned, because Petitioners had perfected their security interest before the filing of the bankruptcy petition, Petitioners had priority over the Trustee's claim in the patent and deserved relief from the stay. Accordingly, the bankruptcy court granted Petitioners' motion. The BAP affirmed.

Petitioners then filed this timely appeal.

DISCUSSION

Article 9 of the UCC, as adopted in California, governs the method for perfecting a security interest in personal property. Article 9 applies to "general intangibles," a term that includes intellectual property. The parties do not dispute that Petitioners complied with Article 9's general filing requirements and, in the case of most types of property, would have priority over a subsequent lien creditor. The narrower question in this case is whether Petitioners' actions were sufficient to perfect their interest when the "general intangible" to which the lien attached is a patent. The parties also do not dispute that, *if* Petitioners were required to file notice of their security interest in the patent with the PTO, then the Trustee, as a hypothetical lien creditor under, has a superior right to the patent.

The Trustee makes two arguments. First, the Trustee contends that the Patent Act preempts Article 9's filing requirements. Second, the Trustee argues that Article 9 itself provides that a security interest in a patent can be perfected only by filing it with the PTO. We discuss each argument in turn.

A. Preemption

1. The Analytical Framework

"[T]he Supremacy Clause, U.S. Const., Art. VI, cl. 2, invalidates state laws that "interfere with, or are contrary to," federal law." Congress may preempt state law in several different ways. Congress may do so expressly (express preemption). Even in the absence of express preemptive text, Congress' intent to preempt an entire field of state law may be inferred "where the scheme of federal regulation is sufficiently comprehensive to make reasonable the inference that Congress "left no room" for supplementary state regulation" (field preemption). State law also is preempted "when compliance with both state and federal law is impossible," or if the operation of state law "stands as an obstacle to the accomplishment and execution of the full purposes and objectives of Congress" (conflict preemption).

The Patent Act does not contain preemptive text, so express preemption is not an issue here. Concerning field and conflict preemption, the Supreme Court has adopted a "pragmatic" approach to deciding whether the Patent Act preempts a particular state law. Congress, in the Patent Act, "has balanced innovation incentives against promoting free competition, and state laws upsetting that balance are preempted."

Using this form of analysis, the Supreme Court has held, on numerous occasions, that the Patent Act preempts a state law that grants patent-like protection to a product. Those cases do not control, however, because we are confronted not with a state law that grants patent-like protection to a product but, rather, with a state commercial law that provides a method for perfecting a security interest in a federally protected patent.

That distinction is key because the Supreme Court has instructed clearly that the Patent Act does not preempt every state commercial law that touches on intellectual property. For example, in *Aronson v. Quick Point Pencil Co.* the Supreme Court observed that commercial agreements "traditionally are the domain of state law. State law is not displaced merely because the contract relates to intellectual property which may or may not be patentable; the states are free to regulate the use of such intellectual property in any manner not inconsistent with federal law."

The Court also has held that the Patent Act does not preempt a state's trade secret law even though the practical effect of the state law is to prohibit the public dissemination of information that, under the Patent Act, is not eligible for protection. *Kewanee Oil*, In *Kewanee*, the Court examined the purposes of the Patent Act and the state trade secret law at issue and concluded that the state law did not stand " "as an obstacle to the accomplishment and execution of the full purposes and objectives of Congress." " The Court observed that the state law also encouraged invention, but did so by protecting a subject matter that was beyond the Patent Act's horizon; therefore, "the two systems are not and never would be in conflict."

It is within this framework that we evaluate the Trustee's claim. The Trustee argues that the recording provision found in 35 U.S.C. § 261 requires that the holder of a security interest in a patent record that interest with the PTO in order to perfect as to a subsequent lien creditor. Section 261 provides:

> Ownership; assignment
>
> Subject to the provisions of this title, patents shall have the attributes of personal property.
>
> Applications for patent, patents, or any interest therein, shall be assignable in law by an instrument in writing. The applicant, patentee, or his assigns or legal representatives may in like manner grant and convey an exclusive right under his application for patent, or patents, to the whole or any specified part of the United States.
>
> A certificate of acknowledgment under the hand and official seal of a person authorized to administer oaths within the United States, or, in a foreign country, of a diplomatic or consular officer of the United States or an officer authorized to administer oaths whose authority is proved by a certificate of a diplomatic or consular officer of the United States, or apostle of an official designated by a foreign country which, by treaty or convention, accords like effect to apostles of designated officials in the United States, shall be prima facie evidence of the execution of an assignment, grant or conveyance of a patent or application for patent.
>
> An assignment, grant or conveyance shall be void as against any subsequent purchaser or mortgagee for a valuable consideration, without notice, unless it is recorded in the Patent and Trademark Office within three

months from its date or prior to the date of such subsequent purchase or mortgage.

If the Trustee's reading of the relevant portion of § 261 is correct, then to the extent that Article 9 allows a different method of perfection, it would be preempted under either a "field" or "conflict" preemption theory. That is because recording systems increase a patent's marketability and thus play an integral role in the incentive scheme created by Congress. Recording systems provide notice and certainty to present and future parties to a transaction; they work "by virtue of the fact that interested parties have a specific place to look in order to discover with certainty whether a particular interest has been transferred." If, as the Trustee argues, the Patent Act expressly delineates the place where a party must go to acquire notice and certainty about liens on patents, then a state law that requires the public to look elsewhere unquestionably would undercut the value of the Patent Act's recording scheme. If, on the other hand, § 261 does not cover liens on patents, then Article 9's filing requirements do not conflict with any policies inherent in the Patent Act's recording scheme.

2. The Patent Act Requires Parties to Record with the PTO Only Ownership Interest in Patents.

As noted, the Patent Act's recording provision provides that an "assignment, grant or conveyance shall be void as against any subsequent purchaser or mortgagee for a valuable consideration, without notice, unless it is recorded in the [PTO]." 35 U.S.C. § 261. In order to determine whether Congress intended for parties to record with the PTO the type of interest that is at issue in this case, we must give the words of the statute the meaning that they had in 1870, the year in which the current version of § 261 was enacted.

Our task is not an easy one because security interests, and the words used to describe them, have changed significantly since the 19th Century. For example, before Article 9, a party could secure property using a pledge, an assignment, a chattel mortgage, a chattel trust, a trust deed, a factor's lien, or a conditional sale. Each type of device carried with it elaborate rules that controlled its use, and each conferred different rights and liabilities upon the contracting parties. Article 9, which was first enacted in 1962, brought the "long history of the proliferation of independent security devices . . . to an end." It did so in part by introducing a body of law that would govern a "single, "unitary" security device": the Article 9 security interest.

With that history in mind, we must determine whether Congress intended to include the kind of transaction at issue in this case within the scope of 35 U.S.C. § 261. The first phrase in § 261's recording provision — "assignment, grant or conveyance" — refers to different types of transactions. The neighboring clause — "shall be void as against any subsequent purchaser or mortgagee" — refers to the status of the party that receives an interest in the patent. Therefore, for the Trustee to prevail in this case, (1) Petitioners' transaction with Debtor must have been the type of "assignment, grant or conveyance" referred to in § 261, and (2) the Trustee, who has the status of a hypothetical lien creditor, must be a "subsequent purchaser or mortgagee." We hold that neither condition is met.

As we will discuss next, our conclusion finds support in the text of § 261, keeping in view the historical definitions of the terms used in the recording provision; the context, structure, and policy behind § 261; Supreme Court precedent; and PTO regulations. We will begin by analyzing the statute's text and context, as interpreted by the Supreme Court. For the sake of clarity, we will discuss the two relevant phrases in the recording provision of § 261 separately.

a. The Phrase "Assignment, Grant or Conveyance" Concerns Transfers of Ownership Interests Only.

The historical meanings of the terms "assignment, grant or conveyance" all involved the transfer of an ownership interest. A patent "assignment" referred to a transaction that transferred specific rights in the patent, all involving the patent's title.

A "grant," historically, also referred to a transfer of an ownership interest in a patent, but only as to a specific geographic area.

Although older cases defining the term "conveyance" in the context of intangible property are sparse, and its historic meaning tended to vary, the common contemporaneous definition was "to transfer the legal title . . . from the present owner to another."

That Congress intended to incorporate the common, contemporaneous meanings of the words "assignment," "grant," and "conveyance" into the Patent Act's recording provision can be seen when § 261 is examined in its entirety. The first clue is the provision's title: "Ownership; assignment." By using the unambiguous words "ownership; assignment," Congress must have intended to introduce the subject that was to follow: the ownership of patents and the assignment thereof.

Continuing through § 261, the second paragraph states that patents shall be assignable by an instrument in writing. That paragraph goes on to provide that the patentee or the patentee's assigns "may in like manner *grant and convey an exclusive right* under his application for patent . . . to the whole or any specified part of the United States." (Emphasis added.) The types of transactions referred to in § 261's second paragraph — (1) the assignment of a patent, and (2) the grant or conveyance of an exclusive right in a patent in the whole or part of the United States — track the historical definitions of assignment, grant, and conveyance that we just discussed — transactions that all involve the transfer of an ownership interest in a patent.

Moreover, we presume that words used more than once in the same statute have the same meaning throughout. Here, the second paragraph of § 261 uses the words "grant and convey" to signify the transfer of an "exclusive right [in a patent] . . . to the whole or any specified part of the United States." We presume, then, that when Congress used the words "grant or conveyance" two paragraphs later in the same statute, Congress still intended to refer to ownership interests only.

Supreme Court precedent supports our view that the terms "assignment, grant or conveyance" refer to ownership interests only. In *Waterman*, the Supreme Court analyzed the nature of a patent "assignment" and "mortgage." The plaintiff in

Waterman assigned to his wife a patent for an improvement in fountain pens. The plaintiff's wife then granted back to the plaintiff a license to use the patent. That license was never recorded. The wife then assigned the patent to a third party as collateral for a debt; the document concerning this arrangement was filed with the PTO. Finally, the wife assigned the patent back to the plaintiff. The question for the Court was whether the plaintiff had standing to bring an action for infringement of the patent. The Court held that only the third party had standing.

In resolving the matter, the Court noted that a patent's owner may convey, assign, or grant one of three interests:

> [1] the whole patent, comprising the exclusive right to make, use and vend the invention throughout the United States; or [2] an undivided part or share of that exclusive right; or [3] the exclusive right under the patent within and throughout a specified part of the United States. A transfer of either of these three kinds of interests is an *assignment*, properly speaking, and vests in the assignee a *title* in so much of the patent itself, with a right to sue infringers . . . . Any assignment or transfer, short of one of these, is a *mere license*, giving the licensee no title in the patent, and no right to sue at law in his own name for an infringement.

Whether a particular conveyance qualifies as an assignment or a license "does not depend upon the name by which it calls itself, but upon the legal effect of its provisions," that is, whether title is passed depends on the rights that were transferred by the contracting parties. Only the holder of an ownership interest in the patent had standing to sue.

Waterman contains no explicit holding that 35 U.S.C. § 261 applies only to a secured transaction that effects a transfer of ownership, but it does imply as much. The Court in *Waterman* expressly differentiated between three kinds of transfers of ownership interests — all of which it labeled as versions of "assignments" — and everything else, which it referred to as "mere licenses." The Court did not discuss "grants" or "conveyances" separately, but (1) as a matter of logic, they must fall into one of the two overarching and mutually exclusive categories that the Court created: assignments (ownership interests) or licenses (less than ownership interests); and (2) the kinds of transfers of ownership interests discussed by the Court (and labeled "assignments") correspond neatly to the historical definitions of the transactions delineated in the statute. It is clear, then, that the transactions that the Court referred to as effecting a transfer of ownership are the same transactions that Congress referred to as an "assignment, grant or conveyance."

In the present case, the parties do not dispute that the transaction that gave Petitioners their interest in the patent did not involve a transfer of an ownership interest in the patent. Petitioners held a "mere license," which did not have to be recorded with the PTO.

b. The Phrase "Subsequent Purchaser or Mortgagee" does not Include Subsequent Lien Creditors.

The Trustee's argument fails not only because a security interest that does not transfer ownership is not an "assignment, grant or conveyance," but also because he is not a subsequent "purchaser or mortgagee." Congress intended for parties to record their ownership interests in a patent so as to provide constructive notice only to subsequent holders of an ownership interest. Again, we derive our conclusion from the historical definitions of the words, from the context and structure of § 261, and from Supreme Court precedent.

The historical meaning of "purchaser or mortgagee" proves that Congress intended for the recording provision to give constructive notice only to subsequent holders of an ownership interest. For the sake of convenience, we begin with the definition of "mortgagee."

Historically, a "mortgagee" was someone who obtained title to property used to secure a debt. A "mortgage" must be differentiated from a "pledge," a term that is absent from the Patent Act. Professor Gilmore, in his treatise, Security Interests in Personal Property § 1.1, at 8, notes that the historical distinction between a pledge and a mortgage was that "the mortgagee got title or an estate whereas the pledgee got merely possession with a right to foreclose on default." Similarly, Judge Learned Hand wrote, in 1922, that it "is everywhere agreed that the significant distinction between a pledge and a mortgage is that in the first the creditor gets no title, . . . while in the second he does."

That the Patent Act refers to securing a patent through a "mortgage" but not through a "pledge" is significant, for both were common methods of using a patent as collateral. Generally, the inclusion of certain terms in a statute implies the exclusion of others. It seems then, that by using the term "mortgagee," but not "lien" or "pledge," Congress intended in 1870 for the Patent Act's recording provision to protect only those who obtained title to a patent.

The term "purchaser" does not detract from this conclusion. Section 261 instructs that an unrecorded "assignment, grant or conveyance" shall be void as against a subsequent "purchaser . . . for a valuable consideration, without notice." The historical definition of a "purchaser for value and without notice" was a "*bona fide* purchaser. A purchaser . . . who takes a conveyance purporting to pass the entire title, legal and equitable," who pays value and does not have notice of the rights of others to the property.

Congress, by stating that certain transactions shall be void as against a subsequent "purchaser or mortgagee" intended for the words to be read together: A "purchaser" is one who buys an ownership interest in the patent, while a "mortgagee" is one who obtains an ownership interest in a patent as collateral for a debt.

Our previous comments about the context and structure of § 261 support our conclusion that Congress intended to protect only subsequent holders of an ownership interest. As noted, the title of § 261 is "Ownership; assignment," which suggests that the recording provision is concerned only with ownership interests.

In summary, the historical definitions of the terms "purchaser or mortgagee," taken in context and read in the light of Supreme Court precedent, establish that Congress was concerned only with providing constructive notice to subsequent parties who take an ownership interest in the patent in question.

The Trustee is not a subsequent "mortgagee," as that term is used in 35 U.S.C. § 261, because the holder of a patent mortgage holds title to the patent itself. The Patent Act does not require parties to record documents in order to provide constructive notice to subsequent lien creditors who do not hold title to the patent.

3. Public Policies that Underlie Recording Provisions Cannot Override the Text of the Patent Act.

The Trustee argues that requiring lien creditors to record their interests with the PTO is in line with the general policy behind recording statutes. It may be, as the Trustee argues, that a national system of filing security interests is more efficient and effective than a state-by-state system. However, there is no statutory hook upon which to hang the Trustee's policy arguments. Moreover, we are not concerned with the policy behind recording statutes generally but, rather, with the policy behind 35 U.S.C. § 261 specifically.

We must interpret § 261 in the light of the purposes that Congress was seeking to serve. Congress simply was not concerned with non-ownership interests in patents, and this limitation was well understood at the time. As explained in a venerable treatise on the law of patents:

A license is not such a conveyance of an interest in the patented invention as to affect its ownership, and hence is not required to be recorded . . . . The value of the patented invention to the vendee may be impaired by such outstanding licenses, but of this he must inform himself at his own risk as best he may. The record of a license, not being legally required, is not constructive notice to any person for any purpose. 2 Robinson § 817, at 602–03.

Cases Interpreting the Copyright Act do not Control.

The Trustee's final argument is that this court should follow *Peregrine*, in which a district court held that the Copyright Act preempts state methods of perfecting security interests in copyrights. The court in *Peregrine* observed that the "federal copyright laws ensure predictability and certainty of copyright ownership, promote national uniformity and avoid the practical difficulties of determining and enforcing an author's rights under the differing laws and in the separate courts of the various States." The court reasoned that allowing state methods to stand would conflict with those goals.

Of course, *Peregrine* is not binding on this court although, in the present case, we have no occasion to pass on its correctness as an interpretation of the Copyright Act. We note, however, that the Copyright Act, by its terms, governs security interests. The Copyright Act governs any "transfer" of ownership, which is defined by statute to include any "hypothecation." A "hypothecation" is the "pledging of something as security without delivery of title or possession."

By contrast, the Patent Act does not refer to a "hypothecation" and, as we have demonstrated, does not refer to security interests at all. The fact that one federal intellectual property statute with a recording provision expressly refers to security interests (the Copyright Act), while another does not (the Patent Act), is more evidence that security interests are *outside* the scope of 35 U.S.C. § 261.

****

5. PTO Regulations Require Only the Recording of Documents that Transfer Ownership in a Patent.

It is worthy of mention that the applicable PTO regulations parallel our interpretation of 35 U.S.C. § 261. Title 37 C.F.R. § 3.11(a) provides that "assignments" must be recorded in the PTO. That regulation also states that "[o]ther documents *affecting title* to applications, patents, or registrations, will be recorded at the discretion of the Commissioner" of Patents and Trademarks. (Emphasis added.) Section 313 of the Manual of Patent Examining Procedure (7th ed.1998) explains that "[o]ther documents" that may be filed include "agreements which convey a security interest. Such documents are recorded in the public interest in order to give third parties notification of equitable interests . . . ."

Title 37 C.F.R. § 3.11 is illuminating because it shows that the PTO does not consider security interests to be "assignments, grants or conveyances." Under 35 U.S.C. § 261, certain conveyances — those that transfer an ownership interest — *must* be recorded to be effective as against a subsequent purchaser or mortgagee. If security interests *were* "assignments, grants or conveyances," then they would *have* to be filed to provide constructive notice to a subsequent purchaser or mortgagee, consistent with the Patent Act. As a matter of law and logic, the Commissioner would not have the "discretion" to reject federal filing.

CONCLUSION

Because 35 U.S.C. § 261 concerns only transactions that effect a transfer of an ownership interest in a patent, the Patent Act does not preempt Article 9. Consequently, Petitioners perfected their security interest in Debtor's patent by recording it with the California Secretary of State. They have priority over the Trustee's claim because they recorded their interest before the filing of the bankruptcy petition.

AFFIRMED.

QUESTIONS

1.   How does the court distinguish the holding in *In re Peregrine*? Is the federal interest in ensuring predictability and certainty of intellectual property ownership through a uniform, national recording system greater in the case of copyrights than patents?

2.   If the security interest in *Cybernetic Services* was labeled a "mortgage" and recorded under Article 9, would it have priority over a subsequent lien creditor?

3.   May a security interest in a patent be filed with the PTO? Would such a filing give constructive notice to subsequent lien creditors?

4. Recall that in the *Stanford* case, discussed in section 3.6 of the materials, the Federal Circuit held that the present assignment of patent rights to Roche in patents not yet applied for, or issued, was a valid assignment which had priority over Stanford's future patent assignment agreement. Could Roche have filed its assignment agreement for patents not yet applied for, or issued, with the PTO under section 261 of the Patent Act? How would such a filing be catalogued by the PTO?

5. If you were counsel to a bank planning to take a security interest in a debtor's patent portfolio, what would you advise the bank regarding recordation of the security interest?

CASE NOTES

1. Pasteurized Eggs Corporation (PEC) is the debtor-in-possession in a Chapter 11 bankruptcy proceeding, and BDJV is the successor in interest to the inventors of a patented process for the pasteurization of fresh in shell eggs ("Technology"). In January 1997, BDJV entered into a Patent Purchase Agreement with PEC under which BDJV agreed "to transfer and assign to [PEC] all of its respective rights, titles and interests" in the Technology. PEC agreed to pay $1,465,000 in option payments in thirteen quarterly installments beginning on the date of the agreement and extending through October 1999. The agreement provided that, upon completion of the option payments, the option will be fully exercised and the assignment of all rights in the Technology will be vested in PEC. Under the agreement, BDJV retained certain rights in the Technology, including the right to object to BDJV's choice of patent counsel, the right to file patents on improvements to the Technology, and the right to prosecute patents and defend patent infringement claims. Prepetition, PEC made all of the required option payments and BDJV and recorded the Patent Purchase Agreement with the PTO. During the Chapter 11 bankruptcy proceeding, PEC claimed it had acquired ownership rights in the Technology pursuant to the Patent Purchase Agreement and that the patents should be included in the bankruptcy estate. BDJV argued that because it retained certain rights in the Technology under the Patent Purchase Agreement, the agreement conveyed a mere license to the Technology, not title to the Technology. The parties also disagreed on whether BDJV had perfected a security interest in the Technology. Under section 544 of the Bankruptcy Code, the debtor is allowed to assume the role of a hypothetical lien creditor and avoid any unperfected security interests. BDJV argued that even if the Patent Purchase Agreement was a transfer of title in the Technology, it still retained a security interest in the Technology to ensure PEC's satisfaction of other obligations under the Patent Purchase Agreement, and that it had perfected this security interest by recording this interest with the PTO. What result. *See* In re Pasteurized Eggs Corp., 296 B.R. 283 (Bankr. D.N.H. 2003).

2. *See also* In re Tower Tech. Inc., 67 Fed. Appx. 521 (10th Cir. 2003) (Perfection of security interest in patent in Oklahoma is governed by the state's version of the Uniform Commercial Code, which was not preempted by the recording provisions of the Patent Act); In re Coldwave Systems, LLC, 368 B.R. 91 (Bankr. D. Mass. 2007) (Creditor's security interest in patent did not involve a transfer of ownership

rights and was a mere "license" which was not an assignment, grant or conveyance; therefore, the security interest could not be perfected by recording it with the Patent and Trademark Office).

Additional Information

1. JOHN FRANCIS HILSON, ASSET-BASED LENDING: A PRACTICAL GUIDE TO SECURED Financing § 17:3 (2006).

2. CORPORATE COUNSEL'S GUIDE TO BANKRUPTCY LAWS § 18:5 (2009).

3. 1 SECURITY INTERESTS IN PERSONAL PROPERTY § 16:13 (2009).

4. HOWARD C. ANAWALT, IP STRATEGY: COMPLETE INTELLECTUAL PROPERTY PLANNING, ACCESS, AND PROTECTION § 1:12 (2009).

5. RAYMOND T. NIMMER, JEFF DODD, MODERN LICENSING LAW § 16:23 (2009).

6. Aleksandar Nikolic, *Securitization of Patents and Its Continued Viability in Light of the Current Economic Conditions*, 19 ALB. L.J. SCI. & TECH. 393 (2009).

7. Jason A. Kidd, *The Ninth Circuit Falls Short While Establishing the Proper Perfection Method for Security Interests in Patents in In re Cybernetic Services*, 36 CREIGHTON L. REV. 669 (2003).

8. Stephen Dirksen, Kyle Grimshaw, *Cybernetic Implications for the U.C.C.*, 2001 DUKE L. & TECH. REV. 40 (2001).

9. Xuan-Thao Nguyen, *Collateralizing Intellectual Property*, 42 GA. L. REV. 1 (2007).

10. Kesavalu M. Bafawandoss, *Security Interests in Intellectual Property-Patents*, 33 S.U. L. REV. 93 (2005).

11. Pauline Stevens, *Security Interests in Patents and Patent Applications?*, 6 U. PITT. J. TECH. L. & POL'Y 2 (2005).

Chapter 7

LICENSING AND ANTITRUST LAW

There is an inherent tension between patent law and antitrust law. Patent law grants a patentee the exclusive right to exclude others from practicing a patent and allows this right to be transferred subject to numerous restrictions, including restrictions on how the patent may be practiced, the field, territory and period of time in which the patent may be practiced, and the consideration structure for the practice of the patent. The exclusive right of the patentee to control the use of the patent limits competition in the patent's application market and, therefore, is often referred to as the "patent monopoly." The antitrust laws, on the other hand, seek to eliminate restraints on market competition. The three main sources of antitrust law are the Sherman Act, the Clayton Act and the Federal Trade Commission Act.

Section 1 of the Sherman Act provides that: "[e]very contract, combination . . . or conspiracy, in restraint of trade or commerce among the several States, or with foreign nations, is declared to be illegal." 15 U.S.C. § 1. Section 2 of the Sherman Act makes it unlawful to "monopolize, or attempt to monopolize, or combine or conspire with any other person or persons, to monopolize any part of the trade or commerce among the several States, or with foreign nations . . . ." 15 U.S.C. § 2. Section 3 of the Clayton Act makes it unlawful "for any person engaged in commerce . . . to lease or make a sale or contract for sale of goods . . ., whether patented or unpatented . . ., or fix a price charged therefore, or discount from, or rebate upon, such price, on the condition . . ., that the lessee or purchaser thereof shall not use or deal in the goods . . ., of a competitor or competitors of the lessor or seller, where the effect of such lease, sale, or contract for sale or such condition . . ., may be to substantially lessen competition or tend to create a monopoly in any line of commerce." 15 U.S.C. § 14. Finally, Section 5 of the Federal Trade Commission Act makes it illegal to engage in "unfair methods of competition in commerce . . ."

Given the generality of the antitrust statutes, it should not be surprising that antitrust doctrine has been almost entirely developed by the federal courts. It should also not be surprising that, over the course of the hundred-plus years that federal courts have been interpreting antitrust laws, antitrust doctrine has changed with the composition of the Supreme Court, and with the changing political and economic perspectives of the times. Nonetheless, certain core antitrust concepts have remained consistent despite differing applications.

Some of the core antitrust concepts that you will encounter in this chapter include the *per se* and rule-of-reason analyses of alleged antitrust violations, actual market power and presumed market power, patent misuse and tie-in arrangements.

Under the *per se* analysis of an alleged antitrust violation, the plaintiff need only show that illegal conduct has occurred. The plaintiff need not prove that the defendant had some requisite degree of market power or that the conduct restrained competition in the relevant market. The conduct itself is irrebuttably presumed to be anticompetitive. An often-cited *per se* violation of the antitrust laws is price-fixing where competitors conspire among themselves to offer goods or services at the same, or nearly the same, price. Under the rule-of-reason analysis of an alleged antitrust violation, the plaintiff must show that the defendant had actual market power and that the conduct resulted in lessening competition in the relevant market. In applying the rule-of-reason analysis to an alleged antitrust violation, courts weigh the anti-competitive and pro-competitive effects of the defendant's conduct. If a court determines that the anti-competitive effects are greater than the pro-competitive effects, the court will find the defendant's conduct violated the antitrust laws; if a court determines that the pro-competitive effects are greater than the anti-competitive effects, the court will find the defendant's conduct did not violate the antitrust laws.

Actual market power is most often measured by a firm's market share. In general, courts have found that firms with thirty percent or less market share do not have market power, and firms with fifty percent or more market share do have market power. However, a firm will not be punished simply because it has a large market share if its market share is due to a superior product, superior marketing or superior management. Determination of a firm's market share depends entirely upon the definition of the market; and the definition of the market, in turn, depends upon the definition of the *product market* and the *geographic market*. The more broadly the product market is defined (e.g., including aluminum and steel in the building structural support market) and the more broadly the geographic market is defined (e.g., including the U.S. and Canada in the domestic market), the lower a firm's market share will be. Likewise, the converse is true; the more narrowly the product market and geographic market are defined, the higher a firm's market share will be.

Presumed market power arose in the context of a sale or license of a product or service protected by intellectual property. For many years, courts found that a firm which sold or licensed products or services protected by intellectual property was presumed to have market power in the product or service market; and, thus, the plaintiff did not have to prove actual market power to sustain an alleged antitrust violation. More recent court cases, as well as administrative rules, have done away with the presumption of market power based solely on the ownership of intellectual property. Today, a plaintiff must establish actual market power in the case of a firm which owns intellectual property just as it would in the case of firm which did not own intellectual property.

Patent misuse was a judicially created doctrine that operated outside of the antitrust laws; a patent misuse violation did not necessarily have to be an antitrust violation. Patent misuse was not an affirmative cause of action, but a defense to a patent infringement suit. The rationale behind the patent misuse doctrine was that the patentee should not be allowed to expand the scope of a patent through the imposition of onerous contract terms. We considered patent misuse earlier in the materials with respect to licensing patent pools in subsection 2.2.10 and with respect to royalties which extend beyond the patent term in subsection 2.3.9. As with other antitrust doctrines, patent misuse has undergone significant changes over the years.

Finally, tie-in sales involve situations in which the seller sells a *tying* product on the condition that the buyer also buys a *tied* product. Similar to patent misuse, the concern with tie-in sales is that the patentee is extending the scope of its patent by requiring the buyer to purchase an unpatented and unwanted product in order to acquire a patented, wanted product. To establish a tie-in sale violation of the antitrust laws, the plaintiff must prove that the defendant seller had sufficient market power in the tying product market to lessen competition in the tied product market. Here again, the issue of whether the plaintiff must prove actual market power, or whether market power will be presumed from the ownership of intellectual property, arises.

7.1   SHERMAN, CLAYTON AND FEDERAL TRADE COMMISSION ACTS

In the *Illinois Tool Works* case, the Supreme Court reviews and revises its approach to the determination of market power in the case of tie-in sales when the tying product is patented. As you read the case, consider how the Court weaves together cases that did not involve intellectual property and cases that did involve intellectual property, and cases that presumed market power and cases that did not presume market power.

ILLINOIS TOOL WORKS v. INDEPENDENT INK
547 U.S. 28 (2006)

JUSTICE STEVENS.

In *Jefferson Parish Hospital Dist. No. 2 v. Hyde* we repeated the well-settled proposition that "if the Government has granted the seller a patent or similar monopoly over a product, it is fair to presume that the inability to buy the product elsewhere gives the seller market power." This presumption of market power, applicable in the antitrust context when a seller conditions its sale of a patented product (the "tying" product) on the purchase of a second product (the "tied" product), has its foundation in the judicially created patent misuse doctrine. In 1988, Congress substantially undermined that foundation, amending the Patent Act to eliminate the market power presumption in patent misuse cases. See 35 U.S.C. § 271(d). The question presented to us today is whether the presumption of market power in a patented product should survive as a matter of antitrust law despite its demise in patent law. We conclude that the mere fact that a tying product is patented does not support such a presumption.

I

Petitioners, Trident, Inc., and its parent, Illinois Tool Works Inc., manufacture and market printing systems that include three relevant components: (1) a patented piezoelectric impulse ink jet printhead; (2) a patented ink container, consisting of a bottle and valved cap, which attaches to the printhead; and (3) specially designed, but unpatented, ink. Petitioners sell their systems to original equipment manufacturers (OEMs) who are licensed to incorporate the printheads and containers into printers that are in turn sold to companies for use in printing barcodes on cartons and packaging materials. The OEMs agree that they will purchase their ink exclusively from petitioners, and that neither they nor their customers will refill the patented containers with ink of any kind.

Respondent, Independent Ink, Inc., has developed an ink with the same chemical composition as the ink sold by petitioners. After an infringement action brought by Trident against Independent was dismissed for lack of personal jurisdiction, Independent filed suit against Trident seeking a judgment of non-infringement and invalidity of Trident's patents. In an amended complaint, it alleged that petitioners are engaged in illegal tying and monopolization in violation of §§ 1 and 2 of the Sherman Act.

After discovery, the District Court granted petitioners' motion for summary judgment on the Sherman Act claims. It rejected respondent's submission that petitioners "necessarily have market power in the market for the tying product as a matter of law solely by virtue of the patent on their printhead system, thereby rendering [the] tying arrangements *per se* violations of the antitrust laws." Finding that respondent had submitted no affirmative evidence defining the relevant market or establishing petitioners' power within it, the court concluded that respondent could not prevail on either antitrust claim. The parties settled their other claims, and respondent appealed.

After a careful review of the "long history of Supreme Court consideration of the legality of tying arrangements," the Court of Appeals for the Federal Circuit reversed the District Court's decision as to respondent's § 1 claim. Placing special reliance on our decisions in *International Salt Co. v. United States* and Loew's as well as our *Jefferson Parish* dictum, and after taking note of the academic criticism of those cases, it concluded that the "fundamental error" in petitioners' submission was its disregard of "the duty of a court of appeals to follow the precedents of the Supreme Court until the Court itself chooses to expressly overrule them." We granted certiorari to undertake a fresh examination of the history of both the judicial and legislative appraisals of tying arrangements. Our review is informed by extensive scholarly comment and a change in position by the administrative agencies charged with enforcement of the antitrust laws.

II

Over the years, however, this Court's strong disapproval of tying arrangements has substantially diminished. Rather than relying on assumptions, in its more recent opinions the Court has required a showing of market power in the tying product. Our early opinions consistently assumed that "[t]ying arrangements serve hardly any purpose beyond the suppression of competition." In 1962, in *Loew's*, the Court relied on this assumption despite evidence of significant competition in the market for the tying product. And as recently as 1969, Justice Black, writing for the majority, relied on the assumption as support for the proposition "that, at least when certain prerequisites are met, arrangements of this kind are illegal in and of themselves, and no specific showing of unreasonable competitive effect is required." Explaining the Court's decision to allow the suit to proceed to trial, he stated that "decisions rejecting the need for proof of truly dominant power over the tying product have all been based on a recognition that because tying arrangements generally serve no legitimate business purpose that cannot be achieved in some less restrictive way, the presence of any appreciable restraint on competition provides a sufficient reason for invalidating the tie."

Reflecting a changing view of tying arrangements, four Justices dissented in *Fortner I*, arguing that the challenged "tie" — the extension of a $2 million line of credit on condition that the borrower purchase prefabricated houses from the defendant — might well have served a legitimate purpose. In his opinion, Justice White noted that promotional tie-ins may provide "uniquely advantageous deals" to purchasers. And Justice Fortas concluded that the arrangement was best characterized as "a sale of a single product with the incidental provision of financing."

The dissenters' view that tying arrangements may well be procompetitive ultimately prevailed; indeed, it did so in the very same lawsuit. After the Court remanded the suit in *Fortner I*, a bench trial resulted in judgment for the plaintiff, and the case eventually made its way back to this Court. Upon return, we unanimously held that the plaintiff's failure of proof on the issue of market power was fatal to its case — the plaintiff had proved "nothing more than a willingness to provide cheap financing in order to sell expensive houses."

The assumption that "[t]ying arrangements serve hardly any purpose beyond the suppression of competition," rejected in *Fortner II*, has not been endorsed in any opinion since. Instead, it was again rejected just seven years later in *Jefferson Parish*, where, as in *Fortner II*, we unanimously reversed a Court of Appeals judgment holding that an alleged tying arrangement constituted a *per se* violation of § 1 of the Sherman Act. Like the product at issue in the *Fortner* cases, the tying product in *Jefferson Parish* — hospital services — was unpatented, and our holding again rested on the conclusion that the plaintiff had failed to prove sufficient power in the tying product market to restrain competition in the market for the tied product — services of anesthesiologists.

In rejecting the application of a *per se* rule that all tying arrangements constitute antitrust violations, we explained:

> "[W]e have condemned tying arrangements when the seller has some special ability — usually called "market power" — to force a purchaser to do something that he would not do in a competitive market . . . .

> "*Per se* condemnation — condemnation without inquiry into actual market conditions — is only appropriate if the existence of forcing is probable. Thus, application of the *per se* rule focuses on the probability of anticompetitive consequences . . . .

> "For example, if the Government has granted the seller a patent or similar monopoly over a product, it is fair to presume that the inability to buy the product elsewhere gives the seller market power. Any effort to enlarge the scope of the patent monopoly by using the market power it confers to

restrain competition in the market for a second product will undermine competition on the merits in that second market. Thus, the sale or lease of a patented item on condition that the buyer make all his purchases of a separate tied product from the patentee is unlawful."

Notably, nothing in our opinion suggested a rebuttable presumption of market power applicable to tying arrangements involving a patent on the tying good. Instead, it described the rule that a contract to sell a patented product on condition that the purchaser buy unpatented goods exclusively from the patentee is a *per se* violation of § 1 of the Sherman Act.

Justice O'Connor wrote separately in *Jefferson Parish*, concurring in the judgment on the ground that the case did not involve a true tying arrangement because, in her view, surgical services and anesthesia were not separate products. In her opinion, she questioned not only the propriety of treating any tying arrangement as a *per se* violation of the Sherman Act, but also the validity of the presumption that a patent always gives the patentee significant market power, observing that the presumption was actually a product of our patent misuse cases rather than our antitrust jurisprudence. It is that presumption, a vestige of the Court's historical distrust of tying arrangements, that we address squarely today.

****

IV

Although the patent misuse doctrine and our antitrust jurisprudence became intertwined in *International Salt*, subsequent events initiated their untwining. This process has ultimately led to today's reexamination of the presumption of *per se* illegality of a tying arrangement involving a patented product, the first case since 1947 in which we have granted review to consider the presumption's continuing validity.

Three years before we decided *International Salt*, this Court had expanded the scope of the patent misuse doctrine to include not only supplies or materials used by a patented device, but also tying arrangements involving a combination patent and "unpatented material or [a] device [that] is itself an integral part of the structure embodying the patent." In reaching this conclusion, the Court explained that it could see "no difference in principle" between cases involving elements essential to the inventive character of the patent and elements peripheral to it; both, in the Court's view, were attempts to "expand the patent beyond the legitimate scope of its monopoly."

Shortly thereafter, Congress codified the patent laws for the first time. At least partly in response to our *Mercoid* decision, Congress included a provision in its codification that excluded some conduct, such as a tying arrangement involving the sale of a patented product tied to an "essential" or "nonstaple" product that has no use except as part of the patented product or method, from the scope of the patent misuse doctrine. § 271(d). Thus, at the same time that our antitrust jurisprudence continued to rely on the assumption that "tying arrangements generally serve no legitimate business purpose," Congress began chipping away at the assumption in the patent misuse context from whence it came.

It is Congress' most recent narrowing of the patent misuse defense, however, that is directly relevant to this case. Four years after our decision in *Jefferson Parish* repeated the patent-equals-market-power presumption, Congress amended the Patent Code to eliminate that presumption in the patent misuse context. The relevant provision reads:

> "(d) No patent owner otherwise entitled to relief for infringement or contributory infringement of a patent shall be denied relief or deemed guilty of misuse or illegal extension of the patent right by reason of his having done one or more of the following: . . . (5) conditioned the license of any rights to the patent or the sale of the patented product on the acquisition of a license to rights in another patent or purchase of a separate product, *unless, in view of the circumstances, the patent owner has market power in the relevant market for the patent or patented product on which the license or sale is conditioned.*" 35 U.S.C. § 271(d)(5) (emphasis added).

The italicized clause makes it clear that Congress did not intend the mere existence of a patent to constitute the requisite "market power." Indeed, fairly read, it provides that without proof that Trident had market power in the relevant market, its conduct at issue in this case was neither "misuse" nor an "illegal extension of the patent right."

While the 1988 amendment does not expressly refer to the antitrust laws, it certainly invites a reappraisal of the *per se* rule announced in *International Salt*. A rule denying a patentee the right to enjoin an infringer is significantly less severe than a rule that makes the conduct at issue a federal crime punishable by up to 10 years in prison. It would be absurd to assume that Congress intended to provide that the use of a patent that merited punishment as a felony would not constitute "misuse." Moreover, given the fact that the patent misuse doctrine provided the basis for the market power presumption, it would be anomalous to preserve the presumption in antitrust after Congress has eliminated its foundation.

After considering the congressional judgment reflected in the 1988 amendment, we conclude that tying arrangements involving patented products should be evaluated under the standards applied in cases like *Fortner II* and *Jefferson Parish* rather than under the *per se* rule applied in *Morton Salt* and *Loew's*. While some such arrangements are still unlawful, such as those that are the product of a true monopoly or a marketwide conspiracy, that conclusion must be supported by proof of power in the relevant market rather than by a mere presumption thereof.

V

Rather than arguing that we should retain the rule of *per se* illegality, respondent contends that we should endorse a rebuttable presumption that patentees possess market power when they condition the purchase of the patented product on an agreement to buy unpatented goods exclusively from the patentee. Respondent recognizes that a large number of valid patents have little, if any, commercial significance, but submits that those that are used to impose tying arrangements on unwilling purchasers likely do exert significant market power. Hence, in respondent's view, the presumption would have no impact on patents of only slight value and would be justified, subject to being rebutted by evidence offered by the patentee, in cases in which the patent has sufficient value to enable the patentee to insist on acceptance of the tie.

Respondent also offers a narrower alternative, suggesting that we differentiate between tying arrangements involving the simultaneous purchase of two products that are arguably two components of a single product — such as the provision of surgical services and anesthesiology in the same operation, or the licensing of one copyrighted film on condition that the licensee take a package of several films in the same transaction, — and a tying arrangement involving the purchase of unpatented goods over a period of time, a so-called "requirements tie." According to respondent, we should recognize a presumption of market power when faced with the latter type of arrangements because they provide a means for charging large volume purchasers a higher royalty for use of the patent than small purchasers must pay, a form of discrimination that "is strong evidence of market power."

The opinion that imported the "patent equals market power" presumption into our antitrust jurisprudence, however, provides no support for respondent's proposed alternative. In *International Salt*, it was the existence of the patent on the tying product, rather than the use of a requirements tie, that led the Court to presume market power. Moreover, the requirements tie in that case did not involve any price discrimination between large volume and small volume purchasers or evidence of noncompetitive pricing. Instead, the leases at issue provided that if any competitor offered salt, the tied product, at a lower price, "the lessee should be free to buy in the open market, unless appellant would furnish the salt at an equal price."

As we have already noted, the vast majority of academic literature recognizes that a patent does not necessarily confer market power. Similarly, while price discrimination may provide evidence of market power, particularly if buttressed by evidence that the patentee has charged an above-market price for the tied package, it is generally recognized that it also occurs in fully competitive markets. We are not persuaded that the combination of these two factors should give rise to a presumption of market power when neither is sufficient to do so standing alone. Rather, the lesson to be learned from *International Salt* and the academic commentary is the same: Many tying arrangements, even those involving patents and requirements ties, are fully consistent with a free, competitive market. For this reason, we reject both respondent's proposed rebuttable presumption and their narrower alternative.

It is no doubt the virtual consensus among economists that has persuaded the enforcement agencies to reject the position that the Government took when it supported the *per se* rule that the Court adopted in the 1940's. In antitrust guidelines issued jointly by the Department of Justice and the Federal Trade Commission in 1995, the enforcement agencies stated that in the exercise of their prosecutorial discretion they "will not presume that a patent, copyright, or trade secret necessarily confers market power upon its owner." While that choice is not binding on the Court, it would be unusual for the Judiciary to replace the normal rule of lenity that is applied in criminal cases with a rule of severity for a special category of antitrust cases.

Congress, the antitrust enforcement agencies, and most economists have all reached the conclusion that a patent does not necessarily confer market power upon the patentee. Today, we reach the same conclusion, and therefore hold that, in all cases involving a tying arrangement, the plaintiff must prove that the defendant has market power in the tying product.

VI

In this case, respondent reasonably relied on our prior opinions in moving for summary judgment without offering evidence defining the relevant market or proving that petitioners possess power within it. When the case returns to the District Court, respondent should therefore be given a fair opportunity to develop and introduce evidence on that issue, as well as any other issues that are relevant to its remaining § 1 claims. Accordingly, the judgment of the Court of Appeals is vacated, and the case is remanded for further proceedings consistent with this opinion.

It is so ordered.

QUESTIONS

1.   Did the *Fortner II* case involve a patented tying product? If not, what is its relevance to the Court's analysis of presumed market power in the case of patented tying products?

2.   The Court notes that Congress amended the Patent Act to provide that a tying arrangement in which a nonstaple, unpatented product is tied to the sale of a patented product does not constitute patent misuse. What is a nonstaple product? Doesn't the tying of an unpatented product to a patented product, by definition, extend the scope of the patented product patent? Why would Congress allow this type of tying arrangement?

3.   What is a "requirements tying" arrangement? If a company sold a patented product on the condition that the buyer purchase from the company unpatented, staple supplies to use with the product, would this violate the antitrust laws? Would this constitute patent misuse?

4.   How does the Court view the relationship between tie-in arrangements under the antitrust laws and under the patent misuse doctrine? What does the Court deduce regarding tie-in arrangements under the antitrust laws from Congress' exclusion of tie-in arrangements under the patent misuse doctrine?

In the following case, *Static Control Components*, the court provides a thorough tutorial on the operation of the antitrust laws in a case which is factually and procedurally quite complex.

STATIC CONTROL COMPONENTS, INC. v. LEXMARK INTERNATIONAL, INC.
487 F.Supp.2d 861 (E.D. Ky. 2007)

Van Tatenhove, District Judge.

This matter is before the Court on Lexmark International, Inc.'s Motion for Summary Judgment on the Remanufacturers' Claims of affirmative antitrust and Lanham Act violations. Also before the Court is Wazana Brothers International, Inc.'s Motion for Summary Judgment on three of its Lanham Act claims.

Lexmark's Motion must be largely denied. It is granted only to the extent that the Remanufacturers have failed to produce sufficient evidence from which a reasonable jury could find that certain distribution contracts at issue are horizontal, *per se* restraints on trade and on the issue of the *per se* tying claim. Wazana's Motion is granted only to the extent that the Court holds that, as a matter of law, the allegedly false or deceptive statements at issue are not ambiguous. The remainder of Wazana's Motion must be denied since Lexmark has presented sufficient facts from which a reasonable jury could find that the statements were not false or deceptive.

I. BACKGROUND

A. FACTS

Defendant, Lexmark International, Inc. ("Lexmark"), is a manufacturer of laser printers. It controls approximately 10%–15% of the national and international laser printer market, whereas its largest competitor, Hewlett-Packard ("HP") controls between 50%–75% of the national and international markets. In addition to being in the laser printer business, Lexmark also manufactures and sells the toner cartridges for its printers. Sometimes these toner cartridges are sold under Lexmark labels. Other times, Lexmark sells its cartridges to resellers, and the cartridges are sold under those companies' labels. One of these resale agreements is with IBM, under which IBM and Lexmark entered into "a multinational procurement relationship under which Lead Buyer [IBM] and its Affiliates may purchase or license from Lead Supplier [Lexmark]." The procurement contract was not limited simply to the cartridges, but also includes equipment. Under the IBM-Lexmark contract, if IBM, while selling Lexmark products, sold compatible cartridges or re-fill cartridge kits, IBM would face contractual penalties.

B. ANTITRUST CLAIMS

1. Relevant Antitrust Law

Wazana and Pendl have asserted three separate, statutory antitrust claims against Lexmark. The first of these, Sherman Act section 1, provides, in pertinent part: "[e]very contract, combination in the form of trust or otherwise, or conspiracy, in restraint of trade or commerce among the several States, or with foreign nations, is declared to be illegal." 15 U.S.C. § 1.

The second claim asserted is a violation of Sherman Act section 2, which makes it unlawful to "monopolize, or attempt to monopolize, or combine or conspire with any other person or persons, to monopolize any part of the trade or commerce among the several States, or with foreign nations . . . ." 15 U.S.C. § 2.

Finally, Pendl and Wazana argue that Lexmark has violated section 3 of the Clayton Act:

> It shall be unlawful for any person engaged in commerce, in the course of such commerce, to lease or make a sale or contract for sale of goods, wares, merchandise, machinery, supplies, or other commodities, whether patented or unpatented, for use, consumption, or resale within the United States or any Territory thereof or the District of Columbia or any insular possession or other place under the jurisdiction of the United States, or fix a price charged therefore, or discount from, or rebate upon, such price, on the condition, agreement, or understanding that the lessee or purchaser thereof shall not use or deal in the goods, wares, merchandise, machinery, supplies, or other commodities of a competitor or competitors of the lessor or seller, where the effect of such lease, sale, or contract for sale or such condition, agreement, or understanding may be to substantially lessen competition or tend to create a monopoly in any line of commerce. 15 U.S.C. § 14.

4. The Relevant Market, Market Power, and Other Factors: Sherman Act Section 1

i. Market Power

" Market power is the power to force a purchaser to do something that he would not do in a competitive market," and it entails the ability of one seller to restrict output or raise prices. In order for a Sherman Act claim to lie against a defendant, there must be a finding of market power. Determining market power is, thus, critical to this Court's inquiry. A toner cartridge is nothing more than a part which is purchased in order to make a machine function. As such, this Court must begin its market power examination with the line of case law examining market power in the context of a machine repair market.

The line of on-point cases traces back to *Eastman Kodak*. In *Eastman Kodak*, the Supreme Court looked to whether Kodak affected an illegal tying agreement when it entered into a contract with its copy machine parts suppliers. The contract was formed after Kodak sold the original copiers, and it prevented the parts suppliers from selling replacement parts to copy machine repairmen. This prohibition essentially allowed Kodak to corner the repair market through its control of the parts markets. The issue in *Eastman Kodak* was whether the service market could be tied to the parts market, not whether the service or parts markets were tied to the equipment market. The Court distinguished between two possible markets within an aftermarket, one for service and the other for parts, and it left to the jury the issue of whether these two aftermarkets were separate. Ultimately, the Court held that a company need not have market power in the primary, i.e., copier, market in order to have market power in the tying, i.e., copy machine parts, market.

Out of this broad holding grew a Sixth Circuit case, which at first seems analogous to the current action. In *PSI Repair Services, Inc.*, the issue was whether Honeywell, an industrial control equipment manufacturer, should be allowed to prevent customers from seeking outside service repair by requiring that customers purchase a repair part, a circuit board, from Honeywell. Only a small percentage of the parts on the circuit board were made exclusively by Honeywell, and the rest of the board was made for Honeywell by outside contractors. In effect, Honeywell's policy devastated the third party repair industry by cutting off the supply of replacement parts.

The Sixth Circuit took a two step approach to determine if Honeywell possessed market power sufficient to support Sherman Act claims. First, the court decided that the primary equipment market was the relevant market for an antitrust analysis. Second, the court decided that Honeywell could not, as a matter of law, have sufficient power within the primary market to support Sherman Act claims.

In distinguishing the holding in *Eastman Kodak* from that of *PSI Repair Services*, the Sixth Circuit set out the following language, which is instructive to this Court's query:

> We likewise agree that the change in policy in *Kodak* was the crucial factor in the Court's decision. By changing its policy after its customers were "locked in," Kodak took advantage of the fact that its customers lacked the information to anticipate this change. Therefore, it was Kodak's own actions that increased its customers' information costs. In our view, this was the evil condemned by the Court . . . .

> . . . [W]e thus hold that an antitrust plaintiff cannot succeed on a *Kodak*-type theory when the defendant has not changed its policy after locking-in some of its customers, and the defendant has been otherwise forthcoming about its pricing structure and service policies . . . .

> . . . . If there were any evidence in the record that Honeywell took advantage of its customers' imperfect information in order to reap supra-competitive profits in the aftermarkets for its equipment, we would not hesitate to allow a *Kodak*-type theory to be submitted to the jury.

The factual underpinnings of *PSI Repair Services* elucidate the Sixth Circuit's reasoning. There were "no allegations that Honeywell changed its parts-restrictive policy," and the seller's policy was generally known. Prior to sale, there were lengthy negotiations, during which various service plans were offered and estimates of service costs and parts' failure rates were provided upon request. The evidence of information availability, specifically information provided and limited by the manufacturer as opposed to the general information costs imposed by a functioning marketplace, was the crucial distinction from *Kodak* which lead the court to ultimately determine that there was insufficient market power as a matter of law. Under this Sixth Circuit precedent, in order for a plaintiff to succeed on a

Kodak-type theory — that a lack of market power in the equipment market does not necessarily preclude market power sufficient for a section 1 claim — there must be some evidence that the defendant has changed its policy after locking-in customers and that the defendant has not "been otherwise forthcoming about its pricing structure and service policies."

Though the Motion before the Court involves a myriad of alleged anticompetitive behavior going well beyond the scope of the *PSI Repair Services* and *Kodak* holdings (i.e., tying), these cases remain relevant to the determination of market power. First, the Court notes that implicit in both parties' discussions of the instant motion was the assumption that the cartridge and printer markets are separate. However, even if the parties' were to contest this issue, their dispute would leave a question of fact. Second, it is clear under both *Eastman Kodak* and *PSI Repair Services* that the printer market is, at least initially, the relevant market for the determination of market power.

The seminal question, then, is whether Lexmark possesses sufficient market power when applying the rule of *PSI Repair Services.* It is undisputed that Lexmark does not hold a sufficient grasp on the printer market such that an inference of market power can be drawn. Thus, the issue becomes whether the Remanufacturers have submitted sufficient evidence of a change in Lexmark's policy such that market power may still be present.

The Remanufacturers have presented several pieces of evidence in favor of a finding of market power. Especially important to the disposition of this Motion are the following facts: (1) imperfect ability to determine life-time, or life-cycle, costs for printers; (2) Lexmark was able to increase the price of remanufactured cartridges; and (3) Lexmark did not actually always provide non-prebate cartridges. To the extent that Lexmark argues that these facts are incorrect, there is a disputed issue of fact that, for the purposes of summary judgment, must be resolved in favor of the Remanufacturers. When the Remanufacturers' facts are taken as true, they are sufficient under the *Kodak*-theory, as developed by *PSI Repair Services*, to create a genuine issue of fact best left for the jury. Stated alternatively, a reasonable jury could find that the Remanufacturers have presented more than a mere scintilla of evidence that Lexmark misled customers into believing that non-prebate cartridges would be available; lifetime costs were impossible to calculate; and that Lexmark caused an increase in the overall price of available cartridges. To wit, the Remanufacturers' have presented evidence which falls squarely within the factors outlined and decried by *Kodak* and *PSI Repair Services.* If a jury finds that Lexmark did, in fact, not provide non-prebate cartridges when it claimed that those cartridges were available, the jury could also find that Lexmark used market power to take advantage of its customers' imperfect knowledge in order to corner the remanufactured cartridge market. In sum, this Court cannot determine, at this stage, that Lexmark does not possess market power. Summary judgment on Sherman Act section 1 cannot be granted based on an absence of market power.

The Court should caution, however, that situations such as this, wherein market power does not automatically flow from market share, are difficult to prove. The Supreme Court's cautionary language is instructive:

[i]n the end, of course, [the defendant]'s . . . argument[ ] may prove to be correct. It may be . . . that the equipment market does discipline the aftermarkets so that [both] are priced competitively overall, or that any anti-competitive effects of [the defendant]'s behavior are outweighed by its competitive effects. But [this Court] cannot reach these conclusions as a matter of law on [this] record.

The disputed issues of fact must first go to the jury.

ii. Remaining Section 1 Factors

While the Court has concluded its analysis under the market share argument made by Lexmark, it has by no means addressed all the arguments raised by Lexmark. Lexmark makes specific arguments under both a *per se* and a *rule-of-reason* approach. For the purposes of analysis under those approaches, the Court assumes that there is sufficient market power.

Several additional reasons supporting summary judgment were woven into Lexmark's argument on market power. Specifically, Lexmark argues that there is insufficient evidence for finding anticompetitive behavior under any of the Sherman Act section 1 standards. There are two standards for determining whether actions violate section 1 of the Sherman Act: (1) *per se* violations and (2) violations subject to the *rule of reason*. *Per se* violations do not require a finding that the defendant's actions were anticompetitive, but they do require the plaintiff to show that the defendant "possesses market power or unique access to a business element necessary for effective competition."

If the facts do not sustain a finding of a *per se* violation, then the Court will apply the *rule-of-reason* approach. A "*rule-of-reason*" analysis involves, inter alia, a study of consequences of the conduct on the affected market before imposition of antitrust sanctions.

(a) *Per Se* Violations

(1) Tying

A per se tying arrangement is "an agreement by a party to sell one product but only on the condition that the buyer also purchases a different (or tied) product, or at least agrees that he will not purchase that product from any other supplier." In a tying claim, a party is able to exclude competitors from a market because of its "power or leverage in another market." In order to present a *per se* tying claim, a "seller must possess substantial market power in the tying product market." If there is appreciable power in the tying market, then a court must determine whether the defendant's conduct is pro-competitive or anticompetitive. Determining whether a party's actions have an anticompetitive effect requires use of the Sixth Circuit's three step analysis: "(1) the seller must have power in the tying product market; (2) there must be a substantial threat that the tying seller will acquire market power in the tied-product market; and (3) there must be a coherent economic basis for treating the tying and tied products as distinct."

As to the first prong, the Supreme Court reexamined the market power of patent holders within the context of a tying claim. *Ill. Tool Works, Inc.* The issue before the Court was whether there was an automatic presumption of market power with patented goods. The Supreme Court rejected a *per se* approach to patented good tying claims and held that patented products should be examined under a case-by-case, market based approach.

Lexmark is seeking summary judgment on the issue of whether the Remanufacturers can prove that there is impermissible tying between Lexmark's printers and its printer cartridges. Regardless of any *Kodak-PSI* theory that might ultimately lead to a finding of market power, the *per se* approach is no longer an appropriate means by which a patented good can be found to be an illegal tying agreement. The means available to the Remanufacturers is through applying the *rule of reason*. To the extent that Lexmark seeks summary judgment on the issue of a *per se* tying arrangement, this Court will grant the Motion.

(2) Contracts

The next issue before the Court is whether Lexmark's distribution contracts are *per se* restraints of trade. When looking to whether a contract in restraint of trade is anticompetitive under section 1 of the Sherman Act, the key issue is whether that contract addresses a horizontal or vertical market. Horizontal conspiracies are "agreements among competitors at the same level of market structure to stifle trade, such as agreements among manufacturers or among distributors to fix prices for a given product." Vertical conspiracies are "agreements among actors at different levels of market structure to restrain trade, "such as agreements between a manufacturer and its distributors to exclude another distributor from a given product and geographic market." " While horizontal restraints of trade fall under *per se* analysis, a vertical restraint will be analyzed pursuant to the *rule of reason*.

The Remanufacturers state that Lexmark's contracts with certain resellers, specifically Dell and IBM, are horizontal restraints of trade, which are *per se* anticompetitive. The Remanufacturers do not, however, cite to any evidence submitted in support of this position. In contrast, Lexmark has submitted examples of six separate resale agreements, none of which are with Dell or IBM, and has referred the Court to a copy of the IBM agreement, which was submitted by SCC. Though this Court must presume that the Remanufacturers' version of the facts are correct, they must still present some affirmative evidence to support their position. Because the Remanufacturers have not presented any evidence in support of their allegation of a horizontal restraint of trade, Lexmark's evidence must be taken as true.

A review of the contracts provided by Lexmark reveals that these are not horizontal restraints of trade. They go well beyond "naked restraints of trade with no purpose except stifling competition." The contracts are specifically designated as "resale" agreements that provide for sale of goods under the purchaser's label. The IBM contract is "for a multinational procurement relationship." Lexmark's agreements, therefore, "involve agreements among actors at different levels of market structure to restrain trade." To the extent that Lexmark seeks summary judgment that the agreements between it and IBM, Dell, and any other reseller are not horizontal restraints of trade which are *per se* anticompetitive, summary judgment is appropriate. As vertical trade agreements, they are subject to the *rule of reason.*

(b) The Rule of Reason

When applying the *rule of reason,* "an agreement limiting consumer choice by impeding the "ordinary give and take of the market place" cannot be sustained." The general test for whether there is an antitrust violation under the *rule of reason* "is whether the restraint imposed is such as merely regulates and perhaps thereby promotes competition or whether it is such as may suppress or even destroy competition."

The parties do not clearly distinguish between the *rule of reason* and the *per se* arguments within Lexmark's Motion. Because Lexmark is clearly seeking summary judgment on the tying and contract claims, regardless of whether Lexmark is clear in its *rule-of-reason* argument, this Court will address both of those issues.

(1) Tying

As already addressed, whether a patented good has created an illegal tying agreement under section 1 of the Sherman Act is a question to be analyzed under a case-by-case, *rule-of-reason* analysis. Here, the issue of market power cannot be decided on summary judgment because there remain disputed issues of fact. Because Lexmark relies only on market power, and the issue of market power cannot be decided at this stage of the litigation, Lexmark's Motion must be denied insofar as it relates to the Remanufacturers' tying claim under the *rule-of-reason,* case-by-case, analysis articulated by the Supreme Court in *Illinois Tool Works, Inc.*

(2) Contract

The IBM contract cited by Lexmark contains the following clause:

> In addition, if Buyer promotes or sells non-Supplier business printer cartridges or re-fill kits that function in Eligible Printers, Buyer will notify Supplier, in which case Supplier will not be required to pay any Consideration for the annual period in which the non-Supplier inkjet cartridge or re-fill kits were promoted or sold by Buyer.

The contract later adds the following at the end of that clause: "and Supplier shall have the right to immediately terminate this Appendix G."

This record is very limited, but it is the only evidence that the Court has before it. This contract prohibits the reseller from also selling or promoting non-Lexmark cartridges, albeit inkjet cartridges, and its enforcement tool is the threat of lost consideration. On this very limited record, this prohibition might ultimately be found to be a device through which trade was suppressed. That is to say, it is not clear that the Lexmark-IBM contract simply dictates the methods whereby trade will be effectuated. Therefore, the Court cannot hold as a matter of law that Lexmark did not unreasonably destroy competition through unreasonable, contractual market restraints.

5. The Relevant Market and Monopoly Power: Sherman Act Section 2

In order to prevail on a Section 2 claim, the Remanufacturers must demonstrate "(1) the possession of monopoly power in a relevant market; and (2) the willful acquisition, maintenance, or use of that power by anti-competitive means as opposed to "growth or development resulting from a superior product, business acumen, or historical accident." Section 2 claims are examined under a fact specific analysis, and in proving its claim, a plaintiff must first "define the relevant product and geographic markets in which it competes with the alleged monopolizer, and with respect to the monopolization claim, to show that the defendant, in fact, possesses monopoly power." "

"To establish the offense of monopolization a plaintiff must demonstrate that a defendant either unfairly attained or maintained monopoly power. To have monopoly power, a defendant must have "the power to control prices or exclude competition. "[W]hen a competitor, with a dangerous probability of success, engages in anti-competitive practices the specific design of which are, to build a monopoly or exclude or destroy competition," there is an attempted monopolization. Section 2 monopoly power "requires . . . something greater than market power under Section 1." "

The standard for monopoly power is, in fact, very high, and is typically defined by the market share. For example, in *Eastman Kodak*, the Supreme Court held that there was a triable issue of fact as to whether Kodak held monopoly power when Kodak controlled 80% to 95% of the service market and 100% of the parts market. In *Grinnell*, the Court held that 87% of market power could constitute monopoly power, and in American Tobacco Co. v. United States the Court determined that control of over two-thirds of the market could amount to monopoly power.

While market share might, in many instances, lead to an inference of monopoly power, it is not, in and of itself, the only factor to consider. "[M]arket share is only a starting point for determining whether monopoly power exists, and the inference of monopoly power does not automatically follow from the possession of a commanding market share." Within the context of an aftermarket monopolization, there are special factors to consider.

When there is an allegation of aftermarket monopolization, the analysis is more complex, "because market share data standing alone is not necessarily a reliable proxy for monopoly power." It is to be expected that a company will supply a large percentage of its aftermarket parts and services. It is only when there are "significant information and switching costs that the "link between the primary market and the aftermarket" is severed for monopolization purposes. In sum, "[o]nly a careful factual analysis of the market in question will reveal whether monopoly power, in fact, exists."

The Remanufacturers have presented a triable issue of fact as to whether Lexmark enjoyed monopoly power. Summary judgment in *Eastman Kodak* was inappropriate because questions of fact remained regarding supracompetitive pricing, indeterminate lifecycle costs, and high switching costs. The Remanufacturers have submitted evidence that would satisfy three of these factors: that Lexmark controlled, at a minimum, 75% of the market for remanufactured sales and 80% of the overall market for Lexmark-compatible toner cartridges; that Lexmark was able to charge a higher price for its remanufactured cartridges than the remanufacturers charged; and that determining a life-cycle cost for a printer is nearly impossible. As a result, this Court cannot, at this stage of litigation, hold that the market reality was such that Lexmark was not able to gain monopoly power.

Lexmark appears to have rested its entire section 2 argument on the issue of monopoly power. Since Lexmark does not argue whether the Remanufacturers have presented sufficient evidence that it willfully acquired, maintained, or used potential monopoly power through the use of anti-competitive means, this Court need not address this issue. Even if addressed, there is evidence that Lexmark engaged in the Prebate program in order to achieve total control over the remanufactured cartridge market. Suffice it to say, neither prong one or prong two under a Sherman Act § 2 analysis is sufficient to grant summary judgment for Lexmark.

6. The Relevant Market and Market Power: Clayton Act

The Clayton Act addresses the legality of exclusive dealing contracts. An exclusive dealing contract is formed when a good is sold on the condition that the buyer not deal with competitors of the seller. In order to be an illegal exclusive dealing contract, a court must engage in a three-part inquiry. First, a court must determine "line of commerce, i.e. the type of goods . . ." that are involved. Second, the court must determine that there is a relationship between the anticompetitive actions and the market. Third, "the competition foreclosed by the contract must be found to constitute a substantial share of the relevant market."

Under the Clayton Act, "the relevant market is the prime factor in relation to which the ultimate question, whether the contract forecloses competition in a substantial share of the line of commerce involved, must be decided." Clayton Act claims are generally analyzed in conjunction with a Sherman Act section 1 discussion, and the same facts are relevant to a market power determination under both statutes. As the Court has previously discussed, the Remanufacturers have presented sufficient evidence to proceed on the question of whether Lexmark has used its power in the market to foreclose a significant amount of competition. Summary judgment is inappropriate on this issue.

****

III. CONCLUSION

Accordingly, for the foregoing reasons and being sufficiently advised, it is hereby ORDERED as follows:

1. that Defendant's Motion for Summary Judgment is DENIED in part and GRANTED in part;

2. that Counterclaim-Defendant's Motion for Summary Judgment is DENIED in part and GRANTED in part; [and]

3. that Counterclaim-Defendant's Motion for Hearing on its Motion for Summary Judgment is DENIED as moot.

QUESTIONS

1. The court found that Lexmark controlled approximately 10–15% of the national and international laser printer market, whereas Lexmark's largest competitor, Hewlett-Packard, controlled 50–75% of the national and international laser printer market. Nonetheless, the court found that Lexmark may have monopoly market power sufficient to support a Sherman Act Section 2 claim? How did the court define the relevant potential monopoly market?

2. Why did the court grant Lexmark's motion for summary judgment on the issue of whether Remanufactures can show a *per se* unlawful tying of Lexmark's printers and its print cartridges?

3. The court states that, in order to present a *per se* tying claim, a seller must possess substantial market power in the tying product market and the court must determine whether the defendant's conduct is pro-competitive or anticompetitive. How is this definition of a *per se* tying claim different from a rule-of-reason definition of a tying claim? Is the court's definition of a *per se* tying claim consistent with its grant of Lexmark's motion for summary judgment on the issue of whether Remanufactures can show a *per se* unlawful tying of Lexmark's printers and print cartridges?

4. What is the difference between market power under the *Kodak* and *PSI Repair Services* holdings and market power based on market share? Did the evidence Remanufactures presented on the imperfect ability to determine life-cycle costs for printers, Lexmark's price increases on remanufactured cartridges, and Lexmark's failure to always provide non-prebate cartridges show that Lexmark had changed its policy on tying its printers and print cartridges after the sale of its printers?

5. If Lexmark had not required purchasers of its printers to also purchase its print cartridges, but instead provided that the use of non-Lexmark print cartridges would void all warranties on its Lexmark printers, would this have been an unlawful tie-in arrangement?

6. Why are horizontal restraints of trade *per se* anticompetitive and vertical restraints of trade subject to the rule-of-reason analysis?

7. How much of the court's decision can be explained simply by the fact that it was deciding on motions for summary judgment?

CASE NOTES

1. Over-end takeoff (OETO) devices are used in the manufacture of disposable diapers. In 1998, Diaper Producer A developed an OETO device for use in its manufacturing processes. Accratec, another disposable diaper manufacturer, performed testing on Diaper Producer A's device and eventually developed an OETO device of its own that was based on, and substantially similar to, Diaper Producer

A's device. Accratec filed a patent application on is device in 2001 and subsequently assigned its rights in the patent to Du Pont. Du Pont filed additional patent applications on the OETO device but concealed from the PTO the true identity of the inventors and knowledge of prior art. The '054 patent issued to Du Pont, and Du Pont then reassigned the patent to Invista, a Du Pont subsidiary, which then granted Accratec the exclusive right to manufacture and sell the patented OETO device. OverEnd claimed it developed its own, non-infringing OETO device in 2004, but has been unable to market its device because Invista has used the '054 patent to obtain injunctions prohibiting OverEnd from showing its device at trade shows and has advised all potential customers that it owned all patent rights to OETO devices and will vigorously enforce them. Invista currently has 70–80% market share in the OETO device market. OverEnd brought suit against Invista alleging four causes of action: a declaration of non-infringement of the '054 patent; a declaration that the '054 patent is invalid; an allegation that Invista and Accratec have conspired to restrain trade in the OETO device market by using the fraudulently obtained '054 patent to obtain injunctions and threaten law suits against OverEnd; and an allegation that Invista has attempted to monopolize the market for OETO devices. In defense, Invista argued that OverEnd has failed to plead facts explaining why the market alleged is the relevant and economically significant product market, and that OverEnd has failed to plead an antitrust injury stemming from reduced competition. What result? *See* OverEnd Technologies, LLC v. Invista S.A.R.L., 431 F. Supp. 2d 925 (E.D. Wis. 2006.)

2.   *See also* Walker Process Equip., Inc. v. Food Machinery and Chemical Corp., 382 U.S. 172 (1965) (Enforcement of a patent procured by fraud on the PTO may violate the Sherman Act provided other elements necessary to a Sherman Act violation are present; under these facts, a violation of the Sherman Act could give rise to treble damages under Section 4 of the Clayton Act); Schor v. Abbott Laboratories, 378 F. Supp. 2d 850 (N.D. Ill. 2005) (In a consumer class action filed under the Sherman Act alleging pharmaceutical manufacturer used its monopoly over its patented AIDS drug to unreasonably inflate prices of competitor's drug combinations that included the patented AIDS drug, manufacturer could not be held liable under monopoly leveraging theory for violation of Section 2 of the Sherman Act); Monsanto Co. v. Scruggs, 459 F. 3d 1328 (Fed. Cir. 2006) (Patentee's "no replant" policy was a valid exercise of its rights under the patent laws, not a violation of antitrust laws).

Additional Information

1.   Louis Altman & Malla Pollack, Callman On Unfair Comp., Tr. & Mono. § 10:19 (4th ed.) (2010).

2.   Robert A. Matthews, Jr., 5 Annotated Patent Digest § 34:43 (2010).

3.   Corp. Counsel's Antitrust Deskbook § 14:16 (2009).

4.   Thomas V. Vakerics, Antitrust Basics §§ 7.11, 11:02 (2009).

5.   Robert S. Chaloupka, Sp Study for Corp Couns on Major Supply Agrmts § 15:10 (2009).

6. WILLIAM C. HOLMES, 1 HOLMES, INTELLECTUAL PROPERTY AND ANTITRUST LAW § 8:2 (2010).

7. WILLIAM C. HOLMES, 2 HOLMES, INTELLECTUAL PROPERTY AND ANTITRUST LAW §§ 20:2, 28:2 (2010).

8. Robert S. Chaloupka, *From Salt to Ink: The Perplexing Problem of Market Power in Tying Cases*, 135 ANTITRUST COUNSELOR ARTICLE I (2006).

9. Anne Layne-Farrar, *Antitrust and Intellectual Property Rights: Assessing the Link Between Standards and Market Power*, 21 SUM ANTITRUST 42 (2007).

10. Kevin D. McDonald, *Moving Forward While Facing Backward: Illinois Tool Rejects the Presumption of Market Power in Patent Tying Cases*, 20 SUM ANTITRUST 33 (2006).

11. Puneet V. Kakkar, *Still Tied Up: Illinois Tool v. Independent Ink*, 22 BERKELEY TECH. L.J. 47 (2007).

12. Harvey I. Saferstein, *Patent Licensing and the Antitrust Laws*, 899 PLI/PAT 913 (2007).

13. Kathleen A. Dorton, *Intellectual Property Tying Arrangements: Has the Market Power Presumption Reached the End of Its Rope*, 57 DEPAUL L. REV. 539 (2008).

7.2 DOJ-FTC ANTITRUST LICENSING GUIDELINES

ANTITRUST GUIDELINES FOR THE LICENSING OF INTELLECTUAL PROPERTY
1995 WL 1146232 (D.O.J.)
Issued By The U.S. Department Of Justice And The Federal Trade Commission

1. Intellectual property protection and the antitrust laws

1.0 These Guidelines state the antitrust enforcement policy of the U.S. Department of Justice and the Federal Trade Commission (individually, "the Agency," and collectively, "the Agencies") with respect to the licensing of intellectual property protected by patent, copyright, and trade secret law, and of know-how. By stating their general policy, the Agencies hope to assist those who need to predict whether the Agencies will challenge a practice as anticompetitive. However, these Guidelines cannot remove judgment and discretion in antitrust law enforcement. Moreover, the standards set forth in these Guidelines must be applied in unforeseeable circumstances. Each case will be evaluated in light of its own facts, and these Guidelines will be applied reasonably and flexibly.

The intellectual property laws and the antitrust laws share the common purpose of promoting innovation and enhancing consumer welfare. The intellectual property laws provide incentives for innovation and its dissemination and commercialization by establishing enforceable property rights for the creators of new and useful products, more efficient processes, and original works of expression. In the absence of intellectual property rights, imitators could more rapidly exploit the efforts of innovators and investors without compensation. Rapid imitation would reduce the commercial value of innovation and erode incentives to invest, ultimately to the detriment of consumers. The antitrust laws promote innovation and consumer welfare by prohibiting certain actions that may harm competition with respect to either existing or new ways of serving consumers.

2. General principles

2.0 These Guidelines embody three general principles: (a) for the purpose of antitrust analysis, the Agencies regard intellectual property as being essentially comparable to any other form of property; (b) the Agencies do not presume that intellectual property creates market power in the antitrust context; and (c) the Agencies recognize that intellectual property licensing allows firms to combine complementary factors of production and is generally pro-competitive.

2.1 Standard antitrust analysis applies to intellectual property

The Agencies apply the same general antitrust principles to conduct involving intellectual property that they apply to conduct involving any other form of tangible or intangible property. That is not to say that intellectual property is in all respects the same as any other form of property. Intellectual property has important characteristics, such as ease of misappropriation, that distinguish it from many other forms of property. These characteristics can be taken into account by standard antitrust analysis, however, and do not require the application of fundamentally different principles.

2.2 Intellectual property and market power

Market power is the ability profitably to maintain prices above, or output below, competitive levels for a significant period of time. The Agencies will not presume that a patent, copyright, or trade secret necessarily confers market power upon its owner. Although the intellectual property right confers the power to exclude with respect to the specific product, process, or work in question, there will often be sufficient actual or potential close substitutes for such product, process, or work to prevent the exercise of market power. If a patent or her form of intellectual property does confer market power, that market power does not by itself offend the antitrust laws. As with any other tangible or intangible asset that enables its owner to obtain significant supra-competitive profits, market power (or even a monopoly) that is solely "a consequence of a superior product, business acumen, or historic accident" does not violate the antitrust laws. Nor does such market power impose on the intellectual property owner an obligation to license the use of that property to others. As in other antitrust contexts, however, market power could be illegally acquired or maintained, or, even if lawfully acquired and maintained, would be relevant to the ability of an intellectual property owner to harm competition through unreasonable conduct in connection with such property.

2.3 Procompetitive benefits of licensing

Intellectual property typically is one component among many in a production process and derives value from its combination with complementary factors. Complementary factors of production include manufacturing and distribution facilities, workforces, and other items of intellectual property. The owner of intellectual property has to arrange for its combination with other necessary factors to realize its commercial value. Often, the owner finds it most efficient to contract with others for these factors, to sell rights to the intellectual property, or to enter into a joint venture arrangement for its development, rather than supplying these complementary factors itself.

Licensing, cross-licensing, or otherwise transferring intellectual property (hereinafter "licensing") can facilitate integration of the licensed property with complementary factors of production. This integration can lead to more efficient exploitation of the intellectual property, benefiting consumers through the reduction of costs and the introduction of new products. Such arrangements increase the value of intellectual property to consumers and to the developers of the technology. By potentially increasing the expected returns from intellectual property, licensing also can increase the incentive for its creation and thus promote greater investment in research and development.

Field-of-use, territorial, and other limitations on intellectual property licenses may serve pro-competitive ends by allowing the licensor to exploit its property as efficiently and effectively as possible. These various forms of exclusivity can be used to give a licensee an incentive to invest in the commercialization and distribution of products embodying the licensed intellectual property and to develop additional applications for the licensed property. The restrictions may do so, for example, by protecting the licensee against free-riding on the licensee's investments by other licensees or by the licensor. They may also increase the licensor's incentive to license, for example, by protecting the licensor from competition in the licensor's own technology in a market niche that it prefers to keep to itself. These benefits of licensing restrictions apply to patent, copyright, and trade secret licenses, and to know-how agreements.

3. Antitrust concerns and modes of analysis

3.1 Nature of the concerns

While intellectual property licensing arrangements are typically welfare-enhancing and pro-competitive, antitrust concerns may nonetheless arise. For example, a licensing arrangement could include restraints that adversely affect competition in goods markets by dividing the markets among firms that would have competed using different technologies. An arrangement that effectively merges the research and development activities of two of only a few entities that could plausibly engage in research and development in the relevant field might harm competition for development of new goods and services. An acquisition of intellectual property may lessen competition in a relevant antitrust market. The

Agencies will focus on the actual effects of an arrangement, not on its formal terms.

The Agencies will not require the owner of intellectual property to create competition in its own technology. However, antitrust concerns may arise when a licensing arrangement harms competition among entities that would have been actual or likely potential competitors in a relevant market in the absence of the license (entities in a "horizontal relationship"). A restraint in a licensing arrangement may harm such competition, for example, if it facilitates market division or price-fixing. In addition, license restrictions with respect to one market may harm such competition in another market by anti-competitively foreclosing access to, or significantly raising the price of, an important input, or by facilitating coordination to increase price or reduce output. When it appears that such competition may be adversely affected, the Agencies will follow the analysis set forth below.

3.2 Markets affected by licensing arrangements

Licensing arrangements raise concerns under the antitrust laws if they are likely to affect adversely the prices, quantities, qualities, or varieties of goods and services either currently or potentially available. The competitive effects of licensing arrangements often can be adequately assessed within the relevant markets for the goods affected by the arrangements. In such instances, the Agencies will delineate and analyze only goods markets. In other cases, however, the analysis may require the delineation of markets for technology or markets for research and development (innovation markets).

3.2.1 Goods markets

A number of different goods markets may be relevant to evaluating the effects of a licensing arrangement. A restraint in a licensing arrangement may have competitive effects in markets for final or intermediate goods made using the intellectual property, or it may have effects upstream, in markets for goods that are used as inputs, along with the intellectual property, to the production of other goods. In general, for goods markets affected by a licensing arrangement, the Agencies will approach the delineation of relevant market and the measurement of market share in the intellectual property area as in section 1 of the U.S. Department of Justice and Federal Trade Commission Horizontal Merger Guidelines.

3.2.2 Technology markets

Technology markets consist of the intellectual property that is licensed (the "licensed technology") and its close substitutes — that is, the technologies or goods that are close enough substitutes significantly to constrain the exercise of market power with respect to the intellectual property that is licensed. When rights to intellectual property are marketed separately from the products in which they are used, the Agencies may rely on technology markets to analyze the competitive effects of a licensing arrangement.

3.2.3 Research and development: innovation markets

If a licensing arrangement may adversely affect competition to develop new or improved goods or processes, the Agencies will analyze such an impact either as a separate competitive effect in relevant goods or technology markets, or as a competitive effect in a separate innovation market. A licensing arrangement may have competitive effects on innovation that cannot be adequately addressed through the analysis of goods or technology markets. For example, the arrangement may affect the development of goods that do not yet exist. Alternatively, the arrangement may affect the development of new or improved goods or processes in geographic markets where there is no actual or likely potential competition in the relevant goods.

An innovation market consists of the research and development directed to particular new or improved goods or processes, and the close substitutes for that research and development. The close substitutes are research and development efforts, technologies, and goods that significantly constrain the exercise of market power with respect to the relevant research and development, for example by limiting the ability and incentive of a hypothetical monopolist to retard the pace of research and development. The Agencies will delineate an innovation market only when the capabilities to engage in the relevant research and development can be associated with specialized assets or characteristics of specific firms.

3.3 Horizontal and vertical relationships

As with other property transfers, antitrust analysis of intellectual property licensing arrangements examines whether the relationship among the parties to the arrangement is primarily horizontal or vertical in nature, or whether it has substantial aspects of both. A licensing arrangement has a vertical component when it affects activities that are in a complementary relationship, as is typically the case in a licensing arrangement. For example, the licensor's primary line of business may be in research and development, and the licensees, as manufacturers, may be buying the rights to use technology developed by the licensor. Alternatively, the licensor may be a component manufacturer owning intellectual property rights in a product that the licensee manufactures by combining the component with other inputs, or the licensor may manufacture the product, and the licensees may operate primarily in distribution and marketing.

In addition to this vertical component, the licensor and its licensees may also have a horizontal relationship. For analytical purposes, the Agencies ordinarily will treat a relationship between a licensor and its licensees, or between licensees, as horizontal when they would have been actual or likely potential competitors in a relevant market in the absence of the license.

The existence of a horizontal relationship between a licensor and its licensees does not, in itself, indicate that the arrangement is anticompetitive. Identification of such relationships is merely an aid in determining whether there may be anticompetitive effects arising from a licensing arrangement. Such a relationship need not give rise to an anticompetitive effect, nor does a purely vertical relationship assure that there are no anticompetitive effects.

4. General principles concerning the Agencies' evaluation of licensing arrangements under the rule of reason

4.1 Analysis of anticompetitive effects

The existence of anticompetitive effects resulting from a restraint in a licensing arrangement will be evaluated on the basis of the analysis described in this section.

4.1.2 Licensing arrangements involving exclusivity

A licensing arrangement may involve exclusivity in two distinct respects. First, the licensor may grant one or more exclusive licenses, which restrict the right of the licensor to license others and possibly also to use the technology itself. Generally, an exclusive license may raise antitrust concerns only if the licensees themselves, or the licensor and its licensees, are in a horizontal relationship. Examples of arrangements involving exclusive licensing that may give rise to antitrust concerns include cross-licensing by parties collectively possessing market power, grantbacks, and acquisitions of intellectual property rights.

A non-exclusive license of intellectual property that does not contain any restraints on the competitive conduct of the licensor or the licensee generally does not present antitrust concerns even if the parties to the license are in a horizontal relationship, because the non-exclusive license normally does not diminish competition that would occur in its absence.

A second form of exclusivity, exclusive dealing, arises when a license prevents or restrains the licensee from licensing, selling, distributing, or using competing technologies. Exclusivity may be achieved by an explicit exclusive dealing term in the license or by other provisions such as compensation terms or other economic incentives. Such restraints may anti-competitively foreclose access to, or increase competitors' costs of obtaining, important inputs, or facilitate coordination to raise price or reduce output, but they also may have pro-competitive effects. For example, a licensing arrangement that prevents the licensee from dealing in other technologies may encourage the licensee to develop and market the licensed technology or specialized applications of that technology. The Agencies will take into account such pro-competitive effects in evaluating the reasonableness of the arrangement.

4.3 Antitrust "safety zone"

Because licensing arrangements often promote innovation and enhance competition, the Agencies believe that an antitrust "safety zone" is useful in order to provide some degree of certainty and thus to encourage such activity. Absent extraordinary circumstances, the Agencies will not challenge a restraint in an intellectual property licensing arrangement if (1) the restraint is not facially anticompetitive and (2) the licensor and its licensees collectively account for no more than twenty percent of each relevant market significantly affected by the restraint. This "safety zone" does not apply to those transfers of intellectual property rights to which a merger analysis is applied.

Whether a restraint falls within the safety zone will be determined by reference only to goods markets unless the analysis of goods markets alone would inadequately address the effects of the licensing arrangement on competition among technologies or in research and development.

5. Application of general principles

5.0 This section illustrates the application of the general principles discussed above to particular licensing restraints and to arrangements that involve the cross-licensing, pooling, or acquisition of intellectual property. The restraints and arrangements identified are typical of those that are likely to receive antitrust scrutiny; however, they are not intended as an exhaustive list of practices that could raise competitive concerns.

5.1 Horizontal restraints

The existence of a restraint in a licensing arrangement that affects parties in a horizontal relationship (a "horizontal restraint") does not necessarily cause the arrangement to be anticompetitive. As in the case of joint ventures among horizontal competitors, licensing arrangements among such competitors may promote rather than hinder competition if they result in integrative efficiencies. Such efficiencies may arise, for example, from the realization of economies of scale and the integration of complementary research and development, production, and marketing capabilities.

Following the general principles outlined in section 3.4, horizontal restraints often will be evaluated under the rule of reason. In some circumstances, however, that analysis may be truncated; additionally, some restraints may merit per se treatment, including price fixing, allocation of markets or customers, agreements to reduce output, and certain group boycotts.

5.2 Resale price maintenance

Resale price maintenance is illegal when "commodities have passed into the channels of trade and are owned by dealers." Consistent with the principles set forth in section 3.4, the Agencies will enforce the per se rule against resale price maintenance in the intellectual property context.

5.3 Tying arrangements

A "tying" or "tie-in" or "tied sale" arrangement has been defined as "an agreement by a party to sell one product . . . on the condition that the buyer also purchases a different (or tied) product, or at least agrees that he will not purchase that [tied] product from any other supplier." Conditioning the ability of a licensee to license one or more items of intellectual property on the licensee's purchase of another item of intellectual property or a good or a service has been held in some cases to constitute illegal tying. Although tying arrangements may result in anticompetitive effects, such arrangements can also result in significant efficiencies and pro-competitive benefits. In the exercise of their prosecutorial discretion, the

Agencies will consider both the anticompetitive effects and the efficiencies attributable to a tie-in. The Agencies would be likely to challenge a tying arrangement if: (1) the seller has market power in the tying product, (2) the arrangement has an adverse effect on competition in the relevant market for the tied product, and (3) efficiency justifications for the arrangement do not outweigh the anticompetitive effects. The Agencies will not presume that a patent, copyright, or trade secret necessarily confers market power upon its owner.

5.4 Exclusive dealing

In the intellectual property context, exclusive dealing occurs when a license prevents the licensee from licensing, selling, distributing, or using competing technologies. Exclusive dealing arrangements are evaluated under the rule of reason. In determining whether an exclusive dealing arrangement is likely to reduce competition in a relevant market, the Agencies will take into account the extent to which the arrangement (1) promotes the exploitation and development of the licensor's technology and (2) anti-competitively forecloses the exploitation and development of, or otherwise constrains competition among, competing technologies.

5.5 Cross-licensing and pooling arrangements

Cross-licensing and pooling arrangements are agreements of two or more owners of different items of intellectual property to license one another or third parties. These arrangements may provide pro-competitive benefits by integrating complementary technologies, reducing transaction costs, clearing blocking positions, and avoiding costly infringement litigation. By promoting the dissemination of technology, cross-licensing and pooling arrangements are often pro-competitive.

Cross-licensing and pooling arrangements can have anticompetitive effects in certain circumstances. For example, collective price or output restraints in pooling arrangements, such as the joint marketing of pooled intellectual property rights with collective price setting or coordinated output restrictions, may be deemed unlawful if they do not contribute to an efficiency-enhancing integration of economic activity among the participants. When cross-licensing or pooling arrangements are mechanisms to accomplish naked price fixing or market division, they are subject to challenge under the per se rule.

5.6 Grantbacks

A grantback is an arrangement under which a licensee agrees to extend to the licensor of intellectual property the right to use the licensee's improvements to the licensed technology. Grantbacks can have pro-competitive effects, especially if they are nonexclusive. Such arrangements provide a means for the licensee and the licensor to share risks and reward the licensor for making possible further innovation based on or informed by the licensed technology, and both promote innovation in the first place and promote the subsequent licensing of the results of the innovation. Grantbacks may adversely affect competition, however, if they substantially reduce the licensee's incentives to engage in research and development and thereby limit rivalry in innovation markets.

A non-exclusive grantback allows the licensee to practice its technology and license it to others. Such a grantback provision may be necessary to ensure that the licensor is not prevented from effectively competing because it is denied access to improvements developed with the aid of its own technology. Compared with an exclusive grantback, a non-exclusive grantback, which leaves the licensee free to license improvements technology to others, is less likely to have anticompetitive effects.

The Agencies will evaluate a grantback provision under the rule of reason, considering its likely effects in light of the overall structure of the licensing arrangement and conditions in the relevant markets. An important factor in the Agencies' analysis of a grantback will be whether the licensor has market power in a relevant technology or innovation market. If the Agencies determine that a particular grantback provision is likely to reduce significantly licensees' incentives to invest in improving the licensed technology, the Agencies will consider the extent to which the grantback provision has offsetting pro-competitive effects, such as (1) promoting dissemination of licensees' improvements to the licensed technology, (2) increasing the licensors' incentives to disseminate the licensed technology, or (3) otherwise increasing competition and output in a relevant technology or innovation market. In addition, the Agencies will consider the extent to which grantback provisions in the relevant markets generally increase licensors' incentives to innovate in the first place.

6. Enforcement of invalid intellectual property rights

The Agencies may challenge the enforcement of invalid intellectual property rights as antitrust violations. Enforcement or attempted enforcement of a patent obtained by fraud on the Patent and Trademark Office or the Copyright Office may violate section 2 of the Sherman Act, if all the elements otherwise necessary to establish a section 2 charge are proved, or section 5 of the Federal Trade Commission Act. Actual or attempted enforcement of patents obtained by inequitable conduct that falls short of fraud under some circumstances may violate section 5 of the Federal Trade Commission Act. Objectively baseless litigation to enforce invalid intellectual property rights may also constitute an element of a violation of the Sherman Act.

QUESTIONS

1.   What are the general pro-competitive effects of intellectual property licensing noted by the Agencies? What are the general anticompetitive effects of intellectual property licensing noted by the Agencies?

2.   What are the potential pro-competitive effects of field-of-use, territorial and other restrictions in intellectual property licenses noted by the Agencies? What are the potential anticompetitive effects of these license limitations?

3. What is a "goods" market? What is a "technology" market? What is an "innovation" market?

4. Which type of licensing arrangement warrants closer antitrust scrutiny, vertical licenses or horizontal licenses? Why?

5. What is the antitrust "safety zone"?

6. Why might a licensor include an exclusive dealing clause in a license agreement? Would it matter whether the license was an exclusive or non-exclusive license?

7. When are cross-licenses and pooling arrangements likely to be pro-competitive? Anticompetitive?

8. When are grantback provisions likely to be pro-competitive? Anticompetitive?

Additional Information

1. 1 MATERIALS ON ANTITRUST COMPL. § 9:5 (2009).

2. CORP. COUNSEL'S ANTITRUST DESKBOOK § 14:3 (2009).

3. WILLIAM M. FLETCHER, 10A FLETCHER CYC. CORP. § 5020.20 (2010).

4. 1 CALLMANN ON UNFAIR COMP., TR. & MONO. § 4:56 (4th Ed.) (2010).

5. Harvey I. Saferstein, *Patent Licensing and the Antitrust Laws*, 899 PLI/PAT 913 (2007).

6. Arnold B. Calmann, *Antitrust Issues in Licensing*, 915 PLI/PAT 449 (2007).

7. Scott D. Russell, *Analytical Framework for Antitrust Counseling on Intellectual Property Licensing*, 950 PLI/PAT 501 (2008).

8. Mark A. McCarty, Matthew D. Kent, *Antitrust Primer: "Licensing Intellectual Property"*, 950 PLI/PAT 561 (2008).

9. Report, George G. Gordon, *Analyzing IP License Restrictions Under the Antitrust Laws: A General Outline of Issues* (2002), available at http://www.dechert.com/library/Analyzing%20IP%20License%20-%GGordon%205-02.PDF.

10. Rita Coco, *Antitrust Liability for Refusal to License Intellectual Property: A Comparative Analysis and the International Setting*, 12 MARQ. INTELL. PROP. L. REV. 1 (2008).

11. Gosta Schindler, *Wagging the Dog? Reconsidering Antitrust-Based Regulations of IP-Licensing*, 12 MARQ. INTELL. PROP. L. REV. 49 (2008).

12. Richard A. Posner, *Transaction Costs and Antitrust Concerns in the Licensing of Intellectual Property*, 4 J. MARSHALL REV. INTELL. PROP. L. 325 (2005).

13. Raymond Klitzke, *Patent Licensing: Concerted Action by Licensees*, 13 DEL. J. CORP. L. 459 (1988).

Chapter 8

TAX EFFECTS OF TECHNOLOGY CREATION AND TRANSFER

The Internal Revenue Code (IRC) defines two types of income — ordinary income and capital gains income. The capital gains tax rate is lower than the ordinary income tax rate. Although the spread between the capital gains and ordinary income tax rates fluctuates with the never-ending amendments to the IRC, in general, the capital gains tax rate (~15%) is about one-half of the ordinary income tax rate (~%35). IRC § 61 provides an all-encompassing definition of ordinary "gross income," and IRC § 61(a)(6) specifically includes royalties as ordinary gross income. Also included within IRC § 61 ordinary gross income are salaries and wages, as well as income received from the sale of property in the ordinary course of the taxpayer's trade or business. A sale of an item from inventory is an example of a sale of property in the ordinary course of trade or business. IRC § 162 provides that the ordinary and necessary trade or business expenses of the taxpayer may be deducted from the taxpayer's gross income.

IRC § 1221 defines the term "capital asset" as property held by the taxpayer other than property which would properly be included in inventory. IRC § 1231 provides the general rules for calculating long-term capital gains and long-term capital losses, and § 1231(b) defines property used in the taxpayer's trade or business as property which is subject to an allowance for depreciation and which is held by the taxpayer for more than one year.

This chapter of the materials considers these IRC provisions as they apply to the creation and transfer of patents. The first section deals with the deductibility of research and experimentation expenses. The second section deals with the rules for obtaining research and experimentation tax credits. A tax credit is more valuable to the taxpayer than a tax deduction. A tax credit is a dollar-for-dollar credit against the taxes otherwise owed by the taxpayer. A tax deduction is a deduction from the taxpayer's gross income. A $50,000 tax credit would save the taxpayer $50,000 in taxes regardless of the taxpayer's tax bracket; a $50,000 tax deduction would save the taxpayer $17,500 in taxes if the taxpayer was in the 35% tax bracket.

The third section in this chapter deals with the tax treatment of property contributed to a start-up company by its founders in exchange for stock. Although the rules here are not unique to patents, we will consider them in the case of patents contributed to a start-up company. The fourth section considers the issuance of stock for services rendered to a company. The fifth section deals with the tax treatment of a license or sale of a patent by the patent owner, and the sixth section deals with the tax treatment of a sale or exchange of a patent by the patent holder. As you will see, a patent holder will always be a patent owner, but a patent owner may not be a patent holder.

The Internal Revenue Code and its accompanying Treasury Regulations are enormously intricate with every section and subsection referring to, and incorporating, numerous other sections and subsections which, in turn, refer to and incorporate numerous additional sections and subsections which, in turn, etc. Of necessity, therefore, this chapter considers the tax effects of technology creation and transfer in a general overview way, omitting considerable detail. The goal is to familiarize the reader with these tax effects as part of a comprehensive understanding of the technology innovation process, not to prepare the reader for the practice of intellectual property tax law. However, even at this level of generality, as you will see, the I.R.C. and Treasury Regulation provisions are challenging to comprehend. As an aid to initial understanding of the readings in this chapter, a general statement of these tax rules is provided below.

Research and development expenses (in IRC language, research and experimental expenses) can either be deducted from gross income in the year in which the expenses are incurred or they can be amortized over a period of not less than 60 months. Intangible assets are amortized by deducting from gross income a portion of their cost each year over the intangible asset's useful life. Taxpayers can obtain a tax credit to the extent that their current year's research and experimentation expenditures exceed their previous years' research and experimentation expenditures, calculated according to various formulas.

The founders' contribution of intellectual property to a start-up company is a tax-free transaction. Whereas, ordinarily, any transfer of property is a taxable event, transfers to start-up companies are exempted from this general rule to support business development. The *quid pro quo* for this tax-free transfer of property is that the founder's stock takes the same basis as the founder's basis in the property which is transferred and the property in the hands of the start-up company also takes the same basis as the founder's basis in the property transferred. The basis of stock or property is the cost of acquiring the stock or property, minus certain deductions. The basis is used to calculate gain or loss on the sale or other disposition of the stock or property. The gain or loss on the sale of stock or property is calculated as the sale price minus the adjusted basis.

Although the contribution of *property* in exchange for stock is a tax-free transaction, the contribution or *services* in exchange for stock is not. Generally, the value of stock received for services is taxed as ordinary income at the time the stock becomes vested in the recipient; the appreciation in the value of the stock between the time it is received and the time it becomes vested is taxed as ordinary income. However, the recipient of stock for services can elect to have the stock taxed as ordinary income at the time the stock is received regardless of whether or not the stock is vested. If the recipient of stock for services makes this election, then the appreciation in the value of the stock between the time of the election and the time of vesting will be taxed as capital gains.

The sale or assignment of a patent by the patent owner is generally considered to be a sale of a capital asset which gives rise to capital gain taxation. On the other hand, the license of a patent by the patent owner is generally considered to be an income-producing transaction which gives rise to ordinary income taxation of the royalties received. In the case of a sale or assignment of a patent, the purchaser or assignee will own the patent as a capital asset which will be amortized over the patent's useful life. In the case of a license of a patent, the licensee will not own the patent, and the licensee will deduct the royalties paid in the year in which they are paid. Whether the patent transfer is determined to be a sale or a license is based on whether the patent owner has transferred all substantial rights in the patent. This determination is similar to the determination of standing to sue for patent infringement considered in subsection 2.2.9 of the materials.

Finally, the IRC provides special rules for the sale or exchange of a patent by the patent "holder," defined as the individual whose efforts created the patent or another individual who acquired the creator's interest in the patent for consideration. These rules are intended to spur invention by providing inventors favorable tax treatment. The special rules for treating the sale or exchange of a patent by the patent holder provide that the transfer will be considered to be a sale or exchange of a capital asset held for more than one year, regardless of whether the actual holding period is less than one year, and regardless of whether payment for the transfer is spread over the period of the transferee's use of the patent, or the payment is contingent on the productivity, use or disposition of the patent. These latter conditions are often considered indicia of a transfer of less than all substantial rights in a patent which would result in ordinary income taxation of the payments.

8.1   RESEARCH AND EXPERIMENTATION EXPENSE DEDUCTIONS

In enacting section 174 of the Internal Revenue Code in 1954, Congress recognized that the allowance of current deductibility of research and development expenses "will greatly stimulate the search for new products and new inventions upon which the future economic and military strength of our Nation depends." Although current deductibility of research and development expenses was already allowed to a limited extent as an ordinary and necessary business expense under I.R.C. section 162, the enactment of section 174 signaled a new commitment to encouraging technology innovation. However, as you will see below, in implementing section 174, the Internal Revenue Service has narrowly defined "research and experimentation expenditures" and has precluded deductibility of downstream expenses for activities which are often closely associated with commercialization of research and experimentation results.

I.R.C. § 174   RESEARCH AND EXPERIMENTAL EXPENDITURES

(a)   Treatment as expenses. —

(1)   In general. — A taxpayer may treat research or experimental expenditures which are paid or incurred by him during the taxable year in connection with his trade or business as expenses which are not chargeable to capital account. The expenditures so treated shall be allowed as a deduction.

(2)   When method may be adopted. —

(A)   Without consent. — A taxpayer may, without the consent of the Secretary, adopt the method provided in this subsection for his first taxable year —

(i) which begins after December 31, 1953, and ends after August 16, 1954, and

(ii) for which expenditures described in paragraph (1) are paid or incurred.

(B)   With consent. — A taxpayer may, with the consent of the Secretary, adopt at any time the method provided in this subsection.

(3)   Scope. — The method adopted under this subsection shall apply to all expenditures described in paragraph (1). The method adopted shall be adhered to in computing taxable income for the taxable year and for all subsequent taxable years unless, with the approval of the Secretary, a change to a different method is authorized with respect to part or all of such expenditures.

(b)   Amortization of certain research and experimental expenditures. —

(1)   In general. — At the election of the taxpayer, made in accordance with regulations prescribed by the Secretary, research or experimental expenditures which are —

(A) paid or incurred by the taxpayer in connection with his trade or business,

(B) not treated as expenses under subsection (a), and

(C) chargeable to capital account but not chargeable to property of a character which is subject to the allowance under section 167 (relating to allowance for depreciation, etc.) or section 611 (relating to allowance for depletion), may be treated as deferred expenses. In computing taxable income, such deferred expenses shall be allowed as a deduction ratably over such period of not less than 60 months as may be selected by the taxpayer (beginning with the month in which the taxpayer first realizes benefits from such expenditures). Such deferred expenses are expenditures properly chargeable to capital account for purposes of section 1016(a)(1) (relating to adjustments to basis of property).

TREAS. REG. § 1.174-1   RESEARCH AND EXPERIMENTAL EXPENDITURES; IN GENERAL.

Section 174 provides two methods for treating research or experimental expenditures paid or incurred by the taxpayer in connection with his trade or business. These expenditures may be treated as expenses not chargeable to capital account and deducted in the year in which they are paid or incurred (see § 1.174-3), or they may be deferred and amortized (see § 1.174-4). Research or experimental expenditures which are neither treated as expenses nor deferred and amortized under section 174 must be charged to capital account. The expenditures to which section 174 applies may relate either to a general research program or to a particular project. See § 1.174-2 for the definition of research and experimental expenditures. The term paid or incurred, as used in section 174 and in §§ 1.174-1 to 1.174-4, inclusive, is to be construed according to the method of accounting used by the taxpayer in computing taxable income. See section

7701(a)(25).

TREAS. REG. § 1.174-2   DEFINITION OF RESEARCH AND EXPERIMENTAL EXPENDITURES.

(a)   In general.

(1) The term research or experimental expenditures, as used in section 174, means expenditures incurred in connection with the taxpayer's trade or business which represent research and development costs in the experimental or laboratory sense. The term generally includes all such costs incident to the development or improvement of a product. The term includes the costs of obtaining a patent, such as attorneys' fees expended in making and perfecting a patent application. Expenditures represent research and development costs in the experimental or laboratory sense if they are for activities intended to discover information that would eliminate uncertainty concerning the development or improvement of a product. Uncertainty exists if the information available to the taxpayer does not establish the capability or method for developing or improving the product or the appropriate design of the product. Whether expenditures qualify as research or experimental expenditures depends on the nature of the activity to which the expenditures relate, not the nature of the product or improvement being developed or the level of technological advancement the product or improvement represents.

(2) For purposes of this section, the term product includes any pilot model, process, formula, invention, technique, patent, or similar property, and includes products to be used by the taxpayer in its trade or business as well as products to be held for sale, lease, or license.

(3) The term research or experimental expenditures does not include expenditures for —

(i) The ordinary testing or inspection of materials or products for quality control (quality control testing);

(ii) Efficiency surveys;

(iii) Management studies;

(iv) Consumer surveys;

(v) Advertising or promotions;

(vi) The acquisition of another's patent, model, production or process; or

(vii) Research in connection with literary, historical, or similar projects.

(4) For purposes of paragraph (a)(3)(i) of this section, testing or inspection to determine whether particular units of materials or products conform to specified parameters is quality control testing. However, quality control testing does not include testing to determine if the design of the product is appropriate.

****

(6) Section 174 applies to a research or experimental expenditure only to the extent that the amount of the expenditure is reasonable under the circumstances. In general, the amount of an expenditure for research or experimental activities is reasonable if the amount would ordinarily be paid for like activities by like enterprises under like circumstances. Amounts supposedly paid for research that are not reasonable under the circumstances may be characterized as disguised dividends, gifts, loans, or similar payments. The reasonableness requirement of this paragraph (a)(6) does not apply to the reasonableness of the type or nature of the activities themselves.

(7) This paragraph (a) applies to taxable years beginning after October 3, 1994.

(8) The provisions of this section apply not only to costs paid or incurred by the taxpayer for research or experimentation undertaken directly by him but also to expenditures paid or incurred for research or experimentation carried on in his behalf by another person or organization (such as a research institute, foundation, engineering company, or similar contractor). However, any expenditures for research or experimentation carried on in the taxpayer's behalf by another person are not expenditures to which section 174 relates, to the extent that they represent expenditures for the acquisition or improvement of land or depreciable property, used in connection with the research or experimentation, to which the taxpayer acquires rights of ownership.

(9) The application of subparagraph (2) of this paragraph may be illustrated by the following examples:

Example 1. A engages B to undertake research and experimental work in order to create a particular product. B will be paid annually a fixed sum plus an amount equivalent to his actual expenditures. In 1957, A pays to B in respect of the project the sum of $150,000 of which $25,000 represents an addition to B's laboratory and the balance represents charges for research and experimentation on the project. It is agreed between the parties that A will absorb the entire cost of this addition to B's laboratory which will be retained by B. A may treat the entire $150,000 as expenditures under section 174.

Example 2. X Corporation, a manufacturer of explosives, contracts with the Y research organization to attempt through research and experimentation the creation of a new process for making certain explosives. Because of the danger involved in such an undertaking, Y is compelled to acquire an isolated tract of land on which to conduct the research and experimentation. It is agreed that upon completion of the project Y will transfer this tract, including any improvements thereon, to X. Section 174 does not apply to the amount paid to Y representing the costs of the tract of land and improvements.

(b)   Certain expenditures with respect to land and other property.

(1) Expenditures by the taxpayer for the acquisition or improvement of land, or for the acquisition or improvement of property which is subject to an allowance for depreciation under section 167 or depletion under section 611, are not deductible under section 174, irrespective of the fact that the property

or improvements may be used by the taxpayer in connection with research or experimentation. However, allowances for depreciation or depletion of property are considered as research or experimental expenditures, for purposes of section 174, to the extent that the property to which the allowances relate is used in connection with research or experimentation. If any part of the cost of acquisition or improvement of depreciable property is attributable to research or experimentation (whether made by the taxpayer or another), see subparagraphs (2), (3), and (4) of this paragraph.

(2) Expenditures for research or experimentation which result, as an end product of the research or experimentation, in depreciable property to be used in the taxpayer's trade or business may, subject to the limitations of subparagraph (4) of this paragraph, be allowable as a current expense deduction under section 174(a). Such expenditures cannot be amortized under section 174(b) except to the extent provided in paragraph (a)(4) of § 1.174-4.

(3) If expenditures for research or experimentation are incurred in connection with the construction or manufacture of depreciable property by another, they are deductible under section 174(a) only if made upon the taxpayer's order and at his risk. No deduction will be allowed (i) if the taxpayer purchases another's product under a performance guarantee (whether express, implied, or imposed by local law) unless the guarantee is limited, to engineering specifications or otherwise, in such a way that economic utility is not taken into account; or (ii) for any part of the purchase price of a product in regular production. For example, if a taxpayer orders a specially-built automatic milling machine under a guarantee that the machine will be capable of producing a given number of units per hour, no portion of the expenditure is deductible since none of it is made at the taxpayer's risk. Similarly, no deductible expense is incurred if a taxpayer enters into a contract for the construction of a new type of chemical processing plant under a turn-key contract guaranteeing a given annual production and a given consumption of raw material and fuel per unit. On the other hand, if the contract contained no guarantee of quality of production and of quantity of units in relation to consumption of raw material and fuel, and if real doubt existed as to the capabilities of the process, expenses for research or experimentation under the contract are at the taxpayer's risk and are deductible under section 174(a). However, see subparagraph (4) of this paragraph.

(4) The deductions referred to in subparagraphs (2) and (3) of this paragraph for expenditures in connection with the acquisition or production of depreciable property to be used in the taxpayer's trade or business are limited to amounts expended for research or experimentation. For the purpose of the preceding sentence, amounts expended for research or experimentation do not include the costs of the component materials of the depreciable property, the costs of labor or other elements involved in its construction and installation, or costs attributable to the acquisition or improvement of the property. For example, a taxpayer undertakes to develop a new machine for use in his business. He expends $30,000 on the project of which $10,000 represents the actual costs of material, labor, etc., to construct the machine, and $20,000 represents research costs which are not attributable to the machine itself.

Under section 174(a) the taxpayer would be permitted to deduct the $20,000 as expenses not chargeable to capital account, but the $10,000 must be charged to the asset account (the machine).

TREAS. REG. § 1.174-3   TREATMENT AS EXPENSES.

(a)   **In general.** Research or experimental expenditures paid or incurred by a taxpayer during the taxable year in connection with his trade or business are deductible as expenses, and are not chargeable to capital account, if the taxpayer adopts the method provided in section 174(a). See paragraph (b) of this section. If adopted, the method shall apply to all research and experimental expenditures paid or incurred in the taxable year of adoption and all subsequent taxable years, unless a different method is authorized by the Commissioner under section 174(a)(3) with respect to part or all of the expenditures. See paragraph (b)(3) of this section. Thus, if a change to the deferred expense method under section 174(b) is authorized by the Commissioner with respect to research or experimental expenditures attributable to a particular project or projects, the taxpayer, for the taxable year of the change and for subsequent taxable years, must apply the deferred expense method to all such expenditures paid or incurred during any of those taxable years in connection with the particular project or projects, even though all other research and experimental expenditures are required to be deducted as current expenses under this section. In no event will the taxpayer be permitted to adopt the method described in this section as to part of the expenditures relative to a particular project and adopt for the same taxable year a different method of treating the balance of the expenditures relating to the same project.

TREAS. REG. § 1.174-4   TREATMENT AS DEFERRED EXPENSES.

(a)   **In general.**

(1) If a taxpayer has not adopted the method provided in section 174(a) of treating research or experimental expenditures paid or incurred by him in connection with his trade or business as currently deductible expenses, he may, for any taxable year beginning after December 31, 1953, elect to treat such expenditures as deferred expenses under section 174(b), subject to the limitations of subparagraph (2) of this paragraph. If a taxpayer has adopted the method of treating such expenditures as expenses under section 174(a), he may not elect to defer and amortize any such expenditures unless permission to do so is granted under section 174(a)(3). See paragraph (b) of this section.

(2) The election to treat research or experimental expenditures as deferred expenses under section 174(b) applies only to those expenditures which are chargeable to capital account but which are not chargeable to property of a character subject to an allowance for depreciation or depletion under section 167 or 611, respectively. Thus, the election under section 174(b) applies only if the property resulting from the research or experimental expenditures has no determinable useful life. If the property resulting from the expenditures has a determinable useful life, section 174(b) is not applicable, and the capitalized expenditures must be amortized or depreciated over the determinable useful life. Amounts treated as deferred expenses are properly chargeable to capital

account for purposes of section 1016(a)(1), relating to adjustments to basis of property. See section 1016(a)(14). See section 174(c) and paragraph (b)(1) of § 1.174-2 for treatment of expenditures for the acquisition or improvement of land or of depreciable or depletable property to be used in connection with the research or experimentation.

(3) Expenditures which are treated as deferred expenses under section 174(b) are allowable as a deduction ratably over a period of not less than 60 consecutive months beginning with the month in which the taxpayer first realizes benefits from the expenditures. The length of the period shall be selected by the taxpayer at the time he makes the election to defer the expenditures. If a taxpayer has two or more separate projects, he may select a different amortization period for each project. In the absence of a showing to the contrary, the taxpayer will be deemed to have begun to realize benefits from the deferred expenditures in the month in which the taxpayer first puts the process, formula, invention, or similar property to which the expenditures relate to an income-producing use. See section 1016(a)(14) for adjustments to basis of property for amounts allowed as deductions under section 174(b) and this section. See section 165 and the regulations thereunder for rules relating to the treatment of losses resulting from abandonment.

QUESTIONS

1.   When would a taxpayer choose to deduct research and experimentation expenses in the year in which the expenses are incurred? When would a taxpayer choose to amortize research and experimentation expenses? As between deduction and amortization of research and experimentation expenses, which do you think taxpayers most often prefer?

2.   Would the expenses incurred by a taxpayer in seeking to improve upon an existing patent not owned by the taxpayer qualify as research or experimentation expenditures?

3.   Do you see any relationship between the activities excluded from § 174 and the activities that fall outside the scope of the experimental use exception to the public use statutory bar?

4.   In Treasury Regulation § 1.174-2 Example 1, why may A treat the entire $150,000 as expenditures under § 174?

5.   Treasury Regulation § 1.174-2(b) provides that expenditures by the taxpayer for the acquisition or improvement of land, or for the acquisition or improvement of property are not deductible under § 174 "irrespective of the fact that the property or improvements may be used by the taxpayer in connection with research or experimentation." However, § 1.174-2(b) also provides that "allowances for depreciation or depletion of property are considered as research or experimental expenditures, for purposes of section 174, to the extent that the property to which the allowances relate is used in connection with research or experimentation." What is the difference between these two provisions?

6. Is a taxpayer's expenditure to develop an assay to screen for chemical compounds that may result in a product offered for sale by the taxpayer deductible under § 174?

7. Can a taxpayer elect to deduct expenditures on Research Project A under § 174(a) and amortize expenditures on Research Project B under § 174(b)?

8. What must a taxpayer do to change from deducting expenditures under § 174(a) to amortizing expenditures under § 174(b)?

LDL RESEARCH & DEVELOPMENT II, LTD. v COMMISSIONER OF INTERNAL REVENUE
124 F.3d 1338 (10th Cir. 1997)

LUCERO, CIRCUIT JUDGE

Section 174(a) of the Internal Revenue Code allows "[a] taxpayer [to] treat research or experimental expenditures which are paid or incurred by him during the taxable year in connection with his trade or business as expenses which are not chargeable to capital account. The expenditures so treated shall be allowed as a deduction." In this case we are required to determine when a partnership's expenditures made to third parties to engage in research are "in connection with [the partnership's] trade or business" and consequently deductible as current expenses pursuant to 26 U.S.C. § 174(a).

I

At issue in the present case are three claimed deductions made by a Utah limited partnership, LDL Research and Development II ("LDL II"), for research and development expenditures paid to a Utah corporation, Larson-Davis Laboratories ("Larson-Davis"). The deductions were claimed on LDL II's tax returns for 1983, 1984, and 1985, and total some $1,111,210. Larson-Davis was founded in 1981 by two engineers, Brian Larson and Larry Davis, to research, develop, manufacture, and market acoustic and vibration testing electronic equipment. Both Larson and Davis had extensive prior experience in these areas of expertise. In contrast, the general partners of LDL II had only minimal experience in researching, developing, manufacturing and marketing such equipment.

In November 1983, Larson-Davis concluded a number of written agreements with LDL II, including a "Development Agreement," "Cross-License Option Agreement," and "Purchase Option Agreement." Under the terms of the Development Agreement, LDL-II was to pay Larson-Davis $975,000 in three annual installments in return for Larson-Davis developing various electronic testing devices. Larson-Davis was to send LDL-II monthly and quarterly reports regarding the status of research and development of the devices. Under the Development Agreement, which was to terminate on the earlier of October 1, 1986 or the date the devices were ready for commercial production, LDL-II would be the exclusive owner of the technology developed by Larson-Davis.

While the Development Agreement suggests LDL-II would own the resulting technology, the other agreements indicate that its ownership was not absolute. Under the terms of the Cross-License Option Agreement, Larson-Davis held an option on a non-exclusive license to manufacture and market developed devices for 14 months. If the option were exercised, LDL-II would receive a 12% royalty fee. Finally, under the terms of the Purchase Option Agreement, Larson-Davis held an option to buy all rights in the technology outright from LDL-II. If exercised, LDL-II would receive a 15% royalty fee up to a total of $6.35 million. At that point, Larson-Davis would transfer 5% of its stock to LDL-II. All rights in the technology were to pass to Larson-Davis at the time the Purchase Option was exercised.

Simultaneous with these agreements, LDL-II published a "Private Placement Memorandum" (or "PPM") designed to attract investors to the partnership. The PPM stated that Larson-Davis would research, develop, manufacture and market two specific electronic devices. The PPM further stated that the general partners of LDL-II were not significantly experienced in researching, developing, manufacturing, or marketing such devices, and that LDL-II had done no study on the marketability of the proposed devices. By the terms of the PPM, LDL's limited partners would obtain tax benefits from 1983 to 1985 as § 174(a) deductions reported by LDL II were passed through to investors. Limited partners would also have the prospect of cash distributions from 1986 onward. The PPM anticipated that a total of $1,905,300 in capital would be raised, principally from the sale of limited partnership units and promissory notes. Some $975,000 would be paid to Larson-Davis by the terms of the Development Agreement, while $905,000 would go to LDL-II for salaries, administrative costs, and interest payments on the promissory notes, and $139,149 would be held as a cash reserve. The limited partnership shares sold would allow LDL II to raise a further $224,000 from its limited partners as needed.

In 1985, Larson-Davis developed the "Series 3100 Real Time Analyzer" (the "3100"), which performed the functions of both electronic devices described in the PPM and Development Agreement. In April 1986, LDL-II exercised its option under the Use License Option Agreement. In October of that same year, Larson-Davis exercised its option under the Cross License Option Agreement to market and manufacture the 3100. In November 1987, LDL-II and Larson-Davis entered into a Memorandum of Agreement that extended the terms of the Cross License Option Agreement for a further five months. Though it appears that Larson-Davis never formally exercised its rights under the Purchase Option Agreement, Larson-Davis paid LDL-II the higher 15% royalty fee from June 1988. In total, Larson-Davis paid LDL-II some $236,196 in royalties between 1986 and 1989. Thereafter, sales of the 3100 declined. Because Larson-Davis apparently never exercised its option under the Purchase Option Agreement, LDL-II continues to hold the rights to market and manufacture the 3100. However, it has never pursued these rights.

Following an audit, the Internal Revenue Service disallowed the deductions on grounds that LDL-II was not engaged in a trade or business in connection with the research and development expenditures made to Larson-Davis. LDL-II challenged the Commissioner's ruling in the United States Tax Court. When judgment was entered for the Commissioner, LDL-II appealed to this court. We exercise jurisdiction pursuant to 26 U.S.C. § 7482. We conclude that the tax court properly denied the deductions claimed by the partnership.

II

A taxpayer's research and development expenditures are deductible under § 174(a) only if they are incurred in connection with the taxpayer's trade or business. *Nickeson v. Commissioner.* The taxpayer has the burden of proving that amounts deducted are spent for qualified research and experimental expenditures. Lisa Fagan et al., *Mertens Law of Federal Income Taxation,* § 25.95, at 260. We determine the availability of a deduction pursuant to § 174(a), first, by making "an initial inquiry into whether the activity was undertaken or continued in good faith, with the dominant hope and intent of realizing a profit, i.e., taxable income there from." *Nickeson.* In this case, the Commissioner has conceded that LDL-II's payment of research and development expenditures to Larson-Davis had a bona fide profit motive and was not made merely to reap tax benefits.

To claim a deduction, LDL-II need not carry out any actual research. The Commissioner has interpreted § 174(a)(1) to allow deductions to be taken:

> not only [for] costs paid or incurred by the taxpayer for research and experimentation undertaken directly by him but also for expenditures paid or incurred for research or experimentation carried on in his behalf by another person or organization (such as a research institute, foundation, engineering company, or similar contractor).

Treas. Reg. § 1.174-2(a)(2). Neither the Internal Revenue Code nor Treasury regulations defines "in connection with the taxpayer's trade or business" more specifically.

In this circuit, research expenditures are made "in connection with" the partnership's trade or business if the taxpayer is "actively involved in the [research project] as a trade or business." *Nickeson.* Other circuits also allow research expenditures to be deducted under § 174 if a taxpayer has a "realistic prospect" of such involvement. *See Spellman.* LDL-II claims to satisfy either the "active involvement" or "realistic prospect" tests. The Commissioner disputes both contentions.

In this case, the Tax Court ruled that LDL-II was neither actively engaged in a trade or business nor had a realistic prospect of being so. Its basis for concluding that LDL-II was not actively engaged in a trade or business was the partnership's lack of control over the activities of Larson-Davis. The former could only insist that Larson-Davis spend the $975,000 on 3100 research, and provide the partnership with progress reports. LDL-II's actual activities were limited to "ministerial" functions such as "filing tax returns, receiving status reports from [Larson-Davis], and informing investors of the status of the research, development, manufacture, and marketing of the electronic devices."

The Tax Court also concluded that LDL-II lacked a realistic prospect of engaging in a trade or business in connection with the 3100 technology. First, compared to the principals of Larson-Davis, LDL-II had little or no experience in the research, development, manufacture, and marketing of electronic devices. Second, the written documents made clear that LDL-II was in fact relying on Larson-Davis to perform all these functions; whatever rights LDL-II retained to manufacture or market the devices were purely theoretic. LDL-II had no plans in place to market and manufacture the devices should Larson-Davis not exercise its options to do so. Thus, there was only a "mere possibility" that LDL-II would enter the relevant trade or business. Third, LDL-II lacked the capital and employees necessary to market and manufacture the 3100. Accordingly, the Tax Court regarded LDL-II as a passive investor and unentitled to the deductions claimed.

LDL-II believes that the Tax Court erred in crediting the "form" of its relationship with Larson-Davis over its actual "substance." According to LDL-II, the latter should control the tax consequences of their deal with Larson-Davis. LDL-II also contends that because the Commissioner conceded the partnership had a profit motive, it must have been more than a passive investor in Larson-Davis. Both arguments fit within LDL-II's contention that its day-to-day activities in connection with the 3100 project demonstrate entitlement to the § 174(a)(1) deductions because LDL-II was actively engaged in a "trade or business" as required by the statute.

We review the Tax Court's factual findings under the clearly erroneous standard and purely legal questions de novo. That court's "ultimate determination that the partnership's expenditures were not "research or experimental expenditures . . . in connection with [a] trade or business" involves the application of law to fact, and calls for de novo review by this court. We therefore reject the Commissioner's contention that we should review the ultimate facts of this case — whether the taxpayer satisfied either the active involvement or realistic prospect tests — under a clear error standard."

III

A

To be actively involved in the 3100 project as a trade or business, LDL-II must be more than a passive investor in the 3100 project. We have not definitively established the boundary between passive investment and active involvement. In prior cases, the primary determinant between involvement and investment was the degree of taxpayer control over, or regular and substantial participation in, the project in question.

The Tax Court's conclusion that LDL-II's involvement in the project at the time the deductions were claimed was insufficient to justify the deductions claimed under the active involvement test is based on the factual finding that LDL-II's on-going activities toward the project during the years in question were limited to "filing tax returns, receiving status reports from the Lab [i.e. Larson-Davis], and informing investors of the status of the research, development, manufacture, and marketing of the electronic devices." Noting the partnership's agreements with Larson-Davis, the Tax Court found that the only indicia of LDL-II's control over the 3100 project were its "right . . . to receive reports and the limitation on the Lab [Larson-Davis] in the use of the $ 975,000."

Unless these findings are clearly erroneous, we must affirm the tax court's determination that LDL-II was not actively engaged in the 3100 project. Appellant argues that many of the Tax Court's factual findings proceed from erroneously elevating the "form" of the relationship between LDL-II and Larson-Davis above its "substance." Appellant views the written agreements between itself and Larson-Davis as the "form" of their relationship. The true substance of that relationship, appellant contends, is revealed in unrebutted oral testimony given at trial by CFS employees who worked for LDL-II and by employees of Larson-Davis who were familiar with the interactions between the two firms. This testimony allegedly indicates that LDL-II exercised a far greater degree of control over Larson-Davis and was far more actively engaged in connection with the 3100 business than the Tax Court found on the basis of the formal relationship between the two.

LDL-II incorrectly characterizes the basis of the Tax Court's factual findings. A close reading of the decision below reveals that the lower court credited the "form" of the relationship over what appellants view as its substance only inasmuch as it perceived the written agreements between Larson-Davis and LDL-II to be more revealing of the true substance of the relationship than the oral testimony presented at trial. The Tax Court explicitly recognized that to determine the taxpayer's entitlement to a deduction under § 174(a)(1), "all of the surrounding facts and circumstances are relevant." Moreover, it expressly found the oral testimony offered by LDL-II at trial to be "vague," and concluded that the appellant had failed to produce "documentary evidence *or other credible testimony* that would indicate that the general partners of LDL exercised any significant direction or control over the Lab."

"If the district court's account of the evidence is plausible in light of the record viewed in its entirety, the court of appeals may not reverse it even though convinced that had it been sitting as the trier of fact, it would have weighed the evidence differently. Where there are two permissible views of the evidence, the fact finder's choice between them cannot be clearly erroneous." Reviewing the testimony offered, we conclude that the tax court's decision to credit the substance of the relationship as established by the written agreements between LDL-II and Larson-Davis, and by the PPM, was not clearly erroneous.

Applying the facts to the law, the right to receive reports and monitor the use of the contributed funds cannot render LDL-II actively involved in the electronic acoustic testing equipment business. To suppose otherwise would mean that a "bond debenture entitling the debenture trustee to inspect the books and plants of the corporation issuing the bonds would make the bondholders joint venturers with the corporation." At least as to a start-up R & D partnership, the right to require contributed funds to be spent on a specified research project cannot establish active involvement in a trade or business. Such funding may constitute the R & D partnership's initial steps into the trade or business in question — but that will only be the case where the partnership will ultimately control the commercial exploitation of the fruits of the research. If the partnership will not exercise such control, then the initial research funding will be merely a passive investment in a specific research project. Ear-marking funding cannot, without more, establish active involvement in a trade or business. That is the case regardless of whether LDL-II expended energy and resources in determining which research project should receive its prospective investment. Managing investments, no matter how time-consuming or lucrative, does not constitute a trade or business.

Supreme Court precedent strongly suggests that any non-financial contributions LDL-II may have provided Larson-Davis would not in and of themselves establish LDL-II's active involvement in the 3100 trade or business. In *Whipple*, the Supreme Court stated:

> Devoting one's time and energies to the affairs of a corporation is not of itself, and without more, a trade or business of the person so engaged. Though such activities may produce income, profit or gain in the form of dividends or enhancement in the value of an investment, this return is distinctive to the process of investing and is generated by the successful operation of the corporation's business as distinguished from the trade or business of the taxpayer himself. When the only return is that of an investor, the taxpayer has not satisfied his burden of demonstrating that he is engaged in a trade or business since investing is not a trade or business and the return to the taxpayer, though substantially the product of his services, legally arises not from his own trade or business but from that of the corporation.

Of course, LDL-II might have provided certain services to Larson-Davis for purposes other than protecting its pre-existing investment in the 3100 company. For instance, the two firms might have negotiated for LDL-II to have provided such services for compensation separate from return on investment. If that were the case, then LDL-II might be able to establish its services were provided in connection with a trade or business, and leave open the possibility that its research expenditures would be deductible. However, the written agreements between Larson-Davis and LDL-II provide no indication whatever that LDL-II was expected or required to provide anything more than research funds. Even the oral testimony offered by LDL-II-discounted though it was by the Tax Court does not suggest that LDL-II's legal, accounting, or other business services were factored into the overall bargain negotiated between the two concerns. Thus, even if Larson-Davis came to rely on LDL-II for such services, there is no record to support a finding that the partnership was doing more than promoting or protecting its investment. Such is not "active involvement" for the purposes of § 174(a).

B

Many start-up R & D partnerships that contract out research work will not qualify for § 174(a)(1) deductions under the "active involvement" test. In the years the deductions are claimed, such partnerships will often have too limited a connection to a trade or business to establish the kind of proprietorial control that can validate the deduction of research expenditures under § 174(a)(1). The "realistic prospect" test, which is in effect a specific form of the active engagement test, arises from the Supreme Court's determination that, in order to qualify for a deduction under § 174(a)(1), a taxpayer need not be actively engaged in a trade or business at the time research expenditures are made. *See Snow v. Commissioner.* On the basis of legislative history, the *Snow* Court held that § 174(a)(1) was partly intended to benefit start-up research and development companies. The Court upheld the deductibility of research expenditures by a taxpayer who had reported no sales during the year for which the deduction was claimed, but whose expectations of entering the market with a developed product were at that time high and, indeed, subsequently realized.

Snow "fairly invited the creation of R&D tax shelters," and has been interpreted narrowly to require that deducted research and development expenditures be directed at projects with "realistic prospects" of "developing a new product that will be exploited in a business of the taxpayer," "If those prospects are not realistic, the expenditure cannot be "in connection with" a business of the taxpayer," who therefore remains merely a passive investor. In light of *Snow*, a taxpayer demonstrates a "realistic prospect" of entering its own business in connection with the research project, by "manifesting both the objective intent to enter such a business and the capability of doing so." Hence, the mere possibility of engaging in a project-connected trade or business does not satisfy the requirements of § 174(a). By the same token, the bare contractual right to enter such a business does not entitle the taxpayer to a § 174(a)(1) deduction. Rather, the "right question" is "whether the partnership[ ] reasonably anticipated availing [itself] of the privileges [it] possessed on paper."

Snow does not question an investor's lack of entitlement to § 174 deductions. "Tax law draws a fundamental distinction between engaging in a business of one's own and investing in the business of another." By its plain language, § 174(a)(1) is limited to expenditures made by the taxpayer in connection with *his* trade or business. Accordingly, the IRS has consistently and reasonably maintained that investors in R & D partnerships should receive the same tax treatment as investors in other enterprises, and should not be able to avail themselves of § 174(a)(1). Thus, investment risk from a project's potential failure is not enough to confer entitlement to a research deduction under the "realistic prospect" test. Rather, the taxpayer who funds research activities by another party can only claim such a deduction if it will own the results of the research project at its completion, and will thereby accede to the benefits and costs of proprietary control. By assuming an expectation of ownership before the research has been conducted, the taxpayer ensures that its research payments to another party are potentially in connection with its own future trade or business. The question is not wholly determined by ownership because the taxpayer's intended commercial exploitation must still meet the definition of a "trade or business." But unless it assumes a realistic expectation of owning the resulting technology for purposes of commercial ownership, the taxpayer's research expenditures will be made in connection with another party's trade or business, and will not be deductible.

The risks of investing in a research endeavor and of assuming its ownership, including the risk associated in carrying on a trade or business from any technology that it may produce, are not readily separable. At the extremes, the differences are apparent. A taxpayer that funds research by another party in return for royalties is clearly no more than an investor making a capital contribution to the trade or business of another. Conversely, a profit-motivated taxpayer that funds research by another party in return for full ownership of the research results assumes the risks associated with the expectation of ownership. It is accountable for any liabilities generated by the research product, and stands to reap the entire financial benefit of the research project proving successful. Assuming that the taxpayer objectively manifests its intention to exploit the fruits of the research product in an adequately commercial capacity, it presumptively makes the research expenditure in connection with its trade or business.

LDL-II clearly believes that as the stated "owner" of the results of the 3100 research venture, it is entitled to the deductions. Had the partnership simply engaged Larson-Davis to perform certain research, LDL-II would have had an entirely realistic expectation of assuming the full benefits and costs of ownership; all the returns and liabilities of the final product would have been its own. But by granting Larson-Davis the two options contained in the Cross-License and Purchase Option Agreements, LDL-II's expectations of ownership were far different. In effect, the options show that it was Larson-Davis that bargained for an expectation of ownership, thereby assuming the risks and rewards of proprietary control.

Thus, should the completed research have proven marketable, Larson-Davis would likely have exercised its option rights. In return for its earlier financial contributions, LDL-II would have been left with the prospect of royalty returns, a reduced exposure to products liability, and, for the fourteen month period of the Cross-License Agreement, the opportunity to sell non-exclusive, short-term licenses to parties other than Larson-Davis. These are not the indicia of ownership that would indicate a realistic prospect of entering a business in connection with the 3100. Royalty returns on funding a fortiori flow to investors. Larson-Davis's indemnification responsibilities under the Purchase Option Agreement were "not those of a licensee, but of the owner of the ultimate product." At trial, LDL-II provided no evidence that there was any market for non-exclusive 14-month licenses to the technology, or that it intended to enter such a market, or that it would be able to do so in and for such a short time frame.

In the event Larson-Davis concluded that the results of the research were not marketable, and accordingly chose not to exercise its options, LDL-II would accede to ownership. But in such circumstances, LDL-II would be left with a marginal asset and few prospects for entering a trade or business in connection with the fruits of the research. Where Larson-Davis chose not to exploit the law of contracts to assume ownership of the completed research, the laws of economics would likely preclude commercial exploitation.

LDL-II claims its expectations of ownership were far broader. It tells us it insisted on retaining ownership of the resultant technology so that had Larson-Davis failed as a commercial enterprise, the partnership would have been able to enter the business of selling 3100 products itself — a proposition that amounts to "putting in good money after the bad." LDL-II has not shown that this retained interest was based on anything more than the possibility of Larson-Davis's failure. The partnership's possible succession to an ownership interest it never intended to exploit would not automatically put it in the 3100 trade or business any more than "foreclosing on a real estate mortgage would make a bank a real estate company." Tom Christopolous, who was an analyst at CFS Properties during 1983-85, stated that "if Larson-Davis couldn't make it," the firm contemplated "prop[ping] up Larson-Davis" and "hiring the existing salespeople and bringing them inside CFS," but admitted that the plans for this "purely hypothetical" contingency were not "real finite." Moreover, he stressed that plans were limited "because the project, basically, with the exception of the initial period, hit its numbers."

As the tax court noted, the PPM suggests LDL-II intended from the outset that the marketing and manufacturing of the resultant technology be performed by Larson-Davis pursuant to the terms of the Cross-License and Purchase Option agreements. The first documentary evidence of LDL-II's actually evaluating the potential for entering the 3100 business through potential licensees other than Larson-Davis dates from 1989, four years after the final deductions were claimed. Subsequent investigations confirmed the economic difficulties of proceeding with any such operation, and concluded that LDL-II should continue to allow Larson-Davis to market and manufacture the technology for a dwindling royalty return despite Larson-Davis's actual failure to purchase the technology outright. These facts support the conclusion that LDL-II had sought to deduct "a capital contribution to a company that was in the business of developing new products," and not "a development expense in connection with its own . . . prospective business." Such a deduction must be disallowed.

At best, then, the record shows no more than that LDL-II briefly made vague, worst-case plans. Even were we to find clear error in the Tax Court's refusal to credit the oral testimony offered, the partnership has not shown that it ever had an objectively realistic prospect of entering the 3100 business. Without a far stronger evidentiary showing that the partnership regarded its takeover of the 3100 business as probable, and planned with serious intent for that probability, we cannot conclude that the Tax Court erred in its "realistic prospect" analysis.

IV

Section 174(a)(1) was expressly intended to encourage businesses to carry out research, and we are sympathetic to the view that "[w]ithout R & D partnerships, many of today's new technologies would still be on the drawing board." Certainly, "[t]he uncertain contours of "trade and business" create opportunities for fair debate." Ultimately, however, "[f]air debates about fact-bound matters of characterization are resolved on appeal in favor of the solution the trier of facts reaches." Before making any research expenditures, LDL-II negotiated a set of structured agreements that undermined its proprietary control of the completed research, and leave it now unable to overcome the obvious inference that it contractually assumed the role of an investor.

AFFIRMED.

QUESTIONS

1. What is a Private Placement Memorandum? How does it factor into the court's decision?

2. Why did the Commissioner concede that LDL-II's payment of research and development expenditures to Larson-Davis had a *bona fide* profit motive? How could LDL II earn a profit on its research and development expenditures to Larson-Davis?

3.   The court notes that there are two different tests to determine whether research expenditures are made in "conjunction with" a taxpayer's trade or business — the active involvement test and the realistic prospect test. What facts are necessary to satisfy each test? Why did the court find that LDL-II failed to satisfy either test?

4.   The court suggests that if LDL-II had provided legal, accounting or other business services to Larson-Davis for compensation, this may have constituted active involvement in Larson-Davis' trade or business, which may allow LDL-II to deduct the research expenditures under § 174(a). How would the provision of legal, marketing or other business services relate to the trade or business of manufacturing and marketing acoustic electrical devices? Would Larson-Davis' law firm or accounting firm have been entitled to deduct research expenditures under § 174(a)?

5.   The public policy underlying § 174 is to encourage investment in research and development by allowing current-year deductions of research and development expenditures. Why would it matter whether this investment came from LDL-II or Larson-Davis? Would limiting the § 174 deduction to Larson-Davis have advanced this public policy if Larson-Davis did not have $975,000 to invest in research? Can R&D partnerships be distinguished from other forms of investment?

6.   Based on the court's holding, how would you advise a new R&D limited partnership to structure its relationship to a research-based company to increase the likelihood that the R&D limited partnership could pass through the § 174(a) deductions to its limited partners?

CASE NOTES

1.   In 1981, Bauer and Leith developed a plan to finance their continued research on a new cement-type composite for use in the aerospace industry. First, Bauer and Leith formed a new corporation, CemCom Research Associates (CemCom) to conduct the research and to license the final technology to other firms that would manufacture and sell end-user products. Second, Bauer and Leith retained an investment advisor to form a limited partnership, Research One Limited Partnership (Partnership) that would sell partnership shares to the public. Third, the Partnership entered into a Research and Development Agreement (R&D Agreement) with CemCom under which CemCom would perform all the necessary research and the rights in any technology resulting from the research would vest in the Partnership. The R&D Agreement expressly provided that CemCom would undertake all research activities "on behalf" of the Partnership. Under the R&D Agreement, the Partnership would pay CemCom a total of $5,050,000 for the research services. Fourth, the Partnership and CemCom entered into a Technology Transfer Agreement (TTA) under which CemCom received an option to obtain a perpetual exclusive license to any technology resulting from the research. In the event CemCom exercised the option, CemCom would pay the partnership substantial royalties. In the event CemCom did not exercise the option, CemCom, Bauer and Leith would be prohibited from engaging in any research, development or business activity involving the cement technology for a period of five years. Between 1984 and 1986, CemCom assigned six patents on the cement technology to the Partnership. In 1986, CemCom granted an exclusive sublicense for the technology

to a chemical company for twenty-five years. At this time, CemCom also renegotiated the royalty agreement with the Partnership to provide for lower minimum royalties and higher maximum royalties. One of the limited partners in the Partnership, Harris, deducted his distributive share of the research expenses paid by the Partnership to CemCom. The IRS disallowed the deduction and the Tax Court affirmed the IRS's decision. Harris appealed. What result? *See* Harris v. Commissioner of Internal Revenue, 16 F.3d 75 (5th Cir. 1994).

2. *See also* Snow v. Commissioner of Internal Revenue, 416 U.S. 500 (1974) (Allowance of deduction for experimental expenditures in connection with a taxpayer's trade or business should be interpreted to encourage research and experimentation; taxpayer should be allowed to deduct distributive share of operating loss of partnership formed to develop special purpose incinerator, even though partnership had no product for sale in the year in question); Kantor v. Commissioner of Internal Revenue, 998 F.2d 1514 (9th Cir. 1992) (Taxpayer does not need to be engaged in trade or business at time deductible research expenditure is made, but must demonstrate both objective intent of entering trade or business and capability of doing so; generally, start-up companies may not deduct pre-operational research expenditures as ordinary business expenses, but must instead capitalize such expenditures); Diamond v. Commissioner of Internal Revenue, 930 F.2d 372 (4th Cir. 1991) (Sole general partner of project partnership, a public held corporation under Israeli law, had complete control over research and development phase of project and, therefore, partnership was more properly classified as an investor in partnership activities).

Additional Information

1. Christopher M. Sove, Jason A. Fiske, 6 Mertens Law of Fed. Income Tax'n § 25:117 (2011).

2. Carina Bryant, 8 Mertens Law of Fed. Income Tax'n § 32A:34 (2011).

3. Alan S. Gutterman, 2 Corp. Couns. Gd. to Strategic Alliances § 20:13 (2011).

4. Steven Z. Szczepanski, David M. Epstein, 2 Eckstrom's Licensing in For. & Dom. Opps. § 9:29 (2010).

5. Calvin H. Johnson, *Why Do Venture Capital Funds Burn Research and Development Deduction*, 29 Va. Tax Rev. 29 (2009).

6. Brian K. Buchheit, *Examination of I.R.C. Section 174 in a Post-State Street Bank Environment: Redefining Tax Benefits for Research and Experimentation with Respect to Patents*, 2 Fla. St. U. Bus. Rev. 213 (2001).

7. Vsevolod L. Maksin, *Assets in Wonderland: The IRS's Inconsistent Policy on Software Costs*, 21 Cardozo L. Rev. 959 (1999).

8. Michael E. Hara, *Driggs v. United States — Should a Reasonableness Requirement Be Imposed on Section 174 of the Internal Revenue Code?*, 66 U. Det. L. Rev. 621 (1989).

9.   Matthew B. Krasner, *Tax Benefit Rule and Related Doctrines as Applied to the Recapture of Research and Other Intangible Development Costs*, 60 ST. JOHN'S L. REV. 26 (1985).

10. Jennifer L. Venghaus, *Tax Incentives: A Means of Encouraging Research and Development for Homeland Security*, 37 U. RICH. L. REV. 1213 (2003).

11. Xuan-Thao Nguyen, Jeffrey A. Maine, *Acquiring Innovation*, 57 AM. U. L. REV. 775 (2008).

12. J. William Callison, *Tax Aspects of Computer Software Development*, 13 COLO. LAW 959 (1984).

13. Jonathan Pavluk, *Computer Software and Tax Policy*, 84 COLUM. L. REV. 1992 (1984).

14. William Natbony, *The Tax Incentives for Research and Development: An Analysis and a Proposal*, 76 GEO. L. J. 347 (1987).

15. Richard S. Markovits, *On the Economic Efficiency of Using Law to Increase Research and Development: A Critique of Various Tax, Antitrust, Intellectual Property and Tort Law Rules and Policy Proposals*, 39 HARV. J. ON LEGIS. 63 (2002).

16. Belinda L. Heath, *The Importance of Research and Development Tax Incentives in the World Market*, 11 MSU-DCL J. INT'L L. 351 (2002).

17. Neal Lipschitz, *R&D Deductions*, 3/28/94 Nat'l L.J. A7, (col. 1) (1994).

18. Gerald W. Heller, *Leaky Shelter? "R&D" Law Yields Few Advantages*, 11/25/91 Nat'l L.J. 23, (col. 4) (1991).

19. James S. Kaplan, *Use of Limited Partnerships Provides Financing for R&D*, 6/18/84 Nat'l L.J. 23, (col. 3) (1984).

20. Patrick J. Ellingsworth, *The R&D Limited Partnership*, 7/25/83 Nat'l L.J. 21, (col. 1) (1983).

21. Patrick J. Ellingsworth, *Investing in Research and Development Limited Partnerships*, 7/18/83 Nat'l L.J. 38, (col. 1) (1983).

8.2   RESEARCH AND EXPERIMENTATION TAX CREDITS

The research tax credit under I.R.C. section 41 is similar in many respects to the current deductibility of research expenses under I.R.C. section 174. Both are intended to stimulate R&D activity, and both contain similar, narrow definitions of qualifying research expenses. There are, however, important differences between section 41 and section 174. First and foremost, section 41 provides for a research tax credit, whereas section 174 only provides for a research expense deduction. As noted in the beginning of this chapter, a research tax credit is much more valuable to a taxpayer than a research expense deduction. Section 41 also contains provisions not included in section 174. Section 41 provides for a research tax credit for expenditures on basic research which is conducted by universities or non-profit research laboratories, and for expenditures to energy consortia for purposes of energy research. Finally, section 41 contains special provisions for start-up companies to ensure that they can benefit from the research tax credit.

Despite the importance of the research tax credit in encouraging increased levels of research spending, the research tax credit has never been a permanent provision in the I.R.C. The research tax credit has expired and been extended 13 times since its inception in 1981. The latest research tax credit extension expires on December 31, 2011.

I.R.C. § 41.   CREDIT FOR INCREASING RESEARCH ACTIVITIES

(a)   **General rule.** — For purposes of section 38, the research credit determined under this section for the taxable year shall be an amount equal to the sum of —

(1) 20 percent of the excess (if any) of —

(A) the qualified research expenses for the taxable year, over

(B) the base amount,

(2) 20 percent of the basic research payments determined under subsection (e)(1)(A), and

(3) 20 percent of the amounts paid or incurred by the taxpayer in carrying on any trade or business of the taxpayer during the taxable year (including as contributions) to an energy research consortium for energy research.

(b)   **Qualified research expenses.** — **For purposes of this section** —

(1)   Qualified research expenses. — The term "qualified research expenses" means the sum of the following amounts which are paid or incurred by the taxpayer during the taxable year in carrying on any trade or business of the taxpayer —

(A) in-house research expenses, and

(B) contract research expenses.

(2)   In-house research expenses. —

(A)   In general. — The term "in-house research expenses" means —

(i) any wages paid or incurred to an employee for qualified services performed by such employee,

(ii) any amount paid or incurred for supplies used in the conduct of qualified research, and

(iii) under regulations prescribed by the Secretary, any amount paid or incurred to another person for the right to use computers in the conduct of qualified research.

(3)   Contract research expenses. —

(A)   In general. — The term "contract research expenses" means 65 percent of any amount paid or incurred by the taxpayer to any person (other than an employee of the taxpayer) for qualified research.

(4) Trade or business requirement disregarded for in-house research expenses of certain startup ventures. — In the case of in-house research expenses, a taxpayer shall be treated as meeting the trade or business requirement of paragraph (1) if, at the time such in-house research expenses are paid or incurred, the principal purpose of the taxpayer in making such expenditures is to use the results of the research in the active conduct of a future trade or business —

(A) of the taxpayer, or

(B) of 1 or more other persons who with the taxpayer are treated as a single taxpayer under subsection (f)(1).

(c) Base amount. —

(1) In general. — The term "base amount" means the product of —

(A) the fixed-base percentage, and

(B) the average annual gross receipts of the taxpayer for the 4 taxable years preceding the taxable year for which the credit is being determined (hereinafter in this subsection referred to as the "credit year").

(2) Minimum base amount. — In no event shall the base amount be less than 50 percent of the qualified research expenses for the credit year.

****

(C) Maximum fixed-base percentage. — In no event shall the fixed-base percentage exceed 16 percent.

(4) Election of alternative incremental credit. —

(A) In general. — At the election of the taxpayer, the credit determined under subsection (a)(1) shall be equal to the sum of —

(i) 3 percent of so much of the qualified research expenses for the taxable year as exceeds 1 percent of the average described in subsection (c)(1)(B) but does not exceed 1.5 percent of such average,

(ii) 4 percent of so much of such expenses as exceeds 1.5 percent of such average but does not exceed 2 percent of such average, and

(iii) 5 percent of so much of such expenses as exceeds 2 percent of such average.

(5) Election of alternative simplified credit. —

(A) In general. — At the election of the taxpayer, the credit determined under subsection (a)(1) shall be equal to 14 percent (12 percent in the case of taxable years ending before January 1, 2009) of so much of the qualified research expenses for the taxable year as exceeds 50 percent of the average qualified research expenses for the 3 taxable years preceding the taxable year for which the credit is being determined.

(d) Qualified research defined. — For purposes of this section —

(1)   In general. — The term "qualified research" means research —

(A) with respect to which expenditures may be treated as expenses under section 174,

(B) which is undertaken for the purpose of discovering information —

(i) which is technological in nature, and

(ii) the application of which is intended to be useful in the development of a new or improved business component of the taxpayer, and

(C) substantially all of the activities of which constitute elements of a process of experimentation for a purpose described in paragraph (3).

Such term does not include any activity described in paragraph (4).

****

(3)   Purposes for which research may qualify for credit. — For purposes of paragraph (1)(C) —

(A)   In general. — Research shall be treated as conducted for a purpose described in this paragraph if it relates to —

(i) a new or improved function,

(ii) performance, or

(iii) reliability or quality.

(B)   Certain purposes not qualified. — Research shall in no event be treated as conducted for a purpose described in this paragraph if it relates to style, taste, cosmetic, or seasonal design factors.

(4)   Activities for which credit not allowed. — The term "qualified research" shall not include any of the following:

(A)   Research after commercial production. — Any research conducted after the beginning of commercial production of the business component.

(B)   Adaptation of existing business components. — Any research related to the adaptation of an existing business component to a particular customer's requirement or need.

(C)   Duplication of existing business component. — Any research related to the reproduction of an existing business component (in whole or in part) from a physical examination of the business component itself or from plans, blueprints, detailed specifications, or publicly available information with respect to such business component.

(D)   Surveys, studies, etc. — Any —

(i) efficiency survey,

(ii) activity relating to management function or technique,

(iii) market research, testing, or development (including advertising or promotions),

(iv) routine data collection, or

(v) routine or ordinary testing or inspection for quality control.

(E)   Computer software. — Except to the extent provided in regulations, any research with respect to computer software which is developed by (or for the benefit of) the taxpayer primarily for internal use by the taxpayer, other than for use in —

(i) an activity which constitutes qualified research (determined with regard to this subparagraph), or

(ii) a production process with respect to which the requirements of paragraph (1) are met.

(F)   Foreign research. — Any research conducted outside the United States, the Commonwealth of Puerto Rico, or any possession of the United States.

(G)   Social sciences, etc. — Any research in the social sciences, arts, or humanities.

(H)   Funded research. — Any research to the extent funded by any grant, contract, or otherwise by another person (or governmental entity).

(e)   Credit allowable with respect to certain payments to qualified organizations for basic research. — For purposes of this section —

(1)   In general. — In the case of any taxpayer who makes basic research payments for any taxable year —

(A) the amount of basic research payments taken into account under subsection (a)(2) shall be equal to the excess of —

(i) such basic research payments, over

(ii) the qualified organization base period amount, and

(B) that portion of such basic research payments which does not exceed the qualified organization base period amount shall be treated as contract research expenses for purposes of subsection (a)(1).

(2)   Basic research payments defined. — For purposes of this subsection —

(A)   In general. — The term "basic research payment" means, with respect to any taxable year, any amount paid in cash during such taxable year by a corporation to any qualified organization for basic research but only if —

(i) such payment is pursuant to a written agreement between such corporation and such qualified organization, and

(ii) such basic research is to be performed by such qualified organization.

****

(6)   Qualified organization. — For purposes of this subsection, the term "qualified organization" means any of the following organizations:

(A)   Educational institutions. — Any educational organization which —

(i) is an institution of higher education (within the meaning of section 3304(f)), and

(ii) is described in section 170(b)(1)(A)(ii).

(B)   Certain scientific research organizations. — Any organization not described in subparagraph (A) which —

(i) is described in section 501(c)(3) and is exempt from tax under section 501(a),

(ii) is organized and operated primarily to conduct scientific research, and

(iii) is not a private foundation.

(7)   Definitions and special rules. — For purposes of this subsection —

(A)   Basic research. — The term "basic research" means any original investigation for the advancement of scientific knowledge not having a specific commercial objective, except that such term shall not include —

(i) basic research conducted outside of the United States, and

(ii) basic research in the social sciences, arts, or humanities.

(6)   Energy research consortium. —

(A)   In general. — The term "energy research consortium" means any organization —

(i) which is —

(I) described in section 501(c)(3) and is exempt from tax under section 501(a) and is organized and operated primarily to conduct energy research, or

(II) organized and operated primarily to conduct energy research in the public interest (within the meaning of section 501(c)(3)),

(ii) which is not a private foundation,

(iii) to which at least 5 unrelated persons paid or incurred during the calendar year in which the taxable year of the organization begins amounts (including as contributions) to such organization for energy research, and

(iv) to which no single person paid or incurred (including as contributions) during such calendar year an amount equal to more than 50 percent of the total amounts received by such organization during such calendar year for energy research.

TREAS. REG. § 1.41-2   QUALIFIED RESEARCH EXPENSES.

(a)   Trade or business requirement —

(1)   In general. An in-house research expense of the taxpayer or a contract research expense of the taxpayer is a qualified research expense only if the expense is paid or incurred by the taxpayer in carrying on a trade or business of the taxpayer. The phrase "in carrying on a trade or business" has the same meaning for purposes of section 41(b)(1) as it has for purposes of section 162; thus, expenses paid or incurred in connection with a trade or business within the meaning of section 174(a) (relating to the deduction for research and experimental expenses) are not necessarily paid or incurred in carrying on a trade or business for purposes of section 41. A research expense must relate to a particular trade or business being carried on by the taxpayer at the time the expense is paid or incurred in order to be a qualified research expense. For purposes of section 41, a contract research expense of the taxpayer is not a qualified research expense if the product or result of the research is intended to be transferred to another in return for license or royalty payments and the taxpayer does not use the product of the research in the taxpayer's trade or business.

(2)   New business. Expenses paid or incurred prior to commencing a new business (as distinguished from expanding an existing business) may be paid or incurred in connection with a trade or business but are not paid or incurred in carrying on a trade or business. Thus, research expenses paid or incurred by a taxpayer in developing a product the sale of which would constitute a new trade or business for the taxpayer are not paid or incurred in carrying on a trade or business.

****

(4)   Partnerships —

(i)   In general. An in-house research expense or a contract research expense paid or incurred by a partnership is a qualified research expense of the partnership if the expense is paid or incurred by the partnership in carrying on a trade or business of the partnership, determined at the partnership level without regard to the trade or business of any partner.

(ii)   Special rule for certain partnerships and joint ventures.

(A) If a partnership or a joint venture (taxable as a partnership) is not carrying on the trade or business to which the research relates, then the general rule in paragraph (a)(4)(i) of this section would not allow any of such expenditures to qualify as qualified research expenses.

(b)   Supplies and personal property used in the conduct of qualified research —

(1)   In general. Supplies and personal property (except to the extent provided in paragraph (b)(4) of this section) are used in the conduct of qualified research if they are used in the performance of qualified services (as defined in section 41(b)(2)(B), but without regard to the last sentence thereof) by an

employee of the taxpayer (or by a person acting in a capacity similar to that of an employee of the taxpayer; see example (6) of § 1.41-2(e)(5)). Expenditures for supplies or for the use of personal property that are indirect research expenditures or general and administrative expenses do not qualify as in-house research expenses.

(d) Wages paid for qualified services —

(1) In general. Wages paid to or incurred for an employee constitute in-house research expenses only to the extent the wages were paid or incurred for qualified services performed by the employee. If an employee has performed both qualified services and nonqualified services, only the amount of wages allocated to the performance of qualified services constitutes an in-house research expense. In the absence of another method of allocation that the taxpayer can demonstrate to be more appropriate, the amount of in-house research expense shall be determined by multiplying the total amount of wages paid to or incurred for the employee during the taxable year by the ratio of the total time actually spent by the employee in the performance of qualified services for the taxpayer to the total time spent by the employee in the performance of all services for the taxpayer during the taxable year.

(e) Contract research expenses —

(1) In general. A contract research expense is 65 percent of any expense paid or incurred in carrying on a trade or business to any person other than an employee of the taxpayer for the performance on behalf of the taxpayer of —

(i) Qualified research as defined in § 1.41-4 or 1.41-4A, whichever is applicable, or

(ii) Services which, if performed by employees of the taxpayer, would constitute qualified services within the meaning of section 41(b)(2)(B).

Where the contract calls for services other than services described in this paragraph (e)(1), only 65 percent of the portion of the amount paid or incurred that is attributable to the services described in this paragraph (e)(1) is a contract research expense.

Research Credit Calculation Examples

The following are simplified examples of calculating the research credits under I.R.C. § 41(a), the elective alternative incremental credit under § 41(c)(4) and the elective alternative simplified credit under § 41(c)(5). We will use the same facts for each calculation.

ACorp has $40M in qualified research expenditures for tax year 2008. ACorp has aggregate qualified research expenditures for tax years 1995 — 2007 of $20B and aggregate gross receipts for tax years 1995 — 2007 of $150B. ACorp's average annual gross receipts for tax years 2004 — 2007 is $200M and ACorp's average qualified research expenditures for tax years 2005-2007 is $30M. ACorp had no basic research expenditures and no expenditures to energy research consortia for energy research.

ACorp's research credit under § 41(a) would be calculated as follows:

§ 41(a)(1)(A): Qualified research expenses for 2008 = $40M

§ 41(c)(1): Base amount = $26M (13% × $200M)

§ 41(c)(3)(A): Fixed-base percentage = 13% ($20B/$150B)

Excess of 2008 qualified research expenses over base amount = $13M ($40M — $26M)

§ 41(a) Research tax credit = $2.6M (20% × $13M)

ACorp's elective alternative incremental research credit under § 41(c)(4) would be calculated as follows:

§ 41(c)(4)(i): 3% of 2008 qualified research expenditures = $1.2M (3% × $40M)

1% of average gross receipts for preceding 4 taxable years = $2.0M (1% × $200M)

Excess of 2008 qualified research expenditures over 1% of average gross receipts for preceding 4 taxable years = − $.8M

The same negative research credit would result under subparagraphs (ii) and (iii). ACorp, therefore, would not elect the alternative incremental research credit under § 41(c)(4).

ACorp's elective alternative simplified research credit under § 41(c)(5) would be calculated as follows:

§ 41(c)(5): 2008 qualified research expenditures = $40M

Average qualified research expenditure for preceding 3 taxable years = $30M

50% of average qualified research expenditures for preceding 3 taxable years = $15M (50% × $30M)

2008 qualified research expenditures — 50% of average qualified research expenditures for preceding 3 taxable years = $25M ($40M — $15M)

Alternative simplified research credit = $3.5M (14% × $25M)

Under the facts of the example, ACorp would elect the alternative simplified research credit of $3.5M under § 41(c)(5) over the research credit of $2.6M under § 41(a).

QUESTIONS

1. I.R.C. § 41(b)(4) provides that, in the case of in-house research expenses of startup companies, the trade or business requirement is satisfied if, "at the time such in-house research expenses are paid or incurred, the principal purpose of the taxpayer in making such expenditures is to use the results of the research in the active conduct of a future trade or business." Is there a similar provision in I.R.C. § 174? Why would Congress treat small businesses more favorably with respect to tax credits than tax deductions?

2.   Are there any differences between the treatment of "contract research expenses" in calculating research credits under § 41 and in calculating tax deductions under § 174?

3.   Are there any differences between "qualified research expenses" under § 41 and under § 174?

4.   Would a company that sponsors a basic science research project at a university be entitled to a research tax credit under § 41?

5.   Must a taxpayer be engaged in an energy-related trade or business in order to be eligible to receive research tax credits for payments to an energy consortium for energy research? What is an "energy consortium"?

EUSTACE v. COMMISSIONER OF INTERNAL REVENUE
312 F.3d 905 (11th Cir. 2002)

EASTERBROOK, CIRCUIT JUDGE.

Applied Systems, a Subchapter S corporation, develops and sells software that independent insurance agencies use to manage their businesses. During the early 1990s Applied Systems improved its software package, and its investors (the taxpayers in this case) want to take a tax credit under 26 U.S.C. § 41 based on the amount by which Applied Systems increased its R & D expenses during these years. Taxpayers who have sought a credit under § 41 for commercial software development have been uniformly unsuccessful. The only exception — on which the taxpayers in this case principally rely — is the district court's decision in *Tax & Accounting v. United States* which the tenth circuit reversed after they filed their brief. Applied Systems' claim is no better than the others.

The evidence at trial in the Tax Court shows that Applied Systems engaged in normal software development. During the early 1990s it enhanced its software package so that it could handle additional ratings computations, so that it could handle transactions between insurers and agencies, so that multiple people could work on the same customer file simultaneously without corrupting or overwriting each others' changes, and so that more functions could be handled in a given amount of random access memory. It discarded a word processing module licensed from another vendor, replacing it with a simple text editor with reduced memory demands but good form-letter-generation features. These are not the only changes, but they show the character of the work. None of it was pioneering; all of it entailed variations on themes long used by other developers. The Commissioner conceded that this work met many of the requirements in § 41 but contested several others, of which only two require attention: that the research be "undertaken for the purpose of discovering information which is technological in nature" (§ 41(d)(1)(B)(i)), and that the activities "constitute elements of a process of experimentation" (§ 41(d)(1)(C)). The Tax Court concluded that Applied Systems flunked both tests — the former because it did not produce an "innovation in underlying principle" and the latter because the research in question was not designed to dispel uncertainty about the technological possibility of developing software of this kind.

Taxpayers concede that if § 41 means what the Tax Court thought, then they lose. Applied Systems has not tried to show that its software embodies any leap in information technology or that there was any doubt about the technological ability to produce software of this kind. But it contends that § 41 does not set so high a standard and that industrious development of software through a process of trial and error meets the statutory standard. The difficulty with this position is that the Tax Court did not get its legal views out of thin air. This court announced them in *United Stationers*, and *Wicor* declined an opportunity to revisit the subject. *United Stationers* held that software development satisfies the statutory technological-information requirement only if "the research is intended to expand or refine existing principles of computer science" and the resulting information is "of broad effect." As for experimentation, we held that the taxpayer must formulate and test hypotheses in order to dissipate uncertainty about the possibility of success, a standard that fine-tuning (or debugging) of computer programs does not satisfy.

Although the word "experiment" has many shadings in common speech, we held that as used in § 41 it has the *scientific* sense of forming and testing hypotheses rather than the lay (or even engineering) sense of trial and error. Galileo engaged in experiments about acceleration when he rolled balls down an inclined plane. An auto manufacturer trying different nozzles from those on hand to find the one that applies the smoothest coat of paint is not engaged in "experimentation" under this view, nor is a software developer trying different methods to implement a feature accompanied by maximum execution speed and minimum demand on system resources such as RAM. Tinkering differs from experimentation in the vocabulary of research — and § 41 is about research, and thus about use of the scientific method. Authors and movie makers playing with sentences and scenes to find what most impresses the public are not doing scientific research using "experimentation." Just so with software. Developers are authors too; that they write lines of code readable by machines rather than lines of words readable by people does not fundamentally change the nature of the task and make one form of writing "experimentation" when the other is not. Experimentation is a subset of all steps taken to resolve uncertainty; otherwise searching for a place to park a car would be a "process of experimentation."

The tenth circuit has disagreed with our understanding of § 41. It held in *Tax & Accounting Software* that the technological-information requirement can be satisfied by new knowledge that is less a step forward than *United Stationers* required — but that "information must be separate from the product that is actually developed." With respect to experimentation, the tenth circuit was not receptive to the idea that only hypothesis formulation and testing fits, but it still held that the taxpayer must establish that testing was designed to overcome uncertainty about whether the desired end result was technologically feasible. Applied Systems cannot meet these definitions any more than those in *United Stationers*.

In the long run, neither our view nor the tenth circuit's has staying power. Both *United Stationers* and *Tax & Accounting Software* analyzed § 41 without the benefit of the regulations that are supposed to illuminate the path to decision. Section 41's predecessor was enacted in 1981, and § 41 has been on the books in its current form since 1986, but the Internal Revenue Service has yet to promulgate the regulations that are important to this statutory design. (Section 41 refers ten times to regulations that the Secretary of the Treasury is to develop and issue.) The most recent draft was published almost a year ago, 66 Fed. Reg. 66,362 (Dec. 26, 2001), and has not been made final. Applied Systems asks us to discard the approach of *United Stationers* and use the one found in the draft regulations. That would not be sound, for two reasons: first, proposed regulations have no legal effect; second, the draft says that when final the regulations will apply only to taxable years ending on or after December 21, 2001. So Applied Systems gets no solace from this source even if the regulatory approach would favor its position (which we doubt, given that the regulations essentially track *United Stationers'* definition of "experimentation" as use of the scientific method).

One other line of argument requires only brief mention. Applied Systems thinks that we should disregard *Wicor* and *United Stationers* on the ground that the credit sought by those taxpayers was covered by § 41(d)(4)(E), which disqualifies the costs of internal-use software except to the extent allowed by (nonexistent) regulations. In both *Wicor* and *United Stationers* the taxpayer contracted with a consulting firm to develop software that the taxpayer would use in its own business, while Applied Systems developed software for sale to customers. Yet § 41(d)(4)(E) has nothing to do with the definitions in § 41(d)(1), and *Wicor* stopped there. *United Stationers* held that the taxpayer lost under both § 41(d)(1) and § 41(d)(4)(E). That an opinion contains multiple grounds of decision does not justify disregarding any of them; it would be no more sound to throw out *United Stationers'* interpretation of § 41(d)(1) than to disregard its interpretation of § 41(d)(4)(E) (which was that contracting-out the development of software for in-house use fits within the § 41(d)(4)(E) disqualification). Sections 41(d)(1) and (d)(4) are independent rules, which deserve, and have received, independent constructions.

Whether we apply the definitions articulated in *United Stationers* or the competing interpretation from *Tax & Accounting Software*, simple industrious software development does not qualify for the § 41 tax credit. Accordingly, the judgment of the Tax Court is

AFFIRMED.

QUESTIONS

1.   What is a Subchapter S corporation?

2.   Isn't there always some degree of uncertainty regarding the results of a research project? Stated differently, if the results of the research are known beforehand, can the activity properly be called "research"?

3.   Do you agree with the court that writing a computer program is fundamentally no different than writing a book? Do you think searching for a place to park a car is in any way similar to developing a software program?

4.   Would the fact that a patent was issued on a computer program be dispositive on the question of whether "the research . . . expanded[ed] or refine[d] existing principles of computer science"? What problems do you see in using patent issuance

to determine satisfaction of the experimentation requirement under § 41?

TAX AND ACCOUNTING SOFTWARE CORP. v. UNITED STATES
301 F.3d 1254 (10th Cir. 2002)

LUCERO, CIRCUIT JUDGE.

Plaintiff taxpayers filed a refund suit seeking money allegedly owed them from a tax credit for research and development expenses under I.R.C. § 41. In a matter of first impression in this circuit, we interpret the scope of "qualified research" under I.R.C. § 41, including the requirement in § 41(d)(1) that the taxpayer must intend to "discover[ ] information" using a "process of experimentation." The district court granted summary judgment to the taxpayers and the government appealed. Our review of this case was abated from January 18, 2002, until May 24, 2002, pursuant to the government's request. We have jurisdiction under 28 U.S.C. § 1291, and we reverse and remand.

I

Plaintiffs-Tim Kloehr, his wholly owned Subchapter S corporation, Tax and Accounting Software Corporation ("TAASC"), and Mr. Kloehr's wife Sheryl Kloehr-filed suit seeking a refund of taxes paid by Mr. Kloehr for his 1993 tax year and by him and his wife for 1994. TAASC is an Oklahoma corporation that develops and sells software for use by tax and accounting professionals. In 1993 and 1994, TAASC developed four computer software products for sale to its customers: EasyACCT, EasyMICR, Professional Tax System, and EasyTEL. The research and development expenses for these four products are at issue in this suit.

EasyACCT is an integrated accounting program that collects data for the preparation of financial statements and allows for the transfer of this information to TAASC's tax-preparation software. The parties agree that at the time of its introduction to the public EasyACCT was unique in the functions that it provided.

EasyMICR is a software program designed to print magnetic-ink-character banking transit codes on blank check stock. It was developed in both DOS and Windows versions. A commercial failure, EasyMICR was subsequently integrated into EasyACCT.

Professional Tax System integrates a number of tax-preparation software programs into a single, seamless package and allows for the preparation of tax returns for both state and federal tax forms using the same data. It was the first commercial software program to allow for electronic filing with state and federal governments. The program was also designed to run with minimal memory and therefore is able to run on a wide range of computers.

EasyTEL is an automated, multi-task call-processing system that allows businesses to answer and transfer calls, take messages, provide information over the phone, convert faxes to e-mails, and distribute faxes automatically. EasyTEL is unusual because it was designed to run on low-cost computer hardware and requires little maintenance.

In 1993, TAASC incurred a total of $1,838,756 in research and development expenses for the development of these software products; in 1994, it incurred a total of $2,444,938 in expenses. TAASC claimed a portion of these expenses as research and development tax credits under I.R.C. § 41, but the Internal Revenue Service ("IRS") disallowed those tax credits. As a result, Mr. Kloehr faced tax deficiencies of $123,764 in 1993 and $192,510 in 1994. Mr. Kloehr paid the deficiencies and brought a refund suit on May 14, 1998 under I.R.C. § 7422(a) and 28 U.S.C. § 1346(a)(1). On the parties' cross-motions for summary judgment, the district court granted summary judgment for TAASC.

****

II

Central to the parties' dispute in this case is what constitutes "qualified research," which entitles a business to a tax credit under I.R.C. § 41. We begin our analysis with an overview of the provisions of I.R.C. § 41(d)(1), which defines "qualified research," and a brief history of the § 41 tax credit.

We initially note that the provision in question, I.R.C. § 41, is separate from the tax code provision that provides for a *deduction* for any "research or experimental expenditures" made by a business. I.R.C. § 174(a)(1). The latter expenditures have been defined by regulation as expenditures for "activities intended to discover information that would eliminate uncertainty concerning the development or improvement of a product." Treas. Reg. § 1.174-2. Our interpretation of the proper scope of the tax credit under § 41 has no bearing on the scope or applicability of the deduction under § 174.

A

Section 41(d)(1) lays out five separate requirements for "qualified research":

(1) The research must qualify as expenses under I.R.C. § 174, the tax code provision providing for deductions of research expenses.

(2) The research must be "undertaken for the purpose of discovering information."

(3) The information discovered must be "technological in nature."

(4) The "application" of the information described above must be "intended to be useful in the development of a new or improved business component of the taxpayer."

(5) "Substantially all" of the research must "constitute elements of a process of experimentation" for a valid purpose under the tax credit.

The government concedes that TAASC has met the first and fourth requirements. The parties also do not dispute that the research undertaken by TAASC was "technological in nature" as required by I.R.C. § 41(d)(1)(B)(i). Thus, we consider only the proper interpretation of requirements two (the "discovering information" requirement) and five (the "process of experimentation" requirement).

****

C

TAASC's interpretation of the "discovering information" test is that it only requires a taxpayer to "discover[ ] technological information that led it to develop innovative . . . products." Alternatively, TAASC argues that the "discovering information" test in § 41 should have the same meaning as it has in the definition of research for purposes of § 174 of the tax code. TAASC also implies that because its products were new and innovative compared with the other commercially available products in the field of tax and accounting software, its research and development expenses for those products therefore must qualify for the tax credit.

The government argues that the 1986 amendments, including the addition of the "discovering information" requirement, were intended to narrow the scope of the tax credit significantly. As a result, to meet the "discovering information" requirement, qualified research must "rely upon, and expand or refine, principles of the physical or biological sciences, engineering or computer science." According to the government, TAASC's research did not "expand or refine" principles of computer science, a point that TAASC conceded before the district court.

The district court, however, agreed with TAASC that § 41(d)(1) does not require the taxpayer to expand or refine principles of science or engineering in order to qualify for the tax credit. It added that the "emphasis should be on whether the information qualifies as being "technological in nature" . . ., not whether the work could be considered a revolutionary discovery in the scientific sense." Indeed, the court reasoned that the allegation that there is a separate requirement that the taxpayer "discover" information is erroneous and a "strained and improper reading without any support in the legislative history to back it up." It concluded that as a matter of law TAASC had met the requirements of "discovering information" for purposes of § 41(d)(1), relying in part on the fact that TAASC's products were "new and more efficient combination[s] of software that [were] not available to the public."

The parties also disagree whether TAASC's software development process qualifies as a "process of experimentation." TAASC argues that by trying various programming methods in order to achieve its desired results, it undertook a process of experimentation. The government responds that because TAASC used generally known computer programming skills to achieve its final objective, there was no "experimentation," even if TAASC was unsure which particular technique would allow it to achieve its goal.

The government also contends that TAASC did not use a "process of experimentation" because TAASC believed at the outset that the final results of its research — the development of the software — were certain to be technically feasible. According to the government, the "process of experimentation" requirement requires the taxpayer to be uncertain as to whether the final result can be feasibly achieved. The district court concluded that TAASC's research satisfied the "process of experimentation" requirement.

III

We first analyze what Congress intended when it required that taxpayers "discover" information in order to qualify for the tax credit. In doing so, we apply traditional tools of statutory construction and interpretation, starting with an overview of the applicable principles.

****

B

In interpreting a statute we begin with its plain language. "In ascertaining the plain meaning of the statute, the court must look to the particular statutory language at issue, as well as the language and design of the statute *as a whole.*"

The word "information" has a broad meaning. *See Webster's Third New International Dictionary Unabridged* 1160 (1993) (defining "information" as, for example, "knowledge communicated by others or obtained from investigation, study, or instruction," or "knowledge of a particular event or situation"). Among other definitions, "discover" can mean "to make known (something secret, hidden, unknown, or previously unnoticed)," "to reveal the identity of," or "to disclose to view (something hidden, covered, or previously unseen)." *Id.* at 647; *see also id.* (stating that the word discover "means to come to know something not previously known, either by purposive search and investigation or by accident"). In the present statutory context, i.e., as one of the requirements for "research" that the government would have an interest in encouraging through a tax credit, we conclude that the word "discover" requires that what is "discovered" — in this case, information — be something new or previously unknown.

Moreover, the new information that is discovered must also be information that is "intended to be useful in the development of a new or improved business component of the taxpayer." § 41(d)(1)(B)(ii). The new information therefore cannot merely be the product itself but must also have independent value that can be applied in the development of a new product.

In short, the statute requires that the taxpayer's research, in order to qualify, must have developed new information that is applied towards the development of a product. This is the "discovery" requirement of § 41. Contrary to TAASC's arguments, mere evidence that the taxpayer has developed a new and useful product in and of itself will not qualify. Contrary to the government's argument, the new information need not "expand, or refine, principles of the physical or biological sciences, engineering, or computer science." In other words, each of the positions of the parties is incorrect.

More importantly, for our purposes, the district court erred when it held that any "discovery" test was based on a "strained and improper reading without any support," a holding that essentially read the "discovering information" language out of the statute. The district court also erred when it rejected the argument that the "discovering information" language requires "newness and expansion of existing knowledge." The term "discovery" means that the researcher must find new information or, in other words, must expand existing knowledge. Finally, the district court erred when it relied on the mere newness and innovation of the product itself, without determining that TAASC discovered new information separate from that product, in concluding that TAASC met the requirements of § 41.

To summarize, the "discovering information" language of § 41 establishes a separate requirement that the taxpayer must meet in order to qualify for the tax credit. Under that requirement, the taxpayer must show that he discovered new information and that information must be separate from the product that is actually developed.

IV

The next issue is whether TAASC's work amounted to a "process of experimentation." We analyze both (1) whether the "process of experimentation" test allows a taxpayer to use methods that are generally known, and (2) whether the test requires the taxpayer initially to believe that there is uncertainty as to whether the final result is feasible.

A

In construing the "process of experimentation" requirement, we again start with the language of the statute. "Process" has a broad meaning that supports TAASC's interpretation. *See Webster's Third New International Dictionary Unabridged* at 1808 (defining process in this context as "a progressive forward movement from one point to another on the way to completion," "the action of passing through continuing development from a beginning to a contemplated end," "the action of continuously going along through each of a succession of acts, events or developmental stages," or "a particular method or system of doing something, producing something, or accomplishing a specific result").

The definition of "experiment" is "a test or trial," "a tentative procedure or policy," or "an act or operation carried out under conditions determined by the experimenter (as in a laboratory) in order to discover some unknown principle or effect or to test, establish, or illustrate some suggested or known truth." *Id.* at 800.

Here, the definition of "experiment" is ambiguous with respect to the questions at issue. Concerning the first issue, none of the definitions clarifies whether the methods may be generally known. Regarding the second issue, whether the taxpayer must initially believe that there is uncertainty as to whether the final result is feasible, the first two definitions would best fit with TAASC's broad reading of the term. The last definition could support either the government's argument that the final results of the experimental process must be uncertain as to feasibility — the final result being an "unknown principle or effect" — or TAASC's position that the final results may be certain as to feasibility — the final result may also be a "known truth." Given that the "process of experimentation" must be used to discover new information (as we discussed above), however, the government's position regarding this last definition is stronger. New information cannot be a "known truth."

In light of the conflicting definitions, we conclude that the term "process of experimentation" is ambiguous as to the points at issue: namely, whether the final results must be certain as to feasibility and whether the methods to be used in the "process of experimentation" may be generally known. Because of this ambiguity, legislative history may properly be invoked in construing the "process of experimentation" requirement.

B

By all indications, the government has consistently argued in § 41(d)(1) litigation that there must be uncertainty as to whether the final result can be achieved for the "process of experimentation" test to be satisfied. However, the government has apparently not raised the issue of whether generally known techniques may be used in the "process of experimentation" in any of these cases.

In the various versions of the regulations implementing § 41(d)(1), the government implies that the end result may be certain so long as the method of achieving that result is uncertain at the outset. Over time, however, the government has apparently changed its view regarding whether the converse is true — i.e., whether the method of achieving the result may be certain provided that the end result itself is uncertain.

As for the issue of whether generally known techniques may be used in the "process of experimentation," the government has not addressed that question at all in any of the proposed or final regulations. Because the government has either taken no position or has altered its position on both issues, its interpretation of the "process of experimentation" requirement is entitled to little deference.

C

We conclude that the term "process of experimentation" can include research in which the taxpayer tries alternative methods to achieve a result and all of the methods are already commonly known, but it is uncertain which method will allow the taxpayer to achieve the result. As noted above, the definition of "experiment" does not seem to prohibit the use of commonly or generally known methods. The government has apparently not made the argument that the methods cannot be commonly or generally known in previous litigation, nor has it discussed or considered this interpretation of the statute in its evolving regulations. Nor does the legislative history reflect a contrary legislative intent. Congress stated that a "process of experimentation" would include efforts to "develop, test, and choose among *viable alternatives*." Viable alternative methods need not be new to the taxpayer nor must they be generally unknown to the public.

Moreover, as the Treasury Department itself noted in discussing the regulations implementing § 41 early in 2001, "virtually all research utilizes existing scientific principles and technology." Most scientific research requires the use of known methodologies to determine whether or not particular results are achievable. Although Congress intended to narrow the scope of the research tax credit in 1986, we conclude that the government's position in this case overstates how narrow Congress intended the research credit to be. Congress did not intend to eliminate the use of already known techniques in the discovery of new information through its narrowing of the tax credit clause.

D

The second issue is whether the taxpayer must show that it was uncertain about whether the end result of the "process of experimentation" was technically feasible at the time that it commenced the research. Courts that have previously decided this issue have generally agreed with the government's position.

The government substantially relies on the legislative history. The 1986 House Report defines "process of experimentation" as:

> a process of scientific experimentation or engineering activities to design a business item *where the design of the item as a whole is uncertain at the outset*, but instead must be determined by developing one or more hypotheses for specific design decisions, testing and analyzing those hypotheses (through, for example, modeling or simulation), and refining or discarding the hypotheses as part of a sequential design process to develop the overall item.

[C]osts of developing a new or improved business item are not eligible for the credit if the method of reaching the desired objective (the new or improved product characteristics) is *readily discernible and applicable as of the beginning of the research activities*, so that true experimentation in the scientific or laboratory sense would not have to be undertaken to develop, test, and choose among viable alternatives.

The 1986 Senate Report language is substantially identical and the 1986 Conference Report used slightly different language. This legislative history suggests that the credit is inapplicable when the final design is certain at the outset or the taxpayer knows how to achieve the result at the beginning of the claimed research.

TAASC cites subsequent legislative history from 1998 and 1999 to support its position on the issue. Specifically, it notes that during the 1998 reenactment of the tax credit, the conference committee stated that the process of experimentation test included research "even if the taxpayer knows at the outset that it may be technically possible to achieve the result." However, we cannot consider this subsequent legislative history.

In *Pierce v. Underwood*, the Supreme Court considered whether legislative history included with the 1985 reenactment of the Equal Access to Justice Act ("EAJA") would control the interpretation of a provision of the 1980 version of the EAJA that was reenacted without change in 1985. The legislative history indicated that Congress approved of the interpretation of that provision of the EAJA by some courts, but not by other courts. The Court held that Congress could not control the interpretation of a statute in that way.

****

As was the case in *Pierce*, neither the 1998 nor the 1999 reenactments of the tax credit substantively changed the definition of "qualified research" in the text of the statute. The only reference to the definition was in the legislative history, and that legislative history does not indicate any intent to change the textual meaning of the "process of experimentation" requirement. Congress cannot retroactively change the meaning and intent of previously enacted statutory language through the introduction of legislative history which purports to state what the original meaning of that statutory language was. Congress must change the wording of the statute itself if it wishes to change the meaning of the statute. Following *Pierce*, we will not consider the subsequent legislative history urged upon us by TAASC.

Looking to the legislative history for § 44F, the predecessor to § 41, it appears that at least part of the goal of the tax credit is to provide incentives for companies to invest in research that might not otherwise be undertaken because of its high risks. Thus, the very uncertainty of the research is a rationale for the tax credit in the first place. Allowing experimentation to qualify for the tax credit where the feasibility of the final result was certain would undermine that rationale, and might encourage companies to be more conservative in their allocation of resources, concentrating on problems with a solution that is evident from the outset.

TAASC's interpretation of the statute would allow relatively basic activities, such as debugging software, to be included as "experimentation" within the scope of § 41. Debugging software often requires the utilization of multiple known methods to eliminate the bug from the software. The software developer often has little or no doubt that one of the methods will eliminate the bug. Thus, without the government's limitation on what "experimentation" can mean, all debugging would qualify for the tax credit. The legislative history quoted above indicates that Congress did not intend such a result. We are further persuaded by the maxim that tax credits are to be narrowly interpreted. In enacting the § 41 credit, Congress did not repeal the deduction under § 174, suggesting that less risky research activities were to remain deductible, not creditable.

V

We now apply our legal analysis to the record before us. With respect to the "discovering information" test, much of the record is filled with the conclusory assertions of both parties that the evidence clearly demonstrates that TAASC has, or has not, met the formulation of the test advanced by that party. TAASC's evidence emphasized that its products were new and innovative, and therefore must meet the test; the government's evidence minimized the innovations in TAASC's work. But a crucial question, as shown by our analysis of the plain language of the statute, is whether any new information that TAASC discovered in the course of its research was independent and separate from the new products that it developed. This issue was never developed by either party below, and thus summary judgment for TAASC was inappropriate on this issue.

As for the "process of experimentation" requirement, the affidavits submitted by TAASC under seal indicate to us that TAASC did explore a variety of alternatives to achieve the result in question. However, TAASC has also conceded in its briefs that "TAASC believed . . . [its] goal was technically feasible," at least with respect to the Professional Tax Software project. And before the district court, TAASC "acknowledge[d] that its programmers did not question the technical feasibility of the products" in question. TAASC therefore cannot, as a matter of law, meet this requirement.

VI

The judgment of the district court is REVERSED, and the case REMANDED.

QUESTIONS

1.   The court holds that in order to satisfy the "discovering information" requirement of § 41, TAASC must show that it discovered new information separate from the new software products it developed. The court also found that at least one of TAASC's software programs was unique in the functions it provided. Wouldn't the development of unique software functions generate new information and knowledge that could be reused in the development of subsequent generations of software programs? Wouldn't this new information and knowledge exist separately from the software program TAASC developed?

2.   The court finds that the term "process of experimentation" can include the use of already known research methods when it is uncertain which research methods will allow the taxpayer to achieve the desired result. The court also finds that "experimentation" requires that the feasibility of the final result not be certain? Would the use of known research methods guarantee the feasibility of the final result? Would TAASC spend $2,444,938 on research if it did not believe the desired result of the research was feasible? Would any company invest in research if it believed the desired result of the research was not feasible?

3.   Can debugging of a software program be clearly distinguished from developing the software program in the first instance? Why do you think the court used debugging as an example of non-qualifying research under section 41?

4.   How exactly do the holdings in *Eustice* and *Tax and Accounting* differ?

5.   If you were counsel to a software development firm located in the Tenth Circuit, how would you advise the firm to proceed with its research and development activities in order to increase its chances of obtaining section 41 tax credits? Would careful maintenance of research notebooks be part of your advice?

CASE NOTES

1. *See* Union Carbide Corp. v. Commissioner of Internal Revenue, T.C. Memo-50 (U.S. Tax Ct. 2009) ("Process of experimentation" requirement under § 41 was intended to prevent taxpayers from receiving tax credits for expenses relating to new product development as opposed to new high technology development; case discusses a number of different manufacturing processes and considers which constitute qualified research and which do not); Fairchild Industries Inc. v. United States, 71 F.3d 868 (Fed. Cir. 1996) (Progress payments paid to firm by federal government prior to completion of entire research project, but which firm had no rights to until completion of each research phase, did not constitute government funded research that would disqualify the research for tax credits under § 41(d)(4)(H) of the tax code); TSR, Inc. v. Commissioner of Internal Revenue, 96 T.C. 903 (U.S. Tax Ct. 1991) (Expenses related to research and development of computer games, such as "Dungeons & Dragons," are not scientific or technological in nature and, therefore, do not qualify for section 44 tax credits).

Additional Information

1. ANN K. WOOSTER, 177 A.L.R. FED. 245 (2011).

2. ROBERT J. HAFT, PETER M. FASS, 4B TAX-ADVANTAGED SECURITIES §§ 21:37–21-58 (2010).

3. ALAN S. GUTTERMAN, 1 CORP. COUNS. GD. TO STRATEGIC ALLIANCES § 11:67 (2011).

4. 33A AM. JUR. 2D FEDERAL TAXATION ¶¶ 15106, 15107, 15108, 15111 (2010).

5. William R. Swindle, *Recent Cases Provide Relief for Substantiating Research Tax Credit Claims*, 84 PRACTXST 316 (2010).

6. Evan Wamsley, *The Definition of Qualified Research Under the Section 41 Research and Development Tax Credit: Its Impact on the Credit's Effectiveness*, 87 VA. L. REV. 165 (2001).

7. Kreig Mitchell, *Section 41 Research and Experimentation Tax Credit Audit Considerations*, 37-MAR COLO. LAW. 49 (2008).

8. David L. Cameron, *Research Tax Credit: Statutory Construction, Regulatory Interpretation and Policy Incoherence*, 9 COMPUTER L. REV. & TECH. J. 63 (2004).

9. *Industry Group Objects to Proposed IRS Research Tax Credit Rule*, 41 No. 11 GOV'T CONTRACTOR P 125 (1999).

10. Patricia J. Sweeney, Regan G. Reeves, *Revisiting the Funding Exclusion of the Research Tax Credit After Lockheed Martin v. U.S.*, 41 No. 2 GOV'T CONTRACTOR P 14 (1999).

8.3 FOUNDERS' CAPITAL CONTRIBUTIONS

The general rule for taxation upon the sale or exchange of property is set forth in I.R.C. § 1001. Gain or loss on the sale or exchange of property is recognized in the tax year in which the sale or exchange occurred. The exception to this general rule for the transfer of property to a corporation in exchange for stock is set forth in I.R.C. § 351. Section 351 reflects a public policy of encouraging the formation of new companies by not imposing a tax upon the transfer of property in order to create a new company. However, as noted in the beginning of this chapter, § 351 only postpones the time of taxation; it does eliminate taxation. By providing for a carry-over basis of the property transferred and the stock received, the full amount of the gain will be taxed upon the sale or exchange of the property or stock.

I.R.C. § 1001. DETERMINATION OF AMOUNT OF AND RECOGNITION OF GAIN OR LOSS

(a) Computation of gain or loss. — The gain from the sale or other disposition of property shall be the excess of the amount realized therefrom over the adjusted basis provided in section 1011 for determining gain, and the loss shall be the excess of the adjusted basis provided in such section for determining loss over the amount realized.

****

(c) Recognition of gain or loss. — Except as otherwise provided in this subtitle, the entire amount of the gain or loss, determined under this section, on the sale or exchange of property shall be recognized.

(d) Installment sales. — Nothing in this section shall be construed to prevent (in the case of property sold under contract providing for payment in installments) the taxation of that portion of any installment payment representing gain or profit in the year in which such payment is received.

I.R.C. § 351. TRANSFER TO CORPORATION CONTROLLED BY TRANSFEROR

(a) General rule. — No gain or loss shall be recognized if property is transferred to a corporation by one or more persons solely in exchange for stock in such corporation and immediately after the exchange such person or persons are in control (as defined in section 368(c)) of the corporation.

(b) Receipt of property. — If subsection (a) would apply to an exchange but for the fact that there is received, in addition to the stock permitted to be received under subsection (a), other property or money, then —

(1) gain (if any) to such recipient shall be recognized, but not in excess of —

(A) the amount of money received, plus

(B) the fair market value of such other property received; and

(2) no loss to such recipient shall be recognized.

(c) Special rules where distribution to shareholders. —

(1)   In general. — In determining control for purposes of this section, the fact that any corporate transferor distributes part or all of the stock in the corporation which it receives in the exchange to its shareholders shall not be taken into account.

(d)   Services, certain indebtedness, and accrued interest not treated as property. — For purposes of this section, stock issued for —

(1) services,

(2) indebtedness of the transferee corporation which is not evidenced by a security, or

(3) interest on indebtedness of the transferee corporation which accrued on or after the beginning of the transferor's holding period for the debt, shall not be considered as issued in return for property.

TREAS. REG. § 1.351-1   TRANSFER TO CORPORATION CONTROLLED BY TRANSFEROR.

(a) (1) Section 351(a) provides, in general, for the nonrecognition of gain or loss upon the transfer by one or more persons of property to a corporation solely in exchange for stock or securities in such corporation, if immediately after the exchange, such person or persons are in control of the corporation to which the property was transferred. As used in section 351, the phrase "one or more persons" includes individuals, trusts, estates, partnerships, associations, companies, or corporations (see section 7701(a)(1)). To be in control of the transferee corporation, such person or persons must own immediately after the transfer stock possessing at least 80 percent of the total combined voting power of all classes of stock entitled to vote and at least 80 percent of the total number of shares of all other classes of stock of such corporation (see section 368(c)). In determining control under this section, the fact that any corporate transferor distributes part or all of the stock which it receives in the exchange to its shareholders shall not be taken into account. The phrase "immediately after the exchange" does not necessarily require simultaneous exchanges by two or more persons, but comprehends a situation where the rights of the parties have been previously defined and the execution of the agreement proceeds with an expedition consistent with orderly procedure. For purposes of this section —

(i) Stock or securities issued for services rendered or to be rendered to or for the benefit of the issuing corporation will not be treated as having been issued in return for property, and

(ii) Stock or securities issued for property which is of relatively small value in comparison to the value of the stock and securities already owned (or to be received for services) by the person who transferred such property, shall not be treated as having been issued in return for property if the primary purpose of the transfer is to qualify under this section the exchanges of property by other persons transferring property.

For the purpose of section 351, stock rights or stock warrants are not included in the term "stock or securities."

(2) The application of section 351(a) is illustrated by the following examples:

Example (1). C owns a patent right worth $25,000 and D owns a manufacturing plant worth $75,000. C and D organize the R Corporation with an authorized capital stock of $100,000. C transfers his patent right to the R Corporation for $25,000 of its stock and D transfers his plant to the new corporation for $75,000 of its stock. No gain or loss to C or D is recognized.

Example (2). B owns certain real estate which cost him $50,000 in 1930, but which has a fair market value of $200,000 in 1955. He transfers the property to the N Corporation in 1955 for 78 percent of each class of stock of the corporation having a fair market value of $200,000, the remaining 22 percent of the stock of the corporation having been issued by the corporation in 1940 to other persons for cash. B realized a taxable gain of $150,000 on this transaction.

Example (3). E, an individual, owns property with a basis of $10,000 but which has a fair market value of $18,000. E also had rendered services valued at $2,000 to Corporation F. Corporation F has outstanding 100 shares of common stock all of which are held by G. Corporation F issues 400 shares of its common stock (having a fair market value of $20,000) to E in exchange for his property worth $18,000 and in compensation for the services he has rendered worth $2,000. Since immediately after the transaction, E owns 80 percent of the outstanding stock of Corporation F, no gain is recognized upon the exchange of the property for the stock. However, E realized $2,000 of ordinary income as compensation for services rendered to Corporation F.

I.R.C. § 358.   BASIS TO DISTRIBUTEES

(a) General rule. — In the case of an exchange to which section 351, 354, 355, 356, or 361 applies--

(1) Nonrecognition property. — The basis of the property permitted to be received under such section without the recognition of gain or loss shall be the same as that of the property exchanged —

(A) decreased by —

(i) the fair market value of any other property (except money) received by the taxpayer,

(ii) the amount of any money received by the taxpayer, and

(iii) the amount of loss to the taxpayer which was recognized on such exchange, and

(B) increased by —

(i) the amount which was treated as a dividend, and

(ii) the amount of gain to the taxpayer which was recognized on such exchange (not including any portion of such gain which was treated as a dividend).

(2) Other property. — The basis of any other property (except money) received by the taxpayer shall be its fair market value.

TREAS. REG. § 1.358-1 BASIS TO DISTRIBUTEES.

(a) In the case of an exchange to which section 351 or 361 applies in which, under the law applicable to the year in which the exchange was made, only nonrecognition property is received, the basis of all the stock and securities received in the exchange shall be the same as the basis of all property exchanged therefor. If in an exchange or distribution to which section 351, 356, or 361 applies both nonrecognition property and "other property" are received, the basis of all the property except "other property" held after the transaction shall be determined as described in the preceding three sentences decreased by the sum of the money and the fair market value of the "other property" (as of the date of the transaction) and increased by the sum of the amount treated as a dividend (if any) and the amount of the gain recognized on the exchange, but the term gain as here used does not include any portion of the recognized gain that was treated as a dividend. In any case in which a taxpayer transfers property with respect to which loss is recognized, such loss shall be reflected in determining the basis of the property received in the exchange. The basis of the "other property" is its fair market value as of the date of the transaction.

(b) The application of paragraph (a) of this section may be illustrated by the following example:

Example. A purchased a share of stock in Corporation X in 1935 for $150. Since that date A has received distributions out of other than earnings and profits (as defined in section 316) totaling $60, so that A's adjusted basis for the stock is $90. In a transaction qualifying under section 356, A exchanged this share for one share in Corporation Y, worth $100, cash in the amount of $10, and other property with a fair market value of $30. The exchange had the effect of the distribution of a dividend. A's ratable share of the earnings and profits of Corporation X accumulated after February 28, 1913, was $5. A realized a gain of $50 on the exchange, but the amount recognized is limited to $40, the sum of the cash received and the fair market value of the other property. Of the gain recognized, $5 is taxable as a dividend, and $35 is taxable as a gain from the exchange of property. The basis to A of the one share of stock of Corporation Y is $90, that is, the adjusted basis of the one share of stock of Corporation X ($90), decreased by the sum of the cash received ($10) and the fair market value of the other property received ($30) and increased by the sum of the amount treated as a dividend ($5) and the amount treated as a gain from the exchange of property ($35). The basis of the other property received is $30.

QUESTIONS

1. In Treas. Reg. § 1.351-1, Example (1), why was there no gain or loss recognized to C and D on their transfer of the patent and manufacturing plant to R Corporation in exchange for stock? Would it make a difference if C received $10,000 of R Corporation's stock and D received $90,000 of R Corporation's stock?

2. In Example (2), why did B recognize a taxable gain of $150,000 on his transfer of land to N Corporation in exchange for stock? Would it make a difference if B received 100% of the voting stock in N Corporation?

3.   In Example (3), what is E's basis in the stock of Corporation F?

4.   In the Example in Treas. Reg. § 1.358-1(b), how is A's realized gain of $50 calculated? How is A's recognized gain of $40 calculated? How is A's basis in the stock of Corporation Y calculated?

5.   A and B are co-inventors of a new DNA extraction technology for which they have filed a patent application. To date, A and B have incurred $5,000 of patent prosecution costs. While the patent application is still pending, A and B formed ExTech and transferred their pending patent application to ExTech in exchange for 50% of ExTech's common stock. ExTech's remaining shares of common stock are held in a treasury reserve fund for future issue. Is the transfer by A and B of the patent application to ExTech a taxable transaction? Assuming A and B each received 25% of the transferred stock, what are their bases in the stock? What is ExTech's basis in the patent application?

6.   Following the same facts as in question 5 above, A and B decide to pay themselves "sweat equity" for their research services on behalf of ExTech. They agree that they each will receive 10 shares of ExTech common stock for every month they work for ExTech. Is the transfer of ExTech common stock in exchange for A's and B's research services a taxable transaction? If so, how would the gain on the stock transfers to A and B be calculated? What would be the basis of the stock received by A and B in exchange for their research services?

[Editor's Note: The following case is a very lucid and witty explication of Section 351 exchanges of property for stock.]

PERACCHI v. COMMISSIONER OF INTERNAL REVENUE
143 F.3d 487 (10th Cir. 1998)

KOZINSKI, CIRCUIT JUDGE:

We must unscramble a Rubik's Cube of corporate tax law to determine the basis of a note contributed by a taxpayer to his wholly-owned corporation.

The Transaction

The taxpayer, Donald Peracchi, needed to contribute additional capital to his closely-held corporation (NAC) to comply with Nevada's minimum premium-to-asset ratio for insurance companies. Peracchi contributed two parcels of real estate. The parcels were encumbered with liabilities which together exceeded Peracchi's total basis in the properties by more than half a million dollars. As we discuss in detail below, under section 357(c), contributing property with liabilities in excess of basis can trigger immediate recognition of gain in the amount of the excess. In an effort to avoid this, Peracchi also executed a promissory note, promising to pay NAC $1,060,000 over a term of ten years at 11% interest. Peracchi maintains that the note has a basis equal to its face amount, thereby making his total basis in the property contributed greater than the total liabilities. If this is so, he will have extracted himself from the quicksand of section 357(c) and owe no immediate tax on the transfer of property to NAC. The IRS, though, maintains that (1) the note is not genuine indebtedness and should be treated as an unenforceable gift; and (2) even if the note is genuine, it does not increase Peracchi's basis in the property contributed.

The parties are not splitting hairs: Peracchi claims the basis of the note is $1,060,000, its face value, while the IRS argues that the note has a basis of zero. If Peracchi is right, he pays no immediate tax on the half a million dollars by which the debts on the land he contributed exceed his basis in the land; if the IRS is right, the note becomes irrelevant for tax purposes and Peracchi must recognize an immediate gain on the half million. The fact that the IRS and Peracchi are so far apart suggests they are looking at the transaction through different colored lenses. To figure out whether Peracchi's lens is rose-tinted or clear, it is useful to take a guided tour of sections 351 and 357 and the tax law principles undergirding them.

Into the Lobster Pot: Section 351

"Decisions to embrace the corporate form of organization should be carefully considered, since a corporation is like a lobster pot: easy to enter, difficult to live in, and painful to get out of." Boris I. Bittker & James S. Eustice, Federal Income Taxation of Corporations and Shareholders ¶ 2.01[3] (6th ed. 1997) (hereinafter Bittker & Eustice).

The Code tries to make organizing a corporation pain-free from a tax point of view. A capital contribution is, in tax lingo, a "nonrecognition" event: A shareholder can generally contribute capital without recognizing gain on the exchange. It's merely a change in the form of ownership, like moving a billfold from one pocket to another. So long as the shareholders contributing the property remain in control of the corporation after the exchange, section 351 applies: It doesn't matter if the capital contribution occurs at the creation of the corporation or if — as here — the company is already up and running. The baseline is that Peracchi may contribute property to NAC without recognizing gain on the exchange.

Gain Deferral: Section 358(a)

Peracchi contributed capital to NAC in the form of real property and a promissory note. Corporations may be funded with any kind of asset, such as equipment, real estate, intellectual property, contracts, leaseholds, securities or letters of credit. The tax consequences can get a little complicated because a shareholder's basis in the property contributed often differs from its fair market value. The general rule is that an asset's basis is equal to its "cost." But when a shareholder like Peracchi contributes property to a corporation in a nonrecognition transaction, a cost basis does not preserve the unrecognized gain. Rather than take a basis equal to the fair market value of the property exchanged, the shareholder must substitute the basis of that property for what would otherwise be the cost basis of the stock. This preserves the gain for recognition at a later day: The gain is built into the shareholder's new basis in the stock, and he will recognize income when he disposes of the stock.

The fact that gain is deferred rather than extinguished doesn't diminish the importance of questions relating to basis and the timing of recognition. In tax, as in comedy, timing matters. Most taxpayers would much prefer to pay tax on contributed property years later — when they sell their stock — rather than when they contribute the property. Thus what Peracchi is seeking here is gain deferral: He wants the gain to be recognized only when he disposes of some or all of his stock.

Continuity of Investment: Boot and section 351(b)

Continuity of investment is the cornerstone of nonrecognition under section 351. Nonrecognition assumes that a capital contribution amounts to nothing more than a nominal change in the form of ownership; in substance the shareholder's investment in the property continues. But a capital contribution can sometimes allow a shareholder to partially terminate his investment in an asset or group of assets. For example, when a shareholder receives cash or other property in addition to stock, receipt of that property reflects a partial termination of investment in the business. The shareholder may invest that money in a wholly unrelated business, or spend it just like any other form of personal income. To the extent a section 351 transaction resembles an ordinary sale, the nonrecognition rationale falls apart.

Thus the central exception to nonrecognition for section 351 transactions comes into play when the taxpayer receives "boot" — money or property other than stock in the corporation — in exchange for the property contributed. Boot is recognized as taxable income because it represents a partial cashing out. It's as if the taxpayer contributed part of the property to the corporation in exchange for stock, and sold part of the property for cash. Only the part exchanged for stock represents a continuation of investment; the part sold for cash is properly recognized as yielding income, just as if the taxpayer had sold the property to a third party.

Peracchi did not receive boot in return for the property he contributed. But that doesn't end the inquiry: We must consider whether Peracchi has cashed out in some other way which would warrant treating part of the transaction as taxable boot.

Assumption of Liabilities: Section 357(a)

The property Peracchi contributed to NAC was encumbered by liabilities. Contribution of leveraged property makes things trickier from a tax perspective. When a shareholder contributes property encumbered by debt, the corporation usually assumes the debt. And the Code normally treats discharging a liability the same as receiving money: The taxpayer improves his economic position by the same amount either way. NAC's assumption of the liabilities attached to Peracchi's property therefore could theoretically be viewed as the receipt of money, which would be taxable boot.

The Code takes a different tack. Requiring shareholders like Peracchi to recognize gain any time a corporation assumes a liability in connection with a capital contribution would greatly diminish the nonrecognition benefit section 351 is meant to confer. Section 357(a) thus takes a lenient view of the assumption of liability: A shareholder engaging in a section 351 transaction does not have to treat the assumption of liability as boot, even if the corporation assumes his obligation to pay.

This nonrecognition does not mean that the potential gain disappears. Once again, the basis provisions kick in to reflect the transfer of gain from the shareholder to the corporation: The shareholder's substitute basis in the stock received is decreased by the amount of the liability assumed by the corporation. The adjustment preserves the gain for recognition when the shareholder sells his stock in the company, since his taxable gain will be the difference between the (new lower) basis and the sale price of the stock.

Sasquatch and The Negative Basis Problem: Section 357(c)

Highly leveraged property presents a peculiar problem in the section 351 context. Suppose a shareholder organizes a corporation and contributes as its only asset a building with a basis of $50, a fair market value of $100, and mortgage debt of $90. Section 351 says that the shareholder does not recognize any gain on the transaction. Under section 358, the shareholder takes a substitute basis of $50 in the stock, then adjusts it downward under section 357 by $90 to reflect the assumption of liability. This leaves him with a basis of minus $40. A negative basis properly preserves the gain built into the property: If the shareholder turns around and sells the stock the next day for $10 (the difference between the fair market value and the debt), he would face $50 in gain, the same amount as if he sold the property without first encasing it in a corporate shell.

But skeptics say that negative basis, like Bigfoot, doesn't exist. Basis normally operates as a cost recovery system: Depreciation deductions reduce basis, and when basis hits zero, the property cannot be depreciated farther. At a more basic level, it seems incongruous to attribute a negative value to a figure that normally represents one's investment in an asset. Some commentators nevertheless argue that when basis operates merely to measure potential gain (as it does here), allowing negative basis may be perfectly appropriate and consistent with the tax policy underlying nonrecognition transactions. Whatever the merits of this debate, it seems that section 357(c) was enacted to eliminate the possibility of negative basis.

Section 357(c) prevents negative basis by forcing a shareholder to recognize gain to the extent liabilities exceed basis. Thus, if a shareholder contributes a building with a basis of $50 and liabilities of $90, he does not receive stock with a basis of minus $40. Instead, he takes a basis of zero and must recognize a $40 gain.

Peracchi sought to contribute two parcels of real property to NAC in a section 351 transaction. Standing alone the contribution would have run afoul of section 357(c): The property he wanted to contribute had liabilities in excess of basis, and Peracchi would have had to recognize gain to the extent of the excess, or $566,807.

The Grift: Boosting Basis with a Promissory Note

Peracchi tried to dig himself out of this tax hole by contributing a personal note with a face amount of $1,060,000 along with the real property. Peracchi maintains that the note has a basis in his hands equal to its face value. If he's right, we must add the basis of the note to the basis of the real property. Taken together, the aggregate basis in the property contributed would exceed the aggregate liabilities.

Under Peracchi's theory, then, the aggregate liabilities no longer exceed the aggregate basis, and section 357(c) no longer triggers any gain. The government argues, however, that the note has a zero basis. If so, the note would not affect the tax consequences of the transaction, and Peracchi's $566,807 in gain would be taxable immediately.

Are Promises Truly Free?

Which brings us (phew!) to the issue before us: Does Peracchi's note have a basis in Peracchi's hands for purposes of section 357(c)? The language of the Code gives us little to work with. The logical place to start is with the definition of basis. Section 1012 provides that "[t]he basis of property shall be the cost of such property . . . ." But "cost" is nowhere defined. What does it cost Peracchi to write the note and contribute it to his corporation? The IRS argues tersely that the "taxpayers in the instant case incurred no cost in issuing their own note to NAC, so their basis in the note was zero." Building on this premise, the IRS makes Peracchi out to be a grifter: He holds an unenforceable promise to pay himself money, since the corporation will not collect on it unless he says so.

It's true that all Peracchi did was make out a promise to pay on a piece of paper, mark it in the corporate minutes and enter it on the corporate books. It is also true that nothing will cause the corporation to enforce the note against Peracchi so long as Peracchi remains in control. But the IRS ignores the possibility that NAC may go bankrupt, an event that would suddenly make the note highly significant. Peracchi and NAC are separated by the corporate form, and this gossamer curtain makes a difference in the shell game of C Corp organization and reorganization. Contributing the note puts a million dollar nut within the corporate shell, exposing Peracchi to the cruel nutcracker of corporate creditors in the event NAC goes bankrupt. And it does so to the tune of $1,060,000, the full face amount of the note. Without the note, no matter how deeply the corporation went into debt, creditors could not reach Peracchi's personal assets. With the note on the books, however, creditors can reach into Peracchi's pocket by enforcing the note as an unliquidated asset of the corporation.

The key to solving this puzzle, then, is to ask whether bankruptcy is significant enough a contingency to confer substantial economic effect on this transaction. If the risk of bankruptcy is important enough to be recognized, Peracchi should get basis in the note: He will have increased his exposure to the risks of the business — and thus his economic investment in NAC — by $1,060,000. If bankruptcy is so remote that there is no realistic possibility it will ever occur, we can ignore the potential economic effect of the note as speculative and treat it as merely an unenforceable promise to contribute capital in the future.

When the question is posed this way, the answer is clear. Peracchi's obligation on the note was not conditioned on NAC's remaining solvent. It represents a new and substantial increase in Peracchi's investment in the corporation. The Code

954 TAX EFFECTS OF TECHNOLOGY CREATION AND TRANSFER CH. 8

seems to recognize that economic exposure of the shareholder is the ultimate measuring rod of a shareholder's investment. Peracchi therefore is entitled to a step-up in basis to the extent he will be subjected to economic loss if the underlying investment turns unprofitable.

The economics of the transaction also support Peracchi's view of the matter. The transaction here does not differ substantively from others that would certainly give Peracchi a boost in basis. For example, Peracchi could have borrowed $1 million from a bank and contributed the cash to NAC along with the properties. Because cash has a basis equal to face value, Peracchi would not have faced any section 357(c) gain. NAC could then have purchased the note from the bank for $1 million which, assuming the bank's original assessment of Peracchi's creditworthiness was accurate, would be the fair market value of the note. In the end the corporation would hold a million dollar note from Peracchi — just like it does now — and Peracchi would face no section 357(c) gain. The only economic difference between the transaction just described and the transaction Peracchi actually engaged in is the additional costs that would accompany getting a loan from the bank. Peracchi incurs a "cost" of $1 million when he promises to pay the note to the bank; the cost is not diminished here by the fact that the transferor controls the initial transferee. The experts seem to agree: "Section 357(c) can be avoided by a transfer of enough cash to eliminate any excess of liabilities over basis; and since a note given by a solvent obligor in purchasing property is routinely treated as the equivalent of cash in determining the basis of the property, it seems reasonable to give it the same treatment in determining the basis of the property transferred in a § 351 exchange." Bittker & Eustice ¶ 3.06[4][b].

We are aware of the mischief that can result when taxpayers are permitted to calculate basis in excess of their true economic investment. For two reasons, however, we do not believe our holding will have such pernicious effects. First, and most significantly, by increasing the taxpayer's personal exposure, the contribution of a valid, unconditional promissory note has substantial economic effects which reflect his true economic investment in the enterprise. The main problem with attributing basis to nonrecourse debt financing is that the tax benefits enjoyed as a result of increased basis do not reflect the true economic risk. Here Peracchi will have to pay the full amount of the note with after-tax dollars if NAC's economic situation heads south. Second, the tax treatment of nonrecourse debt primarily creates problems in the partnership context, where the entity's loss deductions (resulting from depreciation based on basis inflated above and beyond the taxpayer's true economic investment) can be passed through to the taxpayer. It is the pass-through of losses that makes artificial increases in equity interests of particular concern. We don't have to tread quite so lightly in the C Corp context, since a C Corp doesn't funnel losses to the shareholder.

We find further support for Peracchi's view by looking at the alternative: What would happen if the note had a zero basis? The IRS points out that the basis of the note in the hands of the corporation is the same as it was in the hands of the taxpayer. Accordingly, if the note has a zero basis for Peracchi, so too for NAC. But what happens if NAC — perhaps facing the threat of an involuntary petition for bankrupt cy — turns around and sells Peracchi's note to a third party for its fair market value? According to the IRS's theory, NAC would take a carryover basis of zero in the note and would have to recognize $1,060,000 in phantom gain on the subsequent exchange, even though the note did not appreciate in value one bit. That can't be the right result.

Accordingly, we hold that Peracchi has a basis of $1,060,000 in the note he wrote to NAC. The aggregate basis exceeds the liabilities of the properties transferred to NAC under section 351, and Peracchi need not recognize any section 357(c) gain.

****

Conclusion

We hold that Peracchi has a basis of $1,060,000 in the note, its face value. As such, the aggregate liabilities of the property contributed to NAC do not exceed its basis, and Peracchi does not recognize any section 357(c) gain. The decision of the Tax Court is REVERSED. The case is remanded for entry of judgment in favor of Peracchi.

QUESTIONS

1.   Assume a taxpayer obtains an assignment of a patent portfolio for $1 million. The taxpayer amortizes the patent portfolio in the amount of $500,000. After the fair market value of the patent portfolio increases to $1.5 million as a result of a series of lucrative licenses, the taxpayer borrows $750,000 using the patent portfolio as collateral for the loan. The taxpayer then transfers the patent portfolio to NewCo, a C corporation he forms, in exchange for 100% of the voting stock in NewCo. Would the taxpayer realize any gain under section 357(c)? If so, in what amount? What would be NewCo's basis in the patent portfolio?

2.   Assume X, the founder and 100% owner of TechCo, obtains an exclusive license to a university patent for the life of the patent. Under the terms of the license, X pays the university's patent prosecution costs of $25,000 and agrees to pay the university 4% royalties on the net sales of all products produced using the patent. If X transferred the exclusive license to TechCo solely in exchange for stock, what would be X's basis in the stock?

3.   Assume the same facts as above, except X arranges for the university to grant the exclusive license directly to TechCo. Because TechCo has very little cash, X gives the university a promissory note in the amount of $25,000 to secure the payment of the patent prosecution costs. Under the terms of the promissory note, X will pay the university $5,000 a year for 5 years at a 10% interest rate. How would X's promissory note affect X's basis in TechCo stock?

4.   Would the result in *Peracchi* be different if NAV was an S Corporation or a partnership? Why? What if NAV was a limited liability company (LLC)?

5.   What is "boot"? What is a "negative basis"? What is "grift"? Why are promises not "truly free"?

CASE NOTES

1. In 1959, DuPont was manufacturing patented urea herbicides in the United States. DuPont also held French patents on the urea herbicides and was selling the herbicides in France. Under French patent law, a company owning French patents must manufacture the patented product in France within three years of obtaining the patent or risk being required to grant a compulsory license to a French manufacturer. To avoid this risk, DuPont established a wholly-owned subsidiary in France to manufacture and sell the patented herbicides. DuPont granted the French subsidiary a royalty-free, non-exclusive license to make, use and sell the urea herbicides under the French patents for the life of the patents. The license allowed the subsidiary to sublicense the manufacturing of the herbicides for its own sales, but any other sublicenses required DuPont's consent. In exchange for the license, DuPont received stock in its French subsidiary which it valued at $411,500. DuPont claimed the receipt of the stock was not subject to taxation under section 351 and did not include the value of the stock as income in the 1959 tax year. The IRS claimed the grant of the non-exclusive license did constitute an "exchange" under section 351. In making this claim, the IRS equated the "exchange" requirement under section 351 with the "sale or exchange" requirement of the IRC for capital gains treatment. According to the IRS, the grant of a non-exclusive license does not result in a capital gains transaction under the provisions of the IRC governing capital gains treatment and, therefore, does not constitute an "exchange" for purposes of section 351 non-recognition. What result? *See* E. I. DuPont de Nemours and Co. v. U.S., 471 F.2d 1211 (Cl. Ct. 1973).

2. *See also* Rubber Research, Inc. v. Commissioner of Internal Revenue, 422 F.2d 1402 (8th Cir. 1970) (Section 351 nonrecognition is not available to taxpayer that did not control 80% of transferre corporation voting stock immediately after the transfer; the proper measure of income tax gain where one company transfers a sublicense to another company in exchange for the other company's stock is the difference between the value of the stock received in the exchange and the adjusted basis of the sublicense granted in the exchange).

Additional Information

1. WILLIAM S. MCKEE ET AL., FED. TAX'N PARTERSHIPS AND PARTNERS ¶ 18.01–18.02 (2011).

2. 33 AM. JUR. 2D FEDERAL TAXATION ¶¶ 4904, 5251–5256 (2011).

3. GEORGE D. SMOLEN, 5 MERTENS LAW OF FED. INCOME TAX'N § 23:92 (2011).

4. RICHARD D. BLAU, BRUCE N. LEMONS, THOMAS P. ROHMAN, 1 S CORPORATIONS FEDERAL TAXATION §§ 5:21–5:26, 5:29 (2010).

5. 47B C.J.S. INTERNAL REVENUE § 372 (2010).

6. 758 § III (BNA), 20XX WL 4741850, BASIC REQUIREMENTS OF § 351 (2010).

7. John A. Townsend, *Reconciling Section 482 and the Other Nonrecognition Provisions*, 50 TAX LAW. 701 (1997).

8.   Note, *Losing Control: Toward a New Understanding of the Taxation of Post-Incorporation Stock Sales*, 108 HARV. L. REV. 1661 (1995).

8.4 STOCK IN EXCHANGE FOR SERVICES

The issuance of stock to employees is a common form of compensation. For companies, the advantages of compensating employees by means of stock include avoiding salary payments when cash is short, incentivizing employees to contribute to the success of the company, assuring key employees remain with the company and compensating employees under non-competition agreements after employment is terminated. For employees, the advantages of receiving stock include benefiting from the discount spread between the price paid for the stock and its fair market value at the time of sale, and participating directly in the financial growth of the company over time. The payment of stock for services is especially useful in the case of start-up and early-stage companies that need to recruit and retain highly qualified personnel, but have little cash with which to do this.

Section 83 of the Internal Revenue Code describes the tax consequences to employees and employers when stock is issued in exchange for the performance of services. As a general rule, an employee who receives stock in exchange for services must report the value of the stock, less the amount paid for the stock, as ordinary income compensation in the year in which the stock is received. Likewise, an employer who issues stock in exchange for services is allowed to deduct the value of the stock, less the amount paid for the stock, from gross income in the year in which the stock is issued. The employee's inclusion of the stock value in the employee's gross income as compensation for services, and the employer's deduction of the stock value from its gross income as compensation, are reciprocal; that is, one cannot occur without the other.

The question that complicates the application of IRC § 83 is not whether stock received in exchange for services is taxable to the employee, and deductible to the employer, as compensation, but when the tax event occurs. IRC Section 83 provides that the employee does not realize compensation income at the time the stock is received if the stock is subject to a substantial risk of forfeiture *and* the stock cannot be transferred. The recognition of compensation income is deferred until the stock is no longer subject to a substantial risk of forfeiture or the stock can be transferred, whichever occurs first. The Treasury Regulations under § 83 define in detail "transfer," "substantially vested and substantially nonvested," and "substantial risk of forfeiture."

Under § 83(a), an employee can realize income compensation from issued stock even if the employee does not sell the stock to another person. For example, if company X issued employee E 100 shares of stock valued at $500 per share and the stock contract provided that 10 shares of stock would become vested each year for the next 10 years, E would have to report income compensation in the amount of $5000 at the end of year one whether or not E sold the stock. The employee's dilemma of having to pay tax on the stock received when the employee has not received cash from the sale of stock is mitigated by § 83(b). Section 83(b) allows the employee to elect to include in gross income the value of the stock in the year it is received even if the stock is subject to a substantial risk of forfeiture. If the employee elects to include the value of the stock as compensation income in the year in which it is received, the employee will pay tax on the difference between the value of the stock at the time of transfer, and the amount paid for the stock, at ordinary income rates. If the employee later sells the stock, the gain or loss on the sale, measured as the difference between the amount reported as ordinary income and the amount received in exchange for the sale of stock, will be taxed at capital gains rates.

This section includes IRC Section 83 and the accompanying regulations. I forewarn you that there is considerable IRS-speak in the regulations. The two cases in this section, *Robinson* and *Pagal*, deal with the questions of when stock is transferrable and when stock options are taxable.

I.R.C. § 83 PROPERTY TRANSFERRED IN CONNECTION WITH PERFORMANCE OF SERVICES

(a) **General rule.** — If, in connection with the performance of services, property is transferred to any person other than the person for whom such services are performed, the excess of —

(1) the fair market value of such property (determined without regard to any restriction other than a restriction which by its terms will never lapse) at the first time the rights of the person having the beneficial interest in such property are transferable or are not subject to a substantial risk of forfeiture, whichever occurs earlier, over

(2) the amount (if any) paid for such property,

shall be included in the gross income of the person who performed such services in the first taxable year in which the rights of the person having the beneficial interest in such property are transferable or are not subject to a substantial risk of forfeiture, whichever is applicable. The preceding sentence shall not apply if such person sells or otherwise disposes of such property in an arm's length transaction before his rights in such property become transferable or not subject to a substantial risk of forfeiture.

(b) **Election to include in gross income in year of transfer.** —

(1) In general. — Any person who performs services in connection with which property is transferred to any person may elect to include in his gross income, for the taxable year in which such property is transferred, the excess of —

(A) the fair market value of such property at the time of transfer (determined without regard to any restriction other than a restriction which by its terms will never lapse), over

(B) the amount (if any) paid for such property.

If such election is made, subsection (a) shall not apply with respect to the transfer of such property, and if such property is subsequently forfeited, no deduction shall be allowed in respect of such forfeiture.

(2) Election. — An election under paragraph (1) with respect to any

transfer of property shall be made in such manner as the Secretary prescribes and shall be made not later than 30 days after the date of such transfer. Such election may not be revoked except with the consent of the Secretary.

(c) Special rules. — For purposes of this section —

(1) Substantial risk of forfeiture. — The rights of a person in property are subject to a substantial risk of forfeiture if such person's rights to full enjoyment of such property are conditioned upon the future performance of substantial services by any individual.

(2) Transferability of property. — The rights of a person in property are transferable only if the rights in such property of any transferee are not subject to a substantial risk of forfeiture.

(3) Sales which may give rise to suit under section 16(b) of the Securities Exchange Act of 1934. — So long as the sale of property at a profit could subject a person to suit under section 16(b) of the Securities Exchange Act of 1934, such person's rights in such property are —

(A) subject to a substantial risk of forfeiture, and

(B) not transferable.

(4) For purposes of determining an individual's basis in property transferred in connection with the performance of services, rules similar to the rules of section 72(w) shall apply.

(d) Certain restrictions which will never lapse. —

(1) Valuation. — In the case of property subject to a restriction which by its terms will never lapse, and which allows the transferee to sell such property only at a price determined under a formula, the price so determined shall be deemed to be the fair market value of the property unless established to the contrary by the Secretary, and the burden of proof shall be on the Secretary with respect to such value.

(2) Cancellation. — If, in the case of property subject to a restriction which by its terms will never lapse, the restriction is canceled, then, unless the taxpayer establishes —

(A) that such cancellation was not compensatory, and

(B) that the person, if any, who would be allowed a deduction if the cancellation were treated as compensatory, will treat the transaction as not compensatory, as evidenced in such manner as the Secretary shall prescribe by regulations, the excess of the fair market value of the property (computed without regard to the restrictions) at the time of cancellation over the sum of —

(C) the fair market value of such property (computed by taking the restriction into account) immediately before the cancellation, and

(D) the amount, if any, paid for the cancellation,

shall be treated as compensation for the taxable year in which such cancellation occurs.

(e)   Applicability of section. — This section shall not apply to —

(1) a transaction to which section 421 applies,

(2) a transfer to or from a trust described in section 401(a) or a transfer under an annuity plan which meets the requirements of section 404(a)(2),

(3) the transfer of an option without a readily ascertainable fair market value,

(4) the transfer of property pursuant to the exercise of an option with a readily ascertainable fair market value at the date of grant, or

(5) group-term life insurance to which section 79 applies.

(f)   Holding period. — In determining the period for which the taxpayer has held property to which subsection (a) applies, there shall be included only the period beginning at the first time his rights in such property are transferable or are not subject to a substantial risk of forfeiture, whichever occurs earlier.

(g)   Certain exchanges. — If property to which subsection (a) applies is exchanged for property subject to restrictions and conditions substantially similar to those to which the property given in such exchange was subject, and if section 354, 355, 356, or 1036 (or so much of section 1031 as relates to section 1036) applied to such exchange, or if such exchange was pursuant to the exercise of a conversion privilege —

(1) such exchange shall be disregarded for purposes of subsection (a), and

(2) the property received shall be treated as property to which subsection (a) applies.

(h)   Deduction by employer. — In the case of a transfer of property to which this section applies or a cancellation of a restriction described in subsection (d), there shall be allowed as a deduction under section 162, to the person for whom were performed the services in connection with which such property was transferred, an amount equal to the amount included under subsection (a), (b), or (d)(2) in the gross income of the person who performed such services. Such deduction shall be allowed for the taxable year of such person in which or with which ends the taxable year in which such amount is included in the gross income of the person who performed such services.

QUESTIONS

1.   On April 1, 2005, company X sells employee E 100 shares of common stock for $10 per share. At the time of the sale, the fair market value of the common stock is $100 per share. Under the terms of the sale, E must sell the common stock back to X for $10 per share in the event E terminates employment with X prior to April 1, 2015. The stock certificates issued to E are stamped with the legend "Non-Transferrable." What amount must E include as compensation in tax year 2005?

2. Assume the same facts as above, except the stock certificates are not stamped with the legend "Non-Transferrable" and E sells the stock in an arm's length transaction to B for $50 per share on April 1, 2010. What amount must E include as compensation in tax year 2010?

3. Assume the same facts as in question 1. If E does not terminate employment with X prior to April 1, 2015, at which time the value of X common stock is $250 per share, what amount must E include as compensation in tax year 2015?

4. Taxpayers generally prefer to defer payment of taxes as long as possible, because future dollars used to pay taxes are less valuable than current dollars. Why would a taxpayer elect to pay ordinary income taxes under § 83(b) on stock received for services that is substantially nonvested and nontransferable?

TREAS. REG. § 1.83-1 PROPERTY TRANSFERRED IN CONNECTION WITH THE PERFORMANCE OF SERVICES.

(a) Inclusion in gross income —

(1) General rule. Section 83 provides rules for the taxation of property transferred to an employee or independent contractor (or beneficiary thereof) in connection with the performance of services by such employee or independent contractor. In general, such property is not taxable under section 83(a) until it has been transferred (as defined in § 1.83-3(a)) to such person and become substantially vested (as defined in § 1.83-3(b)) in such person. In that case, the excess of —

(i) The fair market value of such property (determined without regard to any lapse restriction, as defined in § 1.83-3(i)) at the time that the property becomes substantially vested, over

(ii) The amount (if any) paid for such property, shall be included as compensation in the gross income of such employee or independent contractor for the taxable year in which the property becomes substantially vested. Until such property becomes substantially vested, the transferor shall be regarded as the owner of such property, and any income from such property received by the employee or independent contractor (or beneficiary thereof) or the right to the use of such property by the employee or independent contractor constitutes additional compensation and shall be included in the gross income of such employee or independent contractor for the taxable year in which such income is received or such use is made available. This paragraph applies to a transfer of property in connection with the performance of services even though the transferor is not the person for whom such services are performed.

****

(b) Subsequent sale, forfeiture, or other disposition of nonvested property.

(1) If substantially nonvested property (that has been transferred in connection with the performance of services) is subsequently sold or otherwise disposed of to a third party in an arm's length transaction while still

substantially nonvested, the person who performed such services shall realize compensation in an amount equal to the excess of —

(i) The amount realized on such sale or other disposition, over

(ii) The amount (if any) paid for such property.

Such amount of compensation is includible in his gross income in accordance with his method of accounting. Two preceding sentences also apply when the person disposing of the property has received it in a non-arm's length transaction described in paragraph (c) of this section. In addition, section 83(a) and paragraph (a) of this section shall thereafter cease to apply with respect to such property.

(2) If substantially nonvested property that has been transferred in connection with the performance of services to the person performing such services is forfeited while still substantially nonvested and held by such person, the difference between the amount paid (if any) and the amount received upon forfeiture (if any) shall be treated as an ordinary gain or loss. This paragraph (b)(2) does not apply to property to which § 1.83-2(a) applies.

(3) This paragraph (b) shall not apply to, and no gain shall be recognized on, any sale, forfeiture, or other disposition described in this paragraph to the extent that any property received in exchange therefore is substantially nonvested. Instead, section 83 and this section shall apply with respect to such property received (as if it were substituted for the property disposed of).

(c) **Dispositions of nonvested property not at arm's length.** If substantially nonvested property (that has been transferred in connection with the performance of services) is disposed of in a transaction which is not at arm's length and the property remains substantially nonvested, the person who performed such services realizes compensation equal in amount to the sum of any money and the fair market value of any substantially vested property received in such disposition. Such amount of compensation is includible in his gross income in accordance with his method of accounting. However, such amount of compensation shall not exceed the fair market value of the property disposed of at the time of disposition (determined without regard to any lapse restriction), reduced by the amount paid for such property. In addition, section 83 and these regulations shall continue to apply with respect to such property, except that any amount previously includible in gross income under this paragraph (c) shall thereafter be treated as an amount paid for such property. For example, if in 1971 an employee pays $50 for a share of stock which has a fair market value of $100 and is substantially nonvested at that time and later in 1971 (at a time when the property still has a fair market value of $100 and is still substantially nonvested) the employee disposes of, in a transaction not at arm's length, the share of stock to his wife for $10, the employee realizes compensation of $10 in 1971. If in 1972, when the share of stock has a fair market value of $120, it becomes substantially vested, the employee realizes additional compensation in 1972 in the amount of $60 (the $120 fair market value of the stock less both the $50 price paid for the stock and the $10 taxed as compensation in 1971). For purposes of this paragraph, if substantially nonvested property has been transferred to a person other than the person who performed the services, and the transferee dies holding the property while the property is still substantially nonvested and while the person who performed the services is alive, the transfer which results by reason of the death of such transferee is a transfer not at arm's length.

****

(e) Forfeiture after substantial vesting. If a person is taxable under section 83(a) when the property transferred becomes substantially vested and thereafter the person's beneficial interest in such property is nevertheless forfeited pursuant to a lapse restriction, any loss incurred by such person (but not by a beneficiary of such person) upon such forfeiture shall be an ordinary loss to the extent the basis in such property has been increased as a result of the recognition of income by such person under section 83(a) with respect to such property.

(f) Examples. The provisions of this section may be illustrated by the following examples:

Example (1). On November 1, 1978, X corporation sells to E, an employee, 100 shares of X corporation stock at $10 per share. At the time of such sale the fair market value of the X corporation stock is $100 per share. Under the terms of the sale each share of stock is subject to a substantial risk of forfeiture which will not lapse until November 1, 1988. Evidence of this restriction is stamped on the face of E's stock certificates, which are therefore nontransferable (within the meaning of § 1.83-3(d)). Since in 1978 E's stock is substantially nonvested, E does not include any of such amount in his gross income as compensation in 1978. On November 1, 1988, the fair market value of the X corporation stock is $250 per share. Since the X corporation stock becomes substantially vested in 1988, E must include $24,000 (100 shares of X corporation stock × $250 fair market value per share less $10 price paid by E for each share) as compensation for 1988. Dividends paid by X to E on E's stock after it was transferred to E on November 1, 1973, are taxable to E as additional compensation during the period E's stock is substantially nonvested and are deductible as such by X.

Example (2). Assume the facts are the same as in example (1), except that on November 1, 1985, each share of stock of X corporation in E's hands could as a matter of law be transferred to a bona fide purchaser who would not be required to forfeit the stock if the risk of forfeiture materialized. In the event, however, that the risk materializes, E would be liable in damages to X. On November 1, 1985, the fair market value of the X corporation stock is $230 per share. Since E's stock is transferable within the meaning of § 1.83-3(d) in 1985, the stock is substantially vested and E must include $22,000 (100 shares of X corporation stock × $230 fair market value per share less $10 price paid by E for each share) as compensation for 1985.

Example (3). Assume the facts are the same as in example (1) except that, in 1984 E sells his 100 shares of X corporation stock in an arm's length sale to I, an investment company, for $120 per share. At the time of this sale each share of X corporation's stock has a fair market value of $200. Under paragraph (b) of this section, E must include $11,000 (100 shares of X corporation stock × $120 amount realized per share less $10 price paid by E per share) as compensation for 1984 notwithstanding that the stock remains nontransferable and is still subject to a substantial risk of forfeiture at the time of such sale. Under § 1.83-4(b)(2), I's basis in the X corporation stock is $120 per share.

QUESTIONS

1.   If a company pays dividends to an employee on stock issued for services that is substantially nonvested and nontransferable, how must the employee report these dividends?

2.   On May 1, 2004, company X sells to employee E 100 shares of stock for $25 per share for future services to be performed. At the time of the sale, the fair market value of the stock $250 per share. The sales contract provides that the stock will be forfeited if E does not achieve a specified amount of sales by May 1, 2006. If E fails to achieve the specified amount of sales by May 1, 2006 and the 100 shares of common stock are forfeited to X, how should E report the forfeited shares in tax year 2006?

3.   If an employee sells stock received for services, which is subject to a substantial risk of forfeiture, to another person, and the stock continues to be subject to a substantial risk of forfeiture in the hands of the transferee, must the employee report the amount realized in the sale as compensation in the year of the sale?

TREAS. REG. § 1.83-2 ELECTION TO INCLUDE IN GROSS INCOME IN YEAR OF TRANSFER.

(a) **In general.** If property is transferred (within the meaning of § 1.83-3(a)) in connection with the performance of services, the person performing such services may elect to include in gross income under section 83(b) the excess (if any) of the fair market value of the property at the time of transfer (determined without regard to any lapse restriction, as defined in § 1.83-3(i)) over the amount (if any) paid for such property, as compensation for services. The fact that the transferee has paid full value for the property transferred, realizing no bargain element in the transaction, does not preclude the use of the election as provided for in this section. If this election is made, the substantial vesting rules of section 83(a) and the regulations thereunder do not apply with respect to such property, and except as otherwise provided in section 83(d)(2) and the regulations thereunder (relating to the cancellation of a nonlapse restriction), any subsequent appreciation in the value of the property is not taxable as compensation to the person who performed the services. Thus, property with respect to which this election is made shall be includible in gross income as of the time of transfer, even though such property is substantially nonvested (as defined in § 1.83-3(b)) at the time of transfer, and no compensation will be includible in gross income when such property becomes substantially vested (as defined in § 1.83-3(b)). In computing the gain or loss from the subsequent sale or exchange of such property, its basis shall be the amount paid for the property increased by the amount included in gross income under section 83(b). If property for which a section 83(b) election is in effect is forfeited while substantially nonvested, such forfeiture shall be treated as a sale or exchange upon which there is realized a loss equal to the excess (if any) of —

(1) The amount paid (if any) for such property, over,

(2) The amount realized (if any) upon such forfeiture.

If such property is a capital asset in the hands of the taxpayer, such loss shall be a capital loss. A sale or other disposition of the property that is in substance a forfeiture, or is made in contemplation of a forfeiture, shall be treated as a forfeiture under the two immediately preceding sentences.

****

QUESTIONS

1. On June 1, 2007, company X sells employee E 100 shares of common stock for $50 per share. At the time of the sale, the fair market value of X common stock is $100 per share. If E makes an election under section 83(b), how much will E include in gross income in tax year 2007? How will this income be taxed?

2. Assume the same facts as in question 1. If E sells the stock on July 15, 2010 for $300 per share, what amount will E include in gross income in tax year 2010? How will this income be taxed?

TREAS. REG. § 1.83-3   MEANING AND USE OF CERTAIN TERMS.

(a)   Transfer —

(1)   In general. For purposes of section 83 and the regulations thereunder, a transfer of property occurs when a person acquires a beneficial ownership interest in such property (disregarding any lapse restriction, as defined in § 1.83-3(i)). For special rules applying to the transfer of a life insurance contract (or an undivided interest therein) that is part of a split-dollar life insurance arrangement (as defined in § 1.61-22(b)(1) or (2)), see § 1.61-22(g).

(2)   Option. The grant of an option to purchase certain property does not constitute a transfer of such property. However, see § 1.83-7 for the extent to which the grant of the option itself is subject to section 83. In addition, if the amount paid for the transfer of property is an indebtedness secured by the transferred property, on which there is no personal liability to pay all or a substantial part of such indebtedness, such transaction may be in substance the same as the grant of an option. The determination of the substance of the transaction shall be based upon all the facts and circumstances. The factors to be taken into account include the type of property involved, the extent to which the risk that the property will decline in value has been transferred, and the likelihood that the purchase price will, in fact, be paid. See also § 1.83-4(c) for the treatment of forgiveness of indebtedness that has constituted an amount paid.

(3)   Requirement that property be returned. Similarly, no transfer may have occurred where property is transferred under conditions that require its return upon the happening of an event that is certain to occur, such as the termination of employment. In such a case, whether there is, in fact, a transfer

depends upon all the facts and circumstances. Factors which indicate that no transfer has occurred are described in paragraph (a)(4), (5), and (6) of this section.

(4)   Similarity to option. An indication that no transfer has occurred is the extent to which the conditions relating to a transfer are similar to an option.

(5)   Relationship to fair market value. An indication that no transfer has occurred is the extent to which the consideration to be paid the transferee upon surrendering the property does not approach the fair market value of the property at the time of surrender. For purposes of paragraph (a)(5) and (6) of this section, fair market value includes fair market value determined under the rules of § 1.83-5(a)(1), relating to the valuation of property subject to nonlapse restrictions. Therefore, the existence of a nonlapse restriction referred to in § 1.83-5(a)(1) is not a factor indicating no transfer has occurred.

(6)   Risk of loss. An indication that no transfer has occurred is the extent to which the transferee does not incur the risk of a beneficial owner that the value of the property at the time of transfer will decline substantially. Therefore, for purposes of this (6), risk of decline in property value is not limited to the risk that any amount paid for the property may be lost.

(7)   Examples. The provisions of this paragraph may be illustrated by the following examples:

Example (1). On January 3, 1971, X corporation sells for $500 to S, a salesman of X, 10 shares of stock in X corporation with a fair market value of $1,000. The stock is nontransferable and subject to return to the corporation (for $500) if S's sales do not reach a certain level by December 31, 1971. Disregarding the restriction concerning S's sales (since the restrictions is a lapse restriction), S's interest in the stock is that of a beneficial owner and therefore a transfer occurs on January 3, 1971.

Example (2). On November 17, 1972, W sells to E 100 shares of stock in W corporation with a fair market value of $10,000 in exchange for a $10,000 note without personal liability. The note requires E to make yearly payments of $2,000 commencing in 1973. E collects the dividends, votes the stock and pays the interest on the note. However, he makes no payments toward the face amount of the note. Because E has no personal liability on the note, and since E is making no payments towards the face amount of the note, the likelihood of E paying the full purchase price is in substantial doubt. As a result E has not incurred the risks of a beneficial owner that the value of the stock will decline. Therefore, no transfer of the stock has occurred on November 17, 1972, but an option to purchase the stock has been granted to E.

Example (3). On January 3, 1971, X corporation purports to transfer to E, an employee, 100 shares of stock in X corporation. The X stock is subject to the sole restriction that E must sell such stock to X on termination of employment for any reason for an amount which is equal to the excess (if any) of the book value of the X stock at termination of employment over book value on January 3, 1971. The stock is not transferable by E and the restrictions on transfer are stamped on the certificate. Under these facts and circumstances, there is no transfer of the X stock within the meeting of section 83.

Example (4). Assume the same facts as in example (3) except that E paid $3,000 for the stock and that the restriction required E upon termination of employment to sell the stock to M for the total amount of dividends that have been declared on the stock since September 2, 1971, or $3,000 whichever is higher. Again, under the facts and circumstances, no transfer of the X stock has occurred.

Example (5). On July 4, 1971, X corporation purports to transfer to G, an employee, 100 shares of X stock. The stock is subject to the sole restriction that upon termination of employment G must sell the stock to X for the greater of its fair market value at such time or $100, the amount G paid for the stock. On July 4, 1971 the X stock has a fair market value of $100. Therefore, G does not incur the risk of a beneficial owner that the value of the stock at the time of transfer ($100) will decline substantially. Under these facts and circumstances, no transfer has occurred.

(b) **Substantially vested and substantially nonvested property.** For purposes of section 83 and the regulations thereunder, property is substantially nonvested when it is subject to a substantial risk of forfeiture, within the meaning of paragraph (c) of this section, and is nontransferable, within the meaning of paragraph (d) of this section. Property is substantially vested for such purposes when it is either transferable or not subject to a substantial risk of forfeiture.

(c) **Substantial risk of forfeiture —**

(1) In general. For purposes of section 83 and the regulations thereunder, whether a risk of forfeiture is substantial or not depends upon the facts and circumstances. A substantial risk of forfeiture exists where rights in property that are transferred are conditioned, directly or indirectly, upon the future performance (or refraining from performance) of substantial services by any person, or the occurrence of a condition related to a purpose of the transfer, and the possibility of forfeiture is substantial if such condition is not satisfied.

Property is not transferred subject to a substantial risk of forfeiture to the extent that the employer is required to pay the fair market value of a portion of such property to the employee upon the return of such property. The risk that the value of property will decline during a certain period of time does not constitute a substantial risk of forfeiture. A nonlapse restriction, standing by itself, will not result in a substantial risk of forfeiture.

(2) Illustrations of substantial risks of forfeiture. The regularity of the performance of services and the time spent in performing such services tend to indicate whether services required by a condition are substantial. The fact that the person performing services has the right to decline to perform such services without forfeiture may tend to establish that services are insubstantial. Where stock is transferred to an underwriter prior to a public offering and the full enjoyment of such stock is expressly or impliedly conditioned upon the successful completion of the underwriting, the stock is subject to a substantial risk of forfeiture. Where an employee receives property from an employer subject to a requirement that it be returned if the total earnings of the

employer do not increase, such property is subject to a substantial risk of forfeiture. On the other hand, requirements that the property be returned to the employer if the employee is discharged for cause or for committing a crime will not be considered to result in a substantial risk of forfeiture. An enforceable requirement that the property be returned to the employer if the employee accepts a job with a competing firm will not ordinarily be considered to result in a substantial risk of forfeiture unless the particular facts and circumstances indicate to the contrary. Factors which may be taken into account in determining whether a covenant not to compete constitutes a substantial risk of forfeiture are the age of the employee, the availability of alternative employment opportunities, the likelihood of the employee's obtaining such other employment, the degree of skill possessed by the employee, the employee's health, and the practice (if any) of the employer to enforce such covenants. Similarly, rights in property transferred to a retiring employee subject to the sole requirement that it be returned unless he renders consulting services upon the request of his former employer will not be considered subject to a substantial risk of forfeiture unless he is in fact expected to perform substantial services.

(3) Enforcement of forfeiture condition. In determining whether the possibility of forfeiture is substantial in the case of rights in property transferred to an employee of a corporation who owns a significant amount of the total combined voting power or value of all classes of stock of the employer corporation or of its parent corporation, there will be taken into account (i) the employee's relationship to other stockholders and the extent of their control, potential control and possible loss of control of the corporation, (ii) the position of the employee in the corporation and the extent to which he is subordinate to other employees, (iii) the employee's relationship to the officers and directors of the corporation, (iv) the person or persons who must approve the employee's discharge, and (v) past actions of the employer in enforcing the provisions of the restrictions. For example, if an employee would be considered as having received rights in property subject to a substantial risk of forfeiture, but for the fact that the employee owns 20 percent of the single class of stock in the transferor corporation, and if the remaining 80 percent of the class of stock is owned by an unrelated individual (or members of such an individual's family) so that the possibility of the corporation enforcing a restriction on such rights is substantial, then such rights are subject to a substantial risk of forfeiture. On the other hand, if 4 percent of the voting power of all the stock of a corporation is owned by the president of such corporation and the remaining stock is so diversely held by the public that the president, in effect, controls the corporation, then the possibility of the corporation enforcing a restriction on rights in property transferred to the president is not substantial, and such rights are not subject to a substantial risk of forfeiture.

(4) Examples. The rules contained in paragraph (c)(1) of this section may be illustrated by the following examples. In each example it is assumed that, if the conditions on transfer are not satisfied, the forfeiture provision will be enforced.

Example (1). On November 1, 1971, corporation X transfers in connection with the performance of services to E, an employee, 100 shares of corporation X stock for $90 per share. Under the terms of the transfer, E will be subject to a binding commitment to resell the stock to corporation X at $90 per share if he leaves the employment of corporation X for any reason prior to the expiration of a 2-year period from the date of such transfer. Since E must perform substantial services for corporation X and will not be paid more than $90 for the stock, regardless of its value, if he fails to perform such services during such 2-year period, E's rights in the stock are subject to a substantial risk of forfeiture during such period.

****

Example (3). On November 25, 1971, corporation X gives to E, an employee, in connection with his performance of services to corporation X, a bonus of 100 shares of corporation X stock. Under the terms of the bonus arrangement E is obligated to return the corporation X stock to corporation X if he terminates his employment for any reason. However, for each year occurring after November 25, 1971, during which E remains employed with corporation X, E ceases to be obligated to return 10 shares of the corporation X stock. Since in each year occurring after November 25, 1971, for which E remains employed he is not required to return 10 shares of corporation X's stock, E's rights in 10 shares each year for 10 years cease to be subject to a substantial risk of forfeiture for each year he remains so employed.

****

Example (5). On January 7, 1971, corporation X, a computer service company, transfers to E, 100 shares of corporation X stock for $50. E is a highly compensated salesman who sold X's products in a three-state area since 1960. At the time of transfer each share of X stock has a fair market value of $100. The stock is transferred to E in connection with his termination of employment with X. Each share of X stock is subject to the sole condition that E can keep such share only if he does not engage in competition with X for a 5-year period in the three-state area where E had previously sold X's products. E, who is 45 years old, has no intention of retiring from the work force. In order to earn a salary comparable to his current compensation, while preventing the risk of forfeiture from arising, E will have to expend a substantial amount of time and effort in another industry or market to establish the necessary business contacts. Thus, under these facts and circumstances E's rights in the stock are subject to a substantial risk of forfeiture.

(d) **Transferability of property.** For purposes of section 83 and the regulations thereunder, the rights of a person in property are transferable if such person can transfer any interest in the property to any person other than the transferor of the property, but only if the rights in such property of such transferee are not subject to a substantial risk of forfeiture. Accordingly, property is transferable if the person performing the services or receiving the property can sell, assign, or pledge (as collateral for a loan, or as security for the performance of an obligation, or for any other purpose) his interest in the property to any person other than the transferor of such property and if the transferee is not required to give up the property or its value in the event the substantial risk of forfeiture materializes. On the other hand, property is not considered to be transferable merely because the person performing the services or receiving the property may designate a beneficiary to receive the property in the event of his death.

(e) **Property.** For purposes of section 83 and the regulations thereunder, the term "property" includes real and personal property other than either money or an unfunded and unsecured promise to pay money or property in the future. The term also includes a beneficial interest in assets (including money) which are transferred or set aside from the claims of creditors of the transferor, for example, in a trust or escrow account. See, however, § 1.83-8(a) with respect to employee trusts and annuity plans subject to section 402(b) and section 403(c). In the case of a transfer of a life insurance contract, retirement income contract, endowment contract, or other contract providing life insurance protection, or any undivided interest therein, the policy cash value and all other rights under such contract (including any supplemental agreements thereto and whether or not guaranteed), other than current life insurance protection, are treated as property for purposes of this section. However, in the case of the transfer of a life insurance contract, retirement income contract, endowment contract, or other contract providing life insurance protection, which was part of a split-dollar arrangement (as defined in § 1.61-22(b)) entered into (as defined in § 1.61-22(j)) on or before September 17, 2003, and which is not materially modified (as defined in § 1.61-22(j)(2)) after September 17, 2003, only the cash surrender value of the contract is considered to be property. Where rights in a contract providing life insurance protection are substantially nonvested, see § 1.83-1(a)(2) for rules relating to taxation of the cost of life insurance protection.

(f) **Property transferred in connection with the performance of services.** Property transferred to an employee or an independent contractor (or beneficiary thereof) in recognition of the performance of, or the refraining from performance of, services is considered transferred in connection with the performance of services within the meaning of section 83. The existence of other persons entitled to buy stock on the same terms and conditions as an employee, whether pursuant to a public or private offering may, however, indicate that in such circumstances a transfer to the employee is not in recognition of the performance of, or the refraining from performance of, services. The transfer of property is subject to section 83 whether such transfer is in respect of past, present, or future services.

(g) **Amount paid.** For purposes of section 83 and the regulations thereunder, the term "amount paid" refers to the value of any money or property paid for the transfer of property to which section 83 applies, and does not refer to any amount paid for the right to use such property or to receive the income therefrom. Such value does not include any stated or unstated interest payments. For rules regarding the calculation of the amount of unstated interest payments, see § 1.483-1(c). When section 83 applies to the transfer of property pursuant to the exercise of an option, the term "amount paid" refers to any amount paid for the grant of the option plus any amount paid as the exercise price of the option. For rules regarding the forgiveness of indebtedness treated as an amount paid, see § 1.83-4(c).

(h) Nonlapse restriction. For purposes of section 83 and the regulations thereunder, a restriction which by its terms will never lapse (also referred to as a "nonlapse restriction") is a permanent limitation on the transferability of property —

(1) Which will require the transferee of the property to sell, or offer to sell, such property at a price determined under a formula, and

(2) Which will continue to apply to and be enforced against the transferee or any subsequent holder (other than the transferor).

A limitation subjecting the property to a permanent right of first refusal in a particular person at a price determined under a formula is a permanent nonlapse restriction. Limitations imposed by registration requirements of State or Federal security laws or similar laws imposed with respect to sales or other dispositions of stock or securities are not nonlapse restrictions. An obligation to resell or to offer to sell property transferred in connection with the performance of services to a specific person or persons at its fair market value at the time of such sale is not a nonlapse restriction. See § 1.83-5(c) for examples of nonlapse restrictions.

(i) Lapse restriction. For purposes of section 83 and the regulations thereunder, the term "lapse restriction" means a restriction other than a nonlapse restriction as defined in paragraph (h) of this section, and includes (but is not limited to) a restriction that carries a substantial risk of forfeiture.

****

QUESTIONS

1. In Example (1) under § 1.83-3(a)(7), the stock sold to S is nontransferable and subject to return to X corporation for the purchase price paid by S in the event S does not reach a certain sales level by a certain date. Why does this constitute a transfer of stock on the date of sale?

2. In Example (3) under § 1.83-3(a)(7), why is there no transfer of X stock to E on January 3, 1971?

3. When does a substantial risk of forfeiture exist for stock transferred to an employee for services? If a company is required to pay an employee some portion of the fair market value of stock transferred for services upon the employee's return of the stock to the company, is there a substantial risk of forfeiture?

4. In Example (5) under § 1.83-3(c)(4), why is there a substantial risk of forfeiture of E's stock?

5. What is a "nonlapse restriction" on stock issued in exchange for services?

TREAS. REG. § 1.83-5 RESTRICTIONS THAT WILL NEVER LAPSE.

(a) Valuation. For purposes of section 83 and the regulations thereunder, in the case of property subject to a nonlapse restriction (as defined in § 1.83-3(h)), the price determined under the formula price will be considered to be the fair market value of the property unless established to the contrary by the Commissioner, and the burden of proof shall be on the commissioner with respect to such value. If stock in a corporation is subject to a nonlapse restriction which requires the transferee to sell such stock only at a formula price based on book value, a reasonable multiple of earnings or a reasonable combination thereof, the price so determined will ordinarily be regarded as determinative of the fair market value of such property for purposes of section 83. However, in certain circumstances the formula price will not be considered to be the fair market value of property subject to such a formula price restriction, even though the formula price restriction is a substantial factor in determining such value. For example, where the formula price is the current book value of stock, the book value of the stock at some time in the future may be a more accurate measure of the value of the stock than the current book value of the stock for purposes of determining the fair market value of the stock at the time the stock becomes substantially vested.

(b)   Cancellation —

(1)   In general. Under section 83(d)(2), if a nonlapse restriction imposed on property that is subject to section 83 is cancelled, then, unless the taxpayer establishes —

(i) That such cancellation was not compensatory, and

(ii) That the person who would be allowed a deduction, if any, if the cancellation were treated as compensatory, will treat the transaction as not compensatory, as provided in paragraph (c)(2) of this section, the excess of the fair market value of such property (computed without regard to such restriction) at the time of cancellation, over the sum of —

(iii) The fair market value of such property (computed by taking the restriction into account) immediately before the cancellation, and

(iv) The amount, if any, paid for the cancellation, shall be treated as compensation for the taxable year in which such cancellation occurs. Whether there has been a noncompensatory cancellation of a nonlapse restriction under section 83(d)(2) depends upon the particular facts and circumstances. Ordinarily the fact that the employee or independent contractor is required to perform additional services or that the salary or payment of such a person is adjusted to take the cancellation into account indicates that such cancellation has a compensatory purpose. On the other hand, the fact that the original purpose of a restriction no longer exists may indicate that the purpose of such cancellation is noncompensatory. Thus, for example, if a so-called "buy-sell" restriction was imposed on a corporation's stock to limit ownership of such stock and is being cancelled in connection with a public offering of the stock, such cancellation will generally be regarded as noncompensatory. However, the mere fact that the employer is willing to forego a deduction under section 83(h) is insufficient evidence to establish a noncompensatory cancellation of a nonlapse restriction. The refusal by a corporation or shareholder to repurchase stock of the corporation which is subject to a permanent right of first refusal will generally be treated as a cancellation of a nonlapse restriction. The preceding sentence shall not apply where there is no nonlapse restriction, for example, where the price to be paid for the stock subject to the right of first refusal is the fair market value of the stock. Section 83(d)(2) and this (1) do not apply where immediately after the cancellation of a nonlapse restriction the property is still substantially nonvested and no section 83(b) election has been made with respect to such property. In such a case the rules of section 83(a) and § 1.83-1 shall apply to such property.

(2)   Evidence of noncompensatory cancellation. In addition to the information necessary to establish the factors described in paragraph (b)(1) of this section, the taxpayer shall request the employer to furnish the taxpayer with a written statement indicating that the employer will not treat the cancellation of the nonlapse restriction as a compensatory event, and that no deduction will be taken with respect to such cancellation. The taxpayer shall file such written statement with his income tax return for the taxable year in which or with which such cancellation occurs.

(c)   **Examples.** The provisions of this section may be illustrated by the following examples:

Example (1). On November 1, 1971, X corporation whose shares are closely held and not regularly traded, transfers to E, an employee, 100 shares of X corporation stock subject to the condition that, if he desires to dispose of such stock during the period of his employment, he must resell the stock to his employer at its then existing book value. In addition, E or E's estate is obligated to offer to sell the stock at his retirement or death to his employer at its then existing book value. Under these facts and circumstances, the restriction to which the shares of X corporation stock are subject is a nonlapse restriction. Consequently, the fair market value of the X stock is includible in E's gross income as compensation for taxable year 1971. However, in determining the fair market value of the X stock, the book value formula price will ordinarily be regarded as being determinative of such value.

Example (2). Assume the facts are the same as in example (1), except that the X stock is subject to the condition that if E desires to dispose of the stock during the period of his employment he must resell the stock to his employer at a multiple of earnings per share that is in this case a reasonable approximation of value at the time of transfer to E. In addition, E or E's estate is obligated to offer to sell the stock at his retirement or death to his employer at the same multiple of earnings. Under these facts and circumstances, the restriction to which the X corporation stock is subject is a nonlapse restriction. Consequently, the fair market value of the X stock is includible in E's gross income for taxable year 1971. However, in determining the fair market value of the X stock, the multiple-of-earnings formula price will ordinarily be regarded as determinative of such value.

Example (3). On January 4, 1971, X corporation transfers to E, an employee, 100 shares of stock in X corporation. Each such share of stock is subject to an agreement between X and E whereby E agrees that such shares are to be held solely for investment purposes and not for resale (a so-called investment letter restriction). E's rights in such stock are substantially vested upon transfer, causing the fair market value of each share of X corporation stock to be includible in E's gross income as compensation for taxable year 1971. Since such an investment letter restriction does not constitute a nonlapse restriction, in determining the fair market value of each share, the investment letter restriction is disregarded.

Example (4). On September 1, 1971, X corporation transfers to B, an independent contractor, 500 shares of common stock in X corporation in exchange for B's agreement to provide services in the construction of an office building on property owned by X corporation. X corporation has 100 shares of preferred stock outstanding and an additional 500 shares of common stock outstanding. The preferred stock has a liquidation value of $1,000x, which is equal to the value of all assets owned by X. Therefore, the book value of the common stock in X corporation is $0. Under the terms of the transfer, if B wishes to dispose of the stock, B must offer to sell the stock to X for 150 percent of the then existing book value of B's common stock. The stock is also subject to a substantial risk of forfeiture until B performs the agreed-upon services. B makes a timely election under section 83(b) to include the value of the stock in gross income in 1971. Under these facts and circumstances, the restriction to which the shares of X corporation common stock are subject is a nonlapse restriction. In determining the fair market value of the X common stock at the time of transfer, the book value formula price would ordinarily be regarded as determinative of such value. However, the fair market value of X common stock at the time of transfer, subject to the book value restriction, is greater than $0 since B was willing to agree to provide valuable personal services in exchange for the stock. In determining the fair market value of the stock, the expected book value after construction of the office building would be given great weight. The likelihood of completion of construction would be a factor in determining the expected book value after completion of construction.

QUESTIONS

1. When is the cancellation of a nonlapse restriction compensation to an employee? How is the amount of this compensation calculated?

2. In Example (1) under § 1.83-5(c), why is the restriction to which the shares of X stock are subject a nonlapse restriction? What difference does the nonlapse restriction make in determining whether the value of X stock is includible in E's gross income in the year the stock is received? How does the nonlapse restriction affect the valuation of X stock?

TREAS. REG. § 1.83-6   DEDUCTION BY EMPLOYER.

(a) Allowance of deduction —

(1) General rule. In the case of a transfer of property in connection with the performance of services, or a compensatory cancellation of a nonlapse restriction described in section 83(d) and § 1.83-5, a deduction is allowable under section 162 or 212 to the person for whom the services were performed.

The amount of the deduction is equal to the amount included as compensation in the gross income of the service provider under section 83(a), (b), or (d)(2), but only to the extent the amount meets the requirements of section 162 or 212 and the regulations thereunder. The deduction is allowed only for the taxable year of that person in which or with which ends the taxable year of the service provider in which the amount is included as compensation. For purposes of this paragraph, any amount excluded from gross income under section 79 or section 101(b) or subchapter N is considered to have been included in gross income.

****

(4)   Capital expenditure, etc. No deduction is allowed under section 83(h) to the extent that the transfer of property constitutes a capital expenditure, an item of deferred expense, or an amount properly includible in the value of inventory items. In the case of a capital expenditure, for example, the basis of the property to which such capital expenditure relates shall be increased at the same time and to the same extent as any amount includible in the employee's gross income in respect of such transfer. Thus, for example, no deduction is allowed to a corporation in respect of a transfer of its stock to a promoter upon its organization, notwithstanding that such promoter must include the value of such stock in his gross income in accordance with the rules under section 83.

****

(b)   Recognition of gain or loss. Except as provided in section 1032, at the time of a transfer of property in connection with the performance of services the transferor recognizes gain to the extent that the transferor receives an amount that exceeds the transferor's basis in the property. In addition, at the time a deduction is allowed under section 83(h) and paragraph (a) of this section, gain or loss is recognized to the extent of the difference between (1) the sum of the amount paid plus the amount allowed as a deduction under section 83(h), and (2) the sum of the taxpayer's basis in the property plus any amount recognized pursuant to the previous sentence.

(c)   Forfeitures. If, under section 83(h) and paragraph (a) of this section, a deduction, an increase in basis, or a reduction of gross income was allowable (disregarding the reasonableness of the amount of compensation) in respect of a transfer of property and such property is subsequently forfeited, the amount of such deduction, increase in basis or reduction of gross income shall be includible in the gross income of the person to whom it was allowable for the taxable year of forfeiture. The basis of such property in the hands of the person to whom it is forfeited shall include any such amount includible in the gross income of such person, as well as any amount such person pays upon forfeiture.

QUESTIONS

1.   On January 5, 2002, company X sells 100 shares of common stock to employee E for $50 per share. At the time of the sale, X common stock has a fair market value of $200 per share. The sales contract imposes no restrictions on the

transferability of the 100 shares of X common stock. How much can X deduct as compensation paid to E?

2.   Assume the same facts as in question 1, except the sales contract provided that the stock would be forfeited in the event E terminated employment with X within five years of the date on which the stock was transferred. If E terminated employment with X prior to the five year period and the stock was forfeited to X, how would X report the stock forfeiture?

TREAS. REG. § 1.83-7   TAXATION OF NONQUALIFIED STOCK OPTIONS.

(a)   **In general.** If there is granted to an employee or independent contractor (or beneficiary thereof) in connection with the performance of services, an option to which section 421 (relating generally to certain qualified and other options) does not apply, section 83(a) shall apply to such grant if the option has a readily ascertainable fair market value (determined in accordance with paragraph (b) of this section) at the time the option is granted. The person who performed such services realizes compensation upon such grant at the time and in the amount determined under section 83(a). If section 83(a) does not apply to the grant of such an option because the option does not have a readily ascertainable fair market value at the time of grant, sections 83(a) and 83(b) shall apply at the time the option is exercised or otherwise disposed of, even though the fair market value of such option may have become readily ascertainable before such time. If the option is exercised, sections 83(a) and 83(b) apply to the transfer of property pursuant to such exercise, and the employee or independent contractor realizes compensation upon such transfer at the time and in the amount determined under section 83(a) or 83(b). If the option is sold or otherwise disposed of in an arm's length transaction, sections 83(a) and 83(b) apply to the transfer of money or other property received in the same manner as sections 83(a) and 83(b) would have applied to the transfer of property pursuant to an exercise of the option. The preceding sentence does not apply to a sale or other disposition of the option to a person related to the service provider that occurs on or after July 2, 2003. For this purpose, a person is related to the service provider if —

(1) The person and the service provider bear a relationship to each other that is specified in section 267(b) or 707(b)(1), subject to the modifications that the language "20 percent" is used instead of "50 percent" each place it appears in sections 267(b) and 707(b)(1), and section 267(c)(4) is applied as if the family of an individual includes the spouse of any member of the family; or

(2) The person and the service provider are engaged in trades or businesses under common control (within the meaning of section 52(a) and (b)); provided that a person is not related to the service provider if the person is the service recipient with respect to the option or the grantor of the option.

(b)   **Readily ascertainable defined** —

(1)   Actively traded on an established market. Options have a value at the time they are granted, but that value is ordinarily not readily ascertainable unless the option is actively traded on an established market. If an option is actively traded on an established market, the fair market value of such option is readily ascertainable for purposes of this section by applying the rules of

valuation set forth in § 20.2031-2.

(2)   Not actively traded on an established market. When an option is not actively traded on an established market, it does not have a readily ascertainable fair market value unless its fair market value can otherwise be measured with reasonable accuracy. For purposes of this section, if an option is not actively traded on an established market, the option does not have a readily ascertainable fair market value when granted unless the taxpayer can show that all of the following conditions exist:

(i) The option is transferable by the optionee;

(ii) The option is exercisable immediately in full by the optionee;

(iii) The option or the property subject to the option is not subject to any restriction or condition (other than a lien or other condition to secure the payment of the purchase price) which has a significant effect upon the fair market value of the option; and

(iv) The fair market value of the option privilege is readily ascertainable in accordance with paragraph (b)(3) of this section.

(3)   Option privilege. The option privilege in the case of an option to buy is the opportunity to benefit during the option's exercise period from any increase in the value of property subject to the option during such period, without risking any capital. Similarly, the option privilege in the case of an option to sell is the opportunity to benefit during the exercise period from a decrease in the value of property subject to the option. For example, if at some time during the exercise period of an option to buy, the fair market value of the property subject to the option is greater than the option's exercise price, a profit may be realized by exercising the option and immediately selling the property so acquired for its higher fair market value. Irrespective of whether any such gain may be realized immediately at the time an option is granted, the fair market value of an option to buy includes the value of the right to benefit from any future increase in the value of the property subject to the option (relative to the option exercise price), without risking any capital. Therefore, the fair market value of an option is not merely the difference that may exist at a particular time between the option's exercise price and the value of the property subject to the option, but also includes the value of the option privilege for the remainder of the exercise period. Accordingly, for purposes of this section, in determining whether the fair market value of an option is readily ascertainable, it is necessary to consider whether the value of the entire option privilege can be measured with reasonable accuracy. In determining whether the value of the option privilege is readily ascertainable, and in determining the amount of such value when such value is readily ascertainable, it is necessary to consider —

(i) Whether the value of the property subject to the option can be ascertained;

(ii) The probability of any ascertainable value of such property increasing or decreasing; and

(iii) The length of the period during which the option can be exercised.

QUESTIONS

1.   Under what circumstances is the value of a stock option granted in exchange for services includible as compensation to the optionee in the tax year in which the option is granted?

2.   If a stock option is not includible as compensation to the optionee in the tax year in which the option is granted, when would it be includible as compensation?

ROBINSON v. COMMISSIONER OF INTERNAL REVENUE
805 F.2d 38 (1st Cir. 1986)

TORRUELLA, CIRCUIT JUDGE.

This appeal concerns the meaning of the timing provisions of Section 83 of the Internal Revenue Code, 26 U.S.C. § 83, which governs the taxation of property transferred in connection with a performance of services.

I. The Stock Option Agreement

Appellant Prentice Robinson held an option to purchase stock, at a below market price, in Centronics Data Computer Corp., a Delaware corporation with its principal place of business in New Hampshire. Robinson received the option as part of his employment package when he became a Centronics employee during the spring of 1969.

The distinguishing feature of the stock option agreement that leads to this dispute is a provision that required Robinson to sell his shares back to Centronics, at his original cost, if he wished to dispose of them in less than one year from the day he exercised the stock option. The effect of this sellback provision was similar to the insider trading rule of the Securities Exchange Act of 1934, 15 U.S.C. § 78p(b) ("Rule 16b"), which requires the insider to disgorge to the corporation any profit made on a short term sale.

The option agreement also required that the stock certificate issued to Robinson carry the following legend:

> The shares represented by this certificate have not been registered under the Securities Act of 1933 and may not be sold, offered for sale or otherwise transferred or disposed unless a registration statement under such Act is in effect with respect thereto or unless the company has received an opinion of counsel satisfactory to it, that an exemption from such registration is applicable to said shares.

To further protect its interests, Centronics placed a "stop transfer order" with the corporation's transfer agent. The stop transfer order required the agent to notify Centronics of any request to transfer Robinson's stock to a new owner and prohibited the agent from transferring the shares without Centronics' approval and without an opinion of Centronics' counsel that the transfer did not violate securities laws.

On March 4, 1974, Robinson exercised the option. The present appeal requires us to determine when Robinson realized a benefit from the option agreement and when, not whether, he should have paid Federal income taxes on it.

II. Section 83

Section 83 of the Internal Revenue Code, 26 U.S.C. § 83, states that the value of property transferred in connection with the performance of services shall be taxable income "in the first taxable year in which the rights of the person having the beneficial interest in such property *are transferable or are not subject to a substantial risk of forfeiture*, whichever is applicable." I.R.C. § 83(a) (emphasis added). Appellant contends that the sellback provision of the option agreement, combined with the legend on the stock certificate and the stop transfer order, (1) subjected his stock to a substantial risk of forfeiture and (2) rendered it non-transferable until 1975. We agree and therefore reverse the opinion of the Tax Court below.

III. "Substantial Risk of Forfeiture"

While not defining the term "substantial risk of forfeiture," Congress offered some guidance as to its meaning in § 83(c)(1) in the legislative history of that section. I.R.C. § 83(c)(1) is a "special rule" that states "[t]he rights of a person in property are subject to a substantial risk of forfeiture if such person's rights to full enjoyment of such property are conditioned upon the future performance of substantial services by any individual." The Committee Reports on the Bill enacting § 83 explain that "[i]n other cases the question of whether there is a substantial risk of forfeiture depends upon the facts and circumstances." Congress thus left further definition of the term to the Treasury Department and the courts.

The Treasury Regulations pursuant to § 83, like § 83 itself, do not define what constitutes a substantial risk of forfeiture. They recapitulate the "special rule" and the facts and circumstances test and then add an additional rule: "A substantial risk of forfeiture exists where rights in property that are transferred are conditioned, directly or indirectly, . . . upon the occurrence of a condition *related to a purpose of the transfer*, and the possibility of forfeiture is substantial if such condition is not satisfied." 26 C.F.R. 1.83-3(c)(1) (emphasis added). Satisfaction of either the § 83(c)(1) special rule or the Treasury regulation additional rule indicates a substantial risk. In other cases the "facts and circumstances" may still be such that there is a substantial risk of forfeiture.

Neither the statutory nor the regulatory rule fit appellant's situation. We, therefore, must resort to logic and common sense. The sellback provision of the stock option agreement contemplates a forfeiture of Robinson's beneficial interest in the stock transfer if he sells the stock in less than a year. But the forfeiture is not conditioned on his future performance of any services. And the Tax Court found that the sellback provision was not related to the purpose of the transfer.

Accordingly, we are left with the question of whether, in the facts and circumstances of Robinson's case, the risk of forfeiture was "substantial." The Tax Court found that the risk was insubstantial, because the sellback provision would expire in one year. We cannot agree with this logic.

Whether a condition creates a substantial risk of forfeiture is not a function of time, nor, as the Commissioner urges in this appeal, is it a function of the likelihood of triggering the event that will require the forfeiture to take place. To the extent that the substantiality of the risk depends on probability, the probability should be measured by the likelihood of the forfeiture taking place once the triggering event occurs. Here, the likelihood of the triggering event (sale of the stock in less than a year) was very low; Robinson would not be so foolish as to risk the forfeiture. But, if he had sold the stock in less than a year, the probability of Centronics enforcing the sellback provision was very high. The company had a fiduciary duty to its shareholders to do so.

This probability alone, however, does not satisfy § 83(a). Otherwise, a clever draftsman could evade the purpose of § 83 by adding a formula forfeiture provision to transfers of property in exchange for services. Congress enacted § 83 to curb the use of sales restrictions to defer taxes on property given in exchange for services. Congress drafted a broad rule that declares property to be vested and taxable as soon as it can be transferred or is not subject to a "*substantial* risk of forfeiture." The use of the modifier *substantial* indicates that the risk must be real; it must serve a significant business purpose apart from the tax laws.

The § 83(c)(1) special rule providing that conditions based on future performance of services create a substantial risk illustrates this requirement. Conditioning the right to property on future performance of services serves an important business purpose: ensuring continued performance and loyalty. The Treasury regulation additional rule, that conditions related to the purpose of the transfer of the property create a substantial risk, is consistent with this principle as well. Section 83 property is transferred for some reason that has an existence apart from the tax laws: for example, the transferee invented a new device, performed some essential task, or brought some needed expertise to the organization. If the risk of forfeiture relates to this reason, it is substantial.

Applying the same principle to this case we find that Robinson's stock was subject to a substantial risk of forfeiture until the sellback provision elapsed. The tax court found as fact that Centronics imposed the sellback provision to prevent Robinson from engaging in insider trading. The officers of the corporation wanted to prevent Robinson from using his knowledge of the company to make a profit on a short term change in the corporation's position. The sellback condition thus served a significant business purpose.

IV. "Transferable"

We now turn to the analysis of whether Robinson's stock was transferable according to § 83(a) prior to the expiration of the sellback provision. Under § 83, rights in property are transferable "only if the rights in such property of any transferee are not subject to a substantial risk of forfeiture." § 83(c)(2). We have already held that the sellback provision subjected Robinson's interest in the stock to a substantial risk of forfeiture. The transferability question hinges on whether Robinson can transfer the stock free of this risk.

Under Delaware law a purchaser of stock who has knowledge of a sale restriction on the stock is bound by the restriction. Accordingly, only a purchaser who was unaware of the sellback provision would not be bound by it. In order to sell the stock to an unknowing purchaser, the Tax Court found that Robinson would have faced several hurdles which he could have surmounted in only extraordinarily unusual circumstances.

First, he would have had to violate the option agreement forbidding him to sell the shares to anyone without offering them first to Centronics at his original cost. Robinson testified, and the Commission does not dispute, that such a breach would have threatened his continued employment with Centronics. Second, the stock certificate carried a legend that the Tax Court concluded limited "lawful transfer of the restricted securities . . . [to] an exempt private resale unless the Option Stock were registered." As the Tax Court found, "a purchaser in a private resale must be an informed person, frequently represented by counsel." Finally, the stop transfer order prohibited the transfer of the official stock certificate without Centronics' approval.

These hurdles rendered the stock nontransferable until the sellback provision lapsed. The Tax Court's contrary finding was not based upon evidence of the practical workings of the securities markets, but rather upon a hypothetical, back-door transfer in breach of the option agreement. This was error. Transferability under § 83(a) depends on standard practices and assumes observance of contracts, not hypothetical *sub rosa* violations.

Accordingly, the order of the Tax Court is *reversed*.

QUESTIONS

1. What is the difference between the probability that a substantial risk of forfeiture may occur and the probability that a substantial risk of forfeiture may be enforced? Which of the two probabilities did the court find to be determinative of whether compensation has been received?

2. What significant business purpose did the stock sellback provision serve other than delaying the imposition of taxation?

3. Why did the court find that Robinson's stock was not transferrable prior to the expiration of the sellback period?

PAGEL, INC. v. COMMISSIONER OF INTERNAL REVENUE
905 F.2d 1190 (8th Cir. 1990)

FAGG, CIRCUIT JUDGE.

Pagel, Inc. (Pagel) appeals from a United States Tax Court decision that income derived from Pagel's sale of a stock option was taxable as ordinary income under 26

U.S.C. § 83 (1976). We affirm.

Pagel received a nonqualified stock option in 1977 as partial compensation for underwriting a stock offering on behalf of Immuno Nuclear Corp. (Immuno). This option gave Pagel the right to buy Immuno shares at scheduled prices but restricted Pagel from exercising or disposing of the option for thirteen months after its grant. At the time of receipt, Immuno options were not publicly traded. Pagel sold the Immuno option in 1981 and reported the sale as a capital gain.

Section 83 provides that the excess of the fair market value of property received in compensation for services over the amount, if any, paid for the property shall be taxed as ordinary income. 26 U.S.C. § 83(a) (1976). If an option received as compensation is not publicly traded and the optionee is restricted from immediately exercising or disposing of the option, the option has no readily ascertainable fair market value. Treas. Reg. § 1.83-7(b)(2) (1978). In that case, section 83 will apply at the time the option is exercised or disposed of. Because the Immuno option had no readily ascertainable fair market value at the time Pagel received it, the Commissioner of Internal Revenue (the Commissioner) rejected Pagel's claimed capital gain treatment, instead treating the proceeds of the sale as ordinary income and assessing a deficiency against Pagel.

Pagel contends sale of the Immuno option should not be taxed as ordinary income because subsection 83(e)(3) provides "section [83] shall not apply to . . . the [grant] of an option without a readily ascertainable fair market value" at the time of the grant. We reject this contention. Pagel mistakenly reads subsection 83(e)(3) in isolation from the remainder of the statute. Here subsections 83(e)(3) and 83(e)(4) must be read together.

Subsection 83(e)(4) provides that "section [83] shall not apply to . . . the [exercise or disposal] of an option with a readily ascertainable fair market value" at the time it is granted. When read together, it is clear subsections 83(e)(3) and 83(e)(4) provide a blueprint for determining when section 83 shall apply to compensatory options and for avoiding income recognition both at the time of grant and at exercise or disposition. Under subsections 83(e)(3) and (e)(4), if an option has a readily ascertainable fair market value when granted, the recipient must recognize ordinary income at the time of grant but not at the time of exercise or disposal; if an option does not have a readily ascertainable fair market value when granted, the recipient must recognize ordinary income at the time of exercise or disposal but not at the time of grant. We conclude the Commissioner properly determined the sale of the Immuno option was taxable as ordinary income in Pagel's 1981-82 tax year.

Pagel argues in the alternative it should have reported the option as ordinary income in its 1977-78 tax year because a number of recognized formulas are capable of measuring the fair market value of a restricted option at the time of the option's grant. Pagel contends the Commissioner's definition of "readily ascertainable fair market value" in Treas. Reg. § 1.83-7(b)(2) arbitrarily prevents restricted options from being taxed under section 83 at their true value as determined by the formulas. Pagel thus claims the regulation is inconsistent with the language of section 83. We cannot agree.

The Tax Court correctly observed that "Congress has delegated to the Commissioner, not to the courts, the task of prescribing all needful rules and regulations for the enforcement of the Internal Revenue Code." The Tax Court also observed that respect for Congress's delegation suggests "Treasury regulations [should not] be rejected unless they are unreasonable and plainly inconsistent with the [revenue] statute[s]." The Tax Court recognized Treas. Reg. § 1.83-7(b)(2) "further[s] a policy under which there is reasonable accuracy in the valuation of nonpublicly traded options." We agree this policy is neither plainly contrary to the language of section 83 nor inconsistent with the statute's legislative aims.

Noting that Treas. Reg. § 1.83-7(b)(2) adopted the definition of "readily ascertainable fair market value" contained in Treas. Reg. § 1.421-6(c)(3)(i) (1961), the Tax Court carefully tracked Congress's activity in adopting and amending statutory provisions concerning compensatory options. When Congress enacted section 83 in 1969 and amended the statute relating to qualified employee options in 1976, Congress was aware of the regulations' definition, but did not enact any provisions to alter the regulation. Because the regulatory definition of readily ascertainable fair market value has been in place since 1961, the Tax Court concluded that Congress's failure to amend the definition shows "[Congress has] not perceive[d] the regulat[ion] to be unreasonable or plainly contrary to congressional intent." We agree.

Having carefully considered Pagel's contentions, we affirm the decision of the Tax Court.

QUESTIONS

1.   If a stock option has a readily ascertainable fair market value at the time it is granted, the recipient must include the value of the option at the time of the grant as ordinary income in the same tax year as the grant. If the recipient later sells the option for an amount greater than the amount included in ordinary income, how should the recipient treat the gain from the sale of the option?

2.   If a stock option does not have a readily ascertainable fair market value at the time of the grant, the recipient must recognize ordinary income at the time the stock option is exercised or sold. What amount of ordinary income must the recipient recognize if the stock option is exercised? What amount of ordinary income must the recipient recognize if the stock option is sold?

CASE NOTES

1.   General Digital Corporation (Company) was formed in April 1970 to manufacture micro-electronic circuits. At the Company's first board meeting, the directors approved a resolution to issue 90,000 shares of common stock to the Company's president, 66,000 shares of common stock to the Company's underwriter, and 264,000 shares of common stock to seven key employees including Lawrence Alves who joined the company as vice-president for finance and administration. The stock purchase agreement provided that the Company would sell Alves 40,000 shares of common stock for ten cents per share. The stock purchase

agreement divided Alves' shares into three groups; one-third of the shares were subject to repurchase by the Company at ten cents per share if Alves terminated his employment in less than four years, one-third of the stock was subject to the same restriction if Alves terminated his employment in less than five years, and one-third of the stock was unrestricted. Alves did not make an election under section 83(b) to include the excess of the fair market value of the stock over the ten cents per share he paid for the stock as ordinary income for the 1970 tax year. Alves also did not report this excess amount as ordinary income in 1974 and 1975 when the repurchase restrictions terminated. The IRS determined that this excess amount should have been reported as ordinary income in 1974 and 1975. Alves claimed he had paid the full fair market value for the stock in 1970 and, therefore, was not required to pay any additional tax on the stock until such time as he sold the stock. The Tax Court upheld the IRS' deficiency determination and Alves appealed. What result? *See* Alves v. Commissioner of Internal Revenue, 734 F.2d 478 (9th Cir. 1984).

2. *See also* MacNaughton v. U.S., 888 F.2d 418 (6th Cir. 1989) (Stock certificates issued to physician in exchange for services that did not contain a restriction legend and could have been transferred to a third party at any time under Tennessee law; however, there was clear evidence that the shares were intended to be subject to restriction on transfer and failure to properly legend certificates would not remove restriction for tax purposes); Grant v. U.S., 15 Cl.Ct. 38 (Cl. Ct. 1988) (Restrictions imposed on the transfer of unregistered stock under the federal securities laws were not restrictions which will never lapse; amount of compensation for services included in income will be calculated without regard to any restrictions other than restrictions that will never lapse); Sakol v. Commissioner of Internal Revenue, 574 F.2d 694 (2d Cir. 1978) (IRC § 83(a) requiring employees receiving stock in exchange for services to include in gross income the excess of the fair market value of the stock over the amount paid for the stock as soon as the stock is no longer subject to a substantial risk of forfeiture, ignoring other restrictions on the transferability of the stock that might diminish its value, does not violate Fifth and Sixteenth Amendments).

Additional Information

1. 47B C.J.S. INTERNAL REVENUE § 318 (2011).

2. 33A AM. JUR. 2D FEDERAL TAXATION §§ 7055, 7063 (2011).

3. RICHARD A. BOOTH, FINANCING THE CORPORATION § 10:5 (2010).

4. CHARLES C. SHULMAN, 2 QUAL. RETIREMENT PLANS § 24:57 (2010).

5. JOSEPH W. BARTLETT, EQUITY FIN. § 5,5 (2011).

6. WILLIAM R. CHRISTIAN, IRVING M. GRANT, SUBCHAPTER S. TAX. ¶ 9.08 (2011).

7. JAMES S. EUSTICE, JOEL D. KUNTZ, FED. INCOME TAX'N OF S CORP. ¶ 6.05 (2011).

8. FRANCES B. JONES, BRENT A. PETERS, ERIC S. KRACOV, 3 SUCCESSFUL PARTNERING BETWEEN INSIDE AND OUTSIDE COUNSEL § 55A:29 (2011).

9. Andre L. Smith, *Do NFL "Signing Bonuses" Carry a Substantial Risk of Forfeiture Within the Meaning of Section 83 of the Internal Revenue Code?*,

19 Seton Hall J. Sports & Ent. L. (2009).

10.   David R. Herwitz, *Allocation of Stock Between Services and Capital in the Organization of a Close Corporation*, 75 Harv. L. Rev. 1098 (1962).

8.5   LICENSE OR SALE BY THE PATENT OWNER

A patent is a "capital asset" under I.R.C. § 1221. The transfer of rights in a patent can give rise to either ordinary income or capital gains. If the patent is licensed, the royalty payments will constitute ordinary income to the licensor and an ordinary and necessary current business expense to the licensee. If a patent is sold or assigned, the payment(s) to the seller-assignor will constitute capital gains or capital losses, and the patent in the hands of the buyer-assignee will constitute a capital asset used in the trade or business of the buyer/assignee which will be amortized over the useful life of the patent. The I.R.C. and Treasury Regulation provisions in this subsection further define the differences between ordinary income and capital gains treatment of money or property received in exchange for the grant of patent rights. The *Bailey* case considers whether an exchange of patent rights constitutes a license, sale or assignment.

I.R.C. § 61   GROSS INCOME DEFINED

(a)   **General definition.** — Except as otherwise provided in this subtitle, gross income means all income from whatever source derived, including (but not limited to) the following items:

(1) Compensation for services, including fees, commissions, fringe benefits, and similar items;

(2) Gross income derived from business;

(3) Gains derived from dealings in property;

(4) Interest;

(5) Rents;

(6) Royalties;

(7) Dividends;

(8) Alimony and separate maintenance payments;

(9) Annuities;

(10) Income from life insurance and endowment contracts;

(11) Pensions;

(12) Income from discharge of indebtedness;

(13) Distributive share of partnership gross income;

(14) Income in respect of a decedent; and

(15) Income from an interest in an estate or trust.

TREAS. REG. § 1.61-6   GAINS DERIVED FROM DEALINGS IN PROPERTY.

(a)   **In general.** Gain realized on the sale or exchange of property is included in gross income, unless excluded by law. For this purpose property includes tangible items, such as a building, and intangible items, such as goodwill. Generally, the gain is the excess of the amount realized over the unrecovered cost or other basis for the property sold or exchanged. The specific rules for computing the amount of gain or loss are contained in section 1001 and the regulations thereunder. When a part of a larger property is sold, the cost or other basis of the entire property shall be equitably apportioned among the several parts, and the gain realized or loss sustained on the part of the entire property sold is the difference between the selling price and the cost or other basis allocated to such part. The sale of each part is treated as a separate transaction and gain or loss shall be computed separately on each part. Thus, gain or loss shall be determined at the time of sale of each part and not deferred until the entire property has been disposed of. This rule may be illustrated by the following examples:

Example (1). A, a dealer in real estate, acquires a 10-acre tract for $10,000, which he divides into 20 lots. The $10,000 cost must be equitably apportioned among the lots so that on the sale of each A can determine his taxable gain or deductible loss.

(b)   Nontaxable exchanges. Certain realized gains or losses on the sale or exchange of property are not "recognized," that is, are not included in or deducted from gross income at the time the transaction occurs. Gain or loss from such sales or exchanges is generally recognized at some later time. Examples of such sales or exchanges are the following:

(1) Certain formations, reorganizations, and liquidations of corporations, see sections 331, 333, 337, 351, 354, 355, and 361;

(2) Certain formations and distributions of partnerships, see sections 721 and 731;

(3) Exchange of certain property held for productive use or investment for property of like kind, see section 1031;

(4) A corporation's exchange of its stock for property, see section 1032;

(5) Certain involuntary conversions of property if replaced, see section 1033;

(6) Sale or exchange of residence if replaced, see section 1034;

(7) Certain exchanges of insurance policies and annuity contracts, see section 1035; and

(8) Certain exchanges of stock for stock in the same corporation, see section 1036.

(c)   **Character of recognized gain.** Under subchapter P, chapter 1 of the Code, relating to capital gains and losses, certain gains derived from dealings in property are treated specially, and under certain circumstances the maximum rate of tax on such gains is 25 percent, as provided in section 1201. Generally, the property subject to this treatment is a "capital asset," or treated as a "capital asset." For definition of such assets, see sections 1221 and 1231, and the regulations thereunder. For some of the rules either granting or denying this special treatment, see the following sections and the regulations thereunder:

(1) Transactions between partner and partnership, section 707;

(2) Sale or exchange of property used in the trade or business and involuntary conversions, section 1231;

(3) Payment of bonds and other evidences of indebtedness, section 1232;

(4) Gains and losses from short sales, section 1233;

(5) Options to buy or sell, section 1234;

(6) Sale or exchange of patents, section 1235;

(7) Securities sold by dealers in securities, section 1236;

(8) Real property subdivided for sale, section 1237;

(9) Amortization in excess of depreciation, section 1238;

(10) Gain from sale of certain property between spouses or between an individual and a controlled corporation, section 1239;

(11) Taxability to employee of termination payments, section 1240.

TREAS. REG. § 1.61-8   RENTS AND ROYALTIES.

(a)   **In general.** Gross income includes rentals received or accrued for the occupancy of real estate or the use of personal property. For the inclusion of rents in income for the purpose of the retirement income credit, see section 37 and the regulations thereunder. Gross income includes royalties. Royalties may be received from books, stories, plays, copyrights, trademarks, formulas, patents, and from the exploitation of natural resources, such as coal, gas, oil, copper, or timber. Payments received as a result of the transfer of patent rights may under some circumstances constitute capital gain instead of ordinary income. See section 1235 and the regulations thereunder. For special rules for certain income from natural resources, see Subchapter I (section 611 and following), Chapter 1 of the Code, and the regulations thereunder.

I.R.C. § 1221.   CAPITAL ASSET DEFINED

(a)   **In general.** — For purposes of this subtitle, the term "capital asset" means property held by the taxpayer (whether or not connected with his trade or business), but does not include —

(1) stock in trade of the taxpayer or other property of a kind which would properly be included in the inventory of the taxpayer if on hand at the close of the taxable year, or property held by the taxpayer primarily for sale to customers in the ordinary course of his trade or business;

(2) property, used in his trade or business, of a character which is subject to

the allowance for depreciation provided in section 167, or real property used in his trade or business;

(3) a copyright, a literary, musical, or artistic composition, a letter or memorandum, or similar property, held by —

(A) a taxpayer whose personal efforts created such property,

(B) in the case of a letter, memorandum, or similar property, a taxpayer for whom such property was prepared or produced, or

I.R.C. § 1231. PROPERTY USED IN THE TRADE OR BUSINESS AND INVOLUNTARY CONVERSIONS

(a) General rule. —

(1) Gains exceed losses. — If —

(A) the section 1231 gains for any taxable year, exceed

(B) the section 1231 losses for such taxable year, such gains and losses shall be treated as long-term capital gains or long-term capital losses, as the case may be.

(2) Gains do not exceed losses. — If —

(A) the section 1231 gains for any taxable year, do not exceed

(B) the section 1231 losses for such taxable year, such gains and losses shall not be treated as gains and losses from sales or exchanges of capital assets.

(3) Section 1231 gains and losses. — For purposes of this subsection —

(A) Section 1231 gain. — The term "section 1231 gain" means —

(i) any recognized gain on the sale or exchange of property used in the trade or business, and

(ii) any recognized gain from the compulsory or involuntary conversion (as a result of destruction in whole or in part, theft or seizure, or an exercise of the power of requisition or condemnation or the threat or imminence thereof) into other property or money of —

(I) property used in the trade or business, or

(II) any capital asset which is held for more than 1 year and is held in connection with a trade or business or a transaction entered into for profit.

(B) Section 1231 loss. — The term "section 1231 loss" means any recognized loss from a sale or exchange or conversion described in subparagraph (A).

(b) Definition of property used in the trade or business. — For purposes of this section —

(1) General rule. — The term "property used in the trade or business"

means property used in the trade or business, of a character which is subject to the allowance for depreciation provided in section 167, held for more than 1 year, and real property used in the trade or business, held for more than 1 year, which is not —

(A) property of a kind which would properly be includible in the inventory of the taxpayer if on hand at the close of the taxable year,

(B) property held by the taxpayer primarily for sale to customers in the ordinary course of his trade or business,

(C) a copyright, a literary, musical, or artistic composition, a letter or memorandum, or similar property, held by a taxpayer described in paragraph (3) of section 1221(a), or

(D) a publication of the United States Government (including the Congressional Record) which is received from the United States Government, or any agency thereof, other than by purchase at the price at which it is offered for sale to the public, and which is held by a taxpayer described in paragraph (5) of section 1221(a).

QUESTIONS

1.   ACorp acquired BCorp's entire patent portfolio consisting of 500 patents for $1,000,000. Two years later, ACorp assigned 200 of these patents to CCorp for $500,000. What is ACorp's long-term capital gain from this transaction?

2.   APartners is a research and development limited partnership. APartners employs 15 scientists who are actively engaged in researching nanoparticle drug delivery systems. APartners deducts the scientists' salaries and certain lab costs under I.R.C. § 174 as current business expenses incurred in connection with its trade or business. APartners also has received research tax credits under I.R.C § 41 for the four prior tax years. APartners assigns title to its patents to large pharmaceutical companies for further development and marketing. Is the money received from these assignments taxable as ordinary income or capital gains? Would it matter if APartners did not claim expense deductions under § 174 and tax credits under § 41? Would it matter if APartners' research was for the purpose of developing proprietary drug delivery systems that it would market directly?

3.   Under I.R.C. § 1231(a)(1), if § 1231 gains for any taxable year exceed § 1231 losses for the same taxable year, the gains or losses shall be treated as long-term capital gains or losses. If § 1231 gains for any taxable year do not exceed § 1231 losses for the same taxable year, how are such gains or losses treated?

WILLIAM M. BAILEY v. COMMISSIONER OF INTERNAL REVENUE

1950 U.S. Tax Ct. LEXIS 69 (U.S. Tax Ct. 1950)

OPPER, JUDGE:

Petitioner seeks redetermination of a deficiency of $1,467.57 in income tax for 1946. Some adjustments are not contested. The only question is whether $3,533.40 which petitioner received from William M. Bailey Company, the petitioner in a related proceeding in Docket No. 22615, is taxable in full or as a long-term capital gain.

The case was heard on a stipulation of facts and other evidence.

FINDINGS OF FACT

The stipulated facts are hereby found.

Petitioner filed a Federal income tax return on a cash basis for the calendar year 1946 with the collector of internal revenue for the twenty-third district of Pennsylvania at Pittsburgh.

He was employed by Carnegie Steel Company from 1900 to 1915 as office boy, stenographer, and secretary to the president; and by Midvale Steel Company from 1915 to 1919 as secretary and assistant to the president. In 1920, petitioner was an incorporator of Bailey-Lewis Company. The name was changed in 1921 to William M. Bailey Company, hereinafter called the company. Petitioner has been president and a majority stockholder of the company since its organization.

The company has never engaged in manufacturing. From 1921 to 1926 its business consisted of selling the products of New York Blower Company, Chicago, and Vulcan Iron Works, Wilkes-Barre, Pennsylvania. On March 27, 1926, petitioner as "licensee" entered into a written agreement with Frank R. McGee and Arthur R. Schulze as "licensors," under which petitioner was granted the "exclusive right and license to make, use and sell" chimney and goggle valves for blast furnaces. The valves were protected by three United States patents issued to McGee and Schulze. Petitioner agreed to pay the licensors royalties equal to ten per cent of the "gross selling price" of the patented apparatus. The licensors agreed to prosecute suits for infringement of the patents at petitioner's request, the cost of litigation to be paid by petitioner. The agreement was to continue for the full terms of the patents, unless earlier revoked by the parties, and petitioner agreed upon expiration of the patents to pay McGee and Schulze a 5 per cent commission on gross sales.

By a written instrument dated November 5, 1927, reciting a consideration of $25,000 which was paid in capital stock of the company, petitioner assigned to the company his rights under the agreement of March 27, 1926.

The chimney and goggle valves protected by the three McGee and Schulze patents contained four thermal expansion tubes, and were designed for installation in the hot gas main between blast furnaces and dust catcher. Their basic principle of operation was the expansion of the tubes when heated by steam, causing two flanges to move apart. When the steam was shut off, the tubes contracted, and the flanges closed against the valve's plate.

The company did not sell any of the four-tube valves. Its chief engineer, Andrew Bowland, prepared drawings redesigning the valves to contain only three tubes. The action of the valve plate was also changed from a vertical operation to a swing from a point of suspension. The drawings were shown to McGee and Schulze. On July 31, 1928, a patent was issued to McGee covering the valve as improved.

Each valve was equipped with a steel plate with one open and one closed side. The function of the plate was to permit or prevent the flow of gas through the main, depending upon which side of the plate was exposed. Plates varied from 48 to 108 inches in diameter, and would cause gas leakage unless machined to within 15/1000 of an inch of the required thickness. The company had difficulty in obtaining plates machined to this specification. At that time, plates were shaped out of solid rolled steel.

While visiting Vulcan Iron Works, petitioner watched the manufacture of parts for lime kilns. The track on which kilns revolve is made from a steel section in the shape of the letter "T." Petitioner saw a "T" section rolled in a machine to form a circle, and was informed by Vulcan's superintendent that the same machine could roll a two-inch steel bar into any shape and thickness desired. The same day petitioner told Bowland of his intention to design a satisfactory plate for the valve by rolling in the same manner, two two-inch steel bars. This method enabled the plate manufacturers to machine each side of the bar to within 2/1000 of an inch of the specified thickness, and resulted in a gas-tight valve. A patent covering the plate was applied for on July 31, 1931, and was issued to petitioner on February 20, 1934.

Soon after they were designed, two of the plates were installed in the plants of Carnegie Steel Company and Bethlehem Steel Company. Petitioner did not receive royalties from their sale.

The company has never enforced its "shop rights" to use inventions of its employees. It has a mutual understanding with its employees that it will pay them royalties of 5 per cent on any inventions of theirs that it markets. By a written agreement with Bowland dated June 27, 1933, the company agreed to pay him royalties of 5 per cent on sales of steel stove bottoms covered by his patent. This was the company's first written agreement to pay royalties to an employee or officer.

In 1934, under an oral agreement, the company began to make "royalty" payments of 5 per cent to petitioner on sales of the plates covered by his patent. A written "memorandum agreement" between the company and petitioner, dated April 8, 1943, provided: "The William M. Bailey Company agrees to pay William M. Bailey, Five (5%) per cent Royalty on the net selling price of each and every Goggle Plate manufactured in accordance with his design as shown on above patent. This agreement to hold good during the life of the patent or as long as this Plate is manufactured and is being sold by The William M. Bailey Company." This royalty has been paid since the patent was issued but no formal agreement was ever signed. It is now felt that some form of agreement should be prepared and signed as a protection both to the Patentee and the Company.

The thermal expansion valve could not be operated successfully on gas mains smaller than 48 inches in diameter. The chief engineer of the company, Bowland, began working in 1931 to design a satisfactory valve for small gas mains. On October 14, 1936, he applied for a patent on a mechanical valve for that purpose. A written agreement dated October 6, 1936, between Bowland and the company provided, in part:

> In lieu of the assignment of the Patent Application of Andrew Bowland and patent when it is granted on the design of our American Mechanical Goggle Valve, The William M. Bailey Company agrees to pay Andrew Bowland 3% on the net selling price of each and every valve of this design as long as it is necessary to pay F. E. Kling on his patent No. 1,334,248. After this patent is run out in 1937, The Bailey Company agrees to pay Andrew Bowland 5% on the net selling price on this valve.

A written agreement of September 29, 1937, between the same parties, recited that the Kling patent had expired and that the company would thereafter pay Bowland "a royalty of 5% on the American Mechanical Goggle Valves."

A United States patent on the mechanical valve, reciting that the application had been made by Andrew Bowland, assignor to William M. Bailey Company, was issued to the company on July 26, 1938.

On May 1, 1936, the company agreed in writing:

> (3) to pay William M. Bailey, Three (3%) per cent Royalty on the net selling price on each and every Mechanical Goggle Valve manufactured in which the Goggle Plate as covered by the above patent is used. This agreement to hold good during the life of the patent or as long as the plate is used on the Mechanical Goggle Valves and sold by the William M. Bailey Company.

On November 8, 1945, petitioner as "licensor" and the company as "licensee" entered into a written agreement reciting that "the Licensor is the owner of the entire right, title, and interest" in a United States and an English patent on the plate, and that "the Licensor, by oral agreement, heretofore gave the Licensee the right and license to make, use and sell apparatus embodying the inventions' protected by the patents." The stated purpose of the agreement was "to provide for the licensing by the Licensor of the Licensee to make, use and sell apparatus embodying the inventions described and claimed in said license patent and also to confirm and ratify their past oral or informal agreements, to the same effect." The agreement called for "royalties" of 5 per cent and 10 per cent on products covered by the United States and English patents, respectively, and provided in part:

> (1) The Licensor hereby grants and gives the Licensee the sole and exclusive right and license to make, use and sell apparatus embodying the inventions described and claimed in the aforesaid letters patent to the full and of the terms for which such patents are granted.

The company was required to obtain petitioner's written consent "to assign this license or any part thereof," but was entitled to prosecute or defend at its own expense infringement suits connected with the patents. If the company declined, petitioner was authorized to prosecute and defend infringement suits. Either party could terminate the agreement on sixty days' notice "for sufficient cause, such as lack of development of designs of the Licensor to keep pace with competition, or improper conduct or neglect of business by the Licensee."

The three agreements between petitioner and the company dated May 1, 1936, April 8, 1943, and November 8, 1945, were each signed twice by petitioner, as president of the company and in his individual capacity.

Petitioner did not sell inventions or patents in the regular course of business. The plate covered by the patents in question is his only invention.

The company paid petitioner "royalties" aggregating $3,533.40 in 1946, which he reported in his return as a long-term capital gain. In his notice of deficiency, respondent "determined that the amount of $3,533.40, representing royalties received by you in the taxable year and reported by you in your return as a long-term capital gain in the amount of $1,766.73, is not a long-term gain as reported but rather, is ordinary income."

OPINION

We are satisfied that the arrangement between petitioner and his corporation was a license and not a sale under the original oral agreements and the first reductions to writing in prior years; and we have so held in the related case of William M. Bailey Company, promulgated this day, where the question was whether the corporation was entitled under that agreement to deduct royalty payments as license fees paid for property of which it was not the owner.

Petitioner at no time contends that the final formal agreement of 1945 did any more than to incorporate the previous arrangements in a writing and to formalize them. He says in his briefs: "The assignment was formally made in writing by agreement dated November 8, 1945, in which all prior oral or informal agreements were ratified and confirmed," and "The only logical conclusion is that sometime after July, 1933, petitioner orally assigned his invention to the company, which was confirmed in writing on November 8, 1945."

While it is true that the 1945 agreement uses the language "make, use and sell," and that if this is the true effect of the agreement for the full term of the patent it constitutes a complete assignment, nevertheless the use of particular words is not necessarily decisive as petitioner himself asserts. The intent of the agreement governs. And in Federal Laboratories, Inc., 8 T.C. 1150, where an exclusive license "to make, use and sell" was involved, it was nevertheless held that the intention of the assignor to retain title appeared unmistakably from the instrument.

Here we conclude from the document as a whole, from the obvious intention of the parties to incorporate the terms of the prior oral agreements, and from the limitations placed upon the term of the assignment and upon the rights of the assignee, that what petitioner granted to the corporation was something less than an outright sale of the patent. Under these circumstances, what he received was more nearly royalties than the proceeds of the sale of a capital asset, and is accordingly taxable as ordinary income.

Decision will be entered for the respondent.

QUESTIONS

1.   What rights in the patent did William M. Bailey retain that led the court to find that the transaction with the William M. Bailey Company was a license rather than an assignment? Can the purchase price of a capital asset be paid in installment payments? How do installment payments differ from "royalties"?

2.   If the payments to William M. Bailey are taxed as ordinary income, how will these payments be treated by the William M. Bailey Company?

GABLE v. COMMISSIONER OF INTERNAL REVENUE
T.C. Memo 1974-312 (1974)

TANNENWALD, JUDGE:

****

Petitioner asserts an overpayment for the year 1969. Because of concessions by the parties, the sole issue remaining for decision is whether the amount of $40,000 received by petitioner in 1969 constituted compensation for services or payment in exchange for patent rights or an option to acquire such rights.

FINDINGS OF FACT

Some of the facts are stipulated and are found accordingly. The stipulation of facts and accompanying exhibits are incorporated herein by this reference.

Petitioner resided in Kansas City, Missouri, at the time the petition was filed. His Federal income tax return and amended return and a second amended return were filed with the Internal Revenue Service Center at Kansas City, Missouri.

In 1959, petitioner became interested in water soluble compounds having magnetic properties. He began investigating them in that year and in 1965 applied for a patent covering the invention of such compounds, as well as processes for their production. No patent has yet been issued with respect to this application. In 1969, petitioner approached Chemetron Corporation (Chemetron) with a view to interesting it in his invention. On July 11, 1969, Chemetron and petitioner executed a "Secrecy Agreement."

****

Chemetron did develop an interest, and it and petitioner entered into a series of negotiations.

Chemetron ultimately agreed to acquire an option to purchase petitioner's rights in his invention and to supply the funding necessary for a program of further research and development designed to make the invention commercially marketable.

****

A copy of the License Agreement later entered into by the parties was attached to the Option Agreement (hereinafter sometimes referred to as the Option) as Exhibit B at the time the latter was signed. Both documents were drafted by Chemetron's patent counsel. The Option was formally executed on October 1, 1969, although the parties had approved its terms somewhat earlier. On August 29, 1969, in anticipation of the agreement, Chemetron loaned petitioner $20,000 on a note due 31 days after date. This amount was subsequently applied against Chemetron's obligation under the Option and the note was cancelled on October 1, 1969. On October 22, 1969, Chemetron made a further payment of $20,000. These two payments, aggregating $40,000, represent the entire amount received by petitioner in 1969 under the Option. The balance was paid in 1970.

On September 1, 1970, Chemetron notified petitioner that it was exercising its option to acquire his invention, and a License Agreement (hereinafter sometimes referred to as the License) was executed between them on September 15, 1970. The License contained substantially the same recitations and definitions as the Option.

****

ULTIMATE FINDING OF FACT

The $40,000 received by petitioner from Chemetron in 1969 constituted payment for the transfer of patent rights and not compensation for services.

OPINION

Petitioner reported the $40,000 received under the Option in 1969 as ordinary income. By an amendment to his petition, he now claims that these payments were in exchange for the transfer of patent rights and should be treated as capital gain under section 1235. Document1zzB00111974002275 Respondent contends that these amounts were compensation for services and therefore properly reported as ordinary income; otherwise he concedes that section 1235 applies.

The difficulty in resolving the purely factual issue thus presented stems from the nature of an invention and a recognition that it is to a large degree no more than the embodiment of the inventor's inspiration and labor so that the payments an inventor receives are, at least in part, inevitably in recompense for his "services." Indeed, respondent's own regulations take into account the dual characteristics of payments in respect of inventions. Thus, section 1.1235 — 1(c), Income Tax Regs., provides in part:

(2) Payments to an employee. Payments received by an employee as compensation for services rendered as an employee under an employment contract requiring the employee to transfer to the employer the rights to any invention by such employee are not attributable to a transfer to which section 1235 applies. However, whether payments received by an employee from his employer (under an employment contract or otherwise) are attributable to the transfer by the employee of all substantial rights to a patent (or an undivided interest therein) or are compensation for services rendered the employer by the employee is a question of fact. In determining which is the case, consideration shall be given not only to all the facts and circumstances of the employment relationship but also to whether the amount of such payments depends upon the production, sale, or use by, or the value to, the employer of the patent rights transferred by the employee. If it is determined that payments are attributable to the transfer of patent rights, and all other requirements of section 1235 are met, such payments shall be treated as proceeds derived from the sale of a patent.

The fact that petitioner was obligated to perform services by the terms of the Option does not, as respondent believes, dispose of this case. If the essence of a transaction is the sale of a patent or the grant of an option and the performance of services is only a step in developing the property transferred or to be transferred, the special nature of patents for tax purposes requires that the consideration paid be treated as received for the patent or, as in this case, the option to acquire the patent.

Against the foregoing background, we proceed to analyze the true nature of the transaction between petitioner and Chemetron. Of the three writings in evidence, the Option Agreement is the most pertinent, since the $40,000 payment was made pursuant to it.

The wording of the Option shows that the parties bargained over the rights to petitioner's invention and improvements thereon, and not over his services. The introductory paragraphs recite that petitioner "represents that he is the owner of the entire and unencumbered right, title and interest in and to the * * * inventions," that "Chemetron desires to obtain an exclusive license from Gable under said inventions," and that "Chemetron is willing to advance certain funds for certain further investigation." By clause 2, Chemetron agrees "to provide funds * * * for research and development * * * in accordance with written directions and program provided by Gable * * * and consented to by Chemetron." Petitioner's research obligation is described as an "80% program" by which petitioner in clause 4 "agrees to continue to devote 80% of his time * * * in carrying out further work, development and experiments to solve technical problems." Clause 3 grants an option to Chemetron to acquire the invention within thirteen months. The gist of this language is that Chemetron acquired, not an option plus services, but an option plus a research program designed to make that option (and the underlying patent) more valuable. From Chemetron's point of view, it was making an investment in property sought to be acquired; from petitioner's, the program was intended to enhance the value of the patent and hence (through the percentage royalty agreement) the purchase price.

Most significant is the section of clause 4 relating to the effect of termination of the agreement without the exercise of Chemetron's option. In that event, petitioner was entitled to retain not only the result of his own development work, but also any work performed by Chemetron with respect to his invention. This strongly suggests that the patent rights, and not petitioner's personal services, were the focus of the agreement. It also negates the existence of any strict employment relationship, since if such a relationship existed, Chemetron as employer normally could assert ownership of petitioner's work product and would necessarily be under no obligation to surrender its own.

A further indication that amounts received under the Option should not be treated as compensation is found in clause 6 of the License, incorporated by reference in the Option Agreement, requiring the advances to be repaid out of royalties under certain conditions. Petitioner was to receive royalties calculated as a varying percentage of quarterly sales, depending on the source of the sale, but royalties were never to be less than a specified yearly minimum dollar amount. Chemetron could recoup its development expenditures made under the Option by a reduction of up to 25 percent in the percentage royalty (but not the minimum royalty) payable each year. Respondent would have us disregard this deduction feature; from the fact that no royalties in excess of the minimum have been paid, he infers that none were anticipated and that the pay-back provision was, in effect, a sham. We cannot follow respondent's lead on this issue. First, the presence of technical problems when the License was drafted in 1969 inhibited an evaluation of the still-unexplored potential of the commercial exploitation of the compounds. It is unlikely the parties would have been able to agree on a fixed liquidated amount as the sole compensation for the patent transfer. Further, while Chemetron made no commitment at that time, a year later it executed the License according to the originally contemplated terms. This is persuasive that in 1970 Chemetron considered the invention to be worth at least the minimum royalty amount, which, in turn, strongly indicates that the 1969 agreement in good faith anticipated the possibility of royalties in excess of the minimum. It is, to say the least, curious that, if the reduction for payments under the Option was never intended to take effect, the parties would have taken the trouble to erect an elaborate royalty schedule and then limited reductions to 25 percent of such additional royalties. The record is devoid of any evidence indicating that these provisions were disingenuously inserted to bolster for tax purposes the credibility of a sham agreement and we think it unlikely that any such literary posturing was contemplated.

We think that, to the extent that services were involved herein, they were subsidiary to the grant of the option and the transfer of the petitioner's invention. It is an established rule that a contract to assign patent rights can require the transferor to furnish services in connection with the sale without affecting the capital nature of the entire proceeds. The principle underlying these decisions, which are not limited to situations involving section 1235, reflects the recognition that a patent transfer is, in large part, a transfer of knowledge. In any sale of technical information and know-how, the buyer is likely to require the assistance of the seller in implementing the acquired knowledge and developing its full potential. The rule is applied to exempt from treatment as "services" not only the communication of existing know-how, but the development of further information as long as it relates to the property transferred and constitutes assistance rendered in connection with the transfer. To be sure, all of the above-cited decisions involved the furnishing of assistance and know-how after the transfer of the patent rights. But we think that the fact that petitioner's services were rendered in the pre-acquisition period does not necessarily deprive him of the benefit of the principle to be derived from those decisions, where the development of the underlying invention had progressed to such a point that only "technical problems" relating to commercial marketability remained. Thus, the situation herein is to be sharply distinguished from that which would exist if the invention in question did not exist or was in a clearly embryonic stage and the payments were made for services to be rendered in creating or further developing the invention.

The situation herein is also distinguishable from that involved in cases where the payments are found to have been intended as compensation for services unrelated to, or merely tangential to, the transfer of patent rights, as contrasted with being an integral part of, and subsidiary to, such a transfer. This contrast is dramatized in Arthur C. Ruge, 26 T.C. 138 (1956). There, the taxpayer and his co-inventor sold a patent covering electrical strain gages and agreed to furnish up to 60 days of consulting services per year to assist the buyer in the "establishment, or subsequent control, of its manufacturing operations of electrical strain gages or applications thereof or of rendering consulting services relating to or embodying strain responsive apparatus." Separate consideration was allocated to their undertaking to supply their "best efforts and thoughts for promoting the strain gage business." Payments under the first clause were held to be capital in nature, while those made under the "best efforts" provision were compensation for services and taxable as ordinary income. We believe that the research work performed here by petitioner is more closely analogous to the services called for by the first clause in Ruge, for the reason that it related to the development and implementation of the particular invention transferred rather than the general advancement of the purchaser's business.

Although the issue is not entirely free from doubt, we conclude, on the basis of all the facts and circumstances revealed by the record herein, that the $40,000 received by petitioner from Chemetron in 1969 did not constitute compensation for services but rather was payment for an interest in the product of petitioner's work and that to the extent that Petitioner's services were involved they were subsidiary to the option and transfer involved herein.

To reflect our conclusion and the concessions of the parties on other issues,

Decision will be entered under Rule 155.

QUESTIONS

1. On what basis did the court distinguish the instant case from *Ruge*? What does this distinction suggest in terms of structuring the transfer of patent rights where the transferee desires the patent owner to perform further research and development services, and to assist in marketing the invention embodied in the patent?

2. If the patent owner and transferee enter into an agreement under which the patent owner will assist the transferee in designing and installing the equipment necessary to manufacture the licensed technology in exchange for a fixed payment, would the payment be treated as capital gains or ordinary income? What if the agreement were structured as a consulting agreement? What if the assistance with design and installation of manufacturing equipment was included as a term in the patent license?

3. If the patent owner and transferee enter into an agreement under which the patent owner will provide the transferee's customers with training and support in the use of the licensed technology in exchange for a fixed payment, would the payment be treated as capital gains of ordinary income? What if the customer training and support was included as a term in the license agreement?

CASE NOTES

1. Farris invented a needle-less syringe which made it possible to fill a medical syringe without exposing the liquid contents to airborne contaminants. Farris received four patents on his invention. In March 2004, Farris assigned the needle-less syringe patents to Cardinal Health, a pharmaceutical manufacturing company. The assignment agreement stated that "for $1 and other good and valuable consideration Farris hereby assigns said patents to Cardinal Health." The assignment agreement did not define "other good and valuable consideration" and did not provide for any other compensation to Farris. The parties recorded the assignment with the PTO in July 2005. Three months after executing the patent assignment, Farris entered into a sales representative agreement with Cardinal Health. Under the sales representative agreement, Farris agreed to devote approximately forty hours per week, for two years, performing services for Cardinal Health as an independent contractor. All of the services were related to "Cardinal Health's Smart Amp Products" which were not defined in the agreement. The agreement, however, did state that Farris had "extensive knowledge and experience" regarding such products and would use his "best efforts" to perform all normal and routine services of a sales representative, and would train Cardinal Health personnel on the use of the Smart Amp Products. Other services enumerated in the agreement included developing a sales strategy for Smart Amp Products and cultivating relationships with potential customers. Farris received a total of $37,500 in 2006 under the agreement. Farris did not report these payments on his 2006 tax return and, when the IRS issued a deficiency notice, Farris claimed the payments were capital gains from his assignment of his patents to Cardinal Health. The IRS claimed these payments were ordinary income for services. What result? *See* Farris v. Commissioner of Internal Revenue, T.C. Memo. 2010-222 (U.S. Tax Ct. 2010).

2. *See also* General Spring Corp. v. Commissioner of Internal Revenue, 12 T.C.M. (CCH) 847 (Tax Ct. 1953) (Transfer of patent rights was a sale of capital assets even though proceeds were not received in single payment, there was a qualification on assignee's right to sue for infringement, and assignee's right to reassign was restricted; in addition, the fact that taxpayer deducted depreciation on patents after assignment, listed its business as "licensing under royalty contracts"

and expended large sums in further development of patent after assignment, did not change conclusion that transfer of patent rights was a sale of capital assets); Dreymann v. Commissioner of Internal Revenue, T.C.M. (P-H) P 50,045 (Tax Ct. 1950) (Taxpayer received capital gains income from assignment of patent despite fact he had sold a previous patent, was employed by the transferee corporation to perfect the patent, and received a percentage of gross sales from product manufactured under patent); Hessert v. Commissioner of Internal Revenue, T.C.M. (P-H) P 47,301 (Tax Ct. 1947) (Personal services provided by patent owner were ancillary and subsidiary to the sale of patents and were advisory in nature, not unusual in the sale of highly technical and intricate device; service provided beyond those supporting the sale were subject to separate contract and income was segregated and distinct from sale; fact that minimum payment for sale was based on percentage of sales does not convert sale agreement into contract for personal services); Kelly v. Commissioner of Internal Revenue, T.C.M. (P-H) P 47,252 (Tax Ct. 1947) (Taxpayer-employee who was not originally hired as inventor and who assigned his patent rights to employer was entitled to capital gains treatment of proceeds from assignment; payment for assignment of patent rights and payment for employee provision of services were separate).

Additional Information

1. STEVEN Z. SZCZEPANSKI, DAVID M. EPSTEIN, 2 ECKSTROM'S LICENSING IN FOR. & DOM. OPS. Appendix 9J (2010).

2. M. T. BRUNNER, 46 A.L.R.2d 615 (2010).

3. 33A AM. JUR. 2D FEDERAL TAXATION, ¶. 10851, 11403 (2010).

4. 47A C.J.S. INTERNAL REVENUE § 128 (2010).

5. *Payments to Patent Holder Were Ordinary Income, Not Capital Gains*, 86 PRACTICAL TAX STRATEGIES 41 (2011).

6. Madelyn S. Cantor, *Tax Policy: Copyrights and Patents*, 31 VILL. L. REV. 931 (1986).

7. William D. Jordan, *Captial Gains Tax — Corporation Taxation — Federal Income Taxation — An Exclusive Contract Right to Practice a Patent is a Capital Asset and Its Surrender Results in Capital Gains Taxation of the Proceeds. United States v. Dresser Indus. Inc., 324 F.2d 56 (5th Cir. 1963)*, 42 TEX. L. REV. 738 (1964).

8.6   SALE OR EXCHANGE BY THE PATENT HOLDER

The public policy underlying I.R.C § 1235 is similar to that of I.R.C. § 41. Whereas § 41 seeks to promote R&D activities by companies by providing tax credits for increased levels of R&D spending, § 1235 seeks to promote inventive activities by individuals by providing capital gains treatment for the transfer of patent rights by the inventor or a person who has acquired the inventor's patent rights. Section 1235 capital gains treatment is more liberal in a number of respects than capital gains treatment under §§ 1221 and 1231. Section 1235 eliminates the 1-year holding period required by §§ 1221 and 1231. Section 1235 allows for capital gain treatment even if payment for the patent is spread over the transferee's use of the patent or is contingent on the productivity of the patent transferred. Both of these provisions can negate capital gains treatment under §§ 1221 and 1231. Finally, § 1235 does not exclude capital gains treatment for property primarily held for sale as does § 1221. Under § 1235, an inventor can engage in a regular course of business of selling patents without loss of capital gain treatment.

As you will see, however, § 1235 does limit the availability of capital gains treatment to a specific type of transfer and to a select group of favored individuals. To be eligible for § 1235 treatment, the transfer must include all substantial rights in the patent. Section 1235 treatment is only available to individual inventors or to individuals who are "holders" of a patent. Section 1235 treatment is not available for transfers of patent rights by employees to their employers or to transfers of patent rights to "related persons," which includes certain relatives of the inventor and corporations in which the inventor owns a certain percentage of stock.

The Internal Revenue Code and Treasury Regulation provisions in this section further define a § 1235 transfer. The *Busse* case considers the relationship of § 1235 to a number of other Code provisions, and the *McClain* case considers who is an "employee" for purposes of § 1235. Finally, the I.R.S. Technical Advice Memorandum considers § 1235 in the context of a university faculty inventor.

I.R.C. § 1235. SALE OR EXCHANGE OF PATENTS

(a) **General.** — A transfer (other than by gift, inheritance, or devise) of property consisting of all substantial rights to a patent, or an undivided interest therein which includes a part of all such rights, by any holder shall be considered the sale or exchange of a capital asset held for more than 1 year, regardless of whether or not payments in consideration of such transfer are —

(1) payable periodically over a period generally coterminous with the transferee's use of the patent, or

(2) contingent on the productivity, use, or disposition of the property transferred.

(b) **"Holder" defined.** — For purposes of this section, the term "holder" means —

(1) any individual whose efforts created such property, or

(2) any other individual who has acquired his interest in such property in exchange for consideration in money or money's worth paid to such creator prior to actual reduction to practice of the invention covered by the patent, if such individual is neither —

(A) the employer of such creator, nor

(B) related to such creator (within the meaning of subsection (d)).

TREAS. REG. § 1.1235-1 SALE OR EXCHANGE OF PATENTS.

(a) **General rule.** Section 1235 provides that a transfer (other than by gift, inheritance, or devise) of all substantial rights to a patent, or of an undivided interest in all such rights to a patent, by a holder to a person other than a related person constitutes the sale or exchange of a capital asset held for more than 1 year (6 months for taxable years beginning before 1977; 9 months for taxable years beginning in 1977), whether or not payments therefor are:

(1) Payable periodically over a period generally coterminous with the transferee's use of the patent, or

(2) Contingent on the productivity, use, or disposition of the property transferred.

(b)   Scope of section 1235. If a transfer is not one described in paragraph (a) of this section, section 1235 shall be disregarded in determining whether or not such transfer is the sale or exchange of a capital asset. For example, a transfer by a person other than a holder or a transfer by a holder to a related person is not governed by section 1235. The tax consequences of such transfers shall be determined under other provisions of the internal revenue laws.

(c)   Special rules —

(1)   Payments for infringement. If section 1235 applies to the transfer of all substantial rights to a patent (or an undivided interest therein), amounts received in settlement of, or as the award of damages in, a suit for compensatory damages for infringement of the patent shall be considered payments attributable to a transfer to which section 1235 applies to the extent that such amounts relate to the interest transferred. For taxable years beginning before January 1, 1964, see section 1304, as in effect before such date, and § 1.1304A-1 for treatment of compensatory damages for patent infringement.

(2)   Payments to an employee. Payments received by an employee as compensation for services rendered as an employee under an employment contract requiring the employee to transfer to the employer the rights to any invention by such employee are not attributable to a transfer to which section 1235 applies. However, whether payments received by an employee from his employer (under an employment contract or otherwise) are attributable to the transfer by the employee of all substantial rights to a patent (or an undivided interest therein) or are compensation for services rendered the employer by the employee is a question of fact. In determining which is the case, consideration shall be given not only to all the facts and circumstances of the employment relationship but also to whether the amount of such payments depends upon the production, sale, or use by, or the value to, the employer of the patent rights transferred by the employee. If it is determined that payments are attributable to the transfer of patent rights, and all other requirements under section 1235 are met, such payments shall be treated as proceeds derived from the sale of a patent.

(d)   Payor's treatment of payments in a transfer under section 1235. Payments made by the transferee of patent rights pursuant to a transfer satisfying the requirements of section 1235 are payments of the purchase price for the patent rights and are not the payment of royalties.

TREAS. REG. § 1.1235-2   DEFINITION OF TERMS.

For the purposes of section 1235 and § 1.1235-1:

(a)   Patent. The term patent means a patent granted under the provisions of title 35 of the United States Code, or any foreign patent granting rights generally similar to those under a United States patent. It is not necessary that the patent or patent application for the invention be in existence if the requirements of section 1235 are otherwise met.

(b)   All substantial rights to a patent.

(1) The term all substantial rights to a patent means all rights (whether or not then held by the grantor) which are of value at the time the rights to the patent (or an undivided interest therein) are transferred. The term all substantial rights to a patent does not include a grant of rights to a patent:

(i) Which is limited geographically within the country of issuance;

(ii) Which is limited in duration by the terms of the agreement to a period less than the remaining life of the patent;

(iii) Which grants rights to the grantee, in fields of use within trades or industries, which are less than all the rights covered by the patent, which exist and have value at the time of the grant; or

(iv) Which grants to the grantee less than all the claims or inventions covered by the patent which exist and have value at the time of the grant.

The circumstances of the whole transaction, rather than the particular terminology used in the instrument of transfer, shall be considered in determining whether or not all substantial rights to a patent are transferred in a transaction.

(2) Rights which are not considered substantial for purposes of section 1235 may be retained by the holder. Examples of such rights are:

(i) The retention by the transferor of legal title for the purpose of securing performance or payment by the transferee in a transaction involving transfer of an exclusive license to manufacture, use, and sell for the life of the patent;

(ii) The retention by the transferor of rights in the property which are not inconsistent with the passage of ownership, such as the retention of a security interest (such as a vendor's lien), or a reservation in the nature of a condition subsequent (such as a provision for forfeiture on account of nonperformance).

(3) Examples of rights which may or may not be substantial, depending upon the circumstances of the whole transaction in which rights to a patent are transferred, are:

(i) The retention by the transferor of an absolute right to prohibit sublicensing or subassignment by the transferee;

(ii) The failure to convey to the transferee the right to use or to sell the patent property.

(4) The retention of a right to terminate the transfer at will is the retention of a substantial right for the purposes of section 1235.

(c) Undivided interest. A person owns an undivided interest in all substantial rights to a patent when he owns the same fractional share of each and every substantial right to the patent. It does not include, for example, a right to the income from a patent, or a license limited geographically, or a license which covers some, but not all, of the valuable claims or uses covered by the patent. A transfer limited in duration by the terms of the instrument to a period less than the remaining life of the patent is not a transfer of an undivided interest in all substantial rights to a patent.

(d) Holder.

(1) The term holder means any individual:

(i) Whose efforts created the patent property and who would qualify as the original and first inventor, or joint inventor, within the meaning of title 35 U.S.C., or

(ii) Who has acquired his interest in the patent property in exchange for a consideration paid to the inventor in money or money's worth prior to the actual reduction of the invention to practice (see paragraph (e) of this section), provided that such individual was neither the employer of the inventor nor related to him (see paragraph (f) of this section). The requirement that such individual is neither the employer of the inventor nor related to him must be satisfied at the time when the substantive rights as to the interest to be acquired are determined, and at the time when the consideration in money or money's worth to be paid is definitely fixed. For example, if prior to the actual reduction to practice of an invention an individual who is neither the employer of the inventor nor related to him agrees to pay the inventor a sum of money definitely fixed as to amount in return for an undivided one-half interest in rights to a patent and at a later date, when such individual has become the employer of the inventor, he pays the definitely fixed sum of money pursuant to the earlier agreement, such individual will not be denied the status of a holder because of such employment relationship.

(2) Although a partnership cannot be a holder, each member of a partnership who is an individual may qualify as a holder as to his share of a patent owned by the partnership. For example, if an inventor who is a member of a partnership composed solely of individuals uses partnership property in the development of his invention with the understanding that the patent when issued will become partnership property, each of the inventor's partners during this period would qualify as a holder. If, in this example, the partnership were not composed solely of individuals, nevertheless, each of the individual partners' distributive shares of income attributable to the transfer of all substantial rights to the patent or an undivided interest therein, would be considered proceeds from the sale or exchange of a capital asset held for more than 1 year (6 months for taxable

years beginning before 1977; 9 months for taxable years beginning in 1977).

(3) An individual may qualify as a holder whether or not he is in the business of making inventions or in the business of buying and selling patents.

(e)   Actual reduction to practice. For the purposes of determining whether an individual is a holder under paragraph (d) of this section, the term actual reduction to practice has the same meaning as it does under section 102(g) of title 35 of the United States Code. Generally, an invention is reduced to actual practice when it has been tested and operated successfully under operating conditions. This may occur either before or after application for a patent but cannot occur later than the earliest time that commercial exploitation of the invention occurs.

(f)   Related person.

(1) The term related person means one whose relationship to another person at the time of the transfer is described in section 267(b), except that the term does not include a brother or sister, whether of the whole or the half blood. Thus, if a holder transfers all his substantial rights to a patent to his brother or sister, or both, such transfer is not to a related person.

(2) If, prior to September 3, 1958, a holder transferred all his substantial rights to a patent to a corporation in which he owned more than 50 percent in value of the outstanding stock, he is considered as having transferred such rights to a related person for the purpose of section 1235. On the other hand, if a holder, prior to September 3, 1958, transferred all his substantial rights to a patent to a corporation in which he owned 50 percent or less in value of the outstanding stock and his brother owned the remaining stock, he is not considered as having transferred such rights to a related person since the brother relationship is to be disregarded for purposes of section 1235.

(3) If, subsequent to September 2, 1958, a holder transfers all his substantial rights to a patent to a corporation in which he owns 25 percent or more in value of the outstanding stock, he is considered as transferring such rights to a related person for the purpose of section 1235. On the other hand if a holder, subsequent to September 2, 1958, transfers all his substantial rights to a patent to a corporation in which he owns less than 25 percent in value of the outstanding stock and his brother owns the remaining stock, he is not considered as transferring such rights to a related person since the brother relationship is to be disregarded for purposes of section 1235.

(4) If a relationship described in section 267(b) exists independently of family status, the brother-sister exception, described in subparagraphs (1), (2), and (3) of this paragraph, does not apply. Thus, if a holder transfers all his substantial rights to a patent to the fiduciary of a trust of which the holder is the grantor, the holder and the fiduciary are related persons for purposes of section 1235(d). (See section 267(b)(4).) The transfer, therefore, would not qualify under section 1235(a). This result obtains whether or not

the fiduciary is the brother or sister of the holder since the disqualifying relationship exists because of the grantor-fiduciary status and not because of family status.

QUESTIONS

1.   Under what circumstances will § 1235 apply to amounts received as damages in a patent infringement suit? What is the rationale for providing § 1235 treatment for infringement damages? Does § 1235 treatment of infringement damages promote individual inventive activities?

2.   How is the determination made as to whether payments by an employer to an employee are for the transfer of patent rights or are compensation for services? How does the fact that the amount of such payments is dependent on the value of the patent rights to the employer affect this determination?

3.   How are payments by the transferee of an inventor's patent rights treated?

4.   Is it necessary for a patent or patent application to exist in order to qualify for § 1235 treatment? What is the "property" transferred if no patent or patent application exists?

5.   What rights in a patent may an inventor retain and still qualify for § 1235 treatment? Would the retention by the patent owner of the right to prohibit sublicensing or subassignment of the patent constitute a transfer of less than all substantial rights in the patent? What if the transfer agreement provided that sublicensing or subassignment is allowed, but only with transferor's permission? Only with the transferor's permission which permission will not be "unreasonably" withheld?

6.   What is the transfer of an "undivided interest" in a patent?

7.   Why does § 1235 require that a "holder" of a patent must acquire the rights in the patent prior to actual reduction to practice? Can an actual reduction to practice occur after a patent application has been filed?

BUSSE v. UNITED STATES
437 F.Supp. 928 (E.D. Wis. 1977)

WARREN, DISTRICT JUDGE.

This is a suit by three taxpayers, Busse Brothers, Inc., Marcella Busse, and Curtis Busse, to recover income taxes in the total sum of $115,940.25 assessed by the Internal Revenue Service against all three during the calendar years 1968 and 1969. The assessments were made by the IRS on the premise that certain amounts received by the individual taxpayers from Busse Brothers in payment for the transfer of a patent were dividends rather than royalties, that such payments could not be properly deducted by the corporation and constituted ordinary income to the individual taxpayers. The IRS also decided that portions of the payments to the individual defendants were "imputed-interest" under 26 U.S.C. § 483 and as such were ordinary income to these individuals.

All three taxpayers paid the assessments under protest and filed timely claims for refund which were denied. Plaintiffs then filed suit.

FINDINGS OF FACT

1. Busse Brothers was originally a partnership of Curtis and Gilbert Busse in Randolph, Wisconsin. It engaged in the filling station, auto repair, auto wrecking business, and other similar activities. During World War II the auto wrecking business collapsed and Curtis worked for various area canners while Gilbert was employed as a machinist. In 1946, the brothers reactivated their partnership and began the manufacture and sale of retort crate loaders and unloaders for canning companies. They had two part-time employees. By 1949, the enterprise had grown to the point where it employed 25 people.

2. During the 1950's, the can manufacturing and canning industry was expanding tremendously. The handling, transporting, and storage of the vast quantities of cans involved, led to a great deal of experimentation as the industry sought to mechanize its can handling methods. A general trend developed toward automatic bulk handling with an entire layer of containers on a "pallet" of wood or other material being treated and handled as a single unit. This required a system for automatically arranging cans on the support structure (palletizing) and also taking the containers off (de-palletizing). Several manufacturing concerns had developed prototypes of automatic can palletizers-but the testimony of representative industry users leads to the inescapable conclusion that competing machines were difficult to sustain in operation and generally unsatisfactory.

3. Standard Knapp Company, a division of Emhardt Corporation had developed a embryonic palletizing device and in the winter of 1956, the Busse Brothers were invited to the Mankato, Minnesota, plant of Green Giant to observe the machine in action. Both brothers felt the standard Knapp equipment was unsatisfactory. Upon returning to Randolph, they conferred with agents of a customer, Continental Can Company, and started developing, in conjunction with Continental Can, a device to do the job.

4. Six weeks of effort were unsuccessful, but the partnership nonetheless advised Continental Can that they were prepared to produce an effective machine for Continental Can.

5. Early discussions indicated that Continental Can was discouraged by these initial failures and not prepared to make it a joint venture whereupon it was agreed that if Curtis and Gilbert Busse could build a machine that worked, Continental Can would buy it. A prototype was thereafter developed, built and demonstrated in a period between 60 and 90 days thereafter. This machine was the embodiment of the claims of the subsequent "Busse patent."

6. The first sale of a Busse palletizer occurred in 1957, and immediately thereafter began a rapid growth of sales and profits by the partnership. Total company sales increased from $355,751 in 1957 to $2,340,385 in 1968 and $2,449,811 in 1969; sales of the palletizer itself from $35,894 in 1957 to $1,233,108 in 1968 and $1,308,810 in 1969. The palletizer success also stimulated the sale of allied products manufactured by the concern.

7. In 1958, Curtis Busse assigned one-half of his invention of the palletizer to his brother Gilbert. A patent was applied for in 1958, and in 1960, the patent involved in this case was issued.

8. The patent (No. 2,949,179) claims covered the palletizer and a U-shaped hydraulic power sweep. They did not cover a de-palletizer nor a variety of systems and devices that were a part of, or utilized with, both the patented palletizer and the non-patented de-palletizer.

9. The palletizing and de-palletizing processes were so interrelated that even though Busse Brothers held no patent on a de-palletizer, the upsurge in sales of palletizers created a comparable growth in sales of de-palletizers, kits and appurtenances.

10. The success of the Busse palletizer did generate a number of competing entries into the field which sought to avoid the protected claims of the Busse machine, but none of these had any significant success in cutting the commanding share of the market for both palletizers and de-palletizers which Busse held. In the years 1957 through 1970, Busse sold 75 percent to 90 percent of the palletizers in use in the nation.

11. Gilbert Busse died in 1962 and his interest in the partnership passed to his wife, Marcella. A new corporation, Busse Brothers, Inc. was formed on January 1, 1966 and some of the partnership assets were contributed to the corporation in exchange for stock. The partnership retained the real estate and certain other assets. On January 13, 1966, the first corporate meeting was held and, among other items of business, the directors authorized the corporation to purchase from Curtis Busse and Marcella Busse their interests in the patent.

12. Extended consultation with counsel and various advisers resulted in the execution on April 28, 1967 of a formal assignment of the patent pursuant to which Curtis and Marcella conveyed all of their respective interests in the patent in consideration of periodic installment payments of 5 percent of the corporation's "net selling price (. . .) of palletizers and de-palletizers (including parts and kits therefor) sold by assignee which are covered by any claim of said Patent No. 2,949,179." The assignment did not establish any down payment nor any minimum payment.

13. After Gilbert Busse's death in 1962, it was necessary to arrive at a value, for tax purposes, of his share of the partnership. After negotiations, it was ultimately agreed between counsel for the estate and the IRS that the total value of the partnership intangibles including both the patent and the good will was $390,000. For estate tax purposes, Gilbert's interest was thus $195,000. For purposes of determining Marcella's 1967 income tax purposes, it was necessary to determine a date-of-death value for Gilbert's patent interest so that the appropriate value could be depreciated over the remaining life of the patent. Again, after negotiations between Marcella's accountant and the IRS, it was agreed that the value of the patent at the time of Gilbert's death was to be established, for income tax purposes, at $240,000 with his share thereof thus set at $120,000.

14. Subsequent to the 1966 agreement to sell the patent (embodied formally in the 1967 Assignment), the corporation continued to enjoy substantial and

increasing sales of both palletizers, de-palletizers, and the kits for each. In 1968 and 1969, the following payments were made pursuant to the assignment:

	CURTIS	MARCELLA
1968	$43,525.92	$43,525.92
1969	$46,993.35	$46,993.35

15. For the years 1968 and 1969, Curtis and Marcella each reported these payments as long-term capital gains. Curtis, as inventor, had no basis and the total of the payments was treated as a long-term gain. Marcella, as a result of negotiations with the IRS, had a basis of $120,000 at the time of Gilbert's death. From then until 1966, she had deducted $27,845.30 thereof. Thus, at the time of the assignment, her basis was $92,154.70, which she then began spreading over the remaining life of the patent. This resulted in an annual deduction of $7,955.80.

16. For the years 1968 and 1969, Busse Brothers, Inc. deducted the installment payments as a deductible amortization of the purchase price. The IRS determined that only 44.5 percent of the installments ($38,751 in 1968; $41,886 in 1969) constituted "reasonable" payments for the patent and disallowed the balance as a "dividend," hence, non-deductible to the corporation and ordinary income (not long-term capital gain) to Curtis and Marcella.

17. The IRS further determined that of such "reasonable" amounts, the sums of $2,374.51 in 1968 and $3,575.70 in 1969 paid to Curtis and also to Marcella constituted "imputed interest" under Section 483 of the Internal Revenue Code such that although deductible by the corporation, both Curtis and Marcella must have said amounts treated as ordinary income. At the time of trial, the government abandoned this position with regard to the payments made to Curtis. It maintained its contention concerning payments made to Marcella.

18. The IRS also determined that $6,659.18 of the 1969 installment payments to Marcella should be treated as "depreciation recapture" to her under Section 1245 of the Internal Revenue Code. This would make it ordinary income to her. Marcella Busse has conceded this issue and it need not be further addressed by the Court except as it may affect the judgment to be rendered herein.

CONCLUSIONS OF LAW

Thus, the ultimate issues presented to the Court in the bench trial are essentially, (A) whether or not the 1968 and 1969 installment payments made to Curtis Busse and to Marcella Busse were "reasonable" so as to make the sale of the patent to the corporations deductible to the corporation and eligible for capital gains treatment to the taxpayers, and (B) whether or not the 1968 and 1969 payments to Marcella are subject to the "imputed interest" requirements of 26 U.S.C. § 483(f)(4) such that a portion of the payment to Marcella in each year would be ordinary income to her. As to all other issues originally in the case, one side or the other has conceded.

A. "REASONABLENESS"

As a general backdrop to this opinion, the Court would note and generally agree with the government that transactions of tax significance between a taxpayer and his closely held or controlled corporation are to be viewed with close scrutiny so as to avoid abuse of the tax laws. However, it is equally true that sanctions or implication of wrongdoing should not attach to a citizen who arranges his affairs so as to minimize the tax impact. In fact, as plaintiff notes in a footnote of his brief, it is clear that when it comes to the tax treatment of patent sales, there is an affirmative public policy to encourage invention through favorable tax provisions.

In dealing with taxpayers and their controlled corporations whether or not a given transaction is what it appears to be-or whether it is a masked scheme to distribute corporate earnings under artificial tax devices must be judged by what is "reasonable," Merrit v. Commissioner, 39 T.C. 257 (1962), and that ubiquitous term is deemed to be what an unrelated party would have paid under the same or similar circumstances. What the naked terms of the contract call for does not determine the issue for the Court.

It seems abundantly clear that this particular transaction does not fall within the purview of 26 U.S.C. § 1235 which implements Congressional intent to give inventors and certain financial backers capital gains treatment on patent sales even though the asset is not held for six months. Curtis Busse was the inventor; Marcella was not. But, the transfer was to a corporation in which each owned more than 25 percent of the stock. The transfer could not qualify under § 1235. Nonetheless, the patent was held by Curtis and Marcella Busse more than six months and transferred to a corporation in which each held less than 80 percent of the stock. Hence, although not qualifying under § 1235, the sale was nonetheless entitled to long-term capital gains treatment under the general provisions applicable to the sale or transfer of any capital asset. 26 U.S.C. § 1239 (assuming the payments pursuant to the sale were not disguised dividends).

Despite the fact that § 1235 does not govern the transaction its content and legislative history were frequently referred to in the arguments on the issue of "reasonableness."

In its brief the government attacks the formula of the sale contract which measured the sale price of the patent by 5 percent of the sales of palletizers and de-palletizers (as well as kits and appurtenances). It argues that 26 U.S.C. § 1235 permits the transfer of the patent to be treated as a long-term capital gain even when the payments in consideration of such transfer are:

contingent on the productivity, use, or disposition of the property transferred.

Arguing that long-term capital gains treatment for a patent sale under § 1239 should not be any more favorable than it would be under § 1235, if applicable, the government takes the position that the patent was the property transferred and that there is something inherently wrong with the transaction because the sale price is determined by the sales of both palletizers and de-palletizers. In fact, the government's evaluation expert opined that different markets exist for the two kinds of machines and that since the patent covered only the palletizers, it was unreasonable to measure the patent price by the sales of both devices. Counsel for defendant regards the wording quoted above from § 1235 as a limitation requiring that capital gains treatment can only be extended when the payments are contingent on the productivity of the patent itself and cannot be measured by the productivity of non-patented items. The Court finds a number of faults with this argument. It overlooks the wording of s 1235(a) which applies capital gains treatment (when certain conditions are met), regardless of whether or not payments in consideration of such transfer are . . . (1) payable periodically . . . or (2) contingent on the productivity . . . (emphasis supplied). Additionally, it is the Court's opinion that the term "productivity" is broad enough to cover the profits from sales of both palletizers and de-palletizers because of the proven close relationship between the two. Finally, the Court notes the parallel which can be drawn to the "entire market value rule" from the realm of patent law, permitting recovery based on the value of an entire mechanism containing a variety of features only one of which is patented.

The evidence shows that the invention of the palletizer seems to have immediately created a market for de-palletizers. Although any given purchaser of palletizers would not require an equal number of de-palletizers, the record establishes that the technologies of the two devices were so much alike that palletizer purchasers frequently drew upon the engineering sales service of Busse in solving their own or their customers' de-palletizing problems; that palletizer buyers did in fact purchase large numbers of Busse de-palletizers; and that the invention of the palletizer created immediate and substantial sales of de-palletizers by Busse.

Nor is the Court aware of any rules of law, custom or usage requiring that the measure of a sale price can be only the sale of patented devices.

The owner of the monopolistic property right granted under a patent who for some reason transfers that interest would be influenced by so many factors that the judgment as to what is a reasonable price becomes highly subjective and tailored to the specifics of the situation. Mr. Reak testified regarding the newspaper stacker where the royalties were 55 percent on the first five units; 28 percent on units 6 through 15; 14 percent on 16 through 25; 10 percent on units 26 through 125; 7 percent on units 126 through 225; and 5 percent on the balance. That unique formula was tailored to the realities of that situation.

Many of the factors that must perforce be considered were discussed by the experts for each party during their testimony. The strength of the patent, industry rates, saturation of the market, exclusivity of the sales, comparables, contribution of the patented product to other sales, and profitability of the patent after making the payments were all covered in testimony and in extensive briefs.

The government points to the language on page 2 of the assignment calling for the payment of 5 percent of the selling price of "palletizers and de-palletizers . . . which are covered by any claim of said Patent" as an ambiguity that should be construed in favor of the defendants' interpretation since the drafter stands on both sides of the bargain in this instance. That argument appears inapplicable to the Court. We are here concerned not with construing the language of an ambiguous contract to establish the rights of the parties, but rather with deciding whether the terms of a clear contract (which may well be factually inaccurate inasmuch as the de-palletizers were not covered by the patent) which has been interpreted in the same way by both parties, is in fact "reasonable" from the point of view of a third party, i. e., the government.

The contention by defendant that the assignment formula, tying the royalty rate to sales of palletizers and the non-patented de-palletizers, raises the possibility of patent misuse or antitrust violations is not convincing to the Court. Misuse of patent and antitrust laws focus on impairing the operation of the free market place and the lessening of competition. Here the monopoly enjoyed by the owner is government created and government sanctioned. The measure of the price for the patent, i. e., sales of palletizers and de-palletizers was not forced upon an unwilling purchaser who had to buy A and B to get A; nor was competition in the de-palletizer market affected in any way by this assignment. The Automatic Radio Mfg. Co. v. Hazeltine Research, Inc and Glen Mfg., Inc. v. Perfect Fit Industries, Inc. cases cited by defendant, and Zenith Corp. v. Hazeltine, convince the Court that while patentees do not have carte blanche authority to condition the grant of patent licenses upon the payment of royalties on unpatented articles, neither is it per se a misuse of patents to measure the consideration by a percentage of the sales of items covered by the patent and not covered by the patent. Under the facts of this case, the Court cannot find patent misuse or antitrust implications. This finding is buttressed by the realization that the resolution of this issue takes us no closer to the crucial question of the case at bar — whether the amounts paid under the assignment were such that they were unreasonable and were really dividends in disguise.

After consideration of the full record, the Court is satisfied that the Busse patent was strong; that it was not successfully avoided by competitors; that the transfer was a sale of what amounted to an exclusive license for a substantial remaining patent life; that the development of the patented product had an immediate and sustained positive impact on the total sales of the company, and that when the rule of thumb which both sides appeared to agree upon (25 to 33 percent of "profits") is applied against the gross profit of sales of palletizers and de-palletizers, the payments were "reasonable."

The valuation placed upon the one-half interest in the patent in Gilbert's estate in 1966 is urged by the government as constituting a frozen figure which should estop the taxpayer from asserting any other value insofar as the reasonableness of the sale is concerned. This value was established arbitrarily, and primarily as a compromise in the preparation of Marcella's income tax returns, at $120,000 for Gilbert's one-half of the patent. Then, using this value, the government seeks to calculate a "reasonable flow of income for that assumed value pursuant to the reverse application of Haskold's Formula." The Court can perceive of no rationale that warrants this procedure and justifies holding the taxpayer who has sold under a contingent percentage of sales formula to the rigidities of a figure born in negotiation or to a valuation formulary that pre-supposes equal annual installments. The Court found the terms of the Canadian licensing agreement (5 percent of sales of palletizers and de-palletizers), an admitted arm's length transaction, much more persuasive on the issue of reasonableness. To be sure it was a license to manufacture and not a sale of all patent rights. The fact that it also covers the manufacture of unpatented crate unloaders is offset by the fact that the license also provided for exchange of manufacturing "know-how." It is highly probative, it appears to the Court, as to reasonableness.

****

Because certain of the issues have been disposed of by action of the parties and others by this memorandum, and because the various resolutions require computation as to the financial result, it is ORDERED that the parties within thirty (30) days, present to the Court an agreed computation embodying resolutions of all issues as made herein.

SO ORDERED.

QUESTIONS

1. Why did Curtis Busse's transfer of his patent rights not qualify for § 1235 treatment? Why did Marcella Busse's transfer of her patent rights not qualify for § 1235 treatment?

2. The court notes that in 1958, Curtis Busse assigned one-half of his invention rights to his brother Gilbert. Gilbert's interest in the patent passed to his wife, Marcella, upon his death in 1962. Nonetheless, the payments to Curtis and Marcella in 1968 and 1969 were the same. Why?

3. Why does the court reject the government's argument that basing the patent sale price on the sales of both patented and unpatented products would not itself disqualify the transaction from § 1235 treatment?

4. On what basis does the court conclude that the payments to Curtis and Marcella Busse for the transfer of their patent rights were "reasonable" under the circumstances?

5. Section 1235 allows for payments contingent on sales attributable to the patent transferred, similar to royalties. The payments to Curtis and Marcella were contingent on sales of both the patented and unpatented products. However, the payments to Curtis and Marcella did not qualify for § 1235 treatment. Why would these payments not be considered royalties taxed as ordinary income rather than installment payments taxed as capital gains?

McCLAIN v. COMMISSIONER OF INTERNAL REVENUE
40 T.C. 841 (U.S. Tax Ct. 1963)

FORRESTER, JUDGE:

Respondent determined deficiencies in petitioners' income taxes for the calendar years 1957 and 1958 in the amounts of $2,913.62 and $1,756.27, respectively. Petitioners assert an overpayment of such taxes for 1958 of $999.31. The sole issue for decision is whether certain income received from his employer by petitioner Thomas H. McClain (hereinafter referred to as McClain or petitioner) was ordinary income or capital gain.

All of the facts have been stipulated and are so found.

Petitioners are husband and wife residing in La Canada, Calif. They filed joint Federal income tax returns, computed on the cash basis, with the district director of internal revenue at Los Angeles, Calif., for the calendar years 1957 and 1958.

McClain entered the employ of Lockheed Aircraft Corp. (hereinafter referred to as Lockheed) on October 16, 1936. He was initially employed as a file clerk and blueprint sorter. In 1937 he was made a layout draftsman, a position held by him until July 1, 1941, when we was assigned to the position of junior research engineer. McClain worked as a junior research engineer until August 1942, at which time he was designated a design engineer, and he occupied that position until he was promoted to design specialist on October 16, 1961.

Except for a period of 4 months in 1954 when he was on a temporary leave of absence while president of the Lockheed Section of the Engineers and Architects Association, now known as the Engineers and Scientists Guild, McClain has been continuously employed by Lockheed since 1936. His formal education prior to employment at Lockheed included a high school diploma and 1 1/2 years of junior college study in the field of aviation mechanics and design.

Lockheed is today and for a number of years has been a major company in the development and production of aircraft, missiles, and related equipment. The common stock of Lockheed is listed on the New York Stock Exchange. McClain has never owned, and does not now own, directly, indirectly, constructively, or otherwise, 25 percent or more of any class of the outstanding stock of Lockheed.

Early in 1938, Lockheed adopted the practice of requiring every employee, as a condition of employment, to execute an agreement in favor of Lockheed, which agreement pertained in part to possible future inventions of the employee. The agreement became known within Lockheed as the "Assignment of Inventions Agreement" (hereinafter referred to as the agreement). Initially, this agreement was placed by Lockheed on the bottom of each employee's application for employment. At the time this practice was adopted in 1938, each existing employee of Lockheed, including McClain, was required to file a new application for employment and execute the agreement which appeared on the bottom thereof as a condition of his continued employment.

McClain executed such a new application for employment on April 15, 1938. The application contained the agreement in the following form:

> In event of my employment by Lockheed Aircraft Corporation, I agree fully to the following: * * * (4) In part consideration for the wages to be paid to me in the event of my employment, I hereby agree to assign to Lockheed Aircraft Corporation, its successors or appointees, all my right, title and interest in and to any inventions, improvements, and new methods of manufacture or process, together with any patents that may be issued thereon, both in the United States of America and all foreign countries, that I may invent, discover, or produce, or cause to be invented, discovered or produced in any manner whatsoever, relating to aircraft, aeronautical equipment or to machines, methods, operations or processes used in their manufacture or relating in any way to the field of aviation, whether during

my regular working hours, or at the suggestion or request of my employer, or whether solely or jointly with others. I further agree to execute all documents necessary to the issuance of patents therefor, both in the United States of America and all foreign countries and to the assignment thereof to Lockheed Aircraft Corporation, its successors or appointees. The word "invention" as herein used includes "make," "discover," or "produce," or any of them; "invention includes the phrase "any new or useful original art, machine, manufacture, process, composition of matter, design, or configuration of any kind" " and the words "improvement," "discovery" or "production" or any of them; "patent" includes "letters patent" and "all the extensions, renewals, modifications, improvements and reissues of such patent" "appointee" includes "whomsoever the first party may designate." This agreement shall be effective during the entire period of my employment and for a period of six (6) months thereafter.

During the years 1940 and 1941, while employed by Lockheed, McClain conceived, invented, and perfected a new and different windshield construction (hereinafter referred to as the invention) to be used on aircraft. This involved the use of both a laminated glass windshield, the plastic filler of which extends beyond the glass on all sides, and a special type of mounting or bracket into which the glass is laid when installed on the aircraft.

The basic idea for the invention was conceived by McClain in 1940 and disclosed to Lockheed by means of drawings and a written description prepared by him. An application for patent was prepared by Lockheed's attorneys and filed by McClain under Lockheed's supervision and control in the U.S. Patent Office during 1940. This application was abandoned because McClain had not adequately described therein the type of material to be used between the windshield glass.

McClain originally conceived of polymerized vinyl butyral for use between the windshield glass. The Pittsburgh Plate Glass Co., at the request of Lockheed, prepared working models of the McClain concept, using his glass. These models were tested by McClain to determine which material was best suited to his concept. These tests of the working models were conducted by him during 1941, using Lockheed equipment and facilities, at Lockheed's direction, and with Lockheed's approval. McClain concluded that polymerized vinyl butyral, the type of material originally considered, was the preferred material to be employed between the layers of glass.

During the period in 1940 in which the basic idea for the McClain invention first was conceived by him, McClain was assigned by Lockheed, as a layout draftsman, to design the window installations for the cockpit section of the fuselage of the model 44 aircraft then being developed by Lockheed. In performing this assignment it was anticipated by Lockheed that McClain would use the existing state of the art (that is to say, the then-available materials and techniques).

McClain was not originally assigned by Lockheed specifically to invent a new windshield construction for the model 44 or any other aircraft. However, after he had conceived of the invention he was assigned as a junior research engineer in a structural research group at Lockheed for a relatively short time to determine which material was best suited to his concept.

The invention was determined to involve two separate patentable ideas. The two patentable ideas involved were the subject of documents entitled "Assignment" which were signed by McClain on December 31, 1941, and on June 12, 1942. The assignments read in pertinent part as follows:

ASSIGNMENT

WHEREAS, I, THOMAS H. McCLAIN, residing at Altadena, County of Los Angeles, State of California, have invented a new and useful TRANS-PARENT CLOSURE AND MOUNTING for which I am about to make application for Letters Patent of the United States; and

WHEREAS, LOCKHEED AIRCRAFT CORPORATION, of Burbank, County of Los Angeles, State of California, is desirous of acquiring an interest therein:

NOW, THEREFORE, for a valuable consideration, the receipt of which is hereby acknowledged I, THOMAS H. McCLAIN, do hereby sell, assign and transfer unto said LOCKHEED AIRCRAFT CORPORATION, its successors and assigns, the full and exclusive right for the territory of the United States of America and for all foreign countries, in and to the said invention as described in the specification executed by me on the * * * (date of execution hereof) preparatory to obtaining Letter Patent of the United States therefor; said invention, application and Letters Patent to be held and enjoyed by the said LOCKHEED AIRCRAFT CORPORATION for its own use and behalf, and for its legal representative, to the full end of the term for which said Letters Patent may be granted, as fully and entirely as the same would have been held by me had this assignment and sale not been made.

The assignments executed by McClain in 1941 and 1942 were recorded in the U.S. Patent Office on January 3, 1942, and June 15, 1942, respectively.

The two patentable ideas comprising the invention related to aircraft and the field of aviation and were hence covered by the provisions of the agreement executed by McClain in favor of Lockheed on April 15, 1938.

With respect to each patentable idea comprising the invention, a patent application was filed by McClain, with Lockheed bearing the costs of making such application. The applications were prepared by attorneys employed by Lockheed. With respect to the first patentable idea contained in McClain's invention, patent No. 2,293,656 was issued by the U.S. Patent Office on August 18, 1942. With respect to the second patentable idea contained in McClain's invention, the U.S. Patent Office issued patent No. 2,351,991 on June 20, 1944. The invention described by the patents has also been patented in seven foreign countries.

All legal steps toward the procurement of the patents in the United States and the various foreign countries were handled either by attorneys directly employed within Lockheed or by outside counsel retained by Lockheed.

Lockheed has executed licensing agreements covering the invention with three licensees, including the Pittsburgh Plate Glass Co. and the Libbey-Owens-Ford Co., and has derived very substantial royalties from such license agreements. All negotiations with respect to these license agreements were handled by Lockheed personnel other than McClain, who took no part therein. The license agreement between Lockheed and the Libbey-Owens-Ford Co. was executed on May 25, 1942. The license agreement between Lockheed and the Pittsburgh Plate Glass Co. was executed on November 18, 1940.

In October 1942, Lockheed adopted a plan now known as the Lockheed patent plan (hereinafter referred to as the plan). The idea for this plan was originally conceived by Lockheed's patent counsel, who recommended it to the company's management. The McClain invention, which was recognized by Lockheed as a valuable invention and a contribution to the aviation industry, was a factor which caused the management of Lockheed to recognize the desirability of such a program and which influenced the decision of Lockheed's management to adopt the plan. McClain did not participate in any way in the discussions of the various Lockheed officials which ultimately culminated in the decision to adopt the plan.

The terms of the plan were first promulgated to all Lockheed employees in October 1942, in a booklet entitled "Lockheed and Vega Plan for Recognizing Constructive Employee Ideas." The plan as enumerated in that booklet provided that an employee who developed a patentable idea would receive $25 at the time the application for patent was filed and would receive a second $25 at the time the patent was issued. In addition to these initial payments, it was provided that if Lockheed granted licenses or made sales of whole or partial rights under the patent, the employee would receive 10 percent of the money received from such licensing or sale. These latter payments were not to exceed an aggregate of $5,000, except that in unusual cases the maximum payment might be exceeded upon special consideration by the president of Lockheed.

The 1942 booklet describing the plan contained the following statement:

> The company reserves the right to change or discontinue this plan at any time after published notice. Awards for proposals and patents granted but not paid preceding the change or discontinuance of this plan will not be affected.

****

For the calendar years 1957 and 1958, petitioners reported the salary paid to McClain in the amounts of $11,729.34 and.$12,203.09 respectively, as ordinary income on their Federal income tax returns.

Through the year 1961, McClain received the following royalty payments from Lockheed pursuant to the plan, all of which were paid out of royalties received by Lockheed pursuant to the aforementioned license agreements:

McClain received no payments pursuant to the plan in 1957 and 1958 other than those paid out of royalties received by Lockheed and mentioned above.

For the years 1942 through 1956, petitioners reported all payments made under the plan to McClain on their Federal income tax returns as ordinary income, as part of McClain's compensation from Lockheed.

1018   TAX EFFECTS OF TECHNOLOGY CREATION AND TRANSFER   CH. 8

On their Federal income tax returns for the taxable years 1957 and 1958, petitioners reported the amounts of $16,674.35 and $11,316.55, respectively, paid by Lockheed to McClain under the plan as capital gain. Petitioners commenced to report such payments as capital gain pursuant to the advice of their legal counsel.

From the inception of the plan in October of 1942, payments made by Lockheed to employees, including McClain, pursuant to the plan were paid by means of checks separate from checks issued for the salary paid to employees. Such payments made to employee-inventors who at the time of such payments were still employed by Lockheed were issued by the payroll department of Lockheed and carried the payroll code of "P" with the account number of the employee. Such payments made to employee-inventors who at the time of such payments were no longer employed by Lockheed were issued by the accounts payable department of Lockheed and did not carry the payroll code number.

From the inception of the plan, all withholding and employment taxes were deducted by Lockheed from the amount of all payments under the plan to employee-inventors who at the time of such payments continued to be employees of Lockheed, and all such payments were included on forms W-2 issued by Lockheed with respect to such employees.

No withholding or employment taxes were deducted by Lockheed from payments made pursuant to the plan to employee-inventors who at the time of such payments were no longer employed by Lockheed.

The amounts received by McClain from Lockheed in 1957 and 1958 pursuant to the plan were in consideration for the transfer of all substantial rights to patents.

Respondent determined that the amounts received by McClain in the years in question pursuant to the plan constitutes ordinary income under section 61 of the Internal Revenue Code, and he argues on brief that said amounts were in consideration of services rendered Lockheed by McClain, and therefore did not constitute consideration for the transfer of the patents.

The sole issue is whether the disputed payments are within section 1235, which provides in relevant part as follows:

SEC. 1235, SALE OR EXCHANGE OF PATENTS.

(a) GENERAL. — A transfer (other than by gift, inheritance, or devise) of property consisting of all substantial rights to a patent, or an undivided interest therein which includes a part of all such rights, by any holder shall be considered the sale or exchange of a capital asset held for more than 6 months, regardless of whether or not payments in consideration of such transfer are-

(1) payable periodically over a period generally coterminous with the transferee's use of the patent, or

(2) contingent on the productivity, use, or disposition of the property transferred.

(b) "HOLDER" DEFINED. — FOR purposes of this section, the term "holder" means-

(1) any individual whose efforts created such property, or . . . ..

The regulations provide that the question of whether payments to an employee are compensation for services, or are attributable to the transfer of patent rights, is one of fact. Respondent argues that the regulation is not applicable because the transfer in this case was fully supported by the consideration of petitioner's employment. Respondent concludes that petitioner had no remaining substantial rights to transfer and that consequently the disputed payments were simply additional salary.

We perceive no substantial differences between this case and Roland Chilton, 40 T.C. 552. The differences that do exist favor this petitioner, for Chilton was expressly hired to "render * * * engineering work relating to the improvement of existing types of aircraft engines * * * and to the development of new types * * * (and to) apply his experience and his inventive ability to the problems, improvements, and developments relating to the company's products * * *." Thus Chilton was far closer to having been hired to invent than this petitioner.

It is true that in Roland Chilton, supra, the employment contract provided for the royalty payments there in dispute, while here such contract is silent as to any payments over and above wages. But we regard this as a distinction without a difference. It is clear that petitioner was not hired to invent, and Lockheed, without quibble, paid him the amounts in dispute in full compliance with its successive patent plans. These amounts were not gifts, Commissioner v. Duberstein, 363 U.S. 278, and it is equally clear from the facts that they were not mere wages, but were attributable to the transfer of the patent rights and at least a part of the consideration for such transfer just as surely as the bonuses paid in Lucas v. Ox Fibre Brush Co., 281 U.S. 115, were additional compensation for services and deductible by the corporate payor.

Decision will be entered for the petitioner.

QUESTIONS

1. McClain was an employee of Lockheed and he signed an agreement with Lockheed which obligated him to assign any inventions he made during his employment and for six months after his employment terminated. Nonetheless, the court found that McClain was not an employee of Lockheed for purposes of § 1235. Why?

2. How did Lockheed's accounting for employee invention payments affect the outcome of the case? Did it matter that Lockheed deducted withholding and employment taxes from its payments to employee-inventors, and included all such payments on the employee's W-2 form?

3. Employers typically pay bonuses to employees for their patentable inventions. How are bonuses taxed? How can employers structure payments to employee-inventors to lessen the taxes on these payments?

INTERNAL REVENUE SERVICE TECHNICAL ADVICE MEMORANDUM
TAM 2002 49002, 2002 WL 31736299 (2002)

ISSUE(S):

Whether Taxpayer is entitled to capital gains treatment under § 1235 of the Internal Revenue Code for royalties received from University.

CONCLUSION:

Taxpayer is entitled to capital gains treatment under § 1235 for royalties received from University, which are in exchange for all substantial rights in the patent to Invention.

FACTS:

Taxpayer has been a professor at University since Date. University is part of the State University System. Taxpayer's responsibilities have involved teaching, conducting research, and administrative tasks in varying degrees, with between fifty and one hundred percent of Taxpayer's efforts devoted to research during any given academic term. Taxpayer receives a salary for Taxpayer's employment with University.

The collective bargaining agreement, to which Taxpayer is a party, incorporates State's Administrative Code provisions relating to inventions by University employees. The State Administrative Code provides, in part, that an invention which is made in the field or discipline in which the employee is employed by University, or by using University support, is the property of University and the employee shall share in the proceeds therefrom. It further directs the University Vice President to conduct an investigation which assesses the respective equities of the inventor and University in the invention, and determines its importance and the extent to which University should be involved in its protection, development and promotion. The Vice President will then inform the inventor of University's decision on whether or not to assert rights in the invention. If University wishes to own the invention, the division, between University and the inventor, of proceeds generated by the licensing or assignment of patent rights or trade secrets, will be set out in a written contract between University and the inventor. If University decides to not exercise its rights, the invention becomes the sole property of the employee.

In the course of Taxpayer's research, Taxpayer developed Invention. Taxpayer filed patent applications for Invention. Taxpayer then executed assignment agreements which assigned Taxpayer's interest in the patent applications to University. Taxpayer also entered into a royalty distribution agreement with University regarding Invention. The royalty agreement provided that Taxpayer would receive x percent of the first $y in royalties resulting from University's licensing of the patents, and z percent of royalties in excess of $yyyyy. University licensed the patents to Manufacturer, who has produced Invention for sale. Taxpayer's share of the royalties paid by Manufacturer for the years in question amounts to $a, $b and $c, respectively. University has treated these amounts as royalty payments, and not as part of Taxpayer's salary.

LAW AND ANALYSIS:

Section 1235(a) provides that a transfer (other than by gift, inheritance, or devise) of property consisting of all substantial rights to a patent, or an undivided interest therein which includes a part of all such rights, by any holder shall be considered the sale or exchange of a capital asset held for more than 1 year, regardless of whether or not payments in consideration of such transfer are — (1) payable periodically over a period generally coterminous with the transferee's use of the patent, or (2) contingent on the productivity, use, or disposition of the property transferred.

Section 1235(b) defines a "holder" as: (1) any individual whose efforts created such property, or (2) any other individual who has acquired his interest in such property in exchange for consideration in money or money's worth paid to such creator prior to actual reduction to practice of the invention covered by the patent, if such individual is neither — (A) the employer of such creator, nor (B) related to such creator (within the meaning of § 1235(d)).

Section 1.1235-1(c)(2) of the Income Tax Regulations provides that payments received by an employee as compensation for services rendered as an employee under an employment contract requiring the employee to transfer to the employer the rights to any invention by such employee are not attributable to a transfer to which § 1235 applies. However, whether payments received by an employee from his employer (under an employment contract or otherwise) are attributable to the transfer by the employee of all substantial rights to a patent (or an undivided interest therein) or are compensation for services rendered the employer by the employee is a question of fact. In determining which is the case, consideration shall be given not only to all the facts and circumstances of the employment relationship but also to whether the amount of such payments depends upon the production, sale, or use by, or the value to, the employer of the patent rights transferred by the employee. If it is determined that payments are attributable to the transfer of patent rights, and all other requirements under § 1235 are met, such payments shall be treated as proceeds derived from the sale of a patent.

Section 1.1235-2(a) states that the term "patent" means a patent granted under the provisions of Title 35 of the United States Code, or any foreign patent granting rights generally similar to those under a United States patent. It is not necessary that the patent or patent application for the invention be in existence if the requirements of § 1235 are otherwise met.

Initially, it appears that Taxpayer is entitled to § 1235 treatment. Section 1235(a) allows long term capital gains treatment for payments received for the transfer, by a holder, of all substantial rights to a patent. It is undisputed that Taxpayer qualifies as a holder under § 1235(b), as it was Taxpayer's efforts that created Invention. However, because Invention arose from Taxpayer's employment with University, the requirements of § 1.1235-1(c)(2) must be satisfied. All of the facts and circumstances of the employment relationship must be considered to determine whether payments to Taxpayer were compensation for services or payment for the transfer of Taxpayer's patent rights. Also, whether the amount of payments depends on the production, sale, use or value of the patent must be considered.

In *Chilton v. Commissioner*, the taxpayer was employed as an engineer, responsible for the design of aircraft engines. His employment contract stated that, if the taxpayer invented anything related to aircraft engines or accessories, "all said inventions and improvements shall belong to and be the sole and exclusive property of [employer] in and for all countries of the world." The taxpayer invented several things, many of which his employer selected to have assigned to it. The taxpayer patented these inventions, assigned them to his employer, and received various additional payments.. His employer treated these additional amounts as royalties, rather than including them in with the taxpayer's regular salary. The Tax Court rejected the Commissioner's argument that, because of the quoted language in the taxpayer's employment contract, the taxpayer never owned any substantial rights to transfer. Further, the taxpayer was not "hired to invent," because he was hired to apply his inventive ability, rather than to invent a specific product, and was therefore permitted to treat the royalty payments as long term capital gains under § 1235.

In *McClain v. Commissioner*, the taxpayer also was employed as a design engineer for an aircraft company. The taxpayer's employment contract contained similar language as in *Chilton* about inventions. The Tax Court found no substantial difference between *McClain* and *Chilton*, stating that the taxpayer had an even better claim under § 1235, because the taxpayer in *Chilton* had been hired to improve engine designs and develop new ones. In contrast, the Tax Court rejected the taxpayer's § 1235 argument in *Beausoleil v. Commissioner. Beausoleil* involved an invention incentive program, in which employee inventions earned points toward reward plateaus. The Tax Court found that there was no connection between the eventual achievement award money and the assignments of the rights to individual inventions. Further, the employer treated these awards as salary. The payments also bore no relation to the usefulness of the invention. The payments were given ordinary income treatment. The U.S. Court of Appeals for the Second Circuit, in applying these cases, also stressed that an important factor to consider in receiving § 1235 treatment is whether the payments would continue beyond the employment relationship, for the entire life of the patent.

The facts of Taxpayer's case are essentially equivalent to the facts of *Chilton* and *McClain*. Looking to the facts and circumstances of the employment relationship, the payments in question are connected to the transfer of the rights to Invention, rather than compensation for services. The compensation received for the rights to Invention are in addition to and separate from Taxpayer's salary, pursuant to a separate agreement with University. Taxpayer executed a separate assignment of rights document as well. University treats the payments as royalties, and not as salary. It appears that the right to continued receipt of these payments is not contingent on continued employment with University. The amount of the payments received by Taxpayer are dependent on the use or value of the licensing of the patent. The royalty agreement provides that the amount of the payment is a percentage of what University receives in royalties from its licensing of the patent.

The amount received varied substantially during the years in question.

There is a question of whether the provisions of the State Administrative Code pertaining to research at University preclude Taxpayer from ever having acquired any interest in Invention. If this were so, § 1235 treatment would be precluded, because Taxpayer would have no rights to transfer. The well established principle is that initial patent rights vest with the inventor. *See* 35 U.S.C. § 111. State contract and property law may govern with respect to determining who has acquired rights from the inventor, but it cannot supplant the creation of such rights under federal law. There is no dispute that University acquired a property interest in Invention from Taxpayer, but state statutes cannot operate to extinguish inventorship.

The provisions in the State Administrative Code should be read as having the same effect as similar contract provisions in the cases cited above. Any other reading would leave the statute preempted. This reading is consistent with the reading of the Administrative Code itself, which acts as a handbook of University policy. Because University is an organ of State, the policies of University have been codified, along with the policies of all the schools in the State university system. The State Administrative Code has been included in the collective bargaining agreement between University professors and University. The State Administrative Code sections themselves do not appear to attempt to abrogate the inventor's initial property rights. The provisions are contractual in nature, calling for the assignment of rights in order to share in the proceeds. University must exercise its rights if it wishes to take full ownership of a particular invention. In situations in which University decides not to obtain a particular invention, the employee may keep it. This reading is consistent with the submitted opinion of the University Office of General Counsel. Thus, even if state law could extinguish any possible rights an employee may acquire through creation of an invention, this statute does not do that.

It is of no concern that the transfer of rights to future inventions took place in the adoption of Taxpayer's employment contract. Section 1.1235-2(a) states that the patent need not be in existence at the time of the transfer for § 1235 to apply. In an analogous case regarding an independent contractor, the Tax Court explained the relating back concept. *See Gilson v. Commissioner*, T.C. Memo 1984-447 (1984). ". . . [T]he taxpayer's obligation from the outset to assign his invention to the other party does not render unavailable the benefits of section 1235 — it is unimportant whether the contract to assign is viewed as executory, so that no "transfer" occurs until formal assignment and payment, or whether the payment is viewed as relating back to the previous transfer of patent rights." *Id.* It is irrelevant for the purposes of § 1235 whether the substantial rights are viewed as having been transferred in the original employment contract, or in the later assignment document.

For the foregoing reasons, we conclude that Taxpayer is entitled to capital gains treatment under § 1235 for royalty payments received in exchange for all substantial rights to the patents for Invention.

CAVEAT(S)

A copy of this technical advice memorandum is to be given to the taxpayer(s). Section 6110(k)(3) of the Code provides that it may not be used or cited as precedent.

This document may not be used or cited as precedent. Section 6110(j)(3) of the Internal Revenue Code.

QUESTIONS

1.   Under the reasoning in the TAM, would a faculty member ever be considered as an employee hired to invent?

2.   Would it matter whether the faculty invention was made using federal funds, industry-sponsored research funds, or university funds?

3.   Why could the State Administrative Code not preclude a faculty member from ever having acquired title in an invention?

4.   Why is it irrelevant under § 1235 whether the transfer of all substantial rights in a patent occurs at the time of the original employment contract or at the time of an actual assignment agreement? Would this result also follow in the case of non-faculty inventor?

CASE NOTES

1.   Lee and Golner were employed as tool and die makers on the night shift at the A. O. Smith Corporation (Smith) in Milwaukee. Lee and Golner shared a mutual hobby of shotgun shooting and decided to make a shotgun reloading tool for their own use. After some experimentation, they invented the Lee Loader for Shotgun Shells (Lee Loader) which was simpler and less expensive than any competing device on the market. Lee and Golner filed a joint patent application on the invention and began selling the Lee Loader in 1958. They filed a partnership return in 1958 reporting net income in the amount of $3,479. In 1959, Lee was laid off from Smith and began working full time on the partnership which was now called Lee Custom Engineering (LCE). Lee and Golner terminated their partnership in May 1959 without a written termination agreement. Under the termination arrangement, the partnership profits to date were split between the two men, Golner gave Lee all of his rights in the patent application and Lee agreed to hold Golner harmless from any liability arising from the partnership business. They also agreed that if Lee went broke, he would owe Golner nothing, but if Lee "made it big," he would pay Golner "something." Lee continued to operate the business from 1959-1962 as a sole proprietorship, during which time sales grew from $26,000 to $98,000. In 1962, on the advice of his accountant, Lee decided to incorporate LCE. At this time, Golner had resigned from Smith and the men entered into a pre-incorporation agreement under which Lee would pay $2,500 for 250 shares of LCE stock (24%) and Golner would receive 190 shares of LCE stock (76%) in exchange for Golner's services to LCE. The pre-incorporation agreement also provided that Lee would assign LCE the exclusive right to manufacture, sell and

distribute the Lee Loader for the life of the patent in exchange for running royalty payments. The Lee Loader patent issued in September 1962. In his tax returns for 1963 and 1964, Lee reported his income from the license agreement as long term capital gains. After an audit, the IRS determined that the income was taxable as ordinary income and assessed Lee $34,500 in additional taxes and interest. Lee appealed the IRS determination. What result? *See* Lee v. United States, 302 F.Supp. 945 (E.D. Wis. 1969).

2. *See also* Eickmeyer v. Commissioner of Internal Revenue, 580 F.2d 395 (10th Cir. 1978) (The grant of 12 separate licenses to a patented process, each called an "exclusive license of an undivided interest in the patent," was, in fact, a grant of 12 non-exclusive licenses and royalties received from these licenses were not entitled to capital gains treatment under section 1235; the term "undivided interest" means a fractional interest in all of the rights of patent ownership, not the division of the rights of patent ownership); E.I. du Pont de Nemours and Co. v. United States, 432 F.2d 1052 (3rd Cir. 1970) (Retention of right to import U.S. manufactured nylon into Brazil as part of an agreement granting foreign company exclusive license to manufacture nylon in Brazil under licensor's Brazilian patents was not so substantial as to deny capital gains treatment of proceeds from license); Kueneman v. Commissioner of Internal Revenue, 628 F.2d 1196 (9th Cir. 1980) (Taxpayer failed to establish that license which was limited to a specific geographic area transferred substantially all rights to their patents that would entitle them to capital gains treatment of license proceeds; in order to qualify for capital gains treatment, patent owner must transfer right to make, use and sell the patented invention throughout the United States); Charlson v. United States, 525 F.2d 1046 (Ct. Cl. 1975) (Taxpayer's sale of patents to corporation formed by personal friends and business associates in exchange for corporation's promise to pay taxpayer 80% of all royalties did not disqualify royalties from capital gain treatment unless taxpayer was in reality conducting business affairs of corporation); Mros v. Commissioner of Internal Revenue, 493 F.2d 813 (9th Cir. 1974) (License of patent rights subject to a field of use restriction was not a transfer of substantially all patent owner rights and proceeds from license not entitled to capital gains treatment); Fawick v. Commissioner of Internal Revenue, 436 F.2d 655 (6th Cir. 1971) (Exclusive license for manufacture limited to marine service was not a transfer of substantially all patent owner rights and proceeds not entitled to capital gain treatment); Kirby v. United States, 297 F.2d 466, 5th Cir. 1961 (Exclusive license in which licensee was granted right to manufacture patented product for lease, and licensor retained right to manufacture patented product for sale, was not a transfer of substantially all of patent owner's rights).

Additional Information

1. Steven Z. Szczepanski, David M. Epstein, 2 Eckstrom's Licensing in For. & Dom. Ops. §§ 9:16–9:25 (2010).

2. Kathleen Quirsfeld, 4 Mertens Law of Fed. Income Tax'n 22C:05–22C:09 (2011).

3. 33A Am. Jur. 2d Federal Taxation ¶ 11052 (2011).

4. 47A C.J.S. Internal Revenue § 140 (2011).

5. William A. Drennan, *Changing Invention Economics by Encouraging Corporate Inventors to Sell Patents*, 58 U. Miami L. Rev. 1045 (2004).

6. William A. Drennan, *A Method of Analysis for the Unlikely Asked to Perform the Amazing: Determining "Patentability" Without a Patent Application Under Section*, 22 Va. Tax. Rev. 443 (2003).

7. Madelyn S. Cantor, *Tax Policy: Copyright and Patents*, 31 Vill. L. Rev. 931 (1986).

8. Note, *A Comparison of the Tax Treatment of Authors and Inventors*, 70 Harv. L. Rev. 1419 (1957).

Chapter 9

U.S. TECHNOLOGY EXPORT CONTROLS

The export of high technology from the United States is important for two conflicting reasons. First, high-technology exports are one of the few areas in which the United States enjoys a positive balance of trade. Second, high-technology exports pose threats to U.S. national security, foreign policy and global competitiveness. These conflicting priorities have resulted in a regulatory system of export controls that a recent Government Accounting Office report calls "inherently complex." This chapter considers "dual-use" technology export controls. Dual-use technologies are technologies that are primarily for civilian use, but can also be used for military purposes.

The first section of this chapter provides an overview of the U.S. export control system. This section explains how to use the Export Administration Regulations (EAR), how items controlled under the EAR are classified on the Commerce Control List (CCL), and how export license requirements and export license exceptions are determined. The second section considers "deemed exports." Deemed exports are communications to foreign nationals that are "deemed" to be exports of technologies to the foreign national's home country. The third section looks at two selected technology exports: encryption technologies and software programs. The final section provides a summary of recent cases which have been brought to enforce the EAR.

Before proceeding to consider controls on the export of dual-use technologies, it is helpful to put these dual-use controls in the context of the broader U.S. export control system.

There are three primary federal agencies involved in regulating exports from the United States: the Department of State, the Department of Commerce and the Treasury Department. The Department of State regulates the export of defense items through its Directorate of Defense Trade Controls. The governing statute for the export of defense items is the Arms Export Control Act, and the implementing regulations are the International Traffic in Arms Regulations (ITAR). The U.S. Munitions List (USML) specifies the defense items, services and technical data subject to export controls.

The Department of Commerce regulates the export of dual-use items through its Bureau of Industry and Security (BIS). The governing statute for the export of dual-use items is the Export Administration Act, and the implementing regulations are the Export Administration Regulations (EAR). The Commerce Control List (CCL) specifies the dual-use items, services and technologies subject to export control.

The Treasury Department administers trade sanctions and embargoes through its Office of Foreign Assets Control (OFAC). The OFAC requires companies to obtain a license prior to entering into financial transactions with any "target country" designated by the Treasury Department. There is no list of controlled transactions comparable to the USML and CCL. Instead, the Code of Federal Regulations contains provisions specifying sanctions against individual target countries or entities.

There are five federal agencies involved in enforcing export controls: Customs and Border Protection (CBP), Immigration and Customs Enforcement (ICE), the Federal Bureau of Investigation (FBI), and the U.S. Attorneys Office have responsibility for enforcing both the ITAR and EAR regulations. The Office of Export Enforcement (OEE) within Commerce's BIS also has responsibility for enforcing the EAR regulations. These federal agencies and the OEE sometimes cooperate in enforcement activities and sometimes do not.

Since 9/11, the enforcement of export regulations, and the severity of penalties, have increased dramatically. A former BIS official has stated that criminal convictions have quadrupled over the past five years and that civil enforcement activities have also increased significantly. The maximum criminal fine that can be levied on a company for violation of the EAR is $1M or five times the value of the illegal export; proposed changes would increase this to $5M or ten times the value of the illegal export. The maximum criminal penalty that can be levied on an individual for violation of the EAR is $250K and/or 10 years in prison; proposed changes would increase this to $1M. Civil fines for violation of the EAR range from $10K–$120K, and proposed changes would increase this to a maximum of $500K. Penalties for violation of the ITAR regulations are even more severe.

The majority of the readings in this chapter are contained in the Code of Federal Regulations (15 C.F.R. Parts 730–772). These readings have been obtained from the Department of Commerce's very useful BIS website — http://www.bis.doc.gov/. The summary of recent cases was also obtained from the BIS website.

9.1 OVERVIEW OF EXPORT CONTROL SYSTEM

The first reading in this section provides an overview of the scope of the EAR, the general prohibitions, license exceptions, record-keeping and reporting requirements. The following readings provide more detailed information on these subjects.

15 C.F.R. PART 732: STEPS FOR USING THE EAR

§ 732.1 STEPS OVERVIEW

(a) (1) Introduction

In this part, references to the EAR are references to 15 CFR chapter VII, subchapter C. This part is intended to help you determine your obligations under the EAR by listing logical steps in § 732.2 through § 732.5 of this part that you can take in reviewing these regulations. A flow chart describing these steps is contained in Supplement No. 1 to part 732. By cross-references to the relevant provisions of the EAR, this part describes the suggested steps for you to determine applicability of the following:

(i) The scope of the EAR (part 734 of the EAR);

(ii) Each of the general prohibitions (part 736 of the EAR);

(iii) The License Exceptions (part 740 of the EAR); and

(iv) Other requirements such as clearing your export with the U.S. Customs Service, keeping records, and completing and documenting license applications.

(2) These steps describe the organization of the EAR, the relationship among the provisions of the EAR, and the appropriate order for you to consider the various provisions of the EAR.

(b)   Facts about your transaction

The following five types of facts determine your obligations under the EAR and will be of help to you in reviewing these steps:

(1) What is it? What an item is, for export control purposes, depends on its *classification*, which is its place on the Commerce Control List (see part 774 of the EAR).

(2) Where is it going? The *country of ultimate destination* for an export or reexport also determines licensing requirements (see parts 738 and 774 of the EAR concerning the Country Chart and the Commerce Control List).

(3) Who will receive it? The *ultimate end-user* of your item cannot be a bad end-user. See General Prohibition Four (Denial Orders) in § 736.2(b)(4) and parts 744 and 764 of the EAR for a reference to the list of persons you may not deal with.

(4) What will they do with it? The *ultimate end-use* of your item cannot be a bad end-use. See General Prohibition Five (End-Use End-User) in § 736.2(b)(5) and part 744 of the EAR for general end-use and end-user restrictions.

(5) What else do they do? *Conduct* such as contracting, financing, and freight forwarding in support of a proliferation project (as described in § 744.6 of the EAR) may prevent you from dealing with someone.

(c)   Are your items and activities subject to the EAR?

You should first determine whether your commodity, software, or technology is subject to the EAR (see part 734 of the EAR concerning scope), and Steps 1 through 6 help you do that. For exports from the United States, only Steps 1 and 2 are relevant. If you already know that your item or activity is subject to the EAR, you should go on to consider the ten general prohibitions in part 736 of the EAR. If your item or activity is not subject to the EAR, you have no obligations under the EAR and may skip the remaining steps.

(d)   Does your item or activity require a license under one or more of the ten general prohibitions?

(1) Brief summary of the ten general prohibitions. The general prohibitions are found in part 736 of the EAR and referred to in these steps. They consist,

very briefly, of the following:

(i) General Prohibition One (Exports and Reexports): Export and reexport of controlled items to listed countries.

(ii) General Prohibition Two (Parts and Components Reexports): Reexport and export from abroad of foreign-made items incorporating more than a de minimis amount of controlled U.S. content.

(iii) General Prohibition Three (Foreign produced Direct Product Reexports): Reexport and export from abroad of the foreign-produced direct product of U.S. technology and software.

(iv) General Prohibition Four (Denial Orders): Engaging in actions prohibited by a denial order.

(v) General Prohibition Five (End-Use End-User): Export or reexport to prohibited end-user or end-users.

(vi) General Prohibition Six (Embargo): Export or reexport to embargoed destinations.

(vii) General Prohibition Seven (U.S. Person Proliferation Activity): Support of proliferation activities.

(viii) General Prohibition Eight (In-Transit): In-transit shipments and items to be unladen from vessels and aircraft.

(ix) General Prohibition Nine (Orders, Terms and Conditions): Violation of any orders, terms, or conditions.

(x) General Prohibition Ten (Knowledge Violation to Occur): Proceeding with transactions with knowledge that a violation has occurred or is about to occur.

(2) *Controls on items on the Commerce Control List (CCL)*. If your item or activity is subject to the EAR, you should determine whether any one or more of the ten general prohibitions require a license for your export, reexport, or activity. Steps 7 through 11 refer to classification of your item on the Commerce Control List (CCL) (part 774 of the EAR) and how to use the Country Chart (Supplement No. 1 to part 738 of the EAR) to determine whether a license is required based upon the classification of your item. These steps refer to General Prohibitions One (Exports and Reexports), Two (Parts and Components Reexports), and Three (Foreign-Produced Direct Product Reexports) for all countries except: Cuba, Iran, and North Korea. For these countries, you may skip Steps 7 through 11 and go directly to Step 12.

(3) *Controls on activities*. Steps 12 through 18 refer to General Prohibitions Four through Ten. Those general prohibitions apply to all items subject to the EAR, not merely those items listed on the CCL in part 774 of the EAR. For example, they refer to the general prohibitions for persons denied export privileges, prohibited end-uses and end-users, countries subject to a comprehensive embargo (e.g., Cuba, Iran, and North Korea), prohibited activities of U.S. persons in support of proliferation of weapons of mass destruction,

prohibited unlading of shipments, compliance with orders, terms and conditions, and activities when a violation has occurred or is about to occur.

(4) *General prohibitions*. If none of the ten general prohibitions applies, you should skip the steps concerning License Exceptions and for exports from the United States, review Steps 27 through 29 concerning Shipper's Export Declarations to be filed with the U.S. Customs Service, Destination Control Statements for export control documents, and recordkeeping requirements.

(e) Is a License Exception available to overcome the license requirement?

If you decide by reviewing the CCL in combination with the Country Chart that a license is required for your destination, you should determine whether a License Exception will except you from that requirement. Steps 20 through 24 help you determine whether a License Exception is available. Note that generally License Exceptions are not available to overcome General Prohibitions Four through Ten. However, selected License Exceptions for embargoed destinations are specified in part 746 of the EAR and License Exceptions for short supply controls are specified in part 754 of the EAR. If a License Exception is available and the export is from the United States, you should review Steps 26 through 28 concerning Shipper's Export Declarations to be filed with the U.S. Customs Service, Destination Control Statements for export control documents and recordkeeping requirements. If a License Exception is not available, go on to Steps 25 through 29.

(f) How do you apply for a license?

If you must file a license application, you should review the requirements of part 748 of the EAR as suggested by Step 26. Then you should review Steps 27 through 29 concerning Shipper's Export Declarations to be filed with the U.S. Customs Service, Destination Control Statements for export control documents, and record keeping requirements.

§ 732.2 STEPS REGARDING SCOPE OF THE EAR

Steps 1 through 6 are designed to aid you in determining the scope of the EAR. A flow chart describing these Steps is contained in Supplement No. 2 to part 732.

(a) Step 1: Items subject to the exclusive jurisdiction of another Federal agency

This step is relevant for both exports and reexports. Determine whether your item is subject to the exclusive jurisdiction of another Federal Agency as provided in § 734.3 of the EAR.

(1) If your item is subject to the exclusive jurisdiction of another federal agency, comply with the regulations of that agency. You need not comply with the EAR and may skip the remaining steps.

(2) If your item is not subject to the exclusive jurisdiction of another federal agency, then proceed to Step 2 in paragraph (b) of this section.

(b) Step 2: Publicly available technology and software

This step is relevant for both exports and reexports. Determine if your technology or software is publicly available as defined and explained at part 734 of the EAR. Supplement No. 1 to part 734 of the EAR contains several practical examples describing publicly available technology and software that are outside the scope of the EAR. The examples are illustrative, not comprehensive. Note that encryption software controlled for EI reasons under ECCN 5D002 on the Commerce Control List (refer to Supplement No.1 to Part 774 of the EAR) and mass market encryption software with symmetric key length exceeding 64-bits classified under ECCN 5D992 shall be subject to the EAR even if publicly available. Accordingly, the provisions of the EAR concerning the public availability of items are not applicable to encryption items controlled for "EI" reasons under ECCN 5D002 and mass market encryption software with symmetric key length exceeding 64-bits classified under ECCN 5D992.

(1) If your technology or software is publicly available, and therefore outside the scope of the EAR, you may proceed with the export or reexport if you are not a U.S. person subject to General Prohibition Seven. If you are a U.S. person, go to Step 15 at § 732.3(j) of this part. If you are a U.S. person and General Prohibition Seven concerning proliferation activity of U.S. persons does not apply, then you may proceed with the export or reexport of your publicly available technology or software. Note that all U.S. persons are subject to the provisions of General Prohibition Seven.

(2) If your technology or software is not publicly available and you are exporting from the United States, skip to the Step 7 in § 732.3(b) of this part concerning the general prohibitions.

(3) If you are exporting items from a foreign country, you should then proceed Step 3 in paragraph (c) of this section and the other steps concerning the scope of the EAR.

(c) Step 3: Reexport of U.S.-origin items

This step is appropriate only for reexporters. For an item in a foreign country, you should determine whether the item is of U.S.-origin. If it is of U.S.-origin, skip to Step 7 in § 732.3(b) of this part. If it is not of U.S.-origin, then proceed to Step 4 in paragraph (d) of this section.

(d) Step 4: Foreign-made items incorporating controlled U.S.-origin items

This step is appropriate only for items that are made outside the United States and not currently located in the United States. Special requirements and restrictions apply to foreign-made items that incorporate U.S.-origin encryption items (see § 734.4(a)(2), (b), and (g) of the EAR).

(1) Determining whether your foreign made item is subject to the EAR. Using the guidance provided in Supplement No. 2 to part 734 of the EAR, determine whether controlled U.S.-origin items are incorporated into the foreign-made item and are above the *de minimis* level set forth in § 734.4 of the EAR

(2) If no U.S.-origin controlled items are incorporated or if the percentage of incorporated U.S.-origin controlled items are equal to or below the *de minimis* level described in § 734.4 of the EAR, then the foreign-made item is not subject to the EAR by reason of the *de minimis* rules, and you should go on to consider Step 6 regarding the foreign-produced direct product rule.

(3) If the foreign-made item incorporates more than the *de minimis* level of U.S.-origin items, then that item is subject to the EAR and you should skip to Step 7 at § 732.3 of this part and consider the steps regarding all other general prohibitions, license exceptions, and other requirements to determine applicability of these provisions to the foreign-made item.

(e) **[RESERVED]**

(f) Step 6: Foreign-made items produced with certain U.S. technology for export to specified destinations

This step is appropriate for foreign-made items in foreign countries.

(1) If your foreign-produced item is described in an entry on the CCL and the Country Chart requires a license to your export or reexport destination for national security reasons, you should determine whether your item is subject to General Prohibition Three (Foreign-Produced Direct Product Reexports) (§ 736.2(b)(3) of the EAR). Your item is subject to the EAR if it is captured by General Prohibition Three (Foreign-Produced Direct Product Reexports), and that prohibition applies if your transaction meets each of the following conditions:

(i) *Country scope of prohibition.* Your export or reexport destination for the direct product is Cuba or a destination in Country Group D:1 (see Supplement No. 1 to part 740 of the EAR) (reexports of foreign-produced direct products exported to other destinations are not subject to General Prohibition Three);

(ii) *Scope of technology or software used to create direct products subject to the prohibition.* Technology or software that was used to create the foreign-produced direct product, and such technology or software that was subject to the EAR and required a written assurance as a supporting document for a license or as a precondition for the use of License Exception TSR in § 740.6 of the EAR (reexports of foreign-produced direct products created with other technology and software are not subject to General Prohibition Three); and

(iii) *Scope of direct products subject to the prohibition.* The foreign-produced direct products are subject to national security controls as designated on the proper ECCN of the Commerce Control List in part 774 of the EAR (reexports of foreign-produced direct products not subject to national security controls are not subject to General Prohibition Three).

(2) ***License Exceptions.*** Each License Exception described in part 740 of the EAR overcomes this General Prohibition Three if all terms and

conditions of a given License Exception are met by the exporter or reexporter.

(3) **_Subject to the EAR_**. If your item is captured by the foreign-produced direct product control at General Prohibition Three, then your export from abroad is subject to the EAR. You should next consider the steps regarding all other general prohibitions, License Exceptions, and other requirements. If your item is not captured by General Prohibition Three, then your export from abroad is not subject to the EAR. You have completed the steps necessary to determine whether your transaction is subject to the EAR, and you may skip the remaining steps. Note that in summary, items in foreign countries are subject to the EAR when they are:

(i) U.S.-origin commodities, software and technology unless controlled for export exclusively by another Federal agency or unless publicly available;

(ii) Foreign-origin commodities, software, and technology that are within the scope of General Prohibition Two (Parts and Components Reexports), or General Prohibition Three (Foreign-Produced Direct Product Reexports). (However, such foreign-made items are also outside the scope of the EAR if they are controlled for export exclusively by another Federal Agency or publicly available.)

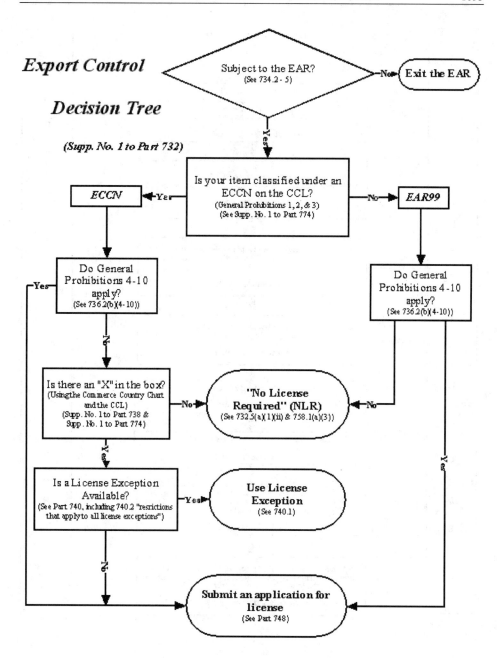

Export Control

Decision Tree

(Supp. No. 1 to Part 732)

Subject to the EAR?
(See 734.2 - 5)

No → Exit the EAR

Yes

Is your item classified under an ECCN on the CCL?
(General Prohibitions 1, 2, & 3)
(See Supp. No. 1 to Part 774)

Yes → *ECCN*

No → *EAR99*

Do General Prohibitions 4-10 apply?
(See 736.2(b)(4-10))

Do General Prohibitions 4-10 apply?
(See 736.2(b)(4-10))

Yes

No

Is there an "X" in the box?
(Using the Commerce Country Chart and the CCL)
(Supp. No. 1 to Part 738 & Supp. No. 1 to Part 774)

No → **"No License Required" (NLR)**
(See 732.5(a)(1)(ii) & 758.1(a)(3))

No

Yes

Is a License Exception Available?
(See Part 740, including 740.2 "restrictions that apply to all license exceptions")

Yes → **Use License Exception**
(See 740.1)

No

Yes

Submit an application for license
(See Part 748)

Subject to the EAR?

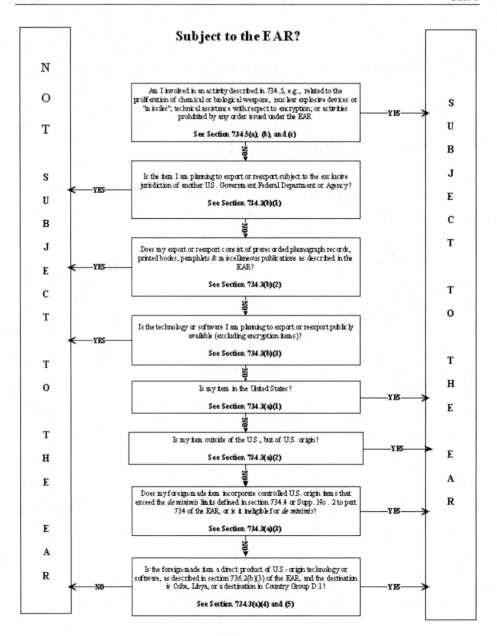

NOT SUBJECT TO THE EAR

Am I involved in an activity described in 734.5, e.g., related to the proliferation of chemical or biological weapons, nuclear explosive devices or "missiles"; technical assistance with respect to encryption; or activities prohibited by any order issued under the EAR

See Section 734.5(a), (b), and (c) — YES →

Is the item I am planning to export or reexport subject to the exclusive jurisdiction of another U.S. Government Federal Department or Agency?

See Section 734.3(b)(1) — ← YES

Does my export or reexport consist of prerecorded phonograph records, printed books, pamphlets & miscellaneous publications as described in the EAR?

See Section 734.3(b)(2) — ← YES

Is the technology or software I am planning to export or reexport publicly available (excluding encryption items)?

See Section 734.3(b)(3) — ← YES

Is my item in the United States?

See Section 734.3(a)(1) — YES →

Is my item outside of the US., but of U.S. origin?

See Section 734.3(a)(2) — YES →

Does my foreign-made item incorporate controlled U.S. origin items that exceed the *de minimis* limits defined in section 734.4 or Supp. No . 2 to part 734 of the EAR, or is it ineligible for *de minimis*?

See Section 734.3(a)(3) — YES →

Is the foreign-made item a direct product of U.S.-origin technology or software, as described in section 736.2(b)(3) of the EAR, and the destination is Cuba, Libya, or a destination in Country Group D:1?

See Section 734.3(a)(4) and (5) — ← NO — YES →

SUBJECT TO THE EAR

QUESTIONS

1.　How do General Prohibitions One, Two and Three differ from General Prohibitions Four through Ten? Do you think this difference may affect the availability of license exceptions?

2.　What items are not subject to the EAR? Why are these items not subject to the EAR?

The next reading provides more detailed information on the ten General Prohibitions.

15 C.F.R. PART 736 — GENERAL PROHIBITIONS

§ 736.1　INTRODUCTION

In this part, references to the EAR are references to 15 CFR chapter VII, subchapter C. A person may undertake transactions subject to the EAR without a license or other authorization, unless the regulations affirmatively state such a requirement. As such, if an export, reexport, or activity is subject to the EAR, the general prohibitions contained in this part and the License Exceptions specified in part 740 of the EAR must be reviewed to determine if a license is necessary. In the case of all exports from the United States, you must document your export as described in part 762 of the EAR regarding recordkeeping and clear your export through the U.S. Customs Service as described in part 758 of the EAR regarding export clearance requirements. Also note that for short supply controls all prohibitions and License Exceptions are in part 754 of the EAR.

(a) In this part we tell you:

(1) The facts that make your proposed export, reexport, or conduct subject to these general prohibitions, and

(2) The ten general prohibitions.

(b) Your obligations under the ten general prohibitions and under the EAR depend in large part upon the five types of information described in § 736.2(a) of this part and upon the general prohibitions described in § 736.2(b) of this part. The ten general prohibitions contain cross-references to other parts of the EAR that further define the breadth of the general prohibitions. For that reason, this part is not freestanding. In part 732, we provide certain steps you may follow in proper order to help you understand the general prohibitions and their relationship to other parts of the EAR.

(c) If you violate any of these ten general prohibitions, or engage in other conduct contrary to the Export Administration Act, the EAR, or any order, license, License Exception, or authorization issued thereunder, as described in part 764 of the EAR regarding enforcement, you will be subject to the sanctions described in that part.

§ 736.2   GENERAL PROHIBITIONS AND DETERMINATION OF APPLICABILITY

(a)   Information or facts that determine the applicability of the general prohibitions

The following five types of facts determine your obligations under the ten general prohibitions and the EAR generally:

(1)   Classification of the item. The classification of the item on the Commerce Control List (see part 774 of the EAR);

(2)   Destination. The country of ultimate destination for an export or reexport (see parts 738 and 774 of the EAR concerning the Country Chart and the Commerce Control List);

(3)   End-user. The ultimate end user (see General Prohibition Four (paragraph (b)(4) of this section) and Supplement No. 1 to part 764 of the EAR for references to persons with whom your transaction may not be permitted; see General Prohibition Five (Paragraph (b)(5) of this section) and part 744 for references to end-users for whom you may need an export or reexport license).

(4)   End-use. The ultimate end-use (see General Prohibition Five (paragraph (b)(5) of this section) and part 744 of the EAR for general end-use restrictions); and

(5)   Conduct. Conduct such as contracting, financing, and freight forwarding in support of a proliferation project as described in part 744 of the EAR.

(b)   General prohibitions

The following ten general prohibitions describe certain exports, reexports, and other conduct, subject to the scope of the EAR, in which you may not engage unless you either have a license from the Bureau of Industry and Security (BIS) or qualify under part 740 of the EAR for a License Exception from each applicable general prohibition paragraph. The License Exceptions at part 740 of the EAR apply only to General Prohibitions One (Exports and Reexports in the Form Received), Two (Parts and Components Reexports), and Three (Foreign-Produced Direct Product Reexports); however, selected License Exceptions are specifically referenced and authorized in part 746 of the EAR concerning embargo destinations and in § 744.2(c) of the EAR regarding nuclear end-uses.

(1) General Prohibition One — Export and reexport of controlled items to listed countries (Exports and Reexports). You may not, without a license or License Exception, export any item subject to the EAR to another country or reexport any item of U.S.-origin if each of the following is true:

(i) The item is controlled for a reason indicated in the applicable Export Control Classification Number (ECCN), and

(ii) Export to the country of destination requires a license for the control reason as indicated on the Country Chart at part 738 of the EAR. (The scope of this prohibition is determined by the correct classification of your item and the ultimate destination as that combination is reflected on the Country Chart). Note that each License Exception described at part 740 of the EAR supersedes General Prohibition One if all terms and conditions of a given License Exception are met by the exporter or reexporter.

(2) General Prohibition Two — Reexport and export from abroad of foreign-made items incorporating more than a *de minimis* amount of controlled U.S. content (U.S. Content Reexports).

(i) You may not, without a license or license exception, reexport or export from abroad foreign-made commodities that incorporate controlled U.S.-origin commodities, foreign-made commodities that are "bundled" with controlled U.S.-origin software, foreign-made software that is commingled with controlled U.S.-origin software, or foreign-made technology that is commingled with controlled U.S.-origin technology if such items require a license according to any of the provisions in the EAR and incorporate or are commingled with more than a *de minimis* amount of controlled U.S. content, as defined in § 734.4 of the EAR concerning the scope of the EAR.

(A) It incorporates more than the *de minimis* amount of controlled U.S. content, as defined in § 734.4 of the EAR concerning the scope of the EAR;

(B) It is controlled for a reason indicated in the applicable ECCN; and

(C) Its export to the country of destination requires a license for that control reason as indicated on the Country Chart. (The scope of this prohibition is determined by the correct classification of your foreign-made item and the ultimate destination, as that combination is reflected on the Country Chart.)

(3) General Prohibition Three — Reexport and export from abroad of the foreign-produced direct product of U.S. technology and software (Foreign-Produced Direct Product Reexports).

(i) *Country scope of prohibition.* You may not, without a license or License Exception, reexport, or export from abroad items subject to the scope of this General Prohibition Three to Cuba, or a destination in Country Group D.

(ii) *Product scope of foreign-made items subject to prohibition.* This General Prohibition 3 applies if an item meets either the Conditions defining the direct product of technology or the Conditions defining the direct product of a plant in paragraph (b)(3)(ii)(A) of this section:

(A) *Conditions defining direct product of technology.* Foreign-made items are subject to this General Prohibition 3 if they meet both of the following conditions:

(1) They are the direct product of technology or software that requires a written assurance as a supporting document for a license, as defined in paragraph (o)(3)(i) of Supplement No. 2 to part 748 of the EAR, or as a precondition for the use of License Exception TSR at § 740.6 of the EAR, and

(2) They are subject to national security controls as designated on the applicable ECCN of the Commerce Control List at part 774 of the EAR.

(B) *Conditions defining direct product of a plant.* Foreign-made items are also subject to this General Prohibition 3 if they are the direct product of a complete plant or any major component of a plant if both of the following conditions are met:

(1) Such plant or component is the direct product of technology that requires a written assurance as a supporting document for a license or as a precondition for the use of License Exception TSR at § 740.6 of the EAR, and

(2) Such foreign-made direct products of the plant or component are subject to national security controls as designated on the applicable ECCN of the Commerce Control List at part 774 of the EAR.

(iii) *License Exceptions.* Each License Exception described at part 740 of the EAR supersedes this General Prohibition Three if all terms and conditions of a given exception are met by the exporter or reexporter.

(4) General Prohibition Four (Denial Orders) — Engaging in actions prohibited by a denial order.

(i) You may not take any action that is prohibited by a denial order issued under part 766 of the EAR, Administrative Enforcement Proceedings. These orders prohibit many actions in addition to direct exports by the person denied export privileges, including some transfers within a single country, either in the United States or abroad, by other persons. You are responsible for ensuring that any of your transactions in which a person who is denied export privileges is involved do not violate the terms of the order. Orders denying export privileges are published in the *Federal Register* when they are issued and are the legally controlling documents in accordance with their terms. BIS also maintains compilations of persons denied export privileges on its Web site at *http://www.bis.doc.gov.* BIS may, on an exceptional basis, authorize activity otherwise prohibited by a denial order. See Sec. 764.3(a)(2) of the EAR.

(ii) There are no License Exceptions described in part 740 of the EAR that authorize conduct prohibited by this General Prohibition Four.

(5) General Prohibition Five — Export or reexport to prohibited end-uses or end-users (End-Use End-User).

You may not, without a license, knowingly export or reexport any item subject to the EAR to an end-user or end-use that is prohibited by part 744 of the EAR.

(6) General Prohibition Six — Export or reexport to embargoed destinations (Embargo).

(i) You may not, without a license or License Exception authorized under part 746, export or reexport any item subject to the EAR to a country that is embargoed by the United States or otherwise made subject to controls as both are described at part 746 of the EAR.

(ii) License Exceptions to General Prohibition Six are described in part 746 of the EAR, on Embargoes and Other Special Controls. Unless a License Exception or other authorization is authorized in part 746 of the EAR, the License Exceptions described in part 740 of the EAR are not available to overcome this general prohibition.

(7) General Prohibition Seven — Support of Proliferation Activities (U.S. Person Proliferation Activity).

(i) *Support of Proliferation Activities (U.S. Person Proliferation Activity).*

(A) If you are a U.S. person as that term is defined in § 744.6(c) of the EAR, you may not engage in any activities prohibited by § 744.6(a) or (b) of the EAR, which prohibits the performance, without a license from BIS, of certain financing, contracting, service, support, transportation, freight forwarding, or employment that you know will assist in certain proliferation activities described further in part 744 of the EAR. There are no License Exceptions to this General Prohibition Seven in part 740 of the EAR unless specifically authorized in that part.

(B) If you are a U.S. person as that term is defined in § 744.6(c) of the EAR, you may not export a Schedule 1 chemical listed in Supplement No. 1 to part 745 without first complying with the provisions of §§ 742.18 and 745.1 of the EAR.

(C) If you are a U.S. person as that term is defined in § 744.6(c) of the EAR, you may not export a Schedule 3 chemical listed in Supplement No. 1 to part 745 to a destination *not* listed in Supplement No. 2 to part 745 without complying with the End-Use Certificate requirements in § 745.2 of the EAR that apply to Schedule 3 chemicals controlled for CW reasons in ECCN 1C350, ECCN 1C355, and ECCN 1C395.

(8) General Prohibition Eight — In transit shipments and items to be unladen from vessels or aircraft (Intransit).

(i) *Unlading and shipping in transit.* You may not export or reexport an item through or transit through a country listed in paragraph (b)(8)(ii) of this section unless a License Exception or license authorizes such an export or reexport directly to such a country of transit, or unless such an export or reexport is eligible to such a country of transit without a license.

(ii) *Country scope.* This General Prohibition Eight applies to Armenia, Azerbaijan, Belarus, Cambodia, Cuba, Georgia, Kazakhstan, Kyrgyzstan, Laos, Mongolia, North Korea, Russia, Tajikistan, Turkmenistan, Ukraine, Uzbekistan, Vietnam.

(9) General Prohibition Nine — Violation of any order, terms, and conditions (Orders, Terms, and Conditions).

You may not violate terms or conditions of a license or of a License Exception issued under or made a part of the EAR, and you may not violate any order issued under or made a part of the EAR. There are no License Exceptions to this General Prohibition Nine in part 740 of the EAR.

(10) **General Prohibition Ten** — Proceeding with transactions with knowledge that a violation has occurred or is about to occur (Knowledge Violation to Occur).

You may not sell, transfer, export, reexport, finance, order, buy, remove, conceal, store, use, loan, dispose of, transport, forward, or otherwise service, in whole or in part, any item subject to the EAR and exported or to be exported with knowledge that a violation of the Export Administration Regulations, the Export Administration Act or any order, license, License Exception, or other authorization issued thereunder has occurred, is about to occur, or is intended to occur in connection with the item. Nor may you rely upon any license or License Exception after notice to you of the suspension or revocation of that license or exception. There are no License Exceptions to this General Prohibition Ten in part 740 of the EAR.

QUESTIONS

1. What is a reexport?

2. What facts determine the applicability of General Prohibition One?

3. What is a U.S. content reexport?

4. What is a foreign-produced direct product reexport?

5. What is the concern underlying General Prohibition Eight?

6. What are the license exceptions to General Prohibition Ten?

The next reading explains the relationship between the Commerce Control List and the Country Chart.

15 C.F.R. PART 738 — COMMERCE CONTROL LIST OVERVIEW AND THE COUNTRY CHART

§ 738.1   INTRODUCTION

(a)   *Commerce Control List scope*

(1) In this part, references to the EAR are references to 15 CFR chapter VII, subchapter C. The Bureau of Industry and Security (BIS) maintains the Commerce Control List (CCL) within the Export Administration Regulations (EAR), which includes items (i.e., commodities, software, and technology) subject to the export licensing authority of BIS. The CCL does not include those items exclusively controlled for export or reexport by another department or agency of the U.S. Government. In instances where agencies other than the Department of Commerce administer controls over related items, entries in the CCL contain a reference to these controls.

(2) The CCL is contained in Supplement No. 1 to part 774 of the EAR. Supplement No. 2 to part 774 of the EAR contains the General Technology and Software Notes relevant to entries contained in the CCL.

(b)   Commerce Country Chart scope

BIS also maintains the Commerce Country Chart. The Commerce Country Chart, located in Supplement No. 1 to part 738, contains licensing requirements based on destination and Reason for Control. In combination with the CCL, the Commerce Country Chart allows you to determine whether a license is required for items on the CCL to any country in the world.

§ 738.2   COMMERCE CONTROL LIST (CCL) STRUCTURE

(a)   Categories

The CCL is divided into 10 categories, numbered as follows:

0-Nuclear Materials, Facilities and Equipment and Miscellaneous

1-Materials, Chemicals, "Microorganisms," and Toxins

2-Materials Processing

3-Electronics

4-Computers

5-Telecommunications and Information Security

6-Lasers and Sensors

7-Navigation and Avionics

8-Marine

9-Propulsion Systems, Space Vehicles and Related Equipment

(b)   Groups

Within each category, items are arranged by group. Each category contains the same five groups. Each Group is identified by the letters A through E, as follows:

A-Equipment, Assemblies and Components

B-Test, Inspection and Production Equipment

C-Materials D-Software E-Technology

D-Software

E-Technology

(c)   Order of review

In order to classify your item against the CCL, you should begin with a review of the general characteristics of your item. This will usually guide you to the appropriate category on the CCL. Once the appropriate category is identified, you should match the particular characteristics and functions of your item to a specific ECCN. If the ECCN contains a list under the "*Items*" heading, you should review the list to determine within which subparagraph(s) your items are identified.

(d)   Entries

(1)   **Composition of an entry.** Within each group, individual items are identified by an Export Control Classification Number (ECCN). Each number

consists of a set of digits and a letter. The first digit identifies the general category within which the entry falls (e.g., *3* A001). The letter immediately following this first digit identifies under which of the five groups the item is listed (e.g., 3 *A* 001). The second digit differentiates individual entries by identifying the type of controls associated with the items contained in the entry (e.g., 3A *0* 01). Listed below are the Reasons for Control associated with this second digit.

0: National Security reasons (including Dual Use and Wassenaar Arrangement Munitions List) and Items on the NSG Dual Use Annex and Trigger List

1: Missile Technology reasons

2: Nuclear Nonproliferation reasons

3: Chemical & Biological Weapons reasons

9: Anti-terrorism, Crime Control, Regional Stability, Short Supply, UN Sanctions, etc.

(i) Since Reasons for Control are not mutually exclusive, numbers are assigned in order of precedence. As an example, if an item is controlled for both National Security and Missile Technology reasons, the entry's third digit will be a "0." If the item is controlled only for Missile Technology the third digit will be "1."

(ii) The numbers in either the second or third digit (e.g., 3A *00* 1) serve to differentiate between multilateral and unilateral entries. An entry with the number "9" as the second digit, identifies the entire entry as controlled for a unilateral concern (e.g., 2B991 for anti-terrorism reasons). If the number "9" appears as the third digit, the item is controlled for unilateral purposes based on a proliferation concern (e.g., 2A292 is controlled for unilateral purposes based on nuclear nonproliferation concerns).

(iii) The last digit within each entry (e.g., 3A00*1*) is used for the sequential numbering of ECCNs to differentiate between entries on the CCL.

(2) Reading an ECCN. A brief description is provided next to each ECCN. Following this description is the actual entry containing "License Requirements," "License Exceptions," and "List of Items Controlled" sections. A brief description of each section and its use follows:

(i) *License Requirements*. This section contains a separate line identifying of all possible Reasons for Control in order of precedence, and two columns entitled "Control(s)" and "Country Chart."

(A) The "Controls" header identifies all applicable Reasons for Control, in order of restrictiveness, and to what extent each applies (e.g., to the entire entry or only to certain subparagraphs). Those requiring licenses for a larger number of countries and/or items are listed first. As you read down the list, the number of countries and/or items requiring a license declines. Since Reasons for Control are not mutually exclusive, items controlled within a particular ECCN may be controlled for more than one reason. The following is a list of all possible Reasons for Control:

AT-Anti-Terrorism

CB-Chemical & Biological Weapons

CC-Crime Control

CW-Chemical Weapons Convention

EI-Encryption Items

FC-Firearms Convention

MT-Missile Technology

NS-National Security

NP-Nuclear Nonproliferation

RS-Regional Stability

SS-Short Supply

UN-United Nations Embargo

SI-Significant Items

SL-Surreptitious Listening

(B) The "Country Chart" header identifies, for each applicable Reason for Control, a column name and number (e.g., CB Column 1). These column identifiers are used to direct you from the CCL to the appropriate column identifying the countries requiring a license. Consult part 742 of the EAR for an in-depth discussion of the licensing requirements and policies applicable to each Country Chart column.

(ii) *License Exceptions*. This section provides a brief eligibility statement for each ECCN-driven License Exception that may be applicable to your transaction, and should be consulted only AFTER you have determined a license is required based on an analysis of the entry and the Country Chart. The brief eligibility statement in this section is provided to assist you in deciding which ECCN-driven License Exception related to your particular item and destination you should explore prior to submitting an application. The term "Yes" (followed in some instances by the scope of Yes) appears next to each available ECCN-driven License Exception. The term "N/A" will be noted for License Exceptions that are not available within a particular entry. If one or more License Exceptions appear to apply to your transaction, you must consult part 740 of the EAR to review the conditions and restrictions applicable to each available License Exception. The list of License Exceptions contained within each ECCN is not an all-exclusive list. Other License Exceptions, not based on particular ECCNs, may be available. Consult part 740 of the EAR to determine eligibility for non-ECCN-driven License Exceptions.

(iii)   List of Items Controlled.

(A) *Units*. The unit of measure applicable to each entry is identified in the "Units" header. Most measurements used in the CCL are expressed in metric units with an inch-pound conversion where appropriate. Note that in some ECCNs the inch-pound unit will be listed first.

In instances where other units are in general usage or specified by law, these will be used instead of metric. Generally, when there is a difference between the metric and inch-pound figures, the metric standard will be used for classification and licensing purposes.

(B) *Related definitions*. This header identifies, where appropriate, definitions or parameters that apply to all items controlled by the entry. The information provided in this section is unique to the entry, and hence not listed in the definitions contained in part 772 of the EAR.

(C) *Related controls*. If another U.S. government agency or department has export licensing authority over items related to those controlled by an entry, a statement is included identifying the agency or department along with the applicable regulatory cite. An additional cross-reference may be included in instances where the scope of controls differs between a CCL entry and its corresponding entry on list maintained by the European Union. This information is provided to assist readers who use both lists.

(D) *Items*. This header contains a positive list of all items controlled by a particular entry and must be reviewed to determine whether your item is controlled by that entry. In some entries, the list is contained within the entry heading. In these entries a note is included to direct you to the entry heading.

§ 738.3　COMMERCE COUNTRY CHART STRUCTURE

(a)　Scope

The Commerce Country Chart allows you to determine the Commerce Control List (CCL) export and reexport license requirements for most items listed on the CCL. Such license requirements are based on the Reasons for Control listed in the Export Control Classification Number (ECCN) that applies to the item. Some ECCNs, however, impose license requirements either without reference to a reason for control code that is listed on the Commerce Country Chart, or in addition to such a reference. Those ECCNs may state their license requirements in full in their "Reasons for Control" sections or they may refer the reader to another provision of the EAR for license requirement information. In addition, some ECCNs do not impose license requirements, but refer the reader to the regulations of another government agency that may impose license requirements on the items described in that ECCN.

(1) ECCNs 0A983, 5A980, 5D980, and 5E980. A license is required for all destinations for items controlled under these entries. For items controlled by 0A983 and 5E980, no License Exceptions apply. For items controlled by 5A980 and 5D980, License Exception GOV may apply if your item is consigned to and for the official use of an agency of the U.S. Government (see § 740.2(a)(3)). If your item is controlled by 0A983, 5A980, 5D980, or 5E980 you should proceed directly to part 748 of the EAR for license application instructions and § 742.11 or § 742.13 of the EAR for information on the licensing policy relevant to these types of applications.

(2)   [RESERVED]

(b)   Countries

The first column of the Country Chart lists all countries in alphabetical order. There are a number of destinations that are not listed in the Country Chart contained in Supplement No. 1 to part 738. If your destination is not listed on the Country Chart and such destination is a territory, possession, or department of a country included on the Country Chart, the EAR accords your destination the same licensing treatment as the country of which it is a territory, possession, or department. For example, if your destination is the Cayman Islands, a dependent territory of the United Kingdom, consult the United Kingdom on the Country Chart for licensing requirements.

(c)   Columns

Stretching out to the right are horizontal headers identifying the various Reasons for Control. Under each Reason for Control header are diagonal column identifiers capping individual columns. Each column identifier consists of the two letter Reason for Control and a column number (e.g., CB Column 1). The column identifiers correspond to those listed in the "Country Chart" header within the "License Requirements" section of each ECCN.

(d)   Cells

The symbol "X" is used to denote licensing requirements on the Country Chart. If an "X" appears in a particular cell, transactions subject to that particular Reason for Control/Destination combination require a license. There is a direct correlation between the number of "X"s applicable to your transaction and the number of licensing reviews your application will undergo.

§ 738.4   DETERMINING WHETHER A LICENSE IS REQUIRED

(a)   Using the CCL and the Country Chart

(1)   Overview. Once you have determined that your item is classified under a specific ECCN, you must use information contained in the "License Requirements" section of that ECCN in combination with the Country Chart to decide whether a license is required. Note that not all license requirements set forth under the "License Requirements" section of an ECCN refer you to the Commerce Country Chart, but in some cases this section will contain references to a specific section in the EAR for license requirements. In such cases, this section would not apply.

(2)   License decision making process. The following decision making process must be followed in order to determine whether a license is required to export or reexport a particular item to a specific destination:

(i)   *Examine the appropriate ECCN in the CCL.* Is the item you intend to export or reexport controlled for a single Reason for Control?

(A) If *yes*, identify the single Reason for Control and the relevant Country Chart column identifier (e.g., CB Column 1).

(B) If *no*, identify the Country Chart column identifier for each applicable Reason for Control (e.g., NS Column 1, NP Column 1, etc.).

(ii) *Review the Country Chart.* With each of the applicable Country Chart Column identifiers noted, turn to the Country Chart (Supplement No. 1 to part 738). Locate the correct Country Chart column identifier on the diagonal headings, and determine whether an "X" is marked in the cell next to the country in question for each Country Chart column identified in the applicable ECCN.

If your item is subject to more than one reason for control, repeat this step using each unique Country Chart column identifier.

(A) If *yes*, a license application must be submitted based on the particular reason for control and destination, unless a License Exception applies. If "Yes" is noted next to any of the listed License Exceptions, you should consult part 740 of the EAR to determine whether you can use any of the available ECCN-driven License Exceptions to effect your shipment, rather than applying for a license. Each affirmative license requirement must be overcome by a License Exception. If you are unable to qualify for a License Exception based on each license requirement noted on the Country Chart, you must apply for a license. Note that other License Exceptions, not related to the CCL, may also apply to your transaction (See part 740 of the EAR).

(B) If no, a license is not required based on the particular Reason for Control and destination. Provided that General Prohibitions Four through Ten do not apply to your proposed transaction and the License Requirement section does not refer you to any other part of the EAR to determine license requirements. For example, any applicable review requirements described in § 742.15(b) of the EAR must be met for certain mass market encryption items to effect your shipment using the symbol "NLR." Proceed to parts 758 and 762 of the EAR for information on export clearance procedures and recordkeeping requirements. Note that although you may stop after determining a license is required based on the first Reason for Control, it is best to work through each applicable Reason for Control. A full analysis of every possible licensing requirement based on each applicable Reason for Control is *required* to determine the most advantageous License Exception available for your particular transaction and, if a license is required, ascertain the scope of review conducted by BIS on your license application.

(b) Sample analysis using the CCL and Country Chart

(1) *Scope.* The following sample entry and related analysis is provided to illustrate the type of thought process you must complete in order to determine whether a license is required to export or reexport a particular item to a specific destination using the CCL in combination with the Country Chart.

(2)   Sample CCL entry.

2A000: Entry heading.

LICENSE REQUIREMENTS:

Reason for Control: NS, NP, AT

Control(s)	*Country Chart*
NS applies to entire entry	NS Column 2
NP applies to 2A000.b	NP Column 1
AT applies to entire entry	AT Column 1

LICENSE EXCEPTIONS
LVS: $5,000
GBS: Yes
CIV: N/A

LIST OF ITEMS CONTROLLED:
Unit: Number
Related Definition: N/A
Related Controls: N/A *Items*:
a. Having x.
b. Having z.

(3)   Sample analysis. After consulting the CCL, I determine my item, valued at $10,000, is classified under ECCN 2A000.a. I read that the entire entry is controlled for national security, and anti-terrorism reasons. Since my item is classified under paragraph.a, and not.b, I understand that though nuclear nonproliferation controls apply to a portion of the entry, they do not apply to my item. I note that the appropriate Country Chart column identifiers are NS Column 2 and AT Column 1. Turning to the Country Chart, I locate my specific destination, India, and see that an "X" appears in the NS Column 2 cell for India, but not in the AT Column 1 cell. I understand that a license is required, unless my transaction qualifies for a License Exception or Special Comprehensive License. From the License Exception LVS value listed in the entry, I know immediately that my proposed transaction exceeds the value limitation associated with LVS. Noting that License Exception GBS is "Yes" for this entry, I turn to part 740 of the EAR to review the provisions related to use of GBS.

Sample Country Chart Page

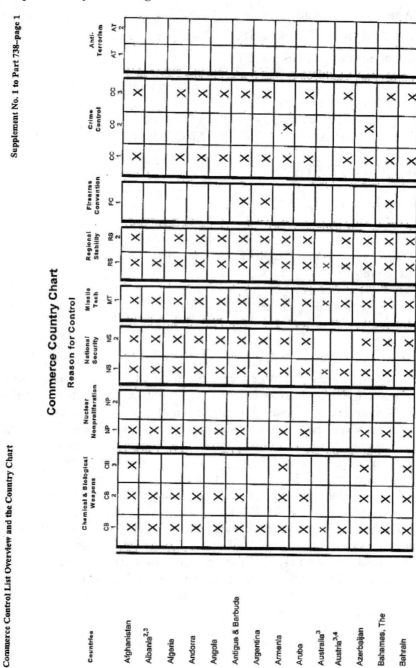

Commerce Control List Overview and the Country Chart

Supplement No. 1 to Part 738—page 1

Commerce Country Chart

Reason for Control

December 23, 2009

Export Administration Regulations

QUESTIONS

1.　What is the relationship between an item's Export Control Classification Number, the Commerce Country Chart and the requirement to obtain an export license?

2.　What does the first digit in the ECCN identify? What does the first letter in the ECCN identify? What does the third digit in the ECCN identify?

3.　ECCN 3A001 includes electronic components. Different types of electronic components are controlled for different reasons, including National Security, Missile Technology, Nuclear Non-proliferation and Anti-terrorism reasons. Would the export of an ECCN 3A001 item controlled for Nuclear Non-proliferation reasons to Australia require a license? Would the export of the same item to Bahrain require a license?

4.　Must an export license be obtained for each Reason for Control? Does BIS consider each Reason for Control when reviewing a license application for an export to a particular country?

5.　Would the export of an item controlled for Chemical and Biological Weapons, Nuclear Non-proliferation and National Security to Azerbaijan be subject to a higher level of review than the export of the same item to Afghanistan?

The next reading in this section covers license exceptions. This reading has been significantly edited to reduce its length and complexity; however, essential descriptions of some of these license exceptions have been preserved.

15 C.F.R. Part 740 — LICENSE EXCEPTIONS

§ 740.1　INTRODUCTION

In this part, references to the EAR are references to 15 CFR chapter VII, subchapter C.

(a)　Scope

A "License Exception" is an authorization contained in this part that allows you to export or reexport under stated conditions, items subject to the Export Administration Regulations (EAR) that would otherwise require a license under General Prohibition One, Two, Three, or Eight as indicated under one or more of the Export Control Classification Numbers (ECCNs) in the Commerce Control List (CCL) in Supplement No. 1 to part 774 of the EAR and items subject to the EAR that would require a license based on the embargo policies described in part 746 of the EAR. If your export or reexport is subject to General Prohibition Six for embargoed destinations, refer to part 746 of the EAR to determine the availability of any License Exceptions. Special commodity controls apply to short supply items. License Exceptions for items listed on the CCL as controlled for Short Supply reasons are found in part 754 of the EAR. If your export or reexport is to subject to General Prohibition Five, consult part 744 of the EAR. If your export or reexport is subject to General Prohibitions Four, Seven, Nine, or Ten, then no License Exceptions apply.

(b) Certification

By using any of the License Exceptions you are certifying that the terms, provisions, and conditions for the use of the License Exception described in the EAR have been met. Please refer to part 758 of the EAR for clearance of shipments and documenting the use of License Exceptions.

(c) License Exception symbols

Each License Exception bears a three letter symbol that will be used for export clearance purposes (see paragraph (d) of this section).

(d) Shipper's Export Declaration or Automated Export System Record

You must enter on any required Shipper's Export Declaration (SED) or Automated Export System (AES) record the correct License Exception symbol (e.g., LVS, GBS, CIV) and the correct Export Control Classification Number (ECCN) (e.g., 4A003, 5A002) for all shipments of items exported under a License Exception. Items temporarily in the United States meeting the provisions of License Exception TMP, under § 740.9(b)(3), are excepted from this requirement. See § 758.1 of the EAR for Shipper's Export Declaration requirements or Automated Export System (AES) requirements.

(e) Destination Control Statement

You may be required to enter an appropriate Destination Control Statement on commercial documents in accordance with Destination Control Statement requirements of § 758.6 of the EAR.

(f) Recordkeeping

Records of transactions involving exports under any of the License Exceptions must be maintained in accordance with the recordkeeping requirements of part 762 of the EAR.

§ 740.2 RESTRICTIONS ON ALL LICENSE EXCEPTIONS

(a) You may not use *any* License Exception if any one or more of the following apply:

(1) Your authorization to use a License Exception has been suspended or revoked, or your intended export does not qualify for a License Exception.

(2) The export or reexport is subject to one of the ten General Prohibitions, is not eligible for a License Exception, and has not been authorized by BIS.

(3) The item is primarily useful for surreptitious interception of wire, oral, or electronic communications, or related software, controlled under ECCNs 5A980 or 5D980, unless the item is consigned to and for the official use of an agency of the U.S. Government (see § 740.11(b)(2)(ii) of this part, Governments (GOV)).

(4) The item being exported or reexported is subject to the license requirements described in § 742.7 of the EAR and the export or reexport is not:

(i) Being made to Australia, Japan, New Zealand, or a NATO (North

Atlantic Treaty Organization) member state (see NATO membership listing in § 772.1 of the EAR);

(ii) Authorized by § 740.11(b)(2)(ii) (official use by personnel and agencies of the U.S. government); or

(iii) Authorized by § 740.14(e) of the EAR (certain shotguns and shotgun shells for personal use).

(5) (i) The item is controlled for missile technology (MT) reasons, except that the items described in ECCNs 6A008, 7A001, 7A002, 7A004, 7A101, 7A102, 7A103, 7A104, 7B001, 7D001, 7D002, 7D003, 7D101, 7D102, 7E003, or 7E101, may be exported as part of a manned aircraft, land vehicle or marine vehicle or in quantities appropriate for replacement parts for such applications under § 740.9(a)(2)(ii) (License Exception TMP for kits consisting of replacement parts), § 740.10 (License Exception RPL), § 740.13 (License Exception TSU), or § 740.15(c) (License Exception AVS for equipment and spare parts for permanent use on a vessel or aircraft).

(ii) MT controlled commodities described in ECCN 2A001 may be exported or reexported under § 740.9(a)(2)(ii) (License Exception TMP) or § 740.10 (License Exception RPL) as one-for-one replacement for equipment previously legally exported or reexported.

(6) The export or reexport is to a comprehensively embargoed destination (Cuba, Iran, and North Korea), unless a license exception or portion thereof is specifically listed in the license exceptions paragraph pertaining to a particular embargoed country in part 746 of the EAR.

****

§ 740.3 SHIPMENTS OF LIMITED VALUE (LVS)

(a) Scope

License Exception LVS authorizes the export and reexport in a single shipment of eligible commodities as identified by "LVS — $(value limit)" on the CCL.

(b) Eligible Destinations

This License Exception is available for all destinations in Country Group B (see Supplement No. 1 to part 740), provided that the net value of the commodities included in the same order and controlled under the same ECCN entry on the CCL does not exceed the amount specified in the LVS paragraph for that entry.

****

§ 740.4 SHIPMENTS TO COUNTRY GROUP B COUNTRIES (GBS)

License Exception GBS authorizes exports and reexports to Country Group B (see Supplement No. 1 to part 740) of those commodities where the Commerce Country Chart (Supplement No. 1 to part 738 of the EAR) indicates a license requirement to the ultimate destination for national security reasons only and identified by "GBS — Yes" on the CCL. See § 743.1 of the EAR for reporting requirements for exports of certain commodities under License Exception GBS.

§ 740.5 CIVIL END-USERS (CIV)

(a) Scope

License Exception CIV authorizes exports and reexports of items on the Commerce Control List (CCL) (Supplement No. 1 to part 774 of the EAR) that have a license requirement to the ultimate destination pursuant to the Commerce Country Chart (Supplement No. 1 to part 738 of the EAR) for NS reasons only; and identified by "CIV Yes" in the License Exception section of the Export Control Classification Number (ECCN), provided the items are destined to civil end-users for civil end-uses in Country Group D:1, except North Korea (Supplement No. 1 to part 740 of this part).

****

§ 740.6 TECHNOLOGY AND SOFTWARE UNDER RESTRICTION (TSR)

(a) Scope

License Exception TSR permits exports and reexports of technology and software where the Commerce Country Chart (Supplement No. 1 to part 738 of the EAR) indicates a license requirement to the ultimate destination for national security reasons only and identified by "TSR — Yes" in entries on the CCL, provided the software or technology is destined to Country Group B. (See Supplement No. 1 to part 740.) A written assurance is required from the consignee before exporting under this License Exception. [More information on the TSR exception is provided in subsection 9.3.2.]

****

§ 740.7 COMPUTERS (APP)

(a) Scope

(1) Commodities. License Exception APP authorizes exports and reexports of computers, including "electronic assemblies" and specially designed components therefore controlled by ECCN 4A003, *except* ECCN 4A003.e (equipment performing analog-to-digital conversions exceeding the limits in ECCN 3A001.a.5.a), exported or reexported separately or as part of a system for consumption in Computer Tier countries as provided by this section. When evaluating your computer to determine License Exception APP eligibility, use the APP parameter to the exclusion of other technical parameters in ECCN 4A003.

(2) Technology and software. License Exception APP authorizes exports of technology and software controlled by ECCNs 4D001 and 4E001 specially designed or modified for the "development," "production," or "use" of computers, including "electronic assemblies" and specially designed components therefore classified in ECCN 4A003, *except* ECCN 4A003.e (equipment

performing analog-to-digital conversions exceeding the limits in ECCN 3A001.a.5.a), to Computer Tier countries as provided by this section.

(b) Restrictions

(1) Related equipment controlled under ECCN 4A003.g may not be exported or reexported under this License Exception when exported or reexported separately from eligible computers authorized under this License Exception.

(2) Access and release restrictions.

(i) *Computers and software*. Computers and software eligible for License Exception APP may not be accessed either physically or computationally by nationals of Cuba, Iran, North Korea, Sudan, or Syria, except that commercial consignees described in Supplement No. 3 to part 742 of the EAR are prohibited only from giving such nationals user-accessible programmability.

(ii) *Technology and source code*. Technology and source code eligible for License Exception APP may not be released to nationals of Cuba, Iran, North Korea, Sudan, or Syria.

(3) Computers and software eligible for License Exception APP may not be reexported or transferred (in country) without prior authorization from BIS, *i.e.*, a license, a permissive reexport, another License Exception, or "No License Required." This restriction must be conveyed to the consignee, via the Destination Control Statement, see § 758.6 of the EAR. Additionally, the end-use and end-user restrictions in paragraph (b)(5) of this section must be conveyed to any consignee in Computer Tier 3.

(4) You may not use this License Exception to export or reexport items that you know will be used to enhance the APP beyond the eligibility limit allowed to your country of destination.

(5) License Exception APP does not authorize exports, reexports and transfers (in-country) for nuclear, chemical, biological, or missile end-users and end-uses subject to license requirements under § 744.2, § 744.3, § 744.4, and § 744.5 of the EAR. Such exports, reexports and transfers (in-country) will continue to require a license and will be considered on a case-by-case basis. Reexports and transfers (in-country) to these end-users and end-uses in eligible countries are strictly prohibited without prior authorization.

(6) Foreign nationals in an expired visa status are not eligible to receive deemed exports of technology or source code under this License Exception. It is the responsibility of the exporter to ensure that, in the case of deemed exports, the foreign national maintains a valid U.S. visa, if required to hold a visa from the United States.

****

§ 740.9 TEMPORARY IMPORTS, EXPORTS, AND REEXPORTS (TMP)

This License Exception authorizes various temporary exports and reexports;

exports and reexports of items temporarily in the United States; and exports and reexports of beta test software.

(a)   Temporary exports

(1)   Scope. You may export and reexport commodities and software for temporary use abroad (including use in international waters) subject to the conditions and restrictions described in paragraphs (a)(2) through (a)(5) of this section. U.S. persons, as defined in paragraph (a)(2)(i)(C), may export and reexport technology for temporary use abroad under paragraph (a)(2)(i) of this section to U.S. persons or their employees traveling or temporarily assigned abroad (including use in international waters) subject to the conditions and restrictions described in paragraphs (a)(2) through (a)(5) of this section. Paragraph (a) does *not* authorize any new release of technology. Persons receiving technology exported or reexported under paragraph (a)(2)(i) must already be authorized to receive the same technology in accordance with the EAR (e.g., through a license or license exception), or, alternatively, not require such authorization on account of the technology's NLR status. Technology exports and reexports authorized under this paragraph (a) may be made as actual shipments, transmissions, or releases. Exports and reexports of encryption items controlled under ECCN 5E002 are *not* permitted pursuant to this paragraph (a). Items shipped as temporary exports and reexports under the provisions of this paragraph (a) must be returned to the country from which they were exported or reexported as soon as practicable but, except in circumstances described in this section, no later than one year from the date of export or reexport. This requirement does not apply if the items are consumed or destroyed in the normal course of authorized temporary use abroad or an extension or other disposition is permitted by the EAR or in writing by BIS.

****

§ 740.10   SERVICING AND REPLACEMENT OF PARTS AND EQUIPMENT (RPL)

This License Exception authorizes exports and reexports associated with one-for-one replacement of parts or servicing and replacement of equipment.

*****

§ 740.11   GOVERNMENTS, INTERNATIONAL ORGANIZATIONS, AND INTERNATIONAL INSPECTIONS UNDER THE CHEMICAL WEAPONS CONVENTION (GOV)

This License Exception authorizes exports and reexports for international nuclear safeguards; U.S. government agencies or personnel, and agencies of cooperating governments; and international inspections under the Chemical Weapons Convention.

****

§ 740.13   TECHNOLOGY AND SOFTWARE — UNRESTRICTED (TSU)

This license exception authorizes exports and reexports of operation technology and software; sales technology and software; software updates (bug fixes); "mass market" software subject to the General Software Note; and encryption source code (and corresponding object code) that would be considered publicly available under § 734.3(b)(3) of the EAR. Note that encryption software subject to the EAR is not subject to the General Software Note (see paragraph (d)(2) of this section). [More information on the TSU exception is provided in subsection 9.3.2.]

****

§ 740.17   ENCRYPTION COMMODITIES, SOFTWARE AND TECHNOLOGY (ENC)

License Exception ENC authorizes export and reexport of software and commodities and components therefore that are classified under ECCNs 5A002.a.1, a.2, a.5, a.6 or a.9, 5B002, 5D002, and technology that is classified under ECCN 5E002. This License Exception ENC does not authorize export or reexport to, or provision of any service in any country listed in Country Group E:1 in Supplement No. 1 to part 740 of the EAR, or release of source code or technology to any national of a country listed in Country Group E:1. Reexports and transfers under License Exception ENC are subject to the criteria set forth in paragraph (c) of this section. Paragraph (d) of this section sets forth information about review requests required by this section. Paragraph (e) sets forth reporting required by this section. [More information on the ENC exception is provided in subsection 9.3.1 below.]

****

§ 740.19   CONSUMER COMMUNICATIONS DEVICES (CCD)

(a)   Authorization

This License Exception authorizes the export or reexport of commodities and software described in paragraph (b) to Cuba subject to the conditions in paragraphs (c) and (d) of this section. This section does not authorize U.S.-owned or -controlled entities in third countries to engage in reexports of foreign produced commodities to Cuba for which no license would be issued by the Treasury Department pursuant to 31 CFR 515.559. Cuba is the only eligible destination under this License Exception.

QUESTIONS

1.   What restrictions are imposed on all license exceptions? Can you explain the restriction in § 740.2(4)?

2.   Throughout the EAR, Cuba, Iran, North Korea, Sudan and Syria are subject to highly restrictive export rules and, in some instances, complete export prohibi-

tions. Are U.S. interests the same with respect to all four countries? What may be the difference between U.S. interests regarding Cuba and Iran?

The final reading in this section describes the record keeping required for exporters of dual-use technologies.

15 C.F.R. PART 762: RECORDKEEPING

§ 762.1   SCOPE

In this part, references to the EAR are references to 15 CFR chapter VII, subchapter C.

(a)   Transactions subject to this part

The recordkeeping provisions of this part apply to the following transactions:

(1) Transactions involving restrictive trade practices or boycotts described in part 760 of the EAR;

(2) Exports of commodities, software, or technology from the United States and any known reexports, transshipment, or diversions of items exported from the United States;

(3) Exports to Canada, if, at any stage in the transaction, it appears that a person in a country other than the United States or Canada has an interest therein, or that the item involved is to be reexported, transshipped, or diverted from Canada to another foreign country; or

(4) Any other transactions subject to the EAR, including, but not limited to, the prohibitions against servicing, forwarding and other actions for or on behalf of end-users of proliferation concern contained in §§ 736.2(b)(7) and 744.6 of the EAR. This part also applies to all negotiations connected with those transactions, except that for export control matters a mere preliminary inquiry or offer to do business and negative response thereto shall not constitute negotiations, unless the inquiry or offer to do business proposes a transaction that a reasonably prudent exporter would believe likely lead to a violation of the EAA, or any order, license or authorization issued thereunder.

(b)   Persons subject to this part

Any person subject to the jurisdiction of the United States who, as principal or agent (including a forwarding agent), participates in any transaction described in paragraph (a) of this section, and any person in the United States or abroad who is required to make and maintain records under any provision of the EAR, shall keep and maintain all records described in § 762.2 of this part that are made or obtained by that person and shall produce them in a manner provided by § 762.6 of this part.

§ 762.2 RECORDS TO BE RETAINED

(a) Records required to be retained

The records required to be retained under this part 762 include the following:

(1) Export control documents, as defined in part 772 of the EAR;

(2) Memoranda;

(3) Notes;

(4) Correspondence;

(5) Contracts;

(6) Invitations to bid;

(7) Books of account;

(8) Financial records;

(9) Restrictive trade practice or boycott documents and reports; and

(10) Other records pertaining to the types of transactions described in § 762.1(a) of this part, which are made or obtained by a person described in § 762.1(b) of this part.

****

§ 762.4 ORIGINAL RECORDS REQUIRED

The regulated person must maintain the original records in the form in which that person receives or creates them unless that person meets all of the conditions of § 762.5 of this part relating to reproduction of records. If the original record does not meet the standards of legibility and readability described in § 762.5 of this part and the regulated person intends to rely on that record to meet the recordkeeping requirements of the EAR, that person must retain the original record.

§ 762.5 REPRODUCTION OF ORIGINAL RECORDS

(a) The regulated person may maintain reproductions instead of the original records provided all of the requirements of paragraph (b) of this section are met.

(b) In order to maintain the records required by § 762.2 of this part, the regulated persons defined in § 762.1 of this part may use any photographic, photostatic, miniature photographic, micrographic, automated archival storage, or other process that completely, accurately, legibly and durably reproduces the original records (whether on paper, microfilm, or through electronic digital storage techniques). The process must meet all of the following requirements, which are applicable to all systems:

(1) The system must be capable of reproducing all records on paper.

(2) The system must record and be able to reproduce all marks, information, and other characteristics of the original record, including both obverse and reverse sides of paper documents in legible form.

(3) When displayed on a viewer, monitor, or reproduced on paper, the records must exhibit a high degree of legibility and readability. (For purposes of this section, legible and legibility mean the quality of a letter or numeral that enable the observer to identify it positively and quickly to the exclusion of all other letters or numerals. Readable and readability mean the quality of a group of letters or numerals being recognized as complete words or numbers.)

(4) The system must preserve the initial image (including both obverse and reverse sides of paper documents) and record all changes, who made them and when they were made. This information must be stored in such a manner that none of it may be altered once it is initially recorded.

(5) The regulated person must establish written procedures to identify the individuals who are responsible for the operation, use and maintenance of the system.

(6) The regulated person must establish written procedures for inspection and quality assurance of records in the system and document the implementation of those procedures.

(7) The system must be complete and contain all records required to be kept by this part or the regulated person must provide a method for correlating, identifying and locating records relating to the same transaction(s) that are kept in other record keeping systems.

(8) The regulated person must keep a record of where, when, by whom, and on what equipment the records and other information were entered into the system.

(9) Upon request by the Office of Export Enforcement, the Office of Antiboycott Compliance, or any other agency of competent jurisdiction, the regulated person must furnish, at the examination site, the records, the equipment and, if necessary, knowledgeable personnel for locating, reading, and reproducing any record in the system.

(c) Requirements applicable to systems based on the storage of digital images

For systems based on the storage of digital images, the system must provide accessibility to any digital image in the system. With respect to records of transactions, including those involving restrictive trade practices or boycott requirements or requests. The system must be able to locate and reproduce all records relating to a particular transaction based on any one of the following criteria:

(1) The name(s) of the parties to the transaction;

(2) Any country(ies) connected with the transaction; or

(3) A document reference number that was on any original document.

(d) Requirements applicable to a system based on photographic processes.

For systems based on photographic, photostatic, or miniature photographic processes, the regulated person must maintain a detailed index of all records in the system that is arranged in such a manner as to allow immediate location of any particular record in the system.

§ 762.6 PERIOD OF RETENTION

(a) Five year retention period

All records required to be kept by the EAR must be retained for five years from the latest of the following times:

(1) The export from the United States of the item involved in the transaction to which the records pertain or the provision of financing, transporting or other service for or on behalf of end-users of proliferation concern as described in §§ 736.2(b)(7) and 744.6 of the EAR;

(2) Any known reexport, transshipment, or diversion of such item;

(3) Any other termination of the transaction, whether formally in writing or by any other means; or

(4) I n the case of records of pertaining to transactions involving restrictive trade practices or boycotts described in part 760 of the EAR, the date the regulated person receives the boycott-related request or requirement.

(b) Destruction or disposal of records

If the Bureau of Industry and Security or any other government agency makes a formal or informal request for a certain record or records, such record or records may not be destroyed or disposed of without the written authorization of the agency concerned. This prohibition applies to records pertaining to voluntary disclosures made to BIS in accordance with § 764.5(c)(4)(ii) and other records even if such records have been retained for a period of time exceeding that required by paragraph (a) of this section.

§ 762.7 PRODUCING AND INSPECTING RECORDS

(a) Persons located in the United States

Persons located in the United States may be asked to produce records that are required to be kept by any provision of the EAR, or any license, order, or authorization issued thereunder and to make them available for inspection and copying by any authorized agent, official, or employee of the Bureau of Industry and Security, the U.S. Customs Service, or any other agency of the U.S. Government, without any charge or expense to such agent, official, or employee. The Office of Export Enforcement and the Office of Antiboycott Compliance encourage voluntary cooperation with such requests. When voluntary cooperation is not forthcoming, the Office of Export Enforcement and the Office of Antiboycott Compliance are authorized to issue subpoenas requiring persons to appear and testify, or produce books, records, and other writings. In instances where a person does not comply with a subpoena, the Department of Commerce may petition a district court to have a subpoena enforced.

(b) Persons located outside of the United States

Persons located outside of the United States that are required to keep records by any provision of the EAR or by any license, order, or authorization issued thereunder shall produce all records or reproductions of records required to be kept, and make them available for inspection and copying upon request by an authorized agent, official, or employee of the Bureau of Industry and Security, the U.S. Customs Service, or a Foreign Service post, or by any other accredited representative of the U.S. Government, without any charge or expense to such agent, official or employee.

CASE NOTE

1.   U.S. v. Posey, 864 F.2d 1487 (9th Cir. 1989) (Although substantive offense of violating the Arms Export Control Act required defendant to actually export Munitions List items not in the public domain, such export was not necessary for a conspiracy conviction; even if all items taken out of the country were lawfully exported, defendant could be found guilty of conspiracy; the fact that technical arms information exported to Union of South Africa was available under the Freedom of Information Act did not decriminalize its exportation under the Arms Export Control Act).

Additional Information

1. MARK S. HOLMES, EXPORTING TECHNOLOGY: SCOPE OF FEDERAL REGULATIONS, PATENT LICENSING: STRATEGY, NEGOTIATIONS AND FORMS § 9:1–9:7 (2009).

2. Cecil Hunt, U.S. Export Controls and Economic Sanctions — An Overview, SN056 ALI-ABA 193 (2008).

3. Mark A. Kirsch, Jason A. D'Angelo, Export Control Cases on the Rise — The U.S. Government No Longer Views Violations As Merely Technical Or Regulatory Offenses, 7/23/2007 Nat'l L.J. S1, col. 1 (2007).

4. Export Enforcement & Fines Soar in Last Months of 2008, MANAGING IMPORTS AND EXPORTS (January, 2009).

5. Jamie L. Keith, Vice President and General Counsel, University of Florida, Fundamentals of Export Controls and Trade Sanctions and Embargoes for Research Universities, available at http://www.admin.ufl.edu/DDD/attach07-08/19May08_1.doc.

6. Rowena Rega, Universities Should Implement Internal Control Programs To Monitor Compliance With Export Control Laws, 35 J.L. & EDUC. 199 (2006).

7. John R. Liebman, Kevin J. Lombardo, A Guide to Export Controls for the Non-Specialist, 28 LOY. L.A. INT'L & COMP. L. REV. 497 (2006).

8. Linda M. Weinberg, Lynn Van Buren, The Impact of U.S. Export Controls and Sanctions on Employment, 35 PUB. CONT. L.J. 537 (2006).

9. Tara L. Dunn, *Surviving United States Export Controls Post 9/11: A Model Compliance Program*, 33 Denv. J. Int'l L. & Pol'y 435 (2005).

10. Gregory W. Bowman, *E-Mails, Servers, and Software: U.S. Export Controls for the Modern Era*, 35 Geo. J. Int'l L. 319 (2004).

11. Michael D. Klaus, *Dual-Use Free Trade Agreements: The Contemporary Alternative to High-Tech Export Controls*, 32 Denv. J. Int'l L. & Pol'y 105 (2003).

12. Press Release, U.S. Bureau of Industry and Security, *DHL Signs $9.44 Million Joint Settlement Agreement with BIS and OFAC*, available at www.bis.doc.gov., August 6th, 2009.

13. Frederick P. Waite, M. Roy Goldberg, *Responsible Export Controls or "Nets to Catch the Wind"? The Commerce Department's New U.S. Controls on Exports of Chemical Precursors, Equipment and Technical Data Intended to Prevent Development of Chemical and Biological Weapons*, 22. Cal. W. Int'l L.J. 193 (1991-1992).

14. James E. Bartlett, et al., *Export Controls and Economic Sanctions*, 43 Int'l Law. 311 (2009).

9.2 DEEMED EXPORTS

Deemed exports are a source of considerable concern for companies which have employees who are foreign nationals and for universities which have students who are foreign nationals. A deemed export of technology or source code to a foreign national requires a license from the BIS in the same way as an actual shipment of items subject to the EAR. Under the EAR, technology that is required for the development, production or use of controlled items also constitutes controlled technology subject to the same export restrictions as the related items listed in the CCL. "Use" technology consists of information which would permit a person to operate, install, maintain, repair, overhaul and refurbish items subject to the EAR. "Use" technology also constitutes controlled technology subject to the same export restrictions as the related technology listed in the CCL. The CFR Part below sets forth the definitions of a deemed export and a deemed reexport.

15 CFR PART 734 — SCOPE OF EXPORT ADMINISTRATION REGULATIONS

§ 734.2 IMPORTANT EAR TERMS AND PRINCIPLES

(a) *Subject to the EAR — Definition*

(1) "Subject to the EAR" is a term used in the EAR to describe those items and activities over which BIS exercises regulatory jurisdiction under the EAR. Conversely, items and activities that are *not* subject to the EAR are outside the regulatory jurisdiction of the EAR and are not affected by these regulations. The items and activities subject to the EAR are described in § 734.2 through § 734.5 of this part. You should review the Commerce Control List (CCL) and any applicable parts of the EAR to determine whether an item

or activity is subject to the EAR. However, if you need help in determining whether an item or activity is subject to the EAR, see § 734.6 of this part. Publicly available technology and software not subject to the EAR are described in § 734.7 through § 734.11 and Supplement No. 1 to this part.

(2) Items and activities subject to the EAR may also be controlled under export-related programs administered by other agencies. Items and activities subject to the EAR are not necessarily exempted from the control programs of other agencies. Although BIS and other agencies that maintain controls for national security and foreign policy reasons try to minimize overlapping jurisdiction, you should be aware that in some instances you may have to comply with more than one regulatory program.

(3) The term "subject to the EAR" should not be confused with licensing or other requirements imposed in other parts of the EAR. Just because an item or activity is subject to the EAR does not mean that a license or other requirement automatically applies. A license or other requirement applies only in those cases where other parts of the EAR impose a licensing or other requirement on such items or activities.

(b)   *Export and reexport*

(1)   Definition of export. "Export" means an actual shipment or transmission of items subject to the EAR out of the United States, or release of technology or software subject to the EAR to a foreign national in the United States, as described in paragraph (b)(2)(ii) of this section. See paragraph (b)(9) of this section for the definition that applies to exports of encryption source code and object code software subject to the EAR.

(2)   Export of technology or software. (See paragraph (b)(9) for provisions that apply to encryption source code and object code software.) "Export" of technology or software, excluding encryption software subject to "EI" controls, includes:

(i) Any release of technology or software subject to the EAR in a foreign country; or

(ii) Any release of technology or source code subject to the EAR to a foreign national. Such release is deemed to be an export to the home country or countries of the foreign national. This deemed export rule does not apply to persons lawfully admitted for permanent residence in the United States and does not apply to persons who are protected individuals under the Immigration and Naturalization Act (8 U.S.C. 1324b(a)(3)). Note that the release of any item to any party with knowledge a violation is about to occur is prohibited by § 736.2(b)(10) of the EAR.

(3)   Definition of "release" of technology or software. Technology or software is "released" for export through:

(i) Visual inspection by foreign nationals of U.S.-origin equipment and facilities;

(ii) Oral exchanges of information in the United States or abroad; or

(iii) The application to situations abroad of personal knowledge or technical experience acquired in the United States.

(4) Definition of reexport. "Reexport" means an actual shipment or transmission of items subject to the EAR from one foreign country to another foreign country; or release of technology or software subject to the EAR to a foreign national outside the United States, as described in paragraph (b)(5) of this section.

(5) Reexport of technology or software. Any release of technology or source code subject to the EAR to a foreign national of another country is a deemed reexport to the home country or countries of the foreign national. However, this deemed reexport definition does not apply to persons lawfully admitted for permanent residence. The term "release" is defined in paragraph (b)(3) of this section. Note that the release of any item to any party with knowledge or reason to know a violation is about to occur is prohibited by § 736.2(b)(10) of the EAR.

****

QUESTIONS

1. Is a person who is lawfully in the United States with an H1-B visa a foreign national? Is a person who is not a U.S. citizen, but who has been issued a green card and granted permanent residence status, a foreign national?

2. Is the release of software subject to the EAR to a foreign national a deemed export?

DEEMED EXPORT NOTES

1. The means by which technology or software is released does not matter in determining export license requirements. The technology or software can be hand-delivered, sent as an email attachment or uploaded or downloaded from an Internet site. Therefore, source code subject to the EAR that is made available to a foreign national in the U.S. by means of a local network server is a deemed export. However, as you saw earlier, publicly available technology and software such as information that has been, or will be, published is not subject to the EAR. Nor is information that results from fundamental research, that is provided in an academic course or teaching laboratory, or that is contained in certain patent applications. However, if research information is withheld from publication or treated as a proprietary trade secret, the research information will be subject to the EAR and require a license before it can be released to a foreign national.

License exceptions apply to deemed exports in the same way they apply to tangible items. License exception CIV, which allows the export of dual-use technology to civil end-users for civil end-uses, is available for technology and source code released to foreign nationals. In this case, the deemed exporter must submit a foreign national review application to the BIS. This application is similar to an export license. Likewise, license exception TSR, which allows the export of certain technology and source code, is available for releases to foreign nationals in the U.S. However, the foreign national must provide the deemed exporter with a letter of assurance that he or she will not engage in any further release the technology or source code. Finally, license exception APP, which allows the release of national security controlled high performance computer technology and source code, is available in the case of a deemed export. However, this license exception also requires a foreign national review application be submitted to the BIS.

Deemed exports can also occur in the context of General Prohibitions 4, 5, 6, 7, 9 and 10. Deemed exports of technology or source code in violation of denial orders, to prohibited end-users or for prohibited end-uses, to embargoed countries, in support of proliferation activity, in violation of orders, terms or conditions, and with knowledge that a violation of the EAR has occurred or will occur, are all unlawful.

Finally, in the case of foreign nationals who have dual citizenship, the BIS bases its license determination on the persons' most recent country of citizenship or permanent residence.

2. A committee established to provide independent advice to the Secretary of Commerce, undertook a major reexamination of the deemed export controls. In its final report issued in December 2007, the committee found that: "Leadership in science and technology today is a globally shared and highly interdependent perishable asset;" and that "In this new world, a nation that attempts to build a "wall" around its scientific and technologic communities simply denies itself the opportunity to fully benefit from the vast body of knowledge being accumulated elsewhere — and thereby virtually assures itself of an inferior competitive position in the knowledge world." The committee made a number of specific findings and provided two broad recommendations. Among the committee's findings were the following.

The current deemed export regulations have become increasingly irrelevant because most scientific and technological knowledge that cannot be exported from the U.S. can be obtained from other countries.

The current Commerce Control List is too encompassing covering many unimportant items ranging from police handcuffs to hunting rifles and from conventional radios to mass market computers.

The existing regulations are excessively complex and vague.

Many academic and industrial organizations are unaware of the deemed export rules.

Some regulations appear to be illogical and the criteria for assessing the threat posed by a release of technology or source code to a foreign national appears to be superficial.

In light of these findings, the Advisory Committee made two broad recommendations.

Replace the current deemed export licensing process with a simplified new process that will both enhance national/homeland security and strengthen America's economic competitiveness.

Extend the educational outreach program currently conducted by BIS to assure that all parties potentially subject to deemed export control rules are familiar with those rules.

See Deemed Export Advisory Committee, *The Deemed Export Rule in the Era of Globalization* (2007) (report prepared for the U.S. Department of Commerce) available at http://tac.bis.gov./2007/deacreport.pdf.

To date, these recommendations have not been acted upon.

CASE NOTES

1. *Video Amplifiers to China/National Security Controlled Technology to Chinese Nationals.* On July 25, 2005, Charlie Kuan, former president of Suntek Microwave, Newark, California, was sentenced to 12 months and one day in prison and two years of supervised release for failure to obtain required export licenses for shipments of detector log video amplifiers (DLVA), items controlled for national security reasons, to Chedgdu Jeway Microwave Telecommunications, a company controlled by the Chinese government. Suntek, which was also charged with failing to obtain export licenses under the deemed export provisions of the EAR, was sentenced to a $339,000 criminal fine. BIS additionally assessed administrative penalties of $275,000 against Suntek, $187,000 against Kuan, and 20-year denials of export privileges against both parties in connection with these violations. BIS, Major Case List, October 2009 available at http://www.bis.doc.gov./complianceandenforcement/majorcaselist/mc1102009.pdf.

2. *National Security Controlled Technology to Chinese and Ukrainian Nationals.* In November 2004, BIS assessed Fujitsu Network Communications, Inc. an administrative penalty of $125,000 as part of an agreement with Fujitsu to settle charges related to unlicensed deemed exports to foreign nationals. In particular, BIS alleged that Fujitsu failed to obtain the export licenses required for transferring commercial digital fiber-optic transmission and broadband switching technology to Chinese and Ukrainian nationals that were subject to national security controls. BIS, Major Case List, October 2009 available at http://www.bis.doc.gov./complianceandenforcement/majorcaselist/mc1102009.pdf.

3. WASHINGTON — John Reece Roth, 72, of Knoxville, Tenn., was sentenced to 48 months in prison for violating the Arms Export Control Act by conspiring to illegally export, and actually exporting, technical information relating to a U.S. Air Force (USAF) research and development contract. The sentencing, which was announced by U.S. Attorney Russ Dedrick of the Eastern District of Tennessee and David Kris, Assistant Attorney General for National Security, took place in U.S. District Court in Knoxville before Judge Thomas Varlan, Jr. A former University of Tennessee professor, Roth will serve a term of two years supervised release after completing his prison term.

The illegal exports by Dr. Roth of technical information, known as "technical data," related to his illegal disclosure and transport of restricted military information associated with the USAF contract to develop specialized plasma technology for use on an advanced form of an unmanned aerial vehicle (UAV), also known as a drone.

The illegal exports of military technical information involved specific information about advanced plasma technology that had been designed and was being tested for use on the wings of drones operating as weapons or surveillance systems. The Arms Export Control Act prohibits the export of defense-related materials, including the technical data, to a foreign national or a foreign nation.

After a trial in September 2008, Dr. Roth was convicted of conspiring with Atmospheric Glow Technology, Inc., a Knoxville technology company, of unlawfully exporting in 2005 and 2006 fifteen different "defense articles" to a citizen of the People's Republic of China in violation of the Arms Export Control Act. This law prohibits the export of defense-related materials, including the technical data, to a foreign national or a foreign nation. These defense articles related to different specific military technical data that had been restricted and was associated with the USAF project to develop plasma technology for use on weapons system drones.

Dr. Roth was also convicted of one count of wire fraud relating to defrauding the University of Tennessee of his honest services by illegally exporting sensitive military information relating to this USAF research and development contract.

The Federal Bureau of Investigation (FBI) led the investigation and was joined in its efforts by U.S. Immigration and Customs Enforcement (ICE), the U.S. Air Force Office of Special Investigations, and the Department of Commerce's Office of Export Enforcement. The case was prosecuted by Assistant U.S. Attorneys Jeffrey Theodore and Will Mackie of the U.S. Attorney's Office for the Eastern District of Tennessee.

U.S. Attorney Dedrick commended the efforts of the special agents from the agencies supporting the investigation. He noted that this case was quickly brought to trial and sentencing through the excellent work of the Department of Justice's National Security Division and the Assistant U.S. Attorneys and support staff from his office. Dedrick added, "This case should send a stern warning to those who would betray the trust of our nation by violating the export control laws by providing our military information to foreign nationals."

David Kris, Assistant Attorney General for National Security, stated, "I applaud the agents and prosecutors who worked tirelessly to bring about this result. The illegal export of restricted military data represents a serious threat to national security. We know that foreign governments are actively seeking this information for their own military development. Today's sentence should serve as a warning to anyone who knowingly discloses restricted military data in violation of our laws."

FBI Special Agent in Charge Richard Lambert added: "Safeguarding sensitive military technology vital to our nation's defense remains a top priority of the FBI. We are grateful to the University of Tennessee for its invaluable partnership in this important investigation."

Press Release, Department of Justice, *Retired University Professor Sentenced To Four Years In Prison For Arms Export Violations Involving Citizen of China*, Wednesday, July 1, 2009, WLNR 12560298.

As you will see in the case below, the Sixth Circuit Court of Appeals affirmed Roth's conviction.

U.S. v. ROTH
628 F.3d 827 (6th Cir. 2011)

BOYCE F. MARTIN, JR., CIRCUIT JUDGE.

This case involves violations of the Arms Export Control Act, which imposes export controls on "defense articles and services" without a license. Defendant-appellant John Roth worked as a consultant on a United States Air Force defense research project, which had been awarded to Atmospheric Glow Technologies, Inc. in Knoxville, Tennessee. The project entailed developing plasma technology for use on military aircraft. The government charged Roth with exporting data from the project on a trip to China and allowing two foreign nationals in Knoxville access to certain data and equipment in violation of the Act. A jury in United States District Court for the Eastern District of Tennessee convicted him of one count of conspiracy, fifteen counts of exporting defense articles and services without a license, and one count of wire fraud. He appeals his convictions. For the following reasons, we AFFIRM.

I. BACKGROUND

Roth is a published author in the field of plasma technology and was a professor of electrical engineering at the University of Tennessee at Knoxville during the events underlying this case. His former student, Daniel Sherman, was a principal at Atmospheric, of which Roth was a minority owner. The two men had co-authored a paper explaining how plasma technology devices can be used to affect electrohydrodynamic flow, a topic relating to aircraft flight.

In October 2003, the Air Force solicited contract proposals to develop plasma actuators that could be used to control the flight of small, subsonic, unmanned, military drone aircraft. The project would be broken down into Phase I, which entailed developing the design of the actuators, and Phase II, which entailed testing the actuators in a wind tunnel and on a non-military aircraft.

Atmospheric submitted the winning Phase I proposal and the Air Force awarded it the contract in May 2004 with Roth working as a consultant for the project. At or around that time, Sherman told Roth that the project would be paid for with "6.2" funds, which Roth knew implied that the research would be subject to export control laws that prohibit allowing access to the research outside of the United States or to foreign nationals unless a license has been obtained.

When Phase I was completed, Roth assisted Atmospheric in drafting the contract proposal for Phase II, which the Air Force also assigned to Atmospheric. Roth also assisted in writing, and signed, Task Order 102, a subcontract between him and Atmospheric acknowledging that Phase II work was subject to export controls. The Air Force identified some of the technical data reports in the Phase II contract as being export controlled, such as the Quarterly Reports, Technology Transfer Reports, Final Report, and Test Plan. Jesse Crump, who worked for the Department of Defense, testified at trial that the data contained in the Weekly Reports and Quarterly Reports was unquestionably export controlled information, partly because it could only be intended for military use. Additionally, the contract and the subcontract incorporated federal regulations prohibiting foreign nationals from working on the project. Nevertheless, Roth proposed that two of his graduate research assistants — Truman Bonds, an American, and Xin Dai, a Chinese national — would work with him on the project. Sherman originally protested Dai's involvement, so it was decided that Bonds was to work at Atmospheric on the export controlled data and Dai would work at the University without access to the export controlled data. Bonds testified at trial that the main reason for the separation of work was because of Dai's foreign citizenship and the export controlled data. Roth did not think that Dai needed to be shielded from the data and Dai eventually gained access to the Weekly Reports from Atmospheric.

As part of the testing of the plasma actuators, a device called the Force Stand was developed for the project and installed in labs at Atmospheric and the University in the fall of 2005. It was used to test the actuators and gather data before proceeding to the stage in which the actuators would be tested in a wind tunnel. Dai worked with the Force Stand, and another graduate student named Sirous Nourgostar, an Iranian national, had access to it multiple times. Crump testified that the Force Stand was a defense article because it was designed specifically to collect data for this project, which had a military purpose.

In anticipation of Dai's completion of his doctorate, Roth informed Sherman and Atmospheric that he intended to replace Dai with Nourgostar. After meeting with reluctance and opposition from Sherman because of Nourgostar's foreign citizenship, and especially because of America's contentious affairs with Iran, Roth sought support from Carolyn Webb, an administrator at the University who supervised research contracts. Webb worried that some parts of the project might concern export controlled data and referred Roth to Robin Witherspoon, the University's officer in charge of export controls. At their initial meeting, Roth explained to Witherspoon that the project was military in nature, but that the subject of the research was part of the public domain, which meant it was publicly available, and, thus, not export controlled. Witherspoon indicated that she was concerned that the data from the research was export controlled. She later followed up with Roth via e-mail and phone to explain that she had concluded that the data was export controlled. At that time, Dai was removed from the project. Additionally, knowing of Roth's upcoming trip to lecture in China, Witherspoon warned him that he could not take anything from Phase II abroad. In a similar vein, Sherman obtained agreement from Roth that he would not take any data from the project to China.

Aside from the Phase II project, Sherman and Atmospheric submitted another contract proposal in May 2005 to the Defense Advanced Research Projects Agency, an arm of the Department of Defense that assigns and funds advanced weapons projects. Roth and Sherman spoke about Roth working on the project, and Roth sent Sherman a plan for part of the project that was incorporated into the Agency Proposal. Sherman e-mailed Roth a completed copy of the Proposal, which contained export controlled information from the Boeing Company's weapons division, and marked all but one of the pages with "Proprietary and Export Controlled Information."

On May 16, 2006, Roth traveled to China to lecture at universities regarding his work. He took with him a paper copy of a Phase II Weekly Report, a flash drive with electronic copies of Phase II reports, and a laptop computer on which was stored a copy of the Agency Proposal. Neither Roth nor anyone else accessed any of the electronic files stored on the thumb drive or the laptop, but Roth had Dai send him a copy of a paper containing Phase II data by way of a Chinese professor's e-mail address. Roth later gave Nourgostar access to the paper in the fall of 2007.

On May 20, 2008, a grand jury in United States District Court for the Eastern District of Tennessee returned an indictment against Roth and Atmospheric claiming that Roth had taken Phase II data and the Agency Proposal to China, and both Roth and Atmospheric had allowed Dai and Nourgostar access to the data and the Force Stand. Roth was charged with one count of conspiracy to export defense articles in violation of the Act, fifteen counts of exporting defense articles in violation of the Act, and one count of wire fraud. Before the court delivered instructions to the jury, Roth requested an instruction regarding willfulness that required the government to prove beyond a reasonable doubt that he knew the data and items he allegedly exported were listed on the United States Munitions List. Additionally, he requested a separate instruction regarding ignorance of the law as a defense. However, the district court declined to deliver a separate instruction on ignorance of the law as an affirmative defense, and gave the jury the following instruction regarding willfulness:

> To prove that defendant acted knowingly and willfully, the government must prove beyond a reasonable doubt that the defendant voluntarily and intentionally violated a known legal duty. In other words, the defendant must have acted voluntarily and intentionally and with the specific intent to do something he knew was unlawful, that is to say, with intent either to disobey or disregard the law. Negligent conduct, or conduct by mistake or accident, or with a good faith belief that the conduct was lawful, is not sufficient to constitute willfulness.

The jury found Roth guilty of all counts on September 3. He timely filed a motion for judgment of acquittal on grounds of legal and factual insufficiency. He also filed a motion for a new trial, arguing that the district court's jury instructions were improper because the court failed to read to the jury the proper instruction for willfulness and declined to give a separate instruction on ignorance of the law as a defense. The district court denied both motions.

II. DISCUSSION

On appeal, Roth claims that: (1) the Phase II data and the data included in the Agency Proposal are not defense articles or services as a matter of law; (2) the district court incorrectly instructed the jury as to willfulness and improperly failed to deliver his proposed instruction regarding ignorance of the law; and (3) there was insufficient evidence to support the jury's conclusion that he willfully exported the Agency Proposal.

A. Defense Articles and Services Under the Act

We review questions of statutory interpretation de novo.

The Act allows for the President of the United States to identify "defense articles and defense services" on the United States Munitions List that cannot be exported without a license from the United States. 22 U.S.C. § 2778(a)–(b) (2006). Furthermore, section 2778(c) imposes criminal penalties for "[a]ny person who willfully violates any provision of [the Act]." In part, the Munitions List identifies as defense articles:

> (a) Aircraft, including . . . drones . . . which are specifically designed, modified, or equipped for military purposes.

> (h) Components, parts, accessories, attachments, and associated equipment (including ground support equipment) specifically designed or modified for the articles in paragraphs (a) through (d) of this category, excluding aircraft tires and propellers used with reciprocating engines.

> (i) Technical data (as defined in § 120.10) and defense services (as defined in § 120.9) directly related to the defense articles enumerated in paragraphs (a) through (h) of this category (see § 125.4 for exemptions), except for hot section technical data associated with commercial aircraft engines. Technical data directly related to the manufacture or production of any defense articles enumerated elsewhere in this category that are designated as Significant Military Equipment (SME) shall itself be designated SME. 22 C.F.R. § 121.1, Category VIII (2010).

Section 120.10 of the Code of Federal Regulations proceeds to define "technical data" as:

> (1) Information . . . which is required for the design, development, production, manufacture, assembly, operation, repair, testing, maintenance or modification of defense articles. This includes information in the form of blueprints, drawings, photographs, plans, instructions or documentation.

And section 120.09 instructs that a "defense service" is, in relevant part, "[t]he furnishing to foreign persons of any technical data controlled under this subchapter (see § 120.10), whether in the United States or abroad."

Initially, we take note that courts may not review whether items are properly designated as defense articles on the Munitions List. 22 U.S.C. § 2778(h). Our query, therefore, is not whether technical data and components are defense articles, but whether the data from Phase II and the Agency Proposal and the Force Stand fall under the definitions of technical data and components.

Roth argues that the Phase II data, Agency Proposal, and Force Stand were not defense articles because they were not developed to put plasma actuators on anything designated on the Munitions List. He draws this conclusion because during the time he worked on the project, future stages of Phase II envisioned testing actuators on commercially available aircraft, which are not covered on the Munitions List, before incorporating the actuators into military aircraft. He asserts that his removal from Phase II before actuators were ever applied to any aircraft signifies that his actions could have no connection to a military aircraft.

However, the federal regulations extend export controls to all stages of defense projects that are covered by the Act, not just the final stages when military devices are directly involved. In pertinent part, the federal regulations define "technical data," which is a category of defense article, as "[i]nformation . . . which is required for the design, development, production, manufacture, [and] assembly . . . of defense articles" such as drones. 22 C.F.R. §§ 120.10, 121.1. These terms envision that research requires multiple stages before a project reaches completion, and apply export controls to all those phases. Furthermore, the regulations define "components" as "parts, accessories, attachments, and associated equipment . . . specifically designed or modified for the articles" such as drones. The regulations have been written to cover a broad range of articles at all stages of research and development in projects covered by the Act.

Somehow, Roth ignores the fact that the final goal of Phase II was to incorporate plasma actuators on military drone aircraft. While the project might have called for the data to be tested on a commercially available drone plane at some point in the project, Roth admits that all the data collected, as well as the Force Stand that was developed to collect it, were derived for eventual military use. What is more, he does not argue that the data and Force Stand would not have been defense articles once they were used in conjunction with a military aircraft. This omission implies that the data and the Force Stand would have qualified as defense articles at some point. It seems that Roth thinks that barriers exist between the stages of the project that prevent the defense article qualification from being imputed from one stage to another, which is incorrect according to 22 C.F.R. §§ 120.10, 121.1.

Because the final objective of this project was incorporating plasma actuators into military drones, the district court properly concluded that the underlying data and component were defense articles and services pursuant to 22 C.F.R. § 121.1, Category VIII.

B. Jury Instructions

When a party claims a jury instruction improperly or inaccurately stated the law, we review that claim de novo. On the other hand, "[a] district court's refusal to give a jury instruction is reviewed for abuse of discretion." Roth's claim that the court instructed the jury on the incorrect definition of willfulness is reviewed de novo. His claim that the court erred by not giving the jury an instruction on ignorance of the law as a separate and complete defense is reviewed for abuse of discretion.

1. Willfulness

Neither the Supreme Court nor our Court has defined "willfulness" under section 2778(c). Roth argues that it requires the defendant to intentionally export defense articles or services that he specifically knows are on the Munitions List. The government counters that willfulness under the statute only requires a defendant to know of the general unlawfulness of his conduct, not to know of the specific statutory provision he is violating.

"[A] fundamental canon of statutory construction is that "when interpreting statutes, the language of the statute is the starting point for interpretation, and it should also be the ending point if the plain meaning of that language is clear." "Here, the language cannot be our ending point as the Supreme Court has commented that willfulness can be " "a word of many meanings" whose construction is often dependent on the context in which it appears." " Generally though, in criminal cases, "in order to establish a "willful" violation of a statute, "the Government must prove that the defendant acted with knowledge that his conduct was unlawful." " "

Other circuits have interpreted the willfulness element of section 2778(c) and produced different results. Multiple circuits have interpreted willfulness as requiring a defendant to know generally that the act of exporting the underlying items is unlawful without requiring that the defendant know the items are on the Munitions List. *See United States v. Murphy*, (holding that willfulness was sufficiently established under section 2778(c) if the defendant "knew he had a legal duty not to export the weapons"); *see also United States v. Hsu*, (rejecting the defendants' argument that "the [jury] instructions as to "willfulness" were deficient because the "jury was not instructed that the government had to show that the defendants knew that the KIV-7HS was covered by the Munitions List . . . [or that] the device was designed for military use" "); *United States v. Tsai*, (affirming court's instructions that the defendant did not have to have read the Munitions List or know all the details of the law, and holding that the "[district] court did not err in instructing the jury that it could convict if it found that defendant knew that the export was illegal"); *United States v. Smith*, (finding jury instructions were proper because "[t]he jury was told that defendant must have known that the helicopters to be exported were subject to the licensing requirements of the Arms Export Control Act and that he intended to export them in a manner inconsistent therewith" even though the Munitions List was not referenced).

Conversely, in *United States v. Gregg*, the Eighth Circuit appears to have interpreted willfully to require that a defendant knew the underlying exported items were on the Munitions List. In applying section 2778(c), the court approved of a jury instruction that "plainly directed acquittal if the jury was not satisfied beyond a reasonable doubt that the *defendant knew that the items exported were on the Munitions List* and required license."

Additionally, it is helpful to consider *Bryan*, in which the Supreme Court decided the meaning of willfulness in a statute analogous to section 2778(c). In *Bryan*, the defendant was convicted of conspiring to willfully deal firearms without a license in violation of the Federal Firearms Statute, 18 U.S.C. §§ 922(a)(1)(A), 924(a)(1)(D). At that time, the statute criminalized multiple types of acts, but in pertinent part, it made it illegal for anyone to "willfully violate[ ] any other provision of this chapter." 18 U.S.C. § 924(a)(1)(D) (1994). The Supreme Court held that the willfulness requirement of section 924(a)(1)(D) only required that a defendant know his act was unlawful. The defendant argued that the Court should extend to section 924(a)(1)(D) the exception from *Ratzlaf* and *Cheek v. United States*, that requires knowledge of a law to satisfy willfulness requirements. The Court refused, however, and distinguished those cases by explaining that they involved "highly technical statutes," such as tax laws and banking regulations, "that presented the danger of ensnaring individuals engaged in apparently innocent conduct." The Court stated that those cases could not apply to the defendant in *Bryan* because a jury had already found that he knew what he did was unlawful, therefore, precluding him from mistaking his action as innocent.

In our view, the arguments in the multiple cases from the other circuits deciding the section 2778(c) willfulness issue and the Supreme Court's interpretation of analogous section 924(a)(1)(D) are persuasive. All that section 2778(c) expressly requires is that someone willfully violate a provision of the Act. Congress did not instruct courts to apply the willfulness requirement to any specific provision, let alone the Munitions List, even though it could have. Furthermore, no court has conclusively held that willfulness requires knowledge that an item is on the Munitions List. Additionally, as in *Bryan*, the underlying conduct concerned in the Act — exporting defense articles and services without a license — is not innocent in the way an everyday, uninformed citizen may unintentionally violate complex, confusing tax laws. Rather, exporting defense articles can only be achieved by educated parties with atypical access to proprietary military weapons, systems, and data. By Roth's own admission, he knew that receiving "6.2" funds from the Air Force imposed regulations on his research. Finally, the Federal Firearms Act considered in *Bryan* is extremely similar to the statute considered here. Both impose criminal sanctions for actions involving highly regulated weapons, and both have similar willfulness requirements that apply broadly to violations of their respective statutes. It follows, then, that the Supreme Court's analysis in *Bryan* applies to the Act.

Accordingly, following *Bryan* and the swath of cases from other circuits interpreting section 2778(c), we hold that section 2778(c) does not require a defendant to know that the items being exported are on the Munitions List. Rather, it only requires knowledge that the underlying action is unlawful.

The instruction given by the district court defined willfulness as doing something intentionally that the defendant knew was unlawful, which falls in line with *Bryan*, the other circuits' interpretations of section 2778(c), and now our holding here. As a result, the district court's jury instruction regarding willfulness was proper.

2. Ignorance of the law

When a district court refuses to give a requested jury instruction, we will reverse that decision "only when (1) the requested instruction is a correct statement of the law; (2) the requested instruction is not substantially covered by other instructions actually delivered; and (3) the failure to give the requested instruction impairs the defendant's theory of the case."

The ignorance of the law as a defense instruction would not have been a correct statement of law. Roth incorrectly asserts that multiple circuits have held that ignorance of the law is a separate defense to charges under the Act. In fact, no circuit court has decided this issue. Indeed, the Supreme Court has identified only a few areas, such as tax law, where "ignorance of the law is a defense," and that is because the tax system is so complex. Only when "highly technical statutes . . . present[ ] the danger of ensnaring individuals engaged in apparently innocent conduct," as in the example of tax laws and banking regulations, has the Supreme Court "held that . . . statutes "carve out an exception to the traditional rule" that ignorance of the law is no excuse."

It should be noted that two cases from the Fifth Circuit have addressed ignorance of the law in the context of charges brought under the Act. In *United States v. Davis*, the court noted that, with specific intent crimes, juries should not be instructed that ignorance of the law is not a defense. Later, in *United States v. Hernandez*, the Fifth Circuit cited *Davis* and commented that a "court should put squarely before the jury the relevance of ignorance of the law" in cases charging specific intent crimes. Both cases instructed that ignorance can be critical when instructing a jury about the defendant's state of mind when specific intent is an element of the crime. However, neither case went so far as to hold that ignorance is a separate, affirmative defense that juries must be instructed about when considering specific intent crimes. They left open the possibility that a court may instruct a jury regarding ignorance of the law in some other fashion, such as when explaining the required *mens rea* of the crime.

Furthermore, it appears that the instruction given by the district court regarding willfulness substantially covered Roth's proposed ignorance instruction. Roth admits as much in his brief. The first two sentences of the proposed instruction actually concern willfulness as an element of the crime. It is not until the third and fourth sentences of the proposed instruction that Roth really addresses and explains ignorance of the law as an affirmative and separate defense. There, he would have instructed the jury that:

> An innocent or negligent mistake by the Defendant is insufficient to support a finding of a knowing and willful export. So if Defendant was ignorant of the requirements of the Arms Export Control Act or was aware of the requirements of the Act but believed that he was complying with those requirements, he did not act knowingly or willfully, and you must find him not guilty.

This, however, is extremely similar to the court's instruction that "[n]egligent conduct, or conduct by mistake or accident, or with a good faith belief that the conduct was lawful, is not sufficient to constitute willfulness," which was delivered to the jury through the willfulness instruction. Both the proposed and actual instructions address negligence, mistake, and a good faith belief regarding compliance with the law.

Roth's proposed instruction was not a correct statement of the law, and the portion that was correct was substantially covered by another instruction. Furthermore, because the district court addressed much of the proposed instruction in the willfulness instruction, failing to deliver Roth's proposed ignorance of the law instruction to the jury impaired his case only slightly, if at all. Therefore, the district court did not abuse its discretion in declining to deliver Roth's proposed instruction on ignorance of the law as a separate defense.

****

III. CONCLUSION

The data from Phase II and the Agency Proposal, as well as the Force Stand, are defense articles and services as a matter of law because the ultimate objective of the project was to apply plasma actuators to military aircraft. Additionally, the district court did not err in its jury instructions. Finally, there was sufficient evidence to support Roth's conviction for exporting the Agency Proposal. Accordingly, we AFFIRM.

QUESTIONS

1. Was Roth found guilty of violating the "deemed export" regulations or of directly violating the prohibition on export of defense articles and services without a license?

2. On what basis did the court reject Roth's contention that the Phase II data, Agency Proposal and Force Stand were not defense articles because at the time he worked on the project the future stages of Phase II envisioned testing the actuators on commercial aircraft?

3. What is the difference between knowing that certain conduct is generally unlawful and knowing that certain conduct violates specific statutory prohibitions? Which type of conduct did Roth engage in?

4. Under what circumstances is a defendant's ignorance of the law a defense to a crime charged?

Additional Information

1. L. J. KUTTEN 3 COMPUTER SOFTWARE § 13:14 (2009).

2. *New Deemed Exports' Reality in on the Horizon*, Managing Imports and Exports (April, 2008).

3. Jamie L. Keith, Vice President and General Counsel University of Florida, *Update On Developments In "Deemed" Export Controls In The University Context*, available at http://www.generalcounsel.ufl.edu/downloads?Update DevelopmentsDeemedExportControlsInTheUniversityContext.pdf (2006).

4. Benjamin C. Findley, *Revisions to the United States Deemed-Export Regulations: Implications for Universities, University Research, and Foreign Faculty, Staff and Students*, 2006 WIS. L. REV. 1223 (2006).

5. Report, Deemed Export Advisory Committee, *The Deemed Export Rule In The Era Of Globalization* (2007) (report prepared for the U.S. Department of Commerce) available at http://www.fas.org/sgp/library/deeemedexports.pdf.

6. *Request for Public Comments on Deemed Export Advisory Committee Recommendations*, 73 Fed. Reg. 28795 (May 19, 2008).

7. Christopher R. Wall, *Controlling the Flow of Technology in Global Operations: Deemed Exports*, 901 PLI/COMM. 295 (2007).

8. Gerard Morales, Matthew Goldstein, *"Deemed Exports" of Technology: How Safe is Your Client's Company?*, 54 No. 2 PRAC. LAW. 29 (2008).

9. Sandra F. Sperino, *Complying with Export Laws Without Importing Discrimination Liability: An Attempt to Integrate Employment Discrimination Laws and the Deemed Export Rules*, 52 ST. LOUIS U. L.J. 375 (2008).

9.3 SELECTED EXPORT CONTROLS

This section considers two ubiquitous dual-use items: encryption technology and software programs. Because of their importance in both civilian and military applications, and because the line between their civilian and military applications is very fine, export control of these items is especially challenging.

9.3.1 Encryption Technology

Encryption is a process which involves transforming readable information, known as "plaintext," into unreadable information, known as "ciphertext." The transformation of plaintext into ciphertext is accomplished by means of an algorithm that precisely converts each plaintext symbol into a corresponding ciphertext symbol. Decryption is the transformation of the ciphertext symbols back to the plaintext symbols by use of a reverse algorithm, know as a "key." Although encryption systems have existed for hundreds, if not thousands, of years, in the last thirty years or so, encryption has become a rapidly advancing science due in part to the demand for increasing levels of information security and in part to the increasing power of computers.

In the civilian sector, encryption is important to protect the privacy of personal and commercial communications, as well as to assure data integrity in banking and financial transactions. Encryption is important in the military sector for both defensive and offensive purposes. Governments need access to state-of-the-art encryption technology to learn of threats to national security from hostile countries and terrorist groups. Governments also need access to state-of-the art encryption technology to gather intelligence on actors and activities that may undermine its foreign policy or weaken its global position.

The first readings in this subsection cover the definitions of encryption technologies, the CCL-based controls on encryption technologies and the license exceptions for the export of encryption technologies. The final reading in this subsection, *Junger v. Daley*, considers the First Amendment implications of encryption export controls. In a computer program format, encryption technology can take the form of either object code, the series of 0s and 1s which provide direct instructions to the computer hardware, or source code, a higher-level computer programming language which represents a shorthand expression for the object code. Source code can also exist in two forms. One form of source code is executable source code, which can be converted directly into object code by a complier to provide instructions to the computer hardware. The other form of source code is printed source code, which can be read and understood by computer scientists but cannot be directly converted into object code. *Junger* explores the difference between these two forms of source code in the context of the First Amendment.

15 C.F.R. PART 772 DEFINITIONS OF TERMS

"Asymmetric algorithm." (Cat 5) means a cryptographic algorithm using different, mathematically-related keys for encryption and decryption.

Technical Note: *A common use of "asymmetric algorithms" is key management.*

"Cryptography." (Cat 5) — The discipline that embodies principles, means and methods for the transformation of data in order to hide its information content, prevent its undetected modification or prevent its unauthorized use. "Cryptography" is limited to the transformation of information using one or more "secret parameters" (e.g., crypto variables) and/or associated key management.

"Encryption Component." Any encryption commodity or software (except source code), including encryption chips, integrated circuits, application specific encryption toolkits, or executable or linkable modules that alone are incapable of performing complete cryptographic functions, and is designed or intended for use in or the production of another encryption item.

"Encryption items." The phrase encryption items includes all encryption commodities, software, and technology that contain encryption features and are subject to the EAR. This does not include encryption items specifically designed, developed, configured, adapted or modified for military applications (including command, control and intelligence applications) which are controlled by the Department of State on the U.S. Munitions List.

"Encryption licensing arrangement." A license that allows the export of specified products to specified destinations in unlimited quantities. In certain cases, exports are limited to specified end-users for specified end-uses. Generally, reporting of all sales of the specified products is required at six month intervals. This includes sales made under distribution arrangements and distribution and warehousing agreements that were previously issued by the Department of State for encryption items.

"Encryption object code." Computer programs containing an encryption source code that has been compiled into a form of code that can be directly executed by a computer to perform an encryption function.

"Encryption software." Computer programs that provide capability of encryption functions or confidentiality of information or information systems. Such software includes source code, object code, applications software, or system software.

"Encryption source code." A precise set of operating instructions to a computer that, when compiled, allows for the execution of an encryption function on a computer.

QUESTIONS

1. In the lexicon of the EAR, which is the more encompassing definition of "encryption" — encryption component, encryption items or encryption software?

2. Is encryption source code in printed form included in the definition of encryption software?

15 C.F.R. § 742 — CONTROL POLICY — CCL BASED CONTROLS

§ 742.15   ENCRYPTION ITEMS

Encryption items can be used to maintain the secrecy of information, and thereby may be used by persons abroad to harm U.S. national security, foreign policy and law enforcement interests. The United States has a critical interest in ensuring that important and sensitive information of the public and private sector is protected. Consistent with our international obligations as a member of the Wassenaar Arrangement, the United States has a responsibility to maintain control over the export and reexport of encryption items. As the President indicated in Executive Order 13026 and in his Memorandum of November 15, 1996, exports and reexports of encryption software, like exports and reexports of encryption hardware, are controlled because of this functional capacity to encrypt information, and not because of any informational or theoretical value that such software may reflect, contain, or represent, or that its export or reexport may convey to others abroad. For this reason, export controls on encryption software are distinguished from controls on other software regulated under the EAR.

(a)   Licensing requirements and policy

(1) Licensing requirements. A license is required to export or reexport encryption items ("EI") classified under ECCN 5A002.a.1, a.2, a.5, a.6 and a.9; 5D002.a or c.1 for equipment controlled for EI reasons in ECCN 5A002; or 5E002 for "technology" for the "development," "production," or "use" of commodities or "software" controlled for EI reasons in ECCNs 5A002 or 5D002 to all destinations, except Canada. Refer to part 740 of the EAR, for license exceptions that apply to certain encryption items, and to § 772.1 of the EAR for definitions of encryption items and terms. Most encryption items may be exported under the provisions of License Exception ENC set forth in § 740.17 of the EAR. Before submitting a license application, please review License Exception ENC to determine whether this license exception is available for your item or transaction. For exports and reexports of encryption items that are not eligible for a license exception, exporters must submit an application to obtain authorization under a license or an Encryption Licensing Arrangement.

(2) Licensing policy. Applications will be reviewed on a case-by-case basis by BIS, in conjunction with other agencies, to determine whether the export or reexport is consistent with U.S. national security and foreign policy interests. Encryption Licensing Arrangements (ELAs) may be authorized for exports and reexports of unlimited quantities of encryption commodities and software to national or federal government bureaucratic agencies for

civil use, and to state, provincial or local governments, in all destinations, except countries listed in Country Group E:1 of Supplement No. 1 to part 740. ELAs are valid for four years and may require post-export reporting or pre-shipment notification. Applicants seeking authorization for Encryption Licensing Arrangements must specify the sales territory and class of end-user on their license applications.

(b)   Review requirement for mass market encryption commodities and software exceeding 64 bits:

Mass market encryption commodities and software employing a key length greater than 64 bits for the symmetric algorithm (including such products previously reviewed by BIS and exported under ECCN 5A002 or 5D002) are subject to the EAR and require review by BIS and the ENC Encryption Request Coordinator (Ft. Meade, MD), prior to export or reexport. Encryption commodities and software that are described in § 740.17(b)(2) of the EAR do not qualify for mass market treatment. A new product review is required if a change is made to the cryptographic functionality (*e.g.*, algorithms) or other technical characteristics affecting mass market eligibility (*e.g.*, performance enhancements to provide network infrastructure services, or customizations to end-user specifications) of the originally reviewed product However, a new product review is not required when a change involves: the subsequent bundling, patches, upgrades or releases of a product; name changes; or changes to a previously reviewed encryption product where the change is limited to updates of encryption software components where the product is otherwise unchanged.

(1)   Procedures for requesting review. To request review of your mass market encryption products, you must submit to BIS and the ENC Encryption Request Coordinator the information described in paragraphs (a) through (e) of Supplement No. 6 to this part 742, and you must include specific information describing how your products qualify for mass market treatment under the criteria in the Cryptography Note (Note 3) of Category 5, Part 2 ("Information Security"), of the Commerce Control List (Supplement No. 1 to part 774 of the EAR). Review requests must be submitted to BIS in accordance with §§ 748.1 and 748.3 of the EAR. See paragraph (r) of Supplement No. 2 to part 748 of the EAR for special instructions about this submission. Submissions to the ENC Encryption Request Coordinator should be directed to the mailing address indicated in § 740.17(e)(1)(ii) of the EAR. BIS will notify you if there are any questions concerning your request for review (e.g., because of missing or incompatible support documentation).

****

(3)   Exclusions from review requirements. The following commodities and software do not require review prior to export or reexport as mass market products.

(i)   Short-range wireless encryption functions. Commodities and software not otherwise controlled in Category 5, but that are classified under ECCN 5A992 or 5D992 only because they incorporate components or software that provide short-range wireless encryption functions (*e.g.*, with a nominal operating range not exceeding 100 meters according to the manufacturer's specifications). Commodities and software included in this description include those designed to comply with the Institute of Electrical and Electronic Engineers (IEEE) 802.11 wireless LAN standard (35 meters) for short-range use and those designed to comply with the IEEE 802.15.1 standard that provide only the short-range wireless encryption functionality, and would not be classified under Category 5, part 1 of the CCL (telecommunications) absent this encryption functionality. Certain items excluded from review by this paragraph may also be excluded from review under paragraph (b)(3)(iii) of this section (commodities and software that provide "ancillary cryptography").

(ii)   [RESERVED]

(iii)   "Ancillary cryptography." Commodities and software that perform "ancillary cryptography." See Nota Bene of definition of "ancillary cryptography" in § 772.1 of the EAR.

(4) Commodities and software that activate or enable cryptographic functionality.

Commodities, software, and components that allow the end-user to activate or enable cryptographic functionality in encryption products which would otherwise remain disabled, are controlled according to the functionality of the activated encryption product.

(5) Examples of mass market encryption products. Subject to the requirements of the Cryptography Note (Note 3) in Category 5, Part 2, of the Commerce Control List, mass market encryption products include, but are not limited to, general purpose operating systems and desktop applications (e.g., e-mail, browsers, games, word processing, database, financial applications or utilities) designed for use with computers classified as ECCN 4A994 or EAR99, laptops, or hand-held devices; commodities and software for client Internet appliances and client wireless LAN devices; home use networking commodities and software (*e.g.*, personal firewalls, cable modems for personal computers, and consumer set top boxes); and portable or mobile civil telecommunications commodities and software (*e.g.*, personal data assistants (PDAs), radios, or cellular products).

****

QUESTIONS

1.   The regulations state that the purpose for controlling the export of encryption items is to avoid harm to U.S. national security, foreign policy and law enforcement interests "and not because of any informational or theoretical value that such software may reflect, contain, or represent, or that its export or reexport may convey to others abroad." What is the difference between these two rationales for controlling encryption exports? Are you persuaded that the United States has

no interests at stake under the second rationale?

2. What is the difference between an Encryption Licensing Arrangement and an encryption export license?

3. Does an encryption chip in a cell phone require an export license?

4. What is an example of a mass market encryption product?

15 C.F.R. PART 740 — LICENSE EXCEPTIONS

§ 740.17 ENCRYPTION COMMODITIES, SOFTWARE AND TECHNOLOGY (ENC)

License Exception ENC authorizes export and reexport of software and commodities and components therefore that are classified under ECCNs 5A002 .a.1, a.2, a.5, a.6 or a.9, 5B002, 5D002, and technology that is classified under ECCN 5E002. This License Exception ENC does not authorize export or reexport to, or provision of any service in any country listed in Country Group E:1 in Supplement No. 1 to part 740 of the EAR, or release of source code or technology to any national of a country listed in Country Group E:1. [Country Group E:1 includes Cuba, Iran, North Korea, Sudan and Syria.] Reexports and transfers under License Exception ENC are subject to the criteria set forth in paragraph (c) of this section. Paragraph (d) of this section sets forth information about review requests required by this section. Paragraph (e) sets forth reporting required by this section.

(a)   No prior review or post export reporting required

(1)   Internal "development" or "production" of new products. License Exception ENC authorizes exports and reexports of items described in paragraph (a)(1)(i) of this section, to end-users described in paragraph (a)(1)(ii) of this section, for the intended end-use described in paragraph (a)(1)(iii) of this section without prior review by the U.S. Government.

(i)   *Eligible items.* Eligible items are those classified under ECCNs 5A002.a.1, .a.2, .a.5, .a.6, or .a.9, 5B002, 5D002, or 5E002.

(ii)   *Eligible End-users.* Eligible end-users are "private sector end-users" wherever located, except to countries listed in Country Group E:1 (see Supplement No. 1 to part 740 of the EAR) that are headquartered in a country listed in Supplement No. 3 of this part.

(1) An individual who is not acting on behalf of any foreign government; or

(2) A commercial firm (including its subsidiary and parent firms, and other subsidiaries of the same parent) that is not wholly owned by, or otherwise controlled by or acting on behalf of, any foreign government.

(iii)   *Eligible End-use.* The eligible end-use is internal "development" or "production" of new products by those end-users.

****

(2) Exports and reexports to "U.S. Subsidiaries." License Exception ENC authorizes export and reexport of items classified under ECCNs 5A002.a.1, .a.2, .a.5, .a.6, or .a.9, 5B002, 5D002, or 5E002 to any "U.S. subsidiary," wherever located, except to countries listed in Country Group E:1 (see Supplement No. 1 to part 740 of the EAR), without prior review by the U.S. Government. License Exception ENC also authorizes export or reexport of such items by a U.S. company and its subsidiaries to foreign nationals who are employees, contractors or interns of a U.S. company or its subsidiaries if the items are for internal company use, including the "development" or "production" of new products, without prior review by the U.S. Government.

****

QUESTIONS

1. Who are eligible end-users under license exception ENC?

2. What are eligible end-uses under license exception ENC?

JUNGER v. DALEY
209 F.3d 481 (6th Cir. 2000)

BOYCE F. MARTIN, JR., CHIEF JUDGE.

This is a constitutional challenge to the provisions of the Export Administration Regulations, 15 C.F.R. Parts 730-74, that regulate the export of encryption software. Peter D. Junger appeals the district court's grant of summary judgment in favor of Secretary Daley and the other defendants.

The district court found that encryption source code is not sufficiently expressive to be protected by the First Amendment, that the Export Administration Regulations are permissible content-neutral restrictions, and that the Regulations are not subject to a facial challenge as a prior restraint on speech. Subsequent to the district court's holding and the oral arguments before this Court, the Bureau of Export Administration issued an interim final rule amending the regulations at issue. Having concluded that the First Amendment protects computer source code, we reverse the district court and remand this case for further consideration of Junger's constitutional claims in light of the amended regulations.

ENCRYPTION AND SOFTWARE BACKGROUND

Encryption is the process of converting a message from its original form ("plaintext") into a scrambled form ("ciphertext"). Most encryption today uses an algorithm, a mathematical transformation from plaintext to ciphertext, and a key that acts as a password. Generally, the security of the message depends on the strength of both the algorithm and the key.

Encryption has long been a tool in the conduct of military and foreign affairs. Encryption has many civil applications, including protecting communication and data sent over the Internet. As technology has progressed, the methods of encryption have changed from purely mechanical processes, such as the Enigma machines of Nazi Germany, to modern electronic processes. Today, messages can be encrypted through dedicated electronic hardware and also through general-purpose computers with the aid of encryption software.

For a general-purpose computer to encrypt data, it must use encryption software that instructs the computer's circuitry to execute the encoding process. Encryption software, like all computer software, can be in one of two forms: object code or source code. Object code represents computer instructions as a sequence of binary digits (0s and 1s) that can be directly executed by a computer's microprocessor. Source code represents the same instructions in a specialized programming language, such as BASIC, C, or Java. Individuals familiar with a particular computer programming language can read and understand source code. Source code, however, must be converted into object code before a computer will execute the software's instructions. This conversion is conducted by compiler software. Although compiler software is typically readily available, some source code may have no compatible compiler.

REGULATORY BACKGROUND

The Export Administration Regulations create a comprehensive licensing scheme to control the export of nonmilitary technology, software, and commodities. In 1996, the President transferred export jurisdiction over nonmilitary encryption items from the State Department to the Commerce Department's Bureau of Export Administration.

The Regulations are structured around the Commodity Control List, which lists items subject to export control. *See* 15 C.F.R. Part 774. Each item on the List is given an Export Control Classification Number that designates the category of the controlled item and the reasons why the government controls the item's export. *See* 15 C.F.R. § 738.2. The reasons for control affect the nature and scope of the export controls.

Encryption software, including both source code and object code, is regulated under Export Control Classification Number 5D002 for national security reasons. In addition, encryption technology and encryption hardware are regulated for national security reasons under different Classification Numbers. Generally, the Regulations require a license for the export of all encryption items to all foreign destinations, except Canada. Although the regulations provide some exceptions, most encryption software in electronic form remains subject to the license requirements for export. Encryption software in printed form, however, is not subject to the Regulations. *See* 15 C.F.R. § 734.3(b)(2).

The Regulations define "export" as the "actual shipment or transmission of items subject to the EAR out of the United States." For encryption software, the definition of "export" also includes publication of the software on the Internet, unless steps are taken to restrict foreign access to the Internet site.

FACTUAL BACKGROUND

Peter Junger is a professor at the Case Western University School of Law. Junger maintains sites on the World Wide Web that include information about courses that he teaches, including a computers and the law course. Junger wishes to post on his web site encryption source code that he has written to demonstrate how computers work. Such a posting is defined as an export under the Regulations.

On June 12, 1997, Junger submitted three applications to the Commerce Department, requesting determinations of commodity classifications for encryption software programs and other items. On July 4, the Export Administration told Junger that Classification Number 5D002 covered four of the five software programs he had submitted. Although it found that four programs were subject to the Regulations, the Export Administration found that the first chapter of Junger's textbook, *Computers and the Law*, was an allowable unlicensed export. Though deciding that the printed book chapter containing encryption code could be exported, the Export Administration stated that export of the book in electronic form would require a license if the text contained 5D002 software. Since receiving the classification determination, Junger has not applied for a license to export his classified encryption source code.

Junger filed this action to make a facial challenge to the Regulations on First Amendment grounds, seeking declaratory and injunctive relief that would permit him to engage in the unrestricted distribution of encryption software through his web site. Junger claims that encryption source code is protected speech. The district court granted summary judgment in favor of the defendants, holding that encryption source code is not protected under the First Amendment, that the Regulations are permissible content-neutral regulations, and that the Regulations are not subject to facial challenge on prior restraint grounds.

We review the grant of summary judgment *de novo*.

The issue of whether or not the First Amendment protects encryption source code is a difficult one because source code has both an expressive feature and a functional feature. The United States does not dispute that it is possible to use encryption source code to represent and convey information and ideas about cryptography and that encryption source code can be used by programmers and scholars for such informational purposes. Much like a mathematical or scientific formula, one can describe the function and design of encryption software by a prose explanation; however, for individuals fluent in a computer programming language, source code is the most efficient and precise means by which to communicate ideas about cryptography.

The district court concluded that the functional characteristics of source code overshadow its simultaneously expressive nature. The fact that a medium of expression has a functional capacity should not preclude constitutional protection. Rather, the appropriate consideration of the medium's functional capacity is in the analysis of permitted government regulation.

The Supreme Court has explained that "all ideas having even the slightest redeeming social importance," including those concerning "the advancement of truth, science, morality, and arts" have the full protection of the First Amendment. *Roth v. United States.* This protection is not reserved for purely expressive communication. The Supreme Court has recognized First Amendment protection for symbolic conduct, such as draft-card burning, that has both functional and expressive features. *See United States v. O'Brien.*

The Supreme Court has expressed the versatile scope of the First Amendment by labeling as "unquestionably shielded" the artwork of Jackson Pollack, the music of Arnold Schoenberg, or the Jabberwocky verse of Lewis Carroll. *Hurley v. Irish-American Gay, Lesbian and Bisexual Group.* Though unquestionably expressive, these things identified by the Court are not traditional speech. Particularly, a musical score cannot be read by the majority of the public but can be used as a means of communication among musicians. Likewise, computer source code, though unintelligible to many, is the preferred method of communication among computer programmers.

Because computer source code is an expressive means for the exchange of information and ideas about computer programming, we hold that it is protected by the First Amendment.

The functional capabilities of source code, and particularly those of encryption source code, should be considered when analyzing the governmental interest in regulating the exchange of this form of speech. Under intermediate scrutiny, the regulation of speech is valid, in part, if "it furthers an important or substantial governmental interest." In *Turner Broadcasting System v. FCC*, the Supreme Court noted that although an asserted governmental interest may be important, when the government defends restrictions on speech "it must do more than simply "posit the existence of the disease sought to be cured."" The government "must demonstrate that the recited harms are real, not merely conjectural, and that the regulation will in fact alleviate these harms in a direct and material way." We recognize that national security interests can outweigh the interests of protected speech and require the regulation of speech. In the present case, the record does not resolve whether the exercise of presidential power in furtherance of national security interests should overrule the interests in allowing the free exchange of encryption source code.

Before any level of judicial scrutiny can be applied to the Regulations, Junger must be in a position to bring a facial challenge to these regulations. In light of the recent amendments to the Export Administration Regulations, the district court should examine the new regulations to determine if Junger can bring a facial challenge.

For the foregoing reasons, we REVERSE the district court and REMAND the case to the district court for consideration of Junger's constitutional challenge to the amended regulations.

QUESTIONS

1.   The court held that "computer source code" is protected by the First Amendment. Did the court mean that executable computer source code is protected by the First Amendment, or only printed computer source code?

2.   Export Administration determined that the printed book chapter containing encryption code could be exported without a license, but that the export of the book in electronic form would require a license if the text contained encryption software source code. What is the difference?

3.   If executable computer source code is expression protected under the First Amendment, would printed diagrams, data, instructions, etc. pertaining to CCL-controlled items also be protected under the First Amendment?

ENCRYPTION NOTE

BIS Updates Encryption Export Rule;
Revised Rule Streamlines Review Process, Enhances National Security
June 25, 2010

WASHINGTON — The U.S. Department of Commerce's Bureau of Industry and Security (BIS) today revised its rules regarding the export of most mass market electronic products that contain encryption functions and other encryption products.

"This revised rule enhances our national security and cuts red tape by eliminating the review of readily available encryption items, like cell phones and household appliances, and allows the Government to focus its resources on more sensitive encryption items," Assistant Secretary of Commerce for Export Administration Kevin Wolf said.

The new rule ends the U.S. government's 30-day technical review requirement to export most mass market and other types of encryption products. "Mass market" electronic products containing encryption include cell phones, laptops, and disk drives. Exporters and manufacturers of the encryption products may now self-classify the products and then export them without a license if they register on-line with BIS. BIS also requires that they submit an annual self-classification report. This rule is expected to decrease technical reviews by approximately 70 percent and semi-annual reporting by up to 85 percent.

The rule also extends the scope of License Exception ENC authorizations to most encryption technology exports, following a technical review. In addition, it adds a decontrol note for items that perform "ancillary" cryptography, which covers items such as games, robotics, business process automation, and other products that contain encryption capabilities but do not have communication, computing, networking or information security as a primary function.

"This rule is the first step in the President's effort to fundamentally reform U.S. encryption export controls," Assistant Secretary Wolf said. "The Administration will continue to review the encryption rules to further enhance national security and ensure the continued competitiveness of U.S. encryption products. This effort will include a review of the current controls on publicly available encryption software, integrated circuits with encryption functionality, high-speed routers, and other types of restricted encryption products."

Available at http://www.bis.doc.gov/news/2010/bis_press06252010.htm

Additional Information

1. KURTIS A. KEMPER, 2 COMPUTER AND INFORMATION LAW DIGEST § 10:6 (2d ed.) (2010).

2. KATHERYN A. ANDERSEN, 1 LAW AND BUSINESS OF COMPUTER SOFTWARE § 6:20 (2d ed.) (2010).

3. L. J. KUTTEN, 3 COMPUTER SOFTWARE § 13:8 (2010).

4. TERRENCE F. MACLAREN, 1 ECKSTROM'S LICENSING: JOINT VENTURES § 5:13 (2011).

5. 1 L. OF INTL TRADE §§ 25:15, 27:15 (2011).

6. LILLIAN V. BLAGEFF, 1 CORP COUNS GD TO EXPORT CONTROLS §§ 1:14, 2:14 (2010).

7. Katherine A. Moeke, *Free Speech to a Machine? Encryption Software Source Code Is Not Constitutionally Protected "Speech" Under First Amendment*, 84 MINN. L. REV. 1007 (2000).

8. Mark T. Pasko, *Re-Defining National Security in the Technology Age: The Encryption Export Debate*, 26 J. LEGIS. 337 (2000).

9. Daniel R. Rua, *Cryptobabble: How Encyrption Export Disputes Are Shaping Free Speech for the New Millennium*, 24 N.C. J. INT'L L. & COM. REG 125 (1998).

9.3.2 Software Programs

This subsection describes the two principal license exceptions for computer software: Technology and Software Under Restriction (TSR) and Technology and Software Unrestricted (TSU).

15 C.F.R. § 740.6 — TECHNOLOGY AND SOFTWARE UNDER RESTRICTION (TSR)

(a) Scope

License Exception TSR permits exports and reexports of technology and software where the Commerce Country Chart (Supplement No. 1 to part 738 of the EAR) indicates a license requirement to the ultimate destination for national security reasons only and identified by "TSR — Yes" in entries on the CCL, provided the software or technology is destined to Country Group B. (See Supplement No. 1 to part 740.) A written assurance is required from the consignee before exporting under this License Exception.

(1) Required assurance for export of technology. You may not export or

reexport technology under this License Exception until you have received from the importer a written assurance that, without a BIS license or License Exception, the importer will not:

(i) Reexport or release the technology to a national of a country in Country Groups D:1 or E:2; or

(ii) Export to Country Groups D:1 or E:2 the direct product of the technology, if such foreign produced direct product is subject to national security controls as identified on the CCL (See General Prohibition Three, § 736.2(b)(3) of the EAR); or

(iii) If the direct product of the technology is a complete plant or any major component of a plant, export to Country Groups D:1 or E:2 the direct product of the plant or major component thereof, if such foreign produced direct product is subject to national security controls as identified on the CCL or is subject to State Department controls under the U.S. Munitions List (22 CFR part 121).

(2) Required assurance for export of software. You may not export or reexport software under this License Exception until you have received from the importer a written assurance that, without a BIS license or License Exception, the importer will neither:

(i) Reexport or release the software or the source code for the software to a national of a country in Country Groups D:1 or E:2; nor

(ii) Export to Country Groups D:1 or E:2 the direct product of the software, if such foreign produced direct product is subject to national security controls as identified on the CCL. (See General Prohibition Three, § 736.2(b)(3) of the EAR).

(3) Form of written assurance. The required assurance may be made in the form of a letter or any other written communication from the importer, including communications via facsimile, or the assurance may be incorporated into a licensing agreement that specifically includes the assurances. An assurance included in a licensing agreement is acceptable only if the agreement specifies that the assurance will be honored even after the expiration date of the licensing agreement. If such a written assurance is not received, License Exception TSR is not applicable and a license is required. The license application must include a statement explaining why assurances could not be obtained.

(4) Other License Exceptions. The requirements in this License Exception do not apply to the export of technology or software under other License Exceptions, or to the export of technology or software included in an application for the foreign filing of a patent, provided the filing is in accordance with the regulations of the U.S. Patent Office.

(b) Reporting requirements

See § 743.1 of the EAR for reporting requirements for exports of certain items under License Exception TSR. Note that reports are not required for release of technology or source code subject to the EAR to foreign nationals in the U.S.

under the provisions of License Exception TSR.

QUESTIONS

1. What is a written assurance? What does a written assurance cover?

2. Why are reports not required for release of technology or source code to foreign nationals in the United States under the provisions of license exception TSR?

15 C.F.R. § 740.13 — TECHNOLOGY AND SOFTWARE — UNRESTRICTED (TSU)

This license exception authorizes exports and reexports of operation technology and software; sales technology and software; software updates (bug fixes); "mass market" software subject to the General Software Note; and encryption source code (and corresponding object code) that would be considered publicly available under § 734.3(b)(3) of the EAR. Note that encryption software subject to the EAR is not subject to the General Software Note (see paragraph (d)(2) of this section).

(a) Operation technology and software

(1) **Scope.** The provisions of paragraph (a) permit exports and reexports of operation technology and software. "Operation technology" is the minimum technology necessary for the installation, operation, maintenance (checking), and repair of those commodities or software that are lawfully exported or reexported under a license, a License Exception, or NLR. The "minimum necessary" operation technology does not include technology for development or production and includes use technology only to the extent required to ensure safe and efficient use of the commodities or software. Individual entries in the software and technology subcategories of the CCL may further restrict the export or reexport of operation technology.

(2) **Provisions and Destinations.**

(i) *Provisions.* Operation software may be exported or reexported provided that both of the following conditions are met:

(A) The operation software is the minimum necessary to operate equipment authorized for export or reexport; and

(B) **The operation software is in object code.**

(ii) *Destinations.* Operation software and technology may be exported or reexported to any destination to which the equipment for which it is required has been or is being legally exported or reexported.

(b) Sales technology

(1) **Scope.** The provisions of paragraph (b) authorize exports and reex-

ports of sales technology. "Sales technology" is data supporting a prospective or actual quotation, bid, or offer to sell, lease, or otherwise supply any item.

(2) Provisions and destinations.

(i) *Provisions.* Sales technology may be exported or reexported provided that:

(A) The technology is a type customarily transmitted with a prospective or actual quotation, bid, or offer in accordance with established business practice; and

(B) Neither the export nor the reexport will disclose the detailed design, production, or manufacture technology, or the means of reconstruction, of either the quoted item or its product. The purpose of this limitation is to prevent disclosure of technology so detailed that the consignee could reduce the technology to production.

(ii) *Destinations.* Sales technology may be exported or reexported to any destination.

NOTE:

Neither this section nor its use means that the U.S. Government intends, or is committed, to approve a license application for any commodity, plant, software, or technology that may be the subject of the transaction to which such quotation, bid, or offer relates. Exporters are advised to include in any quotations, bids, or offers, and in any contracts entered into pursuant to such quotations, bids, or offers, a provision relieving themselves of liability in the event that a license (when required) is not approved by the Bureau of Industry and Security.

(c) Software updates

The provisions of paragraph (c) authorize exports and reexports of software updates that are intended for and are limited to correction of errors ("fixes" to "bugs") in software lawfully exported or reexported (original software). Such software updates may be exported or reexported only to the same consignee to whom the original software was exported or reexported, and such software updates may not enhance the functional capacities of the original software. Such software updates may be exported or reexported to any destination to which the software for which they are required has been legally exported or reexported.

(d) General Software Note: mass market software

(1) Scope. The provisions of paragraph (d) authorize exports and reexports of mass market software subject to the General Software Note (see Supplement No. 2 to part 774 of the EAR; also referenced in this section).

(2) Exclusions. The provisions of this paragraph (d) are not available for encryption software controlled for "EI" reasons under ECCN 5D002 or for encryption software with symmetric key length exceeding 64-bits that qualifies as mass market encryption software under the criteria in the Cryptography Note (Note 3) of Category 5, Part 2, of the Commerce Control List (Supplement No. 1 to part 774 of the EAR). (Once such mass market encryption software has been reviewed by BIS and released from "EI" and "NS" controls pursuant to § 742.15(b) of the EAR, it is controlled under ECCN 5D992.c and is thus outside the scope of License Exception TSU.) See § 742.15(b) of the EAR for exports and reexports of mass market encryption products controlled under ECCN 5D992.c.

(3) Provisions and destinations.

(i) *Destinations.* Mass market software is available to all destinations except destinations in Country Group E:1 (see Supplement No. 1 to this "Mass market" software may fall under the classification of "general use" software for export clearance purposes. Exporters should consult the Census Bureau FTSR for possible SED or AES requirements.)

(ii) *Provisions.* Mass market treatment is available for software that is generally available to the public by being:

(A) Sold from stock at retail selling points, without restriction, by means of:

(*1*) Over the counter transactions;

(*2*) Mail order transactions; or

(*3*) Telephone call transactions; *and*

(B) Designed for installation by the user without further substantial support by the supplier.

(e) Encryption source code (and corresponding object code)

(1) Scope and eligibility. This paragraph (e) authorizes exports and reexports, without review, of encryption source code controlled by ECCN 5D002 that, if not controlled by ECCN 5D002, would be considered publicly available under § 734.3(b)(3) of the EAR. Such source code is eligible for License Exception TSU under this paragraph (e) even if it is subject to an express agreement for the payment of a licensing fee or royalty for commercial production or sale of any product developed using the source code. This paragraph also authorizes the export and reexport of the corresponding object code (i.e., that which is compiled from source code that is authorized for export and reexport under this paragraph) if both the object code and the source code from which it is compiled would be considered publicly available under § 734.3(b)(3) of the EAR, if they were not controlled under ECCN 5D002.

(2) Restrictions. This paragraph (e) does not authorize:

(i) Export or reexport of any encryption software controlled under ECCN 5D002 that does *not* meet the requirements of paragraph (e)(1), even if the software incorporates or is specially designed to use other encryption software that meets the requirements of paragraph (e)(1) of this section; or

(ii) Any knowing export or reexport to a country listed in Country Group E:1 in Supplement No. 1 to part 740 of the EAR.

(3) Notification requirement. You must notify BIS and the ENC Encryption Request Coordinator via e-mail of the Internet location (e.g., URL or Internet address) of the source code or provide each of them a copy of the source code at or before the time you take action to make the software publicly available as that term is described in § 734.3(b)(3) of the EAR. If you elect to meet this requirement by providing copies of the source code to BIS and the ENC Encryption Request Coordinator, you must provide additional copies to each of them each time the cryptographic functionality of the software is updated or modified. If you elect to provide the Internet location of the source code, you must notify BIS and the ENC Encryption Request Coordinator each time the Internet location is changed, but you are not required to notify them of updates or modifications made to the encryption software at the previously notified location. In all instances, submit the notification or copy to *crypt@bis.doc.gov* and to *enc@nsa.gov.*

Note to paragraph (e). Posting encryption source code and corresponding object code on the Internet (e.g., FTP or World Wide Web site) where it may be downloaded by anyone neither establishes "knowledge" of a prohibited export or reexport for purposes of this paragraph, nor triggers any "red flags" necessitating the affirmative duty to inquire under the "Know Your Customer" guidance provided in Supplement No. 3 to part 732 of the EAR.

(f) Special Recordkeeping Requirements: ECCNs 2D983 and 2E983

In addition to any other recordkeeping requirements set forth elsewhere in the EAR, exporters are required to maintain records, as specified in this paragraph, when exporting operation software or technology controlled under ECCNs 2D983 and 2E983, respectively, under License Exception TSU. Records maintained pursuant to this section may be requested at any time by an appropriate BIS official as set forth in § 762.7 of the EAR. The following information must be specially maintained for each export or reexport transaction, under License Exception TSU, of operation software and technology controlled by ECCNs 2D983 and 2E983:

(1) A description of the software or technology exported or reexported, including the ECCN, as identified on the CCL;

(2) A description of the equipment for which the software or technology is intended to be used, including the ECCN, as identified on the CCL;

(3) The intended end-use of the software or technology;

(4) The name and address of the end-user;

(5) The quantity of software shipped; and

(6) The location of the equipment for which the software or technology is intended to be used, including the country of destination.

QUESTIONS

1. What is Operation Technology and Software? To what extent does Operation Technology and Software include "use" technology?

2. What is an example of Sales Technology?

3. What destinations are not eligible for mass market software license exception TSU?

4. Is publicly available mass market encryption source code eligible for the TSU license exception if it is available only for a fee, royalty or sales payment?

5. What is the purpose of the notification requirement for using the TSU license exception for mass market encryption source code?

CASE NOTES

1. Bernstein v. United States DOJ, 176 F.3d 1132 (9th Cir. 1999) (Encryption software in its source code form is "expression" for First Amendment purposes and thus is entitled to the protections of the prior restraint doctrine; mathematician could bring a facial challenge on prior restraint grounds against regulations that imposed restrictions on export of encryption software in source code form, including requirement of prepublication license, because licensing scheme vested unbridled discretion in government officials and directly jeopardized scientific expression; *Bernstein v. U.S. Dep't of Justice*, 192 F.3d 1308 (9th Cir. 1999) (Three-judge panel decision withdrawn; case to be reheard by en banc court); Karn v. U.S. Dep't of State, 925 F.Supp. 1 (D.C., 1996) (Designation of computer diskette containing encryption software as a "defense article" was not subject to judicial review; regulation of cryptographic software was narrowly tailored to the goal of limiting proliferation of cryptographic products and did not violate exporter's free speech rights).

Additional Information

1. LILLIAN V. BLAGEFF, 1 CORP COUNS GD TO EXPORT CONTROLS § 2:15 (2008).

2. Benjamin H. Flower, Jr., *Exporting Technology and Software, Particularly Encryption*, 910 PLI/COMM. 279 (2008).

3. Cindy Cohn, Lee Tien, *Peter Junger, Digital Freedom Fighter*, 58 CASE W. RES. L. REV. 315 (2008).

4. Ray C. Fox, *Old Law and New Technology: The Problem of Computer Code and the First Amendment*, 49 U.C.L.A. L. REV. 871 (2002).

5. Norman A. Crain, *Bernstein, Karn and Junger: Constitutional Challenges to Cryptographic Regulations*, 50 ALA. L. REV. 869 (1999).

6. Mitchell A. Goodkin, David H Goodkin, Software Export Rules, 86-JUN MICH. B.J. 30 (2007).

6. Mathew P. Voors, *Encryption Regulation in the Wake of September 11, 2001: Must We Protect National Security at the Expense of the Economy*, 55 FED. COMM. L.J. 331 (2003).

7. Peter K. Hoffmann, *Cracking the Department of Commerce's Encryption Export Regulations*, 6 B.U. J. SCI. & TECH. L. 15 (2001).

9.4   SELECTED RECENT ENFORCEMENT CASES

The cases summarized below are illustrative of the range of technologies involved in export control violations, the diversity of persons and companies against whom civil and criminal actions have been brought for violations of export controls, and the severity of the civil and criminal fines and penalties imposed for export control violations.

BIS EXPORT ENFORCEMENT MAJOR CASES LIST

October 2009

The mission of the Commerce Department's Bureau of Industry and Security (BIS) is to advance U.S. national security, foreign policy and economic objectives by ensuring an effective export control and treaty compliance system and promoting continued U.S. strategic technology leadership.

BIS integrates its export licensing, outreach and enforcement activities to effectively regulate international trade in sensitive dual-use items, prevent violations and combat illicit trafficking and proliferation. BIS's enforcement arm, the Office of Export Enforcement (OEE), is an elite law enforcement organization recognized for its expertise, professionalism, integrity and accomplishments in export enforcement. OEE's export enforcement goal is to *keep the most sensitive goods out of the most dangerous hands.*

BIS's export enforcement activities target the most significant threats facing the United States today: the proliferation of Weapons of Mass Destruction (WMD) and missile delivery systems, terrorism and state sponsors of terror, and diversions of dual-use goods to unauthorized military end-uses. During Fiscal Year 2008 (October 1, 2007 through September 30, 2008), OEE investigations resulted in 40 criminal convictions resulting in criminal fines totaling $2.7 million, $800,000 in forfeitures and 218 months imprisonment. During that same time period, BIS has also imposed more than $3.6 million in administrative penalties and other administrative sanctions as a result of 56 closed administrative enforcement cases.

Below are some of BIS's most significant cases. The Major Cases List is comprised of two sections: new additions to the List are highlighted first, followed by major cases from over the last several years grouped by case focus.

New to the Major Cases List This Month

Goods to Syria, Iran, and Sudan — On August 6, 2009, DPWN Holdings (USA), Inc. (formerly known as DHL Holdings (USA), Inc.) and DHL Express (USA), Inc. (collectively "DHL"), agreed to pay a civil penalty of $9,444,744 to settle allegations that DHL unlawfully aided and abetted the illegal export of goods to Iran, Syria and Sudan, and failed to comply with record keeping requirements of the Export Administration Regulations and Office of Foreign Assets Control (OFAC) Regulations. DHL also agreed to conduct external audits covering exports to Iran, Syria and Sudan from March 2007 through December 2011. OEE and OFAC jointly conducted this investigation. (Terrorism/State Sponsors of Terrorism)

Sighting Devices to Taiwan and Afghanistan — On September 18, 2009, Aaron Henderson, doing business as Valhalla Tactical Supply, in U.S. District Court in the Southern District of Iowa, pled guilty to violating the International Emergency Economic Powers Act and was sentenced to time served followed by two years of supervised release, and a $100 payment to the Crime Victims Fund. The guilty plea related to the export of sighting devices to Taiwan and Afghanistan without the required export licenses from the Department of Commerce. OEE, U.S. Immigration and Customs Enforcement, and the Bureau of Alcohol Tobacco and Firearms jointly conducted the investigation. (Other Dual Use)

Riflescopes to Russia — On September 16, 2009, Lev Steinberg, a resident of Brooklyn, NY, pled guilty in U.S. District Court in the Southern District of New York to violating the International Emergency Economic Powers Act and the Foreign Corrupt Practices Act. Steinberg was arrested in March 2009 for illegally exporting Department of Commerce controlled riflescopes to Russia. (Other Dual Use)

Aircraft Components to Iran — On September 24, 2009, Aviation Services International BV (ASI), an aircraft supply company in the Netherlands, Robert Kraaipoel, Director of ASI, Neils Kraaipoel, sales manager of ASI, and Delta Logistics pled guilty in U.S. District Court in Washington, DC to charges related to a conspiracy to illegally export aircraft components and other U.S.-origin commodities to entities in Iran, via the Netherlands, the United Arab Emirates and Cyprus. Between October 2005 and October 2007, the defendants received orders from customers in Iran for U.S.-origin items, then contacted companies in the United States and negotiated purchases on behalf of the Iranian customers. The defendants provided false end-user certificates to U.S. companies to conceal the true end-users in Iran. The defendants caused U.S. companies to ship items to ASI in the Netherlands or other locations in the United Arab Emirates and Cyprus which were then repackaged and transshipped to Iran. OEE, U.S. Immigration and Customs Enforcement, Defense Criminal Investigative Service and the Federal Bureau of Investigation jointly conducted the investigation. (Terrorism/State Sponsors of Terrorism)

Major Cases

WMD and Missile Proliferation

Electronic Components to China — On May 14, 2009, Joseph Piquet was sentenced in U.S. District Court to 60 months in prison and two years of probation. On March 5, 2009, a federal trial jury in Fort Pierce, Florida found Joseph Piquet, President of Alphatronx Inc., guilty of Conspiracy and violations of the Arms Export Control Act and the International Emergency Economics Powers Act following a four day trial. Piquet was convicted based on his role in a conspiracy to purchase high-tech, military-use electronic components from a domestic corporation, and to then ship the items to Hong Kong and the People's Republic of China without first obtaining the required export licenses. Among the commodities involved in this conspiracy were high power amplifiers designed for use by the U.S. military in early warning radar and missile target acquisition systems, and low noise amplifiers that have both commercial and military use. OEE and U.S.

Immigration and Customs Enforcement jointly conducted this investigation.

Electronic Sensors to a Listed Entity — On May 11, 2009, Sam Peng was sentenced in U.S. District Court in the Central District of California to three years of probation, five months of home confinement, 400 hours of community service, and a $6,000 fine. Peng pled guilty in September 2007 to exporting electronic sensors and vibration test equipment to a listed entity in India while acting as the Export Compliance Manager for Endevco Corporation.

Electronic Components to List Entities in India — On August 11, 2008, Mythli Gopal was sentenced in U.S. District Court for the District of Columbia to a $5,000 fine, four years of probation with the condition of 60 days of home confinement, and 200 hours of community service. On June 16, 2008, Parthasarathy Sudarshan was sentenced in U.S. District Court for the District of Columbia to 35 months in prison, two years of supervised release, a $60,000 fine, and a $100 special assessment. Sudarshan will receive credit for time served, which at the time of sentencing was approximately 15 months. Gopal and Sudarshan, along with Akn Prasad and Sampath Sundar, illegally exported controlled electronic components to government entities in India that participate in the development of ballistic missiles, space launch vehicles, and fighter jets. Prasad and Sundar remain at large overseas. Sudarshan previously conducted business as Cirrus Electronics, and, between 2002 and 2006, the co-conspirators used the business to illegally procure and export the controlled items to listed Indian Entities, specifically the Vikram Sarabhai Space Center and Bharat Dynamics Limited. This investigation was conducted by OEE and the Federal Bureau of Investigation, with assistance from U.S. Immigration and Customs Enforcement.

Cryogenic Submersible Pumps to Iran — On July 17, 2008, Cryostar SAS, formerly known as Cryostar France (Cryostar), was sentenced in the U.S. District for the District of Columbia to a $500,000 criminal fine and two years of probation for its involvement in a conspiracy to illegally export U.S.-origin cryogenic submersible pumps to Iran. On April 10, 2008, Cryostar pled guilty to three felony counts charging one count of Conspiracy, one count of Export Without an Export License, and one count of Attempted Export Without an Export License. The conspirators, Cryostar France, Ebara International Corporation, and another French company, developed a plan to conceal the export of cryogenic pumps to Iran. The plan was that Ebara would sell and export the pumps to Cryostar France, which would then resell the pumps to another French company, with the ultimate and intended destination being the 9th and 10th Olefin Petrochemical Complexes in Iran. Ebara and its former president pled guilty and were sentenced in 2004.

Nuclear Detonators to Pakistan — On August 1, 2006, BIS issued a 10 year denial of export privileges against Asher Karni and related parties Pakland PME Corporation and Humayun Khan in connection with their exports of electrical equipment and components with nuclear weapons applications to Pakistan. On August 4, 2005, Karni, a South African businessman was sentenced to three years in prison as part of his guilty plea to conspiracy and export violations arising out of his unlawful exports to Pakistan and India of U.S. origin goods controlled for nuclear nonproliferation reasons. On April 8, 2005, the U.S. Attorney for the District of Columbia announced that Khan, of Islamabad, Pakistan, had been indicted for conspiring to violate, and, on three occasions, violating U.S. export restrictions. Khan, operating through his company Pakland PME, is alleged to have arranged, through Karni, the purchase and export to Pakistan of U.S. origin triggered spark gaps, which can be used as nuclear weapons detonators. Khan falsely indicated that the goods were intended for medical use. Khan is believed to be currently in Pakistan. OEE, the Federal Bureau of Investigation, and the U.S. Immigration and Customs Enforcement jointly conducted this investigation.

Omission of Nuclear End-Use in Submission of License Applications to the Department — On March 12, 2008, MTS Systems Corporation of Eden Prairie, Minnesota, pled guilty to two counts of Title 18 United States Code Section 1018, False Certification or Writing, in connection with MTs' submission of two license applications to the Department of Commerce. In March 2003, MTS submitted a license application to the Department to export seismic testing equipment valued at $525,000 to the Electrical Research and Development Association in Makarpura, India. The stated end-use was "for seismic vibration testing facility to test motors and other electronic equipment under earthquake conditions." The end-use statement did not reflect the corporate knowledge that the system would be used in a nuclear power plant. In November 2003, MTS submitted a second license application for approximately $3 million of seismic testing equipment that would be used at the Structural Engineering Research Center (SERC) in Chennai, India. In filing this license application, MTS did not include information that SERC was receiving funding from India's Department of Atomic Energy for this transaction and the end-use of this system would involve seismic testing for Indian nuclear facilities. As part of this plea agreement MTS was fined $400,000, placed on probation for two years and ordered to provide an export compliance seminar. As part of a global settlement, MTS was also administratively fined $400,000 by the Department of Commerce for these two violations. In 2006, MTS was also administratively fined $36,000 for having exported a thermal fatigue testing machine to India which was ultimately destined for the Indira Gandhi Center for Atomic Research. Six Indian parties involved in this earlier export and diversion were also denied export privileges ranging from 10 to 15 years for each party.

Industrial Furnace to China — On October 4, 2006, William Kovacs, president of Elatec Technology Corporation, was sentenced to 12 months and one day in prison, three years of supervised release, and 300 hours community service in connection with the export of an industrial furnace to a proliferation entity of concern in China. On May 28, 2004, Kovacs and Elatec pled guilty to charges that they conspired to violate U.S. export licensing requirements in connection with this export. Elatec's export license application for this transaction had previously been denied by BIS due to missile technology concerns. An associate, Stephen Midgley, separately pled guilty on January 10, 2005, to falsely stating in export documents that the furnace did not require an export license when the goods were shipped to China. Midgley was sentenced to one year probation, 120 hours community service and a $1,500 criminal fine. BIS assessed Midgley a $5,000 ($4,000 suspended) administrative penalty as part of an agreement with Midgley to settle charges related to this unlicensed export. OEE and U.S. Immigration and Customs Enforcement jointly conducted this investigation.

Nickel Powder to Taiwan — On October 11, 2007, Theresa Chang was sentenced to three years of probation and to pay a $5,000 criminal fine. On June 21, 2007, Chang pled guilty to one count of making false statements related to the export of nickel powder controlled for nuclear proliferation reasons to Taiwan without an export license.

Carbon-Carbon Industrial Manufacturing Equipment to Missile Laboratory in India — On November 18, 2005, Fiber Materials Inc. of Maine; its wholly owned subsidiary, Materials International of Massachusetts; and the companies' two top officers, Walter Lachman and Maurice Subilia, were sentenced for conspiracy and export violations related to the unlicensed export to India of equipment used to manufacture carbon-carbon components with applications in ballistic missiles. On March 31, 1995, all four defendants were convicted of one count of violating the Export Administration Act and one count of conspiracy by a federal trial jury. The equipment, a specially designed control panel for the operation of a hot isostatic press used to produce carbon-carbon items, was exported to the Defense Research Development Laboratory in India and delivered to Agni, the defense laboratory developing India's principal nuclear-capable ballistic missile. Lachman was sentenced to three years of probation, the first year of which is to be spent in home detention. Subilia was sentenced to three years of probation, the first six months of which was to be spent in community confinement, to be followed by one year of home detention. A criminal fine of $250,000 was imposed on Lachman, Subilia, and Fiber Materials; no fine was imposed on Materials International because it is a wholly-owned subsidiary of Fiber Materials. Additionally, on March 14, 2007, 10 year Denial Orders were issued to Subilia, Lachman, and Fiber Materials, Inc. relating to their November 18, 2005 conviction. OEE and U.S. Immigration and Customs Enforcement jointly conducted this investigation.

Controlled Items to Ballistic Missile Facility in Iran — In September 2005, Mohammed Farajbakhsh was sentenced to seven months in prison and two years of probation following his April 2005 guilty plea to one count each of conspiracy and violation of the International Emergency Economic Powers Act for conspiring to illegally export goods to Iran via the United Arab Emirates (UAE). Farajbakhsh, Hamid Fatholoomy, and their UAE-based companies Diamond Technology and Akeed Trading were indicted in February 2005 for allegedly shipping computer goods from a U.S. supplier to an entity affiliated with Iran's ballistic missile program, as well as satellite communications equipment and other goods. OEE, Defense Criminal Investigative Service, and U.S. Immigration and Customs Enforcement jointly conducted this investigation.

Chemical and Biological Weapons Controlled Toxins to Syria — On August 5, 2005, Maine Biological Labs was sentenced to a criminal fine of $500,000 and five years of probation for illegal exports and false statements in connection with unlicensed exports of virus toxins to Syria. On July 22, 2005, six individuals, all former employees of Maine Biological Labs, were sentenced in connection with various charges including conspiracy, illegal exports, smuggling, false statements, aiding and abetting, and anti-boycott offenses. One former employee was sentenced to two years of probation; the remaining five were each sentenced to terms of imprisonment ranging from nine months to 12 months and one day. The court also imposed criminal fines ranging from $5,000 to $30,000 on the defendants. Two other former employees were previously convicted on similar charges and sentenced to probation. OEE, the U.S. Department of Agriculture, and U.S. Immigration and Customs Enforcement jointly conducted this investigation.

Thermal Insulation Blankets to China — On May 17, 2005, Vladimir Alexanyan, owner of Valtex International, was ordered to pay a $12,000 criminal fine, was sentenced to three years of probation, and was ordered to refrain from any international activities or trade for the term of his probation. Valtex International was ordered to pay a $250,000 criminal fine. In February 2005, Vladimir Alexanyan and Valtex pled guilty to export violations and false statements in connection with the attempted export of satellite/missile insulation blankets to the Chinese Academy of Space Technology in Beijing. BIS had previously rejected Valtex's application for an export license for these items. The goods were seized in San Francisco before their shipment from the U.S. BIS assessed Alexanyan an $88,000 administrative penalty and Valtex a $77,000 administrative penalty to settle charges related to this attempted unlicensed export. Both Valtex and Alexanyan are also subject to five year denials of export privileges to China. Further, Valtex agreed to implement an export management system. OEE and U.S. Immigration and Customs Enforcement jointly conducted this investigation.

Digital Oscilloscopes Controlled for Nuclear Nonproliferation Reasons to Israel — On March 21, 2005, Metric Equipment Sales pled guilty in the Northern District of California to one count of exporting digital oscilloscopes to Israel without a BIS license. The oscilloscopes, with sampling rates exceeding 1 GHz, are capable of being utilized in WMD development and missile delivery fields and are controlled for nuclear nonproliferation reasons. Metric was sentenced to a $50,000 criminal fine, three years of probation, and 250 hours of community service. BIS assessed Metric a $150,000 administrative penalty and a five year suspended denial of export privileges as part of an agreement with Metric to settle charges related to these unlicensed exports.

Computer Chips with Guidance System Applications to China — On October 6, 2004, Ting-Ih Hsu, a naturalized U.S. citizen and president of Azure Systems, Inc., and Hai Lin Nee, a Chinese citizen and an employee of Azure, were sentenced to three years of probation for false statements in connection with the illegal export of low-noise amplifier chips to China. The defendants falsely described the goods as "transistors" in export documents. These goods have application in the U.S. Hellfire missile. OEE and U.S. Immigration and Customs Enforcement jointly conducted this investigation.

Pulse Generators to India — On June 6, 2004, BNC Corp. of San Rafael, California (previously Berkeley Nucleonics Corporation) was sentenced to five years of probation and a $300,000 criminal fine for illegally exporting pulse generators to two entities in India without the required export licenses. The end-users were listed on BIS's entity list for nuclear non-proliferation reasons. Two former employees of BNC, Richard Hamilton and Vincent Delfino, were convicted in December 2003 for their role in these exports. Each was sentenced to two years of probation, a $1,000 criminal fine, and 100 hours of community service and was prohibited from engaging in or facilitating export transactions. BIS assessed BNC a $55,000 administrative penalty and a five year suspended denial of export privileges as part of an agreement with BNC to settle charges related to these unlicensed exports.

Bubonic Plague to Tanzania — On March 10, 2004, Thomas Campbell Butler, MD, a professor at Texas Tech University, was sentenced to two years in prison, three years of supervised release, and criminal fines and restitution totaling more than $50,000 for export violations, false statements, theft, embezzlement, fraud, and mail and wire fraud. Butler was arrested in January 2003 for falsely reporting to the FBI that 30 vials of bubonic plague bacteria that had been destroyed by Butler were missing and presumed stolen from his university laboratory. An investigation into Butler's report uncovered that Butler had earlier exported a related set of bubonic plague bacteria to Tanzania in September 2002 without the required licenses. In addition, on September 1, 2006, Dr. Butler agreed to pay a $37,400 administrative penalty and his export privileges were denied for a period of 10 years. OEE conducted this investigation as a member of the North Texas Joint Terrorism Task Force.

Biological Research Products to Indian Government Organizations on the Entity *List* — On December 28, 2005, Becton, Dickinson, & Co., of Franklin Lakes, New Jersey was ordered to pay a $123,000 administrative fine, and was subjected to an audit requirement to settle charges of 36 violations of the Export Administration Regulations (EAR) involving the export of various life sciences research products to listed entities from the Indian Department of Atomic Energy and Indian Department of Defense.

Exports of Chemical and Biological Weapons Controlled Chemicals to Multiple Locations — On August 9, 2005, BIS assessed a $142,450 administrative penalty against BJ Services Company of Tomball, Texas as part of an agreement that settled charges that between 1999 and 2002, BJ Services made 13 exports of items controlled for chemical and biological weapons reasons to various destinations without obtaining the required export licenses. The settlement agreement also requires that BJ Services must perform an audit of its internal compliance program that is required to be submitted to OEE.

Illegal Exports of Biotoxins to Canada — On May 9, 2005, EMD Biosciences, Inc. (EMD) of San Diego, California, was order to pay a $904,500 administrative penalty to settle charges that it exported biological toxins to Canada in violation of the EAR. EMD also received a two year suspended denial of export privileges. Between June 2002 and July 2003, EMD committed 134 violations of the EAR stemming from 67 exports of biological toxins to Canada that were made without obtaining required Department of Commerce export licenses. EMD, formerly known as CN Biosciences, Inc., in 1999, paid administrative fines for unlicensed exports of the same and similar toxins.

Diaphragm Pumps to Iran, Syria Israel and China — On April 27, 2005, Wilden Pump and Engineering Co., LLC (Wilden), Grand Terrace, California, was ordered to pay a $700,000 administrative penalty to settle charges that it violated the EAR in connection with unauthorized exports of diaphragm pumps from the U.S. to Iran, Israel, China, Syria, and the United Arab Emirates without the required Department of Commerce export licenses. Between 2000 and 2003, Wilden committed 71 violations of the EAR. Specifically, BIS found that Wilden committed

26 violations by exporting diaphragm pumps without the required licenses. In connection with 22 of the exports, Wilden violated the EAR by transferring diaphragm pumps with knowledge that violations of the EAR would occur. BIS also charged that Wilden committed 23 violations of the EAR by making false statements on export control documents. The majority of the pumps that were exported are controlled for export and re-export for due chemical and biological weapons proliferation reasons.

Deemed Exports

Video Amplifiers to China/National Security Controlled Technology to Chinese Nationals — On July 25, 2005, Charlie Kuan, former president of Suntek Microwave, Newark, California, was sentenced to 12 months and one day of prison and two years of supervised release for failure to obtain required export licenses for shipments of detector log video amplifiers (DLVA), items controlled for national security reasons, to Chengdu Jeway Microwave Telecommunications, a company controlled by the Chinese government. Suntek, which was also charged with failing to obtain export licenses under the deemed export provisions of the EAR, was sentenced to a $339,000 criminal fine. BIS additionally assessed administrative penalties of $275,000 against Suntek, $187,000 against Kuan, and 20 year denials of export privileges against both parties in connection with these violations.

National Security Controlled Technology to Chinese and Ukrainian Nationals — In November 2004, BIS assessed Fujitsu Network Communications, Inc. an administrative penalty of $125,000 as part of an agreement with Fujitsu to settle charges related to unlicensed deemed exports to foreign nationals. In particular, BIS alleged that Fujitsu failed to obtain the export licenses required for transferring commercial digital fiber-optic transmission and broadband switching technology to Chinese and Ukrainian nationals. The applicable technology is subject to national security controls.

National Security Controlled Items and Technology to China — In September 2004, BIS assessed a $560,000 administrative penalty against Lattice Semiconductor Corporation as part of an agreement to settle charges of unlicensed exports of extended range programmable logic devices and technical data to China and the deemed export of controlled technology to Chinese nationals. The items and technology are controlled for national security reasons.

National Security Controlled Technology to Chinese and Iranian Nationals — In April 2004, BIS assessed New Focus, Inc., an administrative penalty of $200,000 as part of an agreement with New Focus to settle charges related to unlicensed deemed exports to foreign nationals and other exports. In particular, BIS alleged that New Focus failed to obtain the export licenses required for transferring technology to two Iranian nationals and one Chinese national who, in the course of their employment in the U.S., were exposed to national security controlled manufacturing technology. BIS also alleged that New Focus failed to obtain the required export licenses for shipments of national security controlled amplifiers to the Czech Republic, Singapore, and Chile.

Other Dual Use

Electronic Components to China — On August 3, 2009, William Tsu of Cheerway Corporation was sentenced in U.S. District Court in the Central District of California. Tsu was sentenced to 40 months in prison, three years of supervised probation, and a $200 special assessment. On March 13, 2009, Tsu pled guilty to exporting and attempting to export semiconductors and integrated circuits to China without the required export license.

Cameras to China — On July 27, 2009 and August 3, 2009, Zhi Yong Guo and Tah Wei Chao, respectively, were sentenced in U.S. District Court in the Central District of California. Chao was sentenced to 20 months in prison, three years of supervised probation, a $3,000 fine, and issued a special assessment of $300. Guo was sentenced to 60 months in prison, three years of supervised probation, a $12,500 fine, and issued a special assessment of $200. On February 23, 2009, a federal jury in the Central District of California found Guo guilty of conspiracy and exporting and/or attempting to export restricted items related to a plot to procure and export thermal imaging cameras to the People's Republic of China without obtaining the required licenses. On July 17, 2008, Chao pled guilty in the Central District of California to conspiracy and violating the International Emergency Economic Powers Act. Both Chao and Guo were arrested at the Los Angeles International Airport in April 2008 after authorities recovered 10 thermal imaging cameras that had been hidden in their suitcases, stuffed in shoes and concealed in clothing. On August 25, 2008, Evan Zhang pled guilty in the Central District of California to one count of violating the International Emergency Economic Powers Act and the Export Administration Regulations for his involvement in the conspiracy. This was a joint investigation with U.S. Immigration and Customs Enforcement, the Federal Bureau of Investigation, Customs and Border Protection, the Diplomatic Security Service, and the Transportation Security Administration.

Night Vision Rifle Scopes — On May 12, 2009, Donald Wayne Hatch was sentenced in U.S. District Court in the Southern District of Iowa to two years of probation and a $5,000 fine for causing false statements to be made. At the same proceeding, a fine of $90,000 was levied against Rigel Optics, Inc. for the unlicensed export of Generation II night vision goggles. On July 31, 2008, Donald Wayne Hatch and Rigel Optics Inc. entered a guilty plea before a U.S. Magistrate Judge in the Southern District of Iowa. Hatch pled guilty to one count of Making False Statements, and also entered a guilty plea on behalf of the corporation to one count of violating the Arms Export Control Act. Hatch and Rigel Optics Inc. sold night vision optical equipment to various foreign customers. OEE and U.S. Immigration and Customs Enforcement jointly conducted this investigation.

Thermal Imaging Cameras to South Korea — On March 25, 2009, David Lee, a.k.a. David Young, owner and sole operator of Lucena Technology Inc., pled guilty in U.S. District Court in the Northern District of Illinois to violating the International Emergency Economic Powers Act. On December 16, 2008, Lee was indicted on charges that he knowingly and willfully exported seven thermal imaging cameras to South Korea. This investigation was conducted jointly by OEE and U.S. Immigration and Customs Enforcement.

Optical Sighting Devices to Various Locations — Cabela's Incorporated, an outdoor equipment outfitter based in Sidney, Nebraska, has agreed to pay a civil penalty of $680,000 to settle allegations that it committed 152 violations of the Export Administration Regulations involving the export of controlled optical sighting devices to various countries worldwide. The allegations involved 76 exports of optical sighting devices for firearms in 2004 and 2005 to Argentina, Brazil, Canada, Chile, Finland, Ireland, Malaysia, Malta, Mexico, Pakistan, the Philippines, South Africa, Sweden, and Taiwan. These devices are controlled on the Commerce Control List for crime control and firearms convention reasons and require a license to export to the various destinations at issue. BIS also alleged that Cabela's failed to file the required Shipper's Export Declaration for each of the 76 exports in question. In 2005, Cabela's settled similar allegations made by BIS that, on 685 occasions between April 1999 and September 2000, Cabela's made unlicensed exports of optical sighting devices to a number of countries, including Argentina, Brazil, Canada, Chile, and Mexico.

Export of Rifle Scopes — On July 24, 2008, Euro Optics Inc. was sentenced in the Middle District of Pennsylvania to a $10,000 corporate fine, $800 special assessment, and five years of corporate probation. On March 17, 2008, Euro Optics Inc. pled guilty to violating the International Emergency Economic Powers Act and the International Trafficking in Arms Regulations related to exports of Department of Commerce and Department of State-controlled rifle scopes to various countries without the required licenses. This was a joint case with the U.S. Immigration and Customs Enforcement/Philadelphia.

Power Amplifiers to China — On June 6, 2008, WaveLab, Inc. was sentenced in U.S. District Court for the Eastern District of Virginia to one year of supervised probation and a $15,000 fine for the unlawful export of power amplifiers to the People's Republic of China. WaveLab was previously ordered to forfeit $85,000 in this case. On March 7, 2008, WaveLab pled guilty to violating the International Emergency Economic Powers Act in connection with these unlicensed exports. The investigation identified 11 occasions between October 2004 and February 2006 where WaveLab exported power amplifiers from Reston, Virginia to the People's Republic of China without obtaining the required Department of Commerce license.

Export of Navigation Equipment Components — On January 25, 2008, Northrop Grumman Corporation of Los Angeles, California, agreed to pay a $400,000 administrative penalty to settle allegations that it committed 131 violations of the Export Administration Regulations, both in its own capacity and as successor to Litton Industries, Inc., which Northrop acquired in April 2001. BIS alleged that Northrop Grumman committed unlicensed exports of specially designed components for navigation equipment and module manufacturing data that were to destinations in the Philippines, Singapore, Malaysia, Italy, and the United Kingdom between January 1998 and September 2002. Northrop Grumman voluntarily self-disclosed the violations and cooperated fully in the investigation.

Exports of Night Vision to Various Locations — On January 22, 2008, Green Supply Inc. was sentenced in U.S. District Court in the Eastern District of Missouri to two years of probation, a $17,500 fine, and $800 special assessment for violations of export controls. On November 2, 2007, Green Supply pled guilty to one count of violating the International Emergency Economic Powers Act and one count of violating the International Trafficking in Arms Regulations. The charges are the result of an investigation that identified approximately 66 illegal exports in violation of the International Emergency Economic Powers Act and eight illegal exports in violation of the International Trafficking in Arms Regulations between 2002 and 2006. Green Supply is a wholesale distributor of hunting and camping equipment to include restraint devices, shotgun barrels, global positioning systems, firearm scopes and sights, and other items controlled for export. OEE and U.S. Immigration and Customs Enforcement jointly conducted this investigation.

False Statements on Shipper's Export Declarations — On August 8, 2007, P.R.A. World Wide Trading Co., Inc. (PRA), of Brooklyn, N.Y., agreed to pay $250,000 in administrative penalties to settle charges that it violated the Export Administration Regulations government the export of dual-use items. Specifically, BIS alleged that PRA conspired to make false statements to the U.S. Government and made false or misleading representations on export control documents. BIS will suspend $90,000 of this figure for one year and subsequently waive this amount if PRA does not commit any violations during the suspension period. BIS charged that between June 1, 2001 and December 20, 2002, PRA, a freight forwarder, on 41 occasions conspired to make false statements in violation of the EAR and falsely represented the value of the items subject to the EAR on Shipper's Export Declarations (SEDs). On December 19, 2006, criminal sanctions were imposed on the owner and President of PRA, Igor Cherkassky after he pled guilty to one count of conspiracy to make false statements on SEDs. Cherkassky admitted that between 1998 and 2004, while serving as the President of PRA, he instructed employees to prepare and submit SEDs that contained false information about the true value of exported items. Pursuant to the plea, Cherkassky was sentenced to two months in prison, three years of supervised release, a $5,000 criminal fine, and a $100 special assessment.

Chapter 10

BUSINESS ORGANIZATIONS AND MANAGEMENT RESPONSIBILITIES

Thus far in these materials, we have considered the technology innovation process without regard to the organizational and managerial contexts within which the technology innovation process takes place. This chapter discusses these matters. The first section of this chapter provides a summary overview of the different forms of business organizations which can be used to commercialize new technologies. The business forms covered in this section include limited partnerships, Subchapter C corporations, Subchapter S corporations and limited liability companies. Formation, management, investor liability, continuity of existence, transferability of interests and taxation are considered for each of these different forms of business organizations.

The second section in this chapter considers management responsibilities in different business organizations. This section covers the fiduciary duties of directors, officers and majority shareholders in business organizations with respect to one another and with respect to the business organization itself. This section also covers shareholder direct and derivative causes of action, usurpation of corporate opportunities and piercing the corporate veil. As you will see, the law in these areas is rooted in state statutes which are subject to a substantial degree of judicial interpretation.

10.1 CHOICE OF BUSINESS ORGANIZATION

The choice of business organization determines fundamental operating features of the business, including the requirements for the formation of the business, control and management of the business, investor liability for the debts and torts of the business, the continuity of existence of the business, the transfer of ownership interests in the business, and the federal and state taxation of the business. There are two general types of business organizations — "pass-through" business organizations and "independent-entity" business organizations. In "pass-through" business organizations, the owners and the business organization are one and the same. The "pass-through" business organization has no separate legal status, and the debts, liabilities and taxes incurred by the "pass-through" business organization pass directly to the owners. Sole proprietorships, which are business organizations in which an individual conducts the business in his or her own name, and general partnerships, which are business organizations in which a group of individuals conducts business as a collection of individuals, are examples of "pass-through" business organizations. "Pass-through" business organizations can be created without filing any documents with the state.

"Independent-entity" business organizations, on the other hand, have a legal existence separate from their owners. An "independent-entity" business organization is itself individually liable for the debts, torts and taxes incurred by the business organization; and the owners of "independent-entity" business organizations are liable for the debts, torts and taxes of the business organization only to the extent of their investment in the business organization. Corporations and limited partnerships, which conduct business in the name of the corporation or the limited partnership, are examples of "independent-entity" business organizations. "Independent-entity" business organizations are created only by filing specified documents with the state.

As you will see below, there are also hybrid business organizations which have some features of "pass-through" business organizations and some features of "independent-entity" business organizations. Subchapter S corporations and limited liability companies are examples of hybrid business organizations in which taxes can be passed through to the owners while liability for debts and torts remains with the business organization.

This section considers the legal attributes of limited partnerships, subchapter C corporations, subchapter S corporations and limited liability companies — the four principal forms of business organizations for commercializing new technologies.

10.1.1 Limited Partnership

Although general partnerships are rarely used in commercialization of new technologies, it is useful to consider general partnerships briefly in order to provide a context for the other business organizations that are used in technology commercialization. As noted above, a general partnership is an association of two or more persons who conduct the business as co-owners. Individual partners in a general partnership are liable for all partnership obligations to the extent of their investment in the partnership and, importantly, to the extent of their personal assets. Individual partners in a general partnership are also jointly and severally liable; one individual partner may be held liable for the unpaid partnership obligations of other partners. For tax purposes, a general partnership is not taxed as a separate entity; all tax gains, losses, deductions and credits are passed through to the individual partners in accordance with their *pro rata* ownership interests. No formal, written agreement is required to create a general partnership. Indeed, a general partnership can be formed by an oral agreement or by the parties' course of conduct.

In contrast to a general partnership, a limited partnership has two classes of partners: general partners who have the same personal and investment liability for the obligations of the limited partnership as general partners do in a general partnership, and limited partners who are liable only to the extent of their investment in the partnership. As a general rule, control and management of a limited partnership rests in the hands of the general partners, who often charge the limited partnership a fee for their management services. Limited partners do not participate in the day-to-day management of the limited partnership, but may participate in major partnership decisions, such as the sale of the partnership or its major assets. If a limited partner becomes too active in the management of the limited partnership, he or she can lose the limited liability protection.

A limited partnership is a legislatively authorized business organization. A limited partnership is formed by filing a certificate of limited partnership with the Office of Secretary of State. The certificate of limited partnership includes the name and address of the general partner, the nature of the business to be conducted by the limited partnership, and designation of a state-resident for service of process on the limited partnership. The certificate of limited partnership also includes procedures and processes for managing the partnership.

A limited partnership continues in existence until it is dissolved by either the time or event specified in the partnership agreement, the consent of all the partners, or the withdrawal of the general partner without provision for a successor general partner. Withdrawal of a limited partner does not affect the continuing existence of the partnership.

Limited partners have the right to share in the profits, losses and asset distributions of the partnership according to their percentage ownership of the partnership. Limited partner ownership shares are often designated as partnership "units." Limited partners may assign their partnership interests unless prohibited from doing so in the partnership agreement, which is usually the case. Assignment of a partnership interest does not relieve the assignor partner of pre-assignment obligations owed to the partnership.

For taxation purposes, limited partnerships are treated substantially the same as general partnerships — tax profits, losses, deductions and credits are passed through to the partners, both general and limited. It is important to note, however, that partners will be taxed on partnership net income even if the partnership does not distribute the net income to the partners. This may occur, for example, when a partnership generates taxable net income, but must use the net income to pay off the principal on a loan.

Limited partnerships are often used as tax-shelter vehicles where the limited partners are primarily seeking to shelter other income with potential partnership pass-through losses and the general partners are primarily seeking appreciation of the partnership assets. Venture capital funds are almost always structured as limited partnerships. High-wealth individuals invest in venture capital funds as limited partners to obtain pass-through tax losses to apply against other income. A $1000 pass-through tax loss to a limited partner in the 35% tax bracket generally results in a tax savings of $35 for the limited partner. (Of course, limited partners expect a positive return on their investment at some point in time; tax losses alone cannot generate a positive investment return.) The general partner in a venture capital fund performs due diligence investigations on potentially "investable" companies, decides which companies to invest in, and manages the fund's portfolio of companies. For these services, the general partner typically charges the fund a management fee. The general partner is most interested in the cash-out value of the fund at its termination.

Given the differing interests of the limited partners and general partner in a venture capital fund, a fund is often structured to pass all losses to the limited partners until the limited partners have recovered their investment in the fund and, thereafter, divide the losses and profits *pro rata* with the limited and general partners. Note that when limited partners receive pass-through tax losses from the partnership, these losses reduce the limited partners' investment basis in the partnership units dollar-for-dollar. Thus, when the partnership is terminated and the partnership units are redeemed, the limited partners will pay a higher tax due to their reduced investment basis in the partnership units. However, this is still a profitable investment strategy for limited partners because the pass-through tax losses are used to offset income taxed at higher ordinary income rates while the tax on the appreciated partnership units at the termination of the partnership are taxed at lower capital gains rates.

Additional Information

1. Arthur B. Willis, John S. Pennell, Philip F. Postlewaite, Parntership Tax ¶ 3.01 (2011).

2. William P. Streng, Fed. Income Tax'n of Corp. & Shareholders Form ¶ 2.02 (2011).

3. Robert J. Haft, Peter M. Fass, 4 Tax-Advantaged Securities § 5:37 (2011).

4. Robert J. Haft, 2 Venture Cap. & Bus. Fin. § 3:37 (2011).

5. Robert L. Haig, 7 Bus. & Com. Litig. Fed. Cts. § 83:54 (2d ed.) (2010).

10.1.2   Subchapter C Corporation

A Subchapter C corporation, named for the subchapter in the Internal Revenue Code which generally governs the tax attributes of corporations, is a separate, incorporated legal entity formed pursuant to a state-enabling statute. Although every state has its own incorporation statute, these statutes generally follow closely the Model Revised Business Corporation Act. This subsection will discuss subchapter C corporations in reference to the Model Revised Business Corporation Act.

The incorporation process usually begins with a search of the state's list of names of all domestic corporations, and all foreign corporations registered to do business in the state, to determine whether the proposed corporate name is deceptively similar to the name of an already listed corporation. If the proposed new corporation is contemplating doing business in multiple states, the same name search must be done in each state in which the proposed new corporation will register to do business. Today, these searches can be performed easily online. Once the name for the new corporation has been determined to be sufficiently dissimilar from the names of the other listed corporations, the name can be applied for and reserved, usually for a period of ninety days.

The proposed new corporation is created by the preparation and filing of a document, generally called a "certificate of incorporation" or "corporate charter," with the state office charged with the responsibility of administering corporate filings. In New York, for example, this office is the New York State Division of Corporations, which operates under the office of the New York Secretary of State. The corporate charter is prepared and filed by one or more persons who act as the initial "incorporators" of the corporation; sometimes, these persons are the actual principals in the proposed new corporation, sometimes, they are attorneys or staff working in the law firm handling the incorporation. Incorporation filing services, including name searches, are also provided by companies specializing in this work that are located in every state capital. These companies also generally provide a corporate seal, a corporate stock book and a boiler plate corporate charter and by-laws. The charge for these services is generally around $200–300.

The corporate charter is the fundamental document governing the operation of the corporation and includes, among other items, the corporation's name (many states require the inclusion of the word "Corporation," "Corp.," "Ltd." or "Inc." in the name), its principal place of business, the name of a resident person who will receive service of process on behalf of the corporation, the purpose for which the corporation is being formed (the purpose clause generally includes a catch-all phrase providing for "any other lawful business in the state"), the different classes of the corporation's stock, the par value of and means of payment for the corporation's stock, any restrictions on the transfer of the corporation's stock, indemnification of officers and directors, and the names and addresses of the initial officers and directors of the corporation. In essence, the corporate charter sets forth the most basic features of the corporation and, ultimately, governs the relationships among the directors, officers, shareholders and creditors.

The next step following the filing of the corporate charter is holding the initial corporation meeting. At the initial meeting, the first issuance of the corporation's stock is authorized, the corporation's charter is adopted, the corporation's directors are elected, the corporation's officers are appointed, and the corporation's by-laws are adopted. The corporation's by-laws set forth the details of the corporation's operation and include such items as how the meetings of directors and shareholders will be called, the time and place of the corporation's annual meeting, what constitutes a quorum for meetings, what votes are necessary to adopt various motions, the corporation's fiscal year, any standing committees of the directors, and the duties of the principal officers.

As suggested above, control of a corporation is ultimately in the hands of the shareholders. The shareholders elect the corporation's directors, the directors appoint the corporation's officers, and the officers hire the corporation's managers. As you will see in the next section, the relationship between and among the directors, officers and shareholders is based on a fairly complex set of fiduciary duties, and attendant procedural and substantive rules of corporate law.

Corporations have a perpetual existence and can only be terminated by a vote of the shareholders, a judicial dissolution order, or a decree by the Secretary of State. The ownership interests of shareholders in corporations are freely transferrable unless restricted in some way by the corporate charter, the corporate by-laws or a shareholder agreement. Restrictions on ownership transfers generally take the form of first refusal restrictions and right of first offer restrictions. A first refusal restriction generally provides for repurchase of shares by the company, if the company elects to do so, either at a price set in advance, at a price that varies according to some formula, at a price that matches the price offered by a third party, or at an indeterminate price labeled "fair market value." Right of first offer restrictions generally provide that the corporation must be offered the shares for purchase prior to the shares being offered for sale to a third party. The corporation usually has a stated period of time in which to exercise its first option to purchase shares. If the corporation exercises its option to purchase the shares, the shares can still be offered to a third party but only at a price higher than the price offered by the corporation. First offer restrictions sometimes provide that, in the latter case, the corporation can revise its offer to meet the price offered by the third party. Restrictions on ownership transfers are invariably included in the charter or by-laws of closely held corporations (corporations with a limited number of shareholders having a fiduciary relationship to one another) and rarely included in the charter or by-laws of larger private and public corporations.

As a separate legal entity formed pursuant to a state statute, corporations are liable for all federal and state taxes levied on their net income, for all debts owed to creditors and for all torts committed by agents of the corporation. Again, the shareholders are liable for the corporation's taxes, debts and torts only to the extent of their investment in the corporation. The shareholders' personal assets are beyond the reach of tax authorities, creditors and tort plaintiffs unless the corporation is determined to be a "sham," in which case the court may "pierce the corporate veil." Subsection 10.2.6 below considers instances in which the corporate veil may be pierced. In the case of start-up and early-stage companies, the shareholders' immunity from creditors is often illusory. Very often, creditors such as banks and suppliers will not extend credit to start-up and early-stage companies unless repayment is guaranteed by the shareholders personally. In some cases, this guarantee will be required to be backed by mortgages on the shareholders' real or personal property.

As you saw in the tax section of the materials, corporations can deduct interest paid on loans and bonds, but cannot deduct dividends paid to shareholders. Moreover, dividends paid to shareholders, above a certain amount, are taxed to the shareholders at ordinary income tax rates. This is the source of the often-criticized "double taxation" of corporate income; corporate income is taxed first at the corporate level and then taxed again at the shareholder level when the corporation distributes the income as dividends. However, there are some fairly straightforward ways to deal with the problem of double taxation. The corporation can refrain from paying dividends, in which case the retained income will increase the value of the corporation. If the corporation is sold and the proceeds distributed to the shareholders, then the appreciated value of the corporation due to the retained income will be taxed to the shareholders at capital gains rates. In a sense, the corporation has converted ordinary income into capital gains.

Another way in which a corporation, especially a closed corporation, can avoid double taxation is to pay most of its net income to shareholders as salaries and wages. Although the shareholders will be taxed on the salaries and wages at ordinary income tax rates, the corporation will minimize its tax liability because salaries and wages are deductible ordinary and necessary business expenses. If the corporation requires retained income for operating purposes, the shareholders can lend the corporation the necessary amount in exchange for a stated interest payment. Although the interest payments the shareholders will be taxed at ordinary income rates, the interest payments will be deductible business expenses to the corporation.

Finally, it should be noted that, under a long line of Supreme Court cases, corporations have well-recognized first amendment rights. Corporate first amendment rights include political speech, as well as commercial speech and campaign contributions.

Additional Information

1. Vincent Di Lorenzo, Clifford R. Ennico, Basic Legal Transactions § 14:5 (2010).

2. Scott D. Shimick, 9 Mertens Law of Fed. Income Tax'n §§ 35A:6–35A:7, 35A:13 (2011).

3. Vasilios T. Nacopoulos, *Whither (Wither) Subchapter C?: The Effect of the Double-Tax System's Progeny (the LLC, Check-the-Box and Subchapter S)*, 17 J.L. & Com. 159 (1997).

10.1.3   Subchapter S Corporation

Operationally, Subchapter S corporations, also named for the subchapter of the Internal Revenue Code which governs their formation, are the same as Subchapter C corporations. Subchapter S corporations are treated as separate entities for purposes of shareholder liability for corporate debts and torts, they have a perpetual continuity of existence, and their stock is freely transferable unless restricted by the corporate charter, by-laws or shareholder agreements. Subchapter S corporations are also formed by filing a corporate charter with the Secretary of State, and they have the same management, control and interlocking fiduciary duties as Subchapter C corporations. However, Subchapter S corporations differ from Subchapter C corporations in one very important respect — for purposes of federal and state taxation, Subchapter S corporations are pass-through entities. All taxable income, losses, deductions and credits are passed through directly to the shareholders of Subchapter S corporations.

The statutory requirements for the formation of Subchapter S corporations are quite specific. A Subchapter S corporation may not have more than 75 shareholders, all of whom must be natural persons who are not nonresident aliens. Subchapter S corporation also can only have one class of stock, and switching from Subchapter S status to Subchapter C status may result in the imposition of additional taxes.

Use of a Subchapter S corporation is often beneficial during the early stages of business development when a corporation has tax losses but no taxable income against which to apply the tax losses. However, when the corporation becomes profitable, the situation is reversed and the shareholders may be obligated to pay taxes on the Subchapter S net income even though the corporation does not distribute any of the net income to the shareholders. The single class of stock requirement for Subchapter S corporations can also pose problems down the line if the corporation seeks to obtain venture capital investment. As you will see in the next chapter, venture capital investors invariably seek to invest in companies through the use of some form of preferred stock. If the one class of stock authorized when the Subchapter S corporation was formed was common stock, which is almost always the case, the Subchapter S corporation will have to be converted to a Subchapter C corporation in order to authorize the issuance of a second class of preferred stock. Finally, the tax benefits of a Subchapter S corporation have become less important with the advent of limited liability companies, which are not subject to the same formation restrictions as Subchapter S corporations, but can nonetheless pass through the limited liability company's taxable net income, losses, deductions and credits to the members of the limited liability company.

Additional Information

1. Dana Shilling, L. Desk Book § 1.05 (2011).

2. Scott D. Shimick, 11 Mertens Law of Fed. Income Tax'n § 41B:96 (2011).

3. Vincent Di Lorenzo, Clifford R. Ennico, Basic Legal Transactions § 14:6 (2010).

4. Alan S. Gutterman, Organizational Management and Administration § 12:51 (2010).

10.1.4   Limited Liability Company

A limited liability company (LLC) is a hybrid corporation/partnership. An LLC possesses all of the characteristics of a corporation, including limited liability of its members for LLC debts and torts, continuity of existence until terminated by a vote of its members or a termination event, and transferability of members' ownership interests unless restricted. The IRS allows an LLC to elect to be taxed as either a corporation or a partnership. A limited liability company can form a corporation and transfer its assets to the corporation without tax consequences, assuming that the members contributing cash or property to the new corporation own 80% or more of the new corporation's voting stock after the formation of the new corporation. However, if a corporation wants to reorganize as a limited liability company, there is a double tax — appreciated assets are taxed at the corporate level, and the shareholders are taxed on the corporation's liquidation distributions.

An LLC is formed by filing "articles of organization" or a "certificate of formation" with the Secretary of State. The certificate of formation generally contains the same information included in a corporate charter, such as the name of the LLC (again, a name search must be done to ensure the selected name is not deceptively similar to an already listed name, and the words "Limited Liability Company" or "LLC" generally must be included in the name), the name and address of a resident registered agent for service of process, the names and addresses of the initial members, and the purposes for which the LLC is being organized. A number of states require that the formation of an LLC be published in local papers a specified number of times over a specified period of time.

The members of an LLC may directly manage the company or, more commonly, the members may delegate all or specific management tasks to "managers," the LLC counterpart to corporate directors or partnership general partners. The day-to-day business of the LLC is generally conducted pursuant to an operating agreement. The operating agreement may contain any provisions not inconsistent with the LLC statute. Typically, the operating agreement provides for member voting, delegation of management functions, and distribution of profits and losses. In an LLC, profits and losses can be distributed to members disproportionately to their contributions of capital or ownership interests.

As noted above, unless restricted by the certificate of formation, members may transfer their membership interests to third parties; however, a transfer of a member's interest does not entitle the transferee to participate in the voting or management of the LLC. Unless the operating agreement provides otherwise, new members may be admitted to the LLC only with the unanimous consent of existing members.

Additional Information

1. James S. Eustice, Fed. Income Tax'n of Corp. & Shareholders ¶ 2.05 (2011).

2. Carter G. Bishop, Daniel S. Kleinberger, Limited Liab. Co. ¶ 1.01 (2010).

3. William Meade Fletcher, 1 Fletcher Cyc. Corp. § 20 (2011).

4. Scott D. Shimick, 9 Mertens Law of Fed. Income Tax'n § 35A:7 (2011).

5. James S. Eustice, Joel D. Kuntz, Fed. Income Tax'n of S Corp. ¶ 2.03 (2011).

6. Arthur B. Willis, John S. Pennell, Philip F. Postlewaite, Partnership Tax ¶ 3.01 (2011).

10.1.5   Comparison of Corporations and Limited Liability Companies

Many practitioners think shares of corporate stock are more liquid (i.e., more easily transferred) than membership interests in LLCs. This perception is based on the fact that corporate stock is generally intended to be transferrable and ultimately, hopefully, publicly traded; whereas LLC membership interests are generally not intended to be transferrable because of the smaller number and closer relationships of the members. To the extent that corporate stock is more liquid than LLC membership interests, the corporate form of business organization is more desirable. However, as noted earlier, transfer of corporate stock can easily be restricted by the corporate charter, by-laws or shareholder agreements. Such restrictions are especially common in start-up and early-stage companies and close corporations. If this is the case, the ownership liquidity advantage of corporate business organizations is nullified.

As a general rule, the corporate form of business organization is more formal and structured than the LLC. State corporate law statutes invariably prescribe such things as the means for electing boards of directors, notice and conduct of stockholder meetings, maintenance of corporate records, and duties and responsibilities of corporate directors and officers. In addition, state corporate law statutes generally provide default rules for such things as shareholder voting, classes of stock and dividend distributions. State LLC statutes are generally far more flexible, allowing the members to structure the management, finance and members' relationships to suit the unique needs of the LLC. To the extent that the LLC is a more flexible form of business organization, it offers benefits over the corporate form of business organization. However, state corporate law statutes are generally permissive and allow shareholders a good deal of discretion in drafting the corporate charter, by-laws and shareholder agreements to tailor the corporation for particular purposes.

Finally, because corporations have existed since the founding of the United States, whereas LLCs were first recognized by the IRS in 1988, there is far, far more jurisprudence on corporate law than LLC law. This is especially the case in Delaware, the favored state of incorporation for a great number of corporations, where the Delaware Chancery Court and Delaware Supreme Court have decided thousands of corporate law cases over many, many years. Corporate lawyers and businesspersons greatly value legal predictability and, therefore, generally prefer the corporate form of business organization.

Additional Information

1. PETER M. FASS, BARBARA S. GERRARD, THE S CORPORATION HANDBOOK § 4:37 (2010).

2. CORP. COUNS. GD TO DOMESTIC JT. VENTURES § 8:3 (2010).

3. VINCENT DI LORENZO, CLIFFORD R. ENNICO, BASIC LEGAL TRANSACTIONS §§ 35:9–35:16 (2010).

4. Thomas E. Geu, *Understanding the Limited Liability Company: A Basic Comparative Primer (Part One)*, 37 S.D.L. REV. 44 (1991/1992).

5. Thomas E. Geu, *Understanding the Limited Liability Company: A Basic Comparative Primer (Part Two)*, 37 S.D.L. REV. 467 (1991/1992).

10.2   MANAGEMENT RESPONSIBILITIES

The management of a business organization is entrusted to its directors and officers. When the actions of directors or officers are challenged by investors, courts grant directors and officers substantial deference under the so-called "business judgment rule." However, as you will see, this deference is not *carte blanche*, and when a director or officer is found to have placed his or her personal interests above those of the business organization, or to have acted in a way that grossly disregarded the best interests of the business organization, courts have not hesitated to impose personal financial liability on directors and officers. The delicate balancing act here is to protect the business and its investors from unscrupulous conduct by directors and officers without having the court become too deeply involved in the management of the business enterprise.

10.2.1   Directors' Fiduciary Duties

The *Weiss* case below considers the practice of corporate directors in granting stock options prior to the issuance of quarterly earnings reports when the reports were positive and after the issuance of quarterly reports when the reports were negative. As you read this case, consider who exactly may be harmed by this practice and what the appropriate remedy may be. In the course of the opinion, the court also discusses the theories of "unjust enrichment" and "waste." How do these theories of liability relate to a claim of breach of fiduciary duty?

WEISS v. SWANSON
948 A.2d 433 (Del. Ch. 2008)

LAMB, VICE CHANCELLOR.

In this derivative action, the plaintiff challenges option grants made by directors pursuant to stockholder-approved option plans. According to the plaintiff, the board of directors adopted a policy of using material, inside information to time option grants, but never disclosed the practice. Specifically, the plaintiff alleges that the board of directors routinely granted options prior to quarterly earnings releases containing positive information, and after releases containing negative information. On this motion to dismiss for failure to adequately plead demand excusal and for failure to state a claim upon which relief can be granted, the court takes the particularized well-pleaded allegations of the complaint as true and draws all reasonable inferences in favor of the plaintiff. Applying that standard, the court concludes that the complaint adequately pleads a claim of breach of fiduciary duty against a majority of the company's board of directors based on the alleged issuance and receipt of options not authorized by the company's plans. Therefore, the motion to dismiss will be denied.

I.

A. The Parties

The plaintiff, Frederick Weiss, has been a stockholder of Linear Technology Corporation since January 12, 1996. Weiss brings this action derivatively on behalf of Linear, the nominal defendant. Linear was founded in 1981 as a manufacturer of high performance linear integrated circuits, including high performance amplifiers, voltage references, battery chargers, and RF signal conditioning circuits.

The individual defendants are certain former and current Linear directors and officers. At the time the challenged option grants were approved, defendants Robert H. Swanson Jr., David S. Lee, Richard M. Moley, Thomas S. Volpe, and Leo T. McCarthy (collectively, the "Director Defendants") constituted Linear's board of directors. Defendant Lothar Maier became a director in September 2005. McCarthy left the board in November 2006, and Linear has since had a five-person board. At all relevant times, Lee, Moley, Volpe, and McCarthy constituted the Compensation Committee. The five named officers who allegedly received challenged option grants are Paul Coghlan, David B. Bell, Robert C. Dobkin, Donald Paulus, and Alexander McCann (collectively, the "Officer Defendants").

B. Facts

Weiss filed his first complaint on March 23, 2007, and filed an amended derivative complaint on August 10, 2007 in response to a motion to dismiss filed on May 5, 2007. The defendants filed the pending motion to dismiss on September 19, 2007.

In his complaint, Weiss challenges 22 option grants the company made between July 1996 and July 2005 pursuant to three stockholder-approved option plans: the 1988 Stock Option Plan, the 1996 Incentive Stock Option Plan, and the 2005 Equity Incentive Plan. The plans set out the general terms by which options may be granted. Notably, the plans authorize the board of directors to approve grants made to directors. Thus, according to Weiss, the Director Defendants approved all option grants made to themselves. Weiss also alleges that the plans authorize the Compensation Committee to approve option grants made to officers.

Under Linear's stockholder-approved option plans, the administrators are authorized to grant options as part of a compensation system designed to "attract and retain the best available personnel" and "to provide additional incentive to Employees, Directors, and Consultants." Two types of options are authorized — incentive stock options designed to comply with section 422 of the Internal Revenue Code of 1986, and non-statutory stock options. All options Weiss challenges are non-statutory options. Paragraph 9 of the 1996 Plan provides:

> In the case of a Non-statutory Stock Option, the per Share exercise price shall be determined by the Administrator. In the case of a Non-statutory Stock Option intended to qualify as "performance-based compensation" within the meaning of Section 162(m) of the Internal Revenue Code, the per Share exercise price shall be no less than 100% of the Fair Market Value per Share on the date of grant.

Thus, under the plans, the directors had full discretion to grant "in the money" options by setting exercise prices lower than the fair market value of Linear's stock price on the date of grant. The plans also provide that "[t]he date of grant of an Option shall be, for all purposes, the date on which the Administrator makes the determination granting such Option, or such other later date as is determined by the Administrator."

Weiss alleges that from July 1996 to June 2005, the directors granted options that violated the purposes, intent, spirit, and objectives of these plans. Specifically, Weiss alleges that the Director Defendants knew the company's quarterly earnings releases were highly anticipated by Linear investors, and that Linear's stock was dramatically affected by these announcements. Weiss claims that the directors had advance knowledge of the contents of the quarterly earnings releases, and used this information to time each of the 22 challenged grants on terms favorable to the defendants. According to the complaint, when the quarterly earnings release contained materially adverse information expected to drive down the market price of Linear's shares, the Director Defendants "bullet-dodged" the options, delaying their grant until after the release of the information. Conversely, when the quarterly earnings release contained material information expected to drive up the market price of Linear's shares, the Director Defendants allegedly "spring-loaded" the options, granting them just prior to the quarterly earnings release. Weiss also alleges that the Director Defendants never disclosed to stockholders that they timed option grants in this manner.

Weiss recognizes that granting and receiving spring-loaded and bullet-dodged options might be an appropriate exercise of business judgment in some circumstances. However, he asserts the Director Defendants' policy of timing options as alleged in this case was inconsistent with the expectations of the stockholders who approved the plans. Therefore, Weiss reasons, the defendants breached their fiduciary duties by authorizing, receiving, or (by abdication of duty) permitting grants not authorized by the stockholders. Weiss also contends that this timing policy harmed the corporation by artificially lowering the exercise price of the options, causing the company to receive too little money when the options are eventually exercised.

Weiss further alleges that the Director Defendants breached their fiduciary duties by causing Linear to issue the 1996 Proxy Statement, the 1998 Proxy Statement, the 2000 Proxy Statement, and the 2005 Proxy Statement without disclosing material information-namely, that options had been spring-loaded and bullet-dodged. Finally, Weiss brings a waste claim against the Director Defendants, and a claim for unjust enrichment against all the defendants.

In response, the defendants assert that Weiss neither made demand nor adequately pleads reasons for demand excusal. The defendants also argue that the complaint fails to state a claim for breach of fiduciary duty. According to the defendants, the complaint is devoid of allegations that Linear's directors had material inside knowledge, or acted with the intent to circumvent the restrictions contained in the plans, both necessary elements of a breach of duty claim premised on the grant of spring-loaded and bullet-dodged options. The Officer Defendants further argue that the complaint fails to state a claim against them because mere receipt of timed options does not represent a breach of fiduciary duty. Finally, the defendants argue that claims relating to 14 of the 22 grants are time-barred.

For the reasons set forth below, the defendants' motion to dismiss will be denied.

II.

****

B. Failure To State A Claim

1. Breach Of Fiduciary Duty

The defendants argue that the complaint fails to state a breach of fiduciary duty claim under Court of Chancery Rule 12(b)(6) as to the Director Defendants for approving the challenged grants. "[W]here [the] plaintiff alleges particularized facts sufficient to prove demand futility under the second prong of *Aronson*, that plaintiff *a fortiori* rebuts the business judgment rule for the purpose of surviving a motion to dismiss pursuant to Rule 12(b)(6)." Therefore, the complaint states a claim against the Director Defendants for breach of fiduciary duty as a result of approving the challenged option grants.

The defendants also contend that the complaint fails to state a claim against the Director Defendants for breach of fiduciary duty in connection with improper disclosures. The defendants note that under Delaware law, improper disclosure leads to a breach of fiduciary duty only when the disclosure is made in connection with a request for stockholder action. According to the defendants, Weiss has not identified any specific stockholder action connected to the disclosures.

This argument clearly lacks merit. Weiss alleges that the Director Defendants omitted that they would grant spring-loaded and bullet-dodged options from both the 1996 proxy statement seeking stockholder approval of the 1996 option plan and the 1998 proxy statement seeking stockholder approval of an amendment to the 1996 plan increasing the number of shares of common stock reserved for issuance. Weiss also alleges that in connection with proxy solicitations seeking reelection to Linear's board of directors, the Director Defendants made statements giving the impression that they had implemented the option plans in accordance with the plans' terms, when in fact they implemented a policy of timing grants that was not authorized under the plans. Therefore, Weiss has adequately pleaded a claim against the Director Defendants for breach of fiduciary duty based upon improper disclosures.

Weiss has also stated a claim against the Officer Defendants and Maier for receiving the challenged grants. Here, the complaint alleges that these individuals knew or, absent recklessness, should have known that the grants violated the stockholder-approved option plans. Under the liberal pleading standards of this court, this knowledge may be averred generally. Such allegations, taken as true, support an inference that the Officer Defendants and Maier, via their receipt of the options, breached their fiduciary duties.

2. Unjust Enrichment

The defendants further argue that Weiss has not stated a claim for unjust enrichment as to any defendant because Weiss has not explained how the alleged timing of option grants enriched grantees. This argument is wholly without merit. Weiss posits that timing option grants ensures that the exercise price of a grantee's option is lower than it otherwise would be. Thus, upon exercise of the option, the grantee receives more value, and the company less, than he should.

The defendants argue that they have not been unjustly enriched as to options that remain unexercised. However, as the court stated in *Ryan*, this fact alone does not lead to a conclusion that there is no reasonably conceivable set of circumstances under which the defendants might be unjustly enriched. Indeed, the defendants retain something of value-the challenged options-at the expense of the corporation. Nothing suggests that the defendants are prevented from exercising their options once they fully vest. Thus, "one can imagine a situation where [the defendants] exercise[ ] the options and benefit[ ] from the low exercise price." Moreover, even if the defendants do not exercise any options at all, the court may still be able to fashion an appropriate remedy, such as repricing or rescinding the options. Thus, the motion to dismiss the unjust enrichment claim will be denied.

3. Waste

Waste has been defined as follows:

> Roughly, a waste entails an exchange of corporate assets for consideration so disproportionately small as to lie beyond the range at which any reasonable person might be willing to trade. Most often the claim is associated with a transfer of corporate assets that serves no corporate purpose; or for which no consideration at all is received. Such a transfer is in effect a gift. If, however, there is any substantial consideration received by the corporation, and if there is a good faith judgment that in the circumstances the transaction is worthwhile, there should be no finding of waste, even if the fact finder would conclude *ex post* that the transaction was unreasonably risky.

In *Desimone*, Vice Chancellor Strine stated that stock option manipulation could lead to a claim for waste.

The defendants argue that Weiss has failed to plead a claim for waste because he does not allege that the defendants should not have received any options, only that the option grants were excessive by some unarticulated amount. The defendants mischaracterize Weiss's allegations. Weiss alleges that the defendants should not have received any of the timed options at all, and that the grants were approved without any valid corporate purpose.

The court recognizes that a claim for waste must meet "an extreme test, very rarely satisfied by shareholder plaintiff." However, in this case, the court cannot conclude that there is no reasonably conceivable set of facts under which Weiss could prove a claim of waste. Therefore, Weiss has pleaded a claim for waste.

****

IV.

For the foregoing reasons, the defendants' motion to dismiss is DENIED. IT IS SO ORDERED.

QUESTIONS

1. How did the defendants benefit from the grant of stock options prior to quarterly earnings reports when the earnings reports were positive and from the grant of stock options after quarterly earnings reports when the earnings reports were negative?

2. How did this practice of granting options harm Linear?

3. What conduct of the director defendants did the court find sufficient to constitute a request for stockholder action to support the improper disclosure claim?

4. On what basis did the court find that the officer defendants may have breached their fiduciary duties?

5. Why did the court find that the defendants may have been unjustly enriched even with respect to unexercised options?

6. Would charitable gifts by a corporation constitute waste? Would expenditures on pollution control technology not mandated by law constitute waste?

CASE NOTES

1. Nemec retired from Booz Allen (the Company) in March 2006 after nearly 30 years. During Nemec's employment with Booz Allen, he was elected three times to the Company's board of directors and held a number of senior officer positions. At the time of his retirement, Nemec ranked third in seniority among all Booz Allen partners. Schrader was a member of the Booz Allen board of directors at the time Booz Allen redeemed Nemec's stock. Booz Allen had a Stock Option Plan under which officers of Booz Allen were compensated annually with grants of stock rights that were convertible into common stock of the Company. Under the Stock Option Plan, retired officers had the right to sell their stock (put rights) back to the Company at book value for two years from the date of retirement. After the two year period, the Company had the right to redeem, at any time, all or part of the retired officers' stock at book value. Nemec did not exercise his put right within the two year period. In April 2008, in anticipation of the sale of Booz Allen's government consulting business to a private equity firm, the Booz Allen directors opted to redeem Nemec's stock. At the time of redemption Nemec owned about 2.6% of the Company stock and its book value was approximately $162 per share. After the sale of its government consulting business in May 2008, the book value of Booz Allen stock rose to over $700 per share. It was estimated that the pre-transaction redemption of Nemec's stock added nearly $60 million to the value of the existing officers' and directors' stock. Nemec sued Schrader and other directors individually claiming they had breached their fiduciary duty to the retired officers and unjustly enriched themselves by redeeming Nemec's stock prior to the sale of the Company's consulting business. What result? *See* Nemec v. Shrader, 991 A.2d 1120 (Del. 2010).

2. *See also,* Bezirdjian v. O'Reilly, 183 Cal.App.4th 316 (Cal. Ct. App.2010) (Under Delaware law, the decision as to whether or not to file a lawsuit on behalf of a corporation is a management decision to be made by the board of directors; when board of directors refuses stockholder's demand to file a lawsuit, courts will review the board's refusal under the business judgment rule; to rebut presumption of lawful exercise of business judgment, plaintiff in shareholder derivative action must plead specific facts that would create a reasonable doubt that the board's decision was made in good faith); Wahlcometroflex v. Baldwin, 991 A. 2d 44 (Me. 2010) (Breach of fiduciary duty can negate protection of business judgment rule; when business judgment rule is negated, officers and directors must show the challenged transaction was completely fair to the corporation; in determining breach of

fiduciary duty, when business judgment rule applies, standard is gross negligence defined as reckless indifference or deliberate disregard of stockholders); Miyashiro v. Roehrig, Roehrig, Wilson & Hara, 228 P.3d 341 (Haw. Ct. App. 2010) (In legal malpractice, breach of fiduciary duty action against attorney who represented former shareholder and corporate president in shareholder derivative suit, and against escrow company which delivered shares given to former shareholder and corporate president in settlement of shareholder derivative suit to ex-wife of former shareholder and corporate president, issues of material fact precluded summary judgment on malpractice, breach of fiduciary duty claim against attorney, but escrow company did not breach any duties owed to former shareholder and corporate president); Tsutsui v. Barasch, 67 A.D.3d 896 (N.Y. App. Div. 2009) (Shareholder demand on directors prior to filing a derivative action excused when shareholder sufficiently alleged self-interest of majority of board; chairman of board and chief executive officer accused of benefiting by engaging in insider trading, three directors benefited by affiliation with business that profited through sale of stock on basis of inside information, and another director lacked independence by virtue of nearly $1 million paid to his three-attorney law firm over two years prior to filing complaint); Berg & Berg Enterprises, LLC v. Boyle, 178 Cal. App. 4th 1020 (Cal. Ct. App. 2010) (Breach of fiduciary duty under the "trust fund doctrine," where corporate assets become a trust fund for benefit of creditors immediately upon corporate insolvency, generally applies to cases where directors or officers have diverted assets for benefit of insiders or preferred creditors; under California law, there is no broad fiduciary duty that directors owe to creditors solely because the corporation has become insolvent); Ferer v. Aaron Ferer & Sons Co., 770 N.W. 2d 608 (Neb. 2009) (Minority shareholders' suit against directors for breach of fiduciary duty in purchasing company stock from minority shareholders and receiving consulting fees while acting as directors is a derivative claim that must be filed in the name of the corporation; minority shareholders could not adequately represent the interests of the company in a derivative action because the personal interests of minority shareholders were the primary focus of the suit); Sherman v. Ryan, 911 N.E.2d 378 (Ill. App. Ct. 2009) (Shareholders' allegations in derivative action were not sufficient to allege "bad faith" breach of fiduciary duty by directors of insurance broker for sending insurance business to the carrier that offered broker highest contingent commissions; allegation that one director made a public apology for "improper" commissions did not constitute a sufficient allegation to show directors knew the commissions were illegal); Yates v. Holt-Smith, 768 N.W.2d 213 (Wis. Ct. App. 2009) (Director was motivated by her own self-interest in attempting to pressure shareholder into selling her shares by withholding payment of year-end dividend; business judgment rule does not apply to shield director who has acted in bad faith); Straight v. Goss, 678 S.E.2d 443 (S.C. Ct. App. 2009) (Directors' purchase of new manufacturing facility and lease of the facility to corporation did not violate state corporate conflict of interest statute where original facility was damaged by two fires, landlord decided to take over original facility, corporation did not have financial ability to obtain mortgage and shareholder derivative suit plaintiff was unwilling to guarantee mortgage on corporation's behalf).

Additional Information

1. Elizabeth T. Tsai, 39 A.L.R.3d 428 (2010).

2. 4 Causes of Action 569 (2009).

3. Laura H. Dietz Et al., 18B Am. Jur. 2D Corporations §§ 1553, 1588 (2010).

4. Aaron Rachelson, Corporate Acquisitions §§ 11:107–11:110 (2010).

5. Joseph Warren Bishop, Law of Corp. Officers & Dir.: Indemn. & Ins. §§ 4:8, 7:80 (2010).

6. John F. Olson Et al., Dir. & Off. Liab. § 1:38 (2009).

7. Brent A. Olson, 1 Publicly Traded Corporations: Governance & Reg. § 3:7 (2010).

8. Catherine G. Dearlove, Jennifer J. Veet, *Loyal to Whom? Recent Delaware Decisions Clarifying Common Stockholders Are Primary Beneficiaries of Directors' Fiduciary Duties*, 1853 PLI/Corp 915 (2010).

9. Morton A. Pierce, Chang-Do Gong, Gregory R. Daddario, *Fiduciary Duties of Corporate Directors — 2010 Update*, 1786 PLI/corp 295 (2010).

10. Randy J. Holland, *Delaware Directors' Fiduciary Duties: The Focus on Loyalty*, 11 U. Pa. J. Bus. 675 (2009).

11. Alissa Mickels, *Beyond Corporate Social Responsibility: Reconciling the Ideals of a For-Benefit Corporation with Director Fiduciary Duties in the U.S. and Europe*, 32 Hastings Int'l & Comp. L. Rev. 271 (2009).

12. Paula J. Dalley, *Shareholder (and Director) Fiduciary Duties and Shareholder Activism*, 8 Hous. Bus. & Tax L. J. 301 (2008).

13. Ralph C. Ferrara, *Directors' Fiduciary Duties and the Business Judgment Rule*, 1634 PLI/Corp 407 (2007).

14. Remus D. Valsan, Moin A. Yahya, *Shareholders, Creditors, and Dircectors' Fiduciary Dutites: A Law and Finance Approach*, 2 Va. L. & Bus. Rev. 1 (2007).

15. Nadelle Grossman, *Director Compliance with Elusive Fiduciary Duties in a Climate of Corporate Governance Reform*, 12 Fordham J. Corp. & Fin. L. 393 (2007).

16. Lisa M. Fairfax, *Spare the Rod, Spoil the Director? Revitalizing Directors' Fiduciary Duty Through Legal Liability*, 42 Hous. L. Rev. 393 (2005).

10.2.2 Officers' Fiduciary Duties

The *Wahlcometroflex* case involves the failure of a company's president and chief executive officer to file financial statements as required under the terms of a commercial loan to the business. In the course of its decision, the court discusses the subtle interrelationships among the concepts of fiduciary duty, the duty of care, the business judgment rule and unjust enrichment.

WAHLCOMETROFLEX, INC. v. BALDWIN,
991 A.2d 44 (Me. 2010)

JABAR, J.

Alexander G. Baldwin, former president and director of WahlcoMetroflex, Inc., appeals from a judgment entered in favor of the company in the Superior Court (Androscoggin County, *Wheeler, J.*) following a jury trial. Baldwin argues that the court erred in instructing the jury on the fiduciary duty of care and, on the nonjury count, erred in finding that he had been unjustly enriched. Because we agree that the jury was improperly instructed, we vacate the jury's verdict of breach of fiduciary duty and remand this issue for a new trial. We also vacate the portion of the judgment finding unjust enrichment.

I. BACKGROUND

WahlcoMetroflex is a Delaware corporation located in Lewiston that designs and manufactures industrial dampers and expansion joints. Alexander Baldwin and six other shareholders formed the company in 2001. Each shareholder held a management position, with Baldwin as the president and chief executive officer (CEO).

At WahlcoMetroflex's inception, Baldwin was one of two individuals responsible for negotiating the terms of a credit and security agreement between the company and Wells Fargo Business Credit. WahlcoMetroflex obtained a loan and a line of credit from Wells Fargo, and this financing was secured by personal guaranties from all seven shareholders. The guaranties obligated each shareholder to prepare an annual financial statement listing personal assets, liabilities, and net worth as of December 31, and to forward the statement to Wells Fargo no later than January 31 of the following year. If a shareholder did not provide his personal financial statement by April 30, Wells Fargo could fine WahlcoMetroflex $200 per day for each late financial statement.

For the years 2001 and 2002, Wells Fargo received Baldwin's financial documents. For 2003 and 2004, Baldwin inadvertently failed to submit his statements. Because of Baldwin's inaction, Wells Fargo fined WahlcoMetroflex.

Due to financial difficulties at the company, in late 2003 every shareholder took a twenty percent pay cut. Then, towards the end of December 2003, Baldwin announced that he was cutting his salary by seventy-five percent and stepping back from the company. He did, however, retain the position of president and CEO.

In January or early February 2004, Baldwin accepted a consultant position with British Petroleum. British Petroleum is not a competitor of WahlcoMetroflex, and Baldwin did not usurp any of WahlcoMetroflex's customers or business opportunities when he began consulting for British Petroleum. As a consultant, Baldwin worked for British Petroleum on an as-needed basis.

After Baldwin stepped back from the company and began working for British Petroleum, he had minimal contact with the other shareholders. At the end of

March 2004, WahlcoMetroflex sent Baldwin a letter informing him that the company had elected a new president but inviting him to stay involved with the company. In response, Baldwin resigned.

WahlcoMetroflex initiated this action in May 2007 and filed a seven-count amended complaint several months later. The complaint was organized around two types of conduct: Baldwin's failure to provide his personal financial statements in 2003 and 2004, and Baldwin's employment with British Petroleum while still an employee and officer of WahlcoMetroflex. The company alleged that the failure to provide his financial statements resulted in a breach of fiduciary duty (Count 1), a breach of contract with WahlcoMetroflex (Count 2), a breach of contract to which WahlcoMetroflex was a third-party beneficiary (Count 3), negligence (Count 4), and tortious interference (Count 5). In addition, WahlcoMetroflex asserted that Baldwin's work for British Petroleum resulted in a breach of fiduciary duty (Count 6), and unjust enrichment (Count 7).

Following a two-day trial, Baldwin moved, pursuant to M.R. Civ. P. 50(a), for judgment as a matter of law as to all counts. The court granted the motion on the second, fourth, and fifth counts. The court then instructed the jury on all remaining claims except unjust enrichment, which was a nonjury count.

On the first count, the court instructed the jury that, based on Delaware law, Baldwin could breach his fiduciary duty by failing to act in accordance with the duties of loyalty, good faith, or care. Addressing the duty of care, the court explained:

> You may also find that Mr. Baldwin breached a duty of care if you determine that he failed to provide Wells Fargo with personal financial statements and, in doing so, acted with reckless indifference to or a deliberate disregard [of] the company's shareholders or engaged in actions which are without the bounds of reason, *or if you find that he did not act with care, competence and diligence* when he failed to provide Wells Fargo with personal financial statements. (Emphasis added.)

At the completion of the jury instructions, Baldwin objected to the "care, competence and diligence" language, arguing that it was "almost tantamount to [a] negligence instruction."

The jury found that Baldwin breached his fiduciary duty by failing to provide his financial statements and awarded WahlcoMetroflex $10,000 in compensatory damages. The jury returned a verdict in Baldwin's favor on the third-party beneficiary claim. The jury also found that Baldwin was not "liable for breach of fiduciary duty for having worked for British Petroleum while also serving as WahlcoMetroflex's [p]resident, CEO or director[.]"

After the jury's verdict, the court took the unjust enrichment count under advisement. The court found that Baldwin failed to perform his duties as president and CEO of WahlcoMetroflex after he began working at British Petroleum. Because Baldwin received a salary from WahlcoMetroflex during this period, the court determined that he had been unjustly enriched. The court awarded WahlcoMetroflex damages representing the full amount that it paid Baldwin in 2004.

Baldwin filed a motion for reconsideration, which the Superior Court denied. He then filed this appeal.

II. DISCUSSION

A. Duty of Care Instruction

Baldwin argues that the court erred in instructing the jury that he could breach the duty of care he owed as a corporate officer by acting with negligence. We review jury instructions "in their entirety to determine whether they fairly and correctly apprised the jury in all necessary respects of the governing law." When a party preserves an objection to a jury instruction pursuant to M.R. Civ. P. 51(b), an error in the instruction is reversible if it results in prejudice.

The parties agree that Delaware substantive law applies to the issues on appeal. The general principles applicable to corporate officers and directors are well-known: they owe the fiduciary duties of good faith, loyalty, and care to their corporation; their actions are ordinarily presumed proper and entitled to the protection of the business judgment rule; a breach of a fiduciary duty can eliminate the protection afforded by the business judgment rule; and once the presumption of the business judgment rule is rebutted, the officers and directors must prove that the challenged transaction was entirely fair.

When the business judgment rule applies, the standard to determine a breach of the fiduciary duty of care is gross negligence. Gross negligence is defined as "reckless indifference to or a deliberate disregard of the whole body of stockholders or actions which are without the bounds of reason."

The business judgment rule, however, does not apply when officers "have either abdicated their functions, or absent a conscious decision, failed to act." In the instant case, the business judgment rule did not apply to Baldwin's failure to provide his personal financial statements. Thus, the question on appeal is whether negligence or gross negligence is required to breach the fiduciary duty of care when the business judgment rule is inapplicable.

Addressing this same question, the Delaware Court of Chancery concluded that the duty of care is breached by gross negligence. The court noted that one Delaware case, *Rabkin v. Philip A. Hunt Chem. Corp.*, held that ordinary negligence is the appropriate standard when the business judgment rule does not apply. The court went on to explain that later cases appear to have "eclipsed *Rabkin* by implicitly accepting that gross negligence is the appropriate standard even in cases of director inaction and lack of oversight."

Thus, Delaware law requires gross negligence to establish a breach of the duty of care even when the protections of the business judgment rule do not apply. The Superior Court erred in instructing the jury that Baldwin could breach the duty of care by failing to act with "care, competence and diligence." Further, because the instruction allowed the jury to assess Baldwin's conduct against a lesser standard than what was actually required for a violation of the law, the court's error was prejudicial. Accordingly, we vacate the jury's verdict on this count and remand this issue for a new trial.

B. Unjust Enrichment

Two claims centered on Baldwin's simultaneous employment by British Petroleum and WahlcoMetroflex: a legal claim for breach of fiduciary duty and an equitable claim for unjust enrichment. Under Delaware law, "[u]njust enrichment is defined as the unjust retention of a benefit to the loss of another, or the retention of money or property of another against the fundamental principles of justice or equity and good conscience." Unjust enrichment is recognized both (1) as a substantive cause of action and (2) as a prerequisite to an equitable or legal restitutionary remedy for another cause of action. When used as a substantive cause of action, it is limited to circumstances where no wrongdoing is present and it provides the only ground for any recovery.

Such limitations on the use of unjust enrichment as a substantive cause of action can be understood, at least in part, as measures to prevent the circumvention of an applicable legal claim through the use of a more general unjust enrichment claim. Moreover, in tort often "an unjust enrichment claim is essentially another way of stating a traditional tort claim (i.e., if defendant is permitted to keep the benefit of his tortious conduct, he will be unjustly enriched)." Therefore, if the tort claim fails, the unjust enrichment claim must fail as well.

As a further limitation, to pursue unjust enrichment in equity, the plaintiff must lack an adequate remedy at law. A remedy at law is adequate if it "(1) is as complete, practical and as efficient to the ends of justice and its prompt administration as the remedy in equity, and (2) is obtainable as of right." "[W]hether a litigant seeking equitable relief has an adequate remedy at law is a question of law."

Here, WahlcoMetroflex cannot succeed on its unjust enrichment claim. The claim was based on the same facts as the company's claim for breach of fiduciary duty. There is no detectable difference between the company's tort claim for breach of fiduciary duty and its unjust enrichment claim in which the enrichment is claimed to be unjust because it was accomplished through a breach of fiduciary duty. Accordingly, the unjust enrichment claim cannot survive as an independent cause of action and must be dismissed.

The entry is:

Judgment vacated in part. Remanded for a new trial limited to the issue of Baldwin's breach of fiduciary duty for the failure to provide personal financial statements (Count 1) and for dismissal of the unjust enrichment claim. In all other respects, the judgment is affirmed.

QUESTIONS

1. What is the business judgment rule?

2. Why did the business judgment rule not apply to Baldwin's failure to provide his personal financial statements?

3. What conduct can eliminate the protection afforded by the business judgment rule?

4. If the business judgment rule is rebutted, what is the burden of proof on the officers and directors?

5. What is required under Delaware law to establish a breach of fiduciary duty when the business judgment rule applies? What is required under Delaware law to establish a breach of fiduciary duty when the business judgment rule does not apply? What is the relevance of the business judgment rule to establishing a breach of fiduciary duty?

6. When is a substantive cause of action for unjust enrichment permitted? Why? When is an equitable cause of action for unjust enrichment permitted? Why?

CASE NOTES

1. Astra is a pharmaceutical company incorporated in New York. In 1981, Bildman became president and chief executive officer of Astra. Bildman and Astra entered into an employment agreement in July 1993 which remained in effect until Bildman's employment was terminated in June 1996. In December 1995, Bildman learned that *Business Week* was investigating allegations of sexual harassment at Astra committed by Bildman and other senior managers. Bildman formed a task force to investigate the *Business Week* investigation and the task force reported back to Astra that they were "positive" there is no basis for the *Business Week* investigation. In April 1996, the Astra board of directors retained the law firm of Winthrop Stimson to investigate the charges of sexual harassment and voted unanimously to suspend Bildman with pay. The board asked Bildman to cooperate with the Winthrop Stimson investigators and to refrain from contacting any current or former Astra employees. Bildman did neither and, in addition, formed a five-employee satellite office to shred numerous Astra documents. *Business Week* published the article in May 1996 and reported that it had interviewed more than 70 former and current Astra employees and had found "a dozen cases of women who claimed they were either fondled or solicited for sexual favors by Bildman or other [Astra] executives." In June 1996, Astra's board of directors voted to rescind Bildman's employment agreement and to terminate Bildman's employment for cause. Astra claimed that Bildman, as president and chief executive officer, had breached his fiduciary duties to Astra and requested that Bildman be required to forfeit all of his salary and bonuses from 1991 — 1996, an amount in excess of $5 million. The trial court held that New York's "faithless servant" doctrine would impose a "disproportionately harsh" penalty on Bildman if he was required to forfeit all of his salary and bonuses. Instead, the trial court held Bildman should only be required to forfeit his salary and bonuses in excess of the value of his services to Astra from 1991 — 1996. Astra appealed the trial court's holding. What result? *See* Astra USA, Inc. v. Bildman, 914 N.E.2d 36 (Mass. 2009).

2. *See also* Kaplan v. O.K. Technologies, *L.L.C.*, 675 S.E.2d 133 (N.C. Ct. App. 2009) (Members of a limited liability company are like shareholders in a corporation and do not owe a fiduciary duty to each other or to the company; member's status as sole investor in limited liability company does not create fiduciary duty between

investor member and other members; limited liability company member did not have fiduciary duty to corporation which assigned all of its intellectual property to limited liability company); Somers v. Crane, 295 S.W.3d 5 (Tex. App.2009) (Corporation's chief executive officer and board members do not owe a fiduciary duty to shareholders absent a separate contract with CEO or board members, or a confidential relationship; fiduciary relationships are "extraordinary" and should not be recognized lightly); Pride Int'l., Inc. v. Bragg, 259 S.W.3d 839 (Tex. App. 2009) (Under Delaware law, a director's fiduciary duty consists of due care, good faith and loyalty; directors have a duty of disclosure, but do not have to disclose speculative information; a corporate officer has no fiduciary duty in negotiating his own employment contract because it is clear that the officer and company have adverse interests); Shenker, et al. v. Laureate Education Inc., 983 A.2d 408 (Md. 2009) (Directors in cash-out merger assume a different role than when managing the general business affairs of the corporation and have fiduciary duties to shareholders; common law imposes on directors negotiating a cash-out merger duties to make full disclosure of all material facts and to negotiate to maximize shareholder value); Clark v. Sims, 219 P.3d 20 (N.M. Ct. App. 2009) (A close corporation is one which has (1) a small number of stockholders; (2) no ready market for the corporate stock; and (3) substantial majority stockholder participation in the management of the corporation; president of close corporation breached his fiduciary duty when he transferred corporate property to himself, leaving vice president and secretary with worthless stock in a defunct corporation); In the Matter of Bear Stearns Litigation, 870 N.Y.S.2d 709 (N.Y. Supp. Ct. 2008) (Under Delaware law, to rebut presumption of business judgment rule, shareholder plaintiffs must show directors breached their fiduciary duty of care, or duty of loyalty, or acted in bad faith; lack of loyalty may be shown by showing directors were interested in decision, lack of care may be shown by showing directors' grossly negligent failure to consider all material facts available, and bad faith may be shown by showing directors intentionally acted with purpose other than to advance best interests of the corporation); UnitedHealth Group, Inc. Shareholder Derivative Litigation, 754 N.W.2d 544 (Minn. 2008) (Special litigation committees allow corporations to determine whether to dismiss or settle derivative suits despite conflicts of interest on the part of some of the directors; special litigation committees must satisfy the requirements of the business judgment rule before courts will defer to their decisions); Mona v. Mona Electric Group, Inc., 934 A.2d 450 (Md. Ct. Spec. App. 2007) (No evidence that decision by directors to terminate minority shareholder chief executive officer (son) and replace him with majority shareholder CEO (father) was not undertaken in good faith and therefore entitled to the business judgment rule presumption; minority shareholder does not have a breach of fiduciary duty claim against board regarding majority shareholder's compensation).

Additional Information

1. WILLIAM MEADE FLETCHER, 3 FLETCHER CYC. CORP. §§ 837.50, 837.60 (2010).

2. LAURA H. DIETZ ET AL., 18B AM. JUR. 2D CORPORATIONS §§ 1460, 1480, 1483 (2010).

3. FRANCIS C. AMENDOLA ET AL., 19 C.J.S. CORPORATIONS § 564 (2010).

4. WILLIAM MEADE FLETCHER, 31 FLETCHER CYC. CORP. §§ 1036–1040 (2010).

5. JOSEPH W. BISHOP, LAW OF CORP. OFFICERS & DIR.: INDEMN. & INS. § 3:23 (2010).

6. EDWARD BRODSKY & M. PATRICIA ADAMSKI, LAW OF CORP. OFFS. & DIRS.: RTS., DUTIES & LIABS. § 2:10 (2009).

7. David Rosenberg, *Supplying the Adverb: The Future of Corporate Risk-Taking and the Business Judgment Rule*, 6 BERKELEY BUS. L.J. 216 (2009).

8. Clark W. Furlow, *Good Faith, Fiduciary Duties, and the Business Judgment Rule in Delaware*, 2009 UTAH L. REV. 1061 (2009).

9. Fred W. Triem, *Judicial Schizophrenia in Corporate Law: Confusing the Standard of Care with the Business Judgment Rule*, 24 ALASKA L. REV. 23 (2007).

10. Jeremy Telman, *The Business Judgment Rule, Disclosure, and Executive Compensation*, 81 TUL. L. REV. 829 (2007).

11. David Rosenberg, *Galactic Stupidity and the Business Judgment Rule*, 32 J. CORP. L. 310 (2007).

12. Andrew S. Gold, *A Decision Theory Approach to the Business Judgment Rule: Reflections on Disney, Good Faith, and Judicial Uncertainty*, 6 MD. L. REV. 398 (2007).

13. Lyman P. O. Johnson, *Corporate Officers and the Business Judgment Rule*, 60 BUSINESS LAW. 439 (2005).

10.2.3   Majority Shareholders' Fiduciary Duties

Majority shareholders in a "close corporation," defined generally as a corporation which has few shareholders who participate actively in the management of the corporation, have a fiduciary duty to the minority shareholders. The *Pointer* case considers the fiduciary duties of the majority shareholders to the ex-CEO of the company under a claim of self-dealing by the ex-CEO.

POINTER v. CASTELLANI,
918 N.E.2d 805 (Mass. 2009)

IRELAND, J.

The plaintiff, Bernard J. Pointer, was part owner of Fletcher Granite Company, LLC, a closely held corporate entity. The case commenced in the Superior Court in Middlesex County and was transferred to the business litigation session, where a Superior Court judge presided over a jury-waived trial, lasting some twenty-three days, in which over 750 exhibits were admitted. In a forty-seven page written decision containing findings of fact and rulings of law, the judge found for Pointer on his claims against the defendants for a freeze-out and breach of fiduciary duty; for breach of an employment contract and of the covenant of good faith and fair dealing; and for interference with an advantageous relationship. He also found for the plaintiff on the defendants' counterclaims. We granted the parties' applications for direct appellate review. Because we conclude that there was no error in the judge's conclusions and we see no reason to revisit our holding in *Brodie v. Jordan*, 447 Mass. 866, 857 N.E.2d 1076 (2006), we affirm the judgment. However, we remand the case for a determination of damages or other equitable remedy for the plaintiff on his claim of a freeze-out and further proceedings consistent with this opinion.

Background and Facts

Proper understanding of this case requires a somewhat lengthy discussion of the essential facts that we gleaned from the findings of the judge. We also present only so much of the lengthy procedural history in this case as is necessary to understand the issues raised. In our review, we do not set aside a judge's findings of fact unless they are clearly erroneous. The burden is on the appellant to show that a finding is clearly erroneous. *Id.* "Where there are two permissible views of the evidence, the fact finder's choice between them cannot be clearly erroneous."

1. Fletcher Granite Company, LLC (FGC), was formed on February 25, 1999, by Pointer and defendants Victor Castellani, Paul Woodberry, and Kathleen Herbert to take ownership of the assets of a granite company we shall call Pioneer. Pioneer's granite business included the operation of several quarries, the sale of rough granite to others, the fabrication of granite into various building and landscape items including curbing, and certain real estate that included quarries and abutting properties. One of the pieces of real estate significant for our purposes was an approximately sixty-four acre parcel in Milford that contained wetlands and an abandoned quarry.

Pointer had been president of Pioneer, and his initial involvement in the sale of the business was in that capacity. Ultimately, however, he joined with Castellani, Woodberry, and Herbert. The group had agreed that, when FGC assumed ownership of Pioneer, they would continue to operate the quarry business and sell the real estate.

FGC's operating agreement provided that Castellani and Woodberry together would own a fifty-one per cent interest in the business and Pointer would own a forty-three per cent interest. Pointer, Castellani, Woodberry, and Herbert became members of FGC. Pointer, Castellani, and Herbert were the initial managers. The initial managers could not be removed except for a "willful or intentional violation or reckless disregard of the Manager's duties . . . [or] a material breach of the Operating Agreement without cure after twenty days notice [by] the Board of Managers." Pointer became FGC's president; he was the only one experienced in operating a granite business. Herbert acted as the chief financial officer, and Woodberry and Castellani, "for the most part, were merely passive investors."

Through a wholly owned subsidiary, Pioneer also owned a residential subdivision called Greystone Estates, Inc. (Greystone). Pioneer was unwilling to sell its granite business unless it also sold Greystone. Pointer and another individual, Lou Frank, had decided to purchase Greystone. To that end, just before FGC was formed, he and Frank formed Stone Ridge Investments, LLC (SRI), of which Pointer owned fifty per cent. The other members of FGC were interested only in the quarry business and not in Greystone. The other members knew Pointer was involved in

SRI, as he conducted SRI business while he was president of FGC. Pointer told the others that he would assist Frank in the Greystone transaction, but Pointer did not disclose that he was a substantial (fifty per cent) owner. Implicit in the judge's findings however, which also has support in the record, is that the others knew he was a principal of SRI. The others learned of the extent of Pointer's ownership only after Pointer's employment was terminated. It is important to note that, as discussed *infra*, Pointer and Frank formed another entity, Stone Ridge Management, LLC (SRM), in 2000.

FGC closed on Pioneer's quarry, mill, and certain real estate on March 30, 1999. All but Woodberry were present at the closing. On April 1, 1999, SRI closed on Greystone. Pointer was the only member of FGC present.

The judge found that, at the time the parties entered into the transaction to acquire Pioneer's businesses, Pointer's intention was to stay with FGC as president and ultimately to control FGC. Pointer had a further expectation that he would be involved in the real estate development part of the transaction. The judge found that Castellani and Woodberry had expectations "primarily as investors in the FGC quarrying and granite sales business. They had little interest or expectation in actually running FGC." Herbert's expectations were that she continue her position as financial officer of FGC and own a "small piece of the company." The judge further found that neither Herbert, Castellani, nor Woodberry had any "interest in real estate purchase, sale or development."

2. We now provide some preliminary information about FGC's operating agreement and Pointer's employment contract. Under § 2.3 of the operating agreement, FGC was organized to "own and operate a quarry business and to engage in any other lawful act or activity permitted under the [l]aw." In addition, under § 5.1.4.7 of the operating agreement, the approval of 66.7 per cent of the managers was required for FGC to engage in any business other than that related to quarrying. Furthermore, § 5.4.3 of the operating agreement states:

> "[N]othing in this Agreement shall be deemed to restrict in any way the rights of any Member, or any affiliate of any Member, to conduct any other business or activity whatsoever, and no Member shall be accountable to [FGC] or to any other Member with respect to that business or activity. The organization of [FGC] shall be without prejudice to the Members' respective rights (or the rights of their respective Affiliates) to maintain, expand, or diversify such other interests and activities and to receive and enjoy profits or compensation therefrom. Each Member waives any rights the Member might otherwise have to share or participate in such other interests or activities of any other Member or the Member's Affiliates."

The operating agreement explicitly anticipated that "the conduct of [FGC]'s business may involve business dealings and undertakings with Members and their Affiliates" and required that, "in those cases, . . . dealings and undertakings shall be at arm's length and on commercially reasonable terms."

****

4. In 2003, issues began to arise at FGC related to "FGC's deteriorating operating profits and its then precarious cash position." FGC had a revolving credit agreement with Citizens Bank that allowed FGC to borrow operating funds when cash sales were at a low point. There was a limit on the amount FGC could borrow based on the value of FGC's receivables and inventory (borrowing base). When FGC bought inventory, the bank gave FGC a letter of credit, thereby reducing its borrowing base.

As part of its landscaping business, FGC bought cobblestones imported from India that required such a letter of credit. In early 2003, the members and managers of FGC, concerned about having enough cash to operate their business in the first three quarters of 2003, decided to defer cobblestone orders until the fall of 2003. Nonetheless, Pointer, concerned that the business would have an insufficient supply of cobblestones for the landscaping season, decided on his own to order a "half ship" of them. The minutes of the board meetings in February and May, 2003, reveal that this shipment was known to the members. In any event, the resulting letter of credit reduced FGC's borrowing base by over $700,000. In addition, the order placed an additional $170,000 cash demand on FGC.

In order to deal with the cash shortage, Pointer took two steps. First, he decided to use a billing method known as "cut-and-store," which was a way to send invoices to customers in advance of shipment, in hopes that payment would be more prompt. In March, 2003, Pointer decided to include the cut-and-store bills in FGC's receivable records (and thereby in the receivable amounts reported to the bank). This was contrary to FGC's agreement with the bank, although Pointer contended that he was unaware of this fact. There is record support for the judge's finding that, "[d]espite concerns expressed by Castellani at trial, it appears that the bank was aware of the cut-and-store situation and was not seriously concerned about it."

Second, Pointer caused FGC to borrow $300,000 from SRI's affiliate, SRM, at an interest rate of fifteen per cent, approximately three times the prime rate. Herbert was aware of the transaction because Pointer, after depositing the check from SRM to FGC, presented her with a copy of it. Castellani and Woodberry were not informed of the loan. The loan was contrary to the bank covenants, and could have constituted an event of default that would have permitted the bank to call in the loan. It also violated the operating agreement. Herbert, the chief financial officer, did not know the loan violated bank covenants. In addition, the judge found that, at the time Pointer made the loan, Herbert had "hear[d] from the bank about overdrawn checks and called both Castellani and Pointer in a panic. Neither Castellani, Woodberry, nor Herbert, however, offered to loan any money to FGC." Pointer then told Herbert that he did not have money and would ask Frank (i.e., SRI/SRM) for the loan. In any event, Pointer repaid any excess interest to FGC.

When Castellani and Woodberry learned of Pointer's actions, they were concerned about his judgment and ability to manage FGC, but they did not discuss their concerns with him. Instead, they concluded that Pointer deliberately reported the receivables to the bank and had concealed financial problems by borrowing from SRM. In addition, FGC, on a pure performance basis, was projecting a loss for 2003, and was in difficulties with its bank.

As majority owners, Castellani and Woodberry secretly decided to find someone to replace Pointer as the top executive of FGC. In November, 2003, the pair began communicating with the defendant Jonathan Maurer, culminating in Maurer's hiring in January, 2004, as FGC's chief executive officer. The contract Maurer signed stated that Castellani and Woodberry would "use their best efforts to cause the operating agreement to be modified" to allow Maurer to purchase shares up to forty per cent of FGC. Pointer was not informed of the decision to hire Maurer until February, 2004. In addition, Pointer and Castellani executed a memorandum, in February, 2004, that provided that Pointer's employment agreement could continue until at least March 31, 2006. Maurer became a manager of FGC, and started working on March 15, 2004. The record shows that Maurer had Pointer removed from all of FGC's interoffice distribution lists as of March 18, 2004.

In March, 2004, two other actions by Pointer came to the attention of Castellani and Woodberry. During a four-year period, Pointer made political contributions in the amount of $4,825. He wrote personal checks for which he was reimbursed by FGC. This practice had the effect of concealing from Federal and State election authorities contributions by FGC, and predated the sale of the granite business to FGC. In March, 2004, Castellani and Woodberry learned about the contributions. However, the judge found that Pointer's practice was not hidden from FGC, and that in 2003, FGC instituted a company policy, drafted with the assistance of Castellani, that allowed such contributions if either the chairman or the president (i.e., Pointer) approved. The judge concluded that the political contributions were an "exceptionally minor issue." In any event, Pointer reimbursed FGC for the contributions.

The second action by Pointer involved a report done by FGC's accountants concerning the cut-and-store billing activity. The judge found "although [the bank was] somewhat concerned [it] took no action other than to assist FGC and provide it with acceptable forms to accomplish the same thing. The bank never called its loan . . . ."

At a meeting on March 29, 2004, the managers and members tried to talk about these issues with Pointer, but he refused to participate because it was not on the agenda he had submitted for the meeting. Pointer was informed that he was suspended with full pay and benefits. He was also barred from the facility unless there was a prior arrangement with one of the managers.

Without notice to Pointer, the managers had a meeting where they terminated Pointer's employment as of June 30, 2004, by means of a resolution that set forth several allegations (resolution). Pointer was given no opportunity to respond. After Pointer's termination, Maurer told Pointer that he could no longer represent FGC in any official capacity and would not be allowed direct access to his FGC electronic mail messages.

Pointer sued the defendants, alleging, in relevant part, that the defendants engaged in a freeze-out, committed a breach of their fiduciary duty, violated his employment contract and the covenant of good faith and fair dealing, and interfered with an advantageous relationship. The judge found for Pointer on his claims, and on the defendants' counterclaims, which alleged, insofar as relevant here, breach of fiduciary duty by misappropriating a corporate opportunity and self-dealing; breach of contract; and breach of the implied covenant of good faith and fair dealing in relation to the operating agreement and his employment agreement. The judge found for SRI/SRM on the defendants' counterclaim charging aiding and abetting fiduciary breaches.

The defendants appealed, and Pointer cross-appealed concerning the appropriate remedy for the freeze-out.

Discussion

It is uncontested that FGC is a close corporation in that it has "(1) a small number of stockholders; (2) no ready market for the corporate stock; and (3) substantial majority stockholder participation in the management, direction and operations of the corporation." "Because of the fundamental resemblance . . . to [a] partnership . . . stockholders in the close corporation owe one another substantially the same fiduciary duty in the operation of the enterprise that partners owe to one another[, that is,] the "utmost good faith and loyalty." "

1. *The freeze-out and termination of employment.* The defendants argue that the judge erred in finding for Pointer on his claims of a freeze-out and wrongful termination of his employment. There was no error.

Whatever the advantages of the corporate form, it's very structure may "suppl[y] an opportunity for the majority stockholders to oppress or disadvantage minority stockholders [through] a variety of oppressive devices, termed "freeze-outs." " Means employed to effectuate a freeze-out include depriving the minority shareholder of offices or employment in the corporation. In *Wilkes v. Springside Nursing Home, Inc.*, this court stated:

> "The denial of employment to the minority at the hands of the majority is especially pernicious in some instances. A guaranty of employment with the corporation may have been one of the "basic reason[s] why a minority owner has invested capital in the firm . . . ." The minority stockholder typically depends on his salary as the principal return on his investment, since the "earnings of a close corporation . . . are distributed in major part in salaries . . . ." Other noneconomic interests of the minority stockholder are likewise injuriously affected by barring him from corporate office . . . .
> In sum, by terminating a minority stockholder's employment . . . the majority effectively frustrate the minority stockholder's purposes in entering on the corporate venture and also deny him equal return on his investment."

A breach of fiduciary duty through a freeze-out also occurs when the reasonable expectations of a shareholder are frustrated.

Nevertheless, majority shareholders "have certain rights to what has been termed "selfish ownership" in the corporation which should be balanced against the concept of their fiduciary obligation to the minority" permitting them "room to maneuver" and "a large measure of discretion" in, among other things, hiring and firing corporate employees. Therefore, where there is an allegation of a breach of fiduciary duty, the court must allow the controlling group to demonstrate a "legitimate business purpose for its action." The minority stockholder is then allowed to "demonstrate that the same legitimate objective could have been achieved through an alternative course less harmful to the minority's interest."

Applying these principles to the facts in this case, the judge did not err in concluding that Pointer was subject to a freeze-out when Castellani and Woodberry, in violation of their fiduciary duty, secretly hired Maurer in January, 2004, barred Pointer from the FGC, and ultimately fired him as president in June, 2004. In addition, for the reasons cited above, the judge also did not err in concluding that Pointer's actions did not require his termination because less harmful alternatives outweighed "any of the asserted business purposes for the actions that Castellani and Woodberry took in secretly engaging Maurer." The judge stated:

> "[Castellani and Woodberry] attempted to excuse this failure [to inform Pointer about discussions with Maurer] by expressing concern that Pointer would react badly to news that an effort was underway to find someone who would be senior to him in the operations of FGC. If Pointer were to leave before a new executive could be located, [they] knew that there was no one immediately able to step into his role. Certainly neither of them was equipped, nor interested, in doing so. Further, they were concerned that the bank might move their account to workout or call the loan if Pointer left the company."

There is no merit to the defendants' argument, without citation to authority, that they did not commit a breach of their fiduciary duty because, even though he was barred from FGC without an invitation from another manager, Pointer continued to be a manager and member, hold an equity interest, and receive detailed financial information. At the very least, as the judge found, the freeze-out frustrated Pointer's reasonable expectation that ultimately he would be able to be the owner of FGC. Moreover, Pointer did not have full access to his electronic mail messages or interoffice memoranda. There also is no merit to the defendants' argument that termination cannot be a freeze-out. Nor did the judge err in stating that Pointer had a reasonable expectation of employment as president. The judge found that when Castellani and Woodberry secretly decided to replace Pointer, one of the reasons they kept the information from Pointer was because they needed someone to run FGC in the interim and neither Castellani nor Woodberry was equipped or interested. Although it is true that the employment contract could be terminated and was extended only until March, 2006, as discussed *infra*, here it was wrongfully terminated and thus frustrated Pointer's reasonable expectation in remaining president.

The defendants claim that the judge also erred in holding that Pointer did not commit a breach of his employment contract. This argument has no merit.

The resolution terminating Pointer's employment enumerated the grounds on which that termination was based. In relevant part, it stated that Pointer had violated his employment agreement and the operating agreement, and engaged in acts of malfeasance that materially injured FGC by forming a fifty per cent ownership in SRI/SRM and engaging in certain real estate transactions; inadequately compensating for resources FGC provided to Pointer while he conducted SRI/SRM business; causing FGC to borrow $300,000 from SRM at exorbitant interest rates; including cut-and-store billing in the receivables that resulted in false reports to the bank; and reimbursing himself for political contributions. Given the judge's findings recited *supra*, he did not err in concluding, inter alia, that the $300,000 loan helped FGC; Pointer had a right, even under his employment contract, to conduct SRI/SRM business to the extent he reasonably determined was necessary and everyone at FGC was aware of this; the cut-and-store reporting was known to the bank and FGC was not harmed thereby; and, although the political contributions should not have been handled in the way they were, Pointer had the power to make contributions in FGC's behalf and all the other owners had to do was talk to Pointer about his practices.

The judge also did not err in determining that the defendants' claim that Pointer should have revealed to the other members and managers that the purchase of FGC's parcel was part of a larger real estate venture and that Pointer was a fifty per cent owner of SRI/SRM was contrived. The judge found that no one from FGC other than Pointer had any interest in real estate development; that under FGC's operating agreement, for FGC to engage in real estate transactions, approval of 66.7 per cent of the members was required, and the defendants presented no evidence that demonstrated that FGC was deviating from its operating agreement; and that Castellani knew that SRM was aggregating land for development. In fact, the others knew that there was discussion about using some land for a golf course. Castellani sent Pointer a newspaper article involving a golf course developer sued over "turtles."

The defendants argue that they could not have demonstrated that FGC was interested in real estate when they did not know that Pointer was a fifty per cent owner of SRM, and thus, they argue, they did not know that the opportunity was even available to them. However, the judge implicitly found that they knew Pointer was an owner of SRI and that SRM was buying the parcel; indeed, Pointer signed the purchase and sale agreement and deed for FGC's parcel as a manager of SRM.

As the judge found, Castellani, Woodberry, Herbert and Maurer owed Pointer, who was a forty-three per cent owner of FGC, "real substance and communication, including efforts to resolve *supposed* complaints by less drastic measures than termination. But such efforts never truly were attempted." (Emphasis added.) The judge called some of the charges "contrived" or not "credible," and concluded that, by the time the resolution was written, the others were simply trying "to find a way to get rid of Pointer."

The defendants argue that because Pointer was president under an employment contract, the terms of the contract control rather than their fiduciary duty. Even assuming that this assertion has merit, the cases on which the defendants rely are easily distinguished. One involved a corporation whose stock was publicly traded. Two concerned terminations that were consistent with applicable employment contracts. Here, there is support for the judge's conclusion that Pointer did not violate his employment agreement.

****

Remedy for freeze-out

Having found Castellani, Woodberry, Herbert, and Maurer individually liable to Pointer for a freeze-out, the judge gave the parties ninety days to try to reach a binding agreement under which one side or the other would buy out the shareholder interests of the other. Failing that, he ordered FGC to be liquidated by a receiver and each party to be awarded the net proceeds in accordance with their respective shareholder interests under the operating agreement. The defendants appealed from the judge's entire judgment, including the remedy; Pointer did not appeal. The parties did not agree to a buyout. The judge stayed that portion of the judgment ordering liquidation, pending the appeal. In his order, the judge noted that he was aware of our decisions in *Brodie v. Jordan* (remedy for freeze-out is to put minority shareholder in same position he or she would have been in had freeze-out not occurred; absent agreement between shareholders, court cannot force buyout of minority shareholder's stock), and *Bernier v. Bernier*, (discussing valuation of shares of S corporation).

In July, 2008, approximately eight months after judgment entered, Pointer filed a motion for relief from judgment. He asked the judge to modify the remedy for the freeze-out because, he argued, FGC was insolvent and, therefore, a forced sale would yield him nothing. He requested that the remedy be modified to order the defendants to pay him approximately $3.6 million dollars, which, according to an expert who testified for Pointer at trial, was 43.3 per cent of the value of FGC when the freeze-out occurred. In return, Pointer would tender his stock.

Because the trial judge had retired, another judge ruled that the relief Pointer sought was contrary to the *Brodie* decision. As the judge stated, the operating agreement does not require any buyout during the lifetime of a shareholder.

Both sides make numerous arguments concerning the appropriate remedy for the freeze-out. We need not discuss them because we conclude that the trial judge's order for a forced sale of FGC violated our holding in the *Brodie* decision. Because we held that a forced buyout of a shareholder was improper without some authorization from shareholders, it would be inconsistent for us now to hold that a forced sale is proper. Nevertheless, Pointer is entitled to damages or other equitable relief from Castellani, Woodberry, Herbert, and Maurer, which will put him in the position he would have been in had the freeze-out not occurred, and compensates him for the denial of his reasonable expectations.

Anticipating that this court would conclude that a forced sale of FGC violated the holding in the *Brodie* decision, the trial judge fashioned an alternative remedy, stating he "would grant to Pointer an order for his reinstatement as [p]resident of FGC, together with back pay for salary lost at the rate he was earning at the time of his discharge to the date of his reinstatement, indemnification for his reasonable attorney's fees and costs in litigating this action, along with appropriate injunctive relief to enable him to resume and continue in the future, under reasonable regulation by the FGC members and managers, in his position as [p]resident." However, since the trial judge fashioned this remedy, it appears that circumstances have changed, not the least of which is that FGC may have been sold. We are constrained in fashioning a remedy here, as Pointer sought both monetary damages and equitable relief, and the appropriate remedy depends on further factual findings. Therefore, the case is remanded for further proceedings to determine whether it is possible to implement the trial judge's alternative remedy. If not, the judge should fashion another remedy, one that presumably would include monetary damages and other equitable relief that the judge deems appropriate.

Conclusion

For the reasons set forth above, we affirm the decision of the trial judge insofar as he found for Pointer on his claims and on the defendants' counterclaims. We affirm the denial of Pointer's motion for relief from judgment that requested a forced buyout of his shares of FGC. The case is remanded for further proceedings consistent with this opinion concerning an appropriate remedy for the freeze-out.

QUESTIONS

1. How do courts balance the legitimate business purposes of majority stockholders and the reasonable expectations of minority stockholders in the case of a claimed breach of fiduciary duty by the majority?

2. How did the court find that Pointer was subject to a freeze-out when he continued to own the same equity interest after his termination as he did prior to his termination?

3. Why did the court find that Pointer had not violated his employment contract by his fifty percent ownership in SRI/SRM and engaging in real estate activities on behalf of SRI/SRM?

4. In the case of minority stockholders working under an employment contract, which controls the relationship between the majority and minority stockholders — the employment contract or the majority stockholders' fiduciary duty to the minority stockholders?

5. What remedies are available to a minority stockholder in the event that a freeze-out is proven?

CASE NOTES

1. Cookietree is a privately owned Utah corporation that produces and sells baked goods. Cookietree was founded in 1981 by Greg Schenk and his father, Boyd Schenk. Greg Schank was named president of Cookietree at the time of its founding and continued to hold that position. In 1992, Greg Schenk recruited McLaughlin, a former executive at Pillsbury and Quaker Oats, to be the chief operating officer and vice president of Cookietree. McLaughlin's employment contract included a guaranteed minimum salary and options to acquire up to 200,000 shares of common stock in Cookietree. The employment contract also provided that McLaughlin was an at-will employee of Cookietree. In 1993, Cookietree and McLaughlin entered into a Stock Option Agreement that allowed McLaughlin to purchase an additional

200,000 shares of Cookietree. The Stock Option Agreement also provided that any shareholder selling stock must first offer the stock to Cookietree, and that, if Cookietree did not elect to purchase the stock, Cookietree would provide written notice to the other shareholders that the stock was available for purchase. In 1998, just before he died, Boyd Schenk transferred 818,000 shares of Cookietree stock to Greg Schenk which gave Greg Schenk 49% ownership of Cookietree. In 1999, after Boyd Schenk's death, his wife sold 545,200 shares of stock to Greg Schenk, giving him 65% ownership of Cookietree's stock. This transaction was not recorded in Cookietree's minutes or written records, nor was written notice of the transaction provided to Cookietree's board or other shareholders. In 2003, Greg Schenk said he was interested in selling Cookietree and McLaughlin said he was interested in purchasing Cookietree. However, McLaughlin was never able to raise funds sufficient to complete the purchase. Greg Schenk then entered into negotiations with another cookie company, Otis Spunkmeyer. McLaughlin refused to agree to various terms in the Otis Spunkmeyer purchase offer, including a noncompete agreement, and demanded his right of first refusal for any stock sold to Otis Spunkmeyer. Thereafter, the relationship between Greg Schenk and McLaughlin deteriorated rapidly. In August 2004, Greg Schenk fired McLaughlin. The notice of termination stated it was without cause. McLaughlin refused to leave the Cookietree offices and the police were called to escort him from the property. In November 2004, McLauglin sued Cookietree and Greg Schenk for breach of contract and breach of fiduciary duty. In May 2005, during an unnoticed meeting of Cookietree's board of directors, the board ratified the 1999 purchase of stock by Greg Schenk and voted to waive the corporation's right of first refusal in this transaction. The trial court granted summary judgment in favor of Greg Schenk and Cookietree. McLaughlin appealed. What result? *See* McLaughlin v. Schenk, 220 P.3d 146 (Utah 2009).

2. *See also* Horbal v. Cannizzaro, 2009 Mass. Super. LEXIS 372 (Mass. Super. 2009) (Majority shareholders who have no economic interest contrary to the interests of the corporation or who have no monetary interests that were not shared by all of the shareholders cannot be found to have breached any claimed fiduciary duty); Rossman v. Morasco, 974 A.2d 1 (Conn. App. Ct. 2009) (Evidence sufficient to support jury finding of breach of fiduciary duty by majority shareholder in failing to notify minority shareholder of emergency meeting to approve sale of business assets, but minority shareholder did not suffer damages because majority shareholder owned 75 percent of corporation and could approve the sale of corporate assets without consent of minority shareholder; evidence sufficient to support jury finding that minority shareholder committed tortious interference with contract rights of corporation by starting a competing company and soliciting corporation's customers to switch to competing company, offering corporation's customers reduced rates, and claiming security issues regarding an employee of corporation who was a convicted felon but never posed a security risk and no longer worked for corporation); Blohm v. Kelly, 765 N.W.2d 147 (Minn. Ct. App. 2009) (Claim by minority shareholder that majority shareholder abused his position by paying himself excessive compensation and using corporate assets to pay personal debts was a derivative claim, not a direct claim, because alleged wrongful conduct would directly impair assets of corporation and only indirectly impair capital distributions to minority shareholder; trial court acted within its discretion in staying minority

shareholder's suit against majority shareholder pending findings of corporation's special litigation committee); Notz v. Everett Smith Group, Ltd., 764 N.W.2d 904 (Wis. 2009) (Claimed breach of fiduciary duty by minority shareholder against majority shareholder based on sale of subsidiary with high growth potential involved harm primarily to corporation and thus minority shareholder could not bring a direct claim); Mazloom v. Mazloom, 675 S.E.2d 746 (S.C. Ct. App. 2009) (By signing and filing document with Secretary of State that minority shareholder owned 25 percent of shares of stock in successor corporation, majority shareholders were estopped from denying minority shareholder's ownership interest; minority shareholder relied upon filing with Secretary of State and took no further legal actions to establish his ownership interest); Whitehorn v. Whitehorn Farms, 195 P.3d 836 (Mont. 2008) (Where minority shareholder has converted corporate property, family corporation's termination of minority shareholder from his positions as employee and officer did not constitute breach of corporation's fiduciary duty to minority shareholder; shareholders in a close corporation owe the duty of utmost good faith and loyalty to one another, but majority shareholders should not be stymied by a minority shareholder's grievances if there is a legitimate business purpose for the majority shareholders' actions); Pasquale v. Casale, 893 N.E.2d 1263 (Mass. App. Ct. 2008) (Order requiring majority shareholder to repurchase stock of minority shareholder to award damages for wrongfully withholding retained earnings was not an abuse of discretion by trial court); Kortum v. Johnson, 755 N.W.2d 432 (N.D. 2008) (In a claim of shareholder oppression by virtue of termination of employment, the threshold question is whether minority shareholder had a reasonable expectation of continued employment in the close corporation, even though she signed a shareholder agreement acknowledging her status as an at-will employee; shareholders of close corporation still owed fiduciary duty to shareholder whose employment was terminated; trial court failed to make findings as to whether shareholders breached fiduciary duty to terminated shareholder, whether the shareholder agreement reflected the reasonable expectations of the shareholders, and whether terminated shareholder had a reasonable expectation of continued employment as partial return on her investment); Schulman v. Wolff & Samson, PC, 951 A.2d 1051 (N.J. Super. Ct. App. Div. 2008) (Minority shareholders could pursue breach of contract and fraud claims against attorneys and law firms which they alleged assisted majority shareholders in scheme to deprive minority shareholders of their lawful interests in corporation; action against attorneys and law firms was a separate cause of action from the shareholder litigation); Saunders v. Firtel, 2008 Conn. Super. LEXIS 1249 (Conn. Super. Ct. 2008) (No fiduciary relationship exists as between shareholders who possess mutual knowledge and skill regarding the corporation; there is no unequal bargaining position in a relationship between two successful and astute businessmen; shareholders were fully aware of contents of all contracts, and the personal needs, interest and talents of the other shareholder); Williams v. Stanford, 977 So.2d 722 (Fla. Dist. Ct. App. 2008) (Genuine issue of material fact existed regarding minority shareholder's claim of fraud, misrepresentation and breach of fiduciary duty against majority shareholder in connection with transfer of corporate assets to another company; in cases of fraud or material misrepresentation, shareholder is entitled to equitable remedies in addition to statutory appraisal rights); Davis v. Brockamp & Jaeger, Inc., 174 P.3d 607 (Or. Ct. App.) (Low bonuses paid to minority shareholder did not demonstrate minority shareholder oppression where bonuses were based on objective measure of profits generated by construction project managed by minority shareholder; bonus representing 12.5 percent return on equity to minority shareholder employee in lieu of dividend was not insufficient benefit even though president, sole director and majority shareholder granted himself a bonus that was 26.3 times as much as granted to minority shareholder employee; minority shareholders have no right to participate in management decisions unless specifically granted in corporation's articles of incorporation or other agreement).

Additional Information

1. William Meade Fletcher, 12b Fletcher Cyc. Corp. §§ 5810, 5811, 5811.05, 5811.10, 5811.20, 5811.50 (2010).

2. Laura H. Dietz Et al., 18A Am. Jur. 2d Corporations §§ 644, 651, 655 (2010).

3. Michael A. Rosenhouse, 39 A.L.R. 6th 1 (2010).

4. Francis C. Amendola Et al., 18 C.J.S. Corporations § 378 (2010).

5. Thomas M. Madden, *Do Fiduciary Duties of Managers and Members of Limited Liability Companies Exist as with Majority Shareholders of Closely Held Corporations?*, 12 Duq. Bus. L.J. 211 (2010).

6. Iman Anabtawi, Lynn Stout, *Fiduciary Duties for Activist Shareholders*, 60 Stan. L. Rev. 1255 (2008).

7. Margaret H. Paget, *Corporate Law — Shareholder Breach of Fiduciary Duty in Close Corporations*, 91 Mass. L. Rev. 32 (2207).

8. Robert C. Art, *Shareholder Rights and Remedies in Close Corporations: Oppression, Fiduciary Duties, and Reasonable Expectations*, 28 J. Corp. L. 371 (2003).

9. Regina M. Giannini, *"Punctilio of Honor" or "Disintegrating Erosion"? The Fiduciary Duty to Disclose for Partners, Corporate Directors, and Majority Shareholders*, 27 Sw. U. L. Rev. 73 (1997).

10. Mark B. Barta, *Is the Imposition of Fiduciary Responsibilities Running From Managers, Directors, and Majority Shareholders to Minority Shareholders Economically Efficient*, 38 Clev. St. L. Rev. 559 (1990).

11. L. Clark Hicks, Jr., *Corporations — Fiduciary Duty — In a Close Corporation, A Majority Shareholder Owes a Fiduciary Duty Towards the Minority When Seeking a Controlling Share*, 60 Miss. L.J. 425 (1990).

10.2.4   Shareholder Direct and Derivative Suits

Shareholders can bring two types of suits against directors and officers of a corporation — a direct suit and a derivative suit. In a direct suit, the shareholders allege personal harm and seek to recover personally. In a derivative suit, the shareholders allege harm to the corporation and seek to recover on behalf of the corporation. The *Metcoff* case considers both direct and derivative claims asserted in the same suit. Before shareholders can file a derivative suit, they must first demand that the directors file the derivative suit on behalf of the corporation, unless they can show that such a demand would be futile. The *In Re Comverse Technology* case discusses the factors considered in determining whether a demand would be futile. The case also discusses how the directors' appointment of a special committee to consider whether or not to file a derivative suit affects the determination of demand futility.

METCOFF v. LEBOVICS,
977 A.2d 285 (Conn. Super. Ct. 2007)

STEVENS, J.

STATEMENT OF THE CASE

This action was instituted by the plaintiffs, Jerrold M. Metcoff and David Wilson, against the defendants, Irene Lebovics, Cy E. Hammond, John J. McCloy II, Sam Oolie and Michael J. Parrella. All the defendants are officers or directors of a corporation named NCT Group, Inc. (NCT Group). NCT Group is incorporated under the laws of the state of Delaware. The operative complaint is the revised complaint dated December 20, 2006. This complaint asserts two causes of action against the defendants-one for breach of fiduciary duty and the other for violation of the Connecticut Unfair Trade Practices Act (CUTPA), General Statutes § 42-110a et seq. Pending before the court is the defendants' motion to strike. As will be explained, the motion to strike is granted.

The claims at issue emanate from a merger agreement executed by NCT Group, NCT Midcore, Inc., now known as Midcore Software, Inc. (NCT Midcore), and Midcore Software. The plaintiffs were the major stockholders of Midcore Software, and the agreement called for a merger between Midcore Software and NCT Midcore, with NCT Midcore being the surviving corporation. As part of the merger, the plaintiffs were to receive shares of NCT Group stock and certain royalties. Most of the 256 paragraphs of the complaint address how NCT Group and NCT Midcore breached this agreement and, in the process, committed other sundry, wrongful acts. Neither NCT Group nor NCT Midcore is a defendant in this action and, therefore, the allegations about their breach of the agreement are peripheral to the substance of the plaintiffs' complaints against the defendants, except to the extent that they support the plaintiffs' claim that they are creditors of NCT Group.

Count one of the complaint alleges that NCT Group became insolvent and that the defendants, as officers or directors of NCT Group, owed fiduciary duties to the corporation's creditors, such as the plaintiffs. This count further alleges that the defendants committed various acts in violation of these fiduciary duties and contrary to any valid exercise of business judgment. These acts included the defendants' authorizing fraudulent transfers of NCT Group assets, receiving exorbitant compensation, including bonuses and stock options, and engaging in self-dealing (apparently involving NCT Group or its subsidiary dealing with entities controlled by certain of the defendants). The plaintiffs also claim that the defendants breached their fiduciary duties by not causing the delivery to the plaintiffs of the NCT Group shares that the plaintiffs were entitled to receive under the merger agreement. The plaintiffs further allege that the defendants' actions "demonstrated a marked degree of animus, ill will and spite" toward the plaintiffs.

In count two of the complaint, the plaintiffs allege that the defendants' conduct in breach of their fiduciary duties indicates that they were engaged in an "unfair, deceptive, immoral oppressive and/or unscrupulous practice in the conduct of their primary business, trade or commerce" in violation of CUTPA. According to the complaint, each defendant's primary business, trade or commerce includes "performing the functions of an NCT Group director and/or officer."

In their demand for relief, the plaintiffs seek "money damages," as well as "interest pursuant to [General Statutes] § 37-3a." The plaintiffs also seek punitive damages and attorney's fees under CUTPA, General Statutes § 42-110g.

DISCUSSION

A motion to strike tests the legal sufficiency of a pleading. "The purpose of a motion to strike is to contest . . . the legal sufficiency of the allegations of any complaint . . . to state a claim upon which relief can be granted. In ruling on a motion to strike, the court is limited to the facts alleged in the complaint. The court must construe the facts in the complaint most favorably to the plaintiff." The trial court deciding a motion to strike must consider as true the well pleaded facts, but not the legal conclusions, set forth in the complaint. The court should view the facts in a broad fashion, on one hand, to include facts that are necessarily implied by and fairly provable by the allegations but, on the other hand, to avoid enlarging the allegations of the complaint by assuming facts that are clearly not alleged.

I

FIRST COUNT-BREACH OF FIDUCIARY DUTY

A. Direct Claim

In the first count of the complaint, the plaintiffs assert claims against the defendants for breaching the fiduciary duties that the defendants, as officers and directors of NCT Group, allegedly owed to the corporation's creditors generally, and to the plaintiffs, as creditors, particularly. The first claim may be characterized as a derivative claim on behalf of the corporation and the second claim may be characterized as a direct claim by the plaintiffs.

As to their direct claim, the plaintiffs allege that because NCT Group was insolvent and the defendants' actions evidenced hostility directly toward them as creditors, the defendants, as officers and directors of NCT Group, owed the plaintiffs fiduciary duties on which they may base personal claims for monetary compensation against the defendants. In support of this position, the plaintiffs primarily rely on *Production Resources Group, L.L.C. v. NCT Group, Inc.* In support of their motion to strike, the defendants contend that as a matter of law, they do not owe the plaintiffs any such fiduciary duties and, even if they did, the plaintiffs have failed to assert allegations sufficient to bring a direct claim against them under the holding of *Production Resources Group, L.L.C.*

As a general rule, officers and directors of a corporation owe fiduciary duties to the corporation and its shareholders, not to any individual creditor. However, the court in *Production Resources Group, L.L.C. v. NCT Group, Inc.* opined that directors may owe a fiduciary duty to a corporate creditor when the corporation is insolvent, the creditor's claim is liquidated or "imminently" due and the directors' actions against the creditor evince direct animus or hostility.

After the parties' oral argument on the motion to strike, the Delaware Supreme Court issued the decision in *North American Catholic Educational Programming Foundation, Inc. v. Gheewalla*, rejecting the holding and reasoning of *Production Resources Group, L.L.C.*, regarding a director's exposure to direct claims of creditors when a corporation is insolvent or in the "zone of insolvency." The court held that "creditors of a Delaware corporation that is either insolvent or in the zone of insolvency have no right, as a matter of law, to assert direct claims for breach of fiduciary duty against its directors."

In a supplemental memorandum of law filed in response to the Delaware court's decision in *North American Catholic Educational Programming Foundation, Inc.*, the plaintiffs emphasize that this issue is one of first impression in Connecticut, and they urge the court to reject that court's holding and adopt the reasoning of courts in other jurisdictions recognizing direct claims by creditors of insolvent corporations against the corporations' directors. The court rejects this invitation, finding that the reasoning of *North American Catholic Educational Programming Foundation, Inc.*, is persuasive and dispositive:

> "It is well established that the directors owe their fiduciary obligations to the corporation and its shareholders. While shareholders rely on directors acting as fiduciaries to protect their interests, creditors are afforded protection through contractual agreements, fraud and fraudulent conveyance law, implied covenants of good faith and fair dealing, bankruptcy law, general commercial law and other sources of creditor rights. Delaware courts have traditionally been reluctant to expand existing fiduciary duties. Accordingly, the general rule is that directors do not owe creditors duties beyond the relevant contractual terms."

> "Recognizing that directors of an insolvent corporation owe direct fiduciary duties to creditors, would create uncertainty for directors who have a fiduciary duty to exercise their business judgment in the best interest of the insolvent corporation. To recognize a new right for creditors to bring direct fiduciary claims against those directors would create a conflict between those directors' duty to maximize the value of the insolvent corporation for the benefit of all those having an interest in it, and the newly recognized direct fiduciary duty to individual creditors. Directors of insolvent corporations must retain the freedom to engage in vigorous, good faith negotiations with individual creditors for the benefit of the corporation."

Thus, the court holds that as a matter of law, the general rule is that whether a corporation is solvent or insolvent, directors of the corporation do not owe a fiduciary duty to a corporate creditor that would expose them to personal liability to the creditor for an alleged breach of such duty. The officers and directors of a corporation owe their fiduciary duties to the corporation and its shareholders, and corporate creditors are afforded rights and remedies under existing and extensive contract, tort and statutory protections.

B. Derivative Claim

The parties agree that the plaintiffs' derivative claim is controlled by Delaware law. As was just discussed, the Delaware Supreme Court in *North American Catholic Educational Programming Foundation, Inc.*, held that a creditor of an insolvent corporation cannot assert a direct claim against the corporation's directors. The court also stated that such a creditor may assert a derivative claim against the directors for breach of the directors' fiduciary duties owed to the corporation. Although such an action is brought by a creditor of an insolvent corporation, the essential nature of this claim is derivative and is therefore the same as a shareholder derivative action — the action is to remedy harm to the corporation, and any recovery must go to the corporation. Any benefit to the complaining creditor is, therefore, derivative or indirect in the sense that the recovery increases the assets or the economic viability of the insolvent corporation as a whole.

A "cardinal precept" of Delaware corporate law is that a corporation's directors manage the business and affairs of the corporation, and "[b]y its very nature the derivative action impinges on the managerial freedom of directors." Although derivative actions recognize a need for a mechanism to hold directors and officers accountable to the corporation for their own wrongdoing, such actions still may not be pursued if the corporation is willing and able to pursue the suit itself. Consequently, under Delaware law, before the institution of a derivative action, the complainant must give the directors the opportunity to manage the litigation and satisfy various prerequisites to mitigate "the potentially disruptive effects of derivative litigation on the ability of a board of directors to direct the business and affairs of a corporation." Determining whether an action is direct or derivative is important because derivative claims, but not direct claims, are subject to these procedural prerequisites and impinge on the managerial role of the corporation's directors.

The defendants concede that the plaintiffs complain about matters indicating corporate injury. The defendants argue, however, that the plaintiffs have not truly asserted derivative claims because they seek relief to benefit themselves and not NCT Group, namely, damages for the defendants' failure to "cause delivery" of the shares of NCT Group due and owing to the plaintiffs under the merger agreement. In response, the plaintiffs contend that they properly have asserted derivative claims, and they have either met all the requirements for asserting such claims or are not required to meet these requirements. The court agrees with the defendants to the extent that the derivative claims are not pleaded with sufficient particularity to survive a motion to strike.

"The distinction between direct and derivative claims is frustratingly difficult to describe with precision." As a consequence, the distinction between direct and derivative claims is often difficult to discern. This task is made more arduous in this case because rather than separating their direct and derivative claims into separate counts, plaintiffs combine both these causes of action into a hodgepodge of allegations contained in a single count.

Under Delaware law, the test for determining whether a claim is direct or derivative is stated simply as follows: "Who suffered the alleged harm — the corporation or the suing stockholder individually — and who would receive the benefit of the recovery or other remedy"? The parties agree that the complaint's allegations involve claims of self-dealing and bad faith that directly affect NCT Group. What is less clear from the complaint's allegations is how the corporation has been harmed and what precise relief the plaintiffs are seeking to rectify any such harm.

To determine "who would receive the benefit of the recovery or other remedy" as required under the test articulated by *Tooley v. Donaldson, Lufkin & Jenrette*, the complaint must clearly indicate what relief is being sought. Viewing the complaint broadly in favor of the plaintiffs, one could guess or possibly assume what relief the plaintiffs are seeking derivatively, but in the face of the plaintiffs' somewhat convoluted allegations and the Practice Book's fact pleading requirements this is not a matter that the court (or the defendants) should have to guess or make assumptions about. In many instances in which the relief sought is unclear from the language of the complaint, it may be reasonably discerned from the claims being asserted or the gravamen of the complaint. However, the allegations of the plaintiffs' complaint, described nicely, are all over the place, possibly because the plaintiffs have combined their direct and derivative causes of action into one count.

For example, most of the complaint addresses the plaintiffs' claims against NCT Group and NCT Midcore, and describes the various causes of action the plaintiffs have against these corporations, including breach of contract, breach of warranties, negligent and intentional misrepresentation, fraudulent transfers, civil conspiracy and CUTPA claims. As indicated previously, except for supporting the plaintiffs' point that they are creditors of NCT Group, these allegations are not particularly material to the plaintiffs' derivative claim.

The complaint contains two allegations that support the claim that the defendants have engaged in "self-dealing." The first is that the defendants have "preferred themselves in the form of large salaries, reimbursements and payment of other contingencies and benefits" when the corporation was insolvent. The complaint does not indicate whether the plaintiffs seek to repudiate these arrangements and have the payments disgorged or whether the plaintiffs are seeking some other form of damages (for example, a determination of reasonable compensation and a recovery of what was received in excess of this amount).

Second, the complaint alleges that the defendants authorized NCT Group to enter into business arrangements with other companies that are controlled by one or more of the defendants or by a de facto shareholder. The complaint does not allege that these associations were unfair to NCT Group and, more particularly, the complaint neither alleges that any harm or losses were sustained by NCT Group as a result of these associations, nor explains the extent or nature of such harm. As a general rule, corporate transactions in which a director has a financial interest are not per se void or voidable.

The complaint also alleges that contrary to the exercise of valid business judgment, the defendants authorized transfers of stock and promissory notes to insiders for no or inadequate consideration in violation of General Statutes §§ 52-552e or 52-552f. The complaint does not appear to seek any relief under the fraudulent conveyance statute, General Statutes § 52-552h; at least, the plaintiffs do not make any express demand for any such relief, and the court does not address the applicability of that statute to the allegations of this complaint. The appropriate corporate relief to address the alleged transactions might involve either the recovery of the transferred property (which would require naming the transferees as additional defendants) or a recovery of an amount representing the difference between what was paid and what should have been paid as the fair cost for the transferred assets. The latter is what the plaintiffs may be seeking by their general "damages" demand, but the court agrees with the defendants that there is nothing expressly asserted in the body of the complaint indicating that the plaintiffs have any interest in such a recovery.

The defendants appear to make a cogent argument that the plaintiffs only assert a very general, vague claim for derivative damages because the only relief they quite clearly express and actually seek is damages for their direct claims. Regardless of whether the complaint's vagueness may be explained for this reason, the court concludes that to assert a derivative claim in a manner sufficient to distinguish this cause of action from a direct claim, the complaint must clearly describe the relief being sought for the benefit of the corporation in a particularized manner so that this determination is not controlled by surmise, assumption or conjecture.

The defendants' next argument is that the plaintiffs cannot assert derivative claims because, in that these claims emanate from the plaintiffs' failure to acquire NCT Group shares under the merger agreement, the plaintiffs are not "true" creditors and should be treated as shareholders. The defendants reason that "to permit [the] plaintiffs to assert entitlement to an enhanced position by an equitable construct designed to favor true creditors over shareholders would place [the] plaintiffs in a far better position than that in which they would have been but for the alleged breach of the alleged contractual obligation to receive stock." As to the plaintiffs' derivative claim, the defendants' argument is rejected as emphasizing a difference without legal significance.

Even as to an insolvent corporation, directors still owe fiduciary duties to shareholders. Insolvency "simply changes the class of those eligible to press the claim derivatively, by *expanding* it to include creditors." Appreciating the general proposition that stockholders and creditors of an insolvent corporation may have vastly different interests and preferences, the court has not located any authority precluding a plaintiff who may be a stockholder, a creditor or both from filing a derivative action on behalf of the corporation, especially when the claim is based on self-dealing or bad faith conduct by the directors.

The defendants' last argument regarding the plaintiffs' derivative claims is that the plaintiffs have failed to satisfy the procedural prerequisites necessary for the filing of a derivative action under Delaware law. See footnote 5. Specifically, the defendants claim that the plaintiffs were not shareholders during the entire time period during which the transactions at issue took place; that the plaintiffs did not make a pre-suit demand on the NCT Group directors to take action on the matters of the complaint; and the plaintiffs are not adequate representatives to assert the derivative claims. In response, the plaintiffs contend that these pre-suit requirements apply to derivative actions filed by shareholders and not to those filed by creditors such as the plaintiffs. In addition, the plaintiffs maintain that pre-suit demand is excused because they allege personal interest and self-dealing on the part of the defendants.

There are relatively few cases discussing derivative actions instituted by creditors, and there are no Delaware cases delineating the pre-suit requirements for such actions. The Chancery Court's decision in *Production Resources Group, L.L.C. v. NCT Group, Inc.* discusses the pre-suit requirements for such cases, but does not reach a conclusion on the precise issues presented here because these issues were either not raised or fully addressed by the parties in *Production Resources Group, L.L.C.*

The plaintiffs are correct that the textual requirements of Del. Code Ann. tit. 8, § 327 (2001), and rule § 23.1 of the Delaware Chancery Court rules apply to shareholder derivative actions. Contrary to the plaintiffs' position, however, it would be very anomalous for the parameters for the filing of derivative actions to be broader for a creditor when a corporation is insolvent than for a shareholder when the corporation is solvent.

The court agrees with the plaintiffs that because they are asserting derivative claims as creditors, they need not satisfy the rule requiring them to be shareholders when the contested transactions took place. On the other hand, the court agrees with the defendants that the representation and demand requirements are applicable here because they are integral aspects of derivative claims. A well established, judicially imposed rule is that "the plaintiff in a derivative action must be qualified to serve in a fiduciary capacity as a representative of a class, whose interest is dependent upon the representative's adequate and fair prosecution." Similarly, the pre-suit demand requirement facilitates the balance between the protection of corporate interests through derivative actions and the deference given to corporate directors' managerial discretion:

> "The demand requirement serves a salutary purpose. First, by requiring exhaustion of intracorporate remedies, the demand requirement invokes a species of alternative dispute resolution procedure which might avoid litigation altogether. Second, if litigation is beneficial, the corporation can control the proceedings. Third, if demand is excused or wrongfully refused, the stockholder will normally control the proceedings."

The plaintiffs make a strong argument that the complaint's allegations of self-interest and self-dealing by the defendants as directors of NCT Group operate to excuse them from the demand requirement. The defendants do not squarely address whether these allegations of the complaint are sufficient to excuse the demand requirement. The plaintiffs, on the other hand, do not address whether they are adequate representatives to maintain this derivative action. The plaintiffs' reliance on *Production Resources Group, L.L.C. v. NCT Group, Inc.* to argue that the representative requirement is inapplicable to creditor derivative actions is misplaced because, as previously stated, *Production Resources Group, L.L.C.,* does not reach this question. In any event, the court rejects the plaintiffs' position and concludes that the plaintiffs, as creditors of an insolvent corporation, should be adequate class representatives for a derivative action. The case law indicates that the defendants have the burden of proof on this issue.

Despite the numerous and extensive memoranda of law filed by the parties, the court is not satisfied that they have fully and squarely addressed whether the plaintiffs are excused from the pre-suit demand requirement and whether the plaintiffs are adequate representatives to maintain a derivative action. Especially because the court has already ruled that the plaintiffs must revise the complaint to describe more clearly what derivative relief they are seeking, the court will not now resolve these issues regarding the demand and representation requirements. The defendants have leave to reassert these objections in response to any substitute complaint filed by the plaintiffs asserting derivative claims.

****

CONCLUSION

Therefore, for the foregoing reasons, the defendants' motion to strike the revised complaint is granted.

QUESTIONS

1.   What is the difference between direct and derivative claims against the directors of a corporation?

2.   What is the rationale for not allowing creditors to file direct claims against corporate directors, but allowing creditors to file derivative claims against corporate directors? What benefit, if any, might creditors gain by filing derivative claims against corporate directors?

3.   What is the pre-suit demand requirement for filing derivative causes of action? What is the purpose of the pre-suit demand requirement? When may the pre-suit demand requirement be excused?

4.   What is the adequate representation requirement for filing derivative causes of action? What is the purpose of the adequate representation requirement?

5.   How does the relief sought by plaintiffs in suits against corporate directors affect the determination of whether the suit is a direct or derivative claim?

MATTER OF COMVERSE TECH., INC. DERIVATIVE LITIG.,
56 A.3d 49 (N.Y. App. Div. 2008)

Saxe, J.

This appeal involves the concept of demand futility in the context of shareholder derivative litigation. Specifically, the question presented is whether appointment by a board of directors of a special committee to inquire into the challenged conduct by directors and take whatever steps it deemed necessary to rectify the problem, and whether the actions taken by the committee establish as a matter of law that before this litigation began, the board showed itself willing to take the appropriate corrective measures, rendering the litigation unnecessary.

Facts

On March 18, 2006, the Wall Street Journal published an article reporting on an SEC investigation exploring the possibility that grants of stock options to high-level employees at approximately a dozen large corporations were being illegally backdated. (Forelle and Bandler, *The Perfect Payday*, Wall Street Journal, March 18, 2006, at A1). While proper stock option grants set the option price as of the dates the options are granted, backdated option grants give their recipients the right to purchase company stock at the lower price at which the stock had sold on an earlier date. This practice, the Wall Street Journal article explained, can earn millions of extra dollars for the grantee executives, because when grantees sell stock obtained with backdated stock options, they earn not only any increase in the market value of the stock between the time the option was granted and the time the stock is sold, but also the windfall created by the difference between the stock's value on the date the option was actually awarded and its lower value on the date to which the option was backdated.

A variety of violations of law may result from the practice of awarding backdated options. Typically, companies grant options under a shareholder-approved plan filed with the SEC that states that any stock options awarded will carry the stock price on the day the company awards them; under these circumstances, the use of any different date and price could constitute securities fraud. In addition, when options are priced below the stock's fair market value on the day they are awarded, the recipient receives a value that is equivalent to extra pay; yet these backdated options are not acknowledged as an additional cost to the company, which consequently may be overstating its profits.

The Wall Street Journal article described the Journal's own analysis, the results of which strongly suggested that backdating of stock options was a widespread practice. Among the companies whose questionable stock option grants were named in the article was the nominal defendant here, Comverse Technology, Inc. Specifically, the article discussed two stock option grants awarded to Comverse founder and CEO Jacob "Kobi" Alexander that purportedly were issued on dates on which the price of Comverse stock dipped briefly.

As plaintiffs allege in this shareholder derivative action, the investigation by the

Wall Street Journal in the weeks preceding its publication of the article set in motion the events leading to this action. After receiving inquiries from the Wall Street Journal in early March 2006, Comverse held a number of meetings with in-house counsel, and ultimately, on March 10, 2006, Comverse's board of directors formed a special committee to investigate the timing of the company's stock option grants and to take appropriate action to deal with any problems uncovered. The committee was comprised of two directors, one of whom, Ron Hiram, had been a director and compensation committee member since June 2001, which included part of the period in which the granting of backdated options is alleged to have occurred. On March 14, 2006, a press release issued by Comverse announced the formation of the special committee and the possibility that the company might need to revise previous years' financial statements. On March 16, 2006, the committee formally interviewed Alexander, who admitted that, with the assistance of defendant David Kreinberg, at various times Comverse's CFO, vice president of finance and vice president of financial planning, and defendant William F. Sorin, a director and corporate secretary of Comverse, he had backdated option grants. The committee soon thereafter interviewed Kreinberg and Sorin as well.

Complaint

This shareholders' derivative action was commenced on April 11, 2006. At that time, Comverse's board consisted of defendants Kobi Alexander, William F. Sorin, Itzik Danziger, John H. Friedman, Sam Oolie, and Ron Hiram, as well as nonparty Raz Alon. The complaint names as defendants a number of current and former Comverse officers and directors, as well as the company's auditor, and seeks restitution and money damages against each defendant, on behalf of Comverse and its shareholders.

The complaint alleges that, beginning in 1991, Kobi Alexander and David Kreinberg, with the assistance of William F. Sorin, repeatedly awarded themselves backdated stock options, despite the company's approved option plan authorizing the award of options with an exercise price not less than the fair market value of the company's common stock on the date of the option.

Sorin is said to have orchestrated the paperwork by which the approval of the compensation committee was obtained for the backdated option grants; the compensation committee signed the necessary consents forwarded to them by Sorin, despite the use of an "as of" date earlier than the date on which it actually approved the option grants. To conceal the improper backdating, some of the individual defendants caused proxy statements to be disseminated that falsely reported the dates of stock option grants, representing that they were granted at fair market value during the relevant period. In addition, when asked directly about the reports pointing toward backdating, defendants Alexander, Kreinberg and Sorin initially falsely stated that Comverse had simply acted quickly on the dates on which Comverse stock prices dipped, so as to provide for and obtain board approval for stock option grants on those dates.

As to those defendants who were members of the company's compensation committee, John H. Friedman, Ron Hiram, and Sam Oolie, it is alleged that they failed to fulfill their fiduciary obligation to administer the company's stock option plans and instead, as a practical matter, ceded the administration of option plans to Alexander and Kreinberg. It is alleged that the compensation committee knowingly or recklessly approved these backdated stock options engineered by Alexander beginning in 1991.

Finally, the complaint asserted that a demand of the board of directors would have been futile because the backdating of options is so egregious that it could not have been the product of sound business judgment.

Comverse successfully moved to dismiss the complaint on the ground that plaintiffs had not complied with the requirement of Business Corporation Law § 626(c) that the complaint "set forth with particularity the efforts of the plaintiff to secure the initiation of such action by the board or the reasons for not making such effort." This appeal followed.

Discussion

"Derivative claims against corporate directors belong to the corporation itself," since "[t]he remedy sought is for wrong done to the corporation," and the recovery sought is for "the benefit of the corporation" The Court of Appeals has "historically been reluctant to permit shareholder derivative suits, noting that the power of courts to direct the management of a corporation's affairs should be exercised with restraint" In fact, the requirement of Business Corporation Law § 626(c) that the complaint in a shareholders' derivative action set forth with particularity either "the efforts of the plaintiff to secure the initiation of such action by the board or the reasons for not making such effort" is intended to balance the right of a board to manage the corporation's business with the need for shareholders to be able to safeguard the company's interests when its officers or directors fail to discharge their responsibilities.

The controlling case in New York on demand futility establishes that there are three types of circumstances in which shareholders may proceed with derivative claims in the absence of a demonstrated attempt to persuade the board to initiate an action itself. The complaint must allege with particularity that "(1) a majority of the directors are interested in the transaction, or (2) the directors failed to inform themselves to a degree reasonably necessary about the transaction, or (3) the directors failed to exercise their business judgment in approving the transaction."

The initial question is therefore whether plaintiffs' allegations support their assertion that a majority of the board was so interested or so culpable regarding the complained-of conduct that it would have been futile to demand that the board take legal action to make the company whole.

Interest

Under New York law, a director may be interested under either of two scenarios: self-interest in the transaction or loss of independence due to the control of an interested director. The self-interest of Alexander and Sorin is undeniable and undisputed. We agree with plaintiffs that the requisite self-interest is shown also as to director Itzik Danziger by the allegation that he was a recipient of backdated options worth millions of dollars, whether or not he took part in the actual backdating process.

However, the board as it existed at the time the action was commenced was composed of seven individuals, and we are not convinced that the allegations of the complaint establish that any directors other than the three previously mentioned fall into the category of "interested." Plaintiffs claim that directors Oolie, Hiram and Friedman personally benefitted from the backdating scheme, in that they approved false financial statements as members of the audit committee and approved the backdated options as members of the compensation committee, and then sold some of their own shares of Comverse stock at prices that were artificially inflated due to the backdating and false financial statements. However, the alleged benefit obtained from selling Comverse stock does not appear to differ from a benefit that may have accrued to Comverse shareholders generally. "Directors are self-interested in a challenged transaction where they will receive a direct financial benefit from the transaction which is different from the benefit to shareholders generally."

Failure to Stay Informed

We agree with plaintiffs that the allegations are sufficient to satisfy the second ground for demand futility described. "Demand is excused because of futility when a complaint alleges with particularity that the board of directors did not fully inform themselves about the challenged transaction to the extent reasonably appropriate under the circumstances." The complaint alleges with particularity that the board and its compensation committee failed to exercise reasonably appropriate oversight of the stock option granting process, not even informing themselves to a reasonable degree about the dates assigned to company stock option grants, and approving backdated option grants without reviewing or taking any note of the date on which they were ostensibly awarded or to whom the options were given. Specifically, it is asserted that "unanimous written consents" for grants of stock options were sometimes presented to the compensation committee for signature more than a month after the grant date, in circumstances where the stock price had risen dramatically in the intervening period, and yet were approved unquestioningly. The compensation committee members often approved option grants orally, in direct violation of the company's bylaws. In addition, the compensation committee had a list of individuals who received option grants in 2001 that contained more than two dozen names of individuals who were not Comverse employees but ostensibly received grants totaling 250,000 options; it is claimed that these options were placed by Alexander in a "slush fund" for later use. Yet not even a cursory check or inquiry was made by the compensation committee; nor was that list even compared against the list of Comverse employees. Even a minimal review would have prompted members of the board and the compensation committee to perform some sort of additional inquiry into the corporation's use of option grants. The allegations therefore establish that there were grounds for inquiry by these directors and officers, and that no inquiry was made, rendering demand futile under the second test.

While the magnitude of the illegal transactions here is not nearly that of the

$900 million scheme considered in *Miller v. Schreyer*, we nevertheless consider applicable that decision's ruling that a demand is properly considered futile when "[i]n view of the illegal purpose of the transactions, their magnitude and duration, their timing, and the identity of their beneficiary, the matter should have come to the attention of senior management even on a rudimentary audit."

Failure to Exercise Business Judgment

The third test of holds that demand on the Board is excused because of futility when "the challenged transaction was so egregious on its face that it could not have been the product of sound business judgment of the directors" The business judgment rule "bars judicial inquiry into actions of corporate directors taken in good faith and in the exercise of honest judgment in the lawful and legitimate furtherance of corporate purposes," not actions taken in furtherance of illegitimate purposes.

Although the courts of this state have not yet addressed this issue with regard to backdated stock options, it is instructive that Delaware courts have expressly held that backdating stock options is so egregious that it could not have been the product of the sound business judgment of the directors.

We agree with these Delaware courts: the approval of a decade's worth of backdated stock options simply does not qualify as a legitimate exercise of business judgment. As the motion court observed, passively rubber-stamping the acts of the active corporate managers does not exempt directors from culpability, and the business judgment rule does not protect them.

Ramification of Appointment of Special Committee

Despite its conclusion that plaintiffs sufficiently pleaded with particularity facts establishing at least two prongs of the demand futility test, the motion court concluded that demand futility was not established, because by the time the action was commenced, the corporation had appointed a special committee to conduct its own investigation into the backdating of options, which indicated the board's willingness to take the actions necessary to protect the interests of the corporation.

We disagree with the motion court's reasoning. First, the mere creation of a special committee does not in itself necessarily establish the board's willingness to take all the necessary and appropriate steps to obtain the relief available. Indeed, in a case where a corporation did not even seek dismissal but merely sought a stay of shareholder derivative litigation pending the investigation by its appointed special litigation committee, this Court specifically observed that the mere creation of the committee did not alone justify a stay of the shareholder derivative action.

Here, director Ron Hiram, one of the two appointed members of the special committee, was a director and member of the compensation committee for part of the period at issue, and he allegedly failed to take any steps reasonably necessary to oversee the awarding of options. His appointment as one of the two members of the special committee arguably creates a conflict at the outset, calling into question the committee's ability to fully investigate the conduct of all potentially liable parties.

In any event, in arguing that the appointment of the special committee definitively shows that a demand to the Board would not have been futile, Comverse relies upon case law from other jurisdictions in which approaches to the demand futility issue differ greatly from that adopted in *Marx v. Akers*. In this jurisdiction, it is *Marx v. Akers* that provides the framework for determining whether demand futility has been established.

In addition, the actual steps taken by the special committee fail to establish Comverse's entitlement to dismissal of this action. While it is true that the special committee was promptly appointed once the board was made aware of the Wall Street Journal's planned exposure of wrongdoing within Comverse, and the committee promptly took certain steps to obtain admissions from the perpetrators of the scheme and to remove them from the board, the complaint's allegations call into question the special committee's willingness to take appropriate actions to protect the company and obtain recompense. For example, although Comverse had obtained the resignations of Alexander, Kreinberg and Sorin by May 1, 2006, it continued to retain these individuals as advisors. It was only when the SEC filed civil charges against the three in August 2006, and the United States Attorney for the Eastern District of New York instituted a criminal prosecution against these men, accusing them of conspiracy to violate the federal securities laws' anti-fraud, wire fraud and mail fraud provisions and demanding restitution in the amount of $51 million, that Comverse severed all remaining ties to them and terminated all agreements with them. Moreover, when director Itzik Danziger, who had allegedly received backdated stock options worth millions of dollars, resigned from the board in September 2006, he was allowed to keep his unexercised backdated options.

Plaintiffs, on behalf of the corporation, contend that relief should be sought not only against the three directors who carried out the scheme, but also against others whose acts or omissions constituted a breach of their fiduciary obligations to the corporation and caused it financial injury. Yet the three directors who carried out the scheme have been the sole focus of the special committee's actions. Defendants argue that since the special committee has shown a willingness to take action against those placed highest in the corporate order, there can be no question that it would fairly consider the possibility of suing less senior individuals, former directors and officers, and the company's outside auditors. However, nothing in the record supports this bare assertion. There is no indication that the special committee showed a willingness to go beyond its initial acts of questioning and ultimately removing the three who planned and carried out the scheme-acts that in any event the board was essentially forced to take in the wake of the initial reporting and the subsequent SEC investigation and criminal prosecutions against those individuals.

Defendants assert that it is not for the shareholders to decide which directors to sue, inasmuch as "the decision whether and to what extent to explore and prosecute [claims against corporate directors] lies within the judgment and control of the corporation's board of directors." However, once the plaintiffs have made a showing that the directors not only failed to inform themselves to a degree reasonably necessary about the challenged conduct, but indeed failed to exercise their business judgment when they rubber-stamped the transactions, the board and its chosen committee members will not be fully shielded by the tenets of the business judgment rule (*id.*). "[T]he rule shields the deliberation and conclusions of the chosen representatives of the board only if they possess a disinterested independence and do not stand in a dual relation which prevents an unprejudicial exercise of judgment." Since the allegations of the complaint raise legitimate questions as to the committee's disinterested independence, defendants' reliance on the directors' discretion in choosing the direction of litigation does not create grounds for dismissal of the complaint here.

In conclusion, the picture presented in the complaint is that of a special committee taking a tepid rather than a vigorous approach to the misconduct and the resultant harm. Under such circumstances, the board should not be provided with any special protection. Therefore, because we cannot conclude that the appointment of the special committee, and the steps it has so far undertaken, establish as a matter of law the board's willingness to take appropriate action to protect the interests of the corporation, we hold that the grant of Comverse's motion to dismiss this shareholder derivative action pursuant to CPLR 3211 was erroneous.

Accordingly, the judgment of the Supreme Court, New York County (Richard B. Lowe III, J.), entered October 28, 2007, dismissing this shareholders' derivative action, should be reversed, on the law, without costs, and the complaint reinstated. The appeal from the order of the same court and Justice, entered August 14, 2007, which granted the motion to dismiss the complaint should be dismissed, without costs, as subsumed within the appeal from the judgment.

Judgment, Supreme Court, New York County (Richard B. Lowe III, J.), entered October 28, 2007, reversed, on the law, without costs, and the complaint reinstated. Appeal from order, same court and Justice, entered August 14, 2007, dismissed, without costs, as subsumed within the appeal from the judgment.

All concur.

QUESTIONS

1. How does the requirement of a demand upon directors prior to filing a derivative action balance the rights of boards to manage corporate business and the rights of shareholders to safeguard corporate interests against directors' failure to discharge their responsibilities?

2. Must demand futility be established with respect to each individual director?

3. On what basis did the court find that a demand was excused under the facts of this case?

4. How did the business judgment rule factor into the court's decision?

5. If you were advising Comverse on the appointment of a special committee to investigate the backdated stock options, what would you advise them?

CASE NOTES

1.   Feldman is a former stockholder, officer and board member of Telx. When Feldman left Telx in 2002, he owned 1,499,574 shares of Telx common stock. In 2003, the Telx board approved an Employee Stock Option Plan (ESOP) which provided for the issuance of stock options to the Telx board members and senior managers. Telx effected a ten-for-one reverse stock split in August 2004 and Feldman then sold 148,000 of his Telx shares to one of the Telx directors for $3.36 per share. Feldman retained 1000 shares of Telx stock after this sale. In 2005, Feldman filed a derivative action against the Telx board members arguing that the ESOP stock options were invalid and that they diluted his equity ownership percentage. In September 2006, while this litigation was proceeding, Telx closed a merger with GI Partners Fund (GI Partners) in which GI Partners acquired all of Telx outstanding stock for $15 per share. The Telx board members then moved to have Feldman's derivative action dismissed because Feldman was no longer shareholder in Telx. After the Telx board members filed the motion to dismiss, Feldman amended his complaint to be a direct shareholder action against the board members, arguing the board members had breached their fiduciary duty to Feldman by not reconsidering the validity of the ESOP stock options. The trial court dismissed Feldman's amended complaint, finding that it was solely a derivative claim. Feldman appealed. What result? *See* Feldman v. Cutaia, 951 A.2d 727 (Del. 2008)

2.   *See also* Hribar v. Marsh & McLennan Companies, Inc., 73 A.D.3d 859 (N.Y. App. Div. 2010) (Under Delaware law, a court is required to look to the nature of the wrong and to whom the relief should go when distinguishing between direct and derivative actions; shareholder's claimed direct injury must be independent from any injury to the corporation; in a direct cause of action, shareholder must show that a duty owed to the shareholder was breached and that shareholder can prevail without showing an injury to the corporation); Karten v. Woltin, 23 So.3d 839 (Fla. Dist. Ct. App. 2009) (Shareholders may bring a direct suit only if they sustained individual harm; shareholder's allegations did not constitute individual harm and, thus, were required to be asserted in a shareholder derivative action); Bader v. Anderson, 179 Cal. App.4th 775 (Cal. Ct. App. 2009) (A shareholder's derivative suit is essentially two causes of action in equity; one by the shareholder against the corporation's directors to require them to sue the wrongdoers, and the other by the corporation against the wrongdoers; a shareholder must exhaust all means to induce the corporation's directors to take action before bringing a shareholder derivative action; to evaluate a claim of demand futility, the court must determine on a director-by-director basis whether or not each can fairly evaluate the challenged transaction); Angel Investors, LLC v. Garrity, 216 P.3d 944 (Utah 2009) (Utah Rule of Civil Procedure on shareholder derivative suits governs derivative actions brought on behalf of limited liability companies; for purposes of standing in a shareholder derivative suit, a sole dissenting shareholder in a closely held corporation can qualify as a class of one if the shareholder seeks to enforce a right of the corporation and there does not appear to be another similarly situated shareholder; shareholder's direct action against limited liability company for dissolution and damages did not create a conflict of interest that would prevent shareholder from adequately representing limited liability company in derivative action against majority shareholders for malfeasance); Orrock v. Appleton, 213 P.3d 398 (Idaho

2009) (In determining demand futility in shareholder derivative action, a court must decide whether plaintiff's allegations create a reasonable doubt that the directors are disinterested and independent or that the challenged transaction is not a valid exercise of business judgment); Long v. Biomet, Inc., 901 N.E.2d 37 (Ind. Ct. App. 2009) (When a corporation is merged out of existence, the shareholders' interests in the merged corporation come to an end and any derivative cause of action passes to the surviving corporation along with all the other assets of the merged corporation; former shareholders of merged company lacked standing to maintain derivative action against former officers and directors of merged company; if merger is solely for purpose of shielding wrongdoers from liability, merger can be attacked by former shareholder as devoid of a legitimate corporate purpose); Lemenestrel v. Warden, 964 A.2d 902 (Pa. Super. Ct. 2009) (Trial court did not abuse its discretion by treating minority shareholders' suit as a derivative rather than a direct claim because minority shareholders did not produce any evidence showing that, by treating their claims as direct claims, corporation would not be exposed to multiple actions, corporation's creditors would not be prejudiced and distribution of recovery would not be unfair); Kingston v. Breslin, 56 A.D.3d 430 (N.Y. App. Div. 2008) (In a derivative action challenging the sale of a corporation, shareholder is not permitted to claim equitable relief for alleged fraudulent inducement in signing consent agreement for sale); McPadden v. Sidhu, 964 A.2d 1262 (Del. Ch. 2008) (Shareholder excused from making demand on board of directors prior to bringing a derivative action when challenged sale of corporation subsidiary was to corporation's vice president, and board assigned task of soliciting bids and offers for subsidiary to vice president, knowing vice president was interested in buying subsidiary); Levy v. Reiner, 659 S.E.2d 848 (Ga. Ct. App. 2008) (The purposes of derivative actions are to prevent multiple shareholder suits, to protect corporate creditors by assuring recovery goes to corporation, and to protect the interests of all shareholders by assuring recovery does not go to one or a few shareholders; minority shareholders in a close corporation cannot bring direct action against officers or directors for breach of fiduciary duty based on excessive salaries).

Additional Information

1. William Meade Fletcher, 12b Fletcher Cyc. Corp. §§ 5908, 5911, 5914, 5924, 5933 (2010).

2. Laura H. Dietz Et al., 19 Am. Jur. 2d Corporations §§ 1946, 1948, 1982, 2045 (2010).

3. Edward Brodsky, M. Patricia Adamski, Law of Corp. Offs. & Dirs.: Rts., Duties & Liabs. §§ 9:4, 10:15 (2009).

4. John F. Olson Et al., Dir. & Off. Liab. §§ 2:13.50, 2:15 (2009).

5. Seth Aronson et al., *Shareholder Derivative Actions: From Cradle to Grave*, 1762 PLI/Corp 163 (2009).

6. Allan B. Cooper, Kim R. Greenhalgh, Melanie S. Williams, *Too Close for Comfort: Application of Shareholder" Derivative Actions to Disputes Involving Closely Held Corporations*, 9 U.C. Davis Bus. L.J. 171 (2009).

7. Christy L. Abbott, *The Shareholder Derivative Suit as a Response to Stock Option Backdating*, 53 St. Louis U. L.J. 593 (2009).

8. Ann M. Scarlett, *A Better Approach for Balancing Authority and Accountability in Shareholder Derivative Litigation*, 57 Kan. L. Rev. 39 (2008).

9. Ann M. Scarlett, *Confusion and Unpredictability in Shareholder Derivative Litigation: The Delaware Courts' Response to Recent Corporate Scandals*, 60 Fla. L. Rev. 589 (2008).

10. Elizabeth Dunshee, *Multiple Representation in Shareholder Derivative Suits: Do the Current Rules Do Enough to Promote Informed Consent*, 9 Del. L. Rev. 213 (2007).

10.2.5   Usurpation of Corporate Opportunities

Directors and officers of a corporation are permitted to enter into transactions with the corporation, and to pursue opportunities in the same line of business as the corporation, so long as the directors and officers do not treat the corporation unfairly, and their dealings are transparent and known to the corporation. The *Texlon* case considers a claim of usurpation of corporate opportunity by a person who first served as the CEO of the corporation and later served as a highly-paid consultant to the corporation. In deciding the case, the court distinguishes between a misappropriation of corporate assets claim and a usurpation of corporate opportunity claim, and, in passing, sharply criticizes the plaintiff's attorney for failing to make this distinction in the complaint.

TELXON CORP. v. MEYERSON,
802 A.2d 257 (Del. 2002)

Walsh, Justice:

In this appeal, we consider the propriety of the Court of Chancery's decision to grant summary judgment in a derivative action subsequently pursued by a successor corporate entity against its former directors. The complaint, originally asserted as a stockholders' derivative action, challenged the level of compensation that Directors had been receiving as well as Directors' decision for the corporation to acquire a minority interest, and later 100%, of a company owned by the corporation's then-Board Chairman. Following cross-motions for summary judgment, the Court of Chancery granted judgment to the Directors on the excessive compensation claims and the duty of loyalty claims, but denied summary judgment as to two duty of care claims in which there were disputes of fact. Because the corporation's charter contains an exculpation provision, the plaintiff chose to forego prosecution of the duty of care claims in order to convert the Court of Chancery's dismissal order into an appealable final judgment.

Upon a full review of an enlarged record, we conclude that the unsettled nature of that record does not permit resolution through summary judgment. Accordingly, we reverse the decision of the Court of Chancery granting summary judgment and remand this case for further proceedings to resolve factual differences apparent in the record.

I

Telxon is a Delaware corporation that develops and markets portable hand-held computers for retailers and wholesalers in various industries. Between 1991 and 1993 (the time period relevant to this action), the Telxon board of directors consisted of Raymond Meyo, Dan Wipff, Robert Meyerson, Raj Reddy, Norton Rose and Robert Goodman. Meyerson was also the CEO of Telxon from 1978 to 1985. During the late 1980s and early 1990s, Meyerson continued to serve as the Chairman of the Board, and provided part-time consulting services to Telxon. The parties continue to dispute whether Meyerson was an executive at this time, or served as a non-executive Chairman.

In 1985, Meyo succeeded Meyerson as CEO and continued as Telxon's CEO until he resigned in October, 1992. Director Wipff was Telxon's Chief Financial Officer from December 1991 through January 1995. Beginning in October 1992, Wipff also served as its President and Chief Operating Officer. Director Goodman was the senior partner of Goodman Weiss Miller LLP, a Cleveland, Ohio law firm that provided legal services to Telxon and, in the past, had also provided services both to Meyerson personally and to another company that Meyerson owned. Director Reddy was the Dean of the School of Computer Science at Carnegie Mellon University and a well recognized leader in the field of computer science. Director Rose was the President and Principal/Owner of Norton W. Rose & Co., a Cleveland, Ohio consulting firm.

Telxon began experiencing operational problems in 1989, and the board decided that Meyerson should be engaged to assist Meyo in managing the corporation. To that end, Telxon entered into a consulting agreement with Meyerson's wholly-owned company, Accipiter Corporation ("Accipiter"). Under the 1989 consulting agreement, Accipiter (through Meyerson) agreed to perform technical and marketing services necessary for the planning and development of new products. The agreement further provided that Accipiter's work product, created pursuant to the contract, would become the property of Telxon, and Accipiter could not "render similar consulting services to any direct competitors of Telxon in the PTC market." On March 6, 1992, Telxon entered into a new three-year consulting agreement with Accipiter, under which Accipiter agreed to provide management consulting, corporate and financial analysis, and marketing development services, as requested by Telxon. Specifically, Accipiter would provide Telxon with "140 eight hour days per year of consulting services, the majority to be provided by Meyerson." In return, Accipiter would receive $840,000 annually, plus $240,000 for general administrative and overhead costs, plus reimbursement for its travel and other out-of-pocket expenses.

In August of 1991, Meyerson began to explore the possibility of developing a product known as "pen based computers" ("PBCs"). The parties continue to dispute whether Meyerson offered this opportunity to the Telxon board. The Court of Chancery determined that Meyerson did offer PBC technology to the Telxon board, and the board decided that Telxon should not develop its own PBC product directly, because of the expense involved, but should allow Meyerson to develop it while retaining a stake in Meyerson's work. At oral argument before this Court, Directors asserted that there are board minutes reflecting the consideration, and rejection, by the board of a proposal by Meyerson for Telxon to develop PBCs. Because the record developed in the Court of Chancery did not include such minutes, and in view of Telxon's strenuous argument that the minutes reflect no such consideration by the board, Directors were required to supplement the record on appeal to sustain their contentions. Directors have been unable to produce any such documentation, but continue to allege that then-CEO Meyo considered and rejected the opportunity for Telxon to develop PBCs.

Despite the absence of supporting minutes, it is undisputed that in August or September of 1991, Meyerson (who at that point was consulting for Telxon part-time) chose to pursue development of PBC technology on his own and formed Teletransaction for that purpose. At some point (the timing of which is disputed), the Telxon board decided that it should acquire some interest in Teletransaction. The Court of Chancery found that, at a February 12, 1992 board meeting, the board approved a plan for Telxon to invest in Teletransaction in incremental steps. First, Telxon would acquire a 15% interest in Teletransaction. Second, upon the successful completion of a PBC prototype, Telxon would acquire an additional 30% interest for $3 million, increasing its ownership interest to 45%. Third, after Teletransaction had PBC products that were ready for sale, Telxon would purchase an additional 35% stock interest for $3.5 million, bringing its total ownership interest in Teletransaction to 80%. Although Telxon agrees that the board did seek to acquire Teletransaction, it disputes the reasoning and timing attributed to the board by the Court of Chancery. The parties agree, however, that Meyerson abstained from any discussions of the Teletransaction acquisition.

In March 1992, Telxon began its acquisition of Teletransaction by purchasing 15% of Teletransaction's stock for $1.7 million, the bulk of which was distributed directly to Meyerson and members of his family. Again, it is unclear whether this transaction was part of a larger scheme to acquire Teletransaction incrementally. Six months later, however, on October 14, 1992, Meyo suddenly resigned as CEO. The Court of Chancery found that the Telxon board then concluded that the emergency caused by Meyo's resignation made it advisable for Telxon to acquire 100% of Teletransaction, rather than 80% in three stages, so that Meyerson would agree to resume his post as CEO of Telxon. Accordingly, on October 20, 1992, the board authorized Telxon to acquire an additional 30% of Teletransaction for $3 million "as a down payment and a part of the process of negotiation for the acquisition of all, or substantially all of the stock of [Teletransaction], and as part of the inducement to Mr. Meyerson to accept the role as full-time Chief Executive Officer of Telxon . . . ."

In November 1992, during negotiations between Meyerson and Telxon over the terms of Meyerson's return to Telxon, Meyerson demanded an additional $5 million above the initially agreed price for Telxon's purchase of 80% of Teletransaction. Meyerson told the board that the additional $5 million would compensate him for (i) his sale of the 20% residual equity in Teletransaction he had originally intended to retain, and (ii) his commitment to become full-time CEO of Telxon, rather than a part-time consultant. After discussing Meyerson's proposal and receiving a fairness opinion from an independent financial advisor, Unterberg Harris, the board, without Meyerson present, approved that proposal subject to certain conditions. The total consideration for the 100% purchase of Teletransaction, as consummated in 1993, would be $17.3 million.

This action followed soon thereafter. The complaint challenged the acquisition of Teletransaction both at the point that the initial 15% interest was acquired and when the purchase was consummated. Telxon argues that since it already owned all rights to the PBC developed by Meyerson under the consulting agreement, the decision to later purchase Teletransaction, whose only asset was the PBC technology, was a breach of the Directors' fiduciary duties and, as to Meyerson, a misappropriation of a corporate asset and usurpation of a corporate opportunity.

The complaint also challenged the compensation paid to Directors during this time frame. Directors Rose, Reddy, and Goodman, as non-executive directors, received an annual retainer of $20,000 and a fee of $2,500 for each board meeting and committee meeting attended in person and $1,250 for each meeting attended by telephone. During fiscal year 1993, the board met twenty-four times and committees served on by Directors Rose, Reddy and Goodman met fourteen times. The compensation for each of these three directors was therefore approximately $90,000. In addition, they were each retained as a consultant and paid $30,000, $25,000, and $10,000, respectively. Meyerson's compensation under the consulting agreements with Accipiter was also challenged as excessive.

The Court of Chancery granted summary judgment in favor of Directors on the compensation claims and the duty of loyalty claims. This appeal followed.

II

Initially, Telxon contends that it was entitled to have summary judgment granted in its favor. There is no "right" to a summary judgment. A trial court's denial of summary judgment is entitled to a high level of deference and is, therefore, rarely disturbed. Additionally, we have determined that the existence of factual disputes makes this case an inappropriate one for summary judgment in favor of either party.

III

Telxon alternatively argues that the Court of Chancery erred when it found, as a matter of law, that Meyerson was free to develop PBC technology on his own. It is unclear whether Telxon is urging a misappropriation theory or a corporate opportunity theory, or both. Directors argue that Telxon raised neither theory below and are therefore barred from raising them on appeal. In its complaint, however, Telxon did make a claim that Meyerson "misappropriated a corporate asset," and that issue was briefed in the trial court. Accordingly, although it was not addressed by the trial court in its decision, the issue was fairly presented to that court and thus properly a subject of appeal.

The corporate opportunity theory, too, was implicitly raised below, in the argument that Meyerson breached his duty of loyalty by usurping an opportunity for himself that rightfully belonged to Telxon. As we have previously recognized, this Court may rule on an issue fairly presented to the trial court, even if it was not addressed by that court below. Furthermore, on this record we need not necessarily reach the merits of either the misappropriation or the corporate opportunity claim, if we are satisfied that facts bearing on the claims remain in dispute and should not have been the subject of a summary judgment.

We agree with Telxon, however, that the Court of Chancery erred when it found that Meyerson was free to develop PBC technology on his own because "the Board made a business decision that Telxon should not develop directly its own PBC product." The question of whether Meyerson ever presented the opportunity to develop PBCs to the Telxon board remains a hotly disputed one. At oral argument before this Court, we attempted to have the parties clarify their disparate views reflected in their briefs. Despite their claims of board participation, Directors could not produce board minutes reflecting that Meyerson had presented the PBC opportunity to the board. Following supplemental briefing on the effect of this omission, and an expanded record, Directors continue to argue that Meyo, as the CEO, decided that Telxon should not pursue development of PBCs directly and that the board deferred to Meyo's judgment on the issue.

While presentation of a purported corporate opportunity to a board of directors, and the board's refusal thereof, creates a safe harbor for an interested director, that safe harbor does not extend to an opportunity presented only to the corporation's CEO. Rejection of a corporate opportunity by the CEO is not a valid substitute for consideration by the full board of directors. This proposition is aptly illustrated by the record before us. We do not know the basis of Meyo's decision, if there was such a decision, not to develop PBCs. There is no record reflecting what information Meyo may have relied on to make his decision, or who supplied that information. If Meyerson was Meyo's source of information, his decision cannot be considered an informed one.

The expansion of the record to include previously redacted board minutes also revealed that the board considered purchasing Teletransaction from Meyerson as early as September of 1991, just one month after Meyerson created Teletransaction to begin development of PBCs, leaving little time for the Telxon board to have rejected the opportunity to develop PBCs directly. This evidence sheds doubt on any factual conclusion that Meyerson presented the opportunity to the Telxon board, which it refused. It surely precludes the grant of summary judgment premised on the establishment of that fact. Resolution of whether Meyerson offered Telxon the opportunity to develop PBCs may well depend upon the testimony of various witnesses. Resolving conflicting testimony is the province of a fact finder at a trial, not a judge on summary judgment. Furthermore, the determination of "[w]hether or not the director has appropriated for himself something that in fairness should belong to his corporation is a factual question to be decided by reasonable inference from objective facts."

IV

Telxon also contends that there are disputed issues of material fact as to whether Directors were independent, acted independently, and whether Meyerson deceived the board. Directors argue that the trial court properly found that a majority of the Directors were independent, thereby ratifying the interested purchase of Teletransaction from Meyerson. The Court of Chancery found that four out of five of the Directors were independent from Meyerson, but determined that it was unnecessary to pass on the independence of Director Goodman. Telxon also argues that the Court of Chancery analyzed this claim under a business judgment standard of review when it warranted an entire fairness analysis because Meyerson was concededly interested in the transaction.

Directors must not only be independent, but must act independently. As this Court has previously stated in defining director independence: "[i]t is the care, attention and sense of individual responsibility to the performance of one's duties . . . that generally touches on independence." Where only one director has an interest in a transaction, however, a plaintiff seeking to rebut the presumption of the business judgment rule under the duty of loyalty must show that "the interested director controls or dominates the board as a whole."

A party alleging domination and control of a company's board of directors bears the burden of proving such control by showing a lack of independence on the part of a majority of the directors. Theoretically, a director can be "controlled" by another, for purposes of determining whether the director lacked the independence necessary to consider the challenged transaction objectively. A controlled director is one who is dominated by another party, whether through close personal or familial relationship or through force of will. A director may also be deemed "controlled" if he or she is beholden to the allegedly controlling entity, as when the entity has the direct or indirect unilateral power to decide whether the director continues to receive a benefit upon which the director is so dependent or is of such subjective material importance that its threatened loss might create a reason to question whether the director is able to consider the corporate merits of the challenged transaction objectively.

It is undisputed that Meyerson, an obviously interested party, abstained from voting on the Teletransaction matter. Nonetheless, Telxon argues a majority of the other Directors were beholden to Meyerson, as Telxon's executive Chairman of the Board and "most senior executive," because he was in a position to affect their livelihood. Meyerson did play an integral role in Telxon's management for many years, both during and after his stint as CEO, and it is clear that the other Directors respected his business acumen and often relied upon his counsel. Additionally, Director Goodman's law firm derived a substantial portion of its revenue from Meyerson and his businesses. Given the state of the record, however, we cannot say whether or not the other Directors acted independently or were beholden to Meyerson such that they deferred to his will in the Teletransaction matter.

As previously noted, we allowed the record to be expanded to include previously omitted board minutes showing that Meyerson headed the slate of new corporate officers as Chairman of the Board. Telxon argues that these minutes refute the conclusion reached by the Court of Chancery that Meyerson was merely a non-executive Chairman with no control over the other officers. It is unclear what impact, if any, this revelation would have had on the trial court's analysis, but we believe that it represents a disputed fact that should be resolved only after a trial at which all the facts are presented and the credibility of all the witnesses tested. Only after a full picture of Meyerson's relationship with the other Directors is developed can their independence be ascertained.

V

Finally, Telxon challenges the grant of summary judgment in favor of Directors on the compensation claims. The Court of Chancery granted Directors' motion for summary judgment from the bench, stating only:

> In determining that there's no triable issue of fact and that this claim-that summary judgment should be granted in defendants' favor on this claim, I am not relying on the affidavit of defendants' expert. I'm relying solely upon the other facts and the absence of any facts that would indicate-that is, the absence of any other evidence from the plaintiff's side that would indicate that the level of compensation was so high that the claim should be tried. I cannot see what a trial would accomplish in these circumstances.

Like any other interested transaction, directoral self-compensation decisions lie outside the business judgment rule's presumptive protection, so that, where properly challenged, the receipt of self-determined benefits is subject to an affirmative showing that the compensation arrangements are fair to the corporation. As former Chancellor Allen noted in an earlier stage of this case, director compensation, fixed by the board, is contemplated by Section 141(h) of the Delaware General Corporation Law. The former Chancellor further explained that there is "no single template for how corporations should be governed and no single compensation scheme for corporate directors; amount alone is not the most salient aspect of director compensation, but certainly $100,000 a year or more would not be inappropriate where board service was demanding; and where the number of other boards a director could serve on was carefully limited." The Chancellor refused, however, to dismiss Telxon's breach of loyalty claim with regard to the Directors' compensation. Although "these amounts seem quite within a range that could be paid in good faith by a company seeking to attract competent, committed directors," the Chancellor felt that Directors would likely be required to prove the reasonableness of this compensation.

Here, the trial court seems to have imposed the burden on Telxon to produce evidence that the Directors' compensation was unreasonable. Although the trial court was unable to see "what a trial would accomplish" here, it would certainly resolve the parties' disputed evidence regarding the Directors' contribution to the corporation, which obviously bears on the question of whether or not their compensation was reasonable. Furthermore, the trial court did not consider the interplay between the Directors' compensation and the possible breach of their fiduciary duties. This claim, too, was decided prematurely.

Accordingly, we reverse the judgment of the Court of Chancery and remand for further proceedings consistent with this Opinion.

QUESTIONS

1.   In what way could Meyerson be found to have "misappropriated a corporate (Telxon) asset"?

2.   In what way could Meyerson be found to have usurped a Telxon corporate opportunity?

3.   What is the difference between a claimed misappropriation of a corporate asset and a claimed usurpation of a corporate opportunity?

4.   Under what circumstances can director(s) be "controlled" by another person? Why may the Telxon directors be under the control of Meyerson?

5.   What is the standard for determining the reasonableness of directoral self-compensation? What party bears the burden of proof on whether this standard has been met?

CASE NOTES

1.   Taser develops and manufactures stun guns and other electronic control accessories including a personal video and audio recording device called the Taser Cam. Ward was employed by Taser from January 2004 — July 2007 as vice president of marketing. Ward was an at-will employee, and did not sign an employment, non-compete or non-disclosure agreement. During Ward's employment, he had access to Taser's proprietary information and trade secrets; he also participated with other executives and vice-presidents in evaluating new product ideas and concepts. In December 2006, Ward began considering whether he could develop, on his own, an eyeglass-mounted camera. Ward sought legal advice on his obligations to Taser and retained patent counsel to perform a patent search on his idea. From April 2007 until his retirement from Taser, Ward continued to pursue a patent on his eyeglass-mounted camera, communicated extensively with a product development company about designing and manufacturing his eyeglass-mounted camera, and completed substantial work on a business plan to develop and market the eyeglass-mounted camera. Ward never informed Taser about any of these activities. Ward formed a new company, Vievu, in August 2007 which began marketing the eyeglass-mounted camera. Ten months after Ward's resignation, Taser introduced a new audio-video product. Taser sued Ward in October 2007 claiming misappropriation of trade secrets, breach of duty of loyalty, tortuous interference with contract and other wrongs. The trial court granted Taser's motion of summary judgment and Ward appealed. What result? *See* Taser Int'l., Inc. v. Ward, 231 P.3d 921 (Ariz. Ct. App. 1 2010).

2.   *See also* Marzec v. NYE, 690 S.E.2d 537 (N.C. Ct. App. 2010) ("Continuing wrong doctrine" provides that statute of limitations does not start running until unlawful activity ceases; dismissal based on running of statute of limitations was not correct in claim by vice president against president alleging president usurped corporate opportunity by working for a competitor when no indication in the complaint as to when vice president knew, or should have known, that president was working for competitor); Owen v. Hamilton, 44 A.D.3d 452 (N.Y. App. Div. 2007) (Fact that corporation was financially unable to purchase competing corporation,

and that competing corporation would not have approved sale to corporation, did not preclude finding that purchase of competing corporation by two of corporation's directors usurped a corporate opportunity; decision by corporation's board to consent to purchase of competing corporation by two individual directors was within board's scope of authority and made in good faith); Venturetek, L.P. v. Rand Publishing Co., Inc., 39 A.D.3d 317 (N.Y. App. Div. 2007) (Under Delaware law, defendants did not usurp corporation's opportunities in buying properties when corporation was financially unable to buy properties); Bender v. Schwartz, 917 A.2d 142 (Md. Ct. Spec. App. 2006) (Corporate officer or director may not take a business opportunity for his own if: (1) the corporation is financially able to exploit the opportunity; (2) the opportunity is within the corporation's line of business; (3) the corporation has an interest or expectancy in the opportunity; and (4) by taking the opportunity for his own, the officer's or director's interests will be inimical to his duties to the corporation); Cooper Linse Hallman Capital Management, Inc. v. Hallman, 856 N.E.2d 585 (Ill. App. Ct. 2006) (Former officer and office manager who started competing business after leaving corporation did not usurp corporation's opportunity to sell corporation's sector fund because corporation was still able to sell its sector fund despite competitor's solicitations for its sector fund); Trieweiler v. Sears, 689 N.W.2d 807 (Neb. 2004) (Directors were jointly and severally liable in shareholder derivative suit for misappropriation and usurpation of corporate opportunity from closely held corporation; constructive trust is the traditional remedy imposed for misappropriation of a corporate opportunity; constructive trust subjects person who holds title to property wrongfully obtained to an equitable duty to convey property to its rightful owner).

Additional Information

1. Laura H. Dietz Et al., 18A Am. Jur. 2d Corporations § 666 (2010).

2. Laura H. Dietz Et al., 18B Am. Jur. 2d Corporations §§ 1540–1541, 1544, 1573 (2010).

3. William Meade Fletcher, 3 Fletcher Cyc. Corp. §§ 861.10, 862 (2010).

4. 16 A.L.R. 4th 185, 784 (2010).

5. James L. Rigelhaupt, 77 A.L.R.3d 961 (2010).

6. Joseph W. Bishop, Law of Corp. Officers & Dir.: Indemn. & Ins. § 3:10 (2010).

7. Edward Brodsky, M. Patricia Adamski, Law of Corp. Offs. & Dirs.: Rts., Duties & Liabs. §§ 4:7, 4:12 (2009).

8. Jonathan Rosenberg, Kendall Burr, *Making Sense of New York's Corporate Opportunity Doctrine*, 80-Jun N.Y. St. B.J. 10 (2008).

9. David Kershaw, *Lost in Translation: Corporate Opportunities in Comparative Perspective*, 25 Oxford J. Legal Stud. 603 (2005).

10. Matthew R. Salzwedel, *A Contractual Theory of Corporate Opportunity and a Proposed Statute*, 23 Pace L. Rev. 83 (2002).

11. Terrence Woolf, *The Venture Capitalist's Corporate Opportunity Problem*, 2001 Colum. Bus. L. Rev. 473 (2001).

12. Kenneth B. Davis, *Coporate Opportunity and Competitive Advantage*, 84 Iowa L. Rev. 211 (1999).

13. Eric G. Orlinsky, *Corporate Opportunity Doctrine and Interested Director Transactions: A Framework for Analysis in an Attempt to Restore Predictability*, 24 Del. J. Corp. L 451 (1999).

14. Eric Talley, *Turning Servile Opportunities to Gold: A Strategic Analysis of the Corporate Opportunities Doctrine*, 108 Yale L.J. 277 (1998).

10.2.6   Piercing The Corporate Veil

As noted a number of times earlier, corporations are separate legal entities, and shareholders are not liable for corporate debts, torts or taxes, beyond their investment in the corporation. However, under some circumstances, courts will ignore the corporate form and hold shareholders directly liable. This is known as "piercing the corporate veil." The *McCallum Family* case considers the burden of proof, who may be liable, the types of conduct giving rise to liability, and when a corporate shareholder may breach a fiduciary duty to creditors in a "piercing the corporate veil" suit.

McCALLUM FAMILY L.L.C. v. WINGER,
221 P.3d 69 (Colo. App. 2009)

Opinion by Judge Terry.

In this appeal, we address four issues relating to potential personal liability of a corporate shareholder and another corporate insider who is not a shareholder, officer, or director. We first apply section 13-25-127(1), C.R.S.2009, and conclude that the burden of proof in an action to pierce the corporate veil is by a preponderance of the evidence, not by clear and convincing evidence, as has sometimes been incorrectly stated. Next, we conclude that, in appropriate circumstances, the corporate veil may be pierced to impose personal liability on a corporate insider who is not a shareholder, officer, or director. We then address the types of conduct that constitute defeating the rightful claims of creditors, such that the veil may be pierced. Finally, we discuss the circumstances in which a corporate shareholder may be liable to a creditor for breach of fiduciary duty.

Plaintiff, McCallum Family, L.L.C. (McCallum), appeals the judgment, entered after a trial to the court, in favor of defendants, Marc Winger and Karen Winger. We affirm in part, reverse in part, and remand for further proceedings.

I. Undisputed Facts

McCallum presented the following evidence at trial, and defendants did not contest it:

Marc Winger managed Manitoba Investment Advisors, Inc., a Wyoming corporation authorized to do business in Colorado. During Manitoba's corporate existence, Marc Winger was married to Vicki Winger, who was a director, 50%

shareholder, and president of Manitoba. Marc Winger's mother, Karen Winger, was a director, 50% shareholder, vice president, and secretary of Manitoba.

Although Marc Winger was not a shareholder, officer, or director of Manitoba, he admittedly "managed the entire business." He routinely used corporate funds to pay his personal bills, including $95,400 paid to the State of California as a result of his felony conviction there for failure to pay sales taxes.

Manitoba entered into a commercial triple-net lease, with McCallum as lessor, for real property in Grand Junction, Colorado, from which it ran a mobile home sales operation. Manitoba did not pay Mesa County property taxes as required by the lease for 2003, 2004, and part of 2005, and it vacated the property seven months before the end of the lease term, defaulting on the remaining rent. McCallum obtained a judgment against Manitoba for $76,224.

The parties stipulated that Manitoba was insolvent beginning in September 2004. The corporation was administratively dissolved on May 31, 2006.

II. Burden of Proof

McCallum asserted a claim to pierce the corporate veil and hold Marc Winger personally liable for the debt owed by Manitoba. McCallum contends the trial court erred in applying a clear and convincing burden of proof, rather than a preponderance of the evidence burden, to this claim. We agree.

The proper burden of proof is a question of law which we review de novo. We apply section 13-25-127(1), which states that "the burden of proof in any civil action shall be by a preponderance of the evidence," and conclude that this burden is applicable in cases where a party seeks to pierce the corporate veil, in the absence of issues of constitutional concern.

Here, the trial court relied on language in *In re Phillips* to determine that the burden of proof for McCallum's veil-piercing claim was "clear and convincing" evidence. In *Phillips*, the supreme court answered a question that had been certified by the United States District Court for Colorado. Given that the opinion does not discuss section 13-25-127(1), it is fair to assume the parties did not raise it and the court did not consider it. In any event, because the proper burden of proof was outside the scope of the question certified by the federal court and decided by the supreme court, the court's statement that the burden of proof is by "clear and convincing evidence," is mere dictum which is not binding on us. We are not persuaded otherwise by *Contractors Heating & Supply Co. v. Scherb*, "[t]he corporate form . . . will not be disregarded unless a clear showing is made that it was used to perpetrate a fraud or defeat a rightful claim"), because that decision predated the 1972 adoption of section 13-25-127(1).

When the Colorado Supreme Court faced a conflict between the "preponderance" burden of proof set forth in section 13-25-127(1) and its own precedent applying a different burden, it held that the statute prevails over conflicting appellate case law. In *Gerner*, the court noted that it would decline to apply the statutory burden of proof only if there were issues of constitutional concern.

Because section 13-25-127(1) provides that, with certain exceptions not relevant here, the applicable burden of proof is a preponderance of the evidence, and no issues of constitutional concern were raised in the trial court, that court erred by not applying the preponderance burden of proof. As discussed below, McCallum established the first two prongs of the veil-piercing test, leaving only the determination of whether the third prong was proved. Therefore, we remand to the trial court so that it may determine whether McCallum met its burden to prove, by a preponderance of the evidence, the third prong for piercing the corporate veil.

III. McCallum's Piercing the Corporate Veil Claim

McCallum next argues that the trial court erred by declining to pierce the corporate veil to hold Marc Winger personally liable for the judgment against Manitoba. We conclude, based on the undisputed evidence presented at trial, that McCallum established a prima facie case for piercing the corporate veil against Marc Winger. Therefore, we remand to the trial court for further findings under the correct burden of proof.

A. Requirements for Piercing the Corporate Veil

In a typical case, a determination whether to pierce the corporate veil is a mixed question of law and fact. When faced with such a mixed question, we normally defer to the trial court's findings of historical fact, and review de novo its application of the law to those facts.

This, however, is the unusual case where the controlling facts pertinent to the first two prongs of the three-pronged veil-piercing analysis are undisputed. Thus, we do not defer to the trial court's conclusions of law based on those facts, but rather make an independent judgment on the merits concerning those two prongs.

In general, a corporation is treated as a legal entity separate from its shareholders, officers, and directors. This permits shareholders to invest with the assurance that they will not be held personally liable for the corporation's debts.

The fiction of the corporate veil isolates "the actions, profits, and debts of the corporation from the individuals who invest in and run the entity." Only extraordinary circumstances justify disregarding the corporate entity to impose personal liability.

To determine whether it is appropriate to pierce the corporate veil, a court must make a three-part inquiry.

First, the court must determine whether the corporate entity is the "alter ego" of the person or entity in issue. Courts consider a variety of factors in determining status as an alter ego, including whether (1) the corporation is operated as a distinct business entity; (2) funds and assets are commingled; (3) adequate corporate records are maintained; (4) the nature and form of the entity's ownership and control facilitate misuse by an insider; (5) the business is thinly capitalized; (6) the corporation is used as a "mere shell"; (7) legal formalities are disregarded; and (8) corporate funds or assets are used for noncorporate purposes. This inquiry looks to the specific facts of each case, and not all of the listed factors need to be shown in order to establish alter ego status.

Second, the court must determine whether justice requires recognizing the substance of the relationship between the person or entity sought to be held liable and the corporation over the form because the corporate fiction was "used to perpetrate a fraud or defeat a rightful claim."

Third, the court must consider whether an equitable result will be achieved by disregarding the corporate form and holding a shareholder or other insider personally liable for the acts of the business entity.

All three prongs of the analysis must be satisfied. The paramount goal of piercing the corporate veil is to achieve an equitable result.

B. Piercing the Corporate Veil as to One Who is Not a Shareholder, Officer, or Director

McCallum contends that, although Marc Winger was not a shareholder, officer, or director, the corporate veil should be pierced to impose personal liability on him for the judgment against Manitoba. We conclude that the veil-piercing doctrine may be applied to include corporate insiders such as Marc Winger.

The doctrine of corporate veil piercing is most often applied to impose liability on corporate shareholders, because that is the context in which the issue usually arises. However, "the mere existence or nonexistence of formal stock ownership is not necessarily conclusive" in determining whether the corporate veil may be pierced.

Colorado precedents have recognized that the doctrine may be employed to impose individual liability on non-shareholder corporate insiders, including corporate officers and managers of limited liability companies. In *LaFond v. Basham*, a division of this court expanded the doctrine to impose personal liability on a defendant who was not a corporate shareholder, but was an officer and member of the board of directors of the two corporations in issue; controlled all the policy and activity of the corporations; dominated his wife and son, who were the only shareholders; solely determined when he would draw money from the corporations; and insisted that his loans to the corporations be repaid in preference to other creditors. Another division of this court recently held that the corporate veil could be pierced to hold liable a non-member manager of a limited liability company who appropriated corporate assets as his own.

LaFond and *Sheffield* are consistent with the rationale underlying corporate veil piercing. As numerous cases and commentators have established, the veil may be pierced and the corporation treated as an alter ego where the corporate form has been abused; the corporate entity has been used as a subterfuge and to observe it would work an injustice; the party sought to be held liable has dominance and control over the corporation and uses the corporate entity as a mere instrumentality for the transaction of that party's own affairs; there is such a unity of interest and ownership that the separate personalities of the corporation and the party do not exist; and to allow the corporate fiction to persist would promote injustice or protect fraud. Where the party sought to be held liable exercises an extensive level of control over the corporation, such control may be an important factor in determining whether to pierce the veil.

Where a corporate insider exercises substantial control over the corporation, uses the corporate form to transact his personal business, and treats corporate funds as though they were his own, as the undisputed evidence shows Marc Winger did here, it would elevate form over substance to allow him to avoid personal liability merely because he has avoided owning stock in his own name and assuming a corporate title such as officer or director. Here, he functioned essentially as a shareholder, officer, or director, was closely related to the shareholders, and used the assets of the corporation fundamentally as his own. Under these circumstances, if the other prongs of the veil-piercing test have been met, the mere fact that Marc Winger did not hold the title of shareholder, officer, or director would not preclude the imposition of personal liability on him.

Our holding is consistent with the tenor of Colorado precedents, as well as with decisions of courts in other jurisdictions that have considered the issue. Those other jurisdictions have concluded that where an individual sought to be held liable for corporate debts exercises sufficient dominion and control over the corporation, that person may be deemed an "equitable owner," and thus an alter ego of the corporation.

In *Labadie Coal Co. v. Black*, the court observed that while a person who controls a corporation may seek to avoid personal liability by not becoming a shareholder, that person's lack of shareholder status is not determinative as to whether the veil will be pierced to hold him or her liable. Instead, the key to determining whether an individual is a corporate alter ego is his or her degree of control. Although the defendant had no formal control over any corporate shares because the stock was in his wife's and children's names, he was the "dominant figure" in the corporation and "[held] the reins," and it was "by his actions alone that a relationship with [the] plaintiff was established and business transacted." These facts, combined with an indication of inadequate capitalization and failure to maintain corporate records and observe corporate formalities, formed the basis of the court's decision to remand for reconsideration of the plaintiff's veil-piercing claim.

Other jurisdictions that have adopted the equitable ownership doctrine include:

• Illinois: *Fontana v. TLD Builders, Inc.*, [362 Ill.App.3d 491, 298 Ill.Dec. 654]840 N.E.2d 767, 778–79 (2005) (corporate veil pierced against non-shareholder who exercised degree of ownership and control over corporation such that there was no separate personality between him and the corporation, and sole shareholder was his wife, who was a "non-functioning" officer or director); *Macaluso v. Jenkins*, [95 Ill.App.3d 461, 50 Ill.Dec. 934]420 N.E.2d 251, 255–56 (1981) (sufficient unity of interest existed to pierce corporate veil where the defendant, who did not own shares in not-for-profit corporation, intended to "profit" from the corporation and exercised such a degree of ownership and control that separate personalities of corporation and the defendant did not exist; because veil piercing is an equitable remedy, it is proper to look to substance rather than form in determining whether to hold a non-shareholder personally liable for a corporation's debts).

• Minnesota: *Equity Trust Co. Custodian ex rel. Eisenmenger IRA v. Cole*, 766 N.W.2d 334, 339–40 (Minn.Ct.App.2009) (allowing veil piercing against parties who were not corporate shareholders or members, where they were treated like officers or directors, and were actively involved in managing the entities in issue; reasoning that courts favor reality over form in determining a party's involvement in a corporate enterprise and that otherwise "unscrupulous parties could avoid personal liability" by avoiding formal ownership interests).

• New York: *Freeman v. Complex Computing Co.*, 119 F.3d 1044, 1051 (2d Cir.1997) (applying New York law) ("an individual who exercises sufficient control over the corporation may be deemed an "equitable owner," notwithstanding the fact that the individual is not a shareholder of the corporation" (citing *Guilder v. Corinth Constr. Corp.*, [235 A.D.2d 619]651 N.Y.S.2d 706, 707 (N.Y.App.Div.1997))) (although the *Freeman* defendant was not an actual shareholder, officer, director, or employee, the court treated him as an equitable owner because he " "exercise[d] considerable authority over [the corporation] . . . to the point of completely disregarding the corporate form and acting as though [its] assets [were] his alone to manage and distribute" " (quoting *Lally v. Catskill Airways, Inc.*, [198 A.D.2d 643]603 N.Y.S.2d 619, 621 (N.Y.App.Div.1993))).

We conclude that an individual should not be able to defeat the alter ego prong of the veil-piercing analysis merely because he or she has no formal ownership interest in the corporation, and does not hold the title of officer or director. The proper inquiry is into the substance of the corporation's governance as well as its form. When an individual demonstrates great dominion and control over a corporation, and especially over corporate assets, the lack of such a formal role or title will not necessarily impede a finding of personal liability for corporate activities. An individual who acts as a de facto shareholder, officer, or director may be treated as an equitable owner and held to be the alter ego of a corporation.

Here, the undisputed evidence showed that Marc Winger essentially functioned as an owner, and "managed the whole affair." As in *Labadie* and *Fontana*, he was closely related to both shareholders of the company, his mother and his wife, the latter of whom he admitted was a shareholder and officer in name only. Together with his wife, he made decisions as to how much to pay to himself and creditors. The undisputed testimony at trial was that neither of the nominal shareholders properly supervised his activities.

Although Marc Winger did not sign the lease in issue here, his father signed it under the pseudonym "John Warner." No evidence established that the father had any legitimate role in the business. A reasonable fact finder could conclude that the father signed the lease under a pseudonym for improper reasons, such as to give an appearance that Marc Winger was not the alter ego of the corporation and to assist him in evading personal liability for the lease obligation. In any case, Marc Winger conducted nearly all of Manitoba's business with McCallum, including signing checks and handling lease renegotiations.

In addition, Marc Winger took a number of "distributions" from Manitoba even though he was not a shareholder. This is another indication that he was a de facto owner, because, ordinarily, distributions are paid to corporate shareholders.

He routinely used corporate funds to pay personal bills for himself and his wife, including payment of his California sales tax obligation and outlays for a boat, cell phone, and personal credit cards. McCallum's expert witness in public accounting opined that corporate funds invested in outside real estate projects appeared to have garnered profits that should have been applied to business operations but were not, and that the commingling of Marc Winger's personal funds and company funds was "relatively rampant . . . through the whole existence of Manitoba." The expert stated, "Winger treated the company as one of his pockets and wrote checks as he needed money[;] from time to time [he] would put some money back in, but overall [he] treated the company as if it didn't exist." He further opined that "the Wingers ultimately removed all available funds from Manitoba."

This undisputed evidence showed that the corporation lacked "economic substance."

The evidence adduced at trial established that:

- Marc Winger exercised such a degree of control and dominance over Manitoba's affairs that he should be treated as an equitable owner;

- Manitoba was not operated as a distinct business entity;

- corporate funds were commingled with personal funds, and were used for noncorporate purposes;

- the nature and form of Manitoba's ownership and control facilitated misuse by Marc Winger as an insider;

- the corporation lacked economic substance; and

- the corporation was used as a mere shell.

Therefore, we conclude Marc Winger was the alter ego of Manitoba.

This does not end the veil-piercing inquiry, however. A finding that a party is the alter ego of a corporation satisfies only the first prong of the three-part veil-piercing test. We now address the latter two prongs of the test.

C. Using the Corporate Fiction to Perpetrate a Fraud or Defeat a Rightful Claim

The second prong of the veil-piercing test is whether justice requires recognizing the substance of the relationship between the corporation and the person or entity sought to be held liable over the form because the corporate fiction was "used to perpetrate a fraud or defeat a rightful claim."

The trial court declined to pierce the corporate veil as to Marc Winger because it concluded McCallum was required to prove that Winger had used the corporation to perpetrate a fraud or wrong "in the transaction at issue," and McCallum had presented no evidence that Winger used Manitoba to perpetrate a fraud or wrong against McCallum. McCallum contends this ruling was error, and we agree. As discussed below, the undisputed facts show that McCallum established that Marc Winger used the corporate form to defeat McCallum's rightful claim.

The second prong of the veil-piercing inquiry reflects a recognition that the corporate veil may be pierced "[o]nly when the corporate form was used to shield a dominant shareholder's improprieties." The mere fact that corporate creditors would go unsatisfied because they cannot reach a shareholder's personal assets does not, alone, justify piercing the corporate veil.

Here, the trial court noted that Marc Winger did not sign the lease; no evidence was presented that he conspired with his father or anyone else to mismanage Manitoba or divert its assets to avoid its liability under the lease; there was no evidence that McCallum had investigated Manitoba's financial circumstances before renting to it; and "Manitoba apparently lived up to its obligations under the lease (except for paying . . . property taxes) for four or five years."

Citing *Angelo Tomasso, Inc.* and *Walk-In Medical Ctrs.*, the trial court stated that "[a] plaintiff must show that the defendant used the corporation to perpetrate a fraud or wrong in the transaction in issue."

While we agree with the principle cited by the trial court, it applied the principle too narrowly here. To satisfy this second prong of the test, a plaintiff may show *either* fraud *or* that the corporate form was abused to defeat the rightful claims of creditors. There is no additional requirement to prove any conduct specifically *directed at the plaintiff-creditor.* However, the creditor seeking to pierce the veil must show an *effect* on its lawful rights as a creditor resulting from abuse of the corporate form.

Here, McCallum showed that the corporate form was abused in a manner that defeated its rightful claim as a creditor of Manitoba. It presented evidence, through its accounting expert, that "the Wingers ultimately removed all available corporate funds from Manitoba," thus leaving no funds in that corporation to satisfy the debt owed to McCallum. It demonstrated that profits garnered from real estate in which corporate funds had been invested should have been applied to business operations, but were not. Defendants did not contest any of the evidence showing that Marc Winger's actions placed what should have been corporate funds out of McCallum's reach, thereby defeating its rightful claim. We conclude this uncontested evidence satisfied the second veil-piercing prong, without any additional showing that Marc Winger's activity was directed specifically at defeating McCallum's rights.

D. The Equity Prong

McCallum argues that equity requires piercing the corporate veil as to Marc Winger. By establishing the first two prongs of the veil-piercing analysis, McCallum made a prima facie case for application of the trial court's equitable discretion to pierce the veil. However, whether to exercise that discretion must be determined in the first instance by the trial court, and thus we remand for the trial court to consider this issue.

Because the paramount goal of piercing the corporate veil is to achieve an equitable result, the determination whether to pierce is entirely within the trial court's equitable discretion. In applying this third prong, the court must inquire whether "an equitable result will be achieved by disregarding the corporate form and holding the shareholder personally liable for the acts of the business entity."

This prong emphasizes that corporate veil piercing is a fact-specific, equity-based doctrine.

McCallum demonstrated that the first two veil-piercing prongs were satisfied, and presented a prima facie case for the application of the court's equitable discretion to pierce the corporate veil. However, because the trial court must determine in the first instance whether the equities of the situation merit veil piercing here, we remand to the trial court to make this determination, applying the principles of law we have set forth herein.

The judgment against McCallum on its claims against Marc Winger is reversed, and the case is remanded for further proceedings as directed. In all other respects, the judgment is affirmed.

QUESTIONS

1.   Why might a "clear and convincing" burden of proof be more appropriate in a veil-piercing claim than a "preponderance" burden of proof? In what, if any, ways is a veil-piercing action different from civil actions for breach of contract or tortious harm?

2.   What factors does a court consider in determining whether the corporate entity is the "alter ego" of the person sought to be held personally liable in a veil-piercing action? How did the court apply these factors with respect to Marc Winger?

3.   What is the rationale for holding persons who are not shareholders, directors or officers liable in a veil-piercing action? On what basis did the court find that Marc Winger was an equitable owner of Manitoba?

4.   What is the difference between the second prong of the veil-piercing test (i.e., whether the corporate fiction has been used to perpetuate fraud or defeat a rightful claim) and the third prong of the veil-piercing test (i.e., whether piercing the corporate veil would produce an equitable result)? When would remedying the use of a corporation to perpetuate fraud or defeat a rightful claim not be an equitable result?

CASE NOTES

1.   Schema Inc. is a real estate development company. Longhi, an architect, is a shareholder and officer of Schema Inc. Louis and Lorraine Mazzoni (Mazzonis) were family friends of Longhi. Louis had known Lognhi's parents for 50–60 years and known Lognhi since he was born. Longhi contacted the Mazzonis about building a house in a new residential subdivision being developed by Schema Inc. Louis told Longhi that they could not afford a new house and Longhi then offered to build a new house for the Mazzonis at 50 percent off the list price. The Mazzonis decided to accept Longhi's offer. Later, Longhi informed the Mazzonis that, in order to receive the discount offer, they would have to give Longhi a $50,000 down payment. In January 1996, the Mazzonis signed a Purchase Agreement and a Promissory Note in the amount of $50,000. The Promissory Note provided that the Seller shall

deposit all cash or checks received under the Promissory Note into a Broker's trust account. In February 1996, the Mazzonis delivered a cashier's check to Longhi in the amount of $50,000. Longhi deposited the cashier's check into Schema Inc.'s bank account. In late 1997, the Mazzonis became concerned that construction had not started on their new house. Longhi explained that a certain number of houses had to be sold before construction could begin. In June 1998, the Mazzonis requested the return of their $50,000 down payment. The Mazzonis never received a refund of their $50,000 down payment nor a deed to the lot they had selected. In July 1999, the Mazzonis filed a complaint against Schema Inc. and, in March 2001, they amended their complaint alleging Longhi was personally liable for repayment of the down payment. In October 2008, the trial court found that Longhi was personally liable for the return of the down payment and awarded the Mazzonis treble damages in the amount of $150,000 plus attorney fees. Longhi appealed. What result? *See* Longhi v. Mazzoni, 914 N.E.2d 834 (Ind. Ct. App. 2009).

2. *See also* Bear, Inc. v. Smith, 303 S.W.3d 137 (Ky. Ct. App. 2010) (Some of the factors to be considered in determining whether to pierce the corporate veil include: (1) whether the corporation is adequately capitalized; (2) whether the owners observe corporate formalities; (3) whether there is a comingling of corporate and personal assets; (4) whether the owners deal with the corporation at arm's length; (5) whether the corporation is insolvent at the time of the challenged transaction; (6) whether corporate records have been properly maintained; and (7) whether there are third-party guarantors of the corporation's debts; genuine issue of material fact existed as to whether sole shareholder of corporation abused corporate form to thwart supplier's attempt to recover unpaid account and precluded summary judgment in supplier's action to pierce corporate veil and hold shareholder personally liable for debt); Fisher Investment Capital, Inc. v. Catawba, 689 S.E. 2d 143 (N.C. Ct. App. 2009) (Courts will pierce the corporate veil whenever necessary to prevent fraud or to achieve equity; lender sufficiently alleged that majority shareholder and director controlled corporation in order to defraud lender as required to state a claim to pierce corporate veil); Daniels v. CDB, LLC, 300 S.W.3d 204 (Ky. Ct. App. 2009) (Decision as to whether to pierce corporate veil is an equity decision to be decided by the trial judge, not a jury; the three prongs of the instrumentality theory of piercing the corporate veil are that the corporation was a mere instrumentality of the shareholder, that the shareholder exercised control over the corporation to defraud or to harm the plaintiff, and refusal to disregard corporate entity would subject plaintiff to unjust loss); RDM Holdings, LTD v. Continental Plastics Co., 762 N.W.2d 529 (Mich. Ct. App. 2008) (Claim by lessor against lessee's shareholder seeking to pierce corporate veil could not be litigated in lessee's Chapter 7 bankruptcy because it was not property in the bankruptcy estate and thus the lessor was not precluded by *res judicata* from litigating the claim in a breach-of-lease action against the shareholder); Dombroski v. Wellpoint, Inc., 895 N.E.2d 538 (Ohio 2008) (Corporate veil will not be pierced where control of corporation was exercised to commit unjust or inequitable acts that do not rise to the level of fraud or an illegal act; alleged bad faith in denying insured's claim for a cochlear implant was not fraud or an illegal act sufficient to pierce corporate veil); Pamperin v. Streamline Mfg., 276 S.W.3d 428 (Tenn. Ct. App. 2008) (Hot tub buyer presented sufficient evidence to establish that it was necessary to pierce corporate veil in order to hold individual shareholder liable for corporation's failure to deliver

hot tub or return her $3,000 deposit; shareholder received all of the corporation's assets as a secured creditor and used the corporation's assets that remained after the satisfaction of the secured obligations to start a new business rendering the corporation insolvent); Semande v. Estes, 871 N.E.2d 268 (Ill. App. Ct. 2007) (The corporate veil will generally not be pierced for the benefit of shareholders or directors); Milk v. Total Pay and HR Solutions, Inc., 634 S.E.2d 208 (Ga. Ct. App. 2006) (Evidence did not establish that member undercapitalized limited liability company with an intent to avoid paying future debts improperly, thus undercapitalization did not allow corporate veil to be pierced); Advanced Telephone Systems, Inc. v. Com-Net Professional Mobile Radio, LLC, 846 A.2d 1264 (Pa. Super. Ct. 2004) (In Pennsylvania, there is no state constitutional right to a jury trial in claim seeking to pierce the corporate veil of a limited liability company; even though Pennsylvania precedent established that juries routinely decided corporate piercing claims, there is no state constitutional right to jury trial in corporate piercing claim).

Additional Information

1. 2 CORP. COUNS. GD TO ACQ. & DIVEST. §§ 18:2–18-11, 18:18–18:19 (2010).

2. LAURA H. DIETZ ET AL., 18 AM. JUR.2D CORPORATIONS §§ 47, 49, 51 (2010).

3. WILLIAM MEADE FLETCHER, 1 FLETCHER CYC. CORP. §§ 41, 41.10, 41.28 (2010).

4. FRANCIS C. AMENDOLA ET AL., 18 C.J.S. CORPORATIONS §§ 16, 30 (2010).

5. L. S. TELLIER, 63 A.L.R.2D 1051 (2010).

6. FERDINAND S. TINIO, 46 A.L.R.3D 428 (2010).

7. Thomas K. Cheng, *Form and Substance of the Doctrine of Piercing the Corporate Veil*, 80 MISS. L.J. 497 (2010).

8. Richmond McPherson, Nader Raja, *Corporate Justice: An Empirical Study of Piercing Rates and Factors Courts Consider When Piercing the Corporate Veil*, 45 WAKE FOREST L. REV. 931 (2010).

9. John H. Matheson, *Why Courts Pierce: An Empirical Study of Piercing the Corporate Veil*, 7 BERKELEY BUS. L.J. 1 (2010).

10. David Millon, *Piercing the Corporate Veil, Financial Responsibility, and the Limits of Limited Liability*, 56 EMORY L.J. 1305 (2007).

11. Joseph M. Sauer, *A Tear in the Corporate Veil: The Liability of Corporate Officers for Patent Infringement*, 37 DUQ. L. REV. 89 (1998).

Chapter 11

FINANCING TECHNOLOGY INNOVATION

Technology innovation requires capital investment. Capital investment is needed for many purposes, including funding for research and development, the payment of salaries and operating expenses, the acquisition of plant and equipment, the launch of marketing activities, and the establishment of distribution channels and service networks. This chapter of the materials considers the different means by which capital can be raised to finance technology innovation. The primary focus of the chapter is on the development of new technologies in the hands of start-up and early-stage companies. The sections in the chapter are organized roughly in chronological order, beginning with earlier means, and concluding with later means, of raising capital for technology innovation.

The first section in this chapter looks at the two most popular federal programs available to support research and development by small business companies — the Small Business Innovation Research Program (SBIR) and the Small Business Technology Transfer Program (STTR). This section includes the federal authorizing legislation and the Small Business Administration's policy directives for the SBIR and STTR programs. The final subsection in this section considers data rights and government contract award rights under the SBIR program.

The second section considers private offerings of securities under the Securities Act of 1933. This section covers equity investments by founders, family and friends, and by angel investors. The section also includes materials on securities registration exemptions and private placement memoranda. The following section considers the potential for fraud claims in the context of private securities offerings.

The fourth section considers venture capital investments. The section includes a discussion of the size of the venture capital market, the structure of venture capital firms, the ways in which a venture capital investment can be structured, a sample venture capital term sheet and two cases highlighting the potential for venture capital investment disputes, one case in which the venture capital firm is the plaintiff and one case in which the intended recipient of the venture capital investment is the plaintiff. This section concludes with a glossary of private equity investment terms compiled by the Tuck School of Business at Dartmouth University reprinted with permission.

The fifth section discusses other means of financing technology innovation including bank loans, monetization of intellectual property, securitization of intellectual property and letters of credit.

The sixth section covers initial public offerings (IPOs) — the first offerings of securities to the public which are registered with the Securities and Exchange Commission (SEC). This section includes materials on the IPO process, the registration of securities under the Securities Act of 1933 and the Form S-1 registration statement that must be filed with, and approved by, the SEC prior to the time securities can be offered for sale to the public. This section also includes Google's Form S-1 Registration Statement.

The final two sections consider claims of fraud in public securities offerings and the "due diligence" defense to fraud claims. These sections cover both federal and state securities fraud claims, and federal and state "due diligence" defenses.

11.1 SMALL BUSINESS INNOVATION RESEARCH (SBIR) AND SMALL BUSINESS TECHNOLOGY TRANSFER (STTR) PROGRAMS

The SBIR and STTR Programs were established by Congress and are administered by the SBA. The research awards are made by federal agencies and competition for awards is intense. SBIR and STTR awards not only provide start-up and small companies critical early-stage research funding, they also signal to the investment community that the recipient company is developing potentially valuable, and investment-worthy, technologies. Although this section does not consider comparable state programs, the majority of states also have funds available to support start-up and small companies in their early research efforts.

11.1.1 Overview of SBIR and STTR Programs

For most start-up technology companies, the greatest financial challenge is obtaining funding for research and development. The SBIR and STTR programs are excellent sources of funding to support start-up companies' early research and development. Awards under the SBIR and STTR programs range from $500,000 to $1.5 million over approximately three years for research and development. The awards are in the form of grants or contracts so there are no payback requirements and no relinquishment of equity; the Small Business Concern (SBC) awardee retains complete equity ownership. In addition, the SBC awardee is permitted to retain all data and intellectual property rights resulting from the SBIR or STTR funded research and development, subject to limited use rights by the federal government.

The SBIR and STTR programs require federal agencies with extramural (external) research and development budgets over a specified amount to set aside a percentage of their extramural budgets for research and development awards to SBCs. In general, SBCs are defined as for-profit companies having fewer than 500 employees. Under the SBIR program, federal agencies having extramural budgets over $100M are required to set aside 2.5% of their extramural budgets for awards to SBCs. Under the STTR program, federal agencies having extramural budgets over $1B are required to set aside .3% of their extramural budgets for awards to SBCs. The table on the next page lists the federal agencies participating in the SBIR and STTR programs, and their approximate funding amounts.

Funding under both the SBIR and STTR programs is awarded in three phases. Under the SBIR program, Phase I funding of up to $150,000 is awarded for a six-month period to demonstrate the scientific and technical feasibility (proof of concept) of a new technology; and Phase II funding of up to $1M or more is awarded for up to two years to refine the proof of concept and develop a technology prototype. Under the STTR program, Phase I funding of up to $100,000 is awarded for up to one year to demonstrate the proof of concept of a new technology; and Phase II funding of up to $750,000 is awarded for two or more years to develop a technology prototype. Under both the SBIR and STTR programs, Phase III funding is not provided under the SBIR or STTR programs. Rather, Phase III funding is provided by commercial investors in the SBC or by a federal agency that awards a contract to the SBC which is separate from SBIR or STTR funding.

SBIR / STTR Agencies

Agency	SBIR	STTR	Approx. Funding Amt. — FY 2009
Department. of Agriculture	X		$18,000,000
Department of Commerce National Oceanic and Atmospheric Administration National Institute on Standard and Technology	X		$7,000,000
Department of Defense Army, Navy, Air Force	X	X	$1,000,000,000
Department of Education	X		$9,000,000
Department of Energy	X	X	$102,000,000
Department of Homeland Security	X		$33,000,000
Department of Health and Human Services National Institutes of Health Centers for Disease Control	X	X	$574,000,000
Department of Transportation	X		$4,000,000
Environmental Protection Agency	X		$8,000,000
National Aeronautics and Space Administration	X	X	$108,000,000
National Science Foundation	X	X	$94,000,000

The materials in this section first consider the federal legislation which authorizes the SBIR and STTR programs, then the Policy Directives on the SBIR and STTR programs issued by the Small Business Administration and, finally, an important case which involves an SBC awardee's proprietary data rights and Phase III contract rights under a SBIR award.

11.1.2   Federal Legislation

The SBIR program dates back to 1982 when Congress passed the Small Business Innovation Development (SBID) Act. Congress reauthorized the SBID Act in 1986 and extended the Act to create the STTR program in 1992. In 2000, Congress extended the SBIR program until March 20, 2009, and in 2001, Congress extended the STTR program until September 30, 2009. The SBIR and STTR programs are currently operating under Congressional Continuing Resolutions. Reauthorization bills are currently pending in the House and Senate. The House and Senate reauthorization bills differ on a number of significant points, including the participation of venture capital firms in the SBIR and STTR programs and the length of the reauthorization term. The current version of the legislation is set forth below.

SMALL BUSINESS INNOVATION DEVELOPMENT ACT
15 USCA § 638 (1982)

(a) Declaration of policy

Research and development are major factors in the growth and progress of industry and the national economy. The expense of carrying on research and development programs is beyond the means of many small-business concerns, and such concerns are handicapped in obtaining the benefits of research and development programs conducted at Government expense. These small-business concerns are thereby placed at a competitive disadvantage. This weakens the competitive free enterprise system and prevents the orderly development of the national economy. It is the policy of the Congress that assistance be given to small-business concerns to enable them to undertake and to obtain the benefits of research and development in order to maintain and strengthen the competitive free enterprise system and the national economy.

(b) Assistance to small-business concerns

It shall be the duty of the [Small Business] Administration, and it is empowered —

(1) to assist small-business concerns to obtain Government contracts for research and development;

(2) to assist small-business concerns to obtain the benefits of research and development performed under Government contracts or at Government expense;

(3) to provide technical assistance to small-business concerns to accomplish the purposes of this section; and

(4) to develop and maintain a source file and an information program to assure each qualified and interested small business concern the opportunity to participate in Federal agency small business innovation research programs [SBIR] and small business technology transfer programs [STTR];

(5) to coordinate with participating agencies a schedule for release of SBIR and STTR solicitations, and to prepare a master release schedule so as to maximize small businesses' opportunities to respond to solicitations;

(6) to independently survey and monitor the operation of SBIR and STTR programs within participating Federal agencies;

(7) to report not less than annually to the Committee on Small Business of the Senate, and to the Committee on Science and the Committee on Small Business of the House of Representatives, on the SBIR and STTR programs of the Federal agencies and the Administration's information and monitoring efforts related to the SBIR and STTR programs, including the data on output and outcomes collected pursuant to subsections (g)(10), (o)(9), and (o)(15) of this section, the number of proposals received from, and the number and total amount of awards to, HUB Zone small business concerns under each of the SBIR and STTR programs, and a description of the extent to which Federal agencies are providing in a timely manner information needed to maintain the database described in subsection (k) of this section; and

(8) to provide for and fully implement the tenets of Executive Order No. 13329 (Encouraging Innovation in Manufacturing).

(c) Consultation and cooperation with Government agencies; studies and recommendations

The Administration is authorized to consult and cooperate with all Government agencies and to make studies and recommendations to such agencies, and such agencies are authorized and directed to cooperate with the Administration in order to carry out and to accomplish the purposes of this section.

(d) Joint programs; approval of agreements; withdrawal of approval; publication in Federal Register

(1) The Administrator is authorized to consult with representatives of small-business concerns with a view to assisting and encouraging such firms to undertake joint programs for research and development carried out through such corporate or other mechanism as may be most appropriate for the purpose. Such joint programs may, among other things, include the following purposes:

(A) to construct, acquire, or establish laboratories and other facilities for the conduct of research;

(B) to undertake and utilize applied research;

(C) to collect research information related to a particular industry and disseminate it to participating members;

(D) to conduct applied research on a protected, proprietary, and contractual basis with member or nonmember firms, Government agencies, and others;

(E) to prosecute applications for patents and render patent services for participating members; and

(F) to negotiate and grant licenses under patents held under the joint program, and to establish corporations designed to exploit particular patents obtained by it.

(2) The Administrator may, after consultation with the Attorney General and the Chairman of the Federal Trade Commission, and with the prior written approval of the Attorney General, approve any agreement between small-business firms

providing for a joint program of research and development, if the Administrator finds that the joint program proposed will maintain and strengthen the free enterprise system and the economy of the Nation. The Administrator or the Attorney General may at any time withdraw his approval of the agreement and the joint program of research and development covered thereby, if he finds that the agreement or the joint program carried on under it is no longer in the best interests of the competitive free enterprise system and the economy of the Nation. A copy of the statement of any such finding and approval intended to be within the coverage of this subsection, and a copy of any modification or withdrawal of approval, shall be published in the Federal Register. The authority conferred by this subsection on the Administrator shall not be delegated by him.

(3) No act or omission to act pursuant to and within the scope of any joint program for research and development, under an agreement approved by the Administrator under this subsection, shall be construed to be within the prohibitions of the antitrust laws or the Federal Trade Commission Act [15 U.S.C.A. § 41 et seq.]. Upon publication in the Federal Register of the notice of withdrawal of his approval of the agreement granted under this subsection, either by the Administrator or by the Attorney General, the provisions of this subsection shall not apply to any subsequent act or omission to act by reason of such agreement or approval.

(e) Definitions

For the purpose of this section —

(1) the term "extramural budget" means the sum of the total obligations minus amounts obligated for such activities by employees of the agency in or through Government-owned, Government-operated facilities, except that for the Department of Energy it shall not include amounts obligated for atomic energy defense programs solely for weapons activities or for naval reactor programs, and except that for the Agency for International Development it shall not include amounts obligated solely for general institutional support of international research centers or for grants to foreign countries;

(2) the term "Federal agency" means an executive agency as defined in section 105 of Title 5 or a military department as defined in section 102 of such title, except that it does not include any agency within the Intelligence Community (as the term is defined in section 3.4(f) of Executive Order 12333 or its successor orders);

(3) the term "funding agreement" means any contract, grant, or cooperative agreement entered into between any Federal agency and any small business for the performance of experimental, developmental, or research work funded in whole or in part by the Federal Government;

(4) the term "Small Business Innovation Research Program" or "SBIR" means a program under which a portion of a Federal agency's research or research and development effort is reserved for award to small business concerns through a uniform process having —

(A) a first phase for determining, insofar as possible, the scientific and technical merit and feasibility of ideas that appear to have commercial potential, as described in subparagraph (B), submitted pursuant to SBIR program solicitations;

(B) a second phase, to further develop proposals which meet particular program needs, in which awards shall be made based on the scientific and technical merit and feasibility of the proposals, as evidenced by the first phase, considering, among other things, the proposal's commercial potential, as evidenced by —

(i) the small business concern's record of successfully commercializing SBIR or other research;

(ii) the existence of second phase funding commitments from private sector or non-SBIR funding sources;

(iii) the existence of third phase, follow-on commitments for the subject of the research; and

(iv) the presence of other indicators of the commercial potential of the idea; and

(C) where appropriate, a third phase —

(i) in which commercial applications of SBIR-funded research or research and development are funded by non-Federal sources of capital or, for products or services intended for use by the Federal Government, by follow-on non-SBIR Federal funding awards; or

(ii) for which awards from non-SBIR Federal funding sources are used for the continuation of research or research and development that has been competitively selected using peer review or scientific review criteria;

(5) the term "research" or "research and development" means any activity which is (A) a systematic, intensive study directed toward greater knowledge or understanding of the subject studied; (B) a systematic study directed specifically toward applying new knowledge to meet a recognized need; or (C) a systematic application of knowledge toward the production of useful materials, devices, and systems or methods, including design, development, and improvement of prototypes and new processes to meet specific requirements;

(6) the term "Small Business Technology Transfer Program" or "STTR" means a program under which a portion of a Federal agency's extramural research or research and development effort is reserved for award to small business concerns for cooperative research and development through a uniform process having —

(A) a first phase, to determine, to the extent possible, the scientific, technical, and commercial merit and feasibility of ideas submitted pursuant to STTR program solicitations;

(B) a second phase, to further develop proposed ideas to meet particular program needs, in which awards shall be made based on the scientific, technical, and commercial merit and feasibility of the idea, as evidenced by the first phase and by other relevant information; and

(C) where appropriate, a third phase —

(i) in which commercial applications of STTR-funded research or research and development are funded by non-Federal sources of capital or, for products or services intended for use by the Federal Government, by follow-on non-STTR Federal funding awards; and

(ii) for which awards from non-STTR Federal funding sources are used for the continuation of research or research and development that has been competitively selected using peer review or scientific review criteria;

(7) the term "cooperative research and development" means research or research and development conducted jointly by a small business concern and a research institution in which not less than 40 percent of the work is performed by the small business concern, and not less than 30 percent of the work is performed by the research institution;

(8) the term "research institution" means a nonprofit institution, as defined in section 3703(5) of this title, and includes federally funded research and development centers, as identified by the National Scientific Foundation in accordance with the government wide Federal Acquisition Regulation issued in accordance with section 421(c)(1) of Title 41 (or any successor regulation thereto); and

(9) the term "commercial applications" shall not be construed to exclude testing and evaluation of products, services, or technologies for use in technical or weapons systems, and further, awards for testing and evaluation of products, services, or technologies for use in technical or weapons systems may be made in either the second or the third phase of the Small Business Innovation Research Program and of the Small Business Technology Transfer Program, as defined in this subsection.

(f) Federal agency expenditures for SBIR program

(1) Required expenditure amounts

Each Federal agency which has an extramural budget for research or research and development in excess of $100,000,000 for fiscal year 1992, or any fiscal year thereafter, shall expend with small business concerns —

(A) not less than 1.5 percent of such budget in each of fiscal years 1993 and 1994;

(B) not less than 2.0 percent of such budget in each of fiscal years 1995 and 1996; and

(C) not less than 2.5 percent of such budget in each fiscal year thereafter,

specifically in connection with SBIR programs which meet the requirements of this section, policy directives, and regulations issued under this section.

(2) Limitations

A Federal agency shall not —

(A) use any of its SBIR budget established pursuant to paragraph (1) for the purpose of funding administrative costs of the program, including costs associated with salaries and expenses; or

(B) make available for the purpose of meeting the requirements of paragraph (1)

an amount of its extramural budget for basic research which exceeds the percentages specified in paragraph (1).

(3) Exclusion of certain funding agreements

Funding agreements with small business concerns for research or research and development which result from competitive or single source selections other than an SBIR program shall not be considered to meet any portion of the percentage requirements of paragraph (1).

(g) Administration of small business innovation research programs by Federal agencies required to establish such programs

Each Federal agency required by subsection (f) of this section to establish a small business innovation research program shall, in accordance with this chapter and regulations issued hereunder —

(1) unilaterally determine categories of projects to be in its SBIR program;

(2) issue small business innovation research solicitations in accordance with a schedule determined cooperatively with the Small Business Administration;

(3) unilaterally determine research topics within the agency's SBIR solicitations, giving special consideration to broad research topics and to topics that further 1 or more critical technologies, as identified by —

(A) the National Critical Technologies Panel (or its successor) in the 1991 report required under section 6683 of Title 42, and in subsequent reports issued under that authority; or

(B) the Secretary of Defense, in the 1992 report issued in accordance with section 2522 of Title 10, and in subsequent reports issued under that authority;

(4) unilaterally receive and evaluate proposals resulting from SBIR proposals;

(5) subject to subsection (l) of this section, unilaterally select awardees for its SBIR funding agreements and inform each awardee under such an agreement, to the extent possible, of the expenses of the awardee that will be allowable under the funding agreement;

(6) administer its own SBIR funding agreements (or delegate such administration to another agency);

(7) make payments to recipients of SBIR funding agreements on the basis of progress toward or completion of the funding agreement requirements and, in all cases, make payment to recipients under such agreements in full, subject to audit, on or before the last day of the 12-month period beginning on the date of completion of such requirements;

(8) make an annual report on the SBIR program to the Small Business Administration and the Office of Science and Technology Policy;

(9) include, as part of its annual performance plan as required by subsections (a) and (b) of section 1115 of Title 31, a section on its SBIR program, and shall submit such section to the Committee on Small Business of the Senate, and the Committee

on Science and the Committee on Small Business of the House of Representatives;

(10) collect, and maintain in a common format in accordance with subsection (v) of this section, such information from awardees as is necessary to assess the SBIR program, including information necessary to maintain the database described in subsection (k) of this section; and

(11) provide for and fully implement the tenets of Executive Order No. 13329 (Encouraging Innovation in Manufacturing).

(h) Establishment of goals for funding agreements for research or research and development to small business concerns by agencies having budgets for research and development

In addition to the requirements of subsection (f) of this section, each Federal agency which has a budget for research or research and development in excess of $20,000,000 for any fiscal year beginning with fiscal year 1983 or subsequent fiscal year shall establish goals specifically for funding agreements for research or research and development to small business concerns, and no goal established under this subsection shall be less than the percentage of the agency's research or research and development budget expended under funding agreements with small business concerns in the immediately preceding fiscal year.

****

(j) Small Business Administration policy directives for the general conduct of small business innovation research programs

(1) Policy directives

The Small Business Administration, after consultation with the Administrator of the Office of Federal Procurement Policy, the Director of the Office of Science and Technology Policy, and the Intergovernmental Affairs Division of the Office of Management and Budget, shall, within one hundred and twenty days of July 22, 1982, issue policy directives for the general conduct of the SBIR programs within the Federal Government, including providing for —

(A) simplified, standardized, and timely SBIR solicitations;

(B) a simplified, standardized funding process which provides for (i) the timely receipt and review of proposals; (ii) outside peer review for at least phase two proposals, if appropriate; (iii) protection of proprietary information provided in proposals; (iv) selection of awardees; (v) retention of rights in data generated in the performance of the contract by the small business concern; (vi) transfer of title to property provided by the agency to the small business concern if such a transfer would be more cost effective than recovery of the property by the agency; (vii) cost sharing; and (viii) cost principles and payment schedules;

(C) exemptions from the regulations under paragraph (2) if national security or intelligence functions clearly would be jeopardized;

(D) minimizing regulatory burden associated with participation in the SBIR program for the small business concern which will stimulate the cost-effective conduct of Federal research and development and the likelihood of commercialization of the results of research and development conducted under the SBIR program;

(E) simplified, standardized, and timely annual report on the SBIR program to the Small Business Administration and the Office of Science and Technology Policy;

(F) standardized and orderly withdrawal from program participation by an agency having a SBIR program; at the discretion of the Administration, such directives may require a phased withdrawal over a period of time sufficient in duration to minimize any adverse impact on small business concerns; and

(G) the voluntary participation in a SBIR program by a Federal agency not required to establish such a program pursuant to subsection (f) of this section.

(2) Modifications

****

(3) Additional modifications

****

(k) Database

(1) Public database

Not later than 180 days after December 21, 2000, the Administrator shall develop, maintain, and make available to the public a searchable, up-to-date, electronic database that includes —

(A) the name, size, location, and an identifying number assigned by the Administrator, of each small business concern that has received a first phase or second phase SBIR or STTR award from a Federal agency;

(B) a description of each first phase or second phase SBIR or STTR award received by that small business concern, including —

(i) an abstract of the project funded by the award, excluding any proprietary information so identified by the small business concern;

(ii) the Federal agency making the award; and

(iii) the date and amount of the award;

(C) an identification of any business concern or subsidiary established for the commercial application of a product or service for which an SBIR or STTR award is made;

(D) information regarding mentors and Mentoring Networks, as required by section 657e(d) of this title; and

(E) with respect to assistance under the STTR program only —

(i) whether the small business concern or the research institution initiated their collaboration on each assisted STTR project;

(ii) whether the small business concern or the research institution originated any technology relating to the assisted STTR project;

(iii) the length of time it took to negotiate any licensing agreement between the small business concern and the research institution under each assisted STTR project; and

(iv) how the proceeds from commercialization, marketing, or sale of technology resulting from each assisted STTR project were allocated (by percentage) between the small business concern and the research institution.

****

(n) Required expenditures for STTR by Federal agencies

(1) Required expenditure amounts

(A) In general

(i) Federal agencies generally

Except as provided in clause (ii), with respect to each fiscal year through fiscal year 2009, each Federal agency that has an extramural budget for research, or research and development, in excess of $1,000,000,000 for that fiscal year, shall expend with small business concerns not less than the percentage of that extramural budget specified in subparagraph (B), specifically in connection with STTR programs that meet the requirements of this section and any policy directives and regulations issued under this section.

(ii) Department of Defense

The Secretary of Defense and the Secretary of each military department shall carry out clause (i) with respect to each fiscal year through fiscal year 2010.

(B) Expenditure amounts

The percentage of the extramural budget required to be expended by an agency in accordance with subparagraph (A) shall be —

(i) 0.15 percent for each fiscal year through fiscal year 2003; and

(ii) 0.3 percent for fiscal year 2004 and each fiscal year thereafter.

****

(p) STTR policy directive

(1) Issuance

The Administrator shall issue a policy directive for the general conduct of the STTR programs within the Federal Government. Such policy directive shall be issued after consultation with —

(A) the heads of each of the Federal agencies required by subsection (n) of this section to establish an STTR program;

(B) the Under Secretary of Commerce for Intellectual Property and Director of the United States Patent and Trademark Office; and

(C) the Director of the Office of Federal Procurement Policy.

(2) Contents

The policy directive required by paragraph (1) shall provide for —

(A) simplified, standardized, and timely STTR solicitations;

(B) a simplified, standardized funding process that provides for —

(i) the timely receipt and review of proposals;

(ii) outside peer review, if appropriate;

(iii) protection of proprietary information provided in proposals;

(iv) selection of awardees;

(v) retention by a small business concern of the rights to data generated by the concern in the performance of an STTR award for a period of not less than 4 years;

(vi) continued use by a small business concern, as a directed bailment, of any property transferred by a Federal agency to the small business concern in the second phase of the STTR program for a period of not less than 2 years, beginning on the initial date of the concern's participation in the third phase of such program;

(vii) cost sharing;

(viii) cost principles and payment schedules; and

(ix) 1-year awards for the first phase of an STTR program, generally not to exceed $100,000, and 2-year awards for the second phase of an STTR program, generally not to exceed $750,000, greater or lesser amounts to be awarded at the discretion of the awarding agency, and shorter or longer periods of time to be approved at the discretion of the awarding agency where appropriate for a particular project;

(C) minimizing regulatory burdens associated with participation in STTR programs;

(D) guidelines for a model agreement, to be used by all agencies, for allocating between small business concerns and research institutions intellectual property rights and rights, if any, to carry out follow-on research, development, or commercialization;

****

(r) Third phase agreements

(1) In general

In the case of a small business concern that is awarded a funding agreement for the second phase of an SBIR or STTR program, a Federal agency may enter into a third phase agreement with that business concern for additional work to be performed during or after the second phase period. The second phase funding agreement with the small business concern may, at the discretion of the agency awarding the agreement, set out the procedures applicable to third phase agreements with that agency or any other agency.

(2) "Third phase agreement" defined

In this subsection, the term "third phase agreement" means a follow-on, non-SBIR or non-STTR funded contract as described in paragraph (4)(C) or paragraph (6)(C) of subsection (e) of this section.

(3) Intellectual property rights

Each funding agreement under an SBIR or STTR program shall include provisions setting forth the respective rights of the United States and the small business concern with respect to intellectual property rights and with respect to any right to carry out follow-on research.

****

QUESTIONS

1.   For what purposes may the SBA Administrator authorize SBCs to undertake joint research and development programs? What is required for approval of joint SBC programs?

2.   What federal agencies are specifically excluded from the SBIR and STTR programs? Why are these agencies excluded?

3.   What factors are considered in determining the commercial potential of a Phase II application?

4.   How is the eligibility of research projects for SBIR or STTR funding determined? How is the availability of these research projects made known to SBCs?

5.   How are SBIR and STTR projects administered? What is the role of the Small Business Administration in the SBIR and STTR programs?

6. What does the Act provide regarding SBC intellectual property rights and SBC rights to conduct follow-on research?

11.1.3 SBA SBIR Policy Directive

As seen above, 15 USCA § 638(j) provides that the Small Business Administration (SBA) shall issue policy directives for the general conduct of the federal agencies' SBIR programs. Section 638(j) further provides that these policy directives shall be developed by the SBA after consultation with the Administrator of the Office of Federal Procurement Policy (grants and contracts issued under the SBIR program are treated as federal procurements and subject to the Federal Acquisition Regulations or FARs), the Director of the Office of Science and Technology Policy, and the Intergovernmental Affairs Division of the Office of Management and Budget. The fundamental objectives of the SBA SBIR policy directives are to establish a simplified, standardized and timely process for the issuance of SBIR solicitations, the selection of SBIR awardees, and the funding of SBIR projects. Below is the SBA SBIR Policy Directive issued in 2002.

SBIR POLICY DIRECTIVE
67 Fed. Reg. 60072 (2002)

Small Business Administration

Small Business Innovation Research Program Policy Directive

SUMMARY: This document revises the Small Business Innovation Research (SBIR) Program Policy Directive. This revised Policy Directive reflects statutory amendments to the SBIR Program and provides guidance to Federal agencies for the general conduct of the program.

****

Notice of Final Policy Directive; Small Business Innovation Research Program

To: The Small Business Innovation Research Program Directors.

Subject: Small Business Reauthorization Act of 2000 (Reauthorization Act) — Amendments to the Small Business Innovation Research Program.

1. Purpose. Section 9(j)(3) of the Small Business Act (15 U.S.C. 638(j)(3)) (as amended by Public Law 106-554) requires the Administrator of the U.S. Small Business Administration (SBA) to modify its Small Business Innovation Research (SBIR) Program Policy Directive, issued for the general conduct of the SBIR Program.

2. Authority. This Policy Directive is issued pursuant to 15 U.S.C. 638(j).

3. Procurement Regulations. It is recognized that the Federal Acquisition Regulations may need to be modified to conform to the requirements of the Reauthorization Act and the final Policy Directive. SBA's Administrator or designee

must review and concur with any regulatory provisions that pertain to areas of SBA responsibility. SBA's Office of Technology coordinates such regulatory actions.

4. Personnel Concerned. This Policy Directive serves as guidance for all federal government personnel who are involved in the administration of the SBIR Program, issuance and management of funding agreements or contracts pursuant to the SBIR Program, and the establishment of goals for small business concerns in research or research and development acquisition or grants.

Contents

Section

1. Purpose

2. Summary of Legislative Provisions

3. Definitions

4. Competitively Phased Structure of the Program

5. Program Solicitation Process

6. Eligibility and Application (Proposal) Requirements

7. SBIR Funding Process

8. Terms of Agreement Under SBIR Awards

9. Responsibilities of SBIR Participating Agencies and Departments

10. Annual Report to the Small Business Administration (SBA)

11. Responsibilities of SBA

12. Federal and State Technology (FAST) Partnership Program and Outreach Program

Appendix I: Instructions for SBIR Program Solicitation Preparation

Appendix II: Tech-Net Data Fields for Public Database

1. Purpose

(a) Section 9(j) of the Small Business Act (Act) requires that the Small Business Administration (SBA) issue an SBIR Program Policy Directive for the general conduct of the SBIR Program within the Federal Government.

(b) This Policy Directive fulfills SBA's statutory obligation to provide guidance to the participating Federal agencies for the general operation of the SBIR Program. Additional or modified instructions may be issued by the SBA as a result of public comment or experience.

(c) The statutory purpose of the SBIR Program is to strengthen the role of innovative small business concerns (SBCs) in Federally-funded research or research and development (R/R&D). Specific program purposes are to: (1)

Stimulate technological innovation; (2) use small business to meet Federal R/R&D needs; (3) foster and encourage participation by socially and economically disadvantaged SBCs, and by SBCs that are 51 percent owned and controlled by women, in technological innovation; and (4) increase private sector commercialization of innovations derived from Federal R/R&D, thereby increasing competition, productivity and economic growth.

(d) Federal agencies participating in the SBIR Program (SBIR agencies) are obligated to follow the guidance provided by this Policy Directive. Each agency is required to review its rules, policies, and guidance on the SBIR Program to ensure consistency with this Policy Directive and to make any necessary changes in accordance with each agency's normal procedures. This is consistent with the statutory authority provided to the SBA concerning the SBIR Program.

****

3. Definitions

****

(c) Small Business Concern. A concern that, on the date of award for both Phase I and Phase II funding agreements:

(1) Is organized for profit, with a place of business located in the United States, which operates primarily within the United States or which makes a significant contribution to the United States economy through payment of taxes or use of American products, materials or labor;

(2) Is in the legal form of an individual proprietorship, partnership, limited liability company, corporation, joint venture, association, trust or cooperative, except that where the form is a joint venture, there can be no more than 49 percent participation by foreign business entities in the joint venture;

(3) Is at least 51 percent owned and controlled by one or more individuals who are citizens of, or permanent resident aliens in, the United States, except in the case of a joint venture, where each entity to the venture must be 51 percent owned and controlled by one or more individuals who are citizens of, or permanent resident aliens in, the United States; and

(4) Has, including its affiliates, not more than 500 employees

****

4. Competitively Phased Structure of the Program

The SBIR Program is a phased process, uniform throughout the Federal Government, of soliciting proposals and awarding funding agreements for R/R&D, production, services, or any combination, to meet stated agency needs or missions. In order to stimulate and foster scientific and technological innovation, including increasing commercialization of Federal R/R&D, the program must follow a uniform competitive process of the following three phases:

(a) Phase I. Phase I involves a solicitation of contract proposals or grant applications (hereinafter referred to as proposals) to conduct feasibility-related experimental or theoretical R/R&D related to described agency requirements. These requirements, as defined by agency topics contained in a solicitation, may be general or narrow in scope, depending on the needs of the agency. The object of this phase is to determine the scientific and technical merit and feasibility of the proposed effort and the quality of performance of the SBC with a relatively small agency investment before consideration of further Federal support in Phase II.

(1) Several different proposed solutions to a given problem may be funded.

(2) Proposals will be evaluated on a competitive basis. Agency criteria used to evaluate SBIR proposals must give consideration to the scientific and technical merit and feasibility of the proposal along with its potential for commercialization. Considerations may also include program balance or critical agency requirements.

(3) Agencies may require the submission of a Phase II proposal as a deliverable item under Phase I.

(b) Phase II. The object of Phase II is to continue the R/R&D effort from the completed Phase I. Only SBIR awardees in Phase I are eligible to participate in Phases II and III. This includes those awardees identified via a "novated" or "successor in interest" or similarly-revised funding agreement, or those that have reorganized with the same key staff, regardless of whether they have been assigned a different tax identification number. Agencies may require the original awardee to relinquish its rights and interests in an SBIR project in favor of another applicant as a condition for that applicant's eligibility to participate in the SBIR Program for that project.

(1) Funding must be based upon the results of Phase I and the scientific and technical merit and commercial potential of the Phase II proposal. Phase II awards may not necessarily complete the total research and development that may be required to satisfy commercial or Federal needs beyond the SBIR Program. The Phase II funding agreement with the awardee may, at the discretion of the awarding agency, establish the procedures applicable to Phase III agreements. The Government is not obligated to fund any specific Phase II proposal.

(2) The SBIR Phase II award decision process requires, among other things, consideration of a proposal's commercial potential. Commercial potential includes the potential to transition the technology to private sector applications, Government applications, or Government contractor applications. Commercial potential in a Phase II proposal may be evidenced by:

(i) the SBC's record of successfully commercializing SBIR or other research;

(ii) the existence of Phase II funding commitments from private sector or other non-SBIR funding sources;

(iii) the existence of Phase III, follow-on commitments for the subject of the research; and

(iv) other indicators of commercial potential of the idea.

(c) Phase III. SBIR Phase III refers to work that derives from, extends, or logically concludes effort(s) performed under prior SBIR funding agreements, but is funded by sources other than the SBIR Program. Phase III work is typically oriented towards commercialization of SBIR research or technology.

(1) Each of the following types of activity constitutes SBIR Phase III work:

(i) commercial application of SBIR-funded R/R&D financed by non-Federal sources of capital (Note: The guidance in this Policy Directive regarding SBIR Phase III pertains to the non-SBIR federally-funded work described in (ii) and (iii) below. It does not address the nature of private agreements the SBIR firm may make in the commercialization of its technology.);

(ii) SBIR-derived products or services intended for use by the Federal Government, funded by non-SBIR sources of Federal funding;

(iii) continuation of R/R&D that has been competitively selected using peer review or scientific review criteria, funded by non-SBIR Federal funding sources.

(2) A Phase III award is, by its nature, an SBIR award, has SBIR status, and must be accorded SBIR data rights. (See Section 8(b)(2) regarding the protection period for data rights.) If an SBIR awardee wins a competition for work that derives from, extends, or logically concludes that firm's work under a prior SBIR funding agreement, then the funding agreement for the new, competed work must have all SBIR Phase III status and data rights. A Federal agency may enter into a Phase III SBIR agreement at any time with a Phase II awardee. Similarly, a Federal agency may enter into a Phase III SBIR agreement at any time with a Phase I awardee. An agency official may determine, using the criteria set forth in the Directive as guidance, whether a contract or agreement is a Phase III award.

(3) The competition for SBIR Phase I and Phase II awards satisfies any competition requirement of the Armed Services Procurement Act, the Federal Property and Administrative Services Act, and the Competition in Contracting Act. Therefore, an agency that wishes to fund an SBIR Phase III project is not required to conduct another competition in order to satisfy those statutory provisions. As a result, in conducting actions relative to a Phase III SBIR award, it is sufficient to state for purposes of a Justification and Approval pursuant to FAR 6.302-5, that the project is a SBIR Phase III award that is derived from, extends, or logically concludes efforts performed under prior SBIR funding agreements and is authorized under 10 U.S.C. 2304(b)(2) or 41 U.S.C. 253(b)(2).

(4) Phase III work may be for products, production, services, R/R&D, or any combination thereof.

(5) There is no limit on the number, duration, type, or dollar value of Phase III awards made to a business concern. There is no limit on the time that may elapse between a Phase I or Phase II award and Phase III award, or between a Phase III award and any subsequent Phase III award.

(6) The small business size limits for Phase I and Phase II awards do not apply to Phase III awards.

(7) For Phase III, Congress intends that agencies or their Government-owned, contractor-operated facilities, Federally-funded research and development centers, or Government prime contractors that pursue R/R&D or production developed under the SBIR Program, give preference, including sole source awards, to the awardee that developed the technology. In fact, the Act requires reporting to SBA of all instances in which an agency pursues research, development, or production of a technology developed by an SBIR awardee, with a concern other than the one that developed the SBIR technology. (See Section 4(c)(7) immediately below for agency notification to SBA prior to award of such a funding agreement and Section 9(a)(12) regarding agency reporting of the issuance of such award.) SBA will report such instances, including those discovered independently by SBA, to Congress.

(8) For Phase III, agencies, their Government-owned, contractor-operated facilities, or Federally-funded research and development centers, that intend to pursue R/R&D, production, services, or any combination thereof of a technology developed by an SBIR awardee of that agency, with an entity other than that SBIR awardee, must notify SBA in writing prior to such an award. This notice requirement also applies to technologies of SBIR awardees with SBIR funding from two or more agencies where one of the agencies determines to pursue the technology with an entity other than that awardee. This notification must include, at a minimum: (a) The reasons why the follow-on funding agreement with the SBIR awardee is not practicable; (b) the identity of the entity with which the agency intends to make an award to perform research, development, or production; and (c) a description of the type of funding award under which the research, development, or production will be obtained. SBA may appeal the decision to the head of the contracting activity. If SBA decides to appeal the decision, it must file a notice of intent to appeal with the contracting officer no later than 5 business days after receiving the agency's notice of intent to make award. Upon receipt of SBA's notice of intent to appeal, the contracting officer must suspend further action on the acquisition until the head of the contracting activity issues a written decision on the appeal. The contracting officer may proceed with award if he or she determines in writing that the award must be made to protect the public interest. The contracting officer must include a statement of the facts justifying that determination and provide a copy of its determination to SBA. Within 30 days of receiving SBA's appeal, the head of the contracting activity must render a written decision setting forth the basis of his or her determination.

5. Program Solicitation Process

(a) At least annually, each agency must issue a program solicitation that sets forth a substantial number of R/R&D topics and subtopic areas consistent with stated agency needs or missions. Both the list of topics and the description of the topics and subtopics must be sufficiently comprehensive to provide a wide range of opportunities for SBCs to participate in the agency R&D programs. Topics and subtopics must emphasize the need for proposals with advanced concepts to meet specific agency R/R&D needs. Each topic and subtopic must describe the needs in sufficient detail to assist in providing on-target responses, but cannot involve detailed specifications to prescribed solutions of the problems.

(b) The Act requires issuance of SBIR (Phase I) Program solicitations in accordance with a Master Schedule coordinated between SBA and the SBIR agency. The SBA office responsible for coordination is: Office of Technology, Office of Government Contracting, Office of Government Contracting and Business Development, U.S. Small Business Administration, 409 Third Street, SW., Washington, DC 20416. Phone: (202) 205-6450. Fax: (202) 205-7754. E-mail: technology@sba.gov. Internet site: www.sba.gov/sbir.

(c) For maximum participation by interested SBCs, it is important that the planning, scheduling and coordination of agency program solicitation release dates be completed as early as practicable to coincide with the commencement of the fiscal year on October 1. Bunching of agency program solicitation release and closing dates may prohibit SBCs from preparation and timely submission of proposals for more than one SBIR project. SBA's coordination of agency schedules minimizes the bunching of proposed release and closing dates. Participating agencies may elect to publish multiple program solicitations within a given fiscal year to facilitate in-house agency proposal review and evaluation scheduling.

****

6. Eligibility and Application (Proposal) Requirements

(a) Eligibility Requirements:

(1) To receive SBIR funds, each awardee of a SBIR Phase I or Phase II award must qualify as an SBC.

(2) For Phase I, a minimum of two-thirds of the research or analytical effort must be performed by the awardee. Occasionally, deviations from this requirement may occur, and must be approved in writing by the funding agreement officer after consultation with the agency SBIR Program Manager/Coordinator.

(3) For Phase II, a minimum of one-half of the research or analytical effort must be performed by the awardee. Occasionally, deviations from this requirement may occur, and must be approved in writing by the funding agreement officer after consultation with the agency SBIR Program Manager/Coordinator.

(4) For both Phase I and Phase II, the primary employment of the principal investigator must be with the SBC at the time of award and during the conduct of the proposed project. Primary employment means that more than one-half of the principal investigator's time is spent in the employ of the SBC. This precludes full-time employment with another organization. Occasionally, deviations from this requirement may occur, and must be approved in writing by the funding agreement officer after consultation with the agency SBIR Program Manager/Coordinator. Further, an SBC may replace the principal investigator on an SBIR Phase I or Phase II award, subject to approval in writing by the funding agreement officer. For purposes of the SBIR Program, personnel obtained through a Professional Employer Organization or other similar personnel leasing company may be considered employees of the awardee. This is consistent with SBA's size regulations, 13 CFR 121.106 — Small Business Size Regulations.

(5) For both Phase I and Phase II, the R/R&D work must be performed in the United States. However, based on a rare and unique circumstance, agencies may approve a particular portion of the R/R&D work to be performed or obtained in a country outside of the United States, for example, if a supply or material or other item or project requirement is not available in the United States. The funding agreement officer must approve each such specific condition in writing.

(b) Proposal Requirements:

(1) Documentation of commercialization record of firms with multiple Phase II awards. An SBC submitting a proposal for a funding agreement for Phase I of an SBIR Program that has received more than 15 Phase II SBIR awards during the preceding 5 fiscal years must document the extent to which it was able to secure Phase III funding to develop concepts resulting from previous Phase II SBIR awards.

(2) Commercialization Plan. A succinct commercialization plan must be included with each proposal for an SBIR Phase II award moving toward commercialization. Elements of a commercialization plan may include the following:

(i) Company information: Focused objectives/core competencies; size; specialization area(s); products with significant sales; and history of previous Federal and non-Federal funding, regulatory experience, and subsequent commercialization.

(ii) Customer and Competition: Clear description of key technology objectives, current competition, and advantages compared to competing products or services; description of hurdles to acceptance of the innovation.

(iii) Market: Milestones, target dates, analyses of market size, and estimated market share after first year sales and after 5 years; explanation of plan to obtain market share.

(iv) Intellectual Property: Patent status, technology lead, trade secrets or other demonstration of a plan to achieve sufficient protection to realize the commercialization stage and attain at least a temporal competitive advantage.

(v) Financing: Plans for securing necessary funding in Phase III.

(vi) Assistance and mentoring: Plans for securing needed technical or business assistance through mentoring, partnering, or through arrangements with state assistance programs, SBDCs, Federally-funded research laboratories, Manufacturing Extension Partnership centers, or other assistance providers.

(3) Data Collection: Each Phase II applicant will be required to provide information to the Tech-Net Database System (http://technet.sba.gov). See Appendix I, Section 3(c), "Data Collection Requirement," for additional information.

7. SBIR Funding Process

Because the Act requires a "simplified, standardized funding process," specific attention must be given to the following areas of SBIR Program administration:

(a) Timely Receipt and Review of Proposals.

(1) Participating agencies must establish appropriate dates and formats for review of proposals.

(i) All activities related to Phase I proposal reviews must normally be completed and awards made within 6 months from the closing date of the program solicitation. However, agencies may extend that period up to 12 months based on agency needs.

(ii) Program solicitations must establish proposal submission dates for Phase I and may establish proposal submission dates for Phase II. However, agencies may also negotiate mutually acceptable Phase II proposal submission dates with individual Phase I awardees, accomplish proposal reviews expeditiously, and proceed with Phase II awards. While recognizing that Phase II arrangements between the agency and applicant may require more detailed negotiation to establish terms acceptable to both parties, agencies must not sacrifice the R/R&D momentum created under Phase I by engaging in unnecessarily protracted Phase II proceedings.

(iii) SBIR participants often submit duplicate or similar proposals to more than one soliciting agency when the work projects appear to involve similar topics or requirements, which are within the expertise and capability levels of the applicant. To the extent feasible, more than one agency should not fund "essentially equivalent work" under the SBIR or other Federal programs. For this purpose, the standardized program solicitation will require applicants to indicate the name and address of the agencies to which essentially equivalent work proposals were made, or anticipated to be made, and to identify by subject the projects for which the proposal was submitted and the dates submitted. The same information will be required for any previous Federal Government awards. To assist in avoiding duplicate funding, each agency must provide to SBA and to each SBIR agency a listing of Phase I and Phase II awardees, their complete address, and the title of each SBIR project. This information should be distributed no later than release of the funding agreement award information to the public.

(b) Review of SBIR Proposals. SBA encourages SBIR agencies to use their routine review processes for SBIR proposals whether internal or external evaluation is used. A more limited review process may be used for Phase I due to the larger number of proposals anticipated. Where appropriate, "peer" reviews external to the agency are authorized by the Act. SBA cautions SBIR agencies that all review procedures must be designed to minimize any possible conflict of interest as it pertains to applicant proprietary data. The standardized SBIR solicitation advises potential applicants that proposals may be subject to an established external review process and that the applicant may include company designated proprietary information in its proposal.

(c) Selection of Awardees. Normally, SBIR agencies must establish a proposal review cycle wherein successful and unsuccessful applicants will be notified of final award decisions within 6-months of the agency's Phase I proposal closing date. However, agencies may extend that period up to 12 months based on agency needs.

(1) The standardized SBIR Program solicitation must:

(i) Advise Phase I applicants that additional information may be requested by the awarding agency to evidence awardee responsibility for project completion.

(ii) Advise applicants of the proposal evaluation criteria for Phase I and Phase II.

(2) The SBIR agency and each Phase I awardee considered for a Phase II award must arrange to manage Phase II proposal submissions, reviews, and selections.

(d) Cost Sharing. Cost sharing can serve the mutual interests of the SBIR agencies and certain SBIR awardees by assuring the efficient use of available resources. However, cost sharing on SBIR projects is not required, although it may be encouraged. Therefore, cost sharing cannot be an evaluation factor in the review of proposals. The standardized SBIR Program solicitation (Appendix I) will provide information to prospective SBIR applicants concerning cost sharing.

(e) Payment Schedules and Cost Principles.

(1) SBIR awardees may be paid under an applicable, authorized progress payment procedure or in accordance with a negotiated/definitized price and payment schedule. Advance payments are optional and may be made under appropriate law. In all cases, agencies must make payment to recipients under SBIR funding agreements in full, subject to audit, on or before the last day of the 12-month period beginning on the date of completion of the funding agreement requirements.

(2) All SBIR funding agreements must use, as appropriate, current cost principles and procedures authorized for use by the SBIR agencies. At the time of award, agencies must inform each SBIR awardee, to the extent possible, of the applicable Federal regulations and procedures that refer to the costs that, generally, are allowable under funding agreements.

(f) Funding Agreement Types and Fee or Profit. Statutory requirements for uniformity and standardization require consistency in application of SBIR Program provisions among SBIR agencies. However, consistency must allow for flexibility by the various agencies in missions and needs as well as the wide variance in funds required to be devoted to SBIR Programs in the agencies. The following instructions meet all of these requirements:

(1) Funding Agreement. The type of funding agreement (contract, grant, or cooperative agreement) is determined by the awarding agency, but must be consistent with 31 U.S.C. 6301–6308.

(2) Fee or Profit. Except as expressly excluded or limited by statute, awarding agencies must provide for a reasonable fee or profit on SBIR funding agreements, consistent with normal profit margins provided to profit-making firms for R/R&D work.

(g) Periods of Performance and Extensions.

(1) In keeping with the legislative intent to make a large number of relatively small awards, modification of funding agreements to extend periods of performance, to increase the scope of work, or to increase the dollar amount should be kept to a minimum, except for options in original Phase I or II awards.

(2) Phase I. Period of performance normally should not exceed 6 months. However, agencies may provide a longer performance period where appropriate for a particular project.

(3) Phase II. Period of performance under Phase II is a subject of negotiation between the awardee and the issuing agency. The duration of Phase II normally should not exceed 2 years. However, agencies may provide a longer performance period where appropriate for a particular project.

(h) Dollar Value of Awards.

(1) Generally, a Phase I award may not exceed $100,000 and a Phase II award may not exceed $750,000. SBA may adjust these amounts once every 5 years to reflect economic adjustments and programmatic considerations. There is no dollar level associated with Phase III SBIR awards.

(2) An awarding agency may exceed those award values where appropriate for a particular project. After award of any funding agreement exceeding $100,000 for Phase I or $750,000 for Phase II, the agency's SBIR representative must provide SBA with written justification of such action. This justification must be submitted with the agency's Annual Report data. Similar justification is required for any modification to a funding agreement that would bring the cumulative dollar amount to a total in excess of the amounts set forth above.

(i) National Security Exemption. The Act provides for exemptions related to the simplified standardized funding process "* * * if national security or intelligence functions clearly would be jeopardized." This exemption should not be interpreted as a blanket exemption or prohibition of SBIR participation related to the acquisition of effort on national security or intelligence functions except as specifically defined under section 9(e)(2) of the Act, 15 U.S.C. 638(e)(2). Agency technology managers directing R/R&D projects under the SBIR Program, where the project subject matter may be affected by this exemption, must first make a determination on which, if any, of the standardized proceedings clearly place national security and intelligence functions in jeopardy, and then proceed with an acceptable modified process to complete the SBIR action. SBA's SBIR Program monitoring activities, except where prohibited by security considerations, must include a review of nonconforming SBIR actions justified under this public law provision.

8. Terms of Agreement Under SBIR Awards

(a) Proprietary Information Contained in Proposals. The standardized SBIR Program solicitation will include provisions requiring the confidential treatment of any proprietary information to the extent permitted by law. Agencies will discourage SBCs from submitting information considered proprietary unless the information is deemed essential for proper evaluation of the proposal. The solicitation will require that all proprietary information be identified clearly and marked with a prescribed legend. Agencies may elect to require SBCs to limit proprietary information to that essential to the proposal and to have such information submitted on a separate page or pages keyed to the text. The Government, except for proposal review purposes, protects all proprietary information, regardless of type, submitted in a contract proposal or grant application for a funding agreement under the SBIR Program, from disclosure.

(b) Rights in Data Developed Under SBIR Funding Agreement. The Act provides for "retention by an SBC of the rights to data generated by the concern in the performance of an SBIR award."

(1) Each agency must refrain from disclosing SBIR technical data to outside the Government (except reviewers) and especially to competitors of the SBC, or from using the information to produce future technical procurement specifications that could harm the SBC that discovered and developed the innovation.

(2) SBIR agencies must protect from disclosure and non-governmental use all SBIR technical data developed from work performed under an SBIR funding agreement for a period of not less than four years from delivery of the last deliverable under that agreement (either Phase I, Phase II, or Federally-funded SBIR Phase III) unless, subject to (b)(3) of this section, the agency obtains permission to disclose such SBIR technical data from the awardee or SBIR applicant. Agencies are released from obligation to protect SBIR data upon expiration of the protection period except that any such data that is also protected and referenced under a subsequent SBIR award must remain protected through the protection period of that subsequent SBIR award. For example, if a Phase III award is issued within or after the Phase II data rights protection period and the Phase III award refers to and protects data developed and protected under the Phase II award, then that data must continue to be protected through the Phase III protection period. Agencies have discretion to adopt a protection period longer than four years. The Government retains a royalty-free license for Government use of any technical data delivered under an SBIR award, whether patented or not. This section does not apply to program evaluation.

(3) SBIR technical data rights apply to all SBIR awards, including subcontracts to such awards, that fall within the statutory definition of Phase I, II, or III of the SBIR Program, as described in Section 4 of this Policy Directive. The scope and extent of the SBIR technical data rights applicable to Federally-funded Phase III awards is identical to the SBIR data rights applicable to Phases I and II SBIR awards. The data rights protection period lapses only: (i) Upon expiration of the protection period applicable to the SBIR award, or (ii) by agreement between the awardee and the agency.

(4) Agencies must insert the provisions of (b)(1), (2), and (3) immediately above as SBIR data rights clauses into all SBIR Phase I, Phase II, and Phase III awards. These data rights clauses are non-negotiable and must not be the subject of negotiations pertaining to an SBIR Phase III award, or diminished or removed during award administration. An agency must not, in any way, make issuance of an SBIR Phase III award conditional on data rights. If the SBIR awardee wishes to transfer its SBIR data rights to the awarding agency or to a third party, it must do so in writing under a separate agreement. A decision by the awardee to relinquish, transfer, or modify in any way its SBIR data rights must be made without pressure or coercion by the agency or any other party. Following issuance of an SBIR Phase III award, the awardee may enter into an agreement with the awarding agency to transfer or modify the data rights contained in that SBIR Phase III award. Such a

bilateral data rights agreement must be entered into only after the SBIR Phase III award, which includes the appropriate SBIR data rights clause, has been signed. SBA must immediately report to the Congress any attempt or action by an agency to condition an SBIR award on data rights, to exclude the appropriate data rights clause from the award, or to diminish such rights.

(c) Title Transfer of Agency-Provided Property. Under the Act, the Government may transfer title to equipment provided by the SBIR agency to the awardee where such transfer would be more cost effective than recovery of the property.

(d) Continued Use of Government Equipment. The Act directs that an agency allow an SBIR awardee participating in the third phase of the SBIR Program continued use, as a directed bailment, of any property transferred by the agency to the Phase II awardee. The Phase II awardee may use the property for a period of not less than 2 years, beginning on the initial date of the concern's participation in the third phase of the SBIR Program.

(e) Grant Authority. The Act does not, in and of itself, convey grant authority. Each agency must secure grant authority in accordance with its normal procedures.

(f) Conflicts of Interest. SBA cautions SBIR agencies that awards made to SBCs owned by or employing current or previous Federal Government employees may create conflicts of interest in violation of FAR Part 3 and the Ethics in Government Act of 1978, as amended. Each SBIR agency should refer to the standards of conduct review procedures currently in effect for its agency to ensure that such conflicts of interest do not arise.

(g) American-Made Equipment and Products. Congress intends that the awardee of a funding agreement under the SBIR Program should, when purchasing any equipment or a product with funds provided through the funding agreement, purchase only American-made equipment and products, to the extent possible, in keeping with the overall purposes of this program. Each SBIR agency must provide to each awardee a notice of this requirement.

QUESTIONS

1. To whom is the SBA SBIR Policy Directive directed?

2. The Policy Directive states "The statutory purpose of the SBIR Program is to strengthen the role of innovative small business concerns (SBCs) in Federally-funded research or research and development (R/R&D)." It then sets forth a list of more specific SBIR program purposes. What are these more specific SBIR program purposes?

3. Can a foreign business entity participate in the SBIR program?

4. In evaluating Phase I proposals, what criteria does the Policy Directive require the reviewing agency to consider? Are these criteria consistent? If not, how does the Policy Directive instruct the reviewing agency to prioritize these criteria?

5. In evaluating the commercial potential of Phase II proposals, what criteria does the Policy Directive suggest the reviewing agencies use?

6. What types of work may qualify as Phase III work? Must a federal agency that wants to award a Phase III contract to a SBC first submit the contract for competitive bidding?

7. What is a SBIR program solicitation Master Schedule? Who is responsible for developing a Master Schedule?

8. How much time must the Principal Investigator (PI) in a Phase I and Phase II project devote to the SBC? Could a university faculty member retain a tenured position while serving as a PI on a Phase I or Phase II project?

9. A Phase II proposal must include a commercialization plan. What should be included in a Phase II commercialization plan?

10. What is the normal review and notification cycle for Phase I proposals?

11.1.4   SBA STTR Policy Directive

The provisions of the STTR Policy Directive are similar in most respects to the provisions of the SBIR Policy Directive and, therefore, are not repeated here. Some of the differences between the SBIR program and the STTR program are the following: eleven federal agencies participate in the SBIR program, while only five federal agencies participate in the STTR program; under the SBIR program, a minimum of 66.6% of awarded funds must be spent on work performed by the SBC whereas, under the STTR program, a minimum of 40% of awarded funds must be spent on work performed by the SBC; the Phase I period in the SBIR program is generally six months, while the Phase I period in the STTR program can be up to one year; the principal investigators in the SBIR program must devote the majority of their time (>50%) to work with the SBC, while the principal investigators in the STTR program can share their time in any amount between the SBC and the collaborating research institution.

Probably the most significant difference between the STTR Program and the SBIR Program is that the STTR Program requires the SBC to enter into a research partnership with a research institution, which is most often a university. As part of this research partnership, the SBC and the research institution must enter into an Allocation of Rights agreement prior to receiving an STTR award. The excerpt below sets forth the terms of an SBC agreement with a partnering research institution.

STTR POLICY DIRECTIVE
70 Fed. Reg. 74926 (2005)

Small Business Administration

Small Business Technology Transfer Program Policy Directive

8. Terms of Agreement Under STTR Award

****

(c) Allocation of Rights.

(1) An SBC, before receiving an STTR award, must negotiate a written agreement between the SBC and the single, partnering research institution, allocating intellectual property rights and rights, if any, to carry out follow-on research, development, or commercialization. The SBC must submit this agreement to the awarding agency upon request — either with the proposal or any time thereafter. The SBC must certify in all proposals that the agreement is satisfactory to the SBC.

(2) The awarding agency may accept an existing agreement between the two parties if the SBC certifies its satisfaction with the agreement, and such agreement does not conflict with the interests of the Government. Each agency participating in the STTR Program shall provide a model agreement to be used as guidance by the SBC in the development of an agreement with the research institution. The model agreement should direct the parties to, at a minimum:

(i) State specifically the degree of responsibility, and ownership of any product, process, or other invention or innovation resulting from the cooperative research. The degree of responsibility shall include responsibility for expenses and liability, and the degree of ownership shall also include the specific rights to revenues and profits.

(ii) State which party may obtain United States or foreign patents or otherwise protect any inventions resulting from the cooperative research.

(iii) State which party has the right to any continuation of research, including non-STTR follow-on awards.

The Government will not normally be a party to any agreement between the SBC and the research institution. Nothing in the agreement is to conflict with any provisions setting forth the respective rights of the United States and the SBC with respect to intellectual property rights and with respect to any right to carry out follow-on research.

QUESTION

1. Recall Revenue Procedure 2007-47 and its prohibition on transferring intellectual property rights resulting from sponsored research conducted in facilities developed with tax-exempt bonds at the commencement of the sponsored research project. Can you reconcile the Revenue Procedure 2007-47 prohibition with the STTR required Allocation of Rights agreement between the SBC and a partnering research institution, prior to receipt of the STTR award, if the research will be conducted in tax-exempt bond facilities?

11.1.5   SBIR Data Rights and Phase III Rights

You saw in the SBIR Policy Directive that SBC awardees are granted extensive rights in the data they generate in the course of a Phase I, Phase II or Phase III SBIR project. You also saw in the SBIR Policy Directive that SBCs and SBIR agencies have a great deal of discretion in planning for a Phase III award at the time of a Phase II award. Although the SBIR Policy Directive does not specifically state that a Phase II awardee will receive a Phase III award in the event a Phase III award is issued, the Policy Directive clearly anticipates this result. The *Night Vision* case below is a cautionary tale for SBIR awardees on how to protect their data rights and how to ensure receipt of a Phase III award if one is issued.

NIGHT VISION CORP. v. The UNITED STATES
68 Fed. Cl. 368 (Fed. Cl. 2005)

BLOCK, JUDGE.

Ever since Joshua commanded the sun to stop in the sky so that tribes of Israel could have enough light to destroy the Amorites, mankind has sought ways to overcome the disadvantages the darkness of night pose in warfare. The operations of armies have always been degraded at night, as the darkness presents great difficulty in moving soldiers and identifying the enemy. To fight effectively at night, soldiers traditionally relied on artificial illumination, but this tactic often gave away their tactical position and informed the enemy of their maneuvers.

Today, due to technological advances, the U.S. military no longer relies on artificial illumination, let alone dreams of stopping the sun. In fact, it has almost become clich, to say that the United States military "Owns the Night." The phrase is a boast of the military's near perfect night time operations, which have been achieved in part by technological advances over the last fifty years. The widespread use of one technology in particular — night vision goggles ("NVGs") — has allowed the members of our armed forces to overcome the handicap of darkness and operate effectively at night.

The NVGs we are familiar with from combat footage in Afghanistan and Iraq are electro-optical devices that intensify existing light instead of creating an artificial light source. NVGs first capture ambient light, such as light from the stars, moon or sky glow from man-made sources. This light is then amplified thousands of times by electronic means and displayed via a phosphor screen. The phosphor screen is purposefully colored green because the human eye can differentiate more shades of green than other phosphor colors. Users thus do not look "through" NVGs, but instead look at an amplified electronic image on a phosphor screen.

To maintain its tactical advantage in night fighting capability, the U.S. military constantly seeks to improve existing night vision technology. One area of focus has been in improving the field-of-view of existing NVGs. Historically, the view through NVGs was similar to looking down a tunnel. While a person's natural field-of-view, or peripheral vision, is about 190 degrees, existing NVG technology is limited to roughly 40 degrees of field-of-view. To compensate for this complete absence of peripheral vision, the wearer of NVGs must constantly turn his head side to side. It was the military's desire to mitigate this problem and widen the field-of-vision in NVGs that led to the parties' dispute before this court.

The plaintiff, Night Vision Corporation ("NVC"), is a small business concern that obtained contracts with the United States Air Force for research and development of wide field-of-view NVG technology. NVC successfully developed prototype night vision goggles that expand the field-of-view to 100 degrees without compromising image quality — a technology NVC calls "Panoramic Night Vision Goggles" ("PNVG") — under the Small Business Innovation Research ("SBIR") program. The SBIR program requires certain federal agencies to reserve a portion of their research and development budgets for small business concerns. Generally speaking, fully successful contractors in the SBIR program proceed in three distinct phases. In Phase I, a small business concern is awarded limited funding to determine "the scientific and technical merit and feasibility of ideas that appear to have commercial potential." Following the successful completion of Phase I, a Phase II contract may be awarded, which permits further development of the original idea. Phase III envisions a commercial application of the research and development from the prior phases funded by either "non-Federal sources of capital" or "non-SBIR Federal funding."

NVC successfully completed both a Phase I and a Phase II contracts under the SBIR program. Nevertheless, the Air Force eventually decided not to award a SBIR Phase III contract. Instead, the Air Force conducted a competitive procurement, ultimately awarding a contract for additional development of the wide field-of-view night vision goggle concept to Insight Technology, Inc. ("Insight"), which had served as NVC's subcontractor under its Phase II contract.

This competitive award to Insight bitterly disappointed NVC and its principals. NVC felt that, based upon its successful completion of the SBIR Phase I and II contracts, it was entitled to receive a Phase III contract. Indeed, NVC was convinced that Air Force officials had promised as much while NVC was developing the PNVG prototype. The award to Insight was particularly irksome because NVC and Insight had a troubled relationship as prime and sub-contractors under the Phase II contract.

NVC's conflicts and competition with Insight — and particularly the actions of Air Force employees with respect to these conflicts and competition — form the factual basis of plaintiff's claims. Plaintiff seeks relief on five separate counts. In count I, plaintiff contends that the Air Force breached its SBIR contracts with

NVC by disclosing proprietary technical data to Insight in violation of certain regulations. In count II, plaintiff alleges that the Air Force breached a statutory provision allegedly incorporated by law into NVC's SBIR contracts when the Air Force decided not to award NVC an SBIR Phase III contract. In count III, plaintiff claims that the Air Force breached an implied contract with NVC when it decided not to award NVC an SBIR Phase III contract. In count IV, plaintiff claims that the Air Force violated a duty of good faith and fair dealing that it owed to NVC "in all facets of the procurement process." Finally, count V consists of a bid protest challenging the award of contract no. F33615-00-C-6000 to Insight instead of NVC.

The parties have filed numerous motions, all of which are opposed, regarding each of plaintiff's claims. As will be explained more fully below, the court grants summary judgment to defendant on count I, since plaintiff failed to present evidence that it affixed data rights legends to the goggles, resulting in a waiver of the protection from disclosure plaintiff seeks to invoke here. The court dismisses count II under RCFC 12(b)(6) because the statute plaintiff seeks to incorporate into the contract, imposes no obligation or duty on either party to the contract. The court grants summary judgment to defendant on count III because plaintiff has failed to produce evidence that a government representative with contracting authority made a contract with plaintiff. The court dismisses count IV under RCFC 12(b)(6) because a key element of this claim must involve a violation of a particular contractual term and the plaintiff's claim assumes there was no contractual obligation to award the Phase III contract. Finally, the court grants defendant's motion for judgment on the administrative record on count V because plaintiff has failed to prove the defendant's evaluation of the bids were arbitrary, capricious, or an abuse an discretion, a threshold issue in a bid protest.

I. Factual Background

NVC, whose founder and president is Danny Filiopovich, designs "optical image intensification systems" for night vision goggles, which "enable the wearer to see in low-light and no light conditions." On May 12, 1995, the Air Force awarded NVC a SBIR Phase I contract under which NVC developed a single prototype of its PNVG design.

On July 12, 1996, the Air Force awarded NVC a SBIR Phase II contract under which NVC arranged for the production of twelve developmental night vision goggle prototypes with the help of a subcontractor. Seven of these prototypes were in a configuration called PNVG I and five were in a configuration called PNVG II. Both configurations expanded the field-of-vision provided by existing night vision goggle technologies while maintaining similar image resolutions

The Air Force Research Laboratory ("AFRL") at Wright-Patterson Air Force Base administered NVC's SBIR contracts. NVC worked with several AFRL employees, including: Jeffrey Craig, an engineer and night vision technology specialist; Randy Brown, an AFRL program manager; Dr. H. Lee Task, the senior scientist advisor for NVC's SBIR contracts; and two contracting officers, Judith Demos, who served as the contracting officer throughout most of NVC's performance of its SBIR contracts, and Mary Jones, who succeeded Ms. Demos late in the process.

Sometime after July 1996, Insight agreed to serve as NVC's primary subcontractor under the SBIR Phase II contract. Insight was founded in 1987 by a former Army employee named Kenneth Solinsky, who currently serves as the company's president. Among other things, this subcontract (hereinafter "Phase II subcontract") required Insight to "assist in the design and manufacture of the plastic housings and bridge assembly for the PNVG I units," convert NVC's design "into engineering drawings suitable for manufacture," and "fabricate and assemble the goggle assembly." Unfortunately, the record reveals that NVC and Insight did not work well together, and the two companies maintained a tenuous relationship.

Long before NVC completed performance of its Phase II contract, the Air Force considered the possibility of awarding NVC an SBIR Phase III contract. For instance, in early 1997, Mr. Filipovich stated that Air Force personnel instructed him to prepare NVC for performance of an SBIR Phase III contract. In particular, Air Force personnel indicated that because NVC lacked any production capability it needed to either "develop the production capability that would be required for production in a SBIR Phase III," or subcontract with a company capable of producing the PNVG system.

It was the potential work under a future SBIR Phase III contract that was grist for much of the dispute between Insight and NVC. In April 1998, Mr. Solinsky demanded that Insight "be granted exclusive manufacturing rights" for any SBIR Phase III contract, and threatened to stop work under the Phase II subcontract (thus threatening NVC's ability to perform) until Insight received this guarantee.

Although it initially resisted, NVC sent a letter to Insight on May 8, 1998 promising that "during . . . Phase III, [Insight] will be the exclusive manufacturer for both the PNVG I and PNVG II." After obtaining this promise, Mr. Solinsky sought a further guarantee that Insight would have a role in production beyond Phase III. Contemporaneous with this demand, Insight stopped work and also withheld from NVC a set of drawings that it was required to deliver to NVC under the Phase II subcontract.

By July 1998, the disputes between NVC and Insight threatened completion of the Phase II contract. On July 8, 1998, in an attempt to resolve the conflicts between NVC and Insight, Air Force personnel met with representatives of the two companies. At this meeting, Mr. Solinsky renewed both his demand for a guarantee that Insight would be NVC's exclusive manufacturer beyond any SBIR Phase III contract and his threat that until it received this guarantee, Insight would not perform under the Phase II subcontract. The parties at the meeting discussed and drafted a teaming agreement to be executed by NVC and Insight. The next day, NVC and Insight executed this agreement, which (among other things) guaranteed that if the Phase II contract led to a Phase III contract, Insight would be NVC's manufacturer; the teaming agreement also protected Insight's proprietary data from disclosure to third parties.

Throughout the rest of 1998, the Air Force and NVC continued to discuss the possibility of work under an SBIR Phase III contract. For instance, on December

FINANCING TECHNOLOGY INNOVATION

15–16, 1998, Air Force personnel, met with NVC to discuss "acquisition strategy" related to the PNVG program. At that time, Air Force employees discussed with NVC how the development and production of NVC's night vision goggle technology would proceed under an SBIR Phase III contract.

It appears that by the Spring of 1999, however, the Air Force was considering alternatives to awarding NVC an SBIR Phase III contract. In April 1999, Mr. Brown apparently asked Insight for quotes for the manufacture of 500 PNVG I and 1,000 PNVG II units. In an email dated April 19, 1999, Mr. Solinsky responded with the requested quotes; an email exchange elaborating on these quotes between Solinsky and Mr. Brown followed.

As the completion of the SBIR Phase II approached, all of the parties' focus turned more to determining how the development of the PNVG would proceed. On June 24, 1999, Mr. Filipovich took part in a conference call with Air Force employees, including Mr. Brown, Mr. Craig, Dr. Task, and Mr. Kocian, regarding the possibility of an SBIR Phase III contract. According to Mr. Filipovich, Mr. Brown told him that "the Air Force did not want to offer Phase III to NVC, but, instead, wanted NVC to sell its technology to Insight and become a consultant to Insight." Mr. Filipovich also stated that Mr. Kocian told him: "[y]our only option is to sell [your technology] to Insight. Otherwise, you will never get another contract from the Air Force." Further, Mr. Filipovich claims that Mr. Brown and Dr. Task confirmed that "NVC has no option but to sell NVC or its technology to Insight." Mr. Brown's notes related to this call indicate that the Air Force "probably would not pursue" awarding the SBIR Phase III contract to NVC and that awarding the SBIR Phase III contract to Insight as the prime contractor with NVC as a subcontractor was the "preferred approach."

Mr. Filipovich sent a letter the next day to Mr. Brown and Mr. Craig, summarizing his understanding of what he had been told in the previous day's phone call. Mr. Filipovich wrote he had been told the Air Force would not offer NVC a SBIR Phase III contract. Moreover, Mr. Filipovich wrote, he was told that NVC should not submit — and the Air Force would not accept — a SBIR Phase III contract proposal from NVC. Mr. Filipovich also wrote that he had been encouraged to sell the PNVG program and the related technology to Insight, who would then serve as the prime contractor.

On June 28, 1999, the Air Force officially announced that it was considering a competitive procurement instead of issuing a SBIR Phase III contract to NVC. On that date the Air Force published a notice entitled "Potential Sources Sought," seeking possible developers of a "night vision goggle" offering "a wider field of view (at least 100 degree horizontal by 40 vertical . . .) and high resolution." This document publicized that the Air Force would seek to develop two versions of the goggles. The related descriptions in the document seem to correspond with NVC's PNVG I and PNVG II configurations.

At this time, Insight was preparing to compete directly against NVC for a contract to develop the PNVG system. On July 1, 1999, Insight executed an agreement with ITT Industries, Inc. ("ITT") to work together towards obtaining a PNVG competitive procurement contract. ITT was another indispensable subcontractor to NVC under its SBIR contracts, supplying the "image intensifier tubes" for the PNVG system.

On July 7, 1999, representatives from Insight and ITT met with Air Force personnel to present a sales pitch they called "PNVG: Road to Production." Among other things, this presentation addressed potential legal issues related to the Air Force's decision to proceed with a competitive procurement instead of awarding NVC a SBIR Phase III contract. Specifically, Insight and ITT claimed that pursuant to 48 C.F.R. § 252.227-7018 Insight and ITT enjoyed some data rights related to the PNVG program as subcontractors to NVC. Still, Insight and ITT's presentation ultimately recommended that the "Government should acquire unlimited data rights and provide [those rights] to all competitors."

On July 13, 1999, the Air Force sent a letter to NVC directing it to incorporate into its subcontracts 48 C.F.R. § 52.227-11, a provision regarding data rights protections afforded to subcontractors of federal government contracts. On July 14, 1999, the Air Force sent another letter to NVC announcing its intention to pursue development of the PNVG through a competitive procurement. This letter also stated that the Air Force would like to obtain "government purpose rights" to NVC's proprietary data.

Later that month, it appears that Insight and ITT began actual work on a night vision goggle system that would compete with NVC's PNVG. Based on this preliminary work on or about July 22, 1999, personnel from the Army Night Vision Laboratory requested a cost estimate for the development of up to 20,000 PNVG.

On July 30, 1999, Insight delivered to NVC the drawings it was required to generate under the SBIR Phase II subcontract. The same day, NVC delivered the final data package for its SBIR Phase II contract to the Air Force which included both technical information (such as drawing and schematics) and prototypes of the goggles. NVC claims that it marked all technical data that it delivered to the Air Force with data rights legends indicating that the data was proprietary. Nonetheless, it is uncontroverted that NVC did *not* affix such legends to the actual goggles that it delivered to the Air Force along with the technical documents (a significant factor discussed at length below).

As a contract monitor under NVC's SBIR Phase II contract, Mr. Craig received the goggles that NVC delivered to the Air Force under the contract. Mr. Craig stated that none of these goggles were marked with a restrictive data rights legend, nor were they accompanied by a transmittal document or storage container bearing any such restrictive data rights legend. Mr. Craig stated his belief that all the goggles were marked "patent pending."

With the delivery of the final data package, NVC's SBIR Phase II performance was complete. According to plaintiff, NVC "fully and satisfactorily performed all of its obligations" under both its SBIR Phase I and Phase II contracts. Also, the results that NVC obtained under both of its SBIR contracts "met the Air Force's expectations."

Despite the successful completion of the SBIR Phase II contract, the Air Force remained reluctant to award NVC a Phase III contract. This was apparent from a meeting of Air Force personnel on August 23, 1999. Materials from a presentation given in that meeting stated that the Air Force "did not see any value in NVC conducting a Phase III." This presentation was concluded with the following text: "Recommendation: Acquire Government Purpose Data Rights to PNVG Phase 2 data. Conduct full and open competition for PNVG follow-on contract. Provide PNVG data as a baseline for design." Plaintiff has produced typed notes by an unidentified author, apparently related to this meeting, that contain the words: "Laboratory does not want to award to NVC." Concerning a NVC SBIR Phase III proposal, the notes indicate that the Air Force would "allow NVC to submit," and "if acceptable, award to NVC, if not acceptable, do one of two things, pursue purchase of data rights from NVC or issue a [Program Research and Development Announcement] for the technology."

On August 27, 1999, Air Force and NVC representatives met at Wright-Patterson Air Force Base. At that meeting, Ms. Jones stated that the Air Force was considering either "issuing a Phase III or pursuing full and open competition." Mr. Filipovich asked if the Air Force would consider evaluating a SBIR Phase III proposal from NVC. According to a file memorandum regarding the meeting, Ms. Jones replied that "should [NVC] choose to submit a Phase III proposal the government would evaluate it." Ms. Jones also explained that the Air Force would not request such a proposal or guarantee an award. When Mr. Filipovich replied that NVC would not want to submit a proposal if a SBIR Phase III contract was not a valid option, Ms. Jones stated that "the government cannot guarantee that we will award a Phase III contract just because a Phase III proposal is submitted." Similarly, according to Dr. Task, Mr. Filipovich asked if "he would be guaranteed of getting the contract" if he submitted a Phase III proposal. Dr. Task responded that "there is no guarantee to getting a [Phase III] until after we see the proposal and can evaluate [it]." It is important to note that NVC did not submit a proposal for a SBIR Phase III contract.

****

The Air Force made its final decision against awarding NVC a SBIR Phase III contract in December 1999. An Air Force "Acquisition Strategy Panel" met on December 1, 1999 to discuss the Air Force's plan for future development of the PNVG program. The Acquisition Strategy Panel reviewed factors for and against pursuing either full and open competition or a SBIR Phase III contract with NVC.

The panel specifically cited the reasons against pursuing a SBIR Phase III with NVC that were listed in the November 3, 1999, Information Brief. The panel also noted that "[NVC] had difficulty in managing the Phase II contract which is less of a management challenge than a new Phase III contract would be." The panel ultimately recommended that the Air Force procure further PNVG development through full and open competition using the Program Research & Development Announcement ("PRDA") procedure.

On December 10, 1999, Donald L. Utendorf, then Chief of the Research and Development Contracting Office for the Technology Directorates at Wright-Patterson Air Force Base, decided that the Air Force would issue the PRDA instead of awarding a SBIR Phase III contract to NVC. In reaching this conclusion, Mr. Utendorf adopted the recommendation of Maris Vikmanis, an

AFRL technical management leader, and the AFRL Acquisition Strategy Panel.

On December 16, 1999, the AFRL, in conjunction with the United States Army Night Vision and Electronic Sensors Directorate, posted Program Research and Development Announcement ("PRDA") No. 00-01-HE. The purpose of the PRDA was "to award a negotiated, 24-month Advanced Technology Demonstration ("ATD") contract" for what the Air Force called Integrated Panoramic Night Vision Goggles ("IPNVG").

****

Three companies submitted bids in response to the PRDA: NVC, Insight, and Litton. On March 22, 2000, following technical evaluations of the proposals, the evaluation team ranked Insight first, based upon technical merit, followed by Litton. NVC's proposal was ranked as "Category III" and ineligible for award, because it did not meet agency needs.

The technical evaluation team's summary of comments regarding NVC's bid concluded that "[t]he majority of the program team has not been identified and there is no supporting documentation from any of the subcontractors, showing cost or commitment to perform. Therefore, NVC's proposal does not meet agency needs."

> The technical evaluators' overall summary with respect to Insight was much more favorable: "Insight addresses all of the important aspects of their approach for developing a well conceived Integrated PNVG/ANVG. They provided detailed information of the design approach they plan to pursue and this made it easier to address the amount of risk associated with their effort."

The Air Force entered into negotiations with Insight on April 3, 2000 and awarded Insight contract number F33615-00-C-6000 on April 7, 2000.

****

III. Discussion

Risking a bit of redundancy for the ease of reading, the court restates the grounds of plaintiff's complaint. It consists of five claims for relief, each to be addressed in turn. Count I alleges that defendant breached the SBIR contracts with plaintiff by disclosing proprietary technical data to Insight. Count II alleges that defendant breached a provision allegedly incorporated by law into the SBIR contracts with plaintiff, which required defendant to award plaintiff a SBIR Phase III contract. Count III alleges defendant breached an oral contract with plaintiff by not awarding plaintiff a SBIR Phase III contract. Count IV alleges defendant violated a duty of good faith and fair dealing owed to plaintiff throughout the procurement process. Finally, count V consists of a bid protest challenging the award of contract no. F33615-00-C-6000 to Insight instead of NVC.

A. Did Defendant Breach Plaintiff's SBIR Data Rights?

The parties have filed cross-motions for summary judgment on count I, in which plaintiff claims that defendant violated a prohibition against disclosing plaintiff's proprietary data when defendant sent PNVG prototypes to Insight. Plaintiff argues that PNVG prototype units themselves constitute proprietary "technical data" and are entitled to protection from government disclosure under 48 C.F.R. § 252.227-7018 (2005). Defendant argues that plaintiff waived any legal protection from disclosure of data rights since the plaintiff delivered the goggles to defendant without protective markings that are required by the regulation as a condition to the protection it offers. Defendant further argues that the legal protection plaintiff seeks does not apply to the actual goggle prototypes, since tangible products delivered under a SBIR contract are not "technical data." The court essentially concurs with defendant.

****

The parties' SBIR Phase II contract incorporates by reference 48 C.F.R. § 252.227-7018, the SBIR limited data rights provision. This provision generally prohibits the government from releasing or disclosing "SBIR data to any person other than its support service contractors." 48 C.F.R. § 252.227-7018(b)(4)(ii). On its face, this regulation would prohibit defendants from leasing protected "data" to Insight. Nevertheless, this same provision requires that a contractor clearly mark data with a prescribed legend that the contractor wishes to protect from disclosure. § 252.227-7018(f). In particular, the FAR provides:

> "The Contractor . . . may only assert restrictions on the Government's rights to use, modify, reproduce, release, perform, display, or disclose technical data . . . to be delivered under this contract by marking the deliverable data . . . subject to restriction."

Contractors must use the legend provided in the same provision to preserve the protection of their data from disclosure.

The SBIR data rights legend prescribed by the FAR requires the contractor to list information such as the contract name and number and the expiration date of the SBIR data rights period. The legend must also include the following language:

> "The Government's rights to use, modify, reproduce, release, perform, display, or disclose technical data . . . marked with this legend are restricted during the period shown . . . . No restrictions apply after the expiration date shown above." § 252.227-7018(f)(4).

By its own language, § 252.227-7018(f) indicates that a contractor may only restrict the government's use and disclosure of technical data by marking the deliverable data with the appropriate data legend. A failure to use the appropriate legend results in the government receiving complete, unrestricted use. Other sections of the FAR which limit the government's rights in proprietary data developed by contractors have consistently been interpreted in this vein.

The court finds persuasive the reasoning of the Armed Services Board of Contract Appeals ("ASBCA") in *General Atronics Corp.* There the Navy requested that a contractor include proprietary computer software along with technical hardware called for in the contract. The contractor argued that the Navy's use of the software should be restricted and brought a claim for software licensing fees to cover the Navy's additional use of the software. The ASBCA noted that the contract incorporated 48 C.F.R. § 252.227-7013, which covers rights in technical data and requires a legend to be placed on all data to restrict the governments use. The ASBCA pointed out that the contractor delivered the software to the Navy without the restricted rights legend required by § 252.227-7013. The ASBCA also found immaterial the fact the contractor had delivered technical manuals for the hardware with an appropriate restricted right legend, since those manuals had not specifically made any assertions regarding the software. As a result, the ASBCA concluded that the Navy had acquired unlimited rights to the software and denied the contractor's claim.

As in *General Atronics Corp.*, it is undisputed that neither the prototypes that plaintiff delivered to defendant nor the packaging in which those prototypes arrived were marked with proprietary data legends. This failure to use an appropriate data legend gave the government unrestricted use to the PNVG prototypes. Plaintiff's argument that it was sufficient to have affixed the legend to the "technical drawings and documentation" associated with the goggles is not persuasive. To allow an exception to § 252.227-7018 as the plaintiff advocates would be contrary to the language of the regulation, contradict its intent, and ultimately render the regulatory protection of data unworkable. There simply is no provision in 48 C.F.R. § 252.227-7018 for the extension of the data rights protection from properly marked data to unmarked delivered data. The interpretation of similar sections of the FAR have also not found such extensions of protection.

To read an exception into the regulation as the plaintiff advocates would undermine the entire purpose of restrictive legends. Restrictive legends alert all government officials — even those unfamiliar with the data rights of the contractor — that data is considered proprietary and is inappropriate for dissemination. Creating exceptions to the restrictive rights requirement would place government officials in the difficult position of being unsure which data was subject to restrictions and which was not. The least cost burden in such instances rests with the contractor, who can easily apply an appropriate legend to the proprietary data. Crafting a workable exception to the restrictive legend requirement is beyond the court's constitutional function of interpreting, and not legislating, law. It could also result in the exception consuming the rule. Parties would be left unsure how many items of data could escape without a restrictive legend and still be covered by the legend placed on another item. To be sure, the only result from such an exception would be additional litigation as parties argued about which unlabeled data was covered by which labeled data.

Since plaintiff did not attach the SBIR data rights legend to the PNVG prototypes, no restrictions applied to defendant's use of the prototypes. Defendant was thus within its rights when it shipped the PNVG prototypes to Insight and is therefore entitled to summary judgment on count I.

B. Was Plaintiff Entitled to a SBIR Phase III Contract?

Plaintiff seeks summary judgment while defendant seeks dismissal under RCFC 12(b)(6) on count II, plaintiff's claim that a statutory provision required defendant to award plaintiff a SBIR Phase III contract. Plaintiff argues that 15 U.S.C. § 638(j)(2)(C) operates here to create a contractual entitlement to a SBIR Phase III contract and that the Air Force breached this provision when it decided not to award plaintiff a SBIR Phase III contract. However, a close examination of plaintiff's arguments reveals § 638(j)(2)(C) creates no contractual obligation for a Phase III as a matter of law and, therefore, the statutory provisions on which plaintiff relies cannot form the grounds of any breach of contract claim in this court. Accordingly, dismissal under 12(b)(6) is only proper.

1. The Statutory and Regulatory Guidelines for SBIR Phase III

To properly understand why the plaintiff's claim for a breach of contract fails as a matter of law, a brief examination of the statutory language of 15 U.S.C. § 638 is necessary. To begin with, that section sets out the definition for a SBIR Phase III:

(e) Definitions

(C) where appropriate, a third phase-

(i) in which commercial applications of SBIR-funded research or research and development are funded by non-Federal sources of capital or, for products or services intended for use by the Federal Government, by follow-on non-SBIR Federal funding awards; and

(ii) for which awards from non-SBIR Federal funding sources are used for the continuation of research or research and development that has been competitively selected using peer review or scientific review criteria;

15 U.S.C. § 638(e)(4)(C)(i)–(ii).

The SBIR Phase III contracts are further explained in § 638(r):

(r) Third phase agreements

(1) In general. In the case of a small business concern that is awarded a funding agreement for the second phase of a SBIR or STTR program, a Federal agency may enter into a third phase agreement with that business concern for additional work to be performed during or after the second phase period. The second phase funding agreement with the small business concern may, at the discretion of the agency awarding the agreement, set out the procedures applicable to third phase agreements with that agency or any other agency.

(2) Definition. In this subsection, the term "third phase agreement" means a follow-on, non-SBIR or non-STTR funded contract as described in paragraph (4)(C) or paragraph (6)(C) of subsection (e) of this section.

15 U.S.C. § 638(r)(1)–(2).

As the plaintiff has noted, § 638 also requires the Small Business Administration

("SBA") Administrator to establish policy directives that provide administrative procedures so that agencies taking part in the SBIR program award follow-on contracts to SBIR-program participants. In relevant part this section provides that:

(j) Small Business Administration policy directives for the general conduct of small business innovation research program

(2) Modifications. Not later than 90 days after October 28, 1992, the Administrator shall modify the policy directives issued pursuant to this subsection to provide for-

(C) procedures to ensure, to the extent practicable, that an agency which intends to pursue research, development, or production of a technology developed by a small business concern under a SBIR program enters into follow-on, non-SBIR funding agreements with the small business concern for such research, development, or production;

15 U.S.C. § 638(j)(2)(C).

Pursuant to this section, the SBA Administrator issued the Small Business Innovation Research Program Policy Directive on January 26, 1993. This Policy Directive was intended to provide guidance to Federal agencies on the general conduct of the SBIR program. Concerning the SBIR Phase III, the Policy Directive stated:

7. Small Business Innovation Research Program

(3) Phase III. The term third phase agreement means to follow-on, non-SBIR funded award as described in 1, 2 and 3 below. A federal agency may enter into a third phase agreement with a small business concern for additional work to be performed during or after the second phase period. The second phase funding agreement with the small business concern may, at the discretion of the agency awarding the agreement, set out the procedures applicable to third phase agreements. The competition for Phase I and Phase II awards satisfies any competition requirement of the Competition in Contracting Act.

(a) Where appropriate, there will be a third phase which is funded by:

1. Non-federal sources of capital for commercial applications of SBIR funded research or research and development,

2. The federal government by follow-on non-SBIR awards for SBIR derived products and processes for use by the federal government,

3. Non-SBIR federal sources for the continuation of research or research and development that has been competitively selected using peer review or scientific review criteria.

(b) Agencies which intend to pursue research, research and development or production developed under the SBIR Program will give special acquisition preference including sole source awards to the SBIR company which developed the technology. The Phase III funding agreement will be with non-SBIR funds.

58 FR 6144-02 at 6149.

2. Is There a Contractual Obligation for a SBIR Phase III Contract?

Plaintiff argues that § 638(j)(2)(C) was incorporated by operation of law into the parties' Phase II contract and thereby entitled plaintiff to a SBIR Phase III contract given the underlying circumstances, namely plaintiff's successful completion of SBIR Phase I and II obligations. As defendant points out — and is clear from the above cited section — the statute merely directs a government official to establish certain *procedures* to ensure that "follow-on" Phase III contracts will be awarded *"to the extent practicable."* 15 U.S.C. § 638(j)(2)(C) (emphasis added). While § 638(j)(2)(C) clearly directs the SBA Administrator to take action in issuing procedures, nowhere does it impose an obligation directly upon a procuring agency nor does it create any enforceable rights under a SBIR contract. Moreover, the Policy Directive issued by the SBA in January 1993 in accordance with § 638(j)(2)(C) contains no requirements obligating an agency to award a Phase III contract.

Not only does § 638(j)(2)(C) not impose any contractual obligation to award a Phase III contract, other portions § 638 clearly indicate that such awards are not mandatory. Throughout § 638 the description of procedures for the award of a Phase III is repeatedly qualified with terms such as: *"where appropriate"* in § 638(e)(4)(C); *"may enter into"* in § 638(r)(1); and *"to the extent practicable"* in § 638(j)(2)(C). The plain language of these sections indicates that the awarding of a Phase III contract is not obligatory for the contracting agency, but instead entrusted to a contracting agency's discretion based on the totality of circumstances. Although not controlling when the language of the statute is clear, as is the case here, this conclusion is buttressed by legislative history confirming that SBIR Phase III awards are discretionary.

Accordingly, because the provision upon which plaintiff's claim rests creates no contractual obligations, count II must fail as a matter of law and shall be dismissed under RCFC 12(b)(6).

****

IV. Conclusion

For all of the foregoing reasons, plaintiff's motion for partial summary judgment on counts I, II and IV is DENIED, defendant's motion for summary judgment on counts I and III is GRANTED, defendant's motion to dismiss counts II and IV is GRANTED, and defendant's motion for judgment on the administrative record on count V is GRANTED.

JUDGMENT for Defendant.

QUESTIONS

1.   What could Mr. Filiopvich have done to strengthen his claims that the Air Force breached its SBIR contract with NVC by disclosing proprietary data to Insight and by not awarding a Phase III contract to NVC?

2.   As a subcontractor to NVC, Insight prepared the technical drawings for the PNGV prototype. If Insight had prior possession of the technical data, how would this bear on NVC's claim of unauthorized disclosure by the Air Force?

3.   Why would the proprietary rights legend affixed to the technical data not cover the goggle prototype described in the technical data?

4.   The Air Force contract monitor under NVC's SBIR Phase II contract testified that he believed all the goggles delivered were marked "patent pending." Why would the "patent pending" mark not suffice to give notice of NVC's claim of proprietary rights in the goggles delivered?

5.   It does not appear from the facts in the case that NVC, in fact, ever filed a patent application on the PNVG technology. Why might NVC not have filed a patent application on the PNVG technology? If NVC had filed a patent application on the PNVG technology, how might this have affected the outcome of the case?

6.   How is the Air Force's interest in NVC performing research and development of the PNVG technology different from the Air Force's interest in NVC supplying the PNVG goggles?

CASE NOTE

1.   R & D Dynamics Corp. v. U.S., 80 Fed. Cl. 715 (Fed. Cl. 2007) (Small business which submitted unsuccessful SBIR Phase II proposal filed a post-award bid protest under the Tucker Act; court held SBIR Phase II research and development award is not a "procurement" within the meaning of the Tucker Act and, therefore, challenge to a SBIR Phase II research and development award does not come within the court's bid protest jurisdiction).

Additional Information

1.   2 WEST'S FED. ADMIN. PRAC. § 2112 (4th ed.) (2010).

2.   PETER A. PLUMRIDGE, 1 ADVISING SMALL BUSINESSES § 14:27.10 (2010).

3.   STEVEN Z. SZCZEPANSKI, DAVID M. EPSTEIN, 3 ECKSTROM'S LICENSING IN FOR. & DOM. OPS. § 14:12 (2010).

4.   STEVEN W. FELDMAN, 2 GOVERNMENT CONTRACT AWARDS: NEGOTIATION AND SEALED BIDDING § 25:13 (2009).

5.   LEE R. RETILLION, ROBERT JOE HULL, REPRESENTING START-UP COMPANIES § 5:21 (2009).

6.   Clara Asmail, *Use of Small Business Innovation (SBIR) Program in Support of Technology Transfer*, 45 LES NOUVELLES 135 (2010).

7. David M.G. Ross, *Leveraging Federal Programs to Boost Local Innovation and Encourage Venture Capital Investment: Considering the Small Business Innovation Development Act and Derivative State-Level Incentives, with Specific Implications for Innovators and Legislators in Louisiana and the Southern States*, 11 TUL. J. TECH. & INTELL. PROP. 115 (2008).

8. Damien C. Specht, *Recent SBIR Extension Debate Reveals Venture Capital Influence*, 45-SPG PROCUREMENT LAW 1 (2010).

9. Mary Ann Lieber, *Who Is Eligible for SBIR Grants? — Biotechnology Firms Disagree at SBA Hearing*, 24 BIOTECHNOLOGY L. REP. 598 (2005).

10. Gail and Jim Greenwood, *SBIR & STTR Programs: Almost Free Money to Start and Grow Nanotechnology Businesses*, 2 NANOTECHNOLOGY L. & BUS. 183 (2005).

11.2 PRIVATE SECURITIES OFFERINGS

The different definitions of companies' stages of development sometimes cause confusion. Throughout the book, I have referred to "start-up" and "early-stage" companies. My definition of a "start-up" company is a company that has recently been formed and is in the process of reducing a technology to practice, either actually, by building a physical prototype, or constructively, by filing a patent application. My definition of an "early-stage" company is a company that has moved beyond reduction to practice, and is engaging in commercial scale-up of the technology, research on potential market applications and, possibly, generating some initial customer sales.

Other definitions of companies' development stages are more refined. For example, a set of definitions developed by Theresa Mazzullo, CEO of Excell Partners of Rochester, New York and James Senall, President of High Tech Rochester, for use in conjunction with a federal grant proposal to support entrepreneurship in Upstate New York, includes the following company stages.

Concept Stage — Idea / Research. Company has new technology or product being developed in a laboratory and some general ideas about potential market applications;

Pre-Seed Stage — Prototyping / Opportunity Assessment. Company is proving functionality of technology with proof of concept prototype, is defining specific market opportunities and is preparing value propositions for each of these markets;

Seed Stage — Development / Customer Validation. Company has developed a beta product based on market input and is defining its business model and business plan;

Early-Stage — Market Entry / Revenues. Company has completed a final product, is manufacturing with pilot production capabilities, and is launching sales to paying customers;

Growth Stage — Ramp Up / Profitability. Company has developed scalable manufacturing and distribution channels, and has grown beyond break-even profitability;

Mature Stage — Sustainable Growth. Company is engaged in productivity and operational improvements, in product line extensions, in market expansion, and is realizing increasing profitability.

Using the more refined Muzzullo/Senall definitions, this section will first focus on financing for Concept, Pre-Seed and Seed Stage companies, which, for simplicity, I will continue to call start-up companies. Section 11.4 will focus on venture capital financing for Early-Stage and Growth companies, which I will continue to call early-stage companies, and Section 11.6 will focus on public financing for Mature companies, which I will call initial public offering or IPO companies.

11.2.1 Founders, Family and Friends

The initial investment in a start-up company is most often provided by the company's founders, and the founders' family members and friends. Depending upon the wealth and the number of founders, the founders' cash investment in the company can range anywhere from $5,000 to $50,000. If the founders own patents, or hold exclusive rights to patents, these patents, or patent rights, can also be part of the founders' initial investment in a start-up company. However, in the great majority of cases, the founders' most important investment contribution to a start-up company is not cash or intellectual property rights, but rather the founders' contribution of time and expertise. In exchange for their time and expertise, founders are often issued "sweat equity." Sweat equity almost always consists of common stock issued to the founders in exchange for their services to the company.

Determining the timing and amount of sweat equity to issue to founders can be complicated. If the founders are issued sweat equity at the time the company is formed, in anticipation of their future services, there is a moral hazard problem. That is, the founders have already received their common stock and, therefore, their incentive to contribute time and expertise in the future may be somewhat diminished. On the other hand, if the founders are issued common stock over time, in some proportion to their contribution of time, there is a different type of moral hazard problem. That is, the founders may have an incentive to log excessive time in order to receive additional common stock. This moral hazard can be dealt with by issuing common stock to the founders based upon their completion of enumerated tasks. The problems with issuing common stock in exchange for the completion of tasks is defining the tasks and assigning a common stock value to the tasks. Finally, sweat equity poses a challenge in valuing the expertise of the founders. How is a Ph.D. founder's expertise valued in comparison to a masters degree founder's expertise? How is a senior faculty founder's expertise valued in comparison to a junior faculty founder's expertise? How is the practical experience of a seasoned entrepreneur valued in comparison to the academic experience of research faculty and students? Despite these problems, issuing sweat equity is frequently the only way to compensate founders before the company has revenue from grants or sales, or has additional funds from subsequent investors.

Stock issued to the founders' family members and friends also almost always takes the form of common stock. Although investments by family and friends in a start-up company is usually motivated by a mix of personal, emotional and financial considerations, it is still necessary to place a value on the company in order to determine the percentage of equity to be given away in exchange for a certain amount of investment. Although rarely will a start-up company at this investment stage have a fully prepared business plan, or private offering memorandum, with detailed financial projections, it is nonetheless important to communicate in writing the company's business purpose, its market challenges and opportunities, the basis for determining the company's current value, and the risks associated with the investment. Such a written communication benefits the founders as well as the family and friends investors. For the founders, it provides some protection against future misunderstandings and law suits; for the family and friends investors, it provides some context for their expectations of the company.

Although there is no requirement that the company provide investors at this stage with any specific information, the company, and its officers and directors, are always subject to liability for fraud in the event they make knowing, or grossly negligent, oral or written misrepresentations of material fact.

11.2.2 Angel Investors

So called "angel investors" are usually high net-worth individuals with a high level of tolerance for risk. Angel investors frequently have prior entrepreneurial experience with start-up companies in the same, or a similar, field. A typical angel investment round involves four or five individuals investing a total of around $500,000. In the past, angel investors were most often identified through chance encounters with founders and families in social relationships, or attendance at social functions or professional meetings. Today, angel investing has become considerably more organized and a number of angel investment groups have been formed to share information about potential investments and to provide a central forum for start-up companies to present their new ideas and technologies. One of the most famous of these angel investment groups is the Band of Angels in Silicon Valley.

CASE NOTES

1.   Cummings v. Paramount Partners, LP, 715 F. Supp. 2d 880 (D. Minn. 2010) (By alleging that individuals and entities affiliated with limited partnership hedge fund were involved in the day-to-day operation of the fund and exercised control over solicitation of fund's unregistered securities, investors stated claims for violations of Securities Act sections creating private remedy for buyers of unregistered securities where prospectus or oral communication contained untrue statements or omitted material facts; where investors alleged that manager of hedge fund had access to information that contradicted false statements made in soliciting investors, investors alleged sufficient facts to raise a strong inference of scienter on part of hedge fund manager); Braddock v. Braddock, 60 A.D.3d 84 (N.Y. App. Div. 2009) (Investment banker's allegations satisfied claim of common law fraudulent inducement against cousin who represented that banker would become co-owner of new company when banker raised investment capital to form new company; banker's reliance on cousin's representations that banker would be issued founder's shares equal to half of the cousin's shares evidenced by banker's acceptance of greatly reduced commissions, quitting his job and uprooting his

home); Hughes v. BCI International Holdings, Inc., 452 F.Supp.2d 290 (S.D.N.Y. 2006) (Allegations of misrepresentations in private placement memorandum were sufficient to plead fraud against company founder; claim for fraudulent concealment under New York law requires a duty to disclose based on either a fiduciary relationship or defendant's possession of superior knowledge not readily available to the plaintiff; where founder met personally with investor to solicit investment, and possessed unique and specialized expertise with respect to industry and company's operations, investor sufficiently alleged negligent misrepresentation against founder of privately-held start-up company); Access Cardiosystems, Inc., 404 B.R. 592 (D. Mass. 2009) (While not imposing strict liability on the seller of securities for untrue statements, Massachusetts Blue Sky Law places heavy burden of proof on seller that he did not know, and could not have known with exercise of reasonable care, the untruth or omission; under Massachusetts Blue Sky Law, once plaintiff shows defendant made an untrue statement, or omission, of material fact, burden of proof shifts to defendant to show that plaintiff knew of falsity or omission, or that defendant did not know, or could not have known, of the falsity or omission with exercise of reasonable care; generally, an affirmative false statement to be actionable must relate to facts; however, statements of opinion, belief, prediction or future intention may be actionable if speaker knew the statement was false when it was made; the "bespeaks caution" doctrine provides that when statements of soft information such as forecasts, estimates and projections are accompanied by cautionary language warning that actual results may turn out differently than soft information, a claim that the statement was materially misleading may fail).

Additional Information

1. EQUITY FIN. CH. 9 (2010); EQUITY FIN. FORM 26-15 (2010).

2. JOSEPH W. BARTLETT, EQUITY FIN. § 2.5 (2011).

3. STEVEN C. ALBERTY, ADVISING SMALL BUSINESSES §§ 15:6, 15:12–15:13 (2011).

4. LEE R. PETILLON & ROBERT JOE HULL, REPRESENTING START-UP COMPANIES § 5:17 (2009).

5. ALAN S. GUTTERMAN, ORGANIZATIONAL MANAGEMENT AND ADMINISTRATION § 25:46 (2010).

6. Jeffrey Sohl, *The Angel Investor Market in 2009: Holding Steady But Changes in Seed and Startup Investment*, 1876 PLI/CORP 33 (2011).

7. Gunter Festel, Alexander Schicker, Roman Boutellier, *Importance and Best Practice of Early Stage Nanotechnology Investments*, 7 NANOTECHNOLOGY L. & BUS. 50 (2010).

8. Darian M. Ibrahim, *The (Not So) Puzzling Behavior of Angel Investors*, 61 VAND. L. REV. 1405 (2008).

9. Tom Eikenberry, *A Tennesee Seed Capital Qualified Investment Tax Credit: A Survey and Concrete Proposal for Legislative Action*, 4 TRANSACTIONS: TENN. J. BUS. L. 105 (2003).

10. Kelly L. Mccarty, *Iowa — New Seed Capital Credit Encourages Investment*, 1 JMTAX 58 (1991).

11.2.3 Securities Registration Exemptions

Q&A: SMALL BUSINESS AND THE SEC
A guide to help you understand how to raise capital and comply with the federal securities laws
Available at http://www.sec.gov./info/smallbs/qasbsec.htm

****

I. What Are the Federal Securities Laws?

In the chaotic securities markets of the 1920s, companies often sold stocks and bonds on the basis of glittering promises of fantastic profits — without disclosing any meaningful information to investors. These conditions contributed to the disastrous Stock Market Crash of 1929. In response, the U.S. Congress enacted the federal securities laws and created the Securities and Exchange Commission (SEC) to administer them.

There are two primary sets of federal laws that come into play when a company wants to offer and sell its securities to the public. They are:

* the Securities Act of 1933 (Securities Act), and

* the Securities Exchange Act of 1934 (Exchange Act).

Securities Act

The Securities Act generally requires companies to give investors "full disclosure" of all "material facts," the facts investors would find important in making an investment decision. This Act also requires companies to file a registration statement with the SEC that includes information for investors. The SEC does not evaluate the merits of offerings, or determine if the securities offered are "good" investments. The SEC staff reviews registration statements and declares them "effective" if companies satisfy our disclosure rules.

Exchange Act

The Exchange Act requires publicly held companies to disclose information continually about their business operations, financial conditions, and management. These companies, and in many cases their officers, directors and significant shareholders, must file periodic reports or other disclosure documents with the SEC. In some cases, the company must deliver the information directly to investors.

****

VI. Are There Legal Ways To Offer and Sell Securities Without Registering With the SEC?

Yes! Your company's securities offering may qualify for one of several exemptions from the registration requirements. We explain the most common ones below. You must remember, however, that all securities transactions, even exempt transactions, are subject to the antifraud provisions of the federal securities laws. This means that you and your company will be responsible for false or misleading statements, whether oral or written. The government enforces the federal securities laws through criminal, civil and administrative proceedings. Some enforcement proceedings are brought through private law suits. Also, if all conditions of the exemptions are not met, purchasers may be able to obtain refunds of their purchase price. In addition, offerings that are exempt from provisions of the federal securities laws may still be subject to the notice and filing obligations of various state laws. Make sure you check with the appropriate state securities administrator before proceeding with your offering.

A. Intrastate Offering Exemption

Section 3(a)(11) of the Securities Act is generally known as the "intrastate offering exemption." This exemption facilitates the financing of local business operations. To qualify for the intrastate offering exemption, your company must:

> be incorporated in the state where it is offering the securities; carry out a significant amount of its business in that state; and make offers and sales only to residents of that state.

There is no fixed limit on the size of the offering or the number of purchasers. Your company must determine the residence of each purchaser. If any of the securities are offered or sold to even one out-of-state person, the exemption may be lost. Without the exemption, the company could be in violation of the Securities Act registration requirements. If a purchaser resells any of the securities to a person who resides outside the state within a short period of time after the company's offering is complete (the usual test is nine months), the entire transaction, including the original sales, might violate the Securities Act. Since secondary markets for these securities rarely develop, companies often must sell securities in these offerings at a discount.

It will be difficult for your company to rely on the intrastate exemption unless you know the purchasers and the sale is directly negotiated with them. If your company holds some of its assets outside the state, or derives a substantial portion of its revenues outside the state where it proposes to offer its securities, it will probably have a difficult time qualifying for the exemption.

You may follow Rule 147, a "safe harbor" rule, to ensure that you meet the requirements for this exemption. It is possible, however, that transactions not meeting all requirements of Rule 147 may still qualify for the exemption.

B. Private Offering Exemption

Section 4(2) of the Securities Act exempts from registration "transactions by an issuer not involving any public offering." To qualify for this exemption, the purchasers of the securities must:

> have enough knowledge and experience in finance and business matters to evaluate the risks and merits of the investment (the "sophisticated investor"), or be able to bear the investment's economic risk;

> have access to the type of information normally provided in a prospectus; and agree not to resell or distribute the securities to the public.

In addition, you may not use any form of public solicitation or general advertising in connection with the offering.

The precise limits of this private offering exemption are uncertain. As the number of purchasers increases and their relationship to the company and its management becomes more remote, it is more difficult to show that the transaction qualifies for the exemption. You should know that if you offer securities to even one person who does not meet the necessary conditions, the entire offering may be in violation of the Securities Act.

Rule 506, another "safe harbor" rule, provides objective standards that you can rely on to meet the requirements of this exemption. Rule 506 is a part of Regulation D.

C. Regulation A

Section 3(b) of the Securities Act authorizes the SEC to exempt from registration small securities offerings. By this authority, we created Regulation A, an exemption for public offerings not exceeding $5 million in any 12-month period. If you choose to rely on this exemption, your company must file an offering statement, consisting of a notification, offering circular, and exhibits, with the SEC for review.

Regulation A offerings share many characteristics with registered offerings. For example, you must provide purchasers with an offering circular that is similar in content to a prospectus. Like registered offerings, the securities can be offered publicly and are not "restricted," meaning they are freely tradable in the secondary market after the offering. The principal advantages of Regulation A offerings, as opposed to full registration, are:

> The financial statements are simpler and don't need to be audited;

> There are no Exchange Act reporting obligations after the offering unless the company has more than $10 million in total assets and more than 500 shareholders;

> Companies may choose among three formats to prepare the offering circular, one of which is a simplified question-and-answer document; and

> You may "test the waters" to determine if there is adequate interest in your securities before going through the expense of filing with the SEC.

All types of companies which do not report under the Exchange Act may use Regulation A, except "blank check" companies, those with an unspecified business, and investment companies registered or required to be registered under the Investment Company Act of 1940. In most cases, shareholders may use Regulation A to resell up to $1.5 million of securities.

If you "test the waters," you can use general solicitation and advertising prior to filing an offering statement with the SEC, giving you the advantage of determining whether there is enough market interest in your securities before you incur the full range of legal, accounting, and other costs associated with filing an offering statement. You may not, however, solicit or accept money until the SEC staff completes its review of the filed offering statement and you deliver prescribed offering materials to investors.

D. Regulation D

Regulation D establishes three exemptions from Securities Act registration. Let's address each one separately.

Rule 504

Rule 504 provides an exemption for the offer and sale of up to $1,000,000 of securities in a 12-month period. Your company may use this exemption so long as it is not a blank check company and is not subject to Exchange Act reporting requirements. Like the other Regulation D exemptions, in general you may not use public solicitation or advertising to market the securities and purchasers receive "restricted" securities, meaning that they may not sell the securities without registration or an applicable exemption. However, you can use this exemption for a public offering of your securities and investors will receive freely tradable securities under the following circumstances:

> You register the offering exclusively in one or more states that require a publicly filed registration statement and delivery of a substantive disclosure document to investors;

> You register and sell in a state that requires registration and disclosure delivery and also sell in a state without those requirements, so long as you deliver the disclosure documents mandated by the state in which you registered to all purchasers; or,

> You sell exclusively according to state law exemptions that permit general solicitation and advertising, so long as you sell only to "accredited investors," a term we describe in more detail below in connection with Rule 505 and Rule 506 offerings.

Even if you make a private sale where there are no specific disclosure delivery requirements, you should take care to provide sufficient information to investors to avoid violating the antifraud provisions of the securities laws. This means that any information you provide to investors must be free from false or misleading statements. Similarly, you should not exclude any information if the omission makes what you do provide investors false or misleading.

Rule 505

Rule 505 provides an exemption for offers and sales of securities totaling up to $5 million in any 12-month period. Under this exemption, you may sell to an unlimited number of "accredited investors" and up to 35 other persons who do not need to satisfy the sophistication or wealth standards associated with other exemptions. Purchasers must buy for investment only, and not for resale. The issued securities are "restricted." Consequently, you must inform investors that they may not sell for at least a year without registering the transaction. You may not use general solicitation or advertising to sell the securities.

An "accredited investor" is:

a bank, insurance company, registered investment company, business development company, or small business investment company;

an employee benefit plan, within the meaning of the Employee Retirement Income Security Act, if a bank, insurance company, or registered investment adviser makes the investment decisions, or if the plan has total assets in excess of $5 million;

a charitable organization, corporation or partnership with assets exceeding $5 million;

a director, executive officer, or general partner of the company selling the securities;

a business in which all the equity owners are accredited investors;

a natural person with a net worth of at least $1 million;

a natural person with income exceeding $200,000 in each of the two most recent years or joint income with a spouse exceeding $300,000 for those years and a reasonable expectation of the same income level in the current year; or

a trust with assets of at least $5 million, not formed to acquire the securities offered, and whose purchases are directed by a sophisticated person.

It is up to you to decide what information you give to accredited investors, so long as it does not violate the antifraud prohibitions. But you must give non-accredited investors disclosure documents that generally are the same as those used in registered offerings. If you provide information to accredited investors, you must make this information available to the non-accredited investors as well. You must also be available to answer questions by prospective purchasers.

Here are some specifics about the financial statement requirements applicable to this type of offering:

Financial statements need to be certified by an independent public accountant;

If a company other than a limited partnership cannot obtain audited financial statements without unreasonable effort or expense, only the company's balance sheet, to be dated within 120 days of the start of the offering, must be audited; and

Limited partnerships unable to obtain required financial statements without unreasonable effort or expense may furnish audited financial statements prepared under the federal income tax laws.

Rule 506

As we discussed earlier, Rule 506 is a "safe harbor" for the private offering exemption. If your company satisfies the following standards, you can be assured that you are within the Section 4(2) exemption:

You can raise an unlimited amount of capital;

You cannot use general solicitation or advertising to market the securities;

You can sell securities to an unlimited number of accredited investors (the same group we identified in the Rule 505 discussion) and up to 35 other purchasers. Unlike Rule 505, all non-accredited investors, either alone or with a purchaser representative, must be sophisticated — that is, they must have sufficient knowledge and experience in financial and business matters to make them capable of evaluating the merits and risks of the prospective investment;

It is up to you to decide what information you give to accredited investors, so long as it does not violate the antifraud prohibitions. But you must give non-accredited investors disclosure documents that generally are the same as those used in registered offerings. If you provide information to accredited investors, you must make this information available to the non-accredited investors as well;

You must be available to answer questions by prospective purchasers;

Financial statement requirements are the same as for Rule 505; and

Purchasers receive "restricted" securities. Consequently, purchasers may not freely trade the securities in the secondary market after the offering.

****

VII. Are There State Law Requirements in Addition to Federal Ones?

The federal government and state governments each have their own securities laws and regulations. If your company is selling securities, it must comply with federal and state securities laws. If a particular offering is exempt under the federal securities laws, that does not necessarily mean that it is exempt from any of the state laws.

Historically, most state legislatures have followed one of two approaches in regulating public offerings of securities, or a combination of the two approaches. Some states review small businesses' securities offerings to ensure that companies disclose to investors all information needed to make an informed investment decision. Other states also analyze public offerings using substantive standards to assure that the terms and structure of the offerings are fair to investors, in addition to the focus on disclosure.

To facilitate small business capital formation, the North American Securities Administrators Association, or NASAA, in conjunction with the American Bar Association, developed the Small Company Offering Registration, also known as SCOR. SCOR is a simplified "question and answer" registration form that companies also can use as the disclosure document for investors. SCOR was primarily designed for state registration of small business securities offerings conducted under the SEC's Rule 504, for sale of securities up to $1,000,000. Currently, over 45 states recognize SCOR. To assist small business issuers in completing the SCOR Form, NASAA has developed a detailed "Issuer's Manual." This manual is available through NASAA's Web site at http://www.nasaa.org.

In addition, a small company can use the SCOR Form, called Form U-7, to satisfy many of the filing requirements of the SEC's Regulation A exemption, for sales of securities of up to $5,000,000, since the company may file it with the SEC as part of the Regulation A offering statement.

To assist small businesses offering in several states, many states coordinate SCOR or Regulation A filings through a program called regional review. Regional reviews are available in the New England, Mid-Atlantic, Midwest and Western regions.

Companies seeking additional information on SCOR, regional reviews or the "Issuer's Manual" should contact NASAA.

****

NOTES

1. Form D must be filed with the SEC in conjunction with any exempt securities offering. Among the information provided to the SEC in Form D are the name of the issuer, the type of entity, principal place of business, industry group, issuer revenue size range, issuer net asset value range, offering exemption(s) claimed, duration of the offering, types of securities being offered, total amount of the offering and the number of non-accredited investors to be solicited.

2. Rule 144 provides for the sale of restricted stock purchased in an exempt private offering. Filing with the SEC is required prior to selling restricted stock, and the number of shares that can be sold within certain time periods is limited. Rule 144A provides a safe harbor exemption from registration for sales of certain restricted securities to qualified institutional buyers. Rule 144A is not available to the original issuer of the securities. Rule 144A provides that sales in compliance with the rule are not "distributions" and the seller of the restricted securities, therefore, is not an "underwriter" within the meaning of the Securities Act.

QUESTIONS

1. On what basis does the SEC review registration statements to declare them effective?

2. Why may securities offered under the intrastate offering exemption have to be sold at a discount?

3. What are the benefits of offering securities under the Regulation A exemption as opposed to offering securities through a full registration using a S-1 Registration Statement?

4. When may investors receive freely tradable securities under a Rule 504 securities offering?

5. When is a natural person an accredited investor? When is a business an accredited investor? Why are the directors and officers of the company selling the securities accredited investors?

6. What is the difference between an "accredited investor" and a "sophisticated investor"?

7. Under the Rule 505 exemption, to how many accredited investors may the company sell? Under the Rule 505 exemption, to how many non-accredited investors may the company sell? Are there any differences between the information provided to accredited investors and non-accredited investors under the Rule 505 exemption?

8. What is the difference between non-accredited investors under Rule 505 and non-accredited investors under Rule 506?

9. What are "restricted" securities?

10. Does an exempt public offering of securities limit the liability of the company, and its officers and directors, for federal securities fraud?

11. What is the general relationship between the federal securities laws and the state securities laws?

CASE NOTES

1. Hamby v. Clearwater Consulting Concepts, LLP, 428 F.Supp. 2d 915 (E.D. Ark. 2006) (Filing of Form D is not a prerequisite condition for registration exemption under Regulation D, Rule 506; statement in partnership agreement that securities sales are made pursuant to federal registration exemption is insufficient to exempt sale under Arkansas securities law without showing of actual compliance with the exemption); Ligon v. Deloitte, Haskins & Sells, 957 F.2d 546 (8th Cir. 1992) (Where jury determined that investors did not rely on offeror's representation of net worth there was no cognizable injury under securities law; there can be no primary violation of securities laws without showing of reliance and there can be no claim of aiding and abetting without primary violation); Parker v. Broom, 820 F.2d 966 (8th Cir. 1987) (Issuer bears burden of proof on private offering exemption and must show that offerees had access to the kind of information registration statement would disclose; jury could reasonably conclude that oil company had

conducted private offering, even though company sold investment interests to several parties, because company essentially only dealt with business associate who was an experienced investor); Sorrell v. SEC, 679 F.2d 1323 (9th Cir. 1982) (Private offering exemption depends on number of offerees, offerees' sophistication, conduct of offering, offerees' relationship to issuer and offerees' access to information which would be found in registration statement; registration exemptions are construed narrowly and burden of proof is on person claiming exemption; where broker offered no evidence of the number of offerees or of their access to registration-type information broker failed to meet burden of proof that sale of limited partnership interests was exempt as a private offering exemption); Mary S. Krech Trust v. Lakes Apartments, 642 F.2d 98 (5th Cir. 1981) (Whether offering is public or private is a question of fact which must be resolved under the particular facts of the case; the critical question in determining the validity of a private offering defense is whether the offerees need the protection of the Securities Act; evidence as to number of offerees, their financial wealth and information provided to offerees was sufficient for jury to conclude offering was exempt from registration under the private offering exemption); Swenson v. Engelstad, 626 F.2d 421 (5th Cir. 1980) (Majority shareholder of hockey franchise who conveyed 50 shares of stock in exchange for a sum of money was a "seller" within the meaning of the Securities Act which prohibits the sale of unregistered securities; concession that stock was not registered creates a *prima facie* case of violation of securities laws; majority shareholder of hockey franchise was liable to purchasers of unregistered securities as a controlling person where shares were sold by public relations person and hockey team's manager).

Additional Information

1. William Meade Fletcher, 14 Fletcher Cyc. Corp. § 6796 (2010).

2. Raising Cap. Private Placement Forms & Tech. Form 8.05 (2010).

3. John C. Williams, 84 A.L.R.3d 1009 (2010).

4. 2 West's Fed. Admin. Prac. § 2279 (4th ed.) (2010).

5. Aaron Rachelson, Corporate Acquisitions §§ 2:40-246 (2010).

6. James Buchwalter Et al. 79A C.J.S. Securities Regulation §§ 58, 514 (2010).

7. John R. Kennel, 69 Am. Jur. 2d Securities Regulation — State § 120 (2010).

8. Clifford R. Ennico, Closely Held Corp § 6:44 (2010).

9. Harold S. Bloomenthal & Samuel Wolff, 1 Going Public Handbook § 2:45 (2009).

10. Richard A. Booth, Financing The Corporation § 8:9 (2010).

11. Stuart R. Cohn, 1 Sec. Counseling for Small & Emerging Companies §§ 6:28, 630 (2009).

12. Stuart R. Cohn, 2 Sec. Counseling for Small & Emerging Companies § 15:3 (2009).

13. HAROLD S. BLOOMEHTHAL, SAMUEL WOLFF, 3 SEC. & FED. CORP. LAW §§ 3:39, 3:44, 3:50 (2d ed.) (2010).

14. FRANCIS C. AMENDOLA ET AL. 69 AM. JUR. 2D SECURITIES REGULATION — FEDERAL § 127, 151 (2010).

15. ELIZABETH T. TSAI, 6 A.L.R. FED 536 (2010).

11.2.4   Private Placement Memorandum

The private placement memorandum (PPM) is a multifaceted document. For the company issuing the securities, the PPM is in part a sales document, describing the company and its financial prospects in the most favorable light, and in part a protection document, minimizing the company's future liability in suits brought by disappointed investors. For prospective investors, the PPM is an information document containing the terms of the offering and providing some of the information needed to make a decision whether or not to purchase the securities. Professional investors read a PPM with a good deal of skepticism, other investors sometimes never read a PPM. For potential plaintiffs, and possibly the SEC, the PPM is an indictment document which is compared very carefully to the PPM requirements in cases which have imposed liability on companies, and their officers and directors. This section summarizes the main content of a typical PPM.

SUMMARY OF TYPICAL PRIVATE PLACEMENT MEMORANDUM CONTENTS

As you saw under the private offering exemptions, the company offering the securities must often provide investors information that is very similar to that provided under a registered securities offering. The private placement memorandum (PPM) is the document invariably used to provide this information to investors.

A PPM usually begins with boilerplate language that describes the nature of the stock offering and provides numerous caveats regarding the PPM. Typical boilerplate language would include the following:

> The PPM is being used in conjunction with a private offering of securities pursuant to the registration exemption under Section 4(2) of the Securities Act and Rule 506 promulgated pursuant to Section 4(2), as well as applicable state private offering exemptions;

> The content of the PPM is confidential and solely for use in considering the purchase of the offered securities, and the PPM may not be reproduced or disclosed to any third party without prior written approval;

> The offered securities are subject to restrictions on transfer and resale, and investors agree that they will not transfer or resell the securities except pursuant to an effective registration statement or an exemption from registration;

> The PPM is not an offer to sell or a solicitation to buy any securities other than the securities offered under the PPM, and the PPM is not an offer to

sell or a solicitation to buy securities in any state in which such an offer or solicitation would be unlawful;

Statements in the PPM are made as of the date of the PPM and are subject to change or amendment without notice;

The company has established investor suitability standards for the purchase of the securities and each investor must represent to the company that (a) the investor has the knowledge and experience in financial and business matters to evaluate the merits and risks associated with the purchase of the securities, and the investor is able to bear the economic risks associated with the purchase of the securities; (b) the investor is acquiring the securities solely for the purpose of investment and has no intention to resell the securities; and (c) the investor has had access to all of the financial and business information necessary to make an informed decision regarding the purchase of the securities;

Prospective investors should not consider the contents of the PPM as legal or investment advice, and in making the decision to purchase the securities prospective investors must rely on their own due diligence regarding the company and the terms of the securities offering;

The offer to sell the securities is subject to withdrawal, cancelation or modification at any time prior to the acceptance of the offer by investors according to the terms established by the company for acceptance of the offer.

The first substantive section of a PPM is usually a summary of the securities offering. The offering summary includes among other information:

The minimum and maximum number of shares being offered;

The price per share;

The total dollar amount of the offering;

The description of the shares being offered — common stock, preferred stock, convertible preferred stock, preferences among different classes of stock in payment of dividends and in liquidation of the company; [These different classes of stock will be discussed in the subsection on Venture Capital Investment.]

The number of shares outstanding in each class of stock;

The use of the proceeds received from the sale of the stock; and

The definition of eligible investors.

Following the offering summary, a PPM typically presents the company's financial statements, most often in the form of unaudited income statements and balance sheets for certain accounting periods prior to the offering. Although the financial statements presented by the company may not be audited, they should be prepared according to Generally Accepted Accounting Practices. In addition, any knowing misstatements or omissions of information in the financial statements can be the basis for civil and/or criminal liability of the company and its officers and directors.

Other information included in a typical PPM includes:

A description of the industry in which the company will compete including size, trends, horizontal and vertical relationships, and dominant firms and market shares;

A description of the company's business model including the company's competitive advantages and disadvantages, strategic plans for future growth, and potential future partnering and supply chain relationships;

A description of the competition in the company's market and a discussion of how the company plans to prevail in competing with the firms in the market;

A description of the company's technology(ies) and a discussion of the technology(ies) price and performance advantages relative to other technology(ies) available in the market;

A description of the company's intellectual property portfolio with special attention to the intellectual property protection of the company's key products and services;

A description of all technical, managerial, marketing, intellectual property and legal risks that could affect the value of the investment;

A description of any specific, unresolved legal matters that could affect the value of the investment; and

A description of the company's senior management team including educational background, prior industry experience, published papers and books, patents, and professional recognition and awards.

CASE NOTES

1. Paco Development Partners (PDP) was a limited partnership, created by Paco Pharmaceutical Services (Paco), to engage in research and development of new transdermal pharmaceutical products. Five hundred and seventy-seven investors purchased limited partnership units in PDP, investing a total of $25 million. Each investor received a Private Placement Memorandum (PPM) prior to signing the unit purchase agreement. The PPM was prepared by Dean Witter, the private placement agent, in collaboration with a law firm that served as a technical consultant. Sales of the limited partnership units were restricted to individuals who had a net worth exceeding $1 million or an individual income exceeding $200,000 for the past two years. The PPM advised prospective investors to consult their personal financial advisors to determine whether this investment was suitable for them. The PPM contained many warnings regarding the risky nature of the investment. The inside cover of the PPM stated "Investment in the Units offered hereby involves a high degree of risk. No person should invest in the Units who is not in a position to lose his entire investment." The PPM noted numerous risk factors including the uncertainty of research and development activities, difficulties in obtaining patent

protection and maintaining trade secrets, competition and uncertain product sales, and uncertainty of timely regulatory approval. Prospective investors were also warned that there was no assurance that products could be developed or marketed, that necessary scientific and technical personnel could be recruited, and that the necessary sales and marketing force could be established. Unfortunately, PDP was not successful and seventy-three investors joined in an action against Paco and Dean Witter claiming securities fraud. What result? *See* Barrios v. Paco Pharmaceutical Services, Inc., 816 F.Supp. 243 (S.D.N.Y. 1993).

2. *See also* United States v. Ayers, 2010 U.S. App. LEXIS 15714 (6th Cir. 2010) (PPM provided to prospective bond purchasers that stated proceeds would be used to purchase accounts receivable from healthcare providers, when proceeds were actually used to advance funds to healthcare providers, warranted a jury finding that the PPM contained misrepresentations that were both false and material; principal in bond issuer who attended meetings in which problems of advancing funds to healthcare providers were discussed and who received numerous documents which discussed the fraud knew the PPM representations were false and was guilty of securities fraud); Whirlpool Financial Corp. v. GN Holdings, Inc., 67 F.3d 605 (7th Cir. 1995) (Statute of limitations on securities fraud action expired one year after the discrepancies between the private placement memorandum and actual performance put plaintiff on inquiry notice; inquiry notice arises when victim of alleged fraud becomes aware of facts that would lead a reasonable person to investigate whether there might be a valid claim of fraud; if inquiry notice arises, plaintiff must exercise reasonable diligence in investigating facts); Block v. First Blood Associates, 988 F.2d 344 (2d Cir. 1993) (Investors' securities fraud claim arose when investors had sufficient knowledge to put them on notice that the PPM contained material misrepresentations, not when investment actually failed to produce profits stated in PPM; investors were sophisticated and should have realized that investment was tax-motivated and not intended to return a profit); Wilson v. Saintine Exploration and Drilling Corp., 872 F.2d 1124 (2d Cir. 1989) (Law firm that prepared PPM in connection with a private securities offering by one of its clients could not be held liable for securities fraud, regardless of a material misstatement in the PPM, because law firm was non-selling, collateral participant in the securities offering); Hughes v. BCI Int'l Holdings, Inc., 452 F. Supp. 2d 290, 2006) (Investor's allegations of misrepresentations in PPM were sufficient to plead fraud against company founder individually when investor alleged founder knew company was in dire financial condition at time PPM was provided; New York law imposes a duty to disclose on persons who possess special expertise or who have a special position of trust with another party such that the person knows the other party will rely upon the misrepresentation); Kunzweiler v. Zero.Net, Inc., 2002 U.S. Dist. LEXIS 12080 (N.D. Tex. 2002) (Question of whether reasonable person reading PPM of internet holding company may have been left with misleading impression that company CEO was an unbiased securities trader presented fact questions that could not be resolved on motion to dismiss investor's securities fraud claim against company and its CEO; internet holding company did not have duty to disclose that the CEO controlled the company through another holding company owned by the CEO and his wife absent any contrary affirmative statements in PPM); Kolson v. Vembu, 869 F. Supp. 1315 (N.D. Ill. 1994) (When sophisticated lenders who provided financing for commercial development should have become

aware of alleged misrepresentations in the PPM was a material question of fact which precluded entry of summary judgment for developer on its statute of limitations defense to lenders' fraud claims); Sable v. Southmark/Envicon Capital Corp., 819 F.Supp. 324 (S.D.N.Y. 1993) (Allegedly misleading financial projections in PPM were not sufficient to support claim of securities fraud where PPM contained numerous warnings about financial projections, estimates of tax benefits and profits, and investors presented no evidence that defendants knew at time PPM was provided that projected profits and benefits would not be realized); Adler v. Berg Harmon Assocs., 816 F. Supp. 919 (S.D.N.Y. 1993) (Allegations by investors in real estate tax shelter limited partnership that PPM falsely asserted that partnership properties had sufficient revenues to cover operating costs and debt service created a question of fact sufficient to deny defendants' motion to dismiss in securities fraud action).

Additional Information

1. Joseph W. Bartlett, Equity Fin. Ch. 8; §§ 8.1–8.2; Form 26-2 (2010).

2. Robert Brown, Jr., Herbert B. Max, Raising Cap. Private Placement Forms & Tech. Form 19.23 (2010).

3. Gerald T. Lins Et al., Hedge Funds and Other Private Funds: Reg and Comp § 5:4 (2009).

4. William M. Prifti, 24C Securities Pub. & Priv. Offerings, Appendix E42 (2010).

5. William Jordan, 35 No. 8 Professional Liability Reporter Art. 9 (2010).

6. Kimberly V. Mann, SPO38 ALI-ABA 153 (2009).

11.3 FRAUD IN PRIVATE SECURITIES OFFERINGS

OHIO BUREAU OF WORKERS' COMPENSATION v. MDL ACTIVE DURATION FUND, LTD.
476 F.Supp.2d 809 (S.D. Ohio 2007)

Graham, District Judge.

This is an action filed by the Ohio Bureau of Workers' Compensation, an agency of the state of Ohio, against the MDL Active Duration Fund, Ltd. ("the Fund"), MDL Capital Management Inc. ("MDL Capital"), and Mark D. Lay. The complaint alleges violations of Ohio law, and jurisdiction in this court is based on diversity of citizenship. Other defendants named in the complaint were previously dismissed from this action due to lack of personal jurisdiction in an opinion and order filed on June 1, 2006.

This matter is before the court on the motion of the remaining defendants to dismiss the complaint pursuant to Fed.R.Civ.P. 12(b)(6) for failure to state a claim for which relief may be granted. A complaint may be dismissed for failure to state a claim only where it appears beyond doubt that the plaintiff can prove no set of facts in support of its claim which would entitle it to relief. The court must construe the complaint in a light most favorable to the plaintiff and accept all well-pleaded allegations in the complaint as true. A motion to dismiss under Rule 12(b)(6) will be granted if the complaint is without merit due to an absence of law to support a claim of the type made or of facts sufficient to make a valid claim, or where the face of the complaint reveals that there is an insurmountable bar to relief.

****

I. Common Law Fraud (Count I) and Fraudulent Inducement (Count II)

Defendants allege that the allegations of common law fraud alleged in Count I and fraudulent inducement alleged in Count II fail to state a claim. Defendants also argue that these allegations fail to satisfy the particularity requirement of Fed.R. Civ. P. 9(b).

While state law governs the burden of proving fraud at trial in a diversity action, the procedure for pleading fraud is governed by the pleading requirements of Rule 9(b). Rule 9(b) requires that averments of fraud must be stated with particularity. The Sixth Circuit requires a plaintiff, at a minimum, to allege the time, place, and content of the alleged misrepresentation relied upon, the fraudulent scheme, the fraudulent intent of the defendants, and the injury resulting from the fraud. Allegations of fraudulent misrepresentation must be made with sufficient particularity and with a sufficient factual basis to support an inference that they were knowingly made.

However, when deciding a motion to dismiss for failure to comply with Rule 9(b), this court must also consider the policy favoring simplicity in pleading codified in Fed.R.Civ.P. 8, which requires a "short and plain statement of the claim." The threshold test is whether the complaint places the defendant on sufficient notice of the misrepresentation, thus allowing the defendants to answer and address the plaintiff's claim of fraud in an informed manner.

The elements of a claim of fraud under Ohio law are: (1) a representation, or, where there is a duty to disclose, concealment of a fact; (2) which is material to the transaction at hand; (3) made falsely, with knowledge of its falsity, or with such utter disregard and recklessness as to whether it is true or false that knowledge may be inferred; (4) with the intent of misleading another into relying upon it; (5) justifiable reliance upon the representation or concealment; and (6) a resulting injury proximately caused by the reliance.

The complaint includes allegations of the alleged misrepresentations and concealment of facts on the part of the defendants which form the basis for plaintiff's fraud claims. The alleged misrepresentations include statements in the Private Placement Memorandum ("PPM") submitted by the Fund, as well as other statements and correspondence. The complaint alleges the nature of these statements and omissions, as well as the approximate time and place of these statements and omissions.

Defendants argue that the plaintiff could not have reasonably relied on the language concerning the leverage guideline contained in the PPM in deciding to invest in the Fund. The leverage provision states:

> The Fund is expected to leverage the Fund's investment portfolio as a means to increase yield and enhance total return. Up to 150% of the Fund's assets, at the time of investment, may be leveraged (*i.e.*, the combined value of borrowings and short positions). Leveraging will include, but is not limited to, short selling of securities, reverse repurchase agreements, certain option and futures transactions plus any borrowings to leverage the Fund's assets. Although the use of leverage may enhance returns on the Fund's portfolio and increase the number of investments that may be made by the Fund, it may also substantially increase the risk of loss. The percentage included above is intended as a guideline and may be changed from time to time at the sole discretion of the Board of Directors.

Defendants argue that in light of the language that the limit on leveraging of 150% "is intended as a guideline and may be changed from time to time at the sole discretion of the Board of Directors," the limit was not a sufficiently definite representation to form the basis for a fraud claim. However, this argument is based on defendants' interpretation of the leveraging provision. The leveraging provision is arguably subject to different interpretations. Further, plaintiff's allegations are sufficient to allege that the leveraging guideline provision, even as interpreted by defendants, was not followed. Plaintiff alleges that the Fund's board of directors never took any action to change the leverage percentage. In other words, the board never exercised its discretion to change the PPM guideline of 150%, yet the funds were leveraged well beyond the 150% guideline. Plaintiff has alleged that from April 2004 through December 2004, the Fund frequently exceeded the leverage guideline, without disclosure of this fact to plaintiff. Plaintiff also argues that the 150% figure was so far exceeded that it could not reasonably have been deemed to have been used as a "guideline." It cannot be said that the plaintiff's fraud claim, insofar as it is based on the leverage percentage in the PPM, is insufficient to allege justifiable reliance as a matter of law. In addition, there are other alleged representations and omissions described in the complaint which form a basis for plaintiff's fraud claims.

Defendants also argue that the complaint fails to adequately allege intent or scienter. Rule 9(b) provides that "[m]alice, intent, knowledge, and other condition of mind of a person may be averred generally." Plaintiff has alleged that the defendants knowingly made false representations and knowingly failed to disclose facts concerning the amount being leveraged and the investment strategies of the Fund, and that such representations and concealment of facts were made with knowledge of falsity and with the intent to deceive. Plaintiff has adequately alleged the necessary element of intent.

The court finds that Counts I and II of the amended complaint comply with the requirements of Rule 9(b). However, even if plaintiff's allegations fail to satisfy those requirements, dismissal on this basis alone would not be appropriate in the absence of a motion for a more definite statement under Fed.R.Civ.P. 12(e). No such motion has been filed in this case.

II. Ohio Securities Law Violations (Counts III, IV and V)

Defendants have moved to dismiss Counts III, IV and V, which allege violations of Ohio's securities laws. Count III alleges a violation of Ohio Rev.Code § 1707.41(A), which provides:

> In addition to the other liabilities imposed by law, any person that, by a written or printed circular, prospectus, or advertisement, offers any security for sale, or receives the profits accruing from such sale, is liable, to any person that purchased the security relying on the circular, prospectus, or advertisement, for the loss or damage sustained by the relying person by reason of the falsity of any material statement contained therein or for the omission of material facts, unless the offeror or person that receives the profits establishes that the offeror or person had no knowledge of the publication prior to the transaction complained of, or had just and reasonable grounds to believe the statement to be true or the omitted facts to be not material.

All the defendants are named in this count.

Count IV alleges a violation of Ohio Rev.Code § 1707.42(B) against MDL Capital. Section 1707.42(B) provides that an investment adviser is liable for damages resulting from acts of an investment advisor which violate Ohio Rev.Code Chapter 1707. Count V, which names all defendants, invokes Ohio Rev.Code § 1707.43(A), which provides for a rescission remedy at the election of the purchaser.

The above sections create no new civil liabilities beyond those established by common law, and do not limit or restrict common law liabilities for deception or fraud other than as specified in those sections.

Defendants argue that the complaint fails to comply with the requirements of Rule 9(b) that the fraud which is the underlying basis for the above statutory violations be pleaded with particularity. Defendants rely on *Nickels v. Koehler Management Corp.*,541 F.2d 611, 616–17 (6th Cir.1976), in which the court stated that an action under § 1707.41 required either knowledge of the falsity of the representation or lack of diligence in ascertaining its truth or falsity on the part of the seller. However, as noted previously, the court has determined that the complaint complies with Rule 9(b), and adequately pleads facts supporting the elements of fraud, including knowledge and intent.

Defendants argue that a securities fraud claim cannot be based on the leveraging language in the PPM because the PPM does not contain a representation that leveraging would always be capped at 150%. Defendants point to their later disclosures to the plaintiff that the leveraging limit had been exceeded as evidence that they did not intend from the time of the initial investment to exceed the leveraging limit in the PPM.

This argument is based on defendants' interpretation of the leveraging language. The PPM states that "[u]p to 150% of the Fund's assets, at the time of investment, may be leveraged." Although the PPM states that the leveraging limit of 150% is a guideline which could be modified at the discretion of the board of directors, plaintiff has alleged in the complaint that the leveraging limit was never changed by the board, and was never actually followed as a guideline. Plaintiff has also alleged in the amended complaint that at the time the plaintiff's investment was solicited by means of the PPM, the defendants did not intend to follow the investment strategies and leverage guideline set forth in the PPM, and knowingly concealed facts regarding the true amount of leverage actually employed from the inception of the investment.

The allegations that defendants at some point disclosed that the investments in the fund had been leveraged in excess of 150% do not establish as a matter of law that defendants did not intend to exceed the leveraging guideline from its inception. Hypothetically, a trier of fact could conclude that the disclosures about the leverage guideline being exceeded were made when they were because discovery of that fact by plaintiff was inevitable due to losses to the Fund. In addition, plaintiff has alleged that while Lay disclosed at a meeting on September 16, 2004, that the Fund's assets had been leveraged by approximately 900%, the plaintiff later learned that the Fund's assets had actually been leveraged by approximately 1,900%. These are evidentiary matters which would more appropriately be addressed on summary judgment or at trial.

The complaint is sufficient to allege claims for securities fraud under Ohio law, as opposed to a mere breach of contract. The complaint is adequate to state a claim under §§ 1707.41 and 1707.42.

****

X. Conclusion

In accordance with the foregoing, defendants' motion to dismiss Count VII, as to all defendants, and Count IX as it applies to the defendant Fund, is granted. In all other respects, the motion to dismiss is denied.

QUESTIONS

1.   What is the court's threshold test in balancing the "particularity" requirement of Fed. R. Civ. P. 9(b) and the policy of favoring "short and plain" statements of claims in Fed. R. Civ. P. 8?

2.   The fifth element in a claim of common law fraud under Ohio law is justifiable reliance upon the representation or concealment. Do you think the plaintiff was justified in relying upon the representation that up to 150% of the fund's assets will be leveraged when the representation stated it was intended as a guideline that may be changed at the sole discretion of the Board of Directors?

3.   Did the PPM state that formal action by the Board of Directors was required to change the leverage percentage?

4.   How is a cause of action under Ohio's securities laws different from a cause of action under Ohio's common law fraud law?

5.   Do you think a leverage guideline of 150% could be stretched to 1,900% even with approval of the Board of Directors?

H-M WEXFORD LLC v. ENCORP, INC.
832 A.2d 129, (Del. Ch. 2003)

LAMB, VICE CHANCELLOR.

I.

An investor who bought securities as part of a larger private placement is suing the issuer and the issuer's former CEO, making claims that information it received in connection with that transaction was materially misleading. The plaintiff is also asserting claims against the issuer and its board of directors arising out of the issuer's later efforts to reach a settlement with the plaintiff and the others who invested in the private placement. The plaintiff refused the issuer's proposal to issue additional securities in exchange for a release, but nearly all of the other investors agreed to this proposal and exchanged releases for additional shares of stock. The plaintiff alleges that the structure and effect of this settlement was coercive and discriminatory as to it. In addition, the plaintiff complains that the issuer did not comply fully with the provisions of Section 228 of the Delaware General Corporation Law when it solicited the stockholder written consents necessary to effectuate the terms of the settlement proposal.

In this opinion, the court grants a motion made by most of the defendants to dismiss the misrepresentation claims insofar as they relate to information furnished to the plaintiff that was not incorporated into the fully integrated written agreement by which it purchased the shares. The court will not dismiss other claims for misrepresentation that relate to information referred to or warranted by the purchase agreement. The court also dismisses the claims of unfairness or breach of fiduciary duty alleged with respect to the settlement transaction, as the allegations of the complaint fail to overcome the normal presumption of the business judgment rule. Finally, the court concludes that the complaint adequately alleges a failure to comply with the technical requirements of Section 228.

II.

A. The Parties

1. The Plaintiff

Plaintiff H-M Wexford, LLC is a Delaware limited liability company with its principal place of business in Greenwich, Connecticut. Wexford is in the business of making investments, and represents itself as an "accredited investor" as defined under the federal securities regulations.

2. The Defendants

a. Encorp And Its Executives

Defendant Encorp, Inc. is a Delaware corporation with its principal place of business in Windsor, Colorado. The company provides products, services and solutions to commercial and industrial customers with respect to on-site power systems. Defendant Jeffrey Whitham founded Encorp in 1993 and until recently served as the company's President, CEO and Chairman of the board of directors. Defendant Dennis Orwig has been the President and CEO of Encorp since February 19, 2002. On or about July 26, 2002, Orwig purportedly became a director of Encorp.

b. The Board Of Directors

There are five members of Encorp's board of directors, all of whom are defendants in this case. They are Steven Ballentine, Joseph Iannucci, Jesse Neyman, William Patterson, and George Schreck (collectively, the "Board of Directors"). Ballentine has been a director of Encorp since February 2001, and is a managing member of Ballentine Capital Partners Fund, L.P. Iannucci has been a director of Encorp since December 1997. Neyman is director of Encorp, and is affiliated with AES Holdings, L.P. Patterson has been a director of Encorp since January 1998, and is President of Enstar Management Corporation. Schreck has been a director of Encorp since July 1997. He is Vice President of Pacificorp Energy Services, Inc., and owns 5,000 shares of Encorp Series A preferred stock.

B. The February 2001 Offering

1. The Series D Offering And The Purchase Agreement

On or about February 9, 2001, Wexford and a number of other persons (collectively, the "Purchasers") entered into a Stock and Warrant Purchase Agreement (the "Purchase Agreement") with Encorp for the purchase of certain Encorp stock and warrants (the "February 2001 Offering"). Defendant Whitham signed the Purchase Agreement on behalf of Encorp. The Purchase Agreement provided for Delaware law to govern the transaction.

On or about February 9, 2001, Wexford paid $1,999,800 to Encorp in exchange for 909 units of Encorp stock and warrants (the "Units"), pursuant to the Purchase Agreement. Each Unit that Wexford purchased consisted of one share of Encorp's Series D Convertible Preferred Stock (the "Series D Stock") and one warrant to purchase a share of Series D Stock. An automatic conversion of the warrants later occurred, and, as a result, the Units purchased by Wexford currently consist of 1,808 shares of Series D Stock.

In Section 3.05 of the Purchase Agreement, Encorp stated that it had delivered to the Purchasers the company's unaudited balance sheet as of September 30, 2000, as well as audited balance sheets as of December 31, 1998 and December 31, 1999.

Encorp also provided statements of operations, stockholders equity, and cash flows for those periods (collectively, the "Company Financial Statements"). All of these documents were provided to the Purchasers before the execution of the Purchase Agreement.

In Section 3.05 of the Purchase Agreement, Encorp represented that the Company Financial Statements presented the financial position of Encorp fairly, except where adjusted by notes or schedules. Encorp also represented in Section 3.14 and 3.18 thereof that all books and records were complete and correct and, since the date of the latest balance sheet, there was no material adverse change in its financial condition, contractual arrangements, or any other event or condition that would have a material adverse effect on Encorp's business.

2. The Private Placement Memorandum

Before it signed the Purchase Agreement, Wexford received a copy of a Private Placement Memorandum ("PPM") dated January 11, 2001. The PPM included audited financial information for the year ending December 31, 1999, and unaudited financial information for the eleven-month period ending November 30, 2000. Additionally, the PPM contained projections for the years ending December 31, 2001 and December 31, 2002. The projected figures in the PPM indicated that the sales for the twelve-month period ending December 31, 2000 would be $10.7 million, with a 31% gross margin of $3.3 million. The actual sales for the twelve months ending December 31, 2000 were $9.6 million, and Encorp only had an 11% gross margin of $1.1 million. There also were significant differences in the projections for the year ending December 31, 2001 and the actual results.

The complaint alleges that, before the Purchase Agreement was executed, Encorp and Whitham knew about Encorp's actual sales revenues, and the corresponding gross margins for December 2000 and January 2001, and knew the results for the year ending December 31, 2000. The defendants also allegedly knew that Encorp had lost a significant customer. After the closing, the complaint alleges, Wexford realized that Encorp's financial condition was significantly worse than had been represented in the PPM.

C. The Settlement Proposals And Related Transactions

1. The May 17 Proposal

On or about May 17, 2002, Wexford received a package of documents that set forth the terms of a proposal by Encorp to effectively reprice the Series D Stock (the "May 17 Proposal"). The proposal was an attempt by Encorp, the Board of Directors, and Orwig to resolve informal complaints from Purchasers relating to the February 2001 Offering, and Encorp's ensuing poor financial performance. The documents show that the Board of Directors and Orwig approved the May 17 Proposal. Under the May 17 Proposal, Encorp proposed to issue a sufficient number of additional shares of the Series D Stock in order to effectively reprice the February 2001 Offering at $625 per share.

The May 17 Proposal contemplated that, as part of the transaction, Encorp would grant each Purchaser additional Series D Stock in exchange for a release from any and all claims and obligations related to the February 2001 Offering. The release applied to Encorp, as well as its past and present directors and officers (except Whitham) and Encorp's affiliates and agents. In addition, it was contemplated that Encorp would also grant releases in favor of its directors. Iannucci, Patterson and Schreck constituted a majority of Encorp's directors both at the time of the February 2001 Offering and at the time of the May 17 Proposal and, therefore, allegedly would have benefited from these releases. In his letter to the Purchasers, Orwig stated that the board strongly recommended the May 17 Proposal, but he did not disclose the apparent potential benefit that any such release may have afforded the directors.

The terms of the May 17 Proposal required that Purchasers holding at least 98% of the Series D Stock approve and participate in the settlement. If that condition were satisfied, then all Purchasers would receive additional shares of Series D Stock, *pro rata*, regardless of whether or not they approved and participated in the settlement. Wexford told Encorp that it was not interested in participating in the proposal. Because Wexford holds more than 2% of the Series D Stock, its refusal to participate "killed" the May 17 Proposal.

2. The June 7 Proposal

On or about June 7, 2002, Encorp issued a second proposal (the "June 7 Proposal") in a further effort to settle the dispute about the Series D Stock. Like the first proposal, the June 7 Proposal was approved by the Board of Directors and Orwig. Unlike the May 17 Proposal, however, the June 7 Proposal required participation by only 80% of the Series D shareholders. In a letter accompanying the June 7 Proposal, Orwig explained that the terms of the proposed settlement were revised because Wexford refused to accept the May 17 Proposal. By reducing the required percentage of participating Purchasers, Encorp obviated the need to gain Wexford's agreement in order to settle with the other Purchasers.

Under the June 7 Proposal, the Purchasers who participated in the settlement would receive additional shares of Series D Stock. Those who did not accept the Proposal would not receive additional shares; rather, they would retain their shares and whatever claim they had with regard to the February 2001 Offering. The June 7 Proposal also contemplated several amendments to Encorp's certificate of incorporation that were necessary to affect the transaction. Among other things, these amendments permitted the issuance of additional shares of Series D stock to those Purchasers who agreed to accept the Proposal without implicating preemptive rights of other Purchasers. In addition, the number of authorized shares of Series D Stock was increased from 40,500 to 75,000.

****

III.

Wexford filed its complaint against the defendants on August 19, 2002. The complaint makes claims that the defendants breached the terms of the original Purchase Agreement, and committed fraud against Wexford and the other Purchasers. The complaint also alleges that the defendants' efforts to reprice the Series D Stock through settlement have compromised the value of Wexford's stake in Encorp.

The focus of Wexford's complaint is two-fold. First, it alleges that the financial information provided by Encorp (particularly in the PPM) was materially misleading. Wexford claims that Encorp represented in the Purchase Agreement that it was in better financial condition than it actually was, and that these representations caused Wexford to purchase shares of the Series D Stock. Second, Wexford alleges that the June 7 Proposal represents an attempt by the defendants to force Wexford to agree to the terms of settlement (*i.e.*, the repricing of the Series D Stock issued in the February 2001 Offering). It claims that the June 7 Proposal was issued in response to Wexford's rejection of the May 17 Proposal, in order to discriminate against Wexford in the event that it did not settle. Wexford contends that the defendant members of the Board of Directors who approved the transaction were not disinterested, and that the implementation of the June 7 Proposal and the related transactions benefited the defendants at Wexford's expense.

Count I of the complaint alleges fraudulent inducement by Encorp, its Board of Directors and its then CEO Whitham. Specifically, Wexford claims that it was fraudulently induced into purchasing the Series D Stock. Count II of the complaint alleges equitable fraud against the same defendants. Count III alleges negligent misrepresentation by the defendants and Whitham with regard to the inaccuracy of the information that they provided to Wexford. Count IV alleges a breach of contract by Encorp with regard to the Purchase Agreement entered into by Wexford in relation to the February 2001 Offering. With regard to Counts I through IV, Wexford seeks rescission of the Purchase Agreement, requiring Encorp to return the entire sum Wexford paid for the Units it purchased in the February 2001 Offering — or, in the alternative, an award of damages-plus interest, attorneys fees, and costs.

Count V alleges that there was no proper stockholder approval of the June 7 Proposal because the date on which each stockholder signed the Consent was not properly recorded and the transactions associated with the June 7 Proposal (the Fourth Restated Certificate and other actions approved by the Consent) are therefore invalid. Wexford asks the court to declare invalid the transactions executed pursuant to the June 7 Proposal, and award equitable relief in the form of rescission and cancellation, or damages, plus interest, attorneys' fees, and reasonable cost of suit.

Count VI alleges a breach of fiduciary duty by the director defendants and Orwig. Specifically, Wexford charges that the defendants breached their fiduciary duty of loyalty to Wexford because of inherent conflicts of interest with respect to the June 7 Proposal and the transactions implemented in connection therewith. Wexford seeks damages, interest, attorneys' fees and reasonable costs of suit.

****

V.

A. Claims Relating To The February 2001 Offering

Wexford's claims regarding the February 2001 Offering rest on two basic contentions. First, Wexford claims that the representations made in the PPM, and particularly the accompanying financial statements, were materially misleading. Second, Wexford alleges that the defendants knew that Encorp had suffered an adverse change in financial condition and had lost one of its largest customers, but concealed those facts in order to enhance the appearance of the company's financial position before the execution of the Purchase Agreement. Based on these allegations, Wexford argues that the defendants breached the Purchase Agreement and perpetrated a fraud. Wexford has also alleged negligent misrepresentation against the defendants. While the legal standards used to evaluate breach of contract and fraud claims are quite different, the operative facts that give rise to Wexford's claims are the same. Therefore, the court will examine these claims concurrently.

1. Claims Related To The PPM And Attached Financial Statements

The defendants have moved to dismiss Wexford's claims for breach of contract and fraud (with regard to the ostensibly misleading financial statements) essentially for the same reason. They argue that the PPM cannot serve as a basis for Wexford's claims because it is excluded from the parties' agreement by the integration clause in Section 9.15 of the Purchase Agreement. Therefore, the defendants reason, there could not have been any contractual obligation with regard to the PPM, and thus none could be breached. Likewise, the defendants suggest that, in light of the exclusionary provisions of Section 9.15, Wexford's reliance on the PPM is not justifiable, and therefore the fraud claims based on the PPM must also fail as a matter of law.

The court agrees with the defendants' assessment of these claims, and will therefore dismiss Wexford's breach of contract and fraud claims as they relate to the PPM.

a. Breach Of Contract Claims Relating To The PPM

Under Delaware law, the elements of a breach of contract claim are: 1) a contractual obligation; 2) a breach of that obligation by the defendant; and 3) a resulting damage to the plaintiff. Here, the Purchase Agreement does not give rise to any contractual obligation predicated on the financial information set forth in the

PPM. On the contrary, it is clear from the Purchase Agreement, that Encorp agreed to warrant a different set of financial information, defined in the Purchase Agreement. Thus, its contractual liability will be limited to the warranted financials.

The thrust of Wexford's claim for breach of the Purchase Agreement relates to the Encorp financial statements that were included with the PPM but not in the Purchase Agreement. Specifically, the complaint alleges that the actual and projected Encorp financial information furnished in the PPM to Wexford and relied upon by it, were materially inaccurate and misleading. It then alleges that the deficiencies in the information provided in the PPM constitute a breach of the obligations created by the representations and warranties made in the Purchase Agreement.

In asserting this claim, Wexford relies on Section 3.26 of the Purchase Agreement, which is entitled *Disclosure* and reads in pertinent part:

> Neither this Agreement nor any other document, certificate or written statement delivered or required to be delivered by [Encorp] to each of the Purchasers *under this Agreement*, contains any untrue statement of a material fact or omits to state a material fact necessary in order to make the statements contained herein and therein not misleading.

At oral argument, the plaintiff's counsel suggested that the phrase "under this Agreement" modifies the term "Purchaser" in this Section. But the term "Purchaser" is itself defined in the Purchase Agreement and means a purchaser under the Purchase Agreement. Thus, to read the phrase "under this Agreement" as modifying "Purchaser" would obviously render the phrase meaninglessly redundant and surplusage. To avoid this result, the court reads that phrase as modifying the phrase "delivered or required to be delivered." So construed, it is clear that the warranty of accuracy of information provided by Encorp applies only to documents, certificates or other written statements "delivered or required to be delivered" pursuant to the Purchase Agreement. The PPM was not "delivered or required to be delivered" to Wexford "under" any provision of the Purchase Agreement; therefore, the financial information found in it does not fall within the scope of the warranty in Section 3.26.

This conclusion is supported by reference to the comprehensive integration clause found in Section 9.15 of the Purchase Agreement. Section 9.15 is entitled *Entire Agreement*, and reads:

> This Agreement, including documents, Schedules, instruments and agreements referred to herein, and the agreements and documents executed contemporaneously herewith embody the entire agreement and understanding of the parties hereto in respect to the subject matter hereof. There are no restrictions, promises, representations, warranties, covenants, or undertakings, other than those *expressly set forth or referred to herein* or therein. This Agreement supersedes all prior agreements and understandings between the parties with respect to such subject matter.

The defendants argue correctly that the effect of this clause is to exclude from the Purchase Agreement any representation or warranty not expressly set forth or referred to therein. The PPM is not expressly referred to anywhere in the Purchase Agreement. Therefore, it cannot serve as a basis for a claim that the defendants breached the Purchase Agreement.

Wexford argues that because the Purchase Agreement and the PPM both contain financial statements, the PPM was "referred to" in the Purchase Agreement within the meaning of the integration clause. This argument is unpersuasive for two reasons. First, the financial statements provided with the Purchase Agreement did not cover the same time periods as the financial documents included with the PPM. Second, the clear intent of the parties was that the defendants should warrant only the accuracy of the financial statements as of the period ending September 30, 2000, which were delivered pursuant to the Purchase Agreement. If the parties had agreed that the defendants should warrant the unaudited financial statements through November 30, 2000, which were included in the PPM, they could easily have done so. They did not. This confirms that the PPM and the information delivered therewith cannot serve as a basis for a breach of contract claim. Accordingly, the court will grant the defendants' motion to dismiss with respect to Wexford's breach of contract claims arising from the PPM.

b. Fraud And Negligent Misrepresentation Claims Relating To The PPM

In general terms, Wexford alleges that the defendants knowingly or negligently misrepresented Encorp's financial position, both in the PPM and in the Purchase Agreement. More specifically, Wexford asserts that the financial statements and projections initially provided by the defendants as attachments to the PPM were misleading. It alleges that the results of operations reflected in those financial statements are misleading because the defendants accelerated profits from the first quarter of 2001 into the fourth quarter of 2000 in order to boost Encorp's fourth quarter and year-end numbers before the February 2001 Offering.

As previously discussed, however, the PPM is not a document delivered under the Purchase Agreement. In fact, no projections were delivered under the Purchase Agreement, and it is not alleged that the Company Financial Statements delivered pursuant to the Purchase Agreement omitted any material facts, or were otherwise inaccurate.

Even if the PPM were considered for purposes of the misrepresentation claims, the financial information and projections section of the PPM contains an explicit disclaimer regarding the projections printed in bold type, stating that the projections had not been reviewed and no assurances were given with regard to the projections, and, furthermore, the projections should be read in conjunction with the enumerated risk factors and schedules discussing the projections attached thereto.

Moreover, in the Purchase Agreement, Wexford represented itself as an "accredited investor" as defined by federal securities regulations. As such, Wexford presumptively understood the ramifications of the integration clause in the Purchase Agreement and the disclaimer clause in the PPM. Wexford cannot now profess ignorance with respect to these clauses, and state that it justifiably relied on the information in the PPM when it entered into the Purchase Agreement. To say this differently, if Wexford wanted to be able to rely upon the PPM or particular facts represented therein, it had an obligation to negotiate to have those matters included within the scope of the integration clause of the contract.

Justifiable reliance is an element of common law fraud, equitable fraud, and negligent misrepresentation under Delaware law. Because Wexford cannot claim that it justifiably relied on the information in the PPM, these claims must fail as a matter of law. Therefore, the court will grant the defendants' motion to dismiss the misrepresentation claims with respect to the information contained in the PPM.

****

VI.

For the foregoing reasons, the motion to dismiss with respect to Counts I, II, III, and IV will be GRANTED in part and DENIED in part. The motion to dismiss with respect to Count V is GRANTED in part and DENIED in part. The motion to dismiss with respect to Count VI is GRANTED.

QUESTIONS

1. How could Wexford have assured that the PPM was incorporated into the Purchase Agreement? Why did Wexford not take these steps?

2. Could Wexford have argued a breach of fiduciary duty by the directors and majority shareholders of Encorp? Did Wexford suffer a distinct harm from the other Encorp shareholders?

3. As you saw above, provision of a PPM is required as a condition of a private offering exemption. The PPM is intended to provide purchasers with same basic information as contained in a registration statement. How is this federal disclosure policy affected by allowing the Stock Purchase Agreement to negate the PPM under state contract law?

4. If the PPM is required to be delivered to purchasers under Federal securities laws, why was it not a document "required to be delivered by [Encorp] to each of the Purchasers *under this Agreement*" and, therefore, covered by the warranty that it did not contain any untrue statement of material fact?

CASE NOTES

1. MCG is a Virginia-based venture capital firm that invests in small and mid-size companies in the media, communications, technology and information services sectors. Mitchell helped found MCG in 1998 and served as the company's CEO and Chairman of the Board. In late 2001, as part of its Initial Public Offering, MCG filed a Prospectus with the Securities and Exchange Commission. Based on information provided by Mitchell, the Biographical Information section of the Prospectus stated that "Mr. Mitchell earned a B.A. in Economics from Syracuse University." In fact, Mitchell had attended Syracuse University for three years and

studied economics, but never graduated from Syracuse University. Financial reporters covering MCG discovered the misrepresentation in the Prospectus and Mitchell immediately told the MCG board the truth about his educational background. On November 1, 2002, MCG issued a press release which corrected the information on Mitchell's educational background. A securities analyst immediately downgraded MCG's stock from "Buy" to "Hold" and reporters on CNN's Lou Dobbs Moneyline discussed MCG, saying Mitchell was "another CEO that lied about his resume." MCG's stock dropped from $11.85 to $8.40 per share on November 1, 2002, but recovered the losses within about a month. On November 3, 2002, the MCG board voted to withhold Mitchell's 2001 and 2002 bonuses and to remove him as Chairman of the Board. However, Mitchell continued to serve as CEO. Investors brought a class action suit against MCG and Mitchell, claiming they engaged in securities fraud. The district court granted MCG's motion to dismiss finding Mitchell's misrepresentations were not "material." The investors appealed. What result? *See* Greenhouse v. MCG Capital Corp., 392 F.3d 650 (4th Cir. 2004).

2. *See also* Holland v. Gexa Corp., 161 Fed. Appx. 364 (5th Cir. 2005) (Under Securities Act provision imposing liability on anyone who offers or sells securities by means of a prospectus containing material misrepresentations, plaintiff must plead reliance on the information that induced purchase; action could not be maintained for allegedly fraudulent private placement memorandum under Securities Act provision imposing liability on anyone who offers or sells securities by means of a prospectus containing material misrepresentations); Kunz v. SEC, 64 Fed. Appx. 659 (10th Cir. 2003) (Substantial evidence supported SEC finding of material misstatement in private placement memoranda; where broker and brokerage firm were aware of numerous "red flags" regarding company's financial condition broker and brokerage firm could not rely on independent auditor inspection of company's financial statements); In re Prison Realty Securities Litigation, 117 F.Supp.2d 681 (M.D. Tenn. 2000) (Plaintiff investors satisfied scienter requirement for securities fraud claim under § 10(b) of Securities Act when they alleged knowledge of facts contradicting public statements, deliberate timing of misrepresentations, and withholding of information regarding the financial relationship between companies involved in merger; plaintiff investors may overcome safe harbor provisions of Private Securities Litigation Reform Act for forward-looking statements by proving statements were material, were not coupled with adequate warnings, or speakers had actual knowledge that statements were false); Zobrist v. Coal-X, Inc., 708 F.2d 1511 (10th Cir. 1983) (Justifiable reliance in securities fraud action insures that there is a causal connection between the misrepresentation and the plaintiff's loss; plaintiff may not justifiably rely on a misrepresentation where falsity of misrepresentation is palpable; knowledge of information contained in a prospectus or private offering memorandum is imputed to investor even if investor fails to read prospectus or private offering memorandum); Ahmed v. Trupin, 809 F.Supp. 1100 (S.D.N.Y. 1993) (Under New York law, professional defendant who did not owe plaintiffs a fiduciary duty cannot be held liable to plaintiffs for negligence; under New York law attorney may not be held liable in negligence to investors with whom lawyer is not in relationship of privity; lawyer who prepares opinion letter addressed to investors, or which expressly invites investors' reliance, may engage in a form of limited representation and may be held liable in negligence).

Additional Information

1. J. WILLIAM HICKS, 7B EXEMPTED TRANS. UNDER SECURITIES ACT 1933 §§ 11:198–11:200 (2010).

2. JAMES D. COX, THOMAS L. HAZEN, 3 TREATISE ON THE LAW OF CORPORATIONS § 16:20 (3d) (2011).

3. ROGER J. MAGNUSON, 3 SHAREHOLDER LITIGATION §§ 24:14–24:15, 24:32 (2010).

4. Mellisa C. Nunziato, *Aiding and Abetting, A Madoff Family Affair: Why Secondary Actors Should be Held Accountable for Securities Fraud Through the Restoration of the Private Right of Action for Aiding and Abetting Liability Under the Federal Securities Laws*, 73 ALB. L. REV. 603 (2010).

5. Hon. D. W. Hunt, *Sizing Up Private Securities Fraud Litigation in California State Courts*, 49-SEP ORANGE COUNTY LAW. 23 (2007).

6. Alexander F. Cohen et al., *Zacharias And Section 5 Liability, Current Issues in Exchange Offers, And Current Public And Private Offerings*, 1804 PLI/CORP 317 (2010).

7. Hugh H. Makens, Warner Norcross, *Blue Sky Practice — Part I: Doing It Right: Avoiding Liability Arising From State Private Offerings Under ULOE And Limited Offering Exemptions*, SPO38 ALI-ABA 305 (2009).

8. Jean E. Harris, *Blue Sky Practice Part I: Liability Arising From State Private Offerings Under ULOE and Limited Offering Exemptions*, C993 ALI-ABA 297 (1995).

9. Ira M. Dansky, *Securities Issues: Private Placements; Disclosure; Blue Sky And Other State Laws; Fraud Situations*, 458 PLI/CORP 2005 (1984).

11.4   VENTURE CAPITAL INVESTMENTS

Venture capital firms typically form limited partnership funds with wealthy, highly risk-tolerant investors. The venture capital firm serves as the general partner and manager of the venture fund and the venture investors are passive, limited partners. The fund is charged a management fee by the venture capital firm, usually around 2% of the fund's capital. The management fee is used to cover the very high transaction costs associated with reviewing hundreds of potential "investable" companies and the operational costs of helping to manage the companies after an investment has been made. Depending upon its size, a venture capital firm may form multiple funds, and each fund is managed as a separate legal entity.

A new fund is commenced when a venture capital firm obtains the necessary commitments from investors, generally around $100 million. Minimum investment in a venture fund is most often $100,000 or more. A typical venture fund invests in 10–15 companies and is terminated (liquidated) in 5–7 years. Depending upon the invested company's stage of development, venture funds expect returns on their investment ranging from 25% to 70% per year. In addition to great risk, as noted above, venture investing also entails very high transaction costs. For every 100 business plans reviewed by a venture capital firm for funding, only about 10 get serious consideration, and only one ends up being funded. Of the funded companies, one company may yield sufficient gains to cover repayment of the majority of the venture fund, three or four companies may fail, and the remainder may yield minimal to reasonable rates of return.

11.4.1 Venture Capital Industry

SIZE AND STRUCTURE OF THE VENTURE CAPITAL MARKET

[Editor's Note: Much of the information in this subsection comes from the National Venture Capital Association Yearbook 2010 prepared by Thomson Reuters and The Introduction to Venture Capital and Private Equity Finance published by VC Experts.]

The venture capital industry is critical to the economic growth of the U.S. A recent study found that while venture capital investment represents only 0.2% of U.S. GDP, the revenue of companies funded by venture capital represented 21% of GDP in 2008. Some of the notable companies launched with venture capital include, The Home Depot, Starbucks, Staples, Whole Foods, eBay, Microsoft, Intel, Medtronic, Apple, Google and JetBlue.

Venture capital investments are equity investments in a company's stock at a time when the stock is totally illiquid and, therefore, worthless. Venture investments are generally made in "rounds" every year or two. Venture rounds are often called A Series, B Series, C Series, etc. Within a venture round, funds may be advanced in stages measured by time periods or performance milestones. Venture investments made according to time periods or milestones are called "tranches" and referred to as the first tranche, second tranche, third tranche, etc. In the great majority of cases, the return on a venture investment is only realized at the time the company goes public in an initial public offering (IPO), or at the time the company is acquired or merged into another company. During periods of recession, there are few opportunities for IPOs, mergers and acquisitions, making it very difficult for venture funds to "cash out" or "exit" their investment.

Venture capital firms generally prefer investments in companies that have an established market presence and strong revenue streams. In 2009, venture capital funds invested 9% of fund capital in startup or seed stage companies, 26% in early stage companies, 31% in companies undergoing significant expansion, and 34% in later stage companies preparing for an IPO or positioning for a merger or acquisition. As noted many times in the materials, the earlier the investment, the greater the risk and the higher the required rate of return.

Venture capital firms specialize in industry sectors drawing on the expertise and experience of the firms' managers in these sectors. In 2009, 20% of venture investment was in biotechnology, 18% in software, 14% in medical devices and equipment, 13% in industrial/energy, 6% in information technology services, 7% in media and entertainment, 4% in networking and equipment, and 4% in semiconductors. The remainder of the 2009 venture investment was spread over computers and peripherals (2%), electronics/instrumentation (2%), consumer products and services (2%), financial services (2%), health care services (1%), business products and services (1%), and retail and distribution (1%).

There is general consensus that for a company to be eligible for venture capital investment it must possess a majority of the following characteristics:

> A highly experienced management team and a well-respected board of directors or advisory board;

> A breakthrough technology that directly addresses an urgent need of the customers, is past the prototype stage and has intellectual property protection;

> A practical business model that provides above-average profit margins;

> Double-digit sales growth for the past 4–5 years and the prospect of returning ten times the investment in five to seven years;

> A pipeline of future products or services and a strategic plan for bringing these products or services to market; and

> A decided and distinct competitive advantage over other firms in the market.

Unfortunately, the venture capital industry has been hard-hit by the recent economic downturn. Venture capital under management in the U.S. decreased 11.9% in 2009 from its 2008 level, and more than 35% from its peak in 2006. In 2009, 794 venture capital firms managed 1,188 funds, down from peaks of 1,023 firms in 2005 and 1,883 managed funds in 2001. Investment in venture funds also decreased 46% in 2009 from 2008, with funds raising $15.4 billion in 2009 compared to $28.5 billion in 2008. Fundraising in 2009 was down 57% from the peak fundraising of $36.1 billion in 2007. The decrease in venture capital fundraising is reflected in the decrease in venture capital investments. Total venture investments in 2009 decreased 37% from $27.9 billion in 2008 to $17.7 million in 2009.

Finally, the decline in venture capital investments is also attributable to the decline in venture-backed IPOs and acquisitions, the only two ways in which venture funds receive a return on their investments. In 2009, there were only 12 venture-backed IPOs which raised $1.6 billion and only 270 acquisitions totaling $14.1 billion. The IPOs in 2008 and 2009 are the worst and second-worst numbers of IPOs since 1980. The number of venture-backed company acquisitions continued to decline in 2009 (270) from 2008 (349) and 2007 (379). It is estimated that 38% of these venture-backed acquisitions occurred at a price less than the total venture investment in the company.

Financial markets are inherently cyclical, experiencing regular periods of over-investment and under-investment. However, the number of entrepreneurs and ingenious new business ideas in the U.S. are not cyclical and there are a number of good reasons to believe that the environment is right for both to grow at an accelerating pace. As this occurs, the balance between the supply of, and demand for, venture capital will be restored.

Additional Information

1. Joseph W. Bartlett, Equity Fin. §§ 1.1–1.3, 6.13, 24.1A (2010).

2. Edmond T. Fitzgerald & Erin K. Cho, Advising Private Funds §§ 5:22, 18:2, 24:3, 26:22 (2010).

3. Gary M. Lawrence & Carl Baranowski, Representing High Tech Companies § 2.17 (2009).

4. Joseph C. Long, 12 Blue Sky Law § 3:78 (2010).

4. Steven C. Alberty, Advising Small Business §§ 15:2–15:3 (2010).

5. Brian O'Neal, Mod. Corp. Checklists § 2:8 (2010).

6. Stuart R. Cohn, 1 Sec. Counseling for Small & Emerging Companies § 2:2 (2009).

7. Gerald T. Lins Et al., Hedge Funds and Other Private Funds: Reg and Comp § 12:2 (2009).

8. Robert B. Hughes, 2 Legal Compliance Checkups § 14:4 (2009).

9. Robert J. Haft, 2 Venture Cap. & Bus. Fin. § 1:24 (2010).

10. William M. Prifti, 24 Securities Pub. & Priv. Offerings §§ 3:3–3:13 (2010).

11. Lee R. Petillon & Robert Joe Hull, Representing Start-Up Companies § 5:13, Appendix 2-A (2009).

12. Sarah Reed, *National Venture Capital Association Yearbook, Appendix A: Glossary*, 1799 PLI/Corp 55 (2010).

13. Curtis L. Mo, *2009 Venture Capital Report*, 1799 PLI/Corp 93 (2010).

14. William B. Asher, *Network Effects: Ethical Issues In Venture Capital Lawyering*, 1799 PLI/Corp 199 (2010).

15. Rod J. Howard, *Recent Trends In Sales Of Venture-Capital-Backed Companies*, 1780 PLI/Corp 147 (2010).

14. Brannan W. Reaves, *Minority Shareholder Oppression In The Venture Capital Industry: What You Can Do To Protect Yourself*, 61 Ala. L. Rev. 649 (2010).

15. Calvin H. Johnson, *Why Do Venture Capital Funds Burn Research And Development Deductions?*, 29 Va. Tax Rev. 29 (2009).

16. Jason Doren, *Oasis In The Desert: Investors Search For Liquidity*, 1735 PLI/Corp 45 (2009).

17. Kate Litvak, *Venture Capital Limited Partnership Agreements: Understanding Compensation Arrangements*, 76 u. Chi. L. Rev. 161 (2009).

18. Stephane DuPont, *Venture Impact: The Economic Importance Of Venture Capital Backed Companies To The U.S. Economy*, 1616 PLI/Corp 57 (2007).

11.4.2   Structuring A Venture Capital Investment

PRIMER ON STOCKS AND BONDS

There are two basic types of securities used to finance a company — equity securities and debt securities. Equity securities generally consist of common stock, preferred stock and convertible preferred stock. Within each of these classes of equity securities there may be different series, for example Series A preferred stock and Series B preferred stock, which provide the equity investors with different sets of rights and obligations. The company founders, managers and employees are generally issued common stock. Common stock is the lowest rung on the ladder in the event a company is liquidated or becomes bankrupt. The claims of secured and unsecured creditors, bondholders and preferred stockholders take precedence over common stockholders. On the other hand, the common stockholders enjoy a preference over creditors, bondholders and preferred stockholders in the profits of a company, although preferred stockholders may sometimes enjoy a preference in profits up to certain amount.

Preferred stockholders have special rights that common stockholders do not have. These special rights may include, among others, a preference in the payment of dividends, in participation in the company's management, in the liquidation of the company's assets, in anti-dilution protection (discussed below), and in veto rights over certain company decisions. Private equity investors usually purchase preferred stock when investing in a company.

Convertible preferred stockholders have the right to convert their stock to common stock at certain times or upon certain events, according to a set price or conversion ratio. Convertible preferred stock generally converts automatically to common stock if the company makes an initial public offering (IPO), is acquired by another company in exchange for cash and/or other securities, or undergoes some other type of "liquidity" event (an event in which the company's common stock becomes liquid and, therefore, can be sold for cash or an equivalent of cash). Nearly 95% of all venture capital investments are made using convertible preferred stock. Convertible preferred stock allows venture investors to have the protection of preferences in the event the company does not do well and to convert to more valuable common stock in the event the company does do well.

Debt securities, or bonds, are contractual obligations of a company to repay the principal and interest on the bond at specified times. Whereas a company is not contractually obligated to repay the common or preferred stock investment, or to pay dividends on the stock, the company is required to pay the principal and interest on a bond at the specified times or risk being forced into bankruptcy or some other draconian event. As noted above, bond holders have precedence over common stockholders and preferred stockholders in the event of the company's liquidation or bankruptcy. However, bond holders have no right to share in the company's profits. Bond holders are only entitled to repayment of the principal and interest stated in the bond indenture.

Bonds can also be convertible into common stock or preferred stock at specified times or events, according to a set price or ratio. Convertible bond holders do not have the rights of common and preferred stockholders until such time as the conversion right is exercised.

The ratio between the amount of debt and the amount of equity a company uses to finance its operations is very important. The debt/equity ratio determines the degree of financial leverage of a company. The higher a company's debt/equity ratio, the more highly the company is leveraging its equity investment. The more highly a company leverages its equity investment, the higher the potential value of its equity investment. If a company is financed with 1% equity and 99% debt, 100% of the company's profits go to the equity investors and none of the profits, other than the payment of principal and interest, goes to the debt holders. Stated differently, all of the company's profits, above what is required to pay the principal and interest to the bond holders, go to the equity investors. In essence, the equity investors are receiving 100% of the profits while contributing only 1% of the company's equity capital.

However, the attraction of leverage is offset by risk. The higher the degree of leverage, the higher the degree of risk. Recall that a company is not required to repay equity investors, or to pay dividends to common and preferred stockholders. However, the company is contractually obligated to repay principal and interest to the bond holders. In the example above, if the company is unable to pay the principal and interest on the 99% of debt, the company will become insolvent and will be forced into liquidation or bankruptcy. The equity investment in a company serves as a protective cushion against the prospect of liquidation or bankruptcy by providing the company operating capital without an obligation to repay the equity investment or to pay dividends.

KEY ISSUES IN VENTURE CAPITAL INVESTMENTS

There are many important issues that must be addressed in venture capital investments. Among the most important are the valuation of the company, the stock purchase and stockholder agreements, and the investors' anti-dilution protection.

Valuation of the Company

The valuation of the company will determine the percentage of the company that the venture capital firm will acquire for its investment in the company. For example, if a company's current valuation (pre-money valuation) is $1 million and the venture firm invests $1 million in the company, the company's post-money valuation will be $2 million and the venture firm will own 50% of the company.

Company valuation is affected by a number of factors, some external to the transaction, some internal to the transaction. As you saw above, the state of the economy greatly affects the aggregate amount of venture capital available for investment, and the ability and willingness of venture capital firms to make venture investments. When the economy is strong and growing, the amount of venture capital under management is larger and the ability, and willingness, of venture firms to make venture investments is greater. Under these circumstances, company valuations are likely to be higher. Under the reverse circumstances, such as now, company valuations are likely to be lower or non-existent.

Company valuations are also affected by industry segment. In 2009, the average company valuation in biotechnology was $49 million, in computers and peripherals $18.2 million, in IT services $103.9 million, in medical devices and equipment $40.7 million, in semiconductors $23.3 million, and in telecommunications $30.7 million. The amount of venture capital investment in different industry segments also varies. In 2009, 20% of the total venture investment dollars went to biotechnology companies, 14% went to medical devices and equipment and 1% went to healthcare. The fastest growing industry segment, not surprisingly, is clean technology. In 2009, venture investment in clean technology was $2.2 billion, 12% of the total investment dollars, and four times the amount of investment four years earlier.

Yet another external factor affecting company valuations is the companies' home state. In 2009, California received 50% of the total venture capital investment, New York 5%, Washington 3%, Colorado 3%, Georgia 2%, and the remaining 45 states shared 15%, or an average of 0.3% per state.

Among the internal factors affecting company valuations are the stage of the investment (A Series, B Series, etc.), the profitability of the company, the number of other potential venture investors, the number of other potential venture investments, and the urgency of the company's need for cash. In addition, as noted above, company valuations will be affected by the assessment of the quality of the company's management team and board of directors, the company's core technology and technical expertise, sales growth over time, planned future products or services, and the company's decided and distinct competitive advantage over other firms in the market.

There are a number of means by which to value private companies. The most common valuation method is based on comparable public companies. A comparable public company is a company in the same industry segment with a similar technology. Comparisons are generally made using multiples of the public company's EBIT (Earnings Before Interest and Taxes) or EBITA (Earnings Before Interest Taxes and Amortization). For example, if the market values the comparable public company at two times its EBIT, the private company would be valued at two times its EBIT. However, the valuation of the private company would have to be discounted from the valuation of the public company because the private company securities cannot be sold on the open market. This discount is known as the "liquidity discount." Valuation of a private company can also be done using the price/earnings ratio of comparable public companies. The price earnings ratio is the price paid for the stock of the public company divided by the company's annual earnings. Again, this valuation would have to be adjusted for a liquidity discount.

In addition to valuing the company, the venture firm must determine the percentage ownership of the company it must obtain in order to meet its required internal rate of return (IRR). IRR is a non-compounded interest calculation on the amount of the venture investment. For example, if the venture firm's IRR is 40% per year for A Series investments, the venture firm is considering investing $2 million in the company, and the company's predicted value in 5 years is $8 million, the venture firm would have to own 75 % of the company to meet its IRR.

$$40\% \times 5 \text{ years} = 200\% \text{ (non-compounded rate of return)}$$

$$200\% \times \$2 \text{ million} = \$4 \text{ million (required return on investment)}$$

$$\$4 \text{ million} + \$2 \text{ million (initial investment)} = \$6 \text{ million (total amount returned)}$$

$$\$6 \text{ million} \div \$8 \text{ million (predicted value of company in 5 years)} = 75\%$$

The fact that the founders' percentage ownership in a company is reduced by the venture capital investment does not mean that the value of the founders' investment in the company is lower. The table below illustrates the appreciation in the value of the founders' investment while their percentage ownership is being reduced.

Founders' Increase in Value and Decrease in Ownership

	Founder Investment	Pre-Seed Investment	Seed Round Investment	Series A Venture Capital Investment
Amount Raised	$5,000	$25,000	$250,000	$2,000,000
Share Price	$0.01	$0.25	$1.00	$4.00
New Shares	500,000	100,000	300,000	500,000
Total Shares	500,000	600,000	900,000	1,400,000
Post-Issue Valuation	$5,000	$150,000	$900,000	$5,600,000
Founder Percentage	100%	83%	55%	35%
Founder Value	$5,000	$125,000	$500,000	$1,960,000

Stock Purchase and Stockholder Agreements

A summary of the initial terms and conditions of a venture capital investment are generally set forth in a term sheet. Subsection 11.4.3 below provides a sample venture capital investment term sheet. Negotiations between the parties usually takes place by means of exchanging term sheets setting forth different proposed provisions. Unless the parties clearly indicate otherwise, an agreement reached on a term sheet is not a binding legal agreement. Rather, the binding legal agreement between the parties comes in the form of the stock purchase agreement and the shareholder agreement that embody the provisions of the term sheet.

The stock purchase agreement sets forth who, is buying what, at what price, and when. The "who" consists of the investors usually listed separately in an appendix.

There may be multiple investors listed in a single stock purchase agreement appendix. However, unless indicated otherwise, the multiple investors are individually, not jointly, responsible under the stock purchase agreement. The "what" describes the securities being issued. These securities can be in the form of preferred stock, convertible preferred stock, debt, convertible debt, warrants, puts, calls or any combination of these securities, which are called investment "units." (Warrants, puts and calls will be discussed below.) The stock purchase agreement will describe the features of these securities such as conversion ratios and interest on debt. However, these features will also be set forth in the security instrument itself and it is, obviously, very important that the features set forth in the stock purchase agreement and security instrument be consistent. One way to ensure this is to include the security instrument(s) as an appendix attachment to the stock purchase agreement and include it by reference in the agreement.

The "price" is the most straight-forward provision in the stock purchase agreement unless the investor is paying for the stock in property rather than cash. Here, of course, the property would have to be valued and the terms of the capital contribution described. The "when" sets forth the closing date on which the cash is paid, the securities delivered and the final agreements signed. The stock purchase agreement may provide for multiple closing dates in conjunction with the company achieving different financial or operational milestones. As noted earlier, multiple closing dates are called tranches. Typical operational milestones for an early-stage technology company may be development of a product prototype, successful laboratory testing and beta testing with a limited number of users.

The stock purchase agreement also includes representations and warranties, and affirmative and negative covenants. Representations and warranties are statements of fact, for example the balance sheet provided to the prospective investors is accurate to the best of the company's knowledge, or there are no outstanding legal actions against the company. A misrepresentation in the company's representations and warranties gives rise to a tort cause of action. Affirmative and negative covenants are promissory statements such as the company will maintain a certain debt/equity ratio and will not issue new stock without investor consent. Failure to perform an affirmative or negative covenant gives rise to a breach of contract cause of action.

The stockholder agreement is an agreement between the founders and investors that governs the relationship between the founders, the investors, the company and key employees. The stockholder agreement may cover such terms as the issuance of stock options to key employees, and actions which the company may not take without approval of the investors. However, the most important provision in the stockholder agreement is often the election and composition of the board of directors. Recall that the board of directors has ultimate decision-making authority in a company and, therefore, control of the board of directors is of paramount importance to the founders and investors. The stockholder agreement may set forth the size and operation of the board of directors, including operating subcommittees, how the seats on the board are to be allocated between the founders and investors, and events that might alter the operation of the board or the allocation of board seats.

Control of the board of directors is frequently a highly contentious point between the founders and investors. The founders recognize that losing control of the board is tantamount to losing control of "their" company. The investors recognize that if they do not control the board they cannot protect "their" investment in the company. There are a number of ways in which the interests of the founders and directors can be, at least partially, reconciled. One of the key powers of the board of directors is the right to appoint, dismiss and direct company managers. The stockholder agreement may provide for some check on this power by the founders. The stockholder agreement can provide for X% of the directors to be elected by the investors and Y% by the founders which percentages can change over time depending upon events. The stockholder agreement can also provide that a super-majority of the board, or founder consent, is required for certain major company decisions such as hiring senior company managers or selling company assets.

Other provisions that may be included in the stockholder agreement include:

Pre-emptive rights. The right to purchase additional shares of future stock necessary to preserve the pre-issuance ownership percentage; the exercise of pre-emptive rights may be tied to a stated price or to the price of the new shares;

Right of first refusal. The right to purchase stock at a price offered by a third party;

Right of first offer. The right to make the first offer on stock before it is offered to a third party;

Conversion rights. The right to convert one type of security into another type of security according to a predetermined price or conversion formula;

Puts. The right of investors to require the company to purchase their stock usually at the purchase price plus an accrued annual interest; puts are usually triggered by time or events, and are only useful if the company has cash;

Calls. The right of the company, or founders, to require investors to sell back stock usually at the purchase price plus an accrued annual interest; again usually triggered by time or events, and only useful if the company has cash; and

Warrants. The right to buy additional shares of stock at a fixed or formula price; the exercise price is called the "strike" price.

Investors' Anti-Dilution Protection

Dilution, or reduction in value, of current investors' stock occurs when the company issues new shares of stock at a price lower than the price paid by the current investors. New stock must be issued at a price higher than the average price paid for the existing outstanding stock, or the new stock will dilute the value of the existing outstanding stock. In order to issue new stock at a price higher than the price paid for existing stock, the company must have a higher value than it had when the existing stock was issued. If the company's value is lower when the new stock is issued than it was when the existing stock was issued, the company will have to issue the new stock at a lower price, thus diluting the value of the existing stock. In venture capital investments, this is known as a "down round." Although current investors will never want to see new stock issued at a price that is lower than the price they paid, the current investors often have no choice. If the company must have an infusion of new capital to remain financially viable, the current investors will accept dilution of their stock value rather than having the company fail and having their investment wiped out entirely.

The formula for calculating the anti-dilution tipping point is:

$$AD\% = NI/(NI + EI)$$

$$AD\% = \text{anti-dilution percentage tipping point}$$

$$NI = \text{new investment amount}$$

$$EI = \text{existing investment amount}$$

If the existing investment in a company is $1,000,000 and the company is seeking new investment in the amount of $250,000, the anti-dilution tipping point is 20%.

$$AD\% = \$250,000/(\$250,000 + \$1,000,000)$$

$$AD\% = \$250,000/\$1,250,000$$

$$AD\% = 20\%$$

If the company issues more than 20% of the current stock for the $250,000 investment, or issues 20% of the current stock for less than $250,000, the company will dilute the value of the current stock.

There are a number of ways to protect investors against dilution of their stock value. These include "full ratchet" anti-dilution and "weighted average" anti-dilution. Full ratchet anti-dilution reprices the existing stock at the same price as the new stock. Weighted average anti-dilution prices the existing stock at the weighted average price of the existing stock and the new stock. The net effect of repricing existing stock is that the current investors receive additional shares of stock so that their percentage ownership is not diluted at all, or is diluted to a lesser extent.

Additional Information

1. GARY M. LAWRENCE, CARL BARANOWSKI, REPRESENTING HIGH TECH COMPANIES §§ 2.11–2.14, 2.16 (2009).

2.   STEVEN C. ALBERTY, 1 ADVISING SMALL BUSINESSES § 15:13 (2010).

3.   BRIAN O'NEAL, MODERN CORPORATION CHECKLISTS § 2:9 (2010).

4.   CLIFFORD R. ENNICO, FORMS FOR SMALL BUSINESS ENTITIES §§ 13:9–13:10 (2010).

5.   RICHARD A. BOOTH, FINANCING THE CORPORATION §§ 2:33–2:34 (2010).

6.   ROBERT J. HAFT, 2 VENTURE CAP. & BUS. FIN. §§ 1:5–1:9; §§ 6:2–6:14 (2010).

7.   RICHARD H. ROWE, FINANCIAL PRODUCT FUNDAMENTAL § 1:2.2 (2009).

8.   TED A. DONNER, ATTORNEY'S PRACTICE GUIDE TO NEGOTIATIONS § 32:4 (2009).

9.   Curtis L. Mo, *Clean Tech, Inc. — A Hypothetical Venture Capital Investment*, 1799 PLI/CORP 75 (2010).

10.   Ronald J. Gilson, David M. Schizer, *Understanding Venture Capital Structure: A Tax Explanation For Convertible Preferred Stock*, 889 PLI/TAX 1249 (2009).

11.   *Report On Selected Legal Opinion Issues in Venture Capital Financing Transactions*, 65 BUS. LAW 161 (2009).

12.   Richard R. Plumridge, Kelly N. Matthews, *Typical Venture Capital Transaction Documents*, 1733 PLI/CORP 529 (2009).

13.   Gordon K. Davidson, *Friendbook, Inc. A Hypothetical "Down Round" Venture Capital Financing*, 1733 PLI/CORP 611 (2009).

14.   C. Stephen Bigler, Pamela H. Sudell, *Recent Developments In Delaware Corporate Law Relevant To Venture Capital Practice*, 1616 PLI/CORP 89 (2007).

11.4.3   Sample Venture Capital Term Sheet

NATIONAL VENTURE CAPITAL ASSOCIATION SAMPLE TERM SHEET
Available at http://www.nvca.org/#

This sample document is the work product of a national coalition of attorneys who specialize in venture capital financings, working under the auspices of the NVCA. This document is intended to serve as a starting point only, and should be tailored to meet your specific requirements. This document should not be construed as legal advice for any particular facts or circumstances. Note that this sample document presents an array of (often mutually exclusive) options with respect to particular deal provisions.

TERM SHEET
FOR SERIES A PREFERRED STOCK FINANCING OF
[INSERT COMPANY NAME], INC.
[_____, 20_____]

This Term Sheet summarizes the principal terms of the Series A Preferred Stock Financing of [_____], Inc., a [Delaware] corporation (the

"Company"). In consideration of the time and expense devoted and to be devoted by the Investors with respect to this investment, the No Shop/Confidentiality [and Counsel and Expenses] provisions of this Term Sheet shall be binding obligations of the Company whether or not the financing is consummated. No other legally binding obligations will be created until definitive agreements are executed and delivered by all parties. This Term Sheet is not a commitment to invest, and is conditioned on the completion of due diligence, legal review and documentation that is satisfactory to the Investors. This Term Sheet shall be governed in all respects by the laws of the [State of Delaware].

Offering Terms

Closing Date:	As soon as practicable following the Company's acceptance of this Term Sheet and satisfaction of the Conditions to Closing (the "Closing"). [*provide for multiple closings if applicable*]
Investors:	Investor No. 1: [_____] shares ([_____]%), $[_____] Investor No. 2: [_____] shares ([_____]%), $[_____] [as well other investors mutually agreed upon by Investors and the Company]
Amount Raised:	$[_____], [including $[_____] from the conversion of principal [and interest] on bridge notes].
Price Per Share:	$[_____] per share (based on the capitalization of the Company set forth below) (the "Original Purchase Price").
Pre-Money Valuation:	The Original Purchase Price is based upon a fully-diluted pre-money valuation of $[_____] and a fully-diluted post-money valuation of $[_____] (including an employee pool representing [_____]% of the fully-diluted post-money capitalization).
Capitalization:	The Company's capital structure before and after the Closing is set forth on Exhibit A.

CHARTER

Dividends:	[*Alternative 1:* Dividends will be paid on the Series A Preferred on an as-converted basis when, as, and if paid on the Common Stock]

Offering Terms

[*Alternative 2*: The Series A Preferred will carry an annual [_____]% cumulative dividend [payable upon a liquidation or redemption]. For any other dividends or distributions, participation with Common Stock on an as-converted basis.]

[*Alternative 3*: Non-cumulative dividends will be paid on the Series A Preferred in an amount equal to $[_____] per share of Series A Preferred when and if declared by the Board.]

Liquidation Preference:

In the event of any liquidation, dissolution or winding up of the Company, the proceeds shall be paid as follows:

[*Alternative 1 (non-participating Preferred Stock)*: First pay [one] times the Original Purchase Price [plus accrued dividends] [plus declared and unpaid dividends] on each share of Series A Preferred. The balance of any proceeds shall be distributed pro rata to holders of Common Stock.]

[*Alternative 2 (full participating Preferred Stock)*: First pay [one] times the Original Purchase Price [plus accrued dividends] [plus declared and unpaid dividends] on each share of Series A Preferred. Thereafter, the Series A Preferred participates with the Common Stock pro rata on an as-converted basis.]

[*Alternative 3 (cap on Preferred Stock participation rights)*: First pay [one] times the Original Purchase Price [plus accrued dividends] [plus declared and unpaid dividends] on each share of Series A Preferred. Thereafter, Series A Preferred participates with Common Stock pro rata on an as-converted basis until the holders of Series A Preferred receive an aggregate of [_____] times the Original Purchase Price (including the amount paid pursuant to the preceding sentence).]

A merger or consolidation (other than one in which stockholders of the Company own a majority by voting power of the outstanding shares of the surviving or acquiring corporation) and a sale, lease, transfer, exclusive license or other disposition of all or substantially all of the assets of the Company will be treated as a liquidation event (a "Deemed Liquidation Event"), thereby triggering payment of the liquidation preferences described

Offering Terms

above [unless the holders of [_____
]% of the Series A Preferred elect otherwise].
[The Investors' entitlement to their liquidation preference shall not be abrogated or diminished in the event part of the consideration is subject to escrow in connection with a
Deemed Liquidation Event.]

Voting Rights: The Series A Preferred shall vote together
with the Common Stock on an as-converted
basis, and not as a separate class, except (i)
[so long as [*insert fixed number, or %, or
"any"*] shares of Series A Preferred are outstanding,] the Series A Preferred as a class
shall be entitled to elect [_____]
[(_____)] members of the Board
(the "Series A Directors"), and (ii) as required
by law. The Company's Certificate of Incorporation will provide that the number of authorized shares of Common Stock may be increased or decreased with the approval of a
majority of the Preferred and Common Stock,
voting together as a single class, and without
a separate class vote by the Common Stock.

Protective Provisions: [So long as [*insert fixed number, or %, or
"any"*] shares of Series A Preferred are out-
standing,] in addition to any other vote or approval required under the Company's Charter
or By-laws, the Company will not, without the
written consent of the holders of at least
[_____]% of the Company's Series A
Preferred, either directly or by amendment,
merger, consolidation, or otherwise:

(i) liquidate, dissolve or wind-up the affairs of
the Company, or effect any merger or consolidation or any other Deemed Liquidation
Event; (ii) amend, alter, or repeal any provision of the Certificate of Incorporation or By-
laws [in a manner adverse to the Series A
Preferred]; (iii) create or authorize the creation of or issue any other security convertible into or exercisable for any equity security, having rights, preferences or privileges
senior to or on parity with the Series A Preferred, or increase the authorized number of
shares of Series A Preferred; (iv) purchase or
redeem or pay any dividend on any capital
stock prior to the Series A Preferred, [other
than stock repurchased from former employees or consultants in connection with the cessation of

Offering Terms

their employment/services, at the lower of fair market value or cost;] [other than as approved by the Board, including the approval of [_____] Series A Director(s)]; or (v) create or authorize the creation of any debt security [if the Company's aggregate indebtedness would exceed $[_____][other than equipment leases or bank lines of credit][unless such debt security has received the prior approval of the Board of Directors, including the approval of [_____] Series A Director(s)]; (vi) create or hold capital stock in any subsidiary that is not a wholly-owned subsidiary or dispose of any subsidiary stock or all or substantially all of any subsidiary assets; [or (vii) increase or decrease the size of the Board of Directors].

Optional Conversion: The Series A Preferred initially converts 1:1 to Common Stock at any time at option of holder, subject to adjustments for stock dividends, splits, combinations and similar events and as described below under "Anti-dilution Provisions."

Anti-dilution Provisions: In the event that the Company issues additional securities at a purchase price less than the current Series A Preferred conversion price, such conversion price shall be adjusted in accordance with the following formula:

[*Alternative 1:* "Typical" weighted average:

$$CP2 = CP1 * (A+B) / (A+C)$$

CP2 = Series A Conversion Price in effect immediately after new issue

CP1 = Series A Conversion Price in effect immediately prior to new issue

A = Number of shares of Common Stock deemed to be outstanding immediately prior to new issue (includes all shares of outstanding common stock, all shares of outstanding preferred stock on an as-converted basis, and all outstanding options on an as-exercised basis; and does not include any convertible securities converting into this round of financing)

B = Aggregate consideration received by the Corporation with respect to the new issue divided by CP1

C = Number of shares of stock issued in the subject transaction]

[*Alternative 2:* Full-ratchet — the conversion price will be reduced to the price at which the new shares are issued.]

Offering Terms

[*Alternative 3*: No price-based anti-dilution protection.]

The following issuances shall not trigger anti-dilution adjustment:

(i) securities issuable upon conversion of any of the Series A Preferred, or as a dividend or distribution on the Series A Preferred; (ii) securities issued upon the conversion of any debenture, warrant, option, or other convertible security; (iii) Common Stock issuable upon a stock split, stock dividend, or any subdivision of shares of Common Stock; and (iv) shares of Common Stock (or options to purchase such shares of Common Stock) issued or issuable to employees or directors of, or consultants to, the Company pursuant to any plan approved by the Company's Board of Directors [including at least [_____] Series A Director(s)].

Mandatory Conversion:

Each share of Series A Preferred will automatically be converted into Common Stock at the then applicable conversion rate in the event of the closing of a [firm commitment] underwritten public offering with a price of [_____] times the Original Purchase Price (subject to adjustments for stock dividends, splits, combinations and similar events) and [net/gross] proceeds to the Company of not less than $[_____], or (ii) upon the written consent of the holders of [_____]% of the Series A Preferred.

Pay-to-Play:

[Unless the holders of [_____]% of the Series A elect otherwise,] on any subsequent [down] round all [Major] Investors are required to purchase their pro rata share of the securities set aside by the Board for purchase by the [Major] Investors. All shares of Series A Preferred of any [Major] Investor failing to do so will automatically [lose anti-dilution rights] [lose right to participate in future rounds] [convert to Common Stock and lose the right to a Board seat if applicable].

Offering Terms

Redemption Rights: The Series A Preferred shall be redeemable from funds legally available for distribution at the option of holders of at least [_____]% of the Series A Preferred commencing any time after [_____] at a price equal to the Original Purchase Price [plus all accrued but unpaid dividends]. Redemption shall occur in three equal annual portions. Upon a redemption request from the holders of the required percentage of the Series A Preferred, all Series A Preferred shares shall be redeemed [(except for any Series A holders who affirmatively opt-out)].

STOCK PURCHASE AGREEMENT

Representations and Warranties: Standard representations and warranties by the Company. [Representations and warranties by Founders regarding [technology ownership, etc.].

Conditions to Closing: Standard conditions to Closing, which shall include, among other things, satisfactory completion of financial and legal due diligence, qualification of the shares under applicable Blue Sky laws, the filing of a Certificate of Incorporation establishing the rights and preferences of the Series A Preferred, and an opinion of counsel to the Company.

Counsel and Expenses: Holders of Preferred Stock and the Founders

Company Counsel: [_____]

Investor Counsel: [_____]

INVESTORS' RIGHTS AGREEMENT

Registration Rights:

Registrable Securities: All shares of Common Stock issuable upon conversion of the Series A Preferred [and [any other Common Stock held by the Investors] will be deemed "Registrable Securities."

Offering Terms

Demand Registration: Upon earliest of (i) [three-five] years after the Closing; or (ii) [six] months following an initial public offering ("IPO"), persons holding [_____]% of the Registrable Securities may request [one][two] (consummated) registrations by the Company of their shares. The aggregate offering price for such registration may not be less than $[5–**15**] million. A registration will count for this purpose only if (i) all Registrable Securities requested to be registered are registered and (ii) it is closed, or withdrawn at the request of the Investors (other than as a result of a material adverse change to the Company).

Registration on Form S-3:   The holders of [10–30]% of the Registrable Securities will have the right to require the Company to register on Form S-3, if available for use by the Company, Registrable Securities for an aggregate offering price of at least $[1–5 million]. There will be no limit on the aggregate number of such Form S-3 registrations, provided that there are no more than [two] per year.

Piggyback Registration: The holders of Registrable Securities will be entitled to "piggyback" registration rights on all registration statements of the Company, subject to the right, however, of the Company and its underwriters to reduce the number of shares proposed to be registered to a minimum of [20–30]% on a pro rata basis and to complete reduction on an IPO at the underwriter's discretion. In all events, the shares to be registered by holders of Registrable Securities will be reduced only after all other stockholders' shares are reduced.

Expenses: The registration expenses (exclusive of stock transfer taxes, underwriting discounts and commissions will be borne by the Company. The Company will also pay the reasonable fees and expenses[, not to exceed $_____ ,] of one special counsel to represent all the participating stockholders.

Offering Terms

Lock-up:

Investors shall agree in connection with the IPO, if requested by the managing underwriter, not to sell or transfer any shares of Common Stock of the Company [(including/excluding shares acquired in or following the IPO)] for a period of up to 180 days [plus up to an additional 18 days to the extent necessary to comply with applicable regulatory requirements] following the IPO (provided all directors and officers of the Company [and [1–5]% stockholders] agree to the same lock-up). [Such lock-up agreement shall provide that any discretionary waiver or termination of the restrictions of such agreements by the Company or representatives of the underwriters shall apply to Investors, pro rata, based on the number of shares held.

Termination:

Upon a Deemed Liquidation Event, [and/or] when all shares of an Investor are eligible to be sold without restriction under Rule 144(k) [and/or] the [_____] anniversary of the IPO.

No future registration rights may be granted without consent of the holders of a [majority] of the Registrable Securities unless subordinate to the Investor's rights.

Management and Information Rights:

A Management Rights letter from the Company, in a form reasonably acceptable to the Investors, will be delivered prior to Closing to each Investor that requests one.

Any [Major] Investor [(who is not a competitor)] will be granted access to Company facilities and personnel during normal business hours and with reasonable advance notification. The Company will deliver to such Major Investor (i) annual, quarterly, [and monthly] financial statements, and other information as determined by the Board; (ii) thirty days prior to the end of each fiscal year, a comprehensive operating budget forecasting the Company's revenues, expenses, and cash position on a month-to-month basis for the upcoming fiscal year[; and (iii) promptly following the end of each quarter an up-to-date capitalization table. A "Major Investor" means any Investor who purchases at least $[_____] of Series A Preferred.

Offering Terms

Right to Participate Pro Rata in Future Rounds:

All [Major] Investors shall have a pro rata right, based on their percentage equity ownership in the Company (assuming the conversion of all outstanding Preferred Stock into Common Stock and the exercise of all options outstanding under the Company's stock plans), to participate in subsequent issuances of equity securities of the Company (excluding those issuances listed at the end of the "Anti-dilution Provisions" section of this Term Sheet. In addition, should any [Major] Investor choose not to purchase its full pro rata share, the remaining [Major] Investors shall have the right to purchase the remaining pro rata shares.

Matters Requiring Investor Director Approval:

[So long as the holders of Series A Preferred are entitled to elect a Series A Director, the Company will not, without Board approval, which approval must include the affirmative vote of [one/both] of the Series A Director(s): (i) make any loan or advance to, or own any stock or other securities of, any subsidiary or other corporation, partnership, or other entity unless it is wholly owned by the Company; (ii) make any loan or advance to any person, including, any employee or director, except advances and similar expenditures in the ordinary course of business or under the terms of a employee stock or option plan approved by the Board of Directors; (iii) guarantee, any indebtedness except for trade accounts of the Company or any subsidiary arising in the ordinary course of business; (iv) make any investment inconsistent with any investment policy approved by the Board; (v) incur any aggregate indebtedness in excess of $[_____] that is not already included in a Board-approved budget, other than trade credit incurred in the ordinary course of business; (vi) enter into or be a party to any transaction with any director, officer or employee of the Company or any "associate" (as defined in Rule 12b-2 promulgated under the Exchange Act) of any such person [except transactions resulting in payments to or by the Company in an amount less than $[60,000] per year], [or transactions made in the ordinary course of business and pursuant to reasonable requirements of the Company's business and upon fair and reasonable terms that

Offering Terms

are approved by a majority of the Board of Directors]; (vii) hire, fire, or change the compensation of the executive officers, including approving any option grants; (viii) change the principal business of the Company, enter new lines of business, or exit the current line of business; (ix) sell, assign, license, pledge or encumber material technology or intellectual property, other than licenses granted in the ordinary course of business; or (x) enter into any corporate strategic relationship involving the payment contribution or assignment by the Company or to the Company of assets greater than [$100,000.00].

Non-Competition and Non-Solicitation Agreements:

Each Founder and key employee will enter into a [one] year non-competition and non-solicitation agreement in a form reasonably acceptable to the Investors.

Non-Disclosure and Developments Agreement:

Each current and former Founder, employee and consultant will enter into a non-disclosure and proprietary rights assignment agreement in a form reasonably acceptable to the Investors.

Board Matters:

[Each Board Committee shall include at least one Series A Director.]

The Board of Directors shall meet at least [monthly][quarterly], unless otherwise agreed by a vote of the majority of Directors.

The Company will bind D&O insurance with a carrier and in an amount satisfactory to the Board of Directors. Company to enter into Indemnification Agreement with each Series A Director [and affiliated funds] in form acceptable to such director. In the event the Company merges with another entity and is not the surviving corporation, or transfers all of its assets, proper provisions shall be made so that successors of the Company assume the Company's obligations with respect to indemnification of Directors.

Employee Stock Options:

All employee options to vest as follows: [25% after one year, with remaining vesting monthly over next 36 months].

Offering Terms

[Immediately prior to the Series A Preferred Stock investment, [_____] shares will be added to the option pool creating an unallocated option pool of [_____] shares.]

Key Person Insur-   Company to acquire life insurance on Found-
ance: ers [*name each Founder*] in an amount satis-
                             factory to the Board. Proceeds payable to the
                             Company.

RIGHT OF FIRST REFUSAL/CO-SALE AGREEMENT

Right of first Refusal/   Company first and Investors second (to the
Right of Co-Sale   extent assigned by the Board of Directors,)
(Take-me-Along):   will have a right of first refusal with respect
                                   to any shares of capital stock of the Company
                                   proposed to be transferred by Founders [and
                                   future employees holding greater than [1]% of
                                   Company Common Stock (assuming conver-
                                   sion of Preferred Stock and whether then
                                   held or subject to the exercise of options)],
                                   with a right of oversubscription for Investors
                                   of shares unsubscribed by the other Inves-
                                   tors. Before any such person may sell Com-
                                   mon Stock, he will give the Investors an op-
                                   portunity to participate in such sale on a basis
                                   proportionate to the amount of securities held
                                   by the seller and those held by the participat-
                                   ing Investors.

VOTING AGREEMENT

Board of Directors: At the initial Closing, the Board shall consist
                               of [_____] members comprised of (i)
                               [*Name*] as [the representative designated by
                               [_____], as the lead Investor, (ii)
                               [*Name*] as the representative designated by
                               the remaining Investors, (iii) [*Name*] as the
                               representative designated by the Founders,
                               (iv) the person then serving as the Chief Ex-
                               ecutive Officer of the Company, and (v)
                               [_____] person(s) who are not em-
                               ployed by the Company and who are mutually
                               acceptable [to the Founders and Investors][to
                               the other directors].

Offering Terms

Drag Along: Holders of Preferred Stock and the Founders [and all future holders of greater than [1]% of Common Stock (assuming conversion of Preferred Stock and whether then held or subject to the exercise of options)] shall be required to enter into an agreement with the Investors that provides that such stockholders will vote their shares in favor of a Deemed Liquidation Event or transaction in which 50% or more of the voting power of the Company is transferred and which is approved by [the Board of Directors] [and the holders of _____% of the outstanding shares of Preferred Stock, on an as-converted basis (the "Electing Holders")], so long as the liability of each stockholder in such transaction is several (and not joint) and does not exceed the stockholder's pro rata portion of any claim and the consideration to be paid to the stockholders in such transaction will be allocated as if the consideration were the proceeds to be distributed to the Company's stockholders in a liquidation under the Company's then-current Certificate of Incorporation.]

Sale Rights: Upon written notice to the Company from the Electing Holders, the Company shall initiate a process intended to result in a sale of the Company.]

OTHER MATTERS

Founders' Stock: All Founders to own stock outright subject to Company right to buyback at cost. Buyback right for [_____]% for first [12 months] after Closing; thereafter, right lapses in equal [monthly] increments over following [_____] months.

Existing Preferred Stock: The terms set forth above for the Series [_] Preferred Stock are subject to a review of the rights, preferences and restrictions for the existing Preferred Stock. Any changes necessary to conform the existing Preferred Stock to this term sheet will be made at the Closing.]

Offering Terms

No Shop/
Confidentiality:

The Company agrees to work in good faith expeditiously towards a closing. The Company and the Founders agree that they will not, for a period of [_____] weeks from the date these terms are accepted, take any action to solicit, initiate, encourage or assist the submission of any proposal, negotiation or offer from any person or entity other than the Investors relating to the sale or issuance, of any of the capital stock of the Company [or the acquisition, sale, lease, license or other disposition of the Company or any material part of the stock or assets of the Company] and shall notify the Investors promptly of any inquiries by any third parties in regards to the foregoing. [In the event that the Company breaches this no-shop obligation and, prior to [_____], closes any of the above-referenced transactions [without providing the Investors the opportunity to invest on the same terms as the other parties to such transaction], then the Company shall pay to the Investors $[_____] upon the closing of any such transaction as liquidated damages.] The Company will not disclose the terms of this Term Sheet to any person other than officers, members of the Board of Directors and the Company's accountants and attorneys and other potential Investors acceptable to [_____], as lead Investor, without the written consent of the Investors.

Expiration:

This Term Sheet expires on [_____ _____ , 20_____] if not accepted by the Company by that date.

EXECUTED THIS [_____] Day of [_____], 20 [_____].

[SIGNATURE BLOCKS]

EXHIBIT A
Pre and Post-Financing Capitalization

Security	Pre-Financing		Post-Financing	
	# of Shares	%	# of Shares	%
Common — Founders				
Common — Employee Stock				
Pool				
Issued				
Unissued				
[Common — Warrants]				
Series A Preferred				
Total				

Additional Information

1. STEVEN C. ALBERTY, 1 ADVISING SMALL BUSINESSES: FORMS § 15:2 (2009).

2. CARL BARANOWSKI, REPRESENTING HIGH TECH COMPANIES § 2.07 (2009).

3. ALAN E. SALZMAN, L. JOHN DOERR, START-UP AND EMERGING COMPANIES § 7.05 (2009).

4. WILLIAM M. PRIFTI, 24 SECURITIES: PUB. & PRIV. OFFERINGS § 3:38 (2010).

5. LEE R. PETILLON, ROBERT JOE HULL, REPRESENTING START-UP COMPANIES Appendix 7-L (2009).

6. JOSEPH W. BARTLETT, EQUITY FIN. § 1.2 (2011).

7. BRIAN O'NEAL, MOD. CORP. CHECKLISTS § 2:9 (2011).

8. RICHARD A. BOOTH, FINANCING THE CORPORATION §§ 2:33–2:34 (2010).

9. Ellen B. Corenswet, *Introduction To Venture Capital Deal Terms*, 1799 PLI/CORP 35 (2010).

10. Sarah Reed, *What Are The NVCA Model Venture Capital Financing Documents?*, 1730 PLI/CORP 21 (2009).

11. Curtis L. Mo, *Overview Of Due Diligence Investigations For Venture Capital Deals*, 1666 PLI/CORP 363 (2008).

12. Lori S. Hoberman, *Due Diligence In Venture Capital Deals*, 1660 PLI/CORP 477 (2008).

13. Robert J. Brigham, *National Venture Capital Association Forms*, 1642 PLI/CORP 159 (2008).

14. Stephen Marcovich, Amand B. Sanders, *Documentation for a Venture Capital Investment in a Private Company (With Forms)*, 52 No. 3 PRAC. LAW. 49 (2006).

15. Curtis L. Mo, *Venture Capital Financing: Current Terms, Down Round and Cram-Down Financing*, 1457 PLI/CORP 677 (2004).

16. Joseph L. Lemon, *Don't Let Me Down (Round): Avoiding Illusory Terms in Venture Capital Financing in the Post-Internet Bubble Era*, 39 Tex. J. Bus. L. 1 (2003).

17. Curtis L. Mo, *Recent Trends in Venture Capital Financing Terms*, 1267 PLI/CORP 651 (2001).

18. Francis S. Currie, *Venture Capital Financing: Structure, Terms of Preferred Stock, Stock Purchase Agreements, Due Diligence, and Impact of Rule 19c-4*, 539 PLI/COMM 169 (1990).

11.4.4 Venture Capital Investment Disputes

SPENCER TRASK SOFTWARE v. RPOST INTERNATIONAL
383 F. Supp. 2d 428 (S.D.N.Y. 2003)

LEISURE, DISTRICT JUDGE.

Defendants RPost International Limited, Zafar Kahn, Terry Tomkow, and Ken Barton (collectively "RPost") move to dismiss this action brought by Spencer Trask Software and Information Services, LLC and Spencer Trask Ventures, Inc. (collectively "Spencer Trask"), pursuant to Federal Rule of Civil Procedure 12(b)(6). For the reasons stated below, defendants' motion to dismiss is granted in part and denied in part.

BACKGROUND

On a motion to dismiss, the plaintiffs' well-pleaded allegations in their Amended Complaint are assumed to be true. Therefore the relevant facts, as alleged by the plaintiffs in their Amended Complaint, are as follows. Spencer Trask is an experienced venture capital investor that provides financing for emerging companies, particularly in the technology sector, and in return, Spencer Trask generally receives company stock. RPost is a start-up internet company which aims to provide an electronic mail service for sending "registered e-mails" with security similar to registered mail sent through traditional postal services. In July 2001, RPost circulated an offering memorandum (the "July Memorandum") among investors, seeking investors to complete its Series B round of financing — a private placement of convertible debt of up to $2 million. The proposed terms for investment called for the Series B notes to convert into shares in RPost at a 50% discount to the closing price in RPost's later Series C round of financing. The July Memorandum made numerous representations about the company: listing the "Directors and Advisors" of RPost and describing their backgrounds, and including in that group Marvin Runyon, a former Postmaster General of the United States.

The July Memorandum also listed Brigadier General Richard W. Pryor (Ret.), a former President of Worldcom, as the "Interim CEO" of RPost, and included him in the list of people identified under a heading titled "Team — Founders and Leadership Team." The July Memorandum made representations concerning RPost's relationship with the United States Postal Service (USPS), stating that RPost offered registered e-mail "in partnership with the USPS," and representing that their "partnership was on the cusp of completion." Furthermore, the July Memorandum made representations concerning RPost's capitalization, stating that the authorized capital stock of the company consisted of 120,000,000 "ordinary" shares, of which approximately 21,000,000 were issued and outstanding.

On August 13, 2001, Kevin Kimberlin, Chairman of Spencer Trask & Co., and Danny Zottoli, Chief Executive Officer of Information Services, met with defendants Kahn and Barton, two of the three founders of RPost. Kahn explained that RPost was raising a "Series B" round of financing, but was in need of further financing to close out that round. Kahn represented that RPost expected to sign in 60 days a final operational contract with the USPS, which would give RPost the exclusive use of the USPS brand for the provision of USPS electronic registered mail. Spencer Trask expressed its willingness to provide financing, but only if terms could be reached that ensured that Spencer Trask would have a sufficient stake in the company to justify the risk it would be taking. On August 22, 2001, the parties met again, and reached an agreement on terms for the investment by Spencer Trask ("August Agreement"). The proposed terms for the investment provided that: (1) Spencer Trask would provide RPost with $500,000 in Series B financing, subject only to Spencer Trask's due-diligence review; (2) Information Services would purchase, subject to due diligence, 6% of the fully-diluted outstanding capital stock from each of the three founders for $1.8 million, with Spencer Trask having the right to purchase the shares in three separate tranches over an 18 month period; (3) Spencer Trask would raise or invest $1 million for RPost in its subsequent Series C round of financing provided that two conditions were met: (a) RPost did in fact enter into an exclusive contract with the USPS; and (b) that before March 1, 2002, RPost also raised $1 million of Series C financing from other investors at a pre-money valuation of $30 million or less; and (4) Spencer Trask agreed to make a non-binding commitment to use its best efforts to raise funds for RPost's Series D round of financing. The overall result of the agreed structure was to give Spencer Trask the right to acquire over 20% of RPost stock. Kahn and Kimberlin shook hands on the deal and Kimberlin congratulated Kahn on becoming a partner with Spencer Trask. That same day, in response to a request by Spencer Trask, Kahn sent an e-mail representing that "[t]he total issued and outstanding shares in the company, RPost International Limited . . . are 22,336,000." Spencer Trask relied on this figure in calculating how many shares would be purchased from each founder in the August Agreement.

After Kimberlin and Kahn shook hands on the August Agreement, Kimberlin asked Zottoli to draw up the terms to which they had agreed. David Hochman, a Managing Director at Spencer Trask & Co., drew up four short letter agreements to document the deal; and Hochman and Zottoli then telephoned Kahn and walked him through each sentence reflected in the letter agreements. Kahn told them that the terms in the letters were satisfactory. Hochman then sent the draft letter agreements to Kahn via e-mail on August 23, 2001. These proposed letter agreements summarized the parties' discussions regarding Spencer Trask's purchase of the founders' shares in RPost, provided for payment of $200,000 in cash by Spencer Trask "[o]n execution," and concluded with the sentence, "We are prepared to move promptly to consummate this transaction following the execution of this letter."

Over the next two months, RPost proposed some revisions to the terms of the August Agreement, some of which were material, but Spencer Trask did not accept the material changes. The parties never signed or executed any of the four letter agreements written by Hochman. RPost did not provide Spencer Trask with due-diligence materials until the second week of October, a full month after RPost had assured Spencer Trask that those materials would be sent, and those materials did not include several of the documents needed by Spencer Trask in order to complete their due diligence. In a telephone call on October 26, 2001, Kahn emphasized the urgency of closing Spencer Trask's Series B investment due to the imminence of RPost's signing an exclusive agreement with the USPS. On October 30, 2001, Kahn sent Spencer Trask a letter urging Spencer Trask to provide the Series B financing right away, stating that it was closing financing that week; and on November 1, 2001, Spencer Trask invested $500,000 in RPost's Series B round of financing. In exchange, Spencer Trask received a subordinated promissory note (the "Promissory Note") that was convertible into preferred shares of RPost, the amount of which would be determined by the Series C financing, and the parties executed a Subordinated Convertible Debt Agreement (the "Debt Agreement") on November 1, 2001. In the October 30, 2001 letter, RPost represented that it had 9,624,000 "authorized options in stock option reserve"; but in the Debt Agreement signed on November 1, 2001, RPost represented that it had 3,630,000 authorized options in reserve.

On December 20, 2001, RPost sent Spencer Trask another offering memorandum, which was dated November 2001 (the "November Memorandum"). Like the July Memorandum, the November Memorandum made various representations concerning RPost's management; its relationship with the USPS; and its capital structure.

Despite Spencer Trask's repeated reminders of the need to receive additional information from RPost in order to complete the due diligence needed in order to close the August Agreement, defendants delayed providing that information and scheduling interviews, such that the due diligence was only finalized on January 9, 2002. However, on January 15, 2002, when Kimberlin met with Khan and Barton and stated that Spencer Trask was ready to proceed to the final closing of the remaining phases of the August Agreement, Barton told Kimberlin that their circumstances had changed and that they "did not need" that deal anymore.

In February 2002, Spencer Trask asked RPost a series of questions concerning its capitalization structure and corporate governance. Spencer Trask (sic — RPost) responded to those questions in a letter dated February 22, 2002, via its counsel Hill & Barlow, with the following information: (1) RPost had 21,645,000 shares of common stock issued and outstanding; (2) RPost had outstanding options exercisable for 686,000 shares of common stock; (3) RPost had reserved 9,564,000

additional shares under its option plan; (4) the three founders of the company —
defendants Tomkow, Khan and Barton-were the only members of RPost's board of
directors; (5) RPost did not have an "Executive Committee"; (6) neither Mr.
Runyon nor General Pryor were "current statutory officers" of RPost. In addition,
the plaintiffs alleged that they learned information about the qualifications and
background of Kahn and Barton that made RPost's representations regarding
these individuals in the July and November appear misleading. Plaintiffs continue
to allege that as of March 12, 2002, RPost had still not finalized any agreement with
the USPS.

DISCUSSION

****

B. Claim I: Breach of Contract

Spencer Trask asserts several claims seeking to enforce the alleged August
Agreement with RPost: breach of contract, breach of implied contract, promissory
estoppel, unjust enrichment, and breach of the duty of good faith and fair dealing.
Defendants argue that all of Spencer Trask's contract-based claims fail for two
reasons: (1) the Amended Complaint and incorporated documents conclusively
establish the absence of any claims as matter of law; and (2) the Statute of Frauds
bars all of those claims. The Court will first address whether the Amended
Complaint and the incorporated documents establish a claim upon which relief can
be granted.

Defendants contend that the facts as alleged in the Amended Complaint and the
documents incorporated by reference into the complaint show, as a matter of law,
that RPost did not manifest an intent to enter into a binding agreement in their
conversations with Spencer Trask on August 22, 2001, and therefore, Spencer
Trask and RPost did not enter into a binding agreement as result of their oral
discussions and handshake on that date. Consequently, defendants contend that
plaintiffs cannot state a claim for breach of contract. While plaintiffs assert that the
parties did enter into a binding preliminary agreement in their conversation on
August 22, 2001, they argue that the issue of whether or not the parties intended to
be bound in their August Agreement, and consequently, whether the August
Agreement constitutes an enforceable contract, cannot be determined as a matter
of law at this early stage of the litigation. While the Court can make the
determination of whether the parties intended to be bound in an alleged
preliminary agreement on a motion to dismiss, courts are often reluctant to rule on
the issue of intent to form a binding agreement in a judgment on the pleadings, and
must be cautious in making such determinations.

Under New York contract law, parties may enter into a contract orally, even
though they contemplate later memorializing their agreement in writing. In such a
case, the mere intention to commit the agreement to writing will not prevent
contract formation prior to the execution of that writing. If, however, either party
communicates an intent not to be bound until he achieves a fully executed

document, "no amount of negotiation or oral agreement to specific terms will result in the formation of a binding contract."

In general, "preliminary manifestations of assent that require further negotiation and further contracts do not create binding obligations." However, the Second Circuit has recognized that in some rare instances, if a preliminary agreement clearly manifests the intent of the parties, it can create a binding obligation. Noting that it is a rare instance in which a preliminary agreement clearly manifests such an intention as to create a binding obligation, Judge Pierre N. Leval, then a District Court judge, helpfully outlined two separate categories of such binding preliminary contracts. The first type is a fully binding preliminary agreement, which is created when the parties have agreed upon all essential terms, but agree to memorialize their agreement in a more formal document. "A binding preliminary agreement binds both sides to their ultimate contractual objective in recognition that, "despite the anticipation of further formalities," a contract has been reached." The second type of preliminary agreement, termed by Judge Leval as a "binding preliminary commitment," is created when the parties agree on certain major terms but leave other terms open for negotiation, accepting "a mutual commitment to negotiate together in good faith in an effort to reach final agreement." "In contrast to a fully binding preliminary agreement, a "binding preliminary commitment" does not commit the parties to their ultimate contractual objective but rather to the obligation to negotiate the open issues in good faith in an attempt to reach the . . . objective within the agreed framework."

The key issue, in finding that the plaintiffs have stated a claim for either type of agreement, is whether the parties intended to be bound by that preliminary agreement. In ascertaining whether the parties evinced this intention to be bound, the court must look to "the words and deeds [of the parties] which constitute objective signs in a given set of circumstances." Subjective evidence of intent, however, is generally not considered. Instead, "[w]hat matters are the parties' expressed intentions, the words and deeds which constitute objective signs in a given set of circumstances." The analysis must not put "disproportionate emphasis . . . on any single act, phrase or other expression, but, instead, [should consider] the totality of all of these, given the attendant circumstances, the situation of the parties, and the objectives they were striving to attain."

Plaintiffs have alleged that the parties entered into a fully binding preliminary agreement in their oral agreement on August 22, 2001. In the alternative, plaintiffs argue that if the Court finds they have failed to state a claim that the parties entered into a fully binding preliminary agreement, the August Agreement represented a binding preliminary commitment between the parties, and as such that the defendants have breached their duty to negotiate in good faith under such a commitment.

1) August Agreement Is Not a Binding Preliminary Agreement

The Court has identified four factors to be considered in determining whether parties to a preliminary agreement, which calls for the execution of a formal instrument, intended to be bound in the absence of such an executed final instrument. In *Winston*, the Court looked at the following four factors in determining whether the preliminary agreement between the parties represented a binding preliminary agreement: (1) whether the parties have expressly reserved the right not to be bound without a written contract; (2) whether there has been partial performance of the contract; (3) whether the parties have agreed to all terms of the alleged contract; and (4) whether the alleged agreement is the type that is usually committed to writing. This Court has also found the *Winston* factors to be instructive in determining whether a preliminary agreement should be considered binding as a preliminary commitment to negotiate in good faith, altering the factors considered only slightly and placing less of a focus on the existence of unresolved terms between the parties. In the analysis of both these types of binding agreements, the Court has found the language of the agreements to be the most important factor in discerning the parties' manifested intent. In this case, that is a bit more difficult since the alleged agreement was an oral agreement and the only evidence we have of its language is the language of the draft agreements, which the plaintiffs allege embody the terms of the alleged oral agreement.

a) Express Reservation of Right Not to Be Bound Absent a Writing

While there was not an express reservation of the right not to be bound in the draft Agreements, there was such a reservation in the July Memorandum, and there were several expressions of the mutual intent not to be bound prior to the execution of the draft agreements. The draft agreements, the terms of which were allegedly agreed to by both parties over the telephone after Hochman and Zottoli "walked Kahn through each sentence reflected in the agreements," were sent via e-mail to the defendants the day after the alleged oral agreement. Those agreements laid out the terms agreed to in the alleged oral contract, and concluded with the sentence, "We are prepared to move promptly to consummate this transaction *following the execution of this letter.*" That is not the only reference to execution in these agreements, as the agreements include a requirement that Spencer Trask make a payment of $200,000 "[o]n execution." *Id.* Plaintiffs do not allege that they paid this money. Lastly, all four draft agreements contained blank signature lines with an open agreement date: "Agreed, as of August _____, 2001." These provisions of the draft agreements, each sentence of which the plaintiffs allege were agreed to by both parties, "appear to place importance on the formalities of execution," thereby reflecting a mutual intent on the part of both parties not to be bound to the terms of the agreement until the agreement was executed. Of those three provisions in the draft agreements, the critical language at the end of the agreements, indicating that the plaintiffs "were prepared to move promptly to consummate this transaction *following the execution of this letter,*" is the strongest indication that the parties did not evince an intent to be bound prior to execution. This language is indistinguishable from terms that courts have found preclude a binding preliminary agreement as a matter of law.

Furthermore, the defendants did include an explicit reservation of their right not to be bound in the absence of a written agreement in the July Memorandum provided by RPost to Spencer Trask, which lay out the terms for deals involving investment in RPost's Series B round of financing. In that Memorandum, RPost states, "We may not sell the convertible debt or accept any offer to purchase the convertible debt until we have delivered to you and you have executed the agreement reflecting the definitive terms and conditions of the offering." Plaintiffs have alleged that their investment in the Series B financing was part of the August Agreement, therefore the provision of the July Memorandum, which applied to the sale or purchase of convertible debt for that financing and explicitly reserved the defendants' right not to be bound absent a written agreement, is indicative of the defendants' objective intent not to be bound to a sale or purchase of convertible debt in the absence of a written agreement.

b) Partial Performance

The second factor looks to whether one party has partially performed, and that performance has been accepted by the party disclaiming the contract. Plaintiffs contend that there has been partial performance of the August Agreement: Spencer Trask by investing $500,000 in RPost's Series B financing round and RPost by providing Spencer Trask with due diligence through January 2001. Partial performance requires some actual performance of the contract, such that the plaintiffs must have conferred something of value upon the defendants which the defendants accepted. While it is clear that the plaintiffs' investment of $500,000 did confer a benefit upon the defendants, the defendants assert that that investment was part of the contract signed by the parties in the Debt Agreement and therefore not indicative of the plaintiffs' performance of the August Agreement. Defendants argue that language in the Debt Agreement, stating that "This Agreement constitutes the entire agreement among the parties hereto with respect to the subject matter hereof," indicates that the plaintiffs' Series B investment was not part of a package deal, and should not be seen as partial performance of the August Agreement. Plaintiffs assert that this language does not preclude the Series B investment from being part of a larger package deal, because the language merely indicates that the Debt Agreement was the entire agreement with respect to the "subject matter hereof" — meaning the Series B round of financing that it governed. Accordingly, it is not appropriate for the Court to make a conclusive determination of whether or not the language in the Debt Agreement bars the plaintiffs' investment from being seen as partial performance of the August Agreement at this early stage. Therefore, making all reasonable inferences in favor of the plaintiffs, the Court finds that the second factor slightly favors the plaintiffs.

c) Agreement on All Terms

Turning to the third factor, plaintiffs alleged that the parties reached an oral "agreement on terms," and that RPost thereafter proposed material revisions to those terms. While the Court must take as true the plaintiffs' allegation that the parties reached an agreement on terms, it appears from further allegations in the Amended Complaint that the parties were still negotiating several of these material terms. It seems clear from the negotiations that ensued that the plaintiffs' alleged "agreement on terms" was not an agreement to all terms, and even drawing all reasonable inferences in favor of the plaintiffs, the Court cannot find that this factor weighs in favor of the plaintiffs.

d) Agreement Is Type Usually Committed To Writing

The fourth and final factor is whether the August Agreement is the type that is usually committed to writing. The alleged oral agreement was a complex, multi-stage package deal whereby Spencer Trask would invest or raise at least $1.5 million in Series B and C financing, subject to extensive due diligence and to various pre-conditions and milestones for the Series C round; Spencer Trask would have options to purchase $5.4 million worth of RPost founders' stock at three separate points over an 18-month period; and would have the right of first refusal on a Series D round at some point in the future. The Court agrees with the defendants that it "defies common sense that any sophisticated investor would ever expect to be able to agree to such a deal, or to be able to carry out and ever enforce such a deal, without a written contract."

In sum, three of the four factors strongly point to the conclusion that the parties did not intend to be bound to the terms of the August Agreement in the absence of a written document. Even drawing all reasonable inferences from the partial performance alleged by the plaintiffs, the Court finds that that factor alone is insufficient to state a claim for relief. Therefore, based on the facts alleged in the Amended Complaint and the incorporated documents, the Court finds that the plaintiffs have failed to state a claim that the parties intended the August Agreement to be a binding preliminary agreement.

2) August Agreement May Represent a Binding Preliminary Commitment

In considering whether the August Agreement resulted in the second type of binding preliminary agreement — "a binding preliminary commitment" — the Court looks to the following factors examined by Judge Leval in determining whether the parties evinced an intent to be bound: (1) the language of the agreement; (2) the context of the negotiations; (3) the existence of open terms; (4) any partial performance; and (5) the necessity of putting the agreement in final form, as indicated by the customary form of such transactions. In seeking to determine whether such a preliminary binding commitment was established, "a court's task is, once again, to determine the intentions of the parties at the time of their entry into the understanding, as well as their manifestations to one another by which the understanding was reached." Just as for the first type of binding agreement, the parties must manifest a mutual intent to be bound in order for the Court to find that a binding preliminary commitment has been made. While the Court does find from the language of the draft agreements and the July Memorandum that the parties did not manifest a mutual intent to be bound by the terms of the August Agreement, as was alleged by the plaintiffs, the Court cannot conclusively determine, from the language of these documents, that the parties did not manifest an intent to be bound "to negotiate together in good faith in an effort to reach final agreement within the scope" of the terms laid out in the August Agreement. Therefore this factor is neutral, weighing neither in favor of the plaintiffs nor the defendants.

Looking to the second factor — the context of the negotiations-the one factor not considered in the analysis for the first type of binding agreement, the Court looks to where the parties alleged oral agreement fell within the course of the negotiations. The plaintiffs allege that the parties had at least two meetings and several conversations regarding the deal prior to their oral agreement on August 22, 2001. Therefore, the Court cannot say that the negotiations were at such a preliminary stage that the parties conclusively could have evinced no intent to be bound to a preliminary commitment. Accordingly, drawing all reasonable inferences in favor of the plaintiffs, this factor weighs slightly in favor of the plaintiffs.

In most cases where the courts have found a binding preliminary commitment, the parties have purposely left open terms to be negotiated in good faith. In this case, the plaintiffs have not alleged that the parties purposely left terms open to be negotiated in good faith, however, it is clear from the facts alleged both that the parties did not reach an agreement on all terms in the August Agreement and that the parties did engage in some negotiations about those open terms after they reached their alleged oral agreement. While courts have found the existence of open terms to indicate the parties' intention not to be bound to the terms of a preliminary agreement, courts have found that factor to play a less significant role in the determination of whether the parties evinced an intent to be bound to a negotiate those open terms in good faith.

For the reasons stated in the analysis above, the partial performance factor weighs slightly in favor of the plaintiffs, and the final factor — whether the agreement is one that would have normally been committed to writing-weighs in favor of the defendants. While the defendants have a strong argument that the parties evinced no intention to be bound, either to the terms of the agreement or to a duty to negotiate that agreement in good faith, drawing all reasonable inferences in favor of the plaintiffs, the Court must deny defendants' motion to dismiss plaintiffs' claim alleging a breach of contract, and allow the plaintiffs to submit evidence in support their claim that such a binding preliminary commitment resulted from the parties' alleged oral agreement on August 22, 2001.

C. Claim II: Breach of Implied Contract

The law recognizes two types of implied contracts, those which are implied by the facts and those which are implied by the law. A contract implied from the facts is found where the consent of the parties to the agreement may be inferred from the acts of the parties and all of the surrounding circumstances. An implied-in-fact contract arises in the absence of an express agreement, and is based on the conduct of the parties from which a fact-finder may infer the existence and terms of a contract. Since the Court cannot conclusively determine that the parties did not make a binding preliminary commitment in their alleged oral agreement, the Court cannot dismiss the plaintiffs' claim for breach of implied contract. Moreover, whether certain conduct gives rise to an implied contract is a question of fact, to be determined under the circumstances of the case. As such, it would not be appropriate to dismiss the plaintiffs' claim for breach of implied contract at this point.

D. Claim III: Promissory Estoppel

Under New York law, promissory estoppel has three elements: "a clear and unambiguous promise; a reasonable and foreseeable reliance by the party to whom the promise is made; and injury sustained by the party asserting the estoppel by reason of his reliance." While the defendants have pointed to evidence that indicates that the plaintiffs' $500,000 investment in the Series B financing did not represent reasonable reliance on the defendants' alleged promise, pointing to the portion of the Debt Agreement which provided that it was the "entire agreement among the parties hereto with respect to the subject matter hereof," such evidence cannot conclusively establish at this stage the issue of whether or not the $500,000 constituted reasonable reliance. Therefore, plaintiffs have adequately pled all three elements of promissory estoppel, and the defendants' motion to dismiss the plaintiffs' claim for promissory estoppel is denied.

E. Claim VIII: Unjust Enrichment

Under New York law, "a plaintiff seeking an equitable recovery based on unjust enrichment must first show that a benefit was conferred upon the defendant, and then show that as between the two parties, enrichment of the defendant was unjust." Plaintiffs have alleged that allowing the defendants to retain the benefit of the $500,000 investment and the value of the plaintiffs' reputation and good name as an investor, without honoring the balance of their alleged August agreement would be unjust. Since plaintiffs have adequately pled that a benefit was conferred upon the defendants and that the defendants' enrichment was unjust and at the plaintiffs' expense, the defendants' motion to dismiss the unjust enrichment claim is denied.

F. Claim IX: Breach of Duty of Good Faith and Fair Dealing

The covenant of good faith and fair dealing, implied in every contract under New York law, "includes "an implied undertaking on the part of each party that he will not intentionally and purposely do anything to prevent the other party from carrying out the agreement on his part." " Since this Court is not willing to dismiss the plaintiffs' claim for breach of contract at this juncture, the Court also denies the defendants' motion to dismiss the plaintiffs' claim for breach of duty of good faith and fair dealing.

QUESTIONS

1. Why might RPost have no longer needed, or wanted, the Spencer Trask venture investment?

2. What is the difference between a "binding preliminary agreement" and a "binding preliminary commitment"? How do the tests for these two types of non-formal contract agreements differ?

3. Why did the court find that Spencer Trask's investment of $500,000 in RPost did not conclusively establish partial performance by Spencer Trask?

4. What type of agreement is not "usually committed to writing"?

5. Why did the court find that the August Agreement may represent a binding preliminary commitment?

6. How is a claim of breach of implied contract related to a claim of breach of a binding preliminary commitment?

7. How is a claim of promissory estoppel related to a claim of unjust enrichment?

INFOSAGE v. MELLON VENTURES
896 A.2d 616 (Pa. Super. Ct. 2006)

OPINION BY McCAFFERY, J.

1. Appellant, InfoSAGE, Inc., a Pennsylvania corporation, appeals from the order of the Honorable R. Stanton Wettick, Jr., entered October 19, 2004, in the Court of Common Pleas of Allegheny County, granting summary judgment in favor of Appellees and dismissing in its entirety Appellant's amended complaint. Specifically, Appellant asks us to determine whether genuine issues of material fact exist to support its counts sounding in tortious interference with prospective business relations, breach of fiduciary duty, and aiding and abetting a breach of fiduciary duty. Because we conclude that Appellant has failed to adduce sufficient evidence establishing necessary elements showing a tortious interference with prospective business relations and breach of fiduciary duty, we affirm.

2. The trial court's factual recitation, construing the evidence most favorably to Appellant, is as follows:

> [Appellant] was a software development company. The development of its products and services was financed by an initial round of founder financing of approximately $5 million and two rounds of venture capital financing that provided another $5 million. [Appellee] Mellon Ventures, L.P. ("Mellon") provided the initial round of the venture capital financing. Mellon, Draper Triangle Partners, and Russell, Rea, Zappalla ["RRZ"] provided the second round of venture capital financing.

In the spring of 2001, Appellant had a five-member board of directors. The members were Anthony J. Bonidy (President and CEO — .9% owner), Robert Capretto (Chairman of the Board and 26.5% owner), Robert L. Reed (22.1% owner), Donald H. Jones, and Appellee Charles J. Billerbeck. Draper was a 7.9% owner of Appellant; Donald Jones was a member of Appellant's board of directors as a result of Draper's investment. Mellon was a 20.4% owner of Appellant; Appellee Charles J. Billerbeck, a director of Mellon, was a member of Appellant's board of directors as a result of Mellon's investment.

Evidence favorable to Appellant will support a finding that by early 2001, Appellant had completed the development and testing phase for its software product. In late 2000, Appellant's board of directors approved a business plan predicated upon Appellant's securing a third round of financing that would be used for its marketing efforts. Appellant needed to promptly secure this financing because it would be running out of money by the summer of 2001. In January 2001, Appellant retained Ms. Elizabeth M. Audley, an investment banker with Morgan, Franklin & Co., to assist Appellant in its search for financing. A pre-money valuation of Appellant of $23 million was agreed to be appropriate by all members of the board of directors. Appellant was seeking an equity investment of $5 million.

As of June 2001, the financing had not materialized. The board of directors (other than Mr. Jones and Mr. Billerbeck) voted to enter into a bridge loan contract with Mellon and Draper in order that Appellant could continue doing business while attempting to obtain a third round of financing. The contract was executed on June 22, 2001.

Appellant was never able to obtain a third round of financing. It ceased doing business in October 2001 because it could not obtain additional financing. On January 31, 2002, it filed Chapter 11 proceedings in the United States Bankruptcy Court for the Western District of Pennsylvania.

Several weeks before Appellant entered into the bridge loan, Appellant's principals (Tony Bonidy and Robert Capretto) accused Mr. Billerbeck and Mellon of interfering with Appellant's efforts to obtain financing. They claimed that Mellon was taking steps to dissuade potential investors from participating in the third round of financing.

On August 16, 2001, Appellant filed this lawsuit against Mellon and Mr. Billerbeck, alleging that both.. had tortiously interfered with prospective business relations. The complaint also alleged that both had breached their fiduciary duties to Appellant by interfering with its financing efforts. The accusations against Appellees included their setting an unreasonably low valuation of Appellant and communicating the low valuation to venture capitalists and other third parties.

Subsequently, Appellant amended its complaint to add Mellon Ventures, Inc. ("MVI") and Burton B. Goldstein, Jr. as defendants, and to add a count for aiding and abetting the breach of a fiduciary duty. The Complaint identified MVI as the investment manager for Mellon, and Mr. Goldstein as an employee of MVI. Appellant claims that Mr. Goldstein and MVI assisted Mr. Billerbeck and Mellon in dissuading venture capital firms from providing financing to Appellant by directly contacting these firms and asking them to stay out of the financing efforts of Mellon.

Appellant contends that Appellees interfered with Appellant's efforts to obtain financing because Appellees wanted (i) to force Appellant to obtain the third round of financing from Mellon at terms which Mellon would dictate, (ii) to force Appellant's board of directors to sell Appellant prematurely and/or (iii) to trigger a liquidation preference that would wipe out the ownership interests of the initial investors.

Appellant's Complaint identifies the following third parties as potential third round investors that were dissuaded from investing in Appellant because of actions taken by Appellees that were intended to dissuade them from doing so: Pa. Early Stage, Pennsylvania Technology Investment Authority (PTIA), Liberty Ventures, Cross-Atlantic, Grotech, Gabriel Ventures, Rahn Group, Trinity Ventures, and Phoenician Ventures.

3. Following the close of the pleadings, the parties undertook extensive, indeed exhaustive discovery. At the conclusion of discovery, Appellees filed their motion for summary judgment, contending that the evidence failed to show that they had in any manner interfered with Appellant's efforts to obtain third-round financing. The trial court agreed, and granted Appellees' motion for summary judgment.

4. In arriving at its decision, the court noted that affidavits and testimony given by principals and key witnesses from the nine (9) venture capital firms identified in the amended complaint uniformly revealed that these entities had declined to invest in Appellant for independent business reasons, and that these entities had not been deterred or dissuaded from investing in Appellant by Appellees or any act performed by Appellees. The court further noted that Appellant had adduced evidence indicating potential interference with only four (4) of these firms: Phoenician Ventures I, L.P. ("Phoenician"), Liberty Venture Partners ("Liberty"), PTIA, and Pa. Early Stage. For purposes of its summary judgment review, the court properly rejected any evidence that denied interference by Appellees with these four entities and examined only the evidence arguably supporting Appellant's allegations.

5. Concerning Phoenician, Appellant produced evidence that this firm was aware that Mellon had placed an "unreasonably low valuation" upon Appellant, that the firm was in agreement with this valuation, and that Phoenician understood that Mellon was doing a "down round" for the third round of financing. The court concluded, however, that this evidence failed to establish that (1) Mellon was the source of Phoenician's determination of a low valuation for Appellant and (2) Phoenician would have invested in Appellant but for the acts of Appellees.

6. With respect to Liberty, the court took note of the deposition testimony of Bonidy and Audley indicating that Liberty had showed interest in Appellant at an initial business meeting, after which a principal from Liberty stated that Liberty would "definitely . . . be moving forward." The court then noted evidence showing that two weeks after the meeting, Liberty notified Appellant that it would not be pursuing the investment opportunity with Appellant. In the interim, Billerbeck had become aware that Liberty was interested in Appellant as an investment. Audley also testified that her research revealed that Liberty had co-invested in projects with Mellon and that Liberty "probably knew" Mellon. The court determined that this evidence, taken as a whole, could not support a jury finding that it was more likely than not that Appellees had contacted Liberty to discourage it from investing in Appellant.

Concerning PTIA, the uncontradicted evidence of record established that PTIA had entertained only the *possibility* that it would supply the final twenty (20) percent of the financing which Appellant was seeking, provided that Appellant would first obtain eighty (80) percent of its financing needs from other sources. Therefore, the court concluded that, as Appellant had been unable to obtain third-round financing from any other entity, its failure to obtain financing from PTIA could not be attributable to Appellees.

****

8. The most extensive evidence adduced by the parties concerns Appellees' alleged interference with a possible business relationship between Appellant and Pa. Early Stage. The trial court examined this evidence at length, quoting large portions of relevant testimony in its opinion. We also quote this evidence at length in order to give a full frame of reference to the trial court's decision and the arguments now raised by Appellant in the present appeal.

9. Michael Bolton, the manager of Pa. Early Stage, and Jason Mahoney, a principal employee of the firm, testified by deposition that the decision not to invest in Appellant was based on independent business reasons; that Appellees did not attempt to dissuade or deter Pa. Early Stage from investing in Appellant (in fact just the opposite); and that Appellees did not provide Pa. Early Stage with a value for Appellant. In fact, Pa. Early Stage independently came to believe that Appellant had placed too high a value upon itself. The trial court did *not* consider this testimony for purposes of its summary judgment review.

****

I. Interference with Prospective Business Relations

20. Appellant's first three arguments concern the question of whether Appellant had adduced sufficient evidence to contradict or challenge the array of evidence brought forth by Appellees showing that Appellees had not tortiously interfered with Appellant's prospective business relations. Appellant first contends that Billerbeck's statements and actions made at the May 30, 2001 Duquesne Club meeting, as recalled by Bonidy in his deposition testimony, are tantamount to an admission that he and the other Appellees tortiously interfered with Appellant's attempts to obtain financing from a number of venture capital firms, notably Pa. Early Stage. Appellant further contends that the trial court erred by striking as inadmissible hearsay Kohler's testimony that Goldstein informed Pa. Early Stage that Mellon would take care of Appellant's present financing needs, obviating the need, then, for Pa. Early Stage to invest. Appellant argues that this evidence should survive a hearsay challenge because it was offered only to show Pa. Early Stage's "state of mind" regarding its decision to decline investing in Appellant.

21. Appellant also contends that the trial court, instead of separately and hermetically examining the evidence as to each potential investor, should have viewed the evidence as a whole and provided Appellant with all reasonable inferences arising from that evidence. Appellant argues that had the court done so, it would have detected a pattern revealing (1) an initial interest by numerous venture capital firms in Appellant's prospects; (2) the strength of Appellant's prospects as evidenced by a possible partnership between Appellant and an IBM business program; (3) a sudden and uniform demonstration of a lack of interest by the venture capital firms; (4) coincidentally with the latter, Billerbeck's devising an "unreasonably low" valuation for Appellant, one that was many millions below that devised by Appellant's board of directors; (5) knowledge of Mellon's valuation by at least one venture capital firm (Phoenician); (6) evidence that Goldstein had

contacted Bolton; (7) Goldstein purportedly asking Bolton to keep Pa. Early Stage out of Appellant's third-round of financing; (8) Billerbeck's acknowledgement that Goldstein's alleged action was "fodder for a lawsuit"; (9) Billerbeck's failure to deny any wrongdoing at the Duquesne Club meeting; (10) Billerbeck's offer of a bridge loan "to make the lawsuit go away"; (11) Billerbeck's statement that he would now be on the same team, would get out of the way, and would be proactive; (12) Billerbeck discovering that Liberty was the only firm then interested in investing in Appellant; (13) Liberty's sudden decision not to invest in Appellant approximately one week after Billerbeck had learned of Liberty's interest; and (14) Mellon's offer of a bridge loan with terms so onerous that other venture capital firms would decline any investment with the borrower. Appellant also argues that most, if not all, of the evidence relied upon by Appellees in support of their summary judgment motion involves witness testimony, and thus a jury, not a court reviewing a summary judgment motion, must determine the credibility of this oral evidence.

(a) Elements of the Tort

22. In order for Appellant to prove the tort of interference with prospective business relations, it must establish the following:

(1) a prospective contractual relation;

(2) the purpose or intent to harm the plaintiff by preventing the relation from occurring;

(3) the absence of privilege or justification on the part of the defendant; and

(4) the occasioning of actual damages resulting from the defendant's conduct.

Regarding the first element of this tort, *i.e.*, whether the evidence establishes a prospective contractual relation, our Supreme Court observed:

> Defining a "prospective contractual relation" is admittedly problematic. To a certain extent, the term has an evasive quality, excluding precise definition. It is something less than a contractual right, something more than a mere hope. Nevertheless, a working definition of the term is provided by *Glenn v. Point Park College* wherein it was stated that:

> . . . anything that is prospective in nature is necessarily uncertain. We are not dealing with certainties, but with *reasonable likelihood or probability.* This must be something more than a mere hope or the innate optimism of the salesman. As the Superior Court of New Jersey has put it, ". . . the rule to be applied . . . is that the broker may recover when the jury is satisfied that but for the wrongful acts of the defendant it is *reasonably probable* that the plaintiff would have effected the sale of the property and received a commission . . . ." This is *an objective standard* which of course *must be supplied by adequate proof.*

25. In the case *sub judice*, our comprehensive review of the evidence as a whole, giving Appellant all reasonable inferences from the evidence as we must establishes that Appellant *cannot* show that it had a *reasonable probability* of entering into a contractual relationship with the venture capital firms identified in the lawsuit. First, it is undisputed that Appellant had no contractual relationship with any of the

potential investors for its third-round of financing, nor was any such contract in negotiation. Second, Appellant was unable to present evidence sufficient to challenge the broad array of evidence which Appellees adduced in support of their motion for summary judgment. All evidence in this case, in the form of testimony and affidavits, clearly showed that Appellant's efforts to obtain third-round financing had failed to advance to a point where a reasonable probability of a contractual relation was realistic.

****

II. Breach of Fiduciary Duty

52. Appellant next argues that Billerbeck and Mellon breached their fiduciary duty to Appellant and that Goldstein and MVI aided and abetted this breach. Although the trial court did not address these issues, because our scope of review of a grant of summary judgment is plenary and our standard is the same as that of the trial court, we will address Appellant's arguments in the interests of judicial economy.

53. Section 1712(a) of the Business Corporation Law of 1988, as amended, provides in relevant part:

> A director of a business corporation shall stand in a fiduciary relation to the corporation and shall perform his duties as a director . . . in good faith, in a manner he reasonably believes to be in the best interests of the corporation and with such care . . . as a person of ordinary prudence would use under similar circumstances.

Our Supreme Court has stated with regard to the statutorily-imposed fiduciary duties of corporate directors and officers:

> [Directors and officers] must devote themselves to the corporate affairs with a view to promote the common interests and not their own, and they cannot, either directly or indirectly, utilize their position to obtain any personal profit or advantage other than that enjoyed also by their fellow shareholders . . . . In short, there is demanded of the officer or director of a corporation that he furnish to it his undivided loyalty; if there is presented to him a business opportunity which is within the scope of its own activities and of present or potential advantage to it, the law will not permit him to seize the opportunity for himself; if he does so, the corporation may elect to claim all of the benefits of the transaction. Nor is it material that his dealings may not have caused a loss or been harmful to the corporation; *the test of his liability is whether he has unjustly gained enrichment.*

54. Appellant essentially posits three theories supporting its claim that Billerbeck and Mellon breached their fiduciary duty. First, it argues that Billerbeck and Mellon did "all that [they] could to deter others from investing in [Appellant's third] round [of financing] so as to permit Mellon.. to receive unreasonably favorable terms in connection with Appellant's third round of financing." Second, Appellant argues that the evidence shows that Billerbeck proposed such onerous terms for a

1338 FINANCING TECHNOLOGY INNOVATION CH. 11

bridge loan that had Appellant accepted them, all other venture capital firms would have declined to invest in Appellant, paving the way for Mellon to propose third-round financing on terms advantageous to itself. Third, Appellant argues that Billerbeck devised and "published" an "unreasonably low" valuation of Appellant with the aim of discouraging other investors so that the third-round of financing would be met "on Billerbeck's terms[,] . . . greatly increase[ing Mellon's] percentage interest in Appellant while greatly diminishing the percentage interest of the individual investors. Billerbeck's interest in providing an opportunity for Mellon.. to grab the lion's share of the proceeds of any sale is the motive behind the misconduct." Totally unexplained, however, is why Mellon did not act upon the scheme alleged; *i.e.*, it never provided third-round financing such that it could reap the benefit of all of its alleged nefarious dealings, instead allowing Appellant to succumb to bankruptcy.

55. Appellant's first contention is essentially a restatement of its argument that Appellees tortiously interfered with Appellant's prospective business relations. As we previously have determined, Appellant has failed to produce evidence that, but for the actions of Appellees, it would have entered into its sought-for investment contracts with one or more venture capital firms. Moreover, Appellees never provided third-round financing to Appellant on *any* terms, whether favorable to them or not, and Appellant has admitted that Mellon and the other Appellees were under no obligation to provide third-round financing. Also, Appellant does not identify or even suggest how Billerbeck or Mellon was unjustly enriched by Appellant's failure to obtain third-round financing.

56. Appellant's second contention relates to the onerous terms of Mellon's proposed bridge loan. Without citation to authority, Appellant baldly asserts that it is immaterial for purposes of its count in breach of fiduciary duty that Appellant rejected the onerous terms. However, Appellant is required to prove that the individual breaching his or her fiduciary duty was *unjustly* enriched.

57. Here, Appellant did not make *any* allegation or adduce *any* evidence of fraud. Although Appellant contends that the proposed bridge loan was unfair, Appellant rejected the terms set by Mellon for such a loan, and through its representation by a prestigious Philadelphia law firm, negotiated new terms for a bridge loan that Appellant's board of directors (Billerbeck and Jones not voting) accepted. Because Appellant willingly entered into a loan with Mellon in an arms-length transaction on terms negotiated by counsel, there is no justifiable conclusion that Mellon or Billerbeck was *unjustly* enriched by the transaction. Again, Appellant admits that none of the Appellees was under any obligation to lend or invest any further funds to or in Appellant. Further, we note that the bridge loan, in the amount of $750,000, was made not only by Mellon, who loaned $375,000, but also by Draper (which loaned $225,000) and RRZ (which loaned $150,000).

58. Appellant's last contention regards Billerbeck's alleged scheme to "drive down" the value of Appellant so that Mellon could finance Appellant with favorable terms, achieve a greater ownership share in Appellant, and then "flip" its investment with a quick sale of Appellant. We are compelled to conclude that a jury could not return a verdict in favor of Appellant for breach of fiduciary duty on these allegations because *there is absolutely no evidence in the record to support them,*

even in light of the suspicious statements made by Billerbeck to Bonidy and Capretto, which statements we accept as true for purposes of our review. Once again, Appellant offers no explanation for Mellon's failure to carry out its alleged plan of taking over Appellant and selling it.

59. Appellant appears to be arguing that Billerbeck, by the simple act of computing a valuation of Appellant below $10 million when Appellant's board had agreed on a value of $23 million, and by concluding that Appellant's third-round of financing would have to be a "down round," even though Billerbeck had a factual financial basis for reaching these conclusions, breached his fiduciary duty. However, there is no basis to read Section 1712(a) of the Business Corporation Law so strictly. Appellant is on safer ground in arguing that fiduciary duties were breached based on the allegation that the low valuation was "published" to prospective venture capital firms with the aim of discouraging them from investing in Appellant. Unfortunately for Appellant, this argument must then fail because the record lacks proof of any such publication. The lone piece of evidence in the record concerns a statement purportedly made to Audley by an individual from Phoenician that Phoenician "agreed" with Mellon's valuation.

QUESTIONS

1.   In a "down round" the value of the current stockholder shares is diluted. How could Mellon have benefited from an Infosage "down round"?

2.   Why did the court find that there could be no tortious interference with Infosage's prospective contractual relations with other venture capital firms?

3.   Why did the court find that Billerbeck did not breach his fiduciary duty to Infosage? Could Billerbeck have breached his fiduciary duty to Infosage if it was Mellon who was unjustly enriched?

4.   What relevance did Mellon's bridge loan to Infosage have on Infosage's claim of breach of fiduciary duty? What relevance did Mellon's failure to invest in Infosage's third round financing have on Infosage's claim of breach of fiduciary duty?

CASE NOTES

1.   Capital is a venture capital firm and Whitehall is a meat processing company. In early 1972, Whitehall became interested in acquiring a meat processing facility in South Dakota and sought financing from Capital to complete this acquisition. In December 1972, Capital and Whitehall entered into a financing agreement called an "Agreement Respecting First Mortgage Notes and Warrants for the Purchase of Common Stock." Under the Agreement, Capital would lend Whitehall $1,100,000, partially in exchange for warrants to purchase Whitehall common stock. Also under the Agreement, Capital would have the right to designate two of the five members of the Whitehall board of directors and the Capital-designated directors would have veto and decision-making authority regarding certain Whitehall transactions. The Agreement, which was drafted by Capital's legal counsel, provided in Article 5 that the Agreement shall remain in effect "so long as any portion of the [Whitehall] stock

is held by any of the Purchasers" (who exercise their stock warrants). However, Article 14 of the Agreement provided that the Agreement shall be binding upon the parties "so long as any of the [loan] notes or warrants are outstanding." In March 1975, Whitehall paid off the loan notes and Capital exercised all of its stock warrants, purchasing 243 shares of Whitehall common stock, slightly more than 15% of Whitehall's outstanding common stock. In June 1976, the Whitehall board of directors refused to reelect the two Capital-designated directors. Capital sued Whitehall for specific performance of Capital's right to have two Capital-designated directors elected to the Whitehall board of directors. The trial court rejected Whitehall's claim that Articles 5 and 14 rendered the Agreement ambiguous and entered judgment for Capital. Whitehall appealed. What result? *See* Capital Investments, Inc. v. Whitehall Packing Company, Inc., 91 Wis.2d 178 (Wis. 1979).

2. TechTrader (TT) is a start-up company providing software for on-line business-to-business companies. In late 1999, TT required additional financing to continue operations and sought help from CIBC, an investment bank, in obtaining this financing. In January 2000, the parties executed a "Final Agreement" under which TT retained CIBC as its exclusive financial advisor in connection with a possible sale, merger or acquisition of TT. The Final Agreement provided:

> CIBC will act as exclusive financial advisor to TT in connection with the possible sale or other transfer, directly or indirectly, and whether in one or a series of transactions, of all or a significant portion of the assets or securities of TT or any extraordinary corporate transaction involving a change in control of TT, regardless of the form or structure of such transaction (the "Transaction").

> In connection with this engagement, TT agrees to pay CIBC (a) an agreement fee equal to the greater of $250,000 or 0.5% of the Transaction Value, payable in cash upon the earlier of the close of a Transaction or termination of an agreement for a Transaction, plus (b) a transaction fee equal to the greater of $750,000 or 1.5% of the Transaction Value, payable in cash on the closing date of a Transaction, if, during the term of this engagement or within six (6) months thereafter, a Transaction is consummated or an agreement is entered into that subsequently results in a Transaction.

In June 2000, TT accepted venture capital financing from three venture capital funds in the amount of $19 million in exchange for Series-B Preferred Stock. None of the Series-B venture investors were identified or introduced to TT by CIBC. As a result of the Series-B Investment, the allocation of TT shares and the composition of the TT board of directors were changed. TT claimed that CIBC was not entitled to any fees under the Final Agreement because CIBC played no role in facilitating the Series-B financing. CIBC acknowledged that its role in the Series-B financing was minor, but claimed, nonetheless, it was entitled to the fees set forth in the Final Agreement. When TT refused to pay these fees, CIBC brought a breach of contract action against TT. What result? CIBC World Markets Corp. v. TechTrader, Inc., 183 F.Supp.2d 605 (S.D.N.Y. 2001).

3. *See also* Advent Oil & Operating, Inc. v. S&E Enterprises, LLC., 48 So.3d 70 (Fla. Dist. Ct. App. 2010) (Joint venture agreement between venture capital

investor and oil well operator that provided oil well operator would construct and operate a "salt water disposal well" (SDW) with minimum capacity to return venture investment plus 7% interest for four years was breached by oil well operator when it constructed the SDW, but abandoned the SDW within the four year period); Tampa Bay Financial, Inc. v. Nordeen, 272 Ga.App. 529 (Ga. Ct. App. 2005) (Venture capital investment firm failed to show that consulting contract between venture-backed start-up company and third party was a material fact in making venture investment which is an essential element in a claim of fraudulent concealment; stockholder in start-up company could not reasonably rely on venture capital firm's failure to respond to questions regarding redemption of stockholder's shares after reverse merger as a waiver of an express merger clause in the written investment agreement); Metro Communication Corp. BVI v. Advanced Mobilecomm Technologies, 854 A.2d 121 (Del. Ch. 2004) (Eight percent member of venture capital limited liability company (LLC) stated a common law fraud claim against majority members and managers of LLC by alleging that distributed management reports indicating LLC was attempting to obtain digging permits for fiber optic lines, without disclosing that some of these permits were being obtained through bribery; damages claim was supported by eight percent member's allegation of reliance on fraudulent management reports when contributing additional capital to LLC); Botwinick v. Duck Corp., 700 N.Y.S.2d 143 (N.Y. App. Div. 1999) (Evidence that the employee withheld information from the employer regarding an investment proposal from a venture capital firm constituted a breach of his duty of loyalty and provided employer "good cause" for terminating the employee); Hoag v. Chancellor, Inc., 677 N.Y.S.2d 531 (N.Y. App. Div. 1998) (Allegations by former executives of venture capital firm that officers of firm had intentionally diminished former executives' responsibilities and prospects for future incentive fee compensation and frozen their salaries, were sufficient to state a claim for tortuous interference with contract against officers); Foster v. Churchill, 626 N.Y.S.2d 115 (N.Y. App. Div. 1995) (Executive officers discharged by venture capital investment firm could not claim tortious interference with contract because venture firm discharged executives to save money when company was effectively bankrupt); Parks v. Macro-Dynamics, Inc., 121 Ariz. 517 (Ariz. Ct. App. 1979) (Allegation that defendants knowingly and materially misrepresented themselves as a venture capital investment firm without any intent to provide venture capital, which plaintiff relied upon to its detriment and without any knowledge of the falsity of the representations, was sufficient to support a claim of statutory fraud); United States v. Pace, 313 Fed. Appx. 603 (4th Cir. 2009) (Allegations of multiple written communications from venture capital fund managers to investors telling investors that their money would only be invested in the IPO stock of a named portfolio company when, in fact, funds were used to cover unsuccessful investments in other portfolio companies, were sufficient for rational trier of fact to conclude managers acted with specific intent to defraud investors); Rosenbluth, M.D. v. Prudential Securities, Inc., 134 Fed. Appx. 124 (9th Cir. 2005) (Draft documents containing open material terms were not sufficient to create binding contract for formation of venture capital fund; a completed written contract would be expected in the creation of a $200 million venture capital fund; testimony of investment banker that in 27 years he had never seen a venture capital fund formed on the basis of an oral agreement supported finding of no binding contract); Koninklijke Philips Electronics N.V. v. The ADS Group, 694 F.Supp.2d

246 (S.D.N.Y. 2010) (Venture capital firm that had ownership interest in company that was sued for infringement of CD-ROM patents was not liable for inducing infringement by directing alleged infringing firm to produce products that infringed patent).

Additional Information

1. RESTATEMENT (SECOND) OF CONTRACTS § 90 (2010).

2. RESTATEMENT (SECOND) OF TORTS § 766B (2010).

3. TOM MUSKUS, 44B AM. JUR. 2D INTERFERENCE §§ 1, 48 (2010).

4. 5 A.L.R.4TH 9 (2010).

5. Stephen L. Brodsky, *Federal Courts in New York Provide Framework for Enforcing Preliminary Agreements*, 73-APR N.Y. St. B.J. 9 (2001).

6. Alan Schwartz, Robert E. Scott, *Precontractual Liability and Preliminary Agreements*, 120 HARV. L. REV. 661 (2007).

7. Sundeep Patel, *Securities Litigation Under The Securities Act of 1933 And The Securities Exchange Act of 1934 — Venture Capital*, 5 BUS. L. BRIEF (AM. U.) 23 (2008).

8. Elizabeth Cosenza, *Co-Invest At Your Own Risk: An Exploration Of Potential Remedial Theories For Breaches Of Rights Of First Refusal In The Venture Capital Context*, 55 AM. U. L. REV. 87 (2005).

9. Douglas Cumming, Jeffrey MacIntosh, *Boom, Bust, and Litigation in Venture Capital Finance*, 40 WILLAMETTE L. REV. 867 (2004).

10. Shannon W. Stevenson, *The Venture Capital Solution To The Problem Of Close Corporation Shareholder Fiduciary Duties*, 15 DUKE L.J. 1139 (2001).

11. Bruce A. Mann, Marcus D. Wilkinson, *The Role of Counsel in Venture Capital Transactions If Disputes Arise*, 46 BUS. LAW. 759 (1991).

11.4.5   Glossary of Selected Private Equity Investment Terms

PRIVATE EQUITY GLOSSARY

Copyright, Center for Private Equity and Entrepreneurship, Tuck School of Business at Dartmouth University, Reprinted with Permission
Updated June 21, 2010

"A" round — a financing event whereby angel groups and / or venture capitalists become involved in a fast growth company that was previously financed by founders and their friends and families.

Accredited investor — a person or legal entity, such as a company or trust fund, that meets certain net worth and income qualifications and is considered to be sufficiently sophisticated to make investment decisions in private offerings. Regulation D of the Securities Act of 1933 exempts accredited investors from the protection of the Securities Act. The Securities and Exchange Commission has proposed revisions to the accredited investor qualifying rules, which may or may not result in changes for venture investors. The current criteria for a natural person are: $1 million net worth or annual income exceeding $200,000 individually or $300,000 with a spouse. Directors, general partners and executive officers of the issuer are considered to be accredited investors.

Airball — a loan whose value exceeds the value of the collateral.

Angel — a wealthy individual that invests in companies in relatively early stages of development. Usually angels invest less than $1 million per startup.

Anti-dilution — a contract clause that protects an investor from a substantial reduction in percentage ownership in a company due to the issuance by the company of additional shares to other entities. The mechanism for making an adjustment that maintains the same percentage ownership is called a **Full Ratchet.** The most commonly used adjustment provides partial protection and is called **Weighted Average.**

"B" round — a financing event whereby investors such as venture capitalists and organized angel groups are sufficiently interested in a company to provide additional funds after the "A" round of financing. Subsequent rounds are called "C," "D" and so on.

Balloon payment — a relatively large principal payment due at a specific time as required by a lender.

Blue sky — regulations in individual states regarding the sale of securities and mutual funds. These laws are intended to protect investors from purposely fraudulent transactions.

Book value — the book value of a company is the value of the common stock as shown on its balance sheet. This is defined as total assets minus liabilities minus preferred stock minus intangible assets. The book value of an asset of a company is typically based on its original cost minus accumulated depreciation.

Bootstrapping — the actions of a startup to minimize expenses and build cash flow, thereby reducing or eliminating the need for outside investors.

Broad-based weighted average anti-dilution — A weighted average anti-dilution method adjusts downward the price per share of the preferred stock of investor A due to the issuance of new preferred shares to new investor B at a price lower than the price investor A originally received. Investor A's preferred stock is repriced to a weighted average of investor A's price and investor B's price. A broad-based anti-dilution method uses all common stock outstanding on a fully diluted basis (including all convertible securities, warrants and options) in the denominator of the formula for determining the new weighted average price. See **Narrow-based weighted average anti-dilution.**

Bullet payment — a payment of all principal due at a time specified by a bank or a bond issuer.

Burn rate — the rate at which a startup with little or no revenue uses available cash to cover expenses. Usually expressed on a monthly or weekly basis.

Business Development Company (BDC) — a publicly traded company that invests in private companies and is required by law to provide meaningful support and assistance to its portfolio companies.

Buy-sell agreement — a contract that sets forth the conditions under which a shareholder must first offer his or her shares for sale to the other shareholders before being allowed to sell to entities outside the company.

Call date — when a bond issuer has the right to retire part or all of a bond issuance at a specific price.

Call premium — the premium above par value that an issuer is willing to pay as part of the redemption of a bond issue prior to maturity.

Call price — the price an issuer agrees to pay to bondholders to redeem all or part of a bond issuance.

Capital Asset Pricing Model (CAPM) — a method of estimating the cost of equity capital of a company. The cost of equity capital is equal to the return of a risk-free investment plus a premium that reflects the risk of the company's equity.

Capital call — when a private equity fund manager (usually a "general partner" in a partnership) requests that an investor in the fund (a "limited partner") provide additional capital. Usually a limited partner will agree to a maximum investment amount and the general partner will make a series of capital calls over time to the limited partner as opportunities arise to finance startups and buyouts.

Capital gap — the difficulty faced by some entrepreneurs in trying to raise between $2 million and $5 million. Friends, family and angel investors are typically good sources for financing rounds of less than $2 million, while many venture capital funds have become so large that they are only interested in investing amounts greater than $5 million.

Catch-up — a clause in the agreement between the general partner and the limited partners of a private equity fund. Once the limited partners have received a certain portion of their expected return, the general partner can then receive a majority of profits until the previously agreed upon profit split is reached.

Clawback — a clause in the agreement between the general partner and the limited partners of a private equity fund. The clawback gives limited partners the right to reclaim a portion of disbursements to a general partner for profitable investments based on significant losses from later investments in a portfolio.

Closing — the conclusion of a financing round whereby all necessary legal documents are signed and capital has been transferred.

Collateral — hard assets of the borrower, such as real estate or equipment, for which a lender has a legal interest until a loan obligation is fully paid off.

Common stock — a type of security representing ownership rights in a company. Usually, company founders, management and employees own common stock while investors own preferred stock. In the event of a liquidation of the company, the claims of secured and unsecured creditors, bondholders and preferred stockholders take precedence over common stockholders. See **Preferred stock.**

Comparable — a publicly traded company with similar characteristics to a private company that is being valued. For example, a telecommunications equipment manufacturer whose market value is 2 times revenues can be used to estimate the value of a similar and relatively new company with a new product in the same industry. See **Liquidity discount.**

Conversion — the right of an investor or lender to force a company to replace the investor's preferred shares or the lender's debt with common shares at a preset conversion ratio. A conversion feature was first used in railroad bonds in the 1800's.

Convertible debt — a loan which allows the lender to exchange the debt for common shares in a company at a preset conversion ratio. Also known as a "convertible note."

Convertible preferred stock — a type of stock that gives an owner the right to convert to common shares of stock. Usually, preferred stock has certain rights that common stock doesn't have, such as decision-making management control, a promised return on investment (dividend), or senior priority in receiving proceeds from a sale or liquidation of the company. Typically, convertible preferred stock automatically converts to common stock if the company makes an initial public offering (IPO). Convertible preferred is the most common tool for private equity funds to invest in companies.

Convertible security — a security that gives its owner the right to exchange the security for common shares in a company at a preset conversion ratio. The security is typically preferred stock, warrants or debt.

Co-sale right — a contractual right of an investor to sell some of the investor's stock along with the founder's or majority shareholder's stock if either the founder or majority shareholder elects to sell stock to a third-party. Also known as **Tag-along right.**

Coverage ratio — describes a company's ability to pay debt from cash flow or profits. Typical measures are EBITDA/Interest, (EBITDA minus Capital Expenditures)/Interest, and EBIT/Interest.

Cram down round — a financing event upon which new investors with substantial capital are able to demand and receive contractual terms that effectively cause the issuance of sufficient new shares by the startup company to significantly reduce ("dilute") the ownership percentage of previous investors.

Cumulative dividends — the owner of preferred stock with cumulative dividends has the right to receive accrued (previously unpaid) dividends in full before dividends are paid to any other classes of stock.

Current ratio — the ratio of current assets to current liabilities.

Debt service ratio — the ratio of a required loan payment amount ("debt service") to available cash flow earned during a specific period. Typically lenders insist that a company maintain a certain debt service ratio or else risk penalties such as having to pay off the loan immediately.

Demand rights — a type of registration right. Demand rights give an investor the right to force a startup to register its shares with the SEC and prepare for a public sale of stock (IPO).

Dilution — the reduction in the ownership percentage of current investors, founders and employees caused by the issuance of new shares to new investors.

Discount rate — the interest rate used to determine the present value of a series of future cash flows.

Discounted cash flow (DCF) — a valuation methodology whereby the present value of all future cash flows expected from a company is calculated.

Dividends — payments made by a company to the owners of certain securities. Typically, dividends are paid quarterly, by approval of the board of directors, to owners of preferred stock.

Down round — a round of financing whereby the valuation of the company is lower than the value determined by investors in an earlier round.

Drag-along rights — the contractual right of an investor in a company to force all other investors to agree to a specific action, such as the sale of the company.

Drawdown schedule — an estimate of the gradual transfer of committed investment funds from the limited partners of a private equity fund to the general partners.

Due diligence — the investigatory process performed by investors to assess the viability of a potential investment and the accuracy of the information provided by the target company.

Dutch auction - a method of conducting an IPO whereby newly issued shares of stock are committed to the highest bidder, then, if any shares remain, to the next highest bidder, and so on until all the shares are committed. Note that the price per share paid by all buyers is the price commitment of the buyer of the last share.

Early stage — the state of a company after the seed (formation) stage but before middle stage (generating revenues). Typically, a company in early stage will have a core management team and a proven concept or product, but no positive cash flow.

Earnings before interest and taxes (EBIT) — a measurement of the operating profit of a company. One possible valuation methodology is based on a comparison of private and public companies' value as a multiple of EBIT.

Earnings before interest, taxes, depreciation and amortization (EBITDA) — a measurement of the cash flow of a company. One possible valuation methodology is based on a comparison of private and public companies' value as a multiple of EBITDA.

Elevator pitch — a concise presentation, lasting only a few minutes (an elevator ride), by an entrepreneur to a potential investor about an investment opportunity.

Exit strategy — the plan for generating profits for owners and investors of a company. Typically, the options are to merge, be acquired or make an initial public offering (IPO). An alternative is to recapitalize (re-leverage the company and then pay dividends to shareholders).

Expansion stage — the stage of a company characterized by a complete management team and a substantial increase in revenues.

Fair value — a financial reporting principle for valuing assets and liabilities, for example, portfolio companies in venture capital fund portfolios. This has received much recent attention as the Financial Accounting Standards Board (FASB) has issued definitive guidance (FAS 157) on this long standing principle.

Firm commitment — a commitment by a syndicate of investment banks to purchase all the shares available for sale in a public offering of a company. The shares will then be resold to investors by the syndicate.

First refusal — the right of a privately owned company to purchase any shares that employees would like to sell.

Flipping — the act of selling shares immediately after an initial public offering.

Investment banks that underwrite new stock issues attempt to allocate shares to new investors that indicate they will retain the shares for several months. Often management and venture investors are prohibited from selling IPO shares until a "lock-up period" (usually 6 to 12 months) has expired.

Founder — a person who participates in the creation of a company. Typically, founders manage the company until it has enough capital to hire professional managers.

Founders stock — nominally priced common stock issued to founders, officers, employees, directors, and consultants.

Friends and family financing — capital provided by the friends and family of founders of an early stage company. Founders should be careful not to create an ownership structure that may hinder the participation of professional investors once the company begins to achieve success.

Full ratchet — an anti-dilution protection mechanism whereby the price per share of the preferred stock of investor A is adjusted downward due to the issuance of new preferred shares to new investor B at a price lower than the price investor A originally received. Investor A's preferred stock is repriced to match the price of investor B's preferred stock. Usually as a result of the implementation of a ratchet, company management and employees who own a fixed amount of common shares suffer significant dilution. See **Narrow-based weighted average anti-dilution** and **Broad-based weighted average anti-dilution.**

Fully diluted basis — a methodology for calculating any per share ratios whereby the denominator is the total number of shares issued by the company on the assumption that all warrants and options are exercised and preferred stock converted.

Growth stage — the state of a company when it has received one or more rounds of financing and is generating revenue from its product or service. Also known as **Middle stage.**

Hedge fund — an investment fund that has the ability to use leverage, take short positions in securities, or use a variety of derivative instruments in order to achieve a return that is relatively less correlated to the performance of typical indices (such as the S&P 500) than traditional long-only funds. Hedge fund managers are typically compensated based on assets under management as well as fund performance.

High yield debt — debt issued via public offering or public placement (Rule 144A) that is rated below investment grade by S&P or Moody's. This means that the debt is rated below the top four rating categories (i.e. S&P BB+, Moody's Ba2 or below). The lower rating is indicative of higher risk of default, and therefore the debt carries a higher coupon or yield than investment grade debt. Also referred to as **Junk bonds** or **Sub-investment grade debt.**

Hockey stick — the general shape and form of a chart showing revenue, customers, cash or some other financial or operational measure that increases dramatically at some point in the future. Entrepreneurs often develop business plans with hockey stick charts to impress potential investors.

Holding period — amount of time an investment remains in a portfolio.

Hot issue — stock in an initial public offering that is in high demand.

Hot money — capital from investors that have no tolerance for lack of results by the investment manager and move quickly to withdraw at the first sign of trouble.

Hurdle rate — a minimum rate of return required before an investor will make an investment.

Incubator — a company or facility designed to host startup companies. Incubators help startups grow while controlling costs by offering networks of contacts and shared backoffice resources.

Indenture — the terms and conditions between a bond issuer and bond buyers.

In-kind distribution — a distribution to limited partners of a private equity fund that is in the form of publicly traded shares rather than cash.

Inside round — a round of financing in which the investors are the same investors as the previous round. An inside round raises liability issues since the valuation of the company has no third party verification in the form of an outside investor. In addition, the terms of the inside round may be considered self-dealing if they are onerous to any set of shareholders or if the investors give themselves additional preferential rights.

Institutional investor — professional entities that invest capital on behalf of companies or individuals. Examples are: pension plans, insurance companies and university endowments.

Interest coverage ratio — earnings before interest and taxes (EBIT) divided by interest expense. This is a key ratio used by lenders to assess the ability of a company to produce sufficient cash to pay its debt obligation.

Internal rate of return (IRR) — the interest rate at which a certain amount of capital today would have to be invested in order to grow to a specific value at a specific time in the future.

Investment thesis / Investment philosophy — the fundamental ideas which determine the types of investments that an investment fund will choose in order to achieve its financial goals.

Issuer — the company that chooses to distribute a portion of its stock to the public.

J curve — a concept that during the first few years of a private equity fund, cash flow or returns are negative due to investments, losses, and expenses, but as investments produce results the cash flow or returns trend upward. A graph of cash flow or returns versus time would then resemble the letter "J."

Junior debt — a loan that has a lower priority than a senior loan in case of a liquidation of the asset or borrowing company. Also known as **Subordinated debt.**

Later stage — the state of a company that has proven its concept, achieved significant revenues compared to its competition, and is approaching cash flow break even or positive net income. Typically, a later stage company is about 6 to 12 months away from a liquidity event such as an IPO or buyout. The rate of return for venture capitalists that invest in later stage, less risky ventures is lower than in earlier stage ventures.

Lead investor — the venture capital investor that makes the largest investment in a financing round and manages the documentation and closing of that round. The lead investor sets the price per share of the financing round, thereby determining the valuation of the company.

Letter of intent — a document confirming the intent of an investor to participate in a round of financing for a company. By signing this document, the subject company agrees to begin the legal and due diligence process prior to the closing of the transaction. Also known as a **Term sheet.**

Leverage — the use of debt to acquire assets, build operations and increase revenues. By using debt, a company is attempting to achieve results faster than if it only used its cash available from pre-leverage operations. The risk is that the increase in assets and revenues does not generate sufficient net income and cash flow to pay the interest costs of the debt.

Leveraged buyout (LBO) — the purchase of a company or a business unit of a company by an outside investor using mostly borrowed capital.

Leveraged recapitalization — the reorganization of a company's capital structure resulting in more debt added to the balance sheet. Private equity funds can recapitalize a portfolio company and then direct the company to issue a one-time dividend to equity investors. This is often done when the company is performing well financially and the debt markets are expanding.

Liquidation — the sale of a company. This may occur in the context of an acquisition by a larger company or in the context of selling off all assets prior to cessation of operations (Chapter 7 bankruptcy). In a liquidation, the claims of secured and unsecured creditors, bondholders and preferred stockholders take precedence over common stockholders.

Liquidation preference — the contractual right of an investor to priority in receiving the proceeds from the liquidation of a company. For example, a venture capital investor with a "2x liquidation preference" has the right to receive two times its original investment upon liquidation.

Liquidity discount — a decrease in the value of a private company compared to the value of a similar but publicly traded company. Since an investor in a private company cannot readily sell his or her investment, the shares in the private company must be valued less than a comparable public company.

Liquidity event — a transaction whereby owners of a significant portion of the shares of a private company sell their shares in exchange for cash or shares in another, usually larger company. For example, an IPO is a liquidity event.

Lock-up agreement — investors, management and employees often agree not to sell their shares for a specific time period after an IPO, usually 6 to 12 months. By avoiding large sales of its stock, the company has time to build interest among potential buyers of its shares.

London Interbank Offered Rate (L.I.B.O.R.) — the average rate charged by large banks in London for loans to each other. LIBOR is a relatively volatile rate and is typically quoted in maturities of one month, three months, six months and one year.

Management buyout (MBO) — a leveraged buyout controlled by the members of the management team of a company or a division. Often an MBO is conducted in partnership with a buyout fund.

Management fee — a fee charged to the limited partners in a fund by the general partner. Management fees in a private equity fund usually range from 0.75% to 3% of capital under management, depending on the type and size of fund. For venture capital funds, 2% is typical.

Management rights — the rights often required by a venture capitalist as part of the agreement to invest in a company. The venture capitalist has the right to consult with management on key operational issues, attend board meetings and review information about the company's financial situation.

Market capitalization — the value of a publicly traded company as determined by multiplying the number of shares outstanding by the current price per share.

Mezzanine — a layer of financing that has intermediate priority (seniority) in the capital structure of a company. For example, mezzanine debt has lower priority than senior debt but usually has a higher interest rate and often includes warrants. In venture capital, a mezzanine round is generally the round of financing that is designed to help a company have enough resources to reach an IPO. See **Bridge financing.**

Middle stage — the state of a company when it has received one or more rounds of financing and is generating revenue from its product or service. Also known as **Growth stage.**

Milestones — operational or financial goals of a company that are often used to determine whether a company will receive additional financing or whether management will receive additional compensation.

Multiples — a valuation methodology that compares public and private companies in terms of a ratio of value to an operations figure such as revenue or net income. For example, if several publicly traded computer hardware companies are valued at approximately 2 times revenues, then it is reasonable to assume that a startup computer hardware company that is growing fast has the potential to achieve a valuation of 2 times its revenues. Before the startup issues its IPO, it will likely be valued at less than 2 times revenue because of the lack of liquidity of its shares. See **Liquidity discount.**

Narrow-based weighted average anti-dilution — a type of anti-dilution mechanism. A weighted average ratchet adjusts downward the price per share of the preferred stock of investor A due to the issuance of new preferred shares to new investor B at a price lower than the price investor A originally received. Investor A's preferred stock is repriced to a weighted average of investor A's price and investor B's price. A narrow-based ratchet uses only common stock outstanding in the denominator of the formula for determining the new weighted average price.

Net operating income (NOI) — a measure of cash flow that excludes the effects of financing decisions. NOI is calculated as earnings before interest and taxes multiplied by one minus the tax rate. Also known as **net operating profit after taxes.**

No-shop clause — a section of an agreement to purchase a company whereby the seller agrees not to market the company to other potential buyers for a specific time period.

Non-cumulative dividends — dividends that are payable to owners of preferred stock at a specific point in time only if there is sufficient cash flow available after all company expenses have been paid. If cash flow is insufficient, the owners of the preferred stock will not receive the dividends owed for that time period and will have to wait until the board of directors declares another set of dividends.

Non-interference — an agreement often signed by employees and management whereby they agree not to interfere with the company's relationships with employees, clients, suppliers and sub-contractors within a certain time period after termination of employment.

Non-solicitation — an agreement often signed by employees and management whereby they agree not to solicit other employees of the company regarding job opportunities.

Operating cash flow — the cash flow produced from the operation of a business, not from investing activities (such as selling assets) or financing activities (such as issuing debt). Calculated as net operating income (NOI) plus depreciation.

Optics — the way a concept is presented. Sometimes entrepreneurs' presentations are strong on optics but weak in content.

Option pool — a group of options set aside for long term, phased compensation to management and employees.

Orphan — a startup company that does not have a venture capitalist as an investor.

Outstanding shares — the total amount of common shares of a company, not including treasury stock, convertible preferred stock, warrants and options.

Oversubscription — when demand exceeds supply for shares of an IPO or a private placement.

Pay to play — a clause in a financing agreement whereby any investor that does not participate in a future round agrees to suffer significant dilution compared to other investors. The most onerous version of "pay to play" is automatic conversion to common shares, which in essence ends any preferential rights of an investor, such as the right to influence key management decisions.

Pari passu — a legal term referring to the equal treatment of two or more parties in an agreement. For example, a venture capitalist may agree to have registration rights that are pari passu with the other investors in a financing round.

Participating dividends — the right of holders of certain preferred stock to receive dividends and participate in additional distributions of cash, stock or other assets.

Participating preferred stock — a unit of ownership composed of preferred stock and common stock. The preferred stock entitles the owner to receive a predetermined sum of cash (usually the original investment plus accrued dividends) if the company is sold or has an IPO. The common stock represents additional continued ownership in the company. Participating preferred stock has been characterized as "having your cake and eating it too."

Piggyback rights — rights of an investor to have his or her shares included in a registration of a startup's shares in preparation for an IPO.

Placement agent — a company that specializes in finding institutional investors that are willing and able to invest in a private equity fund. Sometimes a private equity fund will hire a placement agent so the fund partners can focus on making and managing investments in companies rather than on raising capital.

Portfolio company — a company that has received an investment from a private equity fund.

Post-money valuation — the valuation of a company including the capital provided by the current round of financing. For example, a venture capitalist may invest $5 million in a company valued at $2 million "pre-money" (before the investment was made). As a result, the startup will have a post-money valuation of $7 million.

Preemptive rights — the rights of shareholders to maintain their percentage ownership of a company by buying shares sold by the company in future financing rounds.

Preference — seniority, usually with respect to dividends and proceeds from a sale or dissolution of a company.

Preferred return — a minimum return per annum that must be generated for limited partners of a private equity fund before the general partner can begin receiving a percentage of profits from investments.

Preferred stock — a type of stock that has certain rights that common stock does not have. These special rights may include dividends, participation, liquidity preference, anti-dilution protection and veto provisions, among others. Private equity investors usually purchase preferred stock when they make investments in companies.

Pre-money valuation — the valuation of a company prior to the current round of financing. For example, a venture capitalist may invest $5 million in a company valued at $2 million pre-money. As a result, the startup will have a "post-money" valuation of $7 million.

Price earnings ratio (PE ratio) — the ratio of a public company's price per share and its net income after taxes on a per share basis.

Primary shares — shares sold by a corporation (not by individual shareholders).

Private equity — equity investments in non-public companies, usually defined as being made up of venture capital funds and buyout funds. Real estate, oil and gas, and other such partnerships are sometimes included in the definition.

Private securities — securities that are not registered with the Securities and Exchange Commission and do not trade on any exchanges. The price per share is negotiated between the buyer and the seller (the "issuer").

Prudent man rule — a fundamental principle for professional money management which serves as a basis for the Prudent Investor Act. The principle is based on a statement by Judge Samuel Putnum in 1830: "Those with the responsibility to invest money for others should act with prudence, discretion, intelligence and regard for the safety of capital as well as income." In the 1970s a favorable interpretation of this rule enabled pension fund managers to invest in venture capital for the first time.

Quartile — one fourth of the data points in a data set. Often, private equity investors are measured by the results of their investments during a particular period of time.

Institutional investors often prefer to invest in private equity funds that demonstrate consistent results over time, placing in the upper quartile of the investment results for all funds.

Ratchet — a mechanism to prevent dilution. An anti-dilution clause is a contract clause that protects an investor from a reduction in percentage ownership in a company due to the future issuance by the company of additional shares to other entities.

Realization ratio — the ratio of cumulative distributions to paid-in capital. The realization ratio is used as a measure of the distributions from investment results of a private equity partnership compared to the capital under management.

Red herring — a preliminary prospectus filed with the Securities and Exchange Commission and containing the details of an IPO offering. The name refers to the disclosure warning printed in red letters on the cover of each preliminary prospectus advising potential investors of the risks involved.

Redeemable preferred — preferred stock that can be redeemed by the owner (usually a venture capital investor) in exchange for a specific sum of money.

Redemption rights — the right of an investor to force the startup company to buy back the shares issued as a result of the investment. In effect, the investor has the right to take back his/her investment and may even negotiate a right to receive an additional sum in excess of the original investment.

Return on investment (ROI) — the proceeds from an investment, during a specific time period, calculated as a percentage of the original investment. Also, net profit after taxes divided by average total assets.

Rights offering — an offering of stock to current shareholders that entitles them to purchase the new issue, usually at a discount.

Rights of co-sale with founders — a clause in venture capital investment agreements that allows the VC fund to sell shares at the same time that the founders of a startup chose to sell.

Right of first refusal — a contractual right to participate in a transaction. For example, a venture capitalist may participate in a first round of investment in a startup and request a right of first refusal in any following rounds of investment.

Risk-free rate — a term used in finance theory to describe the return from investing in a riskless security. In practice, this is often taken to be the return on US Treasury Bills.

Scalability — a characteristic of a new business concept that entails the growth of sales and revenues with a much slower growth of organizational complexity and expenses. Venture capitalists look for scalability in the startups they select to finance.

Scale-down — a schedule for phased decreases in management fees for general partners in a limited partnership as the fund reduces its investment activities toward the end of its term.

Scale-up — the process of a company growing quickly while maintaining operational and financial controls in place. Also, a schedule for phased increases in management fees for general partners in a limited partnership as the fund increases its investment activities over time.

Secondary market — a market for the sale of limited partnership interests in private equity funds. Sometimes limited partners chose to sell their interest in a partnership, typically to raise cash or because they cannot meet their obligation to invest more capital according to the takedown schedule. Certain investment companies specialize in buying these partnership interests at a discount.

Secondary shares — shares sold by a shareholder (not by the corporation).

Secured debt — debt that has seniority in case the borrowing company defaults or is dissolved and its assets sold to pay creditors.

Seed capital — investment provided by angels, friends and family to the founders of a startup in seed stage.

Seed stage — the state of a company when it has just been incorporated and its founders are developing their product or service.

Senior debt — a loan that has a higher priority in case of a liquidation of the asset or company.

Series A preferred stock — preferred stock issued by a fast growth company in exchange for capital from investors in the "A" round of financing. This preferred stock is usually convertible to common shares upon the IPO or sale of the company.

Small Business Investment Company (SBIC) — a company licensed by the Small

Business Administration to receive government capital in the form of debt or equity in order to use in private equity investing.

Spin out — a division of an established company that becomes an independent entity. Also known as a spin-off.

Stock option — a right to purchase or sell a share of stock at a specific price within a specific period of time. Stock purchase options are commonly used as long term incentive compensation for employees and management of fast growth companies.

Strategic investor — a relatively large corporation that agrees to invest in a young company in order to have access to a proprietary technology, product or service. By having this access, the corporation can potentially achieve its strategic goals.

Sub-investment grade debt — see **High yield debt.**

Subordinated debt — a loan that has a lower priority than a senior loan in case of a liquidation of the asset or company. Also known as **Junior debt.**

Sweat equity — ownership of shares in a company resulting from work rather than investment of capital.

Syndicate — a group of investors that agree to participate in a round of funding for a company. Alternatively, a syndicate can refer to a group of investment banks that agree to participate in the sale of stock to the public as part of an IPO.

Syndication — the process of arranging a syndicate.

Tag-along right — the right of a minority investor to receive the same benefits as a majority investor. Usually applies to a sale of securities by investors. Also known as a **Co-sale right.**

Takedown — a schedule of the transfer of capital in phases in order to complete a commitment of funds. Typically, a takedown is used by a general partner of a private equity fund to plan the transfer of capital from the limited partners.

Takeover — the transfer of control of a company.

Ten bagger — an investment that returns 10 times the initial capital.

Tender offer — an offer to public shareholders of a company to purchase their shares.

Term loan — a bank loan for a specific period of time, usually up to ten years in leveraged buyout structures.

Term sheet — a document confirming the intent of an investor to participate in a round of financing for a company. By signing this document, the subject company agrees to begin the legal and due diligence process prior to the closing of the transaction. Also known as a **Letter of intent.**

Tranche — a portion of a set of securities. Each tranche may have different rights or risk characteristics.

Turnaround — a process resulting in a substantial increase in a company's revenues, profits and reputation.

Two x — an expression referring to 2 times the original amount. For example, a preferred stock may have a "two x" liquidation preference, so in case of liquidation of the company, the preferred stock investor would receive twice his or her original investment.

Under water option — an option is said to be under water if the current fair market value of a stock is less than the option exercise price.

Underwriter — an investment bank that chooses to be responsible for the process of selling new securities to the public. An underwriter usually chooses to work with a syndicate of investment banks in order to maximize the distribution of the securities.

Unsecured debt — debt which does not have any priority in case of dissolution of the company and sale of its assets.

Venture capital — a segment of the private equity industry which focuses on investing in new companies with high growth rates.

Venture capital method — a valuation method whereby an estimate of the future value of a company is discounted by a certain interest rate and adjusted for future anticipated dilution in order to determine the current value. Usually, discount rates for the venture capital method are considerably higher than public stock return rates, representing the fact that venture capitalists must achieve significant returns on investment in order to compensate for the risks they take in funding unproven companies.

Vesting — a schedule by which employees gain ownership over time of a previously agreed upon amount of retirement funding or stock options.

Vintage — the year that a private equity fund stops accepting new investors and begins to make investments on behalf of those investors.

Voting rights — the rights of holders of preferred and common stock in a company to vote on certain acts affecting the company. These matters may include payment of dividends, issuance of a new class of stock, merger or liquidation.

WACC — see **Weighted average cost of capital.**

Warrant — a security which gives the holder the right to purchase shares in a company at a pre-determined price. A warrant is a long term option, usually valid for several years or indefinitely. Typically, warrants are issued concurrently with preferred stocks or bonds in order to increase the appeal of the stocks or bonds to potential investors.

Washout round — a financing round whereby previous investors, the founders and management suffer significant dilution. Usually as a result of a washout round, the new investor gains majority ownership and control of the company.

Weighted average cost of capital (WACC) — the average of the cost of equity and the after-tax cost of debt. This average is determined using weight factors based on the ratio of equity to debt plus equity and the ratio of debt to debt plus equity.

Weighted average anti-dilution — an anti-dilution protection mechanism whereby the conversion rate of preferred stock is adjusted in order to reduce an investor's loss due to an increase in the number of shares in a company. Without anti-dilution protection, an investor would suffer from a reduction of his or her percentage ownership. Usually as a result of the implementation of a weighted average anti-dilution, company management and employees who own a fixed amount of common shares suffer significant dilution, but not as badly as in the case of a full ratchet.

Wipeout round — see **Washout round.**

Wipeout bridge — a short term financing that has onerous features whereby if the company does not secure additional long term financing within a certain time frame, the bridge investor gains ownership control of the company. See **Bridge financing.**

Write-down — a decrease in the reported value of an asset or a company.

Write-off — a decrease in the reported value of an asset or a company to zero.

Write-up — an increase in the reported value of an asset or a company.

Zombie — a company that has received capital from investors but has only generated sufficient revenues and cash flow to maintain its operations without significant growth. Typically, a venture capitalist has to make a difficult decision as to whether to kill off a zombie or continue to invest funds in the hopes that the zombie will become a winner.

11.5   OTHER FORMS OF FINANCING

Other forms of financing available to a company include bank loans, monetization of intellectual property, securitization of intellectual property and letters of credit. This section considers the nature and use of each of these forms of financing.

11.5.1   Bank Loans

SECURED AND UNSECURED LOANS

There are two basic types of bank loans — unsecured and secured. In an unsecured loan, the bank relies upon the borrower's honesty and business acumen. Unsecured loans are only available to borrowers with very high credit ratings or borrowers with whom the bank has a long-standing relationship. Unsecured loans are rarely available to start-up and early-stage companies, and banks almost always require the personal guarantee of the companies' principals, or third parties, when lending to start-up and early-stage companies. In a secured loan, the borrower pledges assets as collateral for the loan. The bank perfects its security interest in the pledged assets by filing a UCC-1 financing statement with the designated county or state office. In the event of a default on the loan, the bank will foreclose on the assets and sell them to recover as much of the outstanding balance on the loan as possible.

Two common forms of secured loans are loans secured by accounts receivable and loans secured by inventory. In an accounts receivable secured loan, the borrower gives the bank a security interest in its accounts receivable and the bank perfects the security interest through a UCC-1 financing statement. The loan amount is calculated as a percentage of eligible receivables. The types of receivables and the average age of the receivables (the amount of time from invoicing to payment) determines the loan-to-receivable ratio which generally ranges between 70% — 80% of the total receivables. In an accounts receivable loan, the bank lends funds to the borrower as receivables are generated and the borrower repays the bank as receivables are paid.

Inventory-backed loans are secured by a lien on the borrower's inventory. Because inventory is less liquid than receivables, the loan-to-value ratio is lower, generally ranging between 40%–60% of the value of the inventory. Finished goods can be financed at higher value than raw materials and works-in-progress, which often can only be financed at 10% or less of their value. As sales take place, the borrower repays the loan and replenishes the inventory. The borrower's purchasers take title free of the bank lien and the borrower's suppliers take a lien superior to the bank. Inventory-backed loans are subject to the risk of fraud by borrowers who overstate the value of their inventory. Finally, if the finished goods securing the loan are protected by intellectual property, the bank must obtain an assignment of the intellectual property in order to sell the finished goods.

TERM LOANS, REVOLVING LOANS AND LINES OF CREDIT

The three most common forms of bank loans are term loans, revolving loans and lines of credit.

Term loans are generally used to finance the acquisition of fixed assets, such as equipment and computers, and improvements to real estate. In a term loan, the borrower receives the full amount of the loan at closing along with a loan agreement which sets forth a schedule of payments of principal and interest. The length of a term loan varies depending upon the assets purchased. The amount of a term loan is based on some percentage of the value of the purchased assets. Term loans can sometimes include "balloon" payments, payments that are higher than the regularly scheduled payments, and "bullet" payments, payments that are required to pay off the balance of the loan. Depending on the financial strength of the borrowing company, the bank may seek to have the loaned guaranteed by the Small Business Administration (SBA). SBA guaranteed loans are discussed below.

Revolving loans are generally used to bridge cash flow gaps between payment of expenses and receipt of revenue. A revolving loan is made available to the borrower up to a specified amount, for a specified period of time. However, there is no fixed repayment schedule. The borrower may draw-down the loan as needed to pay expenses and repay the loan in increments as revenues are received. Interest on a revolving loan is usually based on the average outstanding balance of the loan. Revolving loans also frequently include a charge for the loan itself separate from the interest charge.

A line of credit is generally used to assist companies with pre-approved financing for capital asset acquisitions. A line of credit is issued to a borrower up to a specified amount for a specified period of time. The borrower utilizes the line of credit as needed to purchase capital assets. The interest on a line of credit is generally based on the amount of the line of credit used by the borrower. Lines of credit also often include charges for the line of credit itself separate from the interest charge.

The documents in a bank loan include a commitment letter, in which the bank commits to make the loan, and the loan agreement. Among the more important provisions in the loan agreement are the amount of the loan, when funds will be available to the buyer, the repayment schedule, the events of default (non-payment, insolvency, breach of covenants), the interest rate (fixed or variable) and the fees (for the commitment letter and closing costs usually stated as a percentage of the loan). Loan agreements invariably include various representations and warranties by the borrower (accuracy of financial statements, other indebtedness, etc.), conditions that must be satisfied prior to closing, general covenants (waiver of right to jury trial, indemnification of bank, etc.) and financial covenants (maintaining a certain financial status, no further mortgages or security interests, no disposition of assets, provision of audited or unaudited financial statements, etc.).

SMALL BUSINESS ADMINISTRATION LOAN PROGRAMS

The Small Business Administration can assist small companies with financing through a number of different programs. The SBA does this by working with banks and other lending institutions to help small companies obtain loans that would otherwise not be available through normal lending channels. The two main SBA financing programs are:

The 7(a) Loan Guaranty Program. This is the SBA's primary lending program. Under the 7(a) Loan Guaranty Program, the SBA guarantees repayment of loans made to small businesses by banks up to a specified percentage of the loan. The SBA Loan Guaranty Program helps small businesses in two ways. First, it allows small businesses to obtain loans that banks would not otherwise provide without the SBA guarantee. Second, it allows small businesses to borrow at lower interest rates because the loan repayment is guaranteed; and

The Small Business Investment Company Program. Small Business Investment Companies (SBICs) are privately owned and managed investment firms that are licensed and regulated by the SBA. The SBA lends funds to the SBICs at below-market interest rates so that the SBICs can provide venture capital and start-up financing to small businesses.

Additional Information

1. Joseph C. Long, 12 Blue Sky Reporter § 6:51 (2010).

2. Lee R. Petillon, Robert J. Hill, Representing Start-Up Companies §§ 10:4–10:5 (2010).

3. Steven C. Alberty, 1 Advising Small Businesses §§ 12:14, 13:24–13:26 (2010).

4. Nathaniel Hansford, 4 UCC Trans. Gd. § 32:43 (2010).

5. Joseph W. Bartlett, Equity Finance § 6.5 (2011).

6. Peter A. Alces, The Law of Suretyship and Guaranty §§ 8:3, 8:5–8:8, 8:16 (2010).

7. 2 West's Fed. Admin. Prac. §§ 2016–2027, 2153 (4th ed.) (2010).

8. Vincent Di Lorenzo, Clifford R. Ennico, Basic Legal Transactions § 12:56 (2010).

9. Hon. Joan N. Feeney, Bankruptcy Law Manual § 11A:21 (2010).

10. Raymond T. Nimmer, 1 Com. Asset-Based Fin. § 1:9 (2011).

11. Raymond T. Nimmer, 3 Com. Asset-Based Fin. §§ 19:3–19:4 (2011).

12. Robert J. Haft, 2 Venture Cap. & Bus. Fin. § 7:1 (2011).

13. Lawrence R. Ahern, 14a West's Legal Forms, Commercial Transactions § 15:30 (3d ed.) (2010).

14. Nathaniel Hansford, 4 UCC Trans Gd. § 31:23.50 (2010).

15. Carolyn E.C. Paris, PLIREF-CORPFIN § 3:2.7 (2007).

16. Thomas S. Hemmendinger, *Form 10.5 Loan and Security Agreement (Accounts Receivable and Inventory Financing with all Personal Property and Fixtures as Collateral*, PLIREF-COMLOAN 10 Form 10.5 (2010).

17. Thomas S. Hemmendinger, *SBA and Other Agency-Guaranteed Loans*, PLIREF-COMLOAN § 8:4 (2010).

18. Michael A. Walters, *Accounts Receivable Financing*, The Florida Bar (1996).

19.   Robin E. Phelan, Terry W. Conner, Joseph L. Kinsella, *Word Wars: Structuring and Documenting Secured Term Loans Under the Bankruptcy Code*, 427 PLI/COMM 127 (1987).

11.5.2 Monetization of Intellectual Property

THE MONETIZATION PROCESS

In general, monetization is the process by which assets, for example securities, are converted into cash or cash-equivalents. A particularly important form of monetization is the conversion of a stream of future income into a current payment of cash, or cash-equivalent. The income stream that is monetized can come from many different sources, for example patent license royalties, music copyright royalties and litigation settlement payments.

In a simple monetization transaction, the "sponsor" (the party seeking to monetize its future income) would transfer the assets generating the future income, as well as the rights to the future income, to a special purpose entity (a trust or corporation). The special purpose entity (SPE) would issue debt securities to "investors" in exchange for the investors' payment of cash to the SPE. The SPE would then pay the cash to the "sponsor." The SPE would pay interest to the bondholders during the monetization period. Depending upon how the monetization is structured, the SPE could accumulate the income and repay the bond principal at the termination of the monetization, or the SPE could make periodic principal payments during the course of the monetization. Monetization can be structured in many different ways: the sponsor can monetize the future income for any period of time; the sponsor can monetize any percentage of future income; the sponsor can monetize the future income up to a specified amount and receive the future income above this amount; and the sponsor can recover the rights to the assets and future income upon the expiration of the monetization transaction.

Monetization provides very favorable tax consequences to the sponsor. There is no tax imposed on the cash payment to the sponsor because it is treated as a loan, and the interest the sponsor pays to the SPE is a deductible expense.

It is critical in a monetization transaction that the revenue stream be stable. The more unstable the revenue stream, the more the investors will discount its value and the less the investors will be willing to pay for rights to the revenue stream. The stability of the revenue stream can be increased by providing for a reserve fund in the SPE, by providing default insurance or by providing third-party repayment guarantees. Especially important to the stability of the revenue stream is the "bankruptcy remoteness" of the assets transferred to the SPE. In the event of the sponsor's bankruptcy, the assets transferred to the SPE must not be includable in the bankruptcy estate. In order for a monetization to make financial sense, the interest rate paid by the sponsor to the SPE must be lower than what the sponsor would have to pay for conventional bank financing.

The loan-to-value ratio in monetizing future revenue streams ranges between 90% in the case of extremely stable revenue streams and 60% in the case of less stable revenue streams.

The figure below depicts a simplified intellectual property monetization transaction.

Figure 5: Monetization of Intellectual Property

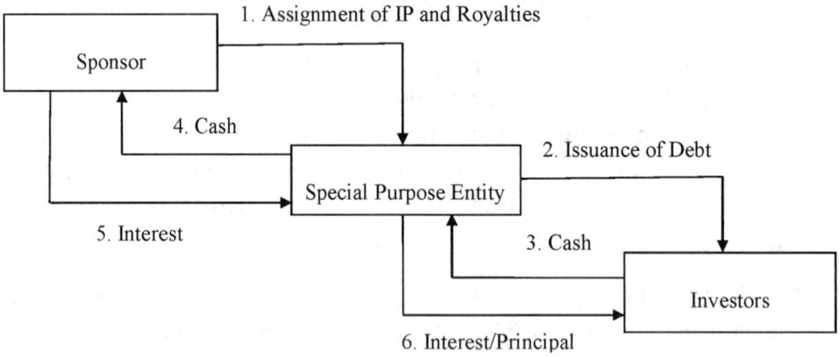

MONTETIZATION EXAMPLES

One of the most notable intellectual property monetizations is the "Bowie Bonds." During the 1990s, David Bowie was receiving approximately $5 million / year in royalty revenues from a portfolio of around 300 song and performance copyrights. In 1997, Bowie wanted to raise $55 million in cash. To do this, he assigned the song and performance copyrights to an SPE which then issued bonds to investors having a face value of $55 million and carrying an interest rate of 7.9% / year. The SPE paid Bowie the $55 million and then accumulated sufficient royalty payments to repay the $55 million, plus 7.9% compound interest, to the bond holders. At the termination of the monetization, Bowie received back the copyrights and royalty rights. Since then, a number of other companies holding intellectual property income-producing assets have sought to monetize those assets. These companies include film studios monetizing movie revenues, Bill Blass monetizing licensing fees, and Dunkin' Donuts monetizing brand names and franchise fees. *See* Nicole Chu, *Bowie Bonds: A Key to Unlocking the Wealth of Intellectual Property*, 21 HASTINGS COMM/ENT L.J. 409 (1999); Jennifer B. Sylva, *Bowie Bonds Sold for Far More Than a Song: The Securitization of Intellectual Property as a Super-Charged Vehicle for High Technology Financing*, 15 SANTA CLARA COMPUTER & HIGH TECH. L.J. 195 (1999).

A far less publicized monetization involved Sears Holdings Company and its Chairman, Edward (Eddie) Lampert. Sears transferred the trademarks to its three most popular brands, Kenmore, Craftsman and DieHard, to an SPE which then issued $1.8 billion in bonds called KCD bonds after the three brand names. Sears created the income stream to support these bonds by entering into a licensing agreement with the SPE under which Sears would pay the SPE royalties for the right to continue using the Kenmore, Craftsman and DieHard brand name. However, the SPE never sold these bonds to the public. Instead, the SPE transferred the bonds to Sears' wholly-owned Bermuda insurance company. According to Sears, the purpose of the monetization was to provide its Bermuda insurance subsidiary greater liquidity to protect against sudden, unanticipated financial troubles. *See* Robert Berner, *The New Alchemy At Sears*, BusinessWeek, April 16, 2007.

Royalties associated with the licensing of pharmaceutical patents have recently also become popular monetization targets. One of the first pharmaceutical patent monetizations occurred in 2000. Yale University researchers developed a new, very promising HIV drug, Zerit. Yale licensed the Zerit patents to Bristol-Myers Squib for running royalties on the sales of Zerit. Around the same time, Yale was in the process of building a $176 million new medical teaching and research complex, and needed cash to complete the construction. Yale, along with its underwriter Royalty Pharma AG, formed an SPE, the BioPharma Royalty Trust. Yale assigned 70% of its patent and royalty rights to the BioPharma Royalty Trust and the BioPharma Royalty Trust issued debt and equity securities in the amount of $115 million of which it paid Yale $100 million. Unfortunately, the sales of Zerit fell far short of expectations and the BioPharma Royalty Trust was prematurely terminated. Nonetheless, Yale retained its $100 million payment and was able to put about $60 million into its new medical complex. *See* Malcolm S. Dorris, Joshua A.O. Stratham, Kira N. Brereton, *Securitization of Pharmaceutical Royalties — A Prescription for Market Growth*, Intellectual Property Today, Tuesday, February 8, 2011, available at http://www.iptoday.com/news-article.asp?id=7039&type=ip. *See also* David Edwards, *Patent Backed Securitization: Blueprint For a New Asset Class* available at www.securitization.net/pdf/gerling_new_0302 pdf.

Additional Information

1. Jose A. Esteves, *Overview of Monetization Techniques*, 1004 PLI/Pat 39 (2010).

2. Ron Laurie, Raymond Millien, *A Survey of Established and Evolving IP Monetization Models*, 1004 PLI/Pat 187 (2010).

3. Joseph Yang, *Recent Case Law Relevant to Patent Monetization*, 1004 PLI/Pat 405 (2010).

4. Jose A. Esteves, *Considerations for Enhancing an In-House IP Monetization Program*, 1004 PLI/Pat 461 (2010).

5. Victor Siber, *Monetizing Intellectual Property, The Nuts and Bolts of Running an IP Business*, 1001 PLI/Pat 301 (2010).

6. Kurt Maschoff, Dean Alderucci, *Patents as Assets: Monetization Strategies for Business Method Patents*, 609 PLI/Pat 249 (2000).

11.5.3   Securitization of Intellectual Property

"Securitization" and "monetization" of intellectual property are often used interchangeably. Although they are similar in many ways, securitization is different from monetization in two important respects; securitization does not involve the issuance of any securities and securitization does not depend upon a stream of future income associated with the intellectual property. In a securitization transaction, intellectual property is used as collateral to secure a loan from a bank or other lending institution. The intellectual property owner/borrower gives the lender a security interest in its intellectual property assets. The lender must then perfect its security interest in the intellectual property assets.

You will recall from Chapter 6 that perfecting security interests in copyrights is different from perfecting security interests in patents. In the case of copyrights, if the copyright has been registered with the Copyright Office, perfection of the security interest in the copyright can only be done by filing the security interest with the Copyright Office. If the copyright has not been registered with the Copyright Office, perfection of the security interest can only be done by filing a UCC-1 financing statement with the appropriate state office. In the case of patents, security interests must be perfected by filing a UCC-1 financing statement with the appropriate state office. However, even though a security interest is not considered to be an assignment under the Patent Act, the Patent and Trademark Office may still accept a security interest for filing. The PTO filing may be used to supplement the UCC filing, but it cannot substitute for the UCC filing.

As noted above, the intellectual property used to securitize a loan does not have to be associated with future royalty income. However, the intellectual property must have some determinable value so that the lender can predict the amount that can be realized upon foreclosure on the intellectual property in the case of a default. Valuation experts are used to establish the value of intellectual property collateral. The valuation process is similar to that used to establish patent damages in intellectual property infringement suits. Because of the uncertain value of intellectual property collateral, and because of its low liquidity, lenders discount the loan-to-value ratio to a far greater extent than in monetizing future income. The loan-to-value ratio in securitization transactions generally ranges between 25% — 30%. The loan-to-value ratio can be increased by insuring the value of the intellectual property collateral or by obtaining third-party guarantors of the loan repayment. There are a number of intellectual property insurance companies. The largest is Intellectual Property Insurance Services Corporation in Louisville, Kentucky. *See* http://www.patentinsurance.com/.

Additional Information

1. KINNEY & LANGE, P.A., INTELL. PROP. L. BUS. LAW § 13:30 (2010 ed.).

2. THOMAS M. WARD, INTELLECTUAL PROPERTY IN COMMERCE §§ 2:4, 2:16–2:32, 2:35–2:52 (2010).

3. CORP. COUNS. GD. TO INTELL. PROP. §§ 14:2–14:6 (2010).

4. RAYMOND T. NIMMER, JEFF DODD, MODERN LICENSING LAW §§ 16:30–16:32 (2010).

5. RAYMOND T. NIMMER, 2 INFORMATION LAW §§ 14:43–14:45 (2010).

6. Harry C. Sigman, Steven O. Weise, *Security Interests in Intellectual Property*, SR036 ALI-ABA 169 (2010).

7.   Kyle Tondo-Kramer, *Increasing Access to Startup Financing Through Intellectual Property Securitization*, 27 J. Marshall J. Computer & Info. L. 613 (2010).

8.   Brian Feit, *Intellectual Property Securitization*, 891 PLI/Comm 759 (2006).

9.   John M. Gabala, *"Intellectual Alchemy": Securitization of Intellectual Property as an Innovative Form of Alternative Financing*, 3 J. Marshall Rev. Intell. Prop. L. 307 (2004).

11.5.4   Letters of Credit

LETTER OF CREDIT PROCESS

Although letters of credit are not generally considered to be financing transactions, they do share some things in common with traditional financing transactions. First, in a letter of credit transaction, the seller of goods receives payment for the goods prior to the time the buyer receives and remits payment for the goods. In essence, in a letter of credit transaction, the seller receives payment for the goods upfront, similar to a seller of goods financing its accounts receivables discussed above. Second, in a letter of credit transaction, the seller is guaranteed payment for the goods. In this sense, the seller in a letter of credit transaction is similar to a sponsor in a monetization transaction that exchanges rights to potentially uncertain future income for the certainty of a upfront, lump-sum payment. Letters of credit are also important to consider because they are crucial in many international business transactions, and in any transaction in which a seller has concerns about a buyer's ability to pay for goods after they are delivered.

The essence of a letter of credit transaction is the commitment of the buyer's bank to pay the seller's bank upon the seller's bank's presentation of certain documents to the buyer's bank. A simplified letter of credit transaction would proceed as follows:

— The buyer and seller enter into a contract for the sale of goods;

— The buyer opens a letter of credit at the buyer's bank on behalf of the seller;

— The buyer's bank informs the seller's bank that the letter of credit has been issued and the seller's bank confirms the letter of credit to the seller;

— The seller then delivers the goods to a carrier and the carrier gives the seller a bill of lading which represents title to the goods;

— The seller then presents the bill of lading to the seller's bank and the seller's bank pays the seller for the goods;

— The seller's bank forwards the bill of lading to the buyer's bank and the buyer's bank pays the seller's bank upon receipt of the bill of lading;

— The buyer then pays the buyer's bank for the letter of credit and the buyer's bank gives the buyer the bill of lading;

— The buyer then presents the bill of lading to the carrier and the carrier gives the buyer the goods.

The seller's bank charges the seller, and the buyer's bank charges the buyer, fees for performing these various letter of credit services.

The drawing below depicts a simplified letter of credit transaction.

Figure 6: Simplified Letter of Credit Transaction

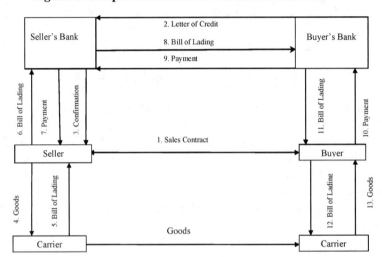

Additional Information

1.   Tracey B. Farrell, 50 Am. Jur. 2d Letters of Credit § 9 (2010).

2.   Corp. Couns. Gd. to Letters of Credit (2010).

3.   James E. Byrne, International Letter of Credit Law and Practice (2011).

4.   Michael P. Malloy, Banking Law & Reg. §§ 4A.4, 4A.4.2 (2011).

5.   A. Sidney Holderness, Et al., Legal Opinion Letters Formbook § 9.01 (2010).

6.   Dana Shilling, L. Desk Book § 2.08 (2011).

7.   Bradford Stone, Lawrence R. Ahern, 15 West's Legal Forms, Commercial Transactions §§ 8:1, 8:30, 8:98 (3d ed.) (2010).

8.   Albert Kritzer, 1 International Contract Manual §§ 10:15–10:20 (2011).

9.   Alan J. Jacobs, Et al, 68A Am. Jur. 2d Secured Transactions § 15 (2011).

10.   Richard A. Lord, 1 Williston on Contracts §§ 1:11, 2:23 (4th ed.) (2011).

11.   Steven C. Alberty, 1 Advising Small Businesses § 13:51 (2011).

12.   Peter Siviglia, Comm. Agreements §§ 14:3A-14:4, 14:7 (2010).

13. TRACEY B. FARRELL, 49 TEX. JUR. 3D LETTERS OF CREDIT (2011).

14. MARY G. LEARY, 20 N.C. INDEX 4TH LETTERS OF CREDIT (2011).

15. ALYS MASEK, 42A CAL. JUR. 3D LETTERS OF CREDIT (2011).

16. Penelope L. Christophorou, *Special Collateral Types: Deposit Accounts, Securities Accounts and Letters of Credit*, 932 PLI/COMM 83 (2011).

17. Xiango Gao, *The Fraud Rule Under the UN Convention on Independent Guarantees and Standby Letters of Credit: A Significant Contribution From an International Perspective*, 1 GEO. MASON J. INT'L COM. L. 48 (2010).

18. James G. Barnes, James E. Byrne, *Letters of Credit*, 65 BUS. LAW. 1267 (2010).

19. Peter H. Weil, Edwin E. Smith, *Letters of Credit*, 925 PLI/COMM 437 (2010).

20. Anthony R. Callobre, *A Primer on Letters of Credit*, SR036 ALI-ABA 243 (2010).

11.6 INITIAL PUBLIC OFFERINGS (IPOS)

An initial public offering of stock is considered the Holy Grail for most early-stage companies. Although it is sometimes said that IPOs make company founders and key employees "overnight millionaires," this glib depiction ignores the years of work and mountains of risk undertaken by the founders and key employees to bring the company to the point of an IPO. As discussed in the SEC Guide below, "going public" carries both benefits and obligations. Among the benefits are increased access to capital, stock liquidity and public recognition. Among the obligations are new reporting and management requirements, and new risks of liability to shareholders. This section discusses the IPO process, the Securities Acts, and the SEC S-1 Registration Statement. The section also includes the S-1 Registration Statement filed by Google for its initial public offering of stock in 2004.

11.6.1 Overview of IPO Process

The participants in the IPO process include investment bank underwriters, lawyers, accountants and the IPO company (issuer) management team. Generally, a lead underwriter forms an underwriter syndicate with other investment banks. The syndication of an IPO spreads the risk and lowers the cost of the IPO for each of the investment banks in the syndicate. The lead underwriter tests the waters for the IPO and obtains "indications of interest" from public and private investment funds. The lead underwriter's "inquiries of interest" to investment funds are not offers of sale of the IPO stock, and the investment funds' indication of interest are not offers to purchase the IPO stock. As you will see below, no offer or purchase of the IPO stock can be made prior to the approval of the company's Registration Statement by the SEC. Based on the indications of interest, the lead underwriter generally recommends to the company the total amount of the IPO offering and the price of the IPO stock.

The IPO company does not sell its stock directly to the public. Rather, the underwriter syndicate buys the stock from the company and resells the stock to public. The purchase of the stock by the underwriter syndicate benefits the company because it guarantees the company a fixed sum of money for the issued stock. The purchase of the stock by the underwriter syndicate benefits the underwriters because the stock is purchased at a discount from the price at which it will ultimately be offered to the public. This discount is generally around 15 percent of the public offering price. The underwriters also receive commissions on sales of stock.

Securities lawyers are involved in every detail of the IPO process. Securities lawyers prepare all SEC filings, most importantly the IPO prospectus, handle all communications with the SEC staff regarding the IPO, and opine on all legal matters affecting the IPO. If the IPO issuer is a technology company reliant on intellectual property, IP lawyers will also be involved in the IPO process. The IP lawyers generally opine on questions such as intellectual property validity, infringement and litigation. The accountants prepare and audit all financial statements of the company. In doing so, the accountants must perform their own due diligence investigation of the company's finances and cannot simply rely on information provided by the company's management. As you will see later is this chapter, the underwriters, lawyers, accountants and IPO company management can be held civilly and criminally liable for any knowing material misrepresentations or omissions in the materials filed with the SEC. The legal and accounting expenses of an IPO generally run about 10 percent of the total IPO offering.

The IPO company management team members directly involved in the IPO process generally include the president or CEO, the treasurer or CFO, and, for technology-based companies, the lead scientist or CTO. The IPO company management team is intimately involved with the underwriters, lawyers and accountants in all facets of the IPO. The IPO company management team also visits potential purchasers of its stock to promote the quality of its management, the superiority of its products or services, and its compelling competitive advantage. These on-site presentations to potential purchasers are often referred to as the "road show."

There are significant transaction costs in undertaking an IPO. As noted above, the underwriters receive about a 15 percent discount on the purchase of stock plus commissions, and the lawyers and accountants receive about 10 percent in fees. When you factor in the value of company management time that is diverted from the daily operation of the company during the IPO process, the total transaction costs of an IPO can easily exceed 35 percent or more of the offering amount.

The first step in the IPO process is the preparation of the Registration Statement called the SEC Form S-1. The SEC provides detailed instructions in Regulation S-K on the information that must be included in the S-1 Registration Statement. Among the information the SEC requires to be included in the S-1 Registration Statement are:

— The number of shares, description of shares, price of shares, selling commission, use of proceeds and company capitalization;

— Background of the company officers, directors, key personnel and major stockholders;

— The company's business model, markets, competitors, critical intellectual property and all risks associated with the company's business operations; and

— Litigation, tax liabilities, audited financial statements, and projections of future income and expenses ("forward looking statements" provided with explicit caveats regarding the potential discrepancies between the projections and the actual results).

Preparation of a draft S-1 Registration Statement generally takes between 60 and 90 days.

The draft S-1 Registration Statement is then filed with the SEC for review by the SEC staff. While the draft S-1 Registration Statement is pending review, the IPO lawyers prepare a draft prospectus based on the information contained in the S-1 Registration Statement. The draft prospectus, referred to as a "Red Herring" prospectus, is a shortened version of the S-1 Registration Statement which does not contain the complete details on the price of the securities and the amount of the offering. The name "Red Herring" comes from the disclosure statement printed in red bold type on the cover of the draft prospectus which explicitly states that the company is not offering securities for sale by virtue of providing persons with the information contained in the draft prospectus. The boiler plate Red Herring disclosure generally states: "A Registration Statement relating to these securities has been filed with the Securities and Exchange Commission but has not yet become effective. Information contained herein is subject to completion or amendment of the Registration Statement. These securities may not be sold, nor may offers to buy these securities be accepted, prior to the time the Registration Statement becomes effective."

As noted, the Red Herring prospectus is a shortened version of the S-1 Registration Statement. The Red Herring prospectus generally contains the following information: the purpose of the issue; the proposed offering price range; disclosure of any option agreements; the underwriters' commissions and discounts; promotion expenses; net proceeds to the issuing company; the company's balance sheet; earnings statements for the last three years, if available; the names and addresses of all officers, directors, underwriters and stockholders owning more than 10% of the current outstanding stock; a copy of the underwriting agreement; a legal opinion on the stock offering; and copies of the articles of incorporation of the company.

The SEC review of the S-1 Registration Statement generally takes between 25 and 30 days. At the conclusion of the SEC review, the SEC either approves the Registration Statement, in which case sales of the securities can commence immediately, or disapproves the Registration Statement, in which case the Registration Statement must be revised and resubmitted.

During the initial market trading period, the underwriters "make a market" for the stock by buying and selling shares of the stock in order to stabilize the stock's price. Very often the underwriters prohibit the company founders and other large shareholders, such as venture capital investors, from selling stock in the market for a certain period of time. This prohibition is called a "lock-up agreement" and usually lasts for 6 to 12 months from the date of the first stock sales. The "lock-up agreement" assures that a large number of shares will not be offered for sale immediately after the first public sales, which would depress the price of the stock.

The factors affecting the IPO stock price are similar to the factors affecting a venture capital investor's valuation of a company. These factors include comparable recent IPO offerings, projected revenues and earnings, the terms of the securities' offer, and the market supply and demand for IPO stock. An attractive IPO company generally has a well-established financial history, high levels of sales growth (~25%/year), high levels of profit margin relative to its industry, growth market opportunities (such as biotechnology, information technology, green technology), a highly successful and experienced management team, and a high quality lead underwriter such as Goldman Sachs, JPMorgan Chase, Merrill Lynch or Credit Suisse.

Additional Information

1. TIMOTHY S. FARBER, WESLEY S. WALTON, CORP. COMMUNICATIONS HANDBOOK Appendix B:1 (2009-2010).

2. GERALD T. LINS, ET AL., HEDGE FUNDS AND OTHER PRIVATE FUNDS: REG AND COMP Appendix 14 (2009).

3. ROBERT J. HAFT, 2B VENTURE CAP. & BUS. FIN. § 19:4 (2010).

4. WILLIAM M. PRIFTI, 24 SECURITIES PUB. & PRIV. OFFERINGS § 2:6 (2010).

5. NICK J. VIZY, 3 CORP COUNS GD TO ACQ & DIVEST § 40:27 (2010).

6. HAROLD S. BLOOMENTHAL, 10 INT'L CAP. MARKETS & SEC. REG. § 8:61 (2010).

7. HAROLD S. BLOOMENTHAL, SAMUEL WOLFF, 1 GOING PUBLIC CORP. § 2:11 (2011).

8. Eric W. Wooley, *How to Prepare an Initial Public Offering: The Underwriters' Perspective*, 1872 PLI/CORP 219 (2011).

9. Deanna L. Kirkpatrick, *How to Prepare an Initial Public Offering: Negotiating Comfort Letters*, 1872 PLI/CORP 281 (2011).

10. William F. Kuntz, *In Re Initial Public Offering Securities Litigation*, 199 PLI/NY 133 (2010).

11. Deanna L. Kirkpatrick, *How To Prepare An Initial Public Offering: The Registration Process — Overview And Selected Considerations*, 1798 PLI/CORP 43 (2010).

12. John L. Clarke, Lisa Firenze, *How To Prepare An Initial Public Offering: Due Diligence And Potential Liabilities*, 1798 PLI/CORP 85 (2010).

13. Brian Korn, *How To Prepare An Initial Public Offering 2010 — The Underwriting Agreement*, 1798 PLI/CORP 135 (2010).

14. Patrick J. Rondeau, *Initial Public Offering: Tasks In IPO Process*, 1660 PLI/CORP 435 (2008).

15. Chee Keong Low, *The Duties Of Directors In "Irrationally Exuberant" Initial Public Offerings*, 28 VA. L. & BUS. REV. 89 (2007).

16. William A. Candelaria, *Initial Public Offering of Shares of Common Stock Time Schedule and Assignments*, 1568 PLI/CORP 7 (2006).

17. John J. Clark, Jr., *Potential Liabilities In Initial Public Offerings*, 1568 PLI/CORP 165 (2006).

18. Thomas W. Van Dyke, Bryan Cave, *Preparing For The Initial Public Offering*, SLO54 ALI-ABA 607 (2005).

19. Christine Hurt, *Moral Hazard And The Initial Public Offering*, 26 CARDOZO L. REV. 711 (2005).

20. Laird H. Simons, *Considerations In Selecting The Managing Underwriter(s) For An Initial Public Offering*, 1450 PLI/CORP 83 (2004).

11.6.2 Securities Acts

Q&A: SMALL BUSINESS AND THE SEC
A guide to help you understand how to raise capital and comply with the federal securities laws
Available at http://www.sec.gov./info/smallbs/qasbsec.htm

I. What Are the Federal Securities Laws?

In the chaotic securities markets of the 1920s, companies often sold stocks and bonds on the basis of glittering promises of fantastic profits — without disclosing any meaningful information to investors. These conditions contributed to the disastrous Stock Market Crash of 1929. In response, the U.S. Congress enacted the federal securities laws and created the Securities and Exchange Commission (SEC) to administer them.

There are two primary sets of federal laws that come into play when a company wants to offer and sell its securities to the public. They are:

• the Securities Act of 1933 (Securities Act), and

• the Securities Exchange Act of 1934 (Exchange Act)

Securities Act

The Securities Act generally requires companies to give investors "full disclosure" of all "material facts," the facts investors would find important in making an investment decision. This Act also requires companies to file a registration statement with the SEC that includes information for investors. The SEC does not evaluate the merits of offerings, or determine if the securities offered are "good" investments. The SEC staff reviews registration statements and declares them "effective" if companies satisfy our disclosure rules.

Exchange Act

The Exchange Act requires publicly held companies to disclose information continually about their business operations, financial conditions, and managements. These companies, and in many cases their officers, directors and significant shareholders, must file periodic reports or other disclosure documents with the SEC. In some cases, the company must deliver the information directly to investors.

****

III. Should My Company "Go Public"?

When your company needs additional capital, "going public" may be the right choice, but you should weigh your options carefully. If your company is in the very early stages of development, it may be better to seek loans from financial institutions or the Small Business Administration. Other alternatives include raising money by selling securities in transactions that are exempt from the registration process.

There are benefits and new obligations that come from raising capital through a public offering registered with the SEC. While the benefits are attractive, be sure you are ready to assume these new obligations:

Benefits

Your access to capital will increase, since you can contact more potential investors.

Your company may become more widely known.

You may obtain financing more easily in the future if investor interest in your company grows enough to sustain a secondary trading market in your securities.

Controlling shareholders, such as the company's officers or directors, may have a ready market for their shares, which means that they can more easily sell their interests at retirement, for diversification, or for some other reason.

Your company may be able to attract and retain more highly qualified personnel if it can offer stock options, bonuses, or other incentives with a known market value.

The image of your company may be improved.

New Obligations

You must continue to keep shareholders informed about the company's business operations, financial condition, and management, incurring additional costs and new legal obligations.

You may be liable if you do not fulfill these new legal obligations.

You may lose some flexibility in managing your company's affairs, particularly when shareholders must approve your actions.

Your public offering will take time and money to accomplish.

IV. How Does My Small Business Register a Public Offering?

If you decide on a registered public offering, the Securities Act requires your company to file a registration statement with the SEC before the company can offer its securities for sale. You cannot actually sell the securities covered by the registration statement until the SEC staff declares it "effective," even though registration statements become public immediately upon filing.

Registration statements have two principal parts:

Part I is the prospectus, the legal offering or "selling" document. Your company — the "issuer" of the securities — must describe in the prospectus the important facts about its business operations, financial condition, and management. Everyone who buys the new issue, as well as anyone who is made an offer to purchase the securities, must have access to the prospectus.

Part II contains additional information that the company does not have to deliver to investors. Anyone can see this information by requesting it from one of the SEC's public reference rooms or by looking it up on the SEC Web site.

The Basic Registration Form — Form S-1

All companies can use Form S-1 to register their securities offerings. You should not prepare a registration statement as a fill-in-the-blank form, like a tax return. It should be similar to a brochure, providing readable information. If you file this form, your company must describe each of the following in the prospectus:

its business;

its properties;

its competition;

the identity of its officers and directors and their compensation;

material transactions between the company and its officers and directors;

material legal proceedings involving the company or its officers and directors;

the plan for distributing the securities; and the intended use of the proceeds of the offering.

Information about how to describe these items is set out in SEC rules. Registration statements also must include financial statements audited by an independent certified public accountant.

In addition to the information expressly required by the form, your company must also provide any other information that is necessary to make your disclosure complete and not misleading. You also must clearly describe any risks prominently in the prospectus, usually at the beginning. Examples of these risk factors are:

lack of business operating history;

adverse economic conditions in a particular industry;

lack of a market for the securities offered; and

dependence upon key personnel.

Alternative Registration Forms for Small Business Issuers

If your company qualifies as a "small business issuer," it can choose to file its registration statement using one of the simplified small business forms. A small business issuer is a United States or Canadian issuer:

that had less than $25 million in revenues in its last fiscal year, and

whose outstanding publicly-held stock is worth no more than $25 million.

Form SB-1 — To Raise $10 Million or Less

Small business issuers offering up to $10 million worth of securities in any 12-month period may use Form SB1. This form allows you to provide information in a question and answer format, similar to that used in Regulation A offerings, a type of exempt offering. Unlike Regulation A filings, Form SB-1 requires audited financial statements.

Form SB-2 — To Raise Capital in Any Amount

If your company is a "small business issuer," it may register an unlimited dollar amount of securities using Form SB-2, and may use this form again and again so long as it satisfies the "small business issuer" definition.

One advantage of Form SB-2 is that all its disclosure requirements are in Regulation S-B, a set of rules written in simple, non-legalistic terminology. Form SB-2 also permits the company to:

Provide audited financial statements, prepared according to generally accepted accounting principles, for two fiscal years. In contrast, Form S-1 requires the issuer to provide audited financial statements, prepared according to more detailed SEC regulations, for three fiscal years; and

Include less extensive narrative disclosure than Form S-1 requires, particularly in the description of your business, and executive compensation.

Staff Review of Registration Statements

SEC staff examines registration statements for compliance with disclosure requirements. If a filing appears incomplete or inaccurate, the staff usually informs the company by letter. The company may file correcting or clarifying amendments.

Once the company has satisfied the disclosure requirements, the staff declares the registration statement effective. The company may then begin to sell its securities. The SEC can refuse or suspend the effectiveness of any registration statement if it concludes that the document is misleading, inaccurate, or incomplete.

V. If My Company Becomes Public, What Disclosures Must I Regularly Make?

Your company can become "public" in one of two ways — by issuing securities in an offering registered under the Securities Act or by registering the company's outstanding securities under Exchange Act requirements. Both types of registration trigger ongoing reporting obligations for your company. In some cases, the Exchange Act also subjects your company's officers, directors and significant shareholders to reporting requirements. Let's discuss these requirements individually.

Reporting obligations because of Securities Act registration

Once the staff declares your company's Securities Act registration statement effective, the Exchange Act requires you to file reports with the SEC. The obligation to file reports continues at least through the end of the fiscal year in which your registration statement becomes effective. After that, you are required to continue reporting unless you satisfy the following "thresholds," in which case your filing obligations are suspended:

> your company has fewer than 300 shareholders of the class of securities offered; or

> your company has fewer than 500 shareholders of the class of securities offered and less than $10 million in total assets for each of its last three fiscal years.

If your company is subject to the reporting requirements, it must file information with the SEC about:

> its operations;

> its officers, directors, and certain shareholders, including salary, various fringe benefits, and transactions between the company and management;

> the financial condition of the business, including financial statements audited by an independent certified public accountant; and

> its competitive position and material terms of contracts or lease agreements.

All of this information becomes publicly available when you file your reports with the SEC. As is true with Securities Act filings, small business issuers may choose to use small business alternative forms and Regulation S-B for registration and reporting under the Exchange Act.

Obligations because of Exchange Act registration

Even if your company has not registered a securities offering, it must file an Exchange Act registration statement if:

it has more than $10 million total assets and a class of equity securities, like common stock, with 500 or more shareholders; or

it lists its securities on an exchange or on Nasdaq.

If a class of your company's securities is registered under the Exchange Act, the company, as well as its shareholders and management, are subject to various reporting requirements, explained below.

Ongoing Exchange Act periodic reporting

If your company registers a class of securities under the Exchange Act, it must file the same annual, periodic, and current reports that are required as a result of Securities Act registration, as explained above. This obligation continues for as long as the company exceeds the reporting thresholds previously outlined. If your company's securities are traded on an exchange or on Nasdaq, the company must continue filing these reports as long as the securities trade on those markets, even if your company falls below the thresholds.

Proxy rules

A company with Exchange Act registered securities must comply with the SEC's proxy rules whenever it seeks a shareholder vote on corporate matters. These rules require the company to provide a proxy statement to its shareholders, together with a proxy card when soliciting proxies. Proxy statements discuss management and executive compensation, along with descriptions of the matters up for a vote. If the company is not soliciting proxies but will take a vote on a matter, the company must provide to its shareholders an information statement that is similar to a proxy statement. The proxy rules also require your company to send an annual report to shareholders if there will be an election of directors. These reports contain much of the same information found in the Exchange Act annual reports that a company must file with the SEC, including audited financial statements. The proxy rules also govern when your company must provide shareholder lists to investors and when it must include a shareholder proposal in the proxy statement.

Beneficial ownership reports

If your company has registered a class of its equity securities under the Exchange Act, persons who acquire more than five percent of the outstanding shares of that class must file beneficial owner reports until their holdings drop below five percent. These filings contain background information about the beneficial owners as well as their investment intentions, providing investors and the company with information about accumulations of securities that may potentially change or influence company management and policies.

Tender offers

A public company with Exchange Act registered securities that faces a takeover attempt, or third party tender offer, should be aware that the SEC's tender offer rules will apply to the transaction. The same is true if the company makes a tender offer for its own Exchange Act registered securities. The filings required by these rules provide information to the public about the person making the tender offer. The company that is the subject of the takeover must file with the SEC its responses to the tender offer. The rules also set time limits for the tender offer and provide other protections to shareholders.

Transaction reporting by officers, directors and ten percent shareholders

Section 16 of the Exchange Act applies to your company's directors and officers, as well as shareholders who own more than 10% of a class of your company's equity securities registered under the Exchange Act. It requires these persons to report their transactions involving the company's equity securities to the SEC. Section 16 also establishes mechanisms for a company to recover "short swing" profits, those profits an insider realizes from a purchase and sale of a company security within a six-month period. In addition, Section 16 prohibits short selling by these persons of any class of the company's securities, whether or not that class is registered under the Exchange Act.

****

IX. Where Can I Go for More Information?

The staff of the SEC's Office of Small Business and the SEC's Small Business Ombudsman will be glad to assist you with any questions you may have regarding federal securities laws. For information about state securities laws, contact NASAA or your state's securities administrator, whose office is usually located in your capital city.

The entire text of the SEC's rules and regulations is available through the U.S. Government Printing Office or from several private publishers of legal information. In addition, numerous books on this subject have been published, and some are available at public libraries. As of this writing, the following volumes of Title 17 of the Code of Federal Regulations (the SEC's rules and regulations) were available from the Government Printing Office:

Vol. II — Parts 200 to 239. SEC Organization; Conduct and Ethics; Information and Requests; Rules of Practice; Regulation S-X and Securities Act of 1933.

Vol III — Parts 240 to End. Securities Exchange Act of 1934; Public Utility Holding Company, Trust Indenture, Investment Company, Investment Advisers, and Securities Investor Protection Corporation Acts.

****

11.6.3   Securities Registration

SEC FORM S-1 REGISTRATION STATEMENT UNDER THE SECURITIES
ACT OF 1933

(Exact name of registrant as specified in its charter)

(State or other jurisdiction of incorporation or organization)

(Primary Standard Industrial Classification Code Number)

(I.R.S. Employer Identification Number)

(Address, including zip code, and telephone number, including area code, of
registrant's principal executive offices)

(Name, address, including zip code, and telephone number, including area code,
of agent for service)

(Approximate date of commencement of proposed sale to the public)

GENERAL INSTRUCTIONS

I. Eligibility Requirements for Use of Form S-1

This Form shall be used for the registration under the Securities Act of 1933
("Securities Act") of securities of all registrants for which no other form is
authorized or prescribed, except that this Form shall not be used for securities of
foreign governments or political subdivisions thereof.

II

PART I — INFORMATION REQUIRED IN PROSPECTUS

Item 1. Forepart of the Registration Statement and Outside Front Cover Page
of Prospectus.

Set forth in the forepart of the registration statement and on the outside front
cover page of the prospectus the information required by Item 501 of Regulation S-
K (§ 229.501 of this chapter).

Item 2. Inside Front and Outside Back Cover Pages of Prospectus.

Set forth on the inside front cover page of the prospectus or, where permitted, on the outside back cover page, the information required by Item 502 of Regulation S-K (§ 229.502 of this chapter).

Item 3. Summary Information, Risk Factors and Ratio of Earnings to Fixed Charges.

Furnish the information required by Item 503 of Regulation S-K (§ 229.503 of this chapter).

Item 4. Use of Proceeds.

Furnish the information required by Item 504 of Regulation S-K (§ 229.504 of this chapter).

Item 5. Determination of Offering Price.

Furnish the information required by Item 505 of Regulation S-K (§ 229.505 of this chapter).

Item 6. Dilution.

Furnish the information required by Item 506 of Regulation S-K (§ 229.506 of this chapter).

Item 7. Selling Security Holders.

Furnish the information required by Item 507 of Regulation S-K (§ 229.507 of this chapter).

Item 8. Plan of Distribution.

Furnish the information required by Item 508 of Regulation S-K (§ 229.508 of this chapter).

Item 9. Description of Securities to be Registered.

Furnish the information required by Item 202 of Regulation S-K (§ 229.202 of this chapter).

Item 10. Interests of Named Experts and Counsel.

Furnish the information required by Item 509 of Regulation S-K (§ 229.509 of this chapter).

Item 11. Information with Respect to the Registrant.

Furnish the following information with respect to the registrant:

(a) Information required by Item 101 of Regulation S-K (§ 229.101 of this chapter), description of business;

(b) Information required by Item 102 of Regulation S-K (§ 229.102 of this chapter), description of property;

(c) Information required by Item 103 of Regulation S-K (§ 229.103 of this chapter), legal proceedings;

(d) Where common equity securities are being offered, information required by Item 201 of Regulation S-K (§ 229.201 of this chapter), market price of and dividends on the registrant's common equity and related stockholder matters;

(e) Financial statements meeting the requirements of Regulation S-X (17 CFR Part 210) (Schedules required under Regulation SX shall be filed as "Financial Statement Schedules" pursuant to Item 15, Exhibits and Financial Statement Schedules, of this Form), as well as any financial information required by Rule 3-05 and Article 11 of Regulation S-X. A smaller reporting company may provide the information in Rule 8-04 and 8-05 of Regulation S-X in lieu of the financial information required by Rule 3-05 and Article 11 of Regulation S-X;

(f) Information required by Item 301 of Regulation S-K (§ 229.301 of this chapter), selected financial data;

(g) Information required by Item 302 of Regulation S-K (§ 229.302 of this chapter), supplementary financial information;

(h) Information required by Item 303 of Regulation S-K (§ 229.303 of this chapter), management's discussion and analysis of financial condition and results of operations;

(i) Information required by Item 304 of Regulation S-K (§ 229.304 of this chapter), changes in and disagreements with accountants on accounting and financial disclosure;

(j) Information required by Item 305 of Regulation S-K (§ 229.305 of this chapter), quantitative and qualitative disclosures about market risk.

(k) Information required by Item 401 of Regulation S-K (§ 229.401 of this chapter), directors and executive officers;

(l) (l) Information required by Item 402 of Regulation S-K (§ 229.402 of this chapter), executive compensation, and information required by paragraph (e)(4) of Item 407 of Regulation S-K (§ 229.407 of this chapter), corporate governance;

(m) Information required by Item 403 of Regulation S-K (§ 229.403 of this chapter), security ownership of certain beneficial owners and management; and

(n) Information required by Item 404 of Regulation S-K (§ 229.404 of this chapter), transactions with related persons, promoters and certain control persons, and Item 407(a) of Regulation S-K (§ 229.407(a) of this chapter), corporate governance.

Item 11A. Material Changes.

If the registrant elects to incorporate information by reference pursuant to General Instruction VII., describe any and all material changes in the registrant's affairs which have occurred since the end of the latest fiscal year for which audited financial statements were included in the latest Form 10-K and that have not been described in a Form 10-Q or Form 8-K filed under the Exchange Act.

****

SIGNATURES

Pursuant to the requirements of the Securities Act of 1933, the registrant has duly caused this registration statement to be signed on its behalf by the undersigned, thereunto duly authorized in the City of _____, State of _____, on_____ , 20_____ .

(Registrant)
By (Signature and Title)

Additional Information

1. 2 WEST'S FED. ADMIN. PRAC. §§ 2256, 2285, 2286–2290, 2292–2293 (4th ed.), (2010).

2. WILLIAM MEADE FLETCHER, 14 FLETCHER CYC. CORP. § 6825 (2010).

3. JASON H.P. KRAVITT, ELIZABETH A. RAYMOND, TRENT M. MURCH, SECURITIZATION FIN. ASSETS § 11.01 (2005).

4. STEPHEN G. CHRISTIANSON, 134 A.L.R. FED. 289 (2010).

5. MELISSA K. STULL, 113 A.L.R. FED. 575 (2010).

6. MELISSA K. STULL, 112 A.L.R. FED. 387 (2010).

7. MARTHA M. CLEARY, 110 A.L.R. FED. 97 (2010).

8. GEORGE F. GABEL, 109 A.L.R. FED. 444 (2010).

9. GEORGE K. CHAMBERLIN, 58 A.L.R. FED. 408 (2010).

10. ELAINE K. ZIPP, 56 A.L.R. FED. 659 (2010).

11. MICHAEL J. KAPLAN, 39 A.L.R. FED 357 (2010).

12. WILLIAM E. AIKEN, 9 A.L.R. FED. 639 (2010).

13. F. S. TINIO, 1 A.L.R. FED. 1007 (2010).

14. JAMES BUCHWALTER ET AL., 79A C.J.S. SECURITIES REGULATION § 373 (2010).

15. FRANCIS C. AMENDOLA ET AL., 69 AM. JUR. 2D SECURITIES REGULATION — Federal § 284 (2010).

16. HAROLD S. BLOOMENTHAL, SAMUEL WOLFF, 1 GOING PUBLIC HANDBOOK § 1:1 (2009).

17. STEVEN C. ALBERTY, MARY ANN FRANTZ, 1 ADVISING SMALL BUSINESSES § 16:7 (2010).

18. STUART R. COHN, 2 SEC. COUNSELING FOR SMALL & EMERGING COMPANIES Appendix 8 (2009).

19.   STUART R. COHN, 2 SEC. COUNSELING FOR SMALL & EMERGING COMPANIES Appendix 9 (2009).

20.   Gary M. Brown, *Approaching Securities Law*, 1618 PLI/CORP 15 (2007).

GOOGLE FORM S-1 REGISTRATION STATEMENT

As filed with the Securities and Exchange Commission on April 29, 2004
Registration No. 333

SECURITIES AND EXCHANGE COMMISSION
Washington, D.C. 20549

————

FORM S-1

REGISTRATION STATEMENT

Under

The Securities Act of 1933

————

————

GOOGLE INC.

(Exact name of Registrant as specified in its charter)

————

Delaware	7375	77-0493581
(State or other jurisdiction of incorporation or organization)	(Primary Standard Industrial Classification Code Number)	(I.R.S. Employer Identification Number)

1600 Amphitheatre Parkway

Mountain View, CA 94043

(650) 623-4000

(Address, including zip code, and telephone number, including area code, of Registrant's principal executive offices)

————

Eric Schmidt

Chief Executive Officer

Google Inc.

1600 Amphitheatre Parkway

Mountain View, CA 94043

(650) 623-4000

(Name, address, including zip code, and telephone number, including area code, of agent for service)

———

Copies to:

Larry W. Sonsini, Esq.	David C. Drummond, Esq.	William H. Hinman, Jr., Esq.
David J. Segre, Esq.	Jeffery L. Donovan, Esq.	Simpson Thacher & Bartlett LLP
Wilson Sonsini Goodrich & Rosati, P.C.	Anna Itoi, Esq.	3330 Hillview Avenue
650 Page Mill Road	Google Inc.	Palo Alto, California 94304
Palo Alto, California 94304-1050	1600 Amphitheatre Parkway	(650) 251-5000
(650) 493-9300	Mountain View, CA 94043	
	(650) 623-4000	

———

Approximate date of commencement of proposed sale to the public: As soon as practicable after the effective date of this Registration Statement.

The information in this prospectus is not complete and may be changed. We may not sell these securities until the registration statement filed with the Securities and Exchange Commission is effective. This prospectus is not an offer to sell these securities and we are not soliciting any offer to buy these securities in any jurisdiction where the offer or sale is not permitted.

Prospectus (Subject to Completion)

Dated April 29, 2004

Shares

Class A Common Stock

———

Google Inc. is offering _____ shares of Class A common stock and the selling stockholders are offering _____ shares of Class A common stock. We will not receive any proceeds from the sale of shares by the selling stockholders. This is our initial public offering and no public market currently exists for our shares. We anticipate that the initial public offering price will be between $_____ and $_____ per share.

Following this offering, we will have two classes of authorized common stock, Class A common stock and Class B common stock. The rights of the holders of Class A common stock and Class B common stock are identical, except with respect to voting and conversion. Each share of Class A common stock is entitled to one vote per share. Each share of Class B common stock is entitled to ten votes per share and is convertible at any time into one share of Class A common stock.

We expect to apply to list our Class A common stock on either the New York Stock Exchange or the Nasdaq National Market under the symbol "_____."

Investing in our Class A common stock involves risks. See "Risk Factors" beginning on page 4.

Price $_____ A Share

Google has granted the underwriters the right to purchase up to an additional _____ shares to cover over-allotments.

The price to the public and allocation of shares will be determined primarily by an auction process. As part of this auction process, we are attempting to assess the market demand for our Class A common stock and to set the size and price to the public of this offering to meet that demand. Buyers hoping to capture profits shortly after our Class A common stock begins trading may be disappointed. The method for submitting bids and a more detailed description of this process are included in "Auction Process" beginning on page 25.

The Securities and Exchange Commission and state securities regulators have not approved or disapproved of these securities, or determined if this prospectus is truthful or complete. Any representation to the contrary is a criminal offense.

LETTER FROM THE FOUNDERS
"AN OWNER'S MANUAL" FOR GOOGLE'S SHAREHOLDERS

INTRODUCTION

Google is not a conventional company. We do not intend to become one. Throughout Google's evolution as a privately held company, we have managed Google differently. We have also emphasized an atmosphere of creativity and challenge, which has helped us provide unbiased, accurate and free access to information for those who rely on us around the world.

Now the time has come for the company to move to public ownership. This change will bring important benefits for our employees, for our present and future shareholders, for our customers, and most of all for Google users. But the standard structure of public ownership may jeopardize the independence and focused objectivity that have been most important in Google's past success and that we consider most fundamental for its future. Therefore, we have designed a corporate structure that will protect Google's ability to innovate and retain its most distinctive characteristics. We are confident that, in the long run, this will bring Google and its shareholders, old and new, the greatest economic returns. We want to clearly explain our plans and the reasoning and values behind them. We are delighted you are considering an investment in Google and are reading this letter.

Sergey and I intend to write you a letter like this one every year in our annual report. We'll take turns writing the letter so you'll hear directly from each of us. We ask that you read this letter in conjunction with the rest of this prospectus.

SERVING END USERS

Sergey and I founded Google because we believed we could provide a great service to the world — instantly delivering relevant information on any topic. Serving our end users is at the heart of what we do and remains our number one priority.

Our goal is to develop services that improve the lives of as many people as possible — to do things that matter. We make our services as widely available as we can by supporting over 97 languages and by providing most services for free. Advertising is our principal source of revenue, and the ads we provide are relevant and useful rather than intrusive and annoying. We strive to provide users with great commercial information.

We are proud of the products we have built, and we hope that those we create in the future will have an even greater positive impact on the world.

LONG TERM FOCUS

As a private company, we have concentrated on the long term, and this has served us well. As a public company, we will do the same. In our opinion, outside pressures too often tempt companies to sacrifice long-term opportunities to meet quarterly market expectations. Sometimes this pressure has caused companies to manipulate financial results in order to "make their quarter." In Warren Buffett's words, "We won't "smooth" quarterly or annual results: If earnings figures are lumpy when they reach headquarters, they will be lumpy when they reach you."

If opportunities arise that might cause us to sacrifice short term results but are in the best long term interest of our shareholders, *we will take those opportunities.* We will have the fortitude to do this. We would request that our shareholders take the long term view.

Many companies are under pressure to keep their earnings in line with analysts' forecasts. Therefore, they often accept smaller, but predictable, earnings rather than larger and more unpredictable returns. Sergey and I feel this is harmful, and we intend to steer in the opposite direction.

----

[1] Much of this was inspired by Warren Buffett's essays in his annual reports and his "An Owner's Manual" to Berkshire Hathaway shareholders.

i

Google has had adequate cash to fund our business and has generated additional cash through operations. This gives us the flexibility to weather costs, benefit from opportunities and optimize our long term earnings. For example, in our ads system we make many improvements that affect revenue in both directions. These are in areas like end user relevance and satisfaction, advertiser satisfaction, partner needs and targeting technology. We release improvements immediately rather than delaying them, even though delay might give "smoother" financial results. You have our commitment to execute quickly to achieve long term value rather than making the quarters more predictable.

We will make decisions on the business fundamentals, not accounting consider-ations, and always with the long term welfare of our company and shareholders in mind.

Although we may discuss long term trends in our business, we do not plan to give earnings guidance in the traditional sense. We are not able to predict our business within a narrow range for each quarter. We recognize that our duty is to advance our shareholders' interests, and we believe that artificially creating short term target numbers serves our shareholders poorly. We would prefer not to be asked to make such predictions, and if asked we will respectfully decline. A management team distracted by a series of short term targets is as pointless as a dieter stepping on a scale every half hour.

RISK VS REWARD IN THE LONG RUN

Our business environment changes rapidly and needs long term investment. We will not hesitate to place major bets on promising new opportunities.

We will not shy away from high-risk, high-reward projects because of short term earnings pressure. Some of our past bets have gone extraordinarily well, and others have not. Because we recognize the pursuit of such projects as the key to our long term success, we will continue to seek them out. For example, we would fund projects that have a 10% chance of earning a billion dollars over the long term. Do not be surprised if we place smaller bets in areas that seem very speculative or even strange. As the ratio of reward to risk increases, we will accept projects further outside our normal areas, especially when the initial investment is small.

We encourage our employees, in addition to their regular projects, to spend 20% of their time working on what they think will most benefit Google. This empowers them to be more creative and innovative. Many of our significant advances have happened in this manner. For example, AdSense for content and Google News were both prototyped in "20% time." Most risky projects fizzle, often teaching us something. Others succeed and become attractive businesses.

We may have quarter-to-quarter volatility as we realize losses on some new projects and gains on others. If we accept this, we can all maximize value in the long term. Even though we are excited about risky projects, we expect to devote the vast majority of our resources to our main businesses, especially since most people naturally gravitate toward incremental improvements.

EXECUTIVE ROLES

We run Google as a triumvirate. Sergey and I have worked closely together for the last eight years, five at Google. Eric, our CEO, joined Google three years ago. The three of us run the company collaboratively with Sergey and me as Presidents. The structure is unconventional, but we have worked successfully in this way.

To facilitate timely decisions, Eric, Sergey and I meet daily to update each other on the business and to focus our collaborative thinking on the most important and immediate issues. Decisions are often made by one of us, with the others being briefed later. This works because we have tremendous trust and respect for each other and we generally think alike. Because of our intense long term working relationship, we can often predict differences of opinion among the three of us. We know that when we disagree, the correct decision is far from obvious. For important decisions, we discuss the issue with the larger team. Eric, Sergey and I run the company without any significant internal conflict, but with healthy debate. As different topics come up, we often delegate decision-making responsibility to one of us.

We hired Eric as a more experienced complement to Sergey and me to help us run the business. Eric was CTO of Sun Microsystems. He was also CEO of Novell and has a Ph.D. in computer science, a very unusual and important combination for Google given our scientific and technical culture. This partnership among the three of us has worked very well and we expect it to continue. The shared judgments and extra energy available from all three of us has significantly benefited Google.

Eric has the legal responsibilities of the CEO and focuses on management of our vice presidents and the sales organization. Sergey focuses on engineering and business deals. I focus on engineering and product management. All three of us devote considerable time to overall management of the company and other fluctuating needs. We are extremely fortunate to have talented management that has grown the company to where it is today — they operate the company and deserve the credit.

CORPORATE STRUCTURE

We are creating a corporate structure that is designed for stability over long time horizons. By investing in Google, you are placing an unusual long-term bet on the team, especially Sergey and me, and on our innovative approach.

We want Google to become an important and significant institution. That takes time, stability and independence. We bridge the media and technology industries, both of which have experienced considerable consolidation and attempted hostile takeovers.

In the transition to public ownership, we have set up a corporate structure that will make it harder for outside parties to take over or influence Google. This structure will also make it easier for our management team to follow the long term, innovative approach emphasized earlier. This structure, called a dual class voting structure, is described elsewhere in this prospectus.

The main effect of this structure is likely to leave our team, especially Sergey and me, with significant control over the company's decisions and fate, as Google shares change hands. New investors will fully share in Google's long term growth but will have less influence over its strategic decisions than they would at most public companies.

While this structure is unusual for technology companies, it is common in the media business and has had a profound importance there. The New York Times Company, the Washington Post Company and Dow Jones, the publisher of *The Wall Street Journal,* all have similar dual class ownership structures. Media observers frequently point out that dual class ownership has allowed these companies to concentrate on their core, long-term interest in serious news coverage, despite fluctuations in quarterly results. The Berkshire Hathaway company has applied the same structure, with similar beneficial effects. From the point of view of long-term success in advancing a company's core values, the structure has clearly been an advantage.

Academic studies have shown that from a purely economic point of view, dual class structures have not harmed the share price of companies. The shares of each of our classes have identical economic rights and differ only as to voting rights.

Google has prospered as a private company. As a public company, we believe a dual class voting structure will enable us to retain many of the positive aspects of being private. We understand some investors do not favor dual class structures. We have considered this point of view carefully, and we have not made our decision lightly. We are convinced that everyone associated with Google — including new investors — will benefit from this structure.

To help us govern, we have recently expanded our Board of Directors to include three additional members. John Hennessy is the President of Stanford and has a Doctoral degree in computer science. Art Levinson is CEO of Genentech and has a Ph.D. in biochemistry. Paul Otellini is President and COO of Intel. We could not be more excited about the caliber and experience of these directors.

We have a world class management team impassioned by Google's mission and responsible for Google's success. We believe the stability afforded by the dual-class structure will enable us to retain our unique culture and continue to attract and retain talented people who are Google's life blood. Our colleagues will be able to trust that they themselves and their labors of hard work, love and creativity will be well cared for by a company focused on stability and the long term.

As an investor, you are placing a potentially risky long term bet on the team, especially Sergey and me. The two of us, Eric and the rest of the management team recognize that our individual and collective interests are deeply aligned with those of the new investors who choose to support Google. Sergey and I are committed to Google for the long term. The broader Google team has also demonstrated an extraordinary commitment to our long term success. With continued hard work and good fortune, this commitment will last and flourish.

When Sergey and I founded Google, we hoped, but did not expect, it would reach its current size and influence. Our intense and enduring interest was to objectively help people find information efficiently. We also believed that searching and organizing all the world's information was an unusually important task that should be carried out by a company that is trustworthy and interested in the public good. We believe a well functioning society should have abundant, free and unbiased access to high quality information. Google therefore has a responsibility to the world. The dual-class structure helps ensure that this responsibility is met. We believe that fulfilling this responsibility will deliver increased value to our shareholders.

BECOMING A PUBLIC COMPANY

Google should go public soon.

We assumed when founding Google that if things went well, we would likely go public some day. But we were always open to staying private, and a number of developments reduced the pressure to change. We soon were generating cash, removing one important reason why many companies go public. Requirements for public companies became more significant in the wake of recent corporate scandals and the resulting passage of the Sarbanes-Oxley Act. We made business progress we were happy with. Our investors were patient and willing to stay with Google. We have been able to meet our business needs with our current level of cash.

A number of factors weighed on the other side of the debate. Our growth has reduced some of the advantages of private ownership. By law, certain private companies must report as if they were public companies. The deadline imposed by this requirement accelerated our decision. As a smaller private company, Google kept business information closely held, and we believe this helped us against competitors. But, as we grow larger, information becomes more widely known. As a public company, we will of course provide you with all information required by law, and we will also do our best to explain our actions. But we will not unnecessarily disclose all of our strengths, strategies and intentions. We have transferred significant ownership of Google to employees in return for their efforts in building the business. And, we benefited greatly by selling $26 million of stock to our early investors before we were profitable. Thus, employee and investor liquidity were significant factors.

We have demonstrated a proven business model and have designed a corporate structure that will make it easier to become a public company. A large, diverse, enthusiastic shareholder base will strengthen the company and benefit from our continued success. A larger cash balance will provide Google with flexibility and protection against adversity. All in all, going public now is the right decision.

IPO PRICING AND ALLOCATION

Informed investors willing to pay the IPO price should be able to buy as many shares as they want, within reason, in the IPO, as on the stock market.

It is important to us to have a fair process for our IPO that is inclusive of both small and large investors. It is also crucial that we achieve a good outcome for Google and its current shareholders. This has led us to pursue an auction-based IPO for our entire offering. Our goal is to have a share price that reflects a fair market valuation of Google and that moves rationally based on changes in our business and the stock market. (The auction process is discussed in more detail elsewhere in this prospectus.)

Many companies have suffered from unreasonable speculation, small initial share float, and boom-bust cycles that hurt them and their investors in the long run. We believe that an auction-based IPO will minimize these problems.

An auction is an unusual process for an IPO in the United States. Our experience with auction-based advertising systems has been surprisingly helpful in the auction design process for the IPO. As in the stock market, if people try to buy more stock than is available, the price will go up. And of course, the price will go down if there aren't enough buyers. This is a simplification, but it captures the basic issues. Our goal is to have an efficient market price — a rational price set by informed buyers and sellers — for our shares at the IPO and afterward. Our goal is to achieve a relatively stable price in the days following the IPO and that buyers and sellers receive a fair price at the IPO.

We are working to create a sufficient supply of shares to meet investor demand at IPO time and after. We are encouraging current shareholders to consider selling some of their shares as part of the offering. These shares will supplement the shares the company sells to provide more supply for investors and hopefully provide a more stable fair price. Sergey and I, among others, are currently planning to sell a fraction of our shares in the IPO. The more shares current shareholders sell, the more likely it is that they believe the price is not unfairly low. The supply of shares available will likely have an effect on the clearing price of the auction. Since the number of shares being sold is likely to be larger at a high price and smaller at a lower price, investors will likely want to consider the scope of current shareholder participation in the IPO. We may communicate from time to time that we would be sellers rather than buyers.

We would like you to invest for the long term, and to do so only at or below what you determine to be a fair price. We encourage investors not to invest in Google at

IPO or for some time after, if they believe the price is not sustainable over the long term.

We intend to take steps to help ensure shareholders are well informed. We encourage you to read this prospectus. We think that short term speculation without paying attention to price is likely to lose you money, especially with our auction structure.

GOOGLERS

Our employees, who have named themselves Googlers, are everything. Google is organized around the ability to attract and leverage the talent of exceptional technologists and business people. We have been lucky to recruit many creative, principled and hard working stars. We hope to recruit many more in the future. We will reward and treat them well.

We provide many unusual benefits for our employees, including meals free of charge, doctors and washing machines. We are careful to consider the long term advantages to the company of these benefits. Expect us to add benefits rather than pare them down over time. We believe it is easy to be penny wise and pound foolish with respect to benefits that can save employees considerable time and improve their health and productivity.

The significant employee ownership of Google has made us what we are today. Because of our employee talent, Google is doing exciting work in nearly every area of computer science. We are in a very competitive industry where the quality of our product is paramount. Talented people are attracted to Google because we empower them to change the world; Google has large computational resources and distribution that enables individuals to make a difference. Our main benefit is a workplace with important projects, where employees can contribute and grow. We are focused on providing an environment where talented, hard working people are rewarded for their contributions to Google and for making the world a better place.

DON'T BE EVIL

Don't be evil. We believe strongly that in the long term, we will be better served — as shareholders and in all other ways — by a company that does good things for the world even if we forgo some short term gains. This is an important aspect of our culture and is broadly shared within the company.

Google users trust our systems to help them with important decisions: medical, financial and many others. Our search results are the best we know how to produce. They are unbiased and objective, and we do not accept payment for them or for inclusion or more frequent updating. We also display advertising, which we work hard to make relevant, and we label it clearly. This is similar to a newspaper, where the advertisements are clear and the articles are not influenced by the advertisers' payments. We believe it is important for everyone to have access to the best information and research, not only to the information people pay for you to see.

MAKING THE WORLD A BETTER PLACE

We aspire to make Google an institution that makes the world a better place. With our products, Google connects people and information all around the world for free. We are adding other powerful services such as Gmail that provides an efficient one gigabyte Gmail account for free. By releasing services for free, we hope to help bridge the digital divide. AdWords connects users and advertisers efficiently, helping both. AdSense helps fund a huge variety of online web sites and enables authors who could not otherwise publish. Last year we created Google Grants — a growing program in which hundreds of non-profits addressing issues, including the environment, poverty and human rights, receive free advertising. And now, we are in the process of establishing the Google Foundation. We intend to contribute significant resources to the foundation, including employee time and approximately 1% of Google's equity and profits in some form. We hope someday this institution may eclipse Google itself in terms of overall world impact by ambitiously applying innovation and significant resources to the largest of the world's problems.

SUMMARY AND CONCLUSION

Google is not a conventional company. Eric, Sergey and I intend to operate Google differently, applying the values it has developed as a private company to its future as a public company. Our mission and business description are available in the rest of the prospectus; we encourage you to carefully read this information. We will optimize for the long term rather than trying to produce smooth earnings for each quarter. We will support selected high-risk, high-reward projects and manage our portfolio of projects. We will run the company collaboratively with Eric, our CEO, as a team of three. We are conscious of our duty as fiduciaries for our shareholders, and we will fulfill those responsibilities. We will continue to attract creative, committed new employees, and we will welcome support from new shareholders. We will live up to our "don't be evil" principle by keeping user trust and not accepting payment for search results. We have a dual-class structure that is biased toward stability and independence and that requires investors to bet on the team, especially Sergey and me.

In this letter we have explained our thinking on why Google is better off going public. We have talked about our IPO auction method and our desire for stability and access for all investors. We have discussed our goal to have investors who determine a rational price and invest for the long term only if they can buy at that price. Finally, we have discussed our desire to create an ideal working environment that will ultimately drive the success of Google by retaining and attracting talented Googlers.

We have tried hard to anticipate your questions. It will be difficult for us to respond to them given legal constraints during our offering process. We look forward to a long and hopefully prosperous relationship with you, our new investors. We wrote this letter to help you understand our company.

We have a strong commitment to our users worldwide, their communities, the web sites in our network, our advertisers, our investors, and of course our employees. Sergey and I, and the team will do our best to make Google a long term success and the world a better place.

PROSPECTUS SUMMARY

This summary highlights information contained elsewhere in this prospectus and does not contain all of the information you should consider in making your investment decision. You should read this summary together with the more detailed information, including our financial statements and the related notes, elsewhere in this prospectus. You should carefully consider, among other things, the matters discussed in "Risk Factors."

Google Inc.

Google is a global technology leader focused on improving the ways people connect with information. Our innovations in web search and advertising have made our web site a top Internet destination and our brand one of the most recognized in the world. We maintain the world's largest online index of web sites and other content, and we make this information freely available to anyone with an Internet connection. Our automated search technology helps people obtain nearly instant access to relevant information from our vast online index.

We generate revenue by delivering relevant, cost-effective online advertising. Businesses use our AdWords program to promote their products and services with targeted advertising. In addition, the thousands of third-party web sites that comprise our Google Network use our Google AdSense program to deliver relevant ads that generate revenue and enhance the user experience.

Our mission is to organize the world's information and make it universally accessible and useful. We believe that the most effective, and ultimately the most profitable, way to accomplish our mission is to put the needs of our users first. We have found that offering a high-quality user experience leads to increased traffic and strong word-of-mouth promotion. Our dedication to putting users first is reflected in three key commitments we have made to our users:

- We will do our best to provide the most relevant and useful search results possible, independent of financial incentives. Our search results will be objective and we will not accept payment for inclusion or ranking in them.
- We will do our best to provide the most relevant and useful advertising. Whenever someone pays for something, we will make it clear to our users. Advertisements should not be an annoying interruption.
- We will never stop working to improve our user experience, our search technology and other important areas of information organization.

We believe that our user focus is the foundation of our success to date. We also believe that this focus is critical for the creation of long-term value. We do not intend to compromise our user focus for short-term economic gain.

Corporate Information

We were incorporated in California in September 1998. In August 2003, we reincorporated in Delaware. Our principal executive offices are located at 1600

Amphitheatre Parkway, Mountain View, California 94043, and our telephone number is (650) 623-4000. We maintain a number of web sites including www.google-.com. The information on our web sites is not part of this prospectus.

Google® is a registered trademark in the U.S. and several other countries. Our unregistered trademarks include: AdSense, AdWords, Blogger, Froogle, Gmail, I'm Feeling Lucky and PageRank. All other trademarks, trade names and service marks appearing in this prospectus are the property of their respective holders.

The Offering

Class A common stock offered:

By Google	_____	Shares
By the selling stockholders	_____	Shares
Total	_____	Shares
Class A common stock to be outstanding after this offering	_____	Shares
Class B common stock to be outstanding after this offering	_____	Shares
Total common stock to be outstanding after this offering	_____	Shares
Use of proceeds	We intend to use the net proceeds from this offering for general corporate purposes, including working capital and capital expenditures. We may also use a portion of the net proceeds to acquire businesses, technologies or other assets. We will not receive any of the proceeds from the sale of shares by the selling stockholders. See "Use of Proceeds" for additional information.	

Proposed symbol

The number of shares of Class A and Class B common stock that will be outstanding after this offering is based on the number of shares outstanding at March 31, 2004 and excludes:

- shares of Class B common stock issuable upon the exercise of warrants outstanding at March 31, 2004, at a weighted average exercise price of $_____ per share.

- shares of Class A common stock issuable upon the exercise of options outstanding at March 31, 2004, at a weighted average exercise price of $_____ per share.

- shares of Class B common stock issuable upon the exercise of options outstanding at March 31, 2004, at a weighted average exercise price of $_____ per share.

- shares of common stock available for future issuance under our stock option plans at March 31, 2004.

Unless otherwise indicated, all information in this prospectus assumes that the underwriters do not exercise the over-allotment option to purchase _____ additional shares of Class A common stock in this offering and that all shares of our Class A Senior common stock and preferred stock are converted into Class B common stock and all shares of our common stock are converted into Class A common stock prior to this offering.

The Auction Process

The auction process being used for our initial public offering differs from methods that have been traditionally used in most other underwritten initial public offerings in the U.S. In particular, the initial public offering price and the allocation of shares will be determined primarily by an auction conducted by our underwriters on our behalf. For more information about the auction process see "Auction Process."

Summary Consolidated Financial Data

The following table summarizes financial data regarding our business and should be read together with "Management's Discussion and Analysis of Financial Condition and Results of Operations" and our consolidated financial statements and the related notes included elsewhere in this prospectus.

RISK FACTORS

An investment in Google involves significant risks. You should read these risk factors carefully before deciding whether to invest in our company. The following is a description of what we consider our key challenges and risks.

Risks Related to Our Business and Industry

We face significant competition from Microsoft and Yahoo.

We face formidable competition in every aspect of our business, and particularly from other companies that seek to connect people with information on the web and provide them with relevant advertising. Currently, we consider our primary competitors to be Microsoft and Yahoo. Microsoft has announced plans to develop a new web search technology that may make web search a more integrated part of the Windows operating system. We expect that Microsoft will increasingly use its financial and engineering resources to compete with us. Yahoo has become an increasingly significant competitor, having acquired Overture Services, which offers Internet advertising solutions that compete with our AdWords and AdSense programs, as well as the Inktomi, AltaVista and AllTheWeb search engines. Since June 2000, Yahoo has used, to varying degrees, our web search technology on its web site to provide web search services to its users. We have notified Yahoo of our election to terminate our agreement, effective July 2004. This agreement with Yahoo accounted for less than 3% of our net revenues for the year ended December 31, 2003 and less than 3% for the three months ended March 31, 2004.

Both Microsoft and Yahoo have more employees than we do (in Microsoft's case, currently more than 20 times as many). Microsoft also has significantly more cash resources than we do. Both of these companies also have longer operating histories and more established relationships with customers. They can use their experience and resources against us in a variety of competitive ways, including by making acquisitions, investing more aggressively in research and development and competing more aggressively for advertisers and web sites. Microsoft and Yahoo also may have a greater ability to attract and retain users than we do because they operate Internet portals with a broad range of products and services. If Microsoft or Yahoo are successful in providing similar or better web search results compared to ours or leverage their platforms to make their web search services easier to access than ours, we could experience a significant decline in user traffic. Any such decline in traffic could negatively affect our net revenues.

We face competition from other Internet companies, including web search providers, Internet advertising companies and destination web sites that may also bundle their services with Internet access.

In addition to Microsoft and Yahoo, we face competition from other web search providers, including companies that are not yet known to us. We compete with Internet advertising companies, particularly in the areas of pay-for-performance and keyword-targeted Internet advertising. Also, we may compete with companies that sell products and services online because these companies, like us, are trying to attract users to their web sites to search for information about products and services.

We also compete with destination web sites that seek to increase their search-related traffic. These destination web sites may include those operated by Internet access providers, such as cable and DSL service providers. Because our users need to access our services through Internet access providers, they have direct relationships with these providers. If an access provider or a computer or computing device manufacturer offers online services that compete with ours, the user may find it more convenient to use the services of the access provider or manufacturer. In addition, the access provider or manufacturer may make it hard to access our services by not listing them in the access provider's or manufacturer's own menu of offerings. Also, because the access provider gathers information from the user in connection with the establishment of a billing relationship, the access provider may be more effective than we are in tailoring services and advertisements to the specific tastes of the user.

There has been a trend toward industry consolidation among our competitors, and so smaller competitors today may become larger competitors in the future. If our competitors are more successful than we are at generating traffic, our revenues may decline.

We face competition from traditional media companies, and we may not be included in the advertising budgets of large advertisers, which could harm our operating results.

In addition to Internet companies, we face competition from companies that offer traditional media advertising opportunities. Most large advertisers have set advertising budgets, a very small portion of which is allocated to Internet advertising. We expect that large advertisers will continue to focus most of their advertising efforts on traditional media. If we fail to convince these companies to spend a portion of their advertising budgets with us, or if our existing advertisers reduce the amount they spend on our programs, our operating results would be harmed.

We expect our growth rates to decline and anticipate downward pressure on our operating margin in the future.

We expect that in the future our revenue growth rate will decline and anticipate that there will be downward pressure on our operating margin. We believe our revenue growth rate will decline as a result of anticipated changes to our advertising program revenue mix, increasing competition and the inevitable decline in growth rates as our net revenues increase to higher levels. We believe our operating margin will decline as a result of increasing competition and increased expenditures for all aspects of our business as a percentage of our net revenues, including product development and sales and marketing expenses. We also expect that our operating margin may decline as a result of increases in the proportion of our net revenues generated from our Google Network members. The margin on revenue we generate from our Google Network members is generally significantly less than the margin on revenue we generate from advertising on our web sites. Additionally, the margin we earn on revenue generated from our Google Network could decrease in the future if our Google Network members require a greater portion of the advertising fees.

Our operating results may fluctuate.

Our operating results may fluctuate as a result of a number of factors, many of which are outside of our control. The following factors may affect our operating results:

- Our ability to compete effectively.
- Our ability to continue to attract users to our web sites.
- The level of use of the Internet to find information.
- Our ability to attract advertisers to our AdWords program.
- Our ability to attract web sites to our AdSense program.
- The mix in our net revenues between those generated on our web sites and those generated through our Google Network.
- The amount and timing of operating costs and capital expenditures related to the maintenance and expansion of our businesses, operations and infrastructure.
- Our focus on long term goals over short-term results.
- The results of our investments in risky projects.
- General economic conditions and those economic conditions specific to the Internet and Internet advertising.
- Our ability to keep our web sites operational at a reasonable cost and without service interruptions.
- The success of our geographical and product expansion.
- Our ability to attract, motivate and retain top-quality employees.
- Foreign, federal, state or local government regulation that could impede our ability to post ads for various industries.

- Our ability to upgrade and develop our systems, infrastructure and products.
- New technologies or services that block the ads we deliver and user adoption of these technologies.
- The costs and results of litigation that we face.
- Our ability to protect our intellectual property rights.
- Our ability to forecast revenue from agreements under which we guarantee minimum payments.
- Our ability to manage click-through fraud and other activities that violate our terms of services.
- Our ability to successfully integrate and manage our acquisitions.
- Geopolitical events such as war, threat of war or terrorist actions.

Because our business is changing and evolving, our historical operating results may not be useful to you in predicting our future operating results. In addition, advertising spending has historically been cyclical in nature, reflecting overall economic conditions as well as budgeting and buying patterns. For example, in 1999, advertisers spent heavily on Internet advertising. This was followed by a lengthy downturn in ad spending on the web. Also, user traffic tends to be seasonal. Our rapid growth has masked the cyclicality and seasonality of our business. As our growth slows, we expect that the cyclicality and seasonality in our business may become more pronounced and may in the future cause our operating results to fluctuate.

For these reasons, comparing our operating results on a period-to-period basis may not be meaningful, and you should not rely on past results as an indication of future performance. Quarterly and annual expenses as a percentage of net revenues may be significantly different from historical or projected rates. Our operating results in future quarters may fall below expectations, which could cause our stock price to fall.

If we do not continue to innovate and provide products and services that are useful to users, we may not remain competitive, and our revenues and operating results could suffer.

Our success depends on providing products and services that people use for a high quality Internet experience. Our competitors are constantly developing innovations in web search, online advertising and providing information to people. As a result, we must continue to invest significant resources in research and development in order to enhance our web search technology and our existing products and services and introduce new high-quality products and services that people will use. If we are unable to predict user preferences or industry changes, or if we are unable to modify our products and services on a timely basis, we may lose users, advertisers and Google Network members. Our operating results would also suffer if our innovations are not responsive to the needs of our users, advertisers and Google Network members, are not appropriately timed with market opportunity or are not effectively brought to market. As search technology continues to develop, our competitors may be able to offer search results that are, or that are perceived to be, substantially similar or better than those generated by our search services. This may force us to compete on bases in addition to quality of search results and to expend significant resources in order to remain competitive.

We generate our revenue almost entirely from advertising, and the reduction in spending by or loss of advertisers could seriously harm our business.

We generated approximately 95% of our net revenues in 2003 from our advertisers. Our advertisers can generally terminate their contracts with us at any time. Advertisers will not continue to do business with us if their investment in advertising with us does not generate sales leads, and ultimately customers, or if we do not deliver their advertisements in an appropriate and effective manner. If we are unable to remain competitive and provide value to our advertisers, they may stop placing ads with us, which would negatively affect our net revenues and business.

We rely on our Google Network members for a significant portion of our net revenues, and otherwise benefit from our association with them, and the loss of these members could adversely affect our business.

We provide advertising, web search and other services to members of our Google Network. The net revenues generated from the fees advertisers pay us when users click on ads that we have delivered to our Google Network members' web sites represented approximately 15% of our net revenues in 2003, and approximately 21% of our net revenues for the three months ended March 31, 2004, and we expect this percentage to increase in the future. We consider this network to be critical to the future growth of our net revenues. However, some of the participants in this network may compete with us in one or more areas. Therefore, they may decide in the future to terminate their agreements with us. If our Google Network members decide to use a competitor's or their own web search or advertising services, our net revenues would decline.

Our agreements with a few of the largest Google Network members account for a significant portion of net revenues derived from our AdSense program. In addition, certain of our key network members operate high-profile web sites, and we derive tangible and intangible benefits from this affiliation. If one or more of these key relationships is terminated or not renewed, and is not replaced with a comparable relationship, our business would be adversely affected.

Our business and operations are experiencing rapid growth. If we fail to manage our growth, our business and operating results could be harmed.

We have experienced, and continue to experience, rapid growth in our headcount and operations, which has placed, and will continue to place, significant demands on our management, operational and financial infrastructure. If we do not effectively manage our growth, the quality of our products and services could suffer, which could negatively affect our brand and operating results. To effectively manage this growth, we will need to continue to improve our operational, financial and management controls and our reporting systems and procedures. These systems enhancements and improvements will require significant capital expenditures and allocation of valuable management resources. If the improvements are not implemented successfully, our ability to manage our growth will be impaired and we may have to make significant additional expenditures to address these issues, which could harm our financial position. The required improvements include:

- Enhancing our information and communication systems to ensure that our offices around the world are well coordinated and that we can effectively communicate with our growing base of users, advertisers and Google Network members.

- Enhancing systems of internal controls to ensure timely and accurate reporting of all of our operations.

- Documenting all of our information technology systems and our business processes for our ad systems and our billing systems.

- Improving our information technology infrastructure to maintain the effectiveness of our search systems.

If we fail to maintain an effective system of internal controls, we may not be able to accurately report our financial results or prevent fraud. As a result, current and potential stockholders could lose confidence in our financial reporting, which would harm our business and the trading price of our stock.

Effective internal controls are necessary for us to provide reliable financial reports and effectively prevent fraud. If we cannot provide reliable financial reports or prevent fraud, our brand and operating results could be harmed. We have in the past discovered, and may in the future discover, areas of our internal controls that need improvement. For example, during our 2002 audit, our external auditors brought to our attention a need to increase restrictions on employee access to our advertising system and automate more of our financial processes. The auditors identified these issues together as a "reportable condition," which means that these were matters that in the auditors' judgment could adversely affect our ability to record, process, summarize and report financial data consistent with the assertions of management in the financial statements. In 2003, we devoted significant resources to remediate and improve our internal controls. Although we believe that these efforts have strengthened our internal controls and addressed the concerns that gave rise to the "reportable condition" in 2002, we are continuing to work to improve our internal controls, including in the areas of access and security. We cannot be certain that these measures will ensure that we implement and maintain adequate controls over our financial processes and reporting in the future. Any failure to implement required new or improved controls, or difficulties encountered in their implementation, could harm our operating results or cause us to fail to meet our reporting obligations. Inferior internal controls could also cause investors to lose confidence in our reported financial information, which could have a negative effect on the trading price of our stock.

We are migrating critical financial functions to a third-party provider. If this transition is not successful, our business and operations could be disrupted and our operating results would be harmed.

We are in the process of transferring to a third-party service provider our worldwide billing, collection and credit evaluation functions. The third-party provider will also track, on an automated basis, our growing number of AdSense revenue share agreements. These functions are critical to our operations and involve sensitive interactions between us and our users, advertisers and members of our Google Network. If we do not successfully implement this project, our business, reputation and operating results could be harmed. We have no experience managing and implementing this type of large-scale, cross-functional, international infrastructure project. We also may not be able to integrate our systems and processes with those of the third-party service provider on a timely basis, or at all. Even if this integration is completed on time, the provider may not perform to agreed upon service levels. Failure of the service provider to perform satisfactorily could result in customer dissatisfaction, disrupt our operations and adversely affect operating results. We will have significantly less control over the systems and processes than if we maintained and operated them ourselves, which increases our risk. If we need to find an alternative source for performing these functions, we may have to expend significant resources in doing so, and we cannot guarantee this would be accomplished in a timely manner or without significant additional disruption to our business.

Our business depends on a strong brand, and if we are not able to maintain and enhance our brand, our business and operating results would be harmed.

We believe that the brand identity that we have developed has significantly contributed to the success of our business. We also believe that maintaining and enhancing the "Google" brand is critical to expanding our base of users, advertisers and Google Network members. Maintaining and enhancing our brand may require us to make substantial investments and these investments may not be successful. If we fail to promote and maintain the "Google" brand, or if we incur excessive expenses in this effort, our business, operating results and financial condition will be materially and adversely affected. We anticipate that, as our market becomes increasingly competitive, maintaining and enhancing our brand may become increasingly difficult and expensive. Maintaining and enhancing our brand will depend largely on our ability to be a technology leader and to continue to provide high quality products and services, which we may not do successfully. To date, we have engaged in relatively little direct brand promotion activities. This enhances the risk that we may not successfully implement brand enhancement efforts in the future.

People have in the past expressed, and may in the future express, objections to aspects of our products. For example, people have raised privacy concerns relating to the ability of our recently announced Gmail email service to match relevant ads to the content of email messages. Some people have also reacted negatively to the fact that our search technology can be used to help people find hateful or derogatory information on the web. Aspects of our future products may raise similar public concerns. Publicity regarding such concerns could harm

our brand. In addition, members of the Google Network and other third parties may take actions that could impair the value of our brand. We are aware that third parties, from time to time, use "Google" and similar variations in their domain names without our approval, and our brand may be harmed if users and advertisers associate these domains with us.

Proprietary document formats may limit the effectiveness of our search technology by excluding the content of documents in such formats.

An increasing amount of information on the Internet is provided in proprietary document formats such as Microsoft Word. The providers of the software application used to create these documents could engineer the document format to prevent or interfere with our ability to access the document contents with our search technology. This would mean that the document contents would not be included in our search results even if the contents were directly relevant to a search. These types of activities could assist our competitors or diminish the value of our search results. The software providers may also seek to require us to pay them royalties in exchange for giving us the ability to search documents in their format. If the software provider also competes with us in the search business, they may give their search technology a preferential ability to search documents in their proprietary format. Any of these results could harm our brand and our operating results.

New technologies could block our ads, which would harm our business.

Technologies may be developed that can block the display of our ads. Most of our net revenues are derived from fees paid to us by advertisers in connection with the display of ads on web pages. As a result, ad-blocking technology could, in the future, adversely affect our operating results.

Our corporate culture has contributed to our success, and if we cannot maintain this culture as we grow, our business may be harmed.

We believe that a critical contributor to our success has been our corporate culture, which we believe fosters innovation, creativity and teamwork. As our organization grows, and we are required to implement more complex organizational management structures, we may find it increasingly difficult to maintain the beneficial aspects of our corporate culture. This could negatively impact our future success. In addition, this offering may create disparities in wealth among Google employees, which may adversely impact relations among employees and our corporate culture in general.

Our intellectual property rights are valuable, and any inability to protect them could reduce the value of our products, services and brand.

Our patents, trademarks, trade secrets, copyrights and all of our other intellectual property rights are important assets for us. There are events that are outside of our control that pose a threat to our intellectual property rights. For example, effective intellectual property protection may not be available in every country in which our products and services are distributed or made available through the Internet. Also, the efforts we have taken to protect our proprietary rights may not be sufficient or effective. Any significant impairment of our intellectual property rights could harm our business or our ability to compete. Also, protecting our intellectual property rights is costly and time consuming. Any increase in the unauthorized use of our intellectual property could make it more expensive to do business and harm our operating results.

We seek to obtain patent protection for our innovations. It is possible, however, that some of these innovations may not be protectable. In addition, given the costs of obtaining patent protection, we may choose not to protect certain innovations that later turn out to be important. Furthermore, there is always the possibility, despite our efforts, that the scope of the protection gained will be insufficient or that an issued patent may be deemed invalid or unenforceable.

We also face risks associated with our trademarks. For example, there is a risk that the word "Google" could become so commonly used that it becomes synonymous with the word "search." If this happens, we could lose protection for this trademark, which could result in other people using the word "Google" to refer to their own products, thus diminishing our brand.

We also seek to maintain certain intellectual property as trade secrets. The secrecy could be compromised by third parties, or intentionally or accidentally by our employees, which would cause us to lose the competitive advantage resulting from these trade secrets.

We are, and may in the future be, subject to intellectual property rights claims, which are costly to defend, could require us to pay damages and could limit our ability to use certain technologies in the future.

Companies in the Internet, technology and media industries own large numbers of patents, copyrights, trademarks and trade secrets and frequently enter into litigation based on allegations of infringement or other violations of intellectual property rights. As we face increasing competition, the possibility of intellectual property rights claims against us grows. Our technologies may not be able to withstand any third-party claims or rights against their use. Any intellectual property claims, with or without merit, could be time-consuming, expensive to litigate or settle and could divert management resources and attention. In addition, many of our agreements with members of our Google Network require us to indemnify these members for third-party intellectual property infringement claims, which would increase our costs as a result of defending such claims and may require that we pay damages if there were an adverse ruling in any such claims. An adverse determination also could prevent us from offering our products and services to others and may require that we procure substitute products or services for these members.

With respect to any intellectual property rights claim, we may have to pay damages or stop using technology found to be in violation of a third party's rights. We may have to seek a license for the technology, which may not be available on reasonable terms and may significantly increase our operating expenses. The technology also may not be available for license to us at all. As a result, we may also be required to develop alternative non-infringing technology, which could require significant effort and expense. If we cannot license or develop technology for the infringing aspects of our business, we may be forced to limit our product and service offerings and may be unable to compete effectively. Any of these results could harm our brand and operating results.

From time to time, we receive notice letters from patent holders alleging that certain of our products and services infringe their patent rights. Some of these have resulted in litigation against us. For example, Overture Services (now owned by Yahoo) has sued us, claiming that the Google AdWords program infringes certain claims of an Overture Services patent. It also claims that the patent relates to Overture Services' own bid-for-ad placement business model and its pay-for-performance technologies. We are currently litigating this case. If Overture Services wins, it may significantly limit our ability to use the AdWords program, and we also may be required to pay damages.

Companies have also filed trademark infringement and related claims against us over the display of ads in response to user queries that include trademark terms. The outcomes of these lawsuits have differed from jurisdiction to jurisdiction. A court in France has held us liable for allowing advertisers to select certain trademarked terms as keywords. We have appealed this decision. We were also sued in Germany on a similar matter where a court held that we are not liable for the actions of our advertisers prior to notification of trademark rights. We are litigating similar issues in other cases in the U.S., France and Germany.

In order to provide users with more useful ads, we have recently revised our trademark policy in the U.S. and Canada. Under our new policy, we no longer disable ads due to selection by our advertisers of trademarks as keyword triggers for the ads. As a result of this change in policy, we may be subject to more trademark infringement lawsuits. Defending these lawsuits could take time and resources. Adverse results in these lawsuits may result in, or even compel, a change in this practice which could result in a loss of revenue for us, which could harm our business.

We have also been notified by third parties that they believe one of our products or services violates their copyrights. Generally speaking, any time that we have a product or service that links to or hosts material in which others allege to own copyrights, we face the risk of being sued for copyright infringement or related claims. Because these products and services comprise the majority of our products and services, the risk of potential harm from such lawsuits is substantial.

Expansion into international markets is important to our long-term success, and our inexperience in the operation of our business outside the U.S. increases the risk that our international expansion efforts will not be successful.

We opened our first office outside the U.S. in 2001 and have only limited experience with operations outside the U.S. Expansion into international markets requires management attention and resources. In addition, we face the following additional risks associated with our expansion outside the U.S.:

- Challenges caused by distance, language and cultural differences.
- Longer payment cycles in some countries.
- Credit risk and higher levels of payment fraud.
- Legal and regulatory restrictions.
- Currency exchange rate fluctuations.
- Foreign exchange controls that might prevent us from repatriating cash earned in countries outside the U.S.
- Political and economic instability and export restrictions.
- Potentially adverse tax consequences.
- Higher costs associated with doing business internationally.

These risks could harm our international expansion efforts, which would in turn harm our business and operating results.

We compete internationally with local information providers and with U.S. competitors who are currently more successful than we are in various markets.

We face different market characteristics and competition outside the U.S. In certain markets, other web search, advertising services and Internet companies have greater brand recognition, more users and more search traffic than we have. Even in countries where we have a significant user following, we may not be as successful in generating advertising revenue due to slower market development, our inability to provide attractive local advertising services or other factors. In order to compete, we need to improve our brand recognition and our selling efforts internationally and build stronger relationships with advertisers. We also need to better understand our international users and their preferences. If we fail to do so, our global expansion efforts may be more costly and less profitable than we expect.

Our business may be adversely affected by malicious third-party applications that interfere with the Google experience.

Our business may be adversely affected by malicious applications that make changes to our users' computers and interfere with the Google experience. These applications have in the past attempted, and may in the future attempt, to change our users' Internet experience, including hijacking queries to Google.com, altering or replacing Google search results, or otherwise interfering with our ability to connect with our users. The interference often occurs without disclosure to or consent from users, resulting in a negative experience that users may associate with Google. These applications may be difficult or impossible to uninstall or disable, may reinstall themselves and may circumvent other applications' efforts to block or remove them. The ability to reach users and provide them with a superior experience is critical to our success. If our efforts to combat these malicious applications are unsuccessful, our reputation may be harmed, and our communications with certain users could be impaired. This could result in a decline in user traffic and associated ad revenues, which would damage our business.

If we fail to detect click-through fraud, we could lose the confidence of our advertisers, thereby causing our business to suffer.

We are exposed to the risk of fraudulent clicks on our ads. We have regularly paid refunds related to fraudulent clicks and expect to do so in the future. If we are unable to stop this fraudulent activity, these refunds may increase. If we find new evidence of past fraudulent clicks we may have to issue refunds retroactively of amounts previously paid to our Google Network members. This would negatively affect our profitability, and these types of fraudulent activities could hurt our brand. If fraudulent clicks are not detected, the affected advertisers may experience a reduced return on their investment in our advertising programs because the fraudulent clicks will not lead to potential revenue for the advertisers. This could lead the advertisers to become dissatisfied with our advertising programs, which could lead to loss of advertisers and revenue.

We are susceptible to index spammers who could harm the integrity of our web search results.

There is an ongoing and increasing effort by "index spammers" to develop ways to manipulate our web search results. For example, because our web search technology ranks a web page's relevance based in part on the importance of the web sites that link to it, people have attempted to link a group of web sites together to manipulate web search results. We take this problem very seriously because providing relevant information to users is critical to our success. If our efforts to combat these and other types of index spamming are unsuccessful, our reputation for delivering relevant information could be diminished. This could result in a decline in user traffic, which would damage our business.

Our ability to offer our products and services may be affected by a variety of U.S. and foreign laws.

The laws relating to the liability of providers of online services for activities of their users are currently unsettled both within the U.S. and abroad. Claims have been threatened and filed under both U.S. and foreign law for defamation, libel, invasion of privacy and other data protection claims, tort, unlawful activity, copyright or trademark infringement, or other theories based on the nature and content of the materials searched and the ads posted or the content generated by our users. From time to time we have received notices from individuals who do not want their names or web sites to appear in our web search results when certain keywords are searched. It is also possible that we could be held liable for misinformation provided over the web when that information appears in our web search results. If one of these complaints results in liability to us, it could be potentially costly, encourage similar lawsuits, distract management and harm our reputation and possibly our business. In addition, increased attention focused on these issues and legislative proposals could harm our reputation or otherwise affect the growth of our business.

The application to us of existing laws regulating or requiring licenses for certain businesses of our advertisers, including, for example, distribution of pharmaceuticals, adult content, financial services, alcohol or firearms, can be unclear. Existing or new legislation could expose us to substantial liability, restrict our ability to deliver services to our users, limit our ability to grow and cause us to incur significant expenses in order to comply with such laws and regulations.

Several other federal laws could have an impact on our business. Compliance with these laws and regulations is complex and may impose significant additional costs on us. For example, the Digital Millennium Copyright Act has provisions that limit, but do not eliminate, our liability for listing or linking to third-party web sites that include materials that infringe copyrights or other rights, so long as we comply with the statutory requirements of this act. The Children's Online Protection Act and the Children's Online Privacy Protection Act restrict the distribution of materials considered harmful to children and impose additional restrictions on the ability of online services to collect information from minors. In addition, the Protection of Children from Sexual Predators Act of 1998 requires online service providers to report evidence of violations of federal child pornography laws under certain circumstances. Any failure on our part to comply with these regulations may subject us to additional liabilities.

We also face risks associated with international data protection. The interpretation and application of data protection laws in Europe and elsewhere are still uncertain and in flux. It is possible that these laws may be interpreted and applied in a manner that is inconsistent with our data practices. If so, in addition to the possibility of fines, this could result in an order requiring that we change our data practices, which in turn could have a material effect on our business.

If we were to lose the services of Eric, Larry, Sergey or our senior management team, we may not be able to execute our business strategy.

Our future success depends in a large part upon the continued service of key members of our senior management team. In particular, our CEO Eric Schmidt and our founders Larry Page and Sergey Brin are critical to the overall management of Google as well as the development of our technology, our culture and our strategic direction. All of our executive officers and key employees are at-will employees, and we do not maintain any key-person life insurance policies. The loss of any of our management or key personnel could seriously harm our business.

The initial option grants to many of our senior management and key employees are fully vested. Therefore, these employees may not have sufficient financial incentive to stay with us.

Many of our senior management personnel and other key employees have become, or will soon become, substantially vested in their initial stock option grants. While we often grant additional stock options to management personnel and other key employees after their hire dates to provide additional incentives to remain employed by us, their initial grants are usually much larger than follow-on grants. Employees may be more likely to leave us after their initial option grant fully vests, especially if the shares underlying the options have significantly appreciated in value relative to the option exercise price. We have not given any additional grants to Eric, Larry or Sergey. Larry and Sergey are fully vested, and only a small portion of Eric's stock is subject to future vesting.

If we are unable to retain or motivate key personnel or hire qualified personnel, we may not be able to grow effectively.

Our performance is largely dependent on the talents and efforts of highly skilled individuals. Our future success depends on our continuing ability to identify, hire, develop, motivate and retain highly skilled personnel for all areas of our organization. Competition in our industry for qualified employees is intense, and we are aware that certain of our competitors have directly targeted our employees. Our continued ability to compete effectively depends on our ability to attract new employees and to retain and motivate our existing employees.

We have in the past maintained a rigorous, highly selective and time-consuming hiring process. We believe that our approach to hiring has significantly contributed to our success to date. As we grow, our hiring process may prevent us from hiring the personnel we need in a timely manner. In addition, as we become a more mature company, we may find our recruiting efforts more challenging. The incentives to attract, retain and motivate employees provided by our option grants or by future arrangements, such as through cash bonuses, may not be as effective as in the past. If we do not succeed in attracting excellent personnel or retaining or motivating existing personnel, we may be unable to grow effectively.

Our CEO and our two founders run the business and affairs of the company collectively, which may harm their ability to manage effectively.

Eric, our CEO, and Larry and Sergey, our founders and presidents, currently provide leadership to the company as a team. Our bylaws provide that our CEO and our presidents will together have general supervision, direction and control of the company, subject to the control of our board of directors. As a result, Eric, Larry and Sergey tend to operate the company collectively and to consult extensively with each other before significant decisions are made. This may slow the decision-making process, and a disagreement among these individuals could prevent key strategic decisions from being made in a timely manner. In the event our CEO and our two founders are unable to continue to work well together in providing cohesive leadership, our business could be harmed.

We have a short operating history and a relatively new business model in an emerging and rapidly evolving market. This makes it difficult to evaluate our future prospects and may increase the risk of your investment.

We first derived revenue from our online search business in 1999 and from our advertising services in 2000, and we have only a short operating history with our cost-per-click advertising model, which we launched in 2002. As a result, we have very little operating history for you to evaluate in assessing our future prospects. Also, we derive nearly all of our net revenues from online advertising, which is an immature industry that has undergone rapid and dramatic changes in its short history. You must consider our business and prospects in light of the risks and difficulties we will encounter as an early-stage company in a new and rapidly evolving market. We may not be able to successfully address these risks and difficulties, which could materially harm our business and operating results.

We may have difficulty scaling and adapting our existing architecture to accommodate increased traffic and technology advances or changing business requirements.

To be successful, our network infrastructure has to perform well and be reliable. The greater the user traffic and the greater the complexity of our products and services, the more computing power we will need. In 2004, we expect to spend substantial amounts to purchase or lease data centers and equipment and to upgrade our technology and network infrastructure to handle increased traffic on our web sites and to roll out new products and services. This expansion is going to be expensive and complex and could result in inefficiencies or operational failures. The costs associated with these adjustments to our architecture could harm our operating results. Cost increases, loss of traffic or failure to accommodate new technologies or changing business requirements could harm our operating results and financial condition.

Problems with bandwidth providers, data centers or other third parties could harm us.

We rely on third-party vendors, including data center and bandwidth providers. Any disruption in the network access or co-location services provided by these third-party providers or any failure of these third-party providers to handle current or higher volumes of use could significantly harm our business. Any financial or other difficulties our providers face may have negative effects on our business, the nature and extent of which we cannot predict. We exercise little control over these third party vendors, which increases our vulnerability to problems with the services they provide. We license technology and related databases from third parties to facilitate aspects of our data center and connectivity operations including, among others, Internet traffic management services. We have experienced and expect to continue to experience interruptions and delays in service and availability for such elements. Any errors, failures, interruptions or delays experienced in connection with these third-party technologies and information services could negatively impact our relationship with users and adversely affect our brand and our business and could expose us to liabilities to third parties.

Our systems are also heavily reliant on the availability of electricity, which also comes from third-party providers. If we were to experience a major power outage, we would have to rely on back-up generators. These back-up generators may not operate properly through a major power outage and their fuel supply could also be inadequate during a major power outage. This could result in a disruption of our business.

System failures could harm our business.

Our systems are vulnerable to damage or interruption from earthquakes, terrorist attacks, floods, fires, power loss, telecommunications failures, computer viruses, computer denial of service attacks or other attempts to harm our system, and similar events. Some of our data centers are located in areas with a high risk of major earthquakes. Our data centers are also subject to break-ins, sabotage and intentional acts of vandalism, and to potential disruptions if the operators of these facilities have financial difficulties. Some of our systems are not fully redundant, and our disaster recovery planning cannot account for all eventualities. The occurrence of a natural disaster, a decision to close a facility we are using without adequate notice for financial reasons or other unanticipated problems at our data centers could result in lengthy interruptions in our service. Any damage to or failure of our systems could result in interruptions in our service. Interruptions in our service could reduce our revenues and profits, and our brand could be damaged if people believe our system is unreliable.

We have experienced system failures in the past and may in the future. For example, in November 2003 we failed to provide web search results for approximately 20% of our traffic for a period of about 30 minutes. Any unscheduled interruption in our service puts a burden on our entire organization and would result in an immediate loss of revenue. If we experience frequent or persistent system failures on our web sites, our reputation and brand could be permanently harmed. The steps we have taken to increase the reliability and redundancy of our systems are expensive, reduce our operating margin and may not be successful in reducing the frequency or duration of unscheduled downtime.

More individuals are using non-PC devices to access the Internet, and versions of our web search technology developed for these devices may not be widely adopted by users of these devices.

The number of people who access the Internet through devices other than personal computers, including mobile telephones, hand-held calendaring and email assistants, and television set-top devices, has increased dramatically in the past few years. The lower resolution, functionality and memory associated with alternative devices make the use of our products and services through such devices difficult. If we are unable to attract and retain a substantial number of alternative device users to our web search services or if we are slow to develop products and technologies that are more compatible with non-PC communications devices, we will fail to capture a significant share of an increasingly important portion of the market for online services.

If we account for employee stock options using the fair value method, it could significantly reduce our net income.

There has been ongoing public debate whether stock options granted to employees should be treated as a compensation expense and, if so, how to properly value such charges. On March 31, 2004, the Financial Accounting Standard Board (FASB) issued an Exposure Draft, *Share-Based Payment: an amendment of FASB statements No. 123 and 95*, which would require a company to recognize, as an expense, the fair value of stock options and other stock-based compensation to employees beginning in 2005 and subsequent reporting periods. If we elect or are required to record an expense for our stock-based compensation plans using the fair value method as described in the Exposure Draft, we could have significant and ongoing accounting charges. See Note 1 of Notes to Consolidated Financial Statements included in this prospectus for a more detailed presentation of accounting for stock-based compensation plans.

We have recognized cost of revenue, and may continue to recognize cost of revenue, in connection with minimum fee guarantee commitments with our Google Network members.

We have entered into, and may continue to enter into, minimum fee guarantee agreements with a small number of Google Network members. In these agreements, we promise to make minimum payments to the Google Networks member for a pre-negotiated period of time, typically from three months to a year or more. If the fees we earn under an agreement are less than the fees we are obligated to pay to a Google Network member, we recognize cost of revenue to the extent of the difference. It is difficult to forecast with certainty the fees that we will earn under our agreements, and sometimes the fees we earn fall short of the minimum guarantee payment amounts. In each period to date, the aggregate fees we have earned under these agreements have exceeded the aggregate amounts we have been obligated to pay to the Google Network members. However, individual agreements have resulted in our recognition of cost of revenues as a result of our minimum fee guarantees. In 2003, we recognized an aggregate of approximately $22.5 million in cost of revenue related to those agreements. In the three-month period ending March 31, 2004, we recognized an aggregate of approximately $9.0 million in cost of revenue related to those agreements. At December 31, 2003, our aggregate outstanding minimum guarantee commitments totaled approximately $527.4 million. At March 31, 2004 our aggregate outstanding minimum guarantee commitments totaled approximately $544.8 million. These commitments expire between 2004 and 2007. We may recognize cost of revenues in the future in connection with these agreements, which could adversely affect our profitability.

We face risks associated with currency exchange rates fluctuations.

As we expand our international operations, more of our customers may pay us in foreign currencies. Conducting business in currencies other than U.S. dollars subjects us to fluctuations in currency exchange rates that could have a negative impact on our reported operating results. Hedging strategies we may implement to mitigate this risk may not eliminate our exposure to foreign exchange fluctuations. Additionally, hedging programs expose us to risks that could adversely affect our operating results, including the following:

- We have limited experience in implementing or operating hedging programs. Hedging programs are inherently risky and we could lose money as a result of poor trades.
- We may be unable to hedge currency risk for some transactions because of a high level of uncertainty or the inability to reasonably estimate our foreign exchange exposures.
- We may be unable to acquire foreign exchange hedging instruments in some of the geographic areas where we do business, or, where these derivatives are available, we may not be able to acquire enough of them to fully offset our exposure.

It has been and may continue to be expensive to obtain and maintain insurance.

We contract for insurance to cover potential risks and liabilities. In the current environment, insurance companies are increasingly specific about what they will and will not insure. It is possible that we may not be able to get enough insurance to meet our needs, may have to pay very high prices for the coverage we do get or may not be able to acquire any insurance for certain types of business risk. This could leave us exposed to potential claims. If we were found liable for a significant claim in the future, our operating results could be negatively impacted.

Acquisitions could result in operating difficulties, dilution and other harmful consequences.

We do not have a great deal of experience acquiring companies and the companies we have acquired have been small. We have evaluated, and expect to continue to evaluate, a wide array of potential strategic transactions. From time to time, we may engage in discussions regarding potential acquisitions. Any of these transactions could be material to our financial condition and results of operations. In addition, the process of integrating an acquired company, business or technology may create unforeseen operating difficulties and expenditures and is risky. The areas where we may face risks include:

- The need to implement or remediate controls, procedures and policies appropriate for a larger public company at companies that prior to the acquisition lacked these controls, procedures and policies.
- Diversion of management time and focus from operating our business to acquisition integration challenges.
- Cultural challenges associated with integrating employees from the acquired company into our organization.

- Retaining employees from the businesses we acquire.

- The need to integrate each company's accounting, management information, human resource and other administrative systems to permit effective management.

Foreign acquisitions involve unique risks in addition to those mentioned above, including those related to integration of operations across different cultures and languages, currency risks and the particular economic, political and regulatory risks associated with specific countries. Also, the anticipated benefit of many of our acquisitions may not materialize. Future acquisitions or dispositions could result in potentially dilutive issuances of our equity securities, the incurrence of debt, contingent liabilities or amortization expenses, or write-offs of goodwill, any of which could harm our financial condition. Future acquisitions may require us to obtain additional equity or debt financing, which may not be available on favorable terms or at all.

We occasionally become subject to commercial disputes that could harm our business.

From time to time we are engaged in disputes regarding our commercial transactions. These disputes could result in monetary damages or other remedies that could adversely impact our financial position or operations. Even if we prevail in these disputes, they may distract our management from operating our business.

We have to keep up with rapid technological change to remain competitive.

Our future success will depend on our ability to adapt to rapidly changing technologies, to adapt our services to evolving industry standards and to improve the performance and reliability of our services. Our failure to adapt to such changes would harm our business. New technologies and advertising media could adversely affect us. In addition, the widespread adoption of new Internet, networking or telecommunications technologies or other technological changes could require substantial expenditures to modify or adapt our services or infrastructure.

Our business depends on the growth and maintenance of the Internet infrastructure.

Our success will depend on the continued growth and maintenance of the Internet infrastructure. This includes maintenance of a reliable network backbone with the necessary speed, data capacity and security for providing reliable Internet services. Internet infrastructure may be unable to support the demands placed on it if the number of Internet users continues to increase, or if existing or future Internet users access the Internet more often or increase their bandwidth requirements. In addition, viruses, worms and similar programs may harm the performance of the Internet. The Internet has experienced a variety of outages and other delays as a result of damage to portions of its infrastructure, and it could face outages and delays in the future. These outages and delays could reduce the level of Internet usage as well as our ability to provide our solutions.

Shares issued, and option grants made, under our stock plans exceeded limitations in the federal and state securities laws.

Shares issued and options granted under our 1998 Stock Plan and our 2003 Stock Plan were not exempt from registration or qualification under federal and state securities laws and we did not obtain the required registrations or qualifications. Shares issued and options granted under our 2003 Stock Plan (No. 2) and our 2003 Stock Plan (No. 3) were not exempt from registration or qualification under federal securities laws and we did not obtain the required registrations or qualifications. As a result, we intend to make a rescission offer to the holders of these shares and options beginning approximately 30 days after the effective date of this registration statement. If this rescission is accepted, we could be required to make aggregate payments to the holders of these shares and options of up to $34 million plus statutory interest. Federal securities laws do not expressly provide that a rescission offer will terminate a purchaser's right to rescind a sale of stock that was not registered as required. If any or all of the offerees reject the rescission offer, we may continue to be liable under federal and state securities laws for up to an aggregate amount of approximately $34 million plus statutory interest. See "Rescission Offer."

****

Risks Related to Our Offering

Our stock price may be volatile, and you may not be able to resell shares of our Class A common stock at or above the price you paid.

Prior to this offering, our common stock has not been traded in a public market. We cannot predict the extent to which a trading market will develop or how liquid that market might become. The initial public offering price may not be indicative of prices that will prevail in the trading market. The trading price of our Class A common stock following this offering is therefore likely to be highly volatile and could be subject to wide fluctuations in price in response to various factors, some of which are beyond our control. These factors include:

- Quarterly variations in our results of operations or those of our competitors.
- Announcements by us or our competitors of acquisitions, new products, significant contracts, commercial relationships or capital commitments.
- Disruption to our operations or those of our Google Network members or our data centers.
- The emergence of new sales channels in which we are unable to compete effectively.
- Our ability to develop and market new and enhanced products on a timely basis.
- Commencement of, or our involvement in, litigation.
- Any major change in our board or management.
- Changes in governmental regulations or in the status of our regulatory approvals.
- Changes in earnings estimates or recommendations by securities analysts.
- General economic conditions and slow or negative growth of related markets.

In addition, the stock market in general, and the market for technology companies in particular, have experienced extreme price and volume fluctuations that have often been unrelated or disproportionate to the operating performance of those companies. Such fluctuations may be even more pronounced in the trading market shortly following this offering. These broad market and industry factors may seriously harm the market price of our Class A common stock, regardless of our actual operating performance. In addition, in the past, following periods of volatility in the overall market and the market price of a company's securities, securities class action litigation has often been instituted against these companies. This litigation, if instituted against us, could result in substantial costs and a diversion of our management's attention and resources.

We may apply the proceeds of this offering to uses that do not improve our operating results or increase the value of your investment.

We intend to use the net proceeds from this offering for general corporate purposes, including working capital and capital expenditures. We may also use a portion of the net proceeds to acquire or invest in companies and technologies that we believe will complement our business. However, we do not have more specific plans for the net proceeds from this offering and will have broad discretion in how we use the net proceeds of this offering. These proceeds could be applied in ways that do not improve our operating results or increase the value of your investment.

Purchasers in this offering will experience immediate and substantial dilution in the book value of their investment.

The initial public offering price of our Class A common stock is substantially higher than the net tangible book value per share of our Class A common stock immediately after this offering. Therefore, if you purchase our Class A common stock in this offering, you will incur an immediate dilution of $ in net tangible book value per share from the price you paid, based on the initial offering price of $ per share. The exercise of outstanding options and warrants will result in further dilution. For a further description of the dilution that you will experience immediately after this offering, please see "Dilution."

We do not intend to pay dividends on our common stock.

We have never declared or paid any cash dividend on our capital stock. We currently intend to retain any future earnings and do not expect to pay any dividends in the foreseeable future.

We will incur increased costs as a result of being a public company.

As a public company, we will incur significant legal, accounting and other expenses that we did not incur as a private company. We will incur costs associated with our public company reporting requirements. We also anticipate that we will incur costs associated with recently adopted corporate governance requirements, including requirements under the Sarbanes-Oxley Act of 2002, as well as new rules implemented by the Securities and Exchange Commission and the NYSE and Nasdaq. We expect these rules and regulations to increase our legal and financial compliance costs and to make some activities more time-consuming and costly. We also expect these new rules and regulations may make it more difficult and more expensive for us to obtain director and officer liability insurance and we may be required to accept reduced policy limits and coverage or incur substantially higher costs to obtain the same or similar coverage. As a result, it may be more difficult for us to attract and retain qualified individuals to serve on our board of directors or as executive officers. We are currently evaluating and monitoring developments with respect to these new rules, and we cannot predict or estimate the amount of additional costs we may incur or the timing of such costs.

The concentration of our capital stock ownership with our founders, executive officers, employees, and our directors and their affiliates will limit your ability to influence corporate matters.

After our offering, our Class B common stock will have ten votes per share and our Class A common stock, which is the stock we are selling in this offering, will have one vote per share. We anticipate that our founders, executive officers, directors (and their affiliates) and employees will together own approximately _____ % of our Class B common stock, representing approximately _____ % of the voting power of our outstanding capital stock. In particular, following this offering, our two founders and our CEO, Larry, Sergey and Eric, will control approximately _____ % of our outstanding Class B common stock, representing approximately _____ % of the voting power of our outstanding capital stock. Larry, Sergey and Eric will therefore have significant influence over management and affairs and over all matters requiring stockholder approval, including the election of directors and significant corporate transactions, such as a merger or other sale of our company or its assets, for the foreseeable future. In addition, because of this dual class structure, our founders, directors, executives and employees will continue to be able to control all matters submitted to our stockholders for approval even if they come to own less than 50% of the outstanding shares of our common stock. This concentrated control will limit your ability to influence corporate matters and, as a result, we may take actions that our stockholders do not view as beneficial. As a result, the market price of our Class A common stock could be adversely affected.

Provisions in our charter documents and under Delaware law could discourage a takeover that stockholders may consider favorable.

Provisions in our certificate of incorporation and bylaws, as amended and restated upon the closing of this offering, may have the effect of delaying or preventing a change of control or changes in our management. These provisions include the following:

- Our certificate of incorporation provides for a dual class common stock structure. As a result of this structure our founders, executives and employees will have significant influence over all matters requiring stock-holder approval, including the election of directors and significant corporate transactions, such as a merger or other sale of our company or its assets. This concentrated control could discourage others from initiating any potential merger, takeover or other change of control transaction that other stockholders may view as beneficial.

- Our board of directors has the right to elect directors to fill a vacancy created by the expansion of the board of directors or the resignation, death or removal of a director, which prevents stockholders from being able to fill vacancies on our board of directors.

- Our stockholders may not act by written consent. As a result, a holder, or holders, controlling a majority of our capital stock would not be able to take certain actions without holding a stockholders' meeting.

- Our certificate of incorporation prohibits cumulative voting in the election of directors. This limits the ability of minority stockholders to elect director candidates.

- Stockholders must provide advance notice to nominate individuals for election to the board of directors or to propose matters that can be acted upon at a stockholders' meeting. These provisions may discourage or deter a potential acquiror from conducting a solicitation of proxies to elect the acquiror's own slate of directors or otherwise attempting to obtain control of our company.

- Our board of directors may issue, without stockholder approval, shares of undesignated preferred stock. The ability to authorize undesignated preferred stock makes it possible for our board of directors to issue preferred stock with voting or other rights or preferences that could impede the success of any attempt to acquire us.

As a Delaware corporation, we are also subject to certain Delaware anti-takeover provisions. Under Delaware law, a corporation may not engage in a business combination with any holder of 15% or more of its capital stock unless the holder has held the stock for three years or, among other things, the board of directors has approved the transaction. Our board of directors could rely on Delaware law to prevent or delay an acquisition of us. For a description of our capital stock, see "Description of Capital Stock."

Future sales of shares by could cause our stock price to decline.

We cannot predict the effect, if any, that market sales of shares or the availability of shares for sale will have on the market price prevailing from time to time. Sales of our Class A common stock in the public market after the restrictions described in this prospectus lapse, or the perception that those sales may occur, could cause the trading price of our stock to decrease or to be lower than it might be in the absence of those sales or perceptions. Based on shares outstanding as of _____ 2004, upon completion of this offering, we will have outstanding _____ shares of common stock, assuming no exercise of the underwriters' over-allotment option. Of these shares, only the shares of Class A common stock sold in this offering will be freely tradable, without restriction, in the public market. We may, in our sole discretion, permit our officers, directors, employees and current stockholders who are subject to contractual lock-up agreements with us to sell shares prior to the expiration of their lock-up agreements.

After the selling restriction agreements pertaining to this offering expire, additional shares will be eligible for sale in the public market as follows:

Days After the Date of this Prospectus	Number of Shares Eligible for Sale in U.S. Public Market/ Percent of Outstanding Common Stock	Comment
At _____ days after the date of this prospectus and various times thereafter		
At _____ days after the date of this prospectus and various times thereafter		
At _____ days after the date of this prospectus and various times thereafter		
At _____ days after the date of this prospectus and various dates thereafter		

_____ of these shares are held by directors, executive officers and other affiliates and will be subject to volume limitations under Rule 144 under the Securities Act and various vesting agreements. In addition, the _____ shares issuable upon exercise of outstanding warrants and the _____ shares issuable upon exercise of outstanding options and reserved for future issuance under our stock plans will become eligible for sale in the public market to the extent permitted by the provisions of various vesting agreements, the selling restriction agreements and Rules 144 and 701 under the Securities Act of 1933, as amended, or the Securities Act. If these additional shares are sold, or if it is perceived that they will be sold, in the public market, the trading price of our common stock could decline.

In addition, we have agreed with our underwriters not to sell any shares of our common stock for a period of 180 days after the date of this prospectus. However, this agreement is subject to a number of exceptions, including an exception that allows us to issue an unlimited number of shares in connection with mergers and acquisition transactions, joint ventures or other strategic transactions. Morgan Stanley & Co. Incorporated and Credit Suisse First Boston LLC, on behalf of the underwriters, may release us from this lock-up arrangement without notice at any time. After the expiration of the 180-day period, there is no contractual restriction on our ability to issue additional shares. Any sales of common stock by us, or the perception that such sales could occur, could cause our stock price to decline.

SPECIAL NOTE REGARDING FORWARD-LOOKING STATEMENTS

This prospectus includes forward-looking statements. All statements other than statements of historical facts contained in this prospectus, including statements regarding our future financial position, business strategy and plans and objectives of management for future operations, are forward-looking statements. The words "believe," "may," "will," "estimate," "continue," "anticipate," "intend," "expect" and similar expressions are intended to identify forward-looking statements. We have based these forward-looking statements largely on our current expectations and projections about future events and financial trends that we believe may affect our financial condition, results of operations, business strategy, short term and long term business operations and objectives, and financial needs. In addition, a number of our "objectives," "intentions," "expectations" or "goals" described in "Auction Process" for qualification of bidders, the bidding process, the auction closing process, the pricing process and the allocation process are also forward-looking statements. These statements are based on current expectations or objectives of the auction process being used for our initial public offering that are inherently uncertain. These forward-looking statements are subject to a number of risks, uncertainties and assumptions, including those described in "Risk Factors."

In light of these risks, uncertainties and assumptions, the forward-looking events and circumstances discussed in this prospectus may not occur and actual results could differ materially and adversely from those anticipated or implied in the forward-looking statements.

Additional Information

1. HAROLD S. BLOOMENTHAL, SAMUEL WOLFF, 1 GOING PUBLIC HANDBOOK § 7:60 (2009).

2. HAROLD S. BLOOMENTHAL, SAMUEL WOLFF, 2 GOING PUBLIC HANDBOOK Appendix 13-1 (2009).

3. HAROLD S. BLOOMENTHAL, SAMUEL WOLFF, 2 GOING PUBLIC HANDBOOK Appendix 18-1 (2009).

4. HAROLD S. BLOOMENTHAL, SAMUEL WOLFF, 3A SEC. & FED. CORP. LAW § 5:48 (2d ed.) (2010).

5. HAROLD S. BLOOMENTHAL, SAMUEL WOLFF, 3B SEC. & FED. CORP. LAW §§ 9:30–9:31, 9:36, 9:46 (2d ed.) (2010).

6. AARON RACHELSON, CORPORATE ACQUISITIONS §§ 2:36–2:38, 11:18 (2010).

7. 2 WEST'S FED. ADMIN. PRAC. § 2291 (4th ed.) (2010).

8. STUART R. COHN, 2 SEC. COUNSELING FOR SMALL & EMERGING COMPANIES Appendix 6, Appendix 7 (2009).

9. FERDINAND S. TINIO, 28 A.L.R. FED. 811 (2010).

10. C.C. MARVEL, 50 A.L.R.2D 1228 (2010).

11. MELISSA K. STULL, 106 A.L.R. FED. 753 (2010).

12. RICHARD CORDERO, 111 A.L.R. FED. 83 (2010).

13. RICHARD J. LINK, 114 A.L.R. FED. 551 (2010).

14. LizabethAnn R. Eisen, *SEC Release: SEC Charges Google and its General Counsel David C. Drummond with Failure to Register Over $80 Million in Employee Stock Options Prior to IPO*, 1879 PLI/CORP 113 (2011).

15. Alan J. Berkeley, *Some Background and Simple FAQS About Dutch Auctions and the Google IPO*, SR043 ALI-ABA 353 (2010).

16.   Matthias Hild, *Google: An Intersection of Business and Technology*, 3 J. Bus. & Tech. L. 41 (2008).

17.   Eugene Choo, *Going Dutch: The Google IPO*, 20 Berkeley Tech. L.J. 405 (2005).

11.7   FRAUD IN PUBLIC SECURITIES OFFERINGS

As noted earlier, one of the risks of public securities offerings is increased exposure to liability in the form of shareholder suits claiming that information provided to investors was fraudulent. The first case in this section, *In Re Stac*, deals with a claim of fraud under federal securities laws. The second case, *Reardon*, deals with a claim of fraud under a state's securities laws.

11.7.1   Federal Securities Fraud

Recall the Securities Act of 1933 (Securities Act) deals with the initial registration and sale of securities and the Securities Exchange Act of 1934 (Exchange Act) deals with the dissemination of false and misleading information in conjunction with the purchase or sale of securities. Both the Securities Act and the Exchange Act provide for private causes of action. The private cause of action under the Securities Act is provided in Section 11. Section 11 provides a private remedy to any purchaser of securities who can prove that the registration statement contained a material omission or misrepresentation of information that a reasonable investor would rely upon in making an investment decision. Section 11 imposes strict liability on issuers and covers material omissions and misrepresentations regardless of whether they were made negligently or innocently. The private cause of action under the Exchange Act is provided in Section 10(b) and SEC Rule 10(b)(5). Section 10(b) provides generally that it is unlawful for any person to use manipulative or deceptive practices in conjunction with the purchase or sale of any security. Rule 10(b)(5) elaborates on Section 10(b) and provides that it is unlawful for any person:

(1) To employ any device, scheme or artifice to defraud; or

(2) To make any untrue statement of material fact or to omit to state a material fact necessary in order to make the statements made, in light of the circumstances under which they were made, not misleading; or

(3) To engage in any act, practice or course of business which operates or would operate as a fraud or deceit upon any person,

(4) In connection with the purchase or sale of any security.

Violations of Section 10(b) and Rule 10(b)(5) require the plaintiff to prove *scienter* — that the defendant knew the falsity of the statement made, or that the defendant acted in reckless disregard of the truth of the statement made.

Liability under Section 11 of the Securities Act, and Section 10(b) and Rule 10(b)(5) of the Exchange Act, can extend beyond the seller of securities and include underwriters, accountants and law firms that have been involved in the alleged wrongful activities.

The case below deals with an IPO and a plaintiff's claim that the Registration Statement and Prospectus issued in conjunction with the IPO violated both Section 11 of the Securities Act, and Section 10(b) and Rule 10(b)(5) of the Exchange Act.

IN RE STAC ELECTRONICS SECURITIES LITIGATION
89 F.3d 1399 (9th Cir. 1996)

T.G. NELSON, CIRCUIT JUDGE:

OVERVIEW

Timothy J. Anderson and other class representatives (collectively "Anderson") who purchased stock in Stac Electronics ("Stac") between May 7 and July 20, 1992, appeal the district court's dismissal of their class action under Sections 11 and 15 of the Securities Act of 1933, and Sections 10(b) and 20 of the Securities Exchange Act of 1934. Anderson alleges that Stac, certain of its officers and directors, and its lead underwriters, Alex. Brown & Sons, Inc., and Montgomery Securities ("Alex. Brown" and "Montgomery," respectively; collectively, "Underwriters"), made material misrepresentations or omissions regarding Stac's initial public offering ("IPO") of May 7, 1992.

FACTS AND PROCEDURAL HISTORY

This case arises from Stac's May 7, 1992, IPO of stock in its computer products company. Stac's most prominent product was the "Stacker," a data-compressing device which doubles storage capacity of disk drives in computers using Microsoft's MS-DOS and compatible systems.

The district court related the following facts, which are not disputed by the parties:

Before it went public, Stac's performance was mixed: it reported net losses per share in 1988, 1989, and 1990, and a net income per share of $.01 in 1991. It also reported revenues hovering around three quarters of a million dollars for 1988 and 1989, with increased revenues in 1990 (to $1.7 million) and 1991 (to $8.3 million).

There was a pronounced move upward-in both revenues and earnings per share-immediately prior to the initial public offering of Stac stock. While Stac reported revenues of $2.3 million and a loss of $.04 per share in the six months prior to March 31, 1991, it reported revenues of $17 million and earnings of $.21 per share in the six months prior to March 31, 1992. The increased revenues and earnings for the 1992 six month period derived from sales of Stacker.

On May 7, 1992, Stac went public, with an initial offering of 3,000,000 shares of common stock. The stock was sold to the public at $12.00 a share, with the individual named Defendants — except for Hoff, Finch and Robelen — selling some 508,000 shares. Neither Hoff, Finch, Robelen nor any of the venture capital Defendants is alleged to have sold any Stac stock during the class period [May 7 to July 20, 1992]. Defendants Alex. Brown & Sons, Inc. and Montgomery Securities acted as co-lead underwriters for the offering; they received substantial fees — some $2.5 million-for their services.

In connection with the IPO, Stac issued a Registration Statement and Prospectus ("Prospectus"), dated May 7, 1992, which included a four-page section on risk factors warning investors, *inter alia*, of Stac's competition, its dependence on Stacker, its reliance on distributors, its limited source of supply, and the potential volatility of its stock price. The Prospectus specifically discussed Microsoft's competitive threat, Stac's return policy and return allowances, and the possible effects on revenues of "channel fill," or heavy purchasing by distributors immediately following the introduction of a new product.

Apart from the Prospectus, information about Stac was disseminated to the public through "roadshow" presentations preceding the IPO and through analysts' reports and press statements by Stac officers and Underwriters following the IPO. All of these portrayed Stac as a good investment. While these portrayals at first seemed accurate — Stac rose to $15 after the IPO — success was short-lived. Stac's stock price fell on July 2, 1992, on the heels of another computer software company's announcement of poor third quarter results.

Stac Director Gary Clow ("Clow") and both Underwriters made statements to *Dow Jones News Wire* distinguishing Stac from the faltering software company. While Alex. Brown continued to rate Stac highly, Montgomery reduced its rating and earnings estimate for Stac on July 6, 1992. On July 20, 1992, Stac disclosed a disappointing third quarter performance, and on July 21, 1992, Stac stock declined to $5.50 per share. Within two days, plaintiffs filed suit. This initial suit was consolidated in the First Amended Class Action Complaint ("the FAC"), filed December 4, 1992.

The FAC asserted four claims for relief: I) against all defendants, alleging violation of Section 11 of the Securities Act, II) against all individual defendants and venture capital defendants, alleging controlling person liability under Section 15 of the Securities Act, III) against all defendants, alleging violations of Section 10(b) of the Exchange Act, and Rule 10b-5 of the Securities and Exchange Commission ("SEC"), and IV) against all individual defendants and venture capital defendants, alleging controlling person liability under Section 20(a) of the Exchange Act.

The complaint basically alleged that Stac went public knowing, but without disclosing, that Microsoft was about to come out with a competitive product (a new version of DOS incorporating Stacker-like data compression capabilities) that would take away Stac's market; that Stac engaged in sham licensing negotiations with Microsoft in order to stall introduction of its new product until Stac could make an IPO and unload stock; and that Stac insiders artificially inflated Stac's stock price prior to the IPO through channel "stuffing" and other fraudulent practices.

The district court dismissed the FAC with leave to amend in a detailed order dated September 17, 1993. The district court held that plaintiffs had failed to state a claim against Stac, the Underwriters, or any other named defendant, primarily on the basis of its finding that, to the extent it was required to do so, Stac had adequately disclosed all purported omissions in its Prospectus in a way that rendered the Prospectus not misleading. The order also stayed discovery.

I. DISCUSSION

Primary Liability.

Anderson argues that by "falsifying" its financial statements and failing to disclose pertinent information in its possession regarding Microsoft's plans to include data compression in its newest version of DOS, Stac misled investors and violated Section 11 of the Securities Act of 1933, Section 10(b) of the Exchange Act of 1934, and Rule 10b-5 of the Securities and Exchange Commission ("SEC"). The district court held that the SAC [Second Amended Complaint] failed to state a claim under Section 11, Section 10(b), or Rule 10b-5. It further held that the SAC failed to plead with sufficient particularity its Section 10(b) and Rule 10b-5 claims, as required by Fed.R.Civ.P. 9(b). We address the adequacy of Anderson's claims *de novo.*

On appeal, Anderson stresses the following: Stac and its officers: 1) failed to disclose imminent competition from Microsoft and deliberately stalled licensing negotiations with Microsoft in order to delay Microsoft's market entry; and 2) falsified its financial statements by artificially inflating reported results through channel "stuffing," accomplished by offering customers "special terms," including discounts and exceptional rights of return; understating its existing reserves; and failing to disclose Stac's "inevitable" impending decline.

Both Section 11 of the Securities Act and Section 10(b) of the Exchange Act require a plaintiff "adequately [to] allege a material misrepresentation or omission." Section 11 creates a private remedy for any purchaser of a security if any part of the registration statement,

when such part became effective, contained an untrue statement of a material fact or omitted to state a material fact required to be stated therein or necessary to make the statements therein not misleading . . . .

The plaintiff in a § 11 claim must demonstrate (1) that the registration statement contained an omission or misrepresentation, and (2) that the omission or misrepresentation was material, that is, it would have misled a reasonable investor about the nature of his or her investment. No scienter is required for liability under § 11; defendants will be liable for innocent or negligent material misstatements or omissions.

In contrast to Section 11, Section 10(b) requires scienter and covers statements made not only in the registration statement or prospectus but also in other documents and in oral communications. Section 10(b) of the Exchange Act of 1934 makes it unlawful "for any person . . . [t]o use or employ, in connection with the purchase or sale of any security . . . any manipulative or deceptive device or contrivance in contravention of such rules and regulations as the Commission may prescribe." SEC Rule 10b-5, promulgated under the authority of Section 10(b) provides that:

It shall be unlawful for any person . . .

(a) To employ any device, scheme, or artifice to defraud,

(b) To make any untrue statement of a material fact or to omit to state a material fact necessary in order to make the statements made, in light of the circumstances under which they were made, not misleading, or

(c) To engage in any act, practice, or course of business which operates or would operate as a fraud or deceit upon any person,

in connection with the purchase or sale of any security.

It is well established that claims brought under Rule 10b-5 and Section 10(b) must meet the particularity requirements of Fed.R.Civ.P. 9(b). Rule 9(b) states that, "[i]n all averments of fraud or mistake, the circumstances constituting fraud or mistake shall be stated with particularity. Malice, intent, knowledge, and other condition of mind of a person may be averred generally."

We closely examined the role of Rule 9(b) in the securities law context in our recent en banc decision, *In re GlenFed, Inc. Sec. Litig.*, ("*GlenFed II*") (discussing pleadings in the context of § 10(b) claims). With respect to scienter, we held that plaintiffs need only "say[ ] [it] existed." However, we went on to hold that plaintiffs "must aver with particularity the circumstances constituting the fraud." We explained that time, place and content allegations, while necessary, are insufficient by themselves to state a claim for fraud. "The plaintiff must set forth what is false or misleading about a statement, and why it is false. In other words, the plaintiff must set forth an explanation as to why the statement or omission complained of was false or misleading." Further, the statement or omission must be shown to have been false or misleading *when made.*

We agree with Anderson that our clarification of the scienter requirement in *GlenFed II* nullifies the district court's conclusion that Anderson's Section 10(b) and Rule 10b-5 claims must fail because Anderson did not plead scienter with particularity. The SAC sufficiently avers fraudulent intent on the part of Stac and its officers for the purpose of Rule 9(b). However, the remainder of our decision in *GlenFed II* supports the conclusion that Anderson's claims must nevertheless fail if, as the district court found, Anderson failed to plead the underlying fraud with particularity.

A. Stac's Prospectus.

The district court found that all of the omissions alleged by Anderson were either actually disclosed, or need not have been disclosed, in Stac's prospectus. The "materiality" of an omission is a fact-specific determination that should ordinarily be assessed by a jury. "[O]nly if the adequacy of the disclosure or the materiality of the statement is so obvious that reasonable minds could not differ are these issues appropriately resolved as a matter of law."

1. Microsoft's plans to include data compression.

The gravamen of Anderson's complaint concerns Stac's alleged failure to disclose its knowledge of Microsoft's plans to introduce data compression in its upcoming version of DOS. According to Anderson, Stac entered into "sham" licensing negotiations with Microsoft merely to stall Microsoft's introduction of its new product. In the SAC, Anderson also alleged that Stac's patents were inadequate to prevent others from using its technology to create competitive products. Prior to the district court's ruling, however, Stac won a $120 million judgment against Microsoft for patent infringement relating to Stacker. The district court properly took judicial notice of this judgment in determining that the proprietary and patent information provided in the Prospectus was not misleading. Anderson does not raise the patent issue on appeal.

Regarding the threat of Microsoft "looming," the district court correctly observed that the Prospectus makes detailed disclosures concerning the risk of competition. For instance, the Prospectus states that "[a] number of competitors offer products that currently compete with [Stac's] products" and that these companies "could seek to expand their product offerings by designing and selling products using data compression or other technology that could render obsolete or adversely affect sales of [Stac's] products." After noting Stac's dependence on sales of DOS-compatible products, the Prospectus observes that:

> One developer of a compatible operating system has licensed a competitive data compression product for incorporation into the latest version of the operating system. *There can be no assurance that Microsoft . . . will not incorporate a competitive data compression technology* in their products or that such a technology will not emerge as an industry standard.

Further, the Prospectus reveals that "[Stac] has licensed and intends to license portions of its core technology to others," a practice which it cautions could result in more competition and price reductions.

Anderson alleges that the "no assurance" language is inadequate and that Stac committed fraud because it *knew* that Microsoft was going to come out with a competitive product, but masked this knowledge as a contingency. Anderson quotes repeatedly the following statement: " "To warn that the untoward may occur when the event is contingent is prudent; to caution that it is only possible for the unfavorable events to happen when they have already occurred is deceit." "

We have rephrased this principle as follows: " "There is a difference between knowing that any product-in-development may run into a few snags, and knowing that a particular product has already developed problems so significant as to require months of delay." " The latter scenario characterizes the situation we encountered in *Warshaw v. Xoma Corp.* Corporate officers of Xoma, a biotech company which had yet to make a profit on its research, assured stockholders that FDA approval of its new drug was imminent, in spite of knowledge that the drug might not work and was unlikely to receive such approval. Anderson has not alleged any such contradictory statements here.

Anderson argues that Stac should have explicitly disclosed its ongoing negotiations with Microsoft and its knowledge that Microsoft intended to introduce data compression technology in its new version of DOS. In short, Anderson suggests that Stac was obliged not only to report on its own product line and marketing plans, but to report on and make predictions regarding *Microsoft's* intentions.

Stac counters, and we have held, that a company is not required to forecast future events or to caution "that future prospects [may not be] as bright as past performance."

We agree with Stac that another company's plans cannot be known to a certainty. Even assuming, as we must, that Microsoft had informed Stac that it planned to introduce data compression, Stac could not have known whether or not Microsoft would truly do so. As Stac points out, the contingency of the event is underscored by the fact that a competitive product was liable to violate Stacker's patent, as borne out by the state judgment against Microsoft. Also, the market already knew of the potential for Microsoft's inclusion of data compression technology, as Anderson alleged in the FAC.

Stac's financial statements.

Anderson also argues that Stac falsified its financial statements in the Prospectus by failing to disclose its channel — "stuffing" practices, its inadequate reserves, and its liberal distribution terms, all of which Anderson characterizes as illegitimate "borrowing" against the future to inflate its returns in the quarter prior to the public offering.

As the district court found, however, the Prospectus describes the phenomenon of channel-filling with its attendant risks, spells out Stac's liberal return policy, warns investors of Stac's exposure to the risk of product returns, and advises investors not to predict future returns on the basis of the results of any single quarter. The following excerpts from the Prospectus are instructive.

a. Channel fill:

> The Company's results of operation are subject to significant quarterly variations as a result of a number of factors and risks, including . . . the phenomenon of "channel fill . . . ." Channel fill often occurs following the introduction of a new product or a new version of a product as distributors buy significant quantities of a new product or version in anticipation of sales of such product or version. Following such purchases, the rate of distributor's purchases may decline.

b. Return policy, risk of returns, and return allowances:

> During the first six months of fiscal 1992 the Company's distributors and software reseller returned substantial quantities of the initial version of Stacker in exchange for version 2.0 of Stacker. Such returns did not materially impact operating results for the first six months of 1992, however, as allowances for returns of the initial version of Stacker had been established in fiscal 1991.

. . . .

Like other manufacturers of packaged software products, the Company is
exposed to the risk of product returns from distributors and direct reseller
customers.

The Company's return policy allows its distributors to return any new,
unused product in the distributor's inventory within . . . 60 days from the
notice of discontinuance of any product, or any version of a product, for a
credit or cash refund. Although the Company believes that it provides
adequate allowances for returns, there can be no assurance that actual
returns in excess of recorded allowances will not result in a material
adverse effect on business, operating results and financial condition.

c. Quarterly results:

The Company has historically experienced significant fluctuations in its
operating results, including net income, and anticipates that these fluctuations will continue. The Company operates with relatively little backlog,
and the majority of its revenues in each quarter results form orders
received in that quarter. Consequently, if near-term demand for the
Company's product weakens in a given quarter, the Company's operating
results for that quarter would be adversely affected . . . As a result, the
Company believes that period-to-period comparisons of its operating
results should not be relied upon as an indication of future performance.

The parties dispute whether, as a matter of law, these statements can be said to
disclose purported omissions and adequately caution investors as to specific risks.
We have recognized that the "bespeaks caution" doctrine "provides a mechanism by
which a court can rule as a matter of law that defendants' forward-looking
representations contained enough cautionary language or risk disclosure to protect
the defendant against claims of securities fraud." " The doctrine serves to "minimize
the chance that a plaintiff with a largely groundless claim will bring a suit and
conduct extensive discovery in the hopes of obtaining an increased settlement."

However, "[i]nclusion of *some* cautionary language is not enough to support a
determination as a matter of law that defendants' statements were not misleading."
"A motion to dismiss for failure to state a claim will succeed only when the
statements containing defendants' challenged documents include *enough* cautionary
language or risk disclosure that reasonable minds could not disagree that the
challenged statements were not misleading."

The district court did not rely on the bespeaks caution doctrine here because it
found that the Prospectus contained no forward-looking representations. By
definition, the bespeaks caution doctrine applies only to affirmative, forward-
looking statements. However, we have observed that the doctrine "merely represents the pragmatic application of two fundamental concepts in the law of securities
fraud: materiality and reliance."

Here, Anderson characterizes certain claims regarding Stac's Prospectus as both
material omissions and misstatements. For example, Anderson alleges that Stac

failed to disclose its inadequate reserves for returns. At the same time, Anderson characterizes the Prospectus's statement that "the Company believes it provides adequate allowances for returns" as an affirmative misstatement. The quoted sentence reads in full: "Although the Company believes it provides adequate allowances for returns, there can be no assurance that actual returns in excess of recorded allowances will not result in a material adverse effect on business, operating results, and financial condition."

Anderson further charges that Stac attributes its increase in revenues in the second quarter of 1992 to awards and favorable reviews, when in fact the increase was due to channel-fill, or what Anderson terms channel — "stuffing." In fact, Stac's conjecture that the 1992 increases were due "partially" to awards and reviews appears in the context of a section on "quarterly trends" which leads off with an explanatory and cautionary statement about the effects of channel fill on revenue. Analyzing the quoted statements in context leads to the inexorable conclusion that investors were specifically and adequately cautioned about the relevant risks. Insofar as Stac's alleged misstatements can be viewed as "optimistic projections," they are more than adequately covered by the bespeaks caution doctrine.

Bespeaks caution aside, Anderson fails to make precise allegations explaining how the alleged misstatements were misleading or untrue when made. "The plaintiff must set forth what is false or misleading about a statement, and why it is false. In other words, the plaintiff must set forth an explanation as to why the statement or omission complained of was false or misleading." Statements which imply factual assertions are actionable if any one of the following statements is inaccurate: "(1) that the statement is genuinely believed, (2) that there is a reasonable basis for that belief, and (3) that the speaker is not aware of any undisclosed facts tending to seriously undermine the accuracy of the statement." To the extent that Anderson alleges that Stac's Prospectus includes affirmative misstatements, it fails to make any showing that any of the implied assertions are inaccurate.

In light of the foregoing, we hold that the district court properly dismissed Anderson's Prospectus-based claims.

C. Pre-offering statements — roadshows.

The district court found that Anderson's allegations concerning roadshow presentations were not stated with adequate particularity under Rule 9(b). We agree with the district court's assessment.

Anderson states time, place and content of the roadshows in the broadest of terms, and suggests that Stac officers made positive forecasts to promote the Stac offering. This does not suffice under Rule 9(b) or *GlenFed II*, especially given that Anderson had fourteen months in which to undertake discovery prior to the stay. We hold that the district court properly dismissed these claims under Rule 9(b).

II

Underwriters' liability.

Anderson alleges that Stac, its outside directors, and other venture capital defendants, schemed with the Underwriters to project false reports following the IPO. But it provides no specific facts — no names, no meetings, no internal memoranda or documents, no specific conduct or statement-in support of its theory. Nor does it explain the disparity in the projections offered by Alex. Brown, which remained positive in its forecast, and by Montgomery, which lowered its rating of Stac after the failure of another computer company.

"In order to be liable for unreasonably disclosed third-party forecasts, defendants must have put their imprimatur, express or implied, on the projections." The facts must be stated with particularity as required by Fed.R.Civ.P. 9(b). "Plaintiffs must show why the projection disclosed lacked a reasonable basis." Finally, "Issuers need not reveal all projections. Any firm generates a range of estimates internally or through consultants. It may reveal the projection it thinks best while withholding others, so long as the one revealed has a "reasonable basis" — a question on which other estimates may reflect without automatically depriving the published one of foundation."

Anderson cannot rely on the group published information exception to Rule 9(b) because the SAC contains no allegations that outside directors or underwriters "either participated in the day-to-day corporate activities, or had a special relationship with the corporation, such as participation in preparing or communicating group information at particular times."

We agree with the district court that "[b]ecause the group pleading doctrine is not available, and because the roles of the underwriter, outside director, and venture capital defendants in propounding the allegedly fraudulent statements are left unspecified, it follows that Plaintiffs have not met the specificity requirements of Rule 9(b)."

For the reasons stated above, the district court's opinion is affirmed.

QUESTIONS

1. What are the differences between a claim under Section 11 of the Securities Act and a claim under Section 10(b) of the Exchange Act?

2. How did Stack's $120 million judgment against Microsoft bear on Anderson's claim that Stack engaged in "sham" licensing negotiations with Microsoft? How did Stack's judgment against Microsoft compare to Stack's 1990 and 1991 revenues? Why did Stack's judgment against Microsoft not increase the value of Stack's stock?

3. What is the difference between cautioning against an adverse event when the adverse event is uncertain and cautioning against an adverse event when the adverse event is likely?

4. What is "channel fill"? Why did Anderson's claim that Stack engaged in "channel fill" fail?

5. What is the "bespeaks caution" doctrine? How does the "bespeaks caution" doctrine serve the interests of the issuer and investor?

6. Why did the court find that the underwriters were not liable? Could underwriters be found liable if the issuer is not found liable? Could underwriters be found not liable if the issuer is found liable?

CASE NOTES

1. Inspire is a biopharmaceutical company that develops prescription drugs to treat diseases of the eyes, lungs and sinuses. Diquafosol, one of the company's leading products, is used to treat dry eye disease. Before Inspire could market Diquafosol, it had to prove to the FDA that the drug was safe and effective. The FDA requires clinical trials of a drug before it grants approval. In the clinical trials, a drug company must meet predetermined goals or "end points." Endpoints can be either subjective or objective. A subjective endpoint depends upon patients' reported experience, such as reduced itchiness of the eyes. An objective endpoint depends upon a repeatable, verifiable test. A common objective test for dry eye drugs is known as "corneal staining." A corneal staining test yields a score from zero to five. A score of zero indicates that patients' dry eyes have been completely eliminated, known as corneal clearing. In Study 105, Inspire undertook to demonstrate that Diquafosol was effective in a large patient population sample. Study 105 demonstrated that patients using Diquafosol had a statistically significant improvement in their corneal staining scores; Diquafosol improved patients' dry eyes, but did not eliminate the disease. However, Study 105 did not meet the subjective endpoint of patients' reduced sense of itchiness.

Because of the mixed results of Study 105, the FDA required Inspire to conduct further clinical tests which Inspire did by means of Study 109. Inspire was very secretive about Study 109 because it claimed it did not want to divulge the FDA's approval requirements information which could help Inspire's competitors plan their own clinical studies. During the course of Study 109, in July and November 2004, Inspire issued prospectuses in conjunction with two stock offerings. The prospectuses mentioned Study 109 only in very general, favorable terms. Also in July and August 2004, a number of Inspire directors sold off some of their shares in the company. On February 9, 2005, Inspire announced that Diquafosol had failed to meet its primary endpoint in Study 109. Inspire's stock price immediately dropped 45% from $16.00 to $8.88 per share. Shareholders in Inspire filed a class action suit alleging that Inspire had violated Sections 10(b) and 10(b)(5) of the Securities Exchange Act by fraudulently misleading investors as to the likelihood of success of Study 109 when it issued its prospectuses. A United States Magistrate Judge granted Inspire's motion to dismiss the investors' suit. The investors appealed. What result? *See* Cozzarelli v. Inspire Pharmaceuticals, Inc., 549 F.3d 618 (4th Cir. 2008).

2. *See also* Garber v. Legg Mason Inc., 2009 U.S. App. LEXIS 21404 (2nd Cir. 2009) (Nondisclosure of manager's departure along with $8.5 billion of client assets

was not materially misleading in registration statement and prospectus when information was available to investors in public domain in three newspaper articles and three statements filed with SEC prior to offering); Wagner v. First Horizon Pharmaceutical Corp., 464 F.3d 1273 (11th Cir. 2006) (There is no state of mind element to claim under Securities Act for preparing and signing materially misleading registration statements; liability under Securities Act for misleading registration statements is virtually absolute, even for innocent misstatements; pleading particularity requirement in fraud claims ensures defendant has sufficient information to formulate a defense); Med Safe Northwest, Inc. v. Medvial, Inc., 2001 U.S. App. LEXIS 127 (10th Cir. 2001) (Law firm that represented patent owner in negotiation of exclusive worldwide license to manufacture products pursuant to license, and filed security interest in patent with Patent and Trademark Office to ensure payment of legal fees, did not have a duty to disclose to investors the existence of its security interest because filing of security interest gave investors constructive notice of security interest; liability for the unlawful sale of unregistered securities under the Securities Act does not extend to attorneys whose involvement in transaction is only the performance of their professional services); Lilley v. Charren, 2001 U.S. App. LEXIS 19430 (9th Cir. 2001) (Statements in prospectuses regarding commercial viability of wind turbine project were not false and misleading sufficient to support securities fraud claims under Section 11 of Securities Act and Section 10(b) of Exchange Act even though some lower level employees expressed their belief that wind turbine project was not economically viable; corporate executives could reasonably rely on senior engineering personnel in making statements in prospectuses where there were not undisclosed material facts; company's statements in prospectuses regarding anticipated technical and commercial viability of wind turbine project were predictive and forward-looking; under "bespeaks caution" doctrine, prospectuses contained ample and comprehensive risk disclosures); Gill v. Three Dimension Systems, Inc., 87 F.Supp.2d 1278 (M.D. Fla. 2000) (Securities fraud action brought by inventor against venture capital firm alleging inventor was told orally that inventor would remain president of corporation satisfied particularity requirement for fraudulent inducement complaint); In re Nationsmart Corporation Securities Litigation, 130 F.3d 309 (8th Cir. 1997) (Particularity requirement for pleading fraud does not apply to claims under Section 11 of Securities Act because proof of fraud or mistake is not a prerequisite to establishing liability; to establish prima facie claim under Section 11 of Securities Act, plaintiff need only show he purchased security and that there was a material misstatement or omission; cautionary statements in stock offering materials cannot be general risk warnings or mere boilerplate, but must be detailed and specific to invoke "bespeaks caution" doctrine; seller's only defense in Section 11 Securities Act claim is that he did not know of the false material misstatement and could not have discovered misstatement with exercise of due diligence); In re Worlds of Wonder Securities Litigation, 694 F.Supp. 1427 (N.D. Calif. 1988) (Liability under Section 11 of Securities Act for giving false and misleading information in registration statement is limited to persons who signed registration statement, directors of issuer, underwriters of offering, and experts named as preparing or certifying portions of the registration statement; accountants cannot be held liable under Section 11 of Securities Act unless false or misleading information in registration statement can be expressly attributed to them; underwriter and securities brokerage firm could be held liable under Section 12(2) of Securities Act if purchasers sufficiently alleged that underwriter and brokerage firm were sellers within meaning of Section 12(2)); Aaron v. SEC, 446 U.S. 680 (1980) (Scienter is an element of a violation of Section 10(b) of the Exchange Act and Rule 10b-5; scienter is an element of a violation of the Securities Act section which makes it unlawful "to employ any device, scheme, or artifice to defraud" purchasers of securities; scienter is not an element of a violation of the Securities Act section which prohibits obtaining money or property "by means of any untrue statement of material fact or any omission to state a material fact;" scienter is not an element of a violation of the Securities Act section which makes it unlawful "to engage in any transaction, practice or course of business which operates or would operate as a fraud or deceit").

Additional Information

1. FRANCIS C. AMENDOLA ET AL., 69A AM. JUR. 2D SECURITIES REGULATION — Federal §§ 1388–1391, 1464, 1467 (2010).

2. KEITH A. ROWLEY, 11 CAUSES OF ACTION 2D 1 (2010).

3. KEITH A. ROWLEY, 9 CAUSES OF ACTION 2D 271 (2010).

4. DONALD J. LIDDLE, 9 AM. JUR. PROOF OF FACTS 2D 577 (2010).

5. JAMES L. RIGELHAUPT, 11 AM. JUR. PROOF OF FACTS 2D 271 (2010).

6. JOHN M. KLAMANN & BERT S. BRAUD, 45 AM. JUR. TRIALS 113 (2010).

7. F. S. TINIO, 1 A.L.R. FED. 1007 (2010).

8. MELISSA K. STULL, 105 A.L.R. FED 725 (2010).

9. GEORGE F. GABEL, 109 A.L.R. FED. 444 (2010).

10. MELISSA K. STULL, 112 A.L.R. FED. 387 (2010).

11. RICHARD J. LINK, 114 A.L.R. FED. 551 (2010).

12. MICHAEL J. KAUFMAN, EXPERT WITNESSES: SECURITY CASES § 1:7 (2009).

13. MICHAEL J. KAUFMAN, 26 SEC. LIT. DAMAGES § 6:31 (2009).

14. RICHARD CORDERO, 111 A.L.R. FED. § 83 (2010).

15. RONALD E. MALLEN, JEFFREY M. SMITH, 2 LEGAL MALPRACTICE §§ 13:7, 13:18–13:31 (2011).

16. HAROLD S. BLOOMENTHAL, SAMUEL WOLFF, 2 GOING PUBLIC HANDBOOK § 11:102 (2011).

17. ARNOLD S. JACOBS, 5F DISCLOSURE & REMEDIES UNDER THE SEC. LAWS Appendix A1 (2011).

18. ALSTON & BIRD LLP, 27 SEC. LIT. FORMS AND ANALYSIS § 4:8 (2010).

19. JASON H.P. KRAVITT, ELIZABETH A. RAYMOND, SECURITIZATION FIN. ASSETS § 11.01 (2010).

20. JOHN F. OLSON, ET AL, DIR. & OFF. LIAB. §§ 3:42–3:45 (2010).

21. ELIZABETH WILLIAMS, 191 A.L.R. FED. 623 (2011).

22. WESLEY KOBYLAK, 66 A.L.R. FED. 848 (2011).

23. KURTIS A. KEMPER, 49 A.L.R. FED. 392 (2011).

24. PATRICIA J. LAMKIN, 32 A.L.R. FED. 714 (2011).

25. E. H. SCHOPLER, 37 A.L.R.2D 649 (2011).

26. JAMES D. COX, THOMAS L. HAZEN, 2 TREATISE ON THE LAW OF CORPORATIONS § 12:9 (3d) (2011).

11.7.2   State Securities Fraud

Private securities actions under state law can be based on a state's securities statutes, common law fraud, negligent misrepresentation, breach of fiduciary duty and breach of a duty to disclose, among others. Securities fraud under states' securities statutes generally incorporate the elements of common law fraud and require (1) a false representation or concealment of a material fact, (2) designed to deceive another person, (3) made with the intent to deceive, (4) which does in fact deceive, (5) resulting in damage to the deceived person.

Just as with federal securities laws, liability under state securities laws can extend to underwriters, accountants and law firms that have been involved in the alleged wrongful transactions.

The case below deals with a claim of fraud under Texas securities law.

REARDON v. LIGHTPATH TECHNOLOGIES
183 S.W.3d 429 (Tex. App. 2005)

KEM THOMPSON FROST, JUSTICE.

In this complex securities fraud case, forty-five plaintiffs appeal from an adverse summary judgment. Appellants, shareholders in a technology company, brought suit against the company and others asserting a number of fraud-based claims, including common law fraud, statutory fraud under section 27.01 of the Texas Business and Commerce Code, securities fraud under the Texas Securities Act, and negligent misrepresentation, as well as a claim for breach of fiduciary duty. The trial court disposed of all claims by granting summary judgment on both traditional and no-evidence grounds. We affirm.

I. INTRODUCTION

The shareholders challenge the trial court's disposition of their fraud-based claims. They assert that the company's representations fraudulently induced them to consent to a transaction that dispossessed them of a part of their ownership in the company in exchange for a type of share, "the E share," the value of which depended upon the company's achievement of certain milestones based on the company's stock price and pretax income. The shareholders allege that the company misrepresented and failed to disclose material facts that would have shown the shareholders that the E shares were highly unlikely to convert to shares of Class A common stock because LightPath was highly unlikely to achieve the necessary milestones. The trial court found, among other things, that the shareholders failed to produce evidence that they suffered damages. We, too, conclude there is no genuine issue of material fact as to whether the shareholders suffered recoverable damages.

II. FACTUAL AND PROCEDURAL BACKGROUND

In the 1980s, Leslie Danziger created a type of optical glass she named "GRADIUM." This glass, Danziger believed, would make it possible to do with one lens, or fewer lenses, what it takes conventional glass multiple lenses to do. Danziger founded LightPath, a company incorporated in Delaware, to design, develop, manufacture, and market GRADIUM to the optics and related industries. However, GRADIUM was a new product that presented many challenges, one of which was that it had never been produced commercially. From 1985 through 1994, LightPath solicited private funding from investors for research and development. During this period, investors were advised that LightPath had limited capitalization and significant debts, and that the commercialization of LightPath's technology was a "highly speculative venture." By 1994, it became apparent to the company that it could not survive without a major infusion of capital. At that time, LightPath had generated no significant revenue. Despite continual undercapitalization, the company made progress with its technology. In 1994, LightPath brought a single type of lens to market. Anticipating a production scale-up, LightPath sought to expand the number and type of lenses the company was creating.

To generate much-needed capital, LightPath pursued the idea of an IPO with a number of investment banking firms, ultimately settling on D.H. Blair. In August 1995, D.H. Blair executed a letter of intent to underwrite an IPO for LightPath. D.H. Blair proposed an offering that initially would raise $8 million through the sale of stock and up to an additional $63 million through future warrant sales.

Recapitalization Plan

As a condition of the IPO, LightPath sought to recapitalize. In proposing this transaction to its existing shareholders, LightPath presented a two-part recapitalization plan in a proxy statement seeking approval of the transaction:

(1) Reverse Stock Split. The number of shares of existing LightPath stock (including those allocated for debt conversion and stock options) would be reduced through a 1-to-5.5 reverse stock split, which would effectively reduce the number of outstanding shares from 5.5 million to 1 million. If a majority of LightPath shareholders approved the reverse split, Class A common stock ("A shares") would be issued to effect this stock split.

Following a 1-to-5.5 reverse stock split, a shareholder with ninety-nine pre-split shares would have eighteen post-split shares, but both her share of ownership of the company and the total worth of her investment would remain the same.

(2) E Shares. LightPath would distribute, as a "non-taxable stock dividend," escrow shares — called "E shares" — to pre-IPO shareholders. All holders of A shares were to receive four E shares for every post-split A share. The E shares would retain voting power, but they would be non-tradeable unless and until LightPath reached certain performance milestones. These milestones would be triggered should LightPath achieve certain targets for the price of it's a shares and/or for its pretax income. The E shares would be redeemed for nominal value unless they converted to A shares by 2000.

LightPath, through Danziger, who was then its President and Chairman of the Board, told the Investors that the company could not effectively market and sell GRADIUM products or fund the planned expansion of its manufacturing operations without the IPO. In September 1995, a majority of shareholders approved the proposed recapitalization plan, and the reverse stock split was accomplished. Every 5.5 shares of Class A stock were redeemed for one share, and LightPath distributed E shares to its existing shareholders.

The IPO offered 1.6 million units. A single unit in the IPO was sold for $5.00. Purchasers received one A share and two warrants per unit, and all 1.6 million units, plus 240,000 in over allotment, were sold. The IPO raised $9.2 million in capital for LightPath. After the IPO, shareholders exercised their warrants, and the IPO raised more than $65 million. Despite the success of the IPO, LightPath did not achieve the E share financial milestones set forth in the proxy statement. Consequently, the E shares did not convert to A shares. The Investors filed suit in June 2000.

The Investors' Claims

The Investors asserted claims of fraud, statutory fraud under Section 27.01 of the Texas Business and Commerce Act, securities fraud under the Texas Securities Act, negligent misrepresentation, and breach of fiduciary duty. The Investors alleged that LightPath misrepresented and failed to disclose material information that the Investors would have found important in approving the recapitalization and IPO transaction, fraudulently inducing the Investors to consent to a transaction that decreased their interest in LightPath. The Investors assert that LightPath misrepresented and failed to disclose facts that would have shown the Investors that the E shares were highly unlikely to convert to A shares because LightPath was highly unlikely to achieve the necessary milestones. The Investors also alleged that LightPath made a material misrepresentation that the post-IPO value of the E shares would be five dollars per share.

LightPath's Motions for Summary Judgment

LightPath moved for traditional and no-evidence summary judgment, asserting the following grounds:

LightPath did not make any material misrepresentations or omissions.

The Texas Securities Act does not apply because any alleged material misrepresentations or omissions by LightPath did not occur in the context of a sale of securities.

The Investors cannot recover because they have suffered no damages.

LightPath did not owe the Investors a fiduciary duty.

The trial court granted this motion and rendered a final judgment dismissing all of the Investors' claims against LightPath. The trial court specifically based its judgment on all of the above-stated summary-judgment grounds.

III. ISSUES PRESENTED

The Investors raise the following issues for appellate review:

Misrepresentation

Did the trial court err in granting summary judgment in favor of LightPath on the ground that LightPath conclusively disproved the making of a material misrepresentation or omission?

Did the trial court err in granting summary judgment in favor of LightPath on the ground that the Investors failed to produce evidence that LightPath made a material misrepresentation or omission?

Texas Securities Act

Did the trial court err in granting summary judgment in favor of LightPath against the Investors' securities fraud claim on the ground that LightPath conclusively disproved that an alleged material misrepresentation or omission occurred in the context of a sale of securities?

Did the trial court err in granting summary judgment in favor of LightPath against the Investors' securities fraud claim on the ground that the Investors failed to produce evidence that an alleged material misrepresentation or omission occurred in the context of a sale of securities?

Damages

Did the trial court err in granting summary judgment in favor of LightPath on the ground that LightPath conclusively disproved that the Investors suffered damages?

Did the trial court err in granting summary judgment in favor of LightPath on the ground that the Investors failed to produce evidence that they suffered damages?

V. ANALYSIS

If the trial court was correct in its determination that summary judgment on all of the Investors' claims is appropriate because the Investors suffered no damages, then it would not be necessary for this court to reach most of the Investors' other issues. Therefore, we will focus on the issue of whether the evidence raises a genuine issue of material fact regarding the Investors' alleged damages, after first addressing a liability issue.

A. Is there a genuine issue of material fact as to whether LightPath represented that the post-IPO value of the E shares would be five dollars per share?

The Investors assert that there is a genuine issue of material fact as to whether LightPath represented that the post-IPO value of the E shares would be five dollars per share. The Investors base this argument on the proxy solicitation letter that LightPath sent the Investors regarding the IPO ("Proxy Letter") and alleged admissions by Danziger at her deposition that LightPath made such a representation. The Proxy Letter states:

> We are pleased to inform you that LightPath has entered into a Letter of Intent for a "firm commitment" underwriting with New York City-based D.H. Blair Investment Banking Corporation for a public offering of LightPath Units. Each Unit will consist of one share of Class A Common Stock and two warrants, as explained in detail in the enclosed Notice and Proxy Statement . . . .

> The Board of Directors is very enthusiastic about this proposed [IPO]. The deal structure as proposed by the Letter of Intent, which is described in the enclosed Proxy Statement, with A shares and E shares and a $5.00 Unit Offering price, is not unusual for this type of "early stage company" financing. The Board is pleased with the small reduction in the aggregate number of shares held by current LightPath shareholders (10% from 5,500,000 to 5,000,000) and that, following the Offering and until warrants are exercised, the current shareholders as a group retain voting control over the affairs of our Company . . .

The structure of this financing, as proposed by the Letter of Intent, is detailed in the enclosed Notice and Proxy Statement. The following summarizes the terms:

> 1.) 1.6 Million Units, consisting of one share of Class A Common Stock and two warrants, will be offered for a Unit price of $5.00 for a total of $8,000,000, with an option to the underwriter to sell an over-allotment of up to an additional 15% of the Units offered, or an additional 240,000 Units. If the over-allotment is sold in full, the gross proceeds will be $9,200,000. Based on the $5.00 Unit price, the post-IPO market valuation is estimated at $33–34.2 Million depending upon the sale of the over-allotment . . . .

> 6.) The Class E-1, E-2, and E-3 shares will automatically convert to Class A Common shares (on a one-for-one basis) upon the achievement by the Company of specific performance milestones (described in the enclosed Proxy Statement) which have been set by the underwriter and agreed to by

the Company; they are based on discounted net profit targets from our Business Plan. The E shares may not be sold, assigned or transferred until converted to A shares. If certain milestones are not met, the corresponding Class E stock is subject to redemption in September, 2000.

The proxy statement enclosed with the proxy letter accurately stated the milestones that had to be met before any of the E shares would convert into A shares. It also stated that on September 30, 2000, all E shares not previously converted into A shares would be redeemed by LightPath for $.00001 per share.

After reviewing the record under the applicable standard of review, we conclude that there is no genuine issue of material fact as to whether the Proxy Letter contains a representation that E shares would have a five dollar per share value after the IPO. The Proxy Letter does not contain such a representation. The Proxy Letter states that the units to be sold in the IPO will consist of one A share and two warrants to purchase A shares, priced at five dollars per unit. The Proxy Letter states that the anticipated IPO would generate $8 million to $9.2 million depending on sale of the over-allotment. In the sentence that the Investors claim constitutes a representation that the E shares would have a value of five dollars per share, the Proxy Letter states that, based on an IPO price of five dollars per unit, "the post-IPO market valuation is estimated at $33–34.2 Million depending upon the sale of the over-allotment." As a matter of law, this statement is not a representation that the E shares will be worth five dollars per share. The Proxy Letter does not state a value for the A shares or for the E shares. The Proxy Letter does not state who estimated "the post-IPO market valuation" of LightPath to be $33–34.2 million. Using a five dollar per unit price, the sale of 1.6 million units would generate $8 million. The underwriter also had an option to sell an over-allotment of up to 240,000 more units, which would generate up to an additional $1.2 million. Even if one subtracts from this range the range of amounts that might be raised in the IPO, that would only indicate that, other than this amount, "the post-IPO market valuation" is estimated to be $25 million. The Proxy Letter and enclosed Proxy Statement state that the E shares may not be sold or assigned until converted into A shares and that they will not convert to A shares unless specific milestones are achieved. As a matter of law, the Proxy Letter does not contain a representation that the E shares would be worth five dollars a share.

The Investors assert that Danziger admitted at her deposition that LightPath made such a representation. At the time of her deposition, Danziger was no longer an officer of LightPath, although she was a director. First, the testimony in question consists of Danziger's answers to questions from the Investors' counsel regarding the Proxy Letter. Danziger does not testify regarding any allegation of the post-IPO value of the E shares not contained in the Proxy Letter. Second, Danziger states that she is not sure how the calculation of $33–34.2 million was done and that she does not remember the basis for it. Danziger also states that the E shares were clearly not tradeable. In a series of leading questions, counsel for the Investors elicited affirmative answers from Danziger as to the following propositions:

> The old shareholders in the reverse stock split were going to get one million A shares at five dollars per share, which totals $5 million.

$5 million of the $33 million valuation comes from the value of the old shareholders' stock.

$8 million would be generated from the IPO.

Subtracting $5 million and $8 million from $33 million leaves $20 million, which divided by four million E shares is five dollars per E share.

Danziger then testified, in answer to leading questions, that the Proxy Letter stated that the E shares would have a value of five dollars per share. Although Danziger signed the Proxy Letter, her testimony more than five years later does not add words to the document. The Investors base their argument on deductions and inferences from the $33–34.2 million market valuation mentioned in the letter; however, at her deposition, Danziger stated she did not remember the basis of the calculation of $33–34.2 million. Furthermore, her admissions are not binding on LightPath as a judicial admission, and they are conclusory statements about the Proxy Letter that do not raise a genuine issue of material fact. Therefore, the trial court correctly granted summary judgment as to the alleged misrepresentation by LightPath in the Proxy Letter that the E shares would have a post-IPO value of five dollars per share. In addressing the Investors' arguments that they raised a genuine issue of material fact as to damages, we presume for the sake of argument that they raised a genuine issue of material fact as to their other allegations of fraud.

VI. CONCLUSION

The trial court correctly granted summary judgment as to the alleged misrepresentation by LightPath in the Proxy Letter that the E shares would have a post-IPO value of five dollars per share. Therefore, that alleged misrepresentation cannot provide a basis for the Investors' alleged damages. Under the applicable standard of review, the damage evidence upon which the Investors rely is speculative, conclusory, and does not raise a genuine issue of material fact as to the essential element of the Investors' alleged damages. Having concluded that the Investors did not establish a genuine issue of material fact as to damages, we overrule the Investors' issue in this regard. Under the law-of-the-case doctrine, we overrule the Investors' issue regarding the trial court's ability to exercise personal jurisdiction over D.H. Blair. Given these rulings, it is not necessary to reach the Investors' remaining issues. We affirm the trial court's judgment.

QUESTIONS

1. Following the reverse stock split, the pre-IPO shareholders held 1 million shares of Class A Common Stock. In the IPO, 1.84 million shares of Class A Common stock were issued (1.6 million plus 240,000 over-allotment). The conversion of the unit warrants to Class A Common Stock resulted in the issuance of another 3.68 million shares of Class A Common Stock (1.84 million shares × 2 warrants/ share). The total issued and outstanding Class A Common Stock in June 2000 when the investors filed suit was 6.52 million shares (1 million + 1.84 million + 3.68 million). Valued at $5 per share, the value of LightPath in June 2000 would be $32.6 million (6.52 million shares × $5 per share) close to the value estimated by the directors of $33 — $34.2 million). However, if, as the investors claimed, the 4 million

E shares were also valued at $5 per share, the value of LightPath in June 2000 would be $52.6 million ($32.6 million + $20 million), nearly double the value estimated by the directors. Do the numbers speak for themselves in terms of the investors' claim that the directors had valued the E shares at $5 per share?

2.   Danziger, who was president and chairman of the board of LightPath at the time of the proxy solicitation, testified that the Proxy Letter stated that the E shares would have a value of five dollars per share. Why did the court dismiss Daniziger's testimony?

3.   Ms. Danziger's personal narrative is very interesting. See http://www.gracecathedral.org/enrichment/dispatches/dis_19980706.shtml

CASE NOTES

1.   Cobalt raised capital through the sale of securities to members of the public. Cobalt was operated by two persons with extensive criminal histories — Shapario and Stitsky. Shapario was a convicted felon and Stitsky, who served 33 months in prison, had been indicted for tax fraud, money laundering and securities fraud. Lum, Danzis is a New Jersey law firm that represented Cobalt, and Chapman is a partner in Lum, Danzis. Lum, Danzis prepared three PPMs for Cobalt which Shapario and Stitsky used to perpetrate a Ponzi scheme resulting in over $22 million in losses to investors. In the PPMs, Lum, Danzis failed to disclose Shapario's and Stitsky's criminal histories and, after an FBI raid on Cobalt's offices, Lum, Danzis attempted to back-date and amend one of the PPMs to disclose Shapario's and Stitsky's criminal background. Lum, Danzis also served as escrow agent for Cobalt's stock subscription documents. After Cobalt collapsed in March 2006, investors filed suit against Lum, Danzis alleging the law firm had actual knowledge of the fraud perpetrated by Cobalt and substantially assisted Cobalt in perpetrating the fraudulent Ponzi scheme. Documents uncovered during an SEC proceeding revealed that it was Shapario who hired Chapman and the Lum law firm, and that Chapman was well aware of Shapario and Stitsky's extensive criminal backgrounds. The Lum law firm asserted that all they did was draft PPMs for a client and that any misrepresentations in the PPMs were irrelevant to the question of whether they had actual knowledge of the Ponzi scheme operated by Cobalt. The trial court granted Lum, Danzis' motion to dismiss. The investors appealed. What result? *See* Oster v. Kirschner, 905 N.Y.S.2d 69 (N.Y. App. Div. 2010).

2.   *See also* Solow v. Heard McElroy & Vestal, L.L.P., 7 So.3d 1269 (La. Ct. App. 2009) (Accounting firm licensed under Accounting Act owes duty only to persons who engage firm to provide financial statements, to compile, review, certify or audit financial information, or to render an opinion on financial statements or financial information; accounting firm was not a seller of, or substantial contributor to, sale of securities, but merely participated in events leading up the sale by conducting an audit); Apollo Capital Fund, LLC v. Roth Capital Partners, LLC, 158 Cal.App.4th 226 (Cal. Ct. App. 2007) (Allegations that broker-dealer, who was placement agent for internet service company's bridge notes, told investors that early pre-payment of bridge notes was "guaranteed," and that preferred stock placement to re-pay bridge notes was mostly complete and would close within three weeks, satisfied reliance requirement of investors' common law fraud claim against broker-dealer,

despite statement in purchase agreement that investors were not relying on any other oral or written representations; allegation that purchase agreement failed to disclose conditions in placement agent agreement to proceed with preferred stock offering stated with particularity a claim against broker-dealer for fraud); Sullivan v. Mebane Packaging Group, Inc., 158 N.C. App. 19 (N.C. Ct. App. 2003) (Corporation's waiver of its call right to departing shareholder's stock was not material to shareholder's agreement to sell stock to chief financial officer and could not form basis of fraud claim against chief financial officer; increase in stock value after shareholder agreed to sell shares could not be a factor in shareholder's decision to sell and thus was not material so as to support fraud claim against buyer of stock; evidence that shareholder obtained outside advice throughout process of negotiating sale of stock rebutted presumption under theory of constructive trust against directors and officers as fiduciaries); Greenberg Traurig of New York, P.C. v. Moody, 161 S.W.3d 56 (Tex. App. 2004) (Under New York law, claim of fraud based on fraudulent omission of information can only be maintained when defendant had a duty to disclose omitted material information; under New York law, no fiduciary relationship exists between attorneys and investors absent a contractual relationship between them; under New York law, law firm that assisted company in initial public offering had no attorney-client relationship with investors); Olczyk v. Cerion Technologies, Inc., 308 Ill.App.3d 905 (Ill. App. Ct. 1999) (Corporation's failure to disclose in its prospectus at time of offering that its two largest customers, accounting for over 80% of sales, had informed corporation that it was being eliminated as a supplier, stated a claim for securities fraud; bespeaks caution doctrine applies only to statements concerning future plans, forecasts and projections; bespeaks caution doctrine cannot shield defendant from liability where it is alleged that defendant possessed material adverse information which defendant failed to disclose at time of securities offering).

Additional Information

1. WILLIAM JORDAN, 33 No. 2 PROFESSIONAL LIABILITY REPORTER ART. 25 (2008).

2. ROGER J. MAGNUSON, 3 SHAREHOLDER LITIGATION §§ 24:14, 24:32 (2010).

3. D. W. Hunt, *Sizing Up Private Securities Fraud Litigation In California State Courts*, 49 SEP Orange County Law. 23 (2007).

4. Matthew D. Haydo, *A Class Action Securities Fraud Claim Brought Under State Law By Holders Of Securities Is Preempted By A Federal Act Purporting To Encompass Claims Brought By Purchasers And Sellers: Merrill Lynch, Pierce, Fenner & Smith, Inc. v. Dabit*, 45 DUQ. L. REV. 325 (2007).

5. Erin M. O'Gara, *Comfort With The Majority: The Eighth Circuit Weighs In On The Proper Pleading Test For A Securities Fraud Claim In Florida State Board Of Administration v. Green Tree Financial Corporation, 270 F.3D 645 (8th Cir. 2001)*, 82 NEB. L. REV. 1276 (2004).

6. Kathy Patrick, *The Liability Of Lawyers For Fraud Under The Federal And State Securities Laws*, 34 ST. MARY'S L.J. 915 (2003).

7. *Calif. High Court Oks Ruling That Bars Coverage For State Securities Fraud Pact*, 12 No. 21 Andrews Ins. Coverage Litig. Rep. 3 (2002).

8. Joseph P. Borg, *"Criminalization" Of Securities Fraud On The State Level: New York And Beyond*, 1273 PLI/Corp 287 (2001).

9. Securities Fraud, *Securities Fraud Suit Eligible For State Court Venue, D DE Rules*, 14 No. 6 Andrews Del. Corp. Litig. Rep. 7 (2000).

10. Michael G. Dailey, *Preemption Of State Court Class Action Claims For Securities Fraud: Should Federal Law Trump?*, 67 U. Cin. L. Rev. 587 (1999).

11. Richard W. Painter, *Responding To A False Alarm: Federal Preemption Of State Securities Fraud Causes Of Action*, 84 Cornell L. Rev. 1 (1998).

12. Michael A. Perino, *Fraud And Federalism: Preempting Private State Securities Fraud Causes Of Action*, 50 Stan. L. Rev. 273 (1998).

13. Hope V. Samborn, *Fear Of Filing: Securities Fraud Plaintiffs Steering Clear of Federal Restrictions by Suing In State Court, Study Says*, 83-May A.B.A. J. 28 (1997).

14. Ira M. Dansky, *Securities Issues: Private Placements: Disclosure; Blue Sky And Other State Laws; Fraud Situations*, 458 PLI/Corp 205 (1984).

11.8 DUE DILIGENCE

Due diligence requires that persons undertake reasonable efforts to determine the true facts of a transaction. In the context of securities law, due diligence is primarily important in four situations. First, corporate directors and officers who establish their due diligence in undertaking a securities transaction have a defense to claims of fraud and breach of fiduciary duty. Second, underwriters, banks, accountants and law firms who establish due diligence in performing their portion of a securities transaction have a defense to claims of secondary securities liability. Third, plaintiffs in a securities action who establish their due diligence in investigating the facts of a securities transaction can rebut claims that their reliance on misrepresentations or omissions of fact was unreasonable. Finally, due diligence often marks the time at which the statute of limitations on a securities action commences. A plaintiff must file a securities action within the prescribed statute of limitations period beginning on the date the plaintiff discovered the alleged wrong, or should have discovered the alleged wrong through the exercise of due diligence.

11.8.1 Due Diligence Under Federal Securities Law

The *Software Toolworks* case below addresses the question of the due diligence of an underwriter and accounting firm involved in a secondary public offering of stock.

SOFTWARE TOOLWORKS v. PAINEWEBBER
50 F.3d 615 (9th Cir. 1995)

CYNTHIA HOLCOMB HALL, CIRCUIT JUDGE:

In this case, we again consider the securities-fraud claims raised by disappointed investors in Software Toolworks, Inc., who appeal the district court's summary judgment in favor of auditors Deloitte & Touche and underwriters Montgomery Securities and PaineWebber, Inc. We affirm in part, reverse in part, and remand.

I.

In July 1990, Software Toolworks, Inc., a producer of software for personal computers and Nintendo game systems, conducted a secondary public offering of common stock at $18.50 a share, raising more than $71 million. After the offering, the market price of Toolworks' shares declined steadily until, on October 11, 1990, the stock was trading at $5.40 a share. At that time, Toolworks issued a press release announcing substantial losses and the share price dropped another fifty-six percent to $2.375.

The next day, several investors ("the plaintiffs") filed a class action alleging that Toolworks, auditor Deloitte &Touche ("Deloitte"), and underwriters Montgomery Securities and PaineWebber, Inc. ("the Underwriters") had issued a false and misleading prospectus and registration statement in violation of sections 11 and 12(2) of the Securities Act of 1933 ("the 1933 Act") and had knowingly defrauded and assisted in defrauding investors in violation of section 10(b) and Rule 10b-5 of the Securities Exchange Act of 1934 ("the 1934 Act"). Specifically, the plaintiffs claimed that the defendants had (1) falsified audited financial statements for fiscal 1990 by reporting as revenue sales to original equipment manufacturers ("OEMs") with whom Toolworks had no binding agreements, (2) fabricated large consignment sales in order for Toolworks to meet financial projections for the first quarter of fiscal 1991 ("the June quarter"), and (3) lied to the Securities Exchange Commission ("SEC") in response to inquiries made before the registration statement became effective.

Toolworks and its officers quickly settled with the plaintiffs for $26.5 million. After the completion of discovery, the district court granted summary judgment in favor of the Underwriters on all claims and in favor of Deloitte on all claims other than one cause of action under section 11. The district court held that (1) the Underwriters had established a "due diligence" defense under sections 11 and 12(2) as a matter of law, (2) Deloitte had made no material misrepresentations or omissions, other than the OEM revenue statements, on which liability under sections 11 and 12(2) could attach, and (3) the plaintiffs had failed to establish that any defendant acted with scienter, a necessary element of liability under section 10(b).

II.

We first address the plaintiffs' claims against the Underwriters under sections 11 and 12(2) of the 1933 Act. Section 11 imposes liability "[i]n case any part of [a] registration statement . . . contain[s] an untrue statement of a material fact or omit[s] to state a material fact required to be stated therein or necessary to make the statements therein not misleading." Similarly, section 12(2) imposes liability for using a prospectus "which includes an untrue statement of a material fact or omits to state a material fact necessary in order to make the statements, in light of the circumstances under which they were made, not misleading."

Liability under sections 11 and 12(2) properly may fall on the underwriters of a public offering. Underwriters, however, may absolve themselves from liability by establishing a "due diligence" defense. Under section 11, underwriters must prove that they "had, after reasonable investigation, reasonable ground to believe and did believe . . . that the statements therein were true and that there was no omission to state a material fact required to be stated therein or necessary to make the statements therein not misleading." Similarly, under section 12(2), underwriters must show that they "did not know, and in the exercise of reasonable care, could not have known, of [the] untruth or omission."

Because section 11's "reasonable investigation" standard is similar, if not identical, to section 12(2)'s "reasonable care" standard, the analysis of each on summary judgment is the same. In determining whether an underwriter meets the due diligence test under either provision, "the standard of reasonableness shall be that required of a prudent man in the management of his own property."

The district court held that the Underwriters had established due diligence as a matter of law and, accordingly, issued summary judgment against the plaintiffs on the section 11 and 12(2) claims. On appeal, the plaintiffs contend that due diligence is so fact-intensive that summary judgment is inappropriate even where underlying historical facts are undisputed. The plaintiffs further contend that, in any event, the district court erred by ignoring disputed issues of material fact in this case. We hold that, in appropriate cases, summary judgment may resolve due diligence issues but that, in this case, the district court erred by granting summary judgment in favor of the Underwriters on several claims.

A.

The plaintiffs first argue that "due diligence . . . [and] the reasonableness of the defendants' investigation . . . is a question for the jury, even on undisputed facts." We agree, of course, that summary judgment is generally an inappropriate way to decide questions of reasonableness because "the jury's unique competence in applying the "reasonable man" standard is thought ordinarily to preclude summary judgment." We have, however, squarely rejected the contention that "reasonableness is *always* a question of fact which precludes summary judgment." Rather, reasonableness "becomes a question of law and losses its triable character if the undisputed facts leave no room for a reasonable difference of opinion." Accordingly, "reasonableness [is] appropriate for determination on [a] motion for summary judgment when only one conclusion about the conduct's reasonableness is possible."

Courts therefore may resolve questions of due diligence in those cases where no rational jury could conclude that the defendant had not acted reasonably. Several courts have, in fact, done just that.

The district court, therefore, properly held that "the adequacy of due diligence may be decided on summary judgment when the underlying historical facts are undisputed."

B.

The plaintiffs next assert that, even if summary judgment may resolve due diligence issues in some cases, the district court erred in this case because three "hotly disputed" issues of material fact preclude summary judgment on the question of the Underwriters' due diligence. We consider each in turn.

1.

The plaintiffs first argue that the Underwriters failed to investigate properly Toolworks' Nintendo business. Specifically, the plaintiffs assert that the Underwriters should have discovered that, in contravention of statements in the prospectus, Toolworks had lowered prices on its Nintendo games and had "sold" significant inventory on a consignment basis, giving buyers an unqualified right to return unsold merchandise.

The district court disagreed, noting that the Underwriters had obtained written representations from Toolworks and Deloitte that the prospectus was accurate, had confirmed with Toolworks' customers that the company did not accept returns of non-defective cartridges, and had surveyed retailers to ensure that the company had not lowered its prices. Thus, the court concluded that the Underwriters had, as a matter of law, "performed a thorough and reasonable investigation of Toolworks' Nintendo business." For the following reasons, we agree.

a.

The plaintiffs argue that the prospectus was false and misleading because it stated that Toolworks' "Nintendo software products have not been subject to price reductions," when, in fact, Toolworks had begun a price-cutting promotion days before the offering. The plaintiffs, however, presented no direct evidence that the Underwriters knew of this promotion. Indeed, the record illustrates that Toolworks' management consistently assured the Underwriters that the company would not reduce prices. The plaintiffs nevertheless assert that summary judgment was inappropriate because a jury might infer that the Underwriters knew about the price cuts because Toolworks' management discussed the promotion while on a private plane with the Underwriters. All personnel who were on the plane, however, testified that no conversations regarding price cutting reached the Underwriters. As such, any inference that the Underwriters knew about the sales would not be based in fact and would be unreasonable. The district court properly granted summary judgment in favor of the Underwriters on this issue.

b.

The plaintiffs also claim that the prospectus was false and misleading because it stated that Toolworks "does not currently provide any product return rights to its retail Nintendo customers," when, in fact, the company had booked several consignment sales prior to the offering. Again, however, the plaintiffs offered no direct evidence that the Underwriters knew about the sales, which represented a significant departure from prior Toolworks' policy. In fact, the record illustrates that the Underwriters made a substantial effort to ascertain Toolworks' return policy, both before and after the consignment sales occurred. The plaintiffs nevertheless assert that circumstantial evidence permits an inference that the Underwriters knowingly "watered down" the prospectus' risk-disclosure statement about merchandise returns and ignored a memorandum from one Toolworks customer ("Walmart") describing an unlimited right-of-return. This argument, however, misconstrues the full record.

In the process of drafting the prospectus, the Underwriters did change the risk-disclosure statement. An original draft stated that, "[i]n light of increased competition among the [Nintendo] entertainment titles on the market, it may be necessary for [Toolworks] to modify its return policy." The final version stated only that "[t]here can be no assurance that [Toolworks] will not be subject to product returns in the future." This change, however, is not sufficient to permit a reasonable inference that the Underwriters knew or should have known that Toolworks actually had changed its return policy. In fact, the Underwriters changed the disclosure statement in direct response to assertions by Toolworks' management that the company would *never* offer return rights and that the prospectus as originally written could prompt customers to seek such concessions in the future.

Moreover, although the Underwriters did receive a memorandum from Walmart describing an unqualified right to return non-defective merchandise, the record illustrates that Walmart never actually had such rights. Upon receiving the Walmart memorandum, the Underwriters called the retailer and confirmed that the statement regarding returns was erroneous (it should have said that Walmart had an unqualified right to return *defective* merchandise). Thus, in light of this correction, the fact that the actual contract between Toolworks and Walmart provided only for the return of defective items, and the fact that Walmart never returned any undamaged products, an inference that the Underwriters attempted to conceal Toolworks' return policy would be unreasonable. The district court properly granted summary judgment in favor of the Underwriters on this issue.

2.

The plaintiffs next assert that a material issue of fact exists regarding whether the Underwriters diligently investigated, or needed to investigate, Toolworks' recognition of OEM revenue on its financial statements. The plaintiffs claim that the Underwriters "blindly rel[ied]" on Deloitte in spite of numerous "red flags" indicating that the OEM entries were incorrect and that, as a result, the district court erred in granting summary judgment.

An underwriter need not conduct due diligence into the "expertised" parts of a prospectus, such as certified financial statements. Rather, the underwriter need only show that it "had no reasonable ground to believe, and did not believe . . . that the statements therein were untrue or that there was an omission to state a material fact required to be stated therein or necessary to make the statements therein not misleading." The issue on appeal, therefore, is whether the Underwriters' reliance on the expertised financial statements was reasonable as a matter of law.

a.

As the first "red flag," the plaintiffs point to Toolworks' "backdated" contract with Hyosung, a Korean manufacturer. During the fourth quarter of fiscal 1990, Toolworks recognized $1.7 million in revenue from an OEM contract with Hyosung. In due diligence, the Underwriters discovered a memorandum from Hyosung to Toolworks stating that Hyosung had "backdated" the agreement to permit Toolworks to recognize revenue in fiscal 1990. The plaintiffs claim that, after discovering this memorandum, the Underwriters could no longer rely on Deloitte because the accountants had approved revenue recognition for the transaction.

If the Underwriters had done nothing more, the plaintiffs' contention might be correct. The plaintiffs, however, ignore the significant steps taken by the Underwriters after discovery of the Hyosung memorandum to ensure the accuracy of Deloitte's revenue recognition. The Underwriters first confronted Deloitte, which explained that it was proper for Toolworks to book revenue in fiscal 1990 because the company had contracted with Hyosung in March, even though the firms did not document the agreement until April. The Underwriters then insisted that Deloitte reconfirm, in writing, the Hyosung agreement and Toolworks' other OEM contracts. Finally, the Underwriters contacted other accounting firms to verify Deloitte's OEM revenue accounting methods.

Thus, with regard to the Hyosung agreement, the Underwriters did not "blindly rely" on Deloitte. The district court correctly held that, as a matter of law, the Underwriters' "investigation of the OEM business was reasonable."

b.

The plaintiffs next assert that the Underwriters could not reasonably rely on Deloitte's financial statements because Toolworks' counsel, Riordan & McKinzie, refused to issue an opinion letter stating that the OEM agreements were binding contracts. This contention has no merit because, contrary to the plaintiffs' assertions, Toolworks had never requested the law firm to render such an opinion. The plaintiffs attempt to infer wrongdoing in such circumstances is patently unreasonable. The district court correctly granted summary judgment in favor of the Underwriters on this issue.

c.

Finally, the plaintiffs assert that, by reading the agreements, the Underwriters should have realized that Toolworks had improperly recognized revenue. Specifically, the plaintiffs claim that several of the contracts were contingent and that it was facially apparent that Toolworks might not receive any revenue under them. As the Underwriters explain, this contention misconstrues the nature of a due diligence investigation:

> [The Underwriters] reviewed the contracts to verify that there was a written agreement for each OEM contract mentioned in the Prospectus — not to analyze the propriety of revenue recognition, which was the responsibility of [Deloitte]. Given the complexity surrounding software licensing revenue recognition, it is absurd to suggest that, in perusing Toolworks' contracts, [the Underwriters] should have concluded that [Deloitte] w[as] wrong, particularly when the OEM's provided written confirmation.

We recently confirmed precisely this point in a case involving analogous facts: "[T]he defendants relied on Deloitte's *accounting decisions* (to recognize revenue) about the sales. Those expert decisions, which underlie the plaintiffs' attack on the financial statements, represent precisely the type of "certified" information on which section 11 permits non-experts to rely."

Thus, because the Underwriters' reliance on Deloitte was reasonable under the circumstances, the district court correctly granted summary judgment on this issue.

3.

The plaintiffs next attack the Underwriters' due diligence efforts for the period after Toolworks filed a preliminary prospectus and before the effective date of the offering. During this time, several significant events transpired. First, *Barron's* published a negative article about Toolworks that questioned the company's "aggressive accounting." Second, in response to the *Barron's* article, the SEC initiated a review of Toolworks' prospectus. Third, Toolworks sent two letters responding to the SEC. And, fourth, Toolworks booked several consignment sales that made the company appear to have a prosperous quarter, thereby ensuring success of the offering.

The district court held that the Underwriters satisfied their due diligence obligations during this period primarily by relying on Toolworks' representations to the SEC. For the following reasons, we conclude that disputed issues of material fact exist regarding the Underwriters' efforts and, accordingly, we reverse and remand for a trial on the merits.

a.

The plaintiffs first contend that the Underwriters should have done more to investigate the *Barron's* allegations of slumping sales and improper accounting. The Underwriters established, however, that they contacted a representative of Nintendo and several large retailers to confirm the strength of the market in response to the *Barron's* article. Moreover, as explained above, the Underwriters' reliance on Deloitte's accounting decisions was reasonable as a matter of law. Summary judgment was appropriate on this issue.

b.

Next, the plaintiffs raise the issue of Toolworks' July 4, 1990 letter to the SEC, which described the company's June quarter performance. In the letter, Toolworks represented that, although preliminary financial data was not available, Toolworks anticipated revenue for the quarter between $21 and $22 million. The plaintiffs claim that Toolworks deliberately falsified these estimates and that the Underwriters knew of this deceit.

The Underwriters claim that they were not involved in drafting the July 4 SEC letter and that, as a result, they have no responsibility for its contents. The plaintiffs presented evidence, however, that the letter was a joint effort of all professionals working on the offering, including the Underwriters. In fact, a Riordan & McKinzie partner specifically testified that, "[w]hen the letter finally went to the SEC, all parties had been involved in the process of creating it. There had been conference calls discussing it and comments and changes made by a lot of different members of the working group." Others similarly testified that the Underwriters were actively involved in discussions of how to respond to the SEC's inquiries regarding the June quarter.

The Underwriters argue that, even if they participated in initial discussions about the letter, they never knew that Toolworks' financial data actually was available and that, as a result, they could not have known that the letter (and the prospectus) were misleading. Given the Underwriters participation in drafting both documents, however, we think this is an unresolved issue of material fact. A reasonable factfinder could infer that, as members of the drafting group, the Underwriters had access to all information that was available and deliberately chose to conceal the truth. We therefore hold that summary judgment was inappropriate on this issue.

c.

After suffering lagging sales in the first two months of the June quarter, Toolworks booked several large consignment sales in late June, the quarter's final month, thereby enabling the company to meet its earnings projections. Toolworks later had to reverse more than $7 million of these sales in its final financial statements for the quarter. The plaintiffs presented evidence that the Underwriters knew that Toolworks had performed poorly in April, that Toolworks had no orders for the month as of June 8, that the June quarter is traditionally the slowest of the year for Nintendo sales, and that the late June sales accounted for more revenue than the cumulative total of Toolworks' Nintendo sales for the prior two and a half months. For its due diligence investigation of these sales, however, the Underwriters did little more than rely on Toolworks' assurances that the transactions were legitimate. A reasonable inference from this evidence is that Toolworks fabricated the June sales to ensure that the offering would proceed and that the Underwriters knew, or should have known, of this fraud. As a result, we conclude that summary judgment regarding the Underwriters' diligence on this issue was also inappropriate.

C.

Thus, we hold that the district court properly granted summary judgment in favor of the Underwriters on the section 11 and 12(2) issues regarding their due diligence investigation into Toolworks' Nintendo sales practices and description of OEM revenue. The district court erred, however, by granting summary judgment on the section 11 and 12(2) claims regarding the July 4 SEC letter and Toolworks' June quarter results. We remand for a trial on the merits of those claims.

QUESTIONS

1.   What is the difference between the Securities Act Section 11's due diligence defense of "reasonable investigation" and Section 12(2)'s due diligence defense of "reasonable care"?

2.   When may due diligence issues be resolved in summary judgment proceedings?

3.   What due diligence steps did the underwriters take after learning of the backdated Hyosung agreement?

4.   Under what circumstances may underwriters rely on accounting decisions regarding recognition of revenue from sales? Can underwriters be held liable in reviewing agreements if they fail to note contingencies in the agreements?

5.   Why was summary judgment not appropriate on the underwriters' liability regarding Toolworks' letter to the SEC which misstated Toolworks' fourth quarter revenue?

CASE NOTES

1.   Nathel owns a wholesale fruit and vegetable company. Between 2001-2005, Nathel invested over $1.6 million in nine oil and gas drilling partnerships. Siegal was the creator and promoter of these partnerships; Howard was a close colleague of Siegel who served as an officer in the partnerships; Coleman and Trevisani, purported oil and gas experts, served as managing partners; and Josephson was Nathel's trusted accountant and financial advisor. Siegal and Howard told Nathel that his investments in the partnerships would earn him returns in the form of tax deductions and oil revenues. These representations were also included in written offering memoranda provided to Nathel. Josephson strongly encouraged Nathel to invest in the partnership telling him that he was familiar with the partnerships and that Siegal was a competent businessman. In November, 2006, Nathel received written notice from the IRS that his investments in the partnership were being audited because the partnerships were taking illegal tax deductions. Upon further investigation, Nathel learned that Siegal and Howard had access to drilling reports

and other information that showed the oil wells proposed to be drilled were already dry or abandoned and, therefore, could not provide oil revenues or tax deductions. Nathel also learned that Coleman and Trevisani were not oil and gas experts; Coleman ran a children's day camp and Trevisani was a practicing attorney. Nathel sued Siegal, Howard, Coleman, Trevisani and Josephson, alleging securities fraud under Section 10(b) of the Securities and Exchange Act. One of the many defenses asserted by the defendants was that Nathel failed to perform basic due diligence into the oil and gas investment partnerships and that, if he had, he would have discovered with minimal effort the truth about the partnerships. Defendants also argued that oil and gas partnership investments are notoriously risky and that Nathel could not reasonably rely on an assumption that he would not lose money in the investments. What result? *See* Nathel v. Siegal, 592 F.Supp.2d 452 (S.D.N.Y. 2008).

2. *See also* Dronsejko v. Thornton, 632 F.3d 658 (10th Cir. 2011) (Investors failed to show that they could not have independently discovered evidence underlying official sanction against independent auditor; corporation's extensive cooperation with shareholders would have allowed shareholders to learn of auditor's allegedly reckless approval of corporation's revenue recognition practices, if shareholders had exercised due diligence); Ruso v. Morrison, 695 F.Supp.2d 33 (S.D.N.Y. 2010) (Investor failed to exercise due diligence in negligence claim against attorney that is required under New York law for equitable tolling of three year statute of limitations); Pension Committee of University of Montreal Pension Plan v. Banc of America Securities, LLC, 691 F.Supp.2d 448 (S.D.N.Y. 2010) (Expert on hedge fund due diligence could explain to jury information disclosed in documents relevant to expert's opinion regarding adequacy of investors' due diligence); South Cherry Street, LLC v. Hennessee Group LLC, 573 F.3d 98 (2nd Cir. 2009) (Investor's allegations that investment advisor failed to fulfill his contractual obligation to perform initial and continuing due diligence in conjunction with a hedge fund investment recommended by investment advisor were not sufficient to give rise to a strong inference of fraudulent intent or reckless disregard that is required to show scienter under section 10(b) of Securities Exchange Act); American High-Income Trust v. AlliedSignal, 329 F.Supp.2d 534 (S.D.N.Y. 2004) (Speculative allegations by buyers of corporate bonds that lead underwriter of private placement of bonds used to finance corporation's purchase of subsidiary should have uncovered fraud in subsidiary were not sufficient to support Rule 10(b)-5 and common law fraud claims); Thompson v. Smith Barney, Harris Upham & Co., Inc., 709 F.2d 1413 (11th Cir. 1983) (In securities fraud claim, investor must establish actual reliance on broker's misrepresentations or omissions and that this reliance was justifiable because investor could not have uncovered truth through exercise of due diligence); Edwards & Hanley v. Wells Fargo Sec. Clearance Corp., 602 F.2d 478 (2nd Cir. 1979) (Brokerage firm which was defrauded by trader who was selling short failed to exercise due diligence as a matter of law by not discovering that massive selling by trader was for trader's own account and that frequent late deliveries of securities indicated short selling); Ernst & Ernst v. Hochfelder, 425 U.S. 185 (1976) (Accountants who have prepared registration statements may avoid civil liability if they can show that, after performing due diligence, they had reasonable grounds to believe that the representations in the registration statements were true and there was no omission of material facts).

Additional Information

1. EUNICE A. EICHELBERGER, 54 A.L.R. FED 11 (2011).

2. FRANCIS C. AMENDOLA ET AL., 69 AM. JUR. 2D SECURITIES REGULATION — FEDERAL §§ 798–799, 1446, 1448 (2010).

3. ARNOLD S. JACOBS, 5D DISCLOSURE & REMEDIES UNDER THE SEC. LAWS § 19:11 (2011).

4. Jack C. Auspitz, Susan E. Quinn, *Litigators' View of Due Diligence*, 1368 PLI/CORP 107 (2003).

5. Herbert S. Wander, Orrin J. Edidin, *Civil Liabilities Under the Federal Securities Laws — June 1990*, C533 ALI-ABA 867 (1990).

6. Robert C. Ruckh, Patrick J. Donoghue, Richard C. Lee, *Financial Due Diligence and the Accountant's Role*, 1119 PLI/CORP 987 (1999).

7. Mark L. Gordon, *Due Diligence, the High Technology Client and Intellectual Property*, 1119 PLI/CORP 933 (1999).

8. Robert B. Robbins, Shaw Pittman, *Due Diligence in Private Placement Offerings*, SE68 ALI-ABA 467 (2000).

11.8.2 Due Diligence Under State Securities Law

Due diligence under state securities laws is important for the same reasons it is important under federal securities laws: as a defense for corporate officers and directors, underwriters, accountants and law firms to claims of fraud or negligence regarding information they provide; as a rebuttal by plaintiffs to claims that the plaintiffs could not reasonably have relied upon the misinformation; and to ensure timely plaintiff filing of securities claims within the prescribed statute of limitations.

The case below deals with a plaintiff's duty of due diligence in an action based upon alleged misrepresentations by the sellers.

SUMMERS v. WELLTECH
935 S.W.2d 228 (Tex. App. 1996)

TAFT, JUSTICE.

This case is based upon allegations of securities fraud during the sale of stock between two companies. The trial court rendered judgment for the plaintiff, WellTech, Inc., and ordered the defendants, control persons of Vanguard Environmental, Inc. (Vanguard), to pay approximately 1.5 million dollars. The control persons appeal that judgment. Among other issues presented, we address whether a control person may be held jointly and severally liable for securities fraud, without the joinder of the controlled entity as a defendant to the lawsuit. We affirm.

Facts

In 1991, appellants, Peter Abadie, Jr., Robert A. Parma, and B. Wayne Summers, formed a company named Vanguard Environmental, Inc. Vanguard was an environmental remediation company, and its key asset was a machine, the TDS-10, designed to measure soil contamination. Summers was the inventor of the TDS-10. Parma and Abadie controlled the finances, management, and marketing of Vanguard.

In late 1991, Vanguard commenced negotiations to secure investors in the company. Abadie had the responsibility of negotiating with all prospective investors. WellTech, through its president, Doug Thompson, negotiated with all three defendants. They agreed that WellTech would pay 1.25 million dollars for 50 percent of Vanguard's stock.

In 1992, Vanguard management discovered that Summers had diverted company funds. On December 9, 1991, Summers diverted approximately $167,000. On March 17, 1992, he diverted over $209,000. Parma testified that he knew the Environmental Protection Agency (EPA) was investigating Summers as of October 15, 1991, but did not believe the allegations and did not inform WellTech or Abadie of the investigation.

Vanguard allegedly made misrepresentations to WellTech regarding the TDS-10 machine's capacity and Vanguard's financial statements, overstating Vanguard's assets in the amount of $250,000. Furthermore, Parma testified that the Vanguard officers could have known about the misrepresentations made to WellTech.

WellTech discovered these misrepresentations after the February 5, 1992, closing. WellTech filed suit on December 3, 1992, seeking rescission of the security sale. After a bench trial, the trial court rendered judgment for WellTech, and Vanguard was ordered to pay WellTech the amount it paid in consideration for the stock plus interest and attorneys' fees. Before rendition of judgment, WellTech executed a document entitled "Tender of Securities," indicating a return of the stock to Vanguard.

Vanguard control persons appeal this judgment.

Vanguard's Liability

Parma and Summers argue in their first point of error that the trial court erred by finding them secondarily and jointly and severally liable for WellTech's claims without pleadings, allegations, or judgment finding that the corporate defendant, Vanguard, had violated the Securities Act. The record reflects the trial court actually held appellants "jointly and severally liable," not "secondarily" liable.

The Securities Act provides:

> A person who directly or indirectly controls a seller, buyer or issuer of a security is liable under Section 33A, 33B, or 33C jointly and severally with the seller, buyer, or issuer, and to the same extent as if he were the seller, buyer, or issuer, unless the controlling person sustains the burden of proof

that he did not know and in the exercise of reasonable care could not have known, of the existence of facts by reason of which liability is alleged to exist.

Parma and Summers propose that this statute precludes a control person's liability in the absence of pleadings alleging the controlled entity's liability. While Vanguard was alleged as a nominal defendant, no relief was sought against Vanguard, which was in bankruptcy. No Texas case has addressed this issue. However, in *Keys v. Wolfe, rev'd on other grounds*, the court addressed this issue and held it was unnecessary to join the seller as a party as long the evidence showed the defendant's control over the seller and a violation of the Securities Act by the seller.

Parma and Summers' brief quotes from the commentary accompanying article 581-33(F) in which the rationale for control person liability is stated: "a control person is in a position to prevent the violation and may be able to compensate the injured investor when the primary violator (e.g. a corporate issuer which has gone bankrupt) is not." This is exactly the situation here. Article 581-33(F) provides for joint and several liability, and does not require a plaintiff to seek affirmative relief against the controlled entity before such relief may be sought from a control person. We decline to impose such an additional requirement. We overrule Parma and Summers' first point of error.

Partial Rescission

In their fourth and fifth points of error, Parma and Summers claim the trial court erred by ordering partial rescission of an indivisible contract. The agreements between Vanguard and WellTech included several loans to Vanguard from WellTech, totaling over one million dollars. The trial court's judgment does not address the loans. Parma and Summers argue that a stock sale transaction is indivisible and the court should have rescinded the entire transaction or none of it. In support of their argument, Parma and Summers cite cases that discuss the indivisibility of property settlement agreements.

A contract is indivisible when by its terms, nature, and purpose it contemplates and intends that each and all parts and the consideration shall be common to each other and interdependent. Vanguard and WellTech executed several agreements at the same time. However, each agreement constituted a separate transaction. There was a sale of stock, a term loan, an equipment loan, and others. The contract between the parties plainly treats these agreements as independent. All agreements were supported by independent consideration and all were executed with distinct and identifiable purposes independent of each other. Therefore, the trial court correctly rescinded only the agreement to sell securities; the balance of the agreements can remain intact because they are separate and distinct agreements.

Accordingly, we overrule Parma and Summers' fourth and fifth points of error.

Equitable Rescission

Parma and Summers' seventh point of error alleges the trial court erred in ignoring the rules applicable to equitable rescission when it ordered rescission under the Securities Act. Parma and Summers claim the rescission was improper because they were not restored to the position they were in prior to the sale.

The federal statute provides that the buyer of securities "may sue either at law or in equity . . . to recover the consideration paid for such security with interest thereon, less the amount of any income received thereon, upon the tender of such security, or for damages if he no longer owns the security." The Texas statute similarly states the buyer "may sue either at law or in equity for rescission, or for damages if the buyer no longer owns the security." The similar wording in the federal and state statutes allows us to look to federal cases as a guide to interpreting this statute.

Federal securities law generally interprets rescission as an exchange to return the parties to a status quo. However, restoration to the status quo is not a "binding prerequisite to the remedy of rescission." In fact, the main concern of courts should be to restore the *plaintiff* to the status quo, not necessarily the defendant. Therefore, the trial court did not err when it decided rescission was the correct remedy to restore WellTech to the status quo.

We overrule Parma and Summers' seventh point of error.

Purchaser Status

In his first point of error, Abadie alleges WellTech was not the buyer of the stock and does not have standing to sue the control persons. Abadie bases his claim on WellTech's use of funds from investors to purchase the majority of the stock.

The Fifth Circuit Court of Appeals held that an individual was considered the "buyer" even though he purchased the stock with his relatives' money. In *Lewis*, an individual bought stock and intended to distribute the stock to each relative according to the amount paid. The court held that the individual was recognized as the "purchaser" because the stock was in his name and a letter of investment intent showed he was the sole purchaser.

Likewise, a federal district court held that a plaintiff did not have to be an owner to be considered the purchaser, but had to have "sufficient indicia of ownership to effectuate a tender of the securities." The plaintiff in *Monetary Management* purchased the bonds in question for a customer, and the court found this sufficient to establish the plaintiff as the purchaser and as the proper party to bring an action for rescission.

WellTech negotiated with the control persons for the purchase of Vanguard stock and was the record holder of the stock. Regardless of who actually funded the sale, WellTech had sufficient indicia of ownership to tender the securities, which it apparently did.

We overrule Abadie's first point of error.

WellTech's Burden

Abadie's fifth point of error alleges WellTech failed to state it would not have bought the Vanguard stock had it known of the alleged adverse material facts.

The Securities Act provides:

A. Liability of Sellers.

(2) Untruth or Omission. A person who offers or sells a security (whether or not the security or transaction is exempt under Section 5 or 6 of this Act) by means of an untrue statement of a material fact or an omission to state a material fact necessary in order to make the statements made, in the light of the circumstances under which they are made, not misleading, is liable to the person buying the security from him, who may sue either at law or in equity for rescission, or for damages if the buyer no longer owns the security. However, a person is not liable if he sustains the burden of proof that either (a) the buyer knew of the untruth or omission or (b) he (the offeror or seller) did not know, and in the exercise of reasonable care could not have known, of the untruth or omission.

The statute does not include a requirement that the plaintiff show he would not have purchased the stock if he had known of the alleged adverse material facts. Absent some authority requiring such proof, Abadie fails to sustain this point.

We overrule Abadie's fifth point of error.

WellTech's Knowledge

Abadie's sixth point of error states that WellTech bought Vanguard's stock knowing of the problems WellTech now deems material. Abadie's argument is based on the expertise of WellTech and WellTech's duty to exercise due diligence to discover the true situation of the company.

WellTech had no duty of due diligence; the statute merely requires proof of a misrepresentation by the seller. It is not a defense to fraud that the defrauded person might have discovered the truth by the exercise of ordinary care.

Furthermore, Abadie argues WellTech knew of the management problems in Vanguard. This is not disputed. However, WellTech's complaints of misrepresentation concerned the embezzlement, EPA investigation, Summers' integrity, and the capacity of the TDS-10, not the general disorganization of the company.

We overrule Abadie's sixth point of error.

Conclusion

We affirm the trial court's judgment.

QUESTIONS

1. Why can control persons be held jointly and severally liable if the entity which they control is not joined as a defendant in the suit? Can control persons be held jointly and severally liable if the entity which they control is not held to be liable? How can the controlled entity be held liable if the controlled entity is not joined as a defendant in the suit?

2. Why did WellTech seek only a partial rescission of their contract with Vanguard?

3. Why did Parma and Summers claim equitable rescission was the proper remedy? What would Parma and Summers gain if they were restored to the status quo prior to the WellTech agreement?

4. The Texas Securities statute provides that a seller of securities is not liable if he sustains the burden of proof that "the buyer knew of the untruth or omission." Do you agree that a buyer of securities should have no obligation of due diligence prior to purchasing the securities? What may be the unintended consequences of relieving buyers of securities of any obligation of due diligence?

CASE NOTES

1. In 1956, Puchner opened an investment account at Prudential-Bache with stockbroker Goodstein. Puchner continued his account with Prudential-Bache until 1978 when Goodstein left to work with Drexel Burnham, at which time he transferred his account to Drexel Burnham. Several years later, Goodstein moved to Thomson McKinnon Securities and Puchner transferred his account to Thomson McKinnon. In August 1983, Puchner sued Prudential-Bache, Drexel Burnham, Thomson McKinnon and Goodstein for fraud, breach of fiduciary duty, negligence and violations of state securities laws. The complaint alleged that from 1958-1982 Goodstein had been defrauding Puchner by buying and selling securities in his account without his knowledge or consent. As part of the fraud, Goodstein had forged Puchner's name and opened a post office box in Puchner's name. The brokerage firms' monthly statements were mailed to the post office box where they were picked up by Goodstein. Goodstein then personally delivered fake statements to Puchner. The complaint further alleged that Goodstein was able to perpetrate this fraud for so many years because Puchner was a professional musician who travelled frequently and because, over the years, Puchner had come to trust and rely on Goodstein to handle all of his personal business affairs, as well as those of his elderly mother. Puchner claimed he first became aware of the fraud when he was contacted by a manager at Thomson McKinnon who had found a check payable to Purchner on Goodstein's desk. The defendants argued that Puchner's fraud action was barred by Florida's statutes of limitations (two years for securities violations; four years for fraud claims; four years for breach of fiduciary duty; and four years for negligence). All of the statutes of limitations commenced on the date the plaintiff discovered, or should have discovered through the exercise of reasonable due diligence, the acts on which the cause of action was based. The defendants claimed Puchner was put on notice of the fraud in 1973 when he discovered Goodstein had opened a post office box in his name without his knowledge or consent. Puchner

responded that he had cultivated a long relationship of trust and confidence with Goodstein and that, when he asked Goodstein about the post office box, Goodstein explained that the post office box was opened to assist Goodstein in managing Puchner's business affairs, by keeping track of Puchner's mail while Puchner was out of town. The trial court granted the brokers' motion for summary judgment. Puchner appealed. What result? *See* Puchner v. Bache Halsey Stuart, Inc., 553 So.2d 216 (Fla. Dist. Ct. App. 1989).

2. Conlan was president of Shawnee Capital Corporation (Shawnee) and LaLonde was president of Killarney Breeding Sales (Killarney). Conners, Frank, Saunders and Johnson (investors) were limited partners in a limited partnership in which Shawnee and Killarney were listed as general partners in the prospectus filed with the Ohio Division of Securities. The purpose of the partnership was to purchase a mare, Falina Angel, owned by LaLonde, for breeding with a stallion called State Dinner and to sell the offspring for a profit on the limited partners' investment of $56,000. The prospectus failed to note that there were outstanding stud-fee liens on Falina Angel which had to be satisfied before the horse could be sold and that LaLonde had previously been convicted of bank fraud. The partnership quickly failed when foreclosure proceedings against LaLonde resulted in a Kentucky county sheriff taking custody of Falina Angel and when Conlan and Shawnee issued a check against insufficient funds in payment of a stallion share in State Dinner. After the investors learned of the partnership's setbacks, they demanded return of their investment and shortly thereafter filed a complaint alleging fraud and state securities law violations by Killarney and LaLonde, and by Shawnee and Conlan. Shawnee and Conlan filed a motion for summary judgment arguing that the facts failed to show their participation in, or awareness of, the fraud perpetrated by Killarney and LaLonde. The trial court found that Conlan and Shawnee were indistinguishable and that they had recklessly failed to exercise due diligence in the preparation of the prospectus and that the investors were entitled to damages from Conlan and Shawnee under the Ohio Securities Act. Conlan and Shawnee appealed. What result? *See* Baker v. Conlan, 66 Ohio App.3d 454 (Ohio Ct. App. 1990).

3. *See also* Ives v. Ramsden, 142 Wash. App. 369 (Wash. Ct. App. 2008) (Statute of limitations for common law fraud and securities fraud began when investor discovered, or should have discovered through exercise of due diligence, acts constituting common law fraud or securities fraud); Ex parte Bernard J. Ebbers, 871 So.2d 776 (Ala. 2003) (Investment banks for bankrupt telecommunications company may be in better position to establish due diligence defense if telecommunications CEO and CFO are not parties to the action and, therefore, could not contradict banks' claims of reasonable inquiries and investigations of companies' activities); Stricker v. Epstein, 213 Ga.App.226 (Ga. Ct. App. 1994) (Purchasers of stock alleging fraud would have discovered fraud more than two years prior to filing fraud claim if they had exercised due diligence; purchasers were put on notice of potential fraud when they stopped receiving monthly checks; there was no relationship of trust between purchasers and corporation that would excuse failure to exercise due diligence); McGrath v. Dougherty, 224 Iowa 216 (Iowa 1937) (Purchasers of corporate bonds claiming fraud could not be excused from performing due diligence by requesting trustees who certified deposit of securities as collateral for bonds to provide statement of deposited securities claiming request

would have been made to the same parties perpetrating the fraud).

Additional Information

1. LISA M. BROWNLEE, IP DUE DILIGENCE IN CORP. TRANSACTIONS § 13:11 (2010).

2. GARY M. LAWRENCE, DUE DILIGENCE IN BUS. TRANSACTIONS § 2.02 (2010).

3. ROBERT J. HAFT, MICHELE H. HUDSON, LIAB. ATTY. & ACCT. FOR SEC TRANSACT. § 5:19 (2010).

4. ROBERT J. HAFT, MICHELE H. HUDSON, DUE DILIGENCE — PER REP & SEC OFFER § 4:6 (2009).

5. ROBERT J. HAFT, 2A VENTURE CAP. & BUS. FIN. §§ 14:32, 14:34, 14:74, 14:106, 14:141 (2010).

6. GREGORY A. MARKEL, GREGORY G. BALLARD, 12 No. 17 ANDREWS SEC. LITIG. & REG. REP. 2 (2006).

7. Jonathan K. Youngwood, *Due Diligence As A Defense In Securities Litigation*, 1746 PLI/CORP 57 (2009).

8. Julia K. Cowles, *Due Diligence For Securities Offerings: A Roadmap For Effective Document Review*, 1746 PLI/CORP 193 (2009).

9. William K. Sjostrom, Jr., *The Due Diligence Defense Under Section 11 Of The Securities Act Of 1933*, 44 BRANDEIS L.J. 540 (2006).

10. 1506 PLI/CORP 49, Third Annual Directors' Institute on Corporate Governance, *Corporate Securities: Due Diligence After Worldcom* (2005).

11. Joseph McLaughlin, Andrew W. Stern, *Remedies In Securities Transactions And Sellers' "Due Diligence" Defenses*, 1304 PLI/CORP 145 (2002).

12. Joseph McLaughlin, Andrew W. Stern, *The Statutory Basis For Due Diligence Under The Federal Securities Laws*, 1247 PLI/CORP 345 (2001).

13. L. Markus Wiltshire, *Ethical Issues Arising In Connection With The Conduct Of Due Diligence In Securities Offerings*, 1176 PLI/CORP 1003 (2000).

Appendix

PSA-X VALUATION EXERCISE

PSA-X Valuation Exercise

For the purposes of this exercise, you are to assume the following facts about the technology, the market and the company. If you need to assume additional facts, please state these additional facts in your valuation.

Introduction

The American Cancer Society estimated that, in 2007, over 260,000 people in the United States were diagnosed with prostate cancer and that over 33,000 people died from the disease. The key to successful treatment of prostate cancer is early and accurate detection. Research has shown that cancer tumors produce biomarkers that can be detected in serum, which is the clear liquid portion of blood that is present after coagulation has taken place. Currently, there is only one serum biomarker known for prostate cancer — the prostate-specific antigen or PSA. The PSA test, which is widely used to detect prostate cancer, measures the level of prostate-specific antigen present in a serum sample. However, the PSA test has two significant limitations.

First, non-cancerous inflammation or infection of the prostate can sometimes yield positive PSA test results for prostate cancer. For patients, false-positive PSA test results often require them to undergo unnecessary biopsy procedures. For the health care system, false-positive PSA test results unnecessarily increase health care costs. Approximately 20% of PSA tests yield false-positive test results. Second, early-stage prostate tumors often produce too little prostate-specific antigen to be detected by the PSA test. This causes false-negative PSA test results. For patients, false-negative PSA test results allow the prostate tumor to continue to grow, lessening the chances for successful treatment. For the health care system, false-negative PSA test results increase the cost of therapeutic procedures. Approximately 30% of PSA tests yield false-negative test results.

The Technology

A combination of research breakthroughs in molecular biology and nanotechnology have produced a new PSA test that could be far superior to the current PSA test. In pre-clinical tests, the new PSA test, known as PSA-X, has shown a false-positive rate of 5% and a false-negative rate of 10%. There is no difference in the time it takes to administer and analyze the PSA and PSA-X tests. However, the micro-chip system used in the PSA-X test is slightly more expensive than the chemical reagent kit used in the PSA test. The average cost to the patient of the current PSA test is $50. The average cost to the patient of the new PSA-X test is estimated to be $60.

The chemical reagent kit used in the current PSA test is sold to laboratories and hospitals for approximately $25, and the cost to manufacture and distribute the current PSA test is approximately $12. It is estimated that the price to laboratories and hospitals of the micro-chip system that will be used in the PSA-X test will be approximately $30, and that the long-term cost to manufacture and distribute the PSA-X micro-system chip will be approximately $15. PSA-X Phase I clinical testing began in Spring _____ and is almost completed. The results of the Phase I clinical testing have been very positive and FDA approval for the PSA-X test could be granted as early as Spring _____. Because it embodies fundamental advances in two fields of science, if the PSA-X test does receive FDA approval, it is estimated that the PSA-X test will be competitive in the prostate cancer test market for at least 10 years and possibly as many as 20 years.

The Market

In 2007, there were approximately 20 million men in the United States over the age of 45 and approximately 200 million men outside the United States over the age of 45. The over 45 age group in the United States and the world is projected to double in the next 20 years. The World Health Organization suggests that men over the age of 45 be tested for prostate cancer annually. However, less than 25% of men in the United States, and less than 10% of men outside the United States, have annual prostate cancer tests. There were approximately 6 million PSA tests performed in the United States in 2007 and approximately 24 million tests performed outside the United States. Four firms dominate the prostate cancer test market, accounting for nearly 100% of market share. These firms are BioMark (40%), K&K (25%), Fitzer (20%) and SureTest (13%). The average financial ratios for these firms are as follows.

Average Financial Ratios

Sales, General & Administrative Expenses	25% of Revenue
Research & Development Expenses	15% of Revenue
Advertising Expenses	10% of Revenue

The Company

The PSA-X test is being developed by a small, university spin-off company — NanoRx. The principals in NanoRx are two medical researchers, a business development manager and an operations manager. Since the founding of NanoRx in 2003, five U.S. patents have been issued and assigned to the company and six U.S. patent applications are currently pending. NanoRx has also obtained three patents in Europe and three patents in Japan on the core features of the PSA-X technology. The average number of independent claims in patents in the field of biomarkers is approximately 4 and the average number of independent claims in the NanoRx issued and pending patents is 7.

To date, NanoRx has invested over $6 million in the development of the PSA-X test through funds raised in a series A venture capital investment, SBIR awards and NIH grants. The NanoRx researchers estimate that it will cost an additional $12 million to complete the development of the PSA-X test through Phase III clinical trials.

Valuation Purposes

NanoRx has requested a valuation of the PSA-X test for two purposes. *First,* for use in securing potential additional private investment in order to conduct further clinical testing of the PSA-X test. For this purpose, NanoRx has asked that valuations be done for the PSA-X test at its current stage of development and at the conclusion of Phase II clinical testing, assuming the Phase II clinical tests are successful. NanoRx hopes to show potential investors the incremental return on investment from progressing from Phase I to Phase II clinical tests. *Second,* for use in negotiating a potential license of the PSA-X test to one of the firms currently in the market. For this purpose, NanoRx has asked that the valuation take into account the further investment needed to made by the licensee, the rate of return on investment to NanoRx and the licensee, and alternative license structures including lump sum payments and running royalties.

Assignment

Please prepare a valuation of the PSA-X test using Excel spreadsheets so that input data can be changed to observe changes in the valuation results. Please also explain how you determined the valuation of the PSA-X test either in notes in the Excel spreadsheets or in a separate document. Your valuation of the PSA-X test should use the Competitive Advantage Valuation method and one, or more, other valuation methods discussed in class. Each team will present its valuation results in class on _____. The class presentation will include both electronic and hardcopies of the spreadsheets and explanation documents.

Note: In adjusting the value of the PSA-X test for technical, market and intellectual property risks using CAV, the risk discount for each of these risks cannot be greater than 95% or less than 5%.

BioFilter Negotiation and Drafting Exercises
BioFilter Facts

Introduction

Blood is big business. It is estimated that the global market for whole blood and blood products was over $12 billion in 2008, with approximately $6 billion of these sales in the U.S. and $3 billion in Europe. The largest suppliers of whole blood and blood products are the national Red Cross organizations. In the U.S., the American Red Cross collects, processes and distributes approximately 12 million units of whole blood annually, which is about one-half of the total annual units donated in the U.S. The Red Cross organizations operating in other countries, which are independent of the American Red Cross and of one another, also account for approximately one-half of the blood supplies in their respective countries. The other half of the blood supplies in the U.S. and other countries is provided by a combination of for-profit companies and regional hospital groups.

The largest for-profit blood supplier in the U.S. is Harris & Harris Corporation, which sold slightly over 5 million units of blood in 2005, and the largest for-profit blood supplier in Europe is Longstreet, Ltd., which sold approximately 6 million units of blood in 2005. Harris & Harris sales were solely in the U.S., while Longstreet had sales in every country in Europe. The great majority of the other for-profit companies and hospital groups in the U.S. and Europe operate on a local basis and had average annual sales of around 200,000 units of blood.

BioFilter, Incorporated

BioFilter, Inc. was founded in 2007 by three research physicians (Drs. Martinez, Fahaud and Chung) at Central State Medical Center of New York (CSMC-NY) for the purpose of commercializing a major advance in blood filtration technology, known as leukocyte reduction filtration. The founders formed a Subchapter C corporation with 5,000,000 authorized shares of common stock with a par value of $.01 per share. Each of the three founders invested $25,000 and were issued 25,000 shares of BioFilter common stock. CSMC-NY, through its non-profit research foundation, granted BioFilter a 10 year exclusive license to the six issued patents and five pending patents on the leukocyte reduction filtration technology in exchange for running royalties in the amount of 3% of net sales, a license fee of $15,000 and 7,500 shares of BioFilter common stock. The patent license is renewable at the end of the initial 10 year term for the remaining life of the patents if the leukocyte reduction filtration technology has received FDA pre-market approval as a medical device.

The leukocyte reduction filtration technology is embodied in a single machine that includes pumps, in-flow and out-flow ports, pressure and flow regulators, filter and storage housings, software, touch screen controls and a power source. The inventors have named the technology "LRF-1000." Although the test results have been extremely positive, to date the LRF-1000 has only been tested in in-vitro laboratory tests. Because it is a new technology and could pose a risk of harm to a donor, the founders expect the LRF-1000 will be classified as a Class III medical device which will require a Pre-market Approval (PMA) by the FDA before the technology can be marketed. The PMA process requires clinical testing to establish the safety and efficacy of a medical device. The founders estimate that the Phase I clinical testing will cost approximately $12 million and take approximately 2 years. The BioFilter business plan is to complete the pre-clinical testing and begin the Phase I clinical testing of the LRF-1000 technology using private equity funds, and then to license the LRF-1000 technology to a major medical device manufacturer in order to complete the more expensive later-stage clinical testing and to take the technology to market. The founders have also discussed the possibility of selling the company to a medical device manufacturer at some point in time, if the price is right.

Leukocyte Reduction Filtration Technology

Whole blood is a mixture of components that includes red blood cells that supply oxygen to the body, white blood cells that protect the body from disease and plasma that contains platelets and various proteins used in, among other biological processes, wound healing. Although all components of blood are useful for different medical purposes, the most common need for blood is in blood transfusions during surgery and emergency room care. Blood transfusions are used to replace patients' lost red blood cells so that body tissue does not die from lack of oxygen. However, when patients are transfused with whole blood, the patients also receive the donor's white blood cells (leukocytes) and plasma, both of which can be harmful and, in a some cases, fatal to the patients.

Leukocytes are critical to fight infection in the body; however, when leukocytes are transfused from one person to another, there are two potential adverse consequences. First, about 10% of patients who receive whole blood transfusions containing leukocytes develop fevers, headaches, nausea and shortness of breath, which can extend their hospital stay by more than a week. Second, some patients develop antibodies against transfused leukocytes which can cause the patient's immune system to destroy transfused platelets as well; this is a life-threatening complication for people with chronic diseases such as leukemia. Currently, only about 20% of whole blood is filtered to remove leukocytes and plasma.

CSMC-NY received a $5 million NIH grant in 2003 to research methods for filtration of leukocytes and plasma from whole blood. At the time of the NIH grant, the only method available to remove leukocytes and plasma from whole blood was by means of a centrifuge, which is a very costly and time-consuming process that often results in the rupture and destruction of up to 20% of the red blood cells that are centrifuged. The three principal researchers on the NIH grant were Doctors Martinez, Fahaud and Chung. The researchers experimented with numerous ultra-fine membranes to separate red blood cells from leukocytes and plasma. Because the hemoglobin molecule that carries oxygen is a large molecule, red blood cells are considerably larger than the other components of whole blood. (The diameter of a red blood cell is approximately 8 micrometers. A micrometer is one-millionth of a meter and is designated by the symbol μm.)

The obstacle to separating red blood cells from other blood components was not finding membranes with pores smaller than 8μm, but rather with what became known as the "filter cake" problem. As the leukocytes and plasma passed through the membrane, the separated red blood cells tended to accumulate on the other side of the membrane, which slowed the flow rate through the membrane, ultimately leading to a complete blockage of the membrane filter. The researchers solved this problem by developing a method for flowing the whole blood through spiral micro-channels parallel to the membrane surface to ensure continuous circulation of the whole blood. By using these spiral micro-channels, and very carefully regulating the flow rate and pressure of the whole blood as it passed through the system to avoid rupturing cells, the researchers were able to eliminate completely the red blood cell filter cake on the membrane surface.

The LRF-1000 technology invented by Doctors Martinez, Fahaud and Chung has many advantages. LRF-1000 is faster and less expensive than the centrifuge method and does not destroy any red blood cells. LRF-1000 also allows for two units of red blood cells to be collected in a single donor session (double the amount that currently can be collected) by collecting only the red blood cells and returning the white blood cells and plasma to the donor. Finally, because the LRF-1000 also filters out plasma that can contain viruses, it eliminates the need for many of the safety tests that currently have to be run on each unit of whole blood collected. These benefits are explained further below.

The Economics of Blood

The human body contains approximately 5 liters (5.3 quarts) of whole blood. Approximately 3 liters are plasma and the remaining amount is cellular matter — primarily red blood cells, leukocytes and platelets. Red blood cells comprise about 40%-45% of whole blood cellular matter. A unit of blood is 1 pint or 450 milliliters. (A milliliter is one-thousandth of a liter and designated as ml.) Generally, a blood donor must be at least 17 years old, healthy and weigh over 110 pounds. A blood donor can donate 1 unit of whole blood every eight weeks. A typical donor session takes about 40 minutes — 10 minutes to check the donor's health, 20 minutes to collect the blood and 10 minutes for kit set-up and take-down. The price of blood varies considerably depending upon the supplier, the geographic region and the nature of the supply arrangement. For many years, the American Red Cross has offered blood at discounted prices to hospitals willing to enter into exclusive supply contracts with the Red Cross. Although this practice has been challenged on antitrust grounds by a number of hospitals and private blood suppliers, no court has yet ruled on this question.

The national average price charged by the American Red Cross is $150 for a unit of whole blood and $200 for a unit of leukocyte-reduced blood. The Red Cross estimates its direct costs per unit of leukocyte-reduced blood are $10 for the blood collection kit, $25 for blood testing, $50 for leukocyte centrifuge removal and $30 for handling, storage and distribution. The remaining costs are indirect, consisting primarily of advertising, administrative salaries, real estate payments and debt charges. The Red Cross does not pay donors. Although private blood supply companies and hospitals do pay donors about $25 per session, and incur the same direct costs as the Red Cross, they generally charge around $10 per unit less than the Red Cross. The challenge confronting private blood supply companies and hospitals, as well as the entire industry, is maintaining an adequate supply of blood.

It is estimated that the blood transfusion supply shortfall in 2008 was nearly 6 million units.

The LRF-1000 technology has the potential to significantly reduce the blood supply shortfall. The LRF-1000 collects whole blood from the donor and separates it into red blood cells, and white blood cells and plasma. The red blood cells are retained in a storage packet while the white blood cells and plasma are returned to the donor along with a saline solution to compensate for the lost blood volume. By means of this process, the LRF-1000 technology is able to collect two units of leukocyte reduced red blood cells in a single donor session. However, the LRF-1000 collection method also requires slightly more time than the current whole blood collection method. The blood collection time is approximately 30 minutes, the kit set-up and take-down time is approximately 15 minutes, and it still takes about 10 minutes to check the donor's health.

The LRF-1000 Technology

The LRF-1000 technology consists of the stationary components described above and a disposable donor collection kit for each donor session. The disposable donor collection kit includes the micro-channel filter membrane, a red blood cell collection bag, plastic tubes and needles. A manufacturing consultant, who was hired by BioFilter, estimates that it will cost approximately $10,000 to manufacture each LRF-1000 collection machine and that it will cost approximately $20 to manufacture each donor collection kit. These estimates were based on an annual sales volume of 500 LRF-1000 collection machines and 200,000 donor kits. Preliminary market research suggests that the LRF-1000 collection machine can be sold for $20,000 each and that the donor collection kits can be sold for $30 each. For a high-end medical device manufacturer, manufacturing the LRF-1000 collection machine would not involve a major investment in new manufacturing equipment. The start-up costs to manufacture the LRF-1000 collection machine are estimated to be under $5 million. However, the manufacture of the micro-channel filter membranes included in the disposable donor collection kits would require significant investment in new equipment. The cost of this new equipment could be as high as $10 million. In addition, because the manufacturing process would be completely new, a substantial portion of the filters produced during the first year or so might be defective. It is not uncommon in precision manufacturing for the early defect rate to be as high as 40%.

LRF-1000 Intellectual Property

CSMC-NY has aggressively sought patent protection for the LRF-1000 technology. Currently, six patents have been issued on the LRF Collection machine and five more are pending. The most important of the issued patents is patent #447 — "Blood collection system using a micro-channel porous membrane filter." Other issued patents cover the housing for the filters, the process of regulating blood flow rate and pressure, a method for blood processing that employs a mounted leukocyte filter and a plastic container for storing red blood cells. The pending patents include pumping devices, a method for collecting plasma, and a system for separating the platelets and proteins in plasma. CSMC-NY's patent firm has indicated that it would be willing to write a "strong" opinion letter regarding the validity of the issued patents on the LRF-1000 technology. CSMC-NY has also obtained patents on the "Blood collection system using a micro-channel porous membrane filter" in Britain, France, Germany, Japan and Switzerland.

Regulation of Blood Safety

In March _____, the U.S. Food and Drug Administration held hearings on a proposed regulation that would require leukocyte filtered blood to be used in all transfusions. The testimony at the hearings was conflicting. On the one hand, many experts testified that leukocyte reduced blood would reduce both morbidity and mortality rates in surgical patients, and shorten the length of hospital stays. These experts cited research studies that found that colorectal surgery patients who received leukocyte reduced blood experience a significant reduction in the incidence of postoperative pneumonia (reduced from 23% to 3%) and this reduced their average hospital stay by six days. These studies also found that patients who receive unfiltered whole blood have a significantly higher rate of wound infection (12% vs. 0%), re-operation (16.9% vs. 3.5%), and intra-abdominal abscess formation (5% vs. 0%) compared to patients who were given leukocyte filtered blood. The experts supporting the proposed regulation estimated that requiring leukocyte filtered blood in transfusions for surgical patients would save the U.S. health care system between $6 billion and $12 billion annually while adding only about $20 to the cost of each unit of blood.

On the other hand, many experts opposed the proposed regulation. The American Red Cross, private blood supply companies and numerous hospital groups testified that the added cost of leukocyte filtration was not justified by the medical benefits and that the proposed regulation would unnecessarily increase national health care costs. These experts did not deny the potential harm which unfiltered whole blood transfusions could cause some patients, but insisted that patients who were vulnerable to these harms could be identified in advance and transfused with leukocyte filtered blood. According to these experts, the great majority of surgical and emergency room patients are not harmed by transfusion of unfiltered whole blood, and the small number who might be harmed could easily be identified beforehand.

The FDA concluded the hearings without making a decision on the proposed regulation and, as of this date, the regulation is still pending. However, the European Union has taken a very different approach to the question and currently Britain, Germany, France, Italy and Spain require the use of leukocyte filtered blood in all transfusions. There are strong indications that other European Union countries will soon also require leukocyte filtered blood in all transfusions.

The Blood Collection Equipment Market

The blood collection kit and blood processing centrifuge markets are a subset of the medical device market. Conventional blood collection kits sell for approximately $10, can be manufactured for approximately $4, and require no accompanying equipment. Blood processing centrifuges sell for approximately $5000, can be manufactured for approximately $3000, and can process approximately 300 units of whole blood per day. The annual world-wide blood collection kit market is estimated to be $350 million, and the annual world-wide blood processing centrifuge market is estimated to be $100 million.

The three largest U.S. blood collection kit manufacturers are Astor Laboratories (55% market share), Harris & Harris (25% market share) and PlasmaScience (10% market share). Astor is currently the exclusive supplier of blood collection kits to the American Red Cross and many large hospital groups. Harris & Harris primarily manufactures blood collection kits for its own blood collection centers, but also sells to some of the other smaller private blood collection companies. PlasmaScience, a new entrant into this market, sells primarily to small private companies and hospital groups. Astor Laboratories and Harris & Harris are also the two largest sellers of blood processing centrifuges and both also provide blood processing services (mainly leukocyte filtration) on a contract basis. Astor Laboratories is the exclusive provider of blood processing services for the American Red Cross, and Harris & Harris provides blood processing services for its own collection centers and for a large number of private companies.

Harris & Harris has sued Astor Laboratories and the American Red Cross alleging that they are engaged in an attempt to monopolize the blood processing market. The suit is still in the discovery phase.

The European market is similar to the U.S. market in many ways. Most of the national Red Cross organizations have exclusive contracts for the provision of blood collection kits and blood processing services with one large domestic firm. Longstreet, Ltd. is the only European firm which sells blood collection kits and blood processing services in multiple EU countries. Over 50% of Longstreet's sales are outside of the United Kingdom. Longstreet, Ltd. is also the largest seller of blood processing centrifuges in Europe.

BioFilter Venture Capital Investment Exercise

The Venture Capital Facts

In the wake of a television network report on the death and injury caused by whole blood transfusions, the FDA announced last week that it would again hold hearings on whether to mandate the use of leukocyte filtered blood. In preparation for the hearings, an FDA official contacted Dr. Fahaud to inquire about the development status of the LRF-1000. During the course of the conversation, the official stated that, if the FDA did mandate the use of leukocyte filtered blood in all blood transfusions, it would be "imperative to get new equipment on line as quickly as possible" and that "the FDA would work closely with developers of new equipment to expedite the review process." Dr. Fahaud immediately shared this information with the other BioFilter principals and they decided to complete the pre-clinical testing and begin the Phase I clinical testing as soon as possible. Dr. Fahaud and his colleagues originally planned to seek another NIH grant to further develop the LRF-1000 prior to commencing clinical tests. In light of the decision to begin clinical testing as soon as possible, the BioFilter principals decided that they would need approximately $12M of private investment primarily to build prototype equipment, conduct the clinical trials, and pay legal and consulting fees for FDA filings. BioFilter has recently obtained an investment commitment of $500K from a local angel investment group. The planned private investment schedule for the remaining $11.5M calls for a $2M Series A investment in Q2 ___, a $4M Series B investment in Q4 ___, and a $5.5M Series C investment in Q2 ____. The CSMC-NY patent lawyer suggested that BioFilter contact Wintergreen Ventures, the largest venture capital investment firm in New York State, and Seed-Stage Partners, a medium-sized venture capital firm in California, to discuss its investment needs.

BioFilter has had initial meetings with both Wintergreen Ventures and Seed-Stage Partners that went very well. Wintergreen Ventures and Seed-Stage Partners were both enthusiastic about the LRF-1000 technology and its financial potential, and BioFilter thought both investment firms could be very helpful in growing their company. At the conclusion of the meetings, BioFilter, Wintergreen Ventures and Seed-Stage Partners each agreed that they would draft a term sheet outlining the major points of a $11.5M, Series A, B and C investments in BioFilter, with special attention to the pre-investment valuation of BioFilter and the percentage ownership of BioFilter that would be sold in each of the three investment rounds; the structure of the investment (common stock, preferred stock, debt, warrants); conversion, preference and redemption features of the investment; anti-dilution provisions; tranches and milestones, and governance control of Bio-Filter. BioFilter has told Wintergreen Ventures about its meeting with Seed-Stage Partners and has told Seed-Stage Partners about its meeting with Wintergreen Ventures. BioFilter has assured both firms that it does not intend to create a bidding war between them and would hold their respective investment proposals in the strictest confidence.

*****

Each team should meet at least two times prior to _____ to discuss the negotiation facts and plan negotiation strategies. I will meet with each team on _____ for confidential briefings on their planned negotiation strategies.

To begin the negotiation exercise, the BioFilter team should prepare an initial written investment term sheet proposal to present to Wintergreen Ventures and Seed-State Partners, and the Wintergreen Ventures and Seed-Stage Partners teams should each prepare an initial written investment term sheet proposal to present to BioFilter. These initial term sheet proposals should be exchanged no later than ____. Although informal discussions can be held anytime during the negotiation period (___ — ___, formal negotiation sessions, which the professor will observe, will be scheduled during class time on ___ and ___. These negotiation sessions will be held in Room ____. BioFilter will negotiate separately with Wintergreen Ventures and Seed-Stage Partners in each of the two formal negotiation sessions for approximately one hour each. Because of the relatively short negotiation time periods, it will be important for the parties to prepare thoroughly for the negotiation meetings, including preparation of a meeting agenda. Additional term sheet proposals can be exchanged any time prior to ___. Please copy the professor on all inter-party written communications at ____@____.___

For the ____ class, each team will prepare a written memo for distribution to the class that (i) summarizes the terms and conditions agreed to, or rejected, in the venture capital investment negotiations; (ii) comments on the team's strategies and goals going into the negotiations; (iii) assesses how each team conducted itself during the negotiations; and (iv) lists lessons learned from the negotiation that could be used in future negotiations.

BioFilter License Agreement Exercise

BioFilter License Facts

Fast forward to November ____. BioFilter has received its venture capital investment commitment of $11.5 million and, thanks to the FDA's expedited review procedures, has nearly completed the Phase One clinical trial of the LRF-1000. The Phase One clinical trial has been very successful and BioFilter believes that there is a good chance that it can complete Phase Two and Phase Three clinical trials by January ____. However, the cost of the clinical trials has been much higher than originally estimated and BioFilter now believes that it will need approximately $20 million in additional funds to complete the Phase Two and Phase Three clinical trials. The founders of BioFilter met last week with their venture capital investment firm and they jointly decided that the time was right to explore the possibility of licensing, or possibly selling, the rights in the LRF-1000 technology. BioFilter and its VC investor agreed that BioFilter could not independently develop the manufacturing, marketing, sales, distribution and support capabilities necessary to commercialize the LRF-1000 technology by the completion of the clinical trials; and that the LRF-1000 technology would lose valuable market lead time if market entry were delayed until BioFilter could develop these capabilities. In addition to losing sales revenue during the period that BioFilter would be independently developing the capabilities necessary for commercialization of the LRF-1000 technology, there was concern that a competing, and possibly superior, technology might be developed during this delay. One specific concern was a published research report on the development of a synthetic blood product that could eliminate the risk of leukocyte induced infection from blood transfusions.

Based upon preliminary market research and recommendations from the venture capital investor, BioFilter has decided that the two most promising potential licensees, or buyers, are Astor Laboratories and Harris & Harris. (Information on Astor Laboratories, Harris & Harris and other firms active in the blood collection equipment market is provided in the *BioFilter, Inc. Negotiation Exercises* memorandum at pages 7–8.) BioFilter has met with Astor Laboratories and Harris & Harris to begin preliminary discussions on the future commercialization of the LRF-1000 technology. BioFilter has informed each company of its discussions with the other company. BioFilter has agreed to draft a proposed term sheet for the license, or sale, of the LRF-1000 technology for review by Astor Laboratories and Harris & Harris; and Astor Laboratories and Harris & Harris have, in turn, agreed to do the same.

Each team should draft a proposed term sheet and exchange these proposals no later than ____. Please copy the professor on all proposed terms sheets and any other communications between teams. The proposed term sheets should be factually and financially specific, reflecting the information provided in the *BioFilter, Inc. Negotiation Exercises* memorandum. Although informal negotiations can

occur at anytime during the negotiation period (___ — ___), formal negotiation
sessions will be scheduled during class time on ___ and ___. The professor will
meet with each team during the ___ class to learn about their proposed term sheet
terms and negotiation strategies. Each team should plan to meet as a group at least
once prior to the ___ class. During the ___ class, each team will present a written
memo that (i) summarizes the terms and conditions agreed to, or rejected, in the
term sheets; (ii) comments on the team's strategies and goals going into the
negotiations; (iii) assesses how each team conducted itself during the negotiations;
and (iv) lists lessons learned from the negotiations that could be used in future
negotiations.

The objective of this negotiation exercise is not to win or lose, or to pit one
company against another. The objective is to develop creative technology commercialization structures and strategies that will maximize the benefits to the parties.

TABLE OF CASES

[References are to pages]

A

A.C. Aukerman Co. v. R.L. Chaides Construction Co. 142
Aaron v. SEC. 1391
Abbott Lab. v. Diamedix Corp.. 226
Adams v. Burke 353; 369
Adenta GmbH v. OrthoArm, Inc.. 178
Adler v. Berg Harmon Assocs. 1241
The Adm'r of the Tulane University Educational Fund v. Debio Holding, S.A. 407
Adobe Sys. v. Stargate Software, Inc. 361
Advanced Bionics Corp. v. Medtronic, Inc.. . . 795
Advanced Micro Devices, Inc. v. Altera Corp.. .351
Advanced Telephone Systems, Inc. v. Com-Net Professional Mobile Radio, LLC. 1180
Advent Oil & Operating, Inc. v. S&E Enterprises, LLC.. .1300
AEG Acquisition Corp., In re. 860-61
Aerobox Composite Structures, In re. 845
Aerocon Eng'g, Inc., v. Silicon Valley Bank (In re World Aux. Power Co.) 853
Ahmed v. Trupin. 1255
Allan Block Corp. v. County Materials Corp.. . . 197
Allied Colloids Inc. v. American Cyanamid Co..805
Alves v. Commissioner of Internal Revenue. . .984
American High-Income Trust v. Alliedsignal. .1410
American Securit Co. v. Shatterproof Glass Corp.. .407
American Sterilizer Co. v. Sybron Corp.. 217
AMP, Inc. v. United States 158
Anderson v. Clow (In re Stac Elecs. Sec. Litig.). 1380
Andreaggi v. Relis. 716
Angel Investors, LLC v. Garrity. 1159
Apollo Capital Fund LLC v. Roth Capital Partners, LLC. .1399
Apple Computer v. Microsoft Corp.. . . . 271; 282
Applera Corp. v. MJ Research Inc.. 818
Application of (see name of party). . . . .
Applied Materials, Inc. v. Advanced Micro-Fabrication Equip. (Shanghai) Co. 757
Arcade Inc. v. Minnesota Min. and Mfg. Co.. . . 237
Arizona Retail Systems, Inc. v. Software Link, Inc.. .437
Armorlite Lens Co. v. Campbell 757
Aronson v. Quick Point Pencil Co.. 136
Astra USA, Inc. v. Bildman 1129
Atlanta Attachment Co. v. Leggett & Platt Inc. . 805

Atlas Chemical Industries, Inc. v. Moraine Products 225
Automatic Radio Mfg. Co. v. Hazeltine Research 135; 167
Ayers; United States v.. 1240
Aymes v. Bonelli 714

B

Bader v. Anderson. 1159
Baker v. Conlan 1417
Bandag Inc. v. Al Bolser's Tire Stores, Inc.. . . .158
Barazzotto v. Intelligent Systems, Inc.. 306
Barrios v. Paco Pharmaceutical Services, Inc. . 1240
Baxter International Inc. v. Cobe Laboratories Inc.. 805
Bayer AG v. Housey Pharms., Inc.. 401
Bd. of Trs. v. Roche Molecular Sys. . 662; 665; 673
Bear, Inc. v. Smith. 1179
Bear Stearns Litigation, In the Matter of 1130
Beckman Instruments, Inc. v. Technical Dev. Corp. 407
Bender v. Schwartz. 1169
Bendix Corp. v. Balax, Inc.. 160
Beraha v. Baxter Health Care Corp. 270; 394
Berg & Berg Enterprises, LLC v. Boyle 1123
Bernard J. Ebbers, Ex parte 1417
Bernstein v. United States DOJ 1095
Bezirdjian v. O'Reilly 1122
Bilski v. Kappos 11
Biopolymers, Inc., Matter of 850
Block v. First Blood Associates. 1240
Blohm v. Kelly. 1141
Bloomer v. Millinger 369
Board of Regents of the State of Florida v. Taborsky 625
Bonito Boats, Inc. v. Thunder Craft Boats, Inc.. 141
Botwinick v. Duck Corp. 1301
Bowers v. Baystate Techs., Inc.. 444
Braddock v. Braddock. 1226
Bristol-Myers Squibb Co. v. Rhone-Poulenc Rorer, Inc.. 829
Broadcast Music, Inc. v. Hirsch 860
Brodie v. Jordan 1132
Brown v. Alcatel USA, Inc.. 728
Brulotte v. Thys Co.. . . . . 136; 397
Bunge Corp. v. Northern Trust Co.. 306
Busse v. United States. 1006

[References are to pages]

C

Cadence Design Sys., Inc. v. Bhandari 735

California E. Labs., Inc. v. Gould 703

Campbell Plastics Eng'g & Mfg. v. Brownlee . .496

Capital Investments, Inc. v. Whitehall Packing Company, Inc.. 1300

Carter v. Helmsley-Spear, Inc. 714

Carter-Wallace, Inc. v. Tambrands, Inc. 426

Cascade Health Solutions v. PeaceHealth 266

Caspi v. The Microsoft Network, LLC. 461

CBS, Inc. v. American Society of Composers, Authors and Publishers 325

CBS Inc. v. Ziff-Davis Pub. Co. 306

Celeritas Techs. v. Rockwell Int'l Corp. 771

Cencor, Inc. v. Tolman 661

Central Admixture Pharmacy Services, Inc. v. Advanced Cardiac Solutions. 529

Century Envelope Co., Inc.. 307

CFLC, Inc., In re 850

Charlson v. United States 1025

Chatlos Systems, Inc. v. National Cash Register Corp.. 283

Chemagro Corporation v. Universal Chemical Co.. 134

Chilton v. Internal Revenue Commissioner. . . .1019

Ciba-Geigy Corp. v. Alza Corp. 530

CIBC World Markets Corp. v. TechTrader, Inc.. 1300

Cincom Systems Inc. v. Novelis Corp.. 352

City of (see name of city). . . . .

Clark v. Sims. 1130

Clark Equip. Co. v. Keller 178

Classen Immunotherapies, Inc. v. Biogen IDEC.829

Classen Immunotherapies, Inc. v. King Pharmaceuticals, Inc.. 829

Clock Spring, L.P. v. Wrapmaster, Inc.. 798

Coldwave Systems, LLC, In re 871

Columbia Univ. Patent Litig., In re 642

Commissioner v. (see name of defendant) . . . . . .

Commonwealth Sci. & Indus. Research Organisation v. Buffalo Tech. Inc.. 215

Compco Corp. v. Day-Brite Lighting. 136

Compton v. Metal Products Inc. 407

Compuserve Inc. v. Patterson. 461

Consolidated Data Terminals v. Applied Digital Data Systems, Inc.. 306

Continental Group, Inc. v. Kinsley 795

Contour Chair Lounge Co. v. True-Fit Chair, Inc.. 160

Cook Biotech Inc. v. Acell, Inc. 651

Cook Inc. v. Boston Sci. Corp.. 338

Cooper Linse Hallman Capital Management, Inc. v. Hallman. 1169

Cordance Corp. v. Amazon.Com, Inc. 250

Cordis Corp. v. Medtronic, Inc.. 220

Core Laboratories, Inc. v. Hayward-Wolff Research Corp.. 325

Corebrace LLC v. Star Seismic LLC. 197

Cornell Univ. v. Hewlett-Packard Co. 650

Cornell University v. Hewlett-Packard Co. 68

Cozzarelli v. Inspire Pharmaceuticals, Inc. 1389

Crown Cork & Seal Co. of Baltimore City v. Brooklyn Bottle Stopper Co. 135

Cummings v. Paramount Partners, LP. 1226

Cyrix Corp. v. Intel Corp.. 281

D

Daniels v. CDB, LLC 1179

Dannenberg v. PaineWebber Inc. (In re Software Toolworks Sec. Litig.) 1402

Davidson & Associates v. Jung. 451

Davis v. Brockamp & Jaeger, Inc.. 1142

DDB Techs., L.L.C. v. MLB Advanced Media, L.P.. .729

De Long Corp. v. Lucas. 416

Deering Milliken Research Corp. v. Leesona Corp.. .416

Diamond v. Commissioner of Internal Revenue . 922

Diamond Scientific Co. v. Ambico, Inc. . . . 143; 160

Digeo, Inc. v. Audible, Inc.. 189

Dillard Dep't Stores, Inc. v. Application Art Laboratories Co.. 178

Doe v. Yale Univ.. 661

Dombroski v. Wellpoint, Inc. 1179

Dorr-Oliver, Inc. v. United States. 757

Dronsejko v. Thornton. 1410

Duberstein; Commissioner v. 1019

Dubilier Condenser Corp.; United States v.. . . .665; 666; 673; 694

Duval Wiedmann, LLC v. Inforocket.Com, Inc.. .197

E

E.I. Du Pont de Nemours & Co. v. Okuley.607; 692

E.I. du Pont de Nemours and Co. v. United States 956; 1025

E.I. du Pont de Nemours and Comp., Inc. v. Shell Oil Comp.. 282

Eagle Comtronics, Inc. v. Pico Prods. 319

Eaton Corp. v. Appliance Valves Corp.. 795

[References are to pages]

eBay Inc. v. MercExchange, L.L.C.. . . . .210; 216

Edwards & Hanly v. Wells Fargo Sec. Clearance Corp.. .1410

Ehrenfried Technologies, Inc., In re 850

Eickmeyer v. Commissioner of Internal Revenue.. 1025

Eisenmenger IRA, Equity Trust Co. Custodian ex rel. v. Cole.. 1175

Eli Lilly & Co. v. Genetech, Inc.. 253

Eli Lilly & Co. v. Medtronic, Inc.. 829

Eli Lilly & Co. v. Zenith Goldline Pharms., Inc.. 805

Eli Lilly and Company v. Emisphere Technologies, Inc.. 269

Eli Lilly Co. v. Aradigm Corp.. 180

Elizabeth, City of v. American Nicholson Paving Co.. 797

EMSL Analytical, Inc. v. Younker 791

Eolas Techs. Inc. v. Microsoft Corp.. 650

Epic Sys. Corp. v. Allcare Health Mgmt. Sys.. .308

Ernst & Ernst v. Hochfelder. 1410

Ethicon, Inc. v. United States Surgical Corp. . . 181

Eustace v. Comm'r 932

Ex parte (see name of relator) . . . .

Ex rel. (see name of relator) . . . .

F

Fairchild Industries Inc. v. United States. 944

Farris v. Comm'r 999

Fawick v. Commissioner of Internal Revenue . 1025

Feldman v. Cutaia 1159

Feldman v. Google, Inc.. 461

Fenn v. Yale Univ.. . . . . .540; 583; 692

Ferer v. Aaron Ferer & Sons Co.. 1123

FilmTec Corp. v. Allied-Signal, Inc.. 672

First Union Nat. Bank v. Steele Software Sys. Corp.. 395

Fisher Investment Capital, Inc. v. Catawba. . . 1179

Flex-Foot, Inc. v. CRP, Inc.. 178

Florida State Board Of Administration v. Green Tree Financial Corporation. 1400

Fontana v. TLD Builders, Inc.. 1174

Forest v. Verizon Communications, Inc.. 461

Foster v. Churchill. 1301

Francklyn v. Guilford Packing Co.. 702

Frederick B. Stevens, Inc. v. Steel & Tubes . . . 269

Freeman v. Complex Computing Co.. 1175

FutureSource LLC v. Reuters, Ltd.. 843

G

G. Golden Associates of Oceanside, Inc. v. Arnold Foods Co., Inc.. 395

Gable v. Commissioner. 994

Garber v. Legg Mason Inc. 1389

Gayler v. Wilder. 665

Gen-Probe v. Center for Neurologic Study. . . .529

Genencor Intern., Inc. v. Novo Nordisk 281

Genentech, Inc. v. Insmed, Inc.. 829

General Signal Corp. v. Primary Flow Signal, Inc.. 757

General Spring Corp. v. Commissioner of Internal Revenue 999

General Talking Pictures Corp. v. Western Electric Co.. . . . . 125; 373

Georgia-Pacific Corp. v. U.S. Plywood Corp.. . . 48; 198

Gill v. Three Dimension Systems, Inc.. 1390

Gilson v. Commissioner. 1023

Gjerlov v. Schuyler Laboratories, Inc.. 214

Gonser v. Leland Detroit Mfg. Co.. 409

Graham v. John Deere Co.. 170

Grant v. U.S.. 984

Great Lakes Intellectual Prop. v. Sakar Int'l, Inc.. 237

Greenberg Traurig of New York, P.C. v. Moody.. 1400

Greenhouse v. MCG Capital Corp.. 1255

Guilder v. Corinth Constr. Corp.. 1175

Gupta v. New Britain General Hospital 661

H

H-M Wexford LLC v. Encorp, Inc.. 1246

Hamby v. Clearwater Consulting Concepts, LLLP 1235

Harris v. Commissioner of Internal Revenue. . .922

Harsco Corp. v. Zlotnicki. 728

Havel v. Kelsey-Hayes Co.. 270

Heidelberg Harris Inc. v. Loebach 352

Hill v. Gateway 2000, Inc.. 437

Hirsch-Chemie Ltd. v. Johns Hopkins Univ.. . .257

Hoag v. Chancellor, Inc.. 1301

Holland v. Gexa Corp.. 1255

Horbal v. Cannizzaro. 1141

Hribar v. Marsh & McLennan Companies, Inc..1159

Hughes v. BCI International Holdings, Inc. . . . 1227; 1240

[References are to pages]

Hull v. Brunswick Corp. 417

I

I.Lan Sys. v. NetScout Serv. Level Corp. 461
IDX Sys. Corp. v. Epic Sys. Corp. 778
IGEN Int'l, Inc. v. Roche Diagnostics GmbH . . 377
IIT Research Institute v. United States 565
Ill. Tool Works Inc. v. Indep. Ink, Inc. 875
In re (see name of party) . . . .
In the Matter of (see name of party) . . . .
InfoSAGE, Inc. v. Mellon Ventures, L.P. 1292
Ingersoll-Rand Co. v. Ciavatta 743
Institut Pasteur v. Cambridge Biotech Corp. (In re
　　Cambridge Biotech Corp.) 190; 850
Int'l Gamco, Inc. v. Multimedia Games, Inc. . . 381
Intel Corp. v. ULSI Sys. Technology 281; 352
Intel Corp. v. United States Int'l Trade
　　Comm'n 276
Intel Corp. v. VIA Techs., Inc. 281
Interconnect Planning Corp. v. Feil. 178
Intergraph Corp. v. Intel Corp. 328
InternetAd Systems, L.L.C. v. Opodo Ltd. 238
Intervisual Communs. v. Volkert 383
Iowa State Univ. Research Found., Inc. v. Wiley
　　Organics, Inc. 650
Israel Bio-Engineering Project v. Amgen Inc. . . 189
Ives v. Ramsden 1417

J

Jacobs v. Nintendo of Am., Inc. 154
Jacobsen v. Katzer. 483
Jamesbury Corp. v. Worcester Valve Co. 725
Jazz Photo Corp. v. Int'l Trade Com'n. 135
Johnson v. Schmitz, et. al. 661
Jordache Enterprise, Inc. v. Global Union Bank .426
Junger v. Daley. 1084

K

Kantor v. Commissioner of Internal Revenue . . 922
Kaplan v. O.K. Technologies, L.L.C. 1129
Kara Technology Inc. v. Stamps.Com Inc. 778
Kardios Systems Corp. v. Perkin-Elmer Corp. . .395
Karn v. U.S. Dep't of State 1095
Karten v. Woltin 1159
Kendall Co. v. Progressive Medical Technology,
　　Inc. 354
Kennedy v. Wright 728
Kewanee Oil Co. v. Bicron Corp. 136
Kingston v. Breslin. 1160

Kirby v. United States. 1025
Kiwanis Intern. v. Ridgewood Kiwanis Club . . 141
Klocek v. Gateway, Inc. 437
Kolmes v. World Fibers Corp. 805
Kolson v. Vembu. 1240
Koninklijke Philips Electronics N.V. v. The ADS
　　Group 1301
Kortum v. Johnson. 1142
Kucharczyk v. Regents of the Univ. of Cal. . . .682
Kueneman v. Commissioner of Internal
　　Revenue. 1025
Kunz v. SEC. 1255
Kunzweiler v. Zero.Net, Inc. 1240

L

Lally v. Catskill Airways, Inc. 1175
LDL Research & Dev. II v. Commissioner. . . .912
Lear, Inc. v. Adkins 161
Lee v. United States 1025
Lemelson v. Synergistics Research Corp. 178
Lemenestrel v. Warden. 1160
Levin v. Septodont Inc. 426
Levy v. Reiner 1160
Ligon v. Deloitte, Haskins & Sells 1235
Lilley v. Charren. 1390
Long v. Biomet, Inc. 1160
Longhi v. Mazzoni. 1179
Lough v. Brunswick Corp. 805
Lubrizol Enterprises v. Richmond Metal
　　Finishers 832
Lucas v. Ox Fibre Brush Co. 1019
Lucent Technologies, Inc. v. Gateway, Inc. 68
Lucent Technologies, Inc. v. Microsoft Corp. . . 250

M

M.A. Mortenson Company, Inc. v. Timberline
　　Software Corp. 437
Macaluso v. Jenkins 1174
MacLean Assoc., Inc. v. Wm. M. Mercer-Meidinger-
　　Hansen, Inc. 704
MacNaughton v. U.S. 984
Madey v. Duke Univ. 807
Madison River Management Company v. Business
　　Management Software Corporation 451
Mallinckrodt, Inc. v. Medipart, Inc. 127; 354
Mary S. Krech Trust v. Lakes Apartments . . . 1236
Marzec v. NYE. 1168
Mass Engineered Design, Inc. v. Ergotron, Inc. . 426
Matter of (see name of party). . . . .

Mazloom v. Mazloom 1142
McCallum Family L.L.C. v. Winger. 1170
McClain v. Commissioner. 1013
McElmurry v. Arkansas Power & Light Co.. . .702
McGrath v. Dougherty. 1417
McLaughlin v. Schenk. 1141
McNeilab, Inc. v. Scandipharm, Inc.. 232
McPadden v. Sidhu. 1160
Meadow River Lumber Co. v. University of Georgia
 Research Found.. 297
Mechanical Ice Tray Corp. v. General Motors
 Corp.. 270
Med Safe Northwest, Inc. v. Medvial, Inc.. . .1390
MedImmune, Inc. v. Genentech, Inc.. 170
Meehan v. PPG Industries, Inc.. 407
Meijer, Inc. v. Abbott Labs.. 266
Mentor H/S, Inc. v. Medical Device Alliance,
 Inc.. .237
Merck KGaA v. Integra Lifesciences I, Ltd.. . .822
Meridian Project Systems, Inc. v. Hardin
 Construction Company, LLC 450
Merrit v. Commissioner. 1010
Metabolite Labs., Inc. v. Lab. Corp. of Am.
 Holdings 426
Metcoff v. Lebovics 1144
Metro Communication Corp. BVI v. Advanced
 Mobilecomm Technologies. 1301
Midwest Research Inst. v. United States. 565
Milk v. Total Pay and HR Solutions, Inc.. . . .1180
Mission I-Tech Hockey, Ltd. v. Oakley, Inc.. . .238
Miyashiro v. Roehrig, Roehrig, Wilson &
 Hara. 1123
Modern Controls, Inc. v. Andreadakis 778
Moldo v. Matsco, Inc. (In re Cybernetic Servs.).862
Mona v. Mona Electric Group, Inc.. 1130
Monsanto Co. v. McFarling 199; 200; 215
Monsanto Co. v. Scruggs 375; 892
Moraine Products v. ICI America, Inc.. 327
Morton Salt Co. v. G.S. Suppiger Co.. 238
Motorola, Inc. v. Lemko Corp.. 742
Mros v. Commissioner of Internal Revenue . . 1025

N

N.V. Philips' Gloeilampenfabrieken v. Atomic
 Energy Commission 190
Nano-Proprietary, Inc. v. Canon, Inc.. . . .197; 215
Nashua Corp. v. RCA Corp. 216
Nathel v. Siegal 1410
Nemec v. Shrader 1122

Netscape Communs. Corp. v. Konrad 805
New Britain Machine Co. v. W. Lloyd Yeo . . .416
Nickels v. Koehler Management Corp.. 1244
Night Vision Corp. v. United States. 1210
Nippon Elec. Glass Co., Ltd. v. Sheldon. 426
Notz v. Everett Smith Group, Ltd. 1142
Nutrition 21 v. United States 523

O

Ohio Bureau of Workers' Comp. v. MDL Active
 Duration Fund, LTD.. 1241
Olan Mills, Inc. v. Linn Photo Co.. 426
Olczyk v. Cerion Technologies, Inc.. 1400
Orrock v. Appleton. 1159
Ortho Pharmaceutical Corp. v. Genetics Institute,
 Inc.. .237
Oster v. Kirschner 1399
OverEnd Technologies, LLC v. Invista S.A.R.L..892
Owen v. Hamilton 1168

P

Pace; United States v.. 1301
Pagel, Inc. v. Commissioner 981
Pamperin v. Streamline Mfg.. 1179
Parker v. Broom 1235
Parks v. Macro-Dynamics, Inc.. 1301
Pasquale v. Casale 1142
Penalty Kick Management, Ltd. v. Coca Cola
 Comp.. 778
Pension Committee of University of Montreal
 Pension Plan v. Banc of America Securities,
 LLC. .1410
Peracchi v. Commissioner. 949
Permanence Corp. v. Kennametal, Inc.. 389
Petur U.S.A. Instrument Co., Inc., In re 843
Pioneer Hi-Bred Int'l v. Ottawa Plant Food. . .135;
 354
Pittsburg State University v. Kansas Board of
 Regents. 581
Planetary Motion, Inc. v. Techsplosion, Inc.. . .483
Platzer v. Sloan-Kettering Inst. for Cancer
 Research 530
Pointer v. Castellani 1131
Pollstar v. Gigmania Ltd.. 461
Pope Mfg. Co. v. Gormully & Jeffery Mfg. Co..225
Posey; U.S. v.. 1062
PPG Industries, Inc. v. Guardian Industries
 Corp.. . . . . 159; 332

PPG Industries, Inc. v. Westwood Chemical, Inc. 178

Precision Shooting Equipment, Inc. v. Holless W. Allen, Inc. 225

Pride Int'l., Inc. v. Bragg 1130

Prima Tek II, L.L.C. v. A-Roo Co. 237

Princo Corp. v. I.T.C. 250

Prison Realty Securities Litigation, In re 1255

Prize Frize, Inc, In re 843

ProCD, Inc. v. Zeidenberg 438

Proveris Scientific Corp. v. Innovasystems, Inc. . 829

Prudential Ins. Co. of America v. Premit Group, Inc. 307

Puchner v. Bache Halsey Stuart, Inc. 1417

Q

Qualcomm Inc. v. Texas Instruments Inc. 325

Quanta Computer, Inc. v. LG Elecs., Inc. 366

R

R & D Dynamics Corp. v. U.S. 1223

R.B. Jenkins & Co. v. Southern Suction and Equipment Co. 416

Rambus Inc. v. Samsung Electronics Co. 325

RDM Holdings, LTD v. Continental Plastics Co. 1179

Reardon v. Lightpath Techs., Inc. 1392

Red Hat, Inc. v. SCO Group, Inc. 483

Regents of the University of New Mexico v. Knight 613

Register.com, Inc. v. Verio, Inc. 461

ResQNet.Com Inc. v. Lansa, Inc. 68

Revere Transducers, Inc. v. Deere & Co.. 759

RFR Indus. v. Rex-Hide Indus. 419

Rhone-Poulenc Agro, S.A. v. DeKalb Genetics Corp. 345

Rite-Nail Packaging Corp. v. Berryfast, Inc.. . .217

Roach Products Inc. v. Bolar Pharmaceuticals Co. 820

Robinson v. Commissioner 978

Rocform Corp. v. Acitelli-Standard Concrete Wall, Inc. 407

Ron Matusalem, In re 843

Rosenbluth, M.D. v. Prudential Securities, Inc. .1301

Rossman v. Morasco. 1141

Roth; United States v. 1069

Rubber Research, Inc. v. Commissioner of Internal Revenue 956

Ruso v. Morrison. 1410

Rutgers Council of AAUP Chapters v. Rutgers University 581

S

S.M. Wilson & Co. v. Smith Int'l., Inc. 306

Sable v. Southmark/Envicon Capital Corp. 1241

Sakol v. Commissioner of Internal Revenue . . .984

Salco Distribs. LLC v. Icode, Inc. 450

Sanders v. Mount Sinai School of Medicine . . .613

SanDisk Corp. v. STMicroelectronics, Inc.. . . .178

Santa Fe-Pomeroy, Inc. v. P & Z Co. 417

SAS Institute, Inc. v. S & H Computer Systems, Inc. 451

Saunders v. Firtel. 1142

Scheiber v. Dolby Labs., Inc.. 397

Schering Corp. v. Roussel-UCLAF SA and Zeneca Inc. 189

Schiller & Schmidt, Inc. v. Nordisco Corp. . . . 714

Schlumberger Res. Mgmt. Servs. v. CellNet Data Sys. (In re CellNet Data Sys.) 833

Schor v. Abbott Laboratories 892

Schroeder v. Tracor, Inc. 698

Schulman v. Wolff & Samson, PC 1142

SCO Group, Inc. v. Novell, Inc. 469

The SCO Group v. IBM 483

Sears, Roebuck & Co. v. Stiffel Co. 135

Semande v. Estes. 1180

Sensabaugh v. Farmers Ins. Exchange 795

Service Eng'g Corp. v. USDA 518

Shaw v. E.I. DuPont De Nemours & Co.. .190; 269

Shaw v. Regents of the University of California. 675

Shenker, et al. v. Laureate Education Inc.. 1130

Sherman v. Ryan. 1123

Sicom Systems, Ltd. v. Agilent Technologies, Inc.. 237

Sinskey v. Pharmacia Ophthalmics Inc. 806

Snow v. Commissioner of Internal Revenue . . .922

Softman Products Co. v. Adobe Systems Inc. . . 461

Solomons v. United States 665

Solow v. Heard McElroy & Vestal, L.L.P. . . . 1399

Somers v. Crane 1130

Sony Electronics, Inc. v. Guardian Media Technologies, Ltd. 178

Sorrell v. SEC 1236

South Cherry Street, LLC v. Hennessee Group LLC. 1410

Southern Research Institute v. Griffin Corp. . . .530

Sparton Corp. v. U.S. 805

Specht v. Netscape Communs. Corp.. 453

[References are to pages]

Speck v. North Carolina Dairy Foundation. . . .613

Spencer Trask Software & Info. Servs. LLC v. RPost Int'l Ltd.. 1282

Spindelfabrik Suessen-Schurr Stahlecker & Grill GmbH v. Schubert & Salzer Maschinenfabrik Aktiengesellschaft 143

St. Clair Intellectual Property Consultants, Inc. v. Matsushita Electronic Industrial Co., Ltd. . . . 742

Stanford v. Roche. 196

State Street Bank & Trust Co. v. Signature Financial Group 10

Static Control Components, Inc. v. Darkprint Imaging, Inc.. 795

Static Control Components, Inc. v. Lexmark Int'l, Inc.. . . . . 375; 882

Step-Saver Data Systems, Inc. v. Wyse Technology. 428

Storm Tech., Inc., In re 843

Straight v. Goss 1123

Stricker v. Epstein 1417

Studiengesell Schaft Kohle; U.S. v. 381

Studiengesellschaft Kohle, m.b.H. v. Hercules, Inc.. 314

Studiengesellschaft Kohle, M.B.H. v. Shell Oil Co.. 216

Sullivan v. Mebane Packaging Group, Inc.. . . .1400

Summers v. Welltech, Inc.. 1411

Sunterra Corp., In re 850

SuperGuide Corp. v. DirectTV Enterprises, Inc..381

Swenson v. Engelstad 1236

Szombathy v. Controlled Shredders, Inc.. 843

T

Tampa Bay Financial, Inc. v. Nordeen 1301

Taser Int'l., Inc. v. Ward. 1168

Tax & Accounting Software Corp. v. United States. .935

TDS Healthcare Systems Corp. v. Humana Hosp. Illinois, Inc.. 394

Telxon Corp. v. Meyerson. 1161

Textile Productions, Inc. v. Mead Corp.. 237

Therien v. Trs. of the Univ. of Pa.. 536

Thompson v. Smith Barney, Harris Upham & Co., Inc.. .1410

TM Patents v. International Business Machines Corporation. 503

Tower Tech. Inc., In re 871

Transitron Electronic Co. v. Hughes Aircraft Co.. 216; 225

Transparent-Wrap Machine Corp. v. Stokes & Smith Co.. 417

Transport Corp. of Am. v. IBM Corp.. 291

Travelers Express Co. v. American Express Integrated Payment Sys., Inc.. 148

Trieweiler v. Sears. 1169

Triple Point Tech., Inc. v. D.N.L. Risk Mgmt., Inc.. .306

Troxel Mfg. Co. v. Schwinn Bicycle Co.. 216

TSR, Inc. v. Commissioner of Internal Revenue.944

Tsutsui v. Barasch 1123

Tuskos Engineering Corp. v. Tuskos. 217

TXO Production Co. v. M.D. Mark, Inc.. 352

U

U.S. v. (see name of defendant) . . . .

U.S. Philips Corp. v. ITC. 240

U.S. Valves. Inc. v. Dray 197; 416

Ultra-Precision Mfg., Ltd. v. Ford Motor Co.. . . 141

Unidisco, Inc. v. Schattner 282

Uniloc USA, Inc. v. Microsoft Corp.. . . . .56; 198

United States v. (see name of defendant). . . . . .

UnitedHealth Group, Inc. Shareholder Derivative Litigation 1130

Univ. of Rochester v. G.D. Searle & Co.. 636

Univ. of W. Va. v. Van Voorhies 615

Universal Gym Equipment v. ERWA Exercise Equipment Ltd.. 215

University of Pittsburgh v. Townsend 613

University Patents, Inc. v. Kligman. 596

Univis Lens Co.; U.S. v. 353; 369

V

V-Formation, Inc. v. Benetton Group SPA 352

Va. Panel Corp. v. MAC Panel Co.. 408

Vacuum Concrete Corp. of America v. American Mach. & Foundry Co.. 270

Vault Corporation v. Quaid Software Limited . . 451

VEC Technology, L.L.C. v. Acrylon Plastics, Inc.. .742

Venturetek, L.P. v. Rand Publishing Co., Inc.. .1169

Verizon Communs., Inc. v. Pizzirani 780

Vermont Microsystems Inc. v. Autodesk Inc. . . 778

Vernor v. Autodesk, Inc. 375

VRT, Inc. v. Dutton-Lainson Co.. 302

W

Wachter Management Company v. Dexter & Chaney, Inc.. .437

Wagner v. First Horizon Pharmaceutical Corp..1390

Wahlcometroflex v. Baldwin 1122; 1125

[References are to pages]

Walker Process Equip., Inc. v. Food Machinery and Chemical Corp.. 892
Wallace v. IBM 483
Wang Lab. v. Oki Elec. Indus. Co.. 321
Warner-Jenkinson Co. v. Allied Chemical Corp..224
Warren v. Fox Family Worldwide, Inc.. 714
Waterjet Tech., Inc. v. Flow Int'l Corp.. 730
Waterman v. Mackenzie. 180; 225
Weed Eater, Inc. v. Dowling 795
Weiss v. Swanson 1117
Wellington Print Works, Inc. v. Magid 702
Western Elec. Co. v. Pacent Reproducer Corp. . 225
Western Geophysical Co. of America, Inc. v. Bolt Associates, Inc.. 270
Whirlpool Financial Corp. v. GN Holdings, Inc.. 1240
Whitehorn v. Whitehorn Farms 1142
Whittemore v. Cutter 807
William Hodges & Co., Inc. v. Sterwood Corp..394
William M. Bailey Co. v. Commissioner.. 990
Williams v. Stanford 1142
Williams v. White Mountain Constr. Co.. 426
Wilson v. Saintine Exploration and Drilling Corp.. 1240
Winbond Elecs. Corp. v. ITC. 159

Windsurfing Int'l Inc. v. AMF Inc.. 250
Wis. Alumni Research Found. v. Xenon Pharms., Inc.. 566
Wommack v. Durham Pecan Co., Inc.. 703
Wordtech Sys. v. Integrated Networks Solutions, Inc.. 68
Worlds of Wonder Securities Litigation, In re . 1390

X

XCO Int'l, Inc. v. Pac. Sci. Co.. 205

Y

Yates v. Holt-Smith 1123
Yeda Research and Development Co., Ltd. v. ImClone 352
Yeshiva University v. Greenberg 581

Z

Zahodnick v. International Business Machines Corp.. 778
Zapata Industries, Inc. v. W.R. Grace & Co.. . .158
Zila, Inc. v. Tinnell 407
Zobrist v. Coal-X, Inc.. 1255

INDEX

[References are to sections.]

A

ACCOUNTING PRINCIPLES (See FINANCING TECHNOLOGY INNOVATION, subhead: Accounting principles)

ANTITRUST LAW
Clayton Act . . . 7.1
Department of Justice . . . 7.2
Federal Trade Commission Act . . . 7.1; 7.2
Sherman Act . . . 7.1

B

BANK LOANS
Financing technology innovation . . . 11.5.1

BANKRUPTCY
Copyrights, perfecting security interests in . . . 6.3
Licensee bankruptcy . . . 6.2
Licensor bankruptcy . . . 6.1
Patents, perfecting security interests in . . . 6.4

BAYH-DOLE ACT
Generally . . . 3.1
Faculty-university relationship, effect on . . . 3.1.4
Legislation . . . 3.1.1
March-in rights . . . 3.1.2
Standing to sue . . . 3.1.3
University-faculty relationship, effect on . . . 3.1.4

BEST EFFORTS CLAUSES
Licenses, in . . . 2.3.8

BIOTECHNOLOGY LICENSES
Generally . . . 2.1.3

BOX-TOP LICENSES
Generally . . . 2.4.1

BREACH OF LICENSES
Generally . . . 2.2.6
Remedies for . . . 2.2.7

BUSINESS ORGANIZATION (See CHOICE OF BUSINESS ORGANIZATION)

C

CHOICE OF BUSINESS ORGANIZATION
Generally . . . 10.1
Corporations and limited liability companies, comparison of . . . 10.1.5
Limited liability companies
    Generally . . . 10.1.4
    Corporations and, comparison of . . . 10.1.5
Limited partnership . . . 10.1.1
Subchapter C corporation . . . 10.1.2
Subchapter S corporation . . . 10.1.3

CLAYTON ACT
Antitrust law . . . 7.1

CLICK-WRAP LICENSES
Generally . . . 2.4.3

COMMERCIALIZATION OF UNIVERSITY TECHNOLOGIES (See UNIVERSITY TECHNOLOGIES COMMERCIALIZATION)

CONTRACT LAW, PATENT LICENSES AND
Generally . . . 2.2.2

CO-OWNER LICENSES
Generally . . . 2.2.5

COPYRIGHTS
Intellectual property . . . 1.5.2
Perfecting security interests in . . . 6.3

D

DEPARTMENT OF JUSTICE
Antitrust licensing guidelines . . . 7.2

DUE DILIGENCE
Generally . . . 11.8
Federal securities law, under . . . 11.8.1
State securities law, under . . . 11.8.2

E

ECONOMIC CONCEPTS
Generally . . . 1.6
Intellectual property, unique economic characteristics of . . . 1.6.2
Macro-economics . . . 1.6.1
Market structures . . . 1.6.3
Micro-economics . . . 1.6.1

EMPLOYEE INTELLECTUAL PROPERTY RIGHTS (See INDUSTRY EMPLOYER-EMPLOYEE INTELLECTUAL PROPERTY RIGHTS)

EMPLOYER INTELLECTUAL PROPERTY RIGHTS (See INDUSTRY EMPLOYER-EMPLOYEE INTELLECTUAL PROPERTY RIGHTS)

EMPLOYMENT CONTRACTS
Employer intellectual property rights under . . . 4.3

ENCRYPTION TECHNOLOGY
Generally . . . 9.3.1

ESTOPPEL
Licensee estoppel . . . 2.2.4

EXPERIMENTAL USE OF NEW TECHNOLOGY
Hatch-Waxman Act infringement safe harbor . . . 5.3

EXPERIMENTAL USE OF NEW TECHNOLOGY—Cont.
Patent infringement, experimental use exemption to . . . 5.2
Public use statutory bar, experimental use exception to . . . 5.1

EXPORT CONTROLS
Overview . . . 9.1
Deemed exports . . . 9.2
Encryption technology . . . 9.3.1
Enforcement cases . . . 9.4
Selection of . . . 9.3
Software programs . . . 9.3.2

F

FACULTY-UNIVERSITY RELATIONSHIP
Bayh-Dole Act effect on . . . 3.1.4
Employment contracts . . . 3.6
Intellectual property ownership disputes . . . 3.3.2

FEDERAL TRADE COMMISSION ACT
Antitrust law . . . 7.1; 7.2

FIDUCIARY DUTIES
Directors, of . . . 10.2.1
Majority shareholders, of . . . 10.2.3
Officers, of . . . 10.2.2

FIELD-OF-USE RESTRICTIONS
Licenses . . . 2.3.7

FINANCING TECHNOLOGY INNOVATION
Accounting principles
    Generally . . . 1.7
    Assets, types of . . . 1.7.1
    Financial reports, types of . . . 1.7.2
Bank loans . . . 11.5.1
Due diligence (See DUE DILIGENCE)
Fraud (See FRAUD)
Initial public offerings (See INITIAL PUBLIC OFFERINGS (IPOs))
Intellectual property
    Monetization of . . . 11.5.2
    Securitization of . . . 11.5.3
Letters of credit . . . 11.5.4
Other forms of . . . 11.5
Private securities offerings (See PRIVATE SECURITIES OFFERINGS)
Public securities offerings (See FRAUD, subhead: Public securities offerings)
Small Business Innovation Research Program (See SMALL BUSINESS INNOVATION RESEARCH PROGRAM (SBIR))
Small Business Technology Transfer Program (See SMALL BUSINESS TECHNOLOGY TRANSFER PROGRAM (STTR))
Venture capital investments (See VENTURE CAPITAL INVESTMENTS)

FRAUD
Private securities offerings . . . 11.3

FRAUD—Cont.
Public securities offerings
    Generally . . . 11.7
    Federal securities fraud . . . 11.7.1
    State securities fraud . . . 11.7.2

G

GRANT CLAUSES
Licenses, in . . . 2.3.2

H

HATCH-WAXMAN ACT
Infringement safe harbor . . . 5.3

HOLD-OVER AGREEMENTS
Industry employer-employee intellectual property rights . . . 4.5

I

IMPLIED LICENSES
Generally . . . 2.2.3; 2.3.1

INDEMNIFICATION
Generally . . . 2.3.11

INDUSTRY EMPLOYER-EMPLOYEE INTELLECTUAL PROPERTY RIGHTS
Employment contracts, employer intellectual property rights under . . . 4.3
Hold-over agreements . . . 4.5
Non-competition agreements . . . 4.7
Non-disclosure agreements . . . 4.6
Shop rights, employer . . . 4.1
State statutory restrictions on employer intellectual property rights . . . 4.4
Works made for hire . . . 4.2

INDUSTRY SPONSORED RESEARCH (See UNIVERSITY TECHNOLOGIES COMMERCIALIZATION, subhead: University-industry sponsored research)

INITIAL PUBLIC OFFERINGS (IPOs)
Overview . . . 11.6; 11.6.1
Securities Acts . . . 11.6.2
Securities registration . . . 11.6.3

INTELLECTUAL PROPERTY
Overview . . . 1.5
Copyrights . . . 1.5.2
Industry employer-employee intellectual property rights (See INDUSTRY EMPLOYER-EMPLOYEE INTELLECTUAL PROPERTY RIGHTS)
Monetization of . . . 11.5.2
Patents . . . 1.5.1
Scope of . . . 1.11.3
Securitization of . . . 11.5.3
Trade secrets . . . 1.5.3
Unique economic characteristics of . . . 1.6.2

[References are to sections.]

INTELLECTUAL PROPERTY—Cont.

University intellectual property ownership (See
UNIVERSITY TECHNOLOGIES COMMER-
CIALIZATION, subhead: Intellectual property
ownership)

Valuation of . . . 1.8.2

IPOs (See INITIAL PUBLIC OFFERINGS (IPOs))

L

LETTERS OF CREDIT

Financing technology innovation . . . 11.5.4

LICENSE AGREEMENTS

Generally . . . 2.1

Biotechnology licenses . . . 2.1.3

Product licenses . . . 2.1.2

Software licenses . . . 2.1.1

LICENSEES, RIGHTS OF (See LICENSORS
AND LICENSEES, RIGHTS OF)

LICENSES

Best efforts clauses . . . 2.3.8

Biotechnology licenses . . . 2.1.3

Breach of licenses

     Generally . . . 2.2.6

     Remedies for . . . 2.2.7

Contract law, patent licenses and . . . 2.2.2

Field-of-use restrictions . . . 2.3.7

Grant clauses . . . 2.3.2

Implied licenses . . . 2.2.3; 2.3.1

Improvements, to . . . 2.3.10

Indemnification . . . 2.3.11

Most-favored licensee clauses . . . 2.3.4

Patent licenses

     Contract law and . . . 2.2.2

     Valuations . . . 1.8.3

Patent owner, by . . . 8.5

Post-sale restrictions . . . 2.3.6

Product licenses . . . 2.1.2

Property rights, as . . . 1.4

Royalties . . . 2.3.9

Software licenses . . . 2.1.1

Terms . . . 2.3

Transfers . . . 2.3.5

Unilateral licenses (See UNILATERAL LICENSES)

Warranties . . . 2.3.3

LICENSING LAW

Antitrust law and (See ANTITRUST LAW)

License agreements (See LICENSE AGREE-
MENTS)

Licensees, rights of (See LICENSORS AND LI-
CENSEES, RIGHTS OF)

Licensors and licensees, rights of (See LICENSORS
AND LICENSEES, RIGHTS OF)

Unilateral licenses (See UNILATERAL LICENSES)

LICENSORS AND LICENSEES, RIGHTS OF

Generally . . . 2.2

Bankruptcy

     Licensee bankruptcy . . . 6.2

     Licensor bankruptcy . . . 6.1

LICENSORS AND LICENSEES, RIGHTS OF—
Cont.

Breach of licenses

     Generally . . . 2.2.6

     Remedies for . . . 2.2.7

Contract law, patent licenses and . . . 2.2.2

Co-owner licenses . . . 2.2.5

Implied licenses . . . 2.2.3

Licensee estoppel . . . 2.2.4

Most-favored licensee clauses . . . 2.3.4

Patent invalidity . . . 2.2.8

Patent licenses and contract law . . . 2.2.2

Patent misuse . . . 2.2.10

Scope of licensor rights . . . 2.2.1

Standing to sue . . . 2.2.9

LIMITED LIABILITY COMPANIES

Generally . . . 10.1.4

Corporations and, comparison of . . . 10.1.5

LIMITED PARTNERSHIP

Generally . . . 10.1.1

M

MACRO-ECONOMICS

Generally . . . 1.6.1

MANAGEMENT RESPONSIBILITIES

Generally . . . 10.2

Corporate opportunities, usurpation of . . . 10.2.5

Directors' fiduciary duties . . . 10.2.1

Fiduciary duties (See FIDUCIARY DUTIES)

Majority shareholders' fiduciary duties . . . 10.2.3

Officers' fiduciary duties . . . 10.2.2

Piercing the corporate veil . . . 10.2.6

Shareholder direct and derivative suits . . . 10.2.4

Usurpation of corporate opportunities . . . 10.2.5

MICRO-ECONOMICS

Generally . . . 1.6.1

MOST-FAVORED LICENSEE CLAUSES

Generally . . . 2.3.4

N

NON-COMPETITION AGREEMENTS

Industry employer-employee intellectual property
     rights . . . 4.7

NON-DISCLOSURE AGREEMENTS

Industry employer-employee intellectual property
     rights . . . 4.6

O

OPEN SOURCE LICENSES

Generally . . . 2.4.4

P

PATENT INFRINGEMENT

Damages . . . 1.8.3

[References are to sections.]

PATENT INFRINGEMENT—Cont.
Experimental use exemption to . . . 5.2

PATENT INVALIDITY
Generally . . . 2.2.8

PATENT LICENSES
Contract law and . . . 2.2.2
Valuations . . . 1.8.3

PATENT MISUSE
Generally . . . 2.2.10

PATENTS
Exchange by patent holder . . . 8.6
Intellectual property . . . 1.5.1
License by patent owner . . . 8.5
Perfecting security interests in . . . 6.4
Sale
 Patent holder, by . . . 8.6
 Patent owner, by . . . 8.5
Sources of information on . . . 1.11.8
University patent enforcement . . . 3.4

PIERCING THE CORPORATE VEIL
Management responsibilities . . . 10.2.6

POST-SALE RESTRICTIONS
Licenses . . . 2.3.6

PRIVATE SECURITIES OFFERINGS
Generally . . . 11.2
Angel investors . . . 11.2.2
Family . . . 11.2.1
Founders . . . 11.2.1
Fraud in . . . 11.3
Friends . . . 11.2.1
Private placement memorandum . . . 11.2.4
Securities registration exemptions . . . 11.2.3

PRODUCT LICENSES
Generally . . . 2.1.2

PUBLIC SECURITIES OFFERINGS (See
 FRAUD, subhead: Public securities offerings)

PUBLIC USE STATUTORY BAR
Experimental use exception to . . . 5.1

R

ROYALTIES
Generally . . . 2.3.9

S

SBA (See SMALL BUSINESS ADMINISTRATION
 (SBA))

SBIR (See SMALL BUSINESS INNOVATION RE-
 SEARCH PROGRAM (SBIR))

SECURITIES ACTS
Initial public offerings . . . 11.6.2

SHERMAN ACT
Antitrust law . . . 7.1

SHOP RIGHTS, EMPLOYER
Industry employer-employee intellectual property
 rights . . . 4.1

SHRINK-WRAP LICENSES
Generally . . . 2.4.2

SMALL BUSINESS ADMINISTRATION (SBA)
Small Business Innovation Research Program Policy
 Directive . . . 11.1.3
Small Business Technology Transfer Program Policy
 Directive . . . 11.1.4

**SMALL BUSINESS INNOVATION RESEARCH
PROGRAM (SBIR)**
Overview . . . 11.1; 11.1.1
Data rights . . . 11.1.5
Federal legislation . . . 11.1.2
Phase III rights . . . 11.1.5
Small Business Administration Policy Directive
 . . . 11.1.3

**SMALL BUSINESS TECHNOLOGY TRANS-
FER PROGRAM (STTR)**
Overview . . . 11.1; 11.1.1
Federal legislation . . . 11.1.2
Small Business Administration Policy Directive
 . . . 11.1.4

SOFTWARE LICENSES
Generally . . . 2.1.1

SOFTWARE PROGRAMS
Generally . . . 9.3.2

STATE STATUTORY RESTRICTIONS
Employer intellectual property rights, on . . . 4.4

STTR (See SMALL BUSINESS TECHNOLOGY
 TRANSFER PROGRAM (STTR))

STUDENT-UNIVERSITY RELATIONSHIP
Intellectual property ownership disputes . . . 3.3.3
Research responsibilities . . . 3.5

SUBCHAPTER C CORPORATION
Generally . . . 10.1.2

SUBCHAPTER S CORPORATION
Generally . . . 10.1.3

T

**TAX EFFECTS OF TECHNOLOGY CRE-
ATION AND TRANSFER**
Exchange by patent holder . . . 8.6
Experimentation and research
 Credit . . . 8.2
  Expense deductions . . . 8.1
Founders' capital contributions . . . 8.3
License by patent owner . . . 8.5
Patent holder, sale or exchange by . . . 8.6
Patent owner, license or sale by . . . 8.5
Research and experimentation
 Credit . . . 8.2
  Expense deductions . . . 8.1

[References are to sections.]

**TAX EFFECTS OF TECHNOLOGY CRE-
ATION AND TRANSFER**—Cont.
Sale
     Patent holder, by . . . 8.6
     Patent owner, by . . . 8.5
Stock in exchange for services . . . 8.4

TECHNOLOGY INNOVATION (GENERALLY)
Accounting principles (See FINANCING TECH-
     NOLOGY INNOVATION, subhead: Accounting
     principles)
Business of
     Generally . . . 1.8
     Intellectual property, valuation of . . . 1.8.2
     Patent infringement damages . . . 1.8.3
     Patent license valuations . . . 1.8.3
     Return . . . 1.8.1
     Risk . . . 1.8.1
Defined . . . 1.2
Economics (See ECONOMIC CONCEPTS)
Financing (See FINANCING TECHNOLOGY IN-
     NOVATION)
Intellectual property (See INTELLECTUAL PROP-
     ERTY)
Licenses as property rights . . . 1.4
Nature of . . . 1.3
Strategy, formulation of
     Generally . . . 1.11
     Advantages . . . 1.11.4
     Companies, sources of information on
         . . . 1.11.8
     Conditions, terms and . . . 1.11.7
     Disadvantages . . . 1.11.4
     Identification . . . 1.11.1
     Intellectual property protection, scope of
         . . . 1.11.3
     Markets
         Definition . . . 1.11.5
         Profiles of firms in . . . 1.11.6
         Sources of information on . . . 1.11.8
     Patents, sources of information on . . . 1.11.8
     Potential applications, consideration of
         . . . 1.11.2
     Terms and conditions . . . 1.11.7
Tax effects of (See TAX EFFECTS OF TECHNOL-
     OGY CREATION AND TRANSFER)
Technology value . . . 1.9.1
Transferee perspective . . . 1.9; 1.9.3
Transferor perspective . . . 1.9; 1.9.2

TECHNOLOGY TRANSFERS
Advantages . . . 1.10; 1.10.1
Disadvantages . . . 1.10; 1.10.2
Etymology of . . . 1.1
Tax effects of (See TAX EFFECTS OF TECHNOL-
     OGY CREATION AND TRANSFER)

TRADE SECRETS
Intellectual property . . . 1.5.3

U

UNILATERAL LICENSES
Generally . . . 2.4
Box-top licenses . . . 2.4.1
Click-wrap licenses . . . 2.4.3
Open source licenses . . . 2.4.4
Shrink-wrap licenses . . . 2.4.2

**UNITED STATES TECHNOLOGY EXPORT
     CONTROLS** (See EXPORT CONTROLS)

**UNIVERSITY TECHNOLOGIES COMMER-
     CIALIZATION**
Bayh-Dole Act (See BAYH-DOLE ACT)
Faculty-university relationship (See FACULTY-
     UNIVERSITY RELATIONSHIP)
Industry sponsored research (See subhead:
     University-industry sponsored research)
Intellectual property ownership
     Generally . . . 3.3
     Faculty-university intellectual property owner-
         ship disputes . . . 3.3.2
     Licensing policies . . . 3.3.4
     Policy . . . 3.3.1
     Student-university intellectual property owner-
         ship disputes . . . 3.3.3
Patent enforcement . . . 3.4
Student-university relationship
     Intellectual property ownership disputes
         . . . 3.3.3
     Research responsibilities . . . 3.5
University-industry sponsored research
     Generally . . . 3.2
     Agreements . . . 3.2.1
     Disputes . . . 3.2.3
     Income tax limitations on sponsored research
         . . . 3.2.2

V

VENTURE CAPITAL INVESTMENTS
Generally . . . 11.4
Disputes . . . 11.4.4
Private equity glossary . . . 11.4.5
Structure of . . . 11.4.2
Term sheet, sample . . . 11.4.3
Venture capital industry . . . 11.4.1

W

WARRANTIES
Licenses, of . . . 2.3.3

WORKS MADE FOR HIRE
Industry employer-employee intellectual property
     rights . . . 4.2